Molecular and Cellular Biology

Custom Edition for University of Illinois

Taken from:
Biological Science, Fifth Edition
by Scott Freeman, Lizabeth Allison, Michael Black, Greg Podgorski,
Kim Quillin, Jon Monroe, and Emily Taylor

Becker's World of the Cell, Eighth Edition
by Jeff Hardin, Gregory Bertoni, and Lewis J. Kleinsmith

Front cover art courtesy of MedicalRF.com/Alamy, Jennifer Waters/Science Source.

Back cover art courtesy of Ingram Publishing/Getty, Maciej Frolow/Getty, Laguna Design/Getty, Victor Habbick Visions/Getty, W Fawcett Don/Getty.

Taken from:

Biological Science, Fifth Edition
by Scott Freeman, Lizabeth Allison, Michael Black, Greg Podgorski, Kim Quillin, Jon Monroe, and Emily Taylor
Copyright © 2014, 2011, 2008 by Pearson Education, Inc.
Upper Saddle River, New Jersey 07458

Becker's World of the Cell, Eighth Edition
by Jeff Hardin, Gregory Bertoni, and Lewis J. Kleinsmith
Copyright © 2012, 2009, 2006 by Pearson Education, Inc.
Published by Benjamin Cummings
San Francisco, California 94111

This special edition published in cooperation with Pearson Learning Solutions.

Pearson Learning Solutions, 501 Boylston Street, Suite 900, Boston, MA 02116
A Pearson Education Company
www.pearsoned.com

Printed in the United States of America

1 2 3 4 5 6 7 8 9 10 V092 16 15 14 13

000200010271786152

MC/MM

ISBN 10: 1-269-38244-6
ISBN 13: 978-1-269-38244-1

Brief Contents

Part 1

Taken from: *Biological Science*, Fifth Edition
by Scott Freeman, Lizabeth Allison, Michael Black, Greg Podgorski, Kim Quillin,
Jon Monroe, and Emily Taylor

Part 2

Taken from: *Becker's World of the Cell*, Eighth Edition
by Jeff Hardin, Gregory Bertoni, and Lewis J. Kleinsmith

Part I

Taken from: *Biological Science*, Fifth Edition
by Scott Freeman, Lizabeth Allison, Michael Black, Greg Podgorski, Kim Quillin,
Jon Monroe, and Emily Taylor

A Note from the Authors

You are about to embark on an amazing journey of discovery. The study of life spans from the inner workings of cells to the complex interactions of entire ecosystems, through the information stored in DNA to the ways genetic information evolves over time. At the same time that our understanding of biology is growing in leaps and bounds, so too are great insights into how learners acquire new knowledge and skills. We are thrilled to join Scott Freeman on *Biological Science*, a book dedicated to active, research-based learning and to exploring the experimental evidence that informs what we know about biology. The next few pages highlight the features in this book and in MasteringBiology® that will help you succeed.

From left to right: Michael Black, Emily Taylor, Jon Monroe,
Lizabeth Allison, Greg Podgorski, Kim Quillin

To the Student: How to Use This Book

New chapter-opening Roadmaps visually group and organize information to help you anticipate key ideas as well as recognize meaningful relationships and connections between them.

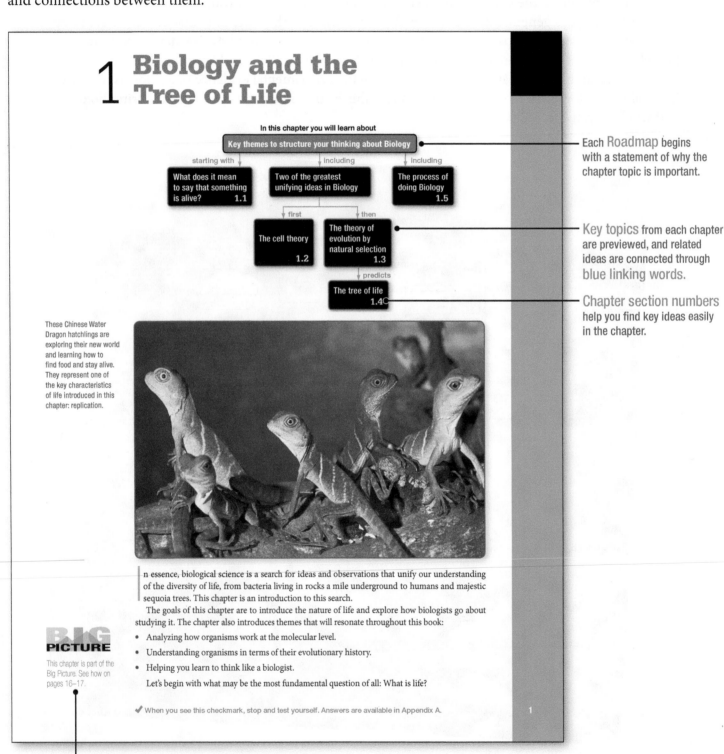

1 Biology and the Tree of Life

In this chapter you will learn about

Key themes to structure your thinking about Biology

starting with — *including* — *including*

What does it mean to say that something is alive? **1.1**

Two of the greatest unifying ideas in Biology

The process of doing Biology **1.5**

first — *then*

The cell theory **1.2**

The theory of evolution by natural selection **1.3**

predicts

The tree of life **1.4**

These Chinese Water Dragon hatchlings are exploring their new world and learning how to find food and stay alive. They represent one of the key characteristics of life introduced in this chapter: replication.

BIG PICTURE

This chapter is part of the Big Picture. See how on pages 16–17.

In essence, biological science is a search for ideas and observations that unify our understanding of the diversity of life, from bacteria living in rocks a mile underground to humans and majestic sequoia trees. This chapter is an introduction to this search.

The goals of this chapter are to introduce the nature of life and explore how biologists go about studying it. The chapter also introduces themes that will resonate throughout this book:

- Analyzing how organisms work at the molecular level.
- Understanding organisms in terms of their evolutionary history.
- Helping you learn to think like a biologist.

Let's begin with what may be the most fundamental question of all: What is life?

✔ When you see this checkmark, stop and test yourself. Answers are available in Appendix A.

1

Each Roadmap begins with a statement of why the chapter topic is important.

Key topics from each chapter are previewed, and related ideas are connected through blue linking words.

Chapter section numbers help you find key ideas easily in the chapter.

Big Picture Concept Maps are referenced on the opening page of related chapters, pointing you to summary pages that help you synthesize challenging topics.

Big Picture Concept Maps integrate visuals and words to help you synthesize information about challenging topics in biology that span multiple chapters and units.

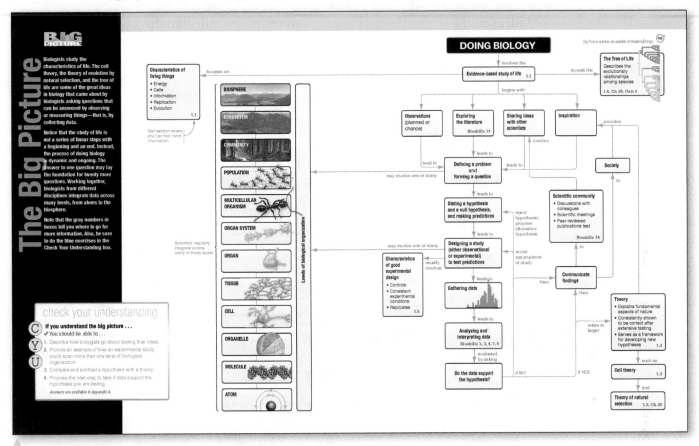

Three New Big Picture topics have been added to the Fifth Edition:

- NEW! Doing Biology
- NEW! The Chemistry of Life
- Energy for Life
- Genetic Information
- Evolution
- NEW! Plant and Animal Form and Function
- Ecology

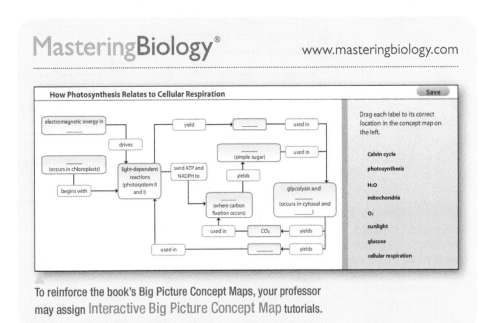

To reinforce the book's Big Picture Concept Maps, your professor may assign Interactive Big Picture Concept Map tutorials.

Practice for success
on tests and exams

Intertwined color-coded "active learning threads" are embedded in the text. The gold thread helps you to identify important ideas, and the blue thread helps you to test your understanding.

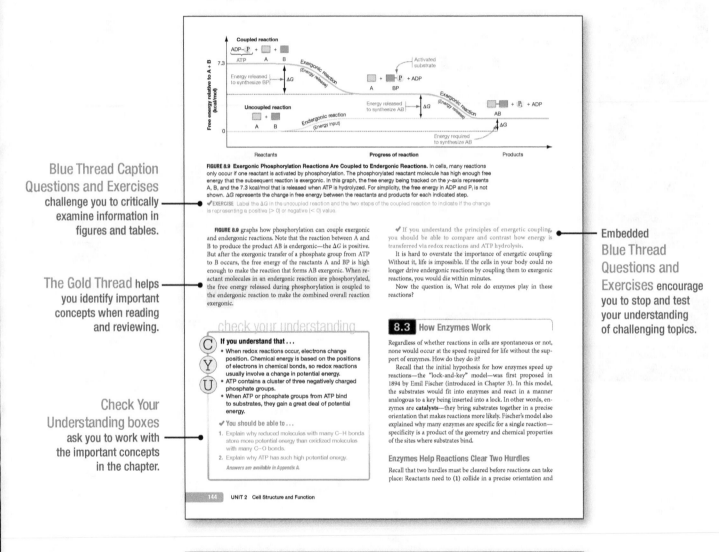

FIGURE 8.9 Exergonic Phosphorylation Reactions Are Coupled to Endergonic Reactions. In cells, many reactions only occur if one reactant is activated by phosphorylation. The phosphorylated reactant molecule has high enough free energy that the subsequent reaction is exergonic. In this graph, the free energy being tracked on the y-axis represents A, B, and the 7.3 kcal/mol that is released when ATP is hydrolyzed. For simplicity, the free energy in ADP and Pᵢ is not shown. ΔG represents the change in free energy between the reactants and products for each indicated step.

✔ **EXERCISE** Label the ΔG in the uncoupled reaction and the two steps of the coupled reaction to indicate if the change is representing a positive (> 0) or negative (< 0) value.

Blue Thread Caption Questions and Exercises challenge you to critically examine information in figures and tables.

FIGURE 8.9 graphs how phosphorylation can couple exergonic and endergonic reactions. Note that the reaction between A and B to produce the product AB is endergonic—the ΔG is positive. But after the exergonic transfer of a phosphate group from ATP to B occurs, the free energy of the reactants A and BP is high enough to make the reaction that forms AB exergonic. When reactant molecules in an endergonic reaction are phosphorylated, the free energy released during phosphorylation is coupled to the endergonic reaction to make the combined overall reaction exergonic.

The Gold Thread helps you identify important concepts when reading and reviewing.

✔ If you understand the principles of energetic coupling, you should be able to compare and contrast how energy is transferred via redox reactions and ATP hydrolysis.

It is hard to overstate the importance of energetic coupling: Without it, life is impossible. If the cells in your body could no longer drive endergonic reactions by coupling them to exergonic reactions, you would die within minutes.

Now the question is, What role do enzymes play in these reactions?

Embedded Blue Thread Questions and Exercises encourage you to stop and test your understanding of challenging topics.

check your understanding

Ⓒ Ⓨ Ⓤ **If you understand that . . .**
* When redox reactions occur, electrons change position. Chemical energy is based on the positions of electrons in chemical bonds, so redox reactions usually involve a change in potential energy.
* ATP contains a cluster of three negatively charged phosphate groups.
* When ATP or phosphate groups from ATP bind to substrates, they gain a great deal of potential energy.

✔ **You should be able to . . .**
1. Explain why reduced molecules with many C–H bonds store more potential energy than oxidized molecules with many C–O bonds.
2. Explain why ATP has such high potential energy.

Answers are available in Appendix A.

Check Your Understanding boxes ask you to work with the important concepts in the chapter.

8.3 How Enzymes Work

Regardless of whether reactions in cells are spontaneous or not, none would occur at the speed required for life without the support of enzymes. How do they do it?

Recall that the initial hypothesis for how enzymes speed up reactions—the "lock-and-key" model—was first proposed in 1894 by Emil Fischer (introduced in Chapter 3). In this model, the substrates would fit into enzymes and react in a manner analogous to a key being inserted into a lock. In other words, enzymes are **catalysts**—they bring substrates together in a precise orientation that makes reactions more likely. Fischer's model also explained why many enzymes are specific for a single reaction—specificity is a product of the geometry and chemical properties of the sites where substrates bind.

Enzymes Help Reactions Clear Two Hurdles

Recall that two hurdles must be cleared before reactions can take place: Reactants need to (1) collide in a precise orientation and

8.2 Nonspontaneous Reactions May Be Driven Using Chemical Energy

* Redox reactions transfer energy by coupling exergonic oxidation reactions to endergonic reduction reactions.
* High-energy C–H bonds may be formed during the reduction step of a redox reaction when an H⁺ is combined with a transferred electron.
* The hydrolysis of ATP is an exergonic reaction and may be used to drive a variety of cellular processes.
* When a phosphate group from ATP is added to a substrate that participates in an endergonic reaction, the potential energy of the substrate is raised enough to make the reaction exergonic and thus spontaneous.

✔ You should be able to explain what energetic coupling means, and why life would not exist without it.

8.3 How Enzymes Work

* Enzymes are protein catalysts. They speed reaction rates but do not affect the change in free energy of the reaction.
* The structure of an enzyme has an active site that brings sub-

End-of-Chapter Blue Thread Exercises, integrated in the chapter summary, help you review the major themes of the chapter and synthesize information.

* Protein cleavage and phosphorylation are examples of how enzymes may be regulated by modifying their primary structure.

✔ You should be able to compare and contrast the effect of allosteric regulation versus phosphorylation on enzyme function.

8.5 Enzymes Can Work Together in Metabolic Pathways

* In cells, enzymes often work together in metabolic pathways that sequentially modify a substrate to make a product.
* A pathway may be regulated by controlling the activity of one enzyme, often the first in the series of reactions. Feedback inhibition results from the accumulation of a product that binds to an enzyme in the pathway and inactivates it.
* Metabolic pathways were vital to the evolution of life, and new pathways continue to evolve in cells.

✔ You should be able to predict how the removal of the intermediate in a two-step metabolic pathway would affect the enzymatic rates of the first and last.

Ⓜ🅑 www.masteringbiology.com

1. MasteringBiology Assignments

Identify gaps in your understanding, then fill them

The Fifth Edition provides many opportunities for you to test yourself and offers helpful learning strategies.

Analyze: Can I recognize underlying patterns and structure?

Evaluate: Can I make judgments on the relative value of ideas and information?

Create: Can I put ideas and information together to generate something new?

Apply: Can I use these ideas in the same way or in a new situation?

Understand: Can I explain this concept in my own words?

Remember: Can I recall the key terms and ideas?

Bloom's Taxonomy describes six learning levels: Remember, Understand, Apply, Analyze, Evaluate, and Create. Questions in the book span all levels, including self-testing at the higher levels to help you develop higher-order thinking skills that will prepare you for exams.

Steps to Building Understanding
Each chapter ends with three groups of questions that build in difficulty:

✓ TEST YOUR KNOWLEDGE
Begin by testing your basic knowledge of new information.

✓ TEST YOUR UNDERSTANDING
Once you're confident with the basics, demonstrate your deeper understanding of the material.

✓ TEST YOUR PROBLEM-SOLVING SKILLS
Work towards mastery of the content by answering questions that challenge you at the highest level of competency.

BIOSKILL 16 using Bloom's taxonomy

Most students have at one time or another wondered why a particular question on an exam seemed so hard, while others seemed easy. The explanation lies in the type of cognitive skills required to answer the question. Let's take a closer look.

NEW! BioSkill Covering Bloom's Taxonomy helps you to recognize question types using the Bloom's cognitive hierarchy, and it provides specific strategies to help you study for questions at all six levels.

Answer Appendix Includes Bloom's Taxonomy Information
Answers to all questions in the text now include the Bloom's level being tested. You can simultaneously practice assessing your understanding of content and recognizing Bloom's levels. Combining this information with the guidance in the BioSkill on Bloom's Taxonomy will help you form a plan to improve your study skills.

✓ Test Your Problem-Solving Skills

13. `analyze` A scientific theory is not a guess—it is an idea whose validity can be tested with data. Both the cell theory and the theory of evolution have been validated by large bodies of observational and experimental data.
14. `apply` If all eukaryotes living today have a nucleus, then it is logical to conclude that the nucleus arose in a common ancestor of all eukaryotes, indicated by the arrow you should have added to the figure. See **FIGURE A1.2.** If it had arisen in a common ancestor of Bacteria or Archaea, then species in those groups would have had to lose the trait—an unlikely event.
15. `evaluate` The data set was so large and diverse that it was no longer reasonable to argue that noncellular life-forms would be discovered. **16.** `apply` b

---

MasteringBiology®
www.masteringbiology.com

NEW! End-of-chapter questions from the book are now available for your professor to assign as homework in MasteringBiology.

Practice scientific thinking and scientific skills

A unique emphasis on the process of scientific discovery and experimental design teaches you how to think like a scientist as you learn fundamental biology concepts.

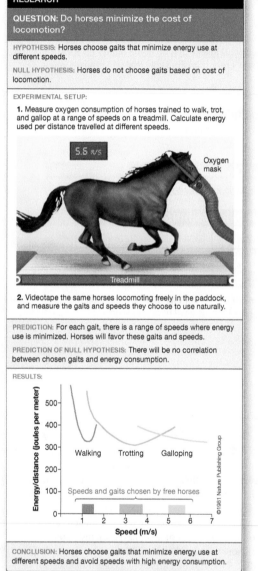

RESEARCH

QUESTION: Do horses minimize the cost of locomotion?

HYPOTHESIS: Horses choose gaits that minimize energy use at different speeds.

NULL HYPOTHESIS: Horses do not choose gaits based on cost of locomotion.

EXPERIMENTAL SETUP:

1. Measure oxygen consumption of horses trained to walk, trot, and gallop at a range of speeds on a treadmill. Calculate energy used per distance travelled at different speeds.

5.8 R/S

Oxygen mask

Treadmill

2. Videotape the same horses locomoting freely in the paddock, and measure the gaits and speeds they choose to use naturally.

PREDICTION: For each gait, there is a range of speeds where energy use is minimized. Horses will favor these gaits and speeds.

PREDICTION OF NULL HYPOTHESIS: There will be no correlation between chosen gaits and energy consumption.

RESULTS:

©1981 Nature Publishing Group

Walking   Trotting   Galloping

Speeds and gaits chosen by free horses

CONCLUSION: Horses choose gaits that minimize energy use at different speeds and avoid speeds with high energy consumption.

FIGURE 48.16 Horses Minimize the Cost of Locomotion by Choosing Appropriate Gaits.
SOURCE: Hoyt, D. F., and C. R. Taylor. 1981. Gait and the energetics of locomotion in horses. *Nature* 292: 239–240.

✔ **QUANTITATIVE** Use the graph to estimate the relative energy expense of galloping rather than trotting at 3.5 meters/second (m/s).

All of the Research Boxes cite the original research paper and include a question that asks you to analyze the design of the experiment or study.

Research Boxes explain how research studies are designed and give you additional practice interpreting data. Each Research Box consistently models the scientific method, presenting the research question, hypotheses, experimental setup, predictions, results, and conclusion. 15 Research Boxes are new to the Fifth Edition.

MasteringBiology®
www.masteringbiology.com

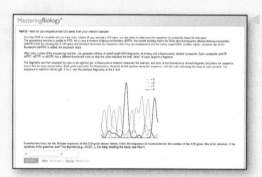

NEW! Solve It Tutorials are available for homework assignments in MasteringBiology and give you an opportunity to work like a scientist through a simulated investigation that requires you to analyze and interpret data.

Experimental Inquiry Tutorials based on some of biology's most seminal experiments give you a chance to analyze data and the reasoning that led scientists from the data to their conclusions.

Experimental Inquiry tutorial topics include:

- What Can You Learn About the Process of Science from Investigating a Cricket's Chirp?
- Which Wavelengths of Light Drive Photosynthesis?
- What Is the Inheritance Pattern of Sex-Linked Traits?
- Does DNA Replication Follow the Conservative, Semiconservative, or Dispersive Model?
- How Do Calcium Ions Help to Prevent Polyspermy During Egg Fertilization?

- Did Natural Selection of Ground Finches Occur When the Environment Changed?
- What Effect Does Auxin Have on Coleoptile Growth?
- What Role Do Genes Play in Appetite Regulation?
- Can a Species' Niche Be Influenced by Interspecific Competition?
- What Factors Influence the Loss of Nutrients from a Forest Ecosystem?

Build important skills scientists use to perform, evaluate, and communicate scientific research.

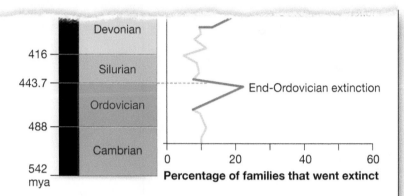

FIGURE 28.14 The Big Five Mass Extinction Events. This graph shows the percentage of lineages called families that went extinct over each interval in the fossil record since the Cambrian explosion. Over 50 percent of families and 90 percent of species went extinct during the end-Permian extinction.

DATA: Benton, M. J., 1995. *Science* 268: 52–58.

✔**QUANTITATIVE** Which extinction event ended the era of the dinosaurs 65 million years ago? About what percentage of families went extinct?

NEW! Graphs and tables now include their data sources, emphasizing the research process that leads to our understanding of biological ideas.

NEW! Quantitative questions are identified throughout the text, helping you practice computational problem solving and data analysis.

Expanded BioSkills Appendix helps you build skills that will be important to your success in biology. At relevant points in the text, you'll find references to the BioSkills appendix that will help you learn and practice foundational skills.

BioSkills Topics include:

- The Metric System and Significant Figures
- Some Common Latin and Greek Roots Used in Biology
- Reading Graphs
- Using Statistical Tests and Interpreting Standard Error Bars
- Combining Probabilities

- Using Logarithms
- Reading a Phylogenetic Tree
- Reading Chemical Structures
- Separating and Visualizing Molecules
- Separating Cell Components by Centrifugation
- Biological Imaging: Microscopy and X-ray Crystallography

- Cell and Tissue Culture Methods
- Model Organisms
- NEW! Primary Literature and Peer Review
- Making Concept Maps
- NEW! Using Bloom's Taxonomy

MasteringBiology®
www.masteringbiology.com

You can access self-paced BioSkills activities in the Study Area, and your instructor can assign additional activities in MasteringBiology.

Visualize biology processes and structures

A carefully crafted visual program helps you gain a better understanding of biology through accurate, appropriately detailed figures.

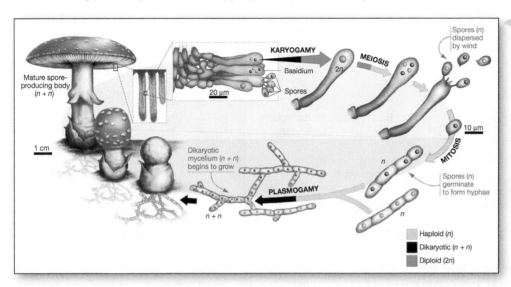

◄ NEW! Redesigned Life Cycle diagrams in Unit 6 and 7 help you compare and contrast processes among different organisms.

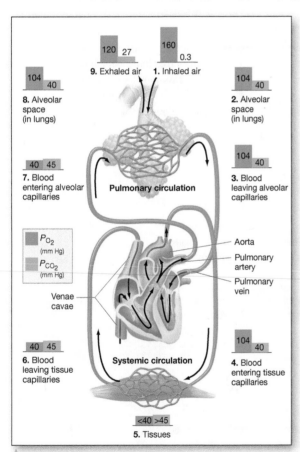

▲ Informative figures help you think through complex biological processes in manageable steps.

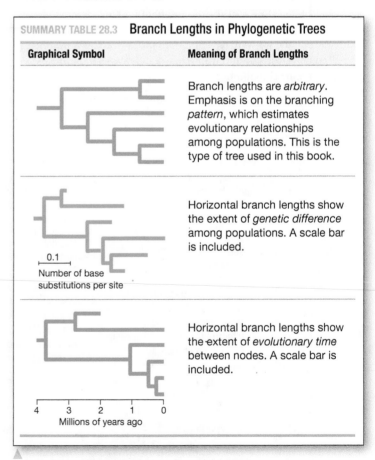

▲ Visual Summary Tables pull together important information in a format that allows for easy comparison and review.

Instructor and Student Resources

For Instructors

Instructor Resource DVD-ROM
978-0-321-86112-2 • 0-321-86112-4

Everything you need for lectures in one place, including video segments that demonstrate how to incorporate active-learning techniques into your own classroom. Enhanced menus make locating and assessing the digital resources for each chapter easy. The Instructor Resource CD/DVD-ROM includes PowerPoint® Lecture Outlines that integrate figures and animations for classroom presentations. All textbook figures, art, and photos are in JPEG format, and all PowerPoint slides and JPEGs have editable labels. Over 300 Instructor Animations accurately depict complex topics and dynamic processes described in the book.

Instructor Guide (Download only)
Available in the instructor resource area of MasteringBiology.®

TestGen® (Download only)
All of the exam questions in the Test Bank have been peer reviewed and student tested, providing questions that set the standard for quality and accuracy. To improve the Test Bank, Metadata from MasteringBiology users has been incorporated directly into the software. Test questions that are ranked according to Bloom's taxonomy and improved TestGen® software makes assembling tests that much easier.

For Students

Study Guide
978-0-321-85832-0 • 0-321-85832-8

The Study Guide presents a breakdown of key biological concepts, difficult topics, and quizzes to help students prepare for exams. Unique to this study guide are four introductory, stand-alone chapters that introduce students to foundational ideas and skills necessary for classroom success: Introduction to Experimentation and Research in the Biological Sciences, Presenting Biological Data, Understanding Patterns in Biology and Improving Study Techniques, and Reading and Writing to Understand Biology. "Looking Forward" and "Looking Back" sections help students make connections across the chapters instead of viewing them as discrete entities.

Practicing Biology: A Student Workbook
978-0-321-88647-7 • 0-321-88647-X

This workbook focuses on key ideas, principles, and concepts that are fundamental to understanding biology. A variety of hands-on activities such as mapping and modeling suit different learning styles and help students discover which topics they need more help on. Students learn biology by doing biology. An instructors guide can be down-loaded from the Instructor Area of MasteringBiology.

MasteringBiology®

www.masteringbiology.com

MasteringBiology is an online homework, tutorial, and assessment system that delivers self-paced tutorials that provide individualized coaching, focus on your course objectives, and respond to each student's progress. The Mastering system helps instructors maximize class time with customizable, easy-to-assign, and automatically graded assessments that motivate students to learn outside of class and arrive prepared for lecture. MasteringBiology is also available with a complete Pearson eText edition of *Biological Science*.

Highlights of the Fifth Edition Item Library include:

* NEW! **assignment options** include Solve It activities, end-of-chapter problems, and questions that accompany new BioSkills and new Big Picture Interactive Concept Maps.
* NEW! **"best of" homework pre-built assignments** help professors assign popular, key content quickly, including a blend of tutorials, end-of-chapter problems, and test bank questions.

* *Get Ready for Biology* and Chemistry Review **assignment options** help students get up to speed with activities that review chemistry, mathematics, and basic biology.

MasteringBiology® Virtual Labs

978-0-321-88644-6 • 0-321-88644-5

MasteringBiology: Virtual Labs is an online environment that promotes critical-thinking skills using virtual experiments and explorations that might be difficult to perform in a wet-lab environment due to time, cost, or safety concerns. MasteringBiology: Virtual Labs offers unique learning experiences in the areas of microscopy, molecular biology, genetics, ecology, and systematics.

For more information, please visit www.pearsonhighered.com/virtualbiologylabs

Detailed Contents

About the Authors

A Letter from Scott:

I started working on *Biological Science* in 1997 with a simple goal: To help change the way biology is taught. After just shy of 20,000 hours of work on four editions of this text, that goal still gets me out of bed in the morning. But instead of focusing my energies on textbook writing, I've decided to devote myself full-time to research on student learning and developing new courses for undergraduate and graduate students at the University of Washington.

So with this edition I am passing the torch—to an all-star cast of leading scientists and educators who have enthusiastically taught from, and contributed to, previous editions of *Biological Science*. Working with them, I have seen the new team bring their passion, talent, and creativity to the book, with expertise that spans the breadth of the life sciences. Just as important, they work beautifully together because they think alike. They are driven by a shared concern for student learning, a commitment to the craft of writing, and a background in evidence-based teaching.

These pages provide a brief introduction to Liz Allison, Michael Black, Greg Podgorski, Kim Quillin, Jon Monroe, and Emily Taylor. As a group, they've built on the book's existing strengths and infused this edition with fresh energy, perspective, and ideas. I'm full of admiration for what they have accomplished, and excited about the impact this edition will have on biology students from all over the world.—*Scott Freeman*

Lizabeth A. Allison is professor and chair of the Biology Department at the College of William & Mary. She received her Ph.D. in Zoology from the University of Washington, specializing in molecular and cellular biology. Before coming to William & Mary, she spent eight years as a faculty member at the University of Canterbury in New Zealand. Liz teaches introductory biology for majors and upper-division molecular biology courses. She has mentored graduate students and more than 80 undergraduate research students, many of them coauthoring papers with her on intracellular trafficking of the thyroid hormone receptor in normal and cancer cells. The recipient of numerous awards, including a State Council for Higher Education in Virginia (SCHEV) Outstanding Faculty Award in 2009, Liz received one of the three inaugural Arts & Sciences Faculty Awards for Teaching Excellence in 2011, and a Plumeri Award for Faculty Excellence in 2012. In addition to her work on this text, she is author of *Fundamental Molecular Biology*, now in its second edition.
Lead Author; Chapter 1 and BioSkills
laalli@wm.edu

Scott Freeman received a Ph.D. in Zoology from the University of Washington and was subsequently awarded an Alfred P. Sloan Postdoctoral Fellowship in Molecular Evolution at Princeton University. He has done research in evolutionary biology on topics ranging from nest parasitism to the molecular systematics of the blackbird family and is coauthor, with Jon Herron, of the standard-setting undergraduate text *Evolutionary Analysis*. Scott is the recipient of a Distinguished Teaching Award from the University of Washington and is currently a Senior Lecturer in the UW Department of Biology, where he teaches introductory biology for majors, a writing-intensive course for majors called The Tree of Life, and a graduate seminar in college science teaching. Scott's current research focuses on how active learning affects student learning and academic performance.

Michael Black received his Ph.D. in Microbiology & Immunology from Stanford University School of Medicine as a Howard Hughes Predoctoral Fellow. After graduation, he studied cell biology as a Burroughs Wellcome Postdoctoral Fellow at the MRC Laboratory of Molecular Biology in Cambridge, England. His current research focuses on the use of molecules to identify and track the transmission of microbes in the environment. Michael is a professor of Cell & Molecular Biology at California Polytechnic State University in San Luis Obispo, where he teaches introductory and advanced classes for majors in cell biology and microbiology. In addition to his teaching and research activities, Michael serves as the director of the Undergraduate Biotechnology Lab, where he works alongside undergraduate technicians to integrate research projects and inquiry-based activities into undergraduate classes.
Chapters 2–12, 36, and 51
mblack@calpoly.edu

Greg Podgorski received his Ph.D. in Molecular and Cellular Biology from Penn State University and has been a postdoctoral fellow at the Max Plank Institute for Biochemistry and Columbia University. His research interests are in biology education, developmental genetics, and computational biology. Greg's most recent work has been in mathematical modeling of how patterns of different cell types emerge during development and how tumors recruit new blood vessels in cancer. Greg has been teaching at Utah State University for more than 20 years in courses that include introductory biology for majors and for nonmajors, genetics, cell biology, developmental biology, and microbiology, and he has offered courses in nonmajors biology in Beijing and Hong Kong. He's won teaching awards at Utah State University and has been recognized by the National Academies as a Teaching Fellow and a Teaching Mentor.

Chapters 13–24
greg.podgorski@usu.edu

Jon Monroe is professor of Biology at James Madison University in Harrisonburg, Virginia. Jon completed his undergraduate work in Botany at the University of Michigan and his graduate work in Plant Physiology at Cornell University. He began his current position after a postdoc in biochemistry at Michigan State University. He currently teaches Plant Biology, and Cell and Molecular Biology. Jon's interest in plants is broad, ranging from systematics and taxonomy to physiology and biochemistry. His research, mostly with undergraduates, uses Arabidopsis thaliana to study the functions of a family of β-amylase genes in starch metabolism. Jon has been active in promoting undergraduate research through his work with the American Society of Plant Biologists (ASPB) and the Council on Undergraduate Research. He has received ASPB's Excellence in Teaching award and James Madison University Alumni Association's Distinguished Faculty Award.

Chapters 29–32; 37–41
monroejd@jmu.edu

Kim Quillin received her B.A. in Biology at Oberlin College *summa cum laude* and her Ph.D. in Integrative Biology from the University of California, Berkeley (as a National Science Foundation Graduate Fellow). Kim has worked in the trenches with Scott Freeman on every edition of *Biological Science*, starting with the ground-up development of the illustrations in the first edition in 1999 and expanding her role in each edition, always with the focus of helping students to think like biologists. Kim currently teaches introductory biology at Salisbury University, a member of the University System of Maryland, where she is actively involved in the ongoing student-centered reform of the concepts-and-methods course for biology majors. Her current research focuses on the scholarship of teaching and learning with an emphasis on measuring science process skills and the advantages and pitfalls of active multimedia learning.

Chapters 25–28; 33–35; 48; 52–57
kxquillin@salisbury.edu

Emily Taylor earned a B.A. in English at the University of California, Berkeley followed by a Ph.D. in Biological Sciences from Arizona State University, where she conducted research in the field of environmental physiology as a National Science Foundation Graduate Research Fellow. She is currently an associate professor of Biological Sciences at the California Polytechnic State University in San Luis Obispo, California. Her student-centered research program focuses on the endocrine and reproductive physiology of free-ranging reptiles, especially rattlesnakes. She teaches numerous undergraduate and graduate courses, including introductory biology, anatomy and physiology, and herpetology, and received the California Faculty Association's Distinguished Educator Award in 2010 and Cal Poly's Distinguished Teaching Award in 2012. Her revision of Unit 8 is her first foray into textbook writing.

Chapters 42–50
etaylor@calpoly.edu

Preface to Instructors

The first edition of *Biological Science* was visionary in its unique emphasis on the process of scientific discovery and experimental design—teaching how we know what we know. The goal was for students not only to learn the language of biology and understand fundamental concepts but also to begin to apply those concepts in new situations, analyze experimental design, synthesize results, and evaluate hypotheses and data—to learn how to think like biologists. Each edition since has proudly expanded on this vision. The Fifth Edition is no exception.

A team of six dedicated teacher-scholars has joined Scott to build on and refine the original vision, and by so doing, make the book an even better teaching and learning tool. The pace of biological discovery is rapid, and with each novel breakthrough it becomes even more challenging to decide what is essential to include in an introductory biology text. Pulling together an author team with firsthand expertise from molecules to ecosystems has ensured that the content of the Fifth Edition reflects cutting-edge biology that is pitched at the right level for introductory students and is as accurate and as exciting as ever for instructors and students alike.

New findings from education research continue to inform and inspire the team's thinking about *Biological Science*—we know more today than ever before about how students learn. These findings demand that we constantly look for new ways to increase student engagement in the learning process, and to help instructors align course activities and learning goals with testing strategies.

The New Coauthors

The new coauthor team brings a broad set of talents and interests to the project, motivated by a deep commitment to undergraduate teaching, whether at a small liberal arts college or a large university. Kim Quillin has been a partner in this textbook in every edition. For the Fifth Edition, she revised chapters across three units in addition to spearheading the continued effort to enhance the visual-teaching program. Michael Black, Greg Podgorski, Jon Monroe, and Emily Taylor, who served as unit advisors on the Fourth Edition, were already familiar with the book. And most of the authorial team have been avid users of previous editions for many years.

Core Values

Together, the coauthor team has worked to extend the vision and maintain the core values of *Biological Science*—to provide a book for instructors who embrace the challenge of boosting students to higher levels of learning, and to provide a book for students that helps them each step of the way in learning to think like scientists. Dedicated instructors have high expectations of their students—the Fifth Edition provides scaffolding to help students learn at the level called for by the National Academy of Sciences, the Howard Hughes Medical Institute, the American Association of Medical Academies, and the National Science Foundation.

What's New in This Edition

The Fifth Edition contains many new or expanded features, all of them targeted at ways to help students learn to construct their own knowledge and think like biologists.

- **Road Maps** The new Road Maps at the beginning of each chapter pair with the Big Picture concept maps introduced in the Fourth Edition. Together they help students navigate chapter content and see the forest for the trees. Each Road Map starts with a purpose statement that tells students what they can expect to learn from each chapter. It then goes on to visually group and organize information to help students anticipate key ideas as well as recognize meaningful relationships and connections between the ideas.

- **The Big Picture** Introduced in the Fourth Edition, Big Picture concept maps integrate words and visuals to help students synthesize information about challenging topics that span multiple chapters and units. In response to requests from instructors and students, three new Big Pictures focused on additional tough topics have been added: Doing Biology, The Chemistry of Life, and Plant and Animal Form and Function. In addition, the Ecology Big Picture is completely revised to reflect changes to that unit.

- **New Chapters** Two new chapters are added to better serve instructors and students. Unit 2 now contains a new Chapter 8, Energy and Enzymes: An Introduction to Metabolic Pathways. This chapter consolidates these critical topics in a place where students and instructors need it most—right before the chapters on cellular respiration and photosynthesis. In the Fourth Edition, animal movement was discussed in a chapter largely focused on animal sensory systems. In the Fifth Edition, this important topic is treated in depth in a new Chapter 48, Animal Movement, that explores how muscle and skeletal systems work together to produce locomotion.

- **New BioSkills** Instructors recognize that biology students need to develop foundational science skills in addition to content knowledge. While these skills are emphasized throughout the book, *Biological Science*, beginning with the Third

Edition, has provided a robust set of materials and activities to guide students who need extra help. To promote even fuller use of this resource, the BioSkills are now updated, expanded, and reorganized. New in this edition are a discussion of significant figures within the BioSkills on the Metric System, and two new BioSkills on Primary Literature and Peer Review and Using Bloom's Taxonomy. BioSkills are located in Appendix B, and practice activities can be assigned online in MasteringBiology®.

- **Promotion of Quantitative Skills** Reports like *Biology 2010, Scientific Foundations for Future Physicians*, and *Vision and Change* all place a premium on quantitative skills. To infuse a quantitative component throughout the text, new and existing quantitative questions are flagged in each chapter to encourage students to work on developing their ability to read or create a graph, perform or interpret a calculation, or use other forms of quantitative reasoning.

- **Bloom's Taxonomy** In the Fifth Edition, all questions in the text are assigned a Bloom's Taxonomy level to help both students and instructors understand whether a question requires higher-order or lower-order cognitive skills. Questions span all six Bloom's levels. (Bloom's levels are identified in Appendix A: Answers.) The coauthors were trained by experts Mary Pat Wenderoth and Clarissa Dirks[1] to ensure we followed a process that would result in high inter-rater reliability—or agreement among raters—in assigning Bloom's levels to questions. The new BioSkill, Using Bloom's Taxonomy, explains the six Bloom's levels to students and offers a practical guide to the kinds of study activities best suited for answering questions at each level.

- **Expanded Emphasis on "Doing Biology"** A constant hallmark of this text is its emphasis on experimental evidence—on teaching how we know what we know. To reflect the progress of science, in the Fifth Edition, the coauthor team replaced many experiments with fresh examples and added new Research Boxes. And as noted earlier, they added a new Big Picture on Doing Biology, focusing on the process of science and the organizational levels of biology. Data sources are now cited for all graphs and data tables to model the importance of citing data sources to students. Updated Research Box questions continue to encourage students to analyze some aspect of experimental design. Also new to this edition is a BioSkill on Primary Literature and Peer Review.

- **Art Program** The art program is further enhanced in this edition by the addition of more illustrated summary tables. These tables make subject areas more accessible to visual learners and reinforce key concepts of the chapter. Many of the life-cycle figures in Unit 6 are significantly overhauled.

[1] Crowe, A., C. Dirks, and M. P. Wenderoth. 2008. Biology in Bloom: Implementing Bloom's Taxonomy to enhance student learning in biology. *CBE–Life Sciences Education* 7: 368–381.

Updated Blue Thread Scaffolding

In the Third and Fourth editions of *Biological Science*, a metacognitive tool was formulated as the now popular feature known as "Blue Thread"—sets of questions designed to help students identify what they do and don't understand. The fundamental idea is that if students really understand a piece of information or a concept, they should be able to do something with it.

In the Fifth Edition, the Blue Thread is revised to reflect changes in chapter content, and to incorporate user feedback. Blue-Thread questions appear in the following locations:

- **In-text "You should be able to's"** offer exercises on topics that professors and students have identified as the most difficult concepts in each chapter.

- **Caption questions and exercises** challenge students to examine the information in a figure or table critically—not just absorb it.

- **Check Your Understanding boxes** present two to three tasks that students should be able to complete in order to demonstrate a mastery of summarized key ideas.

- **Chapter summaries** include "You should be able to" problems or exercises related to each key concept.

- **End-of-chapter** questions are organized in three levels of increasing difficulty so students can build from lower to higher-order cognitive questions.

Integration of Media

The textbook continues to be supported by MasteringBiology®, the most powerful online homework, tutorial, and assessment system available. Tutorials follow the Socratic method, coaching students to the correct answer by offering feedback specific to a student's misconceptions as well as providing hints students can access if they get stuck. Instructors can associate content with publisher-provided learning outcomes or create their own. Content highlights include the following:

- **NEW! Solve It Tutorials** These activities allow students to act like scientists in simulated investigations. Each tutorial presents an interesting, real-world question that students will answer by analyzing and interpreting data.

- **Experimental Inquiry Tutorials** The call to teach students about the process of science has never been louder. To support such teaching, there are 10 interactive tutorials on classic scientific experiments—ranging from Meselson–Stahl on DNA replication to the Grants' work on Galápagos finches and Connell's work on competition. Students who use these tutorials should be better prepared to think critically about experimental design and evaluate the wider implications of the data—preparing them to do the work of real scientists in the future.

- **BioFlix® Animations and Tutorials** BioFlix are movie-quality, 3-D animations that focus on the most difficult core topics and are accompanied by in-depth, online tutorials that provide hints and feedback to guide student learning. Eighteen BioFlix animations and tutorials tackle topics such as meiosis, mitosis, DNA replication, photosynthesis, homeostasis, and the carbon cycle.

- **NEW! End-of-Chapter Questions** Multiple choice end-of-chapter questions are now available to assign in MasteringBiology.

- **Blue-Thread Questions** Over 500 questions based on the Blue-Thread Questions in the textbook are assignable in MasteringBiology.

- **Big Picture Tutorials** Interactive concept map activities based on the Big Picture figures in the textbook are assignable in MasteringBiology, including tutorials to support the three new Big Pictures: Doing Biology, The Chemistry of Life, and Plant and Animal Form and Function.

- **BioSkills Activities** Activities based on the BioSkills content in the textbook are assignable in MasteringBiology, including activities to support the new BioSkills on Primary Literature and Peer Review and Using Bloom's Taxonomy.

- **Reading Quiz Questions** Every chapter includes reading quiz questions you can assign to ensure students read the textbook and understand the basics. These quizzes are perfect as a pre-lecture assignment to get students into the content before class, allowing you to use class time more effectively.

Serving a Community of Teachers

All of us on the coauthor team are deeply committed to students and to supporting the efforts of dedicated teachers. Doing biology is what we love. At various points along our diverse paths, we have been inspired by our own teachers when we were students, and now are inspired by our colleagues as we strive to become even better teacher-scholars. In the tradition of all previous editions of *Biological Science*, we have tried to infuse this textbook with the spirit and practice of evidence-based teaching. We welcome your comments, suggestions, and questions.

Thank you for your work on behalf of your students.

Content Highlights of the Fifth Edition

As discussed in the preface, a major focus of this revision is to enhance the pedagogical utility of *Biological Science*. Another major goal is to ensure that the content reflects the current state of science and is accurate. The expanded author team has scrutinized every chapter to add new, relevant content, update descriptions when appropriate, and adjust the approach to certain topics to enhance student comprehension. In this section, some of the key content improvements to the textbook are highlighted.

Chapter 1 Biology and the Tree of Life A concept map summarizing the defining characteristics of life is added. The process of doing biology coverage is expanded to include discussion of both experimental and descriptive studies, and more rigorous definitions of the terms hypothesis and theory.

Chapter 2 Water and Carbon: The Chemical Basis of Life A stronger emphasis on chemical evolution is threaded throughout the chapter to bring chemistry to life for the student reader. Two prominent models for chemical evolution are introduced; the historic Miller prebiotic soup experiment was moved here. Advanced discussion of energy and chemical reactions was moved to a new chapter (see Chapter 8).

Chapter 3 Protein Structure and Function The chapter is reorganized to emphasize the link between structure and function, from amino acids to folded proteins. Updated content illustrates that protein shapes are flexible and dynamic, and may remain incompletely folded until the protein interacts with other molecules or ions. Details of how enzymes work were moved to Chapter 8.

Chapter 4 Nucleic Acids and the RNA World New experimental results concerning the synthesis of nucleotides and nucleic acids in a prebiotic environment are discussed. The section on the RNA world is expanded to include the artificial evolution of a novel ribozyme involved in nucleotide synthesis.

Chapter 5 An Introduction to Carbohydrates The molecular basis for resistance of structural polymers, such as cellulose, to degradation is clarified. A new research box illustrates the role of carbohydrates in cellular recognition and attachment using the egg and sperm of mice as a model system.

Chapter 6 Lipids, Membranes, and the First Cells New content on lipid and membrane evolution and the proposed characteristics of the first protocell is introduced. The aquaporin and potassium channel figures are updated; how key amino acids serve as selectivity filters is now highlighted.

Chapter 7 Inside the Cell Several new electron micrographs were selected to more clearly illustrate cell component structure and function. A new figure is added to better depict the pulse–chase assay used to identify the secretory pathway. Coverage of nuclear transport is expanded to differentiate between passive diffusion and active nuclear import. Updated content emphasizes the role of the cytoskeleton in localizing organelles, and how polarity of microtubules and microfilaments influences their growth rate.

Chapter 8 Energy and Enzymes: An Introduction to Pathways This new chapter pulls together concepts in energy, chemical reactions, and enzymes that previously were covered in three different chapters. Oxidation and reduction reactions are emphasized to prepare students for Chapters 9 and 10. The energetics behind ATP hydrolysis and its role in driving endergonic reactions is discussed, and figures are revised to better illustrate the process. Updated content on enzyme regulation and a new process figure show a model for how metabolic pathways may have evolved.

Chapter 9 Cellular Respiration and Fermentation Two new summary tables for glycolysis and the citric acid cycle are added that provide the names of the enzymes and the reaction each catalyzes. New content is introduced to propose a connection between the universal nature of the proton motive force and the story of the chemical evolution of life.

Chapter 11 Cell–Cell Interactions Coverage of extracellular matrix structure and function is expanded, including its role in intercellular adhesions and cell signaling. The plant apoplast and symplast are now introduced as key terms in the text and illustrated in a new figure. New content and a new figure on unicellular models for intercellular communication via pheromone sensing (yeast) and quorum sensing (slime mold) are added.

Chapter 12 The Cell Cycle A new figure helps explain the pulse–chase assay for identifying phases of the cell cycle. Content is added to the text and to a figure that illustrates the similarities between chromosome segregation in eukaryotes and prokaryotes. A revised description of anaphase emphasizes how microtubule fraying at the kinetochore can drive chromosome movement. The explanation of how phosphorylation and dephosphorylation turns on MPF activity is updated to reflect current research.

Chapter 15 DNA and the Gene: Synthesis and Repair A new research figure is added that focuses on the relationship between telomere length and senescence in cultured somatic cells.

Chapter 16 How Genes Work Coverage of the evolving concept of the gene and of different types of RNA is expanded. A figure showing the karyotype of a cancer cell is revised to improve clarity.

Chapter 17 Transcription, RNA Processing, and Translation The sections on transcription in bacteria and eukaryotes are now separated, and content on charging tRNAs was moved to a new section. The discussion of translation is reorganized, first to emphasize the process in bacteria and then to highlight differences in eukaryotes.

Chapter 18 Control of Gene Expression in Bacteria Coverage of *lac* operon positive regulation is updated to reflect current research. A new section and new process figure on global gene regulation are added, using the *lexA* regulon as an example.

Chapter 19 Control of Gene Expression in Eukaryotes Extensive updates to the discussion of epigenetics include a new research box and a section on DNA methylation. Coverage of transcription initiation is updated to reflect current science. A new figure illustrates the role of p53 in the cell cycle in normal and cancerous cells.

Chapter 20 Analyzing and Engineering Genes The material on sequencing the Neanderthal genome is updated, including evidence of limited Neanderthal genetic material in some modern human populations. New information on current generation sequencing technologies and massive parallelism is added. Recent advances in gene therapy are highlighted.

Chapter 21 Genomics and Beyond Extensive updates throughout reflect recent advances in genomics. Changes include sequence database statistics, genomes that have been sequenced to study evolutionary relationships, and new figures illustrating gene count versus genome size in prokaryotes and eukaryotes and functional classes of human DNA sequences. A new section on systems biology is added. Also included are notes on the discovery of widespread transcription of eukaryotic genomes, deep sequencing, and the spectrum of mutations in human tumors.

Chapter 29 Bacteria and Archaea The chapter is updated to include a description of metagenomic experiments with an emphasis on the role of gut bacteria in digestion. A newly recognized phylum of Archaea, the Thaumarchaeota, is included, and the table comparing key characteristics of the Bacteria, Archaea, and Eukarya is streamlined.

Chapter 30 Protists For simplicity, protist lineages are now referred to throughout the chapter by their more familiar common names. Also, some key lineage boxes were consolidated to trim the number to one box per major lineage. Discussion of the origin of the nuclear envelope and mitochondria is expanded to reflect new thinking on the evolution of eukaryotic cells. Protist life cycle figures are significantly overhauled.

Chapter 36 Viruses New content focuses on how viruses contribute to evolution via lateral gene transfer and direct addition of genes to cellular genomes. Content is updated and expanded on viral structure and function, and on lytic and latent infections. Three new figures are added, including a comparison of replication of viruses and cells, how pandemic strains of influenza arise via reassortment, and the devastating impact of the 1918 influenza pandemic.

Chapter 48 Animal Movement This new chapter introduces the importance of movement in animals, building from small to large scale. The mechanism of muscle contraction (with revised figures) is covered, followed by discussions of types of muscle tissue (with new content on skeletal-muscle fiber types and parallel- versus pennate-muscle fiber orientation), and skeletal systems (hydrostatic skeletons, exoskeletons, endoskeletons). A completely new final section discusses how biologists study locomotion on land, in the air, and in the water.

Acknowledgments

Reviewers

The peer review system is the key to quality and clarity in science publishing. In addition to providing a filter, the investment that respected individuals make in vetting the material—catching errors or inconsistencies and making suggestions to improve the presentation—gives authors, editors, and readers confidence that the text meets rigorous professional standards.

Peer review plays the same role in textbook publishing. The time and care that this book's reviewers have invested is a tribute to their professional integrity, their scholarship, and their concern for the quality of teaching. Virtually every paragraph in this edition has been revised and improved based on insights from the following individuals.

Tamarah Adair, *Baylor University*
Sandra D. Adams, *Montclair State University*
Marc Albrecht, *University of Nebraska at Kearney*
Larry Alice, *Western Kentucky University*
Leo M. Alves, *Manhattan College*
David R. Angelini, *American University*
Dan Ardia, *Franklin & Marshall College*
Paul Arriola, *Elmhurst College*
Davinderjit K. Bagga, *University of Montevallo*
Susan Barrett, *Wheaton College*
Donald Baud, *University of Memphis*
Vernon W. Bauer, *Francis Marion University*
Robert Bauman, *Amarillo College*
Christopher Beck, *Emory University*
Vagner Benedito, *West Virginia University*
Scott Bingham, *Arizona State University*
Stephanie Bingham, *Barry University*
Wendy Birky, *California State University, Northridge*
Jason Blank, *California Polytechnic State University*
Kristopher A. Blee, *California State University, Chico*
Margaret Bloch-Qazi, *Gustavus Adolphus College*
Lanh Bloodworth, *Florida State College at Jacksonville*
Catherine H. Borer, *Berry College*
James Bottesch, *Brevard Community College*
Jacqueline K. Bowman, *Arkansas Tech University*
John Bowman, *University of California, Davis*
Chris Brochu, *University of Iowa*
Matthew Brown, *Dalhousie University*
Mark Browning, *Purdue University*
Carolyn J. W. Bunde, *Idaho State University*
David Byres, *Florida State College at Jacksonville*
Michael Campbell, *Penn State Erie*
Manel Camps, *University of California, Santa Cruz*
Geralyn M. Caplan, *Owensboro Community and Technical College*
Richard Cardullo, *University of California, Riverside*

David Carlini, *American University*
Dale Casamatta, *University of North Florida*
Deborah Chapman, *University of Pittsburgh*
Joe Coelho, *Quincy University*
Allen Collins, *Smithsonian Museum of Natural History*
Robert A. Colvin, *Ohio University*
Kimberly L. Conner, *Florida State College at Jacksonville*
Karen Curto, *University of Pittsburgh*
Clarissa Dirks, *Evergreen State College*
Peter Ducey, *SUNY Cortland*
Erastus Dudley, *Huntingdon College*
Jeffrey P. Duguay, *Delta State University*
Tod Duncan, *University of Colorado, Denver*
Joseph Esdin, *University of California, Los Angeles*
Brent Ewers, *University of Wyoming*
Amy Farris, *Ivy Tech Community College*
Bruce Fisher, *Roane State Community College*
Ryan Fisher, *Salem State University*
David Fitch, *New York University*
Elizabeth Fitch, *Motlow State Community College*
Michael P. Franklin, *California State University, Northridge*
Susannah French, *Utah State University*
Caitlin Gabor, *Texas State University*
Matthew Gilg, *University of North Florida*
Kendra Greenlee, *North Dakota State University*
Patricia A. Grove, *College of Mount Saint Vincent*
Nancy Guild, *University of Colorado, Boulder*
Cynthia Hemenway, *North Carolina State University*
Christopher R. Herlihy, *Middle Tennessee State University*
Kendra Hill, *South Dakota State University*
Sara Hoot, *University of Wisconsin, Milwaukee*
Kelly Howe, *University of New Mexico*
Robin Hulbert, *California Polytechnic State University*
Rick Jellen, *Brigham Young University*
Russell Johnson, *Colby College*
William Jira Katembe, *Delta State University*
Elena K. Keeling, *California Polytechnic State University*
Jill B. Keeney, *Juniata College*
Greg Kelly, *University of Western Ontario*
Scott L. Kight, *Montclair State University*
Charles Knight, *California Polytechnic State University*
Jenny Knight, *University of Colorado, Boulder*
William Kroll, *Loyola University Chicago*
Dominic Lannutti, *El Paso Community College*
Brenda Leady, *University of Toledo*
David Lindberg, *University of California, Berkeley*
Barbara Lom, *Davidson College*
Robert Maxwell, *Georgia State University*
Marshall D. McCue, *St. Mary's University*
Kurt A. McKean, *SUNY Albany*
Michael Meighan, *University of California, Berkeley*
John Merrill, *Michigan State University*

Richard Merritt, *Houston Community College*
Alan Molumby, *University of Illinois at Chicago*
Jeremy Montague, *Barry University*
Chad E. Montgomery, *Truman State University*
Kimberly D. Moore, *Lone Star College System, North Harris*
Michael Morgan, *Berry College*
James Mulrooney, *Central Connecticut State University*
John D. Nagy, *Scottsdale Community College*
Margaret Olney, *St. Martin's University*
Nathan Okia, *Auburn University at Montgomery*
Robert Osuna, *SUNY Albany*
Daniel Panaccione, *West Virginia University*
Stephanie Pandolfi, *Michigan State University*
Michael Rockwell Parker, *Monell Chemical Senses Center*
Lisa Parks, *North Carolina State University*
Nancy Pelaez, *Purdue University*
Shelley W. Penrod, *Lone Star College System, North Harris*
Andrea Pesce, *James Madison University*
Raymond Pierotti, *University of Kansas*
Melissa Ann Pilgrim, *University of South Carolina Upstate*
Paul Pillitteri, *Southern Utah University*
Debra Pires, *University of California, Los Angeles*
P. David Polly, *Indiana University, Bloomington*
Vanessa Quinn, *Purdue University North Central*
Stacey L. Raimondi, *Elmhurst College*
Stephanie Randell, *McLennan Community College*
Marceau Ratard, *Delgado Community College*
Flona Redway, *Barry University*
Srebrenka Robic, *Agnes Scott College*
Dave Robinson, *Bellarmine University*
George Robinson, *SUNY Albany*
Adam W. Rollins, *Lincoln Memorial University*
Amanda Rosenzweig, *Delgado Community College*
Leonard C. Salvatori, *Indian River State College*
Dee Ann Sato, *Cypress College*
Leena Sawant, *Houston Community College*
Jon Scales, *Midwestern State University*
Oswald Schmitz, *Yale University*
Joan Sharp, *Simon Fraser University*
Julie Schroer, *North Dakota State University*
Timothy E. Shannon, *Francis Marion University*
Lynnette Sievert, *Emporia State University*
Susan Skambis, *Valencia College*
Ann E. Stapleton, *University of North Carolina, Wilmington*
Mary-Pat Stein, *California State University, Northridge*
Christine Strand, *California Polytechnic State University*
Denise Strickland, *Midlands Technical College*
Jackie Swanik, *Wake Technical Community College*
Billie J. Swalla, *University of Washington*
Zuzana Swigonova, *University of Pittsburgh*
Briana Timmerman, *University of South Carolina*
Catherine Ueckert, *Northern Arizona University*
Sara Via, *University of Maryland, College Park*
Thomas J. Volk, *University of Wisconsin–La Crosse*
Jeffrey Walck, *Middle Tennessee State University*
Andrea Weeks, *George Mason University*
Margaret S. White, *Scottsdale Community College*
Steven D. Wilt, *Bellarmine University*
Candace Winstead, *California Polytechnic State University*
James A. Wise, *Hampton University*

Correspondents

One of the most enjoyable interactions we have as textbook authors is correspondence or conversations with researchers and teachers who take the time and trouble to contact us to discuss an issue with the book, or who respond to our queries about a particular data set or study. We are always amazed and heartened by the generosity of these individuals. They care, deeply.

Lawrence Alice, *Western Kentucky University*
David Baum, *University of Wisconsin–Madison*
Meredith Blackwell, *Louisiana State University*
Nancy Burley, *University of California, Irvine*
Thomas Breithaupt, *University of Hull*
Philip Cantino, *Ohio University*
Allen Collins, *Smithsonian Museum of Natural History*
Robert Full, *University of California, Berkeley*
Arundhati Ghosh, *University of Pittsburgh*
Jennifer Gottwald, *University of Wisconsin–Madison*
Jon Harrison, *Arizona State University*
David Hawksworth, *Natural History Museum, London*
Jim Herrick, *James Madison University*
John Hunt, *University of Exeter*
Doug Jensen, *Converse College*
Scott Kight, *Montclair State University*
Scott Kirkton, *Union College*
Mimi Koehl, *University of California, Berkeley*
Rodger Kram, *University of Colorado*
Matthew McHenry, *University of California, Irvine*
Alison Miyamoto, *California State University, Fullerton*
Sean Menke, *Lake Forest College*
Rich Mooi, *California Academy of Sciences*
Michael Oliver, *MalawiCichlids.com*
M. Rockwell Parker, *Monell Chemical Senses Center*
Andrea Pesce, *James Madison University*
Chris Preston, *Monterey Bay Aquarium Research Institute*
Scott Sakaluk, *Illinois State University*
Kyle Seifert, *James Madison University*
Jos Snoeks, *Royal Museum for Central Africa*
Jeffrey Spring, *University of Louisiana*
Christy Strand, *California Polytechnic State University, San Luis Obispo*
Torsten Struck, *University of Osnabrueck, Germany*
Oswald Schmitz, *Yale University*
Ian Tattersal, *American Museum of Natural History*
Robert Turgeon, *Cornell University*
Tom Volk, *University of Wisconsin–La Crosse*
Naomi Wernick, *University of Massachusetts, Lowell*

Supplements Contributors

Instructors depend on an impressive array of support materials—in print and online—to design and deliver their courses. The student experience would be much weaker without the study guide, test bank, activities, animations, quizzes, and tutorials written by the following individuals.

Brian Bagatto, *University of Akron*
Scott Bingham, *Arizona State University*
Jay L. Brewster, *Pepperdine University*

Mirjana Brockett, *Georgia Institute of Technology*
Warren Burggren, *University of North Texas*
Jeff Carmichael, *University of North Dakota*
Tim Christensen, *East Carolina University*
Erica Cline, *University of Washington—Tacoma*
Patricia Colberg, *University of Wyoming*
Elia Crisucci, *University of Pittsburgh*
Elizabeth Cowles, *Eastern Connecticut State University*
Clarissa Dirks, *Evergreen State College*
Lisa Elfring, *University of Arizona, Tucson*
Brent Ewers, *University of Wyoming*
Rebecca Ferrell, *Metropolitan State University of Denver*
Miriam Ferzli, *North Carolina State University*
Cheryl Frederick, *University of Washington*
Cindee Giffen, *University of Wisconsin–Madison*
Kathy M. Gillen, *Kenyon College*
Linda Green, *Georgia Institute of Technology*
Christopher Harendza, *Montgomery County Community College*
Cynthia Hemenway, *North Carolina State University*
Laurel Hester, *University of South Carolina*
Jean Heitz, *University of Wisconsin–Madison*
Tracey Hickox, *University of Illinois, Urbana–Champaign*
Jacob Kerby, *University of South Dakota*
David Kooyman, *Brigham Young University*
Barbara Lom, *Davidson College*
Cindy Malone, *California State University, Northridge*
Jim Manser, retired, *Harvey Mudd College*
Jeanette McGuire, *Michigan State University*
Mark Music, *Indian River State College*
Jennifer Nauen, *University of Delaware*
Chris Pagliarulo, *University of California, Davis*
Stephanie Scher Pandolfi, *Michigan State University*
Lisa Parks, *North Carolina State University*
Debra Pires, *University of California, Los Angeles*
Carol Pollock, *University of British Columbia*
Jessica Poulin, *University at Buffalo, the State University of New York*
Vanessa Quinn, *Purdue University North Central*
Eric Ribbens, *Western Illinois University*
Christina T. Russin, *Northwestern University*
Leonard Salvatori, *Indian River State College*
Joan Sharp, *Simon Fraser University*
Chrissy Spencer, *Georgia Institute of Technology*
Mary-Pat Stein, *California State University, Northridge*
Suzanne Simon-Westendorf, *Ohio University*
Fred Wasserman, *Boston University*
Cindy White, *University of Northern Colorado*
Edward Zalisko, *Blackburn College*

Book Team

Anyone who has been involved in producing a textbook knows that many people work behind the scenes to make it all happen. The coauthor team is indebted to the many talented individuals who have made this book possible.

Development editors Mary Catherine Hager, Moira Lerner-Nelson, and Bill O'Neal provided incisive comments on the revised manuscript. Fernanda Oyarzun and Adam Steinberg used their artistic sense, science skills, and love of teaching to hone the figures for many chapters.

The final version of the text was copyedited by Chris Thillen and expertly proofread by Pete Shanks. The final figure designs were rendered by Imagineering Media Services and carefully proofread by Frank Purcell. Maureen Spuhler, Eric Schrader, and Kristen Piljay researched images for the Fifth Edition.

The book's clean, innovative design was developed by Mark Ong and Emily Friel. Text and art were skillfully set in the design by S4Carlisle Publishing Services. The book's production was supervised by Lori Newman and Mike Early.

The extensive supplements program was managed by Brady Golden and Katie Cook. All of the individuals mentioned—and more—were supported with cheerful, dedicated efficiency by Editorial Assistant Leslie Allen for the first half of the project; Eddie Lee has since stepped in to skillfully fill this role.

Creating MasteringBiology® tutorials and activities also requires a team. Media content development was overseen by Tania Mlawer and Sarah Jensen, who benefited from the program expertise of Caroline Power and Caroline Ross. Joseph Mochnick and Daniel Ross worked together as media producers. Lauren Fogel (VP, Director, Media Development), Stacy Treco (VP, Director, Media Product Strategy), and Laura ensured that the complete media program that accompanies the Fifth Edition, including MasteringBiology, will meet the needs of the students and professors who use our offerings.

Pearson's talented sales reps, who listen to professors, advise the editorial staff, and get the book in students' hands, are supported by tireless Executive Marketing Manager Lauren Harp and Director of Marketing Christy Lesko. The marketing materials that support the outreach effort were produced by Lillian Carr and her colleagues in Pearson's Marketing Comunications group. David Theisen, national director for Key Markets, tirelessly visits countless professors each year, enthusiastically discussing their courses and providing us with meaningful editorial guidance.

The vision and resources required to run this entire enterprise are the responsibility of Vice President and Editor-in-Chief Beth Wilbur, who provided inspirational and focused leadership, and President of Pearson Science Paul Corey, who displays unwavering commitment to high-quality science publishing.

Becky Ruden recruited the coauthor team, drawing us to the project with her energy and belief in this book. The editorial team was skillfully directed by Executive Director of Development Deborah Gale. Finally, we are deeply grateful for three key drivers of the Fifth Edition. Project Editor Anna Amato's superb organizational skills and calm demeanor assured that all the wheels and cogs of the process ran smoothly to keep the mammoth project steadily rolling forward. Supervising Development Editor Sonia DiVittorio's deep expertise, creative vision, keen attention to detail, level, and clarity, and inspiring insistence on excellence kept the bar high for everyone on every aspect of the project. Lastly, Senior Acquisitions Editor Michael Gillespie's boundless energy and enthusiasm, positive attitude, and sharp intellect have fueled and united the team and also guided the book through the hurdles to existence. The coauthor team thanks these exceptional people for making the art and science of book writing a productive and exhilarating process.

1 Biology and the Tree of Life

In this chapter you will learn about

Key themes to structure your thinking about Biology

starting with

What does it mean to say that something is alive? 1.1

including

Two of the greatest unifying ideas in Biology

including

The process of doing Biology 1.5

first

The cell theory 1.2

then

The theory of evolution by natural selection 1.3

predicts

The tree of life 1.4

These Chinese water dragon hatchlings are exploring their new world and learning how to find food and stay alive. They represent one of the key characteristics of life introduced in this chapter—replication.

In essence, biological science is a search for ideas and observations that unify our understanding of the diversity of life, from bacteria living in rocks a mile underground to humans and majestic sequoia trees. This chapter is an introduction to this search.

The goals of this chapter are to introduce the nature of life and explore how biologists go about studying it. The chapter also introduces themes that will resonate throughout this book:

- Analyzing how organisms work at the molecular level.

- Understanding organisms in terms of their evolutionary history.

- Helping you learn to think like a biologist.

Let's begin with what may be the most fundamental question of all: What is life?

This chapter is part of the Big Picture. See how on pages 16–17.

✔ When you see this checkmark, stop and test yourself. Answers are available in Appendix A.

1.1 What Does It Mean to Say That Something Is Alive?

An **organism** is a life-form—a living entity made up of one or more cells. Although there is no simple definition of life that is endorsed by all biologists, most agree that organisms share a suite of five fundamental characteristics.

- *Energy*   To stay alive and reproduce, organisms have to acquire and use energy. To give just two examples: plants absorb sunlight; animals ingest food.

- *Cells*   Organisms are made up of membrane-bound units called cells. A cell's membrane regulates the passage of materials between exterior and interior spaces.

- *Information*   Organisms process hereditary, or genetic, information encoded in units called genes. Organisms also respond to information from the environment and adjust to maintain stable internal conditions. Right now, cells throughout your body are using information to make the molecules that keep you alive; your eyes and brain are decoding information on this page that will help you learn some biology, and if your room is too hot you might be sweating to cool off.

- *Replication*   One of the great biologists of the twentieth century, François Jacob, said that the "dream of a bacterium is to become two bacteria." Almost everything an organism does contributes to one goal: replicating itself.

- *Evolution*   Organisms are the product of evolution, and their populations continue to evolve.

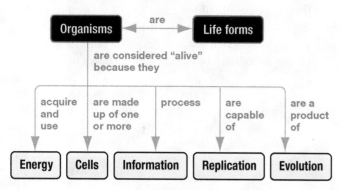

You can think of this text as one long exploration of these five traits. Here's to life!

1.2 The Cell Theory

Two of the greatest unifying ideas in all of science laid the groundwork for modern biology: the cell theory and the theory of evolution by natural selection. Formally, scientists define a **theory** as an explanation for a very general class of phenomena or observations that are supported by a wide body of evidence. The cell theory and theory of evolution address fundamental questions: What are organisms made of? Where do they come from?

When these concepts emerged in the mid-1800s, they revolutionized the way biologists think about the world. They established

two of the five attributes of life: Organisms are cellular, and their populations change over time.

Neither insight came easily, however. The cell theory, for example, emerged after some 200 years of work. In 1665 the Englishman Robert Hooke devised a crude microscope to examine the structure of cork (a bark tissue) from an oak tree. The instrument magnified objects to just 30× (30 times) their normal size, but it allowed Hooke to see something extraordinary. In the cork he observed small, pore-like compartments that were invisible to the naked eye. Hooke coined the term "cells" for these structures because of their resemblance to the cells inhabited by monks in a monastery.

Soon after Hooke published his results, a Dutch scientist named Anton van Leeuwenhoek succeeded in developing much more powerful microscopes, some capable of magnifications up to 300×. With these instruments, van Leeuwenhoek inspected samples of pond water and made the first observations of a dazzling collection of single-celled organisms that he called "animalcules." He also observed and described human blood cells and sperm cells, shown in **FIGURE 1.1**.

In the 1670s an Italian researcher who was studying the leaves and stems of plants with a microscope concluded that plant tissues were composed of many individual cells. By the early 1800s, enough data had accumulated for a German biologist to claim that *all* organisms consist of cells. Did this claim hold up?

All Organisms Are Made of Cells

Advances in microscopy have made it possible to examine the amazing diversity and complexity of cells at higher and higher magnifications. Biologists have developed microscopes that are tens of thousands of times more powerful than van Leeuwenhoek's and have described over a million new species. The basic conclusion made in the 1800s remains intact, however: All organisms are made of cells.

The smallest organisms known today are bacteria that are barely 200 nanometers wide, or 200 *billionths* of a meter. (See **BioSkills 1** in Appendix B to review the metric system and its prefixes.[1]) It would take 5000 of these organisms lined up side by side to span a millimeter. This is the distance between the smallest hash marks on a metric ruler. In contrast, sequoia trees can be over 100 meters tall. This is the equivalent of a 20-story building. Bacteria and sequoias are composed of the same fundamental building block, however—the cell. Bacteria consist of a single cell; sequoias are made up of many cells.

Today a **cell** is defined as a highly organized compartment that is bounded by a thin, flexible structure called a plasma membrane and that contains concentrated chemicals in an aqueous (watery) solution. The chemical reactions that sustain life take place inside cells. Most cells are also capable of reproducing by dividing—in effect, by making a copy of themselves.

The realization that all organisms are made of cells was fundamentally important, but it formed only the first part of the cell

---

[1]BioSkills are located in the second appendix at the back of the book. They focus on general skills that you'll use throughout this course. More than a few students have found them to be a life-saver. Please use them!

(a) van Leeuwenhoek built his own microscopes—which, while small, were powerful. They allowed him to see, for example . . .

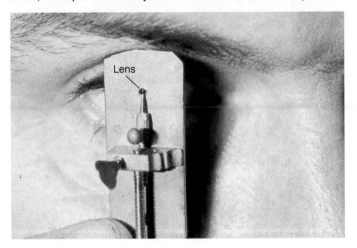

Lens

(b) . . . human blood cells (this modern photo was shot through one of van Leeuwenhoek's original microscopes) . . .

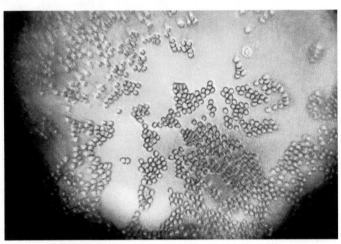

(c) . . . and animal sperm (drawing by van Leeuwenhoek of canine sperm cells on left, human on right).

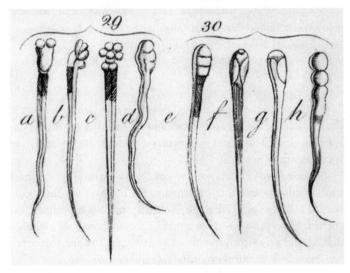

FIGURE 1.1 Van Leeuwenhoek's Microscope Made Cells Visible.

theory. In addition to understanding what organisms are made of, scientists wanted to understand how cells come to be.

Where Do Cells Come From?

Most scientific theories have two components: The first describes a pattern in the natural world; the second identifies a mechanism or process that is responsible for creating that pattern. Hooke and his fellow scientists articulated the pattern component of the cell theory. In 1858, a German scientist named Rudolph Virchow added the process component by stating that all cells arise from preexisting cells.

The complete **cell theory** can be stated as follows: All organisms are made of cells, and all cells come from preexisting cells.

Two Hypotheses   The cell theory was a direct challenge to the prevailing explanation of where cells come from, called spontaneous generation. In the mid-1800s, most biologists believed that organisms could arise spontaneously under certain conditions. For example, the bacteria and fungi that spoil foods such as milk and wine were thought to appear in these nutrient-rich media of their own accord—springing to life from nonliving materials. In contrast, the cell theory maintained that cells do not spring to life spontaneously but are produced only when preexisting cells grow and divide. The all-cells-from-cells explanation was a **hypothesis:** a testable statement to explain a phenomenon or a set of observations.

Biologists usually use the word theory to refer to proposed explanations for broad patterns in nature and prefer hypothesis to refer to explanations for more tightly focused questions. A theory serves as a framework for the development of new hypotheses.

An Experiment to Settle the Question   Soon after Virchow's all-cells-from-cells hypothesis appeared in print, a French scientist named Louis Pasteur set out to test its predictions experimentally. An experimental **prediction** describes a measurable or observable result that must be correct if a hypothesis is valid.

Pasteur wanted to determine whether microorganisms could arise spontaneously in a nutrient broth or whether they appear only when a broth is exposed to a source of preexisting cells. To address the question, he created two treatment groups: a broth that was not exposed to a source of preexisting cells and a broth that was.

The spontaneous generation hypothesis predicted that cells would appear in both treatment groups. The all-cells-from-cells hypothesis predicted that cells would appear only in the treatment exposed to a source of preexisting cells.

FIGURE 1.2 (on page 4) shows Pasteur's experimental setup. Note that the two treatments are identical in every respect but one. Both used glass flasks filled with the same amount of the same nutrient broth. Both were boiled for the same amount of time to kill any existing organisms such as bacteria or fungi. But because the flask pictured in Figure 1.2a had a straight neck, it was exposed to preexisting cells after sterilization by the heat treatment. These preexisting cells are the bacteria and fungi that cling to dust particles in the air. They could drop into the nutrient broth because the neck of the flask was straight.

In contrast, the flask drawn in Figure 1.2b had a long swan neck. Pasteur knew that water would condense in the crook of the swan neck after the boiling treatment and that this pool of water

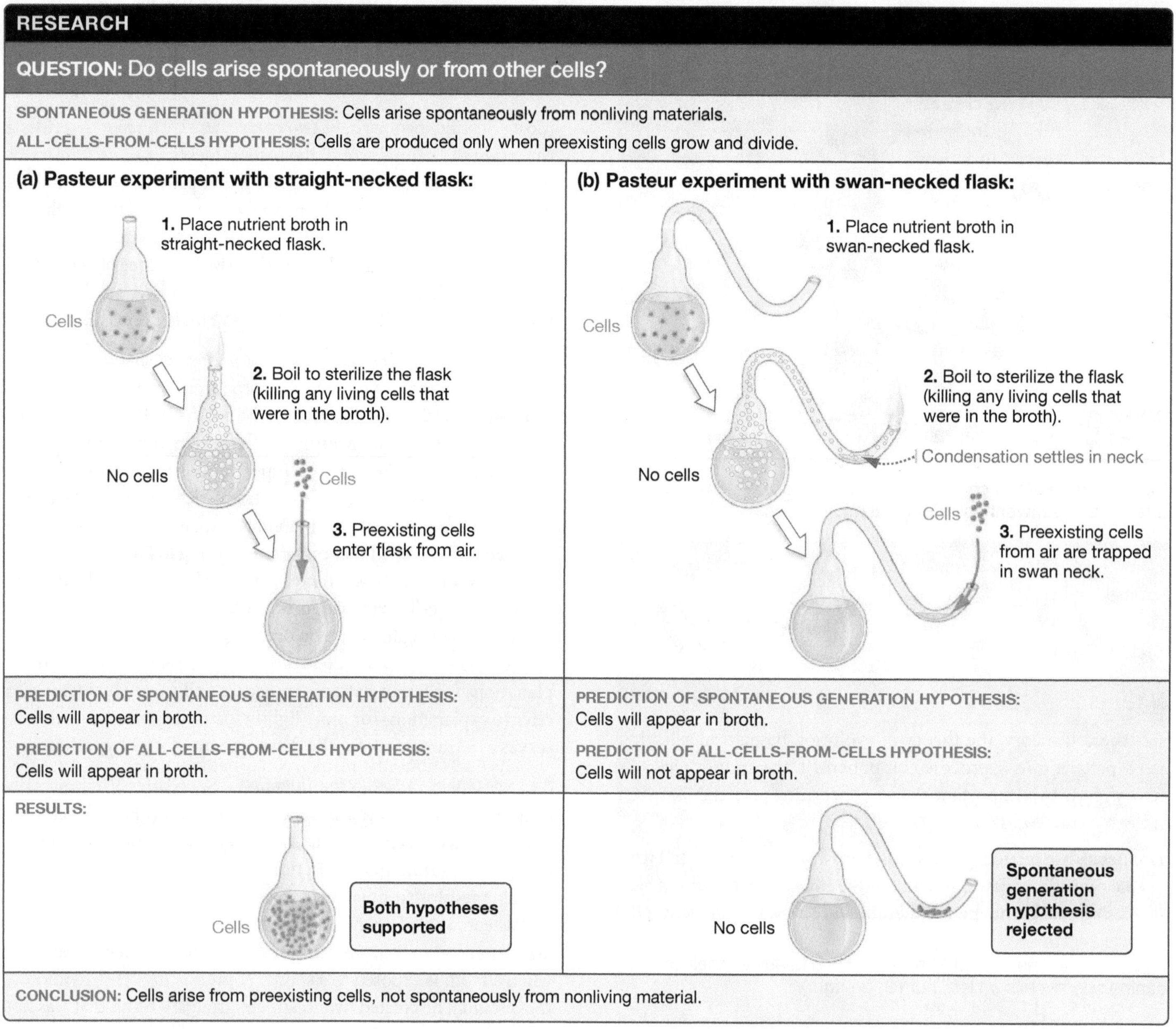

QUESTION: Do cells arise spontaneously or from other cells?

SPONTANEOUS GENERATION HYPOTHESIS: Cells arise spontaneously from nonliving materials.

ALL-CELLS-FROM-CELLS HYPOTHESIS: Cells are produced only when preexisting cells grow and divide.

(a) Pasteur experiment with straight-necked flask:

1. Place nutrient broth in straight-necked flask.

Cells

2. Boil to sterilize the flask (killing any living cells that were in the broth).

No cells

Cells

3. Preexisting cells enter flask from air.

(b) Pasteur experiment with swan-necked flask:

1. Place nutrient broth in swan-necked flask.

Cells

2. Boil to sterilize the flask (killing any living cells that were in the broth).

No cells

Condensation settles in neck

Cells

3. Preexisting cells from air are trapped in swan neck.

PREDICTION OF SPONTANEOUS GENERATION HYPOTHESIS: Cells will appear in broth.

PREDICTION OF ALL-CELLS-FROM-CELLS HYPOTHESIS: Cells will appear in broth.

PREDICTION OF SPONTANEOUS GENERATION HYPOTHESIS: Cells will appear in broth.

PREDICTION OF ALL-CELLS-FROM-CELLS HYPOTHESIS: Cells will not appear in broth.

RESULTS:

Cells

Both hypotheses supported

No cells

Spontaneous generation hypothesis rejected

CONCLUSION: Cells arise from preexisting cells, not spontaneously from nonliving material.

FIGURE 1.2 The Spontaneous Generation and All-Cells-from-Cells Hypotheses Were Tested Experimentally.

✔**QUESTION** What problem would arise in interpreting the results of this experiment if Pasteur had (1) put different types of broth in the two treatments, (2) heated them for different lengths of time, or (3) used a ceramic flask for one treatment and a glass flask for the other?

would trap any bacteria or fungi that entered on dust particles. Thus, the contents of the swan-necked flask were isolated from any source of preexisting cells even though still open to the air.

Pasteur's experimental setup was effective because there was only one difference between the two treatments and because that difference was the factor being tested—in this case, a broth's exposure to preexisting cells.

One Hypothesis Supported   And Pasteur's results? As Figure 1.2 shows, the treatment exposed to preexisting cells quickly filled with bacteria and fungi. This observation was important because it showed that the heat sterilization step had not altered the nutrient broth's capacity to support growth.

The broth in the swan-necked flask remained sterile, however. Even when the flask was left standing for months, no organisms appeared in it. This result was inconsistent with the hypothesis of spontaneous generation.

Because Pasteur's data were so conclusive—meaning that there was no other reasonable explanation for them—the results persuaded most biologists that the all-cells-from-cells hypothesis was correct. However, you will see that biologists now have evidence that life did arise from nonlife early in Earth's history, through a process called chemical evolution (Chapters 2–6).

The success of the cell theory's process component had an important implication: If all cells come from preexisting cells, it follows that all individuals in an isolated population of single-celled organisms are related by common ancestry. Similarly, in you and most other multicellular individuals, all the cells present are descended from preexisting cells, tracing back to a fertilized egg. A fertilized egg is a cell created by the fusion of sperm and egg—cells that formed in individuals of the previous generation. In this way, all the cells in a multicellular organism are connected by common ancestry.

The second great founding idea in biology is similar, in spirit, to the cell theory. It also happened to be published the same year as the all-cells-from-cells hypothesis. This was the realization, made independently by the English scientists Charles Darwin and Alfred Russel Wallace, that all species—all distinct, identifiable types of organisms—are connected by common ancestry.

1.3 The Theory of Evolution by Natural Selection

In 1858 short papers written separately by Darwin and Wallace were read to a small group of scientists attending a meeting of the Linnean Society of London. A year later, Darwin published a book that expanded on the idea summarized in those brief papers. The book was called *The Origin of Species*. The first edition sold out in a day.

What Is Evolution?

Like the cell theory, the theory of evolution by natural selection has a pattern and a process component. Darwin and Wallace's theory made two important claims concerning patterns that exist in the natural world.

1. Species are related by common ancestry. This contrasted with the prevailing view in science at the time, which was that species represent independent entities created separately by a divine being.

2. In contrast to the accepted view that species remain unchanged through time, Darwin and Wallace proposed that the characteristics of species can be modified from generation to generation. Darwin called this process descent with modification.

Evolution is a change in the characteristics of a population over time. It means that species are not independent and unchanging entities, but are related to one another and can change through time.

What Is Natural Selection?

This pattern component of the theory of evolution was actually not original to Darwin and Wallace. Several scientists had already come to the same conclusions about the relationships between species. The great insight by Darwin and Wallace was in proposing a process, called **natural selection,** that explains *how* evolution occurs.

Two Conditions of Natural Selection Natural selection occurs whenever two conditions are met.

1. Individuals within a population vary in characteristics that are **heritable**—meaning, traits that can be passed on to offspring.

A **population** is defined as a group of individuals of the same species living in the same area at the same time.

2. In a particular environment, certain versions of these heritable traits help individuals survive better or reproduce more than do other versions.

If certain heritable traits lead to increased success in producing offspring, then those traits become more common in the population over time. In this way, the population's characteristics change as a result of natural selection acting on individuals. This is a key insight: Natural selection acts on individuals, but evolutionary change occurs in populations.

Selection on Maize as an Example To clarify how selection works, consider an example of **artificial selection**—changes in populations that occur when *humans* select certain individuals to produce the most offspring. Beginning in 1896, researchers began a long-term selection experiment on maize (corn).

1. In the original population, the percentage of protein in maize kernels was variable among individuals. Kernel protein content is a heritable trait—parents tend to pass the trait on to their offspring.

2. Each year for many years, researchers chose individuals with the highest kernel protein content to be the parents of the next generation. In this environment, individuals with high kernel protein content produced more offspring than individuals with low kernel protein content.

FIGURE 1.3 shows the results. Note that this graph plots generation number on the *x*-axis, starting from the first generation (0 on the graph) and continuing for 100 generations. The average percentage of protein in a kernel among individuals in this population is plotted on the *y*-axis.

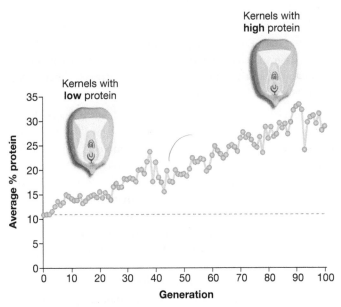

FIGURE 1.3 Response to Selection for High Kernel Protein Content in Maize.

DATA: Moose, S. P., J. W. Dudley, and T. R. Rocheford. 2004. *Trends in Plant Sciences* 9: 358–364; and the Illinois long-term selection experiment for oil and protein in corn (University of Illinois at Urbana–Champaign).

To read this graph, put your finger on the *x*-axis at generation 0. Then read up the *y*-axis, and note that kernels averaged about 11 percent protein at the start of the experiment. Now read the graph to the right. Each dot is a data point, representing the average kernel protein concentration in a particular generation. (A generation in maize is one year.) The lines on this graph simply connect the dots, to make the pattern in the data easier to see. During a few years the average protein content goes down, because of poor growing conditions or chance changes in how the many genes responsible for this trait interact. However, at the end of the graph, after 100 generations of selection, average kernel protein content is about 29 percent. (For more help with reading graphs, see **BioSkills 3** in Appendix B.)

This sort of change in the characteristics of a population, over time, is evolution. Humans have been practicing artificial selection for thousands of years, and biologists have now documented evolution by *natural* selection—where humans don't do the selecting—occurring in thousands of different populations, including humans. Evolution occurs when heritable variation leads to differential success in reproduction.

✔ QUANTITATIVE If you understand the concepts of selection and evolution, you should be able to describe how protein content in maize kernels changed over time, using the same *x*-axis and *y*-axis as in Figure 1.3, when researchers selected individuals with the *lowest* kernel protein content to be the parents of the next generation. (This experiment was actually done, starting with the same population at the same time as selection for high protein content.)

Fitness and Adaptation   Darwin also introduced some new terminology to identify what is happening during natural selection.

- In everyday English, fitness means health and well-being. But in biology, **fitness** means the ability of an individual to produce viable offspring. Individuals with high fitness produce many surviving offspring.

- In everyday English, adaptation means that an individual is adjusting and changing to function in new circumstances. But in biology, an **adaptation** is a trait that increases the fitness of an individual in a particular environment.

Once again, consider kernel protein content in maize: In the environment of the experiment graphed in Figure 1.3, individuals with high kernel protein content produced more offspring and had higher fitness than individuals with lower kernel protein content. In this population and this environment, high kernel protein content was an adaptation that allowed certain individuals to thrive.

Note that during this process, the amount of protein in the kernels of any individual maize plant did not change within its lifetime—the change occurred in the characteristics of the population over time.

Together, the cell theory and the theory of evolution provided the young science of biology with two central, unifying ideas:

1. The cell is the fundamental structural unit in all organisms.

2. All species are related by common ancestry and have changed over time in response to natural selection.

If you understand that . . .

- Natural selection occurs when heritable variation in certain traits leads to improved success in reproduction. Because individuals with these traits produce many offspring with the same traits, the traits increase in frequency and evolution occurs.
- Evolution is a change in the characteristics of a population over time.

✔ **You should be able to . . .**

Using the graph you just analyzed in Figure 1.3, describe the average kernel protein content over time in a maize population where *no* selection occurred.

Answers are available in Appendix A.

1.4   The Tree of Life

Section 1.3 focuses on how individual populations change through time in response to natural selection. But over the past several decades, biologists have also documented dozens of cases in which natural selection has caused populations of one species to diverge and form new species. This divergence process is called **speciation.**

Research on speciation has two important implications: All species come from preexisting species, and all species, past and present, trace their ancestry back to a single common ancestor.

The theory of evolution by natural selection predicts that biologists should be able to construct a **tree of life**—a family tree of organisms. If life on Earth arose just once, then such a diagram would describe the genealogical relationships between species with a single, ancestral species at its base.

Has this task been accomplished? If the tree of life exists, what does it look like?

Using Molecules to Understand the Tree of Life

One of the great breakthroughs in research on the tree of life occurred when American biologist Carl Woese (pronounced *woze*) and colleagues began analyzing the chemical components of organisms as a way to understand their evolutionary relationships. Their goal was to understand the **phylogeny** of all organisms—their actual genealogical relationships. Translated literally, phylogeny means "tribe-source."

To understand which organisms are closely versus distantly related, Woese and co-workers needed to study a molecule that is found in all organisms. The molecule they selected is called small subunit ribosomal RNA (rRNA). It is an essential part of the machinery that all cells use to grow and reproduce.

Although rRNA is a large and complex molecule, its underlying structure is simple. The rRNA molecule is made up of sequences of four smaller chemical components called ribonucleotides. These ribonucleotides are symbolized by the letters A, U, C, and G. In rRNA, ribonucleotides are connected to one another linearly, like the boxcars of a freight train.

Analyzing rRNA Why might rRNA be useful for understanding the relationships between organisms? The answer is that the ribonucleotide sequence in rRNA is a trait that can change during the course of evolution. Although rRNA performs the same function in all organisms, the sequence of ribonucleotide building blocks in this molecule is not identical among species.

In land plants, for example, the molecule might start with the sequence A-U-A-U-C-G-A-G (**FIGURE 1.4**). In green algae, which are closely related to land plants, the same section of the molecule might contain A-U-A-U-G-G-A-G. But in brown algae, which are not closely related to green algae or to land plants, the same part of the molecule might consist of A-A-A-U-G-G-A-C.

The research that Woese and co-workers pursued was based on a simple premise: If the theory of evolution is correct, then rRNA sequences should be very similar in closely related organisms but less similar in organisms that are less closely related. Species that are part of the same evolutionary lineage, like the plants, should share certain changes in rRNA that no other species have.

To test this premise, the researchers determined the sequence of ribonucleotides in the rRNA of a wide array of species. Then they considered what the similarities and differences in the sequences implied about relationships between the species. The goal was to produce a diagram that described the phylogeny of the organisms in the study.

A diagram that depicts evolutionary history in this way is called a phylogenetic tree. Just as a family tree shows relationships between individuals, a phylogenetic tree shows relationships between species. On a phylogenetic tree, branches that share a recent common ancestor represent species that are closely related; branches that don't share recent common ancestors represent species that are more distantly related.

The Tree of Life Estimated from Genetic Data To construct a phylogenetic tree, researchers use a computer to find the arrangement of branches that is most consistent with the similarities and differences observed in the data.

Although the initial work was based only on the sequences of ribonucleotides observed in rRNA, biologists now use data sets that include sequences from a wide array of genetic material. **FIGURE 1.5** shows a recent tree produced by comparing these sequences. Because this tree includes such a diverse array of

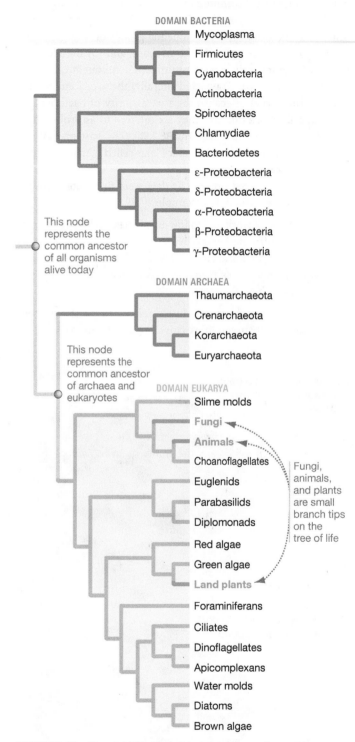

FIGURE 1.5 The Tree of Life. A phylogenetic tree estimated from a large amount of genetic sequence data. The three domains of life revealed by the analysis are labeled. Common names are given for lineages in the domains Bacteria and Eukarya. Phyla names are given for members of the domain Archaea, because most of these organisms have no common names.

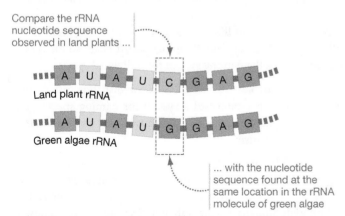

FIGURE 1.4 RNA Molecules Are Made Up of Smaller Molecules. A complete small subunit rRNA molecule contains about 2000 ribonucleotides; just 8 are shown in this comparison.

✔**QUESTION** Suppose that in the same section of rRNA, molds and other fungi have the sequence A-U-A-U-G-G-A-C. Are fungi more closely related to green algae or to land plants? Explain your logic.

species, it is often called the universal tree, or the tree of life. (For help in learning how to read a phylogenetic tree, see **BioSkills 7** in Appendix B.) Notice that the tree's main node is the common ancestor of all living organisms. Researchers who study the origin of life propose that the tree's root extends even further back to the "*last universal common ancestor*" of cells, or **LUCA.**

The tree of life implied by rRNA and other genetic data established that there are three fundamental groups or lineages of organisms: (1) the Bacteria, (2) the Archaea, and (3) the Eukarya. In all **eukaryotes,** cells have a prominent component called the nucleus (**FIGURE 1.6a**). Translated literally, the word eukaryotes means "true kernel." Because the vast majority of bacterial and archaeal cells lack a nucleus, they are referred to as **prokaryotes** (literally, "before kernel"; see **FIGURE 1.6b**). The vast majority of bacteria and archaea are unicellular ("one-celled"); many eukaryotes are multicellular ("many-celled").

When results based on genetic data were first published, biologists were astonished. For example:

- Prior to Woese's work and follow-up studies, biologists thought that the most fundamental division among organisms was between prokaryotes and eukaryotes. The Archaea were virtually unknown—much less recognized as a major and highly distinctive branch on the tree of life.

- Fungi were thought to be closely related to plants. Instead, they are actually much more closely related to animals.

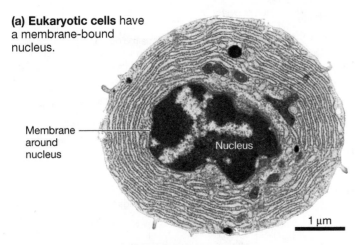

(a) Eukaryotic cells have a membrane-bound nucleus.

Membrane around nucleus

Nucleus

1 μm

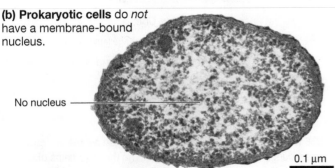

(b) Prokaryotic cells do *not* have a membrane-bound nucleus.

No nucleus

0.1 μm

FIGURE 1.6 Eukaryotes and Prokaryotes.

✔**QUANTITATIVE** How many times larger is the eukaryotic cell in this figure than the prokaryotic cell? (Hint: Study the scale bars.)

- Traditional approaches for classifying organisms—including the system of five kingdoms divided into various classes, orders, and families that you may have learned in high school—are inaccurate in many cases, because they do not reflect the actual evolutionary history of the organisms involved.

The Tree of Life Is a Work in Progress Just as researching your family tree can help you understand who you are and where you came from, so the tree of life helps biologists understand the relationships between organisms and the history of species. The discovery of the Archaea and the accurate placement of lineages such as the fungi qualify as exciting breakthroughs in our understanding of evolutionary history and life's diversity.

Work on the tree of life continues at a furious pace, however, and the location of certain branches on the tree is hotly debated. As databases expand and as techniques for analyzing data improve, the shape of the tree of life presented in Figure 1.5 will undoubtedly change. Our understanding of the tree of life, like our understanding of every other topic in biological science, is dynamic.

How Should We Name Branches on the Tree of Life?

In science, the effort to name and classify organisms is called **taxonomy.** Any named group is called a **taxon** (plural: **taxa**). Currently, biologists are working to create a taxonomy, or naming system, that accurately reflects the phylogeny of organisms.

Based on the tree of life implied by genetic data, Woese proposed a new taxonomic category called the **domain.** The three domains of life are the Bacteria, Archaea, and Eukarya.

Biologists often use the term **phylum** (plural: **phyla**) to refer to major lineages within each domain. Although the designation is somewhat arbitrary, each phylum is considered a major branch on the tree of life. Within the lineage called animals, biologists currently name 30–35 phyla—each of which is distinguished by distinctive aspects of its body structure as well as by distinctive gene sequences. For example, the mollusks (clams, squid, octopuses) constitute a phylum, as do chordates (the vertebrates and their close relatives).

Because the tree of life is so new, though, naming systems are still being worked out. One thing that hasn't changed for centuries, however, is the naming system for individual species.

Scientific (Latin) Names In 1735, a Swedish botanist named Carolus Linnaeus established a system for naming species that is still in use today. Linnaeus created a two-part name unique to each type of organism.

- *Genus* The first part indicates the organism's **genus** (plural: **genera**). A genus is made up of a closely related group of species. For example, Linnaeus put humans in the genus *Homo*. Although humans are the only living species in this genus, at least six extinct organisms, all of which walked upright and made extensive use of tools, were later also assigned to *Homo*.

- *Species* The second term in the two-part name identifies the organism's species. Linnaeus gave humans the species name *sapiens*.

An organism's genus and species designation is called its **scientific name** or Latin name. Scientific names are always italicized. Genus names are always capitalized, but species names are not—as in *Homo sapiens*.

Scientific names are based on Latin or Greek word roots or on words "Latinized" from other languages. Linnaeus gave a scientific name to every species then known, and also Latinized his own name—from Karl von Linné to Carolus Linnaeus.

Linnaeus maintained that different types of organisms should not be given the same genus and species names. Other species may be assigned to the genus *Homo*, and members of other genera may be named *sapiens*, but only humans are named *Homo sapiens*. Each scientific name is unique.

Scientific Names Are Often Descriptive Scientific names and terms are often based on Latin or Greek word roots that are descriptive. For example, *Homo sapiens* is derived from the Latin *homo* for "man" and *sapiens* for "wise" or "knowing." The yeast that bakers use to produce bread and that brewers use to brew beer is called *Saccharomyces cerevisiae*. The Greek root *saccharo* means "sugar," and *myces* refers to a fungus. *Saccharomyces* is aptly named "sugar fungus" because yeast is a fungus and because the domesticated strains of yeast used in commercial baking and brewing are often fed sugar. The species name of this organism, *cerevisiae*, is Latin for "beer." Loosely translated, then, the scientific name of brewer's yeast means "sugar-fungus for beer."

Scientific names and terms often seem daunting at first glance. So, most biologists find it extremely helpful to memorize some of the common Latin and Greek roots. To aid you in this process, new terms in this text are often accompanied by a translation of their Latin or Greek word roots in parentheses. (A glossary of common root words with translations and examples is also provided in **BioSkills 2** in Appendix B.)

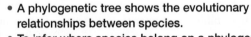
check your understanding

> **Ⓒ Ⓨ Ⓤ**
>
> **If you understand that . . .**
>
> • A phylogenetic tree shows the evolutionary relationships between species.
> • To infer where species belong on a phylogenetic tree, biologists examine genetic and other characteristics of the species involved. Closely related species should have similar characteristics, while less closely related species should be less similar.
>
> ✔ **You should be able to . . .**
>
> Examine the following rRNA ribonucleotide sequences and draw a phylogenetic tree showing the relationships between species A, B, and C that these data imply:
>
> Species A: A A C T A G C G C G A T
> Species B: A A C T A G C G C C A T
> Species C: T T C T A G C G G T A T
>
> *Answers are available in Appendix A.*

This chapter has introduced some of the great ideas in biology. The development of the cell theory and the theory of evolution by natural selection provided cornerstones when the science was young; the tree of life is a relatively recent insight that has revolutionized our understanding of life's diversity.

These theories are considered great because they explain fundamental aspects of nature, and because they have consistently been shown to be correct. They are considered correct because they have withstood extensive testing.

How do biologists go about testing their ideas? Before answering this question, let's step back a bit and consider the types of questions that researchers can and cannot ask.

The Nature of Science

Biologists ask questions about organisms, just as physicists and chemists ask questions about the physical world or geologists ask questions about Earth's history and the ongoing processes that shape landforms.

No matter what their field, all scientists ask questions that can be answered by observing or measuring things—by collecting data. Conversely, scientists cannot address questions that can't be answered by observing or measuring things.

This distinction is important. It is at the root of continuing controversies about teaching evolution in publicly funded schools. In the United States and in Turkey, in particular, some Christian and Islamic leaders have been particularly successful in pushing their claim that evolution and religious faith are in conflict. Even though the theory of evolution is considered one of the most successful and best-substantiated ideas in the history of science, they object to teaching it.

The vast majority of biologists and many religious leaders reject this claim; they see no conflict between evolution and religious faith. Their view is that science and religion are compatible because they address different types of questions.

• Science is about formulating hypotheses and finding evidence that supports or conflicts with those hypotheses.

• Religious faith addresses questions that cannot be answered by data. The questions addressed by the world's great religions focus on why we exist and how we should live.

Both types of questions are seen as legitimate and important.

So how do biologists go about answering questions? After formulating hypotheses, biologists perform experimental studies, or studies that yield descriptive data, such as observing a behavior, characterizing a structure within a cell by microscopy, or sequencing rRNA. Let's consider two recent examples of this process.

Why Do Giraffes Have Long Necks? An Introduction to Hypothesis Testing

If you were asked why giraffes have long necks, you might say based on your observations that long necks enable giraffes to reach food that is unavailable to other mammals. This hypothesis is expressed in African folktales and has traditionally been accepted by many biologists. The food competition hypothesis is so plausible, in fact, that for decades no one thought to test it.

In the mid-1990s, however, Robert Simmons and Lue Scheepers assembled data suggesting that the food competition hypothesis is only part of the story. Their analysis supports an alternative hypothesis—that long necks allow giraffes to use their heads as effective weapons for battering their opponents, and that longer-necked giraffes would have a competitive advantage in fights.

Before exploring these alternative explanations, it's important to recognize that hypothesis testing is a two-step process:

Step 1 State the hypothesis as precisely as possible and list the predictions it makes.

Step 2 Design an observational or experimental study that is capable of testing those predictions.

If the predictions are accurate, the hypothesis is supported. If the predictions are not met, then researchers do further tests, modify the original hypothesis, or search for alternative explanations. But the process does not end here. Biologists also talk to other researchers. Over coffee, at scientific meetings, or through publications, biologists communicate their results to the scientific community and beyond. (You can see the Big Picture of the process of doing biology on pages 16–17.)

Now that you understand more about hypothesis testing, let's return to the giraffes. How did biologists test the food competition hypothesis? What data support their alternative explanation?

The Food Competition Hypothesis: Predictions and Tests   The food competition hypothesis claims that giraffes compete for food with other species of mammals. When food is scarce, as it is during the dry season, giraffes with longer necks can reach food that is unavailable to other species and to giraffes with shorter necks. As a result, the longest-necked individuals in a giraffe population survive better and produce more young than do shorter-necked individuals, and average neck length of the population increases with each generation.

To use the terms introduced earlier, long necks are adaptations that increase the fitness of individual giraffes during competition for food. This type of natural selection has gone on so long that the population has become extremely long necked.

The food competition hypothesis makes several explicit predictions. For example, the food competition hypothesis predicts that:

• neck length is variable among giraffes;

• neck length in giraffes is heritable; and

• giraffes feed high in trees, especially during the dry season, when food is scarce and the threat of starvation is high.

The first prediction is correct. Studies in zoos and natural populations confirm that neck length is variable among individuals.

The researchers were unable to test the second prediction, however, because they studied giraffes in a natural population and were unable to do breeding experiments. As a result, they simply had to accept this prediction as an assumption. In

(a) Most feeding is done at about shoulder height.

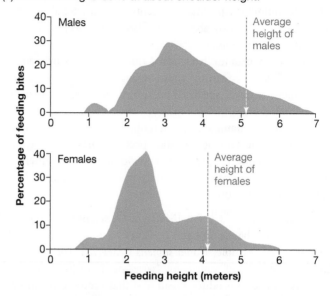

(b) Typical feeding posture in giraffes

FIGURE 1.7 Giraffes Do Not Usually Extend Their Necks Upward to Feed.

DATA: Young, T. P., L. A. Isbell. 1991. *Ethology* 87: 79–89.

general, though, biologists prefer to test every assumption behind a hypothesis.

What about the prediction regarding feeding high in trees? According to Simmons and Scheepers, this is where the food competition hypothesis breaks down.

Consider, for example, data collected by a different research team on the amount of time that giraffes spend feeding in vegetation of different heights. **FIGURE 1.7a** plots the height of vegetation versus the percentage of bites taken by a giraffe, for males and for females from the same population in Kenya. The dashed line on each graph indicates the average height of a male or female in this population.

Note that the average height of a giraffe in this population is much greater than the height where most feeding takes place. In this population, both male and female giraffes spend most of their feeding time eating vegetation that averages just 60 percent of their full height. Studies on other populations of giraffes, during both the wet and dry seasons, are consistent with these data. Giraffes usually feed with their necks bent (**FIGURE 1.7b**).

These data cast doubt on the food competition hypothesis, because one of its predictions does not appear to hold. Biologists have not abandoned this hypothesis completely, though, because feeding high in trees may be particularly valuable during extreme droughts, when a giraffe's ability to reach leaves far above the ground could mean the difference between life and death. Still, Simmons and Scheepers have offered an alternative explanation for why giraffes have long necks. The new hypothesis is based on the mating system of giraffes.

The Sexual Competition Hypothesis: Predictions and Tests Giraffes have an unusual mating system. Breeding occurs year round rather than seasonally. To determine when females are coming into estrus or "heat" and are thus receptive to mating, the males nuzzle the rumps of females. In response, the females urinate into the males' mouths. The males then tip their heads back and pull their lips to and fro, as if tasting the liquid. Biologists who have witnessed this behavior have proposed that the males taste the females' urine to detect whether estrus has begun.

Once a female giraffe enters estrus, males fight among themselves for the opportunity to mate. Combat is spectacular. The bulls stand next to one another, swing their necks, and strike thunderous blows with their heads. Researchers have seen males knocked unconscious for 20 minutes after being hit and have cataloged numerous instances in which the loser died. Giraffes are not the only animals known to fight in this way—male giraffe weevils also use enormously long necks to fight for mating rights.

These observations inspired a new explanation for why giraffes have long necks. The sexual competition hypothesis is based on the idea that longer-necked giraffes are able to strike harder blows during combat than can shorter-necked giraffes. In engineering terms, longer necks provide a longer "moment arm." A long moment arm increases the force of an impact. (Think about the type of sledgehammer you'd use to bash down a concrete wall—one with a short handle or one with a long handle?)

The idea here is that longer-necked males should win more fights and, as a result, father more offspring than shorter-necked males do. If neck length in giraffes is inherited, then the average neck length in the population should increase over time. Under the sexual competition hypothesis, long necks are adaptations that increase the fitness of males during competition for females.

Although several studies have shown that long-necked males are more successful in fighting and that the winners of fights gain access to estrous females, the question of why giraffes have long necks is not closed. With the data collected to date, most biologists would probably concede that the food competition hypothesis needs further testing and refinement and that the sexual competition hypothesis appears promising. It could also be true that both hypotheses are correct. For our purposes, the important take-home message is that all hypotheses must be tested rigorously.

In many cases in biological science, testing hypotheses rigorously involves experimentation. Experimenting on giraffes is difficult. But in the case study considered next, biologists were able to test an interesting hypothesis experimentally.

How Do Ants Navigate? An Introduction to Experimental Design

Experiments are a powerful scientific tool because they allow researchers to test the effect of a single, well-defined factor on a particular phenomenon. Because experiments testing the effect of neck length on food and sexual competition in giraffes haven't been done yet, let's consider a different question: When ants leave their nest to search for food, how do they find their way back?

The Saharan desert ant lives in colonies and makes a living by scavenging the dead carcasses of insects. Individuals leave the burrow and wander about searching for food at midday, when temperatures at the surface can reach 60°C (140°F) and predators are hiding from the heat.

Foraging trips can take the ants hundreds of meters—an impressive distance when you consider that these animals are only about a centimeter long. But when an ant returns, it doesn't follow the same long, wandering route it took on its way away from the nest. Instead, individuals return in a straight line (**FIGURE 1.8**).

Once individuals are close to the nest, they engage in a characteristic set of back-and-forth U-turns until they find their nest hole. How do they do know how far they are from the nest?

The Pedometer Hypothesis Early work on navigation in desert ants showed that they use the Sun's position as a compass—meaning that they always know the approximate direction of the nest relative to the Sun. But how do they know how far to go?

After experiments had shown that the ants do not use landmarks to navigate, Matthias Wittlinger and co-workers set out to test a novel idea. The biologists proposed that Saharan desert ants know how far they are from the nest by integrating information from leg movements.

According to this pedometer hypothesis, the ants always know how far they are from the nest because they track the number

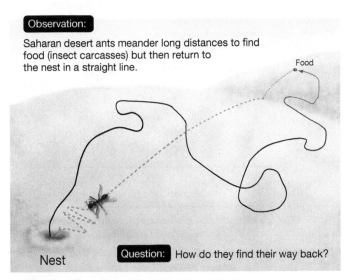

FIGURE 1.8 Navigation in Foraging Desert Ants.

of steps they have taken and their stride length. The idea is that they can make a beeline back toward the burrow because they integrate information on the angles they have traveled *and* the distance they have gone—based on step number and stride length.

If the pedometer hypothesis is wrong, however, then stride length and step number should have no effect on the ability of an ant to get back to its nest. This latter possibility is called a **null hypothesis**. A null hypothesis specifies what should be observed when the hypothesis being tested isn't correct.

Testing the Hypothesis To test their idea, Wittlinger's group allowed ants to walk from a nest to a feeder through a channel—a distance of 10 m. Then they caught ants at the feeder and created three test groups, each with 25 individuals (**FIGURES 1.9** and **1.10**):

- *Stumps* By cutting the lower legs of some individuals off, they created ants with shorter-than-normal legs.

- *Normal* Some individuals were left alone, meaning that they had normal leg length.

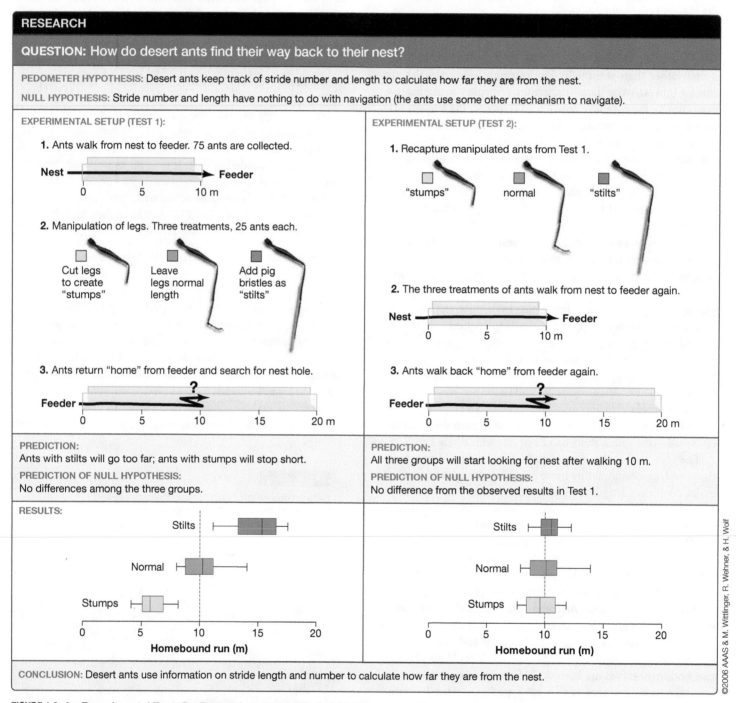

FIGURE 1.9 An Experimental Test: Do Desert Ants Use a "Pedometer"?

SOURCE: Wittlinger, M., R. Wehner, and H. Wolf. 2006. The ant odometer: Stepping on stilts and stumps. *Science* 312: 1965–1967.

✔ **QUESTION** What is the advantage of using 25 ants in each group instead of just one?

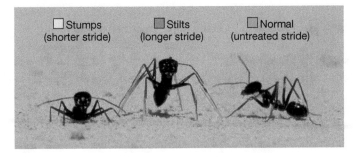

FIGURE 1.10 Manipulation of Desert Ant Stride Length.

- *Stilts* By gluing pig bristles onto each leg, the biologists created ants with longer-than-normal legs.

Next they put the ants in a different channel and recorded how far they traveled in a direct line before starting their nest-searching behavior. To see the data they collected, look at the graph on the left side of the "Results" section in Figure 1.9.

- *Stumps* The ants with stumps stopped short, by about 5 m, before starting to search for the nest opening.
- *Normal* The normal ants walked the correct distance—about 10 m.
- *Stilts* The ants with stilts walked about 5 m too far before starting to search for the nest opening.

To check the validity of this result, the researchers put the test ants back in the nest and recaptured them one to several days later, when they had walked to the feeder on their stumps, normal legs, or stilts. Now when the ants were put into the other channel to "walk back," they all traveled the correct distance—10 m—before starting to search for the nest (see the graph on the right side of the "Results" section in Figure 1.9).

The graphs in the "Results" display "box-and-whisker" plots that allow you to easily see where most of the data fall. Each box indicates the range of distances where 50 percent of the ants stopped to search for the nest. The whiskers indicate the lower extreme (stopping short of the nest location) and the upper extreme (going too far) of where the ants stopped to search. The vertical line inside each box indicates the median—meaning that half the ants stopped above this distance and half below. (For more details on how biologists report medians and indicate the variability and uncertainty in data, see **BioSkills 4** in Appendix B.)

Interpreting the Results The pedometer hypothesis predicts that an ant's ability to walk home depends on the number and length of steps taken on its outbound trip. Recall that a prediction specifies what we should observe if a hypothesis is correct. Good scientific hypotheses make testable predictions—predictions that can be supported or rejected by collecting and analyzing data. In this case, the researchers tested the prediction by altering stride length and recording the distance traveled on the return trip. Under the null hypothesis in this experiment, all the ants—altered and unaltered—should have walked 10 m in the first test before they started looking for their nest.

Important Characteristics of Good Experimental Design In relation to designing effective experiments, this study illustrates several important points:

- It is critical to include **control** groups. A control checks for factors, other than the one being tested, that might influence the experiment's outcome. In this case, there were two controls. Including a normal, unmanipulated individual controlled for the possibility that switching the individuals to a new channel altered their behavior. In addition, the researchers had to control for the possibility that the manipulation itself—and not the change in leg length—affected the behavior of the stilts and stumps ants. This is why they did the second test, where the outbound and return runs were done with the same legs.

- The experimental conditions must be as constant or equivalent as possible. The investigators used ants of the same species, from the same nest, at the same time of day, under the same humidity and temperature conditions, at the same feeders, in the same channels. Controlling all the variables except one—leg length in this case—is crucial because it eliminates alternative explanations for the results.

- Repeating the test is essential. It is almost universally true that larger sample sizes in experiments are better. By testing many individuals, the amount of distortion or "noise" in the data caused by unusual individuals or circumstances is reduced.

✔ If you understand these points, you should be able to explain: (1) What you would conclude if in the first test, the normal individual had not walked 10 m on the return trip before

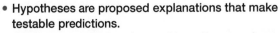

If you understand that . . .

- Hypotheses are proposed explanations that make testable predictions.
- Predictions describe observable outcomes of particular conditions.
- Well-designed experiments alter just one condition—a condition relevant to the hypothesis being tested.

✔ **You should be able to . . .**

Design an experiment to test the hypothesis that desert ants feed during the hottest part of the day because it allows them to avoid being eaten by lizards. Then answer the following questions about your experimental design:

1. How does the presence of a control group in your experiment allow you to test the hypothesis?

2. How are experimental conditions controlled or standardized in a way that precludes alternative explanations of the data?

Answers are available in Appendix A.

looking for the nest; and (2) What you would conclude if the stilts and stumps ants had not navigated normally during the second test.

From the outcomes of these experiments, the researchers concluded that desert ants use stride length and number to measure how far they are from the nest. They interpreted their results as strong support for the pedometer hypothesis.

The giraffe and ant studies demonstrate a vital point: Biologists practice evidence-based decision making. They ask questions about how organisms work, pose hypotheses to answer those questions, and use experimental or observational evidence to decide which hypotheses are correct.

The data on giraffes and ants are a taste of things to come. In this text you will encounter hypotheses and research on questions ranging from how water gets to the top of 100-meter-tall sequoia trees to how the bacterium that causes tuberculosis has become resistant to antibiotics. As you work through this book, you'll get lots of practice thinking about hypotheses and predictions, analyzing the nature of control treatments, and interpreting graphs.

A commitment to tough-minded hypothesis testing and sound experimental design is a hallmark of biological science. Understanding their value is an important first step in becoming a biologist.

CHAPTER 1 REVIEW

For media, go to MasteringBiology

If you understand . . .

1.1 What Does It Mean to Say That Something Is Alive?

- There is no single, well-accepted definition of life. Instead, biologists point to five characteristics that organisms share.

✔ You should be able to explain why the cells in a dead organism are different from the cells in a live organism.

1.2 The Cell Theory

- The cell theory identified the fundamental structural unit common to all life.

✔ You should be able to describe the evidence that supported the pattern and the process components of the cell theory.

1.3 The Theory of Evolution by Natural Selection

- The theory of evolution states that all organisms are related by common ancestry.
- Natural selection is a well-tested explanation for why species change through time and why they are so well adapted to their habitats.

✔ You should be able to explain why the average protein content of seeds in a natural population of a grass species would increase over time, if seeds with higher protein content survive better and grow into individuals that produce many seeds with high protein content when they mature.

1.4 The Tree of Life

- The theory of evolution predicts that all organisms are part of a genealogy of species, and that all species trace their ancestry back to a single common ancestor.

- To construct this phylogeny, biologists have analyzed the sequences in rRNA and in an array of genetic material found in all cells.
- A tree of life, based on similarities and differences in these molecules, has three fundamental lineages, or domains: the Bacteria, the Archaea, and the Eukarya.

✔ You should be able to explain how biologists can determine which of the three domains a newly discovered species belongs to by analyzing its rRNA.

1.5 Doing Biology

- Biology is a hypothesis-driven, experimental science.

✔ You should be able to explain (1) the relationship between a hypothesis and a prediction and (2) why experiments are convincing ways to test predictions.

MB MasteringBiology

1. **MasteringBiology Assignments**

   Tutorials and Activities An Introduction to Graphing; Experimental Inquiry: What Can You Learn about the Process of Science from Investigating a Cricket's Chirp?; Introduction to Experimental Design; Levels of Life Card Game; Metric System Review; The Scientific Method

   Questions Reading Quizzes, Blue-Thread Questions, Test Bank

2. **eText** Read your book online, search, take notes, highlight text, and more.

3. **The Study Area** Practice Test, Cumulative Test, BioFlix® 3-D Animations, Videos, Activities, Audio Glossary, Word Study Tools, Art

You should be able to . . .

1. Anton van Leeuwenhoek made an important contribution to the development of the cell theory. How?
   a. He articulated the pattern component of the theory—that all organisms are made of cells.
   b. He articulated the process component of the theory—that all cells come from preexisting cells.
   c. He invented the first microscope and saw the first cell.
   d. He invented more powerful microscopes and was the first to describe the diversity of cells.

2. What does it mean to say that experimental conditions are controlled?
   a. The test groups consist of the same individuals.
   b. The null hypothesis is correct.
   c. There is no difference in outcome between the control and experimental treatment.
   d. All physical conditions except for one are identical for all groups tested.

3. The term *evolution* means that _____ change through time.

4. What does it mean to say that a characteristic of an organism is heritable?
   a. The characteristic evolves.
   b. The characteristic can be passed on to offspring.
   c. The characteristic is advantageous to the organism.
   d. The characteristic does not vary in the population.

5. In biology, to what does the term *fitness* refer?

6. Could *both* the food competition hypothesis and the sexual competition hypothesis explain why giraffes have long necks? Why or why not?
   a. No. In science, only one hypothesis can be correct.
   b. No. Observations have shown that the food competition hypothesis cannot be correct.
   c. Yes. Long necks could be advantageous for more than one reason.
   d. Yes. All giraffes have been shown to feed at the highest possible height and fight for mates.

7. What would researchers have to demonstrate to convince you that they had discovered life on another planet?

8. What did Linnaeus's system of naming organisms ensure?
   a. Two different organisms never end up with the same genus and species name.
   b. Two different organisms have the same genus and species name if they are closely related.
   c. The genus name is different for closely related species.
   d. The species name is the same for each organism in a genus.

9. What does it mean to say that a species is adapted to a particular habitat?

10. Explain how selection occurs during natural selection. What is selected, and why?

11. The following two statements explain the logic behind the use of molecular sequence data to estimate evolutionary relationships:

    "If the theory of evolution is true, then rRNA sequences should be very similar in closely related organisms but less similar in organisms that are less closely related."

    "On a phylogenetic tree, branches that share a recent common ancestor represent species that are closely related; branches that don't share recent common ancestors represent species that are more distantly related."

    Is the logic of these statements sound? Why or why not?

12. Explain why researchers formulate a null hypothesis in addition to a hypothesis when designing an experimental study.

13. A scientific theory is a set of propositions that defines and explains some aspect of the world. This definition contrasts sharply with the everyday usage of the word theory, which often carries meanings such as "speculation" or "guess." Explain the difference between the two definitions, using the cell theory and the theory of evolution by natural selection as examples.

14. Turn back to the tree of life shown in Figure 1.5. Note that Bacteria and Archaea are prokaryotes, while Eukarya are eukaryotes. On the simplified tree below, draw an arrow that points to the branch where the structure called the nucleus originated. Explain your reasoning.

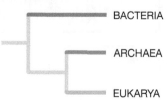

BACTERIA

ARCHAEA

EUKARYA

15. The proponents of the cell theory could not "prove" that it was correct in the sense of providing incontrovertible evidence that all organisms are made up of cells. They could state only that all organisms examined to date were made of cells. Why was it reasonable for them to conclude that the theory was valid?

16. Some humans have heritable traits that make them resistant to infection by HIV. In areas of the world where HIV infection rates are high, are human populations evolving? Explain your logic.
    a. No. HIV infection rates would not affect human evolution.
    b. Yes. The heritable traits that confer resistance to HIV should increase over time.
    c. No. The heritable traits that confer resistance to HIV should decrease over time.
    d. Yes. The heritable traits that confer resistance to HIV should decrease over time.

The Big Picture

Biologists study the characteristics of life. The cell theory, the theory of evolution by natural selection, and the tree of life are some of the great ideas in biology that came about by biologists asking questions that can be answered by observing or measuring things—that is, by collecting data.

Notice that the study of life is not a series of linear steps with a beginning and an end. Instead, the process of doing biology is dynamic and ongoing. The answer to one question may lay the foundation for twenty more questions. Working together, biologists from different disciplines integrate data across many levels, from atoms to the biosphere.

Note that the gray numbers in boxes tell you where to go for more information. Also, be sure to do the blue exercises in the Check Your Understanding box.

Characteristics of living things
- Energy
- Cells
- Information
- Replication
- Evolution

1.1

focuses on

Text section where you can find more information

Scientists regularly integrate across many of these levels

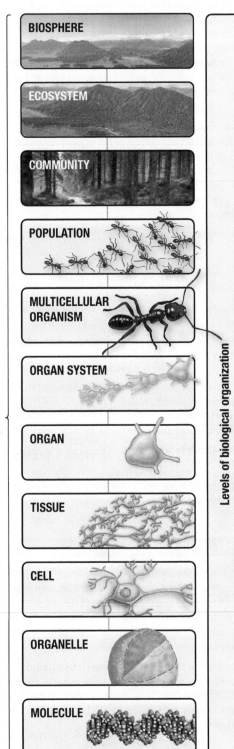

BIOSPHERE

ECOSYSTEM

COMMUNITY

POPULATION

MULTICELLULAR ORGANISM

ORGAN SYSTEM

ORGAN

TISSUE

CELL

ORGANELLE

MOLECULE

ATOM

Levels of biological organization

check your understanding

C Y U

If you understand the big picture . . .

✔ You should be able to . . .

1. Describe how biologists go about testing their ideas.
2. Provide an example of how an experimental study could span more than one level of biological organization.
3. Compare and contrast a hypothesis with a theory.
4. Propose the next step to take if data support the hypothesis you are testing.

Answers are available in Appendix A.

DOING BIOLOGY

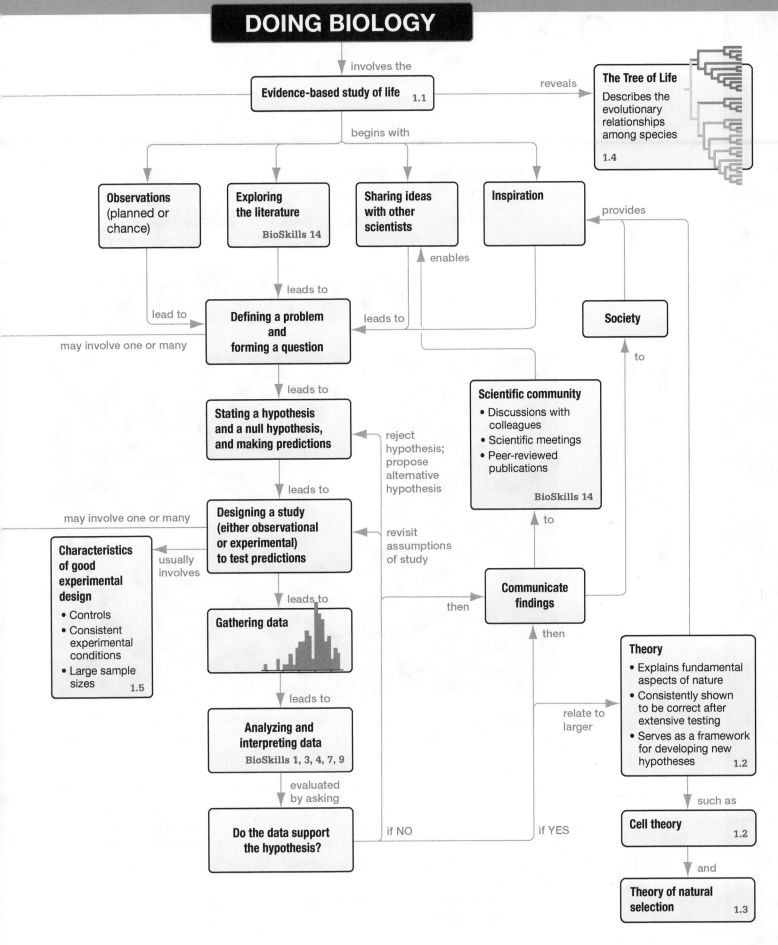

Evidence-based study of life 1.1

involves the

reveals → **The Tree of Life** Describes the evolutionary relationships among species 1.4

begins with

Observations (planned or chance)

Exploring the literature BioSkills 14

Sharing ideas with other scientists

Inspiration

provides

lead to

leads to

may involve one or many

enables

Defining a problem and forming a question

leads to

Society

leads to

Stating a hypothesis and a null hypothesis, and making predictions

reject hypothesis; propose alternative hypothesis

Scientific community
- Discussions with colleagues
- Scientific meetings
- Peer-reviewed publications

BioSkills 14

to

leads to

may involve one or many

Designing a study (either observational or experimental) to test predictions

revisit assumptions of study

Characteristics of good experimental design
- Controls
- Consistent experimental conditions
- Large sample sizes 1.5

usually involves

leads to

Gathering data

then

Communicate findings

then

relate to larger

Theory
- Explains fundamental aspects of nature
- Consistently shown to be correct after extensive testing
- Serves as a framework for developing new hypotheses 1.2

leads to

Analyzing and interpreting data BioSkills 1, 3, 4, 7, 9

evaluated by asking

such as

Do the data support the hypothesis?

if NO

if YES

Cell theory 1.2

and

Theory of natural selection 1.3

17

2 Water and Carbon: The Chemical Basis of Life

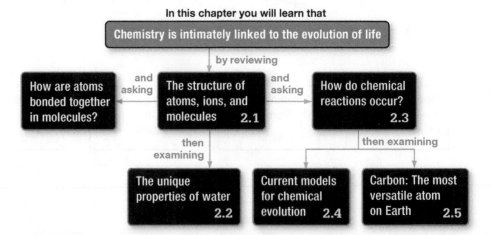

In this chapter you will learn that

Chemistry is intimately linked to the evolution of life

by reviewing

How are atoms bonded together in molecules? — and asking — The structure of atoms, ions, and molecules **2.1** — and asking — How do chemical reactions occur? **2.3**

then examining

The unique properties of water **2.2**

then examining

Current models for chemical evolution **2.4**

Carbon: The most versatile atom on Earth **2.5**

These deep-sea hydrothermal vents produce hydrogen-rich, highly basic fluids at temperatures that range from 40° to 90°C. It has been proposed that life emerged from similar seafloor chimneys early in Earth's history via chemical evolution.

A classic experiment on spontaneous generation by Louis Pasteur tested the idea that life arises from nonliving materials (see Chapter 1). This work helped build a consensus that spontaneous generation does not occur. But for life to exist, spontaneous generation must have occurred at least once, early in Earth's history.

How did life begin? This simple query has been called "the mother of all questions." This chapter examines a theory, called **chemical evolution,** that is the leading scientific explanation for the origin of life. Like all scientific theories, the theory of chemical evolution has a *pattern component* that makes a claim about the natural world and a *process component* that explains that pattern.

This chapter is part of the Big Picture. See how on pages 104–105.

- *The pattern component* In addition to small molecules, complex carbon-containing substances exist and are required for life.

- *The process component* Early in Earth's history, simple chemical compounds combined to form more complex carbon-containing substances before the evolution of life.

✔ When you see this checkmark, stop and test yourself. Answers are available in Appendix A.

The theory maintains that inputs of energy led to the formation of increasingly complex carbon-containing substances, culminating in a compound that could replicate itself. At this point, there was a switch from chemical evolution to biological evolution.

As the original molecule multiplied, the process of evolution by natural selection took over. Eventually a descendant of the original molecule became metabolically active and acquired a membrane. When this occurred, the five attributes of life (discussed in Chapter 1) were fulfilled. Life had begun.

At first glance, the theory of chemical evolution may seem implausible. But is it? What evidence do biologists have that chemical evolution occurred? What approaches do they take to gathering this evidence?

Let's start with the fundamentals—the atoms and molecules that would have combined to get chemical evolution started.

2.1 Atoms, Ions, and Molecules: The Building Blocks of Chemical Evolution

Just four types of atoms—hydrogen, carbon, nitrogen, and oxygen—make up 96 percent of all matter found in organisms today. Many of the molecules found in your cells contain thousands, or even millions, of these atoms bonded together. But early in Earth's history, these elements existed only in simple substances such as water and carbon dioxide, which contain just three atoms apiece.

Two questions are fundamental to understanding how elements could have evolved into the more complex substances found in living cells:

1. What is the physical structure of the hydrogen, carbon, nitrogen, and oxygen atoms found in living cells?

2. What is the structure of the simple molecules—water, carbon dioxide, and others—that served as the building blocks of chemical evolution?

The focus on structure follows from one of the most central themes in biology: *Structure affects function*. To understand how a molecule affects your body or the role it played in chemical evolution, you have to understand how it is put together.

Basic Atomic Structure

FIGURE 2.1a shows a simple way of depicting the structure of an atom, using hydrogen and carbon as examples. Extremely small particles called electrons orbit an atomic nucleus made up of larger particles called protons and neutrons. **FIGURE 2.1b** provides a sense of scale at the atomic level.

Protons have a positive electric charge (+1), neutrons are electrically neutral, and electrons have a negative electric charge (−1). When the number of protons and the number of electrons in an atom are the same, the charges balance and the atom is electrically neutral.

(a) Diagrams of atoms

Hydrogen

Carbon

(b) Most of an atom's volume is empty space.

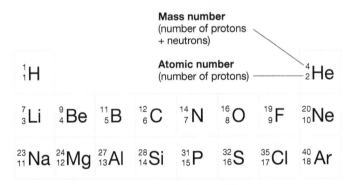

If an atom occupied the same volume as this stadium, the nucleus would be about the size of a pea

FIGURE 2.1 Parts of an Atom. The atomic nucleus, made up of protons and neutrons, is surrounded by orbiting electrons. In reality, electrons do not orbit the nucleus in circles; their actual orbits are complex.

FIGURE 2.2 shows a segment of the periodic table of the elements. Notice that each atom of a given **element** contains a characteristic number of protons, called its **atomic number.** The atomic number is written as a subscript to the left of an element's symbol in Figure 2.2. The sum of the protons and neutrons in an atom is called its **mass number** and is written as a superscript to the left of its symbol.

Mass number
(number of protons
+ neutrons)

$^{1}_{1}H$

Atomic number
(number of protons) — $^{4}_{2}He$

$^{7}_{3}Li$ $^{9}_{4}Be$ $^{11}_{5}B$ $^{12}_{6}C$ $^{14}_{7}N$ $^{16}_{8}O$ $^{19}_{9}F$ $^{20}_{10}Ne$

$^{23}_{11}Na$ $^{24}_{12}Mg$ $^{27}_{13}Al$ $^{28}_{14}Si$ $^{31}_{15}P$ $^{32}_{16}S$ $^{35}_{17}Cl$ $^{40}_{18}Ar$

FIGURE 2.2 A Portion of the Periodic Table. Each element has a unique atomic number and is represented by a unique one- or two-letter symbol. The mass numbers given here are the most common for each element. (Appendix C provides a complete periodic table of elements.)

The number of protons in an element does not vary—if the atomic number of an atom changes, then it is no longer the same element. The number of neutrons present in an element can vary, however. Forms of an element with different numbers of neutrons are known as **isotopes** (literally, "equal-places" in regard to position in the periodic table).

Different isotopes have different masses, yet are the same element. For example, all atoms of the element carbon have 6 protons. But naturally occurring isotopes of carbon can have 6, 7, or even 8 neutrons, giving them a mass number of 12, 13, or 14, respectively. The **atomic weight** of an element is an average of all the mass numbers of the naturally occurring isotopes based on their abundance. This is why the atomic weights for elements are often slightly different from the mass numbers—the atomic weight of carbon, for example, is 12.01.

Most isotopes are stable, but not all. For example, ^{14}C, with 6 protons and 8 neutrons, represents an unstable **radioactive isotope.** Its nucleus will eventually decay and release energy (radiation). When ^{14}C decays, one of its neutrons changes into a proton, converting ^{14}C to the stable ^{14}N isotope of nitrogen, with 7 protons and 7 neutrons. Timing of decay is specific to each radioisotope, a fact that has been very useful in estimating the dates of key events in the fossil record.

Although the masses of protons, neutrons, and electrons can be measured in grams, the numbers involved are so small that biologists prefer to use a special unit called the **dalton.** The masses of protons and neutrons are virtually identical and are routinely rounded to 1 dalton. A carbon atom that contains 6 protons and 6 neutrons has a mass of 12 daltons, while a carbon atom with 6 protons and 7 neutrons would have a mass of 13 daltons. These isotopes would be written as ^{12}C and ^{13}C,

respectively. The mass of an electron is so small that it is normally ignored.

To understand how the atoms involved in chemical evolution behave, focus on how electrons are arranged around the nucleus:

- Electrons move around atomic nuclei in specific regions called **orbitals.**

- Each orbital can hold up to two electrons.

- Orbitals are grouped into levels called **electron shells.**

- Electron shells are numbered 1, 2, 3, and so on, to indicate their relative distance from the nucleus. Smaller numbers are closer to the nucleus.

- Each electron shell contains a specific number of orbitals. An electron shell comprising a single orbital can hold up to two electrons; a shell with four orbitals can contain up to eight electrons.

- The electrons of an atom fill the innermost shells first, before filling outer shells.

To understand how the structures of atoms differ, take a moment to study **FIGURE 2.3**. This chart highlights the elements that are most abundant in living cells. The gray ball in the center of each box represents an atomic nucleus, and the orange circle or circles represent the electron shells around that nucleus. The small orange balls on the circles indicate the number of electrons that are distributed in the shells of each element. Electrons shown as pairs share the same orbital within a shell.

Now focus on the outermost shell of each atom. This is the element's **valence shell.** The electrons found in this shell are referred to as **valence electrons.** Two observations are important:

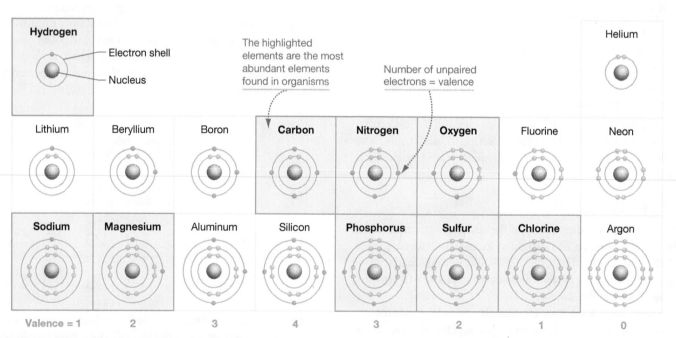

FIGURE 2.3 The Structure of Atoms Found in Organisms.

✔ **QUESTION** If the mass number of phosphorus is 31, how many neutrons exist in the most common isotope of phosphorus?

1. In each of the highlighted elements, the outermost electron shell is not full—not all orbitals in the valence shell have two electrons. The highlighted elements have at least one unpaired valence electron—meaning at least one unfilled valence shell orbital.

2. The number of unpaired valence electrons varies among elements. Carbon, for example, has four valence electrons, all unpaired. Oxygen has six valence electrons; four are paired, two are not. The number of unpaired electrons found in an atom is called its **valence.** Carbon's valence is four, oxygen's is two.

These observations are significant because an atom is most stable when its valence shell is filled. One way that shells can be filled is through the formation of strong **chemical bonds**—attractions that bind atoms together. A strong attraction where two atoms share one or more pairs of electrons is called a **covalent bond.**

How Does Covalent Bonding Hold Molecules Together?

To understand how atoms can become more stable by making covalent bonds, consider hydrogen. The hydrogen atom has just one electron, which resides in a shell that can hold two electrons.

Because it has an unpaired valence electron, the hydrogen atom is not very stable. But when two atoms of hydrogen come into contact, the two electrons become shared by the two nuclei (**FIGURE 2.4**). Both atoms now have a completely filled outer shell. Together, the hydrogen atoms are more stable than the two individual hydrogen atoms.

Shared electrons "glue" two hydrogen atoms together. Substances held together by covalent bonds are called **molecules.** In the case of two hydrogen atoms, the bonded atoms form a single molecule of hydrogen, written as H—H or H_2.

It can also be helpful to think about covalent bonding as electrical attraction and repulsion. Opposite charges attract; like charges repel. As two hydrogen atoms move closer together, their positively charged nuclei repel each other and their negatively charged electrons repel each other. But each proton attracts both electrons, and each electron attracts both protons. Covalent bonds form when the attractive forces overcome the repulsive forces. This is the case when hydrogen atoms interact to form the hydrogen molecule (H_2).

Nonpolar and Polar Bonds   In **FIGURE 2.5a**, the covalent bond between hydrogen atoms is represented by a dash and the electrons are drawn as dots halfway between the two nuclei. This depiction shows that the electrons are shared equally between the two hydrogen atoms, resulting in a covalent bond that is symmetrical.

It's important to note, though, that the electrons participating in a covalent bond are not always shared equally between the atoms involved. This happens because some atoms hold the electrons in covalent bonds much more tightly than do other atoms. Chemists call this property **electronegativity.**

What is responsible for an atom's electronegativity? It's a combination of two things—the number of protons in the nucleus and the distance between the nucleus and the valence shell. If

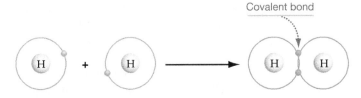

Hydrogen atoms each have one unpaired electron

H_2 molecule has two shared electrons

FIGURE 2.4 Covalent Bonds Result from Electron Sharing. When two hydrogen atoms come into contact, their electrons are attracted to the positive charge in each nucleus. As a result, their orbitals overlap, the electrons are shared by each nucleus, and a covalent bond forms.

you return to Figure 2.3 and move your finger along a row from left to right, you will be moving toward elements that increase in protons and in electronegativity (ignoring the elements in the far right column, which have full outer shells). Each row, however, represents shells of electrons, so if your finger moved down the table, the elements would decrease in electronegativity.

Oxygen, which has eight protons and only two electron shells, is among the most electronegative of all elements. It attracts covalently bonded electrons more strongly than does any other atom commonly found in organisms. Nitrogen's electronegativity is somewhat lower than oxygen's. Carbon and hydrogen, in turn, have relatively low and approximately equal electronegativities. Thus, the electronegativities of the four most abundant elements in organisms are related as follows: $O > N > C \cong H$.

Because carbon and hydrogen have approximately equal electronegativity, the electrons in a C—H bond are shared equally or symmetrically. The result is a **nonpolar covalent bond.** In contrast, asymmetric sharing of electrons results in a **polar covalent bond.** The electrons in a polar covalent bond spend most of their time close to the nucleus of the more electronegative atom. Why is this important?

Polar Bonds Produce Partial Charges on Atoms   To understand the consequences of differences in electronegativity and the formation of polar covalent bonds, consider the water molecule.

Water consists of an oxygen bonded to two hydrogen atoms, and is written H_2O. As **FIGURE 2.5b** illustrates, the electrons

(a) Nonpolar covalent bond in hydrogen molecule

Electrons are halfway between the two atoms, shared equally

(b) Polar covalent bonds in water molecule

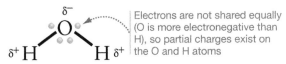

Electrons are not shared equally (O is more electronegative than H), so partial charges exist on the O and H atoms

FIGURE 2.5 Electron Sharing and Bond Polarity. Delta (δ) symbols in polar covalent bonds refer to partial positive and negative charges that arise owing to unequal electron sharing.

involved in the covalent bonds in water are not shared equally but are held much more tightly by the oxygen nucleus than by the hydrogen nuclei. Hence, water has two polar covalent bonds—one between the oxygen atom and each of the hydrogen atoms.

Here's the key observation: Because electrons are shared unequally in each O—H bond, they spend more time near the oxygen atom, giving it a partial negative charge, and less time near the hydrogen atoms, giving them a partial positive charge. These partial charges are symbolized by the lowercase Greek letter delta, δ.

As Section 2.2 shows, the partial charges on water molecules—due simply to the difference in electronegativity between oxygen and hydrogen—are one of the primary reasons that life exists.

Ionic Bonding, Ions, and the Electron-Sharing Continuum

Ionic bonds are similar in principle to covalent bonds, but instead of being shared between two atoms, the electrons in ionic bonds are completely transferred from one atom to the other. The electron transfer occurs because it gives the resulting atoms a full outermost shell.

Sodium atoms (Na), for example, tend to lose an electron, leaving them with a full second shell. This is a much more stable arrangement, energetically, than having a lone electron in their third shell (**FIGURE 2.6a**). The atom that results has a net electric charge of +1, because it has one more proton than it has electrons.

An atom or molecule that carries a full charge, rather than the partial charges that arise from polar covalent bonds, is called an **ion**. The sodium ion is written Na$^+$ and, like other positively charged ions, is called a **cation** (pronounced *KAT-eye-un*).

Chlorine atoms (Cl), in contrast, tend to gain an electron, filling their outermost shell (**FIGURE 2.6b**). The ion has a net charge of −1, because it has one more electron than protons. This

negatively charged ion, or **anion** (pronounced *AN-eye-un*), is written Cl$^-$ and is called chlori*de*.

When sodium and chlorine combine to form sodium chloride (NaCl, common table salt), they pack into a crystal structure consisting of sodium cations and chloride anions (**FIGURE 2.6c**). The electrical attraction between the ions is so strong that salt crystals are difficult to break apart.

This discussion of covalent and ionic bonding supports an important general observation: The degree to which electrons are shared in chemical bonds forms a continuum from equal sharing in nonpolar covalent bonds to unequal sharing in polar covalent bonds to the transfer of electrons in ionic bonds.

As the left-hand side of **FIGURE 2.7** shows, covalent bonds between atoms with exactly the same electronegativity—for example, between the atoms of hydrogen in H$_2$—represent one end of the continuum. The electrons in these nonpolar bonds are shared equally.

In the middle of the continuum are bonds where one atom is much more electronegative than the other. In these asymmetric bonds, substantial partial charges exist on each of the atoms. These types of polar covalent bonds occur when a highly electronegative atom such as oxygen or nitrogen is bonded to an atom with a lower affinity for electrons, such as carbon or hydrogen. Ammonia (NH$_3$) and water (H$_2$O) are examples of molecules with polar covalent bonds.

At the right-hand side of the continuum are molecules made up of atoms with extreme differences in their electronegativities. In this case, electrons are transferred rather than shared, the atoms have full charges, and the bonding is ionic. Sodium chloride (NaCl) is a familiar example of a molecule formed by ionic bonds.

Most chemical bonds that occur in biological molecules are on the left-hand side and the middle of the continuum; in the molecules found in organisms, ionic bonding is less common.

(a) A sodium ion being formed

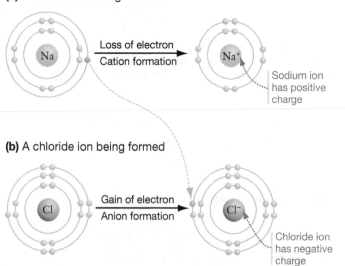

(b) A chloride ion being formed

(c) Table salt (NaCl) is a crystal composed of two ions.

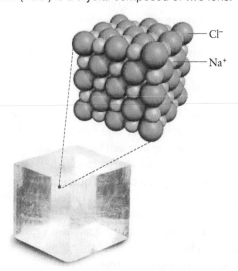

FIGURE 2.6 Ion Formation and Ionic Bonding. The sodium ion (Na$^+$) and the chloride ion (Cl$^-$) are stable because they have full valence shells. In table salt (NaCl), sodium and chloride ions pack into a crystal structure held together by electrical attraction between their positive and negative charges.

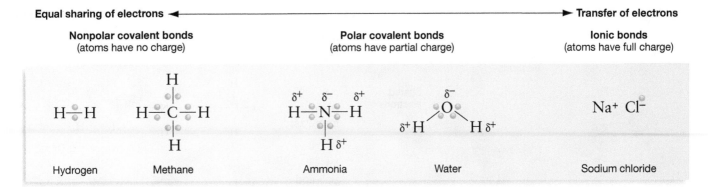

Equal sharing of electrons ◄──────────────────────────────────► Transfer of electrons

| Nonpolar covalent bonds (atoms have no charge) | Polar covalent bonds (atoms have partial charge) | Ionic bonds (atoms have full charge) |

Hydrogen   Methane   Ammonia   Water   Sodium chloride

FIGURE 2.7 The Electron-Sharing Continuum. The degree of electron sharing in chemical bonds can be thought of as a continuum, from equal sharing in nonpolar covalent bonds to no sharing in ionic bonds.

✔ **QUESTION** Why do most polar covalent bonds involve nitrogen or oxygen?

Some Simple Molecules Formed from C, H, N, and O

Look back at Figure 2.3 and count the number of unpaired electrons in the valence shells of carbon, nitrogen, oxygen, and hydrogen atoms. Each unpaired electron in a valence shell can make up half of a covalent bond. It should make sense to you that a carbon atom can form a total of four covalent bonds; nitrogen can form three; oxygen can form two; and hydrogen, one.

When each of the four unpaired electrons of a carbon atom covalently bonds with a hydrogen atom, the molecule that results is written CH_4 and is called methane (**FIGURE 2.8a**). Methane is the most common molecule found in natural gas. When a nitrogen atom's three unpaired electrons bond with three hydrogen atoms, the result is NH_3, or ammonia. Similarly, an atom of oxygen can form covalent bonds with two atoms of hydrogen, resulting in a water molecule (H_2O). As Figure 2.4 showed, a hydrogen atom can bond with another hydrogen atom to form hydrogen gas (H_2).

In addition to forming more than one single bond, atoms with more than one unpaired electron in the valence shell can form double bonds or triple bonds. **FIGURE 2.8b** shows how carbon forms double bonds with oxygen atoms to produce carbon dioxide (CO_2). Triple bonds result when three pairs of electrons are shared. **FIGURE 2.8c** shows the structure of molecular nitrogen (N_2), which forms when two nitrogen atoms establish a triple bond.

✔ If you understand how electronegativity affects covalent bonds, you should be able to draw arrows between the atoms in each molecule shown in Figure 2.8 to indicate the relative position of the shared electrons. If they are equally shared, then draw a double-headed arrow.

The Geometry of Simple Molecules

In many cases, the overall shape of a molecule dictates how it behaves. In chemistry and in biology, function is based on structure.

The shapes of the simple molecules you've just learned about are governed by the geometry of their bonds. Nitrogen (N_2) and

(a) Single bonds

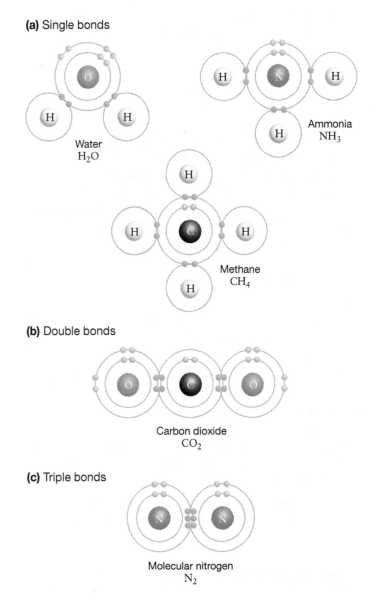

Water H_2O

Ammonia NH_3

Methane CH_4

(b) Double bonds

Carbon dioxide CO_2

(c) Triple bonds

Molecular nitrogen N_2

FIGURE 2.8 Unpaired Electrons in the Valence Shell Participate in Covalent Bonds. Covalent bonding is based on sharing of electrons in the outermost shell. Covalent bonds can be **(a)** single, **(b)** double, or **(c)** triple.

(a) Methane (CH₄)   **(b)** Water (H₂O)

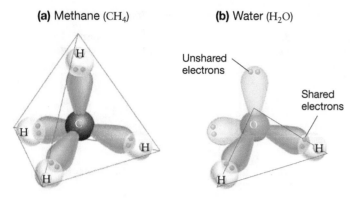

FIGURE 2.9 The Geometry of Methane and Water.

	Methane	Ammonia	Water	Oxygen
(a) Molecular formulas:	CH_4	NH_3	H_2O	O_2

(b) Structural formulas:

H—C—H (with H above and below C)   H—N—H (with H below N)   O with H and H below (bent)   O=O

(c) Ball-and-stick models:

(d) Space-filling models:

FIGURE 2.10 Molecules Can Be Represented Several Ways. Each method of representing a molecule has particular advantages.

carbon dioxide (CO_2), for example, have linear structures (see Figure 2.8). Molecules with more complex geometries include

- Methane (CH_4)—which is tetrahedral, a structure with four triangular faces like a pyramid (**FIGURE 2.9a**). The tetrahedron forms because the electrons in the four C−H bonds repulse each other equally. The electron pairs are as far apart as they can get.

- Water (H_2O)—which is bent and two-dimensional, or planar (**FIGURE 2.9b**). Why? The electrons in the four orbitals of oxygen's valence shell repulse each other, just as they do in methane. But in water, two of the orbitals are filled with electron pairs from the oxygen atom, and two are filled with electron pairs from covalent bonds between oxygen and hydrogen. The shared electrons form a molecule that is V-shaped and flat.

Section 2.2 explores how water's shape, in combination with the partial charges on the oxygen and hydrogen atoms, makes it the most important molecule on Earth.

Representing Molecules

Molecules can be represented in a variety of increasingly complex ways—only some of which reflect their actual shape. Each method has advantages and disadvantages.

- **Molecular formulas** are compact, but don't contain a great deal of information—they indicate only the numbers and types of atoms in a molecule (**FIGURE 2.10a**).

- **Structural formulas** indicate which atoms in a molecule are bonded together. Single, double, and triple bonds are represented by single, double, and triple dashes, respectively. Structural formulas also indicate geometry in two dimensions (**FIGURE 2.10b**). This method is useful for planar molecules such as water and O_2.

- **Ball-and-stick models** take up more space than structural formulas, but provide information on the three-dimensional shape of molecules and indicate the relative sizes of the atoms involved (**FIGURE 2.10c**).

- **Space-filling models** are more difficult to read than ball-and-stick models but more accurately depict the spatial relationships between atoms. (**FIGURE 2.10d**).

In both ball-and-stick and space-filling models, biologists use certain colors to represent certain atoms. A black ball, for

example, always symbolizes carbon. (For more information on interpreting chemical structures, see **BioSkills 8** in Appendix B.)

Some of the small molecules you've just learned about are found in volcanic gases, the atmospheres of nearby planets, and in deep-sea hydrothermal vents, like those shown in the photograph at the start of this chapter. Based on these observations, researchers claim that they were important components of Earth's ancient atmosphere and oceans. If so, then they provided the building blocks for chemical evolution. The question is: How did these simple building blocks combine to form more complex products, early in Earth's history?

Researchers postulate that most of the critical reactions in chemical evolution occurred in an aqueous, or water-based, environment. To understand what happened and why, let's delve into the properties of water and then turn to analyzing the reactions that triggered chemical evolution.

check your understanding

Ⓒ If you understand that . . .

- Covalent bonds are based on electron sharing. Electron sharing allows atoms to fill all the orbitals in their valence shell, making them more stable.
- Covalent bonds can be polar or nonpolar, depending on whether the electronegativities of the two atoms involved are the same or different.

✓ You should be able to . . .

Draw the structural formula of formaldehyde (CH_2O) and add dots to indicate the relative locations of the electrons being shared in each covalent bond, based on the relative electronegativities of C, H, and O.

Answers are available in Appendix A.

2.2 Properties of Water and the Early Oceans

Life is based on water. It arose in an aqueous environment and remains dependent on water today. In fact, 75 percent of the volume in a typical cell is water; water is the most abundant molecule in organisms (**FIGURE 2.11**). You can survive for weeks without eating, but you aren't likely to live more than 3 or 4 days without drinking.

Water is vital for a simple reason: It is an excellent **solvent**—that is, an agent for dissolving substances and getting them into **solution.** The reactions that were responsible for chemical evolution some 3.5 billion years ago, like those occurring inside your body right now, depend on direct, physical interaction between molecules. Substances are most likely to come into contact with one another and react as **solutes**—meaning, when they are dissolved in a solvent like water. The formation of Earth's first ocean, about 3.8 billion years ago, was a turning point in chemical evolution because it gave the process a place to happen.

Why Is Water Such an Efficient Solvent?

To understand why water is such an effective solvent, recall that

1. Both of the O−H bonds in a water molecule are polar, owing to the difference in the electronegativities of hydrogen and oxygen. As a result, the oxygen atom has a partial negative charge and each hydrogen atom has a partial positive charge.

2. The molecule is bent. Consequently, the partial negative charge on the oxygen atom sticks out, away from the partial positive charges on the hydrogen atoms, giving a water molecule an overall polarity (**FIGURE 2.12a**).

FIGURE 2.12b illustrates how water's structure affects its interactions with other water molecules. When two water molecules approach each other, the partial positive charge on hydrogen attracts the partial negative charge on oxygen. This weak electrical attraction forms a **hydrogen bond** between the molecules.

✔ If you understand how water's structure makes hydrogen bonding possible, you should be able to (1) draw a fictional version of Figure 2.12b that shows water as a linear (not bent)

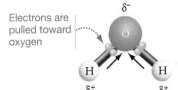 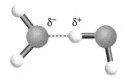

(a) Water is polar.

Electrons are pulled toward oxygen

(b) Hydrogen bonds form between water molecules.

FIGURE 2.12 Water Is Polar and Participates in Hydrogen Bonds. (a) Because of oxygen's high electronegativity, the electrons that are shared between hydrogen and oxygen spend more time close to the oxygen nucleus, giving the oxygen atom a partial negative charge and the hydrogen atom a partial positive charge. **(b)** The electrical attraction that occurs between the partial positive and negative charges on water molecules forms a hydrogen bond.

molecule with partial charges on the oxygen and hydrogen atoms; and (2) explain why electrostatic attractions between such water molecules would be much weaker as a result.

In an aqueous solution, hydrogen bonds also form between water molecules and other polar molecules. Similar interactions occur between water and ions. Ions and polar molecules stay in solution because of their interactions with water's partial charges (**FIGURE 2.13**). Substances that interact with water in this way are said to be **hydrophilic** ("water-loving"). Hydrogen bonding makes it possible for almost any charged or polar molecule to dissolve in water.

In contrast, compounds that are uncharged and nonpolar do not interact with water through hydrogen bonding and do not dissolve in water. Substances that do not interact with water are said to be **hydrophobic** ("water-fearing"). Because their interactions with water are minimal or nonexistent, they are forced to interact with each other (**FIGURE 2.14**, see page 26). The water molecules surrounding nonpolar molecules form hydrogen bonds with one another and increase the stability of these **hydrophobic interactions.**

Although individual hydrogen bonds are not as strong as covalent or ionic bonds, many of them occur in a solution. Hydrogen bonding is extremely important in biology owing to the

FIGURE 2.11 Fruits Shrink When They Are Dried Because They Consist Primarily of Water.

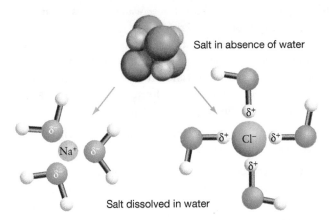

Salt in absence of water

Salt dissolved in water

FIGURE 2.13 Polar Molecules and Ions Dissolve Readily in Water. Water's polarity makes it a superb solvent for polar molecules and ions.

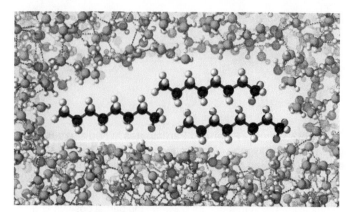

FIGURE 2.14 Nonpolar Molecules Do Not Dissolve in Water. In aqueous solution, nonpolar molecules and compounds are forced to interact with each other. This occurs because water is much more stable when it interacts with itself rather than with the nonpolar molecules.

✔**QUESTION** What is the physical basis of the expression, "Oil and water don't mix"?

(a) A meniscus forms where water meets a solid surface, as a result of two forces.

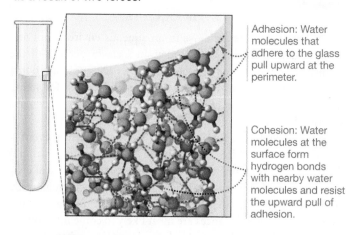

Adhesion: Water molecules that adhere to the glass pull upward at the perimeter.

Cohesion: Water molecules at the surface form hydrogen bonds with nearby water molecules and resist the upward pull of adhesion.

(b) Water has high surface tension.

Because of surface tension, light objects do not fall through the water's surface

FIGURE 2.15 Cohesion, Adhesion, and Surface Tension. **(a)** Meniscus formation is based on hydrogen bonding. **(b)** Water resists forces—like the weight of a spider—that increase its surface area. The resistance is great enough that light objects do not break the surface.

sheer number of hydrogen bonds that form between water and hydrophilic molecules.

What Properties Are Correlated with Water's Structure?

Water's small size, highly polar covalent bonds, and bent shape resulting in overall polarity are unique among molecules. Because the structure of molecules routinely correlates with their function, it's not surprising that water has some remarkable properties, in addition to its extraordinary capacity to act as a solvent.

Cohesion, Adhesion, and Surface Tension Attraction between like molecules is called **cohesion.** Water is cohesive—meaning that it stays together—because of the hydrogen bonds that form between individual molecules.

Attraction between unlike molecules, in contrast, is called **adhesion.** Adhesion is usually analyzed in regard to interactions between a liquid and a solid surface. Water adheres to surfaces that have any polar or charged components.

Cohesion and adhesion are important in explaining how water can move from the roots of plants to their leaves against the force of gravity. But you can also see them in action in the concave surface, or meniscus, that forms in a glass tube (**FIGURE 2.15a**). A meniscus forms as a result of two forces:

1. Water molecules at the perimeter of the surface adhere to the glass, resulting in an upward pull.

2. Water molecules at the surface hydrogen-bond with water molecules next to them and below them, resulting in a net lateral and downward pull that resists the upward pull of adhesion.

Cohesion is also instrumental in the phenomenon known as **surface tension.** When water molecules are at the surface, there

are no water molecules above them for hydrogen bonding. As a result, they exhibit stronger attractive forces between their nearest neighboring molecules. This enhanced attraction between the surface water molecules results in tension that minimizes the total surface area.

This fact has an important consequence: Water resists any force that increases its surface area. More specifically, any force that depresses a water surface meets with resistance. This resistance makes a water surface act like an elastic membrane (**FIGURE 2.15b**).

In water, the "elastic membrane" is stronger than it is in other liquids. Water's surface tension is extraordinarily high because of the stronger hydrogen bonding that occurs between molecules at the surface. This explains why it is better to cut the water's surface with your fingertips when you dive into a pool, instead of doing a belly flop.

Water Is Denser as a Liquid than as a Solid When factory workers pour molten metal or plastic into a mold and allow it to cool to the solid state, the material shrinks. When molten lava pours out of a volcano and cools to solid rock, it shrinks. But when you fill an ice tray with water and put it in the freezer to make ice, the water expands.

Unlike most substances, water is denser as a liquid than it is as a solid. In other words, there are more molecules of water in a given volume of liquid water than there are in the same volume of solid water, or ice. **FIGURE 2.16** illustrates why this is so.

Note that in ice, each water molecule participates in four hydrogen bonds. These hydrogen bonds cause the water molecules to form a regular and repeating structure, or crystal (Figure 2.16a). The crystal structure of ice is fairly open, meaning that there is a relatively large amount of space between molecules.

Now compare the extent of hydrogen bonding and the density of ice with that of liquid water, illustrated in Figure 2.16b. Note that the extent of hydrogen bonding in liquid water is much less than that found in ice, and that the hydrogen bonds in liquid water are constantly being formed and broken. As a result, molecules in the liquid phase are packed much more closely together than in the solid phase.

Normally, heating a substance causes it to expand because molecules begin moving faster and colliding more often and with greater force. But heating ice causes hydrogen bonds to break and the open crystal structure to collapse. In this way, hydrogen bonding explains why water is denser as a liquid than as a solid.

This property of water has an important result: Ice floats (Figure 2.16c). If it didn't, ice would sink to the bottom of lakes, ponds, and oceans soon after it formed. The ice would stay frozen in the cold depths. Instead, ice serves as a blanket, insulating the liquid below from the cold air above. If water weren't so unusual, it is almost certain that Earth's oceans would have frozen solid before life had a chance to start.

Water Has a High Capacity for Absorbing Energy Hydrogen bonding is also responsible for another of water's remarkable physical properties: Water has a high capacity for absorbing energy.

Specific heat, for example, is the amount of energy required to raise the temperature of 1 gram of a substance by 1°C. Water has a high specific heat because when a source of energy hits it, hydrogen bonds must be broken before heat can be transferred and the water molecules begin moving faster. As **TABLE 2.1** indicates, as molecules increase in overall polarity, and thus in their ability to form hydrogen bonds, it takes an extraordinarily large amount of energy to change their temperature.

TABLE 2.1 Specific Heats of Some Liquids

The specific heats reported in this table were measured at 25°C and are given in units of joules per gram of substance per degree Celsius. (The joule is a unit of energy.)

With extensive hydrogen bonding	Specific Heat
Water (H_2O)	4.18
With some hydrogen bonding	
Ethanol (C_2H_6O)	2.44
Glycerol ($C_3H_8O_3$)	2.38
With little or no hydrogen bonding	
Benzene (C_6H_6)	1.74
Xylene (C_8H_{10})	1.72

DATA: D. R. Lide (editor). 2008. Standard Thermodynamic Properties of Chemical Substances, in *CRC Handbook of Physics and Chemistry.* 89th ed. Boca Raton, FL: CRC Press.

(a) In ice, water molecules form a crystal lattice.

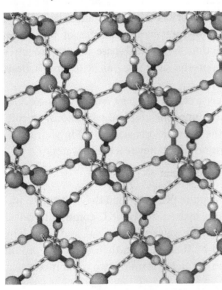

(b) In liquid water, no crystal lattice forms.

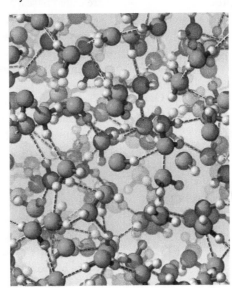

(c) Liquid water is denser than ice. As a result, ice floats.

FIGURE 2.16 Hydrogen Bonding Forms the Crystal Structure of Ice. In ice, each molecule can form four hydrogen bonds at one time. Each oxygen atom can form two; each hydrogen atom can form one.

Property	Cause	Biological Consequences
Solvent for charged or polar compounds	_____ _____ _____ _____	Most chemical reactions important for life take place in aqueous solution.
Denser as a liquid than a solid	As water freezes, each molecule forms a total of four hydrogen bonds, leading to the formation of the low-density crystal structure called ice.	_____ _____ _____
High specific heat	Water molecules must absorb lots of heat energy to break hydrogen bonds and experience increased movement (and thus temperature).	Oceans absorb and release heat slowly, moderating coastal climates.
High heat of vaporization	_____ _____ _____	Evaporation of water from an organism cools the body.

✔ **EXERCISE** You should be able to fill in the missing cells in this table.

Similarly, it takes a large amount of energy to break the hydrogen bonds in liquid water and change the molecules from the liquid phase to the gas phase. Water's **heat of vaporization**—the energy required to change 1 gram of it from a liquid to gas—is higher than that of most molecules that are liquid at room temperature. As a result, water has to absorb a great deal of energy to evaporate. Water's high heat of vaporization is the reason that sweating or dousing yourself with water is an effective way to cool off on a hot day. Water molecules absorb a great deal of energy from your body before they evaporate, so you lose heat.

Water's ability to absorb energy is critical to the theory of chemical evolution. Molecules that were formed in the ocean were well protected from sources of energy that could break them apart, such as intense sunlight. As a result, they would have persisted and slowly increased in concentration over time, making them more likely to react and continue the process.

TABLE 2.2 summarizes some of the key properties of water.

The Role of Water in Acid–Base Reactions

You've seen that water's high specific heat and heat of vaporization tend to keep its temperature and liquid form stable. One other aspect of water's chemistry is important for understanding chemical evolution and how organisms work: Water is not a completely stable molecule. In reality, water molecules continually undergo a chemical reaction with themselves. When a **chemical reaction** occurs, one substance is combined with others or broken down into another substance. Atoms may also be rearranged; in most cases, chemical bonds are broken and new bonds form. The chemical reaction that takes place between water molecules is called a "dissociation" reaction. It can be written as follows:

$$H_2O \rightleftharpoons H^+ + OH^-$$

The double arrow indicates that the reaction proceeds in both directions.

The substances on the right-hand side of the expression are the **hydrogen ion** (H^+) and the **hydroxide ion** (OH^-). A hydrogen ion is simply a proton. In reality, however, protons do not exist by themselves. In water, for example, protons associate with water molecules to form hydronium ions (H_3O^+). Thus, the dissociation of water is more accurately written as:

$$H_2O + H_2O \rightleftharpoons H_3O^+ + OH^-$$

One of the water molecules on the left-hand side of the expression has given up a proton, while the other water molecule has accepted a proton.

Substances that give up protons during chemical reactions and raise the hydronium ion concentration of water are called **acids;** molecules or ions that acquire protons during chemical reactions and lower the hydronium ion concentration of water are called **bases.** Most acids act only as acids, and most bases act only as bases; but water can act as both an acid and a base.

A chemical reaction that involves a transfer of protons is called an acid–base reaction. Every acid–base reaction requires a proton donor and a proton acceptor—an acid and a base, respectively.

Water is an extremely weak acid—very few water molecules dissociate to form hydronium ions and hydroxide ions. In contrast, strong acids like the hydrochloric acid (HCl) in your stomach readily give up a proton when they react with water.

$$HCl + H_2O \rightleftharpoons H_3O^+ + Cl^-$$

Strong bases readily acquire protons when they react with water. For example, sodium hydroxide (NaOH, commonly called lye) dissociates completely in water to form Na^+ and OH^-. The hydroxide ion produced by that reaction then accepts a proton from a hydronium ion in the water, forming two water molecules.

$$NaOH(aq) \longrightarrow Na^+ + OH^-$$
$$OH^- + H_3O^+ \rightleftharpoons 2\,H_2O$$

(The "*aq*" in the first expression indicates that NaOH is in aqueous solution.)

To summarize, adding an acid to a solution increases the concentration of protons; adding a base to a solution lowers the concentration of protons. Water is both a weak acid and a weak base.

Determining the Concentration of Protons In a solution, the tendency for acid–base reactions to occur is largely a function of the number of protons present. The problem is, there's no simple way to count the actual number of protons present in a sample. Researchers solve this problem using the mole concept.

A **mole** refers to the number 6.022×10^{23}—just as the unit called the dozen refers to the number 12 or the unit million refers to the number 1×10^6. The mole is a useful unit because the mass of one mole of any substance is the same as its molecular weight expressed in grams. **Molecular weight** is the sum of the atomic weights of all the atoms in a molecule.

For example, to get the molecular weight of H_2O, you sum the atomic weights of two atoms of hydrogen and one atom of oxygen. Since the atomic weights of hydrogen and oxygen are very close to their mass numbers (see Figure 2.2), the molecular weight of water would be $1 + 1 + 16$, or a total of 18. Thus, if you weighed a sample of 18 grams of water, it would contain around 6×10^{23} water molecules, or about 1 mole of water molecules.

When substances are dissolved in water, their concentration is expressed in terms of molarity (symbolized by "M"). **Molarity** is the number of moles of the substance present per liter of solution. A 1-molar solution of protons in water, for example, means that 1 mole of protons is contained in 1 liter of solution.

Chemists can measure the concentration of protons in a solution directly using molarity and an instrument called a pH meter. In a sample of pure water at 25°C, the concentration of H^+ is $1.0 \times 10^{-7}M$, or 1 ten-millionth molar.

The pH of a Solution Reveals Whether It Is Acidic or Basic Because the concentration of protons in water is such a small number, exponential notation is cumbersome. So chemists and biologists prefer to express the concentration of protons in a solution, and thus whether it is acidic or basic, with a logarithmic notation called **pH**.[1]

By definition, the pH of a solution is the negative of the base-10 logarithm, or log, of the hydrogen ion concentration:

$$pH = -\log[H^+]$$

(To review logarithms, see **BioSkills 6** in Appendix B. The square brackets are a standard notation for indicating "concentration" of a substance in solution.)

Taking antilogs gives

$$[H^+] = \text{antilog}(-pH) = 10^{-pH}$$

Solutions that contain acids have a proton concentration larger than $1 \times 10^{-7}M$ and thus a pH < 7. This is because acidic

molecules tend to release protons into solution. In contrast, solutions that contain bases have a proton concentration less than $1 \times 10^{-7}M$ and thus a pH > 7. This is because basic molecules tend to accept protons from solution.

pH is a convenient way to indicate the concentration of protons in a solution, but take note of what the number represents. For example, if the concentration of H^+ in a sample of water is $1.0 \times 10^{-7}M$, then its pH is 7. If the pH changes to 5, then the sample contains 100 times more protons and has become 100 times more acidic. ✔ QUANTITATIVE If you understand how pH is related to $[H^+]$, you should be able to calculate the concentration of protons in a solution that has a pH of 8.5.

FIGURE 2.17 shows the pH scale and reports the pH of some selected solutions. Pure water is used as a standard, or point of reference, for pH 7 on the pH scale. The solution inside living cells is about pH 7, which is considered neutral—neither acidic nor basic. The normal function of a cell is dependent on maintaining this neutral internal environment. What is responsible for regulating pH?

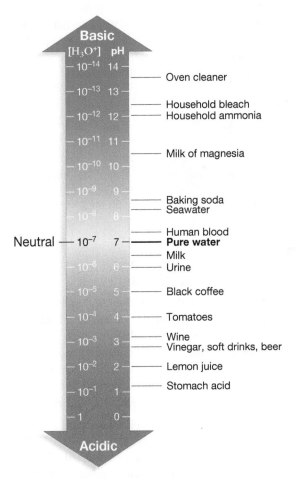

FIGURE 2.17 The pH Scale. Because the pH scale is logarithmic, a change in one unit of pH represents a change in the concentration of hydrogen ions equal to a factor of 10. Coffee has a hundred times more H^+ than pure water has.

✔ QUESTION What happens to the concentration of protons in black coffee after you add milk?

---

[1]The term pH is derived from the French *puissance d'hydrogéne*, or "power of hydrogen."

Buffers Protect Against Damaging Changes in pH   Life is sensitive to changes in pH. Changes in proton concentration affect the structure and function of polar or charged substances as well as the tendency of acid–base reactions to occur.

Compounds that minimize changes in pH are called **buffers** because they reduce the impact of adding acids or bases on the overall pH of a solution. Buffers are important in maintaining relatively constant conditions, or **homeostasis,** in cells and tissues. In cells, a wide array of naturally occurring molecules act as buffers.

Most buffers are weak acids, meaning that they are somewhat likely to give up a proton in solution, but once the proton concentration rises, the acid is regenerated. To see how buffers work, consider the disassociation of carbonic acid in water to form bicarbonate ions and protons:

$$CH_2O_3 \rightleftharpoons CHO_3^- + H^+$$
$$\text{carbonic acid} \qquad \text{bicarbonate}$$

When carbonic acid and bicarbonate are present in about equal concentrations in a solution, they function as a buffering system. If the concentration of protons increases slightly, the protons react with bicarbonate ions to form carbonic acid and pH does not change. If the concentration of protons decreases slightly, carbonic acid gives up protons and pH does not change. ✔ If you understand this concept, you should be able to predict what would happen to the concentration of bicarbonate ions if a base like sodium hydroxide (NaOH) were added to the solution of carbonic acid.

As chemical evolution began, then, water provided the physical environment for key reactions to take place. In some cases water also acted as an important reactant. Although acid–base reactions were not critical to the initial stages of chemical evolution, they became extremely important once the process was under way. Now let's consider what happened in solution, some 3.5 billion years ago.

2.3 Chemical Reactions, Energy, and Chemical Evolution

Proponents of the theory of chemical evolution contend that simple molecules present in the atmosphere and oceans of early Earth participated in chemical reactions that eventually produced larger, more complex organic (carbon-containing) molecules—such as the proteins, nucleic acids, sugars, and lipids introduced in the next four chapters. Currently, researchers are investigating two environments where these reactions may have occurred:

1. *The atmosphere*, which was probably dominated by gases ejected from volcanoes. Water vapor, carbon dioxide (CO_2), and nitrogen (N_2) are the dominant gases ejected by volcanoes today; a small amount of molecular hydrogen (H_2) and carbon monoxide (CO) may also be present.

2. *Deep-sea hydrothermal vents*, where extremely hot rocks contact deep cracks in the seafloor. In addition to gases such as CO_2 and H_2, certain deep-sea vents are rich in minerals containing reactive metals such as nickel and iron.

When gases like CO_2, N_2, H_2, and CO are put together and allowed to interact on their own, however, very little happens. They do not suddenly link together to create large, complex substances like those found in living cells. Instead, their bonds remain intact. To understand why the bonds of these molecules remain unchanged, you must first learn about how chemical reactions proceed.

How Do Chemical Reactions Happen?

Chemical reactions are written in a format similar to mathematical equations: The initial, or **reactant,** molecules are shown on the left and the resulting reaction **product(s)** shown on the right. For example, the most common reaction in the mix of gases and water vapor that emerges from volcanoes results in the production of carbonic acid, which can be precipitated with water as acid rain:

$$CO_2(g) + H_2O(l) \rightleftharpoons CH_2O_3(aq)$$
$$\text{carbonic acid}$$

The physical state of each reactant and product is indicated as gas (*g*), liquid (*l*), solid (*s*), or in aqueous solution (*aq*).

Note that the expression is balanced; that is, 1 carbon, 3 oxygen, and 2 hydrogen atoms are present on each side of the expression. This illustrates the conservation of mass in closed systems—mass cannot be created or destroyed, but it may be rearranged through chemical reactions.

Note also that the expression contains a double arrow, meaning that the reaction is reversible. When the forward and reverse reactions proceed at the same rate, the quantities of reactants and products remain constant, although not necessarily equal. A dynamic but stable state such as this is termed a **chemical equilibrium.**

Changing the concentration of reactants or products can disturb a chemical equilibrium. For example, adding more CO_2 to the mixture would drive the reaction to the right, creating more CH_2O_3 until the equilibrium proportions of reactants and products are reestablished. Removing CO_2 or adding more CH_2O_3 would drive the reaction to the left.

A chemical equilibrium can also be altered by changes in temperature. For example, the water molecules in the following set of interacting elements, or **system,** would be present as a combination of liquid water and water vapor:

$$H_2O(l) \rightleftharpoons H_2O(g)$$

If liquid water molecules absorb enough energy, like the heat released from a volcano, they transform to the gaseous state. (You may recall that water has a high heat of vaporization and requires a large amount of energy to change its state from liquid to gas.) As a result, this change is termed **endothermic** ("within heating") because heat is absorbed during the process. In contrast, the transformation of water vapor to liquid water releases heat and is **exothermic** ("outside heating"). Raising the temperature of this system drives the equilibrium to the right; cooling the system drives it to the left.

In relation to chemical evolution, though, these reactions and changes of physical state are not particularly interesting. Carbonic acid is not an important intermediate in the formation of more complex molecules. However, interesting things do begin to happen when energy is added to mixtures of volcanic gases.

What Is Energy?

Energy can be defined as the capacity to do work or to supply heat. This capacity exists in one of two ways—as a stored potential or as an active motion.

Stored energy is called **potential energy.** An object gains or loses its ability to store energy because of its position. An electron that resides in an outer electron shell will, if the opportunity arises, fall into a lower electron shell closer to the positive charges on the protons in the nucleus. Because of its position farther from the positive charges in the nucleus, an electron in an outer electron shell has more potential energy than does an electron in an inner shell (**FIGURE 2.18**). When stored in chemical bonds, this form of potential energy is called **chemical energy.**

Kinetic energy is energy of motion. Molecules have kinetic energy because they are constantly in motion.

- The kinetic energy of molecular motion is called **thermal energy.**

- The **temperature** of an object is a measure of how much thermal energy its molecules possess. If an object has a low temperature, its molecules are moving slowly. (We perceive this as "cold.") If an object has a high temperature, its molecules are moving rapidly. (We perceive this as "hot.")

- When two objects with different temperatures come into contact, thermal energy is transferred between them. This transferred energy is called **heat.**

There are many forms of potential energy and kinetic energy, and energy can change from one form into another. However, according to the **first law of thermodynamics,** energy is conserved—it cannot be created or destroyed, but only transferred and transformed. (A more thorough explanation of energy transformation is provided in Chapter 8 in the context of cellular metabolism.)

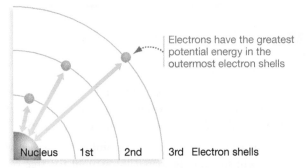

FIGURE 2.18 Potential Energy as a Function of Electron Shells. Electrons in outer shells have more potential energy than do electrons in inner shells, because the negative charges of the electrons in outer shells are farther from the positive charges of the protons in the nucleus. Each shell represents a distinct level of potential energy.

Energy transformation is the heart of chemical evolution. According to the best data available, molecules that were part of the early Earth were exposed to massive inputs of energy. Kinetic energy, in the form of heat, was present in the gradually cooling molten mass that initially formed the planet. The atmosphere and surface of the early Earth were also bombarded with electricity from lightening and radiation from the Sun. Energy stored as potential energy in the chemical bonds of small molecules was also abundant.

Now that you understand that energy transformations are involved in chemical reactions, a big question remains: What determines if a reaction will take place?

What Makes a Chemical Reaction Spontaneous?

When chemists say that a reaction is spontaneous, they have a precise meaning in mind: Chemical reactions are spontaneous if they are able to proceed on their own, without any continuous external influence, such as added energy. Two factors determine if a reaction will proceed spontaneously:

1. Reactions tend to be spontaneous when the product molecules are less ordered than the reactant molecules. For example, nitroglycerin is a single, highly ordered molecule. But when nitroglycerin explodes, it breaks up into gases like carbon dioxide, nitrogen, oxygen, and water vapor. These molecules are much less ordered than the reactant nitroglycerin molecules. The heat that is given off from this explosion also contributes to increasing disorder in the environment. The amount of disorder in a system is called **entropy.** When the products of a chemical reaction are less ordered than the reactant molecules are, entropy increases and the reaction tends to be spontaneous. The **second law of thermodynamics,** in fact, states that entropy always increases in an isolated system.

2. Reactions tend to be spontaneous if the products have lower potential energy than the reactants. If the electrons in the reaction products are held more tightly than those in the reactants, then they have lower potential energy. Recall that highly electronegative atoms such as oxygen or nitrogen hold electrons in covalent bonds much more tightly than do atoms with a lower electronegativity, such as hydrogen or carbon. For example, when hydrogen and oxygen gases react, water is produced spontaneously:

$$2\ H_2(g) + O_2(g) \longrightarrow 2\ H_2O(g)$$

The electrons involved in the O—H bonds of water are held much more tightly by the more electronegative oxygen atom than when they were shared equally in the H—H and O=O bonds of hydrogen and oxygen (see **FIGURE 2.19a** on page 32). As a result, the products have much lower potential energy than the reactants. The difference in chemical energy between reactants and products is given off as heat, so the reaction is exothermic. And although the reaction between hydrogen and oxygen results in less entropy—three molecules of gas produce two molecules of water vapor—the reaction is still spontaneous due to the large drop in potential energy

(a) When hydrogen and oxygen gas react, the product has much lower potential energy than the reactants.

Electrons are held "loosely" in bonds between atoms with equal electronegativities

Electrons are held tightly by highly electronegative atoms

H—H + O═O → H—O—H +

2 Hydrogens (H$_2$)   1 Oxygen (O$_2$)   *Potential energy drops*   2 Waters (H$_2$O)

(b) The difference in potential energy is released as heat and light, which vaporizes the water produced.

Heat and light

Released energy

FIGURE 2.19 Potential Energy May Change during Chemical Reactions. In the Hindenburg disaster of 1937, the hydrogen gas from this lighter-than-air craft reacted with oxygen in the atmosphere, with devastating results.

✔**EXERCISE** Label which electrons have relatively low potential energy and which electrons have relatively high potential energy.

released as heat. Since heat increases disorder in the environment, the second law of thermodynamics remains intact. The Hindenburg disaster of 1937 illustrates the large and terrifying amount of heat energy that is given off from this relatively simple reaction (**FIGURE 2.19b**).

To summarize: In general, physical and chemical processes proceed in the direction that results in increased entropy and lower potential energy (**FIGURE 2.20**). These two factors—potential energy and entropy—are used to figure out whether a reaction is spontaneous (see Chapter 8 for more detail). Were the reactions that led to chemical evolution spontaneous? Section 2.4 explores how researchers address this question.

Reactants:
• high potential energy
• more order (lower entropy)

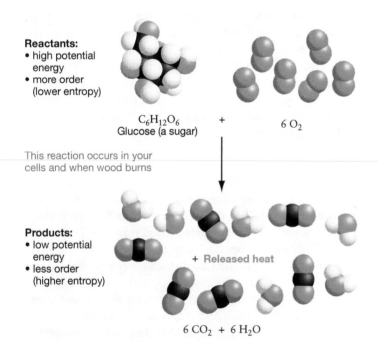

C$_6$H$_{12}$O$_6$
Glucose (a sugar)

+

6 O$_2$

This reaction occurs in your cells and when wood burns

Products:
• low potential energy
• less order (higher entropy)

+ Released heat

6 CO$_2$ + 6 H$_2$O

FIGURE 2.20 Spontaneous Processes Result in Lower Potential Energy, Increased Disorder, or Both.

check your understanding

C
Y
U

If you understand that . . .
• Chemical reactions result in the transformation of energy, either through the release of energy stored in chemical bonds or the uptake of energy from external sources.
• Chemical reactions tend to be spontaneous if they lead to lower potential energy and higher entropy (more disorder).

✔ **You should be able to . . .**
1. Determine if the reaction between methane (CH$_4$) and oxygen (O$_2$) shown here is spontaneous or not, addressing both potential energy and entropy:

$$CH_4 + 2\,O_2 \longrightarrow CO_2 + 2\,H_2O$$

2. Explain how the positions of the valence electrons in carbon and hydrogen change as methane is converted into carbon dioxide and water.

Answers are available in Appendix A.

2.4 Investigating Chemical Evolution: Approaches and Model Systems

To probe the kinds of reactions that may have set chemical evolution in motion, researchers have used two different approaches—one looking from the "top down" and the other from the "bottom up."

1. In the top-down approach, researchers examine modern cells to identify chemistry that is shared throughout the tree of life. Such ancient reactions are prime candidates for being involved in the chemical evolution that led up to **LUCA,** or last universal common ancestor (introduced in Chapter 1).

2. In the bottom-up approach, the primary focus is on the small molecules and environmental conditions that were present in

early Earth. Here, researchers attempt to identify reactions that could build the molecules found in life using only what was available at the time, without regard to reactions used by modern cells.

These approaches have been used to investigate two different model systems that attempt to explain the process component of the theory of chemical evolution:

1. The **prebiotic soup model** proposes that certain molecules were synthesized from gases in the atmosphere or arrived via meteorites. Afterward they would have condensed with rain and accumulated in oceans. This process would result in an "organic soup" that allowed for continued construction of larger, even more complex molecules.

2. The **surface metabolism model** suggests that dissolved gases came in contact with minerals lining the walls of deep-sea vents and formed more complex, organic molecules.

Since it is impossible to directly examine how and where chemical evolution occurred, the next best thing is to re-create the conditions in the lab and test predictions made by these models. In the following sections, you will learn about how biologists used the top-down and bottom-up approaches to identify reactions that support each of these models for chemical evolution.

Early Origin-of-Life Experiments

Chemical evolution was first taken seriously in 1953 when a graduate student named Stanley Miller performed a breakthrough experiment in the study of the prebiotic soup model.

Miller wanted to answer a simple question: Can complex organic compounds be synthesized from the simple molecules present in Earth's early atmosphere? In other words, is it possible to re-create the first steps in chemical evolution by simulating early-Earth conditions in the laboratory?

Miller's experimental setup (**FIGURE 2.21**) was designed to produce a microcosm of early Earth. The large glass flask represented the atmosphere and contained the gases methane (CH_4), ammonia (NH_3), and hydrogen (H_2), all of which have high potential energy. This large flask was connected to a smaller flask by glass tubing. The small flask held a tiny ocean—200 milliliters (mL) of liquid water.

To connect the mini-atmosphere with the mini-ocean, Miller boiled the water constantly. This added water vapor to the mix of gases in the large flask. As the vapor cooled and condensed, it flowed back into the smaller flask, where it boiled again. In this way, water vapor circulated continuously through the system. This was important: If the molecules in the simulated atmosphere reacted with one another, the "rain" would carry them into the mini-ocean, forming a simulated version of the prebiotic soup.

Had Miller stopped at merely boiling the molecules, little or nothing would have happened. Even at the boiling point of water (100°C), the starting molecules used in the experiment are stable and do not undergo spontaneous chemical reactions.

Something did start to happen in the apparatus, however, when Miller sent electrical discharges across the electrodes he'd inserted into the atmosphere. These miniature lightning bolts

QUESTION: Can simple molecules and kinetic energy lead to chemical evolution?

HYPOTHESIS: If kinetic energy is added to a mix of simple molecules, reactions will occur that produce more complex molecules, perhaps including some with C–C bonds.

NULL HYPOTHESIS: Chemical evolution will not occur, even with an input of energy.

EXPERIMENTAL SETUP:

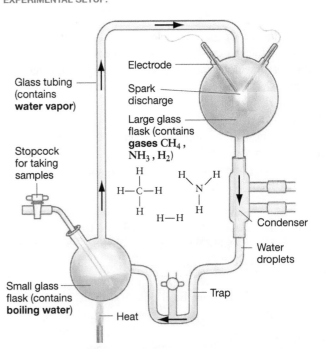

PREDICTION: Complex organic compounds will be found in the liquid water.

PREDICTION OF NULL HYPOTHESIS: Only the starting molecules will be found in the liquid water.

RESULTS

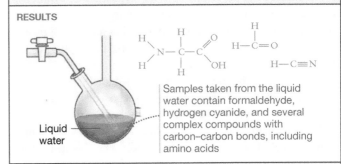

Samples taken from the liquid water contain formaldehyde, hydrogen cyanide, and several complex compounds with carbon–carbon bonds, including amino acids

CONCLUSION: Chemical evolution occurs readily if simple molecules with high free energy are exposed to a source of kinetic energy.

FIGURE 2.21 Miller's Spark-Discharge Experiment. The arrows in the "Experimental setup" diagram indicate the flow of water vapor or liquid. The condenser is a jacket with cold water flowing through it.

SOURCE: Miller, S. L. 1953. A production of amino acids under possible primitive Earth conditions. *Science* 117: 528–529.

✔ **QUESTION** Which parts of the apparatus mimic the ocean, atmosphere, rain, and lightning?

added a crucial element to the reaction mix—pulses of intense electrical energy. After a day of continuous boiling and sparking, the solution in the boiling flask began to turn pink. After a week, it was deep red and cloudy.

When Miller analyzed samples from the mini-ocean, he found large quantities of hydrogen cyanide and formaldehyde. Even more exciting, the sparks and heating had led to the synthesis of additional, more complex organic compounds, including amino acids, which are the building blocks of proteins (see Chapter 3).

Recent Origin-of-Life Experiments

The production of more complex molecules from simple molecules in Miller's experiment supported his claim that the formation of a prebiotic soup was possible. The results came under fire, however, when other researchers pointed out that the early atmosphere was dominated by volcanic gases like CO, CO_2, and H_2, not the CH_4 and NH_3 used in Miller's experiment.

This controversy stimulated a series of follow-up experiments, which showed that the assembly of small molecules into more complex molecules can also occur under more realistic early Earth conditions.

Synthesis of Precursors Using Light Energy
One such reaction that may have played a role in chemical evolution is the synthesis of formaldehyde (CH_2O) from carbon dioxide and hydrogen:

$$CO_2(g) + 2\ H_2(g) \longrightarrow \underset{\text{formaldehyde}}{CH_2O(g)} + H_2O(g)$$

This reaction has not been observed in cells—like Miller's experiment, it represents the bottom-up approach. But researchers have shown that when molecules of formaldehyde are heated, they react with one another to produce larger organic compounds, including energy-rich molecules like sugars (see Chapter 5). Note, however, that this reaction does not occur spontaneously—a large input of energy is required.

To explore the possibility of early formaldehyde synthesis, a research group constructed a computer model of the early atmosphere of Earth. The model consisted of a list of all possible chemical reactions that can occur among the molecules now thought to have dominated the early atmosphere: CO_2, H_2O, N_2, CO, and H_2. In this model, they included reactions that occur when these molecules are struck by sunlight. This was crucial because sunlight represents a source of energy.

The sunlight that strikes Earth is made up of packets of light energy called **photons.** Today, Earth is protected by a blanket of ozone (O_3) in the upper atmosphere that absorbs most of the higher-energy photons in sunlight. But since Earth's early atmosphere was filled with volcanic gases released as the molten planet cooled, and ozone is not among these gases, it is extremely unlikely that appreciable quantities of ozone existed. Based on this logic, researchers infer that when chemical evolution was occurring, large quantities of high-energy photons bombarded the planet.

To understand why this energy source was so important, recall that the atoms in hydrogen and carbon dioxide molecules have full valence shells through covalent bonding. This arrangement makes these molecules largely unreactive. However, energy

from photons can break up molecules by knocking apart shared electrons. The fragments that result, called **free radicals,** have unpaired electrons in their outermost shells and are extremely reactive (**FIGURE 2.22**). To mimic the conditions on early Earth more accurately, the computer model included several reactions that produce highly reactive free radicals.

The result? The researchers calculated that, under conditions accepted as reasonable approximations of early Earth by most scientists, appreciable quantities of formaldehyde would have been produced. The energy in sunlight was converted to chemical energy in the form of new bonds in formaldehyde.

The complete reaction that results in the formation of formaldehyde is written as

$$CO_2(g) + 2\ H_2(g) + \text{sunlight} \longrightarrow CH_2O(g) + H_2O(g)$$

Notice that the reaction is balanced in terms of the atoms *and* the energy involved. The sunlight on the reactant side balances the higher energy required for the formation of formaldehyde and water. This result makes sense if you take a moment to think about it. Energy is the capacity to do work, and building larger, more complex molecules requires work to be done.

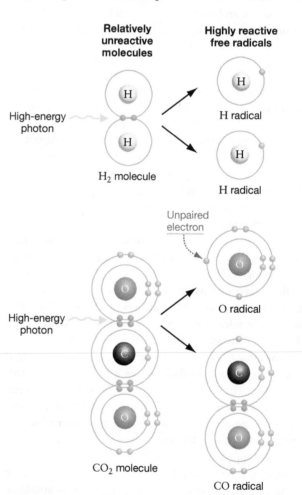

FIGURE 2.22 Free Radicals Are Extremely Reactive. When high-energy photons or pulses of intense electrical energy, such as lightning, strike molecules of hydrogen or carbon dioxide, free radicals can be created. Formation of free radicals is thought to be responsible for some key reactions in chemical evolution.

Using a similar model, other researchers have shown that hydrogen cyanide (HCN)—another important precursor of molecules required for life—could also have been produced in the early atmosphere. According to this research, large quantities of potential precursors for chemical evolution would have formed in the atmosphere and rained out into the early oceans. As a result, organic compounds with relatively high potential energy could have accumulated, and the groundwork would have been in place for the prebiotic soup model of chemical evolution to take off (**FIGURE 2.23a**).

Concentration and Catalysis in Hydrothermal Vents A major stumbling block in the prebiotic soup model is that precursor molecules would have become diluted when they entered the early oceans. Without some means of localized concentration, the formaldehyde and hydrogen cyanide mentioned in the previous section would have been unlikely to meet and react to form larger, more complex molecules. The surface metabolism model offers one possible solution to this dilution effect.

In the surface metabolism model, reactants are recruited to a defined space—a layer of reactive minerals deposited on the

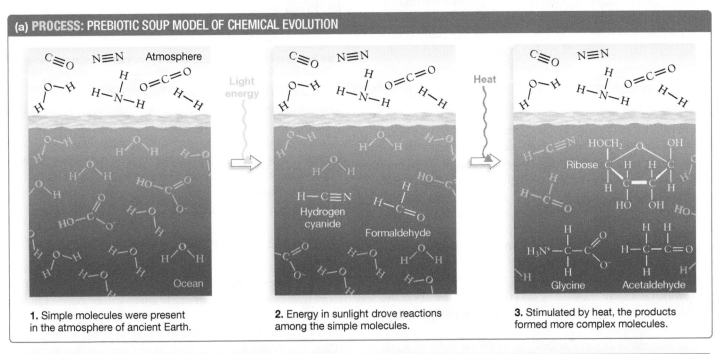

(a) PROCESS: PREBIOTIC SOUP MODEL OF CHEMICAL EVOLUTION

1. Simple molecules were present in the atmosphere of ancient Earth.

2. Energy in sunlight drove reactions among the simple molecules.

3. Stimulated by heat, the products formed more complex molecules.

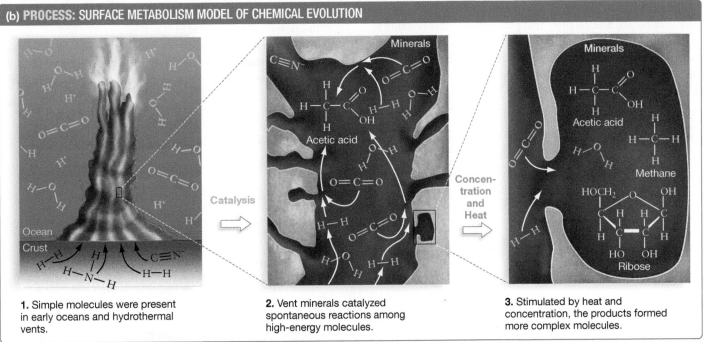

(b) PROCESS: SURFACE METABOLISM MODEL OF CHEMICAL EVOLUTION

1. Simple molecules were present in early oceans and hydrothermal vents.

2. Vent minerals catalyzed spontaneous reactions among high-energy molecules.

3. Stimulated by heat and concentration, the products formed more complex molecules.

FIGURE 2.23 The Start of Chemical Evolution—Two Models. The prebiotic soup and surface metabolism models illustrate how simple molecules containing C, H, O, and N reacted to form organic compounds that served as building blocks for more complex molecules.

walls of deep-sea vent chimneys. Dissolved gases would be attracted by the minerals and concentrated on vent-wall surfaces (**FIGURE 2.23b**).

Here's a key point of this model: Not only would vent-wall minerals bring reactants together, they would also be critical to the rate at which reaction products formed. Even if a potential reaction were spontaneous, it would probably not occur at a level useful for chemical evolution without the support of a **catalyst.** A catalyst provides the appropriate chemical environment for reactants to interact with one another effectively. (You will learn in Chapter 8 that a catalyst only influences the rate of a reaction—it does not provide energy or alter spontaneity.)

A reaction that provides an example of the role catalysts may have played during chemical evolution is the synthesis of acetic acid (CH_3COOH) from carbon dioxide and hydrogen:

$$2\ CO_2(aq) + 4\ H_2(aq) \longrightarrow CH_3COOH(aq) + 2\ H_2O(l)$$
acetic acid

The reaction is driven by chemical energy stored in one of the reactants—H_2—and is spontaneous despite the apparent decrease in entropy. It is employed by certain groups of Bacteria and Archaea today as a step toward building even more complex organic molecules.

This reaction has grabbed wide attention among the chemical evolution research community, for two reasons in particular: **(1)** Acetic acid can be formed under conditions that simulate a hydrothermal vent environment (bottom-up approach). **(2)** It is a key intermediate in an ancient pathway that produces acetyl CoA, which is a molecule used by cells throughout the tree of life (top-down approach). (The role of acetyl CoA in modern cells is discussed in Chapter 9.)

Did vent minerals serve as catalysts in the synthesis of acetic acid in early Earth? Evidence from modern cells suggests the answer may be yes. The catalysts that perform the same reaction in modern cells contain minerals similar to those found in hydrothermal vents. These minerals may represent a form of molecular luggage taken from the deep-sea hydrothermal vents as LUCA evolved its independence.

Research is currently under way to establish laboratory systems to more closely mimic surface metabolism conditions in hydrothermal vents. Preliminary results show that in addition to the production of acetic acid, a variety of larger carbon-based molecules can be formed under early Earth conditions. Among these are precursors for the synthesis of nucleotides, the building blocks for the molecules of inheritance used by every living organism on Earth (see Chapter 4).

2.5 **The Importance of Organic Molecules**

Life has been called a carbon-based phenomenon, and with good reason. Except for water, almost all of the molecules found in organisms contain this atom. Molecules that contain carbon bonded to other elements, such as hydrogen, are called **organic** molecules. (Other types of molecules are referred to as *inorganic* compounds.)

Carbon has great importance in biology because it is the most versatile atom on Earth. Because of its four valence electrons, it will form four covalent bonds. This results in an almost limitless array of molecular shapes, made possible by different combinations of single and double bonds.

Linking Carbon Atoms Together

You have already examined the tetrahedral structure of methane and the linear shape of carbon dioxide. When molecules contain more than one carbon atom, these atoms can be bonded to one another in long chains, as in the component of gasoline called octane (C_8H_{18}; **FIGURE 2.24a**), or in a ring, as in the sugar glucose ($C_6H_{12}O_6$; **FIGURE 2.24b**). Carbon atoms provide the structural framework for virtually all the important compounds associated with life, with the exception of water.

The formation of carbon–carbon bonds was an important event in chemical evolution: It represented a crucial step toward the production of the types of molecules found in living organisms.

(a) Carbons linked in a chain

C_8H_{18} Octane

(b) Carbons linked in a ring

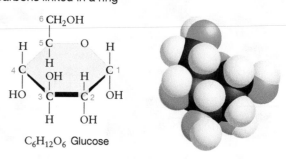

$C_6H_{12}O_6$ Glucose

FIGURE 2.24 The Shapes of Carbon-Containing Molecules. **(a)** Octane is a hydrocarbon chain, and one of the primary ingredients in gasoline. **(b)** Glucose is a sugar that can form a ring-like structure.

Functional Groups

In general, the carbon atoms in an organic molecule furnish a skeleton that gives the molecule its overall shape. But the chemical behavior of the compound—meaning the types of reactions that it participates in—is dictated by groups of H, N, O, P, or S atoms that are bonded to one of the carbon atoms in a specific way.

The critically important H-, N-, O-, P-, and S-containing groups found in organic compounds are called **functional groups**. The composition and properties of six prominent functional groups that are commonly found in organic molecules and recognized by organic chemists are summarized in **TABLE 2.3**. To understand the role that organic compounds play in organisms, it is important to analyze how these functional groups behave.

SUMMARY TABLE 2.3   **Six Functional Groups Commonly Attached to Carbon Atoms**

Functional Group	Formula*	Family of Molecules	Properties of Functional Group	Example
Amino		Amines	Acts as a base—tends to attract a proton to form:	 Glycine (an amino acid)
Carboxyl		Carboxylic acids	Acts as an acid—tends to lose a proton in solution to form:	 Acetic acid
Carbonyl		Aldehydes	Aldehydes, especially, react with certain compounds to produce larger molecules to form:	 Acetaldehyde
		Ketones		 Acetone
Hydroxyl	R—OH	Alcohols	Highly polar, so makes compounds more soluble through hydrogen bonding with water; may also act as a weak acid and drop a proton	 Ethanol
Phosphate		Organic phosphates	Molecules with more than one phosphate linked together store large amounts of chemical energy	 3–Phosphoglyceric acid
Sulfhydryl	R—SH	Thiols	When present in proteins, can form disulfide (S–S) bonds that contribute to protein structure	 Cysteine

*In these structural formulas, "R" stands for the rest of the molecule.

✔ **EXERCISE** Based on the electronegativities of the atoms involved, predict whether each functional group is polar or nonpolar.

- *Amino and carboxyl functional groups* tend to attract or drop a proton, respectively, when in solution. Amino groups function as bases; carboxyl groups act as acids. During chemical evolution and in organisms today, the most important types of amino- and carboxyl-containing molecules are the amino acids (which Chapter 3 analyzes in detail). Amino acids contain both an amino group and a carboxyl group. (It's common for organic compounds to contain more than one functional group.) Amino acids can be linked together by covalent bonds that form between amino and carboxyl groups. In addition, both of these functional groups participate in hydrogen bonding.

- *Carbonyl groups* are found on aldehyde and ketone molecules such as formaldehyde, acetaldehyde, and acetone. This functional group is the site of reactions that link these molecules into larger, more complex organic compounds.

- *Hydroxyl groups* are important because they act as weak acids. In many cases, the protons involved in acid–base reactions that occur in cells come from hydroxyl groups on organic compounds. Because hydroxyl groups are polar, molecules containing hydroxyl groups will form hydrogen bonds and tend to be soluble in water.

- *Phosphate groups* carry two negative charges. When phosphate groups are transferred from one organic compound to another, the change in charge often dramatically affects the structure of the recipient molecule. In addition, phosphates that are bonded together store chemical energy that can be used in chemical reactions (some of these are discussed in Chapter 3).

- *Sulfhydryl groups* consist of a sulfur atom bonded to a hydrogen atom. They are important because sulfhydryl groups can link to one another via disulfide (S–S) bonds.

To summarize, functional groups make things happen. The number and types of functional groups attached to a framework of carbon atoms imply a great deal about how that molecule is going to behave.

When you encounter an organic compound that is new to you, it's important to do the following three things:

1. Examine the overall size and shape provided by the carbon framework.

2. Identify the types of covalent bonds present based on the electronegativities of the atoms. Use this information to estimate the polarity of the molecule and the amount of potential energy stored in its chemical bonds.

3. Locate any functional groups and note the properties these groups give to the molecule.

Understanding these three features will help you to predict the molecule's role in the chemistry of life.

Once carbon-containing molecules with functional groups had appeared early in Earth's history, what happened next? For chemical evolution to continue, small carbon-based molecules had to form still larger, more complex molecules like those found in living cells. How were the molecules of life—proteins, nucleic acids, carbohydrates, and lipids—formed, and how do they function in organisms today? The rest of this unit explores the next steps in chemical evolution, culminating in the formation of the first living cell.

CHAPTER 2   REVIEW

 For media, go to MasteringBiology

If you understand . . .

2.1   Atoms, Ions, and Molecules: The Building Blocks of Chemical Evolution

- When atoms participate in chemical bonds to form molecules, the shared electrons give the atoms full valence shells and thus contribute to the atoms' stability.

- The electrons in a chemical bond may be shared equally or unequally, depending on the relative electronegativities of the two atoms involved.

- Nonpolar covalent bonds result from equal sharing; polar covalent bonds are due to unequal sharing. Ionic bonds form when an electron is completely transferred from one atom to another.

✓ You should be able to compare and contrast the types of bonds found in methane (CH_4), ammonia (NH_3), and sodium chloride (NaCl).

2.2   Properties of Water and the Early Oceans

- The chemical reactions required for life take place in water.

- Water is polar—meaning that it has partial positive and negative charges—because it is bent and has two polar covalent bonds.

- Polar molecules and charged substances, including ions, interact with water and stay in solution via hydrogen bonding and electrostatic attraction.

- Water's ability to participate in hydrogen bonding also gives it an extraordinarily high capacity to absorb heat and cohere to other water molecules.

- Water spontaneously dissociates into hydrogen ions (or protons, H^+) and hydroxide ions (OH^-). The concentration of protons in a solution determines the pH, which can be altered by acids and bases or stabilized by buffers.

✓ You should be able to predict what part of water molecules would interact with amino, carboxyl, and hydroxyl functional groups in solution and the types of bonds that would be involved.

2.3 Chemical Reactions, Energy, and Chemical Evolution

- The first step in chemical evolution was the formation of small organic compounds from molecules such as molecular hydrogen (H_2) and carbon dioxide (CO_2).

- Chemical reactions typically involve bonds being broken, atoms being rearranged, and new bonds being formed. This process involves energy, either from the reactants or external sources (e.g., heat).

- Energy comes in different forms. Although energy cannot be created or destroyed, one form of energy can be transformed into another.

✓ You should be able to explain how the energy in electricity can drive a reaction that is nonspontaneous.

2.4 Investigating Chemical Evolution: Approaches and Model Systems

- Experiments suggest that early in Earth's history, external sources of energy, such as sunlight or lightning, could have driven chemical reactions between simple molecules to form molecules with higher potential energy. In this way, energy in the form of radiation or electricity was transformed into chemical energy.

- The prebiotic soup and surface metabolism models for chemical evolution have been supported by the synthesis of organic molecules in laboratory simulations of the early Earth environment.

✓ You should be able to explain how the surface metabolism model is supported by both the top-down and bottom-up approaches used to investigate reactions involved in chemical evolution.

2.5 The Importance of Organic Molecules

- Carbon is the foundation of organic molecules based on its valence, which allows for the construction of molecules with complex shapes.

- Organic molecules are critical to life because they possess versatility of chemical behavior due to the presence of functional groups.

✓ You should be able to predict how adding hydroxyl groups to the octane molecule in Figure 2.24 would affect the properties of the molecule.

(MB) MasteringBiology

1. MasteringBiology Assignments

Tutorials and Activities Acids, Bases, and pH; Anatomy of Atoms; Atomic Number and Mass Number; BioSkill: Using Logarithms; Carbon Bonding and Functional Groups; Cohesion of Water; Covalent Bonds; Dissociation of Water Molecules; Diversity of Carbon-Based Molecules; Electron Arrangement; Energy Transformations; Functional Groups; Hydrogen Bonding and Water; Hydrogen Bonds; Ionic Bonds; Nonpolar and Polar Molecules; pH Scale; Polarity of Water; Properties of Water; Structure of the Atomic Nucleus

Questions Reading Quizzes, Blue-Thread Questions, Test Bank

2. eText Read your book online, search, take notes, highlight text, and more.

3. The Study Area Practice Test, Cumulative Test, BioFlix® 3-D Animations, Videos, Activities, Audio Glossary, Word Study Tools, Art

You should be able to . . .

✓ TEST YOUR KNOWLEDGE

Answers are available in Appendix A

1. Which of the following occurs when a covalent bond forms?
   a. The potential energy of electrons drops.
   b. Electrons in valence shells are shared between nuclei.
   c. Ions of opposite charge interact.
   d. Polar molecules interact.

2. If a reaction is exothermic, then which of the following statements is true?
   a. The products have lower potential energy than the reactants.
   b. Energy must be added for the reaction to proceed.
   c. The products have lower entropy (are more ordered) than the reactants.
   d. It occurs extremely quickly.

3. Which of the following is most likely to have been the energy source responsible for the formation of acetic acid in deep-sea hydrothermal vents?
   a. heat released from the vents
   b. solar radiation that passed through the ocean water
   c. chemical energy present in the reactants
   d. the increase in entropy in the products

4. What is thermal energy?
   a. a form of potential energy
   b. the temperature increase that occurs when any form of energy is added to a system
   c. mechanical energy
   d. the kinetic energy of molecular motion, measured as heat

5. What factors determine whether a chemical reaction is spontaneous or not?

6. What are the two models that have been proposed to explain the process component of chemical evolution?

7. Which of the following molecules would you predict to have the largest number of polar covalent bonds based on their molecular formulas?
   a. C_2H_6O (ethanol)
   b. C_2H_6 (ethane)
   c. $C_2H_4O_2$ (acetic acid)
   d. C_3H_8O (propanol)

8. Locate fluorine (F) on the partial periodic table provided in Figure 2.2. Predict its relative electronegativity compared to hydrogen, sodium, and oxygen. State the number and type of bond(s) you expect it would form if it reacted with sodium.

9. Oxygen is extremely electronegative, meaning that its nucleus pulls electrons shared in covalent bonds very strongly. Explain the changes in electron position that are illustrated in Figure 2.19 based on oxygen's electronegativity.

10. Draw the electron-sharing continuum and place molecular oxygen (O_2), magnesium chloride ($MgCl_2$), and carbon dioxide (CO_2) on it.

11. Consider the reaction between carbon dioxide and water, which forms carbonic acid:

$$CO_2(g) + H_2O(l) \rightleftharpoons CH_2O_3(aq)$$

In aqueous solution, carbonic acid immediately dissociates to form a proton and bicarbonate ion, as follows:

$$CH_2O_3(aq) \rightleftharpoons H^+(aq) + CHO_3^-(aq)$$

If an underwater volcano bubbled additional CO_2 into the ocean, would this sequence of reactions be driven to the left or the right? How would this affect the pH of the ocean?

12. What is the relationship between the carbon framework in an organic molecule (the "R" in Table 2.3) and its functional groups?

13. When H_2 and CO_2 react, acetic acid can be formed spontaneously while the production of formaldehyde requires an input of energy. Which of the following conclusions may be drawn from this observation?
   a. More heat is released when formaldehyde is produced compared to the production of acetic acid.
   b. Compared to the reactants from which it is formed, formaldehyde has more potential energy than does acetic acid.
   c. Entropy decreases when acetic acid is produced and increases when formaldehyde is produced.
   d. The mineral catalyst involved in acetic acid production provides energy to make the reaction spontaneous.

14. When chemistry texts introduce the concept of electron shells, they emphasize that shells represent distinct potential energy levels.

In introducing electron shells, this chapter also emphasizes that they represent distinct distances from the positive charges in the nucleus. Are these two points of view in conflict? Why or why not?

15. Draw a concept map relating water's structure to its properties. (For an introduction to concept mapping, see **BioSkills 15** in Appendix B.) Your concept map should include the following terms or phrases: polar covalent bonds, polarity (on the water molecule), hydrogen bonding, high heat of vaporization, high specific heat, less dense as a solid, effective solvent, unequal sharing of electrons, high energy input required to break bonds, high electronegativity of oxygen.

16. From what you have learned about water, why do coastal regions tend to have climates with lower annual variation in temperature than do inland areas at the same latitude?

3 Protein Structure and Function

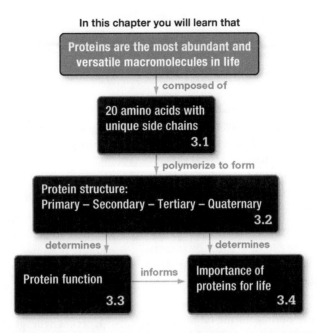

In this chapter you will learn that

Proteins are the most abundant and versatile macromolecules in life

composed of

20 amino acids with unique side chains
3.1

polymerize to form

Protein structure:
Primary – Secondary – Tertiary – Quaternary
3.2

determines

determines

Protein function
3.3

informs

Importance of proteins for life
3.4

A space-filling model of hemoglobin—a protein that is carrying oxygen in your blood right now.

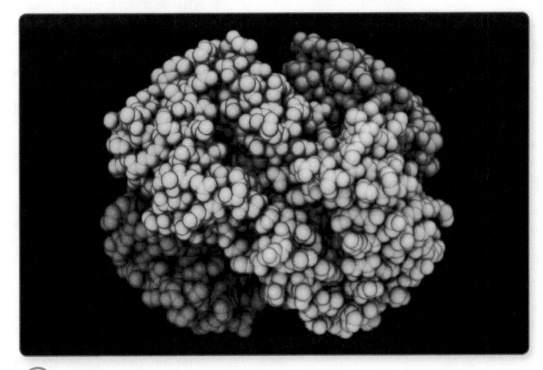

This chapter is part of the Big Picture. See how on pages 104–105.

Chemical reactions in the atmosphere and ocean of ancient Earth are thought to have led to the formation of the first complex carbon-containing compounds. This idea, called chemical evolution, was first proposed by Alexander I. Oparin in 1924. The hypothesis was published again—independently and five years later—by J. B. S. Haldane.

Today, the Oparin–Haldane proposal is considered a formal scientific theory (see Chapter 1). Scientific theories are continuously refined as new information comes to light, and many of Oparin

✔ When you see this checkmark, stop and test yourself. Answers are available in Appendix A.

and Haldane's original ideas have been revised. In its current form, the theory can be broken into four steps.

Step 1 Chemical evolution began with the production of small organic compounds from reactants such as H_2, N_2, NH_3, and CO_2. (Chapter 2 focuses on this step.)

Step 2 These small, simple organic compounds reacted to form mid-sized molecules, such as amino acids, nucleotides, and sugars. (Amino acids are introduced in this chapter. Nucleotides and sugars are discussed in Chapters 4 and 5, respectively.)

Step 3 Mid-sized, building-block molecules linked to form the types of large molecules found in cells today, including proteins, nucleic acids, and complex carbohydrates. Each of these large molecules is composed of distinctive chemical subunits that join together: Proteins are composed of amino acids, nucleic acids are composed of nucleotides, and complex carbohydrates are composed of sugars.

Step 4 Life became possible when one of these large, complex molecules acquired the ability to replicate itself. By increasing in copy number, this molecule would then emerge from the pool of chemicals. At that point, life had begun—chemical evolution gave way to biological evolution.

What type of molecule was responsible for the origin of life? Answering this question is a recurring theme in this and the next three chapters.

To address this question, researchers first designed experiments to identify the types of molecules that could be produced in the waters of prebiotic Earth (Chapter 2). One series of results sparked particular excitement for origin-of-life researchers—the repeated discovery of amino acids among the products of early Earth simulations.

Amino acids have also been found in meteorites and produced in experiments that approximate the environment of interstellar space. Taken together, these observations have led researchers to conclude that amino acids were present and probably abundant during chemical evolution. Since amino acids are the building blocks of proteins, many researchers have therefore asked, Could a protein have been the initial spark of life?

For this question to be valid, proteins would need to possess three of the fundamental attributes of life, namely: information, replication, and evolution. To determine if they do, let's look at the molecules themselves. What are amino acids, and how are they linked to form proteins?

3.1 Amino Acids and Their Polymerization

Modern cells, such as those that make up your body, produce tens of thousands of distinct proteins. Most of these molecules are composed of just 20 different building blocks, called **amino acids.** All 20 of these building blocks have a common structure.

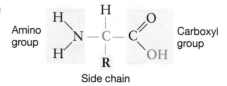

(a) Non-ionized form of amino acid

Amino group

Carboxyl group

Side chain

(b) Ionized form of amino acid

Amino group

Carboxyl group

Side chain

FIGURE 3.1 All Amino Acids Have the Same General Structure. The central α-carbon is shown in red.

The Structure of Amino Acids

To understand how amino acids are put together, recall that carbon atoms have a valence of four—they form four covalent bonds (Chapter 2). All 20 amino acids thus have a common core structure—with a central carbon atom (referred to as the α-carbon) bonded to the four different atoms or groups of atoms diagrammed in **FIGURE 3.1a**:

1. H—a hydrogen atom
2. NH_2—an amino functional group
3. COOH—a carboxyl functional group
4. a distinctive "R-group" (often referred to as a "side chain")

The combination of amino and carboxyl groups not only inspired the name amino acid, but is key to how these molecules behave. In water at pH 7, the concentration of protons causes the amino group to act as a base. It attracts a proton to form NH_3^+ (**FIGURE 3.1b**). The carboxyl group, in contrast, is acidic because its two oxygen atoms are highly electronegative. They pull electrons away from the hydrogen atom, which means that it is relatively easy for this group to lose a proton to form COO^-.

The charges on these functional groups are important for two reasons: (1) They help amino acids stay in solution, where they can interact with one another and with other solutes, and (2) they affect the amino acid's chemical reactivity.

The Nature of Side Chains

What about the R-group? The R-groups, or side chains, on amino acids vary from a single hydrogen atom to large structures containing carbon atoms linked into rings. While all amino acids share the same core structure, each of the 20 R-groups is unique. The properties of amino acids vary because their R-groups vary.

FIGURE 3.2 highlights the R-groups on the 20 most common amino acids found in cells.[1] As you examine these side chains,

---

[1]There are actually 22 amino acids found in proteins that occur in organisms, but two are very rare.

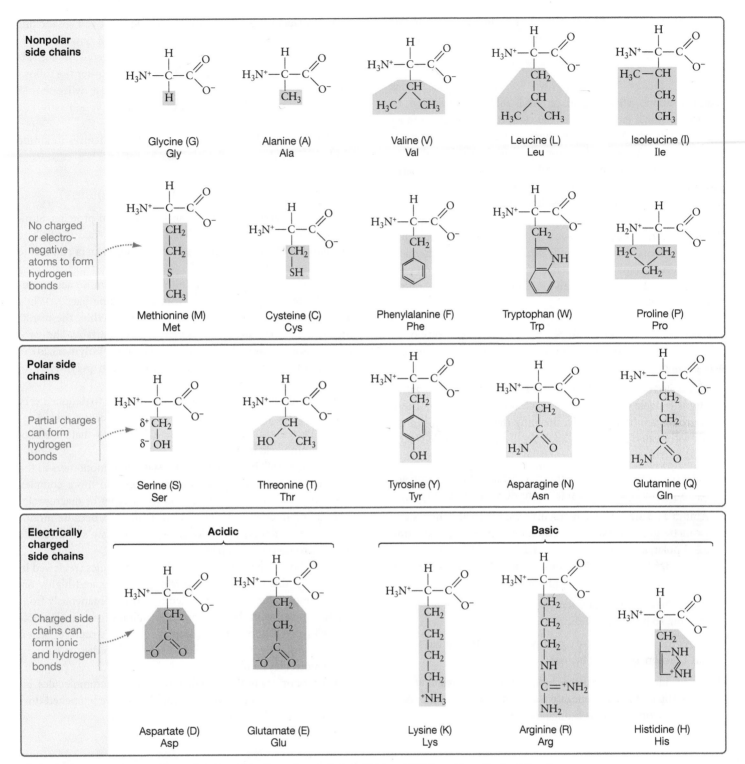

FIGURE 3.2 The 20 Major Amino Acids Found in Organisms. At the pH (about 7.0) found in cells, the 20 major amino acids found in organisms have the structural formulas shown here. The side chains are highlighted, and standard single-letter and three-letter abbreviations for each amino acid are given. For clarity, the carbon atoms in the ring structures of phenylalanine, tyrosine, tryptophan, and histidine are not shown; each bend in a ring is the site of a carbon atom. The hydrogen atoms in these structures are also not shown. A double line inside a ring indicates a double bond.

✔**EXERCISE** Explain why the green R-groups are nonpolar and why the pink R-groups are polar, based on the relative electronegativities of O, N, C, and H (see Chapter 2). Note that sulfur (S) has an electronegativity almost equal to that of carbon and slightly higher than that of hydrogen, making cysteine's side chain mildly hydrophobic.

ask yourself two questions (while referring to Table 2.3): Is this R-group likely to participate in chemical reactions? Will it help this amino acid stay in solution?

Functional Groups Affect Reactivity Several of the side chains found in amino acids contain carboxyl, sulfhydryl, hydroxyl, or amino functional groups. Under the right conditions, these functional groups can participate in chemical reactions. For example, amino acids with a sulfhydryl group (SH) in their side chains can form disulfide (S—S) bonds that help link different parts of large proteins. Such bonds naturally form between the proteins in your hair; curly hair contains many cross-links and straight hair far fewer.

In contrast, some amino acids contain side chains that are devoid of functional groups—consisting solely of carbon and hydrogen atoms. These R-groups rarely participate in chemical reactions. As a result, the influence of these amino acids on protein function depends primarily on their size and shape rather than reactivity.

The Polarity of Side Chains Affects Solubility The nature of its R-group affects the polarity, and thus the solubility, of an amino acid in water.

- Nonpolar side chains lack charged or highly electronegative atoms capable of forming hydrogen bonds with water. These R-groups are **hydrophobic,** meaning that they do not interact with water. Instead of dissolving, hydrophobic side chains tend to coalesce in aqueous solution.

- Polar or charged side chains interact readily with water and are **hydrophilic.** Hydrophilic side chains dissolve in water easily.

Amino acid side chains distinguish the different amino acids and can be grouped into four general types: acidic, basic, uncharged polar, and nonpolar. If given a structural formula for an amino acid, as in Figure 3.2, you can determine which type of amino acid it is by asking three questions:

1. Does the side chain have a negative charge? If so, it has lost a proton, so it must be acidic.

2. Does the side chain have a positive charge? If so, it has taken on a proton, so it must be basic.

3. If the side chain is uncharged, does it have an oxygen atom? If so, the highly electronegative oxygen will result in a polar covalent bond and thus is uncharged polar.

If the answers to all three questions are no, then you are looking at a nonpolar amino acid. ✔ If you understand how the interaction between amino acids and water is affected by the side chains, you should be able to use Figure 3.2 to order the following amino acids from most hydrophilic to most hydrophobic: valine, aspartate, asparagine, and tyrosine. Explain why you have chosen this order.

Now that you have seen the diversity of structures in amino acids, let's put them together to make a protein.

How Do Amino Acids Link to Form Proteins?

Amino acids are linked to one another to form proteins. Similarly, the molecular building blocks called nucleotides attach to one another to form nucleic acids, and simple sugars connect to form complex carbohydrates.

In general, a molecular subunit such as an amino acid, a nucleotide, or a sugar is called a **monomer** ("one-part"). When a large number of monomers are bonded together, the resulting structure is called a **polymer** ("many-parts"). The process of linking monomers together is called **polymerization** (**FIGURE 3.3**). Thus, amino acid monomers can polymerize to form proteins.

Biologists also use the word **macromolecule** to denote a very large molecule that is made up of smaller molecules joined together. Proteins are macromolecules—polymers—that consist of linked amino acid monomers.

The theory of chemical evolution states that monomers in the prebiotic soup polymerized to form larger and more complex molecules, such as the proteins and other types of macromolecules found in organisms. This is a difficult step, because monomers such as amino acids do not spontaneously self-assemble into macromolecules such as proteins.

According to the second law of thermodynamics (reviewed in Chapter 2), this fact is not surprising. Complex and highly organized molecules are not expected to form spontaneously from simpler constituents, because polymerization organizes the molecules involved into a more complex, ordered structure. Stated another way, polymerization decreases the disorder, or entropy, of the molecules involved.

For monomers to link together and form macromolecules, an input of energy is required. How could this have happened during chemical evolution?

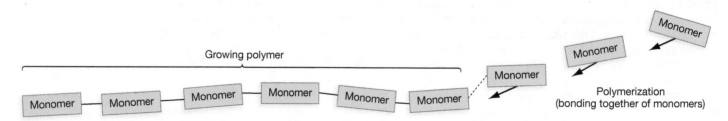

FIGURE 3.3 Monomers Are the Building Blocks of Polymers.

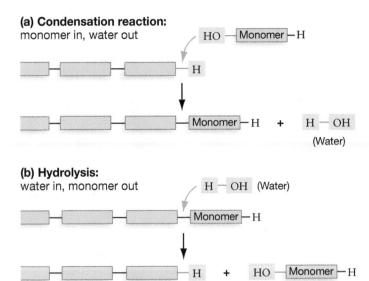

(a) Condensation reaction:
monomer in, water out

HO — Monomer — H

— H

Monomer — H + H — OH

(Water)

(b) Hydrolysis:
water in, monomer out

H — OH (Water)

Monomer — H

— H + HO — Monomer — H

FIGURE 3.4 Polymers Can Be Extended or Broken Apart.

Could Polymerization Occur in the Energy-Rich Environment of Early Earth?

Monomers polymerize through **condensation reactions,** also known as **dehydration reactions.** These reactions are aptly named because the newly formed bond results in the loss of a water molecule (**FIGURE 3.4a**). The reverse reaction, called **hydrolysis,** breaks polymers apart by adding a water molecule (**FIGURE 3.4b**). The water molecule reacts with the bond linking the monomers, separating one monomer from the polymer chain.

In a solution such as the prebiotic soup, condensation and hydrolysis represent the forward and reverse reactions of a chemical equilibrium:

Monomer 1 + Monomer 2 $\underset{\text{hydrolysis}}{\overset{\text{condensation}}{\rightleftharpoons}}$ Monomer 1 — Monomer 2

Hydrolysis dominates because it increases entropy and is favorable energetically.

This means that, in the prebiotic soup, polymerization would occur only if there were a very high concentration of amino acids to push the reaction toward condensation. Since the equilibrium favors free monomers over polymers even under concentrated conditions, a polymer is unlikely to have grown much beyond a short chain.

According to recent experiments, though, there are several ways that amino acids could have polymerized early in chemical evolution.

- Researchers evaluating the surface metabolism model of chemical evolution have been able to generate stable polymers by mixing free amino acids with a source of chemical energy and tiny mineral particles. Apparently, growing macromolecules are protected from hydrolysis if they cling, or adsorb, to a mineral surface. One such experiment produced polymers that were 55 amino acids long.

- In conditions that simulate the hot, metal-rich environments of undersea volcanoes, researchers have observed not only amino acid formation but also their polymerization.

- Amino acids have also joined into polymers in experiments in cooler water if a carbon- and sulfur-containing gas—one that is commonly ejected from undersea volcanoes—is present.

The current consensus is that several mechanisms could have led to polymerization reactions between amino acids, early in chemical evolution. What kind of bond is responsible for linking these monomers?

The Peptide Bond As **FIGURE 3.5** shows, amino acids polymerize when a bond forms between the carboxyl group of one amino acid and the amino group of another. The C–N covalent bond that results from this condensation reaction is called a **peptide bond.** When a water molecule is removed in the condensation reaction, the carboxyl group is converted to a carbonyl functional group (C=O) in the resulting polymer, and the amino group is reduced to an N–H.

Peptide bonds are unusually stable compared to linkages in other types of macromolecules. This is because a pair of valence electrons on the nitrogen is partially shared in the C–N bond (see Figure 3.5). The degree of electron sharing is great enough that peptide bonds actually have some of the characteristics of a double bond. For example, the peptide bond is planar, limiting the movement of the atoms participating in the peptide bond.

When amino acids are linked by peptide bonds into a chain, the amino acids are referred to as residues to distinguish them from free monomers.

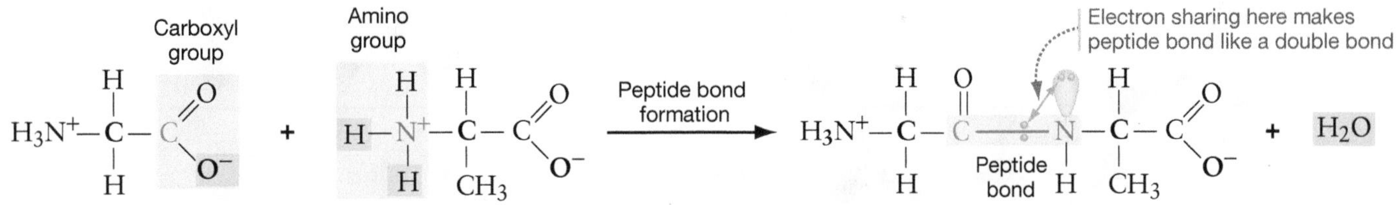

Carboxyl group   Amino group

Peptide bond formation

Electron sharing here makes peptide bond like a double bond

Peptide bond

$+ H_2O$

FIGURE 3.5 Peptide Bonds Form When the Carboxyl Group of One Amino Acid Reacts with the Amino Group of a Second Amino Acid.

(a) Peptide chain

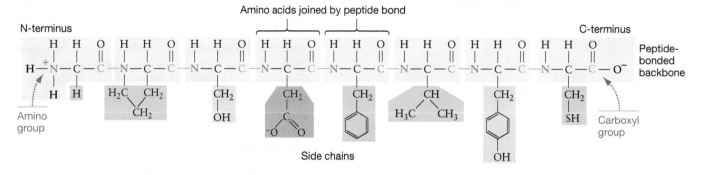

(b) Numbering system

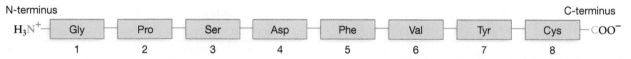

FIGURE 3.6 Amino Acids Polymerize to Form Chains.

FIGURE 3.6a shows how the chain of peptide bonds in a short polymer gives the molecule a structural framework, or a "backbone." There are three key points to note about the peptide-bonded backbone:

1. **R-group orientation** The side chains present in each residue extend out from the backbone, making it possible for them to interact with each other and with water.

2. **Directionality** There is an amino group (NH_3^+) on one end of the backbone and a carboxyl group (COO^-) on the other. The end of the sequence that has the free amino group is called the N-terminus, or amino-terminus, and the end with the free carboxyl group is called the C-terminus, or carboxy-terminus. By convention, biologists always write amino acid sequences from the N-terminus to the C-terminus (**FIGURE 3.6b**), because the N-terminus is the start of the chain when proteins are synthesized in cells.

3. **Flexibility** Although the peptide bond itself cannot rotate because of its double-bond nature, the single bonds on either side of the peptide bond can rotate. As a result, the structure as a whole is flexible (**FIGURE 3.7**).

When fewer than 50 amino acids are linked together in this way, the resulting polymer is called an **oligopeptide** ("few peptides") or simply a **peptide.** Polymers that contain 50 or more amino acids are called **polypeptides** ("many peptides").

The term **protein** is often used to describe any chain of amino acid residues, but formally protein refers to the complete, often

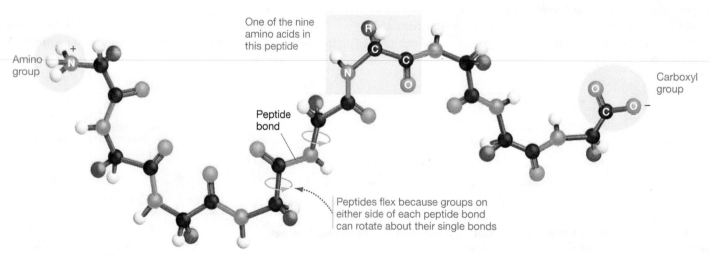

FIGURE 3.7 Peptide Chains Are Flexible.

functional form of the molecule. In Section 3.2, you'll see that some proteins consist of a single polypeptide while others are functional only when multiple polypeptides are bonded to one another.

Proteins are the stuff of life. Let's take a look at how they are put together and then see what they do.

If you understand that . . .

- Amino acids are small molecules with a central carbon atom bonded to a carboxyl group, an amino group, a hydrogen atom, and a side chain called an R-group.
- Each amino acid has distinctive chemical properties because each has a unique R-group.
- Proteins are polymers made up of amino acids.
- When the carboxyl group of one amino acid reacts with the amino group of another amino acid, a strong covalent bond called a peptide bond forms. Small chains are called oligopeptides; large chains are called polypeptides, or proteins.

✔ **You should be able to . . .**

Draw the structural formulas of two glycine residues (glycine's R-group is an H) linked by a peptide bond, and label the amino- and carboxy-terminus.

Answers are available in Appendix A.

3.2 What Do Proteins Look Like?

The unparalleled diversity of proteins—in size, shape, and other aspects of structure—is important because function follows from structure. Proteins can serve diverse functions in cells because they are diverse in size and shape as well as in the chemical properties of their amino acid residues.

FIGURE 3.8 illustrates some of the variety in the sizes and shapes observed in proteins. In the case of the TATA box–binding protein in **FIGURE 3.8a** and the porin protein in **FIGURE 3.8b**, the shape of the molecule has a clear correlation with its function. The TATA box–binding protein has a groove where DNA molecules fit; porin has a hole that forms a pore. The groove in the TATA box–binding protein interacts with specific regions of a DNA molecule, while porin fits in cell membranes and allows certain hydrophilic molecules to pass through. Proteins that provide structural support for cells or tissues, such as the collagen triple helix in **FIGURE 3.8d**, often form long, cable-like fibers.

But many of the proteins found in cells do not have shapes that are noticeably correlated with their functions. For example, the trypsin protein in **FIGURE 3.8c** has an overall globular shape that tells little about its function, which is to bind and cleave peptide bonds of other proteins.

How can biologists make sense of this diversity of protein size and shape? Initially, the amount of variation seems overwhelming. Fortunately, it is not. No matter how large or complex a protein may be, its underlying structure can be broken down into just four basic levels of organization.

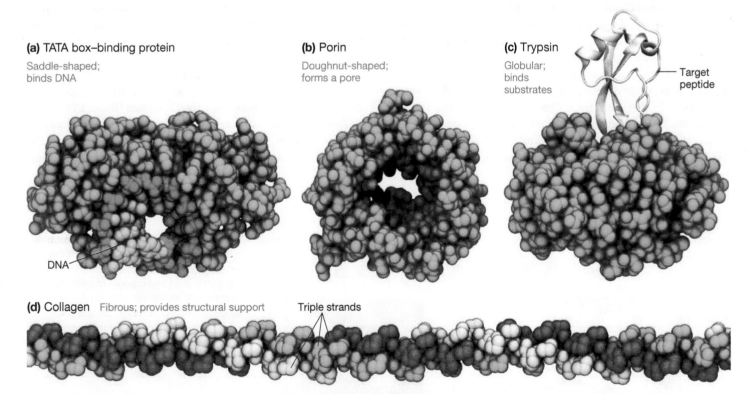

(a) TATA box–binding protein
Saddle-shaped; binds DNA

DNA

(b) Porin
Doughnut-shaped; forms a pore

(c) Trypsin
Globular; binds substrates

Target peptide

(d) Collagen   Fibrous; provides structural support

Triple strands

FIGURE 3.8 In Overall Shape, Proteins Are the Most Diverse Class of Molecules Known.

Primary Structure

Each protein has a unique sequence of amino acids. That simple conclusion was the culmination of 12 years of study by Frederick Sanger and co-workers during the 1940s and 1950s. Sanger's group worked out the first techniques for determining the amino acid sequence of insulin, a hormone that helps regulate sugar concentrations in the blood of humans and other mammals. When other proteins were analyzed, it rapidly became clear that each protein has a definite and distinct amino acid sequence.

Biochemists call the unique sequence of amino acids in a protein the **primary structure** of that protein. The sequence of amino acid residues in Figure 3.6, for example, defines the peptide's primary structure.

With 20 types of amino acids available and length ranging from two amino acid residues to tens of thousands, the number of primary structures that are possible is practically limitless. There may, in fact, be 20^n different combinations of amino acid residues for a polymer with a given length of n. For example, a peptide that is just 10 amino acids long has 20^{10} possible sequences. This is over 10,000 billion.

Why is the order and type of residues in the primary structure of a protein important? Recall that the R-groups present on each amino acid affect its chemical reactivity and solubility. It's therefore reasonable to predict that the R-groups present in a polypeptide will affect that molecule's properties and function.

This prediction is correct. In some cases, even a single change in the sequence of amino acids can cause radical changes in the way the protein as a whole behaves.

As an example, consider hemoglobin, an oxygen-binding protein in human red blood cells. In some individuals, hemoglobin has a valine instead of a glutamate at the 6th position of a strand containing 146 amino acid residues (**FIGURE 3.9a**). Valine's side chain is radically different from the R-group in glutamate. The change in R-group produces hemoglobin molecules that stick to one another and form fibers when oxygen concentrations in the blood are low. Red blood cells that carry these fibers adopt a sickle-like shape (**FIGURE 3.9b**). Sickled red blood cells get stuck in the small blood vessels called capillaries and starve downstream cells of oxygen. A debilitating illness called sickle-cell disease results.

A protein's primary structure is fundamental to its function. Primary structure is also fundamental to the higher levels of protein structure: secondary, tertiary, and quaternary.

Secondary Structure

Even though variation in the amino acid sequence of a protein is virtually limitless, it is only the tip of the iceberg in terms of generating structural diversity.

The next level of organization in proteins—**secondary structure**—is created in part by hydrogen bonding between components of the peptide-bonded backbone. Secondary structures are distinctively shaped sections of proteins that are stabilized largely by hydrogen bonding that occurs between the oxygen on the C=O group of one amino acid residue and the hydrogen on the N—H groups of another (**FIGURE 3.10a**). The oxygen atom in the C=O group has a partial negative charge due to its high electronegativity, while the hydrogen atom in the N—H group has a partial positive charge because it is bonded to nitrogen, which has high electronegativity.

Note a key point: Hydrogen bonding between sections of the same backbone is possible only when a polypeptide bends in a way that puts C=O and N—H groups close together. In most proteins, these polar groups are aligned and form hydrogen bonds with one another when the backbone bends to form one of two possible structures (**FIGURE 3.10b**):

1. an α-**helix** (alpha-helix), in which the polypeptide's backbone is coiled; or

2. a β-**pleated sheet** (beta-pleated sheet), in which segments of a peptide chain bend 180° and then fold in the same plane.

In both structures, the distance between residues that hydrogen-bond to one another is small. In an α-helix, for example, H-bonds form between residues that are just four linear positions apart in the polypeptide's primary sequence (Figure 3.10a).

When biologists use illustrations called ribbon diagrams to represent the shape of a protein, α-helices are shown as coils; β-pleated sheets are shown by groups of arrows in a plane (**FIGURE 3.10c**).

In most cases, secondary structure consists of α-helices and β-pleated sheets. Which one forms, if either, depends on the molecule's primary structure—specifically, the geometry and

(a) Normal amino acid sequence

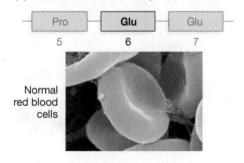

Normal red blood cells

(b) Single change in amino acid sequence

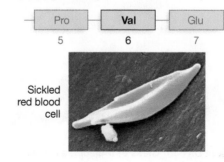

Sickled red blood cell

FIGURE 3.9 Changes in Primary Structure Affect Protein Function. Compare the primary structure of normal hemoglobin **(a)** with that of hemoglobin molecules in people with sickle-cell disease **(b)**. The single amino acid change causes red blood cells to change from their normal disc shape in (a) to a sickled shape in (b) when oxygen concentrations are low.

properties of the amino acids in the sequence. Certain amino acids are more likely to be involved in α-helices than in β-pleated sheets, and vice versa, due to the specific geometry of their side chains. Proline, for example, may be present in β-pleated sheets,

(a) Hydrogen bonds can form between nearby amino and carbonyl groups on the same polypeptide chain.

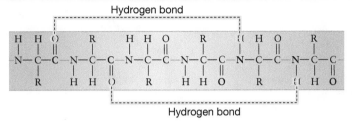

Hydrogen bond

Hydrogen bond

(b) Secondary structures of proteins result.

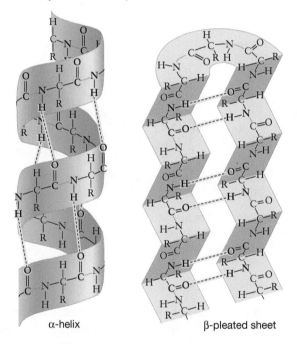

α-helix

β-pleated sheet

(c) Ribbon diagrams of secondary structure

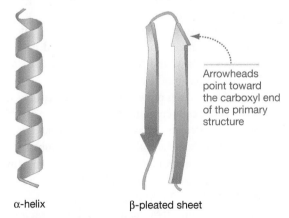

Arrowheads point toward the carboxyl end of the primary structure

α-helix

β-pleated sheet

FIGURE 3.10 Secondary Structures of Proteins. A polypeptide chain can coil or fold in on itself when hydrogen bonds form between N—H and C=O groups on its peptide-bonded backbone.

but it will terminate α-helices due to its unusual side chain. The bond formed between proline's R-group and the nitrogen of the core amino group introduces kinks in the backbone that do not conform to the shape of the helix.

Although each of the hydrogen bonds in an α-helix or a β-pleated sheet is weak relative to a covalent bond, the large number of hydrogen bonds in these structures makes them highly stable. As a result, they increase the stability of the molecule as a whole and help define its shape. In terms of overall shape and stability, though, the tertiary structure of a protein is even more important.

Tertiary Structure

Most of the overall shape, or **tertiary structure,** of a polypeptide results from interactions between R-groups or between R-groups and the backbone. In contrast to the secondary structures, where hydrogen bonds link backbone components together, these side chains can be involved in a wide variety of bonds and interactions. In addition, the amino acid residues that interact with one another are often far apart in the linear sequence. Because each contact between R-groups causes the peptide-bonded backbone to bend and fold, each contributes to the distinctive three-dimensional shape of a polypeptide.

Five types of interactions involving side chains are particularly important:

1. *Hydrogen bonding* Hydrogen bonds form between polar R-groups and opposite partial charges either in the peptide backbone or other R-groups.

2. *Hydrophobic interactions* In an aqueous solution, water molecules interact with the hydrophilic polar side chains of a polypeptide and force the hydrophobic nonpolar side chains to coalesce into globular masses. When these nonpolar R-groups come together, the surrounding water molecules form more hydrogen bonds with each other, increasing the stability of their own interactions.

3. *van der Waals interactions* Once hydrophobic side chains are close to one another, their association is further stabilized by electrical attractions known as **van der Waals interactions.** These weak attractions occur because the constant motion of electrons gives molecules a tiny asymmetry in charge that changes with time. If nonpolar molecules get extremely close to each other, the minute partial charge on one molecule induces an opposite partial charge in the nearby molecule and causes an attraction. Although the interaction is very weak relative to covalent bonds or even hydrogen bonds, a large number of van der Waals attractions can significantly increase the stability of the structure.

4. *Covalent bonding* Covalent bonds can form between the side chains of two cysteines through a reaction between the sulfhydryl groups. These **disulfide ("two-sulfur") bonds** are frequently referred to as bridges, because they create strong links between distinct regions of the same polypeptide or two separate polypeptides.

(a) Interactions that determine the tertiary structure of proteins

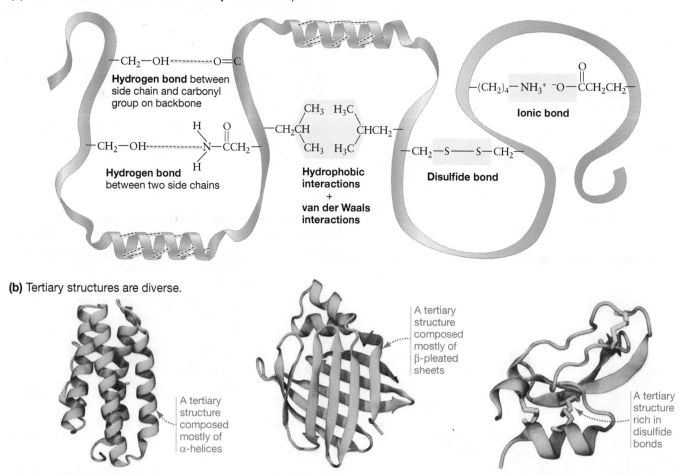

(b) Tertiary structures are diverse.

A tertiary structure composed mostly of α-helices

A tertiary structure composed mostly of β-pleated sheets

A tertiary structure rich in disulfide bonds

FIGURE 3.11 Tertiary Structure of Proteins Results from Interactions Involving R-Groups. (a) The overall shape of a single polypeptide is called its tertiary structure. This level of structure is created by bonds and other interactions that cause it to fold. **(b)** The tertiary structure of these proteins includes interactions between α-helices and β-pleated sheets.

5. **Ionic bonding** Ionic bonds form between groups that have full and opposing charges, such as the ionized acidic and basic side chains highlighted on the right in **FIGURE 3.11a**.

In addition, the overall shape of many proteins depends in part on the presence of secondary structures like α-helices and β-pleated sheets. Thus, tertiary structure depends on both primary and secondary structures.

With so many interactions possible between side chains and peptide-bonded backbones, it's not surprising that polypeptides vary in shape from rod-like filaments to ball-like masses. (See **FIGURE 3.11b**, and look again at Figure 3.8.)

Quaternary Structure

The first three levels of protein structure involve individual polypeptides. But some proteins contain multiple polypeptides that interact to form a single structure. The combination of polypeptides, referred to as subunits, gives a protein **quaternary structure.** The individual polypeptides are held together by the same types of bonds and interactions found in the tertiary level of structure.

In the simplest case, a protein with quaternary structure can consist of just two subunits that are identical. The Cro protein found in a virus called bacteriophage λ (pronounced *LAMB-da*) is an example (**FIGURE 3.12a**). Proteins with two polypeptide subunits are called dimers ("two-parts").

More than two polypeptides can be linked into a single protein, however, and the polypeptides involved may be distinct in primary, secondary, and tertiary structure. For example hemoglobin, an oxygen-binding protein, is a tetramer ("four-parts"). It consists of two copies of two different polypeptides (**FIGURE 3.12b**).

In addition, cells contain **macromolecular machines:** groups of multiple proteins that assemble to carry out a particular function. Some proteins are also found in complexes that include other types of macromolecules. The ribosome (introduced in Chapter 7) provides an example; it consists of several nucleic acid molecules and over 50 different proteins.

TABLE 3.1 summarizes the four levels of protein structure, using hemoglobin as an example. The key thing to note is that protein structure is hierarchical. Quaternary structure is based on tertiary structure, which is based in part on secondary

(a) Cro protein, a dimer

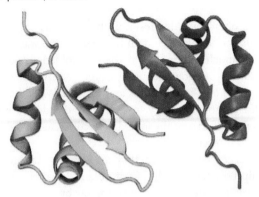

(b) Hemoglobin, a tetramer

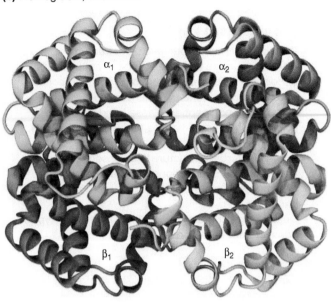

FIGURE 3.12 Quaternary Structures of Proteins Are Created by Multiple Polypeptides. These diagrams represent primary sequences as ribbons. **(a)** The Cro protein is a dimer—it consists of two polypeptide subunits, colored light and dark green. The subunits are identical in this case. **(b)** Hemoglobin is a tetramer—it consists of four polypeptide subunits. The α subunits (light and dark green) are identical; so are the β subunits (light and dark blue).

structure. All three of the higher-level structures are based on primary structure.

The summary table and preceding discussion convey three important messages:

1. The combination of primary, secondary, tertiary, and quaternary levels of structure is responsible for the fantastic diversity of sizes and shapes observed in proteins.

2. Protein folding is directed by the sequence of amino acids present in the primary structure.

3. Most elements of protein structure are based on folding of polypeptide chains.

Does protein folding occur spontaneously? What happens to the function of a protein if normal folding is disrupted? Let's use these questions as a guide to dig deeper into how proteins fold.

SUMMARY TABLE 3.1 Protein Structure

Level	Description	Stabilized by	Example: Hemoglobin
Primary	The sequence of amino acids in a polypeptide	Peptide bonds	Gly — Ser — Asp — Cys
Secondary	Formation of α-helices and β-pleated sheets in a polypeptide	Hydrogen bonding between groups along the peptide-bonded backbone; thus, depends on primary structure	One α-helix
Tertiary	Overall three-dimensional shape of a polypeptide (includes contribution from secondary structures)	Bonds and other interactions between R-groups, or between R-groups and the peptide-bonded backbone; thus, depends on primary structure	One of hemoglobin's subunits
Quaternary	Shape produced by combinations of polypeptides (thus, combinations of tertiary structures)	Bonds and other interactions between R-groups, and between peptide backbones of different polypeptides; thus, depends on primary structure	Hemoglobin consists of four polypeptide subunits

If you understand that . . .

- Proteins have up to four levels of structure.
- Primary structure is the sequence of amino acids.
- Secondary structure results from hydrogen bonds between atoms in the peptide-bonded backbone of the same polypeptide. These bonds produce structures such as α-helices and β-pleated sheets.
- Tertiary structure is the overall shape of a polypeptide. Most tertiary structure is a consequence of bonds or other interactions between R-groups or between R-groups and the peptide-bonded backbone.
- Quaternary structure occurs when multiple polypeptides interact to form a single protein.

✔ **You should be able to . . .**

1. Explain how secondary, tertiary, and quaternary levels of structure depend on primary structure.

2. **QUANTITATIVE** Calculate the number of different primary sequences that could be generated by randomly assembling amino acids into peptides that are five residues long.

Answers are available in Appendix A.

3.3 Folding and Function

If you were able to synthesize one of the polypeptides in hemoglobin from individual amino acids, and you then placed the resulting chain in an aqueous solution, it would spontaneously fold into the shape of the tertiary structure shown in Table 3.1.

In terms of entropy, this result probably seems counterintuitive. Because an unfolded protein has many more ways to move about, it has much higher entropy than the folded version. Folding *does* tend to be spontaneous, however, because the chemical bonds, hydrophobic interactions, and van der Waals forces that occur release enough energy to overcome the decrease in entropy. In terms of energy, the folded molecule is more stable than the unfolded molecule.

Folding is crucial to the function of a completed protein. This relationship between protein structure and function was hammered home in a set of classic experiments by Christian Anfinsen and colleagues during the 1950s.

Normal Folding Is Crucial to Function

Anfinsen studied a protein called ribonuclease that is found in many organisms. Ribonuclease is an enzyme that cleaves ribonucleic acid polymers. Anfinsen found that ribonuclease could be unfolded, or **denatured,** by treating it with compounds that break hydrogen bonds and disulfide bonds. The denatured ribonuclease was unable to function normally—it could no longer break apart nucleic acids (**FIGURE 3.13**).

When the denaturing agents were removed, however, the molecule refolded and began to function normally again. These experiments confirmed that ribonuclease folds spontaneously and that folding is essential for normal function.

More recent work has shown that in cells, folding is often facilitated by specific proteins called **molecular chaperones.** Many molecular chaperones belong to a family of molecules called the heat-shock proteins. Heat-shock proteins are produced in large quantities after cells experience high temperatures or other

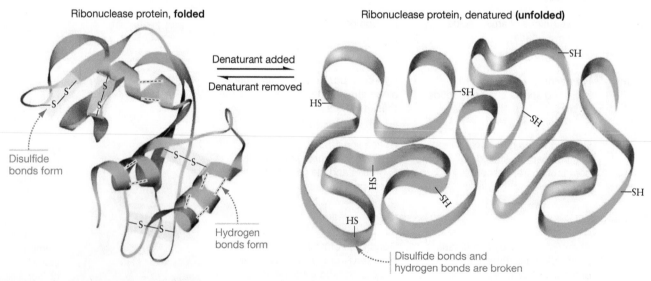

Ribonuclease protein, **folded**

Ribonuclease protein, denatured **(unfolded)**

Denaturant added
Denaturant removed

Disulfide bonds form

Hydrogen bonds form

Disulfide bonds and hydrogen bonds are broken

FIGURE 3.13 Protein Structure Determines Function. (left) Ribonuclease is functional when properly folded via hydrogen and disulfide bonds. **(right)** When the disulfide and various noncovalent bonds are broken, ribonuclease is no longer able to function. The double arrow indicates that this process is reversible.

treatments that make other proteins lose their tertiary structure. Heat-shock proteins recognize denatured proteins by binding to hydrophobic patches that would not normally be exposed in properly folded proteins. This interaction blocks inappropriate interactions with other molecules and allows the proteins to refold.

So what is the "normal shape" of a protein? Is only one shape possible for each protein, or could there be several different folded shapes with only one serving as the functional form?

Protein Shape Is Flexible

Although each protein has a characteristic folded shape that is necessary for its function, most proteins are flexible and dynamic, not rigid and static. As it turns out, many polypeptides are unable to fold into their active shape on their own. Over half of the proteins that have been analyzed to date have been found to contain disordered regions lacking any apparent structure. These proteins exist in an assortment of shapes. Only when they interact with particular ions or molecules, or are chemically modified, will they adopt the shape, or conformation, that allows them to perform their function in the cell.

Protein Folding Is Often Regulated   Since the function of a protein is dependent on its shape, controlling when or where it is folded will regulate the protein's activity.

For example, proteins involved in cell signaling are often regulated by controlling their shape. The inactive form of calmodulin—a protein that helps maintain normal blood pressure—has a disordered shape. When the concentration of calcium ions increases in the cell, calmodulin binds these ions, folds into an ordered, active conformation, and sends a signal to increase the diameter of blood vessels. **FIGURE 3.14** illustrates the major shape change that is induced in calmodulin when it binds to calcium.

Misfolding Can Be "Infectious"   In 1982, Stanley Prusiner published what may be the most surprising result to emerge from research on protein folding: Certain proteins can be folded into infectious, disease-causing agents. These proteins are called **prions** (pronounced *PREE-ons*), or proteinaceous infectious particles.

Infectious prions are alternate forms of normal proteins that are present in healthy individuals. The infectious and normal forms do not necessarily differ in amino acid sequence, but their *shapes* are radically different. The infectious form propagates by inducing conformational changes in normal proteins that cause them to adopt the alternate, infectious shape.

FIGURE 3.15 illustrates the differences in shape observed between the normal and infectious forms of the prion responsible for "mad cow disease" in cattle. The molecule in Figure 3.15a is called the prion protein (PrP) and is a normal component of mammalian cells. The improperly folded version of this protein, like the one in Figure 3.15b, represents the infectious form of the prion.

Prions cause a family of diseases known as the spongiform encephalopathies—literally, "sponge-brain-illnesses." Sheep, cows, goats, and humans afflicted with these diseases undergo massive degeneration of the brain. Although some spongiform encephalopathies

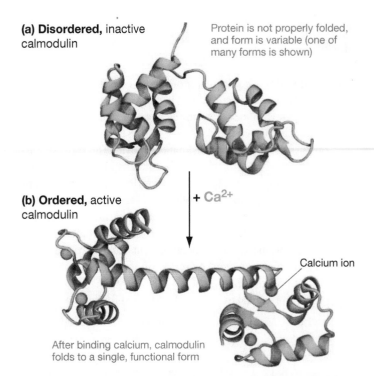

(a) Disordered, inactive calmodulin

Protein is not properly folded, and form is variable (one of many forms is shown)

(b) Ordered, active calmodulin

+ Ca²⁺

Calcium ion

After binding calcium, calmodulin folds to a single, functional form

FIGURE 3.14 Calmodulin Requires Calcium to Fold Properly. Many proteins, like calmodulin, do not complete their folding until after interacting with ions or other molecules. Once calmodulin binds to calcium, it assumes its functional shape.

can be inherited, in many cases the disease is transmitted when individuals eat tissues containing the infectious form of PrP. All the prion illnesses are fatal.

Prions are a particularly dramatic example of how a protein's function depends on its shape as well as how the final shape of a protein depends on folding.

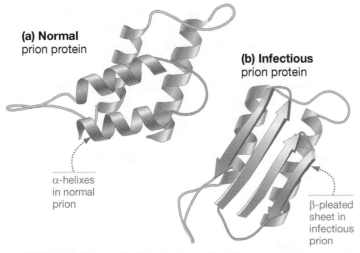

(a) Normal prion protein

(b) Infectious prion protein

α-helixes in normal prion

β-pleated sheet in infectious prion

FIGURE 3.15 Prion Infectivity Is Linked to Structure. Ribbon model of **(a)** a normal, noninfectious prion protein; and **(b)** the infectious form that causes mad cow disease in cattle. Secondary structure is represented by coils (α-helices) and arrows (β-pleated sheets).

3.4 Proteins Are the Most Versatile Macromolecules in Cells

As a group, proteins perform more types of cell functions than any other type of molecule does. It makes sense to hypothesize that life began with proteins, simply because proteins are so vital to the life of today's cells.

Consider the red blood cells that are moving through your arteries right now. Each of these cells contains about 300 million copies of hemoglobin. Hemoglobin carries oxygen from your lungs to cells throughout the body. But every red blood cell also has thousands of copies of a protein called carbonic anhydrase, which is important for moving carbon dioxide from cells back to the lungs, where it can be breathed out. Other proteins form the cell's internal "skeleton" or reside on the cell's membrane to interact with neighboring cells.

Proteins are crucial to most tasks required for cells to exist:

- *Catalysis* Many proteins are specialized to **catalyze,** or speed up, chemical reactions. A protein that functions as a catalyst is called an **enzyme.** The carbonic anhydrase molecules in red blood cells are catalysts. So is the protein called salivary amylase, found in your mouth. Salivary amylase helps begin the digestion of starch and other complex carbohydrates into simple sugars. Most chemical reactions that make life possible depend on enzymes.

- *Defense* Proteins called antibodies and complement proteins attack and destroy viruses and bacteria that cause disease.

- *Movement* Motor proteins and contractile proteins are responsible for moving the cell itself, or for moving large molecules and other types of cargo inside the cell. As you turn this page, for example, specialized proteins called actin and myosin will slide past one another to flex or extend muscle cells in your fingers and arm.

- *Signaling* Proteins are involved in carrying and receiving signals from cell to cell inside the body. If sugar levels in your blood are low, a small protein called glucagon will bind to receptor proteins on your liver cells, triggering enzymes inside to release sugar into your bloodstream.

- *Structure* Structural proteins make up body components such as fingernails and hair, and define the shape of individual cells. Structural proteins keep red blood cells flexible and in their normal disc-like shape.

- *Transport* Proteins allow particular molecules to enter and exit cells or carry them throughout the body. Hemoglobin is a particularly well-studied transport protein, but virtually every cell is studded with membrane proteins that control the passage of specific molecules and ions.

Of all the functions that proteins perform in cells, catalysis may be the most important. The reason is speed. Life, at its most basic level, consists of chemical reactions. But most don't occur fast enough to support life unless a catalyst is present. Enzymes are the most effective catalysts on Earth. Why is this so?

Why Are Enzymes Good Catalysts?

Part of the reason enzymes are such effective catalysts is that they bring reactant molecules—called **substrates**—together in a precise orientation so the atoms involved in the reaction can interact.

The initial hypothesis for how enzymes work was proposed by Emil Fischer in 1894. According to Fischer's "lock-and-key" model, enzymes are analogous to a lock and the keys are substrates that fit into the lock and then react.

Several important ideas in this model have stood the test of time. For example, Fischer was correct in proposing that enzymes bring substrates together in a precise orientation that makes reactions more likely. His model also accurately explained why most enzymes catalyze one specific reaction effectively. Enzyme specificity is a product of the geometry and types of functional groups in the sites where substrates bind.

As researchers began to test Fischer's model, the location where substrates bind and react became known as the enzyme's **active site.** The active site is where catalysis actually occurs.

When techniques for solving the three-dimensional structure of enzymes became available, the active sites were identified as clefts or cavities within the globular shapes. The digestive enzyme trypsin, which is at work in your body now, is a good example. As **FIGURE 3.16** shows, the active site in trypsin is a small notch that contains three key amino acid residues with functional groups that catalyze the cleavage of peptide bonds in other proteins. No other class of macromolecule can match proteins for their catalytic potential. The variety of reactive functional groups present in amino acids is much better suited for this activity than those found in nucleotides or sugars.

The role of enzymes in catalyzing reactions is discussed in more detail in the next unit (see Chapter 8). There you will see that Fischer's model had to be modified as research on enzyme action progressed.

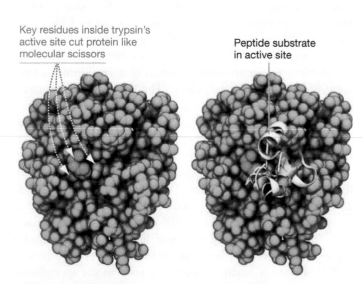

Key residues inside trypsin's active site cut protein like molecular scissors

Peptide substrate in active site

FIGURE 3.16 Substrates Bind to a Specific Location in an Enzyme Called the Active Site. The active site in trypsin, as in many enzymes, is a cleft that contains key amino acid residues that bind substrates and catalyze a reaction.

Was the First Living Entity a Protein Catalyst?

Several observations in the preceding sections could argue that a protein was the first molecule capable of replication. Experimental studies have shown that amino acids were likely abundant during chemical evolution, and that they could have polymerized to form small proteins. In addition, proteins are the most efficient catalysts known.

To date, however, attempts to simulate the origin of life with proteins have not been successful. The only experimental glimpse of a protein's potential to replicate involved an enzyme that could link two oligopeptides together to form a functional duplicate of itself. However, this result required a high concentration of pre-formed, specific oligopeptides that would not have been present during chemical evolution.

Although it is too early to arrive at definitive conclusions, most origin-of-life researchers are increasingly skeptical that life began with a protein. Their reasoning is that to make a copy of something, a mold or template is required. Proteins cannot furnish this information. Nucleic acids, in contrast, *can*. How they do so is the subject of the next chapter.

CHAPTER 3 REVIEW

For media, go to MasteringBiology

If you understand . . .

3.1 Amino Acids and Their Polymerization

- Amino acids have a central carbon bonded to an amino group, a hydrogen atom, a carboxyl group, and an R-group.
- The structure of the R-group affects the chemical reactivity and solubility of the amino acid.
- In proteins, amino acids are joined by a peptide bond between the carboxyl group of one amino acid and the amino group of another amino acid.

✔ You should be able to explain how you could use the structural formula of an amino acid to determine if it is acidic, basic, uncharged polar, or nonpolar.

3.2 What Do Proteins Look Like?

- A protein's primary structure, or sequence of amino acids, is responsible for most of its chemical properties.
- Interactions that take place between C=O and N–H groups in the same peptide-bonded backbone create secondary structures, which are stabilized primarily by hydrogen bonding.
- Tertiary structure results from interactions between R-groups—or R-groups and the peptide-bonded backbone—that stabilize a folded protein into a characteristic overall shape.
- In many cases, a complete protein consists of several different polypeptides, bonded together. The combination of polypeptides represents the protein's quaternary structure.

✔ You should be able to predict where nonpolar amino acid residues would be found in a globular protein, such as the trypsin molecule shown in Figure 3.8c.

3.3 Folding and Function

- Protein folding is a spontaneous process.
- A protein's normal folded shape is essential to its function.
- Many proteins must first bind to other molecules or ions before they can adopt their active conformation.
- Improperly folded proteins can be detrimental to life, and certain proteins even cause deadly infectious diseases.

✔ You should be able to identify one way in which the process of folding in calmodulin and infectious prions is similar.

3.4 Proteins Are the Most Versatile Macromolecules in Cells

- In organisms, proteins function in catalysis, defense, movement, signaling, structural support, and transport of materials.
- Proteins can have diverse functions in cells because they have such diverse structures and chemical properties.
- Catalysis takes place at the enzyme's active site, which has unique chemical properties and a distinctive size and shape.

✔ You should be able to provide the characteristics of proteins that make them especially useful for the following cellular activities: catalysis, defense, and signaling.

MasteringBiology

1. MasteringBiology Assignments

Tutorials and Activities Activation Energy and Enzymes; Amino Acid Functional Groups; Condensation and Hydrolysis Reactions; Enzyme and Substrate Concentrations; Enzyme Inhibition; Factors That Affect Reaction Rate; How Enzymes Function; How Enzymes Work; Levels of Structure in Proteins; Making and Breaking Polymers; Protein Functions, Protein

Structure; Regulating Enzyme Action

Questions Reading Quizzes, Blue-Thread Questions, Test Bank

2. eText Read your book online, search, take notes, highlight text, and more.

3. The Study Area Practice Test, Cumulative Test, BioFlix® 3-D Animations, Videos, Activities, Audio Glossary, Word Study Tools, Art

You should be able to . . .

✓ TEST YOUR KNOWLEDGE
Answers are available in Appendix A

1. What two functional groups are present on every amino acid?
   a. a carbonyl (C=O) group and a carboxyl group
   b. an N–H group and a carbonyl group
   c. an amino group and a hydroxyl group
   d. an amino group and a carboxyl group

2. Twenty different amino acids are found in the proteins of cells. What distinguishes these molecules?

3. By convention, biologists write the sequence of amino acids in a polypeptide in which direction?
   a. carboxy- to amino-terminus
   b. amino- to carboxy-terminus
   c. polar residues to nonpolar residues
   d. charged residues to uncharged residues

4. In a polypeptide, what bonds are responsible for the secondary structure called an α-helix?
   a. peptide bonds
   b. hydrogen bonds that form between the core C=O and N–H groups on different residues
   c. hydrogen bonds and other interactions between side chains
   d. disulfide bonds that form between cysteine residues

5. Where is the information stored that directs different polypeptides to fold into different shapes?

6. What is an active site?
   a. the position in an enzyme where substrates bind
   b. the place where a molecule or ion binds to a protein to induce a shape change
   c. the portion of a motor protein that is involved in moving cargo in a cell
   d. the site on an antibody where it binds to bacterial cells or viruses

✓ TEST YOUR UNDERSTANDING
Answers are available in Appendix A

7. Explain how water participates in the development of the interactions that glue nonpolar amino acids together in the interior of globular proteins.

8. If amino acids were mixed together in a solution, resembling the prebiotic soup, would they spontaneously polymerize into polypeptides? Why or why not?

9. Provide an example of how a specific shape of a protein is correlated with its function.

10. A major theme in this chapter is that the structure of molecules correlates with their function. Use this theme to explain why proteins can perform so many different functions in organisms and why enzymes are such effective catalysts.

11. Why are proteins not considered to be a good candidate for the first living molecule?
    a. Their catalytic capability is insufficient.
    b. Their amino acid monomers were likely not present during chemical evolution.
    c. They cannot serve as a template for replication.
    d. They could not have polymerized on their own from amino acids during chemical evolution.

12. If proteins folded only into rigid, inflexible structures, how might this affect the cell's ability to regulate protein function?

✓ TEST YOUR PROBLEM-SOLVING SKILLS
Answers are available in Appendix A

13. Based on what you know of the peptide bonds that link together amino acid residues, why would proline's side chain reduce the flexibility of the backbone?

14. Make a concept map (see **BioSkills 15** in Appendix B) that relates the four levels of protein structure and shows how they can contribute to the formation of an active site. Your map should include the following boxed terms: Primary structure, Secondary structure, Tertiary structure, Quaternary structure, Active site, Amino acid sequence, R-groups, Helices and sheets, 3-D shape.

15. Proteins that interact with DNA often interact with the phosphates that are part of this molecule. Which of the following types of

amino acids would you predict to be present in the DNA binding sites of these proteins?
    a. acidic amino acids
    b. basic amino acids
    c. uncharged polar amino acids
    d. nonpolar amino acids

16. Some prion-associated diseases are inherited, such as fatal familial insomnia. What is likely to be different between the infectious forms of these inherited prions compared to those that arise via transmission from one animal to another?

4 Nucleic Acids and the RNA World

In this chapter you will learn that

Nucleic acids store the information that encodes life

by asking ↓

What is a nucleic acid? **4.1**

comparing/contrasting

and by asking

| DNA structure and function **4.2** | RNA structure and function **4.3** | Could life have evolved from an RNA? **4.4** |

specialized for

| Stability and storage | Versatility and catalysis |

This is part of the sheet-metal-and-wire model that James Watson and Francis Crick used to figure out the secondary structure of DNA. The large "T" stands for the nitrogen-containing base thymine.

This chapter is part of the Big Picture. See how on pages 104–105.

life began when chemical evolution led to the production of a molecule that could promote its own replication. The nature of this first "living molecule," however, has been the subject of many investigations and heated debates. Even though proteins are the workhorse molecules of today's cells, relatively few researchers favor the hypothesis that life began as a protein molecule. Instead, the vast majority of biologists contend that life began as a polymer called a nucleic acid—specifically, a molecule of ribonucleic acid (RNA). This proposal is called the **RNA world hypothesis.**

The RNA world hypothesis contends that chemical evolution led to the existence of an RNA molecule that could replicate itself. Once this molecule existed, chance errors in the copying process

✔ When you see this checkmark, stop and test yourself. Answers are available in Appendix A.

created variations that would undergo natural selection—the evolutionary process by which individuals with certain attributes are selectively reproduced (see Chapter 1). At this point, chemical evolution was over and biological evolution was off and running.

To test this hypothesis, several groups around the world have been working to synthesize a self-replicating RNA molecule in the laboratory. If they ever succeed, they will have created a lifeform in a test tube.

This chapter focuses on the structure and function of nucleic acids. Let's begin with an analysis of nucleic acid monomers and how they are linked together into polymers. Afterwards, you will learn about the experiments used to determine if a nucleic acid could have triggered the evolution of life on Earth.

4.1 What Is a Nucleic Acid?

Nucleic acids are polymers, just as proteins are polymers. But instead of being made up of monomers called amino acids, **nucleic acids** are made up of monomers called **nucleotides.**

FIGURE 4.1a diagrams the three components of a nucleotide: (1) a phosphate group, (2) a five-carbon sugar, and (3) a nitrogenous (nitrogen-containing) base. The phosphate is bonded to the sugar molecule, which in turn is bonded to the nitrogenous base.

The sugar component of a nucleotide is an organic compound bearing reactive hydroxyl (−OH) functional groups. Notice that the prime symbols (′) in Figure 4.1 indicate that the carbon being referred to is part of the sugar—not of the attached nitrogenous base. The phosphate group in a nucleotide is attached to the 5′ carbon.

Although a wide variety of nucleotides are found in living cells, origin-of-life researchers concentrate on two types: **ribonucleotides,** the monomers of **ribonucleic acid (RNA),** and **deoxyribonucleotides,** the monomers of **deoxyribonucleic acid (DNA).** In ribonucleotides, the sugar is ribose; in deoxyribonucleotides, it is deoxyribose (*deoxy* means "lacking oxygen"). As **FIGURE 4.1b** shows, these two sugars differ by a single oxygen atom. Ribose has an −OH group bonded to the 2′ carbon. Deoxyribose has an H instead at the same location. In both of these sugars, an −OH group is bonded to the 3′ carbon.

In addition to the type of sugar, nucleotides also differ in the type of nitrogenous base. These bases, diagrammed in **FIGURE 4.1c,** belong to structural groups called **purines** and **pyrimidines.** The purines are adenine (A) and guanine (G); the pyrimidines are cytosine (C), uracil (U), and thymine (T). Note that the two rings in adenine and guanine are linked together by nine atoms, compared to the six atoms that make a single ring in each pyrimidine. This makes remembering which bases are purines easy, since both adenine and guanine include "nine" in their names.

As Figure 4.1c shows, ribonucleotides and deoxyribonucleotides also differ in one of their pyrimidine bases. Ribonucleotides

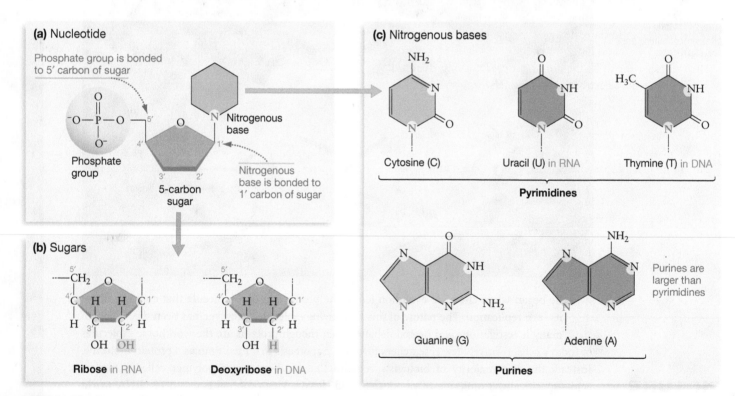

FIGURE 4.1 The General Structure of a Nucleotide. Note that in the bases, the nitrogen that bonds to the sugar is colored blue.

use uracil (U) while deoxyribonucleotides use the closely related base thymine (T).

✔ You should be able to diagram a ribonucleotide and a deoxyribonucleotide. Use a ball for the phosphate group, a pentagon to represent the sugar subunit, and a hexagon to represent the nitrogenous base. Label the 2′, 3′, and 5′ carbons on the sugar molecule, and add the atoms or groups that are bonded to each.

To summarize: After the different sugars and bases are taken into account, eight different nucleotides are used to build nucleic acids—four ribonucleotides (A, G, C, and U) and four deoxyribonucleotides (A, G, C, and T). If nucleic acids played any role in the chemical evolution of life, then at least some of these nucleotides must have been present in the prebiotic oceans. Is there any evidence to suggest that this was possible?

Could Chemical Evolution Result in the Production of Nucleotides?

Based on data from Stanley Miller and researchers who followed (Chapter 2), most biologists contend that amino acids could have been synthesized early in Earth's history. The reactions behind the prebiotic synthesis of nucleotides, however, have been more difficult to identify.

Miller-like laboratory simulations have shown that nitrogenous bases and many different types of sugars can be synthesized readily under conditions that mimic the prebiotic soup. In these experiments, almost all the sugars that have five or six carbons—called pentoses and hexoses, respectively—are produced in approximately equal amounts. If nucleic acids were to form in the prebiotic soup, however, ribose would have had to predominate.

How ribose came to be the dominant sugar during chemical evolution (i.e., what selective process was at work) is still a mystery. Origin-of-life researchers refer to this issue as the "ribose problem." Recent work focusing on the conditions that exist in deep-sea hydrothermal vent systems (see Chapter 2) may point to a possible solution.

Here's the line of reasoning researchers are currently pursuing: Ribose molecules may have been selectively enriched from the mix of sugars in certain early Earth deep-sea vent systems. In one experiment, researchers simulated the conditions that exist in these vents. Then they tested whether minerals that are predicted to have existed in the vent chimneys are able to bind sugars. What they found was striking—the minerals preferentially bound to ribose over other pentoses and hexoses. Did this occur in the ancient vents? If so, the implications are exciting: A high concentration of ribose would be present in the same deep-sea vent environment where chemical evolution is thought to have taken place.

Despite the observed synthesis of nitrogenous bases and the recent discovery of ribose enrichment, the production of nucleotides remains a serious challenge for the theory of chemical evolution. At this time, experiments that attempt to simulate early

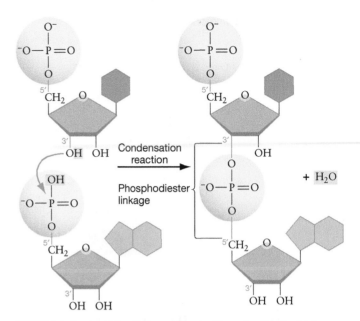

FIGURE 4.2 Nucleotides Polymerize via Phosphodiester Linkages. Ribonucleotides can polymerize via condensation reactions. The resulting phosphodiester linkage connects the 3′ carbon of one ribonucleotide and the 5′ carbon of another ribonucleotide.

Earth environments have yet to synthesize complete nucleotides. But research on this issue continues.

In the meantime, let's consider the next question: Once nucleotides formed, how would they polymerize to form RNA and DNA? This question has an answer.

How Do Nucleotides Polymerize to Form Nucleic Acids?

Nucleic acids form when nucleotides polymerize. As **FIGURE 4.2** shows, the polymerization reaction involves the formation of a bond between a hydroxyl on the sugar component of one nucleotide and the phosphate group of another nucleotide. The result of this condensation reaction is called a **phosphodiester linkage,** or a phosphodiester bond.

A phosphodiester linkage joins the 5′ carbon on the sugar of one nucleotide to the 3′ carbon on the sugar of another. When the nucleotides involved contain the sugar ribose, the polymer that is produced is RNA. If the nucleotides contain the sugar deoxyribose instead, then the resulting polymer is DNA.

DNA and RNA Strands Are Directional **FIGURE 4.3** (see page 60) shows how the chain of phosphodiester linkages in a nucleic acid acts as a backbone, analogous to the peptide-bonded backbone found in proteins.

Like the peptide-bonded backbone of a polypeptide, the sugar-phosphate backbone of a nucleic acid is directional. In a strand of RNA or DNA, one end has an unlinked 5′ phosphate while the other end has an unlinked 3′ hydroxyl—meaning the groups are not linked to another nucleotide. By convention, the

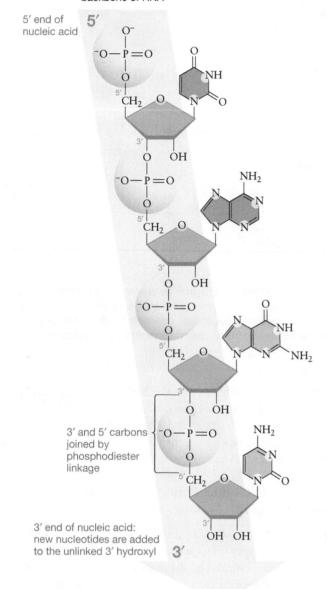

The sugar-phosphate backbone of RNA

5' end of nucleic acid

5'

3' and 5' carbons joined by phosphodiester linkage

3' end of nucleic acid: new nucleotides are added to the unlinked 3' hydroxyl

3'

FIGURE 4.3 RNA Has a Sugar-Phosphate Backbone.

✓**EXERCISE** Identify the four bases in this RNA strand, using Figure 4.1c as a key. Then write down the base sequence, starting at the 5' end.

sequence of bases found in an RNA or DNA strand is always written in the 5'→3' direction. (This system is logical because in cells, RNA and DNA are always synthesized in this direction. Bases are added only at the 3' end of the growing molecule.)

The order of the different nitrogenous bases in a nucleic acid forms the primary structure of the molecule. When biologists write the primary structure of a stretch of DNA or RNA, they simply list the sequence of nucleotides in the 5'→3' direction, using their single-letter abbreviations. For example, a six-base-long DNA sequence might be ATTAGC. It would take roughly

6 billion of these letters to write the primary structure of the DNA in most of your cells.

Polymerization Requires an Energy Source In cells, the polymerization reactions that join nucleotides into nucleic acids are catalyzed by enzymes. Like other polymerization reactions, the process is not spontaneous. An input of energy is needed to tip the energy balance in favor of the process.

Polymerization can take place in cells because the potential energy of the nucleotide monomers is first raised by reactions that add two phosphate groups to the ribonucleotides or deoxyribonucleotides, creating nucleoside triphosphates.[1] In the case of nucleic acid polymerization, researchers refer to these nucleotides as "activated." **FIGURE 4.4a** shows an example of an activated nucleotide; this molecule is called **adenosine triphosphate,** or **ATP.**

Why do added phosphate groups raise the energy content of a molecule? Recall that phosphates are negatively charged and that like charges repel (Chapter 2). Linking two or more phosphates with covalent bonds generates strong repulsive forces. These bonds therefore carry a large amount of potential energy, which can be harvested to power other chemical reactions (**FIGURE 4.4b**). You will see in later chapters that the potential energy stored in ATP is used to drive other cellular activities, independent of nucleotide polymerization.

This is a key point, and one that you will encounter again and again in this text: The addition of one or more phosphate groups raises the potential energy of substrate molecules enough to make an otherwise nonspontaneous reaction possible. (Chapter 8 explains how this happens in more detail.)

Could Nucleic Acids Have Formed in the Absence of Cellular Enzymes? Accumulating data suggest that the answer is yes.

Activation of nucleotides has been observed when prebiotic conditions are simulated experimentally. In a suite of follow-up experiments, researchers have produced RNA molecules by incubating activated nucleotides with tiny mineral particles—in one case, molecules up to 50 nucleotides long were observed. These results support the hypothesis that polymerization of activated nucleotides in the prebiotic world may have been catalyzed by minerals. This model would be in line with the surface metabolism model for chemical evolution (introduced in Chapter 2).

More recent work has shown that under certain conditions, up to 100 nucleotides can be linked together, even without first being activated. To accomplish this, heat was introduced as a source of energy and small nonpolar molecules, called lipids, were added to help the monomers interact. This experiment is particularly interesting with respect to the setting for chemical evolution, because both of these factors—heat and lipids—are thought to have been present in prebiotic hydrothermal vents. (The chemical origins and properties of lipids are covered in Chapter 6.)

[1]A molecule consisting of a sugar and one of the bases in Figure 4.1c is called a nucleoside (a nucleotide is a sugar, a base, and one or more phosphate groups). Thus, a sugar attached to a base and three phosphate groups is called a nucleoside triphosphate.

(a) ATP is an example of an activated nucleotide.

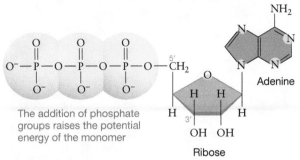

The addition of phosphate groups raises the potential energy of the monomer

Adenine

Ribose

FIGURE 4.4 Activated Monomers Drive Polymerization Reactions. Polymerization reactions are generally nonspontaneous, but those reactions involving nucleoside triphosphates, such as ATP, are spontaneous. The potential energy stored in activated nucleotides is released when the pyrophosphate (PP_i) is removed before the polymerizing condensation reaction shown in Figure 4.2.

(b) Energy is released when phosphates are removed by hydrolysis.

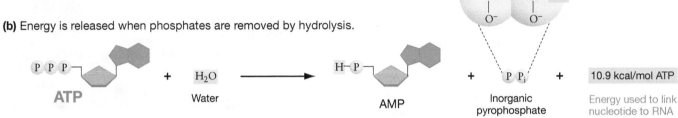

ATP + H_2O ⟶ AMP + Inorganic pyrophosphate + 10.9 kcal/mol ATP

Water

Energy used to link nucleotide to RNA

Based on these results, there is a strong consensus that if ribonucleotides and deoxyribonucleotides were able to form during chemical evolution, they would be able to polymerize into DNA and RNA. Now, what do these nucleic acids look like, and what can they do?

check your understanding

If you understand that . . .

- Nucleotides are monomers that consist of a sugar, a phosphate group, and a nitrogen-containing base.
- Nucleotides polymerize to form nucleic acids through formation of phosphodiester linkages between the 3′ hydroxyl on one nucleotide and the 5′ phosphate on another.
- During polymerization, nucleotides are added only to the 3′ end of a nucleic acid strand.

✔ You should be able to . . .

Draw a simplified diagram of the phosphodiester linkage between two nucleotides, indicate the 5′→3′ polarity, and mark where the next nucleotide would be added to the growing chain.

Answers are available in Appendix A.

4.2 DNA Structure and Function

The primary structure of nucleic acids is somewhat similar to the primary structure of proteins. Proteins have a peptide-bonded backbone with a series of R-groups that extend from it. DNA and RNA molecules have a sugar-phosphate backbone, created by phosphodiester linkages, and a sequence of any of four nitrogenous bases that extend from it.

Like proteins, DNA and RNA also have secondary structure. While the α-helices and β-pleated sheets of proteins are formed by hydrogen bonding between groups in the backbone, the secondary structure of nucleic acids is formed by hydrogen bonding between the nitrogenous bases.

Let's analyze the secondary structure and function of DNA first, and then dig into the secondary structure and function of RNA.

What Is the Nature of DNA's Secondary Structure?

The solution to DNA's secondary structure, announced in 1953, ranks among the great scientific breakthroughs of the twentieth century. James Watson and Francis Crick presented a model for the secondary structure of DNA in a one-page paper published in the scientific journal *Nature*.

Early Data Provided Clues Watson and Crick's finding was a hypothesis based on a series of results from other laboratories. They were trying to propose a secondary structure that could explain several important observations about the DNA found in cells:

- Chemists had worked out the structure of nucleotides and knew that DNA polymerized through the formation of phosphodiester linkages. Thus, Watson and Crick knew that the molecule had a sugar-phosphate backbone.

- By analyzing the nitrogenous bases in DNA samples from different organisms, Erwin Chargaff had established two empirical rules: **(1)** The number of purines in a given DNA molecule is equal to the number of pyrimidines, and **(2)** the number of T's and A's in DNA are equal, and the number of C's and G's in DNA are equal.

- By bombarding DNA with X-rays and analyzing how it scattered the radiation, Rosalind Franklin and Maurice Wilkins had calculated the distances between groups of atoms in the molecule (see **BioSkills 11** in Appendix B for an introduction to this technique, called **X-ray crystallography**). The scattering patterns showed that three distances were repeated many times: 0.34 nanometer (nm), 2.0 nm, and 3.4 nm. Because the measurements repeated, the researchers inferred that DNA molecules had a regular and repeating structure. The pattern of X-ray scattering suggested that the molecule was helical, or spiral, in nature.

Based on this work, understanding DNA's structure boiled down to understanding the nature of the helix involved. What type of helix would have a sugar-phosphate backbone and explain both Chargaff's rules and the Franklin–Wilkins measurements?

DNA Strands Are Antiparallel Watson and Crick began by analyzing the size and geometry of deoxyribose, phosphate groups, and nitrogenous bases. The bond angles and measurements suggested that the distance of 2.0 nm probably represented the width of the helix and that 0.34 nm was likely to be the distance between bases stacked in a spiral.

How could they make sense of Chargaff's rules and the 3.4-nm distance, which appeared to be exactly 10 times the distance between a single pair of bases?

To solve this problem, Watson and Crick constructed a series of physical models like the one pictured in **FIGURE 4.5**. The models allowed them to tinker with different types of helical configurations. After many false starts, something clicked:

- They arranged two strands of DNA side by side and running in opposite directions—meaning that one strand ran in the $5' \rightarrow 3'$ direction while the other strand was oriented $3' \rightarrow 5'$. Strands with this orientation are said to be **antiparallel.**

- If the antiparallel strands are twisted together to form a **double helix,** the coiled sugar-phosphate backbones end up on the outside of the spiral and the nitrogenous bases on the inside.

FIGURE 4.5 **Building a Physical Model of DNA Structure.** Watson (left) and Crick (right) represented the arrangement of the four deoxyribonucleotides in a double helix, using metal plates and wires with precise lengths and geometries.

- For the bases from each backbone to fit in the interior of the 2.0-nm-wide structure, they have to form purine-pyrimidine pairs (see **FIGURE 4.6a**). This is a key point: The pairing allows hydrogen bonds to form between certain purines and pyrimidines. Adenine forms hydrogen bonds with thymine, and guanine forms hydrogen bonds with cytosine (**FIGURE 4.6b**).

- The A-T and G-C bases were said to be complementary. Two hydrogen bonds form when A and T pair, and three hydrogen bonds form when G and C pair. As a result, the G-C interaction is slightly stronger than the A-T bond. In contrast, A-C and G-T pairs allowed no or only one hydrogen bond.

(a) Only purine-pyrimidine pairs fit inside the double helix.

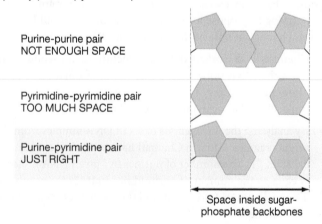

Purine-purine pair
NOT ENOUGH SPACE

Pyrimidine-pyrimidine pair
TOO MUCH SPACE

Purine-pyrimidine pair
JUST RIGHT

Space inside sugar-phosphate backbones

(b) Hydrogen bonds form between G-C pairs and A-T pairs.

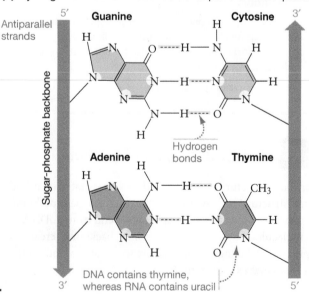

FIGURE 4.6 **Complementary Base Pairing Is Based on Hydrogen Bonding.**

Watson and Crick had discovered **complementary base pairing**. In fact, the term **Watson–Crick pairing** is now used interchangeably with the phrase complementary base pairing. The physical restraints posed by these interactions resulted in a full helical twist every 10 bases, or 3.4 nm.

The Double Helix   **FIGURE 4.7a** shows how antiparallel strands of DNA form when complementary bases line up and form hydrogen bonds. As you study the figure, notice that DNA is put together like a ladder whose ends have been twisted in opposite directions. The sugar-phosphate backbones form the supports of the ladder; the base pairs represent the rungs of the ladder. The twisting allows the nitrogenous bases to line up in a way that makes hydrogen bonding between them possible.

The nitrogenous bases in the middle of the molecule are hydrophobic. This is a key point, because twisting into a double helix minimizes contact between the bases and surrounding water molecules. In addition to hydrogen bonding, van der Waals interactions between the tightly stacked bases in the interior further contribute to the stability of the helix. You see the same forces—hydrogen bonding, hydrophobicity, and van der Waals interactions—play similar roles in protein folding (Chapter 3). But DNA as a whole is hydrophilic and water soluble because the backbones, which face the exterior of the molecule, contain negatively charged phosphate groups that interact with water.

FIGURE 4.7b highlights additional features of DNA's secondary structure. It's important to note that the outside of the helical DNA molecule forms two types of grooves. The larger of the two is known as the major groove, and the smaller one is known as the minor groove. From this figure, you can identify how DNA's secondary structure explains the measurements observed by Franklin and Wilkins.

Since the model of the double helix was published, experimental tests have shown that the hypothesis is correct in almost every detail. To summarize:

- DNA's secondary structure consists of two antiparallel strands twisted into a double helix.

- The molecule is stabilized by hydrophobic interactions in its interior and by hydrogen bonding between the complementary base pairs A-T and G-C.

✔ You should be able to explain why complementary base pairing would not be possible if two DNA strands were aligned in a parallel fashion—instead of the antiparallel alignment shown in Figure 4.6b.

Now the question is, how does this secondary structure affect the molecule's function?

(a) Cartoons of DNA structure

(b) Space-filling model of DNA double helix

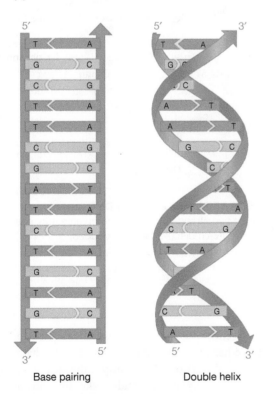

Base pairing   Double helix

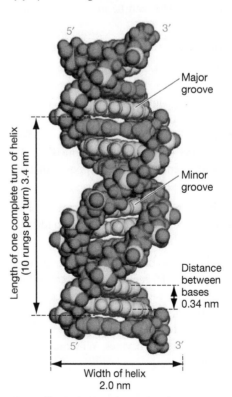

Major groove

Minor groove

Distance between bases 0.34 nm

Length of one complete turn of helix (10 rungs per turn) 3.4 nm

Width of helix 2.0 nm

FIGURE 4.7 The Secondary Structure of DNA Is a Double Helix. (a) The cartoons illustrate complementary base pairing and how strands are twisted into a double helix. **(b)** The space-filling model shows tight packing of the bases inside the double helix. The double-helix structure explains the measurements inferred from X-ray analysis of DNA molecules.

DNA Functions as an Information-Containing Molecule

Watson and Crick's model created a sensation for a simple reason: It revealed how DNA could store and transmit biological information. In literature, information consists of letters on a page. In music, information is composed of the notes on a staff. But inside cells, information consists of a sequence of nucleotides in a nucleic acid. The four nitrogenous bases function like letters of the alphabet. A sequence of bases is like the sequence of letters in a word—it has meaning.

In all organisms that have been examined to date, from tiny bacteria to gigantic redwood trees, DNA carries the information required for the organism's growth and reproduction. Exploring how hereditary information is encoded and translated into action is the heart of several later chapters (Chapters 16 through 19).

Here, however, our focus is on how life began. The theory of chemical evolution holds that life began once a molecule emerged that could make a copy of itself. Does the information contained within DNA allow it to be replicated?

Watson and Crick ended their paper on the double helix with one of the classic understatements in the scientific literature: "It has not escaped our notice that the specific pairing we have postulated immediately suggests a possible copying mechanism." Here's the key insight: DNA's primary structure serves as a mold or template for the synthesis of a complementary strand. DNA contains the information required for a copy of itself to be made. **FIGURE 4.8** shows how a copy of DNA can be made by complementary base pairing.

Step 1 Heating or enzyme-catalyzed reactions can cause the double helix to separate.

Step 2 Free deoxyribonucleotides form hydrogen bonds with complementary bases on the original strand of DNA—also called a **template strand.** As they do, their sugar-phosphate groups form phosphodiester linkages to create a new strand—also called a **complementary strand.** Note that the $5' \rightarrow 3'$ directionality of the complementary strand is opposite that of the template strand.

Step 3 Complementary base pairing allows each strand of a DNA double helix to be copied exactly, producing two identical daughter molecules.

DNA copying is the basis for a second of the five characteristics of life (introduced in Chapter 1): replication. But can DNA catalyze the reactions needed to *self*-replicate? In today's cells and in laboratory experiments, the answer is no. Instead, the molecule is copied through a complicated series of energy-demanding reactions, catalyzed by a large suite of enzymes. Why can't DNA catalyze these reactions itself?

Is DNA a Catalytic Molecule?

The DNA double helix is highly structured. It is regular, symmetric, and held together by hydrogen bonding, hydrophobic

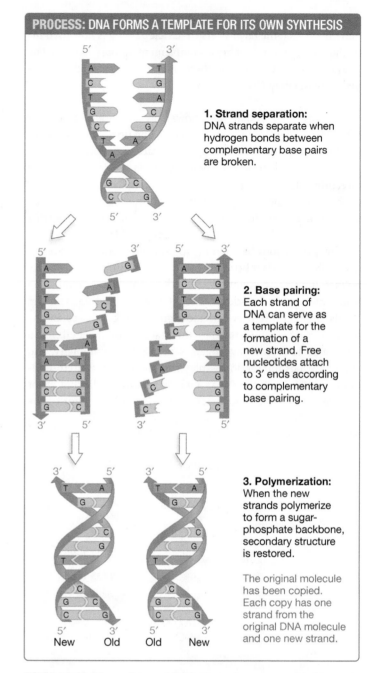

PROCESS: DNA FORMS A TEMPLATE FOR ITS OWN SYNTHESIS

1. Strand separation: DNA strands separate when hydrogen bonds between complementary base pairs are broken.

2. Base pairing: Each strand of DNA can serve as a template for the formation of a new strand. Free nucleotides attach to 3′ ends according to complementary base pairing.

3. Polymerization: When the new strands polymerize to form a sugar-phosphate backbone, secondary structure is restored.

The original molecule has been copied. Each copy has one strand from the original DNA molecule and one new strand.

FIGURE 4.8 Making a Copy of DNA. If new bases are added to each of the two strands of DNA via complementary base pairing, a copy of the DNA molecule can be produced.

✔ **QUESTION** When double-stranded DNA is heated to 95°C, the bonds between complementary base pairs break and single-stranded DNA results. Considering this observation, is the reaction shown in step 1 spontaneous?

interactions, and phosphodiester linkages. In addition, the molecule has few functional groups exposed that can participate in chemical reactions. For example, the lack of a 2′ hydroxyl group on each deoxyribonucleotide makes the polymer much less reactive than RNA, and thus much more resistant to degradation.

Intact stretches of DNA have been recovered from fossils that are tens of thousands of years old. The molecules have the same sequence of bases as the organisms had when they were alive, despite death and exposure to a wide array of pH, temperature, and chemical conditions. DNA's stability is the key to its effectiveness as a reliable information-bearing molecule. DNA's structure is consistent with its function in cells.

The orderliness and stability that make DNA such a dependable information repository also make it extraordinarily inept at catalysis, however. Recall that enzyme function is based on a specific binding event between a substrate and a protein catalyst (Chapter 3). Thanks to variation in reactivity among R-groups in amino acids, and the enormous diversity of shapes found in proteins, a wide array of catalytic activities can be generated. In comparison, DNA's primary and secondary structures are simple. It is not surprising, then, that DNA has never been observed to catalyze any reaction in any organism. Although researchers have been able to construct single-stranded DNA molecules that can catalyze some reactions in the laboratory, the number and diversity of reactions involved is a minute fraction of the activity catalyzed by enzymes.

In short, DNA furnishes an extraordinarily stable template for copying itself and for storing information encoded in a sequence of bases. But owing to its inability to act as an effective catalyst, there is virtually no support for the hypothesis that the first life-form consisted of DNA. Instead, most biologists who are working on the origin of life support the hypothesis that life began with RNA. How does the structure of RNA differ from DNA?

check your understanding

If you understand that . . .

- DNA's primary structure consists of a sequence of deoxyribonucleotides.
- DNA's secondary structure consists of two DNA molecules that run in opposite orientations to each other. The two strands are twisted into a double helix, and they are held together by hydrogen bonds between A-T and G-C pairs and hydrophobic interactions that drive bases into the interior of the helix.
- The sequence of deoxyribonucleotides in DNA contains information. Owing to complementary base pairing, each DNA strand also contains the information required to form its complementary strand.

✔ **You should be able to . . .**

Make a sketch of a double-stranded DNA molecule in the form of a ladder with the sequence of A-G-C-T. Label the 5′ and 3′ ends, the sugar-phosphate backbones, the hydrogen bonds between complementary bases, and the location of hydrophobic interactions.

Answers are available in Appendix A.

4.3 RNA Structure and Function

The first living molecule would have needed to perform two key functions: carry information and catalyze reactions that promoted its own replication. At first glance, these two functions appear to conflict. Information storage requires regularity and stability; catalysis requires variation in chemical composition and flexibility in shape. How is it possible for a molecule to do both? The answer lies in structure.

Structurally, RNA Differs from DNA

Recall that proteins can have up to four levels of structure. Single-chain proteins possess a primary sequence of amino acids, secondary folds that are stabilized by hydrogen bonding between atoms in the peptide-bonded backbone, and tertiary folds that are stabilized by interactions involving R-groups. Quaternary structure is found in proteins consisting of multiple polypeptides.

DNA has only primary and secondary structure. But RNA, like single-chained proteins, can have up to three levels of structure.

Primary Structure Like DNA, RNA has a primary structure consisting of a sugar-phosphate backbone formed by phosphodiester linkages and, extending from that backbone, a sequence of four types of nitrogenous bases. But it's important to recall two significant differences between these nucleic acids:

1. The sugar in the sugar-phosphate backbone of RNA is ribose, not deoxyribose as in DNA.

2. The pyrimidine base thymine does not exist in RNA. Instead, RNA contains the closely related pyrimidine base uracil.

The first point is critical. Look back at Figure 4.1b and compare the functional groups attached to ribose and deoxyribose. Notice the hydroxyl (−OH) group on the 2′ carbon of ribose. This additional hydroxyl is much more reactive than the hydrogen atom on the 2′ carbon of deoxyribose. When RNA molecules fold in certain ways, the hydroxyl group can attack the phosphate linkage between nucleotides, which would generate a break in the sugar-phosphate backbone. While this −OH group makes RNA much less stable than DNA, it can also support catalytic activity by the molecule.

Secondary Structure Like DNA molecules, most RNA molecules have secondary structure that results from complementary base pairing between purine and pyrimidine bases. In RNA, adenine forms hydrogen bonds only with uracil, and guanine again forms hydrogen bonds with cytosine. (Other, non-Watson–Crick base pairs occur, although less frequently.) Three hydrogen bonds form between guanine and cytosine, but only two form between adenine and uracil.

This hydrogen bonding should seem familiar, since DNA bonds together in a similar manner—so how do the secondary structures of RNA and DNA differ? In the vast majority of cases, the purine and pyrimidine bases in RNA undergo hydrogen

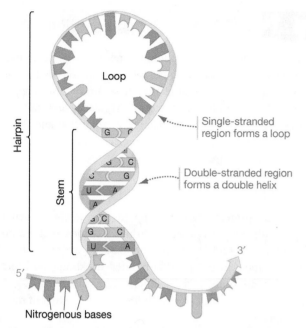

FIGURE 4.9 Complementary Base Pairing and Secondary Structure in RNA: Stem-and-Loop Structures. This RNA molecule has secondary structure. The double-stranded "stem" and single-stranded "loop" form a hairpin. The bonded bases in the stem are antiparallel, meaning that they are oriented in opposite directions.

bonding with complementary bases on the *same strand*, rather than forming hydrogen bonds with complementary bases on a different strand, as in DNA.

FIGURE 4.9 shows how within-strand base pairing works. The key is that when bases on one part of an RNA strand fold over and align with ribonucleotides on another part of the same strand, the two sugar-phosphate strands are antiparallel. In this orientation, hydrogen bonding between complementary bases results in a stable double helix.

If the section where the fold occurs includes unpaired bases, then the stem-and-loop configuration shown in Figure 4.9 results. This type of secondary structure is called a **hairpin.** Several other types of RNA secondary structures are possible, each involving a different length and arrangement of base-paired segments.

Like the α-helices and β-pleated sheets observed in many proteins, RNA secondary structures can form spontaneously. They are directed by hydrophobic interactions and stabilized by hydrogen bonding between the bases. Even though hairpins and other types of secondary structure reduce the entropy of RNA molecules, the energy released in these interactions makes the overall process favorable.

Tertiary Structure   RNA molecules can also have tertiary structure, which arises when secondary structures fold into more complex shapes. As a result, RNA molecules with different base sequences can have very different overall shapes and chemical properties. RNA molecules are much more diverse in size, shape, and reactivity than DNA molecules are. Structurally and chemically, RNA is intermediate between the complexity of proteins and the simplicity of DNA.

TABLE 4.1 summarizes the similarities and differences in the structures of RNA and DNA.

RNA's Structure Makes It an Extraordinarily Versatile Molecule

In terms of structure, you've seen that RNA is intermediate between DNA and proteins. RNA is intermediate in terms of function as well. RNA molecules cannot archive information nearly as efficiently as DNA molecules do, but they do perform key functions in information processing. Likewise, they cannot catalyze as many reactions as proteins do. But as it turns out, the reactions they do catalyze are particularly important.

In cells, RNA molecules function like a jackknife or a pocket tool with an array of attachments: They perform a wide variety of

SUMMARY TABLE 4.1   **DNA and RNA Structure**

Level of Structure	DNA		RNA	
Primary	Sequence of deoxyribonucleotides; bases are A, T, G, C		Sequence of ribonucleotides; bases are A, U, G, C	
Secondary	Two antiparallel strands twist into a double helix, stabilized by hydrogen bonding between complementary bases (A-T, G-C) and hydrophobic interactions		Most common are hairpins, formed when a single strand folds back on itself to form a double-helix "stem" and a single-stranded "loop"	
Tertiary	None*		Folds that form distinctive three-dimensional shapes	Example: tRNA

*In cells, DNA coils around proteins that bind to the double helix. In many cases the DNA-protein complex folds into highly organized, compact structures. But DNA does not form tertiary structure on its own.

tasks reasonably well. Some of the most surprising results in the last decade of biological science, in fact, involve new insights into the diversity of roles that RNAs play in cells. These molecules process information stored in DNA, synthesize proteins, and defend against attack by viruses, among other things.

Next let's focus on the roles that RNA could have played in the origin of life—as an information-containing entity and as a catalyst.

RNA Is an Information-Containing Molecule

Because RNA contains a sequence of bases analogous to the letters in a word, it can function as an information-containing molecule. And because hydrogen bonding occurs specifically between A-U pairs and G-C pairs in RNA, it is possible for RNA to furnish the information required to make a copy of itself.

FIGURE 4.10 illustrates how the information stored in an RNA molecule can be used to direct its own replication.

First, a complementary copy of the RNA is made when free ribonucleotides form hydrogen bonds with complementary bases on the original strand of RNA—the template strand. As they do, their sugar-phosphate groups form phosphodiester linkages to produce a double-stranded RNA molecule (steps 1 and 2).

To make a copy of the original single-stranded RNA, the hydrogen bonds between the double-stranded product must first be broken by heating or by a catalyzed reaction (step 3). The newly made complementary RNA molecule now exists independently of the original template strand. If steps 1–3 were repeated with the new strand serving as a template (steps 4–6), the resulting molecule would be a copy of the original. In this way, the primary sequence of an RNA serves as a mold.

RNA Can Function as a Catalytic Molecule

In terms of diversity in chemical reactivity and overall shape, RNA molecules are no match for proteins. The primary structure of RNA molecules is much more restricted because RNA has only four types of nucleotides versus the 20 types of amino acids found in proteins. Secondary through tertiary structure is more limited as a result, meaning that RNA cannot form the wide array of catalysts observed among proteins.

But because RNA has a degree of structural and chemical complexity, it is capable of catalyzing a number of chemical reactions. Sidney Altman and Thomas Cech shared the 1989 Nobel Prize in chemistry for showing that catalytic RNAs, or **ribozymes,** exist in organisms.

FIGURE 4.11 (on page 68) shows the structure of a ribozyme Cech isolated from a single-celled organism called *Tetrahymena.* This ribozyme catalyzes both the hydrolysis and the condensation of phosphodiester linkages in RNA. Researchers have since discovered a variety of ribozymes that catalyze an array of reactions in cells. For example, ribozymes catalyze the formation of peptide bonds when amino acids polymerize to form polypeptides. Ribozymes are at work in your cells right now.

The three-dimensional nature of ribozymes is vital to their catalytic activity. To catalyze a chemical reaction, substrates must

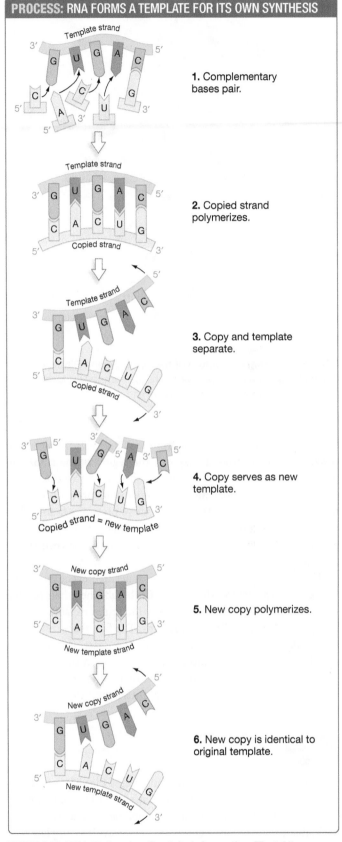

PROCESS: RNA FORMS A TEMPLATE FOR ITS OWN SYNTHESIS

1. Complementary bases pair.

2. Copied strand polymerizes.

3. Copy and template separate.

4. Copy serves as new template.

5. New copy polymerizes.

6. New copy is identical to original template.

FIGURE 4.10 RNA Molecules Contain Information That Allows Them to Be Replicated. For a single-stranded RNA to be copied, it must pass through double-stranded RNA intermediates.

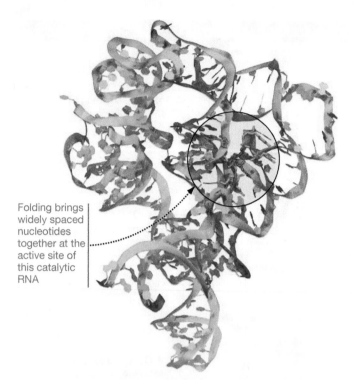

Folding brings widely spaced nucleotides together at the active site of this catalytic RNA

FIGURE 4.11 Tertiary Structure of the *Tetrahymena* Ribozyme.
The folded structure brings together bases from distant locations in the primary structure to form the active site.

be brought together in an environment that will promote the reaction. As with protein enzymes, the region of the ribozyme that is responsible for this activity is called the active site. When the *Tetrahymena* ribozyme was compared to protein enzymes that catalyze similar reactions, their active sites were found to be similar in structure. This observation about two very different molecules demonstrates the critical relationship between structure and function

The discovery of ribozymes was a watershed event in origin-of-life research. Before Altman and Cech published their results, most biologists thought that the only molecules capable of catalyzing reactions in cells were proteins. The fact that a ribozyme in *Tetrahymena* catalyzed a condensation reaction raised the possibility that an RNA molecule could make a copy of itself. Such a molecule could qualify as the first living entity. Is there any experimental evidence to support this hypothesis?

4.4 In Search of the First Life-Form

The theory of chemical evolution maintains that life began as a naked self-replicator—a molecule that existed by itself in solution, without being enclosed in a membrane. To make a copy of itself, that first living molecule had to (**1**) provide a template that could be copied, and (**2**) catalyze polymerization reactions that would link monomers into a copy of that template. Because RNA is capable of both processes, most origin-of-life researchers propose that the first life-form was made of RNA.

No self-replicating RNA molecules have been discovered in nature, however, so researchers test the hypothesis by trying to simulate the RNA world in the laboratory. The eventual goal is to create an RNA molecule that can catalyze its own replication.

How Biologists Study the RNA World

To understand how researchers go about testing the RNA world hypothesis, consider two recent experiments by researchers in David Bartel's laboratory. In one study, the team attempted to generate an RNA molecule that could catalyze the kind of template-directed polymerization needed for RNA replication—an RNA "replicase." Starting with a ribozyme capable of joining two ribonucleotides together, they generated billions of copies into which random mutations were introduced.

Next they incubated the mutants with free ribonucleotides and began selecting for replicase activity. Molecules that exhibited such activity were isolated and copied. After two weeks and 18 rounds of selection, the team succeeded in isolating a ribozyme that could add 14 nucleotides to an existing RNA strand.

Note that the team's experimental protocol was designed to mimic the process of natural selection introduced in Chapter 1. The population of RNAs from each round had variable characteristics that could be replicated and passed on to the next generation of ribozymes. In addition, the researchers were able to select the most efficient RNAs to be the "parents" of the next generation—and in the process introduce new mutations that potentially could make some of the "offspring" even better ribozymes.

This research created considerable excitement among biologists interested in the origin of life, because adding ribonucleotides to a growing strand is a key attribute of an RNA replicase. However, since the maximum product length generated was less than 10 percent of the ribozyme's own length, an RNA replicase capable of making a full-length copy of itself was far from being discovered. In fact, the difficulty in creating an effective RNA replicase has led many researchers to question the idea of a replicase being the first ribozyme to emerge in the RNA world.

In another study, Bartel's group asked a different question: Would it be possible to select for a ribozyme that could make ribonucleotides? This type of ribozyme is not known to exist in nature but would be a key component in the RNA world.

Recall that the direction of a chemical reaction and how much product it makes is influenced by the amount of reactants present (Chapter 2). Since the chemical evolution of nucleotides is thought to have been inefficient, nucleotides would have been a scarce resource on early Earth. Ribozymes that could catalyze the production of nucleotides would be more likely to be copied due to local accumulation of monomers.

Starting with a large pool of randomly generated RNA sequences, the researchers selected for RNAs that could catalyze the addition of a uracil base to a ribose sugar. By round 11, the group had recovered ribozymes that were 50,000 times better at catalyzing the reaction than those found in the fourth round and over 1 million times more efficient than the uncatalyzed reaction. In effect, molecular evolution had occurred in the reaction tubes.

Thanks to similar efforts at other laboratories around the world, biologists have produced an increasingly impressive set of catalytic activities from RNA molecules. The results from each of these studies help clarify our view of what occurred in the RNA world. If a living ribozyme ever existed, then each round of simulated molecular evolution brings us closer to resurrecting it.

The RNA World May Have Sparked the Evolution of Life

Although ribozymes like these lab-generated molecules may have been present in the RNA world, they have not been observed in nature. Of those that have been discovered in modern cells, most play key roles in the synthesis of proteins. This relationship suggests the order of events in chemical evolution—the RNA world preceded proteins.

The evolution of protein enzymes would have marked the end of the RNA world—providing the means for catalyzing reactions necessary for life to emerge in a cellular form. After this milestone, three of the five fundamental characteristics of life (see Chapter 1) were solidly in place:

1. *Information* Proteins and ribozymes were processing information stored in nucleic acids for the synthesis of more proteins.

2. *Replication* Enzymes, and possibly ribozymes, were replicating the nucleic acids that stored the hereditary information.

3. *Evolution* Random changes in the synthesis of proteins, and selective advantages resulting from some of these changes, allowed for the evolution of new proteins and protein families.

If these events occurred in a hydrothermal vent, the molecular assemblages of nucleic acids and proteins would have been constantly fed with thermal and chemical energy. To gain independence from their undersea hatchery, enzymes would have evolved to store this energy as something more portable—carbohydrates. The structure and function of carbohydrates will be the focus of the next chapter.

CHAPTER 4   REVIEW

For media, go to MasteringBiology

If you understand . . .

4.1   What Is a Nucleic Acid?

- Nucleic acids are polymers of nucleotide monomers, which consist of a sugar, a phosphate group, and a nitrogenous base. Ribonucleotide monomers polymerize to form RNA. Deoxyribonucleotide monomers polymerize to form DNA.

- Ribonucleotides have a hydroxyl (−OH) group on their 2′ carbon; deoxyribonucleotides do not.

- Nucleic acids polymerize when condensation reactions join nucleotides together via phosphodiester linkages.

- Nucleic acids are directional: they have a 5′ end and a 3′ end. During polymerization, new nucleotides are added only to the 3′ end.

✔ You should be able to state what cells do to activate nucleotides for incorporation into a polymer and explain why activation is required.

4.2   DNA Structure and Function

- DNA's primary structure consists of a sequence of linked nitrogenous bases. Its secondary structure consists of two DNA strands running in opposite directions that are twisted into a double helix.

- DNA is an extremely stable molecule that serves as a superb archive for information in the form of base sequences. It lacks a reactive 2′ hydroxyl group, and its secondary structure is stabilized by hydrophobic interactions and hydrogen bonds that form between complementary bases stacked on the inside of the helix.

- DNA is readily copied via complementary base pairing. Complementary base pairing occurs between A-T and G-C pairs in DNA.

- DNA's structural stability and regularity are advantageous for information storage, but they make DNA an ineffective catalyst.

✔ You should be able to explain why DNA molecules with a high percentage of guanine and cytosine are particularly stable.

4.3   RNA Structure and Function

- Like DNA, RNA's primary structure consists of a sequence of linked nitrogenous bases. RNA's secondary structure includes short regions of double helices and looped structures called hairpins.

- RNA molecules are usually single stranded. They have secondary structure because of complementary base pairing between A-U and G-C pairs on the same strand.

- Unlike DNA, the secondary structures of RNA can fold into more complex shapes, stabilized by hydrogen bonding, which give the molecule tertiary structure.

- RNA is versatile. The primary function of proteins is to catalyze chemical reactions, and the primary function of DNA is to carry information. But RNA is an "all-purpose" macromolecule that can do both.

✔ You should be able to explain why many RNA molecules exhibit tertiary structure, while most DNA molecules do not.

4.4 In Search of the First Life-Form

- To test the RNA world hypothesis, researchers are attempting to synthesize new ribozymes in the laboratory. Using artificial selection strategies, they have succeeded in identifying RNAs that catalyze several different reactions.

- Ribozymes that catalyze reactions necessary for the production of nucleotides may have preceded the evolution of RNA replicases.

✔ You should be able to provide two examples of activities in the RNA world you expect would benefit from catalysis and justify your choices.

You should be able to . . .

✔ TEST YOUR KNOWLEDGE
Answers are available in Appendix A

1. What are the four nitrogenous bases found in RNA?
   a. uracil, guanine, cytosine, thymine (U, G, C, T)
   b. adenine, guanine, cytosine, thymine (A, G, C, T)
   c. adenine, uracil, guanine, cytosine (A, U, G, C)
   d. alanine, threonine, glycine, cysteine (A, T, G, C)

2. What determines the primary structure of a DNA molecule?
   a. the sugar-phosphate backbone
   b. complementary base pairing and the formation of hairpins
   c. the sequence of deoxyribonucleotides
   d. the sequence of ribonucleotides

3. DNA attains a secondary structure when hydrogen bonds form between the nitrogenous bases called purines and pyrimidines. What are the complementary base pairs that form in DNA?
   a. A-T and G-C
   b. A-U and G-C
   c. A-G and T-C
   d. A-T and G-U

4. Which of the following rules apply to the synthesis of nucleic acids?
   a. Nucleotides are added to the 5′ end of nucleic acids.
   b. The synthesis of nucleic acids cannot occur without the presence of an enzyme to catalyze the reaction.
   c. Strands are synthesized in a parallel direction such that one end of the double-stranded product has the 3′ ends and other has the 5′ ends.
   d. Complementary pairing between bases is required for copying nucleic acids.

5. Nucleic acids are directional, meaning that there are two different ends. What functional groups define the two different ends of a DNA strand?

6. What is responsible for the increased stability of DNA compared to RNA?

✔ TEST YOUR UNDERSTANDING
Answers are available in Appendix A

7. Explain how Chargaff's rules relate to the complementary base pairing seen in the secondary structure of DNA. Would you expect these rules to apply to RNA as well? Explain why or why not.

8. QUANTITATIVE If nucleotides from the DNA of a human were quantified and 30 percent of them consisted of adenine, what percentage of guanine nucleotides would be present?
   a. 20 percent
   b. 30 percent
   c. 40 percent
   d. 70 percent

9. What would be the sequence of the strand of DNA that is made from the following template: 5′-GATATCGAT-3′ (Your answer must be written 5′→3′.) How would this sequence be different if RNA were made from this DNA template?

10. A major theme in this chapter is that the structure of molecules correlates with their function. Explain how DNA's secondary structure limits its catalytic abilities compared with that of RNA. Why is it expected that RNA molecules can catalyze a modest but significant array of reactions?

11. To replicate a ribozyme, a complete complementary copy must be made. Would you expect the double-stranded intermediate to maintain its catalytic activity? Justify your answer with an explanation.

12. Suppose that Bartel's research group succeeded in producing a molecule that could make a copy of itself. Which of the five fundamental characteristics of life (provided in Chapter 1) would support the claim that this molecule is alive?

13. Make a concept map (see **BioSkills 15** in Appendix B) that relates DNA's primary structure to its secondary structure. Your diagram should include deoxyribonucleotides, hydrophobic interactions, purines, pyrimidines, phosphodiester linkages, DNA primary structure, DNA secondary structure, complementary base pairing, and antiparallel strands.

14. Viruses are particles that infect cells. In some viruses, the genetic material consists of two strands of RNA, bonded together via complementary base pairing. Would these antiparallel strands form a double helix? Explain why or why not.

15. Before Watson and Crick published their model of the DNA double helix, Linus Pauling offered a model based on a triple helix. If the three sugar-phosphate backbones were on the outside of such a molecule, would hydrogen bonding or hydrophobic interactions be more important in keeping such a secondary structure together?

16. How would you expect the structure of ribozymes in organisms that grow in very hot environments, such as hot springs or deep-sea vents, to differ from those in organisms that grow in cooler environments?
    a. These ribozymes would have more hairpin secondary structures.
    b. The hairpins would have more G's and C's in the primary structure.
    c. The hairpins would have more A's and U's in the primary structure.
    d. These ribozymes would exhibit no tertiary structure.

5 An Introduction to Carbohydrates

In this chapter you will learn that

The role carbohydrates play in life is based on how they are linked together

by examining

The structure of monosaccharides **5.1**

and how they link to form

Polymers called polysaccharides **5.2**

then asking

What major roles do carbohydrates play? **5.3**

and looking at

Cell structure

Cell identity

Energy storage

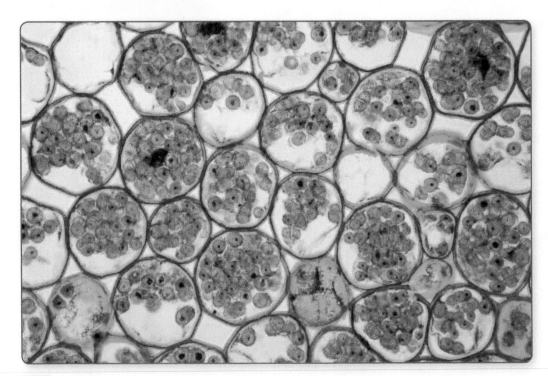

A cross section through a buttercup root. Cellulose-rich cell walls are stained green; starch-filled structures are stained purple. Cellulose is a structural carbohydrate; starch is an energy-storage carbohydrate.

This unit highlights the four types of macromolecules that were key to the evolution of the cell: proteins, nucleic acids, carbohydrates, and lipids. Understanding the structure and function of macromolecules is a basic requirement for exploring how life began and how organisms work. Recall that proteins and nucleic acids could satisfy only three of the five fundamental characteristics of life: information, replication, and evolution (Chapter 4). Carbohydrates, the subject of this chapter, play an important role in a fourth characteristic—energy.

The term **carbohydrate,** or **sugar,** encompasses the monomers called **monosaccharides** (literally, "one-sugar"), small polymers called **oligosaccharides** ("few-sugars"), and the large polymers called **polysaccharides** ("many-sugars"). The name carbohydrate is logical because the molecular formula of many of these molecules is $(CH_2O)_n$, where the n refers to the number of "carbohydrate" groups. The value of n can vary from 3, for the smallest sugar, to well over a thousand for some of the large polymers.

This chapter is part of the Big Picture. See how on pages 104–105.

✔ When you see this checkmark, stop and test yourself. Answers are available in Appendix A.

An aldose
Carbonyl group at
end of carbon chain

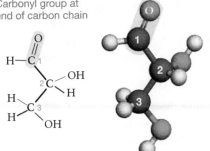

A ketose
Carbonyl group in
middle of carbon chain

The name can also be misleading, though, because carbohydrates do not consist of carbon atoms bonded to water molecules. Instead, they are molecules with a carbonyl (C=O) and several hydroxyl (−OH) functional groups, along with several to many carbon–hydrogen (C−H) bonds. Consider formaldehyde, which was introduced as one of the molecules present in early Earth (Chapter 2). Even though formaldehyde has the same molecular formula as the one given above (CH_2O), it is not a carbohydrate since it does not contain a hydroxyl group.

Let's begin with monosaccharides, put them together into polysaccharides, and then explore how carbohydrates figured in the origin of life and what they do in cells today. As you study this material, be sure to ask yourself the central question of biological chemistry: How does this molecule's structure relate to its properties and function?

5.1 Sugars as Monomers

Sugars are fundamental to life. They provide chemical energy in cells and furnish some of the molecular building blocks required for the synthesis of larger, more complex compounds. Monosaccharides were important during chemical evolution, early in Earth's history. For example, as you've seen, the sugar called ribose is required for the formation of the nucleotides that make up nucleic acids (Chapter 4).

What Distinguishes One Monosaccharide from Another?

Monosaccharides, or simple sugars, are the monomers of carbohydrates. **FIGURE 5.1** illustrates two of the smallest monosaccharides. Although their molecular formulas are identical ($C_3H_6O_3$), their molecular structures are different. The carbonyl group that serves as one of monosaccharides' distinguishing features can be found either at the end of the molecule, forming an aldehyde sugar (an aldose), or within the carbon chain, forming a ketone sugar (a ketose). The presence of a carbonyl group along with multiple hydroxyl groups provides sugars with an array of reactive and hydrophilic functional groups. Based on this observation, it's not surprising that sugars are able to participate in a large number of chemical reactions.

The number of carbon atoms present also varies in monosaccharides. By convention, the carbons in a monosaccharide are numbered consecutively, starting with the end nearest the carbonyl group. Figure 5.1 features three-carbon sugars, or **trioses**. Ribose, which acts as a building block for nucleotides, has five carbons and is called a **pentose;** the glucose that is coursing through your bloodstream right now is a six-carbon sugar, or a **hexose.**

Besides varying in the location of the carbonyl group and the total number of carbon atoms present, monosaccharides can vary in the spatial arrangement of their atoms. There is, for example, a wide array of pentoses and hexoses. Each is distinguished by the configuration of its hydroxyl functional groups. **FIGURE 5.2**

Glucose

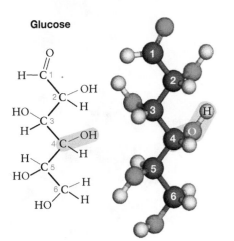

Galactose

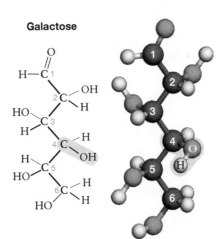

FIGURE 5.2 Sugars May Vary in the Configuration of Their Hydroxyl Groups. The two six-carbon sugars shown here vary only in the spatial orientation of their hydroxyl groups on carbon number 4.

✔**EXERCISE** Mannose is a six-carbon sugar that is identical to glucose, except that the hydroxyl (–OH) group on carbon number 2 is switched in orientation. Circle carbon number 2 in glucose and galactose; then draw the structural formula of mannose.

illustrates glucose and galactose, which are six-carbon sugars. Notice that the two molecules have the same molecular formula ($C_6H_{12}O_6$) but not the same structure. Both are aldose sugars with six carbons, but they differ in the spatial arrangement of the hydroxyl group at the fourth carbon (highlighted in Figure 5.2).

This is a key point: Because the structures of glucose and galactose differ, their functions differ. In cells, glucose is used as a source of carbons for the construction of other molecules and chemical energy that sustains life. But for galactose to be used in these roles, it first has to be converted to glucose via an enzyme-catalyzed reaction. This example underscores a general theme: Even seemingly simple changes in structure—like the location of a single hydroxyl group—can have enormous consequences for function. This is because molecules interact in precise ways, based on their shape.

It's rare for sugars consisting of five or more carbons to exist in the form of the linear chains illustrated in Figure 5.2, however. In aqueous solution they tend to form ring structures. The bond responsible for ring formation occurs only between the carbon containing the carbonyl group and one of the carbons with a hydroxyl group. Glucose serves as the example in **FIGURE 5.3**. When the cyclic structure forms in glucose, the C-1 carbon (the carbon numbered 1 in the linear chain) forms a bond with the oxygen atom of the C-5 hydroxyl and transfers its hydrogen to the C-1 carbonyl, turning it into a hydroxyl group.

Transfer of hydrogen between the C-5 and C-1 functional groups preserves the number of atoms and hydroxyls found in the ring and linear forms. The newly formed C-1 hydroxyl group can be oriented in two distinct ways: above or below the plane of the ring. The different configurations produce the molecules α-glucose and β-glucose.

To summarize, many distinct monosaccharides exist because so many aspects of their structure are variable: aldose or ketose placement of the carbonyl group, variation in carbon number, different arrangements of hydroxyl groups in space, and alternative ring forms. Each monosaccharide has a unique structure and function.

Monosaccharides and Chemical Evolution

Laboratory simulations, like those you read about in Chapter 2, have shown that most monosaccharides are readily synthesized under conditions that mimic the conditions of early Earth. For example, when formaldehyde (CH_2O) molecules are heated in solution, they react with one another to form almost all the pentoses and hexoses.

In addition, researchers have discovered the three-carbon ketose illustrated in Figure 5.1, along with a wide array of compounds closely related to sugars, on a meteorite that struck Murchison, Australia, in 1969. Based on these observations, investigators suspect that sugars are synthesized on dust particles and other debris in interstellar space and could have rained down onto Earth as the planet was forming, as well as being synthesized in the hot water near ancient undersea volcanoes.

More recent evidence suggests that synthesis of sugars could have been catalyzed by minerals found in the walls of deep-sea hydrothermal vents. Most researchers interested in chemical evolution maintain that one or more of the above mechanisms led to the accumulation of monosaccharides in the early oceans.

Modern cells display a wide range of carbohydrates beyond monosaccharides. How do these monomers join together to form polymers? Is the process similar to how amino acids link together to form proteins and nucleotides join to form nucleic acids? Let's explore how the array of functional groups in monosaccharides influences the polymerization of carbohydrates.

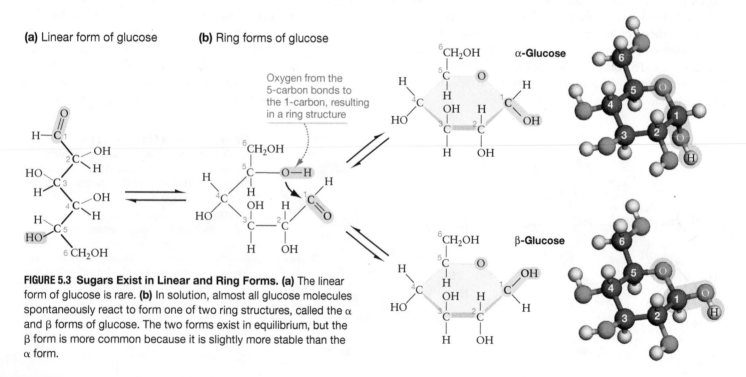

FIGURE 5.3 Sugars Exist in Linear and Ring Forms. (a) The linear form of glucose is rare. **(b)** In solution, almost all glucose molecules spontaneously react to form one of two ring structures, called the α and β forms of glucose. The two forms exist in equilibrium, but the β form is more common because it is slightly more stable than the α form.

If you understand that . . .

- Simple sugars differ from each other in three respects:
  1. the location of their carbonyl group,
  2. the number of carbon atoms present, and
  3. the spatial arrangement of their atoms—particularly the relative positions of hydroxyl (−OH) groups.

✔ **You should be able to . . .**

Draw the structural formula of a three-carbon monosaccharide ($C_3H_6O_3$) in linear form and then draw three other sugars that illustrate the three differences listed above.

Answers are available in Appendix A.

5.2 The Structure of Polysaccharides

Simple sugars can be covalently linked into chains of varying lengths, also known as complex carbohydrates. These chains range in size from small oligomers, or oligosaccharides, to the large polymers called polysaccharides. When only two sugars are linked together, they are known as **disaccharides.**

Similar to proteins and nucleic acids, the structure and function of larger carbohydrates depends on the types of monomers involved and how they are linked together. For example, maltose, also known as malt sugar, and lactose, an important sugar in milk, are two disaccharides that differ by just one monosaccharide. Maltose consists of two identical glucose molecules (**FIGURE 5.4a**), while lactose is made up of glucose and galactose (**FIGURE 5.4b**).

Monosaccharides polymerize when a condensation reaction occurs between two hydroxyl groups, resulting in a covalent interaction called a **glycosidic linkage.** The inverse reaction, hydrolysis, cleaves these linkages. (To review condensation and hydrolysis reactions, see Chapter 3.)

(a) Formation of α-glycosidic linkage

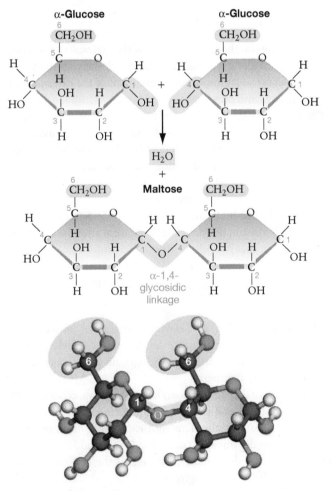

(b) Formation of β-glycosidic linkage

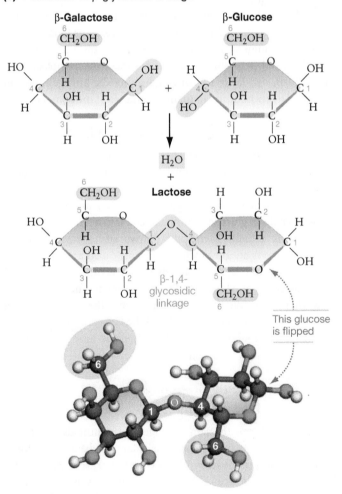

FIGURE 5.4 Monosaccharides Polymerize through Formation of Glycosidic Linkages. A glycosidic linkage occurs when hydroxyl groups on two monosaccharides undergo a condensation reaction. Maltose and lactose are disaccharides.

In that they hold monomers together, glycosidic linkages are analogous to the peptide bonds and phosphodiester linkages in proteins and nucleic acids. There is an important difference, however. Peptide bonds and phosphodiester linkages form between the same locations in their monomers, giving proteins and nucleic acids a standard backbone structure, but this is not the case for polysaccharides. Because glycosidic linkages form between hydroxyl groups, and because every monosaccharide contains at least two hydroxyls, the location and geometry of glycosidic linkages can vary widely among polysaccharides.

Maltose and lactose illustrate two of the most common glycosidic linkages, called the α-1,4-glycosidic linkage and the β-1,4-glycosidic linkage. The numbers refer to the carbons on either side of the linkage, indicating that both linkages are between the C-1 and C-4 carbons. Their geometry, however, is different: α and β refer to the contrasting orientations of the C-1 hydroxyls—on opposite sides of the plane of the glucose rings (i.e., "above" versus "below" the plane).

As Section 5.3 explains, the orientation of this hydroxyl in glycosidic linkages is particularly important in the structure, function, and durability of the molecules. In essence, the difference between polysaccharides used for storage and structural polysaccharides is a simple twist of a link.

To drive this point home, let's consider the structures of the most common polysaccharides found in organisms today: starch, glycogen, cellulose, and chitin, along with a modified polysaccharide called peptidoglycan. Each of these macromolecules is joined by particular α-1,4- or β-1,4-glycosidic linkages and can consist of a few hundred to many thousands of monomers.

Starch: A Storage Polysaccharide in Plants

In plant cells, some monosaccharides are stored for later use in the form of starch. **Starch** consists entirely of α-glucose monomers joined by glycosidic linkages. As the top panel in **TABLE 5.1** shows, the angle of the linkages between C-1 and C-4 carbons causes a chain of glucose subunits to coil into a helix.

Starch is actually a mixture of two such polysaccharides, however. One is an unbranched molecule called amylose, which contains only α-1,4-glycosidic linkages. The other is a branched molecule called amylopectin. The branching in amylopectin occurs when glycosidic linkages form between the C-1 carbon of a glucose monomer on one strand and the C-6 carbon of a glucose monomer on another strand. In amylopectin, branches occur at about one out of every 30 monomers.

Glycogen: A Highly Branched Storage Polysaccharide in Animals

Glycogen performs the same storage role in animals that starch performs in plants. In humans, for example, glycogen is stored in the liver and in muscles. When you start exercising, enzymes begin breaking glycogen into glucose monomers, which are then processed in muscle cells to supply energy. Glycogen is a polymer of α-glucose and is nearly identical to the branched form of starch. However, instead of an α-1,6-glycosidic linkage occurring

in about 1 out of every 30 monomers, a branch occurs in about 1 out of every 10 glucose subunits (see Table 5.1).

Cellulose: A Structural Polysaccharide in Plants

All cells are enclosed by a membrane (Chapter 1). In most organisms living today, the cell is also surrounded by a layer of material called a wall. A **cell wall** is a protective sheet that occurs outside the membrane. In plants, bacteria, fungi, and many other groups, the cell wall is composed primarily of one or more polysaccharides.

In plants, cellulose is the major component of the cell wall. **Cellulose** is a polymer of β-glucose monomers, joined by β-1,4-glycosidic linkages. As Table 5.1 shows, the geometry of the linkage is such that each glucose monomer in the chain is flipped in relation to the adjacent monomer. The flipped orientation is important because **(1)** it generates a linear molecule, rather than the helix seen in starch; and **(2)** it permits multiple hydrogen bonds to form between adjacent, parallel strands of cellulose. As a result, cellulose forms long, parallel strands that are joined by hydrogen bonds. The linked cellulose fibers are strong and give the cell structural support.

Chitin: A Structural Polysaccharide in Fungi and Animals

Chitin is a polysaccharide that stiffens the cell walls of fungi. It is also found in a few types of protists and in many animals. It is, for example, the most important component of the external skeletons of insects and crustaceans.

Chitin is similar to cellulose, but instead of consisting of glucose monomers, the monosaccharide involved is one called *N*-acetylglucosamine (abbreviated as NAG). These NAG monomers are joined by β-1,4-glycosidic linkages (see Table 5.1). As in cellulose, the geometry of these bonds results in every other residue being flipped in orientation.

Like the glucose monomers in cellulose, the NAG subunits in chitin form hydrogen bonds between adjacent strands. The result is a tough sheet that provides stiffness and protection.

Peptidoglycan: A Structural Polysaccharide in Bacteria

Most bacteria, like all plants, have cell walls. But unlike plants, in bacteria the ability to produce cellulose is extremely rare. Instead, a polysaccharide called **peptidoglycan** gives bacterial cell walls strength and firmness.

Peptidoglycan is the most complex of the polysaccharides discussed thus far. It has a long backbone formed by two types of monosaccharides that alternate with each other and are linked by β-1,4-glycosidic linkages (see Table 5.1). In addition, a short chain of amino acids is attached to one of the two sugar types. When molecules of peptidoglycan align, peptide bonds link the amino acid chains on adjacent strands. These links serve the same purpose as the hydrogen bonds between the parallel strands of cellulose and chitin in the cell walls of other organisms.

SUMMARY TABLE 5.1 Polysaccharides Differ in Structure

Polysaccharide	Chemical Structure	Three-dimensional Structure

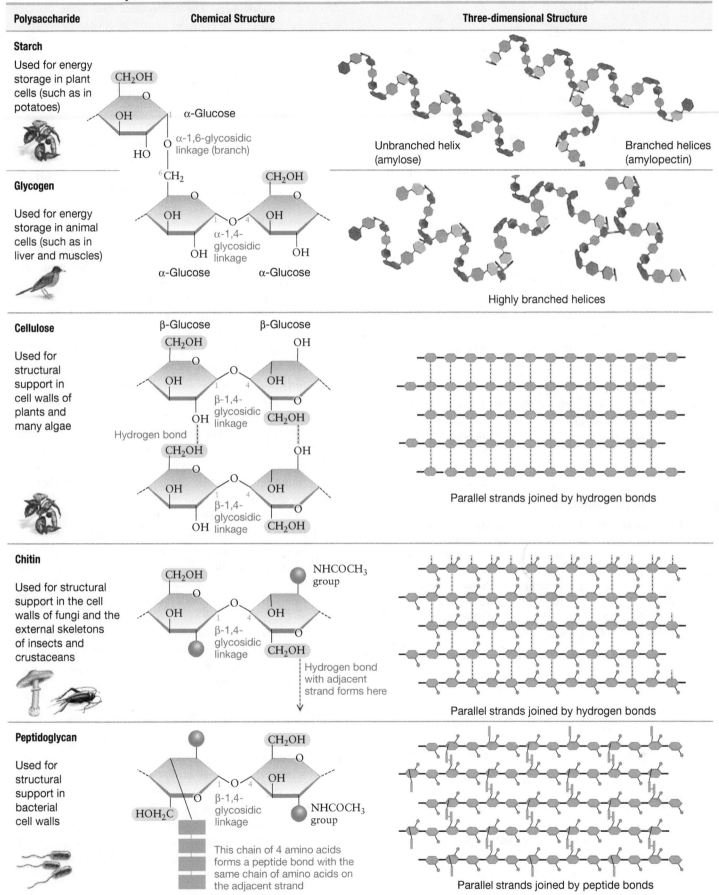

Starch

Used for energy storage in plant cells (such as in potatoes)

α-Glucose
α-1,6-glycosidic linkage (branch)

Unbranched helix (amylose)

Branched helices (amylopectin)

Glycogen

Used for energy storage in animal cells (such as in liver and muscles)

CH_2OH

α-1,4-glycosidic linkage

α-Glucose

α-Glucose

Highly branched helices

Cellulose

Used for structural support in cell walls of plants and many algae

β-Glucose   β-Glucose

CH_2OH

β-1,4-glycosidic linkage

Hydrogen bond

CH_2OH

β-1,4-glycosidic linkage

Parallel strands joined by hydrogen bonds

Chitin

Used for structural support in the cell walls of fungi and the external skeletons of insects and crustaceans

CH_2OH

$NHCOCH_3$ group

β-1,4-glycosidic linkage

CH_2OH

Hydrogen bond with adjacent strand forms here

Parallel strands joined by hydrogen bonds

Peptidoglycan

Used for structural support in bacterial cell walls

CH_2OH

β-1,4-glycosidic linkage

HOH_2C

$NHCOCH_3$ group

This chain of 4 amino acids forms a peptide bond with the same chain of amino acids on the adjacent strand

Parallel strands joined by peptide bonds

Polysaccharides and Chemical Evolution

Cellulose is the most abundant organic compound on Earth today, and chitin is probably the second most abundant by weight. Virtually all organisms depend on glycogen or starch as an energy source. But despite their current importance to life, polysaccharides probably played little to no role in the origin of life. This conclusion is supported by several observations:

- *No plausible mechanism exists for the polymerization of monosaccharides under conditions that prevailed early in Earth's history.* In cells and in laboratory experiments, the glycosidic linkages illustrated in Figure 5.4 and Table 5.1 form only with the aid of protein enzymes. No enzyme-like RNAs are known to catalyze these reactions.

- *To date, no polysaccharide has been discovered that can catalyze polymerization reactions.* Even though polysaccharides contain reactive hydroxyl and carbonyl groups, they lack the structural and chemical complexity that makes proteins, and to a lesser extent RNA, effective catalysts.

- *The monomers in polysaccharides are not capable of complementary base pairing.* Like proteins, but unlike nucleic acids, polysaccharides cannot act as templates for their own replication.

Even though polysaccharides probably did not play a significant role in the earliest forms of life, they became enormously important once cellular life evolved. In the next section, let's take a detailed look at how they function in today's cells.

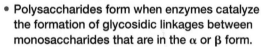

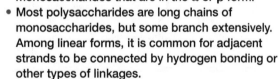

check your understanding

If you understand that . . .

- Polysaccharides form when enzymes catalyze the formation of glycosidic linkages between monosaccharides that are in the α or β form.
- Most polysaccharides are long chains of monosaccharides, but some branch extensively. Among linear forms, it is common for adjacent strands to be connected by hydrogen bonding or other types of linkages.

✓ **You should be able to . . .**

Provide four structural differences that could result in different oligosaccharides consisting of two glucose monomers and two galactose monomers.

Answers are available in Appendix A.

5.3 What Do Carbohydrates Do?

One of the basic functions that carbohydrates perform in organisms is to serve as a substrate for synthesizing more-complex molecules. For example, recall that RNA contains the five-carbon sugar ribose ($C_5H_{10}O_5$) and DNA contains the modified sugar deoxyribose ($C_5H_{10}O_4$). The nucleotides that make up these polymers consist of the ribose or deoxyribose sugar, a phosphate group, and a nitrogenous base (Chapter 4). The sugar itself acts as a subunit of each of these monomers.

In addition, sugars frequently furnish the raw "carbon skeletons" that are used as building blocks in the synthesis of important molecules. Your cells are producing amino acids right now, for example, using sugars as a starting point.

Carbohydrates have diverse functions in cells: In addition to serving as precursors to larger molecules, they **(1)** provide fibrous structural materials, **(2)** indicate cell identity, and **(3)** store chemical energy. Let's look at each function in turn.

Carbohydrates Can Provide Structural Support

Cellulose and chitin, along with the modified polysaccharide peptidoglycan, are key structural compounds. They form fibers that give cells and organisms strength and elasticity.

To appreciate why cellulose, chitin, and peptidoglycan are effective structural molecules, recall that they form long strands and that bonds can form between adjacent strands. In the cell walls of plants, for example, a collection of about 80 cellulose molecules are cross-linked by hydrogen bonding to create a tough fiber. These cellulose fibers, in turn, crisscross to form a tough sheet that is able to withstand pulling and pushing forces—what an engineer would call tension and compression.

Besides being stiff and strong, the structural carbohydrates are durable. Almost all organisms have the enzymes required to break the various α-glycosidic linkages that hold starch and glycogen molecules together, but only a few organisms have enzymes capable of hydrolyzing cellulose, chitin, and peptidoglycan. Due to the strong interactions between strands consisting of β-1,4-glycosidic linkages, water is excluded and the fibers tend to be insoluble. The absence of water within these fibers makes their hydrolysis more difficult. As a result, the structural polysaccharides are resistant to degradation and decay.

Ironically, the durability of cellulose supports digestion. The cellulose that you ingest when you eat plant cells—what biologists call dietary fiber—forms a porous mass that absorbs and retains water. This sponge-like mass adds moisture and bulk that helps fecal material move through the intestinal tract more quickly, preventing constipation and other problems.

The Role of Carbohydrates in Cell Identity

Structural polymers tend to be repetitive, with only one or two types of monosaccharides. The same is not true for all complex carbohydrates. Some types exhibit enormous structural diversity, because their component monomers—and the linkages between them—vary a lot. As a result, they are capable of displaying information to other cells through their structure. More specifically, polysaccharides act as an identification badge on the outer surface of the plasma membrane that surrounds a cell. (Chapter 6 describes plasma membranes in detail.)

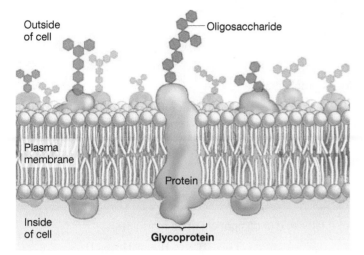

FIGURE 5.5 Carbohydrates Are an Identification Badge for Cells.
Glycoproteins contain sugar groups that project outside the cell from the surface of the plasma membrane enclosing the cell. These sugar groups have distinctive structures that identify the type or species of the cell.

FIGURE 5.5 shows how this information about cell identity is displayed. Molecules called glycoproteins project outward from the cell surface into the surrounding environment. A **glycoprotein** is a protein that has one or more carbohydrates covalently bonded to it—usually relatively short oligosaccharides.

Glycoproteins are key molecules in what biologists call cell–cell recognition and cell–cell signaling. Each cell in your body has glycoproteins on its surface that identify it as part of your body. Immune system cells use these glycoproteins to distinguish your body's cells from foreign cells, such as bacteria. In addition, each distinct type of cell in a multicellular organism—for example, the nerve cells and muscle cells in your body—displays a different set of glycoproteins on its surface.

The identification information displayed by glycoproteins helps cells recognize and communicate with each other.

The key point here is to recognize that the variety in the types of monosaccharides and how they can be linked together makes it possible for an enormous number of unique oligosaccharides to exist. As a result, each cell type and each species can display a unique identity.

During the 1980s, Paul Wassarman and colleagues investigated the role of glycoproteins in one of the most important cell–cell recognition events in the life of a plant or animal—the attachment of sperm to eggs during fertilization. This step guarantees specificity—sperm recognize and bind only to eggs of their own species.

In one experiment, the researchers mixed sperm with purified egg-surface glycoproteins and discovered that most of the sperm lost their ability to attach to eggs (**FIGURE 5.6**). Such loss of function is an example of what researchers call competitive inhibition. The glycoproteins had bound to—and thus blocked—the same structure on the sperm that it uses to bind to eggs. This result showed that sperm attach to eggs via egg glycoproteins.

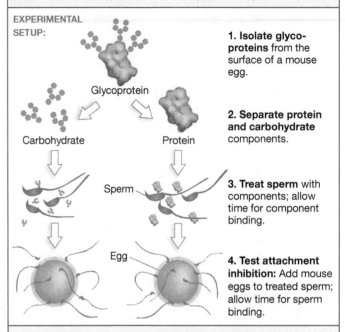

RESEARCH

QUESTION: What part of surface glycoproteins do sperm recognize when they attach to eggs?

HYPOTHESIS: Sperm attach to the carbohydrate component.

NULL HYPOTHESIS: Sperm attach to the protein component.

EXPERIMENTAL SETUP:

Glycoprotein

Carbohydrate   Protein

Sperm

Egg

1. **Isolate glyco-proteins** from the surface of a mouse egg.

2. **Separate protein and carbohydrate** components.

3. **Treat sperm** with components; allow time for component binding.

4. **Test attachment inhibition:** Add mouse eggs to treated sperm; allow time for sperm binding.

PREDICTION: The carbohydrate component of the glycoprotein will bind to sperm and block their attachment to eggs.

PREDICTION OF NULL HYPOTHESIS: The protein component of the glycoprotein will block sperm attachment to eggs.

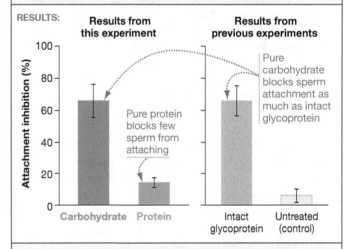

RESULTS:

Results from this experiment

Pure protein blocks few sperm from attaching

Results from previous experiments

Pure carbohydrate blocks sperm attachment as much as intact glycoprotein

CONCLUSION: Sperm recognize and bind to the carbohydrates of egg-surface glycoproteins when they attach to egg cells.

FIGURE 5.6 Carbohydrates Are Required for Cellular Recognition and Attachment.

SOURCES: Florman, H. M., K. B. Bechtol, and P. M. Wassarman. 1984. Enzymatic dissection of the functions of the mouse egg's receptor for sperm. *Developmental Biology* 106: 243–255. Also Florman, H. M., and P. M. Wassarman. 1985. O-linked oligosaccharides of mouse egg ZP3 account for its sperm receptor activity. *Cell* 41: 313–324.

✓**QUANTITATIVE** How would the bars change in the graph if sperm attachment required only the protein portion of egg glycoproteins?

But which part of the egg glycoproteins is essential for recognition and attachment—the protein or the carbohydrate? In follow-up experiments, Wassarman's group used the same type of competitive-binding assay to answer this question. When sperm were mixed with purified carbohydrates alone, most were unable to attach to eggs. In contrast, most sperm treated with purified protein alone were not inhibited and still attached to eggs. Both results show that the carbohydrate component plays a fundamental role in the process of egg-cell recognition.

Carbohydrates and Energy Storage

Candy-bar wrappers promise a quick energy boost, and ads for sports drinks claim that their products provide the "carbs" needed for peak activity. If you were to ask friends or family members what carbohydrates do in your body, they would probably say something like "They give you energy." And after pointing out that carbohydrates are also used in cell identity, as a structural material, and as a source of carbon skeletons for the synthesis of other complex molecules, you'd have to agree.

Carbohydrates store and provide chemical energy in cells. What aspect of carbohydrate structure makes this function possible?

Carbohydrates Store Sunlight as Chemical Energy Recall that the essence of chemical evolution was energy transformations (Chapter 2). For example, it was proposed that the kinetic energy in sunlight may have been converted into chemical energy and stored in bonds of molecules such as formaldehyde (CH_2O).

This same type of transformation from light energy to chemical energy occurs in cells today, but instead of making formaldehyde, cells produce sugars. For example, plants harvest the kinetic energy in sunlight and store it in the bonds of carbohydrates by the process known as **photosynthesis.**

Photosynthesis entails a complex set of reactions that can be summarized most simply as follows:

$$CO_2 + H_2O + \text{sunlight} \longrightarrow (CH_2O)_n + O_2$$

where $(CH_2O)_n$ represents a carbohydrate. The key to understanding the energy conversion that is taking place in this reaction is to compare the positions of the electrons in the reactants to those in the products.

1. The electrons in the C=O bonds of carbon dioxide and the C–O bonds of carbohydrates are held tightly because of oxygen's high electronegativity. Thus, they have relatively low potential energy.

2. The electrons involved in the C–H bonds of carbohydrates are shared equally because the electronegativity of carbon and hydrogen is about the same. Thus, these electrons have relatively high potential energy.

3. Electrons are also shared equally in the carbon–carbon C–C bonds of carbohydrates—meaning that they, too, have relatively high potential energy.

(a) Carbon dioxide

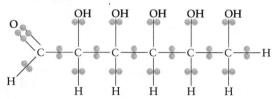

(b) A carbohydrate

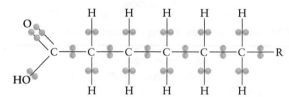

(c) A fatty acid (a component of fat molecules)

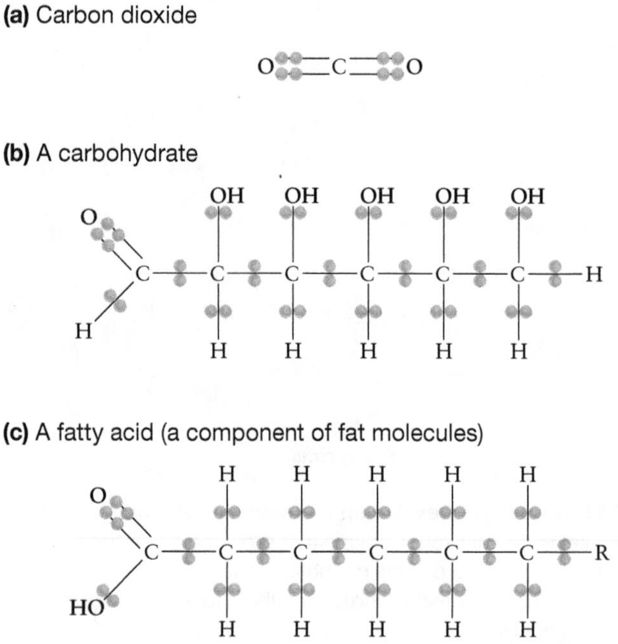

FIGURE 5.7 In Organisms, Potential Energy Is Stored in C–H and C–C Bonds. (a) In carbon dioxide, the electrons involved in covalent bonds are held tightly by oxygen atoms. **(b)** In carbohydrates such as the sugar shown here, many of the covalently bonded electrons are held equally between C and H atoms. **(c)** The fatty acids found in fat molecules have more C–H bonds and fewer C–O bonds than carbohydrates do. ("R" stands for the rest of the molecule.)

✔ **EXERCISE** Circle the bonds in this diagram that have high potential energy.

C–C and C–H bonds have much higher potential energy than C–O bonds have. As a result, carbohydrates have much more chemical energy than carbon dioxide has.

FIGURE 5.7 summarizes and extends these points. Start by comparing the structure of carbon dioxide in Figure 5.7a with the carbohydrate in Figure 5.7b. The main difference is the presence of C–C and C–H bonds in the carbohydrate. Now compare the carbohydrate in Figure 5.7b with the fatty acid—a subunit of a fat molecule—in Figure 5.7c. Compared with carbohydrates, fats contain many more C–C and C–H bonds and many fewer C–O bonds.

This point is important. C–C and C–H bonds have high potential energy because the electrons are shared equally by atoms with low electronegativities. C–O bonds, in contrast, have low potential energy because the highly electronegative oxygen atom holds the electrons so tightly. Both carbohydrates and fats are used as fuel in cells, but fats store twice as much energy per gram compared with carbohydrates. (Fats are discussed in more detail in Chapter 6.)

Enzymes Hydrolyze Polysaccharides to Release Glucose Starch and glycogen are efficient energy-storage molecules because they polymerize via α-glycosidic linkages instead of the β-glycosidic linkages observed in the structural polysaccharides. The α-linkages in storage polysaccharides are readily hydrolyzed to release glucose, while the structural polysaccharides resist enzymatic degradation.

The most important enzyme involved in catalyzing the hydrolysis of α-glycosidic linkages in glycogen molecules is a protein called **phosphorylase.** Many of your cells contain phosphorylase, so they can break down glycogen to provide glucose on demand.

The enzymes involved in breaking the α-glycosidic linkages in starch are called **amylases.** Your salivary glands and pancreas produce amylases that are secreted into your mouth and small intestine, respectively. These amylases are responsible for digesting the starch that you eat.

The glucose subunits that are hydrolyzed from glycogen and starch are processed in reactions that result in the production of chemical energy that can be used in the cell. Glycogen and starch are like a candy bar that has segments, so you can break off chunks whenever you need a boost.

Energy Stored in Glucose is Used to Make ATP When a cell needs energy, reactions lead to the breakdown of the glucose and capture of the released energy through synthesis of the nucleotide adenosine triphosphate (ATP) (introduced in Chapter 4).

More specifically, the energy that is released when sugars are processed is used to synthesize ATP from a precursor called adenosine diphosphate (ADP) plus a free inorganic phosphate (P_i) molecule. The overall reaction can be written as follows:

$$(CH_2O)_n + O_2 + ADP + P_i \longrightarrow CO_2 + H_2O + ATP$$

To put this in words, the chemical energy stored in the C−H and C−C bonds of carbohydrate is transferred to a new bond linking a third phosphate group to ADP to form ATP.

How much energy does it take to form ATP? Consider this example: A cell can use the 10 calories of energy stored in a LifeSavers candy to produce approximately 2×10^{23} molecules of ATP. Although this sounds like a lot of ATP, an average human's energy needs would burn through all of this ATP energy in a little over a minute! The energy in ATP drives reactions like polymerization and cellular processes like moving your muscles.

Carbohydrates are like the water that piles up behind a dam; ATP is like the electricity generated at a dam, which lights up your home. Carbohydrates store chemical energy; ATP makes chemical energy useful to the cell.

Later chapters analyze in detail how cells capture and store energy in sugars and how these sugars are then broken down to provide cells with usable chemical energy in the form of ATP (Chapters 8, 9, and 10). For both of these processes to occur, however, a selectively permeable membrane barrier is required. The following chapter introduces the lipids needed to build these membranes and the role they played in the evolution of the first cell.

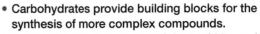

 If you understand that . . .

- Carbohydrates provide building blocks for the synthesis of more complex compounds.
- Polysaccharides such as cellulose, chitin, and peptidoglycan form cell walls, which give cells structural strength.
- Glycoproteins project from the surface of cells. They provide a molecular badge that identifies the cell's type or species.
- Starch and glycogen store sugars for later use in reactions that produce ATP. Sugars contain large amounts of chemical energy because they contain carbon atoms that are bonded to hydrogen atoms or other carbon atoms. The C−H and C−C bonds have high potential energy because the electrons are shared equally by atoms with low electronegativity.

✔ **You should be able to . . .**

1. Identify two aspects of the structures of cellulose, chitin, and peptidoglycan that correlate with their function as structural molecules.

2. Describe how the carbohydrates you ate during breakfast today are functioning in your body right now.

Answers are available in Appendix A.

CHAPTER 5 **REVIEW** *For media, go to MasteringBiology*

If you understand . . .

5.1 **Sugars as Monomers**

- Monosaccharides are organic compounds that have a carbonyl group and several hydroxyl groups. The molecular formula for a sugar is typically $(CH_2O)_n$, but the number of "carbon-hydrate" groups may vary between sugars, as indicated by the *n*.

- Although some monosaccharides may have the same molecular formula, the arrangement of functional groups can lead to differences in the molecular structure of the sugars.

- Individual monosaccharides may form ring structures that differ from one another in the orientation of a hydroxyl group.

✔ You should be able to explain how a relatively small difference in the location of a carbonyl or hydroxyl group can lead to dramatic changes in the properties and function of a monosaccharide.

5.2 The Structure of Polysaccharides

- Monosaccharides can be covalently bonded to one another via glycosidic linkages, which join hydroxyl groups on adjacent molecules.

- In contrast to proteins and nucleic acids, polysaccharides do not always form a single uniform backbone structure. The numerous hydroxyls found in each monosaccharide allow glycosidic linkages to form at different sites and new strands to branch from existing chains.

- The types of monomers involved and the geometries of the glycosidic linkages between monomers distinguish different polysaccharides from one another.

- The most common polysaccharides in organisms today are starch, glycogen, cellulose, and chitin; peptidoglycan is an abundant polysaccharide that has short chains of amino acids attached.

✓ You should be able to compare and contrast glycosidic linkages in polysaccharides with the linkages between monomers in proteins and nucleic acids.

5.3 What Do Carbohydrates Do?

- In carbohydrates, as in proteins and nucleic acids, structure correlates with function.

- Cellulose, chitin, and peptidoglycan are polysaccharides that function in support. They are made up of monosaccharide monomers joined by β-1,4-glycosidic linkages. When individual molecules of these polysaccharides align side by side, bonds form between them—resulting in strong, flexible fibers or sheets that resist hydrolysis.

- The oligosaccharides on cell-surface glycoproteins can function as specific signposts or identity tags because their constituent monosaccharides are so diverse in geometry and composition.

- Both starch and glycogen function as energy-storage molecules. They are made up of glucose molecules that are joined by α-glycosidic linkages. These linkages are readily hydrolyzed to release glucose for the production of ATP.

✓ You should be able to describe four key differences in the structure of polysaccharides that function in energy storage versus structural support.

(MB) **MasteringBiology**

1. MasteringBiology Assignments

Tutorials and Activities Carbohydrates; Carbohydrate Structure and Function; Types of Carbohydrates

Questions Reading Quizzes, Blue-Thread Questions, Test Bank

2. eText Read your book online, search, take notes, highlight text, and more.

3. The Study Area Practice Test, Cumulative Test, BioFlix® 3-D Animations, Videos, Activities, Audio Glossary, Word Study Tools, Art

You should be able to . . .

✓ TEST YOUR KNOWLEDGE
Answers are available in Appendix A

1. What is the difference between a monosaccharide, an oligosaccharide, and a polysaccharide?
   a. the number of carbon atoms in the molecule
   b. the type of glycosidic linkage between monomers
   c. the spatial arrangement of the various hydroxyl residues in the molecule
   d. the number of monomers in the molecule

2. What are three ways monosaccharides differ from one another?

3. What type of bond is formed between two sugars in a disaccharide?
   a. glycosidic linkage
   b. phosphodiester bond
   c. peptide bond
   d. hydrogen bond

4. What holds cellulose molecules together in bundles large enough to form fibers?

   a. the cell wall
   b. peptide bonds
   c. hydrogen bonds
   d. hydrophobic interactions between different residues in the cellulose helix

5. What are the primary functions of carbohydrates in cells?
   a. energy storage, cell identity, structure, and building blocks for synthesis
   b. catalysis, structure, and energy storage
   c. information storage and catalysis
   d. source of carbon, information storage, and energy storage

6. What is responsible for the difference in potential energy between carbohydrates and carbon dioxide?

7. Which of the differences listed here could be found in the same monosaccharide?

  a. different orientation of a hydroxyl in the linear form
  b. different number of carbons
  c. different orientation of a hydroxyl in the ring form
  d. different position of the carbonyl group in the linear form

8. What would most likely occur if the galactose in lactose were replaced with glucose?
  a. It would not be digested by human infants or adults.
  b. It would be digested by most adult humans.
  c. It would be digested by human infants, but not adults.
  d. It would be digested by human adults, but not infants.

9. Explain how the structure of carbohydrates supports their function in displaying the identity of a cell.

10. What is the difference between linking glucose molecules with α-1,4-glycosidic linkages versus β-1,4-glycosidic linkages? What are the consequences?

11. Give three reasons why researchers have concluded that polysaccharides were unlikely to play a large role in the origin of life.

12. Compare and contrast the structures and functions of starch and glycogen. How are these molecules similar? How are they different?

13. A weight-loss program for humans that emphasized minimal consumption of carbohydrates was popular in some countries

in the early 2000s. What was the logic behind this diet? (Note: This diet plan caused controversy and is not endorsed by some physicians and researchers).

14. Galactosemia is a potentially fatal disease that occurs in humans who lack the enzyme that converts galactose to glucose. To treat this disease, physicians exclude the monosaccharide galactose from the diet. Which of the following would you also predict to be excluded from the diet?
  a. maltose   **b.** starch   **c.** mannose   **d.** lactose

15. If you hold a salty cracker in your mouth long enough, it will begin to taste sweet. What is responsible for this change in taste?

16. Lysozyme, an enzyme found in human saliva, tears, and other secretions, catalyzes the hydrolysis of the β-1,4-glycosidic linkages in peptidoglycan. Predict the effect of this enzyme on bacteria, and explain the role its activity plays in human health.

6 Lipids, Membranes, and the First Cells

In this chapter you will learn how

Life's defining barrier—the plasma membrane—
is built of lipids and proteins

by looking at

Lipid structure and function **6.1**

and how

Lipids spontaneously form bilayers **6.2**

then asking

How do substances move across bilayers?

via

Diffusion and osmosis **6.3**

Membrane proteins **6.4**

A space-filling model of a phospholipid bilayer. In single-celled organisms, this cluster of molecules forms part of the boundary between life (inside the cell) and nonlife (outside the cell)—the cell membrane.

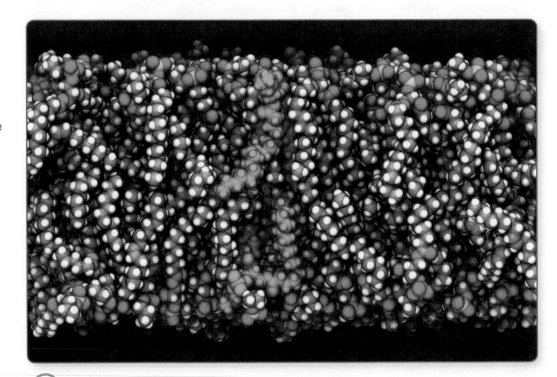

Currently, most biologists support the hypothesis that biological evolution began with a catalytic RNA molecule that could replicate itself. As the offspring of this molecule multiplied, natural selection would have favored the most efficient versions. A second great milestone in the history of life occurred when descendants of these replicators became enclosed within a membrane.

Why is the presence of a membrane so important? The **plasma membrane,** or **cell membrane,** separates life from nonlife. It is a layer of molecules that surrounds the cell interior and separates it from the environment.

- The plasma membrane serves as a selective barrier: It keeps damaging compounds out of the cell and allows entry of compounds needed by the cell.

- Because the plasma membrane sequesters the appropriate chemicals in an enclosed area, reactants collide more frequently—the chemical reactions necessary for life occur much more efficiently.

This chapter is part of the Big Picture. See how on pages 104–105.

✓ When you see this checkmark, stop and test yourself. Answers are available in Appendix A.

While researchers of chemical evolution are currently debating when membranes arose—whether early or late during the emergence of life—there is little argument about the importance of this event. After life secured a membrane, it continued to evolve into an efficient and dynamic reaction vessel—the cell.

How do membranes form? Which ions and molecules can pass through a membrane and which cannot, and why? These are some of the most fundamental questions in all of biological science. Let's delve into them, beginning with the membrane's foundation—lipids.

6.1 Lipid Structure and Function

Lipid is a catchall term for carbon-containing compounds that are found in organisms and are largely nonpolar and hydrophobic—meaning that they do not dissolve readily in water. (Recall from Chapter 2 that water is a polar solvent.) Lipids do dissolve, however, in liquids consisting of nonpolar organic compounds.

To understand why lipids are insoluble in water, examine the five-carbon compound called isoprene, illustrated in **FIGURE 6.1a**. Note that isoprene consists of carbon atoms bonded to hydrogen atoms. The figure also shows the structural formula of a chain of linked isoprenes, called an isoprenoid.

Molecules that contain only carbon and hydrogen are known as **hydrocarbons.** Hydrocarbons are nonpolar because electrons are shared equally in C–H bonds—owing to the approximately equal electronegativity of carbon and hydrogen. Since these bonds form no partial charges, hydrocarbons are hydrophobic. Thus lipids do not dissolve in water, because they have a significant hydrocarbon component.

Bond Saturation Is an Important Aspect of Hydrocarbon Structure

FIGURE 6.1b gives the structural formula of a **fatty acid,** a simple lipid consisting of a hydrocarbon chain bonded to a carboxyl (–COOH) functional group. Fatty acids and isoprenes are key building blocks of important lipids found in organisms. Just as subtle differences in the orientation of hydroxyls in sugars can lead to dramatic effects in their structure and function, the type of C–C bond used in hydrocarbon chains is a key factor in lipid structure.

When two carbon atoms form a double bond, the attached atoms are found in a plane instead of a three-dimensional tetrahedron. The carbon atoms involved are also locked into place. They cannot rotate freely, as they do in carbon–carbon single bonds. As a result, certain double bonds between carbon atoms produce a "kink" in an otherwise straight hydrocarbon chain (Figure 6.1b, left).

Hydrocarbon chains that consist of only single bonds between the carbons are called **saturated.** If one or more double bonds exist in the hydrocarbon chains, then they are **unsaturated.** The choice of terms is logical. If a hydrocarbon chain does not contain a double bond, it is saturated with the maximum number of hydrogen atoms that can attach to the carbon skeleton. If it is unsaturated, then a C–H bond is removed to form a C=C double bond, resulting in fewer than the maximum number of attached hydrogen atoms.

Foods that contain lipids with many double bonds are said to be polyunsaturated and are advertised as healthier than foods with saturated fats. Recent research suggests that polyunsaturated fats help protect the heart from disease. Exactly how this occurs is under investigation.

(a) Isoprenes can be linked into chains called isoprenoids.

(b) Fatty acids can be saturated or unsaturated.

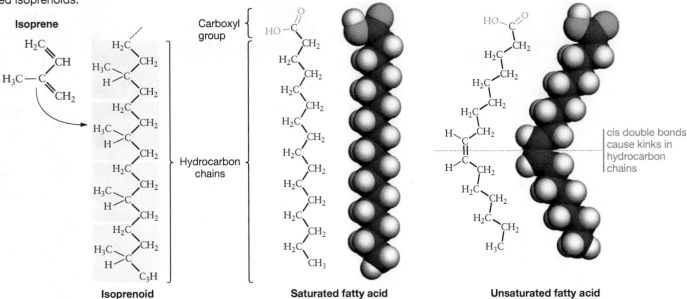

FIGURE 6.1 Hydrocarbon Structure. (a) Isoprene subunits, like the one shown to the left, can be linked to each other, end to end, to form long hydrocarbon chains called isoprenoids. **(b)** Fatty acids typically contain a total of 14–20 carbon atoms, most found in their long hydrocarbon "tails." Unsaturated hydrocarbons contain carbon–carbon double bonds; saturated hydrocarbons do not.

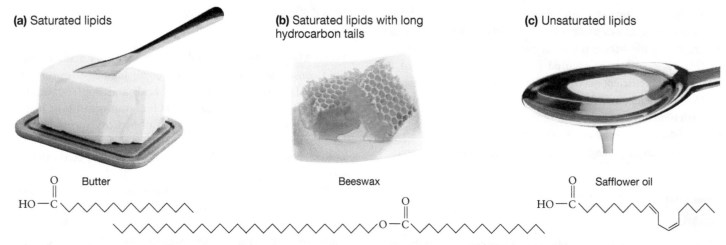

(a) Saturated lipids

Butter

(b) Saturated lipids with long hydrocarbon tails

Beeswax

(c) Unsaturated lipids

Safflower oil

FIGURE 6.2 The Fluidity of Lipids Depends on the Length and Saturation of Their Hydrocarbon Chains. (a) Butter consists primarily of saturated lipids. **(b)** Waxes are lipids with extremely long saturated hydrocarbon chains. **(c)** Oils are dominated by "polyunsaturates"—lipids with hydrocarbon chains that contain multiple C=C double bonds.

Bond saturation also profoundly affects the physical state of lipids. Highly saturated fats, such as butter, are solid at room temperature (**FIGURE 6.2a**). Saturated lipids that have extremely long hydrocarbon tails, like **waxes** do, form particularly stiff solids at room temperature (**FIGURE 6.2b**). Highly unsaturated fats are liquid at room temperature (**FIGURE 6.2c**).

A Look at Three Types of Lipids Found in Cells

Unlike amino acids, nucleotides, and monosaccharides, lipids are characterized by a physical property—their insolubility in water—instead of a shared chemical structure. This insolubility is based on the high proportion of nonpolar C—C and C—H bonds relative to polar functional groups. As a result, the structure of lipids varies widely. For example, consider the most important types of lipids found in cells: fats, steroids, and phospholipids.

Fats **Fats** are nonpolar molecules composed of three fatty acids that are linked to a three-carbon molecule called **glycerol**. Because of this structure, fats are also called triacylglycerols or triglycerides. When the fatty acids are polyunsaturated, they form liquid triacylglycerols called **oils**. In organisms, the primary role of fats is energy storage.

As **FIGURE 6.3a** shows, fats form when a dehydration reaction occurs between a hydroxyl group of glycerol and the carboxyl

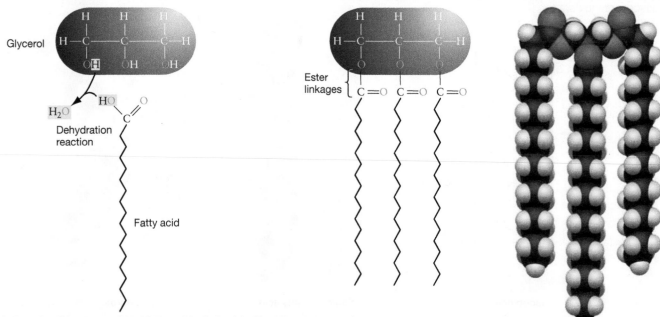

(a) Fats form via dehydration reactions.

Glycerol

Dehydration reaction

Fatty acid

(b) Fats consist of glycerol linked by ester linkages to three fatty acids.

Ester linkages

FIGURE 6.3 Fats Are One Type of Lipid Found in Cells. (a) When glycerol and a fatty acid react, a water molecule leaves. The covalent bond that results from this reaction is termed an ester linkage. **(b)** The structural formula and a space-filling model of tristearin, the most common type of fat in beef.

group of a fatty acid. The glycerol and fatty acid molecules become joined by an **ester linkage.** Fats are not polymers, however, and fatty acids are not monomers. As **FIGURE 6.3b** shows, fatty acids are not linked together to form a macromolecule in the way that amino acids, nucleotides, and monosaccharides are.

Steroids   **Steroids** are a family of lipids distinguished by the bulky, four-ring structure shown in orange in **FIGURE 6.4a**. The various steroids differ from one another by the functional groups or side groups attached to different carbons in those hydrophobic rings. The steroid shown in the figure is cholesterol, which has a hydrophilic hydroxyl group attached to the top ring and an isoprenoid "tail" attached at the bottom. Cholesterol is an important component of plasma membranes in many organisms.

Phospholipids   **Phospholipids** consist of a glycerol that is linked to a phosphate group and two hydrocarbon chains of either isoprenoids or fatty acids. The phosphate group is also bonded to a small organic molecule that is charged or polar (**FIGURE 6.4b**).

Phospholipids composed of fatty acids are found in the domains Bacteria and Eukarya; phospholipids with isoprenoid chains are found in the domain Archaea. (The domains of life were introduced in Chapter 1.) In all three domains, phospholipids are crucial components of the plasma membrane.

The lipids found in organisms have a wide array of structures and functions. In addition to storing chemical energy, lipids act as pigments that capture or respond to sunlight, serve as signals between cells, form waterproof coatings on leaves and skin, and act as vitamins used in many cellular processes. The most prominent function of lipids, however, is their role in cell membranes.

The Structures of Membrane Lipids

Not all lipids can form membranes. Membrane-forming lipids have a polar, hydrophilic region—in addition to the nonpolar, hydrophobic region found in all lipids.

To better understand this structure, take another look at the phospholipid illustrated in Figure 6.4b. Notice that the molecule has a "head" region containing highly polar covalent bonds as well as a negatively charged phosphate attached to a polar or charged group. The charges and polar bonds in the head region interact with water molecules when a phospholipid is placed in solution. In contrast, the long hydrocarbon tails of a phospholipid are nonpolar and hydrophobic. Water molecules cannot form hydrogen bonds with the hydrocarbon tail, so they do not interact extensively with this part of the molecule.

Compounds that contain both hydrophilic and hydrophobic elements are **amphipathic** (literally, "dual-sympathy"). Phospholipids are amphipathic. As Figure 6.4a shows, cholesterol is also amphipathic. Because it has a hydroxyl functional group attached to its rings, it has both hydrophilic and hydrophobic regions. ✔ If you understand these concepts, you should be able to look back at Figure 6.1b and explain why fatty acids are also amphipathic.

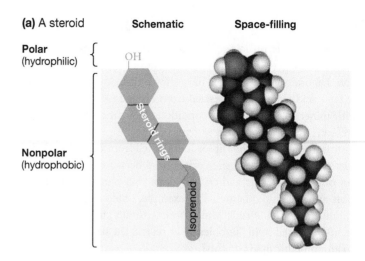

(a) A steroid

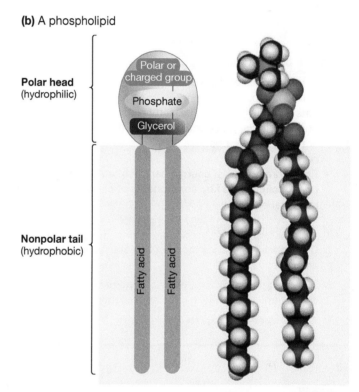

(b) A phospholipid

FIGURE 6.4 Some Lipids Contain Hydrophilic and Hydrophobic Regions. (a) All steroids have the distinctive four-ring structure shown in orange. Cholesterol has a polar hydroxyl group and an isoprenoid chain attached to these rings. **(b)** Most phospholipids consist of two fatty acid or isoprenoid chains that are linked to glycerol, which is linked to a phosphate group, which is linked to a small organic molecule that is polar or charged.

✔QUESTION If cholesterol and phospholipids were in solution, which part of the molecules would interact with water molecules?

The amphipathic nature of phospholipids is far and away their most important feature biologically. It is responsible for life's defining barrier—the plasma membrane. If the membrane defines life, then amphipathic lipids must have existed when life first originated during chemical evolution. Was that possible?

Were Lipids Present during Chemical Evolution?

Like amino acids, nucleic acids, and carbohydrates (Chapters 3–5), there is evidence that lipids were present during chemical evolution. Laboratory experiments have shown that simple lipids, such as fatty acids, can be synthesized from H_2 and CO_2 via reactions with mineral catalysts under conditions thought to be present in prebiotic hydrothermal vent systems (Chapter 2).

It is also possible that lipids literally fell from the sky early in Earth's history. Modern meteorites have been found to contain not only amino acids and carbohydrates but also lipids that exhibit amphipathic qualities. For example, lipids extracted from the meteorite that struck Murchison, Australia, in 1969 spontaneously formed lipid "bubbles" that resembled small cells. Why do amphipathic lipids do this?

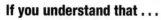

check your understanding

C Y U

If you understand that . . .

- Fats, steroids, and phospholipids differ in structure and function.
- Fats and oils are nonpolar; fatty acids, phospholipids, and certain steroids, like cholesterol, are amphipathic because they have both polar and nonpolar regions.
- Fats store chemical energy; certain steroids and phospholipids are key components of plasma membranes.

✔ **You should be able to . . .**

1. Compare and contrast the structure of a fat, a steroid, and a phospholipid.
2. Based on their structure, explain what makes cholesterol and phospholipids amphipathic.

Answers are available in Appendix A.

6.2 Phospholipid Bilayers

Amphipathic lipids do not dissolve when they are placed in water. Their hydrophilic heads interact with water, but their hydrophobic tails do not. Instead of dissolving in water, then, amphipathic lipids assume one of two types of structures: micelles or lipid bilayers.

- Micelles (**FIGURE 6.5a**) are tiny droplets created when the hydrophilic heads of a set of lipids face the water and form hydrogen bonds, while the hydrophobic tails interact with each other in the interior, away from the water.

- A **lipid bilayer** is created when two sheets of lipid molecules align. As **FIGURE 6.5b** shows, the hydrophilic heads in each layer face the surrounding solution while the hydrophobic tails face one another inside the bilayer. In this way, the hydrophilic heads interact with water while the hydrophobic tails interact with one another.

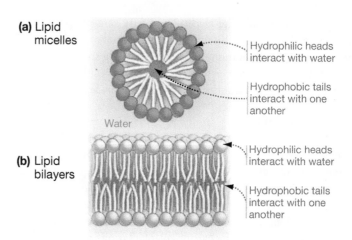

(a) Lipid micelles

Hydrophilic heads interact with water

Hydrophobic tails interact with one another

Water

(b) Lipid bilayers

Hydrophilic heads interact with water

Hydrophobic tails interact with one another

FIGURE 6.5 Lipids Form Micelles and Bilayers in Solution. In **(a)** a micelle or **(b)** a lipid bilayer, the hydrophilic heads of lipids face out, toward water; the hydrophobic tails face in, away from water. Lipid bilayers are the foundation of plasma membranes.

Micelles tend to form from fatty acids or other simple amphipathic hydrocarbon chains. Bilayers tend to form from phospholipids that contain two hydrocarbon tails. For this reason, bilayers are often called phospholipid bilayers.

It's critical to recognize that micelles and phospholipid bilayers form spontaneously—no input of energy is required. This concept can be difficult to grasp because entropy clearly decreases when these structures form. The key is to recognize that micelles and lipid bilayers are much more stable energetically than are independent phospholipids in solution.

Independent lipids are unstable in water because their hydrophobic tails disrupt hydrogen bonds that could otherwise form between water molecules. As a result, the tails of amphipathic molecules are forced together and participate in hydrophobic interactions (introduced in Chapter 2). This point should also remind you of the aqueous behavior of hydrophobic side chains in proteins and bases in nucleic acids.

Artificial Membranes as an Experimental System

When phospholipids are added to an aqueous solution and agitated, lipid bilayers spontaneously form small spherical structures. The hydrophilic heads on both sides of the bilayer remain in contact with the aqueous solution—water is present both inside and outside the vesicle. Artificial membrane-bound vesicles like these are called liposomes (**FIGURE 6.6**).

To explore how membranes work, researchers began creating and experimenting with liposomes and planar bilayers—lipid bilayers constructed across a hole in a glass or plastic wall separating two aqueous solutions (**FIGURE 6.7a**). Some of the first questions they posed concerned the permeability of lipid bilayers. The **permeability** of a structure is its tendency to allow a given substance to pass through it.

Using liposomes and planar bilayers, researchers can study what happens when a known ion or molecule is added to one side of a lipid bilayer (**FIGURE 6.7b**). Does the substance cross the

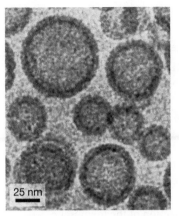
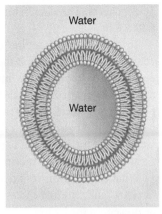

FIGURE 6.6 Liposomes Are Artificial Membrane-Bound Vesicles.
Electron micrograph of liposomes in cross section (left) and a cross-sectional diagram of the lipid bilayer in a liposome (right).

(a) Planar bilayers: Artificial membranes

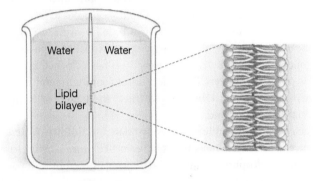

(b) Artificial-membrane experiments

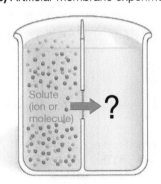

How rapidly can different solutes cross the membrane (if at all) when ...

1. Different types of phospholipids are used to make the membrane?

2. Proteins or other molecules are added to the membrane?

FIGURE 6.7 Use of Planar Bilayers in Experiments. (a) The construction of a planar bilayer across a hole in a wall separating two water-filled compartments. **(b)** A wide variety of experiments are possible with planar bilayers; a few are suggested here.

membrane and show up on the other side? If so, how rapidly does the movement take place? What happens when a different type of phospholipid is used to make the artificial membrane? Does the membrane's permeability change when proteins or other types of molecules become part of it?

Biologists describe such an experimental system as elegant and powerful because it gives them precise control over which factor changes from one experimental treatment to the next.

Control, in turn, is why experiments are such an effective way to explore scientific questions. Recall that good experimental design allows researchers to alter one factor at a time and determine what effect, if any, each has on the process being studied (Chapter 1).

Selective Permeability of Lipid Bilayers

When researchers put molecules or ions on one side of a liposome or planar bilayer and measure the rate at which the molecules arrive on the other side, a clear pattern emerges: Lipid bilayers are highly selective.

Selective permeability means that some substances cross a membrane more easily than other substances do. Small nonpolar molecules move across bilayers quickly. In contrast, large molecules and charged substances cross the membrane slowly, if at all. This difference in membrane permeability is a critical issue because controlling what passes between the exterior and interior environments is a key characteristic of cells.

According to the data in **FIGURE 6.8**, small nonpolar molecules such as oxygen (O_2) move across selectively permeable membranes more than a billion times faster than do chloride ions (Cl^-). In essence, ions cannot cross membranes at all—unless they have "help" in the form of membrane proteins introduced later in the chapter. Very small and uncharged molecules such as water (H_2O) can cross membranes relatively rapidly, even if they are polar. Small polar molecules such as glycerol have intermediate permeability.

The leading hypothesis to explain this pattern is that charged compounds and large polar molecules are more stable dissolved in water than they are in the nonpolar interior of membranes. ✔ If you understand this hypothesis, you should be able to predict where amino acids and nucleotides would be placed in Figure 6.8 and explain your reasoning.

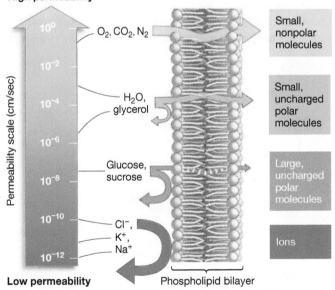

FIGURE 6.8 Lipid Bilayers Show Selective Permeability. Only certain substances cross lipid bilayers readily. Size and polarity or charge affect the rate of diffusion across a membrane.

How Does Lipid Structure Affect Membrane Permeability?

The amphipathic nature of phospholipids allows them to spontaneously form membranes. But not all phospholipid bilayers are the same. The nature of the hydrocarbon tails, in addition to the presence of cholesterol molecules, profoundly influences how a membrane behaves.

Bond Saturation and Hydrocarbon Chain Length Affect Membrane Fluidity and Permeability
The degree of saturation in a phospholipid—along with the length of its hydrocarbon tails—affects key aspects of a lipid's behavior in a membrane.

- When unsaturated hydrocarbon tails are packed into a lipid bilayer, kinks created by double bonds produce spaces among the tails. These spaces reduce the strength of the van der Waals interactions (see Chapter 3) that hold the hydrophobic tails together, weakening the barrier to solutes.

- Packed saturated hydrocarbon tails have fewer spaces and stronger van der Waals interactions. As the length of saturated hydrocarbon tails increases, the forces that hold them together also grow stronger, making the membrane even denser.

These observations have profound impacts on membrane fluidity and permeability—two closely related properties. As **FIGURE 6.9** shows, lipid bilayers are more permeable as well as more fluid when they contain short, kinked, unsaturated hydrocarbon tails. An unsaturated membrane allows more materials to pass because its interior is held together less tightly. Bilayers containing long, straight, saturated hydrocarbon tails are much less permeable and fluid. Experiments on liposomes have shown exactly these patterns.

Cholesterol Reduces Membrane Permeability
Cholesterol molecules are present, to varying extents, in the membranes of every cell in your body. What effect does adding cholesterol have on a membrane? Researchers have found that adding cholesterol molecules to liposomes dramatically reduces the permeability of

lipid bilayers. The data behind this conclusion are presented in **FIGURE 6.10**.

To read the graph in the "Results" section of Figure 6.10, put your finger on the *x*-axis at the point marked 20°C, and note that permeability to glycerol is much higher at this temperature in membranes that contain no cholesterol versus 20 percent or 50 percent cholesterol. Using this procedure at other temperature points should convince you that membranes lacking cholesterol are more permeable than the other two membranes at every temperature tested in the experiment.

What explains this result? Because the steroid rings in cholesterol are bulky, adding cholesterol fills gaps that would otherwise be present in the hydrophobic section of the membrane.

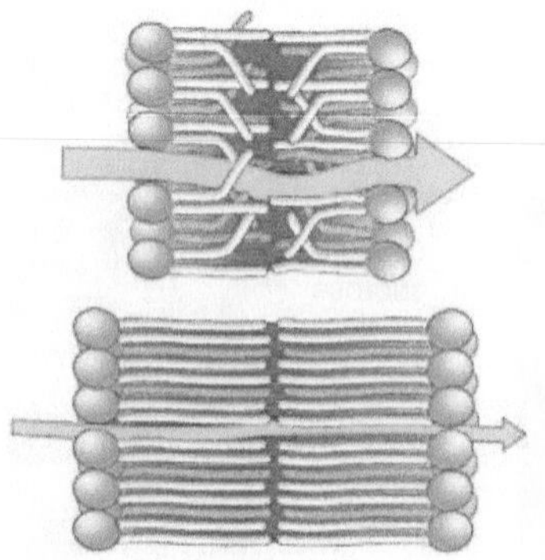

How Does Temperature Affect the Fluidity and Permeability of Membranes?

At about 25°C—or "room temperature"—the phospholipids in a plasma membrane have a consistency resembling olive oil. This fluid physical state allows individual lipid molecules to move laterally within each layer (**FIGURE 6.11**), a little like a person moving about in a dense crowd. By tagging individual phospholipids and following their movement, researchers have clocked average speeds of 2 micrometers (μm)/second at room temperature. At these speeds, a phospholipid could travel the length of a small bacterial cell in a second.

Recall that permeability is closely related to fluidity. As temperature drops, molecules in a bilayer move more slowly. As a result, the hydrophobic tails in the interior of membranes pack together more tightly. At very low temperatures, lipid bilayers even begin to solidify. As the graph in Figure 6.10 indicates, low temperatures can make membranes impervious to molecules that would normally cross them readily. Put your finger on the *x*-axis of that graph, just about the freezing point

If you understand that . . .

- In water, phospholipids form bilayers that are selectively permeable—meaning that some substances cross them much more readily than others do.
- Permeability is a function of the degree of saturation and the length of the hydrocarbon tails in membrane phospholipids, the amount of cholesterol in the membrane, and the temperature.

✓ **You should be able to . . .**

Fill in a chart with columns labeled Factor, Effect on permeability, and Reason and rows under the Factor column labeled Temperature, Cholesterol, Length of hydrocarbon tails, and Saturation of hydrocarbon tails.

Answers are available in Appendix A.

Lipid bilayer with **short** and **unsaturated** hydrocarbon tails

Higher permeability and fluidity

Lipid bilayer with **long** and **saturated** hydrocarbon tails

Lower permeability and fluidity

FIGURE 6.9 Fatty Acid Structure Changes the Permeability of Membranes. Lipid bilayers consisting of phospholipids containing unsaturated fatty acids should have more gaps and be more permeable than those with saturated fatty acids.

QUESTION: Does adding cholesterol to a membrane affect its permeability?

HYPOTHESIS: Cholesterol reduces permeability because it fills spaces in phospholipid bilayers.

NULL HYPOTHESIS: Cholesterol has no effect on permeability.

EXPERIMENTAL SETUP:

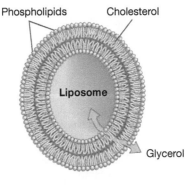

Phospholipids   Cholesterol

Liposome

Glycerol

1. Construct liposomes: Create with no cholesterol, 20% cholesterol, and 50% cholesterol.

2. Measure glycerol movement: Record how quickly glycerol moves across each type of membrane at different temperatures.

PREDICTION: Liposomes with higher cholesterol levels will have reduced permeability.

PREDICTION OF NULL HYPOTHESIS: All liposomes will have the same permeability.

RESULTS:

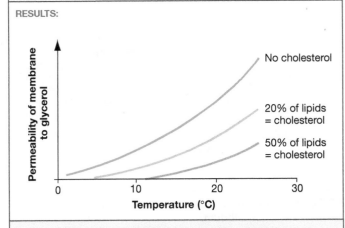

No cholesterol

20% of lipids = cholesterol

50% of lipids = cholesterol

Permeability of membrane to glycerol

Temperature (°C)

CONCLUSION: Adding cholesterol to membranes decreases their permeability to glycerol. The permeability of all membranes analyzed in this experiment increases with increasing temperature.

FIGURE 6.10 The Permeability of a Membrane Depends on Its Composition.

SOURCE: de Gier, J., et al. (1968). Lipid composition and permeability of liposomes. *Biochimica et Biophysica Acta* 150: 666–675.

✔**QUANTITATIVE** Suppose the investigators had instead created liposomes using phospholipids with fully saturated tails and compared them to two other sets of liposomes where either 20 percent or 50 percent of the phospholipids contained polyunsaturated tails. Label the three lines on the graph above with your prediction for the three different liposomes in this new experiment.

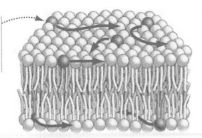

Phospholipids are in constant lateral motion, but rarely flip to the other side of the bilayer

FIGURE 6.11 Phospholipids Move within Membranes. Membranes are dynamic—in part because phospholipid molecules randomly move laterally within each layer in the structure.

of water (0°C), and note that even membranes that lack cholesterol are almost completely impermeable to glycerol. Indeed, trace any of the three lines in Figure 6.10, and as you move to the right (increasing temperature), you also move up (increasing permeability).

These observations on glycerol and lipid movement demonstrate that membranes are dynamic. Phospholipid molecules whiz around each layer, while water and small nonpolar molecules shoot in and out of the membrane. How quickly molecules move within and across membranes is a function of temperature, the structure of hydrocarbon tails, and the number of cholesterol molecules in the bilayer.

6.3 How Molecules Move across Lipid Bilayers: Diffusion and Osmosis

Small uncharged molecules and hydrophobic compounds can cross membranes readily and spontaneously—without an input of energy. The question now is: How is this possible? What process is responsible for movement of molecules across lipid bilayers?

Diffusion

A thought experiment can help explain how substances can cross membranes spontaneously. Suppose you rack up a set of billiard balls in the middle of a pool table and then begin to vibrate the table.

1. Because of the vibration, the billiard balls will move about randomly. They will also bump into one another.

2. After these collisions, some balls will move outward—away from their original position.

3. As movement and collisions continue, the overall or net movement of balls will be outward. This occurs because the random motion of the balls disrupts their original, nonrandom position. As the balls move at random, they are more likely to move away from one another than to stay together.

4. Eventually, the balls will be distributed randomly across the table. The entropy of the billiard balls has increased. Recall that entropy is a measure of the randomness or disorder in

a system (Chapter 2). The second law of thermodynamics states that in an isolated system, entropy always increases.

This hypothetical example illustrates how vibrating billiard balls move at random. More to the point, it also explains how substances located on one side of a lipid bilayer can move to the other side spontaneously. All dissolved molecules and ions, or **solutes,** have thermal energy and are in constant, random motion. Movement of molecules and ions that results from their kinetic energy is known as **diffusion.**

A difference in solute concentrations creates what is called a **concentration gradient.** Solutes move randomly in all directions, but when a concentration gradient exists, there is a net movement from regions of high concentration to regions of low concentration. Diffusion down a concentration gradient, or away from the higher concentration, is a spontaneous process because it results in an increase in entropy.

Once the molecules or ions are randomly distributed throughout a solution, a chemical equilibrium is established. For example, consider two aqueous solutions separated by a lipid bilayer. **FIGURE 6.12** shows how molecules that can pass through the bilayer diffuse to the other side. At equilibrium, these molecules continue to move back and forth across the membrane, but at equal rates—simply because they are equally likely to move in any direction. This means that there is no longer a net movement of molecules across the membrane. ✔ If you understand diffusion, you should be able to predict how a difference in temperature across a membrane would affect the concentration of a solute at equilibrium.

Osmosis

What about water? As the data in Figure 6.8 show, water moves across lipid bilayers relatively quickly. The movement of water is a special case of diffusion that is given its own name: **osmosis.** Osmosis occurs only when solutions are separated by a membrane that permits water to cross, but holds back some or all of the solutes—that is, a selectively permeable membrane.

It's important to note that some of the water molecules in a solution are unavailable to diffuse across the membrane. Recall that solutes form ionic or hydrogen bonds with water molecules (Chapter 2). Water molecules that are bound to a solute that can't cross the membrane are themselves prevented from crossing.

Only unbound water molecules are able to diffuse across the membrane during osmosis. When these unbound water molecules move across a membrane, they flow from the solution with the lower solute concentration into the solution with the higher solute concentration.

To drive this point home, let's suppose the concentration of a particular solute is higher on one side of a selectively permeable membrane than it is on the other side (**FIGURE 6.13**, step 1). Further, suppose that this solute cannot diffuse through the membrane to establish equilibrium. What happens? Water will move from the side with a lower concentration of solute to the side with a higher concentration of solute (Figure 6.13, step 2). Osmosis dilutes the higher concentration and equalizes the concentrations

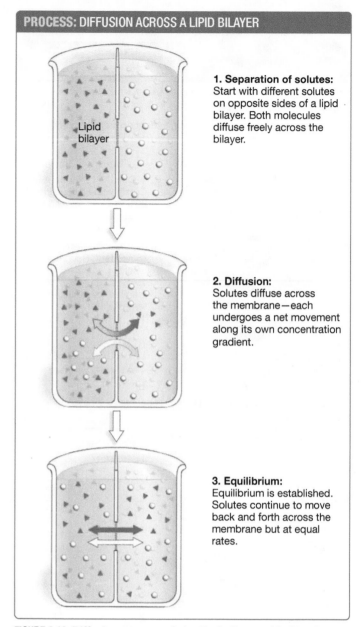

Lipid bilayer

1. Separation of solutes: Start with different solutes on opposite sides of a lipid bilayer. Both molecules diffuse freely across the bilayer.

2. Diffusion: Solutes diffuse across the membrane—each undergoes a net movement along its own concentration gradient.

3. Equilibrium: Equilibrium is established. Solutes continue to move back and forth across the membrane but at equal rates.

FIGURE 6.12 Diffusion across a Selectively Permeable Membrane Establishes an Equilibrium.

on both sides. The movement of water is spontaneous. It is driven by the increase in entropy achieved when solute concentrations are equal on both sides of the membrane.

Movement of water by osmosis is important because it can swell or shrink a membrane-bound vesicle. Consider the liposomes illustrated in **FIGURE 6.14**. (Remember that osmosis occurs only when a solute cannot pass through a separating membrane.)

- *Left* If the solution inside the membrane has a lower concentration of solutes than the exterior has, water moves out of the vesicle into the solution outside. The solution inside is said to be **hypotonic** ("lower-tone") relative to the outside of the vesicle. As water leaves, the vesicle shrinks and the membrane shrivels, resulting in lower vesicle firmness.

PROCESS: OSMOSIS

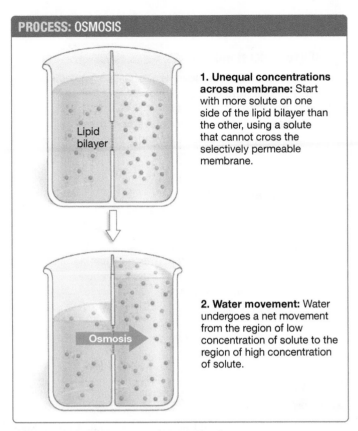

1. Unequal concentrations across membrane: Start with more solute on one side of the lipid bilayer than the other, using a solute that cannot cross the selectively permeable membrane.

2. Water movement: Water undergoes a net movement from the region of low concentration of solute to the region of high concentration of solute.

FIGURE 6.13 Osmosis Is the Diffusion of Water.

✔**QUESTION** Suppose you doubled the number of solute molecules on the left side of the membrane (at the start). At equilibrium, would the water level on the left side be higher or lower than what is shown in the second drawing?

- *Middle* If the solution inside the membrane has a higher concentration of solutes than the exterior has, water moves into the vesicle via osmosis. The inside solution is said to be **hypertonic** ("excess-tone") relative to the outside of the vesicle. The incoming water causes the vesicle to swell and increase in firmness, or even burst.

- *Right* If solute concentrations are equal on both sides of the membrane, the liposome maintains its size. When the inside solution does not affect the membrane's shape, that solution is called **isotonic** ("equal-tone").

Note that the terms hypertonic, hypotonic, and isotonic are relative—they can be used only to express the relationship between a given solution and another solution separated by a membrane. Biologists also commonly use these terms to describe the solution that is exterior to the cells or vesicles.

Membranes and Chemical Evolution

What do diffusion and osmosis have to do with the first membranes floating in the prebiotic soup? Both processes tend to *reduce* differences in chemical composition between the inside and outside of membrane-bound compartments.

If liposome-like structures first arose in the oceans of early Earth, their interiors probably didn't offer a radically different environment from the surrounding solution. In all likelihood, the primary importance of the first lipid bilayers was simply to provide a container for replicating RNA, the macromolecule most likely to have been the first "living" molecule (see Chapter 4). But ribonucleotide monomers would need to be available for these

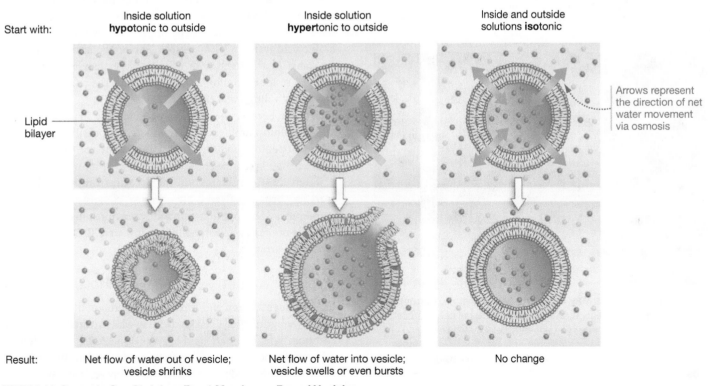

FIGURE 6.14 Osmosis Can Shrink or Burst Membrane-Bound Vesicles.

RNAs to replicate. Can negatively charged ribonucleotides get across lipid bilayers and inside lipid-bounded vesicles?

The answer is yes. Jack Szostak and colleagues first set out to study the permeability of membranes consisting of fatty acids and other simple amphipathic lipids thought to be present in the early oceans. Like phospholipids, fatty acids will spontaneously assemble into lipid bilayers and water-filled vesicles. Their experiments showed that ions, and even ribonucleotides, can diffuse across the fatty acid vesicle membranes—meaning that monomers could have been available for RNA synthesis.

Lending support to this hypothesis, the same minerals found to catalyze the polymerization of RNA from activated nucleotides (see Chapter 4) will also promote the formation of fatty acid vesicles—and in the process, often incorporate themselves and RNA inside. Simple vesicle-like structures that harbor nucleic acids are referred to as **protocells** (**FIGURE 6.15**). Most origin-of-life researchers view protocells as possible intermediates in the evolution of the cell.

Laboratory simulations also showed that free lipids and micelles can become incorporated into fatty acid bilayers, causing protocells to grow. Shearing forces, as from bubbling, shaking, or wave action, cause protocells to divide. Based on these observations, it is reasonable to hypothesize that once replicating RNAs became surrounded by a lipid bilayer, this simple life-form and its descendants would occupy cell-like structures that grew and divided.

Now let's investigate the next great innovation in the evolution of the cell: the ability to create and maintain a specialized internal environment that is conducive to life. What is necessary to construct an effective plasma membrane—one that imports ions and molecules needed for life while excluding ions and molecules that might damage it?

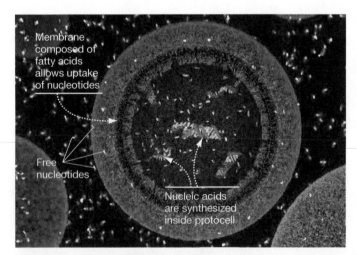

FIGURE 6.15 Protocells May Have Possessed Simple, Permeable Membranes. This image shows a computer model of a protocell. Like this model, the membranes of early cells may have been built of fatty acids. Passive transport of nucleotides across these membranes, as well as replication of nucleic acids inside, has been observed in the laboratory.

Labels within figure: Membrane composed of fatty acids allows uptake of nucleotides; Free nucleotides; Nucleic acids are synthesized inside protocell

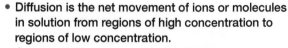

check your understanding

If you understand that . . .

- Diffusion is the net movement of ions or molecules in solution from regions of high concentration to regions of low concentration.
- Osmosis is the movement of water across a selectively permeable membrane, from a region of low solute concentration to a region of high solute concentration.

✓ **You should be able to . . .**

Make a concept map (see **BioSkills 15** in Appendix B) that includes the boxed terms water molecules, solute molecules, osmosis, diffusion, areas of high-to-low concentration, selectively permeable membranes, concentration gradients, hypertonic solutions, hypotonic solutions, and isotonic solutions.

Answers are available in Appendix A.

6.4 Membrane Proteins

What sort of molecule could become incorporated into a lipid bilayer and affect the bilayer's permeability? The title of this section gives the answer away. Proteins that are amphipathic can be inserted into lipid bilayers.

Proteins can be amphipathic because their monomers, amino acids, have side chains that range from highly nonpolar to highly polar or charged (see Figure 3.2). It's conceivable, then, that a protein could have a series of nonpolar amino acid residues in the middle of its primary structure flanked by polar or charged amino acid residues (**FIGURE 6.16a**). The nonpolar residues would be stable in the interior of a lipid bilayer, while the polar or charged residues would be stable alongside the polar lipid heads and surrounding water (**FIGURE 6.16b**).

Further, because the secondary and tertiary structures of proteins are almost limitless in their variety, it is possible for proteins to form openings and thus function as some sort of channel or pore across a lipid bilayer.

From these considerations, it's not surprising that when researchers began analyzing the chemical composition of plasma membranes, they found that proteins were often just as common, in terms of mass, as phospholipids. How were these two types of molecules arranged?

Development of the Fluid-Mosaic Model

In 1935 Hugh Davson and James Danielli proposed that cell membranes were structured like a sandwich in which hydrophilic proteins coat both sides of a pure lipid bilayer (**FIGURE 6.17a**). Early electron micrographs of plasma membranes seemed to be consistent with the sandwich model, and for decades it was widely accepted.

(a) Proteins can be amphipathic.

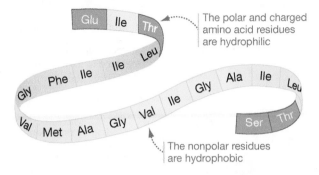

The polar and charged amino acid residues are hydrophilic

The nonpolar residues are hydrophobic

(b) Amphipathic proteins can integrate into lipid bilayers.

Outside cell

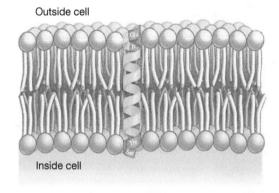

Inside cell

FIGURE 6.16 Amphipathic Proteins Are Anchored in Lipid Bilayers.

(a) Sandwich model

Cell exterior

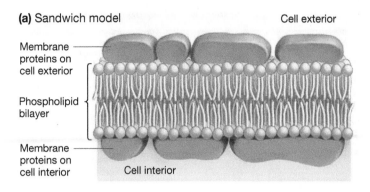

Membrane proteins on cell exterior

Phospholipid bilayer

Membrane proteins on cell interior

Cell interior

(b) Fluid-mosaic model

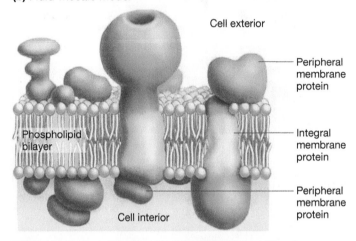

Cell exterior

Peripheral membrane protein

Phospholipid bilayer

Integral membrane protein

Peripheral membrane protein

Cell interior

FIGURE 6.17 Past and Current Models of Membrane Structure Differ in Where Membrane Proteins Reside. (a) The protein-lipid-lipid-protein sandwich model was the first hypothesis for the arrangement of lipids and proteins in cell membranes. **(b)** The fluid-mosaic model was a radical departure from the sandwich hypothesis.

The realization that membrane proteins could be amphipathic, however, led S. Jon Singer and Garth Nicolson to suggest an alternative hypothesis. In 1972, they proposed that at least some proteins span the membrane instead of being found only outside the lipid bilayer. Their hypothesis was called the **fluid-mosaic model (FIGURE 6.17b)**. Singer and Nicolson suggested that membranes are a mosaic of phospholipids and different types of proteins. The overall structure was proposed to be dynamic and fluid.

The controversy over the nature of the cell membrane was resolved in the early 1970s with the development of an innovative technique for visualizing the surface of plasma membranes. The method is called freeze-fracture electron microscopy because the steps involve freezing and fracturing the membrane before examining it with a **scanning electron microscope (SEM),** which produces images of an object's surface (see **BioSkills 11** in Appendix B).

As **FIGURE 6.18** (see page 96) shows, the freeze-fracture technique allows researchers to split cell membranes and view the middle of the structure. The scanning electron micrographs that result show pits and mounds studding the inner surfaces of the lipid bilayer. Researchers interpreted these structures as the locations of membrane proteins. As step 4 in the figure shows, the mounds represent proteins that remained attached to one side of the split lipid bilayer and the pits are the holes they left behind.

These observations conflicted with the sandwich model but were consistent with the fluid-mosaic model. Based on these and subsequent observations, the fluid-mosaic model is now widely accepted.

Notice in Figure 6.17b that some proteins span the membrane and have segments facing both the interior and the exterior surfaces. Proteins like these are called **integral membrane proteins,** or **transmembrane proteins.** Proteins that bind to the membrane without passing through it are called **peripheral membrane proteins.**

Certain peripheral proteins are found only on the interior surface of a cellular membrane, while others are found only on the exterior surface. As a result, the interior and exterior surfaces of the plasma membrane are distinct—the peripheral proteins and the ends of transmembrane proteins differ. Peripheral membrane proteins are often attached to transmembrane proteins.

How do these proteins affect the permeability of membranes? The answer to this question starts with an investigation of the structure of proteins involved in the transport of molecules and ions across the plasma membrane.

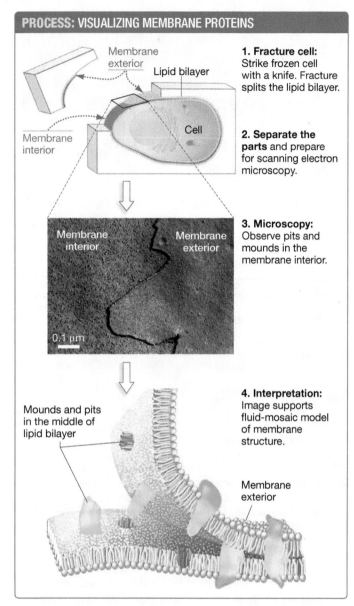

1. **Fracture cell:** Strike frozen cell with a knife. Fracture splits the lipid bilayer.

2. **Separate the parts** and prepare for scanning electron microscopy.

3. **Microscopy:** Observe pits and mounds in the membrane interior.

4. **Interpretation:** Image supports fluid-mosaic model of membrane structure.

FIGURE 6.18 Freeze-Fracture Preparations Allow Biologists to View Membrane Proteins.

✔ **QUESTION** What would be an appropriate control to show that the pits and mounds were not simply irregularities in the lipid bilayer caused by the freeze-fracture process?

Systems for Studying Membrane Proteins

The discovery of transmembrane proteins was consistent with the hypothesis that proteins affect membrane permeability. To test this hypothesis, researchers needed some way to isolate and purify membrane proteins.

FIGURE 6.19 outlines one method that researchers developed to separate proteins from membranes. The key to the technique is the use of detergents. A **detergent** is a small amphipathic molecule. When detergents are added to the solution surrounding a lipid bilayer, the hydrophobic tails of the detergent molecule interact with the hydrophobic tails of the lipids and with the

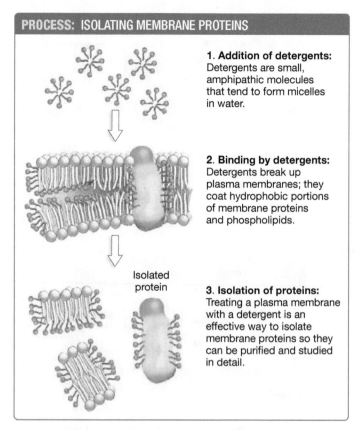

1. **Addition of detergents:** Detergents are small, amphipathic molecules that tend to form micelles in water.

2. **Binding by detergents:** Detergents break up plasma membranes; they coat hydrophobic portions of membrane proteins and phospholipids.

3. **Isolation of proteins:** Treating a plasma membrane with a detergent is an effective way to isolate membrane proteins so they can be purified and studied in detail.

FIGURE 6.19 Detergents Can Be Used to Isolate Proteins from Membranes.

hydrophobic portions of transmembrane proteins. These interactions displace the membrane phospholipids and end up forming water-soluble detergent–protein complexes that can be isolated.

Since intensive experimentation on membrane proteins began, researchers have identified three broad classes of proteins that affect membrane permeability: channels, carriers, and pumps. Let's consider each class in turn.

Facilitated Diffusion via Channel Proteins

As the data in Figure 6.8 show, ions almost never cross pure phospholipid bilayers on their own. But in cells, ions routinely cross membranes through specialized membrane proteins called **ion channels.**

Ion channels form pores, or openings, in a membrane. Ions move through these pores in a predictable direction: from regions of high concentration to regions of low concentration and from areas of like charge to areas of unlike charge.

In **FIGURE 6.20**, for example, a large concentration gradient favors the movement of sodium ions from the outside of a membrane to the inside. But in addition, the inside of this cell has a net negative charge while the outside has a net positive charge. As a result, the combination of these two factors influences the final concentration of sodium ions inside the cell once equilibrium has been established.

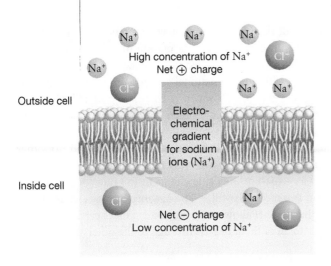

FIGURE 6.20 An Electrochemical Gradient Is a Combined Concentration and Electrical Gradient. Electrochemical gradients are established when ions build up on one side of a membrane.

Ions move in response to a combined concentration and electrical gradient, or what biologists call an **electrochemical gradient.** ✔ If you understand this concept, you should be able to add an arrow to Figure 6.20 indicating the electrochemical gradient for chloride ions.

Is an Ion Channel Involved in Cystic Fibrosis? To understand the types of experiments that biologists do to confirm that a membrane protein is an ion channel, consider work on the cause of cystic fibrosis.

Cystic fibrosis (CF) is the most common genetic disease in humans of Northern European descent. It affects cells that produce mucus, sweat, and digestive juices. Normally these secretions are thin and slippery and act as lubricants. In individuals with CF, however, the secretions become abnormally concentrated and sticky and clog passageways in organs like the lungs.

Experiments published in 1983 suggested that cystic fibrosis is caused by defects in a membrane protein that allow chloride ions (Cl⁻) to move across plasma membranes. It was proposed that reduced chloride ion transport would account for the thick mucus.

How is the transport of chloride ions involved in mucus consistency? Water movement across cell membranes is largely determined by the presence of extracellular ions like chloride. If a defective channel prevents chloride ions from leaving cells, water isn't pulled from cells by osmosis to maintain the proper mucus consistency. In effect, the disease results from the mismanagement of osmosis.

Using molecular techniques introduced in Unit 3 (see Chapter 20), biologists were able to (**1**) find the gene that is defective in people suffering from CF and (**2**) use the gene to produce copies of the normal protein, which was called CFTR (short for cystic fibrosis transmembrane conductance regulator).

Is CFTR a chloride channel? To answer this question, researchers inserted purified CFTR into planar bilayers and

RESEARCH

QUESTION: Is CFTR a chloride channel?

HYPOTHESIS: CFTR increases the flow of chloride ions across a membrane.

NULL HYPOTHESIS: CFTR has no effect on membrane permeability.

EXPERIMENTAL SETUP:

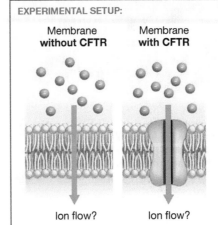

Membrane **without CFTR**

Membrane **with CFTR**

Ion flow?   Ion flow?

1. **Create planar bilayers** with and without CFTR.

2. **Add chloride ions** to one side of the planar bilayer to create an electrochemical gradient.

3. **Record electrical currents** to measure ion flow across the planar bilayers.

PREDICTION: Ion flow will be higher in membrane with CFTR.

PREDICTION OF NULL HYPOTHESIS: Ion flow will be the same in both membranes.

RESULTS:

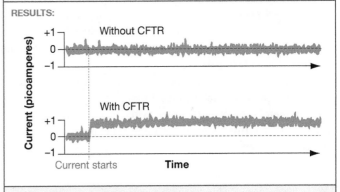

CONCLUSION: CFTR facilitates diffusion of chloride ions along an electrochemical gradient. CFTR is a chloride channel.

FIGURE 6.21 Electric Current Measurements Indicate that Chloride Flows through CFTR.

SOURCE: Bear, C. A., et al. (1992). Purification and functional reconstitution of the cystic fibrosis transmembrane conductance regulator (CFTR). *Cell* 68: 809–818.

✔**QUESTION** The researchers repeated the "with CFTR" treatment 45 times, but recorded a current in only 35 of the replicates. Does this observation negate the conclusion? Explain why or why not.

measured the flow of electric current across the membrane. Because ions carry a charge, ion movement across a membrane produces an electric current.

The graphs in **FIGURE 6.21**, which plot the amount of current flowing across the membrane over time, show the results from this experiment. Notice that when CFTR was absent, no electric current passed through the membrane. But when CFTR was

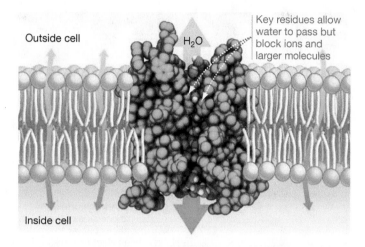

FIGURE 6.22 Membrane Channels Are Highly Selective. A cutaway view looking at the inside of a membrane channel, aquaporin. The key residues identified in the space-filling model selectively filter ions and other small molecules, allowing only water (red and white structures) to pass through.

inserted into the membrane, current began to flow. This was strong evidence that CFTR was indeed a chloride ion channel.

Protein Structure Determines Channel Selectivity Subsequent research has shown that cells have many different types of pore-like **channel proteins** in their membranes, including ion channels like CFTR. Channel proteins are selective. Each channel protein has a structure that permits only a particular type of ion or small molecule to pass through it.

For example, Peter Agre and co-workers discovered channels called **aquaporins** ("water-pores") that allow water to cross the plasma membrane over 10 times faster than it does in the absence of aquaporins. Aquaporins admit water but not other small molecules or ions.

FIGURE 6.22 shows a cutaway view from the side of an aquaporin, indicating how it fits in a plasma membrane. Like other channels that have been studied in detail, aquaporins have a pore that is lined with polar functional groups—in this case, carbonyl groups that interact with water. A channel's pore is hydrophilic relative to the hydrophobic residues facing the phospholipid tails of the membrane.

But how can aquaporin be selective for water and not other polar molecules? The answer was found when researchers examined its structure. Key side chains in the interior of the pore function as a molecular filter. The distance between these groups across the channel allows only those substances capable of interacting with all of them to pass through to the other side.

Movement Through Many Membrane Channels Is Regulated Recent research has shown that many aquaporins and ion channels are **gated channels**—meaning that they open or close in response to a signal, such as the binding of a particular molecule or a change in the electrical voltage across the membrane.

As an example of how voltage-gated channels work, **FIGURE 6.23** shows a potassium channel in closed and open configurations. The electrical charge on the membrane is normally negative on the inside relative to the outside, which causes the channel to adopt a closed shape that prevents potassium ions from passing through. When this charge asymmetry is reversed, the shape changes in a way that opens the channel and allows potassium ions to cross. The key point here is that in almost all cases, the flow of ions and small molecules through membrane channels is carefully controlled.

In all cases, however, the movement of substances through channels is passive—meaning it does not require an input of energy. **Passive transport** is powered by diffusion along an electrochemical gradient. Channel proteins simply enable ions or polar molecules to move across lipid bilayers efficiently, in response to

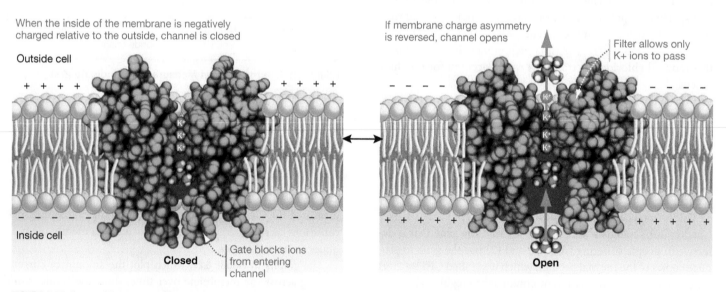

FIGURE 6.23 Some Membrane Channels Are Highly Regulated. A model of a voltage-gated K⁺ channel in the closed and open configurations. The channel filter displaces water molecules that normally surround the K⁺ ions in an aqueous solution.

an existing gradient. They are responsible for **facilitated diffusion:** the passive transport of substances that otherwise would not cross a membrane readily.

Facilitated Diffusion via Carrier Proteins

Facilitated diffusion can also occur through **carrier proteins**—specialized membrane proteins that change shape during the transport process. Perhaps the best-studied carrier protein is one that is involved in transporting glucose into cells.

The Search for a Glucose Carrier Next to ribose, the six-carbon sugar glucose is the most prevalent sugar found in organisms. Virtually all cells alive today use glucose as a building block for important macromolecules and as a source of stored chemical energy (Chapter 5). But as Figure 6.8 shows, lipid bilayers are only moderately permeable to glucose. It is reasonable to expect, then, that plasma membranes have some mechanism for increasing their permeability to this sugar.

This prediction was supported in experiments on pure preparations of plasma membranes from human red blood cells. These plasma membranes turned out to be much more permeable to glucose than are pure lipid bilayers. Why?

After isolating and analyzing many proteins from red blood cell membranes, researchers found one protein that specifically increases membrane permeability to glucose. When they added this purified protein to liposomes, the artificial membrane transported glucose at the same rate as a membrane from a living cell. This experiment convinced biologists that the membrane protein—now called GLUT-1 (short for glucose transporter 1)—was indeed responsible for transporting glucose across plasma membranes.

How Does GLUT-1 Work? Recall that proteins frequently change shape when they bind to other molecules and that such conformational changes are often a critical step in their function (Chapter 3).

FIGURE 6.24 illustrates the current hypothesis for how GLUT-1 works to facilitate the movement of glucose. The idea is that when glucose binds to GLUT-1, it changes the shape of the protein in a way that moves the sugar through the hydrophobic region of the membrane and releases it on the other side.

What powers the movement of molecules through carriers? The answer is diffusion. GLUT-1 facilitates diffusion by allowing glucose to enter the carrier from either side of the membrane. Glucose will pass through the carrier in the direction dictated by its concentration gradient. A large variety of molecules move across plasma membranes via specific carrier proteins.

Pumps Perform Active Transport

Diffusion—whether it is facilitated by proteins or not—is a passive process that will move substances in either direction across a membrane to make the cell interior and exterior more similar. But it is also possible for cells to move molecules or ions in a directed manner, often *against* their electrochemical gradient. Accomplishing this task requires an input of energy, because the cell must counteract the decrease in entropy that occurs when molecules or ions are concentrated. It makes sense, then, that transport against an electrochemical gradient is called **active transport.**

In cells, ATP (adenosine triphosphate) often provides the energy for active transport by transferring a phosphate group (HPO_4^{2-}) to an active transport protein called a **pump.** Recall that ATP contains three phosphate groups (Chapter 4), and that phosphate groups carry two negative charges (Chapter 2). When a phosphate group leaves ATP and binds to a pump, its negative charges interact with charged amino acid residues in the protein. As a result, the protein's potential energy increases and its shape changes.

The Sodium–Potassium Pump A classic example of how structural change leads to active transport is provided in the **sodium–potassium pump,** or more formally, Na+/K+-ATPase. The Na+/K+ part of the name refers to the ions that are transported, ATP indicates that adenosine triphosphate is used, and *–ase* identifies the molecule as an enzyme.

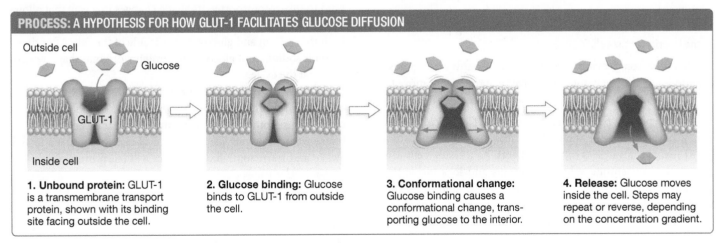

PROCESS: A HYPOTHESIS FOR HOW GLUT-1 FACILITATES GLUCOSE DIFFUSION

Outside cell

Glucose

GLUT-1

Inside cell

1. Unbound protein: GLUT-1 is a transmembrane transport protein, shown with its binding site facing outside the cell.

2. Glucose binding: Glucose binds to GLUT-1 from outside the cell.

3. Conformational change: Glucose binding causes a conformational change, transporting glucose to the interior.

4. Release: Glucose moves inside the cell. Steps may repeat or reverse, depending on the concentration gradient.

FIGURE 6.24 Carrier Proteins Undergo Structural Changes to Move Substances. This model suggests that GLUT-1 binds a glucose molecule, undergoes a conformational change, and releases glucose on the other side of the membrane.

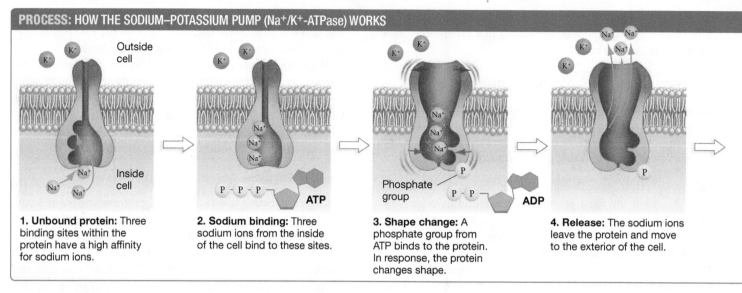

1. Unbound protein: Three binding sites within the protein have a high affinity for sodium ions.

2. Sodium binding: Three sodium ions from the inside of the cell bind to these sites.

3. Shape change: A phosphate group from ATP binds to the protein. In response, the protein changes shape.

4. Release: The sodium ions leave the protein and move to the exterior of the cell.

FIGURE 6.25 The Sodium–Potassium Pump Depends on an Input of Chemical Energy Stored in ATP.

As shown in **FIGURE 6.25**, sodium and potassium ions move in a multistep process:

Step 1 When Na⁺/K⁺-ATPase is in the conformation shown here, binding sites with a high affinity for sodium ions are available.

Step 2 Three sodium ions from the inside of the cell bind to these sites and activate the ATPase activity in the pump.

Step 3 A phosphate group from ATP is transferred to the pump. When the phosphate group attaches, the pump changes its shape in a way that opens the ion-binding pocket to the external environment and reduces its affinity for sodium ions.

Step 4 The sodium ions leave the protein and move to the exterior of the cell.

Step 5 In this conformation, the pump has binding sites with a high affinity for potassium ions facing the external environment.

Step 6 Two potassium ions from outside the cell bind to the pump.

Step 7 When the potassium is bound, the phosphate group is cleaved from the protein and its structure changes in response—back to the original shape with the ion-binding pocket facing the interior of the cell.

Step 8 In this conformation, the pump has low affinity for potassium ions. The potassium ions leave the protein and move to the interior of the cell. The cycle then repeats.

Other types of pumps move protons (H⁺), calcium ions (Ca²⁺), or other ions or molecules across membranes in a directed manner, regardless of the gradients. As a result, cells can import and concentrate valuable nutrients and ions inside the cell despite their relatively low external concentration. They can also expel molecules or ions, even when a concentration gradient favors diffusion of these substances into the cell.

Secondary Active Transport Approximately 30 percent of all the ATP generated in your body is used to drive the Na⁺/K⁺-ATPase cycle. Each cycle exports three Na⁺ ions for every two K⁺ ions it

imports. In this way, the sodium–potassium pump converts energy from ATP to an electrochemical gradient across the membrane. The outside of the membrane becomes positively charged relative to the inside. This gradient favors a flow of anions out of the cell and a flow of cations into the cell.

The electrochemical gradients established by the Na⁺/K⁺-ATPase represent a form of stored energy, much like the electrical energy stored in a battery. How do cells use this energy?

Gradients are crucial to the function of the cell, in part because they make it possible for cells to engage in **secondary active transport**—also known as cotransport. When cotransport occurs, a gradient set up by a pump provides the energy required to power the movement of a different molecule against its particular gradient.

Recall that GLUT-1 facilitates the movement of glucose into or out of cells in the direction of its gradient. Can glucose be moved against its gradient? The answer is yes—a cotransport protein in your gut cells uses the Na⁺ gradient created by Na⁺/K⁺-ATPases to import glucose against its chemical gradient. When Na⁺ ions bind to this cotransporter, its shape changes in a way that allows glucose to bind. Once glucose binds, another shape transports both the sodium and glucose to the inside of the cell. After dropping off sodium and glucose, the protein's original shape returns to repeat the cycle.

In this way, glucose present in the food you are digesting is actively transported into your body. The glucose molecules eventually diffuse into your bloodstream and are transported to your brain, where they provide the chemical energy you need to stay awake and learn some biology. (You will learn more about secondary active transport in Units 7 and 8.)

Plasma Membranes and the Intracellular Environment

Taken together, the selective permeability of the lipid bilayer and the specificity of the proteins involved in passive transport and

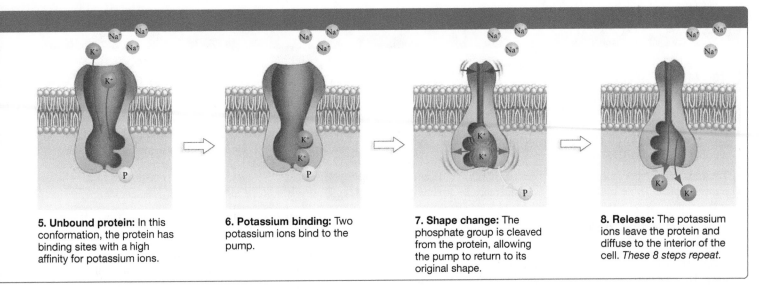

5. Unbound protein: In this conformation, the protein has binding sites with a high affinity for potassium ions.

6. Potassium binding: Two potassium ions bind to the pump.

7. Shape change: The phosphate group is cleaved from the protein, allowing the pump to return to its original shape.

8. Release: The potassium ions leave the protein and diffuse to the interior of the cell. *These 8 steps repeat.*

active transport enable cells to create an internal environment that is much different from the external one (**FIGURE 6.26**).

With the evolution of membrane proteins, the early cells acquired the ability to create an internal environment that was conducive to life—one that contained the substances required for manufacturing ATP and copying ribozymes. Cells with particularly efficient and selective membrane proteins would be favored by natural selection and would come to dominate the population. Cellular life had begun.

Some 3.5 billion years later, cells continue to evolve. What do today's cells look like, and how do they produce and store the chemical energy that makes life possible? Answering these and related questions is the focus of the following unit.

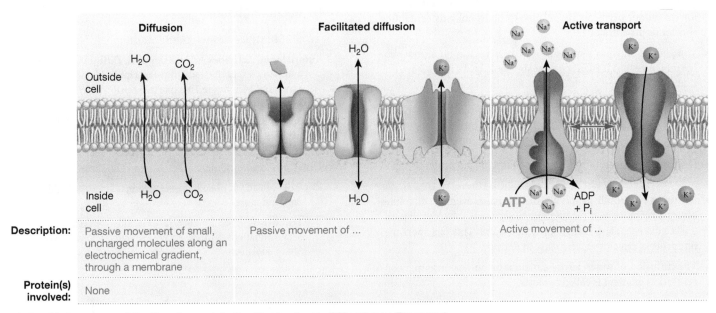

	Diffusion	Facilitated diffusion	Active transport
Description:	Passive movement of small, uncharged molecules along an electrochemical gradient, through a membrane	Passive movement of ...	Active movement of ...
Protein(s) involved:	None		

FIGURE 6.26 Summary of the Passive and Active Mechanisms of Membrane Transport.

✔**EXERCISE** Complete the chart.

If you understand . . .

6.1   Lipid Structure and Function

- Lipids are largely hydrophobic compounds due to their high number of nonpolar C–H bonds.

- The three main types of lipids found in cells are fats, steroids, and phospholipids. These molecules vary considerably in structure and function.

- In hydrocarbon chains, the length and degree of saturation have a profound effect on their physical properties.

- Amphipathic lipids possess a distinct hydrophilic region containing polar or charged groups. Phospholipids have a polar head and a nonpolar tail. The nonpolar tail usually consists of fatty acids or isoprenoids.

✔ You should be able to explain how adding hydrogen (H_2) to vegetable oil, a process called hydrogenation, results in a butter-like solid called margarine.

6.2   Phospholipid Bilayers

- In solution, phospholipids spontaneously assemble into bilayers that can serve as a physical barrier between an internal and external environment.

- Small nonpolar molecules tend to move across lipid bilayers readily; ions cross rarely, if at all.

- The permeability and fluidity of lipid bilayers depend on temperature, on the concentration of steroids, and on the chemical structure of the lipids present, such as the saturation status and length of the hydrocarbon chains. Phospholipids with longer or saturated tails form a dense and highly hydrophobic interior that lowers bilayer permeability, relative to phospholipids containing shorter or unsaturated tails.

✔ You should be able to explain how the structure of a phospholipid bilayer that is highly permeable and fluid differs from one that is highly impermeable and lacking in fluidity.

6.3   How Molecules Move across Lipid Bilayers: Diffusion and Osmosis

- Diffusion is the random movement of ions or molecules owing to their kinetic energy.

- Diffusion can result in the net directional movement of solutes across a membrane, if the membrane separates solutions that differ in concentration, charge, or temperature. This is a spontaneous process driven by an increase in entropy.

- The diffusion of water across a membrane in response to a concentration gradient is called osmosis.

✔ You should be able to imagine a beaker with solutions separated by a planar membrane and then predict what will happen after addition of a solute to one side if the solute (1) crosses the membrane readily or (2) is incapable of crossing the membrane.

6.4   Membrane Proteins

- The permeability of lipid bilayers can be altered significantly by membrane proteins.

- Channel proteins provide pores in the membrane and facilitate the diffusion of specific solutes into and out of the cell.

- Carriers undergo conformational changes that facilitate the diffusion of specific molecules into and out of the cell.

- Pumps use energy to actively move ions or molecules in a single direction, often against the electrical or chemical gradient.

- In combination, the selective permeability of phospholipid bilayers and the specificity of transport proteins make it possible to create an environment inside a cell that is radically different from the exterior.

✔ You should be able to draw and label the membrane of a cell that is placed in a solution containing calcium ions and lactose and show the activity of the following membrane proteins: (1) an H^+ pump that exports protons; (2) a calcium channel; and (3) a lactose carrier. Your drawing should include arrows and labels indicating the direction of solute movement and the direction of the appropriate electrochemical gradients.

MB MasteringBiology

1. MasteringBiology Assignments

Tutorials and Activities Active Transport; Diffusion, Diffusion and Osmosis; Facilitated Diffusion Lipids; Membrane Structure; Membrane Transport: Diffusion and Passive Transport; Membrane Transport: The Sodium–Potassium Pump; Membrane Transport Proteins; Osmosis; Membrane Transport: Cotransport; Osmosis and Water Balance in Cells; Selective Permeability of Membranes

Questions Reading Quizzes, Blue-Thread Questions, Test Bank

2. eText Read your book online, search, take notes, highlight text, and more.

3. The Study Area Practice Test, Cumulative Test, BioFlix® 3-D Animations, Videos, Activities, Audio Glossary, Word Study Tools, Art

You should be able to . . .

1. How is the structure of saturated fats different from that of unsaturated fats?
   a. All of the carbons in the hydrocarbon tails of saturated fats are bonded to one another with double bonds.
   b. Saturated fats have three hydrocarbon tails bonded to the glycerol molecule instead of just two.
   c. The hydrocarbon tails in a saturated fat have the maximum number of hydrogens possible.
   d. Saturated fats have no oxygens present.

2. What distinguishes amphipathic lipids from other lipids?
   a. Amphipathic lipids have polar and nonpolar regions.
   b. Amphipathic lipids have saturated and unsaturated regions.
   c. Amphipathic lipids are steroids.
   d. Amphipathic lipids dissolve in water.

3. If a solution surrounding a cell is hypertonic relative to the inside of the cell, how will water move?
   a. It will move into the cell via osmosis.
   b. It will move out of the cell via osmosis.
   c. It will not move, because equilibrium exists.
   d. It will evaporate from the cell surface more rapidly.

4. When does a concentration gradient exist?
   a. when membranes rupture
   b. when solute concentrations are high
   c. when solute concentrations are low
   d. when solute concentrations differ on the two sides of a membrane

5. What two conditions must be present for the effects of osmosis to occur?

6. In terms of structure, how do channel proteins differ from carrier proteins?

7. If a cell were placed in a solution with a high potassium concentration and no sodium, what would happen to the sodium–potassium pump's activity?
   a. It would stop moving ions across the membrane.
   b. It would continue using ATP to pump sodium out of the cell and potassium into the cell.
   c. It would move sodium and potassium ions across the membrane, but no ATP would be used.
   d. It would reverse the direction of sodium and potassium ions to move them against their gradients.

8. Cooking oil lipids consist of long, unsaturated hydrocarbon chains. Would you expect these molecules to form membranes spontaneously? Why or why not? Describe, on a molecular level, how you would expect these lipids to interact with water.

9. Explain why phospholipids form a bilayer in solution, and why the process is spontaneous.

10. Ethanol (C_2H_5OH) is the active ingredient in alcoholic beverages. Would you predict that this molecule crosses lipid bilayers quickly, slowly, or not at all? Explain your reasoning.

11. Integral membrane proteins are anchored in lipid bilayers. Of the following four groups of amino acids—nonpolar, polar, charged/acidic, charged/basic (see Figure 3.2)—which would likely be found in the portion that crosses the lipid bilayer? Explain your reasoning.

12. Examine the experimental chamber in Figure 6.7a. If the lipid bilayer were to contain the CFTR molecule, what would pass through the membrane if you added a 1-molar solution of sodium chloride on the left side and a 1-molar solution of potassium ions on the right? Assume that there is an equal amount of water on each side at the start of the experiment.

13. In an experiment, you create two groups of liposomes—one made from red blood cell membranes and the other from frog egg cell membranes. When placed in water, those made with red blood cell membranes burst more rapidly than those made from frog membranes. What is the best explanation for these results?
    a. The red blood cell liposomes are more hypertonic relative to water than the frog egg liposomes.
    b. The red blood cell liposomes are more hypotonic relative to water than the frog egg liposomes.
    c. The red blood cell liposomes contain aquaporins, which are not abundant in the frog egg liposomes.
    d. The frog egg liposomes contain ion channels, which are not present in the red blood cell liposomes.

14. When phospholipids are arranged in a bilayer, it is theoretically possible for individual molecules in the bilayer to flip-flop. That is, a phospholipid could turn 180° and become part of the membrane's other surface. From what you know about the behavior of polar heads and nonpolar tails, predict whether flip-flops are frequent or rare. Then design an experiment, using a planar bilayer with one side made up of phospholipids that contain a dye molecule on their hydrophilic head, to test your prediction.

15. Unicellular organisms live in a wide range of habitats, from the hot springs in Yellowstone National Park to the freezing temperatures of the Antarctic. Make a prediction about the saturation status of membrane phospholipids in organisms that live in extremely cold environments versus those that live in extremely hot environments. Explain your reasoning.

16. When biomedical researchers design drugs, they sometimes add methyl (CH_3) groups or charged groups to the molecules. If these groups are not directly involved in the activity of the drug, predict the purpose of these modifications and explain why these strategies are necessary.

THE CHEMISTRY OF LIFE

The first spark of life ignited when simple chemical reactions began to convert small molecules into larger, more complex molecules with novel 3-D structures and activities. According to the theory of chemical evolution, these reactions eventually led to the formation of the four types of macromolecules characteristic of life—proteins, nucleic acids, carbohydrates, and lipids.

As you look through this concept map, consider how the functions of the four types of macromolecules are determined by their structures, and how these structures stem from the chemical properties of the atoms and bonds used to build them.

Note that each box in the concept map indicates the chapters and sections where you can go for review. Also, be sure to do the blue exercises in the **Check Your Understanding** box below.

The Big Picture

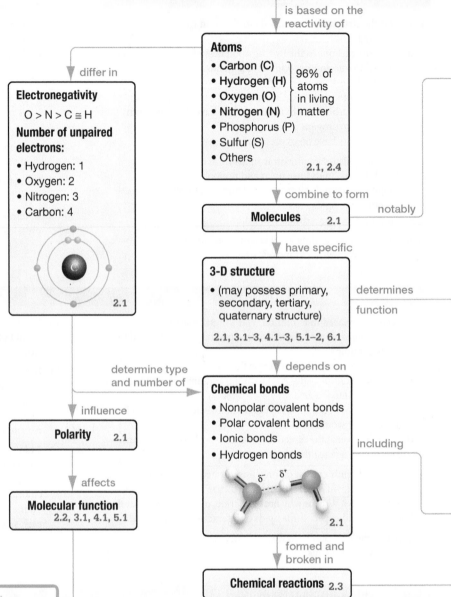

is based on the reactivity of

Atoms
- Carbon (C)
- Hydrogen (H) } 96% of atoms in living matter
- Oxygen (O)
- Nitrogen (N)
- Phosphorus (P)
- Sulfur (S)
- Others

2.1, 2.4

differ in

Electronegativity

$O > N > C \cong H$

Number of unpaired electrons:
- Hydrogen: 1
- Oxygen: 2
- Nitrogen: 3
- Carbon: 4

2.1

combine to form

Molecules 2.1 — notably

have specific

3-D structure
- (may possess primary, secondary, tertiary, quaternary structure)

2.1, 3.1–3, 4.1–3, 5.1–2, 6.1

determines function

depends on

determine type and number of

Chemical bonds
- Nonpolar covalent bonds
- Polar covalent bonds
- Ionic bonds
- Hydrogen bonds

δ^- δ^+

2.1

including

influence

Polarity 2.1

affects

Molecular function
2.2, 3.1, 4.1, 5.1

formed and broken in

Chemical reactions 2.3

as demonstrated by

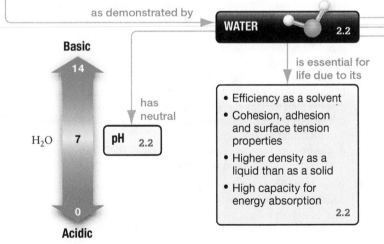

WATER 2.2

is essential for life due to its

- Efficiency as a solvent
- Cohesion, adhesion and surface tension properties
- Higher density as a liquid than as a solid
- High capacity for energy absorption

2.2

has neutral

Basic

14

H_2O 7 **pH** 2.2

0

Acidic

Biological macromolecules

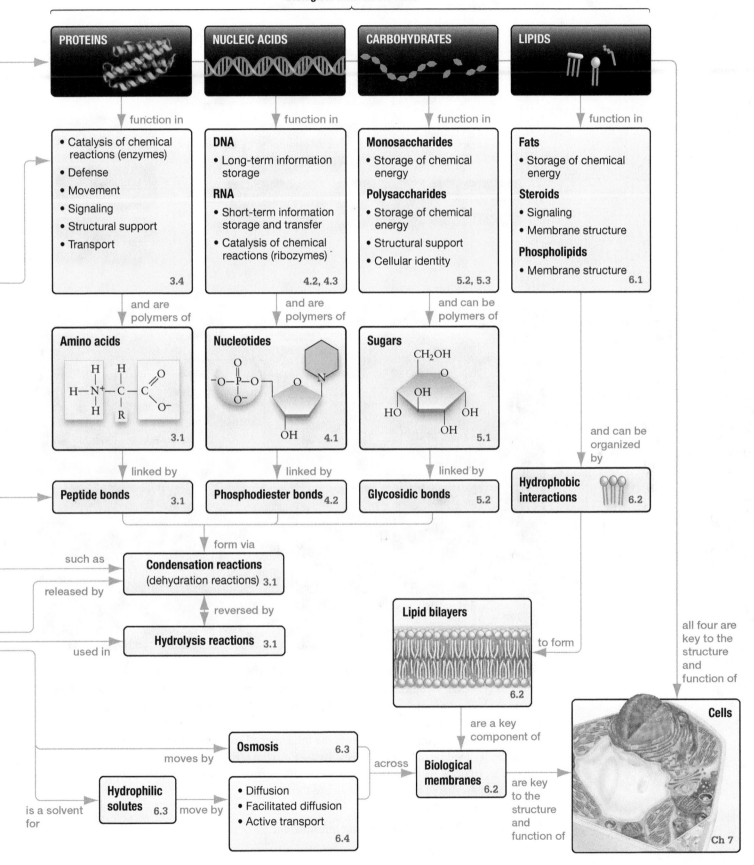

PROTEINS

NUCLEIC ACIDS

CARBOHYDRATES

LIPIDS

function in

function in

function in

function in

Catalysis of chemical reactions (enzymes)
- Defense
- Movement
- Signaling
- Structural support
- Transport

3.4

DNA
- Long-term information storage

RNA
- Short-term information storage and transfer
- Catalysis of chemical reactions (ribozymes)

4.2, 4.3

Monosaccharides
- Storage of chemical energy

Polysaccharides
- Storage of chemical energy
- Structural support
- Cellular identity

5.2, 5.3

Fats
- Storage of chemical energy

Steroids
- Signaling
- Membrane structure

Phospholipids
- Membrane structure

6.1

and are polymers of

and are polymers of

and can be polymers of

Amino acids

3.1

Nucleotides

4.1

Sugars

5.1

linked by

linked by

linked by

and can be organized by

Peptide bonds 3.1

Phosphodiester bonds 4.2

Glycosidic bonds 5.2

Hydrophobic interactions 6.2

form via

such as

Condensation reactions (dehydration reactions) 3.1

released by

reversed by

Lipid bilayers

6.2

Hydrolysis reactions 3.1

used in

to form

all four are key to the structure and function of

are a key component of

Osmosis 6.3

moves by

across

Biological membranes 6.2

Cells

Hydrophilic solutes 6.3

is a solvent for

move by

- Diffusion
- Facilitated diffusion
- Active transport

6.4

are key to the structure and function of

Ch 7

7 Inside the Cell

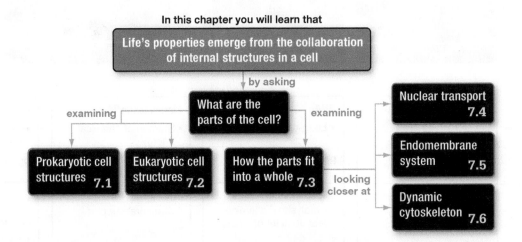

In this chapter you will learn that

Life's properties emerge from the collaboration of internal structures in a cell

↓ by asking

What are the parts of the cell?

examining →

examining →

Prokaryotic cell structures **7.1**

Eukaryotic cell structures **7.2**

How the parts fit into a whole **7.3**

looking closer at →

Nuclear transport **7.4**

Endomembrane system **7.5**

Dynamic cytoskeleton **7.6**

This cell has been treated with fluorescing molecules that bind to its fibrous cytoskeleton. Microtubules (large protein fibers) are yellow; actin filaments (smaller fibers) are blue. The cell's nucleus has been stained green.

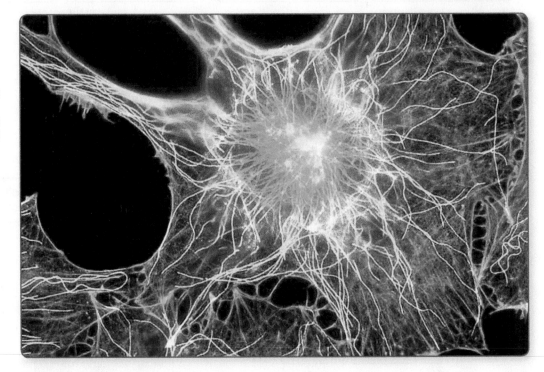

The cell theory states that all organisms consist of cells and all cells are derived from preexisting cells (Chapter 1). Since this theory was initially developed and tested in the 1850s, an enormous body of research has confirmed that the cell is the fundamental structural and functional unit of life. Life on Earth is cellular.

Previous chapters (Unit 1) delved into the fundamental attributes of life by looking at biologists' current understanding of how the cell evolved—from the early chemistry to the assembly and replication of a protocell. As the first cells left the hydrothermal vents, they took with them characteristics that are now shared among all known life-forms.

All cells have

1. nucleic acids that store and transmit information;

2. proteins that perform most of the cell's functions;

✔ When you see this checkmark, stop and test yourself. Answers are available in Appendix A.

3. carbohydrates that provide chemical energy, carbon, support, and identity; and

4. a plasma membrane, which serves as a selectively permeable membrane barrier.

Thanks to the selective permeability of phospholipid bilayers and the activity of membrane transport proteins, the plasma membrane creates an internal environment that differs from conditions outside the cell. Our task now is to explore the structures inside the cell to understand how the properties of life emerged from the combination of these characteristics.

Let's begin by analyzing how the parts inside a cell function individually and then exploring how they work as a unit. This approach is analogous to studying individual organs in the body and then analyzing how they work together to form the nervous system or digestive system. As you study this material, keep asking yourself some key questions: How does the structure of this part or group of parts correlate with its function? What problem does it solve?

7.1 Bacterial and Archaeal Cell Structures and Their Functions

Cells are divided into two fundamental types called eukaryotes and prokaryotes (see Chapter 1). This division is mostly based on cell **morphology** ("form-science")—eukaryotic cells have a membrane-bound compartment called a nucleus, and prokaryotic cells do not.

But according to **phylogeny** ("tribe-source"), or evolutionary history, organisms are divided into three broad domains called (1) Bacteria, (2) Archaea, and (3) Eukarya. Members of the Bacteria and Archaea are prokaryotic; members of the Eukarya—including algae, fungi, plants, and animals—are eukaryotic.

A Revolutionary New View

For almost 200 years, biologists thought that prokaryotic cells were simple in terms of their morphology and that there was little structural diversity among species. This conclusion was valid at the time, given the resolution of the microscopes that were available and the number of species that had been studied.

Things have changed. Recent improvements in microscopy and other research tools have convinced biologists that prokaryotic cells, among which bacteria are the best understood, possess an array of distinctive structures and functions found among millions of species. This conclusion represents one of the most exciting discoveries in cell biology over the past 10 years.

To keep things simple at the start, though, **FIGURE 7.1** offers a low-magnification, stripped-down diagram of a bacterial cell.

Prokaryotic Cell Structures: A Parts List

The labels in Figure 7.1 highlight the components common to all or most bacteria studied to date. Let's explore these elements one by one, and also look at more specialized structures found in particular species, starting from the inside and working out.

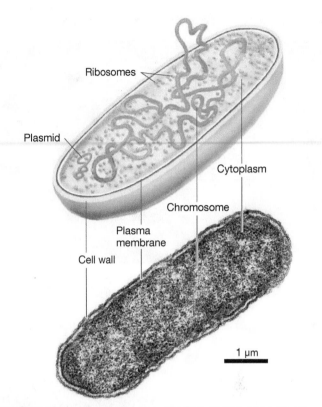

FIGURE 7.1 Overview of a Prokaryotic Cell. Prokaryotic cells are identified by a negative trait—the absence of a membrane-bound nucleus. Although there is wide variation in the size and shape of bacterial and archaeal cells, they all contain a plasma membrane, a chromosome, and protein-synthesizing ribosomes.

The Chromosome Is Organized in a Nucleoid The most prominent structure inside a bacterial cell is the **chromosome.** Most bacterial species have a single, circular chromosome that consists of a large DNA molecule associated with a small number of proteins. The DNA molecule contains information, and the proteins provide structural support for the DNA.

Recall that the information in DNA is encoded in its sequence of nitrogenous bases. Segments of DNA that contain information for building functional RNAs, some of which may be used to make polypeptides, are called **genes** (Chapter 4). Thus, chromosomes contain DNA, which contains genes.

In the well-studied bacterium *Escherichia coli*, the circular chromosome would be over 1 mm long if it were linear—500 times longer than the cell itself (**FIGURE 7.2a**; see page 108). This situation is typical in prokaryotes. To fit into the cell, the DNA double helix coils on itself with the aid of enzymes to form a compact, "supercoiled" structure. Supercoiled regions of DNA resemble a rubber band that has been held at either end and then twisted until it coils back upon itself.

The location and structural organization of the circular chromosome is called the **nucleoid** (pronounced *NEW-klee-oyd*). The genetic material in the nucleoid is often organized by clustering loops of DNA into distinct domains, but it is not separated from the rest of the cell interior by a membrane. The functional role of this organization of the bacterial chromosome and how it changes over time is currently the subject of intense research.

(a) Compared to the cell, chromosomal DNA is very long.

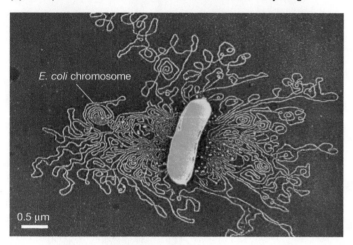

(b) DNA is packaged by supercoiling.

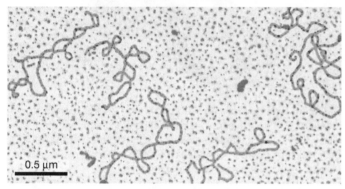

FIGURE 7.2 **Bacterial DNA Is Supercoiled. (a)** The chromosomes of bacteria and archaea are often over 1000 times the length of the cell, as shown in this micrograph of *E. coli* that has been treated to release its DNA. To fit inside cells, this DNA must be highly compacted by supercoiling. **(b)** A colorized electron micrograph showing the effect of supercoiling on the DNA of isolated plasmids.

In addition to one or more chromosomes, bacterial cells may contain from one to about a hundred small, usually circular, supercoiled DNA molecules called **plasmids** (**FIGURE 7.2b**). Plasmids contain genes but are physically independent of the cellular chromosome. In many cases the genes carried by plasmids are not required under normal conditions; instead, they help cells adapt to unusual circumstances, such as the sudden presence of a poison in the environment. As a result, plasmids can be considered auxiliary genetic elements.

Ribosomes Manufacture Proteins **Ribosomes** are observed in all prokaryotic cells and are found throughout the cell interior. It is not unusual for a single cell to contain 10,000 ribosomes, each functioning as a protein-manufacturing center.

Ribosomes are complex structures composed of large and small subunits, each of which contains RNA and protein molecules. Biologists often refer to ribosomes, along with other multicomponent complexes that perform specialized tasks, as "macromolecular machines." (Chapter 17 analyzes the structure and function of ribosomes in detail.)

Photosynthetic Species Have Internal Membrane Complexes In addition to the nucleoid and ribosomes found in all bacteria and archaea studied to date, it is common to observe extensive internal membranes in prokaryotes that perform photosynthesis. Photosynthesis is the suite of chemical reactions responsible for converting the energy in sunlight into chemical energy stored in sugars.

The photosynthetic membranes observed in prokaryotes contain the enzymes and pigment molecules required for these reactions to occur and develop as infoldings of the plasma membrane. In some cases, vesicles pinch off as the plasma membrane folds in. In other cases, flattened stacks of photosynthetic membrane remain connected to the plasma membrane, like those shown in **FIGURE 7.3**. The extensive surface area provided by these internal membranes makes it possible for more photosynthetic reactions to occur and thus increases the cell's ability to make food.

Organelles Perform Specialized Functions Recent research indicates that several bacterial species have internal compartments that qualify as **organelles** ("little organs"). An organelle is a membrane-bound compartment inside the cell that contains enzymes or structures specialized for a particular function.

Bacterial organelles perform an array of tasks, including

- storing calcium ions or other key molecules;

- holding crystals of the mineral magnetite, which function like a compass needle to help cells sense a magnetic field and swim in a directed way;

- organizing enzymes responsible for synthesizing complex carbon compounds from carbon dioxide; and

- sequestering enzymes that generate chemical energy from ammonium ions.

The Cytoskeleton Structures the Cell Interior Recent research has also shown that bacteria and archaea contain long, thin fibers that serve a variety of roles inside the cell. All bacterial species,

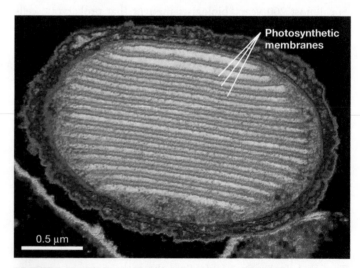

FIGURE 7.3 **Photosynthetic Membranes in Bacteria.** The green stripes in this photosynthetic bacterium are membranes that contain the pigments and enzymes required for photosynthesis. This photo has been colorized to enhance the membranes.

for example, contain protein fibers that are essential for cell division to take place. Some species also have protein filaments that help maintain cell shape. Protein filaments such as these form the basis of the **cytoskeleton** ("cell skeleton").

The discovery of bacterial cytoskeletal elements is so new that much remains to be learned. Currently, researchers are working to understand how the different cytoskeletal elements enable cells to divide and if they play a role in organizing the cell interior into distinctive regions.

The Plasma Membrane Separates Life from Nonlife

The plasma membrane consists of a phospholipid bilayer and proteins that either span the bilayer or attach to one side. Inside the membrane, all the contents of a cell, excluding the nucleus, are collectively termed the **cytoplasm** ("cell-formed").

Because all archaea and virtually all bacteria are unicellular, the plasma membrane creates an internal environment that is distinct from the outside, nonliving environment. The combined effect of a lipid bilayer and membrane proteins prohibits the entry of many substances that would be dangerous to life while allowing the passage of molecules and ions required for life (see Chapter 6).

The Cell Wall Forms a Protective "Exoskeleton"

Because the cytoplasm contains a high concentration of solutes, in most habitats it is hypertonic relative to the surrounding environment. When this is the case, water enters the cell via osmosis and makes the cell's volume expand. In virtually all bacteria and archaea, this pressure is resisted by a stiff **cell wall.**

Bacterial and archaeal cell walls are a tough, fibrous layer that surrounds the plasma membrane. In prokaryotes, the pressure of the plasma membrane against the cell wall is about the same as the pressure in an automobile tire.

The cell wall protects the organism and gives it shape and rigidity, much like the exoskeleton (external skeleton) of a crab or insect. In addition, many bacteria have another protective layer outside the cell wall that consists of lipids with polysaccharides attached. Lipids that contain carbohydrate groups are termed **glycolipids.**

External Structures Enable Movement and Attachment

Besides having a cell wall to provide protection, as just described, many bacteria also interact with their environment via structures that grow from the plasma membrane. The flagella and fimbriae shown in **FIGURE 7.4** are examples that are commonly found on bacterial surfaces.

Bacterial **flagella** (singular: **flagellum**) are assembled from over 40 different proteins at the cell surface of certain species. The base of this structure is embedded in the plasma membrane, and its rotation spins a long, helical filament that propels cells through water. At top speed, flagellar movement can drive a bacterial cell through water at 60 cell lengths per second. In contrast, the fastest animal in the ocean—the sailfish—can swim at a mere 10 body lengths per second.

Fimbriae (singular: **fimbria**) are needlelike projections that extend from the plasma membrane of some bacteria and promote attachment to other cells or surfaces. These structures are

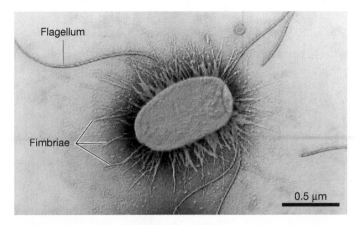

FIGURE 7.4 Extracellular Appendages Found on Bacteria. Some species of bacteria, such as the *E. coli* shown here, assemble large protein structures used for swimming through liquid (flagella) or adhering to surfaces (fimbriae).

more numerous than flagella and are often distributed over the entire surface of the cell. Fimbriae are crucial to the establishment of many infections based on their ability to glue bacteria to the surface of tissues.

The painting in **FIGURE 7.5** shows a cross section of a bacterial cell and provides a close-up view of the internal and external structures introduced in this section. One feature that prokaryotic and eukaryotic cells have in common: They are both packed with dynamic, highly integrated structures.

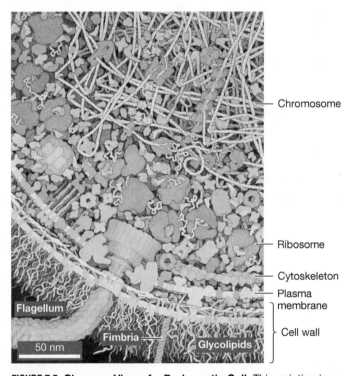

FIGURE 7.5 Close-up View of a Prokaryotic Cell. This painting is David Goodsell's representation of a cross section through part of a bacterial cell. It is based on electron micrographs of bacterial cells and is drawn to scale. Note that the cell is packed with proteins, DNA, ribosomes, and other molecular machinery.

If you understand that . . .

- Each structure in a prokaryotic cell performs a function vital to the cell.

✓ **You should be able to . . .**

Describe the structure and function of (1) the nucleoid, (2) photosynthetic membranes, (3) flagella, and (4) the cell wall.

Answers are available in Appendix A.

7.2 Eukaryotic Cell Structures and Their Functions

The Eukarya includes species that range from microscopic algae to 100-meter-tall redwood trees. Brown algae, red algae, fungi, amoebae, slime molds, green plants, and animals are all eukaryotic. Although multicellularity has evolved several times among eukaryotes (see Chapter 30), many species are unicellular.

The first thing that strikes biologists about eukaryotic cells is how much larger they are on average than bacteria and archaea. Most prokaryotic cells measure 1 to 10 µm in diameter, while most eukaryotic cells range from about 5 to 100 µm in diameter. A micrograph of an average eukaryotic cell, at the same scale as the bacterial cell in Figure 7.3, would fill this page. For many species of unicellular eukaryotes, this size difference allows them to make a living by ingesting bacteria and archaea whole.

Large size has a downside, however. As a cell increases in diameter, its volume increases more than its surface area. In other words, the relationship between them—the surface-area-to-volume ratio—changes. Since the surface is where the cell exchanges substances with its environment, the reduction in this ratio decreases the rate of exchange: Diffusion only allows for rapid movement across very small distances.

Prokaryotic cells tend to be small enough so that ions and small molecules arrive where they are needed via diffusion. The random movement of diffusion alone, however, is insufficient for this type of transport as the cell's diameter increases.

The Benefits of Organelles

How do eukaryotic cells solve the problems that size can engender? The answer lies in their numerous organelles. In effect, the huge volume inside a eukaryotic cell is compartmentalized into many small bins. Because eukaryotic cells are subdivided, the **cytosol**—the fluid portion between the plasma membrane and these organelles—is only a fraction of the total cell volume. This relatively small volume of cytosol reduces the effect of the total cell surface-area-to-volume ratio with respect to the exchange of nutrients and waste products.

Compartmentalization also offers two key advantages:

1. Incompatible chemical reactions can be separated. For example, new fatty acids can be synthesized in one organelle while

excess or damaged fatty acids are degraded and recycled in a different organelle.

2. Chemical reactions become more efficient. First, the substrates required for particular reactions can be localized and maintained at high concentrations within organelles. Second, if substrates are used up in a particular part of the organelle, they can be replaced by substrates that have only a short distance to diffuse. Third, groups of enzymes that work together can be clustered within or on the membranes of organelles instead of floating free in the cytosol. When the product of one reaction is the substrate for a second reaction catalyzed by another enzyme, clustering the enzymes increases the speed and efficiency of both reaction sequences.

If bacteria and archaea can be compared to small, specialized machine shops, then eukaryotic cells resemble sprawling industrial complexes. The organelles and other structures found in eukaryotes are analogous to highly specialized buildings that act as administrative centers, factories, transportation corridors, waste and recycling facilities, warehouses, and power stations.

When typical prokaryotic and eukaryotic cells are compared, four key differences, identified in **TABLE 7.1**, stand out:

1. Eukaryotic chromosomes are found inside a membrane-bound compartment called the **nucleus.**

2. Eukaryotic cells are often much larger than prokaryotes.

3. Eukaryotic cells contain extensive amounts of internal membrane.

4. Eukaryotic cells feature a particularly diverse and dynamic cytoskeleton.

Eukaryotic Cell Structures: A Parts List

FIGURE 7.6 provides a simplified view of a typical animal cell and a plant cell. The artist has removed most of the cytoskeletal elements

SUMMARY TABLE 7.1 How Do the Structures of Prokaryotic and Eukaryotic Cells Differ?

	Bacteria and Archaea	Eukaryotes
Location of DNA	In nucleoid (not membrane bound); plasmids also common	Inside nucleus (membrane bound); plasmids extremely rare
Internal Membranes and Organelles	Extensive internal membranes only in photosynthetic species; limited types and numbers of organelles	Large numbers of organelles; many types of organelles
Cytoskeleton	Limited in extent, relative to eukaryotes	Extensive—usually found throughout volume of cell
Overall Size	Usually small relative to eukaryotes	Most are larger than prokaryotes

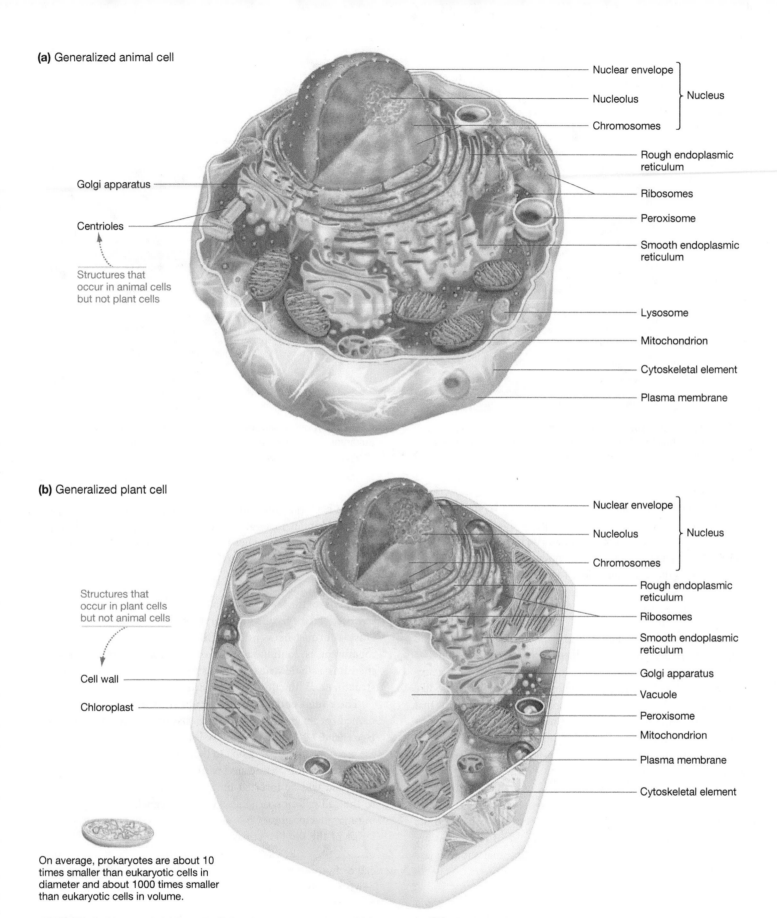

(a) Generalized animal cell

Nuclear envelope ⎱
Nucleolus ⎰ Nucleus
Chromosomes ⎱

Rough endoplasmic reticulum

Ribosomes

Peroxisome

Smooth endoplasmic reticulum

Lysosome

Mitochondrion

Cytoskeletal element

Plasma membrane

Golgi apparatus

Centrioles

Structures that occur in animal cells but not plant cells

(b) Generalized plant cell

Nuclear envelope ⎱
Nucleolus ⎰ Nucleus
Chromosomes ⎱

Rough endoplasmic reticulum

Ribosomes

Smooth endoplasmic reticulum

Golgi apparatus

Vacuole

Peroxisome

Mitochondrion

Plasma membrane

Cytoskeletal element

Structures that occur in plant cells but not animal cells

Cell wall

Chloroplast

On average, prokaryotes are about 10 times smaller than eukaryotic cells in diameter and about 1000 times smaller than eukaryotic cells in volume.

FIGURE 7.6 Overview of Eukaryotic Cells. Generalized images of **(a)** animal and **(b)** plant cells that illustrate the cellular structures in the "typical" eukaryote. The structures have been color-coded for clarity. Compare with the prokaryotic cell, shown at true relative size at bottom left.

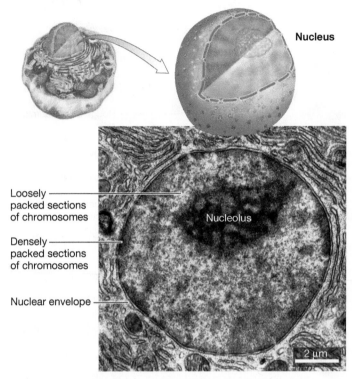

Nucleus

Loosely packed sections of chromosomes

Nucleolus

Densely packed sections of chromosomes

Nuclear envelope

2 μm

FIGURE 7.7 The Nucleus Stores and Transmits Information. The genetic, or hereditary, information is encoded in DNA, which is a component of the chromosomes inside the nucleus.

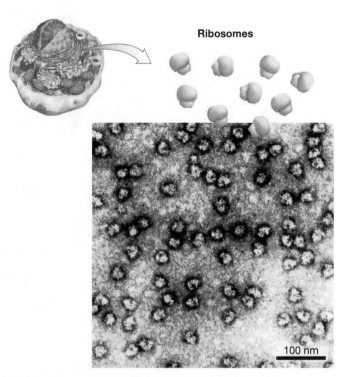

Ribosomes

100 nm

FIGURE 7.8 Ribosomes Are the Site of Protein Synthesis. Eukaryotic ribosomes are larger than bacterial and archaeal ribosomes, but similar in overall structure.

to make the organelles and other cellular parts easier to see. As you read about each cell component in the pages that follow, focus on identifying how its structure correlates with its function. Then use **TABLE 7.2** (see page 117) as a study guide. As with bacterial cells, let's start from the inside and move to the outside.

The Nucleus   The nucleus contains the chromosomes and functions as an administrative center for information storage and processing. Among the largest and most highly organized of all organelles (**FIGURE 7.7**), it is enclosed by a unique structure—a complex double membrane called the **nuclear envelope.** As Section 7.4 will detail, the nuclear envelope is studded with pore-like openings, and the inside surface is linked to fibrous proteins that form a lattice-like sheet called the **nuclear lamina.** The nuclear lamina stiffens the structure and maintains its shape.

Chromosomes do not float freely inside the nucleus—instead, each chromosome occupies a distinct area, which may vary in different cell types and over the course of cell replication. The nucleus also contains specific sites where gene products are processed and includes at least one distinctive region called the **nucleolus,** where the RNA molecules found in ribosomes are manufactured and the large and small ribosomal subunits are assembled.

Ribosomes   In eukaryotes, the cytoplasm consists of everything inside the plasma membrane excluding the nucleus. Scattered throughout this cytoplasm are millions of ribosomes (**FIGURE 7.8**).

Like bacterial ribosomes, eukaryotic ribosomes are complex macromolecular machines that manufacture proteins. They are not classified as organelles because they are not surrounded by membranes.

Endoplasmic Reticulum   The portions of the nuclear envelope extend into the cytoplasm to form an extensive membrane-enclosed factory called the **endoplasmic reticulum** (literally, "inside-formed-network"), or ER. As Figure 7.6 shows, the ER membrane is continuous with the nuclear envelope. Although the ER is a single structure, it has two regions that are distinct in structure and function. Let's consider each region in turn.

The **rough endoplasmic reticulum (RER),** or **rough ER,** is named for its appearance in transmission electron micrographs (see **FIGURE 7.9**, left). The knobby-looking structures in the rough ER are ribosomes that attach to the membrane.

The ribosomes associated with the rough ER synthesize proteins that will be inserted into the plasma membrane, secreted to the cell exterior, or shipped to an organelle. As they are being manufactured by ribosomes, these proteins move to the interior of the sac-like component of the rough ER. The interior of the rough ER, like the interior of any sac-like structure in a cell or body, is called the **lumen.** In the lumen of the rough ER, newly manufactured proteins undergo folding and other types of processing.

The proteins produced in the rough ER have a variety of functions. Some carry messages to other cells; some act as membrane

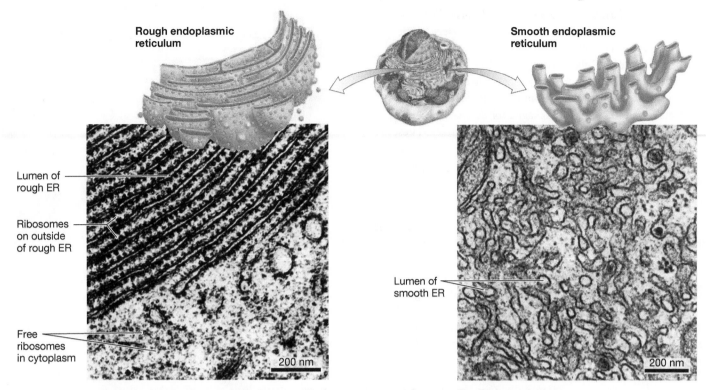

FIGURE 7.9 The Endoplasmic Reticulum Is a Site of Synthesis, Processing, and Storage. The ER is continuous with the nuclear envelope and possesses two distinct regions: on the left, the rough ER is a system of membrane-bound sacs and tubules with ribosomes attached; on the right, the smooth ER is a system of membrane-bound sacs and tubules that lacks ribosomes.

transport proteins or pumps; others are enzymes. The common theme is that many of the rough ER products are packaged into vesicles and transported to various distant destinations—often to the surface of the cell or beyond.

In electron micrographs, parts of the ER that are free of ribosomes appear smooth and even. Appropriately, these parts of the ER are called the **smooth endoplasmic reticulum (SER),** or **smooth ER** (see **FIGURE 7.9**, right).

The smooth ER contains enzymes that catalyze reactions involving lipids. Depending on the type of cell, these enzymes may synthesize lipids needed by the organism or break down lipids and other molecules that are poisonous. For example, the smooth ER is the manufacturing site for phospholipids used in plasma membranes. In addition, the smooth ER functions as a reservoir for calcium ions (Ca^{2+}) that act as a signal triggering a wide array of activities inside the cell.

The structure of the endoplasmic reticulum correlates closely with its function. The rough ER has ribosomes and functions primarily as a protein-manufacturing center; the smooth ER lacks ribosomes and functions primarily as a lipid-processing center.

Golgi Apparatus In many cases, the products of the rough ER pass through the Golgi apparatus before they reach their final destination. The **Golgi apparatus** consists of discrete flattened, membranous sacs called **cisternae** (singular: **cisterna**), which are stacked on top of one another (**FIGURE 7.10**). The organelle also

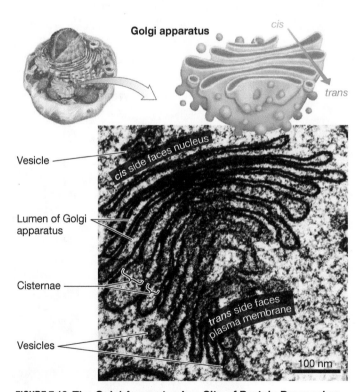

FIGURE 7.10 The Golgi Apparatus Is a Site of Protein Processing, Sorting, and Shipping. The Golgi apparatus is a collection of flattened vesicles called cisternae.

has a distinct polarity, or sidedness. The *cis* ("this side") surface is closest to the nucleus, and the *trans* ("across") surface is oriented toward the plasma membrane.

The *cis* side of a Golgi apparatus receives products from the rough ER, and the *trans* side ships them out to other organelles or the cell surface. In between, within the cisternae, the rough ER's products are processed and packaged for delivery. Micrographs often show "bubbles" on either side of the Golgi stack. These are membrane-bound vesicles that carry proteins or other products to and from the organelle. Section 7.5 analyzes the intracellular movement of molecules from the rough ER to the Golgi apparatus and beyond in more detail.

Lysosomes Animal cells contain organelles called **lysosomes** that function as recycling centers (**FIGURE 7.11**). Lysosomes contain about 40 different enzymes, each specialized for hydrolyzing different types of macromolecules—proteins, nucleic acids, lipids, or carbohydrates. The amino acids, nucleotides, sugars, and other molecules that result from acid hydrolysis leave the lysosome via transport proteins in the organelle's membrane. Once in the cytosol, they can be used as sources of energy or building blocks for new molecules.

These digestive enzymes are collectively called acid hydrolases because under acidic conditions (pH of 5.0), they use water to break monomers from macromolecules. In the cytosol, where the pH is about 7.2, acid hydrolases are less active. Proton pumps in the lysosomal membrane maintain an acidic pH in the lumen of the lysosome by importing hydrogen ions.

Even though lysosomes are physically separated from the Golgi apparatus and the endoplasmic reticulum, these various

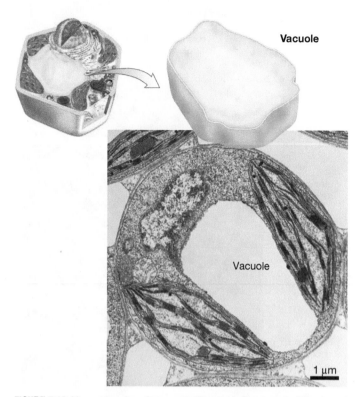

FIGURE 7.12 Vacuoles Are Generally Storage Centers in Plant and Fungal Cells. Vacuoles vary in size and function. Some contain digestive enzymes and serve as recycling centers; most are large storage containers.

✔**QUESTION** Why are toxins like nicotine, cocaine, and caffeine stored in vacuoles instead of the cytosol?

organelles jointly form a key functional grouping referred to as the **endomembrane system.** The endomembrane ("inner-membrane") system is a center for producing, processing, and transporting proteins and lipids in eukaryotic cells. For example, acid hydrolases are synthesized in the ER, processed in the Golgi, and then shipped to the lysosome.

Vacuoles The cells of plants, fungi, and certain other groups lack lysosomes. Instead, they contain a prominent organelle called a vacuole. Compared with the lysosomes of animal cells, the **vacuoles** of plant and fungal cells are large—sometimes taking up as much as 80 percent of a plant cell's volume (**FIGURE 7.12**).

Although some vacuoles contain enzymes that are specialized for digestion, most of the vacuoles observed in plant and fungal cells act as storage depots. In many cases, ions such as potassium (K^+) and chloride (Cl^-), among other solutes, are stored at such high concentrations they draw water in from the environment. As the vacuole expands in volume, the cytoplasm pushes the plasma membrane against the cell wall, which maintains the plant cell's shape. In other cells, vacuoles have more specialized storage functions:

- Inside seeds, cells may contain a large vacuole filled with proteins. When the embryonic plant inside the seed begins to grow, enzymes begin digesting these proteins to provide amino acids for the growing individual.

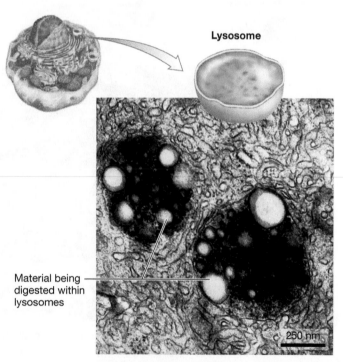

Material being digested within lysosomes

FIGURE 7.11 Lysosomes Are Recycling Centers. Lysosomes are usually oval or globular and have a single membrane.

- In cells that make up flower petals or fruits, vacuoles are filled with colorful pigments.

- Elsewhere, vacuoles may be packed with noxious compounds that protect leaves and stems from being eaten by predators. The type of chemical involved varies by species, ranging from bitter-tasting tannins to toxins such as nicotine, morphine, caffeine, or cocaine.

Peroxisomes Virtually all eukaryotic cells contain globular organelles called **peroxisomes** (**FIGURE 7.13**). These organelles have a single membrane and originate as buds from the ER.

Although different types of cells from the same individual may have distinct types of peroxisomes, these organelles all share a common function: Peroxisomes are centers for reduction–oxidation (redox) reactions. (Chapter 8 explains in detail how redox reactions transfer electrons between atoms and molecules.) For example, the peroxisomes in your liver cells contain enzymes that remove electrons from, or oxidize, the ethanol in alcoholic beverages.

Different types of peroxisomes contain different suites of redox enzymes. In the leaves of plants, specialized peroxisomes called **glyoxysomes** are packed with enzymes that oxidize fats to form a compound that can be used to store energy for the cell. But plant seeds have a different type of peroxisome—one that is packed with enzymes responsible for releasing energy from stored fatty acids. The young plant uses this energy as it begins to grow.

In animals and plants, the products of these reactions often include hydrogen peroxide (H_2O_2), which is highly reactive.

If hydrogen peroxide escaped from the peroxisome, it would quickly react with and damage DNA, proteins, and cellular membranes. This event is rare, however, because inside the peroxisome, the enzyme catalase quickly "detoxifies" hydrogen peroxide by catalyzing its oxidation to form water and oxygen. The enzymes found inside the peroxisome make a specialized set of oxidation reactions possible and safe for the cell.

Mitochondria The energy required to build these organelles and do other types of work comes from adenosine triphosphate (ATP), most of which is produced in the cell's **mitochondria** (singular: **mitochondrion**).

As **FIGURE 7.14** shows, each mitochondrion has two membranes. The outer membrane defines the organelle's surface, while the inner membrane is connected to a series of sac-like **cristae**. The solution enclosed within the inner membrane is called the **mitochondrial matrix.** In eukaryotes, most of the enzymes and molecular machines responsible for synthesizing ATP are embedded in the membranes of the cristae or suspended in the matrix (see Chapter 9). Depending on the type of cell, from 50 to more than a million mitochondria may be present.

Each mitochondrion has many copies of a small, circular chromosome that is independent of the nuclear chromosomes. This mitochondrial DNA contains only around 37 genes in most eukaryotes—most of the genes responsible for the function of the organelle reside in the nuclear DNA.

Among the genes present in mitochondrial DNA are those that encode RNAs for mitochondrial ribosomes. These ribosomes are

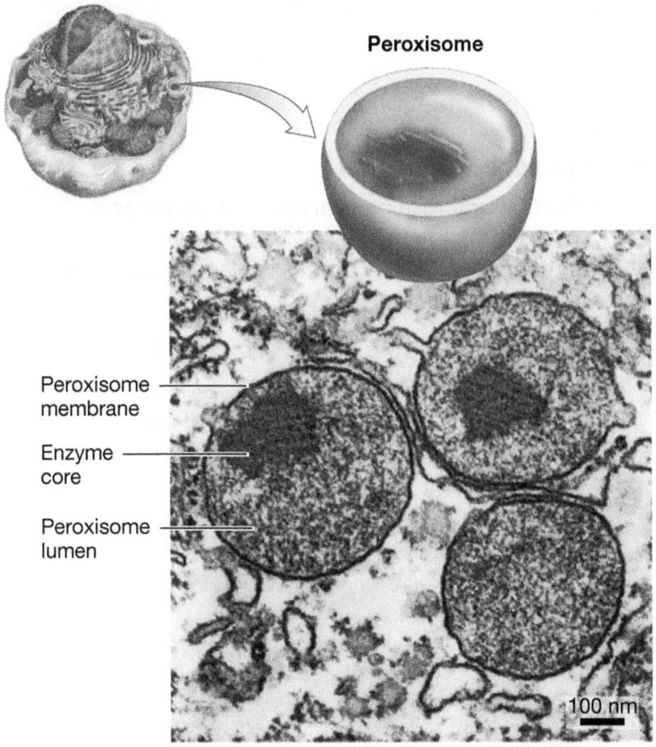

Peroxisome

Peroxisome membrane

Enzyme core

Peroxisome lumen

100 nm

FIGURE 7.13 Peroxisomes Are the Site of Oxidation Reactions. Peroxisomes are globular organelles that are defined by a single membrane.

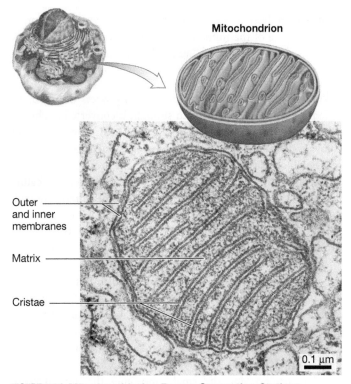

Mitochondrion

Outer and inner membranes

Matrix

Cristae

0.1 μm

FIGURE 7.14 Mitochondria Are Power-Generating Stations. Mitochondria vary in size and shape, but all have a double membrane with sac-like cristae inside.

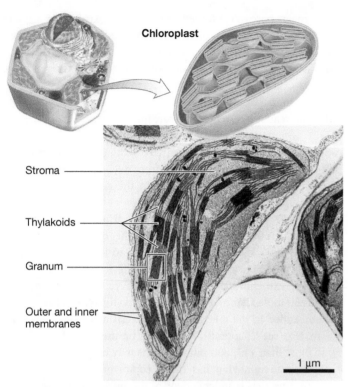

Chloroplast

Stroma

Thylakoids

Granum

Outer and inner
membranes

1 µm

FIGURE 7.15 Chloroplasts Are Sugar-Manufacturing Centers in Plants and Algae. Many of the enzymes and other molecules required for photosynthesis are located in membranes inside the chloroplast. These membranes form thylakoids that consist of discs stacked into grana.

smaller than those found in the cytosol, yet they still function to produce some of the mitochondrial proteins. (Most of the proteins found in mitochondria are produced from ribosomes in the cytosol and imported into the organelle.)

Chloroplasts   Most algal and plant cells possess an organelle called the **chloroplast,** in which sunlight is converted to chemical energy during photosynthesis (**FIGURE 7.15**). The number of chloroplasts per cell varies from none to several dozen.

The chloroplast has a double membrane around its exterior, analogous to the structure of a mitochondrion. Instead of featuring sac-like cristae that connect to the inner membrane, though, the interior of the chloroplast is dominated by a network of hundreds of membrane-bound, flattened, sac-like structures called **thylakoids,** which are independent of the inner membrane.

Thylakoids have stacks, like pancakes, that are called **grana** (singular: **granum**). Many of the pigments, enzymes, and macromolecular machines responsible for converting light energy into chemical energy are embedded in the thylakoid membranes. The region outside the thylakoids, called the **stroma,** contains enzymes that use this chemical energy to produce sugars.

Like mitochondria, each chloroplast contains copies of a circular chromosome and small ribosomes that manufacture some, but not all, of the organelle's proteins. Both mitochondria

and chloroplasts also grow and divide independently of cell division through a process that resembles bacterial fission (see Chapter 12).

These attributes are odd compared with those of the other organelles and have led biologists to propose that mitochondria and chloroplasts were once free-living bacteria. According to the **endosymbiosis theory,** the ancestors of modern eukaryotes ingested these bacteria, but instead of destroying them, established a mutually beneficial relationship with them. (In Chapter 30, you will learn more about the origins of these eukaryotic organelles.)

Cytoskeleton   The final major structural feature that is common to all eukaryotic cells is the cytoskeleton, an extensive system of protein fibers. In addition to giving the cell its shape and structural stability, cytoskeletal proteins are involved in moving the cell itself and moving materials within the cell. In essence, the cytoskeleton organizes all the organelles and other cellular structures into a cohesive whole. Section 7.6 will analyze the structure and functions of the cytoskeleton in detail.

The Cell Wall   In fungi, algae, and plants, cells possess an outer cell wall in addition to their plasma membrane. The cell wall is located outside the plasma membrane and furnishes a durable, outer layer that provides structural support for the cell. The cells of animals, amoebae, and other groups lack a cell wall—their exterior surface consists of the plasma membrane only.

Although the composition of the cell wall varies among species and even among types of cells in the same individual, the general plan is similar: Rods or fibers composed of a carbohydrate run through a stiff matrix made of other polysaccharides and proteins (see Chapter 11 for details).

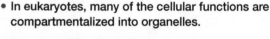

If you understand that . . .

- Each structure in a eukaryotic cell performs a function vital to the cell.
- In eukaryotes, many of the cellular functions are compartmentalized into organelles.

✓ **You should be able to . . .**

1. Explain how the structure of lysosomes and peroxisomes correlates with their function.

2. In Table 7.2, label each component with one of the following roles: administrative/information hub, power station, warehouse, large molecule manufacturing and shipping facility (with subtitles for lipid factory, protein finishing and shipping line, protein synthesis and folding center, waste processing and recycling center), support beams, perimeter fencing with secured gates, protein factory, food-manufacturing facility, and fatty-acid processing and detox center.

Answers are available in Appendix A.

Icons Not to Scale		Structure		Function
		Membrane	**Components**	
	Nucleus	Double ("envelope"); openings called nuclear pores	Chromosomes	Information storage and transmission
			Nucleolus	Ribosome subunit assembly
			Nuclear lamina	Structural support
	Ribosomes	None	Complex of RNA and proteins	Protein synthesis
	Endomembrane system			
	Endoplasmic reticulum: rough	Single; contains receptors for entry of selected proteins	Network of branching sacs	Protein synthesis and processing
			Ribosomes associated	
	Endoplasmic reticulum: smooth	Single; contains enzymes for synthesizing phospholipids	Network of branching sacs	Lipid synthesis and processing
			Enzymes for synthesizing or breaking down lipids	
	Golgi apparatus	Single; contains receptors for products of rough ER	Stack of flattened, distinct cisternae	Protein, lipid, and carbohydrate processing
	Lysosomes	Single; contains proton pumps	Acid hydrolases (catalyze hydrolysis reactions)	Digestion and recycling
	Vacuoles	Single; contains transporters for selected molecules	Varies—pigments, oils, carbohydrates, water, or toxins	Varies—coloration, storage of oils, carbohydrates, water, or toxins
	Peroxisomes	Single; contains transporters for selected macromolecules	Enzymes that catalyze oxidation reactions	Oxidation of fatty acids, ethanol, or other compounds
			Catalase (processes peroxide)	
	Mitochondria	Double; inner contains enzymes for ATP production	Enzymes that harvest energy from molecules to make ATP	ATP production
	Chloroplasts	Double; plus membrane-bound sacs in interior	Pigments	Production of sugars via photosynthesis
			Enzymes that use light energy to make sugars	
	Cytoskeleton	None	Actin filaments	Structural support; movement of materials; in some species, movement of whole cell
			Intermediate filaments	
			Microtubules	
	Plasma membrane	Single; contains transport and receptor proteins	Phospholipid bilayer with transport and receptor proteins	Selective permeability—maintains intracellular environment
	Cell wall	None	Carbohydrate fibers running through carbohydrate or protein matrix	Protection, structural support

7.3 Putting the Parts into a Whole

Within a cell, the structure of each component correlates with its function. In the same way, the overall size, shape, and composition of a cell correlate with its function.

Cells might be analogous to machine shops or industrial complexes, but clothing manufacturing centers are very different in layout and composition from airplane production facilities. How does the physical and chemical makeup of a cell correlate with its function?

Structure and Function at the Whole-Cell Level

Inside an individual plant or animal, cells are specialized for certain tasks and have a structure that correlates with those tasks. For example, the muscle cells in your upper leg are extremely long, tube-shaped structures. They are filled with protein fibers that slide past one another as the entire muscle flexes or relaxes. It is this sliding motion that allows your muscles to contract or extend as you run. Muscle cells are also packed with mitochondria, which produce the ATP required for the sliding motion to occur.

In contrast, nearby fat cells are rounded, globular structures that store fatty acids. They consist of little more than a plasma membrane, a nucleus, and a fat droplet. Neither cell bears a close resemblance to the generalized animal cell pictured in Figure 7.6a.

To drive home the correlation between the overall structure and function of a cell, examine the transmission electron micrographs in **FIGURE 7.16**.

- The animal cell in Figure 7.16a, located in the pancreas, manufactures and exports digestive enzymes. It is packed with rough ER and Golgi, which make these functions possible.

- The animal cell in Figure 7.16b, from the testis, synthesizes and exports the steroid hormone testosterone—a lipid-soluble signal. This cell is dominated by smooth ER, where processing of steroids and other lipids takes place.

- The plant cell in Figure 7.16c, from the leaf of a potato, has hundreds of chloroplasts and is specialized for absorbing light and manufacturing sugar.

- The animal cells in Figure 7.16d come from brown fat. The cells have numerous mitochondria that have been altered so they convert energy stored in fat into heat instead of ATP.

In each case, the types of organelles in each cell and their size and number correlate with the cell's specialized function.

The Dynamic Cell

Biologists study the structure and function of organelles and cells with a combination of tools and approaches. For several decades, a technique called **differential centrifugation** was particularly important because it allowed researchers to isolate particular cell components and analyze their chemical composition. Differential centrifugation is based on breaking cells apart to create a complex mixture and separating components in a centrifuge (see **BioSkills 10** in Appendix B). The individual parts of the cell

(a) Animal pancreatic cell: Exports digestive enzymes.

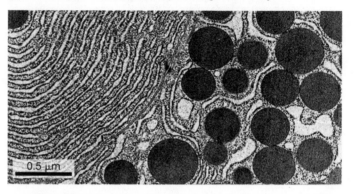

(b) Animal testis cell: Exports lipid-soluble signals.

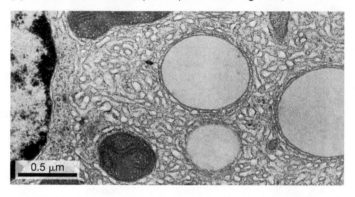

(c) Plant leaf cell: Manufactures ATP and sugar.

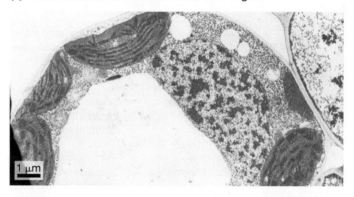

(d) Brown fat cells: Burn fat to generate heat in lieu of ATP.

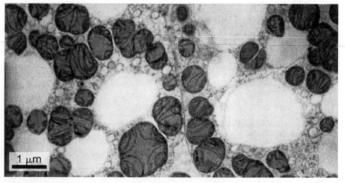

FIGURE 7.16 Cell Structure Correlates with Function.
✔**EXERCISE** In part (a), label the rough ER and the dark, round secretory vesicles. In (b), label the smooth ER. In (c), label the chloroplasts, vacuole, and nucleus. In (d), label the mitochondria.

can then be purified and studied in detail, in isolation from other parts of the cell.

Historically and currently, however, the most important research in cell biology is based on imaging—simply looking at cells. Recent innovations allow biologists to put fluorescing tags or other types of markers on particular cell components and then look at them with increasingly sophisticated light microscopes and electron microscopes. Advances in microscopy provide increasingly high magnification and better resolution.

It's important to recognize, though, that some of these techniques have limitations. Differential centrifugation splits cells into parts that are analyzed independently, and electron microscopy gives a fixed "snapshot" of the cell or organisms being observed. Neither technique allows investigators to explore directly how things move from place to place in the cell or how parts interact. The information gleaned from these techniques can make cells seem static. In reality, cells are dynamic.

The amount of chemical activity and the speed of molecular movement inside cells are nothing short of fantastic. Bacterial ribosomes add up to 20 amino acids per second to a growing polypeptide, and eukaryotic ribosomes typically add 2 per second. Given that there are about 15,000 ribosomes in each bacterium and possibly a million in an average eukaryotic cell, hundreds or even thousands of new protein molecules can be produced each second in every cell. Here are some other remarkable cellular feats:

- In an average second, a typical cell in your body uses an average of 10 million ATP molecules and synthesizes just as many.

- It's not unusual for a cellular enzyme to catalyze 25,000 or more reactions per second; most cells contain hundreds or thousands of different enzymes.

- A minute is more than enough time for each membrane phospholipid in your body to travel the breadth of the organelle or cell where it resides.

- The hundreds of trillions of mitochondria inside you are completely replaced about every 10 days, for as long as you live.

Because humans are such large organisms, it's impossible for us to imagine what life is really like inside a cell. At the scale of a ribosome or an organelle or a cell, gravity is inconsequential. Instead, the dominant forces are the charge- or polarity-based electrostatic attractions between molecules and their energy of motion. At this level, events take nanoseconds, and speeds are measured in micrometers per second. This is the speed of life.

Contemporary methods for studying cells (including some of the imaging techniques featured in **BioSkills 11** in Appendix B) capture this dynamism by tracking how organelles and molecules move and interact over time. The ability to digitize video images of live cells, or take time-lapse photographs of living cells, is allowing researchers to see and study dynamic processes.

The rest of this chapter focuses on this theme of cellular dynamism and movement. Its goal is to put some of the individual pieces of a cell together and ask how they work as systems to accomplish key tasks.

To begin, let's first look at how molecules move into and out of the cell's control center—the nucleus—and then consider how proteins move from ribosomes into the lumen of the rough ER and then to the Golgi apparatus and beyond. The chapter closes by introducing the cytoskeletal elements and their associated motor proteins and how they are used to transport cargo inside the cell or move the cell itself.

7.4 Cell Systems I: Nuclear Transport

The nucleus is the information center of eukaryotic cells—a corporate headquarters, design center, and library all rolled into one. Appropriately enough, its interior is highly organized.

The organelle's overall shape and structure are defined by the mesh-like nuclear lamina. The nuclear lamina provides an attachment point for the chromosomes, each of which occupies a well-defined region in the nucleus.

In addition, specific centers exist where the genetic information in DNA is decoded and processed. At these locations, large suites of enzymes interact to produce RNA messages from specific genes at specific times. Meanwhile, the nucleolus functions as the site of ribosome assembly.

Structure and Function of the Nuclear Envelope

The nuclear envelope separates the nucleus from the rest of the cell. Starting in the 1950s, transmission electron micrographs of cross sections through the nuclear envelope showed that the structure is supported by the fibrous nuclear lamina and bounded by two membranes, each consisting of a lipid bilayer. How does this administrative center communicate with the rest of the cell across the double membrane barrier?

Micrographs like the one in **FIGURE 7.17** (see page 120) show that the nuclear envelope is broken with openings, approximately 60 nanometers (nm) in diameter, called **nuclear pores.** Because these pores extend through both the inner and outer nuclear membranes, they connect the inside of the nucleus with the cytosol. Follow-up research showed that each pore consists of over 50 different proteins. As the diagram on the right side of Figure 7.17 shows, these protein molecules form an elaborate structure called the **nuclear pore complex.**

What substances traverse nuclear pores? Chromosomal DNA clearly does not—it remains in the nucleus as long as the nuclear envelope remains intact. But DNA is used to synthesize RNA inside the nucleus, most of which is exported through nuclear pores to the cytoplasm.

Several types of RNA molecules are produced, each distinguished by size and function. For example, **ribosomal RNAs** are manufactured in the nucleolus, where they bind to proteins to form ribosomes. Molecules called **messenger RNAs (mRNA)** carry the information required to manufacture proteins. Both the newly assembled ribosomes and the mRNAs must be transported from the nucleus to the cytoplasm, where protein synthesis takes place.

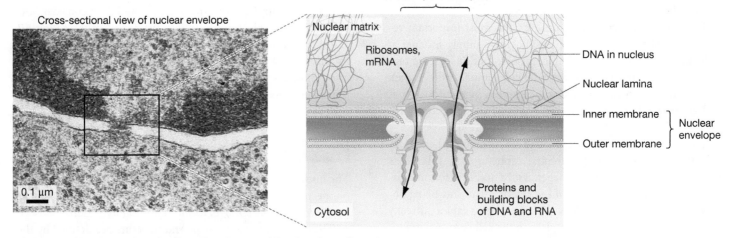

Cross-sectional view of nuclear envelope

Nuclear pore complex

Nuclear matrix

Ribosomes, mRNA

DNA in nucleus

Nuclear lamina

Inner membrane

Outer membrane

Nuclear envelope

0.1 μm

Proteins and building blocks of DNA and RNA

Cytosol

FIGURE 7.17 Structure of the Nuclear Envelope and Nuclear Pore Complex.

Inbound traffic is also impressive. Nucleoside triphosphates that act as building blocks for DNA and RNA enter the nucleus, as do a variety of proteins responsible for copying DNA, synthesizing RNAs, extending the nuclear lamina, or assembling ribosomes.

To summarize, ribosomal subunits and various types of RNAs exit the nucleus; nucleotides and certain proteins enter it. In a typical cell, over 500 molecules pass through each of the 3000–4000 nuclear pores every second. The scale of traffic through the nuclear pores is mind-boggling. How is it regulated and directed?

Experiments in the early 1960s showed that size matters in the passage of molecules through nuclear pores. This conclusion was based on the results from injecting tiny gold particles that varied in diameter and tracking their movement across the pores. In electron micrographs, gold particles show up as defined black dots that can be easily distinguished from cellular structures. Immediately after injection, most of the gold particles were observed in the cytoplasm, and only a few were closely associated with nuclear pores. Ten minutes after injection, only the small particles (< 12.5 nm in diameter) appeared to be distributed throughout both the nucleus and the cytoplasm, and the larger particles were excluded from entering the nucleus.

The fact that the pore opening is almost 5 times larger than this 12.5-nm size limit supports the hypothesis that the nuclear pore complex serves as a gate to control passage through the envelope. If this is the case, then what is required to open these gates so that proteins larger than the size limit, like those responsible for replicating DNA, may pass?

How Do Large Molecules Enter the Nucleus?

It was clear to researchers that size was not the sole factor in selective transport across the nuclear envelope. Certain proteins were concentrated in the nucleus, while others were completely excluded—even if they were similar in size.

A series of experiments on a protein called nucleoplasmin helped researchers understand the nature of nuclear import. Nucleoplasmin is strictly found in the nucleus and plays an important role in the assembly of chromatin. When researchers labeled nucleoplasmin with a radioactive atom and injected it into the cytoplasm of living cells, they found that the radioactive protein was quickly concentrated into the nucleus. Is there a "send-to-nucleus" signal within the nucleoplasmin protein that is responsible for this directed transport?

As shown in **FIGURE 7.18**, the distinctive structure of nucleoplasmin was used to further investigate this process. First, researchers used enzymes called proteases to cleave the core sections of nucleoplasmin from the tails. After separating the tails from the core fragments, they labeled each component with radioactive atoms and injected them into the cytoplasm of different cells.

At various times after the injections, researchers examined the nuclei and cytoplasm of the cells to track down the radioactive label. The results were striking. They found that tail fragments were rapidly transported from the cytoplasm into the nucleus. Core fragments, in contrast, were not allowed to pass through the nuclear envelope and remained in the cytoplasm.

These data led to a key hypothesis: Nuclear proteins are synthesized by ribosomes in the cytosol and contain a "zip code"—a molecular address tag—that marks them for transport through the nuclear pore complex. This zip code allows the nuclear pore complex to open in some way that permits larger proteins and RNA molecules to pass through.

By analyzing different stretches of the tail, the biologists eventually found a 17-amino-acid-long section that had to be present to direct nucleoplasmin to the nucleus. Follow-up work confirmed that other proteins bound for the nucleus, even those expressed by some viruses, have similar amino acid sequences directing their transport. This common sequence came to be called the **nuclear localization signal (NLS).** Proteins that leave the nucleus have a different signal, required for nuclear export.

QUESTION: Does the nucleoplasmin protein contain a "Send to nucleus" signal?

HYPOTHESIS: Nucleoplasmin contains a discrete "Send to nucleus" signal that resides in either the tail or core region.

NULL HYPOTHESIS: Nucleoplasmin does not require a signal to enter the nucleus, or the entire protein serves as the signal.

EXPERIMENTAL SETUP:

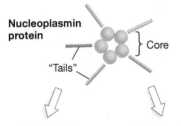

Nucleoplasmin protein

"Tails"

Core

1. Use protease to cleave tails off of nucleoplasmin protein core.

Labeled tails   Labeled cores

2. Attach radioactive labels to protein tails and cores.

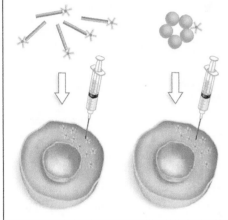

3. Inject labeled tails and cores into cytoplasm of different cells.

4. Wait, then locate labeled fragments ....

PREDICTION:

PREDICTION OF NULL HYPOTHESIS:

RESULTS:

Labeled tail fragments **located in nucleus**   Labeled core fragments still **located in cytoplasm**

CONCLUSION:

FIGURE 7.18 Does the Nucleoplasmin Protein Contain a "Send to Nucleus" Signal?

SOURCES: Mills, A. D., R. A. Laskey, P. Black, et al. 1980. *Journal of Molecular Biology* 139: 561–568; Dingwall, C., S. V. Sharnick, and R. A. Laskey. 1982. *Cell* 30: 449–458.

✔**EXERCISE** Without looking at the text, fill in the prediction(s) and conclusion(s) in this experiment.

More recent research has shown that the movement of proteins and other large molecules into and out of the nucleus is an energy-demanding process that involves special transport proteins. These nuclear transport proteins function like trucks that haul cargo into or out of the nucleus through the nuclear pore complex, depending on whether they have an import or export zip code. Currently, biologists are trying to unravel how all this traffic in and out of the nucleus is regulated to avoid backups and head-on collisions.

✔ If you understand the process of nuclear transport, you should be able to compare and contrast the movement of (1) nucleotides and (2) large proteins through the nuclear pore complex. Which would you expect to require the input of energy?

7.5 Cell Systems II: The Endomembrane System Manufactures, Ships, and Recycles Cargo

The nuclear membrane is not the only place in cells where cargo moves in a regulated and energy-demanding fashion. Most of the proteins found in peroxisomes, mitochondria, and chloroplasts are also actively imported from the cytosol. These proteins contain special signal sequences, like the nuclear localization signal, that target them to the appropriate organelles.

If you think about it for a moment, the need to sort proteins and ship them to specific destinations should be clear. Proteins are produced by ribosomes that are either free in the cytosol or on the surface of the ER. Many of these proteins must be transported to a compartment inside the eukaryotic cell. Acid hydrolases must be shipped to lysosomes and catalase to peroxisomes. To get to the right location, each protein has to have an address tag and a transport and delivery system.

To get a better understanding of protein sorting and transport in eukaryotic cells, let's consider perhaps the most intricate of all manufacturing and shipping complexes: the endomembrane system. In this system, proteins that are synthesized in the rough ER move to the Golgi apparatus for processing, and from there they travel to the cell surface or other destinations.

Studying the Pathway through the Endomembrane System

The idea that materials move through the endomembrane system in an orderly way was inspired by a simple observation. According to electron micrographs, cells that secrete digestive enzymes, hormones, or other products have particularly large amounts of rough ER and Golgi. This correlation led to the idea that these organelles may participate in a "secretory pathway" that starts in the rough ER and ends with products leaving the cell (**FIGURE 7.19**, see page 122). How does this hypothesized pathway work?

Tracking Protein Movement via Pulse–Chase Assay George Palade and colleagues did pioneering research on the secretory

FIGURE 7.19 The Secretory Pathway Hypothesis. The secretory pathway hypothesis proposes that proteins intended for secretion from the cell are synthesized and processed in a highly prescribed series of steps. Note that proteins are packaged into vesicles when they move from the RER to the Golgi and from the Golgi to the cell surface.

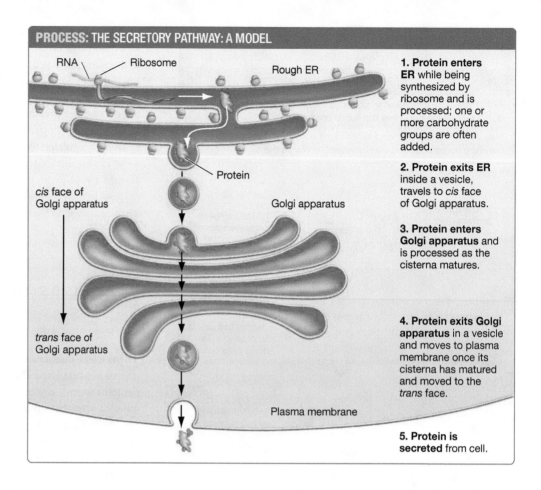

PROCESS: THE SECRETORY PATHWAY: A MODEL

RNA — Ribosome — Rough ER

Protein

cis face of Golgi apparatus

Golgi apparatus

trans face of Golgi apparatus

Plasma membrane

1. Protein enters ER while being synthesized by ribosome and is processed; one or more carbohydrate groups are often added.

2. Protein exits ER inside a vesicle, travels to *cis* face of Golgi apparatus.

3. Protein enters Golgi apparatus and is processed as the cisterna matures.

4. Protein exits Golgi apparatus in a vesicle and moves to plasma membrane once its cisterna has matured and moved to the *trans* face.

5. Protein is secreted from cell.

pathway using a **pulse–chase experiment** to track protein movement. This strategy is based on two steps:

1. *The "Pulse"* Expose experimental cells to a high concentration of a modified amino acid for a short time. For example, if a cell is briefly exposed to a large amount of radioactively labeled amino acid, virtually all the proteins synthesized during that interval will be radiolabeled.

2. *The "Chase"* The pulse ends by washing away the modified amino acid and replacing it with the normal version of the same molecule. The time following the end of the pulse is referred to as the chase. If the chase consists of unlabeled amino acid, then the proteins synthesized during the chase period will *not* be radiolabeled.

The idea is to mark a population of molecules at a particular interval and then follow their fate over time. This approach is analogous to adding a small amount of dye to a stream and then following the movement of the dye molecules.

To understand why the chase is necessary in these experiments, imagine what would happen if you added dye to a stream continuously. Soon the entire stream would be dyed—you could no longer tell where a specific population of dye molecules were moving.

In testing the secretory pathway hypothesis, Palade's team focused on pancreatic cells that were growing in **culture,** or

in vitro.[1] These cells are specialized for secreting digestive enzymes into the small intestine and are packed with rough ER and Golgi.

The basic experimental approach was to pulse the cell culture for 3 minutes with a radiolabeled version of the amino acid leucine, followed by a long chase with nonradioactive leucine (**FIGURE 7.20a**). The pulse produced a population of proteins that were related to one another by the timing of their synthesis. At different points during the chase, the researchers tracked the movement of these proteins by preparing samples of the cells for autoradiography and electron microscopy (see **BioSkills 10** and **11** in Appendix B). The drawings in **FIGURE 7.20b** illustrate what the researchers would have seen in micrographs taken at different times before and after the start of the chase.

Results of the Pulse–Chase Experiment The graph in Figure 7.20b was based on the electron microscopy results, which showed that proteins are trafficked through the secretory pathway in a highly organized and directed manner. Track the movement of proteins through the cell during the chase by covering the graph with a piece of paper and then slowly sliding it off from

---

[1]The term in vitro is Latin for "in glass." Experiments that are performed outside living organisms are done in vitro. The term in vivo, in contrast, is Latin for "in life." Experiments performed with living organisms are done in vivo.

(a) Setup for a pulse-chase experiment

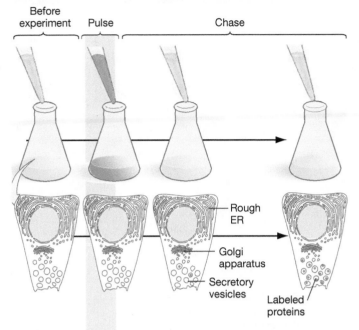

(b) Tracking pulse-labeled proteins during the chase

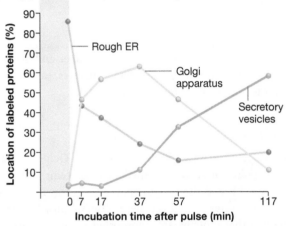

FIGURE 7.20 Tracking Protein Movement in a Pulse–Chase Experiment. Part **(a)** shows how investigators label newly synthesized proteins during the pulse with radioactive amino acids (red). At the start of the chase, this medium is replaced with non-radioactive amino acids (yellow) so only those proteins labeled in the pulse will be tracked. Part **(b)** provides the results of a pulse–chase experiment. The drawings represent micrographs taken that show the radiolabeled proteins (red dots) in the cells. The graph shows the relative abundance of radiolabeled proteins in three different organelles during the chase.

left to right. Notice what is happening to each line at the following three time points:

1. Immediately after the pulse, most of the newly synthesized proteins are inside this cell's rough ER.

2. At 37 minutes into the chase, the situation has changed. Most of the labeled proteins have left the rough ER and entered the

Golgi apparatus, and some of them have accumulated inside structures called secretory vesicles.

3. By the end of the chase, at 117 minutes, most of the labeled proteins have left the Golgi and are either in secretory vesicles or were secreted from the cells.

Over a period of two hours, the labeled population of proteins moved along a defined trail through the rough ER, Golgi apparatus, and secretory vesicles to reach the exterior of the cell. ✔ **QUANTITATIVE** If you understand how the pulse–chase experiment is used to track proteins, use the graph in Figure 7.20b to estimate the time it takes for proteins to pass through the Golgi apparatus.

The results support the hypotheses that a secretory pathway exists and that the rough ER and Golgi apparatus function together as an integrated endomembrane system. Next, let's break this secretory pathway down to examine four of the steps in more detail:

1. How do proteins enter the lumen of the ER?

2. How do the proteins move from the ER to the Golgi apparatus?

3. Once they're inside the Golgi, what happens to them?

4. And finally, how does the Golgi sort out the proteins so each will end up going to the appropriate place?

Entering the Endomembrane System: The Signal Hypothesis

The synthesis of proteins destined to be secreted or embedded in membranes begins in ribosomes free in the cytosol. Günter Blobel and colleagues proposed that at some point these ribosomes become attached to the outside of the ER. But what directs these ribosomes to the ER? The signal hypothesis predicts that proteins bound for the endomembrane system have a molecular zip code analogous to the nuclear localization signal. Blobel proposed that the first few amino acids in the growing polypeptide act as a signal that marks the ribosome for transport to the ER membrane.

This hypothesis received important support when researchers made a puzzling observation: When proteins that are normally synthesized in the rough ER are instead manufactured by isolated ribosomes in vitro—with *no* ER present—they are 20 amino acids longer, on average, than usual.

Blobel seized on these data. He claimed that the extra amino acids are the "send-to-ER" signal, and that the signal is removed inside the organelle. When the same protein is synthesized in vitro, the signal is not removed.

Blobel's group went on to produce convincing data that supported the hypothesis: They identified a sequence of amino acids that will move proteins into the ER lumen, called the **ER signal sequence.**

More recent work has documented the mechanisms responsible for receiving this send-to-ER signal and inserting the

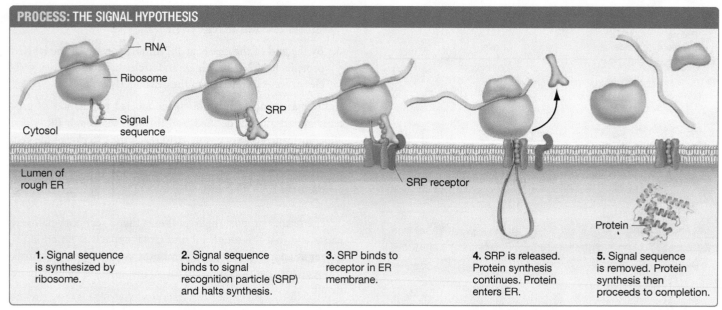

PROCESS: THE SIGNAL HYPOTHESIS

RNA

Ribosome

Signal sequence

Cytosol

SRP

Lumen of rough ER

SRP receptor

Protein

1. Signal sequence is synthesized by ribosome.

2. Signal sequence binds to signal recognition particle (SRP) and halts synthesis.

3. SRP binds to receptor in ER membrane.

4. SRP is released. Protein synthesis continues. Protein enters ER.

5. Signal sequence is removed. Protein synthesis then proceeds to completion.

FIGURE 7.21 The Signal Hypothesis Explains How Proteins Destined for Secretion Enter the Endomembrane System. According to the signal hypothesis, proteins destined for secretion contain a short stretch of amino acids that interact with a signal recognition particle (SRP) in the cytoplasm. This interaction directs the synthesis of the remaining protein into the ER.

protein into the rough ER. **FIGURE 7.21** illustrates the key steps involved.

Step 1 Protein synthesis begins on a free ribosome in the cytosol. The ribosome synthesizes the ER signal sequence.

Step 2 The signal sequence binds to a **signal recognition particle (SRP)**—a complex of RNA and protein. The attached SRP causes protein synthesis to stop.

Step 3 The ribosome + signal sequence + SRP complex moves to the ER membrane, where it attaches to the SRP receptor. Think of the SRP as a key that is activated by an ER signal sequence. The SRP receptor in the ER membrane is the lock.

Step 4 Once the lock (the receptor) and key (the SRP) connect, the SRP is released and protein synthesis continues.

Step 5 The growing protein is fed into the ER lumen through a channel, and the signal sequence is removed.

If the protein will eventually be shipped to the inside of an organelle or secreted from the cell, it is completely transferred into the lumen of the rough ER. If it is an integral membrane protein, part of it remains in the cytosol and rough ER membrane while it is being processed.

Once proteins are inside the rough ER or inserted into its membrane, they fold into their three-dimensional shape with the help of chaperone proteins (see Chapter 3). In addition, proteins that enter the ER lumen interact with enzymes that catalyze the addition of carbohydrate side chains (Figure 7.19). Because carbohydrates are polymers of sugar monomers, the addition of one or more carbohydrate groups is called **glycosylation** ("sugar-together"). The resulting molecule is a **glycoprotein**

("sugar-protein"; see Chapter 5). The number and arrangement of these sugars changes as the protein matures, serving as an indicator for shipment to the next destination.

Moving from the ER to the Golgi

How do proteins travel from the ER to the Golgi apparatus? In Palade's pulse–chase experiment, labeled proteins found between the rough ER and the Golgi apparatus were inside membrane-bound structures. Based on these observations, Palade's group suggested that proteins are transported in vesicles that bud off from the ER, move away, fuse with the membrane on the *cis* face of the Golgi apparatus, and dump their cargo inside.

This hypothesis was supported when other researchers used differential centrifugation to isolate and characterize the vesicles that contained labeled proteins. They found that a distinctive type of vesicle carries proteins from the rough ER to the Golgi apparatus. Ensuring that only appropriate cargo is loaded into these vesicles and that the vesicles dock and fuse only with the *cis* face of the Golgi involves a complex series of events and is an area of active research.

What Happens Inside the Golgi Apparatus?

Section 7.2 indicated that the Golgi apparatus consists of a stack of flattened vesicles called cisternae, and that cargo enters one side of the organelle and exits the other. Recent research has shown that the composition of the Golgi apparatus is dynamic. New cisternae constantly form at the *cis* face of the Golgi, while old cisternae break apart at the *trans* face, to be replaced by the cisternae behind it. In this way a new cisterna follows those formed earlier, advancing toward the *trans* face of the Golgi. As it does, it changes in composition and activity through a process called **cisternal maturation.**

By separating individual cisternae and analyzing their contents, researchers have found that cisternae at various stages of maturation contain different suites of enzymes. Many of these enzymes catalyze glycosylation reactions that further modify the oligosaccharides that were attached to the protein in the ER. As the cisternae slowly move from *cis* to *trans*, these enzymes are replaced with those representing more mature cisternae. The result is that proteins are modified in a stepwise manner as they slowly move through the Golgi.

If the rough ER is like a foundry and stamping plant where rough parts are manufactured, then the Golgi can be considered a finishing area where products are polished, painted, and readied for shipping.

How Do Proteins Reach Their Destinations?

The rough ER and Golgi apparatus constitute an impressive assembly line. Certain proteins manufactured by this process remain in these organelles, replacing worn-out resident molecules. But those proteins that are simply passing through as cargo must be sorted and sent to their intended destination as the *trans* cisterna they are in breaks up into vesicles.

How are these finished products put into the right shipping containers, and how are the different containers addressed?

Studies on enzymes that are shipped to lysosomes have provided some answers to both questions. A key finding was that lysosome-bound proteins have a phosphate group attached to a specific sugar subunit on their surface, forming the compound mannose-6-phosphate. If mannose-6-phosphate is removed from these proteins, they are not transported to a lysosome.

This is strong evidence that the phosphorylated sugar serves as a zip code, analogous to the nuclear localization signal and ER signal sequence discussed earlier. Data indicate that mannose-6-phosphate binds to a receptor protein in the membrane of the *trans*-Golgi cisterna. Regions that are enriched with these receptor–cargo complexes will form vesicles that, in turn, have proteins on their cytosolic surfaces that direct their transport and fusion with pre-lysosomal compartments. In this way, the presence of mannose-6-phosphate targets proteins for vesicles that deliver their contents to organelles that eventually become lysosomes.

FIGURE 7.22 presents a simplified model of how cargo is sorted and loaded into specific vesicles that are shipped to different destinations. Each cargo protein has a molecular tag that directs it to particular vesicle budding sites by interacting with receptors in the *trans* cisterna. These receptors, along with other cytosolic proteins that are not shown, direct the transport vesicles to the correct destinations.

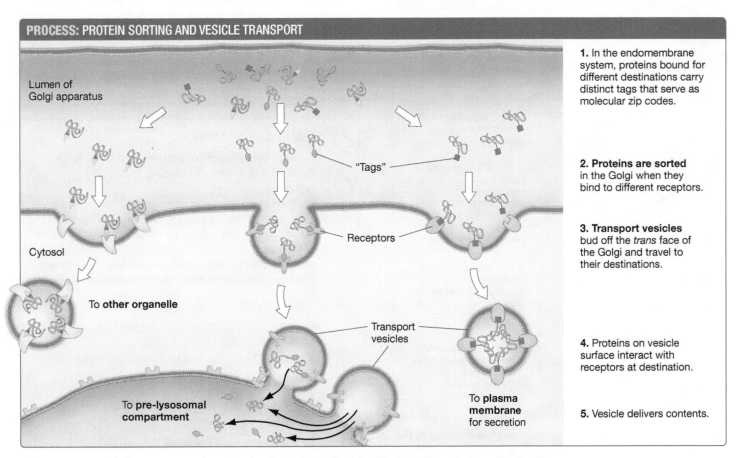

PROCESS: PROTEIN SORTING AND VESICLE TRANSPORT

Lumen of Golgi apparatus

"Tags"

Receptors

Cytosol

To **other organelle**

Transport vesicles

To **pre-lysosomal compartment**

To **plasma membrane** for secretion

1. In the endomembrane system, proteins bound for different destinations carry distinct tags that serve as molecular zip codes.

2. Proteins are sorted in the Golgi when they bind to different receptors.

3. Transport vesicles bud off the *trans* face of the Golgi and travel to their destinations.

4. Proteins on vesicle surface interact with receptors at destination.

5. Vesicle delivers contents.

FIGURE 7.22 In the Golgi Apparatus, Proteins Are Sorted into Vesicles That Are Targeted to a Destination.

In particular, notice that the transport vesicle shown on the right of Figure 7.22 is bound for the plasma membrane, where it will secrete its contents to the outside. This process is called **exocytosis** ("outside-cell-act"). When exocytosis occurs, the vesicle membrane and plasma membrane make contact. As the two membranes fuse, their lipid bilayers rearrange in a way that exposes the interior of the vesicle to the outside of the cell. The vesicle's contents then diffuse into the space outside the cell. This is how cells in your pancreas deliver digestive enzymes to the duct that leads to your small intestine—where food is digested.

Recycling Material in the Lysosome

Now that you have seen how cargo moves out of the cell, let's look at how cargo is brought into the cell. Previously, you learned about how cells import small molecules across lipid bilayers (see Chapter 6), but this is not possible for large molecules like proteins and complex carbohydrates. For these molecules to be recycled and used by the cell, they must first be digested in the lysosome—but how do they get there?

Endocytosis ("inside-cell-act") refers to any pinching off of the plasma membrane that results in the uptake of material from outside the cell. **Receptor-mediated endocytosis** is illustrated in **FIGURE 7.23**. As its name implies, the sequence of events begins when macromolecules outside the cell bind to receptors on the plasma membrane. More than 25 distinct receptors have now been characterized, each specialized for binding to different cargo.

Once receptor binding occurs, the plasma membrane folds in and pinches off to form an endocytic vesicle. These vesicles then drop off their cargo in a transient organelle called the **early endosome** ("inside-body"). The activity of proton pumps in the membrane of this organelle acidifies its lumen, which causes the cargo to be released from their receptors. Many of these emptied cargo receptors are then repackaged into vesicles and returned to the plasma membrane.

As proton pumps continue to lower the early endosome's pH, it undergoes a series of processing steps that cause it to mature into a **late endosome**. The late endosome is the pre-lysosomal compartment introduced earlier (Figure 7.22), where the acid hydrolases from the Golgi apparatus are dropped off. As before, the emptied cargo receptors transported from the Golgi are removed from the late endosome as it matures into a fully active lysosome.

In addition to receptor-mediated endocytosis, the lysosome is involved in recycling material via autophagy and phagocytosis (see **FIGURE 7.24**). During **autophagy** (literally, "same-eating"), damaged organelles are enclosed within an internal membrane and delivered to a lysosome. There the components are digested and recycled. In **phagocytosis** ("eat-cell-act"), the plasma membrane of a cell surrounds a smaller cell or food particle and engulfs it, forming a structure called a phagosome. This structure is delivered to a lysosome, where it is taken in and digested.

Regardless of whether the materials in lysosomes originate via autophagy, phagocytosis, or receptor-mediated endocytosis, the result is similar: Molecules are hydrolyzed. ✔ If you understand the interaction between the endomembrane system

---

PROCESS: RECEPTOR-MEDIATED ENDOCYTOSIS

Recycling of membrane proteins

Endocytic vesicle

H^+

Early endosome

H^+ H^+

Vesicle from Golgi apparatus

Late endosome

Lysosome

1. Macromolecules outside the cell bind to membrane proteins that act as receptors.

2. The plasma membrane folds in and pinches off to form an endocytic vesicle.

3. The endocytic vesicle fuses with an early endosome, activating protons that lower its pH. Cargo is released and empty receptors are recycled to the surface.

4. The early endosome matures into a late endosome that receives digestive enzymes from the Golgi apparatus.

5. The late endosome matures into a functional lysosome and digests the endocytosed macromolecules.

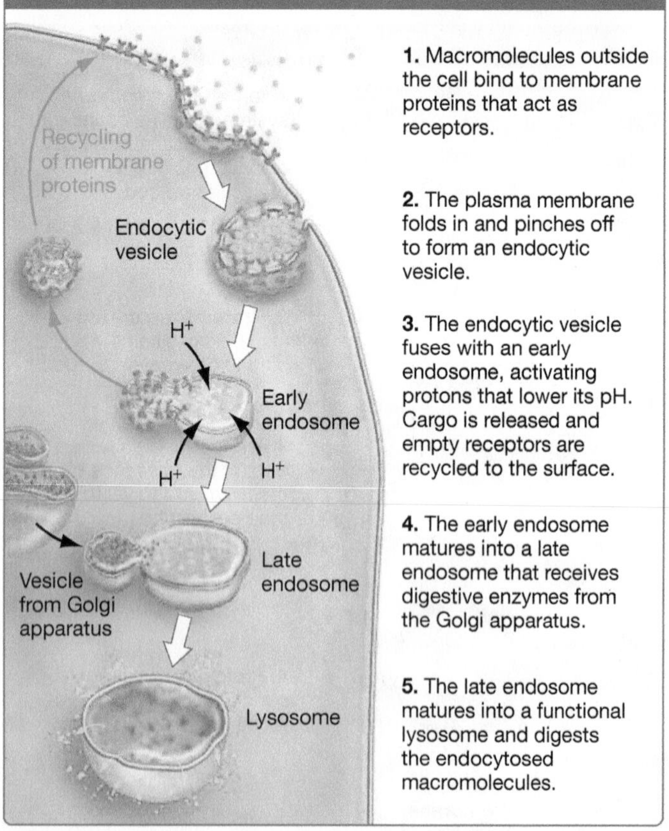

FIGURE 7.23 Receptor-Mediated Endocytosis Is a Pathway to the Lysosome. Endosomes created by receptor-mediated endocytosis will mature into lysosomes.

---

check your understanding

If you understand that . . .

- In cells, the transport of proteins and other large molecules is energy demanding and tightly regulated.
- Proteins must have the appropriate molecular zip code to be directed into the nucleus, the lumen of the rough ER, or vesicles destined for different parts of the cell.
- Vesicles incorporate membrane proteins that direct them to particular target sites for unloading cargo.

✔ **You should be able to . . .**

1. Compare and contrast the movement of proteins into the nucleus versus the ER lumen.

2. Predict the final location of a protein that has been engineered to include an ER signal sequence, mannose-6-phosphate tag, and a nuclear localization signal. Justify your answer by addressing the impact of each signal on its transport.

Answers are available in Appendix A.

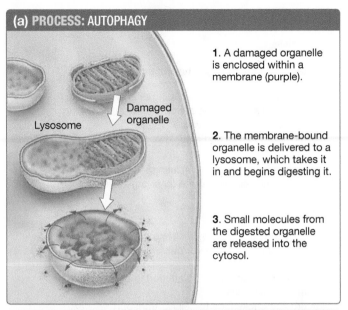

(a) PROCESS: AUTOPHAGY

Lysosome

Damaged organelle

1. A damaged organelle is enclosed within a membrane (purple).

2. The membrane-bound organelle is delivered to a lysosome, which takes it in and begins digesting it.

3. Small molecules from the digested organelle are released into the cytosol.

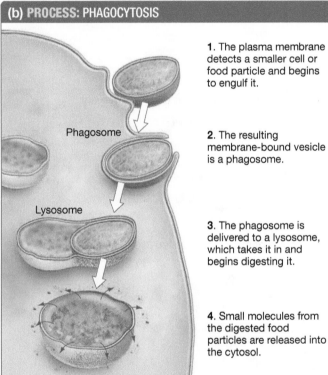

(b) PROCESS: PHAGOCYTOSIS

Phagosome

Lysosome

1. The plasma membrane detects a smaller cell or food particle and begins to engulf it.

2. The resulting membrane-bound vesicle is a phagosome.

3. The phagosome is delivered to a lysosome, which takes it in and begins digesting it.

4. Small molecules from the digested food particles are released into the cytosol.

FIGURE 7.24 Two More Ways to Deliver Materials to Lysosomes. Materials can be transported to lysosomes **(a)** via autophagy or **(b)** after phagocytosis.

and endocytosis, you should be able to predict how the loss of the mannose-6-phosphate receptor would affect receptor-mediated endocytosis.

It is important to note, however, that not all the materials that are surrounded by membrane and taken into a cell end up in lysosomes. In addition to receptor-mediated endocytosis and phagocytosis, small fluid-filled vesicles can be brought into a cell via **bulk-phase endocytosis.** There does not appear to be any cargo selection in bulk-phase endocytosis, and the vesicles are not transported to lysosomes. These tiny vesicles are used elsewhere in the cell and are likely involved in recycling lipids deposited on the plasma membrane during exocytosis.

Throughout this section, vesicles have been key to the transport of cargo. If these transport steps depended on the random movement of diffusion alone, however, then the vesicles and their cargo might never reach their intended destinations. Are there instead defined tracks that direct the movement of these shipping containers? If so, what are these tracks, and what molecule or molecules function to transport the vesicles along them? Let's delve into these questions in the next section.

7.6 Cell Systems III: The Dynamic Cytoskeleton

The endomembrane system may be the best-studied example of how individual organelles work together in a dynamic, highly integrated way. This integration depends in part on the physical relationship of organelles, which is organized by the cytoskeletal system.

The cytoskeleton is a dense and complex network of fibers that helps maintain cell shape by providing structural support. However, the cytoskeleton is not a static structure like the scaffolding used at construction sites. Its fibrous proteins move and change to alter the cell's shape, shift its contents, and even move the cell itself. Like the rest of the cell, the cytoskeleton is dynamic.

As **TABLE 7.3** (see page 128) shows, there are three distinct cytoskeletal elements in eukaryotic cells: actin filaments, intermediate filaments, and microtubules. Recent research has shown structural and functional relationships between these three eukaryotic filaments and cytoskeletal elements in bacteria.

Each of the three cytoskeletal elements found in eukaryotes has a distinct size, structure, and function. Let's look at each one in turn.

Actin Filaments

Sometimes called **microfilaments** because they are the cytoskeletal element with the smallest diameter, **actin filaments** are fibrous structures made of the globular protein actin (Table 7.3). In animal cells, actin is often the most abundant of all proteins—typically it represents 5–10 percent of the total protein in the cell. Each of your liver cells contains about half a billion of these molecules.

Actin Filament Structure A completed actin filament resembles two long strands that coil around each other. Actin filaments form when individual actin protein subunits assemble, or polymerize, from head to tail through the formation of noncovalent bonds.

Because the actin proteins are not symmetrical, this head-to-tail arrangement of actin subunits results in filaments that have two different ends, or polarity. The two distinct ends of an actin filament are referred to as plus and minus ends. The structural difference between these two ends results in different rates of

Filament	Structure	Subunits	Functions
The three types of filaments that make up the cytoskeleton are distinguished by their size, structure, and type of protein subunit.			
Actin filaments (microfilaments)	Strands in double helix 7 nm – end + end	Actin	• maintain cell shape by resisting tension (pull) • move cells via muscle contraction or cell crawling • divide animal cells in two • move organelles and cytoplasm in plants, fungi, and animals
Intermediate filaments	Fibers wound into thicker cables 10 nm	Keratins, lamins, or others	• maintain cell shape by resisting tension (pull) • anchor nucleus and some other organelles
Microtubules	Hollow tube 25 nm – end + end	α- and β-tubulin dimers	• maintain cell shape by resisting compression (push) • move cells via flagella or cilia • move chromosomes during cell division • assist formation of cell plate during plant cell division • move organelles • provide tracks for intracellular transport

assembling new actin subunits: The plus end grows faster than the minus end.

Each filament is generally unstable and will grow or shrink depending on the concentration of free actin subunits. In addition to controlling the availability of free actin, cells regulate the length and longevity of microfilaments via actin-binding proteins that either stabilize or destabilize their structure.

In animal cells, actin filaments are particularly abundant just under the plasma membrane. They are organized into long, parallel bundles or dense, crisscrossing networks in which individual actin filaments are linked to one another by other proteins. The reinforced bundles and networks of actin filaments help stiffen the cell and define its shape.

Actin Filament Function In addition to providing structural support, actin filaments are involved in movement. In several cases, actin's role in movement depends on the protein myosin. Myosin is a **motor protein:** a protein that converts the potential energy in ATP into the kinetic energy of mechanical work, just as a car's motor converts the chemical energy in gasoline into spinning wheels.

The interaction between actin and myosin is frequently presented in the context of how it produces muscle contraction and movement (Chapter 48). For now, it's enough to recognize that when myosin binds and hydrolyzes ATP to ADP, it undergoes a series of shape changes that extends the "head" region, attaches it to actin, and then contracts to pull itself along the actin filament. The shape change of this protein causes the actin and myosin to slide past each other. After repeated rounds of this contraction cycle, the myosin progressively moves toward the plus end of the actin filament (**FIGURE 7.25a**). This type of movement is analogous to an inchworm contracting its body as it moves along a stick.

(a) Actin and myosin interact to cause movement.

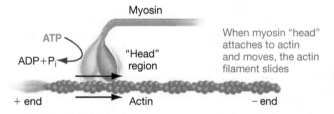

When myosin "head" attaches to actin and moves, the actin filament slides

(b) Examples of movement caused by actin–myosin interactions

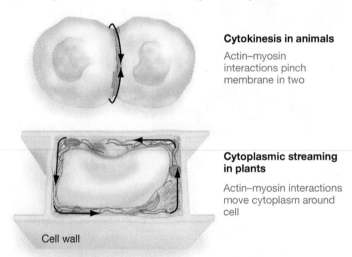

Cytokinesis in animals

Actin–myosin interactions pinch membrane in two

Cytoplasmic streaming in plants

Actin–myosin interactions move cytoplasm around cell

FIGURE 7.25 Many Cellular Movements Are Based on Actin–Myosin Interactions. (a) ATP hydrolysis in the "head" region of myosin causes the protein to attach to actin and change shape. The movement slides the myosin toward the plus end of actin. **(b)** Actin–myosin interactions can divide cells and move organelles and cytoplasm.

As **FIGURE 7.25b** shows, the ATP-powered interaction between actin and myosin is the basis for an array of cell movements:

- **Cytokinesis** ("cell-moving") is the process of cell division. In animals, this occurs by the use of actin filaments that are connected to the plasma membrane and arranged in a ring around the circumference of the cell. Myosin causes the filaments to slide past one another, drawing in the membrane and pinching the cell in two.

- **Cytoplasmic streaming** is the directed flow of cytosol and organelles within plant cells. The movement occurs along actin filaments and is powered by myosin. It is especially common in large cells, where the circulation of cytoplasm facilitates material transport.

In addition, the movement called **cell crawling** occurs when groups of actin filaments grow, creating bulges in the plasma membrane that extend and move the cell. Cell crawling occurs in a wide range of organisms and cell types, including amoebae, slime molds, and certain animal cells.

Intermediate Filaments

Many types of **intermediate filament** exist, each consisting of a different—though similar in size and structure—type of protein (Table 7.3). Humans, for example, have 70 genes that code for intermediate filament proteins. This is in stark contrast to actin filaments and microtubules, which are made from the same protein subunits in all eukaryotic cells.

Moreover, intermediate filaments are not polar; instead, each end of these filaments is identical. They are not involved in directed movement driven by myosin or other motor proteins, but instead serve a purely structural role in eukaryotic cells.

The intermediate filaments that you are most familiar with belong to a family of molecules called the keratins. The cells that make up your skin and line surfaces inside your body contain about 20 types of keratin. These intermediate filaments provide the mechanical strength required for these cells to resist pressure and abrasion. Certain cells in the skin can also produce secreted forms of keratin. Depending on the location of the cell and keratins involved, the secreted filaments form fingernails, toenails, or hair.

Nuclear lamins, which make up the nuclear lamina layer introduced in Section 7.4, also qualify as intermediate filaments. Nuclear lamins form a dense mesh under the nuclear envelope. Recall that in addition to giving the nucleus its shape, they anchor the chromosomes. They are also involved in the breakup and reassembly of the nuclear envelope when cells divide.

Some intermediate filaments project from the nucleus through the cytoplasm to the plasma membrane, where they are linked to intermediate filaments that run parallel to the cell surface. In this way, intermediate filaments form a flexible skeleton that helps shape the cell surface and hold the nucleus in place.

Microtubules

Microtubules are the largest cytoskeletal components in terms of diameter. As Table 7.3 shows, they are assembled from subunits

consisting of two polypeptides, called α-tubulin and β-tubulin, that exist as stable protein **dimers** ("two-parts").

Tubulin dimers polymerize from head to tail to form filaments that interact with one another to create relatively large, hollow tubes. Because of this polarity, these microtubules have α-tubulin polypeptides at one end (the minus end) and β-tubulins at the other end (the plus end). Like actin filaments, microtubules are dynamic and grow faster at their plus ends compared with their minus ends.

Microtubules originate from a structure called the **microtubule organizing center (MTOC).** Their plus ends grow outward, radiating throughout the cell. Although plant cells typically have hundreds of sites where microtubules start growing, most animal and fungal cells have just one site that is near the nucleus.

In animals, the microtubule organizing center has a distinctive structure and is called a **centrosome.** As **FIGURE 7.26** shows, animal centrosomes contain two bundles of microtubules called **centrioles.** Although additional microtubules emanate from these structures in animals, they do not grow directly from the centrioles.

(a) In animals, microtubules originate from centrosomes.

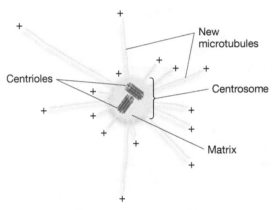

(b) Centrioles consist of microtubules.

Centrosome

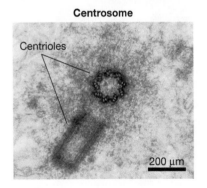

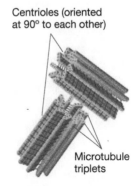

FIGURE 7.26 Centrosomes Are a Type of Microtubule-Organizing Center. (a) Microtubule-organizing centers, such as the centrosomes of animal cells, are the sites where new microtubules are made. Microtubules grow from the matrix surrounding the centrioles, and their positive ends point away from the centrosomes. **(b)** The two centrioles inside a centrosome consist of microtubules as triplets arranged in a circle.

In function, microtubules are similar to actin filaments: They provide stability and are involved in movement. Like steel girders in a skyscraper, the microtubules that radiate from an organizing center stiffen the cell by resisting compression forces. Microtubules also provide a structural framework for organelles. If microtubules are prevented from forming, the network-like configuration of the ER collapses and the Golgi apparatus disappears into vesicles.

Microtubules are best known for their role in separating chromosomes during mitosis and meiosis (see Chapter 12). But microtubules are involved in many other types of cellular movement as well. Let's first consider their role in moving materials inside cells and then explore how microtubules can help cells to swim.

Microtubules Serve as Tracks for Vesicle Transport   Recall from Section 7.5 that vesicles are used to transport materials to a wide array of destinations inside cells. To study how this movement happens, Ronald Vale and colleagues focused on the giant axon, an extremely large nerve cell in squid that runs the length of the animal's body. If the squid is disturbed, the cell signals muscles to contract so it can jet away to safety. The researchers decided to study this particular cell for three reasons.

1. The giant axon is so large that it is relatively easy to see and manipulate.

2. Large numbers of vesicles are transported down the length of the cell. As a result, a large amount of cargo moves a long distance.

(a) Electron micrograph

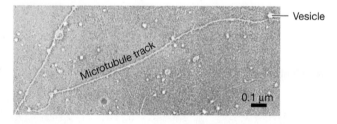

(b) Video image

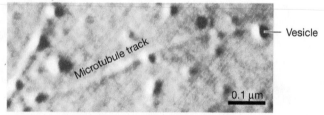

FIGURE 7.27 Transport Vesicles Move along Microtubule Track.
The images show extruded cytoplasm from a squid giant axon.
(a) An electron micrograph that allowed researchers to measure the diameter of the filaments and confirm that they are microtubules. In the upper part of this image, you can see a vesicle on a "track."
(b) A video microscope image using enhanced contrast that allowed researchers to watch vesicles move in real time.

3. The researchers found that if they gently squeezed the cytoplasm out of the cell, vesicle transport still occurred in the extracellular cytoplasmic material. This allowed them to do experiments on vesicle transport without the plasma membrane being in the way.

In short, the squid giant axon provided a system that could be observed and manipulated efficiently in the lab. To watch vesicle transport in action, the researchers mounted a video camera to a microscope. As **FIGURE 7.27** shows, this technique allowed them to document that vesicle transport occurred along filamentous tracks.

To identify the filament involved, the biologists measured the diameter of the tracks and analyzed their chemical composition. Both types of data indicated that the tracks consist of microtubules. Microtubules also appear to be required for movement of materials elsewhere in the cell. For instance, if experimental cells are treated with a drug that disrupts microtubules, the movement of vesicles from the rough ER to the Golgi apparatus is impaired.

The general message of these experiments is that transport vesicles move through the cell along microtubules. How? Do the tracks themselves move, like a conveyer belt, or are vesicles carried along on some sort of molecular vehicle?

Motor Proteins Pull Vesicles Along the Tracks   To study the way vesicles move along microtubules, Vale's group took the squid axon's transport system apart and then determined what components were required to put it back together. A simple experiment convinced the group that this movement is an energy-dependent process: If they depleted the amount of ATP in the cytoplasm, vesicle transport stopped.

To examine this process further, they mixed purified microtubules and vesicles with ATP, but no transport occurred. Something had been left out—but what? To find the missing element or elements, the researchers purified one subcellular part after another and added it to the microtubule + vesicle + ATP system.

Through trial and error, and further purification steps, the researchers finally succeeded in isolating a protein that generated vesicle movement. They named the molecule **kinesin,** from the Greek word *kinein* ("to move").

Like myosin, kinesin is a motor protein. Kinesin converts the chemical energy in ATP into mechanical energy in the form of movement. More specifically, when ATP is hydrolyzed by kinesin, the protein moves along microtubules in a directional manner: toward the plus end.

Biologists began to understand how kinesin works when X-ray diffraction studies showed that it has three major regions: a head section with two globular pieces, a tail associated with small polypeptides, and a stalk that connects the head and tail (**FIGURE 7.28a**).

Follow-up studies confirmed that the head region binds to the microtubule while the tail region binds to the transport vesicle. Recent work has shown that kinesin uses these domains to "walk" along the microtubule through a series of conformational changes as it hydrolyzes ATP (**FIGURE 7.28b**). Amazingly, these motors have been found to "walk" up to 375 steps per second.

Cells contain several different versions of the kinesin motor, each specialized for a different role in the cell. If kinesins move

(a) Structure of kinesin

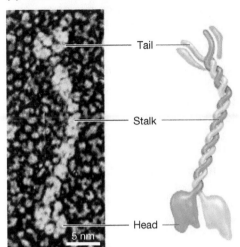

Tail

Stalk

Head

5 nm

(b) Kinesin "walks" along a microtubule track.

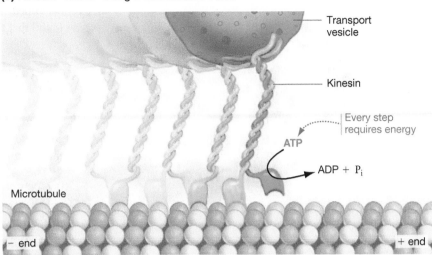

Transport
vesicle

Kinesin

Every step
requires energy

ATP

ADP + P_i

Microtubule

– end

+ end

FIGURE 7.28 Motor Proteins Move Vesicles along Microtubules. (a) Kinesin has three distinct regions.
(b) The current model depicting how kinesin "walks" along a microtubule track to transport vesicles. The two
head segments act like feet that alternately attach, pivot, and release in response to the gain or loss of a phosphate
group from ATP.

only toward the plus ends of microtubules, then what is responsible for moving the cargo in the opposite direction? By studying whole-cell locomotion, researchers discovered a motor that could move toward the minus end of microtubules.

Flagella and Cilia: Moving the Entire Cell

Flagella are long, whiplike projections from the cell surface that function in movement. While many bacteria and eukaryotes have flagella, the structure is completely different in the two groups.

- Bacterial flagella are helical rods made of a protein called flagellin; eukaryotic flagella consist of several microtubules constructed from tubulin dimers.

- Bacterial flagella move the cell by rotating the rod like a ship's propeller; eukaryotic flagella move the cell by undulating—they whip back and forth.

- Eukaryotic flagella are surrounded by the plasma membrane and are considered organelles; bacterial flagella are not.

Based on these observations, biologists conclude that the two structures evolved independently, even though their function is similar.

To understand how some cells move, let's focus on eukaryotic flagella. Eukaryotic flagella are closely related to structures called **cilia** (singular: **cilium**), which are short, hairlike projections that are also found in some eukaryotic cells (**FIGURE 7.29**). Flagella are generally much longer than cilia, and the two structures differ in

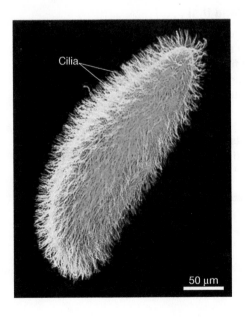

Cilia

50 µm

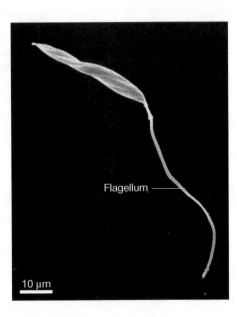

Flagellum

10 µm

FIGURE 7.29 Cilia and Flagella Differ in Length and Number. Cells typically only have 1–4 flagella but may have up to 14,000 cilia. The cells in these scanning electron micrographs have been colorized.

(a) Transmission electron micrograph of axoneme

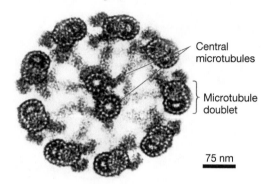

Central microtubules

Microtubule doublet

75 nm

(b) Structure of axoneme

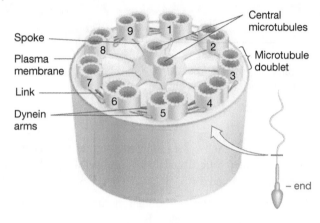

Spoke

Plasma membrane

Link

Dynein arms

9 1

8

7

6 5 4

2

3

Central microtubules

Microtubule doublet

– end

(c) Mechanism of axoneme bending

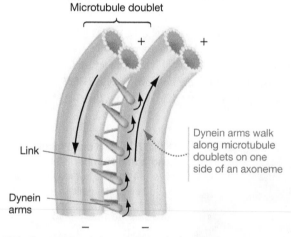

Microtubule doublet

+ +

Link

Dynein arms

Dynein arms walk along microtubule doublets on one side of an axoneme

– –

+ ATP: Causes dynein to walk toward minus end and pull toward plus end

FIGURE 7.30 The Structure and Function of Cilia and Flagella.
(a) Transmission electron micrograph of a cross section through an axoneme. **(b)** The microtubules in cilia and flagella are connected by links and spokes, and the entire structure is surrounded by the plasma membrane. **(c)** When dynein arms walk along the microtubule doublets on one side of a flagellum, force is transmitted to these links and spokes, causing the entire axoneme to bend.

✔**QUESTION** If the links and spokes were removed from the microtubule doublets, what would happen to the axoneme after adding ATP?

their abundance and pattern of movement. But when researchers examined the two structures with an electron microscope, they found that their underlying organization is identical.

How are Cilia and Flagella Constructed? In the 1950s, anatomical studies established that most cilia and flagella have a characteristic "9 + 2" arrangement of microtubules. As **FIGURE 7.30a** shows, nine microtubule pairs, or doublets, surround two central microtubules. The doublets consist of one complete and one incomplete microtubule and are arranged around the periphery of the structure.

The entire 9 + 2 structure is called the **axoneme** ("axle-thread"). The nine doublets of the axoneme originate from a structure called the **basal body.** The basal body is identical in structure with a centriole and plays a central role in the growth of the axoneme.

Through further study, biologists gained a more detailed view of the axoneme's structure. Spoke-like proteins connect each doublet to the central pair of microtubules, and molecular links connect the nine doublets to one another (**FIGURE 7.30b**). Each doublet also has a set of arms that project toward an adjacent doublet.

Axonemes are complex. How do their components interact to generate motion?

What Provides the Force Required for Movement? In the 1960s Ian Gibbons began studying the cilia of a common unicellular eukaryote called *Tetrahymena*. Gibbons found that he could isolate axonemes by using a detergent to remove the plasma membrane that surrounds cilia and then subjecting the resulting solution to differential centrifugation. These steps gave Gibbons a cell-free system for studying how the axonemes in cilia and flagella work. He found that the isolated structures would beat only if he supplied them with ATP, confirming that the beating of cilia is an energy-demanding process.

check your understanding

If you understand that . . .

C Y U

- Each component of the cytoskeleton has a unique structure and set of functions. Actin filaments, intermediate filaments, and microtubules all play a role in structural support. In addition, actin filaments and microtubules work in conjunction with motor proteins to move cytoplasmic materials or the entire cell.
- Most elements of the cytoskeleton are dynamic— they grow and shrink depending on the needs of the cell.

✔ **You should be able to . . .**

Compare and contrast the structure and function of actin filaments, intermediate filaments, and microtubules.

Answers are available in Appendix A.

In another experiment, Gibbons treated the isolated axonemes with a molecule that disrupts interactions between proteins. The resulting axonemes could not beat even after being supplied with ATP. When Gibbons examined them in the electron microscope, he found that the treatment had removed the arms from the doublets. This result suggested that the arms are required for movement. Follow-up work showed that the arms are made of a large protein that Gibbons named **dynein** (from the Greek word *dyne*, meaning "force").

Like myosin and kinesin, dynein is a motor protein that uses ATP to undergo conformational changes. These shape changes move dynein along microtubules toward the minus end. Note that dynein moves in the opposite direction from the kinesin motor, which moves toward the plus end. In the cytoplasm, dynein motors are known to play various roles similar to the other motors, including the transport of vesicles. In the context of the axoneme, however, the outcome of dynein walking in the axoneme is very different.

So what is special about the axoneme? Remember that each of the nine doublets in the axoneme is connected to the central pair of microtubules by a spoke, and all the doublets are connected to each other by molecular links (Figure 7.30b). As a result, the sliding motion produced by dynein walking is constrained—if one doublet slides, it transmits force to the rest of the axoneme via the links and spokes (**FIGURE 7.30c**). If the dynein arms on just one side of the axoneme are activated, then the localized movement results in bending. The bending of cilia or flagella results in a swimming motion.

Scaled for size, flagella-powered swimming can be rapid. In terms of the number of body or cell lengths traveled per second, a sperm cell from a bull moves faster than a human world-record-holder does when swimming freestyle. At the cellular level, life is fast paced.

Taken together, the data reviewed in this chapter can be summed up in six words: Cells are dynamic, highly integrated structures. To maintain the level of organization that is required for life, chemical reactions must take place at mind-boggling speeds. How cells accomplish this feat is taken up elsewhere (see Chapter 8).

If you understand . . .

7.1 Bacterial and Archaeal Cell Structures and Their Functions

- There are two basic cellular designs: prokaryotic and eukaryotic. The single defining characteristic that differentiates prokaryotes from eukaryotes is the absence of a nucleus.

- Structures common to most, if not all, prokaryotes are ribosomes, a cell wall, a plasma membrane, an interior cytoskeleton, and a nucleoid.

- Many prokaryotes also possess flagella, fimbriae, and internal membrane structures, some of which are considered organelles.

✔ You should be able to predict what would happen to cells that are exposed to (1) a drug that prevents ribosomes from functioning, (2) an enzyme that degrades the cell wall, or (3) a drug that prevents the assembly of the cytoskeleton.

7.2 Eukaryotic Cell Structures and Their Functions

- Eukaryotic cells are usually much larger and more structurally complex than prokaryotic cells.

- Eukaryotic cells contain numerous specialized organelles, which allow eukaryotic cells to compartmentalize functions and grow to a large size. Organelles common to most, if not all, eukaryotes are as follows:

  1. The nucleus, which contains the cell's chromosomes and serves as its control center.

  2. The endomembrane system, which consists of a diverse group of interrelated organelles, including the endoplasmic reticulum, Golgi apparatus, lysosomes or vacuoles, and endosomes. These organelles work together to synthesize, process, sort, transport, and recycle material.

  3. Peroxisomes, which are organelles where key reactions take place that often result in the generation of toxic by-products. Specialized enzymes are included that safely disarm these by-products soon after they are generated.

  4. Mitochondria and chloroplasts, which have extensive internal membrane systems where the enzymes responsible for ATP generation and photosynthesis reside.

✔ You should be able to predict what would happen to a plant cell that is exposed to (1) a drug that poisons mitochondria, (2) a drug that inhibits catalase in the peroxisome, or (3) a drug that inhibits the formation of centrioles.

7.3 Putting the Parts into a Whole

- Cells have a tightly organized interior, where the presence and quantity of organelles often reflect the function of the cell.

- The activity in a cell illustrates the dynamic nature of life. Organelles and cytosolic proteins continually bustle about with a seemingly nonstop rush hour.

- Much of what is known about cellular activity has come from advances in cell imaging and techniques for isolating cellular components.

✔ You should be able to predict how a liver cell would differ compared with a salivary gland cell in terms of organelles.

7.4 Cell Systems I: Nuclear Transport

- Cells have sophisticated systems for making sure that proteins and other products end up in the right place.

- Traffic across the nuclear envelope occurs through nuclear pores, which contain a multiprotein nuclear pore complex that serves as gatekeeper.

- Small molecules can passively diffuse through the nuclear pore. Larger molecules enter the nucleus only if they contain a specific molecular signal that directs them through the pore via nuclear transport proteins.

✔ You should be able to propose a hypothesis that would address how certain cytoplasmic proteins can be induced to enter the nucleus by either the addition or the removal of phosphates.

7.5 Cell Systems II: The Endomembrane System Manufactures, Ships, and Recycles Cargo

- Molecules synthesized in the ER may be transported as cargo to the Golgi apparatus and then to a number of different sites, depending on the cargo.

- Before products leave the Golgi, they are sorted by their molecular "zip codes" that direct them to specific vesicles. The vesicles interact with receptor proteins at the target location so that the contents are delivered correctly.

- The lysosome is built from enzymes and membranes that are made and processed through the endomembrane system. These organelles are involved in recycling products via autophagy, phagocytosis, and receptor-mediated endocytosis.

✔ You should be able to justify why proteins (see Chapter 3)—and not RNA, DNA, carbohydrates, or lipids—are the molecules responsible for "reading" the array of molecular zip codes in cells.

7.6 Cell Systems III: The Dynamic Cytoskeleton

- The cytoskeleton is an extensive system of fibers that provides (1) structural support and a framework for arranging and organizing organelles and other cell components; (2) paths for moving vesicles inside cells; and (3) machinery for moving the cell as a whole through the beating of flagella or cilia, or through cell crawling.

- Subunits are constantly being added to or removed from cytoskeletal filaments. Actin filaments and microtubules are polarized, meaning different ends of the filaments are designated as plus or minus ends. The plus ends have a higher growth rate than the minus ends.

- Movement often depends on motor proteins, which use chemical energy stored in ATP to change shape and position. Myosin motors move toward the plus ends of actin filaments. Kinesin and dynein motors move along microtubules toward the plus and minus ends, respectively.

- A specific type of dynein is found in the axonemes of eukaryotic cilia and flagella. These motors move microtubules to generate forces that bend the structures and enable cells to swim or generate water currents.

✔ You should be able to predict which of the three motors presented in this section would be responsible for transporting vesicles from the Golgi to the plasma membrane.

(MB) MasteringBiology

1. MasteringBiology Assignments

Tutorials and Activities Cilia and Flagella; Endomembrane System; Exocytosis and Endocytosis; Form Fits Function; Cells; Membrane Transport: Bulk Transport; Prokaryotic Cell Structure and Function; Pulse–Chase Experiment; Review: Animal Cell Structure and Function; Tour of a Plant Cell: Structures and Functions; Tour of an Animal Cell: Structures and Functions; Tour of an Animal Cell: The Endomembrane System; Transport into the Nucleus

Questions Reading Quizzes, Blue-Thread Questions, Test Bank

2. eText Read your book online, search, take notes, highlight text, and more.

3. The Study Area Practice Test, Cumulative Test, BioFlix® 3-D Animations, Videos, Activities, Audio Glossary, Word Study Tools, Art

You should be able to . . .

1. Which of the following accurately describes a difference between prokaryotic and eukaryotic cells?
   a. Prokaryotic cells have fimbriae that allow the cell to swim whereas eukaryotic cells have flagella.
   b. Eukaryotic cells are generally larger than prokaryotic cells.
   c. Eukaryotic cells have organelles.
   d. Prokaryotic cells have nuclei and eukaryotic cells have nucleoids.

2. What are three attributes of mitochondria and chloroplasts that suggest they were once free-living bacteria?

3. Which of the following is *not* true of secreted proteins?
   a. They are synthesized using ribosomes.
   b. They enter the ER lumen during translation.
   c. They contain a signal that directs them into the lysosome.
   d. They are transported between organelles in membrane-bound vesicles.

4. Which of the following results provided evidence of a nuclear localization signal in the nucleoplasmin protein?
   a. The protein was small and easily slipped through the nuclear pore complex.
   b. After cleavage of the protein, only the tail segments appeared in the nucleus.
   c. Removing the tail allowed the core segment to enter the nucleus.
   d. The SRP bound only to the tail, not the core segment.

5. Molecular zip codes direct molecules to particular destinations in the cell. How are these signals read?
   a. They bind to receptor proteins.
   b. They enter transport vesicles.
   c. They bind to motor proteins.
   d. They are glycosylated by enzymes in the Golgi apparatus.

6. How does the hydrolysis of ATP result in the movement of a motor protein along a cytoskeletal filament?

7. Compare and contrast the structure of a generalized plant cell, animal cell, and prokaryotic cell. Which features are common to all cells? Which are specific to just prokaryotes, or just plants, or just animals?

8. Cells that line your intestines are known to possess a large number of membrane proteins that transport small molecules and ions across the plasma membrane. Which of the following cell structures would you expect to be required for this function of the cells?
   a. the endoplasmic reticulum
   b. peroxisomes
   c. lysosomes
   d. the cell wall

9. Most of the proteins that reside in the nucleus possess a nuclear localization signal (NLS), even if they are small enough to pass

through the pore complex unhindered. Why would a small protein have an NLS, when it naturally diffuses across the pore without one?

10. Make a flowchart that traces the movement of a secreted protein from its site of synthesis to the outside of a eukaryotic cell. Identify all the organelles that the protein passes through. Add notes indicating what happens to the protein at each step.

11. Although all three cytoskeletal fibers constantly replace their subunits, only actin filaments and microtubules demonstrate differences in the rate of growth between the two ends. What is responsible for this difference, and why is this not observed in intermediate filaments?

12. Describe how vesicles move in a directed manner between organelles of the endomembrane system. Explain why this movement requires ATP.

13. Which of the following cell structures would you expect to be most important in the growth of bacteria on the surface of your teeth?
    a. cell wall
    b. fimbriae
    c. flagella
    d. cilia

14. The enzymes found in peroxisomes are synthesized by cytosolic ribosomes. Suggest a hypothesis for how these proteins find their way to the peroxisomes.

15. Propose an experiment that would determine if the NLS in nucleoplasmin is limited to this protein only or if it could direct other structures into the nucleus.

16. George Palade's research group used the pulse–chase assay to dissect the secretory pathway in pancreatic cells. If they had instead performed this assay on muscle cells, which have high energy demands and primarily consist of actin and myosin filaments, where would you expect the labeled proteins to go during the chase?

8 Energy and Enzymes: An Introduction to Metabolic Pathways

In this chapter you will learn how

Enzymes use energy to drive the chemistry of life

looking at energy, asking

What happens to energy in chemical reactions? **8.1**

Can chemical energy drive nonspontaneous reactions? **8.2**

looking at enzymes, asking

How do enzymes help speed chemical reaction rates? **8.3**

What factors affect enzyme function? **8.4**

How do enzymes work together in metabolic pathways? **8.5**

When table sugar is heated in the presence of oxygen, it undergoes the uncontrolled oxidation reaction known as burning. The heat energy in the flame is released as electrons are transferred from sugar to oxygen. Cells use the energy released from this type of reaction to drive the energy-demanding processes required for life.

This chapter is part of the Big Picture. See how on pages 198–199.

Cells are dynamic. Vesicles move cargo from the Golgi apparatus to the plasma membrane and other destinations, enzymes catalyze the synthesis of a complex array of macromolecules, and millions of proteins transport ions and molecules across cellular membranes. These activities change constantly in response to signals from other cells or the environment.

What drives all this action? The answer is twofold—energy and enzymes. Because staying alive takes work, there is no life without energy. Life, at its most basic level, consists of chemical reactions catalyzed by enzymes. By using enzymes to direct which reactions occur and which do not, life possesses the distinguishing feature of creating order from a naturally disordered environment.

✔ When you see this checkmark, stop and test yourself. Answers are available in Appendix A.

This chapter is about how enzymes work to help cells acquire and use energy. It is also your introduction to metabolic pathways—the ordered series of chemical reactions that build up or break down a particular molecule.

Let's begin by reviewing some fundamental concepts about energy and how it is used in cells.

8.1 What Happens to Energy in Chemical Reactions?

When biologists consider energy in chemical reactions, they often use the term **free energy** to describe the amount of energy that is available to do work. Recall that two types of energy exist: kinetic energy or potential energy (Chapter 2). **Kinetic energy** is energy of motion. There are several different forms of kinetic energy—at the molecular level, the energy of motion is called thermal energy. **Potential energy** is energy that is associated with position or configuration. In molecules, this is referred to as chemical energy and is stored in the position of electrons.

Chemical Reactions Involve Energy Transformations

The existence of two types of energy does not mean that energy is locked into either the kinetic or the potential type. Energy is often transformed from one type to the other. To drive this point home, consider a water molecule sitting at the top of a waterfall, as in **FIGURE 8.1**.

Step 1 The molecule has potential energy (E_p) because of its position.

Step 2 As the molecule passes over the waterfall, its potential energy is converted to the kinetic energy (E_k) of motion.

Step 3 When the molecule reaches the rocks below, it undergoes a change in potential energy because it has changed position. The difference in potential energy is transformed into an equal amount of kinetic energy that is manifested in a variety of forms: mechanical energy, which tends to break up the rocks; heat (thermal energy), which raises the temperature of the rocks and the water itself; and sound.

The amount of potential energy in an electron is based on its position relative to other electrons and the protons in the nuclei of nearby atoms (see **FIGURE 8.2a** on page 138). If an electron is close to negative charges on other electrons and far from the positive charges in nuclei, it has high potential energy. In general, the potential energy of a molecule is a function of the way its electrons are configured or positioned.

An electron in an outer electron shell is analogous to the water molecule at the top of a waterfall (**FIGURE 8.2b**). If the electron falls to a lower shell, its potential energy is converted to the kinetic energy of motion. After the electron occupies the lower electron shell, it undergoes a change in potential energy. As panel 3 in Figure 8.1b shows, the change in potential energy is transformed

1. Potential energy
A water molecule sitting at the top of a waterfall has a defined amount of potential energy, E_p.

2. Kinetic energy
As the molecule falls, some of this stored energy is converted to kinetic energy (the energy of motion), E_k.

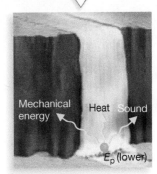

3. Other forms of kinetic energy
When the molecule strikes the rocks below, its energy of motion is converted to thermal, mechanical, and sound energy. The molecule's potential energy is now much lower. The change in potential energy has been transformed into an equal amount of other forms of kinetic energy.

Conclusion: Energy is neither created nor destroyed; it simply changes form.

FIGURE 8.1 Energy Transformations. During an energy transformation, the total amount of energy in the system remains constant.

into an equal amount of kinetic energy—usually thermal energy, but sometimes light.

These examples illustrate the **first law of thermodynamics,** which states that energy is conserved. Energy cannot be created or destroyed, but only transferred and transformed.

The total energy in a molecule is referred to as its **enthalpy** (represented by H). Enthalpy includes the potential energy of the molecule, often referred to as heat content, plus the effect of the molecule on its surroundings in terms of pressure and volume.

(a) The potential energy of an electron is related to its position.

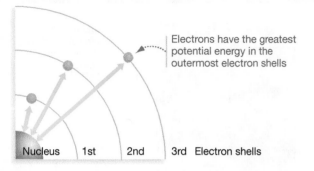

Electrons have the greatest potential energy in the outermost electron shells

Nucleus   1st   2nd   3rd   Electron shells

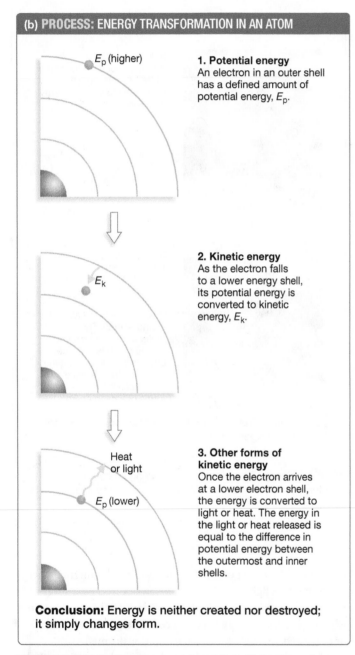

(b) PROCESS: ENERGY TRANSFORMATION IN AN ATOM

E_p (higher)

1. Potential energy
An electron in an outer shell has a defined amount of potential energy, E_p.

E_k

2. Kinetic energy
As the electron falls to a lower energy shell, its potential energy is converted to kinetic energy, E_k.

Heat or light

E_p (lower)

3. Other forms of kinetic energy
Once the electron arrives at a lower electron shell, the energy is converted to light or heat. The energy in the light or heat released is equal to the difference in potential energy between the outermost and inner shells.

Conclusion: Energy is neither created nor destroyed; it simply changes form.

FIGURE 8.2 Chemical energy transformations Potential energy energy stored in atoms or molecules may be transformed into kinetic energy by changes in electron position.

The contributions of heat, pressure, and volume to the enthalpy of a molecule are best understood by observing the changes in enthalpy in a chemical reaction. For example, let's examine the reaction responsible for the explosive bursts of scalding hot liquid a bombardier beetle can produce when provoked, as seen in **FIGURE 8.3**:

$$2 \, H_2O_2(aq) \longrightarrow 2 \, H_2O(l) + O_2(g)$$

In this reaction, hydrogen peroxide (H_2O_2) is broken down into water and O_2 gas, which expands to over 500 times the original volume of the H_2O_2. Heat given off from the reaction also increases the temperature of the liquid dramatically. These massive increases in temperature and volume generate the pressure that propels the boiling liquid out of an opening at the tip of the beetle's abdomen.

Changes in enthalpy in chemical reactions can be measured and are represented by ΔH. (The uppercase Greek letter delta, Δ, is often used in chemical and mathematical notation to represent change.) The value of ΔH is primarily based on the difference in heat content, since—apart from the reaction in the bombardier beetle—most biological reactions do not result in substantial changes in pressure and volume. When a reaction releases heat energy (products have less potential energy than the reactants), it is **exothermic** and the ΔH is negative. If heat energy is taken up during the reaction, generating products that have higher potential energy than the reactants, the reaction is **endothermic** and ΔH is positive.

Another factor that changes during a chemical reaction is the amount of disorder or **entropy** (symbolized by ΔS). When the products of a chemical reaction become less ordered than the reactant molecules were, entropy increases and ΔS is positive. The **second law of thermodynamics,** in fact, states that total entropy always increases in an isolated system. Keep in mind that the isolated system in this case is the universe, which includes the surroundings as well as the products of the reaction.

To determine whether a chemical reaction is spontaneous, it's necessary to assess the combined contributions of changes in heat and disorder. Chemists do this with a quantity called the **Gibbs free-energy change,** symbolized by ΔG.

$$\Delta G = \Delta H - T\Delta S$$

Here, T stands for temperature measured on the Kelvin scale (see **BioSkills 1**, in Appendix B). Water freezes at 273.15 K and boils at 373.15 K.

In words, the free-energy change in a reaction is equal to the change in enthalpy minus the change in entropy multiplied by the temperature. The $T\Delta S$ term simply means that entropy becomes more important in determining free-energy change as the temperature of the molecules increases. Thermal energy increases the amount of disorder in the system, so the faster molecules are moving, the more important entropy becomes in determining the overall free-energy change.

Chemical reactions are spontaneous when ΔG is less than zero. Such reactions are said to be **exergonic.** Reactions are

FIGURE 8.3 Reactions May Be Explosive due to Changes in Enthalpy. When provoked, the bombardier beetle mixes reactants with enzymes in a special chamber near the tip of its abdomen. The enzyme-catalyzed reaction releases heat energy and oxygen gas. The result is the projection of boiling hot liquid at a predator.

nonspontaneous when ΔG is greater than zero. Such reactions are termed **endergonic.** When ΔG is equal to zero, reactions are at equilibrium. ✔ If you understand these concepts, you should be able to explain (1) why the same reaction can be nonspontaneous at low temperature but spontaneous at high temperature, and (2) why some exothermic reactions are nonspontaneous.

Free energy changes when the potential energy and/or entropy of substances change. Spontaneous chemical reactions run in the direction that lowers the free energy of the system. Exergonic reactions are spontaneous and release energy; endergonic reactions are nonspontaneous and require an input of energy to proceed.

Temperature and Concentration Affect Reaction Rates

Even if a chemical reaction occurs spontaneously, it may not happen quickly. The reactions that convert iron to rust or sugar molecules to carbon dioxide and water are spontaneous, but at room temperature they occur very slowly, if at all.

For most reactions to proceed, one or more chemical bonds have to break and others have to form. For this to happen, the substances involved must collide in a specific orientation that brings the electrons involved near each other. (See Chapter 2 to review the forces involved in bond formation.)

The number of collisions occurring between the substances in a mixture depends on their temperature and concentration:

- When the concentration of reactants is high, more collisions should occur and reactions should proceed more quickly.
- When their temperature is high, reactants should move faster and collide more frequently.

Higher concentrations and higher temperatures should speed up chemical reactions. To test this hypothesis, students at Parkland College in Champaign, Illinois, performed the experiments shown in **FIGURE 8.4** (see page 140). Pay special attention to the two graphs in the "Results" section:

- *Temperature versus reaction rate* The graph on the left is based on experiments where the concentration of the reactants was the same, but the temperature varied. Each data point represents one experiment. Notice that the points represent a trend that rises from left to right—meaning, in this case, that the reaction rate speeded up when the temperature of the reaction mixture was higher.

- *Concentration versus reaction rate* The graph on the right is based on experiments where the temperature was constant, but the concentration of reactants varied. Each bar represents the average reaction rate over many replicates of each treatment, or set of concentrations. The thin lines at the top of each bar indicate the standard error of the mean—a measure of variability (see **BioSkills 4** in Appendix B). The take-home message of this graph is that reaction rates are higher when reactant concentrations are higher.

The reactions shown in Figure 8.4 were exergonic, meaning that the products had lower free energy than the reactants, so no input of energy was required. But, what drives nonspontaneous, endergonic reactions? Let's take a closer look.

8.2 Nonspontaneous Reactions May Be Driven Using Chemical Energy

By definition, endergonic reactions require an input of energy to proceed. Recall that radiation from the Sun and electricity from lightning could have driven nonspontaneous reactions during

QUESTION: Do chemical reaction rates increase with increased temperature and concentration?

RATE INCREASE HYPOTHESIS: Chemical reaction rates increase with increased temperature. They also increase with increased concentration of reactants.

NULL HYPOTHESIS: Chemical reaction rates are not affected by increases in temperature or concentration of reactants.

EXPERIMENTAL SETUP:

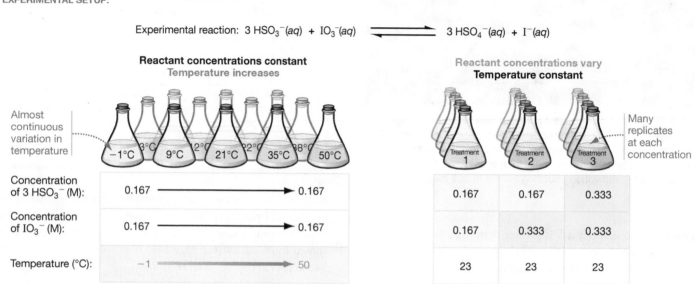

Experimental reaction: $3\ HSO_3^-(aq) + IO_3^-(aq) \rightleftharpoons 3\ HSO_4^-(aq) + I^-(aq)$

Reactant concentrations constant
Temperature increases

Almost continuous variation in temperature

−1°C 3°C 9°C 12°C 21°C 22°C 35°C 38°C 50°C

Reactant concentrations vary
Temperature constant

Treatment 1 Treatment 2 Treatment 3

Many replicates at each concentration

	Reactant concentrations constant		Reactant concentrations vary		
			Treatment 1	Treatment 2	Treatment 3
Concentration of 3 HSO_3^- (M):	0.167 → 0.167		0.167	0.167	0.333
Concentration of IO_3^- (M):	0.167 → 0.167		0.167	0.333	0.333
Temperature (°C):	−1 → 50		23	23	23

PREDICTION: Reaction rate, measured as 1/(time for reaction to go to completion), will increase with increased concentrations of reactants and increased temperature of reaction mix.

PREDICTION OF NULL HYPOTHESIS: There will be no difference in reaction rates among treatments in each setup.

RESULTS:

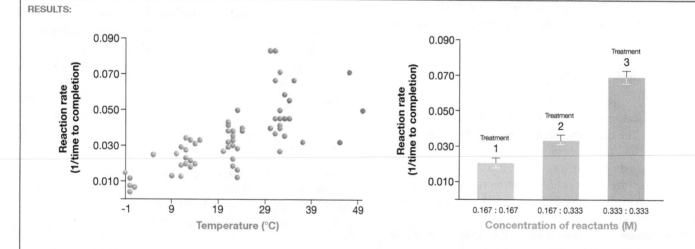

CONCLUSION: Chemical reaction rates increase with increased temperature or concentration.

FIGURE 8.4 Testing the Hypothesis that Reaction Rates Are Sensitive to Changes in Temperature and Concentration.

✓**QUESTION** Use **BioSkills 4** in Appendix B to explain why no error bars are used for the points shown on the graph on the left side of the "Results" section.

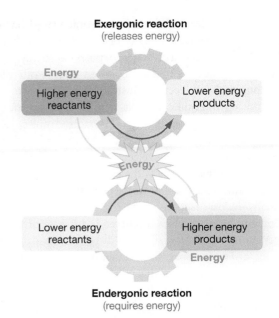

Exergonic reaction
(releases energy)

Energy

Higher energy reactants → Lower energy products

Energy

Lower energy reactants → Higher energy products

Energy

Endergonic reaction
(requires energy)

FIGURE 8.5 Energetic Coupling Allows Endergonic Reactions to Proceed Using the Energy Released from Exergonic Reactions.

chemical evolution (Chapter 2). What source of energy drives these reactions inside cells?

Exergonic reactions release free energy. **FIGURE 8.5** shows how **energetic coupling** between exergonic and endergonic reactions allows chemical energy released from one reaction to drive another. In cells, this process generally occurs in one of two ways, either through the transfer of high-energy electrons or the transfer of a phosphate group.

Redox Reactions Transfer Energy via Electrons

Chemical reactions that involve the loss or gain of one or more electrons are called **reduction–oxidation reactions,** or **redox reactions.** When an atom or molecule loses one or more electrons, it is oxidized. This makes sense if you notice that the term

oxidized sounds as if oxygen has done something to an atom or molecule. Recall that oxygen is highly electronegative and often pulls electrons from other atoms (Chapter 2). On the other hand, when an atom or molecule gains one or more electrons, it is reduced. To keep these terms straight, students often use the mnemonic "OIL RIG"—**Oxidation** *Is Loss* of electrons; **Reduction** *Is Gain* of electrons.

Oxidation events are always paired with a reduction; if one atom loses an electron, another has to gain it, and vice versa. Since electron position is related to energy levels, redox reactions represent the energetic coupling of two half-reactions, one exergonic and one endergonic. Oxidation is the exergonic half-reaction, and reduction is the endergonic half-reaction. Some of the energy that is lost by the oxidized molecule is used to increase potential energy of the reduced molecule. In cases where more free energy is released by the oxidation step than is necessary for the reduction step, the overall reaction is exergonic.

The gain or loss of an electron can be relative, however. During a redox reaction, an electron can be transferred completely from one atom to another, or an electron can simply shift its position in a covalent bond.

An Example of Redox in Action To see how redox reactions work, consider the spontaneous reaction that occurs when reduced carbons in glucose ($C_6H_{12}O_6$) are oxidized as the sugar is burned in the presence of oxygen (O_2) (**FIGURE 8.6**). The orange dots in the illustration represent the positions of the electrons involved in covalent bonds.

Now compare the position of the electrons in the first reactant, glucose, with their position in the first product, carbon dioxide. Notice that many of the electrons have moved farther from the carbon nucleus in carbon dioxide. This means that carbon has been oxidized: it has "lost" electrons. The change occurred because the carbon and hydrogen atoms in glucose share electrons equally, while the carbon and oxygen atoms in CO_2 don't. In CO_2, the high electronegativity of the oxygen atoms pulled electrons away from the carbon atom.

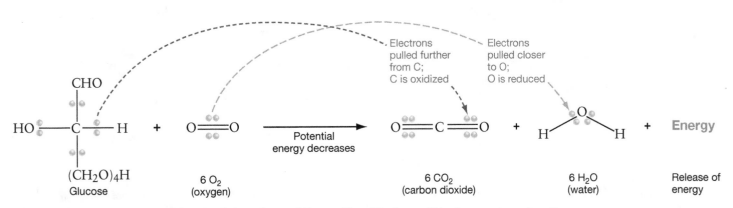

FIGURE 8.6 Redox Reactions Involve the Gain or Loss of One or More Electrons. This diagram shows how the position of electrons changes when glucose reacts with oxygen. The carbons of glucose are oxidized while the oxygen atoms of O_2 are reduced.

Now compare the position of the electrons in the reactant O_2 molecules with their position in the product water molecules. In water, the electrons have moved closer to the oxygen nuclei than they were in the O_2 molecules, meaning that the oxygen atoms have been reduced. Oxygen has "gained" electrons. Thus, when glucose burns, carbon atoms are oxidized while oxygen atoms are reduced.

These shifts in electron position change the amount of chemical energy in the reactants and products. When glucose reacts with oxygen, electrons are held much tighter in the product molecules than in the reactant molecules. This means their potential energy has decreased. The entropy of the products is also much higher than that of the reactants, as indicated by the increase in the number of molecules. As a result, this reaction is exergonic. It releases energy in the form of heat and light.

Another Approach to Understanding Redox During the redox reactions that occur in cells, electrons (e^-) may also be transferred from an atom in one molecule, called the **electron donor,** to an atom in a different molecule, the **electron acceptor.** When this occurs, the electron may be accompanied by a proton (H^+), which would result in the addition of a neutral hydrogen (H) atom to the electron acceptor.

Molecules that obtain hydrogens via redox reactions tend to gain potential energy because the electrons in C−H bonds are equally shared and hence relatively far from the positive charges on the C and H nuclei. This observation should sound familiar,

from what you have learned about carbohydrates (see Chapter 5). Molecules that have a large number of C−H bonds, such as carbohydrates and fats, store a great deal of potential energy.

Conversely, molecules that are oxidized in cells often lose a proton along with an electron. Instead of having many C−H bonds, oxidized molecules in cells tend to have an increased number of C−O bonds (see Figure 8.6). Oxidized molecules tend to lose potential energy. To understand why, remember that oxygen atoms have extremely high electronegativity. Because oxygen atoms hold electrons so tightly, the electrons involved in bonds with oxygen atoms have low potential energy.

In many redox reactions in biology, understanding where oxidation and reduction have occurred is a matter of following hydrogen atoms—reduction often "adds Hs" and oxidation often "removes Hs." For example, **flavin adenine dinucleotide (FAD)** is a cellular electron acceptor that is reduced by two electrons accompanied by two protons to form $FADH_2$ (**FIGURE 8.7a**). $FADH_2$ readily donates these high-energy electrons to other molecules. As a result, it is called an **electron carrier** and is said to have "reducing power."

Another common electron carrier is **nicotinamide adenine dinucleotide (NAD$^+$),** which is reduced to form **NADH.** Like FAD, two electrons reduce NAD$^+$. These two carriers differ, however, in the number of hydrogen atoms transferred. NAD$^+$ acquires only one of the two hydrogens and releases the second into the environment as H$^+$ (**FIGURE 8.7b**).

(a) Flavin adenine dinucleotide

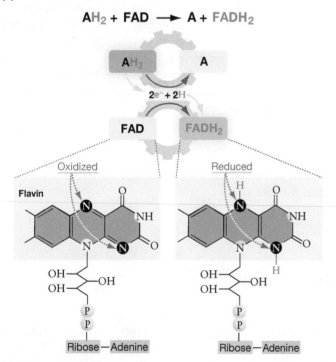

(b) Nicotinamide adenine dinucleotide

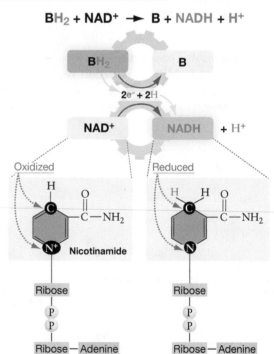

FIGURE 8.7 Redox Reactions May Transfer Protons Along with Electrons. The potential energy of NAD$^+$ and FAD is increased by redox reactions that transfer high-energy electrons, which may or may not be accompanied by protons. The products FADH$_2$ and NADH are important electron carriers.

The two examples in Figure 8.6 illustrate an important point—all redox reactions involve the transfer of electrons, but they do not always involve the transfer of hydrogens. Redox reactions are central in biology—they transfer energy via electrons. The energy released from certain key redox reactions (see Chapter 9) is used to drive the endergonic formation of the nucleotide ATP from ADP and P_i. How is the energy stored in ATP used by the cell?

ATP Transfers Energy via Phosphate Groups

Adenosine triphosphate (ATP) (introduced in Chapter 4) makes things happen in cells because it has a great deal of potential energy. As **FIGURE 8.8a** shows, four negative charges are confined to a small area in the three phosphate groups in ATP. In part because these negative charges repel each other, the potential energy of the electrons in the phosphate groups is extraordinarily high.

ATP Hydrolysis Releases Free Energy When ATP reacts with water during a hydrolysis reaction, the bond between ATP's outermost phosphate group and its neighbor is broken, resulting in the formation of ADP and inorganic phosphate, P_i, which has the formula $H_2PO_4^-$ (**FIGURE 8.8b**). This reaction is highly exergonic. Under standard conditions of temperature and pressure in the laboratory, a total of 7.3 kilocalories of energy per mole of ATP (or 7.3 kcal/mol), is released during the reaction. A **kilocalorie (kcal)** of energy raises 1 kilogram (kg) of water 1°C.

ATP hydrolysis is exergonic because the entropy of the product molecules is higher than that of the reactants, and because there is a large drop in potential energy when ATP breaks down into ADP and P_i. The change in potential energy occurs in part because the electrons from ATP's phosphate groups are now spread across two molecules instead of being clustered on one molecule—meaning that there is now less electrical repulsion.

In addition, the destabilizing effect of the negative charges is reduced in ADP and P_i since these products interact with the partial positive charges on surrounding water molecules more efficiently than the clustered negative charges on ATP did.

How Does ATP Drive Endergonic Reactions? In the time it takes to read this sentence, millions of endergonic reactions have occurred in your cells. This chemical activity is possible, in part, because cells are able to use the energy released from the exergonic hydrolysis of ATP.

If the reaction diagrammed in Figure 8.8b occurred in a test tube, the energy released would be lost as heat. But cells don't lose that 7.3 kcal/mole as heat. Instead, they use it to make things happen. Specifically, the energy that is released when ATP is hydrolyzed may be used to transfer the cleaved phosphate to a target molecule, called a **substrate.**

The addition of a phosphate group to a substrate is called **phosphorylation.** When ATP is used as the phosphate donor, phosphorylation is exergonic because the electrons in ADP and the phosphate added to the substrate have much less potential energy than they did in ATP.

To see how this process works, consider an endergonic reaction between two reactant molecules—compound A and compound B—that results in a product AB needed by your cells. For this reaction to proceed, an input of energy is required.

When a phosphate group from ATP is added to one or both of the reactant molecules, the potential energy of the reactant is increased. This phosphorylated intermediate is referred to as an activated substrate. This is the critical point: Activated substrates have high enough potential energy that the reaction between compound A and, for example, the activated form of compound B is now exergonic. The two compounds then go on to react and form the product molecule AB.

(a) ATP stores a large amount of potential energy.

Phosphate groups

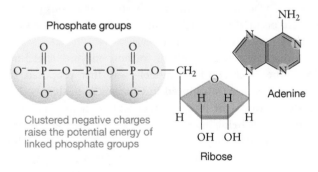

Clustered negative charges raise the potential energy of linked phosphate groups

FIGURE 8.8 Adenosine Triphosphate (ATP) Has High Potential Energy. (a) ATP's high potential energy results, in part, from the four negative charges clustered in its three phosphate groups. The negative charges repel each other, raising the potential energy of the electrons. **(b)** When ATP is hydrolyzed to ADP and inorganic phosphate, a large free-energy change occurs.

(b) Energy is released when ATP is hydrolyzed.

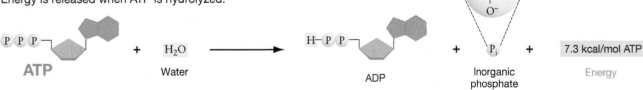

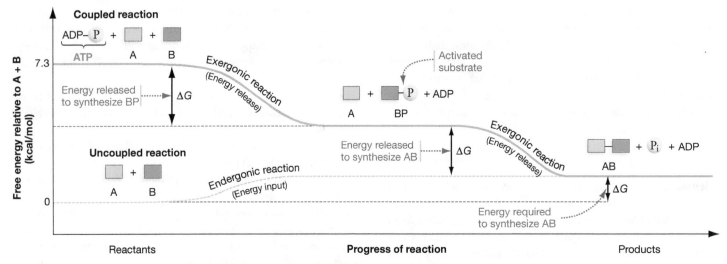

FIGURE 8.9 Exergonic Phosphorylation Reactions Are Coupled to Endergonic Reactions. In cells, many reactions only occur if one reactant is activated by phosphorylation. The phosphorylated reactant molecule has high enough free energy that the subsequent reaction is exergonic. In this graph, the free energy being tracked on the y-axis represents A, B, and the 7.3 kcal/mol that is released when ATP is hydrolyzed. For simplicity, the free energy in ADP and P_i is not shown. ΔG represents the change in free energy between the reactants and products for each indicated step.

✔**EXERCISE** Label the ΔG in the uncoupled reaction and the two steps of the coupled reaction to indicate if the change is representing a positive (> 0) or negative (< 0) value.

FIGURE 8.9 graphs how phosphorylation can couple exergonic and endergonic reactions. Note that the reaction between A and B to produce the product AB is endergonic—the ΔG is positive. But after the exergonic transfer of a phosphate group from ATP to B occurs, the free energy of the reactants A and BP is high enough to make the reaction that forms AB exergonic. When reactant molecules in an endergonic reaction are phosphorylated, the free energy released during phosphorylation is coupled to the endergonic reaction to make the combined overall reaction exergonic.

✔ If you understand the principles of energetic coupling, you should be able to compare and contrast how energy is transferred via redox reactions and ATP hydrolysis.

It is hard to overstate the importance of energetic coupling: Without it, life is impossible. If the cells in your body could no longer drive endergonic reactions by coupling them to exergonic reactions, you would die within minutes.

Now the question is, What role do enzymes play in these reactions?

check your understanding

If you understand that . . .

- When redox reactions occur, electrons change position. Chemical energy is based on the positions of electrons in chemical bonds, so redox reactions usually involve a change in potential energy.
- ATP contains a cluster of three negatively charged phosphate groups.
- When ATP or phosphate groups from ATP bind to substrates, they gain a great deal of potential energy.

✔ You should be able to . . .

1. Explain why reduced molecules with many C–H bonds store more potential energy than oxidized molecules with many C–O bonds.

2. Explain why ATP has such high potential energy.

Answers are available in Appendix A.

8.3 How Enzymes Work

Regardless of whether reactions in cells are spontaneous or not, none would occur at the speed required for life without the support of enzymes. How do they do it?

Recall that the initial hypothesis for how enzymes speed up reactions—the "lock-and-key" model—was first proposed in 1894 by Emil Fischer (introduced in Chapter 3). In this model, the substrates would fit into enzymes and react in a manner analogous to a key being inserted into a lock. In other words, enzymes are **catalysts**—they bring substrates together in a precise orientation that makes reactions more likely. Fischer's model also explained why many enzymes are specific for a single reaction—specificity is a product of the geometry and chemical properties of the sites where substrates bind.

Enzymes Help Reactions Clear Two Hurdles

Recall that two hurdles must be cleared before reactions can take place: Reactants need to (**1**) collide in a precise orientation and

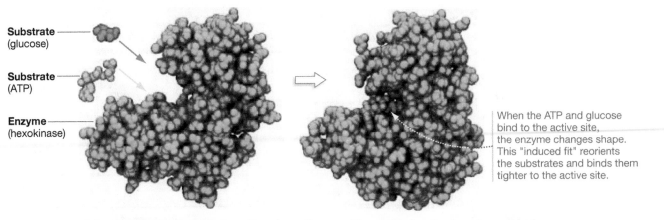

Substrate
(glucose)

Substrate
(ATP)

Enzyme
(hexokinase)

When the ATP and glucose
bind to the active site,
the enzyme changes shape.
This "induced fit" reorients
the substrates and binds them
tighter to the active site.

FIGURE 8.10 Reactant Molecules Bind to Specific Locations in an Enzyme. The reactant molecules, shown in red and yellow, fit into a precise location, called the active site, in the green enzyme. In this enzyme and in many others, the binding event causes the protein to change shape.

(2) have enough kinetic energy to overcome repulsion between electrons that come into contact as a bond forms (Chapter 2). To appreciate how enzymes work, let's consider each hurdle in turn.

Enzymes Bring Substrates Together   Part of the reason enzymes are such effective catalysts is that they bring substrate molecules together in a substrate binding site known as the enzyme's **active site** (Chapter 3). In this way, enzymes help substrates collide in a precise orientation so that the electrons involved in the reaction can interact.

Enzymes generally are very large relative to substrates and roughly globular. The active site is in a cleft or cavity within the globular shape. A good example can be seen in the enzyme glucokinase, which catalyzes the phosphorylation of the sugar glucose. (Many enzymes have names that hint at the identity of the substrate and end with -*ase*.) As the left side of **FIGURE 8.10** shows, the active site in glucokinase is a small notch in an otherwise large, crescent-shaped enzyme.

In Fischer's original lock-and-key model, enzymes were conceived of as being rigid—almost literally as rigid as a lock. As research on enzyme action progressed, however, Fischer's model had to be modified. Perhaps the most important realization was that enzymes are not rigid and static, but flexible and dynamic. In fact, many enzymes undergo a significant change in shape, or conformation, when reactant molecules bind to the active site. You can see this conformational change, called an **induced fit,** in the glucokinase molecule on the right side of Figure 8.10. Once glucokinase binds its substrates—ATP and glucose—the enzyme rocks forward over the active site to bring the two substrates together.

In addition, recent research has clarified the nature of Fischer's key. When one or more substrate molecules enter the active site, they are held in place through hydrogen bonding or other weak interactions with amino acids in the active site. Once the substrate is bound, one or more R-groups in the active site come into play. The degree of interaction between the substrate and enzyme increases and reaches a maximum when a temporary,

unstable, intermediate condition called the **transition state** is formed. When Fischer's key is in its lock, it represents the transition state of the substrate.

There is more to achieving this transition state than simply an enzyme binding to its substrates, however. Even if the reaction is spontaneous, a certain amount of kinetic energy is required to strain the chemical bonds in substrates so they can achieve this transition state—called the **activation energy.** How do enzymes help clear the activation energy hurdle?

Enzymes Lower the Activation Energy   Reactions happen when reactants have enough kinetic energy to reach the transition state. The kinetic energy of molecules, in turn, is a function of their temperature. (This is why reactions tend to proceed faster at higher temperatures.)

FIGURE 8.11 (see page 146) graphs the changes in free energy that take place during the course of a chemical reaction. As you read along the x-axis from left to right, note that a dramatic rise in free energy occurs when the reactants combine to form the transition state—followed by a dramatic drop in free energy when products form. The free energy of the transition state is high because the bonds that existed in the substrates are destabilized—it is the transition point between breaking old bonds and forming new ones.

The ΔG label on the graph indicates the overall change in free energy in the reaction—that is, the energy of the products minus the energy of the reactants. In this particular case, the products have lower free energy than the reactants, meaning that the reaction is exergonic. But because the activation energy for this reaction, symbolized by E_a, is high, the reaction would proceed slowly—even at high temperature.

This is an important point: The more unstable the transition state, the higher the activation energy and the less likely a reaction is to proceed quickly.

Reaction rates, then, depend on both the kinetic energy of the reactants and the activation energy of the particular reaction—meaning the free energy of the transition state. If the kinetic

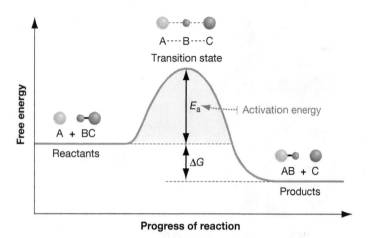

FIGURE 8.11 Changes in Free Energy during a Chemical Reaction. The energy profile shows changes in free energy that occur over the course of a hypothetical reaction between a molecule A and a molecule containing parts B and C. The overall reaction would be written as $A + BC \rightarrow AB + C$. E_a is the activation energy of the reaction.

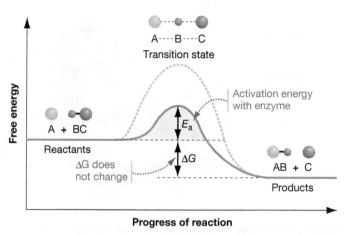

FIGURE 8.12 A Catalyst Changes the Activation Energy of a Reaction. The energy profile for the same reaction diagrammed in Figure 8.11, but now with a catalyst present. Even though the energy barrier to the reaction, E_a, is much lower, ΔG does not change.

✓ **QUESTION** Can a catalyst make a nonspontaneous reaction occur spontaneously? Explain why or why not.

energy of the participating molecules is high, such as at high temperatures, then molecular collisions are more likely to overcome the activation energy barrier. At this point, the transition state is formed and the reaction takes place.

Enzymes don't change the temperature of a solution, though. How do they fit in?

Interactions with amino acid R-groups at the enzyme active site stabilize the transition state and thus lower the activation energy required for the reaction to proceed. At the atomic level, R-groups that line the active site may form short-lived covalent bonds that assist with the transfer of atoms or groups of atoms from one reactant to another. More commonly, the presence of acidic or basic R-groups allows the reactants to lose or gain a proton more readily.

FIGURE 8.12 diagrams how enzymes lower the activation energy for a reaction by lowering the free energy of the transition state. Note that the presence of an enzyme does not affect the overall

energy change, ΔG, or change the energy of the reactants or the products. An enzyme changes only the free energy of the transition state.

Most enzymes are specific in their activity—they catalyze just a single reaction by lowering the activation energy that is required—and many are astonishingly efficient. Most of the important reactions in biology would not occur at all, or else proceed at imperceptible rates, without a catalyst. It's not unusual for enzymes to speed up reactions by a factor of a million; some enzymes make reactions go many *trillions* of times faster than they would without a catalyst.

It's also important to note that an enzyme is not consumed in a chemical reaction, even though it participates in the reaction. The composition of an enzyme is exactly the same after the reaction as it was before.

Enzyme catalysis can be analyzed as a three-step process. **FIGURE 8.13** summarizes this model:

PROCESS: A MODEL OF ENZYME ACTION

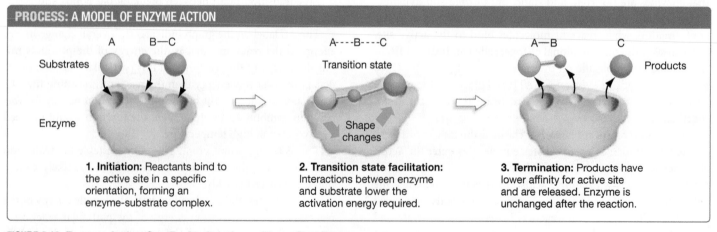

1. Initiation: Reactants bind to the active site in a specific orientation, forming an enzyme-substrate complex.

2. Transition state facilitation: Interactions between enzyme and substrate lower the activation energy required.

3. Termination: Products have lower affinity for active site and are released. Enzyme is unchanged after the reaction.

FIGURE 8.13 Enzyme Action Can Be Analyzed as a Three-Step Process.

1. **Initiation** Instead of reactants occasionally colliding in a random fashion, enzymes orient reactants precisely as they bind at specific locations within the active site.

2. **Transition state facilitation** Inside a catalyst's active site, reactant molecules are more likely to reach their transition state. In some cases the transition state is stabilized by a change in the enzyme's shape. Interactions between the substrate and R-groups in the enzyme's active site lower the activation energy required for the reaction. Thus, the catalyzed reaction proceeds much more rapidly than the uncatalyzed reaction.

3. **Termination** The reaction products have less affinity for the active site than the transition state does. Binding ends, the enzyme returns to its original conformation, and the products are released.

✔ If you understand the basic principles of enzyme catalysis, you should be able to complete the following sentences: (1) Enzymes speed reaction rates by _____ and lowering activation energy. (2) Activation energies drop because enzymes destabilize bonds in the substrates, forming the _____. (3) Enzyme specificity is a function of the active site's shape and the chemical properties of the _____ at the active site. (4) In enzymes, as in many molecules, function follows from _____.

What Limits the Rate of Catalysis?

For several decades after Fischer's model was published, most research on enzymes focused on rates of enzyme action, or what biologists call enzyme kinetics. Researchers observed that, when the amount of product produced per second—indicating the speed of the reaction—is plotted as a function of substrate concentration, a graph like that shown in **FIGURE 8.14** results.

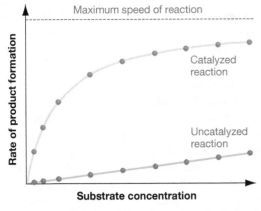

FIGURE 8.14 Enzyme-Catalyzed Reactions Can Be Saturated. At high substrate concentration, enzyme-catalyzed reactions reach a maximum rate. Uncatalyzed reactions slowly increase as substrate concentration increases.

✔**EXERCISE** Label the parts of the *catalyzed reaction curve* that represent where (1) the reaction rate is most sensitive to changes in substrate concentration and (2) most or all of the active sites present are occupied.

In this graph, each data point represents an experiment where reaction rate was measured when substrates were at various concentrations. The two lines represent two series of experiments: one with the reactions catalyzed by an enzyme and the other uncatalyzed. As you read the curve for the catalyzed reaction from left to right, note that it has three basic sections:

1. When substrate concentrations are low, the speed of an enzyme-catalyzed reaction increases in a steep, linear fashion.

2. At intermediate substrate concentrations, the increase in speed begins to slow.

3. At high substrate concentration, the reaction rate plateaus at a maximum speed.

This pattern is in striking contrast to the situation for the uncatalyzed reactions, where the reaction speed is far slower, but tends to show a continuing linear increase with substrate concentration. The "saturation kinetics" of enzyme-catalyzed reactions were taken as strong evidence that the enzyme–substrate complex proposed by Fischer actually exists. The idea was that, at some point, active sites cannot accept substrates any faster, no matter how large the concentration of substrates gets. Stated another way, reaction rates level off because all available enzyme molecules are being used.

Do Enzymes Work Alone?

The answer to this question, in many cases, is no. Atoms or molecules that are not part of an enzyme's primary structure are often required for an enzyme to function normally. These enzyme "helpers" can be divided into three different types:

1. **Cofactors:** Inorganic ions, such as the metal ions Zn^{2+} (zinc), Mg^{2+} (magnesium), and Fe^{2+} (iron), which reversibly interact with enzymes. Cofactors that now participate in key reactions in virtually all living cells are thought to have been involved in catalysis early on in chemical evolution (see Chapter 2).

2. **Coenzymes:** Organic molecules that reversibly interact with enzymes, such as the electron carriers NADH or $FADH_2$.

3. **Prosthetic groups:** Non-amino acid atoms or molecules that are permanently attached to proteins, such as the molecule retinal. Retinal is involved in converting light energy into chemical energy.

In many cases, these enzyme helpers are part of the active site and play a key role in stabilizing the transition state. Their presence is therefore essential for the catalytic activity of many enzymes.

To appreciate why this is important, consider that many of the vitamins in your diet are required for the production of coenzymes. Vitamin deficiencies result in coenzyme deficiencies. Lack of coenzymes, in turn, disrupts normal enzyme function and causes disease. For example, thiamine (vitamin B_1) is required for the production of a coenzyme called thiamine pyrophosphate, which is required by three different enzymes. Lack of thiamine in the diet dramatically reduces the activity of these enzymes and causes an array of nervous system and heart disorders collectively known as beriberi.

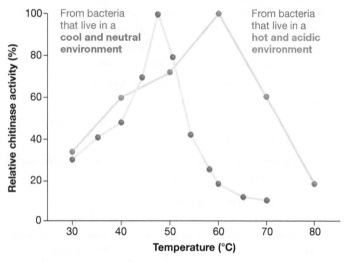

(a) Enzymes from different organisms may function best at different temperatures.

From bacteria that live in a **cool and neutral environment**

From bacteria that live in a **hot and acidic environment**

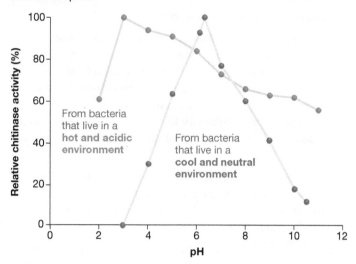

(b) Enzymes from different organisms may function best at different pHs.

From bacteria that live in a **hot and acidic environment**

From bacteria that live in a **cool and neutral environment**

FIGURE 8.15 Enzymes Have an Optimal Temperature and pH. The activity of enzymes is sensitive to changes in temperature **(a)** and pH **(b)**.

DATA: Nawani, N., B. P. Kapadnis, A. D. Das, et al. 2002. *Journal of Applied Microbiology* 93: 865–975. Also Nawani, N., and B. P. Kapadnis. 2001. *Journal of Applied Microbiology* 90: 803–808.

8.4 What Factors Affect Enzyme Function?

Given that an enzyme's structure is critical to its function, it's not surprising that an enzyme's activity is sensitive to conditions that alter protein shape. Recall that protein structure is dependent on the sequence of amino acids and a variety of chemical bonds and interactions that fold the polypeptide into its functional form (Chapter 3).

In particular, the activity of an enzyme often changes drastically as a function of temperature, pH, interactions with other molecules, and modifications of its primary structure. Let's take a look at how enzyme function is affected by, and sometimes even regulated by, each of these factors.

Enzymes Are Optimized for Particular Environments

Temperature affects the folding and movement of an enzyme as well as the kinetic energy of its substrates. The concentration of protons in a solution, as measured by pH, also affects enzyme structure and function. pH affects the charge on carboxyl and amino groups in residue side chains, and also the active site's ability to participate in reactions that involve the transfer of protons or electrons.

Do data support these assertions? **FIGURE 8.15a** shows how the activity of an enzyme, plotted on the *y*-axis, changes as a function of temperature, plotted on the *x*-axis. These data were collected for an enzyme called chitinase, which is used by bacteria to digest cell walls of fungi. In this graph, each data point represents the enzyme's relative activity—meaning the rate of the enzyme-catalyzed reaction, scaled relative to the highest rate observed—in

experiments conducted under conditions that differed only in temperature. Results are shown for two types of bacteria.

Note that, in both bacterial species, the enzyme has a distinct optimum or peak—a temperature at which it functions best. One of the bacterial species lives in the cool soil under palm trees, where the temperature is about 25°C, while the other lives in hot springs, where temperatures can be close to 100°C. The temperature optimum for the enzyme reflects these environments.

The two types of bacteria have different versions of the enzyme that differ in primary structure. Natural selection (introduced in Chapter 1) has favored a structure in each species that is best suited for its distinct environment. The two versions are adaptations that allow each species to thrive at different temperatures.

FIGURE 8.15b makes the same point for pH. The effect of pH on enzyme activity was tested on the same chitinases used in Figure 8.15a, but this time using conditions that varied only in pH. The soil-dwelling bacteria described earlier grow in a neutral pH environment, but the species that lives in hot springs is also exposed to acidic conditions.

Note that the organism that thrives in a hot, acidic environment has a version of the enzyme that performs best at high temperatures and low pH; the organism that lives in the cool soil has a version of the enzyme that functions best at cooler temperatures and nearly neutral pH. Each enzyme is sensitive to changes in temperature and pH, but each species' version of the enzyme has a structure that allows it to function best in its particular environment.

To summarize, the rate of an enzyme-catalyzed reaction depends not only on substrate concentration and the enzyme's intrinsic affinity for the substrate but also on temperature and pH (among other factors). Temperature affects the movement of the substrates and enzyme; pH affects the enzyme's shape and reactivity.

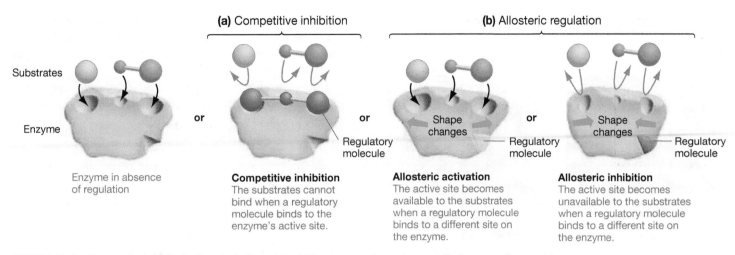

(a) Competitive inhibition

(b) Allosteric regulation

Substrates

Enzyme

or

or

or

Regulatory molecule

Regulatory molecule

Regulatory molecule

Enzyme in absence of regulation

Competitive inhibition
The substrates cannot bind when a regulatory molecule binds to the enzyme's active site.

Allosteric activation
The active site becomes available to the substrates when a regulatory molecule binds to a different site on the enzyme.

Allosteric inhibition
The active site becomes unavailable to the substrates when a regulatory molecule binds to a different site on the enzyme.

FIGURE 8.16 An Enzyme's Activity Is Precisely Regulated. Enzymes are turned on or off when specific regulatory molecules bind to them.

Most Enzymes Are Regulated

Controlling when and where enzymes will function is vital to the work of a cell. While temperature and pH affect the activity of enzymes, they are not often used as a means of regulating enzyme function. Instead, other molecules, in some cases other enzymes, regulate most of the cell's enzymatic activity. These regulatory molecules often change the enzyme's structure in some way, and their activity either activates or inactivates the enzyme.

Regulating Enzymes via Noncovalent Modifications Many molecules that regulate enzyme activity bind non-covalently to the enzyme to either activate or inactivate it. Since the interaction does not alter the enzyme's primary structure, it is often referred to as a "reversible" modification.

Reversible modifications affect enzyme function in one of two ways:

1. The regulatory molecule is similar in size and shape to the enzyme's natural substrate and inhibits catalysis by binding to the enzyme's active site. This event is called **competitive inhibition** because the molecule involved competes with the substrate for access to the enzyme's active site (**FIGURE 8.16a**).

2. The regulatory molecule binds at a location other than the active site and changes the shape of the enzyme. This type of regulation is called **allosteric** ("different-structure") **regulation** because the binding event changes the shape of the enzyme in a way that makes the active site available or unavailable (**FIGURE 8.16b**).

Both strategies depend on the concentration of the regulatory molecule—the more regulatory molecule present, the more likely it will be to bind to the enzyme and affect its activity. The amount of regulatory molecule is often tightly controlled and, as you'll see in Section 8.5, the regulatory molecules themselves often manage the enzymes that produce them.

Regulating Enzymes via Covalent Modifications In some cases, the function of an enzyme is altered by a chemical change in its

primary structure. This change may be reversible or irreversible, depending on the type of modification.

Irreversible changes often result from the cleavage of peptide bonds that make up the primary structure of the enzyme. The enzyme trypsin, for example, is not functional until a small section of the protein is removed by a specific protease.

The most common modification of enzymes is the addition of one or more phosphate groups, similar to what was described for activated substrates in Section 8.2. In this case, however, the enzyme is phosphorylated instead of the substrate molecule. The transfer of a phosphate from ATP to the enzyme may be catalyzed by the enzyme itself or by a different enzyme.

When phosphorylation adds a negative charge to one or more amino acid residues in a protein, the electrons in that part of the protein change configuration. The enzyme's conformation

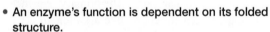
check your understanding

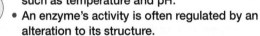

C Y U

If you understand that . . .
- An enzyme's function is dependent on its folded structure.
- Enzymes have been optimized to fold into functional structures at particular environmental conditions, such as temperature and pH.
- An enzyme's activity is often regulated by an alteration to its structure.

✔ **You should be able to . . .**

1. Explain why the relative activity appears to drop off in Figure 8.15b, when it has been shown that reaction rates tend to increase at higher temperatures (Figure 8.4).

2. Predict how the shape change that occurs when an enzyme is phosphorylated would affect its catalytic activity.

Answers are available in Appendix A.

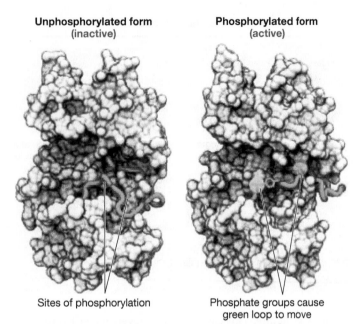

Unphosphorylated form
(inactive)

Phosphorylated form
(active)

Sites of phosphorylation

Phosphate groups cause
green loop to move

FIGURE 8.17 Phosphorylation Changes the Shape and Activity of Proteins. When proteins are phosphorylated, they often change shape in a way that alters their activity. The figure shows the subtle structural change that occurs when mitogen-activated protein kinase (MAPK) is activated by adding two phosphate groups (yellow) to the enzyme.

usually changes as well, which may activate or inactivate its function. Note that although a substrate or an enzyme may be "activated" via phosphorylation, this activation does not represent the same effect. When a substrate is activated, its potential energy has increased, and this energy is used to convert an endergonic reaction to one that is exergonic. When an enzyme is activated, its catalytic function has been turned on—any change in the potential energy of the enzyme is not directly used in driving the reaction.

To see how phosphorylation affects the shape and activity of an enzyme, let's look at an enzyme called mitogen-activated protein kinase (MAPK), which is involved in cell signaling (see Chapter 11). As shown in **FIGURE 8.17**, phosphorylation of amino acid residues in a particular loop of the primary sequence causes a shape change, which functions like a switch to activate the enzyme.

Phosphorylation of an enzyme is a reversible modification to the protein's structure. Dephosphorylation—removal of phosphates—can quickly return the protein to its previous shape. The relative abundance of enzymes that catalyze phosphorylation and dephosphorylation, then, regulates the function of the protein.

8.5 Enzymes Can Work Together in Metabolic Pathways

The eukaryotic cell has been compared to an industrial complex, where distinct organelles are functionally integrated into a cooperative network with a common goal—life (see Chapter 7). Similarly, enzymes often work together in a manner resembling an assembly line in a factory. Each of the molecules of life presented in this book is built by a series of reactions, each catalyzed by a different enzyme. These multistep processes are referred to as **metabolic pathways.**

The following is an example of this type of teamwork, where an initial substrate A is sequentially modified by enzymes 1–3 to produce product D:

$$A \xrightarrow{enzyme\ 1} B \xrightarrow{enzyme\ 2} C \xrightarrow{enzyme\ 3} D$$

The B and C molecules are referred to as intermediates in the pathway—they serve as both a product and a reactant. For example, molecule B is the product of reaction 1 and the reactant for reaction 2.

Although these reactions have been written in a single direction, from left to right, the directionality is dependent on the relative concentrations of the reactants and products. At equilibrium, however, the concentration of the product for each reaction will be higher than the concentration of its respective reactant. Since D is the overall product for this pathway, it will have the highest concentration at equilibrium.

Metabolic Pathways Are Regulated

Since enzymes catalyze the reactions in metabolic pathways, the mechanisms that regulate enzyme function introduced in Section 8.4 also apply to the individual steps in a pathway. For example, to understand how blocking an individual reaction can affect an entire pathway, go back to the three-step model presented earlier and inactivate enzyme 2 by crossing it out. ✔ If you understand the assembly-line behavior of enzymes in a metabolic pathway, you should be able to predict how inactivating enzyme 2 would affect the concentration of molecules A, B, C, and D relative to what they would be if the pathway were fully functional.

When an enzyme in a pathway is inhibited by the product of the reaction sequence, **feedback inhibition** occurs. This is a convenient way for pathways to shut themselves down when their activity is no longer needed. As the concentration of the product molecule becomes abundant, it "feeds back" to stop the reaction sequence (**FIGURE 8.18**). By inhibiting a step early in the pathway, the amount of the initial substrate is not depleted unnecessarily, allowing it to be stored or used for other reactions.

Metabolic Pathways Evolve

While many enzymes are extraordinarily specific, some can catalyze a range of reactions and are able to interact with a family of related substrates. Research suggests that this flexibility allowed new enzymes to evolve and that enzymes specialized for catalyzing key reactions provided cells with a selective advantage. Could the same flexibility also help explain the evolution of the stepwise series of reactions seen in metabolic pathways?

In 1945, Norman Horowitz proposed a simple, stepwise process that could have directed pathway evolution. In Horowitz's model, enzymes first would have evolved to make the building blocks of life from readily available substrates, such as small organic compounds (see Chapter 2).

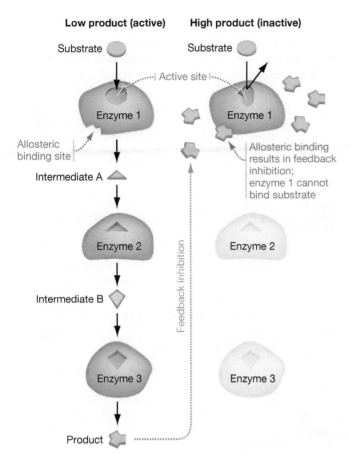

FIGURE 8.18 Feedback Inhibition May Regulate Metabolic Pathways. Feedback inhibition occurs when the product of a metabolic pathway inhibits an enzyme that functions early in the pathway.

If an original substrate were depleted, natural selection would next favor the evolution of a new enzyme to make more of it from other existing molecules. By evolving a new reaction step to produce the original substrate—now serving as an intermediate in a two-step pathway—the original enzyme would have been able to continue its work. **FIGURE 8.19** illustrates this model—referred to as retro-evolution—in which repetition of this backward process produces a multistep metabolic pathway.

Researchers also speculate that as early pathways emerged, early enzymes may have been recruited to new pathways, where they evolved new catalytic activities that performed new tasks. This hypothesis is called patchwork evolution, since the new reaction series would consist of enzymes brought together from different pathways.

Evidence of patchwork evolution has been observed in modern organisms, where new metabolic activities have emerged in response to human-made chemicals. For example, a novel pathway has recently evolved in one species of bacterium to break down the pesticide pentachlorophenol, for use as a source of energy and carbon building blocks. Pentachlorophenol was first introduced into the environment in the 1930s as a timber preservative. The new pathway uses enzymes from two preexisting pathways, which had evolved the ability to work together. The metabolic activity of microbes is now being scrutinized and engineered to clean up a variety of human-made pollutants—giving rise to a new technology called **bioremediation** (see Chapter 29).

Regardless of how they evolved, metabolic pathways are now vital to the function of all cells. Those that break down molecules for sources of energy and carbon building blocks are called **catabolic pathways;** those that use energy and carbon building blocks to synthesize molecules are called **anabolic pathways.**

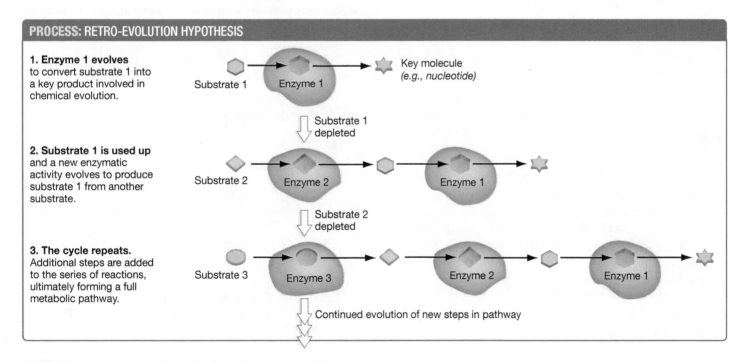

FIGURE 8.19 A Hypothetical Model for Metabolic Pathway Evolution.

You are being kept alive by key catabolic and anabolic pathways. The catabolic pathways of cellular respiration (introduced in Chapter 9) harvest high-energy electrons from reduced carbons (from foods such as starch and sugar) and pass them through redox reactions to generate ATP. These reduced carbons are produced by the anabolic pathways of photosynthesis that are driven by light energy (introduced in Chapter 10). The reactions involved in cellular respiration and photosynthesis perform the most important energy transformations to life on Earth.

CHAPTER 8 REVIEW

For media, go to MasteringBiology

If you understand . . .

8.1 What Happens to Energy in Chemical Reactions?

- Spontaneous reactions do not require an input of energy to occur.

- The Gibbs free energy change, ΔG, summarizes the combined effects of changes in enthalpy and entropy during a chemical reaction.

- Spontaneous reactions have a negative ΔG and are said to be exergonic; nonspontaneous reactions have a positive ΔG and are said to be endergonic.

✓ You should be able to explain why changes in enthalpy and entropy are used to determine whether a reaction is spontaneous.

8.2 Nonspontaneous Reactions May Be Driven Using Chemical Energy

- Redox reactions transfer energy by coupling exergonic oxidation reactions to endergonic reduction reactions.

- High-energy C—H bonds may be formed during the reduction step of a redox reaction when an H^+ is combined with a transferred electron.

- The hydrolysis of ATP is an exergonic reaction and may be used to drive a variety of cellular processes.

- When a phosphate group from ATP is added to a substrate that participates in an endergonic reaction, the potential energy of the substrate is raised enough to make the reaction exergonic and thus spontaneous.

✓ You should be able to explain what energetic coupling means, and why life would not exist without it.

8.3 How Enzymes Work

- Enzymes are protein catalysts. They speed reaction rates but do not affect the change in free energy of the reaction.

- The structure of an enzyme has an active site that brings substrates together. After binding to substrates, the structure of the enzyme changes to stabilize the transition state.

- Activation energy is the amount of kinetic energy required to reach the transition state of a reaction. Enzymes speed up a reaction by lowering the activation energy.

- Many enzymes function only with the help of cofactors, coenzymes, or prosthetic groups.

✓ You should be able to explain how an enzyme's active site can reduce the activation energy of a reaction.

8.4 What Factors Affect Enzyme Function?

- Enzymes are proteins, and thus their activity can be directly influenced by modifications or environmental factors, such as temperature and pH, that alter their three-dimensional structure.

- Most enzymes are regulated by molecules that either compete with substrates to occupy the active site, or alter enzyme shape.

- Protein cleavage and phosphorylation are examples of how enzymes may be regulated by modifying their primary structure.

✓ You should be able to compare and contrast the effect of allosteric regulation versus phosphorylation on enzyme function.

8.5 Enzymes Can Work Together in Metabolic Pathways

- In cells, enzymes often work together in metabolic pathways that sequentially modify a substrate to make a product.

- A pathway may be regulated by controlling the activity of one enzyme, often the first in the series of reactions. Feedback inhibition results from the accumulation of a product that binds to an enzyme in the pathway and inactivates it.

- Metabolic pathways were vital to the evolution of life, and new pathways continue to evolve in cells.

✓ You should be able to predict how the removal of the intermediate in a two-step metabolic pathway would affect the enzymatic rates of the first and last.

(MB) MasteringBiology

1. **MasteringBiology Assignments**

   Tutorials and Activities ATP and Energy; Chemical Reactions and ATP; Energy Transformations; Enzyme and Substrate Concentrations; Enzyme Inhibition; Factors That Affect Reaction Rate; How Enzymes Function; Regulating Enzyme Action; Redox Reactions

   Questions Reading Quizzes, Blue-Thread Questions, Test Bank

2. **eText** Read your book online, search, take notes, highlight text, and more.

3. **The Study Area** Practice Test, Cumulative Test, BioFlix® 3-D Animations, Videos, Activities, Audio Glossary, Word Study Tools, Art

You should be able to . . .

1. The first law of thermodynamics states which of the following?
   a. Energy exists in two forms: kinetic and potential.
   b. Reactions will take place only if energy is released.
   c. Energy is conserved: it cannot be created or destroyed.
   d. Disorder always increases in the universe.

2. If a reaction is exergonic, then which of these statements is true?
   a. The products have lower free energy than the reactants.
   b. Energy must be added for the reaction to proceed.
   c. The products have lower entropy (are more ordered) than the reactants.
   d. The reaction occurs extremely quickly.

3. What is a transition state?
   a. the complex formed as covalent bonds are being broken and re-formed during a reaction
   b. the place where an allosteric regulatory molecule binds to an enzyme
   c. an interaction between reactants with high kinetic energy, due to high temperature
   d. the shape adopted by an enzyme that has an inhibitory molecule bound at its active site

4. What often happens to an enzyme after it binds to its substrate? Is this a permanent change?

5. How does pH affect enzyme-catalyzed reactions?
   a. Protons serve as substrates for most reactions.
   b. Energy stored in protons is used to drive endergonic reactions.
   c. Proton concentration increases the kinetic energy of the reactants, allowing them to reach their transition state.
   d. The concentration of protons affects the folded structure of the enzyme.

6. When does feedback inhibition occur?

7. Explain the lock-and-key model of enzyme activity. What was incorrect about this model?

8. If you were to expose glucose to oxygen on your lab bench, why would you not expect to see it burn as shown in Figure 8.6?
   a. The reaction is endergonic and requires an input of energy.
   b. The reaction is not spontaneous unless an enzyme is added to the substrates.
   c. The sugar must first be phosphorylated to increase its potential energy.
   d. Energy is required for the sugar and oxygen to reach their transition state.

9. Explain why substrate phosphorylation using ATP is an exergonic reaction. How does the phosphorylation of reactants result in driving reactions that would normally be endergonic?

10. **QUANTITATIVE** In Figure 8.9, the energetic coupling of ATP hydrolysis and an endergonic reaction are shown. If the hydrolysis of ATP releases 7.3 kcal of free energy, use the graph in this figure to estimate what you would expect the ΔG values to be for the uncoupled reaction and the two steps in the coupled reaction.

11. Compare and contrast competitive inhibition and allosteric regulation.

12. Using what you have learned about changes in free energy, would you predict the ΔG value of catabolic reactions to be positive or negative? What about anabolic reactions? Justify your answers using the terms enthalpy and entropy.

13. Draw a redox reaction that occurs between compounds AH_2 and B^+ to form A, BH, and H^+. On the drawing, connect the reactant and product forms of each compound and state if it is the reduction or oxidation step and how many electrons are transferred. If this represents an exergonic reaction, identify which of the five substances would have the highest-energy electrons.

14. Researchers can analyze the atomic structure of enzymes during catalysis. In one recent study, investigators found that the transition state included the formation of a free radical (see Chapter 2) and that a coenzyme bound to the active site donated an electron to help stabilize the free radical. How would the reaction rate and the stability of the transition state change if the coenzyme were not available?

15. Recently, researchers were able to measure movement that occurred in a single amino acid in an enzyme as reactions were taking place in its active site. The amino acid that moved was located in the active site, and the rate of movement correlated closely with the rate at which the reaction was taking place. Discuss the significance of these findings, using the information in Figures 8.10 and 8.13.

16. You have discovered an enzyme that appears to function only when a particular sugar accumulates. Which of the following scenarios would you predict to be responsible for activating this enzyme?
   a. The sugar cleaves the enzyme so it is now in an active conformation.
   b. The sugar binds to the enzyme and changes the conformation of the active site.
   c. The sugar binds to the active site and competes with the normal substrate.
   d. The sugar phosphorylates the enzyme, triggering a conformational change.

9 Cellular Respiration and Fermentation

In this chapter you will learn how

Cells make ATP starting from sugars and other high potential energy compounds

by examining ↓   by examining ↓

How cells produce ATP when oxygen is present   **9.1**

How cells produce ATP when oxygen is absent

looking closer at

Glycolysis **9.2**

Pyruvate oxidation **9.3**

Citric acid cycle **9.4**

focusing on

Electron transport and chemiosmosis **9.5**

Fermentation **9.6**

This hydroelectric dam on the Duero river between Spain and Portugal uses pumps to move water from the lower reservoir to the upper reservoir. During periods of high energy demand, the potential energy stored by this activity is used to generate electricity. A similar process is used by cells to produce ATP during cellular respiration.

This chapter is part of the Big Picture. See how on pages 198–199.

ife requires energy. From the very start, chemical evolution was driven by energy from chemicals, radiation, heat, or other sources (see Chapter 2). Harnessing energy and controlling its flow has been the single most important step in the evolution of life.

What fuels life in cells? The answer is the nucleotide adenosine triphosphate (ATP). ATP has high potential energy and allows cells to overcome life's energy barriers (see Chapter 8).

This chapter investigates how cells make ATP, starting with an introduction to the metabolic pathways that harvest energy from high-energy molecules like **glucose**—the most common source of chemical energy used by organisms. The four central pathways of cellular respiration will be

✔ When you see this checkmark, stop and test yourself. Answers are available in Appendix A.

presented with emphasis on how the oxidation of glucose leads to ATP production. Fermentation will also be introduced as an alternative pathway used to make ATP when key reactions in cellular respiration are either shut down or not available.

As cells process sugar, the energy that is released is used to transfer a phosphate group to adenosine diphosphate (ADP), generating ATP. (You can see the Big Picture of how the production of glucose in photosynthesis is related to its catabolism in cellular respiration on pages 198–199.)

9.1 An Overview of Cellular Respiration

In general, a cell contains only enough ATP to last from 30 seconds to a few minutes. Because it has such high potential energy, ATP is unstable and is not stored. Like many other cellular processes, the production and use of ATP is fast. Most cells are making ATP all the time.

Most of the glucose that is used to make ATP is produced by plants and other photosynthetic species. These organisms use the energy in sunlight to reduce carbon dioxide (CO_2) to glucose and other carbohydrates. While they are alive, photosynthetic species use the glucose that they produce to make ATP for themselves. When photosynthetic species decompose or are eaten, they provide glucose to animals, fungi, and many bacteria and archaea.

All organisms use glucose in the synthesis of complex carbohydrates, fats, and other energy-rich compounds. Storage carbohydrates, such as starch and glycogen, act like savings accounts for chemical energy. ATP, in contrast, is like cash. To withdraw chemical energy from the accounts to get cash, storage carbohydrates are first hydrolyzed into their glucose monomers. The glucose is then used to produce ATP through one of two general processes: cellular respiration or fermentation (**FIGURE 9.1**). The primary difference between these two processes lies in the degree to which glucose is oxidized.

What Happens When Glucose Is Oxidized?

When glucose undergoes the uncontrolled oxidation reaction called burning, some of the potential energy stored in its chemical bonds is converted to kinetic energy in the form of heat:

$$C_6H_{12}O_2 + 6\,O_2 \longrightarrow 6\,CO_2 + 6\,H_2O + \text{Heat}$$
$$\text{glucose} \quad \text{oxygen} \quad \text{carbon dioxide} \quad \text{water}$$

More specifically, a total of about 685 kilocalories (kcal) of heat is released when one mole of glucose is oxidized. To put this in perspective, if you burned this amount of glucose, it would give off enough heat to bring almost 2.5 gallons of room-temperature water to a boil.

Glucose does not burn in cells, however. Instead, the glucose in cells is oxidized through a long series of carefully controlled redox reactions. These reactions are occurring, millions of

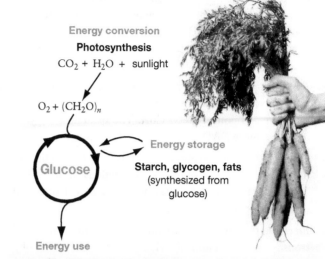

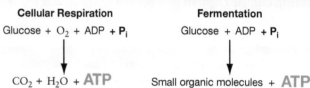

FIGURE 9.1 Glucose Is the Hub of Energy Processing in Cells. Glucose is a product of photosynthesis. Both plants and animals store glucose and oxidize it to provide chemical energy in the form of ATP.

times per minute, in your cells right now. Instead of releasing all of this energy as heat, much of it is being used to make the ATP you need to read, think, move, and stay alive. In cells, the change in free energy (Chapter 8) that occurs during the oxidation of glucose is used to synthesize ATP from ADP and P_i.

So how does fermentation differ from cellular respiration? Respiration, like burning, results in the complete oxidation of glucose into CO_2 and water. Fermentation, on the other hand, does not fully oxidize glucose. Instead, small, reduced organic molecules are produced as waste. As a result, cellular respiration releases more energy from glucose than fermentation.

The complete oxidation of glucose via cellular respiration can be thought of as a four-step process used to convert the chemical energy in glucose to chemical energy in ATP. Each of the four steps consists of a series of chemical reactions, and each step has a distinctive starting molecule and a characteristic set of products.

1. *Glycolysis* During **glycolysis,** one 6-carbon molecule of glucose is broken into two molecules of the three-carbon compound pyruvate. During this process, ATP is produced from ADP, and nicotinamide adenine dinucleotide (NAD^+) is reduced to form NADH.

2. *Pyruvate processing* Pyruvate is processed to release one molecule of CO_2, and the remaining two carbons are used to form the compound acetyl CoA. The oxidation of pyruvate results in more NAD^+ being reduced to NADH.

3. *Citric acid cycle* Acetyl CoA is oxidized to two molecules of CO_2. During this sequence of reactions, more ATP and NADH are produced, and flavin adenine dinucleotide (FAD) is reduced to form $FADH_2$.

4. *Electron transport and oxidative phosphorylation* Electrons from NADH and $FADH_2$ move through a series of proteins called an electron transport chain (ETC). The energy released in this chain of redox reactions is used to create a proton gradient across a membrane; the ensuing flow of protons back across the membrane is used to make ATP. Because this mode of ATP production links the phosphorylation of ADP with the oxidation of NADH and $FADH_2$, it is called **oxidative phosphorylation.**

FIGURE 9.2 summarizes the four steps in cellular respiration. Formally, **cellular respiration** is defined as any suite of reactions that uses electrons harvested from high-energy molecules to produce ATP via an electron transport chain.

The enzymes, products, and intermediates involved in cellular respiration and fermentation do not exist in isolation. Instead, they are part of a huge and dynamic inventory of chemicals inside the cell.

This complexity can be boiled down to a simple essence, however. Two of the most fundamental requirements of a cell are energy and carbon. They need a source of high-energy electrons for generating chemical energy in the form of ATP, and a source of carbon-containing molecules that can be used to synthesize DNA, RNA, proteins, fatty acids, and other molecules. Let's take a closer look at the central role cellular respiration plays in metabolic pathways as a whole.

Cellular Respiration Plays a Central Role in Metabolism

Recall that sets of reactions that break down molecules are called catabolic pathways (Chapter 8). These reactions often harvest stored chemical energy to produce ATP. On the other hand, sets of reactions that synthesize larger molecules from smaller components are called anabolic pathways. Anabolic reactions often use energy in the form of ATP.

How does the process of cellular respiration interact with other catabolic and anabolic pathways? Let's first consider how

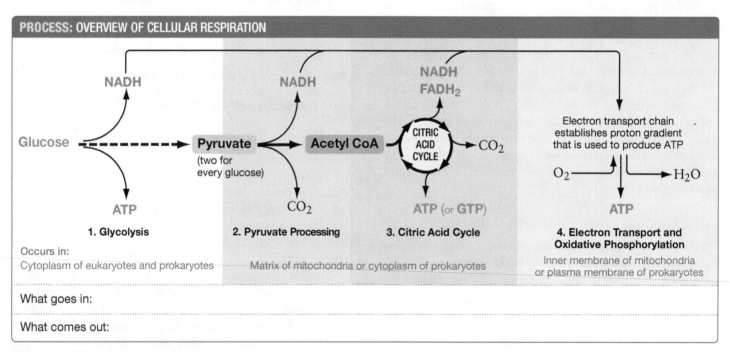

FIGURE 9.2 Cellular Respiration Oxidizes Glucose to Make ATP. Cells produce ATP from glucose via a series of processes: (1) glycolysis, (2) pyruvate processing, (3) the citric acid cycle, and (4) electron transport and oxidative phosphorylation. Each component produces high-energy molecules in the form of nucleotides (ATP or GTP) or electron carriers (NADH or $FADH_2$). Because the four components are connected, glucose oxidation is an integrated metabolic pathway. The first three steps oxidize glucose to produce NADH and $FADH_2$, which then feed the electron transport chain.

✔**EXERCISE** Fill in the chart along the bottom.

eukaryotes extract energy from molecules other than glucose and then examine how intermediates produced in glycolysis and the citric acid cycle are used as building blocks to synthesize cell components.

Catabolic Pathways Break Down a Variety of Molecules Most organisms ingest, absorb, or synthesize many different carbohydrates. These molecules range from sucrose, maltose, and other simple sugars to large polymers such as glycogen and starch (see Chapter 5).

Recall that both glycogen and starch are polymers of glucose, but differ in the way their long chains of glucose branch. Using enzyme-catalyzed reactions, cells can produce glucose from glycogen, starch, and most simple sugars. Glucose and fructose can then be processed in glycolysis.

Carbohydrates are not the only important source of carbon compounds used in catabolic pathways, however. Fats are highly reduced macromolecules consisting of glycerol bonded to chains of fatty acids (see Chapter 6). In cells, enzymes routinely break down fats to release the glycerol and convert the fatty acids into acetyl CoA molecules. Glycerol can be further processed and enter glycolysis. Acetyl CoA enters the citric acid cycle.

Proteins can also be catabolized, meaning that they can be broken down and used to produce ATP. Once they are hydrolyzed to their constituent amino acids, enzyme-catalyzed reactions remove the amino ($-NH_2$) groups. The amino groups are excreted in urine as waste. The carbon compounds that remain are converted to pyruvate, acetyl CoA, and other intermediates in glycolysis and the citric acid cycle.

The top half of **FIGURE 9.3** summarizes the catabolic pathways of carbohydrates, fats, and proteins and shows how their breakdown products feed an array of steps in glucose oxidation and cellular respiration. When all three types of molecules are available in the cell to generate ATP, carbohydrates are used up first, then fats, and finally proteins.

Catabolic Intermediates Are Used in Anabolic Pathways Where do cells get the precursor molecules required to synthesize amino acids, RNA, DNA, phospholipids, and other cell components? Not surprisingly, the answer often involves intermediates in carbohydrate metabolism. For example,

- In humans, about half the required amino acids can be synthesized from molecules siphoned from the citric acid cycle.
- Acetyl CoA is the starting point for anabolic pathways that result in the synthesis of fatty acids. Fatty acids can then be used to build phospholipid membranes or fats.
- Intermediates in glycolysis can be oxidized to start the synthesis of the sugars in ribonucleotides and deoxyribonucleotides. Nucleotides, in turn, are building blocks used in RNA and DNA synthesis.
- If ATP is abundant, pyruvate and lactate (from fermentation) can be used in the synthesis of glucose. Excess glucose may be converted to glycogen or starch and stored.

The bottom half of Figure 9.3 summarizes how intermediates in carbohydrate metabolism are drawn off to synthesize macromolecules. The take-home message is that the same molecule can serve many different functions in the cell. As a result, catabolic and anabolic pathways are closely intertwined.

Metabolism comprises thousands of different chemical reactions, yet the amounts and identities of molecules inside cells are relatively constant. By regulating key reactions involved in catabolic and anabolic pathways, the cell is able to maintain its internal environment even under different environmental conditions—a process referred to as **homeostasis.** Cellular respiration and

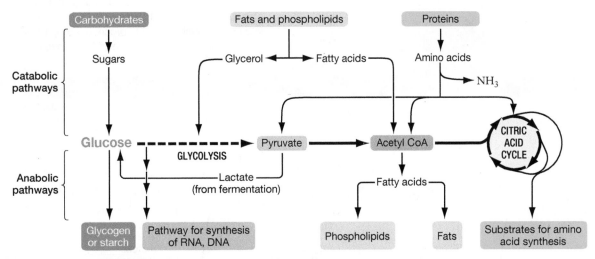

FIGURE 9.3 Cellular Respiration Interacts with Other Catabolic and Anabolic Pathways. A variety of high-energy compounds from carbohydrates, fats, or proteins can be broken down in catabolic reactions and used by cellular respiration for ATP production. Several of the intermediates in carbohydrate metabolism act as precursor molecules in anabolic reactions leading to the synthesis of glycogen or starch, RNA, DNA, fatty acids, and amino acids.

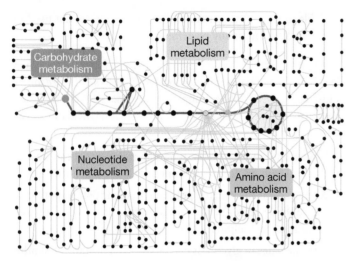

FIGURE 9.4 Pathways of Cellular Respiration Play a Central Role in the Metabolic Activity of Cells. A representation of a few of the thousands of chemical reactions that occur in cells. The dots represent molecules, and the lines represent enzyme-catalyzed reactions. At the center of all this, the first three steps of cellular respiration are emphasized by bold dots and thick lines. For reference, glucose, pyruvate, and acetyl CoA are represented by the distinctive colors used in Figure 9.3.

fermentation pathways may be crucial to the life of a cell, but they also have to be seen as central parts of a whole (**FIGURE 9.4**).

Once you've filled in the chart at the bottom of Figure 9.2, you'll be ready to analyze each of the four steps of cellular respiration in detail. As you delve in, keep asking yourself the same key questions: What goes in and what comes out? What happens to the potential energy that is released? Where does each step occur, and how is it regulated? Then take a look in the mirror. All these processes are occurring right now, in virtually all your cells.

Because the enzymes responsible for glycolysis have been observed in nearly every bacterium, archaean, and eukaryote, it is logical to infer that the ancestor of all organisms living today made ATP by glycolysis. It's ironic, then, that the process was discovered by accident.

In the 1890s Hans and Edward Buchner were working out techniques for breaking open baker's yeast cells and extracting the contents for commercial and medicinal use. (Yeast extracts are still added to some foods as a flavor enhancer or nutritional supplement.) In one set of experiments, the Buchners added sucrose to their extracts. At the time, sucrose was commonly used as a preservative—a substance used to preserve food from decay.

Instead of preserving the yeast extracts, though, the sucrose was quickly broken down and fermented, and alcohol appeared as a by-product. This was a key finding: It showed that metabolic pathways like fermentation could be studied in vitro—outside the organism. Until then, researchers thought that metabolism could take place only in intact organisms.

When researchers studied how the sugar was being processed, they found that the reactions could go on much longer than normal if inorganic phosphate were added to the mixture. This result implied that some of the compounds involved were being phosphorylated. Soon after, a molecule called fructose bisphosphate was isolated. (The prefix *bis*– means that the phosphate groups are attached to the fructose molecule at two different locations.) Subsequent work showed that all but the starting

FIGURE 9.5 Glycolysis Pathway. This sequence of 10 reactions oxidizes glucose to pyruvate. Each reaction is catalyzed by a different enzyme to produce two net ATP (4 ATP are produced, but 2 are invested), two molecules of NADH, and two molecules of pyruvate. In step 4, fructose-1,6-bisphosphate is divided into two products that both proceed through steps 6–10. The amounts for "What goes in" and "What goes out" are the combined totals for both molecules.

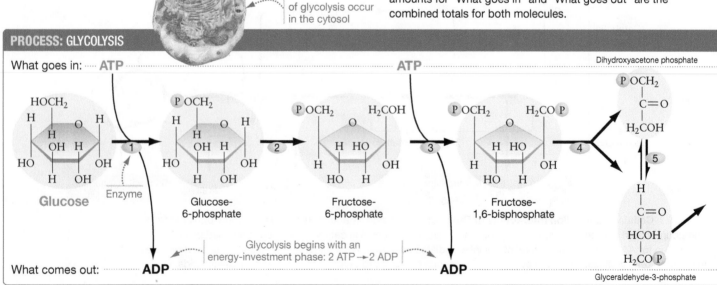

and ending molecules in glycolysis—glucose and pyruvate—are phosphorylated.

In 1905 researchers found that the processing of sugar by yeast extracts stopped if they boiled the reaction mix. Because it was known that enzymes could be inactivated by heat, their discovery suggested that enzymes were involved in at least some of the processing steps. Years later, investigators realized that each step in glycolysis is catalyzed by a different enzyme. Eventually, each of the reactions and enzymes involved was worked out.

Glycolysis Is a Sequence of 10 Reactions

In both eukaryotes and prokaryotes, all 10 reactions of glycolysis occur in the cytosol (**FIGURE 9.5**). Note three key points about this reaction sequence:

1. Glycolysis starts by *using* ATP, not producing it. In the initial step, glucose is phosphorylated to form glucose-6-phosphate. After the second reaction rearranges the sugar to form fructose-6-phosphate, the third reaction adds a second phosphate group, forming the fructose-1,6-bisphosphate observed by early researchers. Thus, two ATP molecules are used up before any ATP is produced.

2. Once the energy-investment phase of glycolysis is complete, the subsequent reactions represent an energy-payoff phase. The sixth reaction in the sequence results in the reduction of two molecules of NAD^+; the seventh produces two molecules of ATP. This is where the energy "debt"—of two molecules of ATP invested early in glycolysis—is paid off. The final reaction in the sequence produces another two ATPs. For each molecule of glucose processed, the net yield is two molecules of NADH, two of ATP, and two of pyruvate.

3. In reactions 7 and 10 of Figure 9.5, an enzyme catalyzes the transfer of a phosphate group from a phosphorylated substrate to ADP, forming ATP. Enzyme-catalyzed reactions that result in

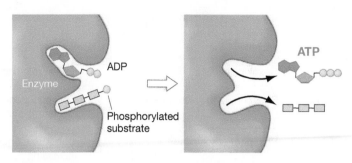

FIGURE 9.6 Substrate-Level Phosphorylation Involves an Enzyme and a Phosphorylated Substrate. Substrate-level phosphorylation occurs when an enzyme catalyzes the transfer of a phosphate group from a phosphorylated substrate to ADP, forming ATP.

ATP production are termed **substrate-level phosphorylation** (**FIGURE 9.6**). The key idea to note here is that the energy to produce the ATP comes from the phosphorylated substrate—not from a proton gradient, as it does when ATP is produced by oxidative phosphorylation.

The discovery and elucidation of the glycolytic pathway ranks as one of the great achievements in the history of biochemistry. For more detail concerning the enzymes that catalyze each step, see **TABLE 9.1** (on page 160). While the catabolism of glucose can occur via other pathways, this set of reactions is among the most ancient and fundamental of all life processes.

How Is Glycolysis Regulated?

An important advance in understanding how glycolysis is regulated occurred when biologists observed that high levels of ATP inhibit a key glycolytic enzyme called phosphofructokinase. **Phosphofructokinase** catalyzes reaction 3 in Figure 9.5—the synthesis of fructose-1,6-bisphosphate from fructose-6-phosphate. This is a crucial step in the sequence.

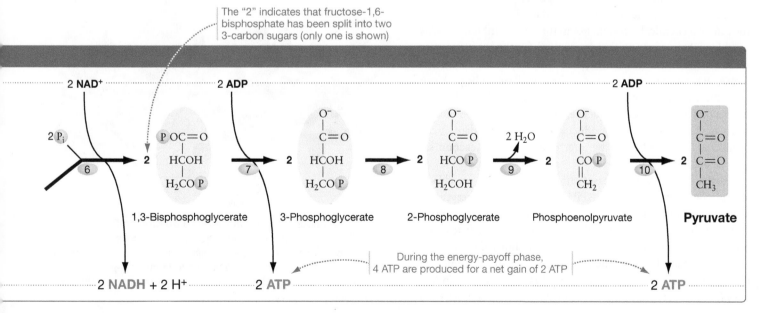

The "2" indicates that fructose-1,6-bisphosphate has been split into two 3-carbon sugars (only one is shown)

During the energy-payoff phase, 4 ATP are produced for a net gain of 2 ATP

2 NADH + 2 H⁺   2 ATP   2 ATP

1,3-Bisphosphoglycerate   3-Phosphoglycerate   2-Phosphoglycerate   Phosphoenolpyruvate   **Pyruvate**

The Reactions of Glycolysis

Step	Enzyme	Reaction
1	Hexokinase	Transfers a phosphate from **ATP** to glucose, increasing its potential energy.
2	Phosphoglucose isomerase	Converts glucose-6-phosphate to fructose-6-phosphate; referred to as an isomer of glucose-6-phosphate.
3	Phosphofructokinase	Transfers a phosphate from **ATP** to the opposite end of fructose-6-phosphate, increasing its potential energy.
4	Fructose-bis-phosphate aldolase	Cleaves fructose-1,6-bisphosphate into two different 3-carbon sugars.
5	Triose phosphate isomerase	Converts dihydroxyacetone phosphate (DAP) to glyceraldehyde-3-phosphate (G3P). Although the reaction is fully reversible, the DAP-to-G3P reaction is favored because G3P is immediately used as a substrate for step 6.
6	Glyceraldehyde-3-phosphate dehydrogenase	A two-step reaction that first oxidizes G3P using the **NAD**$^+$ coenzyme to produce **NADH**. Energy from this reaction is used to attach a P$_i$ to the oxidized product to form 1,3-bisphosphoglycerate.
7	Phosphoglycerate kinase	Transfers a phosphate from 1,3-bisphosphoglycerate to **ADP** to make 3-phosphoglycerate and **ATP**.
8	Phosphoglycerate mutase	Rearranges the phosphate in 3-phosphoglycerate to make 2-phosphoglycerate.
9	Enolase	Removes a water molecule from 2-phosphoglycerate to form a double bond and produce phosphoenolpyruvate.
10	Pyruvate kinase	Transfers a phosphate from phosphoenolpyruvate to **ADP** to make pyruvate and **ATP**.

After reactions 1 and 2 occur, an array of enzymes can reverse the process and regenerate glucose for use in other pathways. Before step 3, then, the sequence is not committed to glycolysis. But once fructose-1,6-bisphosphate is synthesized, there is no point in stopping the process. Based on these observations, it makes sense that the pathway is regulated at step 3. How do cells do it?

As shown in Figure 9.5, ATP serves as a substrate for the addition of a phosphate to fructose-6-phosphate. In the vast majority of cases, increasing the concentration of a substrate would *speed* the rate of a chemical reaction, but in this case, it inhibits it. Why would ATP—a substrate that is required for the reaction—also serve as an inhibitor of the reaction? The answer lies in the fact that ATP is also the end product of the overall catabolic pathway.

Recall that when an enzyme in a pathway is inhibited by the product of the reaction sequence, feedback inhibition occurs (see Chapter 8). When the product molecule is abundant, it can inhibit its own production by interfering with the reaction sequence used to create it.

Feedback inhibition increases efficiency. Cells that are able to stop glycolytic reactions when ATP is abundant can conserve their stores of glucose for times when ATP is scarce. As a result, natural selection should favor individuals who have phosphofructokinase molecules that are inhibited by high concentrations of ATP.

How do high levels of the substrate inhibit the enzyme? As **FIGURE 9.7** shows, phosphofructokinase has two distinct binding sites for ATP. ATP can bind at the enzyme's active site, where it

is used to phosphorylate fructose-6-phosphate, or at a regulatory site, where it turns off the enzyme's activity.

The key to feedback inhibition lies in the ability of the two sites to bind to ATP. When concentrations are low, ATP binds

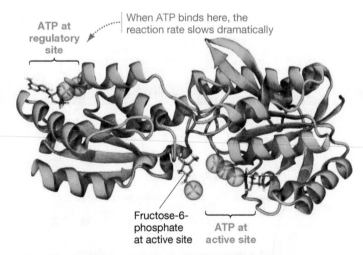

FIGURE 9.7 Phosphofructokinase Has Two Binding Sites for ATP. A model of one of the four identical subunits of phosphofructokinase. In the active site, ATP is used as a substrate to transfer one of its phosphate groups to fructose-6-phosphate. In the regulatory site, ATP binding inhibits the reaction by changing the shape of the enzyme.

only to the active site, which has a greater affinity for ATP than does the regulatory site. As ATP concentrations increase, however, it also binds at the regulatory site on phosphofructokinase. When ATP binds at this second location, the enzyme's conformation changes in a way that dramatically lowers the reaction rate at the active site. In phosphofructokinase, ATP acts as an allosteric regulator (see Chapter 8). ✔ If you understand the principle behind the difference in affinity between the two ATP binding sites, you should be able to predict the consequences if the regulatory site had higher affinity for ATP than the active site did.

To summarize, glycolysis starts with one 6-carbon glucose molecule and ends with two 3-carbon pyruvate molecules. The reactions occur in the cytoplasm, and the energy that is released is used to produce a net total of two ATP and two NADH. Now the question is, what happens to the pyruvate?

9.3 Processing Pyruvate to Acetyl CoA

In eukaryotes, the pyruvate produced by glycolysis is transported from the cytosol to mitochondria. Mitochondria are organelles found in virtually all eukaryotes (see Chapter 7).

As shown in **FIGURE 9.8**, mitochondria have two membranes, called the inner membrane and outer membrane. The interior of the organelle is filled with layers of sac-like structures called **cristae.** Short tubes connect the cristae to the main part of the inner membrane. The region inside the inner membrane but outside the cristae is the **mitochondrial matrix.**

Pyruvate moves across the mitochondrion's outer membrane through small pores, but how it is transported across the inner membrane is still unclear. Current research suggests that either pyruvate is transported directly into the matrix using an unknown

transporter, or it is converted first into lactate, transported across the membrane, and then converted back into pyruvate.

Inside the mitochondrion, pyruvate reacts with a compound called **coenzyme A (CoA).** Coenzyme A is sometimes abbreviated as CoA-SH to call attention to its key sulfhydryl functional group. In this and many other reactions, CoA acts as a coenzyme by accepting and then transferring an acetyl group ($-COCH_3$) to a substrate (the A stands for acetylation). Pyruvate reacts with CoA, through a series of steps, to produce **acetyl CoA.**

The reaction sequence occurs inside an enormous and intricate enzyme complex called **pyruvate dehydrogenase.** In eukaryotes, pyruvate dehydrogenase is located in the mitochondrial matrix. In bacteria and archaea, pyruvate dehydrogenase is located in the cytosol.

As pyruvate is being processed, one of the carbons in the pyruvate is oxidized to CO_2 and NAD^+ is reduced to NADH. The remaining two-carbon acetyl unit is transferred to CoA (**FIGURE 9.9**).

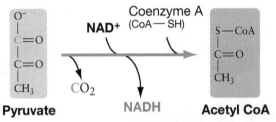

FIGURE 9.9 Pyruvate Is Oxidized to Acetyl CoA. The reaction shown here is catalyzed by pyruvate dehydrogenase.

✔**EXERCISE** Above the reaction arrow, list three molecules whose presence speeds up the reaction. Label them "Positive control." Below the reaction arrow, list three molecules whose presence slows down the reaction. Label them "Negative control by feedback inhibition."

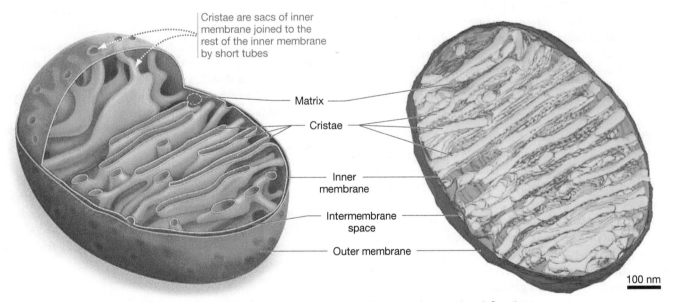

FIGURE 9.8 The Structure of the Mitochondrion. Mitochondria have outer and inner membranes that define the intermembrane space and matrix. Pyruvate processing occurs within the mitochondrial matrix. Recent research using cryo-electron tomography (the colorized micrograph on the right) shows the inner membrane is connected by short tubes to sac-like cristae.

Acetyl CoA is the final product of the pyruvate-processing step in glucose oxidation. Pyruvate, NAD^+, and CoA go in; CO_2, NADH, and acetyl CoA come out.

When supplies of ATP are abundant, however, the process shuts down. Pyruvate processing stops when the pyruvate dehydrogenase complex becomes phosphorylated and changes shape. The rate of phosphorylation increases when other products—specifically acetyl CoA and NADH—are at high concentration.

These regulatory changes are more examples of feedback inhibition. Reaction products feed back to stop or slow down the pathway.

On the contrary, high concentrations of NAD^+, CoA, or adenosine monophosphate (AMP)—which indicates low ATP supplies—*speed up* the reactions catalyzed by the pyruvate dehydrogenase complex.

Pyruvate processing is under both positive and negative control. Large supplies of products inhibit the enzyme complex; large supplies of reactants and low supplies of products stimulate it.

To summarize, pyruvate processing starts with the three-carbon pyruvate molecule and ends with one carbon released as CO_2 and the remaining two carbons in the form of acetyl CoA. The reactions occur in the mitochondrial matrix, and the potential energy that is released is used to produce one NADH for each pyruvate that is processed. Now the question is, what happens to the acetyl CoA?

9.4 The Citric Acid Cycle: Oxidizing Acetyl CoA to CO_2

While researchers were working out the sequence of reactions in glycolysis, biologists in other laboratories were focusing on redox reactions that oxidize small organic acids called **carboxylic acids.** Note that carboxylic acids all have carboxyl functional groups (R-COOH), hence the name.

A key finding emerged from their studies: Redox reactions that involve carboxylic acids such as citrate, malate, and succinate produce carbon dioxide. Recall from Section 9.1 that carbon dioxide is the endpoint of glucose oxidation via cellular respiration. Thus, it was logical for researchers to propose that the oxidation of small carboxylic acids could be an important component of glucose catabolism.

Early researchers identified eight small carboxylic acids that are rapidly oxidized in sequence, from least to most oxidized. What they found next was puzzling. When they added one of the eight carboxylic acids to cells, the rate of glucose oxidation increased, suggesting that the reactions are somehow connected to pathways involved in glucose catabolism. But, the added molecules did not appear to be used up. Instead, virtually all the carboxylic acids added were recovered later. How is this possible?

Hans Krebs solved the mystery when he proposed that the reaction sequence occurs in a cycle instead of a linear pathway. Krebs had another crucial insight when he suggested that the reaction sequence was directly tied to the processing of pyruvate—the endpoint of the glycolytic pathway.

To test these hypotheses, Krebs and a colleague set out to determine if adding pyruvate could link the two ends of the sequence

of eight carboxylic acids. If pyruvate is the key link in forming a cycle, it would need to be involved in the conversion of oxaloacetate, the most oxidized of the eight carboxylic acids, to citrate, the most reduced carboxylic acid. When Krebs added pyruvate, the series of redox reactions occurred. The conclusion? The sequence of eight carboxylic acids is indeed arranged in a cycle (**FIGURE 9.10**).

Many biologists now refer to the cycle as the **citric acid cycle** because it starts with citrate, which is the salt of citric acid after the protons are released. The citric acid cycle is also known as the tricarboxylic acid (TCA) cycle, because citrate has three carboxyl groups, and also as the Krebs cycle, after its discoverer.

When radioactive isotopes of carbon became available in the early 1940s, researchers showed that carbon atoms cycle through the reactions just as Krebs had proposed. For more detail concerning the enzymes that catalyze each step, see **TABLE 9.2** (on page 164). In each cycle, the energy released by the oxidation of one molecule of acetyl CoA is used to produce three molecules of NADH, one of $FADH_2$, and one of **guanosine triphosphate (GTP)**, or ATP, through substrate-level phosphorylation. Whether GTP or ATP is produced depends on the type of cell being considered.[1] For example, GTP appears to be produced in the liver cells of mammals, while ATP is produced in muscle cells.

In bacteria and archaea, the enzymes responsible for the citric acid cycle are located in the cytosol. In eukaryotes, most of the enzymes responsible for the citric acid cycle are located in the mitochondrial matrix. Because glycolysis produces two molecules of pyruvate, the cycle turns twice for each molecule of glucose processed in cellular respiration.

How Is the Citric Acid Cycle Regulated?

By now, it shouldn't surprise you to learn that the citric acid cycle is carefully regulated. The citric acid cycle can be turned off at multiple points, via several different mechanisms of feedback inhibition. Reaction rates are high when ATP is scarce; reaction rates are low when ATP is abundant.

FIGURE 9.11 highlights the major control points. Notice that in step 1, the enzyme that combines acetyl CoA and oxaloacetate to form citrate is shut down when ATP binds to it. This is another example of feedback inhibition, which also regulates enzymes at two additional points in the cycle. In step 3, NADH interferes with the reaction by binding to the enzyme's active site. This is an example of competitive inhibition (see Chapter 8). In step 4, ATP binds to the enzyme at an allosteric regulatory site.

To summarize, the citric acid cycle starts with the two-carbon acetyl molecule in the form of acetyl CoA and ends with the release of two CO_2. The reactions occur in the mitochondrial matrix, and the potential energy that is released is used to produce three NADH, one $FADH_2$, and one ATP or GTP for each acetyl oxidized. But a major question remains.

[1]Traditionally it was thought that the citric acid cycle produced GTP, which was later converted to ATP in the same cell. Recent work suggests that ATP is produced directly in some cell types, while GTP is produced in other cells. See C. O. Lambeth, Reconsideration of the significance of substrate-level phosphorylation in the citric acid cycle. *Biochemistry and Molecular Biology Education* 34 (2006): 21–29.

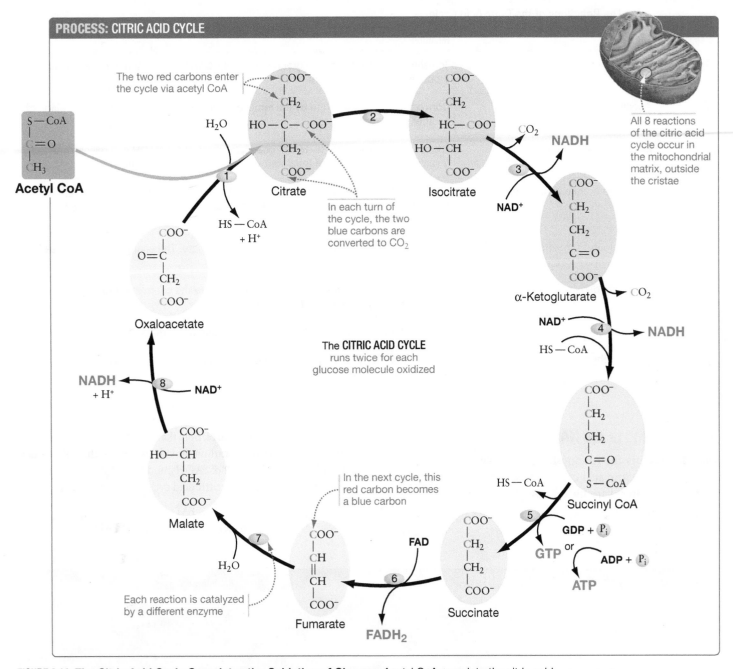

The two red carbons enter the cycle via acetyl CoA

In each turn of the cycle, the two blue carbons are converted to CO_2

All 8 reactions of the citric acid cycle occur in the mitochondrial matrix, outside the cristae

Acetyl CoA

Citrate

Isocitrate

NADH

α-Ketoglutarate

NADH

Oxaloacetate

The CITRIC ACID CYCLE runs twice for each glucose molecule oxidized

NADH

Succinyl CoA

GTP or ATP

Malate

In the next cycle, this red carbon becomes a blue carbon

Succinate

Each reaction is catalyzed by a different enzyme

Fumarate

FADH₂

FIGURE 9.10 The Citric Acid Cycle Completes the Oxidation of Glucose. Acetyl CoA goes into the citric acid cycle, and carbon dioxide, NADH, FADH₂, and GTP or ATP come out. GTP or ATP is produced by substrate-level phosphorylation. If you follow individual carbon atoms around the cycle several times, you'll come to an important conclusion: each of the carbons in the cycle is eventually a "blue carbon" that is released as CO_2.

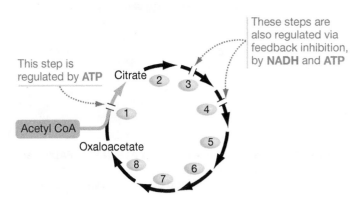

This step is regulated by **ATP**

These steps are also regulated via feedback inhibition, by **NADH** and **ATP**

Acetyl CoA

Citrate

Oxaloacetate

FIGURE 9.11 The Citric Acid Cycle Is Regulated by Feedback Inhibition. The citric acid cycle slows down when ATP and NADH are plentiful. ATP acts as an allosteric regulator, while NADH acts as a competitive inhibitor.

Step	Enzyme	Reaction
1	Citrate synthase	Transfers the 2-carbon acetyl group from acetyl CoA to the 4-carbon oxaloacetate to produce the 6-carbon citrate.
2	Aconitase	Converts citrate to isocitrate by the removal of one water molecule and the addition of another water molecule.
3	Isocitrate dehydrogenase	Oxidizes isocitrate using the **NAD$^+$** coenzyme to produce **NADH** and release one CO_2, resulting in the formation of the 5-carbon molecule α-ketoglutarate.
4	α-Ketoglutarate dehydrogenase	Oxidizes α-ketoglutarate using the **NAD$^+$** coenzyme to produce **NADH** and release one CO_2. The remaining 4-carbon molecule is added to coenzyme A (CoA) to form succinyl CoA.
5	Succinyl-CoA synthetase	CoA is removed, converting succinyl CoA to succinate. The energy released is used to transfer P_i to GDP to form **GTP**, or to ADP to form **ATP**.
6	Succinate dehydrogenase	Oxidizes succinate by transferring two hydrogens to the coenzyme **FAD** to produce **FADH$_2$**, resulting in the formation of fumarate.
7	Fumarase	Converts fumarate to malate by the addition of one water molecule.
8	Malate dehydrogenase	Oxidizes malate by using the **NAD$^+$** coenzyme to produce **NADH**, resulting in the regeneration of the oxaloacetate that will be used in step 1 of the cycle.

What Happens to the NADH and FADH$_2$?

FIGURE 9.12 reviews the relationships of glycolysis, pyruvate processing, and the citric acid cycle and identifies where each process takes place in eukaryotic cells. As the carbons in glucose are oxidized in these steps, the relative changes in free energy are shown in **FIGURE 9.13**.

As you study these figures, note that for each molecule of glucose that is fully oxidized to 6 carbon dioxide molecules, the cell produces 10 molecules of NADH, 2 of FADH$_2$, and 4 of ATP. The overall reaction for glycolysis and the citric acid cycle can be written as

$$C_6H_{12}O_2 + 10\ NAD^+ + 2\ FAD + 4\ ADP + 4\ P_i \longrightarrow$$
$$6\ CO_2 + 10\ NADH + 2\ FADH_2 + 4\ ATP$$

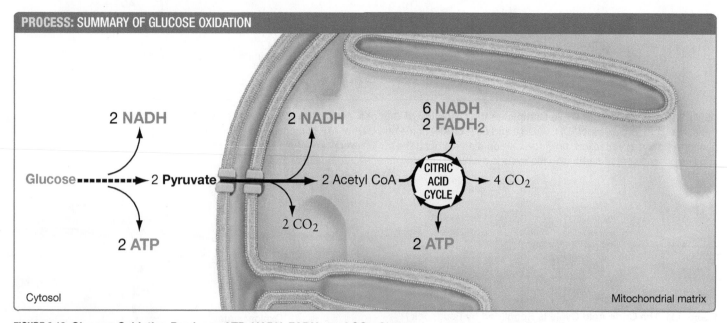

PROCESS: SUMMARY OF GLUCOSE OXIDATION

Cytosol

Mitochondrial matrix

FIGURE 9.12 Glucose Oxidation Produces ATP, NADH, FADH$_2$, and CO$_2$. Glucose is completely oxidized to carbon dioxide via glycolysis, pyruvate processing, and the citric acid cycle. In eukaryotes, glycolysis occurs in the cytosol; pyruvate oxidation and the citric acid cycle take place in the mitochondrial matrix.

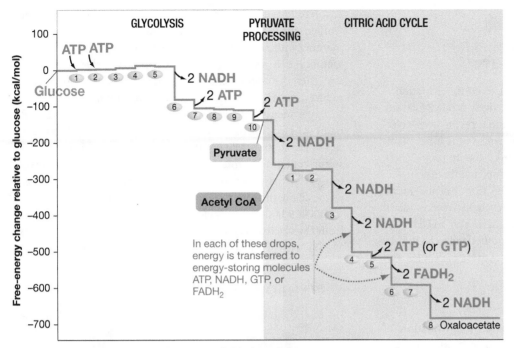

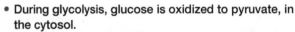

Oxidation of glucose →

FIGURE 9.13 Free Energy Changes as Glucose Is Oxidized. If you read the vertical axis of this graph carefully, it should convince you that about 685 kcal/mol of free energy is released from the oxidation of glucose. Much of the energy is harnessed in the form of ATP, NADH, and $FADH_2$. The numbered green ovals identify the reaction steps in glycolysis and the citric acid cycle (see Tables 9.1 and 9.2).

DATA: Li, X., R. K. Dash, R. K. Pradhan, et al. 2010. *Journal of Physical Chemistry B.* 114: 16068–16082.

✔**QUANTITATIVE** Based on the data in this graph, which of the three high-energy molecules produced during glucose oxidation would you expect to carry the highest amount of chemical energy? Justify your answer.

The ATP molecules are produced by substrate-level phosphorylation and can be used to drive endergonic reactions. The CO_2 molecules are a gas that is disposed of as waste—you exhale it; plants release it or use it as a reactant in photosynthesis.

What happens to the NADH and $FADH_2$ produced by glycolysis, pyruvate processing, and the citric acid cycle? Recall that the overall reaction for glucose oxidation is

$$C_6H_{12}O_6 + 6\,O_2 \longrightarrow 6\,CO_2 + 6\,H_2O + \text{Energy}$$

These three steps account for the glucose, the CO_2, and—because ATP is produced—some of the chemical energy that results from the overall reaction. But the O_2 and the H_2O are still unaccounted for. As it turns out, so is much of the chemical energy. The reaction that has yet to occur is

$$\begin{aligned}\text{NADH} + \text{FADH}_2 + O_2 + \text{ADP} + P_i \longrightarrow \\ \text{NAD}^+ + \text{FAD} + 2\,H_2O + \text{ATP}\end{aligned}$$

In the above reaction, the electrons from NADH and $FADH_2$ are transferred to oxygen. NADH and $FADH_2$ are oxidized to NAD^+ and FAD, and oxygen is reduced to form water.

In effect, glycolysis, pyruvate processing, and the citric acid cycle transfer electrons from glucose to NAD^+ and FAD to form NADH and $FADH_2$. When oxygen accepts electrons from these reduced molecules, water is produced.

At this point, all the components of the overall reaction for glucose oxidation are accounted for, except for the energy. What happens to the energy that is released as electrons are transferred from NADH and $FADH_2$ to the highly electronegative oxygen atoms?

Specifically, how is the transfer of electrons linked to the production of ATP? In the 1960s—decades after the details of glycolysis and the citric acid cycle had been worked out—a startling answer to these questions emerged.

9.5 Electron Transport and Chemiosmosis: Building a Proton Gradient to Produce ATP

The answer to one fundamental question about the oxidation of NADH and $FADH_2$ turned out to be relatively straightforward. By isolating different parts of mitochondria, researchers determined that NADH is oxidized by components in the inner membrane of the mitochondria, including the cristae. In prokaryotes, the oxidation of NADH occurs in the plasma membrane.

Biologists made a key discovery when they isolated membrane components—they were found to cycle between oxidized and reduced states after the addition of NADH and $FADH_2$. The membrane-associated molecules were hypothesized to be the key to processing NADH and $FADH_2$. What are these molecules, and how do they work?

The Electron Transport Chain

Collectively, the molecules responsible for the oxidation of NADH and $FADH_2$ are designated the **electron transport chain (ETC).** As electrons are passed from one molecule to another in the chain, the energy released by the redox reactions is used to move protons across the inner membrane of mitochondria.

Several points are fundamental to understanding how the ETC works:

- Most of the molecules are proteins that contain distinctive cofactors and prosthetic groups where the redox events take place (see Chapter 8). They include iron–sulfur complexes, ring-containing structures called flavins, or iron-containing heme groups called cytochromes. Each of these groups is readily reduced or oxidized.

- The inner membrane of the mitochondrion also contains a molecule called **ubiquinone,** which is not a protein. Ubiquinone got its name because it is nearly ubiquitous in organisms and belongs to a family of compounds called quinones. Also called **coenzyme Q** or simply Q, ubiquinone is lipid soluble and moves efficiently throughout the hydrophobic interior of the inner mitochondrial membrane.

- The molecules involved in processing NADH and $FADH_2$ differ in electronegativity, or their tendency to hold electrons. Some of the molecules pick up a proton with each electron, forming hydrogen atoms, while others obtain only electrons.

Because Q and the ETC proteins can cycle between a reduced state and an oxidized state, and because they differ in electronegativity, investigators realized that it should be possible to arrange them into a logical sequence. The idea was that electrons would pass from a molecule with lower electronegativity to one with higher electronegativity, via a redox reaction.

As electrons moved through the chain, they would be held more and more tightly. A small amount of energy would be released in each reaction, and the potential energy in each successive bond would lessen.

Organization of the Electron Transport Chain Researchers worked out the sequence of compounds in the ETC by experimenting with poisons that inhibit particular proteins in the inner membrane. It was expected that if part of the chain were inhibited, then the components upstream of the block would become reduced, but those downstream would remain oxidized.

Experiments with various poisons showed that NADH donates an electron to a flavin-containing protein (FMN) at the top of the chain, while $FADH_2$ donates electrons to an iron- and sulfur-containing protein (Fe·S) that then passes them directly to Q. After passing through each of the remaining components in the chain, the electrons are finally accepted by oxygen.

FIGURE 9.14 shows how electrons step down in potential energy from the electron carriers NADH and $FADH_2$ to O_2. The x-axis

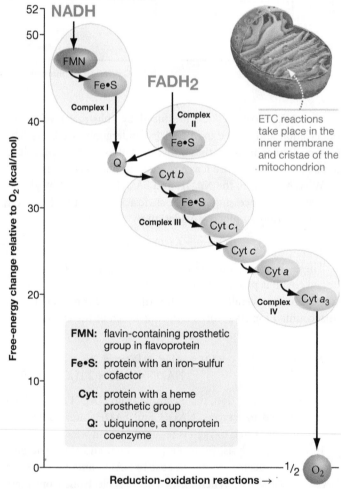

FIGURE 9.14 A Series of Reduction–Oxidation Reactions Occur in an Electron Transport Chain. Electrons step down in potential energy from the electron carriers NADH and $FADH_2$ through an electron transport chain to a final electron acceptor. When oxygen is the final electron acceptor, water is formed. The overall free-energy change of 52 kcal/mol (from NADH to oxygen) is broken into small steps.

DATA: Wilson D. F., M. Erecinska, and P. L. Dutton. 1974. *Annual Review of Biophysics and Bioengineering* 3: 203–230. Also Sled, V. D., N. I. Rudnitzky, Y. Hatefi, et al. 1994. *Biochemistry* 33: 10069–10075.

plots the sequence of redox reactions in the ETC; the y-axis plots the free-energy changes that occur.

The components of the electron transport chain are organized into four large complexes of proteins, often referred to as simply complexes I–IV. Q and the protein **cytochrome c** act as shuttles that transfer electrons between these complexes. Once the electrons at the bottom of the ETC are accepted by oxygen to form water, the oxidation of glucose is complete. Details on the names of the complexes and their role in the electron transport chain are provided in **TABLE 9.3** (on page 168).

Under controlled conditions in the laboratory, the total potential energy difference from NADH to oxygen is a whopping 53 kilocalories/mole (kcal/mol). Oxidation of the 10 molecules of NADH produced from each glucose accounts for almost 80 percent of the total energy released from the sugar. What does the ETC do with all this energy?

Role of the Electron Transport Chain Throughout the 1950s most biologists working on cellular respiration assumed that electron transport chains include enzymes that catalyze substrate-level phosphorylation. Recall that when substrate-level

phosphorylation occurs, a phosphate group is transferred from a phosphorylated substrate to ADP, forming ATP. Despite intense efforts, however, no one was able to find an enzyme among the components of the ETC that would catalyze the phosphorylation of ADP to produce ATP.

What researchers did find, however, is that the movement of electrons through the ETC actively transports protons from the matrix, across the inner membrane, and into the intermembrane space (see **FIGURE 9.15**). The exact route and mechanism used to pump protons is still being worked out. In some cases, it is not clear how the redox reactions taking place inside each complex result in the movement of protons.

The best-understood interaction between electron transport and proton transport takes place in complex III. Research has shown that when Q accepts electrons from complex I or complex II, it picks up protons from the matrix side of the inner membrane. The reduced form of Q then diffuses through the inner

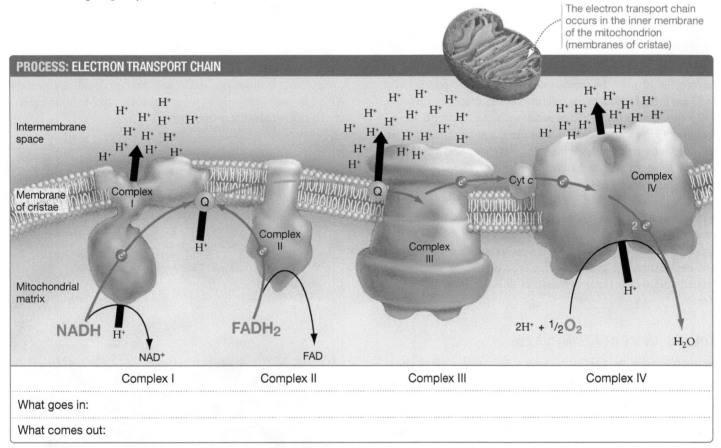

The electron transport chain occurs in the inner membrane of the mitochondrion (membranes of cristae)

FIGURE 9.15 How Does the Electron Transport Chain Work? The individual components of the electron transport chain diagrammed in Figure 9.14 are found in the inner membrane of mitochondria. Electrons are carried from one complex to another by Q and by cytochrome c; Q also shuttles protons across the membrane. The orange arrow indicates Q moving back and forth. Complexes I and IV use the potential energy released by the redox reactions to pump protons from the mitochondrial matrix to the intermembrane space.

✔**EXERCISE** Add an arrow across the membrane and label it "Proton gradient." In the boxes at the bottom, list "What goes in" and "What comes out" for each complex.

ETC Component	Descriptive Name	Reaction
Complex I	NADH dehydrogenase	Oxidizes **NADH** and transfers the two electrons through proteins containing FMN prosthetic groups and Fe·S cofactors to reduce an oxidized form of ubiquinone (Q). Four **H$^+$** are pumped out of the matrix to the intermembrane space.
Complex II	Succinate dehydrogenase	Oxidizes **FADH$_2$** and transfers the two electrons through proteins containing Fe·S cofactors to reduce an oxidized form of Q. This complex is also used in step 6 of the citric acid cycle.
Q	Ubiquinone	Reduced by complexes I and II and moves throughout the hydrophobic interior of the ETC membrane, where it is oxidized by complex III.
Complex III	Cytochrome *c* reductase	Oxidizes Q and transfers one electron at a time through proteins containing heme prosthetic groups and Fe·S cofactors to reduce an oxidized form of cytochrome *c* (cyt *c*). A total of four **H$^+$** for each pair of electrons is transported from the matrix to the intermembrane space.
Cyt *c*	Cytochrome *c*	Reduced by accepting a single electron from complex III and moves along the surface of ETC membrane, where it is oxidized by complex IV.
Complex IV	Cytochrome *c* oxidase	Oxidizes cyt *c* and transfers each electron through proteins containing heme prosthetic groups to reduce oxygen gas (O$_2$), which picks up two **H$^+$** from the matrix to produce water. Two additional **H$^+$** are pumped out of the matrix to the intermembrane space.

membrane, where its electrons are used to reduce a component of complex III near the intermembrane space. The protons held by Q are then released to the intermembrane space.

In this way, through redox reactions alone, Q shuttles electrons and protons from one side of the membrane to the other. The electrons proceed down the transport chain, and the protons contribute to an electrochemical gradient as they are released into the intermembrane space.

Once the nature of the electron transport chain became clear, biologists understood the fate of the electrons and the energy carried by NADH and FADH$_2$. Much of the chemical energy that was originally present in glucose is now accounted for in the proton electrochemical gradient. This is satisfying, except for one crucial question: If electron transport does not make ATP, what does?

The Discovery of ATP Synthase

In 1960 Efraim Racker made several key observations about how ATP is synthesized in mitochondria. When he used mitochondrial membranes to make vesicles, Racker noticed that some vesicles formed with their membrane inside out. Electron microscopy revealed that the inside-out membranes had many large proteins studded along their surfaces. Each protein appeared to have a base in the membrane, from which a lollipop-shaped stalk and a knob project (**FIGURE 9.16**). If the solution was vibrated or treated with a compound called urea, the stalks and knobs fell off.

Racker seized on this technique to isolate the stalks and knobs and do experiments with them. For example, he found that isolated stalks and knobs could hydrolyze ATP, forming ADP and

inorganic phosphate. The vesicles that contained just the base component, without the stalks and knobs, could not process ATP. The base components were, however, capable of transporting protons across the membrane.

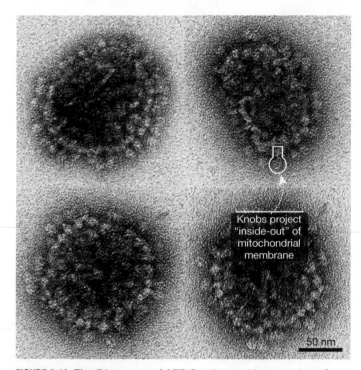

Knobs project "inside-out" of mitochondrial membrane

50 nm

FIGURE 9.16 The Discovery of ATP Synthase. When patches of mitochondrial membrane turn inside out and form vesicles, the lollipop-shaped stalk-and-knob structures of ATP synthase proteins face outward. Normally, the stalk and knob face inward, toward the mitochondrial matrix.

Based on these observations, Racker proposed that the stalk-and-knob component of the protein was an enzyme that both hydrolyzes and synthesizes ATP. To test his idea, Racker added the stalk-and-knob components back to vesicles that had been stripped of them and confirmed that the vesicles regained the ability to synthesize ATP. The entire complex is known as **ATP synthase.** Follow-up work also confirmed his hypothesis that the membrane-bound base component of ATP synthase is a proton channel. Is there a connection between proton transport and ATP synthesis?

The Chemiosmosis Hypothesis

In 1961 Peter Mitchell broke with the prevailing ideas that electron transport produces ATP via substrate phosphorylation. Instead, he proposed something completely new—an indirect connection between electron transport and ATP production. Mitchell's novel hypothesis? The real job of the electron transport chain is to pump protons across the inner membrane of mitochondria from the matrix to the intermembrane space. After a proton gradient is established, an enzyme in the inner membrane, like Racker's ATP synthase, would synthesize ATP from ADP and P_i.

Mitchell introduced the term **chemiosmosis** to describe the use of a proton gradient to drive energy-requiring processes, like the production of ATP. Here, osmosis refers to the force generated from the proton gradient rather than the transport of water. Although proponents of a direct link between electron transport and substrate-level phosphorylation objected vigorously to Mitchell's idea, several key experiments supported it.

FIGURE 9.17 illustrates how the existence of a key element in Mitchell's hypothesis was confirmed: A proton gradient alone can be used to synthesize ATP via ATP synthase. The researchers made vesicles from artificial membranes that contained Racker's ATP synthase isolated from mitochondria. Along with this enzyme, they inserted bacteriorhodopsin, a well-studied membrane protein that acts as a light-activated proton pump.

When light strikes bacteriorhodopsin, it absorbs some of the light energy and changes conformation in a way that pumps protons from the interior of a membrane to the exterior. As a result, the experimental vesicles established a strong electrochemical gradient favoring proton movement to the interior. When the vesicles were illuminated to initiate proton pumping, ATP began to be produced from ADP and P_i inside the vesicles.

Mitchell's prediction was correct: In this situation, ATP production depended solely on the existence of a **proton-motive force,** which is based on a proton electrochemical gradient. It could occur in the *absence* of an electron transport chain. This result, along with many others, has provided strong support for the hypothesis of chemiosmosis. Most of the ATP produced by cellular respiration is made by a flow of protons.

✔ If you understand chemiosmosis, you should be able to explain why ATP production during cellular respiration is characterized as indirect. More specifically, you should be able to explain the relationship between glucose oxidation, the proton gradient, and ATP synthase.

RESEARCH

QUESTION: How are the electron transport chain and ATP production linked?

CHEMIOSMOTIC HYPOTHESIS: The linkage is indirect. The ETC creates a proton-motive force that drives ATP synthesis by the mitochondrial ATP synthase.

ALTERNATIVE HYPOTHESIS: The linkage is direct. The ETC is associated with enzymes that perform substrate-level phosphorylation.

EXPERIMENTAL SETUP:

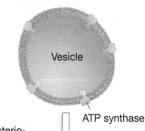

1. Produce vesicles from artificial membranes; add ATP synthase, an enzyme found in mitochondria.

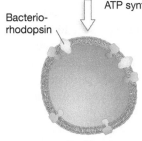

2. Add bacteriorhodopsin, a protein that acts as a light-activated proton pump.

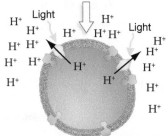

3. Illuminate vesicle so that bacteriorhodopsin pumps protons out of vesicle, creating a proton gradient.

PREDICTION OF CHEMIOSMOTIC HYPOTHESIS: ATP will be produced within the vesicle.

PREDICTION OF ALTERNATIVE HYPOTHESIS: No ATP will be produced.

RESULTS:

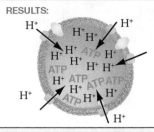

ATP is produced within the vesicle, in the absence of the electron transport chain.

CONCLUSION: The linkage between electron transport and ATP synthesis is indirect; the movement of protons drives the synthesis of ATP.

FIGURE 9.17 Evidence for the Chemiosmotic Hypothesis.

Racker, E., and W. Stoeckenius. 1974. Reconstitution of purple membrane vesicles catalyzing light-driven proton uptake and adenosine triphosphate formation. *Journal of Biological Chemistry.* 249: 662–663.

✔ QUESTION If bacteriorhodopsin were not available, what could the researchers have done with the ATP synthase vesicles to test their hypothesis?

Electron transport chains and ATP synthases are used by organisms throughout the tree of life. They are humming away in your cells now. Let's look in more detail at how they function.

The Proton-Motive Force Couples Electron Transport to ATP Synthesis

As **FIGURE 9.18** shows, the structure of ATP synthase is now well understood. The ATP synthase "knob" component is called the F_1 unit; the membrane-bound, proton-transporting base component is the F_0 unit. The F_1 and F_0 units are connected by a shaft, as well as by a stator, which holds the two units in place.

The F_0 unit serves as a rotor, whose turning is conveyed to the F_1 unit via the shaft. A flow of protons through the F_0 unit causes the rotor and shaft to spin. By attaching long actin filaments to the shaft and examining them with a videomicroscope, researchers have been able to see the rotation, which can reach speeds of 350 revolutions per second. As the shaft spins within the F_1 unit, it is thought to change the conformation of the F_1 subunits in a way that catalyzes the phosphorylation of ADP to ATP.

Chemiosmosis is like the process of generating electricity in a hydroelectric dam (like the one pictured on page 154). The ETC is analogous to a series of gigantic pumps that force water up and behind the dam. The inner mitochondrial membrane functions as the dam, with ATP synthase spinning and generating electricity inside as water passes through—like a turbine. In a mitochondrion, protons are pumped instead of water. When protons move through ATP synthase, the protein spins and generates ATP.

It has been determined that the ETC transports enough protons to produce approximately three ATP for each NADH and two for each $FADH_2$, depending on the type of ATP synthase used. These yields, however, are not observed in cells, since the proton-motive force is also used to drive other processes, such as the import of phosphates into the mitochondrial matrix.

Unlike the turbines in a hydroelectric dam, however, ATP synthase can reverse its direction and hydrolyze ATP to build a proton gradient. If the proton gradient dissipates, the direction of the spin is reversed and ATP is hydrolyzed to pump protons from the matrix to the intermembrane space. Understanding how these reactions occur is currently the focus of intense research. ATP synthase makes most of the ATP that keeps you alive.

The Proton-Motive Force and Chemical Evolution

How was energy first transformed into a usable form during the evolution of life? Since chemiosmosis is responsible for most of the ATP produced by cells throughout the tree of life, it is likely to have arisen early in evolution. But how could a complex electron transport chain evolve to produce the proton-motive force without a proton-motive force to supply the energy?

This apparent conundrum left many of the chemical evolution theorists perplexed until a key discovery was made deep in the ocean along the Mid-Atlantic Ridge—the Lost City hydrothermal vents (see Chapter 2). Researchers propose that the alkaline fluid (low proton concentration) released from these vents in the acidic oceans (high proton concentration) of early Earth may have provided such a gradient.

While there is still considerable debate concerning the role hydrothermal vents may have played in chemical evolution, their discovery has generated much excitement. By harnessing the natural electrochemical gradient deep in the early oceans, the proton-motive force of life may have evolved to mimic the environment of its origin.

Organisms Use a Diversity of Electron Acceptors

FIGURE 9.19 summarizes glucose oxidation and cellular respiration by tracing the fate of the carbon atoms and electrons in glucose. Notice that electrons from glucose are transferred to NADH and $FADH_2$, passed through the electron transport chain, and accepted by oxygen. Proton pumping during electron transport creates the proton-motive force that drives ATP synthesis.

The diagram also indicates the approximate yield of ATP from each component of the process. Recent research shows that about 29 ATP molecules are produced from each molecule of glucose.[2] Of these, 25 ATP molecules are produced by ATP synthase. The fundamental message here? The vast majority of the "payoff" from the oxidation of glucose occurs via oxidative phosphorylation.

Aerobic Versus Anaerobic Respiration

During cellular respiration, oxygen is the electron acceptor used by all eukaryotes and

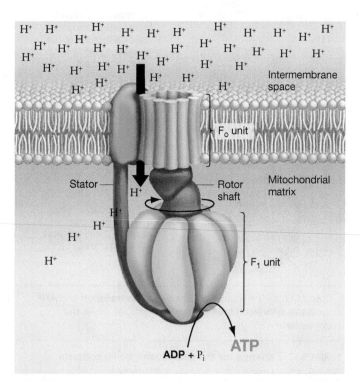

FIGURE 9.18 ATP Synthase Is a Motor. ATP synthase has two major components, designated F_0 and F_1, connected by a shaft. The F_0 unit spins as protons pass through. The shaft transmits the rotation to the F_1 unit, causing it to make ATP from ADP and P_i.

[2]Traditionally, biologists thought that 36 ATP would be synthesized for every molecule of glucose oxidized in eukaryotic cells. More recent work has shown that actual yield is only about 29 ATP [see M. Brand, Approximate yield of ATP from glucose, designed by Donald Nicholson. *Biochemistry and Molecular Biology Education* 31 (2003): 2–4]. Also, it's important to note that yield varies with conditions in the cell.

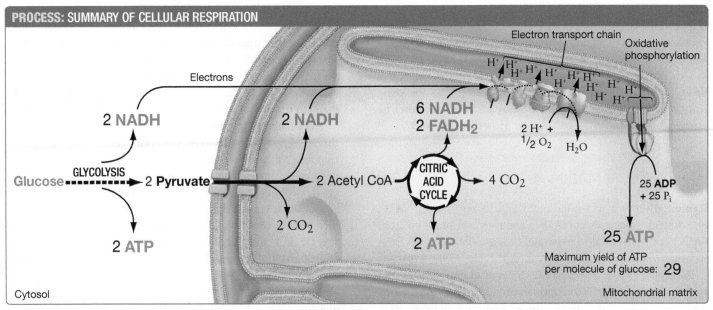

Electron transport chain

Oxidative phosphorylation

Electrons

2 NADH

2 NADH

6 NADH
2 FADH$_2$

Glucose ----GLYCOLYSIS----▶ 2 Pyruvate → 2 Acetyl CoA

CITRIC
ACID
CYCLE

→ 4 CO$_2$

2 H$^+$ +
$\frac{1}{2}$ O$_2$

H$_2$O

25 ADP
+ 25 P$_i$

2 CO$_2$

2 ATP

2 ATP

25 ATP

Maximum yield of ATP
per molecule of glucose: 29

Cytosol

Mitochondrial matrix

FIGURE 9.19 ATP Yield during Cellular Respiration. The actual yield of ATP per glucose (29 ATP) is lower than the theoretical calculation (38 ATP) because of energy required for the import of NADH from the cytoplasm and the use of the proton-motive force to actively transport P$_i$ into the mitochondrial matrix.

a wide diversity of bacteria and archaea. Species that depend on oxygen as an electron acceptor for the ETC use **aerobic** respiration and are called aerobic organisms. (The Latin root *aero* means "air.")

It is important to recognize, though, that cellular respiration can occur without oxygen. Many thousands of bacterial and archaeal species rely on electron acceptors other than oxygen, and electron donors other than glucose. For example, nitrate (NO_3^-) and sulfate (SO_4^{2-}) are particularly common electron acceptors in species that live in oxygen-poor environments (see Chapter 29). In addition, many bacteria and archaea use H_2, H_2S, CH_4, or other inorganic compounds as electron donors—not glucose.

Cells that depend on electron acceptors other than oxygen are said to use **anaerobic** ("no air") respiration. Even though the starting and ending points of cellular respiration differ, aerobic and anaerobic cells still use electron transport chains to create a proton-motive force that drives the synthesis of ATP. In bacteria and archaea, the ETC and ATP synthase are located in the plasma membrane.

Aerobic Respiration Is Most Efficient Even though an array of compounds can serve as the final electron acceptor in cellular respiration, oxygen is the most efficient. Because oxygen holds electrons so tightly, the potential energy of electrons in a bond between an oxygen atom and a non-oxygenic atom, such as hydrogen, is low. As a result, there is a large difference between the potential energy of electrons in NADH and the potential energy of electrons bonded to an oxygen atom, such as found in water (see Figure 9.14). The large differential in potential energy means that the electron transport chain can generate a large proton-motive force.

Cells that do not use oxygen as an electron acceptor cannot generate such a large potential energy difference. As a result, they make less ATP from each glucose molecule than cells that use aerobic respiration. This finding is important: It means that anaerobic organisms tend to grow much more slowly than aerobic organisms. If cells that use anaerobic respiration compete with cells using aerobic respiration, those that use oxygen as an electron acceptor almost always grow faster and reproduce more.

What happens when oxygen or other electron acceptors get used up? When there is no terminal electron acceptor, the electrons in

check your understanding

C Y U

If you understand that . . .
- As electrons from NADH and FADH$_2$ move through the electron transport chain, protons are pumped into the intermembrane space of mitochondria.
- The electrochemical gradient across the inner mitochondrial membrane drives protons through ATP synthase, resulting in the production of ATP from ADP.

✔ **You should be able to . . .**

Add paper squares labeled ETC and ATP synthase and a paper circle labeled ½ O$_2$ → H$_2$O to the model you made in Section 9.4. Explain the steps in electron transport and chemiosmosis using paper triangles to represent electron pairs and dimes to represent protons.

Answers are available in Appendix A.

each of the complexes of the electron transport chain have no place to go and the electron transport chain stops. Without an oxidized complex I, NADH remains reduced. The concentration of NAD^+ drops rapidly as cells continue to convert NAD^+ to NADH.

This situation is life threatening. When there is no longer any NAD^+ to drive glycolysis, pyruvate processing, and the citric acid cycle, then no ATP can be produced. If NAD^+ cannot be regenerated somehow, the cell will die. How do cells cope?

9.6 Fermentation

Fermentation is a metabolic pathway that regenerates NAD^+ by oxidizing stockpiles of NADH. The electrons removed from NADH are transferred to pyruvate, or a molecule derived from pyruvate, instead of an electron transport chain (**FIGURE 9.20**).

In respiring cells, fermentation serves as an emergency back-up that allows glycolysis to continue producing ATP even when the ETC is shut down. It allows the cell to survive and even grow in the absence of electron transport chains.

In many cases, the cell cannot use the molecule that is formed when pyruvate (or another electron acceptor) accepts electrons from NADH. This by-product may even be toxic and excreted from the cell as waste even though it has not been fully oxidized.

Many Different Fermentation Pathways Exist When you run up a long flight of stairs, your muscles begin metabolizing glucose so fast that the supply of oxygen is rapidly used up by their mitochondria. When oxygen is absent, the electron transport chains shut down and NADH cannot donate its electrons there. The pyruvate produced by glycolysis then begins to accept electrons from NADH, and fermentation takes place. This process, called **lactic acid fermentation,** regenerates NAD^+ by forming a product molecule called lactate: a deprotonated form of lactic acid (**FIGURE 9.21a**). Your body reacts by making you breathe faster and increasing your heart rate. By getting more oxygen to your muscle cells, the electron transport chain is revived.

FIGURE 9.21b illustrates a different fermentation pathway, **alcohol fermentation,** which occurs in the fungus *Saccharomyces*

cerevisiae—baker's and brewer's yeast. When yeast cells are placed in an environment such as bread dough or a bottle of grape juice and begin growing, they quickly use up all the available oxygen. Instead of depositing the electrons from NADH into pyruvate, yeast first convert pyruvate to the two-carbon compound acetaldehyde. This reaction gives off carbon dioxide, which causes bread to rise and produces the bubbles in champagne and beer.

Acetaldehyde then accepts electrons from NADH, forming the NAD^+ required to keep glycolysis going. The addition of electrons to acetaldehyde forms ethanol as a waste product. The yeast cells excrete ethanol as waste. In essence, the active ingredient in alcoholic beverages is like yeast urine.

Cells that employ other types of fermentation are used commercially in the production of soy sauce, tofu, yogurt, cheese, vinegar, and other products.

Bacteria and archaea that exist exclusively through fermentation are present in phenomenal numbers in the oxygen-free environment of your small intestine and in the first compartment of a cow's stomach, called the rumen. The rumen is a specialized digestive organ that contains over 10^{10} (10 billion) bacterial and archaeal cells per *milliliter* of fluid. The fermentations that occur in these cells produce an array of fatty acids. Cattle don't actually live off grass directly—they eat it to feed their bacteria and archaea and then use the fermentation by-products from these organisms as a source of energy.

Fermentation as an Alternative to Cellular Respiration Even though fermentation is a widespread type of metabolism, it is extremely inefficient compared with aerobic cellular respiration. Fermentation produces just 2 molecules of ATP for each molecule of glucose metabolized, while cellular respiration produces about 29—almost 15 times more energy per glucose molecule than fermentation. The reason for the disparity is that oxygen has much higher electronegativity than electron acceptors such as pyruvate and acetaldehyde. As a result, the potential energy drop between the start and end of fermentation is a tiny fraction of the potential energy change that occurs during cellular respiration.

Based on these observations, it is not surprising that organisms capable of both processes almost never use fermentation

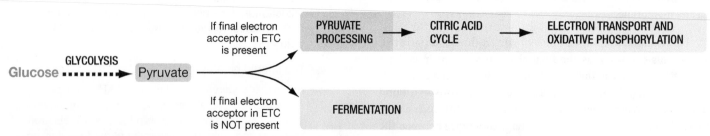

FIGURE 9.20 Cellular Respiration and Fermentation Are Alternative Pathways for Producing Energy. When oxygen or another electron acceptor used by the ETC is present in a cell, the pyruvate produced by glycolysis enters the citric acid cycle and the electron transport system is active. But if no electron acceptor is available to keep the ETC running, the pyruvate undergoes reactions known as fermentation.

(a) Lactic acid fermentation occurs in humans.

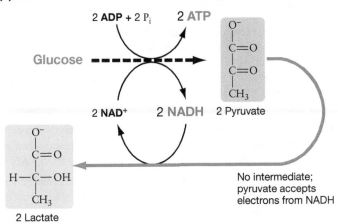

2 Lactate

(b) Alcohol fermentation occurs in yeast.

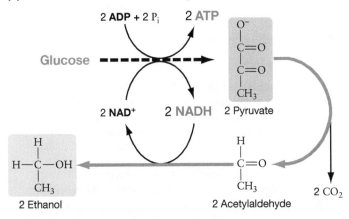

2 Ethanol   2 Acetylaldehyde

FIGURE 9.21 Fermentation Regenerates NAD⁺ So That Glycolysis Can Continue. These are just two examples of the many types of fermentation that occur among bacteria, archaea, and eukaryotes.

when an appropriate electron acceptor is available for cellular respiration. In organisms that usually use oxygen as an electron acceptor, fermentation is an alternative mode of ATP production when oxygen supplies temporarily run out.

Organisms that can switch between fermentation and cellular respiration that uses oxygen as an electron acceptor are called **facultative anaerobes.** The adjective facultative reflects the ability to use cellular respiration when oxygen is present and fermentation when it is absent (anaerobic). Many of your cells can function as facultative anaerobes to a certain extent; however, you cannot survive for long without oxygen. To make this point clear, try holding your breath—it should take only a minute for you to realize how important electron transport is to your cells.

check your understanding

C Y U

If you understand that . . .

- Fermentation occurs in the absence of an electron acceptor at the end of an ETC. It consists of reactions that oxidize NADH to regenerate the NAD⁺ required for glycolysis.

✔ **You should be able to . . .**

Explain why organisms that have an ETC as well as fermentation pathways seldom ferment pyruvate if an electron acceptor at the end of the ETC is readily available.

Answers are available in Appendix A.

CHAPTER 9   REVIEW   *For media, go to MasteringBiology*

If you understand . . .

9.1   An Overview of Cellular Respiration

- Cellular respiration is based on redox reactions that transfer electrons from a compound with high free energy, such as glucose, to a molecule with lower free energy, such as oxygen, through an electron transport chain.

- In eukaryotes, cellular respiration consists of four steps: glycolysis, pyruvate processing, the citric acid cycle, and electron transport coupled to oxidative phosphorylation.

- Glycolysis, pyruvate processing, and the citric acid cycle are central to the metabolism of most cells. Other catabolic pathways feed into them, and the intermediates of the central pathways are used in the synthesis of many key molecules.

✔ You should be able to explain why many different molecules—including lipids, amino acids, and CO_2—are radiolabeled when cells are fed glucose with ^{14}C radioactive carbons.

9.2   Glycolysis: Processing Glucose to Pyruvate

- The glycolytic pathway is a 10-step reaction sequence in which glucose is broken down into two molecules of pyruvate. It takes place in the cytosol, where ATP and NADH are produced.

- Glycolysis slows when ATP binds to phosphofructokinase.

✔ **QUANTITATIVE** You should be able to draw a graph predicting how the rate of ATP production in glycolysis changes as a function of ATP concentration. (Write "ATP concentration" on the x-axis and "ATP production" on the y-axis.)

9.3 Processing Pyruvate to Acetyl CoA

- During pyruvate processing, a series of reactions convert pyruvate to acetyl CoA. NADH is produced and CO_2 is released.

- The pyruvate dehydrogenase complex is inhibited when it is phosphorylated by ATP. It speeds up in the presence of substrates like NAD and ADP.

✔ You should be able to explain why it is not surprising that pyruvate dehydrogenase consists of a large, multi-enzyme complex.

9.4 The Citric Acid Cycle: Oxidizing Acetyl CoA to CO_2

- The citric acid cycle is an eight-step reaction cycle that begins with acetyl CoA. $FADH_2$, NADH, and GTP or ATP are produced; CO_2 is released. By the end of the citric acid cycle, glucose is completely oxidized to CO_2.

- Certain enzymes in the citric acid cycle are inhibited when NADH or ATP binds to them.

✔ You should be able to describe what would happen to NADH levels in a cell in the first few seconds after a drug has poisoned the enzyme that combines acetyl CoA and oxaloacetate to form citrate.

9.5 Electron Transport and Chemiosmosis: Building a Proton Gradient to Produce ATP

- NADH and $FADH_2$ donate electrons to an electron transport chain that resides in the inner membrane of mitochondria and the plasma membrane of many bacteria. The series of redox reactions in these chains gradually steps the electrons down in potential energy until they are transferred to a final electron acceptor (often O_2).

- The energy released from redox reactions in the electron transport chain is used to move protons across the inner mitochondrial membrane, creating an electrochemical gradient. ATP synthase uses the energy stored in this gradient to produce ATP via chemiosmosis—a process called oxidative phosphorylation.

✔ You should be able to predict the effect of a drug that inhibits ATP synthase on the pH in the mitochondrial matrix.

9.6 Fermentation

- In many eukaryotes and bacteria, fermentation occurs when cellular respiration slows down or stops due to an insufficient amount of the final electron acceptor. If the final electron acceptor is absent, then the electron transport chain would no longer oxidize NADH to NAD^+ and ATP could no longer be produced by glycolysis, the citric acid cycle, or oxidative phosphorylation.

- Fermentation pathways regenerate NAD^+, so glycolysis can continue to make ATP and keep the cell alive. This happens when an organic molecule such as pyruvate accepts electrons from NADH.

- Depending on the molecule that acts as an electron acceptor, fermentation pathways produce lactate, ethanol, or other reduced organic compounds as a by-product.

✔ You should be able to explain why you would expect organisms that produce ATP only via fermentation to grow much more slowly than organisms that produce ATP via cellular respiration.

(MB) MasteringBiology

1. MasteringBiology Assignments

Tutorials and Activities Build a Chemical Cycling System; Cellular Respiration (1 of 5): Inputs and Outputs; Cellular Respiration (2 of 5): Glycolysis; Cellular Respiration (3 of 5): Acetyl CoA Formation and the Citric Acid Cycle; Cellular Respiration (4 of 5): Oxidative Phosphorylation; Cellular Respiration (5 of 5): Summary; Citric Acid Cycle; Electron Transport; Fermentation; Glucose Metabolism; Glycolysis; Overview of Cellular Respiration; Pathways for Pyruvate

Questions Reading Quizzes, Blue-Thread Questions, Test Bank

2. eText Read your book online, search, take notes, highlight text, and more.

3. The Study Area Practice Test, Cumulative Test, BioFlix® 3-D animations, Videos, Activities, Audio Glossary, Word Study Tools, Art

You should be able to . . .

✔ TEST YOUR KNOWLEDGE
Answers are available in Appendix A

1. Make a flowchart indicating the relationships among the four steps of cellular respiration. Which steps are responsible for glucose oxidation? Which produce the most ATP?

2. Where does the citric acid cycle occur in eukaryotes?
   a. in the cytosol
   b. in the matrix of mitochondria
   c. in the inner membrane of mitochondria
   d. in the intermembrane space of mitochondria

3. What does the chemiosmotic hypothesis claim?
   a. Substrate-level phosphorylation occurs in the electron transport chain.
   b. Substrate-level phosphorylation occurs in glycolysis and the citric acid cycle.
   c. The electron transport chain is located in the inner membrane of mitochondria.
   d. Electron transport chains generate ATP indirectly, by the creation of a proton-motive force.

4. After glucose is fully oxidized by glycolysis, pyruvate processing, and the citric acid cycle, where is most of the energy stored?

5. What is the function of the reactions in a fermentation pathway?
   a. to generate NADH from NAD^+, so electrons can be donated to the electron transport chain
   b. to synthesize pyruvate from lactate
   c. to generate NAD^+ from NADH, so glycolysis can continue
   d. to synthesize electron acceptors, so that cellular respiration can continue

6. Which of the following would cause cells to switch from cellular respiration to fermentation?
   a. The final electron acceptor in the ETC is not available.
   b. The proton-motive force runs down.
   c. NADH and $FADH_2$ supplies are low.
   d. Pyruvate is not available.

TEST YOUR UNDERSTANDING   Answers are available in Appendix A

7. Describe the relationship between carbohydrate metabolism, the catabolism of proteins and fats, and anabolic pathways.

8. Compare and contrast substrate-level phosphorylation and oxidative phosphorylation.

9. Why does aerobic respiration produce much more ATP than anaerobic respiration?

10. If you were to expose cells that are undergoing cellular respiration to a radioactive oxygen isotope in the form of O_2, which of the following molecules would you expect to be radiolabeled?
    a. pyruvate
    b. water
    c. NADH
    d. CO_2

11. In step 3 of the citric acid cycle, the enzyme isocitrate dehydrogenase is regulated by NADH. Compare and contrast the regulation of this enzyme with what you have learned about phosphofructokinase in glycolysis.

12. Explain the relationship between electron transport and oxidative phosphorylation. What does ATP synthase look like, and how does it work?

TEST YOUR PROBLEM-SOLVING SKILLS   Answers are available in Appendix A

13. Cyanide ($C \equiv N^-$) blocks complex IV of the electron transport chain. Suggest a hypothesis for what happens to the ETC when complex IV stops working. Your hypothesis should explain why cyanide poisoning in humans is fatal.

14. The presence of many sac-like cristae results in a large amount of membrane inside mitochondria. Suppose that some mitochondria had few cristae. How would their output of ATP compare with that of mitochondria with many cristae? Justify your answer.

15. QUANTITATIVE Early estimates suggested that the oxidation of glucose via aerobic respiration would produce 38 ATP. Based on what you know of the theoretical yields of ATP from each step, show how this total was determined. Why do biologists now think this amount of ATP/glucose is not achieved in cells?

16. Suppose a drug were added to mitochondria that allowed protons to freely pass through the inner membrane. Which of the following mitochondrial activities would most likely be inhibited?
    a. the citric acid cycle
    b. oxidative phosphorylation
    c. substrate-level phosphorylation
    d. the electron transport chain

The Big Picture

It takes energy to stay alive. Use this concept map to study how the information on energy and energetics presented in this book fits together.

As you read the map, remember that chemical energy is potential energy. Potential energy is based on the position of matter in space, and chemical energy is all about the position of electrons in covalent bonds. When hydrogen gas reacts explosively with oxygen, all that's happening is that electrons are moving from high-energy positions to lower-energy positions.

In essence, organisms transform energy from the Sun into chemical energy in the C–C and C–H bonds of glucose, and then into chemical energy in the P–P bonds of ATP.

The potential energy in ATP allows cells to do work: pump ions, synthesize molecules, move cargo, and send and receive signals.

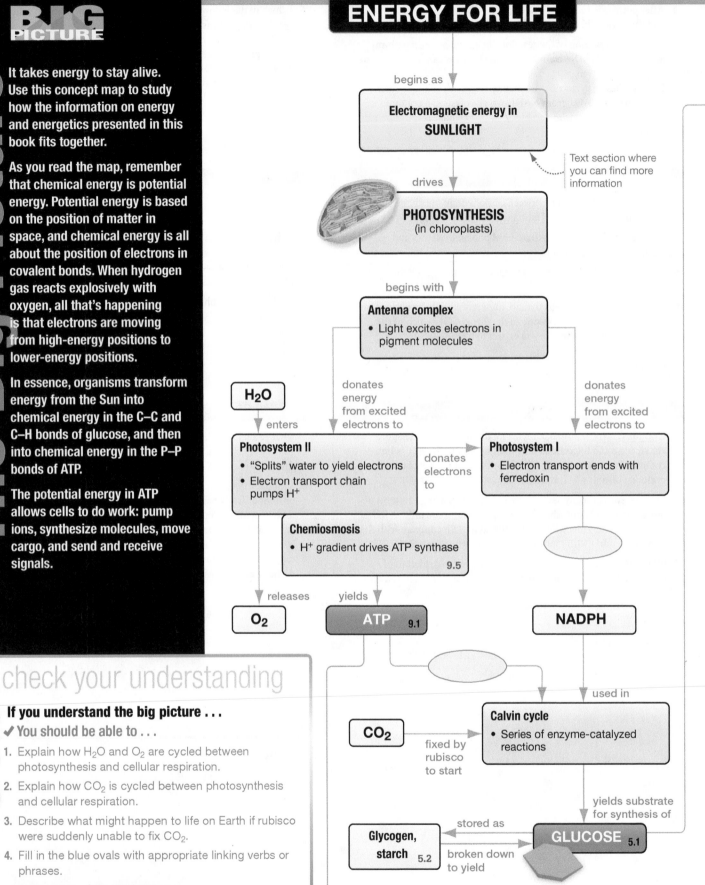

ENERGY FOR LIFE

begins as

Electromagnetic energy in SUNLIGHT

Text section where you can find more information

drives

PHOTOSYNTHESIS
(in chloroplasts)

begins with

Antenna complex
• Light excites electrons in pigment molecules

H_2O

donates energy from excited electrons to

donates energy from excited electrons to

enters

Photosystem II
• "Splits" water to yield electrons
• Electron transport chain pumps H^+

donates electrons to

Photosystem I
• Electron transport ends with ferredoxin

Chemiosmosis
• H^+ gradient drives ATP synthase
9.5

releases

yields

O_2

ATP 9.1

NADPH

used in

CO_2

fixed by rubisco to start

Calvin cycle
• Series of enzyme-catalyzed reactions

yields substrate for synthesis of

stored as

Glycogen, starch 5.2

broken down to yield

GLUCOSE 5.1

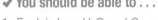

If you understand the big picture . . .

✔ You should be able to . . .

1. Explain how H_2O and O_2 are cycled between photosynthesis and cellular respiration.

2. Explain how CO_2 is cycled between photosynthesis and cellular respiration.

3. Describe what might happen to life on Earth if rubisco were suddenly unable to fix CO_2.

4. Fill in the blue ovals with appropriate linking verbs or phrases.

Answers are available in Appendix A.

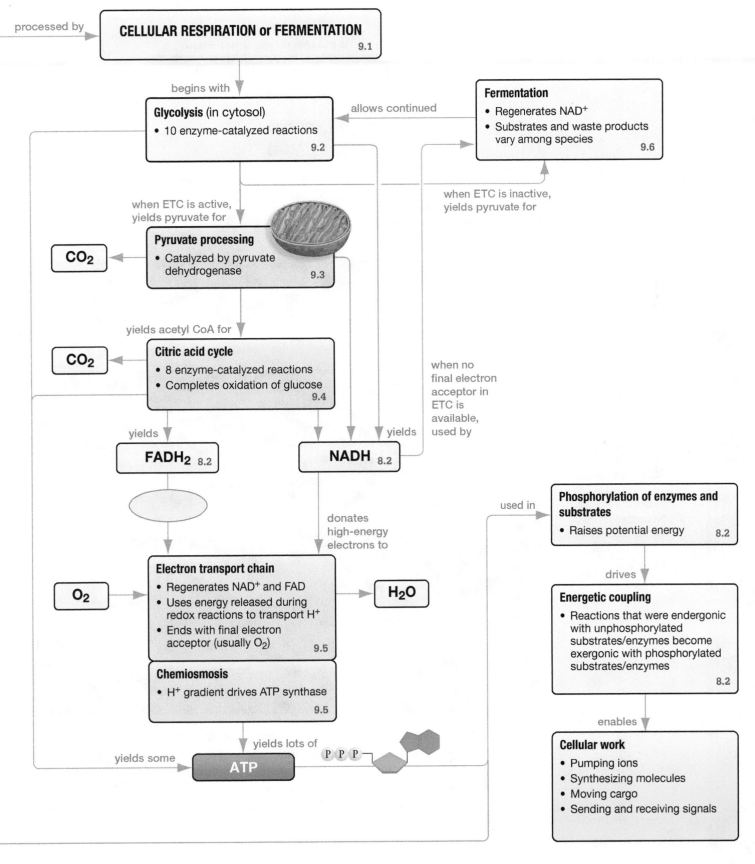

CELLULAR RESPIRATION or FERMENTATION
9.1

processed by →

begins with ↓

Glycolysis (in cytosol)
• 10 enzyme-catalyzed reactions
9.2

← allows continued

Fermentation
• Regenerates NAD⁺
• Substrates and waste products vary among species
9.6

when ETC is active, yields pyruvate for

when ETC is inactive, yields pyruvate for

Pyruvate processing
• Catalyzed by pyruvate dehydrogenase
9.3

CO_2

yields acetyl CoA for

Citric acid cycle
• 8 enzyme-catalyzed reactions
• Completes oxidation of glucose
9.4

CO_2

when no final electron acceptor in ETC is available, used by

yields

FADH₂ 8.2

NADH 8.2

yields

donates high-energy electrons to

Phosphorylation of enzymes and substrates
• Raises potential energy
8.2

used in

drives ↓

Electron transport chain
• Regenerates NAD⁺ and FAD
• Uses energy released during redox reactions to transport H⁺
• Ends with final electron acceptor (usually O_2)
9.5

O_2

H_2O

Energetic coupling
• Reactions that were endergonic with unphosphorylated substrates/enzymes become exergonic with phosphorylated substrates/enzymes
8.2

Chemiosmosis
• H⁺ gradient drives ATP synthase
9.5

enables ↓

yields lots of

ATP

P P P

Cellular work
• Pumping ions
• Synthesizing molecules
• Moving cargo
• Sending and receiving signals

yields some

11 Cell–Cell Interactions

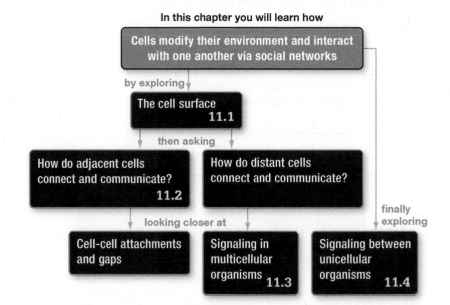

In this chapter you will learn how

Cells modify their environment and interact with one another via social networks

by exploring

The cell surface
11.1

then asking

How do adjacent cells connect and communicate?
11.2

How do distant cells connect and communicate?

looking closer at

Cell-cell attachments and gaps

Signaling in multicellular organisms **11.3**

finally exploring

Signaling between unicellular organisms **11.4**

In this micrograph of cardiac tissue, muscle cells are stained red and their nuclei are stained blue. The green dye highlights a protein called dystrophin, which links the cytoskeleton of muscle cells to proteins that attach to the extracellular matrix. Deficiency in dystrophin leads to muscular dystrophy.

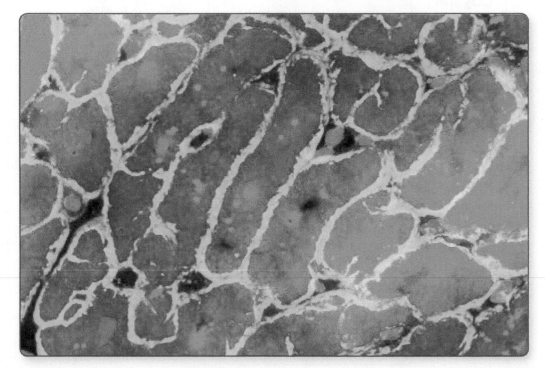

A diversity of events takes place at the cellular level. The plasma membrane surrounds a bustling enterprise consisting of organelles, molecular machines, and cytoskeletal elements (see Chapters 6 and 7). Molecular motors transport cargo throughout the cell at breathtaking speed. It would be a mistake, however, to think that cells are self-contained—that they are worlds in and of themselves. Instead, cells are dependent on interactions with other cells and the surrounding environment.

✓ When you see this checkmark, stop and test yourself. Answers are available in Appendix A.

For most unicellular species, the outside environment is teeming with other organisms. Inside your gut, for example, hundreds of billions of bacterial cells are jostling for space and resources. In addition to interacting with these individuals, every unicellular organism must contend with constant shifts in the physical environment, such as heat, light, ion concentrations, and food supplies. If unicellular organisms are unable to sense these conditions and respond appropriately, they die.

In multicellular species, the environment outside the cell is made up of other cells, both neighboring and distant. The cells that make up a redwood tree, a mushroom, or your body are intensely social. Although biologists often study cells in isolation, an individual tree, fungus, or person is actually an interdependent community of cells. If those cells do not communicate and cooperate, the whole will break into dysfunctional parts and die.

To understand the life of a cell, then, it is critical to analyze how the cell interacts with the world outside its membrane. How do cells obtain information about the world and respond to that information? In particular, how do cells interact with other cells? To answer these questions, let's begin with the cell surface—with the molecules that separate the cell from its environment.

11.1 The Cell Surface

The line between life and nonlife is drawn by the plasma membrane that surrounds every cell. Recall that the structure of this membrane consists of a phospholipid bilayer studded with membrane proteins that are integral, meaning that they are embedded in the bilayer, or peripheral, meaning that they are attached to one surface (see Chapter 6). These proteins participate in the primary function of the plasma membrane: to create an environment inside the cell that is different from conditions outside by regulating the transport of substances.

The plasma membrane does not exist in isolation, however. Cytoskeletal elements attach to the interior face of the bilayer (see Chapter 7), and a complex array of extracellular structures interacts with the membrane's exterior surface. Let's consider the nature of the material outside the cell and then analyze how the cell interacts with it and other cells.

The Structure and Function of an Extracellular Layer

It is actually extremely rare for cells to be bounded simply by a plasma membrane. Most cells secrete products that are assembled into a layer or wall just beyond the membrane. This extracellular material helps define the cell's shape and either attaches it to another cell or acts as a first line of defense against the outside world.

Virtually all types of extracellular structures—from the cell walls of bacteria, algae, fungi, and plants to the extracellular material that surrounds most animal cells—follow the same fundamental design principle. Like reinforced concrete, they are "fiber composites": They consist of a cross-linked network of long

Concrete (the "ground substance") resists compression

Steel rods (the "fibers") resist tension

FIGURE 11.1 Fiber Composites Resist Tension and Compression. Fiber composites, such as reinforced concrete, consist of ground substance that fills spaces between cross-linked rods.

filaments embedded in a stiff surrounding material, or ground substance (**FIGURE 11.1**). The molecules that make up the filaments and the encasing material vary from group to group, but the engineering principle is the same. Why?

- The rods or filaments in a fiber composite are extremely effective at withstanding stretching and straining forces, or tension. The fibers present in extracellular material of most cells are functionally similar to the steel rods in reinforced concrete—they resist being pulled or pushed lengthwise.

- The stiff surrounding substance is effective at withstanding the pressing forces called compression. Concrete performs this function in highways, and a gel-forming mixture of polysaccharides achieves the same end in extracellular material.

Thanks to the combination of tension- and compression-resisting elements, fiber composites are particularly rugged. And in many living cells, the fiber and composite elements are flexible as well as strong.

What molecules make up the rods and ground substance found on the surface of plant and animal cells? How are these extracellular layers synthesized, and what do they do?

The Cell Wall in Plants

Virtually all plant cells are surrounded by a cell wall—a fiber composite that is the basis of major industries. The paper in this book, the threads in your cotton clothing, and the wood in your neighborhood's houses are made up primarily of plant cell walls.

Before analyzing the structure of plant cell walls in detail, it's important to note that these structures are dynamic. If they are damaged by attacking insects, they may release signaling molecules that trigger the reinforcement of walls in nearby cells. Cell walls are also degraded in a controlled way as fruits ripen, making the fruits softer and more digestible for the animals that disperse the seeds inside.

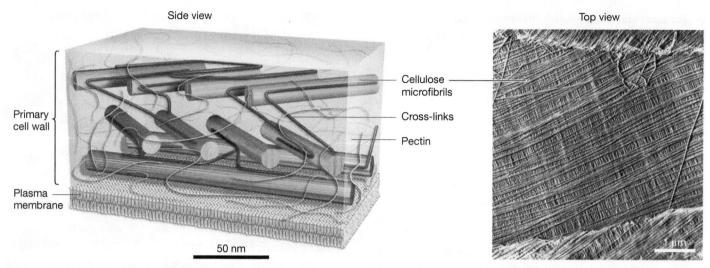

Side view   Top view

Cellulose
microfibrils

Cross-links

Pectin

Primary
cell wall

Plasma
membrane

50 nm   1 µm

FIGURE 11.2 Primary Cell Walls of Plants Are Fiber Composites. In a plant's primary cell wall, cellulose microfibrils are cross-linked by polysaccharide chains. The spaces between the microfibrils are filled with pectin molecules, which form a gelatinous solid.

Primary Cell Walls   When plant cells first form, they secrete an initial fiber composite called a **primary cell wall.**

- The fibrous component of the primary cell wall consists of long strands of cellulose, which are bundled into stout, cable-like structures termed **microfibrils** and then cross-linked by other polysaccharide filaments. The microfibrils are synthesized by a complex of enzymes in the plasma membrane, forming a crisscrossed network (**FIGURE 11.2**).

- The space between microfibrils is filled with gelatinous polysaccharides such as **pectins**—the molecules that are used to thicken jams and jellies. Because the polysaccharides in pectin are hydrophilic, they attract and hold large amounts of water to keep the cell wall moist. The gelatinous components of the cell wall are synthesized in the rough endoplasmic reticulum and Golgi apparatus and secreted to the extracellular space.

The primary cell wall defines the shape of a plant cell. Under normal conditions, the nucleus and cytoplasm fill the entire volume of the cell and push the plasma membrane up against the wall. Because the concentration of solutes is higher inside the cell than outside, water tends to enter the cell via osmosis. The incoming water increases the cell's volume, exerting a force against the wall that is known as **turgor pressure.**

Although plant cells experience turgor pressure throughout their lives, it is particularly important in young cells that are actively growing. Young plant cells secrete proteins named expansins into their cell wall. **Expansins** disrupt hydrogen bonds that cross-link the microfibrils in the wall, allowing them to slide past one another. Turgor pressure then forces the wall to elongate and expand. The result is cell growth.

Secondary Cell Walls   As plant cells mature and stop growing, they may secrete an additional layer of material—a **secondary cell wall**—between the plasma membrane and the primary cell wall. The structure of the secondary cell wall varies from cell to cell in the plant and correlates with that cell's function. Cells on the surface of a leaf have secondary cell walls that are impregnated with waxes that form a waterproof coating; the cells that support the plant's stem have secondary cell walls that contain a great deal of cellulose.

In cells that form wood, the secondary cell wall also includes **lignin,** a complex polymer that forms an exceptionally rigid network. Cells that have thick secondary cell walls of cellulose and lignin help plants withstand the forces of gravity and wind.

Although animal cells do not make a cell wall, they do form a fiber composite outside their plasma membrane. What is this substance, and what does it do?

The Extracellular Matrix in Animals

Most animal cells secrete a fiber composite called the **extracellular matrix (ECM).** Like the extracellular materials found in other organisms, structural support is one of the ECM's most important functions.

ECM design follows the same principles observed in the cell walls of bacteria, archaea, algae, fungi, and plants. There is a key difference, however: The animal ECM contains much more protein relative to carbohydrate than does a cell wall.

- The fibrous component of animal ECM is dominated by a cable-like protein termed **collagen** (**FIGURE 11.3a**).

- The matrix that surrounds collagen and other fibrous components contains gel-forming **proteoglycans** that consist of protein cores with many large polysaccharides attached to them. In some tissues, complexes of proteoglycans may also be produced (**FIGURE 11.3b**).

Most ECM components are synthesized in the rough endoplasmic reticulum (ER), processed in the Golgi apparatus, and

(a) Collagen proteins consist of three polypeptide chains that wind around one another to form the fibrous component of the animal ECM.

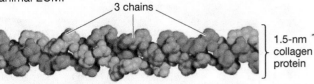

3 chains

1.5-nm collagen protein

(b) Complexes of gelatinous proteoglycans form the ground substance of the animal ECM.

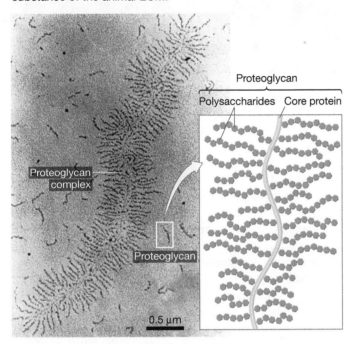

Proteoglycan complex

Proteoglycan

Proteoglycan

Polysaccharides   Core protein

0.5 µm

FIGURE 11.3 The Extracellular Matrix Is a Fiber Composite.
(a) Although several types of fibrous proteins are found in the ECM of animal cells, the most abundant is collagen. Groups of collagen proteins coalesce to form collagen fibrils, and bundles of fibrils link to form collagen fibers. **(b)** The spaces between the collagen fibers are filled with complexes of gelatinous proteoglycans. The proteoglycan subunits consist of a protein core attached to many polysaccharides.

secreted from the cell via exocytosis. After secretion, however, proteins like collagen may then assemble into larger structures, such as the fibrils shown in **FIGURE 11.4**. In addition, the secreted proteoglycans may be attached to long polysaccharides synthesized by cellular enzymes in the extracellular space. These huge complexes, such as the one shown in Figure 11.3b, are responsible for the rubber-like consistency of cartilage.

Even in the same organism, the amount of ECM varies among different types of **tissues,** which consist of similar cells that function as a unit. Bone and cartilage, for example, have relatively few cells surrounded by a large amount of ECM. Skin cells, in contrast, are packed together with a minimal amount of ECM.

The composition of the ECM also varies among tissue types. For example, the ECM surrounding cells in lung tissue contains large amounts of a rubber-like protein called elastin, which allows the ECM to expand and contract during breathing. The structure of a cell's ECM correlates with the function of the tissue.

Although collagen and the other common ECM proteins are much more elastic and bendable than the stiff cell walls of plants, they support cell structure via attachments to the cell surface. As

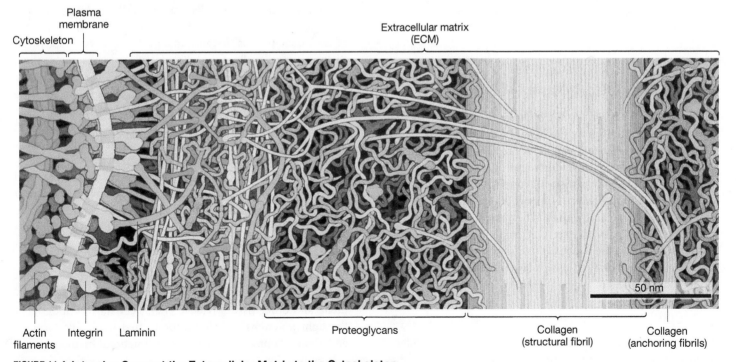

Cytoskeleton

Plasma membrane

Extracellular matrix (ECM)

Actin filaments   Integrin   Laminin

Proteoglycans

Collagen (structural fibril)

Collagen (anchoring fibrils)

50 nm

FIGURE 11.4 Integrins Connect the Extracellular Matrix to the Cytoskeleton.

Figure 11.4 shows, membrane proteins called **integrins** bind to extracellular proteins, including laminins, which in turn bind to other components of the ECM. **Laminins** are ECM crosslinking proteins—not to be confused with lamins, which are intermediate filaments found in the nucleus (see Chapter 7).

The intracellular portions of the integrins also bind to proteins that are connected to the cytoskeleton, effectively forming a bridge between the two support systems. This linkage between the cytoskeleton and ECM is critical. Besides keeping individual cells in place, it helps adjacent cells adhere to each other via their common connection to the ECM.

Cells monitor this cytoskeleton–ECM linkage via signaling pathways that will be introduced in Section 11.3. When integrins bind to the ECM, they transmit signals that inform the cell it is in the right place and properly anchored. If these linkages break down, the signals are not transmitted and cells normally die as a result. For most of the cells in your body, anchorage to the ECM is a matter of life and death.

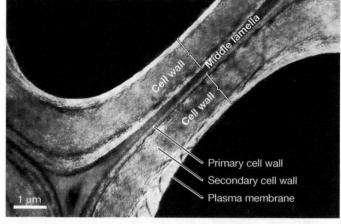

FIGURE 11.5 The Middle Lamella Connects Adjacent Plant Cells. The middle lamella contains gelatinous polysaccharides, called pectins, that help glue together the walls of adjacent cells.

11.2 How Do Adjacent Cells Connect and Communicate?

Intercellular connections are the basis of **multicellularity.** These physical connections between cells—either direct, or indirect via the ECM—are particularly important in the structure and function of tissues. The muscle tissue in your heart, for example, depends on these attachments to support the structure of the cells as they contract and relax with each beat (see the micrograph on the opening page of this chapter).

Let's look first at the structures that attach cells to each other and then examine how they allow adjacent cells to exchange materials and information.

Cell–Cell Attachments in Multicellular Eukaryotes

Materials and structures that bind cells together are particularly important in the **epithelium** (plural: **epithelia**)—a tissue that forms external and internal surfaces. These epithelial layers function as a barrier between the external and internal environments of plants and animals. In animals, epithelial cells also form layers that separate organs to prevent mixing of solutions from adjacent organs or structures.

The adhesive structures that hold cells together vary among multicellular organisms. To illustrate this diversity, consider the intercellular connections observed in the best-studied groups of organisms: plants and animals.

Indirect Intercellular Attachments The extracellular space between adjacent plant cells comprises three layers (**FIGURE 11.5**). The primary cell walls of adjacent plant cells sandwich a central layer designated the middle lamella, which consists primarily of gelatinous pectins. Because this gel layer is continuous with the primary cell walls of the adjacent cells, it serves to glue them together. The two cell walls are like slices of bread; the middle lamella is like a layer of peanut butter. If enzymes degrade the middle lamella, as they do when flower petals and leaves detach and fall, the surrounding cells separate.

In many animal tissues, integrins connect the cytoskeleton of each cell to the extracellular matrix (see Section 11.1). A middle-lamella-like layer of gelatinous polysaccharides and proteoglycans runs between adjacent animal cells. Along with the cytoskeleton–ECM connections, the polysaccharide glue helps hold cells together in tissues. In addition, in certain animal tissues the polysaccharide glue is reinforced by collagen fibrils that span the ECM to connect adjacent cells.

In animals, where cell walls do not exist, a variety of membrane proteins allow for direct cell–cell attachments in epithelia and other tissues (**FIGURE 11.6**). Let's start by looking at the tight junctions and desmosomes that hold cells together and then examine the role of gap junctions in intercellular communication.

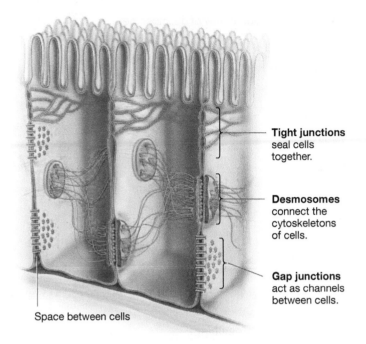

Tight junctions seal cells together.

Desmosomes connect the cytoskeletons of cells.

Gap junctions act as channels between cells.

Space between cells

FIGURE 11.6 An Array of Structures Are Involved in Cell–Cell Adhesion and Communication between Animal Cells.

Tight Junctions Form a Seal between Cells A **tight junction** is a cell–cell attachment composed of specialized proteins in the plasma membranes of adjacent animal cells (**FIGURE 11.7a**). As the drawing in **FIGURE 11.7b** indicates, these proteins line up and bind to one another. The resulting structure resembles quilting, where the proteins "stitch" the membranes of two cells together to form a watertight seal. In this way, tight junctions prevent solutions from flowing through the space between the two cells.

Because tight junctions form a watertight seal, this type of junction is commonly found in cells that form a barrier, such as the epithelial cells lining your stomach and intestines. There, they restrict the passive movement of substances between the contents of your gut and the rest of your body. Instead, only selected nutrients enter and leave the epithelia via specialized transport proteins and channels in the plasma membrane (Chapter 6).

Although tight junctions are indeed tight, they are variable. The tight junctions between the cells lining your bladder draw the cells closer together than those between the cells lining your small intestine, because they consist of different proteins. As a result, small ions can pass between the cells lining the surface of the small intestine more easily than between those lining the bladder—helping you absorb ions in your food and eliminate them in your waste.

Tight junctions are also dynamic. For example, they loosen to permit more transport between epithelial cells lining the small intestine after a meal and then "retighten" later. In this way, tight junctions can open and close in response to changes in environmental conditions.

Although tight junctions are very good at holding cells close together, they are weak adhesions that can be easily broken. Since epithelial cells often experience pulling and shearing forces, other intercellular adhesions are required to help hold cells together in a tissue. What are these other adhesions, and how do they resist being pulled apart?

(a) Electron micrograph of a tight junction in longitudinal section

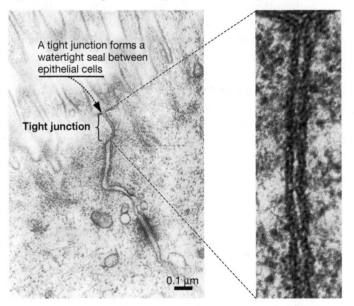

A tight junction forms a watertight seal between epithelial cells

Tight junction

0.1 μm

(b) Three-dimensional view of a tight junction

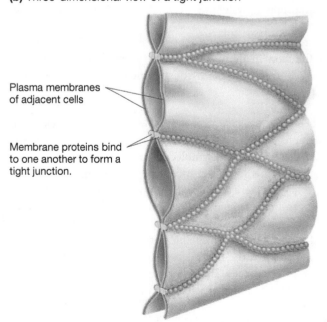

Plasma membranes of adjacent cells

Membrane proteins bind to one another to form a tight junction.

FIGURE 11.7 In Animals, Tight Junctions Form a Seal between Adjacent Cells.

(a) Micrograph of desmosome in longitudinal section

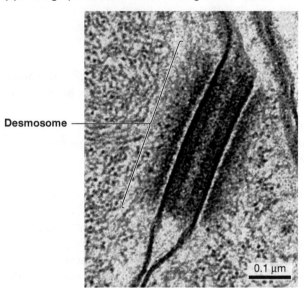

Desmosome

0.1 μm

(b) Three-dimensional view of desmosome

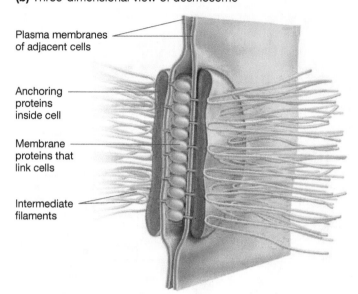

Plasma membranes of adjacent cells

Anchoring proteins inside cell

Membrane proteins that link cells

Intermediate filaments

FIGURE 11.8 Adjacent Animal Cells Are Linked by Desmosomes, Which Bind Cytoskeletons Together.

Desmosomes Form Secure Adhesions **FIGURE 11.8a** illustrates **desmosomes,** cell–cell attachments particularly common in animal epithelial cells and certain muscle cells. The structure and function of a desmosome are analogous to the rivets that hold pieces of sheet metal together.

As **FIGURE 11.8b** indicates, desmosomes are extremely sophisticated cell–cell connections. At their heart are integral membrane attachment proteins that form bridges between anchoring proteins inside adjacent cells. Intermediate filaments help reinforce these connections by attaching to the anchoring proteins in the cytoplasm. In this way, desmosomes help form a continuous structural support system between all the cells in the tissue (see Figure 11.6).

What are the membrane proteins that serve this cell attachment function in desmosomes? The answer to this question traces back to some of the first experiments conducted on cell–cell interactions.

Intercellular Adhesions Are Selective Long before electron micrographs revealed the presence of desmosomes, biologists realized that some sort of molecule must bind animal cells to one another. This insight grew out of experiments from H. V. Wilson's lab that were conducted on sponges in the early 1900s.

Sponges are aquatic animals, and the sponge species used in this study consists of just two basic types of tissues. When Wilson treated adult sponges with chemicals that made the cells separate from one another, the result was a jumbled mass of individual and unconnected cells. But when normal chemical conditions were restored, he noted that the cells gradually began to move and stick together.

As the experiment continued, cells began to aggregate based on their origin—adhering to other cells of the same tissue type.

This phenomenon is now called **selective adhesion.** Eventually the experimental sponge cells re-formed functional adult sponges with two distinct tissues. How could this happen?

The Discovery of Cell–Cell Adhesion Proteins What is the molecular basis of selective adhesion? The initial hypothesis, proposed in the 1970s, was that specialized membrane proteins were involved. The idea was that different types of cells have different types of adhesion proteins in their membranes, and only those with the same or complementary adhesion proteins are able to attach to one another.

This hypothesis was tested through experiments that relied on molecules called antibodies. An **antibody** is a protein produced by an immune response that binds specifically to a unique molecule type, often another protein. When an antibody binds to a protein, it can change the target protein's structure or interfere with its ability to interact with other molecules. This property of antibodies was crucial to these experiments.

FIGURE 11.9 shows how researchers tested the hypothesis that cell–cell adhesion takes place via interactions between membrane proteins:

Step 1 Isolate the membrane proteins from a certain cell type. Produce pure preparations of each protein.

Step 2 Inject one of the membrane proteins into a rabbit. The rabbit's immune system cells respond by creating antibodies to the membrane protein, which is recognized as being foreign. Purify those antibodies. Repeat this procedure for the other membrane proteins that were isolated. In this way, obtain a large collection of antibodies—each of which binds specifically to one (and only one) type of membrane protein.

QUESTION: Do animal cells have adhesion proteins on their surfaces?

HYPOTHESIS: Selective adhesion is due to specific membrane proteins.

NULL HYPOTHESIS: Selective adhesion is not due to specific membrane proteins.

EXPERIMENTAL SETUP:

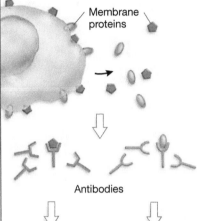

1. **Isolate the membrane proteins** from a certain cell type that adheres to other cells of the same type. (There are many membrane proteins; only two are shown here.)

2. **Produce antibodies** that bind to specific membrane proteins. Purify the antibodies.

3. **Treat cells with an antibody**, one type at a time. Wait; then observe whether cells adhere normally.

PREDICTION:

PREDICTION OF NULL HYPOTHESIS:

RESULTS:

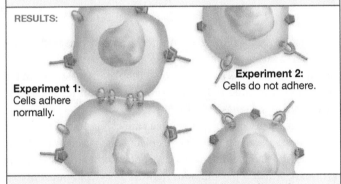

Experiment 1: Cells adhere normally.

Experiment 2: Cells do not adhere.

CONCLUSION: The protein that was blocked in experiment 2 (called a cadherin) is involved in cell–cell adhesion.

FIGURE 11.9 Evidence for Adhesion Proteins on Animal Cells.

SOURCES: Hatta, K., and M. Takeichi. 1986. Expression of N-cadherin adhesion molecules associated with early morphogenetic events in chick development. *Nature* 320: 447–449. Also Takeichi, M. 1988. The cadherins: Cell–cell adhesion molecules controlling animal morphogenesis. *Development* 102: 639–655.

✔**EXERCISE** Fill in the prediction made by each hypothesis.

Step 3 Add one antibody type to a mixture of dissociated cells from a tissue and observe whether the cells reaggregate normally. Repeat this experiment with each of the other antibody types, one type at a time.

If treatment with a particular antibody prevents the cells from attaching to one another, the antibody is probably bound to an adhesion protein. The logic is that if the antibody "shakes hands" with the adhesion protein, the adhesion protein can't shake hands with other adhesion proteins and attach the cells to one another.

This approach allowed biologists to identify several major classes of cell adhesion proteins, including **cadherins**—the attachment molecules in desmosomes. There are various types of cadherins, and cells from different tissues have different forms of cadherin in their plasma membranes. Each cadherin can bind only to cadherins of the same type. In this way, cells of the same tissue type attach specifically to one another.

To summarize: Animal cells attach to one another in a selective manner because different types of cell adhesion proteins can bind and rivet certain cells together. Cadherins provide the physical basis for selective adhesion in many cells and are a critical component of the desmosomes that join mature cells.

✔ If you understand cell–cell attachments, you should be able to predict what would happen if you treated cells in a developing frog embryo with a molecule that blocked a cadherin present in muscle tissue.

In addition to providing structural support to tissues, intercellular connections can direct cell–cell communication. But how can cellular connections pass information between cells?

Cells Communicate via Cell–Cell Gaps

In both plants and animals, direct connections between cells in the same tissue help them to work in a coordinated fashion. One way of accomplishing this is to generate channels in the membranes of adjacent cells, allowing them to communicate via the diffusion of cytosolic ions and small molecules from cell to cell.

How cells respond to this exchange of information varies from signal to signal and from cell to cell, but the result falls into two general categories:

1. Signals may alter which proteins are produced and which are not, by regulating gene expression; or

2. Signals may activate or deactivate particular proteins that already exist in the cell—often those involved in metabolism, membrane transport, secretion, and the cytoskeleton.

Whatever the mechanism, the activity of the cell often changes dramatically after the signal arrives. Let's take a closer look at how these signals are able to travel between adjacent cells connected by gap junctions and plasmodesmata.

Gap Junctions Connect Cells via Protein Channels In most animal tissues, structures called **gap junctions** connect adjacent cells. The key feature of gap junctions is the specialized proteins that assemble in the membranes of adjacent cells, creating

(a) Gap junctions create gaps that connect animal cells.

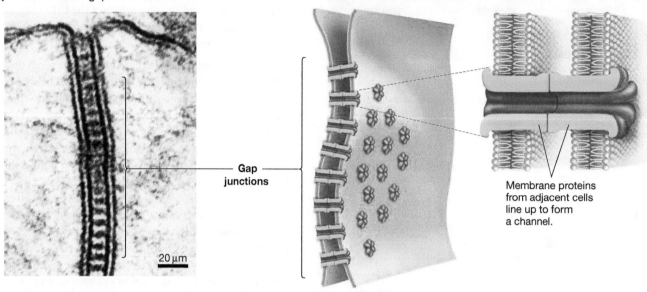

Gap junctions

20 μm

Membrane proteins from adjacent cells line up to form a channel.

(b) Plasmodesmata create gaps that connect plant cells.

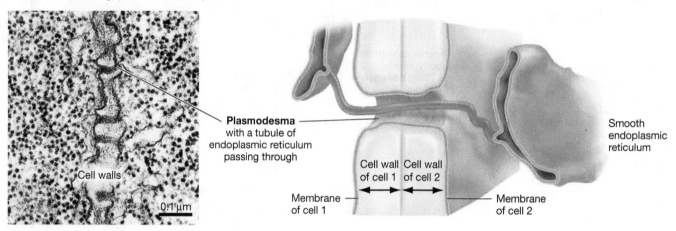

Cell walls

0.1 μm

Plasmodesma with a tubule of endoplasmic reticulum passing through

Cell wall of cell 1

Cell wall of cell 2

Membrane of cell 1

Membrane of cell 2

Smooth endoplasmic reticulum

FIGURE 11.10 Adjacent Animal Cells and Adjacent Plant Cells Communicate Directly.

interconnected pores between the cells (**FIGURE 11.10a**). These channels allow water, ions, and small molecules such as amino acids, sugars, and nucleotides to move between adjacent cells.

Gap junctions are communication portals. The flow of small molecules through gap junctions can help adjacent cells coordinate their activities by allowing the rapid passage of regulatory ions or molecules. In the muscle cells of your heart, for example, a flow of ions through gap junctions acts as a signal that coordinates contractions. Without this cell–cell communication, a normal heartbeat would be impossible.

In plants, direct interactions between membrane proteins are impossible due to the presence of cell walls. How do adjacent plant cells communicate?

Plasmodesmata Connect Cells via Membrane Channels In plants, gaps in cell walls create direct connections between the cytoplasm of adjacent cells. At these connections, named **plasmodesmata** (singular: **plasmodesma**), the plasma membrane and the cytoplasm of the two cells are continuous. Tubular extensions from the smooth endoplasmic reticulum (smooth ER) run through these membrane-lined portals (**FIGURE 11.10b**).

Like gap junctions, plasmodesmata are communication portals through the plasma membrane. In plants, the plasma membrane separates most tissues into two independent compartments: (**1**) the **symplast,** which is a continuous network of cytoplasm connected by plasmodesmata, and (**2**) the **apoplast,** which is the region outside the plasma membrane (**FIGURE 11.11**). The apoplast consists of cell walls, the middle lamella, and air spaces. Small molecules can move through plant tissues in either of these compartments without ever crossing a membrane.

Gap junctions and plasmodesmata allow for adjacent cells to transmit information, like a conversation between neighbors.

But how do multicellular organisms send messages between different tissues, where in most cases there is no direct contact? For example, suppose that the muscle cells in your arm are exercising so hard they run low on sugar or that leaf cells in a maple tree are attacked by caterpillars. How do these cells signal tissues or organs elsewhere in the organism to release materials that are needed to fend off exhaustion or caterpillars? Distant cell communication is the subject of Section 11.3.

11.3 How Do Distant Cells Communicate?

Cells that are not in physical contact communicate with one another. This is true for unicellular organisms, where hundreds or thousands of cells may live in close proximity, as well as for multicellular organisms like humans and maple trees, which typically contain trillions of cells and dozens of tissue types.

Cell–cell communication qualifies as one of the most dynamic and important research areas in biology. Let's begin by analyzing how distant cells in humans and other multicellular eukaryotes exchange information, and then in Section 11.4 explore how unicellular organisms communicate.

Cell–Cell Signaling in Multicellular Organisms

Suppose that cells in your brain sense that you are becoming dehydrated. Brain cells can't do much about the water you lose during urination, but kidney cells can. In response to dehydration, certain brain cells release a signaling molecule that travels to the kidneys. The arrival of this molecule activates specialized membrane channels that prevent water from being lost in urine—an important aspect of fighting dehydration.

Thanks to cell–cell signals, the activities of cells in different parts of a multicellular body are coordinated.

Biologists have classified many different types of signaling molecules that keep distant tissues in touch. For example, neurotransmitters activate membrane channel receptors that open to allow a flow of ions into the cytosol of the cell, changing the electrical properties of the membrane. This type of signal is responsible for the transmission of information along neurons, allowing your brain to control the movements of the rest of your body (see Chapter 48). The best-studied means of distant signaling, however, may be via **hormones**—information-carrying molecules that can act on distant target cells because they are secreted by plant and animal cells into bodily fluids.

Hormones are usually small molecules and are typically present in minute concentrations. Even so, they have a large impact on the activity of target cells and the condition of the body as a whole. Hormones are like a scent or whispered phrase from someone you are attracted to—a tiny signal, but one that makes your cheeks flush and your heart pound.

As **TABLE 11.1** (see page 210) indicates, hormones have a wide array of chemical structures and effects. The important point about a signaling molecule, though, is not whether it is a gas or peptide or steroid, but whether it is lipid soluble or not. The ability of a signaling molecule to pass through lipid bilayers is crucial in determining how a target cell recognizes it. Where does this recognition occur—inside the cell or outside?

- Most lipid-soluble signaling molecules are able to diffuse across the hydrophobic region of the plasma membrane and enter the cytoplasm of their target cells.

- Large or hydrophilic signaling molecules are lipid insoluble and do not cross the plasma membrane. To affect a target cell, they have to be recognized at the cell surface.

How do cells receive and process signals from distant cells? The basic steps are common to all cell–cell signaling systems. Let's consider each step in turn.

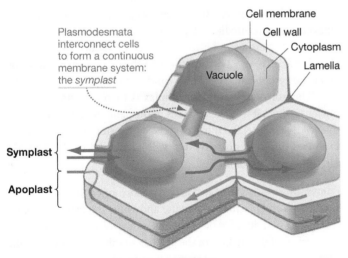

FIGURE 11.11 Most Plant Tissues Are Divided into Two Compartments—Symplast and Apoplast. Small molecules may be transported through plant tissues either within the shared cytoplasm (symplast) or through the extracellular space (apoplast).

TABLE 11.1 Hormones Have Diverse Structures and Functions

Hormone Name	Chemical Structure	Where Is Signal Received?	Function of Signal
Auxin	Small organic compound	At plasma membrane	Signals changes in long axis of plant body
Brassinosteroids	Steroid	At plasma membrane	Stimulate plant cell elongation
Estrogens	Steroid	Inside cell	Stimulate development of female characteristics in animals
Ethylene	C_2H_4 (a gas)	At plasma membrane	Stimulates fruit ripening; regulates aging
FSH	Glycoprotein	At plasma membrane	Stimulates egg maturation, sperm production in animals
Insulin	Protein, 51 amino acids	At plasma membrane	Stimulates glucose uptake in animal bloodstream
Prostaglandins	Modified fatty acid	At plasma membrane	Perform a variety of functions in animal cells
Systemin	Peptide, 111 amino acids	At plasma membrane	Stimulates plant defenses against herbivores
Thyroxine (T4)	Modified amino acid	Inside cell	Regulates metabolism in animals

Signal Reception

Hormones and other types of cell–cell signaling molecules deliver their message by binding to receptor molecules. Even though the molecule that carries the message "We're getting dehydrated—conserve water" is broadcast throughout the body, only certain kidney cells respond because only they have the appropriate receptor. The presence of an appropriate receptor dictates which cells will respond to a particular hormone. Bone and muscle cells don't respond to the "conserve water" message, because they don't have a receptor for it.

Cells in a wide array of tissues may respond to the same signaling molecule, though, if they have the appropriate receptor. If you are startled by a loud noise, cells in your adrenal glands secrete a hormone called adrenaline (also called epinephrine) that carries the message "Get ready to fight or run." In response, your heart rate increases, your breathing rate increases, and cells in your liver release sugars that your muscles can use to power rapid movement. This is the basis of an "adrenaline rush." Heart, lung, and liver cells respond to adrenaline because they each have the receptor that binds to it. Identical receptors in diverse cells and tissues allow long-distance signals to coordinate the activities of cells throughout a multicellular organism.

No matter where signal receptors are located, it's critical to note two important points about these proteins:

1. *Receptors are dynamic.* The number of receptors in a particular cell may decline if hormonal stimulation occurs at high levels over a long period of time. The ability of a receptor molecule to bind tightly to a signaling molecule may also decline in response to intensive stimulation. As a result, the sensitivity of a cell to a particular hormone may change over time.

2. *Receptors can be blocked.* The drugs called beta-blockers, for example, bind to certain receptors for the hormone adrenaline. When adrenaline binds to receptors in heart cells, it stimulates more rapid and forceful contractions. So if a physician wants to reduce a patient's heart cell contraction as a way to lower pressure, she is likely to prescribe a beta-blocker.

Most signal receptors are located in the plasma membrane, where they can bind to signaling molecules that cannot or do not cross the membrane. Other signal receptors exist inside the cell, where they respond to lipid-soluble signaling molecules that readily diffuse through the plasma membrane.

The most important general characteristic of signal receptors, though, is that their conformation—meaning, overall shape—changes when a hormone binds to them. A **signal receptor** is a protein that changes its shape and activity after binding to a signaling molecule.

This is a critical event in cell–cell signaling. The change in receptor structure means that the signal has been received. It's like throwing an "on" switch. What happens next?

Signal Processing

Once a cell receives a signal, something has to happen to initiate the cell's response. This signal processing step happens in one of two ways, depending on whether the signal is received inside the cell or at the membrane surface.

Processing Lipid-Soluble Signals When lipid-soluble signals enter a cell, the information they carry is processed directly—without any intermediate steps. For example, steroid hormones such as testosterone and estradiol (one of a group commonly referred to as estrogens) diffuse through the plasma membrane and enter the cytoplasm, where they bind to a cytosolic receptor protein. The hormone–receptor complex is then transported to the nucleus, where it triggers changes in the genes being expressed in the cell (**FIGURE 11.12**). By altering the expression of genes, the cell produces different proteins that will have a direct effect on the function or shape of the cell.

Processing Lipid-Insoluble Signals Hormones that *cannot* diffuse across the plasma membrane and enter the cytoplasm can't change the activity of genes or pumps directly. Instead, the signal that arrives at the surface of the cell has to initiate an intracellular signal—the signal processing step is indirect.

When a signaling molecule binds at the cell surface, it triggers **signal transduction**—the conversion of a signal from one form to another. A long and often complex series of events ensues, collectively called a signal transduction pathway.

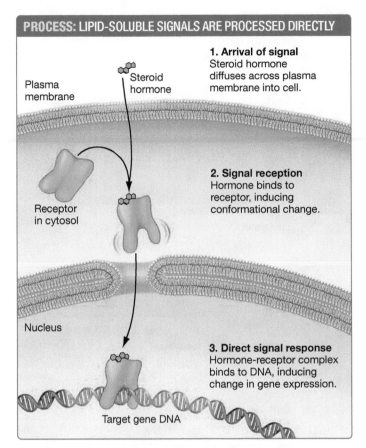

PROCESS: LIPID-SOLUBLE SIGNALS ARE PROCESSED DIRECTLY

Plasma membrane

Steroid hormone

1. Arrival of signal
Steroid hormone diffuses across plasma membrane into cell.

Receptor in cytosol

2. Signal reception
Hormone binds to receptor, inducing conformational change.

Nucleus

3. Direct signal response
Hormone-receptor complex binds to DNA, inducing change in gene expression.

Target gene DNA

FIGURE 11.12 Some Cell–Cell Signaling Molecules Enter the Cell and Bind to Receptors in the Cytoplasm. Because they are lipids, steroid hormones can diffuse across the plasma membrane and bind to signal receptors inside the cell. The hormone–receptor complex is transported to the nucleus and binds to genes, changing their activity.

✔**QUESTION** Based on what you have learned about nuclear transport (see Chapter 7), what type of signal would you expect to be exposed on the cytosolic receptor after the steroid hormone changes the receptor's conformation?

Signal transduction is a common occurrence in everyday life. For example, the e-mail messages you receive are transmitted from one computer to another over cables or wireless transmissions. These electronic signals can be transmitted efficiently over long distances but would be meaningless to you. Software in your computer has to transduce, or convert, the signals into a form that you can understand and respond to, such as words on the screen.

Signal transduction pathways work the same way (**FIGURE 11.13**). In a cell, signal transduction converts an extracellular signal to an intracellular signal. As in an e-mail transmission, a signal that is easy to transmit is converted to a signal that is easily understood and that triggers a response.

Intracellular Signals May Be Amplified Recall that hormones are present in minuscule concentrations but trigger a large response from cells. Signal amplification is one reason this is possible. When a hormone arrives at the cell surface, the message it transmits may be amplified as it changes form. The amplifier

in your portable music player performs an analogous function: Once it is amplified, a tiny sound signal can get a whole roomful of people dancing.

In cells, signal transduction begins at the plasma membrane; amplification occurs inside. Amplification may occur in a variety of ways. In general, the mechanism of amplification correlates with the mechanism of signal transduction. But the general observation is that the arrival of a single signaling molecule may result in a secondary signal that involves many ions or molecules.

For example, one major type of signal transduction system consists of membrane channel receptors that open to allow a flow of ions into the cytosol of the cell. In muscle cells, this type of amplification occurs when calcium ions flood into the cytosol, activating all the myosin filaments so the entire cell contracts as a whole (see Chapter 48).

Here let's focus on two other major types of signal transduction and amplification systems that are distinguished based on how they are initiated:

1. G-protein-coupled receptors initiate the production of intracellular or "second" messengers that then amplify the signal.

2. Enzyme-linked receptors amplify the signal by triggering the activation of a series of proteins inside the cell, through the addition of phosphate groups.

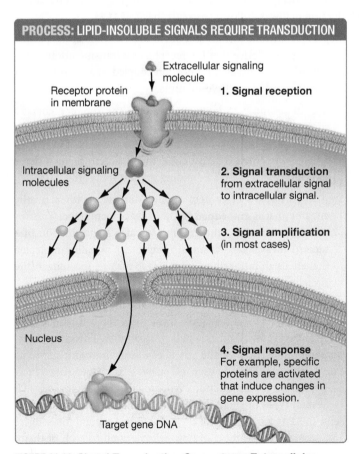

PROCESS: LIPID-INSOLUBLE SIGNALS REQUIRE TRANSDUCTION

Extracellular signaling molecule

Receptor protein in membrane

1. Signal reception

Intracellular signaling molecules

2. Signal transduction
from extracellular signal to intracellular signal.

3. Signal amplification
(in most cases)

Nucleus

4. Signal response
For example, specific proteins are activated that induce changes in gene expression.

Target gene DNA

FIGURE 11.13 Signal Transduction Converts an Extracellular Signal to an Intracellular Signal. Signal transduction is a multistep process.

Although there are many variations in the signaling pathways that fall within these two categories, the common features are emphasized here. Let's look at these two signal transduction systems in turn.

Signal Transduction via G-Protein-Coupled Receptors Many signal receptors span the plasma membrane and are closely associated with membrane-anchored proteins inside the cell called **G proteins.** When G proteins are activated by a signal receptor, they trigger a key step in signal transduction: the production of a messenger inside the cell. They link the receipt of an extracellular signal to the production of an intracellular signal.

G proteins got their name because the type of guanine nucleotide they are bound to regulates their activity: either guanosine triphosphate (GTP) or guanosine diphosphate (GDP). GTP is a nucleoside triphosphate that is similar in structure to adenosine triphosphate (ATP; introduced in Chapter 4). Recall that nucleoside triphosphates have high potential energy because their three phosphate groups have four negative charges close together.

When GTP binds to a G protein, the addition of the negative charges alters the protein's shape. Changes in shape produce changes in activity. G proteins are turned on or activated when they bind GTP; they are turned off or inactivated when a phosphate group, and thus a negative charge, is removed to form GDP. The G protein will remain in this off position until the GDP is removed and the protein binds to a new GTP.

To understand how G proteins fit into an overall signal transduction pathway, follow the events in **FIGURE 11.14**.

Step 1 A hormone arrives and binds to a receptor in the plasma membrane. Notice that the receptor is a transmembrane protein with the intracellular portion coupled to a G protein that is composed of multiple subunits.

Step 2 In response to hormone binding, the receptor changes shape and activates its G protein. Specifically, the receptor kicks out the GDP from the inactive G protein, allowing it to bind to a new GTP. When GTP is bound, the G protein changes shape radically: the active GTP-binding subunit splits off.

Step 3 The active G protein subunit interacts with a nearby enzyme that is embedded in the plasma membrane. This interaction stimulates the enzyme to catalyze production of a **second messenger**—a small, nonprotein signaling molecule that elicits an intracellular response to the first messenger (the signaling molecule that arrived at the cell surface).

Second messengers are effective because they are small and diffuse rapidly to spread the signal throughout the cell. In addition, they can be produced quickly in large quantities. This characteristic is important. Because the arrival of a single hormone molecule can stimulate the production of many second messenger molecules, the signal transduction event amplifies the original signal.

Several types of small molecules act as second messengers in cells. **TABLE 11.2** lists some of the best-studied second messengers and provides an example of how cells respond to each of them. Note that several second messengers activate **protein kinases**—enzymes that activate or inactivate other proteins by adding a phosphate group to them.

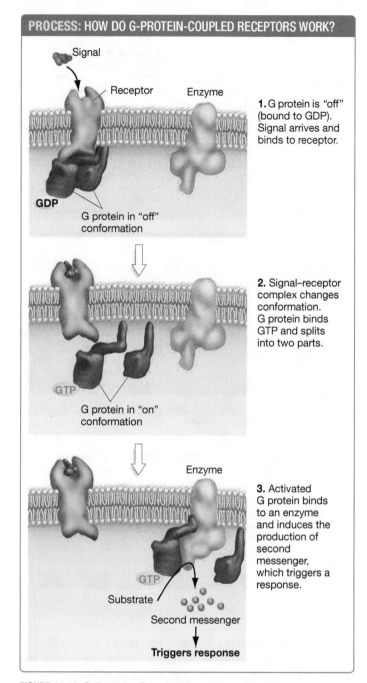

PROCESS: HOW DO G-PROTEIN-COUPLED RECEPTORS WORK?

Signal

Receptor   Enzyme

GDP

G protein in "off" conformation

1. G protein is "off" (bound to GDP). Signal arrives and binds to receptor.

GTP

G protein in "on" conformation

2. Signal–receptor complex changes conformation. G protein binds GTP and splits into two parts.

Enzyme

GTP

Substrate

Second messenger

Triggers response

3. Activated G protein binds to an enzyme and induces the production of second messenger, which triggers a response.

FIGURE 11.14 G-Protein-Coupled Receptors Trigger the Production of a Second Messenger.

It's also important to note two things:

1. Second messengers aren't restricted to a single role or single cell type—the same second messenger can initiate dramatically different events in different cell types; and

2. It is common for more than one second messenger to be involved in triggering a cell's response to the same extracellular signaling molecule.

To make sure that you understand how G proteins and second messengers work, imagine the following movie scene: A spy arrives at a castle gate. The guard receives a note from the spy, but

TABLE 11.2 Examples of Second Messengers

Name	Type of Response
Cyclic guanosine monophosphate (cGMP)	Opens ion channels; activates certain protein kinases
Diacylglycerol (DAG)	Activates certain protein kinases
Inositol trisphosphate (IP_3)	Opens calcium channels to transport stored calcium ions
Cyclic adenosine monophosphate (cAMP)	Activates certain protein kinases
Calcium ions (Ca^{2+})	Binds to a receptor called calmodulin; Ca^{2+}/calmodulin complex then activates proteins

he cannot read the coded message. Instead, the guard turns to the queen. She reads the note and summons the commander of the guard, who sends soldiers throughout the castle to warn everyone of approaching danger. ✔ You should be able to identify which characters in the scene correspond to the second messenger, G protein, hormone, receptor, and enzyme activated by the G protein.

It's difficult to overstate the importance of signal transduction by G-protein-coupled receptors. Biomedical researchers estimate that half of human drugs target signal receptors that are associated with G proteins.

Signal Transduction via Enzyme-Linked Receptors Enzyme-linked receptors transduce hormonal signals by directly catalyzing a reaction inside the cell. **FIGURE 11.15** focuses on the best-studied group of enzyme-linked receptors: the **receptor tyrosine kinases (RTKs).**

Step 1 A hormone binds to an RTK.

Step 2 The protein forms a dimer. In this conformation, the catalytic activity of the receptor is turned on, allowing it to phosphorylate itself using ATP inside the cell.

Step 3 Proteins inside the cell bind to the phosphorylated RTK to form a bridge between the receptor and a peripheral membrane protein called **Ras,** which is a G protein. The formation of the RTK bridge activates Ras by causing it to exchange its GDP for a GTP.

Step 4 When Ras is activated, it triggers the phosphorylation and activation of another protein.

Step 5 The phosphorylated protein is a protein kinase, which then catalyzes the phosphorylation and activation of other kinases, which phosphorylate yet another population of proteins.

This sequence of events is termed a **phosphorylation cascade,** and it culminates in a response by the cell. The enzymes involved are called **mitogen-activated protein kinases (MAPK).** They are so named because many of the signaling molecules that start

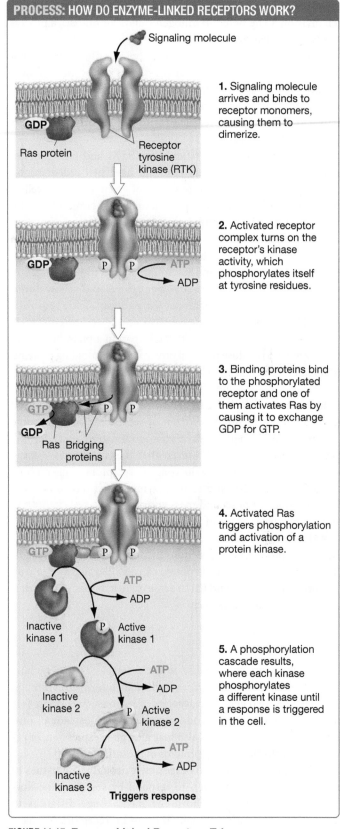

PROCESS: HOW DO ENZYME-LINKED RECEPTORS WORK?

1. Signaling molecule arrives and binds to receptor monomers, causing them to dimerize.

2. Activated receptor complex turns on the receptor's kinase activity, which phosphorylates itself at tyrosine residues.

3. Binding proteins bind to the phosphorylated receptor and one of them activates Ras by causing it to exchange GDP for GTP.

4. Activated Ras triggers phosphorylation and activation of a protein kinase.

5. A phosphorylation cascade results, where each kinase phosphorylates a different kinase until a response is triggered in the cell.

FIGURE 11.15 Enzyme-Linked Receptors Trigger a Phosphorylation Cascade.

these pathways are substances called mitogens, which activate cell division. (The *mito–* in mitogen stands for mitosis, a process involved in eukaryotic cell division.)

In some cases, each copy of an enzyme in the cascade catalyzes the phosphorylation of many copies of the next "downstream" protein, and so on. When this occurs, activated enzymes at a given stage in the cascade exist in greater numbers than the activated enzymes that preceded them, and the original signal is amplified many times over.

To make sure you understand how RTKs and phosphorylation cascades work, imagine that you have two red dominos, one black domino, and a large supply of green, blue, and yellow dominos. The red dominos represent the two subunits of an RTK dimer, and the black domino represents Ras. Each of the other colors represents a different protein kinase in a phosphorylation cascade. ✔ QUANTITATIVE You should be able to (1) explain how you would set up the dominos to simulate a phosphorylation cascade, and (2) state how many green, blue, and yellow dominos would be required to model the pathway if Ras and each protein kinase in the cascade were to activate 10 proteins.

In many cases, the proteins that take part in a phosphorylation cascade are held in close physical proximity by scaffolding proteins. Although this organization limits the amplification of the response, it increases the speed and efficiency of the reaction sequence.

In general, intracellular signals initiated by G-protein-coupled receptors result in the production of second messengers, while enzyme-linked receptors drive phosphorylation cascades. It's important to recognize, however, that these pathways overlap significantly. Some G-protein-coupled receptors trigger phosphorylation cascades, and some enzyme-linked receptors result in the production of second messengers.

To summarize: Many of the key signal transduction events observed in cells occur via G-protein-coupled receptors or enzyme-linked receptors. The signal transduction event has two results: (1) It converts an easily transmitted extracellular message into an intracellular message, and (2) in some cases it amplifies the original message many times over.

Signal Response

What is the ultimate response to the messages carried by hormones? Recall that when adjacent cells share information through cell–cell gaps, two general categories of response may occur (see Section 11.2). Likewise, second messengers or a cascade of protein phosphorylation events also may alter gene expression, or activate or deactivate existing proteins in the target cell.

For example, when plants experience drought, the tissues in the root system are the first to respond by secreting the hormone abscisic acid. This hormone travels huge distances to reach the leaves and eventually bind to its receptors in guard cells that control the stomatal pores that allow for gas exchange. When abscisic acid binds to these receptors, a signal transduction pathway ensues that increases the concentration of calcium inside the guard cells. In response, potassium ions (K^+) move out of the guard cells, creating an osmotic gradient that leads

to the movement of water out of the guard cells. The guard cells deflate and close the pore, which prevents water loss from the plant.

At this point, you've analyzed the first three steps of cell–cell communication: signal reception, signal processing, and the response. Now the question is, how is the signal turned off? Consider the flush of testosterone and estrogens that you experienced during puberty, and the morphological changes these hormones induced. Abnormalities would result if these changes continued indefinitely. What limits the response to a cell–cell signal?

Signal Deactivation

Cells have built-in systems for turning off intracellular signals. For example, once activated G proteins turn on downstream enzymes, the GTP is hydrolyzed to GDP and P_i. When this reaction occurs, the G protein's conformation changes and it returns to an inactive state. Activation of its downstream target stops, and production of the second messenger ceases.

The presence of second messengers in the cytosol is also short lived. For example, pumps in the membrane of the smooth ER return calcium ions to storage, and enzymes called phosphodiesterases convert active cAMP and cGMP (see Table 11.2) to inactive AMP and GMP. When second messengers are cleared from the cytosol, the response stops.

To continue the response from G-protein-coupled receptors, the G proteins must be reactivated by the activated signal receptor to start the process again. Otherwise, the signal transduction system quickly shuts down.

Phosphorylation cascades are also sensitive to the presence of the external signal. Enzymes, called **phosphatases,** that remove phosphate groups from cascade proteins are always present in the cell. If hormone stimulation of a receptor tyrosine kinase ends, phosphatases will dephosphorylate enough components of the phosphorylation cascade that the response ceases.

Although an array of specific mechanisms are involved, here is the general observation: Signal transduction systems trigger a rapid response and can be shut down quickly. As a result, they are exquisitely sensitive to small changes in the concentration of hormones or in the number and activity of signal receptors.

It is critical, though, to appreciate what happens when a signal transduction system does not shut down properly. For example, recall that Ras is active when it binds GTP, but is deactivated once it has hydrolyzed GTP to GDP and P_i. If this hydrolysis activity were defective, however, Ras would stay in the GTP-bound "on" position and continue stimulating a phosphorylation cascade even when the external signal is absent.

Why is continuously active Ras a problem? Recall that the phosphorylation cascade that is activated by Ras involves mitogen-activated protein kinases, many of which induce cell replication. If cells express this type of defective Ras, they would receive a never-ending "divide now" signal that may lead to the development of cancer. An estimated 25–30 percent of all human cancers express this type of defective Ras. (To learn more about the family of diseases called cancer, see Chapters 12 and 19.)

Crosstalk: Synthesizing Input from Many Signals

Although the preceding discussion focused on how cells respond to individual signals, it's crucial to realize that every cell has an array of signal receptors on its plasma membrane and in its cytoplasm, and many cells receive an almost constant stream of different signals. Just as you receive information about your environment via text messages, e-mails, phone calls, and snail mail, cells get an array of chemical signals about changes in their environment.

The signal transduction pathways that are triggered by these signals and receptors intersect and connect. In reality, they are not strictly linear like the pathways illustrated in Figures 11.12 through 11.15. Signal transduction pathways form a network. This complexity is important: It allows cells to respond to many different signals in an integrated way.

The diverse signals that a cell receives are integrated by what biologists call **crosstalk**—meaning, the signals from different pathways interact to modify the cell response (**FIGURE 11.16**). This would be like getting advice from multiple people before making a decision. Here are three key things to note:

1. Elements or products from one pathway may inhibit steps in a different pathway—reducing the cell's response, even though the appropriate signal is present.

2. A response from one pathway may stimulate a greater response by a protein in a different pathway, increasing the cell's response to the other signal.

3. The presence of multiple steps in each signaling pathway provides a series of points where crosstalk can regulate the flow of information. These interactions are important, because they allow the cell to respond appropriately to many signals at the same time.

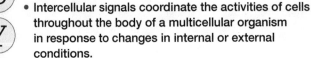

check your understanding

C Y U

If you understand that . . .
- Intercellular signals coordinate the activities of cells throughout the body of a multicellular organism in response to changes in internal or external conditions.
- If intercellular signaling molecules do not enter the cell, they bind to a receptor on the plasma membrane. In response, the intercellular signal is transduced to an intracellular signal that the cell responds to.

✔ **You should be able to . . .**
1. Explain how only certain cells respond to particular signaling molecules that may be sent throughout the body.
2. Explain how some signals are amplified.

Answers are available in Appendix A.

11.4 Signaling between Unicellular Organisms

Cell–cell signaling has been one of the hottest research areas in biological science over the past two decades. Surprisingly, much of what we know about signal transduction in multicellular organisms has come from the study of unicellular organisms. While single-cell microbes communicate with one another in a manner similar to what is observed in multicellular organisms, the topic of conversation often differs. Rather than asking for help, as when a dehydrated brain asks the kidney to conserve water, the conversations between unicellular microbes are often about sex and environmental change.

Responding to Sex Pheromones

While unicellular eukaryotes generally reproduce by cell division, some also are known to undergo sexual reproduction (see Chapters 12 and 13 to learn more about cellular reproduction). At its most basic level, sex involves the fusion of two cells such that genetic material of the two individuals is combined into one nucleus. What attracts individuals of the opposite sex to each other?

In *Saccharomyces cerevisiae*, or baker's yeast, there are two sexes, or mating types, referred to as "**a**" cells and "**α**" cells. By

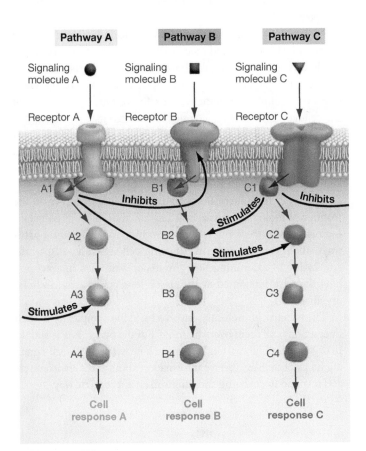

FIGURE 11.16 Signaling Pathways Interact via "Crosstalk."

✔ **EXERCISE** Predict which response would occur in cells exposed to the following signaling molecules: (1) A + B; (2) A + C; (3) C alone.

(a) Yeast cells alter their growth in response to pheromones of the opposite mating type.

(b) Slime mold amoebae aggregate in response to sensing a quorum.

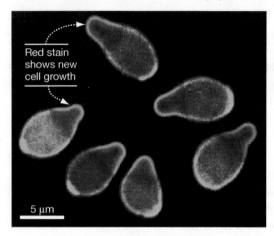

Red stain shows new cell growth

5 µm

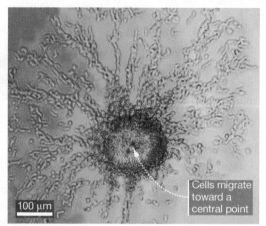

100 µm

Cells migrate toward a central point

FIGURE 11.17 Unicellular Organisms Interact and Respond in a Variety of Ways. (a) Yeast cells respond to pheromone signals from the opposite mating type by growing toward the source of the signal during sexual reproduction. **(b)** Signals secreted by free-living slime mold protists stimulate them to aggregate under high population densities.

studying this eukaryotic model organism, biologists have figured out the cell signaling events that bring yeast of the opposite sex together (to learn more about model organisms, see **BioSkills 13** in Appendix B).

Although the yeast cells are visually indistinguishable, opposite mating types recognize one another via chemical signaling molecules called **pheromones.** The **a** mating type secretes the pheromone **a** factor, and the **α** type secretes the pheromone **α** factor. Receptors on the surface of these cells will bind only to the opposite mating type factor, so when an **a** cell detects the **α** factor, it recognizes that a suitable mate is nearby.

Since yeast cells are not motile, part of the cellular response to the pheromone is to direct new growth toward the signal **(FIGURE 11.17a)**. The signaling pathway that is responsible for this morphological change uses both G-protein-coupled receptors and phosphorylation cascades that were presented in Section 11.3. One of the proteins affected by this signaling pathway is actin, which is used to construct new microfilaments at the site where the G proteins have been activated. These new filaments push out new growth toward the highest concentration of the pheromone to allow the cell to find, and eventually fuse with, its mate.

Responding to Population Density

Within a population of unicellular organisms, widespread communication can occur that closely monitors the environment—in particular, the density of the population. Signaling pathways that respond to population density in microbes are collectively referred to as **quorum sensing.** The name was inspired by the observation that cells of the same species may undergo dramatic

changes in activity when their numbers reach a threshold, or quorum.

Quorum sensing is based on signaling molecules that are secreted by cells and diffuse through the environment. The response to these molecules varies dramatically between species and ranges from bacterial bioluminescence—or light emission—in the light organs of squid to the secretion of molecules that help glue a community of microbes to a surface in biofilms (see Chapter 29).

In effect, quorum sensing allows unicellular organisms to communicate and coordinate activity. When it occurs, these single-celled organisms take on some of the characteristics of multicellular organisms. For example, quorum sensing via a G-protein-coupled receptor recruits the free-living amoebae of the cellular slime mold *Dictyostelium* to aggregate into multicellular mounds **(FIGURE 11.17b)**. Amazingly, the slug-like bodies that are formed from these aggregates can crawl across a surface and eventually organize themselves into a fruiting body that releases spores into the air (see **BioSkills 13** in Appendix B).

This brief introduction to cell–cell signaling brings us to the frontier of biological research. It has taken decades of painstaking research to work out each step in individual signaling pathways. Biologists are now investigating cell signaling at a whole system level—examining how the major pathways interact and how they are integrated at the tissue level within multicellular organisms.

The number of molecules involved and the complexity of their interactions can seem overwhelming, but the punch line is simple: In organisms ranging from bacteria to blue whales, cell–cell signaling helps organisms receive information about their environment and respond to changing conditions in an appropriate way.

If you understand . . .

11.1 The Cell Surface

- The vast majority of cells secrete an extracellular layer.

- In bacteria, archaea, algae, and plants, the extracellular material is stiff and is called a cell wall. In animals, the secreted layer is flexible and is called the extracellular matrix (ECM).

- Extracellular layers are fiber composites. They consist of cross-linked filaments that provide tensile strength and a ground substance that fills space and resists compression.

- In plants, the extracellular filaments are cellulose microfibrils; in animals, the most abundant filaments are made of the protein collagen. In both plants and animals, the ground substance is composed of gel-forming polysaccharides.

✔ You should be able to predict what happens to animal cells when they are treated with an enzyme that (1) cuts integrin molecules, or (2) digests collagen fibrils.

11.2 How Do Adjacent Cells Connect and Communicate?

- In multicellular organisms, molecules in the extracellular layer and plasma membrane mediate interactions between adjacent cells.

- Adjacent cells may be physically bound to one another by glue-like middle lamellae in plants or by tight junctions and desmosomes in animals.

- The cytoplasm of adjacent cells is in direct communication through openings called plasmodesmata in plants and gap junctions in animals.

- Cells may respond to signals by activating certain enzymes, releasing or taking up specific ions or molecules, or changing the activity of target genes. As a result, cells and tissues throughout the body can alter their activity in response to changing conditions, and do so in a coordinated way.

✔ You should be able to predict the consequences of removing the gap junctions between the cells in the cardiac muscle in your heart.

11.3 How Do Distant Cells Communicate?

- Distant cells in multicellular organisms communicate through signaling molecules that bind to receptors found in or on specific target cells.

- Cell–cell signaling molecules that are not lipid soluble bind to receptors in the plasma membrane. The receptor then changes conformation and triggers production of a new type of intracellular signal—a second messenger or phosphorylation cascade.

- Because enzymes inside the cell quickly deactivate the signal and signaling pathways often interact, the cell's response is tightly regulated.

✔ You should be able to explain how the hormone adrenalin can stimulate cells in both the heart and the liver, yet trigger different responses (increasing heart rate versus releasing glucose).

11.4 Signaling between Unicellular Organisms

- Unicellular organisms use chemical signals to sense the pheromones of opposite mating types and population density. Quorum sensing allows closely related cells to coordinate changes in their activity when population density is high.

✔ You should be able to compare and contrast the role of intercellular signaling between unicellular organisms and the cells in a multicellular organism.

MasteringBiology

1. **MasteringBiology Assignments**

   Tutorials and Activities Build a Signaling Pathway; Cell Junctions; Cell Signaling: Reception; Cell Signaling: Transduction and Response; Cellular Responses; Overview of Cell Signaling; Reception; Signal Transduction Pathways

   Questions Reading Quizzes, Blue-Thread Questions, Test Bank

2. **eText** Read your book online, search, take notes, highlight text, and more.

3. **The Study Area** Practice Test, Cumulative Test, BioFlix® 3-D Animations, Videos, Activities, Audio Glossary, Word Study Tools, Art

You should be able to . . .

1. What is a fiber composite? How do cellular fiber composites resemble reinforced concrete?

2. In animals, where are most components of the extracellular material synthesized?
   a. smooth ER
   b. the rough ER
   c. in the extracellular layer itself
   d. in the plasma membrane

3. Treating dissociated cells with certain antibodies makes the cells unable to reaggregate. Why?
   a. The antibodies bind to cell adhesion proteins.
   b. The antibodies bind to the fiber component of the extracellular matrix.
   c. The antibodies bind to the cell surface and inhibit motility.
   d. The antibodies act as enzymes that break down desmosomes.

4. What does it mean to say that a signal is transduced?
   a. The signaling molecule enters the cell directly and binds to a receptor inside.
   b. The physical form of the signal changes between the outside of the cell and the inside.
   c. The signal is amplified, such that even a single molecule evokes a large response.
   d. The signal triggers a sequence of phosphorylation events inside the cell.

5. What characteristics do tight junctions bestow on tissues that use these adhesions to connect adjacent cells?
   a. They allow communication between adjacent cells.
   b. They provide strong connections to resist pulling forces.
   c. They use the extracellular matrix to indirectly connect adjacent cells.
   d. They form a watertight barrier between the cells.

6. What are the two general categories of cellular responses to an intercellular signal?

7. Which of the following statements represents a fundamental difference between the fibers found in the extracellular layers of plants and those of animals?
   a. Plant fibers resist compression forces; animal fibers resist pulling forces.
   b. Animal fibers consist of proteins; plant fibers consist of polysaccharides instead.
   c. Plant extracellular fibers never move; animal fibers can slide past one another.
   d. Cellulose microfibrils run parallel to one another; collagen filaments crisscross.

8. Explain how it is possible for a phosphorylation cascade to amplify an intercellular signal.

9. Compare and contrast the structure and function of tight junctions, desmosomes, and gap junctions.

10. Animal cells adhere to each other selectively. Summarize experimental evidence that supports this statement. Explain the molecular basis of selective adhesion.

11. Make a flowchart summarizing the reception, processing, response, and deactivation steps for a signaling molecule that binds to an intracellular receptor.

12. What is the significance of the observation that many signal transduction pathways create a network, where they intersect or overlap?

13. What would be the impact on the structure of a plant tissue if the cells lacked the ability to modify the extracellular environment?
   a. Cells would swell and burst if placed in a hypotonic environment.
   b. Cells would not be able to adhere to one another.
   c. No defined tissues, consisting of similar cells with coordinated activities, would be possible.
   d. All of the above.

14. Suppose that a particular cell–cell signaling molecule induces a cellular response without requiring signal transduction (i.e., no second messengers or phosphorylation cascades). Compared to the signal transduction pathways you learned about in this chapter, how would an event like this affect (a) the types of responses that are possible, (b) amplification, and (c) regulation?

15. In most species of fungi, chitin is a major polysaccharide found in cell walls. Review the structure of chitin (see Chapter 5), and then describe what would have to take place for the directional growth that occurs when yeast, a type of fungi, respond to sex pheromones.

16. Suppose you created an antibody that bound to the receptor tyrosine kinase illustrated in Figure 11.15. You expected this antibody to inhibit the cell response, but instead it resulted in activating the response, even when no signal was present. Explain this result.

12 The Cell Cycle

In this chapter you will learn how

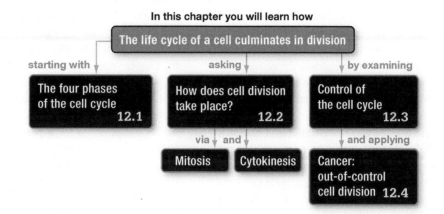

The life cycle of a cell culminates in division

starting with

The four phases of the cell cycle **12.1**

asking

How does cell division take place? **12.2**

via and

Mitosis Cytokinesis

by examining

Control of the cell cycle **12.3**

and applying

Cancer: out-of-control cell division **12.4**

This cell, from a hyacinth plant, is undergoing a type of nuclear division called mitosis. Understanding how mitosis occurs is a major focus of this chapter.

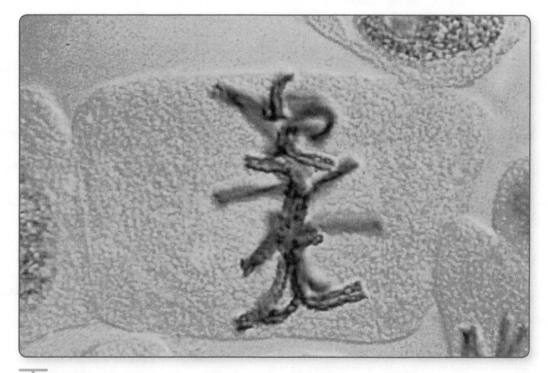

The cell theory maintains that all organisms are made of cells and all cells arise from preexisting cells (Chapter 1). Although the cell theory was widely accepted among biologists by the 1860s, most believed that new cells arose within preexisting cells by a process that resembled the growth of mineral crystals. But Rudolf Virchow proposed that new cells arise by splitting preexisting cells—that is, by **cell division.**

In the late 1800s, microscopic observations of newly developing organisms, or **embryos,** confirmed Virchow's hypothesis. Multicellular eukaryotes start life as single-celled embryos and grow through a series of cell divisions.

Early studies revealed two fundamentally different ways that nuclei divide before cell division: meiosis and mitosis. In animals, **meiosis** leads to the production of sperm and eggs, which are the male and female reproductive cells termed **gametes. Mitosis** leads to the production of all other cell types, referred to as **somatic** (literally, "body-belonging") **cells.** (You can see the Big Picture of

This chapter is part of the Big Picture. See how on pages 366–367.

✔ When you see this checkmark, stop and test yourself. Answers are available in Appendix A.

how these two nuclear divisions are related to each other and the transmission of genetic information on pages 366–367.)

Mitosis and meiosis are usually accompanied by **cytokinesis** ("cell movement")—the division of the cytoplasm into two distinct cells. When cytokinesis is complete, a so-called parent cell has given rise to two daughter cells.

Mitotic and meiotic cell divisions are responsible for one of the five fundamental attributes of life: reproduction (see Chapter 1). But even though mitosis and meiosis share many characteristics, they are fundamentally different. During mitosis, the genetic material is copied and then divided equally between two cells. This is referred to as cellular *replication*, since these daughter cells are genetically identical with the original parent cell. In contrast, meiosis results in daughter cells that are genetically different from each other and that have half the amount of hereditary material as the parent cell.

This chapter focuses on mitotic cell division; meiotic cell division is the subject of the next chapter (Chapter 13). Let's begin with a look at the key events in a cell's life cycle, continue with an in-depth analysis of mitosis and the regulation of the cell cycle, and end by examining how uncontrolled cell division can lead to cancer.

12.1 How Do Cells Replicate?

For life on Earth to exist, cells must replicate. The general requirements for cellular replication are to (**1**) copy the DNA (deoxyribonucleic acid), (**2**) separate the copies, and (**3**) divide the cytoplasm to create two complete cells.

This chapter focuses on eukaryotic cell replication, which is responsible for three key events:

1. *Growth*   The trillions of genetically identical cells that make up your body are the product of mitotic divisions that started in a single fertilized egg.

2. *Wound repair*   When you suffer a scrape, cellular replication generates the cells that repair your skin.

3. *Reproduction*   When yeast cells grow in bread dough or in a vat of beer, they are reproducing by cellular replication. In yeasts and other single-cell eukaryotes, mitotic division is the basis of asexual reproduction. **Asexual reproduction** produces offspring that are genetically identical with the parent.

These events are so basic to life that cell replication has been studied for well over a century. Like much work in biology, the research on how cells divide began by simply observing the process.

What Is a Chromosome?

As studies of cell division in eukaryotes began, biologists found that certain chemical dyes made threadlike structures visible within nuclei. In 1879, Walther Flemming used a dye made from a coal tar to observe these threadlike structures and how they changed in the dividing cells of salamander embryos. The threads first appeared in pairs just before division and then split to produce single, unpaired threads in the daughter cells. Flemming introduced the term mitosis, from the Greek *mitos* ("thread"), to describe this process.

Others studied the roundworm *Ascaris* and noted that the total number of threads in a cell was the same before and after mitosis. All the cells in a roundworm had the same number of threads.

In 1888 Wilhelm Waldeyer coined the term **chromosome** ("colored-body") to refer to these threadlike structures (visible in the chapter-opening photo). A chromosome consists of a single, long DNA double helix that is wrapped around proteins, called **histones,** in a highly organized manner. DNA encodes the cell's hereditary information, or genetic material. A gene is a length of DNA that codes for a particular protein or ribonucleic acid (RNA) found in the cell.

Before mitosis, each chromosome is replicated. As mitosis starts, the chromosomes condense into compact structures that can be moved around the cell efficiently. Then one of the chromosome copies is distributed to each of two daughter cells.

FIGURE 12.1 illustrates unreplicated chromosomes, replicated chromosomes before they have condensed prior to mitosis, and replicated chromosomes that have condensed at the start of mitosis. Each of the DNA copies in a replicated chromosome is called a **chromatid.** Before mitosis, the two chromatids are joined along their entire length by proteins called cohesins. Once mitosis begins, however, many of these connections are removed except for those at a specialized region of the chromosome called the **centromere.** Chromatid copies that remain attached at their centromere are referred to as **sister chromatids.** Even though a replicated chromosome consists of two chromatids, it is still considered a single chromosome.

Cells Alternate between M Phase and Interphase

The division of eukaryotic cells is like a well-choreographed stage performance. The most visually stimulating part of the show occurs when cells are in their dividing phase, called the **M** (*mitotic* or *meiotic*) **phase.** With a light microscope, chromosomes can be stained and observed as discrete units only during M phase, when they condense into compact structures.

The rest of the time, the cell is in **interphase** ("between-phase"). No dramatic changes in the nucleus are visible by light microscopy during interphase. The chromosomes uncoil into the extremely long, thin structures shown in Figure 12.1 and are no longer stained as individual threads. However, this does not mean that the cell is idle. Interphase is an active time: The cell is either growing and preparing to divide or fulfilling its specialized function in a multicellular individual. Cells actually spend most of their time in interphase.

The Discovery of S Phase

Once M phase and interphase were identified by microscopy, researchers could start assigning roles to these distinct phases. They could see that the separation of chromosomes and cytokinesis

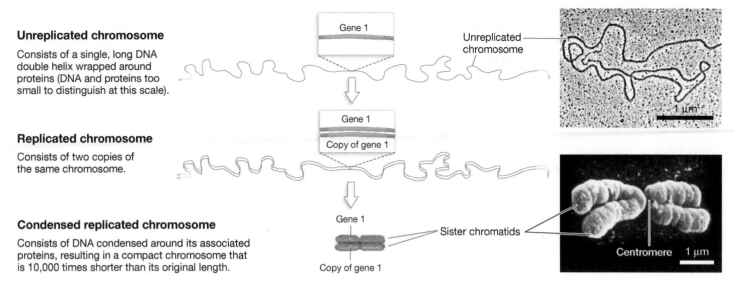

Unreplicated chromosome

Consists of a single, long DNA double helix wrapped around proteins (DNA and proteins too small to distinguish at this scale).

Replicated chromosome

Consists of two copies of the same chromosome.

Condensed replicated chromosome

Consists of DNA condensed around its associated proteins, resulting in a compact chromosome that is 10,000 times shorter than its original length.

Gene 1

Gene 1
Copy of gene 1

Gene 1
Copy of gene 1

Unreplicated chromosome

Sister chromatids

Centromere   1 μm

1 μm

FIGURE 12.1 Changes in Chromosome Morphology. After chromosomes replicate, the two identical copies are attached to each other along their entire length. Early in mitosis, replicated chromosomes condense and sister chromatids remain attached at a region called the centromere.

took place during the M phase, but when are the chromosomes copied?

To answer this question, researchers needed to distinguish cells that were replicating their DNA from those that were not. They were able to do this by adding radioactive phosphorus, in the form of phosphates, to cells. Those cells that were synthesizing DNA would incorporate the radioactive isotope into nucleotides (see Chapter 4 to review where phosphates are in DNA).

The idea was to:

1. label DNA as chromosomes were being copied;

2. wash away any radioactive isotope that hadn't been incorporated and remove RNA, which would also incorporate phosphorus; and then

3. visualize the labeled, newly synthesized DNA by exposing the treated cells to X-ray film. Emissions from radioactive phosphorus create a black dot in the film. This is the technique called autoradiography (see **BioSkills 9** in Appendix B).

In 1951, Alma Howard and Stephen Pelc performed this experiment and looked for cells with black dots—indicating active DNA synthesis—immediately after the exposure to a radioactive isotope ended. They found black dots in some of the interphase cells, but none in M-phase cells. Several years later, these results were verified using radioactive thymidine, which is incorporated into DNA but not RNA. These results were strong evidence that DNA replication occurs during interphase.

Thus, biologists had identified a new stage in the life of a cell. They called it **synthesis** (or **S**) **phase.** S phase is part of interphase. Replication of the genetic material is separated, in time, from the partitioning of chromosome copies during M phase.

Howard and Pelc coined the term **cell cycle** to describe the orderly sequence of events that leads a eukaryotic cell through the duplication of its chromosomes to the time it divides.

The Discovery of the Gap Phases

In addition to discovering the S phase, Howard and Pelc made another key observation—not all the interphase cells were labeled. This meant that there was at least one "gap" in interphase when DNA was not being copied.

Howard and Pelc, along with researchers in other labs, followed up on these early results by asking where S phase was positioned in interphase. There were three possible scenarios:

1. The S phase is immediately before M phase, with a single gap between the end of M and start of S phase;

2. the S phase is immediately after M phase, with a gap between the end of S and the start of M phase; or

3. two gaps exist, one before and one after the S phase.

To address which of these models, if any, is correct, many experiments were done using cells in culture. Cultured cells are powerful experimental tools because they can be manipulated much more easily than cells in an intact organism (see **BioSkills 12** in Appendix B). In most of these studies, researchers used cultures that were asynchronous, meaning that the cells were randomly distributed in the cycle.

To understand the value of these asynchronous cultures, imagine the cell cycle were a clock. Every complete rotation around the clock would represent one cell division, and each tick would represent a different point in the cycle. At any given time, an asynchronous culture would have at least one cell present at each of the ticks on the clock. As time passes, these cells would move around this cell-cycle clock at the same rate and in the same direction.

FIGURE 12.2 The Pulse–Chase Assay Reveals a Gap Phase. Cells labeled with radioactive thymidine during the pulse can be tracked during the chase to identify when they enter M phase. In this assay, a gap between the end of S phase and start of M phase was identified based on the delay observed between the pulse and the presence of labeled mitotic cells.

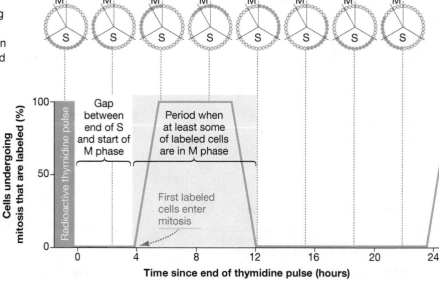

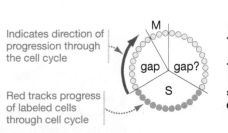

In one experiment, researchers marked the S-phase cells in a human cell culture by exposing it to radioactively labeled thymidine. A short time later, they stopped the labeling by flooding the solution surrounding the cultured cells with nonradioactive thymidine. This pulse–chase approach (introduced in Chapter 7) labeled only those cells that were in S phase during the radioactive pulse. Imagine these marked cells moving like a hand on the clock that could be tracked as they progressed through the cell cycle.

Once the pulse ended, the researchers analyzed samples of the culture at different times during the chase. For each batch of cells, they recorded how many labeled cells were undergoing mitosis, meaning that the cells that were in S phase during the pulse had entered M phase.

One striking result emerged early on: None of the labeled cells started mitosis immediately. Because the cultures were asynchronous, at least some of the cells must have been at the very end of their S phase when exposed to the pulse. If the S phase had been immediately followed by the M phase, some of these labeled cells would have entered M just as the chase began. Instead, it took several hours before any of the labeled cells began mitosis.

The time lag between the end of the pulse and the appearance of the first labeled mitotic nuclei corresponds to a period between the end of S phase and the beginning of M phase. This gap represents the time when chromosome replication is complete, but mitosis has not yet begun. **FIGURE 12.2** shows how cells labeled with radioactive thymidine can be tracked as they progress through the M phase.

After this result, the possibilities for the organization of the cell cycle were narrowed to either one gap between the end of S and start of M phase, or two gaps that flank the S phase. Which of the models best represents the eukaryotic cell cycle? Once researchers determined the lengths of the S and M phases, they found that the combined time, including the gap between these phases, was still short compared with the length of the cell cycle. This discrepancy represents an additional gap phase that is between the end of M and the start of S phase.

The cell cycle was thus finally mapped out. The gap between the end of M and start of S phase is called the **G_1 phase**. The second gap, between the end of S and start of M phase, is called the **G_2 phase.**

The Cell Cycle

FIGURE 12.3 pulls these results together into a comprehensive view of the cell cycle. The cell cycle involves four phases: M phase and an interphase consisting of the G_1, S, and G_2 phases. In the cycle diagrammed here, the G_1 phase is about twice as long as G_2, but the timing of these phases varies depending on the cell type and growth conditions.

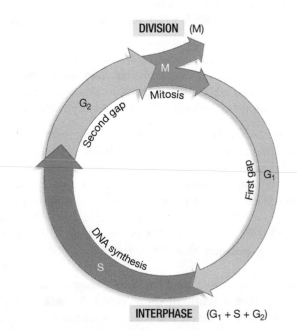

FIGURE 12.3 The Cell Cycle Has Four Phases. A representative cell cycle. The time required for the G_1 and G_2 phases varies dramatically among cells and organisms.

Why do the gap phases exist? Besides needing to copy their chromosomes during interphase, cells also must prepare for division by replicating organelles and increasing in size. Before mitosis can take place, the parent cell must grow large enough to divide into two cells that will be normal in size and function. The two gap phases provide the time required to accomplish these tasks. They allow the cell to complete all the requirements for cell division other than chromosome replication.

Now let's turn to the M phase. Once the genetic material has been copied, how do cells divide it between daughter cells?

12.2 What Happens during M Phase?

The M phase typically consists of two distinct events: the division of the nucleus and the division of the cytoplasm. During cell replication, mitosis divides the replicated chromosomes to form two daughter nuclei with identical chromosomes and genes. Mitosis is usually accompanied by cytokinesis—cytoplasmic division that results in two daughter cells.

FIGURE 12.4 provides an overview of how chromosomes change before, during, and after mitosis and cytokinesis, beginning with a hypothetical plant cell or animal cell in G_1 phase. The first drawing shows a total of four chromosomes in the cell, but chromosome number varies widely among species—chimpanzees and potato plants have a total of 48 chromosomes in each cell; a maize (corn) plant has 20, dogs have 78, and fruit flies have 8.

Eukaryotic chromosomes consist of DNA wrapped around the globular histone proteins. In eukaryotes this DNA–protein material is called **chromatin.** During interphase, the chromatin of each chromosome is in a "relaxed" or uncondensed state, forming long, thin strands (see Figure 12.1, top).

The second drawing in Figure 12.4 shows chromosomes that have been copied before mitosis. Each chromosome now consists of two sister chromatids. Each chromatid contains one long DNA double helix, and sister chromatids represent exact copies of the same genetic information.

At the start of mitosis, then, each chromosome consists of two sister chromatids that are attached to each other at the centromere.

✔ You should be able to explain the relationship between chromosomes and (1) genes, (2) chromatin, and (3) sister chromatids.

Events in Mitosis

As the third drawing in Figure 12.4 indicates, mitosis begins when chromatin condenses to form a much more compact structure. Replicated, condensed chromosomes correspond to the paired threads observed by early biologists.

During mitosis, the two sister chromatids separate to form independent daughter chromosomes. One copy of each chromosome goes to each of the two daughter cells. (See the final drawing in Figure 12.4.) As a result, each cell receives an identical copy of the genetic information that was contained in the parent cell.

Biologists have identified five subphases within M phase based on distinctive events that occur. Interphase is followed by the mitotic subphases of prophase, prometaphase, metaphase, anaphase, and telophase.

Recall that before mitosis begins, chromosomes have already replicated during the S phase of interphase. Now let's look at how cells separate the chromatids in these replicated chromosomes by investigating each subphase of mitosis in turn (**FIGURE 12.5**, on page 224).

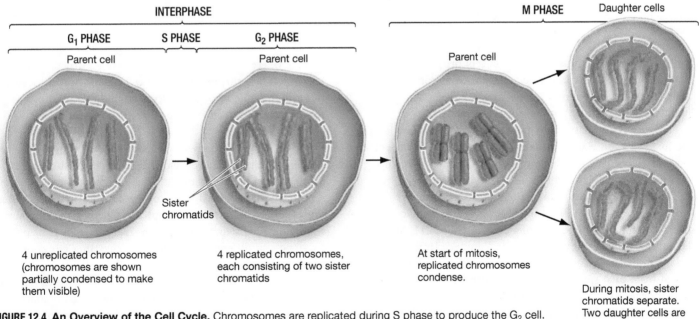

INTERPHASE

| G₁ PHASE | S PHASE | G₂ PHASE |

Parent cell   Parent cell

Sister chromatids

4 unreplicated chromosomes (chromosomes are shown partially condensed to make them visible)

4 replicated chromosomes, each consisting of two sister chromatids

M PHASE   Daughter cells

Parent cell

At start of mitosis, replicated chromosomes condense.

During mitosis, sister chromatids separate. Two daughter cells are formed by cytokinesis.

FIGURE 12.4 An Overview of the Cell Cycle. Chromosomes are replicated during S phase to produce the G_2 cell. During M phase, the replicated chromosomes are partitioned to the two daughter cells. Each daughter cell contains the same complement of chromosomes as the parent cell.

Sister chromatids separate; one chromosome copy goes to each daughter nucleus.

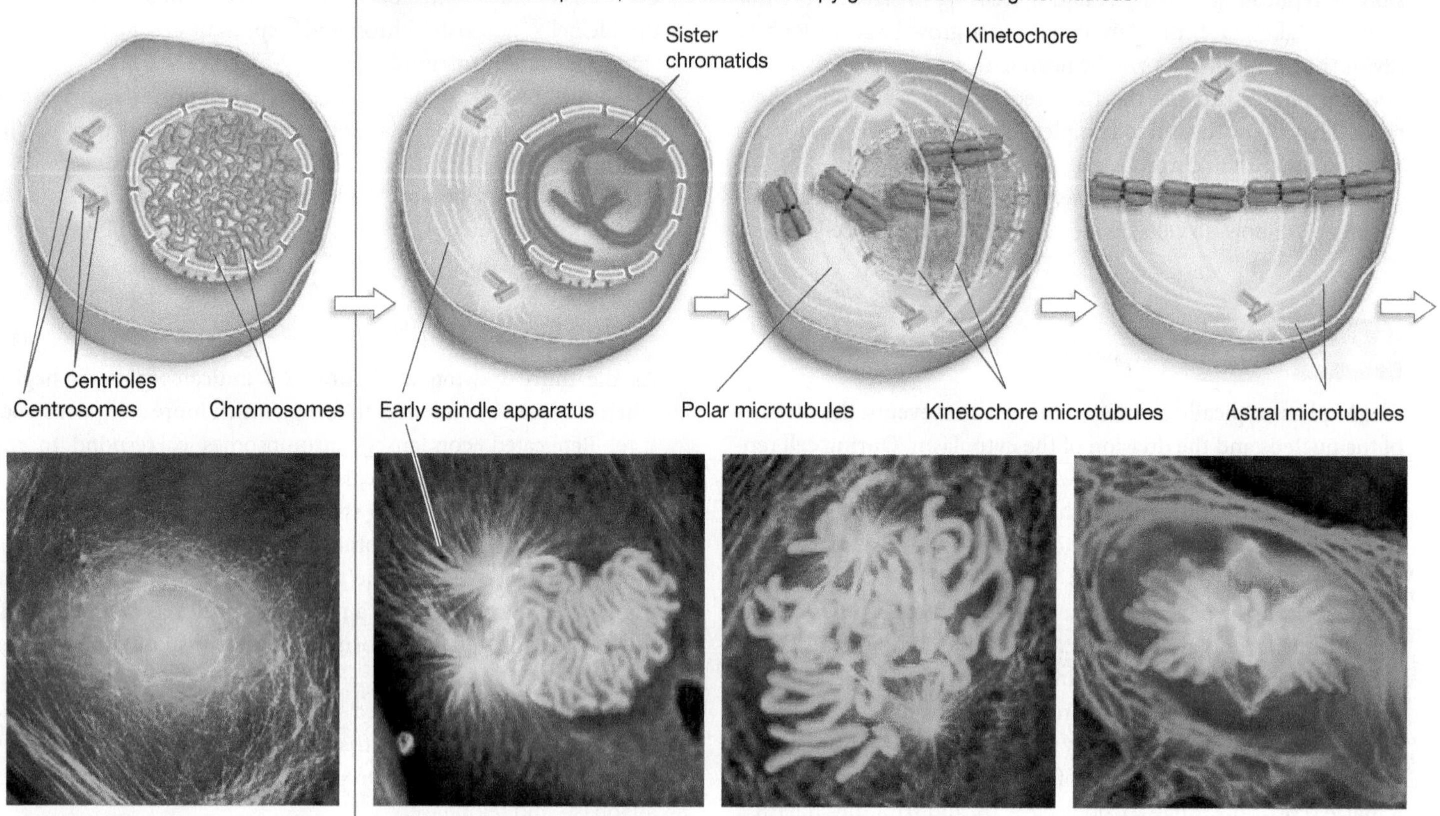

Sister chromatids

Kinetochore

Centrioles
Centrosomes   Chromosomes   Early spindle apparatus   Polar microtubules   Kinetochore microtubules   Astral microtubules

1. Interphase: After chromosome replication, each chromosome is composed of two sister chromatids. Centrosomes have replicated.

2. Prophase: Chromosomes condense, and spindle apparatus begins to form.

3. Prometaphase: Nuclear envelope breaks down. Microtubules contact chromosomes at kinetochores.

4. Metaphase: Chromosomes complete migration to middle of cell.

FIGURE 12.5 **Mitosis and Cytokinesis.** In the micrographs, under the drawings, chromosomes are stained blue, microtubules are yellow/green, and intermediate filaments are red.

✔ QUANTITATIVE: If the model cell in this figure has x amount of DNA and four chromosomes in its G_1 phase, then what is the amount of DNA and number of chromosomes in **(1)** prophase; **(2)** anaphase; **(3)** each daughter cell after division is complete?

Prophase   Mitosis begins with the events of **prophase** ("before-phase," Figure 12.5, step 2), when chromosomes condense into compact structures. Chromosomes first become visible in the light microscope during prophase.

Prophase is also marked by the formation of the spindle apparatus. The **spindle apparatus** is a structure that produces mechanical forces that **(1)** move replicated chromosomes during early mitosis and **(2)** pull chromatids apart in late mitosis.

The spindle consists of microtubules—components of the cytoskeleton (see Chapter 7). In all eukaryotes, microtubules originate from microtubule-organizing centers (MTOCs). MTOCs define the two poles of the spindle and produce large numbers of microtubules. During prophase, some of these microtubules extend from each spindle pole and overlap with one another—these are called **polar microtubules.**

Although the nature of this MTOC varies among plants, animals, fungi, and other eukaryotic groups, the spindle apparatus has the same function. Figure 12.5 illustrates an animal cell undergoing

mitosis, where the MTOC is a **centrosome**—a structure that contains a pair of **centrioles** (see Chapter 7). During prophase in animal cells, the spindle begins to form around the chromosomes by moving centrosomes to opposite sides of the nucleus.

Prometaphase   In many eukaryotes, once chromosomes have condensed, the nuclear envelope disintegrates. Once the envelope has been removed, microtubules are able to attach to chromosomes at specialized structures called **kinetochores.** These events occur during **prometaphase** ("before middle-phase"; see Figure 12.5, step 3). (Organisms that maintain their nuclear envelope use different strategies for separating chromosomes, which will not be discussed here.)

Each sister chromatid has its own kinetochore, which is assembled at the centromere. Since the centromere is also the attachment site for chromatids, the result is two kinetochores on opposite sides of each replicated chromosome. The microtubules that are attached to these structures are called **kinetochore microtubules.**

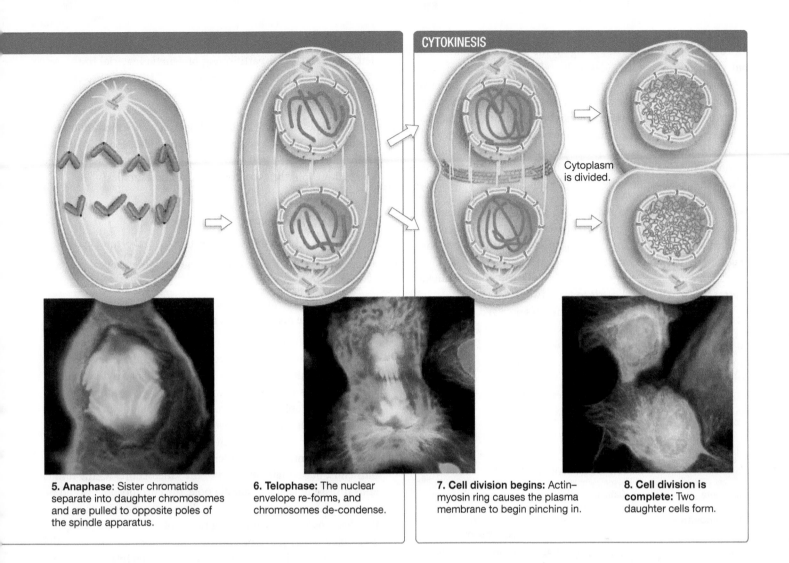

Cytoplasm is divided.

5. Anaphase: Sister chromatids separate into daughter chromosomes and are pulled to opposite poles of the spindle apparatus.

6. Telophase: The nuclear envelope re-forms, and chromosomes de-condense.

7. Cell division begins: Actin–myosin ring causes the plasma membrane to begin pinching in.

8. Cell division is complete: Two daughter cells form.

Early in mitosis, kinesin and dynein motors are recruited to the kinetochore, where they can "walk" the chromosome up and down microtubules. These motors are thought to be very important in the initial attachment of the kinetochore to the plus end of the microtubule. If these ideas are correct, then the process is similar to the way these motors walk along microtubules during vesicle transport (see Chapter 7).

In all eukaryotes, after the kinetochores have attached to microtubules, chromosomes begin to move to the middle of the cell during prometaphase.

Metaphase Once the kinetochore microtubules have moved all the chromosomes to the middle of the spindle (Figure 12.5, step 4), the mitotic cells enter **metaphase** ("middle-phase"). At this point, the chromosomes are lined up along an imaginary plane between the two spindle poles called the **metaphase plate.**

The formation of the spindle apparatus is now complete. The polar microtubules that extend from each spindle pole overlap in the middle of the cell, thereby forming a pole-to-pole connection. Each chromosome is held by kinetochore microtubules reaching out from opposite poles and exerting the same amount of tension, or pull. The spindle poles are held in place partly because of

astral microtubules that extend from the MTOCs and interact with proteins on the cell membrane.

The alignment of these chromosomes results from the growth and shrinkage of the attached kinetochore microtubules. When chromosomes reach the metaphase plate, the shrinkage of these microtubules at the MTOCs is balanced by slow growth of microtubules at the kinetochores. Since the sister chromatids of each chromosome are connected to opposite poles, a tug of war occurs during metaphase that pulls them in opposite directions.

Anaphase At the start of **anaphase** ("against-phase"), the cohesins that are holding sister chromatids together at the centromeres split (Figure 12.5, step 5). Because the chromatids are under tension, each replicated chromosome is pulled apart to create two independent daughter chromosomes. By definition, this separation of chromatids instantly doubles the number of chromosomes in the cell.

Two types of movement occur during anaphase. First, the daughter chromosomes move to opposite poles via the attachment of kinetochore proteins to the shrinking kinetochore microtubules. Second, the two poles of the spindle are pushed and pulled farther apart. The motor proteins in overlapping polar microtubules push the poles away from each other. Different motors on the membrane walk along on the astral microtubules to pull the poles to opposite sides of the cell.

During anaphase, then, replicated chromosomes split into two identical sets of daughter chromosomes. Their separation to opposite poles is a critical step in mitosis because it ensures that each daughter cell receives the same complement of chromosomes.

When anaphase is complete, two complete collections of chromosomes are fully separated, each being identical with those of the parent cell before chromosome replication.

Telophase   During **telophase** ("end-phase"), the nuclear envelope that dissolved in prometaphase reforms around each set of chromosomes, and the chromosomes begin to de-condense (Figure 12.5, step 6). Once two independent nuclei have formed, mitosis is complete. At this point, most cells will go on to divide their cytoplasm via cytokinesis to form two daughter cells.

TABLE 12.1 summarizes the key structures involved in mitosis.

✔ After you've studied the table and reviewed Figure 12.5, you should be able to make a table with rows titled (1) spindle apparatus, (2) nuclear envelope, and (3) chromosomes, and columns titled with the five phases of mitosis. Fill in the table by summarizing what happens to each structure during each phase of mitosis.

SUMMARY TABLE 12.1   **Structures Involved in Mitosis**

Structure	Definition
Chromosome	A structure composed of a DNA molecule and associated proteins
Chromatin	The material that makes up eukaryotic chromosomes; consists of a DNA molecule complexed with histone proteins (see Chapter 19)
Chromatid	One strand of a replicated chromosome, with its associated proteins
Sister chromatids	The two strands of a replicated chromosome. When chromosomes are replicated, they consist of two sister chromatids. The genetic material in sister chromatids is identical. When sister chromatids separate during mitosis, they become independent chromosomes.
Centromere	The structure that joins sister chromatids
Kinetochores	The structures on sister chromatids where microtubules attach
Microtubule-organizing center	Any structure that organizes microtubules (see Chapter 7)
Centrosome	The microtubule-organizing center in animals and some plants
Centrioles	Cylindrical structures that comprise microtubules, located inside animal centrosomes

How Do Chromosomes Move during Anaphase?

The exact and equal partitioning of genetic material to the two daughter nuclei is the most fundamental aspect of mitosis. How does this process occur?

To understand how sister chromatids separate and move to opposite sides of the spindle, biologists have focused on understanding the function of spindle microtubules. How do kinetochore microtubules pull chromatids apart? And how does the kinetochore join the chromosome and microtubules?

Mitotic Spindle Forces   The spindle apparatus is composed of microtubules (see Chapter 7). Recall that:

- microtubules are composed of α-tubulin and β-tubulin dimers,

- microtubules are asymmetric—meaning they have a plus end and a minus end, and

- the plus end is the site where microtubule growth normally occurs while disassembly is more frequent at the minus end.

During mitosis, the microtubules originating from the poles are highly dynamic. Rapid growth and shrinkage ensures that some of the microtubules will be able to attach to kinetochores with their plus ends. Others will be stabilized by different proteins in the cytoplasm and become polar or astral microtubules.

These observations suggest two possible mechanisms for the movement of chromosomes during anaphase. The simplest mechanism would be for microtubules to stop growing at the plus ends, but remain attached to the kinetochore. As the minus ends disassemble at the spindle pole, the chromosome would be reeled in like a hooked fish. An alternative model would have the chromosomes moving along microtubules that are being disassembled at the plus ends at the kinetochore. In this case, the chromosome is like a yo-yo running up a string into your hand.

To test these hypotheses, biologists introduced fluorescently labeled tubulin subunits into prophase or metaphase cells. This treatment made the kinetochore microtubules visible (**FIGURE 12.6,** step 1). Once anaphase began, the researchers marked a region of these microtubules with a bar-shaped beam of laser light. The laser permanently bleached a section of the fluorescently labeled structures, darkening them—although they were still functional (Figure 12.6, step 2).

As anaphase progressed, two things happened: (**1**) The darkened region appeared to remain stationary, and (**2**) the chromosomes moved closer to the darkened regions of the microtubules, eventually overtaking them.

This result suggested that the kinetochore microtubules remain stationary during anaphase, but shorten because tubulin subunits are lost from their plus ends. As microtubule ends shrink back to the spindle poles, the chromosomes are pulled along. But if the microtubule is disassembling at the kinetochore, how does the chromosome remain attached?

Kinetochores Are Linked to Retreating Microtubule Ends   The kinetochore is a complex of many proteins that build a base on the centromere region of the chromosome and a "crown" of fibrous proteins projecting outward. **FIGURE 12.7** shows a current

QUESTION: How do kinetochore microtubules shorten to pull daughter chromosomes apart during anaphase?

HYPOTHESIS: Microtubules shorten at the spindle pole.

ALTERNATIVE HYPOTHESIS: Microtubules shorten at the kinetochore.

EXPERIMENTAL SETUP:

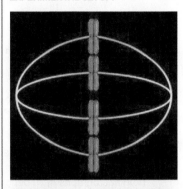

1. Label targets: Use fluorescent labels to make the metaphase chromosomes fluoresce blue and the microtubules fluoresce yellow.

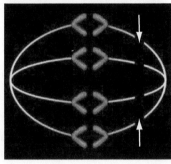

2. Mark microtubules: At the start of anaphase, darken a section of microtubules to mark them without changing their function.

PREDICTION:

PREDICTION OF ALTERNATIVE HYPOTHESIS: Daughter chromosomes will move toward the pole faster than the darkened section.

RESULTS:

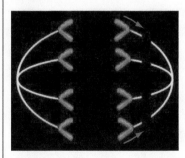

The darkened areas of the microtubules remained stationary as the chromosomes moved through them toward the pole.

CONCLUSION: Kinetochore microtubules shorten at the kinetochore to pull daughter chromosomes apart during anaphase.

FIGURE 12.6 During Anaphase, Microtubules Shorten at the Kinetochore.

SOURCE: Gorbsky, G. J., et al. 1987. Chromosomes move poleward during anaphase along stationary microtubules that coordinately disassemble from their kinetochore ends. *Journal of Cellular Biology* 104: 9–18.

✔**EXERCISE** Complete the prediction for what would occur if chromosome movement were based on microtubules shortening at the spindle pole.

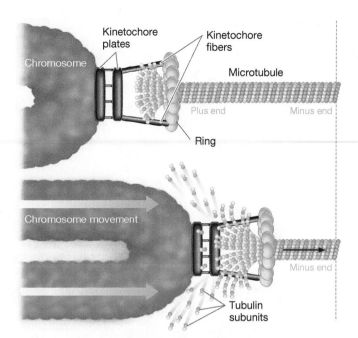

FIGURE 12.7 How Do Microtubules Move Chromosomes during Anaphase? Microtubules are disassembled at the kinetochore during anaphase. In yeast, kinetochore proteins tether the chromosome to a ring that is pushed toward the spindle pole by the fraying plus end of the microtubule.

model for kinetochore structure and function during chromosome movement in anaphase. For simplicity, a yeast kinetochore is shown, which attaches to only one microtubule. (Other eukaryotes can have as many as 30 microtubules attached to each kinetochore.)

Biologists have found that as anaphase gets under way, the plus ends of the kinetochore microtubules begin to fray and disassemble. Fibers that extend from the yeast kinetochore are tethered to this retreating end by attaching to a ring that surrounds the kinetochore microtubule (Figure 12.7, top). As the fraying end widens, its expansion forces the ring, and the attached chromosome, toward the minus end of the microtubule (see Figure 12.7, bottom). The result is that the chromosome is pulled to the spindle pole by the depolymerization of the kinetochore microtubule.

Cytokinesis Results in Two Daughter Cells

At this point, the chromosomes have been replicated in S phase and partitioned to opposite sides of the spindle via mitosis. Now it's time to divide the cell into two daughters that contain identical copies of each chromosome. If these cells are to be viable, however, the parent cell must also ensure that more than just chromosomes make it into each daughter cell.

While the cell is in interphase, the cytoplasmic contents, including the organelles, have increased in number or volume. During cytokinesis (Figure 12.5, steps 7 and 8), the cytoplasm divides to form two daughter cells, each with its own nucleus and complete set of organelles. In most types of cells, cytokinesis directly follows mitosis.

(a) Cytokinesis in plants

Microtubules direct vesicles to center of spindle where they fuse to divide the cell in two

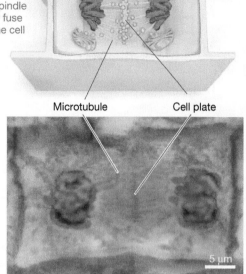

Microtubule   Cell plate

5 µm

(b) Cytokinesis in animals

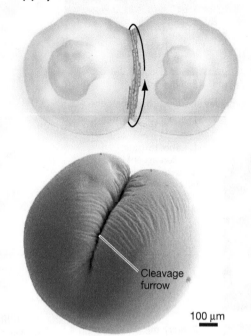

Actin–myosin interactions pinch the membrane in two

Cleavage furrow

100 µm

FIGURE 12.8 The Mechanism of Cytokinesis Varies among Eukaryotes. (a) In plants, the cytoplasm is divided by a cell plate that forms in the middle of the parent cell. **(b)** In animals, the cytoplasm is divided by a cleavage furrow. (The cells in both micrographs have been stained or colorized.)

In plants, polar microtubules left over from the spindle help define and organize the region where the new plasma membranes and cell walls will form. Vesicles from the Golgi apparatus carry components to build a new cell wall to the middle of the dividing cell. These vesicles are moved along the polar microtubules via motor proteins. In the middle of what was the spindle, the vesicles start to fuse together to form a flattened sac-like structure called the **cell plate** (**FIGURE 12.8a**). The cell plate continues to grow as new vesicles fuse with it, eventually contacting the existing plasma membrane. When the cell plate fuses with the existing plasma membrane, it divides the cell into two new daughter cells.

In animals and many other eukaryotes, cytokinesis begins with the formation of a **cleavage furrow** (**FIGURE 12.8b**). The furrow appears because a ring of actin filaments forms just inside the plasma membrane, in the middle of what used to be the spindle. Myosin motor proteins bind to these actin filaments and use adenosine triphosphate (ATP) to contract in a way that causes actin filaments to slide (see Chapter 7).

As myosin moves the ring of actin filaments on the inside of the plasma membrane, the ring shrinks in size and tightens. Because the ring is attached to the plasma membrane, the shrinking ring pulls the membrane with it. As a result, the plasma membrane pinches inward. The actin and myosin filaments continue to slide past each other, tightening the ring further, until the original membrane pinches in two and cell division is complete.

The overall process involved in chromosome separation and cytoplasmic division is a common requirement for all living organisms. The mechanisms involved in accomplishing these events, however, vary depending on the type of cell. What about

bacterial cells? How does chromosomal segregation and cytokinesis compare between prokaryotes and eukaryotes?

Bacterial Cell Replication   Many bacteria divide using a process called **binary fission**. Recent research has shown that chromosome segregation and cytokinesis in bacterial division is strikingly similar to what occurs in the eukaryotic M phase (**FIGURE 12.9**). As the bacterial chromosome is being replicated, protein filaments attach to the copies and separate them to opposite sides of the cell.

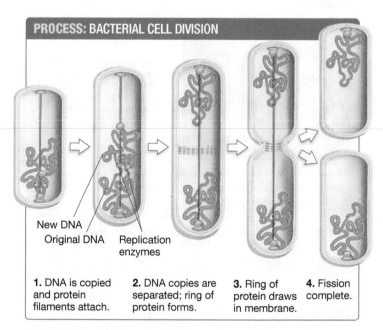

PROCESS: BACTERIAL CELL DIVISION

New DNA
Original DNA   Replication enzymes

1. DNA is copied and protein filaments attach.

2. DNA copies are separated; ring of protein forms.

3. Ring of protein draws in membrane.

4. Fission complete.

FIGURE 12.9 Bacterial Cells Divide but Do Not Undergo Mitosis.

Once the copies of the chromosome have been partitioned to opposite sides of the cell, other filaments, made up of proteins that are similar to eukaryotic tubulin, are responsible for dividing the cytoplasm. These filaments attach to the cell membrane to form a ring between the chromosome copies. A signal from the cell causes the filaments to constrict, drawing in the membrane and eventually cleaving the parent into two genetically identical cells.

Having explored what occurs during cell division, let's focus on how it is controlled in eukaryotes. When does a eukaryotic cell divide, and when does it stop dividing?

check your understanding

If you understand that . . .

- After chromosomes replicate, mitosis separates the copies to generate two nuclei with the same chromosomal complement.
- Microtubules attach to kinetochores and move chromosomes by the addition and subtraction of tubulin dimers.
- Cytokinesis divides the nuclei and cytoplasmic components into two daughter cells that are genetically identical with each other and the parent cell.

✔ **You should be able to . . .**

1. Draw the mitotic spindle for an animal cell that has two chromosomes in metaphase and label the sister chromatids, kinetochores, centrosomes, and the three types of microtubules.

2. Predict how the inhibition of microtubule motors in a plant cell would affect the activities in M phase.

Answers are available in Appendix A.

12.3 Control of the Cell Cycle

Although the events of mitosis are virtually identical in all eukaryotes, other aspects of the cell cycle vary. In humans, for example, intestinal cells routinely divide more than twice a day to replace tissue that is lost during digestion; mature human nerve and muscle cells do not divide at all.

Most of these differences are due to variation in the length of the G_1 phase. In rapidly dividing cells, G_1 is essentially eliminated. Most nondividing cells, in contrast, are permanently stuck in G_1. Researchers refer to this arrested stage as the G_0 state, or simply "G zero." Cells that are in G_0 have effectively exited the cell cycle and are sometimes referred to as post-mitotic. Nerve cells, muscle cells, and many other cell types enter G_0 once they have matured.

A cell's division rate can also vary in response to changing conditions. For example, human liver cells normally replicate about once per year. But if part of the liver is damaged or lost, the remaining cells divide every one or two days until repair is accomplished. Cells of unicellular organisms such as yeasts, bacteria, or archaeans divide rapidly only if the environment is rich in nutrients; otherwise, they enter a quiescent (inactive) state.

To explain these differences, biologists hypothesized that the cell cycle must be regulated in some way. Cell-cycle control is now the most prominent issue in research on cell division—partly because defects in control can lead to uncontrolled, cancerous growth.

The Discovery of Cell-Cycle Regulatory Molecules

The first solid evidence for cell-cycle control molecules came to light in 1970. Researchers found that certain chemicals, viruses, or an electric shock could fuse the membranes of two mammalian cells that were growing in culture, forming a single cell with two nuclei.

How did cell-fusion experiments relate to cell-cycle regulation? When investigators fused cells that were in different stages of the cell cycle, certain nuclei changed phases. For example, when a cell in M phase was fused with one in interphase, the nucleus of the interphase cell immediately initiated mitosis, even if the chromosomes had not been replicated. The biologists hypothesized that the cytoplasm of M-phase cells contains a regulatory molecule that induces interphase cells to enter M phase.

But cell-fusion experiments were difficult to control and left researchers wondering if it was the nucleus or the cytoplasm that was responsible for the induction. To address this issue, they turned to the South African clawed frog, *Xenopus laevis*.

As an egg of these frogs matures, it changes from a cell called an oocyte, which is arrested in a phase similar to G_2, to a mature egg that is arrested in M phase. The large size of these cells—more than 1 mm in diameter—makes them relatively easy to manipulate. Using instruments with extremely fine needles, researchers could specifically examine the effects of the cytoplasm by pulling a sample from a mature egg or an oocyte and injecting it into another.

When biologists purified cytoplasm from M-phase frog eggs and injected it into the cytoplasm of frog oocytes arrested in G_2, the immature oocytes immediately entered M phase (**FIGURE 12.10**, see page 230). But when cytoplasm from interphase cells was injected into G_2 oocytes, the cells remained in the G_2 phase. The researchers concluded that the cytoplasm of M-phase cells—but not the cytoplasm of interphase cells—contains a factor that drives immature oocytes into M phase to complete their maturation.

The factor that initiates M-phase in oocytes was purified and is now called **M phase–promoting factor,** or **MPF.** Subsequent experiments showed that MPF induces M phase in all eukaryotes. For example, injecting M-phase cytoplasm from mammalian cells into immature frog oocytes results in egg maturation, and human MPF can also trigger M phase in yeast cells.

MPF appears to be a general signal that says "Start M phase." How does it work?

QUESTION: Is M phase controlled by regulatory molecules in the cytoplasm?

HYPOTHESIS: Cytoplasmic regulatory molecules control entry into M phase.

NULL HYPOTHESIS: M-phase regulatory molecules are not in the cytoplasm or do not exist.

EXPERIMENTAL SETUP:

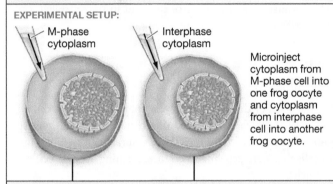

M-phase cytoplasm

Interphase cytoplasm

Microinject cytoplasm from M-phase cell into one frog oocyte and cytoplasm from interphase cell into another frog oocyte.

PREDICTION: Only the oocyte injected with M-phase cytoplasm will begin M phase.

PREDICTION OF NULL HYPOTHESIS: Neither of the frog oocytes will begin M phase.

RESULTS:

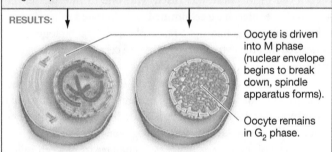

Oocyte is driven into M phase (nuclear envelope begins to break down, spindle apparatus forms).

Oocyte remains in G₂ phase.

CONCLUSION: M-phase cytoplasm contains a regulatory molecule that induces M phase in interphase cells.

FIGURE 12.10 Experimental Evidence for Cell-Cycle Control Molecules. When the cytoplasm from M-phase cells is microinjected into cells in interphase, the interphase chromosomes condense and begin M phase.

SOURCE: Masui, Y., and C. L. Markert. 1971. Cytoplasmic control of nuclear behavior during meiotic maturation of frog oocytes. *Journal of Experimental Zoology* 177: 129–145.

✓**QUESTION** This experiment was done using cells that were undergoing meiosis. What could the investigators do to show that the factor used in meiotic division is the same as used for mitotic division?

MPF Contains a Protein Kinase and a Cyclin MPF is made up of two distinct polypeptide subunits. One subunit is a protein kinase—an enzyme that catalyzes the transfer of a phosphate group from ATP to a target protein. Recall that phosphorylation may activate or inactivate the function of proteins by changing their shape (Chapter 8). As a result, kinases frequently act as regulatory proteins in the cell.

These observations suggested that MPF phosphorylates proteins that trigger the onset of M phase. But research showed that

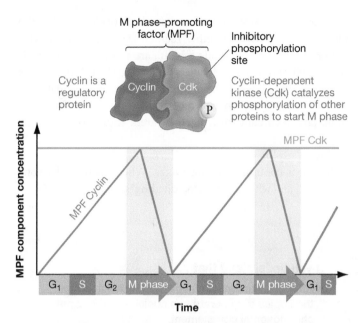

M phase–promoting factor (MPF)

Cyclin is a regulatory protein

Inhibitory phosphorylation site

Cyclin-dependent kinase (Cdk) catalyzes phosphorylation of other proteins to start M phase

FIGURE 12.11 Cyclin Concentration Regulates the Concentration of the MPF Dimer. Cyclin concentrations cycle in dividing cells, reaching a peak in M phase. The activity of MPF, shown in the blue shaded area, requires both cyclin and Cdk components.

✓**QUESTION** Proteins that degrade cyclin are activated by events that MPF initiates. Why is this important?

the concentration of the protein kinase is more or less constant throughout the cell cycle. How can MPF trigger M phase if the protein kinase subunit is always present?

The answer lies in the second MPF subunit, which belongs to a family of proteins called **cyclins.** Cyclins got their name because their concentrations fluctuate throughout the cell cycle.

As **FIGURE 12.11** shows, the concentration of the cyclin associated with MPF builds during interphase and peaks in M phase. The timing of this increase is important because the protein kinase subunit in MPF is functional only when it is bound to the cyclin subunit. As a result, the protein kinase subunit of MPF is called a **cyclin-dependent kinase,** or **Cdk.**

To summarize, MPF is a dimer consisting of a cyclin and a cyclin-dependent kinase. The cyclin subunit regulates the formation of the MPF dimer; the kinase subunit catalyzes the phosphorylation of other proteins to start M phase.

How Is MPF Turned On? According to Figure 12.11, the number of cyclins builds up steadily during interphase. Why doesn't this increasing concentration of MPF trigger the onset of M phase?

The answer is that the activity of MPF's Cdk subunit is further regulated by two phosphorylation events. The phosphorylation of one site in Cdk activates the kinase, but when the second site is phosphorylated, it is inactivated. Both these sites are phosphorylated after cyclin binds to the Cdk. This allows the concentration of the dimer to increase without prematurely starting M phase. Late in G₂ phase, however, an enzyme removes the inhibitory phosphate. This dephosphorylation reaction, coupled with the addition of the activating phosphate, changes the Cdk's shape in a way that turns on its kinase activity.

Once MPF is active, it triggers a chain of events. Although the exact mechanisms involved are still under investigation, the result is that chromosomes begin to condense and the spindle apparatus starts to form. In this way, MPF triggers the onset of M phase.

How Is MPF Turned Off?   During anaphase, an enzyme complex begins degrading MPF's cyclin subunit. In this way, MPF triggers a chain of events that leads to its own destruction.

MPF deactivation illustrates two key concepts about regulatory systems in cells:

- **Negative feedback** occurs when a process is slowed or shut down by one of its products. Thermostats shut down furnaces when temperatures are high; phosphofructokinase is inhibited by ATP (see Chapter 9); MPF is turned off by an enzyme complex that is activated by events in mitosis.

- Destroying specific proteins is a common way to control cell processes. In this case, the enzyme complex that is activated in anaphase attaches small proteins called ubiquitins to MPF's cyclin subunit. This marks the subunit for destruction by a protein complex called the proteasome.

In response to MPF activity, then, the concentration of cyclin declines rapidly. Slowly, it builds up again during interphase. This sets up an oscillation in cyclin concentration.

✔ If you understand this aspect of cell-cycle regulation, you should be able to explain the relationship between MPF and (1) cyclin, (2) Cdk, and (3) the enzymes that phosphorylate MPF, dephosphorylate MPF, and degrade cyclin.

Cell-Cycle Checkpoints Can Arrest the Cell Cycle

The dramatic changes in cyclin concentrations and Cdk activity drive the ordered events of the cell cycle. These events are occurring in your body right now. Over a 24-hour period, you swallow millions of cheek cells and lose millions of cells from your intestinal lining as waste. To replace them, cells in your cheek and intestinal tissue are making and degrading cyclin and pushing themselves through the cell cycle.

MPF is only one of many protein complexes involved in regulating the cell cycle, however. A different cyclin complex triggers the passage from G_1 phase into S phase, and several regulatory proteins maintain the G_0 state of quiescent cells. An array of regulatory molecules holds cells in particular stages or stimulates passage to the next phase.

To make sense of these observations, Leland Hartwell and Ted Weinert introduced the concept of a **cell-cycle checkpoint.** A cell-cycle checkpoint is a critical point in the cell cycle that is regulated.

Hartwell and Weinert identified checkpoints by analyzing yeast cells with defects in the cell cycle. The defective cells kept dividing under culture conditions when normal cells stopped growing, because the defective cells lacked a specific checkpoint. In multicellular organisms, cells that keep dividing in this way may form a mass of cells called a **tumor.**

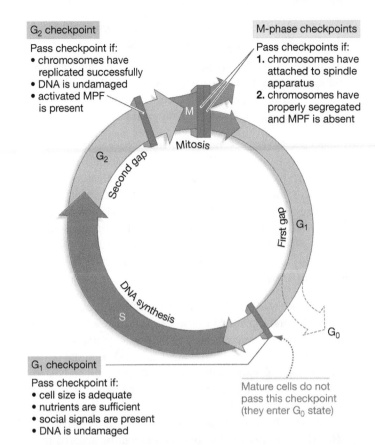

G₂ checkpoint

Pass checkpoint if:
- chromosomes have replicated successfully
- DNA is undamaged
- activated MPF is present

M-phase checkpoints

Pass checkpoints if:
1. chromosomes have attached to spindle apparatus
2. chromosomes have properly segregated and MPF is absent

G₁ checkpoint

Pass checkpoint if:
- cell size is adequate
- nutrients are sufficient
- social signals are present
- DNA is undamaged

Mature cells do not pass this checkpoint (they enter G₀ state)

FIGURE 12.12 The Four Cell-Cycle Checkpoints.

There are distinct checkpoints in three of the four phases of the cell cycle (**FIGURE 12.12**). In effect, interactions among regulatory molecules at each checkpoint allow a cell to "decide" whether to proceed with division or not. If these regulatory molecules are defective, the checkpoint may fail and cells may start dividing in an uncontrolled fashion.

G₁ Checkpoint   The first cell-cycle checkpoint occurs late in G_1. For most cells, this checkpoint is the most important in establishing whether the cell will continue through the cycle and divide, or exit the cycle and enter G_0. What determines whether a cell passes the G_1 checkpoint?

- *Size*   Because a cell must reach a certain size before its daughter cells will be large enough to function normally, biologists hypothesize that some mechanism exists to arrest the cell cycle if the cell is too small.

- *Availability of nutrients*   Unicellular organisms arrest at the G_1 checkpoint if nutrient conditions are poor.

- *Social signals*   Cells in multicellular organisms pass (or do not pass) through the G_1 checkpoint in response to signaling molecules from other cells, which are termed social signals.

- *Damage to DNA*   If DNA is physically damaged, the protein **p53** activates genes that either stop the cell cycle until the damage can be repaired or cause the cell's programmed, controlled destruction—a phenomenon known as **apoptosis.** In this way, p53 acts as a brake on the cell cycle.

If "brake" molecules such as p53 are defective, damaged DNA remains unrepaired. Damage in genes that regulate cell growth can lead to uncontrolled cell division. Consequently, regulatory proteins like p53 are called **tumor suppressors.**

G$_2$ Checkpoint The second checkpoint occurs after S phase, at the boundary between the G$_2$ and M phases. Because MPF is the key signal triggering the onset of M phase, investigators were not surprised to find that it is involved in the G$_2$ checkpoint.

Data suggest that if DNA is damaged or if chromosomes are not replicated correctly, removal of the inactivating phosphate is blocked. When MPF is not turned on, cells remain in G$_2$ phase. Cells at this checkpoint may also respond to signals from other cells and to internal signals relating to their size.

M-Phase Checkpoints The final two checkpoints occur during mitosis. The first regulates the onset of anaphase. Cells in M phase will not split the chromatids until all kinetochores attach properly to the spindle apparatus. If the metaphase checkpoint did not exist, some chromosomes might not separate correctly, and daughter cells would receive either too many or too few chromosomes.

The second checkpoint regulates the progression through M phase into G$_1$. If chromosomes do not fully separate during anaphase, MPF will not decline and the cell will be arrested in M phase. The enzymes that are responsible for cyclin destruction are activated only when all the chromosomes have been properly separated. The presence of MPF activity prevents the cell from undergoing cytokinesis and exiting the M phase.

To summarize, the four cell-cycle checkpoints have the same purpose: They prevent the division of cells that are damaged or that have other problems. The G$_1$ checkpoint also prevents mature cells that are in the G$_0$ state from dividing.

Understanding cell-cycle regulation is fundamental. If one of the checkpoints fails, the affected cells may begin dividing in an uncontrolled fashion. For the organism as a whole, the consequences of uncontrolled cell division may be dire: cancer.

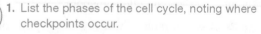

check your understanding

C Y U

If you understand that . . .

- The cell cycle consists of four carefully controlled phases.

✓ **You should be able to . . .**

1. List the phases of the cell cycle, noting where checkpoints occur.
2. Summarize how levels of Cdk and cyclin change over time and how this is related to MPF activity, noting the particular phases that are involved.

Answers are available in Appendix A.

12.4 Cancer: Out-of-Control Cell Division

Fifty percent of American men and 33 percent of American women will develop cancer during their lifetime. In the United States, one in four of all deaths is from cancer. It is the second leading cause of death, exceeded only by heart disease.

Cancer is a general term for disease caused by cells that divide in an uncontrolled fashion, invade nearby tissues, and spread to other sites in the body. Cancerous cells cause disease because they use nutrients and space needed by normal cells and disrupt the function of normal tissues.

Humans suffer from at least 200 types of cancer. Stated another way, cancer is not a single illness but a complex family of diseases that affect an array of organs, including the breast, colon, brain, lung, and skin (**FIGURE 12.13**). In addition, several types of cancer can affect the same organ. Skin cancers, for example, come in multiple forms.

Although cancers vary in time of onset, growth rate, seriousness, and cause, they have a unifying feature: Cancers arise from cells in which cell-cycle checkpoints have failed.

Cancerous cells have two types of defects related to cell division: (**1**) defects that make the proteins required for cell growth active when they shouldn't be, and (**2**) defects that prevent tumor suppressor genes from shutting down the cell cycle.

For example, the protein Ras is a key component in signal transduction systems—including phosphorylation cascades that trigger cell growth (see Chapter 11). Many cancers have defective forms of Ras that do not become inactivated. Instead, the defective Ras constantly sends signals that trigger mitosis and cell division.

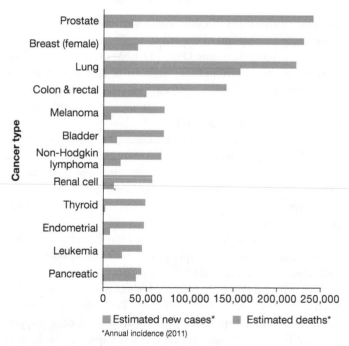

FIGURE 12.13 Cancers Vary in Type and Severity.

DATA: The website of the National Cancer Institute (http://www.cancer.gov), Common Cancer Types, November 2010.

Likewise, a large percentage of cancers have defective forms of the tumor suppressor p53. Instead of being arrested or destroyed, cells with damaged DNA are allowed to continue growing.

Let's review the general characteristics of cancer and then explore how regulatory mechanisms become defective.

Properties of Cancer Cells

When even a single cell in a multicellular organism begins to divide in an uncontrolled fashion, a mass of cells called a tumor may result. If a tumor can be surgically removed without damage to the affected organ, a cure might be achieved. Often, though, surgery doesn't cure cancer. Why?

In addition to uncontrolled replication, cancer cells are invasive—meaning that they are able to spread to adjacent tissues and throughout the body via the bloodstream or the lymphatic vessels, which collect excess fluid from tissues and return it to the bloodstream.

Invasiveness is a defining feature of a **malignant tumor**—one that is cancerous. Masses of noninvasive cells are noncancerous and form **benign tumors.** Some benign tumors are largely harmless. Others grow quickly and can cause problems if they are located in the brain or other sensitive parts of the body.

Cells become malignant and cancerous if they gain the ability to detach from the original tumor and invade other tissues. By spreading from the primary tumor site, cancer cells can establish secondary tumors elsewhere in the body (**FIGURE 12.14**). This process is called **metastasis.**

If metastasis has occurred by the time the original tumor is detected, secondary tumors have already formed and surgical removal of the primary tumor will not lead to a cure. This is why early detection is the key to treating cancer most effectively.

Cancer Involves Loss of Cell-Cycle Control

What causes cancer at the molecular level? Recall that when many cells mature, they enter the G_0 phase—meaning their cell cycle is arrested at the G_1 checkpoint. In contrast, cells that do pass through the G_1 checkpoint are irreversibly committed to replicating their DNA and entering G_2.

Based on this observation, biologists hypothesize that many types of cancer involve defects in the G_1 checkpoint. To understand the molecular nature of the disease, then, researchers have focused on understanding the normal mechanisms that operate at that checkpoint. Cancer research and research on the normal cell cycle have become two sides of the same coin.

Social Control   In unicellular organisms, passage through the G_1 checkpoint is thought to depend primarily on cell size and the availability of nutrients. If nutrients are plentiful, cells pass through the checkpoint and divide rapidly.

In multicellular organisms, however, cells divide in response to signals from other cells. Biologists refer to this as *social control* over cell division. The general idea is that individual cells should be allowed to divide only when their growth is in the best interests of the organism as a whole.

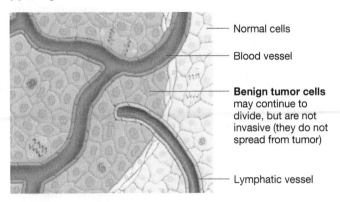

(a) Benign tumor

— Normal cells

— Blood vessel

— **Benign tumor cells** may continue to divide, but are not invasive (they do not spread from tumor)

— Lymphatic vessel

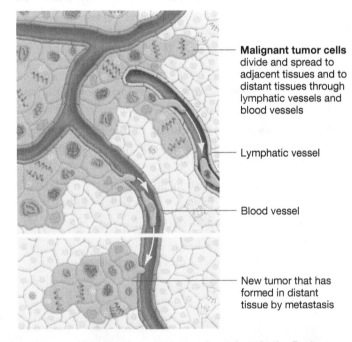

(b) Malignant tumor

— **Malignant tumor cells** divide and spread to adjacent tissues and to distant tissues through lymphatic vessels and blood vessels

— Lymphatic vessel

— Blood vessel

— New tumor that has formed in distant tissue by metastasis

FIGURE 12.14 Cancers Spread to New Locations in the Body.
(a) Benign tumors grow in a single location. **(b)** Malignant tumors are metastatic—meaning that their cells can spread to distant parts of the body and initiate new tumors. Malignant tumors cause cancer.

Social control of the cell cycle is based on **growth factors**—polypeptides or small proteins that stimulate cell division. Many growth factors were discovered by researchers who were trying to grow cells in culture. When isolated mammalian cells were placed in a culture flask and provided with adequate nutrients, they arrested in G_1 phase. The cells began to grow again only when biologists added **serum**—the liquid portion of blood that remains after blood cells and cell fragments have been removed. Researchers identified growth factors as the components in the serum that were responsible for allowing cells to pass through the G_1 checkpoint.

Cancer cells are an exception. They can often be cultured successfully without externally supplied growth factors. This observation suggests that the normal social controls on the G_1 checkpoint have broken down in cancer cells.

How Does the G₁ Checkpoint Work? In G_0 cells, the arrival of growth factors stimulates the production of a key regulatory protein called E2F. When E2F is activated, it triggers the expression of genes required for S phase.

When E2F is first produced, however, its activity is blocked by a tumor suppressor protein called Rb. **Rb protein** is one of the key molecules that enforces the G_1 checkpoint. It is called Rb because a nonfunctional version was first discovered in children with retinoblastoma, a cancer in the light-sensing tissue, or retina, of the eye.

When E2F is bound to Rb, it is in the "off" position—it can't activate the genes required for S phase. As long as Rb stays bound to E2F, the cell remains in G_0. But as **FIGURE 12.15** shows, the situation changes dramatically if growth factors continue to arrive. To understand how growth factors affect E2F activity, think back to how cells progress from G_2 to M phase. As in passage from G_2 to M phase, phosphorylation of other proteins catalyzed by an activated cyclin–Cdk dimer permits passage from G_1 to S.

Step 1 Growth factors arrive from other cells.

Step 2 The growth factors stimulate the production of E2F and of G_1 cyclins, which are different from those used in MPF.

Step 3 Rb binds to E2F, inactivating it. The G_1 cyclins begin forming cyclin–Cdk dimers. Initially, the Cdk component is phosphorylated and inactive.

Step 4 When dephosphorylation turns on the G_1 cyclin–Cdk complexes, they catalyze the phosphorylation of Rb.

Step 5 The phosphorylated Rb changes shape and releases E2F.

Step 6 The unbound E2F is free to activate its target genes. Production of S-phase proteins gets S phase under way.

In this way, growth factors function as a social signal that says, "It's OK to override Rb. Go ahead and pass the G_1 checkpoint and divide."

How Do Social Controls and Cell-Cycle Checkpoints Fail? Cells can become cancerous when social controls fail—meaning, when cells begin dividing in the absence of the go-ahead signal from growth factors. One of two things can go wrong: The G_1 cyclin is overproduced, or Rb is defective.

When cyclins are overproduced and stay at high concentrations, the Cdk that binds to cyclin phosphorylates Rb continuously. This activates E2F and sends the cell into S phase.

Cyclin overproduction results from (1) excessive amounts of growth factors or (2) cyclin production in the absence of growth signals. Cyclins are produced continuously when a signaling pathway is defective. Because this pathway includes the Ras protein (highlighted in Chapter 11), it is common to find overactive Ras proteins in cancerous cells.

What happens if Rb is defective? When Rb is missing or does not bind normally to E2F, any E2F that is present pushes the cell through the G_1 checkpoint and into S phase, leading to uncontrolled cell division.

Because cancer is actually a family of diseases with a complex and highly variable molecular basis, there will be no "magic bullet," or single therapy, that cures all forms of the illness. Still, recent progress in understanding the cell cycle and the molecular basis of cancer has been dramatic, and cancer prevention and early detection programs are increasingly effective. The prognosis for many cancer patients is remarkably better now than it was even a few years ago. Thanks to research, almost all of us know someone who is a cancer survivor.

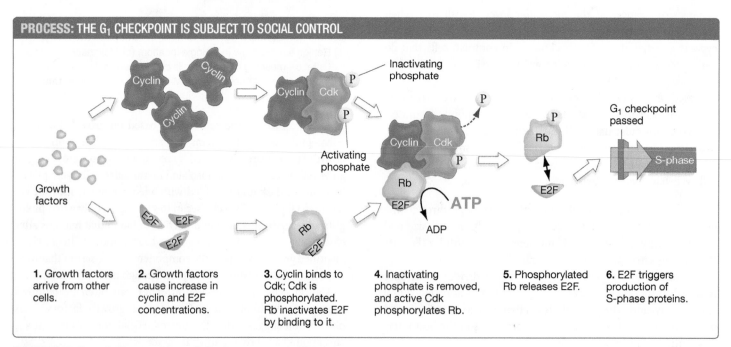

PROCESS: THE G₁ CHECKPOINT IS SUBJECT TO SOCIAL CONTROL

1. Growth factors arrive from other cells.

2. Growth factors cause increase in cyclin and E2F concentrations.

3. Cyclin binds to Cdk; Cdk is phosphorylated. Rb inactivates E2F by binding to it.

4. Inactivating phosphate is removed, and active Cdk phosphorylates Rb.

5. Phosphorylated Rb releases E2F.

6. E2F triggers production of S-phase proteins.

FIGURE 12.15 Growth Factors Move Cells through the G₁ Checkpoint.

If you understand . . .

12.1 How Do Cells Replicate?

- When a cell divides, it must copy its chromosomes, separate the copies, and divide the cytoplasm to generate daughter cells such that each carries the same chromosomal complement as the parent.
- Eukaryotic cells divide by alternating between interphase and M phase.
- Interphase consists of S phase, when chromosomes are replicated, and gap phases called G_1 and G_2, when cells grow and prepare for division.
- Eukaryotic cells divide by cycling through four phases: G_1, S, G_2, and M. Mature cells arrest at G_1 and enter a nonreplicating phase called G_0.

✓ You should be able to explain the roles of each of the four stages of the cell cycle.

12.2 What Happens during M Phase?

- Mitosis and cytokinesis are responsible for the partitioning of chromosomes and division of the parent cell into two daughter cells.
- Mitosis can be described as a sequence of five phases:
  1. *Prophase* Chromosomes condense. The spindle apparatus begins to form, and polar microtubules overlap each other.
  2. *Prometaphase* In cells of many organisms, the nuclear envelope disintegrates. Microtubules attach to the kinetochores of chromosomes and begin moving them to the middle of the spindle.
  3. *Metaphase* All the chromosomes are positioned in the middle of the spindle. The spindle is anchored to the cell membrane by astral microtubules.
  4. *Anaphase* Sister chromatids are pulled apart by the disassembly of kinetochore microtubules at the kinetochore. The separated chromatids are now daughter chromosomes. The spindle poles are moved farther apart to fully separate the replicated chromosomes.
  5. *Telophase* Daughter chromosomes are fully separated and are clustered at opposite poles of the spindle. A nuclear envelope forms around each set and the chromosomes de-condense.
- In most cells, mitosis is followed by cytokinesis—division of all cell contents.

✓ You should be able to predict how mitosis would be different in cells where the nuclear envelope remains intact (e.g., yeast).

12.3 Control of the Cell Cycle

- The onset of S and M phases is primarily determined by the activity of protein dimers consisting of cyclin and cyclin-dependent kinases (Cdks).

- Cyclin concentrations oscillate during the cell cycle, regulating the formation of the dimer. The activity of the Cdk is further regulated by addition of a phosphate in its activating site and removal of one from its inhibitory site.
- Progression through the cell cycle is controlled by checkpoints in three phases.
  1. The G_1 checkpoint regulates progress based on nutrient availability, cell size, DNA damage, and social signals.
  2. The G_2 checkpoint delays progress until chromosome replication is complete and any damaged DNA that is present is repaired.
  3. The two M-phase checkpoints will (1) delay anaphase until all chromosomes are correctly attached to the spindle apparatus and (2) delay the onset of cytokinesis and G_1 until all the chromosomes have been properly partitioned.

✓ You should be able to predict what would happen if the kinase that adds the inhibitory phosphates to Cdk were defective.

12.4 Cancer: Out-of-Control Cell Division

- Cancer is characterized by (1) loss of control at the G_1 checkpoint, resulting in cells that divide in an uncontrolled fashion; and (2) metastasis, or the ability of tumor cells to spread throughout the body.
- The G_1 checkpoint depends in part on Rb, which prevents progression to S phase, and G_1 cyclin–Cdk complexes that trigger progression to S phase. Defects in Rb and G_1 cyclin are common in human cancer cells.

✓ You should be able to compare and contrast the effect of removing growth factors from asynchronous cultures of human cells that are normal versus those that are cancerous.

(MB) **MasteringBiology**

1. **MasteringBiology Assignments**

   Tutorials and Activities Causes of Cancer; Cell Culture Methods; Four Phases of the Cell Cycle; Mitosis (1 of 3): Mitosis and the Cell Cycle; Mitosis (2 of 3): Mechanism of Mitosis; Mitosis (3 of 3): Comparing Cell Division in Animals, Plants, and Bacteria; Mitosis and Cytokinesis Animation; Roles of Cell Division; The Cell Cycle; The Phases of Mitosis

   Questions Reading Quizzes, Blue-Thread Questions, Test Bank

2. **eText** Read your book online, search, take notes, highlight text, and more.

3. **The Study Area** Practice Test, Cumulative Test, BioFlix® 3-D Animations, Videos, Activities, Audio Glossary, Word Study Tools, Art

You should be able to . . .

1. Which statement about the daughter cells following mitosis and cytokinesis is correct?
   a. They are genetically different from each other and from the parent cell.
   b. They are genetically identical with each other and with the parent cell.
   c. They are genetically identical with each other but different from the parent cell.
   d. Only one of the two daughter cells is genetically identical with the parent cell.

2. Progression through the cell cycle is regulated by oscillations in the concentration of which type of molecule?
   a. p53, Rb, and other tumor suppressors
   b. receptor tyrosine kinases
   c. cyclin-dependent kinases
   d. cyclins

3. After the S phase, what comprises a single chromosome?
   a. two daughter chromosomes
   b. a double-stranded DNA molecule
   c. two single-stranded molecules of DNA
   d. two sister chromatids

4. What major events occur during anaphase of mitosis?
   a. Chromosomes replicate, so each chromosome consists of two identical sister chromatids.
   b. Chromosomes condense and the nuclear envelope disappears.
   c. Sister chromatids separate, and the spindle poles are pushed farther apart.
   d. The chromosomes end up at opposite ends of the cell, and two nuclear envelopes form around them.

5. What evidence suggests that during anaphase, kinetochore microtubules shorten at the kinetochore?

6. Under normal conditions, what happens to the cell cycle if the chromosomes fail to separate properly at anaphase?

7. Identify at least two events in the cell cycle that must be completed successfully for daughter cells to share an identical complement of chromosomes.

8. Make a concept map illustrating normal events at the G_1 checkpoint. Your diagram should include p53, DNA damage, Rb, E2F, social signals, G_1 Cdk, G_1 cyclin, S-phase proteins, phosphorylated (inactivated) cyclin–Cdk, dephosphorylated (activated) cyclin–Cdk, phosphorylated (inactivated) Rb.

9. Explain how microinjection experiments supported the hypothesis that specific molecules in the cytoplasm are involved in the transition from interphase to M phase. What was the control for this experiment?

10. Why are most protein kinases considered regulatory proteins?

11. Why are cyclins called cyclins? Explain their relationship to MPF activity.

12. In multicellular organisms, nondividing cells stay in G_0 phase. For the cell, why is it better to be held in G_1 rather than S, G_2, or M phase?
    a. G_1 cells are larger and more likely to perform the normal functions of the cell.
    b. G_1 cells have not replicated their DNA in preparation for division.
    c. G_1 cells are the only ones that do not have their chromatin in a highly condensed state.
    d. MPF is required to enter S phase, so the cell is committed to entering M phase if the cycle moves beyond G_1.

13. **QUANTITATIVE** A particular cell spends 4 hours in G_1 phase, 2 hours in S phase, 2 hours in G_2 phase, and 30 minutes in M phase. If a pulse–chase assay were performed with radioactive thymidine on an asynchronous culture, what percentage of mitotic cells would be radiolabeled after 9 hours?
    a. 0%
    b. 50%
    c. 75%
    d. 100%

14. When fruit fly embryos first begin to develop, a large cell is generated that contains over 8000 nuclei that are genetically identical with one another. What is most likely responsible for this result?

15. What is most likely responsible for the reduction in death rates over the past several years in cancers of the breast and prostate? How is this related to the development of cancer?

16. Cancer is primarily a disease of older people. Further, a group of individuals may share a genetic predisposition to developing certain types of cancer, yet vary a great deal in time of onset—or not get the disease at all. What conclusion could be drawn based on these observations? How does this relate to the requirements for a cell to become cancerous?

15 DNA and the Gene: Synthesis and Repair

15 DNA and the Gene: Synthesis and Repair

In this chapter you will learn how

DNA replication and repair preserve genetic information

by asking

What are genes made of?
15.1

by analyzing

DNA synthesis: early hypotheses
15.2

expanding to

Steps in replication: a model for faithful DNA synthesis
15.3

and ways to

Replicate ends of linear chromosomes
15.4

Correct DNA errors; repair DNA damage
15.5

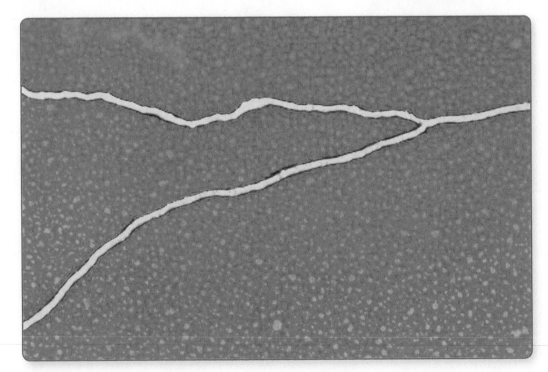

Electron micrograph (with color added) showing DNA in the process of replication. The original DNA double helix (far right) is being replicated into two DNA double helices (on the left). The two helices diverge at the replication fork, which is where DNA synthesis is taking place.

This chapter is part of the Big Picture. See how on pages 366–367.

What are genes made of, and how are they copied so that they are faithfully passed on to offspring? These questions dominated biology during the middle of the twentieth century. Since Mendel's time, the predominant research strategy in genetics had been to conduct a series of experimental crosses, create a genetic model to explain the types and proportions of phenotypes that resulted, and then test the model's predictions through reciprocal crosses, testcrosses, or other techniques. This strategy led to virtually all the discoveries of classical genetics, including Mendel's rules, sex linkage, linkage, and quantitative inheritance.

The chemical composition and molecular structure of Mendel's hereditary factors—which came to be called genes—remained a mystery for the first half of the twentieth century. Although biologists knew that genes and chromosomes were replicated during the cell cycle, with copies distributed

✓ When you see this checkmark, stop and test yourself. Answers are available in Appendix A.

to daughter cells during mitosis and meiosis (see Chapter 12), no one had the slightest clue about how the copying occurred.

The goal of this chapter is to explore how researchers solved these mysteries. The results provided a link between two of the five attributes of life (introduced in Chapter 1): processing genetic information and replication. (You can see how DNA synthesis and repair fits into the Big Picture of Genetic Information on pages 366–367.)

How are genes copied, so they can be passed on to succeeding generations? Let's begin with studies that identified the nature of the genetic material, then explore how genes are copied during the synthesis phase of the cell cycle, and conclude by analyzing how incorrectly copied or damaged genes are repaired. Once the molecular nature of the gene was known, the nature of biological science changed forever.

15.1 What Are Genes Made Of?

The chromosome theory of inheritance proposed that chromosomes contain genes. It had been known since the late 1800s that chromosomes are a complex of DNA and proteins. The question, then, of what genes are made of came down to a simple choice: DNA or protein?

Initially, most biologists backed the hypothesis that genes are made of proteins. The arguments in favor of this hypothesis were compelling. Hundreds, if not thousands, of complex and highly regulated chemical reactions occur in even the simplest living cells. The amount of information required to specify and coordinate these reactions is mind-boggling. With their almost limitless variation in structure and function, proteins are complex enough to contain this much information.

In contrast, DNA was known to be composed of just four types of deoxyribonucleotides (Chapter 4). Early but incorrect evidence suggested that DNA was a simple molecule with some sort of repetitive and uninteresting structure. It seemed impossible that such a simple compound could hold complex information.

DNA or protein? The experiment that settled the question is considered a classic in biological science.

The Hershey–Chase Experiment

In 1952 Alfred Hershey and Martha Chase took up the question of whether genes were made of protein or DNA by studying how a virus called T2 infects and replicates within the bacterium *Escherichia coli*. Nearly 10 years before Hershey and Chase began their study, Oswald Avery and colleagues showed in 1944 that DNA could serve as genetic material, but many scientists remained unconvinced of the finding or its generality. Hershey and Chase knew that T2 infections begin when the virus attaches to the cell wall of *E. coli* and injects its genes into the cell's interior (**FIGURE 15.1a**). These genes then direct the production of a new generation of

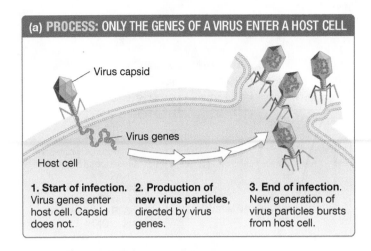

(a) PROCESS: ONLY THE GENES OF A VIRUS ENTER A HOST CELL

Virus capsid

Virus genes

Host cell

1. Start of infection. Virus genes enter host cell. Capsid does not.

2. Production of new virus particles, directed by virus genes.

3. End of infection. New generation of virus particles bursts from host cell.

(b) The virus's capsid stays outside the cell.

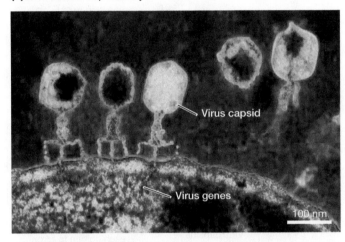

Virus capsid

Virus genes

100 nm

FIGURE 15.1 Viruses Inject Genes into Bacterial Cells and Leave a Capsid Behind. Color has been added to the transmission electron micrograph in (b) to make key structures more visible.

virus particles inside the infected cell, which acts as a host for the virus. (For more information on viruses, see Chapter 36.)

During the infection, the exterior protein coat, or **capsid,** of the original, parent virus is left behind. The capsid remains attached to the exterior of the host cell (**FIGURE 15.1b**). Hershey and Chase also knew that T2 is made up almost exclusively of protein and DNA. Was it protein or DNA that entered the host cell and directed the production of new viruses?

Hershey and Chase's strategy for determining the composition of the viral substance that enters the cell and acts as the hereditary material was based on two biochemical facts: (**1**) Proteins contain sulfur but not phosphorus, and (**2**) DNA contains phosphorus but not sulfur.

As **FIGURE 15.2** (see page 286) shows, the researchers began their work by growing viruses in the presence of either a radioactive isotope of sulfur (^{35}S) or a radioactive isotope of phosphorus (^{32}P). Because these isotopes were incorporated into newly synthesized proteins and DNA, this step produced a population of viruses with radioactive proteins and a population with radioactive DNA.

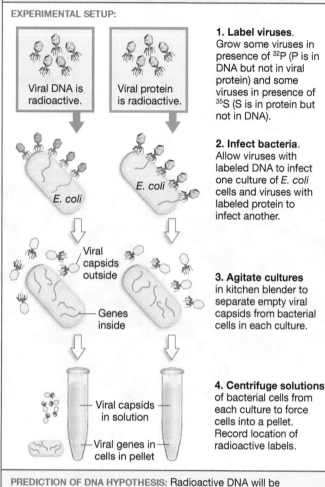

QUESTION: Do viral genes consist of DNA or protein?

DNA HYPOTHESIS: Viral genes consist of DNA.

PROTEIN HYPOTHESIS: Viral genes consist of protein.

EXPERIMENTAL SETUP:

Viral DNA is radioactive.

Viral protein is radioactive.

1. Label viruses. Grow some viruses in presence of ^{32}P (P is in DNA but not in viral protein) and some viruses in presence of ^{35}S (S is in protein but not in DNA).

E. coli

E. coli

2. Infect bacteria. Allow viruses with labeled DNA to infect one culture of *E. coli* cells and viruses with labeled protein to infect another.

Viral capsids outside

Genes inside

3. Agitate cultures in kitchen blender to separate empty viral capsids from bacterial cells in each culture.

Viral capsids in solution

Viral genes in cells in pellet

4. Centrifuge solutions of bacterial cells from each culture to force cells into a pellet. Record location of radioactive labels.

PREDICTION OF DNA HYPOTHESIS: Radioactive DNA will be located within pellet.

PREDICTION OF PROTEIN HYPOTHESIS: Radioactive protein will be located within pellet.

RESULTS:

Radioactive protein is in solution

Radioactive DNA is in pellet

DNA

Protein

CONCLUSION: Viral genes consist of DNA.

FIGURE 15.2 Experimental Evidence that DNA Is the Hereditary Material.

SOURCE: Hershey, A. D., and M. Chase. 1952. Independent functions of viral protein and nucleic acid in growth of bacteriophage. *Journal of General Physiology* 36: 39–56.

✔ **QUESTION** What evidence would these investigators have to produce to convince you that the viral capsids were shaken off the bacterial cells by the agitation step?

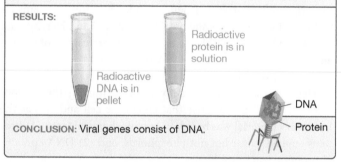

Hershey and Chase allowed each set of radioactive viruses to infect *E. coli* cells. If genes consist of DNA, then radioactive protein should be found only in the capsids outside the infected host cells, while radioactive DNA should be located inside the cells. But if genes consist of proteins, then radioactive protein—and no radioactive DNA—should be inside the cells.

To test these predictions, Hershey and Chase sheared the capsids off the cells by vigorously agitating each of the cultures in kitchen blenders. When the researchers spun the samples in a centrifuge, the small phage capsids remained in the solution while the cells formed a pellet at the bottom of the centrifuge tube (see **BioSkills 10** in Appendix B to review how centrifugation works).

As predicted by the DNA hypothesis, the biologists found that virtually all the radioactive protein was outside cells in the emptied capsids, while virtually all the radioactive DNA was inside the host cells. Because the injected component of the virus directs the production of a new generation of virus particles, this component must represent the virus's genes.

After these results were published, proponents of the protein hypothesis accepted that DNA, not protein, must be the hereditary material. An astonishing claim—that DNA contained all the information for life's complexity—was correct.

The Secondary Structure of DNA

In 1953, one year after Hershey and Chase's landmark results were published, Watson and Crick proposed a model for the secondary structure of DNA. Recall that DNA is typically double-stranded with each strand consisting of a long, linear polymer made up of monomers called deoxyribonucleotides (Chapter 4).

Each deoxyribonucleotide consists of a deoxyribose sugar, a phosphate group, and a nitrogenous base (**FIGURE 15.3a**). Deoxyribonucleotides link together into a polymer when a phosphodiester bond forms between a hydroxyl group on the 3′ carbon of one deoxyribose and the phosphate group attached to the 5′ carbon of another deoxyribose. The two strands together make up one DNA molecule that functions as the genetic information storage molecule of cells.

As **FIGURE 15.3b** shows, the primary structure of each strand of DNA has two major features: (**1**) a "backbone" made up of the sugar and phosphate groups of deoxyribonucleotides and (**2**) a series of bases that project from the backbone. Each strand of DNA has a directionality, or polarity: One end has an exposed hydroxyl group on the 3′ carbon of a deoxyribose, while the other has an exposed phosphate group on a 5′ carbon. Thus, the molecule has distinctly different 3′ and 5′ ends.

As they explored different models for the secondary structure of DNA, Watson and Crick hit on the idea of lining up two of these long strands in opposite directions, or in what is called antiparallel fashion (**FIGURE 15.4a**). They realized that antiparallel strands will twist around each other into a spiral or helix because certain bases fit together snugly in pairs inside the spiral and form hydrogen bonds (**FIGURE 15.4b**). The double-stranded molecule that results is called a **double helix.**

(a) Structure of a deoxyribonucleotide

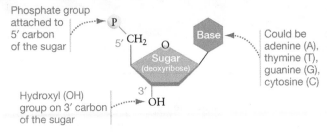

Phosphate group attached to 5′ carbon of the sugar

Base — Could be adenine (A), thymine (T), guanine (G), cytosine (C)

Sugar (deoxyribose)

Hydroxyl (OH) group on 3′ carbon of the sugar

(b) Primary structure of DNA

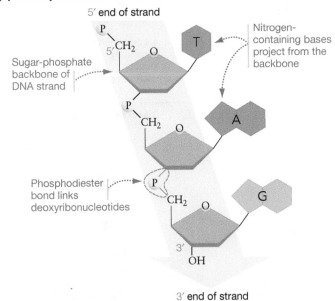

5′ end of strand

Sugar-phosphate backbone of DNA strand

Nitrogen-containing bases project from the backbone

Phosphodiester bond links deoxyribonucleotides

3′ end of strand

FIGURE 15.3 DNA's Primary Structure. (a) Deoxyribonucleotides are monomers that polymerize to form DNA. **(b)** DNA's primary structure is made up of a sequence of deoxyribonucleotides. Notice that the structure has a sugar–phosphate "backbone" with nitrogen-containing bases attached.

✔ **EXERCISE** Write the base sequence of the DNA in part (b), in the 5′ → 3′ direction.

The double-helical DNA is stabilized by hydrogen bonds that form between the bases adenine (A) and thymine (T) and between the bases guanine (G) and cytosine (C), along with hydrophobic interactions that the bases experience inside the helix. Hydrogen bonding of particular base pairs is **complementary base pairing.**

15.2 Testing Early Hypotheses about DNA Synthesis

Watson and Crick realized that the A-T and G-C pairing rules suggested a way for DNA to be copied when chromosomes are replicated during S phase of the cell cycle, before mitosis and meiosis. They suggested that the existing strands of DNA served as a template (pattern) for the production of new strands and that deoxyribonucleotides were added to the new strands according to complementary base pairing. For example, if the template

(a) Complementary base pairing   **(b)** The double helix

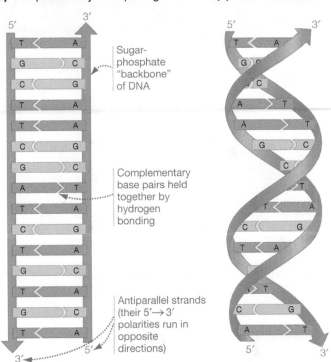

Sugar-phosphate "backbone" of DNA

Complementary base pairs held together by hydrogen bonding

Antiparallel strands (their 5′ → 3′ polarities run in opposite directions)

FIGURE 15.4 DNA's Secondary Structure: The Double Helix. (a) DNA normally consists of two strands, each with a sugar–phosphate backbone. Nitrogen-containing bases project from each strand and form hydrogen bonds. Only A-T and G-C pairs fit together in a way that allows hydrogen bonding to occur between the strands. **(b)** Bonding between complementary bases twists the molecule into a double helix.

strand contained a T, then an A would be added to the new strand to pair with that T. Similarly, a G on the template strand would dictate the addition of a C on the new strand.

Complementary base pairing provided a mechanism for DNA to be copied. But many questions remained about how the copying was done.

Three Alternative Hypotheses

Biologists at the time proposed three alternative hypotheses about how the old and new strands might interact during replication:

1. *Semiconservative replication* If the old, **parental strands** of DNA separated, each could then be used as a template for the synthesis of a new, **daughter strand.** This hypothesis is called **semiconservative replication** because each new daughter DNA molecule would consist of one old strand and one new strand.

2. *Conservative replication* If the bases temporarily turned outward so that complementary strands no longer faced each other, they could serve as a template for the synthesis of an entirely new double helix all at once. This hypothesis, called conservative replication, would result in an intact parental

QUESTION: Is replication semiconservative, conservative, or dispersive?

HYPOTHESIS 1:	HYPOTHESIS 2:	HYPOTHESIS 3:
Replication is semiconservative.	Replication is conservative.	Replication is dispersive.

EXPERIMENTAL SETUP:

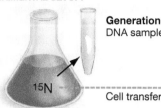 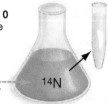 

Generation 0
DNA sample

Generation 1
DNA sample

Generation 2
DNA sample

Cell transfer

1. Grow *E. coli* cells in medium with ^{15}N as sole source of nitrogen for many generations. Collect sample and purify DNA.

2. Transfer cells to medium containing ^{14}N. After cells divide once, collect sample and purify DNA.

3. After cells have divided a second time in ^{14}N medium, collect sample and purify DNA.

4. Centrifuge the three samples separately. Compare the locations of the DNA bands in each sample.

PREDICTIONS:

Semiconservative replication	Conservative replication	Dispersive replication

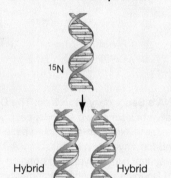 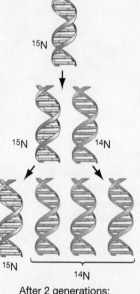 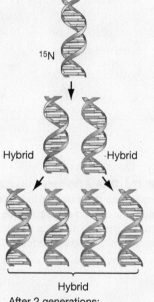

Generation 0

^{15}N

^{15}N

^{15}N

Generation 1

Hybrid   Hybrid

^{15}N ^{14}N

Hybrid   Hybrid

Generation 2

Hybrid ^{14}N Hybrid ^{14}N

^{15}N ^{14}N

Hybrid

After 2 generations:
1/2 low-density DNA (^{14}N)
1/2 intermediate-density DNA (hybrid)

After 2 generations:
1/4 high-density DNA (^{15}N)
3/4 low-density DNA (^{14}N)

After 2 generations:
All intermediate-density DNA (hybrid)

RESULTS:

Top of centrifuge
tube (lower density)

  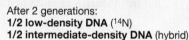 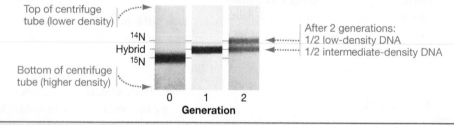

^{14}N
Hybrid
^{15}N

After 2 generations:
1/2 low-density DNA
1/2 intermediate-density DNA

Bottom of centrifuge
tube (higher density)

0   1   2
Generation

CONCLUSION: Data from generation 1 conflict with conservative replication hypothesis. Data from generation 2 conflict with dispersive replication hypothesis. Replication is semiconservative.

FIGURE 15.5 The Meselson–Stahl Experiment.

SOURCE: Meselson, M., and F. W. Stahl. 1958. The replication of DNA in *Escherichia coli*. *Proceedings of the National Academy of Sciences USA* 44: 671–682.

✔**EXERCISE** Meselson and Stahl actually let their experiment run for a fourth generation with cultures growing in the presence of ^{14}N. Explain what data from third- and fourth-generation DNA should look like—that is, where the DNA band(s) should be.

molecule and a daughter DNA molecule consisting entirely of newly synthesized strands.

3. **Dispersive replication** If the parental double helix were cut wherever one strand crossed over another and DNA was synthesized in short sections by extending each of the cut parental strands to the next strand crossover, then there would be a mix of new and old segments along each replicated molecule. This possibility is called dispersive replication—stretches of old DNA would be interspersed with new DNA down the length of each daughter strand.

Matthew Meselson and Franklin Stahl realized that if they could tag or mark parental and daughter strands of DNA in a way that would make them distinguishable from each other, they could determine whether replication was conservative, semiconservative, or dispersive.

The Meselson–Stahl Experiment

Before Meselson and Stahl could do any tagging to distinguish old DNA from new DNA, they needed to choose an organism to study. They decided to work with the bacterium *Escherichia coli*—the same inhabitant of the human gastrointestinal tract that Hershey and Chase used. Because *E. coli* is small and grows quickly and readily in the laboratory, it had become a favored model organism in studies of biochemistry and molecular genetics. (See **BioSkills 13** in Appendix B for more on *E. coli*.)

Like all organisms, bacterial cells copy their entire complement of DNA, or their **genome**, before every cell division. To distinguish parental strands of DNA from daughter strands when *E. coli* replicated, Meselson and Stahl grew the cells for successive generations in the presence of different isotopes of nitrogen: first ^{15}N and later ^{14}N. Because ^{15}N contains an extra neutron, it is heavier than the normal isotope, ^{14}N.

This difference in mass, which creates a difference in density between ^{14}N-containing and ^{15}N-containing DNA, was the key to the experiment summarized in **FIGURE 15.5**. The logic ran as follows:

- If different nitrogen isotopes were available in the growth medium when different generations of DNA were produced, then the parental and daughter strands would have different densities.

- The technique called density-gradient centrifugation separates molecules based on their density (**BioSkills 10** in Appendix B). Low-density molecules cluster in bands high in the centrifuge tube; higher-density molecules cluster in bands lower in the centrifuge tube.

- When intact, double-stranded DNA molecules are subjected to density-gradient centrifugation, DNA that contains ^{14}N should form a band higher in the centrifuge tube; DNA that contains ^{15}N should form a band lower in the centrifuge tube.

In short, DNA containing ^{14}N and DNA containing ^{15}N should form separate bands. How could this tagging system be used to test whether replication is semiconservative, conservative, or dispersive?

Meselson and Stahl began by growing *E. coli* cells with nutrients that contained only ^{15}N. They purified DNA from a sample of these cells and transferred the rest of the culture to a growth medium containing only the ^{14}N isotope. After enough time had elapsed for these cells to divide once—meaning that the DNA had been copied once—they removed a sample and isolated the DNA. After the remainder of the culture had divided again, they removed another sample and isolated its DNA.

As Figure 15.5 shows, the conservative, semiconservative, and dispersive models make distinct predictions about the makeup of the DNA molecules after replication occurs in the first and second generation. Examine the figure carefully to understand these distinct predictions.

The photograph at the bottom of Figure 15.5 shows the experiment's results. After one generation, the density of the DNA molecules was intermediate. These data suggested that the hypothesis of conservative replication was wrong, since it predicted two different densities in the first generation.

After two generations, a lower-density band appeared in addition to the intermediate-density band. This result offered strong support for the hypothesis that DNA replication is semiconservative. Had dispersive replication occurred, the second generation would have produced only a single, intermediate density band. Each newly made DNA molecule comprises one old strand and one new strand—replication is semiconservative.

15.3 A Model for DNA Synthesis

The DNA inside a cell is like an ancient text that has been painstakingly copied and handed down, generation after generation. But while the most ancient of all human texts contain messages that are thousands of years old, the DNA in living cells has been copied and passed down for billions of years. And instead of being copied by monks or clerks, DNA is replicated by molecular scribes. What molecules are responsible for copying DNA, and how do they work?

Meselson and Stahl showed that each strand of DNA is copied in its entirety each time replication occurs, but how does DNA synthesis proceed? Does it require an input of energy in the form of ATP, or it is spontaneous? Is it catalyzed by an enzyme, or does it occur quickly on its own?

The initial breakthrough on DNA replication came with the discovery of an enzyme called **DNA polymerase,** so named because it polymerizes deoxyribonucleotides into DNA. This protein catalyzes DNA synthesis. Follow-up work showed that there are several types of DNA polymerase. DNA polymerase III, for example, is the enzyme that is primarily responsible for copying *E. coli*'s chromosome before cell division.

FIGURE 15.6 (see page 290) illustrates a critical characteristic of DNA polymerases: They can work in only one direction. DNA polymerases can add deoxyribonucleotides only to the 3′ end of a growing DNA chain. As a result, DNA synthesis always proceeds in the 5′ → 3′ direction. ✔ If you understand this

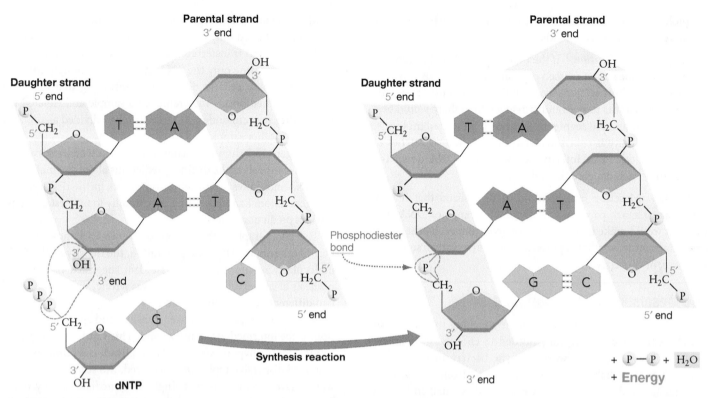

FIGURE 15.6 The DNA Synthesis Reaction. A condensation reaction results in formation of a phosphodiester bond between the 3′ carbon on the end of a DNA strand and the 5′ carbon on an incoming deoxyribonucleoside triphosphate (dNTP) monomer.

concept, you should be able to draw two lines representing a DNA molecule, assign the 3′-to-5′ polarity of each strand, and then label the direction in which DNA synthesis will proceed for each strand.

Figure 15.6 makes another important point about DNA synthesis. You might recall from earlier chapters that polymerization reactions generally are endergonic, meaning they require an input of energy. But for DNA synthesis, the reaction is exergonic (it releases energy) because the monomers that are used in the DNA synthesis reaction are **deoxyribonucleoside triphosphates (dNTPs).** (The *N* in dNTP stands for any of the four bases found in DNA: adenine, thymine, guanine, or cytosine). Because they have three closely spaced phosphate groups, dNTPs have high potential energy—high enough to make the formation of phosphodiester bonds in a growing DNA strand exergonic as two of the phosphates are cleaved off (see Chapter 8).

How Does Replication Get Started?

Another major insight into the mechanism of DNA synthesis emerged when electron microscopy caught DNA replication in action. As **FIGURE 15.7a** shows, a "bubble" forms when DNA is being synthesized. Initially, the replication bubble forms at a specific sequence of bases called the **origin of replication** (**FIGURE 15.7b**). Bacterial chromosomes have only one origin of replication, and thus a single replication bubble forms. Eukaryotes have multiple origins of replication along each chromosome, and thus multiple replication bubbles (**FIGURE 15.7c**).

DNA synthesis is bidirectional—that is, it occurs in both directions at the same time. Therefore, replication bubbles grow in two directions as DNA replication proceeds.

A specific set of proteins are responsible for recognizing sites where replication begins and opening the double helix at those points. These proteins are activated by the proteins that initiate S phase in the cell cycle (see Chapter 12).

Once a replication bubble opens at the origin of replication, a different set of enzymes takes over to start DNA synthesis. Active DNA synthesis takes place at the replication forks of each replication bubble (shown in Figure 15.7c). The **replication fork** is the Y-shaped region where the parent–DNA double helix is split into two single strands and copied.

How Is the Helix Opened and Stabilized?

A large group of enzymes and specialized proteins converge on the point where the double helix opens. The enzyme called **DNA helicase** breaks the hydrogen bonds between the base pairs. This reaction causes the two strands of DNA to separate. **Single-strand DNA-binding proteins (SSBPs)** attach to the separated strands and prevent them from snapping back into a double helix. Working together, DNA helicase and single-strand DNA-binding proteins open up the double helix and maintain the separation of both strands during copying (**FIGURE 15.8**, step 1).

The "unzipping" process that occurs at the replication fork creates tension farther down the helix. To understand why, imagine what would happen if you started to pull apart the twisted

(a) DNA being replicated

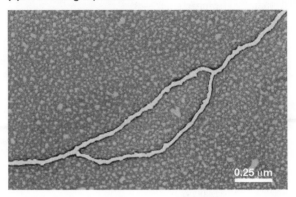

0.25 μm

(b) Bacterial chromosomes have a single origin of replication.

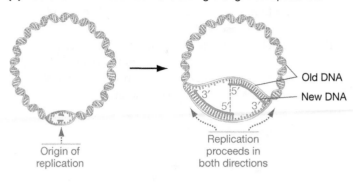

Old DNA
New DNA

Origin of
replication

Replication
proceeds in
both directions

(c) Eukaryotic chromosomes have multiple origins of replication.

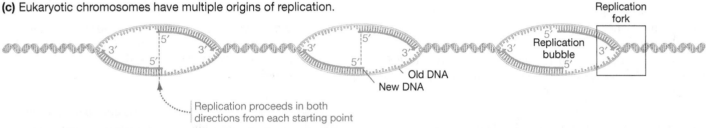

Replication
fork

Replication
bubble

Old DNA
New DNA

Replication proceeds in both
directions from each starting point

FIGURE 15.7 DNA Synthesis Proceeds in Two Directions from an Origin of Replication. Color has been added to the micrograph in part (a).

strands of a rope. The untwisting movements at one end would force the intact section to rotate in response. If the intact end of the rope were fixed in place, it would coil on itself in response to the twisting forces. DNA does not become tightly coiled ahead of the replication fork, because the twisting induced by helicase is relaxed by proteins called topoisomerases. A **topoisomerase** is an enzyme that cuts DNA, allows it to unwind, and rejoins it ahead of the advancing replication fork.

Now, what happens once the DNA helix is open?

How Is the Leading Strand Synthesized?

The keys to understanding what happens at the start of DNA synthesis are to recall that DNA polymerase (**1**) works only in the $5' \rightarrow 3'$ direction and (**2**) requires both a $3'$ end to extend from and a single-stranded template. Both of these properties control how synthesis occurs on both template strands of DNA, and as you'll soon see, they significantly complicate copying one of these. The single-stranded template dictates which

PROCESS: SYNTHESIS OF LEADING STRAND

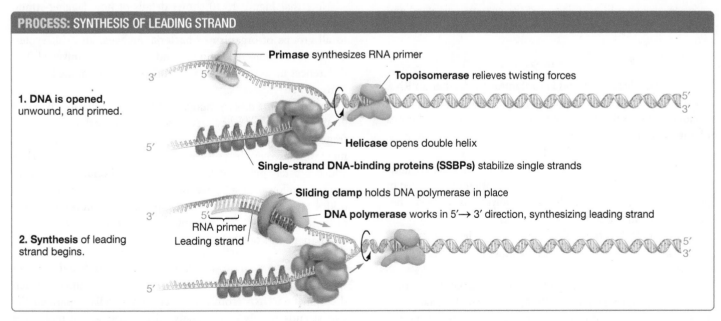

1. **DNA is opened,** unwound, and primed.

Primase synthesizes RNA primer
Topoisomerase relieves twisting forces
Helicase opens double helix
Single-strand DNA-binding proteins (SSBPs) stabilize single strands

2. **Synthesis** of leading strand begins.

Sliding clamp holds DNA polymerase in place
DNA polymerase works in $5' \rightarrow 3'$ direction, synthesizing leading strand
RNA primer
Leading strand

FIGURE 15.8 Leading-Strand Synthesis.

deoxyribonucleotide should be added next. A **primer**—a strand a few nucleotides long that is bonded to the template strand—provides DNA polymerase with a free 3′ hydroxyl (−OH) group that can combine with an incoming deoxyribonucleotide to form a phosphodiester bond. As shown in the figure below and in Figure 15.8, step 2, primers used during cellular DNA synthesis are short RNA strands, not DNA strands.

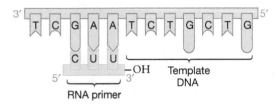

But what adds the primer? Before DNA synthesis can get under way, an enzyme called **primase** synthesizes a short stretch of RNA that acts as a primer for DNA polymerase. The primer is about 10 nucleotides long in *E. coli*. Primase is a type of **RNA polymerase**—an enzyme that catalyzes the polymerization of ribonucleotides into RNA (see Chapter 4 to review RNA's structure). Unlike DNA polymerases, primase and other RNA polymerases do not require a primer to begin synthesis.

Once a primer is present on a single-stranded template, DNA polymerase begins working in the 5′ → 3′ direction and adds deoxyribonucleotides to complete the complementary strand. As Figure 15.8, step 2, shows, DNA polymerase has a shape that grips the DNA strand during synthesis, similar to your hand clasping a rope. Deoxyribonucleotide addition is catalyzed at an active site in a groove between the enzyme's "thumb" and "fingers." As DNA polymerase moves along the DNA molecule, a doughnut-shaped structure behind it, called the sliding clamp, holds the enzyme in place on the template strand.

The enzyme's product is called the **leading strand,** or **continuous strand,** because it leads into the replication fork and is synthesized continuously. ✔ If you understand leading-strand synthesis, you should be able to list the enzymes involved and predict the consequences if any of them are defective.

How Is the Lagging Strand Synthesized?

Synthesis of the leading strand is straightforward. After an RNA primer is in place, DNA polymerase moves along, adding deoxyribonucleotides to the 3′ end of that strand. The enzyme moves into the replication fork, which "unzips" ahead of it. By comparison, events on the opposite strand are more involved.

Recall that the two strands of the DNA double helix are antiparallel—meaning they lie parallel to one another but oriented in opposite directions. The fact that DNA polymerases can synthesize DNA only in the 5′ → 3′ direction creates a paradox. Only one strand of DNA at the replication fork—the leading strand—can be synthesized in a direction that follows the moving replication fork.

The other strand must be synthesized in a direction that runs *away* from the moving replication fork, as illustrated in **FIGURE 15.9**. The strand of DNA that extends in the direction away from the

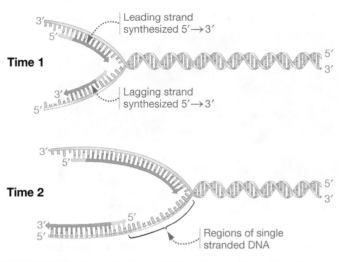

FIGURE 15.9 The Lagging Strand Is Synthesized in a Direction Moving Away from the Replication Fork. This occurs because the DNA strands are antiparallel and DNA polymerase can work only in the 5′ → 3′ direction.

replication fork is called the **lagging strand,** or **discontinuous strand,** because it lags behind the synthesis occurring at the fork. As the replication fork moves, it exposes gaps of single-stranded template DNA (Time 2 in Figure 15.9). How are the growing gaps filled in?

The Discontinuous Replication Hypothesis   The puzzle posed by lagging-strand synthesis was resolved when Reiji Okazaki and colleagues tested a hypothesis called discontinuous replication. This hypothesis held that primase synthesizes new RNA primers for lagging strands as the moving replication fork opens single-stranded regions of DNA, and that DNA polymerase uses these primers to synthesize short lagging-strand DNA fragments that are linked together into a continuous strand. These ideas are illustrated in **FIGURE 15.10**.

Note that Figure 15.10 shows details of how lagging-strand synthesis occurs in *E. coli*. The overall process, however, applies to all groups of organisms—bacteria, archaea, and eukaryotes. The basic reactions of lagging-strand synthesis are universal. The differences lie in the names or specific properties of the key proteins and enzymes.

To explore the discontinuous replication hypothesis, Okazaki's group set out to test a key prediction: Could they find short DNA fragments produced during replication? Their critical experiment was based on the pulse–chase strategy (see Chapter 7). They added a brief "pulse" of radioactive deoxyribonucleotides to *E. coli* cells, followed by a "chase" of nonradioactive deoxyribonucleotides. According to the discontinuous replication model, some of these radioactive deoxyribonucleotides should first appear in short, fragments of DNA.

The Discovery of Okazaki Fragments   As predicted, the researchers succeeded in finding short DNA fragments when they purified DNA from the experimental cells, separated the two strands of DNA, and analyzed the size of the molecules

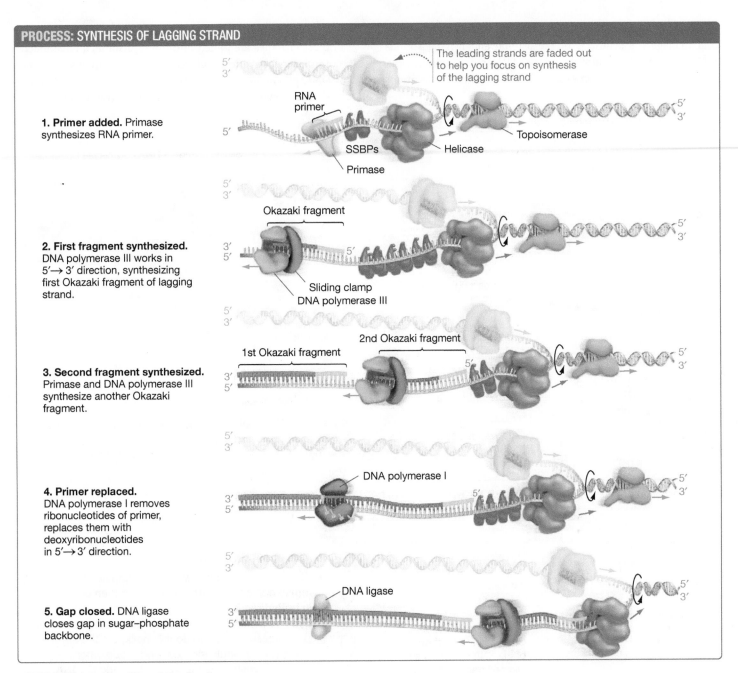

1. Primer added. Primase synthesizes RNA primer.

2. First fragment synthesized. DNA polymerase III works in 5′→ 3′ direction, synthesizing first Okazaki fragment of lagging strand.

3. Second fragment synthesized. Primase and DNA polymerase III synthesize another Okazaki fragment.

4. Primer replaced. DNA polymerase I removes ribonucleotides of primer, replaces them with deoxyribonucleotides in 5′→ 3′ direction.

5. Gap closed. DNA ligase closes gap in sugar–phosphate backbone.

FIGURE 15.10 Lagging-Strand Synthesis.

by centrifugation. A small number of labeled DNA fragments about 1000 base pairs long were present immediately after the pulse. These short DNAs came to be known as **Okazaki fragments** and are shown in steps 2 and 3 of Figure 15.10. These small DNAs became larger during the chase as they were linked together into longer pieces. Subsequent work showed that Okazaki fragments in eukaryotes are even smaller—just 100 to 200 base pairs long.

How are Okazaki fragments connected? First, as step 4 of Figure 15.10 shows, in *E. coli* a specialized DNA polymerase called DNA polymerase I attaches to the 3′ end of an Okazaki fragment. As DNA polymerase I moves along in the 5′ → 3′ direction, it removes that RNA primer ahead of it and replaces the ribonucleotides with the appropriate deoxyribonucleotides.

Once the RNA primer is removed and replaced by DNA, an enzyme called **DNA ligase** catalyzes the formation of a phosphodiester bond between the adjacent fragments (Figure 15.10, step 5). ✔ If you understand lagging-strand synthesis, you should be able to draw what the two newly synthesized molecules of DNA at a single replication fork would look like if DNA ligase were defective.

In eukaryotes, the mechanism for primer removal is different, but the mechanism of synthesizing short Okazaki fragments that are later joined into an unbroken chain of DNA is the same.

Working together, the enzymes that open the replication fork and manage the synthesis of the leading and lagging strands (**TABLE 15.1**) produce faithful copies of DNA before cell division. Although separate enzymes are drawn at different locations around the replication fork in Figures 15.8 and 15.10, in reality, all these enzymes are joined into the **replisome,** a large macromolecular machine. In *E. coli*, the replisome contains two copies of DNA polymerase III that are actively engaged in DNA synthesis. As shown in **FIGURE 15.11**, the lagging strand loops out and

SUMMARY TABLE 15.1 **Proteins Required for DNA Synthesis in Bacteria**

Name	Structure	Function
Opening the helix		
Helicase		Catalyzes the breaking of hydrogen bonds between base pairs to open the double helix
Single-strand DNA-binding proteins (SSBPs)		Stabilizes single-stranded DNA
Topoisomerase		Breaks and rejoins the DNA double helix to relieve twisting forces caused by the opening of the helix
Leading strand synthesis		
Primase		Catalyzes the synthesis of the RNA primer
DNA polymerase III		Extends the leading strand
Sliding clamp		Holds DNA polymerase in place during strand extension
Lagging strand synthesis		
Primase		Catalyzes the synthesis of the RNA primer on an Okazaki fragment
DNA polymerase III		Extends an Okazaki fragment
Sliding clamp		Holds DNA polymerase in place during strand extension
DNA polymerase I		Removes the RNA primer and replaces it with DNA
DNA ligase		Catalyzes the joining of Okazaki fragments into a continuous strand

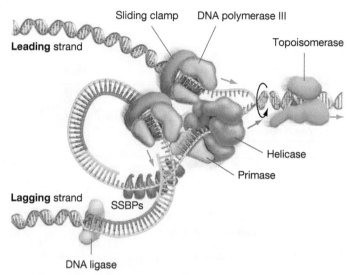

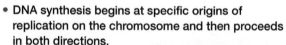

FIGURE 15.11 The Replisome. The enzymes required for DNA synthesis are organized into a macromolecular machine. Note how the lagging strand loops out as the leading strand is being synthesized.

check your understanding

C Y U

If you understand that . . .

- DNA synthesis begins at specific origins of replication on the chromosome and then proceeds in both directions.
- Synthesis at the replication fork occurs in three steps: (1) Helicase opens the double helix, SSBPs stabilize the exposed single strands, and topoisomerase prevents twists downstream of the fork; (2) DNA polymerase synthesizes the leading strand after primase has added an RNA primer; and (3) A series of enzymes synthesize the lagging strand.
- Lagging-strand synthesis cannot be continuous, because it moves away from the replication fork. In bacteria, enzymes called primase, DNA polymerase III, DNA polymerase I, and ligase work in sequence to synthesize Okazaki fragments and link them into a continuous whole.

✔ You should be able to . . .

1. Explain the function of primase.
2. Explain why DNA polymerase I is used predominantly on the lagging strand.

Answers are available in Appendix A.

around the complex, allowing the replisome to move as a single unit as it follows the replication fork. After the DNA polymerase on the lagging strand completes synthesis of an Okazaki fragment, it is released from the DNA and reassembles on the most recently synthesized primer.

15.4 Replicating the Ends of Linear Chromosomes

The circular DNA molecules in bacteria and archaea can be synthesized by the enzymes introduced in Section 15.3, and so can most of the linear DNA molecules found in eukaryotes. But replication at the very ends of linear eukaryotic chromosomes is another story altogether. Replication of chromosome ends requires a specialized DNA replication enzyme that has been the subject of intense research.

The End Replication Problem

The region at the end of a eukaryotic chromosome is called a **telomere** (literally, "end-part"). **FIGURE 15.12** illustrates the problem that arises during the replication of telomeres.

- When the replication fork reaches the end of a linear chromosome, a eukaryotic DNA polymerase synthesizes the leading strand all the way to the end of the parent DNA template (step 1 and step 2, top strand). As a result, leading-strand synthesis results in a double-stranded copy of the DNA molecule.

- On the lagging strand, primase adds an RNA primer close to the tip of the chromosome (see step 2, bottom strand).

- DNA polymerase synthesizes the final Okazaki fragment on the lagging strand (step 3). An enzyme that degrades ribonucleotides removes the primer.

PROCESS: PROBLEMS WITH COPYING THE ENDS OF LINEAR CHROMOSOMES

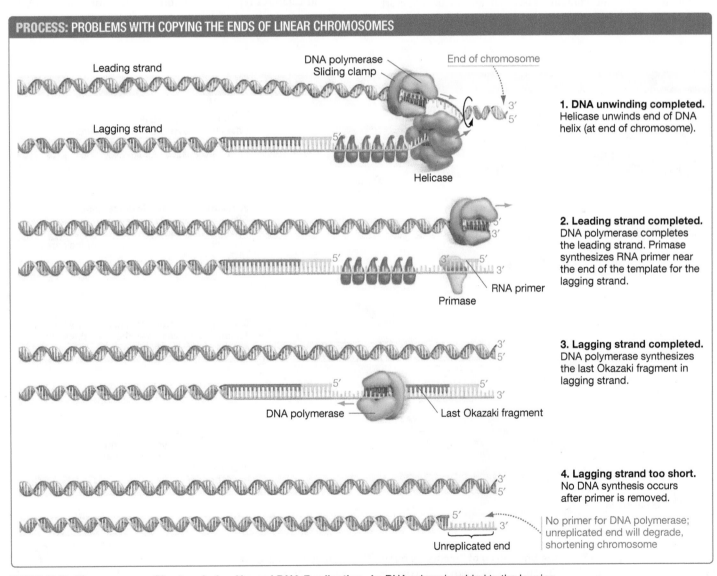

1. DNA unwinding completed. Helicase unwinds end of DNA helix (at end of chromosome).

2. Leading strand completed. DNA polymerase completes the leading strand. Primase synthesizes RNA primer near the end of the template for the lagging strand.

3. Lagging strand completed. DNA polymerase synthesizes the last Okazaki fragment in lagging strand.

4. Lagging strand too short. No DNA synthesis occurs after primer is removed.

No primer for DNA polymerase; unreplicated end will degrade, shortening chromosome

FIGURE 15.12 Chromosomes Shorten during Normal DNA Replication. An RNA primer is added to the lagging strand near the end of the chromosome. Once the primer is removed, it cannot be replaced with DNA. As a result, the chromosome shortens.

- DNA polymerase is unable to add DNA near the tip of the chromosome, because it cannot synthesize DNA without a primer (step 4). As a result, the single-stranded DNA that is left stays single stranded.

The single-stranded DNA at the end of the lagging strand is eventually degraded, which results in the shortening of the chromosome. If this process were to continue unabated, every chromosome would shorten by about 50 to 100 deoxyribonucleotides each time DNA replication occurred. Over time, linear chromosomes would vanish.

Telomerase Solves the End Replication Problem

How do eukaryotes maintain their chromosomes? One answer emerged after Elizabeth Blackburn, Carol Greider, and Jack Szostak reported two striking discoveries:

1. Telomeres do not contain genes but are made of short stretches of bases that are repeated over and over. In human telomeres, for example, the base sequence TTAGGG is repeated thousands of times.

2. A remarkable enzyme called telomerase that carries its own template is involved in replicating telomeres.

Telomerase is extraordinary because it catalyzes the synthesis of DNA from an RNA template that it contains. Telomerase adds DNA onto the end of a chromosome to prevent it from getting shorter.

FIGURE 15.13 shows one model for how telomerase works to maintain the ends of eukaryotic chromosomes.

Step 1 The unreplicated segment of the telomere at the 3′ end of the template for the lagging strand forms a single-stranded "overhang".

Step 2 Telomerase binds to the overhanging single-stranded DNA and begins DNA synthesis. The template for this reaction is a portion of the RNA held within telomerase.

Step 3 Telomerase synthesizes DNA in the 5′ → 3′ direction and catalyzes repeated additions of the same short DNA sequence to the end of the growing single strand.

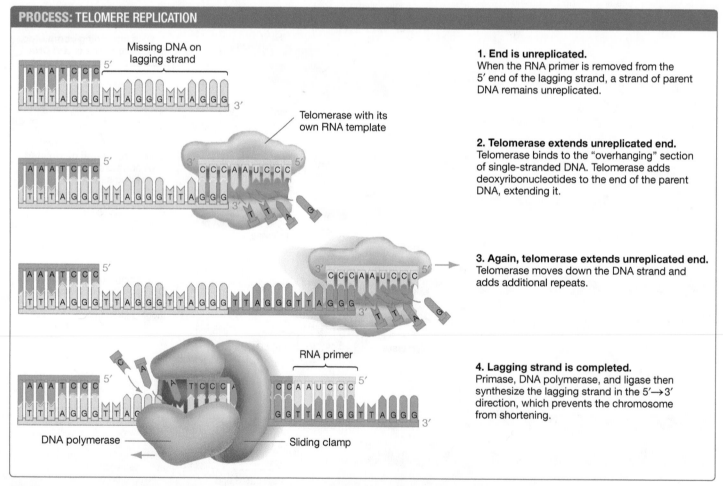

PROCESS: TELOMERE REPLICATION

1. End is unreplicated.
When the RNA primer is removed from the 5′ end of the lagging strand, a strand of parent DNA remains unreplicated.

2. Telomerase extends unreplicated end.
Telomerase binds to the "overhanging" section of single-stranded DNA. Telomerase adds deoxyribonucleotides to the end of the parent DNA, extending it.

3. Again, telomerase extends unreplicated end.
Telomerase moves down the DNA strand and adds additional repeats.

4. Lagging strand is completed.
Primase, DNA polymerase, and ligase then synthesize the lagging strand in the 5′→3′ direction, which prevents the chromosome from shortening.

FIGURE 15.13 Telomerase Prevents Shortening of Telomeres during Replication. By extending the number of repeated sequences in the 5′ → 3′ direction, telomerase provides room for enzymes to add an RNA primer to the lagging-strand template. Normal DNA replication enzymes can then fill in the missing section of the lagging strand.

✔**QUESTION** Would this telomerase work as well if its RNA template had a different sequence?

Step 4 Once the single-stranded overhang on the parent strand is lengthened, the normal enzymes of DNA synthesis use this strand as a template to synthesize a complementary strand. The result is that the lagging strand becomes slightly longer than it was originally.

Telomerase Regulation

The way telomerase is regulated is just as remarkable as the enzyme itself. Telomerase is active in only a limited number of cell types. In humans, for example, active telomerase is found primarily in the cells that produce gametes. Most **somatic cells,** meaning cells that are not involved in gamete formation, lack telomerase activity. As predicted, the chromosomes of somatic cells gradually shorten with each mitotic division, becoming progressively smaller as an individual ages.

These observations led to the hypothesis that the number of cell divisions possible for a somatic cell would be limited by the initial length of its telomeres. Carol Greider and colleagues tested this hypothesis by obtaining cells with a variety of telomere lengths from donors aged newborn to 90 years old and growing these cells in culture. (For an introduction to cell culture, see **BioSkills 12** in Appendix B.) Results of their study are shown in **FIGURE 15.14**. As predicted, there was a positive relationship between initial telomere length and the number of cell divisions before cells stop dividing—longer initial telomere length allowed a greater number of cell divisions, regardless of the donor's age.

You've probably noticed that the data points in Figure 15.14 do not fall perfectly on a line. This scatter or noise is typical in many studies. In interpreting results like these, researchers must consider what might account for the scatter and use statistical tests (see **BioSkills 4** in Appendix B) to determine how reliable the results are likely to be.

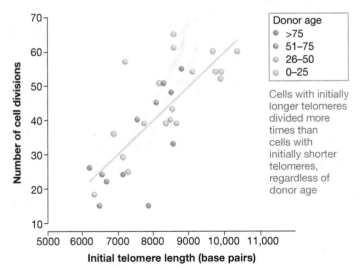

FIGURE 15.14 Telomere Length Predicts the Number of Divisions before Cells Stop Dividing.

DATA: Allsopp, R. C., et al. 1992. *Proceedings of the National Academy of Sciences,* 82: 10114–10118.

If telomere shortening controls the number of divisions possible for a cell, then a related prediction is that by restoring telomerase in somatic cells, these cells should be freed from growth limitations. As predicted, when researchers added telomerase to human cells growing in culture, the cells continued dividing long past the age when otherwise identical cells stop growing. Most biologists are convinced that telomere shortening has a role in limiting the number of cell divisions for somatic cells.

There is a dark side of telomerase activity, however. Unlike the somatic cells they derive from, most cancer cells have active telomerase. Many cancer biologists have proposed that telomerase activity allows the unlimited divisions of cancer cells. A simple prediction is that by inhibiting telomerase, the progression of cancer can be slowed or stopped. When combined with other approaches, could drugs that knock out telomerase be an effective way to fight cancer? Unfortunately, the complexity of cancer often thwarts such simple predictions. So far, answers to this question are unclear. Research continues.

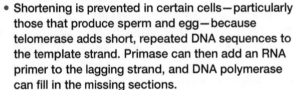

If you understand that . . .

- Linear chromosomes shorten during replication because the end of the lagging strand lacks a primer and cannot be synthesized.
- Shortening is prevented in certain cells—particularly those that produce sperm and egg—because telomerase adds short, repeated DNA sequences to the template strand. Primase can then add an RNA primer to the lagging strand, and DNA polymerase can fill in the missing sections.

✔ **You should be able to . . .**

1. Explain why telomerase is not needed by bacterial cells.
2. Explain why telomerase has to have a built-in template.

Answers are available in Appendix A.

15.5 Repairing Mistakes and DNA Damage

DNA polymerases work fast. In *E. coli*, for example, each replication fork advances about 500 nucleotides per second. But the replication process is also astonishingly accurate. In organisms ranging from *E. coli* to animals, the error rate during DNA replication averages about one mistake per *billion* deoxyribonucleotides.

This level of accuracy is critical. Humans, for example, develop from a fertilized egg that has roughly 12 billion deoxyribonucleotides in its DNA. This DNA is replicated over and over to create the trillions of cells that eventually make up the adult body. If more than one or two mutations occurred during each cell division cycle as a person developed, genes would be riddled with errors by the time the individual reached maturity. Genes that contain errors are often defective.

Based on these observations, it is no exaggeration to claim that the accurate replication of DNA is a matter of life and death. Natural selection favors individuals with enzymes that copy DNA quickly and accurately.

These observations raise a key question. How can the enzymes of DNA replication be as precise as they are?

Correcting Mistakes in DNA Synthesis

As DNA polymerase marches along a DNA template, hydrogen bonding occurs between incoming deoxyribonucleotides and the deoxyribonucleotides on the template strand. DNA polymerases are selective about the bases they add to a growing strand because (1) the correct base pairings (A-T and G-C) are energetically the most favorable, and (2) these correct pairings have a distinct shape. As a result, DNA polymerase inserts an incorrect deoxyribonucleotide (**FIGURE 15.15a**) only about once in every 100,000 bases added.

An error rate of one in 100,000 seems low, but it is much higher than the rate of one in a billion listed at the start of this section. What happens when DNA polymerase makes a mistake?

DNA Polymerase Proofreads Biologists learned more about how DNA synthesis could be so accurate when they found mutant cells in which DNA synthesis was *in*accurate.

Specifically, researchers found *E. coli* mutants with error rates that were 100 times greater than normal. Recall that a mutant is an individual with a novel trait caused by a mutation. In the case of *E. coli* mutants with high error rates in DNA

(a) DNA polymerase adds a mismatched base...

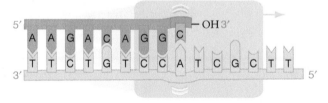

(b) ...but detects the mistake and corrects it.

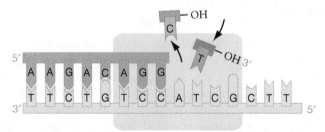

FIGURE 15.15 DNA Polymerase Can Proofread. If a mismatch such as the pairing of A with C occurs **(a)**, DNA polymerase can act as a 3′ → 5′ exonuclease, meaning that it can remove bases in that direction **(b)**. The DNA polymerase then adds the correct base.

replication, biologists found a defect in a portion of the DNA polymerase III enzyme called the ε (epsilon) subunit. Further analyses showed that the ε subunit acts as an exonuclease—meaning an enzyme that removes deoxyribonucleotides from the ends of DNA strands (**FIGURE 15.15b**).

If a newly added deoxyribonucleotide is not correctly paired with a base on the complementary strand, the positioning of the incorrect deoxyribonucleotide provides a poor substrate for DNA polymerase to extend. This is because the geometry of incorrect base pairs differs from that of the correct A-T and G-C pairs. DNA polymerase's active site can detect these shapes and will add a new deoxyribonucleotide only when the previous base pair is correct. In wild-type *E. coli*, the polymerase pauses when it detects the wrong shape, and the exonuclease activity of the ε subunit removes the mismatched deoxyribonucleotide.

These findings led to the conclusion that DNA polymerase III can **proofread**. If the wrong base is added during DNA synthesis, the enzyme pauses, removes the mismatched deoxyribonucleotide that was just added, and then proceeds again with synthesis.

Eukaryotic DNA polymerases have the same type of proofreading ability. Typically, proofreading reduces the overall error rate of DNA synthesis to about one mistake in 10 million bases added. Is this accurate enough? The answer remains no.

Mismatch Repair If—despite its proofreading ability—DNA polymerase leaves a mismatched base behind in the newly synthesized strand, a battery of enzymes springs into action to correct the problem. **Mismatch repair** occurs when mismatched bases are corrected after DNA synthesis is complete.

The proteins responsible for mismatch repair were discovered in the same way proofreading was—by analyzing *E. coli* mutants. In this case, the mutants had normal DNA polymerase III but abnormally high mutation rates.

The first mutation that caused a deficiency in mismatch repair was identified in the late 1960s and was called *mutS*. (The *mut* is short for "mutator.") Twenty years later, researchers had identified 10 proteins involved in the identification and repair of base-pair mismatches in *E. coli*.

These proteins recognize the mismatched base, remove a section containing the incorrect base from the newly synthesized strand, and fill in the correct bases using the older strand as a template. In *E. coli*, chemical marks on the older strand allow the enzymes to distinguish the original strand from the newly synthesized strand. Eukaryotes use a different scheme to recognize the old and new strands of DNA.

This final layer of error detection and correction brings the overall error rate of DNA synthesis down to roughly one mistake per billion deoxyribonucleotides. The mismatch-repair enzymes are like a copy editor who corrects the errors that a writer—DNA polymerase—did not catch.

The importance of mismatch repair is revealed by grim discoveries: Mutations in components of the mismatch repair system are observed in many common human cancers, where they play an important role in cancer development and progression.

Repairing Damaged DNA

Even after DNA is synthesized and proofread and mismatches repaired, the job of ensuring accuracy doesn't end. Genes are under constant assault. DNA is damaged by sunlight, X-rays, and many chemicals like the hydroxyl (OH) radicals produced during aerobic metabolism, aflatoxin B1 found in moldy peanuts and corn, and benzo[α]pyrene in cigarette smoke. If this damage were ignored, mutations would quickly accumulate to lethal levels. To fix problems caused by chemical attack, radiation, or other events, organisms have evolved a wide array of DNA damage-repair systems. As an example, consider the **nucleotide excision repair** system that works on DNA damage caused by ultraviolet light and many different chemicals.

Ultraviolet (UV) light in sunlight—and tanning booths—can cause a covalent bond to form between adjacent pyrimidine bases within the same DNA strand. The thymine-thymine pair illustrated in **FIGURE 15.16** is a common example. This defect, called a thymine dimer, creates a kink in the structure of DNA. The kink stalls standard DNA polymerases, blocking DNA replication. If the damage is not repaired, the cell may die.

Nucleotide excision repair fixes thymine dimers and many other types of damage that distort the DNA helix. In the first step of excision repair, an enzyme recognizes the kink in the DNA helix (step 1 in **FIGURE 15.17**). Once a damaged region is recognized, another enzyme removes a segment of single-stranded DNA containing the defective sequence (step 2). The intact DNA strand provides a template for synthesis of a corrected strand, and the 3′ hydroxyl of the DNA strand next to the gap serves as a primer (step 3). DNA ligase links the newly synthesized DNA to

the original undamaged DNA (step 4). As with mismatch repair, multiple enzymes work together and DNA synthesis plays a central role in repair.

What happens when a human DNA repair system is defective?

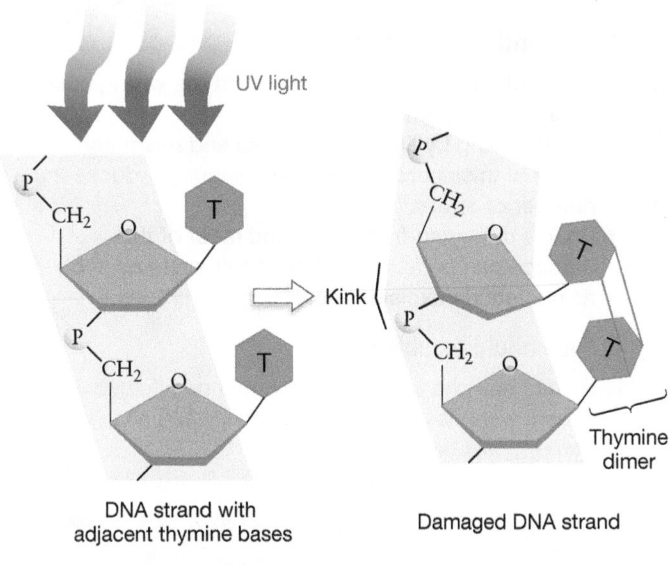

Xeroderma Pigmentosum: A Case Study

Xeroderma pigmentosum (XP) is a rare autosomal recessive disease in humans. Individuals with this condition are extremely sensitive to ultraviolet (UV) light. Their skin develops lesions including rough, scaly patches and irregular dark spots after even slight exposure to sunlight.

In 1968 James Cleaver proposed a connection between XP and DNA nucleotide excision repair. He knew that mutants of *E. coli* had defects in nucleotide excision repair that caused an increased sensitivity to radiation. Cleaver's hypothesis was that people with XP have similar mutations. He proposed that they are extremely sensitive to sunlight because they are unable to repair damage induced by UV light.

Cleaver and other researchers made extensive use of cell cultures (**BioSkills 12**, see Appendix B) to study the hypothesized connection between DNA damage, faulty nucleotide excision repair, and XP. They collected skin cells from people with XP and from people with normal UV light sensitivity. When these cells were grown in culture, the biologists exposed them to increasing amounts of UV radiation and recorded how many survived.

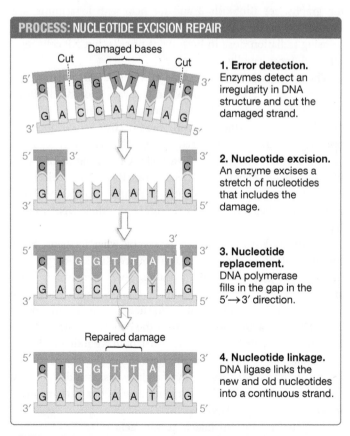

FIGURE 15.17 In Nucleotide Excision Repair, Defective Bases Are Removed and Replaced.

FIGURE 15.16 UV Light Damages DNA. When UV light strikes a section of DNA that has adjacent thymines, the energy can break bonds within each base and lead to the formation of bonds *between* them. The thymine dimer that is produced causes a kink in the DNA.

✔**QUESTION** Why are infrared wavelengths much less likely than UV to damage DNA?

(a) Vulnerability of cells to UV light damage

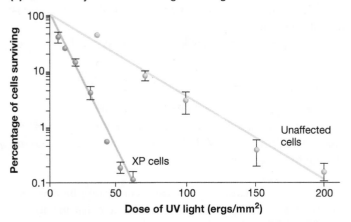

(b) Ability of cells to repair UV light damage

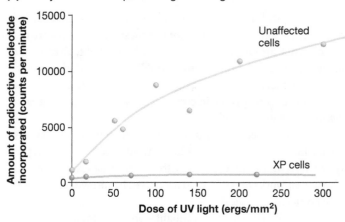

FIGURE 15.18 DNA Damage from UV Light Is Not Repaired Properly in Individuals with XP. (a) When cell cultures from unaffected individuals and XP patients are irradiated with various doses of UV light (expressed here as ergs/mm²), the percentage of cells that survive is strikingly different. **(b)** When cell cultures from unaffected individuals and XP patients are irradiated with various doses of UV light and then provided with a radioactive deoxyribonucleotide, only cells from unaffected individuals incorporate the labeled deoxyribonucleotide into their DNA.

DATA: (a) Cleaver, J. E. 1970. *Int. J. Rad. Biol.* 18: 577–565, Fig 3. (b) Cleaver, J. E. 1972. *J. Invest. Dermatol.* 58: 124–128, Fig 1.

✔ **QUESTION** Why are people who cultivate a sun tan increasing their risk of developing cancer? (Hint: Tanning is a response to UV light.)

FIGURE 15.18a shows the results of one such study by Cleaver. Note that the intensity of the radiation is graphed on the *x*-axis, and the percentage of cells surviving is graphed on the *y*-axis. Note, too, that the *y*-axis is logarithmic. (For help with reading graphs, see **BioSkills 3** and for help with logarithms, see **BioSkills 6**, both in Appendix B.) Cell survival declined with increasing radiation dose in both types of cells, but XP cells died off much more rapidly.

The connection to nucleotide excision repair systems was confirmed in a separate study when Cleaver exposed cells from unaffected and XP individuals to various amounts of UV light and then incubated the cells with a radioactive deoxyribonucleotide to label DNA synthesized during DNA repair. If repair is defective in XP individuals, then their cells should incorporate little radioactive deoxyribonucleotide into their DNA. Cells from unaffected individuals, in contrast, should incorporate large amounts of labeled deoxyribonucleotide into their DNA as it is repaired.

As **FIGURE 15.18b** shows, this is exactly what happens. Here the amount of radioactive deoxyribonucleotides incorporated into DNA is graphed against radiation dose. Increasingly large amounts of radioactivity are found in the DNA of healthy cells as UV dose increases, but almost no such increase occurs in XP cells. These data are consistent with the hypothesis that nucleotide excision repair is virtually nonexistent in XP individuals.

Genetic analyses of XP patients have shown that the condition can result from mutations in any of eight genes. This discovery is not surprising in light of the large number of enzymes involved in repairing damaged DNA.

As you saw for mismatch repair, defects in DNA repair genes are frequently associated with cancer. Individuals with

xeroderma pigmentosum, for example, are 1000 to 2000 times more likely to get skin cancer than are individuals with intact excision repair systems. To explain this pattern, biologists suggest that if DNA damage in the genes involved in the cell cycle goes unrepaired, mutations will result that may allow the cell to grow in an uncontrolled manner. Tumor formation could result. Recall

check your understanding

If you understand that . . .

- DNA polymerases occasionally add the wrong base during DNA synthesis.
- Proofreading by DNA polymerase and mismatch repair of misincorporated bases sharply reduces the number of errors.
- DNA is damaged frequently, and most of this damage can be fixed by DNA repair systems such as nucleotide excision repair.

✔ **You should be able to . . .**

1. Predict how the mutation rate would be affected if there were no differences in stability and shape between all possible base pairs.

2. Predict the effect on mutation rate of a failure in the system for distinguishing old and newly synthesized DNA.

3. State which nucleotide excision repair enzymes are specific for DNA repair and which work in both normal DNA replication and in DNA repair.

Answers are available in Appendix A.

that most cancers develop only after several genes have been damaged (see Chapter 12). If the overall mutation rate in a cell is elevated because of defects in DNA repair, then mutations that trigger cancer become more likely.

At this point, it's clear that genes are made of DNA and that DNA is accurately copied and passed on to offspring. How can information be stored in DNA, and how can this information be used? (These are the topics of the next two chapters.)

If you understand . . .

15.1 What Are Genes Made Of?

- Experiments on viruses that had labeled proteins or DNA showed that DNA is the hereditary material.
- DNA's primary structure consists of a sugar–phosphate backbone and a sequence of nitrogen-containing bases.
- DNA's secondary structure consists of two strands in an antiparallel orientation. The strands twist into a helix and are held together by complementary pairing between bases.

✔ You should be able to interpret an imaginary experiment like the one done by Hershey and Chase that shows that ^{32}P is found only in the pellet and that ^{35}S is found in both the pellet and the solution.

15.2 Testing Early Hypotheses about DNA Synthesis

- By labeling DNA with ^{15}N or ^{14}N, researchers were able to validate the hypothesis that DNA replication is semiconservative.
- In semiconservative replication, each strand of a parent DNA molecule provides a template for the synthesis of a daughter strand, resulting in two complete DNA double helices.

✔ You should be able to write a sequence of double-stranded DNA that is 10 base pairs long, separate the strands, and, without comparing them, write in the bases that are added during DNA replication.

15.3 A Model for DNA Synthesis

- DNA synthesis requires many different enzymes, and it occurs in one direction only.
- DNA synthesis requires both a template and a primer sequence. It takes place at the replication fork where the double helix is opened.
- Synthesis of the leading strand in the $5' \rightarrow 3'$ direction is continuous, but synthesis of the lagging strand is discontinuous because on that strand, the DNA polymerase moves away from the replication fork.

- On the lagging strand, short DNA fragments called Okazaki fragments form and are joined together. Okazaki fragments are primed by a short strand of RNA.

✔ You should be able to draw and label a diagram of a replication bubble that shows (1) the $5' \rightarrow 3'$ polarity of the two parental DNA strands and (2) the leading and lagging daughter strands at each replication fork.

15.4 Replicating the Ends of Linear Chromosomes

- At the ends of linear chromosomes in eukaryotes, the enzyme telomerase adds short, repeated sections of DNA so that the lagging strand can be synthesized without shortening the chromosome.
- Telomerase is active in reproductive cells that eventually undergo meiosis. As a result, gametes contain chromosomes of normal length.
- Chromosomes in cells without telomerase shorten with continued cell division until their telomeres reach a critical length at which cell division no longer occurs.

✔ You should be able to explain the significance of telomerase reactivation in cancer cells.

15.5 Repairing Mistakes and DNA Damage

- DNA replication is remarkably accurate because (1) DNA polymerase selectively adds a deoxyribonucleotide that correctly pairs with the template strand; (2) DNA proofreads each added deoxyribonucleotide; and (3) mismatch repair enzymes remove incorrect bases once synthesis is complete and replace them with the correct base.
- DNA repair occurs after DNA has been damaged by chemicals or radiation.
- Nucleotide excision repair cuts out damaged portions of DNA and replaces them with correct sequences.
- If DNA repair enzymes are defective, mutation rate increases. Because of this, several types of human cancers are associated with defects in the genes responsible for DNA repair.

✔ You should be able to explain the logical connections between failure of repair systems, increases in mutation rate, and high likelihood of cancer developing.

MasteringBiology

1. MasteringBiology Assignments

Tutorials and Activities DNA and RNA Structure; DNA Double Helix; DNA Replication; DNA Replication: A Closer Look; DNA Replication: A Review; DNA Replication: An Overview; DNA Synthesis; Experimental Inquiry: Does DNA Replication Follow the Conservative, Semiconservative, or Dispersive Model; Hershey–Chase Experiment

Questions Reading Quizzes, Blue-Thread Questions, Test Bank

2. eText Read your book online, search, take notes, highlight text, and more.

3. The Study Area Practice Test, Cumulative Test, BioFlix® 3-D Animations, Videos, Activities, Audio Glossary, Word Study Tools, Art

You should be able to . . .

✓ TEST YOUR KNOWLEDGE
Answers are available in Appendix A

1. What does it mean to say that strands in a double helix are antiparallel?
   a. Their primary sequences consist of a sequence of *complementary* bases.
   b. They each have a sugar–phosphate backbone.
   c. They each have a $5' \rightarrow 3'$ directionality.
   d. They have opposite directionality, or polarity.

2. Which of the following is *not* a property of DNA polymerase?
   a. It adds dNTPs only in the $5' \rightarrow 3'$ direction.
   b. It requires a primer to work.
   c. It is associated with a sliding clamp only on the leading strand.
   d. Its exonuclease activity is involved in proofreading.

3. The enzyme that removes twists in DNA ahead of the replication fork is _____.

4. What is the function of primase?
   a. synthesis of the short section of double-stranded DNA required by DNA polymerase
   b. synthesis of a short RNA, complementary to single-stranded DNA
   c. closing the gap at the $3'$ end of DNA after excision repair
   d. removing primers and synthesizing a short section of DNA to replace them

5. How are Okazaki fragments synthesized?
   a. using the leading strand template, and synthesizing $5' \rightarrow 3'$
   b. using the leading strand template, and synthesizing $3' \rightarrow 5'$
   c. using the lagging strand template, and synthesizing $5' \rightarrow 3'$
   d. using the lagging strand template, and synthesizing $3' \rightarrow 5'$

6. An enzyme that uses an internal RNA template to synthesize DNA is _____.

✓ TEST YOUR UNDERSTANDING
Answers are available in Appendix A

7. Researchers design experiments so that only one thing is different between the treatments that are being compared. In the Hershey–Chase experiment, what was this single difference?

8. What is the relationship between defective DNA repair and cancer?

9. Why is the synthesis of the lagging strand of DNA discontinuous? How is it possible for the synthesis of the leading strand to be continuous?

10. Explain how telomerase prevents linear chromosomes from shortening during replication.

11. Predict what would occur in a bacterial mutant that lost the ability to chemically mark the template strand of DNA.
    a. The mutation rate would increase.

    b. The ability of DNA polymerase to discriminate between correct and incorrect base pairs would decrease.
    c. The energy differences between correct and incorrect base pairs would decrease.
    d. The energy differences between correct and incorrect base pairs would increase.

12. What aspect of DNA structure makes it possible for the enzymes of nucleotide excision repair to recognize many different types of DNA damage?
    a. the polarity of each DNA strand
    b. the antiparallel orientation of strands in the double helix
    c. the energy differences between correct and incorrect base pairs
    d. the regularity of DNA's overall structure

13. If you could engineer an activity into DNA polymerase to allow both strands to follow the replication fork, what would this additional activity be?
  a. the ability to begin DNA synthesis without a primer
  b. the ability to proofread in the $5' \rightarrow 3'$ direction
  c. the ability to synthesize DNA in the $3' \rightarrow 5'$ direction
  d. the ability to synthesize DNA without using a template

14. In the late 1950s, Herbert Taylor grew bean root-tip cells in a solution of radioactive thymidine and allowed them to undergo one round of DNA replication. He then transferred the cells to a solution without the radioactive deoxyribonucleotide, allowed them to replicate again, and examined their chromosomes for the presence of radioactivity. His results are shown in the following figure, where red indicates a radioactive chromatid.

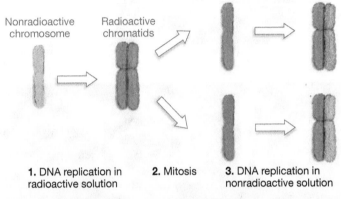

Nonradioactive chromosome   Radioactive chromatids

1. DNA replication in radioactive solution   **2.** Mitosis   **3.** DNA replication in nonradioactive solution

  a. Draw diagrams explaining the pattern of radioactivity observed in the sister chromatids after the first and second rounds of replication.
  b. What would the results of Taylor's experiment be if eukaryotes used a conservative mode of DNA replication?

15. The graph that follows shows the survival of four different *E. coli* strains after exposure to increasing doses of ultraviolet light. The wild-type strain is normal, but the other strains have a mutation in either a gene called *uvrA*, a gene called *recA*, or both.

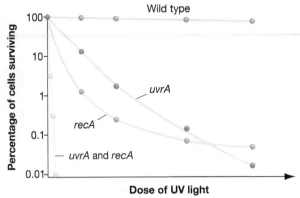

DATA: Howard-Flanders, P., and R. P. Boyce. 1966. *Radiation Research Supplement* 6: 156–184, Fig. 8.

  a. Which strains are most sensitive to UV light? Which strains are least sensitive?
  b. What are the relative contributions of these genes to the repair of UV damage?

16. QUANTITATIVE Assuming that each replication fork moves at a rate of 500 base pairs per second, how long would it take to replicate the *E. coli* chromosome (with 4.6 million base pairs) from a single origin of replication?

16 How Genes Work

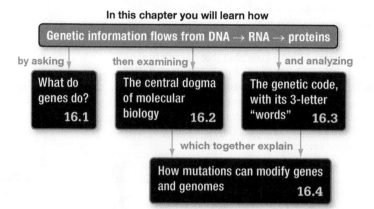

In this chapter you will learn how

Genetic information flows from DNA → RNA → proteins

by asking ↓   *then examining* ↓   *and analyzing* ↓

| What do genes do? **16.1** | The central dogma of molecular biology **16.2** | The genetic code, with its 3-letter "words" **16.3** |

which together explain ↓

How mutations can modify genes and genomes **16.4**

This image shows a normal human male spectral karyotype—a micrograph of metaphase chromosomes stained to show different homologous chromosome pairs. This chapter explores how DNA sequences in chromosomes are related to phenotypes.

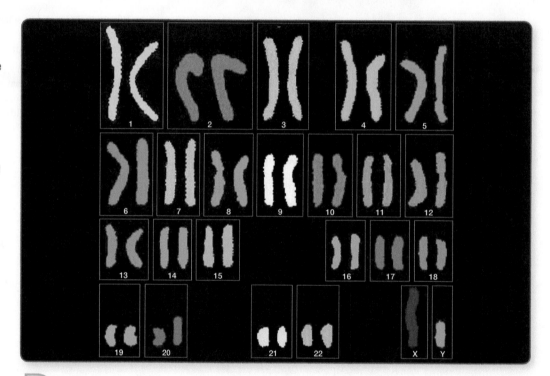

DNA has been called the blueprint of life. If an organism's DNA is like a set of blueprints, then its cells are like construction sites, and the enzymes inside a cell are like construction workers. But how does the DNA inside each cell assemble this team of skilled laborers and specify the materials needed to build and maintain the cell, and remodel it when conditions change?

Mendel provided insights that made the study of these questions possible. He discovered that particular alleles are associated with certain phenotypes and that alleles do not change when transmitted from parent to offspring. Later, the chromosome theory of inheritance established that genes are found in chromosomes, whose movement during meiosis explains Mendel's results.

The science of molecular biology began with the discovery that DNA is the hereditary material and that DNA is a double-helical structure containing sequences of four bases. From these early advances, it was clear that genes are made of DNA and that genes carry the instructions for making and maintaining an individual.

This chapter is part of the Big Picture. See how on pages 366–367.

✔ When you see this checkmark, stop and test yourself. Answers are available in Appendix A.

But biologists still didn't know how the information in DNA is translated into action. How does **gene expression**—the process of converting archived information into molecules that actually do things in the cell—occur?

This chapter introduces some of the most pivotal ideas in all of biology—ideas that connect genotypes to phenotypes by revealing how genes work at the molecular level. They also speak to the heart of a key attribute of life: processing genetic information to produce a living organism. (You can see how these concepts fit into the Big Picture of Genetic Information on pages 366–367.)

Understanding how genes work triggered a major transition in biological science. Instead of thinking about genes solely in relation to their effects on eye color in fruit flies or on seed shape in garden peas, biologists could begin analyzing the molecular composition of genes and their products. The molecular revolution in biology took flight.

16.1 What Do Genes Do?

Although biologists of the early twentieth century made tremendous progress in understanding how genes are inherited, an explicit hypothesis explaining what genes do did not appear until 1941. That year George Beadle and Edward Tatum published a series of breakthrough experiments on a bread mold called *Neurospora crassa*.

Beadle and Tatum's research was inspired by an idea that was brilliant in its simplicity. As Beadle said: "One ought to be able to discover what genes do by making them defective." The idea was to knock out a gene by damaging it and then infer what the gene does by observing the phenotype of the mutant individual.

Today, alleles that do not function at all are called **knock-out, null**, or **loss-of-function alleles.** Creating knock-out mutant alleles and analyzing their effects is still one of the most common research strategies in studies of gene function. But Beadle and Tatum were the pioneers.

The One-Gene, One-Enzyme Hypothesis

To start their work, Beadle and Tatum exposed a large number of *N. crassa* cells to radiation. As described earlier (Chapter 15), radiation can damage the double-helical structure of DNA—often in a way that makes the affected gene nonfunctional.

Their next step was to examine the mutant cells. Eventually they succeeded in finding *N. crassa* mutants that could not make specific compounds. For example, one of the mutants could not make pyridoxine, also called vitamin B_6, even though normal individuals can. Further, Beadle and Tatum showed that the inability to synthesize pyridoxine was due to a defect in a single gene, and that the inability to synthesize other molecules was due to defects in other genes.

These results inspired their **one-gene, one-enzyme hypothesis.** Beadle and Tatum proposed that the mutant *N. crassa* could not make pyridoxine because it lacked an enzyme required to synthesize the compound. They further proposed that the lack of the enzyme was due to a genetic defect. Based on analyses of knock-out mutants, the one-gene, one-enzyme hypothesis claimed that each gene contains the information needed to make an enzyme.

An Experimental Test of the Hypothesis

Three years later, Adrian Srb and Norman Horowitz published a rigorous test of the one-gene, one-enzyme hypothesis. These biologists focused on the ability of *N. crassa* to synthesize the amino acid arginine. In the lab, normal cells of this bread mold grow well on a laboratory culture medium that lacks arginine. This is possible because *N. crassa* cells are able to synthesize their own arginine.

Previous work had shown that organisms synthesize arginine in a series of steps called a **metabolic pathway.** As **FIGURE 16.1** shows, compounds called ornithine and citrulline are intermediate products in the metabolic pathway leading to arginine. Specific enzymes are required to synthesize ornithine, convert ornithine to citrulline, and change citrulline to arginine. Srb and Horowitz hypothesized that specific *N. crassa* genes are responsible for producing each of the three enzymes involved.

To test this idea, Srb and Horowitz used radiation to create a large number of mutant cells. However, radiation is equally likely to damage DNA and mutate genes in any part of the organism's genome, and most organisms have thousands or tens of thousands of genes. Of the many mutants the biologists created, how could they find the handful that specifically knocked out a step in the pathway for arginine synthesis?

To find the mutants they were looking for, the researchers performed what is now known as a genetic screen. A **genetic screen** is any technique for picking certain types of mutants out of many randomly generated mutants.

Srb and Horowitz began their screen by raising colonies of irradiated cells on a medium that included arginine. Then they transferred a sample of each colony to a medium that *lacked* arginine. If an individual could grow in the presence of arginine but failed to grow without arginine, they concluded that it couldn't make its own arginine.

Metabolic pathway for arginine synthesis: Precursor → (Enzyme 1) → Ornithine → (Enzyme 2) → Citrulline → (Enzyme 3) → Arginine

FIGURE 16.1 Different Enzymes Catalyze Each Step in the Metabolic Pathway for Arginine.

✔**QUESTION** If a cell lacked enzyme 2 but was placed in growth medium with ornithine, could it grow? Could it grow if it received citrulline instead?

The biologists followed up by confirming that the offspring of these cells also had this defect. Based on these data, they were confident that they had isolated individuals with mutations in one or more of the genes for the enzymes shown in Figure 16.1.

To test the one-gene, one-enzyme hypothesis, the biologists grew each mutant under four different conditions: on normal media without added arginine, and on normal medium supplemented with ornithine, citrulline, or arginine.

As **FIGURE 16.2** shows, the results from these growth experiments were dramatic. Some of the mutant cells were able to grow on some of these media but not on others. More specifically, the mutants fell into three distinct classes, which the researchers called *arg1*, *arg2*, and *arg3*.

As the "Interpretation" section of the figure shows, the data make sense if each type of mutant lacked a different, specific step in a metabolic pathway because of a defect in a particular gene. In short, Srb and Horowitz had documented a correlation between a specific genetic defect and a defect at a specific point in a metabolic pathway. This experiment convinced most investigators that the one-gene, one-enzyme hypothesis was correct.

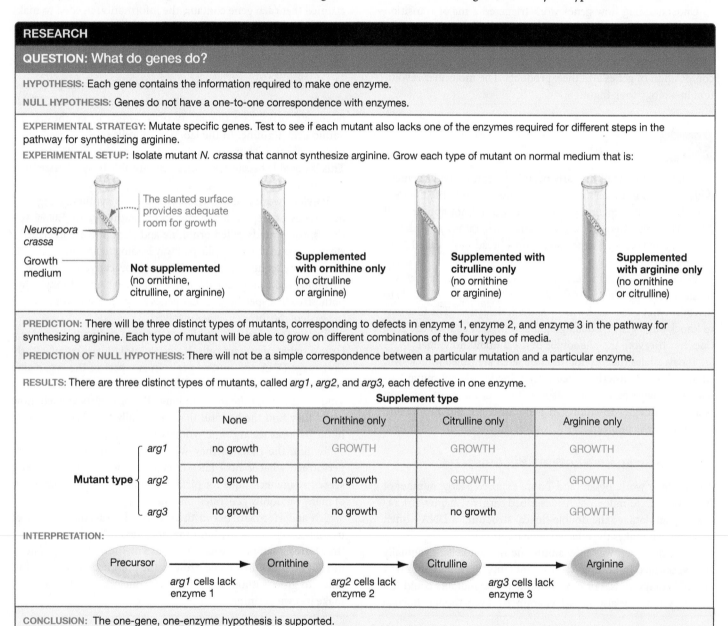

RESEARCH

QUESTION: What do genes do?

HYPOTHESIS: Each gene contains the information required to make one enzyme.

NULL HYPOTHESIS: Genes do not have a one-to-one correspondence with enzymes.

EXPERIMENTAL STRATEGY: Mutate specific genes. Test to see if each mutant also lacks one of the enzymes required for different steps in the pathway for synthesizing arginine.

EXPERIMENTAL SETUP: Isolate mutant *N. crassa* that cannot synthesize arginine. Grow each type of mutant on normal medium that is:

The slanted surface provides adequate room for growth

Neurospora crassa

Growth medium

Not supplemented (no ornithine, citrulline, or arginine)

Supplemented with ornithine only (no citrulline or arginine)

Supplemented with citrulline only (no ornithine or arginine)

Supplemented with arginine only (no ornithine or citrulline)

PREDICTION: There will be three distinct types of mutants, corresponding to defects in enzyme 1, enzyme 2, and enzyme 3 in the pathway for synthesizing arginine. Each type of mutant will be able to grow on different combinations of the four types of media.

PREDICTION OF NULL HYPOTHESIS: There will not be a simple correspondence between a particular mutation and a particular enzyme.

RESULTS: There are three distinct types of mutants, called *arg1*, *arg2*, and *arg3*, each defective in one enzyme.

		Supplement type		
	None	Ornithine only	Citrulline only	Arginine only
arg1	no growth	GROWTH	GROWTH	GROWTH
arg2	no growth	no growth	GROWTH	GROWTH
arg3	no growth	no growth	no growth	GROWTH

Mutant type { arg1, arg2, arg3 }

INTERPRETATION:

Precursor → Ornithine → Citrulline → Arginine

arg1 cells lack enzyme 1

arg2 cells lack enzyme 2

arg3 cells lack enzyme 3

CONCLUSION: The one-gene, one-enzyme hypothesis is supported.

FIGURE 16.2 Experimental Support for the One-Gene, One-Enzyme Hypothesis. The association between specific genetic defects in *N. crassa* and specific defects in the metabolic pathway for arginine synthesis provided evidence that supported the one-gene, one-enzyme hypothesis.

SOURCE: Srb, A. M., and N. H. Horowitz. 1944. The ornithine cycle in *Neurospora* and its genetic control. *Journal of Biological Chemistry* 154: 129–139.

✔**QUESTION** Experimental designs must be repeatable so that other investigators can try the experiment themselves to check the results. Name three things that these researchers would need to describe so that others could repeat this experiment.

Follow-up work showed that genes contain the information for all the proteins produced by an organism—not just enzymes. Biologists finally understood what most genes do: They contain the instructions for making proteins.

In many cases, though, a protein is made up of several different polypeptides, each of which is a product of a different gene. Consequently, for greater accuracy, the one-gene, one-enzyme hypothesis is best called the one-gene, one-polypeptide hypothesis.

16.2 The Central Dogma of Molecular Biology

How does a gene specify the production of a protein? As soon as Beadle and Tatum's hypothesis had been supported in *N. crassa* and a variety of other organisms, this question became a central one.

Part of the answer lay in the molecular structure of the gene. Biochemists knew that the primary components of DNA were four nitrogen-containing bases: the pyrimidines thymine (abbreviated T) and cytosine (C), and the purines adenine (A) and guanine (G). They also knew that these bases were connected in a linear sequence by a sugar–phosphate backbone. Watson and Crick's model for the secondary structure of the DNA molecule (see Chapters 4 and 15) revealed that two strands of DNA are wound into a double helix, held together by hydrogen bonds between the complementary base pairs A-T and G-C.

Given DNA's structure, it appeared extremely unlikely that DNA directly catalyzed the reactions that produce proteins. Its shape was too regular to suggest that it could bind a wide variety of substrate molecules and lower the activation energy for chemical reactions. So how, then, did information translate into action?

The Genetic Code Hypothesis

Crick proposed that the sequence of bases in DNA might act as a code. His idea was that DNA was *only* an information-storage molecule. The instructions it contained would have to be read and then translated into proteins.

Crick offered Morse code as an analogy. Morse code is a message-transmission system using dots and dashes to represent the letters of the alphabet, and in that way it can convey all the complex information of human language. Crick proposed that different combinations of bases could specify the 20 amino acids, just as different combinations of dots and dashes specify the 26 letters of the alphabet. A particular stretch of DNA, then, could contain the information needed to produce the amino acid sequence of a particular polypeptide.

In code form, the tremendous quantity of information required to build and operate a cell could be stored compactly. This information could also be copied through complementary base pairing and transmitted efficiently from one generation to the next.

It soon became apparent, however, that the information encoded in the base sequence of DNA is not translated into the

amino acid sequence of proteins directly. Instead, the link between DNA as information repository and proteins as cellular machines is indirect.

RNA as the Intermediary between Genes and Proteins

The first clue that the biological information in DNA must go through an intermediary in order to produce proteins came from knowledge of cell structure. In eukaryotic cells, DNA is enclosed within a membrane-bound organelle called the nucleus (see Chapter 7). But the cells' ribosomes, where protein synthesis takes place, are outside the nucleus, in the cytoplasm.

To make sense of this observation, François Jacob and Jacques Monod suggested that RNA molecules act as a link between genes and the protein-manufacturing centers. Jacob and Monod's hypothesis is illustrated in **FIGURE 16.3**. They predicted that short-lived molecules of RNA, which they called **messenger RNA,** or **mRNA** for short, carry information out of the nucleus from DNA to the site of protein synthesis. Messenger RNA is one of several distinct types of RNA in cells.

Follow-up research confirmed that the messenger RNA hypothesis is correct. One particularly important piece of evidence was the discovery of an enzyme that catalyzes the synthesis of RNA. This protein is called **RNA polymerase** because it polymerizes ribonucleotides into strands of RNA.

RNA polymerase synthesizes RNA molecules according to the information provided by the sequence of bases in a particular stretch of DNA. Unlike DNA polymerase, RNA polymerase

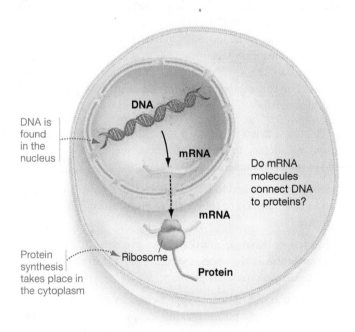

FIGURE 16.3 The Messenger RNA Hypothesis. In cells of eukaryotes such as plants, animals, and fungi, most DNA is found in the nucleus, but proteins are manufactured using ribosomes in the cytoplasm outside the nucleus. Biologists proposed that the information coded in DNA is carried from inside the nucleus out to the ribosomes by messenger RNA (mRNA).

does not require a primer to begin connecting ribonucleotides together to produce a strand of RNA.

To test the mRNA hypothesis, researchers created a reaction mix containing three critical elements: **(1)** the enzyme RNA polymerase; **(2)** ribonucleotides containing the bases adenine (A), uracil (U), guanine (G), and cytosine (C); and **(3)** strands of synthetic DNA that contained deoxyribonucleotides in which the only base was thymine (T).

After allowing the polymerization reaction to proceed, the biologists isolated RNA molecules that contained only the base adenine.

This result supported the hypothesis that RNA polymerase synthesizes RNA according to the rules of complementary base pairing (introduced in Chapter 4), because thymine pairs with adenine. Similar experiments showed that synthetic DNAs containing only cytosine result in the production of RNA molecules containing only guanine.

Dissecting the Central Dogma

Once the mRNA hypothesis was accepted, Francis Crick articulated what became known as the central dogma of molecular biology. The **central dogma** summarizes the flow of information in cells. It simply states that DNA codes for RNA, which codes for proteins:

$$DNA \longrightarrow RNA \longrightarrow proteins$$

Crick's simple statement encapsulates much of the research reviewed in this chapter and the preceding one. DNA is the hereditary material. Genes consist of specific stretches of DNA that code for products used in the cell. The sequence of bases in DNA specifies the sequence of bases in an RNA molecule, which specifies the sequence of amino acids in a protein. In this way, genes ultimately code for proteins.

Proteins are the workers of cells, functioning not only as enzymes but also as motors, structural elements, transporters, and molecular signals.

The Roles of Transcription and Translation   Biologists use specialized vocabulary to summarize the sequence of events captured in the central dogma.

1. DNA is transcribed to RNA by RNA polymerase. **Transcription** is the process of copying hereditary information in DNA to RNA.

2. Messenger RNA is translated to proteins in ribosomes. **Translation** is the process of using the information in nucleic acids to synthesize proteins.

The term transcription is appropriate. In everyday English, transcription simply means making a copy of information. The scientific use is similar because it conveys the idea that DNA acts as a permanent record—an information archive or blueprint. This permanent record is copied, during transcription, to produce the short-lived form called mRNA.

Translation is also an appropriate term. In everyday English, translation refers to converting information from one language

to another. In biology, translation is the transfer of information from one type of molecule to another—from the "language" of nucleic acids to the "language" of proteins. Translation is also referred to simply as protein synthesis.

The following equation summarizes the relationship between transcription and translation as well as the relationships between DNA, RNA, and proteins:

DNA	$\xrightarrow{\text{Transcription}}$	**mRNA**	$\xrightarrow{\text{Translation}}$	**Proteins**
information storage		information carrier		active cell machinery

Gene expression occurs via transcription and translation.

Linking Genotypes and Phenotypes   An organism's genotype is determined by the sequence of bases in its DNA, while its phenotype is a product of the proteins it produces.

To appreciate this point, consider that the proteins encoded by genes are what make the "stuff" of the cell and dictate which chemical reactions occur inside. For example, in populations of the oldfield mouse native to southeastern North America, individuals have a gene for a protein called the melanocortin receptor. Melanocortin is a hormone—an important type of molecular signal (discussed in Chapter 11)—that works through the melanocortin receptor to influence how much dark pigment is deposited in fur. An important aspect of a mouse's phenotype—its coat color—is determined in part by the DNA sequence at the gene for this receptor (**FIGURE 16.4a**).

Later work revealed that alleles of a gene differ in their DNA sequence. As a result, the proteins produced by different alleles of the gene may differ in their amino acid sequence. If the primary structures of proteins vary, their functions are likely to vary as well.

To drive this point home, look at the DNA sequence in the portion of the melanocortin receptor gene shown in **FIGURE 16.4b**, and compare it with the sequence in Figure 16.4a. The sequences differ—meaning that they are different alleles. Now look at the protein products of each allele, and note that one of the amino acids in the protein's primary structure differs—one allele specifies an arginine residue; the other specifies a cysteine residue.

At the protein level, the phenotypes associated with these alleles differ. The consequences for the mouse are striking: Melanocortin receptors that have arginine in this location deposit a large amount of pigment, but receptors that have cysteine in this location deposit small amounts of pigment. Whether a mouse is dark or light depends, largely, on a single base change in its DNA sequence. In this case, a tiny difference in genotype produces a large change in phenotype. The central dogma links genotypes to phenotypes.

Exceptions to the Central Dogma   The central dogma provided an important conceptual framework for the burgeoning field of molecular genetics and inspired a series of fundamental questions about how genes and cells work. But important modifications to the central dogma have occurred in the decades since Frances Crick first proposed it:

(a) Genetic information flows from DNA to RNA to proteins.

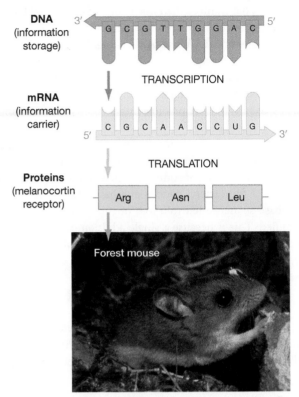

DNA (information storage) 3′ G C G T T G G A C 5′

TRANSCRIPTION

mRNA (information carrier) 5′ C G C A A C C U G 3′

TRANSLATION

Proteins (melanocortin receptor) | Arg | Asn | Leu |

Forest mouse

Mice with this DNA sequence have **dark** coats.

(b) Differences in genotype may cause differences in phenotype.

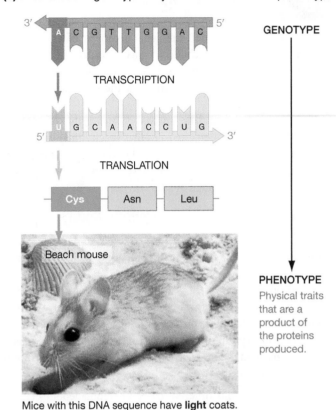

3′ A C G T T G G A C 5′ GENOTYPE

TRANSCRIPTION

5′ U G C A A C C U G 3′

TRANSLATION

| Cys | Asn | Leu |

Beach mouse

Mice with this DNA sequence have **light** coats.

PHENOTYPE
Physical traits that are a product of the proteins produced.

FIGURE 16.4 The Relationship between Genotype and Phenotype. The central dogma revealed the flow of information within the cell. The DNA sequences given in parts **(a)** and **(b)** are from different alleles (genotypes) that influence coat color (phenotypes) in oldfield mice. Forest-dwelling mice are dark, which camouflages them in their forested habitats. Beach-dwelling mice are light, which camouflages them in their sandy habitat.

- Many genes code for RNA molecules that do not function as mRNAs—they are not translated into proteins.

- In some cases, information flows from RNA back to DNA.

The discovery of a wide array of different RNA types ranks among the most profound advances in the past decade of biological science. Some RNAs form major parts of the ribosome, others help to form mRNA from a much longer precursor RNA (Chapter 17), and yet others regulate which genes are expressed (see Chapter 19). New types of RNA are still being discovered. For the genes coding for these types of RNA, information flow would be diagrammed as simply DNA → RNA.

In the early 1970s, the discovery of "reverse" information flow created the kind of excitement now being generated by the discovery of so many kinds of RNA. Some viruses, for example, have genes consisting of RNA. When some RNA viruses infect a cell, a specialized viral polymerase called **reverse transcriptase** synthesizes a DNA version of the RNA genes. In these viruses, information flows from RNA to DNA.

The human immunodeficiency virus (HIV), which causes AIDS, is an RNA virus that uses reverse transcriptase. Several of the most commonly prescribed drugs for AIDS patients fight the infection by poisoning the HIV reverse transcriptase. The drugs prevent viruses from replicating efficiently by disrupting reverse information flow.

The punch line? Crick's hypothesis is a central concept in biology, but cells, viruses, and researchers aren't dogmatic about it.

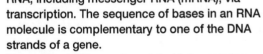

check your understanding

If you understand that . . .

- Genes code for proteins, but they do so indirectly.
- The sequence of bases in DNA is used to produce RNA, including messenger RNA (mRNA), via transcription. The sequence of bases in an RNA molecule is complementary to one of the DNA strands of a gene.
- Messenger RNAs are translated into proteins.
- Differences in DNA sequence can lead to differences in the amino acid sequence of proteins.

✔ **You should be able to . . .**

List the steps that link a change in the base sequence of a gene to a change in the phenotype of an organism.

Answers are available in Appendix A.

16.3 The Genetic Code

Once biologists understood the general pattern of information flow in the cell, the next challenge was to understand the final link between DNA and proteins. Exactly how does the sequence of bases in a strand of mRNA code for the sequence of amino acids in a protein?

If this question could be answered, biologists would have cracked the **genetic code**—the rules that specify the relationship between a sequence of nucleotides in DNA or RNA and the sequence of amino acids in a protein. Researchers from all over the world took up the challenge. A race was on.

How Long Is a Word in the Genetic Code?

The first step in cracking the genetic code was to determine how many bases make up a "word." In a sequence of mRNA, how long is a message that specifies one amino acid?

Based on some simple logic, George Gamow suggested that each code word contains three bases. His reasoning derived from the observation that 20 amino acids are commonly used in cells and from the hypothesis that each amino acid must be specified by a particular sequence of mRNA. **FIGURE 16.5** illustrates Gamow's reasoning:

- There are only four different bases in ribonucleotides (A, U, G, and C), so a one-base code could specify only four different amino acids.

- A two-base code could represent just 4 × 4, or 16, different amino acids.

- A three-base code could specify 4 × 4 × 4, or 64, different amino acids.

A three-base code provides more than enough words to code for all 20 amino acids. A three-base code is known as a **triplet code**.

Gamow's hypothesis suggested that the genetic code could be redundant. That is, more than one triplet of bases might specify the same amino acid. As a result, different three-base sequences in an mRNA—say, AAA and AAG—might code for the same amino acid—say, lysine.

The group of three bases that specifies a particular amino acid is called a **codon**. According to the triplet code hypothesis, many of the 64 codons that are possible might specify the same amino acids.

Work by Francis Crick and Sydney Brenner confirmed that codons are three bases long. Their experiments used chemicals that caused an occasional addition or deletion of a base in DNA. As predicted for a triplet code, a one-base addition or deletion in the base sequence led to a loss of function in the gene being studied. This is because a single addition or deletion mutation throws the sequence of codons, or the **reading frame,** out of register. To understand how a reading frame works, consider the sentence

"The fat cat ate the rat."

The reading frame of this sentence is a three-letter word and a space. If the fourth letter in this sentence—the *f* in *fat*—were deleted, the reading frame would transform the sentence into

"The atc ata tet her at."

This is gibberish.

When the reading frame in a DNA sequence is thrown out of register by the addition or deletion of a base, the composition of each codon changes just like the letters in each word of the example sentence above. The protein produced from the altered DNA sequence has a completely different sequence of amino acids. In terms of its normal function, this protein is gibberish.

Crick and Brenner were also able to produce DNA sequences that had deletions or additions of two base pairs or three base

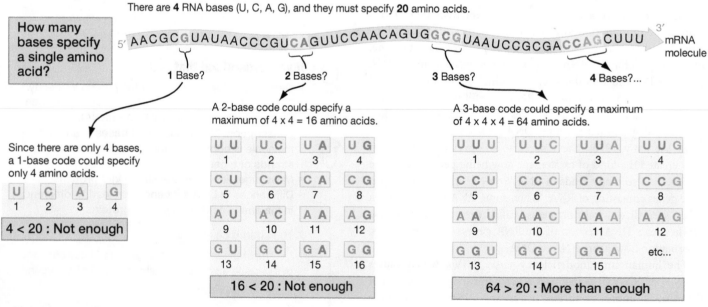

FIGURE 16.5 How Many Bases Form a "Word" in the Genetic Code?

pairs. The only time functional proteins were produced was when three bases were added or removed. In the sentence

> "The fat cat ate the rat."

the combination of removing one letter from each of the first three words might result in

> "Tha tca ate the rat."

Just as the altered sentence still conveys some meaning, genes with three deletion mutations were able to produce a functional protein.

The researchers interpreted these results as strong evidence in favor of the triplet code hypothesis. Most other biologists agreed.

The confirmation of the triplet code launched an effort to determine which amino acid is specified by each of the 64 codons. Ultimately, it was successful.

How Did Researchers Crack the Code?

The initial advance in deciphering the genetic code came in 1961, when Marshall Nirenberg and Heinrich Matthaei developed a method for synthesizing RNAs of known sequence. They began by creating a long polymer of uracil-containing ribonucleotides. These synthetic RNAs were added to an in vitro system for synthesizing proteins. The researchers analyzed the resulting amino acid chain and determined that it was polyphenylalanine—a polymer consisting of the amino acid phenylalanine.

This result provided evidence that the RNA triplet UUU codes for the amino acid phenylalanine. By complementary base pairing, it was clear that the corresponding DNA sequence would be AAA. This initial work was followed by experiments using RNAs consisting of only A or C. RNAs with only AAAAA . . . produced

polypeptides composed of only lysine; poly-C RNAs (RNAs consisting of only CCCCC . . .) produced polypeptides composed entirely of proline.

Nirenberg and Philip Leder later devised a system for synthesizing specific codons. With these they performed a series of experiments in which they added each codon to a cell extract containing the 20 different amino acids, ribosomes, and other molecules required for protein synthesis. Recall that ribosomes are macromolecular machines that synthesize proteins (Chapter 7). Then the researchers determined which amino acid became bound to the ribosomes when a particular codon was present. For example, when the codon CAC was in the reaction mix, the amino acid histidine would bind to the ribosomes. This result indicated that CAC codes for histidine.

These ribosome-binding experiments allowed Nirenberg and Leder to determine which of the 64 codons coded for each of the 20 amino acids.

Researchers also discovered that certain codons are punctuation marks signaling "start of message" or "end of message." These codons indicate that protein synthesis should start at a given codon or that the protein chain is complete.

- There is one **start codon** (AUG), which signals that protein synthesis should begin at that point on the mRNA molecule. The start codon specifies the amino acid methionine.

- There are three **stop codons,** also called termination codons (UAA, UAG, and UGA). The stop codons signal that the protein is complete, they do not code for any amino acid, and they end translation.

The complete genetic code is given in **FIGURE 16.6**. Deciphering it was a tremendous achievement, requiring more than five years of work by several teams of researchers.

SECOND BASE

		U	C	A	G	
F I R S T B A S E	**U**	UUU UUC — Phenylalanine (Phe) UUA UUG — Leucine (Leu)	UCU UCC UCA UCG — Serine (Ser)	UAU UAC — Tyrosine (Tyr) UAA — Stop codon UAG — Stop codon	UGU UGC — Cysteine (Cys) UGA — Stop codon UGG — Tryptophan (Trp)	U C A G
	C	CUU CUC CUA CUG — Leucine (Leu)	CCU CCC CCA CCG — Proline (Pro)	CAU CAC — Histidine (His) CAA CAG — Glutamine (Gln)	CGU CGC CGA CGG — Arginine (Arg)	U C A G
	A	AUU AUC AUA — Isoleucine (Ile) AUG — Methionine (Met) Start codon	ACU ACC ACA ACG — Threonine (Thr)	AAU AAC — Asparagine (Asn) AAA AAG — Lysine (Lys)	AGU AGC — Serine (Ser) AGA AGG — Arginine (Arg)	U C A G
	G	GUU GUC GUA GUG — Valine (Val)	GCU GCC GCA GCG — Alanine (Ala)	GAU GAC — Aspartic acid (Asp) GAA GAG — Glutamic acid (Glu)	GGU GGC GGA GGG — Glycine (Gly)	U C A G

THIRD BASE

FIGURE 16.6 The Genetic Code. To read a codon in mRNA, locate its first base in the red band on the left; then move rightward to the box under the codon's second base in the blue band along the top. Finally, locate the codon's third base in the green band on the right side to learn the amino acid. By convention, codons are always written in the $5' \rightarrow 3'$ direction.

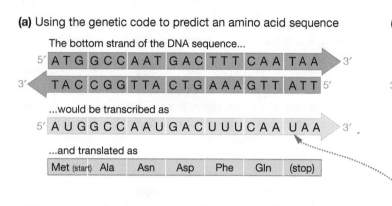

(a) Using the genetic code to predict an amino acid sequence

The bottom strand of the DNA sequence...

5′ ATG GCC AAT GAC TTT CAA TAA 3′
3′ TAC CGG TTA CTG AAA GTT ATT 5′

...would be transcribed as

5′ AUG GCC AAU GAC UUU CAA UAA 3′

...and translated as

| Met (start) | Ala | Asn | Asp | Phe | Gln | (stop) |

(b) Your turn—a chance to practice using the genetic code

The bottom strand of the DNA sequence...

5′ ATG CTG GAG GGG GTT AGA CAT 3′
3′ TAC GAC CTC CCC CAA TCT GTA 5′

...would be transcribed as

5′ ‎ 3′

...and translated as

Remember that RNA contains U (uracil) instead of T (thymine), and that U forms a complementary base pair with A (adenine)

FIGURE 16.7 Using the Genetic Code.

✔**EXERCISE** Fill in the mRNA and amino acid sequences in part (b).

Analyzing the Code   Once biologists had cracked the genetic code, they realized that it has a series of important properties.

- *The code is redundant.*   All amino acids except methionine and tryptophan are coded by more than one codon.

- *The code is unambiguous.*   A single codon never codes for more than one amino acid.

- *The code is non-overlapping.*   Once the ribosome locks onto the first codon, it then reads each separate codon one after another.

- *The code is nearly universal.*   With a few minor exceptions, all codons specify the same amino acids in all organisms.

- *The code is conservative.*   When several codons specify the same amino acid, the first two bases in those codons are almost always identical.

The last point is subtle, but important. Here's the key: If a mutation in DNA or an error in transcription or translation affects the third position in a codon, it is less likely to change the amino acid in the final protein. This feature makes individuals less vulnerable to small, random changes or errors in their DNA sequences. Compared with randomly generated codes, the existing genetic code minimizes the phenotypic effects of small changes in DNA sequence and errors during translation. Stated another way, the genetic code does not represent a random assemblage of bases, like letters drawn from a hat. It has been honed by natural selection and is remarkably efficient.

Using the Code   Using the genetic code and the central dogma, biologists can:

1. Predict the codons and amino acid sequence encoded by a particular DNA sequence (see **FIGURE 16.7a**).

2. Determine the set of mRNA and DNA sequences that would code for a particular sequence of amino acids.

Why is a *set* of mRNA or DNA sequences predicted from a given amino acid sequence? The answer lies in the code's redundancy. If a polypeptide contains phenylalanine, you don't know if the codon responsible is UUU or UUC.

✔ If you understand how to read the genetic code, you should be able to do the following tasks: (1) Identify the codons in Figure 16.4 and decide whether they are translated correctly. (2) Complete the exercise for **FIGURE 16.7b**. (3) Write an mRNA that codes for the amino acid sequence Ala-Asn-Asp-Phe-Gln yet is different from the one given in Figure 16.7a. Indicate the mRNA's 5′ → 3′ polarity. Then write the double-stranded DNA that corresponds to this mRNA. Indicate the 5′ → 3′ polarity of both DNA strands.

Once they understood the central dogma and genetic code, biologists were able to explore and eventually understand the molecular basis of mutation. How do novel traits—such as dwarfing in garden peas and white eye color in fruit flies—come to be?

16.4 How Can Mutation Modify Genes and Chromosomes?

This chapter has explored how the information archived in DNA is put into action in the form of working RNAs and proteins. Now the questions are, what happens if the information in DNA changes? In what ways can this information be changed? What are the consequences for the cell and organism?

A **mutation** is any permanent change in an organism's DNA. It is a modification in a cell's information archive—a change in its genotype. Mutations create new alleles.

Mutations can alter DNA sequences that range in size from a single base pair in DNA to whole sets of chromosomes. Let's look at these different types of mutation and their consequences.

Point Mutation

FIGURE 16.8 shows how a common type of mutation occurs. If a mistake is made during DNA synthesis or DNA repair, a change in the sequence of bases in DNA results. A single-base change such as this is called a **point mutation.**

What happens when point mutations occur in regions of DNA that code for proteins? To answer this question, look back at Figure 16.4 and recall that a change in a single base in DNA is associated with a difference in coat color in populations of oldfield mice. The DNA sequence in Figure 16.4a is found in dark-colored mice that live in forest habitats; the sequence in Figure 16.4b is found in light-colored mice that live in beach habitats.

Because beach-dwelling populations are evolutionarily younger than the nearby forest-dwelling populations, researchers hypothesize the following sequence of events:

1. Forest mice colonized beach habitats.

2. Either before or after the colonization event, a random point mutation occurred in a mouse that altered the melanocortin receptor gene and resulted in some offspring with light coats.

3. Light-colored mice are camouflaged in beach habitats; in sandy environments, they suffer lower predation than dark-colored mice.

4. Over time, the allele created by the point mutation increased in frequency in beach-dwelling populations.

Point mutations that cause these types of changes in the amino acid sequence of proteins are called **missense mutations.** But note that if the same G-to-A change had occurred in the third position of the same DNA codon, instead of the first position, there would have been no change in the protein produced. The mRNA codons CGC and CGU both code for arginine. A point mutation that does not change the amino acid sequence of the gene product is called a **silent mutation.**

Some point mutations disrupt major portions of a protein. Recall that a single addition or deletion mutation throws the sequence of codons out of register and alters the meaning of all subsequent codons. Such mutations are called **frameshift mutations.** Another type of point mutation with a large effect is a **nonsense mutation.** Nonsense mutations occur when a codon that specifies an amino acid is changed by mutation to one that specifies a stop codon. This causes early termination of the polypeptide chain and often results in a non-functional protein.

In terms of the impact on organisms, biologists divide mutations into three categories:

1. **Beneficial** Some mutations increase the fitness of the organism—meaning, its ability to survive and reproduce—in certain environments. The G-to-A mutation is beneficial in beach habitats because it camouflages mice.

2. **Neutral** If a mutation has no effect on fitness, it is termed neutral. Silent mutations are usually neutral.

3. **Deleterious** Because organisms tend to be well adapted to their current habitat, and because mutations are random changes in the genotype, many mutations lower fitness. These mutations are termed harmful or deleterious. The G-to-A mutation would be deleterious in the forest habitat.

Recent studies indicate that the majority of point mutations are slightly deleterious or neutral. **TABLE 16.1** (see page 314) summarizes the types of point mutations that occur in protein-coding sequences of a gene and reviews their consequences for the amino acid sequences of proteins and for fitness.

Point mutations can and do occur in DNA sequences that do not code for proteins. These mutations, however, are not referred to as missense, silent, frameshift, or nonsense mutations

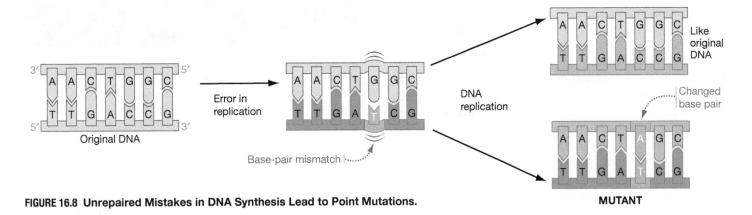

FIGURE 16.8 Unrepaired Mistakes in DNA Synthesis Lead to Point Mutations.

Name	Definition	Example	Consequence
		Original DNA sequence ——— TAT TGG CTA GTA CAT	
		Original mRNA transcript ——— UAU UGG CUA GUA CAU	
		Tyr – Trp – Leu – Val – His ——— Original polypeptide	
Silent	Change in nucleotide sequence that does not change the amino acid specified by a codon	TAC TGG CTA GTA CAT UAC UGG CUA GUA CAU Tyr – Trp – Leu – Val – His	No change in phenotype; neutral with respect to fitness
Missense	Change in nucleotide sequence that changes the amino acid specified by codon	TAT TGT CTA GTA CAT UAU UGU CUA GUA CAU Tyr – Cys – Leu – Val – His	Change in primary structure of protein; may be beneficial, neutral, or deleterious
Nonsense	Change in nucleotide sequence that results in an early stop codon	TAT TGA CTA GTA CAT UAU UGA CUA GUA CAU Tyr – STOP	Leads to mRNA breakdown or a shortened polypeptide; usually deleterious
Frameshift	Addition or deletion of a nucleotide	TAT TCG GCT AGT ACA T UAU UCG GCU AGU ACA U Tyr – Ser – Ala – Ser – Thr	Reading frame is shifted, altering the meaning of all subsequent codons; almost always deleterious

because these terms apply only to mutations that can change the protein-coding potential of a gene. If point mutations alter DNA sequences that are important for *gene expression*, they can have important effects on phenotype even though they do not change the amino acid sequence of a protein.

Chromosome Mutations

Besides documenting various types of point mutations, biologists study larger-scale mutations that change chromosomes. You might recall, for example, that polyploidy is an increase in the number of each type of chromosome, while aneuploidy is the addition or deletion of individual chromosomes.

Polyploidy, aneuploidy, and other changes in chromosome number result from chance mistakes in moving chromosomes into daughter cells during meiosis or mitosis. Polyploidy and aneuploidy are forms of mutation that don't change DNA sequences, but alter the number of chromosome copies.

In addition to changes in overall chromosome number, the composition of individual chromosomes can change in important ways. For example, chromosome segments can become detached when accidental breaks in chromosomes occur. The segments may be flipped and rejoined—a phenomenon known as a chromosome **inversion**—or become attached to a different chromosome, an event called chromosome **translocation.** When a segment of chromosome is lost, this is a **deletion,** and when additional copies of a segment are present, this is a **duplication.**

Like point mutations, chromosome mutations can be beneficial, neutral, or deleterious. For example, more than 200 different inverted sections of chromosomes were found in comparisons

of the DNA from eight phenotypically normal people. These mutations appear to be neutral. Not all chromosome mutations are so harmless, however. Chromosomes of cancer cells exhibit deleterious chromosome mutations that include aneuploidy, inversions, translocations, deletions, and duplications. **FIGURE 16.9**

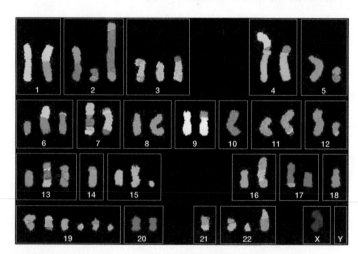

FIGURE 16.9 Chromosome-Level Mutations. A spectral karyotype of a breast cancer cell from a female that shows chromosome rearrangements and aneuploidy typical of cancer. In a normal spectral karyotype, each chromosome is stained a single, solid color, which varies for each chromosome pair.

✔ **EXERCISE** Compare this karyotype to the one shown in the chapter-opening image. Remember that females normally have two X chromosomes and males normally have one X chromosome. Which chromosomes show evidence of aneuploidy? Which chromosomes show evidence of rearrangements?

drives this point home by showing the **karyotype**—the complete set of chromosomes in a cell—of a cancerous human cell.

To summarize, point mutations and chromosome mutations are random changes in DNA that can produce new genes, new alleles, and new traits. At the level of individuals, mutations can cause disease or death or lead to increases in fitness. At the level of populations, mutations furnish the heritable variation that Mendel and Morgan analyzed and that makes evolution possible. The central role of mutation in evolution is explored in depth in Unit 5.

CHAPTER 16 REVIEW

For media, go to MasteringBiology

If you understand . . .

16.1 What Do Genes Do?

- Experiments with mutants of the bread mold *N. crassa* led to the one-gene, one-enzyme hypothesis.

- The original one-gene, one-enzyme hypothesis has been broadened to account for genes that code for proteins other than enzymes and for genes that have RNA as a final product.

✓ You should be able to use Figure 16.1 to explain what compounds could be added to the medium to allow the growth of a mutant unable to synthesize citrulline because of a mutation in the gene for enzyme 1.

16.2 The Central Dogma of Molecular Biology

- DNA is transcribed to messenger RNA (mRNA) by RNA polymerase, and then mRNA is translated to proteins by ribosomes. In this way, genetic information is converted from DNA to RNA to protein.

- The flow of information from DNA to RNA to protein is called the central dogma of molecular biology.

- Many RNAs do not code for proteins. Instead, these RNAs perform other important functions in the cell.

- Reverse transcriptase reverses information flow by copying RNA into DNA. Some viruses with an RNA genome use this enzyme during their replication.

✓ You should be able to explain how a compound that blocks RNA synthesis will affect protein synthesis.

16.3 The Genetic Code

- Each amino acid in a protein is specified by a codon—a group of three bases in mRNA.

- By synthesizing RNAs of known base composition and then observing the results of translation, researchers were able to decipher the genetic code.

- The genetic code is redundant—meaning that most of the 20 amino acids are specified by more than one codon.

- Certain codons signal where translation starts and stops.

✓ Using the genetic code shown in Figure 16.6, you should be able to write all possible mRNA sequences that would produce the following sequence of amino acids: Met-Trp-Lys-Gln.

16.4 How Can Mutation Modify Genes and Chromosomes?

- Mutations are random, heritable changes in DNA that range from changes in a single base to changes in the structure and number of chromosomes.

- Point mutations in protein-coding regions may have no effect on the protein (silent mutation), may change a single amino acid (missense mutation), may shorten the protein (nonsense mutation), or may shift the reading frame and cause many amino acids to be wrong (frameshift mutation).

- Mutations can have beneficial, neutral, or harmful effects on organisms.

✓ You should be able to explain how redundancy in the genetic code allows for silent mutations and whether a silent mutation is likely to be beneficial, neutral, or harmful.

MB **MasteringBiology**

1. **MasteringBiology Assignments**

   Tutorials and Activities Genetic Code; One-Gene One-Enzyme Hypothesis; Overview of Protein Synthesis; Role of the Nucleus and Ribosomes in Protein Synthesis; Triplet Nature of the Genetic Code

   Questions Reading Quizzes, Blue-Thread Questions, Test Bank

2. **eText** Read your book online, search, take notes, highlight text, and more.

3. **The Study Area** Practice Test, Cumulative Test, BioFlix® 3-D Animations, Videos, Activities, Audio Glossary, Word Study Tools, Art

You should be able to . . .

✓ **TEST YOUR KNOWLEDGE** — *Answers are available in Appendix A*

1. What does the one-gene, one-enzyme hypothesis state?
   a. Genes are composed of stretches of DNA.
   b. Genes are made of protein.
   c. Genes code for ribozymes.
   d. A single gene codes for a single protein.

2. Which of the following is an important exception to the central dogma of molecular biology?
   a. Many genes code for RNAs that function directly in the cell.
   b. DNA is the repository of genetic information in all cells.
   c. Messenger RNA is a short-lived "information carrier."
   d. Proteins are responsible for most aspects of the phenotype.

3. DNA's primary structure is made up of just four different bases, and its secondary structure is regular and highly stable. How can a molecule with these characteristics hold all the information required to build and maintain a cell?
   a. The information is first transcribed, then translated.
   b. The messenger RNA produced from DNA has much more complex secondary structures, allowing mRNA to hold much more information.
   c. A protein coded for in DNA has much more complex primary and secondary structures, allowing it to hold much more information.
   d. The information in DNA is in a code form that is based on the sequence of bases.

4. Why did researchers suspect that DNA does not code for proteins directly?

5. Which of the following describes an important experimental strategy in deciphering the genetic code?
   a. comparing the amino acid sequences of proteins with the base sequence of their genes
   b. analyzing the sequence of RNAs produced from known DNA sequences
   c. analyzing mutants that changed the code
   d. examining the polypeptides produced when RNAs of known sequence were translated

6. What is a stop codon?

✓ **TEST YOUR UNDERSTANDING** — *Answers are available in Appendix A*

7. Explain why Morse code is an appropriate analogy for the genetic code.

8. Draw a hypothetical metabolic pathway in *Neurospora crassa* composed of five substrates, five enzymes, and a product called Biological Sciazine. Number the substrates 1–5, and label the enzymes A–E, in order. (For instance, enzyme A catalyzes the reaction between substrates 1 and 2.)
   - Suppose a mutation made the gene for enzyme C nonfunctional. What molecule would accumulate in the affected cells?
   - Suppose a mutant strain can survive if substrate 5 is added to the growth medium but it cannot grow if substrates 1, 2, 3, or 4 are added. Which enzyme in the pathway is affected in this mutant?

9. How did experiments with *Neurospora crassa* mutants support the one-gene, one-enzyme hypothesis?

10. Why does a single-base deletion mutation within a protein-coding sequence usually have a more severe effect than a deletion of three adjacent bases?
    a. because single-base deletions prevent the ribosome from binding to mRNA
    b. because single-base deletions stabilize mRNA
    c. because single-base deletions change the reading frame
    d. because single-base deletions alter the meaning of individual codons

11. When researchers discovered that a combination of three deletion mutations or three addition mutations would restore the function of a gene, most biologists were convinced that the genetic code was read in triplets. Explain the logic behind this conclusion.

12. Explain why all point mutations change the genotype, but why only some point mutations change the phenotype.

✓ **TEST YOUR PROBLEM-SOLVING SKILLS** — *Answers are available in Appendix A*

13. Recall that DNA and RNA are synthesized only in the $5' \rightarrow 3'$ direction and that DNA and RNA sequences are written in the $5' \rightarrow 3'$ direction, unless otherwise noted. Consider the following DNA sequence:

    5′ TTGAAATGCCCGTTTGGAGATCGGGTTACAGCTAGTCAAAG 3′

    3′ AACTTTACGGGCAAACCTCTAGCCCAATGTCGATCAGTTTC 5′

    - Identify bases in the bottom strand that can be transcribed into start and stop codons.
    - Write the mRNA sequence that would be transcribed between start and stop codons if the bottom strand served as the template for RNA polymerase.
    - Write the amino acid sequence that would be translated from the mRNA sequence you just wrote.

14. What problems would arise if the genetic code contained only 22 codons—one for each amino acid, a start signal, and a stop signal?

15. Scientists say that a phenomenon is a "black box" if they can describe it and study its effects but don't know the underlying mechanism that causes it. In what sense was genetics—meaning the transmission of heritable traits—a black box before the central dogma of molecular biology was understood?

16. **QUANTITATIVE** One of the possibilities that researchers interested in the genetic code considered was that the code was overlapping, meaning that a single base could be part of up to three codons. How many amino acids would be encoded in the sequence 5′ AUGUUACGGAAU 3′ by a non-overlapping and maximally overlapping code?
    a. 4 (non-overlapping) and 16 (overlapping)
    b. 4 and 12
    c. 4 and 10
    d. 12 and 4

17 Transcription, RNA Processing, and Translation

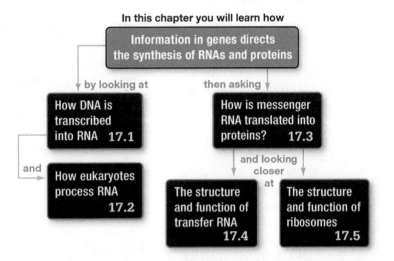

In this chapter you will learn how

Information in genes directs the synthesis of RNAs and proteins

by looking at

How DNA is transcribed into RNA **17.1**

and

How eukaryotes process RNA **17.2**

then asking

How is messenger RNA translated into proteins? **17.3**

and looking closer at

The structure and function of transfer RNA **17.4**

The structure and function of ribosomes **17.5**

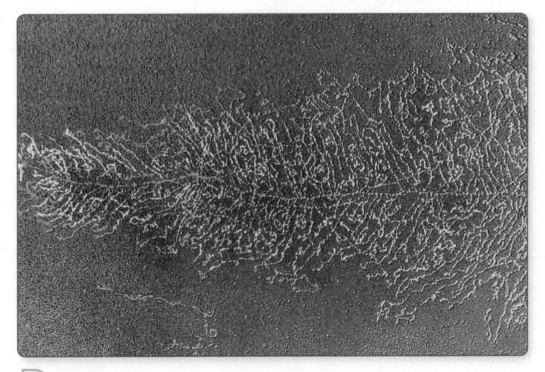

Extensive transcription is occurring along this gene within a frog cell. The horizontal strand in the middle of this micrograph is DNA; the strands that have been colored yellow and red, and that are coming off on either side, are RNA molecules.

Proteins are the stuff of life. They give shape to our cells, control the chemical reactions that go on inside them, and regulate how materials move into, out of, and through them. Some of these proteins may not be produced at all in some types of cells; others may be present in quantities ranging from millions of copies to fewer than a dozen.

A cell builds the proteins it needs from instructions encoded in its DNA. The central dogma of molecular biology states that the flow of information in cells is from DNA to mRNA to protein (Chapter 16). Once this pattern of information flow had been established, biologists puzzled over how cells actually accomplish the two major steps of the central dogma: transcription and

This chapter is part of the Big Picture. See how on pages 366–367.

✓ When you see this checkmark, stop and test yourself. Answers are available in Appendix A.

translation. Specifically, how does RNA polymerase know where to start transcribing a gene, and where to end? And once an RNA message is produced, how is the linear sequence of ribonucleotides translated into the linear sequence of amino acids in a protein?

This chapter delves into the molecular mechanisms of gene expression—the blood and guts of the central dogma. It starts with the monomers that build RNA and ends with a protein.

17.1 An Overview of Transcription

The first step in converting genetic information into proteins is to synthesize an RNA version of the instructions archived in DNA. Enzymes called **RNA polymerases** are responsible for synthesizing mRNA (see Chapter 15).

FIGURE 17.1 shows how the polymerization reaction occurs. Note the incoming monomer—a ribonucleoside triphosphate, or NTP—at the far right of the diagram. NTPs are like dNTPs (introduced in Chapter 15), except that they have a hydroxyl (−OH) group on the 2′ carbon. This makes the sugar in an NTP a ribose instead of the deoxyribose sugar of DNA.

Once an NTP that matches a base on the DNA template is in place, RNA polymerase cleaves off two phosphates and catalyzes the formation of a phosphodiester linkage between the 3′ end of the growing mRNA chain and the new ribonucleoside monophosphate. As this 5′ → 3′ matching-and-catalysis process continues, an RNA that is complementary to the gene is synthesized. This is transcription.

Notice that only one of the two DNA strands is used as a template and transcribed, or "read," by RNA polymerase.

- The strand that is read by the enzyme is the **template strand.**
- The other strand is called the **non-template strand** or **coding strand.** Coding strand is an appropriate name, because, with one exception, its sequence matches the sequence of the RNA that is transcribed from the template strand and codes for a polypeptide.

The coding strand and the RNA don't match exactly, because RNA has uracil (U) rather than the thymine (T) found in the coding strand. Likewise, an adenine (A) in the DNA template strand specifies a U in the complementary RNA strand.

Like DNA polymerases (see Chapter 15), an RNA polymerase performs a template-directed synthesis in the 5′ → 3′ direction. But unlike DNA polymerases, RNA polymerases do not require a primer to begin transcription.

Bacteria have a single RNA polymerase. In contrast, eukaryotes, have at least three distinct types. Let's first take a look at general principles of transcription using bacteria as an example and then examine things that differ in eukaryotes.

Initiation: How Does Transcription Begin in Bacteria?

How does RNA polymerase know where and in which direction to start transcription on the DNA template? The answer to this question defined what biologists call the **initiation** phase of transcription.

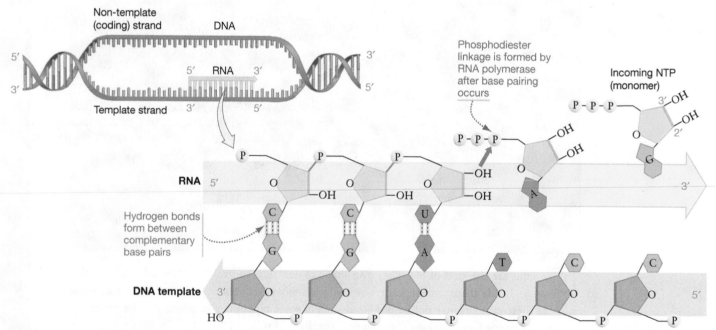

FIGURE 17.1 Transcription Is the Synthesis of RNA from a DNA Template. The reaction catalyzed by RNA polymerase (not shown) results in the formation of a phosphodiester linkage between ribonucleotides. RNA polymerase produces an RNA strand whose sequence is complementary to the bases in the DNA template.

✓**QUESTION** In which direction is RNA synthesized, 5′ → 3′ or 3′ → 5′? In which direction is the DNA template "read"?

Soon after the discovery of bacterial RNA polymerase, researchers found that the enzyme cannot initiate transcription on its own. Instead, a detachable protein subunit called **sigma** must bind to the polymerase before transcription can begin.

Bacterial RNA polymerase and sigma form a **holoenzyme** (literally, "whole enzyme"; **FIGURE 17.2a**). A holoenzyme consists of a **core enzyme** (RNA polymerase, in this case), which contains the active site for catalysis, and other required proteins (such as sigma).

What does sigma do? When researchers mixed the polymerase and DNA together, they found that the core enzyme could bind to any sequence of DNA. When sigma was added to this mixture, the holoenzyme formed and bound only to specific sections of DNA. These binding sites were named **promoters,** because they are sections of DNA that promote the start of transcription.

Most bacteria have alternative sigma proteins that bind to promoters with slightly different DNA base sequences, and may activate a group of genes in response to environmental change. For example, one type of sigma initiates the transcription of genes that help the cell cope with high temperatures. Controlling which sigma proteins are used is one of the ways that bacterial cells regulate which groups of genes are expressed.

The discovery of promoters suggested that sigma was responsible for guiding RNA polymerase to specific locations where transcription should begin. What is the nature of these specific locations? What do promoters look like, and what do they do?

Bacterial Promoters David Pribnow offered an initial answer to these questions in the mid-1970s. When Pribnow analyzed the base sequence of promoters from various bacteria and from viruses that infect bacteria, he found that the promoters were 40–50 base pairs long and had a particular section in common: a series of bases identical or similar to TATAAT. This six-base-pair sequence is now known as the −10 box, because it is centered about 10 bases from the point where bacterial RNA polymerase starts transcription (**FIGURE 17.2b**).

DNA that is located in the direction RNA polymerase moves during transcription is said to be **downstream** from the point of reference; DNA located in the opposite direction is said to be **upstream.** Thus, the −10 box is centered about 10 bases upstream from the transcription start site. The place where transcription begins is called the +1 site.

Soon after the discovery of the −10 box, researchers recognized that the sequence TTGACA also occurred in promoters and was about 35 bases upstream from the +1 site. This second key sequence is called the −35 box. Although all bacterial promoters have a −10 box and a −35 box, the sequences within the promoter but outside these boxes vary.

Events inside the Holoenzyme In bacteria, transcription begins when sigma, as part of the holoenzyme complex, binds to the −35 and −10 boxes. Sigma, and not RNA polymerase, makes the initial contact with DNA of the promoter. Sigma's binding to a promoter determines where and in which direction RNA polymerase will start synthesizing RNA.

Once the holoenzyme is bound to a promoter for a bacterial gene, the DNA helix is opened by RNA polymerase, creating two

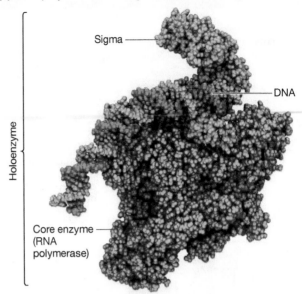

(a) RNA polymerase and sigma form a holoenzyme.

Sigma

DNA

Holoenzyme

Core enzyme
(RNA
polymerase)

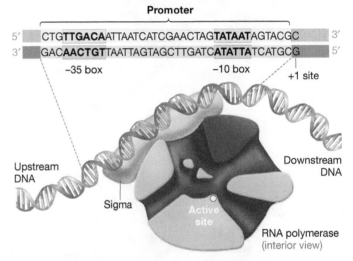

(b) Sigma recognizes and binds to the promoter.

Promoter

5′ CTG**TTGACA**ATTAATCATCGAACTAG**TATAAT**AGTACGC 3′
3′ GAC**AACTGT**TAATTAGTAGCTTGATC**ATATTA**TCATGCG 5′

−35 box   −10 box   +1 site

Upstream
DNA

Downstream
DNA

Sigma   Active site

RNA polymerase
(interior view)

FIGURE 17.2 Sigma Is the Promoter-Recognizing Subunit of Bacterial RNA Polymerase Holoenzyme. (a) A space-filling model of bacterial RNA polymerase holoenzyme. **(b)** A cartoon of bacterial RNA polymerase, showing that sigma binds to the −35 box and −10 box of the promoter.

separated strands of DNA as shown in **FIGURE 17.3** (see page 320), steps 1 and 2. As step 2 shows, the template strand is threaded through a channel that leads to the active site inside RNA polymerase. Ribonucleoside triphosphates (NTPs)—the RNA building blocks—enter a channel in the enzyme and diffuse to the active site.

When an incoming NTP pairs with a complementary base on the template strand of DNA, RNA polymerization begins. The reaction catalyzed by RNA polymerase is exergonic and spontaneous because NTPs have significant potential energy, owing to their three phosphate groups. As step 3 of Figure 17.3 shows, the initiation phase of transcription is complete as RNA polymerase extends the mRNA from the +1 site.

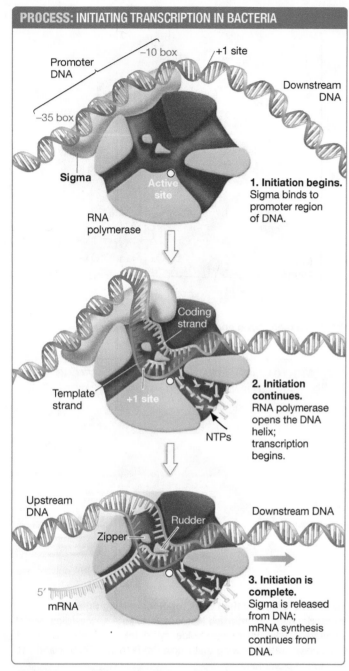

1. Initiation begins. Sigma binds to promoter region of DNA.

2. Initiation continues. RNA polymerase opens the DNA helix; transcription begins.

3. Initiation is complete. Sigma is released from DNA; mRNA synthesis continues from DNA.

FIGURE 17.3 Sigma Orients the DNA Template inside RNA Polymerase. Sigma binds to the promoter, and RNA polymerase opens the DNA helix and threads the template strand through the active site.

Elongation and Termination

Once RNA polymerase begins moving along the DNA template synthesizing RNA, the **elongation** phase of transcription is under way. RNA polymerase is a macromolecular machine with different parts. In the interior of the enzyme, a group of amino acids forms a rudder to help steer the template and non-template strands through channels inside the enzyme (see Figure 17.3, step 3). Meanwhile, the enzyme's active site catalyzes the addition

of nucleotides to the 3′ end of the growing RNA molecule at the rate of about 50 nucleotides per second. A group of projecting amino acids forms a region called the zipper to help separate the newly synthesized RNA from the DNA template.

During the elongation phase of transcription, all the prominent channels and grooves in the enzyme are filled (Figure 17.3, step 3). Double-stranded DNA goes into and out of one groove, ribonucleoside triphosphates enter another, and the growing RNA strand exits to the rear. The enzyme's structure is critical for its function.

Termination ends transcription. In bacteria, transcription stops when RNA polymerase transcribes a DNA sequence that functions as a transcription-termination signal.

The bases that make up the termination signal in bacteria are transcribed into a stretch of RNA with an important property: As soon as it is synthesized, this portion of the RNA folds back on itself and forms a short double helix that is held together by complementary base pairing (**FIGURE 17.4**). Recall that this type of RNA secondary structure is called a hairpin (Chapter 4). The hairpin structure disrupts the interaction between RNA polymerase and the RNA transcript, resulting in the physical separation of the enzyme and its product.

Transcription in Eukaryotes

Fundamental features of transcription are the same in bacteria and eukaryotes. In fact, these similarities provide compelling evidence for a common ancestor of all cells. There are, however, some differences that are worth noting:

- Eukaryotes have three polymerases—RNA polymerase I, II, and III—that are often referred to as pol I, pol II, and pol III. Each polymerase transcribes only certain types of RNA in eukaryotes. RNA pol II is the only polymerase that transcribes protein-coding genes.

- Promoters in eukaryotic DNA are more diverse than bacterial promoters. Most eukaryotic promoters include a sequence called the **TATA box,** centered about 30 base pairs upstream of the transcription start site, and other important sequences that vary more widely.

- Instead of using a sigma protein, eukaryotic RNA polymerases recognize promoters using a group of proteins called **basal transcription factors.** Basal transcription factors assemble at the promoter, and RNA polymerase follows. (This idea, as well as the extensive use of other types of transcription factors to regulate transcription, will be covered in Chapter 19.)

- Termination of eukaryotic protein-coding genes involves a short sequence called the polyadenylation signal or **poly(A) signal.** Soon after the signal is transcribed, the RNA is cut by an enzyme downstream of the poly(A) signal as the polymerase continues to transcribe the DNA template. Eventually RNA polymerase falls off the DNA template and terminates transcription. Bacteria end transcription at a distinct site for each gene, but in eukaryotes, transcription ends variable distances from the poly(A) signal.

PROCESS: ENDING TRANSCRIPTION IN BACTERIA

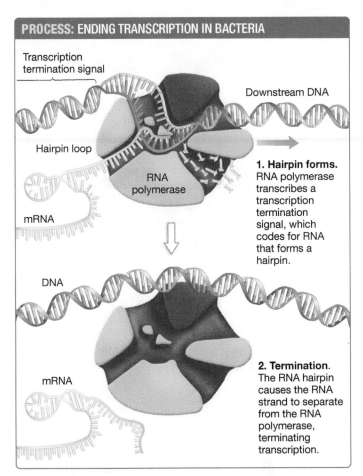

Transcription termination signal

Downstream DNA

Hairpin loop

RNA polymerase

mRNA

1. Hairpin forms. RNA polymerase transcribes a transcription termination signal, which codes for RNA that forms a hairpin.

DNA

mRNA

2. Termination. The RNA hairpin causes the RNA strand to separate from the RNA polymerase, terminating transcription.

FIGURE 17.4 Transcription Terminates When an RNA Hairpin Forms.

17.2 RNA Processing in Eukaryotes

The molecular machinery required for transcription is much more complex in eukaryotes than in bacteria. But these differences are minor when compared with what happens to the eukaryotic RNA after transcription. In bacteria, when transcription terminates, the result is a mature mRNA that's ready to be translated into a protein. In fact, translation often begins while the mRNA is still being transcribed.

The fate of the transcript in eukaryotes is more complicated. When eukaryotic genes of any type are transcribed, the initial product is termed a **primary transcript.** This RNA must undergo multistep processing before it is functional. For protein-coding genes, the primary transcript is called a **pre-mRNA.**

The processing of primary transcripts has important consequences for gene expression in eukaryotes. Let's delve in to see how and why.

The Startling Discovery of Split Eukaryotic Genes

Eukaryotic genes do not consist of one continuous DNA sequence that codes for a product, as do bacterial genes. Instead, the regions in a eukaryotic gene that code for proteins are intermittently interrupted by stretches of hundreds or even thousands of intervening bases.

Although these intervening bases are part of the gene, they do not code for a product. To make a functional RNA, eukaryotic cells must dispose of certain sequences inside the primary transcript and then combine the separated sections into an integrated whole.

What sort of data would provoke such a startling claim? The first evidence came from work that Phillip Sharp and colleagues carried out in the late 1970s to determine the location of genes within the DNA of a virus that infects mammalian cells. Viruses are often used as tools to provide insights into fundamental processes of the cells they infect.

They began one of their experiments by heating the virus' DNA sufficiently to break the hydrogen bonds between complementary bases. This treatment separated the two strands. The single-stranded DNA was then incubated with the mRNA encoded by the virus. The team's intention was to promote base pairing between the mRNA and the single-stranded DNA.

The researchers expected that the mRNA would form base pairs with the DNA sequence that acted as the template for its synthesis—that the mRNA and DNA would match up exactly.

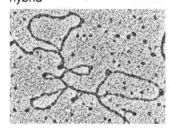

(a) Micrograph of DNA-RNA hybrid

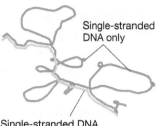

(b) Interpretation of micrograph

Single-stranded DNA only

Single-stranded DNA base paired with mRNA

FIGURE 17.5 The Discovery of Introns. The loops in the micrograph and drawing represent regions of DNA that are transcribed but are not found in the final mRNA. These regions are introns.

✔ **QUESTION** If the noncoding regions of the gene did not exist, what would the micrograph in part (a) look like?

But when the team examined the DNA–RNA hybrid molecules using an electron microscope, they observed the structure shown in **FIGURE 17.5a**. Instead of matching up exactly, parts of the DNA formed loops.

What was going on? As **FIGURE 17.5b** shows, Sharp's group interpreted these loops as stretches of DNA that are present in the template strand but are *not* in the corresponding mRNA.

Sharp's group and a team headed by Richard Roberts then carried out similar studies on eukaryotic genes. The results were the same as for the viral genes. They went on to propose that there is not a one-to-one correspondence between the nucleotide sequence of a eukaryotic gene and its mRNA. As an analogy, it could be said that eukaryotic genes do not carry messages such as "Biology is my favorite course of all time." Instead, they carry messages that read something like:

BIOLτηεπροτεινχοδινγρεγιονσοφγενεσOGY IS MY
FAVORαρειντερρθπτεθβυνονψοθινγθITE COURSE
OF ανθηαωετοβεσπλιχεθτογετηερ ALL TIME

Here the sections of noncoding sequence are represented with Greek letters. They must be removed from the mRNA before it can carry an intelligible message to the translation machinery.

When it became clear that the genes-in-pieces hypothesis was correct, Walter Gilbert suggested that regions of eukaryotic genes that are part of the final mRNA be referred to as **exons** (because they are *ex*pressed) and the sections of primary transcript not in mRNA be referred to as **introns** (because they are *intr*vening). Introns are sections of genes that are not represented in the final RNA product. Because of introns, eukaryotic genes are much larger than their corresponding mature RNAs. Introns were first discovered in genes that produce mRNA, but researchers later found that genes for other types of RNA also could be split.

RNA Splicing

The transcription of eukaryotic genes by RNA polymerase generates a primary transcript (**FIGURE 17.6a**) that contains both exons and introns. As transcription proceeds, the introns are removed

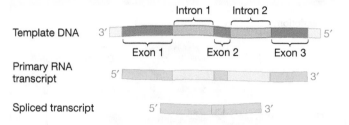

(a) Introns must be removed from eukaryotic RNA transcripts.

Intron 1 Intron 2

Template DNA 3′ [Exon 1 Exon 2 Exon 3] 5′

Primary RNA transcript 5′ 3′

Spliced transcript 5′ 3′

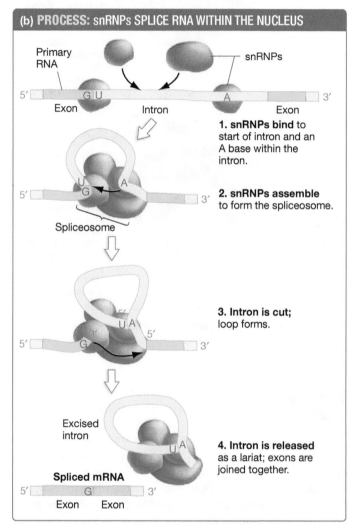

(b) PROCESS: snRNPs SPLICE RNA WITHIN THE NUCLEUS

Primary RNA

snRNPs

5′ G U A 3′

Exon Intron Exon

1. snRNPs bind to start of intron and an A base within the intron.

Spliceosome

2. snRNPs assemble to form the spliceosome.

3. Intron is cut; loop forms.

Excised intron

4. Intron is released as a lariat; exons are joined together.

Spliced mRNA

5′ G 3′

Exon Exon

FIGURE 17.6 Introns Are Spliced Out of the Primary Transcript.

from the growing RNA strand by a process known as **splicing.** In this phase of information processing, pieces of the primary transcript are removed and the remaining segments are joined together. Splicing occurs within the nucleus while transcription is still under way and results in an RNA that contains an uninterrupted genetic message.

FIGURE 17.6b provides more detail about how introns are removed from primary transcripts to form mRNA. Splicing of primary transcripts is catalyzed by RNAs called small nuclear RNAs (snRNAs) working with a complex of proteins. These protein-plus-RNA macromolecular machines are known as **small nuclear ribonucleoproteins,** or **snRNPs** (pronounced "snurps").

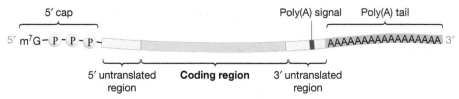

FIGURE 17.7 In Eukaryotes, a Cap and a Tail Are Added to mRNAs. As part of eukaryotic pre-mRNA processing, a cap consisting of a modified guanine (G) nucleotide (symbolized as m⁷G) bonded to three phosphate groups is added to the 5′ end, and a tail made up of a long series of adenine (A) residues is added to the 3′ end after cleavage of the primary transcript.

The snRNAs of the snRNPs recognize RNA sequences critical for splicing. Splicing can be broken into four steps:

1. The process begins when snRNPs bind to the 5′ exon–intron boundary, which is marked by the bases GU, and to a key adenine ribonucleotide (A) near the end the intron.

2. Once the initial snRNPs are in place, other snRNPs arrive to form a multipart complex called a **spliceosome.** The spliceosomes found in human cells contain about 145 different proteins and RNAs, making them the most complex macromolecular machines known.

3. The intron forms a loop plus a single-stranded stem (a lariat) with the adenine at its connecting point.

4. The lariat is cut out, and a phosphodiester linkage links the exons on either side, producing a continuous coding sequence—the mRNA.

Splicing is now complete. In most cases, the excised intron is degraded to ribonucleoside monophosphates.

As you'll see later (Chapter 19), for many genes, the RNA can be spliced in more than one way. This allows the production of different, related mRNAs and proteins from one gene.

Current data suggest that both the cutting and rejoining reactions that occur during splicing are catalyzed by the snRNA molecules in the spliceosome—meaning that the reactions are catalyzed by a ribozyme. Section 17.5 will demonstrate that ribozymes also play a key role in translation. As the RNA world hypothesis (Chapter 4) predicts, proteins are not the only important catalysts in cells.

What is the origin of introns? One hypothesis is that introns in eukaryotes arose from an ancient type of DNA sequence that is present in many bacteria and archaea. These ancient sequences are related to viruses (Chapter 36) and, like viruses, can infect cells and insert into their genomes. Remarkably, when this DNA sequence inserts into a gene and is transcribed, the RNA catalyzes its own splicing out of the primary transcript. This is possible in part because these virus-like elements have sequences similar to snRNAs.

The bacterium that was the source of mitochondria (see Chapter 30) likely carried some of these virus-like DNA sequences. When this bacterium was taken up by an ancestral eukaryote, the virus-like sequences are hypothesized to have spread rapidly. Later in evolution, the portion of the sequence that was a precursor to today's snRNA may have separated from the portion of the sequence that was spliced. This spliced sequence is hypothesized to be the ancestor of the modern eukaryotic intron.

Adding Caps and Tails to Transcripts

For pre-mRNAs, intron splicing is accompanied by other important processing steps.

- As soon as the 5′ end of a eukaryotic pre-mRNA emerges from RNA polymerase, enzymes add a structure called the **5′ cap** (**FIGURE 17.7**). The cap consists of a modified guanine (7-methylguanylate) nucleotide with three phosphate groups.

- An enzyme cleaves the 3′ end of the pre-mRNA downstream of the poly(A) signal (introduced in Section 17.1). Another enzyme adds a long row of 100–250 adenine nucleotides that are not encoded on the DNA template strand. This string of adenines is known as the **poly(A) tail.**

With the addition of the cap and tail and completion of splicing, processing of the pre-mRNA is complete. The product is a mature mRNA.

Figure 17.7 also shows that in the mature RNA molecule, the coding sequence for the polypeptide is flanked by sequences that are not destined to be translated. These 5′ and 3′ untranslated regions (or UTRs) help stabilize the mature RNA and regulate its translation. The mRNAs in bacteria also possess 5′ and 3′ UTRs.

Not long after the caps and tails on eukaryotic mRNAs were discovered, evidence began to accumulate that they protect mRNAs from degradation by ribonucleases—enzymes that

check your understanding

If you understand that . . .

- Eukaryotic genes consist of exons, which are parts of the primary transcript that remain in mature RNA, and introns, which are regions of the primary transcript that are removed in forming mature RNA.
- Macromolecular machines, called spliceosomes, splice introns out of pre-mRNAs.
- Enzymes add a 5′ cap and a poly(A) tail to spliced transcripts, producing a mature mRNA that is ready to be translated.

✔ **You should be able to . . .**

1. Explain why ribonucleoprotein is an appropriate name for the subunits of the spliceosome.

2. Explain the function of the 5′ cap and the poly(A) tail.

Answers are available in Appendix A.

CHAPTER 17 Transcription, RNA Processing, and Translation **323**

degrade RNA—and enhance the efficiency of translation. For example:

- Experimental mRNAs that have a cap and a tail last longer when they are introduced into cells than do experimental mRNAs that lack a cap or a tail.

- Experimental mRNAs with caps and tails produce more proteins than do experimental mRNAs without caps and tails.

Follow-up work has shown that the 5′ cap and the poly(A) tail are bound by proteins that prevent ribonucleases in the cytoplasm from recognizing and destroying the mRNA. The 5′ cap and the poly(A) tail also are important for initiating translation.

RNA processing is the general term for any of the modifications, such as splicing or poly(A) tail addition, needed to convert a primary transcript into a mature RNA. It is summarized in **TABLE 17.1** along with other important differences in how RNAs are produced in eukaryotes as compared with bacteria.

17.3 An Introduction to Translation

To synthesize a protein, the sequence of bases in a messenger RNA molecule is translated into a sequence of amino acids in a polypeptide. The genetic code specifies the correspondence between each triplet codon in mRNA and the amino acid it codes for (see Chapter 16). But how are the amino acids assembled into a polypeptide according to the information in messenger RNA?

(a) Bacterial ribosomes during translation

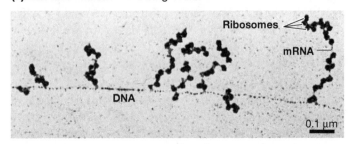

(b) In bacteria, transcription and translation are tightly coupled.

Studies of translation in cell-free systems proved extremely effective in answering this question. Once in vitro translation systems had been developed from human cells, *E. coli*, and a variety of other organisms, biologists could see that the sequence of events is similar in bacteria, archaea, and eukaryotes. As with similarities in transcription across the domains of life, the shared mechanisms of translation argue for a common ancestor of all cells living today.

Ribosomes Are the Site of Protein Synthesis

The first question that biologists answered about translation concerned where it occurs. The answer grew from a simple observation: There is a strong correlation between the number of **ribosomes** in a given type of cell and the rate at which that cell synthesizes proteins. Based on this observation, investigators proposed that ribosomes are the site of protein synthesis.

To test this hypothesis, Roy Britten and collaborators did a pulse–chase experiment similar in design to experiments introduced earlier (Chapter 7). Recall that a pulse–chase experiment labels a population of molecules as they are being produced. The location of the tagged molecules is then followed over time.

In this case, the tagging was done by supplying a pulse of radioactive sulfur atoms that would be incorporated into the amino acids methionine and cysteine, followed by a chase of unlabeled sulfur atoms. If the ribosome hypothesis were correct, the radioactive signal should be associated with ribosomes for a short period of time—when the amino acids are being polymerized into proteins. Later, when translation was complete, all the radioactivity should be found in proteins that are not associated with ribosomes.

This is exactly what the researchers found. Based on these data, biologists concluded that proteins are synthesized at ribosomes and then released.

Translation in Bacteria and Eukaryotes

About a decade after the ribosome hypothesis was confirmed, electron micrographs showed bacterial ribosomes in action (**FIGURE 17.8a**). The images showed that in bacteria, ribosomes

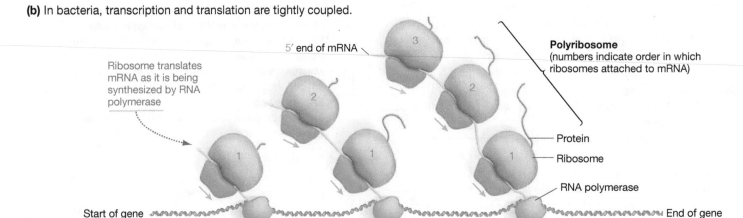

FIGURE 17.8 Transcription and Translation Occur Simultaneously in Bacteria. In bacteria, ribosomes attach to mRNA transcripts and begin translation while RNA polymerase is still transcribing the DNA template strand.

TABLE 17.1 Transcription and RNA Processing in Bacteria and Eukaryotes

Point of Comparison	Bacteria	Eukaryotes
RNA polymerase(s)	One	Three; each produces a different class of RNA
Promoter structure	Typically contains a −35 box and a −10 box	More variable; often includes a TATA box about −30 from the transcription start site
Proteins involved in recognizing promoter	Sigma; different versions of sigma bind to different promoters	Many basal transcription factors
RNA processing	None	Extensive; several processing steps occur in the nucleus before RNA is exported to the cytoplasm: **(1)** Enzyme-catalyzed addition of 5′ cap on mRNAs, **(2)** Splicing (intron removal); by spliceosome to produce mRNA, **(3)** Enzyme-catalyzed addition of 3′ poly(A) tail on mRNAs

attach to mRNAs and begin synthesizing proteins even before transcription is complete. In fact, multiple ribosomes attach to each mRNA, forming a **polyribosome** (**FIGURE 17.8b**). In this way, many copies of a protein can be produced from a single mRNA.

Transcription and translation can occur concurrently in bacteria because there is no nuclear envelope to separate the two processes.

The situation is different in eukaryotes. In these organisms, primary transcripts are processed in the nucleus to produce a mature mRNA, which is then exported to the cytoplasm (**FIGURE 17.9**). This means that in eukaryotes, transcription and translation are separated in time and space. Once mRNAs are outside the nucleus, ribosomes can attach to them and begin translation. As in bacteria, polyribosomes form.

How Does an mRNA Triplet Specify an Amino Acid?

When an mRNA interacts with a ribosome, instructions encoded in nucleic acids are translated into a different chemical language—the amino acid sequences found in proteins. The discovery of the genetic code revealed that triplet codons in mRNA specify particular amino acids in a protein. How does this conversion occur?

One early hypothesis was that mRNA codons and amino acids interact directly. This hypothesis proposed that the bases in a particular codon were complementary in shape or charge to the side group of a particular amino acid (**FIGURE 17.10a**, see page 326). But Francis Crick pointed out that the idea didn't make chemical sense. For example, how could the nucleic acid bases interact with a hydrophobic amino acid side group, which does not form hydrogen bonds?

Crick proposed an alternative hypothesis. As **FIGURE 17.10b** shows, he suggested that some sort of adapter molecule holds amino acids in place while interacting directly and specifically with a codon in mRNA by hydrogen bonding. In essence, Crick predicted the existence of a chemical go-between that produced a physical connection between the two types of molecules. As it turns out, Crick was right.

(a) mRNAs are exported to the cytoplasm.

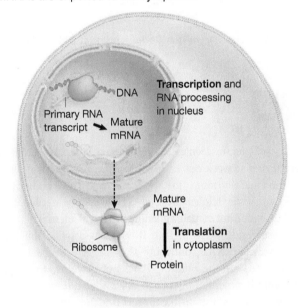

(b) Polypeptides grow from ribosomes translating mRNA.

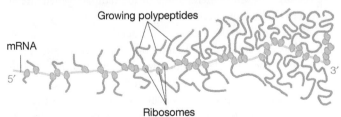

FIGURE 17.9 Transcription and Translation Are Separated in Space and Time in Eukaryotes.

(a) Hypothesis 1: Amino acids interact directly with mRNA codons.

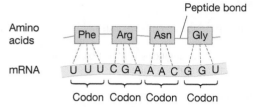

(b) Hypothesis 2: Adapter molecules hold amino acids and interact with mRNA codons.

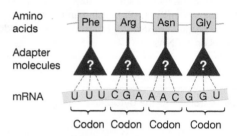

FIGURE 17.10 How Do mRNA Codons Interact with Amino Acids?

17.4 The Structure and Function of Transfer RNA

Crick's adapter molecule was discovered by accident. Biologists were trying to work out an in vitro protein-synthesis system and reasoned that ribosomes, mRNA, amino acids, ATP, and a molecule called guanosine triphosphate, or GTP, would be needed. (GTP is similar to ATP but contains guanine instead of adenine.)

These results were logical: Ribosomes provide the catalytic machinery, mRNAs contribute the message to be translated, amino acids are the building blocks of proteins, and ATP and GTP supply potential energy to drive the endergonic polymerization reactions responsible for forming proteins.

But, in addition, a cellular fraction that contained a previously unknown type of RNA turned out to be indispensable. If this type of RNA is missing, protein synthesis does not occur. What is this mysterious RNA, and why is it essential to translation?

The novel class of RNAs eventually became known as **transfer RNA (tRNA)**. The role of tRNA in translation was a mystery until some researchers happened to add a radioactive amino acid—leucine—to an in vitro protein-synthesis system. The treatment was actually done as a control for an unrelated experiment. To the researchers' amazement, some of the radioactive leucine attached to tRNA molecules.

What happens to the amino acids bound to tRNAs? To answer this question, Paul Zamecnik and colleagues tracked the fate of radioactive leucine molecules that were attached to tRNAs. They found that the amino acids are transferred from tRNAs to proteins.

The data supporting this conclusion are shown in the "Results" section of **FIGURE 17.11**. The graph shows that radioactive amino acids are lost from tRNAs and incorporated into polypeptides synthesized by ribosomes. To understand this conclusion:

RESEARCH

QUESTION: What happens to the amino acids attached to tRNAs?

HYPOTHESIS: Aminoacyl tRNAs transfer amino acids to growing polypeptides.

NULL HYPOTHESIS: Aminoacyl tRNAs do not transfer amino acids to growing polypeptides.

EXPERIMENTAL SETUP:

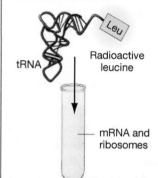

1. Attach radioactive leucine molecules to tRNAs.

2. Add these aminoacyl tRNAs to in vitro translation system. Follow fate of the radioactive amino acids.

PREDICTION: Radioactive amino acids will be found in proteins.

PREDICTION OF NULL HYPOTHESIS: Radioactive amino acids will not be found in proteins.

RESULTS:

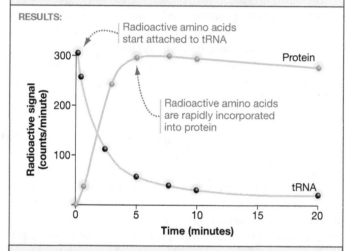

CONCLUSION: Aminoacyl tRNAs transfer amino acids to growing polypeptides.

FIGURE 17.11 Evidence that Amino Acids Are Transferred from tRNAs to Proteins.

SOURCE: Hoagland, M. B., M. L. Stephenson, J. F. Scott, et al. 1958. A soluble ribonucleic acid intermediate in protein synthesis. *Journal of Biological Chemistry* 231: 241–257.

✔ **QUESTION** What would the graphed results look like if the null hypothesis were correct?

1. Put your finger on the point on the *x*-axis that indicates that one minute has passed since the start of the experiment.

2. Read up until you hit the green line and the gray line. The green line represents data from proteins; the gray line represents data from tRNAs.

3. Check the *y*-axis—which indicates the amount of radioactive leucine present—at each point.

4. It should be clear that early in the experiment, almost all the radioactive leucine is attached to tRNA, not protein.

Next, do the same four steps at the point on the *x*-axis labeled 10 minutes (since the start of the experiment). Your conclusion now should be that late in the experiment, almost all the radioactive leucine is attached to proteins, not tRNA.

These results inspired the use of the word transfer in tRNA's name, because amino acids are transferred from the RNA to a growing polypeptide. The experiment also confirmed that tRNAs act as the interpreter during translation: tRNAs are Crick's adapter molecules.

What Do tRNAs Look Like?

Transfer RNAs serve as chemical go-betweens that allow amino acids to interact with an mRNA template. But precisely how does the connection occur?

This question was answered by research on tRNA's molecular structure. The initial studies established the sequence of nucleotides in various tRNAs, or what is termed their primary structure. Transfer RNA sequences are relatively short, ranging from 75 to 85 nucleotides in length.

When biologists studied the primary sequence closely, they noticed that certain parts of the molecules can form secondary structures. Specifically, some sequences of bases in the tRNA molecule can form hydrogen bonds with complementary base sequences elsewhere in the same molecule. As a result, portions of the molecule form stem-and-loop structures (introduced in Chapter 4). The stems are short stretches of double-stranded RNA; the loops are single stranded.

Two aspects of tRNA's secondary structure proved especially important. A CCA sequence at the 3' end of each tRNA molecule offered a site for amino acid attachment, while a triplet on the loop at the other end of the structure could serve as an anticodon. An **anticodon** is a set of three ribonucleotides that forms base pairs with the mRNA codon.

Later, X-ray crystallography studies revealed the tertiary structure of tRNAs. Recall that the tertiary structure of a molecule is the three-dimensional arrangement of its atoms (Chapter 3). As **FIGURE 17.12** shows, tRNAs fold into an L-shaped molecule. The anticodon is at one end of the structure; the CCA sequence and attached amino acid are at the other end.

All the tRNAs in a cell have the same general structure, shaped like an upside-down L. They vary at the anticodon and attached amino acid. The tertiary structure of tRNAs is important because it maintains a precise physical distance between the anticodon and amino acid. As it turns out, this separation is important in positioning the amino acid and the anticodon within the ribosome.

✔ If you understand the structure of tRNAs, you should be able to (1) describe where on the L-shaped structure the amino acid attaches; and (2) explain the relationship between the anticodon of a tRNA and a codon in an mRNA.

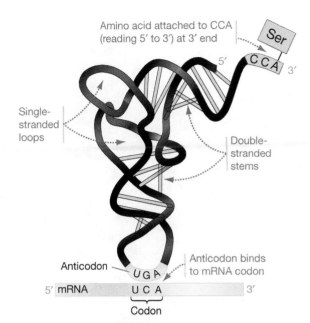

FIGURE 17.12 **The Structure of an Aminoacyl Transfer RNA.** The anticodon forms complementary base pairs with an mRNA codon.

How Are Amino Acids Attached to tRNAs?

How are amino acids linked to tRNAs? Just as important, what allows the right amino acid for a particular tRNA to be attached?

- An input of energy, in the form of ATP, is required to attach an amino acid to a tRNA.

- Enzymes called **aminoacyl-tRNA synthetases** catalyze the addition of amino acids to tRNAs—what biologists call "charging" a tRNA.

- For each of the 20 major amino acids, there is a different aminoacyl-tRNA synthetase and one or more tRNAs.

Each aminoacyl-tRNA synthetase has a binding site for a particular amino acid and a particular tRNA. Subtle differences in tRNA shape and base sequence allow the enzymes to recognize the correct tRNA for the correct amino acid. The combination of a tRNA molecule covalently linked to an amino acid is called an **aminoacyl tRNA. FIGURE 17.13** (see page 328) shows an aminoacyl-tRNA synthetase bound to a tRNA that has just been charged with an amino acid. Note how tightly the two structures fit together—making it possible for the enzyme and its tRNA and amino acid substrates to interact in a precise way.

How Many tRNAs Are There?

After characterizing all the different types of tRNAs, biologists encountered a paradox. According to the genetic code (Chapter 16), the 20 most common amino acids found in proteins are specified by 61 different mRNA codons. Instead of containing 61 different tRNAs with 61 different anticodons, though, most cells contain only about 40. How can all 61 codons be translated with only two-thirds that number of tRNAs?

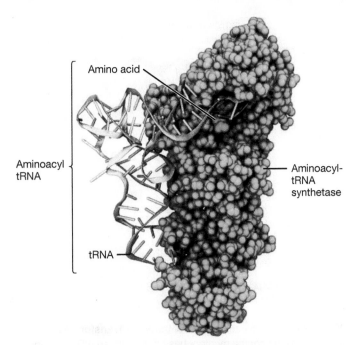

FIGURE 17.13 Aminoacyl-tRNA Synthetases Couple the Appropriate Amino Acid to the Appropriate tRNA.

To resolve this paradox, Francis Crick proposed what is known as the **wobble hypothesis.** Recall that:

1. Many amino acids are specified by more than one codon.

2. Codons for the same amino acid tend to have the same nucleotides at the first and second positions but a different nucleotide at the third position.

For example, both of the codons CAA and CAG code for the amino acid glutamine. Surprisingly, experimental data have shown that a tRNA with an anticodon of GUU can base-pair with both CAA and CAG in mRNA. The GUU anticodon matches the first two bases (C and A) in both codons, but the U in the anticodon's third position forms a nonstandard base pair with a G in the CAG codon.

Crick proposed that inside the ribosome, certain bases in the third position of tRNA anticodons can bind to bases in the third position of a codon in a manner that does not match Watson–Crick base pairing. If so, this would allow a limited flexibility, or "wobble," in the base pairing.

According to the wobble hypothesis, particular nonstandard base pairs—such as G-U—are acceptable in the third position of a codon and do not change the amino acid that the codon specifies. In this way, wobble in the third position of a codon allows just 40 or so tRNAs to bind to all 61 mRNA codons.

17.5 The Structure and Function of Ribosomes

Recall that protein synthesis occurs when the sequence of bases in an mRNA is translated into a sequence of amino acids in a polypeptide. The translation of each mRNA codon begins when the anticodon of an aminoacyl tRNA binds to the codon. Translation of a codon is complete when a peptide bond forms between the tRNA's amino acid and the growing polypeptide chain.

Both of these events take place inside a ribosome. Biologists have known since the 1930s that ribosomes contain many proteins and **ribosomal RNAs (rRNAs).** Later work showed that ribosomes can be separated into two major substructures, called the large subunit and small subunit. Each ribosome subunit consists of a complex of RNA molecules and proteins. The small subunit holds the mRNA in place during translation; the large subunit is where peptide-bond formation takes place.

FIGURE 17.14 shows two views of how the molecules required for translation fit together. Note that during protein synthesis, three distinct tRNAs are lined up inside the ribosome. All three are bound to their corresponding mRNA codons.

- The tRNA that is on the right in the figure, and colored red, carries an amino acid. This tRNA's position in the ribosome is called the A site—"A" for acceptor or aminoacyl.

- The tRNA that is in the middle (green) holds the growing polypeptide chain and occupies the P site, for peptidyl, inside the ribosome. (Think of "P" for peptide-bond formation.)

- The left-hand (blue) tRNA no longer has an amino acid attached and is about to leave the ribosome. It occupies the ribosome's E site—"E" for exit.

Because all tRNAs have similar secondary and tertiary structure, they all fit equally well in the A, P, and E sites.

The ribosome is a macromolecular machine that synthesizes proteins in a three-step sequence:

1. An aminoacyl tRNA diffuses into the A site; if its anticodon matches a codon in mRNA, it stays in the ribosome.

2. A peptide bond forms between the amino acid held by the aminoacyl tRNA in the A site and the growing polypeptide, which was held by a tRNA in the P site.

3. The ribosome moves down the mRNA by one codon, and all three tRNAs move one position within the ribosome. The tRNA in the E site exits; the tRNA in the P site moves to the E site; and the tRNA in the A site switches to the P site.

The protein that is being synthesized grows by one amino acid each time this three-step sequence repeats. The process occurs up to 20 times per second in bacterial ribosomes and about 2 times per second in eukaryotic ribosomes. Protein synthesis starts at the amino end (N-terminus) of a polypeptide and proceeds to the carboxy end (C-terminus; see Chapter 3).

This introduction to how tRNAs, mRNAs, and ribosomes interact during protein synthesis leaves several key questions unanswered. How do mRNAs and ribosomes get together to start the process? Once protein synthesis is under way, how is peptide-bond formation catalyzed inside the ribosome? And how does protein synthesis conclude when the ribosome reaches the end of the message? Let's consider each question in turn.

(a) Diagram of ribosome during translation (interior view)

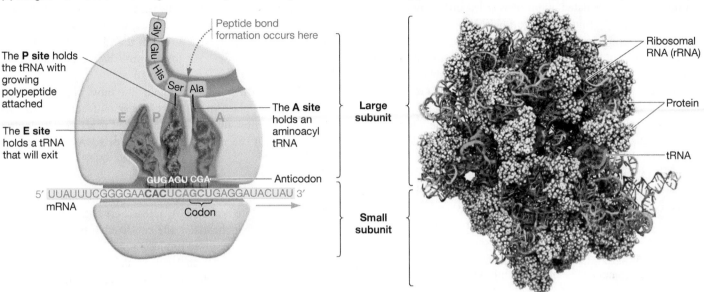

(b) Model of ribosome during translation (exterior view)

The **P site** holds the tRNA with growing polypeptide attached

Peptide bond formation occurs here

The **A site** holds an aminoacyl tRNA

The **E site** holds a tRNA that will exit

Large subunit

Anticodon

5′ UUAUUUCGGGGAA**CAC**UC**AGC**UGAGGAUACUAU 3′

mRNA

Codon

Small subunit

Ribosomal RNA (rRNA)

Protein

tRNA

FIGURE 17.14 The Structure of the Ribosome. Ribosomes have three distinct tRNA binding sites in their interior.

Initiating Translation

To translate an mRNA properly, a ribosome must begin at a specific point in the message, translate the mRNA up to the message's termination codon, and then stop. Using the same terminology that they apply to transcription, biologists call these three phases of protein synthesis initiation, elongation, and termination, respectively.

One key to understanding translation initiation is to recall that a start codon (usually AUG) is found near the 5′ end of all mRNAs and that it codes for the amino acid methionine (Chapter 16).

FIGURE 17.15 shows how translation gets under way in bacteria. The process begins when a section of rRNA in a small ribosomal subunit binds to a complementary sequence on an mRNA. The mRNA region is called the **ribosome binding site,** or **Shine–Dalgarno sequence,** after the biologists who discovered it. The site is about six nucleotides upstream from the start codon.

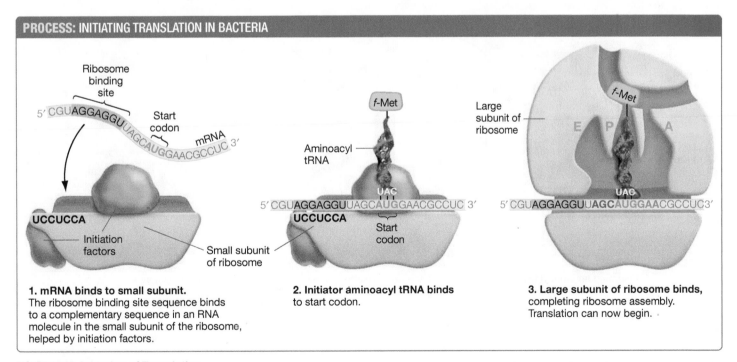

PROCESS: INITIATING TRANSLATION IN BACTERIA

Ribosome binding site

5′ CGU**AGGAGGU**UAGCAUGGAACGCCUC 3′

Start codon

mRNA

UCCUCCA

Initiation factors

Small subunit of ribosome

1. mRNA binds to small subunit.
The ribosome binding site sequence binds to a complementary sequence in an RNA molecule in the small subunit of the ribosome, helped by initiation factors.

f-Met

Aminoacyl tRNA

UAC

5′ CGU**AGGAGGU**UAGCAUGGAACGCCUC 3′

UCCUCCA

Start codon

2. Initiator aminoacyl tRNA binds to start codon.

f-Met

Large subunit of ribosome

E P A

UAC

5′ CGU**AGGAGGU**U**AGC**AUGGAACGCCUC 3′

3. Large subunit of ribosome binds, completing ribosome assembly. Translation can now begin.

FIGURE 17.15 Initiation of Translation.

The interactions between the small subunit, the message, and the tRNA are mediated by proteins called **initiation factors** (Figure 17.15, step 1). Initiation factors help in preparing the ribosome for translation, including binding the first aminoacyl tRNA to the ribosome. In bacteria this initiator tRNA bears a modified form of methionine called *N*-formylmethionine (abbreviated *f*-met) (Figure 17.15, step 2). In eukaryotes, this initiating tRNA carries a normal methionine. Initiation factors also prevent the small and large subunits of the ribosome from coming together until the initiator tRNA is in place at the AUG start codon, and they help bind the mRNA to the small ribosomal subunit.

Initiation is complete when the large subunit joins the complex (Figure 17.15, step 3). When the ribosome is completely assembled, the tRNA bearing *f*-met occupies the P site.

To summarize, translation initiation is a three-step process in bacteria: (1) The mRNA binds to a small ribosomal subunit, (2) the initiator aminoacyl tRNA bearing *f*-met binds to the start codon, and (3) the large ribosomal subunit binds, completing the complex.

In eukaryotes, the details of initiation are different, but they still involve recognition of a start codon, assembly of the ribosome, assistance from initiation factors, and the positioning of a methionine-carrying tRNA in the P site. The cap and poly(A) tail are also important in assembling the ribosome on the mRNA.

Elongation: Extending the Polypeptide

At the start of elongation, the E and A sites in the ribosome are empty of tRNAs. As a result, an mRNA codon is exposed in the A site. As step 1 in **FIGURE 17.16** illustrates, elongation proceeds when an aminoacyl tRNA binds to the codon in the A site by complementary base pairing between the anticodon and codon.

When both the P site and A site are occupied by tRNAs, the amino acids on the tRNAs are in the ribosome's active site. This is where peptide-bond formation—the essence of protein synthesis—occurs.

Peptide-bond formation is one of the most important reactions that take place in cells because manufacturing proteins is among the most fundamental of all cell processes. Biologists wondered, is it the ribosome's proteins or RNAs that catalyze this reaction?

Is the Ribosome an Enzyme or a Ribozyme? Because ribosomes contain both protein and RNA, researchers had argued for decades over whether the active site consisted of protein or RNA. The debate was not resolved until the year 2000, when researchers completed three-dimensional models that were detailed enough to reveal the structure of the active site. These models confirmed that the active site consists entirely of ribosomal RNA. Based on these results, biologists are now convinced that protein synthesis is catalyzed by RNA. The ribosome is a ribozyme—not a protein-based enzyme.

The observation that protein synthesis is catalyzed by RNA is important because it supports the RNA-world hypothesis (Chapter 4). Recall that proponents of this hypothesis claim that life began with RNA molecules and that the presence of DNA and proteins in cells evolved later. If the RNA-world hypothesis is correct, then it would make sense that the production of proteins is catalyzed by RNA.

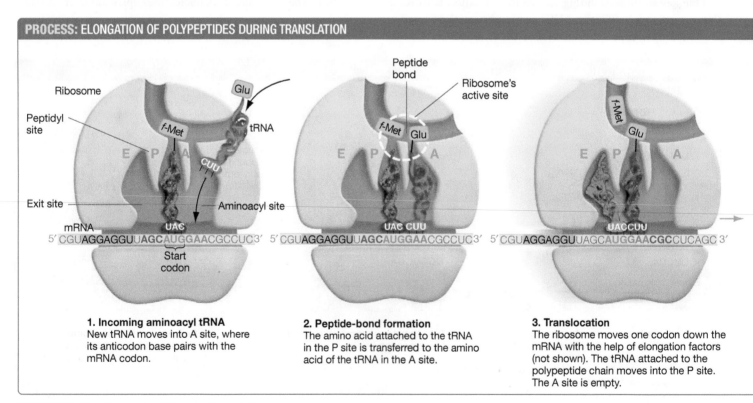

PROCESS: ELONGATION OF POLYPEPTIDES DURING TRANSLATION

1. Incoming aminoacyl tRNA
New tRNA moves into A site, where its anticodon base pairs with the mRNA codon.

2. Peptide-bond formation
The amino acid attached to the tRNA in the P site is transferred to the amino acid of the tRNA in the A site.

3. Translocation
The ribosome moves one codon down the mRNA with the help of elongation factors (not shown). The tRNA attached to the polypeptide chain moves into the P site. The A site is empty.

FIGURE 17.16 The Elongation Phase of Translation.

Moving Down the mRNA What happens after a peptide bond forms? Step 2 in Figure 17.16 shows that when peptide-bond formation is complete, the polypeptide chain is transferred from the tRNA in the P site to the amino acid held by the tRNA in the A site. Step 3 shows the process called **translocation,** which occurs when proteins called **elongation factors** help move the ribosome relative to the mRNA so that translation occurs in the 5′ → 3′ direction. Translocation is an energy-demanding event that requires GTP.

Translocation does several things: It moves the uncharged RNA into the E site; it moves the tRNA containing the growing polypeptide into the P site; and it opens the A site and exposes a new mRNA codon. The empty tRNA that finds itself in the E site is ejected into the cytosol.

The three steps in elongation—(1) arrival of aminoacyl tRNA, (2) peptide-bond formation, and (3) translocation—repeat down the length of the mRNA. Recent three-dimensional models of ribosomes in various stages of translation show that the machine is highly dynamic. The ribosome constantly changes shape as tRNAs come and go and catalysis and translocation occur. The ribosome is a complex and dynamic macromolecular machine.

Terminating Translation

How does protein synthesis end? Recall that the genetic code includes three stop codons: UAA, UAG, and UGA (see Chapter 16). In most cells, no aminoacyl tRNA has an anticodon that binds to these sequences. When the translocating ribosome reaches one of the stop codons, a protein called a **release factor** recognizes the stop codon and fills the A site (**FIGURE 17.17**, see page 333).

Release factors fit tightly into the A site because they have the size and shape of a tRNA coming into the ribosome. However, release factors do not carry an amino acid. When a release factor occupies the A site, the protein's active site catalyzes the hydrolysis of the bond that links the tRNA in the P site to the polypeptide chain. This reaction frees the polypeptide.

The newly synthesized polypeptide and uncharged tRNAs are released from the ribosome, the ribosome separates from the mRNA, and the two ribosomal subunits dissociate. The subunits are ready to attach to the start codon of another message and start translation anew. Termination occurs in very similar ways in bacteria and eukaryotes.

Post-Translational Modifications

Proteins are not fully formed and functional when termination occurs. From earlier chapters, it should be clear that most proteins go through an extensive series of processing steps, collectively called post-translational modification, before they are completely functional. These steps require a wide array of molecules and events and take place in many different locations throughout the cell.

Folding Recall that a protein's function depends on its shape, and that a protein's shape depends on how it folds (see Chapter 3). Although folding can occur spontaneously, it is frequently speeded up by proteins called **molecular chaperones.**

Recent data have shown that in some bacteria, chaperone proteins bind to the ribosome near the "tunnel" where the growing polypeptide emerges from the ribosome. This finding suggests that folding occurs as the polypeptide emerges from the ribosome.

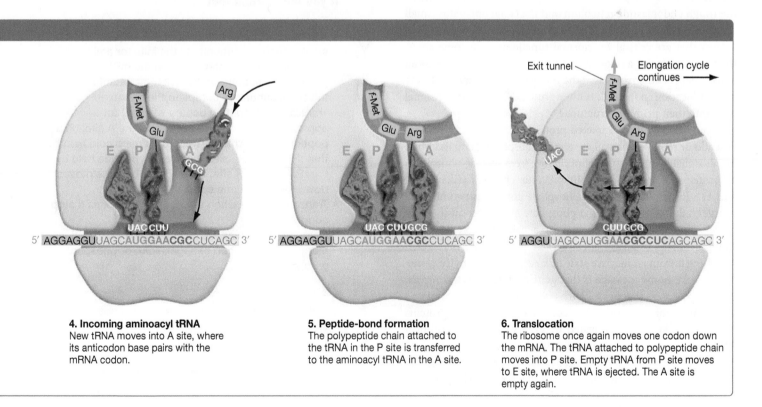

4. Incoming aminoacyl tRNA
New tRNA moves into A site, where its anticodon base pairs with the mRNA codon.

5. Peptide-bond formation
The polypeptide chain attached to the tRNA in the P site is transferred to the aminoacyl tRNA in the A site.

6. Translocation
The ribosome once again moves one codon down the mRNA. The tRNA attached to polypeptide chain moves into P site. Empty tRNA from P site moves to E site, where tRNA is ejected. The A site is empty again.

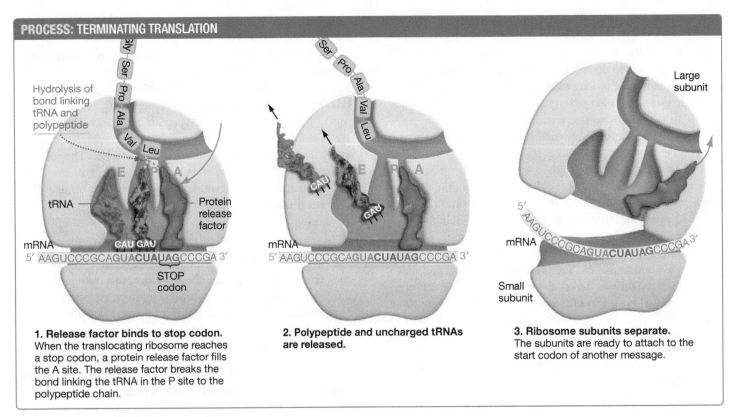

1. Release factor binds to stop codon.
When the translocating ribosome reaches a stop codon, a protein release factor fills the A site. The release factor breaks the bond linking the tRNA in the P site to the polypeptide chain.

2. Polypeptide and uncharged tRNAs are released.

3. Ribosome subunits separate.
The subunits are ready to attach to the start codon of another message.

FIGURE 17.17 Termination of Translation.

Chemical Modifications An earlier chapter pointed out that many eukaryotic proteins are extensively modified after they are synthesized (see Chapter 7). For example, in the organelles called the rough endoplasmic reticulum and the Golgi apparatus, small chemical groups may be added to proteins—often sugar or lipid groups that are critical for normal functioning. In some cases, the proteins receive a sugar-based sorting signal that serves as an address label and ensures that the molecule will be carried to the correct location in the cell. (Other proteins have a sorting signal built into their primary structure.)

In addition, many completed proteins are altered by enzymes that add or remove a phosphate group. Phosphorylation (addition of phosphate) and dephosphorylation (removal of phosphate) of proteins were introduced in previous chapters (Chapters 9 and 11). Recall that because a phosphate group has two negative charges, adding or removing a phosphate group can cause major changes in the shape and chemical reactivity of proteins. These changes have a dramatic effect on the protein's activity—often switching it from an inactive state to an active state, or vice versa.

The take-home message is that gene expression is a complex, multistep process that begins with transcription but may not end with translation. Instead, even completed and folded proteins may be activated or deactivated by events such as phosphorylation. In general, how are genes turned on or off? How does a cell "decide" which of its many genes should be expressed at any time? These questions are the focus of the next two chapters.

check your understanding

If you understand that . . .

- Translation begins when (1) the ribosome binding site on an mRNA binds to an rRNA sequence in the small ribosomal subunit, (2) the initiator aminoacyl tRNA binds to the start codon in the mRNA, and (3) the large subunit of the ribosome attaches to the small subunit to complete the ribosome.
- Translation elongation occurs when (1) an appropriate aminoacyl tRNA enters the A site, (2) a peptide bond forms between the amino acid held by that tRNA in the A site and the polypeptide held by the tRNA in the P site, and (3) the ribosome moves down the mRNA one codon.
- Translation ends when the ribosome reaches a stop codon.
- Completed proteins are modified by folding and, in many cases, addition of sugar, lipid, or phosphate groups.

✔ **You should be able to . . .**

Explain why the E, P, and A sites in the ribosome are appropriately named.

Answers are available in Appendix A.

If you understand . . .

17.1 An Overview of Transcription

- RNA polymerase catalyzes the production of an RNA molecule whose base sequence is complementary to the base sequence of the DNA template strand.

- RNA polymerase binds DNA with the help of other proteins.

- RNA polymerase begins transcription by binding to promoter sequences in DNA.

- In bacteria, this binding occurs in conjunction with a protein called sigma. Sigma associates with RNA polymerase and then recognizes particular sequences within promoters that are centered 10 bases and 35 bases upstream from the start of the actual genetic message.

- Eukaryotic promoters vary more than bacterial promoters.

- In eukaryotes, transcription begins when a large array of proteins called basal transcription factors bind to a promoter. In response, RNA polymerase binds to the site.

- In both bacteria and eukaryotes, the RNA elongates in a 5′ → 3′ direction.

- Transcription in bacteria ends when RNA polymerase encounters a stem-loop structure in the just transcribed RNA; in eukaryotes, transcription terminates after the RNA is cleaved downstream of the poly(A) sequence.

✓ You should be able to predict the consequences of a mutation in bacteria that inserts random nucleotides into the hairpin-coding region near the 3′ end of a transcribed region.

17.2 RNA Processing in Eukaryotes

- In eukaryotes, the primary (initial) transcript must be processed to produce a mature RNA.

- In primary transcripts, stretches of RNA called introns are spliced out and regions called exons are joined together.

- Complex macromolecular machines called spliceosomes splice introns out of pre-mRNA.

- A "cap" is added to the 5′ end of pre-mRNAs, and a poly(A) tail is added to their 3′ end.

- The cap and tail serve as recognition signals for translation and protect the message from degradation by ribonucleases.

- RNA processing occurs in the nucleus.

✓ You should be able to predict whether the protein-coding portion of a gene for an identical protein will be of the same or different lengths in a bacterium and a eukaryote.

17.3 An Introduction to Translation

- Ribosomes translate mRNAs into proteins with the help of adaptor molecules called transfer RNAs.

- In bacteria, an RNA is often transcribed and translated at the same time because there is no nucleus.

- In eukaryotes, transcription and translation of an RNA cannot occur together, because transcription and RNA processing occur in the nucleus and translation occurs in the cytoplasm.

- Experiments with radioactively labeled amino acids showed that transfer RNAs (tRNAs) serve as the chemical bridge between the RNA message and the polypeptide product.

✓ You should be able to explain why it is correct to say that transfer RNAs work as molecular adaptors.

17.4 The Structure and Function of Transfer RNA

- Each transfer RNA carries an amino acid corresponding to the tRNA's three-base-long anticodon.

- tRNAs have an L-shaped, tertiary structure. One leg of the L contains the anticodon, which forms complementary base pairs with the mRNA codon. The other leg holds the amino acid appropriate for that codon.

- Enzymes called aminoacyl-tRNA synthetases link the correct amino acid to the correct tRNA.

- Imprecise pairing—or "wobble pairing"—is allowed in the third position of the codon and anticodon, so only about 40 different tRNAs are required to translate the 61 codons that code for amino acids.

✓ You should be able to predict what would occur if a mutation caused an aminoacyl-tRNA synthetase to recognize two different amino acids.

17.5 The Structure and Function of Ribosomes

- Ribosomes are large macromolecular machines made of many proteins and RNAs.

- In the ribosome, the tRNA anticodon binds to a three-base-long mRNA codon to bring the correct amino acid into the ribosome.

- Peptide-bond formation by the ribosome is catalyzed by a ribozyme (RNA), not an enzyme (protein).

- Protein synthesis occurs in three steps: **(1)** an incoming aminoacyl tRNA occupies the A site; **(2)** the growing polypeptide chain is transferred from a peptidyl tRNA in the ribosome's P site to the amino acid bound to the tRNA in the A site, and a peptide bond is formed; and **(3)** the ribosome is translocated to the next codon on the mRNA, accompanied by ejection of the uncharged RNA from the E site.

- Chaperone proteins help fold newly synthesized proteins into their three-dimensional conformation (tertiary structure).

- Most proteins need to be modified after translation (post-translational modification) to activate them or target them to specific locations.

✔ You should be able to create a concept map (see **BioSkills 15** in Appendix B) that describes the relationships among the following concepts and structures: translation, initiation, elongation, termination, growing polypeptide in P site, start codon, ribosome subunits.

 MasteringBiology

1. MasteringBiology Assignments

Tutorials and Activities Chromosomal Mutations; Following the Instructions in DNA; Point Mutations Protein Synthesis (1 of 3): Overview; Protein Synthesis (2 of 3): Transcription and RNA Processing; Protein Synthesis (3 of 3): Translation and Protein Targeting Pathways; RNA Processing; RNA Synthesis; Synthesizing Proteins; Transcription; Translation; Types of RNA

Questions Reading Quizzes, Blue-Thread Questions, Test Bank

2. eText Read your book online, search, take notes, highlight text, and more.

3. The Study Area Practice Test, Cumulative Test, BioFlix® 3-D Animations, Videos, Activities, Audio Glossary, Word Study Tools, Art

You should be able to . . .

✔ TEST YOUR KNOWLEDGE
Answers are available in Appendix A

1. How did the A site of the ribosome get its name?
   a. It is where amino acids are joined to tRNAs, producing aminoacyl tRNAs.
   b. It is where the amino group on the growing polypeptide chain is available for peptide-bond formation.
   c. It is the site occupied by incoming aminoacyl tRNAs.
   d. It is surrounded by α-helices of ribosomal proteins.

2. Where is the start codon located?
   a. at the very start (5′ end) of the mRNA
   b. at the downstream end of the 3′ untranslated region (UTR)
   c. at the downstream end of the 5′ untranslated region (UTR)
   d. at the upstream end of the 3′ untranslated region (UTR)

3. What is the function of a molecular chaperone?

4. What does a bacterial RNA polymerase produce when it transcribes a protein-coding gene?

   a. rRNA
   b. tRNA
   c. mRNA
   d. pre-mRNA

5. Where is an amino acid attached to a tRNA?

6. Compared with mRNAs that have a cap and tail, what do researchers observe when eukaryotic mRNAs that lack a cap and poly(A) tail are translated within a cell?
   a. The primary transcript cannot be processed properly.
   b. Translation occurs inefficiently.
   c. Enzymes on the ribosome add back a cap and poly(A) tail.
   d. tRNAs become resistant to degradation (being broken down).

✔ TEST YOUR UNDERSTANDING
Answers are available in Appendix A

7. Explain the relationship between eukaryotic promoter sequences, basal transcription factors, and RNA polymerase. Explain the relationship between bacterial promoter sequences, sigma, and RNA polymerase.

8. According to the wobble rules, the correct amino acid can be added to a growing polypeptide chain even if the third base in the mRNA codon is not complementary to the corresponding base in the tRNA anticodon. How do the wobble rules relate to the redundancy of the genetic code?

9. RNases and proteases are enzymes that destroy RNAs and proteins, respectively. Which of the following enzymes when added to a spliceosome is predicted to prevent recognition of pre-mRNA regions critical for splicing?
   a. an RNase specific for tRNAs
   b. an RNase specific for snRNAs
   c. a protease specific for initiation factors
   d. a protease specific for a release factor

10. Describe the sequence of events that occurs during translation as a protein elongates by one amino acid and the ribosome moves down the mRNA. Your answer should specify what is happening in the ribosome's A site, P site, and E site.

11. **QUANTITATIVE** Controlling the rates of transcription and translation is important in bacteria to avoid collisions between ribosomes and RNA polymerases. Calculate the maximum rate of translation by a ribosome in a bacterial cell, provided in units of amino acids per second, so that the ribosome doesn't overtake an RNA polymerase that is transcribing mRNA at a rate of 60 nucleotides per second. How long would it take for this bacterial cell to translate an mRNA containing 1800 codons?

12. In an aminoacyl tRNA, why is the observed distance between the amino acid and the anticodon important?

Answers are available in Appendix A

✓ TEST YOUR PROBLEM-SOLVING SKILLS

13. The 5′ cap and poly(A) tail in eukaryotic mRNAs protect the message from degradation by ribonucleases. But why do ribonucleases exist? What function would an enzyme that destroys messages serve? Answer this question using the example of an mRNA for a hormone that causes human heart rate to increase.

14. The nucleotide shown below is called cordycepin triphosphate.

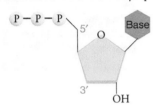

If cordycepin triphosphate is added to a cell-free transcription reaction, the nucleotide is added onto the growing RNA chain but no more nucleotides can be added. The added cordycepin is always found at the 3′ end of an RNA, confirming that synthesis occurs in the 5′ → 3′ direction. Why does cordycepin end transcription?

a. It prevents the association of RNA polymerase and sigma.
b. It irreversibly binds to the active site of RNA polymerase.
c. It cannot be recognized by RNA polymerase.
d. It lacks a 3′ OH.

15. Certain portions of the rRNAs in the large subunit of the ribosome are very similar in all organisms. To make sense of this finding, Carl Woese suggests that the conserved sequences have an important functional role. His logic is that these conserved sequences evolved in a common ancestor of all modern cells and are so important to cell function that any changes in the sequences cause death. In addition to rRNAs, which specific portions of the ribosome would you expect to be identical or nearly identical in all organisms? Explain your logic.

16. Recent structural models show that a poison called α-amanitin inhibits transcription by binding to a site inside eukaryotic RNA polymerase II but not to the active site itself. Based on the model of RNA polymerase in Figure 17.2, predict a place or places where α-amanitin might bind to inhibit transcription.

18 Control of Gene Expression in Bacteria

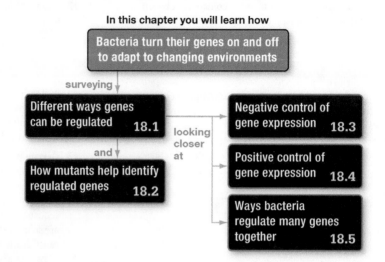

In this chapter you will learn how

Bacteria turn their genes on and off to adapt to changing environments

surveying

Different ways genes can be regulated **18.1**

and

How mutants help identify regulated genes **18.2**

looking closer at

Negative control of gene expression **18.3**

Positive control of gene expression **18.4**

Ways bacteria regulate many genes together **18.5**

The structures that have been colored blue in this scanning electron micrograph are projections from human intestinal cells; the structures colored yellow are the bacterium *Escherichia coli*. In the intestine, the nutrients available to bacteria constantly change. This chapter explores how changes in gene expression help bacteria respond to environmental changes.

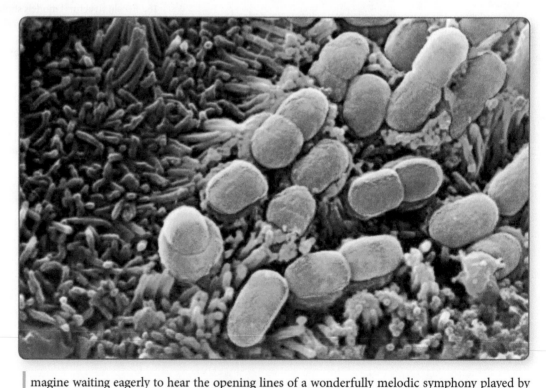

This chapter is part of the Big Picture. See how on pages 366–367.

magine waiting eagerly to hear the opening lines of a wonderfully melodic symphony played by a renowned orchestra. The crowd applauds as the celebrated conductor comes onstage and then hushes as he takes the podium. He cocks the baton; the musicians raise their instruments. As the baton comes down, every instrument begins blaring a different tune at full volume. A tuba plays "Dixie," a violinist renders "In-A-Gadda-Da-Vida," a snare drum lays down beats for Hot Chelle Rae's "Tonight, Tonight," while the bass drum simulates cannons in the "1812 Overture." Instead of music, there is pandemonium. The conductor staggers offstage, clutching his heart.

Cacophony like this would result if a bacterial cell "played" all its genes at full volume all the time. The *Escherichia coli* cells living in your gut right now have over 4300 genes. If all those genes were expressed at the fastest possible rate at all times, the *E. coli* cells would stagger off the stage,

✔ When you see this checkmark, stop and test yourself. Answers are available in Appendix A.

too. But this does not happen. Cells are extremely selective about which genes are expressed, in what amounts, and when.

This chapter explores how bacterial cells control the activity, or expression, of their genes. **Gene expression** is the process of converting information that is archived in DNA into molecules that actually do things in the cell. It occurs when a protein or other gene product is synthesized and active. (You can see on pages 366–367 how gene expression fits into the Big Picture of Genetic Information.)

Previous chapters detailed how genetic information is processed in cells; this chapter focuses on ways to control *when* genetic information is used. Let's begin by reviewing some of the environmental challenges that bacterial cells face and then explore how these organisms meet them.

18.1 An Overview of Gene Regulation and Information Flow

The bacteria that live in and on your body vastly outnumber your own cells. Consider just one of the species present: the gut-dwelling *Escherichia coli*. These cells can use a wide array of carbohydrates to supply the carbon and energy they need. But as your diet changes from day to day, the availability of different sugars in your intestines varies. Each type of nutrient requires a different membrane transport protein to bring the molecule into the cell and a different suite of enzymes to process it. Precise control of gene expression gives *E. coli* the ability to use the available sugars efficiently.

To understand why precise control over gene expression is so important, you have to realize that bacterial cells from an array of species can be densely packed along your intestinal walls. All of these organisms are competing for space and nutrients. In an environment like this, a cell has to use resources efficiently if it's going to be able to survive and reproduce. An individual that synthesizes proteins it doesn't need has fewer resources to devote to making the proteins it does need. Such cells are losers—they compete less successfully for the resources that are required to produce offspring.

Realizing this, biologists predicted that most gene expression is triggered by specific signals from the environment, such as the presence of specific sugars. Did you drink milk at your last meal, or eat French fries and a candy bar? Each type of food contains different sugars. Each sugar should induce a different response from the *E. coli* cells in your intestine. Just as a conductor needs to regulate the orchestra's musicians, cells need to regulate which proteins they produce.

Mechanisms of Regulation

The flow of information from DNA to activation of the final gene product occurs in three steps, represented by arrows in the following diagram:

$$\text{DNA} \longrightarrow \text{mRNA} \longrightarrow \text{protein} \longrightarrow \text{activated protein}$$

Gene expression can be controlled at any of these steps. The arrow from DNA to RNA represents transcription—the making of messenger RNA (mRNA). The arrow from RNA to protein represents translation, in which ribosomes read the information in mRNA and use that information to synthesize a protein. The arrow from protein to activated protein represents post-translational modifications that can lead to changes in shape and activity.

How can a bacterial cell avoid producing proteins that are not needed at a particular time, and thus use resources efficiently? A look at the flow of information from DNA to protein suggests three possible mechanisms:

1. The cell could avoid making the mRNAs for particular enzymes. If there is no mRNA, then ribosomes cannot make the gene product. **Transcriptional control** occurs when regulatory proteins affect RNA polymerase's ability to bind to a promoter and initiate transcription:

$$\text{DNA} \xrightarrow{\quad\times\quad} \text{mRNA} \longrightarrow \text{protein} \longrightarrow \text{activated protein}$$

2. If the mRNA for an enzyme has been made, the cell could prevent the mRNA from being translated into protein. **Translational control** occurs when regulatory molecules alter the length of time an mRNA survives, or affect translation initiation or elongation:

$$\text{DNA} \longrightarrow \text{mRNA} \xrightarrow{\quad\times\quad} \text{protein} \longrightarrow \text{activated protein}$$

3. Many proteins have to be activated by chemical modification, such as the addition of a phosphate group. Regulating this final step is **post-translational control:**

$$\text{DNA} \longrightarrow \text{mRNA} \longrightarrow \text{protein} \xrightarrow{\quad\times\quad} \text{activated protein}$$

Which of these three forms of control occur in bacteria? The short answer is all the above. As **FIGURE 18.1** (see page 338) shows, many factors affect how much active protein is produced from a particular gene.

- Transcriptional control is particularly important due to its efficiency—it saves the most energy for the cell, because it stops the process of gene expression at the earliest possible point.

- Translational control allows a cell to make rapid changes in the amounts of different proteins because the mRNA is already present and available for translation.

- Post-translational control provides the most rapid response of all three mechanisms because only one step is needed to activate an existing protein.

Among these mechanisms of gene regulation, there is a clear trade-off between the speed of response and the conservation of ATP, amino acids, and other resources. Transcriptional control is slow but efficient in resource use; post-translational control is fast but energetically expensive.

Although this chapter focuses almost exclusively on mechanisms of transcriptional control, it is important to keep in mind that bacteria also possess translational and post-translational

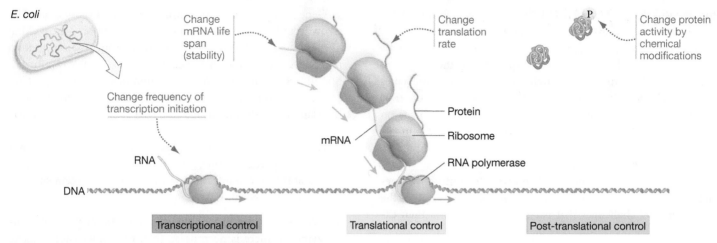

FIGURE 18.1 Gene Expression in Bacteria Can Be Regulated at Three Levels.

✔**EXERCISE** Label the mode of regulation that is slowest in response time and the mode that is fastest. Label the most efficient and least efficient mode in resource use.

controls. Just as important, some genes—such as those that code for the enzymes required for glycolysis—are transcribed all the time, or **constitutively.** Finally, it is critical to realize that gene expression is not an all-or-none proposition. Genes are not just "on" or "off"—instead, the level of expression can vary between these extremes.

The ability to regulate gene expression allows cells to respond to changes in their environment.

Metabolizing Lactose—A Model System

Many of the great advances in genetics have been achieved through the analysis of model systems (see Chapters 15–17). Mendel studied garden peas and discovered the fundamental patterns of gene transmission; Morgan studied fruit flies and confirmed the chromosome theory of inheritance; an array of researchers used *E. coli* and its viruses to work out the mechanisms of DNA synthesis, transcription, and translation. In early studies of gene regulation, a key model system was the metabolism of the sugar lactose in *E. coli*.

Jacques Monod, François Jacob, and many colleagues introduced lactose metabolism in *E. coli* as a model system during the 1950s and 1960s. Although they worked with a single species of bacteria, their results had a profound effect on thinking about gene regulation in all organisms.

E. coli can use a wide variety of sugars for ATP production, via cellular respiration or fermentation. These sugars also serve as raw material in the synthesis of amino acids, vitamins, and other complex compounds. Glucose, however, is *E. coli*'s preferred carbon source—meaning that it is the source of energy and carbon atoms that the organism uses most efficiently.

A preference for glucose makes sense, because glycolysis begins with glucose and is the main pathway for the production of ATP. Lactose, the sugar found in milk, can also be used by *E. coli*, but it is not used until glucose supplies are depleted. Recall that

lactose is a disaccharide made up of one molecule of glucose and one molecule of galactose (see Chapter 5).

To use lactose, *E. coli* must first transport the sugar into the cell. Once lactose is inside the cell, the enzyme β-galactosidase catalyzes a reaction that breaks down the disaccharide into glucose and galactose. The glucose released by this reaction goes directly into the glycolytic pathway; other enzymes convert the galactose to a substance that can also be processed in the glycolytic pathway.

In the early 1950s, biologists discovered that *E. coli* produces high levels of β-galactosidase only when lactose is present in the environment. Based on this observation, researchers proposed that lactose itself regulates the gene for β-galactosidase—meaning that lactose acts as an inducer. An **inducer** is a small molecule that triggers transcription of a specific gene.

In the late 1950s, Jacques Monod wondered how the presence of glucose affects the regulation of the β-galactosidase gene. Would *E. coli* produce high levels of β-galactosidase when both glucose and lactose were present in the surrounding environment? As the experiment summarized in **FIGURE 18.2** shows, the answer was no. Significant amounts of β-galactosidase are produced only when lactose is present and glucose is not present.

Monod teamed up with François Jacob to investigate exactly how lactose and glucose regulate the genes responsible for lactose metabolism—the gene for the membrane protein that imports lactose and the gene for β-galactosidase. Discoveries about how these genes are regulated shed light on how genes in all organisms are controlled. Research on this system is still going strong, over 50 years later.

✔ You should be able to make a chart summarizing the molecules involved in regulating lactose use in *E. coli*. There should be 7 rows and 2 columns. Title the first column "Name" and the second column "Function." The rows are *lacZ, lacY*, operator, promoter, repressor, lactose, and glucose. As you read this chapter, fill in the "Function" column.

QUESTION: *E. coli* produces β-galactosidase when lactose is present. Does *E. coli* produce β-galactosidase when both glucose and lactose are present?

HYPOTHESIS: *E. coli* does not produce β-galactosidase when glucose is present, even if lactose is present. (Glucose is the preferred food source.)

NULL HYPOTHESIS: *E. coli* produces β-galactosidase whenever lactose is present, regardless of the presence or absence of glucose.

EXPERIMENTAL SETUP:

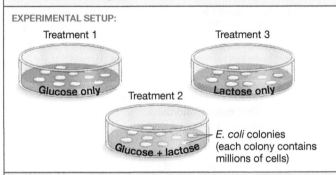

PREDICTION: β-Galactosidase will be produced only in treatment 3.

PREDICTION OF NULL HYPOTHESIS: β-Galactosidase will be produced in treatments 2 and 3.

RESULTS:

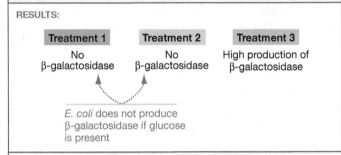

CONCLUSION: Glucose prevents expression of the gene for β-galactosidase. The presence of lactose without glucose stimulates expression of that gene.

FIGURE 18.2 Glucose Affects the Regulation of the β-Galactosidase Gene.

✔ **QUESTION** How would you control growth conditions in the three treatments so that the results of this experiment are valid?

SOURCE: Pardee, A. B., F. Jacob, and J. Monod. 1959. The genetic control and cytoplasmic expression of "inducibility" in the synthesis of β-galactosidase by *E. coli. Journal of Molecular Biology* 1: 165–178.

18.2 Identifying Regulated Genes

To understand how *E. coli* controls production of β-galactosidase and the transport protein that brings lactose into the cell, Jacob and Monod first had to find the genes that code for these proteins. To do this, they employed the same tactic used in the pioneering studies of DNA replication, transcription, and translation reviewed in earlier chapters: They isolated and analyzed mutants. In this case, their goal was to find *E. coli* cells that could not metabolize lactose. Cells that can't use lactose

must lack either β-galactosidase or the lactose transporter protein.

To find mutants that are associated with a particular trait, a researcher has to complete two steps:

1. Generate a large number of individuals with mutations at random locations in their genomes. Monod and colleagues accomplished this step by exposing *E. coli* populations to **mutagens**—X-rays, UV light, or chemicals that damage DNA and increase mutation rates.

2. Screen the treated individuals for mutants with defects in the process or biochemical pathway in question—in this case, defects in lactose metabolism. Recall that a genetic screen is any technique for selecting individuals with certain types of mutations out of a large population, and that a mutant is an individual with a mutation (see Chapter 16).

The researchers were looking for cells that cannot grow in an environment that contains only lactose as an energy source. Normal cells grow well in this environment. How could the researchers select cells on the basis of *lack* of growth?

Replica Plating to Find Lactose Metabolism Mutants

Replica plating and growth on indicator plates were key techniques in the search for mutants with defects in lactose metabolism. **FIGURE 18.3** (see page 6) shows how **replica plating** works.

Step 1 When mutants with defects in lactose metabolism are desired, mutagenized bacteria are spread on a "master plate" filled with a gelatinous growth **medium** containing glucose but no lactose. Growth medium is any liquid or solid that supports the growth of cells. It is important that the mutant cells are capable of growing on the master plate. The bacteria are then allowed to grow, so that each cell produces a colony—a large number of identical cells descended from a single cell.

Step 2 A block covered with a piece of sterilized velvet is pressed onto the master plate. Some cells from each colony on the master plate are transferred to the velvet.

Step 3 The velvet is pressed onto a plate called a replica plate that contains medium that differs from the master plate by a single component. In this case, the second medium has only lactose and no glucose as the source of carbon and energy. Cells from the velvet stick to the replica plate's surface, producing an exact copy of the locations of the colonies on the master plate.

Step 4 After these transferred cells grow, compare the colonies on the replica plate with those on the master plate. In this example, colonies that grow on the master plate but are missing on the replica plate are mutants that cannot metabolize lactose. By picking cells from these colonies on the master plate, researchers build a collection of lactose metabolism mutants.

Several Genes Are Involved in Lactose Metabolism

The initial mutant screen yielded three types of mutants. In one class, the mutant cells were unable to cleave lactose—even when

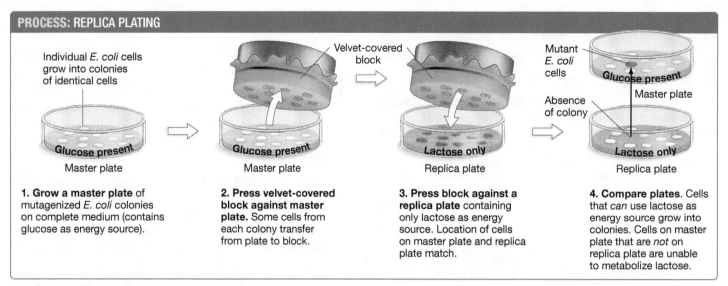

PROCESS: REPLICA PLATING

Individual *E. coli* cells grow into colonies of identical cells

Velvet-covered block

Mutant *E. coli* cells

Glucose present

Absence of colony

Master plate

Glucose present
Master plate

Glucose present
Master plate

Lactose only
Replica plate

Lactose only
Replica plate

1. Grow a master plate of mutagenized *E. coli* colonies on complete medium (contains glucose as energy source).

2. Press velvet-covered block against master plate. Some cells from each colony transfer from plate to block.

3. Press block against a replica plate containing only lactose as energy source. Location of cells on master plate and replica plate match.

4. Compare plates. Cells that *can* use lactose as energy source grow into colonies. Cells on master plate that are *not* on replica plate are unable to metabolize lactose.

FIGURE 18.3 Replica Plating Is a Technique for Identifying Mutants That Cannot Grow in Particular Conditions.
Here, replica plating is used to isolate mutant *E. coli* cells with a deficiency in lactose metabolism.

✔**QUESTION** How would you alter this protocol to isolate mutant cells with a deficiency in the enzymes required to synthesize tryptophan?

lactose was in the medium and transported into cells to induce production of the β-galactosidase protein. Jacob and Monod concluded that these mutants must lack a functioning version of the β-galactosidase protein and, therefore, the gene that encodes β-galactosidase is defective. This gene was designated *lacZ*, and the mutant allele *lacZ⁻*.

In the second class of mutants, the cells failed to accumulate lactose inside the cell. To explain this result, Jacob and Monod hypothesized that the mutant cells had defective copies of the membrane protein responsible for transporting lactose into the cell. This protein was identified and named galactoside permease; the gene that encodes it was designated *lacY*. **FIGURE 18.4** summarizes the functions of β-galactosidase and galactoside permease.

The third and most surprising class of mutants did not show normal regulation of β-galactosidase and galactoside permease expression. Instead, these mutants made the proteins all the

time—even if no lactose was present. **TABLE 18.1** summarizes these three types of mutants.

Cells that are abnormal because they produce a product at all times are called **constitutive mutants.** The gene that was mutated to produce constitutive β-galactosidase and galactoside permease expression was named *lacI*. The letter I signified that these mutants did not need an inducer—lactose—to express β-galactosidase or galactoside permease.

To understand the significance of the *lacI* mutation, recall that in normal cells, the expression of the *lacZ* (β-galactosidase) and *lacY* (galactoside permease) genes is induced by lactose. But in

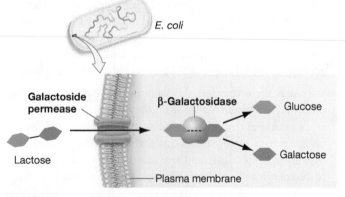

FIGURE 18.4 Two Proteins *E. coli* Needs for Using Lactose.
The membrane protein galactoside permease brings lactose into the cell, and the enzyme β-galactosidase breaks lactose into its glucose and galactose subunits.

TABLE 18.1 Three Types of Lactose Metabolism Mutants in *E. coli*

Observed Phenotype	Interpretation	Genotype
1. Cells cannot cleave lactose, even in the presence of inducer.	No β-galactosidase; gene for β-galactosidase is defective. Call this gene *lacZ*.	*lacZ⁻*
2. Cells cannot accumulate lactose.	No membrane protein (galactoside permease) to import lactose; gene for galactoside permease is defective. Call this gene *lacY*.	*lacY⁻*
3. Cells cleave lactose even if lactose is absent as an inducer.	Constitutive (constant) expression of *lacZ* and *lacY*; gene for regulatory protein that shuts down *lacZ* and *lacY* is defective—it does not need to be induced by lactose. Call this gene *lacI*.	*lacI⁻*

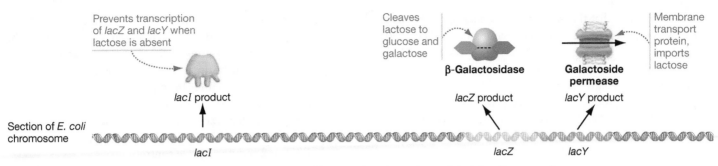

FIGURE 18.5 The *lac* Genes Are in Close Physical Proximity. The associated proteins and their functions are shown above each gene.

cells with a mutant form of *lacI* (*lacI⁻* mutants), gene expression occurs with or without lactose. This means that *lacI⁻* mutants have a defect in gene regulation. In these mutants, the gene remains on when it should be turned off.

To pull these observations together, the researchers hypothesized that the normal product of the *lacI* gene prevents the transcription of *lacZ* and *lacY* when lactose is absent. Because lactose triggers production of β-galactosidase, it was reasonable to expect that the *lacI* gene or gene product interacts with lactose in some way. (Later work showed that the inducer is actually a derivative of lactose called *allolactose*. For historical accuracy and simplicity, however, this discussion refers to lactose itself as the inducer.)

Jacob and Monod had succeeded in identifying three genes involved in lactose metabolism: *lacZ*, *lacY*, and *lacI*. They concluded that *lacZ* and *lacY* code for proteins required for the metabolism and import of lactose, while *lacI* is responsible for some sort of regulatory function. When lactose is absent, the *lacI* gene or gene product shuts down the expression of *lacZ* and *lacY*. But when lactose is present, the opposite occurs—transcription of *lacZ* and *lacY* is induced.

✔ If you understand the genes involved in lactose metabolism, you should be able to describe the specific function of *lacZ* and *lacY*. You should also be able to describe the effect of the *lacI* gene product when lactose is present versus absent and explain why these effects are logical.

Jacob and Monod followed up on these experiments by mapping the location of the three genes on the *E. coli* chromosome (**FIGURE 18.5**). They discovered that the genes are close together. This was a crucial finding because it suggested that *lacZ* and *lacY* might be transcribed together. Could the *lacI* regulatory gene govern both the *lacZ* and *lacY* genes? How does *lacI* actually work? And why do lactose and glucose have opposite effects on gene expression?

18.3 Negative Control of Transcription

In principle, there are two general ways that transcription can be regulated: by negative control or positive control.

1. **Negative control** occurs when a regulatory protein called a **repressor** binds to DNA and shuts down transcription (**FIGURE 18.6a**).

2. **Positive control** occurs when a regulatory protein called an **activator** binds to DNA and triggers transcription (**FIGURE 18.6b**).

When you are driving a car, negative control is exerted by setting the parking brake; positive control occurs when you step on the gas pedal. It turned out that the *lacZ* and *lacY* genes in *E. coli* are controlled by engaging or releasing a parking brake—they are under negative control.

(a) Negative control: Regulatory protein *shuts down* transcription.

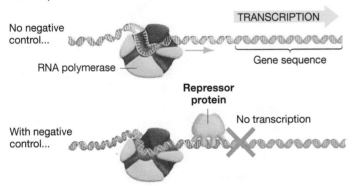

(b) Positive control: Regulatory protein *triggers* transcription.

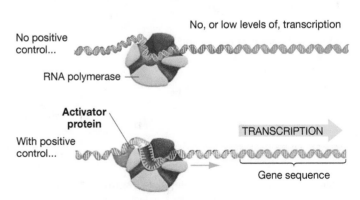

FIGURE 18.6 Genes Are Regulated by Negative Control, Positive Control, or Both. (To review transcription initiation, see Figure 17.3.)

The hypothesis that the *lacZ* and *lacY* genes might be under negative control originated with Leo Szilard in the late 1950s. Szilard suggested to Monod that the *lacI* gene could code for a product that represses transcription of the *lacZ* and *lacY* genes. As it turned out, Szilard was right.

The *lacI* gene produces a repressor protein that exerts negative control over *lacZ* and *lacY* gene transcription. The repressor was proposed to bind directly to DNA at or near the promoter for the *lacZ* and *lacY* genes (**FIGURE 18.7a**).

To explain how lactose triggers transcription, Szilard and Monod proposed that lactose interacts with the repressor in a way that makes the repressor release from its binding site (**FIGURE 18.7b**). In negative control, the repressor is the parking brake; lactose releases the brake.

What about the constitutive mutants? **FIGURE 18.7c** shows that constitutive transcription is observed in *lacI⁻* mutants because a functional repressor is absent—the parking brake is broken.

To test the hypothesis of negative control by a repressor, Jacob, Monod, and co-workers added back a functioning copy of the *lacI* repressor gene to the *lacI⁻* mutants that made β-galactosidase all the time. If these cells were grown using glucose and no lactose, β-galactosidase production declined and then stopped.

This result supported the hypothesis that the repressor codes for a protein that shuts down transcription. Significantly, if the experimental cells were grown using lactose instead of glucose, β-galactosidase activity resumed. This result supported the hypothesis that lactose removes the repressor.

What's the take-home message? The *lacI* gene codes for a repressor protein that exerts negative control on *lacZ* and *lacY*. Lactose acts as an inducer by causing the repressor to release from DNA and ending negative control.

The Operon Model

Jacob and Monod summarized the results of their experiments with a comprehensive model of negative control that was published in 1961. One of their key conclusions was that the genes for β-galactosidase and galactoside permease are controlled together and transcribed into a single mRNA. To encapsulate this idea, they coined the term **operon** for a set of coordinately regulated bacterial genes that are transcribed together into one mRNA. Logically enough, the group of genes involved in lactose metabolism was termed the ***lac* operon**.

Later, a gene called *lacA* was found to be adjacent to *lacY* and *lacZ* and transcribed as part of the same operon. The *lacA* gene

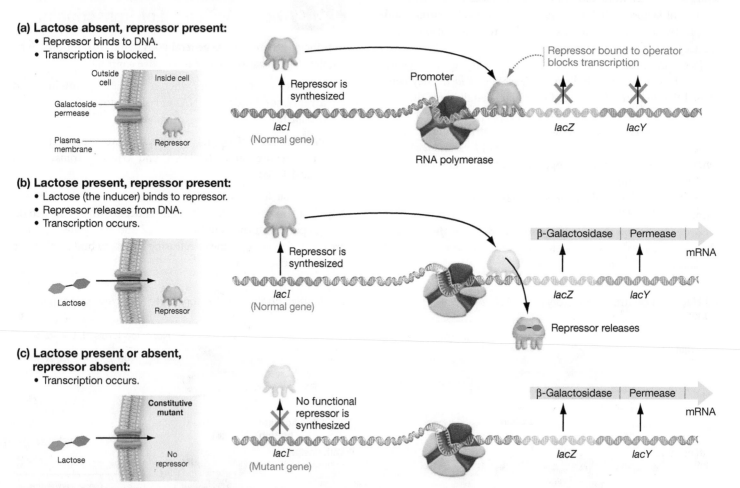

FIGURE 18.7 The Hypothesis of Negative Control of the *lac* Operon. The plasma membrane and galactoside permease are shown as a reminder that lactose comes from outside the cell and controls genes within the *E. coli* chromosome. Repression of the *lac* operon is never complete, so there is always some galactoside permease to transport lactose into the cell and begin induction of the *lac* operon.

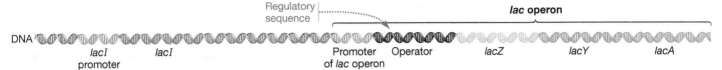

FIGURE 18.8 The *lac* Operon and *lacI* Gene. This view emphasizes the arrangement of genes and regulatory sequences and is not drawn to scale.

✔ **EXERCISE** Using small, colored bits of candy or paper, add the repressor protein to the figure. Next, add RNA polymerase; then add lactose. At each step, explain what happens after the molecule is added.

codes for the enzyme transacetylase. This enzyme catalyzes reactions that allow certain types of sugars to be exported from the cell when they are too abundant and could harm the cell. The components of the *lac* operon are summarized in **FIGURE 18.8**.

Three hypotheses are central to the Jacob–Monod model of *lac* operon regulation:

1. The *lacZ*, *lacY*, and *lacA* genes are adjacent and are transcribed into one mRNA initiated from the single promoter of the *lac* operon. This is known as cotranscription, and it results in the coordinated expression of the three genes.

2. The repressor is a protein encoded by *lacI* that binds to DNA and prevents transcription of the *lac* operon genes (*lacZ*, *lacY*, and *lacA*). Jacob and Monod proposed that *lacI* is expressed constitutively, and that the repressor binds to a section of DNA in the *lac* operon called the **operator.**

3. The inducer (lactose) binds to the repressor. When it does, the repressor changes shape. The shape change causes the repressor to come off the DNA. Recall that this form of control over protein function is **allosteric regulation** (see Chapter 8). In allosteric regulation, a small molecule binds to a protein and causes it to change its shape and activity. When the inducer binds to the repressor, the repressor can no longer bind to DNA and transcription can proceed.

✔ If you understand negative control of the *lac* operon, you should be able to predict the effect of a mutation in the *lacI* gene that alters the repressor so it cannot bind to lactose, and the effect of a mutation in the operator that prevents repressor binding.

How Does Glucose Regulate the *lac* Operon?

The model of *lac* operon control, summarized in Figure 18.7, is elegant and successful in explaining experimental results. But it is not complete. After studying the model, you may think of an important question that it fails to answer: Where does glucose fit in?

Transcription of the *lac* operon is drastically reduced when glucose is present in the environment—even when lactose is available to induce β-galactosidase expression (see Figure 18.2). This makes sense, given that glucose is *E. coli's* preferred carbon source. When glucose is already present, the cell doesn't need to cleave lactose as a way of acquiring glucose.

How can glucose prevent expression of the *lac* operon? Researchers recently discovered that glucose inhibits the lactose

transport activity of galactoside permease through a chain of molecular events. When both glucose and lactose are present in the environment, the transport of lactose into the cell is inhibited. Because lactose does not accumulate in the cytoplasm, the repressor remains bound to the operator. Negative control (as in Figure 18.7a) is in place. In contrast, when glucose levels outside the cell are low, galactoside permease is active. If lactose is present, it is transported into the cell and induces *lac* operon expression (as in Figure 18.7b).

The mechanism of glucose preventing the transport of inducer is known as inducer exclusion. Inducer exclusion affects the activity of many different sugar transporters in addition to galactoside permease. It allows *E. coli* to preferentially use glucose, even when other sugars are also present outside the cell.

This understanding of how glucose regulates the *lac* operon is relatively new. For decades, researchers thought that when glucose levels outside the cell declined, an activator protein called CAP bound to a regulatory sequence in DNA just upstream of the promoter to increase the frequency of transcription initiation. There is strong evidence that binding of CAP to the regulatory sequence is important for efficient transcription of the *lac* operon. However, recent results indicate that CAP is always bound to the regulatory sequence, even in the presence of glucose.

Why Has the *lac* Operon Model Been So Important?

The *lac* operon has been an immensely important model system for two reasons. First, follow-up work showed that many bacterial genes and operons are under negative control by repressor proteins. This means that the findings on the *lac* operon are general. Second, the *lac* operon model introduced a fundamentally important idea: Gene expression is regulated by physical contact between regulatory proteins and specific regulatory sites in DNA. Publication of the *lac* operon model was a watershed event in the history of biological science.

Work on the *lac* operon also offered an important example of post-translational control over gene expression. To understand why, you have to realize that the repressor protein is always present; it is transcribed and translated constitutively. When a rapid change in *lac* operon activity is needed, it does not require changes in the transcription or translation of new repressor proteins. Instead, the activity of *existing* repressor proteins is altered.

This is exactly the prediction made at the beginning of this chapter—post-translational control is best when a rapid response is needed. As it turns out, this is a common type of control. In most cases, the activity of key regulatory proteins is controlled by post-translational modifications.

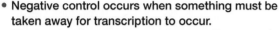
check your understanding

C Y U

If you understand that . . .

- Negative control occurs when something must be taken away for transcription to occur.
- The *lac* operon repressor exerts negative control over three protein-coding genes by binding to the operator site in DNA, near the promoter.
- For transcription to occur in the *lac* operon, an inducer molecule (a derivative of lactose) must bind to the repressor, causing it to change shape and release from the operator.
- The *lac* operon is not transcribed when glucose is available because glucose prevents lactose transport into the cell.

✔ **You should be able to . . .**

1. Explain why lactose should induce transcription of the *lac* operon.

2. Diagram the *lac* operon, showing the relative positions of the operator, the promoter, and the three protein-coding genes; indicate what is happening at the operon in the absence of lactose and in the presence of lactose.

Answers are available in Appendix A.

18.4 Positive Control of Transcription

Positive control is an important way of controlling transcription. In positive control, an activator protein binds to a regulatory sequence in DNA when genes are turned on. When bound to DNA, the activator interacts with RNA polymerase to increase the rate of initiating transcription (see Figure 18.6b).

The ***ara* operon** provides an important example of positive control and of the process of science. The *ara* operon wasn't discovered in the laboratory of a famous scientist. Instead, students working on a project for a laboratory course were the first to uncover it.

This operon contains three genes that allow *E. coli* to use the sugar arabinose. Arabinose is found in many plant cell walls. When you eat vegetables, arabinose is available to the bacteria that inhabit your gut. Without arabinose in the environment, the *ara* operon is not transcribed. But when arabinose is present, transcription of the *ara* operon is turned on by an activator protein called **AraC.** The *ara* operon and an adjacent gene, *araC*, that codes for the araC activator are shown in **FIGURE 18.9**.

FIGURE 18.10 outlines how AraC controls the *ara* operon. The AraC protein is allosterically regulated by arabinose. When bound to arabinose, two copies of the AraC protein attach to a regulatory sequence of DNA called the *ara* initiator that lies just upstream of the promoter (see Figure 18.10a). Once AraC is bound to DNA, it can also bind to RNA polymerase. This interaction between AraC and the RNA polymerase helps to dock the polymerase to the promoter and accelerate the initiation of transcription.

Continued work on the *ara* operon revealed a surprise—AraC is both an activator and a repressor. In the absence of arabinose, the two copies of the AraC protein remain together; but while one araC copy remains bound to the initiator, the other copy now binds to a different regulatory site in DNA, the *ara* operator, as shown in Figure 18.10b. In this configuration, AraC works as a repressor to prevent the transcription of both the *ara* operon and the *araC* gene.

✔ If you understand positive control by the AraC protein, you should be able to predict the effect of a mutation that removes the part of AraC that binds to RNA polymerase.

18.5 Global Gene Regulation

A theme of this chapter is that cells respond to changing environments. To compete for resources, bacteria must be able to coordinate the expression of large sets of genes. As you've seen for the *lac* and *ara* operons, an effective way to express sets of genes together is to group them into an operon and transcribe them into a single mRNA. But there are limits to the size of operons. How can bacterial cells manage responses that require the expression of dozens or even hundreds of genes?

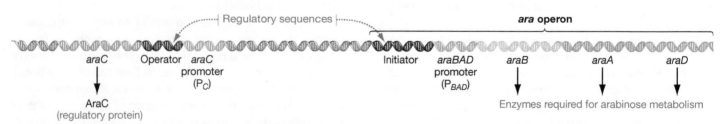

FIGURE 18.9 The *ara* Operon, Regulatory Sequences, and *araC* Gene.

(a) AraC protein is an **activator** when bound to arabinose.

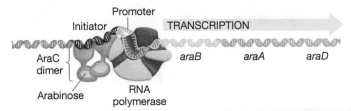

(b) AraC protein is a **repressor** when arabinose is absent.

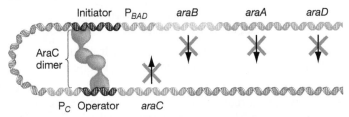

FIGURE 18.10 Positive and Negative Regulation of the *ara* Operon.

Global gene regulation is the coordinated regulation of many genes. You already learned that alternative sigma proteins provide one way for bacteria to turn on large numbers of genes in response to environmental change (Chapter 17). But there are other means of global gene regulation, such as grouping genes into a **regulon**—a set of separate genes or operons that contain the same regulatory sequences and that are controlled by a single type of regulatory protein.

Regulons allow bacteria to respond to challenges that include shortages of nutrients, sudden changes in temperature, exposure to radiation, or shifts in habitat. Let's explore how regulons work in general, and then look at two specific examples.

A general strategy for controlling regulon genes is shown in **FIGURE 18.11**. In this example, the regulon consists of many genes that are scattered across the genome. All of these genes are controlled by the same type of repressor protein that binds to the same operator sequences near the promoter of each gene. When an environmental change triggers the removal of the repressor protein from all the operators, every gene in the regulon is transcribed.

Regulons can be under negative control by a repressor protein or positive control by an activator protein. The regulon in Figure 18.11 is under negative control. The SOS response regulon works exactly this way to allow bacterial cells to repair extensive damage to DNA that can occur when cells are exposed to ultraviolet light, other types of radiation, or some chemicals. Damaged DNA sets off an SOS signal that induces the transcription of more than 40 genes that code for DNA repair enzymes and for DNA polymerases that can use damaged DNA as a template. Without the SOS response, bacteria with massive DNA damage would face almost certain death.

The ToxR regulon of *Vibrio cholera*—the bacterium that causes cholera—is under positive control. This regulon allows *V. cholera* to colonize the human gut and to produce toxins that cause diarrhea. Cholera kills 120,000 people each year and sickens as many as 18 million. ToxR regulon genes are inactive when *V. cholera* lives outside a human host. When bacteria from contaminated drinking water encounter the environment of the human gut, this sets off a signal that activates an activator protein. The activator induces a response by binding to a regulatory DNA sequence near the promoters of all ToxR regulon genes to stimulate their transcription. The diarrhea induced by this regulon is adaptive for *V. cholera* because it spreads more bacteria into the environment to infect new hosts.

What are the general messages of this chapter? Interactions among protein regulators and the DNA sequences they bind produce finely tuned control over gene expression, regulating individual genes, operons, or large sets of genes. With these exquisite controls over gene expression, bacteria have been able to compete, grow, and reproduce for more than 3 billion years of life's history.

Do eukaryotes control their genes the same way as bacteria? If not, what are the differences? These questions are the focus of the next chapter.

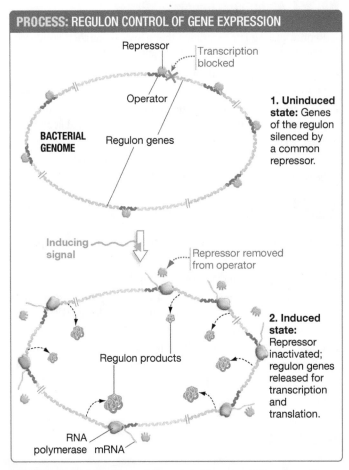

FIGURE 18.11 Genes of a Regulon Are Expressed Together. The "| |" symbols indicate regions of the bacterial genome not shown between regulon genes.

If you understand . . .

18.1 An Overview of Gene Regulation and Information Flow

- Changes in gene expression allow bacterial cells to respond to environmental changes.

- Most gene products are produced or activated only when they are needed.

- Gene expression can be controlled at three levels: transcription, translation, or post-translation (protein activation).

- Transcriptional control can be negative or positive. Negative control occurs when a regulatory protein prevents transcription. Positive control occurs when a regulatory protein increases the frequency of initiating transcription.

✓ You should be able to describe one component of the *lac* operon that is under transcriptional control and one component that is under post-translational control.

18.2 Identifying Regulated Genes

- Replica plating is a technique that allows researchers to identify mutants that cannot grow in a particular condition.

- Replica plating led to the isolation of three types of lactose metabolism mutants.

- Transcription may be constitutive or regulated. Constitutive expression occurs in genes whose products are required at all times, such as genes that encode glycolytic enzymes.

✓ You should be able to propose a strategy to isolate *E. coli* mutants that can grow at 33°C, but not at 42°C.

18.3 Negative Control of Transcription

- The *lac* operon is transcribed efficiently when lactose is present and glucose is absent.

- The *lac* operon is under negative control.

- Negative control occurs because a repressor protein binds to an operator sequence in DNA near the promoter of the protein-encoding genes to prevent their transcription.

- When lactose is present, it binds to the repressor and causes it to fall off the operator, allowing transcription to occur.

- Glucose inhibits transcription of the *lac* operon by inhibiting lactose transport into the cell.

✓ You should be able explain how the operator, repressor, and inducer relate to a car's parking brake.

18.4 Positive Control of Transcription

- Positive control of transcription occurs when a regulatory protein called an activator binds to a regulatory sequence in DNA.

- Activator proteins bind to RNA polymerase in addition to DNA. Binding between the activator and RNA polymerase increases the rate of transcription initiation.

- The *ara* operon codes for genes required for metabolism of the sugar arabinose. The operon is controlled by the AraC regulatory protein. AraC is an activator when bound to arabinose and a repressor when the protein is not bound to arabinose.

✓ You should be able to predict if mutations in the *ara* initiator sequence of the *ara* operon are most likely to affect positive regulation, negative regulation, or both.

18.5 Global Gene Regulation

- Bacterial cells often need to coordinate the expression of large sets of genes in response to changing environments.

- Regulons coordinate the expression of different genes by using a shared regulator that acts on a regulatory sequence found in all genes of the regulon. Regulons can work through negative control using repressors, or through positive control using activators.

✓ You should be able to propose a method that would allow more genes to become part of the SOS regulon.

 MasteringBiology

1. **MasteringBiology Assignments**

   Tutorials and Activities The *lac* Operon

   Questions Reading Quizzes, Blue-Thread Questions, Test Bank

2. **eText** Read your book online, search, take notes, highlight text, and more.

3. **The Study Area** Practice Test, Cumulative Test, BioFlix® 3-D animations, Videos, Activities, Audio Glossary, Word Study Tools, Art

You should be able to . . .

✓ TEST YOUR KNOWLEDGE
Answers are available in Appendix A

1. Replica plating is used to isolate mutants that
   a. can produce an enzyme.
   b. cannot grow in a particular condition.
   c. can utilize lactose.
   d. turn yellow when lactose is broken down.

2. Why are the genes involved in lactose metabolism considered to be an operon?
   a. They occupy adjacent locations on the *E. coli* chromosome.
   b. They have a similar function.
   c. They are all required for normal cell function.
   d. They are all controlled by the same promoter.

3. In the *lac* operon, the repressor inhibits transcription when
   a. the repressor is bound to the inducer.
   b. the repressor is not bound to the inducer.
   c. the repressor is bound to glucose.
   d. the repressor is not bound to the operator.

4. Activators bind to regulatory sequences in _____ and to _____ polymerase.

5. How does inducer exclusion control gene expression in the *lac* operon?

6. A regulon is a set of genes controlled by
   a. one type of regulator of transcription.
   b. two or more different alternative sigma proteins.
   c. many different types of promoters.
   d. glucose.

7. *E. coli* expresses genes for glycolytic enzymes constitutively. Why?

8. Explain the difference between positive and negative control over transcription.

9. Predict what would happen if the *lac* repressor protein were altered so it could not bind inducer.
   a. The repressor could not bind to DNA.
   b. The repressor would always be bound to DNA.
   c. The repressor could bind to DNA only when cells were grown with glucose.
   d. The repressor could bind to DNA only when cells were grown without glucose.

10. Predict what would happen to regulation of the *lac* operon if the *lacI* gene were moved 50,000 nucleotides upstream of its normal location.

11. If any of the following hypothetical drugs could be developed, which would be most effective in preventing cholera?
    a. a drug that increased the amount of the ToxR activator
    b. a drug that blocked the DNA-binding activity of the activator
    c. a drug that increased rates of transcription in *V. cholerae*
    d. a drug that increased rates of translation in *V. cholerae*

12. IPTG is a molecule with a structure very similar to lactose. IPTG can be transported into cells by galactoside permease and can bind to the *lac* repressor protein. However, unlike lactose, IPTG is not broken down by β-galactosidase. Predict what would occur regarding *lac* operon regulation if IPTG were added to *E. coli* growth medium containing arabinose and no glucose or lactose.

13. You are interested in using bacteria to metabolize wastes at an old chemical plant and convert them into harmless compounds. You find bacteria that are able to tolerate high levels of the toxic compounds toluene and benzene, and you suspect that this is because the bacteria can break down these compounds into less-toxic products. If that is true, these toluene- and benzene-resistant strains will be valuable for cleaning up toxic sites. How could you find out whether these bacteria are metabolizing toluene as a source of carbon compounds?

14. QUANTITATIVE Imagine that you are repeating the replica-plating procedure of Jacob and Monod to find mutants that can't grow using lactose. After treating cells with a mutagen, you anticipate a mutation rate of 1×10^{-4} lactose-nonutilizing mutants per mutagen-treated cell. Based on this estimate, how many cells should you replica-plate to have a good chance of finding one mutant?

15. A type of mutation in the *lac* operator known as *lacO^c* prevents repressor binding to DNA and causes constitutive transcription of the *lac* operon. Which of the following secondary mutations might restore normal regulation to the *lac* operon in a *lacO^c* mutant?
    a. a *lacI* mutation that decreases the ability of the repressor to bind the inducer
    b. a *lacI* mutation that produces a repressor than can recognize the mutated *lacO^c* DNA sequence
    c. a promoter mutation that prevents it from being recognized by sigma
    d. an RNA polymerase mutation that allows it to bind to the promoter without using sigma

16. X-gal is a colorless, lactose-like molecule that can be split into two fragments by β-galactosidase. One of these product molecules is blue. The following photograph shows *E. coli* colonies growing in a medium that contains X-gal.

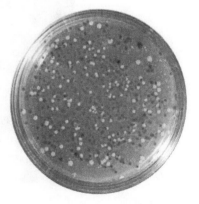

Find three colonies whose cells have functioning copies of β-galactosidase. Find three colonies whose cells might have mutations in the *lacZ* or in the *lacY* genes. Suppose you analyze the protein-coding sequence of the *lacZ* and *lacY* genes of cells from the three mutant colonies and find that these sequences are wild type (normal). What other region of the *lac* operon might be altered to account for the mutant phenotype of these colonies?

19 Control of Gene Expression in Eukaryotes

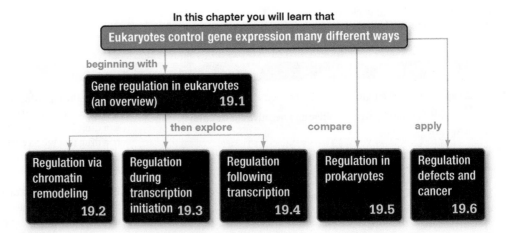

In this chapter you will learn that

Eukaryotes control gene expression many different ways

beginning with

Gene regulation in eukaryotes (an overview)   **19.1**

then explore   *compare*   *apply*

Regulation via chromatin remodeling   **19.2**

Regulation during transcription initiation **19.3**

Regulation following transcription **19.4**

Regulation in prokaryotes **19.5**

Regulation defects and cancer **19.6**

A model of eukaryotic DNA in the condensed state. The DNA (shown in red and pink) is wrapped around proteins (in green). The DNA has to be uncoiled before transcription can take place.

Bacteria regulate gene expression to respond to changes in their environment. *Escherichia coli* thrive best if the genes that are required to import and cleave lactose are expressed only when the cells are relying on lactose as a source of energy (see Chapter 18).

Unicellular eukaryotes face similar challenges. Consider the yeast *Saccharomyces cerevisiae*, which is used extensively in the production of beer, wine, and bread. In nature this species lives on the skins of grapes and other fruits, where the sugars that the cells use as food vary in type and concentration as the fruit ripens, falls, and rots. For yeast cells to grow and reproduce efficiently, gene expression has to be modified in response to these changes.

The cells that make up multicellular eukaryotes face additional challenges. Consider your body, which contains trillions of cells, each with a specialized structure and function. You have heart

This chapter is part of the Big Picture. See how on pages 366–367.

✔ When you see this checkmark, stop and test yourself. Answers are available in Appendix A.

muscle cells, lung cells, nerve cells, skin cells, and so on. Even though these cells are different, they contain the same genes. Your bone cells and blood cells aren't different because of a difference in their genes but because they *express* different genes. Your bone cells have blood-cell genes—they just don't transcribe them.

Why not? The answer is that your cells respond to their environment, just as bacteria and unicellular eukaryotes do. But there's a key difference. The cells in a multicellular eukaryote express different genes in response to changes in the *internal* environment—specifically, to signals from other cells. As a human being or an oak tree develops, cells that are located in different parts of the organism are exposed to different cell–cell signals. As a result, they express different genes. **Differential gene expression** is responsible for creating different cell types, arranging them into tissues, and coordinating their activity to form the multicellular society we call an individual.

How does all of this regulation and differentiation happen? Later chapters introduce the signals that trigger the formation of muscle, bone, leaf, and flower cells. In contrast, this chapter focuses on what happens after a eukaryotic cell receives such a signal. Let's start with an overview of how gene expression can be controlled, and close with a look at how defects in the process can trigger cancer.

19.1 Gene Regulation in Eukaryotes— An Overview

Like bacteria, eukaryotes can control gene expression at the levels of transcription, translation, and post-translation. But as **FIGURE 19.1** shows, three additional levels of control occur in eukaryotes as genetic information flows from DNA to proteins.

The first additional level of control involves the DNA–protein complex at the top of the figure. In eukaryotes, DNA is wrapped around proteins to create a structure called **chromatin.** Eukaryotic genes have promoters, just as bacterial genes do; but before transcription can begin in eukaryotes, the stretch of DNA containing the promoter must be released from tight interactions with proteins, so that RNA polymerase can make contact with the promoter. To capture this idea, biologists say that **chromatin remodeling** must occur before transcription.

The second level of regulation that is unique to eukaryotes is **RNA processing**—the steps required to produce a mature, processed mRNA from a primary RNA transcript. Recall that introns have to be spliced out of primary transcripts (see Chapter 17). In many cases, carefully orchestrated alternative splicing occurs—meaning that different combinations of exons are included in the mRNA. If different cells use different splicing patterns, different gene products result.

Third, mRNA life span is regulated in eukaryotes: mRNAs that remain in the cell for a long time tend to be translated more than mRNAs that have a short life span.

Each of the six potential control points shown in Figure 19.1 is employed in eukaryotic cells. This chapter explores all six—chromatin

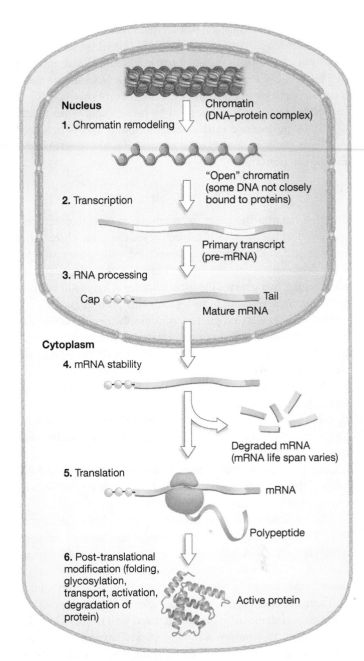

FIGURE 19.1 In Eukaryotes, Gene Expression Can Be Controlled at Many Different Levels.

remodeling, transcription, RNA processing, mRNA stability, translation, and post-translational modification of proteins.

To appreciate the breadth and complexity of gene regulation in eukaryotes, let's follow the series of events that occur as an embryonic cell responds to a developmental signal. Suppose a molecule arrives that specifies the production of a muscle-specific protein. What happens next?

19.2 Chromatin Remodeling

For a molecular signal to trigger the transcription of a particular gene, the chromatin around the target gene must be remodeled.

To appreciate why, consider that a typical cell in your body contains about 6 billion base pairs of DNA. Lined up end to end, these nucleotide pairs would form a double helix about 2 m (6.5 feet) long. But the nucleus that holds this DNA is only about 5 μm in diameter—far less than the thickness of this page. To fit inside the nucleus, the DNA must be packed tightly—so tightly that RNA polymerase can't access it. How is DNA packaged? And how can it be unpacked at particular genes so RNA polymerase can transcribe it?

What Is Chromatin's Basic Structure?

The first data on the chemical composition of chromatin were published in the early 1900s, when researchers established that eukaryotic DNA is intimately associated with proteins. Later work documented that the most abundant DNA-associated proteins belong to a group called the **histones.** Chromatin consists of DNA complexed with histones and other proteins.

In the 1970s electron micrographs like the one in **FIGURE 19.2a** revealed that chromatin has a regular structure. In some preparations for electron microscopy, chromatin looked like beads on a string. The "beads" came to be called **nucleosomes.**

More information emerged in 1984 when researchers determined the three-dimensional structure of eukaryotic chromatin by using X-ray crystallography (see **BioSkills 11** in Appendix B). The X-ray crystallographic data indicated that each nucleosome consists of DNA wrapped almost twice around a core of eight histone proteins. As **FIGURE 19.2b** indicates, a histone called H1 "seals" DNA to each nucleosome. Between each pair of nucleosomes there is a "linker" stretch of DNA.

The intimate association between DNA and histones occurs in part because DNA is negatively charged and histones are positively charged. DNA has a negative charge because of its phosphate groups; histones are positively charged because they contain many lysines and arginines, two positively charged amino acids.

There are additional layers of complexity in packaging DNA. H1 histones interact with one another and with histones in other nucleosomes to produce a tightly packed structure like that shown in Figure 19.2b. Based on its width, this structure is called the 30-nanometer fiber. (Recall that a nanometer is one-billionth of a meter and is abbreviated nm.)

Finally, the 30-nm fibers are attached at intervals along their length to proteins that form a scaffold or framework inside the nucleus. In this way, the entire chromosome is organized and held in place. When chromosomes condense before mitosis or meiosis, the scaffold proteins and 30-nm fibers are folded into still larger and more tightly packed structures.

A eukaryotic chromosome, then, is made up of chromatin that has several layers of organization: The DNA is wrapped around histones to form nucleosomes, nucleosomes are packed into 30-nm fibers, 30-nm fibers are attached to scaffold proteins, and the entire assembly can be folded into the highly condensed structure observed during cell division.

Although research has shown that bacterial DNA interacts with proteins that are organized similarly to nucleosomes,

(a) Nucleosomes in chromatin

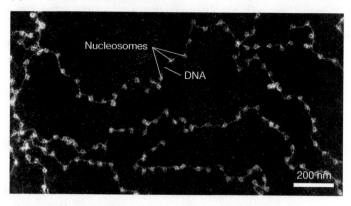

Nucleosomes

DNA

200 nm

(b) Nucleosome structure

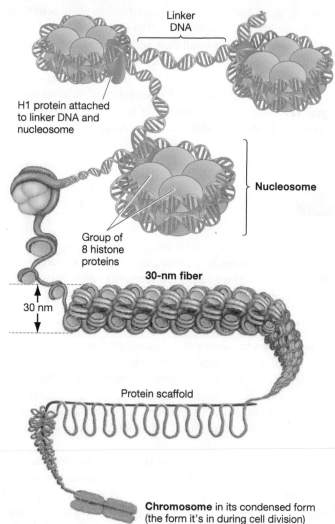

Linker DNA

H1 protein attached to linker DNA and nucleosome

Nucleosome

Group of 8 histone proteins

30-nm fiber

30 nm

Protein scaffold

Chromosome in its condensed form (the form it's in during cell division)

FIGURE 19.2 Chromatin Has Several Levels of Organization.

nothing like the 30-nm fibers or higher-order arrangements has been observed in bacterial chromosomes.

The elaborate structure of eukaryotic chromatin does more than just package DNA so that it fits into the nucleus. Chromatin structure also has profound implications for the control of gene expression. To appreciate this point, consider the 30-nm fiber illustrated in Figure 19.2b. If this tightly packed stretch of DNA contains a promoter, how can RNA polymerase bind to it and initiate transcription?

Evidence that Chromatin Structure Is Altered in Active Genes

Once the nucleosome-based structure of chromatin was established, biologists hypothesized that the close physical interaction between DNA and histones must be altered for RNA polymerase to make contact with DNA. More specifically, biologists hypothesized that a gene could not be transcribed until the condensed chromatin near its promoter was remodeled.

The central idea is that chromatin must be decondensed, to expose the promoter so RNA polymerase can bind to it. If so, then chromatin remodeling would represent the first step in the control of eukaryotic gene expression. Two types of studies have provided strong support for this hypothesis.

DNA in Condensed Chromatin Is Protected from DNase   DNases are enzymes that cut DNA. Some DNases cleave DNA at random locations, and these cannot cut efficiently if DNA is tightly wrapped with proteins. As **FIGURE 19.3** shows, this type of DNase works effectively only if DNA is in a decondensed configuration.

Harold Weintraub and Mark Groudine used this observation to test the hypothesis that the DNA of actively transcribed genes is in an open configuration. In chicken blood cells, they compared chromatin structure in two genes: β-globin and ovalbumin. β-globin is a protein that is part of the hemoglobin found in red blood cells; ovalbumin is a protein found in egg white. In blood cells, the β-globin gene is transcribed at high levels, but the ovalbumin gene is not transcribed at all.

After treating blood cells with DNase and then analyzing the state of chromatin at the β-globin and ovalbumin genes, the researchers found that DNase cut the β-globin gene DNA much more readily than DNA of the ovalbumin gene. They interpreted this finding as evidence that in blood cells, chromatin of the

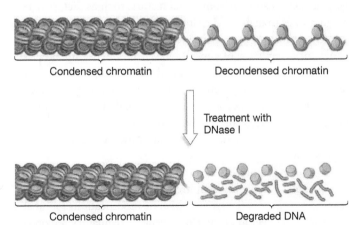

Condensed chromatin   Decondensed chromatin

Treatment with DNase I

Condensed chromatin   Degraded DNA

FIGURE 19.3 DNase Assay for Chromatin Structure. DNase is an enzyme that cuts DNA at random locations. It cannot cut condensed chromatin.

actively transcribed β-globin gene was decondensed; and conversely, chromatin of the non-transcribed ovalbumin gene was condensed. Studies using DNase on different genes in different cell types yielded similar results.

Histone Mutants   The second type of evidence in support of the chromatin-remodeling hypothesis comes from studies of mutant brewer's yeast cells that do not produce the usual complement of histones. In these mutant cells, many genes that are normally never transcribed are instead always transcribed at high levels.

To interpret this finding, biologists hypothesized that the lack of histone proteins prevented the assembly of normal chromatin. If the absence of normal histone–DNA interactions promotes transcription, then the presence of normal histone–DNA interactions must prevent it.

Taken together, the data suggest that in their normal, or default, state, eukaryotic genes are turned off. This is a new mechanism of negative control—different from repressor proteins (introduced in Chapter 18). When DNA is wrapped into a 30-nm fiber, the parking brake is on. If so, then gene expression depends on chromatin being opened up in the promoter region.

How Is Chromatin Altered?

Research on chromatin remodeling has been proceeding at a furious pace, and biologists have succeeded in identifying some of the key players that work to change the state of chromatin condensation. These include enzymes that add methyl groups to DNA, enzymes that chemically modify histones, and macromolecular machines that actively reshape chromatin. Let's examine each of these in turn.

DNA Methylation   A group of enzymes known as **DNA methyltransferases** add methyl groups ($-CH_3$) to cytosine residues in DNA. In mammals, the sequence recognized by these enzymes is a C next to a G in one strand of the DNA. This sequence is abbreviated CpG and is shown below in methylated form within a stretch of DNA.

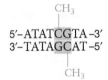

$$CH_3$$
5′–ATAT**CG**TA–3′
3′–TATAG**C**AT–5′
$$CH_3$$

Why is **DNA methylation** important? Methylated CpG sequences are recognized by proteins that trigger chromatin condensation. Actively transcribed genes usually have low levels of methylated CpG near their promoters, and non-transcribed genes usually have high levels of methylated CpG.

Histone Modification   DNA methylation is only one part of the chromatin alteration story. A large set of enzymes adds a variety of chemical groups to specific amino acids of histone proteins. These include phosphate groups, methyl groups, short polypeptide chains, and acetyl groups ($-COCH_3$). Addition of these groups to histones promotes condensed or decondensed chromatin depending on the specific set of modifications.

To account for these effects, researchers have proposed the existence of a **histone code.** The histone code hypothesis postulates that particular combinations of histone modifications set the state of chromatin condensation for a particular gene. In turn, this has an important role in regulating transcription. Let's take a closer look at one way histone modifications can control chromatin structure.

As shown in **FIGURE 19.4**, two different types of enzymes can add or remove acetyl groups from histones. **Histone acetyltransferases (HATs)** add acetyl groups to the positively charged lysine residues in histones, and **histone deacetylases (HDACs)** remove them. **Acetylation** of histones usually results in decondensed chromatin, a state associated with active transcription. How can acetylation of histones promote chromatin decondensation? When HATs add acetyl groups, the acetyl groups neutralize the positive charge on lysine residues and loosens the close association of nucleosomes with the negatively charged DNA. The addition of acetyl groups also creates a binding site for other proteins that help open the chromatin.

In contrast, when HDACs remove acetyl groups from histones, this process usually leads to condensed chromatin, a state associated with no transcription. HATs are an on switch for transcription, and HDACs are an off switch.

Chromatin-Remodeling Complexes   Other major players in chromatin alteration and gene regulation are enzymes that form macromolecular machines called **chromatin-remodeling complexes.** These machines harness the energy in ATP to reshape chromatin. Chromatin-remodeling complexes cause nucleosomes to slide along the DNA or, in some cases, knock the histones completely off the DNA to open up stretches of chromatin and allow gene transcription.

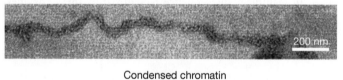

Condensed chromatin

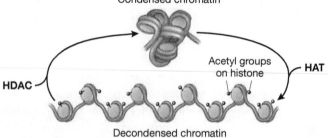

Acetyl groups on histone — **HAT**

HDAC

Decondensed chromatin

200 nm

FIGURE 19.4 Acetyl Groups Decondense Chromatin. Histone acetyltransferases (HATs) cause chromatin to decondense; histone deacetylases (HDACs) cause it to condense.

✓ **QUESTION** Are HAT and HDAC elements in positive control or negative control? Explain your reasoning.

DNA methylation, histone modifications, and chromatin-remodeling complexes work together to fine-tune chromatin condensation at specific genes. The take-home message from work on chromatin remodeling is simple: The condensation state of chromatin is critical in determining whether transcription occurs.

Chromatin Modifications Can Be Inherited

The pattern of chromatin modifications varies from one cell type to another. For example, suppose within an individual you analyzed the same gene in a muscle cell and a brain cell. This and other genes would likely have a different pattern of DNA methylation and histone acetylation in the two cell types.

DNA methylation and histone modifications are an example of **epigenetic inheritance,** the collective term for patterns of inheritance that are due to something other than differences in DNA sequences. The *epi–* of epigenetics comes from the Greek word meaning "upon." It implies another level of inheritance that adds to standard DNA-based mechanisms to explain how different phenotypes are transmitted.

With epigenetic inheritance, if a cell received a "become muscle" signal early in development, it would modify its chromatin in distinctive ways and pass those modifications on to its descendants. Muscle cells are different from brain cells not because they contain different genes, but largely because they have inherited different patterns of DNA methylation and histone modifications during the course of their development.

But the story of epigenetic inheritance involves more than just differentiation of cell types during development. Evidence is emerging that epigenetic mechanisms can record early-life events and that this archive can be difficult to erase. This is the case when prenatal conditions alter the patterns of chromatin modification and the later-life phenotypes of a mother's offspring.

For example, biologists have long known that rats born to mothers fed low-protein diets during pregnancy and while nursing have a greatly increased risk of developing disorders similar to type 2 diabetes. Type 2 diabetes is a serious and increasingly common disease that alters the cellular uptake of glucose. Both genetic factors and environmental factors, such as diet, play important roles in diabetes development.

One significant gene associated with diabetes is *Hnf4a.* *Hnf4a* codes for a regulator of genes involved in glucose uptake. Rats born to protein-deprived mothers develop symptoms of diabetes later in life, even when these rats are fed a normal, healthy diet from the time they are weaned. These diabetic rats also express the *Hnf4a* regulatory gene at lower levels than normal rats. Could epigenetic mechanisms be at work in silencing *Hnf4a* expression?

One team's approach to probing this question is shown in **FIGURE 19.5.** Using a treatment group and a control group, the researchers measured the types of histone modifications found at a key regulatory region of the *Hnf4a* gene. A regulatory region is a section of DNA that, like prokaryotic operators (Chapter 18), is involved in controlling the activity of a gene. The chromatin at this region has to be opened up for transcription to occur. Levels

RESEARCH

QUESTION: Does poor nutrition in a mother produce epigenetic effects in offspring?

HYPOTHESIS: Protein-deprived mothers will produce offspring with abnormal histone modifications.

NULL HYPOTHESIS: Protein-deprived mothers will produce offspring with normal histone modifications.

EXPERIMENTAL SETUP:

1. Provide rat mothers with a normal or a low-protein diet during pregnancy and while nursing.

2. After weaning, feed rat pups a normal diet and raise to old age.

3. Determine types of histone modifications for a regulatory gene involved in diabetes.
(Also measure gene transcription.)

Modifications promoting:

Modifications promoting:

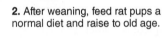

TRANSCRIPTION

Hnf4a

condensed chromatin

decondensed chromatin

PREDICTION: Offspring of mothers fed a low-protein diet will have abnormal histone modifications.

PREDICTION OF NULL HYPOTHESIS: Offspring of mothers fed a low-protein diet will have normal histone modifications.

RESULTS:

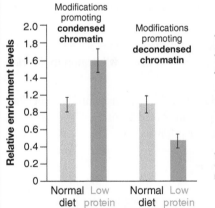

CONCLUSION: A mother's diet influences chromatin modifications and gene expression patterns throughout her offspring's life.

FIGURE 19.5 Events in Early Life Can Be Recorded through Epigenetic Mechanisms.

SOURCE: Sandovici, I., N. H. Smith, and M. D. Nitert. 2011. Maternal diet and aging alter the epigenetic control of a promoter-enhancer interaction at the *Hnf4a* gene in rat pancreatic islets. *Proceedings of the National Academy of Sciences USA* 108: 5449–5454.

✔**QUESTION** What could researchers do to prove that the histone modifications are causing reduced regulatory gene transcription?

---

of *Hnf4a* transcription in the control and treatment groups were also measured. What did the team learn?

As the graph on the left in the "Results" section of Figure 19.5 shows, they found that histone modifications that lead to condensed chromatin were *elevated* in rats born to malnourished mothers compared to control offspring. Conversely, histone modifications associated with decondensed chromatin were significantly *reduced* in the treatment group. The graph on the right confirms that transcription of *Hnf4a* was much lower in the treatment group than the control group. Together these results demonstrate a correlation between altered histone modifications and decreased levels of *Hnf4a* gene expression.

Remember that in this study, all rats were provided a healthy diet after weaning. This finding implies that a mother's nutritional status during pregnancy and nursing is responsible for the types of chromatin modifications seen in rats that develop diabetes.

Chromatin remodeling must occur before transcription. Now the question is, What happens once a section of chromatin is opened and DNA becomes accessible to RNA polymerase?

check your understanding

C Y U

If you understand that . . .

- Eukaryotic DNA is wrapped tightly around histones, forming nucleosomes, which are then coiled into structures called 30-nm chromatin fibers.
- Before transcription can begin, the DNA–protein complex of chromatin must be decondensed so that RNA polymerase can contact the promoter.
- Methylation of DNA and specific chemical modifications of histones play a key role in determining whether chromatin is opened and a gene is expressed.
- In many cases, the patterns of DNA methylation and histone modification in a cell are passed on to its daughter cells.

✔ You should be able to . . .

1. Predict how gene expression will be affected if a cell is grown with compounds that prevent DNA methylation.

2. Explain how certain patterns of histone acetylation or DNA methylation could influence whether a cell became a muscle cell or a brain cell.

Answers are available in Appendix A.

19.3 Initiating Transcription: Regulatory Sequences and Regulatory Proteins

As in bacteria, the **promoter** is a site in DNA where RNA polymerase binds to initiate transcription. Recent findings from genome sequencing projects (see Chapter 20) have shown that there is still much to be learned about eukaryotic promoters. What is known is that promoters in eukaryotes are more complex than bacterial promoters, often containing two or three conserved sequences that serve as binding sites for proteins needed to start transcription. The most intensively studied of these is a sequence known as the **TATA box.**

Once a promoter that contains a TATA box has been exposed by chromatin remodeling, the first step in initiating transcription is binding of the **TATA-binding protein (TBP).** Proteins related to TBP also work on promoters with other conserved sequences. But the binding of TBP or any of its relatives does not guarantee that a gene will be transcribed. In eukaryotes, a wide array of other DNA sequences and proteins work together to allow transcription.

Promoter-Proximal Elements Are Regulatory Sequences Near the Promoter

The first **regulatory sequences** in eukaryotic DNA were discovered in the late 1970s, when Yasuji Oshima and co-workers set out to understand how yeast cells control the metabolism of the sugar galactose.

When galactose is absent, *S. cerevisiae* cells produce only tiny quantities of the enzymes required to metabolize it. But when galactose is present, transcription of the genes encoding these enzymes increases by a factor of 1000.

The team's first major result was the discovery of mutant cells that failed to produce any of the five enzymes required for galactose metabolism, even if galactose was present. To interpret this observation, they hypothesized that

1. the five genes are regulated together, even though they are not on the same chromosome;

2. normal cells have an activator protein that exerts positive control over the five genes;

3. the mutant cells have a mutation that completely disables the activator protein.

Other researchers were able to isolate the regulatory protein and confirm that it binds to a short stretch of DNA located just upstream from the promoter for all five genes required for galactose use.

In bacteria, genes that need to be regulated together are often clustered into a single operon and transcribed into a single mRNA. In contrast, eukaryotes use the strategy uncovered by Oshima's group for the galactose-metabolizing genes in yeast—co-regulated genes are not clustered together, but instead share a regulatory DNA sequence that binds the same regulatory protein.

Regulatory DNA sequences similar to those first discovered in yeast have now been found in a wide array of eukaryotic genes and species. Regulatory sequences like these that are located close to the promoter and bind regulatory proteins are termed **promoter-proximal elements.**

Unlike the promoter itself, promoter-proximal elements have sequences that are unique to specific sets of genes. In this way, they furnish a mechanism for eukaryotic cells to express certain genes but not others.

The discovery of promoter-proximal elements and a mechanism of positive control suggested a satisfying parallel between gene regulation in bacteria and in eukaryotes. This picture changed, however, when researchers discovered a new class of eukaryotic DNA regulatory sequences—sequences unlike anything in bacteria.

Enhancers Are Regulatory Sequences Far from the Promoter

Susumu Tonegawa and colleagues made a startling discovery while exploring how human cells regulate gene expression. The gene studied by Tonegawa's group was broken into many introns and exons. Recall that introns are transcribed sequences that are spliced out of the primary transcript; exons are transcribed regions that are included in the mature RNA once splicing is complete (Chapter 17). The researchers discovered a regulatory sequence within one of the introns that was required for transcription of the gene.

This finding was remarkable for two reasons: (**1**) The regulatory sequence was thousands of bases away from the promoter, and (**2**) it was downstream of the promoter instead of upstream. Regulatory sequences that are far from the promoter and activate transcription are termed **enhancers.** Follow-up work has shown that enhancers occur in all eukaryotes and that they have several key characteristics:

- Enhancers can be more than 100,000 bases away from the promoter. They can be located in introns or in untranscribed sequences on either the 5′ or 3′ side of the gene (See **FIGURE 19.6**).

- Like promoter-proximal elements, many types of enhancers exist.

- Most genes have more than one enhancer.

- Enhancers usually have binding sites for more than one protein.

- Enhancers can work even if their normal 5′→3′ orientation is flipped, or if they are moved to a new location in the vicinity of the gene.

Enhancers are regulatory DNA sequences unique to eukaryotes. When regulatory proteins called **transcriptional activators** bind to enhancers, transcription begins. Thus, enhancers and activators are like a gas pedal—an element in positive control. Eukaryotes also possess regulatory sequences that are similar in structure and share key characteristics with enhancers but work to inhibit transcription. These DNA sequences are called **silencers.** When regulatory proteins called **repressors** bind to silencers, transcription is shut down. Silencers and repressors are like a brake—an element in negative control.

The Role of Transcription Factors in Differential Gene Expression

Follow-up work supported the hypothesis that enhancers and silencers are binding sites for activators and repressors that regulate transcription. Collectively, these proteins are termed

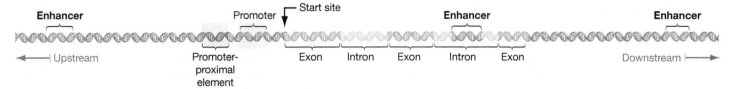

Enhancer Promoter Start site Enhancer Enhancer

← Upstream Promoter-proximal element Exon Intron Exon Intron Exon Downstream →

FIGURE 19.6 Enhancers and Promoter-Proximal Elements Regulate the Expression of Eukaryotic Genes.
Promoter-proximal elements are near the promoter. Enhancers are located farther away, may be upstream or downstream of the promoter, and may even be within introns. Exons and introns are not drawn to scale. They are typically very large compared with regulatory sequences.

✔**EXERCISE** Compare and contrast the structure of this typical eukaryotic gene and the structure of a bacterial operon.

regulatory transcription factors, or often **transcription factors** for short. By analyzing mutant yeast, fruit flies, and roundworms that have defects in the expression of particular genes, biologists have identified a large number of transcription factors that bind to enhancers, silencers, and promoter-proximal elements.

These results support one of the most general statements researchers are able to make about gene regulation in eukaryotes: Different types of cells express different genes because they have different transcription factors. In multicellular species, the transcription factors, in turn, are produced in response to signals that arrive from other cells early in embryonic development.

For example, if a signal that says "become a muscle cell" reaches a cell in the early embryo, it triggers a signal transduction cascade (see Chapter 11) that leads to the production of transcription factors specific to muscle cells. Because different transcription factors bind to specific regulatory sequences, they turn on the production of muscle-specific proteins. But if no "become-a-muscle-cell" signal arrives, then no muscle-specific transcription factors are produced and no muscle-specific gene expression takes place.

Differential gene expression is a result of the production or activation of specific transcription factors. Eukaryotic genes are turned on when transcription factors bind to enhancers and promoter-proximal elements; the genes are turned off when transcription factors bind to silencers or when chromatin is condensed. Distinctive transcription factors are what make a muscle cell a muscle cell and a bone cell a bone cell.

How Do Transcription Factors Recognize Specific DNA Sequences?

Each transcription factor must be able to recognize and bind to a specific DNA sequence. How can it do this?

Recall that DNA bases are partially exposed in the major and minor grooves of the DNA double helix (see Figure 4.7 for a review). The edges of an AT base pair and a GC base pair that project into the grooves of the DNA helix contain different sets of atoms and have different surface shapes (**FIGURE 19.7a**). These differences in composition and shape can be recognized by transcription factors.

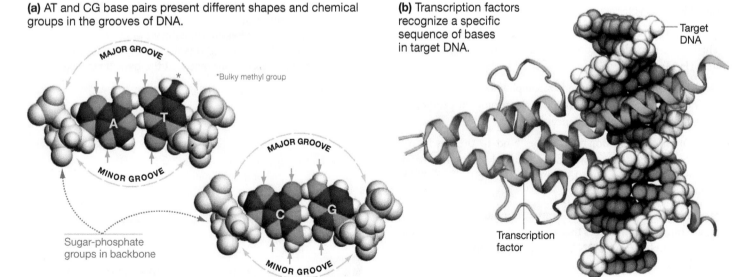

(a) AT and CG base pairs present different shapes and chemical groups in the grooves of DNA.

MAJOR GROOVE
*Bulky methyl group
A T
MINOR GROOVE
Sugar-phosphate groups in backbone

MAJOR GROOVE
C G
MINOR GROOVE

(b) Transcription factors recognize a specific sequence of bases in target DNA.

Target DNA
Transcription factor

FIGURE 19.7 How Transcription Factors Bind to Regulatory Sequences. (a) The edges of base pairs that project into the major and minor grooves of the double helix present a different structure and set of atoms. Atoms that can participate in hydrogen bonding with amino acids of transcription factors are indicated by arrows. The methyl group on thymine (T) is also important in recognition. **(b)** A transcription factor (green) involved in muscle-cell differentiation binding to a regulatory sequence in DNA. The bases recognized by the protein are highlighted in red.

Just as base pairs come together by complementary molecular interactions, so too can proteins and specific DNA sequences. An example is shown in **FIGURE 19.7b**. In this case, a transcription factor that is essential for the development of muscle cells inserts amino acid side chains into two major grooves of DNA. This particular transcription factor binds to a specific enhancer sequence because of complementary interactions between base pairs and its amino acids. Without such specific interactions between transcription factors and DNA, the development of muscle cells—or any other specialized cell type—would not be possible.

A Model for Transcription Initiation

Although gene expression can be controlled at many levels, regulating the start of transcription is at center stage. For a process so important, many questions remain. What is clear is that transcription factors must interact with regulatory sequences to initiate transcription.

Besides the regulatory transcription factors you've learned about that bind to enhancers, silencers, and promoter-proximal elements, there is another type: **basal transcription factors.** These are proteins that interact with the promoter and are not restricted to particular genes or cell types. The term basal implies that these proteins are necessary for transcription to occur, but they do not provide much in the way of regulation. The promoter-recognized TATA-binding protein (TBP) that you learned about earlier is an example of a basal transcription factor that is common to many genes. ✔ If you understand this concept, you should be able to compare and contrast the regulatory and basal transcription factors found in muscle cells versus nerve cells.

In addition to transcription factors, a large complex of proteins called **Mediator** acts as a bridge between regulatory transcription factors, basal transcription factors, and RNA polymerase II.

FIGURE 19.8 summarizes one model for how transcription is initiated in eukaryotes.

Step 1 Transcriptional activators bind to DNA and recruit chromatin-remodeling complexes and histone acetyltransferases (HATs).

Step 2 The chromatin-remodeling complexes and HATs open a swath of chromatin that includes the promoter, promoter-proximal elements, and enhancers.

Step 3 Other transcriptional activators bind to the newly exposed enhancers and promoter-proximal elements; basal transcription factors bind to the promoter and recruit RNA polymerase II.

Step 4 Mediator connects the transcriptional activators and basal transcription factors that are bound to DNA. This step is made possible through DNA looping. RNA polymerase II can now begin transcription.

✔ If you understand this model, you should be able to explain why DNA forms loops near the promoter in order for transcription to begin.

An important point in this model of transcription initiation is the dual role of transcriptional activators. Activators work not only to stimulate transcription but also to bring chromatin-remodeling proteins to the right place at the right time. None of the proteins that remodel chromatin can recognize specific DNA sequences. It is the transcriptional activators that bind to regulatory sequences at particular genes to recruit the proteins needed to remodel chromatin.

The role of transcriptional activators in bringing in proteins that decondense chromatin leads to a chicken-and-egg paradox: How can an activator bind to DNA in the first place if chromatin is condensed? It turns out that except in its most highly condensed forms, chromatin is dynamic. DNA occasionally dissociates from nucleosomes, exposing regulatory sequences to activators that are present in a particular cell type.

Getting RNA polymerase to initiate transcription requires interactions between many proteins, including transcriptional activators that are bound to enhancers and promoter-proximal elements, Mediator, basal transcription factors, and RNA polymerase itself. The result is a large, macromolecular machine that is positioned at a gene's start site and capable of starting transcription.

Compared with what happens in bacteria, where just three to five proteins may interact at the promoter to initiate transcription, the process in eukaryotes is remarkably complicated.

check your understanding

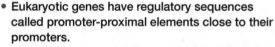
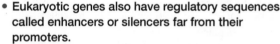

If you understand that . . .

- Eukaryotic genes have regulatory sequences called promoter-proximal elements close to their promoters.
- Eukaryotic genes also have regulatory sequences called enhancers or silencers far from their promoters.
- Transcription initiation is a multistep process that begins when transcriptional activators bind to DNA and recruit proteins that open chromatin.
- Interactions between regulatory transcription factors, Mediator, and basal transcription factors position RNA polymerase II at the gene's start site.

✔ **You should be able to . . .**

1. Compare and contrast the nature of regulatory sequences and regulatory proteins in bacteria versus eukaryotes.

2. Explain why the presence of certain transcription factors could influence whether a cell becomes a muscle cell or a brain cell.

Answers are available in Appendix A.

19.4 Post-Transcriptional Control

Chromatin remodeling and transcription are just the opening to the story of gene regulation. Once a gene is transcribed, a series of events has to occur before a final product appears (see Figure 19.1). Each of these events offers an opportunity

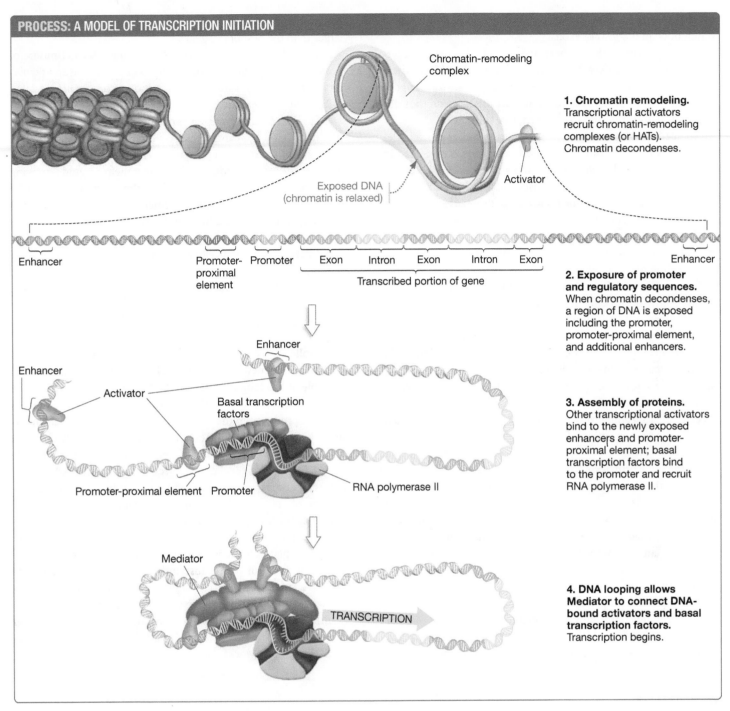

1. Chromatin remodeling. Transcriptional activators recruit chromatin-remodeling complexes (or HATs). Chromatin decondenses.

Chromatin-remodeling complex

Exposed DNA (chromatin is relaxed)

Activator

Enhancer

Promoter-proximal element

Promoter

Exon Intron Exon Intron Exon

Transcribed portion of gene

Enhancer

2. Exposure of promoter and regulatory sequences. When chromatin decondenses, a region of DNA is exposed including the promoter, promoter-proximal element, and additional enhancers.

Enhancer

Enhancer

Activator

Basal transcription factors

Promoter-proximal element   Promoter

RNA polymerase II

3. Assembly of proteins. Other transcriptional activators bind to the newly exposed enhancers and promoter-proximal element; basal transcription factors bind to the promoter and recruit RNA polymerase II.

Mediator

TRANSCRIPTION

4. DNA looping allows Mediator to connect DNA-bound activators and basal transcription factors. Transcription begins.

FIGURE 19.8 Transcription Initiation in Eukaryotes.

to regulate gene expression, and each is used in some cells at least some of the time. These control mechanisms include (1) splicing RNAs in various ways, (2) modifying the life span of mRNAs, (3) altering the rate at which translation is initiated, and (4) activating or inactivating proteins after translation has occurred. Let's consider each in turn.

Alternative Splicing of mRNAs

Introns are spliced out in the nucleus as the primary RNA is transcribed. Recall that the mRNA that results from splicing consists of sequences encoded by exons, and that it is protected by a cap on the 5′ end and a long poly(A) tail on the 3′ end (see Chapter 17). You may also recall that splicing is accomplished by macromolecular machines called **spliceosomes,** and that many primary transcripts can be spliced in more than one way. This turns out to be a major way of regulating eukaryotic gene expression.

During splicing, gene expression is regulated when selected exons are removed from the primary transcript along with the introns. As a result, the same primary RNA transcript can yield more than one kind of mature, processed mRNA, consisting of different combinations of exons.

This is important. Since these mature mRNAs contain differences in their sequences, the polypeptides translated from them will likewise differ. Splicing the same primary RNA transcript in different ways to produce different mature mRNAs and thus different proteins is referred to as **alternative splicing.**

To see how alternative splicing works, consider the muscle-cell protein tropomyosin. The tropomyosin gene is expressed in both skeletal muscle cells and smooth muscle cells. These cells make up two distinct kinds of muscle tissue. Skeletal muscle is responsible for moving your bones; smooth muscle lines many parts of your gut and certain blood vessels.

As **FIGURE 19.9a** shows, the primary transcript from the tropomyosin gene contains 14 exons. In each type of muscle cell, a different subset of the 14 exons are spliced together to produce two different mRNAs (**FIGURE 19.9b**). As a result of alternative splicing, the tropomyosin proteins found in these two cell types are distinct. One reason skeletal muscle and smooth muscle are different is that they contain different types of tropomyosin.

Alternative splicing is controlled by proteins that bind to RNAs in the nucleus and interact with spliceosomes to influence which sequences are used for splicing. When cells that are destined to become skeletal muscle or smooth muscle are developing, they receive signals leading to the production of specific proteins that are active in the regulation of splicing. Instead of transcribing different tropomyosin genes, the cells transcribe a single gene and splice the same primary RNA transcript in different ways.

Before the importance of alternative splicing was widely appreciated, a gene was considered to be a nucleotide sequence that encodes one specific protein or RNA, along with its regulatory sequences. Based on this view, estimates for the number of genes in the human genome were typically in the range of 60,000 to 100,000. But once the complete human genome sequence became available, researchers realized that we may have as few as 20,000 sequences for primary mRNA transcripts.

Even though our genomes contain a relatively low number of genes, recent data indicate that over 90 percent of them undergo alternative splicing to produce multiple products. Thus, the number of different proteins that your cells can produce is far larger than the number of genes.

Given the extent of alternative splicing, the definition of protein-coding genes has been changed to the coding and regulatory sequences that direct the production of one *or more* related mRNAs and polypeptides.

Many alternatively spliced genes produce just a few different products, but some can produce a bewildering array of mRNAs. The current record is the *Dscam* gene of the fruit fly *Drosophila melanogaster*. The products of this gene help to guide growing nerve cells within the embryo. The primary transcript can be spliced into more than 38,000 distinct forms of mRNA, and the *Dscam* gene can produce thousands of different products.

Alternative splicing is a major mechanism in the control of gene expression in multicellular eukaryotes. ✔ If you understand alternative splicing, you should be able to explain why it does not occur in bacteria and describe where it occurs in Figure 19.1.

mRNA Stability and RNA Interference

Once splicing is complete and processed mRNAs are exported to the cytoplasm, new regulatory mechanisms come into play. For example, it has long been known that the life span of an mRNA in a cell can vary. The mRNA for casein—the major protein in milk—is produced in the mammary gland tissue of female mammals. Normally, casein mRNA persists in cells for only about an hour, and little casein protein is produced. But when a female mouse is lactating, regulatory molecules help the mRNAs persist almost 30 times longer—leading to a huge increase in the production of casein. In this instance, shortening of the poly(A) tail decreases the life-span of the mRNA.

More recent discoveries in a variety of organisms, from worms to plants to people, have uncovered a widespread and important form of post-transcriptional gene regulation known as **RNA interference.** RNA interference occurs when a tiny, single-stranded RNA held by a protein complex binds to a complementary sequence in an mRNA. This event unleashes either the destruction of the mRNA or a block to the mRNA's translation. How does it work?

(a) Tropomyosin gene

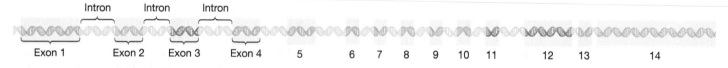

Exon 1   Exon 2   Exon 3   Exon 4   5   6   7   8   9   10   11   12   13   14

(b) Alternative splicing produces more than one mature mRNA.

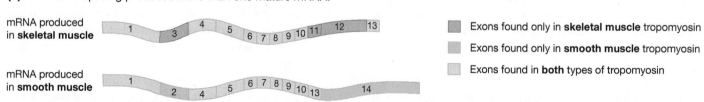

mRNA produced in **skeletal muscle**

mRNA produced in **smooth muscle**

Exons found only in **skeletal muscle** tropomyosin

Exons found only in **smooth muscle** tropomyosin

Exons found in **both** types of tropomyosin

FIGURE 19.9 Alternative Splicing Produces More than One Mature mRNA from the Same Gene.

FIGURE 19.10 walks through the sequence of events.

Step 1 RNA interference begins when RNA polymerase transcribes genes that code for RNAs that double back on themselves to form a hairpin. Hairpin formation occurs because pairs of bases within the RNA transcript are complementary.

Step 2 Some of the RNA is trimmed by enzymes in the nucleus; then the double-stranded hairpin that remains is exported to the cytoplasm.

Step 3 In the cytoplasm, another enzyme cuts out the hairpin loop to form double-stranded RNA molecules that are only about 22 nucleotides long.

Step 4 One of the strands from this short RNA is taken up by a group of proteins called the *RNA-induced silencing complex*, or RISC. The RNA strand held by the RISC is a **microRNA (miRNA).**

Step 5 Once it is part of a RISC, the miRNA binds to its complementary sequences in a target mRNA.

Step 6 If the match between a miRNA and an mRNA is perfect, an enzyme in the RISC destroys the mRNA by cutting it in two. In effect, tight binding by a miRNA is a "kiss of death" for the mRNA. If the match isn't perfect, however, the mRNA is not destroyed. Instead, its translation is inhibited. Either way, miRNAs "interfere" with gene expression.

The first papers on RNA interference were published in the mid-1990s, and the first miRNAs were characterized in 2001. Since then, research on miRNAs and RNA interference has exploded. Current data suggest that a typical animal or plant species has at least 500 genes that code for miRNAs and that each miRNA regulates more than one mRNA. Because of this evidence, it is estimated that a large percentage of all animal and plant genes are controlled by these tiny molecules. miRNAs are critical for normal development, and mutations in miRNA genes are associated with many diseases. RNA interference is increasingly recognized as a key aspect of post-transcriptional control.

Researchers are currently testing whether certain miRNAs could be used to knock out specific genes associated with illness, or to destroy mRNAs produced by viruses during an infection. Research on RNA interference has quickly moved from an exciting new frontier in basic biology to possible applications in medicine.

✔ If you understand RNA interference, you should be able to describe where it occurs in Figure 19.1.

How Is Translation Controlled?

RNA interference is not the only mechanism of gene control that acts on mRNAs and affects whether translation occurs. For example, cells may slow or stop translation in response to a sudden increase in temperature or infection by a virus. The slowdown occurs because regulatory proteins that are activated by the temperature spike or viral invasion add a phosphate group to a protein that is part of the ribosome.

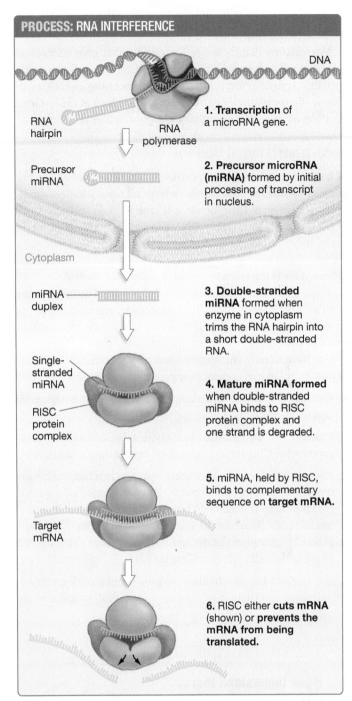

PROCESS: RNA INTERFERENCE

DNA

RNA hairpin

RNA polymerase

1. Transcription of a microRNA gene.

Precursor miRNA

2. Precursor microRNA (miRNA) formed by initial processing of transcript in nucleus.

Cytoplasm

miRNA duplex

3. Double-stranded miRNA formed when enzyme in cytoplasm trims the RNA hairpin into a short double-stranded RNA.

Single-stranded miRNA

RISC protein complex

4. Mature miRNA formed when double-stranded miRNA binds to RISC protein complex and one strand is degraded.

5. miRNA, held by RISC, binds to complementary sequence on **target mRNA.**

Target mRNA

6. RISC either **cuts mRNA** (shown) or **prevents the mRNA from being translated.**

FIGURE 19.10 MicroRNAs Either Target mRNAs for Destruction or Prevent Their Translation. MicroRNAs are held by the RISC protein complex and bind to target mRNAs by complementary base pairing.

You might recall that phosphorylation frequently leads to changes in the shape and chemical reactivity of proteins. In the case of the phosphorylated ribosomal protein, the shape change slows or prevents translation.

For the cell, this dramatic change in gene expression can mean the difference between life and death. High temperatures disrupt protein folding, so shutting down translation prevents the production of improperly folded polypeptides. If the problem is an invading virus, the cell stops the infection because it avoids manufacturing viral proteins.

Mechanisms like these are a reminder that gene expression can be regulated at multiple points: at the level of chromatin structure, transcription initiation, RNA processing, mRNA availability, and translation. But that's not all. Let's look at the last level possible: altering protein activity, after translation is complete.

Post-Translational Control

In bacteria, mechanisms of post-translational regulation are important because they allow cells to respond rapidly to new conditions (see Chapter 18). The same is true for eukaryotes. Instead of waiting for transcription, RNA processing, and translation to occur, the cell can keep an existing but inactive protein waiting in the wings and then quickly activate it in response to altered conditions. This is the essence of post-translational control.

There is a trade-off, however: Speed is gained at the expense of efficiency. Transcription, RNA processing, and translation use up energy and materials; it is wasteful to produce proteins that won't be used.

You have already encountered several important mechanisms of post-translational control over gene expression.

- Proteins are folded into their final, active conformation by chaperone proteins (see Chapters 3 and 17).

- Proteins may be modified by enzymes that add carbohydrate groups (see Chapter 7) or cleave off certain amino acids.

- Phosphorylation is an extremely common mechanism for activating or deactivating proteins. You just learned how a ribosomal protein is deactivated by adding a phosphate. You also might recall discussion of the activation of cyclin–Cdk complexes by phosphorylation and the subsequent entry into M phase of the cell cycle (see Chapter 12).

Yet another key mechanism of post-translational control—the targeted destruction of proteins—was first introduced by

describing the short life span of cyclin proteins. When a protein such as a cyclin needs to be destroyed, enzymes mark it by adding many copies of a small polypeptide called ubiquitin. Ubiquitin got its name because it is ubiquitous in cells. A macromolecular machine called the **proteasome** recognizes proteins that have a ubiquitin tag and cuts them into short segments.

As you can see, the regulation of gene expression in eukaryotes includes everything from opening chromatin in the nucleus to controlling the life span of proteins.

Do bacteria use the same range of regulatory mechanisms? Let's explore this question next.

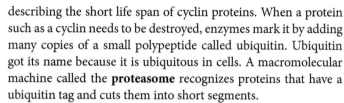

19.5 How Does Gene Expression Compare in Bacteria and Eukaryotes?

Almost as soon as biologists knew that information in DNA is transcribed into RNA and then translated into proteins, they began asking questions about how that flow of information is regulated. **TABLE 19.1** summarizes what biologists have learned over the past half century about how bacterial and eukaryotic gene expression is controlled—organized by the six steps in gene expression introduced in Figure 19.1.

How does the regulation of gene expression differ in bacteria and eukaryotes? Biologists point to five fundamental differences in the control of gene expression in bacteria and eukaryotes:

1. **DNA Packaging** The chromatin of eukaryotic DNA must be decondensed for basal and regulatory transcription factors to gain access to genes and for RNA polymerase to initiate transcription. The tight packaging of eukaryotic DNA means that the default state of transcription in eukaryotes is "off." In contrast, the default state of transcription in bacteria, which lack histone proteins and have freely accessible promoters, is "on." Chromatin structure provides a mechanism of negative control that does not exist in bacteria.

2. **Complexity of transcription** Transcriptional control is much more complex in eukaryotes than in bacteria. The sheer number of eukaryotic proteins involved in regulating transcription dwarfs that in bacteria, as does the complexity of their interactions.

3. **Coordinated transcription** In bacteria, genes that take part in the same cellular response are often organized into operons and transcribed together from a single promoter. In contrast, operons are rare in eukaryotes. Instead, for coordinated gene expression, eukaryotes rely on the strategy used in bacterial regulons—physically scattered genes are expressed together when the same regulatory transcription factors trigger the transcription of genes with the same DNA regulatory sequences.

4. **Greater reliance on post-transcriptional control** Eukaryotes make greater use of post-transcriptional control, such as alternative splicing. Alternative splicing allows eukaryotes to regulate the production of many proteins from each gene.

check your understanding

If you understand that . . .
- Alternative splicing allows a single gene to code for many products.
- RNA interference is one of several mechanisms for controlling an mRNA's life span and translation rate.
- Ubiquitin tagging and destruction by proteasomes is one of many mechanisms for controlling a protein's life span.

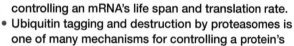

✔ **You should be able to . . .**
1. Explain why the discovery of alternative splicing forced biologists to change their definition of the gene.
2. Explain why RNA interference is aptly named.

Answers are available in Appendix A.

SUMMARY TABLE 19.1 Regulating Gene Expression in Bacteria and Eukaryotes

Level of Regulation	Bacteria	Eukaryotes
Chromatin remodeling	• Limited packaging of DNA • Remodeling not a major issue in regulating gene expression.	• Extensive packaging of DNA • Chromatin must be decondensed for transcription to begin.
Transcription	• Positive and negative control by regulatory proteins that act at sites close to the promoter • Sigma interacts with promoter.	• Positive and negative control by regulatory proteins that act at sites close to *and* far from promoter • Large set of basal transcription factors interact with promoter. • Mediator required.
RNA processing	• Rare	• Extensive processing: alternative splicing of introns
mRNA stability	• Rarely used for control	• Commonly used: RNA interference limits life span or translation rate of many mRNAs.
Translation	• Regulatory proteins bind to mRNAs and ribosomes and affect translation rate.	• Regulatory proteins bind to mRNAs and ribosomes and affect translation rate.
Post-translational modification	• Folding by chaperone proteins • Chemical modification (e.g., phosphorylation) changes protein activity.	• Folding by chaperone proteins • Chemical modification (e.g., phosphorylation) changes protein activity. • Ubiquitination targets proteins for destruction by proteasome.

Alternative splicing, microRNAs, and regulation of mRNA stability are seldom seen in bacteria, but these constitute major elements of control in eukaryotes.

To date, biologists do not have a good explanation for why gene expression is so much more complex in eukaryotes than it is in bacteria. After decades of research, the debate continues.

For multicellular eukaryotes, one hypothesis is that the requirement for complex regulation of gene expression during development has driven the evolution of such complicated and multilayered means of controlling genes.

Normal regulation of gene expression results in the orderly development of an embryo and appropriate responses to environmental change in adults. What happens when gene expression goes awry? Unfortunately, one answer is uncontrolled cell growth and the set of diseases called cancer. Understanding how changes in gene expression can lead to cancer is one of today's great research frontiers.

19.6 Linking Cancer with Defects in Gene Regulation

All cancers involve uncontrolled cell division. What allows this unbridled increase in cell number? Each type of cancer is caused by a different set of mutations that lead to cancer when they affect one of two classes of genes: (1) genes that stop or slow the cell cycle, and (2) genes that trigger cell growth and division by initiating specific phases in the cell cycle. Many of the genes

that are mutated in cancer influence gene regulation. Let's take a closer look at how altered gene regulation can cause uncontrolled cell growth.

The Genetic Basis of Uncontrolled Cell Growth

As you learned in the chapter on the cell cycle (Chapter 12), proteins that stop or slow the cell cycle when conditions are unfavorable for cell division are called tumor suppressors. Logically enough, the genes that code for these proteins are called **tumor suppressor** genes. If the function of a tumor suppressor gene is lost because of mutation, then a key brake on the cell cycle is eliminated.

Genes that stimulate cell division are called **proto-oncogenes** (literally, "first cancer genes"). In normal cells, the proteins produced from proto-oncogenes are active only when conditions are appropriate for growth. In cancerous cells, defects in the regulation of proto-oncogenes can cause these genes to stimulate growth at all times. (In the context of cancer, cell growth refers to an increase in cell numbers, not an increase in the size of individual cells.) In such cases, a mutation has converted the proto-oncogene into an **oncogene**—an allele that promotes cancer development.

For cancers to develop, many mutations are required within a single cell, and these alter both tumor suppressor genes and proto-oncogenes.

The *p53* Tumor Suppressor: A Case Study

To gain a deeper understanding of how defects in gene expression can lead to cancer, consider research on the gene that is most often defective in human cancers. The gene is called *p53* because

(a) Normal cell

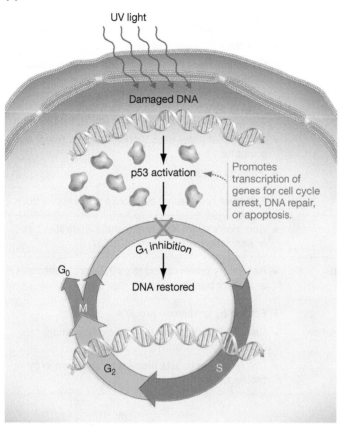

(b) *p53* mutant cell

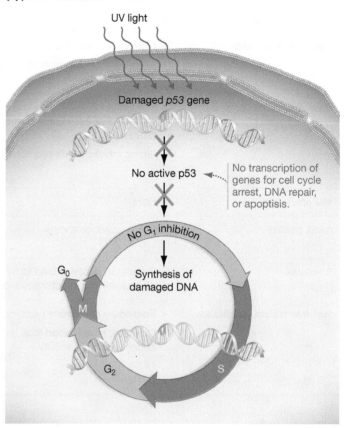

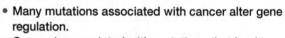

FIGURE 19.11 Consequences of *p53* Mutation.

the protein it codes for has a molecular weight of approximately 53 kilodaltons. Sequencing studies have revealed that mutant, nonfunctional forms of *p53* are found in over half of all human cancers. The *p53* gene codes for a regulatory transcription factor.

Researchers began to understand what *p53* does when they exposed normal, noncancerous human cells to UV radiation and noticed that levels of active *p53* protein increased markedly. Recall that UV radiation damages DNA (see Chapter 15). Follow-up studies confirmed that there is a close correlation between DNA damage and the amount of *p53* in a cell. In addition, analyses of the protein's primary structure suggested that it might contain a DNA-binding region similar to the one shown for the muscle-specific transcription factor in Figure 19.7.

These observations inspired the hypothesis that *p53* is a regulatory transcription factor that serves as a master brake on the cell cycle. In this model, shown in **FIGURE 19.11**, *p53* is activated by DNA damage. Activated *p53* binds to the enhancers of genes that arrest the cell cycle, repair DNA damage, and when all else fails, trigger apoptosis (cell death). Expression of these genes allows the cell to halt the cell cycle in order to repair its DNA, if this is possible, or commit suicide if the DNA damage is too severe. In mutant cells that lack a form of *p53* that can bind to enhancers, DNA damage cannot arrest the cell cycle, the cell cannot kill

check your understanding

If you understand that . . .

- Many mutations associated with cancer alter gene regulation.
- Cancer is associated with mutations that lead to loss of control over the cell cycle.
- Uncontrolled cell growth may result when a mutation in a regulatory gene creates a protein that activates the cell cycle constitutively.
- Uncontrolled cell growth may result when a mutation prevents a tumor suppressor protein from shutting down the cell cycle in damaged cells.

✔ **You should be able to . . .**

1. Explain why cancer has a common pattern of uncontrolled cell growth, but not a common cause. Your answer should refer to the six levels of gene regulation outlined in Figure 19.1.

2. Explain why loss-of-function mutations in *p53* are observed in so many cancers.

Answers are available in Appendix A.

itself, and damaged DNA is replicated. This situation leads to mutations that can move the cell farther down the road to cancer. The *p53* protein is like a quality control officer. If it is missing, errors are made and things go downhill.

Here are some of the results that support this model of *p53* function:

- *p53* activates many different genes, including genes for cell cycle regulation, DNA repair, and apoptosis.

- X-ray crystallography studies show that *p53* binds directly to DNA regulatory sequences of the genes it controls.

- Virtually all the *p53* mutations associated with cancer are located in the protein's DNA-binding region and alter amino acids that interfere with *p53*'s ability to bind to regulatory DNA sequences.

The role of *p53* in preventing cancer is so important that biologists call this gene "the guardian of the genome." Today, biologists are searching for molecules that can restore *p53* activity to protect the genome and act against cancer.

If you understand . . .

19.1 Gene Regulation in Eukaryotes— An Overview

- Changes in gene expression allow eukaryotic cells to respond to changes in the environment and cause distinct cell types to develop.

- In a multicellular eukaryote, cells are different because they express different genes, not because they have different genes.

- Gene expression is regulated at six levels: Chromatin has to be remodeled, the transcription of specific genes may be initiated or repressed, mRNAs may be spliced in different ways to produce a different product, the life span of specific mRNAs may be extended or shortened, translation rate may be increased or decreased, and the life span or activity of particular proteins may be altered.

✔ You should be able to describe how the presence of the nuclear envelope, and the physical separation of transcription and translation, influences the levels of gene regulation observed in eukaryotes versus bacteria and archaea.

19.2 Chromatin Remodeling

- Eukaryotic DNA is packaged with proteins into chromatin that must be opened before transcription can occur.

- Eukaryotic DNA is wrapped around histone proteins to form bead-like nucleosomes that are then coiled into 30-nm fibers and higher-order chromatin structures.

- Transcription cannot be initiated until chromatin around regulatory regions is decondensed.

- The state of chromatin condensation depends on the methylation of cytosines in DNA, acetylation and other modifications of histones, and the action of molecular machines called chromatin-remodeling complexes.

- Patterns of DNA methylation and histone modifications can be passed from mother cells to daughter cells.

- Epigenetic inheritance is the inheritance of different phenotypes due to anything other than differences in alleles; transmitting patterns of chromatin condensation from mother to daughter cells or from parent to offspring is a mechanism of epigenetic inheritance.

✔ You should be able to explain why chromatin remodeling has to be the first step in gene activation.

19.3 Initiating Transcription: Regulatory Sequences and Regulatory Proteins

- In eukaryotes, transcription is triggered by regulatory proteins called transcription factors that bind to sequences both close to and far from the promoter.

- Regulatory transcription factors can be activators or repressors; these bind to regulatory sequences called (1) promoter-proximal sequences that are near promoters or (2) enhancers and silencers that are often located at a distance from gene promoters.

- Amino acids on regulatory transcription factors interact with the projections of base pairs in the grooves of the DNA helix to allow binding to specific regulatory sequences.

- The first regulatory transcription factors that bind to DNA recruit proteins that loosen the interaction between nucleosomes and DNA, making the promoter, promoter-proximal elements, and enhancers accessible to other transcription factors.

- Interactions between regulatory and basal transcription factors occur through a complex of proteins called Mediator and lead to the positioning of RNA polymerase at the promoter and the start of transcription.

✔ You should be able to draw a model of a eukaryotic gene undergoing transcription. Label enhancers, promoter-proximal elements, the promoter, activators, basal transcription factors, Mediator, and RNA polymerase.

19.4 Post-Transcriptional Control

- Once transcription is complete, gene expression is controlled by (1) alternative splicing, (2) RNA interference, and (3) activation or inactivation of protein products.

- Alternative splicing allows a single gene to produce more than one version of an mRNA and more than one kind of protein. It is regulated by proteins that interact with potential splice sites in the primary transcript to control which ones the spliceosome uses.

- RNA interference occurs when tiny strands of complementary RNA bind to mRNAs in association with the protein complex called RISC. This marks the mRNAs for destruction or prevents their translation. If the short RNA strands come from a transcribed cellular gene, they are known as microRNAs (miRNAs).

- Once translation occurs, proteins may be activated or inactivated by the addition or removal of chemical groups such as phosphates, or marked for destruction in the proteasome by adding polypeptides known as ubiquitin.

✔ You should be able to explain why humans can have so few genes.

19.5 How Does Gene Expression Compare in Bacteria and Eukaryotes?

- Examine Table 19.1 Regulating Gene Expression in Bacteria and Eukaryotes.

✔ You should be able to compare and contrast how bacteria and eukaryotes regulate the transcription of genes that need to be turned on together.

19.6 Linking Cancer with Defects in Gene Regulation

- If mutations alter regulatory proteins that promote or inhibit progression through the cell cycle, then uncontrolled cell growth and tumor formation may result.

✔ You should be able to explain why mutations of *p53* that prevent the protein from binding to DNA set the stage for cancer.

(MB) **MasteringBiology**

1. MasteringBiology Assignments

Tutorials and Activities Control of Gene Expression; Control of Transcription; DNA Packing; Overview: Control of Gene Expression; Post-Transcriptional Control Mechanisms; Regulation of Gene Expression in Eukaryotes; Transcription Initiation in Eukaryotes

Questions Reading Quizzes, Blue-Thread Questions, Test Bank

2. eText Read your book online, search, take notes, highlight text, and more.

3. The Study Area Practice Test, Cumulative Test, BioFlix® 3-D Animations, Videos, Activities, Audio Glossary, Word Study Tools, Art

---

You should be able to . . .

✔ **TEST YOUR KNOWLEDGE**   *Answers are available in Appendix A*

1. What is chromatin?
   a. the histone-containing protein core of the nucleosome
   b. the 30-nm fiber
   c. the complex of DNA and proteins found in eukaryotes
   d. the histone *and* non-histone proteins in eukaryotic nuclei

2. What is a tumor suppressor?

3. Which of the following statements about enhancers is correct?
   a. They contain a unique base sequence called a TATA box.
   b. They are located only in 5'-flanking regions.
   c. They are located only in introns.
   d. They are found in a variety of locations and are functional in any orientation.

4. In eukaryotes, what allows only certain genes to be expressed in certain types of cells?

5. What is alternative splicing?
   a. phosphorylation events that lead to different types of post-translational regulation
   b. mRNA processing events that lead to different combinations of exons being spliced together
   c. folding events that lead to proteins with alternative conformations
   d. action by regulatory proteins that leads to changes in the life span of an mRNA

6. What types of proteins bind to promoter-proximal elements?
   a. the basal transcription complex
   b. the basal transcription complex plus RNA polymerase
   c. basal transcription factors such as TBP
   d. regulatory transcription factors such as activators

7. Compare and contrast (a) enhancers and the *E. coli araC* binding site (see Chapter 18), (b) promoter-proximal elements and the operator of the *lac* operon, and (c) basal transcription factors and sigma.

8. Explain how alternative splicing could play a role in changing eukaryotic gene expression in response to changes in the environment.

9. Compare and contrast (a) enhancers and silencers; (b) promoter-proximal elements and enhancers; and (c) regulatory transcription factors and Mediator.

10. Predict how a drug that inhibits histone deacetylase will alter gene expression.

11. Relative to the genetic code, the histone code
    a. has more triplets.
    b. is much simpler to read because of complementary base pairing.
    c. does not depend on particular base sequences.
    d. requires methylated Cs rather than standard Cs in DNA.

12. Predict how a mutation that caused continuous production of active *p53* would affect the cell.

13. In the follow-up work to the experiment shown in Figure 19.5, the researchers used a technique that allowed them to see if two DNA sequences are in close physical proximity (association). They applied this method to examine how often an enhancer and the promoter of the *Hnf4a* regulatory gene were near each other. A logical prediction is that compared with rats born to mothers fed a healthy diet, the *Hnf4a* gene in rats born to mothers fed a protein poor diet would
    a. show no difference in how often the promoter and enhancer associated.
    b. never show any promoter–enhancer association.
    c. show a lower frequency of promoter–enhancer association.
    d. show a higher frequency of promoter–enhancer association.

14. **QUANTITATIVE** Imagine repeating the experiment on epigenetic inheritance that is shown in Figure 19.5. You measure the amount of radioactive uridine (U) incorporated into *Hnf4a* mRNA in counts per minute (cpm) to determine the level of *Hnf4a* gene transcription in rats born to mothers fed either a normal diet or a low protein diet. The results are 11,478 cpm for the normal diet

and 7368 cpm for the low-protein diet conditions. You should prepare a graph similar to the one at the bottom of Figure 19.5 that shows the normalized results relative to the normal diet condition. Normalizing values means that value obtained from one condition is expressed as 1.0 (the norm; the normal diet in this case) and the values obtained from any other conditions (low-protein diet in this case) are expressed as decimal values relative to the norm.

15. After DNA damage, levels of activated p53 protein in the cytoplasm increase. Design an experiment to determine whether this increase is due to increased transcription of the *p53* gene or to activation of preexisting p53 proteins by a post-translational mechanism such as phosphorylation.

16. Researchers have discovered that if a single-stranded mRNA produced by a virus is used as a template to create a double-stranded RNA, that this double-stranded RNA often blocks infection by the virus. Propose an explanation for how infection can be blocked by this type of double-stranded RNA.

The Big Picture

Copying, using, and transmitting genetic information is fundamental to life. Cells use the genetic information archived in their DNA to respond to changes in the environment and, in multicellular organisms, to develop into specific cell types.

Hereditary information is transmitted to offspring with random changes called mutations. Thus, genetic information is dynamic—both within generations and between generations.

Note that each box in the concept map indicates the chapter and section where you can go for review. Also, be sure to do the blue exercises in the Check Your Understanding box below.

check your understanding

(C)(Y)(U)

If you understand the big picture . . .

✔ You should be able to . . .

1. Draw stars next to the three elements of the central dogma of molecular biology.
2. Add arrows and labels indicating what reverse transcriptase does.
3. Draw an E in the corners of boxes that refer only to eukaryotes, not prokaryotes.
4. Fill in the blue ovals with appropriate linking verbs or phrases.

Answers are available in Appendix A.

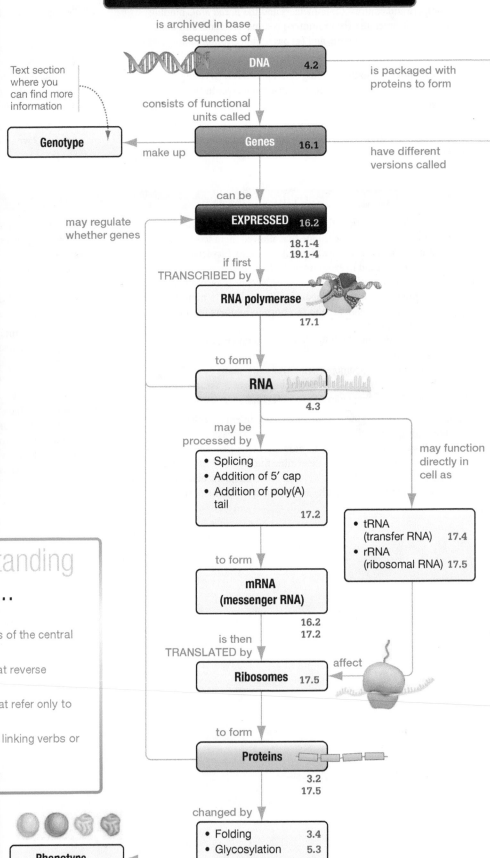

GENETIC INFORMATION

GENETIC INFORMATION is archived in base sequences of **DNA** 4.2

is packaged with proteins to form

consists of functional units called

Text section where you can find more information ⤑ **Genotype**

make up ← **Genes** 16.1

have different versions called

can be **EXPRESSED** 16.2 18.1-4 19.1-4

may regulate whether genes

if first TRANSCRIBED by **RNA polymerase** 17.1

to form **RNA** 4.3

may be processed by
- Splicing
- Addition of 5' cap
- Addition of poly(A) tail 17.2

may function directly in cell as
- tRNA (transfer RNA) 17.4
- rRNA (ribosomal RNA) 17.5

to form **mRNA (messenger RNA)** 16.2 17.2

is then TRANSLATED by **Ribosomes** 17.5 ← affect

to form **Proteins** 3.2 17.5

changed by
- Folding 3.4
- Glycosylation 5.3
- Phosphorylation 8.2
- Degradation 19.4

Phenotype ← produce

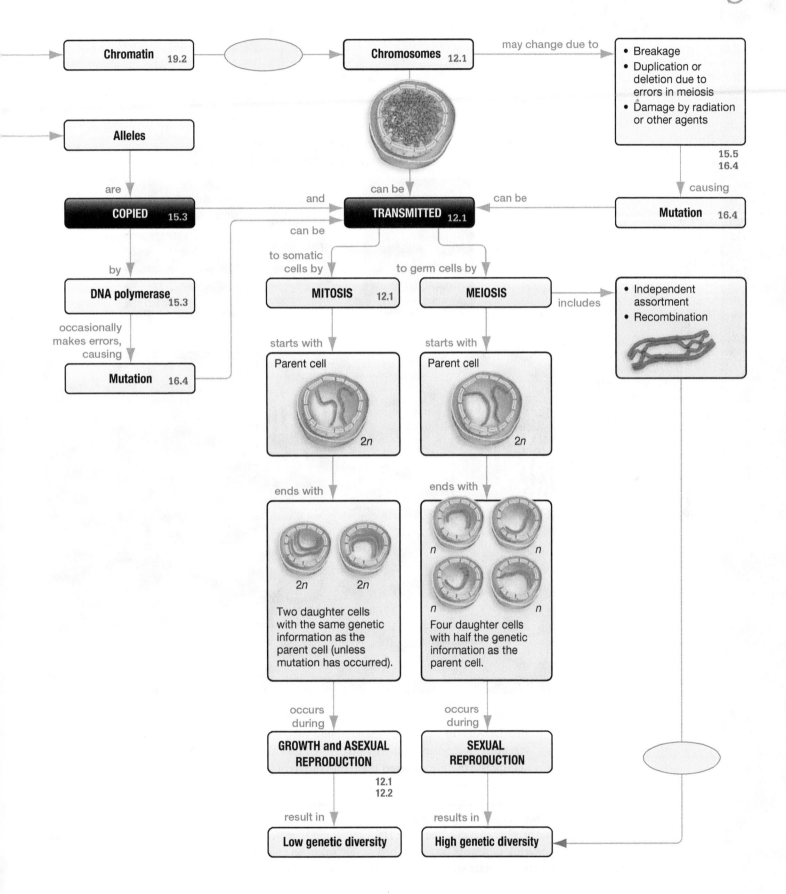

Chromatin 19.2

Chromosomes 12.1 — may change due to →
- Breakage
- Duplication or deletion due to errors in meiosis
- Damage by radiation or other agents

15.5
16.4

Alleles

are ↓

COPIED 15.3 — and → can be ← **TRANSMITTED** 12.1 ← can be ← causing ← **Mutation** 16.4

by ↓

DNA polymerase 15.3

occasionally makes errors, causing ↓

Mutation 16.4

can be

to somatic cells by ↓

to germ cells by ↓

MITOSIS 12.1

MEIOSIS — includes →
- Independent assortment
- Recombination

starts with ↓

starts with ↓

Parent cell 2n

Parent cell 2n

ends with ↓

ends with ↓

2n 2n

n n
n n

Two daughter cells with the same genetic information as the parent cell (unless mutation has occurred).

Four daughter cells with half the genetic information as the parent cell.

occurs during ↓

occurs during ↓

GROWTH and ASEXUAL REPRODUCTION 12.1 12.2

SEXUAL REPRODUCTION

result in ↓

results in ↓

Low genetic diversity

High genetic diversity

367

20 Analyzing and Engineering Genes

In this chapter you will learn that

Biotechnology depends on methods to analyze and alter genomes

by exploring ↓

Case studies of key genetic technologies

applied to

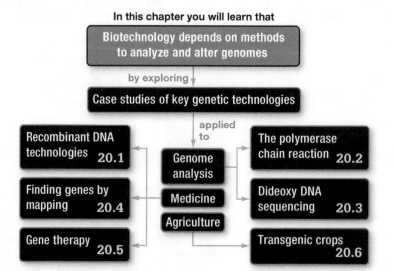

Recombinant DNA technologies **20.1**

Finding genes by mapping **20.4**

Gene therapy **20.5**

Genome analysis

Medicine

Agriculture

The polymerase chain reaction **20.2**

Dideoxy DNA sequencing **20.3**

Transgenic crops **20.6**

The rice plants in these bottles have been genetically engineered—using techniques introduced in this chapter—to produce a molecule needed for a key vitamin.

The molecular revolution in biological science got its start when researchers confirmed that DNA is the hereditary material and succeeded in describing the molecule's secondary structure. But when biologists discovered how to remove DNA sequences from an organism, manipulate them, and insert them into different individuals, the molecular revolution really took off.

Efforts to manipulate DNA sequences in organisms are often referred to as genetic engineering. Genetic engineering became possible with the discovery of enzymes that cut DNA at specific sites and of other enzymes that paste DNA sequences together. These new molecular tools were extremely powerful. Biologists no longer had to rely solely on controlled breeding experiments to change the genetic characteristics of individuals. Instead, they could mix and match specific DNA sequences in

✔ When you see this checkmark, stop and test yourself. Answers are available in Appendix A.

the lab. Because successful efforts to manipulate genes usually result in novel combinations of DNA, techniques used to engineer genes are often referred to as **recombinant DNA technology.**

This chapter uses a series of case histories to introduce basic molecular biology techniques in the context of solving problems. It also considers the ethical and economic issues raised by efforts to manipulate genes. What are the potential perils and benefits of introducing recombinant genes into human beings, food plants, and other organisms? This question, one of the great ethical challenges of the twenty-first century, is a recurrent theme in the following pages.

20.1 Case 1–The Effort to Cure Pituitary Dwarfism: Basic Recombinant DNA Technologies

To understand the basic techniques and tools of genetic engineering, let's consider the role they played in developing a treatment for pituitary dwarfism in humans.

The pituitary gland is a structure at the base of the mammalian brain that produces several important biomolecules, including a protein that stimulates growth. This protein, which was found to be just 191 amino acids long, was named human growth hormone (HGH). In humans, the gene that codes for it is called *GH1.*

The discovery of growth hormone led researchers immediately to suspect that at least some forms of inherited dwarfism might be caused by a defect in the *GH1* gene. This hypothesis was confirmed by studies showing that people with certain types of dwarfism produce little growth hormone or none at all. These people have defective copies of *GH1* and exhibit pituitary dwarfism, type I (**FIGURE 20.1a**).

By studying the pedigrees of families in which dwarfism was common, several teams of researchers established that pituitary dwarfism, type I, is an autosomal recessive trait. In other words, affected individuals have two copies of the defective allele. Individuals who are affected by pituitary dwarfism have normal body proportions but grow more slowly than average people, reach puberty from two to 10 years later than average, and are short in stature as adults—typically no more than 120 cm (4 feet) tall (**FIGURE 20.1b**).

Why Did Early Efforts to Treat the Disease Fail?

Once the molecular basis of pituitary dwarfism was understood, physicians began treating the disease with injections of naturally produced growth hormone. This approach was inspired by the spectacular success that had been achieved in treating type I diabetes mellitus. This form of diabetes is caused by a deficiency of the peptide hormone insulin, and clinicians had been able to alleviate the disease's symptoms by injecting patients with insulin from pigs.

Early trials showed that people with pituitary dwarfism could be treated successfully with growth hormone therapy, but only if the protein came from humans. Growth hormones isolated from pigs, cows, or other animals were ineffective. Until the 1980s, however, the only source of human growth hormone was pituitary glands from human cadavers. As a result, the drug was extremely scarce and expensive.

It turned out that meeting demand was the least of the problems with growth hormone therapy. To understand why, recall that infectious proteins called prions can cause degenerative brain disorders in mammals (see Chapter 3). When some of the children treated with human growth hormone developed a prion disease in their teens and twenties, physicians realized that the supply of growth hormone was contaminated with a prion protein from

(a) *GH1* codes for a pituitary growth hormone.

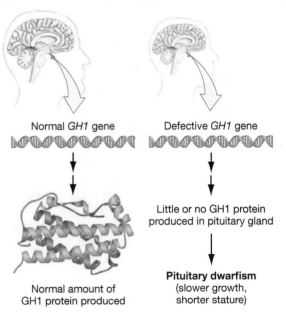

Normal *GH1* gene

Defective *GH1* gene

Little or no GH1 protein produced in pituitary gland

Normal amount of GH1 protein produced

Pituitary dwarfism (slower growth, shorter stature)

(b) Normal versus GH1-deficient

FIGURE 20.1 Pituitary Dwarfism Is a Genetic Disease. (a) If mutations in the human *GH1* sequence are severe enough to inactivate the gene, pituitary dwarfism may result. **(b)** William Harrison and Charles Stratton, in a photo taken about 1860. Harrison and Stratton were both celebrated comedians and performers. Stratton, whose stage name was Tom Thumb, enjoyed audiences in the White House with Abraham Lincoln and Buckingham Palace with Queen Victoria. Stratton had pituitary dwarfism; Harrison had normal height.

some of the cadavers supplying the hormone. In 1984, the use of growth hormone isolated from cadavers was banned.

Steps in Engineering a Safe Supply of Growth Hormone

To replace natural sources of growth hormone, researchers turned to genetic engineering. Their plan was to insert fully functional copies of human *GH1* into the bacterium *Escherichia coli*, which they hoped would then produce huge quantities of recombinant progeny. If the plan worked, the recombinant cells would produce uncontaminated growth hormone in sufficient quantities to meet demand at an affordable price.

The plan required investigators to find *GH1*, obtain many copies of the gene, and insert them into *E. coli* cells. Their ability to do these things hinged on using basic tools of molecular biology.

Using Reverse Transcriptase to Produce cDNAs An enzyme called reverse transcriptase (Chapter 16) is responsible for an exception to the central dogma of molecular biology: It allows information to flow from RNA to DNA. More specifically, reverse transcriptase catalyzes the synthesis of DNA from an RNA template.

DNA that is produced from RNA is called **complementary DNA,** or **cDNA.** Although reverse transcriptase initially produces a single-stranded cDNA, it is also capable of synthesizing the complementary strand to yield a double-stranded DNA. In many cases, however, researchers add a chemically synthesized primer to single-stranded cDNAs and use DNA polymerase to synthesize the second strand (**FIGURE 20.2**).

Reverse transcriptase played a key role in the search for the growth hormone gene. Knowing that *GH1* is actively transcribed in the pituitary gland, researchers isolated mRNAs from pituitary-gland cells and used the enzyme to reverse-transcribe those mRNAs to cDNAs. These reaction products contained double-stranded cDNAs corresponding to each gene that is actively expressed in pituitary cells.

The next move? Isolating each of the cDNAs and making many identical copies of them.

Using Plasmids in Cloning Producing many copies of a gene is referred to as **DNA cloning.** If a researcher says that she has cloned a gene, it means that she has isolated it and then produced many identical copies.

In many cases, researchers can clone a gene by inserting it into a small, circular DNA molecule called a **plasmid.** You might recall that plasmids are common in bacterial cells (see Chapter 7). They are physically separate from the bacterial chromosome and are not required for normal growth and reproduction. Most replicate independently of the chromosome. Some plasmids carry genes for antibiotic resistance or other traits that increase the cell's ability to grow in a particular environment.

Researchers realized that if they could splice a loose piece of DNA into a plasmid and then insert the modified plasmid into a bacterial cell, the engineered plasmid would be replicated and passed on to daughter cells as the bacterium grew and divided. If this recombinant bacterium were then placed in a nutrient broth and allowed to grow and reproduce overnight, billions of copies of the original cell, each containing identical modified plasmid DNA, would result. When a plasmid is used in this way—to make copies of a foreign DNA sequence—it is called a **cloning vector,** or simply a **vector.**

Biologists harvest the recombinant genes by breaking the bacteria open, isolating all the DNA, and then separating the plasmids from the main chromosomes. But how do they insert a gene into a plasmid in the first place?

Using Restriction Endonucleases and DNA Ligase to Cut and Paste DNA To cut a gene out for later insertion into a cloning vector, researchers use enzymes called restriction endonucleases. A **restriction endonuclease** is a bacterial enzyme that cuts DNA molecules at specific base sequences. In bacterial cells, these enzymes cut up DNA from invading viruses and prevent a fatal infection.

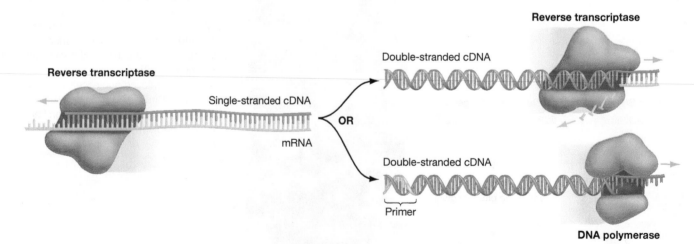

FIGURE 20.2 Reverse Transcriptase Catalyzes the Synthesis of DNA from RNA. The single-stranded DNA produced by reverse transcriptase is complementary to the RNA template. The cDNA can be made double stranded by reverse transcriptase or DNA polymerase. DNA polymerase requires a primer.

More than 800 restriction endonucleases are known, and many of them cut DNA only at sequences that form palindromes. In English, a word or sentence is a palindrome if it reads the same way backward as it does forward. "Madam, I'm Adam" is an example. In biology, a stretch of double-stranded DNA forms a palindrome if the 5'→3' sequence of one strand is identical to the 5'→3' sequence on the antiparallel, complementary strand.

To insert the pituitary-gland cDNAs into plasmids, researchers performed the sequence of steps outlined in **FIGURE 20.3**.

Step 1 The left side of the figure shows a plasmid containing a palindromic sequence, or recognition site, that is cut by a specific restriction endonuclease. As the right side of the figure shows, the researchers attached the same palindromic sequence to the ends of each cDNA in their sample.

Step 2 They cut the recognition sites in each plasmid (left) and at the ends of each cDNA (right) with a restriction endonuclease called EcoRI. (The name comes from the fact that this

enzyme was the first (Roman numeral *I*) restriction endonuclease discovered in *E. coli* strain *R*Y13.)

Step 3 Like most restriction endonucleases, EcoRI makes a staggered cut in the palindrome. The resulting DNA fragments are described as having **sticky ends,** because the single-stranded bases on one fragment are complementary to the single-stranded bases on the other fragment. As a result, the two ends can pair up and hydrogen-bond to each other: The complementary sequences in the sticky ends of the plasmid (in grey) will bind to the sticky ends in the cDNA (in red) by complementary base pairing.

Step 4 Finally, researchers used **DNA ligase**—the enzyme that connects Okazaki fragments during DNA replication (see Chapter 15)—to seal the pieces of DNA together at the arrows marked in green.

The creation of sticky ends in DNA is important. If restriction sites in different DNA sequences are cut with the same restriction

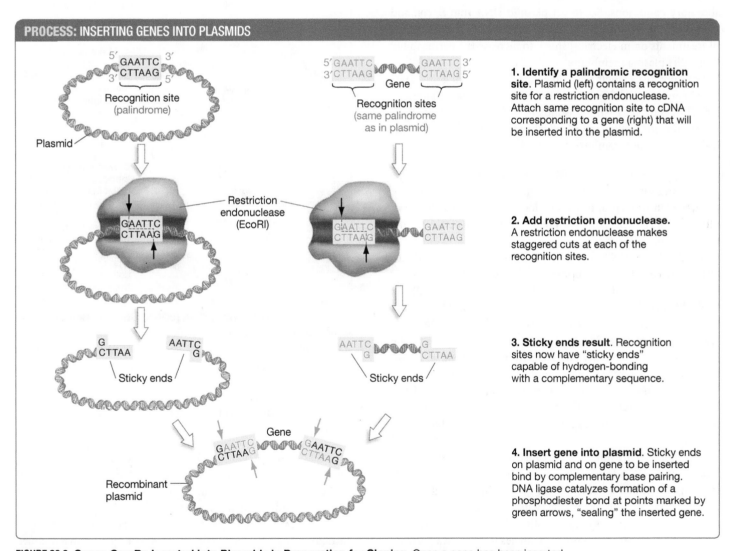

PROCESS: INSERTING GENES INTO PLASMIDS

1. Identify a palindromic recognition site. Plasmid (left) contains a recognition site for a restriction endonuclease. Attach same recognition site to cDNA corresponding to a gene (right) that will be inserted into the plasmid.

2. Add restriction endonuclease. A restriction endonuclease makes staggered cuts at each of the recognition sites.

3. Sticky ends result. Recognition sites now have "sticky ends" capable of hydrogen-bonding with a complementary sequence.

4. Insert gene into plasmid. Sticky ends on plasmid and on gene to be inserted bind by complementary base pairing. DNA ligase catalyzes formation of a phosphodiester bond at points marked by green arrows, "sealing" the inserted gene.

FIGURE 20.3 Genes Can Be Inserted into Plasmids in Preparation for Cloning. Once a gene has been inserted into a plasmid, the recombinant plasmid can be introduced into bacterial cells that grow and divide to produce many identical copies of the gene.

endonuclease, the presence of the same sticky ends in both samples of DNA promotes joining of the resulting fragments. This is the essence of recombinant DNA technology—the ability to create novel combinations of DNA sequences by cutting specific sequences and pasting them into new locations.

After performing this procedure, the researchers who were hunting for the growth hormone gene had a set of recombinant plasmids. Each contained a cDNA made from one of the many human pituitary-gland mRNAs. But the *GH1* gene was still not cloned.

Transformation: Introducing Recombinant Plasmids into Bacterial Cells

If a recombinant plasmid can be inserted into a bacterial or yeast cell, the foreign DNA will be copied and transmitted to new cells as the host cell grows and divides. In short, it can be cloned. In this way, researchers can obtain millions or billions of copies of specific genes. How is the insertion brought about?

Cells that take up DNA from the environment and incorporate it into their genomes are said to undergo **transformation.** Most bacterial cells do not take up DNA on their own under laboratory conditions. So, to get plasmid DNA into *E. coli* and other common laboratory species, researchers use simple chemical treatments or an electrical shock to increase the permeability of the cell's plasma membrane.

Typically, just a single plasmid enters the cell during this treatment. The cells are then spread out on plates under conditions that allow only cells with plasmids to grow into colonies. Each colony contains millions of identical cells, each with many identical copies of the recombinant plasmid.

Producing a cDNA Library

FIGURE 20.4 summarizes the steps covered thus far in the hunt for the growth hormone gene. The result, shown in step 5, is a collection of transformed bacterial cells. Each of the cells contains a plasmid with one cDNA from a pituitary gland mRNA.

A collection of DNA sequences, each of which is inserted into a vector, is called a **DNA library.** If the sequences are cDNAs made from a particular cell type or tissue, the library is called a **cDNA library.** If the sequences are fragments of DNA from the genome of an individual, the library is called a **genomic library.**

DNA libraries are made up of cloned genes. Each gene can be produced in large quantity and isolated in pure form. ✔ If you understand this concept, you should be able to describe how you could make a genomic library starting with DNA from your own cells and using the restriction endonuclease EcoRI to cut the genome into fragments that can be inserted into a plasmid vector.

DNA libraries are important because they provide researchers a way to store DNA fragments from a particular cell type or genome in a form that is accessible for gene cloning. But like a college library, a DNA library isn't very useful unless there is a way to retrieve specific pieces of information. At your school's library, you use call numbers or computer searches to retrieve a particular book or article. How do you go about retrieving a particular gene from a DNA library? For example, how did researchers find

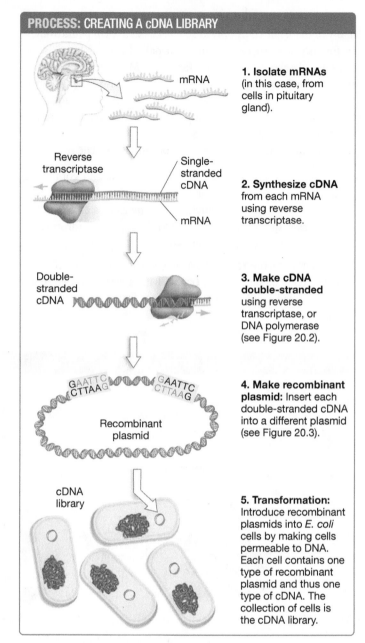

PROCESS: CREATING A cDNA LIBRARY

1. Isolate mRNAs (in this case, from cells in pituitary gland).

Reverse transcriptase
Single-stranded cDNA
mRNA

2. Synthesize cDNA from each mRNA using reverse transcriptase.

Double-stranded cDNA

3. Make cDNA double-stranded using reverse transcriptase, or DNA polymerase (see Figure 20.2).

GAATTC GAATTC
CTTAAG CTTAAG
Recombinant plasmid

4. Make recombinant plasmid: Insert each double-stranded cDNA into a different plasmid (see Figure 20.3).

cDNA library

5. Transformation: Introduce recombinant plasmids into *E. coli* cells by making cells permeable to DNA. Each cell contains one type of recombinant plasmid and thus one type of cDNA. The collection of cells is the cDNA library.

FIGURE 20.4 Complementary DNA (cDNA) Libraries Represent a Collection of the mRNAs in a Cell.

✔**QUESTION** Would each type of cDNA in the library be represented just once? Why or why not?

the growth hormone gene in the cDNA library of the human pituitary gland?

Screening a DNA Library

Molecular biologists are often faced with the task of finding one specific gene in a large collection of DNA fragments. To do this requires a **probe**—a marked molecule that binds to the molecule the biologist is looking for.

A DNA probe is a single-stranded fragment that will bind to a particular single-stranded complementary sequence in a mixture of DNAs. By binding to the target sequence, the probe marks the fragment containing that sequence, distinguishing it from all the other DNA fragments in the sample. As **FIGURE 20.5** shows, a DNA probe must be labeled in some way so that it can be found after it has bound to the complementary sequence in the large sample of fragments.

✔ If you understand the concept of a DNA probe, you should be able to explain why the probe must be single stranded and labeled in order to work, and why it binds to just one specific fragment. You should also be able to indicate where a probe with the sequence AATCG (recall that sequences are always written 5'→3') will bind to a target DNA with the sequence TTTTACCCATTTACGATTGGCCT (again written 5'→3').

To find an appropriate probe for the human growth hormone gene, researchers began by using the genetic code to predict possible DNA sequences of *GH1*. They could do this because they knew the sequence of amino acids in the polypeptide, which they could use to infer the codons that coded for each amino acid. You made similar inferences in some of the exercises in earlier chapters. But recall that there is more than one codon for most amino acids (see Chapter 16). As a result, the researchers could not infer a unique sequence for the growth hormone gene. Instead, they deduced a set of possible sequences that could encode the *GH1* gene.

The next step was to chemically synthesize the set of short, single-stranded DNAs that were complementary to the possible *GH1* sequences. Because one of these sequences would bind to single-stranded fragments from the actual gene by complementary base pairing, it could act as a probe. In this case, the label the researchers attached to the probe was a radioactive atom.

FIGURE 20.6 shows how researchers used this probe to find the plasmid in the cDNA library that contained *GH1*. (For more information on how to use probes, see **BioSkills 9** in Appendix B.) As predicted, the labeled probe bound to its complementary sequence in the cDNA library—identifying the recombinant cell that contained the human growth hormone cDNA.

Mass-Producing Growth Hormone   To accomplish their goal of producing large quantities of the human growth hormone, the investigators used recombinant DNA techniques to transfer the growth hormone cDNA to a new plasmid. The plasmid in question contained a promoter sequence recognized by *E. coli*'s RNA polymerase holoenzyme (see Chapter 17). The recombinant plasmids were then introduced into *E. coli* cells.

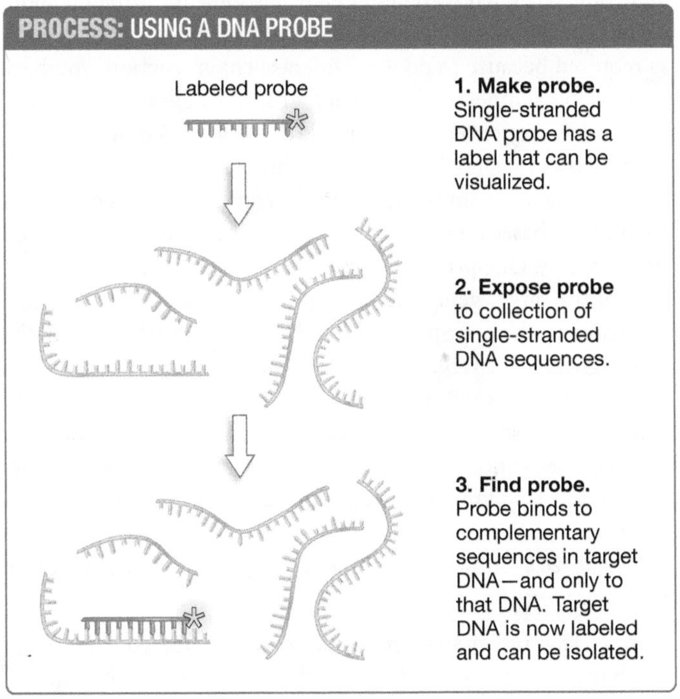

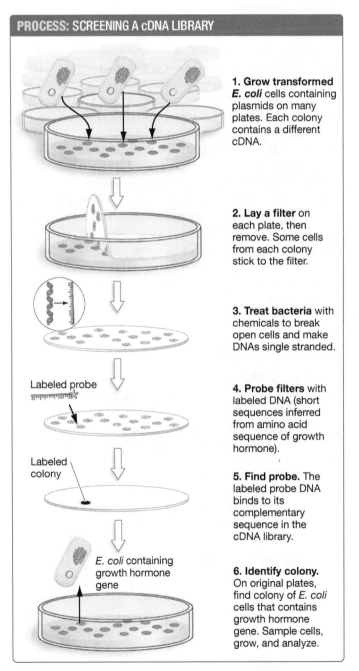

PROCESS: USING A DNA PROBE

Labeled probe

1. Make probe. Single-stranded DNA probe has a label that can be visualized.

2. Expose probe to collection of single-stranded DNA sequences.

3. Find probe. Probe binds to complementary sequences in target DNA—and only to that DNA. Target DNA is now labeled and can be isolated.

FIGURE 20.5 DNA Probes Bind to and Identify Specific Target Sequences.

PROCESS: SCREENING A cDNA LIBRARY

1. Grow transformed *E. coli* cells containing plasmids on many plates. Each colony contains a different cDNA.

2. Lay a filter on each plate, then remove. Some cells from each colony stick to the filter.

3. Treat bacteria with chemicals to break open cells and make DNAs single stranded.

Labeled probe

4. Probe filters with labeled DNA (short sequences inferred from amino acid sequence of growth hormone).

Labeled colony

5. Find probe. The labeled probe DNA binds to its complementary sequence in the cDNA library.

E. coli containing growth hormone gene

6. Identify colony. On original plates, find colony of *E. coli* cells that contains growth hormone gene. Sample cells, grow, and analyze.

FIGURE 20.6 Finding Specific Genes by Probing a cDNA Library.

The resulting transformed *E. coli* cells now contained a gene for human growth hormone attached to a promoter. These cells began to transcribe and translate the human growth hormone gene. Human growth hormone accumulated in the cells and was subsequently isolated and purified.

Today, bacterial cells containing the human growth hormone gene are grown in huge quantities. These cells have proved to be a safe and reliable source of the human growth hormone protein. The effort to cure pituitary dwarfism using recombinant DNA technology was a spectacular success—a triumph of applied biology, or **biotechnology.**

Ethical Concerns over Recombinant Growth Hormone

As supplies of growth hormone increased, physicians used it in treating not only people with pituitary dwarfism but also short children who had no growth hormone deficiency. Even though the treatment requires several injections per week until adult height is reached, growth hormone therapy was popular because it often increased the height of these children by a few centimeters.

In essence, growth hormone was being used as a cosmetic—a way to improve appearance in cultures where height is deemed attractive. But if short people are discriminated against in a culture, is a medical treatment a better solution than education and changes in attitudes? And what if parents wanted a tall child to be even taller, to enhance her potential success as, say, a basketball player?

Currently, the U.S. Food and Drug Administration has approved the use of human growth hormone for only the shortest 1.2 percent of children. These individuals are projected to reach adult heights of less than 160 cm (5′3″) in males and 150 cm (4′11″) in women.

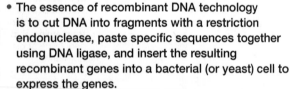

check your understanding

Growth hormone has also become a popular performance-enhancing drug for athletes, because it improves the maintenance of bone density and muscle mass. Part of its popularity stems from the fact that it is difficult to detect in current drug tests.

Should athletes be able to enhance their physical skills by taking hormones or other types of drugs? Is the drug safe at the dosages athletes are using? These questions are being debated by physicians, researchers, agencies that govern sports, and legislative bodies.

In the meantime, it is clear that while solving one important problem, recombinant DNA technology created others. One of this chapter's recurring themes is that genetic engineering has costs that must be carefully weighed against its benefits.

20.2 Case 2–Amplification of Fossil DNA: The Polymerase Chain Reaction

Inserting a gene into a bacterial plasmid is one method for cloning DNA. The polymerase chain reaction is another.

The **polymerase chain reaction (PCR)** is an in vitro DNA synthesis reaction that uses DNA polymerase to replicate a specific section of DNA over and over. It generates many identical copies of a particular region of DNA.

Requirements of PCR

Although PCR is much faster and technologically easier than cloning genes into a DNA library, there is a catch: PCR is possible only when a researcher already has some information about DNA sequences near the gene in question. Sequence information is required because to do a polymerase chain reaction, you have to start by synthesizing short lengths of single-stranded DNA that match sequences on either side of the gene. These short segments act as primers for the DNA synthesis reaction.

As **FIGURE 20.7a** shows, the primer sequences must be complementary to bases on either side of the target gene—the DNA you want to copy. One primer is complementary to a sequence on one side of the target gene; the other primer is complementary to a sequence on the opposite strand of DNA, on the other side of the target gene. If the target DNA molecule is made single stranded, then the primers will bind, or anneal, to their complementary sequences, as shown in **FIGURE 20.7b**. You might recall that DNA polymerase cannot work without a primer. Once the primers are bound, DNA polymerase can extend each new strand of DNA in the 5′→3′ direction.

FIGURE 20.8 shows the sequence of the polymerase chain reaction.

Step 1 The researcher creates a reaction mix containing an abundant supply of the four deoxyribonucleoside triphosphates (dNTPs; see Chapter 15), a DNA sample that includes the gene of interest, many copies of the two primers, and a heat-resistant DNA polymerase called *Taq* polymerase.

(a) PCR primers must bind to sequences on either side of the target sequence, on opposite strands.

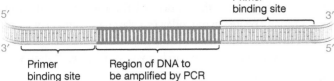

(b) When target DNA is made single stranded, primers bind and allow DNA polymerase to work.

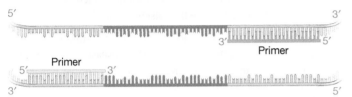

FIGURE 20.7 The Polymerase Chain Reaction Requires Appropriate Primers. (a) To design an appropriate primer, the base sequence at the primer binding sites must be known. **(b)** The primers bind by complementary base pairing to single-stranded target DNA.

✔ **EXERCISE** Indicate where DNA polymerase would begin to work on each strand; add an arrow indicating the direction of DNA synthesis.

Step 2 The reaction mix is heated to 95°C. At this temperature, the double-stranded template DNA denatures. This means that the two DNA strands separate, forming single-stranded templates.

Step 3 The mixture is allowed to cool to 50–60°C. In this temperature range, the primers bind, or anneal, to complementary portions of the single-stranded template DNA. This step is called primer annealing.

Step 4 The reaction mix is heated to 72°C. At this temperature, *Taq* polymerase efficiently synthesizes the complementary DNA strand from the dNTPs, starting at the primer. This step is called *extension*.

Step 5 Repeat steps 2 through 4.

Step 6 Continue repeating steps 2 through 4 until the necessary number of copies is obtained.

The temperature changes required in each step are controlled by automated PCR machines, and there is no need to add more components once the reaction starts.

Taq polymerase is a DNA polymerase found in the thermophilic ("heat-loving") bacterium *Thermus aquaticus*, which was discovered in a hot spring in Yellowstone National Park. Researchers use *Taq* polymerase because the PCR mixture has to be heated, and *Taq* polymerase is heat stable. Enzymes from most organisms are destroyed at high temperature, but *Taq* polymerase functions normally even when heated to 95°C.

The denaturation, primer annealing, and extension steps constitute a single PCR cycle. If one copy of the template sequence existed in the original sample, then two copies are present at the

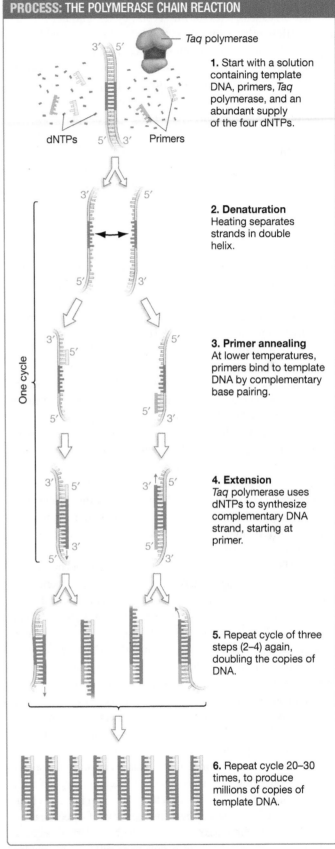

PROCESS: THE POLYMERASE CHAIN REACTION

Taq polymerase

1. Start with a solution containing template DNA, primers, *Taq* polymerase, and an abundant supply of the four dNTPs.

dNTPs   Primers

One cycle

2. Denaturation Heating separates strands in double helix.

3. Primer annealing At lower temperatures, primers bind to template DNA by complementary base pairing.

4. Extension *Taq* polymerase uses dNTPs to synthesize complementary DNA strand, starting at primer.

5. Repeat cycle of three steps (2–4) again, doubling the copies of DNA.

6. Repeat cycle 20–30 times, to produce millions of copies of template DNA.

FIGURE 20.8 The Polymerase Chain Reaction Produces Many Copies of a Specific Sequence. Each PCR cycle (denaturation, primer annealing, and extension) results in a doubling of the number of target sequences.

end of the first cycle (see step 4 in Figure 20.8). These two copies then act as templates for the second cycle—another round of denaturation, primer annealing, and extension—after which four copies of the target gene are present (see step 5).

Each time the cycle repeats, the amount of template sequence in the reaction mixture doubles (step 6). Doubling occurs because each newly synthesized segment of DNA serves as a template in the subsequent cycle, along with the previously synthesized segments. Starting with a single copy, successive cycles result in the production of 2, 4, 8, 16, 32, 64, 128, 256 copies, and so on. A total of n cycles can generate 2^n copies. In just 20 cycles, one sequence can be amplified to over a million copies.

PCR in Action

To understand why PCR is so valuable, consider a study by biologist Svante Pääbo and colleagues, who wanted to analyze DNA recovered from the 30,000-year-old bones of a fossilized human of the species *Homo neanderthalensis*. Their goal was to determine the sequence of bases in the ancient DNA and compare it with DNA from modern humans (*Homo sapiens*).

If modern humans have sequences that are identical or almost identical to the sequences found in Neanderthals, it would suggest that some of us inherited DNA directly from a Neanderthal ancestor. That could happen only if *H. sapiens* and *H. neanderthalensis* interbred while they coexisted in Europe.

The Neanderthal bone was so old, however, that most of the DNA in it had degraded into tiny fragments. The biologists could recover only a minute amount of DNA that was still in even moderate-sized pieces. Fortunately, the Neanderthal DNA sample included a few fragments of the gene region that Pääbo's team wanted to study. The researchers were able to design primers that bracketed this region, based on the sequence of highly conserved sections of the same gene from *H. sapiens*.

Using PCR, the researchers produced millions of copies of the Neanderthal DNA fragment. After analyzing these sequences, the team found that they differ from the same gene segment found in modern humans. Subsequent work with DNA from 14 other Neanderthal fossils, from locations throughout Europe, gave the same result. These data support the hypothesis that Neanderthals never interbred with modern humans—even though the two species lived in the same areas of Europe at the same time.

But a nagging doubt remained—the conclusion was based on the analysis of a small region of the genome, the best that could be done at the time. Would the conclusion hold if more of the genome was analyzed?

To answer this question, Pääbo's team went on to use a form of DNA sequencing that has a DNA amplification step similar to PCR (see Section 20.3). They extracted DNA from fossilized bones and were able to sequence the entire genome of three Neanderthals. The researchers next compared the Neanderthal sequence with the genome sequences of people from different populations living today.

Their conclusion? For African populations there was no evidence of inbreeding with Neanderthals. The story is different,

however, for non-African populations. People from these groups have a small amount of DNA, roughly 1 percent to 4 percent of each person's genome, that is derived from Neanderthal ancestors. So, many people living today can claim just a touch of Neanderthal in their family tree.

PCR has opened new research possibilities in countless areas beyond ancient DNA. For example:

- Forensic scientists, who use biological analyses to help solve crimes, clone DNA from tiny drops of blood or hair. The copied DNA can then be analyzed to identify victims, implicate perpetrators, or exonerate the falsely accused.

- Genetic counselors, who advise couples on how likely their offspring are to suffer from inherited diseases, can use PCR to find out if an embryo conceived by the couple has alleles associated with deadly illness.

Because the complete genomes of a wide array of organisms have now been sequenced, researchers can easily find appropriate primer sequences to use in cloning almost any target gene by PCR. The polymerase chain reaction is now one of the most basic and widely used techniques in biology.

check your understanding

If you understand that . . .

- PCR is a technique for amplifying a specific region of DNA into millions of copies, which can then be sequenced or used for other types of analyses.

✔ **You should be able to . . .**

1. Explain the purpose of the denaturation, annealing, and extension steps in a PCR cycle, and why "chain reaction" is an appropriate part of the term PCR.

2. Write down the sequence of a double-stranded DNA that is 50 base pairs long. Then design 21-base-pair-long primers that would allow you to amplify the segment by PCR.

Answers are available in Appendix A.

20.3 Case 3–Sanger's Breakthrough: Dideoxy DNA Sequencing

Once researchers have cloned a gene from a DNA library or by PCR, determining the gene's base sequence is usually one of the first things they want to do. Learning a gene's sequence is valuable for a variety of reasons. For example:

- Once a gene's sequence is known, the amino acid sequence of its product can be inferred from the genetic code. Knowing a protein's primary structure often provides clues to its function.

- Comparing sequences is fundamental to understanding why alleles vary in function—for example, why one allele causes disease and another doesn't.

- Researchers can infer evolutionary relationships by comparing the sequences of the same gene in different species (see Chapter 1). This information can be used to study an array of questions, ranging from how new traits evolve to where new diseases come from.

How do researchers sequence DNA? In 1977 Frederick Sanger published a technique called dideoxy sequencing that is still in use today.

The Logic of Dideoxy Sequencing

As **FIGURE 20.9** shows, **dideoxy sequencing** is a clever variation on the basic in vitro DNA synthesis reaction. But saying "clever" is an understatement. Sanger had to link three important insights to make his sequencing strategy work.

Dideoxynucleotides Terminate DNA Synthesis   Sanger's first insight was to use monomers for DNA synthesis called dideoxyribonucleoside triphosphates (ddNTPs) along with the normal deoxyribonucleoside triphosphates (dNTPs) (Chapter 15) in the reaction mix. The ddNTPs are identical to dNTPs except that they lack a hydroxyl group at their 3′ carbon. Four types of ddNTPs are used in dideoxy sequencing, each named according to whether it contains adenine (ddATP), thymine (ddTTP), cytosine (ddCTP), or guanine (ddGTP). The use of ddNTPs inspired the name dideoxy sequencing.

Sanger realized that if a ddNTP were added to a growing DNA strand, it would terminate synthesis. Why? After a ddNTP is added, no hydroxyl group is available on a 3′ carbon to link to the 5′ carbon on an incoming dNTP monomer. As a result, DNA polymerization stops once a ddNTP is added.

Fragment Length Correlates with the Location of Each Base
Sanger linked the ability of ddNTPs to stop DNA synthesis to a second fundamental insight: Every time a ddNTP is added to a growing strand, the result is a fragment with a length corresponding to the position in the template of a base complementary to the ddNTP. To produce these fragments, biologists create a reaction mix containing (1) many copies of the template DNA with (2) a primer, (3) DNA polymerase, (4) a large supply of the four dNTPs, and (5) a small amount of the four ddNTPs (Figure 20.9, step 1). Each of the four ddNTPs carries a different fluorescent tag. (In the figure, ddGTP is purple, ddCTP is blue, ddATP is green, and ddTTP is orange.) Fluorescent molecules absorb light at one wavelength and reemit the light at a longer wavelength. As described in **BioSkills 10** (see Appendix B), fluorescent tags provide a very sensitive way of detecting molecules.

Under these conditions, many daughter strands of different lengths are synthesized. All fragments that are the same length end in the same kind of ddNTP.

Step 2 in Figure 20.9 shows why:

- DNA polymerase synthesizes a complementary strand from each template in the reaction mix.

- The synthesis of each one of these complementary strands starts at the same point—the primer.

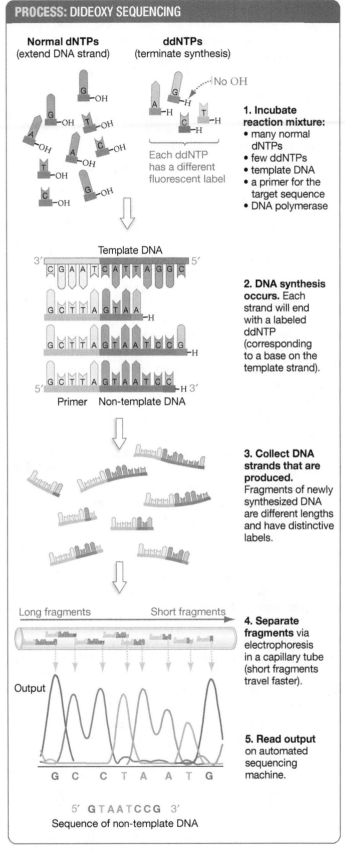

PROCESS: DIDEOXY SEQUENCING

Normal dNTPs (extend DNA strand)

ddNTPs (terminate synthesis)

No OH

Each ddNTP has a different fluorescent label

1. Incubate reaction mixture:
- many normal dNTPs
- few ddNTPs
- template DNA
- a primer for the target sequence
- DNA polymerase

Template DNA

3′ CGAATCATTAGGC 5′

GCTTAGTAA-H

GCTTAGTAATCCG-H

5′ GCTTAGTAATCC-H 3′

Primer   Non-template DNA

2. DNA synthesis occurs. Each strand will end with a labeled ddNTP (corresponding to a base on the template strand).

3. Collect DNA strands that are produced. Fragments of newly synthesized DNA are different lengths and have distinctive labels.

Long fragments   Short fragments

4. Separate fragments via electrophoresis in a capillary tube (short fragments travel faster).

Output

G C   C T A   A T G

5. Read output on automated sequencing machine.

5′ GTAATCCG 3′
Sequence of non-template DNA

FIGURE 20.9 Dideoxy Sequencing Can Determine the Base Sequence of DNA.

- Because there are many dNTPs and relatively few ddNTPs in the reaction mix, dNTPs are usually incorporated opposite each complementary base on the template strand as DNA polymerase works its way along the template strand. Incorporating a dNTP allows DNA synthesis to continue.

- Occasionally, one of the few ddNTPs is incorporated into the growing strand, opposite the corresponding base in the template. The complementary base in the template strand pairs randomly with either a ddNTP or a dNTP.

- The addition of the ddNTP stops further elongation.

- "Stops" of this kind happen for each base in the template strand. As a result, the overall reaction produces a collection of newly synthesized strands (fragments) whose various lengths correspond to the location of each base in the template strand (see step 3 in Figure 20.9). Each fragment will fluoresce in the color of its ddNTP.

DNA Sequence Can Be Read from Fragments Lined Up by Size
Sanger's third insight? When the DNA fragments produced by the synthesis reactions are lined up by size, the dideoxy monomers on the successive fragments reveal the sequence of bases in the template DNA. To line up fragments in order of size, biologists separate them using gel electrophoresis (step 4 in Figure 20.9). As step 5 shows, a machine can read the pattern of fluorescence, indicating the sequence of bases in the newly synthesized strand.

Dideoxy sequencing ranks among the greatest of all technological advances in the history of biological science. Its impact is comparable to the development of light and electron microscopes, microelectrodes for recording membrane potentials, and recombinant gene technology.

"Next Generation" Sequencing

Sequencing technology is advancing at a blindingly fast pace. Dideoxy sequencing is still performed, particularly when relatively long sequences need to be read with great accuracy. But new, "next generation" sequencing approaches now make it possible to sequence much faster and more cheaply.

Most of the newer methods are based on amplification steps related to PCR. These create many copies of each template DNA molecule and allow sequencing of minute quantities of DNA. Even more important, millions of different DNAs can be amplified and sequenced in a single run. Methods that allow simultaneous sequencing or analysis of huge numbers of different molecules are called massively parallel approaches. These sequencing technologies are opening research possibilities that were barely imaginable only a few years ago. Today, instead of sequencing individual genes, researchers often obtain the sequence of entire genomes. A case in point is the sequencing of the Neanderthal genome—this was made possible using a massively parallel approach.

The project to sequence the human genome for the first time took 10 years and cost $3 billion U.S. dollars. Now researchers could sequence your genome in a day for less than $5,000.

If you understand that . . .
- Dideoxy DNA sequencing, which makes use of monomers that stop DNA synthesis in predictable ways, allows researchers to determine the sequence of bases present in a length of DNA.

✓ **You should be able to . . .**
Explain why labeled ddNTPs have to be present in small numbers relative to the number of unlabeled dNTPs.

Answers are available in Appendix A.

20.4 Case 4–The Huntington's Disease Story: Finding Genes by Mapping

Mendel had no idea what a "hereditary determinant" actually was. But now we know. Biology's molecular revolution has allowed researchers to find and characterize individual genes—to explore the connection between genotype and phenotype as explicitly and directly as possible. The question is, How do researchers find the genes associated with certain traits in the first place? How do you find the gene responsible for seed shape in peas, or white eyes in flies, or DNA polymerase III in *E. coli*?

One widely used approach is conceptually simple: You begin with a map of known sites in the genome and then look for an association between one of those known sites and the phenotype you're interested in. The gene that affects the phenotype is probably close to the known site.

In practice, the process is not so simple. As an example of how this type of gene hunt is done, let's consider one of the first successful searches ever conducted for a human gene—the gene associated with Huntington's disease.

How Was the Huntington's Disease Gene Found?

Huntington's disease is a rare but devastating illness. Typically, affected individuals first show symptoms between the ages of 35 and 45. At onset, an individual appears to be clumsier than normal and tends to develop small tics and abnormal movements. As the disease progresses, uncontrollable movements become more pronounced. Eventually the affected individual twists and writhes involuntarily. Personality and intelligence are also compromised—to the extent that the early stage of this disease is sometimes misdiagnosed as the brain disorder schizophrenia. The illness may continue to progress for 10 to 20 years and is eventually fatal.

Because Huntington's disease runs in families, physicians suspected that it was a genetic disease. An analysis of pedigrees from families affected by Huntington's disease suggested that the trait was due to a single, autosomal dominant allele. To understand the molecular basis for the disease, researchers used many of the tools and techniques of genetic engineering that are shown in **TABLES 20.1** and **20.2** (see pages 380–381) as they set out to locate and identify the gene or genes involved. It took over 10 years of intensive effort to reach this goal.

The search for the Huntington's disease gene was led by Nancy Wexler, whose mother had died of the disease. If the trait was indeed due to an autosomal dominant allele, it meant that Wexler had a 50 percent chance of receiving the allele from her mother and would begin to show symptoms when she reached middle age.

Using Genetic Markers

To locate the gene or genes associated with a particular phenotype, such as a disease, researchers traditionally start with a **genetic map,** also known as a **linkage map.** Recall that a genetic map shows the relative positions of genes on the same chromosome, determined by analyzing the frequency of recombination between pairs of genes. Biologists also use **physical maps** of the genome. A physical map shows the absolute position of a gene—in numbers of base pairs—along a chromosome. Genome sequencing (see Chapter 21) has produced physical maps for a wide array of species.

A genetic map is valuable in gene hunts because it contains **genetic markers**—easily identified genes or DNA sequences that have known locations. Each genetic marker provides a landmark—a position along a chromosome that is known relative to other markers. The key is to find where the unknown gene lies relative to the established genetic markers.

To understand how genetic markers can be used, let's use a hypothetical example. Suppose that you knew the position of a hair-color gene in humans relative to other genetic markers. Suppose too that various alleles of this gene contributed to the development of black hair, red hair, blond hair, and brown hair in the group of people you were studying. This variation in phenotype associated with the marker is crucial. To be useful in a gene hunt, a genetic marker has to be **polymorphic,** meaning that the phenotype associated with the marker varies. In our hypothetical example, hair color is a polymorphic genetic marker.

Now suppose that the genetic disease called cystic fibrosis is common among the individuals you were studying and that your goal is to find the gene associated with cystic fibrosis. Further, suppose that people who have cystic fibrosis almost always have black hair—even though they are just as likely as unaffected individuals to have any other inherited trait observed in the study population, such as the presence or absence of a widow's peak or detached earlobes.

If you observe that a certain form of a marker and a certain disease are almost always inherited together, this means that the marker gene and disease gene are physically close to each other on the same chromosome—they are closely linked. If they were not closely linked, then crossing over in between them would be common and they would *not* be inherited together. In this hypothetical study, you could infer that the gene for cystic fibrosis is very close to the hair-color gene. ✔ If you understand this concept, you should be able to explain why it's helpful to hunt for genes using a genetic map with many genetic markers rather than only a few.

Gene hunts in humans boil down to this: Researchers have to find a large number of people who are affected and unaffected. Then they must attempt to locate a genetic marker that almost always occurs in one form in the affected individuals but only rarely in unaffected people. If such a marker is found, the disease gene is almost guaranteed to be nearby.

The types of genetic markers used in gene mapping have changed over time. Today, researchers often have a large catalog of polymorphic genetic markers available, including the particularly abundant markers known as **single nucleotide polymorphisms** (**SNPs,** pronounced *snips*). A SNP is a site in DNA that varies between alleles at a single base pair. Below is an example of a SNP:

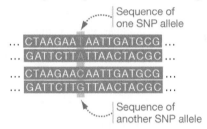

To date, roughly 10 million human SNPs have been identified.

In the late 1970s and early 1980s, when biologists were searching for the Huntington's disease gene, SNPs were unknown. The best genetic markers available were restriction sites—short stretches of DNA where restriction endonucleases cut the double helix. These sequences are also known as restriction endonuclease recognition sites.

The restriction sites that Wexler's team used were polymorphic: Some alleles had a sequence that allowed cuts to occur; but in other alleles, the DNA sequence at the same site varied slightly, and no cuts occurred. Thus, just as an individual might have an A instead of a C at a certain SNP, an individual might have a restriction site allele that allowed cutting or not. Wexler's team was looking for restriction site alleles that were almost always present in diseased individuals but not found any more often than predicted by chance in healthy individuals (**FIGURE 20.10**).

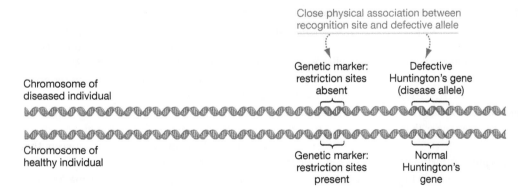

FIGURE 20.10 Genetic Markers Can be Used to Locate Disease Alleles. Because of genetic recombination, genetic markers that are far from the gene of interest are equally likely to be found in both affected and unaffected individuals—there will be no association between particular forms of the marker and either the normal or the disease-causing allele.

Some Common Tools Used in Genetic Engineering

Tool	Description	How Used	Illustration
Reverse transcriptase	Enzyme that catalyzes synthesis of a complementary DNA (cDNA) from an RNA template.	Many applications, including making cDNAs used in constructing a genetic library.	
Restriction endonucleases	Enzymes that cut DNA at a specific sequence—often a palindromic sequence that is six base pairs long.	Allows researchers to cut DNA at specific locations. Cuts in palindromic sites create "sticky ends."	
DNA ligase	An enzyme that catalyzes the formation of a phosphodiester bond between nucleotides on the same DNA strand.	Ligates (joins) sequences that were cut with a restriction endonuclease. Gives researchers the ability to splice fragments of DNA together.	
Plasmids	Small, extrachromosomal circles of DNA found in many bacteria and in some yeast.	After a target gene is inserted into a plasmid, the recombinant plasmid serves as a vector for transferring the gene into a bacterial or yeast cell, so the gene can be cloned.	
Taq polymerase	DNA polymerase from the bacterium *Thermus aquaticus*. Catalyzes synthesis of DNA from a primed DNA template; remains stable at 95°C.	Responsible for the "primer extension" step in the polymerase chain reaction. Heat stability allows enzyme to be active even after the 95°C denaturation step of PCR.	
Single nucleotide polymorphisms (SNPs)	Sites in DNA where the identity of a single base pair varies between alleles.	An important type of polymorphic DNA sequence that is useful in creating the genetic maps required for gene hunts.	

A Linkage Study Once a genetic map containing many genetic markers has been assembled, to find the gene in question, biologists need help from groups of people that include individuals affected by an inherited disease. Recall that the fundamental goal is to find a genetic marker that is almost always inherited along with the disease-causing allele. Biologists call this a linkage study. Gene hunts based on linkage studies are more likely to be successful if large groups are involved. Large sample sizes reduce the possibility that researchers will observe an association between one or more markers and the disease just by chance, rather than because they are closely linked.

Huntington's disease is rare, but Wexler's team was fortunate to find a large, extended family affected with the disease living along the shores of Lake Maracaibo, Venezuela. The researchers followed the inheritance of Huntington's disease and various polymorphic genetic markers within this extended family.

From historical records, the researchers deduced that the Huntington's disease allele was introduced to this family by an English sailor who visited the area in the early 1800s. At the time of the study, over 3000 of his descendants were living in the area. Hundreds of these people had been diagnosed with Huntington's disease. To help in the search for the gene, family members agreed to donate skin or blood samples for DNA analysis.

When Wexler's team looked for associations between the presence or absence of the disease phenotype and genetic markers observed in each family member, they found one marker that

Some Common Techniques Used in Genetic Engineering

Technique	Description	How Used	Illustration
Recombinant DNA technology	Taking a copy of a gene from one individual and placing it in the genome of a different individual (usually of a different species).	Many applications, including DNA cloning, gene therapy (see Section 20.5), and biotechnology (see Sections 20.1 and 20.6).	Inserted gene
DNA libraries	A collection of all DNA sequences present in a particular source. The library consists of individual DNA fragments that are isolated and inserted into a plasmid or other vector, so they can be cloned.	cDNA libraries allow researchers to catalog the genes being expressed in a particular cell type and to work with coding sequences uninterrupted by introns. Genomic libraries allow researchers to archive all the DNA sequences present in a genome. Libraries can be screened to find a particular target gene.	Stored cDNA
Probing/screening a DNA library	Use of a labeled, known DNA fragment to hybridize (by complementary base pairing) with a collection of unlabeled, unknown fragments.	Allows a researcher to find a particular DNA sequence in a large collection of sequences.	Labeled probe
Polymerase chain reaction (PCR)	A DNA synthesis reaction that uses known primer sequences on either side of a target gene. Reaction is based on many cycles of DNA denaturation, primer annealing, and primer extension.	Produces many identical copies of a target sequence. A shortcut method for DNA cloning.	
Dideoxy sequencing	In vitro DNA synthesis reaction that includes dideoxyribo-nucleoside triphosphates (ddNTPs) as monomers.	Determining the base sequence of a gene or other section of DNA.	G C C T A A T G
Genetic mapping	Creation of a map showing the relative positions of genes or specific DNA sequences on chromosomes. Done by analyzing the frequency of recombination between sequences.	Many applications, including use of mapped genetic markers in genetic association studies to find unknown genes associated with diseases or other distinctive phenotypes.	Yellow body / White eyes 1.4 / Ruby eyes 6.1

turned out to be especially important. Four different restriction site alleles (*A, B, C,* and *D*) were present at this location in the genome. The key finding was that the *C* form of the marker was almost always found in diseased individuals. Almost certainly, the English sailor who introduced the Huntington's disease allele had the *C* form of the marker in his DNA. The marker and the Huntington's disease gene are so close together that recombination in between them has been extremely rare. No other genetic marker showed this tight association with Huntington's disease.

From the human genetic map that was available at the time, Wexler's team knew that the marker they had identified was on chromosome 4. Eventually the team succeeded in narrowing down the location of the marker, and thus the Huntington's disease gene, to a region about 500,000 base pairs long. Because the haploid human genome contains over 3 billion base pairs, this was a huge step in focusing the search for the gene.

Pinpointing the Defect Once the general location of the Huntington's disease gene was known, biologists looked in that region for exons that encode an mRNA. Then they used dideoxy sequencing to determine the sequence of exons from diseased and normal individuals, compared the data, and pinpointed specific bases that differed between the two groups.

When this analysis was complete, the research team found that individuals with Huntington's disease have an unusually large number of CAG codons near the 5′ end of one gene. CAG codes for glutamine. Healthy individuals have 11–25 copies of the CAG codon at that location, while affected individuals have 42 or more copies.

When the Huntington's disease research team confirmed that the increased number of CAG codons was always observed in affected individuals, they concluded that the long search for the Huntington's disease gene was over. They named the newly discovered gene *IT15* and its protein product huntingtin. The huntingtin protein is involved in the development of nerve cells. Only later in life do the mutant forms of the protein cause disease.

What Are the Benefits of Finding a Disease Gene?

How have efforts to find disease genes improved human health and welfare? Has the effort to locate the Huntington's disease gene helped researchers and physicians understand and treat the illness? Biomedical researchers point to three major benefits of disease-gene discovery.

Improved Understanding of the Phenotype   Once a disease gene is found and its sequence is known, researchers can usually figure out why its product causes disease. In the case of *IT15*, autopsies of Huntington's patients had shown that their brains decrease in size, and that the brain tissue contains clumps, or aggregates of the protein now called huntingtin.

Huntingtin aggregates are a direct consequence of the increased number of CAG repeats in the *IT15* gene. Long stretches of glutamine are known to promote protein aggregations. The leading hypothesis to explain Huntington's disease proposes that a gradual buildup of huntingtin aggregates triggers neurons to undergo apoptosis, or programmed cell death.

These results explained why Huntington's disease is pleiotropic. Patients suffer from abnormal movements *and* personality changes because neurons throughout the brain are killed. The results also help explain why the disease takes so long to appear, and why it is progressive: The defective huntingtin proteins take time to build up to harmful levels and then continue to increase over time. Finally, understanding the molecular mechanism responsible for the illness explained why the disease allele is dominant. One copy of the defective gene is enough to produce fatal concentrations of huntingtin aggregates.

Therapy   Once *IT15* was found, biologists began a search for new therapies for Huntington's disease by introducing the defective allele into mice, using the types of genetic engineering techniques discussed in Section 20.5. These mice with alleles that have been modified by genetic engineering are called **transgenic** (literally, "across-genes").

Transgenic mice that produce defective versions of the huntingtin protein develop a version of Huntington's disease, exhibiting tremors and abnormal movements, higher-than-normal levels of aggression toward litter and cage mates, and a loss of neurons in the brain. Laboratory animals with disease symptoms that parallel those of a human disease provide an **animal model** of the disease (see **BioSkills 13** in Appendix B).

Animal models are valuable in disease research because they can be used to test potential treatments. For example, research groups are using transgenic mice to test drugs that may prevent or reduce the aggregation of the huntingtin protein.

Genetic Testing   When the Huntington's gene was found and sequenced, biologists used the knowledge to develop a test for the presence of the defective allele. The test consists of obtaining a DNA sample from an individual and using the polymerase chain reaction to amplify the chromosome region that contains the CAG repeats responsible for the disease. If the number of CAG repeats is 35 or less, the individual is not considered at risk. Forty or more repeats results in a positive diagnosis for Huntington's.

Thanks to genetic maps based on SNPs, gene hunts are increasingly successful. Biologists have recently documented alleles associated with a predisposition to developing type I and type II diabetes, breast and ovarian cancer, obesity, coronary heart disease, bipolar disorder, Crohn's disease, and rheumatoid arthritis. Genetic testing for these alleles is now available for both prenatal and adult screens.

Ethical Concerns over Genetic Testing

Knowing the genetic basis of human diseases offers hope, but it also raises difficult ethical issues.

Genetic testing, for example, can create serious moral and legal dilemmas as well as harrowing personal choices. Consider that some people maintain that it is morally wrong to terminate any pregnancy, even if the fetus is certain to be born with a debilitating or fatal genetic disease. Think too about Nancy Wexler's position soon after the discovery of *IT15*: Would you choose to be tested for the defective allele and risk finding out that you were almost certain to develop an incurable disease such as Huntington's?

There are other, equally serious, questions. Should people be tested for any disease that has no cure? Should it be legal for insurance companies to test clients? If so, can companies refuse to insure people at risk for diseases that require expensive treatments? What about employers?

These questions are being debated by political and religious leaders, health-care workers, philosophers, and the public at large. In many cases, we've yet to find answers.

check your understanding

If you understand that . . .

- Genes for particular traits can be located if they are inherited together with a known genetic marker.

✔ You should be able to . . .

Describe how you would design a study aimed at identifying alleles associated with alcoholism.

Answers are available in Appendix A.

Case 5–Severe Immune Disorders: The Potential of Gene Therapy

For physicians who treat inherited disorders such as Huntington's disease, sickle-cell anemia, and cystic fibrosis, the ultimate goal is to cure the disease. This may be done by replacing or augmenting defective copies of the gene with normal alleles. This approach to treatment is called **gene therapy.**

For gene therapy to succeed, two crucial requirements must be met. First, the sequence of the allele associated with the healthy phenotype must be known. Second, a method must be available for introducing this allele into affected individuals and having it be expressed in the correct tissues, in the correct amount, and at the correct time. If the defective allele is dominant, then the introduction step may be even more complicated: In at least some cases, the introduced allele must physically replace or block the expression of the undesirable dominant allele.

How Can Genes Be Introduced into Human Cells?

Section 20.1 reviewed how recombinant DNA sequences are packaged into plasmids and taken up by *E. coli* cells. However, humans and other mammals lack plasmids. How can foreign genes be introduced into human cells?

Researchers have focused on packaging foreign genes into viruses for transport into human cells. These viruses have been engineered so they can deliver genes to cells but cannot replicate to produce new viruses. Viral infection begins when a virus particle attaches to a cell and delivers its genome into the cell (Chapter 36). For some viruses, the viral DNA becomes integrated into a host-cell chromosome. This trait makes it possible to use these viruses as vectors to carry engineered genes into the chromosomes of target cells. Potentially, the genes delivered by the virus could be expressed and produce a product capable of curing a genetic disease.

Vectors used today in gene therapy are often modified retroviruses. Retroviruses have genomes made of single-stranded RNA. When a **retrovirus** infects a human cell, a reverse transcriptase encoded by the virus catalyzes the production of a DNA copy of the virus's RNA genome. Other viral enzymes catalyze the insertion of the viral DNA into a host-cell chromosome. If an RNA version of a human gene can be packaged into a recombinant retrovirus, then the virus will insert a DNA copy of the human gene into a chromosome in a target cell (**FIGURE 20.11**).

Unfortunately, there are problems associated with using retroviruses as agents in gene therapy. For example, if the virus happens to insert the recombinant human gene in a position that disrupts the function of an important gene in the target cell, the consequences may be serious. Despite these risks, modified retroviruses are still among the best vectors currently available for human gene therapy.

Using Gene Therapy to Treat X-Linked Immune Deficiency

In 2000, a research team reported the successful use of gene therapy to treat an illness called severe combined immunodeficiency (SCID). Children who are born with SCID lack a normal immune system and are unable to fight off infections.

The type of SCID the team treated is designated SCID-X1, because it is caused by mutations in a gene on the X chromosome.

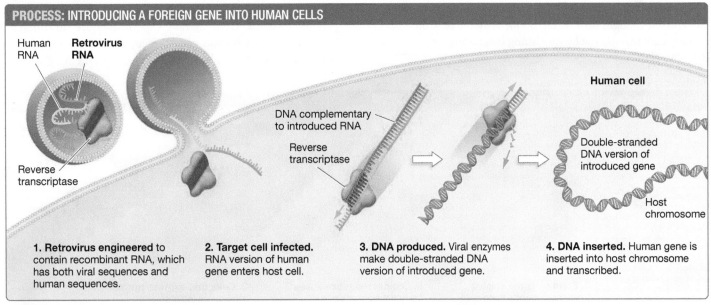

PROCESS: INTRODUCING A FOREIGN GENE INTO HUMAN CELLS

Human RNA

Retrovirus RNA

Reverse transcriptase

DNA complementary to introduced RNA

Reverse transcriptase

Human cell

Double-stranded DNA version of introduced gene

Host chromosome

1. Retrovirus engineered to contain recombinant RNA, which has both viral sequences and human sequences.

2. Target cell infected. RNA version of human gene enters host cell.

3. DNA produced. Viral enzymes make double-stranded DNA version of introduced gene.

4. DNA inserted. Human gene is inserted into host chromosome and transcribed.

FIGURE 20.11 Modified Retroviruses Can Insert a Foreign Gene into a Host-Cell Chromosome. (Many details have been omitted for conceptual clarity.)

✔**QUESTION** What happens if the recombinant DNA is inserted in the middle of a gene that is critical to normal cell function?

FIGURE 20.12 A "Bubble Child." Children with SCID cannot fight off bacterial or viral infections. As a result, such children must live in a sterile environment.

The gene codes for a receptor protein necessary for the development of immune system cells, called T cells, that develop in bone marrow.

Traditionally, physicians have treated SCID-X1 by keeping the patient in a sterile environment, isolated from any direct human contact, until the person could receive a transplant of bone-marrow tissue from a close relative (**FIGURE 20.12**). In most cases, the T cells that the patient needs are produced by the transplanted bone-marrow cells and allow the individual to live normally. In some cases, though, no suitable donor is available. Could gene therapy cure this disease by furnishing functioning copies of the defective gene?

After extensive testing suggested that their treatment plan was safe and effective, the research team gained approval to treat 10 boys, each less than 1 year old, who had SCID-X1 but no suitable bone-marrow donor. The researchers removed bone marrow from each child, collected the stem cells that produce mature T cells, and infected those cells with an engineered retrovirus that delivered the normal receptor gene. Cells that began to produce normal receptor protein were then isolated and transferred back into the patients (**FIGURE 20.13**).

Within four months after reinsertion of the transformed marrow cells, nine of the boys had normal levels of functioning T cells. These patients were removed from germ-free isolation rooms and began residing at home, where they grew and developed normally.

Subsequently, however, four of the boys developed a cancer characterized by unchecked growth of T cells. Follow-up analyses of their bone-marrow cells showed that the normal receptor gene had been inserted either near a gene for a transcription factor that triggers T-cell growth, or near a gene for a cyclin that drives the cell cycle (see Chapter 12). The inserted receptor gene provided an enhancer that led to constitutive (constant) expression of the transcription factor or cyclin.

Three of the four boys responded to cancer chemotherapy and are healthy. The fourth did not respond to treatment and died of cancer.

The tenth boy to receive gene therapy never produced T cells. For unknown reasons, his recombinant stem cells failed to function normally when they were transplanted back into his bone marrow. Fortunately, physicians were later able to find a bone-marrow donor whose cells matched the boy's closely enough to make a successful transplant possible.

Ethical Concerns over Gene Therapy

Throughout the history of medicine, efforts to test new drugs, vaccines, and surgical protocols have always carried a risk for the patients involved. Gene therapy experiments are no different. The researchers who run gene therapy trials must explain the risks clearly and make every effort to minimize them.

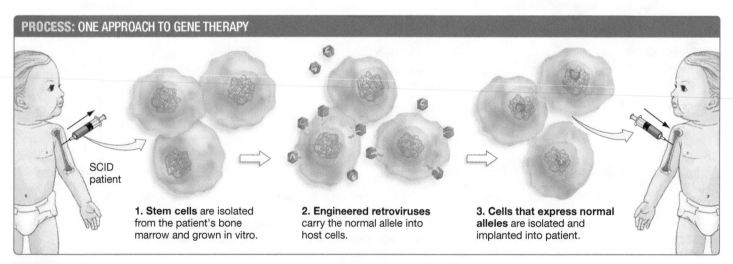

PROCESS: ONE APPROACH TO GENE THERAPY

SCID patient

1. Stem cells are isolated from the patient's bone marrow and grown in vitro.

2. Engineered retroviruses carry the normal allele into host cells.

3. Cells that express normal alleles are isolated and implanted into patient.

FIGURE 20.13 Gene Therapy Can Cure a Genetic Disorder. For gene therapy to work in the case of a loss-of-function allele, copies of a normal allele have to be introduced into a patient's cells and be expressed.

The initial report on the development of cancer in the boys who received gene therapy for SCID-X1 concluded with the following statement: "We have proposed . . . a halt to our trial until further evaluation of the causes of this adverse event and a careful reassessment of the risks and benefits of continuing our study of gene therapy."

When recombinant DNA technology first became possible, many researchers thought they would live to see most or all of the serious inherited diseases caused by single-gene mutations cured by gene therapy. After several decades of rare successes punctuated by tragic failures, that optimism was tempered. In the past few years, however, renewed hope has emerged for gene therapy. Improved vectors have been used successfully to treat two different forms of blindness, a brain disorder, and another type of SCID. Perhaps gene therapy is finally poised to deliver on some of its promises.

20.6 Case 6—The Development of Golden Rice: Biotechnology in Agriculture

Progress in transforming crop plants with recombinant genes has been breathtaking. In 2010, a total 10 percent of all farmland worldwide was planted with transgenic crops—and this number is predicted to show double-digit growth over the foreseeable future. In the same year, roughly 90 percent of soybeans, cotton, and corn grown in the United States were genetically engineered. You almost certainly have eaten food from a genetically modified plant sometime, if not today.

Transgenic crops have been engineered largely to meet three objectives:

1. *Reducing losses from herbivore damage* For instance, researchers have transferred a gene from the bacterium *Bacillus thuringiensis* into corn; the presence of the "Bt toxin" encoded by this gene protects the plant from corn borers and other caterpillar pests.

2. *Reducing competition with weeds* An example is the genetic engineering of soybeans for resistance to an herbicide—a molecule that kills plants—called glyphosate. Soybean fields with the engineered strain can be sprayed with glyphosate to kill weeds without harming the soybeans.

3. *Improving food quality* An important example is engineering soybeans and canola to produce a higher percentage of unsaturated fatty acids relative to saturated fatty acids (Chapter 6). Reducing the amounts of saturated fatty acids helps prevent heart disease, so these crops produce healthier vegetable oils.

How is this work done?

Rice as a Target Crop

Almost half the world's population depends on rice as its staple food. Unfortunately, rice is a poor source of some vitamins and essential nutrients—including vitamin A. Vitamin A deficiency causes blindness in 250,000 Southeast Asian children each year. It also increases susceptibility to diarrhea, respiratory infections, and childhood diseases such as measles.

Humans and other mammals synthesize vitamin A from a precursor molecule known as β-carotene (beta-carotene). β-carotene belongs to a family of orange, yellow, and red plant pigments called the carotenoids.

Rice plants synthesize β-carotene in their chloroplasts but not in the carbohydrate-rich seed tissue called endosperm—the part of the rice seed that you eat. Could genetic engineering produce a strain of rice plants that synthesizes β-carotene in the endosperm?

Synthesizing β-Carotene in Rice

To explore the possibility of genetically engineering rice, a research team searched for compounds in rice endosperm that could serve as precursors for the synthesis of β-carotene. They found that maturing rice endosperm contains a molecule that could be converted to β-carotene in three enzyme-catalyzed reactions. The researchers reasoned that if genes that encode these enzymes could be introduced into rice plants along with regulatory sequences that would trigger their synthesis in endosperm, it should be possible to create a transgenic strain of rice that would contain β-carotene.

Fortunately, genes that encode two of the required enzymes had already been isolated from daffodils, and the gene for the third enzyme had been purified from a bacterium. These genes had been cloned in bacteria. To each of the coding sequences, biologists added regulatory sequences from an endosperm-specific protein. This segment would promote transcription of the recombinant sequences in endosperm cells.

Next, the three sets of sequences had to be inserted into rice plants. How are foreign genes introduced into plants?

The *Agrobacterium* Transformation System

Agrobacterium tumefaciens is a bacterium that infects plant tissues and triggers formation of tumorlike growths called galls. When researchers looked into how these infections occur, they found that a plasmid carried by the *Agrobacterium* cells, called a **Ti (tumor-inducing) plasmid**, plays a key role (**FIGURE 20.14**, see page 386).

Ti plasmids contain several sets of genes. One set encodes products that allow the bacterium to bind to the cell walls of a host. Another set, referred to as the virulence genes, encodes the proteins required to transfer part of the Ti DNA, called T-DNA (transferred DNA), into the plant cell. The T-DNA then travels to the nucleus and integrates into host-cell chromosomes (Figure 20.14, step 1). T-DNA genes are expressed and their products induce the infected cell to grow and divide. This results in the formation of a gall that houses a growing population of *Agrobacterium* cells (Figure 20.14, step 2).

Researchers soon realized that the Ti plasmid offers an efficient way to introduce recombinant genes into plant cells. Follow-up experiments confirmed that recombinant genes could be

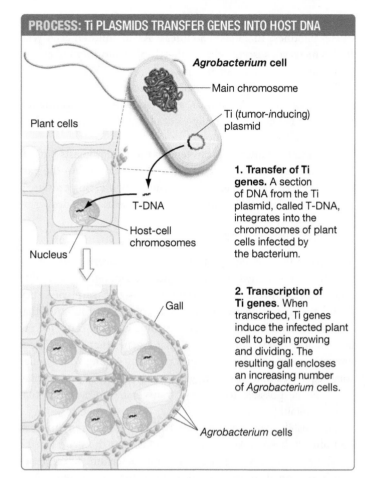

1. Transfer of Ti genes. A section of DNA from the Ti plasmid, called T-DNA, integrates into the chromosomes of plant cells infected by the bacterium.

2. Transcription of Ti genes. When transcribed, Ti genes induce the infected plant cell to begin growing and dividing. The resulting gall encloses an increasing number of *Agrobacterium* cells.

FIGURE 20.14 *Agrobacterium* **Infections Introduce Genes into a Plant Host-Cell Chromosome.** Ti plasmids of *Agrobacterium* cells induce gall formation—a tumorlike growth.

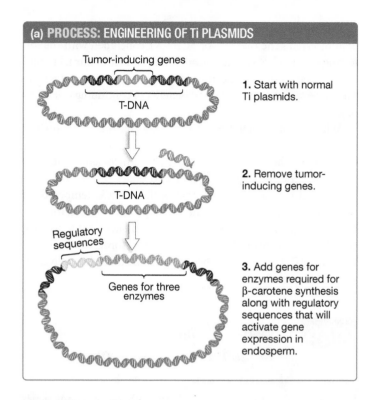

1. Start with normal Ti plasmids.

2. Remove tumor-inducing genes.

3. Add genes for enzymes required for β-carotene synthesis along with regulatory sequences that will activate gene expression in endosperm.

(b) Golden rice (right) is engineered to synthesize β-carotene.

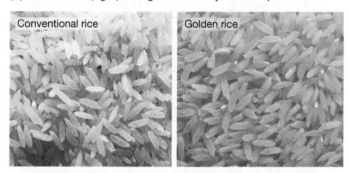

FIGURE 20.15 Constructing a Ti Plasmid to Produce "Golden Rice." Golden rice is a transgenic strain capable of synthesizing β-carotene in the endosperm of its seeds.

added to the T-DNA that integrates into the host chromosome, that the gall-inducing genes could be removed from the T-DNA, and that the resulting sequence is efficiently transferred and expressed in its new host plant.

Using the Ti Plasmid to Produce Golden Rice

To generate a strain of rice that produces all three enzymes needed to synthesize β-carotene in endosperm, the researchers exposed embryos to *Agrobacterium* cells containing genetically modified Ti plasmids (**FIGURE 20.15**). When the transgenic rice plants grew and produced seeds, the researchers found that some rice grains contained so much β-carotene that they were yellow. The biologists called the engineered plants "golden rice."

Follow-up experiments used gene sequences from corn, rather than daffodil, to produce 23 times more β-carotene in rice than the original transformants contained.

Will golden rice help solve a serious public health problem? The answer is not clear. Many environmental groups are strongly opposed to golden rice and any other engineered crops. Regulatory agencies in an array of countries would need to approve the use of golden rice—but there is strong resistance in some nations—and seed would have to be made available to farmers at an affordable price. The barriers to answering the question of whether golden rice can solve health problems are more societal than scientific.

It's important to recognize that each solution offered by genetic engineering introduces new issues to resolve. Biology students and others who are well informed about the techniques and issues involved will be important participants in this debate.

If you understand . . .

20.1   Basic Recombinant DNA Technologies

- In genetic engineering, DNA is added to a cell either to modify the cell's properties or to clone (obtain many identical copies of) the DNA.

- Restriction endonucleases cut DNA at specific locations. The resulting DNA fragments can be inserted into plasmids or other vectors with the help of DNA ligase.

- In many cases, the DNA fragments are inserted into vectors containing regulatory sequences that control expression of inserted genes.

✓ You should be able to explain why a plasmid is needed for gene cloning.

20.2   The Polymerase Chain Reaction

- The polymerase chain reaction (PCR) produces many identical copies of a gene without using cells for cloning.

- PCR depends on having primers that bracket a target stretch of DNA. These allow *Taq* polymerase, a heat-stable DNA polymerase, to amplify a single target DNA sequence to millions of identical copies.

✓ You should be able to list the advantages and disadvantages of cloning in cells versus using PCR to obtain many copies of genes.

20.3   Dideoxy DNA Sequencing

- Dideoxy sequencing determines the sequence of bases in DNA.

- Dideoxy sequencing is based on an in vitro DNA synthesis reaction in which dideoxyribonucleotides stop different DNA replication reactions at different bases in the sequence.

- The DNA fragments of different lengths that are generated by a dideoxy sequencing reaction are separated via gel electrophoresis to determine the sequence of bases.

✓ You should be able to explain how the newly synthesized DNA fragments—when they are lined up by size—can be used to determine the sequence of bases in the template DNA.

20.4   Finding Genes by Mapping

- Genetic maps are often used to find genes associated with phenotypes such as diseases.

- If individuals with a certain phenotype share a particular form of a polymorphic genetic marker (a mapped site with two or more forms in DNA that is unrelated to the phenotype), the gene responsible for the phenotype is likely to be near that marker.

- Once the general area of a gene is known, DNA in the region can be sequenced to determine exactly where the gene is located.

✓ You should be able to explain why genetic markers that are not polymorphic (come in only one form) are not useful in gene hunts.

20.5   The Potential of Gene Therapy

- Researchers are working to cure genetic diseases by gene therapy. This involves inserting normal copies of the defective gene into patients.

- In humans, genes used for gene therapy are often introduced using modified viruses.

- Gene therapy has faced many difficulties but recently has met with some notable successes.

✓ You should be able to describe what makes retroviruses well suited for gene therapy and what the concerns are about their use.

20.6   Biotechnology in Agriculture

- Many important crop plants are genetically engineered for traits that include pest and herbicide resistance, and improved food quality.

- Genes are often introduced into crops by infecting plant cells with bacteria that integrate their plasmid genes into the host-plant genome. By adding recombinant genes to these plasmids, researchers have been able to introduce genes that improve crops.

✓ You should be able to explain how genes are inserted into plants.

(MB) **MasteringBiology**

1. MasteringBiology Assignments

Tutorials and Activities Analyzing DNA Fragments Using Gel Electrophoresis; Cloning a Gene in Bacteria; Gel Electrophoresis of DNA; Making Decisions about DNA Technology: Golden Rice; Producing Human Growth Hormone; Restriction Enzymes; Restriction Enzymes, Recombinant DNA, and Gene Cloning; The Polymerase Chain Reaction

Questions Reading Quizzes, Blue-Thread Questions, Test Bank

2. eText Read your book online, search, take notes, highlight text, and more.

3. The Study Area Practice Test, Cumulative Test, BioFlix® 3-D Animations, Videos, Activities, Audio Glossary, Word Study Tools, Art

You should be able to . . .

1. What do restriction endonucleases do?

2. What is a plasmid?
   a. an organelle found in many bacteria and certain eukaryotes
   b. a circular DNA molecule that often replicates independently of the main chromosome(s)
   c. a type of virus that has a DNA genome and that infects certain types of human cells, including lung and respiratory tract tissue
   d. a type of virus that has an RNA genome, codes for reverse transcriptase, and inserts a cDNA copy of its genome into host cells

3. When present in a DNA synthesis reaction mixture, a ddNTP molecule is added to the growing chain of DNA. No further nucleotides can be added afterward. Why?

4. Once the gene that causes Huntington's disease was found, researchers introduced the defective allele into mice to create an animal model of the disease. Why was this model valuable?
   a. It allowed the testing of potential drug therapies without endangering human patients.
   b. It allowed the study of how the gene is regulated.
   c. It allowed the production of large quantities of the huntingtin protein.
   d. It allowed the study of how the gene was transmitted from parents to offspring.

5. To begin the hunt for the human growth hormone gene, researchers created a cDNA library from cells in the pituitary gland. What did this library contain?
   a. only the sequence encoding growth hormone
   b. DNA versions of all the mRNAs in the pituitary-gland cells
   c. all the coding sequences in the human genome, but no introns
   d. all the coding sequences in the human genome, including introns

6. What does it mean to say that a genetic marker and a disease gene are closely linked?
   a. The marker lies within the coding region for the disease gene.
   b. The sequence of the marker and the sequence of the disease gene are extremely similar.
   c. The marker and the disease gene are on different chromosomes.
   d. The marker and the disease gene are in close physical proximity and tend to be inherited together.

7. Explain how restriction endonucleases and DNA ligase are used to insert foreign genes into plasmids and create recombinant DNA. Make a drawing that shows why sticky ends are sticky and that identifies the location where DNA ligase catalyzes a key reaction.

8. **QUANTITATIVE** If a particular sequence of DNA were amplified using 25 PCR cycles, then the amount of this DNA would be predicted to increase by _____ -fold.

9. What is a cDNA library? Would you expect the cDNA library from a human muscle cell to be different from the cDNA library from a human nerve cell in the same individual? Explain why or why not.

10. What are genetic markers, and how are they used to create a genetic map?

11. Researchers added regulatory sequences from an endosperm-specific gene to the Ti plasmids used in creating golden rice. This was important to
    a. allow inserted genes to integrate into the plant genome.
    b. increase the endosperm growth rate.
    c. prevent the introduced plasmid from harming the endosperm.
    d. promote expression of introduced genes in the rice grain.

12. Compare and contrast PCR with the DNA synthesis that occurs in cells (see Chapter 15).

13. Suppose you had a large amount of sequence data, similar to the data that Nancy Wexler's team had in the region of the Huntington's disease gene, and that you knew that mRNAs of the species being studied typically contain protein-coding regions about 1500 bases long. How would you use the genetic code (see Chapter 16) and information on the structure of promoters (see Chapters 17 and 18) to find the precise location of one or more genes in your sequence?

14. Modifying germ-line or somatic cells for gene therapy involves the same ethical concerns. True or false?

15. Describe similarities between how researchers screen a DNA library and how they perform a genetic screen—for example, for mutant *E. coli* cells that cannot metabolize lactose (see Chapter 18).

16. A friend of yours is doing a series of PCRs and comes to you for advice. She purchased two sets of primers, hoping that one set would amplify the template sequence shown here. (The dashed lines in the template sequence stand for a long sequence of unspecified bases.) Neither of the primer pairs produced any product DNA, however.

	Primer a		Primer b
Primer Pair 1:	5' CAAGTCC 3'	&	5' GCTGGAC 3'
Primer Pair 2:	5' GGACTTG 3'	&	5' GTCCAGC 3'
Template:	5' ATTCGGACTTG---GTCCAGCTAGAGG 3'		
	3' TAAGCCTGAAC---CAGGTCGATCTCC 5'		

a. Explain why each primer pair didn't work. Indicate whether both primers are at fault, or just one of them.
b. Your friend doesn't want to buy new primers. She asks you whether she can salvage this experiment. What do you tell your friend to do?

21 Genomics and Beyond

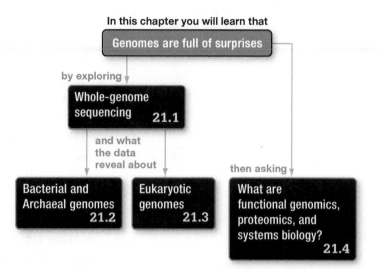

In this chapter you will learn that

Genomes are full of surprises

by exploring

Whole-genome sequencing 21.1

and what the data reveal about

then asking

Bacterial and Archaeal genomes 21.2

Eukaryotic genomes 21.3

What are functional genomics, proteomics, and systems biology? 21.4

A high-throughput robotic genome sequencer. Advances in DNA sequencing technologies are opening new questions to biologists and deepening the understanding of life and its evolution.

The first data sets describing the complete DNA sequence, or **genome,** of humans were published in February 2001. These papers were immediately hailed as a landmark in the history of science. In just 50 years, biologists had gone from not understanding the molecular nature of the gene to knowing the molecular makeup of every gene present in our species.

Years later, knowledge continues to stream from the multinational effort called the **Human Genome Project** and its many spinoffs. It's important to recognize, though, that research on *Homo sapiens* is part of a much larger, ongoing effort to gain insights from the genome sequences of an array of other eukaryotes, bacteria, and archaea. The pace of progress in this field is nothing short of explosive.

The effort to sequence, interpret, and compare whole genomes is **genomics.** While whole-genome sequencing supplies a list of the genes present in an organism, **functional genomics**

✔ When you see this checkmark, stop and test yourself. Answers are available in Appendix A.

answers questions about the functioning of that genome, such as what particular genes do and how they're expressed.

Genomics has spawned a host of related fields. These are often referred to as the –omics—proteomics, metabolomics, and transcriptomics—but also include emerging areas like systems biology. Like genomics, these fields take a holistic approach to learning about the entire set of proteins, metabolites, or RNA transcripts present in a given cell or tissue type at a given time.

As an introductory biology student, you are part of the first generation trained in the genome era. Genomics and the related fields it has generated are revolutionizing biological science. They will almost certainly be an important part of your personal and professional life. Let's delve in.

21.1 Whole-Genome Sequencing

Genomics has moved to the cutting edge of research in biology, largely because of technological advances. These began with the development of dideoxy sequencing and progressed to next-generation sequencing techniques (introduced in Chapter 20). These technical breakthroughs have enabled obtaining immense quantities of high-quality sequence data rapidly and at low cost.

As technology continues to become faster and less expensive, the pace of genome sequencing accelerates. The result is that an almost mind-boggling number of sequences of genes and whole genomes are now being generated. As this book goes to press, the primary international repository for DNA sequence data contained over 425 *billion* nucleotides. By way of comparison, a haploid human genome contains about 3 billion nucleotides on each strand of the DNA double helix.

FIGURE 21.1 gives a visual sense of the growth in sequence data by plotting the number of nucleotides, in billions, versus time. There are three large international online repositories for

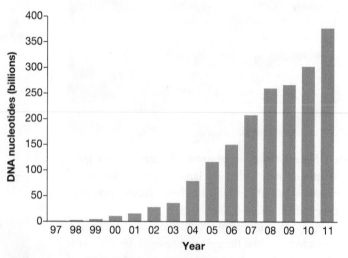

FIGURE 21.1 The Total Number of Bases Sequenced Is Growing Rapidly. Data from the EMBL Nucleotide Sequence Database (also known as EMBL-Bank).

DATA: European Nucleotide Archive/EMBL-Bank Release Notes. Release 110, December 2011. www.ebi.ac.uk/embl/.

sequence data; the numbers plotted here were compiled from one of them. Over 15 years, this database has grown at a staggering average rate of about 46 percent per year.

How Are Complete Genomes Sequenced?

Genomes range in size from about a half million base pairs to several billion. But even under the best conditions, a single dideoxy sequencing reaction can analyze only about 1000 nucleotides. Reads from next-generation sequencing are even shorter. How do investigators break a genome into sequencing-sized pieces and then figure out how the thousands or millions of pieces go back together?

Shotgun Sequencing When researchers first set out to sequence the genome of a species, they usually rely on an approach known as **shotgun sequencing.** In shotgun sequencing, a genome is broken up into a set of overlapping fragments that are small enough to be sequenced completely. The regions of overlap are then used as guides for putting the sequenced fragments back into the correct order (**FIGURE 21.2**).

Step 1 Application of high-frequency sound waves, or sonication, is used to break a genome randomly into pieces about 160 kilobases (kb) long (1 kb = 1000 bases).

Step 2 Each 160-kb piece is inserted into a type of cloning vector called a **bacterial artificial chromosome (BAC).** BACs are able to replicate large segments of DNA. Each BAC is then inserted into a different *Escherichia coli* cell (using techniques introduced in Chapter 20), creating a **BAC library.** A BAC library is a genomic library: a set of all the DNA sequences in a particular genome, split into small segments and inserted into cloning vectors. By allowing each cell to grow into a colony, researchers can isolate large numbers of each 160-kb fragment.

Step 3 After many copies of each 160-kb fragment have been produced, each cloned DNA is again broken into fragments—but this time, into segments about 1 kb long.

Step 4 These small fragments are then inserted into plasmids and placed inside bacterial cells. (Note that by this point the genome has been broken down twice, into increasingly manageable pieces: 160-kb fragments in BACs and 1-kb segments in plasmids.) The plasmids are copied many times as each bacterial cell grows into a large population. Cloned 1-kb fragments are then available for sequencing reactions.

Step 5 Next, the cloned 1-kb fragments from each 160-kb BAC clone are sequenced, and computer programs analyze regions where the ends of different 1-kb segments overlap. Overlaps occur because many copies were made of each 160-kb segment, and these copies were fragmented randomly by sonication.

Step 6 A computer program searches for overlaps between 1-kb fragments from a single BAC clone and stitches the sequences together until a continuous sequence across the BAC has been reconstructed.

Step 7 The ends of the reconstructed BACs are analyzed in a similar way. The goal is to link sequences from each 160-kb

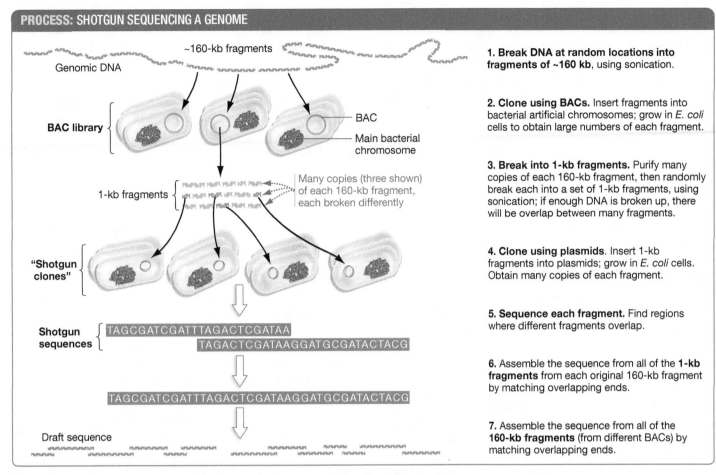

1. Break DNA at random locations into fragments of ~160 kb, using sonication.

2. Clone using BACs. Insert fragments into bacterial artificial chromosomes; grow in *E. coli* cells to obtain large numbers of each fragment.

3. Break into 1-kb fragments. Purify many copies of each 160-kb fragment, then randomly break each into a set of 1-kb fragments, using sonication; if enough DNA is broken up, there will be overlap between many fragments.

4. Clone using plasmids. Insert 1-kb fragments into plasmids; grow in *E. coli* cells. Obtain many copies of each fragment.

5. Sequence each fragment. Find regions where different fragments overlap.

6. Assemble the sequence from all of the 1-kb fragments from each original 160-kb fragment by matching overlapping ends.

7. Assemble the sequence from all of the 160-kb fragments (from different BACs) by matching overlapping ends.

FIGURE 21.2 Shotgun Sequencing Breaks Large Genomes into Many Short Segments.

✓**QUESTION** A shotgun blast produces many small, scattered pieces of shot. Why is "shotgun" an appropriate way to describe this sequencing strategy?

segment based on regions of overlap until the sequence of an entire chromosome is assembled.

In essence, the shotgun strategy consists of breaking a genome into many small fragments, sequencing each fragment, and then putting the sequence data back in the correct order.

✓ If you understand shotgun sequencing, you should be able to explain why it is essential for fragments to have regions of overlap.

The Impact of Next-Generation Sequencing Today, there are approaches that are much faster and cheaper than dideoxy sequencing (see Chapter 20). These next-generation methods are massively parallel, meaning that millions of DNA fragments can be sequenced simultaneously in one run of a sequencing machine. The downside of these methods is that they produce sequence reads of only about 50–200 nucleotides, depending on the particular technology. This is in contrast to the roughly 1000 nucleotides obtained by dideoxy sequencing. For piecing together a whole genome, especially one with many repetitive sequences such as those present in most eukaryotes, these read lengths are too short.

But if a complete genome is already available for the organism, next-generation sequencing offers a remarkably quick and inexpensive way to sequence the entire genome from a particular individual—with all the tiny fragments arranged in the correct order by being compared with the "master genome." This sequencing power has opened up possibilities that were unimaginable even a few years ago.

Consider what was involved in sequencing the human genome. The Human Genome Project required more than 15 years and about $3 billion to assemble the first human genome sequence. In 2011, ten years after the first human genome sequence was available, more than 2700 individual human genomes had been sequenced at a cost as low as $5000 per genome. This is a 2700-fold increase in output and a 600,000-fold drop in price.

What's important is not only the numbers, but what can be done with the information. One illustration is an offshoot of the Human Genome Project, the 1000 Genomes Project. This effort has already sequenced the genomes of over 1000 people selected from diverse populations spread across the planet. An important goal is to assess the genetic similarities and differences among people in order to understand our own evolution. Many similarly ambitious and exciting genomics projects are under way.

Bioinformatics How do researchers piece together the millions of fragments produced by shotgun sequencing? Once a complete genome is assembled, how are the raw sequence data and information about genes and their products made available to the international community of researchers? How can genomes of different species be compared to learn about evolutionary relationships?

The answer is **bioinformatics**—a field that fuses mathematics, computer science, and biology in an effort to manage and analyze sequence data. Researchers in bioinformatics have created searchable databases. These vast repositories hold sequence information that allows investigators to evaluate the similarities between newly discovered genes and genes that have been studied previously in the same or other species.

The World Wide Web has put sequence databases at the fingertips of anyone with an Internet connection. For example, the U.S. National Center for Biotechnology Information (NCBI) is only a click away on your computer. At this free and publicly accessible site, you can search billions of nucleotides by using programs such as BLAST, which can quickly find DNA sequences related to any new gene uncovered in a genomics project.

The vast quantity of data generated by genome sequencing centers makes bioinformatics an indispensable element of genomics.

Which Genomes Are Being Sequenced, and Why?

The first genome to be sequenced from an organism—not a virus—came from a bacterium that lives in the human upper respiratory tract. *Haemophilus influenzae* has one circular chromosome and a total of 1.8 million base pairs of DNA. Its genome was small enough to sequence completely in a reasonable amount of time and within a reasonable budget, given the technology available in the early 1990s. *H. influenzae* was an important research subject because it causes earaches and respiratory tract infections in children. One strain is also capable of infecting the membranes surrounding the brain and spinal cord, causing meningitis.

Publication of the *H. influenzae* genome in 1995 was quickly followed by publication of complete genomes sequenced from an assortment of bacteria and archaea. Sequencing of the first eukaryotic genome, from the yeast *Saccharomyces cerevisiae*, was finished in 1996. Today, the genomes of more than 2000 species from all domains of life have been sequenced. That number is certain to continue climbing in the coming years.

Most of the organisms that have been selected for whole-genome sequencing have interesting biological properties, represent a particular branch of life informative for evolutionary investigations, or cause disease. For example:

- Genomes of bacteria and archaea from hot environments have been sequenced in the hopes of discovering enzymes useful for high-temperature industrial applications.

- A set of more than 50 genomes of diverse bacteria and archaea was sequenced to explore patterns of evolution that are impossible to study by other means.

- Genomes such as those of rice and maize (corn) have been sequenced for crop improvement applications.

- The fruit fly *Drosophila melanogaster*, the roundworm *Caenorhabditis elegans*, the house mouse *Mus musculus*, and the

mustard plant *Arabidopsis thaliana* were analyzed because they serve as model organisms in biology (see **BioSkills 13** in Appendix B). Data from these and other well-studied organisms have helped researchers interpret the human genome.

- The platypus and African elephant genomes have been sequenced to reveal evolutionary relationships among mammals. Although the elephant genomes are not complete, the available data confirmed that there are two distinct species of African elephant. This information is vital to conservation plans.

Which Sequences Are Genes?

Obtaining raw sequence data is just the beginning of the effort to understand a genome. As researchers point out, raw sequence data are analogous to the parts list for a house. The list, however, would read something like "windowwabeborogovestaircasedoorjubjub" because it has no punctuation and contains portions that appear to have no meaning.

Where do the genes for "window," "staircase," and "door" start and end? Are the segments that read "wabeborogove" and "jubjub" important in gene regulation, or are they simply spacers or other types of sequences that have no function at all?

The most basic task in interpreting a genome is to identify which bases constitute genes. This task is called **genome annotation.** Recall the current definition of a gene: A segment of DNA that codes for a functional RNA or protein product—or a series of alternatively spliced products—and that regulates their production. In bacteria and archaea, identifying genes is relatively straightforward. The task is much more difficult in eukaryotes.

Identifying Genes in Bacterial and Archaeal Genomes To interpret bacterial and archaeal genomes, biologists begin with computer programs that scan the sequence of a genome in both directions. These programs identify each reading frame that is possible on the two strands of the DNA. Recall that a reading frame is a continuous sequence of non-overlapping codons (see Chapter 16).

Codons consist of three bases, so three reading frames are possible on each DNA strand, for a total of six possible reading frames (**FIGURE 21.3**). Because randomly generated sequences contain a stop codon at about 1 in every 20 codons on average, a long stretch of codons that lacks a stop codon is a good indication of a protein-coding sequence. The computer programs draw attention to any "gene-sized" stretches of sequence that lack an internal stop codon and are flanked by a stop codon and a start codon. Because polypeptides range in size from a few dozen amino acids to many hundreds of amino acids, gene-sized stretches of sequence range from several hundred bases to thousands of bases. In addition, the computer programs look for sequences typical of promoters, ribosome binding sites, or other regulatory sites. DNA segments that are identified in this way are called **open reading frames,** or **ORFs.**

Once an ORF is found, a computer program compares its sequence with the sequences of known genes from another species.

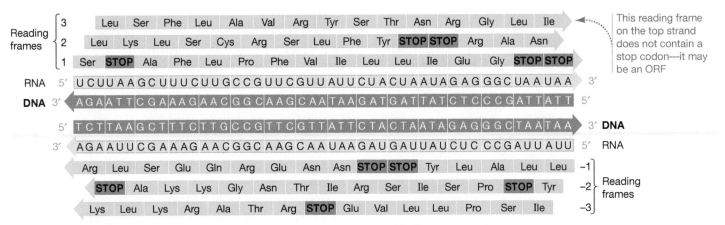

FIGURE 21.3 Open Reading Frames Can Identify Genes. Computer programs use the genetic code to translate the three possible reading frames on each strand of DNA. A long stretch of codons that lacks a stop codon may be an open reading frame (ORF) and identify a gene.

✓**QUESTION** To predict the mRNA codons that would be produced by a particular reading frame, a computer analyzes the DNA in the 3′-to-5′ direction. Why?

If the ORF is unlike any gene that has so far been described in any species, further research is required before it can actually be considered a gene. In contrast, if an ORF shares a significant amount of sequence with a known gene from another species, then it is very likely to be a gene.

Similarities between genes in different species are usually due to **homology.** If genes are homologous, it means they are similar because they are related by descent from a common ancestor. Homologous genes have similar base sequences and frequently the same or a similar function. For example, consider the genes that code for enzymes involved in repairing mismatches in DNA (introduced in Chapter 15). The mismatch-repair genes in *E. coli*, yeast, and humans are similar in DNA sequence and function. To explain this similarity, biologists hypothesize that the common ancestor of all cells living today had mismatch-repair genes—thus, the descendants of this ancestral species also have versions of these genes.

Identifying Genes in Eukaryotic Genomes Mining eukaryotic sequence data for protein-coding genes is complicated. For example, because coding regions are broken up by introns, it is not possible to scan for long ORFs. Instead, researchers combine an array of approaches.

Perhaps the most productive gene-finding strategy has been to isolate mRNAs from cells, use reverse transcriptase to produce a cDNA version of each mRNA, and sequence a portion of the resulting molecule to produce an **expressed sequence tag,** or **EST.** ESTs represent protein-coding genes. To locate the gene, researchers use the EST to find the matching sequence in genomic DNA.

Although ESTs and many other gene-finding strategies have been fruitful, it will likely be many years before biologists are convinced they have identified all the genes in even a single eukaryotic genome. As gene identification efforts continue, researchers are analyzing the data and making some remarkable discoveries. Let's first consider what genome sequencing has revealed about the nature of bacterial and archaeal genomes and then move on to eukaryotes. Is the effort to sequence whole genomes paying off?

21.2 Bacterial and Archaeal Genomes

Biologists have obtained the genome sequences of thousands of distinct bacterial and archaeal species or strains. For example, researchers have sequenced the genome of a laboratory population of *Escherichia coli*—derived from the harmless strain that lives in your gut—as well as the genome of a form that causes severe disease in humans. As a result, researchers can identify genes that differ between these strains and begin experiments to learn what accounts for the infectious properties of some strains.

What general observations have biologists been able to make about the nature of all these bacterial and archaeal genomes?

The Natural History of Prokaryotic Genomes

In a sense, biologists who are working in genomics can be compared to the naturalists of the eighteenth and nineteenth centuries. These early biologists explored the globe, collecting the plants and animals they encountered. Their goals were to describe what existed and identify any patterns. Similarly, the first task of a genome sequencer is to catalog what is in a genome—specifically, the number, type, and organization of genes—and then look for patterns within and between different genomes. Here are some principles that have emerged from analysis of prokaryotic genomes:

- Bacterial and archaeal genomes are compact. They have uninterrupted coding sequences, little space between genes, extensive use of operons, and relatively few regulatory sequences. This structure leads to a linear relationship between genome size and gene number. Look at the graph of bacterial and archaeal genomes in **FIGURE 21.4a**, and notice how genome size and the number of genes increase together in a nearly straight line. In contrast, this simple relationship does not hold for eukaryotic genomes (**FIGURE 21.4b**). Section 21.3 explores these features of eukaryotic genome organization in detail.

- In bacteria, there is a correlation between the size of a genome and the metabolic capabilities of the organism. Species that live in a variety of habitats and use a wide array of molecules for food have large genomes; parasites—species that make use of a host's biochemical machinery rather than synthesizing their own molecules—have small genomes.

- The function of many bacterial and archaeal genes is still unknown. Across a wide range of species, a function cannot yet be assigned to 15 to 30 percent of genes.

- Most of the genes found in one species are not shared widely with others. In a study that sampled the genomes of diverse prokaryotes, every time a new genome was sequenced, more than 1000 new genes were discovered. Only a small set of genes involved in processes such as DNA replication, transcription, and translation are similar across a wide range of bacteria or archaea.

- The content of genomes varies widely even within species. For example, sequencing of 17 different *E. coli* strains revealed a total of about 13,000 different genes. The genome of any one strain has only about 4400 genes, and roughly 2200 of these are shared by all strains. The remaining genes in each genome are found only in some strains but not in others.

- Prokaryotic genomes are frequently rearranged during evolution. Even closely related species show little similarity in gene order.

Perhaps the most surprising observation of all is that in many bacterial and archaeal species, a significant proportion of the genome appears to have been acquired from other, often distantly related, species. The movement of DNA from one species to another is called **lateral gene transfer.** As you'll learn, there are many ways to define a species. But in all traditional definitions, members of one species cannot exchange genes with members of another species. Lateral gene transfer counters this view: Instead of moving vertically from generation to generation within a species, in lateral gene transfer, genes move "laterally" between different coexisting species.

Genomics has shown that lateral gene transfer is more common than ever imagined. This finding is causing many biologists to wonder if conventional evolutionary trees capture the way bacteria and archaea have evolved.

Lateral Gene Transfer in Bacteria and Archaea

The extent of lateral gene transfer is still debated, but genomic data indicate that all bacterial and archaeal species have experienced lateral gene transfer. Lateral gene transfer is a major force in the evolution of bacteria and archaea.

One illustration is the bacterium *Thermotoga maritima*. This species thrives in high-temperature environments near deep-sea vents. Almost 25 percent of the genes in this species are closely related to genes found in archaea that live in the same habitats. The archaea-like genes occur in well-defined clusters within the *T. maritima* genome. These observations support the hypothesis that these sequences were transferred in large pieces from an archaean to a bacterium—organisms in two different domains of life.

How are laterally transferred genes identified? Biologists primarily use two criteria: (**1**) A gene is much more similar to genes in distantly related species than to those in closely related species,

(a) In bacteria (○) and archaea (●), genome size and number of genes increase together in a linear relationship.

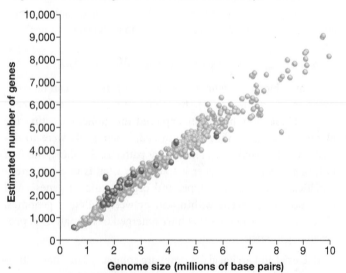

(b) The same relationship does not hold true for eukaryotes (●).

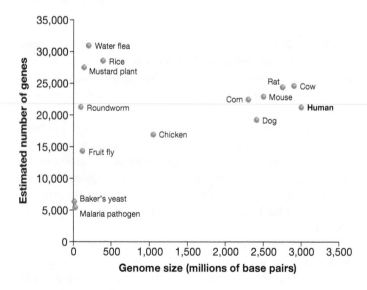

FIGURE 21.4 Relationship Between Genome Size and Gene Number.

DATA: (a) Hou, Y., and S. Lin. 2009. *PLoS ONE* 4(9): e6978, Supplemental Table S1. (b) KEGG: Kyoto Encyclopedia of Genes and Genomes, KEGG Organisms: Complete Genomes. www.genome.jp/kegg/.

and (2) the proportion of G-C base pairs to A-T base pairs in a particular gene or series of genes is markedly different from the base composition of the rest of the genome. This second criterion works because the proportion of G-C base pairs in a genome is characteristic of the particular genus or species.

How can genes move from one species to another? In some cases, plasmids are responsible. For example, most of the genes that are responsible for conferring resistance to antibiotics are found on plasmids. Researchers have documented the transfer of plasmid-borne antibiotic-resistance genes between distantly related bacteria. In many cases of lateral gene transfer, genes from plasmids become integrated into the main chromosome of a bacterium through genetic recombination.

Lateral gene transfer may also occur by transformation—when bacteria and archaea take up raw pieces of DNA from the environment—and by viruses that pick up DNA from one cell and transfer it to another cell.

There is no doubt that lateral gene transfer occurs even between distantly related organisms. What is still debated, however, is how much this shakes the tree of life. If lateral gene transfer is rare, then evolutionary paths in the bacteria and archaea form a set of branches that begin at common ancestors and spread out to descendants. If lateral gene transfer is as widespread as some biologists believe, then evolutionary paths must form a complex interconnected network that links species in a web of vertical and lateral gene transfers. These alternative views are shown in **FIGURE 21.5**.

In light of new genomics findings, will a tree of life stand for bacteria and archaea? Or are the evolutionary relationships in these domains of life best viewed as a web? Stay tuned.

Metagenomics

Biologists continue to gain important insights from sequencing the genomes of individual species and strains. But more recently, some research groups have taken a different approach: cataloging all the genes present in a community of bacteria and archaea. This type of research is called **metagenomics,** or **environmental sequencing.** The subject of these studies is genes—not organisms.

The first environmental sequencing study was conducted in the Sargasso Sea, near the Caribbean island of Bermuda. Researchers chose the spot because it is extremely nutrient poor and species poor—a desert in the ocean. This is a common strategy

in biological science: Start by studying a simple system, then go on to more complex situations. To inventory the complete array of bacterial genes present, the research group collected cells from different water depths and locations, isolated DNA from the samples, and sequenced the DNA.

After analyzing over 1 billion nucleotides, the team concluded that at least 1800 bacterial species were present, of which 148 were previously undiscovered. They also identified more than 1.2 million genes that had never before been characterized. These genes included over 780 sequences that code for proteins similar to the rhodopsin found in the cells of your retina—a molecule that is absorbing the light entering your eye right now. Follow-up work suggests that most of the Sargasso Sea rhodopsin-like molecules are also absorbing light, and that bacterial cells use the energy of the light to pump protons across their plasma membranes—creating a chemiosmotic gradient that can synthesize ATP (see Chapter 9).

Many metagenomics studies are going on today, including one that examined microbes of the human gut (Chapter 29). All these investigations are providing new insights about the living world, from how rhodopsin-like proteins help bacteria thrive in a desert to how your lunch is being digested.

21.3 Eukaryotic Genomes

DNA sequencing has revealed some extraordinary features of eukaryotic genome organization. Genome size varies widely, but the number of genes is much more similar. For example, the genomes shown in Figure 21.4b vary roughly 250-fold in size (from 12 to 3000 million base pairs) but less than sixfold in the number of genes (from 5400 to 30,900). How can gene number be so similar among organisms with vastly different genome sizes and that range in complexity from single-celled parasites to large multicellular plants and animals?

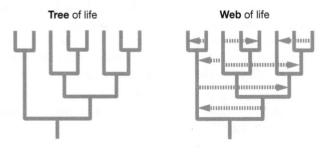

Tree of life   **Web** of life

FIGURE 21.5 Tree of Life and Web of Life Views of Evolution. The broken horizontal arrows indicate lateral gene transfer events.

Before exploring possible answers, let's consider two daunting challenges in sequencing eukaryotic genomes. The first is size. The largest bacterial genome, that of *Sorangium cellulosum,* is slightly more than 13 million base pairs. However, as Figure 21.4b shows, even modest-sized eukaryotic genomes are much larger. The 3-billion-base-pair human genome dwarfs those of bacteria but is miniscule compared with the genome of the Japanese flower *Paris japonica.* This plant's genome contains 149 billion base pairs of DNA—that's 50 times the size of the human genome!

The second challenge in sequencing eukaryotic genes is coping with sequences that are repeated many times. Many eukaryotic genomes are dominated by repeated DNA sequences that occur between genes or inside introns and do not code for products used by the organism. These repeated sequences greatly complicate the work of aligning and interpreting sequence data. They also explain some of the paradox of the immense variation in eukaryotic genome sizes. If repeated sequences don't code for products needed by cells, what do they do?

Transposable Elements and Other Repeated Sequences

In many eukaryotes, the exons and regulatory sequences associated with genes make up a relatively small percentage of the genome. Over 90 percent of a bacterial or archaeal genome consists of genes, but about 50 percent of an average eukaryotic genome consists of repeated sequences that do not code for a product used by the cell.

When repeated sequences were discovered, they were initially considered "junk DNA" that was nonfunctional and probably unimportant and uninteresting. But subsequent work has shown that many of the repeated sequences observed in eukaryotes are actually derived from sequences known as transposable elements.

Transposable elements are segments of DNA that are capable of being inserted into new locations, or transposing, in a genome. They were first discovered in corn by Barbara McClintock and later shown to be present in organisms from every domain of life. Transposable elements behave similarly to some viruses that insert into the genome. In contrast to viruses, however, transposable elements seldom leave their host cell—instead, they make copies of themselves that become inserted in new locations. Transposable elements are passed from mother to daughter cell and from parents to offspring, generation after generation, because they are part of the genome.

A transposable element is an example of what biologists call selfish DNA: a DNA sequence that has invaded a host and persists and reproduces using the resources of the host. Selfish or not, transposable elements play a big role in a species as they move from place to place and cause mutation. Like any mutation, a transposable element insertion into a new site in the genome can have negative, neutral, or positive effects on fitness. Transposable elements are a significant part of almost all cellular genomes and play a major role in evolution. Transposable elements have many effects, disrupting the coding sequence of genes, changing patterns of gene regulation, and promoting gene

duplication and loss. They are genome invaders that also shape the structure and function of genomes in profound ways.

How Do Transposable Elements Work? Transposable elements come in a wide variety of types and spread through genomes in a variety of ways. Different organisms—*E. coli,* fruit flies, yeast, and humans, for example—contain distinct types of transposable elements. Bacterial and archaeal genomes, however, have far fewer transposable elements compared with most eukaryotes. This observation has inspired the hypothesis that bacteria and archaea either have efficient means of removing parasitic sequences or can somehow thwart insertion events.

As an example of how these selfish DNA sequences work, consider a well-studied type of transposable element called a **long interspersed nuclear element (LINE).** LINEs are found in humans and other animals. Because LINEs have a reverse transcriptase like retroviruses (introduced in Chapter 20), biologists hypothesize that they are derived from them evolutionarily. Your genome contains nearly 1 million LINEs, each between 1000 and 5000 bases long. Transposable elements of different types make up over 45 percent of the human genome and 85 percent of the corn (maize) genome. **FIGURE 21.6** illustrates the steps that allow an active LINE to transpose.

Most of the LINEs observed in the human genome do not actually function, however, because they don't contain a promoter or the genes for either reverse transcriptase or integrase. To make sense of this observation, researchers hypothesize that the insertion process illustrated in steps 6 and 7 of Figure 21.6 is often disrupted in some way, leaving the inserted replica of the original LINE incomplete.

Research on transposable elements and lateral gene transfer has revolutionized how biologists view the genome. Many genomes are riddled with transposable elements, and others have undergone radical change in response to lateral gene transfer events. In other words, genomes are much more dynamic and complex than previously thought. Their size and composition can change dramatically over time.

Repeated Sequences and DNA Fingerprinting In addition to containing repeated sequences from transposable elements, many eukaryotic genomes have several thousand loci of relatively short DNA sequences. They are repeated in tandem, one after another, contiguously along part of a chromosome.

These tandem repetitive DNA sequences fall into two major classes:

1. Repeating units that are just 2 to about 6 bases long. These are **microsatellites,** also known as **short tandem repeats (STRs)** or **simple sequence repeats.** The most common type of microsatellite in humans is a repeated stretch of the dinucleotide AC, giving the sequence ACACACAC....

2. Repeating units that are longer, from about 6 to 100 bases long. These are **minisatellites,** or **variable number tandem repeats (VNTRs).**

Microsatellite sequences are thought to originate when DNA polymerase skips or mistakenly adds extra bases during replication;

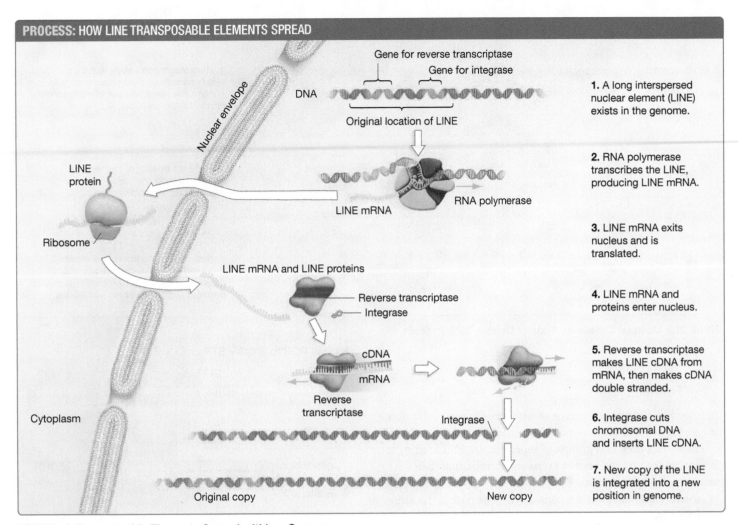

FIGURE 21.6 Transposable Elements Spread within a Genome.

the origin of minisatellites is still unclear. Together, the two types of repeated sequences make up 3 percent of the human genome.

Soon after these sequences were first characterized, Alec Jeffreys and co-workers established that microsatellite and minisatellite loci are "hypervariable," meaning that they vary among individuals much more than any other type of sequence does.

FIGURE 21.7 (see page 398) illustrates one mechanism to explain why microsatellites and minisatellites have so many different alleles: a process called **unequal crossover.** Here's how it works: Homologous chromosomes sometimes align incorrectly during prophase of meiosis I. Instead of lining up in exactly the same location, the two chromosomes pair in a way that matches up bases in different DNA repeats. When crossover occurs, the resulting chromosomes have different numbers of repeats.

Repeated sequences are particularly prone to unequal crossover, because their homologs are so similar that they are likely to misalign. If the region in question has a unique number of repeats, it represents a unique allele. Like any other alleles, microsatellite and minisatellite alleles are transmitted from parents to offspring.

The variation in repeat number among individuals is more than a curious feature of genome organization—it is the basis

of most DNA fingerprinting. **DNA fingerprinting** refers to any technique for identifying individuals based on the unique features of their genomes. Because microsatellite and minisatellite sequences vary so much, they are now the sequences of choice for DNA fingerprinting. How can these sequences be used for DNA fingerprinting?

Investigators obtain a DNA sample and perform the polymerase chain reaction (PCR), using primers that flank a region containing an STR (**FIGURE 21.8**; see page 398). Once the region has been amplified, it can be analyzed to determine the number of repeats present. Primers are now available that allow the analysis of many different STR loci.

These advances have profound impacts on society. Police use DNA fingerprinting to put people behind bars, and DNA fingerprinting has been used to show that people who were accused of crimes were actually innocent. Beyond criminal investigations, DNA fingerprinting has also been used to assign paternity and to identify remains.

Now that some characteristics of eukaryotic genomes have been reviewed, let's consider the genes they contain. Let's start with the most basic question of all: Where do eukaryotic genes come from?

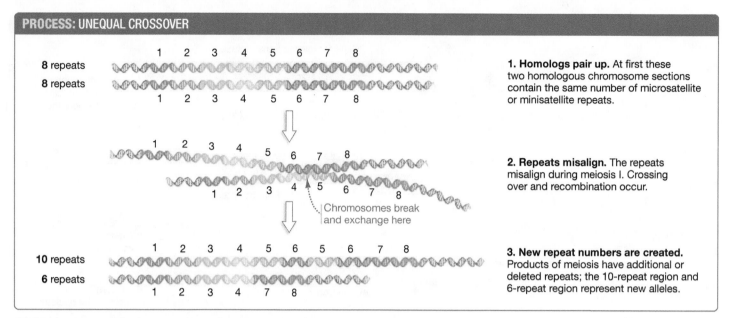

8 repeats
8 repeats

1. Homologs pair up. At first these two homologous chromosome sections contain the same number of microsatellite or minisatellite repeats.

2. Repeats misalign. The repeats misalign during meiosis I. Crossing over and recombination occur.

Chromosomes break and exchange here

10 repeats
6 repeats

3. New repeat numbers are created. Products of meiosis have additional or deleted repeats; the 10-repeat region and 6-repeat region represent new alleles.

FIGURE 21.7 Unequal Crossover Adds or Deletes DNA Repeats.

Gene Families

In eukaryotes, the major source of new genes is the duplication of existing genes. Biologists infer that genes have been duplicated recently when they find groups of genes that are similar in such features as the arrangement of exons and introns, and their base sequence. Within a species, genes that are similar to each other in structure and function are considered to be part of the same **gene family.**

The degree of sequence similarity among members of a gene family varies. In the genes that code for ribosomal RNAs (rRNAs) in vertebrates, the sequences are virtually identical—meaning that each individual has many exact copies of the same gene. In other cases, though, 50 percent or less of the bases are identical.

How Do Gene Families Arise? Genes that make up gene families are hypothesized to have arisen from a common ancestral sequence through gene duplication. When **gene duplication** occurs, an extra copy of a gene is added to the genome.

The most common type of gene duplication results from unequal crossover during meiosis—the same process that resulted in extra microsatellite and minisatellite repeats in Figure 21.7. Gene-sized segments of chromosomes can be deleted or duplicated if homologous chromosomes misalign during prophase of meiosis I and an unequal crossover occurs. Like microsatellites or minisatellites, the duplicated segments are arranged in tandem—one after the other.

New Genes—New Functions? Gene duplication is important because the original gene is still functional and produces a normal product. As a result, the new, duplicated stretches of sequence are redundant. If mutations in the duplicated sequence alter the protein product so that it performs a valuable new function, then an important new gene has been created.

(a) Use PCR to amplify STR loci.

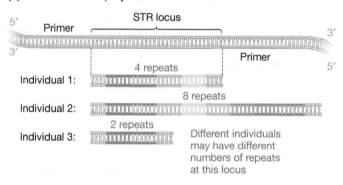

Individual 1:

Individual 2:

Individual 3:

Different individuals may have different numbers of repeats at this locus

(b) Compare number of STR repeats in alleles to test paternity.

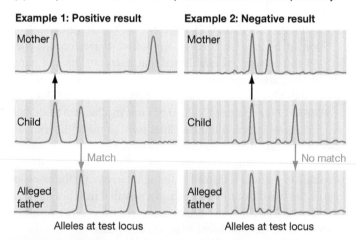

Example 1: Positive result

Mother

Child

Match

Alleged father

Alleles at test locus

Example 2: Negative result

Mother

Child

No match

Alleged father

Alleles at test locus

FIGURE 21.8 DNA Fingerprinting Can Be Used to Identify Parents. **(a)** The lengths of STR loci vary. Only one allele is shown for each individual. Individuals are often heterozygous, so the repeat number varies within and between individuals. **(b)** Here, the position of each peak indicates the number of repeats at a particular locus. Each individual is heterozygous and thus shows two peaks. One of the peaks from the mother and one of the peaks from the father should line up with a peak in the child. Typically 6 to 16 loci are tested to determine paternity.

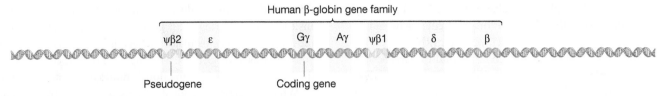

FIGURE 21.9 **Gene Families Are Closely Related Genes.** The β-globin gene family is shown with coding genes in red and pseudogenes in yellow.

✔**EXERCISE** Suppose that during prophase of meiosis I, the β locus on one chromosome aligned with the ψβ2 locus on another chromosome. Then crossing over occurred in the noncoding sequences just to the left (as oriented in the figure) of this β-ψβ2 pairing. List the order of the β-globin-family genes that would result on each chromosome.

As an example of a gene family, consider the human globin genes diagrammed in **FIGURE 21.9**. Collectively, this set of genes is known as the β-globin gene family, and they code for proteins that form part of hemoglobin—the oxygen-carrying molecule in your red blood cells. Each coding gene in the family serves a slightly different function. For example, some genes are transcribed only in the fetus or the adult. The product of the fetal gene binds oxygen more tightly than the proteins expressed in adults. Consequently, oxygen moves from the mother's blood, where it is not as tightly bound to hemoglobin, to the fetus's blood.

In addition to creating genes with new functions, mutations in duplicated regions often make gene expression impossible. For example, a mutation could produce a stop codon in the middle of an exon. A member of a gene family that resembles a working gene but does not code for a functional product because of a mutation is a **pseudogene.** Pseudogenes do not function. Note that the β-globin gene family contains pseudogenes along with several genes that code for oxygen-transporting proteins. The number of pseudogenes is remarkable. In the human genome, for example, there are roughly as many pseudogenes as functional genes.

Lateral Gene Transfer in Eukaryotes

Genome sequencing projects are revealing more and more instances of lateral gene transfer in eukaryotes. What is the role of lateral gene transfer in the evolution of eukaryotes?

There are some clear examples of lateral gene transfer playing pivotal roles in eukaryote evolution. One key example is the capture of bacterial cells that were predecessors of today's mitochondria and chloroplasts and the subsequent transfer of many bacterial genes to the host genome (see Chapter 30). But in general, lateral gene transfer seems to be relatively rare in eukaryotes compared with prokaryotes. While biologists debate whether a tree or a web of life best describes evolution in bacteria and archaea, the eukaryotic tree remains rooted in what appear to be more modest rates of lateral gene transfer.

Insights from the Human Genome Project

More than 10 years ago, President Clinton announced the completion of the human genome sequence as "the most wondrous map ever produced by humankind." What has analysis of human genome sequence revealed? Let's first explore what types of DNA sequences make up the human genome and then examine some questions raised by this wondrous map.

Given biologists' focus on protein-coding genes, the composition of the human genome was unexpected. As **FIGURE 21.10** reveals, less than 2 percent of the genome consists of protein-coding exons, and nearly half is made of transposable elements. Introns make up over one-quarter of the genome and are 17 times more abundant than protein-coding exons.

Of all the observations stemming from the human genome, perhaps the most striking is that organisms with complex morphology, biochemistry, and behavior do not have particularly large numbers of genes. Notice in Figure 21.4b that the total number of genes in humans is only 50 percent more than the number in fruit flies, is about the same as in roundworms, and is substantially lower than the number of genes in water fleas, rice, and the mustard plant *Arabidopsis thaliana*.

Before the human genome was sequenced, many biologists expected that humans would have at least 100,000 genes. But we may only have a fifth of that number. How can this be?

In prokaryotes there is a correlation between genome size, gene number, a cell's metabolic capabilities, and the cell's ability to live in a variety of habitats. But why isn't there a stronger correlation between gene number and morphological, biochemical, and behavioral complexity in eukaryotes?

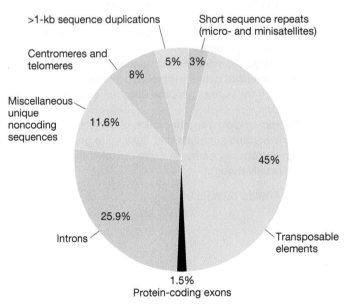

FIGURE 21.10 Composition of the Human Genome.
DATA: Gregory, T. R. 2005. *Nature Reviews Genetics* 6: 699–708.

One hypothesis to explain this observation is based on **alternative splicing.** Recall that the exons of a particular gene can be spliced in ways that produce distinct, mature mRNAs. As a result, a single eukaryotic gene can code for multiple transcripts and thus multiple proteins (see Chapter 19). The alternative-splicing hypothesis claims that multicellular eukaryotes do not need enormous numbers of distinct genes. Instead, more extensive use of alternative splicing in these organisms creates different proteins from the same gene.

In support of the alternative-splicing hypothesis, researchers have analyzed the mRNAs produced by human genes. They estimate that at least 90 percent of genes produce transcripts that are alternatively spliced, with an average of more than three distinct transcripts per gene. This means that the number of different proteins that can be produced is more than triple the gene number. Because of extensive alternative splicing, the number of genes and number of proteins do not have to be tightly linked.

There is likely more to the story, however, than extensive alternative splicing. Accompanying the rapid advances in sequencing technology have been equally dramatic advances in methods for studying how the genome functions. Some of these methods are described later, in Section 21.4. But what's important here are the findings.

Roughly 90 percent of the human genome is transcribed. This is far more than believed even a few years ago. Some of these transcripts code for regulatory RNAs with known roles, such as microRNAs (Chapter 19). Many of these transcripts, however, have no currently known roles. If many of these newly discovered RNAs have a function, then the human genome and the genomes of other complex organisms may not be so gene poor after all. If so,

this would require an adjustment in how we view a typical gene. Instead of considering most genes to code for proteins, perhaps most genes produce regulatory RNAs that are never translated. As you read this, biologists are working hard on this central question that has been opened by functional studies of the human genome.

What are these functional studies, and how are they carried out? The following section considers these questions.

21.4 Functional Genomics, Proteomics, and Systems Biology

Genomics researcher Eric Lander has compared the sequencing of the human genome to the establishment of the periodic table of the elements in chemistry. Once the periodic table was validated, chemists focused on understanding how the elements combine to form molecules. Similarly, biologists now want to understand how the elements of the human genome combine to produce an individual.

Remember that a genome sequence is essentially a parts list. Once that list is assembled, researchers delve deeper to understand how genes interact to produce an organism.

What Is Functional Genomics?

For decades, biologists have worked at understanding how and when individual genes are expressed. Research on the *lac* operon is typical of this type of study (see Chapter 18). But now researchers can ask how and when *all* the genes in an organism are expressed.

Large-scale analysis of gene expression is part of functional genomics—research on how genes work together to produce a phenotype. The effort is motivated by the realization that gene products do not exist in a vacuum. Instead, groups of RNAs and proteins act together to respond to environmental challenges such as extreme heat or drought. Similarly, distinct groups of genes are transcribed at different stages as a multicellular eukaryote grows and develops.

A basic tool of functional genomics is a microarray. A **DNA microarray** consists of as many as 1 million different single-stranded DNA segments that are permanently attached at one end to a glass slide or silicon chip. Each DNA sequence is linked to the slide or chip in a known location and serves as a probe for a specific transcript. For example, the slide pictured in **FIGURE 21.11** contains thousands of spots, each one containing single-stranded DNA from a unique exon found in the human genome.

Microarrays can be used for many applications. The most common use is to learn which genes are expressed as RNAs in a particular cell type under particular conditions. A typical experiment done with a DNA microarray would follow the protocol outlined in **FIGURE 21.12**. For example, if the researchers' goal was to learn how a cell alters its gene expression to meet the challenges of heat stress, the first step would be to isolate mRNAs produced in control cells functioning at normal temperature and in cells of the same kind exposed to high temperatures.

check your understanding

If you understand that . . .

C
Y
U

- Eukaryotic genomes are riddled with transposable elements.
- Relatively short repeated sequences are common in eukaryotic genomes.
- In eukaryotes, many coding sequences are organized into families of genes with related functions.
- Much of the human genome does not code for proteins.
- The recent discovery that much of the genome is transcribed suggests that eukaryotic gene expression may be much more complex than previously thought.

✔ **You should be able to . . .**

1. Explain why there is no simple relationship between the size of a eukaryotic genome and the complexity of the organism.

2. Estimate the ratio of protein-coding portions of the human genome to all transcribed regions of the genome.

Answers are available in Appendix A.

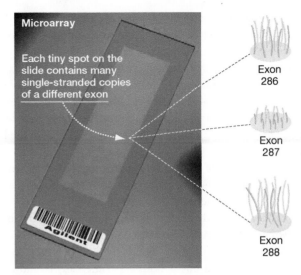

Microarray

Each tiny spot on the slide contains many single-stranded copies of a different exon

Exon 286

Exon 287

Exon 288

FIGURE 21.11 A DNA Microarray. To create this microarray, thousands of short, single-stranded DNA sequences were synthesized in defined positions on a glass plate. In this microarray, the synthesized DNAs represent portions of all exons from a particular species.

Once they had purified mRNAs from the two populations of cells (step 1), investigators would use reverse transcriptase to make a single-stranded cDNA version of each RNA in each of the two samples (see Chapter 20). In addition to the four standard dNTPs, one of the DNA building blocks used in synthesizing the cDNA would carry a fluorescent label (step 2). The label used for the cDNA of the control cells would glow one color (let's say green), while the label chosen for the cDNA of the heat-stressed cells would glow another color (let's say red). The labeled cDNAs of both colors would then be used to bind to the complementary DNA probes on the microarray (step 3). This step is called hybridization because hybrids between probe DNAs and cDNAs will form.

Out of all the exons in the genome, then, only the exons that are being expressed by the two populations of cells will be labeled on the microarray. In this example, genes that are expressed by the control cells under normal conditions will be labeled green, while those expressed by the cells during heat stress will be labeled red. If an exon in the microarray is expressed under both sets of conditions, then both green- and red-labeled cDNAs will bind to the DNA in that spot and make it appear yellow (step 4).

A microarray lets researchers study the expression of thousands of genes at a time. As a result, they can identify which sets of genes are expressed in concert under specific sets of conditions.

Researchers can use microarrays to establish which genes are transcribed in different organs and tissues, in cancers, or—as you saw in Figure 21.12—in response to changes in environmental conditions such as heat stress. ✔ If you understand how microarrays are used, you should be able to explain how you would use a DNA microarray to compare the genes expressed in brain cells versus liver cells of an adult human.

Besides using microarrays, investigators are now able to assess gene expression by directly sequencing cDNAs using next-generation sequencing technologies. For example, if biologists

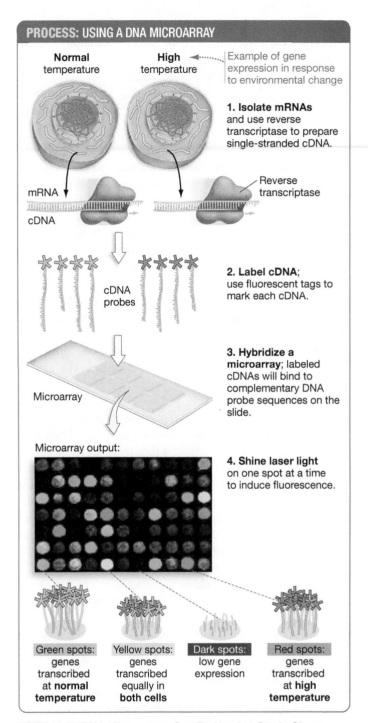

PROCESS: USING A DNA MICROARRAY

Normal temperature

High temperature

Example of gene expression in response to environmental change

1. Isolate mRNAs and use reverse transcriptase to prepare single-stranded cDNA.

mRNA

cDNA

Reverse transcriptase

cDNA probes

2. Label cDNA; use fluorescent tags to mark each cDNA.

Microarray

3. Hybridize a microarray; labeled cDNAs will bind to complementary DNA probe sequences on the slide.

Microarray output:

4. Shine laser light on one spot at a time to induce fluorescence.

| Green spots: genes transcribed at **normal** temperature | Yellow spots: genes transcribed equally in **both cells** | Dark spots: low gene expression | Red spots: genes transcribed at **high** temperature |

FIGURE 21.12 DNA Microarrays Can Be Used to Study Changes in Gene Expression. By probing a microarray with labeled cDNAs synthesized from mRNAs, researchers can identify which sequences are being transcribed. Here mRNAs from cells growing at normal temperature are detected by green color, while mRNAs from cells growing at high temperature are detected by red color.

wanted to learn about gene expression changes induced by heat stress, they would start as they did for the microarray by preparing two different sets of cDNAs, one from control and one from heat-stressed cells. But instead of using these cDNAs to hybridize with microarray probes, biologists would sequence millions of cDNAs from each treatment type. Using bioinformatics tools, they would then determine the frequency of each type of cDNA and compare the frequencies of the two cDNA samples to learn how heat stress alters gene expression.

This approach of extensive sequencing of populations of DNA or cDNA molecules is called **deep sequencing,** and it is quickly becoming an important research approach for functional genomics.

What Is Proteomics?

The Greek root *–ome*, meaning all, inspired the term genome. Similarly, biologists use the term **transcriptome** in referring to the complete set of DNA sequences that are transcribed in a particular cell, and **proteome** in referring to the complete set of proteins that are produced. **Proteomics,** it follows, is the large-scale study of all the proteins in a cell or organism.

Like genomics, proteomic studies begin with a parts list by identifying the proteins present in a cell or organelle. The techniques used for protein identification are distinct from those used in working with DNA. Once individual proteins are identified, researchers then study how the proteins that are present change through time, interact, or vary between different cells. Instead of studying individual proteins or how two proteins might interact, proteomics is based on studying all the proteins present at once.

One approach to studying protein–protein interactions is similar to the use of DNA microarrays, except that large numbers of proteins, rather than DNA sequences, are attached to a glass plate. This microarray of proteins is then treated with an assortment of proteins produced by the same organism. These proteins are labeled with a fluorescent or radioactive tag. If any labeled proteins bind to the proteins in the microarray, the two molecules may also interact in the cell. In this way, researchers can identify proteins that physically bind to one another—like the G proteins and associated enzymes (introduced in Chapter 11), or the cyclin and Cdk molecules (introduced in Chapter 12). Microarray technology is allowing biologists to study protein–protein interactions on a massive scale, opening the door to a new approach to biology.

What Is Systems Biology?

Systems biology is based on the premise that a whole is greater than the sum of its parts. **Systems biology** aims to understand how interactions between the individual parts of a biological system create new properties. For example, how does metabolism come about from the interaction of proteins within a cell? How does cancer arise from the interplay of individual genes? Complex properties that arise from the interaction of simpler elements are **emergent properties.**

DNA replication, metabolism, cancer, and the development of an organism all are emergent properties because they come about from the interactions of simpler elements—genes and proteins. ✔ If you understand this concept, you should be able to explain why cell replication is an emergent property.

Many systems biology investigations focus on mapping the interactions between genes or proteins. Genomics and proteomics provide the parts list needed to start these systems

biology studies. It's the job of a systems biologist to learn how these parts are linked together into networks and how new properties emerge from these interactions.

Let's look at how a systems biology approach was taken to predict all possible interactions between proteins in *Schizosaccharomyces pombe*, a species of yeast. An interaction can mean either that two proteins bind to one another to form a stable complex or that one protein acts on another protein. An example of the first type of interaction is cyclin binding to a cyclin-dependent kinase (Cdk); an example of the second interaction type is when the cyclin–Cdk complex acts as a kinase to add a phosphate to a target protein (see Chapter 12).

To begin their study, the researchers used existing databases of known protein–protein interactions to make predictions about the fission yeast protein interaction network. Then they verified some of the predicted interactions experimentally to show that their prediction method worked. Once they had shown that their prediction method was accurate, they mapped 37,325 possible interactions between 3438 different proteins. If you look at the interaction network in **FIGURE 21.13**, you will see how clusters of interacting proteins emerge from the tangle. These clusters reveal highly connected portions of the network.

The significance? Some of the predicted interactions in this yeast may have implications for human disease. For example, some of the key players in the cluster associated with signal transduction point to previously unexplored relationships that could be important in understanding cancer and neurodegenerative disorders, such as Huntington's disease (see Chapter 20), and for targeted drug design.

Work in genomics, proteomics, and systems biology is opening the door to knowing how cells work in health and disease. These new areas of biology also lay the foundation for understanding one of the most wondrous aspects of life—how a single cell develops into a complete organism. This topic is explored in the unit ahead.

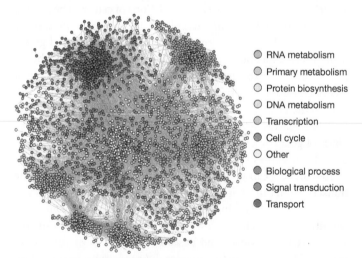

- RNA metabolism
- Primary metabolism
- Protein biosynthesis
- DNA metabolism
- Transcription
- Cell cycle
- Other
- Biological process
- Signal transduction
- Transport

FIGURE 21.13 Yeast Protein Interaction Network. Each circle represents a different protein, with each protein color-coded according to its cellular function. Lines that connect a pair of proteins indicate an interaction.

DATA: V. Pancaldi et al. 2012. *G3: Genes, Genomes, Genetics* 2: 453–467.

If you understand . . .

21.1 Whole-Genome Sequencing

- Advances in DNA sequencing technologies have allowed investigators to sequence DNA more rapidly and cheaply, resulting in a flood of genome data.

- Thousands of genomes have been sequenced to date for many different purposes.

- Bioinformatics is the application of computer science to genome analysis and is essential for genome research.

- Researchers annotate genome sequences by finding genes and determining their function.

- To identify genes in bacteria and archaea, researchers use computers to scan the genome for start and stop codons that are in the same reading frame and that are separated by gene-sized stretches of sequence.

- Genes are also identified based on their homology (similarity due to evolutionary relatedness) to previously identified genes in other species.

- To find genes in eukaryotes, researchers couple the use of computers and study of RNAs to identify transcribed sequences.

✓ You should be able to describe how a research group that discovered a gene for coat color in mice would determine whether a homologous gene exists in the human genome.

21.2 Bacterial and Archaeal Genomes

- Bacterial and archaeal genomes are small relative to many eukaryotic genomes and have tightly spaced genes.

- There is a linear relationship between bacterial and archaeal gene number and genome size, and a similar correspondence in the relationship between metabolic capacity and genome size.

- The function of many of the genes identified in bacteria and archaea is still unknown.

- There is a huge amount of genetic diversity in bacterial and archaeal genomes, even among different strains of the same species.

- Lateral gene transfer is common in bacteria and archaea. It is an important source of new genes in many species.

- Metagenomics allows the analysis of all the genes of all the bacteria or archaea in a community.

✓ You should be able to propose genome characteristics you would look for to distinguish a bacterial parasite from a nonparasitic bacterial species that is found in a range of environments.

21.3 Eukaryotic Genomes

- Eukaryotic genomes tend to be large and complex. They include many sequences that have little to no effect on the fitness of the organism, and many transcribed sequences whose function is not known.

- There is no correlation between morphological complexity and gene number in eukaryotes.

- Because of alternative splicing, the number of distinct transcripts produced in many eukaryotes is much larger than the gene number.

- Gene duplication has been an important source of new genes in eukaryotes.

- Lateral gene transfer occurs in eukaryotes, but appears to play a smaller role than in bacteria and archaea.

- Recent findings show that much more of the eukaryotic genome is transcribed than previously believed, and the function of many noncoding transcripts is unknown.

✓ You should be able to explain what features of eukaryotic genomes result in a lack of correspondence between genome size, gene number, and morphological complexity.

21.4 Functional Genomics, Proteomics, and Systems Biology

- Functional genomics uses tools such as DNA microarrays to learn patterns of gene expression and gene function.

- Proteomics is similar to genomics but works to identify the complete set of proteins expressed in a cell, how this set changes under different conditions, and how it relates to phenotype.

- Systems biology starts with genomics and proteomics data and studies the set of interactions between different genes or proteins to understand how biological systems work.

✓ You should be able to explain how Figure 21.13 indicates that there are networks within networks for interacting proteins associated with particular functions.

(MB) **MasteringBiology**

1. **MasteringBiology Assignments**

   Tutorials and Activities DNA Fingerprinting; Human Genome Project: Genes on Human Chromosome 17; Human Genome Sequencing Strategies; Shotgun Approach to Whole-Genome Sequencing

   Questions Reading Quizzes, Blue-Thread Questions, Test Bank

2. **eText** Read your book online, search, take notes, highlight text, and more.

3. **The Study Area** Practice Test, Cumulative Test, BioFlix® 3-D Animations, Videos, Activities, Audio Glossary, Word Study Tools, Art

You should be able to . . .

1. What is an open reading frame in bacteria?
   a. a gene whose function is already known
   b. a DNA section that is thought to code for a protein because it is similar to a complementary DNA (cDNA)
   c. a DNA section that is thought to code for a protein because it has a start codon and a stop codon flanking hundreds of nucleotides
   d. any member of a gene family

2. What best describes the logic behind shotgun sequencing?
   a. Break the genome into tiny pieces. Sequence each piece. Use overlapping ends to assemble the pieces in the correct order.
   b. Start with one end of each chromosome. Sequence straight through to the other end of the chromosome.
   c. Use a variety of techniques to identify genes and ORFs. Sequence these segments—not the noncoding and repeated sequences.
   d. Break the genome into pieces. Map the location of each piece. Then sequence each piece.

3. A _____ is a 2- to 6-base-pair repeated sequence in DNA.
   a. LINE
   b. restriction site
   c. gene duplication
   d. microsatellite

4. What is a leading hypothesis to explain the paradox that large, morphologically complex eukaryotes such as humans have relatively small numbers of genes?
   a. lateral transfer of genes from other species
   b. alternative splicing of mRNAs
   c. polyploidy, or the doubling of the genome's entire chromosome complement
   d. expansion of gene families through gene duplication

5. What evidence do biologists use to infer that a gene is part of a gene family?

6. What are some characteristics of a pseudogene?

7. Explain how open reading frames are identified in the genomes of bacteria and archaea. Why is it more difficult to find open reading frames in eukaryotes?

8. In a genomics-based search for mutations that caused a patient's cancer, which of the following would provide the most informative comparison with the cancer cell?
   a. the average human DNA sequence available from a database
   b. the DNA sequence of a noncancerous cell from another person
   c. the DNA sequence of a noncancerous cell from the patient
   d. the DNA sequence of a different tumor type from another cancer patient

9. QUANTITATIVE Gene density is the number of genes per unit length of DNA. Most often, gene density is expressed as the number of genes per million base pairs (Mbp). Go to Figure 21.4b and find the approximate number of genes estimated in water fleas and in humans and the size of each genome. What is the gene density per Mbp in water fleas? What is the gene density per Mbp in humans? How much greater is the gene density in water fleas relative to humans?

10. In DNA fingerprinting, why is it an advantage to analyze an STR locus with many different repeat length alleles versus an STR locus with only a few different repeat length alleles?

11. Explain how microarrays of short, single-stranded DNAs that represent many or all of the exons in a genome are used to document changes in the transcription of genes over time or in response to environmental challenges.

12. Explain the concept of homology and how identifying homologous genes helps researchers identify the function of unknown genes.

13. Parasites lack genes for many of the enzymes found in their hosts. Most parasites, however, have evolved from free-living ancestors that had larger genomes. Based on these observations, W. Ford Doolittle claims that the loss of genes in parasites represents an evolutionary trend. He summarizes his hypothesis with the quip "use it or lose it." What does he mean?

14. According to eyewitness accounts, communist revolutionaries executed Nicholas II, the last czar of Russia, along with his wife and five children, the family physician, and about a dozen servants. Many decades after this event, a grave purported to hold the remains of the royal family was discovered. Biologists were asked to analyze DNA from each adult and juvenile skeleton and determine whether the bodies were indeed those of several young siblings, two parents, and several unrelated adults. If the remains of the family were in this grave, predict how similar the DNA fingerprints would be between the parents, the children, and the unrelated individuals in the grave.

15. Pleiotropy occurs when a mutation in one gene results in many different phenotypes. In a study of a gene interaction network, similar to the protein interaction network shown in Figure 21.13, which type of gene would you predict to exhibit the greatest degree of pleiotropy when mutated?
   a. a gene that interacts with one neighbor
   b. a gene that has a duplicate copy
   c. a gene that is the center of interactions with functionally related genes
   d. a gene that is the center of interactions with genes of many different functions

16. One hypothesis for differences between humans and chimps involves differences in gene regulation. A recent study used microarrays to compare the patterns of expression of genes that are active in the brain, liver, and blood of chimpanzees and humans. The overall patterns of gene expression were similar in the liver and blood of the two species, but the expression patterns were strikingly different in the brain. How do these results relate to the hypothesis?

The Big Picture

Geneticist and evolutionary biologist Theodosius Dobzhansky said that "Nothing in biology makes sense except in the light of evolution." Use this concept map to study how ideas introduced in Unit 5 fit together.

The key is to connect the four evolutionary processes that work at the level of populations—natural selection, genetic drift, mutation, and gene flow—to processes, events, and outcomes at higher levels of organization: speciation, adaptive radiation, mass extinction, and the tree of life.

It's all about changes in allele frequencies. Over time, small changes that occur between populations lead to large changes that distinguish major lineages on the tree of life.

Note that each box in the concept map indicates the chapter and section where you can go for review. Also, be sure to do the blue exercises in the **Check Your Understanding box** below.

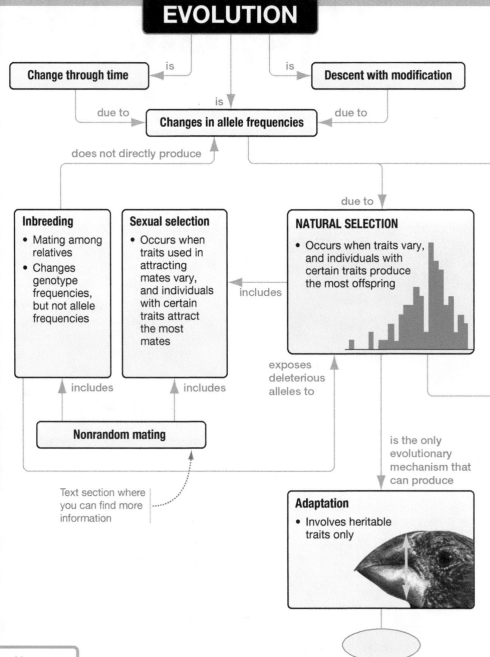

EVOLUTION

Change through time — is — **Changes in allele frequencies** — is — **Descent with modification**

due to / due to / due to

does not directly produce

Inbreeding
- Mating among relatives
- Changes genotype frequencies, but not allele frequencies

Sexual selection
- Occurs when traits used in attracting mates vary, and individuals with certain traits attract the most mates

NATURAL SELECTION
- Occurs when traits vary, and individuals with certain traits produce the most offspring

includes

Nonrandom mating

includes / *includes*

exposes deleterious alleles to

Text section where you can find more information

is the only evolutionary mechanism that can produce

Adaptation
- Involves heritable traits only

Fitness
- Measured by number of viable, fertile offspring produced

usually reduces

check your understanding

If you understand the big picture . . .
✔ You should be able to . . .

1. Draw a circle around the processes that violate the Hardy–Weinberg principle.

2. Fill in the blue ovals with appropriate linking verbs or phrases.

3. Add a box for "Fossil record" with appropriate connections.

4. Draw arrows linking genetic drift, mutation, and gene flow to the appropriate box using the linking phrase "is random with respect to."

Answers are available in Appendix A.

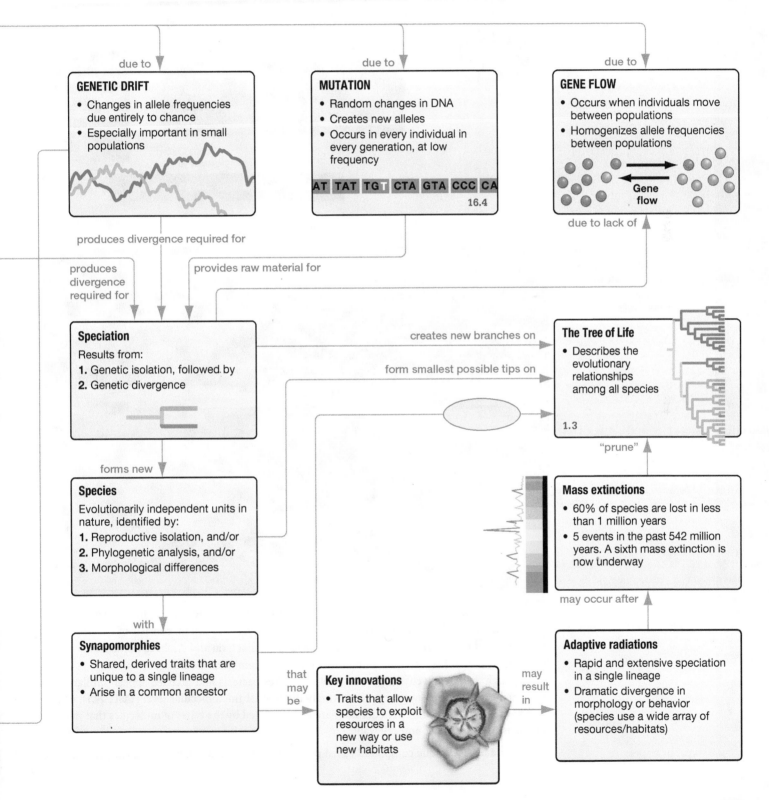

due to ▼

GENETIC DRIFT
- Changes in allele frequencies due entirely to chance
- Especially important in small populations

due to ▼

MUTATION
- Random changes in DNA
- Creates new alleles
- Occurs in every individual in every generation, at low frequency

AT TAT TGT CTA GTA CCC CA
16.4

due to ▼

GENE FLOW
- Occurs when individuals move between populations
- Homogenizes allele frequencies between populations

Gene flow

due to lack of ▲

produces divergence required for

produces divergence required for

provides raw material for

Speciation

Results from:
1. Genetic isolation, followed by
2. Genetic divergence

creates new branches on

form smallest possible tips on

The Tree of Life
- Describes the evolutionary relationships among all species

1.3

"prune" ▲

forms new ▼

Species

Evolutionarily independent units in nature, identified by:
1. Reproductive isolation, and/or
2. Phylogenetic analysis, and/or
3. Morphological differences

Mass extinctions
- 60% of species are lost in less than 1 million years
- 5 events in the past 542 million years. A sixth mass extinction is now underway

may occur after ▲

with ▼

Synapomorphies
- Shared, derived traits that are unique to a single lineage
- Arise in a common ancestor

that may be

Key innovations
- Traits that allow species to exploit resources in a new way or use new habitats

may result in

Adaptive radiations
- Rapid and extensive speciation in a single lineage
- Dramatic divergence in morphology or behavior (species use a wide array of resources/habitats)

29 Bacteria and Archaea

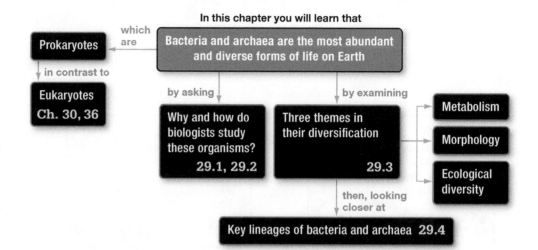

In this chapter you will learn that

Bacteria and archaea are the most abundant and diverse forms of life on Earth

which are → **Prokaryotes**

in contrast to

Eukaryotes Ch. 30, 36

by asking → **Why and how do biologists study these organisms? 29.1, 29.2**

by examining → **Three themes in their diversification 29.3** → **Metabolism** → **Morphology** → **Ecological diversity**

then, looking closer at

Key lineages of bacteria and archaea 29.4

Although this hot spring looks devoid of life, it is actually teeming with billions of bacterial and archaeal cells.

Bacteria and Archaea (usually pronounced *ar-KEE-ah*) form two of the three largest branches on the tree of life (**FIGURE 29.1**). The third major branch, or domain, consists of eukaryotes and is called the Eukarya. Virtually all members of the Bacteria and Archaea domains are unicellular, and all are prokaryotic—meaning that they lack a membrane-bound nucleus.

Although their relatively simple morphology makes bacteria and archaea appear similar to the untrained eye, in some ways they are strikingly different at the molecular level (**TABLE 29.1**). Organisms in the Bacteria and Archaea domains are distinguished by the types of molecules that make up their plasma membranes and cell walls:

- **Bacteria** have a unique compound called peptidoglycan in their cell walls (see Chapter 5).

✓ When you see this checkmark, stop and test yourself. Answers are available in Appendix A.

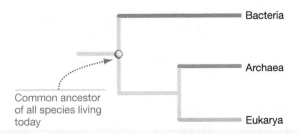

FIGURE 29.1 Bacteria, Archaea, and Eukarya Are the Three Domains of Life. Archaea are more closely related to eukaryotes than they are to bacteria.

✔**QUESTION** Was the common ancestor of all species living today prokaryotic or eukaryotic? Explain your reasoning.

- **Archaea** have unique phospholipids in their plasma membranes—the hydrocarbon tails of the phospholipids are made from isoprene (see Chapter 6).

If you were unicellular, bacteria and archaea would look as different to you as mammals and fish.

In addition, the machinery that bacteria and archaea use to process genetic information is strikingly different. More specifically, the DNA polymerases, RNA polymerases, transcription-initiation proteins, and ribosomes found in Archaea and Eukarya are distinct from those found in Bacteria and similar to each other. These differences have practical consequences: Antibiotics that poison bacterial ribosomes do not affect the ribosomes of archaea or eukaryotes. If all ribosomes were identical, these antibiotics would kill you along with the bacterial species that was supposed to be targeted.

As an introductory biology student, you may know less about bacteria and archaea than about any other group on the tree of life. Before taking this course, it's likely that you'd never even heard of the Archaea. You might be surprised to find out that biologists suspect that the first eukaryotic cells may have formed as a result of a symbiotic event between these two groups of prokaryotes. Notice in Table 29.1 that cells in the domain Eukarya share some features with both Bacteria and Archaea. Studying these shared features has helped biologists understand the early evolution of life on Earth.

This chapter's goal is to convince you that even though bacteria and archaea are tiny, they have an enormous impact on you and the planet in general. By the time you finish reading the chapter, you should understand why a researcher summed up the bacteria and archaea by claiming, "They run this joint."

29.1 Why Do Biologists Study Bacteria and Archaea?

Biologists study bacteria and archaea for the same reasons they study any organisms. First, they are intrinsically fascinating. Discoveries such as finding bacterial cells living a kilometer underground or in 95°C hot springs keep biologists awake at night, staring at the ceiling. They can't wait to get into the lab in the morning and figure out how those cells stay alive.

SUMMARY TABLE 29.1 Characteristics of Bacteria, Archaea, and Eukarya

	Bacteria	Archaea	Eukarya
DNA enclosed by a nuclear envelope? (see Chapter 7)	No	No	Yes
Circular chromosome present?	Yes (but linear in some species)	Yes	No (linear)
Organelles enclosed by membranes present? (see Chapter 7)	No	No	Yes
Rotating flagella present? (see Chapter 7)	Yes	Yes	No (flagella and cilia undulate)
Multicellular species?	No (with some exceptions)	No	Yes
Plasma membrane lipids composed of glycerol bonded to unbranched fatty acids by ester linkages? (see Chapter 6)	Yes	No (branched lipids bonded by ether linkages)	Yes
Cell walls, when present, contain peptidoglycan? (see Chapter 5)	Yes	No	No
RNA polymerase composed of >10 subunits?	No (only 5 subunits)	Yes	Yes
Translation initiated with methionine? (see Chapter 17)	No (initiated with N-formylmethionine; f-met)	Yes	Yes

✔**EXERCISE** Using the data in this table, add labeled marks to Figure 29.1 indicating where the following traits evolved: peptidoglycan in cell wall, archaeal-type plasma membrane, archaeal- and eukaryotic-type translation initiation, and nuclear envelope.

Second, there are practical benefits to understanding the species that share the planet with us. Understanding bacteria and archaea is particularly important—in terms of both understanding life on Earth and improving human health and welfare.

Biological Impact

The lineages in the domains Bacteria and Archaea are ancient, diverse, abundant, and ubiquitous. The oldest fossils of any type found to date are 3.5-billion-year-old carbon-rich deposits derived from bacteria. Because eukaryotes do not appear in the fossil record until 1.75 billion years ago, biologists infer that prokaryotes were the only form of life on Earth for at least 1.7 billion years.

Just how many bacteria and archaea are alive today? Although a mere 5000 species have been formally named and described to date, it is virtually certain that millions exist. Consider that over 1000 species of prokaryotes are living in your large intestine right now, and another 700 species are living in your mouth. Well-known microbiologist Norman Pace points out that there may be tens of millions of different insect species but notes, "If we squeeze out any one of these insects and examine its contents under the microscope, we find hundreds or thousands of distinct microbial species." Most of these **microbes** (microscopic organisms) are bacteria or archaea. Virtually all are unnamed and undescribed. If you want to discover and name new species, then study bacteria or archaea.

Abundance Besides recognizing how diverse bacteria and archaea are in terms of numbers of species, it's critical to appreciate their abundance.

- The approximately 10^{13} (10 trillion) cells in your body are outnumbered ten to one by the bacterial and archaeal cells living on and in you. You are a walking, talking habitat—one that is teeming with bacteria and archaea.

- A mere teaspoon of good-quality soil contains *billions* of microbial cells, most of which are bacteria and archaea.

- In sheer numbers, species in a lineage of marine archaea may be the most successful organisms on Earth. Biologists routinely find these cells at concentrations of over 10,000 individuals per milliliter in most of the world's oceans. At these concentrations, one liter of seawater contains a population equivalent to that of the largest human cities. Yet this lineage was not described until the early 1990s.

- Recent research has found enormous numbers of bacterial and especially archaeal cells in rocks and sediments as much as 1600 meters underneath the world's oceans. Although recently discovered, the bacteria and archaea living under the ocean may make up 10 percent of the world's total mass of living material.

- Biologists estimate the total number of individual bacteria and archaea alive today at over 5×10^{30}. If they were lined up end to end, these cells would make a chain longer than the Milky Way galaxy. They contain 50 percent of all the carbon and 90 percent of all the nitrogen and phosphorus found in organisms.

In terms of the total volume of living material on our planet, bacteria and archaea are dominant life-forms.

Habitat Diversity Bacteria and archaea are found almost everywhere. They live in environments as unusual as oxygen-free mud, hot springs, and salt flats. In seawater they are found from the surface to depths of 10,000 meters (m), and at temperatures over 120°C (well above water's boiling point) near submarine volcanoes.

Although there are far more prokaryotes than eukaryotes, much more is known about eukaryotic diversity than about prokaryotic diversity. Researchers who study prokaryotic diversity are exploring one of the most wide-open frontiers in all of science. So little is known about the extent of these domains that recent collecting expeditions have turned up entirely new **phyla** (singular: **phylum**). These are names given to major lineages within each domain. To a biologist, this achievement is equivalent to the sudden discovery of a new group of eukaryotes as distinctive as flowering plants or animals with backbones.

The physical world has been explored and mapped, and many of the larger plants and animals are named. But in **microbiology**—the study of organisms that can be seen only with the aid of a microscope—this is an age of exploration and discovery.

Some Microbes Thrive in Extreme Environments

Bacteria or archaea that live in high-salt, high-temperature, low-temperature, or high-pressure habitats are **extremophiles** ("extreme-lovers"). Studying them has been extraordinarily fruitful for understanding the tree of life, developing industrial applications, and exploring the structure and function of enzymes.

As an example of these habitats, consider hydrothermal vents at the bottom of the ocean, where water as hot as 300°C emerges and mixes with 4°C seawater. At locations like these, archaea are abundant forms of life.

Researchers recently discovered an archaeon that grows so close to these hydrothermal vents that its surroundings are at 121°C—a record for life at high temperature. This organism can live and grow in water that is heated past its boiling point (100°C) and at pressures that would instantly destroy a human. Since high temperature breaks non-covalent bonds holding macromolecules together, extreme heat usually denatures proteins, makes membranes leaky, and separates the strands of the DNA double helix. Biologists are intrigued by how these unusual archaeal cells can thrive under such extreme conditions.

Other discovered bacteria and archaea can grow

- at a pH less than 1.0;

- at temperatures of 0°C under Antarctic ice;

- in water that is virtually saturated with salt (**FIGURE 29.2**).

Extremophiles have become a hot area of research. The genomes of a wide array of extremophiles have been sequenced, and expeditions regularly seek to characterize new species. Why?

- *Origin of life* Based on models of conditions that prevailed early in Earth's history, it appears likely that the first forms of life lived at high temperature and pressure in environments

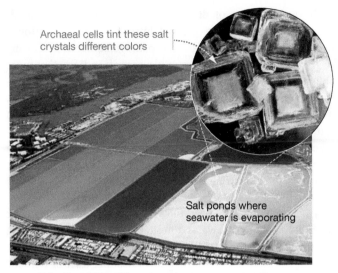

Archaeal cells tint these salt crystals different colors

Salt ponds where seawater is evaporating

FIGURE 29.2 Some Archaeal Cells Live in High-Salt Habitats. The evaporating water is colored red by these photosynthetic cells.

that lacked oxygen—conditions that humans would call extreme. Thus, understanding extremophiles may help explain how life on Earth began.

- *Extraterrestrial life?*   In a similar vein, many astrobiologists ("space-biologists") use extremophiles as model organisms in the search for extraterrestrial life. The idea is that if bacteria and archaea can thrive in extreme habitats on Earth, cells might possibly be found in similar environments on other planets or moons of planets.

- *Commercial applications*   Because enzymes that function at extreme temperatures and pressures are useful in many industrial processes, extremophiles are of commercial interest as well. Recall that *Taq* polymerase—a DNA polymerase that is stable up to 95°C—is used to run the polymerase chain reaction (PCR) in research and commercial settings (see Chapter 20). This enzyme was isolated from a bacterium called *Thermus aquaticus* ("hot water"), which was discovered in a hot spring in Yellowstone National Park.

Bacteria and archaea may be small, but they thrive in an amazing range of conditions.

Medical Importance

The first paper documenting that an archaeon was associated with a human disease—a dental condition called periodontitis—was published in 2004. But biologists have been studying disease-causing bacteria for over a century.

Of the thousands of bacterial species living in and on your body, only a tiny fraction can disrupt normal body functions enough to cause illness. Bacteria that cause disease are said to be **pathogenic** (literally, "disease-producing"). Pathogenic bacteria have been responsible for some of the most devastating epidemics in human history.

TABLE 29.2 lists some of the bacteria that cause illness in humans. Here are the important things to note:

- Pathogenic forms come from several different lineages in the domain Bacteria.

TABLE 29.2 Some Bacteria That Cause Illness in Humans

Lineage	Species	Tissues Affected	Disease
Firmicutes	*Clostridium tetani*	Wounds, nervous system	Tetanus
	Staphylococcus aureus	Skin, urogenital canal	Acne, boils, impetigo, toxic shock syndrome
	Streptococcus pneumoniae	Respiratory tract	Pneumonia
	Streptococcus pyogenes	Respiratory tract	Strep throat, scarlet fever
Spirochaetes	*Borrelia burgdorferi*	Skin and nerves	Lyme disease
	Treponema pallidum	Urogenital canal	Syphilis
Actinobacteria	*Mycobacterium tuberculosis*	Respiratory tract	Tuberculosis
	Mycobacterium leprae	Skin and nerves	Leprosy
	Propionibacterium acnes	Skin	Acne
Chlamydiales	*Chlamydia trachomatis*	Urogenital canal	Genital tract infection
ε-Proteobacteria	*Helicobacter pylori*	Stomach	Ulcer
β-Proteobacteria	*Neisseria gonorrhoeae*	Urogenital canal	Gonorrhea
γ-Proteobacteria	*Haemophilus influenzae*	Ear canal, nervous system	Ear infections, meningitis
	Pseudomonas aeruginosa	Urogenital canal, eyes, ear canal, lungs	Infections of eye, ear, urinary tract, lungs
	Salmonella enterica	Gastrointestinal tract	Food poisoning
	Yersinia pestis	Lymph and blood	Plague

- Pathogenic bacteria tend to affect tissues at the entry points to the body, such as wounds or pores in the skin, the respiratory and gastrointestinal tracts, and the urogenital canal.

Koch's Postulates   Robert Koch was the first person to establish a link between a particular species of bacterium and a specific disease. When Koch began his work on the nature of disease in the late 1800s, microscopists had confirmed the existence of the particle-like organisms people now call bacteria, and Louis Pasteur had shown that bacteria and other microorganisms are responsible for spoiling milk, wine, broth, and other foods. Koch hypothesized that bacteria might also be responsible for causing infectious diseases, which spread by being passed from an infected individual to an uninfected individual.

Koch set out to test this hypothesis by identifying the organism that causes anthrax. Anthrax is a disease of cattle and other grazing mammals that can result in fatal blood poisoning. The disease also occurs infrequently in humans and mice.

To establish a causative link between a specific microbe and a specific disease, Koch proposed that four criteria had to be met:

1. The microbe must be present in individuals suffering from the disease and absent from healthy individuals. By careful microscopy, Koch was able to show that the bacterium *Bacillus anthracis* was always present in the blood of cattle suffering from anthrax, but absent from healthy individuals.

2. The organism must be isolated and grown in a pure culture away from the host organism. Koch was able to grow pure colonies of *B. anthracis* in glass dishes on a nutrient medium, using gelatin as a substrate.

3. If organisms from the pure culture are injected into a healthy experimental animal, the disease symptoms should appear. Koch demonstrated this crucial causative link in mice injected with *B. anthracis*. The symptoms of anthrax infection appeared and then the infected mice died.

4. The organism should be isolated from the diseased experimental animal, again grown in pure culture, and demonstrated by its size, shape, and color to be the same as the original organism. Koch did this by purifying *B. anthracis* from the blood of diseased experimental mice.

These criteria, now called **Koch's postulates,** are still used to confirm a causative link between new diseases and a suspected infectious agent. Microbiologists now recognize that many bacteria cannot be grown in culture, so they use other means of detection for those organisms.

The Germ Theory   Koch's experimental results were the first test of the **germ theory of disease.**

- The pattern component of this theory is that certain diseases are infectious—meaning that they can be passed from person to person.

- The process responsible for this pattern is the transmission and growth of certain bacteria and viruses.

Viruses are acellular particles that parasitize cells (see Chapter 36).

The germ theory of disease laid the foundation for modern medicine. Initially its greatest impact was on sanitation—efforts to prevent transmission of pathogenic bacteria. During the American Civil War, for example, records indicate that more soldiers died of bacterial infections contracted from drinking water contaminated with human feces than from wounds in battle. Also during that conflict it was common for surgeons to sharpen their scalpels on their shoe leather, after walking in horse manure.

Fortunately, improvements in sanitation and nutrition have caused dramatic reductions in mortality rates due to infectious diseases in the industrialized countries.

What Makes Some Bacterial Cells Pathogenic?   Virulence, or the ability to cause disease, is a heritable trait that varies among individuals in a population. Most *Escherichia coli*, for example, are harmless inhabitants of the gastrointestinal tract of humans and other mammals. But some *E. coli* cells cause potentially fatal food poisoning.

What makes some cells of the same species pathogenic, while others are harmless? Biologists have answered this question for *E. coli* by sequencing the entire genome of a harmless lab strain and the pathogenic strain called O157:H7, which is harmful to humans. The genome of the pathogenic strain is slightly larger because it has acquired virulence genes, including one coding for a protein **toxin.** After entering a host cell, this toxin binds to ribosomes and inhibits protein synthesis, killing the host cells. Because of key differences between the ribosomes of bacteria and eukaryotic cells, only host-cell protein synthesis is blocked by the toxin. Cells lining the blood vessels near the host's intestinal epithelium are most affected by the toxin, and the resulting damage leads to bloody diarrhea and possible death. If sanitation is poor, the pathogenic bacteria are likely to infect many new hosts.

Similar types of studies are identifying the genes responsible for virulence in a wide array of pathogenic bacteria.

The Past, Present, and Future of Antibiotics   **Antibiotics** are molecules that kill bacteria or stop them from growing. They are produced naturally by a wide array of soil-dwelling bacteria and fungi. In these environments, antibiotics are hypothesized to help cells reduce competition for nutrients and other resources.

The discovery of antibiotics in 1928, their development over subsequent decades, and widespread use starting in the late 1940s gave physicians effective tools to combat many bacterial infections.

Unfortunately, extensive use of antibiotics in the late twentieth century in clinics and animal feed led to the evolution of drug-resistant strains of pathogenic bacteria. One study found that there are now soil-dwelling bacteria in natural environments that—far from being killed by antibiotics—actually use them as food.

Coping with antibiotic resistance in pathogenic bacteria has become a great challenge of modern medicine. Some researchers even claim that humans may be entering the "post-antibiotic era" in medicine.

New research indicates that bacteria have another advantage: They usually grow as **biofilms,** dense bacterial colonies enmeshed

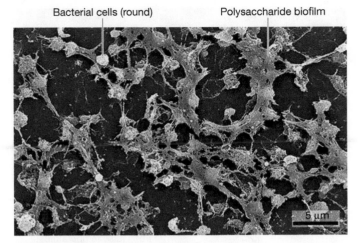

FIGURE 29.3 Biofilm Growing Inside a Catheter. This micrograph shows *Staphylococcus aureus* cells growing inside a catheter—a tube inserted into a body so that fluids can be withdrawn or injected. Bacterial communities that secrete polysaccharides and adhere to surfaces are sometimes more resistant to antibiotics.

FIGURE 29.4 Bacteria and Archaea Can Play a Role in Cleaning Up Pollution. These clean-up workers are spraying nitrogenous nutrients to encourage bacterial and archaeal growth following the 1989 *Exxon Valdez* oil spill in Alaska.

in a polysaccharide-rich matrix that helps shield the bacteria from antibiotics. Antibiotic-resistant biofilms on medical devices such as catheters are a growing problem in hospitals (**FIGURE 29.3**).

Role in Bioremediation

Bacteria are often in the news because of their dire medical effects. However, only a tiny proportion of bacteria and archaea actually cause disease in humans or other organisms. In the vast majority of cases, bacteria and archaea either have no direct impact on humans or are beneficial. For example, microbes play an important role in wastewater treatment efforts, and researchers are using bacteria and archaea to clean up sites polluted with organic solvents—an effort called **bioremediation.**

Throughout the industrialized world, some of the most serious pollutants in soils, rivers, and ponds consist of organic compounds that were originally used as solvents or fuels but leaked or were spilled into the environment. Most of these compounds are highly hydrophobic. Because they do not dissolve in water, they tend to accumulate in sediments. If the compounds are subsequently ingested by burrowing worms or clams or other organisms, they can be passed along to fish, insects, humans, birds, and other species.

At moderate to high concentrations, these pollutants are toxic to eukaryotes. Petroleum from oil spills and compounds that contain ring structures and chlorine atoms, such as the family of compounds called dioxins, are particularly notorious because of their toxicity to humans.

Fortunately, naturally existing populations of bacteria and archaea can grow in spills and degrade the toxins. This growth can be enhanced using two complementary bioremediation strategies:

1. *Fertilizing contaminated sites to encourage the growth of existing bacteria and archaea that degrade toxic compounds.* After several oil spills, researchers added nitrogen to affected sites as a fertilizer (**FIGURE 29.4**). Dramatic increases

occurred in the growth of bacteria and archaea that use hydrocarbons in cellular respiration, probably because the cells used the added nitrogen to synthesize enzymes and other key compounds. In at least some cases, the fertilized shorelines cleaned up much faster than unfertilized sites.

2. *"Seeding," or adding, specific species of bacteria and archaea to contaminated sites.* Seeding shows promise of alleviating pollution in some situations. For example, researchers have recently discovered bacteria that are able to render certain chlorinated, ring-containing compounds harmless. Instead of being poisoned by the pollutants, these bacteria use the chlorinated compounds as electron acceptors during cellular respiration. In at least some cases, the by-product is dechlorinated and nontoxic to humans and other eukaryotes.

To follow up on these discoveries, researchers are now growing the bacteria in quantity, to test the hypothesis that seeding can speed the rate of decomposition in contaminated sediments. Initial reports suggest that seeding may help clean up at least some polluted sites.

29.2 How Do Biologists Study Bacteria and Archaea?

Biologists' understanding of the domains Bacteria and Archaea is advancing more rapidly right now than at any time during the past 100 years—and perhaps faster than our understanding of any other lineages on the tree of life.

As an introduction to the domains Bacteria and Archaea, let's examine a few of the techniques that biologists use to answer questions about them. Some of these research strategies have been used since bacteria were first discovered; some were invented less than 10 years ago.

Using Enrichment Cultures

Which species of bacteria and archaea are present at a particular location, and what do they use as food? To answer questions like these, biologists rely heavily on their ability to culture organisms in the lab. Of the 5000 species of bacteria and archaea described to date, almost all were discovered when they were isolated from natural habitats and grown under controlled conditions in the laboratory.

One classical technique for isolating new types of bacteria and archaea is called **enrichment culture.** Enrichment cultures are based on establishing a specified set of growing conditions—temperature, lighting, substrate, types of available food, and so on. Cells that thrive under the specified conditions increase in numbers enough to be isolated and studied in detail.

To appreciate how this strategy works in practice, consider research on bacteria that live deep below Earth's surface. One study began with samples of rock and fluid from drilling operations in Virginia and Colorado. The samples came from sedimentary rocks at depths ranging from 860 to 2800 meters below the surface, where temperatures are between 42°C and 85°C. The questions posed in the study were simple: Is anything alive down there? If so, what do the organisms use to fuel cellular respiration?

The research team hypothesized that if organisms were living deep below the surface of the Earth, the cells might use hydrogen molecules (H_2) as an electron donor and the ferric ion (Fe^{3+}) as an electron acceptor (**FIGURE 29.5**). Recall that most eukaryotes use sugars as electron donors and use oxygen as an electron acceptor during cellular respiration (see Chapter 9). Fe^{3+} is the oxidized form of iron, and it is abundant in the rocks the biologists collected from great depths. It exists at great depths below the surface in the form of ferric oxyhydroxide, $Fe(OH)_3$. The researchers predicted that if an organism in the samples reduced the ferric ions during cellular respiration, then a black, oxidized, and magnetic mineral called magnetite (Fe_3O_4) would start appearing in the cultures as a by-product of cellular respiration.

What did their enrichment cultures produce? In some cultures, a black compound began to appear within a week. A variety of tests confirmed that the black substance was indeed magnetite. As the "Results" section of Figure 29.5 shows, microscopy revealed the organisms themselves—previously undiscovered bacteria. Because they grow only when incubated at 45°C–75°C, these organisms are considered **thermophiles** ("heat-lovers"). The discovery was spectacular—it was one of the first studies demonstrating that Earth's crust is teeming with organisms to depths of over a mile below the surface. Enrichment culture continues to be a productive way to isolate and characterize new species of bacteria and archaea.

Using Metagenomics

Researchers estimate that of all the bacteria and archaea living today, less than 1 percent have been grown in culture. To augment research based on enrichment cultures, researchers are

---

RESEARCH

QUESTION: Can bacteria live a mile below Earth's surface?

HYPOTHESIS: Bacteria are capable of cellular respiration deep below Earth's surface by using H_2 as an electron donor and Fe^{3+} as an electron acceptor.

NULL HYPOTHESIS: Bacteria from this environment are not capable of using H_2 as an electron donor and Fe^{3+} as an electron acceptor.

EXPERIMENTAL SETUP:

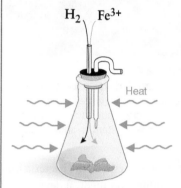

H_2 Fe^{3+}

Heat

Rock and fluid samples

1. Prepare enrichment culture abundant in H_2 and Fe^{3+}; raise temperatures above 45°C.

2. Add rock and fluid samples extracted from drilling operations at depths of about 1000 m below Earth's surface.

PREDICTION: Black, magnetic grains of magnetite (Fe_3O_4) will accumulate because Fe^{3+} is reduced by growing cells and shed as a waste product. Cells will be visible.

PREDICTION OF NULL HYPOTHESIS: No magnetite will appear. No cells will grow.

RESULTS: Cells are visible, and magnetite is detectable.

1 µm

CONCLUSION: At least one bacterial species that can live deep below Earth's surface grew in this enrichment culture. Different culture conditions might result in the enrichment of different species present in the same sample.

FIGURE 29.5 Enrichment Cultures Isolate Large Populations of Cells That Grow under Specific Conditions.

✔**QUESTION** Suppose no organisms had grown in this culture. Explain why the lack of growth would be either strong or weak evidence on the question of whether organisms live a mile below the Earth's surface.

SOURCE: Liu, S. V., J. Zhou, C. Zhang, et al. 1997. Thermophilic Fe(III)-reducing bacteria from the deep subsurface: the evolutionary implications. *Science* 277: 1106–1109.

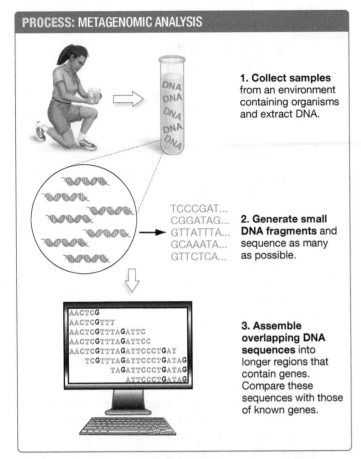

PROCESS: METAGENOMIC ANALYSIS

1. Collect samples from an environment containing organisms and extract DNA.

TCCCGAT...
CGGATAG...
GTTATTTA...
GCAAATA...
GTTCTCA...

2. Generate small DNA fragments and sequence as many as possible.

AACTCG
AACTCGTTT
AACTCGTTTAGATTC
AACTCGTTTAGATTCC
AACTCGTTTAGATTCCCTGAT
    TCGTTTAGATTCCCTGATAG
      TAGATTCCCTGATAG
      ATTCCCTGATAG

3. Assemble overlapping DNA sequences into longer regions that contain genes. Compare these sequences with those of known genes.

FIGURE 29.6 Metagenomics Allows Researchers to Identify Species That Have Never Been Seen. Metagenomic analysis is used to generate DNA sequences from an environmental sample. That information can then be used to identify novel species and investigate biological processes.

employing a technique called **metagenomics** or **environmental sequencing** (see Chapter 21). Metagenomics is employed in part to document the presence of bacteria and archaea in an environmental sample that cannot be grown in culture. It is based on extracting and sequencing much of the DNA from a sample and then identifying species and biochemical pathways by comparing the DNA sequences with those of known genes. **FIGURE 29.6** outlines the steps performed in a metagenomics study.

Metagenomic analysis allows biologists to rapidly identify and characterize organisms that have never been seen. The technique has revealed huge new branches on the tree of life and produced revolutionary data on the habitats where bacteria and archaea are found.

In one recent study biologists extracted DNA from 125 human fecal samples and generated over 500 billion base pairs of sequence, over 150 times more than the entire human genome. The results they obtained are fascinating:

- In total, the samples contained about 1000 different species of bacteria. Some species were found in most of the samples while others were found in only a few of the humans sampled;

- the vast majority of bacterial species identified were from three phyla: Bacteroidetes, Firmicutes, and Actinobacteria;

- the identified bacterial genes that were shared by all of the human subjects suggest that bacteria play important roles in human physiology, including digestion of complex carbohydrates and synthesis of essential amino acids and vitamins.

Results like these make it clear that humans harbor a diverse ecosystem of symbiotic bacteria. Some bacteria may make us sick, but we depend on many others to stay healthy.

In combination with **direct sequencing**—a technique based on isolating and sequencing a specific gene from organisms found in a particular habitat—metagenomics is revolutionizing biologists' understanding of bacterial and archaeal diversity.

Evaluating Molecular Phylogenies

To put data from enrichment culture and metagenomic studies into context, biologists depend on the accurate placement of species on phylogenetic trees. Recall that phylogenetic trees illustrate the evolutionary relationships among species and lineages (see Chapter 1 and **BioSkills 7** in Appendix B). They are a pictorial summary of which species are more closely or distantly related to others.

Some of the most useful phylogenetic trees for the Bacteria and the Archaea have been based on studies of the RNA molecules found in the small subunit of ribosomes, or what biologists call 16S and 18S RNA. (See Chapter 17 for more information on the structure and function of ribosomes.) In the late 1960s Carl Woese and colleagues began a massive effort to determine and compare the base sequences of 16S and 18S RNA molecules from a wide array of species. The result of their analysis was the **tree of life,** illustrated in Figure 29.1.

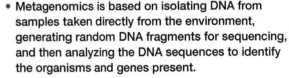
check your understanding

If you understand that . . .

- Enrichment cultures isolate cells that grow in response to specific conditions. They create an abundant sample of bacteria that thrive under particular conditions, allowing further study.
- Metagenomics is based on isolating DNA from samples taken directly from the environment, generating random DNA fragments for sequencing, and then analyzing the DNA sequences to identify the organisms and genes present.

✔ **You should be able to . . .**

1. Design an enrichment culture that would isolate species that could be used to clean up oil spills.
2. Outline a study designed to identify the bacterial and archaeal species present in a soil sample near the biology building on your campus.

Answers are available in Appendix A.

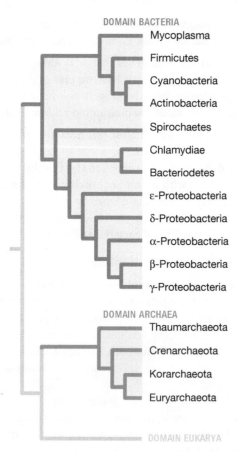

DOMAIN BACTERIA
- Mycoplasma
- Firmicutes
- Cyanobacteria
- Actinobacteria
- Spirochaetes
- Chlamydiae
- Bacteriodetes
- ε-Proteobacteria
- δ-Proteobacteria
- α-Proteobacteria
- β-Proteobacteria
- γ-Proteobacteria

DOMAIN ARCHAEA
- Thaumarchaeota
- Crenarchaeota
- Korarchaeota
- Euryarchaeota

DOMAIN EUKARYA

FIGURE 29.7 Phylogeny of Some Major Lineages in Bacteria and Archaea.

Woese's tree is now considered a classic result. Before its publication, biologists thought that the major division among organisms was between prokaryotes and eukaryotes. But based on data from ribosomal RNA molecules, the major divisions of life-forms are actually the Bacteria, Archaea, and Eukarya. Tracing the early evolutionary history of these domains is extremely difficult since the events distinguishing the lineages took place so long ago. In addition, lateral gene transfer (described in Chapter 21) has blurred the boundaries of the domains. However, recent studies suggest that Eukarya may have formed from a symbiosis between an archaeal cell and a bacterial cell. Traits of both lineages are found within Eukarya (see Chapter 30).

More recent analyses of morphological and molecular characteristics have succeeded in identifying a large series of monophyletic groups within the domains. Recall that a **monophyletic group** consists of an ancestral population and all of its descendants. Monophyletic groups can also be called clades or lineages.

The phylogenetic tree in **FIGURE 29.7** summarizes recent results but is still considered highly provisional. Work on molecular phylogenies continues at a brisk pace. Section 29.4 explores some of these lineages in detail, but for now let's turn to the question of how all this diversification took place.

29.3 What Themes Occur in the Diversification of Bacteria and Archaea?

At first, the diversity of bacteria and archaea can seem almost overwhelming. To make sense of the variation among lineages and species, biologists focus on two themes in diversification: morphology and metabolism. Regarding metabolism, the key question is which molecules are used as food. Bacteria and archaea are capable of living in a wide array of environments because they vary in cell structure and in how they make a living.

Morphological Diversity

Because we humans are so large, it is hard for us to appreciate the morphological diversity that exists among bacteria and archaea. To us, they all look small and similar. But at the scale of a bacterium or archaean, different species are wildly diverse in morphology.

Size, Shape, and Motility   To appreciate how diverse these organisms are in terms of morphology, consider bacteria alone:

- *Size*   Bacterial cells range in size from the smallest of all free-living cells—bacteria called mycoplasmas with volumes as small as 0.15 μm^3—to the largest bacterium known, *Thiomargarita namibiensis*, which has volumes as large as 200 × 10^6 μm^3. Over a billion *Mycoplasma* cells could fit inside an individual *T. namibiensis* (**FIGURE 29.8a**).

- *Shape*   Bacterial cells range in shape from filaments, spheres, rods, and chains to spirals (**FIGURE 29.8b**).

- *Motility*   Many bacterial cells are motile; their swimming movements are powered by rotating flagella. Depending on the direction of rotation, cells either swim ahead or tumble, which allows them to change direction. Gliding movement, which enables cells to creep along a surface, also occurs in several groups, though the molecular mechanism responsible for this form of motility is still unknown (**FIGURE 29.8c**).

Cell-Wall Composition   For single-celled organisms, the composition of the plasma membrane and cell wall are particularly important. The introduction to this chapter highlights the dramatic differences between the plasma membranes and cell walls of bacteria versus archaea.

Within bacteria having cell walls, biologists distinguish two general types of wall using a dyeing system called the **Gram stain.** As **FIGURE 29.9a** shows, Gram-positive cells look purple but Gram-negative cells look pink.

At the molecular level, most cells that are **Gram-positive** have a plasma membrane surrounded by a cell wall with extensive peptidoglycan (**FIGURE 29.9b**). You might recall that peptidoglycan is a complex substance composed of carbohydrate strands that are cross-linked by short chains of amino acids (see Chapter 5). Most cells that are **Gram-negative,** in contrast, have a plasma

(a) Size varies.

Most bacteria are about 1 μm in diameter, but some are much larger.

Smallest (*Mycoplasma mycoides*)

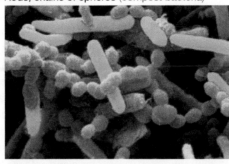

0.3 μm

Compare sizes

100 μm

Largest (*Thiomargarita namibiensis*)

(b) Shape varies...

... from rods to spheres to spirals. In some species, cells adhere to form chains.

Rods, chains of spheres (compost bacteria)

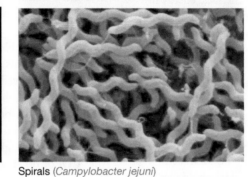

Spirals (*Campylobacter jejuni*)

(c) Motility varies.

Some bacteria are nonmotile, but swimming and gliding are common.

Swimming (*Pseudomonas aeruginosa*)

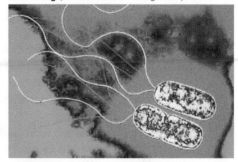

Gliding (*Oscillatoria limosa*)

FIGURE 29.8 Morphological Diversity among Bacteria Is Extensive. Some of the cells in these micrographs have been colorized to make them more visible.

membrane surrounded by a cell wall that has two components—a thin gelatinous layer containing peptidoglycan and an outer phospholipid bilayer (**FIGURE 29.9c**).

Analyzing cell cultures with the Gram stain can be an important preliminary step in treating bacterial infections. Because they contain so much peptidoglycan, Gram-positive cells may respond to treatment by penicillin-like drugs that disrupt peptidoglycan synthesis. Gram-negative cells, in contrast, are more

likely to be affected by erythromycin or other types of drugs that poison bacterial ribosomes.

To summarize, members of the Bacteria and the Archaea are remarkably diverse in their overall size, shape, and motility as well as in the composition of their cell walls and plasma membranes. But when asked to name the innovations that were most responsible for the diversification of these two domains, biologists do not point to their morphological diversity. Instead, they

(a) Gram-positive cells stain more than Gram-negative cells.

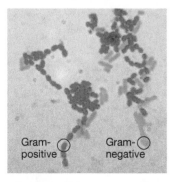

Gram-positive   Gram-negative

(b) Gram-positive cell wall

Cell wall

Polysaccharides

Peptidoglycan

Plasma membrane

Protein

(c) Gram-negative cell wall

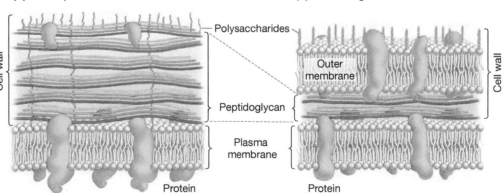

Outer membrane

Cell wall

Protein

FIGURE 29.9 Gram Staining Distinguishes Two Types of Cell Walls in Bacteria. Cells with extensive peptidoglycan retain a large amount of stain and look purple; others retain little stain and look pink, as can be seen in part (a).

point to metabolic diversity—variation in the chemical reactions that go on inside these cells.

Metabolic Diversity

The most important thing to remember about bacteria and archaea is how diverse they are in the types of compounds they can use as food. Bacteria and archaea are the masters of metabolism. Taken together, they can subsist on almost anything—from hydrogen molecules to crude oil. Bacteria and archaea look small and relatively simple to us in their morphology, but their biochemical capabilities are dazzling.

Just how varied are bacteria and archaea when it comes to making a living? To appreciate the answer, recall that all organisms have two fundamental nutritional needs—acquiring chemical energy in the form of adenosine triphosphate (ATP) and obtaining molecules with carbon–carbon bonds that can be used as building blocks for the synthesis of fatty acids, proteins, DNA, RNA, and other large, complex compounds required by the cell.

Bacteria and archaea produce ATP in three ways:

1. **Phototrophs** ("light-feeders") use light energy to excite electrons. ATP is produced by photophosphorylation.

2. **Chemoorganotrophs** oxidize organic molecules with high potential energy, such as sugars. ATP may be produced by cellular respiration—with sugars serving as electron donors—or via fermentation pathways (see Chapter 9).

3. **Chemolithotrophs** ("rock-feeders") oxidize inorganic molecules with high potential energy, such as ammonia (NH_3) or methane (CH_4). ATP is produced by cellular respiration, and inorganic compounds serve as the electron donor.

Bacteria and archaea fulfill their second nutritional need—obtaining building-block compounds with carbon–carbon bonds—in two ways:

1. By synthesizing their own compounds from simple starting materials such as CO_2 and CH_4. Organisms that manufacture their own building-block compounds are termed **autotrophs** ("self-feeders").

2. By absorbing ready-to-use organic compounds from their environment. Organisms that acquire building-block compounds from other organisms are called **heterotrophs** ("other-feeders").

Because there are three distinct ways of producing ATP and two general mechanisms for obtaining carbon, there are a total of six methods for producing ATP and obtaining carbon. The names that biologists use for organisms that employ these six "feeding strategies" are given in **TABLE 29.3**.

Of the six possible ways of producing ATP and obtaining carbon, just two are observed among eukaryotes. But bacteria and archaea do them all. In addition, certain species can switch among modes of living, depending on environmental conditions. In their metabolism, eukaryotes are simple compared with bacteria and archaea. ✔ If you understand the essence of metabolic diversity in bacteria and archaea, you should be able to match the six example species described in **TABLE 29.4** to the appropriate category in Table 29.3.

What makes this remarkable diversity possible? Bacteria and archaea have evolved dozens of variations on the basic processes of respiration and photosynthesis (see Chapter 9). They use compounds with high potential energy to produce ATP via cellular respiration (electron transport chains) or fermentation, they use light to produce high-energy electrons, and they reduce carbon from CO_2 or other sources to produce sugars or other building-block molecules with carbon–carbon bonds.

The story of bacteria and archaea can be boiled down to two sentences: The basic chemistry required for photosynthesis, cellular respiration, and fermentation originated in these lineages. Then the evolution of variations on each of these processes allowed prokaryotes to diversify into millions of species that occupy diverse habitats. Let's take a closer look.

Producing ATP Through Cellular Respiration: Variation in Electron Donors and Acceptors Millions of bacterial, archaeal, and eukaryotic species—including animals and some plants—are chemoorganotrophs. These organisms obtain the energy required to make ATP by breaking down organic compounds such as sugars, starch, or fatty acids.

SUMMARY TABLE 29.3 **Six General Methods for Obtaining Energy and Carbon–Carbon Bonds**

		Source of C–C Bonds (for synthesis of complex organic compounds)	
		Autotrophs: self-synthesized from CO_2, CH_4, or other simple molecules	**Hetero**trophs: from molecules produced by other organisms
Source of Energy (for synthesis of ATP)	**Photo**trophs: from sunlight	photoautotrophs	photoheterotrophs
	Chemoorganotrophs: from organic molecules	chemoorganoautotrophs	chemoorganoheterotrophs
	Chemolithotrophs: from inorganic molecules	chemolitho[auto]trophs	chemolithotrophic heterotrophs

TABLE 29.4 Six Examples of Metabolic Diversity

Example	How ATP Is Produced	How Building-Block Molecules Are Synthesized
Cyanobacteria	via oxygenic photosynthesis	from CO_2 via the Calvin cycle
Clostridium aceticum	via fermentation of glucose	from CO_2 via reactions called the acetyl-CoA pathway
Ammonia-oxidizing archaea (e.g., *Nitrosopumilus* sp.)	via cellular respiration, using ammonia (NH_3) as an electron donor	from CO_2 via the Calvin cycle
Helicobacteria	via anoxygenic photosynthesis	absorb carbon-containing building-block molecules from the environment
Escherichia coli	via fermentation of organic compounds or cellular respiration, using organic compounds as electron donors	absorb carbon-containing building-block molecules from the environment
Beggiatoa	via cellular respiration, using hydrogen sulfide (H_2S) as an electron donor	absorb carbon-containing building-block molecules from the environment

Cellular enzymes can strip electrons from organic molecules that have high potential energy and then transfer these high-energy electrons to the electron carriers NADH and $FADH_2$ (see Chapter 9). These compounds feed electrons to an electron transport chain (ETC), where electrons are stepped down from a high-energy state to a low-energy state (**FIGURE 29.10a**). In eukaryotic cells the ETC is located in the highly folded inner mitochondrial membrane. In bacteria and archaea, this membrane is the plasma membrane.

The energy that is released allows components of the ETC to generate a proton gradient across the plasma membrane (**FIGURE 29.10b**). The resulting flow of protons back through the enzyme ATP synthase results in the production of ATP, via the process called chemiosmosis.

The essence of this process, called **cellular respiration,** is that a molecule with high potential energy serves as an original electron donor and is oxidized, while a molecule with low potential energy serves as a final electron acceptor and becomes reduced. The potential energy difference between the electron donor and electron acceptor is eventually transformed into chemical energy in the form of ATP or is used for other processes (see Chapter 9).

(a) Model of Electron Transport Chain (ETC)

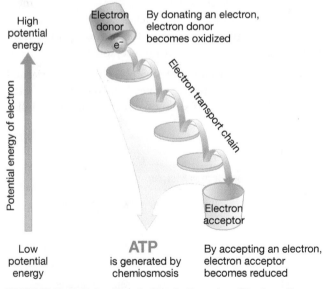

(b) ETC generates proton gradient across plasma membrane.

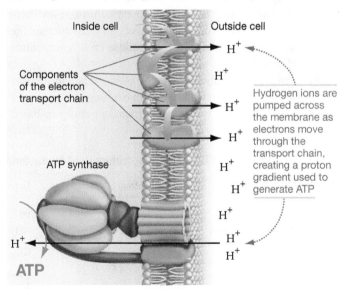

FIGURE 29.10 Cellular Respiration Is Based on Electron Transport Chains. Protons may diffuse away from the cell but a gradient will still form.

✔**EXERCISE** In part (a), add the chemical formula for a specific electron donor, electron acceptor, and reduced by-product for a species of bacteria or archaea. Then write in the electron donor, electron acceptor, and reduced by-product observed in humans.

Most eukaryotes carry out aerobic respiration:

- Organic compounds with high potential energy—often glucose—serve as the original electron donor. When cellular respiration is complete, glucose is completely oxidized to CO_2, which is given off as a by-product.

- Oxygen is the final electron acceptor, and water is also produced as a by-product.

Many bacteria and archaea also rely on these molecules.

It is common, however, to find bacteria and archaea that employ an electron donor other than sugars and an electron acceptor other than oxygen during cellular respiration. These species produce by-products other than carbon dioxide and water (**TABLE 29.5**):

- Molecules with high potential energy serve as electron donors. The substances used as electron donors range from hydrogen molecules (H_2) and hydrogen sulfide (H_2S) to ammonia (NH_3) and methane (CH_4).

- Compounds with relatively low potential energy—including sulfate (SO_4^{2-}), nitrate (NO_3^-), carbon dioxide (CO_2), or ferric ions (Fe^{3+})—act as electron acceptors.

It is only a slight exaggeration to claim that researchers have found bacterial and archaeal species that can use almost any compound with relatively high potential energy as an electron donor and almost any compound with relatively low potential energy as an electron acceptor.

Because the electron donors and electron acceptors used by bacteria and archaea are so diverse, one of the first questions biologists ask about a species is whether it undergoes cellular respiration—and if so, how. The best way to answer this question is through the enrichment culture technique introduced in Section 29.2. Recall that in an enrichment culture, researchers supply specific electron donors and electron acceptors in the medium and try to isolate cells that can use those compounds to support growth.

The remarkable metabolic diversity of bacteria and archaea explains why they play such a key role in cleaning up some types of pollution. Species that use organic solvents or petroleum-based fuels as electron donors or electron acceptors may excrete waste products that are less toxic than the original compounds.

Producing ATP via Fermentation: Variation in Substrates One strategy for making ATP that does not involve electron transport chains is called **fermentation** (see Chapter 9). In fermentation, no outside electron acceptor is used.

Because fermentation is a much less efficient way to make ATP compared with cellular respiration, in many species it occurs as an alternative metabolic strategy when no electron acceptors are available to make cellular respiration possible. In other species, fermentation does not occur at all. But in many bacteria and archaea, fermentation is the only way that cells make ATP.

Although some eukaryotic organisms can ferment glucose to ethanol or lactic acid (see Chapter 9), some bacteria and archaea are capable of using other organic compounds as the starting point for fermentation. Bacteria and archaea that produce ATP via fermentation are still classified as organotrophs, but they are much more diverse in the substrates used. For example:

- The bacterium *Clostridium aceticum* can ferment ethanol, acetate, and fatty acids as well as glucose.

- Other species of *Clostridium* ferment complex carbohydrates (including cellulose or starch), proteins, purines, or amino acids. Species that ferment amino acids produce by-products with names such as cadaverine and putrescine. These molecules are responsible for the odor of rotting flesh.

- Other bacteria can ferment lactose, a prominent component of milk. In some species this fermentation has two end products: propionic acid and CO_2. Propionic acid is responsible for the taste of Swiss cheese; the CO_2 produced during fermentation creates the holes in cheese.

- Many bacterial species in the human digestive tract ferment complex carbohydrates in our diet. The human cells then absorb the by-products and extract even more energy from them using O_2 as the final electron acceptor.

The diversity of enzymatic pathways observed in bacterial and archaeal fermentations extends the metabolic repertoire of these organisms. The diversity of substrates that are fermented also

TABLE 29.5 Some Electron Donors and Acceptors Used by Bacteria and Archaea

Electron Donor	By-Product from Electron Donor	Electron Acceptor	By-Product from Electron Acceptor	Category*
Sugars	CO_2	O_2	H_2O	Organotrophs
H_2 or organic compounds	H_2O or CO	SO_4^{2-}	H_2S or S^{2-}	Sulfate reducers
H_2	H_2O	CO_2	CH_4	Methanogens
CH_4	CO_2	O_2	H_2O	Methanotrophs
H_2S or S^{2-}	SO_4^{2-}	O_2	H_2O	Sulfur bacteria
Organic compounds	CO_2	Fe^{3+}	Fe^{2+}	Iron reducers
NH_3	NO_2^-	O_2	H_2O	Ammonia oxidizers
Organic compounds	CO_2	NO_3^-	N_2O, NO, or N_2	Nitrate reducers

*The name biologists use to identify species that use a particular metabolic strategy.

supports the claim that as a group, bacteria and archaea can use virtually any molecule with relatively high potential energy as a source of high-energy electrons for producing ATP.

Producing ATP via Photosynthesis: Variation in Electron Sources and Pigments

Instead of using molecules as a source of high-energy electrons, phototrophs pursue a radically different strategy: **photosynthesis.** Among bacteria and archaea, photosynthesis can happen in three different ways:

1. Light activates a pigment called bacteriorhodopsin, which uses the absorbed energy to transport protons across the plasma membrane and out of the cell. The resulting flow of protons back into the cell drives the synthesis of ATP via chemiosmosis (see Chapter 9).

2. A recently discovered bacterium that lives near hydrothermal vents on the ocean floor performs photosynthesis not by absorbing light, but by absorbing geothermal radiation.

3. Pigments that absorb light raise electrons to high-energy states. As these electrons are stepped down to lower energy states by electron transport chains, the energy released is used to generate ATP.

An important feature of this last mode of photosynthesis is that the process requires a source of electrons. Recall that in cyanobacteria and plants, the required electrons come from water. When these organisms "split" water molecules apart to obtain electrons, they generate oxygen as a by-product. Species that use water as a source of electrons for photosynthesis are said to complete **oxygenic** ("oxygen-producing") photosynthesis.

In contrast, many phototrophic bacteria use a molecule other than water as the source of electrons. In some cases, the electron donor is hydrogen sulfide (H_2S); a few species can use the ion known as ferrous iron (Fe^{2+}). Instead of producing oxygen as a by-product of photosynthesis, these cells produce elemental sulfur (S) or the ferric ion (Fe^{3+}). This type of photosynthesis is said to be **anoxygenic** ("no oxygen-producing").

The photosynthetic pigments found in plants are chlorophylls *a* and *b*. Cyanobacteria have these two pigments. But researchers have isolated seven additional chlorophylls from different lineages of bacterial phototrophs. Each lineage has one or more of these distinctive chlorophylls, and each type of chlorophyll absorbs light best at a different wavelength. ✔ If you understand that different photosynthetic bacteria contain different kinds of light-absorbing pigments, you should be able to explain how several different photosynthetic species can live in the same habitat without competing for light.

Obtaining Building-Block Compounds: Variation in Pathways for Fixing Carbon

In addition to acquiring energy, organisms must obtain building-block molecules that contain carbon–carbon bonds. Organisms use two mechanisms to procure usable carbon—either making their own or getting it from other organisms (see Chapter 9). Autotrophs make their own building-block compounds; heterotrophs consume them.

In many autotrophs, including cyanobacteria and plants, the enzymes of the Calvin cycle transform carbon dioxide (CO_2) into organic molecules that can be used in synthesizing cell material. The carbon atom in CO_2 is reduced during the process and is said to be "fixed." Animals and fungi, in contrast, obtain carbon from living plants or animals, or by absorbing the organic compounds released as dead tissues decay.

Bacteria and archaea pursue these same two strategies. Some interesting twists occur among bacterial and archaeal autotrophs, however. Not all of them use the Calvin cycle to make building-block molecules, and not all start with CO_2 as a source of carbon atoms. For example, consider these biochemical pathways:

- Some proteobacteria are called **methanotrophs** ("methane-eaters") because they use methane (CH_4) as their carbon source. (They also use CH_4 as an electron donor in cellular respiration.) Methanotrophs process CH_4 into more complex organic compounds via one of two enzymatic pathways, depending on the species.

- Some bacteria can use carbon monoxide (CO) or methanol (CH_3OH) as a starting material.

These observations drive home an important message from this chapter: Compared with eukaryotes, the metabolic capabilities of bacteria and archaea are remarkably complex and diverse.

Ecological Diversity and Global Impacts

The metabolic diversity observed among bacteria and archaea explains why these organisms can thrive in such a wide array of habitats.

- The array of electron donors, electron acceptors, and fermentation substrates exploited by bacteria and archaea allows the heterotrophic species to live just about anywhere.

- The evolution of three distinct types of photosynthesis—based on bacteriorhodopsin, geothermal energy, or pigments that donate high-energy electrons to ETCs—extends the types of habitats that can support phototrophs.

The complex chemistry that these cells carry out, combined with their numerical abundance, has made them potent forces for global change throughout Earth's history. Bacteria and archaea have altered the chemical composition of the oceans, atmosphere, and terrestrial environments for billions of years. They continue to do so today.

The Oxygen Revolution

Today, oxygen represents almost 21 percent of the molecules in Earth's atmosphere. But researchers who study the composition of the atmosphere are virtually certain that no free molecular oxygen (O_2) existed for the first 2.3 billion years of Earth's existence. This conclusion is based on two observations:

1. There was no plausible source of oxygen at the time the planet formed.

2. Chemical analysis of the oldest Earth rocks suggests that they formed in the absence of atmospheric oxygen.

FIGURE 29.11 Cyanobacteria Were the First Organisms to Perform Oxygenic Photosynthesis.

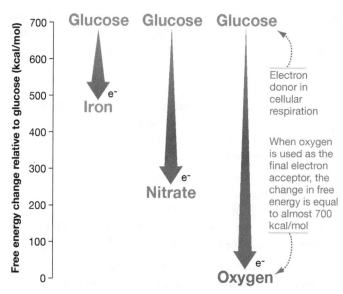

FIGURE 29.12 Cellular Respiration Can Produce More Energy When Oxygen Is the Final Electron Acceptor. More potential energy in glucose can be released when oxygen is the final acceptor compared to other molecules or ions.

DATA: Wilson, D. F., M. Erecińska, and P. L. Dutton. 1974. *Annual Review of Biophysics and Bioengineering* 3: 203–230; Tables 1 and 3.

✔ **QUESTION** Which organisms grow faster—those using aerobic respiration or those using anaerobic respiration? Explain your reasoning.

Early in Earth's history, the atmosphere was dominated by nitrogen and carbon dioxide. Where did the oxygen we breathe come from? The answer is cyanobacteria.

Cyanobacteria is a lineage of photosynthetic bacteria. According to the fossil record, species of cyanobacteria first became numerous in the oceans about 2.7–2.5 billion years ago. Their appearance was momentous because cyanobacteria were the first organisms to perform oxygenic ("oxygen-producing") photosynthesis (**FIGURE 29.11**).

The fossil record and geologic record indicate that oxygen concentrations in the oceans and atmosphere began to increase 2.3–2.1 billion years ago. Once oxygen was common in the oceans, cells could begin to use it as the final electron acceptor during cellular respiration. **Aerobic** respiration was now a possibility. Before that, organisms had to use compounds other than oxygen as a final electron acceptor—only **anaerobic** respiration was possible. (Aerobic and anaerobic respiration are introduced in Chapter 9.)

The evolution of aerobic respiration was a crucial event in the history of life. Because oxygen is extremely electronegative, it is an efficient electron acceptor. Much more energy is released as electrons move through electron transport chains with oxygen as the ultimate acceptor than is released with other substances as the electron acceptor.

To drive this point home, study the graph in **FIGURE 29.12**. Notice that the vertical axis plots free energy changes; the graph shows the energy released when glucose is oxidized with iron, nitrate, or oxygen as the final electron acceptor. Once oxygen was available, then, cells could produce much more ATP for each electron donated by NADH or $FADH_2$. As a result, the rate of energy production rose dramatically.

To summarize, data indicate that cyanobacteria were responsible for a fundamental change in Earth's atmosphere—a high concentration of oxygen. Never before, or since, have organisms done so much to alter the nature of our planet.

Nitrogen Fixation and the Nitrogen Cycle In many environments, fertilizing forests or grasslands with nitrogen results in increased growth. Researchers infer from these results that plant growth is often limited by the availability of nitrogen.

Organisms must have nitrogen to synthesize proteins and nucleic acids. Although molecular nitrogen (N_2) is extremely abundant in the atmosphere, most organisms cannot use it because of the strong triple bond linking the nitrogen atoms. To incorporate nitrogen atoms into amino acids and nucleotides, all eukaryotes and many bacteria and archaea have to obtain N in a form such as ammonia (NH_3) or nitrate (NO_3^-).

Certain bacteria and archaea are the only species that are capable of converting molecular nitrogen to ammonia. The steps in the process, called **nitrogen fixation,** are highly endergonic reduction-oxidation (redox) reactions (see Chapter 9). The key enzyme that catalyzes the reaction—nitrogenase—is found only in selected bacterial and archaeal lineages. Many of these organisms are free living, but some form important relationships with plants:

- Some species of cyanobacteria live in association with a water fern that grows in rice paddies and helps fertilize the plants.

- In terrestrial environments, nitrogen-fixing bacteria live in close association with plants—often taking up residence in special root structures called nodules.

Why is nitrogenase not found in all organisms? The answer lies in an interesting property of the enzyme. When exposed to O_2, nitrogenase is irreversibly poisoned and is degraded. The only organisms with the nitrogenase gene are those that live in anaerobic habitats or are able to protect the enzyme from O_2.

Nitrogen fixation is only the beginning of the story, however. A quick glance back at Table 29.5 should convince you that bacteria and archaea use a wide array of nitrogen-containing

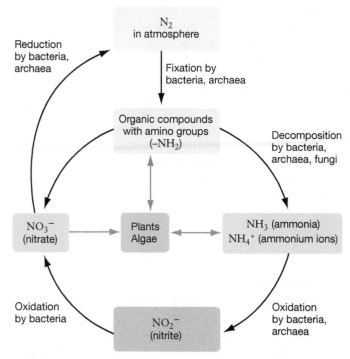

FIGURE 29.13 Bacteria and Archaea Drive the Movement of Nitrogen Atoms through Ecosystems. Nitrogen atoms cycle in different molecular forms.

✔ EXERCISE Add arrows and labels to indicate that animals ingest amino groups from plants or other animals and release amino groups or ammonia.

compounds as electron donors and electron acceptors during cellular respiration.

To understand why this is important, consider that the nitrite (NO_2^-) produced by some bacteria as a by-product of respiration does not build up in the environment. Instead, other species of bacteria and archaea use it as an electron donor, and it is oxidized to molecular nitrate (NO_3^-). Nitrate, in turn, is reduced to molecular nitrogen (N_2) by yet another suite of bacterial and archaeal species. In this way, bacteria and archaea are responsible for driving the movement of nitrogen atoms through ecosystems around the globe in a process called the **nitrogen cycle** (**FIGURE 29.13**).

Similar types of interactions occur with molecules that contain phosphorus, sulfur, and carbon. In this way, bacteria and archaea play a key role in the cycling of nitrogen and other nutrients. ✔ If you understand the role of bacteria and archaea in the nitrogen cycle, you should be able to provide a plausible explanation of what the composition of the atmosphere and what the nitrogen cycle might be like if bacteria and archaea did not exist.

Nitrate Pollution Most crop plants—including corn, rice, and wheat—do not live in association with nitrogen-fixing bacteria. To increase yields of these crops, farmers use fertilizers that are high in nitrogen. In parts of the world, massive additions of nitrogen in the form of ammonia are causing serious pollution problems.

FIGURE 29.14 shows why. When ammonia is added to a cornfield—in midwestern North America, for example—much of

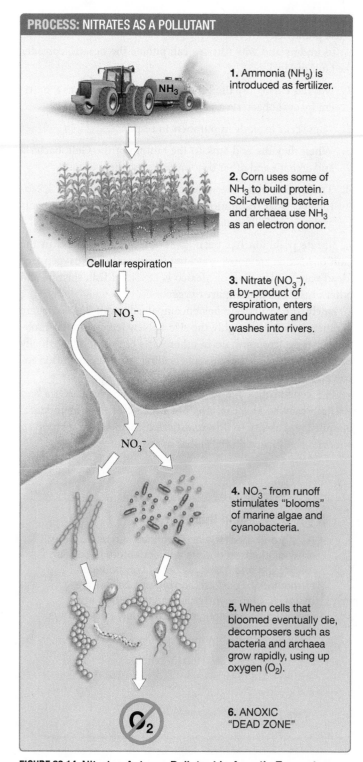

FIGURE 29.14 Nitrates Act as a Pollutant in Aquatic Ecosystems.

it never reaches the growing corn plants. Instead, bacteria and archaea in the soil use a significant fraction of the ammonia as food. Microbes that use ammonia as an electron donor to fuel cellular respiration release nitrite (NO_2^-) as a waste product. Other microbes use nitrite as an electron donor and release nitrate (NO_3^-). Nitrate molecules are extremely soluble in water and tend to be washed out of soils into groundwater or streams.

From there they eventually reach the ocean, where they can cause pollution.

To understand why nitrates can pollute the oceans, consider the Gulf of Mexico:

1. Nitrates carried by the Mississippi River are used as a nutrient by cyanobacteria and algae that live in the Gulf.

2. These cells explode in numbers in response.

3. When they die and sink to the bottom of the Gulf, bacteria and archaea and other decomposers use them as food.

4. The decomposers use so much oxygen as an electron acceptor in cellular respiration that oxygen levels in the sediments and even in Gulf waters decline.

Nitrate pollution has been so severe that large areas in the Gulf of Mexico are anoxic (lacking in oxygen). The oxygen-free "dead zone" in the Gulf of Mexico is devoid of fish, shrimp, and other organisms that require oxygen.

Lately, the dead zone has encompassed about 22,000 square kilometers (km^2)—roughly the size of New Jersey. Similar problem spots are cropping up in other parts of the world. Virtually every link in the chain of events leading to nitrate pollution involves bacteria and archaea.

The general message of this section is simple: Bacteria and Archaea may be small in size, but because of their abundance, ubiquity, and ability to do sophisticated chemistry, they have an enormous influence on the global environment.

check your understanding

If you understand that . . .

• As a group, Bacteria and Archaea can use a wide array of electron donors and acceptors in cellular respiration and a diverse set of compounds in fermentation, perform anoxygenic as well as oxygenic photosynthesis, and fix carbon from several different sources via a variety of pathways.

✔ **You should be able to . . .**

Defend the claim that the metabolism of bacteria and archaea is much more sophisticated than that of eukaryotes.

Answers are available in Appendix A.

29.4 Key Lineages of Bacteria and Archaea

In the decades since the phylogenetic tree identifying the three domains of life was first published, dozens of studies have confirmed the result. It is now well established that all organisms alive today belong to one of the three domains, and that archaea and eukaryotes are more closely related to each other than either group is to bacteria.

Although the relationships among the major lineages within Bacteria and Archaea are still uncertain in some cases, many of the lineages themselves are well studied. Let's survey the attributes of species from selected major lineages within the Bacteria and Archaea, with an emphasis on themes explored earlier in the chapter: their morphological and metabolic diversity, their impacts on humans, and their importance to other species and to the environment.

Bacteria

The name *bacteria* comes from the Greek root *bacter*, meaning "rod" or "staff." The name was inspired by the first bacteria to be seen under a microscope, which were rod shaped. But as the following descriptions indicate, bacterial cells come in a wide variety of shapes.

Biologists who study bacterial diversity currently recognize at least 21 lineages, or phyla, within the domain. Some of these lineages were recognized by distinctive morphological characteristics and others by phylogenetic analyses of gene sequence data. The lineages reviewed here are just a sampling of bacterial diversity.

- Bacteria > Firmicutes
- Bacteria > Cyanobacteria
- Bacteria > Actinobacteria
- Bacteria > Spirochaetes (Spirochetes)
- Bacteria > Chlamydiae
- Bacteria > Proteobacteria

Archaea

The name *archaea* comes from the Greek root *archae*, for "ancient." The name was inspired by the hypothesis that this is a particularly ancient group, which turned out to be incorrect. Also incorrect was the initial hypothesis that archaeans are restricted to hot springs, salt ponds, and other extreme habitats. Archaea live in virtually every habitat known.

Recent phylogenies based on DNA sequence data indicate that the domain is composed of at least four major phyla, called the Thaumarchaeota, Crenarchaeota, Euryarchaeota, and Korarchaeota. The Korarchaeota are known only from direct sequencing studies. They have never been grown in culture, and almost nothing is known about them.

- Archaea > Thaumarchaeota
- Archaea > Crenarchaeota
- Archaea > Euryarchaeota

Bacteria > Firmicutes

The Firmicutes have also been called "low-GC Gram positives" because their cell walls react positively to the Gram stain and because their DNA contains a relatively low percentage of guanine and cytosine (G and C). In some species, G and C represent less than 25 percent of the bases present. There are over 1100 species. ✔ You should be able to mark the origin of the Gram-positive cell wall on Figure 29.7.

Morphological diversity Most are rod shaped or spherical. Some of the spherical species form chains or tetrads (groups of four cells). A few form a durable resting stage called a spore. One subgroup synthesizes a cell wall made of cellulose.

Metabolic diversity Some species can fix nitrogen; some perform anoxygenic photosynthesis. Others make all of their ATP via various fermentation pathways; still others perform cellular respiration, using hydrogen gas (H_2) as an electron donor.

Human and ecological impacts Recent metagenomic studies have shown that members of this lineage are extremely common in the human gut. Species in this group also cause a variety of diseases, including anthrax, botulism, tetanus, walking pneumonia, boils, gangrene, and strep throat. *Bacillus thuringiensis* produces a toxin that is one of the most important insecticides currently used in farming. Species in the lactic acid bacteria group are used to ferment milk products into yogurt or cheese (**FIGURE 29.15**).

Lactobacillus bulgaricus (rods) and *Streptococcus thermophilus*

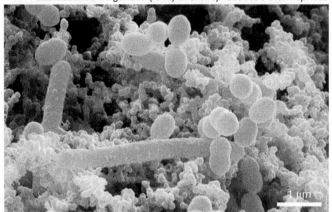

FIGURE 29.15 Firmicutes in Yogurt. (The cells in this scanning electron micrograph have been colorized.)

Bacteria > Cyanobacteria

The cyanobacteria were formerly known as the "blue-green algae"—even though algae are eukaryotes. Only about 80 species of cyanobacteria have been described to date, but they are among the most abundant organisms on Earth. In terms of total mass, cyanobacteria dominate the surface waters in many marine and freshwater environments.

Morphological diversity Cyanobacteria may be found as independent cells, in chains that form filaments (**FIGURE 29.16**), or in the loose aggregations of individual cells called colonies. The shape of *Nostoc* colonies varies from flat sheets to ball-like clusters of cells.

Metabolic diversity All perform oxygenic photosynthesis; many can also fix nitrogen. Because cyanobacteria can synthesize virtually every molecule they need, they can be grown in culture media that contain only CO_2, N_2, H_2O, and a few mineral nutrients. Some species associate with fungi, forming lichens, while others form associations with protists, sponges, or plants. In each case the cyanobacterium provides some form of nutritional benefit to the host. ✔ You should be able to mark the origin of oxygenic photosynthesis on Figure 29.7.

Human and ecological impacts If cyanobacteria are present in high numbers, their waste products can make drinking water smell bad. Some species release molecules called microcystins that are toxic to plants and animals. Cyanobacteria were responsible for the origin of the oxygen atmosphere on Earth. Today they still produce much of the oxygen and nitrogen and many of the organic compounds that feed other organisms in freshwater and marine environments.

Nostoc species

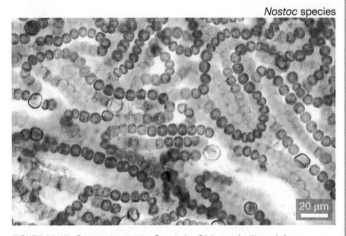

FIGURE 29.16 Cyanobacteria Contain Chlorophyll and Are Green.

Actinobacteria are sometimes called the "high-GC Gram positives" because (1) their cell-wall material appears purple when treated with the Gram stain—meaning that they have a peptidoglycan-rich cell wall and lack an outer membrane—and (2) their DNA contains a relatively high percentage of guanine and cytosine. In some species, G and C represent over 75 percent of the bases present. Over 1100 species have been described to date (**FIGURE 29.17**). ✔ You should be able to mark the origin of this high-GC genome on Figure 29.7.

Morphological diversity Cell shape varies from rods to filaments. Many of the soil-dwelling species are found as chains of cells that form extensive branching filaments called **mycelia.** Because of their morphology they were initially misclassified as fungi, and the incorrect name Actinomyces persists.

Metabolic diversity Many are heterotrophs that use an array of organic compounds as electron donors and oxygen as an electron acceptor. There are several parasitic species that get most of their nutrition from host organisms.

Human and ecological impacts Two serious human diseases, tuberculosis and leprosy, are caused by parasitic *Mycobacterium* species. Over 500 distinct antibiotics have been isolated from species in the genus *Streptomyces*; 60 of these—including streptomycin, neomycin, tetracycline, and erythromycin—are now actively prescribed to treat diseases in humans or domestic livestock. One actinobacterium species is critical to the manufacture of Swiss cheese. Species in the genus *Streptomyces* and *Arthrobacter* are abundant in soil and are vital as decomposers of dead plant and animal material. Some species live in association with plant roots and fix nitrogen; others can break down toxins such as herbicides, nicotine, and caffeine.

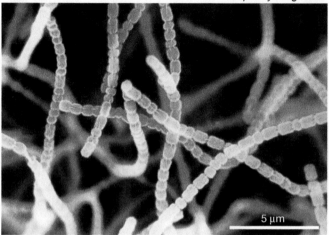

Streptomyces griseus

5 µm

FIGURE 29.17 A *Streptomyces* Species That Produces the Antibiotic Streptomycin.

Based on numbers of species, the spirochetes are one of the smaller bacterial phyla: Only 13 genera and a total of 62 species have been described to date.

Morphological diversity Spirochetes are distinguished by their unique corkscrew shape and flagella (**FIGURE 29.18**). Instead of extending into the water surrounding the cell, spirochete flagella are contained within a structure called the outer sheath, which surrounds the cell. When these flagella beat, the cell lashes back and forth and swims forward. ✔ You should be able to mark the origin of the spirochete flagellum on Figure 29.7.

Metabolic diversity Most spirochetes manufacture ATP via fermentation. The substrate used in fermentation varies among species and may consist of sugars, amino acids, starch, or the pectin found in plant cell walls. A spirochete that lives only in the hindgut of termites can fix nitrogen.

Human and ecological impacts The sexually transmitted disease syphilis is caused by a spirochete. Syphilis is thought to have been brought by European explorers to the Western hemisphere, where it was responsible for killing tens of millions of native people. Lyme disease, also caused by a spirochete, is transmitted to humans by deer ticks. Spirochetes are extremely common in freshwater and marine habitats; many live only under anaerobic conditions.

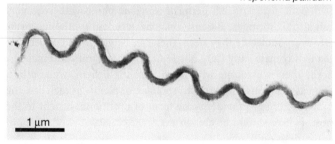

Treponema pallidum

1 µm

FIGURE 29.18 Spirochetes Are Corkscrew-Shaped Cells Inside an Outer Sheath.

In terms of numbers of species living today, Chlamydiae may be the smallest of all major bacterial lineages. Although the group is highly distinct phylogenetically, only 13 species are known. All are Gram-negative.

Morphological diversity Chlamydiae are spherical. They are tiny, even by bacterial standards.

Metabolic diversity All known species in this phylum live as parasites *inside* host cells and are termed **endosymbionts** ("inside-together-living"). Chlamydiae acquire almost all of their nutrition from their hosts. In **FIGURE 29.19**, the chlamydiae have been colored red; the animal cells that they live in are colored brown. ✔ You should be able to mark the origin of the endosymbiotic lifestyle in this lineage on Figure 29.7. (The endosymbiotic lifestyle has also arisen in other bacterial lineages, independently of Chlamydiae.)

Human and ecological impacts *Chlamydia trachomatis* infections are the most common cause of blindness in humans. When the same organism is transmitted from person to person via sexual intercourse, it can cause serious urogenital tract infections. If untreated in women, this disease can lead to ectopic pregnancy, premature births, and infertility. One species causes epidemics of a pneumonia-like disease in birds.

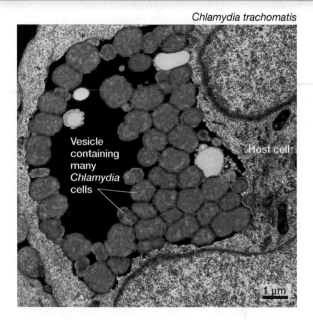

Chlamydia trachomatis

Vesicle containing many *Chlamydia* cells

Host cell

1 µm

FIGURE 29.19 Chlamydiae Live Only Inside Animal Cells.

The approximately 1200 species of proteobacteria form five major subgroups, designated by the Greek letters α (alpha), β (beta), γ (gamma), δ (delta), and ε (epsilon). Because they are so diverse in their morphology and metabolism, the lineage is named after the Greek god Proteus, who could assume many shapes.

Morphological diversity Proteobacterial cells can be rods, spheres, or spirals. Some form stalks (**FIGURE 29.20a**). Some are motile. In one group, cells may move together to form colonies, which then transform into the specialized cell aggregate shown in **FIGURE 29.20b**. This structure is known as a **fruiting body.** At their tips, the fruiting bodies produce cells that are surrounded by a durable coating. These spores sit until conditions improve, and then they resume growth.

Metabolic diversity Proteobacteria make a living in virtually every way known to bacteria—except that none perform oxygenic photosynthesis. Various species may perform cellular respiration by using organic compounds, nitrite, methane, hydrogen gas, sulfur, or ammonia as electron donors and oxygen, sulfate, or sulfur as electron acceptors. Some perform anoxygenic photosynthesis.

Human and ecological impacts *Escherichia coli* may be the best studied of all organisms and is a key species in biotechnology (see Chapter 20, and **BioSkills 13** in Appendix B). Pathogenic proteobacteria cause Legionnaire's disease, cholera, food poisoning, plague, dysentery, gonorrhea, Rocky Mountain spotted fever, typhus, ulcers, and diarrhea. *Wolbachia* infections are common in insects and are often transmitted from mothers to offspring

(a) Stalked bacterium

Caulobacter crescentus

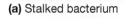

Stalk

1 µm

(b) Fruiting bodies

Chondromyces crocatus

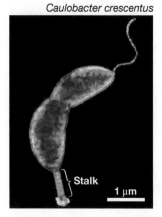

Spores

50 µm

FIGURE 29.20 Some Proteobacteria Grow on Stalks or Form Fruiting Bodies. The stalked bacterium (a) has been colorized.

via eggs. Biologists use *Agrobacterium* cells to transfer new genes into crop plants. Certain acid-loving species of proteobacteria are used in the production of vinegars. Species in the genus *Rhizobium* (α-proteobacteria) live in association with plant roots and fix nitrogen. A group in the δ-proteobacteria, the bdellovibrios, are predators—they drill into other proteobacterial cells and digest them. Because some species use nitrogen-containing compounds as electron acceptors, proteobacteria are critical players in the cycling of nitrogen atoms through terrestrial and aquatic ecosystems.

The Thaumarchaeota were recently recognized as a monophyletic, ancient lineage of archaea. Members of this phylum are extremely abundant in oceans, estuaries, and terrestrial soils. Unlike the extremophiles, species in this lineage are considered mesophilic because they grow best at moderate temperatures.

Morphological diversity Only a few members of this group have been observed, and all consist of rod-shaped cells that are less than 1 micrometer (μm) in length, smaller than typical prokaryotes. One species, *Nitrosopumilus maritimus* (**FIGURE 29.21**), is so abundant it is estimated to constitute possibly 25 percent of the total prokaryotic cell biomass in open oceans.

Metabolic diversity Members of this phylum are called ammonia oxidizers because they use ammonia as a source of electrons and generate nitrite as a by-product. They use the energy from ammonia oxidation to fix CO_2.

Human and ecological impacts Because of their abundance, these organisms are thought to play a major role in Earth's nitrogen and carbon cycles. Their presence in deep ocean waters that lack reduced carbon and sunlight may help explain the productivity of these habitats. The species *Cenarchaeum symbiosum* lives as an endosymbiont inside a marine sponge.

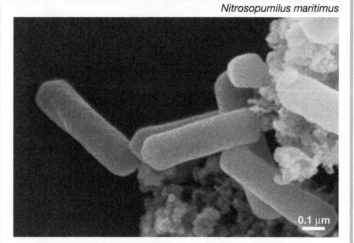

Nitrosopumilus maritimus

0.1 μm

FIGURE 29.21 This Species of Thaumarchaeota Has Rod-Shaped Cells and Is Extremely Abundant in the Open Ocean.

✔**QUANTITATIVE** Use the scale bar in the figure to measure the length of a *N. maritimus* cell. If these cells were placed end to end, how many of them would fit along a meter stick?

The Crenarchaeota got their name because they are considered similar to the oldest archaeans; the word root *cren*– refers to a source or fount. Biologists have named only 37 species so far, but they are virtually certain that thousands are yet to be discovered.

Morphological diversity Crenarchaeota cells can be shaped like filaments, rods, discs, or spheres. One species that lives in extremely hot habitats has a tough cell wall consisting solely of glycoprotein.

Metabolic diversity Depending on the species, cellular respiration can involve organic compounds, sulfur, hydrogen gas, or Fe^{2+} ions as electron donors and oxygen, nitrate, sulfate, sulfur, carbon dioxide, or Fe^{3+} ions as electron acceptors. Some species make ATP exclusively through fermentation pathways.

Human and ecological impacts Crenarchaeota have yet to be used in the manufacture of commercial products. In certain extremely hot, high-pressure, cold, or acidic environments, crenarchaeota may be the only life-form present (**FIGURE 29.22**). Acid-loving species thrive in habitats with pH 1–5; some species are found in ocean sediments at depths ranging from 2500 to 4000 m below the surface.

Sulfolobus species

0.5 μm

FIGURE 29.22 Some Crenarchaeota Live in Sulfur-Rich Hot Springs. The cells in the micrograph have been colorized to make them more visible.

The Euryarchaeota are aptly named, because the word root *eury*– means "broad." Members of this phylum live in every conceivable habitat. Some species are adapted to high-salt habitats with pH 11.5—almost as basic as household ammonia. Other species are adapted to acidic conditions with a pH as low as 0. Species in the genus *Methanopyrus* live near hot springs called black smokers that are 2000 m (over 1 mile) below sea level (**FIGURE 29.23**).

Morphological diversity Euryarchaeota cells can be spherical, filamentous, rod shaped, disc shaped, or spiral. Rod-shaped cells may be short or long or arranged in chains. Spherical cells can be found in ball-like aggregations. Some species have several flagella. Some species lack a cell wall; others have a cell wall composed entirely of glycoproteins.

Metabolic diversity The group includes a variety of methane-producing species. These **methanogens** can use up to 11 different organic compounds as electron acceptors during cellular respiration; all produce CH_4 as a by-product of respiration. In other species of Euryarchaeota, cellular respiration is based on hydrogen gas or Fe^{2+} ions as electron donors and nitrate or sulfate as electron acceptors. Species that live in high-salt environments can use the molecule retinal—which is responsible for light reception in your eyes—to capture light energy and perform photosynthesis.

Human and ecological impacts Species in the genus *Ferroplasma* live in piles of waste rock near abandoned mines. As a by-product of metabolism, they produce acids that drain into streams and pollute them. Methanogens live in the soils of swamps and the guts of mammals (including yours). They are responsible for adding about 2 billion tons of methane to the atmosphere each year. A methanogen in this phylum was also recently implicated in gum disease.

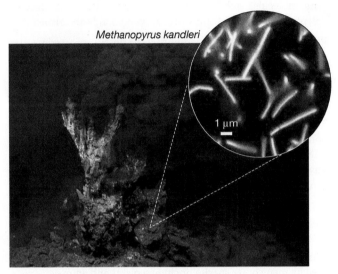

Methanopyrus kandleri

1 μm

FIGURE 29.23 Some Euryarchaeota Cells Live in the Chimneys of "Black Smokers" on the Seafloor.

CHAPTER 29   REVIEW

For media, go to MasteringBiology

If you understand . . .

29.1 Why Do Biologists Study Bacteria and Archaea?

- Bacteria and archaea are the most abundant organisms on Earth and are found in every habitat that has been sampled.

- Bacteria and archaea are very small, prokaryotic cells, and most are unicellular.

- Bacteria and archaea can be distinguished by their different kinds of membrane lipids and cell walls as well as by their different transcription machinery.

- Bacteria play many beneficial roles in animal digestion, bioremediation, and the production of antibiotics.

- Bacteria cause some of the most dangerous human diseases, including plague, syphilis, botulism, cholera, and tuberculosis.

✔ You should be able to explain the difference between a bacterium, an archaeon, and a eukaryote.

29.2 How Do Biologists Study Bacteria and Archaea?

- Enrichment cultures are used to grow large numbers of bacterial or archaeal cells that thrive under specified conditions.

- Using metagenomic analysis, biologists can study bacteria and archaea that cannot be cultured by extracting DNA directly from an environment and then sequencing and characterizing DNA fragments. Information obtained is used to identify biochemical processes and novel organisms that are then placed on the tree of life.

✔ You should be able to explain how metagenomic analysis might be used to reveal whether bacteria carry out nitrogen fixation in the gut of an insect.

29.3 What Themes Occur in the Diversification of Bacteria and Archaea?

- Metabolic diversity and complexity are the hallmarks of the bacteria and archaea, just as morphological diversity and complexity are the hallmarks of the eukaryotes.

- Among bacteria and archaea, a wide array of inorganic or organic compounds with high potential energy may serve as electron donors in cellular respiration, and a wide variety of inorganic or organic molecules with low potential energy may serve as electron acceptors. Dozens of distinct organic compounds are fermented.

- Photosynthesis is widespread in bacteria. In cyanobacteria, water is used as a source of electrons and oxygen gas is generated as a by-product. But in other species, the electron excited by photon capture comes from a source other than water, and no oxygen is produced.

- To acquire building-block molecules containing carbon–carbon bonds, some bacteria and archaea species use the enzymes of the Calvin cycle to reduce CO_2. But several other biochemical pathways found in bacteria and archaea can also reduce simple organic compounds to sugars or carbohydrates.

- Because of their metabolic diversity, bacteria and archaea play a large role in carbon and nitrogen cycling and alter the global atmosphere, oceans, and terrestrial environments.

- Nitrogen-fixing species provide nitrogen in forms that can be used by many other species, including plants and animals.

✓ You should be able to explain why species that release H_2S as a by-product and that use H_2S as an electron donor often live side by side.

29.4 Key Lineages of Bacteria and Archaea

- Prokaryotes can be divided into two lineages, the Bacteria and the Archaea, based on a wide variety of morphological, biochemical, and molecular characters.

- Bacteria are divided into 21 major lineages including organisms that play major roles in ecosystems as primary producers, decomposers, and parasites.

- Archaea are divided into four major lineages and were thought to exist only in extreme environments; they are now recognized to be widespread.

(MB) **MasteringBiology**

1. **MasteringBiology Assignments**

   Tutorials and Activities Classification of Prokaryotes, Diversity in Bacteria, Tree of Life, Water Pollution from Nitrates

   Questions Reading Quizzes, Blue-Thread Questions, Test Bank

2. **eText** Read your book online, search, take notes, highlight text, and more.

3. **The Study Area** Practice Test, Cumulative Test, BioFlix® 3-D Animations, Videos, Activities, Audio Glossary, Word Study Tools, Art

You should be able to . . .

✓ TEST YOUR KNOWLEDGE

Answers are available in Appendix A

1. How do the molecules that function as electron donors and those that function as electron acceptors differ?
   a. Electron donors are almost always organic molecules; electron acceptors are always inorganic.
   b. Electron donors are almost always inorganic molecules; electron acceptors are always organic.
   c. Electron donors have relatively high potential energy; electron acceptors have relatively low potential energy.
   d. Electron donors have relatively low potential energy; electron acceptors have relatively high potential energy.

2. What do some photosynthetic bacteria use as a source of electrons instead of water?
   a. oxygen (O_2)
   b. hydrogen sulfide (H_2S)
   c. organic compounds (e.g., CH_3COO^-)
   d. nitrate (NO_3^-)

3. What is distinctive about the chlorophylls found in different photosynthetic bacteria?
   a. their membranes
   b. their role in acquiring energy
   c. their role in carbon fixation
   d. their absorption spectra

4. What are organisms called that use inorganic compounds as electron donors in cellular respiration?
   a. phototrophs
   b. heterotrophs
   c. organotrophs
   d. lithotrophs

5. True or False. Certain aerobic bacteria in the presence of oxygen can convert nitrogen gas to ammonia.

6. Unlike plant cell walls that contain cellulose, bacterial cell walls are composed of _____.

7. What has metagenomic analysis allowed researchers to do for the first time?
   a. sample organisms from an environment and grow them under defined conditions in the lab
   b. isolate organisms from an environment and sequence their entire genome
   c. study organisms that cannot be cultured (grown in the lab)
   d. identify important morphological differences among species

8. Biologists often use the term energy source as a synonym for "electron donor." Why?

9. The text claims that the tremendous ecological diversity of bacteria and archaea is possible because of their impressive metabolic diversity. Do you agree with this statement? Why or why not?

10. Would you predict that disease-causing bacteria, such as those listed in Table 29.2, obtain energy from light, organic molecules, or inorganic molecules? Explain your answer.

11. The text claims that the evolution of an oxygen atmosphere paved the way for increasingly efficient cellular respiration and higher growth rates in organisms. Explain.

12. From what we know about the evolutionary relationship between the three largest domains, as depicted in Figure 29.1, explain the statement, "Prokaryotes are a paraphyletic group."

13. When using Koch's postulates, which of the following is an essential requirement for the suspected pathogen?
    a. It is present in all organisms with the disease.
    b. It can be cultured on an agar plate.
    c. It is pathogenic on a wide variety of organisms.
    d. It can reproduce sexually within the host.

14. The researchers who observed that magnetite was produced by bacterial cultures from the deep subsurface carried out a follow-up experiment. These biologists treated some of the cultures with a drug that poisons the enzymes involved in electron transport chains. In cultures where the drug was present, no more magnetite was produced. Does this result support or undermine their hypothesis that the bacteria in the cultures perform cellular respiration? Explain your reasoning.

15. *Streptococcus mutans* obtains energy by oxidizing sucrose. This bacterium is abundant in the mouths of Western European and North American children and is a prominent cause of cavities. The organism is virtually absent in children from East Africa, where tooth decay is rare. Propose a hypothesis to explain this observation. Outline the design of a study that would test your hypothesis.

16. Suppose that you've been hired by a firm interested in using bacteria to clean up organic solvents found in toxic waste dumps. Your new employer is particularly interested in finding cells that are capable of breaking a molecule called benzene into less toxic compounds. Where would you go to look for bacteria that can metabolize benzene as an energy or carbon source? How would you design an enrichment culture capable of isolating benzene-metabolizing species?29

30 Protists

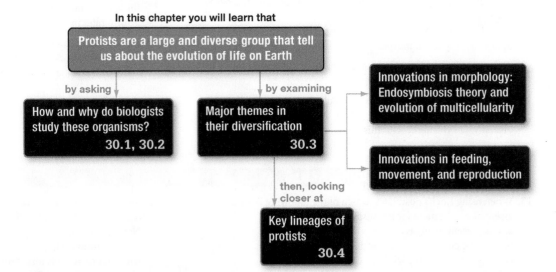

In this chapter you will learn that

Protists are a large and diverse group that tell us about the evolution of life on Earth

by asking → How and why do biologists study these organisms? **30.1, 30.2**

by examining → Major themes in their diversification **30.3**

→ Innovations in morphology: Endosymbiosis theory and evolution of multicellularity

→ Innovations in feeding, movement, and reproduction

then, looking closer at → Key lineages of protists **30.4**

The brown alga (giant kelp) shown here lives attached to rocks in ocean waters. This algae and other species featured in this chapter are particularly abundant in the world's oceans.

This chapter introduces the third domain on the tree of life: the **Eukarya.** Eukaryotes range from single-celled organisms that are the size of bacteria to sequoia trees and blue whales. The largest and most morphologically complex organisms on the tree of life—algae, plants, fungi, and animals—are eukaryotes.

Although eukaryotes are astonishingly diverse, they share fundamental features that distinguish them from bacteria and archaea:

• Compared to bacteria and archaea, most eukaryotic cells are large, have many more organelles, and have a much more extensive system of structural proteins called the cytoskeleton.

✔ When you see this checkmark, stop and test yourself. Answers are available in Appendix A.

- The nuclear envelope is a **synapomorphy** that defines the Eukarya. Recall that a synapomorphy is a shared, derived trait that distinguishes major monophyletic groups.

- Multicellularity is rare in bacteria and unknown in archaea, but has evolved multiple times in eukaryotes.

- Bacteria and archaea reproduce asexually by fission; many eukaryotes reproduce asexually via mitosis and cell division.

- Many eukaryotes undergo meiosis and reproduce sexually.

One of this chapter's fundamental goals is to explore how these morphological innovations—features like organelles and the nuclear envelope—evolved. Another goal is to analyze how morphological innovations allowed eukaryotes to pursue novel ways of performing basic life tasks such as feeding, moving, and reproducing.

In introducing the Eukarya, this chapter focuses on a diverse collection of lineages known as the protists. The term **protist** refers to all eukaryotes that are not land plants, fungi, or animals. Protist lineages are colored orange in **FIGURE 30.1**.

Protists do not make up a monophyletic group. Instead, they refer to a **paraphyletic group**—they represent some, but not all, of the descendants of a single common ancestor. No synapomorphies define the protists. Protists have no trait that is found only in protists and in no other organisms.

By definition, then, the protists are a diverse lot. The common feature among protists is that they tend to live in environments where they are surrounded by water most of the time (**FIGURE 30.2**). Most plants, fungi, and animals are terrestrial, but protists are found in wet soils and aquatic habitats or inside the bodies of other organisms—including, perhaps, you.

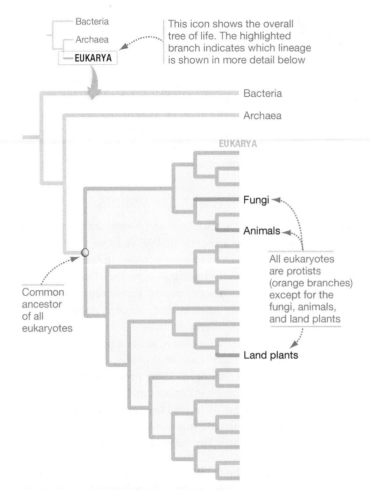

FIGURE 30.1 Protists Are Paraphyletic. The protists include some, but not all, descendants of a single common ancestor.

Open ocean: Surface waters teem with microscopic protists, such as these diatoms.

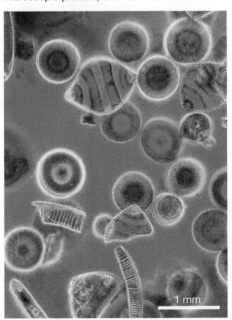

Shallow coastal waters: Gigantic protists, such as these kelp, form underwater forests.

Intertidal habitats: Protists such as these sea palms are particularly abundant in tidal habitats.

FIGURE 30.2 Protists Are Particularly Abundant in Aquatic Environments.

30.1 Why Do Biologists Study Protists?

Biologists study protists for three reasons, in addition to their intrinsic interest: (1) they are important medically, (2) they are important ecologically, and (3) they are critical to understanding the evolution of plants, fungi, and animals. The rest of the chapter focuses on why protists are interesting in their own right and how they evolved. Let's first consider their impact on human health and the environment.

Impacts on Human Health and Welfare

The most spectacular crop failure in history, the Irish potato famine, was caused by a protist. In 1845 most of the 3 million acres that had been planted to grow potatoes in Ireland became infested with *Phytophthora infestans*—a parasite that belongs to a group of protists called water molds. Potato tubers that were infected with *P. infestans* rotted in the fields or in storage.

As a result of crop failures in Ireland for two consecutive years, an estimated 1 million people out of a population of less than 9 million died of starvation or starvation-related illnesses. Several million others emigrated. Many people of Irish heritage living in North America, New Zealand, and Australia trace their ancestry to relatives who left Ireland to evade the famine. As devastating as the potato famine was, however, it does not begin to approach the misery caused by the protist *Plasmodium*.

Malaria Physicians and public health officials point to three major infectious diseases that are currently afflicting large numbers of people worldwide: tuberculosis, HIV, and malaria. Tuberculosis is caused by a bacterium; HIV is caused by a virus (see Chapter 36). Malaria is caused by a protist—specifically, by apicomplexan species in the eukaryotic lineage Alveolata.

Malaria ranks as one of the world's worst infectious diseases. In India alone, over 30 million people each year suffer from debilitating fevers caused by malaria. At least 300 million people worldwide are sickened by it each year, and nearly 1 million die from the disease annually. The toll is equivalent to eight 747s, loaded with passengers, crashing every day. Most of the dead are children of preschool age.

Five species of the protist *Plasmodium* are capable of parasitizing humans. Infections start when *Plasmodium* cells enter a person's bloodstream during a mosquito bite. As **FIGURE 30.3** shows, *Plasmodium* initially infects liver cells; later, some of the *Plasmodium* cells change into a distinctive cell type that infects the host's red blood cells. The *Plasmodium* cells multiply asexually inside the host cells, which are killed as parasite cells exit to infect additional liver cells or red blood cells. Large numbers of *Plasmodium* cells in a human host's blood increase the chance that a mosquito's blood meal will contain some of them.

After blood from an infected human is transferred to a mosquito during a bite, *Plasmodium* cells differentiate to form gametes. Inside the mosquito, gametes fuse to form a diploid zygote, which undergoes meiosis. Sexual reproduction in the mosquito is beneficial to the parasite because it generates genetic diversity to help evade the host's immune system. The haploid cells that result from meiosis can infect a human when the mosquito bites again.

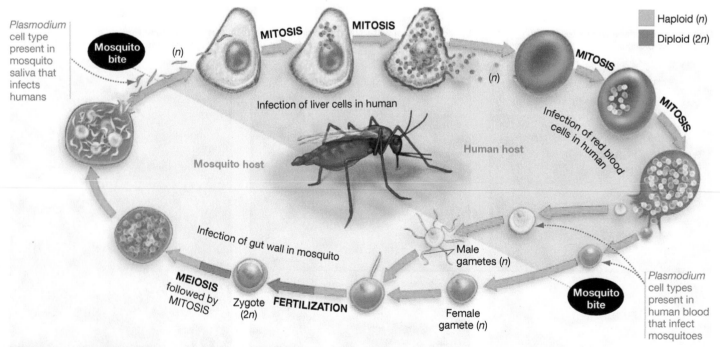

FIGURE 30.3 *Plasmodium* **Lives in Mosquitoes and in Humans, Where It Causes Malaria.** Over the course of its life cycle, *Plasmodium falciparum* alternates between a mosquito host where sexual reproduction takes place, and a human host where asexual reproduction takes place. In humans, it infects and kills liver cells and red blood cells, contributing to anemia and high fever. In mosquitoes, the protist lives in the gut and salivary glands.

TABLE 30.1 Some Human Health Problems Caused by Protists

Species	Disease
Five species of *Plasmodium*, primarily *P. falciparum* and *P. vivax*	Malaria has the potential to affect 40 percent of the world's total population.
Toxoplasma gondii	Toxoplasmosis may cause eye and brain damage in infants and in AIDS patients.
Many species of dinoflagellates	Toxins released during harmful algal blooms accumulate in clams and mussels and poison people if eaten.
Many species of *Giardia*	Diarrhea due to giardiasis (beaver fever) can last for several weeks.
Trichomonas vaginalis	Trichomoniasis is a reproductive tract infection and one of the most common sexually transmitted diseases. About 2 million young women are infected in the United States each year; some of them become infertile.
Several species of *Leishmania*	Leishmaniasis can cause skin sores or affect internal organs—particularly the spleen and liver.
Trypanosoma gambiense and *T. rhodesiense*	Trypanosomiasis ("sleeping sickness") is a potentially fatal disease transmitted through bites from tsetse flies. Occurs in Africa.
Trypanosoma cruzi	Chagas disease affects 16–18 million people and causes 50,000 deaths annually, primarily in South and Central America.
Entamoeba histolytica	Amoebic dysentery results from severe infections.
Phytophthora infestans	An outbreak of this protist wiped out potato crops in Ireland in 1845–1847, causing famine.

Although *Plasmodium* is arguably the best studied of all protists, researchers have still not been able to devise effective and sustainable measures to control it.

- *Plasmodium* has evolved resistance to some of the drugs used to control its growth in infected people.

- Efforts to develop a vaccine against *Plasmodium* have been fruitless to date, in part because the parasite evolves so quickly. Flu virus and HIV pose similar problems.

- Natural selection has favored mosquito strains that are resistant to the insecticides that have been sprayed in their breeding habitats in attempts to control malaria's spread.

Unfortunately, malaria is not the only important human disease caused by protists. **TABLE 30.1** lists some protists that cause human suffering and economic losses.

Harmful Algal Blooms When a unicellular species experiences rapid population growth and reaches high densities in an aquatic environment, it is said to "bloom." Unfortunately, a handful of the many protist species involved in blooms can be harmful.

Harmful algal blooms are usually due to photosynthetic protists called dinoflagellates. Certain dinoflagellates synthesize toxins to protect themselves from predation by small animals called copepods. Because these organisms sometimes have high concentrations of accessory pigments called xanthophylls, their blooms can sometimes discolor seawater (**FIGURE 30.4**).

Algal blooms can be harmful to people because clams and other shellfish filter photosynthetic protists out of the water as food. During a bloom, high levels of toxins can build up in the flesh of these shellfish. Typically, the shellfish themselves are not harmed. But if a person eats contaminated shellfish, several types of poisoning can result.

Paralytic shellfish poisoning, for example, occurs when people eat shellfish that have fed heavily on protists that synthesize poisons called saxitoxins. Saxitoxins block ion channels that have to open for electrical signals to travel through nerve cells.

FIGURE 30.4 Harmful Algal Blooms Are Caused by Dinoflagellates.

In humans, high dosages of saxitoxins cause unpleasant symptoms such as prickling sensations in the mouth or even life-threatening symptoms such as muscle weakness and paralysis.

But like the bacteria and archaea, most species of protists are not harmful. Let's have a look at some protists that are essential to healthy ecosystems.

Ecological Importance of Protists

As a whole, the protists represent just 10 percent of the total number of named eukaryote species. Although the number of named species of protists is relatively low, their abundance is extraordinarily high. The number of individual protists found in some habitats is astonishing.

- One milliliter of pond water can contain well over 500 single-celled protists that swim with the aid of flagella.

- Under certain conditions, dinoflagellates can reach concentrations of 60 thousand cells per milliliter of seawater.

Why is this important?

Protists Play a Key Role in Aquatic Food Chains Photosynthetic protists take in carbon dioxide from the atmosphere and reduce, or "fix," it to form sugars or other organic compounds with high potential energy. Photosynthesis transforms some of the energy in sunlight into chemical energy that organisms can use to grow and produce offspring.

Species that produce chemical energy in this way are called **primary producers.** Diatoms, in the Stramenopila lineage, are photosynthetic protists that rank among the leading primary producers in the oceans simply because they are so abundant. Primary production in the ocean represents almost half of the total carbon dioxide that is fixed on Earth.

Diatoms and other organisms that drift in the open oceans or lakes are called **plankton.** The sugars and other organic compounds produced by photosynthetic plankton are the basis of food chains in freshwater and marine environments.

A **food chain** describes nutritional relationships among organisms, and thus how chemical energy flows within ecosystems. In this case, photosynthetic protists and other primary producers are eaten by primary consumers, many of which are protists. Primary consumers are eaten by fish, shellfish, and other secondary consumers, which in turn are eaten by tertiary consumers—whales, squid, and large fish (such as tuna).

Many of the species at the base of food chains in aquatic environments are protists.

Could Protists Help Limit Global Climate Change? Carbon dioxide levels in the atmosphere are increasing rapidly because humans are burning fossil fuels and forests. Carbon dioxide traps heat that is radiating from Earth, so high CO_2 levels in the atmosphere contribute to the rise in temperatures associated with global climate change—an issue that many observers consider today's most pressing environmental problem.

The carbon atoms in carbon dioxide molecules move to organisms on land or in the oceans and then back to the atmosphere, in what researchers call the **global carbon cycle.** To restrict global climate change, researchers are trying to figure out ways to decrease carbon dioxide concentrations in the atmosphere and increase the amount of carbon stored in terrestrial and marine environments.

To understand how this might be done, consider the marine carbon cycle diagrammed in **FIGURE 30.5**. The cycle starts when CO_2 from the atmosphere dissolves in water and is taken up by primary producers—photosynthetic plankton called phytoplankton—and converted to organic matter. The plankton are eaten by primary consumers, die and are consumed by decomposers or scavengers, or die and sink to the bottom of the ocean. There they may enter one of two long-lived repositories:

1. *Sedimentary rocks* Several lineages of protists have shells made of calcium carbonate ($CaCO_3$). When these shells rain down from the ocean surface and settle in layers at the bottom, the deposits that result are compacted by the weight of the water and by sediments accumulating above them. Eventually the deposits turn into rock. The limestone used to build the pyramids of Egypt consists largely of protist shells.

2. *Petroleum* Although the process of petroleum (oil) formation is not well understood, it begins with accumulations of dead bacteria, archaea, and protists at the bottom of the ocean.

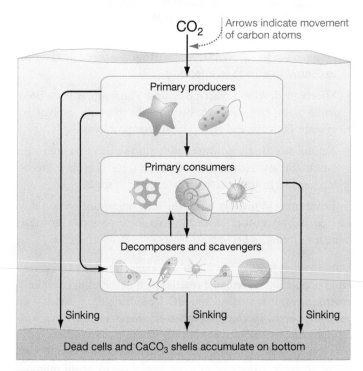

FIGURE 30.5 Protists Play a Key Role in the Marine Carbon Cycle. At the surface, carbon atoms tend to shuttle quickly among organisms. But if carbon atoms sink to the bottom of the ocean in the form of shells or dead cells, they may be locked up for long periods in carbon sinks. (The bottom of the ocean may be miles below the surface.)

Recent experiments have shown that the carbon cycle speeds up when habitats in the middle of the ocean are fertilized with iron. Iron is a critical component of the electron transport chains responsible for photosynthesis and respiration, but it is in particularly short supply in the open ocean. After iron is added to ocean waters, it is not uncommon to see populations of protists and other primary producers increase by a factor of 10.

Some researchers hypothesize that when these blooms occur, the amount of carbon that rains down into carbon sinks in the form of shells and dead cells may increase. If so, then fertilizing the ocean to promote blooms might be an effective way to reduce CO_2 concentrations in the atmosphere.

The effectiveness of iron fertilization is hotly debated, however. Fertilizing the ocean with iron might lead to large accumulations of dead organic matter and the formation of anaerobic dead zones (see Chapter 29). But if further research shows that iron fertilization is safe and effective, it could be added to the list of approaches to limit global climate change.

check your understanding

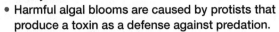

If you understand that . . .

- Malaria is caused by a protist that lives in mosquitoes and in humans in different parts of its life cycle.
- Harmful algal blooms are caused by protists that produce a toxin as a defense against predation.
- Protists are key primary producers in aquatic environments. As a result, they play a key role in the global carbon cycle.

✔ **You should be able to . . .**

1. Explain why public health workers are promoting the use of insecticide-treated sleeping nets as a way of reducing malaria.

2. Make a flowchart showing the chain of events that would start with massive iron fertilization and end with large deposits of carbon-containing compounds on the ocean floor.

Answers are available in Appendix A.

30.2 How Do Biologists Study Protists?

Although biologists have made great strides in understanding pathogenic protists and the role that protists play in the global carbon cycle, they have found it extremely difficult to gain any sort of solid insight into how the group as a whole diversified over time. The problem is that the eukaryotic lineages split over a billion years ago and diverged so much that it is not easy to find any overall patterns in the evolution of the group.

Recently, researchers have made progress in understanding protist diversity by combining data on the morphology of key groups with phylogenetic analyses of DNA sequences. However, despite the progress, significant questions remain about how the Eukarya diversified. Let's analyze how this work is being done, beginning with classical results on the morphological traits that distinguish major eukaryote groups.

Microscopy: Studying Cell Structure

Using light microscopy (see **BioSkills 11** in Appendix B), biologists were able to identify and name many of the protist species known today. For example, the early microscopist Anton van Leeuwenhoek identified the parasite *Giardia intestinalis* by examining samples of his own feces.

When transmission electron microscopes became available, a major breakthrough in understanding protist diversity occurred: Detailed studies revealed that protists could be grouped according to overall cell structure, according to organelles with distinctive features, or both.

For example, both light and electron microscopy confirmed that the species that caused the Irish potato famine has reproductive cells with an unusual type of **flagellum.** Flagella are organelles that project from the cell and whip back and forth to produce swimming movements (see Chapter 7). In reproductive cells of this species, one of the two flagella present has tiny, hollow, hairlike projections. Biologists noted that kelp and other species of brown algae also have cells with this type of flagellum.

To make sense of these results, researchers interpreted these types of distinctive morphological features as synapomorphies. Species that have a flagellum with hollow, hairlike projections became known as stramenopiles (literally, "straw-hairs"); the hairs typically have branches at the tip (**FIGURE 30.6**).

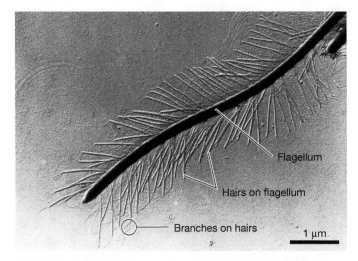

FIGURE 30.6 Species in the Lineage Called Stramenopila Have a Distinctive Flagellum. The unusual, hollow "hairs" that decorate the flagella of stramenopiles often have three branches at the tip.

Lineage	Distinguishing Morphological Features (synapomorphies)
Amoebozoa	Cells lack cell walls. When portions of the cell extend outward to move the cell, they form large lobes.
Opisthokonta	Reproductive cells have a single flagellum at their base. The cristae inside mitochondria are flat, not tube-shaped as in other eukaryotes. (This lineage includes protists as well as the fungi and the animals. Fungi and animals are discussed separately.)
Excavata	Most cells have a pronounced "feeding groove" where prey or organic debris is ingested. Most species lack typical mitochondria, although genes derived from mitochondria are found in the nucleus.
Plantae	Cells have chloroplasts with a double membrane.
Rhizaria	Cells lack cell walls, although some produce an elaborate shell-like covering. When portions of the cell extend outward to move the cell, they are slender in shape.
Alveolata	Cells have sac-like structures called alveoli that form a continuous layer just under the plasma membrane. Alveoli are thought to provide support.
Stramenopila	If flagella are present, cells usually have two—one of which is covered with hairlike projections.

In recognizing the Stramenopila lineage, investigators hypothesized that because an ancestor had evolved a distinctive flagellum, all or most of its descendants also had this trait. The qualifier *most* is important, because it is not unusual for certain subgroups within a lineage to lose particular traits over the course of evolution, much as humans are gradually losing fur and tailbones.

Eventually, seven major groups of eukaryotes came to be identified on the basis of diagnostic morphological characteristics. These groups and the synapomorphies that identify them are listed in **TABLE 30.2**. Notice that in almost every case, the synapomorphies that define eukaryotic lineages are changes in structures that protect or support the cell or that influence the organism's ability to move or feed. The plants, fungi, and animals represent subgroups within two of the seven major eukaryotic lineages.

Evaluating Molecular Phylogenies

When researchers began using DNA sequence data to estimate the evolutionary relationships among eukaryotes, the analyses suggested that the seven groups identified on the basis of distinctive morphological characteristics were indeed monophyletic. This was important support for the hypothesis that the distinctive morphological features were shared, derived characters that existed in a common ancestor of each lineage.

The phylogenetic tree in **FIGURE 30.7** is the current best estimate of the eukaryotes' evolutionary history. As you read this tree, note that:

- The Amoebozoa and the Opisthokonta—which include fungi and animals—form a monophyletic group called the Unikonta.
- The other five major eukaryotic lineages form a monophyletic group called the Bikonta.

Understanding where the root or base of the tree of Eukarya lies has been more problematic. Finding it will help researchers understand what the common ancestor looked like and how eukaryotic lineages evolved over time. One hypothesis suggested that the first eukaryotic split was between unikonts and bikonts—meaning, between eukaryotes that have one flagellum and those with two flagella. This hypothesis is tentative and controversial, however, given the data analyzed to date. Researchers continue to work on the issue of placing the root of the Eukarya.

Discovering New Lineages via Direct Sequencing

The effort to refine the phylogeny of the Eukarya is ongoing. But of all the research frontiers in eukaryotic diversity, the most exciting may be the one based on the technique called direct sequencing.

Direct sequencing is based on sampling soil or water, analyzing the DNA sequence of specific genes in the sample, and using the data to place the organisms in the sample on a phylogenetic tree. Direct sequencing and metagenomics have led to the discovery of previously unknown but major lineages of Archaea (see Chapter 29). To the amazement of biologists all over the world, the same thing happened when researchers used direct sequencing to survey eukaryotes.

The first direct sequencing studies that focused on eukaryotes were published in 2001. One study sampled organisms at depths from 250 to 3000 meters (m) below the surface in waters off Antarctica; another focused on cells at depths of 75 m in the Pacific Ocean, near the equator. Both studies detected a wide array of species that were new to science.

Investigators who examined the samples microscopically were astonished to find that many of the newly discovered eukaryotes were tiny—from 0.2 micrometers (μm) to 5 μm in diameter. Subsequent work has confirmed the existence of many,

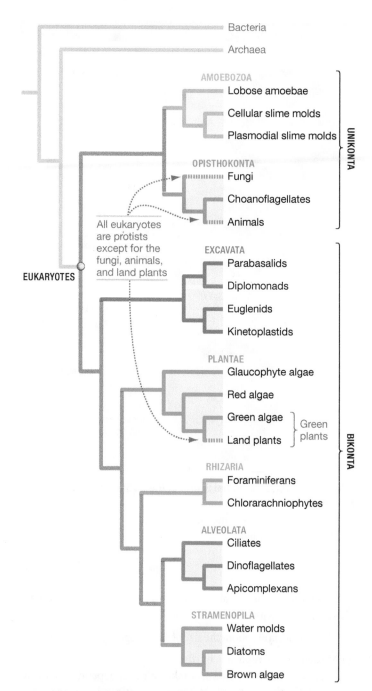

FIGURE 30.7 Phylogenetic Analyses Have Identified Seven Major Lineages of Eukaryotes. This tree shows selected subgroups from the seven major lineages discussed in this chapter. Kinetoplastids are not discussed in detail elsewhere in the chapter, but they include the pathogens *Trypanosoma* and *Leishmania* described in Table 30.1.

diverse species of protists that are less than 0.2 μm in diameter. These cells overlap in size with bacteria, which typically range from 0.5 μm to 2 μm in diameter.

Eukaryotic cells are much more variable in size than previously imagined. A whole new world of tiny protists has only recently been discovered.

30.3 What Themes Occur in the Diversification of Protists?

The protists range in size from bacteria-sized single cells to giant kelp. They live in habitats from the open oceans to the guts of termites. They are almost bewildering in their morphological and ecological diversity. Because they are a paraphyletic group, they do not share derived characteristics that set them apart from all other lineages on the tree of life.

One general theme that can help tie protists together is their amazing diversity. Once an important new innovation arose in protists, it triggered the evolution of species that live in a wide array of habitats and make a living in diverse ways.

What Morphological Innovations Evolved in Protists?

Virtually all bacteria and all archaea are unicellular. Given the distribution of multicellularity in eukaryotes, it is logical to conclude that the first eukaryote was also a single-celled organism.

Further, all eukaryotes alive today have (1) either mitochondria or genes that are normally found in mitochondria, (2) a nucleus and endomembrane system, and (3) a cytoskeleton. Based on the distribution of cell walls in living eukaryotes, it is likely that the first eukaryotes lacked this feature.

Using these observations, biologists hypothesize that the earliest eukaryotes were probably single-celled organisms with mitochondria, a nucleus and endomembrane system, and a cytoskeleton, but no cell wall.

It is also likely that the first eukaryotic cells swam using a novel type of flagellum. Eukaryotic flagella are completely different structures from bacterial flagella and evolved independently.

The eukaryotic flagellum is made up of microtubules, and dynein is the major motor protein. An undulating motion occurs as dynein molecules walk down microtubules (see Chapter 7). The flagella of bacteria and archaea, in contrast, are composed primarily of a protein called flagellin. Instead of undulating, prokaryotic flagella rotate to produce movement.

✔ If you understand the synapomorphies that identify the eukaryotes as a monophyletic group, you should be able to map the origin of the nuclear envelope and the eukaryotic flagellum on Figure 30.7. Once you've done that, let's consider how several of these key new morphological features arose and influenced the subsequent diversification of protists, beginning with one of the traits that define the Eukarya.

Endosymbiosis and the Origin of the Mitochondrion

Mitochondria are organelles that generate adenosine triphosphate (ATP) using pyruvate as an electron donor and oxygen as the ultimate electron acceptor (see Chapter 9).

In 1981 evolutionary biologist Lynn Margulis expanded on a radical hypothesis—first proposed in the nineteenth century—to explain the origin of mitochondria. The **endosymbiosis theory** proposes that mitochondria originated when a bacterial cell took up residence inside another cell about 2 billion years ago.

The theory's name was inspired by the Greek word roots *endo*, *sym*, and *bio* (literally, "inside-together-living"). **Symbiosis** is said to occur when individuals of two different species live in physical contact; **endosymbiosis** occurs when an organism of one species lives inside the cells of an organism of another species.

How and when this momentous event occurred is hotly debated. Some scientists think a primitive amoeba-like eukaryote engulfed a bacterium and simply failed to digest it in its lysosome, allowing it to take up residence. Evidence that was used to support this theory includes the similar feeding habits of today's amoeba, and the existence of some protist species that seem to lack mitochondria.

Recent evidence, however, indicates that all protists originally had mitochondria, and some lost them. A new idea gaining support is that the first eukaryote may have been formed as a result of an endosymbiosis between two prokaryotes—an archaeal host and a bacterium (**FIGURE 30.8**). After this chance union occurred, cells developed nuclei and became much larger. Both of these changes appear to have been triggered by the bacterial invader.

The relationship between the archaeal host and the engulfed bacterial cell was presumed to be stable because a mutual advantage existed between them: The host supplied the bacterium with protection and carbon compounds from its prey, while the bacterium produced much more ATP than the host cell could synthesize on its own.

When Margulis first began promoting the endosymbiosis theory, it met with a storm of criticism—largely because it seemed slightly preposterous. But gradually biologists began to examine it rigorously. For example, endosymbiotic relationships between protists and bacteria exist today. Among the α-proteobacteria alone (see Chapter 29), three major groups are found *only* inside eukaryotic cells. In many cases, the bacterial cells are transmitted to offspring in eggs or sperm and are required for survival.

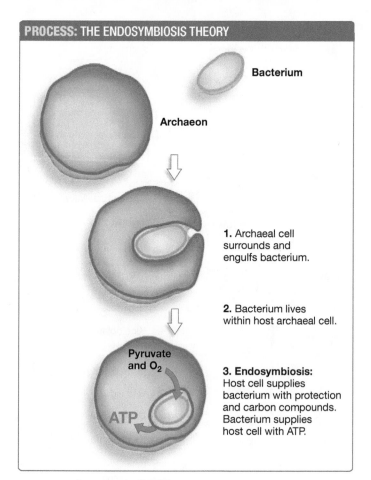

PROCESS: THE ENDOSYMBIOSIS THEORY

Bacterium

Archaeon

1. Archaeal cell surrounds and engulfs bacterium.

2. Bacterium lives within host archaeal cell.

Pyruvate and O₂

ATP

3. Endosymbiosis: Host cell supplies bacterium with protection and carbon compounds. Bacterium supplies host cell with ATP.

FIGURE 30.8 Proposed Initial Steps in the Evolution of the Mitochondrion.

✔ **QUESTION** According to this hypothesis, how many membranes should surround a mitochondrion? Explain your logic.

Several observations about the structure of mitochondria are also consistent with the endosymbiosis theory:

- Mitochondria are about the size of an average α-proteobacterium.

- Mitochondria replicate by fission, as do bacterial cells. The duplication of mitochondria takes place independently of division by the host cell. When eukaryotic cells divide, each daughter cell receives some of the many mitochondria present.

- Mitochondria have their own ribosomes and manufacture some of their own proteins. Mitochondrial ribosomes closely resemble bacterial ribosomes in size and composition and are poisoned by antibiotics such as streptomycin that inhibit bacterial, but not eukaryotic, ribosomes.

- Mitochondria have double membranes, consistent with the engulfing mechanism of origin illustrated in Figure 30.8.

- Mitochondria have their own genomes, which are organized as circular molecules—much like a bacterial chromosome. Mitochondrial genes code for a few of the proteins needed to conduct electron transport and RNAs needed to translate the mitochondrial genome.

Although these data are impressive, they are only consistent with the endosymbiosis theory. Stated another way, they do not exclude other explanations. This is a general principle in science: Evidence is considered strong when it cannot be explained by reasonable alternative hypotheses. In this case, the key was to find data that tested predictions made by Margulis's idea against predictions made by an alternative theory: that mitochondria evolved within eukaryotic cells, separately from bacteria.

A breakthrough occurred when researchers realized that according to the "within-eukaryotes" theory, the genes found in mitochondria are derived from nuclear genes in ancestral eukaryotes. Margulis's theory, in contrast, proposed that the genes found in mitochondria were bacterial in origin.

These predictions were tested by studies on the phylogenetic relationships of mitochondrial genes. Specifically, researchers compared gene sequences isolated from eukaryotic mitochondrial DNA with sequences of similar genes isolated from eukaryotic nuclear DNA and with DNA from several species of bacteria. Exactly as the endosymbiosis theory predicted, mitochondrial gene sequences are much more closely related to the sequences from the α-proteobacteria than to sequences from the nuclear DNA of eukaryotes.

The result diagrammed in **FIGURE 30.9** was considered overwhelming evidence that the mitochondrial genome came from an α-proteobacterium rather than from a eukaryote. The endosymbiosis theory was the only reasonable explanation for the data.

The results were a stunning vindication of a theory that had once been intensely controversial. Mitochondria evolved via endosymbiosis between an α-proteobacterium and an archaeal host.

One intriguing feature of mitochondrial genomes is that they typically encode less than 50 genes, whereas the genomes of their bacterial cousins encode about 1500 genes. Most of the genes from the endosymbiotic bacterium moved into the nuclear genome in what was one of the most spectacular **lateral gene transfer** events in the history of life (see Chapter 21). Some unnecessary genes were lost, but many still encode proteins that are synthesized by cytosolic ribosomes and imported into mitochondria.

✔ If you understand the endosymbiosis theory and the evidence for it, you should be able to describe how the chloroplast—the organelle that is the site of photosynthesis in eukaryotes—could arise via endosymbiosis.

Now let's turn to another distinguishing feature of eukaryotic cells—the nucleus, with its unique double membrane called the nuclear envelope. The origin of the nuclear envelope is also a subject of debate.

The Nuclear Envelope The leading hypothesis to explain the origin of the nuclear envelope is based on infoldings of the plasma membrane. As the drawings in **FIGURE 30.10** show, a stepwise process could give rise to small infoldings that were elaborated

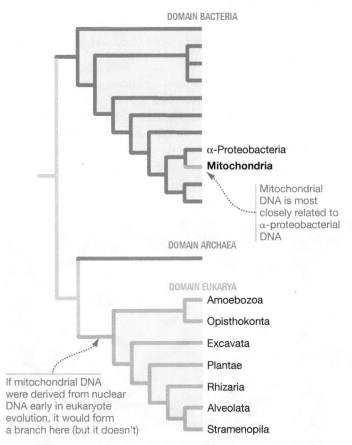

FIGURE 30.9 Phylogenetic Data Support the Endosymbiosis Theory.

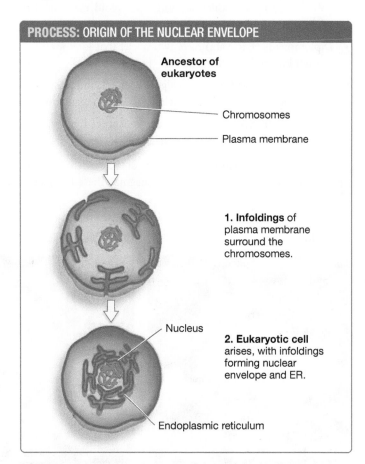

FIGURE 30.10 A Hypothesis for the Origin of the Nuclear Envelope. Infoldings of the plasma membrane, analogous to those shown here, have been observed in bacteria living today.

by mutation and natural selection over time, and the infolding could eventually become detached from the plasma membrane. Note that the infoldings would have given rise to the nuclear envelope and the endoplasmic reticulum (ER) together.

Two lines of evidence support this hypothesis: Infoldings of the plasma membrane occur in some bacteria living today, and the nuclear envelope and ER of today's eukaryotes are continuous (see Chapter 7). ✔ If you understand the infolding hypothesis, you should be able to explain why these observations support it.

According to current thinking, the evolution of the nuclear envelope was advantageous because it separated transcription and translation. Recall that RNA transcripts are processed inside the nucleus but translated outside the nucleus (see Chapter 17). In bacteria and archaea, transcription and translation occur together.

With a simple nuclear envelope in place, alternative splicing and other forms of RNA processing could occur—giving the early eukaryotes a novel way to control gene expression (see Chapter 19). The take-home message here is that an important morphological innovation gave the early eukaryotes a new way to manage and process genetic information.

Once a nucleus had evolved, it underwent diversification. In some cases, unique types of nuclei are associated with the founding of important lineages of protists.

- Ciliates (Alveolata) have a diploid micronucleus that is involved only in reproduction, and a polyploid macronucleus where transcription occurs.

- Diplomonads (Excavata) have two nuclei that look identical; it is not known how they interact.

- In foraminifera (Rhizaria), red algae (Plantae), and plasmodial slime molds (Amoebozoa), certain cells contain many nuclei.

- Dinoflagellates (Alveolata) have chromosomes that lack histones and attach to the nuclear envelope.

In each case, the distinctive structure of the nucleus is a synapomorphy that allows biologists to recognize these lineages as distinct monophyletic groups.

Structures for Support and Protection Many protists have cell walls outside their plasma membrane; others have hard external structures called a **shell;** others have rigid structures inside the plasma membrane. In many cases, these novel structures represent synapomorphies that identify monophyletic groups among protists. For example:

- Diatoms (Stramenopila) are surrounded by a glass-like, silicon-dioxide cell wall (**FIGURE 30.11a**). The cell wall is made up of two pieces that fit together in a box-and-lid arrangement, like the petri plates you may have seen in lab.

- Dinoflagellates (Alveolata) have a cell wall made up of cellulose plates (**FIGURE 30.11b**).

- Within the foraminiferans (Rhizaria), some subgroups secrete an intricate, chambered calcium carbonate shell (**FIGURE 30.11c**).

- Members of other foraminiferan subgroups, and some amoebae, cover themselves with tiny pebbles.

- The parabasalids (Excavata) have a unique internal support rod, consisting of cross-linked microtubules that run the length of the cell.

- The euglenids (Excavata) have a collection of protein strips located just under the plasma membrane. The strips are supported by microtubules and stiffen the cell.

- All alveolates (Alveolata) have distinctive sac-like structures called alveoli, located just under the plasma membrane, that help stiffen the cell.

In many cases, the diversification of protists has been associated with the evolution of innovative structures for support and protection.

Multicellularity One of the most significant changes in the history of life on Earth occurred when organisms containing more than one cell evolved. The mutations leading to **multicellularity** probably first caused cells to simply stick together after cell division. Selection pressures could then act on these larger, colonial organisms, allowing them to evolve and diversify.

(a) Diatom

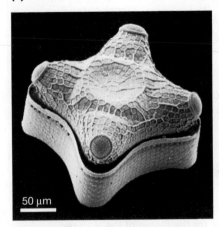

50 μm

Glassy cell wall made of silicon dioxide

(b) Dinoflagellate

10 μm

Tough plates in cell wall made of cellulose

(c) Foraminiferan

50 μm

Chalky, chambered shell made of calcium carbonate

FIGURE 30.11 Hard Outer Coverings in Protists Vary in Composition.

Eventually cells became specialized for different functions. In the simplest multicellular species, certain cells are specialized for producing or obtaining food while other cells are specialized for reproduction. The key point about multicellularity is that not all cells express the same genes.

A few species of bacteria are capable of aggregating and forming structures called fruiting bodies (see Chapter 29). Because cells in the fruiting bodies of these bacteria differentiate into specialized stalk cells and spore-forming cells, they are considered multicellular. But the vast majority of multicellular species are members of the Eukarya.

Multicellularity arose independently in a wide array of eukaryotic lineages, including the green plants, fungi, animals, brown algae, slime molds, and red algae.

To summarize, an array of novel morphological traits played a key role as protists diversified: the mitochondrion, the nucleus and endomembrane system, structures for protection and support, and multicellularity. Evolutionary innovations allowed protists to build and manage the eukaryotic cell in new ways.

Once a new type of eukaryotic cell or multicellular individual existed, subsequent diversification was often triggered by novel ways of finding food, moving, or reproducing. Let's consider each of these life processes in turn.

How Do Protists Obtain Food?

Bacteria and archaea can use a wide array of molecules as electron donors and electron acceptors during cellular respiration (see Chapter 29). Some get these molecules by absorbing them directly from the environment. Other bacteria don't absorb their nutrition—instead, they make their own food via photosynthesis. Many groups of protists are similar to bacteria in the way they find food: They perform photosynthesis or absorb their food directly from the environment.

But one of the most important stories in the diversification of protists was the evolution of a novel method for finding food.

Many protists ingest their food—they eat bacteria, archaea, or even other protists whole. This process is called **phagocytosis** (see Chapter 7). When phagocytosis occurs, an individual takes in packets of food much larger than individual molecules. Thus, protists feed by either (1) ingesting packets of food, (2) absorbing organic molecules directly from the environment, or (3) performing photosynthesis.

Some protists ingest food as well as performing photosynthesis—meaning that they use a combination of feeding strategies. It's also important to recognize that all three lifestyles—ingestive, absorptive, and photosynthetic—can occur within a single lineage.

To drive this last point home, consider the monophyletic group called the alveolates. This lineage has three major subgroups—dinoflagellates, apicomplexans, and ciliates. About half of the dinoflagellates are photosynthetic, but many others are parasitic and absorb nutrients from their hosts. Apicomplexans are parasitic. Ciliates include many species that ingest prey, but some ciliates live in the guts of cattle or the gills of fish. Other ciliate species make a living by holding algae or other types of photosynthetic endosymbionts inside their cells.

The punch line? Within each of the seven major lineages of eukaryotes, different methods for feeding helped trigger diversification.

Ingestive Feeding Ingestive lifestyles are based on eating live or dead organisms or on scavenging loose bits of organic debris. Protists such as the cellular slime mold *Dictyostelium discoideum* are large enough to engulf bacteria and archaea; many protists are large enough to surround and ingest other protists or even microscopic animals.

Feeding by phagocytosis is possible in protists that lack a cell wall. A flexible membrane and dynamic cytoskeleton give these species the ability to surround and "swallow" prey using long, fingerlike projections called **pseudopodia** ("false-feet") (**FIGURE 30.12a**). Phagocytosis was a prerequisite for the endosymbiosis event that led to chloroplasts.

(a) Pseudopodia engulf food.

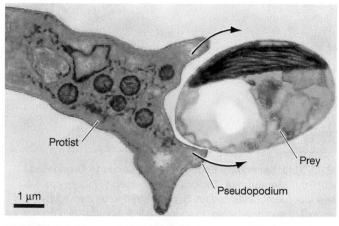

(b) Ciliary currents sweep food into gullet.

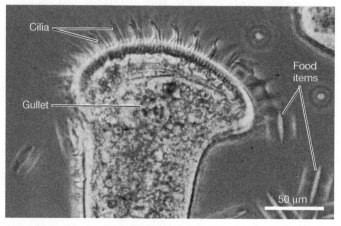

FIGURE 30.12 Ingestive Feeding. Methods of prey capture vary among ingestive protists. **(a)** Some predators engulf prey with pseudopodia; **(b)** other predators sweep them into their gullets with water currents set up by the beating of cilia. Note that the cells in part (a) have been colorized.

Although many ingestive feeders actively hunt down prey and engulf them, others do not. Instead of taking themselves to food, these species attach themselves to a surface. Protists that feed in this way have cilia that surround the mouth and beat in a coordinated way. The motion creates water currents that sweep food particles into the cell (**FIGURE 30.12b**).

Absorptive Feeding   Absorptive feeding occurs when nutrients are taken up directly from the environment, across the plasma membrane, usually through transport proteins. Absorptive feeding is common among protists.

Some protists that live by absorptive feeding are **decomposers,** meaning that they feed on dead organic matter, or **detritus.** But many of the protists that absorb their nutrition directly from the environment live inside other organisms. If an absorptive species damages its host, that species is called a **parasite.**

Photosynthesis—Endosymbiosis and the Origin of Chloroplasts

You might recall that photosystems I and II evolved in bacteria, and that both photosystems occur in cyanobacteria. None of the basic machinery required for photosynthesis evolved in eukaryotes. Instead, they "stole" it—via endosymbiosis.

The endosymbiosis theory contends that the eukaryotic chloroplast originated when a protist engulfed a cyanobacterium. Once inside the protist, the photosynthetic bacterium provided its eukaryotic host with oxygen and glucose in exchange for protection and access to light. If the endosymbiosis theory is correct, today's chloroplasts trace their ancestry to cyanobacteria.

All of the photosynthetic eukaryotes have both chloroplasts and mitochondria. The evidence for an endosymbiotic origin for the chloroplast is persuasive.

- Chloroplasts have the same list of bacteria-like characteristics presented earlier for mitochondria.

- Many examples of endosymbiotic cyanobacteria are living inside the cells of protists or animals today.

- Chloroplasts contain a circular DNA molecule containing genes that are extremely similar to cyanobacterial genes.

- The photosynthetic organelle of one group of protists, the glaucophyte algae, has an outer layer containing the same constituent (peptidoglycan) found in the cell walls of cyanobacteria.

Like mitochondria, the chloroplast genome is very small compared with genomes of living cyanobacteria; most of the original genes were either lost or transferred to the nucleus.

✔If you understand the evidence for the endosymbiotic origin of the chloroplast, you should be able to add a label indicating the location of chloroplast genes on the phylogenetic tree in Figure 30.7.

Photosynthesis—Primary versus Secondary Endosymbiosis

Which eukaryote originally obtained a photosynthetic organelle? Because all species in the Plantae have chloroplasts with two membranes, biologists infer that the original, or primary,

endosymbiosis occurred in these species' common ancestor. That species eventually gave rise to all subgroups in the Plantae lineage—the glaucophyte algae, red algae, and green plants (green algae and land plants).

But chloroplasts also occur in four of the other major lineages of protists—the Excavata, Rhizaria, Alveolata, and Stramenopila. In these species, the chloroplast is surrounded by more than two membranes—usually four.

To explain this observation, researchers hypothesize that the ancestors of these groups acquired their chloroplasts by ingesting photosynthetic protists that already had chloroplasts. This process, called secondary endosymbiosis, occurs when an organism engulfs a photosynthetic eukaryotic cell and retains its chloroplasts as intracellular symbionts. Secondary endosymbiosis is illustrated in **FIGURE 30.13**.

FIGURE 30.14 shows where primary and secondary endosymbiosis occurred on the phylogenetic tree of eukaryotes. Once

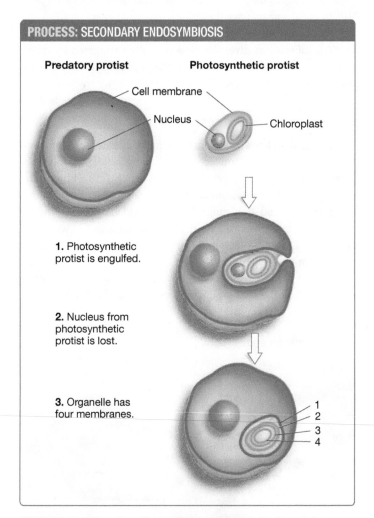

PROCESS: SECONDARY ENDOSYMBIOSIS

Predatory protist   Photosynthetic protist

Cell membrane

Nucleus   Chloroplast

1. Photosynthetic protist is engulfed.

2. Nucleus from photosynthetic protist is lost.

3. Organelle has four membranes.

1
2
3
4

FIGURE 30.13 Secondary Endosymbiosis Leads to Organelles with Four Membranes. The chloroplasts found in some protists have four membranes and are hypothesized to be derived by secondary endosymbiosis. In species where chloroplasts have three membranes, biologists hypothesize that secondary endosymbiosis was followed by the loss of one membrane.

protists obtained the chloroplast, it was "swapped around" to new lineages via secondary endosymbiosis.

✔ If you understand endosymbiosis, you should be able to assess and explain why the primary and secondary endosymbiosis events introduced in this chapter represent the most massive lateral gene transfers in the history of life, in terms of the number of genes moved at once. (To review lateral gene transfer, see Chapter 21.)

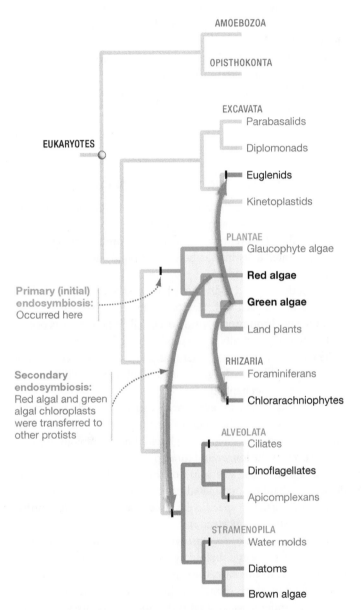

Primary (initial) endosymbiosis: Occurred here

Secondary endosymbiosis: Red algal and green algal chloroplasts were transferred to other protists

FIGURE 30.14 Photosynthesis Arose in Protists by Primary Endosymbiosis and Then Spread among Lineages via Secondary Endosymbiosis. Biochemical similarities link the chloroplasts found in alveolates and stramenopiles with red algae and the chloroplasts found in euglenids and chlorarachniophytes with green algae. Notice that among the alveolates and stramenopiles, only the dinoflagellates, diatoms, and brown algae have photosynthetic species. In ciliates, apicomplexans, and water molds, the chloroplast has been lost or has changed function.

How Do Protists Move?

Many protists actively move to find food. Predators such as the slime mold *Dictyostelium discoideum* crawl over a substrate in search of prey. Most of the unicellular, photosynthetic species are capable of swimming to sunny locations, though others drift passively in water currents. How are these crawling and swimming movements possible?

Amoeboid motion is a sliding movement observed in some protists. In the classic mode illustrated in **FIGURE 30.15**, pseudopodia stream forward over a substrate, and the rest of the cytoplasm, organelles, and plasma membrane follow. The motion requires ATP and involves interactions between proteins called actin and myosin inside the cytoplasm. The mechanism is related to muscle movement in animals (see Chapter 48). But at the level of the whole cell, the precise sequence of events during amoeboid movement is still uncertain. The issue is attracting researchers' attention, because key immune system cells in humans use amoeboid motion as they hunt down and destroy disease-causing agents.

The other major mode of locomotion in protists involves flagella or cilia (**FIGURE 30.16**, see page 566). Recall that flagella and cilia both consist of nine sets of doublet (paired) microtubules arranged around two central, single microtubules (see Chapter 7). Flagella are long and are usually found alone or in pairs; cilia are short and usually occur in large numbers on any one cell.

Amoeboid motion via **pseudopodia**

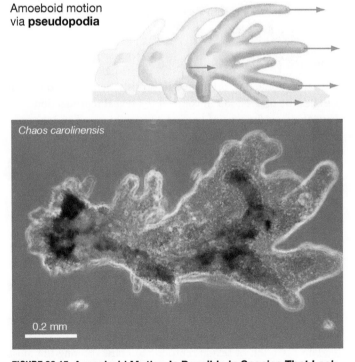

FIGURE 30.15 Amoeboid Motion Is Possible in Species That Lack Cell Walls. In amoeboid motion, long pseudopodia stream out from the cell. The rest of the cytoplasm, organelles, and external membrane follow.

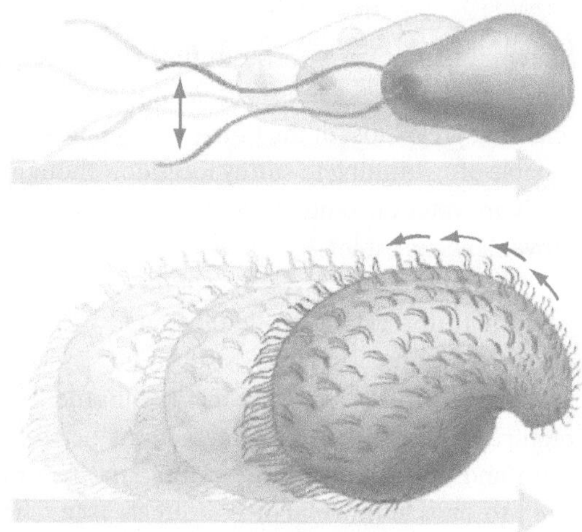

(a) Swimming via **flagella**

(b) Swimming via **cilia**

FIGURE 30.16 Many Protists Swim Using Flagella or Cilia.
(a) Flagella are long and few in number. **(b)** Cilia are short and numerous. In many cases they are used in swimming.

Even closely related protists can use radically different forms of locomotion. For example, within the Alveolata, the ciliates swim by beating their cilia, the dinoflagellates swim by whipping their flagella, and mature apicomplexan cells move by amoeboid motion (though their gametes swim via flagella). It is also common to find protists that do not exhibit active movement, but instead float passively in water currents.

Movement is yet another example of the extensive diversification that occurred within each of the seven major monophyletic groups of eukaryotes.

How Do Protists Reproduce?

Sexual reproduction originated in protists. Sexual reproduction can best be understood in contrast to asexual reproduction. The key issues are the type of nuclear division involved and the consequences for genetic diversity in the offspring produced.

- Asexual reproduction is based on mitosis and cell division in eukaryotic organisms and on fission in bacteria and archaea. It results in daughter cells that are genetically identical to the parent.

- Sexual reproduction is based on meiosis and fusion of gametes. It results in daughter cells that are genetically different from their parents and from each other.

Most protists undergo asexual reproduction routinely. But sexual reproduction occurs only intermittently in many protists—often at one particular time of year, or when individuals are stressed by overcrowding or scarce food supplies.

The evolution of sexual reproduction ranks among the most significant evolutionary innovations observed in eukaryotes.

Sexual versus Asexual Reproduction The leading hypothesis to explain why meiosis evolved states that genetically variable offspring may be able to thrive if the environment changes. For example, offspring with genotypes different from those of their parents may be better able to withstand attacks by parasites that successfully attacked their parents. This is a key point because many types of parasites, including bacteria and viruses, have short generation times and evolve quickly.

Because the genotypes and phenotypes of parasites are constantly changing, natural selection favors host individuals with new genotypes. The idea is that novel genotypes in offspring generated by meiosis may contain combinations of alleles that allow hosts to withstand attack by new strains of parasites. In short, many biologists view sexual reproduction as an adaptation to fight disease.

✔ If you understand the changing-environment hypothesis for the evolution of sex, you should be able to evaluate and explain whether it is consistent with the observation that many protists undergo meiosis when food is scarce or the population density is high.

Life Cycles—Haploid versus Diploid Dominated

A life cycle describes the sequence of events that occur as individuals grow, mature, and reproduce. The evolution of meiosis introduced a new event in the life cycle of protist species; what's more, it created a distinction between haploid and diploid phases in the life of an individual.

Recall that diploid individuals have two of each type of chromosome inside each cell. Haploid individuals have just one of each type of chromosome inside each cell. When meiosis occurs in diploid cells, it results in the production of haploid cells.

The life cycle of most bacteria and archaea is extremely simple: A cell divides, feeds, grows, and divides again. Bacteria and archaea are always haploid.

In contrast, virtually every aspect of a life cycle is variable among protists—whether meiosis occurs, whether asexual reproduction occurs, and whether the haploid or the diploid phase of the life cycle is the longer and more prominent phase.

FIGURE 30.17 illustrates some of this variation. Figure 30.17a depicts the haploid-dominated life cycle observed in many unicellular protists. The specific example given here is the dinoflagellate *Gyrodinium uncatenum*.

To analyze a life cycle, start with **fertilization**—the fusion of two gametes to form a diploid zygote. Then trace what happens to the zygote. In this case, the diploid zygote undergoes meiosis. The haploid products of meiosis then grow into mature cells that eventually undergo asexual reproduction or produce gametes by mitosis and cell division.

Now contrast the dinoflagellate life cycle in Figure 30.17a with the diploid-dominated life cycle in Figure 30.17b. The specific organism shown here is the diatom *Thalassiosira punctigera*. Notice that after fertilization, the diploid zygote develops into a sexually mature, diploid adult cell that can reproduce asexually by dividing mitotically. Meiosis occurs in the adult and results in the formation of haploid gametes, which then fuse to form a diploid zygote. The important contrasts with the

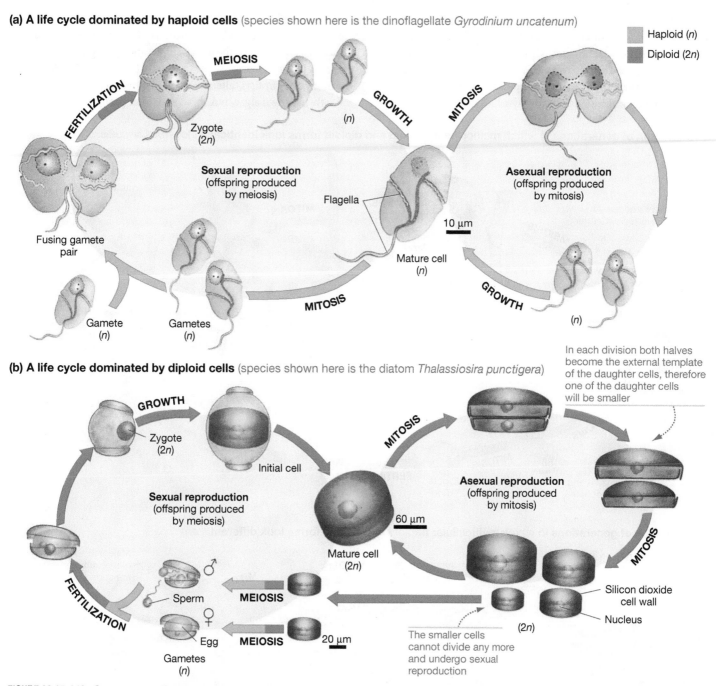

(a) A life cycle dominated by haploid cells (species shown here is the dinoflagellate *Gyrodinium uncatenum*)

Haploid (*n*)
Diploid (2*n*)

MEIOSIS

FERTILIZATION

Zygote (2*n*)

GROWTH

MITOSIS

(*n*)

Sexual reproduction (offspring produced by meiosis)

Asexual reproduction (offspring produced by mitosis)

Flagella

10 μm

Fusing gamete pair

Mature cell (*n*)

Gamete (*n*)

Gametes (*n*)

MITOSIS

GROWTH

(*n*)

(b) A life cycle dominated by diploid cells (species shown here is the diatom *Thalassiosira punctigera*)

GROWTH

Zygote (2*n*)

Initial cell

MITOSIS

In each division both halves become the external template of the daughter cells, therefore one of the daughter cells will be smaller

Sexual reproduction (offspring produced by meiosis)

Asexual reproduction (offspring produced by mitosis)

60 μm

Mature cell (2*n*)

FERTILIZATION

Sperm

MEIOSIS

Egg

MEIOSIS

20 μm

Gametes (*n*)

(2*n*)

Silicon dioxide cell wall

Nucleus

MITOSIS

The smaller cells cannot divide any more and undergo sexual reproduction

FIGURE 30.17 Life Cycles Vary Widely among Unicellular Protists. Many unicellular protists can reproduce by both sexual reproduction and asexual reproduction. The cell may be **(a)** haploid for most of its life or **(b)** diploid for most of its life.

haploid-dominated life cycle are that (**1**) meiosis occurs in the adult cell rather than in the zygote, and (**2**) gametes are the only haploid cells in the life cycle.

Life Cycles—Alternation of Generations In contrast to the relatively simple life cycles of single-celled protists shown in Figure 30.17, many multicellular protists have a multicellular haploid form in one phase of their life cycle alternating with a multicellular diploid form in another phase. This alternation of multicellular haploid and diploid forms is known as **alternation of generations.**

- The multicellular haploid form is called a **gametophyte,** because specialized cells in this individual produce gametes by mitosis and cell division.

- The multicellular diploid form is called a **sporophyte** because it has specialized cells that undergo meiosis to produce haploid cells called spores.

- A **spore** is a single haploid cell that divides mitotically to form a multicellular, haploid gametophyte. A gamete is also a single haploid cell, but its role is to fuse with another gamete to form a zygote.

When alternation of generations occurs, a diploid sporophyte undergoes meiosis and cell division to produce haploid spores. Each spore then divides by mitosis to form a haploid, multicellular gametophyte. The haploid gametes produced mitotically by gametophytes then fuse to form a diploid zygote, which grows into the diploid, multicellular sporophyte.

Gametophytes and sporophytes may be identical in appearance, as in the brown alga called *Ectocarpus siliculosus* (**FIGURE 30.18a**). In many cases, however, the gametophyte and sporophyte look different, as in the brown algae in the genus *Laminaria* (**FIGURE 30.18b**). Among the protists, alternation of generations evolved independently in brown algae, red algae, and other groups.

(a) Alternation of generations in which multicellular haploid and diploid forms look identical (*Ectocarpus siliculosus*)

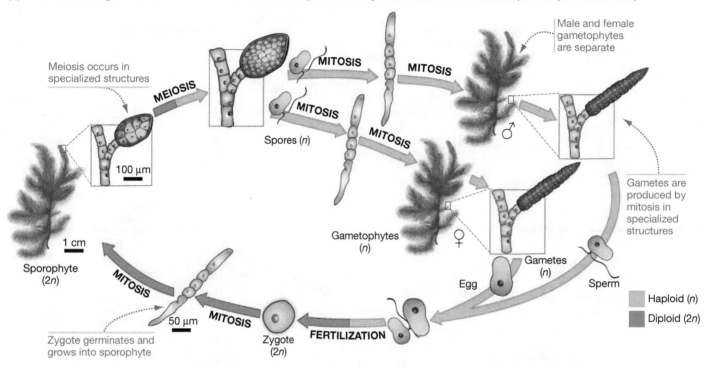

(b) Alternation of generations in which multicellular haploid and diploid forms look different (*Laminaria* sp.)

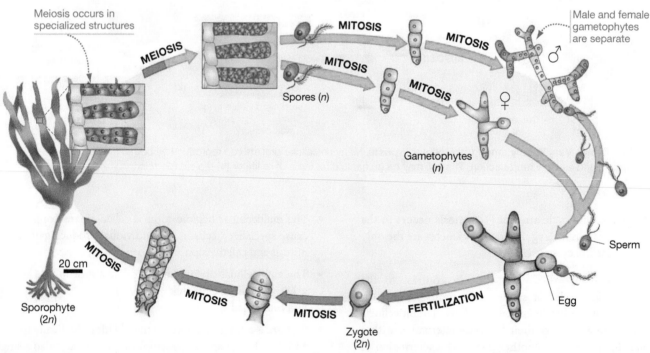

FIGURE 30.18 Alternation of Generations Occurs in Many Multicellular Protists. Compared here, two species of brown algae.

To understand alternation of generations, some students find it helpful to memorize this sentence: Sporophytes produce spores by meiosis; gametophytes produce gametes by mitosis.

✓ If you understand how life cycles vary among multicellular protists, you should be able to (1) define the terms alternation of generations, gametophyte, sporophyte, spore, zygote, and gamete; and (2) diagram a life cycle where alternation of generations occurs, without looking at Figure 30.18.

Why does so much variation occur in the types of life cycles observed among protists? The answer is not known. Variation in life cycles is a major theme in the diversification of protists and is discussed further in the chapter on green algae and land plants. Explaining why that variation exists remains a topic for future research.

30.4 Key Lineages of Protists

Each of the seven major Eukarya lineages has at least one distinctive morphological characteristic. But once an ancestor evolved a distinctive cell structure, its descendants diversified into a wide array of lifestyles. For example, parasitic species evolved independently in all seven major lineages. Photosynthetic species exist in most of the seven, and multicellularity evolved independently in at least four. Similar statements could be made about the evolution of life cycles and modes of locomotion.

In effect, each of the seven lineages represents a similar radiation of species into a wide array of lifestyles. Let's take a more detailed look at some representative taxa from six of the seven major lineages, starting with an overview of each one. The seventh major lineage—the opisthokonts—is featured in the chapters on fungi and the animals. The lineage called green plants is analyzed separately.

Amoebozoa

Species in the Amoebozoa lack cell walls and take in food by engulfing it. They move via amoeboid motion and produce large, lobe-like pseudopodia. They are abundant in freshwater habitats and in wet soils; some are parasites of humans and other animals.

Major subgroups in the lineage are lobose amoebae, cellular slime molds, and plasmodial slime molds. The cellular slime mold *Dictyostelium discoideum* is described in detail in **BioSkills 13** in Appendix B. ✓ You should be able to mark the origin of this lineage's amoeboid form on Figure 30.7 and explain whether it evolved independently of the amoeboid form in Rhizaria.

● Amoebozoa > Plasmodial Slime Molds

Excavata

The unicellular species that form the Excavata are named for the morphological feature that distinguishes them—an "excavated" feeding groove found on one side of the cell. Because some lack recognizable mitochondria, excavates were once thought to trace their ancestry to eukaryotes that existed before the origin of mitochondria. But researchers have found that excavates either have

(1) genes in their nuclear genomes that are of mitochondrial origin, or (2) unusual organelles that appear to be vestigial mitochondria. These observations support the hypothesis that the ancestors of excavates had mitochondria, but that these organelles were lost or reduced over time in this lineage. ✓ You should be able to mark the loss of the mitochondrion on Figure 30.7.

● Excavata > Parabasalids, Diplomonads, and Euglenids

Plantae

Biologists are beginning to use the name **Plantae** to refer to the monophyletic group that includes glaucophyte algae, red algae, green algae, and land plants.

The glaucophyte algae are unicellular or colonial. They live as plankton or attached to substrates in freshwater environments—particularly in bogs or swamps. Some glaucophyte species have flagella or produce flagellated spores, but sexual reproduction has never been observed in the group. The chloroplasts of glaucophytes have a distinct bright blue-green color.

All subgroups within Plantae are descended from a common ancestor that engulfed a cyanobacterium, beginning the endosymbiosis that led to the evolution of the chloroplast—their distinguishing morphological feature. This initial endosymbiosis probably occurred in an ancestor of today's glaucophyte algae. To support this hypothesis, biologists point to several important similarities between cyanobacterial cells and the chloroplasts that are found in the glaucophytes.

- Both have cell walls that contain peptidoglycan and that can be disrupted by the antibacterial compounds lysozyme and penicillin.

- The glaucophyte chloroplast also has a membrane outside its wall that is similar to the membrane found in Gram-negative bacteria (see Chapter 29).

Consistent with these observations, phylogenetic analyses of DNA sequence data place the glaucophytes as the sister group to all other members of the Plantae. ✓ You should be able to mark the origin of the plant chloroplast on Figure 30.7.

Green algae and land plants are described later; here we consider just the red algae in detail.

● Plantae > Red Algae

Rhizaria

The rhizarians are single-celled amoebae that lack cell walls, though some species produce elaborate shell-like coverings. They move by amoeboid motion and produce long, slender pseudopodia. Over 11 major subgroups in this lineage have been identified and named, including the planktonic organisms called actinopods—which synthesize glassy, silicon-rich skeletons—and the chlorarachniophytes, which obtained a chloroplast via secondary endosymbiosis and are photosynthetic. The best-studied and most abundant group is the foraminiferans. ✓ You should be able to mark the origin of the rhizarian amoeboid form on Figure 30.7.

● Rhizaria > Foraminiferans

Alveolata

Alveolates are distinguished by small sacs, called alveoli, that are located just under their plasma membranes. Although all members of this lineage are unicellular, the ciliates, the dinoflagellates, and the apicomplexans are remarkably diverse in morphology and lifestyle. ✔ You should be able to mark the origin of alveoli on Figure 30.7.

● Alveolata > Ciliates, Dinoflagellates, and Apicomplexans

Stramenopila (Heterokonta)

Stramenopiles are sometimes called heterokonts, which translates as "different hairs." At some stage of their life cycle, all stramenopiles have flagella that are covered with distinctive hollow "hairs." The structure of these flagella is unique to the stramenopiles (Figure 30.6). ✔ You should be able to mark the origin of the "hairy" flagellum on Figure 30.7. The lineage includes a large number of unicellular forms, although the brown algae are multicellular and include the world's tallest marine organisms, the kelp.

● Stramenopila > Water Molds, Diatoms, and Brown Algae

Amoebozoa > Plasmodial Slime Molds

The plasmodial slime molds got their name because individuals form a large, weblike structure that consists of a single cell containing thousands of diploid nuclei (**FIGURE 30.19**). Like water molds, the plasmodial slime molds were once considered fungi on the basis of their general morphological similarity.

Morphology The huge "supercell" form, with many nuclei in a single cell, occurs in few protists other than plasmodial slime molds. ✔ You should be able to mark the origin of the supercell on Figure 30.7.

Feeding and locomotion Plasmodial slime molds feed on microorganisms associated with decaying vegetation and move by amoeboid motion or cytoplasmic streaming.

Reproduction Some evidence suggests that when food becomes scarce, part of the amoeba forms a stalk topped by a ball-like structure in which nuclei undergo meiosis and form spores. The spores are then dispersed to new habitats by the wind or small animals. After spores germinate to form amoebae, two amoebae fuse to form a diploid cell that begins to feed and eventually grows into a supercell.

Human and ecological impacts Like cellular slime molds, plasmodial slime molds influence nutrient cycling by feeding on microorganisms. Some species are important model organisms for the study of cell biology and the origin of multicellularity.

Physarum polycephalum

Single cell with many nuclei

5 mm

FIGURE 30.19 Plasmodial Slime Molds Are Important Decomposers in Forests.

The lineage Excavata includes free-living and symbiotic species, and some that are parasites. All are single-celled, and many lack functional mitochondria.

All of the 300 known species of parabasalids live inside animals; some live only in the guts of termites, where they aid in the digestion of cellulose. The relationship between termites and parabasalids is considered mutualistic, because both parties benefit from the symbiosis.

About 100 species of diplomonads have been named. Many live in the guts of animal species without causing harm to their host; other species live in stagnant-water habitats.

There are about 1000 known species of euglenids. Although most live in freshwater, a few are found in marine habitats.

Morphology Parabasalid cells have a distinctive rod of cross-linked microtubules that runs the length of the cell. The rod is attached to the basal bodies where a cluster of flagella arise (**FIGURE 30.20**). Diplomonad cells have two nuclei, which resemble eyes when viewed under the microscope (**FIGURE 30.21**). Each nucleus is associated with four flagella, for a total of eight flagella per cell. Euglenid cells have a unique system of interlocking proteins just inside the plasma membrane that stiffen and support the cell. Some euglenid cells have a light-sensitive "eyespot" and use flagella to swim toward light (**FIGURE 30.22**).

Feeding and locomotion Some euglenids have chloroplasts and perform photosynthesis, and some diplomonads are parasitic, but most other members of the Excavata feed by engulfing bacteria, archaea, and organic matter. Most swim using their flagella. ✔ You should be able to explain how the observation of ingestive feeding in euglenids relates to the hypothesis that this lineage gained chloroplasts via secondary endosymbiosis.

Giardia intestinalis

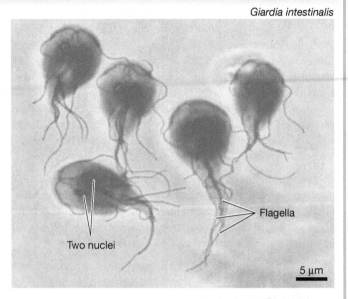

FIGURE 30.21 *Giardia* **Causes Intestinal Infections in Humans.**

Reproduction Nearly all members of the Excavata are known to reproduce only asexually. Sexual reproduction has been observed in just a few species of parabasalids.

Human and ecological impacts Infections of *Trichomonas*, a parabasalid, can sometimes cause reproductive tract problems in humans. However, members of this genus may also live in the gut or mouth of humans without causing harm. The diplomonad *Giardia intestinalis* is a common intestinal parasite in humans and causes giardiasis, or beaver fever. Euglenids are important components of freshwater plankton and food chains.

Trichomonas vaginalis

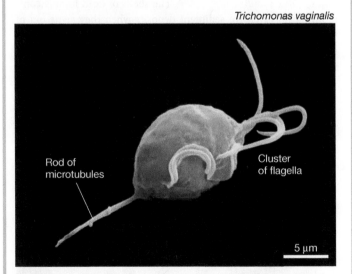

FIGURE 30.20 *Trichomonas* **Causes the Sexually Transmitted Disease Trichomoniasis.** The cell in this micrograph has been colorized.

Euglena velata

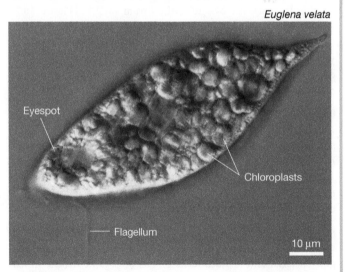

FIGURE 30.22 Euglenids Are Common in Ponds and Lakes.

The 6000 species of red algae live primarily in marine habitats. One species lives over 200 m below the surface; another is the only eukaryote capable of living in acidic hot springs. Although their color varies, many species are red because their chloroplasts contain large amounts of the accessory pigment phycoerythrin, which absorbs strongly in the blue and green portions of the visible spectrum. Because blue light penetrates water better than other wavelengths, red algae are able to live at considerable depth in the oceans. ✔ You should be able to mark the origin of high phycoerythrin concentrations on Figure 30.7.

Morphology Red algae cells have walls that are composed of cellulose and other polymers. A few species are unicellular, but most are multicellular. Many of the multicellular species are filamentous; others grow as thin, hard crusts on rocks or coral. Some species have erect, leaf-like structures called thalli (**FIGURE 30.23**).

Feeding and locomotion The vast majority of red algae are photosynthetic, though a few parasitic species have been identified. Red algae are the only type of algae that lack flagella.

Reproduction Asexual reproduction occurs through production of spores by mitosis. Alternation of generations is common, but the types of life cycles observed in red algae are extremely variable.

Human and ecological impacts On coral reefs, some red algae become encrusted with calcium carbonate. These species contribute to reef building and help stabilize the entire reef structure. Cultivation of *Porphyra* (or nori) for sushi and other foods is a billion-dollar-per-year industry in East Asia. Microbiological agar is also derived from the cell walls of various species of red algae.

Mesophyllum lichenoides

1 cm

FIGURE 30.23 Red Algae Adopt an Array of Growth Forms.

Foraminiferans, or forams, got their name from the Latin *foramen*, meaning "hole." Forams produce shells that have holes (see **FIGURE 30.24**) through which pseudopodia emerge. ✔ You should be able to mark the origin of the foram shell on Figure 30.7. Fossil shells of foraminifera are abundant in marine sediments—a continuous record of fossilized forams dates back 530 million years. A foram species was recently found living in sediments at a depth of 11,000 m below sea level. They are abundant in marine plankton as well as bottom habitats.

Morphology Foraminiferan cells generally have multiple nuclei. The shells of forams are usually made of organic material stiffened with calcium carbonate ($CaCO_3$), and most species have several chambers. One species known from fossils was 12 cm long, but most species are much smaller. The size and shape of the shell are traits that distinguish foram species from each other.

Feeding and locomotion Like other rhizarians, forams feed by extending their pseudopodia and using them to capture and engulf bacterial and archaeal cells or bits of organic debris, which are digested in food vacuoles. Some species have symbiotic algae that perform photosynthesis and contribute sugars to their host. Forams do not move actively but simply float in the water.

Reproduction Members of the foraminifera reproduce asexually by mitosis. When meiosis occurs, the resulting gametes are released into the open water, where pairs fuse to form new diploid individuals.

Human and ecological impacts The shells of dead forams commonly form extensive sediment deposits when they settle out of the water, producing layers that eventually solidify into chalk, limestone, or marble. Geologists use the presence of certain foram species to date rocks—particularly during petroleum exploration.

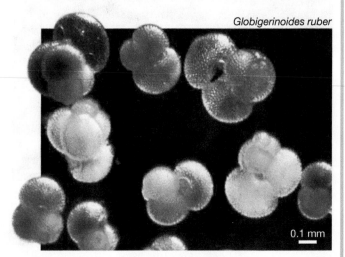

Globigerinoides ruber

0.1 mm

FIGURE 30.24 Forams Are Shelled Amoebae.

Members of the lineage Alveolata comprise three subgroups of single-celled species that are diverse in morphology and nutrition. All alveolates contain flattened, membrane-bound vesicles called alveoli that support the plasma membrane.

Ciliates are named for the cilia that cover them. Some 12,000 species are known from freshwater, marine, and wet soil environments. Most of the 4000 known species of dinoflagellates are marine or freshwater plankton. All of the 5000 known species of apicomplexans are parasitic.

Morphology Ciliate cells have two distinctive nuclei: a polyploid macronucleus that is actively transcribed and a diploid micronucleus that is involved only in gene exchange between individuals (both are stained dark red in **FIGURE 30.25**). ✔ You should be able to mark the origin of the macronucleus/micronucleus structure on Figure 30.7.

Each dinoflagellate species has a distinct shape, in some species maintained by cellulose plates. Apicomplexan cells lack cilia or flagella.

Feeding and locomotion Ciliates may be filter feeders, predators, or parasites. They use cilia to swim and have a mouth area where food is ingested. About half of the dinoflagellates are photosynthetic. They are distinguished by the arrangement of their two flagella, which allows them to swim in a spinning motion: One flagellum projects out from the cell while the other runs around the cell. Some dinoflagellate species are capable of **bioluminescence,** meaning they emit light via an enzyme-catalyzed reaction (**FIGURE 30.26**). Being parasitic, all apicomplexans absorb nutrition directly from their host. Some species can move by amoeboid motion.

Reproduction Ciliates undergo an unusual type of gene exchange called conjugation, in which micronuclei are passed between individuals. Both asexual and sexual reproduction occur in dinoflagellates. In some apicomplexan species, the life cycle involves two distinct hosts, and cells must be transmitted from one host to the next.

Human and ecological impacts Ciliates are abundant marine plankton and are also common in the digestive tracts of mammalian grazers, where they feed on plant matter and help the host animal digest it. Photosynthetic dinoflagellates are important primary producers in marine ecosystems. A few species are responsible for harmful algal blooms (see Figure 30.4). Apicomplexan species in the genus *Plasmodium* cause malaria. *Toxoplasma* is an important pathogen in people infected with HIV (**FIGURE 30.27**).

Paramecium caudatum

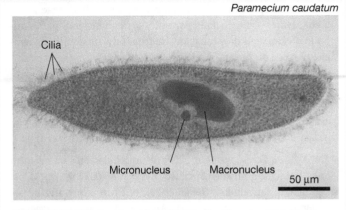

FIGURE 30.25 **Ciliates Are Abundant in Freshwater Plankton.**

Noctiluca scintillans

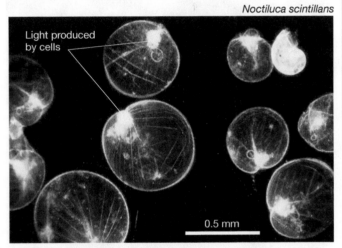

FIGURE 30.26 **Some Dinoflagellate Species Are Bioluminescent.**

Toxoplasma gondii

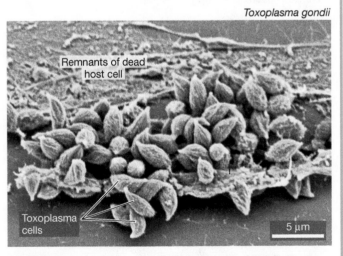

FIGURE 30.27 *Toxoplasma* **Causes Infections in AIDS Patients.**

The stramenopiles are a large and morphologically diverse group of eukaryotes. They include parasitic, saprophytic, and photosynthetic species, and they range in size from tiny, single-celled members to some of the largest multicellular organisms in the oceans.

Several morphological features are shared among the subgroups of stramenopiles, including flagella that are covered with tiny, hollow projections (see Figure 30.6). Photosynthetic diatoms and brown algae contain chloroplasts that originated from a secondary endosymbiosis involving a red alga (see Figure 30.13).

Morphology Some water molds are unicellular and some form long, branching filaments called **hyphae** (**FIGURE 30.28**). Most diatoms are unicellular (**FIGURE 30.29**), often in a box-and-lid arrangement (see Figure 30.11a). All species of brown algae are multicellular; the body typically consists of leaflike blades, a stalk known as a stipe, and a rootlike holdfast (**FIGURE 30.30**). ✔ You should be able to mark the origin of brown algal multicellularity on Figure 30.7.

Feeding and locomotion Most species of water molds feed on decaying organic material; a few are parasitic. Mature individuals are **sessile**—that is, permanently fixed to a substrate. Both diatoms and brown algae are photosynthetic, but diatoms are planktonic whereas brown algae are sessile.

Reproduction Many species of stramenopiles exhibit diploid-dominant life cycles. Several produce spores via asexual or sexual reproduction. Water mold spores form in special structures, like those shown in Figure 30.28. Most species of brown algae exhibit alternation of generations.

Human and ecological impacts Water molds are extremely important decomposers in freshwater ecosystems. Parasitic forms that affect humans indirectly include the organism that caused the Irish potato famine. Other water mold species are responsible for epidemic diseases of trees, including the diebacks currently occurring in oaks.

Diatoms are considered the most important primary producer in fresh and salt water. Their glassy cell walls settle into massive accumulations that are mined and sold as diatomaceous earth, which is used in filtering applications and as an ingredient in polishes, paint, cosmetics, and other products.

In many coastal areas with cool water, brown algae form kelp forests that are important habitats for a wide variety of animals.

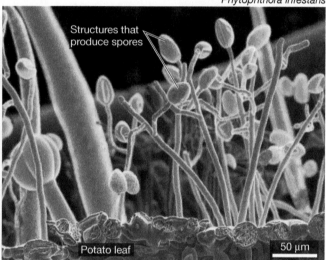

Phytophthora infestans

FIGURE 30.28 *Phytophthora Infestans* **Infects Potatoes.** This is a colorized scanning electron micrograph.

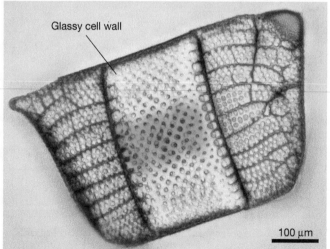

Isthmia nervosa

FIGURE 30.29 **Diatoms Have Glass-Like Cell Walls.**

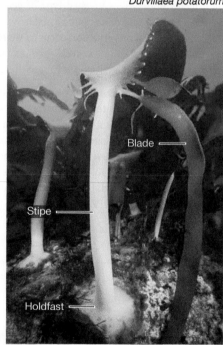

Durvillaea potatorum

FIGURE 30.30 **Many Brown Algae Have a Holdfast, Stalk (Stipe), and Leaflike Blades.**

If you understand . . .

30.1 Why Do Biologists Study Protists?

- Protists include all eukaryotes except the land plants, fungi, and animals.

- Protists are often tremendously abundant in marine and freshwater plankton and other habitats. Protists provide food for many organisms in aquatic ecosystems and fix so much carbon that they have a large impact on the global carbon budget.

- Parasitic protists cause several important diseases in humans, including malaria.

- Toxin-producing protists that grow to high densities can result in a harmful algal bloom.

✓ You should be able to explain what is "primary" about primary production by photosynthetic protists.

30.2 How Do Biologists Study Protists?

- Microscopic investigation of protists led to the understanding that many are single celled. Unlike bacteria, they contain mitochondria, a nucleus and endomembrane system, and a cytoskeleton.

- Direct sequencing has revealed important new groups of protists.

- Phylogenies based on molecular data confirmed that there are seven major lineages of protists and that the group is paraphyletic.

✓ You should be able to describe the major differences between eukaryotic cells and prokaryotic cells.

30.3 What Themes Occur in the Diversification of Protists?

- The first eukaryote probably resulted from an ancient endosymbiosis that occurred when a prokaryotic host cell (likely an archaeal cell) engulfed an α-proteobacterium. This bacterium evolved into today's mitochondria.

- The nuclear envelope probably evolved to spatially separate the processes of transcription and translation.

- Multicellularity evolved in several different protist groups independently.

- Protists vary widely in the way they obtain food. They exhibit predatory, parasitic, or photosynthetic lifestyles, which evolved in many groups independently.

- The evolution of ingestive feeding was important for two reasons: **(1)** It allowed eukaryotes to obtain resources in a new way—by eating bacteria, archaea, and other eukaryotes; and **(2)** it made endosymbiosis and the evolution of mitochondria and chloroplasts possible.

- The chloroplast's size and its circular chromosome, ribosomes, and double membrane are consistent with the hypothesis that this organelle originated as an endosymbiotic cyanobacterium.

- After primary endosymbiosis occurred, chloroplasts were "passed around" to new lineages of protists via secondary endosymbiosis.

- Protists vary widely in the way they reproduce. They undergo cell division based on mitosis and reproduce asexually. Many protists also undergo meiosis and sexual reproduction at some phase in their life cycle.

- Alternation of generations is common in multicellular protist species—meaning the same species has separate haploid and diploid forms. When alternation of generations occurs, haploid gametophytes produce gametes by mitosis; diploid sporophytes produce spores by meiosis.

✓ You should be able to explain the original source of (1) the two membranes in a plant chloroplast and (2) the four membranes in the chloroplast-derived organelle of *Plasmodium*.

30.4 Key Lineages of Protists

- Protists are a highly diverse group of eukaryotic species organized into seven lineages.

- Protist lineages are defined by DNA sequence evidence and morphological traits such as the presence of chloroplasts or unique flagella.

- A wide range of traits including parasitism, autotrophy, and multicellularity evolved independently in several different lineages of protists.

MasteringBiology

1. **MasteringBiology Assignments**

   Tutorials and Activities Alternation of Generations in a Protist; Life Cycles of Protists; Tentative Phylogeny of Eukaryotes

   Questions Reading Quizzes, Blue-Thread Questions, Test Bank

2. **eText** Read your book online, search, take notes, highlight text, and more.

3. **The Study Area** Practice Test, Cumulative Test, BioFlix® 3-D Animations, Videos, Activities, Audio Glossary, Word Study Tools, Art

You should be able to . . .

✓ TEST YOUR KNOWLEDGE

Answers are available in Appendix A

1. Why are protists considered paraphyletic?
   a. They include many extinct forms, including lineages that no longer have any living representatives.
   b. They include some but not all descendants of their most recent common ancestor.
   c. They represent all of the descendants of a single common ancestor.
   d. Not all protists have all of the synapomorphies that define the Eukarya, such as a nucleus.

2. What material is *not* used by protists to manufacture hard outer coverings?
   a. cellulose
   b. lignin
   c. glass-like compounds that contain silicon
   d. mineral-like compounds such as calcium carbonate ($CaCO_3$)

3. What does amoeboid motion result from?
   a. interactions among actin, myosin, and ATP
   b. coordinated beats of cilia
   c. the whiplike action of flagella
   d. action by the mitotic spindle, similar to what happens during mitosis and meiosis

4. According to the endosymbiosis theory, what type of organism is the original ancestor of the chloroplast?
   a. a photosynthetic archaean
   b. a cyanobacterium
   c. an algal-like, primitive photosynthetic eukaryote
   d. a modified mitochondrion

5. True or False: All protists are unicellular.

6. The most important primary producers in marine ecosystems are _____.

✓ TEST YOUR UNDERSTANDING

Answers are available in Appendix A

7. Which of the following is true of the parasite that causes malaria in humans?
   a. It undergoes meiosis immediately following zygote formation.
   b. It is a complex prokaryote.
   c. It makes gametes by meiosis.
   d. It has a diploid-dominant life cycle.

8. Explain the logic behind the claim that the nuclear envelope is a synapomorphy that defines eukaryotes as a monophyletic group.

9. Consider the endosymbiosis theory for the origin of the mitochondrion. What did each partner provide the other, and what did each receive in return?

10. Why was finding a close relationship between mitochondrial DNA and bacterial DNA considered particularly strong evidence in favor of the endosymbiosis theory?

11. The text claims that the evolutionary history of protists can be understood as a series of morphological innovations that established seven distinct lineages, each of which subsequently diversified based on innovative ways of feeding, moving, and reproducing. Explain how the Alveolata support this claim.

✓ TEST YOUR PROBLEM-SOLVING SKILLS

Answers are available in Appendix A

12. Multicellularity is defined in part by the presence of distinctive cell types. At the cellular level, what does this criterion imply?
    a. Individual cells must be extremely large.
    b. The organism must be able to reproduce sexually.
    c. Cells must be able to move.
    d. Different cell types express different genes.

13. Consider the following:
    - *Plasmodium* has an unusual organelle called an apicoplast. Recent research has shown that apicoplasts are derived from chloroplasts via secondary endosymbiosis and have a large number of genes related to chloroplast DNA.
    - Glyphosate is one of the most widely used herbicides. It works by poisoning an enzyme located in chloroplasts.
    - Biologists are testing the hypothesis that glyphosate could be used as an antimalarial drug in humans.

    How are these observations connected?

14. Suppose a friend says that we don't need to worry about the rising temperatures associated with global climate change. Her claim is that increased temperatures will make planktonic algae grow faster and that carbon dioxide (CO_2) will be removed from the atmosphere faster. According to her, this carbon will be buried at the bottom of the ocean in calcium carbonate shells. As a result, the amount of carbon dioxide in the atmosphere will decrease and global warming will decline. Comment.

15. Biologists are beginning to draw a distinction between "species trees" and "gene trees." A species tree is a phylogeny that describes the actual evolutionary history of a lineage. A gene tree, in contrast, describes the evolutionary history of one particular gene, such as a gene required for the synthesis of chlorophyll *a*. In some cases, species trees and gene trees don't agree with each other. For example, the species tree for green algae indicates that their closest relatives are protists and plants. But the gene tree based on chlorophyll *a* from green algae suggests that this gene's closest relative is a bacterium, not a protist. What's going on? Why do these types of conflicts exist?

36 Viruses

In this chapter you will learn that

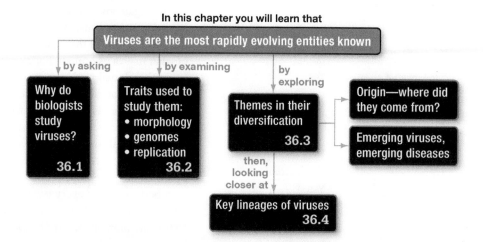

Viruses are the most rapidly evolving entities known

by asking

Why do biologists study viruses?

36.1

by examining

Traits used to study them:
- morphology
- genomes
- replication

36.2

by exploring

Themes in their diversification

36.3

then, looking closer at

Origin—where did they come from?

Emerging viruses, emerging diseases

Key lineages of viruses
36.4

Photomicrograph created by treating seawater with a fluorescing compound that binds to nucleic acids. The smallest, most abundant dots are viruses. The larger, numerous spots are bacteria and archaea. The largest splotches are protists.

f you have ever been laid low by a high fever, cough, scratchy throat, body ache, and debilitating lack of energy, you may have wondered what hit you. What hit you was probably a **virus:** an obligate, intracellular parasite.

Why obligate? Viral replication is *completely* dependent on host cells. Why intracellular? Viruses must enter a host cell for replication to occur. Why parasite? Viruses reproduce at the expense of their host cells.

Viruses can also be defined by what they are not:

- They are not cells and are not made up of cells, so they are not considered organisms.

- They cannot manufacture their own ATP or amino acids or nucleotides, and they cannot produce proteins on their own.

Viruses enter a **host cell,** take over its biosynthetic machinery, and use that machinery to manufacture a new generation of viruses. Outside of host cells, viruses simply exist.

✔ When you see this checkmark, stop and test yourself. Answers are available in Appendix A.

Characteristics	Viruses	Organisms
Hereditary material	DNA or RNA; can be single stranded or double stranded	DNA; always double stranded
Plasma membrane present?	No	Yes
Can carry out transcription independently?	No—even if a viral polymerase is present, transcription of viral genomes requires use of nucleotides provided by host cell	Yes
Can carry out translation independently?	No	Yes
Metabolic capabilities	Virtually none	Extensive—synthesis of ATP, reduced carbon compounds, vitamins, lipids, nucleic acids, etc.

When you have the flu, influenza viruses enter the cells that line your respiratory tract and use the machinery inside to make copies of themselves. Every time you cough or sneeze, you eject millions or billions of their offspring into the environment. If one of those infectious particles is lucky enough to be breathed in by another person, it may enter his or her respiratory tract cells and start a new infection.

Viruses are not organisms. Most biologists would argue that viruses are not alive, because they are dependent on their host cell to satisfy the five attributes of life (see Chapter 1). Yet viruses have a genome, they are superbly adapted to exploit the metabolic capabilities of their host cells, and they evolve. **TABLE 36.1** summarizes some characteristics of viruses and how they differ from organisms.

The diversity and abundance of viruses almost defy description. Each type of virus infects a specific unicellular species or cell type in a multicellular species, and nearly all organisms examined thus far are parasitized by at least one kind of virus. The surface waters of the world's oceans teem with bacteria and archaea, yet viruses outnumber them in this habitat by a factor of 10 to 1. If you leaned over a boat and filled a wine bottle with seawater, it would contain about 10 billion virus particles—close to one and a half times the world's population of humans.

36.1 Why Do Biologists Study Viruses?

Any study of life's diversity would be incomplete unless it included a look at the acellular parasites that contribute to that diversity. Viruses have directly participated in organismal diversity

by introducing foreign genes into cellular genomes. They can pick up cellular genes and shuttle them from one organism to another. In this way, viruses can promote **lateral gene transfer** (see Chapter 21).

In addition, viruses also contribute their own genetic material to organisms. Researchers estimate that 5–8 percent of the human genome consists of remnants of viral genomes from past infections. Some of these viral genes have even evolved to be part of what makes us human. For example, a protein that is encoded by an abandoned viral gene is necessary for proper development and function of the human placenta.

Viruses are also important from a practical standpoint. To health-care workers, agronomists, and foresters, these parasites are a persistent—and sometimes catastrophic—source of misery and economic loss. Much of the research on viruses is motivated by the desire to minimize the damage they can cause. In the human body, virtually every system, tissue, and cell can be infected by at least one kind of virus, and each of these viruses often infects more than one site (**FIGURE 36.1**).

Recent Viral Epidemics in Humans

Physicians and researchers use the term **epidemic** (literally, "upon-people") to describe a disease that rapidly affects a large number of individuals over a widening area.

Viruses have caused the most devastating epidemics in recent human history. During the eighteenth and nineteenth centuries, it was not unusual for Native American tribes to lose 90 percent of their members over the course of a few years to measles, smallpox, and other viral diseases spread by contact with European settlers. To appreciate the impact of these epidemics, think of 10 close friends and relatives—then remove nine.

An epidemic that is worldwide in scope is called a **pandemic.** The influenza outbreak of 1918–1919, called Spanish flu, qualifies as the most devastating pandemic recorded to date. The strain of influenza virus that emerged in 1918 infected people worldwide and was particularly **virulent**—meaning it tended to cause severe disease. The viral outbreak occurred just as World War I was drawing to a close and killed far more people in eight months than did the five-year conflict itself.

FIGURE 36.2 illustrates the impact of this pandemic in relation to the life expectancy in the United States during the twentieth century. Worldwide, the Spanish flu is thought to have killed up to 50 million people. An estimated 20 million died in the first 8 months of the pandemic.

Current Viral Pandemics in Humans: AIDS

In terms of the total number of people affected, the measles and smallpox epidemics and the 1918 influenza pandemic are almost certain to be surpassed by the incidence of **acquired immune deficiency syndrome** (AIDS). AIDS is an affliction caused by the **human immunodeficiency virus (HIV).**

HIV is now the one of the most intensively studied of all viruses. Since the early 1980s, governments and private corporations from around the world have spent hundreds of millions of dollars on

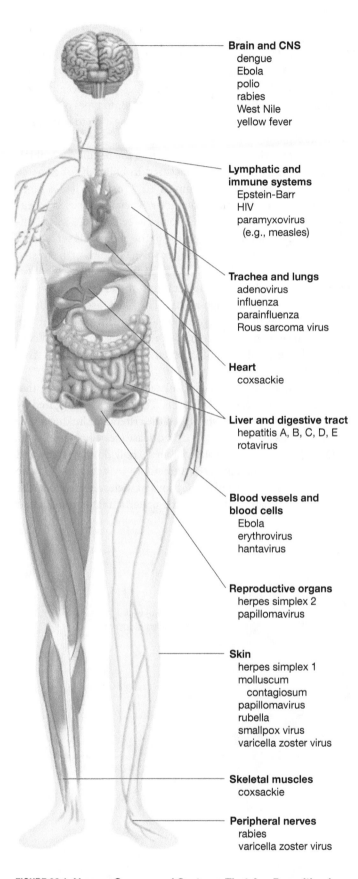

Brain and CNS
dengue
Ebola
polio
rabies
West Nile
yellow fever

Lymphatic and immune systems
Epstein-Barr
HIV
paramyxovirus
(e.g., measles)

Trachea and lungs
adenovirus
influenza
parainfluenza
Rous sarcoma virus

Heart
coxsackie

Liver and digestive tract
hepatitis A, B, C, D, E
rotavirus

Blood vessels and blood cells
Ebola
erythrovirus
hantavirus

Reproductive organs
herpes simplex 2
papillomavirus

Skin
herpes simplex 1
molluscum contagiosum
papillomavirus
rubella
smallpox virus
varicella zoster virus

Skeletal muscles
coxsackie

Peripheral nerves
rabies
varicella zoster virus

FIGURE 36.1 Human Organs and Systems That Are Parasitized by Viruses. Viruses shown in this figure may infect more than one tissue, but for simplicity, usually only one tissue is shown.

(a) Deadly impact of the 1918 influenza pandemic

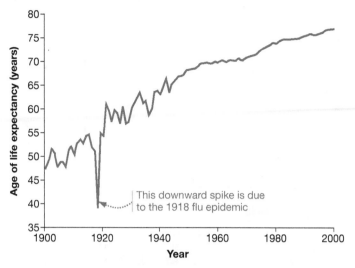

This downward spike is due to the 1918 flu epidemic

(b) Emergency hospital at the start of the 1918 pandemic

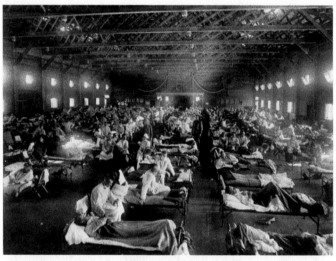

FIGURE 36.2 Life Expectancy of Humans over the 20th Century in the United States. (a) This graph illustrates the dramatic effect of the 1918 influenza pandemic in an otherwise promising trend. **(b)** The first recorded cases of the 1918 Spanish flu were reported at this U.S. Army emergency hospital (Camp Funston, Kansas).

DATA: Arias, E. 2010. United States life tables, 2006. *National Vital Statistics Reports,* 58 (21): 1–40, Table 10. Hyattsville, MD: National Center for Health Statistics.

HIV research. Given this virus's current and projected impact on human populations around the globe, the investment is justified.

How Does HIV Cause Disease? Like other viruses, HIV parasitizes specific types of cells—most notably, the helper T cells of the **immune system,** which is the body's defense system against disease. Helper T cells are crucial to the immune system's response to invading pathogens.

If an HIV particle succeeds in infecting a helper T cell and reproduces inside, the cell will die as hundreds of new progeny particles are released and infect more cells. Although the body continually replaces helper T cells, the number produced does not keep pace with the number being destroyed by HIV. As

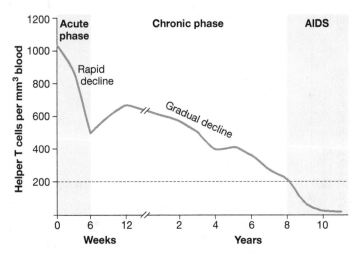

FIGURE 36.3 T-Cell Counts Decline during an HIV Infection.
Graph of changes in the number of helper T cells that are present in the bloodstream over time, based on data from a typical patient infected with HIV. The acute phase may be associated with symptoms such as fever. Few or no disease symptoms occur in the chronic phase. AIDS typically occurs when T-cell counts dip below 200 per mm³ of blood.

DATA: Pantaleo, G., and Fauci, A. S. 1996. *Annual Review of Microbiology* 50: 825-854.

a result, the total number of helper T cells in the bloodstream gradually declines as an HIV infection proceeds (**FIGURE 36.3**).

As the T-cell count drops, the immune system's responses to invading pathogens become less and less effective. Eventually, too few helper T cells are left to fight off pathogens efficiently, allowing bacteria, fungi, protists, or other viruses to multiply unchecked. In almost all cases, one or more of these "opportunistic" infections proves fatal. HIV kills people indirectly—by making them susceptible to diseases that normally do not arise in those with functioning immune systems.

What Is the Scope of the AIDS Pandemic? Researchers with the United Nations AIDS program estimate that AIDS has already killed almost 30 million people worldwide. HIV infection rates have been highest in east and central Africa, where one of the greatest public health crises in history is now occurring. In Botswana, for example, blood-testing programs have confirmed that over 20 percent of the population is HIV positive. Although there may be a lag of as much as 8 to 12 years between the initial infection and the onset of illness, virtually all people who become infected with the virus will die of AIDS.

Currently, the UN estimates the total number of HIV-infected people worldwide at about 34 million. An additional 2.7 million people are infected each year. Most infectious diseases afflict the very young and the very old, but because HIV is primarily a sexually transmitted disease, young adults are most likely to contract the virus and die.

People who become infected with HIV in their late teens or twenties die of AIDS in their twenties or thirties. Tens of millions of people are being lost in the prime of their lives. Physicians, politicians, educators, and aid workers all use the same word to describe the epidemic's impact: staggering.

36.2 How Do Biologists Study Viruses?

Many researchers who study viruses focus on two goals: (**1**) developing vaccines that help hosts fight off disease if they become infected and (**2**) developing antiviral drugs that prevent a virus from replicating efficiently inside the host. Both types of research begin with attempts to isolate the virus in question to learn more about its structure and mode of replication.

Isolating viruses takes researchers into the realm of nanobiology, in which structures are measured in billionths of a meter. (One nanometer, abbreviated nm, is 10^{-9} meter.) Viruses range from about 20 to 300 nm in diameter. They are dwarfed by eukaryotic cells and even by most bacterial cells (**FIGURE 36.4**). Millions of viruses can fit on the period at the end of this sentence.

If virus-infected cells can be grown in culture or harvested from a host individual, researchers can usually isolate the virus by passing solutions of infected cultures or patient samples (e.g., blood, saliva, feces) through a filter. The filters used to study viruses have pores that are large enough for viruses to pass through but are too small to admit cells. If exposing susceptible host cells to the filtrate results in infection, the hypothesis that a virus caused the disease is supported.

In this way, researchers can isolate a virus and confirm that it is the causative agent of infection. These steps are inspired by Koch's postulates, which established the criteria for linking a specific infectious agent with a specific disease (see Chapter 29).

Once biologists have isolated a virus, how do they study and characterize it? The answer is threefold—by analyzing (**1**) the structure of the extracellular infectious particle, referred to as the **virion**; (**2**) the nature of the genetic material that is transmitted

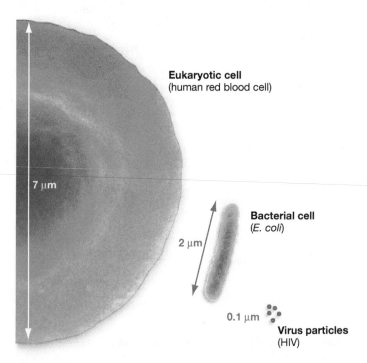

Eukaryotic cell
(human red blood cell)

7 µm

Bacterial cell
(*E. coli*)

2 µm

0.1 µm

Virus particles
(HIV)

FIGURE 36.4 Viruses Are Tiny.

by virions from one host to another; and (3) variations in how viruses replicate. Let's begin with morphological traits.

Analyzing Morphological Traits

To see the virion of a particular virus, researchers usually rely on transmission electron microscopy (see **BioSkills 11** in Appendix B). Only the very largest viruses, such as the smallpox virus, are visible with a light microscope. Electron microscopy has revealed that viruses come in a wide variety of shapes, and many viruses can be identified by shape alone.

In terms of overall structure, most viruses fall into two general categories: **(1)** those that are enclosed by just a shell of protein called a **capsid** and **(2)** those enclosed by both a capsid and a membrane-like **envelope.**

Most viruses produce virions with capsid shapes that are either helical or icosahedral (an icosahedron is a polyhedron with 20 triangular faces) (**FIGURE 36.5a** and **b**). Some viruses, like bacteriophage T4 and the smallpox virus, however, have more complex capsid shapes (**FIGURE 36.5c** and **d**). A virion's capsid serves two functions: it protects the genome while outside the host and is also able to release the genome when infecting a new cell.

Nonenveloped viruses, often called "naked" viruses, use only the capsid shell to protect their genetic material. The naked icosahedral virion illustrated in Figure 36.5b is an adenovirus. You undoubtedly have adenoviruses on your tonsils or in other parts of your upper respiratory passages right now.

Enveloped viruses also have genetic material inside a capsid, or bound to capsid proteins, but the capsid is further enclosed in one or more membranes like the smallpox virus shown in Figure 36.5d. The envelope consists of viral proteins embedded in a phospholipid bilayer derived from a membrane found in a host cell—specifically, the host cell in which the virion was manufactured. Later sections of this chapter will detail how viruses obtain their envelope from an infected host cell.

Analyzing the Genetic Material

In addition to morphology, viruses can be categorized based on the nature of their genome. This is not true for cells. DNA is the hereditary material in all cells, and information flows from DNA to mRNA to proteins (Chapter 16). Although all cells follow this pattern, which is called the central dogma of molecular biology, many viruses break it.

This conclusion traces back to work done in the 1950s, when Heinz Fraenkel-Conrat and colleagues were able to separate the protein and nucleic acid components of a plant virus known as the tobacco mosaic virus, or TMV. Surprisingly, the nucleic acid

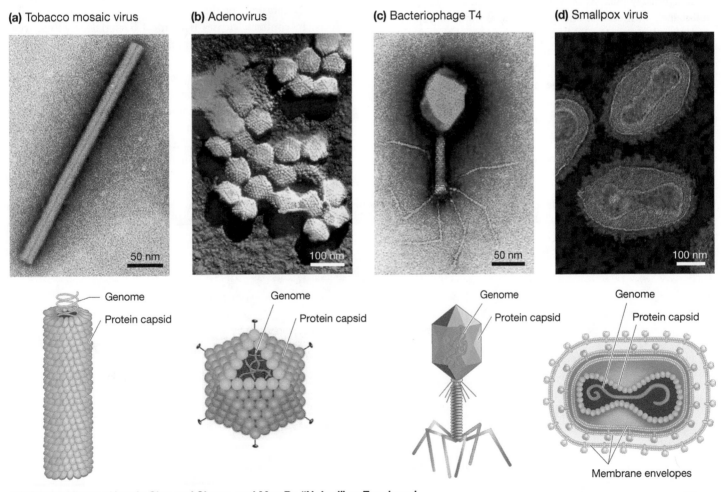

(a) Tobacco mosaic virus   **(b)** Adenovirus   **(c)** Bacteriophage T4   **(d)** Smallpox virus

Genome   Protein capsid   Genome   Protein capsid   Genome   Protein capsid   Genome   Protein capsid   Membrane envelopes

FIGURE 36.5 Viruses Vary in Size and Shape, and May Be "Naked" or Enveloped.

portion of this virus consisted of RNA, and the RNA of TMV, by itself, could infect plant tissues and cause disease. This was a confusing result because it showed that the RNA—not DNA—functions as TMV's genetic material.

Subsequent research revealed an amazing diversity of viral genome types. In some groups of viruses, such as the agents that cause measles and flu, the genome consists of RNA. In others, such as the viruses that cause herpes and smallpox, the genome is DNA. Viral genomes may be linear or circular and may consist of a single molecule or be broken up into several different segments.

Further, the RNA and DNA genomes of viruses can be either single stranded or double stranded. The single-stranded RNA genomes can also be classified as "positive sense" or "negative sense" or "ambisense."

- In a **positive-sense** RNA virus, the genome contains the same sequences as the mRNA required to produce viral proteins.

- In a **negative-sense** RNA virus, the base sequences in the genome are complementary to those in viral mRNAs.

- In an **ambisense** RNA virus, the genome has at least one strand that contains two regions: one is positive sense and the other negative sense.

The nature of viruses has been understood only since the 1940s, but they have been the focus of intense research ever since. Although likely millions of types of virus exist, they all appear to infect their host cells in one of two general ways: via **replicative growth,** which produces the next generation of virions and often kills the host cell, or in a dormant manner that suspends production of virions and allows the virus to coexist with the host for a period of time. Let's look first at the more immediately deadly mode.

Analyzing the Phases of Replicative Growth

Six phases are common to replicative growth in virtually all viruses: (1) attachment to a host cell and entry into the cytosol;
(2) transcription of the viral genome and production of viral proteins; (3) replication of the viral genome; (4) assembly of a new generation of virions; (5) exit from the infected cell; and (6) transmission to a new host.

FIGURE 36.6 shows the replicative growth of a bacteriophage. A **bacteriophage** (literally, "bacteria-eater") is a virus that infects bacterial cells. This cycle is referred to as the **lytic cycle,** since it ends with lysis (destruction) of the cell. One thing should stand out as you examine this process: in a single replicative cycle, one virus particle can produce many progeny.

FIGURE 36.7 shows how a bacteriophage's tremendous capacity for replication results in nonlinear growth that proceeds in a stepwise manner. This growth curve is very different from what is observed in the host cells, where each cell produces only two progeny in each generation.

Each type of virus has a particular way of entering a host cell and completing the subsequent phases of the cycle. Let's take a closer look at each phase.

How Do Viruses Enter a Cell?   The replicative cycle of a virus begins when a free virion enters a target cell. This is no simple task. All cells are protected by a plasma membrane, and many also have a cell wall. How do viruses breach these defenses, insert themselves into the cytosol inside, and begin an infection?

Most plant viruses are inserted directly into the host-cell cytosol via abrasions or the mouthparts of sucking or biting insects. In contrast, viruses that infect bacterial or animal cells must first attach to a specific molecule on the cell wall or plasma membrane.

After a bacteriophage attaches to its host, it uses an enzyme called lysozyme to degrade part of the cell wall and expose the plasma membrane. The genome of the bacteriophage is then transferred to the cytosol in a process referred to as uncoating, which varies depending on the structure of the virus. The T4 bacteriophage shown in Figure 36.6, for example, uncoats its

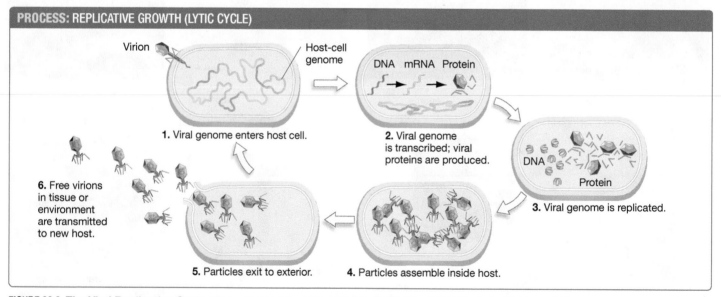

PROCESS: REPLICATIVE GROWTH (LYTIC CYCLE)

Virion
Host-cell genome

1. Viral genome enters host cell.

DNA mRNA Protein

2. Viral genome is transcribed; viral proteins are produced.

DNA
Protein

3. Viral genome is replicated.

4. Particles assemble inside host.

5. Particles exit to exterior.

6. Free virions in tissue or environment are transmitted to new host.

FIGURE 36.6 The Viral Replicative Cycle. Many viruses follow the same general cycle as this bacteriophage model.

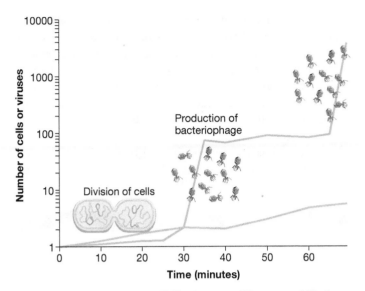

FIGURE 36.7 Growth Patterns Differ between Viruses and Their Host. Cells reproduce in an exponential manner, as indicated by a linear pattern when plotted on a logarithmic scale. The production of virions is not exponential; instead, reproduction of bacteriophage like T4 exhibits a stepwise pattern.

DATA: Courtesy of the Undergraduate Biotechnology Laboratory, California Polytechnic State University, San Luis Obispo.

✔ **QUANTITATIVE** Based on the information and trends in this graph, predict the number of extracellular virions that would be produced after 90 minutes if all of those released by 40 minutes were allowed to infect new host cells. Compare this to the number of cells you would predict to be present after 90 minutes.

genome by injecting it through a hollow needle that is stabbed into the bacterial membrane.

Viruses that attack animal cells must first attach to one or more specific molecules in the host cell's plasma membrane. These molecules, often referred to as virus receptors, are typically either membrane proteins or the carbohydrates attached to glycoproteins or glycolipids.

To appreciate how investigators identify virus receptors, consider research on HIV. In 1981—right at the start of the AIDS epidemic—biomedical researchers realized that people with AIDS had few or no T cells possessing a particular membrane protein called **CD4.** These cells, symbolized as $CD4^+$, are called helper T cells because of their key supportive role in the immune response.

Two research groups hypothesized that CD4 serves as the receptor for HIV attachment. To test this hypothesis, the researchers systematically blocked different membrane proteins on helper T cells and determined which membrane proteins are involved in HIV attachment. They used **antibodies** to specifically bind to host membrane proteins, including several that bound to CD4 (see **BioSkills 9** in Appendix B to review the activity of antibodies).

The key assumption in their experiments was that antibodies directed against the virus receptor would prevent HIV from entering and infecting the cell. After completing their work, both research teams reached exactly the same result: Antibodies to CD4 inhibited HIV from infecting host cells (**FIGURE 36.8**).

RESEARCH

QUESTION: Does CD4 protein function as the receptor HIV uses to enter host cells?

HYPOTHESIS: CD4 is the membrane protein HIV uses to enter cells.

NULL HYPOTHESIS: CD4 is not the membrane protein HIV uses to enter cells.

EXPERIMENTAL SETUP:

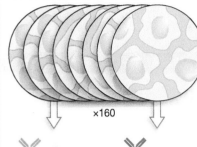

×160

1. **Take 160 identical samples of helper T cells** from a large population of T cells growing in culture.

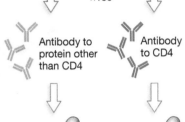

Antibody to protein other than CD4

Antibody to CD4

2. **Add a different antibody to each sample of cells**—each antibody will "block" a specific membrane protein.

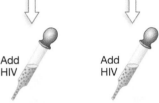

Add HIV   Add HIV

3. **Add a constant number of HIV virions** to all samples. Incubate cultures under conditions optimal for virus entry.

PREDICTION: HIV will not infect cells with antibody to CD4 but will infect other cells.

PREDICTION OF NULL HYPOTHESIS: HIV will infect cells with antibody to CD4.

RESULTS:

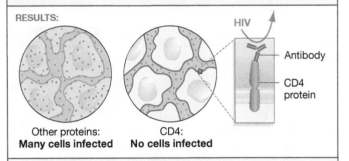

Other proteins: **Many cells infected**

CD4: **No cells infected**

HIV
Antibody
CD4 protein

CONCLUSION: HIV uses CD4 as the receptor to enter helper T cells. Thus, only cells with free, unbound CD4 on their surface can be infected by HIV.

FIGURE 36.8 Experiments Confirmed that CD4 Is the Receptor Used by HIV to Enter Host Cells. In this experiment, the antibodies added to each culture bound to a specific protein found on the surface of helper T cells. Antibody binding blocked the membrane protein, so the protein could not be used by HIV to gain entry to the cells.

SOURCE: Dalgleish, A. G., P. C. Beverley, P. R. Clapham, et al. 1984. The CD4 (T4) antigen is an essential component of the receptor for the AIDS retrovirus. *Nature* 312: 763–767. Also Klatzmann, D., E. Champagne, S. Chamaret, et al. 1984. T-lymphocyte T4 molecule behaves as the receptor for human retrovirus LAV. *Nature* 312: 767–768.

✔ **QUESTION** Does this experiment show that CD4 is the only membrane protein required for HIV entry? Explain why or why not.

Although CD4 is necessary for HIV attachment, uncoating the viral genome will not occur unless the virion also binds to a second membrane protein, called a **co-receptor.** In most individuals, membrane proteins called CXCR4 and CCR5 function as co-receptors. Once the virion binds to both CD4 and a co-receptor, the lipid bilayers of the virion's envelope and the plasma membrane of the T cell fuse (**FIGURE 36.9a**). When fusion occurs, HIV has breached the cell boundary. The viral capsid then enters the cytosol and disassembles to release the genomic RNAs, and infection proceeds.

Another common uncoating process is shown in **FIGURE 36.9b**, where the virion is first internalized via endocytosis (see Chapter 7). After a virion, in this case influenza, attaches to a component on the cell surface, it is pulled into the cell in the form of a vesicle called an endosome. When the endosome acidifies—a normal part of endocytosis—the structure of the viral attachment proteins change in a way that promotes fusion of the viral envelope and the endosomal membrane.

Endocytosis is also commonly used by naked viruses to enter animal cells. As with enveloped viruses, acidification of the

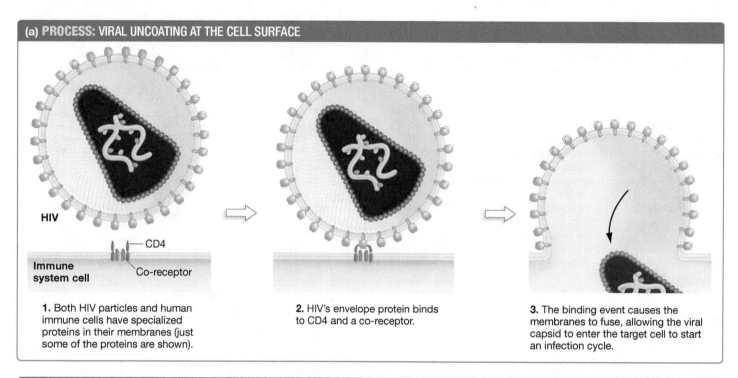

(a) PROCESS: VIRAL UNCOATING AT THE CELL SURFACE

1. Both HIV particles and human immune cells have specialized proteins in their membranes (just some of the proteins are shown).

2. HIV's envelope protein binds to CD4 and a co-receptor.

3. The binding event causes the membranes to fuse, allowing the viral capsid to enter the target cell to start an infection cycle.

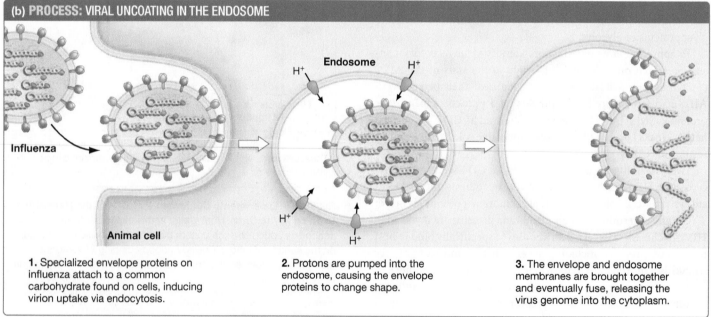

(b) PROCESS: VIRAL UNCOATING IN THE ENDOSOME

1. Specialized envelope proteins on influenza attach to a common carbohydrate found on cells, inducing virion uptake via endocytosis.

2. Protons are pumped into the endosome, causing the envelope proteins to change shape.

3. The envelope and endosome membranes are brought together and eventually fuse, releasing the virus genome into the cytoplasm.

FIGURE 36.9 Enveloped Viruses Bind to Host Membranes and Uncoat via Fusion.

endosome serves as a signal for uncoating the genetic material. In this case, low pH alters the structure of the capsid proteins, which disrupts the endosomal membrane so the viral genetic material may enter the cytosol.

The discovery of virus receptors and requirements for uncoating has inspired a search for compounds that block these early events of the replicative cycle. As a result, drugs have been designed to block attachment and uncoating of HIV by targeting the HIV envelope protein and host CCR5 co-receptor. Drugs that interfere with either viral infection or replication of viruses are called **antivirals.**

How Do Viruses Produce Proteins?   Production of viral proteins begins soon after the virus uncoats its genome. Depending on the virus, transcription of the viral genome may be accomplished by either host or viral RNA polymerases. In all viruses, however, translation of viral transcripts is entirely dependent on the host. Viruses lack the ribosomes, amino acids, ATP, and most of the other biosynthetic machinery required for translating their own mRNAs into proteins.

Viral proteins are produced and processed in one of two ways, depending on whether the proteins end up in the envelope of a virion or in a capsid.

Viral mRNAs that code for envelope proteins are translated as if they were mRNAs for the cell's own membrane proteins. They are translated by ribosomes attached to the rough endoplasmic reticulum (rough ER), where carbohydrates are added to the protein (see Chapter 7). Depending on the virus, the proteins then may be transported to the Golgi apparatus for further processing. In some viruses, such as HIV, the finished glycoproteins are transported to the plasma membrane, where they are assembled into new virions.

A different route is taken by mRNAs that code for proteins that make up the capsid of a virion. These mRNAs are translated by free ribosomes in the cytosol, just as if they were cellular mRNAs for cytosolic proteins.

In some viruses, long polypeptide sequences called polyproteins are cut into individual proteins by viral enzymes called **proteases.** These enzymes cleave viral polyproteins at specific locations—a critical step in the production of finished viral proteins. In HIV, for example, a polyprotein must be cleaved before it can assemble into new viral capsids.

The discovery that HIV produces a protease triggered research for drugs that would inhibit the enzyme. This effort got a huge boost when researchers identified the three-dimensional structure of HIV's protease, using X-ray crystallographic techniques (see **BioSkills 11** in Appendix B). The enzyme has an opening in its interior where the active site is located (**FIGURE 36.10a**). Viral polyproteins fit into the opening and are cleaved at the active site.

Based on these data, researchers immediately began searching for molecules that could fit into the opening and prevent protease from functioning by blocking the active site (**FIGURE 36.10b**). Several HIV protease inhibitors are currently being used to interfere with viral replication.

How Do Viruses Copy Their Genomes?   In addition to transcription and translation, viruses must also copy their genetic material to make a new generation of virions. Viruses depend on the host cell for nucleotide monomers. In addition, some DNA viruses also depend on the host-cell DNA polymerase machinery to replicate their genomes.

In viruses that have an RNA genome, however, the virus must supply its own enzyme to make copies of its genome. Viral enzymes called **RNA replicases** function as *RNA-dependent* RNA polymerases. In other words, RNA replicases synthesize RNA *from an RNA template*, using ribonucleotides provided by the host cell. For example, the RNA replicases of positive-sense single-stranded RNA viruses first convert the genome into double-stranded RNA and then produce multiple positive-sense copies from the negative-sense complementary strand.

(a) HIV's protease enzyme

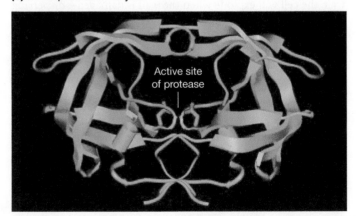

(b) Could a drug block the active site?

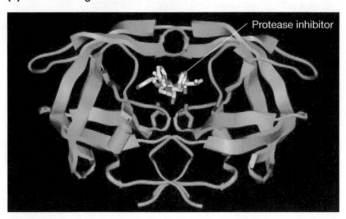

FIGURE 36.10 The Three-Dimensional Structure of HIV's Protease. (a) Ribbon diagram depicting the three-dimensional shape of HIV's protease enzyme. **(b)** Once protease's structure was solved, researchers began synthesizing compounds that were predicted to fit into the active site and prevent the enzyme from working.

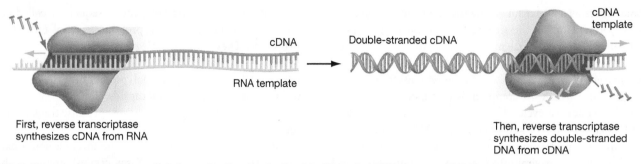

FIGURE 36.11 Reverse Transcriptase Catalyzes Synthesis of a Double-Stranded DNA from an RNA Template. The DNA produced by reverse transcriptase is called a cDNA because its base sequence is complementary to the RNA template.

But not all RNA viruses replicate using RNA replicases. In certain RNA viruses, the genome is first transcribed from RNA to DNA by a viral enzyme called **reverse transcriptase.** This enzyme is an unusual DNA polymerase—one that can make DNA from either an RNA or a DNA template. It first makes **complementary DNA,** or **cDNA,** from a single-stranded RNA template (see Chapter 20). Reverse transcriptase then removes the RNA strand and catalyzes the synthesis of a second, complementary DNA strand, resulting in a double-stranded DNA (**FIGURE 36.11**). The DNA copy is then inserted into the host genome and used as a template for host cellular machinery—including an RNA polymerase—to produce viral mRNAs and genomic RNAs.

Viruses that reverse-transcribe their genome in this way are called **retroviruses** ("backward viruses"). The name is apt because the initial flow of genetic information in this type of virus is RNA → DNA—the opposite of the central dogma (see Chapter 16). HIV is an example of a reverse-transcribing RNA virus.

The first antiviral drugs that were developed to combat HIV act by inhibiting reverse transcriptase. Logically enough, drugs of this type are called reverse transcriptase inhibitors.

How Are New Virions Assembled? Once viral proteins have been produced and the viral genome has been replicated, assembly of a new generation of virions can take place.

During assembly, viral genomes are packaged into capsids. Some viruses also include copies of non-capsid proteins, often enzymes like polymerases, inside the capsid. In many cases, the details of the assembly process are not well understood. Some viruses assemble the capsid first and then use motor proteins to pull the viral genome inside, while others assemble the capsid around the genomic material.

Enveloped viruses use the host endomembrane system (see Chapter 7) to transport their envelope proteins to the appropriate membrane for assembly. For example, virions of HIV and influenza assemble at the host cell's surface and acquire their envelope from its plasma membrane. Other enveloped viruses may assemble at the surface of internal membranes, such as the rough ER or Golgi apparatus.

In most cases, self-assembly occurs—though some viruses produce proteins that provide scaffolding where new virions are put together. To date, researchers have yet to develop drugs that inhibit the assembly process during a viral infection.

How Do Progeny Virions Exit an Infected Cell? Most viruses leave a host cell in one of two ways: by budding from cellular membranes or by bursting out of the cell. In general, enveloped viruses bud; nonenveloped viruses burst.

Viruses that bud from one of the host cell's membranes take some of that membrane with them. As a result, their envelope includes host-cell phospholipids along with envelope proteins encoded by the viral genome. In **FIGURE 36.12a**, HIV is shown budding from the plasma membrane. After the budding step, the HIV capsid is further processed by its protease, giving the virion its characteristic cone-like appearance.

Viruses that bud through internal membranes, such as those of the rough ER or Golgi apparatus, are secreted from the cell by being escorted through the endomembrane system (see Chapter 7). Regardless of the membrane used for producing enveloped viruses, exit from the host cell does not require the death of the host.

In contrast, most nonenveloped viruses release their virions from the cell by lysing it—commonly referred to as the burst. For example, bacteriophages produce lytic enzymes that break down the cell wall of the host. Because the cell exerts pressure on the wall, the cell will explode when the wall is damaged—dispersing a new generation of virions into the environment. **FIGURE 36.12b** shows T4 bacteriophages bursting from an infected *E. coli* cell.

How Are Virions Transmitted to New Hosts? Once the replicative cycle is complete, dozens to several hundred newly assembled virions are in the extracellular space. What happens next?

If the host cell is part of a multicellular organism, the new generation of virions may be transported through the body—often via the bloodstream or lymphatic system. In vertebrates, antibodies produced by the immune system may bind to the virions and mark them for destruction. But if a virion contacts an appropriate host cell before it encounters antibodies, then a new replicative cycle will be started.

The long-term success of the virus, however, is dependent on its ability to be transmitted through the environment from one organism to another. For example, when people cough, sneeze,

(a) Budding of enveloped viruses

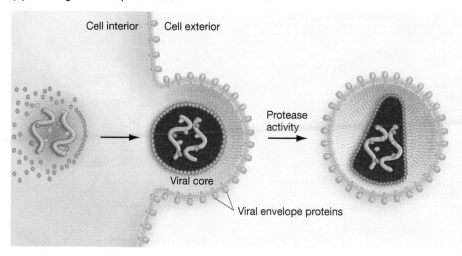
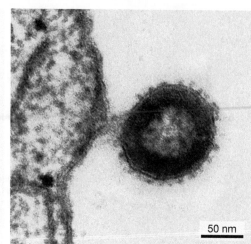

Cell interior   Cell exterior

Protease activity

Viral core

Viral envelope proteins

50 nm

(b) Bursting of nonenveloped viruses

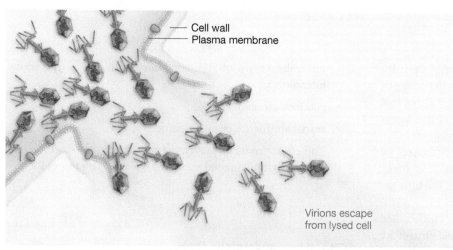
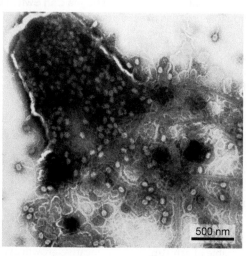

Cell wall
Plasma membrane

Virions escape from lysed cell

500 nm

FIGURE 36.12 Viruses Leave Infected Cells by Budding or Bursting. (a) In enveloped viruses such as HIV, virions are formed as they bud from membranes of the host cell. **(b)** Naked viruses normally exit the host cell by bursting the cell, as in T4 bacteriophage. Bursting kills the host cell; budding does not require cell death to occur.

✔**QUESTION** Propose a hypothesis to explain why cells often die after extensive budding of enveloped viruses.

wipe a runny nose, or defecate, they help rid their body of viruses and bacteria. But they also expel the pathogens into the environment, sometimes directly onto a new host.

From the virus's point of view, a new host represents an unexploited habitat brimming with resources in the form of target cells. The situation is analogous to that of a multicellular animal dispersing to a new habitat and colonizing it. The alleles carried by these successful colonists increase in frequency in the total population. In this way, natural selection favors alleles that allow viruses to do two things: **(1)** replicate within a host and **(2)** be transmitted to new hosts.

✔ If you understand how different types of viruses produce a new generation of virions, you should be able to compare and contrast the replicative cycles of bacteriophage T4 and HIV.

Analyzing How Viruses Coexist with Host Cells

All viruses undergo replicative growth, but some can arrest the replicative cycle and enter a dormant state. Note that only certain types of viruses are capable of switching between replicative growth and dormant coexistence with the host cell. In bacteriophages, this alternate type of infection is called **lysogeny** (**FIGURE 36.13**, page 722).

The onset of lysogeny is triggered by molecular cues in the host that push the virus out of the replicative cycle. Instead of actively transcribing and replicating the viral DNA, it becomes incorporated into the host's chromosome and the expression of most of the viral genes is shut down.

Although no virions are produced during lysogeny, the host's DNA polymerase replicates the viral DNA each time the cell divides. Copies of the viral genome are passed on to daughter cells

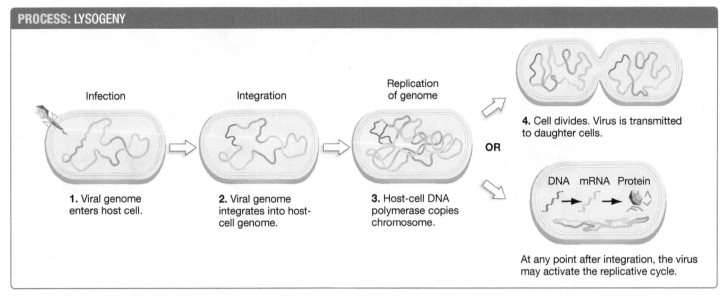

Infection

1. Viral genome enters host cell.

Integration

2. Viral genome integrates into host-cell genome.

Replication of genome

3. Host-cell DNA polymerase copies chromosome.

OR

4. Cell divides. Virus is transmitted to daughter cells.

DNA   mRNA   Protein

At any point after integration, the virus may activate the replicative cycle.

FIGURE 36.13 Some Bacteriophages Can Switch between the Lytic Cycle and Lysogeny. Molecular cues from the host can direct certain bacteriophages toward either lysogeny or the lytic cycle.

just as if it were one of the host's own genes. Some of these introduced genes have been known to significantly alter bacterial hosts. For example, many of the pathogenic strains of *E. coli* that have recently emerged in humans are more virulent due to expression of phage toxins that were introduced via lysogeny.

An integrated bacteriophage genome may be "awakened" by different cues from the host cell, often associated with host stress. Activation leads to excision of the viral DNA from the host genome and reentry into the replicative growth cycle.

In viruses that infect animal cells, the dormant state is called **latency.** As with bacteriophages, only certain animal viruses are capable of arresting their replicative growth cycle. Depending on the virus involved, the genome may or may not be integrated into the host genome.

HIV has a well-characterized latency period that occurs at the start of many new infections. After reverse transcriptase makes a double-stranded DNA version of the viral genome, the viral DNA is inserted into the host-cell genomic DNA. But integration alone is not enough to trigger expression of the viral genes. The helper T cell host must first be activated by the immune response to drive expression of the HIV genome. Until this occurs, HIV remains hidden and silent.

Current antivirals are ineffective against an HIV infection when HIV genes aren't being expressed. For this reason, reducing the likelihood of **transmission**—the spread of pathogens from one individual to another—is presently the most effective way to combat a viral disease like AIDS.

HIV is transmitted from person to person via body fluids such as blood, semen, or vaginal secretions. Faced with decades of disappointing results in drug and vaccine development, public health officials are aggressively promoting preventive medicine, through

- aggressive treatment of venereal diseases—because the lesions caused by chlamydia, genital warts, and gonorrhea encourage

the transmission of HIV-contaminated blood during sexual intercourse;

- condom use; and

- sexual abstinence or monogamy.

The effectiveness of preventive medicine underscores one of this chapter's fundamental messages: Viruses are a fact of life.

check your understanding

C Y U

If you understand that . . .

- Viruses replicate using the energy, substrates, and protein synthesis machinery of their host cells to produce a new generation of virions.
- After infecting a cell, the manner in which viruses proceed through the steps of the replicative cycle will vary depending on the type of virus.

✓ **You should be able to . . .**

Evaluate the claim that the viral replicative cycle more closely resembles the mass production of automobiles than the reproduction of cells.

Answers are available in Appendix A.

36.3 What Themes Occur in the Diversification of Viruses?

The tree of life will never be free of viruses. Mutation and natural selection guarantee that viral genomes will continually adapt to the defenses offered by their hosts, whether those defenses are devised by an immune system or by biomedical researchers.

Two other points are critical to recognize about viral diversity: (1) Biologists do not have a solid understanding of how new viruses originate, but (2) it is certain that viruses will continue to diversify. Because most viral polymerases have high error rates and because viruses lack error repair enzymes, mutation rates are extremely high. Many viruses change constantly—giving them the potential to evolve rapidly.

Where Did Viruses Come From?

No one knows how viruses originated. To address this question, biologists are currently considering three hypotheses to explain where viruses came from.

Origin in Plasmids and Transposable Elements?

Like viruses, plasmids and transposable elements are acellular, mobile genetic elements that replicate with the aid of a host cell (see Chapters 20 and 21). Certain viruses are actually indistinguishable from plasmids except for one feature: They encode proteins that form a capsid and allow the genes to exist outside of a cell.

Some biologists hypothesize that simple viruses represent "escaped gene sets." This hypothesis proposes that mobile genetic elements are descended from clusters of genes that physically escaped from prokaryotic or eukaryotic chromosomes long ago.

According to this hypothesis, the escaped gene sets took on a mobile, parasitic existence because they happened to encode the information needed to replicate themselves at the expense of the genomes that once held them. In the case of viruses, the hypothesis is that the escaped genes included the instructions for making a protein capsid and possibly envelope proteins. According to the escaped-genes hypothesis, it is possible that each of the distinct types of viruses represent distinct "escape events."

To support the escaped-genes hypothesis, researchers would need to discover a virus that had so recently derived from intact prokaryotic or eukaryotic genes that the viral genomes still strongly resembled the DNA sequence of those genes.

Origin in Symbiotic Bacteria?

Some researchers contend that DNA viruses with large genomes trace their ancestry back to free-living bacteria that once took up residence inside eukaryotic cells. The idea is that these organisms degenerated into viruses by gradually losing the genes required to synthesize ribosomes, ATP, nucleotides, amino acids, and other compounds.

Although this idea sounds speculative, it cannot be dismissed lightly. For example, there is evidence that the mitochondria and chloroplasts of eukaryotic cells originated as intracellular symbionts from ancestors that were independent, free-living cells (see Chapter 30). Investigators contend that, instead of evolving into intracellular symbionts that aid their host cell, DNA viruses became parasites capable of replication and transmission from one host to another.

To support the degeneration hypothesis, researchers have pointed to mimivirus, the largest known virus that infects certain protists. In addition to its large size, the genome of this virus was found to contain some of the genes involved in protein synthesis—genes that are common to cells, but had not previously been observed in viruses. It is still not clear, though, whether these genes are remnants from an ancestral cell or were acquired from a host cell that was infected relatively recently. The discovery of a cell that possesses a genome similar to that of the mimivirus would support the degeneration hypothesis for the origin of this virus.

Origin at the Origin of Life?

Recently, some researchers have started to discuss a third alternative to explain the origin of viruses: that they trace their ancestry back to the first, RNA-based forms of life on Earth. If this hypothesis is correct, then the RNA genomes of some viruses are descended from genes found in early inhabitants of the RNA world (see Chapter 4). Some researchers have even suggested that retrovirus-like parasites may have been responsible for transforming the genetic material of cells from RNA to DNA.

To support this hypothesis, advocates point to the ubiquity of viruses—which suggests that they have been evolving along with organisms since life began. The RNA world-origin hypothesis also addresses a problem that weakens the other two hypotheses: Several proteins that are commonly expressed in many viruses are not expressed in any cell examined thus far. If viruses originated at the time of the origin of the cell, then the genes coding for these proteins may have come from an RNA-world pool of genes instead of a cell.

Currently, there is no one widely accepted view of where viruses came from. Because viruses are so diverse, all three hypotheses may be valid.

Emerging Viruses, Emerging Diseases

Although it is not known how the various types of viruses originated, it is certain that viruses will continue to diversify. With alarming regularity, the front pages of newspapers carry accounts of deadly viruses that are infecting humans for the first time.

HIV is an example of a virus responsible for an **emerging disease**: a new illness that suddenly affects significant numbers of individuals in a host population. Another, and perhaps the most infamous of such outbreaks occurred in 1995, when the Ebola virus infected 200 individuals in the Democratic Republic of Congo and had a fatality rate of 80 percent. In both cases, the causative agents were considered emerging viruses because they had switched from their traditional host species to a new host—humans.

Some Emerging Viruses Arise from Genome Reassortment

Each year the World Health Organization worries about a new influenza pandemic, one that might resemble the devastating outbreak of 1918. The small changes that arise from the influenza virus's error-prone RNA replicase are primarily responsible for the need for yearly vaccine updates. But influenza can also acquire alleles that are entirely new to the strain. (A virus **strain** consists of populations that have similar characteristics and is the lowest, or most specific, level of taxonomy for viruses.) How do new strains of influenza originate?

Influenza has a single-stranded RNA genome that consists of eight segments, most of which encode only one protein. If two viruses infect the same cell, the replicated genomic segments

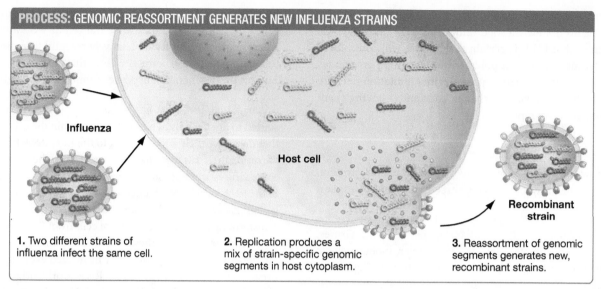

PROCESS: GENOMIC REASSORTMENT GENERATES NEW INFLUENZA STRAINS

Influenza

Host cell

Recombinant strain

1. Two different strains of influenza infect the same cell.

2. Replication produces a mix of strain-specific genomic segments in host cytoplasm.

3. Reassortment of genomic segments generates new, recombinant strains.

FIGURE 36.14 Influenza Can Generate New Strains via Genomic Reassortment.

are randomly shuffled in the cytosol. Thus when the progeny are assembled, many have segments from each parent virus (**FIGURE 36.14**).

The ability to randomly mix genomic segments becomes particularly significant when two different strains infect the same cell. In addition to humans, different strains of influenza can infect other animals, such as birds and pigs. While the avian strains do not efficiently infect humans, they can infect pigs—and so can human viral strains. The last point is key— pigs can serve as mixing vessels to produce new recombinant strains. Pandemic strains are thought to emerge from this type of reassortment.

Using Phylogenetic Trees to Understand Emerging Viruses How do researchers know that an emerging virus has "jumped" to a new host? The answer is to analyze the evolutionary history of the virus in question and then estimate a phylogenetic tree that includes its close relatives.

HIV, for example, belongs to a group of viruses called the lentiviruses, which infect a wide range of mammals including house cats, horses, goats, and primates. (*Lenti* is a Latin root that means "slow"; here it refers to the long period observed between the start of an infection by these viruses and the onset of the diseases they cause.) Consider the conclusions that can be drawn from the phylogenetic tree of HIV, shown in **FIGURE 36.15**.

- *There are immunodeficiency viruses.* Many of HIV's closest relatives parasitize cells that are part of the immune system. Several of them cause diseases with symptoms reminiscent of AIDS. These viruses infect monkeys and chimpanzees and are called simian immunodeficiency viruses (SIVs).

- *There are two HIVs.* There are two distinct types of human immunodeficiency viruses, called HIV-1 and HIV-2. Although both can cause AIDS, HIV-1 is far more virulent and is the better studied of the two.

HIV-1's closest known relatives are immunodeficiency viruses isolated from chimpanzees that live in central Africa. In contrast, HIV-2's closest relatives are immunodeficiency viruses that parasitize monkeys called sooty mangabeys.

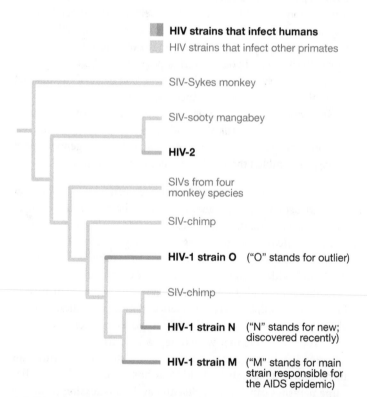

■ HIV strains that infect humans
□ HIV strains that infect other primates

SIV-Sykes monkey

SIV-sooty mangabey

HIV-2

SIVs from four monkey species

SIV-chimp

HIV-1 strain O ("O" stands for outlier)

SIV-chimp

HIV-1 strain N ("N" stands for new; discovered recently)

HIV-1 strain M ("M" stands for main strain responsible for the AIDS epidemic)

FIGURE 36.15 Phylogeny of HIV Strains and Types. Phylogenetic tree showing the evolutionary relationships among some of the immunodeficiency viruses that infect primates—including chimpanzees, humans, and several species of monkeys.

✔ **EXERCISE** On the appropriate branches, indicate where an SIV jumped to humans (draw and label bars across the appropriate branches).

In central Africa, where HIV-1 infection rates first reached epidemic proportions, contact between chimpanzees and humans is extensive. Chimps are hunted for food and kept as pets. Similarly, sooty mangabeys are hunted and kept as pets in western Africa, where HIV-2 infection rates are highest.

- *Multiple "jumps" have occurred.* Several strains of HIV-1 exist. The most important are called O for outlier (meaning, the most distant group relative to other strains), N for new, and M for main. Each of these strains likely represents an independent origin of HIV-1 from a chimp SIV strain.

The last point is particularly important. The existence of distinct strains suggests that HIV-1 has jumped from chimps to humans several times. It may do so again in the future.

Responding to a Virus Outbreak Physicians become alarmed when they see a large number of patients with identical, and unusual, disease symptoms in the same geographic area over a short period of time. The physicians report these cases to public health officials, who take on two urgent tasks: **(1)** identifying the agent that is causing the new illness and **(2)** determining how the disease is being transmitted.

Several strategies can be used to identify the pathogen responsible for an emerging disease. In 1993, an outbreak of an unknown pulmonary syndrome rocked the U.S. Southwest, killing half of the individuals who came down with the disease. Officials recognized strong similarities between symptoms in these cases and symptoms caused by a hantavirus native to northeast Asia, called Hantaan virus. The Hantaan virus rarely causes disease in North America, but it is known to infect rodents.

To determine whether a Hantaan-like virus was responsible for the U.S. outbreak, researchers began capturing mice in the homes and workplaces of afflicted people. About a third of the captured rodents tested positive for the presence of a Hantaan-like virus. Genome sequencing studies confirmed that the virus was a previously undescribed type of hantavirus, and it was aptly named the *sin nombre* virus (Spanish for "no-name virus"). Further, the sequences found in the mice matched those found in infected patients. Based on these results, officials were confident that this rodent-borne hantavirus was causing the wave of human infections.

The next step in the research program, identifying how the agent is being transmitted, is equally critical and takes old-fashioned detective work. By interviewing patients about their activities, researchers called epidemiologists decide how each patient could have acquired the virus. Was there a particular environment or source of food or water shared by those who were infected? Was the illness showing up in health-care workers who were in contact with infected individuals, implying that it was being transmitted from human to human?

If the virus identified as the cause of an illness can be transmitted efficiently from person to person, then the outbreak has the potential to become an epidemic. To date, the sin nombre virus has not been transmitted efficiently from person to person in the United States—only inefficiently from mice to people.

36.4 Key Lineages of Viruses

Because scientists are almost certain that viruses originated more than once throughout the history of life, there is no such thing as the phylogeny of all viruses. Stated another way, unlike the organisms discussed in previous chapters, viruses have no single phylogenetic tree that represents their evolutionary history. Instead, researchers most often focus on comparing base sequences in the genetic material of small, closely related groups of viruses to reconstruct the phylogenies of particular lineages, exemplified by the tree in Figure 36.15.

To organize the genomic diversity of viruses, researchers group them into seven general categories based on the nature of their genetic material and how they replicate. David Baltimore first proposed this approach in 1971; thus, it is called the Baltimore classification. **FIGURE 36.16** (page 726) summarizes the seven classes.

Notice that each of the Baltimore classes has its own unique strategy for transcription and replication of the genetic material. (See Section 36.2 to review how viruses copy their genomes.) All these strategies, however, share the need to produce mRNA, which is then translated by the host cell to make viral proteins.

Within the Baltimore classification system, researchers further distinguish viruses according to **(1)** virion morphology, **(2)** nature of the host species, and **(3)** the type of disease resulting from infection. Using these criteria, biologists identify a total of about 70 virus families.

Although the phylogenetic relationships among viruses is not as clear as what is observed in organisms, those within families are grouped into distinct genera for convenience. Within genera, biologists identify and name types of virus, such as HIV, the measles virus, and smallpox. Within each of these viral types, populations with distinct characteristics may be identified and named as strains.

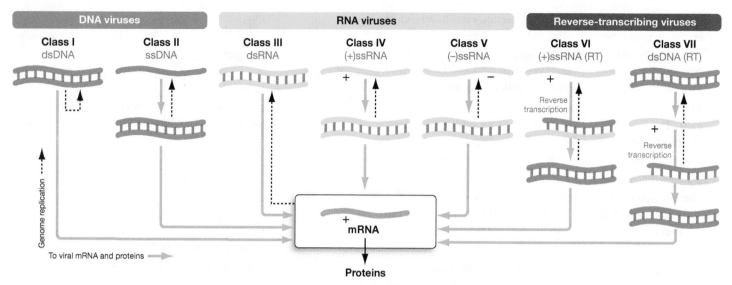

FIGURE 36.16 The Seven Different Strategies for Expression of Viral Genetic Material Converge on the Translation of mRNA. Notice that, although classes I and IV have the same types of genomes as classes VII and VI, they differ in the ways their genomes are replicated.

To get a sense of viral diversity, let's survey some of the most prevalent groups that can be distinguished based on the nature of their genetic material and mode of replication.

● Double-Stranded DNA (dsDNA) Viruses

● Double-Stranded RNA (dsRNA) Viruses

● Positive-Sense Single-Stranded RNA ([+]ssRNA) Viruses

● Negative-Sense Single-Stranded RNA ([−]ssRNA) Viruses

● RNA Reverse-Transcribing Viruses (Retroviruses)

Double-Stranded DNA (dsDNA) Viruses

The double-stranded DNA viruses are a large group, composed of some 21 families and 65 genera. Smallpox is perhaps the most familiar of these viruses (**FIGURE 36.17**). Although smallpox had been responsible for millions of deaths throughout human history, it was eradicated by worldwide vaccination programs. In 1977, smallpox was declared to be extinct in the wild; the only remaining samples of the virus are stored securely in research labs.

Genetic material As their name implies, the genes of these viruses consist of a single molecule of double-stranded DNA. The molecule may be linear or circular.

Host species These viruses parasitize hosts throughout the tree of life, with the notable exception of land plants. They include bacteriophage families called the T-series (T1–T7) and λ, which infect *E. coli*. Other common animal viruses with double-stranded DNA genomes include the human papilloma virus (HPV), herpesviruses, and adenoviruses.

Replicative cycle In most double-stranded DNA viruses that infect eukaryotes, viral genes have to enter the nucleus to be replicated. Often these viruses will replicate their genomes only during S phase, when the host cell's chromosomes are being replicated. Viruses like HPV are able to induce the cells to enter S phase despite the absence of the normal growth signals. This ability may, in fact, be responsible for the link between HPV infections and cervical cancer in women.

FIGURE 36.17 In Humans, Smallpox Can Cause Disease with Easily Recognizable Symptoms.

Double-Stranded RNA (dsRNA) Viruses

There are 7 families of double-stranded RNA viruses and a total of 22 genera. Most of the viruses in this group are nonenveloped.

Genetic material In some families, virions have a genome consisting of 10–12 double-stranded RNA molecules; in other families, the genome is composed of just 1–3 RNA molecules.

Host species A wide variety of organisms, including fungi, land plants, insects, vertebrates, and bacteria, are hosts for viruses with double-stranded RNA genomes. Particularly prominent are viruses that cause disease in rice, corn, sugarcane, and other crops. The bluetongue virus, a double-stranded RNA virus that is transmitted through midges and other biting insects, causes an often fatal disease that has significantly affected the livestock industry (**FIGURE 36.18**). In humans, reovirus and rotavirus infections are the leading cause of infant diarrhea and are responsible for over 110 million cases and a devastating 440,000 infant deaths each year.

Replicative cycle Once inside the cytosol of a host cell, the double-stranded genome of these viruses serves as a template for the synthesis of mRNAs, which are then translated into viral proteins. Some of the proteins form the capsids for a new generation of virions. The genome is copied by a viral enzyme that converts the mRNA transcripts into double-stranded RNA within the newly formed capsids.

FIGURE 36.18 dsRNA Viruses Parasitize a Wide Array of Organisms, Such as Livestock Infected by the Bluetongue Virus.

Positive-Sense Single-Stranded RNA ([+]ssRNA) Viruses

This is the largest group of viruses known. It has 21 families and 81 genera that include both enveloped and nonenveloped morphologies.

Genetic material The sequence of bases in a positive-sense single-stranded RNA virus is the same as that of a viral mRNA. Stated another way, the genome does not need to be transcribed in order for proteins to be produced. Depending on the species, the genome consists of 1–3 double-stranded RNA molecules.

Host species Most of the commercially important plant viruses belong to this group. Because they kill groups of cells in the host plant and turn patches of leaf or stem white, they are often named mottle viruses, spotted viruses, chlorotic (meaning, lacking chlorophyll) viruses, or mosaic viruses. **FIGURE 36.19** shows a healthy cowpea leaf and a cowpea leaf that has been attacked by a positive-sense single-stranded RNA virus. This group of viruses is also known to infect bacteria, fungi, and animals. Viruses within this group that infect humans include the rhinovirus (common cold), polio, SARS CoV, West Nile virus, and hepatitis A, C, and E.

Replicative cycle When the genome of these viruses enters a host cell, the positive-sense single-stranded RNA is immediately translated into a protein, often a polyprotein that is cleaved to generate functionally distinct proteins. These proteins include proteases that process the polypeptides and polymerases that copy the genome and produce mRNA for translation.

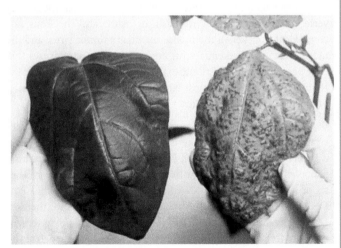

Healthy leaf   Leaf infected with virus

FIGURE 36.19 (+)ssRNA Viruses, Such as the Cowpea Mosaic Virus, Cause Important Plant Diseases.

This group has 7 families and 30 genera. Most members of this group are enveloped, but some negative-sense single-stranded RNA viruses lack an envelope.

Genetic material The sequence of bases in a negative-sense single-stranded RNA virus is opposite in polarity to the sequence in a viral mRNA. Stated another way, the virus genome is complementary to the viral mRNA. Depending on the family, the genome may consist of one single-stranded RNA molecule or up to eight separate RNA molecules.

Host species A wide variety of plants and animals are parasitized by viruses that have negative-sense single-stranded RNA genomes. If you have ever suffered from the flu, the mumps, or the measles, then you are painfully familiar with these viruses (**FIGURE 36.20**). The Ebola, sin nombre, and rabies viruses also belong to this group.

Replicative cycle When the genome of a negative-sense single-stranded RNA virus enters a host cell, a viral RNA-dependent RNA polymerase must accompany it to make new viral RNAs. Some of these transcripts serve as mRNA to be translated into viral proteins, while others function as templates for replicating the viral genome.

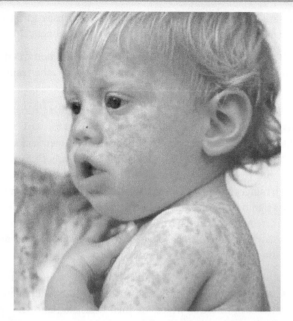

FIGURE 36.20 (−)ssRNA Viruses, Such as the Measles Virus, Cause Some Common Childhood Diseases.

RNA Reverse-Transcribing Viruses (Retroviruses)

The genomes of the RNA reverse-transcribing viruses are composed of positive-sense single-stranded RNA. This group has only one family, called the retroviruses, with 7 genera.

Genetic material Virions have two copies of a positive-sense single-stranded genome.

Host species Species in this group are known to parasitize only vertebrates—specifically birds, fish, or mammals. The Rous sarcoma virus (chickens), the mouse mammary tumor virus, and the murine (mouse) leukemia virus are well-studied retroviruses that have been shown to contribute to the development of cancer. Of the retroviruses, HIV is the most familiar and, in terms of the human population, by far the deadliest virus in this group (**FIGURE 36.21**).

Replicative cycle Although retroviruses have positive-sense single-stranded RNA, their genome is not translated immediately after it enters the host-cell cytosol. Instead, viral reverse transcriptase, which enters the cell along with the genome, catalyzes the synthesis of a double-stranded DNA version of the viral genome. This DNA is transported into the nucleus and integrated into the host genome by a viral protein called integrase. The virus may remain dormant for a period until induced by host-cell signals, such as the activation of HIV via the immune response. Activation starts up the replicative cycle. Genes are transcribed to mRNA to begin the production of a new generation of virions.

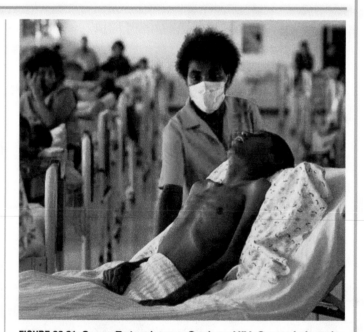

FIGURE 36.21 Some Retroviruses, Such as HIV, Severely Impair the Physiology of the Host.

If you understand . . .

36.1 Why Do Biologists Study Viruses?

- Viruses cause illness and death in organisms from all three domains of life.

- Viruses are specialists—different types of viruses infect particular species and types of cells.

✔ You should be able to explain how HIV causes AIDS and why it takes close to eight years before the clinical signs appear.

36.2 How Do Biologists Study Viruses?

- Most viruses have a capsid made of protein that is either icosahedral or helical in shape. Some viruses are covered by a host-derived membrane called an envelope.

- Viral genomes exhibit considerable diversity. The genetic material may consist of one or more molecules of DNA or RNA that is either double stranded or single stranded.

- Viral entry often depends on specific interactions between viral proteins and molecules on the host-cell surface, called virus receptors. Attachment is followed by uncoating, which is when the viral genome is released into the cytosol.

- The protein-production and genome-replication phases of the replicative cycle depend on biosynthetic machinery, chemical energy, and substrates provided by the host cell.

- Enveloped viruses exit a cell by budding; naked viruses often exit a cell by lysis—killing the host cell in the process.

- Some viruses may enter a dormant phase, when they do not produce virions, but instead coexist with the host cell and transmit genetic material to daughter cells when the host divides.

✔ You should be able to explain how three of the six phases of a viral replicative cycle can be stopped by antivirals, using HIV as an example.

36.3 What Themes Occur in the Diversification of Viruses?

- Three hypotheses have been developed to explain the origin of viruses: (1) They are escaped gene sets from cells; (2) they are the products of degenerate cellular parasites; (3) they coevolved with cells from the RNA world.

- Viruses continue to evolve. Factors influencing rates of viral evolution are errors during genome replication and genomic reassortment.

- Many viruses currently infecting humans are examples of emerging diseases—that is, diseases caused by viruses transmitted from other host species.

✔ You should be able to apply what you know of Darwin's four postulates on natural selection to explain how it is possible for viruses to evolve even though they are not alive.

36.4 Key Lineages of Viruses

- In addition to morphology and the nature of the genetic material, viruses also vary in how the genome is replicated and transcribed to produce mRNA.

✔ You should be able to compare and contrast the transcription and replication of the RNA genomes of class IV and class VI viruses.

MB MasteringBiology

1. **MasteringBiology Assignments**

Tutorials and Activities HIV Replicative Cycle; HIV Reproductive Cycle; Phage Lysogenic and Lytic Cycles; Phage Lytic Cycle; Retrovirus (HIV) Reproductive Cycle; Simplified Viral Reproductive Cycle; Viral Replication

Questions Reading Quizzes, Blue-Thread Questions, Test Bank

2. **eText** Read your book online, search, take notes, highlight text, and more.

3. **The Study Area** Practice Test, Cumulative Test, BioFlix® 3-D Animations, Videos, Activities, Audio Glossary, Word Study Tools, Art

You should be able to . . .

1. What do host cells provide for viruses?
   a. nucleotides and amino acids
   b. ribosomes
   c. ATP
   d. all of the above

2. How do viruses that infect animals enter an animal's cells?
   a. The viruses pass through a wound.
   b. The viruses bind to a membrane component.
   c. The viruses puncture the cell wall.
   d. The viruses lyse the cell.

3. What does reverse transcriptase do?

4. When do most enveloped virions acquire their envelope?
   a. during entry into the host cell
   b. during budding from the host cell
   c. as they burst from the host cell
   d. as they integrate into the host cell's chromosome

5. In the viral replicative cycle, what reaction do viral proteases catalyze?
   a. polymerization of amino acids into peptides
   b. folding of long peptide chains into functional proteins
   c. cutting of polyprotein chains into functional proteins
   d. assembly of virions

6. What features distinguish the seven major categories of viruses?

7. The outer surface of a virion consists of either a membrane-like envelope or a protein capsid. How does the outer surface correlate with a virus's mode of exiting a host cell, and why?

8. Compare and contrast the bacteriophage lytic cycle versus lysogeny by addressing (1) replication of the viral genome, (2) production of virions, and (3) effect on the host cell.

9. Propose a reason why the development of antiviral drugs is more difficult than developing the antibiotics used to treat bacterial infections.

10. How does the diversity of viral genome types support the hypothesis that viruses originated several times independently?

11. What types of data convinced researchers that HIV originated when a simian immunodeficiency virus "jumped" to humans?

12. Of the viruses highlighted in Section 36.4, predict which of the following would be able to make viral proteins by injecting nothing more than its genome into a suitable host cell.
    a. cowpea mosaic ([+]ssRNA) virus
    b. bluetongue (dsRNA) virus
    c. measles ([−]ssRNA) virus
    d. human immunodeficiency (RNA reverse-transcribing) virus

13. Suppose you could isolate a virus that parasitizes the pathogen *Staphylococcus aureus*—a bacterium that causes acne, boils, and a variety of other afflictions in humans. How could you test whether this virus might serve as a safe and effective treatment for a staph infection?

14. If you were in charge of the government's budget devoted to stemming the AIDS epidemic, would you devote most of the resources to drug development or preventive medicine? Defend your answer.

15. Latency is a key adaptation in some animal viruses and likely evolved to prolong the infection by avoiding a strong and effective immune response. Which of the following types of viruses would you expect to require periods of latency?
    a. viruses that have large genomes and require a long time for replication

b. viruses that require a long time for transmission to new host organisms
c. viruses that require a long time for assembling into complex structures
d. viruses that infect cells of the immune system

16. Consider these two contrasting definitions of life: (1) An entity is alive if it is capable of replicating itself via the directed chemical transformation of its environment; (2) An entity is alive if it is an integrated system for the storage, maintenance, replication, and use of genetic information. According to these definitions, are viruses alive? Explain.

The Big Picture

The Big Picture

BIG PICTURE

Plants and animals are diverse lineages of multicellular eukaryotes. They are different in important ways. Each lineage evolved independently from a different single-celled protist—plants with the ability to make their own food by photosynthesis, and animals reliant on obtaining energy from other organisms. Further, plants are sessile, while most animals are capable of complex movements and locomotion.

Yet despite these differences, plants and animals face many of the same challenges to survive and reproduce in water and on land. Use this concept map to explore some of their similarities and differences in form and function.

Note that each box in the concept map indicates the chapters where you can go for more information. Also, be sure to do the blue exercises in the Check Your Understanding box below.

check your understanding

If you understand the big picture . . .
✔ You should be able to . . .

1. Propose one mechanism that both plants and animals use on land to limit the evaporative loss of water.

2. Give an example of a method that both plants and animals use to protect their eggs and sperm from drying out.

3. Explain one constraint of large body size for both plants and animals.

4. Explain where cellular respiration fits into this map.

Answers are available in Appendix A.

Plant and Animal FORM AND FUNCTION

are the product of

Evolutionary processes

including

Abiotic environment
- Temperature
- Light
- Water availability
- pH, salinity, dissolved gases, nutrients
- Habitat structure

create

occurring in

Changing ecological contexts

Biotic environment
- Parental care
- Competitors
- Predators, prey
- Parasites, hosts
- Mutualists

because plants and animals have

Key FUNCTIONS to survive and reproduce

correlate with

including

PLANTS

REGULATION OF WATER AND IONS

- Water moves along a water potential gradient
- Turgor pressure provides structural support
- Terrestrial plants lose water evaporatively by transpiration, regulated by stomata and waxy surfaces

NUTRITION

- Autotrophic; make their own food by photosynthesis

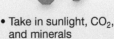

- Take in sunlight, CO_2, and minerals
- Obtain ions from soil, symbiotic fungi, or bacteria

ANIMALS

- Osmotic stress varies in marine, freshwater, and terrestrial habitats
- Urinary system maintains homeostasis of water and electrolytes while managing excretion of nitrogenous wastes
- Terrestrial animals limit evaporative loss

- Heterotrophic; must eat food to acquire energy
- Take in carbohydrates, fats, proteins, vitamins, and minerals
- Obtain nutrients by ingestion, digestion, and absorption

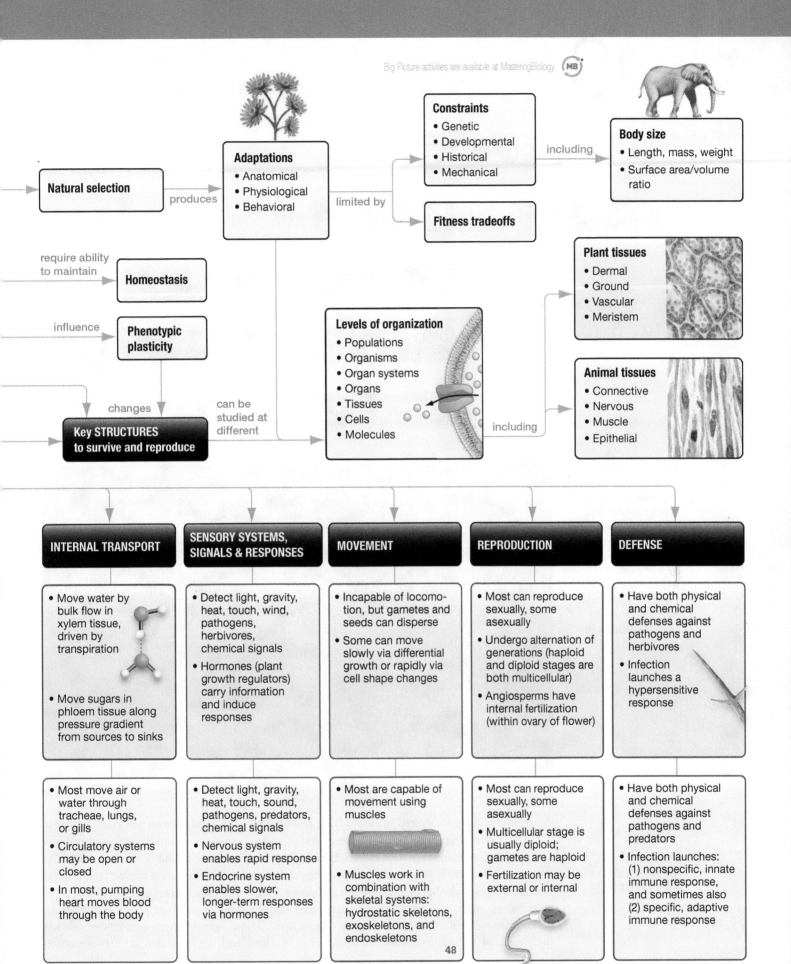

Natural selection → *produces* → **Adaptations**
- Anatomical
- Physiological
- Behavioral

limited by →

Constraints
- Genetic
- Developmental
- Historical
- Mechanical

including →

Body size
- Length, mass, weight
- Surface area/volume ratio

Fitness tradeoffs

require ability to maintain → **Homeostasis**

influence → **Phenotypic plasticity**

changes → **Key STRUCTURES to survive and reproduce**

can be studied at different →

Levels of organization
- Populations
- Organisms
- Organ systems
- Organs
- Tissues
- Cells
- Molecules

Plant tissues
- Dermal
- Ground
- Vascular
- Meristem

including →

Animal tissues
- Connective
- Nervous
- Muscle
- Epithelial

INTERNAL TRANSPORT
- Move water by bulk flow in xylem tissue, driven by transpiration
- Move sugars in phloem tissue along pressure gradient from sources to sinks

- Most move air or water through tracheae, lungs, or gills
- Circulatory systems may be open or closed
- In most, pumping heart moves blood through the body

SENSORY SYSTEMS, SIGNALS & RESPONSES
- Detect light, gravity, heat, touch, wind, pathogens, herbivores, chemical signals
- Hormones (plant growth regulators) carry information and induce responses

- Detect light, gravity, heat, touch, sound, pathogens, predators, chemical signals
- Nervous system enables rapid response
- Endocrine system enables slower, longer-term responses via hormones

MOVEMENT
- Incapable of locomotion, but gametes and seeds can disperse
- Some can move slowly via differential growth or rapidly via cell shape changes

- Most are capable of movement using muscles
- Muscles work in combination with skeletal systems: hydrostatic skeletons, exoskeletons, and endoskeletons

REPRODUCTION
- Most can reproduce sexually, some asexually
- Undergo alternation of generations (haploid and diploid stages are both multicellular)
- Angiosperms have internal fertilization (within ovary of flower)

- Most can reproduce sexually, some asexually
- Multicellular stage is usually diploid; gametes are haploid
- Fertilization may be external or internal

DEFENSE
- Have both physical and chemical defenses against pathogens and herbivores
- Infection launches a hypersensitive response

- Have both physical and chemical defenses against pathogens and predators
- Infection launches: (1) nonspecific, innate immune response, and sometimes also (2) specific, adaptive immune response

48

48 Animal Movement

In this chapter you will learn that

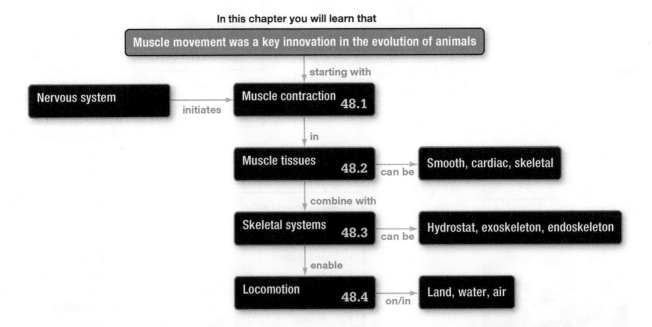

Muscle movement was a key innovation in the evolution of animals

starting with

Nervous system — initiates → Muscle contraction **48.1**

in

Muscle tissues **48.2** — can be → Smooth, cardiac, skeletal

combine with

Skeletal systems **48.3** — can be → Hydrostat, exoskeleton, endoskeleton

enable

Locomotion **48.4** — on/in → Land, water, air

Basilisk lizards are able to run on water—literally. This impressive escape strategy demonstrates the extent to which muscle-generated movements have diversified among animals. For most animals, complex muscle movements make the difference between life and death.

This chapter is part of the Big Picture. See how on pages 840–841.

You may have discovered while studying biology that plants and animals are more similar to each other than they initially appear. For example, plants and animals both require water and nutrients in specific quantities, have highly specialized tissues and complex reproductive structures, and launch defenses against parasites and predators. You can see a comparison of these and other traits in the Big Picture of Plant and Animal Form and Function on pages 840–841.

However, animals possess a quality that clearly distinguishes them from plants and other organisms: movement by virtue of muscle contractions. Muscle-generated movements were a key innovation in animal evolution. Rapid movements, along with sophisticated sensory structures

✔ When you see this checkmark, stop and test yourself. Answers are available in Appendix A.

and complex information processing systems, were vital to animal diversification, and these attributes made animals efficient eating machines in diverse ecosystems.

Muscles generate movement by exerting force and causing shape changes. Movement falls into two general categories:

1. *Movement of the entire organism relative to its environment.* **Locomotion,** movement of an animal under its own power, enables animals to seek food, water, mates, and shelter as well as avoid predators. Modes of locomotion include undulating, jetting, swimming, walking, running, jumping, gliding, and flying.

2. *Movement of one part of the animal relative to other parts (not involved in locomotion).* This type of movement also has important functions—for example, to ventilate gills for gas exchange and to grasp prey. Even sessile organisms like sea anemones and barnacles use complex, muscle-generated movements to survive and reproduce.

How do animals accomplish their spectacular movements? This chapter starts by probing into the mechanism of muscle contraction that serves as the "engine" for most animal movements and then considers how muscle and skeletal systems work together to produce locomotion. The latter discussion introduces a research field called **biomechanics,** in which the principles of physics and engineering are applied to questions about the mechanical structure and function of organisms. Let's jump in.

48.1 How Do Muscles Contract?

The mechanism responsible for the contraction of muscle has fascinated and perplexed scientists for many centuries. Before the advent of microscopes and modern research techniques, scientists could only speculate about what makes muscles contract and relax.

Early Muscle Experiments

In the second century C.E., the Roman physician and philosopher Galen proposed that spirits flowed from nerves into muscles, inflating them and increasing their diameter. This "inflation" hypothesis persisted into the seventeenth century, when the French philosopher René Descartes suggested that nerves carry fluid from the pineal gland—which is in the brain and was considered to be the seat of the soul—to the muscles, making them shorten and swell.

Later that century, Dutch anatomist Jan Swammerdam tested Descartes' inflation hypothesis with a simple yet elegant experiment. He placed a piece of frog muscle into an airtight syringe with the nerve protruding through a small hole in the side and a small drop of water in the tip. He then stimulated the nerve, causing the muscle to contract. If the muscle's volume changed during contraction, the drop of water in the tip of the syringe would move. But it did not. The volume of the muscle remained constant.

Swammerdam's experiment demonstrated an important point: The contraction mechanism is inherent to the muscle itself—muscle is not like a balloon, and the nerve is not like a water hose filling a balloon. This insight was confirmed by Italian scientist Luigi Galvani in the 1790s, when he severed the nerve to a frog's leg muscle and then connected the two sides of the cut with a metal conductor. Contraction occurred. He concluded that the nerve and muscle possess "animal electricity" that can induce contraction.

If the shape of muscle does not change by inflation, what is the mechanism of muscle contraction?

The Sliding-Filament Model

Early microscopists established that the muscle tissue in vertebrate limbs and hearts is composed of slender fibers. A **muscle fiber** is a long, thin muscle cell. Within each of the muscle cells are many threadlike, contractile filaments called **myofibrils.** The myofibrils inside muscle fibers often look striped or striated due to the alternating light–dark units called **sarcomeres,** which repeat along the length of a myofibril (**FIGURE 48.1**).

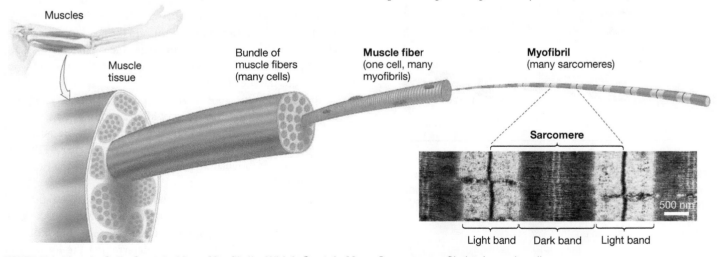

Muscles

Muscle tissue

Bundle of muscle fibers (many cells)

Muscle fiber (one cell, many myofibrils)

Myofibril (many sarcomeres)

Sarcomere

500 nm

Light band   Dark band   Light band

FIGURE 48.1 Muscle Cells Contain Many Myofibrils, Which Contain Many Sarcomeres. Skeletal muscle cells (fibers) have a striped appearance due to repeating sarcomeres, which are units of alternating light–dark bands.

The microscopists observed that sarcomeres shorten as myofibrils contract. Sarcomeres then lengthen when the cell relaxes and an external force stretches the muscle. Based on these observations, it became clear that the question of how muscles contract simplifies to the question of how sarcomeres shorten.

Biologists knew that the answer must involve the two types of protein that had been found in sarcomeres: **actin** and **myosin**. But they did not know the shapes of these molecules or how they were arranged within the sarcomere. Did both types of molecules span the entire length of the sarcomere? Or were the filaments restricted to certain bands within the sarcomere?

In 1952, biologist Hugh Huxley produced electron micrographs of sarcomeres in cross section. He observed that there were two types of filaments, **thin filaments** and **thick filaments**, and that these filaments overlapped in the dark bands but not in the light bands. Huxley and his collaborator Jean Hanson also observed that sarcomeres stripped of their myosin had no dark bands. They concluded that the thick filaments must be composed of myosin, and the thin filaments must be composed of actin.

How did myosin and actin interact to shorten the sarcomere? In 1954, Huxley and Hanson hit on the key insight when they observed how the light and dark bands in sarcomeres changed when the muscles were relaxed versus contracted. Overall, the width of the dark bands did not change during a contraction, but the light bands became narrower.

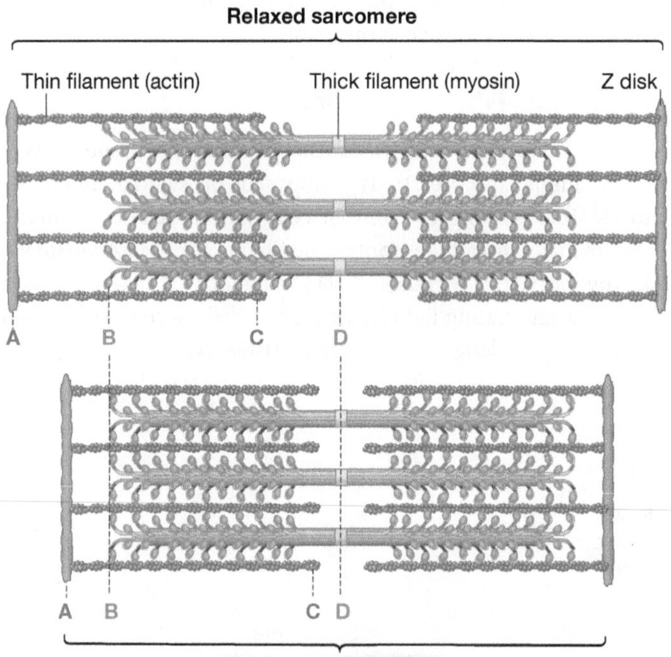

To explain these observations, Huxley and Hanson proposed the **sliding-filament model** illustrated in **FIGURE 48.2**. The hypothesis was that the filaments slide past one another during a contraction. That is, the sarcomere can shorten with no change in lengths of the thin and thick filaments themselves:

- The distance from point A to point C does not change, and the distance from point B to point D does not change.

- Points A and B move closer to each other during contraction, as do points C and D.

Another pair of researchers, Andrew F. Huxley (no relation to Hugh) and Rolf Niedergerke, published the same result at the same time. Follow-up research has shown that the Huxley–Hanson model is correct in almost every detail.

Structurally, thin filaments are composed of two coiled chains of actin, a common component of the cytoskeleton of eukaryotic cells (see Chapter 7). One end of each thin filament is anchored to a structure called the **Z disc,** which forms the end wall of the sarcomere. The other end of a thin filament is free to interact with thick filaments. Thick filaments are composed of multiple strands of myosin. They span the center of the sarcomere and are free at both ends to interact with thin filaments.

To appreciate how the sliding-filament model works, consider the following analogy: Two large trucks are parked 50 m apart, facing each other. Each has a long rope attached to the front bumper. Six burly weightlifters stand in a line in front of each truck, grab onto the rope, and pull, hand over hand, so that the two trucks roll toward one another. ✔ If you understand the model, you should be able to explain which elements in the analogy represent the Z discs, which are the thin filaments, and which elements are the thick filaments.

How Do Actin and Myosin Interact?

How does this sliding action occur at the molecular level? Early work on the three-dimensional structure of myosin revealed that each myosin molecule is made up of a pair of subunits with "tails" coiled around one another and "heads" bent to the side. Each myosin head can bind to actin, and the head region can catalyze the hydrolysis of ATP into adenosine diphosphate (ADP) and a phosphate ion. These results suggested that myosin—not actin—was the site of active movement.

In addition, electron microscopy revealed that myosin and actin are locked together shortly after an animal dies, and its muscles enter the stiff state known as rigor mortis. Because ATP is unavailable in dead tissue, the data suggested that ATP is involved in getting myosin to release from actin once the two molecules have bound to each other.

Later, Ivan Rayment and colleagues solved the detailed three-dimensional structure of the myosin head (**FIGURE 48.3**). Using X-ray crystallographic techniques (see **BioSkills 11** in Appendix B), Rayment's group determined the location of the actin-binding site and examined how myosin's structure

Relaxed sarcomere

Thin filament (actin)   Thick filament (myosin)   Z disk

A   B   C   D

A   B   C D

Contracted sarcomere

FIGURE 48.2 The Sliding-Filament Model Explains Important Aspects of Sarcomere Contraction. When a sarcomere contracts, the lengths of the thin filaments (distance from A to C) and thick filaments (distance from B to D) do not change. Rather, the filaments slide past one another.

✔QUESTION According to the model shown here, why is the dark band in a sarcomere (see Figure 48.1) dark and the light band light?

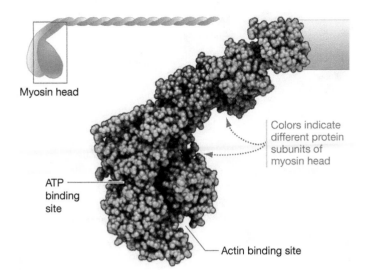

Myosin head

Colors indicate
different protein
subunits of
myosin head

ATP
binding
site

Actin binding site

FIGURE 48.3 Myosin's "Head" Binds ATP and Actin. Each myosin molecule consists of two subunits with their tails coiled together and their two heads exposed. The heads contain binding sites for ATP and actin; when one of these subunits binds, its myosin head changes shape.

changed when ATP or ADP bound to it. As predicted, the protein's conformation changed significantly when bound to ATP versus ADP.

Based on these data, Rayment and co-workers proposed a four-step model for actin–myosin interaction (**FIGURE 48.4**):

Step 1 ATP binds to the myosin head, causing a conformational change that releases the head from the actin in the thin filament.

Step 2 When ATP is hydrolyzed to ADP and inorganic phosphate, the neck of the myosin straightens and the head pivots. The myosin head then binds to a new actin subunit farther down the thin filament. In this position, the myosin head is "cocked" in its high-energy state, ready for the power stroke.

Step 3 When inorganic phosphate is released, the neck bends back to its original position. This bending, called the power stroke, moves the entire thin filament relative to the thick filament.

Step 4 After ADP is released, the myosin head is ready to bind to another molecule of ATP.

As ATP binding, hydrolysis, and release continue, the two ends of the sarcomere are pulled closer together. (The transition from step 4 to step 1 cannot occur after death. Rigor mortis sets in as ATP supplies run out.)

The same basic ratcheting mechanism between actin and myosin is responsible for the amoeboid movement observed in amoebae and slime molds (see Chapter 30) as well as the streaming of cytoplasm observed in algae and land plants. Actin and myosin have played a critical role in the diversification of eukaryotes because they make movement possible in the absence of cilia and flagella.

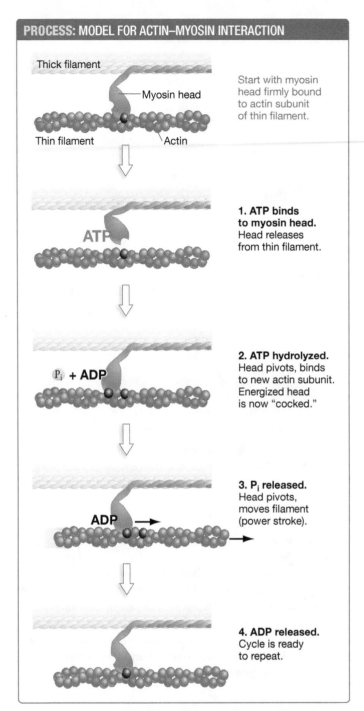

PROCESS: MODEL FOR ACTIN–MYOSIN INTERACTION

Thick filament

Myosin head

Thin filament   Actin

Start with myosin head firmly bound to actin subunit of thin filament.

ATP

1. ATP binds to myosin head. Head releases from thin filament.

P_i + ADP

2. ATP hydrolyzed. Head pivots, binds to new actin subunit. Energized head is now "cocked."

ADP

3. P_i released. Head pivots, moves filament (power stroke).

4. ADP released. Cycle is ready to repeat.

FIGURE 48.4 Myosin and Actin Interact during Muscle Contraction. Summary of the current model of how myosin and actin interact as a sarcomere contracts. The four steps repeat rapidly. (Only one head of the myosin molecule is shown, for simplicity.)

Considering that ATP is almost always available in living muscles, how do muscles ever stop contracting and relax? Besides actin, thin filaments contain two key proteins called **tropomyosin** and **troponin**. Tropomyosin and troponin work together to block the myosin binding sites on actin. The myosin–actin interaction cannot then occur, and thick and thin

(a) Muscle relaxed: Tropomyosin and troponin work together to block the myosin binding sites on actin.

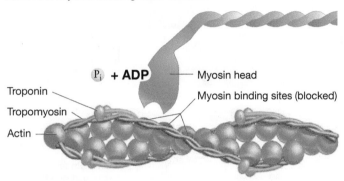

Troponin
Tropomyosin
Actin

P$_i$ + **ADP**

Myosin head
Myosin binding sites (blocked)

(b) Contraction begins: When a calcium ion binds to troponin, the troponin–tropomyosin complex moves, exposing myosin binding sites.

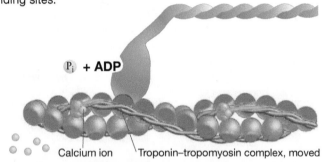

P$_i$ + **ADP**

Calcium ion   Troponin–tropomyosin complex, moved

FIGURE 48.5 Troponin and Tropomyosin Regulate Muscle Activity. Note that the myosin head is in its energized state when a muscle is relaxed.

filaments cannot slide past each other. As a result, the muscle relaxes (**FIGURE 48.5a**).

But when calcium ions bind to troponin, the troponin–tropomyosin complex moves in a way that exposes the myosin binding sites on actin. As **FIGURE 48.5b** shows, myosin then binds and contraction can begin.

How are calcium ions released so that contraction can begin? The process begins with the arrival of an action potential—an electrical signal from a motor neuron.

How Do Neurons Initiate Contraction?

You are probably sitting as you read. If so, contract your calf muscles to point your toes. Your nervous system just played a critical role in controlling the timing of your muscle contractions. First, your central nervous system—your brain—received input from an array of sensory cells in your peripheral nervous system, such as the ones in the retina of your eyes as you read this paragraph. Then your brain integrated this information and triggered action potentials in the motor neurons of the peripheral nervous system of your legs.

FIGURE 48.6 summarizes what happens when an action potential from a motor neuron arrives at a muscle cell:

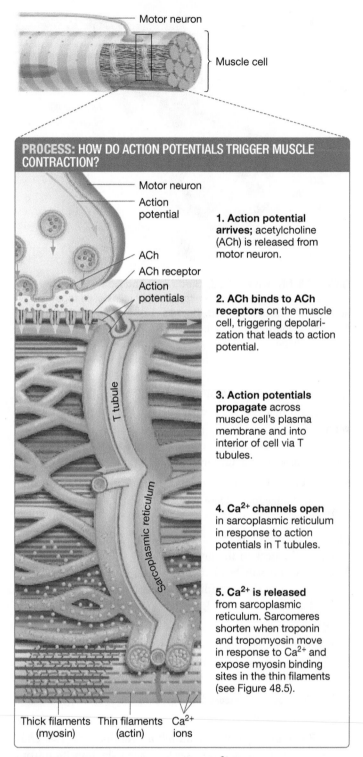

Motor neuron

Muscle cell

PROCESS: HOW DO ACTION POTENTIALS TRIGGER MUSCLE CONTRACTION?

Motor neuron
Action potential

ACh
ACh receptor
Action potentials

T tubule

Sarcoplasmic reticulum

Thick filaments (myosin)   Thin filaments (actin)   Ca^{2+} ions

1. Action potential arrives; acetylcholine (ACh) is released from motor neuron.

2. ACh binds to ACh receptors on the muscle cell, triggering depolarization that leads to action potential.

3. Action potentials propagate across muscle cell's plasma membrane and into interior of cell via T tubules.

4. Ca^{2+} channels open in sarcoplasmic reticulum in response to action potentials in T tubules.

5. Ca^{2+} is released from sarcoplasmic reticulum. Sarcomeres shorten when troponin and tropomyosin move in response to Ca^{2+} and expose myosin binding sites in the thin filaments (see Figure 48.5).

FIGURE 48.6 Action Potentials Trigger Ca^{2+} Release. Action potentials at the neuromuscular junction trigger the release of Ca^{2+}, which binds to troponin–tropomyosin and allows myosin to form a cross-bridge with actin.

1. Action potentials trigger the release of the neurotransmitter **acetylcholine** from the motor neuron into the synaptic cleft between the motor neuron and the muscle cell.

2. Acetylcholine diffuses across the synaptic cleft and binds to acetylcholine receptors on the plasma membrane of the muscle cell. By recording voltage changes in muscle cells, biologists showed that a membrane depolarization occurs in response to the binding of acetylcholine. If enough acetylcholine is applied to a muscle cell, depolarization triggers action potentials in the fiber itself.

3. The action potentials propagate along the length of the muscle fiber and spread into the interior of the fiber via invaginations of the muscle cell membrane called **T tubules.** (The T stands for transverse, meaning extending across.)

4. T tubules intersect with extensive sheets of smooth endoplasmic reticulum called the **sarcoplasmic reticulum.** When an action potential passes down a T tubule and reaches one of these intersections, a protein in the T-tubule membrane changes conformation and opens calcium channels in the sarcoplasmic reticulum.

5. Calcium causes the myosin binding sites on the actin filaments to be exposed, enabling the contraction to begin.

By this series of events, the interaction of the nervous system and muscle tissue at the neuromuscular junction precisely regulates muscle contractions—and thus complex movement.

check your understanding

If you understand that . . .

* Muscles shorten when thick filaments of myosin slide past thin filaments of actin in a series of binding events mediated by the hydrolysis of ATP.
* Muscle cells shorten in response to action potentials, which trigger the release of calcium ions that enable actin and myosin to interact.

✔ **You should be able to . . .**
1. Describe the sliding-filament model.
2. Predict the effect on muscle function of drugs that have the following actions: increase acetylcholine release at the neuromuscular junction, prevent conformational changes in troponin, and block uptake of calcium ions into the sarcoplasmic reticulum.

Answers are available in Appendix A.

48.2 Muscle Tissues

How do muscle cells and muscle tissues vary? After years of careful anatomical study, biologists concluded that animals have three classes of muscle tissue: (1) smooth muscle, (2) cardiac muscle, and (3) skeletal muscle. You, and all other vertebrates, have all three.

Smooth, cardiac, and skeletal muscle share several properties. They all contract as described by the sliding-filament model, and they all contract in response to electrical stimulation. However, the three classes of muscle also differ in important ways, summarized in **TABLE 48.1** (see page 978):

* *Voluntary versus involuntary* **Voluntary muscles** can contract in response to conscious thought (and also by unconscious reflexes) and are stimulated by neurons in the somatic division of the peripheral nervous system. **Involuntary muscles** contract only in response to unconscious electrical activity and are stimulated and inhibited by neurons in the autonomic division of the peripheral nervous system.

* *Multinucleate versus uninucleate* Muscle cells may have one or many nuclei depending on the size of the cells.

* *Striated versus unstriated* In some muscle cells, the actin and myosin filaments are aligned in rows forming sarcomeres, giving the cells and tissues a banded appearance; for this reason, it is often called **striated muscle.** Other muscle cells are unstriated.

Let's apply these characteristics to each class of muscle tissue in more detail.

Smooth Muscle

Smooth muscle cells are unbranched, tapered at each end, and often organized into thin sheets. They lack the sarcomeres that are found in skeletal and cardiac muscle; hence, they are unstriated and appear smooth. Smooth muscle cells are relatively small and have a single nucleus.

Smooth muscle is essential to the function of the lungs, blood vessels, digestive system, urinary bladder, and reproductive system. Bronchioles in the lungs have a layer of smooth muscle that controls the size of airways; similarly, smooth muscles in the blood vessels can contract or relax to alter blood-flow patterns and blood pressure. Layers of smooth muscle in the gastrointestinal tract help mix and move food, and uterine smooth muscle is responsible for expelling the fetus during birth.

Smooth muscle is innervated by autonomic motor neurons, and it is thus involuntary. Acetylcholine from parasympathetic ("rest-and-digest") neurons aids digestion by stimulating contraction of smooth muscle in the stomach and intestine.

In contrast, sympathetic ("fight-or-flight") neurons release the neurotransmitter **norepinephrine;** and the adrenal glands adjacent to the kidneys release the hormone **epinephrine,** also called **adrenaline**. Norepinephrine and epinephrine have the opposite effect to that of acetylcholine: they inhibit contraction of muscle in the stomach and intestine. Different smooth muscles are stimulated or inhibited by autonomic motor neurons depending on the type of neurotransmitter and neuron receptors they have.

Smooth Muscle	Cardiac Muscle	Skeletal Muscle
25 µm	25 µm	25 µm
Location Intestines, arteries, other	Heart	Attached to the skeleton
Function Move food, help regulate blood pressure, etc.	Pump blood	Move skeleton
Cell characteristics	Intercalated discs	Nuclei
Single nucleus	1 or 2 nuclei	Multinucleate
Unstriated	Striated	Striated
Unbranched	Branched; intercalated discs form direct cytoplasmic connection end to end	Unbranched
No sarcomeres	Contains sarcomeres	Contains sarcomeres
Activity is "involuntary," meaning that signal from motor neuron is not required	Activity is "involuntary," meaning that signal from motor neuron is not required	Activity is "voluntary," meaning that signal from somatic motor neuron is required

Cardiac Muscle

Cardiac muscle makes up the walls of the heart and is responsible for pumping blood throughout the body. Unlike smooth muscle, cardiac muscle cells contain sarcomeres and are striated. Further, cardiac muscle cells have a unique branched structure, and they are directly connected end-to-end via specialized regions called intercalated discs. These discs are critical to the flow of electrical signals from cell to cell and thus to the coordination of the heartbeat.

Like smooth muscle, cardiac muscle is involuntary—it contracts following spontaneous depolarizations. During rest, parasympathetic neurons release acetylcholine onto the heart. This neurotransmitter slows down the rate of depolarization of cardiac cells. The result is a slower heart rate.

During exercise, or when an animal is frightened, stressed, or otherwise stimulated, sympathetic neurons release norepinephrine onto the heart, and the adrenal gland releases epinephrine. Norepinephrine and epinephrine have an opposite effect to that of acetylcholine: they increase heart rate and strengthen the force of cardiac muscle contraction. The result is that more blood is pumped from the heart—an essential component of the fight-or-flight response of the sympathetic nervous system.

Skeletal Muscle

Skeletal muscle consists of exceptionally long, unbranched muscle fibers. For example, a muscle fiber of a cat may be 0.4 mm wide and 40 mm long—enormous compared to most cells. These large cells result from the fusion of many smaller embryonic cells during development, accounting for the multiple nuclei spread out along the cell. Each muscle fiber is packed with myofibrils, each of which may contain thousands of sarcomeres, giving skeletal muscle its striated appearance.

Skeletal muscle is so named because it usually attaches to the skeleton. When skeletal muscle contracts, it exerts a pulling force on the skeleton, causing it to move—powering the sprint of cheetahs, the flight of hummingbirds, and the pinch of crab claws. In addition, skeletal muscle encircles the openings of the digestive and urinary tracts and controls swallowing, defecation, and urination.

A significant fraction of the body of many animals is composed of skeletal muscle. For example, 63 percent of the body weight of trout is skeletal muscle, and mammals—including humans—of all sizes are 40 to 45 percent muscle. Clearly, skeletal muscle plays an important role in animal biology. Some of the major skeletal muscles in the human body are shown in **FIGURE 48.7**.

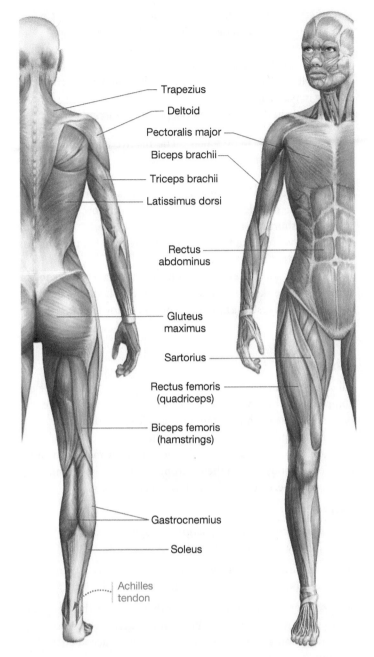

FIGURE 48.7 Major Skeletal Muscles Make Up a Large Portion of the Human Body.

Labels (back view, left figure):
Trapezius
Deltoid
Triceps brachii
Latissimus dorsi
Gluteus maximus
Biceps femoris (hamstrings)
Gastrocnemius
Soleus
Achilles tendon

Labels (front view, right figure):
Pectoralis major
Biceps brachii
Rectus abdominus
Rectus femoris (quadriceps)
Sartorius

Skeletal muscle is distinguished from cardiac and smooth muscle in being voluntary. Skeletal muscle must be stimulated by somatic motor neurons to contract. If these motor neurons are damaged, as can occur with a spinal cord injury, skeletal muscle cannot contract and becomes paralyzed.

Although all muscles contract as described by the sliding-filament model, not all skeletal-muscle fibers have the same contractile properties. The force output of skeletal muscles depends on **(1)** the relative proportion of different fiber types, **(2)** the organization of fibers within the muscle, and **(3)** how the muscle is used. Let's take a closer look at these sources of variation in muscle performance.

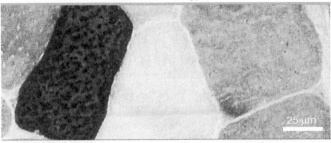

Slow fiber	Fast fiber	Intermediate fiber
Red	White	Pink or red
High myoglobin concentration	Low myoglobin concentration	High myoglobin concentration
Derive most ATP via aerobic respiration (slow oxidative)	Derive most ATP via glycolysis (fast glycolytic)	Derive ATP from glycolysis and aerobic respiration (slow glycolytic)
Many mitochondria	Few mitochondria	Many mitochondria
Slow twitch	Fast twitch	Intermediate twitch
Fatigues slowly	Fatigues quickly	Intermediate fatigue

Skeletal-Fiber Types Skeletal muscle fibers can be divided into general types based on their structural and functional characteristics, summarized in **TABLE 48.2**:

- **Slow muscle fibers** (slow oxidative fibers) appear red because they contain a high concentration of myoglobin, an iron-bearing pigment that carries oxygen (similar to but distinct from hemoglobin in the blood). Slow fibers contract slowly because the myosin hydrolyzes ATP at a slow rate. They also fatigue slowly because they have many mitochondria and can generate steady quantities of ATP using oxidative phosphorylation—that is, aerobic respiration (Chapter 9)—thanks to the plentiful supply of oxygen delivered by myoglobin.

- **Fast muscle fibers** (fast glycolytic fibers) appear white because they have a low myoglobin concentration. They contract rapidly because the myosin hydrolyzes ATP at a rapid rate, but they also fatigue rapidly because their primary source of ATP is glycolysis rather than aerobic respiration.

- **Intermediate muscle fibers** (fast oxidative fibers) appear pink or red. Their contractile properties vary but are intermediate between slow and fast fibers because they derive ATP from both glycolysis and aerobic respiration.

The different fiber types are present in all skeletal muscles, but their relative abundances differ from muscle to muscle. Slow fibers are abundant in muscles specialized for endurance—such as the leg muscles of birds that excel at swimming or walking (the "dark meat" of chicken legs). In humans, the soleus muscle in the back of the calf is an example of a muscle with a high proportion of slow fibers—it helps to keep you upright when you stand.

Fast fibers contract and relax up to three times faster than slow fibers, making them well suited for bursts of activity. The "white meat" of chicken breasts, specialized only for quick bursts of flight to escape predators, are made primarily of fast fibers. The muscles that control your eye movements are another example.

✔If you understand muscle fiber types, you should be able to predict whether the breast meat of pigeons (which are capable of prolonged flights) is composed of dark meat or white meat and explain why there is a color difference between these muscle types.

Can humans change their fiber types through training? Experiments have shown that endurance training can increase the density of blood vessels, mitochondria, and myoglobin in muscle fibers, enabling athletes to improve their muscle performance. However, training does not change slow fibers to fast fibers, nor the reverse. The ratio of muscle-fiber types in muscles is heritable—that is, genetically determined.

Skeletal-Fiber Organization The force of a muscle is proportional to the cross-sectional area of the muscle—the number of sarcomeres lined up side by side exerting a pull in synchrony. By contrast, the length change of the muscle is determined by the length of the muscle fibers—how many sarcomeres are lined up in a row in each fiber. Thus, the arrangement of muscle fibers within a muscle influences the contractile properties of the muscle.

For a given muscle volume, some muscles are organized to maximize length change, because the fibers are parallel to each other in long bands (**FIGURE 48.8**, left)—the longer the chain of

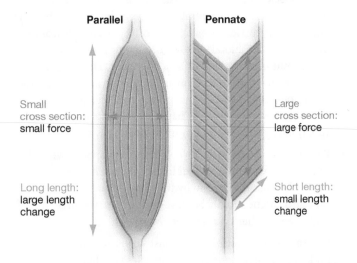

FIGURE 48.8 Muscle-Fiber Patterns Affect Contractile Properties. Most muscles have fibers arranged in either a parallel or pennate pattern. The orientation of muscle fibers affects the contractile properties of the muscle.

sarcomeres in series in the myofibril, the greater the length change. The sartorius muscle in the human thigh has parallel fibers.

Other muscles are organized to maximize force, because the fibers are in a diagonal, or pennate, pattern (penna means feather; **FIGURE 48.8**, right)—the greater the number of sarcomeres pulling in parallel, the greater the force produced. The gastrocnemius muscle in the human calf is a pennate muscle.

Context of Muscle Contraction The relative abundances of fiber types and organization of muscle fibers are not sufficient to account for the diversity of muscle contraction properties of skeletal muscles. Muscle tension also varies according to how extended the muscle is when it contracts and how rapidly it is allowed to shorten—if at all. Muscles like the quadriceps in your thigh can even exert a force while they are lengthening, such as when you ease your weight down a step.

These circumstances depend on the interaction between the muscle and the skeleton. Let's take a closer look at how the muscle and skeletal systems interact to produce movement.

48.3 Skeletal Systems

All a muscle can do is pull. How can complex movements be accomplished using an engine that can only pull? Also, muscles are limited in how much they can shorten. How, then, can they cause dramatic shape changes in animal bodies?

Muscle forces and shape changes are transmitted to other parts of the body and to the environment via the skeleton. Skeletal systems perform four main functions:

1. *Protection* from physical and biological assaults.

2. *Maintenance of body posture* despite the downward pull of gravity and the vagaries of wind and waves.

3. *Re-extension of shortened muscles* If no mechanism of re-extension existed, muscles would shorten only once.

4. *Transfer of muscle forces* to other parts of the body and to the environment, enabling a much greater range of force production and shape change than can be accomplished by muscle alone.

The relative importance of these roles varies among animals according to their lifestyles and environments. For example, natural selection has favored turtles with robust shells in some environments—a skeletal adaptation for protection. In other environments, natural selection has favored highly reduced shells—an adaptation for rapid locomotion. There are trade-offs between protection and mobility.

Despite the stunning diversity in animal bodies, virtually all animals can be considered to have one (or more) of three types of skeletal systems:

1. Hydrostatic skeletons use the hydrostatic pressure of enclosed body fluids or soft tissues to support the body.

2. Endoskeletons have rigid structures inside the body.

3. Exoskeletons have rigid structures on the outside of the body.

Let's consider how each skeletal system transmits muscle forces and shape changes.

Hydrostatic Skeletons

Despite their squishy appearance, soft-bodied animals do have skeletons—hydrostatic skeletons. First let's look at how they are built, and then consider how they function.

Structure **Hydrostatic skeletons** ("still-water skeletons"), or hydrostats, are constructed of an extensible body wall in tension surrounding a fluid or deformable tissue under compression. When fluid is under compression, its pressure increases. The pressurized internal fluid, rather than a rigid structure, enables soft-bodied animals to maintain posture, re-extend muscles, and transfer muscle forces to the environment.

Hydrostatic skeletons occur in diverse animals, from sea anemones and jellyfish to mollusks and many types of worms. Hydrostats also support *parts* of animals, such as the tongues and penises of humans and the tube feet of echinoderms.

The structures of hydrostatic skeletons are diverse as well. The body wall of hydrostats may include different numbers and orientations of muscle layers and fiber-reinforced cuticles or connective tissues. The interior may include seawater, coelomic fluid, blood, or soft organs such as intestines. Hydrostatic skeletons composed mostly of muscle, such as tongues and tentacles, are called muscular hydrostats.

Function How do animals with hydrostatic skeletons move? Consider an earthworm. Its body wall consists of a cuticle reinforced with collagen fibers as well as two layers of muscle—longitudinal muscles, oriented along the length of the animal, and circumferential muscles, oriented in bands around each segment. When the circumferential muscles contract, they make the segments narrower and squeeze the internal coelomic fluid and tissue, thus increasing internal pressure. The pressure pushes outward in all directions, extending the relaxed longitudinal muscles, lengthening the segment (**FIGURE 48.9**).

When the longitudinal muscles contract and the circumferential muscles relax, the reverse occurs—the segments become wider and shorter, pushing sideways against the soil. Alternating contractions of longitudinal and circumferential muscles pass down the earthworm in waves, called **peristalsis.** In this way, earthworms move forward (or backward) within their underground burrows.

Longitudinal and circumferential muscles in earthworms make up an **antagonistic muscle group,** a group of two or more muscles that re-extend one another via the skeleton.

✔ If you understand how a hydrostatic skeleton works, you should be able to explain how earthworms can push laterally against the walls of their burrows despite having muscles that can only pull.

Endoskeletons

Even though parts of you, like your tongue, are supported by a hydrostatic skeleton, your endoskeleton is what keeps you standing up and on the move.

Structure **Endoskeletons** ("inside skeletons") are rigid structures that occur within the body. Even the most ancient of animal lineages, the sponges, secrete spicules—stiff spikes of silica or calcium carbonate ($CaCO_3$)—that provide structural support for the body. In echinoderms, the endoskeleton consists of calcium carbonate plates just beneath the skin—fused into a rigid case in sea urchins, but suspended in a flexible matrix that enables bending of the arms in sea stars.

The vertebrate endoskeleton differs from those of most sponges and echinoderms—and from hydrostatic skeletons—in that it is composed of rigid levers (the bones) separated by joints. Vertebrates change the shapes of their bodies largely by changing the *joint angles* between bones in the limbs and between the limbs and the body, rather than changing the shapes of body segments themselves.

Vertebrate skeletons are composed of four main elements:

1. **Bones** are made up of cells in a hard extracellular matrix of calcium phosphate ($CaPO_4$) with small amounts of calcium carbonate and protein fibers. The adult human body contains 206 bones (**FIGURE 48.10a**, see page 982). The meeting places where adjacent bones interact are called **articulations,** or **joints.** Bones articulate in ways that limit the range of motion, for example enabling a swivel in the shoulder joint but a hinge in the elbow joint (**FIGURE 48.10b**).

2. **Cartilage** is made up of cells scattered in a gelatinous matrix of polysaccharides and protein fibers. Cartilage can be quite rigid, such as in the clam-crushing jaws of some stingrays, or more rubbery, such as in the pads that cushion the joints in your knees and back.

3. **Tendons** are bands of fibrous connective tissue, primarily collagen, that connect skeletal muscles to bones. The ropelike structure of tendons transmits muscle forces to precise locations on the bones, sometimes quite a distance away from the muscle itself.

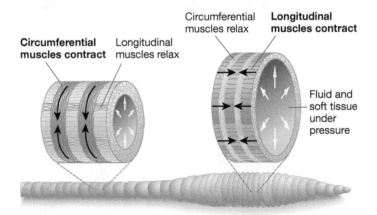

Circumferential muscles contract Longitudinal muscles relax

Circumferential muscles relax **Longitudinal muscles contract**

Fluid and soft tissue under pressure

FIGURE 48.9 Antagonistic Muscle Groups Cause Shape Changes in Hydrostatic Skeletons. The pressure of the internal fluid or tissue transmits forces between muscle groups and between muscles and the environment.

(a) Bones of the human endoskeleton

Cranium
Skull
Mandible

Cervical vertebrae

Clavicle

Scapula

Sternum

Ribs

Thoracic vertebrae

Humerus

Lumbar vertebrae

Pelvic girdle

Sacrum

Ulna

Coccyx

Radius

Spinal column

Carpals

Metacarpals

Phalanges

Femur

Patella

Tibia

Fibula

Tarsals

Metatarsals

Phalanges

FIGURE 48.10 Bones of the Human Endoskeleton. Since bones are rigid and cannot change shape themselves, they articulate at joints that make specific types of movement possible, such as the swiveling and hinging shown here.

(b) Joints enable movement

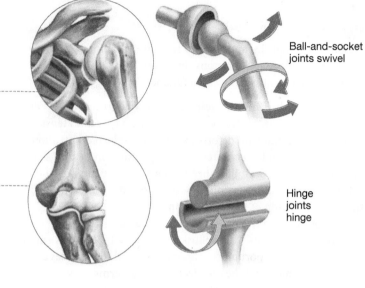

Ball-and-socket joints swivel

Hinge joints hinge

flexors, muscles that pull bones closer together, decreasing the joint angle between them. They swing your lower leg back toward your thigh, reducing the angle of your knee joint. The quadriceps muscles in the front of your thigh are **extensors,** muscles that increase the angle of a joint. They straighten your leg at the knee joint (**FIGURE 48.11**).

The hamstrings and quadriceps muscles accomplish the large swing of the lower leg by inserting into different locations on the tibia (the shin bone). The articulation of the tibia with the femur (the thigh bone) serves as the pivot point for this lever. Along with enabling a shape change, the bone transmits the forces exerted within the thigh muscles to the foot—such as when the extension of your leg enables you to kick a ball.

The role of bones is primarily mechanical, but they also serve several physiological functions. Chief among these is storage of calcium and other minerals. When blood calcium falls to low levels, the bones release calcium to maintain blood–calcium homeostasis. The interior of long bones, called bone marrow, is also

4. **Ligaments** are bands of fibrous connective tissue, primarily collagen, that bind bones to other bones. Ligaments stabilize the joints.

Function Bones and cartilages are structures that do a good job of resisting compression (pushing) and bending, whereas tendons and ligaments do a good job of resisting tension (pulling). These structures combine with muscle in ways that enable the efficient transmission of muscle forces and shape changes.

Vertebrate skeletons move by means of changes in joint angles controlled by antagonistic muscle groups. For example, consider how your thigh muscles flex and extend your knee joint. The hamstring muscles in the back of your thigh are

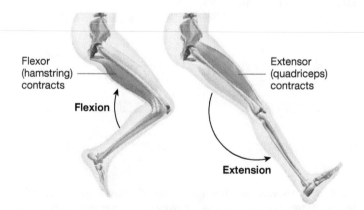

Flexor (hamstring) contracts

Flexion

Extensor (quadriceps) contracts

Extension

FIGURE 48.11 Endoskeletons Move by Contraction and Relaxation of Flexor and Extensor Muscles.

the source of red blood cells needed to carry oxygen in the blood and white blood cells needed for the immune system.

Exoskeletons

The mechanical function of rigid cuticle in exoskeletons is similar in many ways to that of endoskeletons. Exoskeletons occur primarily in arthropod animals, including insects, crustaceans, and arachnids (spiders, ticks, scorpions).

Structure An **exoskeleton** ("outside skeleton") is an exterior skeleton that encloses and protects an animal's body. The origin of the exoskeleton was a key innovation that preceded the spectacular diversification of arthropods. Arthropods, especially insects, are the most diverse and abundant animals on Earth.

The material composition of exoskeletons varies. Insect exoskeletons consist of a cuticle formed from a composite of proteins and the polysaccharide chitin. Chitinous ingrowths of the skeleton form **apodemes,** where muscles attach. Crustaceans such as crabs and lobsters have a cuticle that is mineralized with calcium carbonate, making their shells relatively thick and hard—and heavy. Most crustaceans are marine, so their buoyancy in water helps support their weight.

Function Like vertebrates, arthropods have paired flexor–extensor muscles that operate their jointed skeletons, causing movements that are based on changes in joint angles rather than changes in the dimensions of the segments themselves (**FIGURE 48.12**). Unlike vertebrates, however the muscles of arthropods must be packed *within* the skeletal tubes.

One solution to the problem of the interior placement of muscles is that many arthropod muscles have the pennate, or feather-like arrangement of muscle fibers illustrated in Figure 48.8. This arrangement boosts force output by effectively increasing the muscle cross-sectional area but not the muscle width during a contraction.

The disadvantage of pennate muscles is that their length change is small, so they have limited range of motion. Arthropods compensate for this constraint in part by the placement of their apodemes, which can transduce a small shortening of a muscle into a large change in joint angle.

The rigid levers of vertebrate skeletons can grow continuously as the rest of the body grows. But since the rigid exoskeletons of arthropods encase the growing soft tissue like a suit of armor, they must be shed—molted—periodically and replaced with a bigger one. Arthropods are vulnerable to predation during molts because their skeleton is soft and dysfunctional at that time.

Hydrostatic skeletons, endoskeletons, and exoskeletons all transmit muscle forces and shape changes to other parts of the body and to the environment. While hydrostatic skeletons are the most widespread in terms of the number of animal phyla that contain species with skeletons of this type (virtually all—even arthropods, echinoderms, and vertebrates), the lever-based, segmented, jointed skeletons of arthropods and vertebrates win the prize for overall functional diversity.

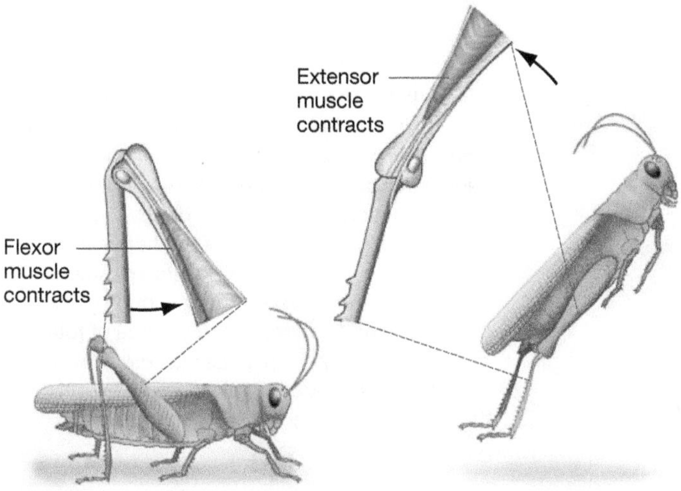

check your understanding

C Y U

If you understand that . . .

- Hydrostatic skeletons, endoskeletons, and exoskeletons transmit muscle forces and shape changes to other parts of the animal and to the environment.
- Antagonistic muscles re-extend one another via the skeleton.
- In contrast to hydrostatic skeletons, shape changes in endoskeletons and exoskeletons involve changes in angles between rigid segments rather than in the segments themselves.

✓ **You should be able to . . .**

1. Compare and contrast the structure and function of hydrostatic skeletons, endoskeletons, and exoskeletons.

2. Predict what would happen if neurons simultaneously stimulated the biceps and triceps muscles to contract.

Answers are available in Appendix A.

Extensor muscle contracts

Flexor muscle contracts

FIGURE 48.12 Exoskeletons Move by Contraction and Relaxation of Flexor and Extensor Muscles.

48.4 Locomotion

The most spectacular capability conferred on animals by the combination of muscle contractions and skeletal systems is efficient locomotion. Animals locomote to seek food, water, mates, and shelter, and to avoid predators. In the process, some animals migrate thousands of miles per year, and others perform astonishing feats of acrobatics. Locomotion has been shaped by natural selection and has been central to complex ecological relationships since the radiation of animals during the Cambrian Explosion more than 500 million years ago.

Many of the diverse modes of locomotion are already familiar to you. Here are some examples.

- **On land** Crawling, walking, running, climbing, hopping, jumping, burrowing
- **In water** Undulating, jetting, swimming, rowing
- **In air** Flying, gliding

What variables do biologists analyze to unlock the secrets of animal locomotion?

How Do Biologists Study Locomotion?

Experimental studies on locomotion have increased exponentially in recent years, partly due to the conceptual breakthrough offered by the field of biomechanics—applying the principles of engineering to quantify the mechanics of organisms. Biomechanics studies the physical act of locomotion at different levels, including

- material properties
- structures
- motions
- forces
- energetics
- ecology and evolution

Let's examine each of these levels, starting with materials.

How Are the Material Properties of Tissues Important to Locomotion?
Because the active contractile properties of skeletal muscle are central to understanding the generation of forces in locomotion, a great deal of research has been devoted to analyzing the contractile properties of muscle, introduced in Section 48.1. However, the passive material properties of the skeletal elements are also essential to understanding the transmission of forces.

Consider how you move. A pioneer of biomechanics, R. McNeill Alexander, observed that the movement and energy exchange of the center of mass of a person walking is mechanically similar to that of an upside-down pendulum, whereas running is mechanically similar to a bouncing ball. Based on this insight, Alexander hypothesized that the large tendons of the lower legs of terrestrial animals—for example, the Achilles tendon at the back of your ankle (see Figure 48.7)—work as springs when animals run.

To test this hypothesis, Alexander measured the elastic properties of tendon by clamping a piece of tendon in an engineering device that measures the pulling force of the tissue as it is stretched to different lengths and released. The tendon returned 93 percent of the energy invested, losing only 7 percent to heat. This high rate of elastic-energy storage explains how tendons add a spring to the steps of runners, reducing the amount of muscle-generated power that must be generated from step to step.

The importance of the material properties of muscles and skeletal tissues is most obvious when they fail, whether in subtle or catastrophic ways. You may have firsthand experience with the debilitating consequences of broken bones or strained tendons.

How Is Musculoskeletal Structure Adapted for Locomotion?
Many biologists begin their study of locomotion by examining the size and shape of the skeletal elements. Careful measurements of skeleton geometries can reveal a great deal about the posture of the organism, range of motion of joints, and skeletal function in general. For example, a team of biologists recently used structural analysis to test the hypothesis that an early tetrapod amphibian, called *Ichthyostega*, could walk on all four limbs like today's salamanders (see **FIGURE 48.13**).

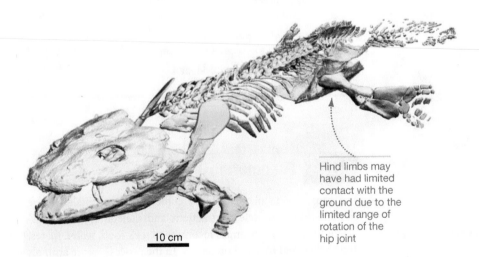

Hind limbs may have had limited contact with the ground due to the limited range of rotation of the hip joint

10 cm

FIGURE 48.13 The Relationship between Structure and Function Can Be Studied Using Computer Models. This computer image of an early tetrapod, *Ichthyostega*, was built using high-resolution scans of fossil bones. The 3D model measures the range of rotation of the major limb joints based on skeleton geometry, determining the overall range of motion of the limbs. The model found that the range of rotation of the shoulder and hip joints was more limited than previously thought, rejecting the hypothesis that these animals could walk on all fours.

FIGURE 48.14 The Motions of Locomotion Can Be Captured on Film. Eadweard Muybridge shot many photo series of animals during locomotion to enable precise analysis of limb and body motions over time.

Similar mechanical principles can be applied to relate the shapes of wings to flying ability, and the shapes of aquatic animals to their ability to swim through water. Sometimes, however, you just have to watch the action itself to understand how an animal uses its body to locomote.

What Does Locomotion Look Like in Living Animals? All the motions of different parts of the skeleton, such as the angular rotation of limbs and the pattern of footfall on the ground, together produce locomotion.

Photographer Eadweard Muybridge is famous for his pioneering photo sequences of locomotion. His work with animals reportedly began when he was commissioned by a racehorse owner to settle a wager on whether horses are ever completely airborne during a gallop. His results are shown in the top sequence of **FIGURE 48.14**. High-speed video and digital images of many other animals have since been recorded, providing insights into many forms of locomotion, such as

- The gait of human sprinters (Figure 48.14, bottom)
- The complex wing-beat patterns of hovering bees and hummingbirds
- The upright, bipedal (two-footed) gait of basilisk lizards running across the surface of water (see chapter opening image)
- The footfall pattern that prevents centipedes from tripping on their own legs
- The aerial undulating of snakes that glide down from treetops
- The limb-like use of fins in lungfish "walking"
- Peristalsis in the muscular feet of crawling snails

For most animals, the pattern of movement during locomotion varies with speed. For example, horses walk at slow speeds, trot at intermediate speeds, and gallop at fast speeds—each gait has a distinct pattern of leg motions.

Computers facilitate the analysis of the many images captured in motion studies. The results are themselves insightful, but they also serve as an important stepping-stone to understanding the forces involved in locomotion.

What Forces Are Involved in Locomotion? If an animal wants to move forward, it must push something backward, as predicted by Newton's third law of motion. Otherwise, the animal could move but not get anywhere, like a person with smooth shoes on slick ice. The types of forces that are important to locomotion vary according to whether the animal is locomoting on land, in water, in air, or some combination of the three.

On land, gravitational forces and inertial forces dominate. The gravitational force experienced by an animal is its weight, which is the product of its mass and the acceleration due to gravity (9.8 m/sec^2 on Earth). Weight is important on land because most terrestrial animals must hold themselves up to move forward. Inertial forces are proportional to mass and velocity, and they represent resistance of bodies and limbs to acceleration and deceleration. Note in the horse and human photo sequences in Figure 48.14 that the arms and legs must swing back and forth dramatically—an energy-intensive process of acceleration and deceleration.

In water, gravitational forces are less important than on land, due to the counteracting buoyant forces supporting the animal's weight in water. However, aquatic animals must overcome drag, the force that resists forward motion through fluids. Convergent evolution of torpedo-shaped bodies has occurred in diverse aquatic animals, from tuna to dolphins and ichthyosaurs, due to the strong selection for bodies that minimize drag during rapid locomotion. Aquatic animals that move more slowly face less drag and thus are morphologically more diverse.

Water and air are both fluids, but air is a thousand times less dense than water. Buoyant forces are therefore negligible in air, making gravitational forces very important to fliers—most animals that locomote by flying or gliding have adaptations that make them lightweight. They must produce a force called lift to counteract gravity, and they must also minimize drag. As a result, fast fliers tend to have very streamlined shapes.

FIGURE 48.15 Visualization of Airflow Is Used to Analyze the Forces Involved in the Hovering of a Bat. The lift and drag forces acting on flying and swimming animals can be measured by observing fluid flow around the animal. The arrows represent the velocity of tiny water droplets illuminated by a laser in front of a high-speed camera.

How are forces measured? Scientists can measure ground force—the force with which a terrestrial animal strikes the substratum during a step—by coaxing an animal to walk, run, or hop upon an instrument called a force plate. Quantifying forces in fluids is more nuanced. It often requires indirect measurement by visualizing the airflow or waterflow around the animal, such as the flow of air around the wings of a hovering bat shown in **FIGURE 48.15**.

What Is the Cost of Locomotion?

Animals must spend energy to find food and mates and escape from predators. However, the more energy an animal spends on locomotion, the less it can spend on producing offspring. There is strong selection pressure to minimize the cost of locomotion. How do biologists measure this cost?

To get a sense of variables that determine the cost of locomotion, consider the classic studies by Alexander on the gait transition from walking to running in humans. Alexander discovered that walking is an efficient mode of transport because you exchange potential energy at the top of your stride with kinetic energy midstride. However, the resulting pendulum-like motion of your center of mass is not efficient at higher speeds, when it becomes more cost effective to run using your spring-like tendons and other skeletal tissues to store energy between strides.

Alexander hypothesized that animals locomote using the most energy-efficient gait at each speed. To test this hypothesis in horses, physiologists Dan Hoyt and Richard Taylor trained horses to walk, trot, and gallop at a range of unnatural speeds—for example, trotting at a speed where the horse would normally have preferred to gallop. Hoyt and Taylor fitted each horse with an oxygen mask and ran it on a treadmill, so that they could measure oxygen consumption and speed simultaneously. The rate of oxygen consumption is a measure of energy use. (Oxygen

consumption is proportional to ATP production during aerobic respiration; see Chapter 9.) The researchers then plotted energy use as a function of speed for each gait.

Hoyt and Taylor also filmed the horses moving freely around their paddock and measured the speeds at which the horses used different gaits when given free choice. The researchers then compared the lab data to the gait preference in the paddock.

The graph in **FIGURE 48.16** shows Hoyt and Taylor's results. The three curves at the top represent the energy used per distance traveled at the three gaits—the dips in the curves indicate the speeds at which the gaits were most efficient. The bars at the bottom of the graph show which gaits and speeds the horses chose when they were able to locomote freely in the paddock. The data support the hypothesis that the horses use the most energy-efficient gaits at different speeds and avoid intermediate speeds where the cost of locomotion is higher.

Similar studies have been conducted for diverse animals running, swimming, and flying, with similar results. Natural selection favors animals that locomote efficiently because they have more energy available for other vital activities.

Evolution and Ecology: What Is the Context? Some biologists study animal locomotion with a strictly mechanistic focus, investigating proximate causes via "how" questions. Alexander's study of the elastic energy storage of the Achilles tendon falls in this category. However, biologists also examine the ultimate causation of locomotion by asking "why" questions, which require an analysis of evolutionary history and ecological context.

For example, why do dolphins and ichthyosaurs have such similar torpedo-like shapes? Both taxa are fast-swimming predators in their marine environments, yet phylogenetic analysis shows that they are not closely related. Rather, the torpedo-like shape evolved independently in both lineages because it substantially reduces drag during rapid locomotion in water, improving the efficiency of locomotion and thus increasing fitness (the number of viable, fertile offspring produced).

But locomotion cannot be "perfected" over evolutionary time. Natural environments are spatially complex and change over time, so the context for locomotion is not static. Further, there are numerous constraints and fitness trade-offs to different aspects of locomotion. Some trade-offs occur within locomotory systems (such as the trade-off between stability and maneuverability) while others occur between locomotion and other aspects of behavior (such as using appendages both for locomotion and feeding). Overall, a thorough study of locomotion requires an integrative approach with evolutionary and ecological context.

Size Matters

Animals that use muscles to power locomotion span a vast range of sizes—an astonishing 10 orders of magnitude (10,000,000,000), from tiny ants to giant whales. Many of these animals also grow over a large size range during their development. As is true for many other aspects of animal structure and function, size matters.

QUESTION: Do horses minimize the cost of locomotion?

HYPOTHESIS: Horses choose gaits that minimize energy use at different speeds.

NULL HYPOTHESIS: Horses do not choose gaits based on cost of locomotion.

EXPERIMENTAL SETUP:

1. Measure oxygen consumption of horses trained to walk, trot, and gallop at a range of speeds on a treadmill. Calculate energy used per distance travelled at different speeds.

2. Videotape the same horses locomoting freely in the paddock, and measure the gaits and speeds they choose to use naturally.

PREDICTION: For each gait, there is a range of speeds where energy use is minimized. Horses will favor these gaits and speeds.

PREDICTION OF NULL HYPOTHESIS: There will be no correlation between chosen gaits and energy consumption.

RESULTS:

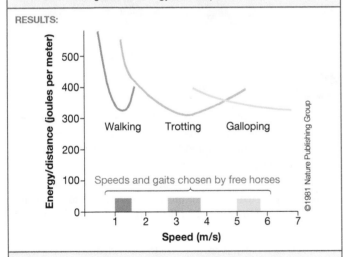

CONCLUSION: Horses choose gaits that minimize energy use at different speeds and avoid speeds with high energy consumption.

FIGURE 48.16 Horses Minimize the Cost of Locomotion by Choosing Appropriate Gaits.

SOURCE: Hoyt, D. F., and C. R. Taylor. 1981. Gait and the energetics of locomotion in horses. *Nature* 292: 239–240.

✔**QUANTITATIVE** Use the graph to estimate the relative energy expense of galloping rather than trotting at 3.5 meters/second (m/s).

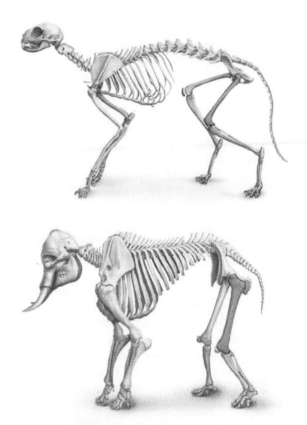

FIGURE 48.17 Size Influences Skeleton Geometry. When scaled to the same size, you can see that the elephant has thicker bones and a more upright stance than a cat does, due to the disproportionate burden of gravity on larger animals. The femurs are highlighted for comparison.

Two organisms may be geometrically similar—that is, they may have exactly the same proportions—but if they are different sizes, they are more different than they seem. To start, the ratio of surface area to volume decreases as the organism gets larger, because surface area is proportional to length squared, while volume is proportional to length cubed. This concept has far-reaching implications for physiology. It also has important mechanical implications.

The weight of an animal is proportional to its volume, and the ability of leg bones to support the weight is proportional to their cross-sectional area. Thus, large terrestrial organisms have disproportionately hefty skeletal elements to avoid breaking their legs—something that Galileo observed 400 years ago when he compared skeletons of small and large organisms (**FIGURE 48.17**).

So, in the late 1980s, it was surprising when Andrew Biewener discovered that animals of different sizes maintain similar stresses in their skeletal tissues. How do they do that?

Biewener observed that posture and behavior are important variables. Small animals locomote in a more crouched posture and make great leaps, while large animals like elephants are more straight-legged, so that their skeletons, rather than their muscles, can support their body weight. Larger animals also locomote more gently. If a house cat were enlarged to be the size of an elephant, it would break its own bones when attempting a pounce.

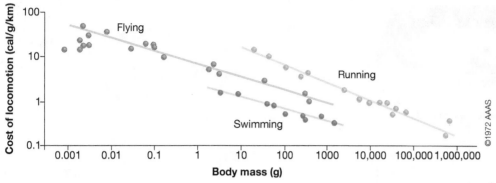

FIGURE 48.18 Cost of Locomotion for Swimming, Running, and Flying Animals Decreases with Mass.

DATA: Schmidt-Nielsen, K. 1972. Locomotion: Energy cost of swimming, flying, and running. *Science* 177: 222–228.

✔**QUANTITATIVE** About how much more costly is it to run than to swim for animals with a body mass of 100 g?

Size is also of paramount importance in determining how organisms locomote through fluids. Fluids have an inherent viscosity, or stickiness, that is of minor concern to animals that are very large and/or fast (thus have high inertia), like dolphins, which can glide through water with little effort. But viscosity is of enormous concern to animals that are very small and/or slow (thus have low inertia), like plankton. If you were the size of a grain of rice and went for a swim in a lake, the water would feel like corn syrup.

Size also affects the cost of locomotion. Physiologist Knut Schmidt-Nielsen, in the early 1970s, was the first to make an energy comparison between different modes of locomotion. To account for widely different body sizes and distances traveled, he normalized all the data to the energy cost in calories per gram of body per kilometer traveled and then plotted the data on a log–log plot (see **BioSkills 6** in Appendix B).

Schmidt-Nielson's data showed that larger organisms use less energy per gram of body tissue per distance traveled than smaller organisms—all the lines slope down to the right (**FIGURE 48.18**). The data also show that for any given body size, running is a more expensive mode of transport than flying, and swimming is the least expensive.

Many other aspects of locomotion can also be plotted as a function of body size. The results reveal general principles that can be used to make predictions for diverse animals, even those that are extinct.

The take-home message? The laws of physics establish very definite constraints on the realm of possible sizes, shapes, and modes of locomotion in animals. Understanding these principles helps illuminate themes and variations among the diversity of animals.

CHAPTER 48 REVIEW

For media, go to MasteringBiology **MB**

If you understand that . . .

48.1 How Do Muscles Contract?

- The muscles of vertebrate limbs are composed of muscle cells, called muscle fibers, that contain threadlike contractile elements called myofibrils, each divided into contractile units called sarcomeres.

- Sarcomeres appear striated, or banded, due to the aligned arrangement of thick filaments (myosin) and thin filaments (actin).

- Sarcomeres shorten when thick filaments of myosin slide past thin filaments of actin in a series of binding events mediated by the hydrolysis of ATP.

- Calcium ions play an essential role in muscle contraction by making the actin in thin filaments available for binding by myosin.

- Acetylcholine released from somatic motor neurons is the neurotransmitter that stimulates contraction of skeletal muscle.

✔ You should be able to predict the primary symptom of botulism, which occurs when a toxin prevents release of acetylcholine from the neuromuscular junction. Explain your answer.

48.2 Muscle Tissues

- Smooth muscle lines bronchioles, blood vessels, the gastrointestinal tract, and certain reproductive organs. Smooth muscle cells are small and unstriated and have a single nucleus. Contractions are involuntary.

- Cardiac muscle occurs in the heart and forces blood through the circulatory system. Cardiac muscle cells are striated, branched, and connected to one another by intercalated discs. Contractions are involuntary.

- Most skeletal muscles are attached to the skeleton and are responsible for voluntary movement of the body. Skeletal muscle cells are long, striated, and multinucleate.

- Skeletal muscle fibers are specialized to contract slowly or quickly and to have a high or low endurance. These properties depend on the concentration of myoglobin present and the use of aerobic respiration and/or glycolysis for the production of ATP.

- Skeletal muscle fibers are organized in a parallel arrangement, which maximizes shortening, or a pennate pattern, which maximizes force production.

✔ You should be able to describe the major structural and functional differences among the three classes of muscle tissue.

48.3 Skeletal Systems

- Hydrostatic skeletons are composed of a body wall in tension surrounding a fluid or soft tissue under compression.

- Endoskeletons are internal skeletons, surrounded by soft tissue. In vertebrates, the jointed endoskeleton is composed of bones, cartilages, tendons, and ligaments.

- Exoskeletons are external skeletons, enclosing soft tissue. In arthropods, the muscles occur within the rigid, jointed cuticle composed of chitin, proteins, and sometimes minerals. Exoskeletons must be shed to enable growth.

- Movement is based on antagonistic muscle groups that act on a skeleton. In vertebrates and arthropods, these muscles are called flexors and extensors. They change the joint angle between rigid skeletal segments—especially in limbs.

✔ You should be able to compare and contrast the types of shape changes that are caused by muscle contractions in the different types of skeletons.

48.4 Locomotion

- Locomotion is movement relative to the environment and requires the transmission of muscle forces to the land, water, or air surrounding the animal.

- Locomotion can be studied at different levels: material properties, structures, motions, forces, and energetics, and within the larger context of evolution and ecology.

- Locomotion on land is usually dominated by gravitational and inertial forces. Swimmers must overcome drag. Fliers must overcome drag and must generate enough lift to overcome gravitational forces.

- Body size is important to the mechanics of locomotion.

✔ You should be able to give general examples of how physical constraints affect the locomotion of animals on land, in water, and in air.

(MB) **MasteringBiology**

1. MasteringBiology Assignments

Tutorials and Activities Muscle Contraction (1 of 2): Muscle Cells and Action Potentials; Muscle Contraction (2 of 2): The Sarcomere and the Sliding-Filament Model; Human Skeleton; Skeletal Muscle Structure; Structure and Contraction of Muscle Fibers

Questions Reading Quizzes, Blue-Thread Questions, Test Bank

2. eText Read your book online, search, take notes, highlight text, and more.

3. The Study Area Practice Test, Cumulative Test, BioFlix® 3-D Animations, Videos, Activities, Audio Glossary, Word Study Tools, Art

You should be able to . . .

✔ **TEST YOUR KNOWLEDGE** 　　　　　　　　　　*Answers are available in Appendix A*

1. Which of the following classes of muscle is/are voluntary?
   a. skeletal muscle
   b. cardiac muscle
   c. smooth muscle
   d. all of the above

2. Which of the following is a neurotransmitter that stimulates contraction of skeletal muscle?
   a. norepinephrine
   b. adrenaline
   c. acetylcholine
   d. calcium

3. In muscle cells, myosin molecules continue moving along actin molecules as long as
   a. ATP is present and troponin is not bound to Ca^{2+}.
   b. ADP is present and tropomyosin is released from intracellular stores.

   c. ADP is present and intracellular acetylcholine is high.
   d. ATP is present and intracellular Ca^{2+} is high.

4. True or false: The postural muscles of your legs are composed mostly of slow muscle fibers.

5. Which of the following is critical to the function of most exoskeletons, endoskeletons, and hydrostatic skeletons?
   a. Muscles interact with the skeleton in antagonistic groups.
   b. Muscles attach to each of these types of skeleton via tendons.
   c. Muscles extend joints by pushing skeletal elements.
   d. Segments of the body or limbs are extended when paired muscles relax in unison.

6. True or false: A large animal will experience twice the gravitational forces of a small animal half its size if their geometries are the same.

7. How did data on sarcomere structure inspire the sliding-filament model of muscle contraction? Explain why the observation that muscle cells contain many mitochondria and extensive smooth endoplasmic reticulum turned out to be logical once the molecular mechanism of muscular contraction was understood.

8. If a sprinter began an endurance running program, which of the following would occur?
   a. Some slow fibers would become fast fibers.
   b. Some fast fibers would become slow fibers.
   c. Some fibers would develop a higher mitochondrial density.
   d. Some fibers would develop a lower mitochondrial density.

9. Acetylcholine has very different effects on cardiac muscle and skeletal muscle. Explain.

10. Rigor mortis is the stiffening of a body after death that occurs when myosin binds to actin but cannot unbind. Why does myosin bind, and what prevents it from unbinding?

11. R. McNeill Alexander discovered that the arch of the human foot operates like a spring during running. Predict how a runner's oxygen consumption would change if a runner wore shoes that prevented the arches from changing shape. Explain your reasoning.

12. Explain how the physical constraints of locomotion on land, in water, and in air influence convergent evolution.

13. Predict the effect of ingestion of the toxin atropine on heart rate. Atropine is a naturally occurring compound in many poisonous nightshade plants. It blocks acetylcholine receptors in the heart. Explain your logic.

14. The force exerted by the shortening of a sarcomere depends on the length of the sarcomere when the stimulus is received. Based on your understanding of the sliding-filament model, predict how force would differ if the sarcomere were in a greatly stretched state at the beginning of the contraction versus in an average resting position. Explain your reasoning.

15. QUANTITATIVE The speed at which you switch from a walk to a run can be predicted using what is called the Froude number, based on the relative importance of gravitational and inertial forces of your pendulum-like walking gait.

$$\text{Froude number} = \frac{(\text{speed of locomotion})^2}{\text{gravitational acceleration} \times \text{leg length}}$$

Most mammals change from a walk to a run at a Froude number of 0.5. If gravitational acceleration is 9.8 m/s^2, and your leg length is 0.9 m, at what speed are you likely to switch from a walk to a run?
   a. 2.0 m
   b. 1.9 m/s
   c. 2.1 m/s
   d. 2.0 m/s^2

16. If you have seen the film *Jurassic Park*, you can imagine the nightmarish sight of *Tyrannosaurus rex* in high-speed pursuit of you as you flee in a jeep. Evaluate whether the data collected on the biomechanics of locomotion in living species are sufficient to determine how fast a large dinosaur like *T. rex* could run.

APPENDIX A Answers

CHAPTER 1

IN-TEXT QUESTIONS AND EXERCISES

p. 4 Fig. 1.2 `analyze` If Pasteur had done any of the things listed, he would have had more than one variable in his experiment. This would allow critics to claim that he got different results because of the differences in broth types, heating, or flask types—not the difference in exposure to preexisting cells. The results would not be definitive.
p. 6 `apply` The average kernel protein content would decline, from 11 percent to a much lower value over time.
p. 6 CYU `apply` The data points would all be about 11 percent, indicating no change in average kernel protein content over time.
p. 7 Fig. 1.4 `apply` Molds and other fungi are more closely related to green algae because they differ from plants at two positions (5 and 8 from left) but differ from green algae at only one position (8).
p. 8 Fig. 1.6 `apply` The eukaryotic cell is roughly 10 times the size of the prokaryotic cell.
p. 9 CYU `evaluate` From the sequence data provided, species A and B differ only in one ribonucleotide of the rRNA sequence (position 10 from left). Species C differs from species A and B in four ribonucleotides (positions 1, 2, 9, and 10). A correctly drawn phylogenetic tree would indicate that species A and B appear to be closely related, and species C is more distantly related. See **FIGURE A1.1**.
p. 13 (1) `analyze` You could conclude that the ants weren't navigating normally, because they had been caught and released and transferred to a new channel. **(2)** `analyze` You could conclude that the ants can't navigate normally on their manipulated legs.
p. 13 CYU The key here is to test predation rates during the hottest part of the day (when desert ants actually feed) versus other parts of the day. The experiment would best be done in the field, where natural predators are present. One approach would be to capture a large number of ants, divide the group in two, and measure predation rates (number of ants killed per hour) when they are placed in normal habitat during the hottest part of the day versus an hour before (or after). **(1)** `analyze` The control group here is the normal condition—ants out during the hottest part of the day. If you didn't include a control, a critic could argue that predation did or did not occur because of your experimental setup or manipulation, not because of differences in temperature. **(2)** `analyze` You would need to make sure that there is no difference in body size, walking speed, how they were captured and maintained, or other traits that might make the ants in the two groups more or less susceptible to predators. They should also be put out in the same habitat, so the presence of predators is the same in the two treatments.
p. 13 Fig. 1.10 `analyze` The interpretation of the experiment would not likely change, but your confidence in the conclusions drawn would be reduced if you used just one ant.

IF YOU UNDERSTAND . . .

1.1. `understand` Dead cells cannot regulate the passage of materials between exterior and interior spaces, replicate, use energy, or process information. **1.2** `understand` Observations on thousands of diverse species supported the claim that all organisms consist of cells. The hypothesis that all cells come from preexisting cells was supported when Pasteur showed that new cells do not arise and grow in a boiled liquid unless they are introduced from the air. **1.3** `understand` If seeds with higher protein content leave the most

offspring, then individuals with low protein in their seeds will become rare over time. **1.4** `understand` A newly discovered species can be classified as a member of the Bacteria if the sequence of its rRNA contains some features found only in Bacteria. The same logic applies to classifying a new species in the Archaea or Eukarya. **1.5** `understand` (1) A hypothesis is an explanation of how the world works; a prediction is an outcome you should observe if the hypothesis is correct. (2) Experiments are convincing because they measure predictions from two opposing hypotheses. Both predicted actions cannot occur, so one hypothesis will be supported while the other will not.

YOU SHOULD BE ABLE TO . . .

✔ Test Your Knowledge

1. `remember` d **2.** `understand` d **3.** `remember` populations **4.** `understand` b **5.** `understand` An individual's ability to survive and reproduce **6.** `understand` c

✔ Test Your Understanding

7. `evaluate` That the entity they discovered replicates, processes information, acquires and uses energy, is cellular, and that its populations evolve. **8.** `understand` a **9.** `understand` Over time, traits that increased the fitness of individuals in this habitat became increasingly frequent in the population. **10.** `understand` Individuals with certain traits are selected, in the sense that they produce the most offspring. **11.** `analyze` Yes. If evolution is defined as "change in the characteristics of a population over time," then those organisms that are most closely related should have experienced less change over time. On a phylogenetic tree, species with substantially similar rRNA sequences would be diagrammed with a closer common ancestor—one that had the sequences they inherited—than the ancestors shared between species with dissimilar rRNA sequences. **12.** `understand` A null hypothesis specifies what a researcher should observe when the hypothesis being tested isn't correct.

✔ Test Your Problem-Solving Skills

13. `analyze` A scientific theory is not a guess—it is an idea whose validity can be tested with data. Both the cell theory and the theory of evolution have been validated by large bodies of observational and experimental data. **14.** `apply` If all eukaryotes living today have a nucleus, then it is logical to conclude that the nucleus arose in a common ancestor of all eukaryotes, indicated by the arrow you should have added to the figure. See **FIGURE A1.2**. If it had arisen in a common ancestor of Bacteria or Archaea, then species in those groups would have had to lose the trait—an unlikely event. **15.** `evaluate` The data set was so large and diverse that it was no longer reasonable to argue that noncellular life-forms would be discovered. **16.** `apply` b

ᴮᴵᴳ PICTURE Doing Biology

p. 16 CYU (1) `understand` Biologists design and carry out a study, either observational or experimental, to test their ideas. As part of this process, they state their ideas as a hypothesis and null hypothesis and make predictions. They analyze and interpret the data they have gathered, and determine whether the data support their ideas. If not, they revisit their ideas and come up with an alternative hypothesis and design another study to test these new predictions. **(2)** `understand` There are many

possible examples. Consider, for example, the experiment on navigation in foraging desert ants (Chapter 1). In addition to testing how the ants use information on stride length and number to calculate how far they are from the nest (multicellular organism and population levels), researchers also could test how the "pedometer" works at the level of cells and molecules. **(3)** `analyze` A hypothesis is a testable statement to explain a specific phenomenon or a set of observations. The word theory refers to proposed explanations for very broad patterns in nature that are supported by a wide body of evidence. A theory serves as a framework for the development of new hypotheses. **(4)** `analyze` The next step is to relate your findings to existing theories and the current scientific literature, and then to communicate your findings to colleagues through informal conversations, presentations at scientific meetings, and eventually publication in peer-reviewed journals.

CHAPTER 2

IN-TEXT QUESTIONS AND EXERCISES

p. 20 Fig. 2.3 `apply` There are 15 electrons in phosphorus, so there must be 15 protons, which is the atomic number. Since the mass number is 31, then the number of neutrons is 16.
p. 23 `understand` *Water:* arrows pointing from hydrogens to oxygen atom; *ammonia:* arrows pointing from hydrogens to nitrogen atom; *methane:* double arrows between carbons and hydrogens; *carbon dioxide:* arrows pointing from carbon to oxygens; *molecular nitrogen:* double arrows between nitrogens.
p. 23 Fig. 2.7 `understand` Oxygen and nitrogen have high electronegativities. They hold shared electrons more tightly than C, H, and many other atoms, resulting in polar bonds.
p. 24 CYU `evaluate` See **FIGURE A2.1**.

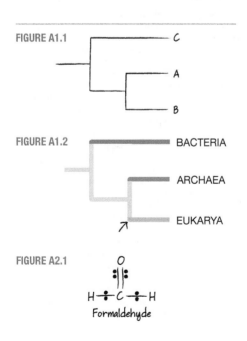

FIGURE A1.1

C
A
B

FIGURE A1.2

BACTERIA
ARCHAEA
EUKARYA

FIGURE A2.1

Formaldehyde

p. 25 (1) (evaluate) δ^+H—O$^{\delta-}$—H$^{\delta+}$ **(2)** (apply) If water were linear, the partial negative charge on oxygen would have partial positive charges on either side. Compared to the actual, bent molecule, the partial negative charge would be much less exposed and less able to participate in hydrogen bonding.

p. 26 Fig. 2.14 (understand) Oils are nonpolar. They have long chains of carbon atoms bonded to hydrogen atoms, which share electrons evenly because their electronegativities are similar. When an oil and water are mixed, the polar water molecules interact with each other via hydrogen bonding rather than with the nonpolar oil molecules, which interact with themselves instead.

p. 28 Table 2.2 (understand) "Cause" (Row 1): electrostatic attractions between partial charges on water and opposite charges on ions; hydrogen bonds; water and other polar molecules. "Biological Consequences" (Row 2): ice to float; freezing solid. "Cause" (Row 4): lots of heat energy; break hydrogen bonds and change water to a gas.

p. 29 (apply) The proton concentration would be 3.2×10^{-9} M.

p. 29 Fig. 2.17 (apply) The concentration of protons would decrease because milk is more basic (pH 6.5) than black coffee (pH 5).

p. 30 (apply) The bicarbonate concentration would increase. The protons (H$^+$) released from carbonic acid would react with the hydroxide ions (OH$^-$) dissociated from NaOH to form H$_2$O, leaving fewer protons free to react with bicarbonate to reform carbonic acid.

p. 32 CYU (1) (apply) The reaction would be spontaneous based on the change in potential energy; the reactants have higher chemical energy than the products. The entropy, however, is not increased based on the number of molecules, although heat given off from the reaction still results in increased entropy. **(2)** (understand) The electrons are shifted farther from the nuclei of the carbon and hydrogen atoms and closer to the nuclei of the more electronegative oxygen atoms.

p. 32 Fig. 2.19 (remember) See FIGURE A2.2.

p. 33 Fig. 2.21 (analyze) The water-filled flask is the ocean; the gas-filled flask is the atmosphere; the condensed water droplets are rain; the electrical sparks are lightning.

p. 37 Table 2.3 (understand) All the functional groups in Table 2.3, except the sulfhydryl group (—SH), are highly polar. The sulfhydryl group is only very slightly polar.

IF YOU UNDERSTAND . . .

2.1. (understand) The bonds in methane and ammonia are all covalent, but differ in polarity: Methane has nonpolar covalent bonds while ammonia has polar covalent bonds. Sodium chloride does not have covalent bonds; instead, ionic bonds hold the ionized sodium and chloride together. **2.2** (understand) Assuming neutral pH, amino and hydroxyl groups would interact with the partial negative charge on water's oxygen, because they both carry a positive charge (partial for the hydrogen in the hydroxyl). The carboxyl group would interact with the partial positive charges on water's hydrogens, since it would carry a negative charge after losing the proton from its hydroxyl. **2.3** (understand) Like solar radiation, the energy in electricity generates free radicals that would promote the reaction. **2.4** (understand) "Top-down" approach: The reaction responsible for synthesizing acetic acid is observed in cells and can serve as an intermediate for the formation of a more complex molecule (acetyl CoA) that is used by cells throughout the tree of life. "Bottom-up" approach: This reaction can also occur under conditions that mimic the early Earth environment in deep-sea vents. **2.5** (apply) The hydroxyls would increase the solubility of octane by introducing polar covalent bonds, which would make the molecule more hydrophilic. The high electronegativity of oxygen would decrease the potential energy of the modified molecule.

YOU SHOULD BE ABLE TO . . .

✓ Test Your Knowledge

1. (understand) b **2.** (remember) a **3.** (remember) c **4.** (remember) d **5.** (remember) Potential energy and entropy. **6.** (remember) The prebiotic soup model and the surface metabolism model.

✓ Test Your Understanding

7. (apply) c. Acetic acid has more highly electronegative oxygen atoms than the other molecules. When bonded to carbon or hydrogen, each oxygen will result in a polar covalent bond. **8.** (apply) Relative electronegativities would be F > O > H > Na. One bond would form with sodium, and it would be ionic. **9.** (understand) When oxygen is covalently bonded to hydrogen, the difference in electronegativities between the atoms causes the electrons to spend more time near the oxygen. In contrast, the atoms in H$_2$ and O$_2$ have the same electronegativities, so they equally share electrons in their covalent bonds. **10.** (apply) See FIGURE A2.3. **11.** (apply) The dissociation reaction of carbonic acid lowers the pH of the solution by releasing extra H$^+$ into the solution. If additional CO$_2$ is added, the sequence of reactions would be driven to the right, which would make the ocean more acidic. **12.** (understand) The carbon framework determines the overall shape of an organic molecule. The functional groups attached to the carbons determine the molecule's chemical behavior, because these groups are likely to interact with other molecules.

✓ Test Your Problem-Solving Skills

13. (analyze) b. **14.** (analyze) No, they don't conflict. Shells that are farther from the protons (positive charges) in the nucleus house electrons that have greater potential energy than shells closer to the nucleus. **15.** (analyze) One possible concept map relating the structure of water to its properties is shown below (see FIGURE A2.4). **16.** (create) In hot weather, water absorbs large amounts of heat due to its high specific heat and high heat of vaporization. In cold weather, water releases the large amount of heat that it has absorbed.

FIGURE A2.2

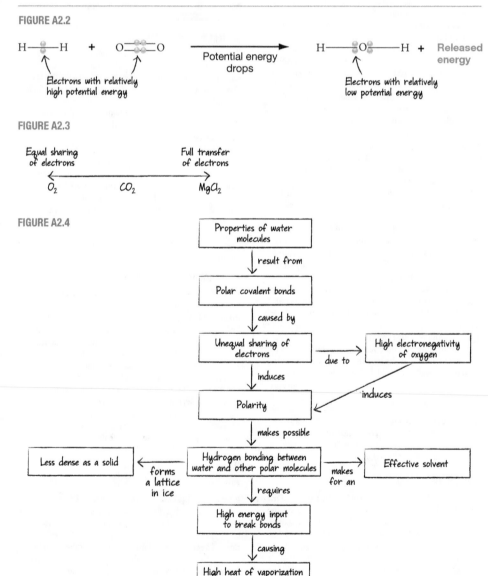

H—H + O=O — Potential energy drops → H—O—H + Released energy

Electrons with relatively high potential energy

Electrons with relatively low potential energy

FIGURE A2.3

Equal sharing of electrons — Full transfer of electrons

O$_2$ CO$_2$ MgCl$_2$

FIGURE A2.4

Properties of water molecules
↓ result from
Polar covalent bonds
↓ caused by
Unequal sharing of electrons → due to → High electronegativity of oxygen
↓ induces   ↓ induces
Polarity ←
↓ makes possible
Less dense as a solid ← forms a lattice in ice — Hydrogen bonding between water and other polar molecules — makes for an → Effective solvent
↓ requires
High energy input to break bonds
↓ causing
High heat of vaporization and high specific heat

CHAPTER 3

IN-TEXT QUESTIONS AND EXERCISES

p. 43 Fig. 3.2 (understand) The green R-groups contain mostly C and H, which have roughly equal electronegativities. Electrons are evenly shared in C−H bonds and C−S bonds, so the groups are nonpolar. Cysteine has a sulfur that is slightly more electronegative than hydrogen, so it will be less nonpolar than the other green groups. All of the pink R-groups have a highly electronegative oxygen atom with a partial negative charge, making them polar. **p. 44** (apply) From most hydrophilic to most hydrophobic: (1) aspartate, (2) asparagine, (3) tyrosine, (4) valine. The most hydrophilic amino acids will have side chains with full charges (ionized), like aspartate, followed by those with the largest number of highly electronegative atoms, like oxygen or nitrogen. Highly electronegative atoms produce polar covalent bonds with carbon or hydrogen. The most hydrophobic will not have oxygen or nitrogen in their side chains, but instead will have the largest number of C−H bonds, which are nonpolar covalent. **p. 47 CYU** (understand) See FIGURE A3.1. **p. 52 CYU (1)** (understand) Secondary, tertiary, and quaternary structure all depend on bonds and other interactions between amino acids that are linked in a chain in a specific order (primary structure). **(2)** (apply) There would be 20^5 different peptides, or 3.2×10^6 different primary sequences. **p. 55 CYU** (apply) Amino acid changes would be expected to be in the active site or in regions that affect the folded structure of this site. Either of these changes could result in a different active site that either binds a new substrate or catalyzes a different reaction.

IF YOU UNDERSTAND . . .

3.1. (understand) Look at the R-group of the amino acid. If there is a positive charge, then it is basic. If there is a negative charge, then it is acidic. If there is not a charge, but there is an oxygen atom, then it is polar uncharged. If there is no charge or oxygen, then it is nonpolar. **3.2** (apply) Nonpolar amino acid residues would be found in the interior of a globular protein, grouped with other nonpolar residues due to hydrophobic interactions. **3.3** (analyze) Both calmodulin and infectious prions require some form of induction to achieve their active conformations. Calcium ions are required for calmodulin to fold into its functional structure while prions are induced to change their shape by other, improperly folded prion proteins. **3.4** (analyze) *Catalysis:* Proteins are made of amino acids, which have many reactive functional groups, and can fold into different shapes that allow the formation of active sites. *Defense:* Similar to catalysis, the chemical properties and capacity for different shapes allows proteins to be made that can attach to virtually any type of invading virus or cell. *Signaling:* The flexibility in protein structure allows protein activities to be quickly turned on or off based on binding to signal molecules or ions.

YOU SHOULD BE ABLE TO . . .

✔ Test Your Knowledge

1. (remember) d **2.** (remember) The atoms and functional groups found in the side chains. **3.** (remember) b **4.** (remember) b **5.** (understand) The order and type of amino acids (i.e., the primary structure) contains the information that directs folding. **6.** (understand) a

✔ Test Your Understanding

7. (understand) Because the nonpolar amino acid residues are not able to interact with the water solvent, they are crowded together in the interior of a protein and surrounded by a network of hydrogen-bonded water molecules. This crowding leads to the development of van der Waals interactions that help glue the nonpolar side chains together. **8.** (understand) No, polymerization is a nonspontaneous reaction because the product molecules have lower entropy than the free form of the reactants and there would be nothing to prevent hydrolysis from reversing the reaction. **9.** (understand) Many possible correct answers, including (1) the presence of an active site in an enzyme that is precisely shaped to fit a substrate or substrates in the correct orientation for a reaction to occur; (2) the doughnut shape of porin that allows certain substances to pass through it; (3) the cable shape of collagen to provide structural support for cells and tissues. **10.** (create) Proteins are highly variable in overall shape and chemical properties due to variation in the composition of R-groups and the array of secondary through quaternary structures that are possible. This variation allows them to fulfill many different roles in the cell. Diversity in the shape and reactivity of active sites also makes them effective catalysts. **11.** (understand) c **12.** (create) In many proteins, especially those involved in cell signaling, their structure is affected by binding to other molecules or ions. Since the shape of the protein is directly involved in its function, the protein's activity is regulated by controlling how it is folded. If proteins were inflexible, this type of control could not occur.

✔ Test Your Problem-Solving Skills

13. (analyze) The side chain of proline is a cyclic structure that is covalently bonded to the nitrogen in the core amino group. This restricts the movement of the side chain relative to the core nitrogen, which further restricts the backbone when the nitrogen participates in a peptide bond with a neighboring amino acid. **14.** (create) See FIGURE A3.2 **15.** (apply) b. Phosphates have a negative charge, so they are most likely to form ionic bonds with the positively-charged side chains of basic amino acid residues. **16.** (apply) The inherited forms likely have some alteration in the primary structure such that the infectious form is spontaneously generated at a higher rate than normal. The amino acid sequence in these prions would likely differ from those transmitted between animals.

CHAPTER 4

IN-TEXT QUESTIONS AND EXERCISES

p. 59 (understand) See FIGURE A4.1.

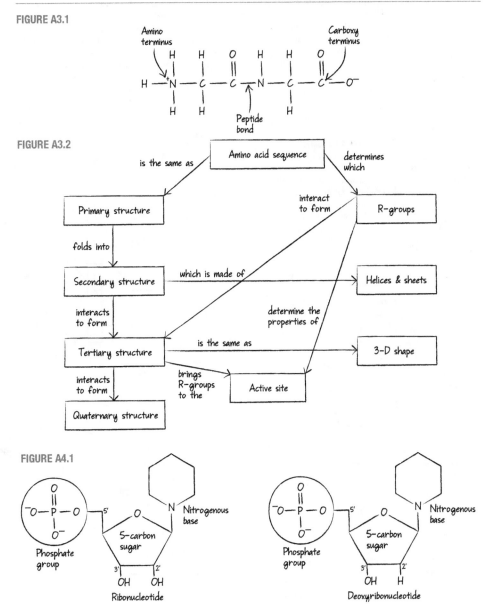

FIGURE A3.1

FIGURE A3.2

FIGURE A4.1

p. 60 Fig. 4.3 (understand) 5'-UAGC-'3

p. 61 CYU (understand) See **FIGURE A4.2**.

p. 63 (understand) If the two strands were parallel, the G-C pairing would align N−H groups together and C=O groups together, which would not allow hydrogen bonds to form.

p. 64 Fig. 4.8 (analyze) It is not spontaneous—energy must be added (as heat) for the reaction to occur.

p. 65 CYU (remember) See **FIGURE A4.3**.

IF YOU UNDERSTAND . . .

4.1. (understand) Cells activate nucleotides by linking additional phosphates to an existing 5' phosphate. Activation increases the chemical energy in the nucleotides enough to offset the decrease in entropy that will result from the polymerization reaction. **4.2** (understand) C-G pairs involve three hydrogen bonds, so they are more stable than A-T pairs with just two hydrogen bonds. **4.3** (analyze) A single-stranded RNA molecule has unpaired bases that can pair with other bases on the same RNA strand, thereby folding the molecule into stem-and-loop configurations. These secondary structures can further fold on themselves, giving the molecule a tertiary structure. Because DNA molecules are double stranded, with no unpaired bases, further internal folding is not possible. **4.4** (understand) Examples would include (1) the production of nucleotides, and (2) polymerization of RNA. It is thought that nucleotides were scarce during chemical evolution, so their catalyzed synthesis by a ribozyme would have been advantageous. Catalysis by an RNA replicase would have dramatically increased the reproductive rate of RNA molecules.

YOU SHOULD BE ABLE TO . . .

✔ Test Your Knowledge

1. (remember) c **2.** (remember) c **3.** (remember) a **4.** (remember) d **5.** (remember) One end has a free phosphate group on the 5' carbon; the other end has a free hydroxyl group bonded to the 3' carbon. **6.** (understand) DNA is a more stable molecule than RNA because it lacks a hydroxyl group on the 2' carbon and is therefore more resistant to cleavage, and because the two sugar-phosphate backbones are held together by many hydrogen bonds between nitrogenous bases.

✔ Test Your Understanding

7. (apply) In DNA, the secondary structure requires that every guanine pairs with a cytosine and every thymine pairs with an adenine, resulting in consistent ratios between the nucleotides. Chargaff's rules do not apply to RNA, since it is single-stranded and the pairing is not consistent throughout the molecules. **8.** (apply) a; if 30 percent is adenine, then 30 percent would be thymine, since they are base-paired together. This means that 40 percent consists of G-C base pairs, which would be equally divided between the two bases. **9.** (apply) The DNA sequence of the new strand would be 5'-ATCGATATC-3'. The RNA sequence would be the same, except each T would be replaced by a U. **10.** (understand) DNA has limited catalytic ability because it (1) lacks functional groups that can participate in catalysis and (2) has a regular structure that is not conducive to forming shapes required for catalysis. RNA molecules can catalyze some reactions because they (1) have exposed hydroxyl functional groups and (2) can fold into shapes that that can function in catalysis. **11.** (apply) No. Catalytic activity in ribozymes depends on the tertiary structure generated from single-stranded molecules. Double-stranded nucleic acids do not form tertiary structures. **12.** (understand) An RNA replicase would undergo replication and be able to evolve. It would process information in the sense of copying itself, and it would use energy to drive polymerization reactions. It would not be bound by a membrane and considered a cell, however, and it would not be able to acquire energy. It would best be considered as an intermediate step between nonlife and true life (as outlined in Chapter 1).

✔ Test Your Problem-Solving Skills

13. (create) See **FIGURE A4.4 14.** (apply) Yes—if the complementary bases lined up over the entire length of the two strands, they would twist into a double helix analogous to a DNA molecule. The same types of hydrogen bonds and hydrophobic interactions would occur as observed in the "stem" portion of hairpins in single-stranded RNA. **15.** (apply) In a triple helix, the bases are unlikely to align properly for hydrogen bonding to occur, so hydrophobic interactions would probably be more important. **16.** (apply) b; the high temperature would make it more likely that the secondary and tertiary structures would be denatured in the ribozymes. To overcome this effect, you would expect the hairpins to possess more G-C pairs, since they consist of three hydrogen bonds compared to the two found in A-T pairs.

CHAPTER 5

IN-TEXT QUESTIONS AND EXERCISES

p. 73 Fig. 5.2 (understand) See the structure of mannose in **FIGURE A5.1**.

p. 75 CYU (apply) See **FIGURE A5.2**.

p. 78 CYU (remember) They could differ in (1) location of linkages (e.g., 1,4 or 1,6); (2) types of linkages (e.g., α or β); (3) the sequence of the monomers (e.g., two galactose and then two glucose, versus alternating galactose and glucose); and/or (4) whether the four monomers are linked in a line or whether they branch.

p. 79 Fig. 5.6 (apply) The percentage of inhibition would not change for the intact glycoprotein bar. The purified

FIGURE A4.2

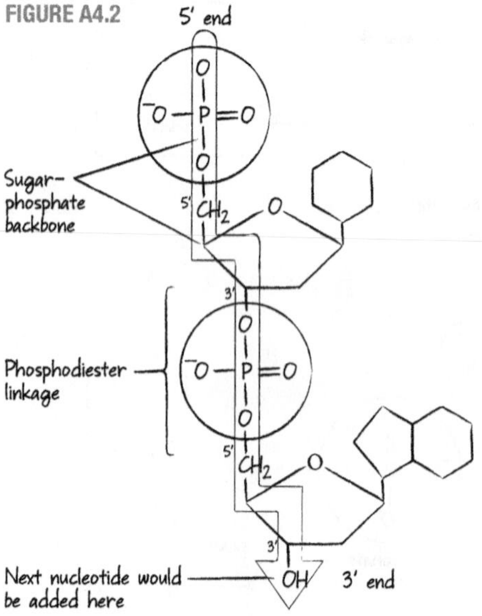

FIGURE A4.3

FIGURE A5.1

FIGURE A4.4

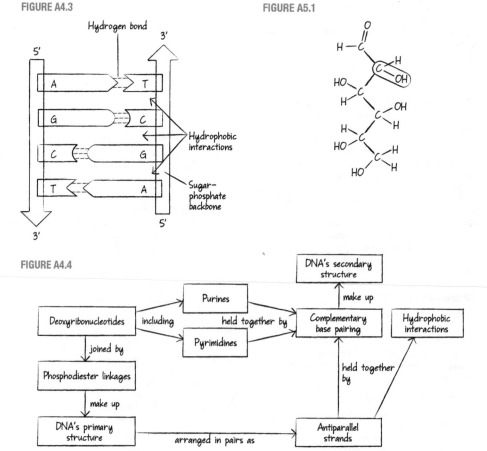

carbohydrate bar would be at zero inhibition, and the glycoprotein with digested carbohydrate bar would be similar to the intact glycoprotein bar.

p. 80 Fig. 5.7 (understand) All of the C–C and C–H bonds should be circled.

p. 81 CYU (1) (understand) *Aspect 1:* The β-1,4-glycosidic linkages in these molecules result in insoluble fibers that are difficult to degrade. *Aspect 2:* When individual molecules of these carbohydrates align, bonds form between them and produce fibers or sheets that resist pulling and pushing forces. **(2)** (apply) Most are probably being broken down into glucose, some of which in turn is being broken down in reactions that lead to the synthesis of ATP. Some will be resistant to digestion, such as the insoluble cellulose that makes up dietary fiber. This will help retain water and support the digestion and passage of fecal material.

IF YOU UNDERSTAND . . .

5.1. (understand) Molecules have to interact in an extremely specific orientation in order for a reaction to occur. Changing the location of a functional group by even one carbon can mean that the molecule will undergo completely different types of reactions. **5.2** (analyze) Glycosidic linkages can vary more in location and geometry than linkages between amino acids and nucleotides do. This variability increases the structural diversity possible in carbohydrates compared to proteins and nucleic acids. **5.3** (understand) (1) Polysaccharides used for energy storage are formed entirely from glucose monomers joined by α-glycosidic linkages; structural polysaccharides are made up of glucose or other sugars joined by β-glycosidic linkages. (2) The monomers in energy-storage polysaccharides are linked in a helical arrangement; the monomers in structural polysaccharides are linked in a linear arrangement. (3) Energy-storage polysaccharides may branch; structural polysaccharides do not. (4) Individual chains of energy-storage polysaccharides do not associate with each other; adjacent chains of structural polysaccharides are linked by hydrogen bonds or covalent bonds.

YOU SHOULD BE ABLE TO . . .

✔ Test Your Knowledge

1. (remember) d **2.** (remember) Monosaccharides can differ from one another in three ways: (1) the location of their carbonyl group; (2) the number of carbon atoms they contain; and (3) the orientations of their hydroxyl groups. **3.** (remember) a **4.** (remember) c **5.** (remember) a **6.** (understand) The electrons in the C=O bonds of carbon dioxide molecules are held tightly by the highly electronegative oxygen atoms, so they have low potential energy. The electrons in the C–C and C–H bonds of carbohydrates are shared equally, so they have much higher potential energy.

✔ Test Your Understanding

7. (understand) c. **8.** (apply) a; lactose is a disaccharide formed from a β-1,4-glycosidic linkage, so if two glucose molecules were linked with this bond, they would resemble units of cellulose and not be digested by human infants or adults. **9.** (understand) Carbohydrates are ideal for displaying the identity of the cell because they are so diverse structurally. This diversity enables them to serve as very specific identity tags for cells. **10.** (understand) When you compare the glucose monomers in an α-1,4-glycosidic linkage versus in a β-1,4-glycosidic linkage, the linkages are located on opposite sides of the plane of the glucose rings, and the glucose monomers are linked in the same orientation versus having every other glucose flipped in orientation. β-1,4-glycosidic linkages are much more likely to form linear fibers and sheets, so they resist degradation. **11.** (remember) Because (1) no mechanism is

known for the prebiotic polymerization of sugars; (2) no catalytic carbohydrates have been discovered that can perform polymerization reactions; and (3) sugar residues in a polysaccharide are not capable of complementary base pairing. **12.** (understand) Starch and glycogen both consist of glucose monomers joined by α-1,4-glycosidic linkages, and both function as storage carbohydrates. Starch is a mixture of unbranched and branched polysaccharides—called amylose and amylopectin, respectively. All glycogen polysaccharides are branched.

✔ Test Your Problem-Solving Skills

13. (analyze) Carbohydrates are energy-storage molecules, so minimizing their consumption may reduce total energy intake. Lack of available carbohydrate also forces the body to use fats for energy, reducing the amount of fat that is stored. **14.** (apply) d; lactose is a disaccharide of glucose and galactose, which can be cleaved by enzymes expressed in the human gut to release galactose. **15.** (analyze) Amylase breaks down the starch in the cracker into glucose monomers, which stimulate the sweet receptors in your tongue. **16.** (apply) When bacteria contact lysozyme, the peptidoglycan in their cell walls begins to degrade, leading to the death of the bacteria. Lysozyme therefore helps protect humans against bacterial infections.

CHAPTER 6

IN-TEXT QUESTIONS AND EXERCISES

p. 87 (understand) Fatty acids are amphipathic because their hydrocarbon tails are hydrophobic but their carboxyl functional groups are hydrophilic.

p. 87 Fig. 6.4 (apply) At the polar hydroxyl group in cholesterol and the polar head group in phospholipids.

p. 88 CYU (1) (analyze) Fats consist of three fatty acids linked to glycerol; steroids have a distinctive four-ring structure with variable side groups attached; phospholipids have a hydrophilic, phosphate-containing "head" region and a hydrocarbon tail. **(2)** (understand) In cholesterol, the hydrocarbon steroid rings and isoprenoid chain are hydrophobic; the hydroxyl group is hydrophilic. In phospholipids, the phosphate-containing head group is hydrophilic; the hydrocarbon chains are hydrophobic.

p. 89 (apply) Amino acids have amino and carboxyl groups that are ionized in water and nucleotides have negatively charged phosphates. Due to their charge and larger size, both would be placed below the small ions at the bottom of the scale (permeability $< 10^{-12}$ cm/sec).

p. 90 CYU (create) See **TABLE A6.1**.

p. 91 Fig. 6.10 (apply) Increasing the number of phospholipids with polyunsaturated tails would increase permeability of the liposomes. Starting from the left, the first line (no cholesterol) would represent liposomes with 50% polyunsaturated phospholipids, the second line would be 20% polyunsaturated phospholipids, and the third line would contain only saturated phospholipids.

p. 92 (apply) If there is a difference in temperature, then there would be a difference in thermal motion. The solute concentration on the side with a higher temperature would decrease because the solute particles would be moving faster and hence be more likely to move to the cooler side of the membrane, where they would slow down.

p. 93 Fig. 6.13 (apply) Higher, because less water would have to move to the right side to achieve equilibrium.

FIGURE A5.2

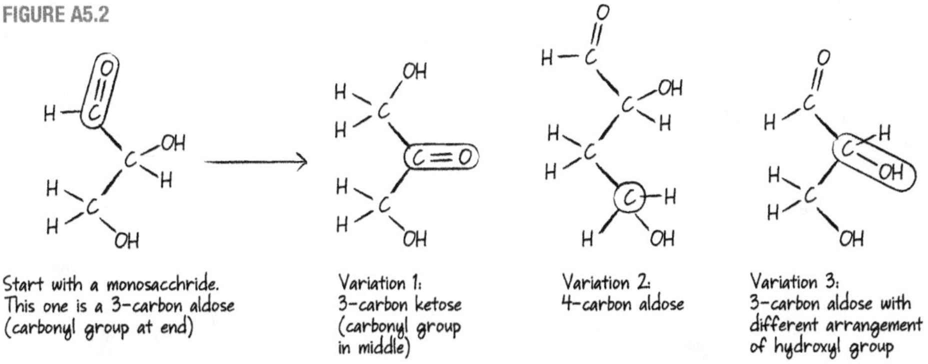

Start with a monosaccharide. This one is a 3-carbon aldose (carbonyl group at end)

Variation 1: 3-carbon ketose (carbonyl group in middle)

Variation 2: 4-carbon aldose

Variation 3: 3-carbon aldose with different arrangement of hydroxyl group

TABLE A6.1

Factor	Effect on permeability	Reason
Temperature	Decreases as temperature decreases.	Lower temperature slows movement of hydrocarbon tails, allowing more interactions (membrane is more dense).
Cholesterol	Decreases as cholesterol content increases.	Cholesterol molecules fill in the spaces between the hydrocarbon tails, making the membrane more tightly packed.
Length of hydrocarbon tails	Decreases as length of hydrocarbon tails increases.	Longer hydrocarbon tails have more interactions (membrane is more dense).
Saturation of hydrocarbon tails	Decreases as degree of saturation increases.	Saturated fatty acids have straight hydrocarbon tails that pack together tightly, leaving few gaps.

p. 96 Fig. 6.18 create Repeat the procedure using a lipid bilayer that is free of membrane proteins, such as synthetic liposomes constructed from only phospholipids. If proteins were responsible for the pits and mounds, then this control would not show these structures.

p. 97 apply Your arrow should point out of the cell. There is no concentration gradient for chloride, but the outside has a net positive charge, which favors outward movement of negative ions.

p. 97 Fig. 6.21 analyze No—the 10 replicates where no current was recorded probably represent instances where the CFTR protein was damaged and not functioning properly. (In general, no experimental method works "perfectly.")

p. 101 CYU understand Passive transport does not require an input of energy—it happens as a result of energy already present in existing concentration or electrical gradients. Active transport is active in the sense of requiring an input of energy from, for example, ATP. In cotransport, a second ion or molecule is transported against its concentration gradient along with (i.e., "co") an ion that is transported along its concentration gradient.

p. 101 Fig. 6.26 understand *Diffusion:* description as given; no proteins involved. *Facilitated diffusion:* Passive movement of ions or molecules that cannot cross a phospholipid bilayer readily along a concentration gradient; facilitated by channel or carrier proteins. *Active transport:* Active movement of ions or molecules that will build a gradient; facilitated by pump proteins powered by an energy source such as ATP.

IF YOU UNDERSTAND . . .

C=C

6.1. analyze Adding H_2 increases the saturation of the oil by converting   bonds into C—C bonds with added hydrogens. Lipids with more C—H bonds tend to be solid at room temperature. **6.2** understand Highly permeable and fluid bilayers possess short, unsaturated hydrocarbon tails while those that are highly impermeable and less fluid contain long, saturated hydrocarbon tails. **6.3** apply (1) The solute will diffuse until both sides are at equal concentrations. (2) Water will diffuse toward the side with the higher solute concentration. **6.4** apply See FIGURE A6.2.

YOU SHOULD BE ABLE TO . . .

✓ Test Your Knowledge

1. understand c **2.** remember a **3.** understand b **4.** understand d **5.** understand For osmosis to occur, a concentration gradient and membrane that allows water to pass, but not the solute, must be present. **6.** analyze Channel proteins form pores in the membrane and carrier proteins undergo conformational changes to shuttle molecules or ions across the membrane.

✓ Test Your Understanding

7. apply b **8.** analyze No, because they have no polar end to interact with water. Instead, these lipids would float on the surface of water, or collect in droplets suspended in water, reducing their interaction with water to a minimum. **9.** understand Hydrophilic, phosphate-containing head groups interact with water; hydrophobic hydrocarbon tails associate with each other. A bilayer is more stable than are independent phospholipids in solution. **10.** apply Ethanol's polar hydroxyl group reduces the speed at which it can cross a membrane, but its small size and lack of charge would allow it to slowly cross membranes—between the rates of water and glucose transport. **11.** understand Only nonpolar, hydrophobic amino acid residues would be found in the portion of the protein that crosses the membrane. In the interior of the bilayer, these residues would be hidden from the water solvent and interact with the nonpolar lipid tails. **12.** apply Chloride ions from sodium chloride will move from the left side to the right through the CFTR. Water

will initially move from the right side to the left by osmosis, but as chloride ions move to the right, water will follow. Na^+ and K^+ ions will not move across the membrane.

✓ Test Your Problem-Solving Skills

13. apply c **14.** create Flip-flops should be rare, because they require a polar head group to pass through the hydrophobic portion of the lipid bilayer. To test this prediction, you could monitor the number of dyed phospholipids that transfer from one side of the membrane to the other in a given period of time. **15.** apply Organisms that live in very cold environments are likely to have highly unsaturated phospholipids. The kinks in unsaturated hydrocarbon tails keep membranes fluid and permeable, even at low temperature. Organisms that live in very hot environments would likely have phospholipids with saturated tails, to prevent membranes from becoming too fluid and permeable. **16.** analyze Adding a methyl group makes a drug more hydrophobic and thus more likely to pass through a lipid bilayer. Adding a charged group makes it hydrophilic and reduces its ability to pass through the lipid bilayer. These modifications would help target the drug to either the inside or outside of cells, respectively.

BIG PICTURE Chemistry of Life

p. 104 CYU (1) understand Oxygen is much more electronegative than hydrogen, so within water, the electrons are unequally shared in the O—H covalent bonds. The resulting partial negative charge around the oxygen and partial positive charges around the hydrogen atoms allow for hydrogen bonds to form among water molecules. **(2)** analyze Unlike other macromolecules, nucleic acids can serve as templates for their own replication. RNA is generally single-stranded and can adopt many different

three-dimensional structures. The flexibility in structure, combined with the presence of reactive hydroxyl groups, contribute to the formation of active sites that catalyze chemical reactions. One or more of these catalytic RNA molecules may have evolved the ability to self-replicate. DNA is not likely to have catalyzed its own replication, as it is most often double-stranded, with no clear tertiary structure, and it lacks the reactive hydroxyl groups. **(3)** remember In the amino acid, the nitrogen in the amino (NH_3^+) group and the carbon in the carboxyl (COO^-) group should be circled. In the nucleotide, the oxygen in the hydroxyl (OH) group and the phosphorus in the phosphate (PO_4^{2-}) group on the nucleotide should be circled. **(4)** understand A line representing a protein should be drawn such that it completely crosses the lipid bilayer at least once. The protein could be involved in a variety of different roles, including transport of substances across the membrane in the form of a channel, carrier, or pump.

CHAPTER 7

IN-TEXT QUESTIONS AND EXERCISES

p. 110 CYU remember (1) The nucleoid compacts the chromosome to fit inside the cell via supercoiling while still keeping it accessible for replication and transmission of information. (2) Photosynthetic membranes increase food production by providing a large surface area to hold the pigments and enzymes required for photosynthesis. (3) Flagella propel cells through liquid, often toward a food source. (4) The layer of thick, strong material stiffens the cell wall and provides protection from mechanical damage.

p. 114 Fig. 7.12 create Storing the toxins in vacuoles prevents the toxins from damaging the plant's own organelles and cells.

FIGURE A6.1

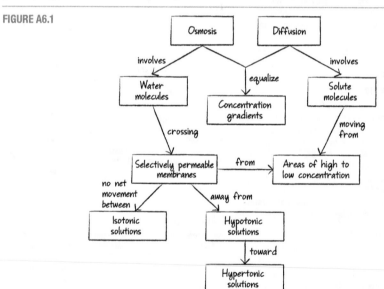

FIGURE A6.2

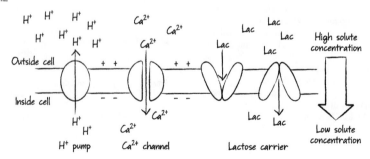

p. 116 CYU (1) (understand) Both organelles contain specific sets of enzymes. Lysosomal enzymes digest macromolecules in the acidic lumen of this organelle, releasing monomers that can be recycled into new macromolecules. Peroxisomes contain catalase and other enzymes that process fatty acids and toxins via oxidation reactions. **(2)** (understand) From top to bottom: administrative/information hub, protein factory, large molecule manufacturing and shipping (protein synthesis and folding center, lipid factory, protein finishing and shipping line, waste processing and recycling center), warehouse, fatty-acid processing and detox center, power station, food-manufacturing facility, support beams, perimeter fencing with secured gates, and leave blank.

p. 118 Fig. 7.16 (remember) See **FIGURE A7.1**.

p. 121 (analyze) (1) Nucleotides are small enough that they would diffuse through the nuclear pore complex along their gradients—a passive process that would not require

energy. (2) Large proteins must be escorted through the nuclear pore complex, which is directional and requires energy, since the protein is concentrated inside the nucleus.

p. 121 Fig. 7.18 (apply) "Prediction": The labeled tail region fragments or the labeled core region fragments of the nucleoplasmin protein will be found in the cell nucleus. "Prediction of null hypothesis": Either both the fragments (no required signal) or neither of them (whole protein signal) will be found in the nucleus of the cell. "Conclusion": The send-to-nucleus signal is in the tail region of the nucleoplasmin protein.

p. 123 (apply) During the chase period, proteins appear to have first entered the Golgi after 7 minutes and then started to move into secretory granules after 37 minutes. This means that in this experiment, it took approximately 30 minutes for the fastest-moving proteins to pass through the Golgi.

p. 126 (apply) In receptor-mediated endocytosis, the conversion of a late endosome to a lysosome is dependent on receiving acid hydrolases from the Golgi. If this receptor is not present, then the enzymes will not be sent and the late endosome will not mature into a lysosome to digest the endocytosed products.

p. 126 CYU (1) (apply) Proteins that enter the nucleus are fully synthesized and have an NLS that interacts with another protein to get it into the organelle. The NLS is not removed. Proteins that enter the ER have a signal sequence that interacts with the SRP during translation. The ribosome is moved to the ER and synthesis continues, moving the protein into the ER. The signal is removed once it enters the organelle. **(2)** (apply) The protein would be in the lysosome. The ER signal would direct the protein into the ER before it is completely synthesized. The M-6-P tag will direct the protein from the Golgi to the late endosome to the lysosome. Thus the complete protein is never free in the cytosol, where the NLS could direct it into the nucleus.

p. 132 CYU (analyze) Actin filaments are made up of two strands of actin monomers, microtubules are made up of tubulin protein dimers that form a tube, and intermediate filaments are made up of a number of different protein subunits. Actin filaments and microtubules exhibit polarity (or directionality), and new subunits are constantly being added or subtracted at either end (but added faster to the plus end). All three elements provide structural support, but only actin filaments and microtubules serve as tracks for motors involved in movement and cell division.

p. 132 Fig. 7.30 (apply) The microtubule doublets of the axoneme would slide past each other completely, but the axoneme would not bend.

IF YOU UNDERSTAND . . .

7.1 (understand) (1) Cells will be unable to synthesize new proteins and will die. (2) In many environments, cells will be unable to resist the osmotic pressure of water entering the cytoplasm and will burst. (3) The cell shape will be different, and cells will not be able to divide. **7.2** (understand) (1) The cell will be unable to produce a sufficient amount of ATP and will die. (2) Reactive molecules, like hydrogen peroxide, will damage the cell, and it will likely die. (3) Nothing will happen, since plants do not have centrioles. **7.3** (analyze) The liver cell would be expected to have more peroxisomes and less rough endoplasmic reticulum than the salivary cells would. **7.4** (create) The addition or removal of phosphates would change the folded structure of the protein, exposing the NLS for nuclear transport. **7.5** (create) As a group, proteins have complex and highly diverse shapes and chemical properties that allow them to recognize a great number of different zip codes in a very specific manner. **7.6** (apply) The Golgi is positioned near the microtubule organizing center, which has microtubules running from the minus end out to the plus end (near the plasma membrane). Kinesin would be used to move these vesicles as it walks toward the plus end.

YOU SHOULD BE ABLE TO . . .

✔ **Test Your Knowledge**

1. (understand) b **2.** (remember) They have their own small, circular chromosomes; they produce their own ribosomes; and they divide in a manner that is similar to bacterial fission, independent of cellular division. **3.** (remember) c **4.** (remember) b **5.** (remember) a **6.** (understand) The phosphate links to the motor protein and causes it to change shape, which results in the protein moving along the filament.

✔ **Test Your Understanding**

7. (analyze) All cells are bound by a plasma membrane, are filled with cytoplasm, carry their genetic information (DNA) in chromosomes, and contain ribosomes

---

FIGURE A7.1

(a) Animal pancreatic cell: Exports digestive enzymes.

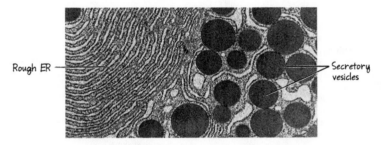

Rough ER

Secretory vesicles

(b) Animal testis cell: Exports lipid-soluble signals.

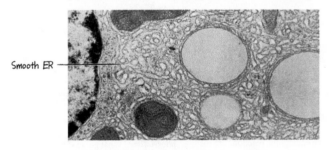

Smooth ER

(c) Plant leaf cell: Manufactures ATP and sugar.

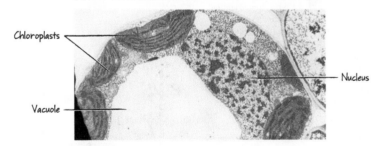

Chloroplasts

Nucleus

Vacuole

(d) Brown fat cells: Burn fat to generate heat in lieu of ATP.

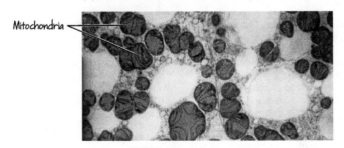

Mitochondria

(the sites of protein synthesis). Some prokaryotes have organelles not found in plants or animals, such as a magnetite-containing structure. Plant cells have chloroplasts, vacuoles, and a cell wall. Animal cells contain lysosomes and lack a cell wall. **8.** analyze a; the endoplasmic reticulum is responsible for synthesizing the membrane proteins required for the transport of solutes across the plasma membrane. **9.** create The NLS will be used to actively import the protein into the nucleus, leaving very little of the protein in the cytoplasm. Diffusion alone would not drive all the protein into the nucleus. **10.** create Ribosome in cytoplasm (signal is synthesized) → Ribosome at rough ER (protein is completed, folded, and glycosylated) → Transport vesicle → Golgi apparatus (protein is processed; has molecular zip code indicating destination) → Transport vesicle → Plasma membrane → Extracellular space. **11.** create This occurs in microfilaments and microtubules because they have ends that differ structurally and functionally—they have different filament growth rates. Intermediate filaments have identical ends, so there is no difference in the rate of assembly between the two ends. **12.** understand Polarized cytoskeletal filaments (microtubules or microfilaments) are present between the organelles. End-directed motor proteins use ATP to move these transport vesicles between them.

✔ Test Your Problem-Solving Skills

13. understand b; fimbriae are involved in bacterial attachment to surfaces and other cells, which would be important in the ability to grow on teeth. **14.** create The proteins must receive a molecular zip code that binds to a receptor on the surface of peroxisomes. They could diffuse randomly to peroxisomes or be transported in a directed way by motor proteins. **15.** create The tails cleaved from nucleoplasmin could be attached to the gold particles that were excluded from crossing the pore complex owing to their size. If these modified particles entered the nucleus, then the tail is not limited to the nucleoplasmin transport alone. **16.** apply The proteins would likely be found in the cytoplasm (e.g., actin and myosin) or imported into the mitochondria. Since there is a high energy demand, you would predict that there are many active mitochondria.

CHAPTER 8

IN-TEXT QUESTIONS AND ANSWERS

p. 139 apply (1) If ΔS is positive (products have more disorder than reactants), then according to the free energy equation, ΔG is more likely to be negative as temperature (T) increases even if ΔH is positive. The increased temperature represents added heat energy that may be used to drive an endothermic reaction to completion, making the reaction spontaneous. (2) Exothermic reactions may be nonspontaneous if they result in a decrease in entropy—meaning that the products are more ordered than the reactants (ΔS is negative).
p. 139 CYU (1) understand Gibbs equation: $\Delta G = \Delta H - T\Delta S$. ΔG symbolizes the change in the Gibbs free energy. ΔH represents the difference in enthalpy (heat, pressure, and volume) between the products and the reactants. T represents the temperature (in degrees Kelvin) at which the reaction is taking place. ΔS symbolizes the change in entropy (amount of disorder). **(2)** understand When ΔH is negative—meaning that the reactants have lower enthalpy than the products—and when ΔS is positive, meaning that the products have higher entropy (are more disordered) than the reactants.
p. 140 Fig. 8.4 understand Each point represents the data from a single test, not an average of many experiments, so it is not possible to calculate the standard error of the average.
p. 144 analyze Redox reactions transfer energy between molecules or atoms via electrons. When oxidized molecules are reduced, their potential energy increases. ATP

hydrolysis is often coupled with the phosphorylation of another molecule. This phosphorylation increases the potential energy of the molecule.
p. 144 CYU (1) understand Electrons in C–H bonds are not held as tightly as electrons in C–O bonds, so they have higher potential energy. **(2)** understand In part, because its three phosphate groups have four negative charges in close proximity. The electrons repulse each other, raising their potential energy.
p. 144 Fig. 8.9 understand The ΔG in the uncoupled reaction would be positive (>0), and each of the steps in the coupled reaction would have a negative (<0) ΔG.
p. 147 remember (1) binding substrates, (2) transition state, (3) R-groups, (4) structure
p. 146 Fig. 8.12 understand No—a catalyst affects only the activation energy, not the overall change in free energy.
p. 147 Fig. 8.14 analyze See **FIGURE A8.1**.
p. 149 CYU (1) create The rate of the reaction is based primarily on the activity of the enzyme. Once the temperature reaches a level that causes unfolding and inactivation of the enzyme, the rate decreases to the uncatalyzed rate. **(2)** apply The shape change would most likely alter the shape of the active site. If phosphorylation activates catalytic activity, the change to the active site would allow substrates to bind and be brought to their transition state. If phosphorylation inhibits catalytic activity, the shape change to the active site would likely prevent substrates from binding or no longer orient them correctly for the reaction to occur.
p. 150 apply The concentration of A and B would be higher than in the fully functional pathway since they are not depleted to produce C. If D is not being depleted by other reactions, then equilibrium would be established between C and D, resulting in lower concentrations of both.

IF YOU UNDERSTAND . . .

8.1 understand Reactions are spontaneous when the free energy in the products is lower than that of the reactants (ΔG is negative). Enthalpy and entropy are measures used to determine free-energy changes. Enthalpy measures the potential energy of the molecules, and entropy measures the disorder. For exergonic, spontaneous reactions, disorder normally increases and the potential energy stored in the products normally decreases relative to the reactants. **8.2** understand Energetic coupling transfers free energy released from exergonic reactions to drive endergonic reactions. Since endergonic reactions are required for sustaining life, without energetic coupling, life would not exist. **8.3** understand Amino acid R-groups lining the active site interact with the substrates, orienting them in a way that stabilizes the transition state, thereby lowering the activation energy needed for the reaction to proceed. **8.4** analyze Allosteric regulation and phosphorylation cause changes in the conformation of the enzyme that affects its catalytic function. Allosteric regulation involves non-covalent bonding, while phosphorylation is a covalent modification of the enzyme's primary structure. **8.5** apply In the first step of the pathway, the rate would increase as the intermediate, which is the product of the first reaction, is removed. In the last step, the rate would decrease due to the loss of the intermediate, which serves as the substrate for the last reaction.

YOU SHOULD BE ABLE TO . . .

✔ Test Your Knowledge

1. remember c **2.** remember a **3.** remember a **4.** remember The enzyme changes shape, but the change is not permanent. The enzyme shape will return to its original conformation after releasing the products. **5.** remember d **6.** remember When the product of a pathway feeds back to interact with an enzyme early in the same pathway to inhibit its function.

✔ Test Your Understanding

7. understand The shape of reactant molecules (the key) fits into the active site of an enzyme (the lock). Fischer's

original model assumed that enzymes were rigid; in fact, enzymes are flexible and dynamic. **8.** understand d. Energy, such as the thermal energy in fire, must be provided to overcome the activation energy barrier before the reaction can proceed. **9.** understand The phosphorylation reaction is exergonic because the electrons in ADP and the phosphate added to the substrate experience less electrical repulsion, and thus have less potential energy, than they did in ATP. A phosphorylated reactant (i.e., an activated intermediate) gains enough potential energy to shift the free energy change for the reaction from endergonic to exergonic. **10.** apply For the coupled reaction, step 1 has a ΔG of about -3 kcal/mol and step 2 has a ΔG of about -3 kcal/mol. The uncoupled reaction has a ΔG of about $+1.3$ kcal/mol. **11.** analyze Both are mechanisms that regulate enzymes; the difference is whether the regulatory molecule binds at the active site (competitive inhibition) or away from the active site (allosteric regulation). **12.** apply Catabolic reactions will often have a negative ΔG based on a decrease in enthalpy and increase in entropy. Anabolic reactions are the opposite—a positive ΔG that is based on an increase in enthalpy and decrease in entropy.

✔ Test Your Problem-Solving Skills

13. create See **FIGURE A8.2**. **14.** apply Without the coenzyme, the free-radical-containing transition state would not be stabilized and the reaction rate would drop dramatically. **15.** analyze The data suggest that the enzyme and substrate form a transition state that requires a change in the shape of the active site, and that each movement corresponds to one reaction. **16.** apply b. The sugar likely functions as an allosteric regulator to activate the enzyme.

CHAPTER 9

IN-TEXT QUESTIONS AND EXERCISES

p. 156 Fig. 9.2 remember Glycolysis: "What goes in" = glucose, NAD^+, ADP, inorganic phosphate; "What comes out" = pyruvate, NADH, ATP. Pyruvate processing: "What goes in" = pyruvate, NAD^+; "What comes out" = NADH, CO_2, acetyl CoA. Citric acid cycle: "What goes in" = acetyl CoA, NAD^+, FAD, GDP or ADP, inorganic phosphate; "What comes out" = NADH, $FADH_2$, ATP or GTP, CO_2. Electron transport and oxidative phosphorylation: "What goes in" = NADH, $FADH_2$, O_2, ADP, inorganic phosphate; "What comes out" = ATP, H_2O, NAD^+, FAD.

FIGURE A8.1

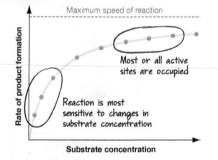

FIGURE A8.2

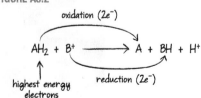

p. 161 If the regulatory site had a higher affinity for ATP than the active site, then ATP would always be bound at the regulatory site, and glycolysis would always proceed at a very slow rate.

p. 161 Fig. 9.9 "Positive control": AMP, NAD⁺, CoA (reaction substrates). "Negative control by feedback inhibition": acetyl CoA, NADH, ATP (reaction products).

p. 165 CYU (1) and (2) are combined with the answer to p. 171 CYU (3) Start with 12 triangles on glucose. (These triangles represent the 12 pairs of electrons that will be moved to electron carriers during redox reactions throughout glycolysis and the citric acid cycle.) Move two triangles to the NADH circle generated by glycolysis and the other 10 triangles to the pyruvate circle. Then move these 10 triangles through the pyruvate dehydrogenase square, placing two of them in the NADH circle next to pyruvate dehydrogenase. Add the remaining eight triangles in the acetyl CoA circle. Next move the eight triangles in the acetyl CoA circle through the citric acid cycle, placing six of them in the NADH circle and two in the FADH₂ circle generated during the citric acid cycle. (4) These boxes are marked with stars in the diagram.

p. 165 Fig. 9.13 NADH would be expected to have the highest amount of chemical energy since its production is correlated with the largest drop in free energy in the graph.

p. 167 Fig. 9.15 The proton gradient arrow should start above in the inner membrane space and point down across the membrane into the mitochondrial matrix. *Complex I:* "What goes in" = NADH; "What comes out" = NAD^+, e^-, transported H^+. *Complex II:* "What goes in" = $FADH_2$; "What comes out" = FAD, e^-, H^+. *Complex III:* "What goes in" = e^-, H^+; "What comes out" = e^-, transported H^+. *Complex IV:* "What goes in" = e^-, H^+, O_2; "What comes out" = H_2O, transported H^+.

p. 169 "Indirect" is accurate because most of the energy released during glucose oxidation is not used to produce ATP directly. Instead, this energy is stored in reduced electron carriers that are used by the ETC to generate a proton gradient across a membrane. These protons then diffuse down their concentration gradient across the inner membrane through ATP synthase, which drives ATP synthesis.

p. 169 Fig. 9.17 They could have placed the vesicles in an acidic solution that has a pH below that of the solution in the vesicle. This would set up a proton gradient across the membrane to test for ATP synthesis.

p. 171 CYU See FIGURE A9.1. To illustrate the chemiosmotic mechanism, take the triangles (electrons) piled on the NADH and FADH₂ circles and move them through the ETC. While moving these triangles, also move dimes from the mitochondrial matrix to the intermembrane space. As the triangles exit the ETC, add them to the oxygen to water circle. Once all the dimes have been pumped by the ETC into the intermembrane space, move them through ATP synthase back into the mitochondrial matrix to fuel the formation of ATP.

p. 173 CYU Electron acceptors such as oxygen have a much higher electronegativity than pyruvate. Donating an electron to O_2 causes a greater drop in potential energy, making it possible to generate much more ATP per molecule of glucose.

IF YOU UNDERSTAND . . .

9.1 The radioactive carbons in glucose can be fully oxidized by the central pathways to generate CO_2, which would be radiolabeled. Other molecules, like lipids and amino acids, would also be expected to be radiolabeled since they are made using intermediates from the central pathways in other anabolic pathways. **9.2** See FIGURE A9.2. **9.3** Pyruvate dehydrogenase accomplishes three different tasks that would be expected to require multiple enzymes and active sites: CO_2 release, NADH production, and linking of an acetyl group to CoA. **9.4** NADH would decrease if a drug poisoned the acetyl CoA and oxaloacetate-to-citrate enzyme, since the citric acid cycle would no longer be able to produce NADH in the steps following this reaction in the pathway. **9.5** The ATP synthase allows protons to reenter the mitochondrial matrix after they have been pumped out by the ETC. By blocking ATP synthase, you would expect the pH of the matrix to increase (decreased proton concentration). **9.6** Organisms that produce ATP by fermentation would be expected to grow more slowly than those that produce ATP via cellular respiration simply because fermentation produces fewer ATP molecules per glucose molecule than cellular respiration does.

YOU SHOULD BE ABLE TO . . .

✔ Test Your Knowledge

1. Glycolysis → Pyruvate processing → citric acid cycle → ETC and chemiosmosis. The first three steps are responsible for glucose oxidation; the final step produces the most ATP. **2.** b **3.** d **4.** Most of the energy is stored in the form of NADH. **5.** c **6.** a

✔ Test Your Understanding

7. Stored carbohydrates can be broken down into glucose that enters the glycolytic pathway. If carbohydrates are absent, products from fat and protein catabolism can be used to fuel cellular respiration or fermentation. If ATP is plentiful, anabolic reactions use

FIGURE A9.1

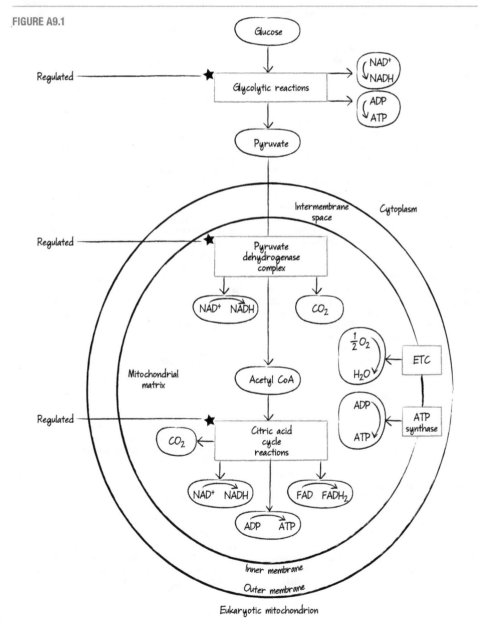

Eukaryotic mitochondrion

FIGURE A9.2

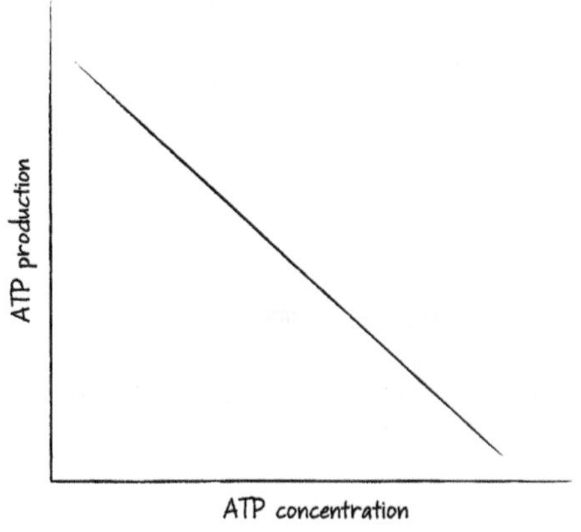

intermediates of the glycolytic pathway and the citric acid cycle to synthesize carbohydrates, fats, and proteins. **8.** (analyze) Both processes produce ATP from ADP and P_i, but substrate-level phosphorylation occurs when enzymes remove a "high-energy" phosphate from a substrate and directly transfer it to ADP, while oxidative phosphorylation occurs when electrons move through an ETC and produce a proton-motive force that drives ATP synthase. **9.** (understand) Aerobic respiration is much more productive because oxygen has extremely high electronegativity compared with other electron acceptors, resulting in a greater release of energy during electron transport and more proton pumping. **10.** (apply) b **11.** (analyze) Both phosphofructokinase and isocitrate dehydrogenase are regulated by feedback inhibition, where the product of the reaction or series of reactions inhibits the enzyme activity. They differ in that phosphofructokinase is regulated by allosteric inhibition while isocitrate dehydrogenase is controlled by competitive inhibition. **12.** (understand) Oxidative phosphorylation is possible via a proton gradient that is established by redox reactions in the ETC. ATP synthase consists of a membrane-associated F_o unit and a F_1 unit joined by a rotor shaft. When protons flow through the F_o unit, it spins the rotor shaft within the fixed F_1 unit. This spinning shaft causes structural changes in the F_1 that drives the synthesis of ATP from ADP and P_i.

✔ Test Your Problem-Solving Skills

13. (create) When complex IV is blocked, electrons can no longer be transferred to oxygen, the final acceptor, and cellular respiration stops. Fermentation could keep glycolysis going, but it is inefficient and unlikely to fuel a cell's energy needs over the long term. Cells that lack the enzymes required for fermentation would die first. **14.** (apply) Because mitochondria with few cristae would have fewer electron transport chains and ATP synthase molecules, they would produce much less ATP than mitochondria with numerous cristae. **15.** (apply) For each glucose molecule, two ATP are produced in glycolysis and two ATP are produced in the citric acid cycle via substrate-level phosphorylation. A total of 10 NADH and 2 $FADH_2$ molecules are produced from glycolysis, pyruvate oxidation, and the citric acid cycle. If each NADH were to yield 3 ATP, and each $FADH_2$ were to yield 2 ATP, then a total of 34 ATP would be produced via oxidative phosphorylation. Adding these totals would result in 38 ATP. A cell will not produce this much ATP, because the proton-motive force is used in other transport steps and because of other issues that may reduce the overall efficiency. **16.** (apply) b

BIG PICTURE Energy

p. 198 CYU (1) (understand) Photosynthesis uses H_2O as a substrate and releases O_2 as a by-product; cellular respiration uses O_2 as a substrate and releases H_2O as a by-product. **(2)** (understand) Photosynthesis uses CO_2 as a substrate; cellular respiration releases CO_2 as a by-product. **(3)** (analyze) CO_2 fixation would essentially stop; CO_2 would continue to be released by cellular respiration. CO_2 levels in the atmosphere would increase rapidly, and production of new plant tissue would cease—meaning that most animals would quickly starve to death. **(4)** (analyze) ATP "is used by" the Calvin cycle; photosystem I "yields" NADPH.

CHAPTER 11

IN-TEXT QUESTIONS AND EXERCISES

p. 204 CYU (analyze) Plant cell walls and animal ECMs are both fiber composites. In plant cell walls the fiber component consists of cross-linked cellulose fibers, and the ground substance is pectin. In animal ECMs the fiber component consists of collagen fibrils, and the ground substance is proteoglycan.
p. 207 (apply) Developing muscle cells could not adhere normally, and muscle tissue would not form properly. The embryo would die.
p. 207 Fig. 11.9 (apply) "Prediction": Cells treated with an antibody that blocks membrane proteins involved in adhesion will not adhere. "Prediction of null hypothesis": All cells will adhere normally.
p. 209 CYU (1) (analyze) The three structures differ in composition, but their function is similar. The middle lamella in plants is composed of pectins that glue adjacent cells together. Tight junctions are made up of membrane proteins that line up and "stitch" adjacent cells together. Desmosomes are "rivet-like" structures composed of proteins that link the cytoskeletons of adjacent cells. **(2)** (understand) The plasma membranes of adjacent plant cells are continuous at plasmodesmata and share portions of the smooth endoplasmic reticulum. Gap junctions connect adjacent animal cells by forming protein-lined pores. Both structures result in openings between the cells that allow cytosol, including ions and small molecules, to be shared.
p. 211 Fig. 11.12 (create) The steroid hormone likely changes the structure of the receptor such that it now exposes a nuclear localization signal, which is required for the protein to be transported into the nucleus.
p. 213 (analyze) The spy is the signaling molecule that arrives at the cell surface (the castle gate). The guard is the G-protein-coupled receptor in the plasma membrane, and the queen is the G protein. The commander of the guard is the enzyme that is activated by the G protein to produce second messengers (the soldiers).
p. 214 (apply) **(1)** The red dominos (RTK components) would be the first two dominos in the chain, followed by the black domino (Ras). This black domino would start two or more new branches, each one represented by a single domino of one color (e.g., green) to represent the activation of one type of kinase. Each of these green dominos would then again branch out, knocking down two or more branches consisting of single dominos of a different color (blue). The same branching pattern would result from each blue domino knocking down two or more yellow dominos. **(2)** Each single black domino (Ras) would require 10 green dominos, 100 blue dominos, and 1000 yellow dominos.
p. 215 CYU (1) (understand) Each cell–cell signaling molecule binds to a specific receptor protein. A cell can respond to a signal only if it has the appropriate receptor. Only certain cell types will have the appropriate receptor for a given signaling molecule. **(2)** (understand) Signals are amplified if one or more steps in a signal transduction pathway, involving either second messengers or a phosphorylation cascade, result in the activation of multiple downstream molecules.
p. 215 Fig. 11.16 (create) **(1)** cell responses A and C **(2)** cell responses A, B, and C **(3)** cell responses B and C.

IF YOU UNDERSTAND . . .

11.1 (apply) (1) Cells without functional integrin molecules would likely die as a result of not being able to send the appropriate anchorage-dependent survival signals. (2) Cells would be more sensitive to pulling or shearing forces; both cells and tissues would be weaker and more susceptible to damage. **11.2** (apply) Cells would not be coordinated in their activity, so the heart tissue would not contract in unison and the heart would not beat.
11.3 (analyze) Adrenalin binds to both heart and liver cells, but the activated receptors trigger different signal transduction pathways and lead to different cell responses.
11.4 (analyze) The signal transduction pathways are similarly organized in both unicellular and multicellular

organisms—consisting of signaling molecules, receptors, and second messengers. There is more variety in the means of transmitting the signal between cells in multicellular organisms compared to unicellular organisms. For example, there are no direct connections such as gap junctions or plasmodesmata in unicellular organisms.

YOU SHOULD BE ABLE TO . . .

✔ Test Your Knowledge

1. (remember) Fiber composites consist of cross-linked fiber components that withstand tension and a ground substance that withstands compression. The cellulose microfibrils in plants and collagen fibrils in animals functionally resemble the steel rods in reinforced concrete. The pectin in plants and proteoglycan in animals functionally resemble the concrete ground substance. **2.** (remember) b **3.** (remember) a **4.** (understand) b **5.** (remember) d **6.** (remember) Responses that affect which proteins are produced and those that affect the activity of existing proteins.

✔ Test Your Understanding

7. (understand) b **8.** (understand) If each enzyme in the cascade phosphorylates many copies of the enzyme in the next step of the cascade, the initial signal will be amplified many times over. **9.** (analyze) All three are made up of membrane-spanning proteins that directly interact between adjacent cells. Tight junctions seal adjacent animal cells together; gap junctions allow a flow of material from the cytosol of one to the other. Desmosomes firmly secure adjacent cells to one another but do not affect the movement of substances between cells or into the cells. **10.** (understand) When dissociated cells from two sponge species were mixed, the cells sorted themselves into distinct aggregates that contained only cells of the same species. By blocking membrane proteins with antibodies and isolating cells that would not adhere, researchers found that specialized groups of proteins, including cadherins, are responsible for selective adhesion. **11.** (create) Signaling molecule crosses plasma membrane and binds to intracellular receptor (reception) → Receptor changes conformation, and the activated receptor complex moves to target site (processing) → Activated receptor complex binds to a target molecule (e.g., a gene or membrane pump), which changes its activity (response) → Signaling molecule falls off receptor or is destroyed; receptor changes to inactive conformation (deactivation). **12.** (understand) Information from different signals may conflict or be reinforcing. "Crosstalk" between signaling pathways allows cells to integrate information from many signals at the same time instead of responding to each signal in isolation.

✔ Test Your Problem-Solving Skills

13. (apply) d **14.** (analyze) (a) The response would have to be extremely local—the activated receptor complex would have to affect nearby proteins. (b) No amplification could occur, because the number of signaling molecules dictates the amount of the response. (c) The only way to regulate the response would be to block the receptor or make it more responsive to the signaling molecule. **15.** (create) Chitin forms chains that can cross-link with one another. This fungal cell wall would likely need to be either relaxed or destroyed, and new cell wall synthesis would be coordinated with the directional growth. **16.** (create) Antibody binding to the two parts of the receptor may be causing them to dimerize. Since dimerization normally results after the signaling molecule binds to the receptor, the antibodies could be activating the receptor by mimicking this interaction. The result would be signal transduction even in the absence of the signaling molecule.

CHAPTER 12

IN-TEXT QUESTIONS AND EXERCISES

p. 223 understand **(1)** Genes are segments of chromosomes that code for RNAs and proteins. **(2)** Chromosomes are made of chromatin. **(3)** Sister chromatids are identical copies of the same chromosome, joined together.

p. 224 Fig. 12.5 apply (1) prophase cells would have 4 chromosomes with 2x DNA. (2) Anaphase cells would have 8 chromosomes and 2x DNA. (3) Each daughter cell will have 4 chromosomes with x DNA.

p. 226 apply See **TABLE A12.1**.

p. 227 Fig. 12.6 apply The chromosome and black bar would move at the same rate toward the spindle pole.

p. 229 CYU (1) apply See **FIGURE A12.1**. **(2)** apply Loss of the motors would result in two problems: (1) It would reduce the ability of chromosomes to attach to microtubules via their kinetochores; (2) cytokinesis would be inhibited since the Golgi-derived vesicles would not be moved to the center of the spindle to build the cell plate.

p. 230 Fig. 12.10 create Inject cytoplasm from an M-phase frog egg into a somatic cell that is in interphase. If the somatic cell starts mitosis, then the meiotic factor is not limited to gametes.

p. 230 Fig. 12.11 analyze In effect, MPF turns itself off after it is activated. If this didn't happen, the cell might undergo mitosis again before the cell has replicated its DNA.

p. 231 understand MPF activates proteins that get mitosis under way. MPF consists of a cyclin and a Cdk, and it is turned on by phosphorylation at the activating site and dephosphorylation at the inhibitory site. Enzymes that degrade cyclin reduce MPF levels.

p. 232 CYU (1) remember $G_1 \rightarrow S \rightarrow G_2 \rightarrow M$. Checkpoints occur at the end of G_1 and G_2 and during M phase. **(2)** understand Cdk levels are fairly constant throughout the cycle, but cyclin increases during interphase and peaks in M phase. This accumulation of cyclin is a prerequisite for MPF activity, which turns on at the end of G_2, initiating M phase, and declines at the end of M phase.

IF YOU UNDERSTAND . . .

12.1 understand The G_1 and G_2 phases give the cell time to replicate organelles and grow before division as well as perform the normal functions required to stay alive. Chromosomes replicate during S phase and are separated from one another during M phase. Cytokinesis also occurs during M phase, when the parent cell divides into two daughter cells. **12.2** apply In cells that do not dissolve the nuclear envelope, the spindle must be constructed inside the nucleus to attach to the chromosomes and separate them. **12.3** apply Cells would prematurely enter M phase, shortening the length of G_2 and resulting in the daughter cells' being smaller than normal. **12.4** analyze The absence of growth factors in normal cells would cause them to arrest in the G_1 phase—eventually all the cells in the culture would be in G_1. The cancerous cells are not likely to be dependent on these growth factors, so the cells would not arrest and would continue through the cell cycle.

YOU SHOULD BE ABLE TO . . .

✓ Test Your Knowledge

1. remember b **2.** remember d **3.** remember d **4.** remember c
5. understand Daughter chromosomes were observed to move toward the pole faster than do the marked regions of fluorescently labeled kinetochore microtubules.
6. remember The cycle would arrest in M phase, and cytokinesis would not occur.

✓ Test Your Understanding

7. apply For daughter cells to have identical complements of chromosomes, all the chromosomes must be replicated during the S phase, the spindle apparatus must connect with the kinetochores of each sister chromatid in prometaphase, and the sister chromatids of each replicated chromosome must be partitioned in anaphase and fully separated into daughter cells by cytokinesis. **8.** create One possible concept map is shown in **FIGURE A12.2**. **9.** understand Microinjection experiments suggested that something in the cytoplasm of M-phase cells activated the transition from interphase to M phase. The control for this experiment was to inject cytoplasm from a G_2-arrested oocyte into another G_2-arrested oocyte. **10.** apply Protein kinases phosphorylate proteins. Phosphorylation changes a protein's shape, altering its function (activating or inactivating it). As a result, protein kinases regulate the function of proteins. **11.** understand Cyclin concentrations change during the cell cycle. At high concentration, cyclins bind to a specific cyclin-dependent kinase (or Cdk), forming a dimer. This dimer becomes active MPF by changing its shape through the phosphorylation (activating site) and dephosphorylation (inhibitory site) of Cdk. **12.** analyze b.

✓ Test Your Problem-Solving Skills

13. analyze a; adding up each phase allows you to determine that the cell cycle is 8.5 hours long. After 9 hours, the radiolabeled cells would have passed through a full cycle and be in either S phase or G_2—none would have entered M phase. **14.** apply The embryo passes through multiple rounds of the cell cycle, but cytokinesis does not occur during M phases. **15.** apply Early detection of cancers leads to a greater likelihood of survival. The widespread implementation of breast and prostate

FIGURE A12.1

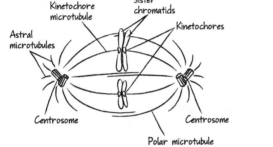

FIGURE A12.2

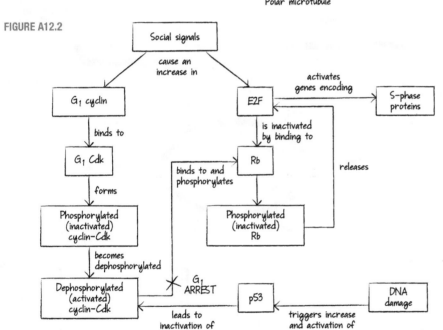

TABLE A12.1

	Prophase	Prometaphase	Metaphase	Anaphase	Telophase
Spindle apparatus	Starts to form	Contacts and moves chromosomes	Anchors poles to membrane and produces tension at kinetochores	Pulls chromatids apart	Defines site of cytokinesis
Nuclear envelope	Present	Disintegrates	Nonexistent	Nonexistent	Re-forms
Chromosomes	Condense	Attach to microtubules	Held at metaphase plate	Sister chromatids separate into daughter chromosomes	Collect at opposite poles

exams allows for the identification and removal of benign tumors before they become malignant. **16.** (analyze) Cancer requires many defects. Older cells have had more time to accumulate defects. Individuals with a genetic predisposition to cancer start out with some cancer-related defects, but this does not mean that the additional defects required for cancer to occur will develop.

CHAPTER 15

IN-TEXT QUESTIONS AND EXERCISES

p. 286 Fig. 15.2 (analyze) The lack of radioactive protein in the pellet (after centrifugation) is strong evidence; they could also make micrographs of infected bacterial cells before and after agitation.

p. 287 Fig. 15.3 (apply) 5′-TAG-3′.

p. 288 Fig. 15.5 (apply) The same two bands should appear, but the upper band (DNA containing only ^{14}N) should get bigger and darker and the lower band (hybrid DNA) should get smaller and lighter in color since each succeeding generation has relatively less heavy DNA.

p. 290 (apply) See **FIGURE A15.1**. The new strands grow in opposite directions, each in the 5′ → 3′ direction.

p. 292 (apply) Helicase, topoisomerase, single-strand DNA-binding proteins, primase, and DNA polymerase are all required for leading-strand synthesis. If any one of these proteins is nonfunctional, DNA replication will not occur.

p. 293 (apply) See **FIGURE A15.2**. If DNA ligase were defective, then the leading strand would be continuous, and the lagging strand would have gaps in it where the Okazaki fragments had not been joined.

p. 294 CYU (1) (understand) DNA polymerase adds nucleotides only to the free 3′ −OH on a strand. Primase synthesizes a short RNA sequence that provides the free 3′ end necessary for DNA polymerase to start working. **(2)** (understand) The need to begin DNA synthesis many times on the lagging strand requires many new primers. Since DNA polymerase I is needed to remove primers, it is required predominantly on the primer-rich lagging strand.

p. 296 Fig. 15.13 (apply) As long as the RNA template could bind to the "overhanging" section of single-stranded DNA, any sequence could produce a longer strand. For example, 5′-CCCAUUCCC-3′ would work just as well.

p. 297 CYU (1) (understand) This is because telomerase is needed only to replicate one end of a linear DNA and bacterial DNAs lack ends because they are circular.

(2) (understand) Since telomerase works by extending one strand of DNA without any external template and because DNA synthesis requires a template, telomerase must contain an internal template to allow it to extend a DNA chain.

p. 299 Fig. 15.16 (analyze) They are lower in energy and not absorbed effectively by the DNA bases.

p. 300 CYU (1) (apply) The mutation rate would be predicted to rise because differences in base-pair stability and shape make it possible for DNA polymerase to distinguish correct from incorrect base pairs during DNA replication. **(2)** (apply) The mutation rate should increase because without a way to distinguish which strand to use as a template for repair, about half of mismatches on average would be repaired using the incorrect strand as a template. **(3)** (remember) The enzyme that removes the dimer and surrounding DNA is specific to nucleotide excision repair. DNA polymerase and DNA ligase work in both nucleotide excision repair and normal DNA synthesis.

p. 300 Fig. 15.18 (apply) Exposure to UV radiation can cause formation of thymine dimers. If thymine dimers are not repaired, they represent mutations. If such mutations occur in genes controlling the cell cycle, cells can grow abnormally, resulting in cancers.

IF YOU UNDERSTAND . . .

15.1 (apply) These results would not allow distinguishing whether DNA or protein was the genetic material.

15.2 (understand) The bases added during DNA replication are shown in red type.

Original DNA:	**CAATTACGGA**
	GTTAATGCCT
Replicated DNA:	**CAATTACGGA**
	GTTAATGCCT
	CAATTACGGA
	GTTAATGCCT

15.3 (understand) See **FIGURE A15.3**. **15.4** (understand) Because cancer cells divide nearly without limit, it's important for these cells to have active telomerase so that chromosomes don't shorten to the point where cell division becomes impossible. **15.5** (understand) If errors in DNA aren't corrected, they represent mutations. When DNA repair systems fail, the mutation rate increases. As the mutation rate increases, the chance that one or more cell-cycle genes will be mutated increases. Mutations in these genes often result in uncontrolled cell division, ultimately leading to cancer.

YOU SHOULD BE ABLE TO . . .

✓ Test Your Knowledge

1. (remember) d **2.** (understand) a **3.** (remember) topoisomerase **4.** (remember) b **5.** (remember) c **6.** (remember) telomerase

✓ Test Your Understanding

7. (remember) Labeling DNA or labeling proteins. **8.** (understand) DNA is constantly damaged, and many pathways have evolved to repair this onslaught of damage. If a DNA repair pathway is inactivated by mutation, damage is inefficiently repaired. Consequently mutation rates increase, and the increased number of mutations increases the probability that cancer-causing mutations will occur.

9. (understand) On the lagging strand, DNA polymerase moves away from the replication fork. When helicase unwinds a new section of DNA, primase must build a new primer on the template for the lagging strand (closer to the fork) and another polymerase molecule must begin synthesis at this point. This makes the lagging-strand synthesis discontinuous. On the leading strand, DNA polymerase moves in the same direction as helicase, so synthesis can continue, without interruption, from a single primer (at the origin of replication).

10. (understand) Telomerase binds to the overhang at the end

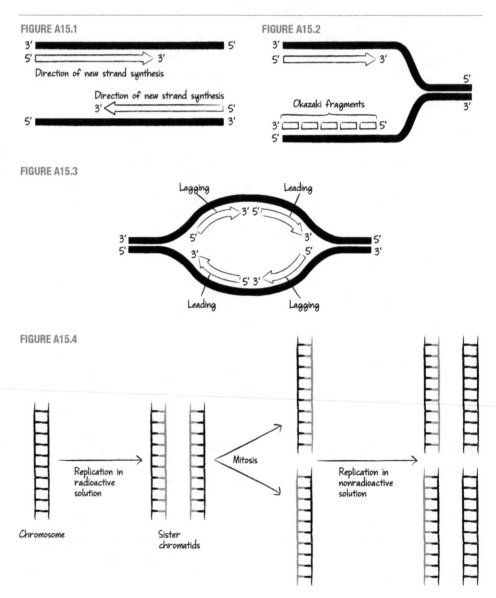

FIGURE A15.1

3′ ◼◼◼◼◼◼◼◼◼◼◼◼ 5′
5′ ◻━━━━━━━━━━▶ 3′

Direction of new strand synthesis

Direction of new strand synthesis
3′ ◀━━━━━━━━━━ 5′
5′ ◼◼◼◼◼◼◼◼◼◼◼◼ 3′

FIGURE A15.2

3′ ◼◼◼◼◼◼◼◼
5′ ◻━━━━━━▶ 3′
                    5′
                    3′
Okazaki fragments
3′ ◻ ◻ ◻ ◻ ◻ 5′
5′

FIGURE A15.3

Lagging   Leading
3′ 5′   3′
3′ ◼◼◼◼◼ 5′   3′ ◼◼◼◼◼ 5′
5′ ◼◼◼◼◼ 3′   5′ ◼◼◼◼◼ 3′
3′   5′
5′ 3′
Leading   Lagging

FIGURE A15.4

Chromosome → Replication in radioactive solution → Sister chromatids → Mitosis → Replication in nonradioactive solution →

of a chromosome. Once bound, it begins catalyzing the addition of deoxyribonucleotides to the overhang in the $5' \rightarrow 3'$ direction, lengthening the overhang. This allows primase, DNA polymerase, and ligase to catalyze the addition of deoxyribonucleotides to the lagging strand in the $5' \rightarrow 3'$ direction, restoring the lagging strand to its original length. **11.** apply a (Because the ability to distinguish which strand contains the incorrect base would be lost). **12.** analyze d (The regularity of DNA's structure allows enzymes to recognize any type of damage that distorts this regular structure.)

✔ Test Your Problem-Solving Skills

13. analyze c (If DNA polymerase could synthesize DNA $3' \rightarrow 5'$ as well as the normal $5' \rightarrow 3'$, then both newly synthesized DNA strands could be extended to follow the replication fork.) **14.** apply (a) In **FIGURE A15.4**, the gray lines represent DNA strands containing radioactivity. (b) After one round of replication in radioactive solution, one double-stranded DNA would be radioactive in both strands and the other would not be radioactive in either strand. After another round of DNA synthesis, this time in nonradioactive solution, one of the four DNA molecules would be radioactive in both strands and the other three DNA molecules would contain no radioactivity in any strand. **15.** analyze (a) The double mutant of both *uvrA* and *recA* is most sensitive to UV light; the single mutants are in between; and the wild type is least sensitive. (b) The *recA* gene contributes more to UV repair through most of the UV dose levels. But at very high UV doses, the *uvrA* gene is somewhat more important than the *recA* gene. **16.** apply About 4600 seconds or 77 minutes. This answer comes from knowing that replication proceeds bidirectionally, so replication from each fork is predicted to replicate half the chromosome. There is 4.6 million base pairs/2 = 2.3 million base pairs. At 500 base pairs per second, this requires 2.3 million base pairs/500 base pairs per second = 4600 seconds. To obtain the time in minutes, divide 4600 seconds by 60 seconds per minute.

CHAPTER 16

IN-TEXT QUESTIONS AND EXERCISES

p. 305 Fig. 16.1 apply No, it could not make citrulline from ornithine without enzyme 2. Yes, it would no longer need enzyme 2 to make citrulline.

p. 306 Fig. 16.2 create Many possibilities: strain of fungi used, exact method for creating mutants and harvesting spores to grow, exact growing conditions (temperature, light, recipe for growth medium—including concentrations of supplements), objective criteria for determining growth or no growth.

p. 309 CYU remember Change in DNA sequence, change in sequence of transcribed mRNA, potential change in amino acid sequence of protein, likely altered protein function (if amino acid sequence was altered), likely change in phenotype.

p. 312 analyze (1) The codons in Figure 16.4 are translated correctly. (2) See **FIGURE A16.1**. (3) There are many possibilities (just pick alternative codons for one or more of the amino acids); one is an mRNA sequence (running $5' \rightarrow 3'$): 5' GCG-AAC-GAU-UUC-CAG 3'. To get the corresponding DNA sequence, write this sequence but substitute Ts for Us: 5' GCG-AAC-GAT-TTC-CAG 3'. Now write the complementary bases, which will be in the $3' \rightarrow 5'$ direction: 3' CGC-TTG-CTA-AAG-GTC 5'. When this second strand is transcribed by RNA polymerase, it will produce the mRNA given with the proper $5' \rightarrow 3'$ orientation.

p. 312 CYU (1) apply Note the $3' \rightarrow 5'$ polarity of the DNA sequences in the accompanying table, and in the subsequent answer. This means that the complementary

mRNA codon will read $5' \rightarrow 3'$. U (rather than T) is the base transcribed from A.

DNA	mRNA Codon	Amino Acid
ATA	UAU	Tyrosine
ATG	UAC	Tyrosine
ATT	UAA	Stop
GCA	UGC	Cysteine

(2) understand The ATA → ATG mutation would have no effect on the protein. The ATA → ATT mutation introduces a stop codon, so the resulting polypeptide would be shortened. This would result in synthesis of a mutant protein much shorter than the original protein. The ATA → GCA mutation might have a profound effect on the protein's conformation because cysteine's structure is different from tyrosine's.

p. 312 Fig. 16.7 apply See **FIGURE A16.1**.

p. 314 Fig. 16.9 analyze Chromosomes 2, 3, 6, 10, 13, 14, 15, 18, 19, 21, 22, and the X chromosome show aneuploidy. Virtually every chromosome has structural rearrangements, and translocations are the most obvious. These are seen when two or more different colors occur on the same chromosome.

IF YOU UNDERSTAND . . .

16.1 understand Ornithine, citrulline or arginine could be added to allow growth. As Figure 16.1 shows, these compounds are made after the steps catalyzed by the enzymes 1, 2, and 3 that are needed to produce arginine. **16.2** understand An inhibitor of RNA synthesis will eventually prevent the synthesis of new proteins because newly synthesized mRNA is needed for translation. **16.3** apply AUG UGG AAA/AAG CAA/CAG **16.4** understand Since redundancy is having more than one codon specify a particular amino acid, redundancy makes it possible for there to be a point mutation without altering the amino acid. This is a silent mutation. A silent mutation is likely to be neutral because there is no change in amino acid sequence.

YOU SHOULD BE ABLE TO . . .

✔ Test Your Knowledge

1. remember d **2.** understand a **3.** understand d **4.** remember Because there is no chemical complementarity between nucleotides and amino acids; and because in eukaryotes, DNA is in the nucleus but translation occurs in the cytoplasm. **5.** understand d **6.** remember A codon that signals the end of translation.

✔ Test Your Understanding

7. understand Because the Morse code and genetic code both use simple elements (dots and dashes; 4 different bases) in different orders to encode complex information (words; amino acid sequences).
8.
Substrate 1 $\xrightarrow{A}$ Substrate 2 $\xrightarrow{B}$ Substrate 3 $\xrightarrow{C}$
Substrate 4 $\xrightarrow{D}$ Substrate 5 $\xrightarrow{E}$ Biological Sciazine
apply Substrate 3 would accumulate. Hypothesis: The individuals have a mutation in the gene for enzyme D.
9. understand They supported an important prediction of the hypothesis: Losing a gene (via mutation) resulted in loss of an enzyme. **10.** understand c **11.** understand In a triplet code, addition or deletion of 1–2 bases disrupts the reading frame "downstream" of the mutation site(s), resulting in a dysfunctional protein. But addition or deletion of 3 bases restores the reading frame—the normal sequence is disrupted only between the first and third mutation. The resulting protein is altered but may still be able to function normally. Only a triplet code would show these patterns. **12.** understand A point mutation changes the nucleotide sequence of an existing allele, creating a new one, so it always changes the genotype. But because the genetic code is redundant, and because point mutations can occur in DNA sequences that do not code for amino acids, these point mutations do not change the protein product and therefore do not change the phenotype.

✔ Test Your Problem-Solving Skills

13. apply See **FIGURE A16.2**. **14.** analyze Every copying error would result in a mutation that would change the amino acid sequence of the protein and would likely affect its function. **15.** analyze Before the central dogma was understood, DNA was known to be the hereditary material, but no one knew how particular sequences of bases resulted in the production of RNA and protein products. The central dogma clarified how genotypes produce phenotypes. **16.** analyze c

CHAPTER 17

IN-TEXT QUESTIONS AND EXERCISES

p. 318 Fig. 17.1 remember RNA is synthesized in the $5' \rightarrow 3'$ direction; the DNA template is "read" $3' \rightarrow 5'$.
p. 321 CYU (1) apply Transcription would be reduced or absent because the missing nucleotides are in the -10 region, one of the two critical parts of the promoter.
(2) understand NTPs are required because the three phosphate groups raise the monomer's potential energy enough to make the polymerization reaction exergonic.

FIGURE A16.1

mRNA sequence:
5' AUG-CUG-GAG-GGG-GUU-AGA-CAU 3'

Amino acid sequence:
Met-Leu-Glu-Gly-Val-Arg-His

FIGURE A16.2

Bottom DNA strand:
3' AACTT-TAC(start)-GGG-CAA-ACC-TCT-AGC-CCA-ATG-TCG-ATC(stop)-AGTTTC 5'

mRNA sequence:
5' AUG-CCC-GUU-UGG-AGA-UCG-GGU-UAC-AGC-UAG 3'

Amino acid sequence:
Met-Pro-Val-Trp-Arg-Ser-Gly-Tyr-Ser

p. 322 Fig. 17.5 (apply) There would be no loops—the molecules would match up exactly.
p. 323 CYU (1) (understand) The subunits contain both RNA (the *ribonucleo–* in the name) and proteins. **(2)** (understand) The cap and tail protect mRNAs from degradation and facilitate translation.
p. 326 Fig. 17.11 (analyze) If the amino acids stayed attached to the tRNAs, the gray line in the graph would stay high and the green line low. If the amino acids were transferred to some other cell component, the gray line would decline but the green line would be low.
p. 327 (understand) (1) The amino acid attaches on the top right of the L-shaped structure. (2) The anticodon is antiparallel in orientation to the mRNA codon, and it contains the complementary bases.
p. 332 CYU (understand) E is for exit—the site where uncharged tRNAs are ejected; P is for peptidyl (or peptide bond)—the site where peptide bond formation takes place; A is for aminoacyl—the site where aminoacyl tRNAs enter.

IF YOU UNDERSTAND . . .

17.1 (apply) Transcription would continue past the normal point because the insertion of nucleotides would disrupt the structure of the RNA hairpin that functions as a terminator. **17.2** (apply) The protein-coding segment of the gene is predicted to be longer in eukaryotes because of the presence of introns. **17.3** (understand) The tRNAs act as adaptors because they couple the information contained in the nucleotides of mRNA to that contained in the amino acid sequence of proteins. **17.4** (apply) An incorrect amino acid would appear often in proteins. This is because the altered synthetase would sometimes add the correct amino acid for a particular tRNA and at other times add the incorrect amino acid. **17.5** (create) One possible concept map is shown in FIGURE A17.1.

YOU SHOULD BE ABLE TO . . .

✔ Test Your Knowledge

1. (understand) c **2.** (remember) c **3.** (understand) To speed the correct folding of newly synthesized proteins **4.** (remember) d **5.** (remember) At the 3′ end **6.** (apply) b

✔ Test Your Understanding

7. (understand) Basal transcription factors bind to promoter sequences in eukaryotic DNA and facilitate the binding of RNA polymerase. As part of the RNA polymerase holoenzyme, sigma binds to a promoter sequence in bacterial DNA and to allow RNA polymerase to initiate at the start of genes. **8.** (analyze) The wobble rules allow a single tRNA to pair with more than one type of mRNA codon. This is distinct from redundancy, in which more than one codon can specify a single amino acid. If the wobble rules did not exist, there would need to be one tRNA for each amino-acid-specifying codon in the redundant genetic code. **9.** (apply) b **10.** (apply) After a peptide bond forms between the polypeptide and the amino acid held by the tRNA in the A site, the ribosome moves down the mRNA. As it does, an uncharged tRNA leaves the E site. The now-uncharged tRNA that was in the P site enters the E site; the tRNA holding the polypeptide chain moves from the A site to the P site, and a new aminoacyl tRNA enters the A site. **11.** (apply) The ribosome's active site is made up of RNA, not protein. **12.** (understand) The separation allows the aminoacyl tRNA to place the amino acid into the ribosome's active site while reaching to the distant codon on the mRNA.

✔ Test Your Problem-Solving Skills

13. (create) Ribonucleases degrade mRNAs that are no longer needed by the cell. If an mRNA for a hormone that increased heart rate were never degraded, the hormone would be produced continuously and heart rate would stay elevated—a dangerous situation. **14.** (apply) d **15.** (analyze)

The regions most crucial to the ribosome's function should be the most highly conserved: the active site, the E, P, and A sites, and the site where mRNAs initially bind. **16.** (analyze) The most likely locations are one of the grooves or channels where RNA, DNA, and ribonucleotides move through the enzyme—plugging one of them would prevent transcription.

CHAPTER 18

IN-TEXT QUESTIONS AND EXERCISES

p. 338 (understand) See TABLE A18.1.
p. 338 Fig. 18.1 (analyze) Write "Slowest response, most efficient resource use" next to the transcriptional control label. Write "Fastest response, least efficient resource use" next to the post-translational control label.
p. 339 Fig. 18.2 (apply) Plates from all three treatments must be identical and contain identical growth medium, except for the presence of the sugars labeled in the figure. Also, all plates must be grown under the same physical conditions (temperature, light) for the same time.
p. 340 Fig. 18.3 (apply) Use a medium with all 20 amino acids when producing a master plate of mutagenized *E. coli* colonies; then use a replica plate that contains all the amino acids except tryptophan. Choose cells from the master plate that did *not* grow on the replica plate.
p. 341 (understand) *lacZ* codes for the β-galactosidase enzyme, which breaks the disaccharide lactose into glucose and galactose. *lacY* codes for the galactoside permease enzyme, which transports lactose into the bacterial cell. *lacI* codes for a protein that shuts down production of the other *lac* products. When lactose is absent, the *lacI* product prevents transcription. This is logical because there is no reason for the cell to make β-galactosidase and galactoside permease if there is no lactose to metabolize. But when lactose is present, it interacts with *lacI* in some way so that *lacZ* and *lacY* are induced (their transcription can occur). When lactose is present, the enzymes that metabolize it are expressed.

FIGURE A17.1

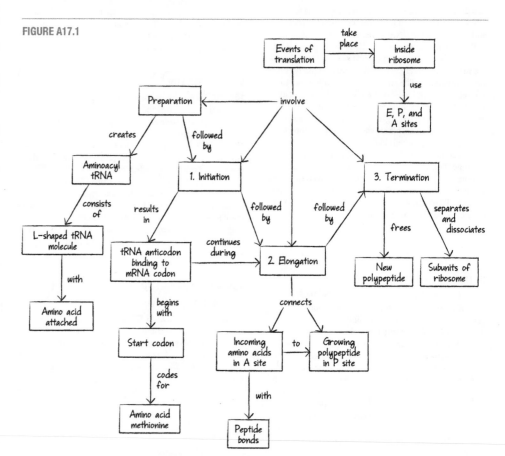

TABLE A18.1

Name	Function
lacZ	Gene for β-galactosidase
lacY	Gene for galactoside permease
Operator	Binding site for repressor
Promoter	Binding site for RNA polymerase
Repressor	Shuts down transcription
Lactose	Binds to repressor and stimulates transcription (removes negative control)
Glucose	At low concentration, increases transcription

p. 343 (apply) A mutation that prevents lactose binding to repressor is predicted to prevent transcription of the *lac* operon under any condition. This is because the repressor would never come off the operator. A mutation in the operator that prevents repressor binding is predicted to lead to constitutive expression of the *lac* operon.

p. 343 Fig. 18.8 (understand) Put the "Repressor protein" on the operator. No transcription will take place. Then put the "RNA polymerase" on the promoter. No transcription will take place. Finally, put "lactose" on the repressor protein and then remove the resulting lactose–repressor complex from the operon. Transcription will begin.

p. 344 CYU (1) (understand) It is logical that the genes for metabolizing lactose should be expressed only when lactose is available. (2) (understand) See **FIGURE A18.1**.

p. 344 (apply) This mutation is predicted to lower rates of transcription initiation because AraC's binding to RNA polymerase is essential for AraC to work as an activator.

IF YOU UNDERSTAND . . .

18.1 (understand) Production of β-galactosidase and galactosidase permease are under transcriptional control—transcription depends on the action of regulatory proteins. The activity of the repressor is under post-translational control. **18.2** (apply) Treat *E. coli* cells with a mutagen, and create a master plate that is grown at 33°C. Replica-plate this master plate and grow the replica plate at 42°C. Look for colonies that are on the master plate at 33°C but not on the replica plate at 42°C. **18.3** (understand) The operator is the parking brake; the repressor locks it in place, and the inducer releases it. **18.4** (apply) *ara* initiator mutations are likely to affect positive and negative control because AraC must bind to the *ara* initiator sequence for both forms of control. **18.5** (create) Mutations that create operators for the SOS regulon repressor protein would put new genes under control of the repressor and incorporate them into the regulon.

YOU SHOULD BE ABLE TO . . .

✓ Test Your Knowledge

1. (remember) b **2.** (understand) d **3.** (apply) b **4.** (remember) DNA; RNA; **5.** (understand) When glucose and another sugar are present in the environment, inducer exclusion prevents the use of the other sugar and allows only use of glucose. **6.** (remember) a

✓ Test Your Understanding

7. (understand) The glycolytic enzymes are always needed in the cell because they are required to produce ATP, and ATP is always needed. **8.** (understand) Positive control means that a regulatory protein, when present, causes transcription to increase. Negative control means that a regulatory protein, when present, prevents transcription. **9.** (apply) b. **10.** (apply) Regulation of the *lac* operon should be normal. The location of the *lacI* gene isn't important, because the gene produces a protein that diffuses within the cell to the operator. **11.** (analyze) b (since the activator needs to bind to regulatory sequences to activate gene expression, preventing DNA binding would cripple the regulon and prevent cholera).**12.** (analyze) The *lac* operon would be strongly induced. Once inside the cell, the IPTG will bind to the repressor, causing it to release from DNA. IPTG cannot be broken down, so its concentration will remain high. Finally, since glucose is absent, there will be no inducer exclusion to inhibit IPTG transport through the galactoside permease transporter.

✓ Test Your Problem-Solving Skills

13. (create) Set up cultures with individuals that all come from the same colony of toluene-tolerating bacteria. Half the cultures should have toluene as the only source of carbon; half should have glucose or another common source of carbon. The glucose-containing medium serves as a control to ensure that cells can be grown in the lab. Cells will grow in both cultures if they are able to use toluene as a source of carbon; they will grow only in glucose-containing medium if toluene cannot be used as a carbon source. **14.** (apply) At a rate of 1×10^{-4} mutants per cell, you would on average find one mutant in every 10,000 (1×10^4) cells. Therefore, you should screen a bit more (~ 2–3 times more) than 10,000 cells to be reasonably sure of finding at least one mutant. **15.** (apply) b **16.** (analyze) Cells with functioning β-galactosidase will produce blue colonies; cells with *lacZ* mutations or *lacY* mutations will not produce β-galactosidase and will produce white colonies. The *lac* promoter could be mutated so that RNA polymerase cannot bind.

CHAPTER 19

IN-TEXT QUESTIONS AND EXERCISES

p. 352 Fig. 19.4 (analyze) Acetylation of histones decondenses chromatin and allows transcription to begin, so HATs are elements in positive control. Deacetylation condenses chromatin and inactivates transcription, so HDACs are elements in negative control.

p. 353 CYU (1) (apply) Many more genes than normal are predicted to be expressed because the inability to methylate DNA would lead to more decondensed chromatin. (2) (understand) Addition of acetyl groups to histones or methyl groups to DNA can cause chromatin to decondense or condense, respectively. Different patterns of acetylation or methylation will determine which genes in muscle cells versus brain cells can be transcribed and which are not available for transcription.

p. 353 Fig. 19.5 (create) They could do something to change histone modifications to see how this affects gene transcription instead of just making the observation that certain histone modifications and low rates of transcription go together.

p. 355 Fig. 19.6 (analyze) A typical eukaryotic gene usually contains introns and is regulated by multiple enhancers. Bacterial operons lack introns and enhancers. The promoter-proximal element found in some eukaryotic genes is comparable to the *araC* binding site in the *ara* operon of bacteria. Bacterial operons have a single promoter but code for more than one protein; eukaryotic genes code for a single product.

p. 356 (analyze) The basal transcription factors found in muscle and nerve cells are similar or identical; the regulatory transcription factors found in each cell type are different.

p. 356 (understand) DNA forms loops when distant regulatory regions, such as silencers and enhancers, are brought close to the promoter through binding of regulatory transcription factors to mediator.

FIGURE A18.1

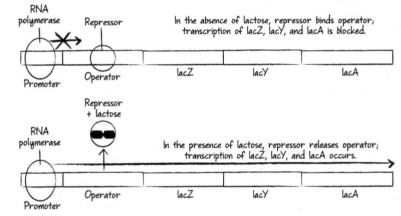

FIGURE A19.1

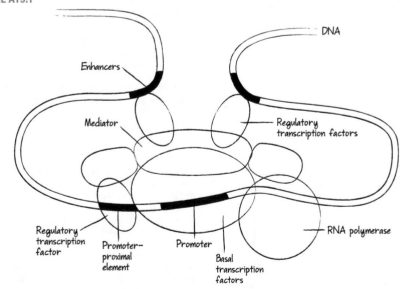

p. 356 CYU (1) (analyze) Bacterial regulatory sequences are found close to the promoter; eukaryotic regulatory sequences can be close to the promoter or far from it. Bacterial regulatory proteins interact directly with RNA polymerase to initiate or prevent transcription; eukaryotic regulatory proteins influence transcription by altering chromatin structure or binding to the basal transcription complex through mediator proteins. **(2)** (understand) Certain regulatory proteins decondense chromatin at muscle- or brain-specific genes and then activate or repress the transcription of cell-type-specific genes. Muscle-specific genes are expressed only if muscle-specific regulatory proteins are produced and activated.

p. 358 (understand) Alternative splicing does not occur in bacteria because bacterial genes do not contain introns—in bacteria, each gene codes for a single product. Alternative splicing is part of step 3 in Figure 19.1.

p. 359 (remember) Step 4 and step 5. RNA interference either **(1)** decreases the life span of mRNAs or **(2)** inhibits translation.

p. 360 CYU (1) (understand) It became clear that a single gene can code for multiple products instead of a single one. **(2)** (understand) The miRNAs interfere with mRNAs by targeting them for destruction or preventing them from being translated.

p. 362 CYU (1) (understand) Many different types of mutations can disrupt control of the cell cycle and initiate cancer. These mutations can affect any of the six levels of control over gene regulation outlined in Figure 19.1. **(2)** (understand) The p53 protein is responsible for shutting down the cell cycle in cells with damaged DNA. If the protein does not function, then cells with damaged DNA—and thus many mutations—continue to divide. If these cells have mutations in genes that regulate the cell cycle, then they may continue to divide in an uncontrolled fashion.

IF YOU UNDERSTAND . . .

19.1 (understand) Because eukaryotic RNAs are not translated as soon as transcription occurs, it is possible for RNA processing to occur, which creates variation in the mRNAs produced from a primary RNA transcript and in their life spans. **19.2** (understand) The default state of eukaryotic genes is "off," because the highly condensed state of the chromatin makes DNA unavailable to RNA polymerase. **19.3** (understand) See **FIGURE A19.1**. **19.4** (understand) Alternative splicing makes it possible for a single gene to code for multiple products. **19.5** (analyze) One difference is that, in bacteria, genes that need to be turned on together are often clustered together in operons. Eukaryotes do not use operons. A similarity is in the way eukaryotes

FIGURE A19.2

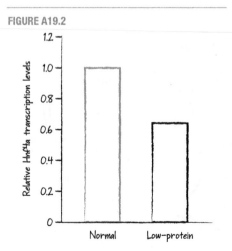

turn on many genes together and the strategy of bacterial regulons. Here, genes that are in many different locations share a DNA regulatory sequence and are activated when a regulatory transcription factor binds to the regulatory sequence. **19.6** (understand) In mutant cells that lack a form of p53 that can bind to enhancers, DNA damage cannot arrest the cell cycle, the cell cannot kill itself, and damaged DNA is replicated. This leads to mutations that can move the cell farther down the road to cancer.

YOU SHOULD BE ABLE TO . . .

✓ Test Your Knowledge

1. (remember) c **2.** (remember) A tumor suppressor is a gene or protein that holds cell division in check unless conditions are right for the cell to divide. **3.** (understand) d **4.** (remember) The set of regulatory transcription factors present in a particular cell, not differences in DNA sequence, are largely responsible for which genes are expressed. **5.** (remember) b **6.** (remember) d

✓ Test Your Understanding

7. (analyze) (a) Enhancers and the *araC* site are similar because both are sites in DNA where regulatory proteins bind. They are different because enhancers generally are located at great distances from the promoter, whereas the *araC* site is located nearer the promoter. (b) Promoter-proximal elements and the *lac* operon operator are both regulatory sites in DNA located close to the promoter. (c) Basal transcription factors and sigma are proteins that must bind to the promoter before RNA polymerase can initiate transcription. They differ because sigma is part of the RNA polymerase holoenzyme, while the basal transcription complex recruits RNA polymerase to the promoter. **8.** (understand) If changes in the environment cause changes in how spliceosomes function, then the RNAs and proteins produced from a particular gene could change in a way that helps the cell cope with the new environmental conditions. **9.** (analyze) (a) Enhancers and silencers are both regulatory sequences located at a distance from the promoter. Enhancers bind regulatory transcription factors that activate transcription; silencers bind regulatory proteins that shut down transcription. (b) Promoter-proximal elements and enhancers are both regulatory sequences that bind positive regulatory transcription factors. Promoter-proximal elements are located close to the promoter; enhancers are far from the promoter. (c) Transcription factors bind to regulatory sites in DNA; mediator does not bind to DNA but instead forms a bridge between regulatory transcription factors and basal transcription factors. **10.** (apply) Inhibition of a histone deacetylase is predicted to leave acetyl groups on histones longer than normal. This is predicted to keep gene transcription going longer than normal, leading to higher levels of particular proteins and a change in the phenotype of the cell. **11.** (analyze) c; this is because there are many more modifications in the histone code relative to the genetic code. **12.** (apply) The cell is predicted to arrest in the cell cycle and most likely will commit suicide through activation of apoptosis genes because of the continually active *p53*.

✓ Test Your Problem-Solving Skills

13. (apply) c; This is because promoters and enhancers are brought into close physical proximity when transcription begins (see Figure 19.8). Since rats of malnourished mothers initiate *Hnf4a* gene transcription infrequently, the promoter and enhancer will be together less often in these animals compared with rats born to well-nourished mothers. **14.** (understand) See **FIGURE A19.2**. The value for the normal diet should be shown as 1.0 and the value for the low-protein diet should be shown as 0.64 (0.64 comes from the ratio of the cpm of the low-protein diet divided by the cpm of the normal diet, or 7368/11,478). **15.** (create) You could treat a culture of

DNA-damaged cells with a drug that stops transcription and then compare them with untreated DNA-damaged cells. If transcriptional control regulates p53 levels, then the p53 level would be lower in the treated cells versus control cells. If control of p53 levels is post-translational, then in both cultures the p53 level would be the same. *Other approaches:* Add labeled NTPs to damaged cells and see if they are incorporated into mRNAs for p53; or add labeled amino acids to damaged cells and see if they are incorporated into completed p53 proteins; or add labeled phosphate groups and see if they are added to p53 proteins. **16.** (create) The double-stranded RNA could be cut by the same enzyme that creates double-stranded miRNAs from miRNA precursors. This double-stranded RNA may be incorporated into RISC and converted into a single-stranded RNA. The single-stranded RNA held by RISC would work in RNA interference to trigger the destruction of the complementary viral mRNA.

BIG PICTURE Genetic Information

p. 366 CYU (1) (remember) Star = DNA, mRNA, proteins. **(2)** (understand) RNA "is reverse transcribed by" reverse transcriptase "to form" DNA. **(3)** (analyze) E = splicing, etc.; E = meiosis and sexual reproduction (along with their links). **(4)** (analyze) Chromatin "makes up" chromosomes; independent assortment and recombination "contribute to" high genetic diversity.

CHAPTER 20

IN-TEXT QUESTIONS AND EXERCISES

p. 372 (understand) Isolate the DNA and cut it into small fragments with EcoRI, which leaves sticky ends. Cut copies of a plasmid or other vector with EcoRI. Mix the fragments and plasmids under conditions that promote complementary base pairing by sticky ends of fragments and plasmids. Use DNA ligase to catalyze formation of phosphodiester bonds and seal the sequences.

p. 372 Fig. 20.4 (apply) No—many times, because many copies of each type of mRNA were present in the pituitary cells, and many pituitary cells were used to prepare the library.

p. 373 (apply) The probe must be single stranded so that it will bind by complementary base pairing to the target DNA, and it must be labeled so that it can be detected. The probe will base-pair only with fragments that include a sequence complementary to the probe's sequence. A probe with the sequence 5′ AATCG 3′ will bind to the region of the target DNA that has the sequence 5′ CGATT 3′ as shown here:

5′ AATCG 3′
3′ TCCGGTTAGCATTACCATTTT 5′

p. 374 CYU (1) (understand) When the endonuclease makes a staggered cut in a palindromic sequence and the strands separate, the single-stranded bases that are left will bind ("stick") to the single-stranded bases left where the endonuclease cut the same palindrome at a different location. **(2)** (understand) The word probe means to examine thoroughly. A DNA probe "examines" a large set of sequences thoroughly and binds to one—the one that has a complementary base sequence.

p. 375 Fig. 20.7 (analyze) The polymerase will begin at the 3′ end of each primer. On the top strand in part (b), it will move to the left; on the bottom strand, it will move to the right. As always, synthesis is in the 5′-to-3′ direction.

p. 376 CYU (1) (understand) Denaturation makes DNA single stranded so the primer can bind to the sequence during the annealing step. Once the primer is in place, *Taq* polymerase can synthesize the rest of the strand during the extension step. It is a "chain reaction" because the products of each reaction cycle are used in the next reaction cycle—this is why the number of copies doubles in each cycle. **(2)** One of many possible answers is shown in **FIGURE A20.1**.

p. 378 CYU If ddNTPs were present at high concentration, they would almost always be incorporated—meaning that only fragments from the first complementary base in the sequence would be produced.

p. 379 Using a map with many markers makes it more likely that there will be one marker that is very tightly linked to the gene of interest—meaning that a form of the marker will almost always be associated with the phenotype you are tracking.

p. 382 CYU Start with a genetic map with as many polymorphic markers as possible. Determine the genotype at these markers for a large number of individuals who have the same type of alcoholism—one that is thought to have a genetic component—as well as a large number of unaffected individuals. Look for particular versions of a marker that is almost always found in affected individuals. Genes that contribute to a predisposition to alcoholism will be near that marker.

p. 383 Fig. 20.11 The insertion will probably disrupt the gene and have serious consequences for the cell and potentially the individual.

IF YOU UNDERSTAND . . .

20.1 Special features of DNA are needed to allow replication in a cell. It is unlikely that any DNA fragment generated by cutting the DNA of one species with a restriction enzyme would replicate when inserted into a bacterial cell. By placing DNA fragments within plasmids that normally replicate in a bacterial cell, the inserted DNA can be replicated along with the plasmid.

20.2 Advantages of cloning in cells: No knowledge of the sequence is required. Disadvantages of cloning in cells: It is slower and technically more difficult than PCR. PCR advantages: It is fast and easy, and it can amplify a DNA sequence that is rare in the sample. PCR disadvantage: It requires knowledge of sequences on either side of the target gene, so primers can be designed.

20.3 The length of each fragment is dictated by where a ddNTP was incorporated into the growing strand, and each ddNTP corresponds to a base on the template strand. Thus the sequence of fragment sizes corresponds to the sequence on the template DNA.

20.4 In this case, both affected and unaffected individuals would have the same marker, so there would be no way to associate a particular form of the marker with the gene and phenotype you are interested in.

20.5 An advantage of using retrovirus vectors is that any foreign genes they carry are integrated into human chromosomes, so delivered genes become a permanent feature of the cell's genome. The concern is that they may integrate at sites that alter gene function in ways that harm cell function, or even worse, lead to cancer. **20.6** Genes can be inserted into the Ti plasmids carried by *Agrobacterium*, and the recombinant plasmids transferred to plant cells infected by the bacterium.

YOU SHOULD BE ABLE TO . . .

✓ Test Your Knowledge

1. They cut DNA at specific sites, known as recognition sites, to produce DNA fragments useful for cloning. **2.** b **3.** ddNTPs lack the −OH (hydroxyl) group on the 3′ carbon of deoxyribose sugar that is required to extend the DNA chain during synthesis. **4.** a **5.** b **6.** d

✓ Test Your Understanding

7. When a restriction endonuclease cuts a "foreign gene" sequence and a plasmid, the same sticky ends are created on the excised foreign gene and the cut plasmid. After the sticky ends on the foreign gene and the plasmid anneal, DNA ligase catalyzes closure of the DNA backbone, sealing the foreign gene into the plasmid DNA (see **FIGURE A20.2**). **8.** If the DNA at each cycle steadily doubles, it is predicted to yield a 33.6 million-fold increase (a 2^{25}-fold increase). **9.** A cDNA library is a collection of complementary DNAs made from all the mRNAs present in a certain group of cells. A cDNA library from a human nerve cell would be different from one made from a human muscle cell, because nerve cells and muscle cells express many different genes that are specific to their cell type. **10.** Genetic markers are genes or other loci that have known locations in the genome. When these locations are diagrammed, they represent the physical relationships between landmarks—in other words, they form a map. **11.** d; these regulatory sequences promote expression of introduced genes in the endosperm—the rice grain eaten as food. **12.** PCR and cellular DNA synthesis are similar in the sense of producing copies of a template DNA. Both rely on primers and DNA polymerase. The major difference between the two is that PCR copies only a specific target sequence, but the entire genome is copied during cellular DNA synthesis.

✓ Test Your Problem-Solving Skills

13. You could use a computer program to identify likely promoter sequences in the sequence data and then look for sequences just downstream that have an AUG start codon and codons that could be part of the protein-coding exons of a potential protein about 500 amino acids (500 codons or 1500 bases) long. **14.** False. Since somatic-cell modifications cannot be passed on to future generations, but germ-line modifications may be passed on to offspring, germ-line modification opens a new set of ethical questions. **15.** In both techniques, researchers use an indicator to identify either a gene of interest or a colony of bacteria with a particular trait. The problem is the same—picking one particular thing (a certain gene or a cell with a particular mutation) out of a large collection. **16.** (a) Primer 1b binds to the top right strand and would allow DNA polymerase to synthesize the top strand across the target gene. Primer 1a, however, binds to the upper left strand and would allow DNA polymerase to synthesize the upper strand *away* from the target gene. Primer 2a binds to the bottom left strand and would allow DNA polymerase to synthesize the bottom strand across the target gene. Primer 2b, however, binds to the bottom right strand and would allow DNA polymerase to synthesize away from the target gene. (b) She could use primer 1b with primer 2a.

FIGURE A20.1

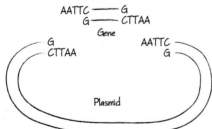

5′ CATGACTATTACGTATCGGGTACTATGCTATCGATCTAGCTACGCTAGCT 3′
3′ GTACTGATAATGCATAGCCCATGATACGATAGCTAGATCGATGCGATCGA 5′

Primer #1, which will anneal to the 3′ end of the top strand:

5′ AGCTAGCGTAGCTAGATCGAT 3′

Primer #2, which will anneal to the 3′ end of the bottom strand:

5′ CATGACTATTACGTATCGGGT 3′

The primers will bind to the separated strands of the parent DNA sequence as follows:

5′ CATGACTATTACGTATCGGGTACTATGCTATCGATCTAGCTACGCTAGCT 3′
                                  3′ TAGCTAGATCGATGCGATCGA 5′

5′ CATGACTATTACGTATCGGGT 3′
3′ GTACTGATAATGCATAGCCCATGATACGATAGCTAGATCGATGCGATCGA 5′

FIGURE A20.2

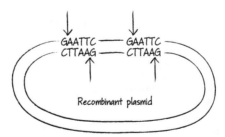

Sticky ends on cut plasmid and gene to be inserted are complementary and can base pair

DNA ligase forms four phosphodiester bonds between gene and plasmid DNA at the points indicated by arrows

CHAPTER 21

IN-TEXT QUESTIONS AND EXERCISES

p. 391 If no overlap occurred, there would be no way of ordering the fragments correctly. You would be able to put fragments only in random order—not the correct order.

p. 391 Fig. 21.2 Shotgun sequencing is based on fragmenting the genome into many small pieces.

p. 393 Fig. 21.3 Because the mRNA codons that match up with each strand are oriented in the 5′-to-3′ direction.

p. 395 CYU (1) Parasites don't need genes that code for enzymes required to synthesize molecules they acquire from their hosts. **(2)** If two closely related

species inherited the same gene from a common ancestor, the genes should be similar. But if one species acquired the same gene from a distantly related species via lateral gene transfer, then the genes should be much less similar. **p. 399 Fig. 21.9** `understand`
Chromosome 1:
ψβ2-ε-Gγ-Aγ-ψβ1-δ-ψβ2-ε-Gγ-Aγ-ψβ1-δ-β
Chromosome 2: β
p. 400 CYU (1) `understand` Eukaryotic genomes have vastly different numbers of transposable elements and other repeated sequences that don't directly contribute to phenotype. So genome size can vary widely without changing the number of coding genes or the complexity of the organism. **(2)** `apply` Because most of the genome is transcribed, this number is very close to the percentage of the genome that codes for exons. In humans, the ratio would be roughly 2%.
p. 401 `understand` Start with a microarray containing exons from a large number of human genes. Isolate mRNAs from brain tissue and liver tissue, and make labeled cDNAs from each. Probe the microarray with cDNA made from each type of tissue, and record where binding occurs. Binding events identify exons that are transcribed in each type of tissue. Compare the results to identify genes that are expressed in brain but not liver, or in liver but not brain.
p. 402 `understand` Cell replication is an emergent property because it is due to the interaction of proteins working in a network, yet is a property that could not be predicted from the analysis of any one of these proteins.

IF YOU UNDERSTAND . . .

21.1 `understand` If a search of human gene sequence databases revealed a gene that was similar in base sequence, and if follow-up work confirmed that the mouse and human genes were similar in their pattern of exons and introns and regulatory sequences, then the researchers could claim that they are homologous. **21.2** `understand` The genome of a parasite is predicted to be smaller and to have fewer genes, particularly for metabolism, than the genome of a nonparasite. **21.3** `understand` These features include variable numbers of transposable elements; noncoding repeated sequences; and noncoding, nonrepetitive DNA. These add to genome size without adding genes that directly influence phenotype. Additionally, mechanisms such as alternative splicing and the possibility of many noncoding regulatory RNAs can create situations in which few protein-coding genes but many different proteins are expressed in intricately regulated ways—features that would increase morphological complexity without increasing gene number. **21.4** `understand` Color-coded clusters shown in Figure 21.13 represent networks of interacting proteins that work together to carry out a particular cellular function. But it's clear from the figure that smaller, clusters are also connected into larger networks.

YOU SHOULD BE ABLE TO . . .

✓ Test Your Knowledge

1. `remember` c **2.** `understand` a **3.** `remember` d **4.** `remember` b **5.** `understand` Finding two or more genes of similar sequence in the genome. **6.** `remember` Having a sequence that is clearly related to a functional gene but with a crippling mutation such as a stop codon or deletion.

✓ Test Your Understanding

7. `analyze` Computer programs are used to scan sequences in both directions to find ATG start codons, a gene-sized logical sequence with recognizable codons, and then a stop codon. One can also look for characteristic promoter, operator, and other regulatory sites. It is more difficult to identify open reading frames in eukaryotes because their genomes are so much larger and because of the presence of introns and repeated sequences.

8. `evaluate` c **9.** `apply` Water flea gene density is about 31,000 genes/200 Mbp = 155 genes/Mbp. In humans, gene density is about 21,000 genes/3000 Mbp = 7 genes/Mbp. The relative gene density of water flea/human = 155/7 = 22. **10.** `analyze` Because with many different alleles, the chance that a match is coincidental is low relative to the chance that they match by identity (they come from the same person). **11.** `understand` A DNA microarray experiment identifies which genes are being expressed in a particular cell at a particular time. If a series of experiments shows that different genes are expressed in cells at different times or under different conditions, it implies that expression was turned on or off in response to changes in age or changes in conditions. **12.** `understand` Homology is a similarity among different species that is due to their inheritance from a common ancestor. If a newly sequenced gene is found to be homologous with a known gene of a different species, it is assumed that the gene products have similar function.

✓ Test Your Problem-Solving Skills

13. `analyze` If "gene A" is not necessary for existence, it can be lost by an event like unequal crossing over (on the chromosome with deleted segments) with no ill effects on the organism. In fact, individuals who have lost unnecessary genes are probably at a competitive advantage, because they no longer have to spend time and energy copying and repairing unused genes. **14.** `apply` If the grave were authentic, it might include two very different parental patterns along with five children whose patterns each represented a mix between the two parents. The other unrelated individuals would have patterns not shared by anyone else in the grave. **15.** `apply` d; mutation of such a central gene is likely to influence the phenotypes associated with all the genes it interacts with. If these interacting genes are involved in many different functions, the effects of mutation of a central gene are likely to be widespread, or pleiotropic. **16.** `apply` You would expect that the livers and blood of chimps and humans would function similarly, but that strong differences occur in brain function. The microarray data support this prediction and suggest chimp and human brains are different because certain genes are turned on or off at different times and expressed in different amounts.

CHAPTER 29

IN-TEXT QUESTIONS AND EXERCISES

p. 529 Fig. 29.1 `analyze` Prokaryotic—it would require just one evolutionary change, the origin of the nuclear envelope in Eukarya. If it were eukaryotic, it would require

that the nuclear envelope was lost in both Bacteria and Archaea—two changes are less parsimonious.
p. 529 Table 29.1 `understand` See **FIGURE A29.2**.
p. 534 Fig. 29.5 `analyze` Weak—different culture conditions may have revealed different species.
p. 535 CYU (1) `create` Conditions should mimic a spill—sand or stones with a layer of crude oil, or seawater with oil floating on top. Add samples, from sites contaminated with oil, that might contain cells capable of using molecules in oil as electron donors or electron acceptors. Other conditions (temperature, pH, etc.) should be realistic. **(2)** `create` Use metagenomic analysis. After isolating DNA from a soil sample, fragment and sequence the DNA. Compare the sequences to those from known organisms and use the data to place the species on the tree of life.
p. 538 `apply` cyanobacteria—photoautotrophs; *Clostridium aceticum*—chemoorganoautotroph; *Nitrosopumilus* sp.—chemolithoautotrophs; helicobacteria— photoheterotrophs; *Escherichia coli*—chemoorganoheterotroph; *Beggitoa*—chemolithotrophic heterotrophs.
p. 539 Fig. 29.10 `apply` Table 29.5 contains the answers. For example, for organisms called sulfate reducers you would have H_2 as the electron donor, SO_4^{2-} as the electron acceptor, and H_2S as the reduced by-product. For humans the electron donor is glucose ($C_6H_{12}O_6$), the electron acceptor is O_2, and the reduced by-product is water (H_2O).
p. 541 `understand` Different species of bacteria that have different forms of bacterial chlorophyll will not absorb the same wavelengths of light and will therefore not compete.
p. 542 Fig. 29.12 `apply` Aerobic respiration. More free energy is released when oxygen is the final electron acceptor than when any other molecule is used, so more ATP can be produced and used for growth.
p. 543 `apply` If bacteria and archaea did not exist, then (1) the atmosphere would have little or no oxygen, and (2) almost all nitrogen would exist in molecular form (the gas N_2).
p. 543 Fig. 29.13 `apply` Add a label for "animals" in the upper right quarter of the circle, and draw arrows leading from "Organic compounds with amino groups" to "animals" and from "animals" to "NH_3."
p. 544 CYU `evaluate` Eukaryotes can only (1) fix carbon via the Calvin–Benson pathway, (2) use aerobic respiration with organic compounds as electron donors, and (3) perform oxygenic photosynthesis. Among bacteria and archaea, there is much more diversity in pathways for carbon fixation, respiration, and photosynthesis, along with many more fermentation pathways.
p. 545a, p. 545b, p. 546a, p. 546b, p. 547 `apply` See **FIGURE A29.1**.

FIGURE A29.1

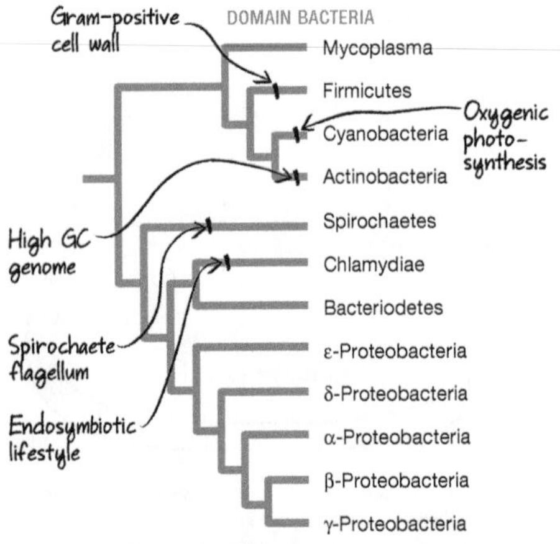

FIGURE A29.2

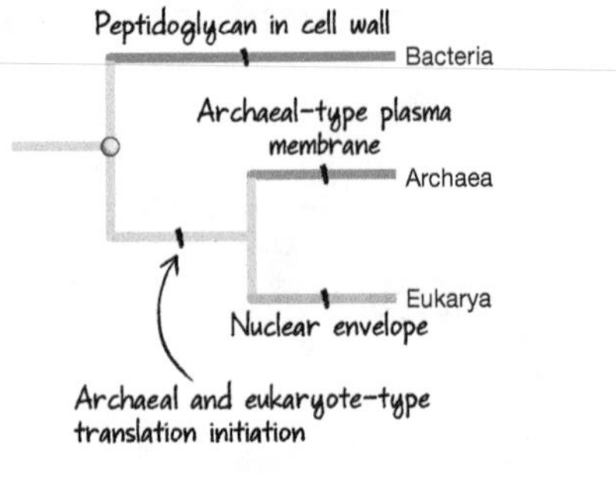

p. 548 Fig. 29.21 (apply) About 600,000 *N. maritimus* cells would fit end to end on a meter stick.

IF YOU UNDERSTAND . . .

29.1 (analyze) Eukaryotes have a nuclear envelope that encloses their chromosomes; bacteria and archaea do not. Bacteria have cell walls that contain peptidoglycan, and archaea have phospholipids containing isoprene subunits in their plasma membranes. Thus, the exteriors of a bacterium and archaeon are radically different. Archaea and eukaryotes also have similar machinery for processing genetic information. **29.2** (apply) After extracting and sequencing DNA from bacteria that live in an insect gut, analyze the resulting sequences for genes that are similar to known genes involved in nitrogen fixation. **29.3** (understand) They are compatible, and thrive in each others' presence—one species' waste product is the other species' food.

YOU SHOULD BE ABLE TO . . .

✓ Test Your Knowledge

1. (understand) c **2.** (remember) b **3.** (remember) d **4.** (remember) d **5.** (remember) False—the enzyme nitrogenase is poisoned by oxygen. **6.** (remember) peptidoglycan

✓ Test Your Understanding

1. (understand) c **2.** (understand) An electron donor provides the potential energy required to produce ATP. **3.** (evaluate) Yes. The array of substances that bacteria and archaea can use as electron donors, electron acceptors, and fermentation substrates, along with the diversity of ways that they can fix carbon and perform photosynthesis, allows them to live just about anywhere. **4.** (apply) They should get energy from reduced organic compounds "stolen" from their hosts. **5.** (understand) Large amounts of potential energy are released and ATP produced when oxygen is the electron acceptor, because oxygen is so electronegative. Large body size and high growth rates are not possible without large amounts of ATP. **6.** (understand) They are paraphyletic because the prokaryotes include some (bacteria and archaea) but not all (eukaryotes) groups derived from the common ancestor of all organisms living today.

✓ Test Your Problem-Solving Skills

1. (understand) c (It is pathogenic on a wide variety of organisms). **2.** (analyze) This result supports their hypothesis because the drug poisons the enzymes of the electron transport chain and prevents electron transfer to Fe^{3+}, which is required to drive magnetite synthesis. If magnetite had still formed, another explanation would have been needed. **3.** (create) Hypothesis: A high rate of tooth cavities in Western children is due to an excess of sucrose in the diet, which is absent from the diets of East African children. To test this hypothesis, switch a group of East African children to a diet that contains sucrose, switch a group of Western children to a diet lacking sucrose, and monitor the presence of *S. mutans* in both groups of children. **4.** (create) Look in waters or soil polluted with benzene-containing compounds. Put samples from these environments in culture tubes where benzene is the only source of carbon. Monitor the cultures and study the cells that grow efficiently.

CHAPTER 30

IN-TEXT QUESTIONS AND EXERCISES

p. 529 CYU (1) (understand) Opisthokonts have a flagellum at the base or back of the cell; alveolate cells contain unique support structures called alveoli; stramenopiles—meaning "straw hairs"—have straw-like hairs on their flagella. **(2)** (understand) In direct sequencing, DNA is isolated directly from the environment and analyzed to place species on the tree of life. It is not necessary to actually see the species being studied. **p. 557 CYU (1)** (understand) *Plasmodium* species are transmitted to humans by mosquitoes. If mosquitoes can be prevented from biting people, they cannot spread the disease. **(2)** (apply) Iron added → primary producers (photosynthetic protists and bacteria) bloom → more carbon dioxide taken up from atmosphere during photosynthesis → consumers bloom, eat primary producers → bodies of primary producers and consumers fall to bottom of ocean → large deposits of carbon-containing compounds form on ocean floor. **p. 560** (apply) See FIGURE A30.1. **p. 560 Fig. 30.8** (analyze) Two—one derived from the original bacterium and one derived from the eukaryotic cell that engulfed the bacterium. **p. 561** (apply) A photosynthetic bacterium (e.g., a cyanobacterium) could have been engulfed by a larger eukaryotic cell. If it was not digested, it could continue to photosynthesize and supply sugars to the host cell. **p. 562** (apply) Membrane infoldings observed in bacterial species today support the hypothesis's plausibility—they confirm that the initial steps actually could have happened. The continuity of the nuclear envelope and ER are consistent with the hypothesis, which predicts that the two structures are derived from the same source (infolded membranes). **p. 564** (apply) The chloroplast genes label should come off of the branch that leads to cyanobacteria. (If you had a phylogeny of just the cyanobacteria, the chloroplast branch would be located somewhere inside.) **p. 565** (analyze) The acquisition of the mitochondrion and the chloroplast represent the transfer of entire genomes, and not just single genes, to a new organism. **p. 566** (apply) Yes—when food is scarce or population density is high, the environment is changing rapidly (deteriorating). Offspring that are genetically unlike their parents may be better able to cope with the new and challenging environment. **p. 569a** (understand) (1) Alternation of generations refers to a life cycle in which there are multicellular haploid phases and multicellular diploid phases. A gametophyte is the multicellular haploid phase that produces gametes; the sporophyte is the multicellular diploid phase that produces spores. A spore is a cell that grows into a multicellular individual but is not produced by fusion of two cells. A zygote is a cell that grows into a multicellular individual but *is* produced by fusion of two cells (gametes). Gametes are haploid cells that fuse to form a zygote. (2) See FIGURE A30.2. **p. 569b** (apply) Most likely, the two types of amoebae evolved independently. The alternative hypothesis is that the common ancestor of alveolates, stramenopiles, rhizarians, plants, opisthokonts, and amoebozoa were amoeboid and that this growth form was lost many times. See FIGURE A30.1. **p. 569c, p. 569d, p. 569e, p. 570a, p. 570b, p. 570c** (apply) See FIGURE A30.1. **p. 571** (analyze) If euglenids could take in food via phagocytosis (ingestive feeding), then that would have provided a mechanism by which a smaller photosynthetic protist could have been engulfed and incorporated into the cell via secondary endosymbiosis. **p. 572a, p. 572b, p. 573, p 574.** (apply) See FIGURE A30.1.

IF YOU UNDERSTAND . . .

30.1 (understand) Photosynthetic protists use CO_2 and light to produce sugars and other organic compounds, so they furnish the first or primary source of organic material in an ecosystem. **30.2** (remember) Eukaryotic cells contain many organelles, including a nucleus, endomembrane system, and an extensive cytoskeleton. Most prokaryotic cells contain few or no organelles, and no nucleus or endomembrane system and lack a complex cytoskeleton.

30.3 (understand) (1) Outside membrane was from host eukaryote; inside from engulfed cyanobacterium. (2) From the outside in, the four membranes are derived from the eukaryote that engulfed a chloroplast-containing eukaryote, the plasma membrane of the eukaryote that was engulfed, the outer membrane of the engulfed cell's chloroplast, and the inner membrane of its chloroplast.

YOU SHOULD BE ABLE TO . . .

✓ Test Your Knowledge

1. (understand) b **2.** (remember) b **3.** (remember) a **4.** (remember) b **5.** (remember) False. **6.** (remember) diatoms.

FIGURE A30.1

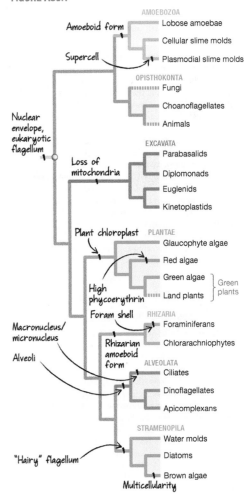

FIGURE A30.2

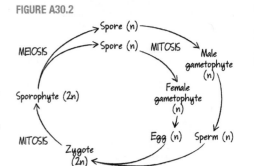

Test Your Understanding

1. (understand) a **2.** (understand) Because all eukaryotes living today have cells with a nuclear envelope, it is valid to infer that their common ancestor also had a nuclear envelope. Because bacteria and archaea do not have a nuclear envelope, it is valid to infer that the trait arose in the common ancestor of eukaryotes. **3.** (understand) The host cell provided a protected environment and carbon compounds for the endosymbiont; the endosymbiont provided increased ATP from the carbon compounds **4.** (understand) It confirmed a fundamental prediction made by the hypothesis and could not be explained by any alternative hypothesis. **5.** (understand) All alveolates have alveoli, which are unique structures that function in supporting the cell. Among alveolates there are species that are (1) ingestive feeders, photosynthetic, or parasitic, and that (2) move using cilia, flagella, or a type of amoeboid movement.

Test Your Problem-Solving Skills

1. (analyze) d **2.** (analyze) If the apicoplast that is found in *Plasmodium* (the organism that causes malaria) is genetically similar to chloroplasts, and if glyphosate poisons chloroplasts, it is reasonable to hypothesize that glyphosate will poison the apicoplast and potentially kill the *Plasmodium.* This would be a good treatment strategy for malaria because humans have no chloroplasts, provided that the glyphosate produces no other effects that would be detrimental to humans. **3.** (evaluate) Primary producers usually grow faster when CO_2 concentration increases, but to date they have not grown fast enough to make CO_2 levels drop—CO_2 levels have been increasing steadily over decades. **4.** (analyze) Given that lateral gene transfer can occur at different points in a phylogenetic history, specific genes can become part of a lineage by a different route from that taken by other genes of the organism. In the case of chlorophyll *a*, its history traces back to a bacterium being engulfed by a protist and forming a chloroplast.

CHAPTER 36

IN-TEXT QUESTIONS AND EXERCISES

p. 717 Fig. 36.7 (apply) Starting with 1 virion, approximately 80 virions were produced after 40 minutes. If all of these virions infected new cells, you expect each of the 80 infected cells to produce 80 virions by 90 minutes, or a total of 6400 virions. The cells appear to replicate once every 30 minutes, which means that they will have replicated 3 times during this period. The total number of cells at 90 minutes would be approximately 2^3, or 8 cells. There would be 800 times as many virions as cells.

p. 717 Fig. 36.8 (analyze) No—it only shows that CD4 is required. (Subsequent work showed that other proteins are involved as well.)

p. 721 (analyze) In T4, the viral genome is injected into the host while HIV inserts its genome via membrane fusion. HIV must first convert its genome into double-stranded DNA before replication, which is not necessary for T4, which has a DNA genome. Both viruses use double-stranded DNA to make mRNA that is translated into viral proteins. T4 virions are made in the cytosol of the cell and are released when the cell bursts. HIV virions bud from the cell surface, which does not require cell death.

p. 721 Fig. 36.12 (create) Budding may disrupt the integrity of the host-cell plasma membrane enough to kill the cell.

p. 722 CYU (analyze) Like cars in the assembly line of an automobile plant, new virions are assembled from premanufactured parts, and large numbers of progeny are produced per generation. Cells, on the other hand, reproduce by the division of a single integrated unit, resulting in only two progeny per generation.

p. 724 Fig. 36.15 (apply) You should have the following bars and labels: on branch to HIV-2 (sooty mangabey to human); on branch to HIV-1 strain O (chimp to human); on branch to HIV-1 strain N (chimp to human); on branch to HIV-1 strain M (chimp to human).

p. 725 CYU (1) (apply) The escaped-genes and degenerate-cell hypotheses state that viruses originated from cells, while the RNA-world hypothesis suggests that viruses originated in parallel with, maybe even influenced, the origin of cells. The escaped-gene and RNA-world hypotheses state that the viruses originated from parasitic molecules. The degenerate-cell hypothesis states that viruses originated from parasitic organisms. **(2)** (apply) A mutation that made transmission between humans more efficient would make it more dangerous. Such mutation could occur via genomic reassortment in pigs, where an avian virus and a human virus could co-infect cells and produce recombinants.

IF YOU UNDERSTAND . . .

36.1 (understand) HIV infects helper T cells. These cells play a central role in the human immune response. As latently infected cells are activated by the immune response, HIV replication causes cell death. Over several years, steady decline in helper T cells leads to a compromised immune response that allows other infections to eventually kill the infected person. **36.2** (understand) (1) Fusion inhibitors block viral envelope proteins or host cell receptors. (2) Protease inhibitors prevent processing/assembly of viral proteins. (3) Reverse transcriptase inhibitors block reverse transcriptase, preventing replication of the genome. **36.3** (apply) There is heritable variation among virions, due to random changes that occur as their genomes are copied. There is also differential reproductive success among virions in their ability to successfully infect host cells. This differential success is due to the presence of certain heritable traits. **36.4** (analyze) Both classes have positive-sense single-stranded RNA genomes. Class IV viruses use an RNA replicase to make a negative-sense copy of the genome, which is then used as a template for producing mRNA and genomic RNAs. Class VI viruses use reverse transcriptase to convert their RNA genome into dsDNA, which is then integrated into the host genome. There it serves as a template to for transcribing viral mRNA and genomic RNAs by host-cell RNA polymerase.

YOU SHOULD BE ABLE TO . . .

Test Your Knowledge

1. (remember) d **2.** (remember) b **3.** (understand) In class VI and VII viruses, reverse transcriptase converts positive-sense single-stranded RNA to double-stranded DNA. **4.** (remember) b **5.** (remember) c **6.** (remember) The unique type of genetic material included in the virion (classes I–V) in addition to the manner in which the genome is replicated (compare classes VI and VII with classes IV and I, respectively).

Test Your Understanding

7. (analyze) A virus with an envelope exits host cells by budding. A virus that lacks an envelope exits host cells by lysis (or other mechanisms that don't involve budding). **8.** (analyze) (1) Rate of viral genome replication is much higher via the lytic cycle. In lysogeny, the viral genome can replicate only when the host cell replicates. (2) Only the lytic cycle produces virions. (3) The lytic cycle results in host cell death, while the host cell continues to survive during lysogeny. **9.** (create) Viruses rely on host-cell enzymes to replicate, whereas bacteria do not. Therefore, many drugs designed to disrupt the virus life cycle cannot be used, because they would kill host cells as well. Only viral-specific proteins are good targets for drug design. **10.** (evaluate) Each major hypothesis to explain the origin of viruses is associated with a different type of genome. Escaped genes: single- and double-stranded DNA or possibly single-stranded RNA. Degenerate cells: double-stranded DNA. RNA world: single- or double-stranded RNA. **11.** (understand) The phylogenies of SIVs and HIVs show that the two shared common ancestors, but that SIVs are ancestral to the HIVs. Also, there are plausible mechanisms for SIVs to be transmitted to humans through butchering or contact with pets, but fewer or no plausible mechanisms for HIVs to be transmitted to monkeys or chimps. **12.** (apply) a; the single-stranded positive-sense RNA genome of this virus can serve as an mRNA to produce viral proteins, while all of the other possibilities require viral enzymes to transcribe the genome into mRNA.

Test Your Problem-Solving Skills

13. (create) Culture the *Staphylococcus* strain outside the human host and then add the virus to determine whether the virus kills the bacterium efficiently. Then test the virus on cultured human cells to determine whether the virus harms human cells. Then test the virus on monkeys or other animals to determine if it is safe. Finally, you could test the virus on human volunteers. **14.** (evaluate) Prevention is currently the most cost-effective program, but it does not help people who are already infected. Treatment with effective drugs not only prolongs lives but also reduces virus loads in infected people, so that they have less chance of infecting others. **15.** (apply) b; by prolonging the infection in this manner, these viruses are more likely to be transmitted to a new host. **16.** (evaluate) Viruses cannot be considered to be alive by the definition given in (1), because viruses are not capable of replicating by themselves. By the definition given in (2), it can be argued that viruses are alive because they store, maintain, replicate, and use genetic information—although they cannot perform all these tasks on their own.

CHAPTER 48

IN-TEXT QUESTIONS AND EXERCISES

p. 974 (understand) The trucks are the Z discs, the ropes are the thin filaments, and the burly weightlifters are the thick filaments.

p. 974 Fig. 48.2 (analyze) The dark band includes thin filaments and a dense concentration of bulbous structures extending from the thick filament; the light band consists of thin filaments only.

p. 977 CYU (1) (understand) In a sarcomere, thick myosin filaments are sandwiched between thin actin filaments. When the heads on myosin contact actin and change conformation, they pull the actin filaments toward one another, shortening the whole sarcomere. **(2)** (apply) Increased acetylcholine release would result in an increased rate of muscle-cell contraction. Preventing conformational changes in troponin would prevent muscle contraction. Blocking the uptake of calcium ions into the sarcoplasmic reticulum would lead to sustained muscle contraction.

p. 980 (apply) The breast meat of pigeons is composed of dark meat because these muscles are specialized for endurance. Their dark color is due to a high concentration of myoglobin.

p. 981 (create) When earthworms shorten their longitudinal muscles, the segment containing these muscles shortens and squeezes the internal fluid, which becomes pressurized and pushes in all directions, expanding the circumference of the segment and pushing laterally against the burrow.

p. 983 CYU (1) (analyze) Exoskeletons are made of chitin, proteins, and other substances like calcium carbonate. Endoskeletons are made of calcium phosphate, calcium carbonate, and proteins. Exoskeletons occur on the outsides of animals, whereas endoskeletons occur on the insides. Both types of skeletons are composed of rigid levers separated by joints such that motions are a result of changes in joint angles. Both types of skeletons attach to skeletal muscle and serve to transmit muscle forces. Hydrostatic skeletons also transmit muscle forces but are made of soft tissues that vary from animal to animal. Shape changes in hydrostatic skeletons occur not from changes in joint angles, but from shape changes of the bodies themselves. **(2)** apply No movement of the arm would occur, because for these antagonistic muscles to produce movement, one of them must be contracted while the other is relaxed.

p. 986 Fig. 48.16 apply Galloping at 3.5 m/s would cost about 75 percent more energy.

p. 987 Fig. 48.18 apply About 10 times more costly.

IF YOU UNDERSTAND . . .

48.1 apply Paralysis, because acetylcholine has to bind to its receptors on the membrane of postsynaptic muscle fibers for action potentials to propagate in the muscle and cause contraction. **48.2** analyze Skeletal muscle is multinucleate, unbranched, striated, and voluntary. Cardiac muscle is branched, striated, and involuntary. Smooth muscle is smooth and involuntary. **48.3** analyze When muscles contract in hydrostatic skeletons, the body deforms by becoming longer and thinner, or shorter and narrower, or by bending side to side. In vertebrates and arthropods, muscle contractions cause changes in the joint angles between rigid segments rather than shape changes in the segments themselves. **48.4** understand On land, an animal is constrained by its weight; larger animals cannot move as freely and are in greater danger of breaking than are smaller animals. In water, animals are constrained by their shapes. Some shapes would cause high drag, which would inhibit locomotion. In air, animals are constrained by their weight. Larger animals must create more lift to overcome gravity.

YOU SHOULD BE ABLE TO . . .

✓ Test Your Knowledge

1. remember a **2.** remember c **3.** understand d **4.** remember True **5.** understand a **6.** understand False.

✓ Test Your Understanding

7. create The key observation was that the banding pattern of sarcomeres changed during contraction. Even though the entire unit became shorter, only some portions moved relative to each other. This observation suggested that some portions of the structure slid past other portions. Muscle fibers have to have many mitochondria because large amounts of ATP are needed to power myosin heads to move along actin filaments; large amounts of calcium stored in smooth ER are needed to initiate contraction by binding to troponin. **8.** apply c **9.** analyze Acetylcholine reduces the rate and force of contraction of cardiac muscle, whereas it stimulates skeletal muscle to contract. **10.** create ATP is no longer produced after death, so calcium cannot be actively transported from the cytosol into the sarcoplasmic reticulum to enable the binding of myosin and actin. The proteins do not unbind, because this process requires ATP. **11.** apply The oxygen consumption of the runner would increase because the arches of his or her feet would no longer store as much elastic energy, which normally reduces the energetic cost of running. **12.** create Because diverse animals experience the same physical constraints where they live, natural selection favors the same kind of adaptations to those constraints, resulting in convergent evolution. For example,

dolphins and ichthyosaurs are distantly related but have a similar body shape due to their similar ability to swim rapidly through water.

✓ Test Your Problem-Solving Skills

13. apply In cardiac muscle, the binding of acetylcholine to its receptors causes the heart rate to slow. Ingestion of nightshade would increase heart rate because it blocks acetylcholine receptors. **14.** apply If the sarcomere is in a stretched state before stimulation, the initial force production would be reduced because less overlap would occur between actin and myosin; thus, fewer myosin heads could engage in the pull. **15.** c:

$$0.5 = v^2/(9.8 \text{ m/s}^2 \times 0.9 \text{ m})$$
$$0.5 = v^2/8.8 \text{ m}^2/\text{s}^2$$
$$v^2 = 0.5 \times 8.8 \text{ m}^2/\text{s}^2$$
$$v = \text{square root of } 4.4 \text{ m}^2/\text{s}^2$$
$$v = 2.1 \text{ m/s}$$

16. evaluate The bones of *T. rex* are available and can be analyzed to determine their structural properties, such as the mechanical advantage of the leg joints and the ability of the bones to withstand the different forces that the skeleton would experience at different speeds based on data from living animals. A very close estimate could be made, but the exact speed would be hard to determine without observing the dinosaur in action, since behavior affects speed.

Bioskills

BIOSKILLS 1; p. B:2 CYU (1) apply 3.1 miles **(2)** apply 37°C **(3)** apply Multiply your weight in pounds by 1/2.2 (0.45). **(4)** apply 4 **(5)** apply 4 **(6)** Two significant figures. When you multiply, the answer can have no more significant figures than the least accurate measurement—in this case, 1.6.

BIOSKILLS 2; p. B:3 CYU (1) apply "different-yoked-together" **(2)** apply "sugary-loosened" **(3)** apply "study-of-form" **(4)** apply "three-bodies"

BIOSKILLS 3; p. B:6 CYU (1) apply about 18% **(2)** apply a dramatic drop (almost 10%) **(3)** understand No—the order of presentation in a bar chart does not matter (though it's convenient to arrange the bars in a way that reinforces the overall message). **(4)** apply 11 **(5)** apply 68 inches

BIOSKILLS 4; p. B:7 CYU apply Test 2, the estimate based on the larger sample—the more replicates or observations you have, the more precise your estimate of the average should be.

BIOSKILLS 5; p. B:8 CYU (1) apply $1/2 \times 1/2 \times 1/2 \times 1/2 = 1/16$ **(2)** apply $1/6 + 1/6 + 1/6 = 1/2$

BIOSKILLS 6; p. B:9 CYU (1) understand exponential **(2)** apply $\ln N_t = \ln N_0 + rt$

BIOSKILLS 7; p. B:9 Fig. B7.1. analyze See **FIGURE BA.1**. **p. B:10 Fig. B7.2.** analyze See **FIGURE BA.2**. **p. B:11 Fig. B7.3.** analyze Figure B7.3d is different.

BIOSKILLS 8; p. B:12 Fig. B8.1. apply See **FIGURE BA.3**.

BIOSKILLS 9; p. B:13 Fig. B9.1 understand DNA and RNA are acids that tend to drop a proton in solution, giving them a negative charge. **p. B:15 CYU** analyze The lane with no band comes from a sample where RNA X is not present. The same size RNA X is present in the next two lanes, but the faint band has very few copies while the dark band has many. In the

fourth lane, the band is formed by a smaller version of RNA X, and relatively few copies are present.

BIOSKILLS 10; p. B:17 CYU (1) understand size and/or density. **(2)** apply Mitochondria, because they are larger in size compared with ribosomes.

BIOSKILLS 11; p. B:19 CYU (1) analyze No—it's just that no mitochondria happened to be present in this section sliced through the cell. **(2)** explain Understanding a molecule's structure is often critical to understanding how it functions in cells.

BIOSKILLS 12; p. B:21 CYU (1) analyze It may not be clear that the results are relevant to noncancerous cells that are not growing in cell culture—that is, that the artificial conditions mimic natural conditions.

FIGURE BA.1

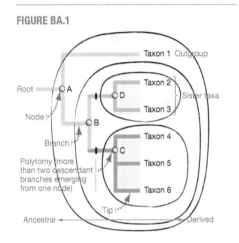

FIGURE BA.2

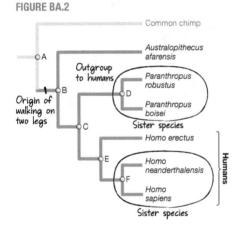

FIGURE BA.3

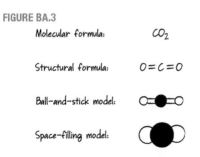

(2) *analyze* It may not be clear that the results are relevant to individuals that developed normally, from an embryo—that is, that the artificial conditions mimic natural conditions.

BIOSKILLS 13; p. B:23 Fig. B13.1 *analyze* This is human body temperature—the natural habitat of *E. coli*.
p. B:24 CYU (1) *analyze* *Caenorhabditis elegans* would be a good possibility, because the cells that normally die have

already been identified. You could find mutant individuals that lacked normal cell death; you could compare the resulting embryos to normal embryos and be able to identify exactly which cells change as a result. **(2)** *analyze* Any of the multicellular organisms in the list would be a candidate, but *Dictyostelium discoideum* might be particularly interesting because cells stick to each other only during certain points in the life cycle. **(3)** *analyze* *Mus musculus*—as the only mammal in the list, it is the

organism most likely to have a gene similar to the one you want to study.

BIOSKILLS 14; p. B:26 CYU *synthesize* Many examples are possible. See Figure 1.9 in Chapter 1, as an example of the format to use for your Research Box.

BIOSKILLS 15; p. B:27 CYU (1) *analyze* See **FIGURE BA.4**.
(2) *analyze* See **FIGURE BA.4**.

FIGURE BA.4

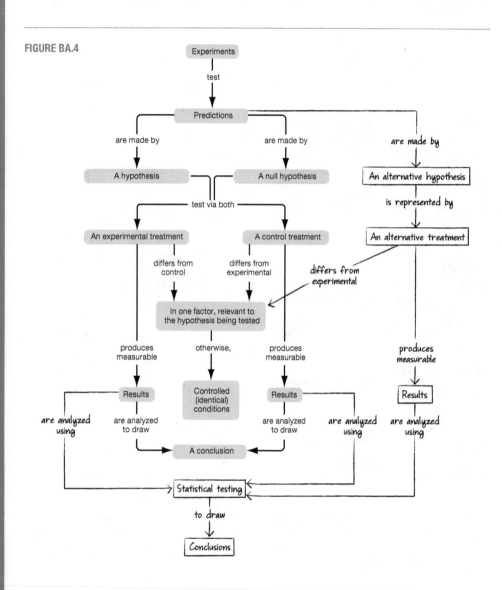

BioSkills

BIOSKILL 1 the metric system and significant figures

Scientists ask questions that can be answered by observing or measuring things—by collecting data. What units are used to make measurements? When measurements are reported, how can you tell how reliable the data are?

The Metric System

The metric system is the system of units of measure used in every country of the world but three (Liberia, Myanmar, and the United States). It is also the basis of the SI system—the International System of Units (abbreviated from the French, *Système international d'unités*)—used in scientific publications.

The popularity of the metric system is based on its consistency and ease of use. These attributes, in turn, arise from the system's use of the base 10. For example, each unit of length in the system is related to all other measures of length in the system by a multiple of 10. There are 10 millimeters in a centimeter; 100 centimeters in a meter; 1000 meters in a kilometer.

Measures of length in the English system, in contrast, do not relate to each other in a regular way. Inches are routinely divided into 16ths; there are 12 inches in a foot; 3 feet in a yard; 5280 feet (or 1760 yards) in a mile.

If you have grown up in the United States and are accustomed to using the English system, it is extremely important to begin developing a working familiarity with metric units and values. **Tables B1.1** and **B1.2** (see B:2) should help you get started with this process.

As an example, consider the following question: An American football field is 120 yards long, while rugby fields are 144 meters

TABLE B1.1 **Metric System Units and Conversions**

Measurement	Unit of Measurement and Abbreviation	Metric System Equivalent	Converting Metric Units to English Units
Length	kilometer (km)	1 km = 1000 m = 10^3 m	1 km = 0.62 mile
	meter (m)	1 m = 100 cm	1 m = 1.09 yards = 3.28 feet = 39.37 inches
	centimeter (cm)	1 cm = 0.01 m = 10^{-2} m	1 cm = 0.3937 inch
	millimeter (mm)	1 mm = 0.001 m = 10^{-3} m	1 mm = 0.039 inch
	micrometer (µm)	1 µm = 10^{-6} m = 10^{-3} mm	
	nanometer (nm)	1 nm = 10^{-9} m = 10^{-3} µm	
Area	hectare (ha)	1 ha = 10,000 m^2	1 ha = 2.47 acres
	square meter (m^2)	1 m^2 = 10,000 cm^2	1 m^2 = 1.196 square yards
	square centimeter (cm^2)	1 cm^2 = 100 mm^2 = 10^{-4} m^2	1 cm^2 = 0.155 square inch
Volume	liter (L)	1 L = 1000 mL	1 L = 1.06 quarts
	milliliter (mL)	1 mL = 1000 µL = 10^{-3} L	1 mL = 0.034 fluid ounce
	microliter (µL)	1 µL = 10^{-6} L	
Mass	kilogram (kg)	1 kg = 1000 g	1 kg = 2.20 pounds
	gram (g)	1 g = 1000 mg	1 g = 0.035 ounce
	milligram (mg)	1 mg = 1000 µg = 10^{-3} g	
	microgram (µg)	1 µg = 10^{-6} g	
Temperature	Kelvin (K)*		K = °C + 273.15
	degrees Celsius (°C)		°C = $\frac{5}{9}$ (°F − 32)
	degrees Fahrenheit (°F)		°F = $\frac{9}{5}$°C + 32

*Absolute zero is −273.15 °C = 0 K.

TABLE B1.2 Prefixes Used in the Metric System

Prefix	Abbreviation	Definition
nano–	n	$0.000\ 000\ 001 = 10^{-9}$
micro–	μ	$0.000\ 001 = 10^{-6}$
milli–	m	$0.001 = 10^{-3}$
centi–	c	$0.01 = 10^{-2}$
deci–	d	$0.1 = 10^{-1}$
–	–	$1 = 10^{0}$
kilo–	k	$1000 = 10^{3}$
mega-	M	$1\ 000\ 000 = 10^{6}$
giga-	G	$1\ 000\ 000\ 000 = 10^{9}$

long. In yards, how much longer is a rugby field than an American football field? To solve this problem, first convert meters to yards: 144 m × 1.09 yards/m = 157 yards (note that the unit "m" cancels out). The difference in yards is thus: 157 – 120 = 37 yards. If you did these calculations on a calculator, you might have come up with 36.96 yards. Why has the number of yards been rounded off? The answer lies in significant figures. Let's take a closer look.

Significant Figures

Significant figures or "sig figs"—the number of digits used to report the measurement—are critical when reporting scientific data. The number of significant figures in a measurement, such as 3.524, is the number of digits that are known with some degree of confidence (3, 5, and 2) plus the last digit (4), which is an estimate or approximation. How do scientists know how many digits to report?

Rules for Working with Significant Figures

The rules for counting significant figures are summarized here:

- All nonzero numbers are always significant.
- Leading zeros are never significant; these zeros do nothing but set the decimal point.
- Embedded zeros are always significant.

- Trailing zeros are significant *only* if the decimal point is specified (Hint: Change the number to scientific notation. It is easier to see the "trailing" zeros.)

Table B1.3 provides examples of how to apply these rules. The bottom line is that significant figures indicate the precision of measurements.

Precision versus Accuracy

If biologists count the number of bird eggs in a nest, they report the data as an exact number—say, 3 eggs. But if the same biologists are measuring the diameter of the eggs, the numbers will be inexact. Just how inexact they are depends on the equipment used to make the measurements. For example, if you measure the width of your textbook with a ruler several times, you'll get essentially the same measurement again and again. Precision refers to how closely individual measurements agree with each other. So, you have determined the length with precision, but how do you know if the ruler was accurate to begin with?

Accuracy refers to how closely a measured value agrees with the correct value. You don't know the accuracy of a measuring device unless you calibrate it, by comparing it against a ruler that is known to be accurate. As the sensitivity of equipment used to

check your understanding

If you understand BioSkill 1

✔ You should be able to . . .

1. **QUANTITATIVE** Calculate how many miles a runner completes in a 5.0-kilometer run.

2. **QUANTITATIVE** Calculate your normal body temperature in degrees Celsius (Normal body temperature is 98.6°F.).

3. **QUANTITATIVE** Calculate your current weight in kilograms.

4. **QUANTITATIVE** Calculate how many liters of milk you would need to buy to get approximately the same volume as a gallon of milk.

5. **QUANTITATIVE** Multiply the measurements 2.8723 and 1.6. How many significant figures does your answer have? Why?

TABLE B1.3 Rules for Working with Significant Figures

Example	Number of Significant Figures	Scientific Notation	Rule
35,200	5	3.52×10^{4}	All nonzero numbers are always significant
0.00352	3	3.52×10^{-3}	Leading zeros are not significant
1.035	4	$1.035\ (\times 10^{0})$	Imbedded zeros are always significant
200	1	2×10^{2}	Trailing zeros are significant only if the decimal point is specified
200.0	4	2.000×10^{2}	Trailing zeros are significant only if the decimal point is specified

make a measurement increases, the number of significant figures increases. For example, if you used a kitchen scale to weigh out some sodium chloride, it might be accurate to 3 ± 1 g (1 significant figure); but an analytical balance in the lab might be accurate to 3.524 ± 0.001 g (4 significant figures).

In science, only the numbers that have significance—that are obtained from measurement—are reported. It is important to follow the "sig fig rules" when reporting a measurement, so that data do not appear to be more accurate than the equipment allows.

Combining Measurements

How do you deal with combining measurements with different degrees of accuracy and precision? The simple rule to follow is that the accuracy of the final answer can be no greater than the least accurate measurement. So, when you multiply or divide measurements, the answer can have no more significant figures than the least accurate measurement. When you add or subtract measurements, the answer can have no more decimal places than the least accurate measurement.

As an example, consider that you are adding the following measurements: 5.9522, 2.065, and 1.06. If you plug these numbers into your calculator, the answer your calculator will give you is 9.0772. However, this is incorrect—you must round your answer off to the nearest value, 9.08, to the least number of decimal places in your data.

It is important to nail down the concept of significant figures and to practice working with metric units and values. The Check Your Understanding questions in this BioSkill should help you get started with this process.

BIOSKILL 2 — some common Latin and Greek roots used in biology

Greek or Latin Root	English Translation	Example Term
a, an	not	anaerobic
aero	air	aerobic
allo	other	allopatric
amphi	on both sides	amphipathic
anti	against	antibody
auto	self	autotroph
bi	two	bilateral symmetry
bio	life, living	bioinformatics
blast	bud, sprout	blastula
co	with	cofactor
cyto	cell	cytoplasm
di	two	diploid
ecto	outer	ectoparasite
endo	inner, within	endoparasite
epi	outer, upon	epidermis
exo	outside	exothermic
glyco	sugary	glycolysis
hetero	different	heterozygous
homo	alike	homozygous
hydro	water	hydrolysis
hyper	over, more than	hypertonic
hypo	under, less than	hypotonic
inter	between	interspecific
intra	within	intraspecific
iso	same	isotonic
logo, logy	study of	morphology
lyse, lysis	loosen, burst	glycolysis
macro	large	macromolecule

Greek or Latin Root	English Translation	Example Term
meta	change, turning point	metamorphosis
micro	small	microfilament
morph	form	morphology
oligo	few	oligopeptide
para	beside	parathyroid gland
photo	light	photosynthesis
poly	many	polymer
soma	body	somatic cells
sym, syn	together	symbiotic, synapsis
trans	across	translation
tri	three	trisomy
zygo	yoked together	zygote

check your understanding

 C Y U

If you understand BioSkill 2

✔ **You should be able to . . .**

Provide literal translations of the following terms:

1. heterozygote
2. glycolysis
3. morphology
4. trisomy

Graphs are the most common way to report data, for a simple reason. Compared to reading raw numerical values in a table or list, a graph makes it much easier to understand what the data mean.

Learning how to read and interpret graphs is one of the most basic skills you'll need to acquire as a biology student. As when learning piano or soccer or anything else, you need to understand a few key ideas to get started and then have a chance to practice—a lot—with some guidance and feedback.

Getting Started

To start reading a graph, you need to do three things: read the axes, figure out what the data points represent—that is, where they came from—and think about the overall message of the data. Let's consider each step in turn.

What Do the Axes Represent?

Graphs have two axes: one horizontal and one vertical. The horizontal axis of a graph is also called the *x*-axis or the abscissa. The vertical axis of a graph is also called the *y*-axis or the ordinate. Each axis represents a variable that takes on a range of values. These values are indicated by the ticks and labels on the axis. Note that each axis should *always* be clearly labeled with the unit or treatment it represents.

FIGURE B3.1 shows a scatterplot—a type of graph where continuous data are graphed on each axis. Continuous data can take an array of values over a range. In contrast, discrete data can take only a restricted set of values. If you were graphing the average height of men and women in your class, height is a continuous variable, but gender is a discrete variable.

For the example in this figure, the *x*-axis represents time in units of generations of maize; the *y*-axis represents the average percentage of the dry weight of a maize kernel that is protein.

To create a graph, researchers plot the independent variable on the *x*-axis and the dependent variable on the *y*-axis (Figure B3.1a). The terms independent and dependent are used because the values on the *y*-axis depend on the *x*-axis values. In our example, the researchers wanted to show how the protein content of maize kernels in a study population changed over time. Thus, the protein concentration plotted on the *y*-axis depended on the year (generation) plotted on the *x*-axis. The value on the *y*-axis always depends on the value on the *x*-axis, but not vice versa.

In many graphs in biology, the independent variable is either time or the various treatments used in an experiment. In these cases, the *y*-axis records how some quantity changes as a function of time or as the outcome of the treatments applied to the experimental cells or organisms.

(a) Read the axes—what is being plotted?

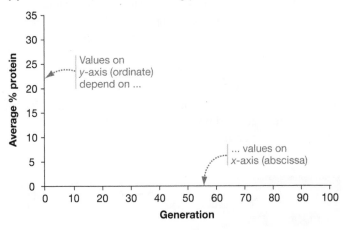

(b) Look at the bars or data points—what do they represent?

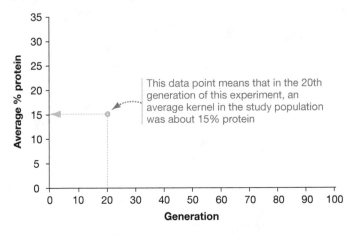

(c) What's the punchline?

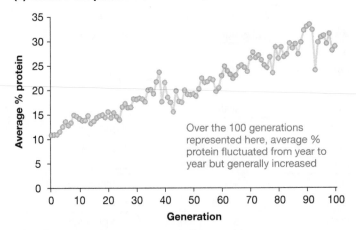

FIGURE B3.1 **Scatterplots Are Used to Graph Continuous Data.**

What Do the Data Points Represent?

Once you've read the axes, you need to figure out what each data point is. In our maize kernel example, the data point in Figure B3.1b represents the average percentage of protein found in a sample of kernels from a study population in a particular generation.

If it's difficult to figure out what the data points are, ask yourself where they came from—meaning, how the researchers got them. You can do this by understanding how the study was done and by understanding what is being plotted on each axis. The *y*-axis will tell you what they measured; the *x*-axis will usually tell you when they measured it or what group was measured. In some cases—for example, in a plot of average body size versus average brain size in primates—the *x*-axis will report a second variable that was measured.

In other cases, a data point on a graph may represent a relative or arbitrary unit of measurement. The data point shows the ratio of the amount of a substance, intensity, or other quantities, relative to a predetermined reference measurement. For example, the *y*-axis might show the percentage of relative activity of an enzyme—the rate of the enzyme-catalyzed reaction, scaled to the highest rate of activity observed (100 percent)—in experiments conducted under conditions that are identical except for one variable, such as pH or temperature (see Figure 8.14).

What Is the Overall Trend or Message?

Look at the data as a whole, and figure out what they mean. Figure B3.1c suggests an interpretation of the maize kernel example. If the graph shows how some quantity changes over time, ask yourself if that quantity is increasing, decreasing, fluctuating up and down, or staying the same. Then ask whether the pattern is the same over time or whether it changes over time.

When you're interpreting a graph, it's extremely important to limit your conclusions to the data presented. Don't extrapolate beyond the data, unless you are explicitly making a prediction based on the assumption that present trends will continue. For example, you can't say that the average percentage of protein content was increasing in the population before the experiment started, or that it will continue to increase in the future. You can say only what the data tell you.

Types of Graphs

Many of the graphs in this text are scatterplots like the one shown in Figure B3.1c, where individual data points are plotted. But you will also come across other types of graphs in this text.

Scatterplots, Lines, and Curves

Scatterplots sometimes have data points that are by themselves, but at other times data points will be connected by dot-to-dot lines to help make the overall trend clearer, as in Figure B3.1c, or may have a smooth line through them.

A *smooth line* through data points—sometimes straight, sometimes curved—is a mathematical "line of best fit." A line of best fit represents a mathematical function that summarizes the relationship between the *x* and *y* variables. It is "best" in the sense of fitting the data points most precisely. The line may pass through some of the points, none of the points, or all of the points.

Curved lines often take on characteristic shapes depending on the relationships between the *x* and *y* variable. For example, a bell-shaped curve depicts a normal distribution in which most data points are clumped near the middle, while a sigmoid or S-shaped curve exhibits small changes at first, which then accelerate and approach maximal value over time. Data from studies on population growth, enzyme kinetics (see Chapter 8), and oxygen–hemoglobin dissociation typically fall on a curved line.

Bar Charts, Histograms, and Box-and-Whisker Plots

Scatterplots, or line-of-best-fit graphs, are the most appropriate type of graph when the data have a continuous range of values and you want to show individual data points. But other types of graphs are used to represent different types of distributions:

- *Bar charts* plot data that have discrete or categorical values instead of a continuous range of values. In many cases the bars might represent different treatment groups in an experiment, as in **FIGURE B3.2a** (see B:6). In this graph, the height of the bar indicates the average value. Statistical tests can be used to determine whether a difference between treatment groups is significant (see **BIOSKILLS 4**).

- *Histograms* illustrate frequency data and can be plotted as numbers or percentages. **FIGURE B3.2b** shows an example where height is plotted on the *x*-axis, and the number of students in a population is plotted on the *y*-axis. Each rectangle indicates the number of individuals in each interval of height, which reflects the relative frequency, in this population, of people whose heights are in that interval. The measurements could also be recalculated so that the *y*-axis would report the proportion of people in each interval. Then the sum of all the bars would equal 100 percent. Note that if you were to draw a smooth curve connecting the top of the bars on this histogram, the smooth curve would represent the shape of a bell.

- *Box-and-whisker plots* allow you to easily see where most of the data fall. Each box indicates where half of the data numbers are. The whiskers indicate the lower extreme and the upper extreme of the data. The vertical line inside each box indicates the median—meaning that half of the data are above this value and half are below (see Figure 1.9 for an example).

When you are looking at a bar chart that plots values from different treatments in an experiment, ask yourself if these values are the same or different. If the bar chart reports averages over discrete ranges of values, ask what trend is implied—as you would for a scatterplot.

(a) Bar chart

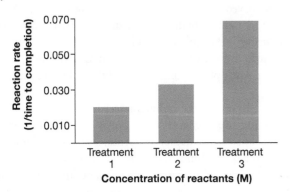

(b) Histogram

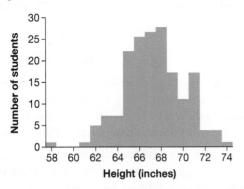

FIGURE B3.2 **Bar Charts and Histograms. (a)** Bar charts are used to graph data that are discontinuous or categorical. **(b)** Histograms show the distribution of frequencies or values in a population.

When you are looking at a histogram, ask whether there is a "hump" in the data—indicating a group of values that are more frequent than others. Is the hump in the center of the distribution of values, toward the left, or toward the right? If so, what does it mean?

Similarly, when you are looking at a box-and-whisker plot, ask yourself what information the graph gives you. What is the range of values for the data? Where are half the data points? Below what value is three quarters of the data?

Getting Practice

Working with this text will give you lots of practice with reading graphs—they appear in almost every chapter. In many cases we've inserted an arrow to represent your instructor's hand at the whiteboard, with a label that suggests an interpretation or draws your attention to an important point on the graph. In other cases, you should be able to figure out what the data mean on your own or with the help of other students or your instructor.

check your understanding

If you understand BioSkill 3

✔ You should be able to . . .

1. **QUANTITATIVE** Determine the total change in average percentage of protein in maize kernels, from the start of the experiment until the end.

2. **QUANTITATIVE** Determine the trend in average percentage of protein in maize kernels between generation 37 and generation 42.

3. Explain whether the conclusions from the bar chart in Figure B3.2a would be different if the data and label for Treatment 3 were put on the far left and the data and label for Treatment 1 on the far right.

4. **QUANTITATIVE** Determine approximately how many students in this class are 70 inches tall, by using Figure B3.2b.

5. **QUANTITATIVE** Determine the most common height in the class graphed in Figure B3.2b.

BIOSKILL 4 using statistical tests and interpreting standard error bars

When biologists do an experiment, they collect data on individuals in a treatment group and a control group, or several such comparison groups. Then they want to know whether the individuals in the two (or more) groups are different. For example, in one experiment student researchers measured how fast a product formed when they set up a reaction with three different concentrations of reactants (introduced in Chapter 8). Each treatment—meaning, each combination of reactant concentrations—was replicated many times.

FIGURE B4.1 graphs the average reaction rate for each of the three treatments in the experiment. Note that Treatments 1, 2, and 3 represent increasing concentrations of reactants. The thin

"I-beams" on each bar indicate the standard error of each average. The standard error is a quantity that indicates the uncertainty in the calculation of an average.

For example, if two trials with the same concentration of reactants had a reaction rate of 0.075 and two trials had a reaction rate of 0.025, then the average reaction rate would be 0.050. In this case, the standard error would be large. But if two trials had a reaction rate of 0.051 and two had a reaction rate of 0.049, the average would still be 0.050, but the standard error would be small.

In effect, the standard error quantifies how confident you are that the average you've calculated is the average you'd observe if

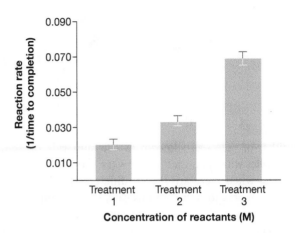

FIGURE B4.1 Standard Error Bars Indicate the Uncertainty in an Average.

you did the experiment under the same conditions an extremely large number of times. It is a measure of precision (see **BIOSKILLS 1**).

Once they had calculated these averages and standard errors, the students wanted to answer a question: Does reaction rate increase when reactant concentration increases?

After looking at the data, you might conclude that the answer is yes. But how could you come to a conclusion like this objectively, instead of subjectively?

The answer is to use a statistical test. This can be thought of as a three-step process.

1. Specify the null hypothesis, which is that reactant concentration has no effect on reaction rate.

2. Calculate a test statistic, which is a number that characterizes the size of the difference among the treatments. In this case, the test statistic compares the actual differences in reaction rates among treatments to the difference predicted by the null hypothesis. The null hypothesis predicts that there should be no difference.

3. The third step is to determine the probability of getting a test statistic at least as large as the one calculated just by chance. The answer comes from a reference distribution—a mathematical function that specifies the probability of getting various values of the test statistic if the null hypothesis is correct. (If you take a statistics course, you'll learn which test

statistics and reference distributions are relevant to different types of data.)

You are very likely to see small differences among treatment groups just by chance—even if no differences actually exist. If you flipped a coin 10 times, for example, you are unlikely to get exactly five heads and five tails, even if the coin is fair. A reference distribution tells you how likely you are to get each of the possible outcomes of the 10 flips if the coin is fair, just by chance.

In this case, the reference distribution indicated that if the null hypothesis of no actual difference in reaction rates is correct, you would see differences at least as large as those observed only 0.01 percent of the time just by chance. By convention, biologists consider a difference among treatment groups to be statistically significant if there is less than a 5 percent probability of observing it just by chance. Based on this convention, the student researchers were able to claim that the null hypothesis is not correct for reactant concentration. According to their data, the reaction they studied really does happen faster when reactant concentration increases.

You'll likely be doing actual statistical tests early in your undergraduate career. To use this text, though, you only need to know what statistical testing does. And you should take care to inspect the standard error bars on graphs in this book. As a *very* rough rule of thumb, averages often turn out to be significantly different, according to an appropriate statistical test, if there is no overlap between two times the standard errors.

check your understanding

If you understand BioSkill 4

✔ **You should be able to . . .**

QUANTITATIVE Determine which of the following tests used to estimate the average height of individuals in a class is likely to have the smallest standard error, and why.

- Measuring the height of two individuals chosen at random to estimate the average.

- Measuring the height of every student who showed up for class on a particular day to estimate the average.

In several cases in this text, you'll need to combine probabilities from different events in order to solve a problem. One of the most common applications is in genetics problems. For example, Punnett squares work because they are based on two fundamental rules of probability. Each rule pertains to a distinct situation.

The Both-And Rule

The both-and rule—also known as the product rule or multiplication rule—applies when you want to know the probability that two or more independent events occur together. Let's use the rolling of two dice as an example. What is the probability of rolling two sixes? These two events are independent, because the probability of rolling a six on one die has no effect on the probability of rolling a six on the other die. (In the same way, the probability of getting a gamete with allele R from one parent has no effect on the probability of getting a gamete with allele R from the other parent. Gametes fuse randomly.)

The probability of rolling a six on the first die is 1/6. The probability of rolling a six on the second die is also 1/6. The probability of rolling a six on *both* dice, then, is $1/6 \times 1/6 = 1/36$. In other words, if you rolled two dice 36 times, on average you would expect to roll two sixes once.

In the case of a cross between two parents heterozygous at the R gene, the probability of getting allele R from the father is 1/2 and the probability of getting R from the mother is 1/2. Thus, the probability of getting both alleles and creating an offspring with genotype RR is $1/2 \times 1/2 = 1/4$.

The Either-Or Rule

The either-or rule—also known as the sum rule or addition rule—applies when you want to know the probability of an event happening when there are several different ways for the same event or outcome to occur. In this case, the probability that the event will occur is the sum of the probabilities of each way that it can occur.

For example, suppose you wanted to know the probability of rolling either a one or a six when you toss a die. The probability of drawing each is 1/6, so the probability of getting one or the other is $1/6 + 1/6 = 1/3$. If you rolled a die three times, on average you'd expect to get a one or a six once.

In the case of a cross between two parents heterozygous at the R gene, the probability of getting an R allele from the father and an r allele from the mother is $1/2 \times 1/2 = 1/4$. Similarly, the probability of getting an r allele from the father and an R allele from the mother is $1/2 \times 1/2 = 1/4$. Thus, the combined probability of getting the Rr genotype in either of the two ways is $1/4 + 1/4 = 1/2$.

check your understanding

If you understand BioSkill 5

✔ **You should be able to . . .**

1. **QUANTITATIVE** Calculate the probability of getting four "tails" if four students each toss a coin.

2. **QUANTITATIVE** Calculate the probability of getting a two, a three, or a six after a single roll of a die.

BIOSKILL 6 using logarithms

You have probably been introduced to logarithms and logarithmic notation in algebra courses, and you will encounter logarithms at several points in this course. Logarithms are a way of working with powers—meaning, numbers that are multiplied by themselves one or more times.

Scientists use exponential notation to represent powers. For example,

$$a^x = y$$

means that if you multiply a by itself x times, you get y. In exponential notation, a is called the base and x is called the exponent. The entire expression is called an exponential function.

What if you know y and a, and you want to know x? This is where logarithms come in. You can solve for exponents using logarithms. For example,

$$x = \log_a y$$

This equation reads, x is equal to the logarithm of y to the base a. Logarithms are a way of working with exponential functions. They are important because so many processes in biology (and chemistry and physics, for that matter) are exponential. To understand what's going on, you have to describe the process with an exponential function and then use logarithms to work with that function.

Although a base can be any number, most scientists use just two bases when they employ logarithmic notation: 10 and e (sometimes called Euler's number after Swiss mathematician Leonhard Euler). What is e? It is a rate of exponential growth shared by many natural processes, where e is the limit of $(1 + \frac{1}{n})^n$ (as n tends to infinity). Mathematicians have shown that the base e is an irrational number (like π) that is approximately equal to 2.718. Like 10, e is just a number; $10^0 = 1$ and, likewise, $e^0 = 1$. But both 10 and e have qualities that make them convenient to use in biology (as well as chemistry and physics).

Logarithms to the base 10 are so common that they are usually symbolized in the form $\log y$ instead of $\log_{10} y$. A logarithm to the base e is called a natural logarithm and is symbolized ln (pronounced *EL-EN*) instead of log. You write "the natural logarithm of y" as $\ln y$.

Most scientific calculators have keys that allow you to solve problems involving base 10 and base e. For example, if you know y, they'll tell you what $\log y$ or $\ln y$ are—meaning that they'll solve for x in our first example equation. They'll also allow you to find a number when you know its logarithm to base 10 or base e. Stated another way, they'll tell you what y is if you know x, and y is equal to e^x or 10^x. This is called taking an antilog. In most cases, you'll use the inverse or second function button on your calculator to find an antilog (above the log or ln key).

To get some practice with your calculator, consider this equation:

$$10^2 = 100$$

If you enter 100 in your calculator and then press the log key, the screen should say 2. The logarithm tells you what the exponent is. Now press the antilog key while 2 is on the screen. The calculator screen should return to 100. The antilog solves the exponential function, given the base and the exponent.

If your background in algebra isn't strong, you'll want to get more practice working with logarithms—you'll see them frequently during your undergraduate career. Remember that once you understand the basic notation, there's nothing mysterious about logarithms. They are simply a way of working with exponential functions, which describe what happens when something is multiplied by itself a number of times—like cells that divide and then divide again and then again.

Using logarithms will also come up when you are studying something that can have a large range of values, like the concentration of hydrogen ions in a solution or the intensity of sound that the human ear can detect. In cases like this, it's convenient to express the numbers involved as exponents. Using exponents makes a large range of numbers smaller and more manageable. For example, instead of saying that hydrogen ion concentration in a solution can range from 1 to 10^{-14}, the pH scale allows you to simply say that it ranges from 1 to 14. Instead of giving the actual value, you're expressing it as an exponent. It just simplifies things.

check your understanding

If you understand BioSkill 6

✔ **You should be able to . . .**

Use the equation $N_t = N_0 e^{rt}$.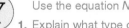

1. Explain what type of function this equation describes.

2. **QUANTITATIVE** Determine how you would write the equation, after taking the natural logarithm of both sides.

Phylogenetic trees show the evolutionary relationships among species, just as a genealogy shows the relationships among people in your family. They are unusual diagrams, however, and it can take practice to interpret them correctly.

To understand how evolutionary trees work, consider **FIGURE B7.1**. Notice that a phylogenetic tree consists of a root (the most ancestral branch in the tree), branches, nodes, and tips.

- Branches represent populations through time. In this text, branches are drawn as horizontal lines. In most cases the length of the branch is arbitrary and has no meaning, but in some cases branch lengths are proportional to time or the extent of genetic difference among populations (if so, there will be a scale at the bottom of the tree). The vertical lines on the tree represent splitting events, where one group broke into two independent groups. Their length is arbitrary—chosen simply to make the tree more readable.

- Nodes (also called forks) occur where an ancestral group splits into two or more descendant groups (see point A in Figure B7.1). Thus, each node represents the most recent common ancestor of the two or more descendant populations that emerge from it. If more than two descendant groups emerge from a node, the node is called a polytomy (see node C). A polytomy usually means that the populations split from one another so quickly that it is not possible to tell which split off earlier or later.

- Tips (also called terminal nodes) are the tree's endpoints, which represent groups living today or a dead end—a branch

ending in extinction. The names at the tips can represent species or larger groups such as mammals or conifers.

Recall that a taxon (plural: taxa) is any named group of organisms (see Chapter 1). A taxon could be a single species, such as *Homo sapiens*, or a large group of species, such as Primates. Tips connected by a single node on a tree are called sister taxa.

The phylogenetic trees used in this text are all rooted. This means that the first, or most basal, node on the tree—the one on the far left in this book—is the most ancient. To determine where the root on a tree occurs, biologists include one or more outgroup species when they are collecting data to estimate a particular phylogeny. An outgroup is a taxonomic group that is known to have diverged before the rest of the taxa in the study. Outgroups are used to establish whether a trait is ancestral or derived. An ancestral trait is a characteristic that existed in an ancestor; a derived trait is a characteristic that is a modified form of the ancestral trait, found in a descendant.

In Figure B7.1, Taxon 1 is an outgroup to the monophyletic group consisting of taxa 2–6. A monophyletic group consists of an ancestral species and all of its descendants. The root of a tree is placed between the outgroup and the monophyletic group being studied. This position in Figure B7.1 is node A. Note that black hash marks are used to indicate a derived trait that is shared among the red branches, and another derived trait that is shared among the orange branches.

Understanding monophyletic groups is fundamental to reading and estimating phylogenetic trees. Monophyletic groups may also be called lineages or clades and can be identified using the "one-snip test": If you cut any branch on a phylogenetic tree, all of the branches and tips that fall off represent a monophyletic group. Using the one-snip test, you should be able to convince yourself that the monophyletic groups on a tree are nested. In Figure B7.1, for example, the monophyletic group comprising node A and taxa 1–6 contains a monophyletic group consisting of node B and taxa 2–6, which includes the monophyletic group represented by node C and taxa 4–6.

To put all these new terms and concepts to work, consider the phylogenetic tree in **FIGURE B7.2**, which shows the relationships between common chimpanzees and six human and humanlike species that lived over the past 5–6 million years. Chimps functioned as an outgroup in the analysis that led to this tree, so the root was placed at node A. The branches marked in red identify a monophyletic group called the hominins.

To practice how to read a tree, put your finger at the tree's root, at the far left, and work your way to the right. At node A, the ancestral population split into two descendant populations. One of these populations eventually evolved into today's chimps; the other gave rise to the six species of hominins pictured. Now

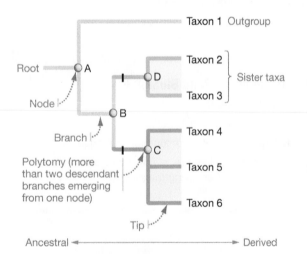

FIGURE B7.1 Phylogenetic Trees Have Roots, Branches, Nodes, and Tips.

✔**EXERCISE** Circle all four monophyletic groups present.

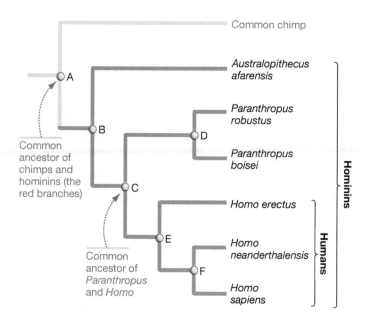

FIGURE B7.2 An Example of a Phylogenetic Tree. A phylogenetic tree showing the relationships of species in the monophyletic group called hominins.

✔**EXERCISE** All of the hominins walked on two legs—unlike chimps and all of the other primates. Add a mark on the phylogeny to show where upright posture evolved, and label it "origin of walking on two legs." Circle and label a pair of sister species. Label an outgroup to the monophyletic group called humans (species in the genus *Homo*).

continue moving your finger toward the tips of the tree until you hit node C. It should make sense to you that at this splitting event, one descendant population eventually gave rise to two *Paranthropus* species, while the other became the ancestor of humans—species in the genus *Homo*. As you study Figure B7.2, consider these two important points:

1. There are many equivalent ways of drawing this tree. For example, this version shows *Homo sapiens* on the bottom. But the tree would be identical if the two branches emerging from node E were rotated 180°, so that the species appeared in the order *Homo sapiens*, *Homo neanderthalensis*, *Homo erectus*. Trees are read from root to tips, not from top to bottom or bottom to top.

2. No species on any tree is any higher or lower than any other. Chimps and *Homo sapiens* have been evolving exactly the same amount of time since their divergence from a common ancestor—neither species is higher or lower than the other. It is legitimate to say that more ancient groups like *Australopithecus afarensis* have traits that are ancestral or more basal—meaning, that appeared earlier in evolution—compared to traits that appear in *Homo sapiens*, which are referred to as more derived.

FIGURE B7.3 presents a chance to test your tree-reading ability. Five of the six trees shown in this diagram are identical in terms of the evolutionary relationships they represent. One differs. The key to understanding the difference is to recognize that the ordering of tips does not matter in a tree—only the ordering of nodes (branch points) matters. You can think of a tree as being like a mobile: The tips can rotate without changing the underlying relationships.

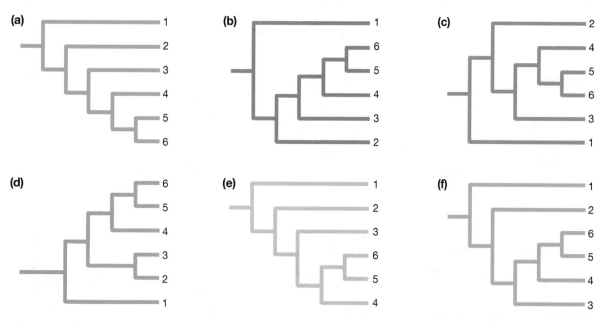

FIGURE B7.3 Alternative Ways of Drawing the Same Tree.

✔**QUESTION** Five of these six trees describe exactly the same relationships among taxa 1 through 6. Identify the tree that is different from the other five.

If you haven't had much chemistry yet, learning basic biological chemistry can be a challenge. One stumbling block is simply being able to read chemical structures efficiently and understand what they mean. This skill will come much easier once you have a little notation under your belt and you understand some basic symbols.

Atoms are the basic building blocks of everything in the universe, just as cells are the basic building blocks of your body. Every atom has a one- or two-letter symbol. **Table B8.1** shows the symbols for most of the atoms you'll encounter in this book. You should memorize these. The table also offers details on how the atoms form bonds as well as how they are represented in some visual models.

When atoms attach to each other by covalent bonding, a molecule forms. Biologists have a couple of different ways of representing molecules—you'll see each of these in the book and in class.

- Molecular formulas like those in **FIGURE B8.1a** simply list the atoms present in a molecule. Subscripts indicate how many of each atom are present. If the formula has no subscript, only one atom of that type is present. A methane (natural gas) molecule, for example, can be written as CH_4. It consists of one carbon atom and four hydrogen atoms.

- Structural formulas like those in **FIGURE B8.1b** show which atoms in the molecule are bonded to each other. Each bond is indicated by a dash. The structural formula for methane in-

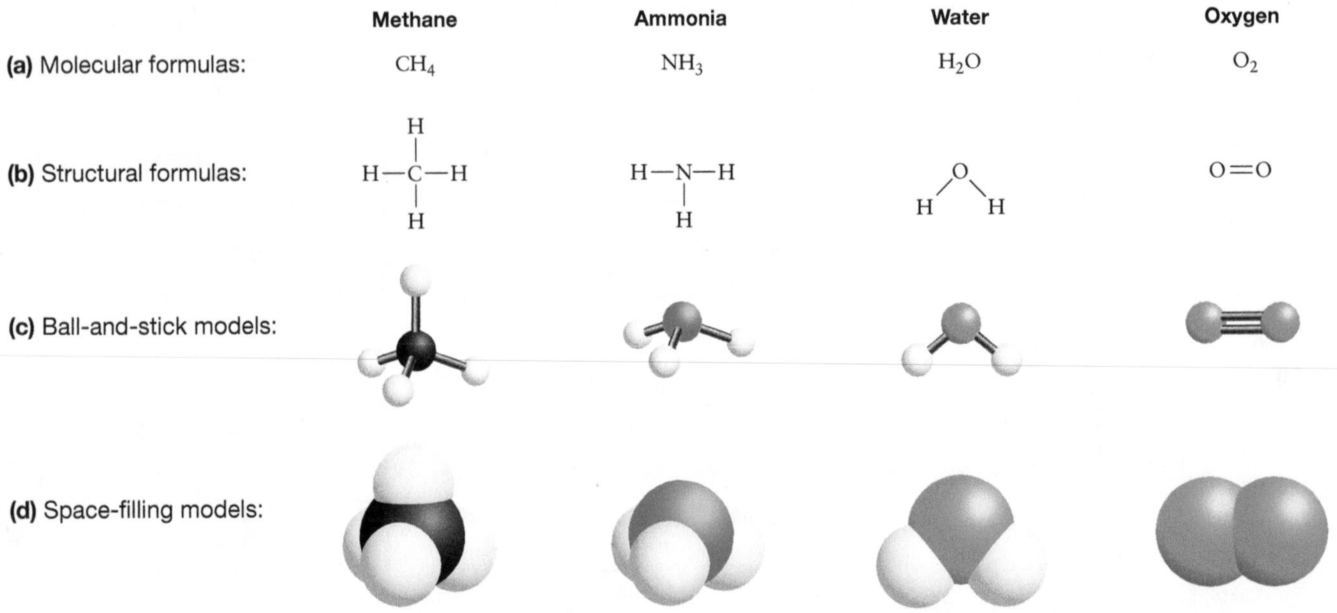

TABLE B8.1 Some Attributes of Atoms Found in Organisms

Atom	Symbol	Number of Bonds It Can Form	Standard Color Code*
Hydrogen	H	1	white
Carbon	C	4	black
Nitrogen	N	3	blue
Oxygen	O	2	red
Sodium	Na	1	—
Magnesium	Mg	2	—
Phosphorus	P	5	orange or purple
Sulfur	S	2	yellow
Chlorine	Cl	1	—
Potassium	K	1	—
Calcium	Ca	2	—

*In ball-and-stick or space-filling models.

	Methane	Ammonia	Water	Oxygen
(a) Molecular formulas:	CH_4	NH_3	H_2O	O_2

FIGURE B8.1 Molecules Can Be Represented in Several Different Ways.

✓**EXERCISE** Carbon dioxide consists of a carbon atom that forms a double bond with each of two oxygen atoms, for a total of four bonds. It is a linear molecule. Write carbon dioxide's molecular formula and then draw its structural formula, a ball-and-stick model, and a space-filling model.

dicates that each of the four hydrogen atoms forms one covalent bond with carbon, and that carbon makes a total of four covalent bonds. Single covalent bonds are symbolized by a single dash; double bonds are indicated by two dashes.

Even simple molecules have distinctive shapes, because different atoms make covalent bonds at different angles. Ball-and-stick and space-filling models show the geometry of the bonds accurately.

- In a ball-and-stick model, a stick is used to represent each covalent bond (see **FIGURE B8.1c**).
- In space-filling models, the atoms are simply stuck onto each other in their proper places (see **FIGURE B8.1d**).

To learn more about a molecule when you look at a chemical structure, ask yourself three questions:

1. *Is the molecule polar—meaning that some parts are more negatively or positively charged than others?* Molecules that contain nitrogen or oxygen atoms are often polar, because these atoms have such high electronegativity (see Chapter 2). This trait is important because polar molecules dissolve in water.

2. *Does the structural formula show atoms that might participate in chemical reactions?* For example, are there charged atoms or amino or carboxyl (−COOH) groups that might act as a base or an acid?

3. *In ball-and-stick and especially space-filling models of large molecules, are there interesting aspects of overall shape?* For example, is there a groove where a protein might bind to DNA, or a cleft where a substrate might undergo a reaction in an enzyme?

BIOSKILLS 9 separating and visualizing molecules

To study a molecule, you have to be able to isolate it. Isolating a molecule is a two-step process: the molecule has to be separated from other molecules in a mixture and then physically picked out or located in a purified form. **BIOSKILLS 9** focuses on the techniques that biologists use to separate nucleic acids and proteins and then find the particular one they are interested in.

Using Electrophoresis to Separate Molecules

In molecular biology, the standard technique for separating proteins and nucleic acids is called gel electrophoresis or, simply, electrophoresis (literally, "electricity-moving"). You may be using electrophoresis in a lab for this course, and you will certainly be analyzing data derived from electrophoresis in this text.

The principle behind electrophoresis is simple. Proteins (when denatured and coated with a special detergent) and nucleic acids carry a charge. As a result, these molecules move when placed in an electric field. Negatively charged molecules move toward the positive electrode; positively charged molecules move toward the negative electrode.

To separate a mixture of macromolecules so that each one can be isolated and analyzed, researchers place the sample in a gelatinous substance. More specifically, the sample is placed in a "well"—a slot in a sheet or slab of the gelatinous substance. The "gel" itself consists of long molecules that form a matrix of fibers. The gelatinous matrix has pores that act like a sieve through which the molecules can pass.

When an electrical field is applied across the gel, the molecules in the well move through the gel toward an electrode. Molecules that are smaller or more highly charged for their size move faster than do larger or less highly charged molecules. As they move, then, the molecules separate by size and by charge. Small and highly charged molecules end up at the bottom of the gel; large, less-charged molecules remain near the top.

An Example "Run"

FIGURE B9.1 (see B:14) shows the electrophoresis setup used in an experiment investigating how RNA molecules polymerize. In this case, the investigators wanted to document how long RNA molecules became over time, when ribonucleoside triphosphates were present in a particular type of solution.

Step 1 shows how they loaded samples of macromolecules, taken on different days during the experiment, into wells at the top of the gel slab. This is a general observation: Each well holds a different sample. In this and many other cases, the researchers also filled a well with a sample containing fragments of known size, called a size standard or "ladder."

In step 2, the researchers immersed the gel in a solution that conducts electricity and applied a voltage across the gel. The molecules in each well started to run down the gel, forming a lane. After several hours of allowing the molecules to move, the researchers removed the electric field (step 3). By then, molecules of different size and charge had separated from one another. In this case, small RNA molecules had reached the bottom of the gel. Above them were larger RNA molecules, which had run more slowly.

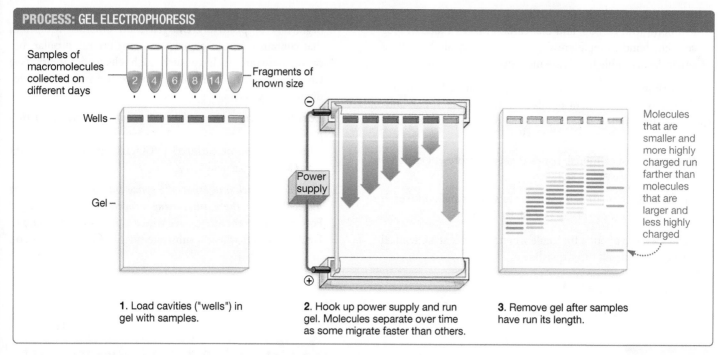

Samples of macromolecules collected on different days

2 4 6 8 14

Fragments of known size

Wells —

Gel —

Power supply

⊖

⊕

Molecules that are smaller and more highly charged run farther than molecules that are larger and less highly charged

1. Load cavities ("wells") in gel with samples.

2. Hook up power supply and run gel. Molecules separate over time as some migrate faster than others.

3. Remove gel after samples have run its length.

FIGURE B9.1 **Macromolecules Can Be Separated via Gel Electrophoresis.**

✓QUESTION DNA and RNA run toward the positive electrode. Why are these molecules negatively charged?

Why Do Separated Molecules Form Bands?

When researchers visualize a particular molecule on a gel, using techniques described in this section, the image that results consists of bands: shallow lines that are as wide as a lane in the gel. Why?

To understand the answer, study **FIGURE B9.2**. The left panel shows the original mixture of molecules. In this cartoon, the size of each dot represents the size of each molecule. The key is to realize that the original sample contains many copies of each specific molecule, and that these copies run down the length of the gel together—meaning, at the same rate—because they have the same size and charge.

It's that simple: Molecules that are alike form a band because they stay together.

Using Thin Layer Chromatography to Separate Molecules

Gel electrophoresis is not the only way to separate molecules. Researchers also use a method called thin layer chromatography. This method was developed in the early 1900s by botanists who were analyzing the different-colored pigments from leaves of a plant, hence the name chromatography from the Greek words khroma for "color" and graphein, "to write."

In this method, rather than loading the sample into the well of a gel, the samples are deposited or "spotted" near the bottom of a stiff support, either glass or plastic, that is coated with a thin layer of silica gel, cellulose, or a similar porous material. The coated support is placed in a solvent solution. As the solvent

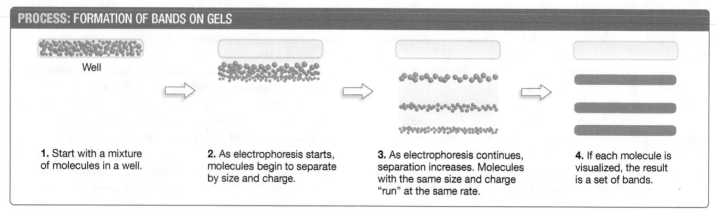

Well

1. Start with a mixture of molecules in a well.

2. As electrophoresis starts, molecules begin to separate by size and charge.

3. As electrophoresis continues, separation increases. Molecules with the same size and charge "run" at the same rate.

4. If each molecule is visualized, the result is a set of bands.

FIGURE B9.2 **On a Gel, Molecules That Are Alike Form Bands.**

wicks upward through the coating by capillary action, it carries the molecules in the mixture with it. Molecules are carried at different rates, based on their size and solubility in the solvent.

Visualizing Molecules

Once molecules have been separated using electrophoresis or thin layer chromatography, they have to be detected. Unfortunately, although plant pigments are colored, proteins and nucleic acids are invisible unless they are tagged in some way. Let's first look at two of the most common tagging systems and then consider how researchers can tag and visualize specific molecules of interest and not others.

Using Radioactive Isotopes and Autoradiography

When molecular biology was getting under way, the first types of tags in common use were radioactive isotopes—forms of atoms that are unstable and release energy in the form of radiation.

In the polymerization experiment diagrammed in Figure B9.1, for example, the researchers had attached a radioactive phosphorus atom to the monomers—ribonucleoside triphosphates—used in the original reaction mix. Once polymers formed, they contained radioactive atoms. When electrophoresis was complete, the investigators visualized the polymers by laying X-ray film over the gel. Because radioactive emissions expose film, a black dot appears wherever a radioactive atom is located in the gel. So many black dots occur so close together that the collection forms a dark band.

This technique for visualizing macromolecules is called autoradiography. The autoradiograph that resulted from the polymerization experiment is shown in **FIGURE B9.3**. The samples, taken on days 2, 4, 6, 8, and 14 of the experiment, are noted along the bottom. The far right lane contains macromolecules of known size; this lane is used to estimate the size of the molecules in the experimental samples. The bands that appear in each sample lane represent the different polymers that had formed.

Reading a Gel

One of the keys to interpreting or "reading" a gel, or the corresponding autoradiograph, is to realize that darker bands contain more radioactive markers, indicating the presence of many radioactive molecules. Lighter bands contain fewer molecules.

To read a gel, then, you look for (1) the presence or absence of bands in some lanes—meaning, some experimental samples—versus others, and (2) contrasts in the darkness of the bands—meaning, differences in the number of molecules present.

For example, several conclusions can be drawn from the data in Figure B9.3. First, a variety of polymers formed at each stage. After the second day, for example, polymers from 12 to 18 monomers long had formed. Second, the overall length of polymers produced increased with time. At the end of the fourteenth day, most of the RNA molecules were between 20 and 40 monomers long.

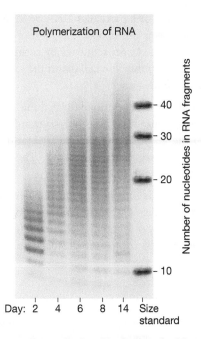

FIGURE B9.3 Autoradiography Is a Technique for Visualizing Macromolecules. The molecules in a gel can be visualized in a number of ways. In this case, the RNA molecules in the gel exposed an X-ray film because they had radioactive atoms attached. When developed, the film is called an autoradiograph.

Starting in the late 1990s and early 2000s, it became much more common to tag nucleic acids with fluorescent tags. Once electrophoresis is complete, fluorescence can be detected by exposing the gel to an appropriate wavelength of light; the fluorescent tag fluoresces or glows in response.

Fluorescent tags have important advantages over radioactive isotopes: (1) They are safer to handle. (2) They are faster—you don't have to wait hours or days for the radioactive isotope to expose a film. (3) They come in multiple colors, so you can tag several different molecules in the same experiment and detect them independently.

Using Nucleic Acid Probes

In many cases, researchers want to find one specific molecule—a certain DNA sequence, for example—in the collection of molecules on a gel. How is this possible? The answer hinges on using a particular molecule as a probe.

You'll learn in more detail about how probes work in this text (Chapter 20). Here it's enough to get the general idea: A probe is a marked molecule that binds specifically to your molecule of interest. The "mark" is often a radioactive atom, a fluorescent tag, or an enzyme that catalyzes a color-forming or light-emitting reaction.

If you are looking for a particular DNA or RNA sequence on a gel, for example, you can expose the gel to a single-stranded probe that binds to the target sequence by complementary base pairing. Once it has bound, you can detect the band through autoradiography or fluorescence.

- **Southern blotting** is a technique for making DNA fragments that have been run out on a gel single stranded, transferring them from the gel to a nylon membrane, and then probing them to identify segments of interest. The technique was named after its inventor, Edwin Southern.

- **Northern blotting** is a technique for transferring RNA fragments from a gel to a nylon membrane and then probing them to detect target segments. The name is a lighthearted play on Southern blotting—the protocol from which it was derived.

Using Antibody Probes

How can researchers find a particular protein out of a large collection of different proteins? The answer is to use an antibody. An antibody is a protein that binds specifically to a section of a different protein.

To use an antibody as a probe, investigators attach a tag molecule—often an enzyme that catalyzes a color-forming reaction—to the antibody and allow it to react with proteins in a mixture. The antibody will stick to the specific protein that it binds to and then can be visualized thanks to the tag it carries.

If the proteins in question have been separated by gel electrophoresis and transferred to a membrane, the result is called a western blot. The name western is an extension of the Southern and northern patterns.

Using Radioimmunoassay and ELISA to Measure Amounts of Molecules

Another important method that makes use of antibodies is called a radioimmunoassay. This method is used when investigators want to measure tiny amounts of a molecule, such as a hormone in the blood. In this case, a known quantity of a hormone is labeled with a radioactive tag. This tagged hormone is then mixed with a known amount of antibody, and the two bind to one another. Next, a sample of blood, containing an unknown quantity of that same hormone, is added. The hormone from the blood and the radiolabeled hormone compete for antibody binding sites. As the concentration of unlabeled hormone increases, more of it binds to the antibody, displacing more of the radiolabeled hormone. The amount of unbound radiolabeled hormone is then measured. Using known standards as a reference, the amount of hormone in the blood can be determined.

Another commonly used technique based on similar principles is called ELISA (enzyme-linked immunosorbent assay). In this case, the amount of a particular molecule is measured using colorimetric signals instead of a radioactive signal.

check your understanding

If you understand BioSkill 9

✓**You should be able to . . .**

Interpret a gel that has been stained for "RNA X." One lane contains no bands. Two lanes have a band in the same location, even though one of the bands is barely visible and the other is extremely dark. The fourth lane has a faint band located below the bands in the other lanes.

Biologists use a technique called differential centrifugation to isolate specific cell components. Differential centrifugation is based on breaking cells apart to create a complex mixture and then separating components in a centrifuge. A centrifuge accomplishes this task by spinning cells in a solution that allows molecules and other cell components to separate according to their density or size and shape. The individual parts of the cell can then be purified and studied in detail, in isolation from other parts of the cell.

The first step in preparing a cell sample for centrifugation is to release the cell components by breaking the cells apart. This can be done by putting them in a hypotonic solution, by exposing them to high-frequency vibration, by treating cells with a detergent, or by grinding them up. Each of these methods breaks apart plasma membranes and releases the contents of the cells.

The resulting pieces of plasma membrane quickly reseal to form small vesicles, often trapping cell components inside. The solution that results from the homogenization step is a mixture of these vesicles, free-floating macromolecules released from the cells, and organelles. A solution like this is called a cell extract or cell homogenate.

When a cell homogenate is placed in a centrifuge tube and spun at high speed, the components that are in solution tend to move outward, along the red arrow in **FIGURE B10.1a**. The effect is similar to a merry-go-round, which seems to push you outward in a straight line away from the spinning platform. In response to this outward-directed force, the cell homogenate exerts a centripetal (literally, "center-seeking") force that pushes the homogenate away from the bottom of the tube. Larger, denser molecules or particles resist this inward force more readily than do smaller, less dense ones and so reach the bottom of the centrifuge tube faster.

To separate the components of a cell extract, researchers often perform a series of centrifuge runs. Steps 1 and 2 of

(a) How a centrifuge works

When the centrifuge spins, the macromolecules tend to move toward the bottom of the centrifuge tube (red arrow)

The solution in the tube exerts a centripetal force, which resists movement of the molecules to the bottom of the tube (blue arrow)

Motor

Very large or dense molecules overcome the centripetal force more readily than smaller, less dense ones. As a result, larger, denser molecules move toward the bottom of the tube faster.

(b) PROCESS: DIFFERENTIAL CENTRIFUGATION

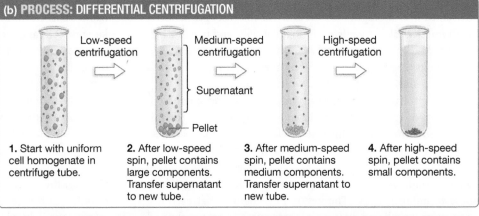

Low-speed centrifugation

Medium-speed centrifugation

Supernatant

Pellet

High-speed centrifugation

1. Start with uniform cell homogenate in centrifuge tube.

2. After low-speed spin, pellet contains large components. Transfer supernatant to new tube.

3. After medium-speed spin, pellet contains medium components. Transfer supernatant to new tube.

4. After high-speed spin, pellet contains small components.

(c) PROCESS: SUCROSE DENSITY–GRADIENT CENTRIFUGATION

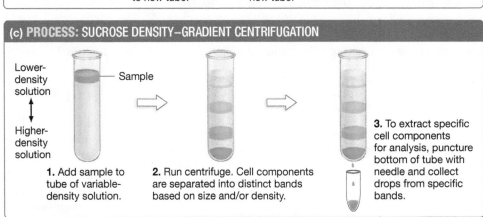

Lower-density solution

Higher-density solution

Sample

1. Add sample to tube of variable-density solution.

2. Run centrifuge. Cell components are separated into distinct bands based on size and/or density.

3. To extract specific cell components for analysis, puncture bottom of tube with needle and collect drops from specific bands.

FIGURE B10.1 Cell Components Can Be Separated by Centrifugation. (a) The forces inside a centrifuge tube allow cell components to be separated. **(b)** Through a series of centrifuge runs made at increasingly higher speeds, an investigator can separate fractions of a cell homogenate by size via differential centrifugation. **(c)** A high-speed centrifuge run can achieve extremely fine separation among cell components by sucrose density–gradient centrifugation.

FIGURE B10.1b illustrate how an initial treatment at low speed causes larger, heavier parts of the homogenate to move below smaller, lighter parts. The material that collects at the bottom of the tube is called the pellet, and the solution and solutes left behind form the supernatant ("above-swimming"). The supernatant is placed in a fresh tube and centrifuged at increasingly higher speeds and longer durations. Each centrifuge run continues to separate cell components based on their size and density.

To accomplish separation of macromolecules or organelles, researchers frequently follow up with centrifugation at extremely high speeds. One strategy is based on filling the centrifuge tube with a series of sucrose solutions of increasing density (**FIGURE B10.1c**). The density gradient allows cell components to separate on the basis of small differences in size, shape, and density. When the centrifuge run is complete, each cell component occupies a distinct band of material in the tube, based on how quickly each component moves through the increasingly

dense gradient of sucrose solution during the centrifuge run. A researcher can then collect the material in each band for further study.

BIOSKILL 11 biological imaging: microscopy and x-ray crystallography

A lot of biology happens at levels that can't be detected with the naked eye. Biologists use an array of microscopes to study small multicellular organisms, individual cells, and the contents of cells. And to understand what individual macromolecules or macromolecular machines like ribosomes look like, researchers use data from a technique called X-ray crystallography.

You'll probably use dissecting microscopes and compound light microscopes to view specimens during your labs for this course, and throughout this text you'll be seeing images generated from other types of microscopy and from X-ray crystallographic data. Among the fundamental skills you'll be acquiring as an introductory student, then, is a basic understanding of how these techniques work. The key is to recognize that each approach for visualizing microscopic structures has strengths and weaknesses. As a result, each technique is appropriate for studying certain types or aspects of cells or molecules.

Light and Fluorescence Microscopy

If you use a dissecting microscope during labs, you'll recognize that it works by magnifying light that bounces off a whole specimen—often a live organism. You'll be able to view the specimen in three dimensions, which is why these instruments are sometimes called stereomicroscopes, but the maximum magnification possible is only about 20 to 40 times normal size (20× to 40×).

To view smaller objects, you'll probably use a compound microscope. Compound microscopes magnify light that is passed *through* a specimen. The instruments used in introductory labs are usually capable of 400× magnifications; the most sophisticated

compound microscopes available can achieve magnifications of about 2000×. This is enough to view individual bacterial or eukaryotic cells and see large structures inside cells, like condensed chromosomes (see Chapter 12). To prepare a specimen for viewing under a compound light microscope, the tissues or cells are usually sliced to create a section thin enough for light to pass through efficiently. The section is then dyed to increase contrast and make structures visible. In many cases, different types of dyes are used to highlight different types of structures.

To visualize specific proteins, researchers use a technique called immunostaining. After preparing tissues or cells for viewing, the specimen is stained with fluorescently tagged antibodies. In this case, the cells are viewed under a fluorescence microscope. Ultraviolet or other wavelengths of light are passed through the specimen. The fluorescing tag emits visible light in response. The result? Beautiful cells that glow green, red, or blue.

Electron Microscopy

Until the 1950s, the compound microscope was the biologist's only tool for viewing cells directly. But the invention of the electron microscope provided a new way to view specimens. Two basic types of electron microscopy are now available: one that allows researchers to examine cross sections of cells at extremely high magnification, and one that offers a view of surfaces at somewhat lower magnification.

Transmission Electron Microscopy

The transmission electron microscope (TEM) is an extraordinarily effective tool for viewing cell structure at high magnification. TEM forms an image from electrons that pass through a specimen, just as a light microscope forms an image from light rays that pass through a specimen.

Biologists who want to view a cell under a transmission electron microscope begin by "fixing" the cell, meaning that they treat it with a chemical agent that stabilizes the cell's structure and contents while disturbing them as little as possible. Then the researcher permeates the cell with an epoxy plastic that stiffens the structure. Once this epoxy hardens, the cell can be cut into extremely thin sections with a glass or diamond knife. Finally, the sectioned specimens are impregnated with a metal—often lead. (The reason for this last step is explained shortly.)

FIGURE B11.1a outlines how the transmission electron microscope works. A beam of electrons is produced by a tungsten filament at the top of a column and directed downward. (All of the air is pumped out of the column, so that the electron beam isn't scattered by collisions with air molecules.) The electron beam passes through a series of lenses and through the specimen. The lenses are actually electromagnets, which alter the path of the beam much like a glass lens in a dissecting or compound microscope bends light. The electromagnet lenses magnify and focus the image on a screen at the bottom of the column. There the electrons strike a coating of fluorescent crystals, which emit visible light in response—just like a television screen. When the microscopist moves the screen out of the way and allows the electrons to expose a sheet of black-and-white film or to be detected by a digital camera, the result is a micrograph—a photograph of an image produced by microscopy.

The image itself is created by electrons that pass through the specimen. If no specimen were in place, all the electrons would pass through and the screen (and micrograph) would be uniformly bright. Unfortunately, cell materials by themselves would also appear fairly uniform and bright. This is because an atom's ability to deflect an electron depends on its mass. In turn, an atom's mass is a function of its atomic number. The hydrogen, carbon, oxygen, and nitrogen atoms that dominate biological molecules have low atomic numbers. This is why cell biologists must saturate cell sections with lead solutions. Lead has a high atomic number and scatters electrons effectively. Different macromolecules take up lead atoms in different amounts, so the metal acts as a "stain" that produces contrast. With TEM, areas of dense metal scatter the electron beam most, producing dark areas in micrographs.

The advantage of TEM is that it can magnify objects up to 250,000×—meaning that intracellular structures are clearly visible. The downsides are that researchers are restricted to observing dead, sectioned material, and they must take care that the preparation process does not distort the specimen.

Scanning Electron Microscopy

The scanning electron microscope (SEM) is the most useful tool biologists have for looking at the surfaces of structures. Materials are prepared for scanning electron microscopy by coating their surfaces with a layer of metal atoms. To create an image of this surface, the microscope scans the surface with a narrow beam of electrons. Electrons that are reflected back from the surface or that are emitted by the metal atoms in response to the beam then strike a detector. The signal from the detector controls a second electron beam, which scans a TV-like screen and forms an image magnified up to 50,000 times the object's size.

Because SEM records shadows and highlights, it provides images with a three-dimensional appearance (**FIGURE B11.1b**). It cannot magnify objects nearly as much as TEM can, however.

(a) Transmission electron microscopy: High magnification of cross sections

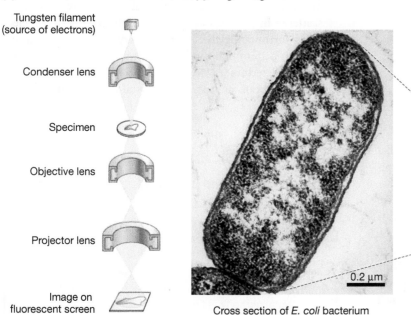

Tungsten filament (source of electrons)

Condenser lens

Specimen

Objective lens

Projector lens

Image on fluorescent screen

0.2 µm

Cross section of *E. coli* bacterium

(b) Scanning electron microscopy: Lower magnification of surfaces

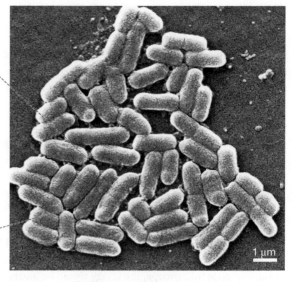

1 µm

Surface view of *E. coli* bacteria

FIGURE B11.1 There Are Two Basic Types of Electron Microscopy.

Studying Live Cells and Real-Time Processes

Until the 1960s, biologists were unable to get clear, high-magnification images of living cells. But a series of innovations over the past 50 years has made it possible to observe organelles and subcellular structures in action.

The development of video microscopy, where the image from a light microscope is captured by a video camera instead of by an eye or a film camera, proved revolutionary. It allowed specimens to be viewed at higher magnification, because video cameras are more sensitive to small differences in contrast than are the human eye or still cameras. It also made it easier to keep live specimens functioning normally, because the increased light sensitivity of video cameras allows them to be used with low illumination, so specimens don't overheat. And when it became possible to digitize video images, researchers began using computers to remove out-of-focus background material and increase image clarity.

A more recent innovation was the use of a fluorescent molecule called green fluorescent protein, or GFP, which allows researchers to tag specific molecules or structures and follow their movement in live cells over time. This was a major advance over immunostaining, in which cells have to be fixed. GFP is naturally synthesized in jellyfish that fluoresce, or emit light. By affixing GFP to another protein (using genetic engineering techniques described in Chapter 20) and then inserting it into a live cell, investigators can follow the protein's fate over time and even videotape its movement. For example, researchers have videotaped GFP-tagged proteins being transported from the rough ER through the Golgi apparatus and out to the plasma membrane. This is cell biology: the movie.

GFP's influence has been so profound that the researchers who developed its use in microscopy were awarded the 2008 Nobel Prize in Chemistry.

Visualizing Structures in 3-D

The world is three-dimensional. To understand how microscopic structures and macromolecules work, it is essential to understand their shape and spatial relationships. Consider three techniques currently being used to reconstruct the 3-D structure of cells, organelles, and macromolecules.

- **Confocal microscopy** is carried out by mounting cells that have been treated with one or more fluorescing tags on a microscope slide and then focusing a beam of ultraviolet or other wavelengths of light at a specific depth within the specimen. The fluorescing tag emits visible light in response. A detector for this light is then set up at exactly the position where the emitted light comes into focus. The result is a sharp image of a precise plane in the cell being studied (**FIGURE B11.2a**). Note that if you viewed the same specimen under a conventional fluorescence microscope, the image would be blurry because it results from light emitted by the entire cell (**FIGURE B11.2b**). By altering the focal plane, a researcher can record images from

(a) Confocal fluorescence image of single cell

(b) Conventional fluorescence image of same cell

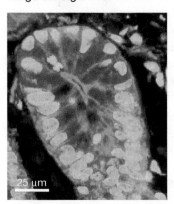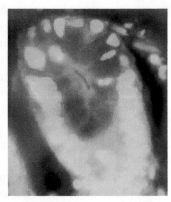

25 μm

FIGURE B11.2 Confocal Microscopy Provides Sharp Images of Living Cells. (a) The confocal image of this mouse intestinal cell is sharp, because it results from light emitted at a single plane inside the cell. **(b)** The conventional image of this same cell is blurred, because it results from light emitted by the entire cell.

an array of depths in the specimen; a computer can then be used to generate a 3-D image of the cell.

- **Electron tomography** uses a transmission electron microscope to generate a 3-D image of an organelle or other subcellular structure. The specimen is rotated around a single axis while the researcher takes many "snapshots." The individual images are then pieced together with a computer. This technique has provided a much more accurate view of mitochondrial structure than was possible using traditional TEM (see Chapter 7).

- **X-ray crystallography, or X-ray diffraction analysis**, is the most widely used technique for reconstructing the 3-D structure of molecules. As its name implies, the procedure is based on bombarding crystals of a molecule with X-rays. X-rays are scattered in precise ways when they interact with the electrons surrounding the atoms in a crystal, producing a diffraction pattern that can be recorded on X-ray film or other types of detectors (**FIGURE B11.3**). By varying the orientation of the X-ray beam as it strikes a crystal and documenting the

If you understand BioSkill 11

✓ You should be able to . . .

1. Interpret whether the absence of mitochondria in a transmission electron micrograph of a cancerous human liver means that the cell lacks mitochondria.

2. Explain why the effort to understand the structure of biological molecules is worthwhile even though X-ray crystallography is time consuming and technically difficult. What's the payoff?

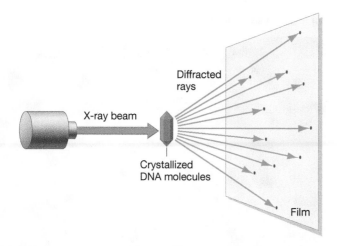

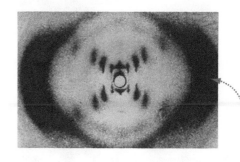

The patterns are determined by the structure of the molecules within the crystal

FIGURE B11.3 X-Ray Crystallography. When crystallized molecules are bombarded with X-rays, the radiation is scattered in distinctive patterns. The photograph at the right shows an X-ray film that recorded the pattern of scattered radiation from DNA molecules.

diffraction patterns that result, researchers can construct a map representing the density of electrons in the crystal. By relating these electron-density maps to information about the primary structure of the nucleic acid or protein, a 3-D model of the molecule can be built. Virtually all of the molecular models used in this book were built from X-ray crystallographic data.

BIOSKILL 12 cell and tissue culture methods

For researchers, there are important advantages to growing plant and animal cells and tissues outside the organism itself. Cell and tissue cultures provide large populations of a single type of cell or tissue and the opportunity to control experimental conditions precisely.

Animal Cell Culture

The first successful attempt to culture animal cells occurred in 1907, when a researcher cultivated amphibian nerve cells in a drop of fluid from the spinal cord. But it was not until the 1950s and 1960s that biologists could routinely culture plant and animal cells in the laboratory. The long lag time was due to the difficulty of re-creating conditions that exist in the intact organism precisely enough for cells to grow normally.

To grow in culture, animal cells must be provided with a liquid mixture containing the nutrients, vitamins, and hormones that stimulate growth. Initially, this mixture was serum, the liquid portion of blood; now, serum-free media are available for certain cell types. Serum-free media are preferred because they are much more precisely defined chemically than serum.

In addition, many types of animal cells will not grow in culture unless they are provided with a solid surface that mimics the types of surfaces that enable cells in the intact organisms to adhere. As a result, cells are typically cultured in flasks (**FIGURE B12.1a**, left; see B:22).

Even under optimal conditions, though, normal cells display a finite life span in culture. In contrast, many cultured cancerous cells grow indefinitely. This characteristic correlates with a key feature of cancerous cells in organisms: Their growth is continuous and uncontrolled.

Because of their immortality and relative ease of growth, cultured cancer cells are commonly used in research on basic aspects of cell structure and function. For example, the first human cell type to be grown in culture was isolated in 1951 from a malignant tumor of the uterine cervix. These cells are called HeLa cells in honor of their donor, Henrietta Lacks, who died soon thereafter from her cancer. HeLa cells continue to grow in laboratories around the world (Figure B12.1a, right).

Plant Tissue Culture

Certain cells found in plants are totipotent—meaning that they retain the ability to divide and differentiate into a complete, mature plant, including new types of tissue. These cells, called parenchyma cells, are important in wound healing and asexual reproduction. But they also allow researchers to grow complete adult plants in the laboratory, starting with a small number of parenchyma cells.

Biologists who grow plants in tissue culture begin by placing parenchyma cells in a liquid or solid medium containing all the

(a) Animal cell culture: immortal HeLa cancer cells

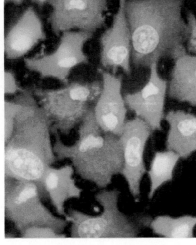

(b) Plant tissue culture: tobacco callus

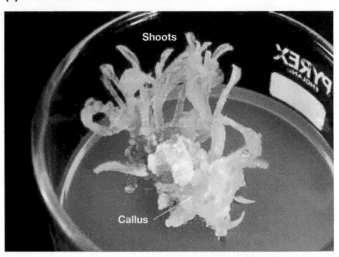

Shoots

Callus

FIGURE B12.1 **Animal and Plant Cells Can Be Grown in the Lab.**

nutrients required for cell maintenance and growth. In the early days of plant tissue culture, investigators found not only that specific growth signals called hormones were required for successful growth and differentiation but also that the relative abundance of hormones present was critical to success.

The earliest experiments on hormone interactions in tissue cultures were done with tobacco cells in the 1950s by Folke Skoog and co-workers. These researchers found that when the hormone called auxin was added to the culture by itself, the cells enlarged but did not divide. But if the team added roughly equal amounts of auxin and another growth signal called cytokinin to the cells, the cells began to divide and eventually formed a callus, or an undifferentiated mass of parenchyma cells.

By varying the proportion of auxin to cytokinins in different parts of the callus and through time, the team could stimulate the growth and differentiation of root and shoot systems and produce whole new plants (**FIGURE B12.1b**). A high ratio of auxin to cytokinin led to the differentiation of a root system, while a high ratio of cytokinin to auxin led to the development of a shoot system. Eventually Skoog's team was able to produce a complete plant from just one parenchyma cell.

The ability to grow whole new plants in tissue culture from just one cell has been instrumental in the development of genetic engineering (see Chapter 20). Researchers insert recombinant genes into target cells, test the cells to identify those that successfully express the recombinant genes, and then use tissue culture techniques to grow those cells into adult individuals with a novel genotype and phenotype.

check your understanding

If you understand BioSkill 12
✔ You should be able to . . .

1. Identify a limitation of how experiments on HeLa cells are interpreted.

2. State a disadvantage of doing experiments on plants that have been propagated from single cells growing in tissue culture.

Research in biological science starts with a question. In most cases, the question is inspired by an observation about a cell or an organism. To answer it, biologists have to study a particular species. Study organisms are often called model organisms, because investigators hope that they serve as a model for what is going on in a wide array of species.

Model organisms are chosen because they are convenient to study and because they have attributes that make them appropriate for the particular research proposed. They tend to have some common characteristics:

- *Short generation time and rapid reproduction* This trait is important because it makes it possible to produce offspring quickly and perform many experiments in a short amount of time—you don't have to wait long for individuals to grow.

- *Large numbers of offspring* This trait is particularly important in genetics, where many offspring phenotypes and genotypes need to be assessed to get a large sample size.

- *Small size, simple feeding and habitat requirements* These attributes make it relatively cheap and easy to maintain individuals in the lab.

The following notes highlight just a few model organisms supporting current work in biological science.

Escherichia coli

Of all model organisms in biology, perhaps none has been more important than the bacterium *Escherichia coli*—a common inhabitant of the human gut. The strain that is most commonly worked on today, called K-12 (**FIGURE B13.1a**; see B:24), was originally isolated from a hospital patient in 1922.

During the last half of the twentieth century, key results in molecular biology originated in studies of *E. coli*. These results include the discovery of enzymes such as DNA polymerase, RNA polymerase, DNA repair enzymes, and restriction endonucleases; the elucidation of ribosome structure and function; and the initial characterization of promoters, regulatory transcription factors, regulatory sites in DNA, and operons. In many cases, initial discoveries made in *E. coli* allowed researchers to confirm that homologous enzymes and processes existed in an array of organisms, often ranging from other bacteria to yeast, mice, and humans.

The success of *E. coli* as a model for other species inspired Jacques Monod's claim that "Once we understand the biology of *Escherichia coli*, we will understand the biology of an elephant." The genome of *E. coli* K-12 was sequenced in 1997, and the strain continues to be a workhorse in studies of gene function, biochemistry, and particularly biotechnology. Much remains to

be learned, however. Despite over 60 years of intensive study, the function of about a third of the *E. coli* genome is still unknown.

In the lab, *E. coli* is usually grown in suspension culture, where cells are introduced to a liquid nutrient medium, or on plates containing agar—a gelatinous mix of polysaccharides. Under optimal growing conditions—meaning before cells begin to get crowded and compete for space and nutrients—a cell takes just 30 minutes on average to grow and divide. At this rate, a single cell can produce a population of over a million descendants in just 10 hours. Except for new mutations, all of the descendant cells are genetically identical.

Dictyostelium discoideum

The cellular slime mold *Dictyostelium discoideum* is not always slimy, and it is not a mold—meaning a type of fungus. Instead, it is an amoeba. Amoeba is a general term that biologists use to characterize a unicellular eukaryote that lacks a cell wall and is extremely flexible in shape. *Dictyostelium* has long fascinated biologists because it is a social organism. Independent cells sometimes aggregate to form a multicellular structure.

Under most conditions, *Dictyostelium* cells are haploid (*n*) and move about in decaying vegetation on forest floors or other habitats. They feed on bacteria by engulfing them whole. When these cells reproduce, they can do so sexually by fusing with another cell then undergoing meiosis, or asexually by mitosis, which is more common. If food begins to run out, the cells begin to aggregate. In many cases, tens of thousands of cells cohere to form a 2-mm-long mass called a slug (**FIGURE B13.1b**). (This is not the slug that is related to snails.)

After migrating to a sunlit location, the slug stops and individual cells differentiate according to their position in the slug. Some form a stalk; others form a mass of spores at the tip of the stalk. (A spore is a single cell that develops into an adult organism, but it is not formed from gamete fusion like a zygote is.) The entire structure, stalk plus mass of spores, is called a fruiting body. Cells that form spores secrete a tough coat and represent a durable resting stage. The fruiting body eventually dries out, and the wind disperses the spores to new locations, where more food might be available.

Dictyostelium has been an important model organism for investigating questions about eukaryotes:

- Cells in a slug are initially identical in morphology but then differentiate into distinctive stalk cells and spores. Studying this process helped biologists better understand how cells in plant and animal embryos differentiate into distinct cell types.

(a) Bacterium *Escherichia coli* (strain K-12)

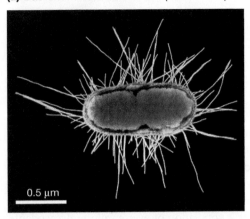

0.5 μm

(b) Slime mold *Dictyostelium discoideum*

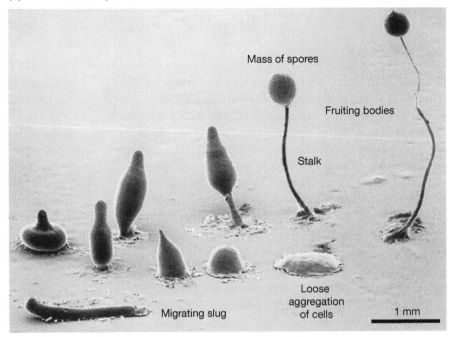

Mass of spores

Fruiting bodies

Stalk

Migrating slug

Loose aggregation of cells

1 mm

(c) Thale cress *Arabidopsis thaliana*

5 cm

(e) Fruit fly *Drosophila melanogaster*

0.5 mm

(f) Roundworm *Caenorhabditis elegans*

0.1 mm

(d) Yeast *Saccharomyces cerevisiae*

5 μm

(g) Mouse *Mus musculus*

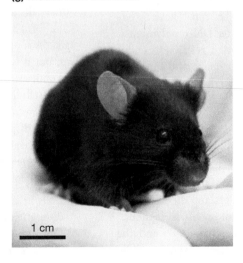

1 cm

FIGURE B13.1 Model Organisms.

✔ **QUESTION** *E. coli* is grown at a temperature of 37°C. Why?

- The process of slug formation has helped biologists study how animal cells move and how they aggregate as they form specific types of tissues.

- When *Dictyostelium* cells aggregate to form a slug, they stick to each other. The discovery of membrane proteins responsible for cell–cell adhesion helped biologists understand some of the general principles of multicellular life (highlighted in Chapter 11).

Arabidopsis thaliana

In the early days of biology, the best-studied plants were agricultural varieties such as maize (corn), rice, and garden peas. When biologists began to unravel the mechanisms responsible for oxygenic photosynthesis in the early to mid-1900s, they relied on green algae that were relatively easy to grow and manipulate in the lab—often the unicellular species *Chlamydomonas reinhardii*—as an experimental subject.

Although crop plants and green algae continue to be the subject of considerable research, a new model organism emerged in the 1980s and now serves as the preeminent experimental subject in plant biology. That organism is *Arabidopsis thaliana*, commonly known as thale cress or wall cress (**FIGURE B13.1c**).

Arabidopsis is a member of the mustard family, or Brassicaceae, so it is closely related to radishes and broccoli. In nature it is a weed—meaning a species that is adapted to thrive in habitats where soils have been disturbed.

One of the most attractive aspects of working with *Arabidopsis* is that individuals can grow from a seed into a mature, seed-producing plant in just four to six weeks. Several other attributes make it an effective subject for study: It has just five chromosomes, has a relatively small genome with limited numbers of repetitive sequences, can self-fertilize as well as undergo cross-fertilization, can be grown in a relatively small amount of space and with a minimum of care in the greenhouse, and produces up to 10,000 seeds per individual per generation.

Arabidopsis has been instrumental in a variety of studies in plant molecular genetics and development, and it is increasingly popular in ecological and evolutionary studies. In addition, the entire genome of the species has now been sequenced, and studies have benefited from the development of an international "*Arabidopsis* community"—a combination of informal and formal associations of investigators who work on *Arabidopsis* and use regular meetings, e-mail, and the Internet to share data, techniques, and seed stocks.

Saccharomyces cerevisiae

When biologists want to answer basic questions about how eukaryotic cells work, they often turn to the yeast *Saccharomyces cerevisiae*.

S. cerevisiae is unicellular and relatively easy to culture and manipulate in the lab (**FIGURE B13.1d**). In good conditions, yeast cells grow and divide almost as rapidly as bacteria. As a result, the species has become the organism of choice for experiments on control of the cell cycle and regulation of gene expression in eukaryotes. For example, research has confirmed that several of the genes controlling cell division and DNA repair in yeast have homologs in humans; and when mutated, these genes contribute to cancer. Strains of yeast that carry these mutations are now being used to test drugs that might be effective against cancer.

S. cerevisiae has become even more important in efforts to interpret the genomes of organisms like rice, mice, zebrafish, and humans. It is much easier to investigate the function of particular genes in *S. cerevisiae* by creating mutants or transferring specific alleles among individuals than it is to do the same experiments in mice or zebrafish. Once the function of a gene has been established in yeast, biologists can look for the homologous gene in other eukaryotes. If such a gene exists, they can usually infer that it has a function similar to its role in *S. cerevisiae*. It was also the first eukaryote with a completely sequenced genome.

Drosophila melanogaster

If you walk into a biology building on any university campus around the world, you are almost certain to find at least one lab where the fruit fly *Drosophila melanogaster* is being studied (**FIGURE B13.1e**).

Drosophila has been a key experimental subject in genetics since the early 1900s. It was initially chosen as a focus for study by T. H. Morgan, because it can be reared in the laboratory easily and inexpensively, matings can be arranged, the life cycle is completed in less than two weeks, and females lay a large number of eggs. These traits made fruit flies valuable subjects for breeding experiments designed to test hypotheses about how traits are transmitted from parents to offspring.

More recently, *Drosophila* has also become a key model organism in the field of developmental biology. The use of flies in developmental studies was inspired largely by the work of Christianne Nüsslein-Volhard and Eric Wieschaus, who in the 1980s isolated flies with genetic defects in early embryonic development. By investigating the nature of these defects, researchers have gained valuable insights into how various gene products influence the development of eukaryotes. The complete genome sequence of *Drosophila* has been available to investigators since the year 2000.

Caenorhabditis elegans

The roundworm *Caenorhabditis elegans* emerged as a model organism in developmental biology in the 1970s, due largely to work by Sydney Brenner and colleagues. (*Caenorhabditis* is pronounced *see-no-rab-DIE-tiss*.)

C. elegans was chosen for three reasons: (**1**) Its cuticle (soft outer layer) is transparent, making individual cells relatively easy to observe (**FIGURE B13.1f**); (**2**) adults have exactly 959 nonreproductive cells; and, most important, (**3**) the fate of each cell in an embryo can be predicted because cell fates are invariant among individuals. For example, when researchers examine a 33-cell *C. elegans* embryo, they know exactly which of the 959 cells in the adult will be derived from each of those 33 embryonic cells.

In addition, *C. elegans* are small (less than 1 mm long), are able to self-fertilize or cross-fertilize, and undergo early development in just 16 hours. The entire genome of *C. elegans* has now been sequenced.

Mus musculus

The house mouse *Mus musculus* is the most important model organism among mammals. For this reason, it is especially prominent in biomedical research, where researchers need to work on individuals with strong genetic and developmental similarities to humans.

The house mouse was an intelligent choice of model organism in mammals because it is small and thus relatively inexpensive to maintain in captivity, and because it breeds rapidly. A litter can contain 10 offspring, and generation time is only 12 weeks—meaning that several generations can be produced in a year. Descendants of wild house mice have been selected for docility and other traits that make them easy to handle and rear; these populations are referred to as laboratory mice (**FIGURE B13.1g**).

Some of the most valuable laboratory mice are strains with distinctive, well-characterized genotypes. Inbred strains are virtually homogenous genetically and are useful in experiments where gene-by-gene or gene-by-environment interactions have to be controlled. Other populations carry mutations that knock out genes and cause diseases similar to those observed in humans. These individuals are useful for identifying the cause of genetic diseases and testing drugs or other types of therapies.

check your understanding

If you understand BioSkill 13

✔ **You should be able to . . .**

Determine which model organisms described here would be the best choice for the following studies. In each case, explain your reasoning.

1. A study of why specific cells in an embryo die at certain points in normal development. One goal is to understand the consequences for the individual when programmed cell death does not occur when it should.

2. A study of proteins that are required for cell–cell adhesion.

3. Research on a gene suspected to be involved in the formation of breast cancer in humans.

BIOSKILL 14 — primary literature and peer review

As part of the process of doing science, biologists communicate their results to the scientific community through publications in scientific journals that report on their original research discoveries (see Chapter 1). These published reports are referred to, interchangeably, as the primary literature, research papers, or primary research articles.

What Is the Primary Literature?

Scientists publish "peer-reviewed" papers. This means that several experts in the field have carefully read the paper and considered its strengths and weaknesses. Reviewers write a critique of the paper and make a recommendation to the journal editor as to whether the paper should be published. Often reviewers will suggest additional experiments that need to be completed before a paper is considered acceptable for publication. The peer review process means that research discoveries are carefully vetted before they go to press.

A primary research paper can be distinguished from secondary sources—such as review articles, textbooks, and magazine articles—by looking for key characteristics. A primary research paper includes a detailed description of methods and results, written by the researchers who did the work. A typical paper contains a Title, Abstract, Introduction, Materials and Methods (or Experimental Design), Results and Discussion (**Table B14.1**), although the order and name of the sections varies among journals.

Getting Started

At first, trying to read the primary literature may seem like a daunting task. A paper may be peppered with unfamiliar terms and acronyms. If you tried to read a research paper from start to finish, like you might read a chapter in this textbook, it would be a frustrating experience. But, with practice, the scientific literature becomes approachable, and it is well worth the effort. The primary literature is the cutting edge, the place to read firsthand about the process of doing science. Becoming skilled at reading and evaluating scientific reports is a powerful way to learn how to think critically—to think like a biologist.

To get started, try breaking down reading the primary research article into a series of steps:

1. Read the authors' names. Where are they from? Are they working as a team or alone? After delving into the literature,

TABLE B14.1 Sections of a Primary Research Paper

Section	Characteristics
Title	Short, succinct, eye-catching
Abstract	Summary of Methods, Results, Discussion. Explains why the research was done and why the results are significant.
Introduction	Background information (what past work was done, why the work was important). States the objectives and hypotheses of the study and explains why the study is important.
Materials and Methods	Explains how the work was done and where it was done.
Results	Explains what the data show.
Discussion	Explains why the data show what they show, how the analysis relates to the objectives from the Introduction, and the significance of findings and how they advance the field.

certain familiar names will crop up again and again. You'll begin to recognize the experts in a particular field.

2. Read the title. It should summarize the key finding of the paper and tell you what you can expect to learn from the paper.

3. Read the abstract. The abstract summarizes the entire paper in a short paragraph. At this point, it might be tempting to stop reading. But sometimes authors understate or overstate the significance and conclusions of their work. You should never cite an article as a reference after having read only the abstract.

4. Read the Introduction. The first couple of paragraphs should make it clear what the objectives or hypotheses of the paper are; the remaining paragraphs will give you the background information you need to understand the point of the paper.

5. Flip through the article and look at the figures, illustrations, and tables, including reading the legends.

6. Read the Results section carefully. Ask yourself these questions: Do the results accurately describe the data presented in the paper? Were all the appropriate controls carried out in an experiment? Are there additional experiments that you think should have been performed? Are the figures and tables clearly labeled?

7. Consult the Materials and Methods section to help understand the research design and the techniques used.

8. Read the Discussion. The first and last paragraphs usually summarize the key findings and state their significance. The Discussion is the part of the paper where the results are explained in the context of the scientific literature. The authors should explain what their results mean.

Getting Practice

The best way to get practice is to start reading the scientific literature as often as possible. You could begin by reading some of the references cited in this textbook. You can get an electronic copy of most articles through online databases such as PubMed, Science-Direct, or Google Scholar, or through your institution's library.

After reading a primary research paper, you should be able to paraphrase the significance of the paper in a few sentences, free of technical jargon. You should also be able to both praise and criticize several points of the paper. As you become more familiar with reading the scientific literature, you're likely to start thinking about what questions remain to be answered. And, you may even come up with "the next experiment."

check your understanding

If you understand BioSkill 14

✔ **You should be able to . . .**

After choosing a primary research paper on a topic in biology that you would like to know more about, select one figure in the Results section that reports on the experiment and construct a Research box (like the ones in this textbook) that depicts this experiment.

A concept map is a graphical device for organizing and expressing what you know about a topic. It has two main elements: **(1)** concepts that are identified by words or short phrases and placed in a box or circle, and **(2)** labeled arrows that physically link two concepts and explain the relationship between them. The concepts are arranged hierarchically on a page with the most general concepts at the top and the most specific ideas at the bottom.

The combination of a concept, a linking word, and a second concept is called a proposition. Good concept maps also have cross-links—meaning, labeled arrows that connect different elements in the hierarchy as you read down the page.

Concept maps, initially developed by Joseph Novak in the early 1970s, have proven to be an effective studying and learning tool. They can be particularly valuable if constructed by a group, or when different individuals exchange and critique concept maps they have created independently. Although concept maps vary widely in quality and can be graded using objective criteria, there are many equally valid ways of making a high-quality concept map on a particular topic.

When you are asked to make a concept map in this text, you will usually be given at least a partial list of concepts to use. As an example, suppose you were asked to create a concept map on experimental design and were given the following concepts: results, predictions, control treatment, experimental treatment, controlled (identical) conditions, conclusions, experiment, hypothesis to be tested, null hypothesis. One possible concept map is shown in **FIGURE B15.1**.

Good concept maps have four qualities:

1. They exhibit an organized hierarchy, indicating how each concept on the map relates to larger and smaller concepts.

2. The concept words are specific—not vague.

3. The propositions are accurate.

4. There is cross-linking between different elements in the hierarchy of concepts.

As you practice making concept maps, go through these criteria and use them to evaluate your own work as well as the work of fellow students.

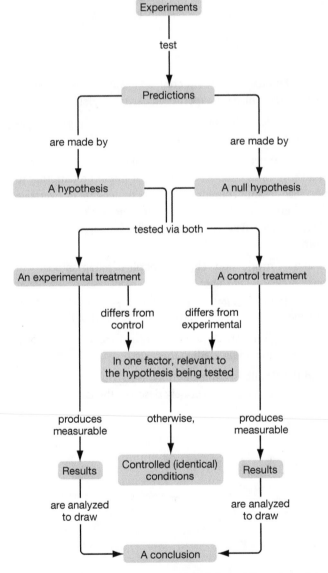

FIGURE B15.1 A Concept Map on Principles of Experimental Design.

check your understanding

If you understand BioSkill 15

✓ **You should be able to . . .**

1. Add an "Alternative hypothesis" concept to the map in Figure B15.1, along with other concepts and labeled linking arrows needed to indicate its relationship to other information on the map. (Hint: Recall that investigators often contrast a hypothesis being tested with an alternative hypothesis that does not qualify as a null hypothesis.)

2. Add a box for the concept "Statistical testing" (see **BIOSKILLS 4**) along with appropriately labeled linking arrows.

Most students have at one time or another wondered why a particular question on an exam seemed so hard, while others seemed easy. The explanation lies in the type of cognitive skills required to answer the question. Let's take a closer look.

Categories of Human Cognition

Bloom's Taxonomy is a classification system that instructors use to identify the cognitive skill levels at which they are asking students to work, particularly on practice problems and exams. Bloom's Taxonomy is also a very useful tool for students to know—it can help you to figure out the appropriate level at which you should be studying to succeed in a course.

Bloom's Taxonomy distinguishes six different categories of human thinking: remember, understand, apply, analyze, evaluate, and create. One of the most useful distinctions lies not in the differences among the six categories, but rather in the difference between high-order cognitive (HOC) and low-order cognitive (LOC) skills. **FIGURE B16.1** shows how the different levels of the taxonomy can be broken into HOC and LOC skills.

Skills that hallmark LOCs include recall, explanation, or application of knowledge in the exact way that you have before (remember, understand, apply), while skills that typify HOCs include the application of knowledge in a new way, as well as the breakdown, critique, or creation of information (analyze, evaluate, and create). Most college instructors will assume students are proficient at solving LOC questions and will expect you to frequently work at the HOC levels. HOC problems usually require use of basic vocabulary and applying knowledge—working at this level helps students to master the LOC levels.

Six Study Steps to Success

Bloom's Taxonomy provides a useful guide for preparing for an exam, using the following six steps:

1. *Answer in-chapter questions while reading the chapter.* All questions in this book have been assigned Bloom's levels, so you can review the question answers and the Bloom's level while you study.

2. *Identify the Bloom's level(s) of the questions that you are having greatest difficulty answering.* While working through

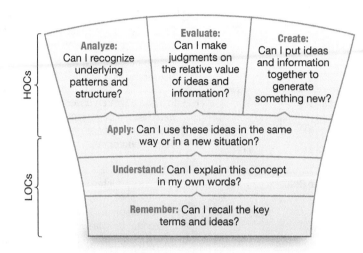

FIGURE B16.1 Bloom's Taxonomy.

the text, take note of the content and Bloom's level(s) that you find the most challenging.

3. *Use the Bloom's Taxonomy Study Guide* (**Table B16.1**; see B:30) *to focus your study efforts at the appropriate Bloom's level.* Table B16.1 lists specific study methods that can help you practice your understanding of the material at both the LOC and HOC levels, whether you are studying alone or with a study group.

4. *Complete the end-of-chapter questions as if you're taking an exam, without looking for the answers.* If you look at the chapter text or jump to the answers, then you really aren't testing your ability to work with the content and have reduced the questions to the lowest Bloom's level of remember.

5. *Grade your answers and note the Bloom's level of the questions you got wrong.* At what level of Bloom's Taxonomy were the questions you missed?

6. *Use the Bloom's Taxonomy Study Guide to focus your study efforts at the appropriate Bloom's level.* If you missed a lot of questions, then spend more time studying the material and find other resources for quizzing yourself.

By following these steps and studying at the HOC levels, you should succeed in answering questions on in-class exams.

TABLE B16.1 Bloom's Taxonomy Study Guide

	Individual Study Activities	Group Study Activities
Create (HOC) Generate something new	• Generate a hypothesis or design an experiment based on information you are studying • Create a model based on a given data set • Create summary sheets that show how facts and concepts relate to each other • Create questions at each level of Bloom's Taxonomy as a practice test and then take the test	• Each student puts forward a hypothesis about biological process and designs an experiment to test it. Peers critique the hypotheses and experiments • Create a new model/summary sheet/concept map that integrates each group member's ideas
Evaluate (HOC) Defend or judge a concept or idea	• Provide a written assessment of the strengths and weaknesses of your peers' work or understanding of a given concept based on previously determined criteria	• Provide a verbal assessment of the strengths and weaknesses of your peers' work or understanding of a given concept based on previously described criteria, and have your peers critique your assessment
Analyze (HOC) Distinguish parts and make inferences	• Analyze and interpret data in primary literature or a textbook without reading the author's interpretation and then compare the authors' interpretation with your own • Analyze a situation and then identify the assumptions and principles of the argument • Compare and contrast two ideas or concepts • Construct a map of the main concepts by defining the relationships of the concepts using one- or two-way arrows	• Work together to analyze and interpret data in primary literature or a textbook without reading the author's interpretation, and defend your analysis to your peers • Work together to identify all of the concepts in a paper or textbook chapter, construct individual maps linking the concepts together with arrows and words that relate the concepts, and then grade each other's concept maps
Apply (HOC or LOC) Use information or concepts in new ways (HOC) or in the same ways (LOC)	• Review each process you have learned and then ask yourself: What would happen if you increase or decrease a component in the system, or what would happen if you alter the activity of a component in the system? • If possible, graph a biological process and create scenarios that change the shape or slope of the graph	• Practice writing out answers to old exam questions on the board, and have your peers check to make sure you don't have too much or too little information in your answer • Take turns teaching your peers a biological process while the group critiques the content
Understand (LOC) Explain information or concepts	• Describe a biological process in your own words without copying it from a book or another source • Provide examples of a process • Write a sentence using the word • Give examples of a process	• Discuss content with peers • Take turns quizzing each other about definitions, and have your peers check your answer
Remember (LOC) Recall information	• Practice labeling diagrams • List characteristics • Identify biological objects or components from flash cards • Quiz yourself with flash cards • Take a self-made quiz on vocabulary • Draw, classify, select, or match items • Write out the textbook definitions	• Check a drawing that another student labeled • Create lists of concepts and processes that your peers can match • Place flash cards in a bag and take turns selecting one for which you must define a term • Do the preceding activities, and have peers check your answers

Periodic Table of Elements

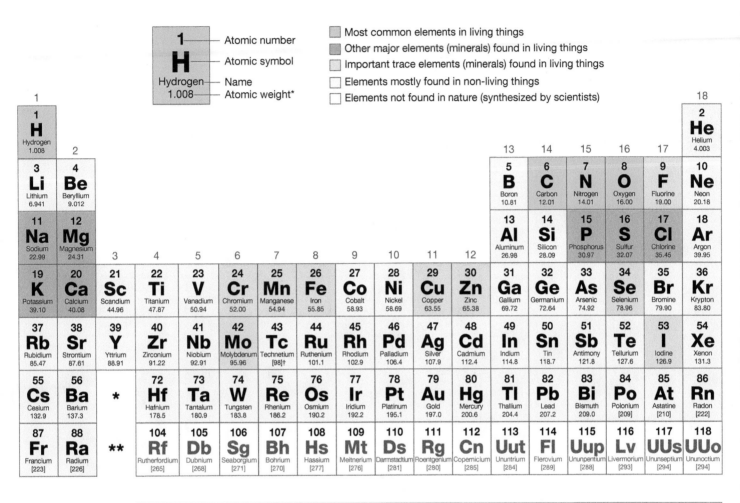

Atomic number — 1
Atomic symbol — H
Name — Hydrogen
Atomic weight* — 1.008

- ☐ Most common elements in living things
- ☐ Other major elements (minerals) found in living things
- ☐ Important trace elements (minerals) found in living things
- ☐ Elements mostly found in non-living things
- ☐ Elements not found in nature (synthesized by scientists)

DATA: Wieser, M. E., and M. Berglund. 2009. *Pure and Applied Chemistry* 81: 2131–2156.

*Atomic weights are reported to four significant figures.

†For elements with a variable number of protons and/or neutrons, the mass number of the longest-lived isotope of the element is reported in brackets.

Glossary

5′ cap A modified guanine (G) nucleotide (7-methylguanylate) added to the 5′ end of eukaryotic mRNAs. Helps protect the mRNA from being degraded and promotes efficient initiation of translation.

abdomen A region of the body; in insects, one of the three prominent body regions called tagmata.

abiotic Not alive (e.g., air, water, and some components of soil). Compare with **biotic**.

aboveground biomass The total mass of living plants in an area, excluding roots.

abscisic acid (ABA) A plant hormone that inhibits growth; it stimulates stomatal closure and triggers dormancy.

abscission In plants, the normal (often seasonal) shedding of leaves, fruits, or flowers.

abscission zone The region at the base of a petiole where cell wall degradation occurs; results in the dropping of leaves.

absorption In animals, the uptake of ions and small molecules, derived from food, across the lining of the intestine and into the bloodstream.

absorption spectrum The amount of light of different wavelengths absorbed by a pigment. Usually depicted as a graph of light absorbed versus wavelength. Compare with **action spectrum**.

acclimation A change in a study organism's phenotype that occurs in response to laboratory conditions.

acclimatization A change in an individual's phenotype that occurs in response to a change in natural environmental conditions.

acetyl CoA A molecule produced by oxidation of pyruvate (the final product of glycolysis) in a reaction catalyzed by pyruvate dehydrogenase. Can enter the citric acid cycle and is used as a carbon source in the synthesis of fatty acids, steroids, and other compounds.

acetylation Addition of an acetyl group ($-COCH_3$) to a molecule. Acetylation of histone proteins is important in controlling chromatin condensation.

acetylcholine (Ach) A neurotransmitter, released by nerve cells at neuromuscular junctions, that triggers contraction of skeletal muscle cells but slows the rate of contraction in cardiac muscle cells. Also used as a neurotransmitter between neurons.

acid Any compound that gives up protons or accepts electrons during a chemical reaction or that releases hydrogen ions when dissolved in water.

acid-growth hypothesis The hypothesis that auxin triggers elongation of plant cells by increasing the activity of proton pumps, making the cell wall more acidic and leading to expansion of the cell wall and an influx of water.

acoelomate A bilaterian animal that lacks an internal body cavity (coelom). Compare with **coelomate** and **pseudocoelomate**.

acquired immune deficiency syndrome (AIDS) A human disease characterized by death of immune system cells (in particular helper T cells) and subsequent vulnerability to other infections. Caused by the human immunodeficiency virus (HIV).

acrosome A caplike structure, located on the head of a sperm cell, that contains enzymes capable of dissolving the outer coverings of an egg.

ACTH See **adrenocorticotropic hormone**.

actin A globular protein that can be polymerized to form filaments. Actin filaments are part of the cytoskeleton and constitute the thin filaments in skeletal muscle cells.

actin filament A long fiber, about 7 nm in diameter, composed of two intertwined strands of polymerized actin protein; one of the three types of cytoskeletal fibers. Involved in cell movement. Also called a *microfilament*. Compare with **intermediate filament** and **microtubule**.

action potential A rapid, temporary change in electrical potential across a membrane, from negative to positive and back to negative. Occurs in cells, such as neurons and muscle cells, that have an excitable membrane.

action spectrum The relative effectiveness of different wavelengths of light in driving a light-dependent process such as photosynthesis. Usually depicted as a graph of some measure of the process versus wavelength. Compare with **absorption spectrum**.

activation energy The amount of energy required to initiate a chemical reaction; specifically, the energy required to reach the transition state.

activator A protein that binds to a DNA regulatory sequence to increase the frequency of transcription initiation by RNA polymerase.

active site The location in an enzyme molecule where substrates (reactant molecules) bind and react.

active transport The movement of ions or molecules across a membrane against an electrochemical gradient. Requires energy (e.g., from hydrolysis of ATP) and assistance of a transport protein (e.g., pump).

adaptation Any heritable trait that increases the fitness of an individual with that trait, compared with individuals without that trait, in a particular environment.

adaptive immune response See **adaptive immunity**.

adaptive immunity Immunity to a particular pathogen or other antigen conferred by activated B and T cells in vertebrates. Characterized by specificity, diversity, memory, and self–nonself recognition. Also called *adaptive immune response*. Compare with **innate immunity**.

adaptive radiation Rapid evolutionary diversification within one lineage, producing many descendant species with a wide range of adaptive forms.

adenosine triphosphate (ATP) A molecule consisting of an adenine base, a sugar, and three phosphate groups that can be hydrolyzed to release energy. Universally used by cells to store and transfer energy.

adhesion The tendency of certain dissimilar molecules to cling together due to attractive forces. Compare with **cohesion**.

adipocyte A fat cell.

adrenal gland Either of two small endocrine glands, one above each kidney. The outer portion (cortex) secretes several steroid hormones; the inner portion (medulla) secretes epinephrine and norepinephrine.

adrenaline See **epinephrine**.

adrenocorticotropic hormone (ACTH) A peptide hormone, produced and secreted by the anterior pituitary, that stimulates release of steroid hormones (e.g., cortisol, aldosterone) from the adrenal cortex.

adult A sexually mature individual.

adventitious root A root that develops from a plant's shoot system instead of from the plant's root system.

aerobic Referring to any metabolic process, cell, or organism that uses oxygen as an electron acceptor. Compare with **anaerobic**.

afferent division The part of the nervous system that transmits information about the internal and external environment to the central nervous system. Consists mainly of sensory neurons. Compare with **efferent division**.

age class All the individuals of a specific age in a population.

age-specific fecundity The average number of female offspring produced by a female in a certain age class.

age structure The proportion of individuals in a population that are of each possible age.

agglutination Clumping together of cells or viruses by antibodies or other cross-linking molecules.

aggregate fruit A fruit (e.g., raspberry) that develops from a single flower that has many separate carpels. Compare with **multiple** and **simple fruit**.

AIDS See **acquired immune deficiency syndrome**.

albumen A solution of water and protein (particularly albumins), found in amniotic eggs, that nourishes the growing embryo. Also called *egg white*.

alcohol fermentation Catabolic pathway in which pyruvate produced by glycolysis is converted to ethanol in the absence of oxygen.

aldosterone A hormone that stimulates the kidney to conserve salt and water and promotes retention of sodium; produced in the adrenal cortex.

allele A particular version of a gene.

allergen Any molecule (antigen) that triggers an allergic response (an allergy).

allergy An IgE-mediated abnormal response to an antigen, usually characterized by dilation of blood vessels, contraction of smooth muscle cells, and increased activity of mucus-secreting cells.

allopatric speciation Speciation that occurs when populations of the same species become geographically isolated, often due to dispersal or vicariance. Compare with **sympatric speciation**.

allopatry Condition in which two or more populations live in different geographic areas. Compare with **sympatry**.

allopolyploidy (adjective: allopolyploid) The state of having more than two full sets of chromosomes (polyploidy) due to hybridization between different species. Compare with **autopolyploidy**.

allosteric regulation Regulation of a protein's function by binding of a regulatory molecule, usually to a specific site distinct from the active site, that causes a change in the protein's shape.

α-amylase See **amylase**.

α-helix (alpha-helix) A protein secondary structure in which the polypeptide backbone coils into a spiral shape stabilized by hydrogen bonding.

alternation of generations A life cycle involving alternation of a multicellular haploid stage (gametophyte) with a multicellular diploid stage (sporophyte). Occurs in most plants and some protists.

alternative splicing In eukaryotes, the splicing of primary RNA transcripts from a single gene in different ways to produce different mature mRNAs and thus different polypeptides.

altruism Any behavior that has a fitness cost to the individual (lowered survival and/or reproduction) and a fitness benefit to the recipient. See **reciprocal altruism**.

alveolus (plural: alveoli) Any of the tiny air-filled sacs of a mammalian lung.

ambisense RNA virus A ssRNA virus whose genome consists of at least one strand that contains both positive-sense and negative-sense regions.

aminoacyl tRNA A transfer RNA molecule that is covalently bound to an amino acid.

aminoacyl-tRNA synthetase An enzyme that catalyzes the addition of a particular amino acid to its corresponding tRNA molecule.

ammonia (NH_3) A small molecule, produced by the breakdown of proteins and nucleic acids, that is very toxic to cells. Is a strong base that gains a proton to form the ammonium ion (NH_4^+).

amnion The innermost of the membranes surrounding the embryo in an amniotic egg.

amniotes A major lineage of vertebrates (Amniota) that reproduce with amniotic eggs. Includes all reptiles (including birds) and mammals—all tetrapods except amphibians.

amniotic egg An egg that has a watertight shell or case enclosing a membrane-bound water supply (the amnion), food supply (yolk sac), and waste sac (allantois).

amoeboid motion See **cell crawling**.

amphibians A lineage of vertebrates, many of which breathe through their skin and feed on land but lay their eggs in water. Represent the earliest tetrapods; include frogs, salamanders, and caecilians.

amphipathic Containing hydrophilic and hydrophobic regions.

ampullae of Lorenzini Structures on the heads of sharks that contain cells with electroreceptors.

amylase Any enzyme that can break down starch by catalyzing hydrolysis of the glycosidic linkages between the glucose residues.

amyloplasts Starch-storing organelles (plastids) in plants. In root cap cells, they settle to the bottom of the cell and may be used as gravity detectors.

anabolic pathway Any set of chemical reactions that synthesizes large molecules from smaller ones. Generally requires an input of energy. Compare with **catabolic pathway**.

anadromous Having a life cycle in which adults live in the ocean (or large lakes) but migrate up freshwater streams to breed and lay eggs.

anaerobic Referring to any metabolic process, cell, or organism that uses an electron acceptor other than oxygen, including fermentation or anaerobic respiration. Compare with **aerobic**.

anaphase A stage in mitosis or meiosis during which chromosomes are moved to opposite poles of the spindle apparatus.

anatomy The study of the physical structure of organisms.

ancestral trait A trait found in the ancestors of a particular group.

aneuploidy (adjective: aneuploid) The state of having an abnormal number of copies of a certain chromosome.

angiosperm A flowering vascular plant that produces seeds within mature ovaries (fruits). The angiosperms form a single lineage. Compare with **gymnosperm**.

animal A member of a major lineage of eukaryotes (Animalia) whose members typically have a complex, large, multicellular body; eat other organisms; and are mobile.

animal model Any disease that occurs in a non-human animal and has parallels to a similar disease of humans. Studied by medical researchers in hopes that findings may apply to human disease.

anion A negatively charged ion.

annelids Members of the phylum Annelida (segmented worms). Distinguished by a segmented body and a coelom that functions as a hydrostatic skeleton. Annelids belong to the lophotrochozoan branch of the protostomes.

annual Referring to a plant whose life cycle normally lasts only one growing season—less than one year. Compare with **perennial**.

anoxygenic Referring to any process or reaction that does not produce oxygen. Photosynthesis in purple sulfur and purple nonsulfur bacteria, which does not involve photosystem II, is anoxygenic. Compare with **oxygenic**.

antagonistic muscle group A set of two or more muscles that reextend one another by transmitting their forces via the skeleton.

antenna (plural: antennae) A long appendage of the head that is used to touch or smell.

antenna complex Part of a photosystem, containing an array of chlorophyll molecules and accessory pigments, that receives energy from light and directs the energy to a central reaction center during photosynthesis.

anterior Toward an animal's head and away from its tail. The opposite of posterior.

anterior pituitary The part of the pituitary gland containing endocrine cells that produce and release a variety of peptide hormones in response to other hormones from the hypothalamus. Compare with **posterior pituitary**.

anther The pollen-producing structure at the end of a stamen in flowering plants (angiosperms).

antheridium (plural: antheridia) The sperm-producing structure in most land plants except angiosperms.

anthropoids One of the two major lineages of primates, including apes, humans, and all monkeys. Compare with **prosimians**.

antibiotic Any substance, such as penicillin, that can kill or inhibit the growth of bacteria.

antibody A protein produced by B cells that can bind to a specific part of an antigen, tagging it for removal by the immune system. All monomeric forms of antibodies consist of two light chains and two heavy chains, which vary between different antibodies. Also called *immunoglobulin*.

anticodon The sequence of three bases (a triplet) in a transfer RNA molecule that can bind to an mRNA codon with a complementary sequence.

antidiuretic hormone (ADH) A peptide hormone, secreted from the posterior pituitary gland, that stimulates water retention by the kidney. Also called *vasopressin*.

antigen Any foreign molecule, often a protein, that can stimulate an innate or adaptive response by the immune system.

antigen presentation Process by which small peptides, derived from ingested particulate antigens (e.g., bacteria) or intracellular antigens (e.g., viruses in infected cell) are complexed with MHC proteins and transported to the cell surface, where they are displayed and can be recognized by T cells.

antiparallel Describing the opposite orientation of nucleic acid strands that are hydrogen bonded to one another, with one strand running in the $5' \rightarrow 3'$ direction and the other in the $3' \rightarrow 5'$ direction.

antiporter A carrier protein that allows an ion to diffuse down an electrochemical gradient, using the energy of that process to transport a different substance in the opposite direction *against* its concentration gradient. Compare with **symporter**.

antiviral Any drug or other agent that can interfere with the transmission or replication of viruses.

aorta In terrestrial vertebrates, the major artery carrying oxygenated blood away from the heart.

aphotic zone Deep water receiving no sunlight. Compare with **photic zone**.

apical Toward the top. In plants, at the tip of a branch. In animals, on the side of an epithelial layer that faces the environment and not other body tissues. Compare with **basal**.

apical–basal axis The shoot-to-root axis of a plant.

apical bud A bud at the tip of a stem or branch, where growth occurs to lengthen the stem or branch.

apical dominance Inhibition of lateral bud growth by the apical meristem at the tip of a plant branch.

apical meristem A group of undifferentiated plant cells, at the tip of a shoot or root, that is responsible for primary growth. Compare with **cambium**.

apodeme Any of the chitinous ingrowths of the exoskeleton to which muscles attach.

apomixis The formation of mature seeds without fertilization occurring; a type of asexual reproduction.

apoplast In plants, the region outside plasma membranes consisting of the porous cell walls and the intervening extracellular air space. Compare with **symplast**.

apoptosis Series of tightly controlled changes that lead to the self-destruction of a cell. Occurs frequently during embryological development and as part of the immune response to remove infected or cancerous cells. Also called *programmed cell death*.

appendix A blind sac (having only one opening) that extends from the cecum in some mammals.

aquaporin A type of channel protein through which water can move by osmosis across a plasma membrane.

aquifer An underground layer of porous rock, sand, or gravel that is saturated with water.

***ara* operon** A set of three genes in *E. coli* that are transcribed into a single mRNA and required for metabolism of the sugar arabinose. Transcription of the *ara* operon is controlled by the AraC regulatory protein.

araC The regulatory gene (written as *araC*) or regulatory protein (when written as AraC) of the *E. coli ara* operon.

arbuscular mycorrhizal fungi (AMF) Fungi from the Glomeromycota lineage whose hyphae enter the root cells of their host plants. Also called *endomycorrhizal fungi*.

Archaea One of the three taxonomic domains of life, consisting of unicellular prokaryotes distinguished by cell walls made of certain polysaccharides not found in bacterial or eukaryotic cell walls, plasma membranes composed of unique isoprene-containing phospholipids, and ribosomes and RNA polymerase similar to those of eukaryotes. Compare with **Bacteria** and **Eukarya**.

archegonium (plural: archegonia) The egg-producing structure in most land plants except angiosperms.

arteriole Any of the many tiny vessels that carry blood from arteries to capillaries.

arteriosclerosis Hardening and loss of elasticity of arteries.

artery Any thick-walled blood vessel that carries blood (oxygenated or not) under relatively high pressure away from the heart to organs throughout the body. Compare with **vein**.

arthropods Members of the phylum Arthropoda. Distinguished by a segmented body; a hard, jointed exoskeleton; paired, jointed appendages; and an extensive body cavity called a hemocoel. Arthropods belong to the ecdysozoan branch of the protostomes.

articulation A movable point of contact between two rigid components of a skeleton, such as between bones of a vertebrate endoskeleton or between segments of cuticle in an arthropod exoskeleton. See **joint**.

artificial selection Deliberate manipulation by humans, as in animal and plant breeding, of the genetic composition of a population by allowing only individuals with desirable traits to reproduce.

ascus (plural: asci) Specialized spore-producing cell found at the ends of hyphae in "sac fungi" (Ascomycota).

asexual reproduction Any form of reproduction where offspring inherit DNA from only one parent. Includes binary fission, budding, and parthenogenesis. Compare with **sexual reproduction**.

astral microtubules Mitotic and meiotic microtubules that have arisen from the two spindle poles and interact with proteins on the plasma membrane.

asymmetric competition Ecological competition between two species in which one species suffers a much greater fitness decline than the other. Compare with **symmetric competition**.

atomic number The number of protons in the nucleus of an atom, giving the atom its identity as a particular chemical element.

atomic weight The average mass of an element that is based on the relative proportions of all the naturally occurring isotopes.

ATP synthase A large membrane-bound protein complex that uses the energy of protons flowing through it to synthesize ATP.

ATP See **adenosine triphosphate**.

atrioventricular (AV) node A region of the heart between the right atrium and right ventricle where electrical signals from the atrium are slowed briefly before spreading to the ventricle. This delay allows the ventricle to fill with blood before contracting. Compare with **sinoatrial (SA) node**.

atrium (plural: atria) A thin-walled chamber of the heart that receives blood from veins and pumps it to a neighboring chamber (the ventricle).

autocrine Relating to a chemical signal that affects the same cell that produced and released it.

autoimmunity A pathological condition in which the immune system attacks self cells or tissues of an individual's own body.

autonomic nervous system The part of the peripheral nervous system that controls internal organs and involuntary processes, such as stomach contraction, hormone release, and heart rate. Includes parasympathetic and sympathetic nerves. Compare with **somatic nervous system**.

autophagy The process by which damaged organelles are surrounded by a membrane and delivered to a lysosome to be recycled.

autopolyploidy (adjective: autopolyploid) The state of having more than two full sets of chromosomes

(polyploidy) due to a mutation that doubled the chromosome number. All the chromosomes come from the same species. Compare with **allopolyploidy**.

autosomal inheritance The inheritance patterns that occur when genes are located on autosomes rather than on sex chromosomes.

autosome Any chromosome other than a sex chromosome (i.e., any chromosome other than the X or Y in mammals).

autotroph Any organism that can synthesize reduced organic compounds from simple inorganic sources such as CO_2 or CH_4. Most plants and some bacteria and archaea are autotrophs. Also called *primary producer*. Compare with **heterotroph**.

auxin Indoleacetic acid (IAA), a plant hormone that stimulates phototropism and cell elongation.

axillary bud A bud that forms at a node and may develop into a lateral (side) branch. Also called *lateral bud*.

axon A long projection of a neuron that can propagate an action potential.

axon hillock The site in a neuron where an axon joins the cell body and where action potentials are first triggered.

axoneme A structure found in eukaryotic cilia and flagella and responsible for their motion; composed of two central microtubules surrounded by nine doublet microtubules (9 + 2 arrangement).

B cell A type of lymphocyte that matures in the bone marrow and, with T cells, is responsible for adaptive immunity. Produces antibodies and also functions in antigen presentation. Also called *B lymphocyte*.

B-cell receptor (BCR) An immunoglobulin protein embedded in the plasma membrane of mature B cells and to which antigens bind. Apart from the transmembrane domain, it is identical in structure to antibodies.

BAC library A collection of all the sequences found in the genome of a species, inserted into **bacterial artificial chromosomes (BACs)**.

background extinction The average rate of low-level extinction that has occurred continuously throughout much of evolutionary history. Compare with **mass extinction**.

Bacteria One of the three taxonomic domains of life, consisting of unicellular prokaryotes distinguished by cell walls composed largely of peptidoglycan, plasma membranes similar to those of eukaryotic cells, and ribosomes and RNA polymerase that differ from those in archaeans or eukaryotes. Compare with **Archaea** and **Eukarya**.

bacterial artificial chromosome (BAC) An artificial version of a bacterial chromosome that can be used as a cloning vector to produce many copies of large DNA fragments.

bacteriophage Any virus that infects bacteria.

baculum A bone inside the penis; usually present in mammals with a penis that lacks erectile tissue.

balancing selection A mode of natural selection in which no single allele is favored in all populations of a species at all times. Instead, there is a balance among alleles in terms of fitness and frequency.

ball-and-stick model A representation of a molecule where atoms are shown as balls—colored and scaled to indicate the atom's identity—and covalent bonds are shown as rods or sticks connecting the balls in the correct geometry.

bar coding The use of well-characterized gene sequences to identify species.

bark The protective outer layer of woody plants, composed of cork cells, cork cambium, and secondary phloem.

baroreceptors Specialized nerve cells in the walls of the heart and certain major arteries that detect changes in blood pressure and trigger appropriate responses by the brain.

basal Toward the base. In plants, toward the root or at the base of a branch where it joins the stem. In animals, on the side of an epithelial layer that abuts underlying body tissues. Compare with **apical**.

basal body The microtubule organizing center for cilia and flagella in eukaryotic cells. Consists of nine triplets of microtubules arranged in a circle and establishes the structure of axonemes. Structurally identical with a centriole.

basal lamina A thick, collagen-rich extracellular matrix that underlies most epithelial tissues in animals and connects it to connective tissue.

basal metabolic rate (BMR) The total energy consumption by an organism at rest in a comfortable environment. For aerobes, often measured as the amount of oxygen consumed per hour.

basal transcription factor Proteins, present in all eukaryotic cells, that bind to promoters and help initiate transcription. Compare with **regulatory transcription factor**.

base Any compound that acquires protons or gives up electrons during a chemical reaction or accepts hydrogen ions when dissolved in water.

basidium (plural: basidia) Specialized spore-producing cell at the ends of hyphae in club fungi, members of the Basidiomycota.

basilar membrane The membrane on which the bottom portion of hair cells sits in the vertebrate cochlea.

basolateral Toward the bottom and sides. In animals, the side of an epithelial layer that faces other body tissues and not the environment.

Batesian mimicry A type of mimicry in which a harmless or palatable species resembles a dangerous or poisonous species. Compare with **Müllerian mimicry**.

beak A structure that exerts biting forces and is associated with the mouth; found in birds, cephalopods, and some insects.

behavior Any action by an organism, often in response to a stimulus.

behavioral ecology The study of how organisms respond to particular abiotic and biotic stimuli from their environment.

beneficial In genetics, referring to any mutation, allele, or trait that increases an individual's fitness.

benign tumor A mass of abnormal tissue that appears due to unregulated growth but does not spread to other organs. Benign tumors are not cancers. Compare with **malignant tumor**.

benthic Living at the bottom of an aquatic environment.

benthic zone The area along the bottom of an aquatic environment.

β-pleated sheet (beta-pleated sheet) A protein secondary structure in which the polypeptide backbone folds into a sheetlike shape stabilized by hydrogen bonding.

bilateral symmetry An animal body pattern in which one plane of symmetry divides the body into a left side and a right side. Typically, the body is long and narrow, with a distinct head end and tail end. Compare with **radial symmetry**.

bilaterian A member of a major lineage of animals (Bilateria) that are bilaterally symmetrical at some point in their life cycle, have three embryonic germ layers, and have a coelom. All protostomes and deuterostomes are bilaterians.

bile A complex solution produced by the liver, stored in the gallbladder, and secreted into the intestine. Contains steroid derivatives called bile salts that are responsible for emulsification of fats during digestion.

binary fission The process of cell division used for asexual reproduction of many prokaryotic cells. The genetic material is replicated and partitioned to opposite sides of a growing cell, which is then divided in half to create two genetically identical cells.

biodiversity The diversity of life considered at three levels: genetic diversity (variety of alleles and/or genes in a population, species, or group of species); species diversity (variety and relative abundance of species present in a certain area); and ecosystem diversity (variety of communities and abiotic components in a region).

biodiversity hotspot A region that is extraordinarily rich in species.

biofilm A complex community of bacteria enmeshed in a polysaccharide-rich, extracellular matrix that allows them to attach to a surface.

biogeochemical cycle The pattern of circulation of an element or molecule among living organisms and the environment.

biogeography The study of how species and populations are distributed geographically.

bioinformatics The field of study concerned with managing, analyzing, and interpreting biological information, particularly DNA sequences.

biological species concept The definition of a species as a population or group of populations that are reproductively isolated from other groups. Members of a species have the potential to interbreed in nature to produce viable, fertile offspring but cannot interbreed successfully with members of other species. Compare with **morphospecies** and **phylogenetic species concepts**.

bioluminescence The emission of light by a living organism via an enzyme-catalyzed reaction.

biomagnification In animal tissues, an increase in the concentration of particular molecules that may occur as those molecules are passed up a food chain.

biomass The total mass of all organisms in a given population or geographical area; usually expressed as total dry weight.

biome A large terrestrial or marine region characterized by distinct abiotic characteristics and dominant types of vegetation.

biomechanics A field of biology that applies the principles of physics and engineering to analyze the mechanical structure and function of organisms.

bioprospecting The effort to find commercially useful compounds by studying organisms—especially species that are poorly studied to date.

bioremediation The use of living organisms, usually bacteria or archaea, to degrade environmental pollutants.

biosphere The thin zone surrounding the Earth where all life exists; the sum of all terrestrial and aquatic ecosystems.

biotechnology The application of biological techniques and discoveries to medicine, industry, and agriculture.

biotic Living, or produced by a living organism. Compare with **abiotic**.

bipedal Walking primarily on two legs; characteristic of hominins.

bipolar cell A type of cell in the vertebrate retina that receives information from one or more photoreceptors and passes it to other bipolar cells or ganglion cells.

bivalent The structure formed by synapsed homologous chromosomes during prophase of meiosis I. Also known as a *tetrad*.

bivalves A lineage of mollusks that have shells made of two parts, or valves, such as clams and mussels.

bladder A mammalian organ that holds urine until it can be excreted.

blade The wide, flat part of a plant leaf.

blastocoel Fluid-filled cavity in the blastula of many animal species.

blastocyst The mammalian blastula. A roughly spherical structure composed of trophoblast cells on the exterior and a cluster of cells (the inner cell mass) that fills part of the interior space.

blastomere A cell created by cleavage divisions in early animal embryos.

blastopore An opening (pore) in the surface of some early embryos, through which cells move during gastrulation.

blastula In vertebrate development, a ball of cells (blastomere cells) typically surrounding a fluid-filled cavity (the blastocoel). The blastula is formed by cleavage of a zygote and undergoes gastrulation. See **blastocyst**.

blood A type of connective tissue consisting of red blood cells and leukocytes suspended in a fluid portion, an extracellular matrix called plasma. Transports materials throughout the vertebrate body.

body mass index (BMI) A mathematical relationship of weight and height used to assess obesity in humans. Calculated as weight (kg) divided by the square of height (m^2).

body plan The basic architecture of an animal's body, including the number and arrangement of limbs, body segments, and major tissue layers.

bog A freshwater wetland that has no or almost no water flow, resulting in very low oxygen levels and acidic conditions.

Bohr shift The rightward shift of the oxygen–hemoglobin equilibrium curve that occurs with decreasing pH. It results in hemoglobin being more likely to release oxygen in the acidic environment of exercising muscle.

bone A type of vertebrate connective tissue consisting of living cells and blood vessels within a hard extracellular matrix composed of calcium phosphate ($CaPO_4$) and small amounts of calcium carbonate ($CaCO_3$) and protein fibers.

bone marrow The soft tissue filling the inside of large bones; contains stem cells that develop into red blood cells and leukocytes throughout life.

Bowman's capsule The hollow, double-walled, cup-shaped portion of a nephron that surrounds a glomerulus in the vertebrate kidney.

brain A large mass of neurons, located in the head region of an animal, that is involved in information processing; may also be called the cerebral ganglion.

brain stem The most posterior portion of the vertebrate brain, connecting to the spinal cord and responsible for autonomic body functions such as heart rate, respiration, and digestion.

braincase See **cranium**.

branch (1) A part of a phylogenetic tree that represents populations through time. (2) Any extension of a plant's shoot system.

brassinosteroids A family of steroid hormones found in plants; stimulate growth.

bronchiole Any of the small tubes in mammalian lungs that carry air from the bronchi to the alveoli.

bronchus (plural: bronchi) In mammals, one of a pair of large tubes that lead from the trachea to each lung.

bryophyte See **non-vascular plants**.

budding Asexual reproduction in which an outgrowth from the parent breaks free as an independent individual; occurs in yeasts and some invertebrates.

buffer A substance that, in solution, acts to minimize changes in the pH of that solution when acid or base is added.

bulbourethral gland In male mammals, either of a small pair of glands at the base of the urethra that secrete an alkaline mucus (part of semen), which lubricates the tip of the penis and neutralizes acids in the urethra during copulation. In humans, also called *Cowper's glands*.

bulk flow The directional mass movement of a fluid due to pressure differences, such as movement of water through plant xylem and phloem, and movement of blood in animals.

bulk-phase endocytosis Nonspecific uptake of extracellular fluid by pinching off the plasma membrane to form small membrane-bound vesicles; considered to be a means of retrieving membrane from the surface following exocytosis. Compare with **receptor-mediated endocytosis**.

bundle-sheath cell A type of cell found around the vascular tissue (veins) of plant leaves.

C$_3$ pathway The most common form of photosynthesis in which atmospheric CO_2 is fixed by rubisco to form 3-phosphoglycerate, a three-carbon molecule. Used in first phase of the Calvin cycle.

C$_4$ pathway A variant type of photosynthesis in which atmospheric CO_2 is first fixed by PEP carboxylase into four-carbon acids, rather than the three-carbon molecules of the classic C$_3$ pathway. Used to concentrate CO_2 to reduce photorespiration in the Calvin cycle while stomata are closed.

C$_4$ photosynthesis A variant type of photosynthesis in which atmospheric CO_2 is first fixed into four-carbon sugars, rather than the three-carbon sugars of classic C$_3$ photosynthesis. Enhances photosynthetic efficiency in hot, dry environments by reducing loss of oxygen due to photorespiration.

cadherin Any of a class of cell-surface proteins involved in selective cell–cell adhesion. Important for coordinating movements of cells and the establishment of tissues during embryological development.

callus In plants, a mass of undifferentiated cells that can generate roots and other tissues necessary to create a mature plant.

Calvin cycle In photosynthesis, the set of reactions that use NADPH and ATP formed in the light-dependent reactions to drive the fixation of CO_2, reduction of the fixed carbon to produce sugar, and the regeneration of the substrate used to fix CO_2. Also called *light-independent reactions*.

calyx All of the sepals of a flower.

CAM See **crassulacean acid metabolism**.

cambium (plural: cambia) In woody plants, tissue that consists of two types of cylindrical meristems that increase the width of roots and shoots through the process of secondary growth. See **vascular cambium** and **cork cambium**.

Cambrian explosion The rapid diversification of animal body types and lineages that occured between the species present in the Doushantuo faunas (around 570 mya), Ediacaran faunas (565–542 mya), and the Early Cambrian faunas (525–515 mya).

cancer General term for any tumor whose cells grow in an uncontrolled fashion, invade nearby tissues, and spread to other sites in the body.

capillarity The tendency of water to move up a narrow tube due to adhesion, cohesion, and surface tension (also called capillary action).

capillary Any of the many small, thin-walled blood vessels that permeate all tissues and organs, and allow exchange of gases and other molecules between blood and body cells.

capillary bed A thick network of capillaries.

capsid A shell of protein enclosing the genome of a virus particle.

carapace In crustaceans, a large platelike section of the exoskeleton that covers and protects the cephalothorax (e.g., a crab's "shell").

carbohydrate Any of a class of molecules that contain a carbonyl group, several hydroxyl groups, and several to many carbon-hydrogen bonds. See **monosaccharide** and **polysaccharide**.

carbon cycle, global The worldwide movement of carbon among terrestrial ecosystems, the oceans, and the atmosphere.

carbon fixation The process of converting gaseous carbon dioxide into an organic molecule, often associated with photosynthesis. See also **PEP carboxylase** and **rubisco**.

carbonic anhydrase An enzyme that catalyzes the formation of carbonic acid (H_2CO_3) from carbon dioxide and water.

carboxylic acids Organic acids with the form R-COOH (a carboxyl group).

cardiac cycle One complete heartbeat cycle, including systole and diastole.

cardiac muscle The muscle tissue of the vertebrate heart; responsible for pumping blood. Consists of long, branched fibers that are electrically connected and that initiate their own contractions; not under voluntary control. Compare with **skeletal** and **smooth muscle**.

cardiovascular disease A group of diseases of the heart and blood vessels caused by poor diet, obesity, inactivity, genetics, tobacco use, age, and other factors.

carnivore (adjective: carnivorous) An animal whose diet consists predominantly of meat, or other animals. Most members of the mammalian taxon Carnivora are carnivores. Some plants are carnivorous, trapping and killing small animals and then absorbing nutrients from the prey's body. Compare with **herbivore** and **omnivore**.

carotenoid Any of a class of accessory pigments, found in chloroplasts, that absorb wavelengths of light not absorbed by chlorophyll; typically appear yellow, orange, or red. Includes carotenes and xanthophylls.

carpel The female reproductive organ in a flower. Consists of the stigma, to which pollen grains adhere; the style, through which the pollen tube grows; and the ovary, which houses the ovule. Compare with **stamen**.

carrier protein A membrane protein that facilitates diffusion of a small molecule (e.g., glucose) across a membrane by a process involving a reversible change in the shape of the protein. Also called *carrier* or *transporter*. Compare with **channel protein**.

carrier A heterozygous individual carrying a normal allele and a recessive allele for an inherited trait; does not display the phenotype of the recessive trait but can pass the recessive allele to offspring.

carrying capacity (*K*) The maximum population size of a certain species that a given habitat can support.

cartilage A type of vertebrate connective tissue that consists of relatively few cells scattered in a stiff matrix of polysaccharides and protein fibers. Provides structural support.

Casparian strip In plant roots, a waxy layer containing suberin, a water-repellent substance that prevents movement of water through the walls of endodermal cells, thus blocking the apoplastic pathway of water and ion movement into the vascular tissue.

cast A type of fossil, formed when the decay of a body part leaves a void that is then filled with minerals that later harden.

catabolic pathway Any set of chemical reactions that breaks down large, complex molecules into smaller ones, releasing energy in the process. Compare with **anabolic pathway**.

catalysis (verb: catalyze) Acceleration of the rate of a chemical reaction due to a decrease in the free energy of the transition state, called the activation energy.

catalyst Any substance that increases the rate of a chemical reaction without itself undergoing any permanent chemical change.

catecholamines A class of small compounds, derived from the amino acid tyrosine, that are used as hormones or neurotransmitters. Include epinephrine, norepinephrine, and dopamine.

cation A positively charged ion.

cation exchange The release (displacement) of cations, such as magnesium and calcium from soil particles, by protons in acidic soil water. The released cations are available for uptake by plants.

CD4 A membrane protein on the surface of some T cells in humans. $CD4^+$ T cells can give rise to helper T cells.

CD8 A membrane protein on the surface of some T cells in humans. $CD8^+$ T cells can give rise to cytotoxic T cells.

Cdk See **cyclin-dependent kinase**.

cDNA See **complementary DNA**.

cDNA library A set of cDNAs from a particular cell type or stage of development. Each cDNA is carried by a plasmid or other cloning vector and can be separated from other cDNAs. Compare with **genomic library**.

cecum A blind sac between the small intestine and the colon. Is enlarged in some species (e.g., rabbits) that use it as a fermentation vat for digestion of cellulose.

cell A highly organized compartment bounded by a thin, flexible structure (plasma membrane) and containing concentrated chemicals in an aqueous (watery) solution. The basic structural and functional unit of all organisms.

cell body The part of a neuron that contains the nucleus; where incoming signals are integrated. Also called the *soma*.

cell crawling A form of cellular movement involving actin filaments in which the cell produces bulges (pseudopodia) that stick to the substrate and pull the cell forward. Also called *amoeboid motion*.

cell cycle Ordered sequence of events in which a eukaryotic cell replicates its chromosomes, evenly partitions the chromosomes to two daughter cells, and then undergoes division of the cytoplasm.

cell-cycle checkpoint Any of several points in the cell cycle at which progression of a cell through the cycle can be regulated.

cell division Creation of new cells by division of preexisting cells.

cell-mediated (immune) response The type of immune response that involves generation of cytotoxic T cells from $CD8^+$ T cells. Defends against pathogen-infected cells, cancer cells, and transplanted cells. Compare with **humoral (immune) response**.

cell membrane See **plasma membrane**.

cell plate A flattened sac-like structure formed in the middle of a dividing plant cell from Golgi-derived vesicles containing cell wall material; ultimately divides the cytoplasm into two separate cells.

cell sap An aqueous solution found in the vacuoles of plant cells.

cell theory The theory that all organisms are made of cells and that all cells come from preexisting cells.

cell wall A fibrous layer found outside the plasma membrane of most bacteria and archaea and many eukaryotes.

cellular respiration A common pathway for production of ATP, involving transfer of electrons from compounds with high potential energy through an electron transport chain and ultimately to an electron acceptor (often oxygen).

cellulase An enzyme that can break down cellulose by catalyzing hydrolysis of the glycosidic linkages between the glucose residues.

cellulose A structural polysaccharide composed of glucose monomers joined by β-1,4-glycosidic linkages. Found in the cell wall of algae, plants, and some bacteria and fungi.

Cenozoic era The most recent interval of geologic time, beginning 65.5 million years ago, during which mammals became the dominant vertebrates and angiosperms became the dominant plants.

central dogma The scheme for information flow in the cell: DNA → RNA → protein.

central nervous system (CNS) Large numbers of neurons aggregated into clusters called ganglia in bilaterian animals. In vertebrates, the central nervous system consists of the brain and spinal cord. Compare with **nerve net** and **peripheral nervous system (PNS)**.

centriole One of two small cylindrical structures found together within the centrosome near the nucleus of a eukaryotic cell (not found in plants). Consists of microtubule triplets and is structurally identical with a basal body.

centromere Constricted region of a replicated chromosome where the two sister chromatids are joined and the kinetochore is located.

centrosome Structure in animal and fungal cells, containing two centrioles, that serves as a microtubule organizing center for the cell's cytoskeleton and for the spindle apparatus during cell division.

cephalization The formation in animals of a distinct anterior region (the head) where sense organs and a mouth are clustered.

cephalochordates One of the three major chordate lineages (Cephalochordata), comprising small, mobile organisms that live in marine sands and suspension feed; also called *lancelets* or *amphioxus*. Compare with **urochordates** and **vertebrates**.

cephalopods A lineage of mollusks including the squid, octopuses, and nautiluses. Distinguished by large brains, excellent vision, tentacles, and a reduced or absent shell.

cerebellum Posterior section of the vertebrate brain; involved in coordination of complex muscle movements, such as those required for locomotion and maintaining balance.

cerebrum The most anterior section of the vertebrate brain. Divided into left and right hemispheres and four lobes: frontal lobe, involved in complex decision making (in humans); occipital lobe, receives and interprets visual information; parietal lobe, involved in integrating sensory and motor functions; and temporal lobe, functions in memory, speech (in humans), and interpreting auditory information.

cervix The bottom portion of the uterus, containing a canal that leads to the vagina.

chaetae (singular: chaeta) Bristle-like extensions found in some annelids.

channel protein A protein that forms a pore in a cell membrane. The structure of most channels allows them to admit just one or a few types of ions or molecules. Compare with **carrier protein**.

character Any genetic, morphological, physiological, or behavioral characteristic of an organism to be studied.

character displacement The evolutionary tendency for the traits of similar species that occupy overlapping ranges to change in a way that reduces interspecific competition.

chelicerae A pair of clawlike appendages found around the mouth of certain arthropods called chelicerates (spiders, mites, and allies).

chemical bond An attractive force binding two atoms together. Covalent bonds, ionic bonds, and hydrogen bonds are types of chemical bonds.

chemical energy The potential energy stored in covalent bonds between atoms.

chemical equilibrium A dynamic but stable state of a reversible chemical reaction in which the forward reaction and reverse reactions proceed at the same rate, so that the concentrations of reactants and products remain constant.

chemical evolution A The theory that simple chemical compounds in the early atmosphere and ocean combined via chemical reactions to form larger, more complex substances, eventually leading to the origin of life and the start of biological evolution.

chemical reaction Any process in which one compound or element is combined with others or is broken down; involves the making and/or breaking of chemical bonds.

chemiosmosis An energetic coupling mechanism whereby energy stored in an electrochemical proton gradient is used to drive an energy-requiring process such as production of ATP.

chemokine Any of a subset of cytokines that acts as a chemical signal attracting leukocytes to a site of tissue injury or infection.

chemolithotroph An organism (bacteria or archaea) that produces ATP by oxidizing inorganic molecules with high potential energy such as ammonia (NH_3) or methane (CH_4). Also called *lithotroph*. Compare with **chemoorganotroph**.

chemoorganotroph An organism that produces ATP by oxidizing organic molecules with high potential energy such as sugars. Also called *organotroph*. Compare with **chemolithotroph**.

chemoreception A sensory system in which receptors are activated in response to the binding of chemicals.

chemoreceptor A sensory cell or organ specialized for detection of specific molecules or classes of molecules.

chiasma (plural: chiasmata) The X-shaped structure formed during meiosis by crossing over between non-sister chromatids in a pair of homologous chromosomes.

chitin A structural polysaccharide composed of *N*-acetyl-glucosamine (NAG) monomers joined end to end by β-1,4-glycosidic linkages. Found in cell walls of fungi and many algae, and in external skeletons of insects and crustaceans.

chitons A lineage of marine mollusks that have a protective shell formed of eight calcium carbonate plates.

chlorophyll Any of several closely related green pigments, found in chloroplasts, that absorb light during photosynthesis.

chloroplast A chlorophyll-containing organelle, bounded by a double membrane, in which photosynthesis occurs; found in plants and photosynthetic protists. Also the location of starch, amino acid, fatty acid, purine, and pyrimidine synthesis.

choanocyte A specialized, flagellated feeding cell found in choanoflagellates (protists that are the closest living relatives of animals) and sponges (the most ancient animal phylum).

cholecystokinin A peptide hormone secreted by cells in the lining of the small intestine. Stimulates the secretion of digestive enzymes from the pancreas and of bile from the liver and gallbladder.

chordate Any member of the phylum Chordata. Chordates are deuterostomes distinguished by a dorsal hollow nerve cord, pharyngeal gill slits, a notochord, and a post-anal tail. Includes vertebrates, cephalochordata, and urochordata.

chromatid One of the two identical double-stranded DNAs composing a replicated chromosome that is connected at the centromere to the other strand.

chromatin The complex of DNA and proteins, mainly histones, that compose eukaryotic chromosomes. Can be highly compact (heterochromatin) or loosely coiled (euchromatin).

chromatin remodeling The process by which the DNA in chromatin is unwound from its associated proteins to allow transcription or replication. May involve chemical modification of histone proteins or reshaping of the chromatin by large multiprotein complexes in an ATP-requiring process.

chromatin remodeling complexes Sets of enzymes that use energy from ATP hydrolysis shift nucleosomes on DNA to expose regulatory sequences to transcription factors.

chromosome theory of inheritance The principle that genes are located on chromosomes and that patterns of inheritance are determined by the behavior of chromosomes during meiosis.

chromosome Gene-carrying structure consisting of a single long molecule of double-stranded DNA and

associated proteins (e.g., histones). Most prokaryotic cells contain a single, circular chromosome; eukaryotic cells contain multiple noncircular (linear) chromosomes located in the nucleus.

cilium (plural: cilia) One of many short, filamentous projections of some eukaryotic cells, containing a core of microtubules. Used to move the cell as well as to circulate fluid or particles around the surface of a stationary cell. See **axoneme**.

circadian clock An internal mechanism found in most organisms that regulates many body processes (sleep–wake cycles, hormonal patterns, etc.) in a roughly 24-hour cycle.

circulatory system The system responsible for moving oxygen, carbon dioxide, and other materials (hormones, nutrients, wastes) within the animal body.

cisternae (singular: cisterna) Flattened, membrane-bound compartments that make up the Golgi apparatus.

cisternal maturation The process of cargo movement through the Golgi apparatus by residing in cisternae that mature from *cis* to *trans* via the import and export of different Golgi enzymes.

citric acid cycle A series of eight chemical reactions that start with citrate (deprotonated citric acid) and ends with oxaloacetate, which reacts with acetyl CoA to form citrate—forming a cycle that is part of the pathway that oxidizes glucose to CO_2. Also known as the *Krebs cycle* or *tricarboxylic acid (TCA) cycle*.

clade See **monophyletic group**.

cladistic approach A method for constructing a phylogenetic tree that is based on identifying the unique traits (shared, derived characters, called synapomorphies) of each monophyletic group.

Class I MHC protein A type of MHC protein that is present on the plasma membrane of virtually all nucleated cells and functions in presenting antigen to $CD8^+$ T cells.

Class II MHC protein A type of MHC protein that is present only on the plasma membrane of certain cells in the immune response, such as dendritic cells, macrophages, and B cells. It functions in presenting epitopes of antigens to $CD4^+$ T cells.

cleavage In animal development, the series of rapid mitotic cell divisions, with little cell growth, that produces successively smaller cells (blastomeres) and transforms a zygote into a multicellular blastula.

cleavage furrow A pinching in of the plasma membrane that occurs as cytokinesis begins in animal cells and deepens until the cytoplasm is divided into two daughter cells.

climate The prevailing, long-term weather conditions in a particular region.

climax community The stable, final community that develops from ecological succession.

clitoris A rod of erectile tissue in the external genitalia of female mammals. Is formed from the same embryonic tissue as the male penis and has a similar function in sexual arousal.

cloaca In a few mammals and many nonmammalian vertebrates, a body cavity opening to the outside and used by both the excretory and reproductive systems.

clonal selection theory The dominant explanation of the generation of an adaptive immune response. According to the theory, the immune system retains a vast pool of inactive lymphocytes, each with a unique receptor for a unique epitope. Lymphocytes that encounter their complementary epitopes are stimulated to divide (selected and cloned), producing daughter cells that combat infection and confer immunity.

clone (1) An individual that is genetically identical to another individual. (2) A lineage of genetically identical individuals or cells. (3) As a verb, to make one or more genetic replicas of a cell or individual.

cloning vector A plasmid or other agent used to transfer recombinant genes into cultured host cells. Also called simply *vector*.

closed circulatory system A circulatory system in which the circulating fluid (blood) is confined to blood vessels and flows in a continuous circuit. Compare with **open circulatory system**.

cnidocyte A specialized stinging cell found in cnidarians (e.g., jellyfish, corals, and anemones) and used in capturing prey.

co-receptor Any membrane protein that acts with some other membrane protein in a cell interaction or cell response.

cochlea The organ of hearing in the inner ear of mammals, birds, and crocodilians. A coiled, fluid-filled tube containing specialized pressure-sensing neurons (hair cells) that detect sounds of different pitches.

coding strand See **non-template strand**.

codominance An inheritance pattern in which heterozygotes exhibit both of the traits seen in each type of homozygous individual.

codon A sequence of three nucleotides in DNA or RNA that codes for an amino acid or a start or stop signal for protein synthesis.

coefficient of relatedness (*r*) A measure of how closely two individuals are related. Calculated as the probability that an allele in two individuals is inherited from the same ancestor.

coelom An internal, usually fluid-filled body cavity that is completely or partially lined with mesoderm.

coelomate An animal that has a true coelom, completely lined with mesoderm. Compare with **acoelomate** and **pseudocoelomate**.

coenocytic Containing many nuclei and a continuous cytoplasm through a filamentous body, without the body being divided into distinct cells. Some fungi are coenocytic.

coenzyme A small organic molecule that is a required cofactor for an enzyme-catalyzed reaction. Often donates or receives electrons or functional groups during the reaction.

coenzyme A (CoA) A molecule that is required for many cellular reactions and that is often transiently linked to other molecules, such as acetyl groups (see **acetyl CoA**).

coenzyme Q A nonprotein molecule that shuttles electrons between membrane-bound complexes in the mitochondrial electron transport chain. Also called **ubiquinone** or *Q*.

coevolution A pattern of evolution in which two interacting species reciprocally influence each other's adaptations over time.

coevolutionary arms race A series of adaptations and counter-adaptations observed in species that interact closely over time and affect each other's fitness.

cofactor An inorganic ion, such as a metal ion, that is required for an enzyme to function normally. May be bound tightly to an enzyme or associate with it transiently during catalysis.

cohesion The tendency of certain like molecules (e.g., water molecules) to cling together due to attractive forces. Compare with **adhesion**.

cohesion-tension theory The theory that water movement upward through plant vascular tissues is due to loss of water from leaves (transpiration), which pulls a cohesive column of water upward.

cohort A group of individuals that are the same age and can be followed through time.

coleoptile A modified leaf that covers and protects the stems and leaves of grass seedlings.

collagen A fibrous, pliable, cable-like glycoprotein that is a major component of the extracellular matrix of animal cells. Various subtypes differ in their tissue distribution, some of which are assembled into large fibrils in the extracellular space.

collecting duct In the vertebrate kidney, a large straight tube that receives filtrate from the distal tubules of several nephrons. Involved in the regulated reabsorption of water.

collenchyma cell In plants, an elongated cell with cell walls thickened at the corners that provides support to growing plant parts; usually found in strands along leaf veins and stalks. Compare with **parenchyma cell** and **sclerenchyma cell**.

colon The portion of the large intestine where feces are formed by compaction of wastes and reabsorption of water.

colony An assemblage of individuals. May refer to an assemblage of semi-independent cells or to a breeding population of multicellular organisms.

commensalism (adjective: commensal) A symbiotic relationship in which one organism (the commensal) benefits and the other (the host) is not harmed. Compare with **mutualism** and **parasitism**.

communication In ecology, any process in which a signal from one individual modifies the behavior of another individual.

community All of the species that interact with each other in a certain area.

companion cell In plants, a cell in the phloem that is connected via many plasmodesmata to adjacent sieve-tube elements. Companion cells provide materials to maintain sieve-tube elements and function in the loading and unloading of sugars into sieve-tube elements.

compass orientation A type of navigation in which movement occurs in a specific direction.

competition In ecology, the interaction of two species or two individuals trying to use the same limited resource (e.g., water, food, living space). May occur between individuals of the same species (intraspecific competition) or different species (interspecific competition).

competitive exclusion principle The principle that two species cannot coexist in the same ecological niche in the same area because one species will outcompete the other.

competitive inhibition Inhibition of an enzyme's ability to catalyze a chemical reaction via binding of a nonreactant molecule that competes with the substrate(s) for access to the active site.

complement system A set of proteins that circulate in the bloodstream and can destroy bacteria by forming holes in the bacterial plasma membrane.

complementary base pairing The association between specific nitrogenous bases of nucleic acids stabilized by hydrogen bonding. Adenine pairs only with thymine (in DNA) or uracil (in RNA), and guanine pairs only with cytosine.

complementary DNA (cDNA) DNA produced in the laboratory using an RNA transcript as a template and reverse transcriptase; corresponds to a gene but lacks introns. Also produced naturally by retroviruses.

complementary strand A newly synthesized strand of RNA or DNA that has a base sequence complementary to that of the template strand.

complete digestive tract A digestive tract with two openings, usually called a mouth and an anus.

complete metamorphosis See **holometabolous metamorphosis**.

compound eye An eye formed of many independent light-sensing columns (ommatidia); occurs in arthropods. Compare with **simple eye**.

concentration gradient Difference across space (e.g., across a membrane) in the concentration of a dissolved substance.

condensation reaction A chemical reaction in which two molecules are joined covalently with the removal of an −OH from one and an −H from another to form water. Also called a *dehydration reaction*. Compare with **hydrolysis**.

conduction (1) Direct transfer of heat between two objects that are in physical contact. Compare with **convection**. (2) Transmission of an electrical impulse along the axon of a nerve cell.

cone cell A photoreceptor cell with a cone-shaped outer portion that is particularly sensitive to bright light of a certain color. Also called simply *cone*. Compare with **rod cell**.

connective tissue An animal tissue consisting of scattered cells in a liquid, jellylike, or solid extracellular matrix. Includes bone, cartilage, tendons, ligaments, and blood.

conservation biology The effort to study, preserve, and restore threatened genetic diversity, populations, communities, and ecosystems.

constant (C) region The invariant amino acid sequence in polypeptides that are used to make antibodies, B-cell receptors, and T-cell receptors. Apart from antibody class types (IgG, IgM, etc.), this region remains constant within an individual. Compare with **variable (V) region**.

constitutive Always occurring; always present. Commonly used to describe enzymes and other proteins that are synthesized continuously or mutants in which one or more genetic loci are constantly expressed due to defects in gene control.

constitutive defense A defensive trait that is always manifested even in the absence of a predator or pathogen. Also called *standing defense*. Compare with **inducible defenses**.

constitutive mutant An abnormal (mutated) strain that produces a product at all times, instead of under certain conditions only.

consumer See **heterotroph**.

consumption Predation or herbivory.

continental shelf The portion of a geologic plate that extends from a continent under seawater.

continuous strand See **leading strand**.

contraception Any of several methods to prevent pregnancy.

control In a scientific experiment, a group of organisms or samples that do not receive the experimental treatment but are otherwise identical to the group that does.

convection Transfer of heat by movement of large volumes of a gas or liquid. Compare with **conduction**.

convergent evolution The independent evolution of similar traits in distantly related organisms due to adaptation to similar environments and a similar way of life.

cooperative binding The tendency of the protein subunits of hemoglobin to affect each other's oxygen binding such that each bound oxygen molecule increases the likelihood of further oxygen binding.

coprophagy The eating of feces.

coral reef A large assemblage of colonial marine corals that usually serves as shallow-water, sunlit habitat for many other species as well.

co-receptor Any membrane protein that acts with some other membrane protein in a cell interaction or cell response.

core enzyme The enzyme responsible for catalysis in a multipart holoenzyme.

cork cambium One of two types of cylindrical meristem, consisting of a ring of undifferentiated plant cells found just under the cork layer of woody stems and roots; produces new cork cells on its outer side. Compare with **vascular cambium**.

cork cell A cell in the protective outermost layer of a woody stem and root that produces and accumulates waxes that make the cell less permeable to water and gases.

corm A rounded, thick underground stem that can produce new plants via asexual reproduction.

cornea The transparent sheet of connective tissue at the very front of the eye in vertebrates and some other animals. Protects the eye and helps focus light.

corolla All of the petals of a flower.

corona The cluster of cilia at the anterior end of a rotifer; in many species it facilitates suspension feeding.

corpus callosum A thick band of neurons that connects the two hemispheres of the cerebrum in the mammalian brain.

corpus luteum A yellowish structure that secretes progesterone in an ovary. Is formed from a follicle that has recently ovulated.

cortex (1) In animals, the outermost region of an organ, such as the kidney or adrenal gland. (2) In plants, a layer of ground tissue found outside the vascular bundles of roots and outside the pith of a stem.

corticotropin-releasing hormone (CRH) A peptide hormone, produced and secreted by the hypothalamus, that stimulates the anterior pituitary to release ACTH.

cortisol A steroid hormone, produced and secreted by the adrenal cortex, that increases blood glucose and prepares the body for stress. The major glucocorticoid hormone in some mammals. Also called *hydrocortisone*.

cost–benefit analysis Decisions or analyses that weigh the fitness costs and benefits of a particular action.

cotransporter A transmembrane protein that facilitates diffusion of an ion down its previously established electrochemical gradient and uses the energy of that process to transport some other substance, in the same or opposite direction, *against* its concentration gradient. Also called *secondary active transporter*. See **antiporter** and **symporter**.

cotyledon The first leaf, or seed leaf, of a plant embryo. Used for storing and digesting nutrients and/or for early photosynthesis.

countercurrent exchanger In animals, any anatomical arrangement that allows the maximum transfer of heat or a soluble substance from one fluid to another. The two fluids must be flowing in opposite directions and have a heat or concentration gradient between them.

covalent bond A type of chemical bond in which two atoms share one or more pairs of electrons. Compare with **hydrogen bond** and **ionic bond**.

cranium A bony, cartilaginous, or fibrous case that encloses and protects the brain of vertebrates. Forms part of the skull. Also called *braincase*.

crassulacean acid metabolism (CAM) A variant type of photosynthesis in which CO_2 is fixed and stored in organic acids at night when stomata are open and then released to feed the Calvin cycle during the day when stomata are closed. Helps reduce water loss and CO_2 loss by photorespiration.

cristae (singular: crista) Sac-like invaginations of the inner membrane of a mitochondrion. Location of the electron transport chain and ATP synthase.

Cro-Magnon A prehistoric European population of modern humans (*Homo sapiens*) known from fossils, paintings, sculptures, and other artifacts.

crop A storage organ in the digestive system of certain vertebrates.

cross A mating between two individuals that is used for genetic analysis.

cross-pollination Pollination of a flower by pollen from another individual, rather than by self-fertilization. Also called *crossing*.

cross-talk Interactions among signaling pathways, triggered by different signals, that modify a cellular response.

crossing over The exchange of segments of non-sister chromatids between a pair of homologous chromosomes that occurs during meiosis I.

crosstalk Interactions among signaling pathways that modify a cellular response.

crustaceans A lineage of arthropods that includes shrimp, lobster, and crabs. Many have a carapace (a platelike portion of the exoskeleton covering the cephalothorax) and mandibles for biting or chewing.

cryptic species A species that cannot be distinguished from similar species by easily identifiable morphological traits.

culture In cell biology, a collection of cells or a tissue growing under controlled conditions, usually in suspension or on the surface of a dish of solid growth medium.

Cushing's disease A human endocrine disorder caused by loss of feedback inhibition of cortisol on ACTH secretion. Characterized by high ACTH and cortisol levels and wasting of body protein reserves.

cuticle A protective coating secreted by the outermost layer of cells of an animal or a plant; often functioning to reduce evaporative water loss.

cyanobacteria A lineage of photosynthetic bacteria formerly known as blue-green algae. Likely the first life-forms to carry out oxygenic photosynthesis.

cyclic AMP (cAMP) Cyclic adenosine monophosphate; a small molecule, derived from ATP, that is widely used by cells in signal transduction and transcriptional control.

cyclic electron flow Path of electrons in which excited electrons of photosystem I are transferred back to plastoquinone (PQ), the start of the electron transport chain normally associated with photosystem II. Instead of reducing $NADP^+$ to make NADPH, the electron energy is used to make ATP via photophosphorylation. Compare with **noncyclic electron flow**.

cyclin One of several regulatory proteins whose concentrations fluctuate cyclically throughout the cell cycle. Involved in the control of the cell cycle via cyclin-dependent kinases.

cyclin-dependent kinase (Cdk) Any of several related protein kinases that are functional only when bound to a cyclin and are activated by other modifications. Involved in control of the cell cycle.

cytochrome *c* (cyt *c*) A soluble protein that shuttles electrons between membrane-bound complexes in the mitochondrial electron transport chain.

cytokine Any of a diverse group of signaling proteins, secreted largely by cells of the immune system, whose effects include stimulating leukocyte production, recruiting cells to the site of infection, tissue repair, and fever. Generally function to regulate the type, intensity, and duration of an immune response.

cytokinesis Division of the cytoplasm to form two daughter cells. Typically occurs immediately after division of the nucleus by mitosis or meiosis.

cytokinins A class of plant hormones that stimulate cell division and retard aging.

cytoplasm All the contents of a cell, excluding the nucleus, bounded by the plasma membrane.

cytoplasmic determinant A regulatory transcription factor or signaling molecule that is distributed unevenly in the cytoplasm of the egg and that directs early pattern formation in an embryo.

cytoplasmic streaming The directed flow of cytosol and organelles that facilitates distribution of materials within some large plant and fungal cells. Occurs along actin filaments and is powered by myosin.

cytoskeleton In eukaryotic cells, a network of protein fibers in the cytoplasm that are involved in cell shape, support, locomotion, and transport of materials within the cell. Prokaryotic cells have a similar but much less extensive network of fibers.

cytosol The fluid portion of the cytoplasm, excluding the contents of membrane-enclosed organelles.

cytotoxic T cell A type of $CD8^+$ effector T cell that induces apoptosis in infected and cancerous cells. Recognizes target cells via interactions with complementary class I MHC–peptide complexes. Also called *cytotoxic T lymphocyte (CTL)* and *killer T cell*. Compare with **helper T cell**.

dalton (Da) A unit of mass equal to 1/12 the mass of one carbon-12 atom; about the mass of 1 proton or 1 neutron.

daughter strand The strand of DNA that is newly replicated from an existing template strand of DNA.

day-neutral plant A plant whose flowering time is not affected by the relative length of day and night (the photoperiod). Compare with **long-day** and **short-day plant**.

dead space Air passages that are not involved in gas exchange with the blood; examples are the trachea and bronchi.

deciduous Describing a plant that sheds leaves or other structures at regular intervals (e.g., each autumn).

decomposer See **detritivore**.

decomposer food chain An ecological network of detritus, decomposers that eat detritus, and predators and parasites of the decomposers.

deep sequencing A method to learn the types of mRNAs or DNA sequences present in cells, and their relative amounts, involving the preparation and sequencing of cDNA libraries.

definitive host The host species in which a parasite reproduces sexually. Compare with **intermediate host**.

dehydration reaction See **condensation reaction**.

deleterious In genetics, referring to any mutation, allele, or trait that reduces an individual's fitness.

deletion In genetics, refers to the loss of part of a chromosome.

demography The study of factors that determine the size and structure of populations through time.

dendrite A short extension from a neuron's cell body that receives signals from other neurons.

dendritic cell A type of leukocyte that ingests and digests foreign antigens, moves to a lymph node, and presents the antigens' epitopes, in the context of MHC proteins on its membrane, to $CD4^+$ and $CD8^+$ T cells.

dense connective tissue A type of connective tissue, distinguished by having an extracellular matrix dominated by collagen fibers. Found in tendons and ligaments.

density dependent In population ecology, referring to any characteristic that varies depending on population density.

density independent In population ecology, referring to any characteristic that does not vary with population density.

deoxyribonucleic acid (DNA) A nucleic acid composed of deoxyribonucleotides that carries the genetic information of a cell. Generally occurs as two intertwined strands, but these can be separated. See also **double helix**.

deoxyribonucleoside triphosphate (dNTP) A monomer used by DNA polymerase to polymerize DNA. Consists of the sugar deoxyribose, a base (A, T, G, or C), and three phosphate groups.

deoxyribonucleotide See **nucleotide**.

depolarization A change in membrane potential from its resting negative state to a less negative or a positive state; a normal phase in an action potential. Compare with **hyperpolarization**.

depolarization Change in membrane potential from its resting negative state to a less negative or to a positive state; a normal phase in an action potential. Compare with **hyperpolarization**.

deposit feeder An animal that eats its way through a food-containing substrate.

derived trait A trait that is clearly homologous with a trait found in an ancestor of a particular group, but that has a new form.

dermal tissue system The tissue forming the outer layer of a plant; also called *epidermis*.

descent with modification The phrase used by Darwin to describe his hypothesis of evolution by natural selection.

desmosome A type of cell–cell attachment structure, consisting of cadherin proteins, that is anchored to intermediate filaments. Serves to link the cytoskeletons of adjacent animal cells and form strong cell–cell attachments throughout a tissue. Compare with **gap junction** and **tight junction**.

detergent A type of small amphipathic molecule used to solubilize hydrophobic molecules in aqueous solution.

determination In development, the commitment of a cell to a particular differentiated fate. Once a cell is fully determined, it can differentiate only into a particular cell type (e.g., liver cell, brain cell).

detritivore An organism whose diet consists mainly of dead organic matter (detritus). Various bacteria, fungi, protists, and animals are detritivores. Also called *decomposer*.

detritus A layer of dead organic matter that accumulates at ground level or on seafloors and lake bottoms.

deuterostomes A major lineage of bilaterian animals that share a pattern of embryological development, including formation of the anus earlier than the mouth, and formation of the coelom by pinching off of layers of mesoderm from the gut. Includes echinoderms and chordates. Compare with **protostomes**.

developmental homology A similarity in embryonic form, or in the fate of embryonic tissues, that is due to inheritance from a common ancestor.

diabetes mellitus A disease caused by defects in insulin production (type 1) or in the response of cells to insulin (type 2). Characterized by abnormally high blood glucose levels and huge amounts of glucose-containing urine.

diaphragm An elastic, sheetlike structure. In mammals, the muscular sheet of tissue that separates the chest and abdominal cavities. It contracts and moves downward during inhalation, expanding the chest cavity.

diastole The portion of the cardiac cycle during which the atria or ventricles of the heart are relaxed. Compare with **systole**.

diastolic blood pressure The force exerted by blood against artery walls during relaxation of the heart's left ventricle. Compare with **systolic blood pressure**.

dicot Any flowering plant (angiosperm) that has two cotyledons (embryonic leaves) upon germination. The dicots do not form a monophyletic group. Also called *dicotyledonous plant*. Compare with **eudicot** and **monocot**.

dideoxy sequencing A laboratory technique for determining the exact nucleotide sequence of DNA. Relies on the use of dideoxynucleoside triphosphates (ddNTPs), which terminate DNA replication.

diencephalon The part of the mammalian brain that relays sensory information to the cerebellum and functions in maintaining homeostasis.

differential centrifugation Procedure for separating cellular components according to their size and density by spinning a cell homogenate in a series of centrifuge runs. After each run, the supernatant is removed from the deposited material (pellet) and spun again at progressively higher speeds.

differential gene expression Expression of different sets of genes in cells with the same genome. Responsible for creating different cell types.

differentiation The process by which any unspecialized cell becomes a distinct specialized cell type (e.g., liver cell, brain cell), usually by changes in gene expression. Also called *cell differentiation*.

diffusion Spontaneous movement of a substance from one region to another, often with a net movement from a region of high concentration to one of low concentration (i.e., down a concentration gradient).

digestion The physical and chemical breakdown of food into molecules that can be absorbed into the body of an animal.

digestive tract The long tube that begins at the mouth and ends at the anus. Also called *alimentary canal* or *gastrointestinal (GI) tract*.

dihybrid cross A mating between two parents that are heterozygous for two different genes.

dikaryotic Describing a cell or fungal mycelium having two haploid nuclei that are genetically distinct.

dimer An association of two molecules that may be identical (homodimer) or different (heterodimer).

dioecious Describing an angiosperm species that has male and female reproductive structures on separate plants. Compare with **monoecious**.

diploblast (adjective: diploblastic) An animal whose body develops from two basic embryonic cell layers

or tissues—ectoderm and endoderm. Compare with **triploblast**.

diploid (1) Having two sets of chromosomes (2*n*). (2) A cell or an individual organism with two sets of chromosomes, one set inherited from the mother and one set from the father. Compare with **haploid**.

direct sequencing A technique for identifying and studying microorganisms that cannot be grown in culture. Involves detecting and amplifying copies of certain specific genes in the microorganisms' DNA, sequencing these genes, and then comparing the sequences with the known sequences from other organisms.

directional selection A mode of natural selection that favors one extreme phenotype with the result that the average phenotype of a population changes in one direction. Generally reduces overall genetic variation in a population. Compare with **disruptive selection** and **stabilizing selection**.

disaccharide A carbohydrate consisting of two monosaccharides (sugar residues) linked together.

discontinuous strand See **lagging strand**.

discrete trait An inherited trait that exhibits distinct phenotypes rather than the continuous variation characteristic of a quantitative trait such as body height.

dispersal The movement of individuals from their place of origin (birth, hatching) to a new location.

disruptive selection A mode of natural selection that favors extreme phenotypes at both ends of the range of phenotypic variation. Maintains overall genetic variation in a population. Compare with **stabilizing selection** and **directional selection**.

distal tubule In the vertebrate kidney, the convoluted portion of a nephron into which filtrate moves from the loop of Henle. Involved in the regulated reabsorption of sodium and water. Compare with **proximal tubule**.

disturbance In ecology, any strong, short-lived disruption to a community that changes the distribution of living and/or nonliving resources.

disturbance regime The characteristic disturbances that affect a given ecological community.

disulfide bond A covalent bond between two sulfur atoms, typically in the side chains of certain amino acids (e.g., cysteine). Often contributes to tertiary and quaternary levels of protein structure.

DNA See **deoxyribonucleic acid**.

DNA cloning Any of several techniques for producing many identical copies of a particular gene or other DNA sequence.

DNA fingerprinting Any of several methods for identifying individuals by unique features of their genomes. Commonly involves using PCR to produce many copies of certain short tandem repeats (microsatellites) and then analyzing their lengths.

DNA helicase An enzyme that breaks hydrogen bonds between nucleotides of DNA, "unzipping" a double-stranded DNA molecule.

DNA library See **cDNA library** and **genomic library**.

DNA ligase An enzyme that joins pieces of DNA by catalyzing the formation of a phosphodiester bond between the pieces.

DNA methylation The addition of a methyl group ($-CH_3$) to a DNA molecule.

DNA methyltransferase A class of eukaryotic enzymes that add a methyl group to cytosines in DNA. Methylation of DNA leads to chromatin condensation and is an important means of regulating gene expression in eukaryotes.

DNA microarray A set of single-stranded DNA fragments, representing thousands of different genes that are permanently fixed to a small glass slide. Can be used to determine which genes are expressed in different cell types, under different conditions, or at different developmental stages.

DNA polymerase Any enzyme that catalyzes synthesis of DNA from deoxyribonucleotide triphosphates (dNTPs).

domain (1) A taxonomic category, based on similarities in basic cellular biochemistry, above the kingdom level. The three recognized domains are Bacteria, Archaea, and Eukarya. (2) A section of a protein that has a distinctive tertiary structure and function.

dominant Referring to an allele that determines the same phenotype when it is present in homozygous or heterozygous form.. Compare with **recessive**.

dormancy A temporary state of greatly reduced metabolic activity and growth in plants or plant parts (e.g., seeds, spores, bulbs, and buds).

dorsal Toward an animal's back and away from its belly. The opposite of ventral.

dorsal hollow nerve chord See **nerve chord**.

double fertilization An unusual form of reproduction seen in flowering plants, in which one sperm cell fuses with an egg to form a zygote and the other sperm cell fuses with two polar nuclei to form the triploid endosperm.

double helix The secondary structure of DNA, consisting of two antiparallel DNA strands wound around each other.

Down syndrome A human developmental disorder caused by trisomy of chromosome 21.

downstream In genetics, the direction in which RNA polymerase moves along a DNA strand. Compare with **upstream**.

duplication In genetics, refers to an additional copy of part of a chromosome.

dynein A class of motor proteins that uses the chemical energy of ATP to "walk" toward the minus end of a microtubule. Dyneins are responsible for bending of cilia and flagella, play a role in chromosome movement during mitosis, and can transport vesicles and organelles.

early endosome A small transient organelle that is formed by the accumulation of vesicles from receptor-mediated endocytosis and is an early stage in the formation of a lysosome.

ecdysone An insect hormone that triggers either molting (to a larger larval form) or metamorphosis (to the adult form), depending on the level of juvenile hormone.

ecdysozoans A major lineage of protostomes (Ecdysozoa) that grow by shedding their external skeletons (molting) and expanding their bodies. Includes arthropods, nematodes, and other groups. Compare with **lophotrochozoans**.

echinoderms A major lineage of deuterostomes (Echinodermata) distinguished by adult bodies with five-sided radial symmetry, a water vascular system, and tube feet. Includes sea urchins, sand dollars, and sea stars.

echolocation The use of echoes from vocalizations to obtain information about locations of objects in the environment.

ecological selection Also known as environmental selection. A type of natural selection that favors individuals with heritable traits that enhance their ability to survive and reproduce in a certain physical and/or biological environment, excluding their ability to obtain a mate. Compare with **sexual selection**.

ecology The study of how organisms interact with each other and with their surrounding environment.

ecosystem All the organisms that live in a geographic area, together with the nonliving (abiotic) components that affect or exchange materials with the organisms; a community and its physical environment.

ecosystem diversity The variety of biotic components in a region along with abiotic components, such as soil, water, and nutrients.

ecosystem function The sum of biological and chemical processes that are characteristic of a given ecosystem—such as primary production, nitrogen cycling, and carbon storage.

ecosystem services All of the benefits that humans derive, directly or indirectly, from ecosystem functions.

ecotourism Tourism that is based on observing wildlife or experiencing other aspects of natural areas.

ectoderm The outermost of the three basic cell layers (germ layers) in most animal embryos; gives rise to the outer covering and nervous system. Compare with **endoderm** and **mesoderm**.

ectomycorrhizal fungi (EMF) Fungi whose hyphae form a dense network that covers their host plant's roots but do not enter the root cells.

ectoparasite A parasite that lives on the outer surface of the host's body.

ectotherm An animal that gains most of its body heat from external sources as opposed to metabolic processes. Compare with **endotherm**.

effector Any cell, organ, or structure with which an animal can respond to external or internal stimuli. Usually functions, along with a sensor and integrator, as part of a homeostatic system.

efferent division The part of the nervous system that carries commands from the central nervous system to the body. Consists primarily of motor neurons.

egg A mature female gamete and any associated external layers (such as a shell). Larger and less mobile than the male gamete. In animals, also called *ovum*.

ejaculation The release of semen from the copulatory organ of a male animal.

ejaculatory duct A short duct through which sperm move during ejaculation; connects the vas deferens to the urethra.

electric current A flow of electrical charge past a point. Also called *current*.

electrical potential Potential energy created by a separation of electrical charges between two points. Also called *voltage*.

electrocardiogram (EKG) A recording of the electrical activity of the heart, as measured through electrodes on the skin.

electrochemical gradient The combined effect of an ion's concentration gradient and electrical (charge) gradient across a membrane that affects the diffusion of ions across the membrane.

electrogenic fish Any of various kinds of fishes having specialized electric organs that emit a current into the water to detect objects.

electrolyte Any compound that dissociates into ions when dissolved in water. In nutrition, any of the major ions necessary for normal cell function.

electromagnetic spectrum The entire range of wavelengths of radiation extending from short wavelengths (high energy) to long wavelengths (low energy). Includes gamma rays, X-rays, ultraviolet, visible light, infrared, microwaves, and radio waves (from short to long wavelengths).

electron acceptor A reactant that gains an electron and is reduced in a reduction–oxidation reaction.

electron carrier Any molecule that readily accepts electrons from and donates electrons to other molecules. Protons may be transferred with the electrons in the form of hydrogen atoms.

electron donor A reactant that loses an electron and is oxidized in a reduction–oxidation reaction.

electron shell A group of orbitals of electrons with similar energies. Electron shells are arranged in roughly concentric layers around the nucleus of an atom, and electrons in outer shells have more energy than those in inner shells. Electrons in the outermost shell, the valence shell, often are involved in chemical bonding.

electron transport chain (ETC) Any set of membrane-bound protein complexes and mobile electron carriers involved in a coordinated series of redox reactions in which the potential energy of electrons is successively decreased and used to pump protons from one side of a membrane to the other.

electronegativity A measure of the ability of an atom to attract electrons toward itself from an atom to which it is bonded.

electroreception A sensory system in which receptors are activated by electric fields.

electroreceptor A sensory cell or organ specialized to detect electric fields.

element A substance, consisting of atoms with a specific number of protons. Elements preserve their identity in chemical reactions.

elongation (1) The process by which RNA lengthens during transcription. (2) The process by which a polypeptide chain lengthens during translation.

elongation factors Proteins involved in the elongation phase of translation, assisting ribosomes in the synthesis of the growing peptide chain.

embryo A young, developing organism; the stage after fertilization and zygote formation.

embryo sac The female gametophyte in flowering plants.

embryogenesis The production of an embryo from a zygote. Embryogenesis is an early event in development of animals and plants.

Embryophyta An increasingly popular name for the lineage called land plants; reflects their retention of a fertilized egg.

embryophyte A plant that nourishes its embryos inside its own body. All land plants are embryophytes.

emergent property A property that stems from the interaction of simpler elements and that is impossible to predict from the study of individual elements.

emergent vegetation Any plants in an aquatic habitat that extend above the surface of the water.

emerging disease Any infectious disease, often a viral disease, that suddenly afflicts significant numbers of humans for the first time; often due to changes in the host species for a pathogen or to radical changes in the genetic material of the pathogen.

emigration The migration of individuals away from one population to other populations. Compare with **immigration**.

emulsification (verb: emulsify) The dispersion of fat into an aqueous solution. Usually requires the aid of an amphipathic substance such as a detergent or bile salts, which can break large fat globules into microscopic fat droplets.

endangered species A species whose numbers have decreased so much that it is in danger of extinction throughout all or part of its range.

endemic species A species that lives in one geographic area and nowhere else.

endergonic Referring to a chemical reaction that requires an input of energy to occur and for which the Gibbs free-energy change (ΔG) is greater than zero. Compare with **exergonic**.

endocrine Relating to a chemical signal (hormone) that is released into the bloodstream by a producing cell and acts on a distant target cell.

endocrine disruptor An exogenous chemical that interferes with normal hormonal signaling.

endocrine gland A gland that secretes hormones directly into the bloodstream or interstitial fluid instead of into ducts. Compare with **exocrine gland**.

endocrine system All of the glands and tissues that produce and secrete hormones into the bloodstream.

endocytosis General term for any pinching off of the plasma membrane that results in the uptake of material from outside the cell. Includes phagocytosis, pinocytosis, and receptor-mediated endocytosis. Compare with **exocytosis**.

endoderm The innermost of the three basic cell layers (germ layers) in most animal embryos; gives rise to the digestive tract and organs that connect to it (liver, lungs, etc.). Compare with **ectoderm** and **mesoderm**.

endodermis In plant roots, a cylindrical layer of cells that separates the cortex from the vascular tissue and location of the Casparian strip.

endomembrane system A system of organelles in eukaryotic cells that synthesizes, processes, transports, and recycles proteins and lipids. Includes the endoplasmic reticulum (ER), Golgi apparatus, and lysosomes.

endomycorrhizal fungi See **arbuscular mycorrhizal fungi (AMF)**.

endoparasite A parasite that lives inside the host's body.

endophyte (adjective: endophytic) A fungus that lives inside the aboveground parts of a plant in a symbiotic relationship. Compare with **epiphyte**.

endoplasmic reticulum (ER) A network of interconnected membranous sacs and tubules found inside eukaryotic cells. See **rough** and **smooth endoplasmic reticulum**.

endoskeleton Bony and/or cartilaginous structures within the body that provide support. Examples are the spicules of sponges, the plates in echinoderms, and the bony skeleton of vertebrates. Compare with **exoskeleton**.

endosperm A triploid ($3n$) tissue in the seed of a flowering plant (angiosperm) that serves as food for the plant embryo. Functionally analogous to the yolk in some animal eggs.

endosymbiont An organism that lives in a symbiotic relationship inside the body of its host.

endosymbiosis An association between organisms of two different species in which one lives inside the cell or cells of the other.

endosymbiosis theory The theory that mitochondria and chloroplasts evolved from prokaryotes that were engulfed by host cells and took up a symbiotic existence within those cells, a process termed primary endosymbiosis. In some eukaryotes, chloroplasts may have originated by secondary endosymbiosis; that is, when a cell engulfed a chloroplast-containing protist and retained its chloroplasts.

endotherm An animal whose primary source of body heat is internally generated. Compare with **ectotherm**.

endothermic Referring to a chemical reaction that absorbs heat. Compare with **exothermic**.

energetic coupling In cellular metabolism, the mechanism by which energy released from an exergonic reaction (commonly, hydrolysis of ATP) is used to drive an endergonic reaction.

energy The capacity to do work or to supply heat. May be stored (potential energy) or available in the form of motion (kinetic energy).

enhancer A regulatory sequence in eukaryotic DNA that may be located far from the gene it controls or within introns of the gene. Binding of specific proteins to an enhancer enhances the transcription of certain genes.

enrichment culture A method of detecting and obtaining cells with specific characteristics by placing a sample, containing many types of cells, under a specific set of conditions (e.g., temperature, salt concentration, available nutrients) and isolating those cells that grow rapidly in response.

enthalpy (H) A quantitative measure of the amount of potential energy, or heat content, of a system plus the pressure and volume it exerts on its surroundings.

entropy (S) A quantitative measure of the amount of disorder of any system, such as a group of molecules.

envelope (viral) A membrane that encloses the capsids of some viruses. Normally includes specialized proteins that attach to host-cell surfaces.

environmental sequencing See **metagenomics**.

enzyme A protein catalyst used by living organisms to speed up and control biological reactions.

epicotyl In some embryonic plants, a portion of the embryonic stem that extends above the cotyledons.

epidemic The spread of an infectious disease throughout a population in a short time period. Compare with **pandemic**.

epidermis The outermost layer of cells of any multicellular organism.

epididymis A coiled tube wrapped around each testis in reptiles, birds, and mammals. The site of the final stages of sperm maturation.

epigenetic inheritance Pattern of inheritance involving differences in phenotype that are not due to differences in the nucleotide sequence of genes.

epinephrine A catecholamine hormone, produced and secreted by the adrenal medulla, that triggers rapid responses related to the fight-or-flight response. Also called *adrenaline*.

epiphyte (adjective: epiphytic) A nonparasitic plant that grows on the trunks or branches of other plants and is not rooted in soil.

epithelial tissues See **epithelium**.

epithelium (plural: epithelia) An animal tissue consisting of sheetlike layers of tightly packed cells that line an organ, a gland, a duct, or a body surface. Also called *epithelial tissue*.

epitope A small region of a particular antigen to which an antibody, B-cell receptor, or T-cell receptor binds.

equilibrium potential The membrane potential at which there is no net movement of a particular ion into or out of a cell.

ER signal sequence A short amino acid sequence that marks a polypeptide for transport to the endoplasmic reticulum, where synthesis of the polypeptide chain is completed and the signal sequence removed. See **signal recognition particle**.

erythropoietin (EPO) A peptide hormone, released by the kidney in response to low blood-oxygen levels, that stimulates the bone marrow to produce more red blood cells.

esophagus The muscular tube that connects the mouth to the stomach.

essential amino acid Any amino acid that an animal cannot synthesize and must obtain from the diet. May refer specifically to one of the eight essential amino acids of adult humans: isoleucine, leucine, lysine, methionine, phenylalanine, threonine, tryptophan, and valine.

essential nutrient Any chemical element, ion, or compound that is required for normal growth, reproduction, and maintenance of a living organism and that cannot be synthesized by the organism.

EST See **expressed sequence tag**.

ester linkage The covalent bond formed by a condensation reaction between a carboxyl group and a hydroxyl group. Ester linkages join fatty acids to glycerol to form a fat or phospholipid.

estradiol The major estrogen produced by the ovaries of female mammals and many other vertebrates. Stimulates development of the female reproductive tract, growth of ovarian follicles, and growth of breast tissue in mammals.

estrogens A class of steroid hormones, including estradiol, estrone, and estriol, that generally promote female-like traits. Secreted by the gonads, fat tissue, and some other organs.

estrous cycle A female reproductive cycle in which the uterine lining is reabsorbed rather than shed in the absence of pregnancy and the female is sexually receptive only briefly during mid-cycle (estrus). It is seen in all mammals except Old World monkeys and apes (including humans). Compare with **menstrual cycle**.

ethylene A gaseous plant hormone associated with senescence that induces fruits to ripen and flowers to fade.

eudicot A member of a monophyletic group (lineage) of angiosperms that includes complex flowering plants and trees (e.g., roses, daisies, maples). All eudicots have two cotyledons, but not all dicots are members of this lineage. Compare with **dicot** and **monocot**.

Eukarya One of the three taxonomic domains of life, consisting of unicellular organisms (most protists, yeasts) and multicellular organisms (fungi, plants, animals) distinguished by a membrane-bound cell nucleus, numerous organelles, and an extensive cytoskeleton. Compare with **Archaea** and **Bacteria**.

eukaryote A member of the domain Eukarya; an organism whose cells contain a nucleus, numerous membrane-bound organelles, and an extensive cytoskeleton. May be unicellular or multicellular. Compare with **prokaryote**.

eusociality A complex social structure in which workers sacrifice most or all of their direct reproduction to help rear the queen's offspring. Common in insects such as ants, bees, wasps, and termites.

eutherians A lineage of mammals (Eutheria) whose young develop in the uterus and are not housed in an abdominal pouch. Also called *placental mammals*.

evaporation The energy-absorbing phase change from a liquid state to a gaseous state. Many organisms evaporate water as a means of heat loss.

evo-devo Popular term for evolutionary developmental biology, a research field focused on how changes in developmentally important genes have led to the evolution of new phenotypes.

evolution (1) The theory that all organisms on Earth are related by common ancestry and that they have changed over time, and continue to change, via natural selection and other processes. (2) Any change in the genetic characteristics of a population over time, especially, a change in allele frequencies.

ex situ conservation Preserving species outside of natural areas (e.g., in zoos, aquaria, or botanical gardens).

excitable membrane A plasma membrane that is capable of generating an action potential. Neurons, muscle cells, and some other cells have excitable membranes.

excitatory postsynaptic potential (EPSP) A change in membrane potential, usually depolarization, at a

neuron dendrite that makes an action potential more likely.

exergonic Referring to a chemical reaction that can occur spontaneously, releasing heat and/or increasing entropy, and for which the Gibbs free-energy change (ΔG) is less than zero. Compare with **endergonic**.

exocrine gland A gland that secretes some substance through a duct into a space other than the circulatory system, such as the digestive tract or the skin surface. Compare with **endocrine gland**.

exocytosis Secretion of intracellular molecules (e.g., hormones, collagen), contained within membrane-bound vesicles, to the outside of the cell by fusion of vesicles to the plasma membrane. Compare with **endocytosis**.

exon A transcribed region of a eukaryotic gene or region of a primary transcript that is retained in the mature RNA. Except for 5′ and 3′ UTRs, mRNA exons code for amino acids. Compare with **intron**.

exoskeleton A hard covering secreted on the outside of the body, used for body support, protection, and muscle attachment. Prominent in arthropods. Compare with **endoskeleton**.

exothermic Referring to a chemical reaction that releases heat. Compare with **endothermic**.

exotic species A nonnative species that is introduced into a new area. Exotic species often are competitors, pathogens, or predators of native species.

expansins A class of plant proteins that break hydrogen bonds between components in the primary cell wall to allow it to expand for cell growth.

exponential population growth The accelerating increase in the size of a population that occurs when the growth rate is constant and density independent. Compare with **logistic population growth**.

expressed sequence tag (EST) A portion of a transcribed gene (synthesized from an mRNA in a cell), used to find the physical location of that gene in the genome.

extant species A species that is living today.

extensor A muscle that pulls two bones farther apart from each other, increasing the angle of the joint, as in the extension of a limb or the spine. Compare with **flexor**.

extinct species A species that has died out.

extracellular digestion Digestion that takes place outside of an organism, as occurs in many fungi that make and secrete digestive enzymes.

extracellular matrix (ECM) A complex meshwork in which animal cells are embedded, consisting of proteins (e.g., collagen, proteoglycan, laminin) and polysaccharides produced by the cells.

extremophile A bacterium or archaean that thrives in an "extreme" environment (e.g., high-salt, high-temperature, low-temperature, or low-pressure).

F₁ generation First filial generation. The first generation of offspring produced from a mating (i.e., the offspring of the parental generation).

facilitated diffusion Passive movement of a substance across a membrane with the assistance of transmembrane carrier proteins or channel proteins.

facilitation In ecological succession, the phenomenon in which early-arriving species make conditions more favorable for later-arriving species. Compare with **inhibition** and **tolerance**.

facultative anaerobe Any organism that can survive and reproduce by performing aerobic respiration when oxygen is available or fermentation when it is not.

FAD/FADH₂ Oxidized and reduced forms, respectively, of flavin adenine dinucleotide. A nonprotein electron carrier that functions in the citric acid cycle and oxidative phosphorylation.

fallopian tube A narrow tube connecting the uterus to the ovary in humans, through which the egg travels after ovulation. Site of fertilization and cleavage. In nonhuman animals, called *oviduct*.

fast muscle fiber Type of skeletal muscle fiber that is white in color, generates ATP by glycolysis, and contracts rapidly but fatigues easily. Also called *fast glycolytic*, or *Type IIb*, *fiber*.

fat A lipid consisting of three fatty acid molecules joined by ester linkages to a glycerol molecule. Also called *triacylglycerol* or *triglyceride*.

fatty acid A lipid consisting of a hydrocarbon chain bonded at one end to a carboxyl group. Used by many organisms to store chemical energy; a major component of animal and plant fats and phospholipids.

fauna All the animal species characteristic of a particular region, period, or environment.

feather A specialized skin outgrowth, composed of β-keratin, present in all birds as well as in some non-avian dinosaurs. Used for flight, insulation, display, and other purposes.

feces The waste products of digestion.

fecundity The average number of female offspring produced by a single female in the course of her lifetime.

feedback inhibition A type of control in which high concentrations of the product of a metabolic pathway inhibit one of the enzymes early in the pathway. A form of negative feedback.

fermentation Any of several metabolic pathways that regenerate oxidizing agents, such as NAD⁺, by transferring electrons to a final electron acceptor in the absence of an electron transport chain. Allows pathways such as glycolysis to continue to make ATP.

ferredoxin In photosynthetic organisms, an iron- and sulfur-containing protein in the electron transport chain of photosystem I. Can transfer electrons to the enzyme NADP⁺ reductase, which catalyzes formation of NADPH.

fertility The average number of surviving children that each woman has during her lifetime.

fertilization Fusion of the nuclei of two haploid gametes to form a zygote with a diploid nucleus.

fertilization envelope A physical barrier that forms around a fertilized egg in many animals. The fertilization envelope prevents fertilization by more than one sperm (polyspermy).

fetal alcohol syndrome (FAS) A condition marked by hyperactivity, severe learning disabilities, and depression. Thought to be caused by exposure of an individual to high blood alcohol concentrations during embryonic development.

fetus In live-bearing animals, the unborn offspring after the embryonic stage. It usually is developed sufficiently to be recognizable as belonging to a certain species.

fiber In plants, a type of elongated sclerenchyma cell that provides support to vascular tissue. Compare with **sclereid**.

Fick's law of diffusion A mathematical relationship that describes the rates of diffusion of gases.

fight-or-flight response Rapid physiological changes that prepare the body for emergencies. Includes increased heart rate, increased blood pressure, and decreased digestion.

filament Any thin, threadlike structure, particularly (1) the threadlike extensions of a fish's gills or (2) part of a stamen: the slender stalk that bears the anthers in a flower.

filter feeder See **suspension feeder**.

filtrate Any fluid produced by filtration, in particular the fluid ("pre-urine") in the Malpighian tubules of insects and the nephrons of vertebrate kidneys.

filtration A process of removing large components from a fluid by forcing it through a filter. Occurs in a renal corpuscle of the vertebrate kidney, allowing water and small solutes to pass from the blood into the nephron.

fimbria (plural: fimbriae) A long, needlelike projection from the cell membrane of prokaryotes that is involved in attachment to nonliving surfaces or other cells.

finite rate of increase (λ) The rate of increase of a population over a given period of time. Calculated as the ending population size divided by the starting population size. Compare with **intrinsic rate of increase**.

first law of thermodynamics The principle of physics that energy is conserved in any process. Energy can be transferred and converted into different forms, but it cannot be created or destroyed.

fission (1) A form of asexual reproduction in which a prokaryotic cell divides to produce two genetically similar daughter cells by a process similar to mitosis of eukaryotic cells. Also called *binary fission*. (2) A form of asexual reproduction in which an animal splits into two or more individuals of approximately equal size; common among invertebrates.

fitness The ability of an individual to produce viable offspring relative to others of the same species.

fitness trade-off See **trade-off**.

fixed action pattern (FAP) Highly stereotyped behavior pattern that occurs in a certain invariant way in a certain species. A form of innate behavior.

flaccid Limp as a result of low internal (turgor) pressure (e.g., a wilted plant leaf). Compare with **turgid**.

flagellum (plural: flagella) A long, cellular projection that undulates (in eukaryotes) or rotates (in prokaryotes) to move the cell through an aqueous environment. See **axoneme**.

flatworms Members of the phylum Platyhelminthes. Distinguished by a broad, flat, unsegmented body

that lacks a coelom. Flatworms belong to the lophotrochozoan branch of the protostomes.

flavin adenine dinucleotide See **FAD/FADH₂**.

flexor A muscle that pulls two bones closer together, decreasing the joint angle, as in the flexing of a limb or the spine. Compare with **extensor**.

floral meristem A group of undifferentiated plant stem cells that can give rise to the four organs making up a flower.

florigen In plants, a protein hormone that is synthesized in leaves and transported to the shoot apical meristem, where it stimulates flowering.

flower In angiosperms, the part of a plant that contains reproductive structures. Typically includes a calyx, a corolla, and one or more stamens and/or carpels. See **perfect** and **imperfect flower**.

fluid connective tissue A type of connective tissue, distinguished by having a liquid extracellular matrix; includes blood.

fluid feeder Any animal that feeds by sucking or mopping up liquids such as nectar, plant sap, or blood.

fluid-mosaic model The widely accepted hypothesis that the plasma membrane and organelle membranes consist of proteins embedded in a fluid phospholipid bilayer.

fluorescence The spontaneous emission of light from an excited electron falling back to its normal (ground) state.

follicle In a mammalian ovary, a sac of supportive cells containing an egg cell.

follicle-stimulating hormone (FSH) A peptide hormone, produced and secreted by the anterior pituitary; it stimulates (in females) growth of eggs and follicles in the ovaries or (in males) sperm production in the testes.

follicular phase In a menstrual cycle, the first major phase, during which follicles grow and estradiol levels increase; ends with ovulation.

food Any nutrient-containing material that can be consumed and digested by animals.

food chain A relatively simple pathway of energy flow through a few species, each at a different trophic level, in an ecosystem. Might include, for example, a primary producer, a primary consumer, a secondary consumer, and a decomposer. A subset of a **food web**.

food web The complex network of interactions among species in an ecosystem formed by the transfer of energy and nutrients among trophic levels. Consists of many food chains.

foot One of the three main parts of the mollusk body; a muscular appendage, used for movements such as crawling and/or burrowing into sediment.

foraging Searching for food.

forebrain One of the three main regions of the vertebrate brain; includes the cerebrum, thalamus, and hypothalamus. Compare with **hindbrain** and **midbrain**.

fossil Any physical trace of an organism that existed in the past. Includes tracks, burrows, fossilized bones, casts, and so on.

fossil record All of the fossils that have been found anywhere on Earth and that have been formally described in the scientific literature.

founder effect A change in allele frequencies that often occurs when a new population is established from a small group of individuals (founder event) due to sampling error (i.e., the small group is not a representative sample of the source population).

fovea In the vertebrate eye, a portion of the retina where incoming light is focused; contains a high proportion of cone cells.

frameshift mutation The addition or deletion of a nucleotide in a coding sequence that shifts the reading frame of the mRNA.

free energy The energy of a system that can be converted into work. It may be measured only through the change in free energy in a reaction. See **Gibbs free-energy change**.

free radicals Any substance containing one or more atoms with an unpaired electron. Unstable and highly reactive.

frequency The number of wave crests per second traveling past a stationary point. Determines the pitch of sound and the color of light.

frequency-dependent selection A pattern of selection in which certain alleles are favored only when they are rare; a form of balancing selection.

fronds The large leaves of ferns.

frontal lobe In the vertebrate brain, one of the four major areas in the cerebrum.

fruit In flowering plants (angiosperms), a mature, ripened plant ovary (or group of ovaries), along with the seeds it contains and any adjacent fused parts; often functions in seed dispersal. See **aggregate**, **multiple**, and **simple fruit**.

fruiting body A structure formed in some prokaryotes, fungi, and protists for spore dispersal; usually consists of a base, a stalk, and a mass of spores at the top.

functional genomics The study of how a genome works; that is, when and where specific genes are expressed and how their products interact to produce a functional organism.

functional group A small group of atoms bonded together in a precise configuration and exhibiting particular chemical properties that it imparts to any organic molecule in which it occurs.

fundamental niche The total theoretical range of environmental conditions that a species can tolerate. Compare with **realized niche**.

fungi A lineage of eukaryotes that typically have a filamentous body (mycelium) and obtain nutrients by absorption.

fungicide Any substance that can kill fungi or slow their growth.

G protein Any of various proteins that are activated by binding to guanosine triphosphate (GTP) and inactivated when GTP is hydrolyzed to GDP. In G-protein-coupled receptors, signal binding directly triggers the activation of a G protein, leading to production of a second messenger or initiation of a phosphorylation cascade.

G₁ phase The phase of the cell cycle that constitutes the first part of interphase before DNA synthesis (S phase).

G₂ phase The phase of the cell cycle between synthesis of DNA (S phase) and mitosis (M phase); the last part of interphase.

gallbladder A small pouch that stores bile from the liver and releases it as needed into the small intestine during digestion of fats.

gametangium (plural: gametangia) (1) The gamete-forming structure found in all land plants except angiosperms. Contains a sperm-producing antheridium and an egg-producing archegonium. (2) The gamete-forming structure of some chytrid fungi.

gamete A haploid reproductive cell that can fuse with another haploid cell to form a zygote. Most multicellular eukaryotes have two distinct forms of gametes: egg cells (ova) and sperm cells.

gametogenesis The production of gametes (eggs or sperm).

gametophyte In organisms undergoing alternation of generations, the multicellular haploid form that arises from a single haploid spore and produces gametes. Compare with **sporophyte**.

ganglion (plural: ganglia) A mass of neurons in a centralized nervous system.

ganglion cell In the retina, a type of neuron whose axons form the optic nerves.

gap junction A type of cell–cell attachment structure that directly connects the cytosolic components of adjacent animal cells, allowing passage of water, ions, and small molecules between the cells. Compare with **desmosome** and **tight junction**.

gastrin A hormone produced by cells in the stomach lining in response to the arrival of food or to a neural signal from the brain. Stimulates other stomach cells to release hydrochloric acid.

gastropods A lineage of mollusks distinguished by a large, muscular foot and a unique feeding structure, the radula. Include slugs and snails.

gastrulation The process of coordinated cell movements, including the moving of some cells from the outer surface of the embryo to the interior, that results in the formation of three germ layers (endoderm, mesoderm, and ectoderm) and the axes of the embryo.

gated channel A channel protein that opens and closes in response to a specific stimulus, such as the binding of a particular molecule or a change in voltage across the membrane.

gemma (plural: gemmae) A small reproductive structure that is produced asexually in some plants during the gametophyte phase and can grow into a mature gametophyte; most common in non-vascular plants, particularly liverworts and club mosses, and in ferns

gene A section of DNA (or RNA, for some viruses) that encodes information for building one or more related polypeptides or functional RNA molecules along with the regulatory sequences required for its transcription.

gene duplication The formation of an additional copy of a gene, typically by misalignment of chromosomes during crossing over. Thought to be an important evolutionary process in creating new genes.

gene expression The set of processes, including transcription and translation, that convert information in DNA into aproduct of a gene, most commonly a protein.

gene family A set of genetic loci whose DNA sequences are extremely similar. Thought to have arisen by duplication of a single ancestral gene and subsequent mutations in the duplicated sequences.

gene flow The movement of alleles between populations; occurs when individuals leave one population, join another, and breed.

gene pool All the alleles of all the genes in a certain population.

gene therapy The treatment of an inherited disease by introducing a normal form of the gene.

generation The average time between a mother's first offspring and her daughter's first offspring.

genetic bottleneck A reduction in allelic diversity resulting from a sudden reduction in the size of a large population (population bottleneck) due to a random event.

genetic code The set of all codons and their meaning.

genetic correlation A type of evolutionary constraint in which selection on one trait causes a change in another trait as well; may occur when the same gene(s) affect both traits.

genetic diversity The diversity of alleles or genes in a population, species, or group of species.

genetic drift Any change in allele frequencies due to random events. Causes allele frequencies to drift up and down randomly over time, and eventually can lead to the fixation or loss of alleles.

genetic equivalence Having all different cell types of a multicellular individual possess the same genome.

genetic homology Similarity in DNA nucleotide sequences, RNA nucleotide sequences, or amino acid sequences due to inheritance from a common ancestor.

genetic map A list of genes on a chromosome that indicates their position and relative distances from one another. Also called a *linkage map*. Compare with **physical map**.

genetic marker A genetic locus that can be identified and traced in populations by laboratory techniques or by a distinctive visible phenotype.

genetic recombination A change in the combination of alleles on a given chromosome or in a given individual. Also called *recombination*.

genetic screen Any technique that identifies individuals with a particular type of mutation.

genetic variation (1) The number and relative frequency of alleles present in a particular population. (2) The proportion of phenotypic variation in a trait that is due to genetic rather than environmental influences in a certain population in a certain environment.

genetics The study of the inheritance of traits.

genital (plural: genitalia) Any external copulatory organ.

genome All the hereditary information in an organism, including not only genes but also stretches of DNA that do not contain genes.

genome annotation The process of analyzing a genome sequence to identify key features such as genes, regulatory sequences, and splice sites.

genomic library A set of DNA segments representing the entire genome of a particular organism. Each segment is carried by a plasmid or other cloning vector and can be separated from other segments. Compare with **cDNA library**.

genomics The field of study concerned with sequencing, interpreting, and comparing whole genomes from different organisms.

genotype All the alleles of every gene present in a given individual. Often specified only for the alleles of a particular set of genes under study. Compare with **phenotype**.

genus (plural: genera) In Linnaeus' system, a taxonomic category of closely related species. Always italicized and capitalized to indicate that it is a recognized scientific genus.

geologic time scale The sequence of eons, eras, and periods used to describe the geologic history of Earth.

germ cell In animals, any cell that can potentially give rise to gametes. Also called *germ-line cells*.

germ layer In animals, one of the three basic types of tissue formed during gastrulation; gives rise to all other tissues. See **endoderm**, **mesoderm**, and **ectoderm**.

germ line In animals, any of the cells that are capable of giving rise to reproductive cells (sperm or egg). Compare with **germ cell**.

germ theory of disease The theory that infectious diseases are caused by bacteria, viruses, and other microorganisms.

germination The process by which a seed becomes a young plant.

gestation The period of development inside the mother, from implantation to birth, in those species that have live birth.

gibberellins A class of hormones, found in plants and fungi, that stimulate growth. Gibberellic acid (GA) is one of the major gibberellins.

Gibbs free-energy change (ΔG) A measure of the change in enthalpy and entropy that occurs in a given chemical reaction. ΔG is less than 0 for spontaneous reactions and greater than 0 for nonspontaneous reactions.

gill Any organ in aquatic animals that exchanges gases and other dissolved substances between the blood and the surrounding water. Typically, a filamentous outgrowth of a body surface.

gill arch In aquatic vertebrates, a curved region of tissue between the gills. Gills are suspended from the gill arches.

gill filament In fish, any of the many long, thin structures that extend from gill arches into the water and across which gas exchange occurs.

gill lamella (plural: gill lamellae) Any of hundreds to thousands of sheetlike structures, each containing a capillary bed, that make up a gill filament.

gland An organ whose primary function is to secrete some substance, either into the blood (endocrine gland) or into some other space such as the gut or skin (exocrine gland).

glia Collective term for several types of cells in nervous tissue that are not neurons and do not conduct electrical signals but perform other functions, such as providing support, nourishment, or electrical insulation. Also called *glial cells*.

global carbon cycle See **carbon cycle, global**.

global climate change The global sum of all the local changes in temperature and precipitation patterns that accompany global warming (or in some past events, global cooling).

global gene regulation The regulation of multiple bacterial genes that are not part of one operon.

global nitrogen cycle See **nitrogen cycle, global**.

global warming A sustained increase in Earth's average surface temperature.

global water cycle See **water cycle, global**.

glomalin A glycoprotein that is abundant in the hyphae of arbuscular mycorrhizal fungi; when hyphae decay, it is an important component of soil.

glomerulus (plural: glomeruli) (1) In the vertebrate kidney, a ball-like cluster of capillaries, surrounded by Bowman's capsule, at the beginning of a nephron. (2) In the brain, a ball-shaped cluster of neurons in the olfactory bulb.

glucagon A peptide hormone produced by the pancreas in response to low blood glucose. Raises blood glucose by triggering breakdown of glycogen and stimulating gluconeogenesis. Compare with **insulin**.

glucocorticoids A class of steroid hormones, produced and secreted by the adrenal cortex, that increase blood glucose and prepare the body for stress. Include cortisol and corticosterone. Compare with **mineralocorticoids**.

gluconeogenesis Synthesis of glucose, often from non-carbohydrate sources (e.g., proteins and fatty acids). In plants, used to produce glucose from products of the Calvin cycle. In animals, occurs in the liver in response to low insulin levels and high glucagon levels.

glucose Six-carbon monosaccharide whose oxidation in cellular respiration is the major source of ATP in animal cells.

glyceraldehyde-3-phosphate (G3P) The phosphorylated three-carbon compound formed as the result of carbon fixation in the first step of the Calvin cycle.

glycerol A three-carbon molecule that forms the "backbone" of phospholipids and most fats.

glycogen A highly branched storage polysaccharide composed of glucose monomers joined by α-1,4- and α-1,6-glycosidic linkages. The major form of stored carbohydrate in animals.

glycolipid Any lipid molecule that is covalently bonded to a carbohydrate group.

glycolysis A series of 10 chemical reactions that oxidize glucose to produce pyruvate, NADH, and ATP.

Used by organisms as part of fermentation or cellular respiration.

glycoprotein Any protein with one or more covalently bonded carbohydrates, typically oligosaccharides.

glycosidic linkage The covalent linkage formed by a condensation reaction between two sugar monomers; joins the residues of a polysaccharide.

glycosylation Addition of a carbohydrate group to a molecule.

glyoxysome Specialized type of peroxisome found in plant cells and packed with enzymes for processing the products of photosynthesis.

gnathostomes Animals with jaws. Most vertebrates are gnathostomes.

Golgi apparatus A eukaryotic organelle, consisting of stacks of flattened membranous sacs (cisternae), that functions in processing and sorting proteins and lipids destined to be secreted or directed to other organelles. Also called *Golgi complex*.

gonad An organ, such as a testis or an ovary, that produces reproductive cells.

gonadotropin-releasing hormone (GnRH) A peptide hormone, produced and secreted by the hypothalamus, that stimulates release of follicle-stimulating hormone (FSH) and luteinizing hormone (LH) from the anterior pituitary.

grade In taxonomy, a group of species that share some, but not all, of the descendants of a common ancestor. Also called a *paraphyletic group*.

Gram-negative Describing bacteria that look pink when treated with a Gram stain. These bacteria have a cell wall composed of a thin layer of peptidoglycan and an outer phospholipid layer. Compare with **Gram-positive**.

Gram-positive Describing bacteria that look purple when treated with a Gram stain. These bacteria have cell walls composed of a thick layer of peptidoglycan and no outer phospholipid later. Compare with **Gram-negative**.

Gram stain A dye that distinguishes the two general types of cell walls found in bacteria. Used to routinely classify bacteria as Gram-negative or Gram-positive.

granum (plural: grana) In chloroplasts, a stack of flattened, membrane-bound thylakoid discs where the light reactions of photosynthesis occur.

gravitropism The growth or movement of a plant in a particular direction in response to gravity.

grazing food chain The ecological network of herbivores and the predators and parasites that consume them.

great apes See **hominids**.

green algae A paraphyletic group of photosynthetic organisms that contain chloroplasts similar to those in green plants. Often classified as protists, green algae are the closest living relatives of land plants and form a monophyletic group with them.

greenhouse gas An atmospheric gas that absorbs and reflects infrared radiation, so that heat radiated from Earth is retained in the atmosphere instead of being lost to space.

gross primary productivity In an ecosystem, the total amount of carbon fixed by photosynthesis (or more

rarely, chemosynthesis), including that used for cellular respiration, over a given time period. Compare with **net primary productivity**.

ground meristem The middle layer of a young plant embryo. Gives rise to the ground tissue system.

ground tissue An embryonic tissue layer that gives rise to parenchyma, collenchyma, and sclerenchyma—tissues other than the epidermis and vascular tissue. Also called *ground tissue system*.

groundwater Any water below the land surface.

growth factor Any of a large number of signaling molecules that are secreted by certain cells and that stimulate other cells to grow, divide, or differentiate.

growth hormone (GH) A peptide hormone, produced and secreted by the mammalian anterior pituitary, that promotes lengthening of the long bones in children and muscle growth, tissue repair, and lactation in adults. Also called *somatotropin*.

guanosine triphosphate (GTP) A nucleotide consisting of guanine, a ribose sugar, and three phosphate groups. Can be hydrolyzed to release free energy. Commonly used in RNA synthesis and also functions in signal transduction in association with G proteins.

guard cell One of two specialized, crescent-shaped cells forming the border of a plant stoma. Guard cells can change shape to open or close the stoma. See also **stoma**.

gustation The perception of taste.

guttation Excretion of water droplets from plant leaves; visible in the early morning. Caused by root pressure.

gymnosperm A vascular plant that makes seeds but does not produce flowers. The gymnosperms include five lineages of green plants (cycads, ginkgoes, conifers, redwoods, and gnetophytes). Compare with **angiosperm**.

H⁺-ATPase See **proton pump**.

habitat degradation The reduction of the quality of a habitat.

habitat destruction Human-caused destruction of a natural habitat, replaced by an urban, suburban, or agricultural landscape.

habitat fragmentation The breakup of a large region of a habitat into many smaller regions, separated from others by a different type of habitat.

Hadley cell An atmospheric cycle of large-scale air movement in which warm equatorial air rises, moves north or south, and then descends at approximately 30° N or 30° S latitude.

hair cell A pressure-detecting sensory cell that has tiny "hairs" (stereocilia) jutting from its surface. Found in the inner ear, lateral line system, and ampullae of Lorenzini.

hairpin A secondary structure in RNA consisting of a stable loop formed by hydrogen bonding between purine and pyrimidine bases on the same strand.

Hamilton's rule The proposition that an allele for altruistic behavior will be favored by natural selection only if $Br\ C$, where B = the fitness benefit to the recipient, C = the fitness cost to the actor, and r = the coefficient of relatedness between recipient and actor.

haploid (1) Having one set of chromosomes (1*n* or *n* for short). (2) A cell or an individual organism with one set of chromosomes. Compare with **diploid**.

haploid number The number of different types of chromosomes in a cell. Symbolized as *n*.

Hardy–Weinberg principle A principle of population genetics stating that genotype frequencies in a large population do not change from generation to generation in the absence of evolutionary processes (e.g., mutation, gene flow, genetic drift, and selection), and nonrandom mating.

haustorium (plural: haustoria) Highly modified stem or root of a parasitic plant. The haustorium penetrates the tissues of a host and absorbs nutrients and water.

hearing The sensation of the wavelike changes in air pressure called sound.

heart A muscular pump that circulates blood throughout the body.

heart murmur A distinctive sound caused by backflow of blood through a defective heart valve.

heartwood The older xylem in the center of an older stem or root, containing protective compounds and no longer functioning in water transport.

heat Thermal energy that is transferred from an object at higher temperature to one at lower temperature.

heat of vaporization The energy required to vaporize 1 gram of a liquid into a gas.

heat-shock proteins Proteins that facilitate refolding of proteins that have been denatured by heat or other agents.

heavy chain The larger of the two types of polypeptide chains in an antibody or B-cell receptor molecule; composed of a variable (*V*) region, which contributes to the antigen-binding site, and a constant (*C*) region. Differences in heavy-chain constant regions determine the different classes of immunoglobulins (IgA, IgE, etc.). Compare with **light chain**.

helper T cell A CD4$^+$ effector T cell that secretes cytokines and in other ways promotes the activation of other lymphocytes. Activated by interacting with complementary class II MHC–peptide complexes on the surface of antigen-presenting cells such as dendritic cells.

heme A small molecule that binds to each of the four polypeptides that combine to form hemoglobin; contains an iron ion that can bind oxygen.

hemimetabolous metamorphosis A type of metamorphosis in which the animal increases in size from one stage to the next, but does not dramatically change its body form. Also called *incomplete metamorphosis*.

hemocoel A body cavity, present in arthropods and some mollusks, containing a pool of circulatory fluid (hemolymph) bathing the internal organs. Unlike a coelom, a hemocoel is not lined in mesoderm.

hemoglobin An oxygen-binding protein consisting of four polypeptide subunits, each containing an oxygen-binding heme group. The major oxygen carrier in mammalian blood.

hemolymph The circulatory fluid of animals with open circulatory systems (e.g., insects) in which the fluid is not confined to blood vessels.

herbaceous Referring to a plant that is not woody.

herbivore (adjective: herbivorous) An animal that eats primarily plants and rarely or never eats meat. Compare with **carnivore** and **omnivore**.

herbivory The practice of eating plant tissues.

heredity The transmission of traits from parents to offspring via genetic information.

heritable Referring to traits that can be transmitted from one generation to the next.

hermaphrodite An organism that produces both male and female gametes.

heterokaryotic Describing a cell or fungal mycelium containing two or more haploid nuclei that are genetically distinct.

heterospory (adjective: heterosporous) In seed plants, the production of two distinct types of spores: microspores, which become the male gametophyte, and megaspores, which become the female gametophyte. Compare with **homospory**.

heterotherm An animal whose body temperature varies markedly. Compare with **homeotherm**.

heterotroph Any organism that cannot synthesize reduced organic compounds from inorganic sources and that must obtain them from other organisms. Some bacteria, some archaea, and virtually all fungi and animals are heterotrophs. Also called *consumer*. Compare with **autotroph**.

heterozygote advantage A pattern of natural selection that favors heterozygous individuals compared with homozygotes. Tends to maintain genetic variation in a population, thus is a form of balancing selection.

heterozygous Having two different alleles of a gene.

hexose A monosaccharide (simple sugar) containing six carbon atoms.

hibernation An energy-conserving physiological state, marked by a decrease in metabolic rate, body temperature, and activity, that lasts for a prolonged period (weeks to months). Occurs in some animals in response to winter cold and scarcity of food. Compare with **torpor**.

hindbrain One of the three main regions of the vertebrate brain, responsible for balance and sometimes hearing; includes the cerebellum and medulla oblongata. Compare with **forebrain** and **midbrain**.

histamine A molecule released from mast cells during an inflammatory response that, at high concentrations, causes blood vessels to constrict to reduce blood loss from tissue damage.

histone One of several positively charged (basic) proteins associated with DNA in the chromatin of eukaryotic cells.

histone acetyltransferases (HATs) A class of eukaryotic enzymes that loosen chromatin structure by adding acetyl groups to histone proteins.

histone code The hypothesis that specific combinations of chemical modifications of histone proteins contain information that influences chromatin condensation and gene expression.

histone deacetylases (HDACs) A class of eukaryotic enzymes that condense chromatin by removing acetyl groups from histone proteins.

holoenzyme A multipart enzyme consisting of a core enzyme (containing the active site for catalysis) along with other required proteins.

holometabolous metamorphosis A type of metamorphosis in which the animal completely changes its form; includes a distinct larval stage. Also called *complete metamorphosis*.

homeobox A DNA sequence of about 180 base pairs that codes for a DNA binding motif called the homeodomain in the resulting protein. Genes containing a homeobox usually play a role in controlling development of organisms from fruit flies to humans.

homeostasis (adjective: homeostatic) The array of relatively stable chemical and physical conditions in an animal's cells, tissues, and organs. May be achieved by the body's passively matching the conditions of a stable external environment (conformational homeostasis) or by active physiological processes (regulatory homeostasis) triggered by variations in the external or internal environment.

homeotherm An animal that has a constant or relatively constant body temperature. Compare with **heterotherm**.

homeotic mutation A mutation that causes one body part to be substituted for another.

hominids Members of the family Hominidae, which includes humans and extinct related forms, chimpanzees, gorillas, and orangutans. Distinguished by large body size, no tail, and an exceptionally large brain. Also called *great apes*.

hominins Any extinct or living species of bipedal apes, such as *Australopithecus africanus*, *Homo erectus*, and *Homo sapiens*.

homologous See **homology**.

homologous chromosomes In a diploid organism, chromosomes that are similar in size, shape, and gene content. Also called *homologs*.

homology (adjective: homologous) Similarity among organisms of different species due to their inheritance from a common ancestor. Features that exhibit such similarity (e.g., DNA sequences, proteins, body parts) are said to be homologous. Compare with **homoplasy**.

homoplasy (adjective: homoplastic) Similarity among organisms of different species due to reasons other than common ancestry, such as convergent evolution. Features that exhibit such similarity (e.g., the wings of birds and bats) are said to be homoplastic, or convergent. Compare with **homology**.

homospory (adjective: homosporous) In seedless vascular plants, the production of just one type of spore. Compare with **heterospory**.

homozygous Having two identical alleles of a gene.

hormone Any of many different signaling molecules that circulate throughout the plant or animal body and can trigger characteristic responses in distant target cells at very low concentrations.

hormone-response element A specific sequence in DNA to which a steroid hormone–receptor complex can bind and affect gene transcription.

host An individual that has been invaded by an organism such as a parasite or a virus, or that provides habitat or resources to a commensal organism.

host cell A cell that has been invaded by a parasitic organism or a virus and provides an environment that is conducive to the pathogen's growth and reproduction.

***Hox* genes** A class of genes found in several animal phyla, including vertebrates, that are expressed in a distinctive pattern along the anterior–posterior axis in early embryos and control formation of specific structures. *Hox* genes code for transcription factors with a DNA-binding sequence called a homeobox.

human Any member of the genus *Homo,* which includes modern humans (*Homo sapiens*) and several extinct species.

human chorionic gonadotropin (hCG) A glycoprotein hormone produced by a human embryo and placenta from about week 3 to week 14 of pregnancy. Maintains the corpus luteum, which produces hormones that preserve the uterine lining.

Human Genome Project The multinational research project that sequenced the human genome.

human immunodeficiency virus (HIV) A retrovirus that causes acquired immune deficiency syndrome (AIDS) in humans.

humoral (immune) response The type of immune response that is mediated through the production and secretion of antibodies, complement proteins, and other soluble factors that eliminate extracellular pathogens. Compare with **cell-mediated (immune) response**.

humus The decayed organic matter in soils.

hybrid The offspring of parents from two different strains, populations, or species.

hybrid zone A geographic area where interbreeding occurs between two species, sometimes producing fertile hybrid offspring.

hydrocarbon An organic molecule that contains only hydrogen and carbon atoms.

hydrogen bond A weak interaction between two molecules or different parts of the same molecule resulting from the attraction between a hydrogen atom with a partial positive charge and another atom (usually O or N) with a partial negative charge. Compare with **covalent bond** and **ionic bond**.

hydrogen ion (H$^+$) A single proton with a charge of 1+; typically, one that is dissolved in solution or that is being transferred from one atom to another in a chemical reaction.

hydrolysis A chemical reaction in which a molecule is split into smaller molecules by reacting with water. In biology, most hydrolysis reactions involve the splitting of polymers into monomers. Compare with **condensation reaction**.

hydrophilic Interacting readily with water. Hydrophilic compounds are typically polar compounds containing partially or fully charged atoms. Compare with **hydrophobic**.

hydrophobic Not readily interacting with water. Hydrophobic compounds are typically nonpolar compounds that lack partially or fully charged atoms. Compare with **hydrophilic**.

hydrophobic interactions Very weak interactions between nonpolar molecules, or nonpolar regions of the same molecule, when exposed to an aqueous solvent. The surrounding water molecules support these interactions by interacting with one another and encapsulating the nonpolar molecules.

hydroponic growth Growth of plants in liquid cultures instead of soil.

hydrostatic skeleton A system of body support involving a body wall in tension surrounding a fluid or soft tissue under compression.

hydroxide ion (OH$^-$) An oxygen atom and a hydrogen atom joined by a single covalent bond and carrying a negative charge; formed by dissociation of water.

hygiene hypothesis The claim that immune disorders arise in individuals less likely to have been exposed to pathogens and parasites, especially in early childhood. Provides an explanation for the increased risk of allergies and autoimmune disease in countries with high levels of sanitation.

hyperosmotic Comparative term designating a solution that has a greater solute concentration, and therefore a lower water concentration, than another solution. Compare with **hyposmotic** and **isosmotic**.

hyperpolarization A change in membrane potential from its resting negative state to an even more negative state; a normal phase in an action potential. Compare with **depolarization**.

hypersensitive reaction An intense allergic response by cells that have been sensitized by previous exposure to an allergen.

hypersensitive response In plants, the rapid death of a cell that has been infected by a pathogen, thereby reducing the potential for infection to spread throughout a plant. Compare with **systemic acquired resistance**.

hypertension Abnormally high blood pressure.

hypertonic Comparative term designating a solution that, if inside a cell or vesicle, results in the uptake of water and swelling or even bursting of the membrane-bound structure. This solution has a greater solute concentration than the solution on the other side of the membrane. Used when the solute is unable to pass through the membrane. Compare with **hypotonic** and **isotonic**.

hypha (plural: hyphae) One of the long, branching strands of a fungal mycelium (the mesh-like body of a fungus). Also found in some protists.

hypocotyl The stem of a very young plant; the region between the cotyledon (embryonic leaf) and the radicle (embryonic root).

hyposmotic Comparative term designating a solution that has a lower solute concentration, and therefore a higher water concentration, than another solution. Compare with **hyperosmotic** and **isosmotic**.

hypothalamic–pituitary axis The functional interaction of the hypothalamus and the anterior pituitary gland, which are anatomically distinct but work together to regulate most of the other endocrine glands in the body.

hypothalamus A part of the brain that functions in maintaining the body's internal physiological state by regulating the autonomic nervous system, endocrine system, body temperature, water balance, and appetite.

hypothesis A testable statement that explains a phenomenon or a set of observations.

hypotonic Comparative term designating a solution that, if inside a cell or vesicle, results in the loss of water and shrinkage of the membrane-bound structure. This solution has a lower solute concentration than the solution on the other side of the membrane. Used when the solute is unable to pass through the membrane. Compare with **hypertonic** and **isotonic**.

immigration The migration of individuals into a particular population from other populations. Compare with **emigration**.

immune system The system whose primary function is to defend the host organism against pathogens. Includes several types of cells (e.g., leukocytes). In vertebrates, several organs are also involved where specialized cells develop or reside (e.g., lymph nodes and thymus).

immunity (adjective: immune) State of being protected against infection by disease-causing pathogens.

immunization The conferring of immunity to a particular disease by artificial means.

immunoglobulin (Ig) Any of the class of proteins that are structurally related to antibodies.

immunological memory The ability of the immune system to "remember" an antigen and mount a rapid, effective adaptive immune response to a pathogen encountered years or decades earlier. Based on the formation of memory lymphocytes.

impact hypothesis The hypothesis that a collision between the Earth and an asteroid caused the mass extinction at the K–P boundary, 65 million years ago.

imperfect flower A flower that contains male parts (stamens) *or* female parts (carpels) but not both. Compare with **perfect flower**.

implantation The process by which an embryo buries itself in the uterine or oviductal wall and forms a placenta. Occurs in mammals and some other viviparous vertebrates.

in situ hybridization A technique for detecting specific DNAs and mRNAs in cells and tissues by use of labeled complementary probes. Can be used to determine where and when particular genes are expressed in embryos.

inbreeding Mating between closely related individuals. Increases homozygosity of a population and often leads to a decline in the average fitness via selection (inbreeding depression).

inbreeding depression In inbred offspring, fitness declines due to deleterious recessive alleles that are homozygous, thus exposed to selection.

inclusive fitness The combination of (1) direct production of offspring (direct fitness) and (2) extra production of offspring by relatives in response to help provided by the individual in question (indirect fitness).

incomplete digestive tract A digestive tract that has just one opening.

incomplete dominance An inheritance pattern in which the heterozygote phenotype is in between the homozygote phenotypes.

incomplete metamorphosis See **hemimetabolous metamorphosis**.

independent assortment, principle of The concept that each pair of hereditary elements (alleles of the same gene) segregates (separates) independently of alleles of other genes during meiosis. One of Mendel's two principles of genetics.

indeterminate growth A pattern of growth in which an individual continues to increase its overall body size throughout its life.

induced fit Change in the shape of the active site of an enzyme, as the result of initial weak binding of a substrate, so that it binds substrate more tightly.

inducer A small molecule that triggers transcription of a specific gene, often by binding to and inactivating a repressor protein.

inducible defense A defensive trait that is manifested only in response to the presence of a consumer (predator or herbivore) or pathogen. Compare with **constitutive defense**.

infection thread An invagination of the plasma membrane of a root hair through which beneficial nitrogen-fixing bacteria enter the roots of their host plants (legumes).

inflammatory response An aspect of the innate immune response, seen in most cases of infection or tissue injury, in which the affected tissue becomes swollen, red, warm, and painful.

ingestion The act of bringing food into the digestive tract.

inhibition In ecological succession, the phenomenon in which early-arriving species make conditions less favorable for the establishment of certain later-arriving species. Compare with **facilitation** and **tolerance**.

inhibitory postsynaptic potential (IPSP) A change in membrane potential, usually hyperpolarization, at a neuron dendrite that makes an action potential less likely.

initiation (1) In an enzyme-catalyzed reaction, the stage during which enzymes orient reactants precisely as they bind at specific locations within the enzyme's active site. (2) In DNA transcription, the stage during which RNA polymerase and other proteins assemble at the promoter sequence and open the strands of DNA to start transcription. (3) In translation, the stage during which a complex consisting of initiation factor proteins, a ribosome, an mRNA, and an aminoacyl tRNA corresponding to the start codon is formed.

initiation factors A class of proteins that assist ribosomes in binding to a messenger RNA molecule to begin translation.

innate behavior Behavior that is inherited genetically, does not have to be learned, and is typical of a species.

innate immune response See **innate immunity**.

innate immunity A set of barriers to infection and generic defenses against broad types of pathogens. Produces an immediate response that involves many different leukocytes, which often activate an inflammatory response. Compare with **acquired immunity**.

inner cell mass (ICM) A cluster of cells, in the interior of a mammalian blastocyst, that eventually develop into the embryo. Contrast with **trophoblast**.

inner ear The innermost portion of the mammalian ear, consisting of a fluid-filled system of tubes that includes the cochlea (which receives sound vibrations from the middle ear) and the semicircular canals (which function in balance).

insects A terrestrial lineage of arthropods distinguished by three tagmata (head, thorax, abdomen), a single pair of antennae, and unbranched appendages.

insulin A peptide hormone produced by the pancreas in response to high levels of glucose (or amino acids) in blood. Enables cells to absorb glucose and coordinates synthesis of fats, proteins, and glycogen. Compare with **glucagon**.

integral membrane protein Any membrane protein that spans the entire lipid bilayer. Also called *transmembrane protein*. Compare with **peripheral membrane protein**.

integrated pest management In agriculture or forestry, systems for managing insects or other pests that include carefully controlled applications of toxins, introduction of species that prey on pests, planting schemes that reduce the chance of a severe pest outbreak, and other techniques.

integrator A component of an animal's nervous system that functions as part of a homeostatic system by evaluating sensory information and triggering appropriate responses. See **effector** and **sensor**.

integrin Any of a class of cell-surface proteins that bind to laminins and other proteins in the extracellular matrix, thus holding cells in place.

intercalated disc A type of specialized connection between adjacent heart muscle cells that contains gap junctions, allowing electrical signals to pass between the cells.

intermediate filament A long fiber, about 10 nm in diameter, composed of one of various proteins (e.g., keratins, lamins); one of the three types of cytoskeletal fibers. Used to form networks that help maintain cell shape and hold the nucleus in place. Compare with **actin filament** and **microtubule**.

intermediate host The host species in which a parasite reproduces asexually. Compare with **definitive host**.

intermediate muscle fiber Type of skeletal muscle fiber that is pink in color, generates ATP by both glycolysis and aerobic respiration, and has contractile properties that are intermediate between slow fibers and fast fibers. Also called fast oxidative fiber.

interneuron A neuron that passes signals from one neuron to another. Compare with **motor neuron** and **sensory neuron**.

internode The section of a plant stem between two nodes (sites where leaves attach).

interphase The portion of the cell cycle between one M phase and the next. Includes the G_1 phase, S phase, and G_2 phase.

intersexual selection The sexual selection of an individual of one gender for mating by an individual of the other gender (usually by female choice).

interspecific competition Competition between members of different species for the same limited resource. Compare with **intraspecific competition**.

interstitial fluid The plasma-like fluid found in the region (interstitial space) between cells.

intertidal zone The region between the low-tide and high-tide marks on a seashore.

intrasexual selection Competition among members of one gender for an opportunity to mate (usually male–male competition).

intraspecific competition Competition between members of the same species for the same limited resource. Compare with **interspecific competition**.

intrinsic rate of increase (r_{max}) The rate at which a population will grow under optimal conditions (i.e., when birthrates are as high as possible and death rates are as low as possible). Compare with **finite rate of increase**.

intron A region of a eukaryotic gene that is transcribed into RNA but is later removed. Compare with **exon**.

invasive species An exotic (nonnative) species that, upon introduction to a new area, spreads rapidly and competes successfully with native species.

inversion A mutation in which a segment of a chromosome breaks from the rest of the chromosome, flips, and rejoins in reversed orientation.

invertebrates A paraphyletic group composed of animals without a backbone; includes about 95 percent of all animal species. Compare with **vertebrates**.

involuntary muscle Muscle that contracts in response to stimulation by involuntary (parasympathetic or sympathetic), but not voluntary (somatic), neural stimulation.

ion An atom or a molecule that has lost or gained electrons and thus carries an electric charge, either positive (cation) or negative (anion), respectively.

ion channel A type of channel protein that allows certain ions to diffuse across a plasma membrane down an electrochemical gradient.

ionic bond A chemical bond that is formed when an electron is completely transferred from one atom to another so that the atoms remain associated due to their opposite electric charges. Compare with **covalent bond** and **hydrogen bond**.

iris A ring of pigmented muscle just behind the cornea in the vertebrate eye that contracts or expands to control the amount of light entering the eye through the pupil.

isosmotic Comparative term designating a solution that has the same solute concentration and water concentration as another solution. Compare with **hyperosmotic** and **hyposmotic**.

isotonic Comparative term designating a solution that, if inside a cell or vesicle, results in no net uptake or loss of water and thus no effect on the volume of the membrane-bound structure. This solution has the same solute concentration as the solution on the other side of the membrane. Compare with **hypertonic** and **hypotonic**.

isotope Any of several forms of an element that have the same number of protons but differ in the number of neutrons.

joint A place where two components (bones, cartilages, etc.) of a skeleton meet. May be movable (an articulated joint) or immovable (e.g., skull sutures).

juvenile An individual that has adult-like morphology but is not sexually mature.

juvenile hormone An insect hormone that prevents larvae from metamorphosing into adults.

karyogamy Fusion of two haploid nuclei to form a diploid nucleus. Occurs in many fungi, and in animals and plants during fertilization of gametes.

karyotype The distinctive appearance of all of the chromosomes in an individual, including the number of chromosomes and their length and banding patterns (after staining with dyes).

keystone species A species that has an exceptionally great impact on the other species in its ecosystem relative to its abundance.

kidney In terrestrial vertebrates, one of a paired organ situated at the back of the abdominal cavity that filters the blood, produces urine, and secretes several hormones.

kilocalorie (kcal) A unit of energy often used to measure the energy content of food. A kcal of energy raises 1 kg of water 1°C.

kin selection A form of natural selection that favors traits that increase survival or reproduction of an individual's kin at the expense of the individual.

kinesin A class of motor proteins that uses the chemical energy of ATP to "walk" toward the plus end of a microtubule. Used to transport vesicles, particles, organelles and chromosomes.

kinetic energy The energy of motion. Compare with **potential energy**.

kinetochore A protein complex at the centromere where microtubules attach to the chromosome. Contains motor proteins and microtubule-binding proteins that are involved in chromosome segregation during M phase.

kinetochore microtubules Microtubules in the spindle formed during mitosis and meiosis that are attached to the kinetochore on a chromosome.

kinocilium (plural: kinocilia) A single cilium that juts from the surface of many hair cells and functions in detection of sound or pressure.

knock-out allele A mutant allele that does not produce a functional product. Also called a *null allele* or *loss-of-function allele*.

Koch's postulates Four criteria used to determine whether a suspected infectious agent causes a particular disease.

labium majus (plural: labia majora) One of two outer folds of skin that surround the labia minora, clitoris, and vaginal opening of female mammals.

labium minus (plural: labia minora) One of two folds of skin inside the labia majora and surrounding the opening of the urethra and vagina.

labor The strong muscular contractions of the uterus that expel the fetus during birth.

***lac* operon** A set of three genes in *E. coli* that are transcribed into a single mRNA and required for lactose metabolism. Studies of the *lac* operon revealed many insights about gene regulation.

lactation (verb: lactate) Production of milk to feed offspring, from mammary glands of mammals.

lacteal A small lymphatic vessel extending into the center of a villus in the small intestine. Receives chylomicrons containing fat absorbed from food.

lactic acid fermentation Catabolic pathway in which pyruvate produced by glycolysis is converted to lactic acid in the absence of oxygen.

lagging strand In DNA replication, the strand of new DNA that is synthesized discontinuously in a series of short pieces that are later joined. Also called *discontinuous strand*. Compare with **leading strand**.

laminins An abundant protein in the extracellular matrix that binds to other ECM components and to integrins in plasma membranes; helps anchor cells in place. Predominantly found in the basal lamina; many subtypes function in different tissues.

large intestine The distal portion of the digestive tract, consisting of the cecum, colon, and rectum. Its primary function is to compact the wastes delivered from the small intestine and absorb enough water to form feces.

larva (plural: larvae) An immature stage of an animal species in which the immature and adult stages have different body forms.

late endosome A membrane-bound vesicle that arises from an early endosome, accepts lysosomal enzymes from the Golgi, and matures into a lysosome.

latency In viruses that infect animals, the ability to coexist with the host cell in a dormant state without producing new virions. The viral genetic material is replicated as the host cell replicates. Genetic material may or may not be integrated in the host genome, depending on the virus.

lateral bud A bud that forms at the nodes of a stem and may develop into a lateral (side) branch. Also called *axillary bud*.

lateral gene transfer Transfer of DNA between two different species.

lateral line system A pressure-sensitive sensory organ found in many aquatic vertebrates.

lateral root A plant root that extends horizontally from another root.

leaching Loss of nutrients from soil via percolating water.

leading strand In DNA replication, the strand of new DNA that is synthesized in one continuous piece. Also called *continuous strand*. Compare with **lagging strand**.

leaf The main photosynthetic organ of vascular plants.

leak channel Ion channel that allows ions to leak across the membrane of a neuron in its resting state.

learning An enduring change in an individual's behavior that results from specific experience(s).

leghemoglobin An iron-containing protein similar to hemoglobin. Found in infected cells of legume root nodules where it binds oxygen, preventing it from poisoning a bacterial enzyme needed for nitrogen fixation.

legumes Members of the pea plant family. Many form symbiotic associations with nitrogen-fixing bacteria in their roots.

lens A transparent structure that focuses incoming light onto a retina or other light-sensing apparatus of an eye.

lenticel Spongy segment in bark that allows gas exchange between cells in a woody stem and the atmosphere.

leptin A hormone produced and secreted by fat cells (adipocytes) that acts to stabilize fat-tissue mass partly by inhibiting appetite and increasing energy expenditure.

leukocyte Any of several types of blood cells, including neutrophils, macrophages, and lymphocytes, that reside in tissues and circulate in blood and lymph. Functions in tissue repair and defense against pathogens. Also called *white blood cell*.

lichen A symbiotic association of a fungus, often in the Ascomycota lineage, and a photosynthetic alga or cyanobacterium.

life cycle The sequence of developmental events and phases that occurs during the life span of an organism, from fertilization to offspring production.

life history The sequence of events in an individual's life from birth to reproduction to death, including how an individual allocates resources to growth, reproduction, and activities or structures that are related to survival.

life table A data set that summarizes the probability that an individual in a certain population will survive and reproduce in any given year over the course of its lifetime.

ligament Connective tissue that joins bones of an endoskeleton together.

ligand Any molecule that binds to a specific site on a receptor molecule.

ligand-gated channel An ion channel that opens or closes in response to binding by a certain molecule. Compare with **voltage-gated channel**.

light chain The smaller of the two types of polypeptide chains in an antibody or B-cell receptor molecule; composed of a variable (*V*) region, which contributes to the antigen-binding site, and a constant (*C*) region. Compare with **heavy chain**.

lignin A substance, found in the secondary cell walls of some plants, that is exceptionally stiff and strong; a complex polymer built from six-carbon rings. Most abundant in woody plant parts.

limiting nutrient Any essential nutrient whose scarcity in the environment significantly reduces growth and reproduction of organisms.

limnetic zone Open water (not near shore) that receives enough sunlight to support photosynthesis.

lineage See **monophyletic group**.

LINEs (long interspersed nuclear elements) The most abundant class of transposable elements in human genomes; can create copies of itself and insert them elsewhere in the genome. Compare with **SINEs**.

lingual lipase An enzyme produced by glands in the tongue. It breaks down fat molecules into fatty acids and monoglycerides.

linkage In genetics, a physical association between two genes because they are on the same chromosome; the inheritance patterns resulting from this association.

linkage map See **genetic map**.

lipid Any organic substance that does not dissolve in water, but dissolves well in nonpolar organic solvents. Lipids include fatty acids, fats, oils, waxes, steroids, and phospholipids.

lipid bilayer The basic structural element of all cellular membranes; consists of a two-layer sheet of phospholipid molecules with their hydrophobic tails oriented toward the inside and their hydrophilic heads toward the outside. Also called *phospholipid bilayer*.

littoral zone Shallow water near shore that receives enough sunlight to support photosynthesis. May be marine or freshwater; often flowering plants are present.

liver A large, complex organ of vertebrates that performs many functions, including storage of glycogen, processing and conversion of food and wastes, and production of bile.

lobe-finned fish Fish with fins supported by bony elements that extend down the length of the structure.

locomotion Movement of an organism under its own power.

locus (plural: loci) A gene's physical location on a chromosome.

logistic population growth The density-dependent decrease in growth rate as population size approaches the carrying capacity. Compare with **exponential population growth**.

long interspersed nuclear elements See **LINEs**.

long-day plant A plant that blooms in response to short nights (usually in late spring or early summer in the Northern Hemisphere). Compare with **day-neutral** and **short-day plant**.

loop of Henle In the vertebrate kidney, a long U-shaped loop in a nephron that extends into the medulla. Functions as a countercurrent exchanger to set up an osmotic gradient that allows reabsorption of water from the collecting duct.

loose connective tissue A type of connective tissue consisting of fibrous proteins in a soft matrix. Often functions as padding for organs.

lophophore A specialized feeding structure found in some lophotrochozoans and used in suspension (filter) feeding.

lophotrochozoans A major lineage of protostomes (Lophotrochozoa) that grow by extending the size of their skeletons rather than by molting. Many phyla have a specialized feeding structure (lophophore) and/or ciliated larvae (trochophore). Includes rotifers, flatworms, segmented worms, and mollusks. Compare with **ecdysozoans**.

loss-of-function allele See **knock-out allele**.

LUCA The *l*ast *u*niversal *c*ommon *a*ncestor of cells. This theoretical entity is proposed to be the product of chemical evolution and provided characteristics of life that are shared by all living organisms on Earth today.

lumen The interior space of any hollow structure (e.g., the rough ER) or organ (e.g., the stomach).

lung Any respiratory organ used for gas exchange between blood and air.

luteal phase The second major phase of a menstrual cycle, after ovulation, when the progesterone levels are high and the body is preparing for a possible pregnancy.

luteinizing hormone (LH) A peptide hormone, produced and secreted by the anterior pituitary, that stimulates estrogen production, ovulation, and formation of the corpus luteum in females and testosterone production in males.

lymph The mixture of fluid and white blood cells that circulates through the ducts and lymph nodes of the lymphatic system in vertebrates.

lymph node Any of many small, oval structures that lymph moves through in the lymphatic system. Filters the lymph and screens it for pathogens and other antigens. Major sites of lymphocyte activation.

lymphatic system In vertebrates, a body-wide network of thin-walled ducts (or vessels) and lymph nodes, separate from the circulatory system. Collects excess fluid from body tissues and returns it to the blood; also functions as part of the immune system.

lymphocyte A cell that circulates through the bloodstream and lymphatic system and is responsible for the development of adaptive immunity. In most cases belongs to one type of leukocyte—either B cells or T cells.

lysogeny In viruses that infect bacteria (bacteriophages), the ability to coexist with the host cell in a dormant state without producing new virions. The viral genetic material is integrated in the host chromosome and is replicated as the host cell replicates. Compare with **lytic cycle**.

lysosome A small, acidified organelle in an animal cell containing enzymes that catalyze hydrolysis reactions and can digest large molecules. Compare with **vacuole**.

lysozyme An enzyme that functions in innate immunity by digesting bacterial cell walls. Occurs in lysosomes of phagocytes and is secreted in saliva, tears, mucus, and egg white.

lytic cycle A type of viral replicative growth in which the production and release of virions kills the host cell. Compare with **lysogeny**.

M phase The phase of the cell cycle during which cell division occurs. Includes mitosis or meiosis and often cytokinesis.

M-phase-promoting factor (MPF) A complex of a cyclin and cyclin-dependent kinase that, when activated, phosphorylates a number of specific proteins needed to initiate mitosis in eukaryotic cells.

macromolecular machine A group of proteins that assemble to carry out a particular function.

macromolecule Any very large organic molecule, usually made up of smaller molecules (monomers) joined together into a polymer. The main biological macromolecules are proteins, nucleic acids, and polysaccharides.

macronutrient Any element (e.g., nitrogen) that is required in large quantities for normal growth, reproduction, and maintenance of a living organism. Compare with **micronutrient**.

macrophage A type of leukocyte in the innate immune system that participates in the inflammatory response by secreting cytokines and phagocytizing invading pathogens and apoptotic cells. Also serves as an antigen-presenting cell to activate lymphocytes.

MADS box A DNA sequence that codes for a DNA-binding motif in proteins; present in floral organ identity genes in plants. Functionally similar sequences are found in some fungal and animal genes.

magnetoreception A sensory system in which receptors are activated in response to magnetic fields.

magnetoreceptor A sensory cell or organ specialized for detecting magnetic fields.

major histocompatibility protein See **MHC protein**.

maladaptive Describing a trait that lowers fitness.

malaria A human disease caused by five species of the protist *Plasmodium* and passed to humans by mosquitoes.

malignant tumor A tumor that is actively growing and disrupting local tissues or is spreading to other organs. Cancer consists of one or more malignant tumors. Compare with **benign tumor**.

Malpighian tubules A major excretory organ of insects, consisting of blind-ended tubes that extend from the gut into the hemocoel. Filter hemolymph to form "pre-urine" and then send it to the hindgut for further processing.

mammals One of the two lineages of amniotes (vertebrates that produce amniotic eggs) distinguished by hair (or fur) and mammary glands. Includes the monotremes (platypuses), marsupials, and eutherians (placental mammals).

mammary glands Specialized exocrine glands that produce and secrete milk for nursing offspring. A diagnostic feature of mammals.

mandibles Any mouthpart used in chewing. In vertebrates, the lower jaw. In insects, crustaceans, and myriapods, the first pair of mouthparts.

mantle One of the three main parts of the mollusk body; the thick outer tissue that protects the visceral mass and may secrete a calcium carbonate shell.

marsh A wetland dominated by grasses and other nonwoody plants.

marsupials A lineage of mammals (Marsupiala) that nourish their young in an abdominal pouch after a very short period of development in the uterus.

mass extinction The extinction of a large number of diverse evolutionary groups during a relatively short period of geologic time (about 1 million years). May occur due to sudden and extraordinary environmental changes. Compare with **background extinction**.

mass feeder An animal that ingests chunks of food.

mass number The total number of protons and neutrons in an atom.

mast cell A type of leukocyte that is stationary (embedded in tissue) and helps trigger the inflammatory response, including secretion of histamine, to infection or injury. Particularly important in allergic responses and defense against parasites.

maternal chromosome A chromosome inherited from the mother.

mechanical advantage The ratio of force exerted on a load to the muscle force of the effort. A measure of the force efficiency of a mechanical system.

mechanoreception A sensory system in which receptors are activated in response to changes in pressure.

mechanoreceptor A sensory cell or organ specialized for detecting distortions caused by touch or pressure. One example is hair cells in the cochlea.

mediator Regulatory proteins in eukaryotes that form a physical link between regulatory transcription factors that are bound to DNA, the basal transcription complex, and RNA polymerase.

medium A liquid or solid that supports the growth of cells.

medulla The innermost part of an organ (e.g., kidney or adrenal gland).

medulla oblongata In vertebrates, a region of the brain stem that along with the cerebellum forms the hindbrain.

medusa (plural: medusae) The free-floating stage in the life cycle of some cnidarians (e.g., jellyfish). Compare with **polyp**.

megapascal (MPa) A unit of pressure (force per unit area) equivalent to 1 million pascals (Pa).

megasporangium (plural: megasporangia) In heterosporous species of plants, a spore-producing structure that produces megaspores, which go on to develop into female gametophytes.

megaspore In seed plants, a haploid (*n*) spore that is produced in a megasporangium by meiosis of a diploid (2*n*) megasporocyte; develops into a female gametophyte. Compare with **microspore**.

meiosis In sexually reproducing organisms, a special two-stage type of cell division in which one diploid (2*n*) parent cell produces haploid (*n*) cells (gametes); results in halving of the chromosome number. Also called *reduction division*.

meiosis I The first cell division of meiosis, in which synapsis and crossing over occur and homologous chromosomes are separated from each other, producing daughter cells with half as many chromosomes (each composed of two sister chromatids) as the parent cell.

meiosis II The second cell division of meiosis, in which sister chromatids are separated from each other. Similar to mitosis.

melatonin A hormone, produced by the pineal gland, that regulates sleep–wake cycles and seasonal reproduction in vertebrates.

membrane potential A difference in electric charge across a cell membrane; a form of potential energy. Also called *membrane voltage*.

memory Retention of learned information.

memory cells A type of lymphocyte responsible for maintaining immunity for years or decades after an infection. Descended from a B cell or T cell activated during a previous infection or vaccination.

meniscus (plural: menisci) The concave boundary layer formed at most air–water interfaces due to adhesion and surface tension.

menstrual cycle A female reproductive cycle seen in Old World monkeys and apes (including humans) in which the uterine lining is shed (menstruation) if no pregnancy occurs. Compare with **estrous cycle**.

menstruation The periodic shedding of the uterine lining through the vagina that occurs in females of Old World monkeys and apes, including humans.

meristem (adjective: meristematic) In plants, a group of undifferentiated cells, including stem cells, which can divide and develop into various adult tissues throughout the life of a plant. See also **apical meristem** and **ground meristem**.

mesoderm The middle of the three basic cell layers (germ layers) in most animal embryos; gives rise to muscles, bones, blood, and some internal organs (kidney, spleen, etc.). Compare with **ectoderm** and **endoderm**.

mesoglea A gelatinous material, containing scattered ectodermal cells, that is located between the ectoderm and endoderm of cnidarians (e.g., jellyfish, corals, and anemones).

mesophyll cell A type of cell, found near the surfaces of plant leaves, that is specialized for the light-dependent reactions of photosynthesis.

Mesozoic era The interval of geologic time, from 251 million to 65.5 million years ago, during which gymnosperms were the dominant plants and dinosaurs the dominant vertebrates. Ended with extinction of the dinosaurs (except birds).

messenger RNA (mRNA) An RNA molecule transcribed from DNA that carries information (in codons) that specifies the amino acid sequence of a polypeptide.

meta-analysis A comparative analysis of the results of many smaller, previously published studies.

metabolic pathway A linked series of biochemical reactions that build up or break down a particular molecule; the product of one reaction is the substrate of the next reaction.

metabolic rate The total energy use by all the cells of an individual. For aerobic organisms, often measured as the amount of oxygen consumed per hour.

metabolic water The water that is produced as a by-product of cellular respiration.

metagenomics The inventory of all the genes in a community or ecosystem by sequencing, analyzing, and comparing the genomes of the component organisms. Also called *environmental sequencing*.

metagenomics The inventory of all the genes in a community or ecosystem by sequencing, analyzing, and comparing the genomes of the component organisms. Sequencing of all or most of the genes present in an environment directly (also called *environmental sequencing*).

metallothioneins Small plant proteins that bind to and prevent excess metal ions from acting as toxins.

metamorphosis Transition from one developmental stage to another, such as from the larval to the adult form of an animal.

metaphase A stage in mitosis or meiosis during which chromosomes line up in the middle of the cell.

metaphase plate The plane along which chromosomes line up in the middle of the spindle during metaphase of mitosis or meiosis; not an actual structure.

metapopulation A population made up of many small, physically isolated populations connected by migration.

metastasis The spread of cancerous cells from their site of origin to distant sites in the body where they may establish additional tumors.

methanogen A prokaryote that produces methane (CH_4) as a by-product of cellular respiration.

methanotroph An organism (bacteria or archaea) that uses methane (CH_4) as its primary electron donor and source of carbon.

methyl salicylate (MeSA) A molecule that is hypothesized to function as a signal, transported among tissues, that triggers systematic acquired resistance in plants—a response to pathogen attack.

MHC protein Any of a large set of mammalian cell-surface glycoproteins involved in marking cells as self and in antigen presentation to T cells. Also called *MHC molecule*. Compare with **Class I** and **Class II MHC protein**.

microbe Any microscopic organism, including bacteria, archaea, and various tiny eukaryotes.

microbiology The field of study concerned with microscopic organisms.

microfibril Bundled strands of cellulose that serve as the fibrous component in plant cell walls.

microfilament See **actin filament**.

micronutrient Any element (e.g., iron, molybdenum, magnesium) that is required in very small quantities for normal growth, reproduction, and maintenance of a living organism. Compare with **macronutrient**.

micropyle The tiny pore in a plant ovule through which the pollen tube reaches the embryo sac.

microRNA (miRNA) A small, single-stranded RNA associated with proteins in an RNA-induced silencing complex (RISC). Processed from a longer premiRNA gene transcript. Can bind to complementary sequences in mRNA molecules, allowing the associated proteins of RISC to degrade the bound mRNA or inhibit its translation. See **RNA interference**.

microsatellite A noncoding stretch of eukaryotic DNA consisting of a repeating sequence 2 to 6 base pairs long. Also called *short tandem repeat* or *simple sequence repeat*.

microsporangium (plural: microsporangia) In heterosporous species of plants, a spore-producing structure that produces microspores, which go on to develop into male gametophytes.

microspore In seed plants, a haploid (*n*) spore that is produced in a microsporangium by meiosis of a diploid (2*n*) microsporocyte; develops into a male gametophyte. Compare with **megaspore**.

microtubule A long, tubular fiber, about 25 nm in diameter, formed by polymerization of tubulin protein dimers; one of the three types of cytoskeletal fibers. Involved in cell movement and transport of materials within the cell. Compare with **actin filament** and **intermediate filament**.

microtubule organizing center (MTOC) General term for any structure (e.g., centrosome and basal body) that organizes microtubules in cells.

microvilli (singular: microvillus) Tiny protrusions from the surface of an epithelial cell that increase the surface area for absorption of substances.

midbrain One of the three main regions of the vertebrate brain; includes sensory integrating and relay centers. Compare with **forebrain** and **hindbrain**.

middle ear The air-filled middle portion of the mammalian ear, which contains three small bones (ossicles) that transmit and amplify sound from the tympanic membrane to the inner ear. Is connected to the throat via the eustachian tube.

migration (1) In ecology, a seasonal movement of large numbers of organisms from one geographic location or habitat to another. (2) In population genetics, movement of individuals from one population to another.

millivolt (mV) A unit of voltage equal to 1/1000 of a volt.

mimicry A phenomenon in which one species has evolved (or learns) to look or sound like another species. See **Batesian mimicry** and **Müllerian mimicry**.

mineral One of various inorganic substances that are important components of enzyme cofactors or of structural materials in an organism.

mineralocorticoids A class of steroid hormones, produced and secreted by the adrenal cortex, that regulate electrolyte levels and the overall volume of body fluids. Aldosterone is the principal one in humans. Compare with **glucocorticoids**.

minisatellite A noncoding stretch of eukaryotic DNA consisting of a repeating sequence that is 6 to 100 base pairs long. Also called *variable number tandem repeat (VNTR)*.

mismatch repair The process by which mismatched base pairs in DNA are fixed.

missense mutation A point mutation (change in a single base pair) that changes one amino acid for another within the sequence of a protein.

mitochondrial matrix Central compartment of a mitochondrion, which is lined by the inner membrane; contains mitochondrial DNA, ribosomes, and the enzymes for pyruvate processing and the citric acid cycle.

mitochondrion (plural: mitochondria) A eukaryotic organelle that is bounded by a double membrane and is the site of aerobic respiration and ATP synthesis.

mitogen-activated protein kinases (MAPK) Enzymes that are involved in signal transduction pathways that often lead to the induction of cell replication. Different types are organized in a series, where one kinase activates another via phosphorylation. See also **phosphorylation cascade**.

mitosis In eukaryotic cells, the process of nuclear division that results in two daughter nuclei genetically identical with the parent nucleus. Subsequent cytokinesis (division of the cytoplasm) yields two daughter cells.

mode of transmission The type of inheritance observed as a trait is passed from parent to offspring. Some common types are autosomal recessive, autosomal dominant, and X-linked recessive.

model organism An organism selected for intensive scientific study based on features that make it easy to work with (e.g., body size, life span), in the hope that findings will apply to other species.

molarity A common unit of solute concentration equal to the number of moles of a dissolved solute in 1 liter of solution.

mole The amount of a substance that contains 6.022×10^{23} of its elemental entities (e.g., atoms, ions, or molecules). This number of molecules of a compound will have a mass equal to the molecular weight of that compound expressed in grams.

molecular chaperone A protein that facilitates the folding of newly synthesized proteins into their correct three-dimensional shape. Usually works by an ATP-dependent mechanism.

molecular formula A notation that indicates only the numbers and types of atoms in a molecule, such as H_2O for the water molecule. Compare with **structural formula**.

molecular weight The sum of the atomic weights of all of the atoms in a molecule; roughly, the total number of protons and neutrons in the molecule.

molecule A combination of two or more atoms held together by covalent bonds.

molting A method of body growth, used by ecdysozoans, that involves the shedding of an external protective cuticle or skeleton, expansion of the soft body, and growth of a new external layer.

monocot Any flowering plant (angiosperm) that has a single cotyledon (embryonic leaf) upon germination. Monocots form a monophyletic group. Also called a monocotyledonous plant. Compare with **dicot**.

monoecious Describing an angiosperm species that has both male and female reproductive structures on each plant. Compare with **dioecious**.

monohybrid cross A mating between two parents that are both heterozygous for one given gene.

monomer A small molecule that can covalently bind to other similar molecules to form a larger macromolecule. Compare with **polymer**.

monophyletic group An evolutionary unit that includes an ancestral population and all of its descendants but no others. Also called a *clade* or *lineage*. Compare with **paraphyletic group** and **polyphyletic group**.

monosaccharide A molecule that has the molecular formula $(CH_2O)_n$ and cannot be hydrolyzed to form any smaller carbohydrates. Also called *simple sugar*. Compare with **oligosaccharide** and **polysaccharide**.

monosomy The state of having only one copy of a particular type of chromosome in an otherwise diploid cell.

monotremes A lineage of mammals (Monotremata) that lay eggs and then nourish the young with milk. Includes just five living species: the platypus and four species of echidna, all with leathery beaks or bills.

morphogen A molecule that exists in a concentration gradient and provides spatial information to embryonic cells.

morphology The shape and appearance of an organism's body and its component parts.

morphospecies concept The definition of a species as a population or group of populations that have measurably different anatomical features from other groups. Also called *morphological species concept*. Compare with **biological species concept** and **phylogenetic species concept**.

motor neuron A nerve cell that carries signals from the central nervous system (brain and spinal cord) to an effector, such as a muscle or gland. Compare with **interneuron** and **sensory neuron**.

motor protein A class of proteins whose major function is to convert the chemical energy of ATP into motion. Includes dynein, kinesin, and myosin.

MPF See **M-phase-promoting factor**.

mRNA See **messenger RNA**.

mucosal-associated lymphoid tissue (MALT) Collective term for lymphocytes and other leukocytes associated with skin cells and mucus-secreting epithelial tissues in the gut and respiratory tract. Plays an important role in preventing entry of pathogens into the body.

mucous cell A type of cell found in the epithelial layer of the stomach; responsible for secreting mucus into the stomach.

mucus (adjective: mucous) A slimy mixture of glycoproteins (called mucins) and water that is secreted in many animal organs for lubrication. Serves as a barrier to protect surfaces from infection.

Müllerian inhibitory substance A peptide hormone, secreted by the embryonic testis, that causes regression (withering away) of the female reproductive ducts.

Müllerian mimicry A type of mimicry in which two (or more) harmful species resemble each other. Compare with **Batesian mimicry**.

multicellularity The state of being composed of many cells that adhere to each other and do not all express the same genes, with the result that some cells have specialized functions.

multiple allelism The existence of more than two alleles of the same gene.

multiple fruit A fruit (e.g., pineapple) that develops from many separate flowers and thus many carpels. Compare with **aggregate** and **simple fruit**.

multiple sclerosis (MS) A human autoimmune disease in which the immune system attacks the myelin sheaths that insulate axons of neurons.

muscle fiber A single muscle cell.

muscle tissue An animal tissue consisting of bundles of long, thin, contractile cells (muscle fibers). Functions primarily in movement.

mutagen Any physical or chemical agent that increases the rate of mutation.

mutant An individual that carries a mutation, particularly a new or rare mutation.

mutation Any change in the hereditary material of an organism (DNA in most organisms, RNA in some viruses). The only source of new alleles in populations.

mutualism (adjective: mutualistic) A symbiotic relationship between two organisms (mutualists) that benefits both. Compare with **commensalism** and **parasitism**.

mutualist Organism that is a participant and partner in a mutualistic relationship. See **mutualism**.

mycelium (plural: mycelia) A mass of underground filaments (hyphae) that form the body of a fungus. Also found in some protists and bacteria.

mycorrhiza (plural: mycorrhizae) A mutualistic association between certain fungi and the roots of most vascular plants, sometimes visible as nodules or nets in or around plant roots.

myelin sheath Multiple layers of myelin, derived from the cell membranes of certain glial cells, wrapped around the axon of a neuron and providing electrical insulation.

myocardial infarction Death of cardiac muscle cells when deprived of oxygen.

myoD A transcription factor that is a master regulator of muscle cell differentiation (short for "*myo*blast *d*etermination").

myofibril Long, slender structure composed of contractile proteins organized into repeating units (sarcomeres) in vertebrate heart muscle and skeletal muscle.

myosin Any one of a class of motor proteins that use the chemical energy of ATP to move along actin filaments in muscle contraction, cytokinesis, and vesicle transport.

myriapods A lineage of arthropods with long segmented trunks, each segment bearing one or two pairs of legs. Includes millipedes and centipedes.

NAD⁺/NADH Oxidized and reduced forms, respectively, of nicotinamide adenine dinucleotide. A nonprotein electron carrier that functions in many of the redox reactions of metabolism.

NADP⁺/NADPH Oxidized and reduced forms, respectively, of nicotinamide adenine dinucleotide phosphate. A nonprotein electron carrier that is reduced during the light-dependent reactions in photosynthesis and extensively used in biosynthetic reactions.

natural experiment A situation in which a natural change in conditions enables comparisons of groups, rather than a manipulation of conditions by researchers.

natural selection The process by which individuals with certain heritable traits tend to produce more surviving offspring than do individuals without those traits, often leading to a change in the genetic makeup of the population. A major mechanism of evolution.

nauplius A distinct planktonic larval stage seen in many crustaceans.

Neanderthal A recently extinct European species of hominin, *Homo neanderthalensis*, closely related to but distinct from modern humans.

nectar The sugary fluid produced by flowers to attract and reward pollinating animals.

nectary A nectar-producing structure in a flower.

negative control Of genes, when a regulatory protein shuts down expression by binding to DNA on or near the gene.

negative feedback A self-limiting, corrective response in which a deviation in some variable (e.g., concentration of some compound) triggers responses aimed at returning the variable to normal. Represents a means of maintaining homeostasis. Compare with **positive feedback**.

negative pressure ventilation Ventilation of the lungs by expanding the rib cage so as to "pull" air into the lungs. Compare with **positive pressure ventilation**.

negative-sense RNA virus An ssRNA virus whose genome contains sequences complementary to those in the mRNA required to produce viral proteins. Compare with **ambisense virus** and **positive-sense virus**.

nematodes See **roundworms**.

nephron One of many tiny tubules inside the kidney that function in the formation of urine.

neritic zone Shallow marine waters beyond the intertidal zone, extending down to about 200 meters, where the continental shelf ends.

nerve A long, tough strand of nervous tissue, typically containing thousands of axons, wrapped in connective tissue; carries impulses between the central nervous system and some other part of the body.

nerve cord In chordate animals, a hollow bundle of nerves extending from the brain along the dorsal (back) side of the animal, with cerebrospinal fluid inside a central channel. One of the defining features of chordates.

nerve net A nervous system in which neurons are diffuse instead of being clustered into large ganglia or tracts; found in cnidarians and ctenophores.

nervous tissue An animal tissue consisting of nerve cells (neurons) and various supporting cells.

net primary productivity (NPP) In an ecosystem, the total amount of carbon fixed by photosynthesis over a given time period minus the amount oxidized during cellular respiration. Compare with **gross primary productivity**.

net reproductive rate (R_0) The growth rate of a population per generation; equivalent to the average number of female offspring that each female produces over her lifetime.

neural tube A folded tube of ectoderm that forms along the dorsal side of a young vertebrate embryo; gives rise to the brain and spinal cord.

neuroendocrine Referring to nerve cells (neurons) that release hormones into the blood or to such hormones themselves.

neurogenesis The birth of new neurons from central nervous system stem cells.

neurohormones Hormones produced by neurons.

neuron A cell that is specialized for the transmission of nerve impulses. Typically has dendrites, a cell body, and a long axon that forms synapses with other neurons. Also called *nerve cell*.

neurosecretory cell A nerve cell (neuron) that produces and secretes hormones into the bloodstream. Principally found in the hypothalamus. Also called *neuroendocrine cell*.

neurotoxin Any substance that specifically destroys or blocks the normal functioning of neurons.

neurotransmitter A molecule that transmits signals from one neuron to another or from a neuron to a muscle or gland. Examples are acetylcholine, dopamine, serotonin, and norepinephrine.

neutral In genetics, referring to any mutation or mutant allele that has no effect on an individual's fitness.

neutrophil A type of leukocyte, capable of moving through body tissues, that engulfs and digests pathogens and other foreign particles; also secretes various compounds that attack bacteria and fungi.

niche The range of resources that a species can use and the range of conditions that it can tolerate. More broadly, the role that species plays in its ecosystem.

niche differentiation The evolutionary change in resource use by competing species that occurs as the result of character displacement.

nicotinamide adenine dinucleotide See **NAD⁺/ NADH**.

nitrogen cycle, global The movement of nitrogen among terrestrial ecosystems, the oceans, and the atmosphere.

nitrogen fixation The incorporation of atmospheric nitrogen (N_2) into ammonia (NH_3), which can be used to make many organic compounds. Occurs in only a few lineages of bacteria and archaea.

nociceptor A sensory cell or organ specialized to detect tissue damage, usually producing the sensation of pain.

Nod factors Molecules produced by nitrogen-fixing bacteria that help them recognize and bind to roots of legumes.

node (1) In animals, any small thickening (e.g., a lymph node). (2) In plants, the part of a stem where leaves or leaf buds are attached. (3) In a phylogenetic tree, the point where two branches diverge, representing the point in time when an ancestral group split into two or more descendant groups. Also called *fork*.

node of Ranvier One of the unmyelinated sections that occurs periodically along a neuron's axon and serves as a site where an action potential can be regenerated.

nodule Globular structure on roots of legume plants that contain symbiotic nitrogen-fixing bacteria.

noncyclic electron flow Path of electron flow in which electrons pass from photosystem II, through an electron transport chain, to photosystem I, and ultimately to NADP⁺ during the light-dependent reactions of photosynthesis. See also **Z scheme**.

nondisjunction An error that can occur during meiosis or mitosis, in which one daughter cell receives two copies of a particular chromosome and the other daughter cell receives none.

nonpolar covalent bond A covalent bond in which electrons are equally shared between two atoms of the same or similar electronegativity. Compare with **polar covalent bond**.

nonsense mutation A point mutation (change in a single base pair) that converts an amino-acid-specifying codon into a stop codon.

non-sister chromatids The chromatids of a particular type of chromosome (after replication) with respect to the chromatids of its homologous chromosome. Crossing over occurs between non-sister chromatids. Compare with **sister chromatids**.

non-template strand The strand of DNA that is not transcribed during synthesis of RNA. Its sequence corresponds to that of the mRNA produced from the other strand. Also called *coding strand*.

non-vascular plants A paraphyletic group of land plants that lack vascular tissue and reproduce using spores. The non-vascular plants include three lineages of green plants (liverworts, mosses, and hornworts). These lineages are sometimes called *bryophytes*.

norepinephrine A catecholamine used as a neurotransmitter in the sympathetic nervous system. Also is produced by the adrenal medulla and functions as a hormone that triggers rapid responses relating to the fight-or-flight response.

notochord A supportive but flexible rod that occurs in the back of a chordate embryo, ventral to the developing spinal cord. Replaced by vertebrae in most adult vertebrates. A defining feature of chordates.

nuclear envelope The double-layered membrane enclosing the nucleus of a eukaryotic cell.

nuclear lamina A lattice-like sheet of fibrous nuclear lamins, which are one type of intermediate filament. Lines the inner membrane of the nuclear envelope, stiffening the envelope and helping to organize the chromosomes.

nuclear lamins Intermediate filaments that make up the nuclear lamina layer—a lattice-like layer inside the nuclear envelope that stiffens the structure.

nuclear localization signal (NLS) A short amino acid sequence that marks a protein for delivery to the nucleus.

nuclear pore An opening in the nuclear envelope that connects the inside of the nucleus with the cytoplasm and through which molecules such as mRNA and some proteins can pass.

nuclear pore complex A large complex of dozens of proteins lining a nuclear pore, defining its shape and regulating transport through the pore.

nuclease Any enzyme that can break down RNA or DNA molecules.

nucleic acid A macromolecule composed of nucleotide monomers. Generally used by cells to store or transmit hereditary information. Includes ribonucleic acid and deoxyribonucleic acid.

nucleoid In prokaryotic cells, a dense, centrally located region that contains DNA but is not surrounded by a membrane.

nucleolus In eukaryotic cells, a specialized structure in the nucleus where ribosomal RNA processing occurs and ribosomal subunits are assembled.

nucleosome A repeating, bead-like unit of eukaryotic chromatin, consisting of about 200 nucleotides of DNA wrapped twice around eight histone proteins.

nucleotide excision repair The process of removing a damaged region in one strand of DNA and replacing it with the correct sequence using the undamaged strand as a template.

nucleotide A molecule consisting of a five-carbon sugar (ribose or deoxyribose), a phosphate group, and one of several nitrogen-containing bases. DNA and RNA are polymers of nucleotides containing deoxyribose (deoxyribonucleotides) and ribose (ribonucleotides), respectively. Equivalent to a nucleoside plus one phosphate group.

nucleus (1) The center of an atom, containing protons and neutrons. (2) In eukaryotic cells, the large organelle containing the chromosomes and surrounded by a double membrane. (3) A discrete clump of neuron cell bodies in the brain, usually sharing a distinct function.

null allele See **knock-out allele**.

null hypothesis A hypothesis that specifies what the results of an experiment will be if the main hypothesis being tested is wrong. Often states that there will be no difference between experimental groups.

nutrient Any substance that an organism requires for normal growth, maintenance, or reproduction.

occipital lobe In the vertebrate brain, one of the four major areas in the cerebrum.

oceanic zone The waters of the open ocean beyond the continental shelf.

odorant Any volatile molecule that conveys information about food or the environment.

oil An unsaturated fat that is liquid at room temperature.

Okazaki fragment Short segment of DNA produced during replication of the lagging strand template. Many Okazaki fragments make up the lagging strand in newly synthesized DNA.

olfaction The perception of odors.

olfactory bulb A bulb-shaped projection of the brain just above the nose. Receives and interprets odor information from the nose.

oligodendrocyte A type of glial cell that wraps around axons of some neurons in the central nervous system, forming a myelin sheath that provides electrical insulation. Compare with **Schwann cell**.

oligopeptide A chain composed of fewer than 50 amino acids linked together by peptide bonds. Often referred to simply as *peptide*.

oligosaccharide A linear or branched polymer consisting of less than 50 monosaccharides joined by glycosidic linkages. Compare with **monosaccharide** and **polysaccharide**.

ommatidium (plural: ommatidia) A light-sensing column in an arthropod's compound eye.

omnivore (adjective: omnivorous) An animal whose diet regularly includes both meat and plants. Compare with **carnivore** and **herbivore**.

oncogene Any gene whose protein product stimulates cell division at all times and thus promotes cancer development. Often is a mutated form of a gene involved in regulating the cell cycle. See **proto-oncogene**.

one-gene, one-enzyme hypothesis The hypothesis that each gene is responsible for making one enzyme. This hypothesis has expanded to include genes that produce proteins other than enzymes or that produce RNAs as final products.

oogenesis The production of egg cells (ova).

oogonium (plural: oogonia) In an ovary, any of the diploid cells that can divide by mitosis to create primary oocytes (which can undergo meiosis) and more oogonia.

open circulatory system A circulatory system in which the circulating fluid (hemolymph) is not confined to blood vessels. Compare with **closed circulatory system**.

open reading frame (ORF) Any DNA sequence, ranging in length from several hundred to thousands of base pairs long, that is flanked by a start codon and a stop codon. ORFs identified by computer analysis of DNA may be functional genes, especially if they have other features characteristic of genes (e.g., promoter sequence).

operator In prokaryotic DNA, a binding site for a repressor protein; located near the start of an operon.

operculum The stiff flap of tissue that covers the gills of teleost fishes.

operon A region of prokaryotic DNA that codes for a series of functionally related genes and is transcribed from a single promoter into one mRNA.

opsin A transmembrane protein that is covalently linked to retinal, the light-detecting pigment in rod and cone cells.

optic nerve A bundle of neurons that runs from the eye to the brain.

optimal foraging The concept that animals forage in a way that maximizes the amount of usable energy they take in, given the costs of finding and ingesting their food and the risk of being eaten while they're at it.

orbital The region of space around an atomic nucleus in which an electron is present most of the time.

organ A group of tissues organized into a functional and structural unit.

organ system Groups of tissues and organs that work together to perform a function.

organelle Any discrete, membrane-bound structure within a cell (e.g., mitochondrion) that has a characteristic structure and function.

organic For a compound, containing carbon and hydrogen and usually containing carbon–carbon bonds. Organic compounds are widely used by living organisms.

organism Any living entity that contains one or more cells.

organogenesis A stage of embryonic development that follows gastrulation and that creates organs from the three germ layers.

origin of replication The site on a chromosome at which DNA replication begins.

osmoconformer An animal that does not actively regulate the osmolarity of its tissues but conforms to the osmolarity of the surrounding environment.

osmolarity The concentration of dissolved substances in a solution, measured in osmoles per liter.

osmoregulation The process by which a living organism controls the concentration of water and salts in its body.

osmoregulator An animal that actively regulates the osmolarity of its tissues.

osmosis Diffusion of water across a selectively permeable membrane from a region of low solute concentration (high water concentration) to a region of high solute concentration (low water concentration).

ossicles, ear In mammals, three bones found in the middle ear that function in transferring and amplifying sound from the outer ear to the inner ear.

ouabain A plant toxin that poisons the sodium–potassium pumps of animals.

out-of-Africa hypothesis The hypothesis that modern humans (*Homo sapiens*) evolved in Africa and spread to other continents, replacing other *Homo* species without interbreeding with them.

outcrossing Reproduction by fusion of the gametes of different individuals, rather than by self-fertilization.

outer ear The outermost portion of the mammalian ear, consisting of the pinna (ear flap) and the ear canal. Funnels sound to the tympanic membrane.

outgroup A taxon that is closely related to a particular monophyletic group but is not part of it.

oval window A membrane separating the fluid-filled cochlea from the air-filled middle ear; sound vibrations pass through it from the middle ear to the inner ear in mammals.

ovary The egg-producing organ of a female animal, or the fruit- and seed-producing structure in the female part of a flower.

overexploitation Unsustainable removal of wildlife from the natural environment for use by humans.

oviduct See **fallopian tube**.

oviparous In animals, producing eggs that are laid outside the body where they develop and hatch. Compare with **ovoviviparous** and **viviparous**.

ovoviviparous In animals, producing eggs that are retained inside the body until they are ready to hatch. Compare with **oviparous** and **viviparous**.

ovulation The release of an egg from an ovary of a female vertebrate. In humans, an ovarian follicle releases an egg at the end of the follicular phase of the menstrual cycle.

ovule In flowering plants, the structure inside an ovary that contains the female gametophyte and eventually (if fertilized) becomes a seed.

ovum (plural: ova) See **egg**.

oxidation The loss of electrons from an atom or molecule during a redox reaction, either by donation of an electron to another atom or molecule, or by the shared electrons in covalent bonds moving farther from the atomic nucleus.

oxidative phosphorylation Production of ATP molecules by ATP synthase using the proton gradient established via redox reactions of an electron transport chain.

oxygen–hemoglobin equilibrium curve The graphed depiction of the percentage of hemoglobin in the blood that is bound to oxygen at various partial pressures of oxygen.

oxygenic Referring to any process or reaction that produces oxygen. Photosynthesis in plants, algae, and cyanobacteria, which involves photosystem II, is oxygenic. Compare with **anoxygenic**.

oxytocin A peptide hormone, secreted by the posterior pituitary, that triggers labor and milk production in females and that stimulates pair bonding, parental care, and affiliative behavior in both sexes.

p53 A tumor-suppressor protein (molecular weight of 53 kilodaltons) that responds to DNA damage by stopping the cell cycle, turning on DNA repair machinery, and, if necessary, triggering apoptosis. Encoded by the *p53* gene.

pacemaker cell Any of a group of specialized cardiac muscle cells in the sinoatrial (SA) node of the vertebrate heart that have an inherent rhythm and can generate an electrical impulse that spreads to other heart cells.

paleontologists Scientists who study the fossil record and the history of life.

Paleozoic era The interval of geologic time, from 542 million to 251 million years ago, during which fungi, land plants, and animals first appeared and diversified. Began with the Cambrian explosion and ended with the extinction of many invertebrates and vertebrates at the end of the Permian period.

pancreas A large gland in vertebrates that has both exocrine and endocrine functions. Secretes digestive enzymes into a duct connected to the intestine and secretes several hormones (notably, insulin and glucagon) into the bloodstream.

pancreatic amylase An enzyme produced by the pancreas that breaks down glucose chains by catalyzing hydrolysis of the glycosidic linkages between the glucose residues.

pancreatic lipase An enzyme that is produced in the pancreas and acts in the small intestine to break bonds in complex fats, releasing small lipids.

pandemic The spread of an infectious disease in a short time period over a wide geographic area and affecting a very high proportion of the population. Compare with **epidemic**.

parabiosis An experimental technique for determining whether a certain physiological phenomenon is regulated by a hormone; consists of surgically uniting two individuals so that hormones can pass between them.

paracrine Relating to a chemical signal that is released by one cell and affects neighboring cells.

paraphyletic group A group that includes an ancestral population and *some* but not all of its descendants. Compare with **monophyletic group**.

parapodia (singular: parapodium) Appendages found in some annelids from which bristle-like structures (chaetae) extend.

parasite An organism that lives on a host species (ectoparasite) or in a host species (endoparasite) and that damages its host.

parasitism (adjective: parasitic) A symbiotic relationship between two organisms that is beneficial to one organism (the parasite) but detrimental to the other (the host). Compare with **commensalism** and **mutualism**.

parasitoid An organism that has a parasitic larval stage and a free-living adult stage. Most parasitoids are insects that lay eggs in the bodies of other insects.

parasympathetic nervous system The part of the autonomic nervous system that stimulates responses for conserving or restoring energy, such as reduced heart rate and increased digestion. Compare with **sympathetic nervous system**.

parenchyma cell In plants, a general type of cell with a relatively thin primary cell wall. These cells, found in leaves, the centers of stems and roots, and fruits, are involved in photosynthesis, storage, and transport. Compare with **collenchyma cell** and **sclerenchyma cell**.

parental care Any action by which an animal expends energy or assumes risks to benefit its offspring (e.g., nest building, feeding of young, defense).

parental generation The adults used in the first experimental cross of a breeding experiment.

parental strand A strand of DNA that is used as a template during DNA synthesis.

parietal cell A cell in the stomach lining that secretes hydrochloric acid.

parietal lobe In the vertebrate brain, one of the four major areas in the cerebrum.

parsimony The logical principle that the most likely explanation of a phenomenon is the most economical or simplest. When applied to comparison of alternative phylogenetic trees, it suggests that the one requiring the fewest evolutionary changes is most likely to be correct.

parthenogenesis Development of offspring from unfertilized eggs; a type of asexual reproduction.

partial pressure The pressure of one particular gas in a mixture of gases; the contribution of that gas to the overall pressure.

particulate inheritance The observation that genes from two parents do not blend together in offspring, but instead remain separate or particle-like.

pascal (Pa) A unit of pressure (force per unit area).

passive transport Diffusion of a substance across a membrane. When this event occurs with the assistance of membrane proteins, it is called *facilitated diffusion*.

patch clamping A technique for studying the electrical currents that flow through individual ion channels by sucking a tiny patch of membrane to the hollow tip of a microelectrode.

paternal chromosome A chromosome inherited from the father.

pathogen (adjective: pathogenic) Any entity capable of causing disease, such as a microbe, virus, or prion.

pattern formation The series of events that determines the spatial organization of an entire embryo or parts of an embryo, for example, setting the major body axes early in development.

pattern-recognition receptor On leukocytes, a class of membrane proteins that bind to molecules commonly associated with foreign cells and viruses and signal responses against broad types of pathogens. Part of the innate immune response.

peat Semi-decayed organic matter that accumulates in moist, low-oxygen environments such as *Sphagnum* (moss) bogs.

pectin A gelatinous polysaccharide found in the primary cell wall of plant cells. Attracts and holds water, forming a gel that resists compression forces and helps keep the cell wall moist.

pedigree A family tree of parents and offspring, showing inheritance of particular traits of interest.

penis The copulatory organ of male mammals, used to insert sperm into a female.

pentose A monosaccharide (simple sugar) containing five carbon atoms.

PEP carboxylase An enzyme that catalyzes addition of CO_2 to phosphoenolpyruvate, a three-carbon compound, forming a four-carbon organic acid. See also **C$_4$ pathway** and **crassulacean acid metabolism (CAM)**.

pepsin A protein-digesting enzyme present in the stomach.

peptide See **oligopeptide**.

peptide bond The covalent bond formed by a condensation reaction between two amino acids; links the residues in peptides and proteins.

peptidoglycan A complex structural polysaccharide found in bacterial cell walls.

perennial Describing a plant whose life cycle normally lasts for more than one year. Compare with **annual**.

perfect flower A flower that contains both male parts (stamens) and female parts (carpels). Compare with **imperfect flower**.

perforation In plants, a small hole in the primary and secondary cell walls of vessel elements that allows passage of water.

pericarp The part of a fruit, formed from the ovary wall, that surrounds the seeds and protects them. Corresponds to the flesh of most edible fruits and the hard shells of most nuts.

pericycle In plant roots, a layer of cells just inside the endodermis that give rise to lateral roots.

peripheral membrane protein Any membrane protein that does not span the entire lipid bilayer and associates with only one side of the bilayer. Compare with **integral membrane protein**.

peripheral nervous system (PNS) All the components of the nervous system that are outside the central nervous system (the brain and spinal cord). Includes the somatic nervous system and the autonomic nervous system.

peristalsis Rhythmic waves of muscular contraction. In the digestive tract, pushes food along. In animals with hydrostatic skeletons, enables crawling.

permafrost A permanently frozen layer of icy soil found in most tundra and some taiga.

permeability The tendency of a structure, such as a membrane, to allow a given substance to diffuse across it.

peroxisome An organelle found in most eukaryotic cells that contains enzymes for oxidizing fatty acids and other compounds, including many toxins, rendering them harmless. See **glyoxysome**.

petal Any of the leaflike organs arranged around the reproductive organs of a flower. Often colored and scented to attract pollinators.

petiole The stalk of a leaf.

pH A measure of the concentration of protons in a solution and thus of acidity or alkalinity. Defined as the negative of the base-10 logarithm of the proton concentration: $pH = -\log[H^+]$.

phagocytosis Uptake by a cell of small particles or cells by invagination and pinching off of the plasma membrane to form small, membrane-bound vesicles; one type of **endocytosis**.

pharyngeal gill slits A set of parallel openings from the throat to the outside that function in both feeding and gas exchange. A diagnostic trait of chordates.

pharyngeal jaw A secondary jaw in the back of the throat; found in some fishes, it aids in food processing. Derived from modified gill arches.

phenology The timing of events during the year, in environments where seasonal changes occur.

phenotype The detectable traits of an individual. Compare with **genotype**.

phenotypic plasticity Within-species variation in phenotype that is due to differences in environmental conditions. Occurs more commonly in plants than animals.

pheophytin The molecule in photosystem II that accepts excited electrons from the reaction center chlorophyll and passes them to an electron transport chain.

pheromone A chemical signal, released by an individual into the external environment, that can trigger changes in the behavior or physiology or both of another member of the same species.

phloem A plant vascular tissue that conducts sugars between roots and shoots; contains sieve-tube elements and companion cells. Primary phloem develops from the procambium of apical meristems; secondary phloem, from the vascular cambium. Compare with **xylem**.

phosphatase An enzyme that removes phosphate groups from proteins or other molecules. Phosphatases are often used in the inactivation of signaling pathways that involve the phosphorylation and activation of proteins.

phosphodiester linkage Chemical linkage between adjacent nucleotide residues in DNA and RNA. Forms when the phosphate group of one nucleotide condenses with the hydroxyl group on the sugar of another nucleotide. Also known as *phosphodiester bond*.

phosphofructokinase The enzyme that catalyzes synthesis of fructose-1,6-bisphosphate from fructose-6-phosphate, a key reaction in glycolysis (step 3). Also called *6-phosphofructokinase*.

phospholipid A class of lipid having a hydrophilic head (including a phosphate group) and a hydrophobic tail (consisting of two hydrocarbon chains). Major components of the plasma membrane and organelle membranes.

phosphorylase An enzyme that breaks down glycogen by catalyzing hydrolysis of the α-glycosidic linkages between the glucose residues.

phosphorylation (verb: phosphorylate) The addition of a phosphate group to a molecule.

phosphorylation cascade A series of enzyme-catalyzed phosphorylation reactions commonly used in signal transduction pathways to amplify and convey a signal inward from the plasma membrane.

photic zone In an aquatic habitat, water that is shallow enough to receive some sunlight (whether or not it is enough to support photosynthesis). Compare with **aphotic zone**.

photon A discrete packet of light energy; a particle of light.

photoperiod The amount of time per day (usually in hours) that an organism is exposed to light.

photoperiodism Any response by an organism to the relative lengths of day and night (i.e., photoperiod).

photophosphorylation Production of ATP molecules by ATP synthase using the proton-motive force generated as light-excited electrons flow through an electron transport chain during photosynthesis.

photoreception A sensory system in which receptors are activated by light.

photoreceptor A molecule, a cell, or an organ that is specialized to detect light.

photorespiration A series of light-driven chemical reactions that consumes oxygen and releases carbon dioxide, basically undoing photosynthesis. Usually occurs when there are high O_2 and low CO_2 concentrations inside plant cells; often occurs when stomata must be kept closed to prevent dehydration.

photoreversibility A change in conformation that occurs in certain plant pigments when they are exposed to the particular wavelengths of light that they absorb; triggers responses by the plant.

photosynthesis The complex biological process that converts the energy of light into chemical energy stored in glucose and other organic molecules. Occurs in most plants, algae, and some bacteria.

photosystem One of two types of units, consisting of a central reaction center surrounded by antenna complexes, that is responsible for the light-dependent reactions of photosynthesis.

photosystem I A photosystem that contains a pair of P700 chlorophyll molecules and uses absorbed light energy to reduce $NADP^+$ to NADPH.

photosystem II A photosystem that contains a pair of P680 chlorophyll molecules and uses absorbed light energy to produce a proton-motive force for the synthesis of ATP. Oxygen is produced as a by-product when water is split to obtain electrons.

phototroph An organism (most plants, algae, and some bacteria) that produces ATP through photosynthesis.

phototropins A class of plant photoreceptors that detect blue light and initiate various responses.

phototropism Growth or movement of an organism in a particular direction in response to light.

phylogenetic species concept The definition of a species as the smallest monophyletic group in a phylogenetic tree. Compare with **biological species concept** and **morphospecies concept**.

phylogenetic tree A branching diagram that depicts the evolutionary relationships among species or other taxa.

phylogeny The evolutionary history of a group of organisms.

phylum (plural: phyla) In Linnaeus' system, a taxonomic category above the class level and below the kingdom level. In plants, sometimes called a *division*.

physical map A map of a chromosome that shows the number of base pairs between various genetic markers. Compare with **genetic map**.

physiology The study of how an organism's body functions.

phytochrome A specialized plant photoreceptor that exists in two shapes depending on the ratio of red to far-red light and is involved in the timing of certain physiological processes, such as flowering, stem elongation, and germination.

pigment Any molecule that absorbs certain wavelengths of visible light and reflects or transmits other wavelengths.

piloting A type of navigation in which animals use familiar landmarks to find their way.

pineal gland An endocrine gland, located in the brain, that secretes the hormone melatonin.

pioneering species Those species that appear first in recently disturbed areas.

pit In plants, a small hole in the secondary cell walls of tracheids and vessel elements that allows passage of water.

pitch The sensation produced by a particular frequency of sound. Low frequencies are perceived as low pitches; high frequencies, as high pitches.

pith In the shoot systems of plants, ground tissue located to the inside of the vascular bundles.

pituitary gland A small gland located directly under the brain and physically and functionally connected to the hypothalamus. Produces and secretes an array of hormones that affect many other glands and organs.

placenta A structure that forms in the pregnant uterus from maternal and fetal tissues. Delivers oxygen to the fetus, exchanges nutrients and wastes between mother and fetus, anchors the fetus to the uterine wall, and produces some hormones. Occurs in most mammals and in a few other vertebrates.

placental mammals See **eutherians**.

plankton Drifting organisms (animals, plants, archaea, or bacteria) in aquatic environments.

Plantae The monophyletic group that includes red, green, and glaucophyte algae, and land plants.

plasma The non-cellular portion of blood.

plasma cell A B cell that produces large quantities of antibodies after being activated by interacting with antigen and a CD4$^+$ T cell via peptide presentation. Also called an *effector B cell*.

plasma membrane A membrane that surrounds a cell, separating it from the external environment and selectively regulating passage of molecules and ions into and out of the cell. Also called *cell membrane*.

plasmid A small, usually circular, supercoiled DNA molecule independent of the cell's main chromosome(s) in prokaryotes and some eukaryotes.

plasmodesmata (singular: plasmodesma) Physical connections between two plant cells, consisting of membrane-lined gaps in the cell walls through which the two cells' plasma membranes, cytoplasm, and smooth ER can connect directly. Functionally similar to gap junctions in animal cells.

plasmogamy Fusion of the cytoplasm of two individuals. Occurs in many fungi.

plastocyanin A small protein that shuttles electrons originating from photosystem II to the reaction center of photosystem I during photosynthesis.

plastoquinone (PQ) A nonprotein electron carrier in the chloroplast electron transport chain. Receives excited electrons from photosystem II (noncyclic) or photosystem I (cyclic) and passes them to more electronegative molecules in the chain. Also transports protons from the stroma to the thylakoid lumen, generating a proton-motive force.

platelet A small membrane-bound cell fragment in vertebrate blood that functions in blood clotting. Derived from large cells in the bone marrow.

pleiotropy (adjective: pleiotropic) The ability of a single gene to affect more than one trait.

ploidy The number of complete chromosome sets present. *Haploid* refers to a ploidy of 1; *diploid,* a ploidy of 2; *triploid,* a ploidy of 3; and *tetraploid,* a ploidy of 4.

point mutation A mutation that results in a change in a single base pair in DNA.

polar (1) Asymmetrical or unidirectional. (2) Carrying a partial positive charge on one side of a molecule and a partial negative charge on the other. Polar molecules are generally hydrophilic.

polar body Any of the tiny, nonfunctional cells that are made as a by-product during meiosis of a primary oocyte, due to most of the cytoplasm going to the ovum.

polar covalent bond A covalent bond in which electrons are shared unequally between atoms differing in electronegativity, resulting in the more electronegative atom having a partial negative charge and the other atom, a partial positive charge. Compare with **nonpolar covalent bond**.

polar microtubules Mitotic and meiotic microtubules that have arisen from the two spindle poles and overlap with each other in the middle of the spindle apparatus.

polar nuclei In flowering plants, the nuclei in the female gametophyte that fuse with one sperm nucleus to produce the endosperm. Most species have two.

pollen grain In seed plants, a male gametophyte enclosed within a protective coat of sporopollenin.

pollen tube In flowering plants, a structure that grows out of a pollen grain after it reaches the stigma, extends down the style, and through which two sperm cells are delivered to the ovule.

pollination The process by which pollen reaches the carpel of a flower (in flowering plants), transferred from anther to stigma, or reaches the ovule directly (in conifers and their relatives).

pollination syndrome Suites of flower characters that are associated with certain types of pollinators and that have evolved through natural selection imposed by the interaction between flowers and pollinators.

poly(A) signal In eukaryotes, a short sequence of nucleotides near the 3′ end of pre-mRNAs that signals cleavage of the RNA and addition of the poly(A) tail.

poly(A) tail In eukaryotes, a sequence of about 100–250 adenine nucleotides added to the 3′ end of newly transcribed messenger RNA molecules.

polygenic inheritance Having many genes influence one trait.

polymer Any long molecule composed of small repeating units (monomers) bonded together. The main biological polymers are proteins, nucleic acids, and polysaccharides.

polymerase chain reaction (PCR) A laboratory technique for rapidly generating millions of identical copies of a specific stretch of DNA. Works by incubating the original DNA sequence of interest with primers, nucleotides, and DNA polymerase.

polymerization (verb: polymerize) The process by which many identical or similar small molecules (monomers) are covalently bonded to form a large molecule (polymer).

polymorphic species A species that has two or more distinct phenotypes in the same interbreeding population at the same time.

polymorphism (adjective: polymorphic) (1) The occurrence of more than one allele at a genetic locus in a population. (2) The occurrence of more than two distinct phenotypes of a trait in a population.

polyp The immotile (sessile) stage in the life cycle of some cnidarians (e.g., jellyfish). Compare with **medusa**.

polypeptide A chain of 50 or more amino acids linked together by peptide bonds. Compare with **oligopeptide** and **protein**.

polyphyletic group An unnatural group based on convergent (homoplastic) characteristics that are not present in a common ancestor. Compare with **monophyletic group**.

polyploidy (adjective: polyploid) The state of having more than two full sets of chromosomes, either from the same species (autopolyploidy) or from different species (allopolyploidy).

polyribosome A messenger RNA molecule along with more than one attached ribosome and their growing peptide strands.

polysaccharide A linear or branched polymer consisting of many monosaccharides joined by glycosidic linkages. Compare with **monosaccharide** and **oligosaccharide**.

polytomy A node in a phylogenetic tree that depicts an ancestral branch dividing into three or more descendant branches; usually indicates that insufficient data were available to resolve which taxa are more closely related.

population A group of individuals of the same species living in the same geographic area at the same time.

population density The number of individuals of a population per unit area.

population dynamics Changes in the size and other characteristics of populations through time and space.

population ecology The study of how and why the number of individuals in a population changes over time and space.

population thinking The ability to analyze trait frequencies, event probabilities, and other attributes of populations of molecules, cells, or organisms.

pore In land plants, an opening in the epithelium that allows gas exchange. See also **stoma**.

positive control Of genes, when a regulatory protein triggers expression by binding to DNA on or near the gene.

positive feedback A physiological mechanism in which a change in some variable stimulates a response that increases the change. Relatively rare in organisms but is important in generation of the action potential. Compare with **negative feedback**.

positive pressure ventilation Ventilation of the lungs by using positive pressure in the mouth to "push" air into the lungs. Compare with **negative pressure ventilation**.

positive-sense RNA virus An ssRNA virus whose genome contains the same sequences as the mRNA required to produce viral proteins. Compare with **ambisense virus** and **negative-sense virus**.

posterior Toward an animal's tail and away from its head. The opposite of anterior.

posterior pituitary The part of the pituitary gland that contains the ends of hypothalamic neurosecretory cells and from which oxytocin and antidiuretic hormone are secreted. Compare with **anterior pituitary**.

postsynaptic neuron A neuron that receives signals, usually via neurotransmitters, from another neuron at a synapse. Compare with **presynaptic neuron**.

post-translational control Regulation of gene expression by modification of proteins (e.g., addition of a phosphate group or sugar residues) after translation.

postzygotic isolation Reproductive isolation resulting from mechanisms that operate after mating of individuals of two different species occurs. The most common mechanisms are the death of hybrid embryos or reduced fitness of hybrids.

potential energy Energy stored in matter as a result of its position or molecular arrangement. Compare with **kinetic energy**.

prebiotic soup model Hypothetical explanation for chemical evolution whereby small molecules reacted with one another in a mixture of organic molecules condensed into a body of water, typically in reference to the early oceans.

Precambrian The interval between the formation of the Earth, about 4.6 billion years ago, and the appearance of most animal groups about 542 million years ago. Unicellular organisms were dominant for most of this era, and oxygen was virtually absent for the first 2 billion years.

pre-mRNA In eukaryotes, the primary transcript of protein-coding genes. Pre-mRNA is processed to form mRNA.

predation The killing and eating of one organism (the prey) by another (the predator).

predator Any organism that kills other organisms for food.

prediction A measurable or observable result of an experiment based on a particular hypothesis. A correct prediction provides support for the hypothesis being tested.

pressure-flow hypothesis The hypothesis that sugar movement through phloem tissue is due to differences in the turgor pressure of phloem sap.

pressure potential (ψ_p) A component of the potential energy of water caused by physical pressures on a solution. It can be positive or negative. Compare with **solute potential** (ψ_s).

presynaptic neuron A neuron that transmits signals, usually by releasing neurotransmitters, to another neuron or to an effector cell at a synapse.

prezygotic isolation Reproductive isolation resulting from any one of several mechanisms that prevent individuals of two different species from mating.

primary active transport A form of active transport in which a source of energy like ATP is directly used to move ions against their electrochemical gradients.

primary cell wall The outermost layer of a plant cell wall, made of cellulose fibers and gelatinous polysaccharides, that defines the shape of the cell and withstands the turgor pressure of the plasma membrane.

primary consumer An herbivore; an organism that eats plants, algae, or other primary producers. Compare with **secondary consumer**.

primary decomposer A decomposer (detritivore) that consumes detritus from plants.

primary growth In plants, an increase in the length of stems and roots due to the activity of apical meristems. Compare with **secondary growth**.

primary immune response An adaptive immune response to a pathogen that the immune system has not encountered before. Compare with **secondary immune response**.

primary meristem In plants, three types of partially differentiated cells that are produced by apical meristems, including protoderm, ground meristem, and procambium. Compare with **apical meristem** and **cambium**.

primary oocyte Any of the large diploid cells in an ovarian follicle that can initiate meiosis to produce a haploid secondary oocyte and a polar body.

primary producer Any organism that creates its own food by photosynthesis or from reduced inorganic compounds and that is a food source for other species in its ecosystem. Also called *autotroph*.

primary spermatocyte Any of the diploid cells in the testis that can initiate meiosis I to produce two secondary spermatocytes.

primary structure The sequence of amino acid residues in a peptide or protein; also the sequence of nucleotides in a nucleic acid. Compare with **secondary**, **tertiary**, and **quaternary structure**.

primary succession The gradual colonization of a habitat of bare rock or gravel, usually after an environmental disturbance that removes all soil and previous organisms. Compare with **secondary succession**.

primary transcript In eukaryotes, a newly transcribed RNA molecule that has not yet been processed to a mature RNA. Called *pre-mRNA* when the final product is a protein.

primase An enzyme that synthesizes a short stretch of RNA to use as a primer during DNA replication.

primates The lineage of mammals that includes prosimians (lemurs, lorises, etc.), monkeys, and great apes (including humans).

primer A short, single-stranded RNA molecule that base-pairs with a DNA template strand and is elongated by DNA polymerase during DNA replication.

probe A radioactively or chemically labeled single-stranded fragment of a known DNA or RNA sequence that can bind to and detect its complementary sequence in a sample containing many different sequences.

proboscis A tubular, often extensible feeding appendage with which food can be obtained.

procambium A primary meristem tissue that gives rise to the vascular tissue.

product Any of the final materials formed in a chemical reaction.

progesterone A steroid hormone produced and secreted by the corpus luteum in the ovaries after ovulation and by the placenta during gestation; protects the uterine lining.

programmed cell death Regulated cell death that is used in development, tissue maintainance, and destruction of infected cells. Can occur in different ways; apoptosis is the best-known mechanism.

prokaryote A member of the domain Bacteria or Archaea; a unicellular organism lacking a nucleus and containing relatively few organelles or cytoskeletal components. Compare with **eukaryote**.

prolactin A peptide hormone, produced and secreted by the anterior pituitary, that promotes milk production in female mammals and has a variety of effects on parental behavior and seasonal reproduction in other vertebrates.

prometaphase A stage in mitosis or meiosis during which the nuclear envelope breaks down and microtubules attach to kinetochores.

promoter A short nucleotide sequence in DNA that binds a sigma factor (in bacteria) or basal transcription factors (in eukaryotes) to enable RNA polymerase to begin transcription. In bacteria, several contiguous genes are often transcribed from a single promoter. In eukaryotes, each gene generally has its own promoter.

promoter-proximal element In eukaryotes, regulatory sequences in DNA that are close to a promoter and that can bind regulatory transcription factors.

proofreading The process by which a DNA polymerase recognizes and removes a wrong base added during DNA replication and then continues synthesis.

prophase The first stage in mitosis or meiosis during which chromosomes become visible and the spindle apparatus forms. Synapsis and crossing over occur during prophase of meiosis I.

prosimians One of the two major lineages of primates, a paraphyletic group including lemurs, pottos, and lorises. Compare with **anthropoids**.

prostate gland A gland in male mammals that surrounds the base of the urethra and secretes a fluid that is a component of semen.

prosthetic group A non-amino acid atom or molecule that is permanently attached to an enzyme or other protein and is required for its function.

protease An enzyme that can break up proteins by cleaving the peptide bonds between amino acid residues.

proteasome A macromolecular machine that destroys proteins that have been marked by the addition of ubiquitin.

protein A macromolecule consisting of one or more polypeptide chains composed of 50 or more amino acids linked together. Each protein has a unique sequence of amino acids and generally possesses a characteristic three-dimensional shape.

protein kinase An enzyme that catalyzes the addition of a phosphate group to another protein, typically activating or inactivating the substrate protein.

proteinase inhibitors Defense compounds, produced by plants, that induce illness in herbivores by inhibiting digestive enzymes.

proteoglycan A type of highly glycosylated protein found in the extracellular matrix of animal cells that attracts and holds water, forming a gel that resists compression forces.

proteome The complete set of proteins produced by a particular cell type.

proteomics The systematic study of the interactions, localization, functions, regulation, and other features of the full protein set (proteome) in a particular cell type.

protist Any eukaryote that is not a green plant, animal, or fungus. Protists are a diverse paraphyletic group. Most are unicellular, but some are multicellular or form aggregations called colonies.

protocell A hypothetical pre-cell structure consisting of a membrane compartment that encloses replicating macromolecules, such as ribozymes.

protoderm The exterior layer of a young plant embryo that gives rise to the epidermis.

proto-oncogene Any gene that encourages cell division in a regulated manner, typically by triggering specific phases in the cell cycle. Mutation may convert it into an oncogene. See **oncogene**.

proton pump A membrane protein that can hydrolyze ATP to power active transport of protons (H^+ ions) across a membrane against an electrochemical gradient. Also called H^+-ATPase.

proton-motive force The combined effect of a proton gradient and an electric potential gradient across a membrane, which can drive protons across the membrane. Used by mitochondria and chloroplasts to power ATP synthesis via the mechanism of chemiosmosis.

protostomes A major lineage of animals that share a pattern of embryological development, including formation of the mouth earlier than the anus, and formation of the coelom by splitting of a block of mesoderm. Includes arthropods, mollusks, and annelids. Compare with **deuterostomes**.

proximal tubule In the vertebrate kidney, the convoluted section of a nephron into which filtrate moves from Bowman's capsule. Involved in the largely unregulated reabsorption of electrolytes, nutrients, and water. Compare with **distal tubule**.

proximate causation In biology, the immediate, mechanistic cause of a phenomenon (how it happens), as opposed to why it evolved. Also called *proximate explanation*. Compare with **ultimate causation**.

pseudocoelomate An animal that has a coelom that is only partially lined with mesoderm. Compare with **acoelomate** and **coelomate**.

pseudogene A DNA sequence that closely resembles a functional gene but is not transcribed. Thought to have arisen by duplication of the functional gene followed by inactivation due to a mutation.

pseudopodium (plural: pseudopodia) A temporary bulge-like extension of certain protist cells used in cell crawling and ingestion of food.

puberty The various physical and emotional changes that an immature human undergoes in reaching reproductive maturity. Also the period when such changes occur.

pulmonary artery A short, thick-walled artery that carries oxygen-poor blood from the heart to the lungs.

pulmonary circulation The part of the circulatory system that sends oxygen-poor blood to the lungs. It is separate from the rest of the circulatory system (the systemic circulation) in mammals and birds.

pulmonary vein A short, thin-walled vein that carries oxygen-rich blood from the lungs to the heart. Humans have four such veins.

pulse–chase experiment A type of experiment in which a population of cells or molecules at a particular moment in time is marked by means of a labeled molecule (pulse) and then their fate is followed over time (chase).

pump Any membrane protein that can hydrolyze ATP and change shape to power active transport of a specific ion or small molecule across a plasma membrane against its electrochemical gradient. See **proton pump**.

pupa (plural: pupae) A metamorphosing insect that is enclosed in a protective case.

pupil The hole in the center of the iris through which light enters a vertebrate or cephalopod eye.

pure line In animal or plant breeding, a strain that produces offspring identical with themselves when self-fertilized or crossed to another member of the same population. Pure lines are homozygous for most, if not all, genetic loci.

purifying selection Selection that lowers the frequency of or even eliminates deleterious alleles.

purines A class of small, nitrogen-containing, double-ringed bases (guanine, adenine) found in nucleotides. Compare with **pyrimidines**.

pyrimidines A class of small, nitrogen-containing, single-ringed bases (cytosine, uracil, thymine) found in nucleotides. Compare with **purines**.

pyruvate dehydrogenase A large enzyme complex, located in the mitochondrial matix, that is responsible for converting pyruvate to acetyl CoA during cellular respiration.

quantitative trait A trait that exhibits continuous phenotypic variation (e.g., human height), rather than the distinct forms characteristic of discrete traits.

quaternary structure In proteins, the overall three-dimensional shape formed from two or more polypeptide chains (subunits); determined by the number, relative positions, and interactions of the subunits. In single stranded nucleic acids, the hydrogen bonding between two or more distinct strands will form from this level of structure through hydrophobic interactions between complementary bases. Compare with **primary**, **secondary**, and **tertiary structures**.

quorum sensing Cell–cell signaling in unicellular organisms, in which cells of the same species communicate via chemical signals. It is often observed that cell activity changes dramatically when the population reaches a threshold size, or quorum.

radial symmetry An animal body pattern that has at least two planes of symmetry. Typically, the body is in the form of a cylinder or disk, and the body parts radiate from a central hub. Compare with **bilateral symmetry**.

radiation Transfer of heat between two bodies that are not in direct physical contact. More generally, the emission of electromagnetic energy of any wavelength.

radicle The root of a plant embryo.

radioactive isotope A version of an element that has an unstable nucleus, which will release radiation energy as it decays to a more stable form. Decay often results in the radioisotope becoming a different element.

radioimmunoassay A competitive binding assay in which the quantity of hormone in a sample can be estimated. Uses radioactively labeled hormones that compete with the unknown hormone to bind with an antibody.

radula A rasping feeding appendage in mollusks such as gastropods (snails, slugs).

rain shadow The dry region on the side of a mountain range away from the prevailing wind.

range The geographic distribution of a species.

Ras protein A type of G protein that is activated by enzyme-linked cell-surface receptors, including receptor tyrosine kinases. Activated Ras then initiates a phosphorylation cascade, culminating in a cell response.

ray-finned fishes Members of the Actinopterygii, a diverse group of fishes with fins supported by bony rods arranged in a ray pattern.

rays In plant shoot systems with secondary growth, a lateral row of parenchyma cells produced by vascular cambium. Transport water and nutrients laterally across the stem.

Rb protein A tumor suppressor protein that helps regulate progression of a cell from the G_1 phase to the S phase of the cell cycle. Defects in Rb protein are found in many types of cancer.

reactant Any of the starting materials in a chemical reaction.

reaction center Centrally located component of a photosystem containing proteins and a pair of specialized chlorophyll molecules. It is surrounded by antenna complexes that transmit resonance energy to excite the reaction center pigments.

reading frame A series of non-overlapping, three-base-long sequences (potential codons) in DNA or RNA. The reading frame for a polypeptide is set by the start codon.

realized niche The portion of the fundamental niche that a species actually occupies given limiting factors such as competition with other species. Compare with **fundamental niche**.

receptor-mediated endocytosis Uptake by a cell of certain extracellular macromolecules, bound to specific receptors in the plasma membrane, by pinching off the membrane to form small membrane-bound vesicles.

receptor tyrosine kinase (RTK) Any of a class of enzyme-linked cell-surface signal receptors that undergo phosphorylation after binding a signaling molecule. The activated, phosphorylated receptor then triggers a signal transduction pathway inside the cell.

recessive Referring to an allele whose phenotypic effect is observed only in homozygous individuals. Compare with **dominant**.

reciprocal altruism Altruistic behavior that is exchanged between a pair of individuals at different times (i.e., sometimes individual A helps individual B, and sometimes B helps A).

reciprocal cross A cross in which the mother's and father's phenotypes are the reverse of that examined in a previous cross.

recombinant Possessing a new combination of alleles. May refer to a single chromosome or DNA molecule, or to an entire organism.

recombinant DNA technology A variety of techniques for isolating specific DNA fragments and introducing them into different regions of DNA or a different host organism.

rectal gland A salt-excreting gland in the digestive system of sharks, skates, and rays.

rectum The last portion of the digestive tract. It is where feces are held until they are expelled.

red blood cell A hemoglobin-containing cell that circulates in the blood and delivers oxygen from the lungs to the tissues.

redox reaction Any chemical reaction that involves either the complete transfer of one or more electrons from one reactant to another, or a reciprocal shift in the position of shared electrons within one or more of the covalent bonds of two reactants. Also called *reduction–oxidation reaction*.

reduction The gain of electrons by an atom or molecule during a redox reaction, either by acceptance of an electron from another atom or molecule, or by the shared electrons in covalent bonds moving closer to the atomic nucleus.

reduction–oxidation reaction See **redox reaction**.

reflex An involuntary response to environmental stimulation. May involve the brain (conditioned reflex) or not (spinal reflex).

refractory No longer responding to stimuli that previously elicited a response. An example is the tendency of voltage-gated sodium channels to remain closed immediately after an action potential.

regulatory sequence Any segment of DNA that is involved in controlling transcription of a specific gene by binding a regulatory transcription factor protein.

regulatory transcription factor General term for proteins that bind to DNA regulatory sequences (eukaryotic enhancers, silencers, and promoter-proximal elements), but not to the promoter itself, leading to an increase or decrease in transcription of specific genes. Compare with **basal transcription factor**.

regulon A large set of genes in bacteria that are controlled by a single type of regulatory molecule. Regulon genes are transcribed in response to environmental cues and allow cells to respond to changing environments.

reinforcement In evolutionary biology, the natural selection for traits that prevent interbreeding between recently diverged species.

release factors Proteins that trigger termination of translation when a ribosome reaches a stop codon.

renal corpuscle In the vertebrate kidney, the ball-like structure at the beginning of a nephron, consisting of a glomerulus and the surrounding Bowman's capsule. Acts as a filtration device.

replacement rate The number of offspring each female must produce over her entire life to "replace" herself and her mate, resulting in zero population growth. The actual number is slightly more than 2 because some offspring die before reproducing.

replica plating A method of identifying bacterial colonies that have certain mutations by transferring cells from each colony on a master plate to a second (replica) plate and observing their growth when exposed to different conditions.

replication fork The Y-shaped site at which a double-stranded molecule of DNA is separated into two single strands for replication.

replicative growth The process by which viruses produce new virions.

replisome The macromolecular machine that copies DNA; includes DNA polymerase, helicase, primase, and other enzymes.

repolarization Return to a resting potential after a membrane potential has changed; a normal phase in an action potential.

repressor (1) In bacteria, a protein that binds to an operator sequence in DNA to prevent transcription when an inducer is not present and that comes off DNA to allow transcription when an inducer binds to the repressor protein. (2) In eukaryotes, a protein that binds to a silencer sequence in DNA to prevent or reduce gene transcription.

reproductive development The phase of plant development that involves development of the flower and reproductive cells. Follows vegetative development and occurs when a shoot apical meristem (SAM) transitions to a flower-producing meristem.

reptiles One of the two lineages of amniotes (vertebrates that produce amniotic eggs) distinguished by adaptations for life and reproduction on land. Living reptiles include turtles, snakes and lizards, crocodiles and alligators, and birds. Except for birds, all are ectotherms.

resilience, community A measure of how quickly a community recovers following a disturbance.

resistance, community A measure of how much a community is affected by a disturbance.

respiratory system The collection of cells, tissues, and organs responsible for gas exchange between an animal and its environment.

resting potential The membrane potential of a cell in its resting, or normal, state.

restriction endonucleases Bacterial enzymes that cut DNA at a specific base-pair sequence (restriction site). Also called *restriction enzymes*.

retina A thin layer of light-sensitive cells (rods and cones) and neurons at the back of a simple eye, such as that of cephalopods and vertebrates.

retinal A light-absorbing pigment that is linked to the protein opsin in rods and cones of the vertebrate eye.

retrovirus A virus with an RNA genome that reverse-transcribes its RNA into a double-stranded DNA sequence, which is then inserted into the host's genome as part of its replicative cycle.

reverse transcriptase An enzyme that can synthesize double-stranded DNA from a single-stranded RNA template.

rhizobia (singular: rhizobium) Members of the bacterial genus *Rhizobium;* nitrogen-fixing bacteria that live in root nodules of members of the pea family (legumes).

rhizoid The hairlike structure that anchors a nonvascular plant to the substrate.

rhizome A modified stem that runs horizontally underground and produces new plants at the nodes (a form of asexual reproduction). Compare with **stolon**.

rhodopsin A transmembrane complex that is instrumental in detection of light by rods of the vertebrate eye. Is composed of the transmembrane protein opsin covalently linked to retinal, a light-absorbing pigment.

ribonucleic acid (RNA) A nucleic acid composed of ribonucleotides that usually is single stranded. Functions include structural components of ribosomes (rRNA), transporters of amino acids (tRNA), and messages of the DNA code required for protein synthesis (mRNA), among others.

ribonucleotide See **nucleotide**.

ribosomal RNA (rRNA) An RNA molecule that forms part of the ribosome.

ribosome A large macromolecular machine that synthesizes proteins by using the genetic information encoded in messenger RNA. Consists of two subunits, each composed of ribosomal RNA and proteins.

ribosome binding site In a bacterial mRNA molecule, the sequence just upstream of the start codon to which a ribosome binds to initiate translation. Also called the *Shine–Dalgarno sequence*.

ribozyme Any RNA molecule that can act as a catalyst, that is, speed up a chemical reaction.

ribulose bisphosphate (RuBP) A five-carbon compound that combines with CO_2 in the first step of the Calvin cycle during photosynthesis.

RNA See **ribonucleic acid**.

RNA interference (RNAi) Degradation of an RNA molecule or inhibition of its translation following its binding by a short RNA (microRNA) whose sequence is complementary to a portion of the mRNA.

RNA polymerase An enzyme that catalyzes the synthesis of RNA from ribonucleotides using a DNA template.

RNA processing In eukaryotes, the changes that a primary RNA transcript undergoes to become a mature RNA molecule. For pre-mRNA it includes the addition of a 5′ cap and poly(A) tail and splicing to remove introns.

RNA replicase A viral enzyme that can synthesize RNA from an RNA template. Also called an *RNA-dependent RNA polymerase*.

RNA world hypothesis Proposal that chemical evolution produced RNAs that could catalyze key reactions involved in their own replication and basic metabolism, which led to the evolution of proteins and the first life-form.

rod cell A photoreceptor cell with a rod-shaped outer portion that is particularly sensitive to dim light but not used to distinguish colors. Also called simply *rod*. Compare with **cone cell**.

root (1) An underground part of a plant that anchors the plant and absorbs water and nutrients. (2) The most ancestral branch in a phylogenetic tree.

root apical meristem (RAM) A group of undifferentiated plant stem cells at the tip of a plant root that can differentiate into mature root tissue.

root cap A small group of cells that covers and protects the root apical meristem. Senses gravity and determines the direction of root growth.

root hair A long, thin outgrowth of the epidermal cells of plant roots, providing increased surface area for absorption of water and nutrients.

root pressure Positive pressure of xylem sap in the vascular tissue of roots. Generated during the night as a result of the accumulation of ions from the soil and subsequent osmotic movement of water into the xylem.

root system The belowground part of a plant.

rotifer Member of the phylum Rotifera. Distinguished by a cluster of cilia, called a corona, used in suspension feeding in marine and freshwater environments. Rotifers belong to the lophotrochozoan branch of the protostomes.

rough endoplasmic reticulum (rough ER) The portion of the endoplasmic reticulum that is dotted with ribosomes. Involved in synthesis of plasma membrane proteins, secreted proteins, and proteins localized to the ER, Golgi apparatus, and lysosomes. Compare with **smooth endoplasmic reticulum**.

roundworms Members of the phylum Nematoda. Distinguished by an unsegmented body with a pseudocoelom and no appendages. Roundworms belong to the ecdysozoan branch of the protostomes. Also called *nematodes*.

rubisco The enzyme that catalyzes the first step of the Calvin cycle during photosynthesis: the addition of a molecule of CO_2 to ribulose bisphosphate. See also **carbon fixation**.

ruminant Member of a group of hoofed mammals (e.g., cattle, sheep, deer) that have a four-chambered stomach specialized for digestion of plant cellulose. Ruminants regurgitate cud, a mixture of partially digested food and cellulose-digesting bacteria, from the largest chamber (the rumen) for further chewing.

salinity The proportion of solutes dissolved in water in natural environments, often designated in grams of solute per kilogram of water (cited as parts per thousand).

salivary amylase An enzyme that is produced by the salivary glands and that can break down starch by catalyzing hydrolysis of the glycosidic linkages between the glucose residues.

salivary gland A type of vertebrate gland that secretes saliva (a mixture of water, mucus-forming glycoproteins, and digestive enzymes) into the mouth.

sampling error The selection of a nonrepresentative sample from some larger population, due to chance.

saprophyte An organism that feeds primarily on dead plant material.

sapwood The younger xylem in the outer layer of wood of a stem or root, functioning primarily in water transport.

sarcomere The repeating contractile unit of a skeletal muscle cell; the portion of a myofibril located between adjacent Z disks.

sarcoplasmic reticulum Sheets of smooth endoplasmic reticulum in a muscle cell. Contains high concentrations of calcium, which can be released into the cytoplasm to trigger contraction.

saturated Referring to lipids in which all the carbon-carbon bonds are single bonds. Such compounds have relatively high melting points. Compare with **unsaturated**.

scanning electron microscope (SEM) A microscope that produces images of the surfaces of objects by reflecting electrons from a specimen coated with a layer of metal atoms. Compare with **transmission electron microscope**.

scarify To scrape, rasp, cut, or otherwise damage the coat of a seed. Necessary in some species to trigger germination.

Schwann cell A type of glial cell that wraps around axons of some neurons outside the brain and spinal cord, forming a myelin sheath that provides electrical insulation. Compare with **oligodendrocyte**.

scientific name The unique, two-part name given to each species, with a genus name followed by a species name—as in *Homo sapiens*. Scientific names are always italicized, and are also known as Latin names.

sclereid In plants, a relatively short type of sclerenchyma cell that usually functions in protection, such as in seed coats and nutshells. Compare with **fiber**.

sclerenchyma cell In plants, a cell that has a thick secondary cell wall and provides support; typically contains the tough structural polymer lignin and usually is dead at maturity. Includes fibers and sclereids. Compare with **collenchyma cell** and **parenchyma cell**.

scrotum A sac of skin containing the testes and suspended just outside the abdominal body cavity of many male mammals.

second law of thermodynamics The principle of physics that the entropy of the universe or any closed system always increases.

second-male advantage The reproductive advantage, in some species, of a male who mates with a female last, after other males have mated with her.

second messenger A nonprotein signaling molecule produced or activated inside a cell in response to stimulation at the cell surface. Commonly used to relay the message of a hormone or other extracellular signaling molecule.

secondary active transport Transport of an ion or molecule in a defined direction that is often against its electrochemical gradient, in company with an ion or molecule being transported along its electrochemical gradient. Also called *cotransport*.

secondary cell wall The thickened inner layer of a plant cell wall formed by certain cells as they mature and have stopped growing; in water-conducting cells, contains lignin. Provides support or protection.

secondary consumer A carnivore; an organism that eats herbivores. Compare with **primary consumer**.

secondary growth In plants, an increase in the width of stems and roots due to the activity of cambium. Compare with **primary growth**.

secondary immune response The adaptive immune response to a pathogen that the immune system has encountered before. Normally much faster and more efficient than the primary response, due to immunological memory. Compare with **primary immune response**.

secondary metabolites Molecules that are closely related to compounds in key synthetic pathways and that often function in defense.

secondary oocyte A cell produced by meiosis I of a primary oocyte in the ovary. If fertilized, will complete meiosis II to produce an ootid (which develops into an ovum) and a polar body.

secondary spermatocyte A cell produced by meiosis I of a primary spermatocyte in the testis. Can undergo meiosis II to produce spermatids.

secondary structure In proteins, localized folding of a polypeptide chain into regular structures (i.e., alpha-helix and beta-pleated sheet) stabilized by hydrogen bonding between atoms of the peptide backbone. In nucleic acids, elements of structure (e.g., helices and hairpins) stabilized by hydrogen bonding and hydrophobic interactions between complementary bases. Compare with **primary**, **tertiary**, and **quaternary structures**.

secondary succession Gradual colonization of a habitat after an environmental disturbance (e.g., fire, windstorm, logging) that removes some or all previous organisms but leaves the soil intact. Compare with **primary succession**.

secretin A peptide hormone produced by cells in the small intestine in response to the arrival of food from the stomach. Stimulates secretion of bicarbonate (HCO_3^-) from the pancreas.

sedimentary rock A type of rock formed by gradual accumulation of sediment, particularly sand and mud, as in riverbeds and on the ocean floor. Most fossils are found in sedimentary rocks.

seed A plant reproductive structure consisting of an embryo, associated nutritive tissue (endosperm), and an outer protective layer (seed coat). In angiosperms, develops from the fertilized ovule of a flower.

seed bank A repository where seeds, representing many different varieties of domestic crops or other species, are preserved.

seed coat A protective layer around a seed that encases both the embryo and the endosperm.

segment A well-defined, repeated region of the body along the anterior–posterior body axis, containing structures similar to other nearby segments.

segmentation Division of the body or a part of it into a series of similar structures; exemplified by the body segments of insects and worms and by the somites of vertebrates.

segmentation genes A group of genes that control the formation and patterning of body segmentation in embryonic development. Includes maternal genes, gap genes, pair-rule genes, and segment polarity genes.

segregation, principle of The concept that each pair of hereditary elements (alleles of the same gene) separate from each other during meiosis. One of Mendel's two principles of genetics.

selective adhesion The tendency of cells of one tissue type to adhere to other cells of the same type.

selective permeability The property of a membrane that allows some substances to diffuse across it much more readily than other substances.

selectively permeable membrane Any membrane across which some solutes can move more readily than others.

self-fertilization The fusion of two gametes from the same individual to form offspring. Also called *selfing*.

self molecule A molecule that is synthesized by an organism and is a normal part of its cells and/or body; as opposed to nonself, or foreign, molecules.

semen The combination of sperm and accessory fluids that is released by male mammals and reptiles during ejaculation.

semiconservative replication The way DNA replicates, in which each strand of an existing DNA molecule serves as a template to create a new complementary DNA strand. It is called semiconservative because each newly replicated DNA molecule conserves one of the parental strands and contains another, newly replicated strand.

seminal vesicle In male mammals, either of a pair of reproductive glands that secrete a sugar-containing fluid into semen, which provides energy for sperm movement.

senescence The genetically programmed, active process of aging.

sensor Any cell, organ, or structure with which an animal can sense some aspect of the external or internal environment. Usually functions, along with an integrator and effector, as part of a homeostatic system.

sensory neuron A nerve cell that carries signals from sensory receptors to the central nervous system. Compare with **interneuron** and **motor neuron**.

sepal One of the protective leaflike organs enclosing a flower bud and later part of the outermost portion of the flower.

septum (plural: septa) Any wall-like structure. In fungi, septa divide the filaments (hyphae) of mycelia into cell-like compartments.

serotonin A neurotransmitter involved in many brain functions, including sleep, pleasure, and mood.

serum The liquid that remains when cells and clot material are removed from clotted blood. Contains water, dissolved gases, growth factors, nutrients, and other soluble substances. Compare with **plasma**.

sessile Permanently attached to a substrate; not capable of moving to another location.

set point A normal or target value for a regulated internal variable, such as body heat or blood pH.

sex chromosome Chromosomes that differ in shape or in number in males and females. For example, the X and Y chromosomes of many animals. Compare with **autosome**.

sex-linked inheritance Inheritance patterns observed in genes carried on sex chromosomes. In this case, females and males have different numbers of alleles of a gene. Often creates situations in which a trait appears more often in one sex. Also called *sex-linkage*.

sexual dimorphism Any trait that differs between males and females.

sexual reproduction Any form of reproduction in which genes from two parents are combined via fusion of gametes, producing offspring that are genetically distinct from both parents. Compare with **asexual reproduction**.

sexual selection A type of natural selection that favors individuals with traits that increase their ability to obtain mates. Acts more strongly on males than females. (Compare with **ecological selection**.)

shell A hard, protective outer structure.

Shine–Dalgarno sequence See **ribosome binding sequence**.

shoot In a plant embryo, the combination of hypocotyl and cotyledons, which will become the aboveground portions of the plant.

shoot apical meristem (SAM) A group of undifferentiated plant stem cells at the tip of a plant stem that can differentiate into mature shoot tissues.

shoot system The aboveground part of a plant comprising stems, leaves, and flowers (in angiosperms).

short-day plant A plant that blooms in response to long nights (usually in late summer or fall in the Northern Hemisphere). Compare with **day-neutral** and **long-day plant**.

short tandem repeats (STRs) Relatively short DNA sequences that are repeated, one after another, down the length of a chromosome. See **microsatellite**.

shotgun sequencing A method of sequencing genomes that is based on breaking the genome into small pieces, sequencing each piece separately, and then figuring out how the pieces are connected.

sieve plate In plants, a pore-containing structure at each end of a sieve-tube element in phloem.

sieve-tube element In plants, an elongated sugar-conducting cell in phloem that lacks nuclei and has sieve plates at both ends, allowing sap to flow to adjacent cells.

sigma A bacterial protein that associates with the core RNA polymerase to allow recognition of promoters.

signal In behavioral ecology, any information-containing behavior or characteristic.

signal receptor Any cellular protein that binds to a particular signaling molecule (e.g., a hormone or neurotransmitter) and triggers a response by the cell. Receptors for lipid-insoluble signals are transmembrane proteins in the plasma membrane; those for many lipid-soluble signals (e.g., steroid hormones) are located inside the cell.

signal recognition particle (SRP) An RNA–protein complex that binds to the ER signal sequence in a polypeptide as it emerges from a ribosome and transports the ribosome–polypeptide complex to the ER membrane, where synthesis of the polypeptide is completed.

signal transduction The process by which a stimulus (e.g., a hormone, a neurotransmitter, or sensory information) outside a cell is converted into an intracellular signal required for a cellular response. Usually involves a specific sequence of molecular events, or signal transduction pathway, that may lead to amplification of the signal.

signal transduction cascade See **phosphorylation cascade**.

silencer A regulatory sequence in eukaryotic DNA to which repressor proteins can bind, inhibiting gene transcription.

silent mutation A point mutation that changes the sequence of a codon without changing the amino acid that is specified.

simple eye An eye with only one light-collecting apparatus (e.g., one lens), as in vertebrates and cephalopods. Compare with **compound eye**.

simple fruit A fruit (e.g., apricot) that develops from a single flower that has a single carpel or several fused carpels. Compare with **aggregate** and **multiple fruit**.

simple sequence repeat See **microsatellite**.

SINEs (short interspersed nuclear elements) The second most abundant class of transposable elements in human genomes; can create copies of itself and insert them elsewhere in the genome. Compare with **LINEs**.

single nucleotide polymorphism (SNP) A site on a chromosome where individuals in a population have different nucleotides. Can be used as a genetic marker to help track the inheritance of nearby genes.

single-strand DNA-binding proteins (SSBP) A protein that attaches to separated strands of DNA during replication or transcription, preventing them from re-forming a double helix.

sink Any tissue, site, or location where an element or a molecule is consumed or taken out of circulation (e.g., in plants, a tissue where sugar exits the phloem). Compare with **source**.

sinoatrial (SA) node In the right atrium of the vertebrate heart, a cluster of cardiac muscle cells that initiates the heartbeat and determines the heart rate. Compare with **atrioventricular (AV) node**.

siphon A tubelike appendage of many mollusks, often used for feeding or propulsion.

sister chromatids The paired strands of a recently replicated chromosome, which are connected at the centromere and eventually separate during anaphase of mitosis and meiosis II. Compare with **non-sister chromatids**.

sister species Closely related species that occupy adjacent branches in a phylogenetic tree.

skeletal muscle The muscle tissue attached to the bones of the vertebrate skeleton. Consists of long, unbranched muscle fibers with a characteristic striped (striated) appearance; controlled voluntarily. Compare with **cardiac** and **smooth muscle**.

sliding-filament model The hypothesis that thin (actin) filaments and thick (myosin) filaments slide past each other, thereby shortening the sarcomere. Shortening of all the sarcomeres in a myofibril results in contraction of the entire myofibril.

slow muscle fiber Type of skeletal muscle fiber that is red in color due to the abundance of myoglobin, generates ATP by oxidative phosphorylation, and contracts slowly but does not fatigue easily. Also called *slow oxidative*, or *Type I, fiber*.

small intestine The portion of the digestive tract between the stomach and the large intestine. The site of the final stages of digestion and of most nutrient absorption.

small nuclear ribonucleoproteins See **snRNPs**.

smooth endoplasmic reticulum (smooth ER) The portion of the endoplasmic reticulum that does not have ribosomes attached to it. Involved in synthesis and secretion of lipids. Compare with **rough endoplasmic reticulum**.

smooth muscle The unstriated muscle tissue that lines the intestine, blood vessels, and some other organs. Consists of tapered, unbranched cells that can sustain long contractions. Not voluntarily controlled. Compare with **cardiac** and **skeletal muscle**.

snRNPs (small nuclear ribonucleoproteins) Complexes of proteins and small RNA molecules that function as components of spliceosomes during splicing (removal of introns from pre-mRNAs).

sodium–potassium pump A transmembrane protein that uses the energy of ATP to move sodium ions out of the cell and potassium ions in. Also called Na^+/K^+-ATPase.

soil organic matter Organic (carbon-containing) compounds found in soil.

solute Any substance that is dissolved in a liquid.

solute potential (ψ_S) A component of the potential energy of water caused by a difference in solute concentrations at two locations. Can be zero (pure water) or negative. Compare with **pressure potential (ψ_P)**.

solution A liquid containing one or more dissolved solids or gases in a homogeneous mixture.

solvent Any liquid in which one or more solids or gases can dissolve.

soma See **cell body**.

somatic cell Any type of cell in a multicellular organism except eggs, sperm, and their precursor cells. Also called *body cells*.

somatic hypermutation Mutation that occurs in the variable regions of immunoglobulin genes when B cells are first activated and in memory cells, resulting in novel variation in the receptors that bind to antigens.

somatic nervous system The part of the peripheral nervous system (outside the brain and spinal cord) that controls skeletal muscles and is under voluntary control. Compare with **autonomic nervous system**.

somatostatin A hormone secreted by the pancreas and hypothalamus that inhibits the release of several other hormones.

somite A block of mesoderm that occurs in pairs along both sides of the developing neural tube in a vertebrate embryo. Gives rise to muscle, vertebrae, ribs, and the dermis of the skin.

sori In ferns, a cluster of spore-producing structures (sporangia) usually found on the underside of fronds.

source Any tissue, site, or location where a substance is produced or enters circulation (e.g., in plants, the tissue where sugar enters the phloem). Compare with **sink**.

space-filling model A representation of a molecule where atoms are shown as balls—color-coded and scaled to indicate the atom's identify—attached to each other in the correct geometry.

speciation The evolution of two or more distinct species from a single ancestral species.

species An evolutionarily independent population or group of populations. Generally distinct from other species in appearance, behavior, habitat, ecology, genetic characteristics, and so on.

species–area relationship The mathematical relationship between the area of a certain habitat and the number of species that it can support.

species diversity The variety and relative abundance of the species present in a given ecological community.

species richness The number of species present in a given ecological community.

specific heat The amount of energy required to raise the temperature of 1 gram of a substance by 1°C; a measure of the capacity of a substance to absorb energy.

sperm A mature male gamete; smaller and more mobile than the female gamete.

sperm competition Competition between the sperm of different males to fertilize eggs inside the same female.

spermatid An immature sperm cell.

spermatogenesis The production of sperm. Occurs continuously in a testis.

spermatogonium (plural: spermatogonia) Any of the diploid cells in a testis that can give rise to primary spermatocytes.

spermatophore A gelatinous package containing sperm cells that is produced by males of species that have internal fertilization without copulation.

sphincter A muscular valve that can close off a tube, as in a blood vessel or a part of the digestive tract.

spicule Stiff spike of silica or calcium carbonate that provides structural support in the body of many sponges.

spindle apparatus The array of microtubules responsible for moving chromosomes during mitosis and meiosis; includes kinetochore microtubules, polar microtubules, and astral microtubules.

spines In plants, modified leaves that are stiff and sharp and that function in defense.

spiracle In insects, a small opening that connects air-filled tracheae to the external environment, allowing for gas exchange.

spleen A dark red organ, found near the stomach of most vertebrates, that filters blood, stores extra red blood cells in case of emergency, and plays a role in immunity.

spliceosome In eukaryotes, a large, complex assembly of snRNPs (small nuclear ribonucleoproteins) that catalyzes removal of introns from primary RNA transcripts.

splicing The process by which introns are removed from primary RNA transcripts and the remaining exons are connected together.

sporangium (plural: sporangia) A spore-producing structure found in seed plants, some protists, and some fungi (e.g., chytrids).

spore (1) In bacteria, a dormant form that generally is resistant to extreme conditions. (2) In eukaryotes, a single haploid cell produced by mitosis or meiosis (not by fusion of gametes) that is capable of developing into an adult organism.

sporophyte In organisms undergoing alternation of generations, the multicellular diploid form that arises from two fused gametes and produces haploid spores. Compare with **gametophyte**.

sporopollenin A watertight material that encases spores and pollen of modern land plants.

stabilizing selection A mode of natural selection that favors phenotypes near the middle of the range of phenotypic variation. Reduces overall genetic variation in a population. Compare with **disruptive selection** and **directional selection**.

stamen The male reproductive structure of a flower. Consists of an anther, in which pollen grains are produced, and a filament, which supports the anther. Compare with **carpel**.

standing defense See **constitutive defense**.

stapes The last of three small bones (ossicles) in the middle ear of vertebrates. Receives vibrations from the tympanic membrane and by vibrating against the oval window passes them to the cochlea.

starch A mixture of two storage polysaccharides, amylose and amylopectin, both formed from α-glucose monomers. Amylopectin is branched, and amylose is unbranched. The major form of stored carbohydrate in plants.

start codon The AUG triplet in mRNA at which protein synthesis begins; codes for the amino acid methionine.

statocyst A sensory organ of many arthropods that detects the animal's orientation in space (e.g., whether the animal is flipped upside down).

statolith A tiny stone or dense particle found in specialized gravity-sensing organs in some animals such as lobsters, and in gravity-sensing tissues of plants.

statolith hypothesis The hypothesis that amyloplasts (dense, starch-storing plant organelles) serve as statoliths in gravity detection by plants.

stem cell Any relatively undifferentiated cell that can divide to produce a daughter cell that remains a stem cell and a daughter cell that can differentiate into specific cell types.

stems Vertical, aboveground structures that make up the shoot system of plants.

stereocilium (plural: stereocilia) One of many stiff outgrowths from the surface of a hair cell that are involved in detection of sound by terrestrial vertebrates or of waterborne vibrations by fishes.

steroid A class of lipid with a characteristic four-ring hydrocarbon structure.

sticky ends The short, single-stranded ends of a DNA molecule cut by a restriction endonuclease. Tend to form hydrogen bonds with other sticky ends that have complementary sequences.

stigma The sticky tip at the end of a flower carpel to which pollen grains adhere.

stolon A modified stem that runs horizontally over the soil surface and produces new plants at the nodes (a form of asexual reproduction). Compare with **rhizome**.

stoma (plural: stomata) Generally, a pore or opening. In plants, a microscopic pore, surrounded by specialized cells that open the pore, on the surface of a leaf or stem through which gas exchange occurs. See also **guard cells**.

stomach A tough, muscular pouch in the vertebrate digestive tract between the esophagus and small intestine. Physically breaks up food and begins digestion of proteins.

stop codon Any of three mRNA triplets (UAG, UGA, or UAA) that cause termination of protein synthesis. Also called a *termination codon*.

strain The lowest, most specific level of taxonomy that refers to a population of individuals that are genetically very similar or identical.

striated muscle Muscle tissue containing protein filaments organized into repeating structures that give the cells and tissues a banded appearance.

stroma The fluid matrix of a chloroplast in which the thylakoids are embedded. Site where the Calvin cycle reactions occur.

structural formula A two-dimensional notation in which the chemical symbols for the constituent atoms are joined by straight lines representing single (−), double (=), or triple (≡) covalent bonds. Compare with **molecular formula**.

structural homology Similarities in adult organismal structures (e.g., limbs, shells, flowers) that are due to inheritance from a common ancestor.

style The slender stalk of a flower carpel connecting the stigma and the ovary.

suberin Waxy substance found in the cell walls of cork tissue and in the Casparian strip of endodermal cells.

subspecies A population that has distinctive traits and some genetic differences relative to other populations of the same species but that is not distinct enough to be classified as a separate species.

substrate (1) A reactant that interacts with a catalyst, such as an enzyme or ribozyme, in a chemical reaction. (2) A surface on which a cell or organism sits.

substrate-level phosphorylation Production of ATP or GTP by the transfer of a phosphate group from an intermediate substrate directly to ADP or GDP. Occurs in glycolysis and in the citric acid cycle.

succession In ecology, the gradual colonization of a habitat after an environmental disturbance (e.g., fire, flood), usually by a series of species. See **primary** and **secondary succession**.

sucrose A disaccharide formed from glucose and fructose. One of the two main products of photosynthesis.

sugar Synonymous with carbohydrate, though usually used in an informal sense to refer to small carbohydrates (monosaccharides and disaccharides).

summation The additive effect of different postsynaptic potentials on a nerve or muscle cell, such that several subthreshold stimulations can cause or inhibit an action potential.

supporting connective tissue A type of connective tissue distinguished by having a firm extracellular matrix. Includes bone and cartilage.

surface metabolism model Hypothetical explanation for chemical evolution whereby small molecules reacted with one another through catalytic activity associated with a surface, such as the mineral deposits found in deep-sea hydrothermal vents.

surface tension The cohesive force that causes molecules at the surface of a liquid to stick together, thereby resisting deformation of the liquid's surface and minimizing its surface area.

survivorship On average, the proportion of offspring that survive to a particular age.

survivorship curve A graph depicting the percentage of a population that survives to different ages.

suspension feeder Any organism that obtains food by filtering small particles or small organisms out of water or air. Also called *filter feeder*.

sustainability The planned use of environmental resources at a rate no faster than the rate at which they are naturally replaced.

sustainable agriculture Agricultural techniques that are designed to maintain long-term soil quality and productivity.

swamp A wetland that has a steady rate of water flow and is dominated by trees and shrubs.

swim bladder A gas-filled organ of many ray-finned fishes that regulates buoyancy.

symbiosis (adjective: symbiotic) Any close and prolonged physical relationship between individuals of two different species. See **commensalism**, **mutualism**, and **parasitism**.

symmetric competition Ecological competition between two species in which both suffer similar declines in fitness. Compare with **asymmetric competition**.

sympathetic nervous system The part of the autonomic nervous system that stimulates fight-or-flight responses, such as increased heart rate, increased blood pressure, and decreased digestion. Compare with **parasympathetic nervous system**.

sympatric speciation The divergence of populations living within the same geographic area into different species as the result of their genetic (not physical) isolation. Compare with **allopatric speciation**.

sympatry Condition in which two or more populations live in the same geographic area, or close enough to permit interbreeding. Compare with **allopatry**.

symplast In plants, the space inside the plasma membranes. The symplast of adjacent cells is often connected through plasmodesmata. Compare with **apoplast**.

symporter A cotransport protein that allows an ion to diffuse down an electrochemical gradient, using the energy of that process to transport a different substance in the same direction *against* its concentration gradient. Compare with **antiporter**.

synapomorphy A shared, derived trait found in two or more taxa that is present in their most recent common ancestor but is missing in more distant ancestors. Useful for inferring evolutionary relationships.

synapse The interface between two neurons or between a neuron and an effector cell.

synapsis The physical pairing of two homologous chromosomes during prophase I of meiosis. Crossing over is observed during synapsis.

synaptic cleft The space between two communicating nerve cells (or between a neuron and effector cell) at a synapse, across which neurotransmitters diffuse.

synaptic plasticity Long-term changes in the responsiveness or physical structure of a synapse that can occur after particular stimulation patterns. Thought to be the basis of learning and memory.

synaptic vesicle A small neurotransmitter-containing vesicle at the end of an axon that releases neurotransmitter into the synaptic cleft by exocytosis.

synaptonemal complex A network of proteins that holds non-sister chromatids together during synapsis in meiosis I.

synthesis (S) phase The phase of the cell cycle during which DNA is synthesized and chromosomes are replicated.

system A defined set of interacting chemical components under observation.

systemic acquired resistance (SAR) A slow, widespread response of plants to a localized infection that protects healthy tissue from invasion by pathogens. Compare with **hypersensitive response**.

systemic circulation The part of the circulatory system that sends oxygen-rich blood from the lungs out to the rest of the body. It is separate from the pulmonary circulation in mammals and birds.

systemin A peptide hormone, produced by plant cells damaged by herbivores, that initiates a protective response in undamaged cells.

systems biology The study of the structure of networks and how interactions between individual network components such as genes or proteins can lead to emergent biological properties.

systole The portion of the cardiac cycle during which the heart muscles are contracting. Compare with **diastole**.

systolic blood pressure The force exerted by blood against artery walls during contraction of the heart's left ventricle. Compare with **diastolic blood pressure**.

T cell A type of lymphocyte that matures in the thymus and, with B cells, is responsible for adaptive immunity. Involved in activation of B cells (CD4+ helper T cells) and destruction of infected cells (CD8+ cytotoxic T cells). Also called *T lymphocytes*.

T-cell receptor (TCR) A type of transmembrane protein found on T cells that can bind to antigens displayed on the surfaces of other cells. Composed of two polypeptides, called the alpha chain and beta chain, that consist of variable and constant regions. See **antigen presentation**.

T tubule Any of the membranous tubes that extend into the interior of muscle cells, propagating action potentials throughout the cell and triggering release of calcium from the sarcoplasmic reticulum.

tagmata (singular: tagma) Prominent body regions in arthropods, such as the head, thorax, and abdomen in insects.

taiga A vast forest biome throughout subarctic regions, consisting primarily of short coniferous trees. Characterized by intensely cold winters, short summers, and high annual variation in temperature.

taproot A large, vertical main root of a plant's root system.

taste bud A sensory structure, found chiefly in the mammalian tongue, containing spindle-shaped cells that respond to chemical stimuli.

TATA-binding protein (TBP) A protein that binds to the TATA box in eukaryotic promoters and is a component of the basal transcription complex.

TATA box A short DNA sequence in many eukaryotic promoters about 30 base pairs upstream from the transcription start site.

taxon (plural: taxa) Any named group of organisms at any level of a classification system.

taxonomy The branch of biology concerned with the classification and naming of organisms.

tectorial membrane A membrane, located in the vertebrate cochlea, that takes part in the transduction of sound by bending the stereocilia of hair cells in response to sonic vibrations.

telomerase An enzyme that adds DNA to the ends of chromosomes (telomeres) by catalyzing DNA synthesis from an RNA template that is part of the enzyme.

telomere The end of a linear chromosome that contains a repeated sequence of DNA.

telophase The final stage in mitosis or meiosis during which daughter chromosomes (homologous chromosomes in meiosis I) have separated and new nuclear envelopes begin to form around each set of chromosomes.

temperate Having a climate with pronounced annual fluctuations in temperature (i.e., warm summers and cold winters) but typically neither as hot as the tropics nor as cold as the poles.

temperature A measurement of thermal energy present in an object or substance, reflecting how much the constituent molecules are moving.

template strand An original nucleic acid strand used to make a new, complementary copy based on hydrogen bonding between nitrogeneous bases.

temporal lobe In the vertebrate brain, one of the four major areas in the cerebrum.

tendon A band of tough, fibrous connective tissue that connects a muscle to a bone.

tentacle A long, thin, muscular appendage typically used for feeling and feeding. Occurs in different forms in diverse animals such as cephalopod mollusks and sea anemones.

termination (1) In enzyme-catalyzed reactions, the final stage in which the enzyme returns to its original conformation and products are released. (2) In transcription, the dissociation of RNA polymerase from DNA. (3) In translation, the dissociation of a ribosome from mRNA when it reaches a stop codon.

territory An area that is actively defended by an animal from others of its species and that provides exclusive or semi-exclusive use of its resources by the owner.

tertiary consumers In a food chain or food web, organisms that feed on secondary consumers. Compare with **primary consumer** and **secondary consumer**.

tertiary structure The overall three-dimensional shape of a single polypeptide chain, resulting from multiple interactions among the amino acid side chains and the peptide backbone. In single-stranded nucleic acids, the three-dimensional shape is formed by hydrogen bonding and hydrophobic interactions between complementary bases. Compare with **primary**, **secondary**, and **quaternary structure**.

testcross The breeding of an individual that expresses a dominant phenotype but has an unknown genotype with an individual having only recessive alleles for the traits of interest. Used to order to infer the unknown genotype from observation of the phenotypes seen in offspring.

testis (plural: testes) The sperm-producing organ of a male animal.

testosterone A steroid hormone, produced and secreted by the testes, that stimulates sperm production and various male traits and reproductive behaviors.

tetrad The structure formed by synapsed homologous chromosomes during prophase of meiosis I. Also known as a *bivalent*.

tetrapod Any member of the lineage that includes all vertebrates with two pairs of limbs (amphibians, mammals, and reptiles, including birds).

texture A quality of soil, resulting from the relative abundance of different-sized particles.

theory An explanation for a broad class of phenomena that is supported by a wide body of evidence. A theory serves as a framework for the development of new hypotheses.

thermal energy The kinetic energy of molecular motion.

thermocline A steep gradient (cline) in environmental temperature, such as occurs in a thermally stratified lake or ocean.

thermophile A bacterium or archaean that thrives in very hot environments.

thermoreception A sensory system in which receptors are activated by changes in heat energy.

thermoreceptor A sensory cell or an organ specialized for detection of changes in temperature.

thermoregulation Regulation of body temperature.

thick filament A filament composed of bundles of the motor protein myosin; anchored to the center of the sarcomere. Compare with **thin filament**.

thigmotropism Growth or movement of an organism in response to contact with a solid object.

thin filament A filament composed of two coiled chains of actin and associated regulatory proteins; anchored at the Z disk of the sarcomere. Compare with **thick filament**.

thorax A region of the body; in insects, one of the three prominent body regions, along with the head and abdomen, called tagmata.

thorn A modified plant stem shaped as a sharp, protective structure. Helps protect a plant against feeding by herbivores.

threshold potential The membrane potential that will trigger an action potential in a neuron or other excitable cell. Also called simply *threshold*.

thylakoid A membrane-bound network of flattened sac-like structures inside a plant chloroplast that functions in converting light energy to chemical energy. A stack of thylakoid discs is a granum.

thymus An organ, located in the anterior chest or neck of vertebrates, in which immature T cells that originated in the bone marrow undergo maturation.

thyroid gland A gland in the neck that releases thyroid hormone (which increases metabolic rate) and calcitonin (which lowers blood calcium).

thyroid hormones Either of two hormones, triiodothyronine (T_3) or thyroxine (T_4), produced by the thyroid gland. See **triiodothyronine** and **thyroxine**.

thyroid-stimulating hormone (TSH) A peptide hormone, produced and secreted by the anterior pituitary, that stimulates release of thyroid hormones from the thyroid gland.

thyroxine (T_4) A lipid-soluble hormone, derived from the amino acid tyrosine, containing four iodine atoms and produced and secreted by the thyroid gland. Acts primarily to increase cellular metabolism. In mammals, T_4 is converted to the more active hormone triiodothyronine (T_3) in the liver.

Ti plasmid A plasmid carried by *Agrobacterium* (a bacterium that infects plants) that can integrate into a plant cell's chromosomes and induce formation of a gall.

tight junction A type of cell–cell attachment structure that links the plasma membranes of adjacent animal cells, forming a barrier that restricts movement of substances in the space between the cells. Most abundant in epithelia (e.g., the intestinal lining). Compare with **desmosome** and **gap junction**.

tip The end of a branch on a phylogenetic tree. Represents a specific species or larger taxon that has not (yet) produced descendants—either a group living today or a group that ended in extinction. Also called *terminal node*.

tissue A group of cells that function as a unit, such as muscle tissue in an animal or xylem tissue in a plant.

tolerance In ecological succession, the phenomenon in which early-arriving species do not affect the probability that subsequent species will become established. Compare with **facilitation** and **inhibition**.

tonoplast The membrane surrounding a plant vacuole.

tool-kit genes A set of key developmental genes that establishes the body plan of animals and plants; present at the origin of the multicellular lineages and elaborated upon over evolutionary time by a process of duplication and divergence. Includes *Hox* genes.

top-down control The hypothesis that population size is limited by predators or herbivores (consumers).

topoisomerase An enzyme that prevents the twisting of DNA ahead of the advancing replication fork by cutting the DNA, allowing it to unwind, and rejoining it.

torpor An energy-conserving physiological state, marked by a decrease in metabolic rate, body temperature, and activity, that lasts for a short period (overnight to a few days or weeks). Occurs in some small mammals when the ambient temperature drops significantly. Compare with **hibernation**.

totipotent Capable of dividing and developing to form a complete, mature organism.

toxin A poison produced by a living organism, such as a plant, animal, or microorganism.

trachea (plural: tracheae) (1) In insects, any of the small air-filled tubes that extend throughout the body and function in gas exchange. (2) In terrestrial vertebrates, the airway connecting the larynx to the bronchi. Also called *windpipe*.

tracheid In vascular plants, a long, thin, water-conducting cell that has pits where its lignin-containing secondary cell wall is absent, allowing water movement between adjacent cells. Compare with **vessel element**.

trade-off In evolutionary biology, an inescapable compromise between two traits that cannot be optimized simultaneously. Also called *fitness trade-off*.

trait Any observable characteristic of an individual.

transcription The process that uses a DNA template to produce a complementary RNA.

transcription factor General term for a protein that binds to a DNA regulatory sequence to influence transcription. It includes both regulatory and basal transcription factors.

transcriptional activator A eukaryotic regulatory transcription factor that binds to regulatory DNA sequences in enhancers or promoter-proximal elements to promote the initiation of transcription.

transcriptional control Regulation of gene expression by various mechanisms that change the rate at which genes are transcribed to form messenger RNA. In negative control, binding of a regulatory protein to DNA represses transcription; in positive control, binding of a regulatory protein to DNA promotes transcription.

transcriptome The complete set of genes transcribed in a particular cell.

transduction The conversion of information from one mode to another. For example, the process by which a stimulus outside a cell is converted into a response by the cell.

transfer RNA (tRNA) An RNA molecule that has an anticodon at one end and an amino acid attachment site at the other. Each tRNA carries a specific amino acid and binds to the corresponding codon in messenger RNA during translation.

transformation (1) Incorporation of external DNA into a cell. Occurs naturally in some bacteria; can be induced in the laboratory. (2) Conversion of a normal mammalian cell to one that divides uncontrollably.

transgenic A plant or animal whose genome contains DNA introduced from another individual, often from a different species.

transition state A high-energy intermediate state of the reactants during a chemical reaction that must be achieved for the reaction to proceed. Compare with **activation energy**.

transitional feature A trait that is intermediate between a condition observed in ancestral (older) species and the condition observed in derived (younger) species.

translation The process by which a polypeptide (a string of amino acids joined by peptide bonds) is synthesized from information in codons of messenger RNA.

translational control Regulation of gene expression by various mechanisms that alter the life span of messenger RNA or the efficiency of translation.

translocation (1) In plants, the movement of sugars and other organic nutrients through the phloem by bulk flow. (2) A type of mutation in which a piece of a chromosome moves to a nonhomologous chromosome. (3) The movement of a ribosome down a messenger RNA during translation.

transmembrane protein See **integral membrane protein**.

transmission The passage or transfer of (1) a disease from one individual to another or (2) electrical impulses from one neuron to another.

transpiration Loss of water vapor from aboveground plant parts. Occurs primarily through stomata.

transporter See **carrier protein**.

transposable elements Any of several kinds of DNA sequences that are capable of moving themselves, or copies of themselves, to other locations in the genome. Include LINEs and SINEs.

tree of life The phylogenetic tree that includes all organisms.

trichome A hairlike appendage that grows from epidermal cells in the shoot system of some plants. Trichomes exhibit a variety of shapes, sizes, and functions depending on species.

triiodothyronine (T₃) A lipid-soluble hormone, derived from the amino acid tyrosine, containing three iodine atoms and produced and secreted by the thyroid gland. Acts primarily to increase cellular metabolism. In mammals, T_3 has a stronger effect than does the related hormone thyroxine (T_4).

triose A monosaccharide (simple sugar) containing three carbon atoms.

triplet code A code in which a "word" of three letters encodes one piece of information. The genetic code is a triplet code because a codon is three nucleotides long and encodes one amino acid.

triploblast (adjective: triploblastic) An animal whose body develops from three basic embryonic cell layers or tissues: ectoderm, mesoderm, and endoderm. Compare with **diploblast**.

trisomy The state of having three copies of one particular type of chromosome in an otherwise diploid cell.

tRNA See **transfer RNA**.

trochophore A larva with a ring of cilia around its middle that is found in some lophotrochozoans.

trophic cascade A series of changes in the abundance of species in a food web, usually caused by the addition or removal of a key predator.

trophic level A feeding level in an ecosystem.

trophoblast The exterior of a blastocyst (the structure that results from cleavage in embryonic development of mammals).

tropomyosin A regulatory protein present in thin (actin) filaments that blocks the myosin-binding sites on these filaments in resting muscles, thereby preventing muscle contraction.

troponin A regulatory protein, present in thin (actin) filaments, that can move tropomyosin off the myosin-binding sites on these filaments, thereby triggering muscle contraction. Activated by high intracellular calcium.

true navigation The type of navigation by which an animal can reach a specific point on Earth's surface. Also called *map orientation*.

trypsin A protein-digesting enzyme present in the small intestine that activates several other protein-digesting enzymes.

tube foot One of the many small, mobile, fluid-filled extensions of the water vascular system of echinoderms; the part extending outside the body is called a podium, while the bulb within the body is the ampulla. Used in locomotion, feeding, and respiration.

tuber A modified plant rhizome that functions in storage of carbohydrates.

tuberculosis A disease of the lungs caused by infection with the bacterium *Mycobacterium tuberculosis*.

tumor A mass of cells formed by uncontrolled cell division. Can be benign or malignant.

tumor suppressor A protein (e.g., p53 or Rb) that prevents cell division, such as when the cell has DNA damage. Mutant genes that code for tumor suppressors are associated with cancer.

tundra The treeless biome in polar and alpine regions, characterized by short, slow-growing vegetation, permafrost, and a climate of long, intensely cold winters and very short summers.

turbidity Cloudiness of water caused by sediments and/or microscopic organisms.

turgid Swollen and firm as a result of high internal pressure (e.g., a plant cell containing enough water for the cytoplasm to press against the cell wall). Compare with **flaccid**.

turgor pressure The outward pressure exerted by the fluid contents of a living plant cell against its cell wall.

turnover In lake ecology, the complete mixing of upper and lower layers of water of different temperatures; occurs each spring and fall in temperate-zone lakes.

tympanic membrane The membrane separating the middle ear from the outer ear in terrestrial vertebrates, or similar structures in insects. Also called the *eardrum*.

ubiquinone See **coenzyme Q**.

ulcer A hole in an epithelial layer, exposing the underlying tissues to damage.

ultimate causation In biology, the reason that a trait or phenomenon is thought to have evolved; the adaptive advantage of that trait. Also called *ultimate explanation*. Compare with **proximate causation**.

umami The taste of glutamate, responsible for the "meaty" taste of most proteins and of monosodium glutamate.

umbilical cord The cord that connects a developing mammalian embryo or fetus to the placenta and through which the embryo or fetus receives oxygen and nutrients.

unequal crossover An error in crossing over during meiosis I in which the two non-sister chromatids match up at different sites. Results in gene duplication in one chromatid and gene loss in the other.

unsaturated Referring to lipids in which at least one carbon-carbon bond is a double bond. Double bonds produce kinks in hydrocarbon chains and decrease the compound's melting point. Compare with **saturated**.

upstream In genetics, opposite to the direction in which RNA polymerase moves along a DNA strand. Compare with **downstream**.

urea The major nitrogenous waste of mammals, adult amphibains, and cartilaginous fishes. Compare with **ammonia** and **uric acid**.

ureter In vertebrates, a tube that transports urine from one kidney to the bladder.

urethra The tube that drains urine from the bladder to the outside environment. In male vertebrates, also used for passage of semen during ejaculation.

uric acid A whitish excretory product of birds, reptiles, and terrestrial arthropods. Used to remove from the body excess nitrogen derived from the breakdown of amino acids. Compare with **ammonia** and **urea**.

urochordates One of the three major chordate lineages (Urochordata), comprising sessile or floating, filter-feeding animals that have a polysaccharide covering (tunic) and two siphons through which water enters and exits; include tunicates and salps. Compare with **cephalochordates** and **vertebrates**.

uterus The organ in which developing embryos are housed in mammals and some other viviparous vertebrates.

vaccination Artificially producing immunological memory against a pathogen by using isolated antigens or altered versions of the pathogen to stimulate an adaptive immune response in the absence of disease.

vaccine A preparation designed to stimulate an immune response against a particular pathogen without causing illness. Vaccines consist of inactivated (killed) pathogens, live but weakened (attenuated) pathogens, or parts of a pathogen (subunit vaccine).

vacuole A large organelle in plant and fungal cells that usually is used for bulk storage of water, pigments, oils, or other substances. Some vacuoles contain enzymes and have a digestive function similar to lysosomes in animal cells.

vagina The birth canal of female mammals; a muscular tube that extends from the uterus through the pelvis to the exterior.

valence The number of unpaired electrons in the outermost electron shell of an atom; often determines how many covalent bonds the atom can form.

valence electron An electron in the outermost electron shell, the valence shell, of an atom. Valence electrons tend to be involved in chemical bonding.

valence shell The outermost electron shell of an atom.

valve In circulatory systems, any of the flaps of tissue that prevent backward flow of blood, particularly in veins and in the heart.

van der Waals interactions A weak electrical attraction between two nonpolar molecules that have been brought together through hydrophobic interactions. Often contributes to tertiary and quaternary structures in proteins.

variable number tandem repeat See **minisatellite**.

variable (V) region The amino acid sequence that changes in polypeptides used to make antibodies, B-cell receptors, and T-cell receptors, This portion of the protein is highly variable within an individual and forms the epitope-binding site. Compare with **constant (C) region**.

vas deferens (plural: vasa deferentia) A muscular tube that stores and transports semen from the epididymis to the ejaculatory duct. Also called the *ductus deferens*.

vasa recta In the vertebrate kidney, a network of blood vessels that runs alongside the loop of Henle of a nephron. Functions in reabsorption of water and solutes from the filtrate.

vascular bundle In a plant stem, a cluster of xylem and phloem strands that run the length of the stem.

vascular cambium One of two types of cylindrical meristem, consisting of a ring of undifferentiated plant cells in the stem and root of woody plants; produces secondary xylem (wood) and secondary phloem. Compare with **cork cambium**.

vascular tissue In plants, tissue that transports water, nutrients, and sugars. Made up of the complex tissues xylem and phloem, each of which contains several cell types. Also called *vascular tissue system*.

vector A biting insect or other organism that transfers pathogens from one species to another. See also **cloning vector**.

vegetative development The phase of plant development that involves growth and the the production of all plant structures except the flower.

vein Any blood vessel that carries blood (oxygenated or not) under relatively low pressure from the tissues toward the heart. Compare with **artery**.

veliger A distinctive type of larva, found in mollusks.

vena cava (plural: venae cavae) Either of two large veins that return oxygen-poor blood to the heart.

ventral Toward an animal's belly and away from its back. The opposite of dorsal.

ventricle (1) A thick-walled chamber of the heart that receives blood from an atrium and pumps it to the body or to the lungs. (2) Any of several small fluid-filled chambers in the vertebrate brain.

venule Any of the body's many small veins (blood vessels that return blood to the heart).

vertebrae (singular: vertebra) The cartilaginous or bony elements that form the backbones of vertebrate animals.

vertebrates One of the three major chordate lineages (Vertebrata), comprising animals with a dorsal column of cartilaginous or bony structures (vertebrae) and a skull enclosing the brain. Includes fishes, amphibians, mammals, and reptiles (including birds). Compare with **cephalochordates** and **urochordates**.

vessel element In vascular plants, a short, wide, water-conducting cell that has gaps through both the primary and secondary cell walls, allowing unimpeded passage of water between adjacent cells. Compare with **tracheid**.

vestigial trait A reduced or incompletely developed structure that has no function or reduced function, but is clearly similar to functioning organs or structures in closely related species.

vicariance The physical splitting of a population into smaller, isolated populations by a geographic barrier.

villi (singular: villus) Small, fingerlike projections (1) of the lining of the small intestine or (2) of the fetal portion of the placenta adjacent to maternal arteries. Function to increase the surface area available for absorption of nutrients and gas exchange.

virion The infectious extracellular particle that is produced from a viral infection; used for transmitting the virus between hosts. It consists of a DNA or RNA genome enclosed within a protein shell (capsid) that may be further enveloped in a phospholipid bilayer. Compare with **virus**.

virulence (adjective: virulent) Referring to the ability of pathogens to cause severe disease in susceptible hosts.

virus An obligate, intracellular parasite that is acellular, but uses host-cell biosynthetic machinery to replicate. Compare with **virion**.

visceral mass One of the three main parts of the mollusk body; contains most of the internal organs and external gill.

visible light The range of wavelengths of electromagnetic radiation that humans can see, from about 400 to 700 nanometers.

vitamin Any of various organic micronutrients that usually function as coenzymes.

vitelline envelope A fibrous sheet of glycoproteins that surrounds mature egg cells in many vertebrates. Surrounded by a thick gelatinous matrix (the jelly layer) in some aquatic species. In mammals, called the *zona pellucida*.

viviparous Producing live young (instead of eggs) that develop within the body of the mother before birth. Compare with **oviparous** and **ovoviviparous**.

volt (V) A unit of electrical potential (voltage).

voltage Potential energy created by a separation of electric charges between two points. Also called *electrical potential*.

voltage clamping A technique for imposing a constant membrane potential on a cell. Widely used to investigate ion channels.

voltage-gated channel An ion channel that opens or closes in response to changes in membrane voltage. Compare with **ligand-gated channel**.

voluntary muscle Muscle that contracts in response to stimulation by voluntary (somatic), but not involuntary (parasympathetic or sympathetic), neural stimulation.

vomeronasal organ A paired sensory organ, located in the nasal region, containing chemoreceptors that bind odorants and pheromones.

wall pressure The inward pressure exerted by a cell wall against the fluid contents of a living plant cell.

Wallace line A line in the Indonesian region that demarcates two areas, each of which is characterized by a distinct set of animal species.

water potential (ψ) The potential energy of water in a certain environment compared with the potential energy of pure water at room temperature and atmospheric pressure. In living organisms, ψ equals the solute potential (ψ_S) plus the pressure potential (ψ_P).

water-potential gradient A difference in water potential in one region compared with that in another region. Determines the direction that water moves, always from regions of higher water potential to regions of lower water potential.

water table The upper limit of the underground layer of soil that is saturated with water.

water vascular system In echinoderms, a system of fluid-filled tubes and chambers that functions as a hydrostatic skeleton.

watershed The area drained by a single stream or river.

Watson–Crick pairing See **complementary base pairing**.

wavelength The distance between two successive crests in any regular wave, such as light waves, sound waves, or waves in water.

wax A class of lipid with extremely long, saturated hydrocarbon tails. Harder and less greasy than fats.

weather The specific short-term atmospheric conditions of temperature, moisture, sunlight, and wind in a certain area.

weathering The gradual wearing down of large rocks by rain, running water, temperature changes, and wind; one of the processes that transform rocks into soil.

weed Any plant that is adapted for growth in disturbed soils.

white blood cell Any of several types of blood cells, including neutrophils, macrophages, and lymphocytes, that circulate in blood and lymph and function in defense against pathogens.

wild type The most common phenotype seen in a wild population.

wildlife corridor Strips of wildlife habitat connecting populations that otherwise would be isolated by human-made development.

wilt To lose turgor pressure in a plant tissue.

wobble hypothesis The hypothesis that some tRNA molecules can pair with more than one mRNA codon by tolerating some non-standard base pairing in the third base, so long as the first and second bases are correctly matched.

wood Xylem resulting from secondary growth; forms strong supporting material. Also called *secondary xylem*.

worm An animal with a long, thin, tubelike body lacking limbs.

Woronin body A dense organelle in certain fungi that plugs pores in damaged septa to prevent leakage of cytoplasm.

X-linked inheritance Inheritance patterns for genes located on the mammalian X chromosome. Also called *X-linkage*.

X-ray crystallography A technique for determining the three-dimensional structure of large molecules, including proteins and nucleic acids, by analysis of the diffraction patterns produced by X-rays beamed at crystals of the molecule.

xenoestrogens Foreign chemicals that bind to estrogen receptors or otherwise induce estrogen-like effects.

xeroderma pigmentosum (XP) A human disease characterized by extreme sensitivity to ultraviolet light. Caused by an autosomal recessive allele that inactivates the nucleotide excision DNA repair system.

xylem A plant vascular tissue that conducts water and ions; contains tracheids and/or vessel elements.

Primary xylem develops from the procambium of apical meristems; secondary xylem, or wood, from the vascular cambium. Compare with **phloem**.

Y-linked inheritance Inheritance patterns for genes located on the mammalian Y chromosome. Also called *Y-linkage*.

yeast Any fungus growing as a single-celled form. Also, a specific lineage of Ascomycota.

yolk The nutrient-rich cytoplasm inside an egg cell; used as food for the growing embryo.

Z disk The structure that forms each end of a sarcomere. Contains a protein that binds tightly to actin, thereby anchoring thin filaments.

Z scheme Model for changes in the potential energy of electrons as they pass from photosystem II to photosystem I and ultimately to NADP$^+$ during the light-dependent reactions of photosynthesis. See also **noncyclic electron flow**.

zero population growth (ZPG) A state of stable population size due to fertility staying at the replacement rate for at least one generation.

zona pellucida The gelatinous layer around a mammalian egg cell. In other vertebrates, called the *vitelline envelope*.

zone of (cellular) division In plant roots, a group of apical meristematic cells just behind the root cap where cells are actively dividing.

zone of (cellular) elongation In plant roots, a group of young cells, derived from primary meristem tissues and located behind the apical meristem, that are increasing in length.

zone of (cellular) maturation In plant roots, a group of plant cells, located several millimeters behind the root cap, that are differentiating into mature tissues.

zygosporangium (plural: zygosporangia) The distinctive spore-producing structure in fungi that are members of the Zygomycota.

zygote The cell formed by the union of two gametes; a fertilized egg.

Credits

Researchers, Inc. **30.12a** Biophoto Associates/Photo Researchers, Inc.
30.12b Photoshot Holdings Ltd./Bruce Coleman **30.15** Eric V. Grave/Photo Researchers, Inc. **30.19** Jeffrey Lepore/Photo Researchers, Inc. **30.20** Eye of Science/ Photo Researchers, Inc. **30.21** Tai-Soon Young/Chungbuk National University College of Medicine **30.22** David J. Patterson **30.23** Francis Abbott/Nature Picture Library **30.24** @Colomban de Vargas, SBRoscoff **30.25** David J. Patterson **30.26** Inra **30.27** Vern B. Carruthers, Dept. of Microbiology & Immunology, U. of Michigan Medical School **30.28** Andrew Syred/SPL/Photo Researchers, Inc. **30.29** Linden Gledhill Photography **30.30** Kelvin Aitken/V&W/Image Quest Marine

Chapter 36 **Opener** Jed Fuhrman, University of Southern California **36.2** Science Source/Photo Researchers, Inc. **36.4** David M. Phillips/Photo Researchers, Inc. **36.5a** Science Source/Photo Researchers, Inc. **36.5b** Biophoto Associates/Photo Researchers, Inc. **36.5c** Oliver Meckes/E.O.S./Max-Planck-Institut-Tubingen/ Photo Researchers, Inc. **36.5d** Eye of Science/Photo Researchers, Inc. **36.12a** Eye of Science/Photo Researchers, Inc. **36.12b** Biozentrum, University of Basel/Photo Researchers, Inc. **36.17** Jean Roy, Centers for Disease Control and Prevention (CDC) **36.18** Infectious Diseases of Livestock. J.A.W. Coetzer and R.C. Tustin, University of Pretoria **36.19** David Parker/SPL/Photo Researchers, Inc. **36.20** Lowell Georgia/ Photo Researchers, Inc. **36.21** David Gray/REUTERS

Chapter 48 **Opener** Bence Mate/Nature Picture Library **48.1** Don W. Fawcett/ Photo Researchers, Inc. **48.T1L** Biophoto Associates/Photo Researchers, Inc. **48.T1M** Manfred Kage/Peter Arnold/Photolibrary/Getty Images **48.T1R** Nina Zanetti/Pearson Education **48.T2** National Library of Medicine **48.12TB** Eadweard Muybridge Collection/Kingston Museum/Photo Researchers, Inc. **48.15** Anders Hedenström, Lund University, Sweden

Appendix A: Answers **A7.1ab** Don W. Fawcett/Photo Researchers, Inc. **A7.1c** Biophoto Associates/Photo Researchers, Inc. **A7.1d** From "*Caveolin-1 expression is essential for proper nonshivering thermogenesis in brown adipose tissue.*" Cohen, A. W., Schubert, W., Brasaemle, D. L., Scherer, P. E., Lisanti, M. P. *Diabetes.* 2005 Mar; 54(3): 679–86, Fig. 6.

Appendix B: BioSkills **B9.3** Reproduced by permission from J. P. Ferris, et al. "Synthesis of long prebiotic oligomers on mineral surfaces." *Nature* 381: 59–61 (1996), Fig. 2. ©1996 Macmillan Magazines Ltd. Image courtesy of James P. Ferris, Rensselaer Polytechnic Institute. **B11.1a** Biology Media/Photo Researchers, Inc. **B11.1b** Janice Carr/Centers for Disease Control and Prevention (CDC) **B11.2ab** Michael W. Davidson/Molecular Expressions **B11.3** Rosalind Franklin/ Photo Researchers, Inc. **B12.1aL** National Cancer Institute **B12.1aR** E.S. Anderson/ Photo Researchers, Inc. **B12.1b** Sinclair Stammers/Photo Researchers, Inc. **B13.1a** Kwangshin Kim/Photo Researchers, Inc. **B13.1b** Richard L. (Larry) Blanton, Ph.D. **B13.1c** Holt Studios International/Photo Researchers, Inc. **B13.1d** Custom Medical Stock Photo, Inc. **B13.1e** Graphic Science/Alamy Images **B13.1f** Sinclair Stammers/Photo Researchers, Inc. **B13.1g** dra_schwartz/iStockphoto

Illustration and Text Credits

Chapter 1 **1.3** Based on S. P. Moose, J. W. Dudley, and T. R. Rocheford. 2004. Maize selection passes the century mark: A unique resource for 21st century genomics. *Trends in Plant Science* 9 (7): 358–364, Fig. 1a; and the Illinois long-term selection experiment for oil and protein in corn (University of Illinois at Urbana–Champaign). **1.7a** Based on T. P. Young and L. A. Isbell. 1991. Sex differences in giraffe feeding ecology: Energetic and social constraints. *Ethology* 87: 79–80, Figs. 5a, 6a. **1.9** Adapted by permission of AAAS and the author from M. Wittlinger, R. Wehner, and H. Wolf. 2006. The ant odometer: Stepping on stilts and stumps. *Science* 312: 1965–1967, Figs. 1, 2, 3. (http://www.sciencemag.org/content/312/5782/1965.short).

Chapter 2 **T2-1** Data: D. R. Lide (editor). 2008. Standard thermodynamic properties of chemical substances. In *CRC Handbook of Physics and Chemistry.* 89th ed. Boca Raton, FL: CRC Press. **2.21** After S. L. Miller. 1953. A production of amino acids under possible primitive Earth conditions. *Science* 117 (3046): 528–529.

Chapter 3 **Opener** PDB ID: 2DN2. S. Y. Park, T. Yokoyama, N. Shibayama, et al. 2006. 1.25 Å resolution crystal structures of human hemoglobin in the oxy, deoxy and carbonmonoxy forms. *Journal of Molecular Biology* 360: 690–701. **3.8a** PDB ID: 1TGH. Z. S. Juo, T. K. Chiu, P. M. Leiberman, et al. 1996. How proteins recognize the TATA box. *Journal of Molecular Biology* 261: 239–254. **3.8b** PDB ID: 2X9K. F. Korkmaz-Ozkan, S. Koster, W. Kuhlbrandt, et al. 2010. Correlation between the OmpG secondary structure and its pH-dependent alterations monitored by FTIR. *Journal of Molecular Biology* 401: 56–67. **3.8c** PDB ID: 2PTC. M. Marquart, J. Walter, J. Deisenhofer, et al. 1983. The geometry of the reactive site and of the peptide groups in trypsin, trypsinogen and its complexes with inhibitors. *Acta Crystallographica* Section B39: 480–490. **3.8d** PDB ID: 1CLG. J. M. Chen, C. D. E. King, S. H. Feairheller, et al. 1991. An energetic evaluation of a "Smith" collagen microfibril model. *Journal of Protein Chemistry* 10: 535–552. **3.11b, left** PDB ID: 2MHR. S. Sheriff, W. A. Hendrickson, and J. L. Smith. 1987. Structure of myohemerythrin in the azidomet state at 1.7/1.3 resolution. *Journal of Molecular Biology* 197: 273–296.

3.11b, middle PDB ID: 1FTP. N. H. Haunerland, B. L. Jacobson, G. Wesenberg, et al. 1994. Three-dimensional structure of the muscle fatty-acid-binding protein isolated from the desert locust *Schistocerca gregaria*. *Biochemistry* 33: 12378–12385. **3.11b, right** PDB ID: 1IXA. M. Baron, D. G. Norman, T. S. Harvey, et al. 1992. The three-dimensional structure of the first EGF-like module of human factor IX: Comparison with EGF and TGF-alpha. *Protein Science* 1: 81–90. **3.12a** PDB ID: 1D1L. P. B. Rupert, A. K. Mollah, M. C. Mossing, et al. 2000. The structural basis for enhanced stability and reduced DNA binding seen in engineered second-generation Cro monomers and dimers. *Journal of Molecular Biology* 296: 1079–1090. **3.12b** PDB ID: 2DN2. S.Y. Park, T. Yokoyama, N. Shibayama, et al. 2006. 1.25 Å resolution crystal structures of human hemoglobin in the oxy, deoxy and carbonmonoxy forms. *Journal of Molecular Biology* 360: 690–701. **3.14a** PDB ID: 1DMO. M. Zhang, T. Tanaka, and M. Ikura. 1995. Calcium-induced conformational transition revealed by the solution structure of apo calmodulin. *Nature Structural Biology* 2: 758–767. **3.14b** PDB ID: 3CLN. Y. S. Babu, C. E. Bugg, and W. J. Cook. 1988. Structure of calmodulin refined at 2.2 Å resolution. *Journal of Molecular Biology* 204: 191–204. **3.16** PDB ID: 2PTC. M. Marquart, J. Walter, J. Deisenhofer, et al. 1983. The geometry of the reactive site and of the peptide groups in trypsin, trypsinogen and its complexes with inhibitors. *Acta Crystallographica* Section B39: 480–490.

Chapter 4 **T4-1** PDB ID: 1EHZ. H. Shi and P. B. Moore. 2000. The crystal structure of yeast phenylalanine tRNA at 1.93 Å resolution: A classic structure revisited. *RNA* 6: 1091–1105. **4.11** PDB ID: 1X8W. F. Guo, A. R. Gooding, and T. R. Cech. 2004. Structure of the *Tetrahymena* ribozyme: Base triple sandwich and metal ion at the active site. *Molecular Cell* 16: 351–362.

Chapter 5 **5.6** H. M. Florman, K. B. Bechtol, and P. M. Wassarman. 1984. Enzymatic dissection of the functions of the mouse egg's receptor for sperm. *Developmental Biology* 106: 243–255. Also H. M. Florman and P. M. Wassarman. 1985. O-linked oligosaccharides of mouse egg ZP3 account for its sperm receptor activity. *Cell* 41: 313–324; J. D. Bleil and P. M. Wassarman. 1988. Galactose at the nonreducing terminus of O-linked oligosaccharides of mouse egg zona pellucida glycoprotein ZP3 is essential for the glycoprotein's sperm receptor activity. *PNAS* 85: 6778–6782.

Chapter 6 **Opener** CHARMM-GUI Archive—Library of Pure Lipid Bilayer (www. charmm-gui.org/?doc=archive&lib=lipid_pure), POPE Bilayer Library (pope_n256. pdb). Reference: S. Jo, T. Kim, and W. Im. 2007. Automated builder and database of protein/membrane complexes for molecular dynamics simulations. *PLoS ONE* 2 (9): e880. **6.10** Data: J. de Gier, J. G. Mandersloot, and L. L. van Deenen. 1968. Lipid composition and permeability of liposomes. *Biochimica et Biophysica Acta* 150: 666–675. **6.21** Data: C. E. Bear, C. Duguay, A. L. Naismith, et al. 1992. Purification and functional reconstitution of the cystic fibrosis transmembrane conductance regulator (CFTR). *Cell* 68: 809–818. **6.22** PDB ID: 2ZZ9. K. Tani, T. Mitsuma, Y. Hiroaki, et al. 2009. Mechanism of aquaporin-4's fast and highly selective water conduction and proton exclusion. *Journal of Molecular Biology* 389: 694–706. **6.23** PDB ID: 1K4C. Y. Zhou, J. H. Morais-Cabral, A. Kaufman, et al. 2001. Chemistry of ion coordination and hydration revealed by a K⁺ channel–Fab complex at 2.0 Å resolution. *Nature* 414: 43–48. **6.23** PDB ID: 3FB7. L. G. Cuello, V. Jogini, D. M. Cortes, et al. Open KcsA potassium channel in the presence of Rb⁺ ion. (To be published.) **7.18** A. D. Mills, R. A. Laskey, P. Black, et al. 1980. An acidic protein which assembles nucleosomes in vitro is the most abundant protein in *Xenopus* oocyte nuclei. *Journal of Molecular Biology* 139: 561–568. Also C. Dingwall, S. V. Sharnick, and R. A. Laskey. 1982. A polypeptide domain that specifies migration of nucleoplasmin into the nucleus. *Cell* 30: 449–458.

Chapter 7 **7.5** Reprinted with kind permission from Springer Science+Business Media B.V. from David S. Goodsell, *The Machinery of Life*. 2nd ed., 2009.

Chapter 8 **8.8** PDB ID: 1Q18. V. V. Lunin, Y. Li, J. D. Schrag, et al. 2004. Crystal structures of *Escherichia coli* ATP-dependent glucokinase and its complex with glucose. *Journal of Bacteriology* 186: 6915–6927. **8.8** PDB ID: 2Q2R. A. T. Cordeiro, A. J. Caceres, D. Vertommen, et al. 2007. The crystal structure of *Trypanosoma cruzi* glucokinase reveals features determining oligomerization and anomer specificity of hexose-phosphorylating enzymes. *Journal of Molecular Biology* 372: 1215–1226. **8.14a&b** Data: N. N. Nawani, B. P. Kapadnis, A. D. Das, et al. 2002. Purification and characterization of a thermophilic and acidophilic chitinase from Microbispora sp. V2. *Journal of Applied Microbiology* 93: 865–975, Figs. 7, 8a. Also N. N. Nawani and B. P. Kapadnis. 2001. One-step purification of chitinase from *Serratia marcescens* NK1, a soil isolate. *Journal of Applied Microbiology* 90: 803–808, Figs. 3, 4. **8.15** PDB ID: 2ERK. B. J. Canagarajah, A. Khokhlatchev, M. H. Cobb, et al. 1997. Activation mechanism of the MAP kinase ERK2 by dual phosphorylation. *Cell* (Cambridge, MA) 90: 859–869. **8.15** PDB ID 3ERK. Z. Wang, B. J. Canagarajah, J. C. Boehm, et al. 1998. Structural basis of inhibitor selectivity in MAP kinases. *Structure* 6: 1117–1128.

Chapter 9 **9.7** PDB ID: 4PFK. P. R. Evans and P. J. Hudson. 1981. Phosphofructokinase: Structure and control. *Philosophical Transactions R. Soc. Lond. B: Biol. Sci.* 293: 53–62. **9.13** Data: X. Li, R. K. Dash, R. K. Pradhan, et al. 2010. A database of thermodynamic quantities for the reactions of glycolysis and the tricarboxylic acid cycle. *Journal of Physical Chemistry B* 114: 16068–16082, Table 4. **9.14** Data: D.F . Wilson, M. Erecinska, and P. L. Dutton. 1974. Thermodynamic relationships in mitochondrial oxidative phosphorylation. *Annual Review of Biophysics and Bioengineering* 3: 203–230, Tables 1, 3. Also V. D. Sled, N. I. Rudnitzky, Y. Hatefit, et al. 1994. Thermodynamic analysis of flavin in mitochondrial NADH: Ubiquinone oxidoreductase (complex I). *Biochemistry* 33: 10069–10075. **9.17** E. Racker and W. Stoeckenius. 1974. Reconstitution of purple membrane vesicles catalyzing light-driven proton uptake and adenosine triphosphate formation. *Journal of Biological Chemistry* 249: 662–663.

Chapter 11 **11.4** Reprinted with kind permission from Springer Science+Business Media B.V. from David S. Goodsell, *The Machinery of Life.* 2nd ed., 2009. **11.7b** B. Alberts, A. Johnson, J. Lewis, et al. 2002. *Molecular Biology of the Cell.* 4th ed., Fig. 19.5, p. 1069. **11.9** K. Hatta and M. Takeichi. 1986. Expression of N-cadherin adhesion molecules associated with early morphogenetic events in chick development. *Nature* 320: 447–449. Also M. Takeichi. 1988. The cadherins: Cell–cell adhesion molecules controlling animal morphogenesis. *Development* 102: 639–655.

Chapter 12 **12.6** G. J. Gorbsky, P. J. Sammack, and G. G. Borisey. 1987. Chromosomes move poleward during anaphase along stationary microtubules that coordinately dissemble from their kinetochore ends. *Journal of Cell Biology* 104: 9–18. **12.9** Based on J. L. Ptacin, S. F. Lee, E. C. Garner, et al. 2010. A spindle-like apparatus guides bacterial chromosome segregation. *Nature Cell Biology* 12: 791–798, Fig. 5. **12.10** Y. Masui and C. L. Markert. 1971. Cytoplasmic control of nuclear behavior during meiotic maturation of frog oocytes. *Journal of Experimental Zoology* 177: 129–145. **12.13** Data: the website of the National Cancer Institute (www.cancer.gov), Common Cancer Types, November 2010.

Chapter 15 **15.2** A. D. Hershey and M. Chase. 1952. Independent functions of viral protein and nucleic acid in growth of bacteriophage. *Journal of General Physiology* 36: 39–56. **15.5** Adapted by permission of Dr. Matthew Meselson after M. Meselson and F. W. Stahl. 1958. The replication of DNA in *Escherichia coli. PNAS* 44: 671–682, Fig. 6. **15.14** Data: R. C. Allsopp, H. Vaziri, C. Patterson, et al. 1992. Telomere length predicts replicative capacity of human fibroblasts. *PNAS* 89: 10114–10118. **15.18a** Data: J. E. Cleaver. 1970. DNA repair and radiation sensitivity in human (xeroderma pigmentosum) cells. *International Journal of Radiation Biology* 18: 557–565, Fig. 3. **15.18b** Data: J .E. Cleaver. 1972. Xeroderma pigmentosum: Variants with normal DNA repair and normal sensitivity to ultraviolet light. *Journal of Investigative Dermatology* 58: 124–128, Fig. 1. **15.UN2** Graph adapted by permission of the Radiation Research Society from P. Howard-Flanders and R. P. Boyce. 1966. DNA repair and genetic recombination: Studies on mutants of *Escherichia coli* defective in these processes. *Radiation Research Supplement* 6: 156–184, Fig. 8.

Chapter 16 **16.2** Data: A. M. Srb and N. H. Horowitz. 1944. The ornithine cycle in *Neurospora* and its genetic control. *Journal of Biological Chemistry* 154: 129–139.

Chapter 17 **17.2a** PDB ID: 3IYD. B. P. Hudson, J. Quispe, S. Lara-Gonzalez, et al. 2009. Three-dimensional EM structure of an intact activator-dependent transcription initiation complex. *PNAS* 106: 19830–19835. **17.11** Based on M. B. Hoagland, M. L. Stephenson, J. F. Scott, et al. 1958. A soluble ribonucleic acid intermediate in protein synthesis. *Journal of Biological Chemistry* 231: 241–257, Fig. 6. **17.13** PDB ID: 1ZJW: I. Gruic-Sovulj, N. Uter, T. Bullock, et al. 2005. tRNA-dependent aminoacyl-adenylate hydrolysis by a nonediting class I aminoacyl-tRNA synthetase. *Journal of Biological Chemistry* 280: 23978–23986. **17.14b** PDB IDs: 3FIK, 3FIH. E. Villa, J. Sengupta, L. G. Trabuco, et al. 2009. Ribosome-induced changes in elongation factor Tu conformation control GTP hydrolysis. *PNAS* 106: 1063–1068.

Chapter 18 **18.2** Data: A. B. Pardee, F. Jacob, and J. Monod. 1959. The genetic control and cytoplasmic expression of "inducibility" in the synthesis of ß-galactosidase by *E. coli. Journal of Molecular Biology* 1: 165–178.

Chapter 19 **Opener** PDB ID: 1ZBB. T. Schalch, S. Duda, D. F. Sargent, et al. 2005. X-ray structure of a tetranucleosome and its implications for the chromatin fibre. *Nature* 436: 138–141. **19.5** I. Sandovici, N. H. Smith, and M. D. Nitert. 2011. Maternal diet and aging alter the epigenetic control of a promoter–enhancer interaction at the *Hnf4a* gene in rat pancreatic islets. *PNAS* 108: 5449–5454. **19.7b** PDB ID: 1MDY. P. C. Ma, M. A. Rould, H. Weintraub, et al. 1994. Crystal structure of MyoD bHLH domain–DNA complex: Perspectives on DNA recognition and implications for transcriptional activation. *Cell* (Cambridge, MA) 77: 451–459.

Chapter 21 **21.1** Data: European Nucleotide Archive/EMBL–Bank Release Notes. Release 110, December 2011 (www.ebi.ac.uk/embl/). **21.4a&b** Data: (a) Y. Hou and S. Lin. 2009. *PLoS ONE* 4 (9): e6978, Supplemental Table S1. (b) KEGG: *Kyoto Encyclopedia of Genes and Genomes*, KEGG Organisms: Complete genomes (www.genome.jp/kegg/). **21.8** Reproduced by permission of GENDIA from www.paternity.be/information_EN.html#identitytest, Examples 1 and 2. **21.10** Based on G. T. Ryan. 2005. Synergy between sequence and size in large-scale genomics. *Nature Reviews Genetics* 6, Box 3, p. 702. **21.13** V. Pancaldi, O. S. Sarac, C. Rallis, et al. 2012. Predicting the fission yeast protein interaction network. *G3: Genes, Genomes, Genetics* 2 (4): 453–567, Fig. 5.

Chapter 29 **29.12** Data: D. F. Wilson, M. Erecinska, and P. L. Dutton. 1974. Thermodynamic relationships in mitochondrial oxidative phosphorylation. *Annual Review of Biophysics and Bioengineering* 3: 203–230, Tables 1, 3. **30.1** S. M. Adl, A. G. Simpson, M. A. Farmer, et al. 2005. The new higher level classification of eukaryotes with emphasis on the taxonomy of protists. *Journal of Eukaryotic Microbiology* 52: 399–451. Also N. Arisue, M. Hasegawa, and T. Hashimoto. 2005. Root of the eukaryota tree as inferred from combined maximum likelihood analyses of multiple molecular sequence data. *Society for Molecular Biology and Evolution, Molecular Biology and Evolution* 22: 409–420; V. Hampl, L. Hug, J. W. Leigh, et al. 2009. Phylogenomic analyses support the monophyly of Excavata and resolve relationships among eukaryotic "supergroups." *PNAS* 106 (10): 3859–3864, Figs. 1, 2, 3; J. D. Hackett, H. S. Yoon, S. Li, et al. 2007. Phylogenomic analysis supports the monophyly of cryptophytes and haptophytes with chromalveolates. *Molecular Biology and Evolution* 24: 1702–1713, Fig. 1; P. Schaap, T. Winckler, M. Nelson, et al. 2006. Molecular phylogeny and evolution of morphology in the social amoebas. *Science* 314: 661–663.

Chapter 30 **30.1, 30.7** S. M. Adl, A. G. Simpson, M. A. Farmer, et al. 2005. The new higher level classification of eukaryotes with emphasis on the taxonomy of protists. *Journal of Eukaryotic Microbiology* 52: 399–451. Also N. Arisue, M. Hasegawa, and T. Hashimoto. 2005. Root of the eukaryota tree as inferred from combined maximum likelihood analyses of multiple molecular sequence data. *Society for Molecular Biology and Evolution, Molecular Biology and Evolution* 22: 409–420; V. Hampl, L. Hug, J. W. Leigh, et al. 2009. Phylogenomic analyses support the monophyly of Excavata and resolve relationships among eukaryotic "supergroups." *PNAS* 106 (10): 3859–3864, Figs. 1, 2, 3; J. D. Hackett, H. S. Yoon, S. Li, et al. 2007. Phylogenomic analysis supports the monophyly of cryptophytes and haptophytes and the association of Rhizaria with chromalveolates. *Molecular Biology and Evolution* 24: 1702–1713, Fig. 1; P. Schaap, T. Winckler, M. Nelson, et al. 2006. Molecular phylogeny and evolution of morphology in the social amoebas. *Science* 314: 661–663.

Chapter 36 **36.2a** Data: E. Arias. 2010. United States life tables, 2006. *National Vital Statistics Reports* 58 (21): 1–40, Table 10. Hyattsville, MD: National Center for Health Statistics. **36.3** Adapted with permission of Annual Reviews from G. Pantaleo and A. S. Fauci. 1996. Immunopathogensis of HIV infection. *Annual Review of Microbiology* 50: 825–854. Fig. 1a, p. 829. **36.7** Data courtesy of the Undergraduate Biotechnology Laboratory, California Polytechnic State University, San Luis Obispo. **36.8** A. G. Dalgleish, P. C. Beverley, P. R. Clapham, et al. 1984. The CD4 (T4) antigen is an essential component of the receptor for the AIDS retrovirus. *Nature* 312: 763–767. Also D. Klatzmann, E. Champagne, S. Chamaret, et al. 1984. T-lymphocyte T4 molecule behaves as the receptor for human retrovirus LAV. *Nature* 312: 767–768. **36.15** F. Gao, E. Bailes, D. L. Robertson, et al. 1999. Origin of HIV-1 in the chimpanzee *Pan troglodytes troglodytes. Nature* 397: 436–441, Fig. 2.

Chapter 48 **48.3** PDB ID: 1KWO. D. M. Himmel, S. Gourinath, L. Reshetnikova, et al. 2002. Crystallographic findings on the internally uncoupled and near-rigor states of myosin: Further insights into the mechanics of the motor. *PNAS* 99: 12645–12650. **48.7** After Exercise Information—Interactive Muscle Map (www.askthetrainer.com/exercise-information/). **48.15** Reprinted by permission from Macmillan Publishers Ltd from D. F. Hoyt and C. R. Taylor. 1981. Gait and the energetics of locomotion in horses. *Nature* 292: 239–240, Fig. 2, p. 240. **48.16** S. Vogel. 2003. *Comparative Biomechanics: Life's Physical World.* 2nd ed. Princeton, NJ: Princeton University Press, Fig. 3.5, p. 60. Reprinted by permission of Princeton University Press. **48.17** Reprinted with permission from AAAS from K. Schmidt-Nielsen. 1972. Locomotion: Energy cost of swimming, flying, and running. *Science* 177: 222–228. (http://www.sciencemag.org/content/177/4045/222.extract).

Appendix B: BioSkills **TB16.1** A. Crowe, C. Dicks, and M. P. Wenderoth. 2008. Biology in bloom: Implementing Bloom's Taxonomy to enhance student learning in Biology. *CBE-Life Sciences Education* 7: 368–381, Table 3.

Index

AIDS (acquired immune deficiency syndrome), 309, **712**–14, **1056**. *See also* HIV (human immunodeficiency virus)

Air
  animal locomotion in, 984
  animal olfaction (smell) and, 965–66
  behavior of oxygen and carbon dioxide in, 903–4
  circulation patterns of, 1065–66
  lichens and quality of, 631 (*see also* Atmosphere)
  nitrogen fixation from, 787–89
  plant essential nutrients from, 780*t*
  water potential in, 758–59

Alarm calling, prairie dog, 1095–97
Albino sea turtle, 465*f*
Albumen, **693**
Alcohol fermentation, **172**–73*f*
Alcohol use, 1033
Alcohols, 37*t*
Aldehydes, 37*t*, 73
Aldoses, 73
Aldosterone, **877**, **1003**
Alexander, R. McNeill, 984, 986

Algae
  blooms of, 555–56, 1148*f*, 1160
  brown, 7, 552*f*, 557, 568–69, 574
  green (*see* Green algae)
  in lichens, 623, 631
  photosynthesis in, 180–81*f*, 184, 190–91
  protist lineages of, 569, 572, 574
  red, 572
  rRNA sequences for, 7

Alkaline mucus, 1023*t*
Alkaline soil, 781–82
Alkalinity, pH scale of, 29
Allantois membrane, 694
All-cells-from-cells hypothesis, 3–5
All-taxa surveys, 1175

Alleles, **238**, **261**
  in central dogma of molecular biology, 308–9
  codominance and incomplete dominance of, 272, 273*f*
  female choice for good, 475–76
  foraging, 1085
  frequencies of, in populations, 465–71*f*
  genes and, 238, 239*f*, 247 (*see also* Genes)
  genetic bottlenecks and, 481–82
  genetic drift and, 479
  in human inheritance, 277–79
  linkage, crossing over, and recombination of, 270–71, 274*f*
  in Mendelian genetics, 258*t*, 277*t*
  multiple alleleism and, 271–72
  mutations and, 305, 313, 483–84, 486
  in particulate inheritance, 261–63
  plant pathogen resistance, 815
  wild-type, 267–69

Allergens, **1055**–56
Allergies, **1055**–56
Alligators, 703
Allolactose, 341
Allopatric speciation, **494**–95
Allopatry, **494**–95, 500
Allopolyploids, **498**–99
Allosteric regulation, **149**, **343**
Aloe vera, 739*f*
α-amylase, **809**
α-glucose, 74, 75*f*, 76

α-glycosidic linkages, 75*f*–76
α-helix (alpha helix), **48**–49
α-tubulin, 129
Alpine skypilots, 831
ALS (Lou Gehrig's disease), 408
Alternate leaves, 738*f*
Alternation of generations, **567**, **588**, **823**
  fungal, 625–26*f*
  in land plants, 588–89, 823–25
  in protists, 567–69
Alternative splicing, RNA, 357–**58**, 360–61, **400**
Altman, Sidney, 67–68
Altruism, **1095**–98
Alvarez, Luis and Walter, 521
Alveolata, 558*t*, 570, 573
Alveoli, 570, **909**, 910*f*
Amazon rain forest, 1168, 1179, 1180. *See also* Tropical wet forests
Ambisense RNA viruses, **716**
American chestnut trees, 815
American elm trees, 613
Amines, 37*t*

Amino acids, **42**. *See also* Proteins
  amphipathic proteins and, 94, 95*f*
  as animal nutrients, 883
  carbohydrates and, 78
  in central dogma of molecular biology, 308
  functional groups and, 38
  genetic code for, 310–12
  hormones as derivatives of, 995–96
  major, found in organisms, 43*t*
  in metabolic pathways, 157
  as neurotransmitters, 941*t*
  in one-gene, one-enzyme hypothesis on gene expression, 305–7
  Oparin–Haldane theory on chemical evolution of, 41–42
  in peptidoglycan, 76
  in point mutations, 313–14
  polymerization of, to form proteins, 44–47
  ribosomal polypeptide synthesis from, in translation, 328–31
  sequences of, in genetic homologies, 450–51
  sequences of, in protein primary structure, 47–48
  side chains (R-groups) of, 42–44
  specification of, in translation, 325–26
  structure of, 42
  transfer of, to proteins by tRNAs, 326–28

Aminoacyl tRNAs, 326–**27**, 328–31
Aminoacyl-tRNA synthetases, **327**, 328*f*
Amino functional group, 37*t*–38, 42, 46, 48–49*f*
Amino-terminus, 46, 328

Ammonia, **865**
  in archaea metabolism, 539*t*
  molecular structure of, B:12*f*
  in nitrogen fixation, 542–44, 787
  as nitrogenous waste, 865, 866*t*
  in origin-of-life experiments, 33–34
  simple molecules of, 23*f*, 24*f*
Amnion, **1032**
Amniotes, **689**
Amniotic eggs, **689**–91, 693–94
Amniotic fluid, 1032
Amoeba, as model organism, B:23–B:25
Amoebic dysentery, 555*t*

Amoeboid motion, **565**
Amoebozoa, 558*t*, 569, 570
AMP (adenosine monophosphate), 162

Amphibians, **696**
  fungal parasites of, 629
  hormones in metamorphosis of, 997–98
  impacts of global climate change on, 1167
  lineages of, 696, 700
  mechanoreception by lateral line system of, 958–59

Amphioxus, 686, 687
Amphipathic compounds, **87**, 87, 94, 95*f*

Amplification
  cell–cell signal, 211–12
  chemical signal, 1010
  sensory signal, 953
Ampullae of Lorenzini, **967**–68
Amylases, **81**, 895*t*
Amylopectin, 76
Amyloplasts, **804**
Amylose, 76
Anabolic pathways, **151**–52, 157–58. *See also* Catabolic pathways
Anadromous organisms, **697**
Anaerobic respiration, 170–71, **542**. *See also* Aerobic respiration; Fermentation
Analyze (Bloom's taxonomy skill), B:29*f*–B:30*t*
Anaphase, **225**–27, 245*f*
Anaphase I, 242*f*, 243–44, 245*f*
Anaphase II, 243*f*, 244
Anaphylactic shock, 1056
Anatomy, **843**. *See also* Animal form and function
Anatomy, levels of organization, 849*f*
Ancestral groups, phylogenetic trees and, B:10–B:11
Ancestral traits, 491–92, **506**–10, B:10–B:11. *See also* Common ancestry
Anchor roots, 734–35*f*
Anemones, 653–54, 887*f*
Anfinsen, Christian, 52
Angiosperms, **581**. *See also* Plant(s); Seed plants
  adaptive radiation of, 517, 595–97*f*
  Anthophyta lineage of, 608–9*f*
  in Cenozoic era, 515
  characteristics of, 581
  diversification of, 582
  flowers in, 592–93, 595*f*
  form and function of, 732 (*see also* Plant form and function)
  fruits in, 594–95
  life cycle of, 824*f*–25
  molecular phylogeny of, 583
  parasitic, 789, 790*f*
  pollination in, 593–94, 608–9*f*
  reproduction in, 823 (*see also* Plant reproduction)

Anguilla, 481
Anhydrite, 522
Animal(s), **637**. *See also* Animal cells; Animal development; Animal form and function; Animal movement; Animal nutrition; Animal reproduction
  appearance of, in Paleozoic era, 515
  biological methods for studying, 637–38
  Cambrian explosion and adaptive radiation of, 518–20, 636–37
  carbohydrate hydrolysis by digestive enzymes in, 80–81
  cell–cell attachments in, 204–7

  chemical signals of, 992–93
  chitin as structural polysaccharide in, 76, 78
  cloning of, 409
  cytokinesis in, 228
  electrolytes of, 862
  endocrine systems and hormones of, 991–92, 993, 994*f*–95 (*see also* Hormones, animal)
  evolutionary innovations of, 637–46
  food sources and feeding strategies of, 646–49
  gap junctions in tissues of, 207–8
  gas exchange and circulation in, 902–3 (*see also* Circulatory systems; Respiratory systems)
  glycogen as storage polysaccharide in, 76
  as heterotrophs, 176
  immune systems of (*see* Immune systems)
  impact of global warming on, 1166–68
  key lineages of non-bilaterian, 652–54
  life cycles of, 651–52
  major phyla of, 638*t*
  mass extinctions of, 520–23
  as models of disease, 382
  nervous systems of (*see* Nervous systems)
  nitrogenous wastes of, 865–66
  osmoregulation by (*see* Osmoregulation)
  phylogenetic relationship of fungi to, 8, 618
  phylogenies of, 637*f*, 639*f*
  pollination by, 593–94, 608–9*f*, 830–32
  populations of (*see* Population[s])
  prions and diseases of, 53
  protostome and deuterostome, 644–45 (*see also* Deuterostomes; Protostomes)
  relative diversity of lineages of, 658*f*
  seed dispersal by, 835–37
  sensory systems of (*see* Sensory systems, animal)
  shared traits of, 637

Animal cells. *See also* Eukaryotic cells
  anatomy and physiology at level of, 849*f*
  blood, 912, 982–83, **1039**–41, 1042*t*
  cultures of, B:21, B:22*f* (*see also* Cultures, cell and tissue)
  extracellular matrix in, 202–4
  lysosomes in, 114
  meiosis and mitosis in cell cycle of, 219–20 (*see also* Cell cycle)
  plant cells vs., 110*f*, 742–43 (*see also* Plant cells)
  sensory, 929
  shared development processes of, 406–9
  whole-cell dynamism of, 118–19

Animal development, 419–31. *See also* Development
  cleavage in, 423–24
  developmental principles in, 419–20
  early marsupial, 1031
  fertilization in, 420–23
  gastrulation in, 424–26
  germ cells in, 438
  germ line in, 433
  hormones in, 997–1000
  Hox genes in, 414–15
  human embryo image, 419*f*
  lophotrochozoan vs. ecdysozoan, 670
  ordered phases of, 420*f*
  organogenesis in, 426–29
  plant development vs., 432–33, 438 (*see also* Plant development)

Boldface page numbers indicate a glossary entry; page numbers followed by an *f* indicate a figure; those followed by *t* indicate a table.

Boldface page numbers indicate a glossary entry; page numbers followed by an
f indicate a figure; those followed by *t* indicate a table.

I:6   INDEX

Boldface page numbers indicate a glossary entry; page numbers followed by an *f* indicate a figure; those followed by *t* indicate a table.

Boldface page numbers indicate a glossary entry; page numbers followed by an
f indicate a figure; those followed by *t* indicate a table.

I:10   INDEX

Boldface page numbers indicate a glossary entry; page numbers followed by an *f* indicate a figure; those followed by *t* indicate a table.

Boldface page numbers indicate a glossary entry; page numbers followed by an
f indicate a figure; those followed by *t* indicate a table.

I:20 INDEX

Boldface page numbers indicate a glossary entry; page numbers followed by an *f* indicate a figure; those followed by *t* indicate a table.

Boldface page numbers indicate a glossary entry; page numbers followed by an *f* indicate a figure; those followed by *t* indicate a table.

Ribosomes (continued)
as ribozymes, 330–31
structure and function of, 117t
termination of translation in, 331, 332f
in translation, 323–25, 328–32
in translocation of mRNA, 331
Ribozymes, **67–69**, 330–31
Ribulose bisphosphate (RuBP), **191**–92
Rice, 368f, 385, 392. *See also* Golden rice
Rickets, vitamin D–resistant, 279
Rieseberg, Loren, 501–2
Rifampin, 455–56
Ring structures, 74, 181f
Rings, tree growth, 751
Ripening, fruit, 812–13f
Ripple, William, 1153
Rivers, 1078, 1155
RNA (ribonucleic acid), **58**, 65–69.
See also DNA (deoxyribonucleic acid); Messenger RNAs (mRNAs); Nucleic acids; Ribosomal RNAs (rRNAs); Transfer RNAs (tRNAs)
as catalytic molecule, 67–68
in central dogma of molecular biology, 308–9
codons in synthesis of, 311
components of, 58–59
directionality of strands of, 59–60
discovery of variety of types of, 309
DNA structure vs. structure of, 66t
in DNA synthesis, 292–94t, 295–97
electron micrograph of, 317f
as first self-replicating molecule, 68–69
gel electrophoresis of, B:13–B:14
genes and, 220
in genetic code, 310–12
genetic homologies and, 450–51
as genetic information-containing molecule, 67
as intermediary between genes and proteins in gene expression, 307–8
metabolic pathways and, 157
nucleolus and eukaryotic, 112
polymerization of ribonucleotides to form, 59–61
ribonuclease enzyme and, 52
RNA world hypothesis on, as first self-replicating molecule, 57–58
structure of, 65–66
sugar-phosphate backbone of, 60f
synthesis of, 67, 119–20
versatility of, 66–67
visualizing, B:15–B:16
RNA-induced silencing complex (RISC), 359
RNA interference, **358**–59, 361t
RNA polymerase, **292**, **307**, **318**
chromatin remodeling and, 349
in DNA synthesis, 292
in eukaryotic transcription initiation, 356, 357f
in recombinant DNA technology, 373–74
in RNA interference, 359
in RNA processing, 325t
in RNA synthesis, 307–8, 318–20
RNA processing, **324**, **349**
bacterial vs. eukaryotic, 361t
eukaryotic, 321–24, 325t, 356–59
RNA replicases, **719**–20
RNA reverse-transcribing viruses. *See* Retroviruses

RNA splicing, 322–23
RNA transcripts, 390
RNA viruses, 715–16, 719–20, 726f, 727–28
RNA world hypothesis, **57**–58, 68–69, 330–31
Roberts, Richard, 322
Robotic genome sequencers, 389f
Robust australopithecines, 706–7, 778–79f
Rock weathering, 778–79f, 1158
Rods, eye, **960**–64
Rohwer, Steve, 500–501
Root apical meristem (RAM), **434**
Root cap, **741**, **803**–4
Root cortex, water transport through, 760–61
Root hairs, **742**, 759–60, **782**–87
Root pressure, 759, **761**
Root systems, **732**
characteristics of, 733
formation of, 434
functions of, 732
modified roots in, 734–35
morphological diversity of, 733–34
organization of primary, 741–42
phenotypic plasticity in, 734
soil retention by, 578
water transport in (*see* Water transport, plant)
Roots, **434**, **603**. *See also* Root systems
auxin and adventitious, 807
formation of, 434
infection of, by nitrogen-fixing bacteria, 787–89
as land plant adaptations, 603
modified, 734–35
movement of water and solutes into, 759–61 (*see also* Water transport, plant)
nutrient uptake by, 782–87
plant nutrition and, 775f
soil composition and, 778–79f
Rosenzweig, Michael, 1086–87
Rotifers, 638t, 665
Rough ER (rough endoplasmic reticulum), **112**
ECM components and, 202–3
endoplasmic reticulum and, 112–13
post-translational protein modifications in, 332
proteins synthesis and transport by, 121–24
structure and function of, 117t
Round dance, honeybee, 1092–93
Roundworms, **674**
apoptosis in, 408
chromosomes of, 238
diversity of, 672
foraging in, 1085
genome of, 392
manipulation of hosts by, 1133
as model organisms, 658, B:24f, B:25–B:26
parasitic, and elephantiasis, 1037f
phylogeny of, 638t, 674
as protostome, 658
terrestrial adaptations of, 659
Rubisco, **192**, 193–95, **766**
RuBP (ribulose bisphosphate), 191–92
Rumen, 172, 891

Ruminants, 172, **891**
Running, Steve, 1168
Rusts, 630

S

S-shaped curves, scatterplot, B:5
S (synthesis) phase, 220–**21**, 223f
Saccharomyces cerevisiae
alcohol fermentation with, 172–73f
complete genome sequence of, 618
economic value of, 614, 632
gene regulation in, 348–49
genome of, 392
glycolysis discovery from extracts of, 158–59
meaning of scientific name of, 9
as model organism, B:24f, B:25
sex pheromones of, 215–16
Sac fungi, 617
Saddle-shaped proteins, 47f
Saharan desert ant, 11–14
St. Martin, Alexis, 890
Sakmann, Bert, 935
Salamanders, 700, 1019
Salinity, aquatic biome, **1074**
Saliva, 888, 889
Salivary amylase, 54, **889**, 895t
Salivary glands, 848f, 887f, **889**
Salmon, 483, 851–52, 868, 1060–61, 1074, 1091
Salmonella, 1042–43
Salps, 688
Salt. *See also* Sodium chloride (table salt)
in aquatic salinity, 1074
freshwater fish import of, 868
shark excretion of, 866–68
Salty habitats, 492–93, 549, 757–58, 786–87
Sampling effects, 1186
Sampling error, **478**
Sand dollars, 684–86f
Sandbox tree, 834–35
Sandwich model, plasma membrane, 94–95
Sanger, Frederick, 47–48, 377–78
Saprophytes, **614**–15, 623–24, 629
Sapwood, **751**
Sarcomeres, **973**–74, 980
Sarcoplasmic reticulum, **977**
Sargasso Sea environmental sequencing, 395
Satiation hormone, 1001–3
Satin bowerbird, 1082f
Saturated fatty acids, 85f, 385
Saturated lipids, **85**–86
Saxitoxins, 555–56
Scaffold proteins, 350
Scallops, 668
Scanning electron microscope, 95–96f
Scanning electron microscopy (SEM)
in biological imaging, B:19
of DNA and RNA, 317f
of DNA synthesis, 284f
of *Escherichia coli*, 336f
of human fertilization, 237f
of human immune system cells, 1037f
Scarified seed coats, **836**
Scatterplots, B:4–B:5
Scents
flower, 593–94
in sympatric speciation, 496–97
Scheepers, Lue, 10–11
Schmidt-Nielsen, Kurt, 988
Schmitz, Oswald, 1191–92

Schooling, fish, 1129f
Schwann cells, **937**
SCID (severe combined immunodeficiency), 383–84, 1056
Science. *See also* Bioskills
Science. *See also* Process boxes; Quantitative Methods boxes
in biological study of life, 1, 9–14 (*see also* Biology)
experimental design in, 11–14
experiments as hypothesis testing in, 3–5, 9–11
pattern and process components of theories of, 445
religious faith vs., 9
taxonomy and, 8–9
theories in, 2, 3, 9
Science-Direct (online database), B:27
Scientific journals, B:26–B:27
Scientific names, 8–**9**
Scientific notation, B:2–B:3
Sclera, 960, 961f
Sclereids, **746**, 747
Sclerenchyma cells, **745**–47, 748t, 749
Scott, J. C., 1175
Screening, DNA library, 372–73, 381t
Scrotum, **1021**, 1023t
Sea anemone, 642
Sea bass, 868
Sea cucumbers, 684
Sea lilies, 684
Sea slugs, 946–48
Sea spiders, 678
Sea squirts, 686–87f, 688
Sea stars, 444f, 684–85, 1018, 1137–38, 1153
Sea turtles, 465f, 1118, 1119f
Sea urchins, 237–38, 420–23, 684–86f, 1018f
Seals, 1086
Seaside sparrows, 492–93
Seasons
global climate change, phenology, and, 1166–67
mating and, 1087–88
migration and, 1091
plant translocation and, 766
weather and, 1066, 1067f
Seawater. *See* Marine biomes
Second law of thermodynamics, **31**, 44, **138**
Second-male advantage, **1019**–20
Second messengers, **212**, **795**, **940**, **1009**
examples of, 213t
in hormonal signal transduction, 1008–10
neurotransmitters and, 940
in plant cell–cell signaling, 795
in signal transduction via G-protein-coupled receptors, 211–13
Secondary active transport (cotransport), **100**, **770**, 864–65
Secondary cell wall, **202**, **585**, **745**, 762–63
Secondary consumers, 556, **1150**
Secondary endosymbiosis, 564–65
Secondary growth, plant, **748**–51
Secondary immune response, **1054**–55
Secondary metabolites, 815
Secondary oocytes, **1017**
Secondary phloem, 748–50
Secondary spermatocytes, **1016**
Secondary structure, **48**
DNA, 57f, 61–63 (*see also* Double helix secondary structure, DNA)
DNA vs. RNA, 66t

Boldface page numbers indicate a glossary entry; page numbers followed by an *f* indicate a figure; those followed by *t* indicate a table.

Boldface page numbers indicate a glossary entry; page numbers followed by an *f* indicate a figure; those followed by *t* indicate a table.

Boldface page numbers indicate a glossary entry; page numbers followed by an *f* indicate a figure; those followed by *t* indicate a table.

I:40 INDEX

Variable number tandem repeats (VNTRs), **396**–98*f*
Variable (V) regions, **1045**–46
Variables, experimental, 13
Vas deferens, **1022**–23*t*
Vasa recta, **876**, 877*f*
Vascular bundles, **742**
Vascular cambium, **748**
  auxin and, 807
  secondary growth functions of, 748–50
Vascular plants. *See* Seedless vascular plants; Seed plants
Vascular tissue, plant, **435**, **580**, **759**. *See also* Phloem tissue; Xylem tissue
  elaboration of, into tracheids and vessel elements, 585–86
  formation of, 435, 437*f*
  in land plants, 580–81, 585
  root and shoot systems and, 732
  translocation (sugar transport) and, 766–72
  water transport and, 759–65
Vascular tissue systems, plant, **740**. *See also* Phloem tissue; Xylem tissue
  embryogenesis and, 833
  phloem structure in, 747
  primary plant body and tissues of, 740–41, 742, 748*t*
  secondary growth of, 748–51
  xylem structure in, 746–47
Vectors, cloning, **370**. *See also* Plasmids
Vegetation, emergent, 1077
Vegetative development, **433**, 436–38
  flexibility of cell determination in, 438
  genetic control of leaf shape in, 436–38
  meristems in lifelong growth and, 436, 437*f*
  reproductive development vs., 433 (*see also* Reproductive development, plant)
Veins, 871, **917**–18, 921, 924
Veliger, **668**
Velvet worms, 672–73
Venae cavae, **921**
Venter, Oscar, 1178
Ventilation. *See also* Respiratory systems
  of fish gills, 906
  in gas exchange, 903
  homeostatic control of, 911–12
  of insect tracheae, 907
  of vertebrate lungs, 909–11*f*
Ventral body axis, **410**
Ventricles, **919**, 921
Venules, **917**–18
Venus flytraps, 790, 806
Vertebrae, **688**
Vertebral column, 688
Vertebrates, **645**, **682**, **688**–703. *See also* Animal(s)
  adaptive immunity in, 1042 (*see also* Adaptive immune response; Immune systems)
  amphibians, 696
  body plan of, 686–87
  closed circulatory systems of, 917 (*see also* Circulatory systems)
  as deuterostome chordates, 682
  endoskeletons of, 981–83
  evolution of, 688–91
  fishes, 696
  in fossil record, 689–91
  hormones in sexual development and activity of, 998–99
  key lineages of, 696–703
  lungs of, 909–12 (*see also* Respiratory systems)

mammals, 696
molecular phylogenies of, 691
morphological innovations of, 692–93
nervous systems of, 942–49 (*see also* Nervous systems)
osmoregulation in terrestrial, 871–79 (*see also* Kidneys)
phylogenetic tree of, 690*f*
primates, hominins, and humans, 704–8 (*see also* Human[s])
relative abundance of species of, 691*f*
reproductive innovations of, 693–94
reptiles, 696–97
segmentation in, 645
sensory systems of (*see* Sensory systems, animal)
vertebrae, cranium, and brain structure of, 688
wings and flight in, 694–95
Vervet monkeys, 1098
Vesicles
  artificial membrane-bound, 88–89
  in chemical evolution, 94
  in cytokinesis, 228
  in electron transport chain, 168–69
  in endomembrane protein transport, 123–27
  microtubules and transport by, 130–31
  osmosis across membrane-bound, 92–93
  prokaryotic, 108
  rough ER in, 114
  secretory, 123
  synaptic, 939
Vessel elements, **586**, **746**–47
Vessels, angiosperm, 596
Vestigial traits, **448**
  of cetaceans, 453
  as evidence for evolutionary change, 448–49
  as nonadaptive, 461
Vicariance, **494**, 495
Video microscopy
  of ATP synthase, 170
  in biological imaging, B:20
  of transport vesicles, 130*f*
Villi, **852**–53*f*, **892**
Virchow, Rudolf, 3, 219
Virions, **714**–15. *See also* Replicative growth, viral
Virulent infections, 532, **712**
Virus vaccines, 1055
Viruses, **711**–30
  abundance and diversity of, 712
  analyzing coexistence of, with host cells, 721–22
  analyzing genetic material of, 715–16
  analyzing morphological traits of, 715
  analyzing phases of replicative growth of lytic cycle of, 716–21
  bacteriophage λ, 50
  Baltimore classification system for, 725–26
  biological methods of studying, 714–22
  biological reasons for studying, 712–14
  characteristics of living organisms vs. characteristics of, 712*t*
  diversification themes of, 722–25
  emerging diseases and emerging, 723–25
  eukaryotic translation and, 359–60
  in gene therapy, 383–85
  Hershey–Chase experiment on DNA in genes of, 285–86

human epidemics and pandemics from, 712–14
  identification of emerging, 725
  infection of host cells by, 711–12
  key lineages of, 725–28
  living organisms vs., 711–12
  nanobiology in isolation of, 714
  origins of, 723
  photomicrograph of, 711*f*
  proteins as defense against, 54
  RNA in, 309
  in splitting eukaryotic genes, 321–22
  vaccines against, 1055
Visceral mass, **662**–63
Viscosity, animal locomotion and fluid, 988
Visible light, **179**
Vision, animal. *See* Photoreception, animal; Sight
Visual communication, 1093
Visual cues, mating and, 1088
Visualization, molecular, B:15–B:16
Vitamin A deficiency, 385
Vitamin B$_1$, 884*t*
Vitamin B$_6$, 305
Vitamin B$_{12}$, 884*t*
Vitamin C, 884*t*
Vitamin D, 884*t*
Vitamin D-resistant rickets (hypophasphatemia), 279
Vitamins, **883**
  coenzymes and, 147
  as essential nutrients for animals and humans, 883, 884*t*
  lipids as, 87
  transgenic crops and deficiencies of, 385
Vitelline envelope, **1017**–18*f*
Viviparous species, **651**, **694**, **1020**–21
Vivipary, 836
Volcanic gases, 24, 30, 34–35, 45
Volt, **930**
Voltage, **783**, **930**
Voltage clamping, **935**
Voltage-gated channels, 98–99, **934**
Volume, in chemical reactions, 138
Volume, metric units and conversions for, B:1*t*
Volume/surface area, animal body, 850–53
Volume/surface area relationships, plant, 732–33
Voluntary muscles, **977**, 979
Vomeronasal organ, **967**
Von Békésy, Georg, 956–57
Von Frisch, Karl, 1084, 1092–93
von Linné, Karl, 9

W

Waggle dance, honeybee, 1092–93
Waldeyer, Wilhelm, 220
Walking, 986
Wall cress. *See* Mustard plant
Wall pressure, **756**
Wallace, Alfred Russel, 5, 444, 446, 453, 1063
Wallace line, **1063**
Warblers, 1062
Wasps, 485, 818–19
Wasserman, Paul, 79–80
Wastes, 883*f*, 888, 896. *See also* Nitrogenous wastes, animal
Water
  absorption of, in large intestines, 896
  absorption of, in small intestines, 896

  in acid-base reactions, 28–30
  angiosperm vessels for conducting, 596
  animal heat exchange by evaporation of, 855
  animal locomotion in, 984, 985, 988
  animal requirements for, 842–43
  aquaporins and transport of, across plasma membranes, 98
  behavior of oxygen and carbon dioxide in, 904–5
  cohesion, adhesion, and surface tension of, 26
  covalent bonds of, 21–23
  in decomposition rates, 1157
  density of, as liquid and as solid, 26–27
  depth and flow of in aquatic biomes, 1074–75, 1077–79
  efficiency of, as solvent, 25–26
  energy absorbing capacity of, 27–28
  green plant holding of, and moderation of climate, 578
  insolubility of lipids in, 85, 86–87
  land plant adaptations to prevent loss of, 584–85
  large intestine absorption of, 888
  lipid bilayers and, 89
  molecular structure of, 24*f*, B:12*f*
  in net primary production of terrestrial biomes, 1155
  nitrate pollution of, 543–44
  noncyclic electron flow between, and NADP$^+$ in Z-scheme model, 188–89
  in nutrient cycling, 1158
  osmosis as diffusion of, across lipid bilayers, 92–93
  oxidation of, in photosystem II, 186
  photosynthetic oxygen production from, 177–78
  plant nutrients from, 780*t*
  plant transport of (*see* Water transport, plant)
  polarity of amino acid side chains and solubility in, 44
  production of, by cellular respiration, 165
  production of, by electron transport chain, 166*f*–67
  properties of, 26–28
  purification of, as ecosystem regulating service, 1188
  in seed germination, 837
  specific heat of, 27*t*
Water balance, animal. *See* Osmoregulation
Water bears, 672–73
Water cycle, global, 1159–60, 1166
Water depth, 1074, 1075*f*, 1077–79
Water flea, 1167
Water flow, 1074–75, 1077–79
Water loss, animal
  terrestrial adaptations to prevent, 662–63
  insect minimization of, 869–70
Water loss, plant
  biochemical pathway adaptations to, 766
  regulation of, 754–55, 765–66
  seed maturation and, 834
  stomata and regulation of, 743–44
  turgor pressure, wilting, and plant, 758
Water molds, 574

Boldface page numbers indicate a glossary entry; page numbers followed by an *f* indicate a figure; those followed by *t* indicate a table.

Part 2

Taken from: *Becker's World of the Cell*, Eighth Edition
by Jeff Hardin, Gregory Bertoni, and Lewis J. Kleinsmith

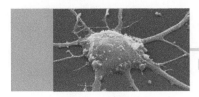

DETAILED CONTENTS

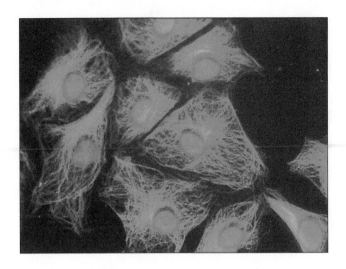

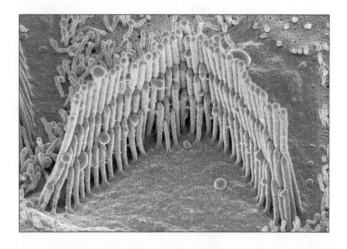

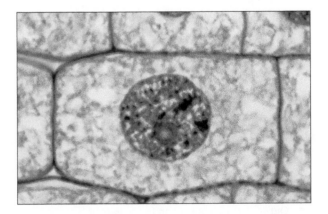

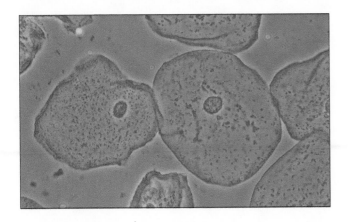

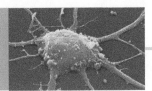

JEFF HARDIN is Professor and Chair of the Zoology Department at the University of Wisconsin-Madison. He is also faculty director of the Biology Core Curriculum, a four-semester honors biology sequence for undergraduates. His research interests center on how cells migrate and adhere to one another to change the shape of animal embryos. Dr. Hardin's teaching is enhanced by his extensive use of digital microscopy and his web-based teaching materials, which are used on many campuses in the United States and other countries. As part of his interest in teaching biology, Dr. Hardin was a founding member of the University of Wisconsin Teaching Academy. His teaching awards include a Lily Teaching Fellowship and a National Science Foundation Young Investigator Award. He is also on the editorial board of *CBE: Life Sciences Education*, and is a curator of WormClassroom, a digital initiative that promotes the use of *C. elegans* in college classrooms and laboratories.

GREGORY BERTONI has been active in teaching, research, and scientific writing for over 25 years. He earned a Ph.D. in Cellular and Molecular Biology from the University of Wisconsin-Madison, where he taught students in introductory and graduate-level biochemistry, sophomore cell biology, and plant physiology. He helped to develop a new course entitled "Ways of Knowing" designed to introduce entering freshmen to a variety of academic fields as well as to the learning process itself. His published research includes studies in bacterial pathogenesis, plant-microbe interactions, and plant gene expression. Dr. Bertoni is a science editor for *The Plant Cell*, a leading international research journal in plant cell and molecular biology. He is also responsible for updating the journal's Teaching Tools in Plant Biology, an online resource for biology instructors. He has been teaching biology and medical microbiology at Columbus State Community College in Columbus, Ohio for most of the past 10 years. In addition, Dr. Bertoni is a freelance scientific writer who contributes to text- and web-based projects in biology, physics, and microbiology and assists authors in preparing manuscripts for publication.

LEWIS J. KLEINSMITH is an Arthur F. Thurnau Professor Emeritus of Molecular, Cellular, and Developmental Biology at the University of Michigan, where he has served on the faculty since receiving his Ph.D. from Rockefeller University in 1968. His teaching experiences have involved courses in introductory biology, cell biology, and cancer biology, and his research interests have included studies of growth control in cancer cells, the role of protein phosphorylation in eukaryotic gene regulation, and the control of gene expression during development. Among his numerous publications, he is the author of *Principles of Cancer Biology* as well as several award-winning educational software programs. His honors include a Guggenheim Fellowship, the Henry Russell Award, a Michigan Distinguished Service Award, citations for outstanding teaching from the Michigan Students Association, an NIH Plain Language Award, and a Best Curriculum Innovation Award from the EDUCOM Higher Education Software Awards Competition.

WAYNE M. BECKER taught cell biology at the University of Wisconsin-Madison for 30 years until his retirement. His interest in textbook writing grew out of notes, outlines, and problem sets that he assembled for his students, culminating in *Energy and the Living Cell*, a paperback text on bioenergetics published in 1977, and *The World of the Cell*, the first edition of which appeared in 1986. He earned all his degrees at the University of Wisconsin-Madison. All three degrees are in biochemistry, an orientation that is readily discernible in his textbooks. His research interests were in plant molecular biology, focused specifically on the regulation of the expression of genes that encode enzymes of the photorespiratory pathway. His honors include a Chancellor's Award for Distinguished Teaching, Guggenheim and Fulbright Fellowships, and a Visiting Scholar Award from the Royal Society of London. This text builds on his foundation, and is inspired by his legacy.

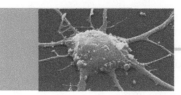

PREFACE

"*Because we enjoy interacting with biology undergrads and think that they should have biology textbooks that are clearly written, make the subject matter relevant to the reader, and help them appreciate not only how much we already know about biology—cell biology, in our case—but also how much more remains to be investigated and discovered.*" That's how any of the authors of this text would likely respond if asked why we've invested so much time in writing and revising *The World of the Cell*. Each of us has an extensive history of teaching undergraduate courses in cell biology and related areas, and each of us treasures our contact with students as one of the most rewarding aspects of being a faculty member.

As we reflect on the changes we've seen in our courses over the years, we realize that the past several decades have seen an explosive growth in our understanding of the properties and functions of living cells. This enormous profusion of information presents us with a daunting challenge as we confront the task of keeping *Becker's World of the Cell* up to date while simultaneously ensuring that it remains both manageable in length and readily comprehensible to students encountering the field of cell and molecular biology for the first time. This eighth edition represents our most recent attempt to rise to that challenge. As with the previous editions, each of us has brought our own teaching and writing experience to the venture in ways that we have found mutually beneficial—a view that we hope our readers will share.

One major objective for this edition has been to update the content of the text, especially in areas where the pace of research is especially brisk and recent findings are particularly significant. At the same time, we have remained committed to the three central goals that have characterized each preceding edition. As always, our primary goal is to introduce students to the fundamental principles that guide cellular organization and function. Second, we think it is important for students to understand some of the critical scientific evidence that has led to the formulation of these central concepts. And finally, we have sought to accomplish these goals in a book of manageable length that can be easily read and understood by beginning cell biology students—and that still fits in their backpacks! To accomplish this third goal, we have necessarily been selective both in the types of examples chosen to illustrate key concepts and in the quantity of scientific evidence included. We have, in other words, attempted to remain faithful to the overall purpose of each previous edition: to present the essential principles, processes, and methodology of molecular and cell biology as lucidly as possible. We have also given careful attention to accuracy, consistency, vocabulary, and readability to minimize confusion and maximize understanding for our readers.

What's New in This Edition

The eighth edition retains the clear writing style from previous editions, and adds new emphasis on modern genetic/genomic/proteomic approaches to cell biology:

- **New, up-to-date information has been added** on the tools that modern cell biologists use, including model organisms, bioinformatics, and genomics/proteomics. This discussion better establishes the modern, 21st century approach to cell biology while retaining the classical emphasis from previous editions.

- **Major reorganization of the cell cycle and apoptosis material,** including moving apoptosis from Chapter 15 to Chapter 19 to better match conventional course syllabi.

- **New discussions of modern genetic and molecular technologies,** such as nanotechnology, bioluminescence, X-ray crystallographic data, and genetic engineering of animals and transgenic plants.

- **Content updates** have been added throughout the book highlighting the most recent advances in the understanding of cell biology (see Content Highlights of the Eighth Edition).

- **New, In-text media callouts** that link chapter content to multimedia resources, such as learning activities, 3D molecular structure tutorials, videos, and animations, that are available on www.thecellplace.com

 VIDEOS www.thecellplace.com   Spindle formation during mitosis

- **New online videos, 3D structure tutorials, animations, and activities** have been added to The Cell Place (www.thecellplace.com) to enhance student learning through dynamic visualization.

- **New Pearson E-text** and Pearson Custom Library options are available.

- **New PowerPoint Lecture Tools,** including pre-made lecture outlines containing all of the figures and photos and embedded animations, and 5–10 personal response system (PRS) clicker questions per chapter.

Content Highlights of the Eighth Edition

Updated material and new information has been added throughout the book. Topics that have been altered, updated, or added include the following:

CHAPTER 3: Streamlined discussion of protein function; improved discussion of peptide bond geometry; introduced CASP—the worldwide test of protein structure modeling programs; added miRNA and siRNA to the discussion of RNA; introduced lipid rafts earlier.

CHAPTER 4: Added discussions of the important functions of what had been called "junk" DNA, how mitochondrial DNA analysis is used to trace genetic lineages and the origin of modern humans, construction of an artificial ribosome in vitro, and how prions cause chronic wasting disease in deer and elk. Presented new results of X-ALD gene therapy clinical trial.

CHAPTER 6: Updated discussion on induced fit; added new figures showing formation of lysozyme active site after protein folding and the changes in the active site of carboxypeptidase following substrate binding; added description of aspirin as an irreversible inhibitor of cyclooxygenase; described cryophilic microorganisms such as *Listeria*.

CHAPTER 7: Added a new paragraph and figure describing the common glycolipids MGDG and DGDG; included a more extensive description of lipid raft composition, formation, and proteomics; added descriptions of how antimicrobial peptides disrupt cell membranes, described membrane receptors for nutrients and for the gaseous hormone ethylene; updated roles of caveolae in human physiology and disease.

CHAPTER 12: Added new paragraph describing mechanism of action and clinical uses of botulinum toxin. Added new material on N-glycosylation and secretion involving interleukin-31 and p53 and new micrographs showing exocytosis and phagocytosis. Added new paragraph describing reactive oxygen species and their detoxification in the peroxisome; included a more detailed description of the reaction mechanism of P-450 monooxygenases.

CHAPTER 15: Katanins are now discussed in the microtubule section. Added significant new information on formins in the actin section, and much more coverage of Rho GTPases, including RhoGEFs, GAPs, and GDIs.

CHAPTER 16: Added new information and a new part of a figure on hair cells, as well as significant new text on intraflagellar transport (IFT) and ciliopathies to Box 16A. Updated the figure on focal contacts and the leading edge to provide an integrated view of actin polymerization at the leading edge.

CHAPTER 18: Added new information on NTF2 in the Ran/importin/exportin section. Updated section on nuclear bodies to be more explicit about types and functions of nuclear bodies (Cajal, GEMs, speckles, etc.). Added a new figure describing the percentage of various types of DNA in the human genome.

CHAPTER 19: Added new information on spindle midzones, as well as new material and a new figure on myosin and Rho during cytokinesis. Added new material on ATR and checkpoint kinases in the cell cycle control section. Reorganized content between Chapter 14 and Chapter 19 to streamline discussion: much of the Ras discussion and Akt/PI3K has been moved out of this chapter. Apoptosis was removed from Chapter 14, and is now in Chapter 19. In addition, the apoptosis figure was redrawn to show a more accurate depiction of the apoptosome based on cryoEM data.

CHAPTER 21: Added information on regulatory role of the C terminus of RNA pol II. Added a discussion of electrophoretic mobility shift assays (EMSAs) as a technique, while the historical method of R loop detection was streamlined and supplemented with an improved schematic diagram.

CHAPTER 22: Added a new figure showing the results of experiments with microsomes, demonstrating that cotranslational import is required for cleavage of the signal sequence. Added a brief discussion of operons in eukaryotes.

APPENDIX: Added mention of photoconvertible and photoswitchable fluorophores. Added a section on various techniques for superresolution microscopy. Streamlined discussion of correlative microscopy. Updated figure on the fluorescence microscope to more accurately reflect modern epifluorescence systems.

Techniques and Methods

Throughout the text, we have tried to explain not only *what* we know about cells but also *how* we know what we know. Toward that end, we have included descriptions of experimental techniques and findings in every chapter, almost always in the context of the questions they address and in anticipation of the answers they provide. For example, polyacrylamide gel electrophoresis is introduced not in a chapter that simply catalogues a variety of methods for studying cells but in Chapter 7, where it becomes important to our understanding of how membrane proteins can be separated from one another. Similarly, equilibrium density centrifugation is described in Chapter 12, where it is essential to our understanding of how lysosomes were originally distinguished from mitochondria and subsequently from peroxisomes as well.

To help readers locate techniques out of context, an alphabetical Guide to Techniques and Methods appears on the inside of the front cover, with references to chapters, pages, tables, figures, and boxed essays, as appropriate. To enhance its usefulness, the Guide to Techniques and Methods includes references not just to laboratory techniques but also to the mathematical determination of values such as ΔG (free energy change) and $\Delta E_0'$ (standard reduction potential), bioinformatics techniques such as BLAST searching, and even to clinical procedures such as the treatment of methanol poisoning.

Microscopy is the only exception to our general approach of introducing techniques in context. The techniques of light and electron microscopy are so pervasively relevant to contemporary cell biology that they warrant special consideration as a self-contained unit, which is included as an Appendix entitled *Visualizing Cells and Molecules*. This Appendix gives students ready access to detailed information on a variety of microscopy techniques, including cutting-edge uses of light microscopy for imaging and manipulating molecular processes.

Building on the Strengths of Previous Editions

We have retained and built upon the strengths of prior editions in four key areas:

1. **The chapter organization focuses on main concepts.**

   - Each chapter is divided into sections that begin with a *concept statement heading*, which summarizes the material and helps students focus on the main points to study and review.

   - Chapters are written and organized in ways that allow instructors to assign the chapters and chapter sections in different sequences to make the book adaptable to a wide variety of course plans.

   - Each chapter culminates with a bulleted *Summary of Key Points* that briefly describes the main points covered in each section of the chapter.

   - Each *Summary of Key Points* is followed by a *Making Connections* paragraph that highlights some of the interrelationships that connect the content of the current chapter to topics covered elsewhere in the book.

2. **The illustrations teach concepts at an appropriate level of detail.**

   - Many of the more complex figures incorporate *minicaptions* to help students grasp concepts more quickly by drawing their focus into the body of an illustration rather than depending solely on a separate figure legend to describe what is taking place.

   - *Overview figures* outline complicated structures or processes in broad strokes and are followed by text and figures that present supporting details.

   - Carefully selected micrographs are usually accompanied by scale bars to indicate magnification.

3. **Important terminology is highlighted and defined in several ways.**

   - **Boldface type** is used to highlight the most important terms in each chapter, all of which are defined in the Glossary.

   - *Italics* are employed to identify additional technical terms that are less important than boldfaced terms but significant in their own right. Occasionally, italics are also used to highlight important phrases or sentences.

   - The Glossary includes definitions and page references for all bold-faced key terms and acronyms in every chapter—more than 1500 terms in all, a veritable "dictionary of cell biology" in its own right.

4. **Each chapter helps students learn the process of science, not just facts.**

   - Text discussions emphasize the experimental evidence that underlies our understanding of cell structure and function, to remind readers that advances in cell biology, as in all branches of science, come not from lecturers in their classrooms or textbook authors at their computers but from researchers in their laboratories.

   - The inclusion of a *Problem Set* at the end of each chapter reflects our conviction that we learn science not just by reading or hearing about it, but by working with it. The problems are designed to emphasize understanding and application, rather than rote recall. Many of the problems are class-tested, having been selected from problem sets and exams we have used in our own courses.

   - To maximize the usefulness of the problem sets, detailed answers for all problems are available for students in a *Solutions Manual* that is available for purchase separately.

   - Each chapter contains one or more *Boxed Essays* to aid students in their understanding of particularly important or intriguing aspects of cell biology. Some of the essays provide *Deeper Insights* into potentially difficult principles, such as the essay that uses the analogy of monkeys shelling peanuts to explain enzyme kinetics (Box 6A). Other essays describe *Tools of Discovery*, some of the important experimental techniques used by cell biologists, as exemplified by the description of

DNA fingerprinting in Box 18C. And yet another role of the boxed essays is to describe *Human Applications* of research findings in cell biology, as illustrated by the discussion of cystic fibrosis and the prospects for gene therapy in Box 8B.

■ A *Suggested Reading* list is included at the end of each chapter, with an emphasis on review articles and carefully selected research publications that motivated students are likely to understand. We have tried to avoid overwhelming readers with lengthy bibliographies of the original literature but have referenced articles that are especially relevant to the topics of the chapter. In most chapters, we have included a few citations of especially important historical publications, which are marked with blue dots to alert the reader to their historical significance.

Supplementary Learning Aids

For Instructors

Instructor Resource DVD-ROM for *Becker's World of the Cell* • 0-321-68959-3/978-0-321-68959-7

Available to adopters, this DVD-ROM includes:

■ PowerPoint Lecture Tools, including pre-made lecture outlines containing all of the figures and photos and embedded animations, and 5–10 Personal Response System (PRS) clicker questions per chapter.

■ JPEG images of all textbook figures and photos, including printer-ready transparency acetate masters.

■ Videos and animations of key concepts, organized by chapter for ease of use in the classroom.

■ The full test bank for *Becker's World of the Cell.*

Computerized Test Bank for *Becker's World of the Cell* • 0-321-68958-5/978-0-321-68958-0

The test bank provides over 1000 multiple-choice, short-answer, and inquiry/activity questions.

For Students

Solutions Manual for *Becker's World of the Cell* • 0-321-68961-5/978-0-321-68961-0

Written by the authors, this is a collection of complete, detailed answers for all of the end-of-chapter questions and problems.

The Cell Place for *Becker's World of the Cell* • 0-321-68960-7/978-0-321-68960-3

The book's companion website, *www.thecellplace.com*, helps students explore a variety of cell biology topics in depth, and includes interactive tutorials, simulations, animations, videos, molecular structure files, and step-by-step problems. Practice quizzes contain 20 multiple-choice questions for each chapter, with instant feedback for correct and incorrect answers.

We Welcome Your Comments and Suggestions

The ultimate test of any textbook is how effectively it helps instructors teach and students learn. We welcome feedback and suggestions from readers and will try to acknowledge all correspondence.

Jeff Hardin
Department of Zoology
University of Wisconsin-Madison
Madison, Wisconsin 53706
e-mail: jdhardin@wisc.edu

Gregory Bertoni
The Plant Cell
American Society of Plant Biologists
Rockville, Maryland 20855
e-mail: gbertoni@aspb.org

Lewis J. Kleinsmith
Department of Molecular, Cellular, and Developmental Biology
University of Michigan
Ann Arbor, Michigan 48109
e-mail: lewisk@umich.edu

ACKNOWLEDGMENTS

We want to acknowledge the contributions of the numerous people who have made this book possible. We are indebted especially to the many students whose words of encouragement catalyzed the writing of these chapters and whose thoughtful comments and criticisms have contributed much to whatever level of reader-friendliness the text may be judged to have. Each of us owes a special debt of gratitude to our colleagues, from whose insights and suggestions we have benefited greatly and borrowed freely. We also acknowledge those who have contributed to previous editions of our textbooks, including David Deamer, Martin Poenie, Jane Reece, John Raasch, and Valerie Kish, as well as Peter Armstrong, John Carson, Ed Clark, Joel Goodman, David Gunn, Jeanette Natzle, Mary Jane Niles, Timothy Ryan, Beth Schaefer, Lisa Smit, David Spiegel, Akif Uzman, and Karen Valentine. Most importantly, we are grateful to Wayne Becker for his incisive writing and vision, which led to the creation of this book and featured so prominently in previous editions. We have tried to carry on his tradition of excellence. In addition, we want to express our appreciation to the many colleagues who graciously consented to contribute micrographs to this endeavor, as well as the authors and publishers who have kindly granted permission to reproduce copyrighted material.

The many reviewers listed below provided helpful criticisms and suggestions at various stages of manuscript development and revision. Their words of appraisal and counsel were gratefully received and greatly appreciated. Indeed, the extensive review process to which this and the prior editions of the book have been exposed should be considered a significant feature of the book. Nonetheless, the final responsibility for what you read here remains ours, and you may confidently attribute to us any errors of omission or commission encountered in these pages.

We are also deeply indebted to the many publishing professionals whose consistent encouragement, hard work, and careful attention to detail contributed much to the clarity of both the text and the art. Special recognition and sincere appreciation go to Anna Amato in her role as project editor, to Gary Carlson, Josh Frost, Lindsay White, Deborah Gale, Lori Newman, Laura Tommasi, Sonia DiVittorio, and Lee Ann Doctor at Benjamin Cummings, to Stephanie Davidson at Dartmouth Publishing, and to Crystal Clifton and her colleagues at Progressive Publishing Alternatives.

Finally, we are grateful beyond measure to our wives, families, graduate students, and postdoctoral associates, without whose patience, understanding, and forbearance this book could not have been written.

Reviewers for The Eighth Edition

Nihal Altan-Bonnet, *Rutgers University*
Stephen E. Asmus, *Centre College*
Manuel Alejandro Barbieri, *Florida International University*
Kenneth D. Belanger, *Colgate University*
Loren A. Bertocci, *Marian University, Indianapolis*
Annemarie Bettica, *Manhattanville College*
Ann C. Billetz, *Massachusetts College of Liberal Arts*
Robert J. Bloch, *University of Maryland School of Medicine*
Olga Boudker, *Weill Cornell Medical College*
Joshua Brumberg, *Queens College, CUNY*
John G. Burr, *University of Texas, Dallas*
Richard Cardullo, *University of California, Riverside*
Catherine P. Chia, *University of Nebraska-Lincoln*
Francis Choy, *University of Victoria*
Garry Davies, *University of Alaska, Anchorage*
Thomas DiChristina, *Georgia Institute of Technology*
Christy Donmoyer, *Allegheny College*
Scott E. Erdman, *Syracuse University*
Kenneth Field, *Bucknell University*
Theresa M. Filtz, *Oregon State University*
Larry J. Forney, *University of Idaho*
Elliott S. Goldstein, *Arizona State University*
Denise Greathouse, *University of Arkansas*
Richard D. Griner, *Augusta State University*
Mike Harrington, *University of Alberta, Edmonton*
Alan M. Jones, *University of North Carolina Chapel Hill*
Thomas C.S. Keller III, *Florida State University*
Gregory Kelly, *University of Western Ontario*
Karen L. Koster, *University of South Dakota*
Darryl Kropf, *University of Utah*
Charles A. Lessman, *University of Memphis*
Jani Lewis, *State University of New York at Geneseo*
Howard L. Liber, *Colorado State University*
Ryan Littlefield, *University of Washington*
Phoebe Lostroh, *Colorado College*

Michelle Malotky, *Guilford College*
Stephen M. Mount, *University of Maryland*
Leisha Mullins, *Texas A&M University*
Hao Nguyen, *California State University, Sacramento*
Joseph Pomerening, *Indiana University*
Joseph Reese, *Pennsylvania State University*
Nancy Rice, *Western Kentucky University*
Thomas M. Roberts, *Florida State University*
Donald F. Slish, *Plattsburgh State University of New York*
Charlotte Spencer, *University of Alberta, Edmonton*
Lesly A. Temesvari, *Clemson University*
Frances E. Weaver, *Widener University*
Gary M. Wessel, *Brown University*
David Worcester, *University of Missouri*

Reviewers of Previous Editions

Amelia Ahern-Rindell, *University of Portland*
Kirk Anders, *Gonzaga University*
Katsura Asano, *Kansas State University*
Steven Asmus, *Centre College*
Karl Aufderheide, *Texas A&M University*
L. Rao Ayyagari, *Lindenwood College*
William Balch, *Scripps Research Institute*
Tim Beagley, *Salt Lake Community College*
Margaret Beard, *Columbia University*
William Bement, *University of Wisconsin-Madison*
Paul Benko, *Sonoma State University*
Steve Benson, *California State University, Hayward*
Joseph J. Berger, *Springfield College*
Gerald Bergtrom, *University of Wisconsin, Milwaukee*
Karen K. Bernd. *Davidson College*
Maria Bertagnolli, *Gonzaga University*
Frank L. Binder, *Marshall University*
Robert Blystone, *Trinity University*
R. B. Boley, *University of Texas at Arlington*
Mark Bolyard, *Southern Illinois University, Edwardsville*
Edward M. Bonder, *Rutgers, the State University of New Jersey*
David Boone, *Portland State University*
Janet Braam, *Rice University*
James T. Bradley, *Auburn University*
Suzanne Bradshaw, *University of Cincinnati*
J. D. Brammer, *North Dakota State University*
Chris Brinegar, *San Jose State University*
Andrew Brittain, *Hawaii Pacific University*
Grant Brown, *University of Toronto*
David Bruck, *San Jose State University*
Alan H. Brush, *University of Connecticut, Storrs*
Patrick J. Bryan, *Central Washington University*
Brower R. Burchill, *University of Kansas*
Ann B. Burgess, *University of Wisconsin-Madison*
John G. Burr, *University of Texas, Dallas*
Thomas J. Byers, *Ohio State University*

David Byres, *Florida Community College, Jacksonville*
P. Samuel Campbell, *University of Alabama, Huntsville*
George L. Card, *University of Montana*
Anand Chandrasekhar, *University of Missouri*
C. H. Chen, *South Dakota State University*
Mitchell Chernin, *Bucknell University*
Edward A. Clark, *University of Washington*
Philippa Claude, *University of Wisconsin-Madison*
Dennis O. Clegg, *University of California, Santa Barbara*
John M. Coffin, *Tufts University School of Medicine*
J. John Cohen, *University of Colorado Medical School*
Larry Cohen, *Pomona College*
Nathan Collie, *Texas Tech University*
Reid S. Compton, *University of Maryland*
Mark Condon, *Dutchess Community College*
Jonathan Copeland, *Georgia Southern University*
Jeff Corden, *Johns Hopkins University*
Bracey Dangerfield, *Salt Lake Community College*
Garry Davies, *University of Alaska, Anchorage*
Maria Davis, *University of Alabama, Huntsville*
David DeGroote, *St. Cloud State*
Arturo De Lozanne, *University of Texas, Austin*
Douglas Dennis, *James Madison University*
Elizabeth D. Dolci, *Johnson State College*
Aris J. Domnas, *University of North Carolina, Chapel Hill*
Michael P. Donovan, *Southern Utah University*
Robert M. Dores, *University of Denver*
Stephen D'Surney, *University of Mississippi*
Ron Dubreuil, *University of Illinois, Chicago*
Diane D. Eardley, *University of California, Santa Barbara*
Lucinda Elliot, *Shippensburg University*
William Ettinger, *Gonzaga University*
Guy E. Farish, *Adams State College*
Mary A. Farwell, *East Carolina University*
David Featherstone, *University of Illinois, Chicago*
Kenneth Field, *Bucknell University*
Margaret F. Field, *St. Mary's College of California*
James E. Forbes, *Hampton University*
Charlene L. Forest, *Brooklyn College*
Carl S. Frankel, *Pennsylvania State University, Hazleton Campus*
David R. Fromson, *California State University, Fullerton*
David M. Gardner, *Roanoke College*
Craig Gatto, *Illinois State University*
Carol V. Gay, *Pennsylvania State University*
Stephen A. George, *Amherst College*
Nabarun Ghosh, *West Texas A&M University*
Swapan K. Ghosh, *Indiana State University*
Susan P. Gilbert, *University of Pittsburgh*
Reid Gilmore, *University of Massachusetts*
Joseph Gindhart, *University of Massachusetts, Boston*
Michael L. Gleason, *Central Washington University*
T. T. Gleeson, *University of Colorado*
James Godde, *Monmouth College*

Ursula W. Goodenough, *Washington University*

Thomas A. Gorell, *Colorado State University*

James Grainger, *Santa Clara University*

Marion Greaser, *University of Wisconsin-Madison*

Karen F. Greif, *Bryn Mawr College*

Richard Griner, *Augusta State University*

Mark T. Groudine, *Fred Hutchinson Cancer Research Center, University of Washington School of Medicine*

Gary Gussin, *University of Iowa*

Karen Guzman, *Campbell University*

Leah T. Haimo, *University of California, Riverside*

Arnold Hampel, *Northern Illinois University*

Laszlo Hanzely, *Northern Illinois University*

Donna Harman, *Lubbock Christian University*

Bettina Harrison, *University of Massachusetts, Boston*

William Heidcamp, *Gustavus Adolphus College*

John Helmann, *Cornell University*

Lawrence Hightower, *University of Connecticut, Storrs*

Chris Holford, *Purdue University*

James P. Holland, *Indiana University, Bloomington*

Johns Hopkins III, *Washington University*

Nancy Hopkins, *Tulane University*

Betty A. Houck, *University of Portland*

Linda S. Huang, *University of Massachusetts, Boston*

Sharon Isern, *Florida Gulf Coast University*

Kenneth Jacobson, *University of North Carolina, Chapel Hill*

Makkuni Jayaram, *University of Texas, Austin*

William R. Jeffery, *University of Texas, Austin*

Kwang W. Jeon, *University of Tennessee*

Jerry E. Johnson Jr., *University of Houston*

Kenneth C. Jones, *California State University, Northridge*

Patricia P. Jones, *Stanford University*

Cheryl L. Jorcyk, *Boise State University*

David Kafkewitz, *Rutgers University*

Martin A. Kapper, *Central Connecticut State University*

Lon S. Kaufman, *University of Illinois, Chicago*

Steven J. Keller, *University of Cincinnati Main Campus*

Greg Kelly, *University of Western Ontario*

Gwendolyn M. Kinebrew, *John Carroll University*

Kirill Kiselyov, *University of Pittsburgh*

Loren Knapp, *University of South Carolina*

Robert Koch, *California State University, Fullerton*

Bruce Kohorn, *Bowdoin College*

Joseph R. Koke, *Southwest Texas State University*

Irene Kokkala, *Northern Georgia College & State University*

Keith Kozminski, *University of Virginia*

Hal Krider, *University of Connecticut, Storrs*

William B. Kristan, Jr., *University of California, San Diego*

David N. Kristie, *Acadia University (Nova Scotia)*

Frederic Kundig, *Towson State University*

Jeffrey Kushner, *James Madison University*

Dale W. Laird, *University of Western Ontario (London, Ontario, Canada)*

Michael Lawton, *Rutgers University*

Elias Lazarides, *California Institute of Technology*

Wei-Lih Lee, *University of Massachusetts, Amherst*

Esther M. Leise, *University of North Carolina, Greensboro*

Charles Lessman, *University of Memphis*

Daniel Lew, *Duke University*

Carol Lin, *Columbia University*

John T. Lis, *Cornell University*

Kenneth Long, *California Lutheran University*

Robert Macey, *University of California, Berkeley*

Albert MacKrell, *Bradley University*

Roderick MacLeod, *University of Illinois, Urbana-Champaign*

Shyamal K. Majumdar, *Lafayette College*

Gary G. Matthews, *State University of New York, Stony Brook*

Douglas McAbee, *California State University, Long Beach*

Mark McCallum, *Pfeiffer University*

Iain McKillop, *University of North Carolina, Charlotte*

Thomas D. McKnight, *Texas A&M University*

JoAnn Meerschaert, *St. Cloud University*

Trevor Mendelow, *University of Colorado*

John Merrill, *Michigan State University*

Robert L. Metzenberg, *University of Wisconsin-Madison*

Teena Michael, *University of Hawaii, Manoa*

Hugh A. Miller III, *East Tennessee State University*

Jeffrey Miller, *University of Minnesota*

Nicole Minor, *Northern Kentucky University*

James Moroney, *Louisiana State University*

Tony K. Morris, *Fairmont State College*

Deborah B. Mowshowitz, *Columbia University*

Amy Mulnix, *Earlham College*

James Mulrooney, *Central Connecticut State University*

Hao Nguyen, *California State University, Sacramento*

Carl E. Nordahl, *University of Nebraska, Omaha*

Richard Nuccitelli, *University of California, Davis*

Donata Oertel, *University of Wisconsin-Madison*

Joanna Olmsted, *University of Rochester*

Laura Olsen, *University of Michigan*

Alan Orr, *University of Northern Iowa*

Donald W. Ott, *University of Akron*

Curtis L. Parker, *Morehouse School of Medicine*

Lee D. Peachey, *University of Colorado*

Debra K. Pearce, *Northern Kentucky University*

Mark Peifer, *University of North Carolina, Chapel Hill*

Howard Petty, *Wayne State University*

Susan Pierce, *Northwestern University*

Joel B. Piperberg, *Millersville University*

William Plaxton, *Queen's University*

George Plopper, *Rensselaer Polytechnic Institute*

Gilbert C. Pogany, *Northern Arizona University*

Archie Portis, *University of Illinois*

Stephen Previs, *Case Western Reserve University*

Mitch Price, *Pennsylvania State University*

Ralph Quatrano, *Oregon State University*

Ralph E. Reiner, *College of the Redwoods*

Gary Reiness, *Lewis and Clark College*

Douglas Rhoads, *University of Arkansas*

John Rinehart, *Eastern Oregon University*

Tom Roberts, *Florida State University*

Michael Robinson, *North Dakota State University*

Adrian Rodriguez, *San Jose State University*

Donald J. Roufa, *Kansas State University*

Donald H. Roush, *University of North Alabama*

Gary Rudnick, *Yale University*

Donald Salter, *Leuther Laboratories*

Edmund Samuel, *Southern Connecticut State University*

Mary Jane Saunders, *University of South Florida*

John I. Scheide, *Central Michigan University*

David J. Schultz, *University of Louisville*

Mary Schwanke, *University of Maine, Farmington*

David W. Scupham, *Valparaiso University*

Edna Seaman, *University of Massachusetts, Boston*

Diane C. Shakes, *University of Houston*

Joel Sheffield, *Temple University*

Sheldon S. Shen, *Iowa State University*

James R. Shinkle, *Trinity University Texas*

Randall D. Shortridge, *State University of New York, Buffalo*

Maureen Shuh, *Loyola University, New Orleans*

Brad Shuster, *New Mexico State University*

Jill Sible, *Virginia Polytechnic Institute and State University*

Esther Siegfried, *Pennsylvania State University*

Michael Silverman, *California State Polytechnic University, Pomona*

Neil Simister, *Brandeis University*

Dwayne D. Simmons, *University of California, Los Angeles*

Robert D. Simoni, *Stanford University*

William R. Sistrom, *University of Oregon*

Donald F. Slish, *Plattsburgh State University of New York*

Roger Sloboda, *Dartmouth College*

Robert H. Smith, *Skyline College*

Juliet Spencer, *University of San Francisco*

Mark Staves, *Grand Valley State University*

John Sternfeld, *State University of New York, Cortland*

Barbara Y. Stewart, *Swarthmore College*

Margaret E. Stevens, *Ripon College*

Bradley J. Stith, *University of Colorado, Denver*

Richard D. Storey, *Colorado College*

Antony O. Stretton, *University of Wisconsin-Madison*

Philip Stukus, *Denison University*

Stephen Subtelny, *Rice University*

Scott Summers, *Colorado State University*

Millard Susman, *University of Wisconsin-Madison*

Brian Tague, *Wake Forest University*

Elizabeth J. Taparowsky, *Purdue University*

Barbara J. Taylor, *Oregon State University*

Bruce R. Telzer, *Pomona College*

Jeffrey L. Travis, *State University of New York, Albany*

John J. Tyson, *Virginia Polytechnic University*

Akif Uzman, *University of Texas, Austin*

Thomas Vandergon, *Pepperdine University*

Quinn Vega, *Montclair State University*

James Walker, *University of Texas, Pan American*

Paul E. Wanda, *Southern Illinois University, Edwardsville*

Fred D. Warner, *Syracuse University*

James Watrous, *St. Joseph's University*

Andrew N. Webber, *Arizona State University*

Cindy Martinez Wedig, *University of Texas, Pan American*

Fred H. Wilt, *University Of California, Berkeley*

James Wise, *Hampton University*

David Worcester, *University of Missouri, Columbia*

Lauren Yaich, *University of Pittsburgh, Bradford*

Linda Yasui, *Northern Illinois University*

Yang Yen, *South Dakota State University*

James Young, *University of Alberta*

Luwen Zhang, *University of Nebraska, Lincoln*

Qiang Zhou, *University of California, Berkeley*

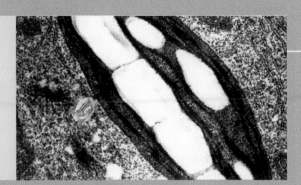

3

The Macromolecules of the Cell

We looked at some of the basic chemical principles of cellular organization. We saw that each of the major kinds of biological macromolecules—proteins, nucleic acids, and polysaccharides—consists of a relatively small number (from 1 to 20) of repeating monomeric units. These polymers are synthesized by condensation reactions in which activated monomers are linked together by the removal of water. Once synthesized, the individual polymer molecules fold and coil spontaneously into stable, three-dimensional shapes. These folded molecules then associate with one another in a hierarchical manner to generate higher levels of structural complexity, usually without further input of energy or information.

We are now ready to examine the major kinds of biological macromolecules. In each case, we will focus first on the chemical nature of the monomeric components and then on the synthesis and properties of the polymer itself. As we will see shortly, most biological macromolecules in cells are synthesized from about 30 common small molecules. We begin our survey with proteins because they play such important and widespread roles in cellular structure and function. We then move on to nucleic acids and polysaccharides. The tour concludes with lipids, which do not quite fit the definition of a polymer but are important cellular components whose synthesis resembles that of true polymers.

Proteins

Proteins are a class of extremely important and ubiquitous macromolecules in all organisms, occurring nearly everywhere in the cell. In fact, their importance is implied by their name, which comes from the Greek word *proteios,* meaning "first place." Whether we are talking about conversion of carbon dioxide to sugar in photosynthesis, oxygen transport in the blood, the regulation of gene expression by transcription factors, cell-to-cell communication, or the motility of a flagellated bacterium, we are dealing with processes that depend crucially on particular proteins with specific properties and functions.

Based on function, proteins fall into nine major classes. Many proteins are *enzymes,* serving as catalysts that greatly increase the rates of the thousands of chemical reactions on which life depends. *Structural proteins,* on the other hand, provide physical support and shape to cells and organelles, giving them their characteristic appearances. *Motility proteins* play key roles in the contraction and movement of cells and intracellular structures. *Regulatory proteins* are responsible for control and coordination of cellular functions, ensuring that cellular activities are regulated to meet cellular needs. *Transport proteins* are involved in the movement of other substances into, out of, and within the cell. *Hormonal proteins* mediate communication between cells in distant parts of an organism, and *receptor proteins* enable cells to respond to chemical stimuli from their environment. Finally, *defensive proteins* provide protection against disease, and *storage proteins* serve as reservoirs of amino acids.

Because virtually everything that a cell is or does depends on the proteins it contains, it is clear we need to understand what proteins are and why they have the properties they do. We begin our discussion by looking at the amino acids present in the proteins, and then we will consider some properties of proteins themselves.

The Monomers Are Amino Acids

Proteins are linear polymers of **amino acids.** Although more than 60 different kinds of amino acids are typically present in a cell, only 20 kinds are used in protein synthesis, as indicated in **Table 3-1**. Some proteins contain more than 20 different kinds of amino acids, but the additional ones usually are a result of modifications that occur after the protein has been synthesized. Although most proteins contain all or most of the 20 amino acids, the

Table 3-1   **Common Small Molecules in Cells**

Kind of Molecules	Number Present	Names of Molecules	Role in Cell	Figure Number for Structures
Amino acids	20	See list in Table 3-2.	Monomeric units of all proteins	3-2
Aromatic bases	5	Adenine	Components of nucleic acids	3-15
		Cytosine		
		Guanine		
		Thymine		
		Uracil		
Sugars	varies	Ribose	Component of RNA	3-15
		Deoxyribose	Component of DNA	
		Glucose	Energy metabolism; component of starch and glycogen	3-21
Lipids	varies	Fatty acids	Components of phospholipids and membranes	3-27a
		Cholesterol		3-27e

Source: Adapted from Wald (1994).

proportions vary greatly, and no two different proteins have the same amino acid sequence.

Every amino acid has the basic structure illustrated in **Figure 3-1**, with a carboxyl group, an amino group, a hydrogen atom, and a side chain known as an R group. All are attached to a central carbon atom known as the *α carbon*. Except for glycine, for which the R group is just a hydrogen atom, all amino acids have an asymmetric α carbon atom and therefore exist in two stereoisomeric forms, called D- and L-amino acids. Both kinds exist in nature, but only L-amino acids occur in proteins.

Because the carboxyl and amino groups shown in Figure 3-1 are common features of all amino acids, the specific properties of the various amino acids vary depending on the chemical nature of their R groups, which range from a single hydrogen atom to relatively complex aromatic groups. Shown in **Figure 3-2** are the structures of the 20 L-amino acids found in proteins. The three-letter abbreviations given in parentheses for each amino acid are widely used by biochemists and molecular biologists. **Table 3-2** lists these three-letter abbreviations and the corresponding one-letter abbreviations that are also commonly used.

Nine of these amino acids have nonpolar, *hydrophobic* R groups (Group A). As you look at their structures, you will notice the hydrocarbon nature of the R groups, with few or no oxygen and nitrogen atoms. These hydrophobic amino acids are usually found in the interior of the molecule as a polypeptide folds into its three-dimensional shape. If a protein (or a region of the molecule) has a preponderance of hydrophobic amino acids, the whole protein (or the hydrophobic portion of the molecule) will be excluded from aqueous environments and will instead be found in hydrophobic locations, such as the interior of a membrane.

The remaining 11 amino acids have *hydrophilic* R groups that are either distinctly polar (Group B) or actually charged at the pH values characteristic of cells (Group C). Notice that the two acidic amino acids are negatively charged, and the three basic amino acids are positively charged. Hydrophilic amino acids tend to occur on the

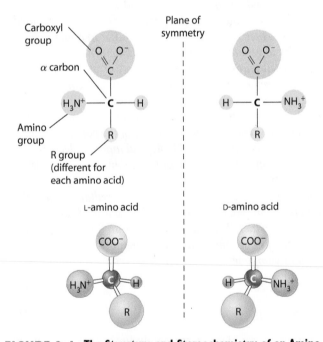

FIGURE 3-1   The Structure and Stereochemistry of an Amino Acid. Because the central carbon atom is asymmetric in all amino acids except glycine, most amino acids can exist in two isomeric forms, designated L and D and shown here as (top) conventional structural formulas and (bottom) ball-and-stick models. The L and D forms are stereoisomers, with the vertical dashed line as the plane of symmetry. Of the two forms, only L-amino acids are present in proteins.

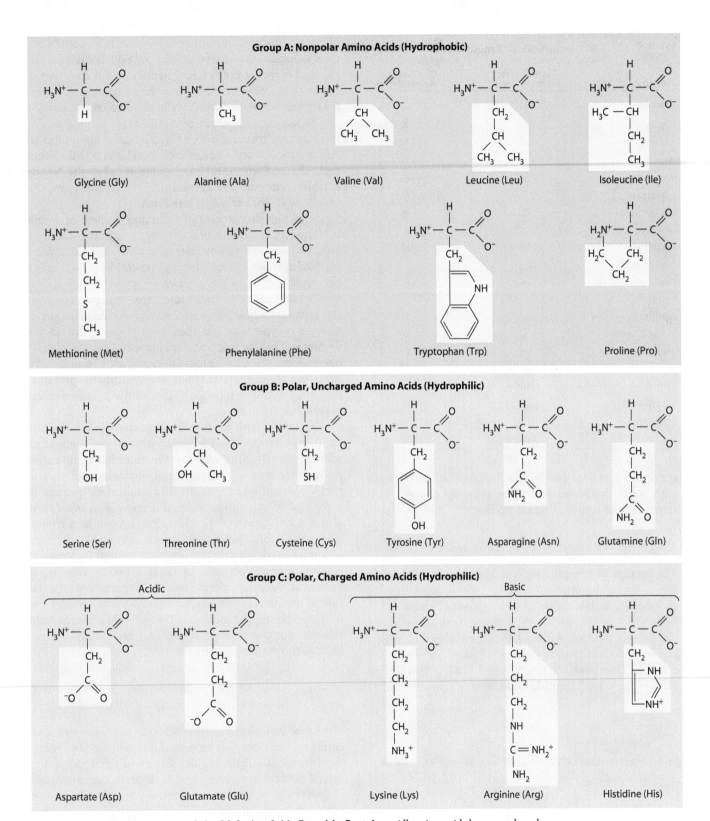

FIGURE 3-2 The Structures of the 20 Amino Acids Found in Proteins. All amino acids have a carboxyl group and an amino group attached to the central (α) carbon, but each has its own distinctive R group (light boxes). Those in Group A have nonpolar R groups and are therefore hydrophobic; notice the hydrocarbon nature of their R groups. The others are hydrophilic, either because the R group is polar (Group B) or because the R group is protonated or deprotonated at cellular pH and thus carries a formal electrostatic charge (Group C). Notice the unusual structure of proline—its R group is covalently linked to the amino nitrogen.

Table 3-2 Abbreviations for Amino Acids

Amino Acid	Three-Letter Abbreviation	One-Letter Abbreviation
Alanine	Ala	A
Arginine	Arg	R
Asparagine	Asn	N
Aspartate	Asp	D
Cysteine	Cys	C
Glutamate	Glu	E
Glutamine	Gln	Q
Glycine	Gly	G
Histidine	His	H
Isoleucine	Ile	I
Leucine	Leu	L
Lysine	Lys	K
Methionine	Met	M
Phenylalanine	Phe	F
Proline	Pro	P
Serine	Ser	S
Threonine	Thr	T
Tryptophan	Trp	W
Tyrosine	Tyr	Y
Valine	Val	V

surface of proteins, thereby maximizing their interactions with water molecules and other polar or charged substances in the surrounding environment.

The Polymers Are Polypeptides and Proteins

The process of stringing individual amino acids together into a linear polymer involves the stepwise addition of each new amino acid to the growing chain by a *dehydration* (or *condensation*) *reaction*. As the three atoms comprising H_2O are removed, the carboxyl carbon of one amino acid and the amino nitrogen of a second are linked directly. This covalent C—N bond linking two amino acids is known as a **peptide bond,** shown below in bold:

$$H_3N^+ - \overset{\overset{\displaystyle R_1}{\displaystyle |}}{CH} - \overset{\overset{\displaystyle O}{\displaystyle \|}}{C} - O^- \quad + \quad H_3N^+ - \overset{\overset{\displaystyle R_2}{\displaystyle |}}{CH} - \overset{\overset{\displaystyle O}{\displaystyle \|}}{C} - O^- \longrightarrow$$

Amino acid 1   Amino acid 2

$$H_3N^+ - \overset{\overset{\displaystyle R_1}{\displaystyle |}}{CH} - \overset{\overset{\displaystyle O}{\displaystyle \|}}{C} - \overset{\overset{\displaystyle |}{\displaystyle N} \atop \underset{\displaystyle H}{\displaystyle |}}{} - \overset{\overset{\displaystyle R_2}{\displaystyle |}}{CH} - \overset{\overset{\displaystyle O}{\displaystyle \|}}{C} - O^- \quad + \quad H_2O$$

Peptide

As each new peptide bond is formed by dehydration, the growing chain of amino acids is lengthened by one amino acid. Peptide bond formation is illustrated schematically in **Figure 3-3** using ball-and-stick models

of the amino acids glycine and alanine. Because of electron delocalization between the peptide bond and the adjacent carbon-oxygen bond, peptide bonds have partial double-bond character, and thus the six nearest atoms are nearly planar (shaded rectangle in Figure 3-3).

Notice that the chain of amino acids formed in this way has an intrinsic *directionality* because it always has an amino group at one end and a carboxyl group at the other end. The end with the amino group is called the **N- (or amino) terminus,** and the end with the carboxyl group is called the **C- (or carboxyl) terminus.**

Although this process of elongating a chain of amino acids is often called *protein synthesis,* the term is not entirely accurate because the immediate product of amino acid polymerization is not a protein but a **polypeptide.** A protein is a polypeptide chain (or a complex of several polypeptides) that has attained a unique, stable, three-dimensional shape and is biologically active as a result. Some proteins consist of a single polypeptide, and their final shape is due to the folding and coiling that occur spontaneously as the chain is being formed. Such proteins are called **monomeric proteins.** Many other proteins are **multimeric proteins,** consisting of two or more polypeptides that are often called polypeptide subunits.

Be careful with the terminology, though: On the one hand, a polypeptide is a *polymer,* with amino acids as its monomeric repeating units; on the other hand, the entire polypeptide may sometimes be a *monomer* unit that is part of a multimeric protein. If a multimeric protein is composed of two polypeptides, it is referred to as a *dimer;* and if it has three polypeptides, it is known as a *trimer.* The hemoglobin that carries oxygen in your bloodstream is a multimeric protein known as a *tetramer* because it contains four polypeptides, two each of two different types known as the α and the β subunits (**Figure 3-4**). In the case of multimeric proteins, protein synthesis involves not only elongation and folding of the individual polypeptide subunits but also their subsequent interaction and assembly into the multimeric protein.

Several Kinds of Bonds and Interactions Are Important in Protein Folding and Stability

The initial folding of a polypeptide into its proper shape, or **conformation,** depends on several different kinds of bonds and interactions, including the covalent disulfide bond and several noncovalent interactions. In addition, the association of individual polypeptides to form a multimeric protein relies on these same bonds and interactions, which are depicted in **Figure 3-5.** These interactions involve the carboxyl, amino, and R groups of the individual amino acids, which are known as *amino acid residues* once they are incorporated into the polypeptide.

Disulfide Bonds. A special type of covalent bond that contributes to the stabilization of protein conformation is the **disulfide bond,** which forms between the sulfur atoms of two cysteine amino acid residues. These become

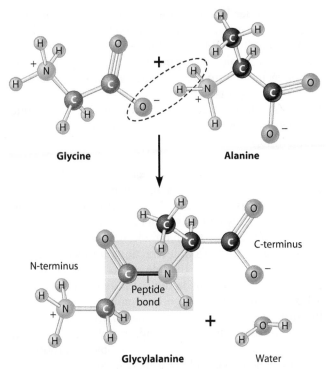

Glycine　　　　　　　**Alanine**

N-terminus　　　　　　　　　　　　C-terminus

Peptide bond

Glycylalanine　　　　Water

FIGURE 3-3 Peptide Bond Formation. Successive amino acids in a polypeptide are linked to one another by peptide bonds that are formed between the carboxyl group of one amino acid and the amino group of the next as a water molecule is removed (dotted oval). Shown here is the formation of a peptide bond between the amino acids glycine and alanine. The six atoms in the shaded rectangle are nearly planar.

covalently linked following an oxidation reaction that removes the two hydrogen atoms from the sulfhydryl groups of the two cysteines, forming a disulfide bond, shown below in bold and in Figure 3-5a:

$$HC-CH_2-SH \quad + \quad HS-CH_2-CH$$

$$\downarrow \quad 2H$$

$$HC-CH_2-S-S-CH_2-CH$$

Once formed, a disulfide bond confers considerable stability to the structure of the protein because of its covalent nature. It can be broken only by reducing it again—by adding two hydrogen atoms and regenerating the two sulfhydryl groups in the reverse of the reaction above. In many cases, the cysteine residues involved in a particular disulfide bond are a part of the same polypeptide. They may be quite distant from each other along the polypeptide but are brought close together by the folding process. Such *intramolecular disulfide bonds* stabilize the conformation of the polypeptide. In the case of multimeric proteins, a disulfide bond may form between cysteine residues located in two different polypeptides. Such *intermolecular disulfide bonds* link the two polypeptides to one another covalently. The hormone insulin is a dimeric protein that has its two subunits linked in this manner.

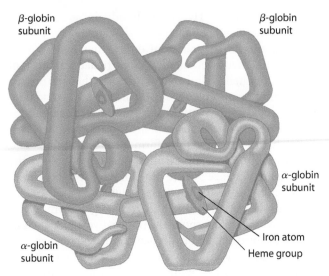

β-globin subunit　　　　　　　β-globin subunit

α-globin subunit

Iron atom
Heme group

α-globin subunit

FIGURE 3-4 The Structure of Hemoglobin. Hemoglobin is a multimeric protein composed of four polypeptide subunits (two α chains and two β chains). Each subunit contains a heme group with an iron atom that can bind a single oxygen molecule.

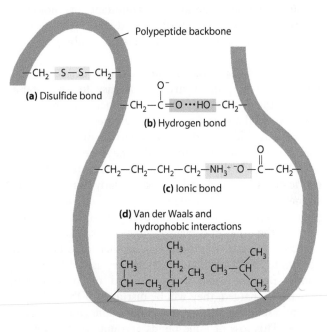

Polypeptide backbone

$-CH_2-S-S-CH_2-$

(a) Disulfide bond

$-CH_2-C=O \cdots HO-CH_2-$

(b) Hydrogen bond

$-CH_2-CH_2-CH_2-CH_2-NH_3^+ \ ^-O-C-CH_2-$

(c) Ionic bond

(d) Van der Waals and hydrophobic interactions

FIGURE 3-5 Bonds and Interactions Involved in Protein Folding and Stability. The initial folding and subsequent stability of a polypeptide depend on **(a)** covalent disulfide bonds as well as on several kinds of noncovalent bonds and interactions, including **(b)** hydrogen bonds, **(c)** ionic bonds, **(d)** van der Waals interactions, and hydrophobic interactions.

In addition to covalent disulfide bonds, **noncovalent bonds and interactions** are also important in maintaining protein structure. Although individually much weaker than covalent bonds, they are diverse and numerous and collectively exert a powerful influence on protein structure and stability. These include *hydrogen bonds, ionic bonds, van der Waals interactions,* and *hydrophobic interactions* (see Figure 3-5).

Proteins　**45**

Hydrogen Bonds. **Hydrogen bonds** in water, forms between a covalently bonded hydrogen atom on one water molecule and an oxygen atom on another molecule. In polypeptides, hydrogen bonding is particularly important in stabilizing helical and sheet structures that are prominent parts of many proteins, as we will soon see. In addition, the R groups of many amino acids have functional groups that are able to participate in hydrogen bonding. This allows hydrogen bonds to form between amino acid residues that may be distant from one another along the amino acid sequence but are brought into close proximity by the folding of the polypeptide (Figure 3-5b).

Hydrogen bond *donors* have a hydrogen atom that is covalently linked to a more electronegative atom, such as oxygen or nitrogen, and hydrogen bond *acceptors* have an electronegative atom that attracts this hydrogen atom. Examples of good donors include the hydroxyl groups of several amino acids and the amino groups of others. The carbonyl and sulfhydryl groups of several other amino acids are examples of good acceptors. An individual hydrogen bond is quite weak (about 2–5 kcal/mol, compared to 70–100 kcal/mol for covalent bonds). But because hydrogen bonds are abundant in biological macromolecules such as proteins and DNA, they become a formidable force when present in large numbers.

Ionic Bonds. The role of **ionic bonds** (or *electrostatic interactions*) in protein structure is easy to understand. Because the R groups of some amino acids are positively charged and the R groups of others are negatively charged, polypeptide folding is dictated in part by the tendency of charged groups to repel groups with the same charge and to attract groups with the opposite charge (Figure 3-5c). Several features of ionic bonds are particularly significant. The strength of such interactions—about 3 kcal/mol—allows them to exert an attractive force over greater distances than some of the other noncovalent interactions. Moreover, the attractive force is nondirectional, so that ionic bonds are not limited to discrete angles, as is the case with covalent bonds. Because ionic bonds depend on both groups remaining charged, they will be disrupted if the pH value becomes so high or so low that either of the groups loses its charge. This loss of ionic bonds accounts in part for the denaturation that most proteins undergo at high or low pH.

Van der Waals Interactions. Interactions based on charge are not limited to ions that carry a discrete charge. Even molecules with nonpolar covalent bonds may have transient positively and negatively charged regions. Momentary asymmetries in the distribution of electrons and hence in the separation of charge within a molecule are called *dipoles*. When two molecules that have such transient dipoles are very close to each other and are oriented appropriately, they are attracted to each other, though for only as long as the asymmetric electron distribution persists in both molecules. This transient attraction of two nonpolar molecules is called a **van der Waals interaction,** or *van der Waals force* (Figure 3-5d). A single such interaction is transient and very weak—typically 0.1–0.2 kcal/mol—and is effective only when the two molecules are quite close together—within 0.2 nm of each other, in fact. Van der Waals interactions are nonetheless important in the structure of proteins and other biological macromolecules, as well as in the binding together of two molecules with complementary surfaces that fit closely together.

Hydrophobic Interactions. The fourth type of noncovalent interaction that plays a role in maintaining protein conformation is usually called a **hydrophobic interaction,** but it is not really a bond or interaction at all. Rather, it is the tendency of hydrophobic molecules or parts of molecules to be excluded from interactions with water (Figure 3-5d). As already noted, the side chains of the 20 different amino acids vary greatly in their affinity for water. Amino acids with hydrophilic R groups tend to be located near the surface of a folded polypeptide, where they can interact maximally with the surrounding water molecules. In contrast, amino acids with hydrophobic R groups are essentially nonpolar and are usually located on the inside of the polypeptide, where they interact with one another because they are excluded by water.

Thus, polypeptide folding to form the final protein structure is, in part, a balance between the tendency of hydrophilic groups to seek an aqueous environment near the surface of the molecule and the tendency of hydrophobic groups to minimize contact with water by associating with each other in the interior of the molecule. If most of the amino acids in a protein were hydrophobic, the protein would be virtually insoluble in water and would be found instead in a nonpolar environment. Membrane proteins, which have many hydrophobic residues, are localized in membranes for this very reason. Similarly, if all or most of the amino acids were hydrophilic, the polypeptide would most likely remain in a fairly distended, random shape, allowing maximum access of each amino acid to an aqueous environment. But precisely because most polypeptide chains contain both hydrophobic and hydrophilic amino acids, hydrophilic regions of the molecule are drawn toward the surface, whereas hydrophobic regions are driven toward the interior.

Overall, then, the stability of the folded structure of a polypeptide depends on an interplay of covalent disulfide bonds and four noncovalent factors: hydrogen bonds between R groups that are good donors and good acceptors, ionic bonds between charged amino acid R groups, transient van der Waals interactions between nonpolar molecules in very close proximity, and hydrophobic interactions that drive nonpolar groups to the interior of the molecule.

The final conformation of the fully folded polypeptide is the net result of these forces and tendencies. Individually, each of these noncovalent interactions is quite low in energy. However, the cumulative effect of many of them—

Table 3-3   Levels of Organization of Protein Structure

Level of Structure	Basis of Structure	Kinds of Bonds and Interactions Involved
Primary	Amino acid sequence	Covalent peptide bonds
Secondary	Folding into α helix, β sheet, or random coil	Hydrogen bonds
Tertiary	Three-dimensional folding of a single polypeptide chain	Disulfide bonds, hydrogen bonds, ionic bonds, van der Waals interactions, hydrophobic interactions
Quaternary	Association of multiple polypeptides to form a multimeric protein	Same as for tertiary structure

involving the side groups of the hundreds of amino acids that make up a typical polypeptide—greatly stabilizes the conformation of the folded polypeptide.

Protein Structure Depends on Amino Acid Sequence and Interactions

The overall shape and structure of a protein are usually described in terms of four hierarchical levels of organization, each building on the previous one: the *primary, secondary, tertiary,* and *quaternary* structures (Table 3-3). Primary structure refers to the amino acid sequence, while the higher levels of organization concern the interactions between the amino acid residues. These interactions give the protein its characteristic *conformation*, or three-dimensional arrangement of atoms in space (Figure 3-6).

Secondary structure involves local interactions between amino acid residues that are close together along the chain, whereas tertiary structure results from long-distance interactions between stretches of amino acid residues from different parts of the molecule. Quaternary structure concerns the interaction of two or more individual polypeptides to form a single multimeric protein. All three of these higher-level structures are dictated by the primary structure, but each is important in its own right in the overall structure of the protein. Secondary and tertiary structures are involved in determining the conformation of the individual polypeptide, while quaternary structure is relevant for proteins consisting of more than one polypeptide.

Primary Structure. As already noted, the **primary structure** of a protein is a formal designation for the amino acid sequence (Figure 3-6a). When we describe the primary structure, we are simply specifying the order in which its amino acids appear from one end of the molecule to the other. By convention, amino acid sequences are

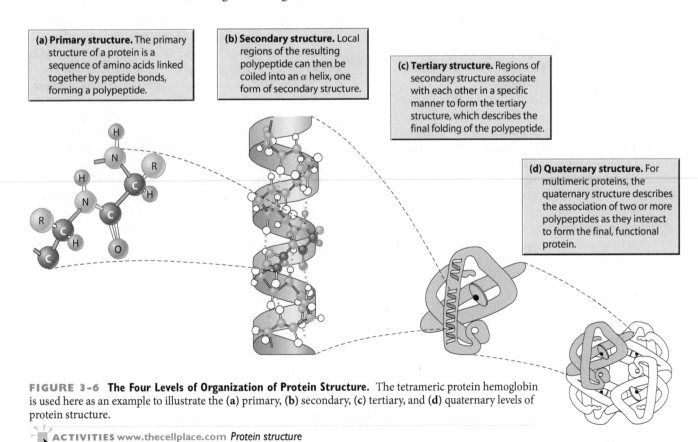

(a) Primary structure. The primary structure of a protein is a sequence of amino acids linked together by peptide bonds, forming a polypeptide.

(b) Secondary structure. Local regions of the resulting polypeptide can then be coiled into an α helix, one form of secondary structure.

(c) Tertiary structure. Regions of secondary structure associate with each other in a specific manner to form the tertiary structure, which describes the final folding of the polypeptide.

(d) Quaternary structure. For multimeric proteins, the quaternary structure describes the association of two or more polypeptides as they interact to form the final, functional protein.

FIGURE 3-6 The Four Levels of Organization of Protein Structure. The tetrameric protein hemoglobin is used here as an example to illustrate the **(a)** primary, **(b)** secondary, **(c)** tertiary, and **(d)** quaternary levels of protein structure.

ACTIVITIES www.thecellplace.com *Protein structure*

always written from the N-terminus to the C-terminus of the polypeptide, which is also the direction in which the polypeptide is synthesized.

The first protein to have its complete amino acid sequence determined was the hormone *insulin*. This important technical advance was reported in 1956 by Frederick Sanger, who eventually received a Nobel Prize for the work. To determine the sequence of the insulin molecule, Sanger cleaved it into smaller fragments and analyzed the amino acid order within individual, overlapping fragments. Insulin consists of two polypeptides, called the *A subunit* and the *B subunit*, with 21 and 30 amino acid residues, respectively. **Figure 3-7** shows the primary structure of insulin, illustrating the primary sequence of each subunit in sequence from its N-terminus (left) to its C-terminus (right). Notice also the covalent disulfide (—S—S—) bond between two cysteine residues within the A chain and the two disulfide bonds linking the A and B chains. As we will see shortly, disulfide bonds play an important role in stabilizing the tertiary structure of many proteins.

Sanger's techniques paved the way for the sequencing of hundreds of other proteins and led ultimately to the design of machines that can determine an amino acid sequence automatically. A more recent approach for determining protein sequences has emerged from the understanding that nucleotide sequences in DNA code for the amino acid sequences of protein molecules. It is now much easier to determine a DNA nucleotide sequence than to purify a protein and analyze its amino acid sequence. Once a DNA nucleotide sequence has been determined, the amino acid sequence of the polypeptide encoded by that DNA segment can be easily determined. Computerized data banks are now available that contain thousands of polypeptide sequences, making it easy to compare sequences and look for regions of similarity between polypeptides.

The primary structure of a protein is important both genetically and structurally. Genetically, it is significant because the amino acid sequence of the polypeptide is determined by the order of nucleotides in the corresponding messenger RNA. The messenger RNA is in turn encoded by the DNA that represents the gene for this protein, so the primary structure of a protein is the result of the order of nucleotides in the DNA of the gene.

Of more immediate significance are the implications of the primary structure for higher levels of protein structure.

In essence, all three higher levels of protein organization are direct consequences of the primary structure. Thus, if synthetic polypeptides are made that correspond in sequence to the α and β subunits of hemoglobin, they will assume the native three-dimensional conformations of these subunits and will then interact spontaneously to form the native $\alpha_2\beta_2$ tetramer that we recognize as hemoglobin (see Figure 3-4).

Secondary Structure. The **secondary structure** of a protein describes local regions of structure that result from hydrogen bonding between NH and CO groups along the polypeptide backbone. These local interactions result in two major structural patterns, referred to as the α **helix** and β **sheet** conformations (**Figure 3-8**).

The α helix structure was proposed in 1951 by Linus Pauling and Robert Corey. As shown in Figure 3-8a, an α helix is spiral in shape, consisting of a backbone of amino acids linked by peptide bonds with the specific R groups of the individual amino acid residues jutting out from it. A helical shape is common to repeating polymers, as we will see when we get to the nucleic acids and the polysaccharides. In the α helix there are 3.6 amino acids per turn, bringing the peptide bonds of every fourth amino acid in close proximity. The distance between these peptide bonds is, in fact, just right for the formation of a hydrogen bond between the NH group adjacent to one peptide bond and the CO group adjacent to the other, as shown in Figure 3-8a.

As a result, every peptide bond in the helix is hydrogen-bonded through its CO group to the peptide bond immediately "below" it in the spiral and through its NH group to the peptide bond just "above" it, even though the amino acid residues involved are not directly adjacent. These hydrogen bonds are all nearly parallel to the main axis of the helix and therefore tend to stabilize the spiral structure by holding successive turns of the helix together.

Another form of common secondary structure in proteins is the β sheet, also initially proposed by Pauling and Corey. As shown in Figure 3-8b, this structure is an extended sheetlike conformation with successive atoms in the polypeptide chain located at the "peaks" and "troughs" of the pleats. The R groups of successive amino acids jut out on alternating sides of the sheet. Because the carbon atoms that make up the backbone of the polypeptide chain are successively located a little above and a little below the plane of the β sheet, such structures are sometimes called

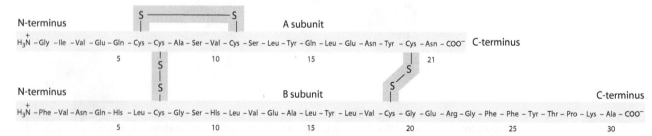

FIGURE 3-7 The Primary Structure of Insulin. Insulin consists of two polypeptides, called the A and B subunits, each shown here from the N-terminus to the C-terminus. The two subunits are covalently linked by two disulfide bonds. (For abbreviations of amino acids, see Table 3-2.)

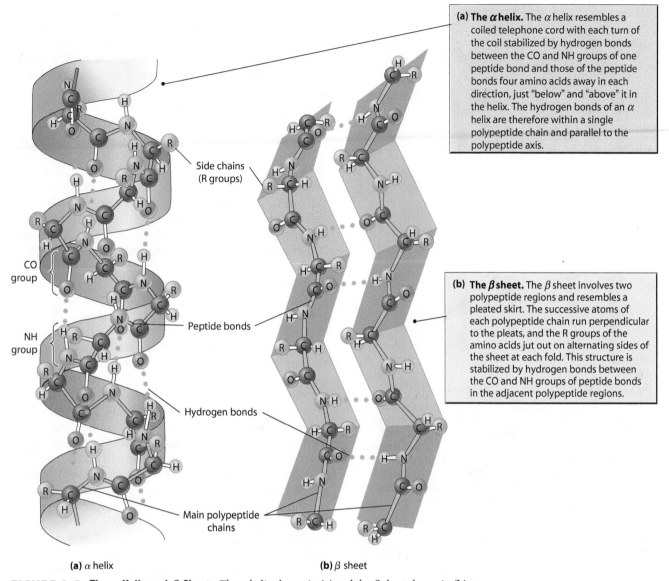

(a) The α helix. The α helix resembles a coiled telephone cord with each turn of the coil stabilized by hydrogen bonds between the CO and NH groups of one peptide bond and those of the peptide bonds four amino acids away in each direction, just "below" and "above" it in the helix. The hydrogen bonds of an α helix are therefore within a single polypeptide chain and parallel to the polypeptide axis.

(b) The β sheet. The β sheet involves two polypeptide regions and resembles a pleated skirt. The successive atoms of each polypeptide chain run perpendicular to the pleats, and the R groups of the amino acids jut out on alternating sides of the sheet at each fold. This structure is stabilized by hydrogen bonds between the CO and NH groups of peptide bonds in the adjacent polypeptide regions.

Side chains (R groups)

CO group

NH group

Peptide bonds

Hydrogen bonds

Main polypeptide chains

(a) α helix

(b) β sheet

FIGURE 3-8   The α Helix and β Sheet. The α helix shown in (**a**) and the β sheet shown in (**b**) are important elements in the secondary structure of proteins. Both are stabilized by hydrogen bonds (blue dots), either within a local region of primary sequence (α helix) or between two separate regions (β sheet).

VIDEOS www.thecellplace.com *An idealized alpha helix; An idealized beta-pleated sheet*

β-pleated sheets. Whether a local amino acid sequence forms an α helix or a β sheet depends on the particular combination of amino acids present.

Like the α helix, the β sheet is characterized by a maximum of hydrogen bonding. In both cases, all of the CO groups and NH groups adjacent to the peptide bonds are involved. However, hydrogen bonding in an α helix is invariably intramolecular (within the same polypeptide), whereas hydrogen bonding in the β sheet can be either intramolecular (between two segments of the same polypeptide) or intermolecular (linking two different polypeptides). The protein regions that form β sheets can interact with each other in two different ways. If the two interacting regions run in the same N-terminus-to-C-terminus direction, the structure is called a *parallel β sheet*; if the two strands run in opposite N-terminus-to-C-terminus directions, the structure is called an *antiparallel β sheet*.

Whether a specific segment of a polypeptide will form an α helix, a β sheet, or neither depends on the amino acids present in that segment. For example, leucine, methionine, and glutamate are strong "α helix formers," meaning they are commonly found in α-helical regions. Isoleucine, valine, and phenylalanine are strong "β sheet formers," often being found in β-sheet regions. Proline is considered a "helix breaker" because its R group is covalently bonded to its amino nitrogen, which therefore lacks the hydrogen atom needed for hydrogen bonding. Proline is rarely found in an α helix and, when present, introduces a bend in the helix.

To depict localized regions of structure within a protein, biochemists have adopted the conventions shown in **Figure 3-9**. An α-helical region is represented as either a spiral or a cylinder, whereas a β-sheet region is drawn as a flat ribbon or arrow with the arrowhead pointing in the

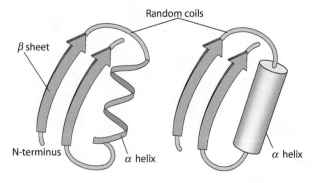

(a) β-α-β motif with α helix represented as a spiral (left) or a cylinder (right)

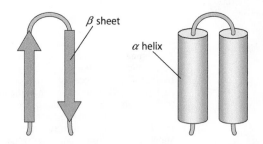

(b) Hairpin loop motif

(c) Helix-turn-helix motif

FIGURE 3-9 Common Structural Motifs. These short sections of polypeptides show three common units of secondary structure: the **(a)** β-α-β, **(b)** hairpin loop, and **(c)** helix-turn-helix motifs. An α helix can be represented as either a spiral or a cylinder, whereas a β sheet is represented as a flat ribbon or arrow pointing toward the C terminus. In (a), the β sheets are parallel; in (b), they are anti-parallel. The short segments (green) connecting α helices and β sheets are called random coils and have no defined secondary structure.

direction of the C-terminus. A looped segment that connects α-helical and/or β-sheet regions is called a *random coil* and is depicted as a narrow cord.

Certain combinations of α helices and β sheets have been identified in many proteins. These units of secondary structure, called **motifs,** consist of small segments of an α helix and/or β sheet connected to each other by looped regions of varying length. Among the most commonly encountered motifs are the β-α-β motif shown in Figure 3-9a and the hairpin loop and helix-turn-helix motifs depicted in Figure 3-9, parts b and c, respectively. When the same motif is present in different proteins, it usually serves the same purpose in each. For example, the helix-turn-helix motif is one of several secondary structure motifs that are characteristic of the DNA-binding proteins we will encounter when we consider the regulation of gene expression.

Tertiary Structure. The **tertiary structure** of a protein can probably be best understood by contrasting it with the secondary structure (Figure 3-6b, c). Secondary structure is a predictable, repeating conformational pattern that derives from the repetitive nature of the polypeptide

because it involves hydrogen bonding between NH and CO groups adjacent to peptide bonds—the common structural elements along every polypeptide chain. If proteins contained only one or a few kinds of similar amino acids, virtually all aspects of protein conformation could probably be understood in terms of secondary structure, with only modest variations among proteins.

Tertiary structure comes about precisely because of the variety of amino acids present in proteins and the very different chemical properties of their R groups. In fact, tertiary structure depends almost entirely on interactions between the various R groups, regardless of where along the primary sequence they happen to be. Tertiary structure therefore reflects the nonrepetitive and unique aspect of each polypeptide because it depends not on the CO and NH groups common to all of the amino acids in the chain but instead on the very feature that makes each amino acid distinctive—its R group.

Tertiary structure is neither repetitive nor readily predictable; it involves competing interactions between side groups with different properties. Hydrophobic R groups, for example, spontaneously seek out a nonaqueous environment in the interior of the molecule while polar amino acids are drawn to the surface. Oppositely charged R groups can form ionic bonds, while similarly charged groups will repel each other. As a result, the polypeptide chain will be folded, coiled, and twisted into the **native conformation**—the most stable three-dimensional structure for that particular sequence of amino acids.

The relative contributions of secondary and tertiary structures to the overall shape of a polypeptide vary from protein to protein and depend critically on the relative proportions and sequence of amino acids in the chain. Broadly speaking, proteins can be divided into two categories: *fibrous proteins* and *globular proteins*.

Fibrous proteins have extensive secondary structure (either α helix or β sheet) throughout the molecule, giving them a highly ordered, repetitive structure. In general, secondary structure is much more important than tertiary interactions are in determining the shape of fibrous proteins, which often have an extended, filamentous structure. Especially prominent examples of fibrous proteins include the *fibroin* protein of silk and the *keratins* of hair and wool, as well as *collagen* (found in tendons and skin) and *elastin* (present in ligaments and blood vessels).

The amino acid sequence of each of these proteins favors a particular kind of secondary structure, which in turn confers a specific set of desirable mechanical properties on the protein. Fibroin, for example, consists mainly of long stretches of antiparallel β sheets, with the polypeptide chains running parallel to the axis of the silk fiber but in opposite directions. The most prevalent amino acids in fibroin are glycine, alanine, and serine. These amino acids have small R groups that pack together well (see Figure 3-2). The result is a silk fiber that is strong and relatively inextensible because the polypeptide chains in a β-sheet conformation are already stretched to nearly their maximum possible length.

Hair and wool fibers, on the other hand, consist of the protein α-keratin, which is almost entirely α helical. The individual keratin molecules are very long and lie with their helix axes nearly parallel to the fiber axis. As a result, hair is quite extensible because stretching of the fiber is opposed not by the covalent bonds of the polypeptide chain, as in β sheets, but by the hydrogen bonds that stabilize the α-helical structure. The individual α helices in a hair are wound together to form a strong, ropelike structure, as shown in **Figure 3-10**. First, two keratin α helices are coiled around each other, and two of these coiled pairs associate to form a protofilament containing four α helices. Groups of eight protofilaments then interact to form intermediate filaments, which bundle together to form the actual hair fiber. Not surprisingly, the α-keratin polypeptides in hair are rich in hydrophobic residues that interact with each other where the helices touch, allowing the tight packing of the filaments in hair.

As important as fibrous proteins may be, they represent only a small fraction of the kinds of proteins present in most cells. Most of the proteins involved in cellular structure are **globular proteins,** so named because their polypeptide chains are folded into compact structures rather than extended filaments. The polypeptide chain of a globular protein is often folded locally into regions with α-helical or β-sheet structures, and these regions of secondary structure are themselves folded on one another to give the protein its compact, globular shape. This folding is possible because regions of α helix or β sheet are interspersed with random coils, irregularly structured regions that allow the polypeptide chain to loop and fold (see Figure 3-9). Thus, every globular protein has its own unique tertiary structure, made up of secondary structural elements (helices and sheets) folded in a specific way that is especially suited to the particular functional role of that protein.

Figure 3-11 shows the native tertiary structure of ribonuclease, a typical globular protein. We encountered ribonuclease in as an example of the denaturation and renaturation of a polypeptide and the spontaneity of its folding. Two different conventions are used in Figure 3-11 to represent the structure of ribonuclease: the *ball-and-stick* model used in Figure 3-8 and the *spiral-and-ribbon* model used in Figure 3-9. For clarity, most of the side chains of ribonuclease have been omitted in both models. The groups shown in gold in Figure 3-11a are the four disulfide bonds that help to stabilize the tertiary structure of ribonuclease.

Globular proteins can be mainly α helical, mainly β sheet, or a mixture of both structures. These categories are illustrated in **Figure 3-12** by the coat protein of tobacco mosaic virus (TMV), a portion of an immunoglobulin (antibody) molecule, and a portion of the enzyme hexokinase, respectively. Helical segments of globular proteins often consist of bundles of helices, as seen for the coat protein of TMV in Figure 3-12a. Segments with mainly β-sheet structure are usually characterized by a barrel-like configuration (Figure 3-12b) or by a twisted sheet (Figure 3-12c).

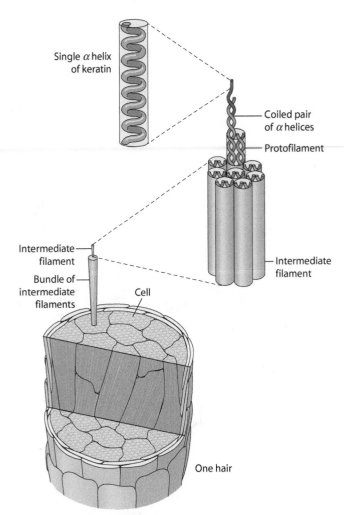

FIGURE 3-10 The Structure of Hair. The main structural protein of hair is α-keratin, a fibrous protein with an α-helical shape. The individual α helices in a hair are wound together to form a strong, ropelike structure. Two keratin α helices are coiled around each other, and two of these coiled pairs associate to form a protofilament containing four α helices. Groups of eight protofilaments then interact to form intermediate filaments, which then bundle together to form the hair fibers (see also Figure 15-23).

Many globular proteins consist of a number of segments called domains. A **domain** is a discrete, locally folded unit of tertiary structure that usually has a specific function. Each domain typically includes 50–350 amino acids, with regions of α helices and β sheets packed together compactly. Small globular proteins are usually folded into a single domain (Figure 3-11b). Large globular proteins usually have multiple domains. The portions of the immunoglobulin and hexokinase molecules shown in Figure 3-12, parts b and c, are, in fact, specific domains of these proteins. **Figure 3-13** shows an example of a protein that consists of a single polypeptide folded into two functional domains.

Proteins that have similar functions (such as binding a specific ion or recognizing a specific molecule) usually have a common domain containing a sequence of identical or very similar amino acid residues. Moreover, proteins

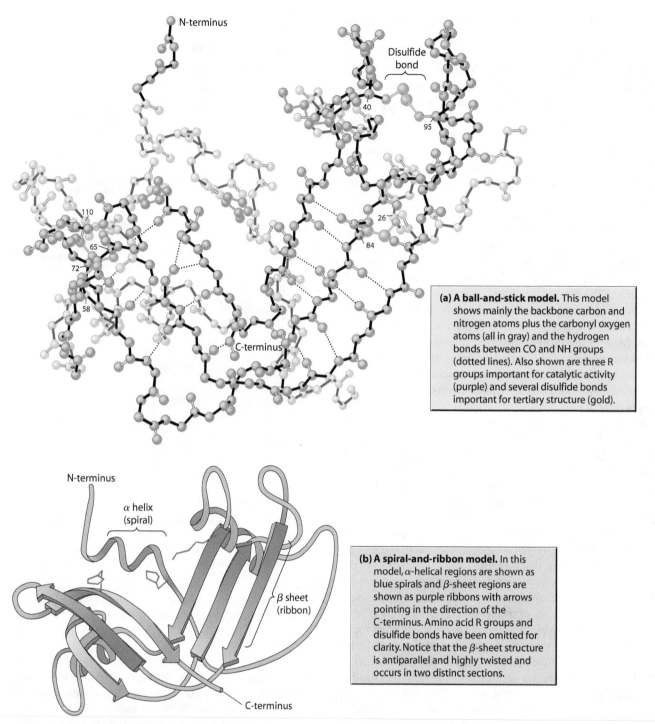

(a) **A ball-and-stick model.** This model shows mainly the backbone carbon and nitrogen atoms plus the carbonyl oxygen atoms (all in gray) and the hydrogen bonds between CO and NH groups (dotted lines). Also shown are three R groups important for catalytic activity (purple) and several disulfide bonds important for tertiary structure (gold).

(b) **A spiral-and-ribbon model.** In this model, α-helical regions are shown as blue spirals and β-sheet regions are shown as purple ribbons with arrows pointing in the direction of the C-terminus. Amino acid R groups and disulfide bonds have been omitted for clarity. Notice that the β-sheet structure is antiparallel and highly twisted and occurs in two distinct sections.

FIGURE 3-11 **The Three-Dimensional Structure of Ribonuclease.** Ribonuclease is a monomeric globular protein with significant α-helical and β-sheet segments connected by random coils. Its tertiary structure can be represented either by (a) a ball-and-stick model or by (b) a spiral-and-ribbon model.

with multiple functions usually have a separate domain for each function. Thus, domains can be thought of as the modular units of function from which globular proteins are constructed. Many different types of domains have been described in proteins and given names such as the immunoglobulin domain, the kringle domain, or the death domain. Each type is composed of a particular combination of α-helix and β-sheet secondary structures that give the domain a specific function.

Before leaving the topic of tertiary structure, we should emphasize again the dependence of these higher levels of organization on the primary structure of the polypeptide. The significance of primary structure is exemplified especially well by the inherited condition *sickle-cell anemia*. People with this trait have red blood cells that are distorted from their normal disk shape into a "sickle" shape, which causes the abnormal cells to clog blood vessels and impede blood flow, limiting oxygen availability in the tissues.

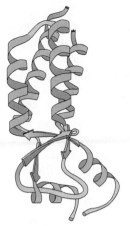

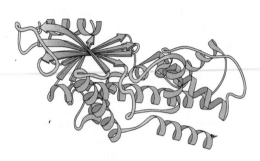

Tobacco mosaic virus coat protein	Immunoglobulin, V₂ domain	Hexokinase, domain 2
(a) Predominantly α helix	**(b)** Predominantly β sheet	**(c)** Mixed α helix and β sheet

FIGURE 3-12 **Structures of Several Globular Proteins.** Shown here are proteins with different tertiary structures: **(a)** a predominantly α-helical structure (blue spirals), the coat protein of tobacco mosaic virus (TMV); **(b)** a mainly β-sheet structure (purple ribbons with arrows), the V₂ domain of immunoglobulin; and **(c)** a structure that mixes α helices and β sheets, domain 2 of hexokinase. The immunoglobulin V₂ domain is an example of an antiparallel β-barrel structure, whereas the hexokinase domain 2 illustrates a twisted β sheet. (Green segments are random coils.)

This condition is caused by a slight change in the hemoglobin molecule within the red blood cells. In people with sickle-cell anemia, the hemoglobin molecules have normal α polypeptide chains, but their β chains have a single amino acid that is different. At one specific position in the chain (the sixth amino acid residue from the N-terminus), the glutamate normally present is replaced by valine. This single substitution (written as E6V) causes enough of a difference in the tertiary structure of the β chain that the hemoglobin molecules tend to crystallize, deforming the cell into a sickle shape. Not all amino acid substitutions cause such dramatic changes in structure and function, but this example underscores the crucial relationship between the amino acid sequence of a polypeptide and the final shape and biological activity of the molecule.

Although we know that the primary sequence of a protein determines its final folded shape, we still are not able to predict exactly how a given protein will fold, especially for large proteins (more than 100 amino acids). In fact, one of the most challenging unsolved problems in structural biochemistry is to predict the final folded tertiary structure of a protein from its known primary structure. Even with all our knowledge of the factors and forces involved in folding, and the availability of supercomputers to do billions of calculations per second, we cannot often predict the most stable conformation for a given protein.

In fact, in every other year since 1994, protein modelers worldwide test their predictive methods in a major modeling experiment known as CASP—the critical assessment of techniques for protein structure prediction. Their predictions are compared to subsequently released three-dimensional protein structures, and the results are published in a special issue of the journal *Proteins: Structure, Function and Bioinformatics.* One of the goals of this modeling research is for drug discovery—the ability to design therapeutic agents able to bind to specific regions of a protein involved in human disease.

FIGURE 3-13 **An Example of a Protein Containing Two Functional Domains.** This model of the enzyme glyceraldehyde phosphate dehydrogenase shows a single polypeptide chain folded into two domains. One domain binds to the substance being metabolized, whereas the other domain binds to a chemical factor required for the reaction to occur. The two domains are indicated by different shadings.

Quaternary Structure. The **quaternary structure** of a protein is the level of organization concerned with subunit interactions and assembly (see Figure 3-6d). Quaternary structure therefore applies only to multimeric proteins. Many proteins are included in this category, particularly those with molecular weights above 50,000. Hemoglobin, for example, is a multimeric protein with two α chains and two β chains (see Figure 3-4). Some multimeric proteins contain identical polypeptide subunits; others, such as hemoglobin, contain two or more different kinds of polypeptides.

The bonds and forces that maintain quaternary structure are the same as those responsible for tertiary structure: hydrogen bonds, electrostatic interactions, van der Waals interactions, hydrophobic interactions, and covalent disulfide bonds. As noted earlier, disulfide bonds may be either within a polypeptide chain or between chains. When they occur within a polypeptide, they stabilize tertiary structure. When they occur between polypeptides, they help maintain quaternary structure, holding the individual polypeptides together (see Figure 3-7). As in the case of polypeptide folding, the process of subunit assembly is often, though not always, spontaneous. Most, if not all, of the requisite information is provided by the amino acid sequence of the individual polypeptides, but often molecular chaperones are required to ensure proper assembly.

In some cases a still higher level of assembly is possible in the sense that two or more proteins (often enzymes) are organized into a **multiprotein complex,** with each protein involved sequentially in a common multistep process. An example of such a complex is an enzyme system called the *pyruvate dehydrogenase complex.* This complex catalyzes the oxidative removal of a carbon atom (as CO_2) from the three-carbon compound pyruvate (or pyruvic acid), a reaction that will be of interest to us. Three individual enzymes and five kinds of molecules called coenzymes constitute a highly organized *multienzyme complex.* The pyruvate dehydrogenase complex is one of the best understood examples of how cells can achieve economy of function by ordering the enzymes that catalyze sequential reactions into a single multienzyme complex. Other multiprotein complexes we will encounter in our studies include ribosomes, proteosomes, the photosystems, and the DNA replication complex.

Nucleic Acids

Next, we come to the **nucleic acids,** macromolecules of paramount importance to the cell because of their role in storing, transmitting, and expressing genetic information. Nucleic acids are linear polymers of nucleotides strung together in a genetically determined order that is critical to their role as informational macromolecules. The two major types of nucleic acids are **DNA (deoxyribonucleic acid)** and **RNA (ribonucleic acid).** DNA and RNA differ in their chemistry and their role in the cell. As the names suggest, RNA contains the five-carbon sugar **ribose** in each of its nucleotides, whereas DNA contains the closely related sugar **deoxyribose.** Functionally, DNA serves primarily as the repository of genetic information, whereas RNA molecules play several different roles in expressing that information—that is, in protein synthesis.

The primary roles of DNA and RNA in a typical plant or animal cell are shown in **Figure 3-14.** Most of the DNA in a cell is located in the nucleus, the major site of RNA synthesis in the cell. ❶ *Transcription*: A specific segment of a DNA molecule known as a gene directs the synthesis of a complementary molecule of *messenger RNA (mRNA)*. Each gene contains the information to produce a specific polypeptide using this mRNA. ❷ *mRNA export*: Following processing to remove introns (and in some cases RNA editing to alter specific bases), the mRNA leaves the nucleus through *nuclear pores*—tiny channels in the nuclear membrane—and enters the cytoplasm. ❸ *Translation (polypeptide synthesis)*: A ribosome, which is a complex of ribosomal proteins and *ribosomal RNA (rRNA)* molecules, attaches to the mRNA to read the coded information. As the ribosome moves down the mRNA, *transfer RNA (tRNA)* molecules bring the correct amino acids to be added to the growing polypeptide chain in the order specified by the information in the mRNA. These roles of DNA and RNA in the storage, transmission, and expression of genetic information will be considered in detail in Chapters 18–22.

In addition to these three main types of RNA, several others have been discovered in recent years. Many, if not all, eukaryotic cells contain a wide variety of *small RNAs* of 20–30 nucleotides that function as regulatory molecules. *MicroRNAs (miRNAs)* are small endogenous RNAs that down-regulate the expression of specific genes by binding to their mRNAs and either promoting mRNA degradation or inhibiting translation. They are important in regulating genes involved in embryonic development and cell proliferation, and abnormal regulation by miRNAs is associated with certain human diseases. Other small RNAs known as *small interfering RNAs (siRNAs)* are derived from exogenous sources (e.g., infection by an RNA virus) and can inhibit either transcription or translation. Use of siRNAs to target specific mRNAs for destruction is being actively explored as a way to silence genes known to contribute to human disease. For now we will focus on the chemistry of nucleic acids and nucleotides.

The Monomers Are Nucleotides

Nucleic acids are informational macromolecules and contain nonidentical monomeric units in a specified sequence. The monomeric units of nucleic acids are called **nucleotides.** Nucleotides exhibit less variety than amino acids do; DNA and RNA each contain only four different kinds of nucleotides. (Actually, there is more variety than this suggests, especially in some RNA molecules in which some nucleotides have been chemically modified after insertion into the chain.)

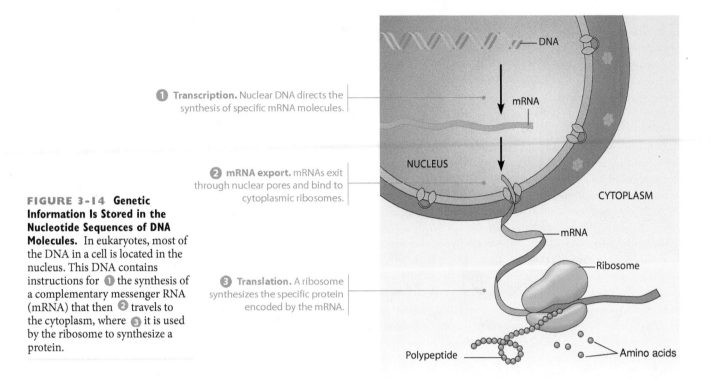

FIGURE 3-14 **Genetic Information Is Stored in the Nucleotide Sequences of DNA Molecules.** In eukaryotes, most of the DNA in a cell is located in the nucleus. This DNA contains instructions for ❶ the synthesis of a complementary messenger RNA (mRNA) that then ❷ travels to the cytoplasm, where ❸ it is used by the ribosome to synthesize a protein.

❶ Transcription. Nuclear DNA directs the synthesis of specific mRNA molecules.

❷ mRNA export. mRNAs exit through nuclear pores and bind to cytoplasmic ribosomes.

❸ Translation. A ribosome synthesizes the specific protein encoded by the mRNA.

As shown in **Figure 3-15**, each nucleotide consists of a five-carbon sugar to which is attached a phosphate group and a nitrogen-containing aromatic base. The sugar is either D-ribose (in RNA) or D-deoxyribose (in DNA). The phosphate is joined by a phosphoester bond to the 5′ carbon of the sugar, and the base is attached to the 1′ carbon. The base may be either a **purine** or a **pyrimidine**. DNA contains the purines **adenine (A)** and **guanine (G)** and the pyrimidines **cytosine (C)** and **thymine (T)**. RNA also has adenine, guanine, and cytosine, but it contains the pyrimidine **uracil (U)** in place of thymine. Like the 20 amino acids present in proteins, these five aromatic bases are among the most common small molecules in cells (see Table 3-1).

Without the phosphate, the remaining base-sugar unit is called a **nucleoside**. Each pyrimidine and purine may therefore occur as the free base, the nucleoside, or the nucleotide. The appropriate names for these compounds are given in **Table 3-4**. Notice that nucleotides and nucleosides containing deoxyribose are specified by a lowercase d preceding the letters identifying the base.

As the nomenclature indicates, a nucleotide can be thought of as a **nucleoside monophosphate** because it is a nucleoside with a single phosphate group attached to it. This terminology can be readily extended to molecules with two or three phosphate groups attached to the 5′ carbon. For example, the nucleoside adenosine (adenine plus ribose) can have one, two, or three phosphates attached and is designated accordingly as **adenosine monophosphate (AMP)**, **adenosine diphosphate (ADP)**, or **adenosine triphosphate (ATP)**. The relationships among these compounds are shown in **Figure 3-16**.

You probably recognize ATP as the energy-rich compound used to drive various reactions in the cell, including the activation of monomers for polymer

Table 3-4	The Bases, Nucleosides, and Nucleotides of RNA and DNA			
	RNA		**DNA**	
Bases	**Nucleoside**	**Nucleotide**	**Deoxynucleoside**	**Deoxynucleotide**
Purines				
Adenine (A)	Adenosine	Adenosine monophosphate (AMP)	Deoxyadenosine	Deoxyadenosine monophosphate (dAMP)
Guanine (G)	Guanosine	Guanosine monophosphate (GMP)	Deoxyguanosine	Deoxyguanosine monophosphate (dGMP)
Pyrimidines				
Cytosine (C)	Cytidine	Cytidine monophosphate (CMP)	Deoxycytidine	Deoxycytidine monophosphate (dCMP)
Uracil (U)	Uridine	Uridine monophosphate (UMP)	—	—
Thymine (T)	—	—	Deoxythymidine	Deoxythymidine monophosphate (dTMP)

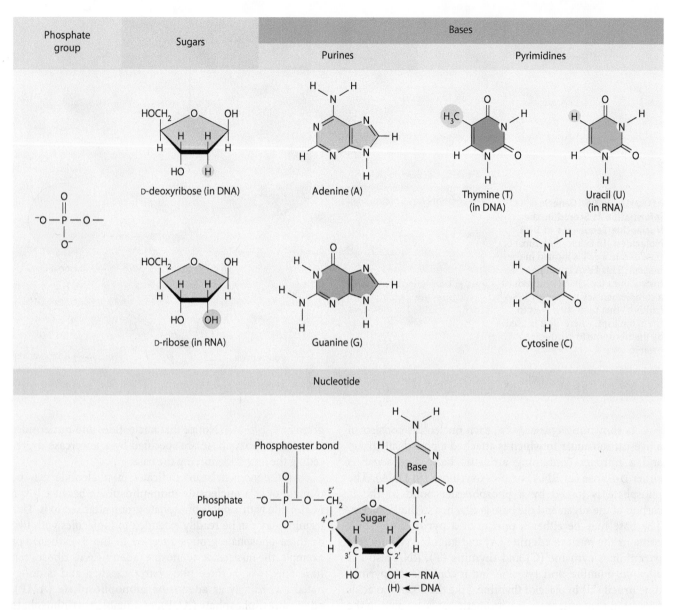

Phosphate group	Sugars	Bases		
		Purines	Pyrimidines	

D-deoxyribose (in DNA)

D-ribose (in RNA)

Adenine (A)

Guanine (G)

Thymine (T) (in DNA)

Uracil (U) (in RNA)

Cytosine (C)

Nucleotide

Phosphoester bond

Base

Phosphate group

Sugar

HO   OH ← RNA
(H) ← DNA

FIGURE 3-15 The Structure of a Nucleotide. In RNA, a nucleotide consists of the five-carbon sugar D-ribose with an aromatic nitrogen-containing base attached to the 1′ carbon and a phosphate group linked to the 5′ carbon by a phosphoester bond. (Carbon atoms in the sugar of a nucleotide are numbered from 1′ to 5′ to distinguish them from those in the base, which are numbered without the prime.) In DNA, the hydroxyl group on the 2′ carbon is replaced by a hydrogen atom, so the sugar is D-deoxyribose. The bases in DNA are the purines adenine (A) and guanine (G) and the pyrimidines thymine (T) and cytosine (C). In RNA, thymine is replaced by the pyrimidine uracil (U).

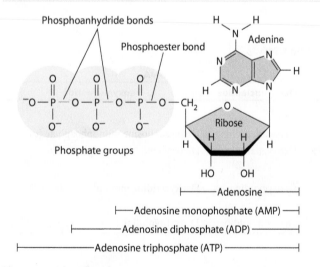

Phosphoanhydride bonds

Phosphoester bond

Adenine

Ribose

Phosphate groups

Adenosine

Adenosine monophosphate (AMP)

Adenosine diphosphate (ADP)

Adenosine triphosphate (ATP)

FIGURE 3-16 The Phosphorylated Forms of Adenosine. Adenosine occurs as the free nucleoside and can also form part of the following three nucleotides: adenosine monophosphate (AMP), adenosine diphosphate (ADP), and adenosine triphosphate (ATP). The bond linking the first phosphate to the ribose of adenosine is a phosphoester bond, whereas the bonds linking the second and third phosphate groups to the molecule are phosphoanhydride bonds. The hydrolysis of a phosphoanhydride bond typically liberates two to three times as much free energy as does the hydrolysis of a phosphoester bond.

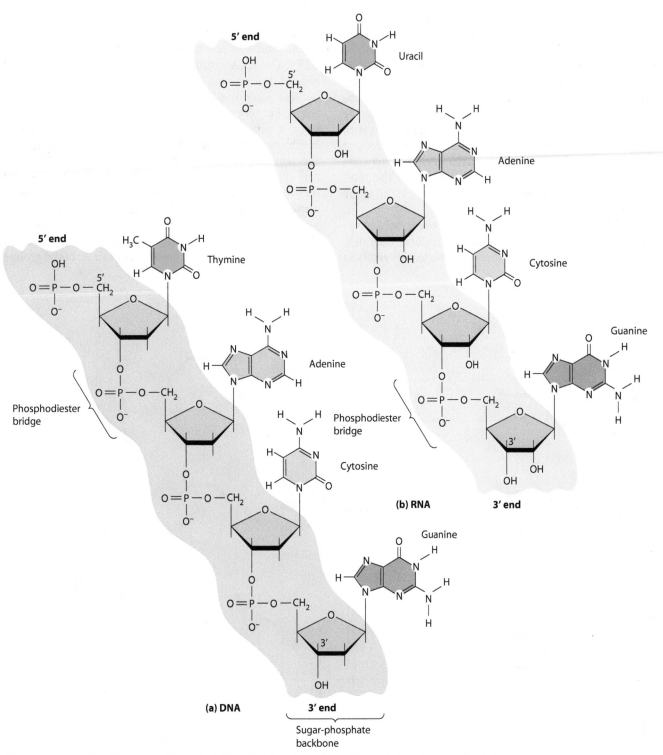

FIGURE 3-17 The Structure of Nucleic Acids. Nucleic acids consist of linear chains of nucleotides, each containing a sugar, a phosphate, and a base. The sugar is **(a)** deoxyribose in DNA and **(b)** ribose in RNA. Successive nucleotides in the chain are joined together by 3′, 5′ phosphodiester bridges. The resulting polynucleotide has an intrinsic directionality, with a 5′ end and a 3′ end. For both DNA and RNA, the backbone of the chain is an alternating sugar-phosphate sequence, from which the bases jut out.

ACTIVITIES www.thecellplace.com *DNA and RNA structure*

formation. As this example suggests, nucleotides play two roles in cells: They are the monomeric units of nucleic acids, and several of them—ATP most notably—serve as intermediates in various energy-transferring reactions.

The Polymers Are DNA and RNA

Nucleic acids are linear polymers formed by linking each nucleotide to the next through a phosphate group, as shown in **Figure 3-17** (see also Figure 19-7). Specifically, the phosphate group already attached by a phosphoester bond to the 5' carbon of one nucleotide becomes linked by a second phosphoester bond to the 3' carbon of the next nucleotide. The resulting linkage is known as a **3',5' phosphodiester bridge,** which consists of a phosphate group linked to two adjacent nucleotides via two phosphoester bonds (one to each nucleotide). The **polynucleotide** formed by this process has an intrinsic directionality, with a 5' phosphate group at one end and a 3' hydroxyl group at the other end. By convention, nucleotide sequences are always written from the 5' end to the 3' end of the polynucleotide because, as we will see in Chapter 19, this is the direction of nucleic acid synthesis in cells.

Nucleic acid synthesis requires both energy and information. To provide the energy needed to form each new phosphodiester bridge, each successive nucleotide enters as a high-energy nucleoside triphosphate. The precursors for DNA synthesis are therefore dATP, dCTP, dGTP, and dTTP. For RNA synthesis, ATP, CTP, GTP, and UTP are needed. Information is required for nucleic acid synthesis because successive incoming nucleotides must be added in a specific, genetically determined sequence. For this purpose, a preexisting molecule is used as a **template** to specify nucleotide order. For both DNA and RNA synthesis, the template is usually DNA. Template-directed nucleic acid synthesis relies on precise and predictable *base pairing* between a template nucleotide and the specific incoming nucleotide that can pair with the template nucleotide.

This recognition process depends on an important chemical feature of the purine and pyrimidine bases shown in **Figure 3-18**. These bases have carbonyl groups

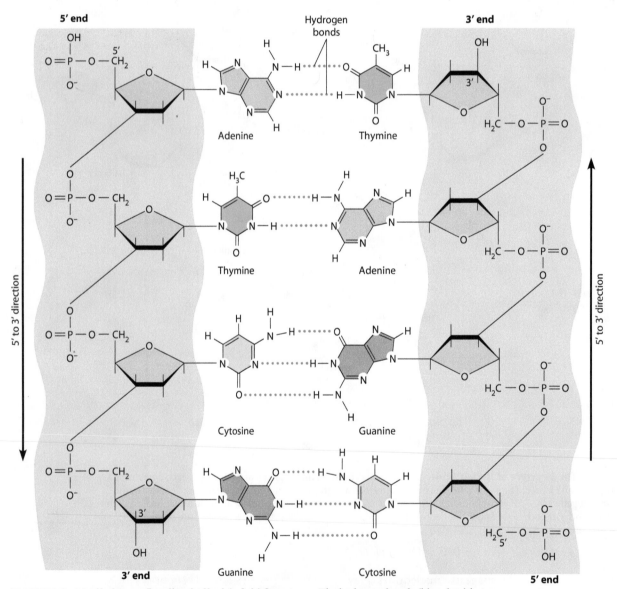

FIGURE 3-18 Hydrogen Bonding in Nucleic Acid Structure. The hydrogen bonds (blue dots) between adenine and thymine and between cytosine and guanine account for the AT and CG base pairing of DNA. Notice that the AT pair is held together by two hydrogen bonds, whereas the CG pair has three hydrogen bonds. If one or both strands were RNA instead, the pairing partner for adenine would be uracil (U).

and nitrogen atoms capable of hydrogen bond formation under appropriate conditions. Complementary relationships between purines and pyrimidines allow A to form two hydrogen bonds with T (or U) and G to form three hydrogen bonds with C, as shown in Figure 3-18. This pairing of A with T (or U) and G with C is a fundamental property of nucleic acids. Genetically, this **base pairing** provides a mechanism for nucleic acids to recognize one another, as we will see in Chapter 18. For now, however, let's concentrate on the structural implications.

A DNA Molecule Is a Double-Stranded Helix

One of the most significant biological advances of the twentieth century came in 1953 in a two-page article in the scientific journal *Nature*. In the article, Francis Crick and James Watson postulated a double-stranded helical structure for DNA—the now-famous **double helix**—that not only accounted for the known physical and chemical properties of DNA but also suggested a mechanism for replication of the structure. Some highlights of this exciting chapter in the history of contemporary biology are related in **Box 3A**.

The double helix consists of two complementary chains of DNA twisted together around a common axis to form a right-handed helical structure that resembles a spiral staircase (**Figure 3-19**). The two chains are oriented in opposite directions along the helix, with one running in the $5' \rightarrow 3'$ direction and the other in the $3' \rightarrow 5'$ direction. The backbone of each chain consists of sugar molecules alternating with phosphate groups (see Figure 3-18). The phosphate groups are charged, and the sugar molecules contain polar hydroxyl groups. Therefore, it is not surprising that the sugar-phosphate backbones of the two strands are on the outside of the DNA helix, where their interaction with the surrounding aqueous environment can be maximized. The pyrimidine and purine bases, on the other hand, are aromatic compounds with less affinity for water. Accordingly, they are oriented inward, forming the base pairs that hold the two chains together.

To form a stable double helix, the two component strands must be *antiparallel* (running in opposite directions) as well as *complementary*. By complementary, we mean that each base in one strand can form specific hydrogen bonds with the base in the other strand directly across from it. From the pairing possibilities shown in Figure 3-18, this means that each A must be paired with a T, and each G with a C. In both cases, one member of the pair is a pyrimidine (T or C) and the other is a purine (A or G). The distance between the two sugar-phosphate backbones in the double helix is just sufficient to accommodate one of each kind of base. If we envision the sugar-phosphate backbones of the two strands as the sides of a circular staircase, then each step or rung of the stairway corresponds to a pair of bases held in place by hydrogen bonding (Figure 3-19).

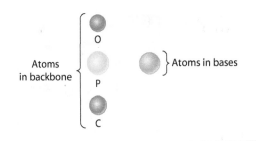

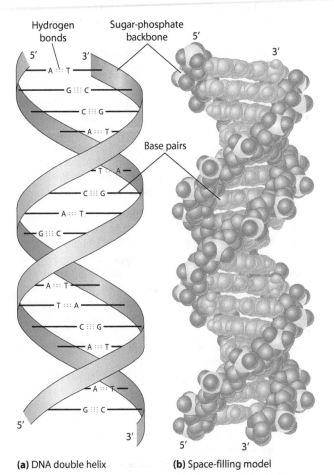

(a) DNA double helix   **(b)** Space-filling model

FIGURE 3-19 The Structure of Double-Stranded DNA.
(a) A schematic representation of the double-helical structure of DNA. The continuously turning strips represent the sugar-phosphate backbones of the molecule, while the horizontal bars represent paired bases of the two strands. **(b)** A space-filling model of the DNA double helix, with color-coded atoms as shown at the top of the figure.

The right-handed Watson-Crick helix shown in Figure 3-19 is actually an idealized version of what is called *B-DNA*. B-DNA is the main form of DNA in cells, but two other forms may also exist, perhaps in short segments interspersed within molecules consisting mainly of B-DNA. *A-DNA* has a right-handed, helical configuration that is shorter and thicker than B-DNA. *Z-DNA*, on the other hand, is a left-handed double helix that derives its name from the zigzag pattern of its longer, thinner sugar-phosphate backbone. (For a comparison of the structures of B-DNA and Z-DNA, see Figure 18-5.)

"I have never seen Francis Crick in a modest mood. Perhaps in other company he is that way, but I have never had reason so to judge him." With this observation as an introduction, James Watson goes on to describe, in a very personal and highly entertaining way, the events that eventually led to the discovery of the structure of DNA. The account, published in 1968 under the title *The Double Helix*, is still fascinating reading for the personal, unvarnished insights it provides into how an immense scientific discovery came about. In the preface, Watson comments on his reasons for writing the book:

> There remains general ignorance about how science is "done." That is not to say that all science is done in the manner described here. This is far from the case, for styles of scientific research vary almost as much as human personalities. On the other hand, I do not believe that the way DNA came out constitutes an odd exception to a scientific world complicated by the contradictory pulls of ambition and the sense of fair play.

As portrayed in Watson's account, Crick and Watson are about as different from each other in nature and background as they could be. But there was one thing they shared, and that was an unconventional but highly productive way of "doing" science. They did little actual experimentation on DNA, choosing instead to draw heavily on the research findings of others and to use their own considerable ingenuities in building models and exercising astute insights (**Figure 3A-1**). Out of it all emerged, in a relatively short time, an understanding of the double-helical structure of DNA that has come to rank as one of the major scientific events of the twentieth century.

To appreciate their findings and their brilliance, we must first understand the setting in which Watson and Crick worked. The early 1950s was an exciting time in biology. It had been only a few years since Avery, MacLeod, and McCarty had published evidence on the genetic transformation of bacteria, but the work of Hershey and Chase that confirmed DNA as the genetic material had not yet appeared in print. Meanwhile, at Columbia University, Erwin Chargaff's careful chemical analyses had revealed that although the relative proportions of the four bases—A, T, C, and G—varied greatly from one species to the next, it was always the same for all members of a single species. Even more puzzling and portentous was Chargaff's second finding: For a given species, A and T always occurred in the same proportions, and so did G and C (that is, %A = %T and %C = %G).

FIGURE 3A-1 James Watson (left) and Francis Crick (right) at work with their model of DNA.

Important clues came from the work of Maurice Wilkins and Rosalind Franklin at King's College in London. Wilkins and Franklin were using the technique of X-ray diffraction to study DNA structure, and they took a rather dim view of Watson and Crick's strategy of model building. X-ray diffraction is a useful tool for detecting regularly occurring structural elements in a crystalline substance because any structural feature that repeats at some fixed interval in the crystal contributes in a characteristic way to the diffraction pattern that is obtained. From Franklin's painstaking analysis of the diffraction pattern of DNA, it became clear that the molecule was long and thin, with some structural element being repeated every 0.34 nm and another being repeated every 3.4 nm. Even more intriguing, the molecule appeared to be some sort of helix.

This stirred the imaginations of Watson and Crick because they had heard only recently of Pauling and Corey's α-helical structure

RNA structure also depends in part on base pairing, but this pairing is usually between complementary regions within the same strand and is much less extensive than the interstrand pairing of the DNA duplex. Of the various RNA species, secondary and tertiary structures occur mainly in rRNA and tRNA, as we will see in Chapter 21. In addition, some infectious viruses consist of double-stranded RNA held together by hydrogen bonding between complementary base pairs.

Polysaccharides

The next macromolecules we will consider are the **polysaccharides,** which are long-chain polymers of sugars and sugar derivatives. Polysaccharides usually consist of a single kind of repeating unit, or sometimes an alternating pattern of two kinds, and are not informational molecules. We will see in Chapter 7, however, that shorter polymers called *oligosaccharides,* when attached to proteins on the

for proteins. Working with models of the bases cut from stiff cardboard, Watson and Crick came to the momentous insight that DNA was also a helix, but with an all-important difference: It was a *double* helix, with hydrogen-bonded pairing of purines and pyrimidines. The actual discovery is best recounted in Watson's own words:

> When I got to our still empty office the following morning, I quickly cleared away the papers from my desk top so that I would have a large, flat surface on which to form pairs of bases held together by hydrogen bonds. Though I initially went back to my like-with-like prejudices, I saw all too well that they led nowhere. When Jerry [Donohue, an American crystallographer working in the same laboratory] came in I looked up, saw that it was not Francis, and began shifting the bases in and out of various other pairing possibilities. Suddenly I became aware that an adenine-thymine pair held together by two hydrogen bonds was identical in shape to a guanine-cytosine pair held together by at least two hydrogen bonds. All the hydrogen bonds seemed to form naturally; no fudging was required to make the two types of base pairs identical in shape. Quickly I called Jerry over to ask him whether this time he had any objections to my new base pairs.
>
> When he said no, my morale skyrocketed, for I suspected that we now had the answer to the riddle of why the number of purine residues exactly equaled the number of pyrimidine residues. Two irregular sequences of bases could be regularly packed in the center of a helix if a purine always hydrogen-bonded to a pyrimidine. Furthermore, the hydrogen-bonding requirement meant that adenine would always pair with thymine, while guanine could pair only with cytosine. Chargaff's rules then suddenly stood out as a consequence of a double-helical structure for DNA. Even more exciting, this type of double helix suggested a replication scheme much more satisfactory than my briefly considered like-with-like pairing. Always pairing adenine with thymine and guanine with cytosine meant that the base sequences of the two intertwined chains were complementary to each other. Given the base sequence of one chain, that of its partner was automatically determined. Conceptually, it was thus very easy to visualize how a single chain could be the template for the synthesis of a chain with the complementary sequence.
>
> Upon his arrival Francis did not get more than halfway through the door before I let loose that the answer to everything was in our hands. Though as a matter of principle he maintained skepticism for a few moments, the similarly shaped AT and GC pairs had their expected impact. His quickly pushing the bases together in a number of different ways did not reveal any other way to satisfy Chargaff's rules. A few minutes later he spotted the fact that the two glycosidic bonds (joining base and sugar) of each base pair were systematically related by a dyad axis perpendicular to the helical axis. Thus, both pairs could be flip-flopped over and still have their glycosidic bonds facing in the same direction. This had the important consequence that a given chain could contain both purines and pyrimidines. At the same time, it strongly suggested that the backbones of the two chains must run in opposite directions.
>
> The question then became whether the AT and GC base pairs would easily fit the backbone configuration devised during the previous two weeks. At first glance this looked like a good bet, since I had left free in the center a large vacant area for the bases. However, we both knew that we would not be home until a complete model was built in which all the stereochemical contacts were satisfactory. There was also the obvious fact that the implications of its existence were far too important to risk crying wolf. Thus, I felt slightly queasy when at lunch Francis winged into the Eagle to tell everyone within hearing distance that we had found the secret of life.[*]

The rest is history. Shortly thereafter, the prestigious journal *Nature* carried an unpretentious two-page article entitled simply "Molecular Structure of Nucleic Acids: A Structure for Deoxyribose Nucleic Acid," by James Watson and Francis Crick. Though modest in length, that paper has had far-reaching implications. In fact, near the end, this article contains what some consider to be one of the greatest scientific understatements ever: "It has not escaped our notice that the specific pairing that we have postulated immediately suggests a possible copying mechanism for the genetic material."[†] The double-stranded model that Watson and Crick worked out in 1953 has proved to be correct in all its essential details, unleashing a revolution in the field of biology.

[*]Excerpted from *The Double Helix*, pp. 194–197. Copyright © 1968 James D. Watson. Reprinted with the permission of the author and Atheneum Publishers, Inc.
[†]From *Nature* 171 (1953): 737–738.

cell surface, play important roles in cellular recognition of extracellular signal molecules and of other cells. As noted earlier, polysaccharides include the storage polysaccharides starch and glycogen and the structural polysaccharide cellulose. Each of these polymers contains the six-carbon sugar glucose as its single repeating unit, but they differ in the nature of the bond between successive glucose units as well as in the presence and extent of side branches on the chains.

The Monomers Are Monosaccharides

The repeating units of polysaccharides are simple sugars called **monosaccharides** (from the Greek *mono,* meaning "single," and *sakkharon,* meaning "sugar"). A sugar can be defined as an aldehyde or ketone that has two or more hydroxyl groups. Thus, there are two categories of sugars: the *aldosugars,* with a terminal carbonyl group (**Figure 3-20a**), and the *ketosugars,* with an internal

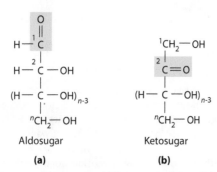

FIGURE 3-20 Structures of Monosaccharides. (a) Aldosugars have a carbonyl group on carbon atom 1. (b) Ketosugars have a carbonyl group on carbon atom 2. The number of carbon atoms in a monosaccharide (*n*) varies from three to seven.

carbonyl group (Figure 3-20b). Within these categories, sugars are named generically according to the number of carbon atoms they contain. Most sugars have between three and seven carbon atoms and thus are classified as *trioses* (three carbons), *tetroses* (four carbons), *pentoses* (five carbons), *hexoses* (six carbons), or *heptoses* (seven carbons). We have already encountered two pentoses—the ribose of RNA and the deoxyribose of DNA.

The single most common monosaccharide in the biological world is the aldohexose D-glucose, represented by the formula $C_6H_{12}O_6$ and by the structure shown in **Figure 3-21**. The formula $C_nH_{2n}O_n$ is characteristic of sugars and gave rise to the general term **carbohydrate** because compounds of this sort were originally thought of as "hydrates of carbon"—$C_n(H_2O)_n$. Although carbohydrates are not simply hydrated carbons, for every CO_2 molecule incorporated into sugar, one water molecule is consumed.

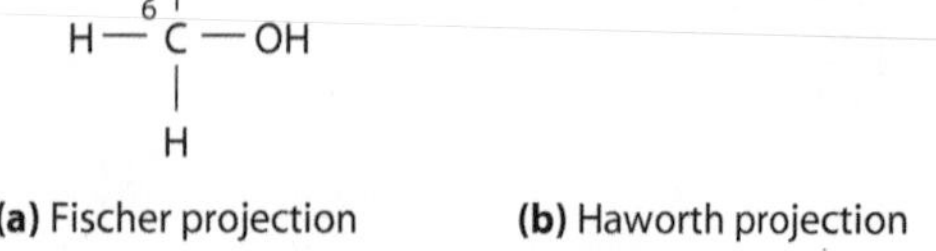

In keeping with the general rule for numbering carbon atoms in organic molecules, the carbons of glucose are numbered beginning with the more oxidized end of the molecule, the carbonyl group. Because glucose has four asymmetric carbon atoms (carbon atoms 2, 3, 4, and 5), there are $2^4 = 16$ different possible stereoisomers of the aldosugar $C_6H_{12}O_6$. Here, we will concern ourselves only with D-glucose, which is the most stable of the 16 isomers.

Figure 3-21a illustrates D-glucose as it appears in what chemists call a **Fischer projection,** with the —H and —OH groups intended to project slightly out of the plane of the paper. This structure depicts glucose as a linear molecule, and it is often a useful representation of glucose for teaching purposes. In reality, however, glucose exists in the cell in a dynamic equilibrium between the linear (or straight-chain) configuration of Figure 3-21a and the ring form shown in Figure 3-21b. This ring forms when the oxygen atom of the hydroxyl group on carbon atom 5 forms a bond with carbon atom 1. Although the bonding of this oxygen atom to carbon atoms 1 and 5 seems unlikely from the Fischer projection, it is actually favored by the tetrahedral nature of each carbon atom in the chain. This ring form is the predominant structure, because it is energetically more stable.

Therefore, the more satisfactory representation of glucose is the **Haworth projection** shown in Figure 3-21b. This shows the spatial relationship of different parts of the molecule and makes the spontaneous formation of a bond between an oxygen atom and carbon atoms 1 and 5 appear more likely. Either of the representations of glucose shown in Figure 3-21 is valid, but the Haworth projection is generally preferred because it indicates both the ring form and the spatial relationship of the carbon atoms.

Notice that formation of the ring structure results in the generation of one of two alternative forms of the molecule, depending on the spatial orientation of the hydroxyl group on carbon atom 1. These alternative forms of glucose are designated α and β. As shown in **Figure 3-22**, α-D-glucose has the hydroxyl group on carbon atom 1

(a) Fischer projection   **(b)** Haworth projection

FIGURE 3-21 The Structure of D-Glucose. The D-glucose molecule can be represented by **(a)** the Fischer projection of the straight-chain form or **(b)** the Haworth projection of the ring form. In the Fischer projection, the —H and —OH groups are intended to project slightly out of the plane of the paper. In the Haworth projection, carbon atoms 2 and 3 are intended to jut out of the plane of the paper, and carbon atoms 5 and 6 are behind the plane of the paper. The —H and —OH groups then project upward or downward, as indicated. Notice that the carbon atoms are numbered from the more oxidized end of the molecule.

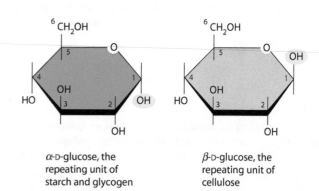

α-D-glucose, the repeating unit of starch and glycogen

β-D-glucose, the repeating unit of cellulose

FIGURE 3-22 The Ring Forms of D-Glucose. The hydroxyl group on carbon atom 1 (blue oval) points downward in the α form and upward in the β form.

pointing downward in the Haworth projection, and β-D-glucose has the hydroxyl group on carbon atom 1 pointing upward. Starch and glycogen both have α-D-glucose as their repeating unit, whereas cellulose consists of strings of β-D-glucose.

In addition to the free monosaccharide and the long-chain polysaccharides, glucose also occurs in **disaccharides,** which consist of two monosaccharide units linked covalently. Three common disaccharides are shown in **Figure 3-23.** *Maltose* (malt sugar) consists of two glucose units linked together, whereas *lactose* (milk sugar) contains a glucose linked to a galactose and *sucrose* (common table sugar) has a glucose linked to a fructose.

Each of these disaccharides is formed by a condensation reaction in which two monosaccharides are linked together by the elimination of water. The resulting **glycosidic bond** is characteristic of linkages between

sugars. In the case of maltose, both of the constituent glucose molecules are in the α form, and the glycosidic bond forms between carbon atom 1 of one glucose and carbon atom 4 of the other. This is called an α *glycosidic bond* because it involves a carbon atom 1 with its hydroxyl group in the α configuration. Lactose, on the other hand, is characterized by a β *glycosidic bond* because the hydroxyl group on carbon atom 1 of the galactose is in the β configuration. Some people lack the enzyme needed to hydrolyze this β glycosidic bond and are considered *lactose intolerant* due to their difficulty in metabolizing this disaccharide. The distinction between α and β again becomes critical when we get to the polysaccharides because both the three-dimensional configuration and the biological role of the polymer depend critically on the nature of the bond between the repeating monosaccharide units.

The Polymers Are Storage and Structural Polysaccharides

Polysaccharides typically perform either storage or structural roles in cells. The most familiar *storage polysaccharides* are **starch,** found in plant cells (**Figure 3-24a**), and **glycogen,** found in animal cells and bacteria (Figure 3-24b). Both of these polymers consist of α-D-glucose units linked together by α glycosidic bonds. In addition to $\alpha(1 \rightarrow 4)$ bonds that link carbon atoms 1 and 4 of adjacent glucose units, these polysaccharides may contain occasional $\alpha(1 \rightarrow 6)$ linkages along the backbone, giving rise to side chains (Figure 3-24c). Storage polysaccharides can therefore be branched or unbranched polymers, depending on the presence or absence of $\alpha(1 \rightarrow 6)$ linkages.

Glycogen is highly branched, with $\alpha(1 \rightarrow 6)$ linkages occurring every 8 to 10 glucose units along the backbone and giving rise to short side chains of about 8 to 12 glucose units (Figure 3-24b). In our bodies, glycogen is stored mainly in the liver and in muscle tissue. In the liver, it is used as a source of glucose to maintain blood sugar levels. In muscle, it serves as a fuel source to generate ATP for muscle contraction. Bacteria also commonly store glycogen as a glucose reserve.

Starch, the glucose reserve commonly found in plant tissue, occurs both as unbranched **amylose** and as branched **amylopectin.** Like glycogen, amylopectin has $\alpha(1 \rightarrow 6)$ branches, but these occur less frequently along the backbone (once every 12 to 25 glucose units) and give rise to longer side chains (lengths of 20 to 25 glucose units are common; Figure 3-24a). Starch deposits are usually 10–30% amylose and 70–90% amylopectin. Starch is stored in plant cells as *starch grains* within the plastids—either within the *chloroplasts* that are the sites of carbon fixation and sugar synthesis in photosynthetic tissue or within the *amyloplasts*, which are specialized plastids for starch storage. The potato tuber, for example, is filled with starch-laden amyloplasts.

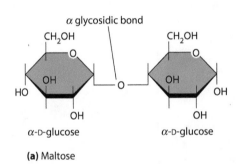

(a) Maltose

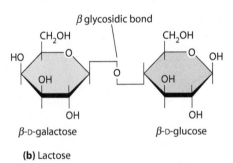

(b) Lactose

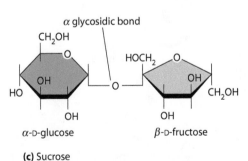

(c) Sucrose

FIGURE 3-23 Some Common Disaccharides. (a) Maltose (malt sugar) consists of two molecules of α-D-glucose linked by an α glycosidic bond. **(b)** Lactose (milk sugar) consists of a molecule of β-D-galactose linked to a molecule of β-D-glucose by a β glycosidic bond. **(c)** Sucrose (table sugar) consists of a molecule of α-D-glucose linked to a molecule of β-D-fructose by an α glycosidic bond.

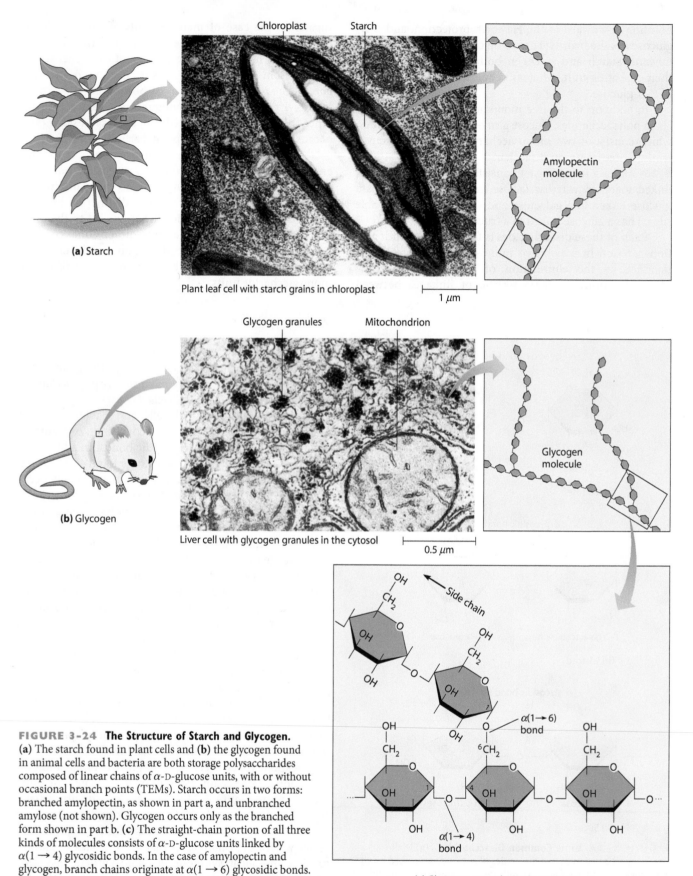

(a) Starch

Plant leaf cell with starch grains in chloroplast

1 μm

Amylopectin molecule

(b) Glycogen

Liver cell with glycogen granules in the cytosol

0.5 μm

Glycogen molecule

Side chain

α(1→6) bond

α(1→4) bond

(c) Glycogen or amylopectin structure

FIGURE 3-24 The Structure of Starch and Glycogen.
(a) The starch found in plant cells and **(b)** the glycogen found in animal cells and bacteria are both storage polysaccharides composed of linear chains of α-D-glucose units, with or without occasional branch points (TEMs). Starch occurs in two forms: branched amylopectin, as shown in part a, and unbranched amylose (not shown). Glycogen occurs only as the branched form shown in part b. **(c)** The straight-chain portion of all three kinds of molecules consists of α-D-glucose units linked by α(1 → 4) glycosidic bonds. In the case of amylopectin and glycogen, branch chains originate at α(1 → 6) glycosidic bonds.

The best-known example of a *structural polysaccharide* is the **cellulose** found in plant cell walls (**Figure 3-25**). Cellulose is an important polymer quantitatively—more than half of the carbon in many plants is typically present in cellulose. Like starch and glycogen, cellulose is a polymer of glucose; however, the repeating monomer is β-D-glucose, and the linkage is therefore $\beta(1 \rightarrow 4)$. This bond has structural consequences that we will get to shortly, but it also has nutritional implications. Mammals do not possess an enzyme that can hydrolyze this $\beta(1 \rightarrow 4)$ bond and therefore cannot utilize cellulose as food. As a result, you can digest potatoes (starch) but not grass and wood (cellulose).

Animals such as cows and sheep might seem to be exceptions because they do eat grass and similar plant products. But they cannot cleave β glycosidic bonds either; they rely on microorganisms (bacteria and protozoa) in their digestive systems to do this for them. The microorganisms digest the cellulose, and the host animal then obtains the end-products of microbial digestion, now in a form the animal can use (glucose). Even termites do not actually digest wood. They simply chew it into small pieces that are then hydrolyzed to glucose monomers by microorganisms in their digestive tracts.

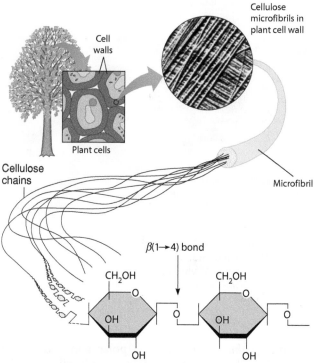

FIGURE 3-25 The Structure of Cellulose. Cellulose consists of long, unbranched chains of β-D-glucose units linked together by $\beta(1 \rightarrow 4)$ glycosidic bonds. Many such chains associate laterally and are held together by hydrogen bonds to form microfibrils. Individual microfibrils can be seen in the micrograph of a primary plant cell wall shown here (TEM). The $\beta(1 \rightarrow 4)$ glycosidic bonds cannot be hydrolyzed by most higher animals.

ACTIVITIES www.thecellplace.com *Carbohydrate structure and function*

Although $\beta(1 \rightarrow 4)$-linked cellulose is the most abundant structural polysaccharide, others are also known. The celluloses of fungal cell walls, for example, contain either $\beta(1 \rightarrow 4)$ or $\beta(1 \rightarrow 3)$ linkages, depending on the species. The cell wall of most bacteria is somewhat more complex and contains two kinds of sugars, *N-acetylglucosamine (GlcNAc)* and *N-acetylmuramic acid (MurNAc)*. As shown in **Figure 3-26a**, GlcNAc and MurNAc are derivatives of *β-glucosamine,* a glucose molecule with the hydroxyl group on carbon atom 2 replaced by an amino group. GlcNAc is formed by acetylation of the amino group, and MurNAc requires the further addition of a three-carbon lactyl group to carbon atom 3. The cell wall polysaccharide is then formed by the linking of GlcNAc and MurNAc in a strictly alternating sequence with $\beta(1 \rightarrow 4)$ bonds (Figure 3-26b). Figure 3-26c shows the structure of yet another structural polysaccharide, the **chitin** found in insect exoskeletons, crustacean shells, and fungal cell walls. Chitin consists of GlcNAc units only, joined by $\beta(1 \rightarrow 4)$ bonds.

Polysaccharide Structure Depends on the Kinds of Glycosidic Bonds Involved

The distinction between the α and β glycosidic bonds of storage and structural polysaccharides has more than just nutritional significance. Because of the difference in linkages and therefore in the spatial relationship between successive glucose units, the two classes of polysaccharides differ markedly in secondary structure. The helical shape already established as a characteristic of both proteins and nucleic acids is also found in polysaccharides. Both starch and glycogen coil spontaneously into loose helices, but often the structure is not highly ordered due to the numerous side chains of amylopectin and glycogen.

Cellulose, by contrast, forms rigid, linear rods. These in turn aggregate laterally into *microfibrils* (see Figure 3-25). Microfibrils are about 5–20 nm in diameter and are composed of about 36 cellulose chains. Plant and fungal cell walls consist of these rigid microfibrils of cellulose embedded in a *noncellulosic matrix* containing a rather variable mixture of several other polymers (*hemicellulose* and *pectin*, mainly) and a protein called *extensin* that occurs only in the cell wall. Cell walls have been aptly compared to reinforced concrete, in which steel rods are embedded in the cement before it hardens to add strength. In cell walls, the cellulose microfibrils are the "rods" and the noncellulosic matrix is the "cement."

Lipids

Strictly speaking, **lipids** differ from the macromolecules we have discussed so far in this chapter because they are not formed by the kind of linear polymerization that gives rise to proteins, nucleic acids, and polysaccharides. However, they are commonly regarded as macromolecules because of their high molecular weights and their presence in important cellular structures, particularly membranes. Also, the final steps in the synthesis of triglycerides, phospholipids,

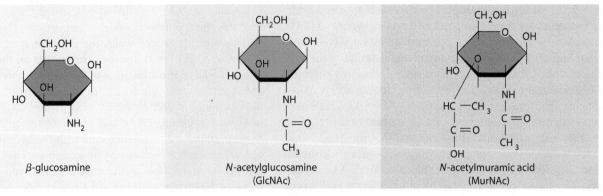

(a) Polysaccharide subunits

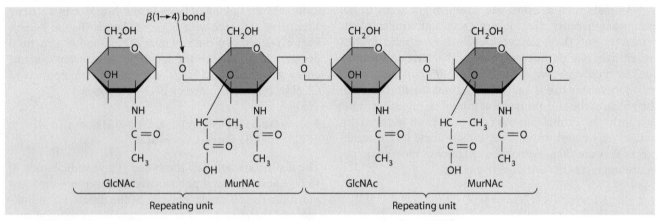

(b) A bacterial cell wall polysaccharide

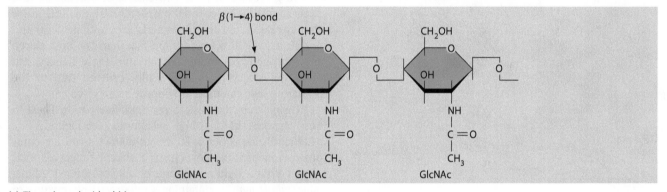

(c) The polysaccharide chitin

FIGURE 3-26 Polysaccharides of Bacterial Cell Walls and Insect Exoskeletons. **(a)** Chemical structures of the monosaccharide subunits glucosamine, *N*-acetylglucosamine (GlcNAc), and *N*-acetylmuramic acid (MurNAc). **(b)** A bacterial cell wall polysaccharide, consisting of alternating GlcNAc and MurNAc units linked by $\beta(1 \rightarrow 4)$ bonds. **(c)** The polysaccharide chitin found in insect exoskeletons and crustacean shells, with GlcNAc as its single repeating unit and successive GlcNAc units linked by $\beta(1 \rightarrow 4)$ bonds.

and other large lipid molecules involve condensation reactions similar to those used in polymer synthesis.

Lipids constitute a rather heterogeneous category of cellular components that resemble one another more in their solubility properties than in their chemical structures. *The distinguishing feature of lipids is their hydrophobic nature.* Although they have little, if any, affinity for water, they are readily soluble in nonpolar solvents such as chloroform or ether. Accordingly, we can expect to find that they are rich in nonpolar hydrocarbon regions and have relatively few polar groups. Some lipids, however,

are *amphipathic,* having both a polar and a nonpolar region. This characteristic has important implications for membrane structure.

Because they are defined in terms of solubility characteristics rather than chemical structure, we should not be surprised to find that lipids as a group include molecules that are quite diverse in terms of structure, chemistry, and function. Functionally, lipids play at least three main roles in cells. Some serve as forms of *energy storage,* others are involved in *membrane structure,* and still others have *specific biological functions,* such as the transmission of chemical signals into and within the cell. We will discuss lipids in terms of six main classes, based on their chemical structure: *fatty acids, triacylglycerols, phospholipids, glycolipids, steroids,* and *terpenes.* Note that, because of the wide variety of lipids and the fact that members of different classes sometimes share structural and chemical similarities,

this is only one of several different ways to classify lipids. The six main classes of lipids as we will discuss them are illustrated in **Figure 3-27,** which includes representative examples of each class. We will look briefly at each of these six kinds of lipids, pointing out their functional roles in the process.

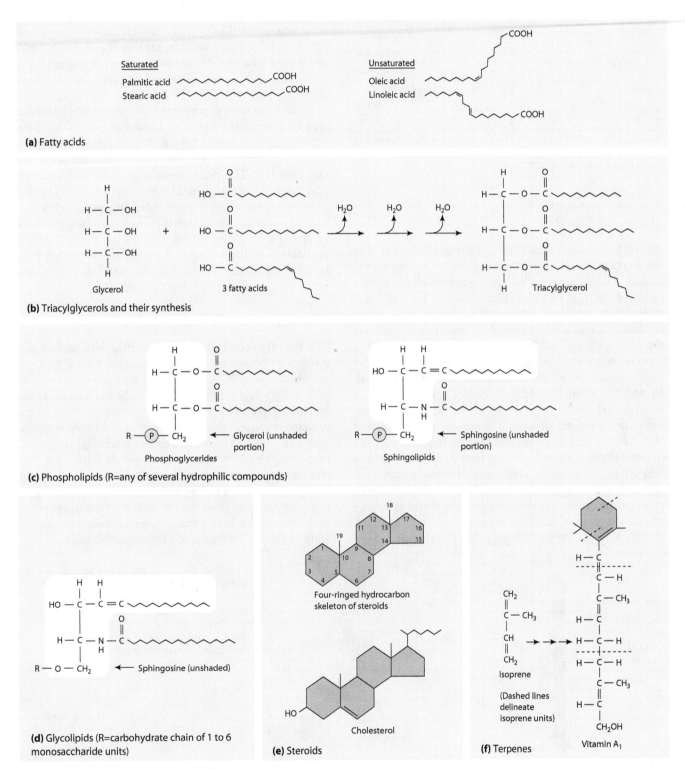

FIGURE 3-27 The Main Classes of Lipids. The zigzag lines in parts a–d represent the long hydrocarbon chains of fatty acids. Each corner of the zigzag lines represents a methylene (—CH₂—) group.

ACTIVITIES www.thecellplace.com *Lipid structure and function*

Table 3-5	Some Common Fatty Acids in Cells	
Number of Carbons	Number of Double Bonds	Common Name*
12	0	Laurate
14	0	Myristate
16	0	Palmitate
18	0	Stearate
20	0	Arachidate
16	1	Palmitoleate
18	1	Oleate
18	2	Linoleate
18	3	Linolenate
20	4	Arachidonate

*Shown are the names for the ionized forms of the fatty acids as they exist at the near-neutral pH of most cells. For the names of the free fatty acids, simply replace the –ate ending with –ic acid.

Fatty Acids Are the Building Blocks of Several Classes of Lipids

We will begin our discussion with **fatty acids** because they are components of several other kinds of lipids. A fatty acid is a long, unbranched hydrocarbon chain with a carboxyl group at one end (Figure 3-27a). The fatty acid molecule is therefore amphipathic; the carboxyl group renders one end (often called the "head") polar, whereas the hydrocarbon "tail" is nonpolar. Fatty acids contain a variable, but usually even, number of carbon atoms. The usual range is from 12 to 20 carbon atoms per chain, with 16- and 18-carbon fatty acids especially common.

Table 3-5 lists some common fatty acids. Fatty acids with even numbers of carbon atoms are greatly favored because fatty acid synthesis involves the stepwise addition of two-carbon units to a growing fatty acid chain. Because they are highly reduced, having many hydrogen atoms but few oxygen atoms, fatty acids yield a great deal of energy upon oxidation and are therefore efficient forms of energy storage—a gram of fat contains more than twice as much usable energy as a gram of sugar or polysaccharide.

Table 3-5 also shows the variability in fatty acids due to the presence of double bonds between carbons. Fatty acids without double bonds are referred to as **saturated fatty acids** because every carbon atom in the chain has the maximum number of hydrogen atoms attached to it (**Figure 3-28a**). The general formula for a saturated fatty acid with n carbon atoms is $C_nH_{2n}O_2$. Saturated fatty acids have long, straight chains that pack together well. By contrast, **unsaturated fatty acids** contain one or more double bonds, resulting in a bend or kink in the chain that prevents tight packing (Figure 3-28b; also see Figure 7-14). Structures and models of several of these fatty acids are shown in Table 7-2, page 168.

There has been much recent concern about a particular type of unsaturated fatty acid known as a *trans fat. Trans* fats contain unsaturated fatty acids with a particular type of double bond that causes less of a bend in the fatty acid chain (see page 171). This causes them to resemble saturated fatty acids both in their shape and in their ability to pack together more tightly than typical unsaturated fatty acids. While naturally present in small amounts in meat and dairy products, *trans* fats are produced artificially during the commercial production of shortening and margarine. *Trans* fats have been linked to changes in blood cholesterol that are associated with increased risk of heart disease.

Triacylglycerols Are Storage Lipids

The **triacylglycerols,** also called *triglycerides,* consist of a glycerol molecule with three fatty acids linked to it. As shown in Figure 3-27b, **glycerol** is a three-carbon alcohol with a hydroxyl group on each carbon. Fatty acids are linked to glycerol by *ester bonds,* which are formed by the removal of water. Triacylglycerols are synthesized stepwise, with one fatty acid added at a time. *Monoacylglycerols* contain a single fatty acid, *diacylglycerols* have two, and *triacylglycerols* have three. The three fatty acids of a given triacylglycerol need not be identical. They can—and generally do—vary in chain length, degree of unsaturation, or both. Each fatty acid in a triacylglycerol is linked to a carbon atom of glycerol by means of a condensation reaction.

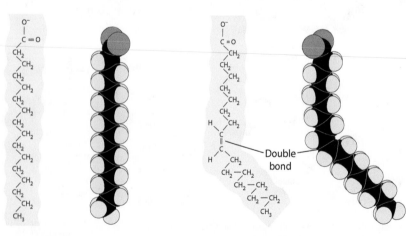

(a) Palmitate (saturated)   **(b)** Oleate (unsaturated)

FIGURE 3-28 Structures of Saturated and Unsaturated Fatty Acids. (a) The saturated 16-carbon fatty acid palmitate. **(b)** The unsaturated 18-carbon fatty acid oleate. The space-filling models are intended to emphasize the overall shape of the molecules. Notice the kink that the double bond creates in the oleate molecule.

The main function of triacylglycerols is to store energy. In some animals, triacylglycerols also provide insulation against low temperatures. Animals such as walruses, seals, and penguins that live in very cold climates store triacylglycerols under their skin and depend on the insulating properties of this fat for survival.

Triacylglycerols containing mostly saturated fatty acids are usually solid or semisolid at room temperature and are called *fats*. Fats are prominent in the bodies of animals, as evidenced by the fat that comes with most cuts of meat, by the large quantity of lard that is obtained as a by-product of the meat-packing industry, and by the widespread concern people have that they are "getting fat." In plants, most triacylglycerols are liquid at room temperature, as the term *vegetable oil* suggests. Because the fatty acids of oils are predominantly unsaturated, their hydrocarbon chains have kinks that prevent an orderly packing of the molecules. As a result, vegetable oils have lower melting temperatures than most animal fats do. Soybean oil and corn oil are two familiar vegetable oils. Vegetable oils can be converted into solid products such as margarine and shortening by hydrogenation (saturation) of the double bonds, a process explored further in Problem 3-15 at the end of the chapter.

Phospholipids Are Important in Membrane Structure

Phospholipids make up a third class of lipids (see Figure 3-27c). They are similar to triacylglycerols in some chemical details but differ strikingly in their properties and their role in the cell. First and foremost, phospholipids are important in membrane structure due to their amphipathic nature. In fact, they are critical to the bilayer structure found in all membranes. Based on their chemistry, phospholipids are classified as *phosphoglycerides* or *sphingolipids* (see Figure 3-27c).

Phosphoglycerides are the predominant phospholipids present in most membranes. Like triacylglycerols, a phosphoglyceride consists of fatty acids that are esterified to a glycerol molecule. However, the basic component of a phosphoglyceride is **phosphatidic acid,** which has just two fatty acids and a phosphate group attached to a glycerol backbone (**Figure 3-29a**). Phosphatidic acid is a key intermediate in the synthesis of other phosphoglycerides but is itself not at all prominent in membranes. Instead, membrane phosphoglycerides invariably have, in addition, a small hydrophilic alcohol linked to the phosphate by an ester bond and represented in Figure 3-29a as an R group. The alcohol is usually *serine, ethanolamine, choline,* or *inositol* (see Figure 3-29b), groups that contribute to the polar nature of the phospholipid head group.

The combination of a highly polar head and two long nonpolar chains gives phosphoglycerides the characteristic amphipathic nature that is so critical to their role in membrane structure. As we saw earlier, the fatty acids can vary considerably in both length and the presence and position of sites of unsaturation. In membranes, 16- and 18-carbon fatty acids are most common, and a typical phosphoglyceride molecule is likely to have one saturated and one unsaturated fatty acid. The length and the degree of unsaturation of fatty acid chains in membrane phospholipids profoundly affect membrane fluidity and can, in fact, be regulated by the cells of some organisms.

In addition to the phosphoglycerides, some membranes contain another class of phospholipid called **sphingolipids,** which are important in membrane structure and cell signaling. When sphingolipids were first discovered by Johann Thudicum in the late nineteenth century, their biological role seemed as enigmatic as the Sphinx, after which he named them. As the name suggests, these lipids are based not on glycerol but on the amine alcohol **sphingosine.** As shown in Figure 3-27c, sphingosine has a long hydrocarbon chain with a single site of unsaturation near the polar end. Through its amino group, sphingosine can form an amide bond to a long-chain fatty acid (up to 34 carbons). The resulting molecule is called a *ceramide* and

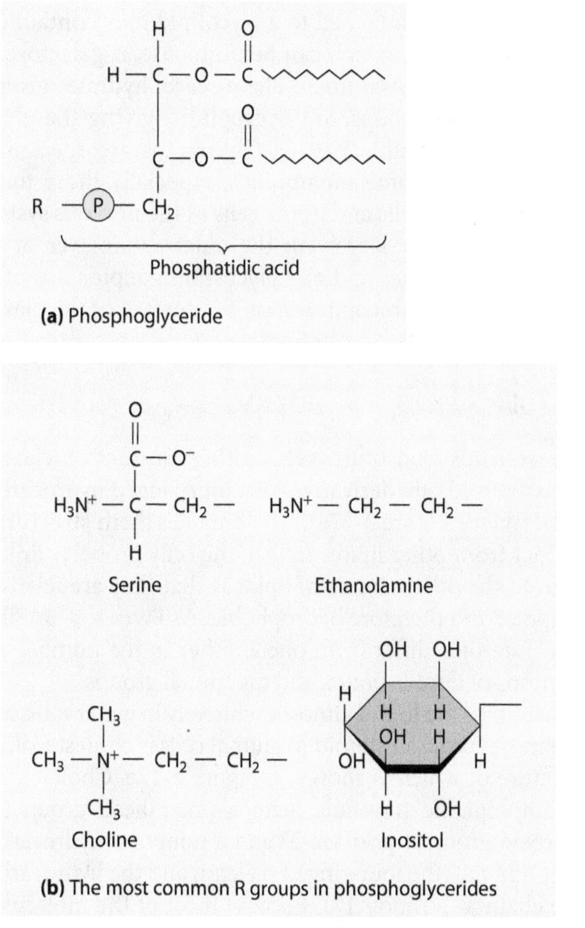

(a) Phosphoglyceride

(b) The most common R groups in phosphoglycerides

FIGURE 3-29 Structures of Common Phosphoglycerides.
(a) A phosphoglyceride consists of a molecule of phosphatidic acid (glycerol esterified to two fatty acids and a phosphate group) with a small polar alcohol, represented as R, also esterified to the phosphate group. **(b)** The four most common R groups found in phosphoglycerides are serine, ethanolamine, choline, and inositol, the first three of which contain a positively charged amino group or nitrogen atom.

consists of a polar region flanked by two long, nonpolar tails, giving it a shape approximating that of the phospholipids.

The hydroxyl group on carbon atom 1 of sphingosine juts out from what is effectively the head of this hairpin molecule. A sphingolipid is formed when any of several polar groups becomes linked to this hydroxyl group. A whole family of sphingolipids exists, differing only in the chemical nature of the polar group attached to the hydroxyl group of the ceramide (the R group of Figure 3-27c). Sphingolipids are present predominantly in the outer leaflet of the plasma membrane bilayer, where they often are found in *lipid rafts*, which, as we will see in Chapter 7, are localized microdomains within a membrane that facilitate communication with the external environment of the cell.

Glycolipids Are Specialized Membrane Components

Glycolipids are lipids containing a carbohydrate group instead of a phosphate group and are typically derivatives of sphingosine or glycerol (see Figure 3-27d). Those containing sphingosine are called *glycosphingolipids*. The carbohydrate group attached to a glycolipid may contain one to six sugar units, which can be D-glucose, D-galactose, or N-acetyl-D-galactosamine. These carbohydrate groups, like phosphate groups, are hydrophilic, giving the glycolipid an amphipathic nature. Glycolipids are specialized constituents of some membranes, especially those found in certain plant cells and in the cells of the nervous system. Glycolipids occur largely in the outer monolayer of the plasma membrane, and the glycosphingolipids are often sites of biological recognition on the surface of the plasma membrane.

Steroids Are Lipids with a Variety of Functions

The **steroids** constitute yet another distinctive class of lipids. Steroids are derivatives of a four-ringed hydrocarbon skeleton (see Figure 3-27e), which makes them structurally distinct from other lipids. In fact, the only property linking them to the other classes of lipids is that they are relatively nonpolar and therefore hydrophobic. As **Figure 3-30** illustrates, steroids differ from one another in the number and positions of double bonds and functional groups.

Steroids are found almost exclusively in eukaryotic cells. The most common steroid in animal cells is **cholesterol,** the structure of which is shown in Figure 3-27e. Cholesterol is an amphipathic molecule, with a polar head group (the hydroxyl group at position 3) and a nonpolar hydrocarbon body and tail (the four-ringed skeleton and the hydrocarbon side chain at position 17). Because most of the molecule is hydrophobic, cholesterol is insoluble and is found primarily in membranes. It occurs in the plasma membrane of animal cells and in most of the membranes of organelles, except the inner membranes of mitochondria and chloroplasts. Similar membrane steroids also occur in other cells, including *stigmasterol* and *sitosterol* in plant cells, *ergosterol* in fungal cells, and related sterols in *Mycoplasma* bacteria.

Cholesterol is the starting point for the synthesis of all the **steroid hormones** (Figure 3-30), which include the male and female *sex hormones,* the *glucocorticoids,* and the *mineralocorticoids.* The sex hormones include the *estrogens* produced by the ovaries of females (*estradiol,* for example) and the *androgens* produced by the testes of males (*testosterone,* for example). The glucocorticoids (*cortisol,* for example) are a family of hormones that promote gluconeogenesis (synthesis of glucose) and suppress inflammation reactions. Mineralocorticoids such as *aldosterone* regulate ion balance by promoting the reabsorption of sodium, chloride, and bicarbonate ions in the kidney.

Terpenes Are Formed from Isoprene

The final class of lipids shown in Figure 3-27 consists of the **terpenes.** Terpenes are synthesized from the five-carbon compound *isoprene* and are therefore also called *isoprenoids.* Isoprene and its derivatives are joined together in various combinations to produce such substances as *vitamin A* (see Figure 3-27f), a required nutrient in our bodies, and *carotenoid pigments,* which are involved in light harvesting in plants during photosynthesis. Other isoprene-based compounds are *dolichols,* which are involved in activating sugar derivatives, and electron carriers such as *coenzyme Q* and *plastoquinone.* Finally, polymers of isoprene units known as polyisoprenoids are found in the cell membranes of Archaea, a unique domain of organisms distinct from eukaryotes and bacteria that we will encounter in Chapter 4.

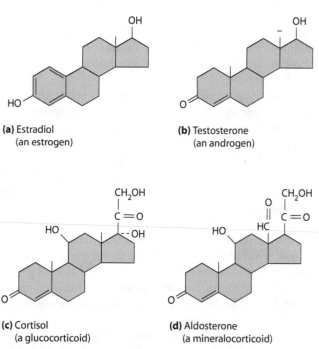

(a) Estradiol (an estrogen)

(b) Testosterone (an androgen)

(c) Cortisol (a glucocorticoid)

(d) Aldosterone (a mineralocorticoid)

FIGURE 3-30 Structures of Several Common Steroid Hormones. Among the many steroids that are synthesized from cholesterol are the hormones **(a)** estradiol, an estrogen; **(b)** testosterone, an androgen; **(c)** cortisol, a glucocorticoid; and **(d)** aldosterone, a mineralocorticoid.

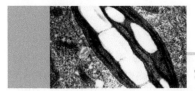

The Macromolecules of the Cell

■ Three classes of macromolecular polymers are prominent in cells: proteins, nucleic acids, and polysaccharides. Lipids are not long, polymeric macromolecules, but they are included in this chapter because of their general importance as constituents of cells (especially membranes) and because their synthesis involves condensation reactions between smaller constituents.

■ Proteins and nucleic acids are macromolecules in which the particular ordering of monomers is critical to their roles in the cell. Polysaccharides, on the other hand, usually contain only one or a few kinds of repeating units and play storage or structural roles instead.

Proteins

■ All of the thousands of different proteins in a cell are linear chains of amino acid monomers. Each of the 20 different amino acids found in proteins has a different R group, which can be either hydrophobic, hydrophilic uncharged, or hydrophilic charged. These amino acids can be linked together in any sequence via peptide bonds to form the wide variety of polypeptides that make up monomeric and multimeric proteins.

■ The amino acid sequence of a polypeptide (its primary structure) usually contains all of the information necessary to specify local folding into α helices and β sheets (secondary structure), overall three-dimensional shape (tertiary structure), and, for multimeric proteins, association with other polypeptides (quaternary structure).

■ Major forces influencing polypeptide folding and stability are covalent disulfide bond formation and several types of noncovalent interactions: hydrogen bonds, ionic bonds, van der Waals interactions, and hydrophobic interactions.

■ Despite extensive knowledge of the forces involved in protein folding, we are still not able to predict the final folded tertiary structure of a protein from its primary amino acid sequence, except in the case of peptides and relatively small proteins.

Nucleic Acids

■ The nucleic acids DNA and RNA are informational macromolecules composed of nucleotide monomers linked together by phosphodiester bridges in a specific order. Each nucleotide is composed of a deoxyribose or ribose sugar, a phosphate, and a purine or pyrimidine base.

■ The base sequence of the nucleotides in a particular segment of DNA known as a gene determines the sequence of the amino acids in the protein encoded by that gene. DNA is the carrier of genetic information in a cell, while mRNA, tRNA, and rRNA function mainly in expression of the information in DNA by their involvement in protein synthesis.

■ While RNA is mainly single stranded, DNA forms a double-stranded helix based on complementary base pairing (A with T and C with G) that is stabilized by hydrogen bonding. Elucidation of the double-helical structure of DNA was a defining biological breakthrough of the twentieth century.

■ In addition to mRNA, tRNA, and rRNA, several other types of RNAs have been discovered in cells, including microRNA (miRNA) and small interfering RNA (siRNA). These RNAs regulate gene expression either by inhibiting translation or by promoting mRNA degradation.

Polysaccharides

■ In contrast to nucleic acids and proteins, polysaccharides show little variation in sequence and serve storage or structural roles. They typically consist either of a single type of monosaccharide or of two alternating monosaccharides linked together by either α or β glycosidic bonds. The type of glycosidic bond determines whether the polysaccharide serves as energy storage or as a structural polysaccharide.

■ The α linkages are readily digestible by animals and are found in storage polysaccharides such as starch and glycogen, which consist solely of glucose monomers. In contrast, the β glycosidic bonds of cellulose and chitin are not digestible by animals and give these molecules a rigid shape suitable to their functions as structural molecules.

Lipids

■ Lipids are not true polymers but are often considered macromolecules due to their high molecular weight and their frequent association with macromolecules, particularly proteins. Lipids vary substantially in chemical structure but are grouped together because they share the common property of being hydrophobic and thus are nearly insoluble in water.

■ Fatty acids are lipids consisting of a long hydrocarbon chain of 12–20 carbon atoms with a carboxylic acid group at one end. They are energy-rich molecules found in the triacylglycerols that make up animal fats and vegetable oils, as well as in the phospholipids found in all cellular membranes.

■ Phosphoglycerides and sphingolipids are types of phospholipids that make up the lipid bilayer of biological membranes. They are amphipathic molecules with two hydrophobic fatty acid chains and a polar phosphate-containing head group.

■ Glycolipids are similar to phospholipids but contain a polar carbohydrate group instead of phosphate. They are often found on the outer surface of membranes, where they play a role in cell recognition.

■ Other important cellular lipids are the steroids (including cholesterol and several sex hormones) and the terpenes (including vitamin A and some important coenzymes).

MAKING CONNECTIONS

Now that you are familiar with the types of macromolecules in cells, where in our upcoming studies do you suppose we will see proteins, nucleic acids, polysaccharides, and lipids again? Not to sound repetitive, but—again the simple answer is "everywhere." For example, in the next chapter we will survey the main structures and organelles of the cell, all of which are composed of macromolecules important to their functions. In the next few chapters, we will see how proteins act as enzyme catalysts in cellular reactions that provide both energy and usable biochemical compounds for the cell. We will also study the structure of phospholipid membranes and the mechanisms used by transport proteins to move material

into and out of the cell across these membranes. In subsequent chapters, we will see how proteins are involved in motility, muscle contraction, structural support, and cell-to-cell communication. Polysaccharides, as you know, serve as storage and structural molecules in cells. Soon, we will see them as components of glycoproteins and glycolipids that have important roles in cell recognition and protein trafficking. Finally, in later chapters, we will study the unique importance of nucleic acids as the carriers of genetic information, and we will see how they interact with proteins in controlling gene expression and cell division in both normal cells and cancer cells.

PROBLEM SET

More challenging problems are marked with a •.

3-1 Polymers and Their Properties. For each of the six biological polymers listed, indicate which of the properties apply. Each polymer has multiple properties, and a given property may be used more than once.

Polymers

(a) Cellulose

(b) Messenger RNA

(c) Globular protein

(d) Amylopectin

(e) DNA

(f) Fibrous protein

Properties

1. Branched-chain polymer
2. Extracellular location
3. Glycosidic bonds
4. Informational macromolecule
5. Peptide bond
6. β linkage
7. Phosphodiester bridge
8. Nucleoside triphosphates
9. Helical structure possible
10. Synthesis requires a template

3-2 Stability of Protein Structure. Several different kinds of bonds or interactions are involved in generating and maintaining the structure of proteins. List five such bonds or interactions, give an example of an amino acid that might be involved in each, and indicate which level(s) of protein structure might be generated or stabilized by that particular kind of bond or interaction.

3-3 Amino Acid Localization in Proteins. Amino acids tend to be localized either in the interior or on the exterior of a globular protein molecule, depending on their relative affinities for water.

(a) For each of the following pairs of amino acids, choose the one that is more likely to be found in the interior of a protein molecule, and explain why:

alanine; glycine	glutamate; aspartate
tyrosine; phenylalanine	methionine; cysteine

(b) Explain why cysteine residues with free sulfhydryl groups tend to be localized on the exterior of a protein molecule, whereas those involved in disulfide bonds are more likely to be buried in the interior of the molecule.

3-4 Sickle-Cell Anemia. Sickle-cell anemia (see page 52) is a striking example of the drastic effect a single amino acid substitution can have on the structure and function of a protein.

(a) Given the chemical nature of glutamate and valine, can you suggest why substitution of valine for glutamate at position 6 of the β chain would be especially deleterious?

(b) Suggest several amino acids that would be much less likely than valine to cause impairment of hemoglobin function if substituted for the glutamate at position 6 of the β chain.

(c) Can you see why, in some cases, two proteins could differ at several points in their amino acid sequence and still be very similar in structure and function? Explain.

3-5 Hair Versus Silk. The α-keratin of human hair is a good example of a fibrous protein with extensive α-helical structure. Silk fibroin is also a fibrous protein, but it consists primarily of β-sheet structure. Fibroin is essentially a polymer of alternating glycines and alanines, whereas α-keratin contains most of the common amino acids and has many disulfide bonds.

(a) If you were able to grab onto both ends of an α-keratin polypeptide and pull, you would find it to be both extensible (it can be stretched to about twice its length in moist heat) and elastic (when you let go, it will return to its normal length). In contrast, a fibroin polypeptide has essentially no extensibility, and it has great resistance to breaking. Explain these differences.

(b) Can you suggest why fibroin assumes a pleated sheet structure, whereas α-keratin exists as an α helix and even reverts spontaneously to a helical shape when it has been stretched artificially?

3-6 The "Permanent" Wave That Isn't. The "permanent" wave that your local beauty parlor offers depends critically on rearrangements in the extensive disulfide bonds of keratin that give your hair its characteristic shape. To change the shape of your hair (that is, to give it a wave or curl), the beautician first treats your hair with a sulfhydryl reducing agent, then uses curlers or rollers to impose the desired artificial shape, and follows this by treatment with an oxidizing agent.

(a) What is the chemical basis of a permanent? Be sure to include the use of a reducing agent and an oxidizing agent in your explanation.

(b) Why do you suppose a permanent isn't permanent? (Explain why the wave or curl is gradually lost during the weeks following your visit to the beautician.)

(c) Can you suggest an explanation for naturally curly hair?

3-7 Features of Nucleic Acids. For each of the following features of nucleic acids, indicate whether it is true of DNA only (D), of RNA only (R), of both DNA and RNA (DR), or of neither (N).

(a) Contains the base adenine.

(b) Contains the nucleotide deoxythymidine monophosphate.

(c) Occurs only in single-stranded form.

(d) Is involved in the process of protein synthesis in the cytoplasm of the cells in the liver.

(e) Is synthesized by a process that involves base pairing.

(f) Is an inherently directional molecule, with an N-terminus on one end and a C-terminus on the other end.

3-8 Wrong Again. For each of the following false statements, change the statement to make it true, and explain why it was false:

(a) Proteins, nucleic acids, polysaccharides, and lipids are all very long polymers that are synthesized by condensation of individual monomer units.

(b) The amino acid proline is not found in α helices because its R group is too large to fit into the α helix.

(c) While a protein can be denatured by high-temperature treatment, extremes of pH generally have no effect on tertiary structure.

(d) Nucleic acids are synthesized from monomers that are activated by linking them to a carrier molecule in an energy-requiring reaction.

(e) α-D-glucose and β-D-glucose are stereoisomers.

(f) Fatty acids are important components of all cellular lipids.

(g) It is easy to predict the final folded structure of a protein from its amino acid sequence using today's powerful supercomputers.

(h) Most cells contain only three types of RNA: mRNA, tRNA, and rRNA.

3-9 Storage Polysaccharides. The only common examples of branched-chain polymers in cells are the storage polysaccharides glycogen and amylopectin. Both are degraded exolytically, which means by stepwise removal of terminal glucose units.

(a) Why might it be advantageous for a storage polysaccharide to have a branched-chain structure instead of a linear structure?

(b) Can you foresee any metabolic complications in the process of glycogen degradation? How do you think the cell handles this?

(c) Can you see why cells that degrade amylose instead of amylopectin have enzymes capable of endolytic (internal) as well as exolytic cleavage of glycosidic bonds?

(d) Why do you suppose the structural polysaccharide cellulose does not contain branches?

3-10 Carbohydrate Structure. From the following descriptions of gentiobiose, raffinose, and a dextran, draw Haworth projections of each:

(a) *Gentiobiose* is a disaccharide found in gentians and other plants. It consists of two molecules of β-D-glucose linked to each other by a $\beta(1 \rightarrow 6)$ glycosidic bond.

(b) *Raffinose* is a trisaccharide found in sugar beets. It consists of one molecule each of α-D-galactose, α-D-glucose, and β-D-fructose, with the galactose linked to the glucose by an $\alpha(1 \rightarrow 6)$ glycosidic bond and the glucose linked to the fructose by an $\alpha(1 \rightarrow 2)$ bond.

(c) *Dextrans* are polysaccharides produced by some bacteria. They are polymers of α-D-glucose linked by $\alpha(1 \rightarrow 6)$ glycosidic bonds, with frequent $\alpha(1 \rightarrow 3)$ branching. Draw a portion of a dextran, including one branch point.

3-11 Telling Them Apart. For each of the following pairs of molecules, specify a property that would distinguish between them, and indicate two different chemical tests or assays that could be used to make that distinction:

(a) The protein insulin and the DNA in the gene that encodes insulin

(b) The DNA that encodes insulin and the messenger RNA for insulin

(c) Starch and cellulose

(d) Amylose and amylopectin

(e) The monomeric protein myoglobin and the tetrameric protein hemoglobin

(f) A triacylglycerol and a phospholipid with a very similar fatty acid content

(g) A glycolipid and a sphingolipid

(h) A bacterial cell wall polysaccharide and chitin

• **3-12 Find an Example.** For each of the following classes of proteins, give two examples of specific proteins, briefly state how each one is important in cells, and mention a type of cell in which each protein would be found. You may use any available resources: later chapters in the text, your notes from other classes, or the Internet. Try to find examples that your professor may not be familiar with. (We love when our students can educate us!)

(a) Enzymes

(b) Structural proteins

(c) Motility proteins

(d) Regulatory proteins

(e) Transport proteins

(f) Hormonal proteins

(g) Receptor proteins

(h) Defensive proteins

(i) Storage proteins

3-13 Cotton and Potatoes. A cotton fiber consists almost exclusively of cellulose, whereas a potato tuber contains mainly starch. Cotton is tough, fibrous, and virtually insoluble in water. The starch present in a potato tuber, on the other hand, is neither tough nor fibrous and can be dispersed in hot water to form a turbid solution. Yet both the cotton fiber and the potato tuber consist primarily of polymers of D-glucose in $(1 \rightarrow 4)$ linkage.

(a) How can two polymers consisting of the same repeating subunit have such different properties?

(b) What is the advantage of the respective properties in each case?

• **3-14 Thinking About Lipids.** You should be able to answer each of the following questions based on the properties of lipids discussed in this chapter:

(a) How would you define a lipid? In what sense is the operational definition different from that of proteins, nucleic acids, or carbohydrates?

(b) Arrange the following lipids in order of decreasing polarity: cholesterol, estradiol, fatty acid, phosphatidyl choline, and triglyceride. Explain your reasoning.

(c) Which would you expect to resemble a sphingomyelin molecule more closely: a molecule of phosphatidyl choline containing two molecules of palmitate acid as its fatty acid side chains or a phosphatidyl choline molecule with one molecule of palmitate and one molecule of oleate as its fatty acid side chains? Explain your reasoning.

(d) Assume you and your lab partner Mort determined the melting temperature for each of the following fatty acids:

arachidic, linoleic, linolenic, oleic, palmitic, and stearic acids. Mort recorded the melting points of each but neglected to note the specific fatty acid to which each value belongs. Assign each of the following melting temperatures (in °C) to the appropriate fatty acid, and explain your reasoning: −11, 5, 16, 63, 70, and 76.5.

(e) For each of the following amphipathic molecules, indicate which part of the molecule is hydrophilic: phosphatidyl serine, sphingomyelin, cholesterol, and triacylglycerol.

3-15 Shortening. A popular brand of shortening has a label on the can that identifies the product as "partially hydrogenated soybean oil, palm oil, and cottonseed oil."

(a) What does the process of partial hydrogenation accomplish chemically?

(b) What did the product in the can look like before it was partially hydrogenated?

(c) What is the physical effect of partial hydrogenation?

(d) Why would it be misleading to say that the shortening is "made from 100% polyunsaturated oils"?

SUGGESTED READING

References of historical importance are marked with a •.
General References and Reviews

Jardetzky, O., and M. D. Finucane. *Dynamics, Structure, and Function of Biological Macromolecules.* Washington, DC: IOS Press, 2001.

Murray, R. K. *Harper's Illustrated Biochemistry,* 26th ed. New York: McGraw-Hill, 2003.

Wald, G. The origins of life. *Proc. Natl. Acad. Sci. USA* 52 (1994): 595.

Proteins

• Bernard, S. A., and F. W. Dahlquist. *Classic Papers on Protein Structure and Function.* Sausalito, CA: University Science, 2002.

Ellis, R. J., ed. *The Chaperonins.* New York: Academic Press, 1996.

Ezzell, C. Proteins rule. *Sci. Amer.* 286 (April 2002): 40.

Flannery, M. C. Proteins: The unfolding and folding picture. *Amer. Biol. Teacher* 61 (1999): 150.

Hartl, F. U., and M. Hayer-Hartl. Converging concepts of protein folding in vitro and in vivo. *Nature Struct. Mol. Biol.* 16 (2009): 574.

Kang, T. S., and R. M. Kini. Structural determinants of protein folding. *Cell. Mol. Life Sci.* 66 (2009): 2341.

Kryshtafovych, A., and K. Fidelis. Protein structure prediction and model quality assessment. *Drug Discov. Today* 14 (2009): 386.

Lesk, A. M. *Introduction to Protein Architecture: The Structural Biology of Proteins.* Oxford: Oxford University Press, 2001.

Moult, J., and E. Melamud. From fold to function. *Curr. Opin. Struct. Biol.* 10 (2000): 384.

Petsko, G. A., and D. Ringe. *Protein Structure and Function.* Sunderland, MA: Sinauer Assoc., 2004.

Ringler, P., and G. E. Schulz. Self-assembly of proteins into designed networks. *Science* 302 (2003): 106.

Nucleic Acids

Cao, X., G. Yeo, A. R. Muotri, T. Kuwabara, and F. H. Gage. Noncoding RNAs in the mammalian central nervous system. *Annu. Rev. Neurosci.* 29 (2006): 77.

Chen, X. Small RNAs and their roles in plant development. *Annu. Rev. Cell Dev. Biol.* 25 (2009): 21.

• Crick, F. H. C. The structure of the hereditary material. *Sci. Amer.* (October 1954): 54.

Davies, K. *Cracking the Genome: Inside the Race to Unlock Human DNA.* New York: The Free Press, 2001.

Ezzell, C. The business of the human genome. *Sci. Amer.* (July 2000): 48.

Forsdye, D. R. Chargaff's legacy. *Gene* 261 (2000): 127.

Frouin, I. et al. DNA replication: A complex matter. *EMBO Rep.* 4 (2003): 666.

Liu, Q., and Z. Paroo. Biochemical principles of small RNA pathways. *Annu. Rev. Biochem.* 79 (2010): 295.

• Portugal, F. H., and J. S. Cohen. *The Century of DNA: A History of the Discovery of the Structure and Function of the Genetic Substance.* Cambridge, MA: MIT Press, 1977.

Venter, J. C. et al. The sequence of the human genome. *Science* 291 (2001): 1304.

• Watson, J. *A Passion for DNA.* Cold Spring Harbor, NY: Cold Spring Harbor Laboratory Press, 2000.

Carbohydrates and Lipids

Akoh, C. C., and D. B. Min. *Food Lipids: Chemistry, Nutrition, and Biotechnology.* Boca Raton, FL: CRC Press, 2008.

Garg, H. G., M. K. Cowman, and C. A. Hales. *Carbohydrate Chemistry, Biology and Medical Applications.* New York: Elsevier, 2008.

Lindhorst, T. K. *Essentials of Carbohydrate Chemistry and Biochemistry,* 3rd ed.. Weinheim, Germany: Wiley-VCH, 2007.

Merrill, A. H., Jr., et al. Sphingolipids—the enigmatic lipid class: Biochemistry, chemistry, physiology, and pathophysiology. *Toxicol. Appl. Pharmacol.* 142 (1997): 208.

Shimizu, T. Lipid mediators in health and disease: Enzymes and receptors as therapeutic targets for the regulation of immunity and inflammation. *Annu. Rev. Pharmacol. Toxicol.* 49 (2009): 123.

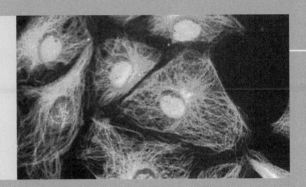

4

Cells and Organelles

*I*n the previous two chapters, we encountered the major kinds of molecules found in cells, as well as some principles governing the assembly of these molecules into the supramolecular structures that make up cells and their organelles. Now we are ready to focus our attention on cells and organelles directly.

Properties and Strategies of Cells

As we begin to consider what cells are and how they function, several general characteristics of cells quickly emerge. These include the organizational complexity and molecular components of cells, the sizes and shapes of cells, and the specializations that cells undergo.

All Organisms Are Bacteria, Archaea, or Eukaryotes

With improvements in microscopy, biologists came to recognize two fundamentally different types of cellular organization: a simpler one characteristic of bacteria and a more complex one found in all other kinds of cells. Based on the structural differences of their cells, organisms have been traditionally divided into two broad groups, the **prokaryotes** (bacteria) and the **eukaryotes** (plants, animals, fungi, algae, and protozoa). The most fundamental distinction between the two groups is that eukaryotic cells have a true, membrane-bounded nucleus (*eu–* is Greek for "true" or "genuine"; *–karyon* means "nucleus"), whereas prokaryotic cells do not (*pro–* means "before," suggesting an evolutionarily earlier form of life).

Recently, however, the term *prokaryote* is becoming less satisfactory to describe these non-nucleated cells, partly because this is a negative classification based on what cells do not have and partly because it wrongly implies a fundamental similarity among all organisms whose cells lack a nucleus. The fact that two organisms lack a particular gross structural feature does not necessarily imply evolutionary

relatedness—cells of humans and *Mycoplasma,* a type of bacterium, both lack cell walls but are not at all closely related. Likewise, sharing a gross structural feature does not necessarily mean a close relationship. Although plants and most bacteria have cell walls, they are only distantly related.

Molecular and biochemical criteria are proving to be more reliable than structural criteria in describing evolutionary relationships among organisms. The more closely related two different organisms are, the more similarities we see in their sequences of particular DNA, RNA, and protein molecules. Especially useful for comparative studies are molecules common to all living organisms that are necessary for universal, basic processes, in which even slight changes in component molecules are not well tolerated. This includes molecules such as the ribosomal RNAs used in protein synthesis and the cytochrome proteins used in energy metabolism.

Based on the pioneering ribosomal RNA sequencing work of Carl Woese, Ralph Wolfe, and coworkers, we now recognize that the group traditionally called the prokaryotes actually includes two widely divergent groups—the **bacteria** and the **archaea,** which are as different from each other as we are from bacteria! Rather than the prokaryote-eukaryote dichotomy, it is more biologically correct to describe all organisms as belonging to one of three *domains*—the bacteria, the archaea, or the **eukarya** (eukaryotes). As shown in **Table 4-1,** cells of each of these domains share some characteristics with cells of the other domains, but all three domains have some unique characteristics.

The bacteria include most of the commonly encountered single-celled, non-nucleated organisms that we have traditionally referred to as bacteria—for example, *Escherichia coli, Pseudomonas,* and *Streptococcus.* The archaea (which were called *archaebacteria* before investigators realized how different they are from bacteria) include many species that live in extreme habitats on Earth and have very diverse metabolic strategies. Members of the archaea include the

Property	Prokaryotes		Eukaryotes	Refer to:
	Bacteria	Archaea		
Typical size	Small (1–5 μm)	Small (1–5 μm)	Large (10–100 μm)	—
Nucleus and organelles	No	No	Yes	Table 4-2
Microtubules and microfilaments	Actin-like and tubulin-like proteins	Actin-like and tubulin-like proteins	Actin and tubulin proteins	Chapter 15
Exocytosis and endocytosis	No	No	Yes	Chapter 12
Cell wall	Peptidoglycan	Varies from proteinaceous to peptidoglycan-like	Cellulose in plants, fungi; none in animals, protozoa	
Mode of cell division	Binary fission	Binary fission	Mitosis or meiosis plus cytokinesis	Chapter 19
Typical form of chromosomal DNA	Circular, few associated proteins	Circular, associated with histone-like proteins	Linear, associated with histone proteins	Chapter 18
RNA processing	Minimal	Moderate	Extensive	Chapter 21
Transcription initiation	Bacterial type	Eukaryotic type	Eukaryotic type	Chapter 21
RNA polymerase	Bacterial type	Some features of both bacterial, eukaryotic types	Eukaryotic type	Chapter 21
Ribosome size and number of proteins	70S with 55 proteins	70S with 65 proteins	80S with 78 proteins	Chapter 22
Ribosomal RNAs	Bacterial type	Archaeal type	Eukaryotic type	Chapter 21
Translation initiation	Bacterial type	Eukaryotic type	Eukaryotic type	Chapter 22
Membrane phospholipids	Glycerol-3-phosphate + linear fatty acids	Glycerol-1-phosphate + branched polyisoprenoids	Glycerol-3-phosphate + linear fatty acids	Chapter 7

[*]This table lists many features that we have not yet discussed in detail. Its main purpose is to point out that, despite some sharing of characteristics, each of the three main cell types has a unique set of properties.

methanogens, which obtain energy from hydrogen while converting carbon dioxide into methane; the *halophiles,* which can grow in extremely salty environments; and the *thermacidophiles,* which thrive in acidic hot springs where the pH can be as low as 2 and the temperature can exceed 100°C! Rather than being considered as an evolutionarily ancient form of prokaryote (*archae–* is a Greek prefix meaning "ancient"), archaea are now considered to be descended from a common ancestor that also gave rise to the eukaryotes long after diverging from the bacteria, as shown here:

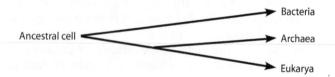

While resembling bacteria in many ways, archaea possess many unique features, as well as features that are found in eukaryotes. They resemble bacteria in cell size and gross structure, in their method of cell division, and in many aspects of basic metabolism and enzyme content. However, they are much more similar to eukaryotes regarding many details of DNA replication, transcription, RNA processing, and initiation of protein synthesis. Unique features of archaea include their ribosomal RNAs and their membrane phospholipids (Table 4-1).

Limitations on Cell Size

Cells come in various sizes and shapes. Some of the smallest bacterial cells, for example, are only about 0.2–0.3 μm in diameter—so small that about 50,000 such cells could fit side by side on your thumbnail. At the other extreme are highly elongated nerve cells, which may extend one or more meters. The nerve cells running the length of a giraffe's neck or legs are especially dramatic examples. So are bird eggs, which are extremely large single cells, although much of their internal volume is occupied by the yolk that nourishes the developing embryo.

Despite these extremes, most cells fall into a rather narrow and predictable range of sizes. Bacterial and archaeal cells, for example, are usually about 1–5 μm in diameter, while most cells of higher plants and animals have dimensions in the range of 10–100 μm. Why are cells so small? Several factors limit cell size, but the three most important are (1) the requirement for an adequate surface area/volume ratio, (2) the rates at which molecules diffuse, and (3) the need to maintain adequate local concentrations of the specific substances and enzymes involved in necessary cellular processes. Let's now look at each of these three factors in turn.

Surface Area/Volume Ratio. In most cases, the main limitation on cell size is set by the need to maintain an adequate **surface area/volume ratio.** Surface area is critical because it is at the cell surface that the needful exchanges between a cell and its environment take place. The cell's internal volume determines the amount of nutrients that will have to be imported and the quantity of waste products that must be excreted. The surface area effectively represents the amount of cell membrane available for such uptake and excretion.

The problem of maintaining adequate surface area arises because the volume of a cell increases with the cube of the cell's length or diameter, whereas its surface area increases only with the square. Thus, large cells have a lower ratio of surface area to volume than small cells do, as illustrated in **Figure 4-1**. This comparison illustrates a major constraint on cell size: As a cell increases in size, its surface area does not keep pace with its volume, and the necessary exchange of substances between the cell and its surroundings becomes more and more problematic. Cell size, therefore, can increase only as long as the membrane surface area is still adequate for the passage of materials into and out of the cell.

Some cells, particularly those that play a role in absorption, have characteristics that maximize their surface area. Effective surface area is most commonly increased by the inward folding or outward protrusion of the cell membrane. The cells lining your small intestine, for example, contain many fingerlike projections called *microvilli* that greatly increase the effective membrane surface area and therefore the nutrient-absorbing capacity of these cells (**Figure 4-2**).

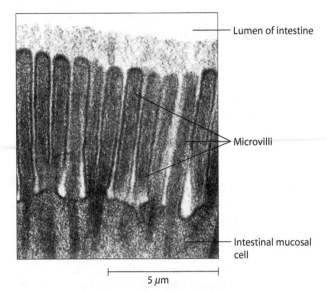

FIGURE 4-2 The Microvilli of Intestinal Mucosal Cells.
Microvilli are fingerlike projections of the cell membrane that greatly increase the absorptive surface area of intestinal mucosal cells, such as those lining the inner surface of your small intestine (TEM).

Volume stays the same, but surface area increases*

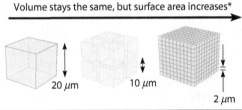

Number of cells	1	8	1000
Length of one side	20 μm	10 μm	2 μm
Total volume	8000 μm³	8000 μm³	8000 μm³
Total surface area	2400 μm²	4800 μm²	24,000 μm²
Surface area to volume ratio	0.3	0.6	3.0

*For a cube having a side with length s, volume = s^3 and surface area = $6s^2$.

FIGURE 4-1 The Effect of Cell Size on the Surface Area/Volume Ratio. The single large cell on the left, the eight smaller cells in the center, and the 1000 tiny cells on the right all have the same total volume (8000 μm³), but the total surface area increases as the cell size decreases. The surface area/volume ratio therefore increases from left to right as the linear dimension of the cell decreases. Note how the eight small cells in the center have the same total volume as the large cell on the left but twice the surface area. Likewise, the 1000 small bacterial cells on the right have the same total volume but a total surface area ten times that of the single large eukaryotic cell on the left.

Diffusion Rates of Molecules. Cell size is also limited by how rapidly molecules can move around in the cell to reach sites of specific cellular activities. Many molecules move through the cell by **diffusion,** which is the free, unassisted movement of a substance from a region of high concentration to a region of low concentration. Molecular movement can therefore be limited by the diffusion rates for molecules of various sizes. And because the rate of diffusion decreases as the size of the molecule increases, this limitation is most significant for macromolecules such as proteins and nucleic acids.

Recent work shows that many eukaryotic cells may be able to bypass this limitation by actively transporting ions, macromolecules, and other materials through the cytoplasm using special carrier proteins. Some cells of higher organisms get around this limitation to some extent by *cytoplasmic streaming* (also called *cyclosis* in plant cells), a process that involves active movement and mixing of cytoplasmic contents rather than diffusion. Other cells move specific molecules through the cell using vesicles that are transported along microtubules, as we will see shortly. In the absence of these mechanisms, however, the size of a cell is limited by the diffusion rates of the molecules it contains.

The Need for Adequate Concentrations of Reactants and Catalysts. A third limitation on cell size is the need to maintain adequate concentrations of the essential compounds and enzymes needed for the various processes that cells must carry out. For a chemical reaction to occur in a cell, the appropriate reactants must collide with and bind to a particular enzyme. The frequency of such collisions will be greatly increased by higher concentrations of the reactants and the enzyme. To maintain the concentration of a specific molecule, the number of molecules must increase proportionately with cell volume. Every time each of the three dimensions of the cell doubles, there is an eightfold increase in cell volume, and thus eight times as many molecules are required to maintain the original concentration. In the absence of a concentrating mechanism, this obviously taxes the cell's synthetic capabilities.

Eukaryotic Cells Use Organelles to Compartmentalize Cellular Function

An effective solution to the concentration problem is the *compartmentalization of activities* within specific regions of the cell. If all the enzymes and compounds necessary for a particular process are localized within a specific region, high concentrations of those substances are needed only in that region rather than throughout the whole cell.

To compartmentalize activities, most eukaryotic cells have a variety of **organelles,** which are membrane-bounded compartments that are specialized for specific functions. For example, the cells in a plant leaf have most of the enzymes, compounds, and pigments needed for photosynthesis compartmentalized together into structures called *chloroplasts.* Such a cell can therefore maintain appropriately high concentrations of everything it requires for photosynthesis within its chloroplasts without having to maintain correspondingly high concentrations of these substances elsewhere in the cell. In a similar way, other processes are localized within other compartments.

Bacteria, Archaea, and Eukaryotes Differ from Each Other in Many Ways

Returning to the distinction between bacteria, archaea, and eukaryotes, we recognize many important structural, biochemical, and genetic differences among these groups. Some of these differences are summarized in Table 4-1 and are discussed here briefly—others will be discussed in

later chapters. For now, it is important to realize that, despite some sharing of characteristics among cells of each of these three domains, each type of cell has a unique set of distinguishing properties.

Presence of a Membrane-Bounded Nucleus. As already noted, a structural distinction has traditionally been made between eukaryotes and prokaryotes (bacteria and archaea) and is reflected in the nomenclature itself. However, as we learn more about the cellular details of the three domains of living organisms, this distinction is becoming less important than other aspects of structure and function. A eukaryotic cell has a true, membrane-bounded nucleus, whereas a prokaryotic cell does not. Instead of being enveloped by a membrane, the genetic information of a bacterial or archaeal cell is folded into a compact structure known as the *nucleoid,* which is attached to the cell membrane in a particular region of the cytoplasm (**Figure 4-3**). Within a eukaryotic cell, on the other hand, most of the genetic information is localized to the nucleus, which is surrounded not by a single membrane but by a *nuclear envelope* consisting of two membranes (**Figure 4-4**). The nucleus also includes the *nucleolus,* which is the site of ribosomal RNA synthesis and ribosome subunit assembly, and it contains the DNA-bearing *chromosomes,* which are dispersed as chromatin throughout the semifluid *nucleoplasm* that fills the internal volume of the nucleus.

Use of Internal Membranes to Segregate Function. As Figure 4-3 illustrates, bacterial (and archaeal) cells generally do not contain internal membranes; most cellular functions occur either in the cytoplasm or on the plasma membrane. However, there is a group of photosynthetic bacteria known as *cyanobacteria* that have extensive internal membranes on which photosynthetic reactions are carried out. Also, some bacteria have membrane-bound structures that resemble organelles, while others have protein-lined compartments that serve

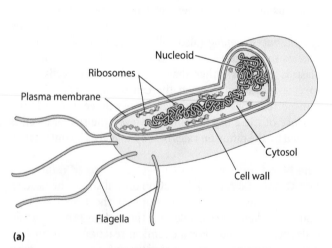

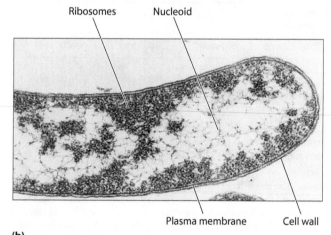

(a)

(b)

FIGURE 4-3 **Structure of a Rod-Shaped Bacterial Cell.** **(a)** A three-dimensional model showing the components of a bacterium. **(b)** An electron micrograph of a bacterial cell with several of the same components labeled. Notice that the nucleoid refers to the folded bacterial chromosome, not a membrane-bounded compartment (TEM).

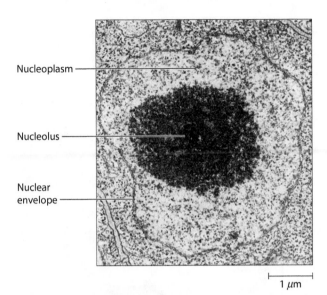

Nucleoplasm

Nucleolus

Nuclear
envelope

1 μm

FIGURE 4-4 The Nucleus of a Eukaryotic Cell. The nucleus is enclosed by a pair of membranes called the nuclear envelope. Because this cell is between divisions, the chromosomes are dispersed as chromatin in the nucleoplasm within the nucleus and are not visible. The nucleolus is involved in the synthesis of ribosomal components (TEM).

as organelles by isolating groups of enzymes involved in specific metabolic pathways. In contrast, nearly all eukaryotic cells make extensive use of internal membranes to compartmentalize specific functions (**Figure 4-5** and **Figure 4-6**), and they often have numerous organelles.

Examples of internal membrane systems in eukaryotic cells include the *endoplasmic reticulum,* the *Golgi complex,* and the membranes surrounding and delimiting organelles such as *mitochondria, chloroplasts, lysosomes,* and *peroxisomes,* as well as various kinds of *vacuoles* and *vesicles.* Each of these organelles is surrounded by its own characteristic membrane (or pair of membranes) that may be similar to other membranes in basic structure but can have a distinctive chemical composition. Localized within each such organelle is the molecular machinery needed to carry out the particular cellular functions for which the structure is specialized. We will meet each of these organelles later in this chapter and then return to each one in its appropriate context in succeeding chapters.

The Cytoskeleton. Also found in the cytoplasm of eukaryotic cells are several nonmembranous, proteinaceous structures that are involved in cellular contraction, motility, and the establishment and support of cellular architecture. These include the *microtubules* found in the cilia and flagella of many cell types, the *microfilaments* found in muscle fibrils and other structures involved in motility, and the *intermediate filaments,* which are especially prominent in cells that are subject to stress. Microtubules, microfilaments, and intermediate filaments are key components of the *cytoskeleton,* which imparts structure and elasticity to almost all eukaryotic cells, as we will learn shortly and explore in more detail in Chapter 15. In addition, the cytoskeleton can provide a scaffolding for

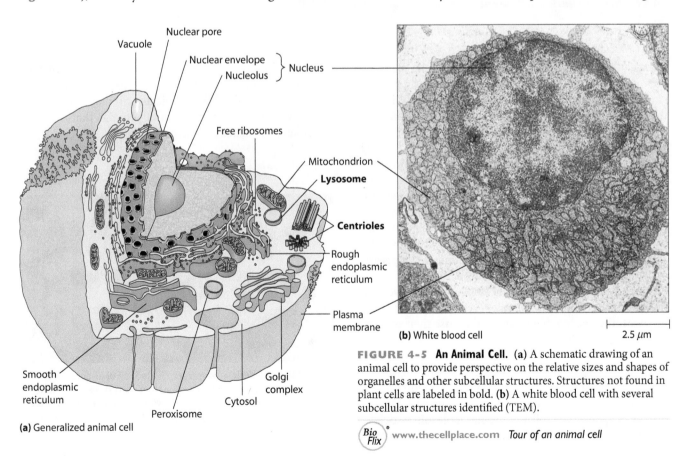

Vacuole

Nuclear pore

Nuclear envelope

Nucleolus

Nucleus

Free ribosomes

Mitochondrion

Lysosome

Centrioles

Rough endoplasmic reticulum

Plasma membrane

Smooth endoplasmic reticulum

Peroxisome

Cytosol

Golgi complex

(a) Generalized animal cell

(b) White blood cell

2.5 μm

FIGURE 4-5 An Animal Cell. (a) A schematic drawing of an animal cell to provide perspective on the relative sizes and shapes of organelles and other subcellular structures. Structures not found in plant cells are labeled in bold. **(b)** A white blood cell with several subcellular structures identified (TEM).

Bio Flix www.thecellplace.com *Tour of an animal cell*

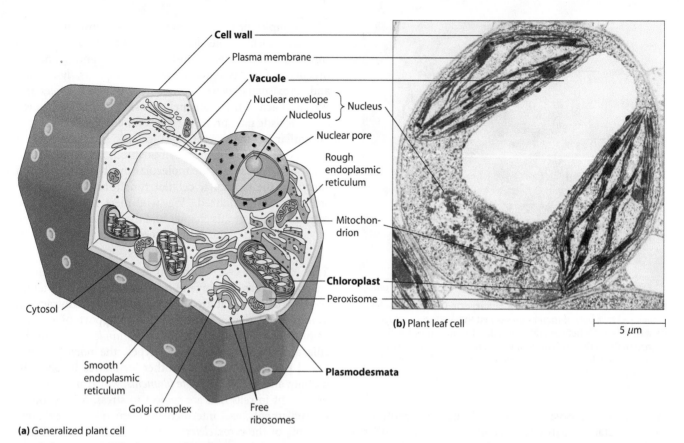

Cell wall
Plasma membrane
Vacuole
Nuclear envelope
Nucleolus
} Nucleus
Nuclear pore
Rough endoplasmic reticulum
Mitochondrion
Chloroplast
Peroxisome

Cytosol

Smooth endoplasmic reticulum

Golgi complex

Free ribosomes

Plasmodesmata

(a) Generalized plant cell

(b) Plant leaf cell

5 μm

FIGURE 4-6 A Plant Cell. **(a)** A schematic drawing of a plant cell. Compare this drawing with the animal cell in Figure 4-5a, and notice that plant cells are characterized by the absence of lysosomes and the presence of chloroplasts, a cell wall, and a large central vacuole. Structures not found in animal cells are labeled in bold. **(b)** A cell from a *Coleus* leaf, with several subcellular structures identified (TEM).

Bio Flix® **www.thecellplace.com** *Tour of a plant cell*

intracellular transport of vesicles to places in the cell where their contents are needed (**Figure 4-7**). Recently, proteins similar to cytoskeleton proteins have been found in bacteria and appear to have a role in maintaining cell shape.

Exocytosis and Endocytosis. A further feature of eukaryotic cells is their ability to exchange materials between the membrane-bounded compartments within the cell and the exterior of the cell. This exchange is possible because of *exocytosis* and *endocytosis*, processes involving membrane fusion events that are unique to eukaryotic cells. In endocytosis, portions of the plasma membrane invaginate and are pinched off to form membrane-bounded cytoplasmic vesicles containing substances that were previously on the outside of the cell. Exocytosis is essentially the reverse of this process: Membrane-bounded vesicles inside the cell fuse with the plasma membrane and release their contents to the outside of the cell.

Organization of DNA. Another distinction among bacteria, archaea, and eukaryotes is the amount and organization of the genetic material. Bacterial DNA is usually present in the cell as a circular molecule associated with relatively few proteins. On the other hand, eukaryotic

DNA exists in the cell as multiple linear molecules that are complexed with large amounts of proteins known as *histones*. Archaeal DNA is typically circular and is complexed with moderate amounts of proteins that resemble the eukaryotic histone proteins.

Microtubule   Vesicles   0.25 μm

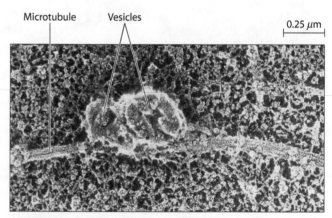

FIGURE 4-7 Vesicle Transport. This SEM of a squid giant axon shows two neurotransmitter-containing vesicles attached to a microtubule. The microtubule provides a "track" to move the molecules in these vesicles through the cell to the axon tips, where they will aid in nerve cell signaling.

The circular DNA molecule of a bacterial or archaeal cell is much longer than the cell itself. It therefore has to be folded and packed together tightly to fit into the cell. For example, the common intestinal bacterium *Escherichia coli* is only about a micrometer or two long, yet it has a circular DNA molecule about 1300 μm in circumference. Clearly, a great deal of folding and packing is necessary to fit that much DNA into such a small cell. By way of analogy, it is roughly equivalent to packing about 60 feet (18 m) of very thin thread into a typical thimble.

But if DNA appears to pose a packaging problem for prokaryotic cells, consider the case of the eukaryotic cell. Most eukaryotic cells have at least 1000 times as much DNA as *E. coli* has but encode only 5–10 times as many proteins. Because scientists did not know the function of the excess, noncoding DNA, it had been often referred to as "junk DNA."

Now, however, it appears that much of this excess DNA may have important functions other than encoding cellular proteins. Some of it is involved in production of regulatory miRNAs, other regions appear to be involved in generation of species diversity during evolution, and some contains repetitive sequences that appear to serve as binding sites for regulatory proteins. A recent study showed that up to 33% of the binding sites for transcription factors with roles in cancer development are found in these regions of repetitive DNA. Thus, we must be careful not to assume that there is no function for certain cellular components just because we currently do not understand their roles in the cell.

Whatever the function of such large amounts of DNA, the problem of packaging all this material is clearly acute. It is solved universally among eukaryotes by the organization of DNA into complex structures called **chromosomes,** which contain at least as much histone protein as DNA (see Figure 18-22). It is as chromosomes that the DNA of eukaryotic cells is packaged, segregated during cell division, and transmitted to daughter cells. **Figure 4-8** shows a chromosome from an animal cell as seen by high-voltage electron microscopy.

Segregation of Genetic Information. A further contrast between prokaryotes and eukaryotes is the way they allocate genetic information to daughter cells upon division. Bacterial and archaeal cells merely replicate their DNA and divide by a relatively simple process called *binary fission,* with one molecule of the replicated DNA and half of the cytoplasm going to each daughter cell. Following DNA replication in eukaryotic cells, the chromosomes are distributed equally to the daughter cells by the more complex processes of *mitosis* and *meiosis,* followed by *cytokinesis,* the division of the cytoplasm.

Expression of DNA. The differences among bacterial, archaeal, and eukaryotic cells extend to the expression of genetic information. Eukaryotic cells tend to transcribe genetic information in the nucleus into large RNA molecules and depend on later processing and transport

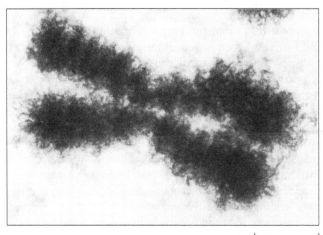

$\vdash\!\!-\!\!-\!\!\dashv$ 1 μm

FIGURE 4-8 A Eukaryotic Chromosome. This chromosome was obtained from a cultured Chinese hamster cell and visualized by high-voltage electron microscopy (HVEM). The cell was undergoing mitosis, and the chromosome is therefore highly coiled and condensed.

processes to deliver RNA molecules of the proper sizes to the cytoplasm for protein synthesis. Each RNA molecule typically encodes one polypeptide.

By contrast, bacteria transcribe very specific segments of genetic information into RNA messages, and often a single RNA molecule contains the information to produce several polypeptides. In bacteria, little or no processing of RNA occurs; a moderate amount is seen in archaea, though less than in eukaryotes. The absence of a nuclear membrane in bacteria and archaea makes it possible for messenger RNA molecules to become involved in the process of protein synthesis even before they are completely synthesized. Bacteria, archaea, and eukaryotes also differ in the size and composition of the ribosomes and ribosomal RNAs used to synthesize proteins (see Table 4-1). We will explore this distinction in more detail later in the chapter.

Cell Specialization Demonstrates the Unity and Diversity of Biology

In their structure and function, cells are characterized by both unity and diversity, as you can see in the generalized animal and plant cells shown in Figures 4-5 and 4-6. By unity and diversity, we simply mean that all cells resemble one another in fundamental ways, yet they differ from one another in other important ways. In upcoming chapters we will concentrate on those aspects of structure and function common to most cell types. We will find, for example, that virtually all cells oxidize sugar molecules for energy, transport ions across membranes, transcribe DNA into RNA, and undergo division to generate daughter cells.

Much the same is true for structural features. All cells are surrounded by a selectively permeable plasma membrane, all cells have ribosomes for protein synthesis, and all contain double-stranded DNA as their genetic information. Clearly, we can be confident that we are dealing with fundamental aspects of cellular organization and function when we consider processes and structures common to most, if not all, cells.

But sometimes our understanding of cellular biology is enhanced by considering not just the unity but also the diversity of cells—the features that are especially prominent in a particular cell type. For example, to understand how the process of protein secretion works, it is advantageous to consider a cell that is highly specialized for that particular function. Cells from the human pancreas are a good choice for studying this process because they secrete large amounts of digestive enzymes.

Similarly, to study functions known to occur in mitochondria, it is clearly an advantage to select a cell type that is highly specialized in the energy-releasing processes occurring in the mitochondrion. Such a cell would likely have a lot of well-developed, highly active mitochondria. In fact, it was for this very reason—to study a cell that is highly specialized for a particular function—that Hans Krebs chose the flight muscle of the pigeon as the tissue for carrying out the now-classic studies on the cyclic pathway of oxidative reactions that we know as the *tricarboxylic acid (TCA)*, or *Krebs, cycle.*

In general, the single cell of unicellular organisms must be capable of carrying out any and all of the functions necessary for survival, growth, and reproduction. It typically does not overemphasize any single function at the expense of others. Multicellular organisms, on the other hand, are characterized by a division of labor among tissues and organs that not only allows for but also depends on specialization of structure and function. Whole groups of cells become highly specialized for a particular task, which then becomes their specific role in the overall functioning of the organism.

The Eukaryotic Cell in Overview: Pictures at an Exhibition

From the preceding discussion, it should be clear that all cells carry out many of the same basic functions and have some of the same basic structural features. However, the cells of eukaryotic organisms are far more complicated structurally than bacterial or archaeal cells, primarily because of the organelles and other intracellular structures that eukaryotes use to compartmentalize various functions. The structural complexity of eukaryotic cells is illustrated by the typical animal and plant cells shown in Figures 4-5 and 4-6.

In reality, of course, there is no such thing as a truly "typical" cell; nearly all eukaryotic cells have features that distinguish them from the generalized cells shown in Figures 4-5 and 4-6. Nonetheless, most eukaryotic cells are sufficiently similar to warrant a general overview of their structural features.

As we have seen, a typical eukaryotic cell has at least four major structural features: an external *plasma membrane* to define its boundary and retain its contents, a *nucleus* to

Table 4-2	Chapter Cross-References for Cellular Structures and Techniques Used to Study Cells

For more detailed information about these cellular structures, see the following chapters:

Cytoskeleton	Chapter 15
Endoplasmic reticulum	Chapter 12
Golgi complex	Chapter 12
Lysosome	Chapter 12
Nucleus	Chapter 18
Peroxisome	Chapter 12
Plasma membrane	Chapter 7
Ribosome	Chapter 22

For more detailed information about techniques used to study cellular structures, see these chapters and the Appendix:

Autoradiography	Chapter 18 and Appendix
Centrifugation	Chapter 12
Electron microscopy	Appendix
Light microscopy	Appendix

house the DNA that directs cellular activities, *membrane-bounded organelles* in which various cellular functions are localized, and the *cytosol* interlaced by a *cytoskeleton* of microtubules and microfilaments. In addition, plant and fungal cells have a rigid *cell wall* external to the plasma membrane. Animal cells do not have a cell wall; they are usually surrounded by an *extracellular matrix* consisting primarily of proteins that provide structural support.

Our intention here is to look at each of these structural features in overview, as an introduction to cellular architecture. For now, we will simply look at each structure as we might look at pictures at an exhibition, moving through the gallery rather quickly just to get a feel for the overall display. Keep in mind, however, that these introductory "pictures" are only static representations of a dynamic cell that can adapt and respond to its environment. We will study each structure in detail in later chapters when we consider the dynamic cellular processes in which these organelles and other structures are involved (Table 4-2).

The Plasma Membrane Defines Cell Boundaries and Retains Contents

Our tour begins with the **plasma membrane** that surrounds every cell (Figure 4-9). The plasma membrane defines the boundaries of the cell, ensuring that its contents are retained. The plasma membrane consists of phospholipids, other lipids, and proteins and is organized into two layers (Figure 4-9b). Typically, each phospholipid molecule consists of two hydrophobic "tails" and a hydrophilic "head" and is therefore an *amphipathic molecule.*

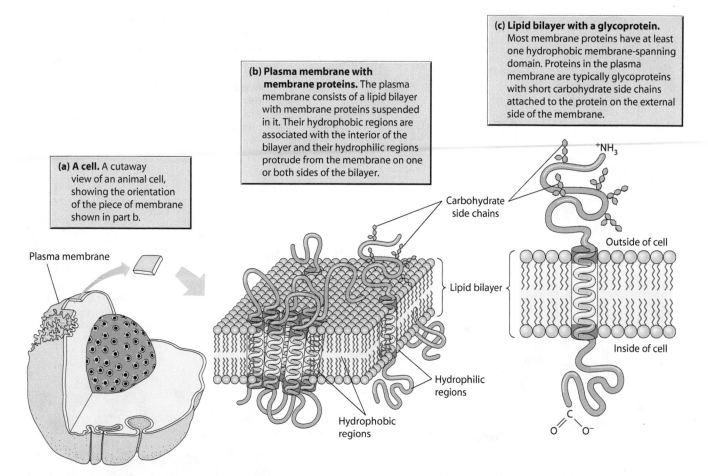

(a) A cell. A cutaway view of an animal cell, showing the orientation of the piece of membrane shown in part b.

(b) Plasma membrane with membrane proteins. The plasma membrane consists of a lipid bilayer with membrane proteins suspended in it. Their hydrophobic regions are associated with the interior of the bilayer and their hydrophilic regions protrude from the membrane on one or both sides of the bilayer.

(c) Lipid bilayer with a glycoprotein. Most membrane proteins have at least one hydrophobic membrane-spanning domain. Proteins in the plasma membrane are typically glycoproteins with short carbohydrate side chains attached to the protein on the external side of the membrane.

Plasma membrane

Carbohydrate side chains

Lipid bilayer

Outside of cell

Inside of cell

Hydrophilic regions

Hydrophobic regions

FIGURE 4-9 **Organization of the Plasma Membrane.** This figure shows successively more detail **(a)**–**(c)** in a section of the plasma membrane that surrounds all cells.

The phospholipid molecules orient themselves in the two layers of the membrane such that the hydrophobic, hydrocarbon tails of each molecule face inward and the hydrophilic, phosphate-containing heads of the molecules face outward (Figure 4-9c). The resulting **lipid bilayer** is the basic structural unit of virtually all membranes and serves as a permeability barrier to most water-soluble substances. Some members of Archaea, however, have an unusual phospholipid membrane that has long hydrophobic tails (twice the normal length) linked to a polar head group on both ends, forming a monolayer.

Membrane proteins are also amphipathic, with both hydrophobic and hydrophilic regions on their surfaces. They orient themselves in the membrane such that hydrophobic regions of the protein are located within the hydrophobic interior of the membrane, whereas hydrophilic regions protrude into the aqueous environment at the surfaces of the membrane. Many of the proteins with hydrophilic regions exposed on the external side of the plasma membrane have carbohydrate side chains known as oligosaccharides attached to them and are therefore called *glycoproteins* (Figure 4-9c).

The proteins present in the plasma membrane play a variety of roles. Some are *enzymes,* which catalyze reactions known to be associated with the membrane—reactions such as cell wall synthesis. Others serve as *anchors* for structural elements of the cytoskeleton that we will encounter later in the chapter. Still others are *transport proteins,* responsible for moving specific substances (ions and hydrophilic solutes, usually) across the membrane. Membrane proteins are also important as *receptors* for external chemical signals that trigger specific processes within the cell. Transport proteins, receptor proteins, and most other membrane proteins are *transmembrane proteins* that have hydrophilic regions protruding from both sides of the membrane. These hydrophilic regions are connected by one or more hydrophobic, membrane-spanning domains.

The Nucleus Is the Information Center of the Eukaryotic Cell

Perhaps the most prominent structure we encounter in a eukaryotic cell is the **nucleus** (**Figure 4-10**). The nucleus serves as the cell's information center. Here, separated from the rest of the cell by a membrane boundary, are the DNA-bearing chromosomes of the cell. Actually, the boundary around the nucleus consists of two membranes, called the *inner* and *outer nuclear membranes.* Taken together, the two membranes make up the **nuclear envelope.** Unique to the membranes of the nuclear envelope are numerous small

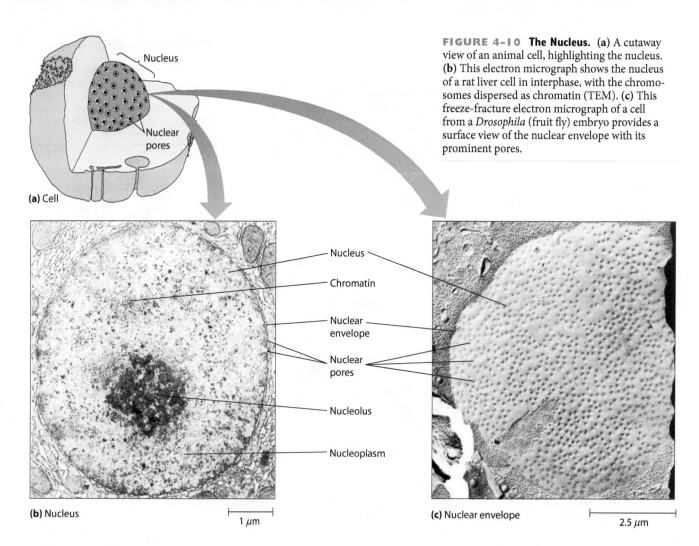

FIGURE 4-10 **The Nucleus.** (a) A cutaway view of an animal cell, highlighting the nucleus. (b) This electron micrograph shows the nucleus of a rat liver cell in interphase, with the chromosomes dispersed as chromatin (TEM). (c) This freeze-fracture electron micrograph of a cell from a *Drosophila* (fruit fly) embryo provides a surface view of the nuclear envelope with its prominent pores.

(a) Cell

Nucleus

Nuclear pores

Nucleus

Chromatin

Nuclear envelope

Nuclear pores

Nucleolus

Nucleoplasm

(b) Nucleus   1 μm

(c) Nuclear envelope   2.5 μm

openings called *pores* (Figure 4-10). Each pore is a channel through which water-soluble molecules and supramolecular complexes can move between the nucleus and cytoplasm. This channel is lined with transport machinery known as a *pore complex* that regulates the movement of macromolecules through the nuclear envelope and is shown in close-up detail in Figures 18-28 and 18-29. Ribosomal subunits, messenger RNA molecules, chromosomal proteins, and enzymes needed for nuclear activities are transported across the nuclear envelope through these nuclear pores.

The number of chromosomes within the nucleus is characteristic of the species. It can be as low as two (in the sperm and egg cells of some grasshoppers, for example), or it can run into the hundreds. Chromosomes are most readily visualized during mitosis, when they are highly condensed and can easily be stained (see Figure 4-8). During the *interphase* between divisions, on the other hand, chromosomes are dispersed as DNA-protein fibers called **chromatin** and are not easy to visualize (Figure 4-10b).

Also present in the nucleus are **nucleoli** (singular: **nucleolus**), structures responsible for synthesizing and assembling some of the RNA and protein components needed to form the ribosomes. Nucleoli are usually associated with specific regions of particular chromosomes that contain the genes encoding ribosomal RNAs.

Intracellular Membranes and Organelles Define Compartments

The internal volume of the cell exclusive of the nucleus is called the *cytoplasm* and is occupied by *organelles* and by the semifluid *cytosol* in which they are suspended. By "semifluid," we mean that the cytosol is not a thin, watery liquid. Instead, it is believed to be a more viscous material with a consistency closer to that of honey or soft gelatin. In this section, we will look at each of the major eukaryotic organelles. In a typical animal cell, these compartments make up almost half of the cell's total internal volume.

As we continue on our tour of the eukaryotic cell and begin to explore its organelles, you may find it helpful to view these subcellular structures from a human perspective by reading **Box 4A** and acquainting yourself with some of the heritable human diseases that are associated with malfunctions of specific organelles. In most cases, these disorders are caused by genetic defects in specific proteins—enzymes and transport proteins, most commonly—that are localized to particular organelles.

The Mitochondrion. Our tour of the eukaryotic organelles begins with a prominent organelle—the **mitochondrion** (plural: **mitochondria**), shown in **Figure 4-11**. Mitochondria

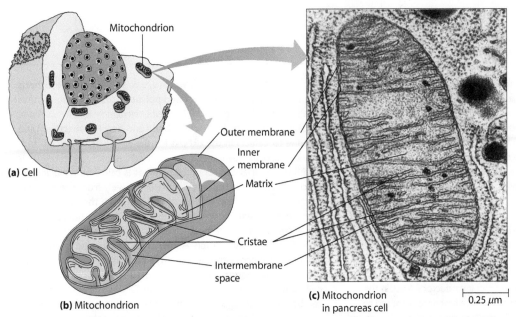

(a) Cell

(b) Mitochondrion

Mitochondrion

Outer membrane

Inner membrane

Matrix

Cristae

Intermembrane space

(c) Mitochondrion in pancreas cell

0.25 μm

FIGURE 4-11 **The Mitochondrion.** (a) A cutaway view showing the relative numbers and size of the mitochondria within a typical animal cell. Remember that plant cells and all other eukaryotic cells also have mitochondria. (b) A schematic illustration of mitochondrial structure. (c) A mitochondrion in a rat pancreas cell (TEM).

VIDEOS www.thecellplace.com *Mitochondria in 3-D*

are found in all eukaryotic cells and are the site of aerobic respiration. Mitochondria are large by cellular standards—up to a micrometer across and usually a few micrometers long. A mitochondrion is therefore comparable in size to a whole bacterial cell. Most eukaryotic cells contain hundreds of mitochondria, and each mitochondrion is surrounded by two membranes, designated the *inner* and *outer mitochondrial membranes*. Also found in mitochondria are small, circular molecules of DNA that encode some of the RNAs and proteins needed in mitochondria, along with the ribosomes involved in protein synthesis. In humans and most animals, mitochondria are inherited only through the mother. Therefore, analysis of mitochondrial DNA sequences has been quite useful in tracing genetic lineages in order, for example, to determine the geographic region(s) of origin and subsequent dispersal of modern humans.

Oxidation of sugars and other cellular "fuel" molecules to carbon dioxide in mitochondria extracts energy from food molecules and conserves it as *adenosine triphosphate (ATP)*. It is within the mitochondrion that the cell localizes most of the enzymes and intermediates involved in such important cellular processes as the TCA cycle, fat oxidation, and ATP generation. Most of the intermediates involved in transporting electrons from oxidizable food molecules to oxygen are located in or on the **cristae** (singular: **crista**), infoldings of the inner mitochondrial membrane. Other reaction sequences, particularly those of the TCA cycle and those involved in fat oxidation, occur in the semifluid **matrix** that fills the inside of the mitochondrion.

The number and location of mitochondria within a cell can often be related directly to their role in that cell.

Tissues with an especially heavy demand for ATP as an energy source can be expected to have cells that are well endowed with mitochondria, and the organelles are usually located within the cell just where the energy need is greatest. This localization is illustrated by the sperm cell in **Figure 4-12**. As the drawing indicates, a sperm cell often

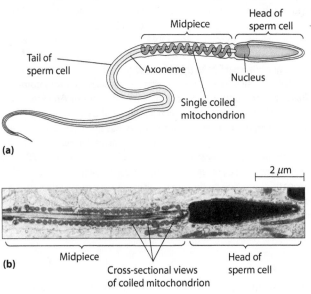

Head of sperm cell

Midpiece

Tail of sperm cell

Axoneme

Nucleus

Single coiled mitochondrion

(a)

2 μm

(b) Midpiece

Cross-sectional views of coiled mitochondrion

Head of sperm cell

FIGURE 4-12 **Localization of the Mitochondrion Within a Sperm Cell.** The single mitochondrion present in a sperm cell is coiled tightly around the axoneme of the tail, reflecting the localized need of the sperm tail for energy. (a) A schematic drawing of a sperm. (b) An electron micrograph of the head and the midpiece of a sperm cell from a marmoset monkey (TEM).

The Eukaryotic Cell in Overview: Pictures at an Exhibition   **85**

Although we may not often acknowledge it—indeed, we may not even be aware of it—many human diseases are actually caused by molecular malfunctions within specific organelles. In fact, several of the organelles that we have encountered on our tour of the "picture exhibition" in this chapter—and that we will encounter in more detail in later chapters—are the sites of a variety of human genetic disorders. Most of them are rare but very serious when they occur. The list of organelle-linked diseases is lengthy, including such diverse mitochondrial disorders as *myopathies* (diseases or disorders of muscle cells), *Leigh syndrome* (a devastating neurodegenerative disorder), and *fatal infantile respiratory defects*. Also included are peroxisomal disorders such as *Zellweger syndrome* and *neonatal adrenoleukodystrophy*, as well as more than 40 *lysosomal storage diseases*, each marked by the harmful accumulation of specific substances. We will consider several of these diseases here, though only at an introductory level. In the process we will anticipate discussions of the functions localized to several organelles, including mitochondria as well as peroxisomes and lysosomes (Chapter 12).

Mitochondrial Disorders

Most of the diseases associated with mitochondrial defects are characteristic of either muscle or nerve tissue. This is not surprising, given the high rates of ATP consumption by these tissues and the essential role of the mitochondrion in ATP synthesis. The list includes at least 35 myopathies, as well as a variety of disorders affecting nerve function. Depending on the specific defect, these disorders range greatly in severity. Some lead to infant death; others result in blindness, deafness, seizures, or stroke-like episodes. Milder forms, on the other hand, are characterized by muscular weakness, intolerance of exercise, muscle deterioration, and, in some cases, infertility due to nonmotile sperm.

These are all genetic disorders; and to understand them, we need to know that mitochondria have a limited amount of their own DNA. The mitochondrion encodes some, though by no means all, of its own proteins. Human mitochondrial DNA (mtDNA) consists of 16,568 base pairs and contains 37 genes: 22 specify transfer RNAs (tRNAs), 2 specify ribosomal RNAs (rRNAs), and the remaining 13 encode polypeptides, all of which are components of the respiratory complexes that carry out oxygen-dependent ATP synthesis. An extensive amount of information regarding mitochondrial DNA, including mutations associated with human diseases, has been compiled by the MITOMAP project at the University of California–Irvine.

Although the respiratory complexes also contain about 70 nuclear-encoded polypeptides, most of the known mitochondrial myopathies are due to defects in mitochondrial rather than in nuclear genes, involving either the deletion or mutation of specific mitochondrial genes. Most of these defects occur in the genes that encode *mitochondrial tRNAs*, which are required for the synthesis of all 13 mitochondrially encoded polypeptides. Examples of these diseases include *mitochondrial encephalomyopathy* and *hypertrophic cardiomyopathy*, which affect the brain and heart, respectively, and are due to defects in the tRNAs for the amino acids leucine and isoleucine, respectively.

Mitochondrial disorders follow what is called *maternal inheritance*, which means that they come exclusively from the mother. Since all human mitochondria are derived from the mitochondria that were present in the egg at the time of fertilization, the sperm cell provides its half of the nuclear genome but makes little or no mitochondrial contribution. A further distinction between nuclear and mitochondrial genes is that a typical human cell contains hundreds of mitochondria, each with 2 to 10 copies of mtDNA, so the cell contains thousands of copies of mtDNA. As a result, mtDNAs can be quite heterogeneous within specific tissues, and mitochondrial disorders are likely to arise only when most of the mitochondria within a given tissue contain a particular mutant gene.

Peroxisomal Disorders

Most of the human diseases associated with peroxisomes are due to the absence of a single peroxisomal protein. Considering the variety of cellular functions that are localized to this organelle, it is not surprising that many disorders are known in which specific peroxisomal proteins are either defective or absent. Unlike mitochondria, peroxisomes contain no DNA; thus, all of these defects are due to mutations in nuclear genes.

There are several well-studied peroxisomal disorders: *Zellweger syndrome (ZS), neonatal adrenoleukodystrophy (NALD), X-linked adrenoleukodystrophy (X-ALD)*, and *infantile Refsum disease (IRD)*. ZS is characterized by a variety of severe neurological, visual, and liver disorders that lead to death during early childhood, often by age one or two. NALD (autosomal recessive) and X-ALD (sex-linked, typically male-only) are less severe than ZS but eventually lead to neurological impairment and death. Patients with NALD or X-ALD usually begin to display symptoms of adrenal failure and neurological debilitation during early childhood. The symptoms of IRD are similar to, but less severe than, those of ZS and NALD.

Although these diseases were discovered independently and not initially considered to be related, we now know that each of these disorders is caused by mutations in any of 11 different human genes. The most severe mutations in these genes cause ZS, moderately severe mutations cause NALD, and the least severe mutations cause IRD.

In some forms of NALD, the defective gene product is a membrane protein involved in the transport of very-long-chain fatty acids into the peroxisomes, where such fatty acids are broken

has a single spiral mitochondrion wrapped around the central shaft, or *axoneme,* of the cell. Notice how tightly the mitochondrion coils around the axoneme, just where the ATP is actually needed to propel the sperm cell. Muscle cells and cells that specialize in the transport of ions also have numerous mitochondria located strategically to meet the special energy needs of such cells (**Figure 4-13**).

The Chloroplast. The next organelle we encounter on our gallery tour is the **chloroplast,** the site of photosynthesis in plants and algae (**Figure 4-14**). Chloroplasts are large organelles, typically a few micrometers in diameter and 5–10 μm long, and can be quite numerous in the leaves of green plants. They are therefore substantially bigger than mitochondria and larger than any other structure in a

down to shorter chain lengths that can be handled by the mitochondrion. When this transport mechanism is impaired or nonfunctional, the very-long-chain fatty acids accumulate in cells and tissues. That accumulation is particularly devastating in the brain, where the very-long-chain fatty acids destroy the myelin sheaths that provide essential insulation for nerve cells, thereby profoundly impairing transmission of neural signals.

Similarly, X-ALD is caused by mutation of a gene encoding a peroxisomal transporter, *ABCD-1*. This transporter is involved in recycling of myelin, a component of the sheath that surrounds neurons. Its deficiency leads to demyelination and neurodegeneration and is typically fatal before adolescence. However, in late 2009, early results of a gene therapy trial showed significant promise: neural degeneration was halted in two X-ALD patients who received an infusion of their own blood cells that had been treated with a modified viral vector containing a functional gene encoding *ABCD-1*.

In ZS, the missing or defective gene product can be any of several proteins that are essential for targeting peroxisomal enzymes for uptake by the organelle. As we will learn in Chapter 12, peroxisomal proteins are encoded by nuclear genes, synthesized on cytoplasmic ribosomes, and then imported into the peroxisome. Individuals with ZS can typically synthesize all of the requisite enzymes, but they have a deficiency in any of several membrane proteins involved in transporting these enzymes into the organelle. As a result, the proteins remain in the cytosol, where they cannot perform their intended functions. Peroxisomes can be detected in the cells of such individuals, but the organelles are empty "ghosts"—membrane-bounded structures without the normal complement of enzymes. Not surprisingly, afflicted individuals develop various neurological, visual, and liver disorders that lead inevitably to death during early childhood.

Lysosomal Disorders

Another organelle subject to a variety of genetic defects is the lysosome, which plays an essential role in the digestion of food molecules and in the recycling of cellular components that are no longer needed. Over 40 heritable *lysosomal storage diseases* are known, each characterized by the harmful accumulation of a specific substance or class of substances—most commonly polysaccharides or lipids—that would normally be catabolized by the hydrolytic enzymes present within the lysosome. In some cases, the defective protein is either a key enzyme in degrading the substance or a protein involved in transporting the degradation products out of the lysosome. In other cases, the requisite enzymes are synthesized in normal amounts but are secreted into the extracellular medium rather than being targeted to the lysosomes.

An example of this latter type of disorder is *I-cell disease*, which is due to a defect in an enzyme called N-acetylglucosamine phospho-

transferase. This enzyme is required to correctly process the portion of the protein that targets, or signals, lysosomal enzymes for import into the organelle. Without the necessary signal, the hydrolytic enzymes are not transported into the lysosomes. Thus, the lysosomes become engorged with undegraded polysaccharides, lipids, and other material. This causes irreversible damage to the cells and tissues.

A well-known example is *Tay-Sachs disease*, which is quite rare in the general population but has a higher incidence among Ashkenazi Jews of eastern European ancestry. After about six months, children who are homozygous for this defect show rapid mental and motor deterioration as well as skeletal, cardiac, and respiratory dysfunction. This is followed by dementia, paralysis, blindness, and death, usually within three years. The disease results from the accumulation in nervous tissue of a particular glycolipid called *ganglioside G_{M2}*. (For the structure of gangliosides, see Figure 7-6.) The missing or defective lysosomal enzyme is *β-N-acetylhexosaminidase A*, which cleaves the terminal N-acetylgalactosamine from the "glyco" (carbohydrate) portion of the ganglioside. G_{M2} is a prominent component of the membranes in brain cells. Not surprisingly, lysosomes from children afflicted with Tay-Sachs disease are filled with membrane fragments containing undigested gangliosides.

All of the known lysosomal storage diseases can be diagnosed prenatally. Even more significant are the prospects for *enzyme replacement therapy* and *gene therapy*. Enzyme replacement therapy has been shown to be effective with a particular lysosomal disorder called *Gaucher disease*, characterized by the absence or deficiency of a specific hydrolase called *glucocerebrosidase*. In the absence of this enzyme, lipids called *glucocerebrosides* accumulate in the lysosomes of macrophages, which are the white blood cells that engulf and digest foreign material or invasive microorganisms as well as cellular debris and whole damaged cells. (The structure of cerebrosides is also shown in Figure 7-6.) Glucocerebroside accumulation typically leads to liver and spleen enlargement, anemia, and mental retardation. In the past, treatment depended on the ability to purify glucocerebrosidase from human placental material, treat it so that it could be taken up by macrophages, and infuse it into the bloodstream. Recently, however, a synthetic form has been produced using recombinant DNA technology, simplifying the treatment protocol. Macrophages that take up this enzyme are able to degrade glucocerebrosides as needed, thereby effectively treating what would otherwise be a fatal disease.

Gene therapy is a somewhat more futuristic prospect for the treatment of lysosomal storage diseases as well as other heritable disorders. This approach involves inserting the genes for the missing enzymes into the appropriate cells, thereby effectively curing the disease rather than simply treating it. For a further consideration of gene therapy.

typical plant cell except the nucleus. (However, in some algae, there is a single large chloroplast that can be larger than the nucleus.) Like mitochondria, chloroplasts are surrounded by both an inner and an outer membrane. Inside the chloroplast there is a third membrane system consisting of flattened sacs called **thylakoids** and the membranes (**stroma thylakoids**), that interconnect them. Thylakoids

are stacked together to form the **grana** (singular: **granum**) that characterize most chloroplasts (Figure 4-14c, d).

Chloroplasts are the site of *photosynthesis*, the light-driven process that uses solar energy and carbon dioxide to manufacture the sugars and other organic compounds from which all life is ultimately fabricated. Chloroplasts are found in leaves and other photosynthetic tissues of higher plants,

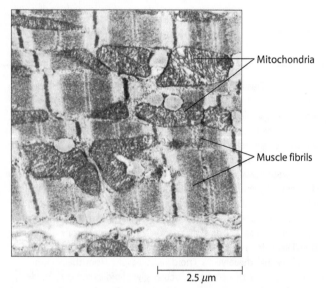

Mitochondria

Muscle fibrils

2.5 μm

FIGURE 4-13 Localization of Mitochondria Within a Muscle Cell. This electron micrograph of a muscle cell from a cat heart shows the intimate association of mitochondria with the muscle fibrils that are responsible for muscle contraction (TEM).

that this reduction process is the reverse of the energy-producing oxidation reactions in mitochondria that convert sugar to carbon dioxide.) Reactions that depend directly on solar energy are localized in or on the thylakoid membrane system. Reactions involved in the reduction of carbon dioxide to sugar molecules occur within the semifluid **stroma** that fills the interior of the chloroplast. Also found in the stroma are chloroplast ribosomes along with small, circular molecules of DNA that encode some of the RNAs and proteins needed in the chloroplast.

Although known primarily for their role in photosynthesis, chloroplasts are also involved in a variety of other chemical processes. They contain enzymes that reduce nitrogen from the oxidation level of soil-derived nitrate ions (NO_3^-) to ammonia (NH_3), the form of nitrogen required for protein synthesis. Enzymes in the chloroplast also catalyze the reduction of sulfate ions (SO_4^{2-}) to hydrogen sulfide (H_2S), which can be incorporated into the amino acid cysteine for use in protein synthesis. Furthermore, the chloroplast is the most prominent example of a class of plant organelles known as the **plastids.** Plastids other than chloroplasts perform a variety of functions in plant cells. *Chromoplasts,* for example, are pigment-containing plastids that are responsible for the characteristic coloration of flowers, fruits, and other plant parts. *Amyloplasts* are plastids that are specialized for the storage of starch (amylose and amylopectin).

as well as in the algae. Located within this organelle are most of the enzymes, intermediates, and light-absorbing pigments needed for photosynthesis—the enzymatic reduction of carbon dioxide to sugar, an energy-requiring process. (Note

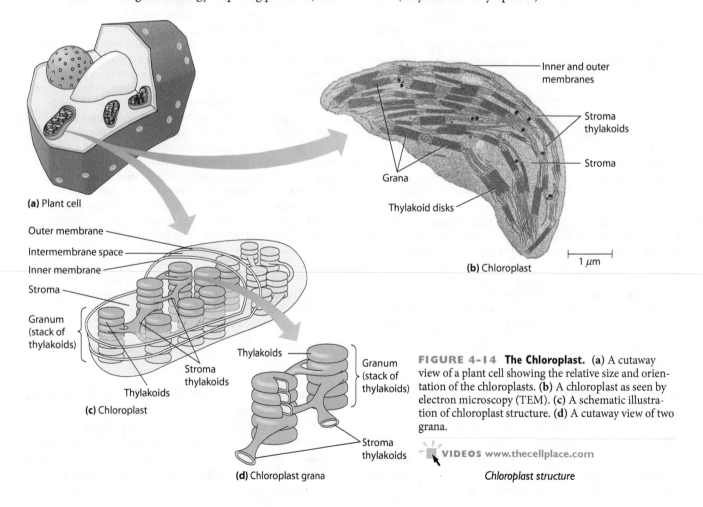

(a) Plant cell

Outer membrane
Intermembrane space
Inner membrane
Stroma
Granum (stack of thylakoids)

Stroma thylakoids
Thylakoids

(c) Chloroplast

Thylakoids

Granum (stack of thylakoids)

Stroma thylakoids

(d) Chloroplast grana

Inner and outer membranes

Stroma thylakoids

Stroma

Grana

Thylakoid disks

1 μm

(b) Chloroplast

FIGURE 4-14 The Chloroplast. (a) A cutaway view of a plant cell showing the relative size and orientation of the chloroplasts. **(b)** A chloroplast as seen by electron microscopy (TEM). **(c)** A schematic illustration of chloroplast structure. **(d)** A cutaway view of two grana.

VIDEOS www.thecellplace.com

Chloroplast structure

The Endosymbiont Theory: Did Mitochondria and Chloroplasts Evolve from Ancient Bacteria? Having just met the mitochondrion and chloroplast as eukaryotic organelles, we pause here for a brief digression concerning the possible evolutionary origins of these organelles. Both mitochondria and chloroplasts contain their own DNA and ribosomes, which enable them to carry out the synthesis of both RNA and proteins (although most of the proteins present in these organelles are in fact encoded by nuclear genes). As molecular biologists studied nucleic acid and protein synthesis in these organelles, they were struck by the many similarities between these processes in mitochondria and chloroplasts and the comparable processes in bacterial cells. Both have circular DNA molecules without associated histones, and both show similarities in rRNA sequences, ribosome size, sensitivity to inhibitors of RNA and protein synthesis, and the type of protein factors used in protein synthesis. In addition to these molecular features, mitochondria and chloroplasts resemble bacterial cells in size and shape, and they have a double membrane in which the inner membrane has bacterial-type lipids.

These similarities led to the **endosymbiont theory** for the evolutionary origins of mitochondria and chloroplasts. This theory proposes that both of these organelles originated from prokaryotes that gained entry to, and established a symbiotic relationship within, the cytoplasm of ancient single-celled organisms called *protoeukaryotes*. The endosymbiont theory proposes that protoeukaryotes ingested bacteria and cyanobacteria by a process known as *phagocytosis* ("cell eating"). Following phagocytosis, these cells were not digested; instead, they took up residence in the cytoplasm and eventually evolved into mitochondria and chloroplasts, respectively.

The Endoplasmic Reticulum. Extending throughout the cytoplasm of almost every eukaryotic cell is a network of membranes called the **endoplasmic reticulum,** or **ER** (**Figure 4-15**). The name sounds complicated, but *endoplasmic* just means "within the plasm" (of the cell), and *reticulum* is simply a fancy word for "network." The endoplasmic reticulum consists of tubular membranes and flattened sacs, or **cisternae** (singular: **cisterna**), that are interconnected. The internal space enclosed by the ER membranes is called the **lumen.** The ER is continuous with the outer membrane of the nuclear envelope (Figure 4-15a).

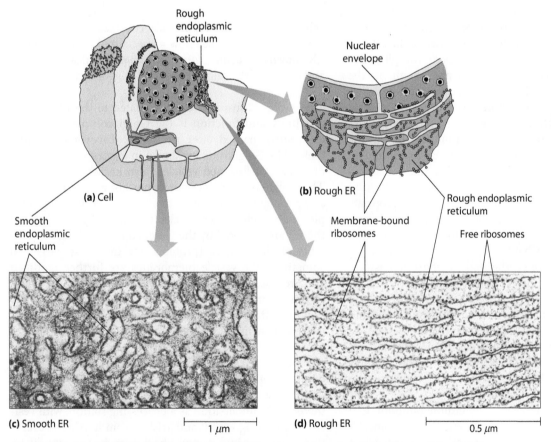

FIGURE 4-15 The Endoplasmic Reticulum. (**a**) A cutaway view of a typical animal cell showing the location and relative size of the endoplasmic reticulum (ER). (**b**) A schematic illustration depicting the organization of the rough ER as layers of flattened membranes. Rough ER membranes are studded on their outer surface with ribosomes and are continuous with the nuclear envelope. (**c**) An electron micrograph of smooth ER in a cell from guinea pig testis (TEM). (**d**) An electron micrograph of rough ER in a rat pancreas cell (TEM); notice that ribosomes are either attached to the ER or free in the cytosol.

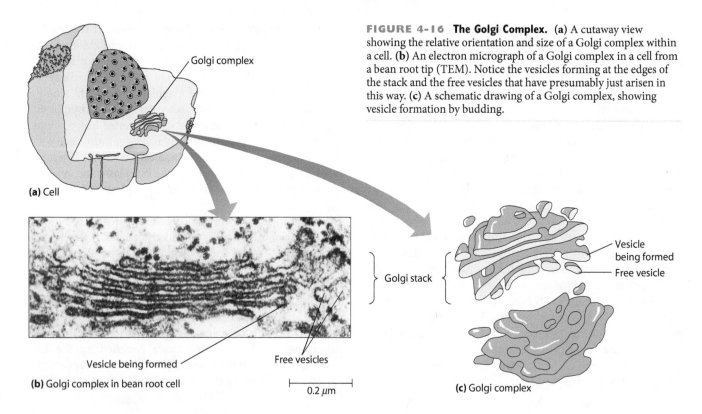

FIGURE 4-16 The Golgi Complex. (a) A cutaway view showing the relative orientation and size of a Golgi complex within a cell. **(b)** An electron micrograph of a Golgi complex in a cell from a bean root tip (TEM). Notice the vesicles forming at the edges of the stack and the free vesicles that have presumably just arisen in this way. **(c)** A schematic drawing of a Golgi complex, showing vesicle formation by budding.

Golgi complex

(a) Cell

(b) Golgi complex in bean root cell

Vesicle being formed

Free vesicles

0.2 μm

Golgi stack

Vesicle being formed

Free vesicle

(c) Golgi complex

The space between the two nuclear membranes is therefore a part of the same compartment as the lumen of the ER.

The ER can be either *rough* or *smooth*. **Rough endoplasmic reticulum (rough ER)** appears "rough" in the electron microscope because it is studded with ribosomes on the side of the membrane that faces the cytosol (Figure 4-15b, d). These ribosomes are actively synthesizing polypeptides that either accumulate within the membrane or are transported across the ER membrane to accumulate in the lumenal space inside the ER. Many membrane proteins and secreted proteins are synthesized in this way. These proteins then travel to the appropriate membrane or to the cell surface via the Golgi complex and secretory vesicles, as described in the following subsection (and in more detail in Chapter 12).

Not all proteins are synthesized by ribosomes associated with membranes of the rough ER, however. Much protein synthesis occurs on free ribosomes that are not attached to the ER but are instead found in the cytosol and are not associated with a membrane (Figure 4-15d). In general, secretory proteins and membrane proteins are made by ribosomes on the rough ER, whereas proteins intended for use within the cytosol or for import into organelles are made on free ribosomes.

The **smooth endoplasmic reticulum (smooth ER)** has no role in protein synthesis and hence no ribosomes. It therefore has a characteristically smooth appearance when viewed by electron microscopy (Figure 4-15c). Smooth ER is involved in the synthesis of lipids and steroids, such as cholesterol and the steroid hormones derived from it. In addition, smooth ER is responsible for inactivating and detoxifying drugs such as barbiturates and other compounds that might otherwise be toxic or harmful to the

cell. When we discuss muscle contraction in detail in Chapter 16, we will see how a specialized type of smooth ER known as the *sarcoplasmic reticulum* is critical for storage and release of the calcium ions that trigger contraction.

The Golgi Complex. Closely related to the ER in both proximity and function is the **Golgi complex** (or *Golgi apparatus*), named after its Italian discoverer, Camillo Golgi. The Golgi complex, shown in **Figure 4-16**, consists of a stack of flattened vesicles (also known as *cisternae*). The Golgi complex plays an important role in processing and packaging secretory proteins and in synthesizing complex polysaccharides. Vesicles that arise by budding off the ER are accepted by the Golgi complex. Here, the contents of the vesicles (proteins, for the most part) and sometimes the vesicle membranes are further modified and processed. The processed contents are then passed on to other components of the cell in vesicles that arise by budding off the Golgi complex (Figure 4-16c).

Most membrane proteins and secretory proteins are glycoproteins. The initial steps in *glycosylation* (addition of short-chain carbohydrates) take place within the lumen of the rough ER, but the process is usually completed within the Golgi complex. The Golgi complex should therefore be understood as a processing station, with vesicles both fusing with it and arising from it. Almost everything that goes into it comes back out—but in a modified, packaged form, often ready for export from the cell.

Secretory Vesicles. Once processed by the Golgi complex, secretory proteins and other substances intended for export from the cell are packaged into **secretory vesicles.** The cells of your pancreas, for example, contain many

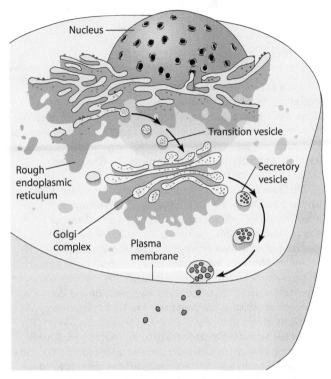

FIGURE 4-17 The Process of Secretion in Eukaryotic Cells. Proteins to be packaged for export are synthesized on the rough ER, passed to the Golgi complex for processing, and eventually compartmentalized into secretory vesicles. These vesicles then make their way to the plasma membrane and fuse with it, releasing their contents to the exterior of the cell.

such vesicles because the pancreas is responsible for the synthesis of several important digestive enzymes. These enzymes are synthesized on the rough ER, packaged by the Golgi complex, and then released from the cell via secretory vesicles, as shown in **Figure 4-17**. These vesicles from the Golgi region move to and fuse with the plasma membrane and discharge their contents to the exterior of the cell by the process of exocytosis. Together, the ER, Golgi, secretory vesicles, and the lysosomes we will discuss shortly constitute the cell's *endomembrane system*. The endomembrane system is responsible for *trafficking* of molecules through the cell, and this process of protein and lipid synthesis, processing, trafficking, and export via the ER, the Golgi complex, and secretory vesicles will be considered in more detail in Chapter 12.

The Lysosome. The next picture at our cellular exhibition is of the **lysosome,** an organelle about 0.5–1.0 μm in diameter and surrounded by a single membrane (**Figure 4-18**). Lysosomes were discovered in the early 1950s by Christian de Duve and his colleagues. The story of that discovery is recounted in **Box 4B** to underscore the significance of chance observations when they are made by astute investigators and to illustrate the importance of new techniques to the progress of science.

Lysosomes are used by the cell as a means of storing *hydrolases,* enzymes capable of digesting specific biological molecules such as proteins, carbohydrates, or fats. While

cells need such enzymes, both to digest food molecules and to break down damaged cellular constituents, these enzymes must be carefully sequestered until actually needed, lest they digest the normal components that were not scheduled for destruction in the cell.

Like secretory proteins, lysosomal enzymes are synthesized on the rough ER, transported to the Golgi complex, and then packaged into vesicles that can become lysosomes. A special carbohydrate covering on the inner surface of the lysosomal membrane protects this membrane (and the cell) from the hydrolytic activities of these enzymes until they are needed. Equipped with its repertoire of hydrolases, the lysosome is able to break down virtually any kind of biological molecule. Eventually, the digestion products are small enough to pass through the membrane into the cytosol of the cell, where they can be used to synthesize more macromolecules—recycling at the cellular level.

The Peroxisome. The next organelle at our exhibition is the **peroxisome.** Peroxisomes resemble lysosomes in size and general lack of obvious internal structure. Like lysosomes, they are surrounded by a single rather than a double membrane. Peroxisomes are found in plant and animal

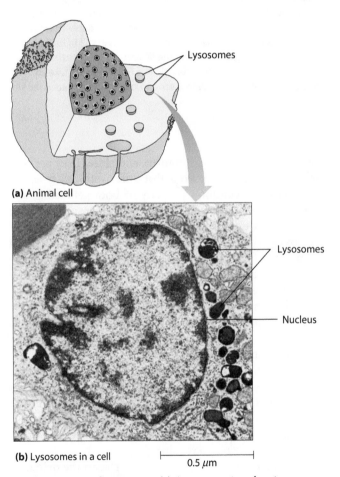

(a) Animal cell

(b) Lysosomes in a cell |——— 0.5 μm ———|

FIGURE 4-18 Lysosomes. (a) A cutaway view showing lysosomes within an animal cell. (b) Lysosomes in an animal cell stained cytochemically for acid phosphatase, a lysosomal enzyme. The cytochemical staining technique results in dense deposits of lead phosphate at the site of acid phosphatase activity (TEM).

The Eukaryotic Cell in Overview: Pictures at an Exhibition   **91**

Discovering Organelles: The Importance of Centrifuges and Chance Observations

Have you ever wondered how the various organelles within eukaryotic cells were discovered? There are almost as many answers to that question as there are kinds of organelles. In general, they were described by microscopists before their role in the cell was understood. As a result, the names of organelles usually reflect structural features rather than physiological roles. Thus, *chloroplast* simply means "green particle" and *endoplasmic reticulum* just means "network within the plasm (of the cell)."

Such is not the case for the *lysosome*, however. This organelle was the first to have its biochemical properties described before it had ever been reported by microscopists. Only after fractionation data had predicted the existence and properties of just such an organelle were lysosomes actually observed in cells. A suggestion of its function is even inherent in the name given to the organelle because the Greek root *lys*– means "to digest." (The literal translation is "to loosen," but that's essentially what digestion does to chemical bonds!)

The lysosome is something of a newcomer on the cellular biology scene; it was not discovered until the early 1950s. The story of that discovery is fascinating because it illustrates how important chance observations can be, especially when made by the right people at the right time. The account also illustrates how significant new techniques can be, since the discovery depended on subcellular fractionation, a technique that was then still in its infancy.

The story begins in 1949 in the laboratory of Christian de Duve, who later received a Nobel Prize for this work. Like so many scientific advances, the discovery of lysosomes depended on a chance observation made by an astute investigator. Because of an interest in the effect of insulin on carbohydrate metabolism, de Duve was attempting at the time to pinpoint the cellular location of *glucose-6-phosphatase*, the enzyme responsible for the release of free glucose in liver cells. For the control enzyme (that is, one not involved in carbohydrate metabolism), de Duve happened to choose *acid phosphatase*.

De Duve first homogenized liver tissue and resolved it into several fractions by the new technique of *differential centrifugation*, which separates cellular components based on differences in size and density. In this way, he was able to show that the glucose-6-phosphatase activity could be recovered with the microsomal fraction. (*Microsomes* are small vesicles that form from ER fragments when tissue is homogenized.) This in itself was an important observation because it helped establish the identity of microsomes, which at the time tended to be dismissed as fragments of mitochondria.

But the acid phosphatase results turned out to be still more interesting, even though they were at first quite puzzling. When de Duve and his colleagues assayed the liver homogenates for this enzyme, they found only a fraction of the expected activity. When assayed again for the same enzyme a few days later, however, the same homogenates had about ten times as much activity.

Speculating that he was dealing with some sort of activation phenomenon, de Duve subjected the homogenates to differential centrifugation to see which subcellular fraction the phenomenon was associated with. He and his colleagues were able to demonstrate

---

cells, as well as in fungi, protozoa, and algae. They perform several distinctive functions that differ with cell type, but they have the common property of both generating and degrading hydrogen peroxide (H_2O_2). Hydrogen peroxide is highly toxic to cells but can be decomposed into water and oxygen by the enzyme *catalase*. Eukaryotic cells protect themselves from the detrimental effects of hydrogen peroxide by packaging peroxide-generating reactions together with catalase in a single compartment, the peroxisome.

In animals, peroxisomes are found in most cell types but are especially prominent in liver and kidney cells (**Figure 4-19**). Beyond their role in detoxifying hydrogen peroxide, animal peroxisomes have several other functions, among them detoxifying other harmful compounds (such as methanol, ethanol, formate, and formaldehyde) and catabolizing unusual substances (such as D-amino acids). Some researchers speculate that peroxisomes may also be involved in regulating oxygen levels within the cell and may play a role in aging.

Animal peroxisomes also play a role in the oxidative breakdown of fatty acids, which are components of triacylglycerols, phospholipids, and glycolipids (see Figure 3-27). Fatty acid breakdown occurs primarily in the mitochondrion. However, fatty acids with

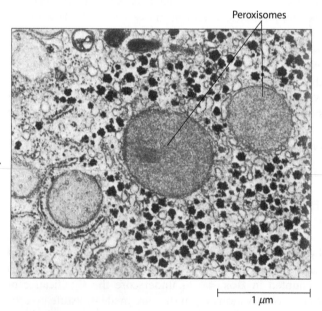

Peroxisomes

1 μm

FIGURE 4-19 Animal Peroxisomes. Several peroxisomes can be seen in this cross section of a liver cell (TEM). Peroxisomes are found in most animal cells but are especially prominent features of liver and kidney cells.

that much of the acid phosphatase activity could be recovered in the mitochondrial fraction and that this fraction showed an even greater increase in activity after standing a few days than did the original homogenates.

To their surprise, they then discovered that, upon recentrifugation, this elevated activity no longer sedimented with the mitochondria but stayed in the supernatant. They went on to show that the activity could be increased and the enzyme solubilized by a variety of treatments, including harsh grinding, freezing and thawing, and exposure to detergents or hypotonic conditions. From these results, de Duve concluded that the enzyme must be present in some sort of membrane-bounded particle that could easily be ruptured to release the enzyme. Apparently, the enzyme could not be detected within the particle, probably because the membrane was not permeable to the substrates used in the enzyme assay.

Assuming that particle to be the mitochondrion, they continued to isolate and study this fraction of the liver homogenates. At that point, another chance observation occurred, this time because of a broken centrifuge. The unexpected breakdown forced one of de Duve's students to use an older, slower centrifuge, and the result was a mitochondrial fraction containing little or no acid phosphatase. Based on this unexpected finding, de Duve speculated that the mitochondrial fraction as they usually prepared it might in fact contain two kinds of organelles: the actual mitochondria, which could be sedimented with either centrifuge, and some sort of more slowly sedimenting particle that came down only in the faster centrifuge.

This led them to devise a fractionation scheme that allowed the original mitochondrial fraction to be subdivided into a rapidly sedimenting component and a slowly sedimenting component. As you might guess, the rapidly sedimenting component contained the mitochondria, as evidenced by the presence of enzymes known to be mitochondrial markers. The acid phosphatase, on the other hand, was in the slowly sedimenting component, along with several other hydrolytic enzymes, such as ribonuclease, deoxyribonuclease, β-glucuronidase, and a protease. Each of these enzymes showed the same characteristic of increased activity upon membrane rupture, a property that de Duve termed *latency*.

By 1955, de Duve was convinced that these hydrolytic enzymes were packaged together in a previously undescribed organelle. In keeping with his speculation that this organelle was involved in intracellular lysis (digestion), he called it a *lysosome*.

Thus, the lysosome became the first organelle to be identified entirely on biochemical criteria. At the time, no such particles had been described by microscopy. But when de Duve's lysosome-containing fractions were examined with the electron microscope, they were found to contain membrane-bounded vesicles that were clearly not mitochondria and were in fact absent from the mitochondrial fraction. Knowing what the isolated particles looked like, microscopists were then able to search for them in fixed tissue. As a result, lysosomes were soon identified and reported in a variety of animal tissues. Within six years, then, the organelle that began as a puzzling observation in an insulin experiment became established as a bona fide feature of most animal cells.

more than 12 carbon atoms are oxidized relatively slowly by mitochondria. In the peroxisomes, on the other hand, fatty acids up to 22 carbon atoms long are oxidized rapidly. The long chains are degraded by the removal of two carbon units at a time until they get to a length (10–12 carbon atoms) that the mitochondria can efficiently handle.

The vital role of peroxisomes in breaking down long-chain fatty acids is underscored by the serious human diseases that result when one or more peroxisomal enzymes involved in degrading long-chain fatty acids are defective or absent. One such disease is neonatal adrenoleukodystrophy (NALD), a sex-linked (male-only) disorder that leads to profound neurological debilitation and eventually to death. (See Box 4A, pages 86–87, for a discussion of NALD and other human diseases associated with deficiencies in peroxisome function.)

The best-understood metabolic roles of peroxisomes occur in plant cells. During the germination of fat-storing seeds, specialized peroxisomes called **glyoxysomes** play a key role in converting stored fat into carbohydrates. In photosynthetic tissue, **leaf peroxisomes** are prominent due to their role in *photorespiration,* the light-dependent uptake of oxygen and release of carbon dioxide. The pho-

torespiratory pathway is an example of a cellular process that involves several organelles. While some of the enzymes that catalyze the reactions in this sequence occur in the peroxisome, others are located in the chloroplast or the mitochondrion. This mutual involvement in a common cellular process is suggested by the intimate association of peroxisomes with mitochondria and chloroplasts in many leaf cells, as shown in **Figure 4-20**.

Vacuoles. Some cells contain another type of membrane-bounded organelle called a **vacuole.** In animal and yeast cells, vacuoles are used for temporary storage or transport. Some protozoa take up food particles or other materials from their environment by phagocytosis. Phagocytosis is a form of endocytosis that involves an infolding of the plasma membrane around the desired substance. This infolding is followed by a pinching-off process that internalizes the membrane-bounded particle as a type of vacuole, known as a phagosome. Following fusion with a lysosome, the contents of a phagosome are hydrolyzed to provide nutrients for the cell.

Plant cells also contain vacuoles. In fact, a single large vacuole is found in most mature plant cells (**Figure 4-21**). This vacuole, sometimes called the **central vacuole,** may

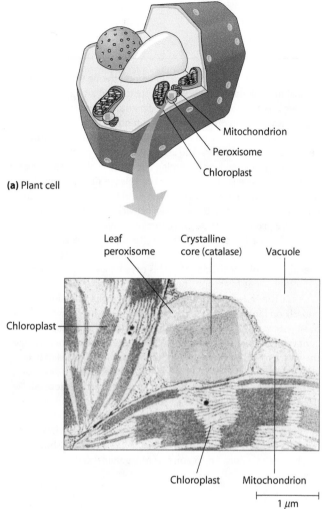

(a) Plant cell

Leaf peroxisome   Crystalline core (catalase)   Vacuole

Chloroplast

Chloroplast   Mitochondrion

1 μm

(b) Organelles in a plant leaf cell

FIGURE 4-20 A Leaf Peroxisome and Its Relationship to Other Organelles in a Plant Cell. (a) A cutaway view showing a peroxisome, a mitochondrion, and a chloroplast within a plant cell. (b) A peroxisome in close proximity to chloroplasts and to a mitochondrion within a tobacco leaf cell (TEM). This is probably a functional relationship because all three organelles participate in the process of photorespiration. The crystalline core frequently observed in leaf peroxisomes is the enzyme catalase, which catalyzes the decomposition of hydrogen peroxide into water and oxygen.

play a limited role in storage and in intracellular digestion. However, its main importance is its role in maintaining the *turgor pressure* that keeps tissue from wilting. The vacuole has a high concentration of solutes; thus, water tends to move into the vacuole, causing it to swell. As a result, the vacuole presses the rest of the cell constituents against the cell wall, thereby maintaining the turgor pressure. The limp appearance of wilted tissue results when the central vacuole does not provide adequate pressure. We can easily demonstrate this by placing a piece of crisp celery in salt water. The high concentration of salt on the outside of the cells will cause water to move out of the cells. As the turgor pressure decreases, the tissue will quickly become limp and lose its crispness.

Ribosomes. The last portrait in our gallery is the **ribosome.** Strictly speaking, the ribosome is not really an organelle because it is not surrounded by a membrane. We will consider it here, however, because ribosomes, like organelles, are the focal point for a specific cellular activity—in this case, protein synthesis. Ribosomes are found in all cells, but bacteria, archaea, and eukaryotes differ from each other in ribosome size and in the number and kinds of ribosomal protein and RNA molecules (see Table 4-1). Bacteria and archaea contain smaller ribosomes than those found in eukaryotes, and all three have different numbers of ribosomal proteins, although there is some similarity between the ribosomal proteins of archaeal and eukaryotic cells. A defining feature is that each of these three cell types has its own unique type of ribosomal RNA, the very molecule whose characteristics were used to define the archaea as a domain distinct from bacteria.

Compared with even the smallest organelles, ribosomes are tiny structures. The ribosomes of eukaryotic and prokaryotic cells have diameters of about 30 and

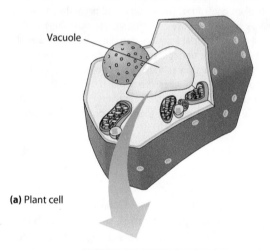

Vacuole

(a) Plant cell

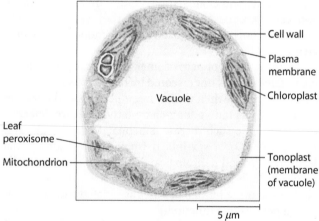

Cell wall

Plasma membrane

Vacuole

Chloroplast

Leaf peroxisome

Mitochondrion

Tonoplast (membrane of vacuole)

5 μm

(b) Large central vacuole

FIGURE 4-21 The Vacuole in a Plant Cell. (a) A cutaway view showing the vacuole in a plant cell. (b) An electron micrograph of a bean leaf cell with a large central vacuole (TEM). The vacuole occupies much of the internal volume of the cell, with the cytoplasm sandwiched into a thin region between the vacuole and the plasma membrane. The membrane of the vacuole is called the tonoplast.

25 nm, respectively. An electron microscope is therefore required to visualize ribosomes (see Figure 4-15d). To appreciate how small ribosomes are, consider that more than 350,000 ribosomes could fit inside a typical bacterial cell, with room to spare!

Another way to express the size of such a small particle is to refer to its **sedimentation coefficient.** The sedimentation coefficient of a particle or macromolecule is a measure of how rapidly the particle sediments in an ultracentrifuge. The rate of sedimentation is expressed in *Svedberg units (S),* as described in Box 12A, pages 327–329 Sedimentation coefficients are widely used to indicate relative size, especially for large macromolecules such as proteins and nucleic acids and for small particles such as ribosomes. Ribosomes from eukaryotic cells have sedimentation coefficients of about 80S, while those from bacteria and archaea are about 70S (see Table 4-1).

A ribosome consists of two subunits differing in size, shape, and composition (**Figure 4-22**). In eukaryotic cells, the **large** and **small ribosomal subunits** have sedimentation coefficients of about 60S and 40S, respectively. For bacterial and archaeal ribosomes, the corresponding values are about 50S and 30S. (Note that the sedimentation coefficients of the subunits do not add up to that of the intact ribosome. This is because sedimentation coefficients depend on both size and shape and are therefore not linearly related to molecular weight.) In early 2009, scientists successfully extracted all 55 ribosomal proteins (plus the three rRNAs) from an *E. coli* cell and then were able to reconstruct a functional "artificial" ribosome capable of synthesizing protein. This is a significant step toward the creation of artificial cells in vitro that have custom-made ribosomes tailored for industrial uses to produce particular desired proteins.

Ribosomes are far more numerous than most other intracellular structures. Prokaryotic cells usually contain thousands of ribosomes, and eukaryotic cells may have hundreds of thousands or even millions of them. Ribosomes are also found in both mitochondria and chloroplasts, where they function in organelle-specific protein synthesis. The ribosomes of these eukaryotic organelles differ in size and composition from the ribosomes found in the cytoplasm of the same cell, but they are strikingly similar to those found in bacteria and cyanobacteria. This similarity is particularly striking when the nucleotide sequences of ribosomal RNA (rRNA) from mitochondria and chloroplasts are compared with those of bacterial and cyanobacterial rRNAs. These similarities provide further support for the endosymbiotic origins of mitochondria and chloroplasts.

The Cytoplasm of Eukaryotic Cells Contains the Cytosol and Cytoskeleton

The **cytoplasm** of a eukaryotic cell consists of that portion of the interior of the cell not occupied by the nucleus. Thus, the cytoplasm includes organelles such as the mitochondria; it also includes the **cytosol,** the semifluid substance in which the organelles are suspended. In a typical animal cell, the cytosol occupies more than half of the cell's total internal volume. Many cellular activities take place in the cytosol, including the synthesis of proteins, the synthesis of fats, and the initial steps in releasing energy from sugars.

In the early days of cell biology, the cytosol was regarded as a rather amorphous, gel-like substance. Its proteins were thought to be soluble and freely diffusible. However, several new techniques have greatly changed this view. We now know that the cytosol of eukaryotic cells, far from being a structureless fluid, is permeated by an intricate three-dimensional array of interconnected microfilaments, microtubules, and intermediate filaments called the **cytoskeleton** (**Figures 4-23** and **4-24**). While the cytoskeleton was initially thought to exist only in

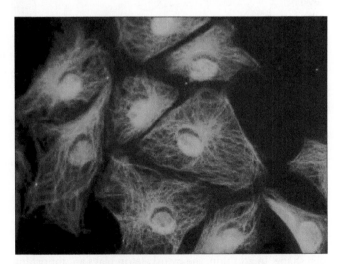

FIGURE 4-23 The Cytoskeleton. This micrograph uses immunofluorescence microscopy to reveal the microtubules in the cytoskeleton of fibroblast cells, which give rise to components of connective tissue and the extracellular matrix. In this image, one fluorescent antibody is directed against the microtubules (green), and a second highlights the nuclei of the cells (blue).

VIDEOS www.thecellplace.com *The cytoskeleton in a neuron growth cone*

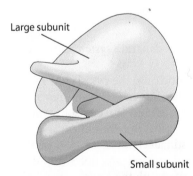

Large subunit

Small subunit

FIGURE 4-22 Structure of a Ribosome. Each ribosome is made up of a large subunit and a small subunit that join together when they attach to a messenger RNA and begin to make a protein. The fully assembled ribosome of a eukaryotic cell has a diameter of about 30 nm. The ribosomes and ribosomal subunits of bacterial and archaeal cells are somewhat smaller than those of eukaryotic cells and consist of their own distinctive protein and RNA molecules.

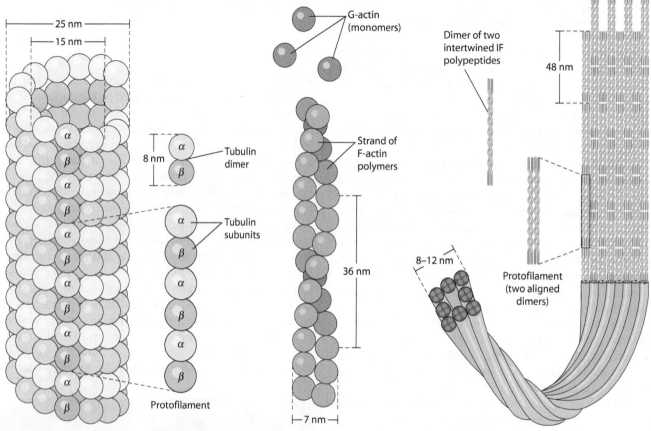

(a) A microtubule. A diagram of a microtubule, showing 13 protofilaments forming a hollow cylinder. Each protofilament is a polymer of tubulin dimers. All the tubulin dimers are oriented in the same direction, giving polarity to the protofilament and hence to the entire microtubule.

(b) A microfilament. A diagram of a microfilament, showing a strand of F-actin twisted into a helical structure. The F-actin polymer consists of monomers of G-actin, all oriented in the same direction to give the microfilament its inherent polarity.

(c) An intermediate filament. A diagram of an intermediate filament. The structural unit is the tetrameric protofilament, consisting of two pairs of coiled polypeptides. Protofilaments assemble by end-to-end and side-to-side alignment, forming an intermediate filament that is thought to be eight protofilaments thick at any point.

FIGURE 4-24 Structures of Microtubules, Microfilaments, and Intermediate Filaments. This figure illustrates the composition and structural details of the three primary elements making up the cytoskeleton of a eukaryotic cell: (**a**) microtubules, (**b**) microfilaments, and (**c**) intermediate filaments. For more information, see Chapter 15.

eukaryotes, proteins related to the eukaryotic cytoskeletal proteins have recently been discovered in bacteria.

As the name suggests, the cytoskeleton is an internal framework that gives a cell its distinctive shape and high level of internal organization. This elaborate array of microfilaments and microtubules forms a highly structured yet dynamic matrix that helps establish and maintain cell shape. In addition, the cytoskeleton plays an important role in cell movement and cell division. As we will see in later chapters, the microfilaments and microtubules that make up the cytoskeleton function in the contraction of muscle cells, the beating of cilia and flagella, the movement of chromosomes during cell division, and, in some cases, the locomotion of the cell itself. We will also see how, rather than being a static framework inside the cell, the

cytoskeleton is a dynamic system that is constantly being remodeled.

In eukaryotic cells, the cytoskeleton serves as a framework for positioning and actively moving organelles and macromolecules within the cytosol. It may also function similarly in regard to ribosomes and enzymes. Some researchers estimate that up to 80% of the proteins and enzymes of the cytosol are not freely diffusible but are instead associated with the cytoskeleton. Even water, which accounts for about 70% of the cell volume, may be influenced by the cytoskeleton. It has been estimated that as much as 20–40% of the water in the cytosol may be bound to the microfilaments and microtubules of the cytoskeleton.

The three major structural elements of the cytoskeleton—*microtubules, microfilaments,* and *intermediate filaments*—are shown in Figure 4-24. They can be visualized by phase-contrast, immunofluorescence, and electron microscopy. Some of the structures they are found in (such as cilia, flagella, or muscle fibrils) can even be seen by ordinary light microscopy. Microfilaments and microtubules are best known for their roles in contraction and motility. In fact, these roles were appreciated well before it became clear that the same structural elements are also integral parts of the pervasive network of microfilaments and microtubules that gives cells their characteristic shape and structure.

Chapter 15 provides a detailed description of the cytoskeleton, followed in Chapter 16 by a discussion of microtubule- and microfilament-mediated contraction and motility. We will also encounter microtubules and microfilaments in Chapter 19 because of their roles in chromosome separation and cell division, respectively. Here, we will focus on the structural features of the three major components of the cytoskeleton: microtubules, microfilaments, and intermediate filaments.

Microtubules. Of the structural elements found in the cytoskeleton, **microtubules** are the largest. A well-known microtubule-based cellular structure is the *axoneme* of cilia and flagella, the appendages responsible for motility of eukaryotic cells. We have already encountered an example of such a structure—the axoneme of the sperm tail shown in Figure 4-12 consists of microtubules. Microtubules also form the *mitotic spindle fibers* that separate chromosomes prior to cell division, as we will see in Chapter 19.

Besides their involvement in motility and chromosome movement, microtubules also play an important role in the organization of the cytoplasm and the intracellular movement of macromolecules and other materials in the cell. They contribute to the overall shape of the cell, the spatial disposition of its organelles, and the distribution of microfilaments and intermediate filaments. Examples of the diverse phenomena governed by microtubules include the asymmetric shapes of animal cells, the plane of cell division in plant cells, the ordering of filaments during muscle development, and the positioning of mitochondria around the axoneme of motile appendages.

As shown in Figure 4-24a, microtubules are hollow cylinders with an outer diameter of about 25 nm and an inner diameter of about 15 nm. Although microtubules are usually drawn as if they are straight and rigid, video microscopy reveals them to be quite flexible in living cells. The wall of the microtubule consists of longitudinal arrays of *protofilaments,* usually 13 of them arranged side by side around the hollow center, called the *lumen.* Each protofilament is a linear polymer of *tubulin.* Tubulin is a dimeric protein consisting of two similar but distinct polypeptide subunits, α-*tubulin* and β-*tubulin.* All of the tubulin dimers in each of the protofilaments are oriented in the same direction, such that all of the subunits face the same end of the microtubule. This uniform orientation gives the microtubule an inherent *polarity.* As we will see in Chapter 15, the polarity of microtubules has important implications for their assembly and for the directional movement of membrane-bounded organelles that microtubules are associated with.

Microfilaments. **Microfilaments** are much thinner than microtubules. They have a diameter of about 7 nm, which makes them the smallest of the major cytoskeletal components. Microfilaments are best known for their role in the contractile fibrils of muscle cells, as we will see in more detail in Chapter 16. However, microfilaments are involved in a variety of other cellular phenomena as well. They can form connections with the plasma membrane and thereby influence locomotion, amoeboid movement, and cytoplasmic streaming. Microfilaments also produce the *cleavage furrow* that divides the cytoplasm of an animal cell after the two sets of chromosomes have been separated by the mitotic spindle fibers. In addition, microfilaments contribute importantly to the development and maintenance of cell shape.

Microfilaments are polymers of the protein *actin* (Figure 4-24b). Actin is synthesized as a monomer called *G-actin* (G for globular). G-actin monomers polymerize into long strands of *F-actin* (F for filamentous), with each strand about 4 nm wide. Each microfilament consists of a chain of actin monomers that are assembled into a filament with a helical appearance and a diameter of about 7 nm. Like microtubules, microfilaments show polarity; all of the subunits are oriented in the same direction. This polarity influences the direction of microfilament elongation; assembly usually proceeds more readily at one end of the growing microfilament, whereas disassembly is favored at the other end.

Intermediate Filaments. **Intermediate filaments** (Figure 4-24c) make up the third structural element of the cytoskeleton. Intermediate filaments have a diameter of about 8–12 nm, larger than the diameter of microfilaments but smaller than that of microtubules. Intermediate filaments are the most stable and the least soluble constituents of the cytoskeleton. Because of this stability, some researchers regard intermediate filaments as a scaffold that supports the entire cytoskeletal framework. Intermediate filaments are also thought to have a tension-bearing role in some cells because they often occur in areas that are subject to mechanical stress.

In contrast to microtubules and microfilaments, intermediate filaments differ in their protein composition from tissue to tissue. Based on biochemical criteria, intermediate filaments from animal cells can be grouped into six classes. A specific cell type usually contains only one or sometimes two classes of intermediate filament proteins. Because of this tissue specificity, animal cells from different tissues can be distinguished on the basis of the intermediate filament proteins present. This *intermediate filament typing* serves as a diagnostic tool in medicine.

Despite their heterogeneity of size and chemical properties, all intermediate filament proteins share common structural features. They all have a central rodlike segment that is remarkably similar from one intermediate filament protein to the other. Flanking the central region of the protein are N-terminal and C-terminal segments that differ greatly in size and sequence, presumably accounting for the functional diversity of these proteins.

Several models have been proposed for intermediate filament structure. One possibility is shown in Figure 4-24c. The basic structural unit is a dimer of two intertwined, intermediate filament polypeptides. Two such dimers align laterally to form a tetrameric *protofilament*. Protofilaments then interact with each other to form an intermediate filament that is thought to be eight protofilaments thick at any point, with protofilaments probably joined end to end in an overlapping manner. We have already seen a similar structure in Figure 3-10 when we looked at the proposed structure of the keratin fibers of hair.

The Extracellular Matrix and the Cell Wall Are "Outside" the Cell

So far, we have considered the plasma membrane that surrounds every cell, the nucleus and cytoplasm within, and the variety of organelles, membrane systems, ribosomes, microtubules, and microfilaments found in the cytoplasm of most eukaryotic cells. While it may seem that our tour of the cell is complete, most cells are also characterized by extracellular structures formed from materials that the cells transport outward across the plasma membrane. These structures often give physical support to the cells making up a particular tissue. For many animal cells, these structures are called the **extracellular matrix (ECM)** and consist primarily of *collagen fibers* and *proteoglycans*. For plant and fungal cells, the extracellular structure is the rigid **cell wall,** which consists mainly of *cellulose microfibrils* embedded in a matrix of other polysaccharides and small amounts of protein.

Most bacteria and archaea are also surrounded by an extracellular structure called a cell wall. However, bacterial cell walls consist not of cellulose but mainly of *peptidoglycans*. Peptidoglycans contain long chains of repeating units of *N*-acetylglucosamine (GlcNAc) and *N*-acetylmuramic acid (MurNAc), amino sugars that we encountered in Chapter 3 (see Figure 3-26). These chains are held together to form a netlike structure by crosslinks composed of about a dozen amino acids linked by peptide bonds—thus the name peptidoglycan. In addition, bacterial cell walls contain a variety of other constituents, some of which are unique to each of the major structural groups of bacteria. Archaeal cell walls vary considerably from species to species—some are mainly proteinaceous, while others have peptidoglycan-like components.

These differences among cells are in keeping with the lifestyles of these groups of organisms. Plants are generally nonmotile, a lifestyle that is compatible with the rigidity that cell walls confer on an organism. Animals, on the other hand, are usually *motile,* an essential feature for an organism that needs not only to find food but also to escape becoming food for other organisms! Accordingly, animal cells are not encased in rigid walls; instead, they are surrounded by a strong but elastic network of collagen fibers. Bacteria and archaea may be motile or nonmotile, but they usually live in hypotonic environments (lower concentrations of external solutes than found in the cells), and their cell walls provide rigid support and protection from bursting due to osmotic pressure as water enters the cell.

The ECM of animal cells can vary in structure depending on the cell type. Micrographs of the ECM from bone, cartilage, and connective tissue. The primary function of the ECM is support, but the kinds of extracellular materials and the patterns they are deposited in may regulate such diverse processes as cell motility and migration, cell division, cell recognition and adhesion, and cell differentiation during embryonic development. The main constituents of animal extracellular structures are the collagen fibers and the network of proteoglycans that surround them. In vertebrates, collagen is such a prominent part of tendons, cartilage, and bone that it is the single most abundant protein of the animal body.

Figure 4-25 illustrates the prominence of the cell wall as a structural feature of a typical plant cell. Although the distinction is not made in the figure, plant cell walls are actually of two types. The wall that is laid down during cell division, called the *primary cell wall,* consists mainly of cellulose fibrils embedded in a gel-like polysaccharide matrix. Primary walls are quite flexible and extensible, which allows them to expand somewhat in response to cell enlargement and elongation. As a cell reaches its final size and shape, a much thicker and more rigid *secondary cell wall* may form by deposition of additional cell wall material on the inner surface of the primary wall. The secondary wall usually contains more cellulose than the primary wall and may have a high content of *lignin,* a major component of wood. Deposition of a secondary cell wall renders the cell inextensible and therefore defines the final size and shape of the cell.

Neighboring plant cells, though separated by the wall between them, are actually connected by numerous cytoplasmic bridges, called **plasmodesmata** (singular: **plasmodesma**), which pass through the cell wall. The plasma membranes of adjacent cells are continuous through each plasmodesma, such that the channel is membrane lined. The diameter of a typical plasmodesma is large enough to allow water and small solutes to pass freely from cell to cell. Most of the cells of the plant are interconnected in this way.

Animal cells can also communicate with each other. But instead of plasmodesmata, they have intercellular connections called *gap junctions,* which are specialized for

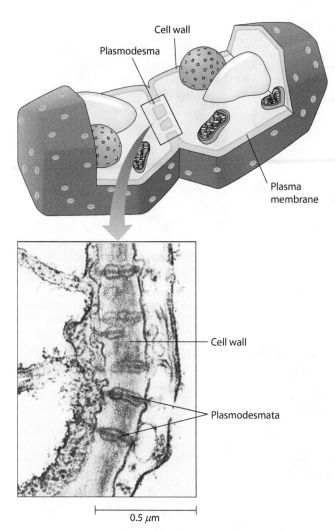

Cell wall

Plasmodesma

Plasma membrane

Cell wall

Plasmodesmata

0.5 µm

FIGURE 4-25 The Plant Cell Wall. The wall surrounding a plant cell consists of rigid microfibrils of cellulose embedded in a noncellulosic matrix of proteins and sugar polymers. Notice how the neighboring cells are connected by plasmodesmata (TEM).

the transfer of material between the cytoplasms of adjacent cells. Two other types of intercellular junctions are also characteristic of animal cells. *Tight junctions* hold cells together so tightly that the transport of substances through the spaces between the cells is effectively blocked. *Adhesive junctions* also link adjacent cells but for the purpose of connecting them tightly into sturdy yet flexible sheets.

Viruses, Viroids, and Prions: Agents That Invade Cells

Before concluding this preview of cellular biology, we will look at several kinds of agents that invade cells, subverting normal cellular functions and often killing their unwilling hosts. These include the *viruses*, which have been studied for over 100 years, and two other agents we know much less about—the *viroids* and *prions*.

A Virus Consists of a DNA or RNA Core Surrounded by a Protein Coat

Viruses are noncellular, parasitic particles that are incapable of a free-living existence. However, they can invade and infect cells and redirect the synthetic machinery of the infected host cell toward the production of more virus particles. Viruses cannot perform all of the functions required for independent existence and must therefore depend on the cells they invade for most of their needs. They are not considered to be living organisms, nor are they made of cells. A virus particle has no cytoplasm, no ribosomes, no organelles, few or no enzymes, and typically consists of only a few different molecules of nucleic acid and protein.

Viruses are, however, responsible for many diseases in humans, animals, and plants and are thus important in their own right. They are also significant research tools for cell and molecular biologists because they are much less complicated than cells. The tobacco mosaic virus (TMV) is a good example of a virus that is important both economically and scientifically—economically because of the threat it poses to tobacco and other crop plants that it can infect and scientifically because it is so amenable to laboratory study. Fraenkel-Conrat's studies on TMV self-assembly described are good examples of the usefulness of viruses to cell biologists.

Viruses are typically named for the diseases they cause. Poliovirus, influenza virus, herpes simplex virus, and TMV are several common examples. Other viruses have more cryptic laboratory names (such as T4, Qβ, λ, or Epstein-Barr virus). Viruses that infect bacterial cells are called *bacteriophages,* or often just *phages* for short. Bacteriophages and other viruses will figure prominently in our discussion of molecular genetics in Chapters 18, 19, 21, 22.

Viruses are smaller than all but the tiniest cells, with most ranging in size from about 25 to 300 nm. They are small enough to pass through a filter that traps bacteria, and the collected filtrate will still be infectious. Because of this, their existence was postulated by Louis Pasteur 50 years before they were able to be seen in the electron microscope! The smallest viruses are about the size of a ribosome, whereas the largest ones are about one-quarter the diameter of a typical bacterial cell. Each virus has a characteristic shape, as defined by its protein capsid. Some of these varied shapes are shown in **Figure 4-26**.

Despite their morphological diversity, viruses are chemically quite simple. Most viruses consist of little more than a *coat* (or *capsid*) of protein surrounding a *core* that contains one or more molecules of either RNA or DNA, depending on the type of virus. This is another feature distinguishing viruses from cells, which always have both DNA and RNA. The simplest viruses, such as TMV, have a single nucleic acid molecule surrounded by a capsid consisting of proteins of a single type. More complex viruses have cores that contain several nucleic acid molecules and

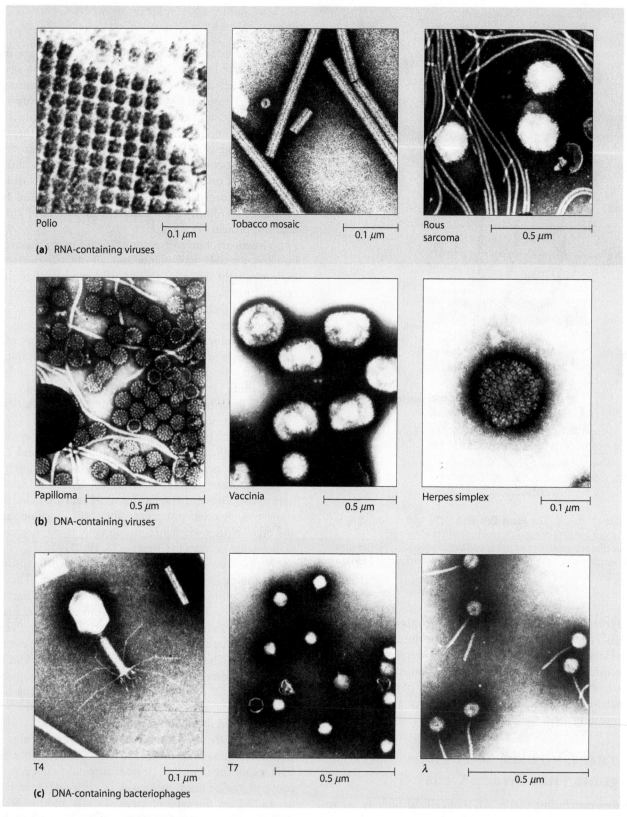

FIGURE 4-26 Sizes and Shapes of Viruses. These electron micrographs illustrate the morphological diversity of viruses. **(a)** RNA-containing viruses (left to right): polio, tobacco mosaic, and Rous sarcoma viruses. **(b)** DNA-containing viruses: papilloma, vaccinia, and herpes simplex viruses. **(c)** DNA-containing bacteriophages: T4, T7, and λ (all TEMs).

capsids consisting of several (or even many) different kinds of proteins. Some viruses are surrounded by a membrane that is derived from the plasma membrane of the host cell in which the viral particles were previously made and assembled. Such viruses are called *enveloped viruses*. Human immunodeficiency virus (HIV), the virus that causes AIDS (acquired immune deficiency syndrome), is an enveloped virus; it is covered by a membrane that it received from the previously infected white blood cell.

Students sometimes ask whether viruses are living. The answer depends crucially on what we mean by "living," and it is probably worth pondering only to the extent that it helps us more fully understand what viruses are—and what they are not. The most fundamental properties of living things are *metabolism* (cellular reactions organized into coherent pathways), *irritability* (perception of, and response to, environmental stimuli), and the *ability to reproduce*. Viruses clearly do not satisfy the first two criteria. Outside their host cells, viruses are inert and inactive. They can, in fact, be isolated and crystallized almost like a chemical compound. It is only in an appropriate host cell that a virus becomes functional, undergoing a cycle of synthesis and assembly that gives rise to more viruses.

Even the ability of viruses to reproduce has to be qualified carefully. A basic tenet of the cell theory is that cells arise only from preexisting cells, but this is not true of viruses. No virus can give rise to another virus by any sort of self-duplication process. Rather, the virus must take over the metabolic and genetic machinery of a host cell, reprogramming it for synthesis of the proteins necessary to package the DNA or RNA molecules that arise by copying the genetic information of the parent virus.

Viroids Are Small, Circular RNA Molecules

As simple as viruses are, there are even simpler noncellular agents that can infect eukaryotic cells (though apparently not prokaryotic cells, as far as we currently know). The **viroids** found in some plant cells represent one class of such agents. Viroids are small, circular RNA molecules, and they are the smallest known infectious agents. These RNA molecules are only about 250–400 nucleotides long and are replicated in the host cell even though they do not code for any protein. Some have been shown to have enzymatic properties that aid in their replication.

Viroids are responsible for diseases of several crop plants, including potatoes and tobacco. A viroid disease that has severe economic consequences is *cadang-cadang disease* of the coconut palm. It is not yet clear how viroids cause disease. They may enter the nucleus and interfere with the transcription of DNA into RNA in a process known as *gene silencing*. Alternatively, they may interfere with the subsequent processing required of most eukaryotic mRNAs, disrupting subsequent protein synthesis.

Viroids do not occur in free form but can be transmitted from one plant cell to another when the surfaces of adjacent cells are damaged and there is no membrane barrier for the RNA molecules to cross. There are also reports that they can be transmitted by seed, pollen, or agricultural implements used in cultivation and harvesting. Recent studies have shown that many plant species harbor latent viroids that cause no obvious symptoms.

Prions Are "Proteinaceous Infective Particles"

Prions represent another class of noncellular infectious agents. The term was coined to describe *proteinaceous infective particles* that are responsible for neurological diseases such as scrapie in sheep and goats, kuru in humans, and mad cow disease in cattle. *Scrapie* is so named because infected animals rub incessantly against trees or other objects, scraping off most of their wool in the process. *Kuru* is a degenerative disease of the central nervous system originally reported among native peoples in New Guinea who consumed infected brain tissue. Patients with this or other prion-based diseases suffer initially from mild physical weakness and dementia; but the effects slowly become more severe, and the diseases are eventually fatal. For a discussion of *mad cow disease*, see Box 22A, page 692.

Prion proteins are abnormally folded versions of normal cellular proteins. Both the normal and variant forms of the prion protein are found on the surfaces of neurons, suggesting that the protein may somehow affect the receptors that detect nerve signals. Some biologists speculate that a similar mechanism is responsible for the plaques of misfolded proteins that are found in the brains of deceased Alzheimer syndrome patients.

Prions are not destroyed by cooking or boiling, so special precautions are recommended in areas where prion-caused diseases are known to occur. For example, a prion disease known as *chronic wasting disease* is found in some deer and elk, especially in the Rocky Mountain region of the western United States. Hunters in areas where this prion is known to occur are cautioned to have meat tested for this prion and to avoid eating meat from any animal that tests positive or appears sick.

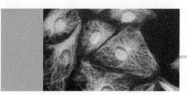

Properties and Strategies of Cells

- Based on gross morphology, cells have traditionally been described as either eukaryotic (animals, plants, fungi, protozoa, and algae) or prokaryotic (bacteria and archaea) based on the presence or absence of a membrane-bounded nucleus. More recently, analysis of ribosomal RNA sequences and other molecular data suggests a tripartite view of organisms, with eukaryotes, bacteria, and archaea as the three main domains.

- A plasma membrane and ribosomes are the only two structural features common to cells of all three groups. Organelles are found only in eukaryotic cells, where they play indispensable roles in the compartmentalization of function. Bacterial and archaeal cells are relatively small and structurally less complex than eukaryotic cells, lacking the internal membrane systems and organelles of eukaryotes.

- Cell size is limited by the need for an adequate amount of surface area for exchange of materials with the environment and the need for high enough concentrations of the compounds necessary to sustain life. Eukaryotic cells are much larger than prokaryotic cells and compensate for their lower surface area/volume ratio by the compartmentalization of materials within membrane-bounded organelles.

The Eukaryotic Cell in Overview

- Besides the plasma membrane and ribosomes common to all cells, eukaryotic cells have a nucleus that houses most of the cell's DNA, a variety of organelles, and the cytosol with its cytoskeleton of microtubules, microfilaments, and intermediate filaments. Also, plant cells have a rigid cell wall, and animal cells are usually surrounded by a strong but flexible extracellular matrix of collagen and proteoglycans.

- The nucleus contains the cell's DNA complexed with protein in the form of chromatin, which condenses during cell division to form the visible structures we call chromosomes. The nucleus is surrounded by a double membrane called the nuclear envelope, which has pores that allow the regulated exchange of macromolecules with the cytoplasm.

- Mitochondria, which are surrounded by a double membrane, oxidize food molecules to provide the energy used to make ATP. Mitochondria also contain ribosomes and their own circular DNA molecules.

- Chloroplasts trap solar energy and use it to "fix" carbon dioxide into organic form and convert it to sugar. Chloroplasts are surrounded by a double membrane and have an extensive system of internal membranes called the thylakoids, in which most of the components involved in ATP generation are found. Chloroplasts also contain ribosomes and circular DNA molecules.

- The endoplasmic reticulum is an extensive network of membranes that are known as either rough ER or smooth ER. Rough ER is studded with ribosomes and is responsible for the synthesis of secretory and membrane proteins, whereas smooth ER is involved in lipid synthesis and drug detoxification. Proteins synthesized on the rough ER are further processed and packaged in the Golgi complex and are then transported either to membranes or to the surface of the cell via secretory vesicles.

- Lysosomes contain hydrolytic enzymes and are involved in cellular digestion. They were the first organelles to be discovered on the basis of their function rather than their morphology. Because of their close functional relationships, the ER, Golgi complex, secretory vesicles, and lysosomes are collectively called the endomembrane system.

- Peroxisomes are about the same size as lysosomes, and both generate and degrade hydrogen peroxide. Animal peroxisomes play an important role in catabolizing long-chain fatty acids. In plants, specialized peroxisomes known as glyoxysomes are involved in the process of photorespiration and in converting stored fat into carbohydrate during seed germination.

- Ribosomes are sites of protein synthesis in all cells. The striking similarities between mitochondrial and chloroplast ribosomes and those of bacteria and cyanobacteria, respectively, lend strong support to the endosymbiont theory that these organelles are of bacterial origin.

- The cytoskeleton is an extensive network of microtubules, microfilaments, and intermediate filaments that gives eukaryotic cells their distinctive shapes. The cytoskeleton is also important in cellular motility and the intracellular movement of cellular structures and materials.

Agents That Invade Cells

- Viruses satisfy some, though not all, of the basic criteria of living things. Viruses are important both as infectious agents that cause diseases in humans, animals, and plants and as laboratory tools, particularly for geneticists. Viroids and prions are infectious agents that are even smaller (and less well understood) than viruses. Viroids are small self-replicating RNA molecules, whereas prions are misfolded proteins that are thought to be abnormal products of normal cellular genes.

MAKING CONNECTIONS

In the first few chapters, we have had an overview of the history and scope of cell biology, a review of chemistry, and a discussion of the macromolecular components of cells. We have just finished an introduction to overall cell structure and the types of organelles found in eukaryotic cells. Next you will see how these cellular components function and interact to give cells the incredible abilities we associate with life. After a discussion of bioenergetics and enzyme function in the next two chapters, you will see how the plasma membrane functions in transport, metabolism, and cell-to-cell communication. As we study the mitochondrion and chloroplast in more detail, you will learn how cells obtain energy to live, grow, and reproduce. We will revisit the roles of the endoplasmic reticulum, Golgi complex, lysosomes, and peroxisomes in studies of protein and membrane trafficking and specialized types of metabolism in Chapter 12. Later, you will learn about the role of the cytoskeleton in cell motility and muscle contraction and how the cytoskeleton interacts with the extracellular matrix. Following that, we will return to the nucleus as we investigate its role as the command center of the cell for genetic information transfer, cell reproduction, and control of nearly all cellular activities.

PROBLEM SET

More challenging problems are marked with a •.

4-1 Wrong Again. For each of the following false statements, change the statement to make it true.

(a) Archaea are ancient bacteria that are the ancestors of modern bacteria.

(b) Bacteria differ from eukaryotes in having no nucleus, mitochondria, chloroplasts, or ribosomes.

(c) Instead of a cell wall, eukaryotic cells have an extracellular matrix for structural support.

(d) All the ribosomes found in a typical human muscle cell are identical.

(e) DNA is found only in the nucleus of a cell.

(f) Because bacterial cells have no organelles, they cannot carry out either ATP synthesis or photosynthesis.

(g) Even the simplest types of infectious agents must have DNA, RNA, and protein.

(h) A large amount of the DNA in eukaryotic cells has no function and is called "junk DNA."

4-2 Cellular Specialization. Each of the cell types listed here is a good example of a cell that is specialized for a specific function. Match each cell type in list A with the appropriate function from list B, and explain why you matched each as you did.

List A	List B
(a) Pancreatic cell	Cell division
(b) Cell from flight muscle	Absorption
(c) Palisade cell from leaf	Motility
(d) Cell of intestinal lining	Photosynthesis
(e) Nerve cell	Secretion
(f) Bacterial cell	Transmission of electrical impulses

4-3 Toward an Artificial Cell. Scientists have recently constructed an artificial ribosome in vitro from purified ribosomal proteins and rRNAs.

(a) What types of intermolecular forces do you think are holding the individual proteins and rRNAs together in this supramolecular complex?

(b) Describe specifically how high temperature, high salt, or low pH would disrupt its structure, causing the ribosome to fall apart.

(c) If you were asked to determine which organism the ribosomal components were from, how could you do this?

(d) What other molecules would you have to add to the test tube in order for the ribosomes to make polypeptides? (This may require some sleuthing in later chapters.)

4-4 Sentence Completion. Complete each of the following statements about cellular structure in ten words or less.

(a) If you were shown an electron micrograph of a section of a cell and were asked to identify the cell as plant or animal, one thing you might do is . . .

(b) A slice of raw apple placed in a concentrated sugar solution will . . .

(c) A cellular structure that is visible with an electron microscope but not with a light microscope is . . .

(d) Several environments in which you are more likely to find archaea than bacteria are . . .

(e) One reason that it might be difficult to separate lysosomes from peroxisomes by centrifugation techniques is that . . .

(f) The nucleic acid of a virus is composed of . . .

4-5 Telling Them Apart. Suggest a way to distinguish between the two elements in each of the following pairs:

(a) Bacterial cells; archaeal cells

(b) Rough ER; smooth ER

(c) Animal·peroxisomes; leaf peroxisomes

(d) Peroxisomes; lysosomes

(e) Viruses; viroids

(f) Microfilaments; intermediate filaments

(g) Polio virus; herpes simplex virus

(h) Eukaryotic ribosomes; bacterial ribosomes

(i) mRNA; miRNA

4-6 Structural Relationships. For each pair of structural elements, indicate with an A if the first element is a constituent part of the second, with a B if the second element is a constituent part of the first, and with an N if they are separate structures with no particular relationship to each other.

(a) Mitochondrion; crista

(b) Golgi complex; nucleus

(c) Cytoplasm; cytoskeleton

(d) Cell wall; extracellular matrix

(e) Nucleolus; nucleus

(f) Smooth ER; ribosome

(g) Lipid bilayer; plasma membrane

(h) Peroxisome; thylakoid

(i) Chloroplast; granum

• **4-7 Protein Synthesis and Secretion.** Although we will not encounter protein synthesis and secretion in detail until later chapters, you already have enough information about these processes to order the seven events that are now listed randomly. Order events 1–7 so that they represent the correct sequence corresponding to steps a–g, tracing a typical secretory protein from the initial transcription (readout) of the relevant genetic information in the nucleus to the eventual secretion of the protein from the cell by exocytosis.

Transcription → (a) → (b) → (c) →
(d) → (e) → (f) → (g) → Secretion

1. The protein is partially glycosylated within the lumen of the ER.

2. The secretory vesicle arrives at and fuses with the plasma membrane.

3. The RNA transcript is transported from the nucleus to the cytoplasm.

4. The final sugar groups are added to the protein in the Golgi complex.

5. As the protein is synthesized, it passes across the ER membrane into the lumen of a Golgi cisterna.

6. The protein is packaged into a secretory vesicle and released from the Golgi complex.

7. The RNA message associates with a ribosome and begins synthesis of the desired protein on the surface of the rough ER.

• **4-8 Disorders at the Organelle Level.** Each of the following medical problems involves a disorder in the function of an organelle or other cell structure. In each case, identify the organelle or structure involved, and indicate whether it is likely to be underactive or overactive.

(a) A girl inadvertently consumes cyanide and dies almost immediately because ATP production ceases.

(b) A boy is diagnosed with neonatal adrenoleukodystrophy (NALD), which is characterized by an inability of his body to break down very-long-chain fatty acids.

(c) A smoker develops lung cancer and is told that the cause of the problem is a population of cells in her lungs that are undergoing mitosis at a much greater rate than is normal for lung cells.

(d) A young man learns that he is infertile because his sperm are nonmotile.

(e) A young child dies of Tay-Sachs disease because her cells lack the hydrolase that normally breaks down a membrane component called ganglioside G_{M2}, which therefore accumulated in the membranes of her brain.

(f) A young child is placed on a milk-free diet because the mucosal cells that line his small intestine do not secrete the enzyme necessary to hydrolyze lactose, the disaccharide present in milk.

• **4-9 Are They Alive?** Biologists sometimes debate whether viruses should be considered as alive. Let's join in the debate.

(a) What are some ways in which viruses resemble cells?

(b) What are some ways in which viruses differ from cells?

(c) Choose either of the two following positions and defend it: (1) Viruses are alive, or (2) Viruses are not alive.

(d) Why do you suppose that viral illnesses are more difficult to treat than bacterial illnesses?

(e) Design a strategy to cure a viral disease without harming the patient.

SUGGESTED READING

References of historical importance are marked with a •.

Eukaryotic, Bacterial, and Archaeal Cells

Bogorad, L. Evolution of early eukaryotic cells: Genomes, proteomes, and compartments. *Photosynth. Res.* 95 (2008): 11.

Brinkmann, H., and H. Philippe. The diversity of eukaryotes and the root of the eukaryotic tree. *Adv. Exp. Med. Biol.* 607 (2007): 20.

Kassen, R., and P. B. Rainey. The ecology and genetics of microbial diversity. *Annu. Rev. Microbiol.* 58 (2004): 207.

Pace, N. R. Time for a change. *Nature* 441 (2006): 289.

Sapp, J. The prokaryote-eukaryote dichotomy: Meanings and mythology. *Microbiol. Mol. Biol. Rev.* 69 (2005): 292.

Tanaka, S., M. R. Sawaya, and T. O. Yeates. Structure and mechanisms of a protein-based organelle in *Escherichia coli*. *Science* 327 (2010): 81.

Trotsenko, Y. A., and V. N. Khmelenina. Biology of extremophilic and extremotolerant methanotrophs. *Arch. Microbiol.* 177 (2002): 123.

• Woese, C. R., and G. E. Fox. Phylogenetic structure of the prokaryotic domain: The primary kingdoms. *Proc. Nat. Acad. Sci. USA* 74 (1977): 5088.

Woese, C. R., O. Kandler, and M. L. Wheelis. Towards a natural system of organisms: Proposal for the domains Archaea, Bacteria, and Eucarya. *Proc. Nat. Acad. Sci. USA* 87 (1990): 4576.

The Nucleus

Burke, B., and C. L. Stewart. The laminopathies: The functional architecture of the nucleus and its contribution to disease. *Annu. Rev. Genomics Hum. Genet.* 7 (2006): 369.

Rippe, K. Dynamic organization of the cell nucleus. *Curr. Opin. Genet. Dev.* 17 (2007): 373.

Tchélidzé P., A. Chatron-Colliet, M. Thiry, N. Lalun, H. Bobichon, and D. Ploton. Tomography of the cell nucleus using confocal microscopy and medium voltage electron microscopy. *Crit. Rev. Oncol. Hematol.* 69 (2009): 127.

Webster, M., K. L. Witkin, and O. Cohen-Fix. Sizing up the nucleus: Nuclear shape, size and nuclear envelope assembly. *J. Cell Sci.* 122 (2009): 1477.

Organelles and Human Diseases

DiMauro, S. Mitochondrial myopathies. *Curr. Opin. Rheumatol.* 18 (2006): 636.

Fan, J., Z. Hu, L. Zeng, W. Lu, X. Tang, J. Zhang, and T. Li. Golgi apparatus and neurodegenerative diseases. *Int. J. Dev. Neurosci.* 26 (2008): 523.

Gould, S. J., and D. Valle. Peroxisome biogenesis disorders: Genetics and cell biology. *Trends Genet.* 16 (2000): 340.

Grabowski, G. A., and R. J. Hopkins. Enzyme therapy for lysosomal storage diseases: Principles, practice, and prospects. *Annu. Rev. Genomics Hum. Genet.* 4 (2003): 403.

Kiselyov, K. et al. Autophagy, mitochondria, and cell death in lysosomal storage diseases. *Autophagy* 3 (2007): 259.

Máximo, V., J. Lima, P. Soares, and M. Sobrinho-Simões. Mitochondria and cancer. *Virchows Arch.* 454 (2009): 481.

Morava, E. et al. Mitochondrial disease criteria: Diagnostic applications in children. *Neurology* 67 (2006): 1823.

Ni, M., and A. S. Lee. ER chaperones in mammalian development and human diseases. *FEBS Lett.* 581 (2007): 3641.

Reeve, A. K., K. J. Krishnan, and D. Turnbull. Mitochondrial DNA mutations in disease, aging, and neurodegeneration. *Ann. NY Acad. Sci.* 1147 (2008):1147.

Wlodkowic, D., J. Skommer, D. McGuinness, C. Hillier, and Z. Darzynkiewicz. ER-Golgi network—a future target for anti-cancer therapy. *Leuk. Res.* 33 (2009): 1440.

Yoshida, H. ER stress and diseases. *FEBS Lett.* 274 (2007): 630.

Intracellular Membranes and Organelles

Allan, V. J., H. M. Thompson, and M. A. McNiven. Motoring around the Golgi. *Nature Cell Biol.* 4 (2002): E236.

Boldogh, I. R., and L. A. Pon. Mitochondria on the move. *Trends Cell Biol.* 17 (2007): 502.

• de Duve, C. The peroxisome in retrospect. *Ann. NY Acad. Sci.* 804 (1996): 1.

Glick, B. S. Organization of the Golgi apparatus. *Curr. Opin. Cell Biol.* 12 (2000): 450.

Jackson, C. L. Mechanisms of transport through the Golgi complex. *J. Cell Sci.* 122 (2009): 443.

Leigh, R. A., and D. Sanders, eds. *The Plant Vacuole.* San Diego: Academic Press, 1997.

Okamoto, K., and J. M. Shaw. Mitochondrial morphology and dynamics in yeast and multicellular eukaryotes. *Annu. Rev. Genet.* 39 (2005): 503.

Reumann, S. The structural properties of plant peroxisomes and their metabolic significance. *Annu. Rev. Genet.* 34 (2000): 623.

• Sabatini, D. D., and G. E. Palade. Charting the secretory pathway. *Trends Cell Biol.* 9 (1999): 413.

Shorter, J., and G. Warren. Golgi architecture and inheritance. *Annu. Rev. Cell Dev. Biol.* 18 (2002): 379.

Voeltz, G. K., M. M. Rolls, and T. A. Rapoport. Structural organization of the endoplasmic reticulum. *EMBO Rep.* 3 (2002): 944.

Waters, M. T., and J. A. Langdale. The making of a chloroplast. *EMBO J.* 28 (2009): 2861.

Yeates, T. O., Crowley, C. S., and S. Tanaka. Bacterial microcompartment organelles: Protein shell structure and evolution. *Annu. Rev. Biophys.* 39 (2010): 185.

The Cytoplasm and the Cytoskeleton

Dillon, C., and Y. Goda. The actin cytoskeleton: Integrating form and function at the synapse. *Annu. Rev. Neurosci.* 28 (2005): 25.

Dinman, J. D. The eukaryotic ribosome: Current status and challenges. *J. Biol. Chem.* 284 (2009): 11761.

Erickson, H. P. Evolution of the cytoskeleton. *Bioessays* 29 (2007): 668.

Hall, A. The cytoskeleton and cancer. *Cancer Metastasis Rev.* 28 (2009): 5.

Howard, J. *Mechanics of Motor Proteins and the Cytoskeleton.* Sunderland, MA: Sinauer Associates, 2001.

Michie, K. A., and J. Lowe. Dynamic filaments of the bacterial cytoskeleton. *Annu. Rev. Biochem.* 75 (2006): 467.

Pogliano, J. The bacterial cytoskeleton. *Curr. Opin. Cell Biol.* 20 (2008): 19.

Schröder M. Engineering eukaryotic protein factories. *Biotechnol. Lett.* 30 (2008): 187.

Strelkov, S. V., H. Herrmann, and U. Aebi. Molecular architecture of intermediate filaments. *BioEssays* 25 (2003): 243.

Strnad, P., C. Stumptner, K. Zatloukal, and H. Denk. Intermediate filament cytoskeleton of the liver in health and disease. *Histochem. Cell Biol.* 129 (2008): 735.

The Extracellular Matrix and the Cell Wall

Bateman, J. F., R. P. Boot-Handford, and S. R. Lamandé. Genetic diseases of connective tissue: Cellular and extracellular effects of ECM mutations. *Nat. Rev. Genet.* 10 (2009): 173.

Bowman, S. M., and S. J. Free. The structure and synthesis of the fungal cell wall. *Bioessays* 28 (2006): 799.

Brett, C. T. Cellulose microfibrils in plants: Biosynthesis, deposition, and integration into the cell wall. *Int. Rev. Cytol.* 199 (2000): 161.

Cosgrove, D. J. Growth of the plant cell wall. *Int. Rev. Mol. Cell Biol.* 6 (2005): 850.

Jamet, E., C. Albenne, G. Boudart, M. Irshad, H. Canut, and R. Pont-Lezica. Recent advances in plant cell wall proteomics. *Proteomics* 8 (2008): 893.

Kreis, T., and R. Vale, eds. *Guidebook to the Extracellular Matrix, Anchor, and Adhesion Proteins,* 2nd ed. Oxford: Oxford University Press, 1999.

Marastoni, S., G. Ligresti, E. Lorenzon, A. Colombatti, and M. Mongiat. Extracellular matrix: A matter of life and death. *Connect. Tissue Res.* 29 (2008): 203.

Viruses, Viroids, and Prions

Aguzzi, A., and M. Polymenidou. Mammalian prion biology: One century of evolving concepts. *Cell* 116 (2004): S109.

Cann, A. J. *Principles of Molecular Virology,* 3rd ed. San Diego: Academic Press, 2001.

Cobb, N. J., and W. K. Surewicz. Prion diseases and their biochemical mechanisms. *Biochemistry* 48 (2009): 2574.

Crozet, C., F. Beranger, and S. Lehmann. Cellular pathogenesis in prion diseases. *Vet. Res.* 39 (2008): 44.

Ding, B., A. Itaya, and X. Zhong. Viroid trafficking: A small RNA makes a big move. *Curr. Opin. Plant Biol.* 8 (2005): 606.

Flores, R. et al. Viroids and viroid-host interactions. *Annu. Rev. Phytopathol.* 43 (2005): 117.

Moore, R. A., L. M. Taubner, and S. A. Priola. Prion protein misfolding and disease. *Curr. Opin. Struct. Biol.* 19 (2009): 14.

Prusiner, S. B., ed. *Prion Biology and Diseases,* 4th ed. Cold Spring Harbor, New York: Cold Spring Harbor Laboratory Press, 2004.

Prusiner, S. B., and M. R. Scott. Genetics of prions. *Annu. Rev. Genet.* 31 (1997): 139.

• Reisner, D., and H. H. Gross. Viroids. *Annu. Rev. Biochem.* 54 (1985): 531.

Stürmer M., H. W. Doerr, and L. Gürtler. Human immunodeficiency virus: 25 years of diagnostic and therapeutic strategies and their impact on hepatitis B and C virus. *Med. Microbiol. Immunol.* 198 (2009): 147.

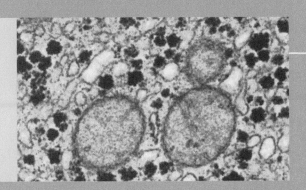

6

Enzymes: The Catalysts of Life

We encountered ΔG′, the change in free energy, and saw its importance as an indicator of thermodynamic spontaneity. Specifically, the sign of ΔG′ tells us whether a reaction is possible in the indicated direction, and the magnitude of ΔG′ indicates how much energy will be released (or must be provided) as the reaction proceeds in that direction. At the same time, we were careful to note that, because it is a thermodynamic parameter, ΔG′ tells us only whether a reaction can go but not about whether it actually will go. For that distinction, we need to know not just the direction and energetics of the reaction, but something about the reaction mechanism and its rate as well.

This brings us to the topic of **enzyme catalysis** because virtually all cellular reactions or processes are mediated by protein (or, in certain cases, RNA) catalysts called enzymes. The only reactions that occur at any appreciable rate in a cell are those for which the appropriate enzymes are present and active. Thus, enzymes almost always spell the difference between "can go" and "will go" for cellular reactions. It is only as we explore the nature of enzymes and their catalytic properties that we begin to understand how reactions that are energetically feasible actually take place in cells and how the rates of such reactions are controlled.

In this chapter, we will first consider why thermodynamically spontaneous reactions do not usually occur at appreciable rates without a catalyst. Then we will look at the role of enzymes as specific biological catalysts. We will also see how the rate of an enzyme-catalyzed reaction is affected by the concentration of available substrate, by the affinity of the enzyme for substrate, and by covalent modification of the enzyme itself. We will also see some of the ways in which reaction rates are regulated to meet the needs of the cell.

Activation Energy and the Metastable State

If you stop to think about it, you are already familiar with many reactions that are thermodynamically feasible yet do not occur to any appreciable extent. An obvious example is the oxidation of glucose. This reaction (or series of reactions, really) is highly exergonic ($\Delta G^{\circ\prime} = -686$ kcal/mol) and yet does not take place on its own. In fact, glucose crystals or a glucose solution can be exposed to the oxygen in the air indefinitely, and little or no oxidation will occur. The cellulose in the paper these words are printed on is another example—and so, for that matter, are *you*, consisting as you do of a complex collection of thermodynamically unstable molecules.

Not nearly as familiar, but equally important to cellular chemistry, are the many thermodynamically feasible reactions in cells that could go but do not proceed at an appreciable rate on their own. As an example, consider the high-energy molecule adenosine triphosphate (ATP), which has a highly favorable $\Delta G^{\circ\prime}$ (-7.3 kcal/mol) for the hydrolysis of its terminal phosphate group to form the corresponding diphosphate (ADP) and inorganic phosphate (P_i):

$$\text{ATP} + \text{H}_2\text{O} \rightleftharpoons \text{ADP} + P_i \qquad \textbf{(6-1)}$$

This reaction is very exergonic under standard conditions and is even more so under the conditions that prevail in cells. Yet despite the highly favorable free energy change, this reaction occurs only slowly on its own, so that ATP remains stable for several days when dissolved in pure water. This property turns out to be shared by many biologically important molecules and reactions, and it is important to understand why.

Before a Chemical Reaction Can Occur, the Activation Energy Barrier Must Be Overcome

Molecules that could react with one another often do not because they lack sufficient energy. For every reaction, there is a specific **activation energy (E_A)**, which is the minimum amount of energy that reactants must have before collisions between them will be successful in giving rise to products. More specifically, reactants need to reach an intermediate chemical stage called the **transition state,** which has a free energy higher than that of the initial reactants. **Figure 6-1a** shows the activation energy required for molecules of ATP and H_2O to reach their transition state. $\Delta G^{\circ\prime}$ measures the difference in free energy between reactants and products (−7.3 kcal/mol for this particular reaction), whereas E_A indicates the minimum energy required for the reactants to reach the transition state and hence to be capable of giving rise to products.

The actual rate of a reaction is always proportional to the fraction of molecules that have an energy content equal to or greater than E_A. When in solution at room temperature, molecules of ATP and water move about readily, each possessing a certain amount of energy at any instant. As Figure 6-1b shows, the energy distribution among molecules will be normally distributed around a mean value (a bell-shaped curve). Some molecules will have very little energy, some will have a lot, and most will be somewhere near the average. The important point is

that the only molecules that are capable of reacting at a given instant are those with enough energy to exceed the *activation energy barrier,* E_A (Figure 6-1b, dashed line).

The Metastable State Is a Result of the Activation Barrier

For most biologically important reactions at normal cellular temperatures, the activation energy is sufficiently high that the proportion of molecules possessing that much energy at any instant is extremely small. Accordingly, the rates of uncatalyzed reactions in cells are very low, and most molecules appear to be stable even though they are potential reactants in thermodynamically favorable reactions. They are, in other words, thermodynamically unstable, but they do not have enough energy to exceed the activation energy barrier.

Such seemingly stable molecules are said to be in a **metastable state.** For cells and cell biologists, high activation energies and the resulting metastable state of cellular constituents are crucial because life by its very nature is a system maintained in a steady state a long way from equilibrium. Were it not for the metastable state, all reactions would proceed quickly to equilibrium, and life as we know it would be impossible. Life, then, depends critically on the high activation energies that prevent most cellular reactions from occurring at appreciable rates in the absence of a suitable catalyst.

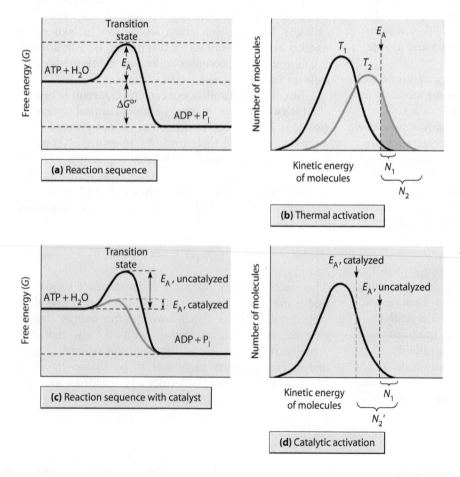

(a) Reaction sequence

(b) Thermal activation

(c) Reaction sequence with catalyst

(d) Catalytic activation

FIGURE 6-1 The Effect of Catalysis on Activation Energy and Number of Molecules Capable of Reaction. (a) The activation energy E_A is the amount of kinetic energy that reactant molecules (here, ATP and H_2O) must possess to reach the transition state leading to product formation. After reactants overcome the activation energy barrier and enter into a reaction, the products have less free energy by the amount $\Delta G^{\circ\prime}$. **(b)** The number of molecules N_1 that have sufficient energy to exceed the activation energy barrier (E_A) can be increased to N_2 by raising the temperature from T_1 to T_2. **(c)** Alternatively, the activation energy can be lowered by a catalyst (blue line), thereby **(d)** increasing the number of molecules from N_1 to N_2' with no change in temperature.

An analogy might help you to understand and appreciate the metastable state. Imagine an egg in a bowl near the edge of a table—its static position represents the metastable state. Although energy would be released if the egg hit the floor, it cannot do so because the edge of the bowl acts as a barrier. A small amount of energy must be applied to lift it up out of the bowl and over the table edge. Then, a much greater amount of energy is released as the egg spontaneously drops to the floor and breaks.

Catalysts Overcome the Activation Energy Barrier

The activation energy requirement is a barrier that must be overcome if desirable reactions are to proceed at reasonable rates. Since the energy content of a given molecule must exceed E_A before that molecule is capable of undergoing reaction, the only way a reaction involving metastable reactants will proceed at an appreciable rate is to increase the proportion of molecules with sufficient energy. This can be achieved either by increasing the average energy content of all molecules or by lowering the activation energy requirement.

One way to increase the energy content of the system is by the input of heat. As Figure 6-1b illustrates, simply increasing the temperature of the system from T_1 to T_2 will increase the kinetic energy of the average molecule, thereby ensuring a greater number of reactive molecules (N_2 instead of N_1). Thus, the hydrolysis of ATP could be facilitated by heating the solution, giving each ATP and water molecule more energy. The problem with using an elevated temperature is that such an approach is not compatible with life because biological systems require a relatively constant temperature. Cells are basically *isothermal* (constant-temperature) systems and require isothermal methods to solve the activation problem.

The alternative to an increase in temperature is to lower the activation energy requirement, thereby ensuring that a greater proportion of molecules will have sufficient energy to collide successfully and undergo reaction. This would be like changing the shape of the bowl holding the egg described earlier into a shallow dish. Now, less energy is needed to lift the egg over the edge of the dish. If the reactants can be bound on some sort of surface in an arrangement that brings potentially reactive portions of adjacent molecules into close juxtaposition, their interaction will be greatly favored and the activation energy effectively reduced.

Providing such a reactive surface is the task of a **catalyst**—an agent that enhances the rate of a reaction by lowering the energy of activation (Figure 6-1c), thereby ensuring that a higher proportion of the molecules possess sufficient energy to undergo reaction without the input of heat (Figure 6-1d). A primary feature of a catalyst is that *it is not permanently changed or consumed as the reaction proceeds*. It simply provides a suitable surface and environment to facilitate the reaction.

Recent work suggests an additional mechanism to overcome the activation energy barrier. This mechanism is known as "quantum tunneling" and sounds like something from a science fiction novel. It is based in part on the realization that matter has both particle-like and wave-like properties. In certain dehydrogenation reactions, the enzyme is believed to allow a hydrogen atom to tunnel *through* the barrier, effectively ending up on the other side without actually going over the top. Unlike most enzyme-catalyzed reactions, these tunneling reactions are temperature independent because an input of thermal energy is not required to ascend the activation energy barrier.

For a specific example of catalysis, let's consider the decomposition of hydrogen peroxide (H_2O_2) into water and oxygen:

$$2H_2O_2 \rightleftharpoons 2H_2O + O_2 \qquad \text{(6-2)}$$

This is a thermodynamically favorable reaction, yet hydrogen peroxide exists in a metastable state because of the high activation energy of the reaction. However, if we add a small number of ferric ions (Fe^{3+}) to a hydrogen peroxide solution, the decomposition reaction proceeds about 30,000 times faster than without the ferric ions. Clearly, Fe^{3+} is a catalyst for this reaction, lowering the activation energy (as shown in Figure 6-1c) and thereby ensuring that a significantly greater proportion (30,000-fold more) of the hydrogen peroxide molecules possess adequate energy to decompose at the existing temperature without the input of added energy.

In cells, the solution to hydrogen peroxide breakdown is not the addition of ferric ions but the enzyme *catalase*, an iron-containing protein. In the presence of catalase, the reaction proceeds about 100,000,000 times faster than the uncatalyzed reaction. Catalase contains iron atoms bound to the enzyme, thus taking advantage of inorganic catalysis within the context of a protein molecule. This combination is obviously a much more effective catalyst for hydrogen peroxide decomposition than ferric ions by themselves. The rate enhancement (catalyzed rate ÷ uncatalyzed rate) of about 10^8 for catalase is not at all an atypical value. The rate enhancements of enzyme-catalyzed reactions range from 10^7 to as high as 10^{17} compared with the uncatalyzed reaction. These values underscore the extraordinary importance of enzymes as catalysts and bring us to the main theme of this chapter.

Enzymes as Biological Catalysts

Regardless of their chemical nature, all catalysts share the following three basic properties:

1. A catalyst increases the rate of a reaction by lowering the activation energy requirement, thereby allowing a thermodynamically feasible reaction to occur at a reasonable rate in the absence of thermal activation.

2. A catalyst acts by forming transient, reversible complexes with substrate molecules, binding them in a manner that facilitates their interaction and stabilizes the intermediate transition state.

3. A catalyst changes only the *rate* at which equilibrium is achieved; it has no effect on the *position* of the equilibrium. This means that a catalyst can enhance the rate of exergonic reactions but cannot somehow change the $\Delta G'$ to allow an endergonic reaction to become spontaneous. Catalysts, in other words, are not thermodynamic wizards.

These properties are common to all catalysts, organic and inorganic alike. In terms of our example, they apply equally to ferric ions and to catalase molecules. However, biological systems rarely use inorganic catalysts. Instead, essentially all catalysis in cells is carried out by organic molecules (proteins, in most cases) called **enzymes.** Because enzymes are organic molecules, they are much more specific than inorganic catalysts, and their activities can be regulated much more carefully.

Most Enzymes Are Proteins

The capacity of cellular extracts to catalyze chemical reactions has been known since the fermentation studies of Eduard and Hans Buchner in 1897. In fact, one of the first terms for what we now call enzymes was *ferments.* However, it was not until 1926 that a specific enzyme, *urease,* was crystallized (from jack beans, by James B. Sumner) and shown to be a protein. This established the protein nature of enzymes and put to rest the belief that biochemical reactions in cells occurred via some unknown "vital force." However, since the early 1980s, biologists have recognized that in addition to proteins, certain RNA molecules, known as *ribozymes,* also have catalytic activity. Ribozymes will be discussed in a later section. Here, we will consider enzymes as proteins—which, in fact, most are.

The Active Site. One of the most important concepts to emerge from our understanding of enzymes as proteins is the **active site.** Every enzyme contains a characteristic cluster of amino acids that form the active site where the substrates bind and the catalytic event occurs. Usually, the active site is an actual groove or pocket with chemical and structural properties that accommodate the intended substrate or substrates with high specificity. The active site consists of a small number of amino acids that are not necessarily adjacent to one another along the primary sequence of the protein. Instead, they are brought together in just the right arrangement by the specific three-dimensional folding of the polypeptide chain as it assumes its characteristic tertiary structure.

Figure 6-2 shows the unfolded and folded structures of the enzyme *lysozyme*, which hydrolyzes the peptido-glycan polymer that makes up bacterial cell walls. The active site of lysozyme is a small groove in the enzyme surface into which the peptidoglycan fits. Lysozyme is a single polypeptide with 129 amino acid residues, but relatively few of these are directly involved in substrate binding and catalysis. Four of these are highlighted in Figure 6-2a. Substrate binding depends on amino acid residues from various positions along the polypeptide, including residues from positions 33–36, 46, 60–64, and 102–110. Catalysis involves two specific residues: a glutamate at position 35 (Glu-35) and an aspartic acid at position 52 (Asp-52). The acid side chain of Glu-35 donates an H^+ to the bond about to be hydrolyzed, and Asp-52 stabilizes the transition state, enhancing cleavage of this bond by an OH^- ion from water. Only as the lysozyme molecule folds to attain its stable three-dimensional conformation are these specific amino acids brought together to form the active site (Figure 6-2b).

Of the 20 different amino acids that make up proteins, only a few are actually involved in the active sites of the many proteins that have been studied. Often, these are cysteine, histidine, serine, aspartate, glutamate, and lysine. All of these residues can participate in binding the substrate to the active site during catalysis, and several also serve as donors or acceptors of protons.

Some enzymes contain specific nonprotein cofactors that are located at the active site and are indispensable for catalytic activity. These cofactors, also called **prosthetic groups,** are usually either metal ions or small organic molecules known as *coenzymes* that are derivatives of vitamins. Frequently, prosthetic groups (especially positively charged metal ions) function as electron acceptors because none of the amino acid side chains are good electron acceptors.

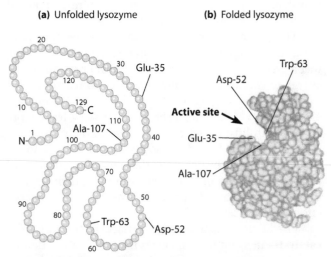

(a) Unfolded lysozyme   **(b)** Folded lysozyme

FIGURE 6-2 The Active Site of Lysozyme. (**a**) Four amino acid residues that are important for substrate binding and catalysis are far apart in the primary structure of unfolded lysozyme. (**b**) These residues are brought together to form part of the active site as lysozyme folds into its active tertiary structure.

3-D Structures www.thecellplace.com *Human lysozyme bound to a ligand*

Where present, prosthetic groups often are located at the active site and are indispensable for the catalytic activity of the enzyme. For example, each catalase enzyme molecule contains a multiring structure known as a *porphyrin ring*, to which an iron atom necessary for catalysis is bound.

The requirement for various prosthetic groups on some enzymes explains our nutritional requirements for trace amounts of vitamins and certain metals. Oxidation of glucose for energy requires two specific coenzymes that are derivatives of the vitamins niacin and riboflavin. Both niacin and riboflavin are essential nutrients in the human diet because our cells cannot synthesize them. These coenzymes, which are bound to the active site of certain enzymes, accept electrons and hydrogen ions from glucose as it is oxidized. Likewise, carboxypeptidase A, a digestive enzyme that degrades proteins, requires a single zinc atom bound to the active site, as we will see later in the chapter. Other enzymes may require atoms of iron, copper, molybdenum, or even lithium. Like enzymes, prosthetic groups are not consumed during chemical reactions, so cells require only minute, catalytic amounts of them.

Enzyme Specificity. Due to the structure of the active site, enzymes display a very high degree of **substrate specificity,** which is the ability to discriminate between very similar molecules. Specificity is one of the most characteristic properties of living systems, and enzymes are excellent examples of biological specificity.

We can illustrate their specificity by comparing enzymes with inorganic catalysts. Most inorganic catalysts are quite nonspecific in that they will act on a variety of compounds that share some general chemical feature. Consider, for example, the *hydrogenation* of (addition of hydrogen to) an unsaturated C=C bond:

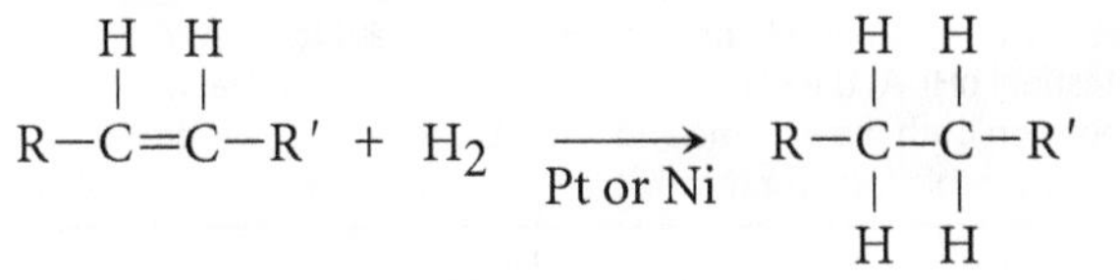

$$R-\overset{\overset{\displaystyle H}{|}}{C}=\overset{\overset{\displaystyle H}{|}}{C}-R' + H_2 \xrightarrow[\text{Pt or Ni}]{} R-\overset{\overset{\displaystyle H}{|}}{\underset{\underset{\displaystyle H}{|}}{C}}-\overset{\overset{\displaystyle H}{|}}{\underset{\underset{\displaystyle H}{|}}{C}}-R' \quad \text{(6-3)}$$

This reaction can be carried out in the laboratory using a platinum (Pt) or nickel (Ni) catalyst, as indicated. These inorganic catalysts are very nonspecific, however; they can catalyze the hydrogenation of a wide variety of unsaturated compounds. In practice, nickel and platinum are used commercially to hydrogenate polyunsaturated vegetable oils in the manufacture of solid cooking fats or shortenings. Regardless of the exact structure of the unsaturated compound, it can be effectively hydrogenated in the presence of nickel or platinum. This lack of specificity of inorganic catalysts during hydrogenation is responsible for the formation of certain *trans* fats (see Chapter 7) that are rare in nature.

In contrast, consider the biological example of hydrogenation as fumarate is converted to succinate, a reaction:

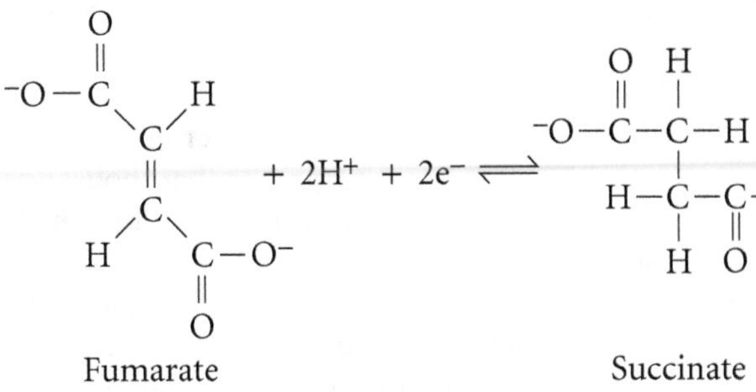

$$+ 2H^+ + 2e^- \rightleftharpoons$$

Fumarate   Succinate   (6-4)

This particular reaction is catalyzed in cells by the enzyme *succinate dehydrogenase* (so named because it normally functions in the opposite direction during energy metabolism). This dehydrogenase, like most enzymes, is highly specific. It will not add or remove hydrogen atoms from any compounds except those shown in Reaction 6-4. In fact, this particular enzyme is so specific that it will not even recognize maleate, which is an isomer of fumarate (**Figure 6-3**).

Not all enzymes are quite that specific. Some accept a number of closely related substrates, and others accept any of a whole group of substrates as long as they possess some common structural feature. Such **group specificity** is seen most often with enzymes involved in the synthesis or degradation of polymers. Since the purpose of carboxypeptidase A is to degrade dietary polypeptide chains by removing the C-terminal amino acid, it makes sense for the enzyme to accept any of a wide variety of polypeptides as substrates. It would be needlessly extravagant of the cell to require a separate enzyme for every different amino acid residue that has to be removed during polypeptide degradation.

In general, however, enzymes are highly specific with respect to substrate, such that a cell must possess almost as many different kinds of enzymes as it has reactions to catalyze. For a typical cell, this means that thousands of different enzymes are necessary to carry out its full metabolic

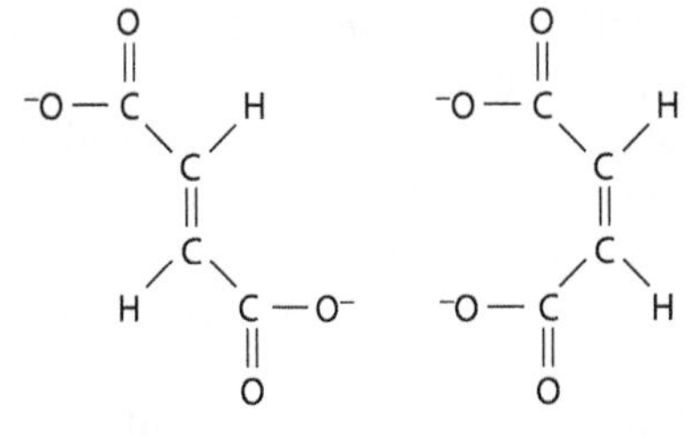

(a) Fumarate   **(b)** Maleate

FIGURE 6-3 Specificity in Enzyme-Catalyzed Reactions. Unlike most inorganic catalysts, enzymes can distinguish between closely related isomers. For example, the enzyme succinate dehydrogenase uses **(a)** fumarate as a substrate but not **(b)** its isomer, maleate.

program. At first, that may seem wasteful in terms of proteins to be synthesized, genetic information to be stored and read out, and enzyme molecules to have on hand in the cell. But you should also be able to see the tremendous regulatory possibilities this suggests—a point we will return to later.

Enzyme Diversity and Nomenclature. Given the specificity of enzymes and the large number of reactions occurring within a cell, it is not surprising that thousands of different enzymes have been identified. This enormous diversity of enzymes led to a variety of schemes for naming enzymes as they were discovered and characterized. Some were given names based on the substrate; *ribonuclease, protease,* and *amylase* are examples. Others, such as *succinate dehydrogenase,* were named to describe their function. Still other enzymes have names like *trypsin* and *catalase* that tell us little about either their substrates or their functions.

The resulting confusion prompted the International Union of Biochemistry to appoint an Enzyme Commission (EC) to devise a rational system for naming enzymes. Using the EC system, enzymes are divided into the following six major classes based on their general functions: *oxidoreductases, transferases, hydrolases, lyases, isomerases,* and *ligases.* The EC system assigns every known enzyme a unique four-part number based on its function—for example, EC 3.2.1.17 is the number for lysozyme. **Table 6-1** provides one representative example of each class of enzymes and the reaction it catalyzes.

Sensitivity to Temperature. Besides their specificity and diversity, enzymes are characterized by their sensitivity to temperature. This temperature dependence is not usually a practical concern for enzymes in the cells of mammals or birds because these organisms are *homeotherms,* "warm-blooded" organisms that are capable of regulating body temperature independent of the environment. However, many organisms (e.g., insects, reptiles, worms, plants, protozoa, algae, and bacteria) function at the temperature of their environment, which can vary greatly. For these organisms, the dependence of enzyme activity on temperature is significant.

At low temperatures, the rate of an enzyme-catalyzed reaction increases with temperature. This occurs because the greater kinetic energy of both enzyme and substrate molecules ensures more frequent collisions, thereby increasing the likelihood of correct substrate binding and sufficient energy to undergo reaction. At some point, however, further increases in temperature result in *denaturation* of the enzyme molecule. It loses its defined tertiary shape as hydrogen and ionic bonds are broken and the native polypeptide assumes a random, extended conformation. During denaturation, the structural integrity of the active site is destroyed, causing a loss of enzyme activity.

The temperature range over which an enzyme denatures varies from enzyme to enzyme and especially from organism to organism. **Figure 6-4a** contrasts the temperature dependence of a typical enzyme from the human body with that of a typical enzyme from a thermophilic bacterium. Not surprisingly, the reaction rate of the human enzyme is maximum at about 37°C (the *optimal temperature* for the enzyme), which is normal body temperature. The sharp decrease in activity at higher temperatures reflects the denaturation of the enzyme molecules. Most enzymes of homeotherms are inactivated by temperatures above about 50–55°C. However, some enzymes are remarkably sensitive to heat. They are denatured and inactivated at temperatures lower than this—in some cases, even by body temperatures encountered in people with high fevers (40°C). This is thought to be part of the beneficial effect of

(a) Temperature dependence. This panel shows how reaction rate varies with temperature for a typical human enzyme (black) and a typical enzyme from a thermophilic bacterium (green). The reaction rate is highest at the optimal temperature, which is about 37°C (body temperature) for the human enzyme and about 75°C (the temperature of a typical hot spring) for the bacterial enzyme. Above the optimal temperature, the enzyme is rapidly inactivated by denaturation.

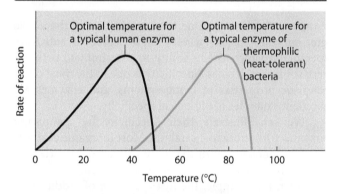

(b) pH dependence. This panel shows how reaction rate varies with pH for the gastric enzyme pepsin (black) and the intestinal enzyme trypsin (red). The reaction rate is highest at the optimal pH, which is about 2.0 for pepsin (stomach pH) and near 8.0 for trypsin (intestinal pH). At the pH optimum for an enzyme, ionizable groups on both the enzyme and the substrate molecules are in the most favorable form for reactivity.

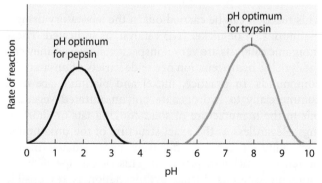

FIGURE 6-4 The Effect of Temperature and pH on the Reaction Rate of Enzyme-Catalyzed Reactions. Every enzyme has an optimum temperature and pH that usually reflect the environment where that enzyme is found in nature.

Table 6-1 The Major Classes of Enzymes with an Example of Each

Class	Reaction Type	Enzyme Name	Example / Reaction Catalyzed
1. Oxidoreductases	Oxidation-reduction reactions	Alcohol dehydrogenase (oxidation with NAD^+)	CH_3-CH_2-OH (Ethanol) $\xrightarrow{NAD^+ \;\; NADH + H^+}$ $CH_3-\overset{O}{\overset{\|}{C}}-H$ (Acetaldehyde)
2. Transferases	Transfer of functional groups from one molecule to another	Glycerokinase (phosphorylation)	$HO-CH_2-\overset{OH}{\overset{\|}{CH}}-CH_2-OH$ (Glycerol) $\xrightarrow{ATP \;\; ADP}$ $HO-CH_2-\overset{OH}{\overset{\|}{CH}}-CH_2-O-PO_3^{2-}$ (Glycerol phosphate)
3. Hydrolases	Hydrolytic cleavage of one molecule into two molecules	Carboxypeptidase A (peptide bond cleavage)	$-NH-\overset{R_{n-1}}{\overset{\|}{CH}}-\overset{O}{\overset{\|}{C}}-NH-\overset{R_n}{\overset{\|}{CH}}-\overset{O}{\overset{\|}{C}}-O^-$ (C-terminus of polypeptide) $\xrightarrow{H_2O}$ $-NH-\overset{R_{n-1}}{\overset{\|}{CH}}-\overset{O}{\overset{\|}{C}}-O^-$ (Shortened polypeptide) $+ H_3N^+-\overset{R_n}{\overset{\|}{CH}}-\overset{O}{\overset{\|}{C}}-O^-$ (C-terminal amino acid)
4. Lyases	Removal of a group from, or addition of a group to, a molecule with rearrangement of electrons	Pyruvate decarboxylase (decarboxylation)	$CH_3-\overset{O}{\overset{\|}{C}}-\overset{O}{\overset{\|}{C}}-O^- + H^+$ (Pyruvate) $\longrightarrow$ $CH_3-\overset{O}{\overset{\|}{C}}-H + CO_2$ (Acetaldehyde)
5. Isomerases	Movement of a functional group within a molecule	Maleate isomerase (cis-trans isomerization)	(Maleate) $\rightleftharpoons$ (Fumarate)
6. Ligases	Joining of two molecules to form a single molecule	Pyruvate carboxylase (carboxylation)	$CH_3-\overset{O}{\overset{\|}{C}}-\overset{O}{\overset{\|}{C}}-O^- + CO_2$ (Pyruvate) $\xrightarrow{ATP \;\; ADP + P_i}$ $^-O-\overset{O}{\overset{\|}{C}}-CH_2-\overset{O}{\overset{\|}{C}}-\overset{O}{\overset{\|}{C}}-O^-$ (Oxaloacetate)

fever when you are ill—the denaturation of heat-sensitive pathogen enzymes.

Some enzymes, however, retain activity at unusually high temperatures. The green curve in Figure 6-4a depicts the temperature dependence of an enzyme from one of the thermophilic archaea mentioned in Chapter 4. Some of these organisms thrive in acidic hot springs at temperatures as high as 80°C, with optimal temperatures close to the boiling point of water, and others live in deep-sea hydrothermal vents at temperatures over 100°C. Other enzymes, such as those of cryophilic ("cold-loving") *Listeria* bacteria and certain yeasts and molds, can function at low temperatures, allowing these organisms to grow slowly even at refrigerator temperatures (4–6°C).

Sensitivity to pH. Enzymes are also sensitive to pH. In fact, most of them are active only within a pH range of about 3–4 pH units. This pH dependence is usually due to the presence of one or more charged amino acids at the active site and/or on the substrate itself. Activity is usually dependent on having such groups present in a specific, either charged or uncharged form. For example, the active site of carboxypeptidase A includes the carboxyl groups from two glutamate residues. These carboxyl groups must be present in the charged (ionized) form, so the enzyme becomes inactive if the pH is decreased to the point where the glutamate carboxyl groups on the enzyme molecules are protonated and therefore uncharged. Extreme changes in pH also disrupt ionic and hydrogen bonds, altering tertiary structure and function.

As you might expect, the pH dependence of an enzyme usually reflects the environment in which that enzyme is normally active. Figure 6-4b shows the pH dependence of two protein-degrading enzymes found in the human digestive tract. Pepsin (black line) is present in the stomach, where the pH is usually about 2, whereas trypsin (red line) is secreted into the small intestine, which has a pH between 7 and 8. Both enzymes are active over a range of almost 4 pH units but differ greatly in their pH optima, consistent with the conditions in their respective locations within the body.

Sensitivity to Other Factors. In addition to temperature and pH, enzymes are sensitive to other factors, including molecules and ions that act as inhibitors or activators of the enzyme. For example, several enzymes involved in energy production via glucose degradation are inhibited by ATP, which inactivates them when energy is plentiful. Other enzymes in glucose breakdown are activated by adenosine monophosphate (AMP) and ADP, which act as signals that energy supplies are low and more glucose should be degraded.

Most enzymes are also sensitive to the ionic strength (concentration of dissolved ions) of the environment, which affects the hydrogen bonding and ionic interactions that help to maintain the tertiary conformation of the enzyme. Because these same interactions are often involved in the interaction between the substrate and the active site, the ionic environment may also affect binding

of the substrate. Several magnesium-requiring chloroplast enzymes required for photosynthetic carbon fixation are active only in the presence of the high levels of magnesium ions that occur when leaves are illuminated.

Substrate Binding, Activation, and Catalysis Occur at the Active Site

Because of the precise chemical fit between the active site of an enzyme and its substrates, enzymes are highly specific and much more effective than inorganic catalysts. As we noted previously, enzyme-catalyzed reactions proceed 10^7 to 10^{17} times more quickly than uncatalyzed reactions do, versus a rate increase of 10^3 to 10^4 times for inorganic catalysts. As you might guess, most of the interest in enzymes focuses on the active site, where binding, activation, and chemical transformation of the substrate occur.

Substrate Binding. Initial contact between the active site of an enzyme and a potential substrate molecule depends on their collision. Once in the active site, the substrate molecules are bound to the enzyme surface in just the right orientation so that specific catalytic groups on the enzyme can facilitate the reaction. Substrate binding usually involves hydrogen bonds or ionic bonds (or both) to charged or polar amino acids. These are generally weak bonds, but several bonds may hold a single molecule in place. The strength of the bonds between an enzyme and a substrate molecule is often in the range of 3–12 kcal/mol. This is less than one-tenth the strength of a single covalent bond. Substrate binding is therefore readily reversible.

For many years, enzymologists regarded an enzyme as a rigid structure, with a specific substrate fitting into the active site like a key fits into a lock. This *lock-and-key model*, first suggested in 1894 by the German biochemist Emil Fischer, explained enzyme specificity but did little to enhance our understanding of the catalytic event. A more refined view of the enzyme-substrate interaction is provided by the **induced-fit model,** first proposed in 1958 by Daniel Koshland. According to this model, substrate binding at the active site distorts both the enzyme and the substrate, thereby stabilizing the substrate molecules in their transition state and rendering certain substrate bonds more susceptible to catalytic attack. In the case of lysozyme, substrate binding induces a conformational change in the enzyme that distorts the peptidoglycan substrate and weakens the bond about to be broken in the reaction.

As shown in **Figure 6-5**, induced fit involves a conformational change in the shape of the enzyme molecule following substrate binding. This alters the configuration of the active site and positions the proper reactive groups of the enzyme optimally for the catalytic reaction. Evidence of such conformational changes upon binding of substrate has come from X-ray diffraction studies of crystallized proteins and nuclear magnetic resonance (NMR) studies of proteins in solution, which can determine the shape of an enzyme molecule with and without bound substrate. Figure 6-5 illustrates the conformational change that

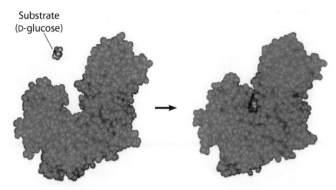

Substrate
(D-glucose)

FIGURE 6-5 The Conformational Change in Enzyme Structure Induced by Substrate Binding. This figure shows a space-filling model for the enzyme hexokinase along with its substrate, a molecule of D-glucose. Substrate binding induces a conformational change in hexokinase, known as induced fit, that improves the catalytic activity of the enzyme.

VIDEOS www.thecellplace.com   *Closure of hexokinase*
                              via induced fit

occurs upon substrate binding to hexokinase, which adds a phosphate group to D-glucose. As glucose binds to the active site, the two domains of hexokinase fold toward each other, closing the binding site cleft about the substrate to facilitate catalysis.

Often, the induced conformational change brings critical amino acid side chains into the active site even if they are not nearby in the absence of substrate. In the active site of carboxypeptidase A (**Figure 6-6**), a zinc ion is tightly bound to three residues of the enzyme (Glu-72, His-69, and His-196) and also loosely binds a water molecule (not shown). Substrate binding to the zinc ion replaces the bound water molecule and induces a conformational change in the enzyme that brings other amino

acid side chains into the active site, including Arg-145, Tyr-248, and Glu-270. These amino acid residues are then in position to participate in catalysis.

Substrate Activation. The role of the active site is not just to recognize and bind the appropriate substrate but also to *activate* it by subjecting it to the right chemical environment for catalysis. A given enzyme-catalyzed reaction may involve one or more means of **substrate activation.** Three of the most common mechanisms are as follows:

1. *Bond distortion.* The change in enzyme conformation induced by initial substrate binding to the active site not only causes better complementarity and a tighter enzyme-substrate fit but also distorts one or more of its bonds, thereby weakening the bond and making it more susceptible to catalytic attack.

2. *Proton transfer.* The enzyme may also accept or donate protons, thereby increasing the chemical reactivity of the substrate. This accounts for the importance of charged amino acids in active-site chemistry, which in turn explains why enzyme activity is so often pH dependent.

3. *Electron transfer.* As a further means of substrate activation, enzymes may also accept or donate electrons, thereby forming temporary covalent bonds between the enzyme and its substrate.

The Catalytic Event. The sequence of events at the active site is illustrated in **Figure 6-7**, using the enzyme sucrase as an example. Sucrase (also known as invertase or β-fructofuranosidase) hydrolyzes the disaccharide sucrose

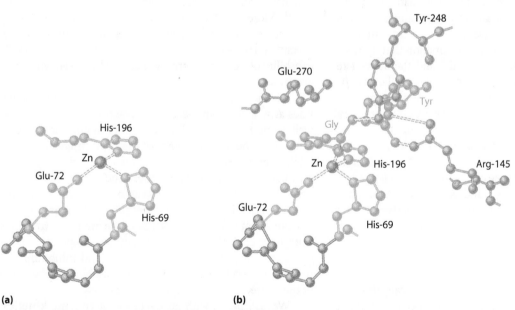

(a)   (b)

FIGURE 6-6 The Change in Active Site Structure Induced by Substrate Binding. (a) The unoccupied active site of carboxypeptidase A contains a zinc ion tightly bound to side chains of three amino acids (cyan). **(b)** Binding of the substrate (the dipeptide shown in orange) to this zinc ion induces a conformation change in the enzyme that brings other amino acid side chains (purple) into the active site to participate in catalysis.

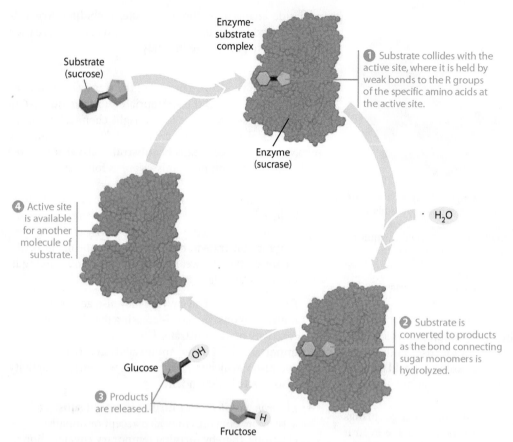

Substrate
(sucrose)

Enzyme-
substrate
complex

1 Substrate collides with the active site, where it is held by weak bonds to the R groups of the specific amino acids at the active site.

Enzyme
(sucrase)

4 Active site is available for another molecule of substrate.

H_2O

2 Substrate is converted to products as the bond connecting sugar monomers is hydrolyzed.

Glucose ─OH

3 Products are released.

Fructose ─H

FIGURE 6-7 The Catalytic Cycle of an Enzyme. In this example, the enzyme sucrase catalyzes the hydrolysis of sucrose to glucose and fructose. The actual structure of this enzyme is shown, but the active site has been modified slightly to emphasize the close fit between enzyme and substrate.

ACTIVITIES www.thecellplace.com *How enzymes work*

into glucose and fructose. The initial random collision of a substrate molecule—sucrose, in this case—with the active site results in its binding to amino acid residues that are strategically positioned there (step **1**). Substrate binding induces a change in the enzyme conformation that tightens the fit between the substrate molecule and the active site and lowers the free energy of the transition state. This facilitates the conversion of substrate into products—glucose and fructose, in this case (step **2**). The products are then released from the active site (step **3**), enabling the enzyme molecule to return to its original conformation, with the active site now available for another molecule of substrate (step **4**). This entire sequence of events takes place in a sufficiently short time to allow hundreds or even thousands of such reactions to occur per second at the active site of a single enzyme molecule!

Enzyme Kinetics

So far, our discussion of enzymes has been basically descriptive. We have dealt with the activation energy requirement that prevents thermodynamically feasible reactions from occurring and with catalysts as a means of reducing the activation energy and thereby facilitating such reactions.

We have also encountered enzymes as biological catalysts and have examined their structure and function in some detail. Moreover, we realize that the only reactions likely to occur in cells at reasonable rates are those for which specific enzymes are on hand, such that the metabolic capability of a cell is effectively specified by the enzymes that are present.

Still lacking, however, is a means of assessing the actual rates at which enzyme-catalyzed reactions will proceed, as well as an appreciation for the factors that influence reaction rates. The mere presence of the appropriate enzyme in a cell does not ensure that a given reaction will occur at an adequate rate. We need to understand the cellular conditions that are favorable for activity of a particular enzyme. We have already seen how factors such as temperature and pH can affect enzyme activity. Now we are ready to appreciate how critically enzyme activity also depends on the concentrations of substrates, products, and inhibitors that prevail in the cell. In addition, we will see how at least some of these effects can be defined quantitatively.

We will begin with an overview of **enzyme kinetics**, which describes quantitative aspects of enzyme catalysis (the word *kinetics* is from the Greek word *kinetikos*, meaning "moving") and the rate of substrate conversion into products. Specifically, enzyme kinetics concerns reaction rates and the manner in which reaction rates are influenced by a variety of factors, including the concentrations of substrates, products, and inhibitors. Most of our attention here will focus on the effects of substrate concentration on the kinetics of enzyme-catalyzed reactions.

We will focus on *initial reaction rates*, the rates of reactions measured over a brief initial period of time during which the substrate concentration has not yet decreased enough to affect the rate of the reaction and the accumulation of product is still too small for the reverse reaction (conversion of product back into substrate) to occur at a significant rate. This resembles the steady-state situation in living cells, where substrates are continually replenished and products are continually removed, maintaining stable concentrations of each. Although this description is somewhat oversimplified compared to the situation in living cells, it nonetheless allows us to understand some important principles of enzyme kinetics.

Enzyme kinetics can seem quite complex at first. To help you understand the basic concepts, **Box 6A** explains how enzymes acting on substrate molecules can be compared to a roomful of monkeys shelling peanuts. You may find it useful to turn to the analogy at this point and then come back to this section.

Most Enzymes Display Michaelis–Menten Kinetics

Here we will consider how the **initial reaction velocity (v)** changes depending on the **substrate concentration ([S])**. The initial reaction velocity is rigorously defined as the rate of change in product concentration per unit time (e.g., mM/min). Often, however, reaction velocities are experimentally measured in a constant assay volume of 1 mL and are reported as μmol of product per minute. At low [S], a doubling of [S] will double v. But as [S] increases, each additional increment of substrate results in a smaller increase in reaction rate. As [S] becomes very large, increases in [S] increase only slightly, and the value of v reaches a maximum.

By determining v in a series of experiments at varying substrate concentrations, the dependence of v on [S] can be shown experimentally to be that of a hyperbola (**Figure 6-8**). An important property of this hyperbolic relationship is that as [S] tends toward infinity, v approaches an upper limiting value known as the **maximum velocity (V_{max})**. This value depends on the number of enzyme molecules and can therefore be increased only by adding more enzyme. The inability of increasingly higher substrate concentrations to increase the reaction velocity beyond a finite upper value is called **saturation**. At saturation, all available enzyme molecules are operating at maximum capacity. Saturation is a fundamental, universal property of enzyme-catalyzed reactions. Catalyzed reactions always become saturated at high substrate concentrations, whereas uncatalyzed reactions do not.

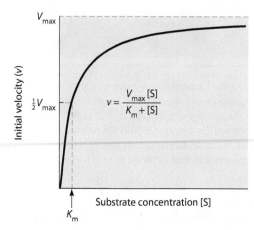

FIGURE 6-8 The Relationship Between Reaction Velocity and Substrate Concentration. For an enzyme-catalyzed reaction that follows Michaelis–Menten kinetics, the initial velocity tends toward an upper limiting velocity V_{max} as the substrate concentration [S] tends toward infinity. The Michaelis constant K_m corresponds to that substrate concentration at which the reaction is proceeding at one-half of the maximum velocity.

Much of our understanding of the hyperbolic relationship between [S] and v is due to the pioneering work of two German enzymologists, Leonor Michaelis and Maud Menten. In 1913, they postulated a general theory of enzyme action that has turned out to be basic to the quantitative analysis of almost all aspects of enzyme kinetics. To understand their approach, consider one of the simplest possible enzyme-catalyzed reactions, a reaction in which a single substrate S is converted into a single product P:

$$S \xrightarrow[\text{Enzyme (E)}]{} P \qquad (6\text{-}5)$$

According to the Michaelis–Menten hypothesis, the enzyme E that catalyzes this reaction first reacts with the substrate S, forming the transient enzyme-substrate complex ES, which then undergoes the actual catalytic reaction to form free enzyme and product P, as shown in the sequence

$$E_f + S \underset{k_2}{\overset{k_1}{\rightleftharpoons}} ES \underset{k_4}{\overset{k_3}{\rightleftharpoons}} E_f + P \qquad (6\text{-}6)$$

where E_f is the free form of the enzyme, S is the substrate, ES is the enzyme-substrate complex, P is the product, and k_1, k_2, k_3, and k_4 are the rate constants for the indicated reactions.

Starting with this model and several simplifying assumptions, including the steady-state conditions, Michaelis and Menten arrived at the relationship between the velocity of an enzyme-catalyzed reaction and the substrate concentration, as follows:

$$v = \frac{V_{max}[S]}{K_m + [S]} \qquad (6\text{-}7)$$

If you found the Mexican jumping beans helpful in understanding free energy you might appreciate an approach to enzyme kinetics based on the analogy of a roomful of monkeys ("enzymes") shelling peanuts ("substrates"), with the peanuts present in varying abundance. Try to understand each step first in terms of monkeys shelling peanuts and then in terms of an actual enzyme-catalyzed reaction.

The Peanut Gallery

For our model, we need a troop of ten monkeys, all equally adept at finding and shelling peanuts. We shall assume that the monkeys are too full to eat any of the peanuts they shell but nonetheless have an irresistible compulsion to go on shelling.

Next, we need the Peanut Gallery, a room of fixed floor space with peanuts scattered equally about on the floor. The number of peanuts will be varied as we proceed, but in all cases there will be vastly more peanuts than monkeys in the room. Moreover, because we know the number of peanuts and the total floor space, we can always calculate the "concentration" (more accurately, the density) of peanuts in the room. In each case, the monkeys start out in an adjacent room. To start an assay, we simply open the door and allow the eager monkeys to enter the Peanut Gallery.

The Shelling Begins

Now we are ready for our first assay. We start with an initial peanut concentration of 1 peanut per square meter, and we assume that, at this concentration of peanuts, the average monkey spends 9 seconds looking for a peanut to shell and 1 second shelling it. This means that each monkey requires 10 seconds per peanut and can thus shell peanuts at the rate of 0.1 peanut per second. Then, since there are ten monkeys in the gallery, the rate (let's call it the velocity v) of peanut-shelling for all the monkeys is 1 peanut per second at this particular concentration of peanuts (which we will call [S] to remind ourselves that the peanuts are really the substrate of the shelling action). All of this can be tabulated as follows:

[S] = Concentration of peanuts (peanuts/m^2)	1
Time required per peanut:	
To find (sec/peanut)	9
To shell (sec/peanut)	1
Total (sec/peanut)	10
Rate of shelling:	
Per monkey (peanut/sec)	0.10
Total (v) (peanut/sec)	1.0

The Peanuts Become More Abundant

For our second assay, we herd all the monkeys back into the waiting room, sweep up the debris, and arrange peanuts about the Peanut Gallery at a concentration of 3 peanuts per square meter. Since peanuts are now three times more abundant than previously, the average monkey should find a peanut three times more quickly than before, such that the time spent finding the average peanut is now only 3 seconds. But each peanut, once found, still takes 1 second to shell, so the total time per peanut is now 4 seconds and the velocity of shelling is 0.25 peanut per second for each monkey, or 2.5 peanuts per second for the roomful of monkeys. This generates another column of entries for our data table:

[S] = Concentration of peanuts (peanuts/m^2)	1	3
Time required per peanut:		
To find (sec/peanut)	9	3
To shell (sec/peanut)	1	1
Total (sec/peanut)	10	4
Rate of shelling:		
Per monkey (peanut/sec)	0.10	0.25
Total (v) (peanut/sec)	1.0	2.5

What Happens to v as [S] Continues to Increase?

To find out what eventually happens to the velocity of peanut-shelling as the peanut concentration in the room gets higher and higher, all you need do is extend the data table by assuming ever-increasing values for [S] and calculating the corresponding v. For example, you should be able to convince yourself that a further tripling of the peanut concentration (from 3 to 9 peanuts/m^2) will bring the time required per peanut down to 2 seconds (1 second to find and another second to shell), which will result in a shelling rate of 0.5 peanut per second for each monkey, or 5.0 peanuts per second overall.

Already you should begin to see a trend. The first tripling of peanut concentration increased the rate 2.5-fold, but the next tripling resulted in only a further doubling of the rate. There seems, in other words, to be a diminishing return on additional peanuts. You can see this clearly if you choose a few more peanut concentrations and then plot v on the y-axis (suggested scale: 0–10 peanuts/sec) versus [S] on the x-axis (suggested scale: 0–100 peanuts/m^2).

What you should find is that the data generate a hyperbolic curve that looks strikingly like Figure 6-8. If you look at your data carefully, you should also see the reason your curve continues to "bend over" as [S] gets higher (i.e., why you get less and less additional velocity for each further increment of peanuts): The shelling time is fixed and therefore becomes a more and more prominent component of the total processing time per peanut as the finding time gets smaller and smaller. You should also appreciate that it is this fixed shelling time that ultimately sets the upper limit on the overall rate of peanut processing because, even when [S] is infinite (i.e., in a world flooded with peanuts), there will still be a finite time of 1 second required to process each peanut. This means that the overall maximum velocity, V_{max}, for the ten monkeys would be 10 peanuts per second.

Finally, you should realize that there is something special about the peanut concentration at which the finding time is exactly equal to the shelling time (it turns out to be 9 peanuts/m^2); this is the point along the curve at which the rate of peanut processing is exactly one-half of the maximum rate. In fact, it is such an important benchmark along the concentration scale that you might even be tempted to give it a special name, particularly if your name were Michaelis and you were monkeying around with enzymes instead of peanuts!

Here, v is the initial reaction velocity, [S] is the initial substrate concentration, V_{max} is the maximum velocity, and K_m is the concentration of substrate that gives exactly half the maximum velocity. V_{max} and K_m (also known as the **Michaelis constant**) are important kinetic parameters that we will consider in more detail in the next section. Equation 6-7 is known as the **Michaelis–Menten equation,** a central relationship of enzyme kinetics. (Problem 6–12 at the end of the chapter gives you an opportunity to derive the Michaelis–Menten equation yourself.)

What Is the Meaning of V_{max} and K_m?

To appreciate the implications of the relationship between v and [S] and to examine the meaning of the parameters V_{max} and K_m, we can consider three special cases of substrate concentration: very low substrate concentration, very high substrate concentration, and the special case of [S] = K_m.

Case 1: Very Low Substrate Concentration ([S] $\ll K_m$). At very low substrate concentration, [S] becomes negligibly small compared with the constant K_m in the denominator of the Michaelis–Menten equation and can be ignored, so we can write

$$v = \frac{V_{max}[S]}{K_m + [S]} \cong \frac{V_{max}[S]}{K_m} \qquad (6\text{-}8)$$

Thus, at very low substrate concentration, the initial reaction velocity is roughly proportional to the substrate concentration. This can be seen at the extreme left side of the graph in Figure 6-8. As long as the substrate concentration is much lower than the K_m value, the velocity of an enzyme-catalyzed reaction increases linearly with substrate concentration.

Case 2: Very High Substrate Concentration ([S] $\gg K_m$). At very high substrate concentration, K_m becomes negligibly small compared with [S] in the denominator of the Michaelis–Menten equation, so we can write

$$v = \frac{V_{max}[S]}{K_m + [S]} \cong \frac{V_{max}[S]}{[S]} = V_{max} \qquad (6\text{-}9)$$

Therefore, at very high substrate concentrations, the velocity of an enzyme-catalyzed reaction is essentially independent of the variation in [S] and is approximately constant at a value close to V_{max} (see the right side of Figure 6-8).

This provides us with a mathematical definition of V_{max}, which is one of the two kinetic parameters in the Michaelis–Menten equation. V_{max} is the upper limit of v as the substrate concentration [S] approaches infinity. In other words, V_{max} is the velocity at saturating substrate concentrations. Under these conditions, every enzyme molecule is occupied in the actual process of catalysis

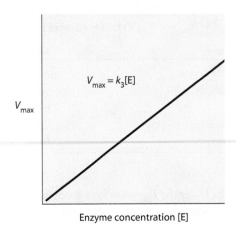

FIGURE 6-9 The Linear Relationship Between V_{max} and Enzyme Concentration. The linear increase in reaction velocity with enzyme concentration provides the basis for determining enzyme concentrations experimentally.

almost all of the time because the substrate concentration is so high that, as soon as a product molecule is released, another substrate molecule arrives at the active site.

V_{max} is therefore an upper limit determined by (1) the time required for the actual catalytic reaction and (2) how many such enzyme molecules are present. Because the actual reaction rate is fixed, the only way that V_{max} can be increased is to increase enzyme concentration. In fact, V_{max} is linearly proportional to the amount of enzyme present, as shown in **Figure 6-9**, where k_3 represents the reaction rate constant.

Case 3: ([S] = K_m). To explore the meaning of K_m more precisely, consider the special case where [S] is exactly equal to K_m. Under these conditions, the Michaelis–Menten equation can be written as

$$v = \frac{V_{max}[S]}{K_m + [S]} \cong \frac{V_{max}[S]}{2[S]} = \frac{V_{max}}{2} \qquad (6\text{-}10)$$

This equation demonstrates mathematically that K_m is that specific substrate concentration at which the reaction proceeds at one-half of its maximum velocity. The K_m is a constant value for a given enzyme-substrate combination catalyzing a reaction under specified conditions. Figure 6-8 illustrates the meaning of both V_{max} and K_m.

Why Are K_m and V_{max} Important to Cell Biologists?

Now that we understand what K_m and V_{max} mean, it is fair to ask why these kinetic parameters are important to cell biologists. The K_m value is useful because it allows us to estimate where along the Michaelis–Menten plot of Figure 6-8 an enzyme is functioning in a cell (providing, of course, that the normal substrate concentration in the cell is known). We can then estimate at what fraction of the maximum velocity the enzyme-catalyzed reaction is likely to be proceeding in

Table 6-2

Table 6-2	K_m and k_{cat} Values for Some Enzymes		
Enzyme Name	**Substrate**	**K_m (M)**	**k_{cat} (s^{-1})**
Acetylcholinesterase	Acetylcholine	9×10^{-5}	1.4×10^4
Carbonic anhydrase	CO_2	1×10^{-2}	1×10^6
Fumarase	Fumarate	5×10^{-6}	8×10^2
Triose phosphate isomerase	Glyceraldehyde-3-phosphate	5×10^{-4}	4.3×10^3
β-lactamase	Benzylpenicillin	2×10^{-5}	2×10^3

the cell. The lower the K_m value for a given enzyme and substrate, the lower the substrate concentration range in which the enzyme is effective. As we will soon see, enzyme activity in the cell can be modulated by regulatory molecules that bind to the enzyme and alter the K_m for a particular substrate. K_m values for several enzyme-substrate combinations are given in Table 6-2 and, as you can see, can vary over several orders of magnitude.

The V_{max} for a particular reaction is important because it provides a measure of the potential maximum rate of the reaction. Few enzymes actually encounter saturating substrate concentrations in cells, so enzymes are not likely to be functioning at their maximum rate under cellular conditions. However, by knowing the V_{max} value, the K_m value, and the substrate concentration in vivo, we can at least estimate the likely rate of the reaction under cellular conditions.

V_{max} can also be used to determine another useful parameter called the **turnover number (k_{cat})**, which expresses the rate at which substrate molecules are converted to product by a single enzyme molecule when the enzyme is operating at its maximum velocity. The constant k_{cat} has the units of reciprocal time (s^{-1}, for example) and is calculated as the quotient of V_{max} over $[E_t]$, the concentration of the enzyme:

$$k_{cat} = \frac{V_{max}}{[E_t]} \qquad (6\text{-}11)$$

Turnover numbers vary greatly among enzymes, as is clear from the examples given in Table 6-2.

The Double-Reciprocal Plot Is a Useful Means of Linearizing Kinetic Data

The classic Michaelis–Menten plot of v versus $[S]$ shown in Figure 6-8 illustrates the dependence of velocity on substrate concentration. However, it is not an especially useful tool for the quantitative determination of the key kinetic parameters K_m and V_{max}. Its hyperbolic shape makes it difficult to extrapolate accurately to infinite substrate concentration in order to determine the critical parameter V_{max}. Also, if V_{max} is not known accurately, K_m cannot be determined.

To circumvent this problem and provide a more useful graphic approach, Hans Lineweaver and Dean Burk in 1934 converted the hyperbolic relationship of the Michaelis–Menten equation into a linear function by inverting both sides of Equation 6-7 and simplifying the resulting expression into the form of an equation for a straight line:

$$\frac{1}{v} = \frac{K_m + [S]}{V_{max}[S]} = \frac{K_m}{V_{max}[S]} + \frac{[S]}{V_{max}[S]}$$

$$= \frac{K_m}{V_{max}}\left(\frac{1}{[S]}\right) + \frac{1}{V_{max}} \qquad (6\text{-}12)$$

Equation 6-12 is known as the **Lineweaver–Burk equation**. When it is plotted as $1/v$ versus $1/[S]$, as in Figure 6-10, the resulting **double-reciprocal plot** is linear in the general algebraic form $y = mx + b$, where m is the slope and b is the y-intercept. Therefore, it has a slope (m) of K_m/V_{max}, a y-intercept (b) of $1/V_{max}$, and an x-intercept ($y = 0$) of $-1/K_m$. (You should be able to convince yourself of these intercept values by setting first $1/[S]$ and then $1/v$ equal to zero in Equation 6-12 and solving for the other value.) Therefore, once the double-reciprocal plot has been constructed, V_{max} can be determined directly from the reciprocal of the y-intercept and K_m from the negative reciprocal of the x-intercept. Furthermore, the slope can be used to check both values.

Thus, the Lineweaver–Burk plot is useful experimentally because it allows us to determine the parameters V_{max}

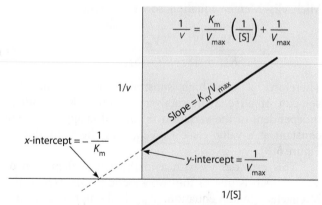

FIGURE 6-10 The Lineweaver–Burk Double-Reciprocal Plot. The reciprocal of the initial velocity, $1/v$, is plotted as a function of the reciprocal of the substrate concentration, $1/[S]$. K_m can be calculated from the x-intercept and V_{max} from the y-intercept.

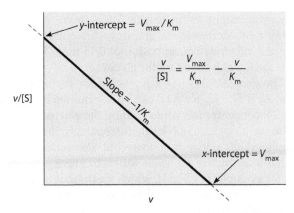

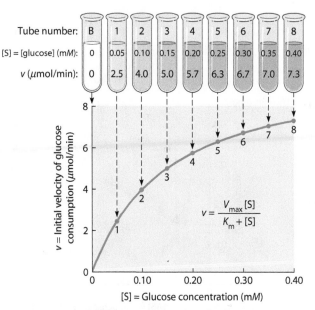

FIGURE 6-11 **The Eadie–Hofstee Plot.** The ratio $v/[S]$ is plotted as a function of v. K_m can be determined from the slope and V_{max} from the x-intercept.

In Figure 6-11:
- $y\text{-intercept} = V_{max}/K_m$
- $\text{Slope} = -1/K_m$
- $x\text{-intercept} = V_{max}$
- $\dfrac{v}{[S]} = \dfrac{V_{max}}{K_m} - \dfrac{v}{K_m}$

In Figure 6-12:
Tube number:	B	1	2	3	4	5	6	7	8
[S] = [glucose] (mM):	0	0.05	0.10	0.15	0.20	0.25	0.30	0.35	0.40
v (μmol/min):	0	2.5	4.0	5.0	5.7	6.3	6.7	7.0	7.3

$$v = \frac{V_{max}[S]}{K_m + [S]}$$

FIGURE 6-12 **Experimental Procedure for Studying the Kinetics of the Hexokinase Reaction.** Test tubes containing graded concentrations of glucose and a saturating concentration of ATP were incubated with a standard amount of hexokinase. The initial rate of product appearance, v, was then plotted as a function of the substrate concentration [S]. The curve is hyperbolic, approaching V_{max} as the substrate concentration gets higher and higher. For the double-reciprocal plot derived from these data, see Figure 6-13.

and K_m without the complication of a hyperbolic shape. It also serves as a useful diagnostic in analyzing enzyme inhibition because the several different kinds of reversible inhibitors affect the shape of the plot in characteristic ways.

The Lineweaver–Burk equation has some limitations, however. The main problem is that a long extrapolation is often necessary to determine K_m, and this may introduce uncertainty in the result. Moreover, the most crucial data points for determining the slope of the curve are the farthest from the y-axis. Because those points represent the samples with the lowest substrate concentrations and lowest levels of enzyme activity, they are the most difficult to measure accurately.

To circumvent these disadvantages, several alternatives to the Lineweaver–Burk equation have come into use to linearize kinetic data. One such alternative is the **Eadie–Hofstee equation,** which is represented graphically as a plot of $v/[S]$ versus v. As **Figure 6-11** illustrates, V_{max} is determined from the x-intercept and K_m from the slope of this plot. (To explore the Eadie–Hofstee plot and another alternative to the Lineweaver–Burk plot further, see Problem 6–13 at the end of this chapter.)

Determining K_m and V_{max}: An Example

To illustrate the value of the double-reciprocal plot in determining V_{max} and K_m, consider a specific example involving the enzyme hexokinase, as illustrated in **Figures 6-12** and **6-13**. Hexokinase is an important enzyme in cellular energy metabolism because it catalyzes the first reaction in the glycolytic pathway. Using the hydrolysis of ATP as a source of both the phosphate group and the free energy needed for the reaction, hexokinase catalyzes the phosphorylation of glucose on carbon atom 6:

$$\text{glucose} + \text{ATP} \xrightarrow{\text{hexokinase}} \text{glucose-6-phosphate} + \text{ADP}$$
$$(6\text{-}13)$$

To analyze this reaction kinetically, we must determine the initial velocity at each of several substrate concentrations.

When an enzyme has two substrates, the usual approach is to vary the concentration of one substrate at a time while holding that of the other one constant at a level near saturation to ensure that it does not become rate limiting. The velocity determination must be made before either the substrate concentration drops appreciably or the product accumulates to the point that the reverse reaction becomes significant.

In the experimental approach shown in Figure 6-12, glucose is the variable substrate, with ATP present at a saturating concentration in each tube. Of the nine reaction mixtures set up for this experiment, one tube is a negative control designated the reagent blank (B) because it contains no glucose. The other tubes contain concentrations of glucose ranging from 0.05 to 0.40 mM. With all tubes prepared and maintained at some favorable temperature (25°C is often used), the reaction in each is initiated by adding a fixed amount of hexokinase.

The rate of product formation in each of the reaction mixtures can then be determined either by continuous spectrophotometric monitoring of the reaction mixture (provided that one of the reactants or products absorbs light of a specific wavelength) or by allowing each reaction mixture to incubate for some short, fixed period of time, followed by chemical assay for either substrate depletion or product accumulation.

As Figure 6-12 indicates, the initial velocity of the glucose consumption reaction for tubes 1–8 ranged from 2.5 to 7.3 μmol of glucose consumed per minute, with no

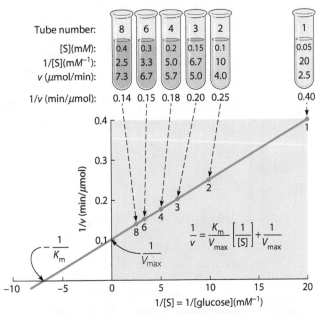

Tube number:	8	6	4	3	2		1
[S](mM):	0.4	0.3	0.2	0.15	0.1		0.05
1/[S](mM^{-1}):	2.5	3.3	5.0	6.7	10		20
v (μmol/min):	7.3	6.7	5.7	5.0	4.0		2.5
1/v (min/μmol):	0.14	0.15	0.18	0.20	0.25		0.40

$$\frac{1}{v} = \frac{K_m}{V_{max}}\left[\frac{1}{[S]}\right] + \frac{1}{V_{max}}$$

FIGURE 6-13 Double-Reciprocal Plot for the Hexokinase Data of Figure 6-12. For each test tube in Figure 6-12, 1/v and 1/[S] were calculated, and 1/v was then plotted as a function of 1/[S]. The y-intercept of 0.1 corresponds to 1/V_{max}, so V_{max} is 10 mM/min. The x-intercept of −6.7 corresponds to −1/K_m, so K_m is 0.15 mM. (Some of the tubes depicted in Figure 6-12 are not shown here due to lack of space.)

detectable reaction in the blank. When these reaction velocities are plotted as a function of glucose concentration, the eight data points generate the hyperbolic curve shown in Figure 6-12. Although the data of Figure 6-12 are idealized for illustrative purposes, most kinetic data generated by this approach do, in fact, fit a hyperbolic curve unless the enzyme has some special properties that cause departure from Michaelis–Menten kinetics.

The hyperbolic curve of Figure 6-12 illustrates the need for some means of linearizing the analysis because neither V_{max} nor K_m can be easily determined from the values as plotted. This need is met by the linear double-reciprocal plot shown in Figure 6-13. To obtain the data plotted here, reciprocals were calculated for each value of [S] and v in Figure 6-12. Thus, the [S] values of 0.05–0.40 mM generate reciprocals of 20–2.5 mM^{-1}, and the v values of 2.5–7.3 μmol/min give rise to reciprocals of 0.4–0.14 min/μmol. Because these are reciprocals, the data point representing the lowest concentration (tube 1) is farthest from the origin, and each successive tube is represented by a point closer to the origin.

When these data points are connected by a straight line, the y-intercept is found to be 0.1 min/μmol, and the x-intercept is −6.7 mM^{-1}. From these intercepts, we can calculate that V_{max} = 1/0.1 = 10 μmol/min and K_m = −(1/−6.7) = 0.15 mM. If we now go back to the Michaelis–Menten plot of Figure 6-12, we can see that both of these values are quite reasonable because we can readily imagine that the plot is rising hyperbolically to a maximum of 10 mM/min. Note that using your eyes

alone, you might estimate the V_{max} to be only 8 or 9 μmol/min. Moreover, the graph reaches one-half of this value at a substrate concentration of 0.15 mM. Therefore, this is the K_m of hexokinase for glucose.

The enzyme also has a K_m value for the other substrate, ATP. The K_m for ATP can be determined by varying the ATP concentration while holding the glucose concentration at a high, fixed level. Interestingly, hexokinase phosphorylates not only glucose but also other hexoses and has a distinctive K_m value for each. The K_m for fructose, for example, is 1.5 mM, which means that it takes ten times more fructose than glucose to sustain the reaction at one-half of its maximum velocity.

Enzyme Inhibitors Act Either Irreversibly or Reversibly

Thus far, we have assumed that substrates are the only substances in cells that affect the activities of enzymes in cells. However, enzymes are also influenced by products, alternative substrates, substrate analogues, drugs, toxins, and a very important class of regulators called *allosteric effectors*. Most of these substances have an inhibitory effect on enzyme activity, reducing the reaction rate with the desired substrate or sometimes blocking the reaction completely.

This **inhibition** of enzyme activity is important for several reasons. First and foremost, enzyme inhibition plays a vital role as a control mechanism in cells. Many enzymes are subject to regulation by specific small molecules other than their substrates. Often this is a means of sensing their immediate environment to respond to specific cellular conditions.

Enzyme inhibition is also important in the action of drugs and poisons, which frequently exert their effects by inhibiting specific enzymes. Inhibitors are also useful to enzymologists as tools in their studies of reaction mechanisms and to doctors for treatment of disease. Especially important inhibitors are *substrate analogues* and *transition state analogues*. These are compounds that resemble the real substrate or transition state closely enough to bind to the active site but cannot undergo reaction to create a functional product.

Substrate analogs are important tools in fighting infectious disease, and many have been developed to inhibit specific enzymes in pathogenic bacteria and viruses, usually targeting enzymes that we humans lack. For example, sulfa drugs resemble the folic acid precursor, PABA. They can bind to and block the active site of the bacterial enzyme used to synthesize folic acid, which is required in DNA synthesis. Likewise, azidothymidine (AZT), which is an antiviral medication, resembles the deoxythymidine molecule normally used by the human immunodeficiency virus (HIV) to synthesize DNA using viral reverse transcriptase. However, after binding to the active site, AZT is incorporated into a growing strand of DNA but forms a "dead-end" molecule of DNA that cannot be elongated.

Inhibitors may be either *reversible* or *irreversible*. An **irreversible inhibitor** binds to the enzyme covalently, causing permanent loss of catalytic activity. Not surprisingly, irreversible inhibitors are usually toxic to cells. Ions of heavy metals are often irreversible inhibitors, as are nerve gas poisons and some insecticides. These substances can bind irreversibly to enzymes such as *acetylcholinesterase,* an enzyme that is vital to the transmission of nerve impulses. Inhibition of acetylcholinesterase activity leads to rapid paralysis of vital functions and therefore to death. One such inhibitor is *diisopropyl fluorophosphate,* a nerve gas that binds covalently to the hydroxyl group of a critical serine at the active site of the enzyme, thereby rendering the enzyme molecule permanently inactive.

Some irreversible inhibitors of enzymes can be used as therapeutic agents. For example, aspirin binds irreversibly to the enzyme cyclooxygenase-1 (COX-1), which produces prostaglandins and other signaling chemicals that cause inflammation, constriction of blood vessels, and platelet aggregation. Thus, aspirin is effective in relieving minor inflammation and headaches, and has been recommended in low doses as a cardiovascular protectant. The antibiotic *penicillin* is an irreversible inhibitor of the enzyme needed for bacterial cell wall synthesis. Penicillin is therefore effective in treating bacterial infections because it prevents the bacterial cells from forming cell walls, thus blocking their growth and division. And because our cells lack a cell wall (and the enzyme that synthesizes it), penicillin is nontoxic to humans.

In contrast, a **reversible inhibitor** binds to an enzyme in a noncovalent, dissociable manner, such that the free and bound forms of the inhibitor exist in equilibrium with each other. We can represent such binding as

$$E + I \rightleftharpoons EI \qquad (6\text{-}14)$$

with E as the active free enzyme, I as the inhibitor, and EI as the inactive enzyme-inhibitor complex. Clearly, the fraction of the enzyme that is available to the cell in active form depends on the concentration of the inhibitor and the strength of the enzyme-inhibitor complex.

The two most common forms of reversible inhibitors are called *competitive inhibitors* and *noncompetitive inhibitors.* A competitive inhibitor binds to the active site of the enzyme and therefore competes directly with substrate molecules for the same site on the enzyme (**Figure 6-14a**). This reduces enzyme activity because many of the active sites of the enzyme molecules are blocked by bound inhibitor molecules and thus cannot bind substrate molecules at the active site. A noncompetitive inhibitor, on the other hand, binds to the enzyme surface at a location *other* than the active site. It does not block substrate binding directly but inhibits enzyme activity indirectly by causing a change in protein conformation that can either inhibit substrate binding to the active site or greatly reduce the catalytic activity at the active site (Figure 6-14b).

Considerable progress has been made in the field of computer-aided drug design. In this approach, the three-dimensional structure of an enzyme active site is analyzed to predict what types of molecules are likely to bind tightly to it and act as inhibitors. Scientists can then design a number of hypothetical inhibitors and test their binding using complex computer models. In this way, we do not have to rely only upon those inhibitors we can discover in

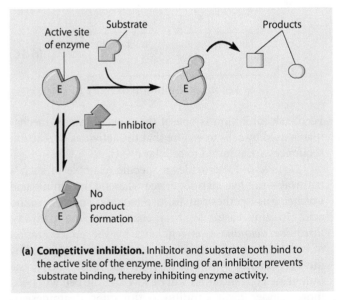

(a) Competitive inhibition. Inhibitor and substrate both bind to the active site of the enzyme. Binding of an inhibitor prevents substrate binding, thereby inhibiting enzyme activity.

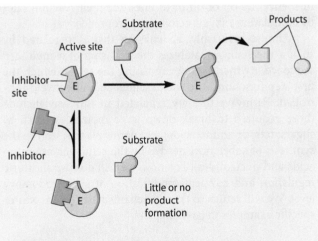

(b) Noncompetitive inhibition. Inhibitor and substrate bind to different sites. Binding of an inhibitor distorts the enzyme, inhibiting substrate binding or reducing catalytic activity.

FIGURE 6-14 Modes of Action of Competitive and Noncompetitive Inhibitors. Both **(a)** competitive and **(b)** noncompetitive inhibitors bind reversibly to the enzyme (E), thereby inhibiting its activity. The two kinds of inhibitors differ in which site on the enzyme they bind to.

nature. Hundreds or even thousands of potential inhibitors can be designed and tested, and only the most promising are actually synthesized and evaluated experimentally.

Enzyme Regulation

To understand the role of enzymes in cellular function, we need to recognize that it is rarely in the cell's best interest to allow an enzyme to function at an indiscriminately high rate. Instead, the rates of enzyme-catalyzed reactions must be continuously adjusted to keep them finely tuned to the needs of the cell. An important aspect of that adjustment lies in the cell's ability to control enzyme activities with specificity and precision.

We have already encountered a variety of regulatory mechanisms, including changes in substrate and product concentrations, alterations in temperature and pH, and the presence and concentration of inhibitors. Regulation that depends directly on the interactions of substrates and products with the enzyme is called **substrate-level regulation.** As the Michaelis–Menten equation makes clear, increases in substrate concentration result in higher reaction rates (see Figure 6-8). Conversely, increases in product concentration reduce the rate at which substrate is converted to product. (This inhibitory effect of product concentration is why v needs to be identified as the *initial* reaction velocity in the Michaelis–Menten equation, as given by Equation 6-7.)

Substrate-level regulation is an important control mechanism in cells, but it is not sufficient for the regulation of most reactions or reaction sequences. For most pathways, enzymes are regulated by other mechanisms as well. Two of the most important of these are *allosteric regulation* and *covalent modification.* These mechanisms allow cells to turn enzymes on or off or to fine-tune their reaction rates by modulating enzyme activities appropriately.

Almost invariably, an enzyme that is regulated by such a mechanism catalyzes the first step of a multistep sequence. By increasing or reducing the rate at which the first step functions, the whole sequence is effectively controlled. Pathways that are regulated in this way include those required to break down large molecules (such as sugars, fats, or amino acids) and pathways that lead to the synthesis of substances needed by the cell (such as amino acids and nucleotides). For now, we will discuss allosteric regulation and covalent modification at an introductory level. We will return to these mechanisms as we encounter specific examples in later chapters.

Allosteric Enzymes Are Regulated by Molecules Other than Reactants and Products

The single most important control mechanism whereby the rates of enzyme-catalyzed reactions are adjusted to meet cellular needs is *allosteric regulation.* To understand this mode of regulation, consider the pathway by which a cell converts some precursor A into some final product P via a series of intermediates B, C, and D in a sequence of reactions catalyzed respectively by enzymes E_1, E_2, E_3, and E_4:

$$A \xrightarrow{E_1} B \xrightarrow{E_2} C \xrightarrow{E_3} D \xrightarrow{E_4} P \qquad (6\text{-}15)$$

Product P could, for example, be an amino acid needed by the cell for protein synthesis, and A could be some common cellular component that serves as the starting point for the specific reaction sequence leading to P.

Feedback Inhibition. If allowed to proceed at a constant, unrestrained rate, the pathway shown in Reaction Sequence 6-15 can convert large amounts of A to P, with possible adverse effects resulting from a depletion of A or an excessive accumulation of P. Clearly, the best interests of the cell are served when the pathway is functioning not at its maximum rate or even some constant rate, but at a rate that is carefully tuned to the cellular need for P.

Somehow, the enzymes of this pathway must be responsive to the cellular level of the product P in somewhat the same way that a furnace needs to be responsive to the temperature of the rooms it is intended to heat. In the latter case, a thermostat provides the necessary regulatory link between the furnace and its "product," heat. If there is too much heat, the thermostat turns the furnace off, inhibiting heat production. If heat is needed, this inhibition is relieved due to the lack of heat. In our enzyme example, the desired regulation is possible because the product P is a specific inhibitor of E_1, the enzyme that catalyzes the first reaction in the sequence.

This phenomenon is called **feedback** (or **end-product**) **inhibition** and is represented by the dashed arrow that connects the product P to enzyme E_1 in the following reaction sequence:

$$A \xrightarrow{E_1} B \xrightarrow{E_2} C \xrightarrow{E_3} D \xrightarrow{E_4} P \qquad (6\text{-}16)$$

Feedback inhibition of E_1 by P

Feedback inhibition is one of the most common mechanisms used by cells to ensure that the activities of reaction sequences are adjusted to cellular needs.

Figure 6-15 provides a specific example of such a pathway—the five-step sequence whereby the amino acid *isoleucine* is synthesized from *threonine*, another amino acid. In this case, the first enzyme in the pathway, *threonine deaminase,* is regulated by the concentration of isoleucine within the cell. If isoleucine is being used by the cell (in the synthesis of proteins, most likely), the isoleucine concentration will be low and the cell will need more. Under these conditions, threonine deaminase is active, and the pathway functions to produce more isoleucine. If the need for isoleucine decreases, isoleucine will begin to accumulate in the cell. This increase in its

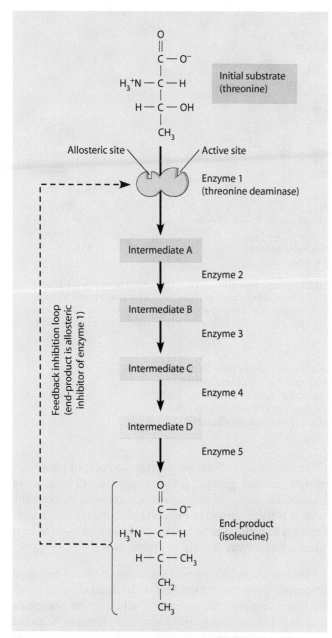

FIGURE 6-15 Allosteric Regulation of Enzyme Activity.
A specific example of feedback inhibition is seen in the pathway
by which the amino acid isoleucine is synthesized from threonine,
another amino acid. The first enzyme in the sequence, threonine
deaminase, is allosterically inhibited by isoleucine, which binds to
the enzyme at a site *other* than the active site.

concentration will lead to inhibition of threonine deaminase and hence to a reduced rate of isoleucine synthesis.

Allosteric Regulation. How can the first enzyme in a
pathway (e.g., enzyme E_1 in Reaction Sequence 6-16) be
sensitive to the concentration of a substance P that is neither its substrate nor its immediate product? The answer
to this question was first proposed in 1963 by Jacques
Monod, Jean-Pierre Changeux, and François Jacob. Their
model was quickly substantiated and went on to become

the foundation for our understanding of **allosteric
regulation.** The term *allosteric* derives from the Greek for
"another shape (or form)," thereby indicating that all
enzymes capable of allosteric regulation can exist in two
different forms.

In one of the two forms, the enzyme has a high affinity
for its substrate(s), leading to high activity. In the other
form, it has little or no affinity for its substrate, giving little
or no catalytic activity. Enzymes with this property are
called **allosteric enzymes.** The two different forms of an
allosteric enzyme are readily interconvertible and are, in
fact, in equilibrium with each other.

Whether the active or inactive form of an allosteric
enzyme is favored depends on the cellular concentration of
the appropriate regulatory substance, called an **allosteric
effector.** In the case of isoleucine synthesis, the allosteric
effector is isoleucine and the allosteric enzyme is threonine
deaminase. More generally, *an allosteric effector is a small
organic molecule that regulates the activity of an enzyme for
which it is neither the substrate nor the immediate product.*

An allosteric effector influences enzyme activity by
binding to one of the two interconvertible forms of the
enzyme, thereby stabilizing it in that state. The effector
binds to the enzyme because of the presence on the enzyme
surface of an **allosteric** (or **regulatory**) **site** that is distinct
from the active site at which the catalytic event occurs.
Thus, a distinguishing feature of all allosteric enzymes (and
other allosteric proteins, as well) is the presence on the
enzyme surface of an *active site* to which the substrate binds
and an *allosteric site* to which the effector binds. In fact,
some allosteric enzymes have multiple allosteric sites, each
capable of recognizing a different effector.

An effector may be either an **allosteric inhibitor** or
an **allosteric activator,** depending on the effect it has
when bound to the allosteric site on the enzyme—that is,
depending on whether the effector is bound to the low-
affinity or high-affinity form of the enzyme (**Figure
6-16**). The binding of an allosteric inhibitor shifts the
equilibrium between the two forms of the enzyme to
favor the low-affinity state (Figure 6-16a). The binding of
an allosteric activator, on the other hand, shifts the equilibrium in favor of the high-affinity state (Figure 6-16b).
In either case, binding of the effector to the allosteric site
stabilizes the enzyme in one of its two interconvertible
forms, thereby either decreasing or increasing the likelihood of substrate binding.

Most allosteric enzymes are large, multisubunit
proteins with an active site or an allosteric site on each
subunit. Thus, quaternary protein structure is important
for these enzymes. Typically, the active sites and allosteric
sites are on different subunits of the protein, which are
referred to as **catalytic subunits** and **regulatory subunits,**
respectively (notice the C and R subunits of the enzyme
molecules shown in Figure 6-16). This means, in turn,
that the binding of effector molecules to the allosteric sites
affects not just the shape of the regulatory subunits but
that of the catalytic subunits as well.

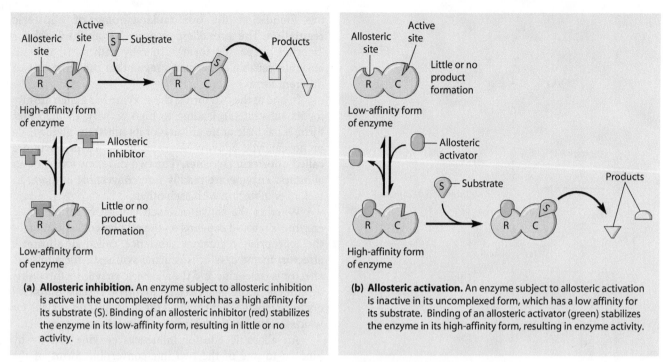

(a) Allosteric inhibition. An enzyme subject to allosteric inhibition is active in the uncomplexed form, which has a high affinity for its substrate (S). Binding of an allosteric inhibitor (red) stabilizes the enzyme in its low-affinity form, resulting in little or no activity.

(b) Allosteric activation. An enzyme subject to allosteric activation is inactive in its uncomplexed form, which has a low affinity for its substrate. Binding of an allosteric activator (green) stabilizes the enzyme in its high-affinity form, resulting in enzyme activity.

FIGURE 6-16 Mechanisms of Allosteric Inhibition and Activation. An allosteric enzyme consists of one or more catalytic subunits (C) and one or more regulatory subunits (R), each with an active site or an allosteric site, respectively. The enzyme exists in two forms, one with a high affinity for its substrate (and therefore a high likelihood of product formation) and the other with a low affinity (and a correspondingly low likelihood of product formation). The predominant form of the enzyme depends on the concentration of its allosteric effector(s).

Allosteric Enzymes Exhibit Cooperative Interactions Between Subunits

Many allosteric enzymes exhibit a property known as **cooperativity.** This means that, as the multiple catalytic sites on the enzyme bind substrate molecules, the enzyme undergoes conformational changes that affect the affinity of the remaining sites for substrate. Some enzymes show *positive cooperativity*, in which the binding of a substrate molecule to one catalytic subunit increases the affinity of other catalytic subunits for substrate. Other enzymes show *negative cooperativity*, in which the substrate binding to one catalytic subunit reduces the affinity of the other catalytic sites for substrate.

The cooperativity effect enables cells to produce enzymes that are more sensitive or less sensitive to changes in substrate concentration than would otherwise be predicted by Michaelis–Menten kinetics. Positive cooperativity causes an enzyme's catalytic activity to increase faster than normal as the substrate concentration is increased, whereas negative cooperativity means that enzyme activity increases more slowly than expected.

Enzymes Can Also Be Regulated by the Addition or Removal of Chemical Groups

In addition to allosteric regulation, many enzymes are subject to control by **covalent modification.** In this form of regulation, an enzyme's activity is affected by the addition or removal of specific chemical groups via covalent bonding.

Common modifications include the addition of phosphate groups, methyl groups, acetyl groups, or derivatives of nucleotides. Some of these modifications can be reversed, whereas others cannot. In each case, the effect of the modification is to activate or to inactivate the enzyme—or at least to adjust its activity upward or downward.

Phosphorylation/Dephosphorylation. One of the most frequently encountered and best understood covalent modifications involves the reversible addition of phosphate groups. The addition of phosphate groups is called **phosphorylation** and occurs most commonly by transfer of the phosphate group from ATP to the hydroxyl group of a serine, threonine, or tyrosine residue in the protein. Enzymes that catalyze the phosphorylation of other enzymes (or of other proteins) are called **protein kinases.** The reversal of this process, **dephosphorylation,** involves the removal of a phosphate group from a phosphorylated protein, catalyzed by enzymes called **protein phosphatases.** Depending on the particular enzyme, phosphorylation may activate or inhibit the enzyme.

Enzyme regulation by reversible phosphorylation/ dephosphorylation was discovered by Edmond Fischer and Edwin Krebs (not Hans Krebs, namesake of the Krebs cycle) at the University of Washington in the 1950s. They were awarded the 1992 Nobel Prize in Physiology or Medicine for their groundbreaking work with *glycogen phosphorylase,* a glycogen-degrading enzyme found in liver and skeletal muscle cells (**Figure 6-17**). In muscle cells, it provides glucose as an energy source for muscle

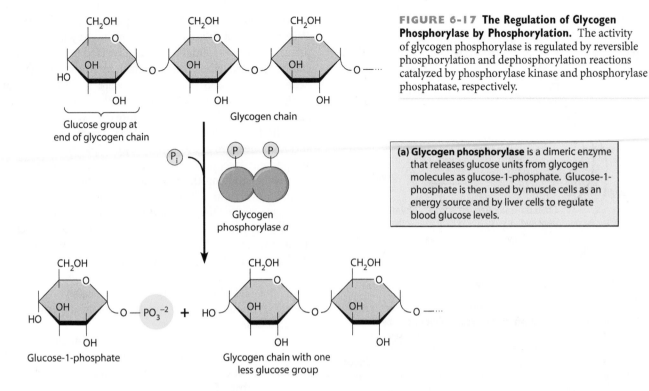

Glucose group at end of glycogen chain

Glycogen chain

Glycogen phosphorylase *a*

Glucose-1-phosphate

Glycogen chain with one less glucose group

(a) Glycogen phosphorylase is a dimeric enzyme that releases glucose units from glycogen molecules as glucose-1-phosphate. Glucose-1-phosphate is then used by muscle cells as an energy source and by liver cells to regulate blood glucose levels.

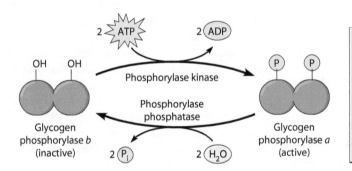

Phosphorylase kinase

Phosphorylase phosphatase

Glycogen phosphorylase *b* (inactive)

Glycogen phosphorylase *a* (active)

(b) Glycogen phosphorylase is regulated in part by a phosphorylation/dephosphorylation mechanism. The inactive form of the enzyme, phosphorylase *b*, can be converted to the active form, phosphorylase *a*, by a dual phosphorylation reaction catalyzed by the enzyme phosphorylase kinase. Removal of the phosphate groups by phosphorylase phosphatase returns the phosphorylase molecule to the inactive *b* form.

contraction and in liver cells it provides glucose for secretion to help maintain a constant blood glucose level. Glycogen phosphorylase breaks down glycogen by successive removal of glucose units as glucose-1-phosphate (Figure 6-17a). Regulation of this dimeric enzyme is achieved in part by the presence of two interconvertible forms of the enzyme—an active form called *phosphorylase a* and an inactive form called *phosphorylase b* (Figure 6-17b).

When glycogen breakdown is required in the cell, the inactive *b* form of the enzyme is converted into the active *a* form by the addition of a phosphate group to a particular serine on each of the two subunits of the phosphorylase molecule. The reaction is catalyzed by *phosphorylase kinase* and results in a conformational change of phosphorylase to the active form. When glycogen breakdown is no longer needed, the phosphate groups are removed from phosphorylase *a* by the enzyme *phosphorylase phosphatase*.

The muscle and liver forms of glycogen phosphorylase, known as isozymes, have subtle differences in their manner of regulation. Besides being regulated by the phosphorylation/dephosphorylation mechanism shown in Figure 6-17, liver glycogen phosphorylase, an allosteric enzyme, is inhibited by glucose and ATP and activated by AMP. Glucose binding to active liver glycogen phosphorylase *a* will inactivate it, blocking glycogen breakdown when glucose accumulates faster than needed. The existence of two levels of regulation for glycogen phosphorylase illustrates an important aspect of enzyme regulation. Many enzymes are controlled by two or more regulatory mechanisms, thereby enabling the cell to make appropriate responses to a variety of situations.

Proteolytic Cleavage. A different kind of covalent activation of enzymes involves the one-time, irreversible removal of a portion of the polypeptide chain by an appropriate proteolytic (protein-degrading) enzyme. This kind of modification, called **proteolytic cleavage,** is exemplified especially well by the proteolytic enzymes of the pancreas, which include trypsin, chymotrypsin, and carboxypeptidase. After being synthesized in the pancreas, these enzymes are secreted in an inactive form into

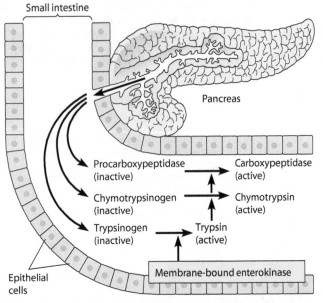

FIGURE 6-18 Activation of Pancreatic Zymogens by Proteolytic Cleavage. Pancreatic proteases are synthesized and secreted into the small intestine as inactive precursors known as zymogens. Procarboxypeptidase, trypsinogen, and chymotrypsinogen are zymogens. Activation of trypsinogen to trypsin requires removal of a hexapeptide segment by enterokinase, a membrane-bound duodenal enzyme. Trypsin then activates other zymogens by proteolytic cleavage. Procarboxypeptidase is activated by a single cleavage event, whereas the activation of chymotrypsinogen is a somewhat more complicated two-step process, the details of which are not shown here.

the duodenum of the small intestine in response to a hormonal signal (**Figure 6-18**). These proteases can digest almost all ingested proteins into free amino acids, which are then absorbed by the intestinal epithelial cells.

Pancreatic proteases are not synthesized in their active form. That would likely cause problems for the cells of the pancreas, which must protect themselves against their own proteolytic enzymes. Instead, each of these enzymes is synthesized as a slightly larger, catalytically inactive molecule called a *zymogen*. Zymogens must themselves be cleaved proteolytically to yield active enzymes. For example, trypsin is synthesized initially as a zymogen called *trypsinogen*. When trypsinogen reaches the duodenum, it is activated by the removal of a hexapeptide (a string of six amino acids) from its N-terminus by the action of *enterokinase,* a membrane-bound protease produced by the duodenal cells. The active trypsin then activates other zymogens by specific proteolytic cleavages.

RNA Molecules as Enzymes: Ribozymes

Until the early 1980s, it was thought that all enzymes were proteins. Indeed, that statement was regarded as a fundamental truth of cellular biology and was found in every textbook. Cell biologists became convinced that all enzymes were proteins because every enzyme isolated in

the 55 years following Sumner's purification of urease in 1926 turned out to be a protein. But biology is full of surprises, and this statement has been revised to include RNA catalysts called **ribozymes.** In fact, many scientists now believe that the earliest enzymes were molecules of catalytic, self-replicating RNA and that these molecules were present in primitive cells even before the existence of DNA.

The first evidence came in 1981, when Thomas Cech and his colleagues at the University of Colorado discovered an apparent exception to the "all enzymes are proteins" rule. They were studying the removal of an internal segment of RNA known as an intron from a specific ribosomal RNA precursor (pre-rRNA) in *Tetrahymena thermophila*, a single-celled eukaryote. In the course of their work, the researchers made the remarkable observation that the process proceeded without the presence of proteins! They showed that the removal of a 413-nucleotide internal segment of RNA from the *Tetrahymena* pre-rRNA is catalyzed by the pre-rRNA molecule itself and is therefore an example of *autocatalysis.*

Two years later, another RNA-based catalyst was discovered in the laboratory of Sidney Altman at Yale University, which was studying *ribonuclease P,* an enzyme that cleaves transfer RNA precursors (pre-tRNAs) to yield functional RNA molecules. It had been known that ribonuclease P consisted of a protein component and an RNA component, and it was generally assumed that the active site was on the protein component. By isolating the components and studying them separately, however, Altman and his colleagues showed unequivocally that only the isolated RNA component was capable of catalyzing the specific cleavage of tRNA precursors on its own. Furthermore, the RNA-catalyzed reaction followed Michaelis–Menten kinetics, further evidence that the RNA component was acting like a true enzyme. (The protein component enhances activity but is not required for either substrate binding or cleavage.)

The significance of these findings was recognized by the Nobel Prize that Cech and Altman shared in 1989 for their discovery of ribozymes. Since these initial discoveries, additional examples of ribozymes have been reported. Of special significance is the active site for a crucial step in protein synthesis by ribosomes. The large ribosomal subunit (see Figure 4-22) is the site of the peptidyl transferase activity that catalyzes peptide bond formation.

The active site for this peptidyl transferase activity was for a long time assumed to be located on one of the protein molecules of the large subunit, with the rRNA providing a scaffold for structural support. However, in 1992, Harry Noller and his colleagues at the University of California, Santa Cruz, demonstrated that, despite the removal of at least 95% of the protein from the large ribosomal subunit, it retained 80% of the peptidyl transferase of the intact subunit. This strongly suggested that one of the rRNA molecules was the catalyst.

Furthermore, the activity was destroyed by treatment with ribonuclease, an enzyme that degrades RNA, but was not affected by proteinase K, an enzyme that degrades protein. Thus, the peptidyl transferase activity responsible for peptide bond formation in ribosomal protein synthesis is due to the rRNA, now known to be a ribozyme. It appears the function of the ribosomal proteins is to provide support and stabilization for the catalytic RNA, not the other way around! This supports the idea that RNA-based catalysis preceded protein-based catalysis.

The discovery of ribozymes has markedly changed the way we think about the origin of life on Earth. For many years, scientists had speculated that the first catalytic macromolecules must have been amino acid polymers resembling proteins. But this concept immediately ran into difficulty because there was no obvious way for a primitive protein to carry information or to replicate itself, which are two primary attributes of life. However, if the first catalysts were RNA rather than protein molecules, it becomes conceptually easier to imagine an "RNA world" in which RNA molecules acted both as catalysts and as replicating systems capable of transferring information from generation to generation.

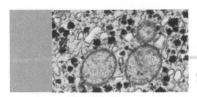

SUMMARY OF KEY POINTS

Activation Energy and the Metastable State

- While thermodynamics allows us to assess the feasibility of a reaction, it says nothing about the likelihood that the reaction will actually occur at a reasonable rate in the cell.

- For a given chemical reaction to occur in the cell, substrates must reach the transition state, which has a higher free energy than either the substrates or products. Reaching the transition state requires the input of activation energy.

- Because of this activation energy barrier, most biological compounds exist in an unreactive, metastable state. To ensure that the activation energy requirement is met and the transition state is achieved, a catalyst is required, which is always an enzyme in biological systems.

Enzymes as Biological Catalysts

- Catalysts, whether inorganic or organic, act by forming transient complexes with substrate molecules that lower the activation energy barrier and rapidly increase the rate of the particular reaction.

- Chemical reactions in cells are catalyzed by enzymes, which in some cases require organic or inorganic cofactors for activity. The vast majority of enzymes are proteins, but a few are composed of RNA and are known as ribozymes.

- Enzymes are exquisitely specific, either for a single specific substrate or for a class of closely related compounds. This is because the actual catalytic process takes place at the active site—a pocket or groove on the enzyme surface that only the correct substrates will fit into.

- The active site is composed of specific, noncontiguous amino acids that become positioned near each other as the protein folds into its tertiary structure. These amino acids are responsible for substrate binding, substrate activation, and catalysis.

- Binding of the appropriate substrate at the active site causes a change in the shape of the enzyme and substrate known as induced fit. This facilitates substrate activation, often by distorting one or more bonds in the substrate, by bringing necessary amino acid side chains into the active site, or by transferring protons and/or electrons between the enzyme and substrate.

Enzyme Kinetics

- An enzyme-catalyzed reaction proceeds via an enzyme-substrate intermediate. Most reactions follow Michaelis–Menten kinetics, characterized by a hyperbolic relationship between the initial reaction velocity v and the substrate concentration [S].

- The upper limit on velocity is called V_{max}, and the substrate concentration needed to reach one-half of this maximum velocity is termed the Michaelis constant, K_m. The hyperbolic relationship between v and [S] can be linearized by a double-reciprocal equation and plot, from which V_{max} and K_m can be determined graphically.

- Enzyme activity is sensitive to temperature, pH, and the ionic environment. Enzyme activity is also influenced by substrate availability, products, alternative substrates, substrate analogues, drugs, and toxins, most of which have an inhibitory effect.

- Irreversible inhibition involves covalent bonding of the inhibitor to the enzyme surface, permanently disabling the enzyme. A reversible inhibitor, on the other hand, binds noncovalently to an enzyme in a reversible manner, either at the active site (competitive inhibition) or elsewhere on the enzyme surface (noncompetitive inhibition).

Enzyme Regulation

- Enzymes must be regulated to adjust their activity levels to cellular needs. Substrate-level regulation involves the effects of substrate and product concentrations on the reaction rate. Additional control mechanisms include allosteric regulation and covalent modification.

- Most allosterically regulated enzymes catalyze the first step in a reaction sequence and are multisubunit proteins with both catalytic subunits and regulatory subunits. Each of the catalytic subunits has an active site that recognizes substrates, whereas each regulatory subunit has one or more allosteric sites that recognize specific effector molecules.

- Allosteric enzymes exist in an equilibrium between a low-activity and a high-activity form. A given effector binds to and stabilizes one of these two forms and therefore will either inhibit or activate the enzyme, depending on which form of the enzyme is bound by the effector.

- Enzyme inhibitors can act either irreversibly or reversibly. Irreversible inhibitors bind covalently to the enzyme, causing a permanent loss of activity. Reversible inhibitors bind noncovalently either to the active site (competitive inhibitors such as substrate analogs) or to a separate site on the enzyme (noncompetitive inhibition).

- Enzymes can also be regulated by covalent modification. The most common covalent modifications include phosphorylation, as seen with glycogen phosphorylase, and proteolytic cleavage, as occurs in the activation of proteolytic pancreatic zymogens.

RNA Molecules as Enzymes: Ribozymes

- Although it was long thought that all enzymes were proteins, we now recognize the catalytic properties of certain RNA molecules called ribozymes.

- These include some rRNA molecules that are able to catalyze the removal of their own introns, RNA components of enzymes that also contain protein components, and the rRNA component of the large ribosomal subunit.

- The discovery of ribozymes has changed the way we think about the origin of life on Earth because RNA molecules, unlike proteins, can both carry information and replicate themselves.

MAKING CONNECTIONS

We learned that thermodynamic principles can be used to tell us whether a particular cellular reaction is feasible but not whether or at what rate the reaction will happen. In this chapter, we have just learned how enzymes make these reactions happen. All the macromolecules we studied in earlier chapters, and most of the cellular components we will learn about later, are produced using enzymes. In the next two chapters, we will take a detailed look at cell membranes and will see that many membranes contain enzymes as integral components. Also, many membrane transporters have enzymatic activities, such as the ATPases that provide energy for moving materials across membranes. We will use our knowledge of enzyme structure, function, and regulation extensively when we study glycolysis, fermentation, aerobic respiration, and photosynthesis in detail. Each of these biochemical pathways is an ordered sequence of highly regulated, enzyme-catalyzed steps. Each step involves the recognition, binding, and activation of specific substrates and the subsequent conversion of substrates to specific products. Throughout the rest of this text, we will encounter enzymes everywhere we look. We will see how they are involved in protein and lipid synthesis, processing, and packaging in Chapter 12, and learn details of their involvement in cell signaling mechanisms in the following two chapters. Later, we will see how assembly of the cytoskeleton and cellular motility likewise depend on enzymatic activities, as do synthesis of the extracellular matrix of animal cells and the cell walls of plants. When we study DNA replication and gene expression, we will see how a number of enzymes are highly regulated to ensure proper transmission of genetic information and precise control of cell function. Finally, when we study the development of cancer, we will see that often it is the result of defects in cellular enzymes such as proteases, protein kinases, and DNA repair enzymes.

PROBLEM SET

More challenging problems are marked with a •.

6-1 The Need for Enzymes. You should now be in a position to appreciate the difference between the thermodynamic feasibility of a reaction and the likelihood that it will actually proceed.

(a) Many reactions that are thermodynamically possible do not occur at an appreciable rate because of the activation energy required for the reactants to achieve the transition state. In molecular terms, what does this mean?

(b) One way to meet this requirement is by an input of heat, which in some cases need only be an initial, transient input. Give an example, and explain what this accomplishes in molecular terms.

(c) An alternative solution is to lower the activation energy. What does it mean in molecular terms to say that a catalyst lowers the activation energy of a reaction?

(d) Organic chemists often use inorganic catalysts such as nickel, platinum, or cations in their reactions, whereas cells use proteins called enzymes. What advantages can you see to the use of enzymes? Can you think of any disadvantages?

(e) Some enzymes can transfer a hydrogen atom without lowering the activation energy barrier. How is this possible?

6-2 Activation Energy. As shown in Reaction 6-2, hydrogen peroxide, H_2O_2, decomposes to H_2O and O_2. The activation energy, E_A, for the uncatalyzed reaction at 20°C is 18 kcal/mol. The reaction can be catalyzed either by ferric ions ($E_A = 13$ kcal/mol) or by the enzyme *catalase* ($E_A = 7$ kcal/mol).

(a) Draw an activation energy diagram for this reaction under catalyzed and uncatalyzed conditions, and explain what it means for the activation energy to be lowered from 18 to 13 kcal/mol by ferric ions but from 18 to 7 kcal/mol by catalase.

(b) Suggest two properties of catalase that make it a more suitable intracellular catalyst than ferric ions.

(c) Suggest yet another way that the rate of hydrogen peroxide decomposition can be accelerated. Is this a suitable means of increasing reaction rates within cells? Why or why not?

6-3 Rate Enhancement by Catalysts. The decomposition of H_2O_2 to H_2O and O_2 shown in Reaction 6-2 can be catalyzed either by an inorganic catalyst (ferric ions) or by the enzyme catalase. Compared with the uncatalyzed rate, this reaction proceeds about 30,000 times faster in the presence of ferric ions but about 100,000,000 times faster in the presence of catalase, an iron-containing enzyme. Assume that 1 μg of catalase can decompose a given quantity of H_2O_2 in 1 minute at 25°C and that all reactions are carried out under sterile conditions.

(a) How long would it take for the same quantity of H_2O_2 to be decomposed in the presence of an amount of ferric ions equivalent to the iron content of 1 μg of catalase?

(b) How long would it take for the same quantity of H_2O_2 to decompose in the absence of a catalyst?

(c) Explain how these calculations illustrate the indispensability of catalysts and the superiority of enzymes over inorganic catalysts.

6-4 Temperature and pH Effects. Figure 6-4 illustrates enzyme activities as functions of temperature and pH. In general, the activity of a specific enzyme is highest at the temperature and pH that are characteristic of the environment in which the enzyme normally functions.

(a) Explain the shapes of the curves in Figure 6-4 in terms of the major chemical or physical factors that affect enzyme activity.

(b) For each enzyme in Figure 6-4, suggest the adaptive advantage of having the enzyme activity profile shown in the figure.

(c) Some enzymes have a very flat pH profile—that is, they have essentially the same activity over a broad pH range. How might you explain this observation?

6-5 Michaelis–Menten Kinetics. Figure 6-19 represents a Michaelis–Menten plot for a typical enzyme, with initial reaction velocity plotted as a function of substrate concentration. Three regions of the curve are identified by the letters A, B, and C.

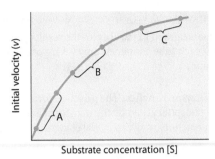

FIGURE 6-19 Analysis of the Michaelis–Menten Plot. See Problem 6-5.

For each of the statements that follow, indicate with a single letter which one of the three regions of the curve fits the statement best. A given letter can be used more than once.

(a) The active site of an enzyme molecule is occupied by substrate most of the time.

(b) The active site of an enzyme molecule is free most of the time.

(c) This is the range of substrate concentration in which most enzymes usually function in normal cells.

(d) This includes the point (K_m, $V_{max}/2$).

(e) Reaction velocity is limited mainly by the number of enzyme molecules present.

(f) Reaction velocity is limited mainly by the number of substrate molecules present.

6-6 Enzyme Kinetics. The enzyme β-galactosidase catalyzes the hydrolysis of the disaccharide lactose into its component monosaccharides:

$$\text{lactose} + H_2O \xrightarrow[\beta\text{-galactosidase}]{} \text{glucose} + \text{galactose} \quad \textbf{(6-17)}$$

To determine V_{max} and K_m of β-galactosidase for lactose, the same amount of enzyme (1 μg per tube) was incubated with a series of lactose concentrations under conditions where product concentrations remained negligible. At each lactose concentration, the initial reaction velocity was determined by assaying for the amount of lactose remaining at the end of the assay. The following data were obtained:

Lactose concentration (mM)	Rate of lactose consumption (M mol/min)
1	10.0
2	16.7
4	25.0
8	33.3
16	40.0
32	44.4

(a) Why is it necessary to specify that product concentrations remained negligible during the course of the reaction?

(b) Plot v (rate of lactose consumption) versus [S] (lactose concentration). Why is it that when the lactose concentration is doubled, the increase in velocity is always less than twofold?

(c) Calculate $1/v$ and $1/[S]$ for each entry on the data table, and plot $1/v$ versus $1/[S]$.

(d) Determine K_m and V_{max} from your double-reciprocal plot.

(e) On the same graph as part b, plot the results you would expect if each tube contained only 0.5 μg of enzyme. Explain your graph.

6-7 More Enzyme Kinetics. The galactose formed in Reaction 6-17 can be phosphorylated by the transfer of a phosphate group from ATP, a reaction catalyzed by the enzyme galactokinase:

$$\text{galactose + ATP} \xrightarrow{\text{galactokinase}} \text{galactose-1-phosphate + ADP} \tag{6-18}$$

Assume that you have isolated the galactokinase enzyme and have determined its kinetic parameters by varying the concentration of galactose in the presence of a constant, high (i.e., saturating) concentration of ATP. The double-reciprocal (Lineweaver–Burk) plot of the data is shown as **Figure 6-20**.

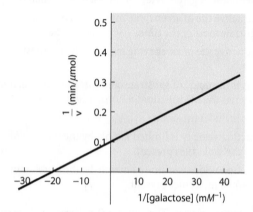

FIGURE 6-20 Double-Reciprocal Plot for the Enzyme Galactokinase. See Problem 6-7.

(a) What is the K_m of galactokinase for galactose under these assay conditions? What does K_m tell us about the enzyme?

(b) What is the V_{max} of the enzyme under these assay conditions? What does V_{max} tell us about the enzyme?

(c) Assume that you now repeat the experiment, but with the ATP concentration varied and galactose present at a constant, high concentration. Assuming that all other conditions are maintained as before, would you expect to get the same V_{max} value as in part b? Why or why not?

(d) In the experiment described in part c, the K_m value turned out to be very different from the value determined in part b. Can you explain why?

6-8 Turnover Number. Carbonic anhydrase catalyzes the reversible hydration of carbon dioxide to form bicarbonate ion:

$$CO_2 + H_2O \rightleftharpoons HCO_3^- + H^+ \tag{6-19}$$

This reaction is important in the transport of carbon dioxide from body tissues to the lungs by red blood cells. Carbonic anhydrase has a molecular weight of 30,000 and a turnover number (k_{cat} value) of $1 \times 10^6 sec^{-1}$. Assume that you are given 1 mL of a solution containing 2.0 μg of pure carbonic anhydrase.

(a) At what rate (in millimoles of CO_2 consumed per second) will you expect this reaction to proceed under optimal conditions?

(b) Assuming standard temperature and pressure, how much CO_2 is that in mL per second?

6-9 Inhibitors: Wrong Again. For each of the following false statements, change the statement to make it true and explain your reasoning.

(a) Diisopropyl fluorophosphate binds covalently to the hydroxyl group of a specific amino acid residue of the target enzyme and is therefore almost certainly an allosteric effector.

(b) The enzyme hexokinase is inhibited by its own product, glucose-6-phosphate, and is therefore an example of feedback inhibition.

(c) Glycogen synthase, like glycogen phosphorylase, is active in the phosphorylated form and inactive in the dephosphorylated form.

(d) An enzyme that is subject to allosteric activation is most likely to catalyze the final reaction in a biosynthetic pathway.

(e) If researchers claim that an enzyme is allosterically activated by compound A and allosterically inhibited by compound B, one of these claims must be wrong.

6-10 What Type of Inhibition? A new mucinase enzyme was recently discovered that breaks down a glycoprotein in mucous membranes and contributes to bacterial vaginosis (*J. Clin. Microbiol.* 43:5504). You are a research pathologist testing a new inhibitor of this enzyme that you have discovered and want to design experiments to understand the nature of this inhibition. You have a supply of the normal glycoprotein substrate, the inhibitor, and an assay to measure product formation.

(a) How might you determine whether inhibition is reversible or irreversible?

(b) If you find that the inhibition is reversible, how would you determine whether the inhibition is competitive or noncompetitive?

6-11 Biological Relevance. Explain the biological relevance of each of the following observations concerning enzyme regulation.

(a) When you need a burst of energy, the hormones epinephrine and glucagon are secreted into your bloodstream and circulated to your muscle cells, where they initiate a cascade of reactions that leads to the phosphorylation of the inactive *b* form of glycogen phosphorylase, thereby converting the enzyme into the active *a* form.

(b) Even in the *a* form, glycogen phosphorylase is allosterically inhibited by a high concentration of glucose or ATP within a specific liver cell.

(c) Your pancreas synthesizes and secretes the proteolytic enzyme carboxypeptidase in the form of an inactive precursor called procarboxypeptidase, which is activated as a result of proteolytic cleavage by the enzyme trypsin in the duodenum of your small intestine.

• 6-12 Derivation of the Michaelis–Menten Equation. For the enzyme-catalyzed reaction in which a substrate S is converted into a product P (see Reaction 6-5), velocity can be defined as the disappearance of substrate or the appearance of product per unit time:

$$v = -\frac{d[S]}{dt} = +\frac{d[P]}{dt} \tag{6-20}$$

Beginning with this definition and restricting your consideration to the initial stage of the reaction when [P] is essentially zero, derive the Michaelis–Menten equation (see Equation 6-7). The following points may help you in your derivation:

(a) Begin by expressing the rate equations for $d[S]/dt$, $d[P]/dt$, and $d[ES]/dt$ in terms of concentrations and rate constants.

(b) Assume a steady state at which the enzyme-substrate complex of Reaction 6-6 is being broken down at the same rate as it is being formed such that the net rate of change, $d[ES]/dt$, is zero.

(c) Note that the total amount of enzyme present, E_t, is the sum of the free form, E_f, plus the amount of complexed enzyme ES: $E_t = E_f + ES$.

(d) When you get that far, note that V_{max} and K_m can be defined as follows:

$$V_{max} = k_3[E_t] \quad K_m = \frac{k_2 + k_3}{k_1} \qquad \textbf{(6-21)}$$

• **6-13 Linearizing Michaelis and Menten.** In addition to the Lineweaver–Burk plot (see Figure 6-10), two other straight-line forms of the Michaelis–Menten equation are sometimes used. The Eadie–Hofstee plot is a graph of $v/[S]$ versus v (see Figure 6-11), and the Hanes–Woolf plot graphs $[S]/v$ versus $[S]$.

(a) In both cases, show that the equation being graphed can be derived from the Michaelis–Menten equation by simple arithmetic manipulation.

(b) In both cases, indicate how K_m and V_{max} can be determined from the resulting graph.

(c) Make a Hanes–Woolf plot, with the intercepts and slope labeled as for the Lineweaver–Burk and Eadie–Hofstee plots (see Figures 6-10 and 6-11). Can you suggest why the Hanes–Woolf plot is the most statistically satisfactory of the three?

SUGGESTED READING

References of historical importance are marked with a •.

General References

Colowick, S. P., and N. O. Kaplan, eds. *Methods Enzymol.* New York: Academic Press, 1955–present (ongoing series).

Copeland, R. A. *Enzymes: A Practical Introduction to Structures, Mechanisms, and Data Analysis.* New York: Wiley, 2000.

Mathews, C. K., K. E. van Holde, and K. G. Ahern. *Biochemistry*, 3rd ed. San Francisco: Benjamin Cummings, 2000.

Nelson, D. L., and M. M. Cox. *Lehninger Principles of Biochemistry*, 5th ed. New York: W. H. Freeman, 2008.

Purich, D. L., and R. D. Allison. *The Enzyme Reference: A Comprehensive Guidebook to Enzyme Nomenclature, Reactions, and Methods.* Boston: Academic Press, 2002.

Historical References

• Changeux, J. P. The control of biochemical reactions. *Sci. Amer.* 212 (April 1965): 36.

• Cori, C. F. James B. Sumner and the chemical nature of enzymes. *Trends Biochem. Sci.* 6 (1981): 194.

• Friedmann, H., ed. *Benchmark Papers in Biochemistry. Vol. 1: Enzymes.* Stroudsburg, PA: Hutchinson Ross, 1981.

• Lineweaver, H., and D. Burk. The determination of enzyme dissociation constants. *J. Amer. Chem. Soc.* 56 (1934): 658.

• Monod, J., J. P. Changeux, and F. Jacob. Allosteric proteins and cellular control systems. *J. Mol. Biol.* 6 (1963): 306.

• Phillips, D. C. The three-dimensional structure of an enzyme molecule. *Sci. Amer.* 215 (November 1966): 78.

• Sumner, J. B. Enzymes. *Annu. Rev. Biochem.* 4 (1935): 37.

Structure and Function of Enzymes

Benkovic, S. J., and S. Hammes-Schiffler. A perspective on enzyme catalysis. *Science* 301 (2003): 1196.

Erlandsen, H., E. E. Abola, and R. C. Stevens. Combining structural genomics and enzymology: Completing the picture in metabolic pathways and enzyme active sites. *Curr. Opin. Struct. Biol.* 10 (2000): 719.

Fersht, A. *Structure and Mechanism in Protein Science: A Guide to Enzyme Catalysis and Protein Folding.* New York: W.H. Freeman, 1999.

Hatzimanikatis, V., C. Li, J. A. Ionita, and L. J. Broadbelt. Metabolic networks: Enzyme function and metabolite structure. *Curr. Opin. Struct. Biol.* 14 (2004): 300.

Minshull, J. et al. Predicting enzyme function from protein sequence. *Curr. Opin. Chem. Biol.* 9 (2005): 202.

Page, M. J., and E. DiCera. Role of Na^+ and K^+ in enzyme function. *Physiol. Rev.* 86 (2006): 1049.

Syed, U., and G. Yona. Enzyme function prediction with interpretable models. *Methods Mol. Biol.* 541 (2009): 373.

Walsh, C. Enabling the chemistry of life. *Nature* 409 (2001): 226.

Mechanisms of Enzyme Catalysis

Fitzpatrick, P. Special issue on enzyme catalysis. *Arch. Biochem. Biophys.* 433 (2005): 1.

Frey, P. A., and D. B. Northrop, eds. *Enzymatic Mechanisms.* Washington, DC: IOS Press, 1999.

Maragoni, A. G. *Enzyme Kinetics: A Modern Approach.* Hoboken, NJ: Wiley Interscience, 2003.

Matthews, J. N., and G. C. Allcock. Optimal designs for Michaelis–Menten kinetic studies. *Stat. Med.* 23 (2004): 477.

Mulholland, A. J. Modeling enzyme reaction mechanisms, specificity and catalysis. *Drug Disc. Today* 10 (2005): 1393.

Murphy, E. F., M. J. C. Crabbe, and S. G. Gilmour. Effective experimental design: Enzyme kinetics in the bioinformatics era. *Drug Disc. Today* 7 (2002): S187.

Sigel, R. K., and A. M. Pyle. Alternative roles for metal ions in enzyme catalysis and the implications for ribozyme chemistry. *Chem. Rev.* 107 (2007): 97.

Ribozymes: RNA as an Enzyme

Baghen, S., and M. Kashani-Sabet. Ribozymes in the age of molecular therapeutics. *Curr. Mol. Med.* 4 (2004): 489.

• Cech, T. R. The chemistry of self-splicing RNA and RNA enzymes. *Science* 236 (1987): 1532.

Khan, A. U. Ribozyme: A clinical tool. *Clin. Chim. Acta* 367 (2006): 20.

Krupp, G., and R. K. Gaur. *Ribozymes: Biochemistry and Biotechnology.* Natick, MA: Eaton Publishing, 2000.

Li, Q. X., P. Tan, N. Ke, and F. Wong-Staal. Ribozyme technology for cancer gene target identification and validation. *Adv. Cancer Res.* 96 (2007): 103.

Lilley, D. M. Structure, folding and mechanisms of ribozymes. *Curr. Opin. Struct. Biol.* 15 (2005): 313.

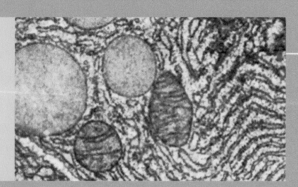

7

Membranes: Their Structure, Function, and Chemistry

An essential feature of every cell is the presence of **membranes** that define the boundaries of the cell and its various internal compartments. Even the casual observer of electron micrographs is likely to be struck by the prominence of membranes around and within cells, especially those of eukaryotic organisms (**Figure 7-1**). In Chapter 3, we encountered the structural molecules that allow membranes to be formed and began to study membranes and membrane-bounded organelles in Chapter 4. Now we are ready to look at membrane structure and function in greater detail. In this chapter, we will examine the molecular structure of membranes and explore the multiple roles that membranes play in the life of the cell.

The Functions of Membranes

We begin our discussion by noting that biological membranes play five related yet distinct roles, as illustrated in **Figure 7-2**. ❶ They define the boundaries of the cell and its organelles and act as permeability barriers. ❷ They serve as sites for specific biochemical functions, such as electron transport during mitochondrial respiration or protein processing in the ER. ❸ Membranes also possess transport proteins that regulate the movement of substances into and out of the cell and its organelles. ❹ In addition, membranes contain the protein molecules that act as receptors to detect external signals. ❺ Finally, they provide mechanisms for cell-to-cell contact, adhesion, and communication. Each of these functions is described briefly in the following five sections.

Membranes Define Boundaries and Serve as Permeability Barriers

One of the most obvious functions of membranes is to define the boundaries of the cell and its compartments and to serve as permeability barriers. The interior of the cell must be physically separated from the surrounding environment, not only to keep desirable substances in the cell but also to keep undesirable substances out. Membranes serve this purpose well because the hydrophobic interior of the membrane is an effective permeability barrier for hydrophilic molecules and ions. The permeability barrier for the cell as a whole is the **plasma** (or **cell**) **membrane,** a membrane that surrounds the cell and regulates the passage of materials both into and out of cells. In addition to the plasma membrane, various **intracellular membranes** serve to compartmentalize functions within eukaryotic cells.

Recently, there has been much interest in a class of *antimicrobial peptides (AMPs),* which are small molecules of 10–50 amino acids that can affect this permeability barrier. Over 1200 different AMPs are known, with more than 20 being produced by human skin alone. One class of AMPs consists of cationic, amphipathic molecules that disrupt bacterial membrane structure by interacting with the negatively charged phospholipids in their cell membranes. These AMPs thus act like detergents and disrupt the membrane structure, causing holes to form that destroy the cell's permeability barrier and kill the cells. Some AMPs have shown promise as antiviral agents in disrupting the outer covering of membrane-enclosed viruses such as the human immunodeficiency virus (HIV).

Membranes Are Sites of Specific Proteins and Therefore of Specific Functions

Membranes have specific functions associated with them because the molecules and structures responsible for those functions—proteins, in most cases—are either embedded in or localized on membranes. One of the most useful ways to characterize a specific membrane, in fact, is to describe the particular enzymes, transport proteins, receptors, and other molecules associated with it.

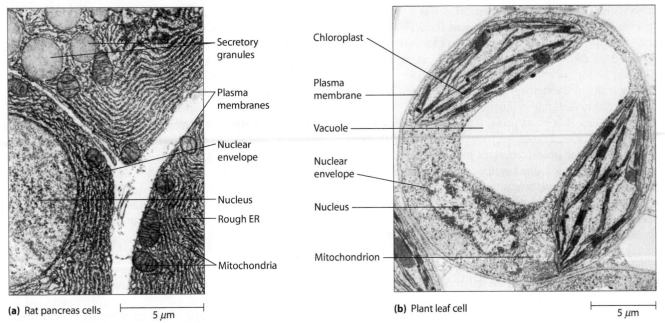

(a) Rat pancreas cells |———— 5 μm ————|

(b) Plant leaf cell |———— 5 μm ————|

FIGURE 7-1 The Prominence of Membranes Around and Within Eukaryotic Cells. Among the structures of eukaryotic cells that involve membranes are the plasma membrane, nucleus, chloroplasts, mitochondria, endoplasmic reticulum (ER), secretory granules, and vacuoles. These structures are shown here in **(a)** portions of three cells from a rat pancreas and **(b)** a plant leaf cell (TEMs).

For example, many distinctive enzymes are present in or on the plasma membrane or the membranes of particular organelles. Such enzymes are often useful as *markers* to identify particular membranes during the isolation of organelles and organelle membranes from suspensions of disrupted cells (see Box 12A, pages 327–329). For example, *glucose-6-phosphatase* is a membrane-bound enzyme found in the endoplasmic reticulum, and its presence in,

say, a preparation of mitochondria would demonstrate contamination with ER membranes.

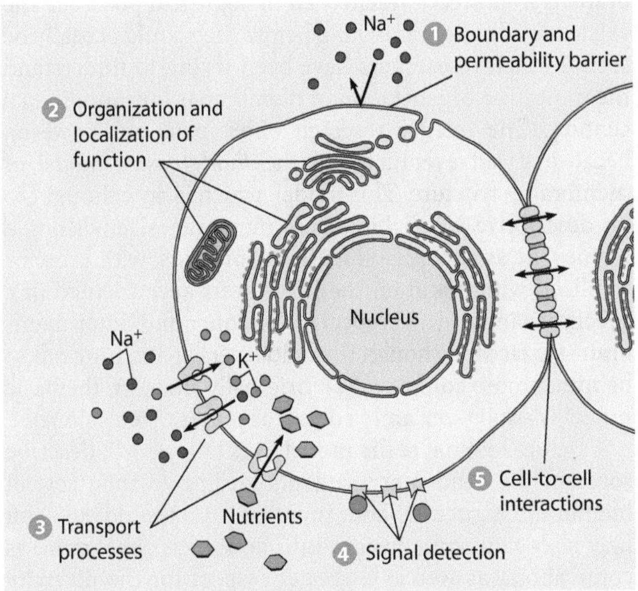

Other functions associated with specific membranes are a direct result of the particular proteins present in these membranes. For example, the plasma membrane contains the enzymes that synthesize the cell wall of plants, fungi, and bacteria. In vertebrate cells, the plasma membrane contains enzymes that secrete the materials that make up the extracellular matrix. Other membrane proteins, such as those in chloroplast and mitochondrial membranes or in the bacterial plasma membrane, are critical for energy-generating processes such as photosynthesis and respiration.

Membrane Proteins Regulate the Transport of Solutes

Another function of membrane proteins is to carry out and regulate the *transport* of substances into and out of cells and their organelles. Nutrients, ions, gases, water, and other substances are taken up into various compartments, and various products and wastes must be removed. While lipophilic molecules, very small molecules, and gases can typically diffuse directly across cellular membranes, most substances needed by the cell require transport proteins that recognize and transport a specific molecule or a group of similar molecules.

For example, cells may have specific transporters for glucose, amino acids, or other nutrients. Your nerve cells transmit electrical signals as Na^+ and K^+ ions are transported across the plasma membrane of neurons by specific ion channel proteins. Transport proteins in muscle cells move calcium ions across membranes to assist in muscle

FIGURE 7-2 Functions of Membranes. Membranes not only define the cell and its organelles but also have a number of important functions, including transport, signaling, and adhesion.

contraction. The chloroplast membrane has a transporter specific for the phosphate ions needed for ATP synthesis, and the mitochondrion has transporters for intermediates involved in aerobic respiration. There is even a specific transporter for water—known as an *aquaporin*—that can rapidly transport water molecules through membranes of kidney cells to facilitate urine production.

Molecules as large as proteins and RNA can be transferred across membranes by transport proteins. Proteins form the nuclear pore complexes in the nuclear envelope through which mRNA molecules and partially assembled ribosomes can move from the nucleus to the cytosol. In some cases, proteins that are synthesized on the endoplasmic reticulum or in the cytosol can be imported into lysosomes, peroxisomes, or mitochondria via transport proteins. In other cases, proteins in the membranes of intracellular vesicles facilitate the movement of molecules such as neurotransmitters either into the cell or out of the cell.

Membrane Proteins Detect and Transmit Electrical and Chemical Signals

Cells receive information from their environment, usually in the form of electrical or chemical signals that impinge on the outer surface of the cell. The nerve impulses being sent from your eyes to your brain as you read these words are examples of such signals, as are the various hormones present in your circulatory system. *Signal transduction* is the term used to describe the specific mechanisms used to transmit such signals from the outer surface of cells to the cell interior.

Many chemical signal molecules bind to specific membrane proteins known as *receptors* on the outer surface of the plasma membrane. Binding of these signal molecules to their receptors triggers specific chemical events on the inner surface of the membrane that lead to changes in cell function. For example, muscle and liver cell membranes contain insulin receptors and can therefore respond to this hormone, which helps cells take in glucose. White blood cells have specific receptors that recognize chemical signals from bacteria and initiate a cellular defense response.

Many plant cells have a transmembrane receptor protein that detects the gaseous hormone ethylene and transmits a signal to the cell that can affect a variety of processes including seed germination, fruit ripening, and defense against pathogens. Bacteria often have plasma membrane receptors that sense nutrients in the environment and can signal the cell to move toward these nutrients. Thus, membrane receptors allow cells to recognize, transmit, and respond to a variety of specific signals in nearly all types of cells.

Membrane Proteins Mediate Cell Adhesion and Cell-to-Cell Communication

Membrane proteins also mediate adhesion and communication between adjacent cells. Although textbooks often depict cells as separate, isolated entities, most cells in multicellular organisms are in contact with other cells. During embryonic development, specific cell-to-cell contacts are critical and, in animals, are often mediated by membrane proteins known as *cadherins*. Cadherins have extracellular sequences of amino acids that bind calcium ions and stimulate adhesion between similar cells in a tissue. However, some pathogenic bacteria, such as some species of *Listeria* and *Shigella*, take advantage of adhesive membrane proteins to attach to and invade intestinal cells and cause disease.

Other types of membrane proteins in animal tissues form *adhesive junctions,* which hold cells together, and *tight junctions,* which form seals that block the passage of fluids between cells. Membrane proteins such as *ankyrin* can also be points of attachment to the cell cytoskeleton, lending rigidity to tissues. In addition, cells within a particular tissue often have direct cytoplasmic connections that allow the exchange of at least some cellular components. This intercellular communication is provided by *gap junctions* in animal cells and by *plasmodesmata* in plant cells. We will learn about all these structures when we move "beyond the cell".

All the functions we have just considered—compartmentalization, localization of function, transport, signal detection, and intercellular communication—depend on the chemical composition and structural features of membranes. It is to these topics that we now turn as we consider how our present understanding of membrane structure developed.

Models of Membrane Structure: An Experimental Perspective

Until electron microscopy was applied to the study of cell structure in the early 1950s, no one had ever seen a membrane. Yet indirect evidence led biologists to postulate the existence of membranes long before they could actually be seen. In fact, researchers have been trying to understand the molecular organization of membranes for more than a century. The intense research effort paid off, however, because it led eventually to the *fluid mosaic model* of membrane structure. This model, which is now thought to be descriptive of all biological membranes, envisions a membrane as two quite fluid layers of lipids, with proteins localized within and on the lipid layers and oriented in a specific manner with respect to the inner and outer membrane surfaces. Although the lipid layers are turning out to be much more complex than originally thought, the basic model is almost certainly correct as presently envisioned.

Before looking at the model in detail, we will describe some of the central experiments leading to this view of membrane structure and function. As we do so, you may also gain some insight into how such developments come about, as well as a greater respect for the diversity of approaches and techniques that are often important in advancing our understanding of biological phenomena. **Figure 7-3** presents a chronology of membrane studies

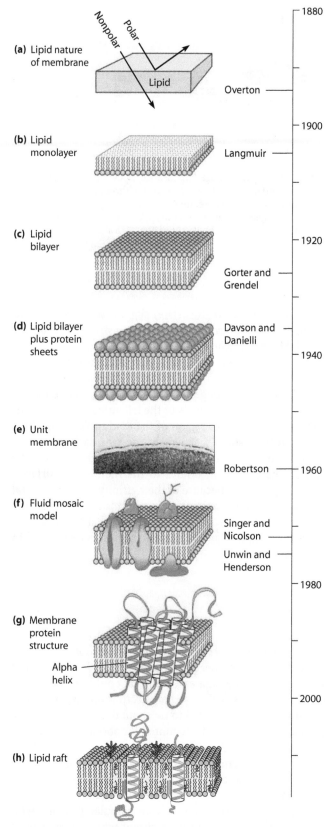

(a) Lipid nature of membrane

Nonpolar Polar

Lipid

Overton — 1880

(b) Lipid monolayer

Langmuir — 1900

(c) Lipid bilayer

Gorter and Grendel — 1920

(d) Lipid bilayer plus protein sheets

Davson and Danielli — 1940

(e) Unit membrane

Robertson — 1960

(f) Fluid mosaic model

Singer and Nicolson

Unwin and Henderson — 1980

(g) Membrane protein structure

Alpha helix — 2000

(h) Lipid raft

FIGURE 7-3 Timeline for Development of the Fluid Mosaic Model. The fluid mosaic model of membrane structure that Singer and Nicolson proposed in 1972 was the culmination of studies dating back to the 1890s (**a**)–(**e**). This model (**f**) has been significantly refined by subsequent studies (**g** and **h**).

that began over a century ago and led eventually to our current understanding of membranes as fluid mosaics.

Overton and Langmuir: Lipids Are Important Components of Membranes

A good starting point for our experimental overview is the pioneering work of German scientist Charles Ernest Overton in the 1890s. Working with cells of plant root hairs, he observed that lipid-soluble substances penetrate readily into cells, whereas water-soluble substances do not. From his studies, Overton concluded that lipids are present on the cell surface as some sort of "coat" (Figure 7-3a). He even suggested that cell coats are probably mixtures of cholesterol and lecithin, an insight that proved to be remarkably farsighted in light of what we now know about the prominence of sterols and phospholipids as membrane components.

A second important advance came about a decade later through the work of Irving Langmuir, who studied the behavior of purified phospholipids by dissolving them in benzene and layering samples of the benzene-lipid solution onto a water surface. As the benzene evaporated, the molecules were left as a lipid film one molecule thick—that is, a "monolayer." Because phospholipids are *amphipathic* molecules, Langmuir reasoned that the phospholipids orient themselves on water such that their hydrophilic heads face the water and their hydrophobic tails protrude away from the water (Figure 7-3b). Langmuir's lipid monolayer became the basis for further thought about membrane structure in the early years of the twentieth century.

Gorter and Grendel: The Basis of Membrane Structure Is a Lipid Bilayer

The next major advance came in 1925 when two Dutch physiologists, Evert Gorter and F. Grendel, extracted the lipids from a known number of erythrocytes (red blood cells) and used Langmuir's method to spread the lipids as a monolayer on a water surface. They found that the area of the lipid film on the water was about twice the estimated total surface area of the erythrocyte. Therefore, they concluded that the erythrocyte plasma membrane consists of not one but *two* layers of lipids.

Hypothesizing a bilayer structure, Gorter and Grendel reasoned that it would be thermodynamically favorable for the nonpolar hydrocarbon chains of each layer to face inward, away from the aqueous milieu on either side of the membrane. The polar hydrophilic groups of each layer would then face outward, toward the aqueous environment on either side of the membrane (Figure 7-3c). Gorter and Grendel's experiment and their conclusions were momentous because this work represented the first attempt to understand membranes at the molecular level. Moreover, the **lipid bilayer** they envisioned became the basic underlying assumption for each successive refinement in our understanding of membrane structure.

Davson and Danielli: Membranes Also Contain Proteins

Shortly after Gorter and Grendel proposed their bilayer model in 1925, it became clear that a simple lipid bilayer, could not explain all the properties of membranes—particularly those related to *surface tension, solute permeability,* and *electrical resistance.* For example, the surface tension of a lipid film was significantly higher than that of cellular membranes but could be lowered by adding protein to the lipid film. Moreover, sugars, ions, and other hydrophilic solutes readily moved into and out of cells even though pure lipid bilayers are nearly impermeable to water-soluble substances.

To explain such differences, Hugh Davson and James Danielli suggested that proteins are present in membranes. They proposed in 1935 that biological membranes consist of lipid bilayers that are coated on both sides with thin sheets of protein (Figure 7-3d). Their model, a protein-lipid-protein "sandwich," was the first detailed representation of membrane organization and dominated the thinking of cell biologists for the next several decades.

The original model was later modified to accommodate additional findings. Particularly notable was the suggestion, made in 1954, that hydrophilic proteins might penetrate into the membrane in places to provide polar pores through an otherwise hydrophobic bilayer. These proteins could then allow water-soluble substances to cross the cell membrane. Specifically, the lipid interior accounted for the hydrophobic properties of membranes, and the protein components explained their hydrophilic properties.

The real significance of the Davson–Danielli model, however, was that it recognized the importance of proteins in membrane structure. This feature, more than any other, made the Davson–Danielli sandwich the basis for much subsequent research on membrane structure.

Robertson: All Membranes Share a Common Underlying Structure

With the advent of electron microscopy in the 1950s, cell biologists could finally verify the presence of a plasma membrane around each cell. They could also observe that most subcellular organelles are bounded by similar membranes. Furthermore, when membranes were stained with osmium, a heavy metal, and then examined closely at high magnification, they were found to have extensive regions of "railroad track" structure that appeared as two dark lines separated by a lightly stained central zone, with an overall thickness of 6–8 nm. This pattern is seen in **Figure 7-4** for the plasma membranes of two adjacent cells that are separated from each other by a thin intercellular space. Because this same staining pattern was observed with many different kinds of

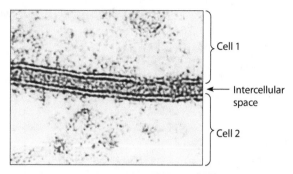

FIGURE 7-4 Trilaminar Appearance of Cellular Membranes. This electron micrograph of a thin section through two adjacent cells shows their plasma membranes separated by a small intercellular space. Each membrane appears as two dark lines separated by a lightly stained central zone in a staining pattern that gives each membrane a trilaminar, or "railroad track," appearance (TEM).

membranes, J. David Robertson suggested that all cellular membranes share a common underlying structure, which he called the *unit membrane* (see Figure 7-3e).

When first proposed, the unit membrane structure seemed to agree remarkably well with the Davson–Danielli model. Robertson suggested that the lightly stained space (between the two dark lines of the trilaminar pattern) contains the hydrophobic region of the lipid molecules, which do not readily stain. Conversely, the two dark lines were thought to represent phospholipid head groups and the thin sheets of protein bound to the membrane surfaces, which appear dark because of their affinity for heavy metal stains. This interpretation appeared to provide strong support for the Davson–Danielli view that a membrane consists of a lipid bilayer coated on both surfaces with thin sheets of protein.

Further Research Revealed Major Shortcomings of the Davson–Danielli Model

Despite its apparent confirmation by electron microscopy and its extension to all membranes by Robertson, the Davson–Danielli model encountered difficulties in the 1960s as more and more data emerged that could not be reconciled with their model. Based on electron microscopy, most membranes were reported to be about 6–8 nm thick—and, of this, the lipid bilayer accounted for about 4–5 nm. That left only about 1–2 nm of space on either surface of the bilayer for the membrane protein, a space that could at best accommodate a thin monolayer of protein. Yet after membrane proteins were isolated and studied, it became apparent that most of them were globular proteins with sizes and shapes that are inconsistent with the concept of thin sheets of protein on the two surfaces of the membrane.

As a further complication, the Davson–Danielli model did not readily account for the distinctiveness of different kinds of membranes. Depending on their source, membranes vary considerably in chemical composition and

Table 7-1 **Protein, Lipid, and Carbohydrate Content of Biological Membranes**

Membrane	Approximate Percentage by Weight			Protein/Lipid Ratio
	Protein	Lipid	Carbohydrate	
Plasma membrane				
Human erythrocyte	49	43	8	1.14
Mammalian liver cell	54	36	10	1.50
Amoeba	54	42	4	1.29
Myelin sheath of nerve axon	18	79	3	0.23
Nuclear envelope	66	32	2	2.06
Endoplasmic reticulum	63	27	10	2.33
Golgi complex	64	26	10	2.46
Chloroplast thylakoids	70	30	0	2.33
Mitochondrial outer membrane	55	45	0	1.22
Mitochondrial inner membrane	78	22	0	3.54
Gram-positive bacterium	75	25	0	3.00

especially in the ratio of protein to lipid (Table 7-1), which can vary from 3 or more in some bacterial cells to only 0.23 for the myelin sheath surrounding nerve axons. Even the two membranes of the mitochondrion differ significantly: The protein/lipid ratio is about 1.2 for the outer membrane and about 3.5 for the inner membrane, which contains all the enzymes and proteins related to electron transport and ATP synthesis. Yet all of these membranes look essentially the same when visualized using electron microscopy.

The Davson–Danielli model was also called into question by studies in which membranes were exposed to *phospholipases,* enzymes that degrade phospholipids by removing their head groups. According to the model, the hydrophilic head groups of membrane lipids should be covered by a layer of protein and therefore protected from phospholipase digestion. However, up to 75% of the membrane phospholipid can be degraded when the membrane is exposed to phospholipases, suggesting that many of the phospholipid head groups are exposed at the membrane surface and not covered by a layer of protein.

Moreover, the surface localization of membrane proteins specified by the Davson–Danielli model was not supported by the experience of scientists who tried to isolate such proteins. Most membrane proteins turned out to be quite insoluble in water and could be extracted only by using organic solvents or detergents. These observations indicated that many membrane proteins are hydrophobic (or at least amphipathic) and suggested that they are located, at least partially, within the hydrophobic interior of the membrane rather than on either of its surfaces.

Singer and Nicolson: A Membrane Consists of a Mosaic of Proteins in a Fluid Lipid Bilayer

The preceding problems with the Davson–Danielli model stimulated considerable interest in the development of new ideas about membrane organization, culminating in 1972 with the **fluid mosaic model** proposed by S. Jonathan Singer and Garth Nicolson. This model, which now dominates our view of membrane organization, has two key features, both implied by its name. Simply put, the model envisions a membrane as a *mosaic* of proteins embedded in, or at least attached to, a *fluid* lipid bilayer (Figure 7-3f). This model retained the basic lipid bilayer structure of earlier models but viewed membrane proteins in an entirely different way—not as thin sheets on the membrane surface but as discrete globular entities within the lipid bilayer (Figure 7-5a).

This way of thinking about membrane proteins was revolutionary when Singer and Nicolson first proposed it, but it turned out to fit the data quite well. Three classes of membrane proteins are now recognized based on differences in how the proteins are linked to the bilayer. *Integral membrane proteins* are embedded within the lipid bilayer, where they are held in place by the affinity of hydrophobic segments of the protein for the hydrophobic interior of the lipid bilayer. *Peripheral proteins* are much more hydrophilic and are therefore located on the surface of the membrane, where they are linked noncovalently to the polar head groups of phospholipids and/or to the hydrophilic parts of other membrane proteins. *Lipid-anchored proteins* are essentially hydrophilic proteins and therefore reside on membrane surfaces, but they are covalently attached to lipid molecules that are embedded within the bilayer.

The fluid nature of the membrane is the second critical feature of the Singer–Nicolson model. Rather than being rigidly locked in place, most of the lipid components of a membrane are in constant motion, capable of lateral mobility (i.e., movement parallel to the membrane surface). Many membrane proteins are also able to move laterally within the membrane, although some proteins are anchored to structural elements such as the cytoskeleton on one side of the membrane or the other and are therefore restricted in their mobility.

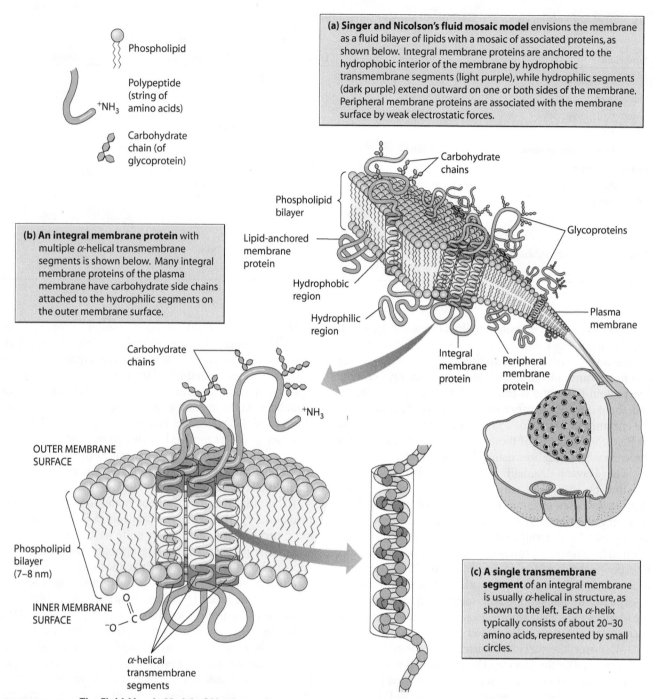

(a) Singer and Nicolson's fluid mosaic model envisions the membrane as a fluid bilayer of lipids with a mosaic of associated proteins, as shown below. Integral membrane proteins are anchored to the hydrophobic interior of the membrane by hydrophobic transmembrane segments (light purple), while hydrophilic segments (dark purple) extend outward on one or both sides of the membrane. Peripheral membrane proteins are associated with the membrane surface by weak electrostatic forces.

Phospholipid

Polypeptide (string of amino acids)

$^+NH_3$

Carbohydrate chain (of glycoprotein)

Carbohydrate chains

Phospholipid bilayer

Lipid-anchored membrane protein

Hydrophobic region

Hydrophilic region

Glycoproteins

Plasma membrane

Integral membrane protein

Peripheral membrane protein

(b) An integral membrane protein with multiple α-helical transmembrane segments is shown below. Many integral membrane proteins of the plasma membrane have carbohydrate side chains attached to the hydrophilic segments on the outer membrane surface.

Carbohydrate chains

$^+NH_3$

OUTER MEMBRANE SURFACE

Phospholipid bilayer (7–8 nm)

INNER MEMBRANE SURFACE

α-helical transmembrane segments

(c) A single transmembrane segment of an integral membrane is usually α-helical in structure, as shown to the left. Each α-helix typically consists of about 20–30 amino acids, represented by small circles.

FIGURE 7-5 The Fluid Mosaic Model of Membrane Structure. These drawings show **(a)** representative phospholipids and proteins in a typical plasma membrane, with closeups of **(b)** an integral membrane protein and **(c)** one of its transmembrane segments.

ACTIVITIES www.thecellplace.com *Membrane structure*

The major strength of the fluid mosaic model is that it readily explains most of the criticisms of the Davson–Danielli model. For example, the concept of proteins partially embedded within the lipid bilayer accords well with the hydrophobic nature and globular structure of most membrane proteins and eliminates the need to accommodate membrane proteins in thin surface layers of unvarying thickness. Moreover, the variability in the protein/lipid ratios of different membranes simply means that different membranes vary in the amount of protein they contain. Also, the exposure of lipid head groups at the membrane surface is obviously compatible with their susceptibility to phospholipase digestion, while the fluidity of the lipid layers and the intermingling of lipids and proteins within the membrane make it easy to envision the mobility of both lipids and proteins.

Unwin and Henderson: Most Membrane Proteins Contain Transmembrane Segments

The next illustration in the timeline (see Figure 7-3g) depicts an important property of integral membrane proteins that cell biologists began to understand in the 1970s: Most such proteins have in their primary structure one or more hydrophobic sequences that span the lipid bilayer (Figure 7-5b, c). These *transmembrane segments* anchor the protein to the membrane and hold it in proper alignment within the lipid bilayer.

The example in Figure 7-3g is *bacteriorhodopsin,* the first membrane protein shown to possess this structural feature. Bacteriorhodopsin is a plasma membrane protein found in archaea of the genus *Halobacterium,* where its presence allows cells to obtain energy directly from sunlight. Nigel Unwin and Richard Henderson used electron microscopy to determine the three-dimensional structure of bacteriorhodopsin and to reveal its orientation in the membrane. Their remarkable finding, reported in 1975, was that bacteriorhodopsin consists of a single peptide chain folded back and forth across the lipid bilayer a total of seven times. Each of the seven transmembrane segments of the protein is a closely packed α helix composed mainly of hydrophobic amino acids. Successive transmembrane segments are linked to each other by short loops of hydrophilic amino acids that extend into or protrude from the polar surfaces of the membrane. Based on subsequent work in many laboratories, membrane biologists currently believe that all transmembrane proteins are anchored in the lipid bilayer by one or more transmembrane segments.

Recent Findings Further Refine Our Understanding of Membrane Structure

Almost from the moment Singer and Nicolson proposed it, the fluid mosaic model revolutionized the way scientists think about membrane structure. The model launched a new era in membrane research that not only confirmed the basic model but also refined and extended it. Moreover, our understanding of membrane structure continues to expand as new research findings further refine and modify the basic model.

Recent developments emphasize the concept that membranes are not homogenous, freely mixing structures. Both lipids and proteins are ordered within membranes, and this ordering often occurs in dynamic microdomains known as *lipid rafts* (Figure 7-3h), which we will discuss later in this chapter. In fact, most cellular processes that involve membranes depend critically on specific structural complexes of lipids and proteins within the membrane. This interaction between a membrane protein and a particular lipid can be highly specific and is often critical for proper membrane protein structure and function.

So, to understand membrane-associated processes, we need more than the original fluid mosaic model with lipids and proteins simply floating around randomly. But the fluid mosaic model is still basic to our understanding of membrane structure, so it is important for us to closely examine its essential features. These features include the chemistry, the asymmetric distribution, and the fluidity of membrane lipids; the relationship of membrane proteins to the bilayer; and the mobility of proteins within the bilayer. We will discuss each of these features in turn, focusing on both the supporting evidence and the implications of each feature for membrane function.

Membrane Lipids: The "Fluid" Part of the Model

We will begin our detailed look at membranes by considering membrane lipids, which are important components of the "fluid" part of the fluid mosaic model.

Membranes Contain Several Major Classes of Lipids

One feature of Singer and Nicolson's fluid mosaic model is that it retains the lipid bilayer initially proposed by Gorter and Grendel, though with a greater diversity and fluidity of lipid components than early investigators recognized. The main classes of membrane lipids are *phospholipids, glycolipids,* and *sterols.* **Figure 7-6** lists the main lipids in each of these categories and depicts the structures of several.

Phospholipids. As we already know from Chapter 3, the most abundant lipids found in membranes are the **phospholipids** (Figure 7-6a). Membranes contain many different kinds of phospholipids, including both the glycerol-based **phosphoglycerides** and the sphingosine-based **sphingolipids.** The most common phosphoglycerides are *phosphatidylcholine, phosphatidylethanolamine, phosphatidylserine,* and *phosphatidylinositol.* A common sphingolipid is *sphingomyelin* (Figure 7-6a), which is one of the main phospholipids of animal plasma membranes but is absent from the plasma membranes of plants and most bacteria. The kinds and relative proportions of phospholipids present vary significantly among membranes from different sources (**Figure 7-7**).

Glycolipids. As their name indicates, **glycolipids** are formed by adding carbohydrate groups to lipids. Some glycolipids are glycerol based, and others are derivatives of sphingosine and are therefore called *glycosphingolipids.* The most common examples are **cerebrosides** and **gangliosides.** Cerebrosides are called *neutral glycolipids* because each molecule has a single uncharged sugar as its head group—galactose, in the case of the galactocerebroside shown in Figure 7-6b. A ganglioside, on the other hand, always has an oligosaccharide head group that

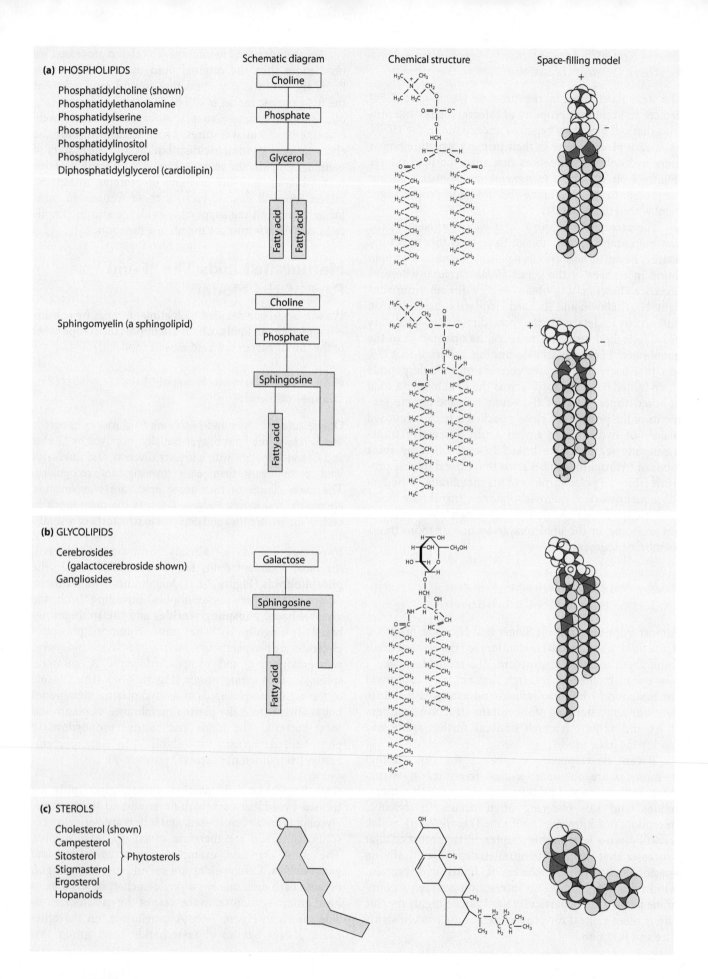

(a) PHOSPHOLIPIDS

Phosphatidylcholine (shown)
Phosphatidylethanolamine
Phosphatidylserine
Phosphatidylthreonine
Phosphatidylinositol
Phosphatidylglycerol
Diphosphatidylglycerol (cardiolipin)

Sphingomyelin (a sphingolipid)

(b) GLYCOLIPIDS

Cerebrosides
  (galactocerebroside shown)
Gangliosides

(c) STEROLS

Cholesterol (shown)
Campesterol
Sitosterol   Phytosterols
Stigmasterol
Ergosterol
Hopanoids

contains one or more negatively charged sialic acid residues and gives the molecule a net negative charge.

Cerebrosides and gangliosides are especially prominent in the membranes of brain and nerve cells. Gangliosides exposed on the surface of the plasma membrane also function as antigens recognized by antibodies in immune reactions, including those responsible for blood group interactions. The human ABO blood groups, for example, involve glycosphingolipids known as A antigen and B antigen that serve as specific cell surface markers of the different groups of red blood cells. Cells of blood type A have the A antigen, and cells of blood type B have the B antigen. Type AB blood cells have both antigen types, and type O blood cells have neither.

Several serious human diseases are known to result from impaired metabolism of glycosphingolipids. The best-known example is *Tay-Sachs disease*, which is caused by the absence of a lysosomal enzyme, β-*N*-acetylhexosaminidase A, that is responsible for one of the steps in ganglioside degradation. As a result of the genetic defect, gangliosides accumulate in the brain and other nervous tissue, leading to impaired nerve and brain function and eventually to paralysis, severe mental deterioration, and death.

Two common glycolipids that do not contain sphingosine are derivatives of glycerol that are abundant in plant and algal chloroplasts. Monogalactosyldiacylglycerol (MGDG) and digalactosyldiacylglycerol (DGDG) have either one or two galactose molecules, respectively, attached to a glycerol backbone that contains two polyunsaturated fatty acid groups (**Figure 7-8**). These two glycolipids constitute up to 75% of the total membrane lipids in leaves, where they are believed to play a role in stabilizing membrane proteins of the photosynthetic apparatus. Together, these two lipids are sometimes considered to be the most abundant glycolipids on Earth. Recently, several studies have shown that MGDG has an inhibitory effect on inflammation and cell proliferation in some human cells and tissues.

Sterols. Besides phospholipids and glycolipids, the membranes of most eukaryotic cells contain significant amounts of **sterols** (Figure 7-6c). The main sterol in animal cell membranes is **cholesterol,** which is necessary for maintaining and stabilizing membranes in our bodies by acting as a fluidity buffer. The membranes of plant cells contain small amounts of cholesterol and larger amounts of **phytosterols,** including campesterol, sitosterol, and stigmasterol. Fungal membranes contain a sterol known as ergosterol that is similar in structure to cholesterol but is not found in humans. Ergosterol is the target of antifungal

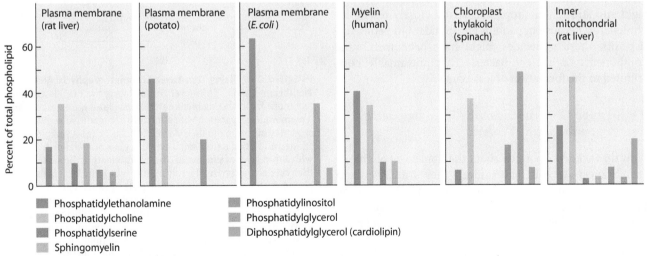

FIGURE 7-7 **Phospholipid Composition of Several Kinds of Membranes.** The relative abundance of different kinds of phospholipids in biological membranes varies greatly with the source of the membrane.

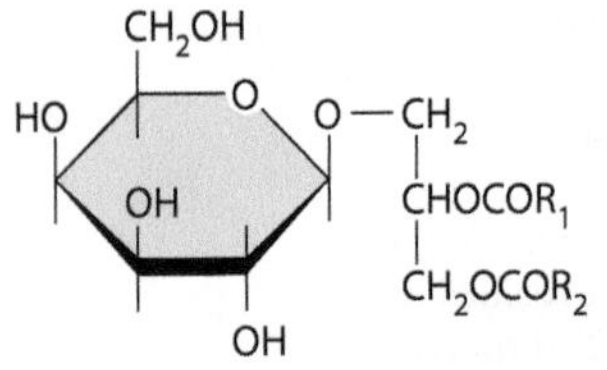

(a) Monogalactosyldiacylglycerol (MGDG)

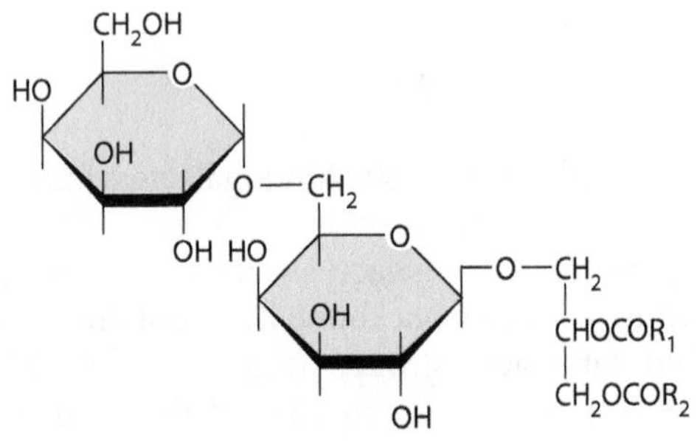

(b) Digalactosyldiacylglycerol (DGDG)

FIGURE 7-8 The Structure of Two Common Glycolipids.
MGDG and DGDG are abundant in plant cell membranes, and are similar in structure to the animal fat triacylglycerol (see Figure 3-27b). They have one or two galactose molecules attached to glycerol in addition to the two fatty acid groups (R_1 and R_2)

medications such as nystatin, which selectively kill fungi but do not harm human cells because they lack ergosterol.

Sterols are not found in the membranes of most bacterial cells. They are, however, found in the plasma membrane of *Mycoplasma* species, which, unlike most bacteria, lack a cell wall. Presumably these *Mycoplasma* bacteria have sterols to add stability and strength to the membrane. Sterols are also absent from the inner membranes of both mitochondria and chloroplasts, which are believed to be derived evolutionarily from the plasma membranes of bacterial cells. However, the plasma membranes of at least some bacteria contain sterol-like molecules called *hopanoids* that appear to substitute for sterols in membrane structure. The hopanoid molecule is rigid and strongly hydrophobic, and it closely resembles cholesterol. Because hopanoids are abundant in petroleum deposits, these molecules might have been membrane components of ancient bacteria that presumably contributed to the formation of fossil fuels.

Thin-Layer Chromatography Is an Important Technique for Lipid Analysis

How do we know so much about the lipid components of membranes? As you may suspect, they are difficult to isolate and study due to their hydrophobic nature. However, using nonpolar solvents such as acetone and chloroform, biologists and biochemists have been isolating, separating, and studying membrane lipids for more than a century. One important technique for the analysis of lipids is **thin-layer chromatography (TLC),** depicted schematically in **Figure 7-9.** This technique is used to separate different kinds of lipids based on their relative polarities.

In this procedure, the lipids are solubilized from a membrane preparation using a mixture of nonpolar organic solvents and separated using a glass plate coated with silicic acid, a polar compound that dries to form a thin film on the glass plate. A sample of the extract is applied to one end of the TLC plate by spotting the extract onto a small area called the *origin* (Figure 7-9a). After the solvent in the sample has evaporated, the edge of the plate is dipped into a solvent system that typically consists of chloroform, methanol, and water. As the solvent moves past the origin and up the plate by capillary action, the lipids are separated based on their polarity—that is, by their relative affinities for the polar silicic acid plate and the less polar solvent.

Nonpolar lipids such as cholesterol have little affinity for the polar silicic acid (the stationary phase) and therefore move up the plate with the solvent system (the mobile phase). Lipids that are more polar, such as phospholipids, interact more strongly with the silicic acid, which slows their movement. In this way the various lipids are separated progressively as the leading edge of the mobile phase continues to move up the plate. When the leading edge, or *solvent front,* approaches the top, the plate is removed from the solvent system and dried. The separated lipids are then recovered from the plate by dissolving each spot or band in a nonpolar solvent such as chloroform for identification and further study.

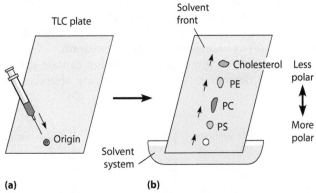

FIGURE 7-9 Using Thin-Layer Chromatography to Analyze Membrane Lipids. Thin-layer chromatography (TLC) is a useful technique for analyzing membrane lipids. Lipids are extracted from a membrane preparation with a mixture of organic solvents and separated according to their degree of polarity. **(a)** A sample is spotted and dried onto a small area of a glass or metal plate coated with a thin layer of silicic acid. **(b)** Components of the sample are then carried upward by the solvent into which the TLC plate is placed. As the solvent moves up the plate by capillary action, the lipids are separated according to their polarity: Less polar lipids such as cholesterol do not adhere strongly to the silicic acid and move further up the plate, while more polar lipids remain closer to the origin. The pattern shown is for lipids of the erythrocyte plasma membrane. The main components are cholesterol, phosphatidylethanolamine (PE), phosphatidylcholine (PC), and phosphatidylserine (PS).

Figure 7-9b shows the TLC pattern seen for the lipids of the erythrocyte plasma membrane. The main components of this membrane are cholesterol (25%) and phospholipids (55%), with phosphatidylethanolamine (PE), phosphatidylcholine (PC), and phosphatidylserine (PS) as the most prominent phospholipids. Other minor components, such as phosphatidylinositol and sphingolipids, are not shown. Control plates are run simultaneously using the same methods and small amounts of known lipids for comparison and identification.

Fatty Acids Are Essential to Membrane Structure and Function

Fatty acids are components of all membrane lipids except the sterols. They are essential to membrane structure because their long hydrocarbon tails form an effective hydrophobic barrier to the diffusion of polar solutes. Most fatty acids in membranes are between 12 and 20 carbon atoms in length, with 16- and 18-carbon fatty acids especially common. This size range appears to be optimal for bilayer formation because chains with fewer than 12 or more than 20 carbons are less able to form a stable bilayer. Thus, the thickness of membranes (about 6–8 nm, depending on the source) is dictated primarily by the chain length of the fatty acids required for bilayer stability.

In addition to differences in length, the fatty acids found in membrane lipids vary considerably in the presence and number of double bonds. **Table 7-2** shows the structures of several fatty acids that are especially common in membrane lipids. *Palmitate* and *stearate* are saturated fatty acids with 16 and 18 carbon atoms, respectively. *Oleate* and *linoleate* are 18-carbon unsaturated fatty acids with one and two double bonds, respectively. Other common unsaturated fatty acids in membranes are *linolenate,* with 18 carbons and three double bonds, and *arachidonate,* with 20 carbons and four double bonds (see Table 3-5, page 68). All unsaturated fatty acids in membranes are in the *cis* configuration, resulting in a sharp bend, or kink, in the hydrocarbon chain at every double bond. Due to the bent nature of their side chains, fatty acids with double bonds do not pack tightly in the membrane.

Membrane Asymmetry: Most Lipids Are Distributed Unequally Between the Two Monolayers

Are the various lipids in a membrane randomly distributed between the two monolayers of lipid that constitute the lipid bilayer? Chemical studies involving membranes derived from a variety of cell types have revealed that most lipids are unequally distributed between the two monolayers. This **membrane asymmetry** includes differences in both the kinds of lipids present and the degree of unsaturation of the fatty acids in the phospholipid molecules.

For example, most of the glycolipids present in the plasma membrane of an animal cell are restricted to the outer monolayer. As a result, their carbohydrate groups protrude from the outer membrane surface, where they are involved in various signaling and recognition events. Phosphatidylethanolamine, phosphatidylinositol, and phosphatidylserine, on the other hand, are more prominent in the inner monolayer, where they are involved in transmitting various kinds of signals from the plasma membrane to the interior of the cell.

Membrane asymmetry is established during membrane biogenesis by the insertion of different lipids, or different proportions of the various lipids, into each of the two monolayers. Once established, asymmetry tends to be maintained because the movement of lipids from one monolayer to the other requires their hydrophilic head groups to pass through the hydrophobic interior of the membrane—an event that is thermodynamically unfavorable. While such "flip-flop," or **transverse diffusion,** of membrane lipids does occur occasionally, it is relatively rare. For instance, a typical phospholipid molecule flip-flops less than once a week in a pure phospholipid bilayer. This movement contrasts strikingly with the **rotation** of phospholipid molecules about their long axis and with the **lateral diffusion** of phospholipids in the plane of the membrane, both of which occur freely, rapidly, and randomly. **Figure 7-10** illustrates these three types of lipid movements.

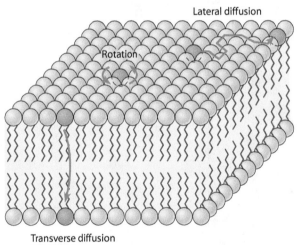

Lateral diffusion

Rotation

Transverse diffusion ("flip-flop")

FIGURE 7-10 Movements of Phospholipid Molecules Within Membranes. A phospholipid molecule is capable of three kinds of movement in a membrane: rotation about its long axis; lateral diffusion by exchanging places with neighboring molecules in the same monolayer; and transverse diffusion, or "flip-flop," from one monolayer to the other. In a pure phospholipid bilayer at 37°C, a typical lipid molecule exchanges places with neighboring molecules about 10 million times per second and can move laterally at a rate of about several micrometers per second. By contrast, an individual phospholipid molecule flip-flops from one layer to the other at a rate ranging from less than once a week in a pure phospholipid bilayer to once every few hours in some natural membranes. The more rapid movement in natural membranes is due to the presence of enzymes called phospholipid translocators, or flippases, that catalyze the transverse diffusion of phospholipid molecules from one monolayer to the other.

Name of Fatty Acid	Number of Carbon Atoms	Number of Double Bonds	Structural Formula	Space-Filling Model
Saturated				
Palmitate	16	0		
Stearate	18	0		
Unsaturated				
Oleate	18	1		
Linoleate	18	2		

While phospholipid flip-flop is relatively rare, it occurs more frequently in natural membranes than in artificial lipid bilayers. This is because some membranes—the smooth endoplasmic reticulum (ER), in particular—have proteins called **phospholipid translocators,** or **flippases,** that catalyze the flip-flop of membrane lipids from one monolayer to the other. Such proteins act only on specific kinds of lipids. For example, one of these proteins in the smooth ER membrane catalyzes the translocation of phosphatidylcholine from one side of the membrane to the other but does not recognize other phospholipids. This ability to move lipid molecules selectively from one side of the bilayer to the other contributes further to the asymmetric distribution of phospholipids across the membrane. The role of smooth ER in the synthesis and selective flip-flop of membrane phospholipids is a topic we will return to in Chapter 12.

The Lipid Bilayer Is Fluid

One of the most striking properties of membrane lipids is that rather than being fixed in place within the membrane, they form a fluid bilayer that permits lateral diffusion of membrane lipids as well as proteins. Lipid molecules move especially fast because they are much smaller than proteins. A typical phospholipid molecule, for example, has a molecular weight of about 800 and can travel the length of a bacterial cell (a few micrometers, in most cases) in one second or less! Proteins move much more slowly than lipids, partly because they are much larger molecules and partly due to their interactions with cytoskeletal proteins on the inside of the cell.

The lateral diffusion of membrane lipids can be demonstrated experimentally by a technique called **fluorescence recovery after photobleaching (Figure 7-11)**. The investigator *tags,* or labels, lipid molecules in the membrane of a living cell by covalently linking them to a fluorescent dye. A high-intensity laser beam is then used to bleach the dye in a tiny spot (a few square micrometers) on the cell surface. If the cell surface is examined immediately thereafter with a fluorescence microscope, a dark, nonfluorescent spot is seen on the membrane. Within seconds, however, the edges of the spot become fluorescent as bleached lipid molecules diffuse out of the laser-treated area and fluorescent lipid molecules from adjoining regions of the membrane diffuse in. Eventually, the spot is indistinguishable from the rest of the cell surface. This technique demonstrates that membrane lipids are in a fluid rather than a static state, and it provides a direct means of measuring the lateral movement of specific molecules.

Membranes Function Properly Only in the Fluid State

As you might guess, membrane fluidity changes with temperature, decreasing as the temperature drops and increasing as it rises. In fact, we know from studies with artificial lipid bilayers that every lipid bilayer has a characteristic **transition temperature** (T_m) at which it becomes fluid ("melts") when warmed from a solid gel-like state. This change in the state of the membrane is called a **phase transition,** and you have probably seen this yourself if you have ever accidentally left a stick of butter on the stove! To function properly, a membrane must be maintained in the fluid state—that is, at a temperature above its T_m value. At a temperature below the T_m value, all functions that depend on the mobility or conformational changes of membrane proteins will be impaired or disrupted. This includes such vital processes as transport of solutes across the membrane, detection and transmission of signals, and cell-to-cell communication (see Figure 7-2).

The technique of **differential scanning calorimetry** is one means of determining the transition temperature of a given membrane. This procedure monitors the uptake of

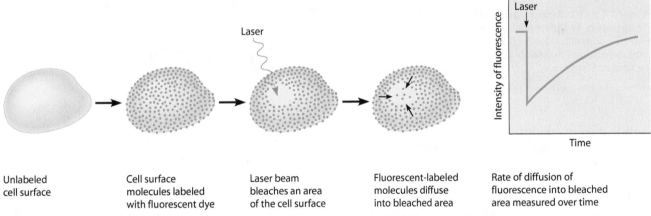

| Unlabeled cell surface | Cell surface molecules labeled with fluorescent dye | Laser beam bleaches an area of the cell surface | Fluorescent-labeled molecules diffuse into bleached area | Rate of diffusion of fluorescence into bleached area measured over time |

FIGURE 7-11 Measuring Lipid Mobility in Membranes by Fluorescence Recovery After Photobleaching. Membrane lipids are labeled with a fluorescent compound, and the fluorescence in a local area is then bleached by irradiating the cell with a laser beam. As fluorescent molecules from surrounding regions diffuse into the bleached area, fluorescence will reappear in the laser-bleached spot. Membrane fluidity is measured by determining the rate of this reappearance of fluorescence. Similar experiments can be carried out to measure the mobility of membrane proteins, as shown in Figure 7-28.

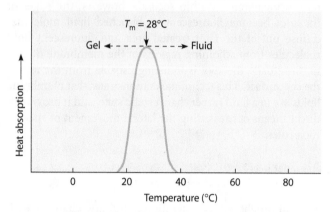

(a) Normal membrane. When the temperature of a typical membrane preparation is increased slowly in a calorimeter chamber, a peak of heat absorption marks the gel-to-fluid transition temperature, T_m.

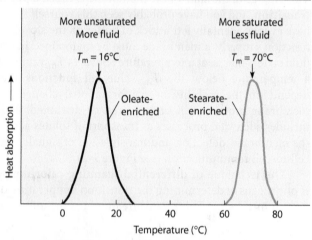

(b) Membranes enriched in unsaturated or saturated fatty acids. Membranes from cells grown in media enriched in the unsaturated fatty acid oleate (left) are more fluid than normal membranes (lower T_m). Membranes from cells grown in media enriched in the saturated fatty acid stearate (right) are less fluid than normal membranes (higher T_m).

FIGURE 7-12 Determination of Membrane Transition Temperature by Differential Scanning Calorimetry. These graphs show T_m determinations for **(a)** a normal membrane from a homeotherm and **(b)** membranes enriched in specific unsaturated or saturated fatty acids.

heat that occurs during the transition from one physical state to another—the gel-to-fluid transition, in the case of membranes. The membrane of interest is placed in a sealed chamber, the *calorimeter,* and the uptake of heat is measured as the temperature is slowly increased. The point of maximum heat absorption corresponds to the T_m (**Figure 7-12**).

Effects of Fatty Acid Composition on Membrane Fluidity. A membrane's fluidity depends primarily on the kinds of lipids it contains. Two properties of a membrane's lipid makeup are especially important in determining

fluidity: the length of the fatty acid side chains and their degree of unsaturation. Long-chain fatty acids have higher transition temperatures than do short-chain fatty acids, which means that membranes enriched in long-chain fatty acids tend to be less fluid.

For example, as the chain length of saturated fatty acids increases from 10 to 20 carbon atoms, the T_m rises from 32°C to 76°C, and the membrane thus becomes progressively less fluid (**Figure 7-13a**). The presence of unsaturation affects the T_m even more markedly. For fatty acids with 18 carbon atoms, the transition temperatures are 70, 16, 5, and −11°C for zero, one, two, and three double bonds, respectively (Figure 7-13b). As a result, membranes containing many unsaturated fatty acids tend to have lower transition temperatures and thus are more fluid than membranes with many saturated fatty acids. Figure 7-12b illustrates this increased fluidity for membranes enriched in oleate (18 carbons, one double bond) versus membranes enriched in stearate (18 carbons, saturated).

The effect of unsaturation on membrane fluidity is so dramatic because the kinks caused by double bonds in fatty acids prevent the hydrocarbon chains from fitting together snugly. Membrane lipids with saturated fatty

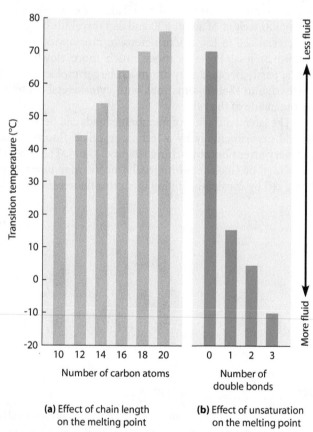

(a) Effect of chain length on the melting point

(b) Effect of unsaturation on the melting point

FIGURE 7-13 The Effect of Chain Length and the Number of Double Bonds on the Melting Point of Fatty Acids. The transition temperature of fatty acids **(a)** increases with chain length for saturated fatty acids, becoming less fluid with longer chains. **(b)** The transition temperature decreases dramatically with the number of double bonds for fatty acids with a fixed chain length, becoming more fluid as more double bonds are present.

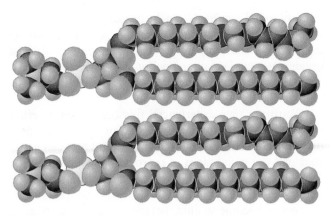

(a) Lipids with saturated fatty acids pack together well in the membrane

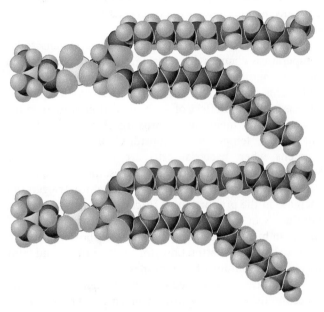

(b) Lipids with a mixture of saturated and unsaturated fatty acids do not pack together well in the membrane

FIGURE 7-14 The Effect of Unsaturated Fatty Acids on the Packing of Membrane Lipids. **(a)** Membrane phospholipids with no unsaturated fatty acids fit together tightly because the fatty acid chains are parallel to each other. **(b)** Membrane lipids with one or more unsaturated fatty acids do not fit together as tightly because the *cis* double bonds cause bends in the chains that interfere with packing. Each structure shown is a phosphatidylcholine molecule, with either two 18-carbon saturated fatty acids (stearate; part a) or two 18-carbon fatty acids, one saturated (stearate) and the other with one *cis* double bond (oleate; part b).

acids pack together tightly (**Figure 7-14a**), whereas lipids with unsaturated fatty acids do not (Figure 7-14b). The lipids of most plasma membranes contain fatty acids that vary in both chain length and degree of unsaturation. In fact, the variability is often intramolecular because membrane lipids commonly contain one saturated and one unsaturated fatty acid. This property helps to ensure that membranes are in the fluid state at physiological temperatures.

Most unsaturated fatty acids found in nature contain *cis* double bonds. In contrast, many commercially processed fats and hydrogenated oils contain significant numbers of *trans* double bonds. The *trans* double bond does not introduce as much of a bend in the fatty acid chain, as shown below (H atoms not shown):

cis configuration   *trans* configuration

Thus, in their overall shape and ability to pack together closely, *trans* fats resemble saturated fats more than *cis* unsaturated fats do. The presence of *trans* fats in membranes increases the transition temperature and decreases the membrane fluidity. As with saturated fats, consuming *trans* fats has been correlated with high blood cholesterol levels and increased risk of heart disease.

Effects of Sterols on Membrane Fluidity. For eukaryotic cells, membrane fluidity is also affected by the presence of sterols—mainly cholesterol in animal cell membranes and phytosterols in plant cell membranes. Sterols are prominent components in the membranes of many cell types. A typical animal cell, for example, contains large amounts of cholesterol—up to 50% of the total membrane lipid on a molar basis. Cholesterol molecules are usually found in both layers of the plasma membrane, but a given molecule is localized to one of the two layers (**Figure 7-15a**). The molecule orients itself in the layer with its single hydroxyl group—the only polar part of an otherwise hydrophobic molecule—close to the polar head group of a neighboring phospholipid molecule, where it can form a hydrogen bond (Figure 7-15b). The rigid hydrophobic steroid rings and the hydrocarbon side chain of the cholesterol molecule interact with the portions of adjacent hydrocarbon chains that are closest to the phospholipid head groups.

This intercalation of rigid cholesterol molecules into the membrane of an animal cell makes the membrane less fluid at higher temperatures than it would otherwise be. However, cholesterol also effectively prevents the hydrocarbon chains of phospholipids from fitting snugly together as the temperature is decreased, thereby reducing the tendency of membranes to gel upon cooling. Thus, cholesterol acts as a fluidity buffer: It has the moderating effect of *decreasing* membrane fluidity at temperatures above the T_m and *increasing* it at temperatures below the T_m. The sterols in the membranes of other eukaryotes and hopanoids in prokaryotes presumably function in the same way.

Besides their effects on membrane fluidity, sterols decrease the permeability of a lipid bilayer to ions and small polar molecules. They probably do so by filling in spaces between hydrocarbon chains of membrane phospholipids, thereby plugging small channels that ions and small molecules might otherwise pass through. In general, a lipid bilayer containing sterols is less permeable to ions and small molecules than is a bilayer lacking sterols.

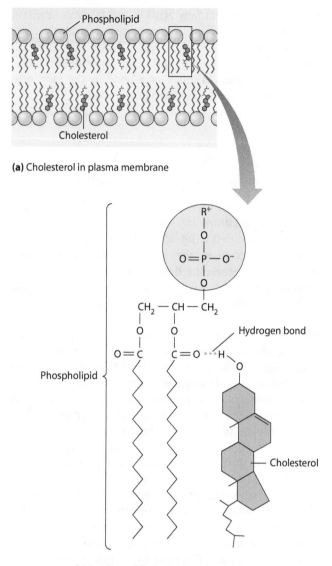

(a) Cholesterol in plasma membrane

(b) Bonding of cholesterol to phospholipid

FIGURE 7-15 Orientation of Cholesterol Molecules in a Lipid Bilayer. **(a)** Cholesterol molecules are present in both lipid monolayers in the plasma membranes of most animal cells, but a given molecule is localized to one of the two layers. **(b)** Each molecule orients itself in the lipid layer so that its single hydroxyl group is close to the polar head group of a neighboring phospholipid molecule. The hydroxyl group of cholesterol forms a hydrogen bond with the oxygen of the ester bond between the glycerol backbone and a fatty acid. The nonpolar steroid rings and hydrocarbon side group of the cholesterol molecule interact with adjacent hydrocarbon chains of the membrane phospholipids.

VIDEOS www.thecellplace.com *Space-filling model of cholesterol*

Most Organisms Can Regulate Membrane Fluidity

Most organisms, whether prokaryotic or eukaryotic, are able to regulate membrane fluidity, primarily by changing the lipid composition of the membranes. This ability is especially important for *poikilotherms*—organisms such as bacteria, fungi, protozoa, algae, plants, invertebrates, and

"cold-blooded" animals such as snakes that cannot regulate their own temperature. Because lipid fluidity decreases as the temperature falls, membranes of these organisms would gel upon cooling if the organism had no way to compensate for decreases in environmental temperature.

You may have experienced this compensating effect even though you are a *homeotherm,* or "warm-blooded" organism: On chilly days, your fingers and toes can get so cold that the membranes of sensory nerve endings cease to function, resulting in temporary numbness. At high temperatures, on the other hand, the lipid bilayers of poikilotherms become so fluid that they no longer serve as an effective permeability barrier. For example, most cold-blooded animals are paralyzed by temperatures that are much above 45°C because nerve cell membranes become so leaky to ions that overall nervous function becomes disabled.

Fortunately, most poikilotherms can compensate for temperature changes by altering the lipid composition of their membranes, thereby regulating membrane fluidity. This capability is called **homeoviscous adaptation** because the main effect of such regulation is to keep the viscosity of the membrane approximately the same despite changes in temperature. Consider, for example, what happens when bacterial cells are transferred from a warmer to a cooler environment. In some species of the genus *Micrococcus,* a drop in temperature triggers an increase in the proportion of 16-carbon versus 18-carbon fatty acids in the plasma membrane. This helps the cell maintain membrane fluidity because the shorter fatty acid chains have less attraction for each other, and this increases the fluidity of membranes.

In this case, the desired increase in membrane fluidity is accomplished by activating an enzyme that removes two terminal carbons from 18-carbon hydrocarbon tails. In other bacterial species, adaptation to environmental temperature involves an alteration in the extent of unsaturation of membrane fatty acids rather than in their length. In the common intestinal bacterium *Escherichia coli,* for example, a decrease in environmental temperature triggers the synthesis of a *desaturase* enzyme that introduces double bonds into the hydrocarbon chains of fatty acids. As these unsaturated fatty acids are incorporated into membrane phospholipids, they decrease the transition temperature of the membrane, thereby ensuring that the membrane remains fluid at the lower temperature.

Homeoviscous adaptation also occurs in yeasts and plants. In these organisms, temperature-related changes in membrane fluidity appear to depend on the increased solubility of oxygen in the cytoplasm at lower temperatures. Oxygen is a substrate for the desaturase enzyme system involved in the generation of unsaturated fatty acids. With more oxygen available at lower temperatures, unsaturated fatty acids are synthesized at a greater rate and membrane fluidity increases, thereby offsetting the temperature effect.

This capability has great agricultural significance because plants that can adapt in this way are cold hardy (resistant to chilling) and can thus be grown in colder environments. Animals such as amphibians and reptiles also adapt to lower temperatures by increasing the proportion of unsaturated fatty acids in their membranes. Furthermore, these animals can increase the proportion of cholesterol in the membrane, thereby decreasing the interaction between hydrocarbon chains and reducing the tendency of the membrane to gel.

Although homeoviscous adaptation is generally most relevant to poikilothermic organisms, it is also important to mammals that hibernate. As an animal enters hibernation, its body temperature often drops substantially—a decrease of more than 30°C for some rodents. The animal adapts to this change by incorporating a greater proportion of unsaturated fatty acids into membrane phospholipids as its body temperature falls.

Lipid Rafts Are Localized Regions of Membrane Lipids That Are Involved in Cell Signaling

Until recently, the lipid component of a membrane was regarded as uniformly fluid and relatively homogeneous within a given monolayer. In recent years, however, the discovery of localized regions of membrane lipids that sequester proteins involved in cell signaling has generated much excitement. These regions are called either *lipid microdomains* or, more popularly, **lipid rafts**—and represent areas of lateral heterogeneity within a membrane monolayer. Lipid rafts are dynamic structures that change in composition as individual lipids and proteins move in and out of them. They were first identified in the outer monolayer of the plasma membrane of eukaryotic cells but have since been detected in the inner monolayer also.

Lipid rafts in the outer membrane monolayer of animal cells are characterized by elevated levels of cholesterol and glycosphingolipids. The glycosphingolipids have longer and more saturated fatty acid tails than those seen in most other membrane lipids. Moreover, the phospholipids present in lipid rafts are more highly saturated than those in the surrounding membrane. These properties, plus the rigidity and hydrophobic nature of cholesterol, allow tight packing of the cholesterol and the hydrocarbon tails of the glycosphingolipids and the phospholipids. As a result, lipid rafts are thicker and less fluid than the rest of the membrane, thereby distinguishing them as discrete lipid microdomains. In addition, these regions are less able to be solubilized by nonionic detergents, a characteristic that facilitates their separation from the rest of the membrane components as intact structures for subsequent analysis.

Initial models of lipid raft formation proposed that localized regions of tightly-associated cholesterol and glycosphingolipid molecules attracted particular raft-associated proteins. Some of these raft-associated proteins are lipoproteins containing a fatty acid such as palmitate attached to a specific cysteine residue, a feature that may facilitate their targeting to lipid rafts. Recent proteomic studies of lipid raft regions have identified over 200 proteins enriched in lipid rafts. Some of these raft-associated proteins can capture and organize particular raft lipids, suggesting an active role of these proteins in lipid raft formation. In addition, lipid rafts contain actin-binding proteins, and some studies have suggested a role of the cytoskeleton in forming and organizing lipid rafts. Studies using inhibitors have shown that both depletion of cholesterol in cells and disruption of the actin cytoskeleton interfere with targeting of proteins to lipid rafts.

Much of the excitement surrounding lipid rafts relates to their role in the detection of, and responses to, extracellular chemical signals. For example, lipid rafts are involved in the transport of nutrients and ions across cell membranes, the binding of activated immune system cells to their microbial targets, and the transport of cholera toxin into intestinal cells. Many receptor proteins involved in the detection of external chemical signals are localized to the outer lipid monolayer of the plasma membrane. When a receptor binds its specific ligands, it can move into particular lipid rafts that are also located in the outer monolayer. Receptor-containing lipid rafts in the outer monolayer are thought to be coupled functionally to specific lipid rafts in the inner monolayer. Some lipid rafts contain specific *kinases,* enzymes that generate second messengers within the cell by catalyzing the phosphorylation of specific substances. In this way, signals that are detected by the receptor proteins in the outer monolayer can be transmitted to the interior of the cell by the functional links between the lipid rafts in the two membrane monolayers.

Closely related to lipid rafts in structure and perhaps in function are *caveolae* (Latin for "little caves"), which are small, flask-shaped invaginations of the plasma membrane of mammalian cells that were first observed more than 50 years ago. They contain the cholesterol-binding protein *caveolin*, which contributes to their curved morphology, and are enriched in cholesterol, sphingolipids, and lipid-anchored proteins. Proposed cellular roles for caveolae include participation in endocytosis and exocytosis, redox sensing, and regulation of airway function in the lungs. In addition, caveolae have been shown to contain proteins important in calcium signaling in heart muscle cells and have been discussed as potential targets for treatment of cardiovascular disease.

Membrane Proteins: The "Mosaic" Part of the Model

Having looked in some detail at the "fluid" aspect of the fluid mosaic model, we come now to the "mosaic" part. That may include lipid rafts and other lipid domains, but the main components of the membrane mosaic are the many membrane proteins as initially envisioned by Singer and Nicolson. We will look first at the confirming evidence that microscopists provided for the membrane as a mosaic of proteins and then consider the major classes of membrane proteins.

The Membrane Consists of a Mosaic of Proteins: Evidence from Freeze-Fracture Microscopy

Strong support for the fluid mosaic model came from studies in which artificial bilayers and natural membranes were prepared for electron microscopy by **freeze fracturing.** In this technique, a lipid bilayer or a membrane (or a cell containing membranes) is frozen quickly and then subjected to a sharp blow from a diamond knife. Because the nonpolar interior of the bilayer is the path of least resistance through the frozen specimen, the resulting fracture often follows the plane between the two layers of membrane lipid. As a result, the bilayer is split into its inner and outer monolayers, revealing the inner surface of each (**Figure 7-16a**).

Electron micrographs of membranes prepared in this way provide striking evidence that proteins are actually suspended within membranes. Whenever a fracture plane splits the membrane into its two layers, particles having the size and shape of globular proteins can be seen adhering to one or the other of the inner membrane surfaces, called the *E* (for *exoplasmic*) and *P* (for *protoplasmic*) *faces* (Figure 7-16b). Moreover, the abundance of such particles correlates well with the known protein content of the particular membrane under investigation. The electron micrographs in **Figure 7-17** illustrate this well: The erythrocyte plasma membrane has a rather low protein/lipid ratio (1.14; see Table 7-1) and a rather low density of particles when subjected to freeze fracture (Figure 7-17a), whereas a chloroplast membrane has a higher protein/lipid ratio (2.33) and a correspondingly higher density of intramembranous particles, especially on the inner lipid layer (Figure 7-17b).

Confirmation that the particles seen in this way really *are* proteins came from work by David Deamer and Daniel Branton, who used the freeze-fracture technique to examine artificial bilayers with and without added protein. Bilayers formed from pure phospholipids showed no

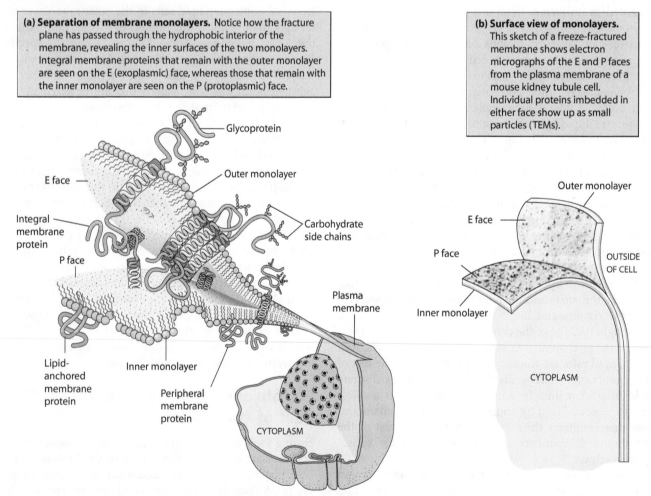

(a) Separation of membrane monolayers. Notice how the fracture plane has passed through the hydrophobic interior of the membrane, revealing the inner surfaces of the two monolayers. Integral membrane proteins that remain with the outer monolayer are seen on the E (exoplasmic) face, whereas those that remain with the inner monolayer are seen on the P (protoplasmic) face.

(b) Surface view of monolayers. This sketch of a freeze-fractured membrane shows electron micrographs of the E and P faces from the plasma membrane of a mouse kidney tubule cell. Individual proteins imbedded in either face show up as small particles (TEMs).

Glycoprotein
E face
Outer monolayer
Integral membrane protein
Carbohydrate side chains
P face
Plasma membrane
Lipid-anchored membrane protein
Inner monolayer
Peripheral membrane protein
CYTOPLASM

Outer monolayer
E face
P face
OUTSIDE OF CELL
Inner monolayer
CYTOPLASM

FIGURE 7-16 Freeze-Fracture Analysis of a Membrane. Sketches of a freeze-fractured membrane showing separation of the two lipid monolayers: **(a)** drawings of representative membrane components and **(b)** an electron micrograph of the surface of each monolayer.

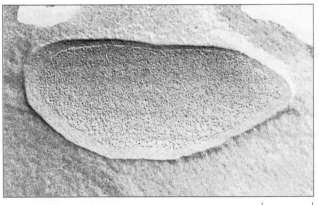

(a) Erythrocyte plasma membrane
0.5 μm

(b) Chloroplast membrane
0.2 μm

FIGURE 7-17 Membrane Proteins Visualized by Freeze-Fracture Electron Microscopy. Membrane proteins appear as discrete particles embedded within the lipid bilayer. The lower density of particles in **(a)** the erythrocyte membrane compared with **(b)** the chloroplast membrane agrees well with the protein/lipid ratios of the two membranes—1.14 and 2.33, respectively (TEMs).

evidence of particles on their interior surfaces (**Figure 7-18a**). When proteins were added to the artificial bilayers, however, particles similar to those seen in natural membranes were readily visible (Figure 7-18b).

Membranes Contain Integral, Peripheral, and Lipid-Anchored Proteins

Membrane proteins differ in their affinity for the hydrophobic interior of the membrane and therefore in the extent to which they interact with the lipid bilayer. That difference in affinity, in turn, determines how easy or difficult it is to extract a given protein from the membrane. Based on the conditions required to extract them—and thus, by extension, on the nature of their association with the lipid bilayer—membrane proteins fall into one of three categories: integral, peripheral, or lipid-anchored. We will

consider each of these in turn, referring in each case to the diagrams shown in **Figure 7-19**.

The plasma membrane of the human erythrocyte, shown in **Figure 7-20**, provides a cellular context for our discussion. This membrane has been one of the most widely studied since the time of Gorter and Grendel, due to the ready availability of red blood cells and how easily pure plasma membrane preparations can be made from them. We will refer to the erythrocyte plasma membrane at several points in the following discussion to note examples of different types of proteins and their roles within the membrane.

Integral Membrane Proteins. Most membrane proteins are amphipathic molecules possessing one or more hydrophobic regions that exhibit an affinity for the hydrophobic interior of the lipid bilayer. These proteins

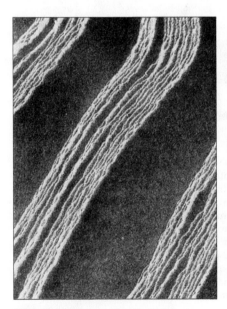

(a) Artificial bilayers without proteins

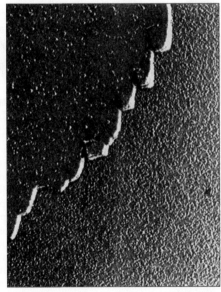

(b) Artificial bilayers with proteins
0.1 μm

FIGURE 7-18 Freeze-Fracture Comparison of Lipid Bilayers With and Without Added Proteins. This figure compares the appearance by freeze-fracture electron microscopy of **(a)** artificial lipid bilayers without proteins and **(b)** artificial bilayers with proteins added. The white lines in the artificial membranes of part a represent individual lipid bilayers in a multilayered specimen, and the gray regions show where single bilayers have split to reveal smooth surfaces. In contrast, the artificial membrane of part b shows large numbers of globular particles in the fracture surface. These are the proteins that were added to the membrane preparation (TEMs).

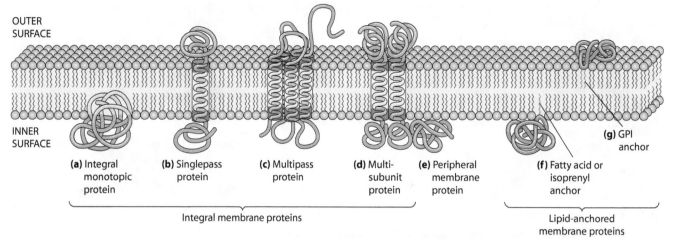

FIGURE 7-19 The Main Classes of Membrane Proteins. Membrane proteins are classified according to their mode of attachment to the membrane. Integral membrane proteins **(a–d)** contain one or more hydrophobic regions that are embedded within the lipid bilayer. **(a)** A few integral proteins appear to be embedded in the membrane on only one side of the bilayer (integral monotopic proteins). However, most integral proteins are transmembrane proteins that span the lipid bilayer either **(b)** once (singlepass proteins) or **(c)** multiple times (multipass proteins). Multipass proteins may consist of either a single polypeptide, as in part c, or **(d)** several associated polypeptides (multisubunit proteins). **(e)** Peripheral membrane proteins are too hydrophilic to penetrate into the membrane but are attached to the membrane by electrostatic and hydrogen bonds that link them to adjacent membrane proteins or to phospholipid head groups. Lipid-anchored proteins **(f–g)** are hydrophilic and do not penetrate into the membrane; they are covalently bound to lipid molecules that are embedded in the lipid bilayer. **(f)** Proteins on the inner surface of the membrane are usually anchored by either a fatty acid or an isoprenyl group. **(g)** On the outer membrane surface, the most common lipid anchor is glycosylphosphatidylinositol (GPI).

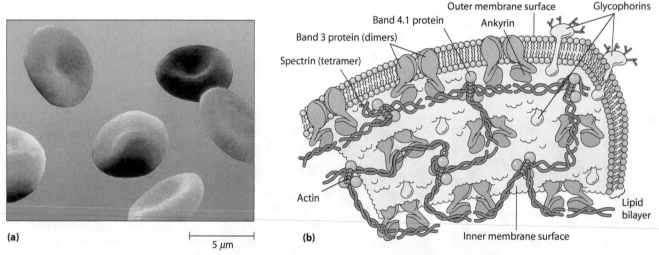

FIGURE 7-20 Structural Features of the Erythrocyte Plasma Membrane. **(a)** An erythrocyte is a small, disk-shaped cell with a diameter of about 7 μm. A mammalian erythrocyte contains no nucleus or other organelles, which makes it easy to obtain very pure plasma membrane preparations without contamination by organelle membranes, as often occurs with plasma membrane preparations from other cell types. **(b)** The erythrocyte plasma membrane as seen from inside the cell. The membrane has a relatively simple protein composition. The two major integral membrane proteins are glycophorin and an anion exchange protein known from its electrophoretic mobility as band 3. The membrane is anchored to the underlying cytoskeleton by long, slender strands of tetrameric spectrin, $(\alpha\beta)_2$, that are linked to glycophorin molecules by band 4.1 protein and to band 3 protein by ankyrin, another peripheral membrane protein. The free ends of adjacent spectrin tetramers are held together by short chains of actin and band 4.1. Not shown is another protein, band 4.2, that assists ankyrin in linking spectrin to band 3 protein. For the electrophoretic fractionation of these proteins, see Figure 7-22.

are called **integral membrane proteins** because their hydrophobic regions are embedded within the membrane interior in a way that makes these molecules difficult to remove from membranes. However, such proteins also have one or more hydrophilic regions that extend outward from the membrane into the aqueous phase on one or both sides of the membrane. Because of their affinity for the lipid bilayer, integral membrane proteins are difficult to isolate and study by standard protein purification techniques, most of which are designed for water-soluble proteins. Treatment with a detergent that disrupts the lipid bilayer is usually necessary to solubilize and extract integral membrane proteins.

A few integral membrane proteins are known to be embedded in, and therefore to protrude from, only one side of the bilayer. These are called **integral monotopic proteins** (Figure 7-19a). However, most integral membrane proteins are **transmembrane proteins,** which means that they span the membrane and have hydrophilic regions protruding from the membrane on both sides. Such proteins cross the membrane either once (*singlepass proteins;* Figure 7-19b) or several times (*multipass proteins;* Figure 7-19c). Some multipass proteins consist of a single polypeptide (Figure 7-19c), whereas others have two or more polypeptides (*multisubunit proteins;* Figure 7-19d).

Most transmembrane proteins are anchored to the lipid bilayer by one or more hydrophobic **transmembrane segments,** one for each time the protein crosses the bilayer. In most cases, the polypeptide chain appears to span the membrane in an α-helical conformation consisting of about 20–30 amino acid residues, most—sometimes even all—of which have hydrophobic R groups. In some multipass proteins, however, several transmembrane segments are arranged as a β sheet in the form of a closed β sheet—the so-called *β barrel.* This structure is especially prominent in a group of pore-forming transmembrane proteins called *porins* that are found in the outer membrane of many bacteria as well as chloroplasts and mitochondria. Regardless of their conformation, transmembrane segments are usually separated along the primary structure of the protein by hydrophilic sequences that protrude or loop out on the two sides of the membrane. Loop regions containing positively charged amino acid residues are more likely to be found on the cytoplasmic side of the membrane. This "positive-inside rule" helps to ensure that all molecules of a particular transmembrane protein are oriented the same way.

Singlepass membrane proteins have just one transmembrane segment, with a hydrophilic carboxyl (C-) terminus extending out of the membrane on one side and a hydrophilic amino (N-) terminus protruding on the other side. Depending on the particular protein, the C-terminus may protrude on either side of the membrane. An example of a singlepass protein is *glycophorin,* a prominent protein in the erythrocyte plasma membrane (Figure 7-20b). Glycophorin is oriented in the membrane so that its C-terminus is on the inner surface of the membrane and its N-terminus is on the outer surface (**Figure 7-21a**).

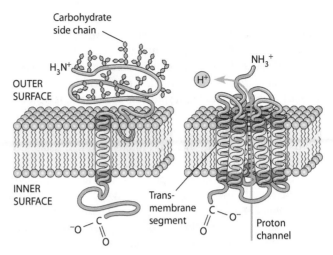

(a) Glycophorin **(b)** Bacteriorhodopsin

FIGURE 7-21 The Structures of Two Integral Membrane Proteins. (a) Glycophorin is a singlepass integral membrane protein in the erythrocyte plasma membrane. Its α-helical transmembrane segment consists entirely of hydrophobic amino acids. The N-terminus protrudes on the outer surface, the C-terminus on the cytoplasmic surface. Glycophorin is a glycoprotein, with 16 carbohydrate chains attached to its outer surface. (b) Bacteriorhodopsin is a multipass integral membrane protein in the plasma membrane of *Halobacterium.* Its seven transmembrane segments, which account for about 70% of its 248 amino acids, are organized into a proton channel. The C- and N-termini of the protein have short hydrophilic segments that protrude on the inner and outer surfaces of the plasma membrane, respectively. Short hydrophilic segments also link each of the transmembrane segments.

Multipass membrane proteins have several transmembrane segments, ranging from 2 or 3 to 20 or more such segments. An example of a multipass protein in the erythrocyte plasma membrane is a dimeric transport protein called *band 3 protein* (also known as the *anion exchange protein*). Each of its two polypeptides spans the lipid bilayer at least six times, with both the C-terminus and the N-terminus on the same side of the membrane. Current models of the dimeric protein assume a total of 12 transmembrane segments.

One of the best-studied examples of a multipass protein is bacteriorhodopsin, the plasma membrane protein that serves halobacteria as a proton pump (see Figure 7-3g). Its three-dimensional structure was reported by Unwin and Henderson in 1975, based on electron microscopy. Bacteriorhodopsin turned out to have seven α-helical, membrane-spanning segments, each corresponding to a sequence of about 20 hydrophobic amino acids in the primary structure of the protein (Figure 7-21b). The seven transmembrane segments are positioned in the membrane to form a channel and thereby to facilitate the light-activated pumping of protons across the membrane.

Peripheral Membrane Proteins. In contrast to integral membrane proteins, some membrane-associated proteins lack discrete hydrophobic sequences and therefore do not penetrate into the lipid bilayer. Instead, these **peripheral**

membrane proteins are bound to membrane surfaces through weak electrostatic forces and hydrogen bonding with the hydrophilic portions of integral proteins and perhaps with the polar head groups of membrane lipids (Figure 7-19e). The presence of aromatic amino acid residues, particularly the hydrophobic tryptophan side chain, is believed to play a role in anchoring proteins at the membrane-water interface. Peripheral proteins are more readily removed from membranes than integral proteins and can usually be extracted by changing the pH or ionic strength.

The main peripheral proteins of the erythrocyte plasma membrane are *spectrin*, *ankyrin*, and a protein called *band 4.1* (see Figure 7-20b). These proteins are bound to the inner surface of the plasma membrane, where they form a skeletal meshwork that supports the plasma membrane and helps maintain the shape of the erythrocyte (see Figure 7-20a).

Lipid-Anchored Membrane Proteins. When Singer and Nicolson initially proposed the fluid mosaic model, they regarded all membrane proteins as either peripheral or integral membrane proteins. However, we now recognize a third class of proteins that are neither specifically peripheral nor integral but have some of the characteristics of both. The polypeptide chains of these **lipid-anchored membrane proteins** are located on one of the surfaces of the lipid bilayer but are covalently bound to lipid molecules embedded within the bilayer (Figure 7-19, parts f and g).

Several mechanisms are employed for attaching lipid-anchored proteins to membranes. Proteins bound to the inner surface of the plasma membrane are attached by covalent linkage either to a fatty acid or to an isoprene derivative called an *isoprenyl* group (Figure 7-19f). In the case of **fatty acid-anchored membrane proteins,** the protein is synthesized in the cytosol and then covalently attached to a saturated fatty acid embedded within the membrane bilayer, usually *myristic acid* (14 carbons) or *palmitic acid* (16 carbons). **Isoprenylated membrane proteins,** on the other hand, are synthesized as soluble cytosol proteins before being modified by addition of multiple 5-carbon isoprenyl groups (see Figure 3-27f), usually in the form of a 15-carbon *farnesyl* group or 20-carbon *geranylgeranyl* group. After attachment, the farnesyl or geranylgeranyl group is inserted into the lipid bilayer of the membrane.

Many lipid-anchored proteins attached to the external surface of the plasma membrane are covalently linked to *glycosylphosphatidylinositol (GPI)*, a glycolipid found in the outer monolayer of the plasma membrane (Figure 7-19g). Lipid rafts are enriched in these **GPI-anchored membrane proteins,** which are made in the endoplasmic reticulum as singlepass transmembrane proteins that subsequently have their transmembrane segments cleaved off and replaced by GPI anchors. The proteins are then transported from the ER to the exterior of the plasma membrane. Once at the cell surface, GPI-anchored proteins can be released from the membrane by the enzyme *phospholipase C,* which is specific for phosphatidylinositol linkages.

Proteins Can Be Separated by SDS–Polyacrylamide Gel Electrophoresis

Before continuing our discussion of membrane proteins, it is useful to consider briefly how membrane proteins are isolated and studied. We will look first at the general problem of solubilizing and extracting proteins from membranes, and we will then learn about an electrophoretic technique that is very useful in the fractionation and characterization of proteins.

Isolation of Membrane Proteins. A major challenge to protein chemists has been the difficulty of isolating and studying membrane proteins, many of which are hydrophobic. Peripheral membrane proteins are in general fairly straightforward to isolate because they are loosely bound to the membrane by weak electrostatic interactions and hydrogen bonding with either the hydrophilic portions of integral membrane proteins or the polar head groups of membrane lipids. Peripheral proteins can be extracted from the membrane by changes in pH or ionic strength. Peripheral membrane proteins can also be solubilized by the use of a chelating (cation-binding) agent to remove calcium or by addition of urea, which breaks hydrogen bonds. Lipid-anchored proteins are similarly amenable to isolation, though with the requirement that the covalent bond to the lipid must first be cleaved. Once extracted from the membrane, most peripheral and lipid-anchored proteins are sufficiently hydrophilic to be purified and studied with techniques commonly used by protein chemists.

Integral membrane proteins, on the other hand, are difficult to isolate from membranes, especially in a manner that preserves their biological activity. In most cases, these proteins can be solubilized only by using detergents that disrupt hydrophobic interactions and dissolve the lipid bilayer. As we will now see, the use of strong ionic detergents such as *sodium dodecyl sulfate (SDS)* allows integral membrane proteins not just to be isolated, but to be fractionated and analyzed by the technique of electrophoresis. However, the use of such strong detergents can affect the function of the protein, and may be suitable only for analytical purposes.

SDS–Polyacrylamide Gel Electrophoresis. Cells contain thousands of different macromolecules that must be separated from one another before the properties of individual components can be investigated. One of the most common approaches for separating molecules from each other is **electrophoresis,** a group of related techniques that utilize an electrical field to separate charged molecules. How quickly any given molecule moves during electrophoresis depends upon its charge as well as its size. Electrophoresis can be carried out using various support media, such as paper, cellulose acetate, starch, polyacrylamide, or agarose (a polysaccharide obtained from seaweed). Of these media, gels made of polyacrylamide or agarose provide the best separation and are most commonly employed for the electrophoresis of nucleic acids and proteins.

When electrophoresis is used to study membrane proteins, membrane fragments are first solubilized with the anionic detergent SDS, which disrupts most protein-protein and protein-lipid associations. The proteins denature, unfolding into stiff polypeptide rods that cannot refold because their surfaces are coated with negatively charged detergent molecules. The solubilized, SDS-coated polypeptides are then layered on the top of a polyacrylamide gel. An electrical potential is then applied across the gel, such that the bottom of the gel is the positively charged anode (**Figure 7-22**). Because the polypeptides are coated with negatively charged SDS molecules, they migrate down the gel toward the anode. The polyacrylamide gel can be thought of as a fine meshwork that

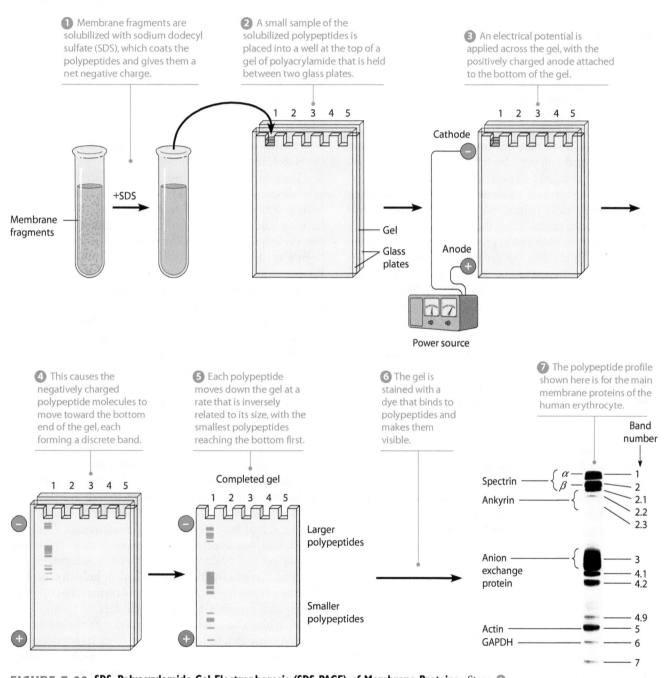

FIGURE 7-22 SDS–Polyacrylamide Gel Electrophoresis (SDS-PAGE) of Membrane Proteins. Steps ❶ through ❻ show the general procedure used to separate membrane proteins using SDS-PAGE. Following step ❶, the procedure is the same as is used for soluble, nonmembrane proteins. Step ❼ shows the individual polypeptides separated from an erythrocyte membrane preparation. The separated bands of protein were initially identified using sequential numbers, as shown on the right. We now know the identity of some of these separated proteins, such as glyceraldehyde-3-phosphate dehydrogenase (GAPDH), shown on the left.

impedes the movement of large molecules more than that of small molecules. As a result, polypeptides move down the gel at a rate that is inversely related to the logarithm of their size.

When the smallest polypeptides approach the bottom of the gel, the process is terminated. The gel is then stained with a dye that binds to polypeptides and makes them visible. (*Coomassie brilliant blue* is commonly used for this purpose.) The particular polypeptide profile shown in Figure 7-22 is for the membrane proteins of human erythrocytes, most of which we have already encountered (see Figure 7-20b). Typically, a set of purified proteins of known molecular weights is run in one lane of the gel alongside the other samples to determine the molecular weights of the polypeptides in the samples.

A more advanced form of electrophoresis known as two-dimensional (2D) SDS-PAGE is often used to separate polypeptides based on both charge and size. Proteins are separated in a thin, nondenaturing, tubular gel so that positively charged polypeptides move to one end of the gel and negatively charged polypeptides move to the other end. Neutral polypeptides will be found in the center. The more charge an individual polypeptide has, the further it will be found from the center. Then, the entire gel is placed at the top of a denaturing SDS-PAGE gel, and proteins move out of the tubular gel and down the denaturing gel based on their molecular sizes. After staining, the individual polypeptides are seen as a set of spots scattered throughout the gel.

Following electrophoresis, individual polypeptides can be detected and identified using a procedure known as **Western blotting.** In this procedure, the polypeptides in a standard SDS-PAGE gel or a 2D SDS-PAGE gel are transferred directly to a nylon or nitrocellulose membrane that is placed flat against the gel. An electric field is used to transfer the proteins from the gel to the membrane, where they remain in the same relative positions that they occupied in the gel. By using labeled antibodies that are known to bind to specific polypeptides, researchers can identify and quantify the polypeptides from the gel. Western blotting is very useful in determining which proteins are present in or on a particular cell. This technique can be used, for example, to identify certain immune system cells or specific types of cancer cells.

Determining the Three-Dimensional Structure of Membrane Proteins Is Becoming More Feasible

Determining the three-dimensional structure of integral membrane proteins has been difficult for many years, primarily because these proteins are generally difficult to isolate and purify due to their hydrophobicity. However, they are proving increasingly amenable to study by *X-ray crystallography*, which determines the structure of proteins that can be isolated in crystalline form. For the many membrane proteins for which no crystal structure is available, an alternative approach called *hydropathic analysis* can be used, provided that the protein or its gene can at least be isolated and sequenced. We will look briefly at each of these techniques.

X-Ray Crystallography. **X-ray crystallography** is widely used to determine the three-dimensional structure of proteins. A description of this technique is included in the Appendix (see page A-27). The difficulty of isolating integral membrane proteins in crystalline form virtually excluded these proteins from crystallographic analysis for many years. The first success was reported by Hartmut Michel, Johann Deisenhofer, and Robert Huber, who crystallized the photosynthetic reaction center from the purple bacterium, *Rhodopseudomonas viridis,* and determined its molecular structure by X-ray crystallography. Based on their detailed three-dimensional structure of the protein, these investigators also provided the first detailed look at how pigment molecules are arranged to capture light energy. In recognition of this work, Michel, Deisenhofer, and Huber shared the Nobel Prize for Chemistry in 1988.

Despite this breakthrough, the application of X-ray crystallography to the study of integral membrane proteins progressed very slowly until the late 1990s, particularly at the level of resolution required to identify transmembrane helices. More recently, however, there has been a veritable explosion of X-ray crystallographic data for integral membrane proteins. According to the data assembled by Stephen White and his colleagues at the University of California, Irvine, there were only 18 proteins whose three-dimensional structures had been determined by 1997. Since then, approximately 200 proteins have been added to the list. Initially, most of these proteins were from bacterial sources, reflecting the relative ease with which membrane proteins are able to be isolated from microorganisms. Increasingly, however, membrane proteins from eukaryotic sources are proving amenable to X-ray crystallographic analysis as well.

Hydropathy Analysis. For the many integral membrane proteins that have not yet yielded to X-ray crystallography, the likely number and locations of transmembrane segments can often be inferred, provided that the protein or its gene can at least be isolated and sequenced. Once the amino acid sequence of a membrane protein is known, the number and positions of transmembrane segments can be inferred from a **hydropathy** (or **hydrophobicity**) **plot**, as shown in **Figure 7-23**. Such a plot is constructed by using a computer program to identify clusters of hydrophobic amino acids. The amino acid sequence of the protein is scanned through a series of "windows," each representing a region of about 10 amino acids, with each successive window one amino acid further along in the sequence.

Based on the known hydrophobicity values for the various amino acids, a **hydropathy index** is calculated for each successive window by averaging the hydrophobicity values of the amino acids in the window. (By convention, hydrophobic amino acids have positive hydropathy values

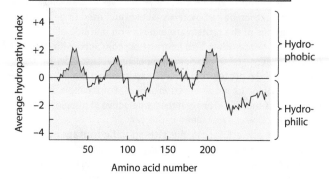

(a) Hydropathy plot of connexin. The hydropathy index on the vertical axis is a numerical measure of the relative hydrophobicity of successive segments of the polypeptide chain based on its amino acid sequence.

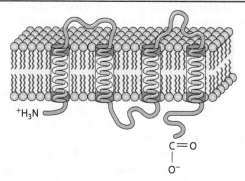

(b) Transmembrane structure of connexin. Connexin has four distinct hydrophobic regions, which correspond to the four α-helical segments that span the plasma membrane.

FIGURE 7-23 Hydropathy Analysis of an Integral Membrane Protein. A hydropathy plot is a means of representing hydrophobic regions (positive values) and hydrophilic regions (negative values) along the length of a protein. This example uses hydropathy data to analyze the plasma membrane protein *connexin*.

and hydrophilic residues have negative values.) The hydropathy index is then plotted against the positions of the windows along the sequence of the protein. The resulting hydropathy plot predicts how many membrane-spanning regions are present in the protein, based on the number of positive peaks. The hydropathy plot shown in Figure 7-23a is for a plasma membrane protein called *connexin*. The plot shows four positive peaks and therefore predicts that connexin has four stretches of hydrophobic amino acids and hence four transmembrane segments, as shown in Figure 7-23b.

Molecular Biology Has Contributed Greatly to Our Understanding of Membrane Proteins

Membrane proteins have not yielded as well as other proteins to biochemical techniques, mainly because of the problems involved in isolating and purifying hydrophobic proteins in physiologically active form. Procedures such as

SDS-PAGE and hydropathy analysis have certainly been useful, as have labeling techniques involving radioisotopes or fluorescent antibodies, which we will discuss later in the chapter. Within the past three decades, however, the study of membrane proteins has been revolutionized by the techniques of molecular biology, especially DNA sequencing and recombinant DNA technology. DNA sequencing makes it possible to deduce the amino acid sequence of a protein without the need to isolate the protein in pure form for amino acid sequencing.

In addition, sequence comparisons between proteins often reveal evolutionary and functional relationships that might not otherwise have been appreciated. DNA pieces can also be used as probes to identify and isolate sequences that encode related proteins. Moreover, the DNA sequence for a particular protein can be altered at specific nucleotide positions to determine the effects of changing specific amino acids on the activity of the mutant protein it codes for. **Box 7A** describes these exciting developments in more detail.

Membrane Proteins Have a Variety of Functions

What functions do membrane proteins perform? Most of what we summarized about membrane function at the beginning of the chapter is relevant here because the functions of a membrane are really just those of its chemical components, especially its proteins.

Some of the proteins in membranes are *enzymes*, which accounts for the localization of specific functions to specific membranes. As we will see in coming chapters, each of the organelles in a eukaryotic cell is in fact characterized by its own distinctive set of membrane-bound enzymes. We encountered an example earlier when we noted the association of glucose-6-phosphatase with the ER. Another example is glyceraldehyde-3-phosphate dehydrogenase (GAPDH), an enzyme involved in the catabolism of blood glucose. GAPDH is a peripheral plasma membrane protein in erythrocytes and other cell types (see Figure 7-22, step ⑦). Closely related to enzymes in their function are *electron transport proteins* such as the cytochromes and iron-sulfur proteins that are involved in oxidative processes in mitochondria, chloroplasts, and the plasma membranes of prokaryotic cells.

Other membrane proteins function in solute transport across membranes. These include *transport proteins*, which facilitate the movement of nutrients such as sugars and amino acids across membranes, and *channel proteins*, which provide hydrophilic passageways through otherwise hydrophobic membranes. Also in this category are *transport ATPases*, which use the energy of ATP to pump ions across membranes.

Numerous membrane proteins are *receptors* involved in recognizing and mediating the effects of specific chemical signals that impinge on the surface of the cell. Hormones, neurotransmitters, and growth-promoting substances are examples of chemical signals that interact with specific

Because membrane proteins mediate a remarkable variety of cellular functions, cell biologists are very interested in these proteins. The study of membrane proteins has begun to yield definitive insights and answers as biochemical techniques commonly used to isolate and analyze cellular proteins have been applied to membrane proteins. This chapter describes several such applications, including SDS–polyacrylamide gel electrophoresis, hydropathy analysis, and procedures for labeling membrane proteins with radioactivity or fluorescent antibodies. Two other biochemical approaches that can be used to study membrane proteins are affinity labeling and membrane reconstitution.

Affinity labeling utilizes radioactive molecules that bind to specific proteins because of known functions of the proteins. For example, *cytochalasin B* is known to be a potent inhibitor of glucose transport. Membranes that have been exposed to radioactive cytochalasin B are therefore likely to contain radioactivity bound specifically to protein molecules involved in glucose transport.

Membrane reconstitution involves the formation of artificial membranes from specific purified components. In this approach, proteins are extracted from membranes with detergent solutions and separated individually. The purified proteins are then mixed together with phospholipids to form liquid-filled membrane vesicles called *liposomes* that can be "loaded" with particular molecules. These reconstituted vesicles can then be tested for their ability to carry out specific membrane protein functions, such as nutrient transport or cell-to-cell communication.

Despite some success with these approaches, membrane biologists are often stymied in their attempts to isolate, purify, and study membrane proteins. Biochemical techniques that work well with soluble proteins are not often useful with hydrophobic proteins. However, the study of membrane proteins has been revolutionized by the techniques of molecular biology, especially *DNA sequencing* and *recombinant DNA technology*. We will consider these techniques in detail in Chapter 18, but we need not wait until then to appreciate the enormous impact of molecular biology on the study of membranes and membrane proteins. **Figure 7A-1** summarizes several approaches that have proven especially powerful for both membrane and nonmembrane proteins.

Vital to these approaches is the isolation (cloning) of a gene or gene fragment that encodes all or part of a specific protein (Figure 7A-1, top). A top priority is to determine the nucleotide sequence of the cloned gene ❶. *DNA sequencing* is one of the triumphs of molecular biology. Determining the nucleotide sequence of a DNA molecule is now far easier than determining the amino acid sequence of the protein it encodes. Moreover, most of the sequencing procedure is carried out quickly and automatically by DNA sequencing machines. Once the DNA for a particular protein has been sequenced, the predicted *amino acid sequence* of the protein can be deduced by using the genetic code (see Figure 21-6) ❷. The predicted amino acid sequence can then be studied using *hydropathy analysis* (see Figure 7-23) to identify likely transmembrane segments of the protein ❸.

Knowing the amino acid sequence of the protein also allows the investigator to prepare synthetic peptides that correspond to specific segments of the protein ❹. Antibodies made against these peptides can then be radioactively labeled and used to determine which regions of the protein are exposed on one side of the membrane or the other. This information, combined with the hydropathy data, often provides compelling evidence for the likely structure of the protein and its orientation within the membrane—and possibly for its mode of action as well. For example, the structure of the CFTR protein that is defective in people with cystic fibrosis was determined in this way.

Another powerful technique, **site-specific mutagenesis,** is used to examine the effect of changing specific amino acids in a protein ❺. The DNA sequence encoding the protein is altered by changing the nucleotides corresponding to a particular amino acid. The mutant DNA is then introduced into living cells, which then synthesize a mutant protein having the altered amino acid. Then, the functional properties of this mutant protein can be studied to determine whether the amino acid is required for proper protein function.

A gene or gene segment can be used as a *DNA probe* to isolate similar DNA sequences ❻. DNA identified in this way is likely to encode proteins similar to the protein that the probe DNA codes for. Such proteins are likely to be related to each other both in evolutionary origin and in their mechanisms of action.

Thanks to the advent of techniques for sequencing whole genomes (discussed in Chapter 18), we can now search whole genomes for nucleotide sequences similar to those already known to encode specific proteins. In this way, various *families,* or groups, of related proteins can be identified. The use of computerized databases, such as GenBank at the National Institutes of Health, has been extremely valuable in suggesting roles for proteins based entirely on their gene sequences.

From studies based on these and other techniques, we now know that cells in the human body need more than 30 families of membrane proteins to facilitate the transport of the great variety of solutes that must be moved across membranes. Each member of such a family may be present in a variety of *isoforms* that differ in such properties as time of expression during development, tissue distribution, or location within the cell. Perhaps it is not so surprising, then, to learn that the genes known to encode transport proteins represent about 10% of the human genome!

Most of these molecular approaches are indirect in the sense that they allow scientists to deduce properties and functions of proteins rather than proving them directly. Still, these techniques are powerful tools that have already significantly expanded our understanding of membrane proteins. And certainly in the future, these and newer techniques of molecular biology, such as proteomics, will continue to revolutionize the study of membranes and their proteins.

FIGURE 7A-1 Application of Molecular Biology Techniques to the Study of Membrane Proteins. These techniques are invaluable for studying membrane proteins, which are often very difficult to isolate.

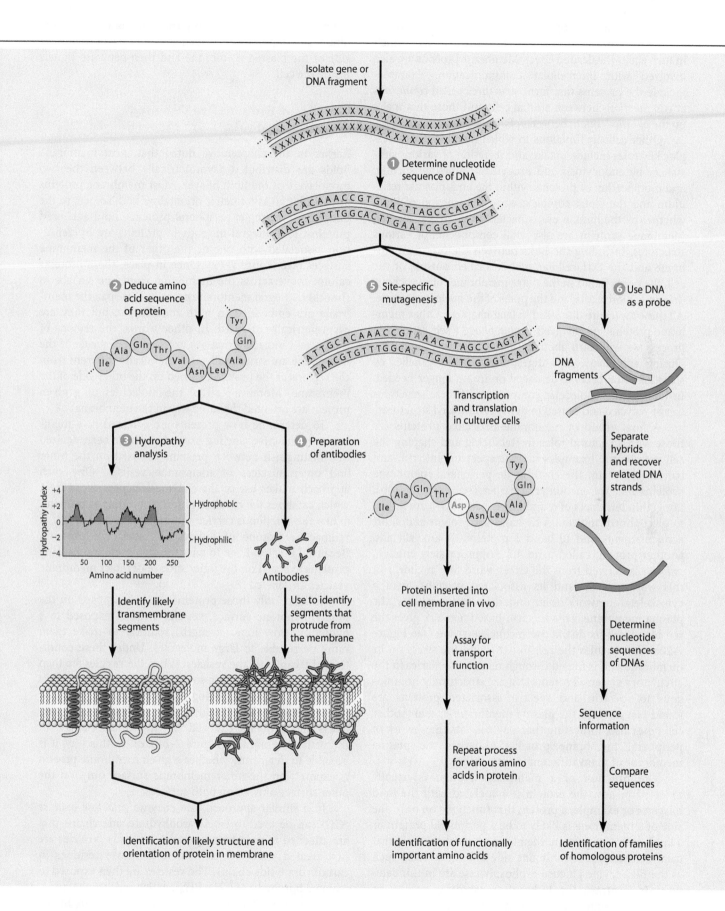

Isolate gene or
DNA fragment

1 Determine nucleotide
sequence of DNA

ATTGCACAAACCGTGAACTTAGCCCAGTAT
TAACGTGTTTGGCACTTGAATCGGGTCATA

2 Deduce amino
acid sequence
of protein

5 Site-specific
mutagenesis

6 Use DNA
as a probe

Tyr
Gln
Ile Ala Gln Thr Val Ala
Asn Leu

ATTGCACAAACCGTAAACTTAGCCCAGTAT
TAACGTGTTTGGCATTTGAATCGGGTCATA

DNA
fragments

Transcription
and translation
in cultured cells

Separate
hybrids
and recover
related DNA
strands

3 Hydropathy
analysis

4 Preparation
of antibodies

+4
+2
0
−2
−4

Hydropathy index

50 100 150 200 250
Amino acid number

Hydrophobic

Hydrophilic

Tyr
Gln
Ile Ala Gln Thr Asp Ala
Asn Leu

Antibodies

Identify likely
transmembrane
segments

Use to identify
segments that
protrude from
the membrane

Protein inserted into
cell membrane in vivo

Determine
nucleotide
sequences
of DNAs

Assay for
transport
function

Sequence
information

Repeat process
for various amino
acids in protein

Compare
sequences

Identification of likely structure and
orientation of protein in membrane

Identification of functionally
important amino acids

Identification of families
of homologous proteins

protein receptors on the plasma membrane of target cells. In most cases, the binding of a hormone or other signal molecule to the appropriate receptor on the membrane surface triggers some sort of intracellular response, which in turn elicits the desired effect. Membrane proteins are also involved with intercellular communication. Examples include the proteins that form structures called *connexons* at *gap junctions* between animal cells and those that make up the *plasmodesmata* between plant cells.

Other cellular functions in which membrane proteins play key roles include uptake and secretion of various substances by endocytosis and exocytosis; targeting, sorting, and modification of proteins within the endoplasmic reticulum and the Golgi complex; and the detection of light, whether by the human eye, a bacterial cell, or a plant leaf. Membrane proteins are also vital components of various structures, including the links between the plasma membrane and the extracellular matrix located outside of the cell, the pores found in the outer membranes of mitochondria and chloroplasts, and the pores of the nuclear envelope. All these topics are discussed in later chapters. Other membrane proteins are involved in *autophagy* ("self eating"), a process we will learn about in more detail in Chapter 12. During autophagy, cells digest their own organelles or structures that become damaged or are no longer needed. In this way, the molecular components of these structures can be recycled and reused in newly synthesized structures.

A final group of membrane-associated proteins are those with structural roles in stabilizing and shaping the cell membrane. Examples include spectrin, ankyrin, and band 4.1 protein, the erythrocyte peripheral membrane proteins that we encountered earlier (see Figure 7-20b). Long, thin tetramers of α and β spectrin, $(\alpha\beta)_2$, are linked to glycophorin molecules by band 4.1 protein and short actin filaments and to band 3 proteins by ankyrin and another protein, called band 4.2. (Appropriately enough, *ankyrin* is derived from the Greek word for "anchor.") In this way, spectrin and its associated proteins form a cytoskeletal network that underlies and supports the plasma membrane. This spectrin-based network gives the red blood cell its distinctive biconcave shape (see Figure 7-20a) and enables the cell to withstand the stress on its membrane as it is forced through narrow capillaries in the circulatory system. Proteins that are structurally homologous to spectrin and spectrin-associated proteins are found just beneath the plasma membrane in many other cell types also, indicating that a cytoskeletal meshwork of peripheral membrane proteins underlies the plasma membrane of many different kinds of cells.

The function of a membrane protein is usually reflected in how the protein is associated with the lipid bilayer. For example, a protein that functions on only one side of a membrane is likely to be a peripheral protein or a lipid-anchored protein. Membrane-bound enzymes that catalyze reactions on only one side of a membrane, such as the ER enzyme glucose-6-phosphatase are in this category. In contrast, the tasks of transporting solutes or transmitting signals across a membrane clearly require

transmembrane proteins. We will examine the role of transmembrane proteins in transport of materials across membranes. We will see how transmembrane receptors bind signaling molecules (such as hormones) on the outside of the plasma membrane and then generate signals inside the cell.

Membrane Proteins Are Oriented Asymmetrically Across the Lipid Bilayer

Earlier in the chapter, we noted that most membrane lipids are distributed asymmetrically between the two monolayers of the lipid bilayer. Most membrane proteins also exhibit an asymmetric orientation with respect to the bilayer. For example, peripheral proteins, lipid-anchored proteins, and integral monotopic proteins are by definition associated with one or the other of the membrane surfaces (see Figure 7-19). Once in place, these proteins cannot move across the membrane from one surface to the other. Integral membrane proteins that span the membrane are embedded in both monolayers, but they are asymmetrically oriented. In other words, the regions of the protein molecule that are exposed on one side of the membrane are structurally and chemically different from the regions of the protein exposed on the other side of the membrane. Moreover, all of the molecules of a given protein are oriented the same way in the membrane.

To determine how proteins are oriented in a membrane, radioactive labeling procedures have been devised that distinguish between proteins exposed on the inner and outer surfaces of membrane vesicles. One such approach makes use of the enzyme *lactoperoxidase (LP)*, which catalyzes the covalent binding of iodine to proteins. When the reaction is carried out in the presence of ^{125}I, a radioactive isotope of iodine, LP labels the proteins. Because LP is too large to pass through membranes, only proteins exposed on the outer surface of intact membrane vesicles are labeled (**Figure 7-24a**).

To label only those proteins that are exposed on the inner membrane surface, vesicles are first exposed to a hypotonic (low ionic strength) solution to make them more permeable to large molecules. Under these conditions, LP can enter the vesicles. When the vesicles are then transferred to an isotonic solution that contains ^{125}I but no external LP, the ^{125}I, being a small molecule, can diffuse into the vesicle where the LP is trapped. Thus, the enzyme labels the proteins exposed on the inner surface of the vesicle membrane (Figure 7-24b, c). In this way, it is possible to determine whether a given membrane protein is exposed on the inner membrane surface only, on the outer surface only, or on both surfaces.

In a similar approach, the enzyme *galactose oxidase (GO)* can be used to label carbohydrate side chains that are attached to membrane proteins or lipids. Vesicles are first treated with GO to oxidize galactose residues in carbohydrate side chains. The vesicles are then exposed to tritiated borohydride ($^3H-BH_4$), which reduces the galactose groups, introducing labeled hydrogen atoms in the

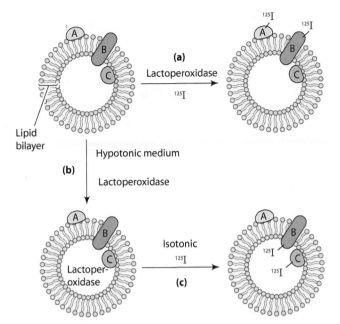

FIGURE 7-24 A Method for Labeling Proteins Exposed on One or Both Surfaces of a Membrane Vesicle. (a) When lactoperoxidase (LP) and ^{125}I are present in the solution outside a membrane vesicle, LP catalyzes the labeling of membrane proteins exposed on the outer membrane surface (i.e., proteins A and B). If membrane vesicles are (b) first incubated in a hypotonic medium to make them permeable to LP and (c) then transferred to an isotonic solution containing ^{125}I but no external LP, proteins exposed on the inner membrane surface (i.e., proteins B and C) become labeled.

process. In both of these approaches, the labeled proteins are typically separated on an SDS-PAGE gel that is then dried and exposed to X-ray film to reveal the locations of the labeled polypeptides.

The orientation of a protein within a membrane can also be determined using antibodies that are designed to recognize specific parts of the protein. Intact cells (or organelles) are exposed to these antibodies and are then tested to determine whether antibodies have bound to the membrane. If so, it can be concluded that the antibody-binding site, or *epitope*, must be on the outer membrane surface.

Many Membrane Proteins Are Glycosylated

In addition to lipids and proteins, most membranes contain small but significant amounts of carbohydrates, except for chloroplast, mitochondrial, and bacterial membranes. The plasma membrane of the human erythrocyte, for example, contains about 49% protein, 43% lipid, and 8% carbohydrate by weight. The glycolipids that we encountered earlier account for a small portion of membrane carbohydrate, but most of the carbohydrate in membranes is found as part of **glycoproteins**—membrane proteins with carbohydrate chains covalently linked to amino acid side chains.

The addition of a carbohydrate side chain to a protein is called **glycosylation**. This process occurs in the ER and Golgi compartments of the cell soon after synthesis. As **Figure 7-25** shows, glycosylation involves linkage of the carbohydrate either to the nitrogen atom of an amino group

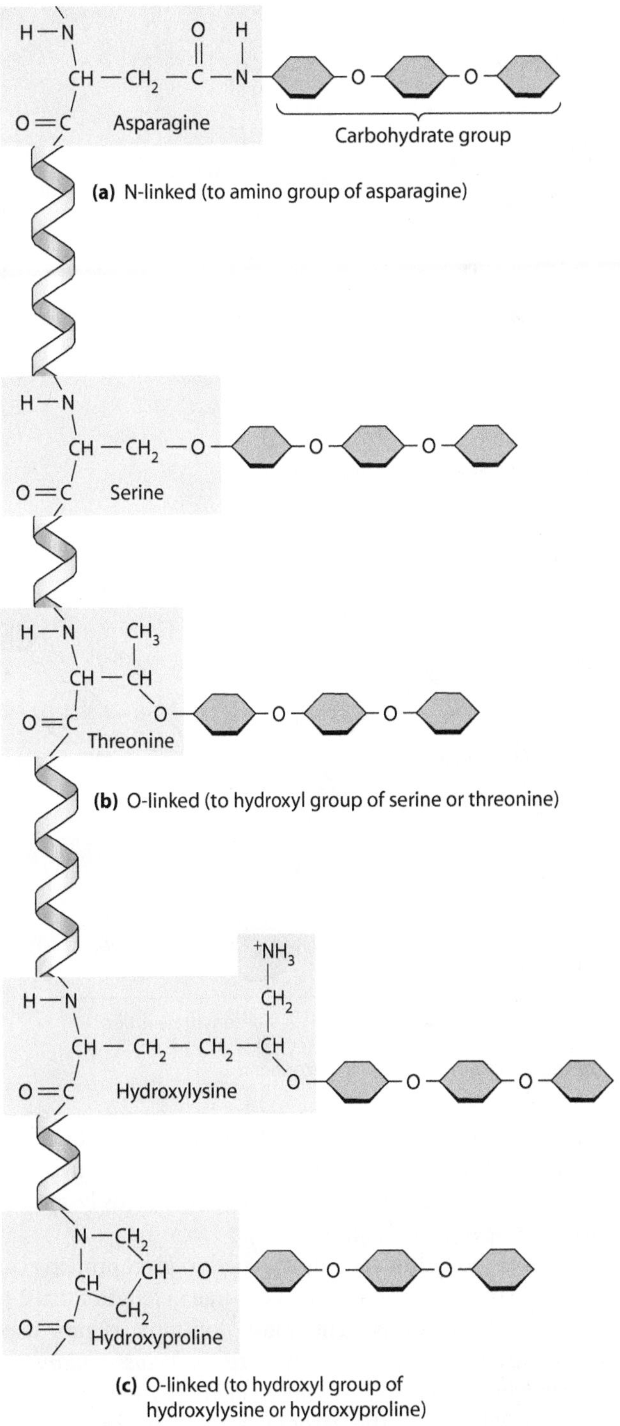

(a) N-linked (to amino group of asparagine)

(b) O-linked (to hydroxyl group of serine or threonine)

(c) O-linked (to hydroxyl group of hydroxylysine or hydroxyproline)

FIGURE 7-25 N-Linked and O-Linked Glycosylation of Membrane Proteins. Carbohydrate groups are linked to specific amino acid residues in membrane proteins in two different ways. (a) N-linked carbohydrates are attached to the amino group of asparagine side chains. (b) O-linked carbohydrates are attached to the hydroxyl group of serine or threonine side chains. (c) In some cases, O-linked carbohydrates are attached to the hydroxyl group of the modified amino acids hydroxylysine and hydroxyproline.

(N-linked glycosylation) or to the oxygen atom of a hydroxyl group *(O-linked glycosylation)*. N-linked carbohydrates are attached to the amino group on the side chain of asparagine (Figure 7-25a), whereas O-linked carbohydrates are usually bound to the hydroxyl groups of either serine or threonine

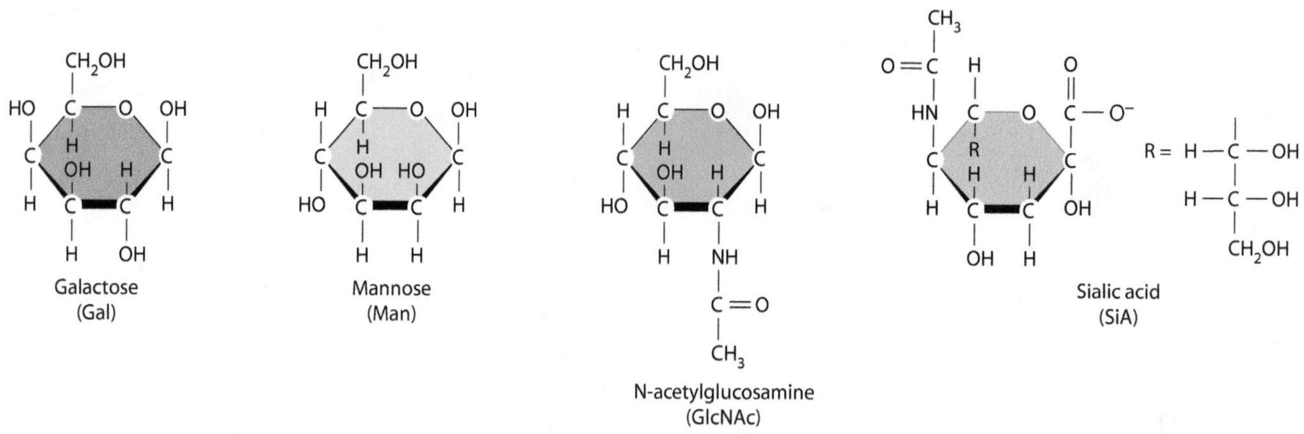

(a) Common sugars found in glycoproteins

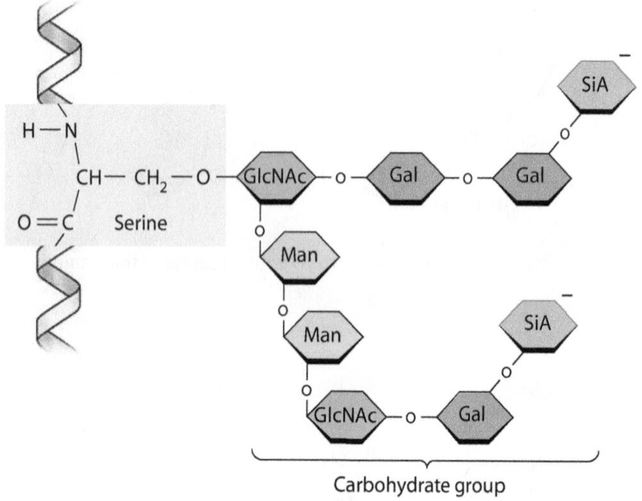

(b) The carbohydrate group of glycophorin

FIGURE 7-26 Examples of Carbohydrates Found in Glycoproteins. (a) The four most common carbohydrates in glycoproteins are galactose (Gal), mannose (Man), *N*-acetylglucosamine (GlcNAc), and sialic acid (SiA). (b) For example, 15 of the 16 carbohydrate chains of glycophorin are linked to the amino acid serine in the hydrophilic portion of the protein on the outer surface of the erythrocyte plasma membrane. Each of these carbohydrate chains consists of three units of Gal and two units each of GlcNAc, Man, and SiA. The two terminal sialic acid groups are negatively charged.

(Figure 7-25b). In some cases, O-linked carbohydrates are attached to the hydroxyl group of hydroxylysine or hydroxyproline, which are derivatives of the amino acids lysine and proline, respectively (Figure 7-25c).

The carbohydrate chains attached to glycoproteins can be either straight or branched and range in length from 2 to about 60 sugar units. The most common sugars used in constructing these chains are *galactose, mannose, N-acetylglucosamine,* and *sialic acid* (**Figure 7-26a**). Figure 7-26b shows the carbohydrate chain found in the erythrocyte plasma membrane protein, glycophorin. This integral membrane protein has 16 such carbohydrate chains attached to the portion of the molecule (the N-terminus) that extends outward from the erythrocyte membrane. Of these 16 chains, 1 is N-linked and 15 are O-linked. Notice that both branches of the carbohydrate chain terminate in a negatively charged sialic acid. Because of these anionic groups on their surfaces, erythrocytes repel each other, thereby reducing blood viscosity.

Glycoproteins are most prominent in plasma membranes, where they play an important role in cell-cell recognition. Consistent with this role, glycoproteins are always positioned so that the carbohydrate groups protrude on the external surface of the cell membrane. This arrangement, which contributes to membrane asymmetry, has been shown experimentally using *lectins,* plant proteins that bind specific sugar groups very tightly. For example, *wheat germ agglutinin,* a lectin found in wheat embryos, binds very specifically to oligosaccharides that terminate in *N*-acetylglucosamine, whereas *concanavalin A,* a lectin from jack beans, recognizes mannose groups in internal positions. Investigators visualize these lectins by linking them to *ferritin,* an iron-containing protein that shows up as an electron-dense spot when viewed with an electron microscope. When such ferritin-linked lectins are used as probes to localize the oligosaccharide chains of membrane glycoproteins, binding is always specifically to the outer surface of the plasma membrane.

In many animal cells, the carbohydrate groups of plasma membrane glycoproteins and glycolipids protrude from the cell surface and form a surface coat called the **glycocalyx** (meaning "sugar coat"). **Figure 7-27** shows the prominent glycocalyx of an intestinal epithelial cell. The carbohydrate groups on the cell surface are important components of the recognition sites of membrane receptors such as those involved in binding extracellular signal

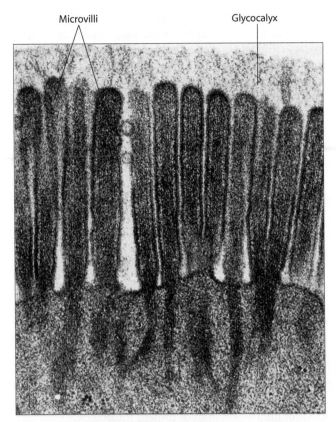

Microvilli Glycocalyx

FIGURE 7-27 The Glycocalyx of an Intestinal Epithelial Cell. This electron micrograph of a cat intestinal epithelial cell shows the microvilli (fingerlike projections that are involved in absorption) and the glycocalyx on the cell surface. The glycocalyx on this cell is about 150 nm thick and consists primarily of oligosaccharide chains about 1.2–1.5 nm in diameter (TEM).

molecules, in antibody-antigen reactions, and in intercellular adhesion to form tissues. In some pathogenic bacteria, such as *Streptococcus pneumoniae*, the presence of a glycocalyx can hide the antigenic surface proteins that would

normally stimulate the immune response. This allows these bacteria to escape detection and subsequent destruction by immune system cells and thus enables them to adhere to target cells and cause disease in the host organism.

Membrane Proteins Vary in Their Mobility

Earlier in the chapter, we noted that lipid molecules can diffuse laterally within the plane of a membrane (see Figure 7-11). Now we can ask the same question about membrane proteins: Are they also free to move within the membrane? In fact, membrane proteins are much more variable than lipids in their mobility. Some proteins appear to move freely within the lipid bilayer. Others are constrained, often because they are anchored to protein complexes located adjacent to one side of the membrane or the other.

Experimental Evidence for Protein Mobility. Particularly convincing evidence for the mobility of at least some membrane proteins has come from *cell fusion experiments* such as those summarized in **Figure 7-28**. In these studies, David Frye and Michael Edidin took advantage of two powerful techniques, one that enabled them to fuse cells from two different species and another that made it possible for them to label specific proteins on the surfaces of cells with antibodies containing fluorescent dye molecules. *Antibodies* are immune system proteins that recognize and bind to specific molecular *antigens* such as cell surface proteins.

Frye and Edidin prepared two **fluorescent antibodies,** each one having a differently-colored dye linked to it, so that the human and mouse proteins could be distinguished. The anti-mouse antibodies were linked to a green fluorescent dye called *fluorescein*, whereas the anti-human antibodies were linked to a red fluorescent dye, *rhodamine*.

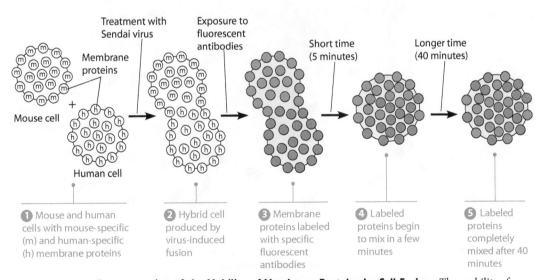

FIGURE 7-28 Demonstration of the Mobility of Membrane Proteins by Cell Fusion. The mobility of membrane proteins can be shown experimentally by the mixing of membrane proteins that occurs when cells from two different species (mouse and human) are fused and the membrane proteins are labeled with specific fluorescent antibodies.

Thus, under a fluorescence microscope, the mouse cells appeared green and the human cells appeared red due to each antibody recognizing and binding to its specific protein antigens on the surface of the cells (Figure 7-28).

Frye and Edidin fused mouse and human cells using Sendai virus, exposed them to the red and green fluorescent antibodies, and observed the fused cells by fluorescence microscopy. At first, the green fluorescent membrane proteins from the mouse cell were localized on one-half of the hybrid cell surface, and the red fluorescent membrane proteins derived from the human cell were restricted to the other half (see Figure 7-28). In a few minutes, however, the proteins from the two parent cells began to intermix. After 40 minutes, the separate regions of green and red fluorescence were completely intermingled.

If the fluidity of the membrane was depressed by lowering the temperature below the transition temperature of the lipid bilayer, this intermixing could be prevented. Frye and Edidin therefore concluded that the intermingling of the fluorescent proteins had been caused by lateral diffusion of the human and mouse proteins through the fluid lipid bilayer of the plasma membrane. Compared to most membrane lipids, however, membrane proteins diffuse through the lipid bilayer much more slowly due to their larger size.

If proteins are completely free to diffuse within the plane of the membrane, then they should eventually become randomly distributed. Support for the idea that at least some membrane proteins behave in this way has emerged from freeze-fracture microscopy, which directly visualizes proteins embedded within the lipid bilayer. When plasma membranes are examined in freeze-fracture micrographs, their embedded protein particles often tend to be randomly distributed. Such evidence for protein mobility is not restricted to the plasma membrane. It has also been found, for example, that the protein particles of the inner mitochondrial membranes are randomly arranged (**Figure 7-29a**). If isolated mitochondrial membrane vesicles are exposed to an electrical potential, the protein particles, which bear a net negative charge, all move to one end of the vesicle (Figure 7-29b). Removing the electrical potential causes the particles to become randomly distributed again, indicating that these proteins are free to move within the lipid bilayer.

Experimental Evidence for Restricted Mobility. Although many types of membrane proteins have been shown to diffuse through the lipid bilayer, their rates of movement vary. A widely used approach for quantifying the rates at which membrane proteins diffuse is fluorescence photobleaching recovery, a technique discussed earlier in the context of lipid mobility (see Figure 7-11). The rate at which unbleached molecules from adjacent parts of the membrane move back into the bleached area can be used to calculate the diffusion rates of various kinds of fluorescent lipid or protein molecules.

Membrane proteins are much more variable in their diffusion rates than lipids are. A few membrane proteins diffuse almost as rapidly as lipids, but most diffuse more

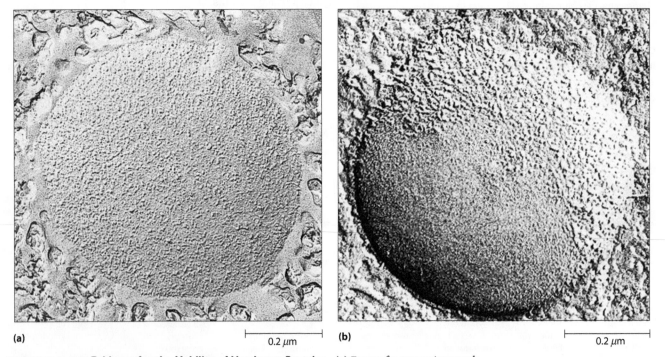

(a)   0.2 μm   (b)   0.2 μm

FIGURE 7-29 Evidence for the Mobility of Membrane Proteins. (a) Freeze-fracture micrograph showing the random distribution of protein particles in vesicles prepared from the inner mitochondrial membrane. (b) Exposure of the vesicles to an electrical field causes the membrane particles to migrate to one end of the vesicle (upper right of micrograph). If membrane proteins were not mobile, this movement of proteins to one side of the vesicle would not happen.

slowly than would be expected if they were completely free to move within the lipid bilayer. Moreover, the diffusion of many membrane proteins is restricted to a limited area of the membrane, indicating that at least some membranes consist of a series of separate *membrane domains* that differ in their protein compositions and hence in their functions. For example, the cells lining your small intestine have membrane proteins that transport solutes such as sugars and amino acids out of the intestine and into the body. These transport proteins are restricted to the side of the cell where the corresponding type of transport is required.

Mechanisms for Restricting Protein Mobility. Several different mechanisms account for restricted protein mobility and hence for cell polarization. In some cases, membrane proteins aggregate within the membrane, forming large complexes that move only sluggishly, if at all. In other cases, membrane proteins form structures that become barriers to the diffusion of other membrane proteins, thereby effectively creating specific membrane domains. The most common restraint on the mobility of membrane proteins, however, is imposed by the binding, or *anchoring,* of such proteins to structures located adjacent to one side of the membrane or the other. For example, many proteins of the plasma membrane are anchored either to elements of the cytoskeleton on the inner surface of the membrane or to extracellular structures such as the extracellular matrix of animal cells. We will encounter both of these anchoring mechanisms.

SUMMARY OF KEY POINTS

The Functions of Membranes

- Cells have a variety of membranes that define the boundaries of the cell and its internal compartments. All biological membranes have the same general structure: a fluid phospholipid bilayer containing a mosaic of embedded proteins.

- While the lipid component of membranes provides a permeability barrier, specific proteins in the membrane regulate transport of materials into and out of cells and organelles.

- Membranes serve as sites for specific proteins and thus can have specific functions. They can detect and transduce external signals, mediate contact and adhesion between neighboring cells, or participate in cell-to-cell communication. They also help to produce external structures such as the cell wall or extracellular matrix.

Models of Membrane Structure: An Experimental Perspective

- Our current understanding of membrane structure represents the culmination of more than a century of studies, beginning with the recognition that lipids are an important membrane component.

- Once proteins were recognized as important components, Davson and Danielli proposed their "sandwich" model—a lipid bilayer surrounded on both sides by layers of proteins. As membranes and membrane proteins were examined in more detail, however, this model was eventually discredited.

- In place of the sandwich model, Singer and Nicolson's fluid mosaic model emerged and is now the universally accepted description of membrane structure. According to this model, proteins with varying affinities for the hydrophobic membrane interior float in and on a fluid lipid bilayer.

- We now know that lipids and proteins are not distributed randomly in the membrane but are often found in microdomains known as lipid rafts that are involved in cell signaling and other interactions.

Membrane Lipids: The "Fluid" Part of the Model

- Prominent lipids in most membranes include numerous types of phospholipids and glycolipids. The proportion of each lipid type can vary considerably depending on the particular membrane or monolayer.

- In eukaryotic cells, sterols are also important membrane components, including cholesterol in animal cells and phytosterols in plant cells. Sterols are not found in the membranes of most prokaryotes, but some bacterial species contain similar compounds called hopanoids.

- Proper fluidity of a membrane is critical to its function. Cells often can vary the fluidity of membranes by changing the length and degree of saturation of the fatty acid chains of the membrane lipids or by the addition of cholesterol or other sterols.

- Long-chain fatty acids pack together well and decrease fluidity. Unsaturated fatty acids contain *cis* double bonds that interfere with packing and increase fluidity.

- Most membrane phospholipids and proteins are free to move within the plane of the membrane unless they are specifically anchored to structures on the inner or outer membrane surface. Transverse diffusion, or "flip-flop," between monolayers is not generally possible, except for phospholipids when catalyzed by enzymes called phospholipid translocators, or flippases.

- As a result, most membranes are characterized by an asymmetric distribution of lipids between the two monolayers and an asymmetric orientation of proteins within the membranes so that the two sides of the membrane are structurally and functionally dissimilar.

Membrane Proteins: The "Mosaic" Part of the Model

- Proteins are major components of all cellular membranes. Membrane proteins are classified as integral, peripheral, or lipid anchored, based on how they are associated with the lipid bilayer.

- Integral membrane proteins have one or more short segments of predominantly hydrophobic amino acids that anchor the protein to the membrane. Most of these transmembrane segments are α-helical sequences of about 20–30 predominantly hydrophobic amino acids.

- Peripheral membrane proteins are hydrophilic and remain on the membrane surface. They are typically attached to the polar head groups of phospholipids by ionic and hydrogen bonding.

- Lipid-anchored proteins are also hydrophilic in nature but are covalently linked to the membrane by any of several lipid anchors that are embedded in the lipid bilayer.

- Membrane proteins function as enzymes, electron carriers, transport molecules, and receptor sites for chemical signals such as neurotransmitters and hormones. Membrane proteins also stabilize and shape the membrane and mediate intercellular communication and cell-cell adhesion.

- Many proteins in the plasma membrane are glycoproteins, with carbohydrate side chains that protrude from the membrane on the external side, where they play important roles as recognition markers on the cell surface.

- Thanks to current advances in SDS-PAGE, molecular biology X-ray crystallography, affinity labeling, and the use of specific antibodies, we are learning much about the structure and function of membrane proteins that were difficult to study in the recent past.

MAKING CONNECTIONS

By now, you should have an appreciation for the molecular basis of membrane structure and the experimental evidence that led to our current understanding of membrane structure. You are also now familiar with many of the types of lipids and proteins that make up these membranes and how they contribute to the functions of specific membranes. In the next chapter, you can apply your knowledge of membrane structure and function as we investigate in detail the mechanisms by which cells can transport molecules across membranes. You will see how the transport of H^+ ions across membranes to create an electrochemical charge gradient is critical for ATP synthesis, both for aerobic respiration in the mitochondrion and for photosynthesis in the chloroplast. We will then study how lipids and proteins are targeted to and inserted into particular membranes in cells in Chapter 12 and how they are processed and sorted to their final destinations, whether it may be into a particular organelle, to the plasma membrane, or out of the cell as a secreted product. We will rely heavily on our understanding of membranes as we investigate electrical and chemical signaling, as you learn about ion channels crucial for nerve impulse transmission, receptor proteins involved in hormonal signaling, and cellular responses to growth factors and other signaling molecules. As we proceed through studies of cell motility, the cytoskeleton, and cell-cell recognition and adhesion in the next few chapters, you will rely extensively on what you have learned about membranes in this chapter. And as we finish our studies in this textbook with detailed looks at the cell nucleus, cell division, and cancer cells, you can better appreciate the important roles of membranes. You will see how defects in cell signaling and adhesion can lead to cancer, and you will learn how we can use our knowledge of membrane proteins to identify and perhaps destroy specific types of cancer cells.

PROBLEM SET

More challenging problems are marked with a •.

7-1 Functions of Membranes. For each of the following statements, specify which one of the five general membrane functions (permeability barrier, localization of function, regulation of transport, detection of signals, or intercellular communication) the statement illustrates.

(a) When cells are disrupted and fractionated into subcellular components, the enzyme cytochrome P-450 is recovered with the endoplasmic reticulum fraction.

(b) On their outer surface tissue, cells of multicellular organisms carry specific glycoproteins that are responsible for cell-cell adhesion.

(c) The interior of a membrane consists primarily of the hydrophobic portions of phospholipids and amphipathic proteins.

(d) Photosystems I and II are embedded in the thylakoid membrane of the chloroplast.

(e) All of the acid phosphatase in a mammalian cell is found within the lysosomes.

(f) The membrane of a plant root cell has an ion pump that exchanges phosphate inward for bicarbonate outward.

(g) The inner mitochondrial membrane contains an ATP-ADP carrier protein that couples outward ATP movement to inward ADP movement.

(h) Insulin does not enter a target cell but instead binds to a specific membrane receptor on the external surface of the membrane, thereby activating the enzyme adenylyl cyclase on the inner membrane surface.

(i) Adjacent plant cells frequently exchange cytoplasmic components through membrane-lined channels called plasmodesmata.

7-2 Elucidation of Membrane Structure. Each of the following observations played an important role in enhancing our understanding of membrane structure. Explain the significance of each, and indicate in what decade of the timeline shown in Figure 7-3 the observation was most likely made.

(a) When a membrane is observed in the electron microscope, both of the thin, electron-dense lines are about 2 nm thick, but the two lines are often distinctly different from each other in appearance.

(b) Ethylurea penetrates much more readily into a membrane than does urea, and diethylurea penetrates still more readily.

(c) The addition of phospholipase to living cells causes rapid digestion of the lipid bilayers of the membranes, which suggests that the enzyme has access to the membrane phospholipids.

(d) When artificial lipid bilayers are subjected to freeze-fracture analysis, no particles are seen on either face.

(e) The electrical resistivity of artificial lipid bilayers is several orders of magnitude greater than that of real membranes.

(f) Some membrane proteins can be readily extracted with 1 M NaCl, whereas others require the use of an organic solvent or a detergent.

(g) When halobacteria are grown in the absence of oxygen, they produce a purple pigment that is embedded in their plasma membranes and has the ability to pump protons outward when illuminated. If the purple membranes are isolated and viewed by freeze-fracture electron microscopy, they are found to contain patches of crystalline particles.

7-3 Wrong Again. For each of the following false statements, change the statement to make it true and explain your reasoning.

(a) Because membranes have a hydrophobic interior, polar and charged molecules cannot pass through membranes.

(b) Proteins typically transmit signals from the outside of the cell to the cytoplasm by flip-flopping from the outer membrane monolayer to the inner monolayer.

(c) O-linked and N-linked glycoproteins are formed when sugar chains are attached to the oxygen and nitrogen atoms of the peptide bonds in proteins.

(d) The three-dimensional structure of a protein cannot be determined unless the protein can be isolated from cells in pure form.

(e) You would expect membrane lipids from tropical plants such as palm and coconut to have short-chain fatty acids with multiple C=C double bonds.

7-4 Gorter and Grendel Revisited. Gorter and Grendel's classic conclusion that the plasma membrane of the human erythrocyte consists of a lipid bilayer was based on the following observations: (i) the lipids that they extracted with acetone from 4.74×10^9 erythrocytes formed a monolayer 0.89 m² in area when spread out on a water surface; and (ii) the surface area of one erythrocyte was about $100 \ \mu m^2$, according to their measurements.

(a) Show from these data how they came to the conclusion that the erythrocyte membrane is a bilayer.

(b) We now know that the surface area of a human erythrocyte is about $145 \ \mu m^2$. Explain how Gorter and Grendel could have come to the right conclusion when one of their measurements was only about two-thirds of the correct value.

7-5 Martian Membranes. Imagine a new type of cell was discovered on Mars in an organism growing in benzene, a non-polar liquid. The cell had a lipid bilayer made of phospholipids, but its structure was very different from that of our cell membranes.

(a) Draw what might be a possible structure for this new type of membrane. What might be characteristic features of the phospholipid head groups?

(b) What properties would you expect to find in membrane proteins embedded in this membrane?

(c) How might you isolate and visualize these unusual membranes?

7-6 That's About the Size of It. From chemistry, we know that each methylene (—CH_2—) group in a straight-chain hydrocarbon advances the chain length by about 0.13 nm. And from studies of protein structure, we know that one turn of an α helix includes 3.6 amino acid residues and extends the long axis of the helix by about 0.56 nm. Use this information to answer the following:

(a) How long is a single molecule of palmitate (16 carbon atoms) in its fully extended form? What about molecules of laurate (12C) and arachidate (20C)?

(b) How does the thickness of the hydrophobic interior of a typical membrane compare with the length of two palmitate molecules laid end to end? What about two molecules of laurate or arachidate?

(c) Approximately how many amino acids must a helical transmembrane segment of an integral membrane protein have if the segment is to span the lipid bilayer defined by two palmitate molecules laid end to end?

(d) The protein bacteriorhodopsin has 248 amino acids and seven transmembrane segments. Approximately what portion of the amino acids are part of the transmembrane segments? Assuming that most of the remaining amino acids are present in the hydrophilic loops linking the transmembrane segments together, approximately how many amino acids are present in each of these loops, on the average?

7-7 Temperature and Membrane Composition. Which of the following responses are *not* likely to be seen when a bacterial culture growing at 37°C is transferred to a culture room maintained at 25°C? Explain your reasoning.

(a) Initial decrease in membrane fluidity

(b) Gradual replacement of shorter-chain fatty acids by longer-chain fatty acids in the membrane phospholipids

(c) Gradual replacement of stearate by oleate in the membrane phospholipids

(d) Enhanced rate of synthesis of unsaturated fatty acids

(e) Incorporation of more cholesterol into the membrane

7-8 Membrane Fluidity and Temperature. The effects of temperature and lipid composition on membrane fluidity are often studied by using artificial membranes containing only one or a few kinds of lipids and no proteins. Assume that you and your lab partner have made the following artificial membranes:

Membrane 1:   Made entirely from phosphatidylcholine with saturated 16-carbon fatty acids.

Membrane 2:   Same as membrane 1, except that each of the 16-carbon fatty acids has a single *cis* double bond.

Membrane 3:   Same as membrane 1, except that each of the saturated fatty acids has only 14 carbon atoms.

After determining the transition temperatures of samples representing each of the membranes, you discover that your lab partner failed to record which membranes the samples correspond to. The three values you determined are –36°C, 23°C, and 41°C. Assign each of these transition temperatures to the correct artificial membrane, and explain your reasoning.

7-9 The Little Bacterium That Can't. *Acholeplasma laidlawii* is a small bacterium that cannot synthesize its own fatty acids and must therefore construct its plasma membrane from whatever fatty acids are available in the environment. As a result, the *Acholeplasma* membrane takes on the physical characteristics of the fatty acids available at the time.

(a) If you give *Acholeplasma* cells access to a mixture of saturated and unsaturated fatty acids, they will thrive at room temperature. Can you explain why?

(b) If you transfer the bacteria of part a to a medium containing only saturated fatty acids but make no other changes in culture conditions, they will stop growing shortly after the change in medium. Explain why.

(c) What is one way you could get the bacteria of part b growing again without changing the medium? Explain your reasoning.

(d) If you were to maintain the *Acholeplasma* culture of part b under the conditions described there for an extended period of time, what do you predict will happen to the bacterial cells? Explain your reasoning.

(e) What result would you predict if you were to transfer the bacteria of part a to a medium containing only unsaturated fatty acids without making any other changes in the culture conditions? Explain your reasoning.

• 7-10 Hydropathy: The Plot Thickens. A hydropathy plot can be used to predict the structure of a membrane protein based on its amino acid sequence and the hydrophobicity values of the amino acids. Hydrophobicity is measured as the standard free energy change, $\Delta G^{\circ\prime}$, for the transfer of a given amino acid residue from a hydrophobic solvent into water, in kilojoules/mole (kJ/mol). The hydropathy index is calculated by averaging the hydrophobicity values for a series of short segments of the polypeptide, with each segment displaced one amino acid further from the N-terminus. The hydropathy index of each successive segment is then plotted as a function of the location of that segment in the amino acid sequence, and the plot is examined for regions of high hydropathy index.

(a) Why do scientists try to predict the structure of a membrane protein by this indirect means when the technique of X-ray crystallography would reveal the structure directly?

(b) Given the way it is defined, would you expect the hydrophobicity index of a hydrophobic residue such as valine or

isoleucine to be positive or negative? What about a hydrophilic residue such as aspartic acid or arginine?

(c) Listed below are four amino acids and four hydrophobicity values. Match the hydrophobicity values with the correct amino acids, and explain your reasoning.

Amino acids: alanine; arginine; isoleucine; serine
Hydrophobicity (in kJ/mol): +3.1; +1.0; −1.1; −7.5

(d) Shown in **Figure 7-30** is a hydropathy plot for a specific integral membrane protein. Draw a horizontal bar over each transmembrane segment as identified by the plot. How long is the average transmembrane segment? How well does that value compare with the number you calculated in Problem 7–6c? How many transmembrane segments do you think the protein has? Can you guess which protein this might be?

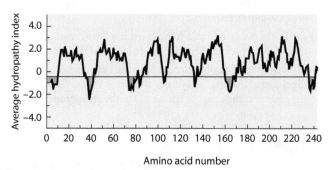

FIGURE 7-30 Hydropathy Plot for an Integral Membrane Protein. See Problem 7-10d.

• 7-11 Inside or Outside? From Figure 7-24, we know that exposed regions of membrane proteins can be labeled with ^{125}I by the lactoperoxidase (LP) reaction. Similarly, carbohydrate side chains of membrane glycoproteins can be labeled with ^{3}H by oxidation of galactose groups with galactose oxidase (GO) followed by reduction with tritiated borohydride (^{3}H—BH$_4$). Noting that both LP and GO are too large to penetrate into the interior of an intact cell, explain each of the following observations made with intact erythrocytes.

(a) When intact cells are incubated with LP in the presence of ^{125}I and the membrane proteins are then extracted and analyzed on SDS–polyacrylamide gels, several of the bands on the gel are found to be radioactive.

(b) When intact cells are incubated with GO and then reduced with ^{3}H—BH$_4$, several of the bands on the gel are found to be radioactive.

(c) All of the proteins of the plasma membrane that are known to contain carbohydrates are labeled by the GO/^{3}H—BH$_4$ method.

(d) None of the proteins of the erythrocyte plasma membrane that are known to be devoid of carbohydrate is labeled by the LP/^{125}I method.

(e). If the erythrocytes are ruptured before the labeling procedure, the LP procedure labels virtually all of the major membrane proteins.

• 7-12 Inside-Out Membranes. It is technically possible to prepare sealed vesicles from erythrocyte membranes in which the original orientation of the membrane is inverted. Such vesicles have what was originally the cytoplasmic side of the membrane facing outward.

(a) What results would you expect if such inside-out vesicles were subjected to the GO/^{3}H — BH$_4$ procedure described in Problem 7-11?

(b) What results would you expect if such inside-out vesicles were subjected to the LP/^{125}I procedure of Problem 7-11?

(c) What conclusion would you draw if some of the proteins that become labeled by the LP/^{125}I method of part b were among those that had been labeled when intact cells were treated in the same way in Problem 7-11a?

(d) Knowing that it is possible to prepare inside-out vesicles from erythrocyte plasma membranes, can you think of a way to label a transmembrane protein with ^{3}H on one side of the membrane and with ^{125}I on the other side?

SUGGESTED READING

References of historical importance are marked with a •.

General References

Peirce, M. J., and R. Wait, eds. *Membrane Proteomics: Methods and Protocols*. New York: Humana Press/Springer Science, 2009.

Quinn., P. J., ed. *Membrane Dynamics and Domains*. New York: Kluwer Academic/Plenum Publishers, 2004.

Vance, D. E., and J. E. Vance, eds. *Biochemistry of Lipids, Lipoproteins, and Membranes*, 5th ed. New York: Elsevier Science, 2008.

Yeagle, P. L., ed. *The Structure of Biological Membranes*, 2nd ed. Boca Raton, Florida: CRC Press LLC, 2005.

Historical References

Davson, H., and J. F. Danielli, eds. *The Permeability of Natural Membranes*. Cambridge, England: Cambridge University Press, 1943.

• Deamer, D. W., A. Kleinzeller, and D. M. Fambrough, eds. *Membrane Permeability: 100 Years Since Ernest Overton*. San Diego: Academic Press, 1999.

• Deisenhofer, J. et al. Structure of the protein subunits in the photosynthetic reaction centre of *Rhodopseudomonas viridis* at 3 Å resolution. *Nature* 318 (1985): 618.

• Gorter, E., and F. Grendel. On bimolecular layers of lipids on the chromocyte of the blood. *J. Exp. Med.* 41 (1925): 439.

• Robertson, J. D. The ultrastructure of cell membranes and their derivatives. *Biochem. Soc. Symp.* 16 (1959): 3.

• Singer, S. J., and G. L. Nicolson. The fluid mosaic model of the structure of cell membranes. *Science* 175 (1972): 720.

• Unwin, N., and R. Henderson. The structure of proteins in biological membranes. *Sci. Amer.* 250 (February 1984): 78.

Membrane Structure and Function

Cossins, A. R. *Temperature Adaptations of Biological Membranes*. London: Portland Press, 1994.

Hanzal-Bayer, M. F., and J. F. Hancock. Lipid rafts and membrane traffic. *FEBS Lett.* 581 (2007): 2098.

Hunte, C., and S. Richers. Lipids and membrane protein structures. *Curr. Opin. Struct. Biol.* 18 (2008): 406.

Ishitsuka, R., S. B. Sato, and T. Kobayashi. Imaging lipid rafts. *J. Biochem (Tokyo)* 137 (2005): 249.

Lai, Y., and R. L. Gallo. AMPed up immunity: How antimicrobial peptides have multiple roles in immune defense. *Trends Immunol.* 30 (2009): 131.

Lindner, R., and H. Y. Naim. Domains in biological membranes. *Exp. Cell Res.* 315 (2009): 2871.

Michel, V., and M. Bakovic. Lipid rafts in health and disease. *Biol. Cell* 99 (2007): 129.

Pani, B., and B. B. Singh. Lipid rafts/caveolae as microdomains of calcium signaling. *Cell Calcium* 45 (2009): 625.

Patra, S. K. Dissecting lipid raft facilitated cell signaling pathways in cancer. *Biochim. Biophys. Acta* 1785 (2008): 182.

Veenhoff, L. M., E. H. M. L. Heuberger, and B. Poolman. Quaternary structure and function of transport proteins. *Trends Biochem. Sci.* 27 (2002): 242.

Yi, F., S. Jin, and P. L. Li. Lipid raft-redox signaling platforms in plasma membrane. *Meth. Mol. Bio.* 580 (2009): 93.

Membrane Lipids

Dowhan, W. Molecular basis for membrane phospholipid diversity: Why are there so many lipids? *Annu. Rev. Biochem.* 66 (1997): 199.

Hawkes, D. J., and J. Mak. Lipid membrane: A novel target for viral and bacterial pathogens. *Int. Rev. Cytol.* 255 (2006): 1.

Katsaros, J., and T. Gutberlet, eds. *Lipid Bilayers: Structure and Interactions*. New York: Springer-Verlag, 2000.

Li, X. A., W. V. Everson, and E. J. Smart. Caveolae, lipid rafts, and vascular disease. *Trends Cardiovasc. Med.* 15 (2005): 92.

Menon, A. Flippases. *Trends Cell Biol.* 5 (1995): 355.

Ohvo-Rekila, H. B. et al. Cholesterol interactions with phospholipids in membranes. *Prog. Lipid Res.* 41 (2002): 66.

Pororsky, T., and A. K. Menon. Lipid flippases and their biological functions. *Cell. Mol. Life Sci.* 63 (2006): 2908.

Stroud, R. M. The state of lipid rafts: From model membranes to cells. *Annu. Rev. Biophys. Biomol. Struct.* 32 (2003): 257.

Zepic, H. H., P. Walde, E. L. Kostoryz, J. Code, and D. M. Yourtee. Lipid vesicles for toxicological assessment of xenobiotics. *Crit. Rev. Toxicol.* 38 (2008): 1.

Zhang, S. C., and C. O. Rock. Membrane lipid homeostasis in bacteria. *Nat. Rev. Microbiol.* 6 (2008): 222.

Membrane Proteins

Bates, I. R., P. W. Wiseman, and J. W. Hanrahan. Investigating membrane protein dynamics in living cells. *Biochem. Cell Biol.* 84 (2006): 825.

Carpenter, E. P., K. Beis, A. D. Cameron, and S. Iwata. Overcoming the challenges of membrane protein crystallography. *Curr. Opin. Struct. Biol.* 18 (2008): 581.

Elofsson, A., and G. von Heijne. Membrane protein structure: Prediction versus reality. *Annu. Rev. Biochem.* 76 (2007): 125.

Engel, A., and H. E. Gaub. Structure and mechanics of membrane proteins. *Annu. Rev. Biochem.* 77 (2008): 127.

Nyholm, T. K., S. Ozdirekcan, and J. A. Killian. How protein transmembrane segments sense the lipid environment. *Biochemistry* 46 (2007): 1457.

Peirce, M. J., J. Saklatvala, A. P. Cope, and R. Wait. Mapping lymphocyte plasma membrane proteins: A proteomic approach. *Methods Molec. Med.* 136 (2007): 361.

Sussman, M. R. Molecular analysis of proteins in the plant plasma membrane. *Annu. Rev. Plant Physiol. Plant Mol. Biol.* 45 (1994): 211.

Werten, P. J. L. et al. Progress in the analysis of membrane protein structure and function. *FEBS Lett.* 529 (2002): 65.

White, S. H. *Membrane Proteins of Known Structure.* http://blanco.biomol.uci.edu/Membrane_Proteins_xtal.html (2010; updated regularly).

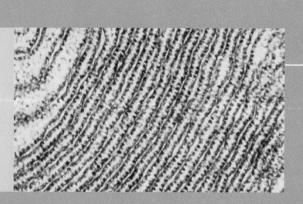

The Endomembrane System and Peroxisomes

A full appreciation of eukaryotic cells depends on an understanding of the prominent role of intracellular membranes and the compartmentalization of function within organelles—intracellular membrane-bounded compartments that house various cellular activities. Whether we consider the storage and transcription of genetic information, the biosynthesis of secretory proteins, the breakdown of long-chain fatty acids, or any of the numerous other metabolic processes occurring within eukaryotic cells, many of the reactions of a particular pathway occur within a distinct type of organelle. Also, the movement of molecules between organelles, known as trafficking, must be tightly regulated to ensure that each organelle has the correct components for its proper structure and function.

We briefly encountered the major organelles found in eukaryotic cells in Chapter 4, and we then learned more about the mitochondrion and chloroplas, respectively. We are now ready to consider several other individual organelles in more detail. We will begin with the rough endoplasmic reticulum, the smooth endoplasmic reticulum, and the Golgi complex, which are sites for protein synthesis, processing, and sorting. Next, we will look at endosomes, organelles that are important for carrying and sorting material brought into the cell. Endosomes help to form lysosomes, which are organelles responsible for digestion of both ingested material and unneeded intracellular components. We will conclude with a look at peroxisomes, which house hydrogen peroxide–generating reactions and perform diverse metabolic functions.

As you study the role of each organelle, keep in mind that the endoplasmic reticulum, the Golgi complex, endosomes, and lysosomes (but not peroxisomes) comprise the **endomembrane system** of the eukaryotic cell, as shown in **Figure 12-1**. (The nuclear envelope, which we will study in Chapter 18, is closely associated with the endomembrane system.) Material flows from the endoplasmic reticulum to and from the Golgi complex, endosomes, and lysosomes by means of transport vesicles that shuttle between the various organelles. These transport vesicles carry membrane lipids and membrane-bound proteins to their proper destinations in the cell, and they also carry soluble materials destined for secretion. Thus, these organelles and the vesicles connecting them make up a single dynamic system of membranes and internal spaces. Currently, one of the most exciting questions in modern cell biology concerns endomembrane trafficking: How does each of the multitude of proteins and lipids in a cell manage to reach its proper destination at the proper time?

The Endoplasmic Reticulum

The **endoplasmic reticulum (ER)** is a continuous network of flattened sacs, tubules, and associated vesicles that stretches throughout the cytoplasm of the eukaryotic cell. Although the name sounds formidable, it is actually quite descriptive. *Endoplasmic* simply means "within the (cyto)plasm," and *reticulum* is a Latin word meaning "network." The membrane-bounded sacs are called **ER cisternae** (singular: **ER cisterna**), and the space enclosed by them is called the **ER lumen** (Figure 12-1). Of the total membrane in a mammalian cell, up to 50–90% surrounds the ER lumen. Unlike more prominent organelles, such as the mitochondrion or chloroplast, however, the ER is not visible by light microscopy unless one or more of its components are stained with a dye or labeled with a fluorescent molecule.

The ER was first observed in the late nineteenth century, when it was noted that some eukaryotic cells, particularly those involved in secretion, contained regions that stained intensely with basic dyes. The significance of these regions remained in doubt until the 1950s, when the resolving power of the electron microscope was improved dramatically. This allowed cell biologists to visualize for the first time the ER's elaborate network of intracellular membranes and to investigate the role of the ER in cellular processes. This is a common

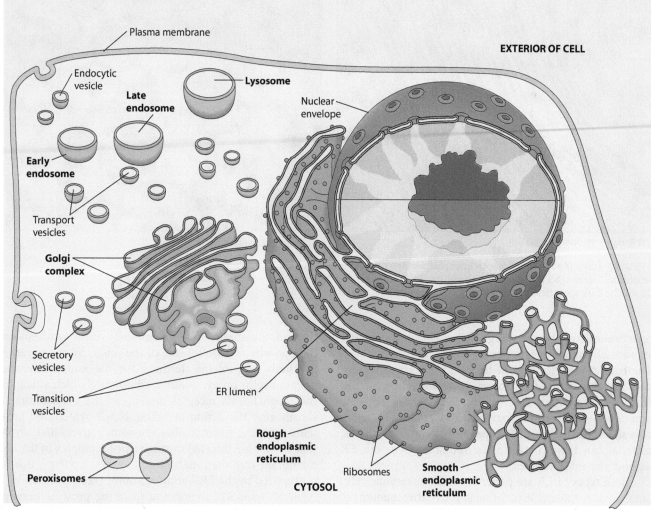

FIGURE 12-1 The Endomembrane System. The endomembrane system of the eukaryotic cell consists of the endoplasmic reticulum (ER), the Golgi complex, endosomes, and lysosomes (but not peroxisomes). It is associated with both the nuclear envelope and the plasma membrane. The ER lumen is linked to the interiors of the Golgi complex, endosomes, and lysosomes by transport vesicles that shuttle material between organelles, as well as to and from the plasma membrane.

theme in scientific discovery—conceptual advances in one field often follow technological advances in a related (or even an unrelated) field.

We now know that enzymes associated with the ER are responsible for the biosynthesis of proteins destined for incorporation into the plasma membrane or into organelles of the endomembrane system and for synthesis of proteins destined for export from the cell. The ER also plays a central role in the biosynthesis of lipids, including triacylglycerols, cholesterol, and related compounds. The ER is the source of most of the lipids that are assembled to form intracellular membranes and the plasma membrane.

The Two Basic Kinds of Endoplasmic Reticulum Differ in Structure and Function

The two basic kinds of endoplasmic reticulum typically found in eukaryotic cells are distinguished from one

another by the presence or absence of ribosomes attached to the ER membrane (**Figure 12-2**). **Rough endoplasmic reticulum (rough ER)** is characterized by ribosomes attached to the cytosolic side of the membrane (the side that faces away from the ER lumen; Figure 12-2a). Translation by these ribosomes occurs in the cytosol, but the newly-synthesized proteins will enter the ER lumen shortly. Because ribosomes contain RNA, it was this RNA that reacted strongly with the basic dyes originally used to identify the rough ER. A subdomain of rough ER, the **transitional elements (TEs),** plays an important role in the formation of **transition vesicles** that shuttle lipids and proteins from the ER to the Golgi complex. In contrast, **smooth endoplasmic reticulum (smooth ER)** appears smooth due to the absence of ribosomes attached to the membrane (Figure 12-2b) and has other roles in the cell.

Rough and smooth ER are easily distinguished morphologically. As illustrated in Figure 12-1, rough ER

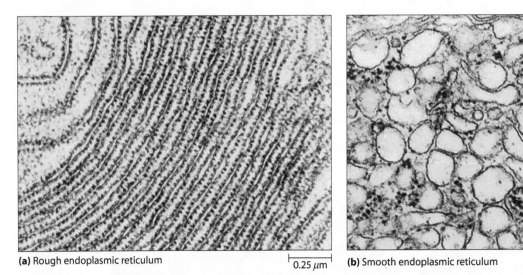

(a) Rough endoplasmic reticulum   ⊢ 0.25 μm ⊣   **(b)** Smooth endoplasmic reticulum   ⊢ 0.25 μm ⊣

FIGURE 12-2 Rough and Smooth Endoplasmic Reticulum. (a) Electron micrograph of endoplasmic reticulum. The rough ER is studded with ribosomes. **(b)** Electron micrograph of smooth endoplasmic reticulum. The dark spots near the smooth ER appear to be glycogen granules (TEMs).

membranes usually form large flattened sheets, whereas smooth ER membranes generally form tubular structures. The transitional elements of the rough ER are an exception to this rule; they often resemble smooth ER. However, the rough and smooth ER are not separate organelles—electron micrographs and studies in living cells show that their lumenal spaces are continuous. Thus, material can travel between the rough and smooth ER without the aid of vesicles.

Both types of ER are present in most eukaryotic cells, but there is considerable variation in the relative amounts of each type, depending on the activities of the particular cell. Cells involved in the biosynthesis of secretory proteins, such as liver cells and cells producing digestive enzymes, tend to have very prominent rough ER networks. On the other hand, cells producing steroid hormones, such as in the testis or ovary, contain extensive networks of smooth ER.

When tissue is homogenized for subcellular fractionation, the ER membranes often break into smaller fragments that spontaneously close to form sealed vesicles known as **microsomes.** Fractions can be isolated with and without attached ribosomes, depending on whether the membrane originated from rough or smooth ER, respectively. Such preparations are tremendously useful for exploring both types of ER. Keep in mind, however, that microsomes do not exist in the cell; they are simply an artifact of the fractionation process. **Box 12A** presents more detailed information about subcellular fractionation by differential centrifugation.

Rough ER Is Involved in the Biosynthesis and Processing of Proteins

The ribosomes attached to the cytosolic side of the rough ER membrane are responsible for synthesizing both membrane-bound and soluble proteins for the endomembrane system. So how do proteins enter the ER lumen and the endomembrane system from their site of synthesis on the opposite (cytosolic) side of the rough ER membrane? Synthesis of proteins destined for the endomembrane system begins on cytoplasmic ribosomes, which attach to the rough ER via receptor proteins in the ER membrane shortly after translation initiation. Newly-synthesized proteins enter the endomembrane system *cotranslationally*— that is, they are inserted through a pore complex in the ER membrane into the rough ER lumen as the polypeptide is synthesized by the ER-bound ribosome (see Figure 22-16). After biosynthesis, membrane-spanning proteins remain anchored to the ER membrane either by hydrophobic regions of the polypeptide or by covalent attachment to membrane lipids. Soluble proteins, including secretory proteins, are released into the ER lumen.

In addition to its role in the biosynthesis of polypeptide chains, the rough ER is the site for several other processes, including the initial steps of addition and processing of carbohydrate groups to glycoproteins, the folding of polypeptides, the recognition and removal of misfolded polypeptides, and the assembly of multimeric proteins. Thus, ER-specific proteins include a host of enzymes that catalyze cotranslational and posttranslational modifications. These modifications include glycosylation, which is important for sorting of proteins to their proper destinations, and disulfide bond formation, which is essential for proper protein folding. We will discuss the topics of protein biosynthesis, targeting, and folding in more detail in Chapter 22.

The ER is also a site for quality control. In *ER-associated degradation (ERAD)*, proteins improperly modified, folded, or assembled are exported from the ER for degradation by cytosolic *proteasomes* before they can move on to the Golgi complex. Several human diseases, including cystic fibrosis and familial hypercholesterolemia, are associated with defects in these processes.

Centrifugation is a procedure used for the isolation and purification of organelles and macromolecules. This method is based on the fact that when a particle is subjected to centrifugal force by spinning a cellular extract at extremely rapid rates in a laboratory centrifuge, the rate of movement of the particle through a specific solution depends on its *size* and *density*, as well as the solution's density and viscosity. The larger or denser a particle is, the higher its **sedimentation rate**, or rate of movement through the solution. Centrifugation is used routinely in labs throughout the world to separate dissolved molecules from cell debris in suspensions of broken cells, to collect precipitated macromolecules such as DNA and proteins from cell suspensions, and to separate different cellular components based on their sedimentation rate.

Because most organelles and macromolecules differ significantly from one another in size and/or density, centrifuging a mixture of cellular components will separate the faster-moving components from the slower-moving ones. This procedure, called **subcellular fractionation,** enables researchers to isolate and purify specific organelles and macromolecules for further manipulation and study in vitro.

Albert Claude, George Palade, and Christian de Duve shared a Nobel Prize in 1974 for their pioneering work in centrifugation and subcellular fractionation. Claude played a key role in developing differential centrifugation as a method of isolating organelles. Palade was quick to use this technique in studies of the endoplasmic reticulum and the Golgi complex, establishing the roles of these organelles in the biosynthesis, processing, and secretion of proteins (see Figure 12-10). De Duve, in turn, used centrifugation in his discovery of two entirely new organelles—lysosomes and peroxisomes.

Centrifugation is also routinely used for isolating and purifying DNA and proteins. Following cell lysis, insoluble cell debris and organelles are removed by centrifugation, and the soluble cytoplasmic portion containing the DNA or protein is recovered. Treatment with the appropriate precipitating agent makes the DNA or protein insoluble so that it can be isolated in a second round of centrifugation.

Centrifuges and Sample Preparation

In essence, a **centrifuge** consists of a rotor—often housed in a refrigerated chamber—spun extremely rapidly by an electric motor. The rotor holds tubes containing solutions or suspensions of particles for fractionation. Centrifugation at very high speeds—above 20,000 revolutions per minute (rpm)—requires an **ultracentrifuge** equipped with a vacuum system to reduce friction between the rotor and air. Some ultracentrifuges reach speeds over 100,000 rpm, subjecting samples to forces exceeding 500,000 times the force of gravity (g).

Tissues must first undergo **homogenization,** or disruption, before the cellular components can be separated by centrifugation. To preserve the integrity of organelles, homogenization is usually done in a cold isotonic solution such as 0.25 M sucrose. Disruption can be achieved by grinding tissue in a mortar and pestle, by forcing cells through a narrow orifice (French press) or by subjecting tissue to ultrasonic vibration, osmotic shock, or enzymatic digestion. The resulting **homogenate** is a suspension of organelles, smaller cellular components, membranes, and molecules. If tissue is homogenized gently enough, most organelles and other structures remain intact and retain their original biochemical properties.

Differential Centrifugation

Differential centrifugation separates organelles based on their size and/or density differences. As illustrated in **Figure 12A-1**, particles that are large or dense (purple spheres) sediment rapidly, those that are intermediate in size or density (blue spheres) sediment less rapidly, and the smallest or least dense particles (black spheres) sediment very slowly.

We can express the relative size and/or density of an organelle or macromolecule in terms of its **sedimentation coefficient,** a measure of how rapidly the particle sediments when subjected to centrifugation. Sedimentation coefficients are expressed in **Svedberg units (S),** in honor of Theodor Svedberg, the Swedish chemist who developed the ultracentrifuge between 1920 and

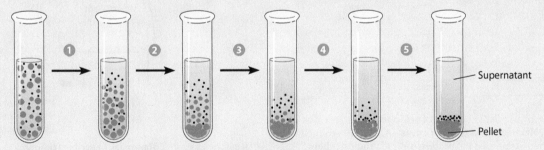

- ● Particles with large sedimentation coefficients
- ● Particles with intermediate sedimentation coefficients
- · Particles with small sedimentation coefficients

FIGURE 12A-1 Differential Centrifugation. Differential centrifugation separates particles based on differences in sedimentation rate, which reflect differences in size and/or density. The technique is illustrated here for three particles that differ significantly in size. The particles, which are initially part of a homogeneous mixture, are subjected to a fixed centrifugal force for five successive time intervals (circled numbers). Particles that are large or dense (purple spheres) sediment rapidly, those that are intermediate in size or density (blue spheres) sediment less rapidly, and the smallest or least dense particles (black spheres) sediment very slowly. Eventually, all of the particles reach the bottom of the tube, unless the process is interrupted after a specific length of time.

1940. The sedimentation coefficients of some organelles, macromolecules, and viruses are shown in **Figure 12A-2**.

An example of differential centrifugation is illustrated in **Figure 12A-3**. The tissue of interest is first homogenized (step ❶). Subcellular fractions are then isolated by subjecting the homogenate and subsequent supernatant fractions to successively higher centrifugal forces and longer centrifugation times (steps ❷– ❺). The **supernatant** is the clarified suspension of homogenate that remains after particles of a given size and density are removed as a **pellet** following each step of the centrifugation process. In each case, the supernatant from one step can be poured off into a new centrifuge tube and then returned to the centrifuge and subjected to greater centrifugal force to obtain the next pellet. In successive steps, the pellets are enriched in nuclei, unbroken cells, and debris (step ❷); mitochondria, lysosomes, and peroxisomes (step ❸); ER and other membrane fragments (step ❹); and free ribosomes and large macromolecules (step ❺). The material in each pellet can be resuspended and used for electron microscopy or biochemical studies. The final supernatant consists mainly of soluble cellular components such as DNA and protein.

Each fraction obtained in this way is enriched for the respective organelles but is also likely contaminated with other organelles and cellular components. Often, most of the contaminants in a pellet can be removed by resuspending the pellet in an isotonic solution and repeating the centrifugation procedure.

Density Gradient Centrifugation

In the previous example of differential centrifugation, the particles about to be separated were uniformly distributed throughout the

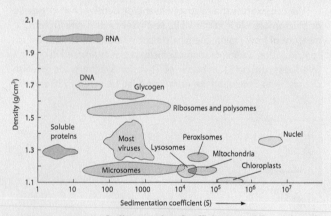

FIGURE 12A-2 Sedimentation Coefficients and Densities of Organelles, Macromolecules, and Viruses. A particle's sedimentation coefficient, expressed in Svedberg units (S), indicates how rapidly it sediments when subjected to a centrifugal force. A higher S value represents more rapid sedimentation. A particle's density (expressed in g/cm³) determines how far it will move during equilibrium density centrifugation.

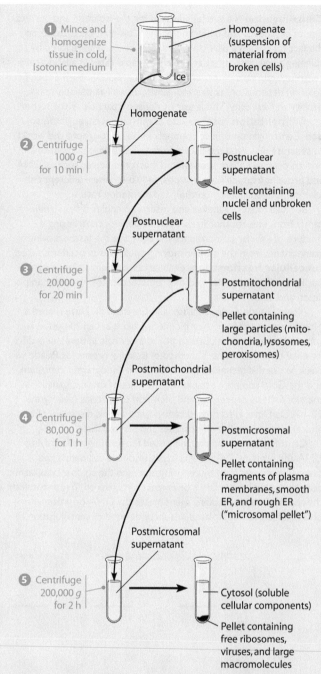

FIGURE 12A-3 Differential Centrifugation and the Isolation of Organelles. To isolate specific cellular components, homogenized tissue is subjected to a series of centrifugation steps. Each step uses the supernatant from the previous step, and subjects it to a higher *g* force for a longer time.

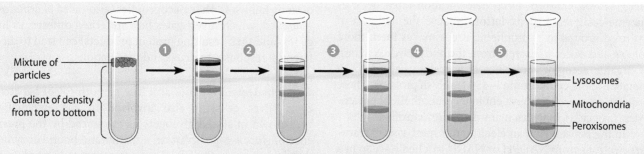

Mixture of particles

Gradient of density from top to bottom

Lysosomes
Mitochondria
Peroxisomes

● Particles with large sedimentation coefficients
● Particles with intermediate sedimentation coefficients
· Particles with small sedimentation coefficients

FIGURE 12A-4 Density Gradient Centrifugation. Density gradient centrifugation, like differential centrifugation (see Figure 12A-1), is a technique for separating particles such as organelles based on differences in sedimentation rate. For this centrifugation method, however, the sample for fractionation is placed as a thin layer on top of a gradient of solute that increases in density from the top of the tube to the bottom. The effect is illustrated here for three organelles that differ significantly in size and/or density. Subjected to a fixed centrifugal force for five successive time intervals (circled numbers), the organelles migrate through the gradient as distinct bands.

solution prior to centrifugation. **Density gradient** (or **rate-zonal**) **centrifugation** is a variation of differential centrifugation in which the sample for fractionation is placed as a thin layer on top of a *gradient of solute*. The gradient consists of an increasing concentration of solute—and therefore density—from the top of the tube to the bottom. When subjected to a centrifugal force, particles differing in size and/or density move downward as discrete *zones*, or bands, that migrate at different rates. Due to the gradient of solute in the tube, the particles at the leading edge of each zone continually encounter a slightly denser solution and are thus slightly impeded. As a result, each zone remains very compact, maximizing the ability to separate different particles.

This process is illustrated in **Figure 12A-4**. Particles that are large or dense (purple) move into the gradient as a rapidly sedimenting band, particles that are intermediate in size or density (blue) sediment less rapidly, and the smallest particles (black) move quite slowly. The centrifuge is stopped after the bands of interest have moved far enough into the gradient to be resolved from each other but *before* any of the bands reach the bottom of the tube. Stopping at this point is essential because all of the particles are denser than the solution in the tube, even at the very bottom of the tube. If centrifugation continues too long, the bands will reach the bottom of the tube one after another, piling up and negating the very purpose of the process.

Density gradient centrifugation can be used to separate lysosomes, mitochondria, and peroxisomes, each of which has a slightly different density. The tissue of interest is first homogenized, and a pellet enriched in these organelles is layered over a gradient of solute that increases in concentration and density from the top of

a tube to the bottom. As shown in Figure 12A-4, the dense peroxisomes move into the gradient as a rapidly sedimenting band. The mitochondria, having intermediate density, form a band above the peroxisomes. The lysosomes are the smallest and least dense and form a band nearer the top of the tube. By assaying each fraction for *marker enzymes* that are unique to each organelle, the fractions containing these organelles can be identified and the extent of cross-contamination can be determined.

Equilibrium Density Centrifugation

Equilibrium density (or **buoyant density**) **centrifugation** is a related method for resolving organelles and macromolecules based on density differences (see Figure 12A-2). Like density gradient centrifugation, this procedure includes a gradient of solute that increases in concentration and density, but in this case the solute is concentrated so that the density gradient spans the range of densities of the organelles or macromolecules about to be separated. Therefore, the material to be purified does not move to the bottom of the tube during centrifugation but instead forms a tight band in a stable equilibrium position where its density is exactly equal to the density of the gradient at that position.

For organelle separation using equilibrium density centrifugation, a gradient of sucrose is often used, and the density range is $1.10–1.30$ g/cm^3 ($0.75–2.3$ M sucrose). This method can also be used to separate different forms of DNA and RNA based on their differing densities. It was used to determine the mechanism of replication of DNA in the classic experiments of Meselson and Stahl (see Figure 19-3).

Smooth ER Is Involved in Drug Detoxification, Carbohydrate Metabolism, Calcium Storage, and Steroid Biosynthesis

Drug Detoxification. Drug detoxification often involves enzyme-catalyzed **hydroxylation** because the addition of hydroxyl groups to hydrophobic drugs makes them more soluble and easier to excrete from the body. Hydroxylation of organic acceptor molecules is typically catalyzed by a member of the **cytochrome P-450** family of proteins. These proteins are especially prevalent in the smooth ER of hepatocytes (liver cells), in which many drugs are detoxified.

In the hepatocytes, an electron transport system transfers electrons from NADPH or NADH to a heme group in a cytochrome P-450 protein, which then donates an electron to molecular oxygen. One atom of molecular oxygen gains two electrons and two H^+, forming H_2O. The other oxygen atom is added to the organic substrate molecule as part of a hydroxyl group. Because one of the two oxygen atoms of O_2 is incorporated into the reaction product, these cytochrome P-450 enzymes are often called *monooxygenases*. The net reaction is shown below, where R represents the organic hydroxyl acceptor:

$$RH + NAD(P)H + H^+ + O_2 \longrightarrow$$
$$ROH + NAD(P)^+ + H_2O \quad \textbf{(12-1)}$$

The elimination of hydrophobic barbiturate drugs, for example, is enhanced by hydroxylation enzymes in the smooth ER. Injection of the sedative phenobarbital into a rat causes a rapid increase in the level of barbiturate-detoxifying enzymes in the liver, accompanied by a dramatic proliferation of smooth ER. However, this means that increasingly higher doses of the drug are necessary to achieve the same sedative effect, an effect known as *tolerance* that is seen in habitual users of phenobarbital. Furthermore, the enzyme induced by phenobarbital can hydroxylate and therefore solubilize a variety of other drugs, including such useful agents as antibiotics, anticoagulants, and steroids. As a result, the chronic use of barbiturates decreases the effectiveness of many other clinically useful drugs.

Another cytochrome P-450 protein found in the smooth ER is part of an enzyme complex called *aryl hydrocarbon hydroxylase*. This complex is involved in metabolizing *polycyclic hydrocarbons,* organic molecules composed of two or more linked benzene rings that are often toxic. Hydroxylation of such molecules is important for increasing their solubility in water, but the oxidized products are often more toxic than the original compounds. Aryl hydrocarbon hydroxylase converts some potential carcinogens into their chemically active forms. Mice synthesizing high levels of this hydroxylase have a higher incidence of spontaneous cancer than normal mice do, whereas mice treated with an inhibitor of aryl hydrocarbon hydrolase develop few tumors. Significantly, cigarette smoke is a potent inducer of aryl hydrocarbon hydroxylase.

Recent work shows that differences in activities and side effects of certain medications can result from differences in the presence or activity of particular cytochrome P-450 genes in different patients. This has led to a new field of study known as **pharmacogenetics** (also called *pharmacogenomics*), which investigates how inherited differences in genes (and their resulting protein products) can lead to differential responses to drugs and medications.

Carbohydrate Metabolism. The smooth ER of hepatocytes (liver cells) is also involved in the enzymatic breakdown of stored glycogen, as evidenced by the presence of *glucose-6-phosphatase,* a membrane-bound enzyme that is unique to the ER. Thus, its presence is used as a marker to identify the ER during subcellular fractionation or to visualize the ER using fluorescent antibodies. Glucose-6-phosphatase hydrolyzes the phosphate group from glucose-6-phosphate to form free glucose and inorganic phosphate (P_i):

$$glucose\text{-}6\text{-}phosphate + H_2O \longrightarrow glucose + P_i \quad \textbf{(12-2)}$$

This enzyme is abundant in the liver because a major role of the liver is to keep the level of glucose in the blood relatively constant. The liver stores glucose as glycogen in granules associated with smooth ER (**Figure 12-3a**). When glucose is needed by the body, especially between meals and in response to increased muscular activity, liver glycogen is broken down by phosphorolysis, producing glucose-6-phosphate (Figure 12-3b). Because membranes are generally impermeable to phosphorylated sugars, the glucose-6-phosphate must be converted to free glucose by glucose-6-phosphatase in order to leave the cell and enter the bloodstream. Free glucose then leaves the liver cell via a glucose transporter (GLUT2) and moves into the blood for transport to other cells that need energy. Significantly, glucose-6-phosphatase activity is present in liver, kidney, and intestinal cells but not in muscle or brain cells. Muscle and brain cells retain glucose-6-phosphate and use it to meet their own substantial energy needs.

Calcium Storage. The *sarcoplasmic reticulum* found in muscle cells is an example of smooth ER that specializes in the storage of calcium. In these cells, the ER lumen contains high concentrations of calcium-binding proteins. Calcium ions are pumped into the ER by *ATP-dependent calcium ATPases* and are released in response to extracellular signals to aid in muscle contraction . Binding of neurotransmitter molecules to receptors on the surface of the muscle cell triggers a signal cascade that leads to the release of calcium from the sarcoplasmic reticulum and causes the contraction of muscle fibers. We will discuss nerve impulse transmission and muscle contraction in more detail in Chapter 16.

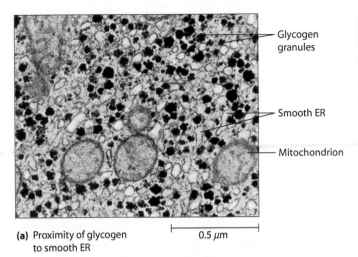

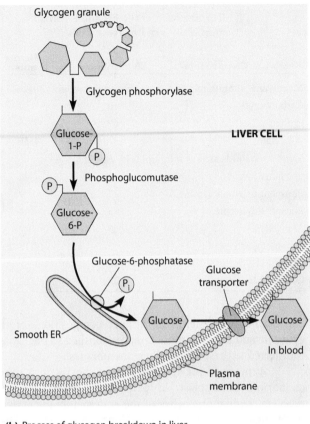

(a) Proximity of glycogen to smooth ER

|—————| 0.5 μm

FIGURE 12-3 **The Role of the Smooth ER in the Catabolism of Liver Glycogen.** **(a)** This electron micrograph of a monkey liver cell shows numerous granules of glycogen closely associated with smooth ER (TEM). **(b)** The breakdown of liver glycogen involves the stepwise removal of glucose units as glucose-1-phosphate, followed by the conversion of glucose-1-phosphate to glucose-6-phosphate by enzymes in the cytosol. Removal of the phosphate group depends on glucose-6-phosphatase, an enzyme associated with the smooth ER membrane. Free glucose is then transported out of the liver cell into the blood by a glucose transporter in the plasma membrane.

(b) Process of glycogen breakdown in liver

Steroid Biosynthesis. The smooth ER in certain cells is the site of biosynthesis of cholesterol and steroid hormones such as cortisol, testosterone, and estrogen. Large amounts of smooth ER are found in the cortisol-producing cells of the adrenal gland; the Leydig cells of the testes, which produce testosterone; the cholesterol-producing cells of the liver; and the follicular cells of the ovary, which produce estrogen. Smooth ER has also been found in close association with plastids in some plants, where it may be involved in phytohormone synthesis.

Cholesterol, cortisol, and the male and female steroid hormones just described share a common four-ring structure but differ in the number and arrangement of carbon side chains and hydroxyl groups (see Figure 3-27e and Figure 3-30). *Hydroxymethylglutaryl-CoA reductase* (*HMG-CoA reductase*), the committed step in cholesterol biosynthesis, is present in large amounts in the smooth ER of liver cells. This enzyme is targeted for inhibition by a class of cholesterol-lowering drugs known as *statins*. In addition, the smooth ER contains a number of P-450 monooxygenases that are important not only in the synthesis of cholesterol but also in its conversion into steroid hormones by hydroxylation.

The ER Plays a Central Role in the Biosynthesis of Membranes

In eukaryotic cells, the ER is the primary source of membrane lipids, including phospholipids and cholesterol. Indeed, most of the enzymes required for the biosynthesis of membrane phospholipids are found nowhere else in the cell. There are, however, important exceptions. Mitochondria synthesize phosphatidylethanolamine by decarboxylating imported phosphatidylserine. Peroxisomes have enzymes to synthesize cholesterol, and chloroplasts contain enzymes for the synthesis of chloroplast-specific lipids.

Biosynthesis of fatty acids for membrane phospholipid molecules occurs in the cytoplasm and incorporation is restricted to the monolayer of the ER membrane facing the cytosol. Cellular membranes, of course, are phospholipid *bilayers,* with phospholipids distributed to both sides. Thus, there must be a mechanism for transferring phospholipids from one layer of the membrane to the other. Because it is thermodynamically unfavorable for phospholipids to flip spontaneously at a significant rate from one side of a bilayer to the other, transfer depends on **phospholipid translocators,** also called **flippases,** which catalyze the translocation of phospholipids through ER membranes (see Figure 7-10).

Phospholipid translocators, like other enzymes, are quite specific and affect only the rate of a process. Therefore, the type of phospholipid molecules transferred across a membrane depends on the particular translocators present, contributing to the *membrane asymmetry* described in Chapter 7. For example, the ER membrane contains a translocator for phosphatidylcholine, and thus it is found in both monolayers of the ER membrane. In contrast, there is no translocator for phosphatidylethanolamine, phosphatidylinositol, or phosphatidylserine, which are therefore confined to the cytosolic monolayer. When vesicles from the ER membrane fuse with other organelles of the

Table 12-1	Composition of the ER and Plasma Membranes of Rat Liver Cells	
Membrane Components	**ER Membrane**	**Plasma Membrane**
Membrane components as % of membrane by weight		
Carbohydrate	10	10
Protein	62	54
Total lipid	27	36
Membrane lipids as % of total lipids by weight		
Phosphatidylcholine	40	24
Phosphatidylethanolamine	17	7
Phosphatidylserine	5	4
Cholesterol	6	17
Sphingomyelin	5	19
Glycolipids	trace	7
Other lipids	27	22

endomembrane system, the distinct compositions of the cytosolic and lumenal monolayers established in the ER are transferred to these other cellular membranes.

Movement of phospholipids from the ER to a mitochondrion, chloroplast, or peroxisome poses a unique problem. Unlike organelles of the endomembrane system, these organelles do not grow by fusion with ER-derived vesicles. Instead, cytosolic **phospholipid exchange proteins** (also called *phospholipid transfer proteins*) convey phospholipid molecules from the ER membrane to the outer mitochondrial and chloroplast membranes. Each exchange protein recognizes a specific phospholipid, removes it from one membrane, and carries it through the cytosol to another membrane. Such transfer proteins also contribute to the movement of phospholipids from the ER to other cellular membranes, including the plasma membrane.

Although the ER is the source of most membrane lipids, the compositions of other cellular membranes vary significantly from the composition of the ER membrane (Table 12-1). A striking feature of the plasma membrane of hepatocytes is the relatively low amount of phosphoglycerides and high amounts of cholesterol, sphingomyelin, and glycolipids. Researchers have observed an increasing gradient of cholesterol content from the ER through the compartments of the endomembrane system to the plasma membrane. This correlates with an increasing gradient of membrane thickness. ER membranes are about 5 nm thick, whereas plasma membranes are about 8 nm thick. The observed change in membrane thickness has implications for sorting and targeting integral membrane proteins, which we will discuss after we look at the Golgi complex and its role in protein processing.

The Golgi Complex

We now turn our attention to the Golgi complex, a component of the endomembrane system that is closely linked, both physically and functionally, to the ER. In the Golgi complex, glycoproteins from the ER undergo further processing and, along with membrane lipids, are sorted and packaged for transport to their proper destinations inside or outside the cell. Thus, the Golgi complex plays a central role in *membrane* and *protein trafficking* in eukaryotic cells.

The **Golgi complex** (or *Golgi apparatus*) derives its name from Camillo Golgi, the Italian biologist who first described it in 1898. He reported that nerve cells soaked in osmium tetroxide showed deposits of osmium in a thread-like network surrounding the nucleus. The same staining reaction was demonstrated with a variety of cell types and other heavy metals. However, no cellular structure could be identified that explained the staining. As a result, the nature—actually, the very existence—of the Golgi complex remained controversial until the 1950s, when its existence was finally confirmed by electron microscopy.

The Golgi Complex Consists of a Series of Membrane-Bounded Cisternae

The Golgi complex is a series of flattened membrane-bounded *cisternae*, disk-shaped sacs that are stacked together as illustrated in **Figure 12-4a**. A series of such cisternae is called a *Golgi stack* and can be visualized by electron microscopy (Figure 12-4b). Usually, there are 3–8 cisternae per stack, though the number and size of Golgi stacks vary with the cell type and with the metabolic activity of the cell. Some cells have one large stack, whereas others—especially active secretory cells—have hundreds or even thousands of Golgi stacks.

The static view of the ER and the Golgi complex presented by electron micrographs such as Figure 12-4b can be misleading. These organelles are actually dynamic structures. Both the ER and Golgi complex are typically surrounded by numerous *transport vesicles* that carry lipids and proteins from the ER to the Golgi complex, between the cisternae of a Golgi stack, and from the Golgi complex to various destinations in the cell, including endosomes, lysosomes, and secretory granules. Thus, the Golgi complex lumen, or *intracisternal space,* is part of the endomembrane system's network of internal spaces (see Figure 12-1).

The Two Faces of the Golgi Stack. Each Golgi stack has two distinct sides, or *faces* (Figure 12-4). The *cis face* is oriented toward the ER. The Golgi compartment closest to the ER is a network of flattened, membrane-bounded tubules referred to as the **cis-Golgi network (CGN)**. Vesicles containing newly synthesized lipids and proteins from the ER continuously arrive at the CGN, where they fuse with CGN membranes. The opposite side of the Golgi complex is called the *trans face*. The compartment on this side of the Golgi complex has similar morphology and is referred to as the **trans-Golgi network (TGN)**. Here, proteins and lipids leave the Golgi in **transport vesicles** that continuously bud from the tips of TGN cisternae. These transport vesicles carry lipids and proteins from the Golgi complex to secretory granules, endosomes, lysosomes, and the plasma membrane. The central sacs between the CGN

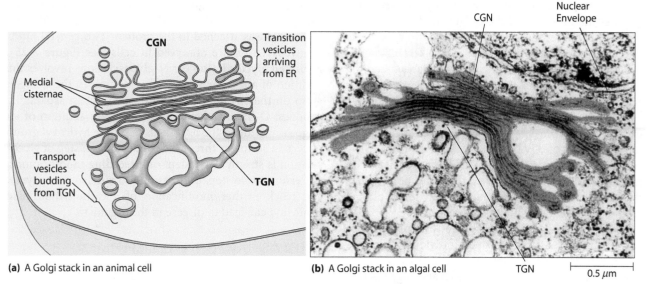

(a) A Golgi stack in an animal cell

(b) A Golgi stack in an algal cell

0.5 µm

FIGURE 12-4 Golgi Structure. A Golgi stack consists of a small number of flattened cisternae. **(a)** At the *cis* face, transition vesicles arriving from the ER fuse with membranes of the *cis*-Golgi network (CGN). At the *trans* face, transport vesicles arise by budding from the *trans*-Golgi network (TGN). The transport vesicles carry lipids and proteins to other components of the endomembrane system or form secretory vesicles. **(b)** This electron micrograph shows a Golgi stack lying next to the nuclear envelope of an algal cell (TEM).

and TGN comprise the **medial cisternae** of the Golgi stack, in which much of the processing of proteins occurs.

The CGN, TGN, and medial cisternae of the Golgi complex are biochemically and functionally distinct. Each compartment contains specific receptor proteins and enzymes necessary for specific steps in protein and membrane processing, as shown by immunological and cytochemical staining techniques. This biochemical *polarity* is illustrated in **Figure 12-5**, which shows a Golgi stack in a rabbit kidney cell. Staining to detect *N-acetylglucosamine transferase I,* an enzyme that modifies carbohydrate side chains of glycoproteins, shows that the enzyme is concentrated in medial cisternae of the Golgi complex.

Two Models Depict the Flow of Lipids and Proteins Through the Golgi Complex

Two models have been proposed to explain the movement of lipids and proteins from the CGN to the TGN via the medial cisternae of the Golgi complex. According to the **stationary cisternae model,** each compartment of the Golgi stack is a stable structure. Trafficking between successive cisternae is mediated by *shuttle vesicles* that bud from one cisterna and fuse with the next cisterna in the *cis*-to-*trans* sequence. Proteins destined for the TGN are simply carried forward by shuttle vesicles, while molecules that belong in the ER and successive Golgi compartments are actively retained or retrieved.

According to the second model, known as the **cisternal maturation model,** the Golgi cisternae are transient compartments that gradually change from CGN cisternae through medial cisternae to TGN cisternae. In this model, transition vesicles from the ER converge to form the CGN, which accumulates specific enzymes for

the early steps of protein processing. Step by step, each *cis* cisterna is transformed first into an intermediate medial cisterna and then into a *trans* cisterna as it acquires additional enzymes. Enzymes that are no longer needed in late compartments return in vesicles to early compartments. In both models, the TGN forms transport vesicles or

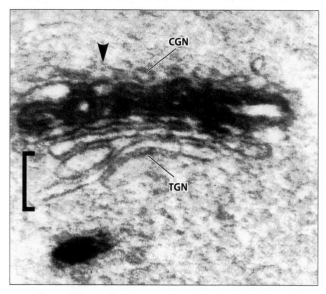

FIGURE 12-5 Immunochemical Staining of a Golgi Complex. This electron micrograph shows a Golgi stack in a rabbit kidney cell. The cell section has been stained to detect the enzyme *N-acetylglucosamine transferase I,* which plays a role in terminal glycosylation of proteins. The arrow and bracket indicate unlabeled cisternae, showing that the enzyme is concentrated in a few medial cisternae close to the *cis* face of the Golgi stack. This indicates that *N*-acetylglucosamine is added to existing oligosaccharides on glycoproteins shortly after the proteins enter the Golgi stack (TEM).

secretory granules containing sorted cargo targeted for various destinations beyond the Golgi complex.

Experimental results suggest that these two models are not necessarily mutually exclusive. It is likely that both apply to some degree, depending on the organism and the role of the cell. While the stationary cisternae model is supported by substantial evidence, some cellular components observed in medial compartments of the Golgi complex are clearly too large to travel by the small shuttle vesicles found in cells. For example, polysaccharide scales produced by some algae first appear in early Golgi compartments. Too large to fit inside transport vesicles, the scales nevertheless reach late Golgi compartments on their way to the plasma membrane for incorporation into the cell wall.

Recently, time-lapse fluorescence microscopy has been used in live yeast cells to study individual Golgi cisternae in real time. Three-dimensional analysis of images supports the cisternal maturation model and suggests that the cisternae mature at a constant rate. In addition, the rate of movement of labeled secretory proteins through the Golgi complex was measured and was shown to match the rate of cisternal maturation.

Anterograde and Retrograde Transport. The movement of material from the ER through the Golgi complex toward the plasma membrane is called **anterograde transport** (*antero* is derived from a Latin word meaning "front," and *grade* is related to a word meaning "step"). Every time a secretory granule fuses with the plasma membrane and discharges its contents by exocytosis, a bit of membrane that originated in the ER becomes a part of the plasma membrane. To balance the flow of lipids toward the plasma membrane and to ensure a supply of components for forming new vesicles, the cell recycles lipids and proteins no longer needed during the late stages of anterograde transport. This is accomplished by **retrograde transport** (*retro* is a Latin word meaning "back"), the flow of vesicles from Golgi cisternae back toward the ER.

In the stationary cisternae model, retrograde flow facilitates both the recovery of ER-specific lipids and proteins that are passed from the ER to the CGN and the transport of compartment-specific proteins back to distinct medial cisternae of the Golgi stack. Material destined for the TGN continues forward. Whether such retrograde traffic occurs directly from all medial cisternae of the Golgi stack back to the ER or by reverse flow through successive cisternae is not yet clear. In the cisternal maturation model, retrograde flow carries material back toward newly forming compartments after receptors and enzymes are no longer needed in the more mature compartments.

Roles of the ER and Golgi Complex in Protein Glycosylation

Much of the protein processing carried out within the ER and Golgi complex involves **glycosylation**—the addition of carbohydrate side chains to specific amino acid residues

of proteins, forming **glycoproteins.** Subsequent enzyme-catalyzed reactions then modify the oligosaccharide side chain that was attached to the protein. Two general kinds of glycosylation are observed in cells (see Figure 7-25). **N-linked glycosylation** (or **N-glycosylation**) involves the addition of a specific oligosaccharide unit to the *nitrogen* atom on the terminal amino group of certain asparagine residues. **O-linked glycosylation** involves addition of an oligosaccharide to the *oxygen* atom on the hydroxyl group of certain serine or threonine residues. Each step of glycosylation is strictly dependent on preceding modifications. An error at one step, perhaps due to a defective enzyme, can block further modification of a carbohydrate side chain and can lead to disease in the organism.

Initial Glycosylation Occurs in the ER

We will focus here on N-glycosylation. **Figure 12-6** describes the steps of glycosylation that may occur as a glycoprotein travels from the ER to the CGN and through the Golgi complex to the TGN. Note that specific enzymes that catalyze various steps of glycosylation and subsequent modifications are present in specific compartments of the ER and Golgi complex. The initial steps of N-glycosylation take place on the cytosolic surface of the ER membrane and later steps occur in the ER lumen (**Figure 12-7**). Despite the variety of oligosaccharides found in mature glycoproteins, all the carbohydrate side chains added to proteins in the ER initially have a common **core oligosaccharide** consisting of two units of N-acetylglucosamine (GlcNAc, see Figure 3-26a), nine mannose units, and three glucose units.

Glycosylation begins as *dolichol phosphate,* an oligosaccharide carrier, is inserted into the ER membrane (Figure 12-7, step ❶). GlcNAc and mannose groups are then added to the phosphate group of dolichol phosphate (step ❷). The growing core oligosaccharide is then translocated from the cytosol to the ER lumen by a *flippase* (step ❸). Once inside the ER lumen, more mannose and glucose units are added (step ❹). The completed core oligosaccharide is then transferred as a single unit from dolichol to an asparagine residue of the recipient protein (step ❺). Finally, the core oligosaccharide attached to the protein is trimmed and modified (step ❻).

Usually, the core oligosaccharide is added to the protein as the polypeptide is being synthesized by a ribosome bound to the ER membrane. We know that this *cotranslational glycosylation* helps to promote proper protein folding because experimental inhibition of glycosylation leads to the appearance of misfolded, aggregated proteins. Addition of a single glucose unit allows other ER proteins to interact with the newly synthesized glycoprotein to ensure its proper folding. One of two ER proteins known as **calnexin** (CNX, membrane-bound) and **calreticulin** (CRT, soluble) can bind to the monoglucosylated glycoprotein and promote disulfide bond formation by forming a complex with the glycoprotein and a thiol oxidoreductase known as *ERp57,* which catalyzes disulfide bond formation. The

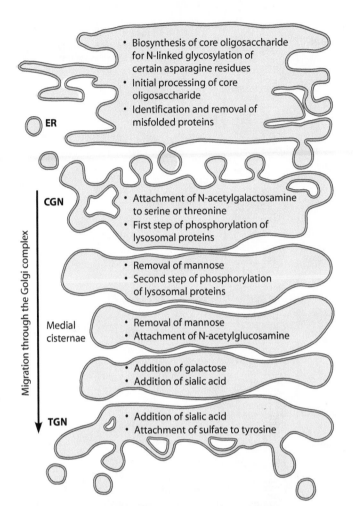

Migration through the Golgi complex

ER
- Biosynthesis of core oligosaccharide for N-linked glycosylation of certain asparagine residues
- Initial processing of core oligosaccharide
- Identification and removal of misfolded proteins

CGN
- Attachment of N-acetylgalactosamine to serine or threonine
- First step of phosphorylation of lysosomal proteins

- Removal of mannose
- Second step of phosphorylation of lysosomal proteins

Medial cisternae
- Removal of mannose
- Attachment of N-acetylglucosamine

- Addition of galactose
- Addition of sialic acid

TGN
- Addition of sialic acid
- Attachment of sulfate to tyrosine

FIGURE 12-6 Compartmentalization of the Steps of Glycosylation and Subsequent Modification of Proteins. Enzymes that catalyze specific steps of glycosylation and further modification of proteins reside in different compartments of the ER and Golgi complex. Processing occurs sequentially as proteins travel from compartment to compartment. The steps listed in the figure are examples of potential modifications and do not necessarily occur with all glycoproteins.

protein complex then dissociates, and the final glucose unit is removed by an enzyme named *glucosidase II.*

At this point, a specific glucosyl transferase in the ER known as *UGGT (UDP-glucose:glycoprotein glucotransferase)* acts as a sensor for proper folding of the newly synthesized glycoprotein. UGGT binds to improperly folded proteins and adds back a single glucose unit, making the protein a substrate for another round of CNX/CRT binding and disulfide bond formation. Once the proper conformation is achieved, UGGT no longer binds the new glycoprotein, which is then free to exit the ER and move to the Golgi.

Further Glycosylation Occurs in the Golgi Complex

Further processing of N-glycosylated proteins happens in the Golgi complex as the glycoproteins move from the *cis* face through the medial cisternae to the *trans* face of the Golgi stack. These **terminal glycosylations** in the Golgi

show remarkable variability among proteins and account for much of the great diversity in structure and function of protein oligosaccharide side chains.

Terminal glycosylation always includes the removal of a few of the carbohydrate units of the core oligosaccharide. In some cases, no further processing occurs in the Golgi complex. In other cases, more complex oligosaccharides are generated by the further addition of GlcNAc and other monosaccharides, including galactose, sialic acid, and fucose (see Figure 7-26a). Some glycoproteins contain galactose units that are added by *galactosyl transferase,* a marker enzyme unique to the Golgi.

Given the role of the Golgi complex in glycosylation, it is not surprising that two of the most important categories of enzymes present in Golgi stacks are *glucan synthetases,* which produce oligosaccharides from monosaccharides, and *glycosyl transferases,* which attach carbohydrate groups to proteins. The ER and Golgi complex contain hundreds of different glycosyl transferases, which indicates the potential complexity of oligosaccharide side chains. Within the Golgi stack, each cisterna contains a distinctive set of processing enzymes.

Notice in the preceding discussion that the mature oligosaccharides in glycoproteins are found only on the lumenal side of the ER and Golgi complex membranes and thus contribute to membrane asymmetry. Because the lumenal side of the ER membrane is topologically equivalent to the exterior surface of the cell, it is easy to see why all plasma membrane glycoprotein oligosaccharides are found on the extracellular side of the membrane.

Roles of the ER and Golgi Complex in Protein Trafficking

Membrane-bound and soluble proteins synthesized in the rough ER must be directed to a variety of intracellular locations, including the ER itself, the Golgi complex, endosomes, and lysosomes. Moreover, once a protein reaches an organelle where it is to remain, there must be a mechanism for preventing it from leaving. Other groups of proteins synthesized in the rough ER are destined for incorporation into the plasma membrane or for release to the outside of the cell. Therefore, each protein contains a specific "tag" targeting the protein to a transport vesicle that will carry material from one specific cellular location to another. Depending on the protein and its destination, the tag may be a short amino acid sequence, an oligosaccharide side chain, a hydrophobic domain, or some other structural feature. Tags may also be involved in excluding material from certain vesicles.

Membrane lipids may also be tagged to help vesicles reach their proper destinations. This tag can be one or more phosphate groups attached to positions 3, 4, and/or 5 of a membrane phosphatidylinositol (PI) molecule by a specific kinase. For example, a functional PI 3-kinase is required for proper sorting of vesicles to the vacuole in yeast. In mammalian cells, inhibition of inositol kinases

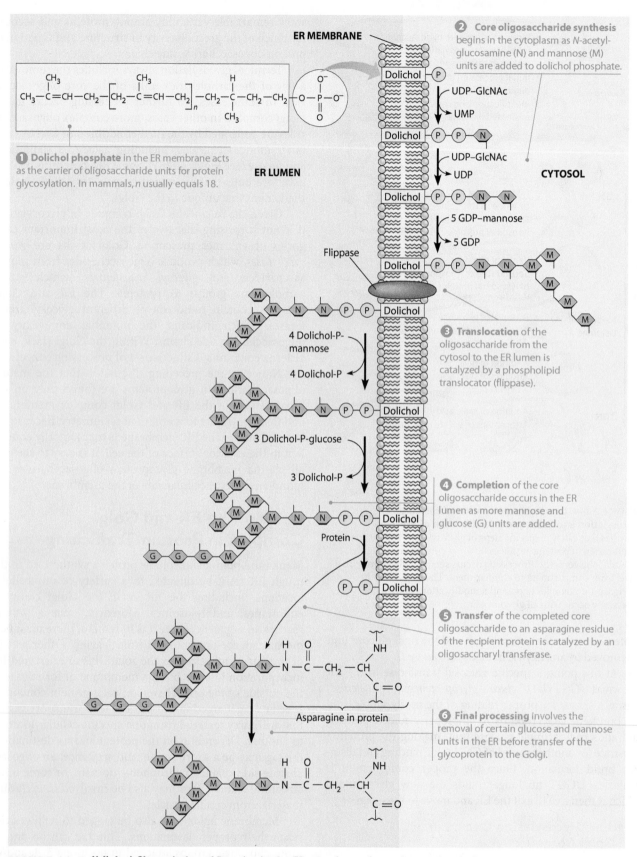

ER MEMBRANE

2 **Core oligosaccharide synthesis** begins in the cytoplasm as *N*-acetyl-glucosamine (N) and mannose (M) units are added to dolichol phosphate.

$$CH_3-C=CH-CH_2-[CH_2-C=CH-CH_2]_n-CH_2-CH-CH_2-CH_2-O-P-O^-$$

1 **Dolichol phosphate** in the ER membrane acts as the carrier of oligosaccharide units for protein glycosylation. In mammals, *n* usually equals 18.

ER LUMEN

CYTOSOL

UDP–GlcNAc
UMP

UDP–GlcNAc
UDP

5 GDP–mannose
5 GDP

Flippase

3 **Translocation** of the oligosaccharide from the cytosol to the ER lumen is catalyzed by a phospholipid translocator (flippase).

4 Dolichol-P-mannose
4 Dolichol-P

3 Dolichol-P-glucose
3 Dolichol-P

4 **Completion** of the core oligosaccharide occurs in the ER lumen as more mannose and glucose (G) units are added.

Protein

5 **Transfer** of the completed core oligosaccharide to an asparagine residue of the recipient protein is catalyzed by an oligosaccharyl transferase.

Asparagine in protein

6 **Final processing** involves the removal of certain glucose and mannose units in the ER before transfer of the glycoprotein to the Golgi.

FIGURE 12-7 N-linked Glycosylation of Proteins in the ER. Synthesis of core oligosaccharides begins in the cytoplasm, using a dolichol phosphate molecule as a carrier. The partially synthesized oligosaccharide is translocated to the ER lumen, where additional monosaccharides are added. The completed oligosaccharide is then transferred to the target protein, and several monosaccharides are removed in final processing.

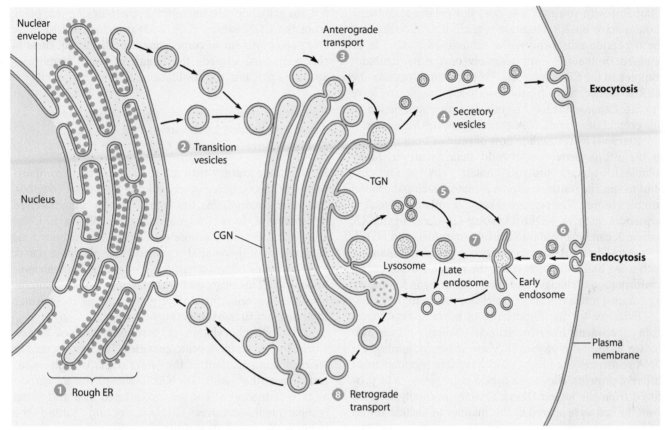

FIGURE 12-8 Trafficking Through the Endomembrane System. Vesicles carry lipids and proteins along several routes from the ER through the Golgi complex to various destinations, including secretory vesicles, endosomes, and lysosomes. ❶ As ribosomes of the rough ER synthesize proteins, the proteins enter the ER lumen, where initial glycosylation steps occur. ❷ Transition vesicles carry glycosylated proteins (and newly synthesized lipids) to the CGN. ❸ Lipids and proteins move through the cisternae of the Golgi stack via shuttle vesicles and cisternae mature as new enzymes are added via vesicles. ❹ At the TGN, some vesicles bud off to form secretory vesicles, which move to the plasma membrane and release their contents by exocytosis. ❺ Other vesicles bud from the TGN to form endosomes that, in turn, help to make lysosomes. ❻ Proteins and other materials are taken into the cell by endocytosis, forming endocytic vesicles that fuse with early endosomes. ❼ Early endosomes containing material for digestion mature to form late endosomes and then lysosomes. ❽ Retrograde traffic returns compartment-specific proteins to earlier compartments.

VIDEOS www.thecellplace.com *ER to Golgi traffic*

disrupts vesicle trafficking to the lysosome. Aside from specific tags on some lipids, the length and degree of saturation of certain membrane lipids have also been shown to be important in vesicle trafficking.

An overview of the trafficking involving the ER and Golgi complex is presented in **Figure 12-8**. Sorting of proteins begins in the ER and early compartments of the Golgi stack, which contain mechanisms for retrieving or retaining compartment-specific proteins. This important step preserves the compartment-specific functions needed to maintain the integrity of glycosylation and processing pathways. The final sorting of material that will leave the Golgi complex occurs in the TGN, where lipids and proteins are selectively packaged into distinct populations of transport vesicles that are destined for different locations in the cell. In some cells, the Golgi complex is also involved in the processing of proteins that enter the cell by endocytosis.

ER-Specific Proteins Contain Retention and Retrieval Tags

The protein composition required in the ER is maintained both by preventing some proteins from escaping when vesicles bud from the ER membrane and by retrieving other proteins that have left the ER and reached the CGN. It is not entirely clear how proteins that never leave the ER are retained, but one theory proposes that they form extensive complexes that are physically excluded from vesicles budding from the ER.

Several proteins localized to the ER contain the tripeptide sequence RXR (Arg-X-Arg, where X is any amino acid), which appears to promote retention in the ER. This *retention tag* is also found in some multisubunit proteins that are destined for the plasma membrane. The *N*-methyl-D-aspartate (NMDA) receptor, which is important in neurotransmission in the mammalian brain, contains such a tag. But why, you may ask, does this plasma membrane protein have an ER retention signal? It is thought that the tripeptide causes individual subunits of NMDA to be retained in the ER until assembly of the multisubunit complex in the ER is complete. Proper assembly masks the RXR sequence, allowing the assembled complex to leave the ER. Other evidence suggests that phosphorylation of this protein near the RXR sequence promotes ER release.

Retrieval by retrograde flow of vesicles from the CGN to the ER is better understood than retention. Many soluble ER-specific proteins contain *retrieval tags* that bind to specific transmembrane receptors facing the Golgi complex lumen. The tags are short C-terminal amino acid sequences such as KDEL (Lys-Asp-Glu-Leu) or KKXX (where X can be any amino acid) in mammals and HDEL (His-Asp-Glu-Leu) in yeast. When a protein containing such a tag binds to its receptor, the receptor undergoes a conformational change, and the receptor-ligand complex is packaged into a transport vesicle for return to the ER.

Evidence for the importance of retrieval tags comes from experiments involving artificial *chimeric proteins,* also known as *fusion proteins.* They are made by joining the DNA sequences encoding two polypeptide segments from different proteins, allowing a hybrid polypeptide to be produced from the joined DNAs. Proteins normally secreted from the cell were altered in this manner to include amino acids representing an ER retrieval tag, and these proteins were subsequently found in the ER rather than being secreted. Interestingly, some of these chimeric proteins found in the ER had undergone partial processing by enzymes found only in the Golgi complex. This finding indicates that the suspected tag did not simply prevent escape of the protein from the ER but actively promoted the retrieval of ER-specific proteins from the Golgi complex.

Golgi Complex Proteins May Be Sorted According to the Lengths of Their Membrane-Spanning Domains

Like resident proteins required in the ER, some resident proteins of the Golgi complex contain retention or retrieval tags. Moreover, in the Golgi complex as in the ER, the formation of large complexes that are excluded from transport vesicles may play a role in maintaining the protein composition of the Golgi complex. In addition, we will next see that a third, distinctly different mechanism is also likely at work in this organelle—a mechanism involving hydrophobic regions of Golgi proteins.

All known Golgi-specific proteins are integral membrane proteins that have one or more hydrophobic membrane-spanning domains anchoring them to Golgi membranes. The length of the hydrophobic domains may determine into which cisterna of the Golgi complex each membrane-bound protein is incorporated as it moves through the organelle. Recall that the thickness of cellular membranes increases progressively from the ER (about 5 nm) to the plasma membrane (about 8 nm). Among Golgi-specific proteins, there is a corresponding increase in the

lengths of hydrophobic membrane-spanning domains going from the CGN to the TGN. Such proteins tend to move from compartment to compartment until the thickness of the membrane exceeds the length of their membrane-spanning domains, thereby blocking further migration.

Targeting of Soluble Lysosomal Proteins to Endosomes and Lysosomes Is a Model for Protein Sorting in the TGN

During their journey through the ER and early compartments of the Golgi complex, soluble lysosomal enzymes, like other glycoproteins, undergo N-glycosylation followed by removal of glucose and mannose units. Within the Golgi complex, however, mannose residues on the carbohydrate side chain of lysosomal enzymes are phosphorylated, forming an oligosaccharide containing mannose-6-phosphate. This oligosaccharide tag distinguishes soluble lysosomal proteins from other glycoproteins and ensures their delivery to lysosomes (**Figure 12-9**).

The phosphorylation of mannose residues is catalyzed by two Golgi-specific enzymes. The first, located in an early compartment of the Golgi stack, is a phosphotransferase that adds GlcNAc-1-phosphate to carbon atom 6 of mannose. The second, located in a mid-Golgi compartment, removes GlcNAc, leaving behind the mannose-6-phosphate residue.

The interior surface of the TGN membrane has mannose-6-phosphate receptors (MPRs) that bind to the mannose-6-phosphate residues of lysosomal proteins. The pH of the TGN is around 6.4, which favors binding of soluble lysosomal enzymes to these receptors. Following binding of tagged lysosomal proteins to the MPRs, the receptor-ligand complexes are packaged into transport vesicles and conveyed to an endosome. In animal cells, lysosomal enzymes needed for degradation of material brought into the cell by endocytosis are transported from the TGN to organelles known as **late endosomes.** These develop from **early endosomes,** which are formed by the coalescence of vesicles from the TGN and plasma membrane.

As an early endosome matures to form a late endosome, the pH of the lumen decreases to about 5.5, causing the bound lysosomal enzymes to dissociate from the MPRs. This prevents the retrograde movement of these enzymes back to the Golgi along with the receptors that are recycled in vesicles that return to the TGN. Finally, the late endosome either matures to form a new lysosome or delivers its contents to an active lysosome.

Strong support for this model of lysosomal enzyme targeting came from studies of a human genetic disorder called *I-cell disease.* Cultured fibroblast cells from patients with I-cell disease synthesize all the expected lysosomal enzymes but then release most of the soluble proteins to the extracellular medium instead of incorporating them into lysosomes. The distinguishing feature of the misdirected proteins is the absence of mannose-6-phosphate residues on their oligosaccharide side chains. The

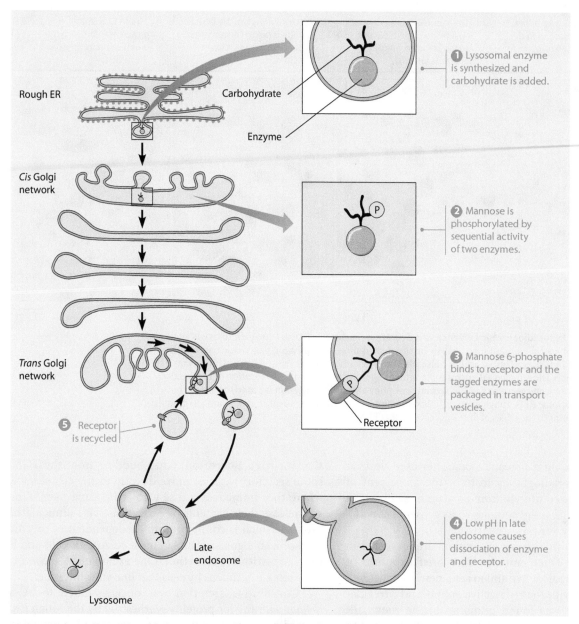

Rough ER

Carbohydrate

Enzyme

1 Lysosomal enzyme is synthesized and carbohydrate is added.

Cis Golgi network

2 Mannose is phosphorylated by sequential activity of two enzymes.

Trans Golgi network

3 Mannose 6-phosphate binds to receptor and the tagged enzymes are packaged in transport vesicles.

Receptor

5 Receptor is recycled

Late endosome

4 Low pH in late endosome causes dissociation of enzyme and receptor.

Lysosome

FIGURE 12-9 Targeting of Soluble Lysosomal Enzymes to Endosomes and Lysosomes by a Mannose-6-Phosphate Tag. **1** In the ER, soluble lysosomal enzymes undergo *N*-glycosylation followed by removal of glucose and mannose units. **2** Within the Golgi complex, mannose residues on the lysosomal enzymes are phosphorylated by two enzymes. The first one adds *N*-acetylglucosamine-1-phosphate to carbon atom 6 of mannose. The second one removes *N*-acetylglucosamine, leaving behind the phosphorylated mannose residue. **3** The tagged lysosomal enzymes bind to mannose-6-phosphate receptors in the TGN and are packaged into coated transport vesicles that convey the enzymes to a late endosome. **4** The acidity of the late endosomal lumen causes the enzymes to dissociate from their receptors. **5** The receptors are recycled in vesicles that return to the TGN. The late endosome either matures to form a lysosome or transfers its contents to an active lysosome.

mannose-6-phosphate tag is clearly essential for targeting soluble lysosomal glycoproteins to the lysosome. As you may have guessed, I-cell disease results from a defective phosphotransferase that is needed to add the mannose-6-phosphate to oligosaccharide chains on lysosomal enzymes. However, while mannose-6-phosphate residues are important for directing traffic from the ER to the lysosome, other pathways appear to be involved as well. For example, in patients with I-cell disease, lysosomal acid hydrolases somehow still reach the lysosomes in liver cells.

Secretory Pathways Transport Molecules to the Exterior of the Cell

Integral to the vesicular traffic shown in Figure 12-8 are **secretory pathways** by which proteins move from the ER through the Golgi complex to **secretory vesicles** and **secretory granules,** which then discharge their contents to the exterior of the cell. The concerted roles of the ER and the Golgi complex in secretion were demonstrated in 1967 by James Jamieson and George Palade in secretory

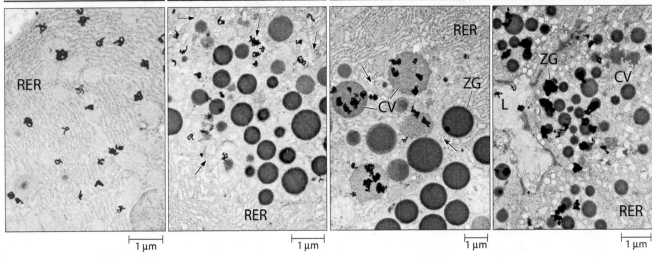

(a) **After 3 minutes,** most of the labeled protein is found in the rough ER where it has just been synthesized.	(b) **After 7 minutes,** most of the new labeled protein has moved into the adjacent Golgi complexes (arrows).	(c) **After 37 minutes,** the labeled protein is being concentrated in condensing vacuoles next to the Golgi.	(d) **After 117 minutes,** the labeled protein is found in zymogen granules, ready for export to the lumen.

FIGURE 12-10 Autoradiographic Evidence of a Secretory Pathway. To trace the path of newly synthesized proteins through a cell, Jamieson and Palade briefly treated slices of guinea pig pancreatic tissue with a small amount of a radioactive amino acid to pulse label newly synthesized proteins. After washing away unincorporated amino acids, they used microscopic autoradiography to determine the location of radioactively labeled protein in pancreatic secretory cells at several time points following injection (**a**) to (**d**) as noted above the panels. Abbreviations: RER, rough endoplasmic reticulum; CV, condensing vacuole; ZG, zymogen granule; L, lumen. Arrows point to the edges of the Golgi complexes (TEMs).

cells from guinea pig pancreatic slices. They used electron microscopic autoradiography to trace the movement of radioactively labeled protein from its place of synthesis in the ER through the Golgi complex to its subsequent packaging in secretory vesicles.

Results from this classic experiment are presented in **Figure 12-10.** Three minutes after brief exposure of tissue slices to a radioactive amino acid, newly synthesized protein labeled with the radioactive amino acid (irregular dark coloration) was found primarily in the rough ER (panel a). A few minutes later, labeled protein began to appear in the Golgi complex (panel b). By 37 minutes, labeled protein was detected in vesicles budding from the Golgi that Jamieson and Palade called *condensing vacuoles* (panel c). After 117 minutes, labeled protein began to accumulate in dense *zymogen granules,* vesicles that discharge secretory proteins to the exterior of the cell (panel d). Some of the radioactively labeled protein was observed in the exterior lumen adjacent to the cell, demonstrating that some of the secretory granules had released their contents from the cell.

Based on this classic experiment and numerous similar studies since then, the secretory pathways shown in Figure 12-8 are now understood in considerable detail. Moreover, we now distinguish two different modes of secretion by eukaryotic cells. *Constitutive secretion* involves the continuous discharge of vesicles at the plasma membrane surface, whereas *regulated secretion* involves controlled, rapid releases that happen in response to an extracellular signal.

Constitutive Secretion. After budding from the TGN, some secretory vesicles move directly to the cell surface, where they immediately fuse with the plasma membrane and release their contents by exocytosis. This unregulated process, which is continuous and independent of specific extracellular signals, occurs in most eukaryotic cells and is called **constitutive secretion.** One example is the continuous release of mucus by cells that line your intestine.

Constitutive secretion was once assumed to be a *default pathway* for proteins synthesized by the rough ER. According to this model, all proteins destined to remain in the endomembrane system must have a tag that diverts them from constitutive secretion. Otherwise, they will move through the endomembrane system and be released outside the cell by default. Support for this model came from studies in which removal of the KDEL retrieval tags on resident ER proteins led to secretion of the modified protein. However, more recent evidence suggests that a variety of short amino acid tags may identify specific proteins for constitutive secretion.

For some proteins, constitutive secretion may require N-glycosylation of the protein, as was recently shown for mouse interleukin-31, a secreted protein involved in extracellular cell-to-cell signaling. Other recent work showed that addition of an N-glycosylation site to the human p53 tumor suppressor protein, a protein that is not normally secreted, caused this altered p53 to be secreted. As you might expect, the secreted protein was N-glycosylated.

Regulated Secretion. While vesicles containing constitutively secreted proteins move continuously and directly from the TGN to the plasma membrane, secretory vesicles involved in **regulated secretion** accumulate in the cell and then fuse with the plasma membrane only in response to specific extracellular signals. An important example is the release of neurotransmitters. Two additional examples of regulated secretion are the release of insulin from pancreatic β cells in response to glucose and the release of *zymogens*—inactive precursors of hydrolytic enzymes—from pancreatic acinar cells in response to calcium or endocrine hormones.

Regulated secretory vesicles form by budding from the TGN as immature secretory vesicles, which undergo a subsequent maturation process. Maturation of secretory proteins involves concentration of the proteins—referred to as *condensation*—and frequently also some proteolytic processing. The mature secretory vesicles then move close to the site of secretion and remain near the plasma membrane until receiving a hormonal or other chemical signal that triggers release of their contents by fusion with the plasma membrane.

Zymogen granules are a type of mature regulated secretory vesicle that are usually quite large and contain highly concentrated protein, as shown in Figure 12-10 and **Figure 12-11**. Note that the zymogen granules are concentrated in the region of the cell between the Golgi stacks from which they arise and the portion of the plasma

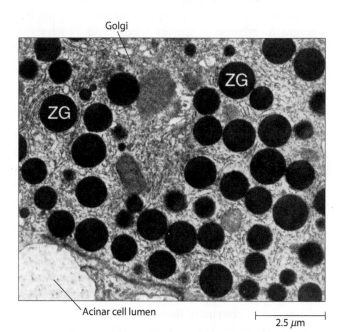

Golgi

ZG

ZG

Acinar cell lumen

2.5 μm

FIGURE 12-11 Zymogen Granules. This electron micrograph of an acinar (secretory) cell from the exocrine pancreas of a rat illustrates the prominence of zymogen granules (ZG), which contain enzymes destined for secretion. They are usually concentrated in the region of the cell between the Golgi complex from which they arise and the portion of the plasma membrane bordering the acinar lumen into which the zymogens will be discharged (TEM).

membrane bordering the lumen into which the contents of the granules are eventually discharged.

The information needed to direct a protein to a regulated secretory vesicle is presumably inherent in the amino acid sequence of the protein, though the precise signals and mechanisms are not yet known. Current evidence suggests that high concentrations of secretory proteins in secretory granules promote the formation of large *protein aggregates* that exclude nonsecretory proteins. This could occur in the TGN, where only aggregates would be packaged in vesicles destined for secretory granules, or it could occur in the secretory granule itself. The pH of the TGN and the secretory granule lumens may serve as a trigger favoring aggregation as material leaves the TGN. The soluble proteins that do not become part of an aggregate in the TGN or a secretory granule would be carried by transport vesicles to other locations.

Exocytosis and Endocytosis: Transporting Material Across the Plasma Membrane

Two methods of transporting materials across the plasma membrane are *exocytosis,* the process by which secretory granules release their contents to the exterior of the cell, and *endocytosis,* the process by which cells internalize external materials. Both processes are unique to eukaryotic cells and are also involved in the delivery, recycling, and turnover of membrane proteins. We will first consider exocytosis because it is the final step in a secretory pathway that began with the ER and the Golgi complex.

Exocytosis Releases Intracellular Molecules Outside the Cell

In **exocytosis,** proteins in a vesicle are released to the exterior of the cell as the membrane of the vesicle fuses with the plasma membrane. A variety of proteins are exported from both animal and plant cells by exocytosis. Animal cells secrete peptide and protein hormones, mucus, milk proteins, and digestive enzymes in this manner. Plant and fungal cells secrete enzymes and structural proteins associated with the cell wall, and carnivorous plants secrete hydrolytic enzymes that are used to digest trapped insects.

The process of exocytosis is illustrated schematically in **Figure 12-12a**. Vesicles containing cellular products destined for secretion move to the cell surface (step ❶), where the membrane of the vesicle fuses with the plasma membrane (step ❷). Fusion with the plasma membrane discharges the vesicle contents to the exterior of the cell (step ❸). In the process, the membrane of the vesicle becomes integrated into the plasma membrane, with the *inner* (lumenal) surface of the vesicle becoming the *outer* (extracellular) surface of the plasma membrane (step ❹). Thus, glycoproteins and glycolipids that were originally formed in the ER and Golgi lumens will face the extracellular space.

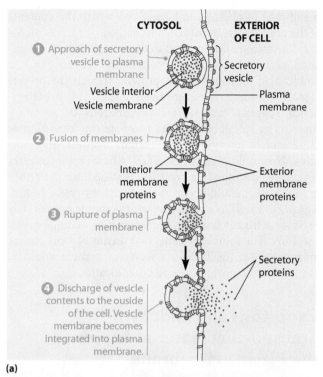

CYTOSOL | EXTERIOR OF CELL

1 Approach of secretory vesicle to plasma membrane

Secretory vesicle

Vesicle interior
Vesicle membrane

Plasma membrane

2 Fusion of membranes

Interior membrane proteins

Exterior membrane proteins

3 Rupture of plasma membrane

Secretory proteins

4 Discharge of vesicle contents to the ouside of the cell. Vesicle membrane becomes integrated into plasma membrane.

(a)

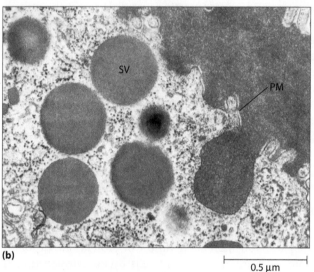

SV

PM

(b)

0.5 µm

FIGURE 12-12 Exocytosis. (a) This illustration shows how a secretory vesicle approaches the plasma membrane, fuses with it, and releases its contents to the exterior of the cell during exocytosis. (b) In this monkey pancreatic cell, secretory vesicles (SV) approach the plasma membrane (PM), where one vesicle has fused with the membrane and secreted its contents.

The mechanism underlying the movement of exocytic vesicles to the cell surface is not yet clear. Current evidence points to the involvement of microtubules in vesicle movement. For example, in some cells, vesicles appear to move from the Golgi complex to the plasma membrane along "tracks" of microtubules that are oriented parallel to the direction of vesicle movement. Moreover, vesicle movement stops when the cells are treated with *colchicine*, a plant alkaloid that prevents microtubule assembly. We

will discuss the intracellular movement of vesicles along microtubules in Chapter 16.

The Role of Calcium in Triggering Exocytosis. Fusion of regulated secretory vesicles with the plasma membrane is generally triggered by a specific extracellular signal. In most cases, the signal is a hormone or a neurotransmitter that binds to specific receptors on the cell surface and triggers the synthesis or release of a *second messenger* within the cell. During regulated secretion, a transient elevation of the intracellular concentration of calcium ions often appears to be an essential step in the signal cascade leading from the receptor on the cell surface to exocytosis. For example, microinjection of calcium into pancreatic cells induces mature secretory granules to discharge their contents to the extracellular medium. The specific role of calcium is not yet clear, but it appears that an elevation in the intracellular calcium concentration leads to the activation of protein kinases whose target proteins are components of either the vesicle membrane or the plasma membrane.

Polarized Secretion. In many cases, exocytosis of specific proteins is limited to a specific surface of the cell. For example, the secretory cells that line your intestine release digestive enzymes only on the side of the cell that faces the interior of the intestine. This phenomenon, called **polarized secretion,** is also seen in nerve cells, which secrete neurotransmitter molecules only at junctions with other nerve cells. Proteins destined for polarized secretion, as well as lipid and protein components of the two different membrane layers, are sorted into vesicles that bind to localized recognition sites on subdomains of the plasma membrane.

Endocytosis Imports Extracellular Molecules by Forming Vesicles from the Plasma Membrane

Most eukaryotic cells carry out one or more forms of **endocytosis** for uptake of extracellular material. A small segment of the plasma membrane progressively folds inward (**Figure 12-13**, step 1), and then it pinches off to form an **endocytic vesicle** containing ingested substances or particles (steps 2 – 4). Endocytosis is important for several cellular processes, including ingestion of essential nutrients by some unicellular organisms and defense against microorganisms by white blood cells.

In terms of membrane flow, exocytosis and endocytosis clearly have opposite effects. Whereas exocytosis adds lipids and proteins to the plasma membrane, endocytosis removes them. Thus, the steady-state composition of the plasma membrane results from a balance between exocytosis and endocytosis. Through endocytosis and retrograde transport, the cell can recycle and reuse molecules deposited in the plasma membrane by secretory vesicles during exocytosis.

The magnitude of the resulting membrane exchange is impressive. For example, the secretory cells in your

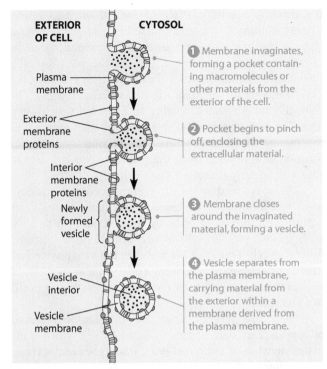

	EXTERIOR OF CELL		CYTOSOL

Plasma membrane

Exterior membrane proteins

Interior membrane proteins

Newly formed vesicle

Vesicle interior

Vesicle membrane

1 Membrane invaginates, forming a pocket containing macromolecules or other materials from the exterior of the cell.

2 Pocket begins to pinch off, enclosing the extracellular material.

3 Membrane closes around the invaginated material, forming a vesicle.

4 Vesicle separates from the plasma membrane, carrying material from the exterior within a membrane derived from the plasma membrane.

FIGURE 12-13 Endocytosis. This illustration shows the uptake of materials from the exterior of the cell during endocytosis. For clarity, the coat proteins at the site of invagination and around the endocytic vesicle have been omitted from this diagram.

pancreas recycle an amount of membrane equal to the whole surface area of the cell within about 90 minutes. Cultured macrophages (large white blood cells) are even faster, replacing an amount of membrane equivalent to the entire plasma membrane within about 30 minutes!

During endocytosis, the membrane of an endocytic vesicle isolates the internalized substances from the cytosol. Most endocytic vesicles develop into early endosomes, which fuse with vesicles from the TGN, acquiring digestive enzymes and maturing to form new lysosomes. A distinction is usually made between *phagocytosis* (Greek for "cellular eating"), in which large solid particles are ingested, and *pinocytosis* ("cellular drinking"), in which liquids containing soluble or suspended molecules are taken up.

Phagocytosis. The ingestion of large particles (>0.5 μm diameter), including aggregates of macromolecules, parts of other cells, and even whole microorganisms or other cells, is known as **phagocytosis.** For many unicellular eukaryotes, such as amoebas and ciliated protozoa, phagocytosis is a routine means for acquiring food. Phagocytosis is also used by some primitive animals, notably flatworms, coelenterates, and sponges, as a means of obtaining nutrients.

In more complex organisms, however, phagocytosis is usually restricted to specialized cells called **phagocytes.** For example, your body contains two classes of white blood cells—*neutrophils* and *macrophages*—which use phagocytosis for defense rather than nutrition. These cells engulf and digest foreign material or invasive microorganisms found in

the bloodstream or in injured tissues. Macrophages have an additional role as scavengers, ingesting cellular debris and whole damaged cells from injured tissues. Under certain conditions, other mammalian cells engage in phagocytosis. For example, fibroblasts found in connective tissue can take up collagen to allow remodeling of the tissue, and dendritic cells in the mammalian spleen can ingest bacteria as part of an immune response.

Phagocytosis has been studied most extensively in the amoeba, which uses it for nutrition. Contact with food particles or smaller organisms triggers the onset of phagocytosis, as shown in **Figure 12-14.** Folds of membrane called *pseudopods* gradually surround the object and then meet and engulf the particle, forming an intracellular **phagocytic vacuole.** This endocytic vesicle, also called a *phagosome,* then fuses with a late endosome or matures directly into a lysosome, forming a large vesicle in which the ingested material is digested. As part of their role in the immune system, human phagocytes generate toxic concentrations of hydrogen peroxide, hypochlorous acid, and other oxidants in the phagocytic vacuole to kill microorganisms.

Receptor-Mediated Endocytosis. Cells can acquire certain soluble and suspended materials by a process known as **receptor-mediated endocytosis** (also called **clathrin-dependent endocytosis**). For this process, cells use specific receptors that are found on the outer surface of the plasma membrane. Receptor-mediated endocytosis is the primary mechanism for the specific internalization of most macromolecules by eukaryotic cells. Depending on the cell type, mammalian cells can ingest hormones, growth factors, enzymes, serum proteins, cholesterol, antibodies, iron, and even some viruses and bacterial toxins by this mechanism.

The discovery of receptor-mediated endocytosis and its role in the internalization of *low-density lipoproteins (LDL)* is highlighted in **Box 12B** (see p. 346). Receptor-mediated endocytosis of LDL carries cholesterol into mammalian cells. An interest in familial hypercholesterolemia, a hereditary predisposition to high blood cholesterol levels and hence to atherosclerosis and heart disease, led Michael Brown and Joseph Goldstein to the discovery of receptor-mediated endocytosis, for which they shared a Nobel Prize in 1986.

Receptor-mediated endocytosis is illustrated in **Figure 12-15.** The process begins with the binding of specific molecules (referred to as ligands) to their *receptors*—specific ligand-binding proteins found on the outer surface of the plasma membrane (step **1**). As the receptor-ligand complexes diffuse laterally in the membrane, they encounter specialized membrane regions called *coated pits* that serve as sites for the collection and internalization of these complexes (step **2**). In a typical mammalian cell, coated pits occupy about 20% of the total surface area of the plasma membrane.

Accumulation of receptor-ligand complexes within the coated pits triggers accumulation of additional proteins on

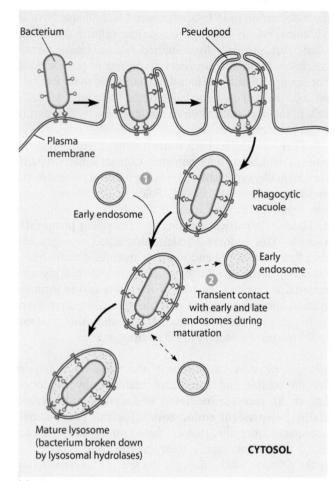

Bacterium

Pseudopod

Plasma membrane

Early endosome

❶

Phagocytic vacuole

Early endosome

❷

Transient contact with early and late endosomes during maturation

Mature lysosome (bacterium broken down by lysosomal hydrolases)

CYTOSOL

(a)

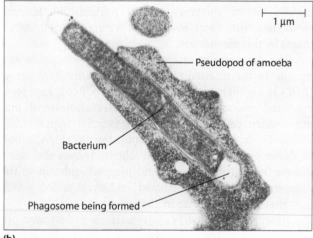

1 μm

Pseudopod of amoeba

Bacterium

Phagosome being formed

(b)

FIGURE 12-14 Phagocytosis. (a) Particles or microorganisms bind to receptors on the cell surface, triggering the onset of phagocytosis. Folds of membrane called *pseudopods* gradually surround the particle. Eventually, the pseudopods meet and engulf the particle, forming a *phagocytic vacuole*. The vacuole then ❶ fuses with an early endosome or ❷ forms transient connections (indicated by dashed lines) with early and late endosomes and matures into a lysosome, in which digestion of the internalized material occurs. **(b)** This micrograph shows a phagosome being formed as an amoeba engulfs a rod-shaped bacterial cell (TEM).

📹 **VIDEOS** www.thecellplace.com *Phagocytosis in action*

the inner (cytosolic) surface of the plasma membrane. These additional proteins—including *adaptor protein, clathrin,* and *dynamin*—are required for promoting membrane curvature and invagination of the pit (step ❸). Invagination continues until the pit pinches off from the plasma membrane, forming a **coated vesicle** (step ❹). The clathrin coat is released, leaving an uncoated vesicle (step ❺). The coat proteins and dynamin are then recycled to the plasma membrane, where they become available for forming new vesicles, while the uncoated vesicle is free to fuse with an early endosome (step ❻).

The speed and scope of receptor-mediated endocytosis are impressive. A coated pit usually invaginates within a minute or so of being formed, and up to 2500 such coated pits invaginate per minute in a cultured fibroblast cell. **Figure 12-16** shows the progressive formation of a coated vesicle from a coated pit as particles of yolk protein are taken up by the maturing oocyte (egg cell) of a chicken.

There are several variations of receptor-mediated endocytosis. Epidermal growth factor (EGF), which stimulates division of epithelial cells, undergoes endocytosis by the mechanism shown in Figure 12-15. Here, endocytosis plays an important role in cell signaling. As EGF receptors are internalized, the cell becomes less responsive to EGF, a process known as *desensitization*. Deficiencies in desensitization caused by defective endocytosis can lead to overstimulation by EGF, resulting in excessive cell growth, cell division, and possible tumor formation.

In another variation of receptor-mediated endocytosis, receptors are concentrated in coated pits independent of formation of receptor-ligand complexes. Binding of ligands to receptors simply triggers internalization. In yet another variation, the receptors are not only constitutively concentrated, but they are also constitutively internalized regardless of whether ligands have bound to the receptors. For example, the LDL receptors described in Box 12B are constitutively internalized.

Following receptor-mediated endocytosis, the uncoated vesicles fuse with vesicles budding from the TGN to form early endosomes in peripheral regions of the cell. *Early endosomes* are sites for the sorting and recycling of extracellular material brought into the cell by endocytosis. Protein molecules essential for new rounds of endocytosis are often—but not always—recycled after separation from the material fated for digestion. The early endosome continues to acquire lysosomal proteins from the TGN and matures to form a late endosome, which then develops into a lysosome. The roles of endosomes in digestion will be discussed in more detail when we examine lysosomes later in the chapter.

Recycling of plasma membrane receptor molecules is facilitated by acidification of the early endosome. The interior of an endocytic vesicle has a pH of about 7.0, whereas the interior of an early endosome has a pH of 5.9–6.5. The lower pH is maintained by an *ATP-dependent proton pump* in the endosomal membrane. The

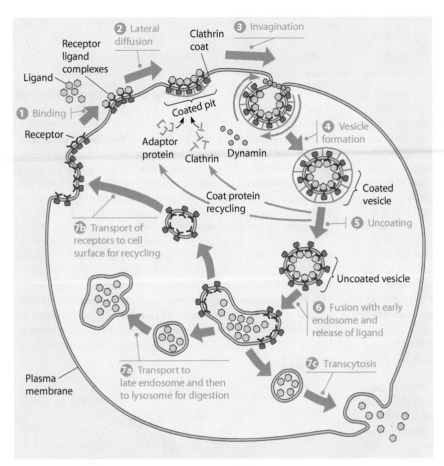

FIGURE 12-15 Receptor-Mediated Endocytosis. During receptor-mediated endocytosis, ❶ the molecules that will be internalized bind to specific receptors on the surface of the plasma membrane. ❷ Receptor-ligand complexes accumulate in coated pits, where ❸ invagination is facilitated by adaptor protein, clathrin, and dynamin on the cytosolic surface of the membrane. The result is ❹ an internalized coated vesicle that ❺ quickly loses its clathrin coat. The uncoated vesicle is now free to ❻ fuse with other intracellular membranes, usually a membrane surrounding an early endosome, where internalized material is sorted. The fate of the receptors and the ingested molecules depends on the nature of the material. Transport vesicles often ❼ᵃ carry material to a late endosome for digestion. Alternative pathways include ❼ᵇ recycling to the plasma membrane or ❼ᶜ transport to another region of the plasma membrane and exocytosis (called transcytosis). For clarity, the nucleus is not shown.

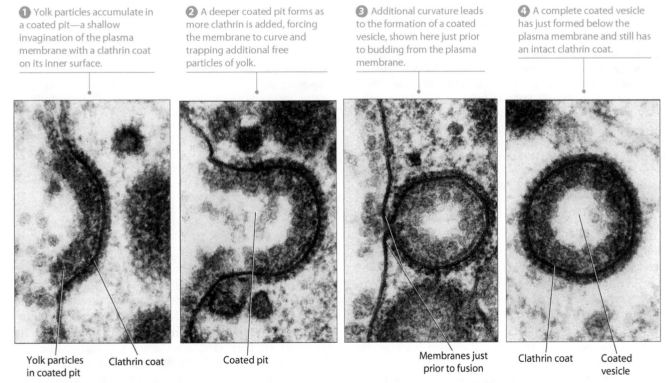

❶ Yolk particles accumulate in a coated pit—a shallow invagination of the plasma membrane with a clathrin coat on its inner surface.

❷ A deeper coated pit forms as more clathrin is added, forcing the membrane to curve and trapping additional free particles of yolk.

❸ Additional curvature leads to the formation of a coated vesicle, shown here just prior to budding from the plasma membrane.

❹ A complete coated vesicle has just formed below the plasma membrane and still has an intact clathrin coat.

Yolk particles in coated pit | Clathrin coat | Coated pit | Membranes just prior to fusion | Clathrin coat | Coated vesicle

FIGURE 12-16 Receptor-Mediated Endocytosis of Yolk Protein by a Chicken Oocyte. This series of electron micrographs illustrates the formation of a coated vesicle from a coated pit during receptor-mediated endocytosis (TEMs).

Receptor-mediated endocytosis is a highly efficient pathway for the uptake of specific macromolecules by eukaryotic cells. Many different kinds of macromolecules can be taken up by this means, and each one is recognized by its own specific receptor on the plasma membrane of the appropriate cell types. As we consider the discovery of receptor-mediated endocytosis, we will focus on a specific receptor—and, as it turns out, on a health issue that many of us are concerned about: the level of cholesterol in our blood.

As you may know, one of the primary factors predisposing a person to heart attacks is an abnormally high level of cholesterol in the blood serum, a condition called *hypercholesterolemia*. Because of its insolubility, cholesterol tends to be deposited on the inside walls of blood vessels, forming the *atherosclerotic plaques* that cause *atherosclerosis*, commonly known as hardening of the arteries. Ultimately, the plaques may block the flow of blood through the vessels, causing strokes and heart attacks. Remember, however, that cholesterol is a normal component of healthy animal cell membranes—a moderate level of cholesterol is required for maintenance of these membranes. Therefore, the body will synthesize cholesterol if dietary amounts are inadequate.

Although a high blood cholesterol level is often linked to diet, some people are genetically predisposed to high blood cholesterol levels and hence to atherosclerosis and heart disease. Individuals with this hereditary predisposition, called **familial hypercholesterolemia (FH),** can have grossly elevated levels of serum cholesterol (about 650–1000 mg/100 mL of blood serum, compared with the normal range of about 130–200 mg/100 mL). They typically develop atherosclerosis early in life and often die from heart disease before the age of 20.

The link between FH and receptor-mediated endocytosis was discovered by Michael Brown and Joseph Goldstein, who began this work in 1972. Their discovery of receptor-mediated endocytosis led to Nobel Prizes for both scientists in 1986. Brown and Goldstein began by culturing fibroblast cells from FH patients in the laboratory and showing that such cells synthesized cholesterol at abnormally high rates compared with normal cells. Their next key observation was that normal cells also synthesized cholesterol at abnormally high rates when they were deprived of the **low-density lipoproteins (LDLs)** that were usually present in the culture medium. LDL is one form in which cholesterol is transported in the blood and taken up into cells.

LDL is one of several types of *blood lipoprotein particles,* which are classified by density. Another class is the **high-density lipoproteins (HDLs),** moderately high levels of which are considered healthy. A lipoprotein particle consists of a monolayer of phospholipid and cholesterol molecules and one or more protein molecules, with the lipids oriented so that their polar head groups face the aqueous medium on the outside and their nonpolar tails extend into the interior of the particle, which contains additional cholesterol molecules esterified to long-chain fatty acids (**Figure 12B-1**). LDLs have the highest cholesterol content—more than 50%.

In addition to phospholipids and cholesterol, each LDL particle has a large protein called *apolipoprotein B-100* embedded in its lipid monolayer. This protein is crucial to our understanding of the difference in the response of FH cells and normal cells to the level of LDL in the medium. Normal fibroblasts maintain a low rate of cholesterol synthesis in the presence of LDL, but when deprived of LDL they make cholesterol at abnormally high rates. Since it was known that cholesterol down-regulates its own synthesis, Brown

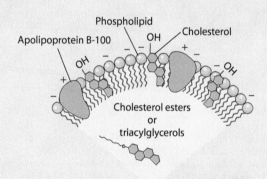

FIGURE 12B-1 LDL Structure. Lipoproteins differ in density depending on the relative amounts of lipid and proteins, with higher lipid amounts resulting in lower density. The low-density lipoprotein (LDL) shown here has a density of 1.02–1.06 g/mL. It contains about 800 phospholipid molecules and 500 free cholesterol molecules in the lipid monolayer plus about 1500 esterified cholesterol molecules in the interior. Apolipoprotein B-100 is embedded in the lipid monolayer and mediates the binding of the LDL to the LDL receptors on the surfaces of cells.

slightly acidic environment of the early endosome decreases the affinity of most receptor-ligand complexes (for example, LDL and its receptor), thereby freeing receptors to be recycled to the plasma membrane while newly ingested material is diverted to other locations. This is similar to the acid-induced recycling of mannose-6-phosphate receptors from the lysosome back to the TGN that we saw previously.

Sorting receptors and ligands is not always as simple as sending the receptors to the plasma membrane and retaining the ligands in the endosome. Depending on the ligand, some receptor-ligand complexes do not dissociate

in the early endosome. While dissociated ligands are swept along to their fate in a lysosome, intact receptor-ligand complexes are still subject to sorting and packaging into transport vesicles. There are at least three alternative fates for these complexes: (1) Some receptor-ligand complexes (for example, epidermal growth factor and its receptor) are carried to a lysosome for degradation. (2) Others are carried to the TGN, where they enter a variety of pathways transporting material throughout the endomembrane system. (3) Receptor-ligand complexes can also travel by transport vesicles to a different region of the plasma membrane, where they are secreted as part of a

and Goldstein hypothesized that LDL was involved in the transport of cholesterol into the cell. Because FH fibroblasts, on the other hand, synthesized cholesterol at a high rate regardless of whether LDL was present in the medium, they thought that these cells might be defective in LDL-dependent cholesterol uptake.

Based on these observations, Brown and Goldstein postulated that the uptake of cholesterol into cells requires a specific receptor for LDL particles on the cell surface. They then tested whether this receptor is absent or defective in FH patients. In a brilliant series of experiments, these investigators and their colleagues demonstrated the existence of an LDL-specific membrane protein, called the **LDL receptor,** and they showed that it recognizes the apolipoprotein B-100 molecule that is present in every LDL particle. They also showed that the cells from FH patients either lacked the LDL receptor entirely or had defective LDL receptors.

To visualize the LDL particles, these scientists conjugated, or linked, them to molecules of ferritin, a protein that binds iron

atoms. Because iron atoms are electron dense, they appear as dark dots in the electron microscope (**Figure 12B-2**). Using this technique, Brown and Goldstein showed that the ferritin-conjugated LDL particles bound to the surface of the cell and clustered at specific locations (Figure 12B-2a). We now recognize these sites as *coated pits*, which are localized regions of the plasma membrane characterized by the presence of *clathrin* on the cytoplasmic side of the membrane and by the accumulation of membrane-bound receptor-ligand complexes on the exterior of the membrane.

Dark dots were also seen on the inside of vesicles that formed by invagination and pinching off of coated pits (Figure 12B-2b). The receptors, in other words, not only bound the LDL on the cell surface but also were apparently involved in the internalization of LDL within vesicles. In short, these workers had discovered a new mechanism by which cells can take up macromolecules from their environment. And since it was an endocytic process involving specific receptors, Brown and Goldstein gave it the name we know it by today—receptor-mediated endocytosis.

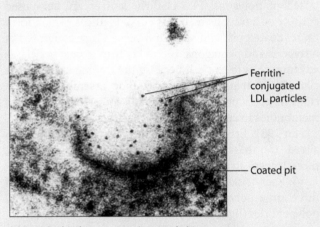

(a) Particles bind to receptors in coated pit

- Ferritin-conjugated LDL particles
- Coated pit

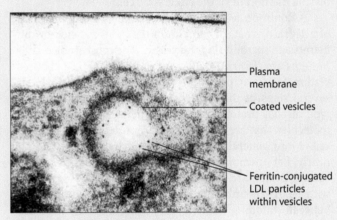

(b) Coated vesicle forms in pit

- Plasma membrane
- Coated vesicles
- Ferritin-conjugated LDL particles within vesicles

FIGURE 12B-2 Visualization of LDL Binding. Conjugation of LDL particles with ferritin, an iron-binding protein, allows visualization of the LDL-ferritin complexes by electron microscopy because of the density of the iron atoms bound to the ferritin. **(a)** LDL-ferritin conjugates, visible as dark dots, bind to receptors concentrated in a coated pit on the surface of a cultured human fibroblast cell. **(b)** The LDL-ferritin conjugates are internalized when a coated vesicle forms from the coated pit region following invagination of the plasma membrane (TEMs).

process called **transcytosis.** This pathway accommodates the transfer of extracellular material from one side of the cell, where endocytosis occurs, through the cytoplasm to the opposite side, where exocytosis occurs. For example, immunoglobulins are transported across epithelial cells from maternal blood to fetal blood by transcytosis.

Clathrin-Independent Endocytosis. An example of a clathrin-independent endocytic pathway is **fluid-phase endocytosis,** a type of pinocytosis for nonspecific internalization of extracellular fluid. Fluid-phase endocytosis, unlike receptor-mediated endocytosis, does not concentrate ingested material. Because the cell engulfs fluid without a mechanism for collecting or excluding particular molecules, the concentration of material trapped in vesicles reflects its concentration in the extracellular environment. In contrast to other forms of endocytosis, fluid-phase endocytosis proceeds at a relatively constant rate in most eukaryotic cells. Because it compensates for the membrane segments that are continuously added to the plasma membrane by exocytosis, it is a means for controlling a cell's volume and surface area. Once inside the cell, fluid-phase endocytic vesicles, like clathrin-dependent endocytic vesicles, are routed to early endosomes.

Coated Vesicles in Cellular Transport Processes

Most of the vesicles involved in lipid and protein transfer are referred to as *coated vesicles* because of the characteristic coats, or layers, of proteins covering their cytosolic surfaces as they form. Coated vesicles are a common feature of most cellular processes that involve the transfer or exchange of substances between specific membrane-bounded compartments of eukaryotic cells or between the inside and the outside of a cell.

Coated vesicles were first reported in 1964 by Thomas Roth and Keith Porter, who described their involvement in the selective uptake of yolk protein by developing mosquito oocytes. Since then, coated vesicles have been shown to play vital roles in diverse cellular processes. Coated vesicles are involved in vesicular traffic throughout the endomembrane system, as well as transport during exocytosis and endocytosis. It is probable that such vesicles participate in most, if not all, vesicular traffic connecting the various membrane-bounded compartments and the plasma membrane of the eukaryotic cell.

A common feature of coated vesicles is the presence of a layer, or coat, of protein on the cytosolic side of the membrane surrounding the vesicle. The most studied coat proteins are *clathrin, COPI,* and *COPII* (COP is an abbreviation for "coat protein."). Coat proteins participate in several steps of the formation of transport vesicles. The type of coat protein on a vesicle helps in the sorting of molecules that are fated for different destinations in the cell. More general roles for COPs may include forcing nearly flat membranes to form spherical vesicles, preventing premature, nonspecific fusion of a budding vesicle with nearby membranes, and regulating the interactions between budding vesicles and microtubules that are important for moving vesicles through the cell.

The specific set of proteins covering the exterior of a vesicle is an indicator of the origin and destination of the vesicle within the cell (**Table 12-2**). *Clathrin-coated vesicles* are involved in the selective transport of proteins from the TGN to endosomes and in the endocytosis of receptor-ligand complexes from the plasma membrane. *COPI-coated vesicles,* on the other hand, facilitate retrograde transport of proteins from the Golgi back to the ER, as well as between cisternae of the Golgi complex. *COPII-coated vesicles* are involved in the transport of material from the ER to the Golgi.

A fourth, more recently discovered coat protein is *caveolin.* The precise role of *caveolin-coated vesicles,* called **caveolae,** is still controversial. Caveolae are small invaginations of the plasma membrane characterized by the presence of the protein *caveolin.* They are a type of lipid raft that is rich in cholesterol and sphingolipids, and they may be involved in cholesterol uptake by cells. Mice deficient in caveolin show dramatic abnormalities in the cardiovascular system, which then becomes enriched in cholesterol. Other studies suggest that these cholesterol-carrying caveolae play a role in signal transduction.

Clathrin-Coated Vesicles Are Surrounded by Lattices Composed of Clathrin and Adaptor Protein

Clathrin-coated vesicles are surrounded by coats composed of two multimeric proteins, *clathrin* and *adaptor protein (AP).* The term **clathrin** comes from *clathratus,* the Latin word for "lattice," and is well chosen because clathrin and AP assemble to form protein lattices composed of polygons. Flat clathrin lattices are composed entirely of hexagons, whereas curved lattices, which form under coated pits and surround vesicles, are composed of hexagons and pentagons. Use of clathrin to coat vesicles is advantageous to the cell because the unique shape of the clathrin proteins and the way they assemble to form clathrin coats provides the driving force that causes flat membranes to curve and form spherical vesicles.

In 1981, Ernst Ungewickell and Daniel Branton visualized the basic structural units of clathrin lattices, three-legged structures called **triskelions** (**Figure 12-17a**). Each triskelion is a multimeric protein composed of three large polypeptides (heavy chains) and three small polypeptides (light chains) radiating from a central vertex, as illustrated in Figure 12-17b. Antibodies that recognize clathrin light chains bind to the legs of the triskelion near the central vertex, suggesting that the light chains are associated with the inner half of each leg.

By combining information gathered from electron microscopy and X-ray crystallography, researchers have assembled the following model for the organization of triskelions into the characteristic hexagons and pentagons of clathrin-coated pits and vesicles (Figure 12-17c). One clathrin triskelion is located at each vertex of the polygonal lattice. Each polypeptide leg extends along two edges of the

Table 12-2	Coated Vesicles Found Within Eukaryotic Cells		
Coated Vesicle	**Coat Proteins***	**Origin**	**Destination**
Clathrin	Clathrin, AP1, ARF	TGN	Endosomes
Clathrin	Clathrin, AP2	Plasma membrane	Endosomes
COPI	COPI, ARF	Golgi complex	ER or Golgi complex
COPII	COPII (Sec13/31 and Sec23/24), Sar1	ER	Golgi complex
Caveolin	Caveolin	Plasma membrane	ER?

*ARF designates ADP ribosylation factor 1; AP1 and AP2 designate different adaptor protein complexes (also called assembly protein complexes).

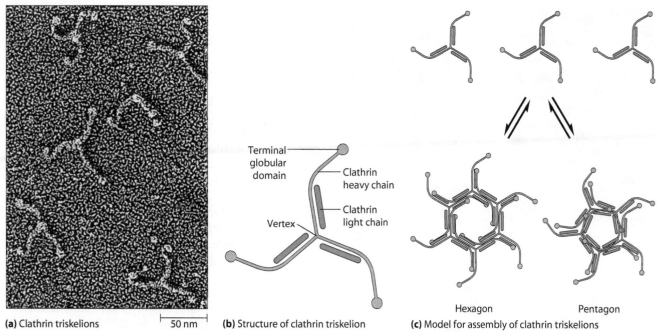

(a) Clathrin triskelions ⊢ 50 nm ⊣ **(b)** Structure of clathrin triskelion **(c)** Model for assembly of clathrin triskelions

FIGURE 12-17 Clathrin Triskelions. Shown above are **(a)** a micrograph of clathrin triskelions (SEM), **(b)** an illustration showing how each triskelion is composed of three clathrin heavy chains and three clathrin light chains, and **(c)** a model for the assembly of triskelions into the characteristic clathrin pentagons and hexagons found in coated pits and vesicles.

lattice, with the knee of the clathrin heavy chain located at an adjacent vertex. This arrangement of triskelions into overlapping networks ensures extensive longitudinal contact between clathrin polypeptides and may confer the mechanical strength needed when a coated vesicle forms.

The second major component of clathrin coats—**adaptor protein (AP)**—was originally identified simply by its ability to promote the assembly of clathrin coats around vesicles and is sometimes called *assembly protein*. We now know that eukaryotic cells contain at least four types of AP complexes, each composed of four polypeptides—two adaptin subunits, one medium chain, and one small chain. The four polypeptides, which are slightly different in each type of AP complex, bind to different transmembrane receptor proteins and confer specificity during vesicle budding and targeting.

In addition to ensuring that appropriate macromolecules will be concentrated in coated pits, AP complexes mediate the attachment of clathrin to proteins embedded in the plasma membrane. Considering the central role of APs, it is not surprising that AP complexes are sites for regulation of clathrin assembly and disassembly. For example, the ability of AP complexes to bind to clathrin is affected by pH, phosphorylation, and dephosphorylation.

The Assembly of Clathrin Coats Drives the Formation of Vesicles from the Plasma Membrane and TGN

The binding of AP complexes to the plasma membrane and the concentration of receptors or receptor-ligand com-

plexes in coated pits require ATP and GTP—though perhaps only for regulation of the process. The assembly of a clathrin coat on the cytosolic side of a membrane appears to provide part of the driving force for formation of a vesicle at the site. Initially, all clathrin units are hexagonal and form a planar, two-dimensional structure (**Figure 12-18a, c**). As more clathrin triskelions are incorporated into the growing lattice, a combination of hexagonal and pentagonal units allows the new clathrin coat to curve around the budding vesicle (Figure 12-18b, d).

As clathrin accumulates around the budding vesicle, at least one more protein—**dynamin**—participates in the process. Dynamin is a cytosolic GTPase required for coated pit constriction and closing of the budding vesicle. This essential protein was first identified in *Drosophila*, a fruit fly used extensively as a genetic model organism. Flies expressing a temperature-sensitive form of dynamin were instantly paralyzed after a temperature shift disrupted the dynamin function. Further investigation revealed an accumulation of coated pits in the membranes of neuromuscular junctions in the affected flies. Formation of the closed vesicle occurs as dynamin forms helical rings around the neck of the coated pit. As GTP is hydrolyzed, the dynamin rings tighten and separate the fully sealed endocytic vesicle from the plasma membrane.

Some mechanism is also required to *uncoat* clathrin-coated membranes. Moreover, uncoating must be done in a regulated manner because, in most cases, the clathrin coat remains intact as long as the membrane is part of a coated pit or budding vesicle but dissociates rapidly once the vesicle is fully formed. Like assembly, dissociation of the clathrin coat

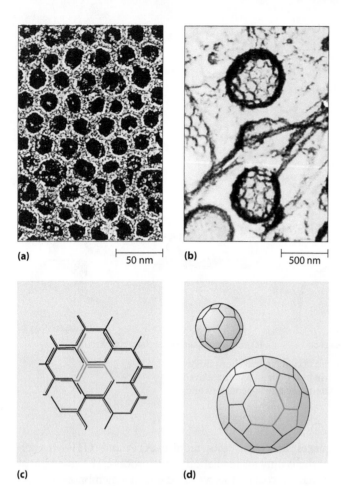

(a) 50 nm

(b) 500 nm

(c)

(d)

FIGURE 12-18 Clathrin Lattices. Each vesicle is surrounded by a cage of overlapping clathrin complexes. **(a)** Freeze-etch electron micrograph of a clathrin lattice in a human carcinoma cell. This flat lattice is composed of hexagonal units. **(b)** Electron micrograph of clathrin cages isolated from a calf brain. Cages include both pentagonal and hexagonal units (TEMs). **(c)** and **(d)** Interpretive drawings of the lattice and clathrin cages shown in (a) and (b).

VIDEOS www.thecellplace.com *Clathrin-coated vesicle formation*

is an energy-consuming process, accompanied by the hydrolysis of about three ATP molecules per triskelion. At least one protein, an *uncoating ATPase,* is essential for this process, though the uncoating ATPase releases only the clathrin triskelions from the APs. The factors responsible for releasing APs from the membrane have not yet been identified.

Clathrin-coated vesicles readily dissociate into soluble clathrin complexes, adaptor protein complexes, and uncoated vesicles that can spontaneously reassemble under appropriate conditions. In a slightly acidic solution containing calcium ions, clathrin complexes will reassemble independently of adaptor protein and membrane-bounded vesicles, resulting in empty shells called *clathrin cages.* Assembly occurs remarkably fast—within seconds, under favorable conditions. Ease of assembly and disassembly is an important feature of the clathrin coat because fusion of the underlying membrane with the membrane of another structure appears to require partial or complete uncoating of the vesicle.

COPI- and COPII-Coated Vesicles Travel Between the ER and Golgi Complex Cisternae

COPI-coated vesicles have been found in all eukaryotic cells examined, including mammalian, insect, plant, and yeast cells. They are involved in retrograde transport from the Golgi complex back to the ER as well as bidirectional transport between Golgi complex cisternae. COPI-coated vesicles are surrounded by coats composed of **COPI** protein and **ADP ribosylation factor (ARF),** a small GTP-binding protein. The major component of the coat, COPI, is a protein multimer composed of seven subunits.

Assembly of a COPI coat is mediated by ARF. In the cytosol, ARF occurs as part of an ARF-GDP complex. However, when ARF encounters a specific *guanine nucleotide exchange factor* associated with the membrane (from which a new coated vesicle is about to form), the GDP is exchanged for GTP. This induces a conformational change in ARF that exposes its hydrophobic N-terminal region, which attaches to the lipid bilayer of the membrane. Once firmly anchored, ARF binds to COPI multimers, and assembly of the coat drives the formation and budding of a new vesicle. After the formation of a free vesicle, a protein in the donor membrane triggers hydrolysis of GTP, and the resulting ARF-GDP releases the coat proteins for another cycle of vesicle budding. Our knowledge of COP-mediated vesicle transport has been aided considerably by using the fungal toxin *brefeldin A,* which inhibits this process by interfering with the ability of the guanine nucleotide exchange factor to produce ARF-GTP from ARF-GDP.

COPII-coated vesicles were first discovered in yeast, where they have a role in transport from the ER to the Golgi complex. Mammalian and plant homologues of some of the components of **COPII** coats have been identified, and the COPII-mediated mechanism of ER export appears to be highly conserved between organisms as different as yeast and humans. The COPII coat found in yeast is assembled from two protein complexes—called *Sec13/31* and *Sec23/24*—and a small GTP-binding protein called *SarI,* which is similar to ARF. By a mechanism resembling formation of a COPI coat, a SarI molecule with GDP bound to it approaches the membrane from which a vesicle is about to form. A peripheral membrane protein then triggers exchange of GTP for GDP, enabling SarI to bind to Sec13/31 and Sec23/24. After the formation of a free vesicle, a component of the COPII coat triggers GTP hydrolysis, and SarI releases Sec13/31 and Sec23/24.

SNARE Proteins Mediate Fusion Between Vesicles and Target Membranes

Much of the intracellular traffic mediated by coated vesicles is highly specific. As we have seen, the final sorting of proteins synthesized in the ER occurs in the TGN when lipids and proteins are packaged into vesicles for transport to various destinations. Recall that when clathrin-coated vesicles form from the TGN, the adaptor complexes include two adaptin subunits. The two adaptin subunits are partly

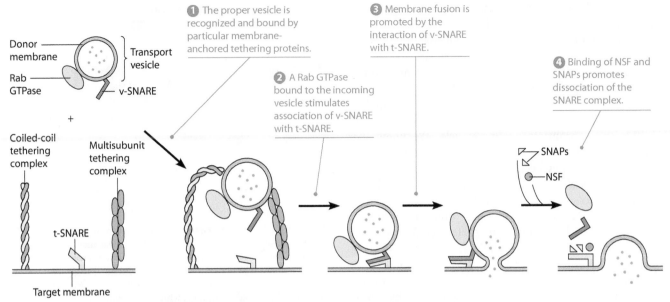

FIGURE 12-19 **The SNARE Hypothesis for Transport Vesicle Targeting and Fusion.** The basic molecular components that mediate sorting and targeting of vesicles in eukaryotic cells include tethering proteins, v-SNAREs on transport vesicles, t-SNAREs on target membranes, Rab GTPase, NSF, and several SNAPs. The exact timing of GTP or ATP hydrolysis is still unclear, but it most likely occurs after vesicle fusion.

responsible for the specificity displayed when receptors are concentrated for inclusion in a budding vesicle.

Once a vesicle forms, however, additional proteins are needed to ensure delivery of the vesicle to the appropriate destination. Therefore, there must be a mechanism to keep the various vesicles in the cell from accidentally fusing with the wrong membrane. The **SNARE hypothesis** provides a working model for this important sorting and targeting step in intracellular transport (**Figure 12-19**).

According to the SNARE hypothesis, the proper sorting and targeting of vesicles in eukaryotic cells involves two families of **SNARE (SNAP receptor) proteins**: the v-SNAREs (vesicle-SNAP receptors) found on transport vesicles and the t-SNAREs (target-SNAP receptors) found on target membranes. The v-SNAREs and t-SNAREs are complementary molecules that, along with additional tethering proteins, allow a vesicle to recognize and fuse with a target membrane. Both v-SNAREs and t-SNAREs were originally investigated because of their role in neuronal exocytosis. Since their discovery in brain tissue, both families of proteins have also been implicated in transport from the ER to the Golgi complex in yeast and other organisms.

When a vesicle reaches its destination, a third family of proteins, the **Rab GTPases,** comes into play. Rab GTPases are also specific: Vesicles fated for different destinations have distinct members of the Rab family associated with them. As illustrated in Figure 12-19, the affinity of complementary v-SNAREs and t-SNAREs for one another enables them to form a stable complex. This ensures that, when these proteins collide, they will remain in contact long enough for a Rab protein associated with the vesicle to lock the complementary t-SNARE and v-SNARE together, facilitating membrane fusion.

Following vesicle fusion, **N-ethylmaleimide-sensitive factor (NSF)** and a group of **soluble NSF attachment proteins (SNAPs)** mediate release of the v- and t-SNAREs of the donor and target membranes. ATP hydrolysis may be involved at this step, but its precise role is unclear. NSF and SNAPs are involved in fusion between a variety of cellular membranes, indicating they are not responsible for specificity during targeting.

SNARE proteins are required for the fusion of neurotransmitter-containing vesicles with the plasma membrane of nerve cells. This fusion event releases the neurotransmitter by exocytosis, leading to an electrical impulse that will initiate muscle contraction. Botulinum toxin (Botox), produced by the bacterium *Clostridium botulinum,* is a protease that cleaves a SNARE protein that is required for this fusion. Thus, the toxin interferes with muscle contraction and can cause paralysis. Although it is one of the most potent biological toxins known, in very small doses Botox can be used therapeutically to control muscle spasms or correct crossed eyes. It is also used cosmetically to remove wrinkles caused by muscle contractions in the skin. Currently, it is being investigated for possible use as a treatment for migraine headaches.

Recent research suggests that SNARE proteins alone cannot account for the specificity observed in vesicle targeting. A different class of proteins known as **tethering proteins** acts over longer distances and provides specificity by connecting vesicles to their target membranes prior to v-SNARE/t-SNARE interaction (Figure 12-19). We know this because experimental toxin-induced cleavage of SNARE proteins in vivo can block SNARE complex formation without blocking vesicle association with the target membrane. Also, in an in vitro reconstituted system, ER-derived vesicles can attach to Golgi membranes without addition of SNARE proteins.

Two main groups of tethering proteins are known at present—*coiled-coil proteins* and *multisubunit complexes.* Coiled-coil proteins such as the **golgins** are important in the initial recognition and binding of COPI- or COPII-coated vesicles to the Golgi. The golgins are anchored by one end to the Golgi membrane and use the other end to contact the appropriate passing vesicle. We know that these proteins are also important in connecting Golgi cisternae to each other because antibodies directed against certain golgins block the action of the golgins and disrupt the structure of the Golgi medial cisternae.

The second class of tethering proteins consists of several families of multisubunit protein complexes containing four to eight or more individual polypeptides. For example, the *exocyst* complex of yeast and mammals is important for protein secretion, binding both to the plasma membrane and to vesicles from the TGN whose contents are destined for export. Other types of multisubunit tethering complexes such as the *COG (conserved oligomeric Golgi)* complex, the *GARP (Golgi-associated retrograde protein)* complex, and the *TRAPP (transport protein particle)* complex are implicated in the initial recognition and specificity of vesicle–target membrane interaction. Most of the proteins in these complexes are highly conserved among organisms as different as yeast and humans. Identifying the functions of these complexes and the roles of their individual subunits is currently one of the most intriguing frontiers of modern cell biology.

Lysosomes and Cellular Digestion

The **lysosome** is an organelle of the endomembrane system that contains digestive enzymes capable of degrading all the major classes of biological macromolecules—lipids, carbohydrates, nucleic acids, and proteins. These hydrolytic enzymes degrade extracellular materials brought into the cell by endocytosis and digest intracellular structures and macromolecules that are damaged or no longer needed. We will first look at the organelle itself and then consider lysosomal digestive processes, as well as some of the diseases that result from lysosomal malfunction.

Lysosomes Isolate Digestive Enzymes from the Rest of the Cell

As we learned in Chapter 4, lysosomes were discovered in the early 1950s by Christian de Duve and his colleagues (see Box 4B, page 92). Differential centrifugation led the researchers to realize that an acid phosphatase initially thought to be located in the mitochondrion was in fact associated with a class of particles that had never been reported before. Along with the acid phosphatase, the new organelle contained several other hydrolytic enzymes, including β-glucuronidase, a deoxyribonuclease, a ribonuclease, and a protease. Because of its apparent role in cellular lysis, de Duve called this newly discovered organelle a *lysosome.*

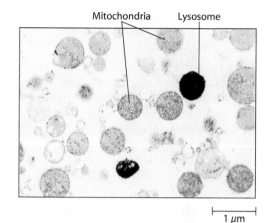

FIGURE 12-20 Cytochemical Localization of Acid Phosphatase, a Lysosomal Enzyme. Tissue was incubated in a medium containing soluble lead nitrate and β-glycerophosphate, which is cleaved by acid phosphatase, producing free glycerol and phosphate anions. The phosphate anions react with lead ions to form insoluble lead phosphate, which precipitates at the site of enzyme activity and reveals the location of acid phosphatase within the cell. The darkly stained organelles shown here are lysosomes highlighted by deposits of the electron-dense lead phosphate. They are surrounded by mitochondria, which lack acid phosphatase and do not become electron dense (TEM).

Only after the lysosome's existence had been predicted, its properties described, and its enzyme content specified was the organelle actually observed by electron microscopy and recognized as a normal constituent of most animal cells. Final confirmation came from cytochemical staining reactions capable of localizing the acid phosphatase and other lysosomal enzymes to specific structures that can be seen by electron microscopy (**Figure 12-20**).

Lysosomes vary considerably in size and shape but are generally about 0.5 μm in diameter. Like the ER and Golgi complex, the lysosome is bounded by a single membrane. This membrane protects the rest of the cell from the hydrolytic enzymes in the lysosomal lumen. The lumenal side of lysosomal membrane proteins is highly glycosylated, forming a nearly continuous carbohydrate coating that appears to protect membrane proteins from lysosomal proteases. ATP-dependent proton pumps in the membrane maintain an acidic environment (pH 4.0–5.0) within the lysosome. This favors enzymatic digestion of macromolecules both by activating acid hydrolases and by partially denaturing the macromolecules targeted for degradation. The products of digestion are then transported across the membrane to the cytosol, where they enter various synthetic pathways or are exported from the cell.

The list of lysosomal enzymes has expanded considerably since de Duve's original work, but all have the common property of being *acid hydrolases*—hydrolytic enzymes with a pH optimum around 5.0. The list includes at least 5 phosphatases, 14 proteases and peptidases, 2 nucleases, 6 lipases, 13 glycosidases, and 7 sulfatases. Taken together, these lysosomal enzymes can digest all the major classes of biological molecules. No wonder, then, that they are sequestered from the rest of the cell, where they cannot quickly destroy the cell itself.

Lysosomes Develop from Endosomes

Lysosomal enzymes are synthesized by ribosomes attached to the rough ER and are translocated through a pore in the ER membrane into the ER lumen before transport to the Golgi complex. After modification and processing in the ER and Golgi complex compartments, the lysosomal enzymes are sorted from other proteins in the TGN. Earlier in the chapter, we described the addition of a unique mannose-6-phosphate tag to soluble lysosomal enzymes. Distinctive sorting signals are also present on membrane-bound lysosomal proteins. The lysosomal enzymes are packaged in clathrin-coated vesicles that bud from the TGN, lose their protein coats, and travel to one of the endosomal compartments (see Figure 12-9).

Lysosomal enzymes are delivered from the TGN to endosomes in transport vesicles, as shown in **Figure 12-21**. Recall that early endosomes are formed by the coalescence of vesicles from the TGN and vesicles from the plasma membrane. Over time, the early endosome matures to form a late endosome, an organelle having a full complement of acid hydrolases but not engaged in digestive activity. As the pH of the early endosomal lumen drops from about 6.0 to 5.5, the organelle loses its capacity to fuse with endocytic vesicles. The late endosome is essentially a collection of newly synthesized digestive enzymes as well as extracellular and intracellular material fated for digestion, packaged in a way that protects the cell from hydrolytic enzymes.

The final step in lysosome development is the activation of the acid hydrolases, which occurs as the enzymes and their substrates encounter a more acidic environment. There are two ways eukaryotic cells accomplish this step. ATP-dependent proton pumps may lower the pH of the late endosomal lumen to 4.0–5.0, transforming the late endosome into a lysosome, thereby generating a new organelle. Alternatively, the late endosome may transfer material to the acidic lumen of an existing lysosome.

Lysosomal Enzymes Are Important for Several Different Digestive Processes

Lysosomes are important for cellular activities as diverse as nutrition, defense, recycling of cellular components, and differentiation. We can distinguish the digestive processes that depend on lysosomal enzymes by the site of their activity and by the origin of the material that is digested, as shown in Figure 12-21. Usually, the site of activity is intracellular. In some cases, though, lysosomes may release their enzymes to the outside of the cell by exocytosis. The materials to be digested are often of extracellular origin, although there are also important processes known to involve lysosomal digestion of internal cellular components.

To distinguish between mature lysosomes of different origins, we refer to those containing substances of extracellular origin as **heterophagic lysosomes,** whereas those with

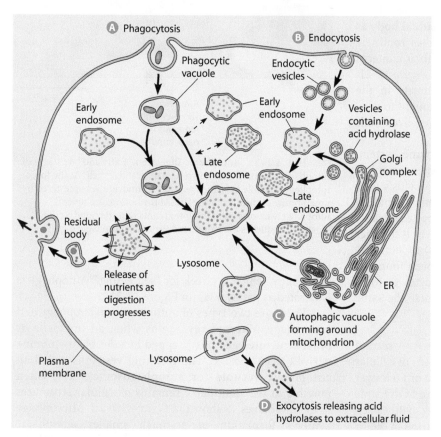

FIGURE 12-21 The Formation of Lysosomes and Their Roles in Cellular Digestive Processes. Illustrated in this composite cell are the major processes in which lysosomes are involved. The pathways depicted are Ⓐphagocytosis, Ⓑ receptor-mediated endocytosis, Ⓒ autophagy, and Ⓓ extracellular digestion. For clarity, the nucleus is not shown.

materials of intracellular origin are called **autophagic lysosomes.** The specific processes in which lysosomal enzymes are involved are *phagocytosis, receptor-mediated endocytosis, autophagy,* and *extracellular digestion.* These are illustrated in Figure 12-21 as pathways Ⓐ, Ⓑ, Ⓒ, and Ⓓ, respectively.

Phagocytosis and Receptor-Mediated Endocytosis: Lysosomes in Defense and Nutrition. One of the most important functions of lysosomal enzymes is the degradation of foreign material brought into eukaryotic cells by *phagocytosis* and *receptor-mediated endocytosis* (see Figures 12-14 and 12-15). Phagocytic vacuoles are transformed into lysosomes by fusing with early endosomes (Figure 12-21, pathway Ⓐ). Depending on the material ingested, these lysosomes can vary considerably in size, appearance, content, and stage of digestion. Vesicles containing material brought into a cell by receptor-mediated endocytosis also form early endosomes (pathway Ⓑ of Figure 12-21). As early endosomes fuse with vesicles from the TGN containing acid hydrolases, they mature to form late endosomes and lysosomes, in which the ingested material is digested.

Soluble products of digestion, such as sugars, amino acids, and nucleotides, are then transported across the lysosomal membrane into the cytosol and are used as a source of nutrients by the cell. Some may cross by facilitated diffusion, whereas others undergo active transport. The acidity of the lysosomal lumen contributes to an electrochemical proton gradient across the lysosomal membrane, which can provide energy for driving transport to and from the cytosol.

Eventually, however, only indigestible material remains in the lysosome, which becomes a **residual body** as digestion ceases. In protozoa, residual bodies routinely fuse with the plasma membrane and expel their contents to the outside by exocytosis, as illustrated in Figure 12-21. In vertebrates, residual bodies may accumulate in the cytoplasm. This accumulation of debris is thought to contribute to cellular aging, particularly in long-lived cells such as those of the nervous system.

Certain white blood cells of the immune system, however, use this residual material. After neutrophils digest invading microorganisms via phagocytosis and lysosome action, they release the debris, which is picked up by scavenging macrophages. These macrophages transport the debris to the lymph nodes and present it to other immune system cells (B and T lymphocytes) to "educate" them regarding what foreign material has been found in the body. This process causes the lymphocytes to form memory cells that will quickly respond in case the same microorganism is encountered in the future.

Autophagy: A Biological Recycling System. A second important task for lysosomes is the breakdown of cellular structures and components that are damaged or no longer needed. Most cellular organelles are in a state of dynamic flux, with new organelles continuously being synthesized while old organelles are destroyed. The digestion of old or unwanted organelles or other cell structures is called

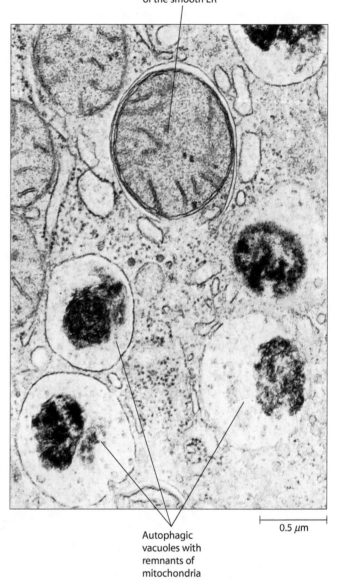

Mitochondrion being sequestered by membrane of the smooth ER

Autophagic vacuoles with remnants of mitochondria

0.5 μm

FIGURE 12-22 Autophagic Digestion. Early and late stages of autophagic digestion are shown here in a rat liver cell. At the top, an autophagic vacuole is formed as a mitochondrion is sequestered by a membrane derived from the ER. At the bottom are several autophagic vacuoles containing remnants of mitochondria (TEM). Most old organelles are eliminated through autophagic digestion.

autophagy, which is Greek for "self-eating." Autophagy is illustrated as pathway Ⓒ in Figure 12-21.

There are two types of autophagy—*macrophagy* and *microphagy.* **Macrophagy** begins when an organelle or other structure becomes wrapped in a double membrane derived from the ER. The resulting vesicle is called an **autophagic vacuole** (or **autophagosome**). It is often possible to see identifiable remains of cellular structures in these vacuoles, as shown in **Figure 12-22. Microphagy** involves formation of a much smaller autophagic vacuole, surrounded by a single phospholipid bilayer that encloses small bits of cytoplasm rather than whole organelles.

Autophagy occurs at varying rates in most cells under most conditions, but it is especially prominent in red blood cell development. As a red blood cell matures, virtually all of the intracellular content is destroyed, including all of the mitochondria. This destruction is accomplished by autophagic digestion. A marked increase in autophagy is also noted in cells stressed by starvation. Presumably, the process represents a desperate attempt by the cell to continue providing for its energy needs, even if it has to consume its own structures to do so.

It has long been suspected that some cancer cells may be deficient in autophagy, but recent work suggests a direct link between autophagy and cancer. The human version of a gene required for autophagy in yeast cells has been shown to be frequently deleted in human breast and ovarian tumors. Knocking out the function of this gene in mice caused a decrease in autophagy and an increase in the number of breast and lung tumors. However, some oncogenes that promote cancer suppress autophagy during tumor development. Clearly, more research is needed.

Extracellular Digestion. While most digestive processes involving lysosomal enzymes occur intracellularly, in some cases lysosomes discharge their enzymes to the outside of the cell by exocytosis, resulting in **extracellular digestion** (Figure 12-21, pathway Ⓓ). One example of extracellular digestion occurs during fertilization of animal eggs. The head of the sperm releases lysosomal enzymes capable of degrading chemical barriers that would otherwise keep the sperm from penetrating the egg surface. Certain inflammatory diseases, such as rheumatoid arthritis, may result from the inadvertent release of lysosomal enzymes by white blood cells in the joints, damaging the joint tissue. The steroid hormones cortisone and hydrocortisone are thought to be effective anti-inflammatory agents because of their role in stabilizing lysosomal membranes and thereby inhibiting enzyme release.

Lysosomal Storage Diseases Are Usually Characterized by the Accumulation of Indigestible Material

The essential role of lysosomes in the recycling of cellular components is clearly seen in disorders caused by deficiencies of specific lysosomal proteins. Over 40 such **lysosomal storage diseases** are known, each characterized by the harmful accumulation of specific substances, usually polysaccharides or lipids (see Box 4A, page 86). In most cases, the substances accumulate because digestive enzymes are defective or missing, but they sometimes accumulate because the proteins that transport degradation products from the lysosomal lumen to the cytosol are defective. In either case, the cells in which material accumulates are severely impaired or destroyed. Skeletal deformities, muscle weakness, and mental retardation commonly result, and are often fatal. Unfortunately, most lysosomal storage diseases are not yet treatable.

The first storage disease to be understood was *type II glycogenosis,* in which young children accumulate excessive amounts of glycogen in the liver, heart, and skeletal muscles and die at an early age. The problem turned out to be a defective form of the lysosomal enzyme *α-1,4-glucosidase,* which catalyzes glycogen hydrolysis in normal cells. Although glycogen metabolism occurs predominantly in the cytosol, a small amount of glycogen can enter the lysosome through autophagy and will accumulate to a damaging level if not broken down to glucose.

Two of the best-known lysosomal storage diseases are *Hurler syndrome* and *Hunter syndrome.* Both arise from defects in the degradation of glycosaminoglycans, which are the major carbohydrate components of the extracellular matrix. The defective enzyme in a patient with Hurler syndrome is *α-L-iduronidase,* which is required for the degradation of glycosaminoglycans. Electron microscopic observation of sweat gland cells from a patient with Hurler syndrome reveals large numbers of atypical vacuoles that stain for both acid phosphatase and undigested glycosaminoglycans. These vacuoles are apparently abnormal late endosomes filled with indigestible material.

Mental retardation is a common feature of lysosomal storage diseases. It can occur due to the impaired metabolism of glycolipids, which are important components of brain tissue and the sheaths of nerve cell axons. One particularly well-known example is *Tay-Sachs disease,* a condition inherited as a recessive trait. Afflicted children show rapid mental deterioration after about six months of age, followed by paralysis and death within three years. The disease results from the accumulation in nervous tissue of a particular glycolipid called a *ganglioside.* The missing lysosomal enzyme in this case is *β-N-acetylhexosaminidase,* which is responsible for cleaving the terminal *N*-acetylgalactosamine from the carbohydrate portion of the ganglioside. Lysosomes from children afflicted with Tay-Sachs disease are filled with membrane fragments containing undigested gangliosides.

The Plant Vacuole: A Multifunctional Organelle

Plant cells contain acidic membrane-enclosed compartments called vacuoles that resemble the lysosomes found in most animal cells but generally serve additional roles. The biogenesis of a vacuole parallels that of a lysosome. Most of the components are synthesized in the ER and transferred to the Golgi complex, where proteins undergo further processing. Coated vesicles then convey lipids and proteins destined for the vacuole to a **provacuole,** which is analogous to an endosome. The provacuole eventually matures to form a functional vacuole that can fill as much as 90% of the volume of a plant cell.

In addition to confining hydrolytic enzymes, plant vacuoles have various other essential functions. Most of these functions reflect the plant's lack of mobility and consequent susceptibility to changes in the surrounding environment. As mentioned in Chapter 4, a major role of the vacuole is to maintain *turgor pressure,* the osmotic pressure that prevents plant cells from collapsing. Turgor pressure prevents a plant from wilting, and it can drive the expansion of cells. During development, softening of the cell wall—accompanied by higher turgor pressure—allows the cell to expand.

Another role of the plant vacuole is the regulation of cytosolic pH. ATP-dependent proton pumps in the vacuolar membrane can compensate for a decline in cytosolic pH (perhaps due to a change in the extracellular environment) by transferring protons from the cytosol to the lumen of the vacuole.

The vacuole also serves as a storage compartment. Seed storage proteins are generally synthesized by ribosomes attached to the rough ER and cotranslationally inserted into the ER lumen. Some of the storage proteins remain in the ER while others are transferred to vacuoles, either by autophagy of vesicles budding from the ER or by way of the Golgi. When the seeds germinate, the storage proteins are available for hydrolysis by vacuolar proteases, thereby releasing amino acids for the biosynthesis of new proteins needed by the growing plant.

Other substances found in vacuoles include malate stored in CAM plants, the anthocyanins that impart color to flowers, toxic substances that deter predators, inorganic and organic nutrients, compounds that shield cells from ultraviolet light, and residual indigestible waste. Storage of soluble as well as insoluble waste is an important function of plant vacuoles. Unlike animals, most plants do not have a mechanism for excreting soluble waste from the organism. The large vacuoles found in plant cells enable the cells to accumulate solutes to a degree that would inhibit or restrict metabolic processes if the material were to remain in the cytosol.

Peroxisomes

Peroxisomes, like the Golgi complex, endosomes, and lysosomes, are bounded by single membranes. However, they are not derived from the endoplasmic reticulum and are therefore not part of the endomembrane system that includes the other organelles discussed in this chapter. Peroxisomes are found in all eukaryotic cells but are especially prominent in mammalian kidney and liver cells, in algae and photosynthetic cells of plants, and in germinating seedlings of plant species that store fat in their seeds. Peroxisomes are somewhat smaller than mitochondria, though there is considerable variation in size, depending on their function and the tissue where they are found.

Regardless of location or size, the defining characteristic of a peroxisome is the presence of *catalase,* an enzyme essential for the degradation of hydrogen peroxide (H_2O_2). Hydrogen peroxide is a potentially toxic compound that is formed by a variety of oxidative reactions catalyzed by *oxidases.* Both catalase and the oxidases are confined to peroxisomes. Thus, the generation and degradation of H_2O_2 occur within the same organelle, thereby protecting other parts of the cell from exposure to this harmful compound. Before discussing the functions of peroxisomes

further, let us look at how peroxisomes were discovered and how they are distinguished from other organelles when viewed by electron microscopy.

The Discovery of Peroxisomes Depended on Innovations in Equilibrium Density Centrifugation

Christian de Duve and his colleagues discovered not only lysosomes, but also peroxisomes. During the course of their early studies on lysosomes, they encountered at least one enzyme, *urate oxidase,* that was associated with lysosomal fractions but was not an acid hydrolase. By using a gradient of sucrose concentration, the researchers found that urate oxidase from rat liver was recovered in a region of the gradient having a slightly higher density than that of other organelles, such as lysosomes and mitochondria (see Figure 12A-4).

Once separation of this new organelle was achieved, additional enzymes were identified in the fractions containing urate oxidase, including catalase and D-*amino acid oxidase.* Catalase, as we have seen, degrades H_2O_2. Like urate oxidase, D-amino acid oxidase generates H_2O_2. Because of its apparent involvement in hydrogen peroxide metabolism, the new organelle became known as a *peroxisome.* Other peroxisomal enzymes have since been identified, and it is now clear that the enzyme complement of the organelle varies significantly from species to species, from organ to organ, and in some cases from one developmental stage to another within the same organ. However, the presence of catalase and one or more hydrogen peroxide–generating oxidases remains a distinguishing characteristic of all peroxisomes.

Once peroxisomes had been identified and isolated biochemically, the existence of organelles with the expected properties was confirmed by electron microscopy. Peroxisomes turned out to be the functional equivalents of organelles that had been seen earlier in electron micrographs of both animal and plant cells. Because their function was not known at the time, these organelles were simply called *microbodies.* In both plant and animal cells, peroxisomes are usually about 0.2–2.0 μm in diameter, are surrounded by a single membrane, and generally have a finely granular or crystalline interior.

As seen in **Figure 12-23,** animal peroxisomes often contain a distinct crystalline core, which usually consists of a crystalline form of urate oxidase. Crystalline cores consisting of catalase may be present in the peroxisomes of plant leaves (see Figure 4-20). When such crystals are present, it is easy to identify peroxisomes, since urate oxidase and catalase are two of the enzymes by which peroxisomes are defined. In the absence of a crystalline core, however, it is not always easy to spot peroxisomes ultrastructurally.

A useful technique in such cases is a cytochemical test for catalase called the *diaminobenzidine (DAB) reaction.* Catalase oxidizes DAB to a polymeric form that causes deposition of electron-dense osmium atoms when the tissue is treated with osmium tetroxide. The resulting electron-dense deposits can be readily seen in cells from

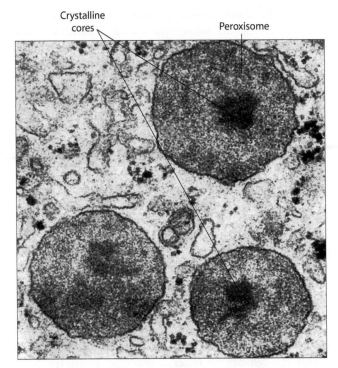

FIGURE 12-23 **Peroxisomes in Animal Cells.** This electron micrograph shows several peroxisomes (microbodies) in the cytoplasm of a rat liver cell. A crystalline core is readily visible in each microbody. In animal microbodies, the cores are almost always crystalline urate oxidase (TEM).

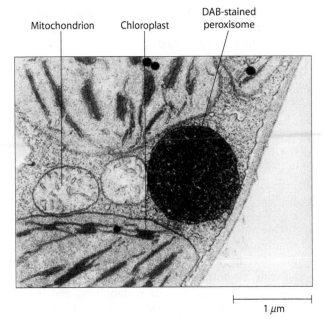

FIGURE 12-24 **Cytochemical Localization of Catalase in Plant Peroxisomes.** Shown here is a tobacco leaf cell similar to the one shown in Figure 4-20, but stained by diaminobenzidine (DAB). The principle of this assay is similar to that of the cytochemical test for acid phosphatase described in Figure 12-20. Catalase oxidizes DAB to a polymeric form that causes the deposition of electron-dense osmium atoms in tissue treated with osmium tetroxide (OsO$_4$). The DAB technique reveals that the deposition of osmium is confined to peroxisomes and thus that catalase is a component of the crystalline core (TEM).

stained tissue. In animal peroxisomes, the entire internal space often stains intensely with DAB, indicating that catalase exists as a soluble enzyme uniformly distributed throughout the matrix of the organelle. Similarly, in plant leaf peroxisomes lacking a crystalline core of catalase, DAB staining is observed through the entire peroxisome (**Figure 12-24**). Because catalase is the single enzyme present in all peroxisomes and does not routinely occur in any other organelle, the DAB reaction is a reliable and specific means of identifying organelles as peroxisomes.

Most Peroxisomal Functions Are Linked to Hydrogen Peroxide Metabolism

Peroxisomes occur widely in animals, plants, algae, and some fungi. In animals, peroxisomes are most prominent in liver and kidney tissue. The essential roles of peroxisomes in eukaryotic cells have become more apparent in recent years, stimulating new research into the metabolic pathways and the disorders arising from defective components of the pathways found in these organelles. There are at least five general categories of peroxisomal functions that we will discuss in the sections below: hydrogen peroxide metabolism, detoxification of harmful compounds, oxidation of fatty acids, metabolism of nitrogen-containing compounds, and catabolism of unusual substances.

Hydrogen Peroxide Metabolism. A significant role of peroxisomes in eukaryotic cells is the detoxification of

H_2O_2 by catalase, which can comprise up to 15% of the total protein in the peroxisome. The oxidases that generate H_2O_2 in peroxisomes transfer electrons plus hydrogen ions (hydrogen atoms) from their substrates to molecular oxygen (O_2), reducing it to H_2O_2. Using RH_2 to represent an oxidizable substrate, the general reaction catalyzed by oxidases can be written as

$$RH_2 + O_2 \longrightarrow R + H_2O_2 \qquad (12\text{-}3)$$

The hydrogen peroxide formed in this manner is broken down by catalase in one of two ways. Usually, catalase functions by detoxifying two molecules of H_2O_2 simultaneously—one is oxidized to oxygen, and a second is reduced to water:

$$2H_2O_2 \longrightarrow O_2 + 2H_2O \qquad (12\text{-}4)$$

Alternatively, catalase can function as a *peroxidase,* in which electrons derived from an organic donor are used to reduce hydrogen peroxide to water:

$$R'H_2 + H_2O_2 \longrightarrow R' + 2H_2O \qquad (12\text{-}5)$$

(The prime on the R group simply indicates that this substrate is likely to be different from the substrate in Reaction 12-3.)

The result is the same in either case: Hydrogen peroxide is degraded without ever leaving the peroxisome. Given the toxicity of hydrogen peroxide (which is the main active ingredient in a variety of disinfectants), it makes good sense for the enzymes responsible for peroxide generation to be compartmentalized together with the catalase that catalyzes its degradation.

Detoxification of Harmful Compounds. As a peroxidase (Reaction 12-5), catalase can use a variety of toxic substances as electron donors, including methanol, ethanol, formic acid, formaldehyde, nitrites, and phenols. Because all of these compounds are harmful to cells, their oxidative detoxification by catalase may be a vital peroxisomal function. The prominent peroxisomes of liver and kidney cells are thought to be important in such detoxification reactions.

In addition, peroxisomal enzymes are important in the detoxification of **reactive oxygen species** such as H_2O_2, superoxide anion (O_2^-), hydroxyl radical (OH$\bullet$ where the dot signifies an unpaired, highly reactive electron), and organic peroxide conjugates. These reactive oxygen species can be formed in the presence of molecular oxygen during normal cellular metabolism, and if they accumulate the cell can suffer from *oxidative stress*. Peroxisomal enzymes such as *superoxide dismutase*, catalase, and peroxidases detoxify these reactive oxygen species, preventing their accumulation and subsequent oxidative damage to cellular components.

Oxidation of Fatty Acids. Peroxisomes found in animal, plant, and fungal cells contain enzymes necessary for oxidizing fatty acids via β *oxidation* to provide energy for the cell. About 25–50% of fatty acid oxidation in animal tissues occurs in peroxisomes, with the remainder localized in mitochondria. In plant and yeast cells, on the other hand, all β oxidation occurs in peroxisomes.

In animal cells, peroxisomal β oxidation is especially important for degrading long-chain (16–22 carbons), very long-chain (24–26 carbons), and branched fatty acids. The primary product of β oxidation, acetyl-CoA, is then exported to the cytosol, where it enters biosynthetic pathways or the TCA cycle. Once fatty acids are shortened to fewer than 16 carbons, further oxidation usually occurs in the mitochondria. Thus, in animal cells, the peroxisome is important for shortening fatty acids in preparation for subsequent metabolism in the mitochondrion rather than completely breaking them down to acetyl-CoA. In plants and yeast, on the other hand, peroxisomes are essential for the complete catabolism of all fatty acids to acetyl-CoA.

Metabolism of Nitrogen-Containing Compounds. Except for primates, most animals require *urate oxidase* (also called *uricase*) to oxidize urate, a purine that is formed during the catabolism of nucleic acids and some proteins. Like other oxidases, urate oxidase catalyzes the direct transfer of hydrogen atoms from the substrate to molecular oxygen, generating H_2O_2:

$$\text{urate} + O_2 \longrightarrow \text{allantoin} + H_2O_2 \quad \textbf{(12-6)}$$

As noted earlier, the H_2O_2 is immediately degraded in the peroxisome by catalase. The allantoin is further metabolized and excreted by the organism, either as allantoic acid or—in the case of crustaceans, fish, and amphibians—as urea.

Additional peroxisomal enzymes involved in nitrogen metabolism include *aminotransferases*. Members of this collection of enzymes catalyze the transfer of amino groups ($-NH_3^+$) from amino acids to α-keto acids:

$$\textbf{(12-7)}$$

Such enzymes play important roles in the biosynthesis and degradation of amino acids by moving amino groups from one molecule to another.

Catabolism of Unusual Substances. Some of the substrates for peroxisomal oxidases are rare compounds for which the cell has no other degradative pathways. Such compounds include D-amino acids, which are not recognized by enzymes capable of degrading the L-amino acids found in polypeptides. In some cells, the peroxisomes also contain enzymes that break down unusual substances called **xenobiotics,** chemical compounds foreign to biological organisms. This category includes *alkanes,* short-chain hydrocarbon compounds found in oil and other petroleum products. Fungi containing enzymes capable of metabolizing such xenobiotics may turn out to be useful for cleaning up oil spills that would otherwise contaminate the environment.

Peroxisomal Disorders. Considering the variety of metabolic pathways found in peroxisomes, it is not surprising that a large number of disorders arise from defective peroxisomal proteins (see Box 4A, page 86). The most common peroxisomal disorder is *X-linked adrenoleukodystrophy.* The defective protein causing this disorder is an integral membrane protein that may be responsible for transporting very long-chain fatty acids into the peroxisome for β oxidation. Accumulation of these long-chain fatty acids in body fluids destroys the myelin sheath in nervous tissues.

Plant Cells Contain Types of Peroxisomes Not Found in Animal Cells

In plants and algae, peroxisomes are involved in several specific aspects of cellular energy metabolism. Here, we will simply introduce several plant-specific peroxisomes and briefly describe their functions.

Leaf Peroxisomes. Cells of leaves and other photosynthetic plant tissues contain characteristic large, prominent **leaf peroxisomes,** which often appear in close contact with chloroplasts and mitochondria (see Figure 12-24; see also

Figure 4-20). The spatial proximity of the three organelles probably reflects their mutual involvement in the *glycolate pathway*, also called the *photorespiratory pathway* because it involves the light-dependent uptake of O_2 and release of CO_2. Several enzymes of this pathway, including a peroxide-generating oxidase and two aminotransferases, are confined to leaf peroxisomes.

Glyoxysomes. Another functionally distinct type of plant peroxisome occurs transiently in seedlings of plant species that store carbon and energy reserves in the seed as fat (primarily triacylglycerols). In such species, stored triacylglycerols are mobilized and converted to sucrose during early postgerminative development by a sequence of events that includes β oxidation of fatty acids as well as a pathway known as the *glyoxylate cycle*. All of the enzymes needed for these processes are localized to specialized peroxisomes called **glyoxysomes**.

Glyoxysomes are found only in the tissues where the fat is stored (endosperm or cotyledons, depending on the species) and are present only for the relatively short period of time required for the seedling to deplete its supply of stored fat. Once they fulfill their role in the seedling, the glyoxysomes are converted to peroxisomes. Glyoxysomes have been reported to appear again in the senescing (aging) tissues of some plant species, presumably to degrade lipids derived from the membranes of the senescent cells. However, the importance of their involvement in senescence is not yet clear.

Other Kinds of Plant Peroxisomes. In addition to their presence in tissues that carry out either photorespiration or β oxidation of fatty acids, peroxisomes are found in other plant tissues. For example, another kind of specialized peroxisome is present in *nodules,* the structures on plant roots in which plant cells and certain bacteria cooperate in the fixation of atmospheric nitrogen (that is, the conversion of N_2 into organic form). The peroxisomes in these cells are involved in the processing of fixed nitrogen.

Peroxisome Biogenesis Occurs by Division of Preexisting Peroxisomes

Like other organelles, peroxisomes increase in number as cells grow and divide. This proliferation of organelles is called *biogenesis,* and the peroxisomal proteins required for this process are known as *peroxins.* Biogenesis of endosomes and lysosomes occurs by fusion of vesicles budding from the Golgi complex, and peroxisomes were once thought to form from vesicles in a similar manner. Later, most investigators believed that peroxisome biogenesis occurred solely from the division of preexisting peroxisomes. Recent evidence suggests that new peroxisomes can be formed by either of these two methods, or perhaps by a combination of the two. Either way, their biogenesis raises two important questions.

First, where do the lipids that make up the newly synthesized peroxisomal membrane come from? We know that some of the lipids are synthesized by peroxisomal enzymes whereas others are synthesized in the ER and carried to the peroxisome by phospholipid exchange proteins. However, there is some evidence that these exchange proteins may not always be efficient enough to account for the rapid incorporation of new lipids and that some direct transfer from ER-derived vesicles may be involved.

Second, where are the new enzymes and other proteins that are present in the peroxisomal membrane and matrix synthesized? Proteins destined for peroxisomes are synthesized on free cytosolic ribosomes and are incorporated into preexisting peroxisomes posttranslationally. This passage of polypeptides across the peroxisomal membrane is an ATP-dependent process mediated by specific membrane peroxins, although the precise role of ATP is unclear.

Figure 12-25 illustrates both the incorporation of membrane components, matrix enzymes, and enzyme cofactors from the cytosol into a peroxisome (steps ❶–❸) and the formation of new peroxisomes by division of a preexisting organelle (step ❹). The protein depicted in the figure is catalase, a tetrameric protein with a heme group bound to each subunit. The subunits are synthesized

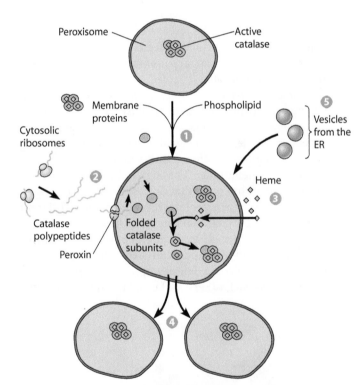

FIGURE 12-25 Biogenesis of Peroxisomes and Protein Import. New peroxisomes typically arise by the division of existing peroxisomes rather than by fusion of vesicles from the Golgi complex. ❶ Lipids and membrane proteins can be added to existing peroxisomes via cytosolic sources. ❷ Polypeptides for peroxisomal matrix enzymes are synthesized on cytosolic ribosomes and are threaded through the membrane via a transmembrane peroxin transport protein. The enzyme shown here is catalase, a tetrameric protein that requires a heme cofactor. ❸ Heme enters the peroxisomal lumen via a separate pathway, and the catalase polypeptides are folded and assembled with heme to form the active tetrameric protein. ❹ After lipids and protein are added, new peroxisomes are formed by the division of the existing peroxisomes. ❺ Some researchers believe that peroxisomes can obtain proteins or form de novo from protoperoxisomal vesicles that are derived from the ER.

individually on cytosolic ribosomes, imported into the peroxisome, refolded, and then assembled, along with heme, into the active tetrameric enzyme. Peroxisomes can also import not only single, unfolded polypeptides but also larger, folded polypeptides and even native oligomeric proteins.

Recent work suggests that some peroxins are synthesized in the cytosol but then travel to the ER in vesicles before being incorporated into peroxisomes (step ⑤). Evidence for this route includes the presence on certain peroxins of N-linked oligosaccharides typical of ER-synthesized proteins. Additionally, treatment of yeast cells with the toxin brefeldin A, which prevents formation of ER-derived vesicles, causes accumulation of the peroxin *Pex3p* in the ER.

Similarly, in plant cells, ascorbate peroxidase appears to be routed to a subdomain of the ER after being synthesized in the cytosol but before being incorporated into the peroxisome. This proposed subdomain of the ER, presumably involved in sorting of cytosolic proteins destined for the peroxisome, has been termed the *peroxisomal ER (pER)*, although its existence is still controversial. Likewise, the existence of the *protoperoxisome,* an ER-derived vesicle considered by some researchers to be capable of developing directly into a peroxisome, is currently the subject of much debate.

For posttranslational import to work, each protein destined for a specific organelle must have some sort of tag or signal that directs, or targets, the protein to the correct organelle. Such a signal functions by recognizing specific receptors or other features on the surface of the appropriate membrane. The signal in each case is a sequence of amino acids that differs in sequence, length, and location for proteins targeted to different organelles. The signal that targets at least some peroxisomal proteins to their destination consists of just three amino acids and is found at or near the carboxyl terminus of the molecule. For example, the most common sequence is SKL (Ser-Lys-Leu), though a limited number of other amino acids are possible at each of the three locations.

This C-terminal tripeptide, known as *PTS-1 (peroxisomal targeting signal-1),* is recognized and bound by the cytosolic peroxin *Pex5p.* A second peroxisomal targeting signal known as *PTS-2* is an N-terminal sequence recognized by the peroxin *Pex7p.* These PTS-binding peroxins deliver the PTS-containing proteins to the peroxisome for import by a mechanism that is not yet fully understood. At the peroxisomal membrane, Pex5p and Pex7p interact with one or more membrane-bound *docking proteins.* Then they are believed to enter the peroxisome carrying their cargo, which they release before they are exported from the peroxisome back to the cytosol to participate in subsequent transport cycles.

Suresh Subramani and others have shown that a protein normally targeted to the peroxisome by PTS-1 will remain in the cytosol if its SKL sequence is removed. Conversely, the addition of an SKL sequence to a cytosolic protein will direct the chimeric protein to the peroxisome. Thus the SKL sequence, or one of the acceptable variants, is both *necessary* and *sufficient* to direct proteins to peroxisomes. Moreover, a peroxisomal targeting sequence identified in one species often functions in other species, even when the organisms are as evolutionarily diverse from one another as plants, yeast, insects, and animals.

In one striking example, the gene for *luciferase,* a peroxisomal enzyme that enables fireflies to emit flashes of light, was transferred into plant cells from which whole plants were then grown. When cells of the genetically transformed plant were carefully examined, the luciferase was found in peroxisomes, the same organelle in which it is located in fireflies. Knowledge of peroxisomal import mechanisms and the identification of numerous peroxins conserved between yeast and humans, coupled with the powerful genetic methods available in yeast model systems, will help us to understand and better treat human diseases caused by faulty peroxisome biogenesis or protein import.

SUMMARY OF KEY POINTS

The Endoplasmic Reticulum

- Especially prevalent within most eukaryotic cells is the endomembrane system, an elaborate array of membrane-bounded organelles derived from the endoplasmic reticulum (ER). The ER itself is a network of sacs, tubules, and vesicles surrounded by a single membrane that separates the ER lumen from the surrounding cytosol.

- The rough ER has ribosomes that synthesize proteins destined for the plasma membrane, for secretion, or for various organelles of the endomembrane system—the nuclear envelope, Golgi complex, endosomes, and lysosomes. Both the rough and smooth ER synthesize lipids for cellular membranes. The smooth ER is also the site of drug detoxification, carbohydrate metabolism, calcium storage, and steroid biosynthesis in some cells.

The Golgi Complex

- The Golgi complex plays an important role in the glycosylation of proteins and in the sorting of proteins for transport to other organelles, for transport to the plasma membrane, or for secretion.

- Transition vesicles that bud from the ER fuse with the *cis*-Golgi network (CGN), delivering lipids and proteins to the Golgi complex. Proteins then move through the Golgi cisternae toward the *trans*-Golgi network (TGN).

Roles of the ER and Golgi Complex in Protein Glycosylation

- Before proteins leave the ER in transition vesicles, they undergo the first few steps of protein modification. ER-specific proteins catalyze core glycosylation and folding of polypeptides, elimination of misfolded proteins, and the assembly of multimeric proteins.

- During their journey through the Golgi complex, proteins are further modified as oligosaccharide side chains are trimmed or further glycosylated in the Golgi lumen.

Roles of the ER and Golgi Complex in Protein Trafficking

- Some ER-specific proteins have a retention signal that prevents them from leaving the ER as vesicles move from the ER to the CGN. Other ER proteins have a retrieval tag that allows them to return to the ER in vesicles that return from the CGN.

- Numerous transport vesicles bud from the TGN Golgi network and carry the processed proteins to their final destinations. The tag that identifies a particular protein and its destination may be a short amino acid sequence, an oligosaccharide side chain, or some other structural feature.

- Hydrolytic enzymes destined for the lysosome are phosphorylated on a mannose residue. Vesicles containing specific receptors for this mannose phosphate group carry these enzymes to the lysosome. During acidification in the lysosome, the enzymes are released from the receptors, which are then recycled back to the TGN.

Exocytosis and Endocytosis

- Exocytosis adds lipids and proteins to the plasma membrane when secretory granules release their contents to the extracellular medium by fusing with the plasma membrane. This addition of material to the plasma membrane is balanced by endocytosis, which removes lipids and proteins from the plasma membrane as extracellular material is internalized in vesicles.

- Phagocytosis is a type of endocytosis involving the ingestion of extracellular particles through invagination of the plasma membrane. Receptor-mediated endocytosis depends on highly specific binding of ligands to corresponding receptors on the cell surface. In both cases, after sorting of receptors and other necessary proteins back to the plasma membrane, ingested material is sent to lysosomes for digestion or to other locations for reuse.

Coated Vesicles in Cellular Transport Processes

- Transport vesicles carry material throughout the endomembrane system. Coat proteins—which include clathrin, COPI, COPII, and caveolin—participate in the sorting of molecules fated for different destinations as well as in the formation of vesicles.

- The specific coat proteins covering a vesicle indicate its origin and help determine its destination within the cell. Clathrin-coated vesicles deliver material from the TGN or plasma membrane to endosomes. COPII-coated vesicles carry materials from the ER to the Golgi, while COPI-coated vesicles transport material from the Golgi back to the ER.

- Once a transport vesicle nears its destination, it is recognized and bound by tethering proteins attached to the target membrane. At this point the v-SNAREs in the transport vesicle membrane and the t-SNAREs in the target membrane interact physically, helping to promote membrane fusion.

Lysosomes and Cellular Digestion

- Extracellular material obtained from phagocytosis or receptor-mediated endocytosis is sorted in early endosomes, which mature to form late endosomes and lysosomes as they fuse with vesicles containing inactive hydrolytic enzymes packaged in the TGN.

- The late endosomal membrane contains ATP-dependent proton pumps that lower the pH of the endosomal lumen and help to transform the late endosome into a lysosome. Then, latent acid hydrolases capable of degrading most biological molecules become active due to the low pH.

- Lysosomes also function in autophagy, the turnover and recycling of cellular structures that are damaged or no longer needed. In some cells, extracellular material is digested by enzymes that lysosomes discharge out of the cell by exocytosis.

The Plant Vacuole: A Multifunctional Organelle

- The plant vacuole is an acidic compartment resembling the animal lysosome. In addition to having hydrolytic enzymes for digestion of macromolecules, it helps the plant cell maintain positive turgor pressure and serves as a storage compartment for a variety of plant metabolites.

Peroxisomes

- Peroxisomes, which are not part of the endomembrane system, appear to increase in number by the division of preexisting organelles rather than by the coalescence of vesicles from the ER or Golgi. However, there is currently a debate concerning the existence of protoperoxisomes, vesicles that some researchers believe bud off from the ER and develop into new peroxisomes.

- Some peroxisomal membrane lipids are synthesized by peroxisomal enzymes, while others are carried from the ER by phospholipid exchange proteins. Most peroxisomal proteins are synthesized by cytosolic ribosomes and are imported posttranslationally. Others are believed to travel via a proposed subdomain of the ER known as the peroxisomal ER (pER).

- The defining enzyme of a peroxisome is catalase, an enzyme that degrades the toxic hydrogen peroxide that is generated by various oxidases in the peroxisome. Animal cell peroxisomes are important for detoxification of harmful substances, oxidation of fatty acids, and metabolism of nitrogen-containing compounds. In plants, peroxisomes play distinctive roles in the conversion of stored lipids into carbohydrate by glyoxysomes and in photorespiration by leaf peroxisomes.

MAKING CONNECTIONS

Now that we are halfway through our studies of cell biology, you should be familiar with many of the basic properties of cells and their components. As in many fields of biology, structure often determines function, and an understanding of cell chemistry and the macromolecules that make up cell structures and organelles is essential. You have learned how enzymes function and how cells get energy from the sun or from organic food molecules. In this chapter, you have used your knowledge of membrane structure and function to understand the movement of materials throughout the cell via the endomembrane system. The second half of the text will focus on more specific aspects of cell biology. Among other things, you will learn how cells respond to external electrical and hormonal signals, how materials move inside cells, how cells themselves move, and how muscle cells contract. We will study how the extracellular matrix in animals and the cell wall in plants join cells together to form specialized tissues. Then we will focus on the roles of DNA and RNA in cell growth and reproduction, on the expression of genetic information, and, finally, on the defects in cell metabolism that can lead to cancer.

PROBLEM SET

More challenging problems are marked with a •.

12-1 Compartmentalization of Function. Each of the following processes is associated with one or more specific eukaryotic organelles. In each case, identify the organelle or organelles, and suggest one advantage of confining the process to the organelle or organelles.

(a) β oxidation of long-chain fatty acids

(b) Biosynthesis of cholesterol

(c) Biosynthesis of insulin

(d) Biosynthesis of testosterone or estrogen

(e) Degradation of damaged organelles

(f) Glycosylation of membrane proteins

(g) Hydroxylation of phenobarbital

(h) Sorting of lysosomal proteins from secretory proteins

12-2 Endoplasmic Reticulum. For each of the following statements, indicate if it is true of the rough ER only (R), of the smooth ER only (S), of both rough and smooth ER (RS), or of neither (N).

(a) Contains less cholesterol than does the plasma membrane.

(b) Has ribosomes attached to its outer (cytosolic) surface.

(c) Is involved in the detoxification of drugs.

(d) Is involved in the breakdown of glycogen.

(e) Is the site for biosynthesis of secretory proteins.

(f) Is the site for the folding of membrane-bound proteins.

(g) Tends to form tubular structures.

(h) Usually consists of flattened sacs.

(i) Visible only by electron microscopy.

12-3 Biosynthesis of Integral Membrane Proteins. In addition to their role in cellular secretion, the rough ER and the Golgi complex are also responsible for the biosynthesis of integral membrane proteins. More specifically, these organelles are the source of glycoproteins commonly found in the outer phospholipid monolayer of the plasma membrane.

(a) In a series of diagrams, depict the synthesis and glycosylation of glycoproteins of the plasma membrane.

(b) Explain why the carbohydrate groups of membrane glycoproteins are always found on the outer surface of the plasma membrane.

(c) What assumptions did you make about biological membranes in order to draw the diagrams in part a and answer the question in part b?

12-4 Coated Vesicles in Intracellular Transport. For each of the following statements, indicate for which coated vesicle the statement is true: clathrin- (C), COPI- (I), or COPII-coated (II). Each statement may be true for one, several, or none (N) of the coated vesicles discussed in this chapter.

(a) Binding of the coat protein to an LDL receptor is mediated by an adaptor protein complex.

(b) Fusion of the vesicle (after dissociation of the coat) with the Golgi membrane is facilitated by specific t-SNARE and Rab proteins.

(c) Has a role in bidirectional transport between the ER and Golgi complex.

(d) Has a role in sorting proteins for intracellular transport to specific destinations.

(e) Has a role in transport of acid hydrolases to late endosomes.

(f) Is essential for all endocytic processes.

(g) Is important for retrograde traffic through the Golgi complex.

(h) Is involved in the movement of membrane lipids from the TGN to the plasma membrane.

(i) The basic structural component of the coat is called a triskelion.

(j) The protein coat dissociates shortly after formation of the vesicle.

(k) The protein coat always includes a specific small GTP-binding protein.

12-5 Interpreting Data. Each of the following statements summarizes the results of an experiment related to exocytosis or endocytosis. In each case, explain the relevance of the experiment and its result to our understanding of these processes.

(a) Addition of the drug colchicine to cultured fibroblast cells inhibits movement of transport vesicles.

(b) Certain pituitary gland cells secrete laminin continuously but secrete adrenocorticotropic hormone only in response to specific signals.

(c) Certain adrenal gland cells can be induced to secrete epinephrine when their intracellular calcium concentration is experimentally increased.

(d) Cells expressing a temperature-sensitive form of dynamin do not display receptor-mediated endocytosis after a temperature shift, yet they continue to ingest extracellular fluid (at a reduced level initially, and then at a normal level within 30–60 minutes).

(e) Brefeldin A inhibits cholesterol efflux in adipocytes (fat cells) without affecting the rate of cellular uptake and re-secretion of apolipoprotein A-I in adipocytes.

12-6 Cellular Digestion. For each of the following statements, indicate the specific digestion process or processes of which the statement is true: phagocytosis (P), receptor-mediated endocytosis (R), autophagy (A), or extracellular digestion (E). Each statement may be true of one, several, or none (N) of these processes.

(a) Can involve exocytosis.

(b) Can involve fusion of vesicles or vacuoles with a lysosome.

(c) Digested material is of extracellular origin.

(d) Digested material is of intracellular origin.

(e) Essential for sperm penetration of the egg during fertilization.

(f) Important for certain developmental processes.

(g) Involves acid hydrolases.

(h) Involves fusion of endocytic vesicles with an early endosome.

(i) Involves fusion of lysosomes with the plasma membrane.

(j) Occurs within lysosomes.

(k) Serves as a source of nutrients within the cell.

12-7 Peroxisomal Properties. For each of the following statements, indicate whether it is true of all (A), some (S), or none (N) of the various kinds of peroxisomes described in this chapter, and explain your answer.

(a) Acquires proteins from the ER and Golgi complex.

(b) Capable of catabolizing fatty acids.

(c) Contains acid hydrolases.

(d) Contains catalase.

(e) Contains peroxide-generating chemical reactions.

(f) Contains the genes coding for luciferase.

(g) Contains urate oxidase.

(h) Is a source of dolichol.

(i) Is surrounded by a lipid bilayer.

12-8 Lysosomal Storage Diseases. Despite a bewildering variety of symptoms, lysosomal storage diseases have several properties in common. For each of the following statements, indicate if you would expect the property to be common to most lysosomal storage diseases (M), to be true of a specific lysosomal storage disease (S), or not to be true of any lysosomal storage diseases (N).

(a) Impaired metabolism of glycolipids causes mental deterioration.

(b) Leads to accumulation of degradation products in the lysosome.

(c) Leads to accumulation of excessive amounts of glycogen in the lysosome.

(d) Results from an inability to regulate the synthesis of glycosaminoglycans.

(e) Results from an absence of functional acid hydrolases.

(f) Results in accumulation of lysosomes in the cell.

(g) Symptoms include muscle weakness and mental retardation.

(h) Triggers proliferation of organelles containing catalase.

12-9 Sorting Proteins. Specific structural features tag proteins for transport to various intracellular and extracellular destinations. Several examples were described in this chapter including: (1) the short peptide Lys-Asp-Glu-Leu, (2) characteristic hydrophobic membrane-spanning domains, and (3) mannose-6-phosphate residues attached to oligosaccharide side chains. For each structural feature, answer the following questions:

(a) Where in the cell is the tag incorporated into the protein?

(b) How does the tag ensure that the protein reaches its destination?

(c) Where would the protein likely go if you were to remove the tag?

• **12-10 Silicosis and Asbestosis.** *Silicosis* is a debilitating miner's disease that results from the ingestion of silica particles (such as sand or glass) by macrophages in the lungs. *Asbestosis* is a similarly serious disease caused by inhalation of asbestos fibers. In both cases, the particles or fibers are found in lysosomes, and fibroblasts, which secrete collagen, are stimulated to deposit nodules of collagen fibers in the lungs, leading to reduced lung capacity, impaired breathing, and eventually death.

(a) How do you think the fibers get into the lysosomes?

(b) What effect do you think fiber or particle accumulation has on the lysosomes?

(c) How might you explain the death of silica-containing or asbestos-containing cells?

(d) What do you think happens to the silica particles or asbestos fibers when such cells die? How can cell death continue almost indefinitely, even after prevention of further exposure to silica dust or asbestos fibers?

(e) Cultured fibroblast cells will secrete collagen and produce connective tissue fibers after the addition of material from a culture of lung macrophages that have been exposed to silica particles. What does this tell you about the deposition of collagen nodules in the lungs of silicosis patients?

• 12-11 What's Happening? Researchers have discovered a group of plant proteins that are related to the exocyst proteins in yeast (*The Plant Cell* 20 (2008): 1330). Explain how the following observations made by these researchers suggest that these plant proteins form a tethering complex similar to the exocyst complex of yeast and mammals.

(a) Following size fractionation of plant protein extracts, antibodies recognizing each of several different plant exocyst proteins bind to the same high-molecular-weight protein fraction.

(b) Mutations in four of the proteins each causes defective pollen germination.

(c) Plants lacking more than one of these proteins have more serious defects in pollen germination than plants lacking only one.

(d) The exocyst proteins all co-localize at the growing tip of elongating pollen cells.

(e) Pollen cells of plants with mutations in exocyst genes are defective in tip growth or germinating pollen cells.

SUGGESTED READING

References of historical importance are marked with a •.

General References

Brown, D. Imaging protein trafficking. *Nephron. Exp. Nephrol.* 103 (2006): 55.

Nunnari, J., and P. Walter. Regulation of organelle biogenesis. *Cell* 84 (1996): 389.

Pan, S., C. J. Carter, and N. V. Raikhel. Understanding protein trafficking in plant cells through proteomics. *Expert Rev. Proteomics* 2 (2005): 781.

Uemura, K., A. Kuzuya, and S. Shimohama. Protein trafficking and Alzheimer's disease. *Curr. Alzheimer Res.* 1 (2004): 1.

The Endoplasmic Reticulum and the Golgi Complex

Dancourt, J., and C. Barlowe. Protein sorting receptors in the early secretory pathway. *Annu. Rev. Biochem.* 79 (2010): 777.

Ellgaard, L., and A. Helenius. ER quality control: Towards an understanding at the molecular level. *Curr. Opin. Cell Biol.* 13 (2001): 431.

• Farquhar, M. G., and G. E. Palade. The Golgi apparatus: 100 years of progress and controversy. *Trends Cell Biol.* 8 (1998): 2.

Glick, B. S., and A. Nakano. Membrane traffic within the Golgi apparatus. *Annu. Rev. Cell Dev. Biol.* 25 (2009): 113.

• Jamieson, J. D., and G. E. Palade. Intracellular transport of secretory proteins in the pancreatic exocrine cell II: Transport to condensing vacuoles and zymogen granules. *J. Cell Biol.* 34 (1967): 597.

Klumperman, J. Transport between ER and Golgi. *Curr. Opin. Cell Biol.* 12 (2000): 445.

Zhao, L., and S. L. Ackerman. Endoplasmic reticulum stress in health and disease. *Curr. Opin. Cell Biol.* 18 (2006): 444.

Exocytosis and Endocytosis

Blázquez, M., and K. I. J. Shennan. Basic mechanisms of secretion: Sorting into the regulated secretory pathway. *Biochem. Cell Biol.* 78 (2000): 181.

Jutras, I., and M. Desjardins. Phagocytosis: At the crossroads of innate and adaptive immunity. *Annu. Rev. Cell Dev. Biol.* 12 (2005): 511.

Lemmon, S. K., and L. M. Traub. Sorting in the endosomal system in yeast and animal cells. *Curr. Opin. Cell Biol.* 12 (2000): 457.

Ng, T. W., E. M. Ooi, G. F. Watts, D. C. Chan, and P. H. Barrett. Genetic determinants of apolipoprotein B-100 kinetics. *Curr. Opin. Lipidol.* 21 (2010): 141.

Pelham, H. R. B. Insights from yeast endosomes. *Curr. Opin. Cell Biol.* 14 (2002): 454.

Tjelle, T. E., T. Lùvdal, and T. Berg. Phagosome dynamics and function. *BioEssays* 22 (2000): 255.

Transport Vesicles

Fielding, C. J. *Lipid Rafts and Caveolae: From Membrane Biophysics to Cell Biology.* New York: Wiley-VCH, 2007.

Hsu, V. W., and J. S. Yang. Mechanisms of COPI vesicle formation. *FEBS Lett.* 583 (2009): 3758.

Lipka, V., C. Kwon, and R. Panstruga. SNARE-ware: The role of SNARE-domain proteins in plant biology. *Annu. Rev. Cell Dev. Biol.* 23 (2007): 147.

Whyte, J. R. C., and S. Munro. Vesicle tethering complexes in membrane traffic. *J. Cell Sci.* 115 (2002): 2627.

Xiang-A. L., W. V. Everson, and E. J. Smart. Caveolae, lipid rafts, and vascular disease. *Trends Cardiovasc. Med.* 15 (2005): 92.

Lysosomes and Vacuoles

• Bainton, D. The discovery of lysosomes. *J. Cell Biol.* 91 (1981): 66s.

Bonifacino, J. S., and L. M. Traub. Signals for sorting of transmembrane proteins to endosomes and lysosomes. *Annu. Rev. Biochem.* 72 (2003): 395.

De, D. N. *Plant Cell Vacuoles: An Introduction.* Collingwood, Victoria: CSIRO Publishing, 2000.

• de Duve, C. The lysosome. *Sci. Amer.* 208 (May, 1963): 64.

Klionsky, D. J., and S. D. Emr. Autophagy as a regulated pathway of cellular degradation. *Science* 290 (2000): 1717.

Marx, J. Autophagy: Is it cancer's friend or foe? *Science* 312 (2006): 1160.

Saftig, P., and J. Klumperman. Lysosome biogenesis and lysosomal membrane proteins: Trafficking meets function. *Nature Rev. Mol. Cell Biol.* 10 (2009): 623.

Peroxisomes

• de Duve, C. The peroxisome: A new cytoplasmic organelle. *Proc. R. Soc. Lond. Ser. B Biol. Sci.* 173 (1969): 71.

Gärtner, J. Organelle disease: Peroxisomal disorders. *Eur. J. Pediatr.* 159 [Suppl. 3] (2000): S236.

Lazarow, P. B. Peroxisome biogenesis: Advances and conundrums. *Curr. Opin. Cell Biol.* 15 (2003): 489.

Ma, C., and S. Subramani. Peroxisome matrix and membrane protein biogenesis. *IUBMB Life.* 61 (2009): 713.

Mullen, R. T., C. R. Flynn, and R. N. Trelease. How are peroxisomes formed? The role of the endoplasmic reticulum and peroxins. *Trends Plant Sci.* 6 (2001): 256.

Smith, J. J., and J. D. Aitchison. Regulation of peroxisome dynamics. *Curr. Opin. Cell Biol.* 21 (2009): 119.

Titorenko, V. I., and R. T. Mullen. Peroxisome biogenesis: The peroxisomal endomembrane system and the role of the ER. *J. Cell Biol.* 174 (2006): 11.

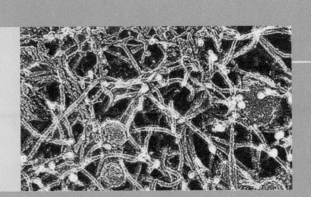

15

Cytoskeletal Systems

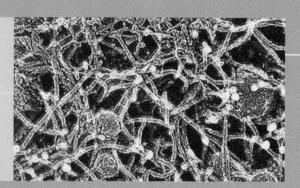

*I*n the preceding chapters, we examined a variety of cellular processes and pathways, many of which occur in the organelles of eukaryotic cells. We also examined signaling events, initiated at the cell surface, that have profound effects on cellular function. We now come to the cytosol, the region of the cytoplasm between and surrounding organelles. Until a few decades ago, the cytosol of the eukaryotic cell was regarded as the generally uninteresting, gel-like substance in which the nucleus and other organelles were suspended. Advances in microscopy and other investigative techniques have revealed that the interior of a eukaryotic cell is highly structured. Part of this structure is provided by the **cytoskeleton:** a complex network of interconnected filaments and tubules that extends throughout the cytosol, from the nucleus to the inner surface of the plasma membrane. The cytoskeleton plays important roles in cell movement and cell division, and in eukaryotes it actively moves membrane-bounded organelles within the cytosol. It also plays a similar role for messenger RNA and other cellular components. The cytoskeleton is also involved in many forms of cell movement and is intimately related to other processes such as cell signaling and cell-cell adhesion. The cytoskeleton is altered by events at the cell surface and, at the same time, appears to participate in and modulate these events.

The term cytoskeleton *accurately expresses the role of this polymer network in providing an architectural framework for cellular function. It confers a high level of internal organization on cells and enables them to assume and maintain complex shapes that would not otherwise be possible. The name does not, however, convey the dynamic, changeable nature of the cytoskeleton and its critical involvement in a great variety of cellular processes.*

Major Structural Elements of the Cytoskeleton

Eukaryotes Have Three Basic Types of Cytoskeletal Elements

The three major structural elements of the cytoskeleton in eukaryotes are *microtubules, microfilaments,* and *intermediate filaments* (Table 15-1). The existence of three distinct systems of filaments and tubules was first revealed by electron microscopy. Biochemical and cytochemical studies then identified the distinctive proteins of each system. The technique of *indirect immunostaining* (see the Appendix, Figure A-12) was especially important in localizing specific proteins to the cytoskeleton.

Each structural element of the cytoskeleton has a characteristic size, structure, and intracellular distribution, and each element is formed by the polymerization of a different kind of subunit (Table 15-1). Microtubules are composed of the protein *tubulin* and are about 25 nm in diameter. Microfilaments, with a diameter of about 7 nm, are polymers of the protein *actin*. Intermediate filaments have diameters in the range of 8–12 nm. Intermediate filament subunits differ depending on the cell type. In addition to its major protein component, each type of cytoskeletal filament has a number of other proteins associated with it. These accessory proteins account for the remarkable structural and functional diversity of cytoskeletal elements.

Bacteria Have Cytoskeletal Systems That Are Structurally Similar to Those in Eukaryotes

Until recently, cytoskeletal proteins were thought to be unique to eukaryotes. However, recent discoveries have shown that bacteria, such as rod-shaped bacteria, and

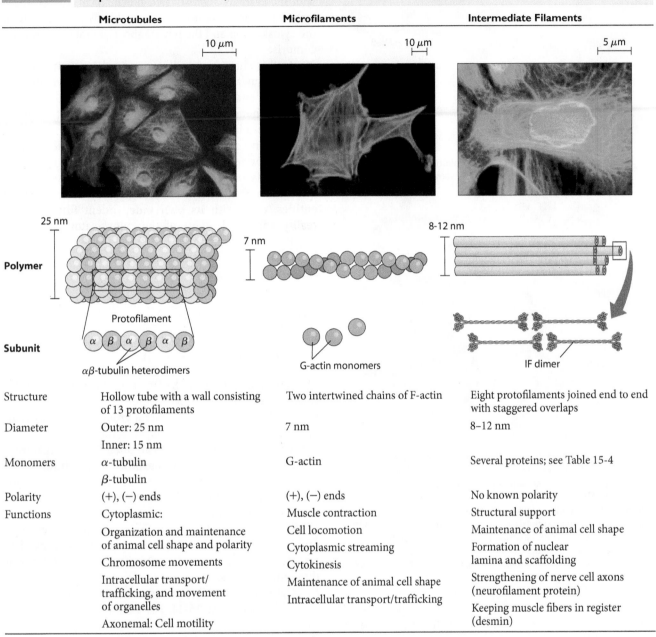

	Microtubules	Microfilaments	Intermediate Filaments
Structure	Hollow tube with a wall consisting of 13 protofilaments	Two intertwined chains of F-actin	Eight protofilaments joined end to end with staggered overlaps
Diameter	Outer: 25 nm	7 nm	8–12 nm
	Inner: 15 nm		
Monomers	α-tubulin	G-actin	Several proteins; see Table 15-4
	β-tubulin		
Polarity	(+), (−) ends	(+), (−) ends	No known polarity
Functions	Cytoplasmic:	Muscle contraction	Structural support
	Organization and maintenance of animal cell shape and polarity	Cell locomotion	Maintenance of animal cell shape
		Cytoplasmic streaming	Formation of nuclear lamina and scaffolding
	Chromosome movements	Cytokinesis	
	Intracellular transport/ trafficking, and movement of organelles	Maintenance of animal cell shape	Strengthening of nerve cell axons (neurofilament protein)
		Intracellular transport/trafficking	
	Axonemal: Cell motility		Keeping muscle fibers in register (desmin)

the Archaea have polymer systems that function in a manner very similar to microfilaments, microtubules, and intermediate filaments (**Figure 15-1**). Based on the effects of mutating these proteins, it is clear that they play roles similar to their eukaryotic counterparts. For example, the actin-like *MreB* protein is involved in DNA segregation, the tubulin-like *FtsZ* protein is involved in determining where bacterial cells will divide, and the intermediate filament-like *crescentin* protein is an important regulator of cell shape. Significantly, the FtsZ protein is produced by certain organelles in some eukaryotes, such as chloroplasts and mitochondria, and localizes to sites where these organelles divide. These findings provide further evidence for the endosymbiont theory discussed in Chapter 4. Although the

bacterial proteins are not very similar to their eukaryotic counterparts at the amino acid level, X-ray crystallography has shown that when they are assembled into polymers, their overall structure is remarkably similar (Figure 15-1e). Moreover, the equivalent proteins bind the same phospho-nucleotides as their eukaryotic equivalents, indicating striking similarities at the biochemical level as well.

The Cytoskeleton Is Dynamically Assembled and Disassembled

The cytoskeleton currently is a topic of great research interest to cell biologists. Microtubules and microfilaments are perhaps best known for their roles in cell motility. For

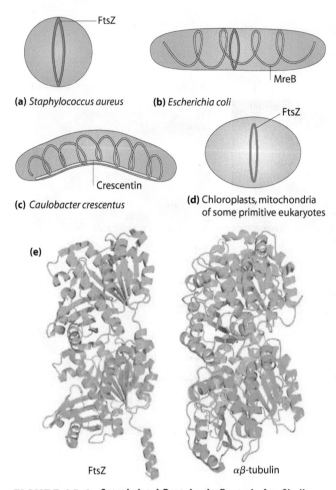

FtsZ

MreB

(a) *Staphylococcus aureus*   **(b)** *Escherichia coli*

FtsZ

Crescentin

(c) *Caulobacter crescentus*   **(d)** Chloroplasts, mitochondria of some primitive eukaryotes

(e)

FtsZ $\alpha\beta$-tubulin

FIGURE 15-1 Cytoskeletal Proteins in Bacteria Are Similar to Those in Eukaryotes. The distribution of several bacterial cytoskeletal proteins are shown in parts a–d. Blue: the microtubule-like FtsZ protein. Orange: the actin-like MreB protein. Yellow: the intermediate-filament-like protein Crescentin. **(a)** *S. aureus.* **(b)** *E. coli.* **(c)** *Caulobacter.* **(d)** Some plastids and mitochondria in some primitive eukaryotes express FtsZ at sites of division. **(e)** Comparison of the structure of FtsZ (left) and an $\alpha\beta$-tubulin heterodimer (X-ray crystallography). Note the similarity in structure.

example, microfilaments are essential components of *muscle fibrils,* and microtubules are the structural elements of *cilia* and *flagella,* appendages that enable certain cells to either propel themselves through a fluid environment or move fluids past the cell. These structures are large enough to be seen by light microscopy and were therefore known and studied long before it became clear that the same structural elements are also integral parts of the cytoskeleton in most cells. With the advent of sophisticated microscopy techniques, it eventually became clear that most cells dynamically regulate where and when specific cytoskeletal structures are assembled and disassembled. Recent progress in understanding cytoskeletal structure relies heavily on a combination of powerful microscopy techniques: various types of *fluorescence microscopy, digital video microscopy,* and various types of *electron microscopy* (Table 15-2). Each technique is described in more detail in the Appendix. In addition, specific drugs can be used to

perturb cytoskeletal function (Table 15-3). In parallel with increasingly sophisticated biochemical studies, these techniques have revealed the incredibly dynamic nature of the cytoskeleton and the remarkably elaborate structures it comprises.

In this chapter, we will focus on the structure of the cytoskeleton and how its components are dynamically assembled and disassembled. In each case, we will consider the chemistry of the subunit(s), the structure of the polymer and how it is polymerized, the role of accessory proteins, and some of the structural and functional roles each component plays within the cell. In doing so, we will be discussing microtubules, microfilaments, and intermediate filaments as though they were separate entities, each with its own independent functions. In reality, the components of the cytoskeleton are linked together both structurally and functionally, as we will see in the last section of this chapter. We begin our discussion with microtubules.

Microtubules

Two Types of Microtubules Are Responsible for Many Functions in the Cell

Microtubules (MTs) are the largest of the cytoskeletal elements (see Table 15-1). Microtubules in eukaryotic cells can be classified into two general groups, which differ in both degree of organization and structural stability.

The first group comprises an often loosely organized, dynamic network of **cytoplasmic microtubules.** The occurrence of cytoplasmic MTs in eukaryotic cells was not recognized until the early 1960s, when better fixation techniques permitted direct visualization of the network of MTs now known to pervade the cytosol of most eukaryotic cells. Since then, fluorescence microscopy has revealed the diversity and complexity of MT networks in different cell types.

Cytoplasmic MTs are responsible for a variety of functions (see Table 15-1). For example, in animal cells they are required to maintain axons, nerve cell extensions whose electrical properties. Some migrating animal cells require cytoplasmic MTs to maintain their polarized shape. In plant cells, cytoplasmic MTs govern the orientation of cellulose microfibrils deposited during the growth of cell walls. Significantly, cytoplasmic MTs form the mitotic and meiotic spindles that are essential for the movement of chromosomes during mitosis and meiosis (see Chapter 19). Cytoplasmic microtubules also contribute to the spatial disposition and directional movement of vesicles and other organelles by providing an organized system of fibers to guide their movement.

The second group of microtubules, **axonemal microtubules,** includes the highly organized, stable microtubules found in specific subcellular structures associated with cellular movement, including cilia, flagella, and the

Table 15-2   Techniques for Visualizing the Cytoskeleton

Technique	Description	Example	
Fluorescence microscopy on fixed specimens*	Fluorescent compounds directly bind to cytoskeletal proteins, or antibodies are used to indirectly label cytoskeletal proteins in chemically preserved cells, causing them to glow in the fluorescence microscope.	A fibroblast stained with fluorescent antibodies directed against actin shows bundles of actin filaments.	
Live cell fluorescence microscopy*	Fluorescent versions of cytoskeletal proteins are made and introduced into living cells. Fluorescence microscopy and video or digital cameras are used to view the proteins as they function in cells.	Fluorescent tubulin molecules were microinjected into living fibroblast cells. Inside the cell, the tubulin dimers become incorporated into microtubules, which can be seen easily with a fluorescence microscope.	
Computer-enhanced digital video microscopy	High-resolution images from a video or digital camera attached to a microscope are computer processed to increase contrast and remove background features that obscure the image.	Two micrographs showing several microtubules were processed to make them visible in detail.	 Unenhanced Enhanced
Electron microscopy	Electron microscopy can resolve individual filaments prepared by thin section, quick-freeze deep-etch, or direct-mount techniques.	A fibroblast cell is prepared by the quick-freeze deep-etch method. Bundles of actin microfilaments are visible.	

*Confocal, deconvolution, multiphoton, and total internal reflection fluorescence (TIRF) microscopy are often used to improve detection of fluorescent signals. See the Appendix for more details.

basal bodies to which these appendages are attached. The central shaft, or *axoneme,* of a cilium or flagellum consists of a highly ordered bundle of axonemal MTs and associated proteins. Given their order and stability, it is not surprising that the axonemal MTs were the first of the two groups to be recognized and studied. We have already encountered an example of such a structure; the axoneme of the sperm tail shown in Figure 4-12 consists of MTs. We will consider axoneme structure and microtubule-mediated motility further in Chapter 16.

Table 15-3   Drugs Used to Perturb the Cytoskeleton

Drug	Source	Affect
Drugs Affecting Microtubules		
Colchicine, colcemid	Autumn crocus, *Colchicum autumnale*	Binds tubulin monomers, inhibiting assembly
Nocadazole	Synthetic benzimidazole	Binds b-tubulin, inhibiting polymerization
Vinblastine, vincristine	Periwinkle plant, *Vinca rosea*	Aggregates tubulin heterodimers
Taxol	Pacific yew tree, *Taxus brevifolia*	Stabilizes microtubules
Drugs Affecting Microfilaments		
Cytochalasin D	Fungal metabolite	Prevents addition of new monomers to plus ends
Latrunculin A	Red sea sponge, *Latrunculia magnifica*	Sequesters actin monomers
Phalloidin	Death cap fungus, *Amanita phalloides*	Binds and stabilizes assembled microfilaments

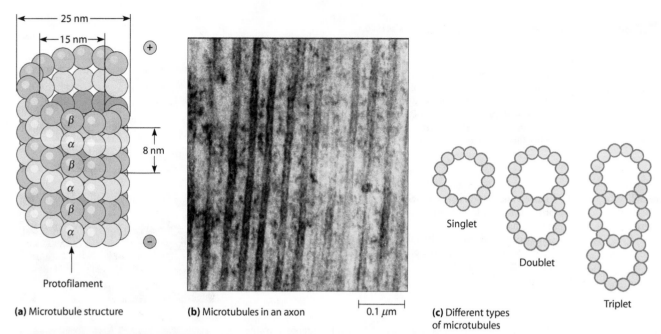

(a) Microtubule structure **(b)** Microtubules in an axon |0.1 μm| **(c)** Different types of microtubules

Singlet

Doublet

Triplet

Protofilament

FIGURE 15-2 Microtubule Structure. **(a)** A schematic diagram showing a microtubule as a hollow cylinder enclosing a lumen. The outside diameter is about 25 nm, and the inside diameter is about 15 nm. The wall of the cylinder consists of 13 protofilaments, one of them indicated by an arrow. A protofilament is a linear polymer of tubulin dimers, each consisting of two polypeptides—α-tubulin and β-tubulin. All heterodimers in the protofilaments have the same orientation, thus accounting for the polarity of the microtubule. **(b)** Microtubules in a longitudinal section of an axon (TEM). **(c)** Microtubules can form as singlets (13 protofilaments around a hollow lumen), doublets, and triplets. Doublets and triplets contain one complete, 13-protofilament microtubule (the *A tubule*) and one or two additional, incomplete tubules (called *B* and *C tubules*) consisting of 10 protofilaments.

Tubulin Heterodimers Are the Protein Building Blocks of Microtubules

MTs are straight, hollow cylinders with an outer diameter of about 25 nm and an inner diameter of about 15 nm (**Figure 15-2**). Microtubules vary greatly in length. Some are less than 200 nm long; others, such as axonemal MTs, can be many micrometers in length. The MT wall consists of longitudinal arrays of linear polymers called **protofilaments.** There are usually 13 protofilaments arranged side by side around the hollow center, or lumen; although some MTs in some animals contain more or less than 13 protofilaments, this number is by far the most common.

As shown in Figure 15-2, the basic subunit of a protofilament is a heterodimer of the protein **tubulin** (for a three-dimensional structure, see Figure 15-1e). The heterodimers that form the bulk of protofilaments are composed of one molecule of **A-tubulin** and one molecule of **B-tubulin.** As soon as individual a- and b-tubulin molecules are synthesized, they bind noncovalently to each other to produce an **AB-heterodimer** that does not dissociate under normal conditions.

Individual a- and b-tubulin molecules have diameters of about 4–5 nm and molecular weights of 55 kDa. Structural studies show that a- and b-tubulins have nearly identical three-dimensional structures, even though they

share only 40% amino acid sequence identity. Each has a GTP-binding domain at the N-terminus, a domain in the middle to which colchicine can bind (colchicine is a MT poison that blocks MT assembly; see below), and a third domain at the C-terminus that interacts with MT-associated proteins (MAPs; we will discuss MAPs later in this chapter).

Within a microtubule, all of the tubulin dimers are oriented in the same direction, such that all of the a-tubulin subunits face the same end. This uniform orientation of tubulin dimers means that one end of the protofilament differs chemically and structurally from the other, giving the protofilament an inherent polarity. Because the orientation of the tubulin dimers is the same for all of the protofilaments in an MT, the MT itself is also a polar structure.

Most organisms have several closely related but nonidentical genes for each of the a- and b-tubulin subunits. These slightly different forms of tubulin are called *tubulin isoforms.* In the mammalian brain, for example, there are five a- and five b-tubulin isoforms. These isoforms differ mainly in the C-terminal domain, which suggests that various tubulin isoforms may interact with different proteins. In addition to different isoforms, tubulin can be chemically modified. For example, acetylated tubulin tends to form more stable MTs than nonacetylated tubulin does.

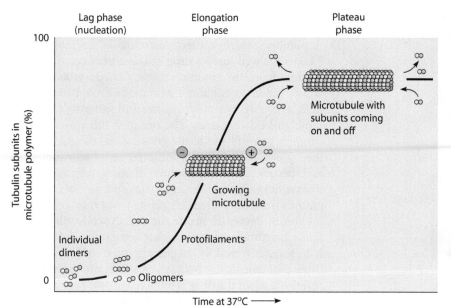

Lag phase (nucleation) | Elongation phase | Plateau phase

FIGURE 15-3 The Kinetics of Microtubule Assembly In Vitro. The kinetics of MT assembly can be monitored by observing the amount of light scattered by a solution containing GTP-tubulin after it is warmed from 0°C to 37°C. (Microtubule assembly is inhibited by cold and activated upon warming.) Such light-scattering measurements reflect changes in the MT population as a whole, not the assembly of individual microtubules. When measured in this way, MT assembly exhibits three phases: lag, elongation, and plateau. The lag phase is the period of nucleation. During the elongation phase, MTs grow rapidly, causing the concentration of tubulin subunits in the solution to decline. When this concentration is low enough to limit further assembly, the plateau phase is reached, during which subunits are added and removed from MTs at equal rates.

Microtubules Can Form as Singlets, Doublets, or Triplets

Cytoplasmic MTs are simple tubes, or *singlet* MTs, built from 13 protofilaments. Some axonemal MTs are more complex, however: they can contain *doublet* or *triplet* MTs. Doublets and triplets contain one complete, 13-protofilament microtubule (the *A tubule*) and one or two additional, incomplete tubules (called *B* and *C tubules*) consisting of 10 or 11 protofilaments (Figure 15-2c). Doublets are found in cilia and flagella; triplets are found in basal bodies and centrioles. We will examine cilia and flagella in much more detail in Chapter 16.

Microtubules Form by the Addition of Tubulin Dimers at Their Ends

Microtubules form by the reversible polymerization of tubulin dimers. The polymerization process has been studied extensively in vitro; a schematic representation of MT assembly in vitro is shown in **Figure 15-3**. When a solution containing a sufficient concentration of tubulin dimers, GTP, and Mg^{2+} is warmed from 0°C to 37°C, the polymerization reaction begins. (MT formation in the solution can be readily measured with a spectrophotometer as an increase in light scattering.) A critical step in the formation of MTs is the aggregation of tubulin dimers into clusters called *oligomers*. These oligomers serve as "nuclei" from which new microtubules can grow, and hence this process is referred to as **nucleation.** Once an MT has been nucleated, it grows by addition of subunits at either end, via a process called **elongation.**

Microtubule formation is initially slow, a period referred to as the *lag phase* of MT assembly. This period reflects the relatively slow process of MT nucleation. The elongation phase of MT assembly—the addition of tubulin dimers—is relatively fast compared with nucleation.

Eventually, the mass of MTs increases to a point where the concentration of free tubulin becomes limiting. This leads to the *plateau phase,* where MT assembly is balanced by disassembly.

Microtubule growth in vitro depends on the concentration of tubulin dimers. The tubulin heterodimer concentration at which MT assembly is exactly balanced with disassembly is called the overall **critical concentration.** MTs tend to grow when the tubulin concentration exceeds the critical concentration and depolymerize when the tubulin concentration falls below the critical concentration.

Addition of Tubulin Dimers Occurs More Quickly at the Plus Ends of Microtubules

The inherent structural polarity of microtubules means that the two ends differ chemically. Another important difference between the two ends of the MT is that one end can inherently grow or shrink much faster than the other. This difference in assembly rate can readily be visualized by mixing the MT-associated structures found at the base of cilia, known as *basal bodies,* with tubulin heterodimers. Assembly of the tubulin heterodimers occurs at both ends, but the MTs grow much faster from one end than the other. (The position of the basal body in the growing MT can be assessed because of its different appearance under the electron microscope; **Figure 15-4.**) The rapidly growing end of the microtubule is called the **plus end,** and the other end is the **minus end.** As we will see below, minus ends of MTs are often anchored at the centrosome; in this case MT dynamics are confined to plus ends.

The different growth rates of the plus and minus ends of microtubules reflect the different critical concentrations required for assembly at the two ends of the MT; the critical concentration for the plus end is lower than that for

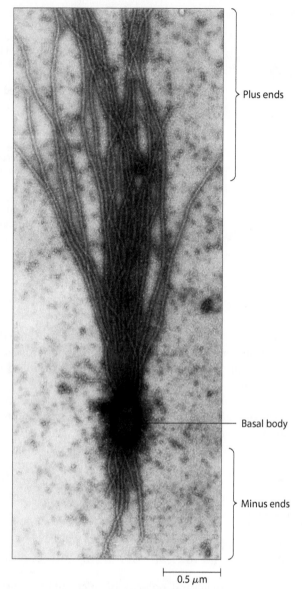

Plus ends

Basal body

Minus ends

0.5 μm

FIGURE 15-4 Polar Assembly of Microtubules in Vitro. The polarity of MT assembly can be demonstrated by adding basal bodies to a solution of tubulin dimers. The tubulin dimers add to the plus and minus ends of the microtubules in the basal body. However, MTs that grow from the plus end are much longer than those growing from the minus end.

the minus end. If the free tubulin concentration is higher than the critical concentration for the plus end but lower than the critical concentration for the minus end, assembly will occur at the plus end while disassembly takes place at the minus end. This simultaneous assembly and disassembly produces the phenomenon known as *treadmilling* (**Figure 15-5**). Treadmilling arises when a given tubulin molecule incorporated at the plus end is displaced progressively along the MT and eventually lost by depolymerization at the opposite end. By examining fluorescent MTs, treadmilling has been observed in living cells, although it is uncertain how important it is to overall MT dynamics.

Drugs Can Affect the Assembly of Microtubules

A number of drugs affect microtubule assembly (Table 15-3). One well-known drug of this sort is **colchicine,** an alkaloid from the autumn crocus, *Colchicum autumnale,* which binds to tubulin monomers, strongly inhibiting their assembly into microtubules and fostering the disassembly of existing ones. The resulting tubulin-colchicine complex can still add to the growing end of an MT, but it then prevents any further addition of tubulin molecules and destabilizes the structure, thereby promoting MT disassembly. *Vinblastine* and *vincristine* are related compounds from the periwinkle plant *(Vinca rosea)* that cause tubulin to aggregate inside the cell. **Nocodazole** (a synthetic benzimidazole) is another compound that inhibits MT assembly and is frequently used in experiments instead of colchicine, because its effects are more readily reversible when the drug is removed.

These compounds are called *antimitotic drugs* because they disrupt the mitotic spindle of dividing cells, blocking the further progress of mitosis. The sensitivity of the mitotic spindle to these drugs is understandable because the spindle fibers are composed of many microtubules. Indeed, vinblastine and vincristine find application in medical practice as anticancer drugs. They are useful for this purpose because cancer cells divide rapidly and are therefore preferentially susceptible to drugs that interfere with the mitotic spindle.

In contrast, **taxol** (from the Pacific yew tree, *Taxus brevifolia*) binds tightly to microtubules and stabilizes them, causing much of the free tubulin in the cell to assemble into microtubules. Within cells, taxol causes free tubulin to assemble into MTs and arrests dividing cells in mitosis. Thus, both taxol and colchicine block cells in mitosis, but

Minus end   Plus end

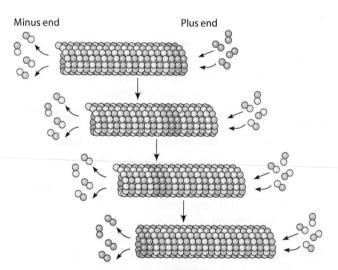

FIGURE 15-5 Treadmilling of Microtubules. Microtubule assembly occurs more readily at the plus end of an MT than at the minus end. When the tubulin concentration is higher than the critical concentration for the plus end but lower than the critical concentration for the minus end, the microtubule can add tubulin heterodimers to its plus end while losing them from its minus end.

they do so by opposing effects on MTs and hence on the fibers of the mitotic spindle. Taxol is also used in the treatment of some cancers, especially breast cancer.

GTP Hydrolysis Contributes to the Dynamic Instability of Microtubules

In the previous section, we saw that tubulin can assemble in vitro in the presence of Mg^{2+} and GTP. In fact, GTP is required for MT assembly. Each tubulin heterodimer binds two GTP molecules. The a-tubulin binds one GTP; the other GTP is bound by b-tubulin and can be hydrolyzed to GDP sometime after the heterodimer is added to an MT. GTP is apparently needed for MT assembly because the association of GDP-bound tubulin heterodimers with each other is too weak to support polymerization. However, hydrolysis of GTP is not necessary for assembly, since MTs polymerize from tubulin heterodimers bound to a nonhydrolyzable analogue of GTP.

Studies of MT assembly in vitro using isolated centrosomes (a structure we will discuss in detail below) as nucleation sites show that some microtubules can grow by polymerization at the same time that others shrink by depolymerization. As a result, some MTs effectively enlarge at the expense of others.

To explain how both polymerization and depolymerization might occur simultaneously, Tim Mitchison and Marc Kirschner proposed the **dynamic instability model.** This model presumes two populations of microtubules, one growing in length by continued polymerization at their plus ends and the other shrinking in length by depolymerization. The distinction between the two populations is that growing MTs have GTP bound to the tubulin at their plus ends, while shrinking MTs have GDP instead. GTP-tubulin molecules are thought to protect MTs by preventing the peeling away of subunits from their plus ends; this *GTP cap* provides a stable MT tip to which further dimers can be added (**Figure 15-6a**). Hydrolysis of GTP by b-tubulin eventually results in an unstable tip, at which point depolymerization may occur rapidly.

The concentration of tubulin bound to GTP is crucial to the dynamic instability model. When GTP-tubulin is readily available, it is added to the microtubule quickly, creating a large GTP-tubulin cap. If the concentration of GTP-tubulin falls, however, the rate of tubulin addition decreases. At a sufficiently low concentration of GTP-tubulin, the rate of hydrolysis of GTP on the b-tubulin subunits near the tip of the MT exceeds the rate of addition of new, GTP-bound tubulin. This results in shrinkage of the GTP cap. When the GTP cap disappears, the MT becomes unstable, and loss of GDP-bound subunits from its tip is favored.

Direct evidence for dynamic instability comes from observation of individual microtubules in vitro via light microscopy. An individual MT can undergo alternating periods of growth and shrinkage (Figure 15-6b). When an MT switches from growth to shrinkage, an event called

microtubule catastrophe, the MT can disappear completely, or it can abruptly switch back to a growth phase, a phenomenon known as *microtubule rescue.* The frequency of catastrophe is inversely related to the free tubulin concentration. High tubulin concentrations make catastrophe less likely, but it can still occur. When catastrophe does

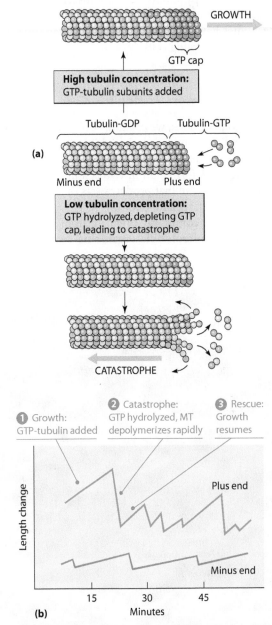

FIGURE 15-6 The GTP Cap and Its Role in the Dynamic Instability of Microtubules. (a) A model illustrating the role of the GTP cap. When the tubulin concentration is high, tubulin-GTP is added to the microtubule tip faster than the incorporated GTP can be hydrolyzed. The resulting GTP cap stabilizes the MT tip and promotes further growth. At lower tubulin concentrations the rate of growth decreases, thereby allowing GTP hydrolysis to catch up. This creates an unstable tip (no GTP cap) that favors MT depolymerization. (b) In an individual MT observed by light microscopy, ❶ growth and ❷ catastrophic shrinkage can occur. The plus and minus ends grow and shrink independently; changes in length are much more dynamic at the plus end. ❸ Rescue involves the switch from shrinkage to growth.

occur, higher tubulin concentrations make the rescue of a shrinking MT more likely. At any tubulin concentration, catastrophe is more likely at the plus end of an MT—that is, dynamic instability is more pronounced at the plus end of the MT. Dynamic instability has been demonstrated in living cells using video-enhanced differential interference contrast microscopy and live-cell fluorescence microscopy to follow the life cycles of individual MTs (**Figure 15-7**). These studies have shown that dynamic instability is a key feature of MTs in living cells.

Microtubules Originate from Microtubule-Organizing Centers Within the Cell

In the previous sections, we primarily discussed the properties that tubulin and microtubules exhibit in vitro, providing a foundation for understanding how MTs function in the cell. However, MT formation in vivo is a more ordered and regulated process, one that produces sets of MTs in specific locations for specific cell functions.

Microtubules commonly originate from a structure in the cell called a **microtubule-organizing center (MTOC).**

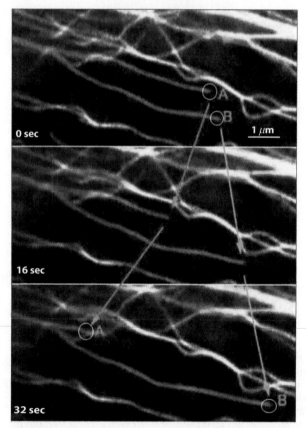

FIGURE 15-7 The Dynamic Instability of Microtubules in Vivo. Microtubules visualized in a living cell by live-cell fluorescence microscopy exhibit dynamic instability in vivo. Here, two individual MTs have been labeled to allow them to be followed over time. MT B grows over a 32-sec time span, whereas A shrinks.

VIDEOS www.thecellplace.com *Interphase microtubule dynamics*

An MTOC serves as a site at which MT assembly is initiated and acts as an anchor for one end of these MTs. Many cells during interphase have an MTOC called the **centrosome** that is positioned near the nucleus. The centrosome in an animal cell is normally associated with two **centrioles** surrounded by a diffuse granular material known as *pericentriolar material* (**Figure 15-8a**). In electron micrographs of the centrosome, MTs originate from the pericentriolar material (Figure 15-8b).

The symmetrical structure of centrioles is remarkable: The walls of centrioles are formed by nine pairs of triplet microtubules (Figure 15-8a). In most cases, centrioles are oriented at right angles to one another; the significance of this arrangement is still unknown. Centrioles are known to be involved in the formation of basal bodies, which are important for the formation of cilia and flagella (see Chapter 16). The role of centrioles in non-ciliated cells is less clear. In animal cells, centrioles may serve to recruit pericentriolar material to the centrosome, which then nucleates growth of microtubules. When centrioles are missing from many animal cells, microtubule-nucleating material disperses, and the MTOC disappears. Cells lacking centrioles can still divide, probably because chromosomes can organize microtubules to some extent on their own. However, the resulting spindles are poorly organized. In contrast to animal cells, the cells of higher plants lack centrioles; their absence indicates that centrioles are not essential for the formation of MTOCs.

Large, ring-shaped protein complexes in the centrosome contain another type of tubulin, **G-tubulin.** In conjunction with a number of other proteins called *GRiPs* (*gamma tubulin ring proteins*), rings of ɣ-tubulin can be seen at the base of MTs that emerge from the centrosome (**Figure 15-9**). These **G-tubulin ring complexes** (**G-TuRCs**) serve to nucleate the assembly of new MTs away from the centrosome. The importance of ɣ-TuRCs has been demonstrated by depleting cells of ɣ-tubulin or other components of the ɣ-TuRC; in the absence of these proteins, centrosomes can no longer nucleate MTs. In addition to the centrosome, some types of cells have other MTOCs. For example, the basal body at the base of each cilium in ciliated cells also serves as an MTOC. During cell division, centrosomes are duplicated, creating new MTOCs for each of the daughter cells. We will discuss mitosis in detail in Chapter 19.

MTOCs Organize and Polarize the Microtubules Within Cells

MTOCs play important roles in controlling the organization of microtubules in cells. The most important aspect of this role is probably the MTOC's ability to nucleate and anchor MTs. Because of this ability, MTs extend out from an MTOC toward the periphery of the cell. Furthermore, they grow out from an MTOC with a fixed polarity—their minus ends are anchored in the MTOC, and their plus ends extend out toward the cell membrane. The

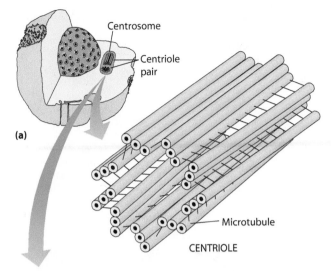

(a)

CENTRIOLE

Centrosome
Centriole pair
Microtubule

FIGURE 15-8 The Centrosome. (a) In animal cells, the centrosome contains two centrioles and associated pericentriolar material. The walls of centrioles are composed of nine sets of triplet microtubules. (b) An electron micrograph of a centrosome showing the centrioles and the pericentriolar material. Notice that microtubules originate from the pericentriolar material. (c) Nucleation and assembly of MTs at a centrosome in vitro.

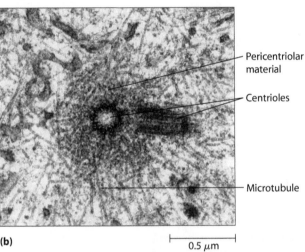

(b)

Pericentriolar material
Centrioles
Microtubule

0.5 μm

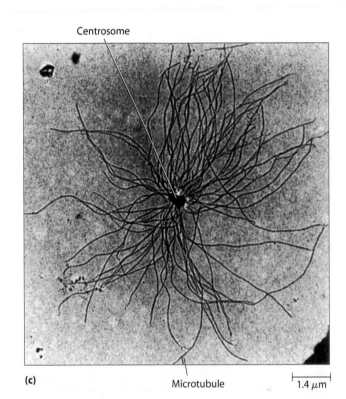

(c)

Centrosome
Microtubule
1.4 μm

relationship between the MTOC and the distribution and polarity of MTs are shown in **Figure 15-10**. The nucleating ability of MTOCs such as the centrosome has an important consequence for microtubule dynamics within cells. Since the minus ends of many MTs are anchored at the centrosome, dynamic growth and shrinkage of these MTs at the plus ends tends to occur at the periphery of cells.

The MTOC also influences the number of microtubules in a cell. Each MTOC has a limited number of nucleation and anchorage sites that seem to control how many MTs can form. However, the MT-nucleating capacity of the MTOC can be modified during certain processes such as mitosis. For example, centrosomes associated with spindle poles in mitotic cells have the highest MT-nucleating activity during prophase and metaphase (see Chapter 19).

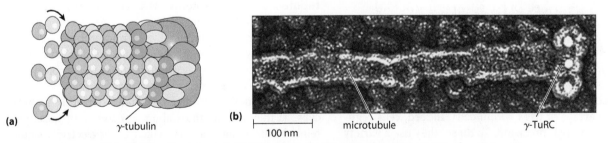

(a)

γ-tubulin

(b)

100 nm

microtubule

γ-TuRC

FIGURE 15-9 γ-Tubulin Ring Complexes (γ-TuRCs) Nucleate Microtubules. (a) γ-TuRCs, found at centrosomes, nucleate microtubule growth. The plus ends of MTs are oriented away from the γ-TuRC. (b) A platinum replica of an MT in vitro. Here, a component of the γ-TuRC (Xgrip109) was labeled with antibodies to which small particles of metal are attached. In the electron micrograph, these antibodies appear as bright spheres (TEM).

Microtubules 431

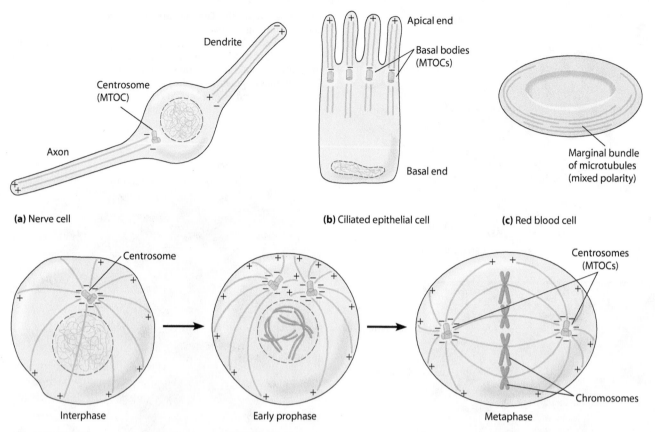

(a) Nerve cell

(b) Ciliated epithelial cell

(c) Red blood cell

(d) Dividing cell

FIGURE 15-10 **The Effects of Microtubule Polarity on MT Orientation in Animal Cells.** In the cell, the distribution of most microtubules is determined by the microtubule-organizing center (MTOC), which is sometimes a centrosome. MT orientation in a cell may vary with that cell's function. Microtubules are shown in orange. **(a)** Nerve cells contain two distinct sets of MTs, those of the axon and those of the dendrite. Axonal MTs are attached at their minus ends to the centrosome, with their plus ends at the tip of the axon. However, dendritic MTs are not associated with the centrosome and are of mixed polarities. **(b)** Ciliated epithelial cells have many MTOCs called basal bodies, one at the base of each cilium. Ciliary MTs originate with their minus ends in the basal bodies and elongate with their plus ends toward the tips of the cilia. **(c)** Mature human red blood cells have no nucleus or MTOC. However, MTs of mixed polarities persist as a circular band at the periphery of the cell. This band helps to maintain the cell's round, disk-like shape. **(d)** Throughout the process of mitosis, MTs in a dividing cell are oriented with their minus ends anchored in the centrosome and their plus ends pointing away from the centrosome. Cell division is preceded by the division of the centrosome. The two centrosomes then separate, each forming one pole of the mitotic spindle. At metaphase, the centrosomes are at opposite sides of the cell. Each centrosome, or spindle pole, forms half of the spindle MTs—some extending from pole to chromosomes, others extending from one pole to the other pole.

Microtubule Stability Is Tightly Regulated in Cells by a Variety of Microtubule-Binding Proteins

We have seen that cellular microtubules exhibit dynamic instability; they grow out from the centrosome and then disassemble. This process could account for randomly distributed and short-lived MTs, but not for organized and stable arrays of MTs within cells. Indeed, cells regulate MTs with great precision. To do so, they use a variety of proteins to regulate MT structure, assembly, and function. Some MT-binding proteins use ATP to drive the transport of vesicles and organelles or to generate sliding forces between MTs. These proteins will be discussed in detail in Chapter 16. Here we focus on proteins that regulate MT structure.

Microtubule-Stabilizing/Bundling Proteins. **Microtubule-associated proteins (MAPs)** account for 10–15% of the mass of MTs isolated from cells. MAPs bind at regular intervals along the wall of a microtubule, allowing interaction with other filaments and cellular structures. Most MAPs have been shown to increase MT stability, and they can affect the density of bundles of MTs.

MAP function has been studied extensively in brain cells, as they are the most abundant source of these proteins. Neurons have axons, which carry electrical signals away from the cell body of the neuron, and dendrites, which receive signals from neighboring cells and carry them to the cell body. The MT bundles are characteristically denser in axons than they are in dendrites. A MAP called *Tau* causes microtubules to form tight bundles in axons. Another MAP, *MAP2*, is present in dendrites and

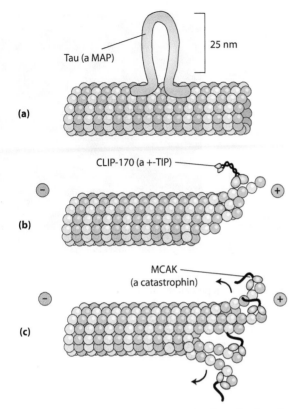

FIGURE 15-11 Microtubule-Interacting Proteins Regulate Microtubule Function in Vivo. Three different MT-interacting proteins are shown. **(a)** Tau is a MAP. Part of Tau binds along the length of an MT; another portion of Tau extends away from the MT, regulating MT spacing. **(b)** +-TIP proteins, such as CLIP-170, bind at or near the plus ends of MTs, stabilizing them. **(c)** Catastrophins, such as MCAK, are kinesin family proteins that destabilize MTs.

causes the formation of looser bundles of MTs. One portion of MAPs such as Tau and MAP2 binds along the length of an MT; another portion extends at right angles to the microtubule, where it can interact with other proteins (**Figure 15-11a**). The length of these "arms" controls the spacing of MTs in bundles; MAP2 has a longer arm than Tau does, and so MAP2 causes MT bundles to form that are less densely packed than with Tau.

The importance of MAPs can be demonstrated by forcing nonneuronal cells to make Tau protein. These cells are normally rounded, but when they express large amounts of Tau, these cells extend single long processes that look remarkably similar to axons. Tau is also important in human disease. Dense tangles of neurites, known as *neurofibrillary tangles,* are a hallmark of several diseases that result in dementia, such as Alzheimer's disease, Pick's disease, and several types of palsy. In the case of Alzheimer's disease, these tangles contain large amounts of hyperphosphorylated Tau protein, which forms paired helical filaments. Human mutations that result in defective Tau protein lead to hereditary predisposition to form such neurofibrillary tangles. Such diseases are therefore sometimes called *tauopathies.*

+-TIP Proteins. MTs are generally too unstable to remain intact for long periods of time and will depolymerize unless they are stabilized in some way. One way to stabilize MTs is to "capture" and protect their growing plus ends. To do so, **+-TIP proteins** (+-end *t*ubulin *i*nteracting *p*roteins) associate with MT plus ends. Some of these proteins, either directly or indirectly, appear to stabilize plus ends, decreasing the likelihood that they will undergo catastrophic subunit loss (**Figure 15-12**). One important example of MT capture involves kinetochores during mitosis, as we will discuss in Chapter 19. Other +-TIPs associate with the cell *cortex,* an actin-based network underneath the plasma membrane, and can stabilize MTs that extend there.

Microtubule-Destabilizing/Severing Proteins. As we have seen, some proteins stabilize microtubules, making them less likely to depolymerize. Other proteins *promote* depolymerization of MTs. For example, the protein *stathmin/Op18* binds to tubulin heterodimers, preventing them from polymerizing. Other proteins act at the ends of MTs once they have polymerized, promoting the peeling of subunits from their ends. Several proteins of the *kinesin* family, called *catastrophins,* act in this way (Figure 15-12c; we will learn more about other kinesins in Chapter 16). By tightly regulating where catastrophins act, a cell can precisely control where and when MTs form and depolymerize. A prime example of such regulation is the mitotic spindle, which we will examine in Chapter 19. Still other proteins sever MTs; one example of such proteins are *katanins.*

Microfilaments

With a diameter of about 7 nm, **microfilaments (MFs)** are the smallest of the cytoskeletal filaments (see Table 15-1). Microfilaments are best known for their role in the contractile fibrils of muscle cells, where they interact with thicker filaments of myosin to cause the contractions characteristic of muscle (see Chapter 16). MFs are not confined to muscle cells, however. They occur in almost all eukaryotic cells and are involved in numerous other phenomena, including a variety of locomotory and structural functions.

Examples of cell movements in which microfilaments play a role include *cell migration* via lamellipodia and filopodia, *amoeboid movement,* and *cytoplasmic streaming,* a regular pattern of cytoplasmic flow in some plant and animal cells. We will discuss all of these phenomena in detail in Chapter 16. MFs also produce the cleavage furrows that divide the cytoplasm of animal cells during cytokinesis (see Chapter 19), and MFs are found at sites of attachment of cells to one another and to the extracellular matrix.

In addition to mediating a variety of cell movements, MFs are important in developing and maintaining cell shape. Most animal cells, for example, have a dense network of microfilaments called the *cell cortex* just beneath the plasma membrane. The cortex confers structural rigidity on the cell surface and facilitates shape changes and cell movement. Parallel bundles of MFs also make up the structural core of *microvilli,* the fingerlike extensions found on the surface of many animal cells (see Figure 4-2).

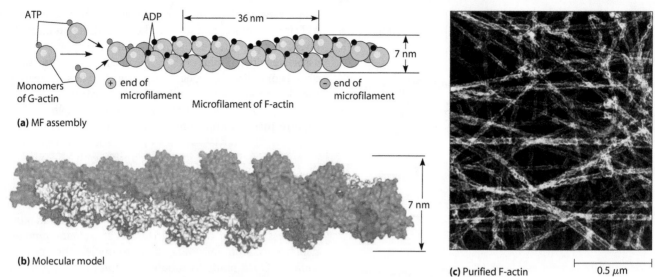

(a) MF assembly

(b) Molecular model

(c) Purified F-actin

0.5 μm

FIGURE 15-12 A Model for Microfilament Assembly in Vitro. (a) Monomers of G-actin polymerize into long filaments of F-actin with a diameter of about 7 nm. A full turn of the helix occurs every 36–37 nm, with about 13.5 monomers required for a full turn. Addition of each G-actin monomer is usually accompanied or followed by hydrolysis of the ATP molecule, although the energy of ATP hydrolysis is not required to drive the polymerization reaction. **(b)** A molecular model of F-actin, based on X-ray crystal structures of G-actin. Two strands of 13 G-actin monomers each are shown. One strand is colored blue, the other gray. **(c)** An electron micrograph of purified F-actin (TEM).

Actin Is the Protein Building Block of Microfilaments

Actin is an extremely abundant protein in virtually all eukaryotic cells, including those of plants, algae, and fungi. Actin is synthesized as a single polypeptide consisting of 375 amino acids, with a molecular weight of about 42 kDa. Once synthesized, it folds into a roughly U-shaped molecule, with a central cavity that binds ATP or ADP. Individual actin molecules are referred to as **G-actin** (globular actin). Under the right conditions, G-actin molecules polymerize to form microfilaments; in this form, actin is referred to as **F-actin** (filamentous actin; see Figure 15-12). Actin in the G or F form also binds to a wide variety of other proteins, collectively known as *actin-binding proteins.*

Different Types of Actin Are Found in Cells

Of the three types of cytoskeletal proteins, actin is the most highly conserved. In functional assays, all actins appear to be identical, and actins from diverse organisms will copolymerize into filaments. Despite this high degree of sequence similarity, actins do differ among different organisms and among tissues of the same organism. Based on sequence similarity, actins can be broadly divided into two major groups: the *muscle-specific actins (a-actins)* and the *nonmuscle actins (b- and g-actins).* b- and g-actin localize to different regions of the cell and appear to have different interactions with actin-binding proteins. For example, in epithelial cells, one end of the cell, the apical end, contains microvilli, whereas the opposite side of the cell, known as the basal

end, is attached to the extracellular matrix. b-actin is predominantly found at the apical end of epithelial cells, whereas g-actin is concentrated at the basal end and sides of the cell.

G-Actin Monomers Polymerize into F-Actin Microfilaments

Like tubulin dimers, G-actin monomers can polymerize reversibly into filaments with a lag phase corresponding to filament nucleation, followed by a more rapid polymer elongation phase. The kinetics of actin polymerization can be studied in solution using fluorescent G-actin. The fluorescence of the labeled F-actin can be measured to yield data similar to that for tubulin. The F-actin filaments that form are composed of two linear strands of polymerized G-actin wound around each other in a helix, with roughly 13.5 actin monomers per turn (Figure 15-12).

Within a microfilament, all the actin monomers are oriented in the same direction, so that an MF, like a microtubule, has an inherent polarity, with one end differing chemically and structurally from the other end. This polarity can be readily demonstrated by incubating MFs with **myosin subfragment 1 (S1),** a proteolytic fragment of myosin (**Figure 15-13**). S1 fragments bind to, or "decorate," the actin MFs to give a distinctive arrowhead pattern, with all the S1 molecules pointing in the same direction (Figure 15-13c). Based on this arrowhead pattern, the terms *pointed end* and *barbed end* are commonly used to identify the minus and plus ends of an MF, respectively. The polarity of the MF is important, because it

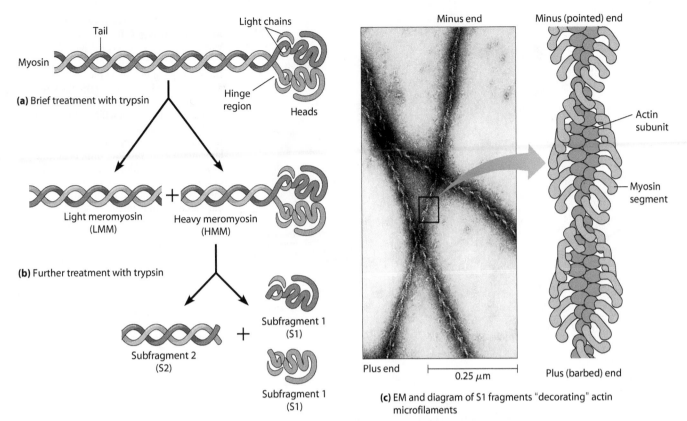

(a) Brief treatment with trypsin

Light meromyosin (LMM) + Heavy meromyosin (HMM)

(b) Further treatment with trypsin

Subfragment 2 (S2) + Subfragment 1 (S1)

Subfragment 1 (S1)

(c) EM and diagram of S1 fragments "decorating" actin microfilaments

FIGURE 15-13 Using Myosin S1 Subfragments to Determine Actin Polarity. Myosin II is part of the contractile machinery found in muscle cells. The globular head of the myosin molecule binds to actin, while the myosin tails can associate with filaments of myosin (the thick myofilaments of muscle cells). **(a)** Myosin II can be cleaved by proteases such as trypsin into two pieces, heavy meromyosin (HMM) and light meromyosin (LMM). **(b)** HMM can be further digested, leaving only the globular head. This fragment, called myosin subfragment 1 (S1), retains its actin-binding properties. **(c)** When actin microfilaments are incubated with myosin S1 and then examined with an electron microscope, the S1 fragments appear to "decorate" the microfilaments like arrowheads. All the S1 arrowheads point toward the minus end, indicating the polarity of the MF.

allows for independent regulation of actin assembly or disassembly at each end of the filament.

The polarity of microfilaments is reflected in more rapid addition or loss of G-actin at the plus end, and slower addition or loss of G-actin at the minus end (see Figure 15-12a). If G-actin is polymerized onto short fragments of S1-decorated F-actin, polymerization proceeds much faster at the barbed end, indicating that the barbed end of the filament is also the plus end. Thus, even when conditions are favorable for adding monomers to both ends of the filament, the plus end will grow faster than the minus end.

As G-actin monomers assemble onto a microfilament, the ATP bound to them is slowly hydrolyzed to ADP, much the same as the GTP bound to tubulin is hydrolyzed to GDP. Thus, the ends of a growing MF tend to have ATP-F-actin, whereas the bulk of the MF is composed of ADP-F-actin. However, ATP hydrolysis is not a strict requirement for MF elongation, since MFs can also assemble from ADP-G-actin or from nonhydrolyzable analogues of ATP-G-actin.

Specific Drugs Affect Polymerization of Microfilaments

As we saw with microtubules, several drugs have been used to perturb the assembly of actin into microfilaments (Table 15-3). Processes that are disrupted in cells treated with these drugs are likely to depend in some way on microfilaments. Several drugs result in depolymerization of microfilaments. The **cytochalasins,** such as *cytochalasin D,* are fungal metabolites that prevent the addition of new monomers to existing polymerized MFs. As subunits are gradually lost from the minus ends of MFs in cytochalasin-treated cells, they eventually depolymerize. In contrast, **latrunculin A,** a marine toxin isolated from the Red Sea sponge *Latrunculia magnifica,* acts by sequestering actin monomers, preventing their addition to the plus ends of growing MFs. In either case, the net result is the loss of MFs within the treated cells. Conversely, the drug *phalloidin,* a cyclic peptide from the death cap fungus *(Amanita phalloides),* stabilizes microfilaments, preventing their depolymerization. Fluorescently labeled phalloidin

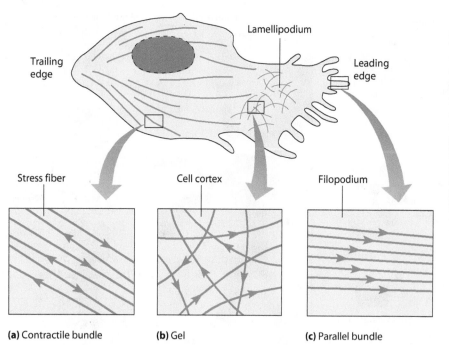

Trailing edge

Lamellipodium

Leading edge

Stress fiber

Cell cortex

Filopodium

(a) Contractile bundle

(b) Gel

(c) Parallel bundle

FIGURE 15-14 The Architecture of Actin in Crawling Cells. Actin is found in a variety of structures in crawling cells such as this macrophage. **(a)** Running from the trailing edge of the cell to the leading edge are contractile bundles of actin, the stress fibers. **(b)** At the periphery of the cell is the cortex, which contains a three-dimensional meshwork of actin filaments crosslinked into a gel. **(c)** The broad leading edge of lamellipodia can produce thin, fingerlike projections called filopodia. Whereas the bulk of lamellipodia contain an actin meshwork, filopodia contain parallel bundles of actin filaments.

is also useful for visualizing F-actin via fluorescence microscopy.

Cells Can Dynamically Assemble Actin into a Variety of Structures

As with microtubules, cells can dynamically regulate where and how G-actin is assembled into microfilaments. For example, cells that crawl have specialized structures called *lamellipodia* and *filopodia* at their leading edge that allow them to move along a surface (we will consider these specialized structures in more detail in Chapter 16). The form of the protrusion appears to depend on the nature of the cell's movement and on the organization of the actin filaments within the cell. In cells that adhere tightly to the underlying substratum and do not move well, organized bundles of actin, called *stress fibers*, stretch from the tail, or trailing edge, of the cell to the front (**Figure 15-14a**). Rapidly moving cells typically do not have such striking actin bundles. In such cells, the cell *cortex*, which lies immediately beneath the plasma membrane and is enriched in actin, is crosslinked into a gel or very loosely organized lattice of microfilaments (Figure 15-14b). At the leading edge, and especially in filopodia, microfilaments form highly oriented, polarized cables, with their barbed (plus) ends oriented toward the tip of the protrusion (Figure 15-14c). The actin in lamellipodia is typically less well organized than in filopodia (**Figure 15-15**). Understanding how cells regulate such a wide variety of actin-based structures requires understanding both how cells can regulate the polymerization of MFs and how MFs, once polymerized, assemble into networks.

Actin bundles in filopodia

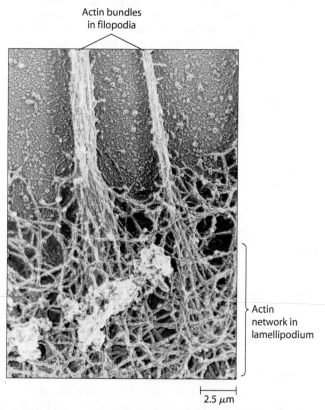

Actin network in lamellipodium

2.5 μm

FIGURE 15-15 Deep-Etch Electron Micrograph Showing Actin Bundles in Filopodia. This view of the periphery of a macrophage shows two prominent actin bundles contained within filopodia that extend from the cell surface. The actin filaments in the filopodia merge with a network of actin filaments lying just beneath the plasma membrane of the lamellipodium.

Actin-Binding Proteins Regulate the Polymerization, Length, and Organization of Microfilaments

As we saw with microtubules, cells can precisely control where actin assembles and the structure of the resulting actin networks. To do so, cells use a variety of **actin-binding proteins** (Figure 15-16). Control of the process of MF polymerization occurs at several steps, including the nucleation of new MFs, the elongation and severing of preexisting MFs, and the association of MFs into networks. We consider each of these briefly here.

Proteins That Regulate Polymerization. In the absence of other factors, the growth of microfilaments depends on the concentration of ATP-bound G-actin. If the concentration of ATP-bound G-actin is high, microfilaments will assemble until the G-actin is limiting. In the cell, however, a large amount of free G-actin is not available for assembly into filaments because it is bound by the protein *thymosin* b4. A second protein called *profilin* appears to compete with thymosin b4 for binding to G-actin monomers. When the profilin concentration is high, polymerization is favored—but only if there are free filament ends available. Yet another protein, known as *ADF/cofilin*, is known to bind to ADP-G-actin and F-actin. ADF/cofilin is thought to increase the rate of turnover of ADP-actin at the minus ends of MFs. The ADP on these G-actin monomers can then be exchanged for a new ATP, and the ATP-G-actin can then be recycled for addition to the growing plus ends of MFs. ADF/cofilin also severs filaments, creating new plus ends as it does so.

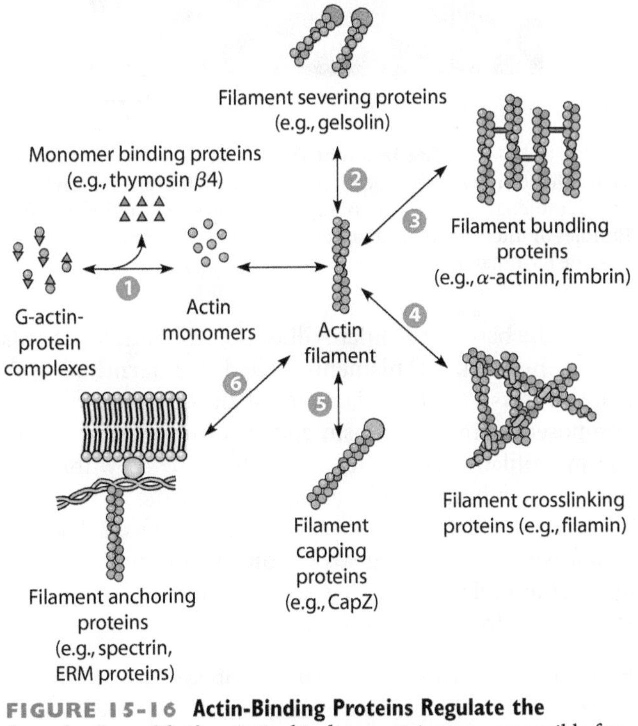

Proteins That Cap Actin Filaments. Whether microfilament ends are available for further growth depends on whether the filament end is *capped*. Capping occurs when a **capping protein** binds the end of a filament and prevents further addition or loss of subunits, thereby stabilizing it. One such protein that functions as a cap for the plus ends of microfilaments is appropriately named *CapZ*. When CapZ is bound to the end of a filament, further addition of subunits at the plus end is prevented; when CapZ is removed, addition of subunits can resume. Another class of proteins called *tropomodulins* bind to the minus ends of actin filaments, preventing loss of subunits from the pointed ends of F-actin. Tropomodulins are found in muscle sarcomeres, as we will see in Chapter 16.

Proteins That Crosslink Actin Filaments. In many cases, actin networks form as loose meshworks of crisscrossing, crosslinked MFs. One of the crosslinking proteins that is important for such networks is *filamin*, a long molecule consisting of two identical polypeptides joined head to head, with an actin-binding site at each tail. Molecules of filamin act as "splices," joining two MFs together where they intersect. In this way, actin MFs are linked to form large three-dimensional networks.

Proteins That Sever Actin Filaments. Other proteins play the opposite role, breaking up the microfilament network and causing the cortical actin gel to soften and liquefy. They do this by severing and/or capping MFs. In some cases, such proteins can serve both functions. One of these severing and capping proteins is *gelsolin*, which functions by breaking actin MFs and capping their newly exposed plus ends, thereby preventing further polymerization.

Proteins That Bundle Actin Filaments. In contrast to the loose organization of the actin at the cell cortex, other actin-containing structures in migrating and nonmigrating cells can be highly ordered. In such cases, actin may be bundled into tightly organized arrays, and a number of actin-binding proteins mediate such bundling. One such protein is *a-actinin*, a protein that is prominent within structures known as *focal contacts* and *focal adhesions*, which are required for cells to make adhesive connections to the extracellular matrix as they migrate. We will consider these structures in more detail in. Another bundling protein, *fascin*, is found in filopodia; fascin keeps the actin within the core of a filopodium tightly bundled, contributing to the spike-like appearance of such protrusions.

FIGURE 15-16 Actin-Binding Proteins Regulate the Organization of Actin. Actin-binding proteins are responsible for converting actin filaments from one form to another. These include ❶ monomer-binding proteins, such as thymosin b4 and profilin; ❷ filament severing proteins, such as gelsolin; ❸ filament bundling proteins, such as a-actinin, fimbrin, and fascin; ❹ filament crosslinking proteins, such as filamin; ❺ filament capping proteins such as CapZ and tropomodulin; and ❻ filament anchoring proteins, such as spectrin and ERM proteins.

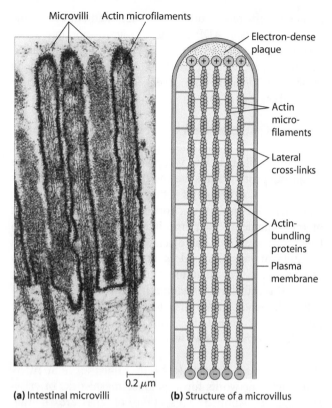

(a) Intestinal microvilli | **(b)** Structure of a microvillus

0.2 μm

Labels in figure: Microvilli, Actin microfilaments, Electron-dense plaque, Actin micro-filaments, Lateral cross-links, Actin-bundling proteins, Plasma membrane

FIGURE 15-17 **Microvillus Structure.** **(a)** An electron micrograph of microvilli from intestinal mucosal cells (TEM). **(b)** A schematic diagram of a single microvillus, showing the core of microfilaments that gives the microvillus its characteristic stiffness. The core consists of several dozen microfilaments oriented with their plus ends facing outward toward the tip and their minus ends facing toward the cell. The plus ends are embedded in an amorphous, electron-dense plaque. The MFs are tightly linked together by actin-bundling (crosslinking) proteins and are connected to the inner surface of the plasma membrane by lateral crosslinks.

Perhaps the best-studied example of ordered actin arrays is the actin bundles found in microvilli. **Microvilli** (singular: **microvillus**) are especially prominent features of intestinal mucosal cells (**Figure 15-17a**). A single mucosal cell in your small intestine, for example, has several thousand microvilli, each about 1–2 μm long and about 0.1 μm in diameter, which increase the surface area of the cell about twentyfold. This large surface area is essential to intestinal function because the uptake of digested food depends on an extensive absorptive surface.

As illustrated in Figure 15-17b, the core of the intestinal microvillus consists of a tight bundle of microfilaments. The plus ends point toward the tip, where they are attached to the membrane through an amorphous, electron-dense plaque. The MFs in the bundle are also connected to the plasma membrane by lateral crosslinks consisting of the proteins *myosin I* and *calmodulin*. These crosslinks extend outward about 20–30 nm from the bundle to contact electron-dense patches on the inner membrane surface. Adjacent MFs in the bundle are bound tightly together at regular intervals by the crosslinking proteins (also called actin-bundling proteins) *fimbrin* and *villin*.

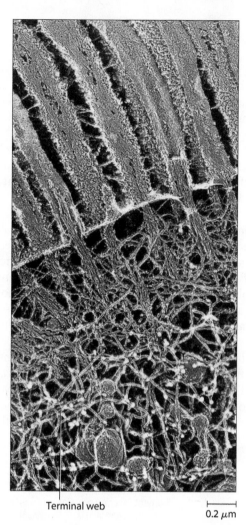

Terminal web

0.2 μm

FIGURE 15-18 **The Terminal Web of an Intestinal Epithelial Cell.** The terminal web beneath the plasma membrane is seen in this freeze-etch electron micrograph of an intestinal epithelial cell. Bundles of microfilaments that form the cores of microvilli extend into the terminal web.

At the base of the microvillus, the MF bundle extends into a network of filaments called the **terminal web** (**Figure 15-18**). The filaments of the terminal web are composed mainly of myosin and spectrin, which connect the microfilaments to each other, to proteins within the plasma membrane, and perhaps also to the network of intermediate filaments beneath the terminal web. The terminal web apparently gives rigidity to the microvilli by anchoring their MF bundles securely so that they project straight out from the cell surface.

Proteins That Link Actin to Membranes. For MFs to exert force on the plasma membrane during events such as cell movement and cytokinesis, they must be connected to the plasma membrane. The connection of MFs to the plasma membrane is indirect and requires one or more linker proteins that anchor MFs to transmembrane proteins embedded within the plasma membrane.

One group of proteins that appears to function widely in linking microfilaments to membranes is the *band 4.1, ezrin, radixin,* and *moesin* family of actin-binding proteins. When these proteins are mutated, a wide variety of cellular processes are affected, including cytokinesis, secretion, and the formation of microvilli. Another example of how actin can be linked to membranes involves the proteins *spectrin* and *ankyrin* (**Figure 15-19**). As we saw in Chapter 7, the plasma membrane of the erythrocyte is supported by a network of spectrin filaments that are crosslinked by very short actin chains. This network is connected to the plasma membrane by molecules of the proteins ankyrin and band 4.1 that link the spectrin filaments to specific transmembrane proteins. Based on mutations in the genes encoding spectrins and ankyrins in *Drosophila* and in the nematode *Caenorhabditis elegans,* these proteins are important in a wide variety of cells for maintenance of cell shape.

Proteins That Promote Actin Branching and Growth. In addition to loose networks and bundles, cells can assemble actin into branched networks that form a treelike, or *dendritic,* network (**Figure 15-20a**). Such dendritic networks are a prominent feature of lamellipodia in migrating cells. A complex of actin-related proteins, the **Arp2/3 complex,** helps branches to form by nucleating new branches on the sides of existing filaments (Figure 15-20b). Proteins we have already discussed, such as profilin, cofilin, and capping proteins, regulate the length of filaments that polymerize from branch points, thereby regulating the length of such structures.

Arp2/3 branching is activated by a family of proteins that includes the *Wiskott-Aldrich syndrome protein,* or *WASP,* and *WAVE/Scar.* Human patients who cannot produce functional WASP have defects in the ability of their platelets to undergo changes in shape and so have difficulties in forming blood clots. A very different kind of disease also involves the Arp2/3 complex: Pathogenic bacteria can "hijack" the actin polymerization machinery of the cell to spread (**Box 15A**).

Branched actin networks are only one type of actin-based structure that cells can produce. For some cellular events, long actin filaments are more useful. Actin polymerization in this case can be regulated independently of the Arp2/3 complex, through proteins known as *formins.* Formins are required to assemble certain unbranched F-actin structures, including actin cables and the contractile ring during cell division (see Chapter 19). Formins appear to be able to act "processively," moving along the end of a growing filament as they stimulate filament growth (Figure 15-20c). Formins can form dimers, binding to the barbed (plus) ends of actin filaments. Some formins have extensions that can bind profilin and are therefore thought to act as "staging areas" for the addition of actin monomers to growing filaments. Plants have a large number of formin-like proteins, which are thought to play similar roles in regulating the actin cytoskeleton.

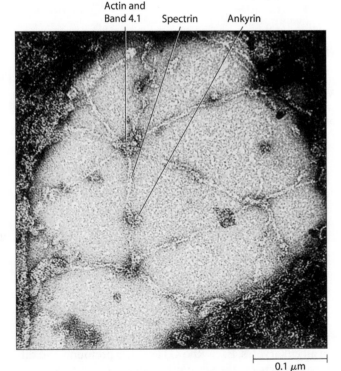

Cell Signaling Regulates Where and When Actin-Based Structures Assemble

We have seen that actin-binding proteins regulate the types of actin-based structures that cells assemble. Cell signaling, in turn, regulates the activity of these proteins. Both plasma membrane lipids and several small G proteins related to Ras regulate the formation, stability, and breakdown of MFs.

FIGURE 15-19 Support of the Erythrocyte Plasma Membrane by a Spectrin-Ankyrin-Actin Network. The plasma membrane of a red blood cell is supported on its inner surface by a filamentous network that gives the cell both strength and flexibility. **(a)** A diagram showing the major components of the spectrin-ankyrin-actin network. Long filaments of spectrin are crosslinked by short actin filaments. The network is anchored to the band 3 transmembrane protein by molecules of the protein ankyrin. **(b)** An electron micrograph of an erythrocyte membrane, showing actual spectrin network components (TEM).

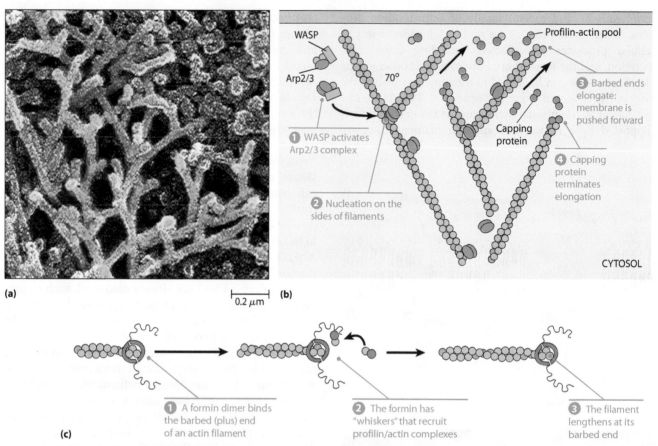

(a)

0.2 μm

(b)

WASP

Arp2/3

70°

Profilin-actin pool

3 Barbed ends elongate: membrane is pushed forward

Capping protein

1 WASP activates Arp2/3 complex

2 Nucleation on the sides of filaments

4 Capping protein terminates elongation

CYTOSOL

(c)

1 A formin dimer binds the barbed (plus) end of an actin filament

2 The formin has "whiskers" that recruit profilin/actin complexes

3 The filament lengthens at its barbed end

FIGURE 15-20 Formation of Actin Networks by Actin Polymerization. Actin networks, like those found in migrating cells, have a characteristic pattern of branching. **(a)** Branched actin filaments in a frog keratocyte. Individual branched actin filaments are colored to make them easier to distinguish (deep-etch TEM). **(b)** Model for Arp2/3-dependent branching. Branching is stimulated by WASP family proteins; capping protein helps regulate the length of new branches. **(c)** Model for formin-induced elongation of an actin filament. Formin dimers bind profilin-actin, serving as a "staging area" for actin polymerization.

VIDEOS www.thecellplace.com *Formation of branched actin*

Inositol Phospholipids. Inositol phospholipids are one type of membrane phospholipid that regulates actin assembly. Recall that *phosphatidylinositol-4,5-bisphosphate* (PIP_2) is important during some signaling events, such as insulin signaling. PIP_2 can bind to profiling, CapZ, and proteins such as ezrin, thereby recruiting them to the plasma membrane, as well as regulating the ability of these proteins to interact with actin. For example, CapZ binds tightly to PIP_2, resulting in its removal from the end of a microfilament, thereby permitting the filament to be disassembled and making its monomers available for assembly into new filaments. Gelsolin is another actin-binding protein that can be regulated by binding to polyphosphoinositides. When gelsolin binds to a specific polyphosphoinositide, it can no longer cap the plus end of an MF, allowing the uncapped end to undergo changes in length.

Rho Family GTPases. One striking case of regulation of the actin cytoskeleton is the dramatic change in the cytoskeleton of cells exposed to certain growth factors. For example, in response to stimulation by platelet-derived

growth factor (PDGF), fibroblasts will begin to grow, divide, and form actin-rich membrane extensions that resemble lamellipodia. Other factors, such as lysophosphatidic acid (LPA), induce cells to form stress fibers.

How do such signals result in such dramatic reorganization of the actin cytoskeleton? Many of these signals result in changes in the actin cytoskeleton through their action on a family of monomeric G proteins known as **Rho GTPases.** Three key members of this family are **Rho, Rac,** and **Cdc42.** Originally identified in yeast, these proteins are important regulators of the actin cytoskeleton in all eukaryotes. Each Rho GTPase has profound and different effects on the actin cytoskeleton (**Figure 15-21**). For example, activation of the Rho pathway results in the formation of stress fibers, and Rho inactivation prevents the appearance of stress fibers following exposure of fibroblasts to LPA. Similarly, Rac activation often results in extension of lamellipodia by cultured cells, and inhibition of Rac prevents this normal response to PDGF. Finally, activation of Cdc42 results in the formation of filopodia. Rho GTPases perform a vast array of function within cells, from formation of protrusions to assembly

One of the most remarkable findings of modern cell motility research is the discovery that disease-causing microorganisms can co-opt the cell's normal cell adhesion and cell motility systems to penetrate a cell's defenses and enter the cell. The best-studied example of such motility is the gram-positive bacterium *Listeria monocytogenes*. One way that *Listeria* attaches to the host's cells involves the binding of a *Listeria* protein known as *internalin A* to *E-cadherin* on the cell surface. Once bound, *Listeria* enter a cell, move through it at a rate of 11 μm/min, and progress to nearby uninfected cells, where they continue the cycle of infection (**Figure 15A-1**). Short actin filaments radiate away from the bacteria, forming "comet tails" of branched F-actin (Figure 15A-1b). By using fluorescently labeled actin, investigators have determined that the tails form by Arp2/3-dependent polymerization of actin, which is nucleated near the surface of the internalized bacterium. The protein on the surface of

Listeria that promotes actin polymerization is known as *ActA*. The microfilaments nucleated by ActA are strikingly similar to those found at the leading edge of migrating cells and are formed using much of the same cellular machinery.

Other bacteria induce different sorts of actin "tails." Bacteria of the genus *Rickettsia* that cause spotted fevers induce long, unbranched actin filaments reminiscent of filopodia. Thus, different pathogens have devised various ways of recruiting the host cytoskeleton for propulsion.

Some pathogens bind to the cell surface but are not internalized. For example, the enteropathogenic form of *E. coli*, which causes diarrhea in infants by forming colonies on the surface of intestinal epithelial cells, attaches to the surface of intestinal cells, where it organizes actin-rich "pedestals" that may function like the actin tails induced by *Listeria*.

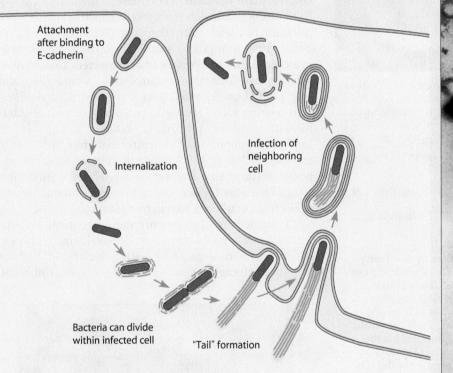

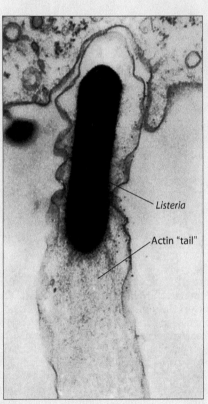

(a)   (b)   0.1 μm

FIGURE 15A-1   Infection of a Macrophage by *Listeria monocytogenes*. (a) Life cycle of *Listeria*. A bacterium attaches to the surface of an uninfected cell. The bacterium then moves inside the cell, where it can divide to produce more bacteria in the infected cell. It then spreads to a nearby cell by producing a "comet tail" of polymerized actin, which propels the bacterium forward. (b) A transmission electron micrograph showing a *Listeria* within an infected macrophage and the "comet tail" of actin filaments that forms behind the bacterium.

VIDEOS www.thecellplace.com *Listeria movement via actin polymerization*

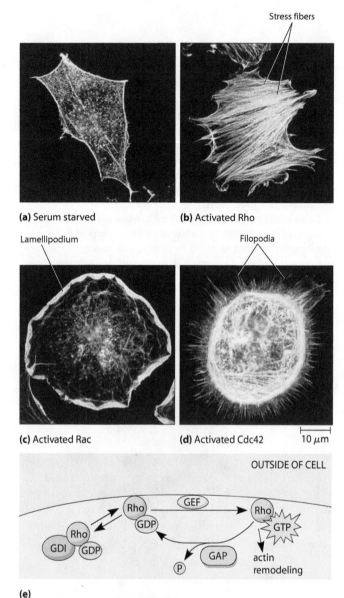

(a) Serum starved **(b)** Activated Rho

Lamellipodium

Filopodia

Stress fibers

(c) Activated Rac **(d)** Activated Cdc42

10 μm

OUTSIDE OF CELL

(e)

FIGURE 15-21 Regulation of Protrusions by Rho Family Proteins. (a) When a cultured fibroblast in the absence of growth factors ("serum starved") is stained for actin, it has few actin bundles and shows little protrusive activity. (b) Under conditions that activate the Rho signaling pathway (such as addition of lysophosphatidic acid, LPA), stress fibers form. (c) When the Rac pathway is activated (in this case by injecting mutated Rac that is always active), lamellipodia form. (d) When Cdc42 is activated (e.g., by injecting a guanine nucleotide exchange factor that activates Cdc42), filopodia form. (e) Regulation of Rho family proteins. Guanine-nucleotide exchanges factors (GEFs) stimulate exchange of a bound GDP for GTP, activating Rho family proteins, and allowing them to stimulate actin remodeling. GTPase activating proteins (GAPs) stimulate Rho GTPases to hydrolyze their bound GTP, thereby inactivating them. Guanine-nucleotide displacement inhibitors (GDIs) can sequester inactive Rho family G proteins, retaining them in the cytosol.

and disassembly of the cytokinetic furrow to regulating endo- and exocytosis. Many of these events are under the control of cell signaling; not surprisingly, then, these proteins are essential for growth factors such as PDGF and LPA to exert their effects.

Like Ras, Rho family GTPases are stimulated by *guanine-nucleotide exchange factors (GEFs),* which foster exchange of a bound GDP for GTP (Figure 15-21e). Corresponding *GTPase activating proteins (GAPs)* stimulate Rho GTPases to hydrolyze their bound GTP, thereby inactivating them. In addition, proteins known as *guanine-nucleotide dissociation inhibitors (GDIs)* can sequester inactive Rho GTPases in the cytosol. All of these events can be modulated by cell signals, allowing fine-tuning of where actin-based structures are assembled. Once active, different Rho GTPases can stimulate different types of actin polymerization. For example, activated Cdc42 can bind to and activate WASP, stimulating actin polymerization by the Arp2/3 complex. Rac can activate another WASP family protein, WAVE. Rho is known to bind to and activate formins, which explains why Rho activation can lead to formation of longer, less branched actin filaments.

Intermediate Filaments

Intermediate filaments (IFs) have a diameter of about 8–12 nm, which makes them intermediate in size between microtubules and microfilaments (see Table 15-1), or between the thin (actin) and thick (myosin) filaments in muscle cells, where IFs were first discovered. To date, most studies have focused on animal cells, where IFs occur singly or in bundles and appear to play a structural or tension-bearing role. One well-known and abundant intermediate filament protein is *keratin.* Keratin is an important component of structures that grow from skin in animals, including hair, claws and fingernails, horns and beaks, turtle shells, feathers, scales, and the outermost layer of the skin. **Figure 15-22** is an electron micrograph of IFs from a cultured human fibroblast cell.

Intermediate filaments are the most stable and the least soluble constituents of the cytoskeleton. Treatment of cells with detergents or with solutions of high or low ionic strength removes most of the microtubules,

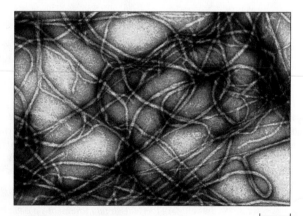

200 nm

FIGURE 15-22 Intermediate Filaments. Electron micrograph of negatively stained keratin 5 and 14 intermediate filaments reconstituted in vitro (TEM).

microfilaments, and other proteins of the cytosol but leaves networks of IFs that retain their original shape. Due to the stability of the IFs, some scientists suggest that they serve as a scaffold to support the entire cytoskeletal framework. In contrast to MTs and MFs, IFs do not appear to be polarized.

Intermediate Filament Proteins Are Tissue Specific

In contrast to microtubules and microfilaments, intermediate filaments differ markedly in amino acid composition from tissue to tissue. Based on the cell type in which they are found, IFs and their proteins can be grouped into six classes (Table 15-4). Classes I and II comprise the *keratins,* proteins that make up the *tonofilaments* found in the epithelial cells covering the body surfaces and lining its cavities. (The IFs visible beneath the terminal web in the intestinal mucosa cell of Figure 15-18 consist of keratin.) Class I keratins are *acidic keratins,* whereas class II are *basic* or *neutral keratins;* each of these classes contains at least 15 different keratins.

Class III IFs include vimentin, desmin, and glial fibrillary acidic protein. *Vimentin* is present in connective tissue and other cells derived from nonepithelial cells. Vimentin-containing filaments are often prominent features in cultured fibroblast cells, in which they form a network that radiates from the center out to the periphery of the cell. *Desmin* is found in muscle cells, and *glial fibrillary acidic (GFA) protein* is characteristic of the glial cells that surround and insulate nerve cells. Class IV IFs are the *neurofilament (NF) proteins* found in the neurofilaments of nerve cells. Class V IFs are *nuclear lamins* A, B, and C, which form a filamentous scaffold along the inner surface of the nuclear membrane of virtually all eukaryotic cells, including those in plants. Neurofilaments found in cells in the embryonic nervous system are made of *nestin,* which constitutes class VI.

As IF proteins and their genes have been sequenced, it has become clear that these proteins are encoded by a single (though large) family of related genes and can therefore be classified according to amino acid sequence relatedness as well. The six classes of IF proteins have been distinguished on this basis (see Table 15-4).

Due to the tissue specificity of intermediate filaments, animal cells from different tissues can be distinguished on the basis of the IF protein present, as determined by immunofluorescence microscopy. This *intermediate filament typing* serves as a diagnostic tool in medicine. IF typing is especially useful in the diagnosis of cancer because tumor cells are known to retain the IF proteins characteristic of the tissue of origin, regardless of where the tumor occurs in the body. Because the appropriate treatment often depends on the tissue of origin, IF typing is especially valuable in cases where diagnosis using conventional microscopic techniques is difficult.

Intermediate Filaments Assemble from Fibrous Subunits

As products of a family of related genes, all IF proteins have some common features, although they differ significantly in size and chemical properties. In contrast to actin and tubulin, all IF proteins are fibrous, rather than globular, proteins. All IF proteins have a homologous central

---

Table 15-4   **Classes of Intermediate Filaments**

Class	IF Protein	Molecular Mass (kDa)	Tissue	Function
I	Acidic cytokeratins	40–56.5	Epithelial cells	Mechanical strength
II	Basic cytokeratins	53–67	Epithelial cells	Mechanical strength
III	Vimentin	54	Fibroblasts; cells of mesenchymal origin; lens of eye	Maintenance of cell shape
III	Desmin	53–54	Muscle cells, especially smooth muscle	Structural support for contractile machinery
III	GFA protein	50	Glial cells and astrocytes	Maintenance of cell shape
IV	Neurofilament proteins		Central and peripheral nerves	Axon strength; determines axon size
	NF-L (major)	62		
	NF-M (minor)	102		
	NF-H (minor)	110		
V	Nuclear lamins		All cell types	Form a nuclear scaffold to give shape to nucleus
	Lamin A	70		
	Lamin B	67		
	Lamin C	60		
VI	Nestin	240	Neuronal stem cells	Unknown

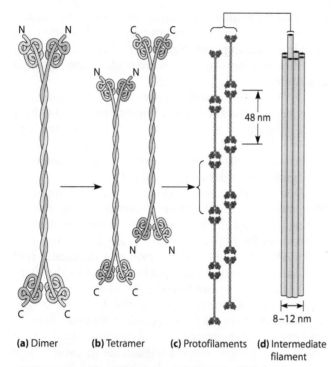

(a) Dimer   **(b)** Tetramer   **(c)** Protofilaments   **(d)** Intermediate filament

FIGURE 15-23 A Model for Intermediate Filament Assembly in Vitro. **(a)** The starting point for assembly is a pair of intermediate filament (IF) polypeptides. The two polypeptides are identical for all IFs except keratin filaments, which are obligate heterodimers with one each of the type I and type II polypeptides. The two polypeptides twist around each other to form a two-chain coiled coil, with their conserved center domain aligned in parallel. **(b)** Two dimers align laterally to form a tetrameric protofilament. **(c)** Protofilaments assemble into larger filaments by end-to-end and side-to-side alignment. **(d)** The fully assembled intermediate filament is thought to be eight protofilaments thick at any point.

rodlike domain of 310–318 amino acids that has been remarkably conserved in size, in secondary structure, and, to some extent, in sequence. This central domain consists of four segments of coiled helices interspersed with three short linker segments. Flanking the central helical domain are N- and C-terminal domains that differ greatly in size, sequence, and function among IF proteins, presumably accounting for the functional diversity of these proteins.

A possible model for IF assembly is shown in **Figure 15-23**. The basic structural unit of intermediate filaments consists of two IF polypeptides intertwined into a *coiled coil.* The central helical domains of the two polypeptides are aligned in parallel, with the N- and C-terminal regions protruding as globular domains at each end. Two such dimers then align laterally to form a tetrameric *protofilament.* Protofilaments interact with each other, associating in an overlapping manner to build up a filamentous structure both laterally and longitudinally. When fully assembled, an intermediate filament is thought to be eight protofilaments thick at any point,

with protofilaments probably joined end to end in staggered overlaps.

Intermediate Filaments Confer Mechanical Strength on Tissues

Intermediate filaments are considered to be important structural determinants in many cells and tissues. Because they often occur in areas of the cell that are subject to mechanical stress, they are thought to have a tension-bearing role. For example, when keratin filaments are genetically modified in the keratinocytes of transgenic mice, the epidermal cells are fragile and rupture easily. In humans, naturally occurring mutations of keratins give rise to a blistering skin disease called *epidermolysis bullosa simplex (EBS).* IF defects are also suspected in other pathological conditions, including *amyotrophic lateral sclerosis (ALS)* and certain types of inherited *cardiomyopathies,* which result from defects in the organization of heart muscle.

Although our discussion of IFs may give the impression that they are static structures, this is not the case. In neurons, for example, IFs are dynamically transported and remodeled. Different IFs form a structural scaffold called the *nuclear lamina* on the inner surface of the nuclear membrane (discussed in detail in Chapters 18 and Chapter 19). The nuclear lamina is composed of three separate IF proteins called *nuclear lamins A, B, and C.* These lamins become phosphorylated and disassemble as a part of nuclear envelope breakdown at the onset of mitosis. After mitosis, lamin phosphatases remove the phosphate groups, allowing the nuclear envelope to form again.

The Cytoskeleton Is a Mechanically Integrated Structure

In the preceding sections, we have looked at the individual components of the cytoskeleton as separate entities. In fact, cellular architecture depends on the unique properties of the different cytoskeletal components working together. Microtubules are generally thought to resist bending when a cell is compressed, while microfilaments serve as contractile elements that generate tension. Intermediate filaments are elastic and can withstand tensile forces.

The mechanical integration of intermediate filaments, microfilaments, and microtubules is made possible by specific linker proteins that connect them, known as *plakins.* One plakin, called *plectin,* is a versatile linker protein that is found at sites where intermediate filaments are connected to microfilaments or microtubules (**Figure 15-24**). Plectin, as well as several other plakins, contains binding sites for intermediate filaments, microfilaments, and microtubules. By linking these major types of polymers, plakins help to integrate them into a mechanically integrated cytoskeletal network. As a result, interconnected cytoskeletal structures can adapt to stretching forces in such a way that the tension-bearing elements become aligned with the direction of stress. These stress-bearing properties of the cytoskeleton are important in epithelial cells such as those that line the gut. These cells are subjected to stress as smooth muscle within the intestinal wall contracts and puts pressure on the contents of the gut.

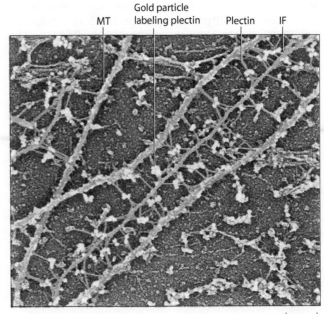

FIGURE 15-24 Connections Between Intermediate Filaments and Other Components of the Cytoskeleton. Intermediate filaments are linked to both microtubules and actin filaments by a protein called plectin. Plectin (red) links IFs (green) to MTs (blue). Gold particles (yellow) label plectin (deep-etch TEM). Plectins can also bind actin MFs (not shown). Here, IFs serve as strong but elastic connectors between the different cytoskeletal filaments.

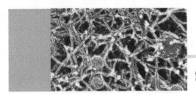

SUMMARY OF KEY POINTS

The Cytoskeleton

- Both prokaryotes and eukaryotes possess an interconnected network of proteins that polymerize from smaller subunits called the cytoskeleton. In eukaryotes, it consists of an extensive three-dimensional network of microtubules (MTs), microfilaments (MFs), and intermediate filaments (IFs) that determines cell shape and allows a variety of cell movements.

- The cytoskeleton is a structural feature of cells that is revealed especially well by digital video, fluorescence, and electron microscopy.

- A variety of drugs can be used to perturb the assembly and disassembly of microtubules and microfilaments in eukaryotes. Such drugs are useful for determining which cellular processes require different cytoskeletal filaments.

Microtubules

- Microtubules (MTs) are hollow tubes with walls consisting of heterodimers of a- and b-tubulin polymerized linearly into protofilaments. Both a- and b-tubulin can bind GTP. First identified as components of the axonemal structures of cilia and flagella and the mitotic spindle of dividing cells, microtubules are now recognized as a general cytoplasmic constituent of most eukaryotic cells.

- MTs are polar structures that elongate preferentially from one end, known as the plus end. MT growth occurs when the concentration of tubulin rises above the critical concentration, the concentration of monomers at which subunit addition is exactly balanced by subunit loss from an MT.

- Drugs such as nocodazole, colchicine, and colcemid cause depolymerization of MTs; taxol stabilizes MTs.

- MTs can undergo cycles of catastrophic shortening and elongation—a phenomenon known as dynamic instability, which involves hydrolysis of GTP by b-tubulin near the plus end, followed by recovery of the GTP-cap at the plus end.

- Within cells, MT dynamics and growth are organized by microtubule-organizing centers (MTOCs). The centrosome is a major MTOC, which contains nucleation sites that are rich in g-tubulin and are used to nucleate MT growth.

- Microtubule-associated proteins (MAPs) stabilize MTs along their length, +-TIP proteins stabilize and anchor their plus ends, and catastrophins hasten their catastrophic depolymerization.

Microfilaments

- Microfilaments (MFs), or F-actin, are double-stranded polymers of G-actin monomers, which bind ATP. Originally discovered because of their role in muscle cells, MFs are components of virtually all eukaryotic cells.

- Like microtubules, MFs are polar structures; G-actin monomers preferentially add to the plus (barbed) ends of MFs; their minus (pointed) ends display far slower subunit addition and loss.

- Actin-binding proteins tightly regulate the polymerization and function of F-actin. These include monomer-binding proteins, which regulate polymerization, and proteins that cap, crosslink, sever, bundle, and anchor F-actin in various ways.

- Microfilament assembly within cells is regulated by cell signaling, which can be mediated by the activity of phosphoinositides and by the monomeric G proteins, Rho, Rac, and Cdc42.

Intermediate Filaments

- Intermediate filaments (IFs) are the most stable and least soluble constituents of the cytoskeleton. They appear to play a structural or tension-bearing role within cells.

- IFs are tissue specific and can be used to identify cell type. Such typing is useful in the diagnosis of cancer.

- All IF proteins have a highly conserved central domain flanked by terminal regions that differ in size and sequence, presumably accounting for the functional diversity of IF proteins.

- IFs, MTs, and MFs are interconnected within cells to form cytoskeletal networks that can withstand tension and compression, providing mechanical strength and rigidity to cells.

MAKING CONNECTIONS

In our overview of the cell in Chapter 4, we saw that the cytoskeleton is a key component of cellular structure and function. In this chapter, you learned that the cytoskeleton is a structural feature of bacterial and eukaryotic cells. The eukaryotic cytoskeleton consists of an extensive three-dimensional network of microtubules, microfilaments, and intermediate filaments that determines cell shape and allows a variety of cell movements. The cytoskeleton is required for a wide variety of cellular events—from the trafficking of vesicles within the cell (see Chapter 12) to the adhesion of cells in animal tissues to the construction of the cell wall in plants. Like other biological polymers, such as the individual proteins, nucleic acids, and carbohydrates we examined in Chapter 3, polymerization of cytoskeletal polymers involves assembly of macromolecules from repeating subunits. Where and when local polymerization of the cytoskeleton occurs is an important

and tightly controlled event. One way polymerization is controlled is through cell signaling; in some cases cell signals activate Rho family GTPases. These are similar to the monomeric G protein Ras, which you saw was a key component of receptor tyrosine kinase signaling. A major event that requires the coordinated activity of the cytoskeleton—cell division—is a major topic in Chapter 19. There we will see that microtubules are crucial for mitosis, and actin is essential for cytokinesis. Because the cytoskeleton is required for cell proliferation, it is a target of chemotherapy for the treatment of cancer.

To understand in more detail how the cytoskeleton is employed in dynamic events such as cell division and cell movement, we need to consider how assembled arrays of cytoskeletal proteins are used in cell movement and to move structures within cells. We will explore these topics in the next chapter.

PROBLEM SET

More challenging problems are marked with a •.

15-1 Filaments and Tubules. Indicate whether each of the following descriptions is true of microtubules (MT), microfilaments (MF), intermediate filaments (IF), or none of these (N). More than one response may be appropriate for some statements.

(a) Involved in muscle contraction.

(b) Involved in the movement of cilia and flagella.

(c) More important for chromosome movements than for cytokinesis.

(d) More important for cytokinesis than for chromosome movements in animal cells.

(e) Most likely to remain when cells are treated with solutions of nonionic detergents or solutions of high ionic strength.

(f) Structurally similar proteins are found in bacterial cells.

(g) Their subunits can bind and catalyze hydrolysis of phosphonucleotides.

(h) Can be detected by immunofluorescence microscopy.

(i) Play well-documented roles in cell movement.

(j) The fundamental repeating subunit is a dimer.

15-2 True or False. Identify each of the following statements as true (T) or false (F). Provide a brief justification for your answer.

(a) The minus end of microtubules and microfilaments is so named because subunits are lost and never added there.

(b) The energy required for tubulin and actin polymerization is provided by hydrolysis of a nucleoside triphosphate.

(c) Microtubules, microfilaments, and intermediate filaments all exist in a typical eukaryotic cell in dynamic equilibrium with a pool of subunit proteins.

(d) Latrunculin A treatment would block intracellular movements of *Listeria*.

(e) An algal cell contains neither tubulin nor actin.

(f) All of the protein subunits of intermediate filaments are encoded by genes in the same gene family.

(g) All microtubules within animal cells have their minus ends anchored at the centrosome.

(h) As long as actin monomers continue to be added to the plus end of a microfilament, the MF will continue to elongate.

15-3 Cytoskeletal Studies. Described here are the results of several recent studies on the proteins of the cytoskeleton. In each case, state the conclusion(s) that can be drawn from the findings.

(a) Small vesicles containing pigment inside of pigmented fish epidermal cells aggregate or disperse in response to treatment with certain chemicals. When nocodazole is added to cells in which the pigment granules have been induced to aggregate, the granules cannot disperse again.

(b) When an animal cell is treated with colchicine, its microtubules depolymerize and virtually disappear. If the colchicine is then washed away, the MTs appear again, beginning at the centrosome and elongating outward at about the rate (1μm/min) at which tubulin polymerizes in vitro.

(c) Extracts from nondividing frog eggs in the G2 phase of the cell cycle were found to contain structures that could induce the polymerization of tubulin into microtubules in vitro. When examined by immunostaining, these structures were shown to contain γ-tubulin.

• **15-4 Stabilization and the Critical Concentration.** Suppose you have determined the overall critical concentration for a sample of purified tubulin. Then you add a preparation of centrosomes (microtubule-organizing centers), which nucleate microtubules so that the minus end is bound to the centrosome and stabilized against disassembly. When you again determine the overall critical concentration, you find it is different. Explain why the overall critical concentration would change.

15-5 Actin' up. The polymerization of G-actin into microfilaments can be followed using pyrene-labeled actin and a device to measure the fluorescence of polymerized actin in a test tube. The increase in fluorescence can then be plotted over time, similar to light-scattering experiments to measure tubulin polymerization (**Figure 15-25**). Examine the graph, and

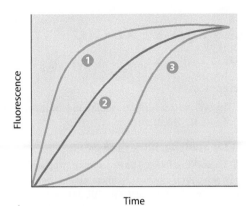

FIGURE 15-25 Actin Polymerization Kinetics Measured by Pyrene Actin Incorporation Under Various Experimental Conditions. See Problem 15-5.

identify which of the curves corresponds to each of the following situations. In each case, state your reasoning.

(a) Pyrene actin is added alone in the presence of buffer.

(b) Pyrene actin is added along with purified Arp2/3 complex proteins.

(c) Pyrene actin is added along with purified Arp2/3 complex proteins and a purified protein fragment that corresponds to active N-WASP (a WASP family protein).

• **15-6 Spongy Actin.** You are interested in the detailed effects of cytochalasin D on microfilaments over time. Based on what you know about the molecular mechanism of action of cytochalasins, draw diagrams of what happens to microfilaments within cells treated with the drug. In particular, explain why existing actin polymers eventually depolymerize.

• **15-7 A New Wrinkle.** Fibroblasts can be placed on thin sheets of silicone rubber. Under normal circumstances, fibroblasts exert sufficient tension on the rubber so that it visibly wrinkles. Explain how the ability of fibroblasts to wrinkle rubber would compare with that of normal cells under the following conditions.

(a) The cells are injected with large amounts of purified gelsolin.

(b) The cells are treated with a permeable form of C3 transferase, a toxin from the bacterium, *Clostridium botulinum*, which covalently modifes an amino acid in Rho by ADP-ribosylation. This renders Rho unable to bind to proteins that it would normally bind to when active.

(c) The cells are treated with taxol.

(d) The cells are treated with latrunculin A, the drug is washed out, and the cells are observed periodically.

(e) A constitutively activated Rho is introduced into the cell.

15-8 Stressed Out. It is now possible, using nanoengineering techniques, to attach magnetic beads to the surface of large cells to measure how mechanically stiff they are. It is also known that acrylamide, which is polymerized to make gels for protein electrophoresis, is very toxic. One effect of acrylamide is to depolymerize intermediate filaments, such as keratin. What effect would you predict acrylamide treatment would have on the mechanical rigidity of a keratinocyte (skin cell)? Explain your answer.

SUGGESTED READING

References of historical importance are marked with a •.

General References

Pollard, T. D. The cytoskeleton, cellular motility and the reductionist agenda. *Nature* 422 (2003): 741.

Techniques for Studying the Cytoskeleton

• Bridgman, P. C., and T. S. Reese. The structure of cytoplasm in directly frozen cultured cells. 1. Filamentous meshworks and the cytoplasmic ground substance. *J. Cell Biol.* 99 (1980): 1655.

• Hirokawa, N., and J. E. Heuser. Quick-freeze, deep-etch visualization of the cytoskeleton beneath surface differentiations of intestinal epithelial cells. *J. Cell Biol.* 91 (1981): 399s.

Prokaryotic Cytoskeleton

Cabeen, M. T., and C. Jacobs-Wagner. Skin and bones: The bacterial cytoskeleton, cell wall, and cell morphogenesis. *J. Cell Biol.* 179 (2007): 381.

Graumann, P. L. Cytoskeletal elements in bacteria. *Annu. Rev. Microbiol.* 61 (2007): 589.

Microtubules

Akhmanova, A., and M. O. Steinmetz. Tracking the ends: A dynamic protein network controls the fate of microtubule tips. *Nat Rev Mol Cell Biol.* 9 (2008): 309.

Gardner, M. K., A. J. Hunt, H. V. Goodson, and D. J. Odde. Microtubule assembly dynamics: New insights at the nanoscale. *Curr. Opin. Cell Biol.* 20 (2008): 64.

Howard, J., and A. A. Hyman. Microtubule polymerases and depolymerases. *Curr. Opin. Cell Biol.* 19 (2007): 31.

• Mitchison, T., and M. Kirschner. Dynamic instability of microtubule growth. *Nature* 312 (1984): 237.

• Nicolaou, K. C. et al. Taxoids: New weapons against cancer. *Sci. Amer.* 274 (1996): 94.

Wiese, C., and Y. Zheng. Microtubule nucleation: Gamma-tubulin and beyond. *J. Cell Sci.* 119 (2006): 4143.

Microfilaments

Baines, A. J. Evolution of spectrin function in cytoskeletal and membrane networks. *Biochem. Soc. Trans.* 37 (2009): 796–803.

Goode, B. L., and M. J. Eck. Mechanism and function of formins in the control of actin assembly. *Annu. Rev. Biochem.* 76 (2007): 593.

Heasman, S. J., and A. J. Ridley. Mammalian Rho GTPases: New insights into their functions from in vivo studies. *Nat. Rev. Mol. Cell Biol.* 9 (2008): 690.

• Heintzelman, M. B., and M. S. Mooseker. Assembly of the intestinal brush border cytoskeleton. *Curr. Top. Dev. Biol.* 26 (1992): 93.

Hughes, S. C., and R. G. Fehon. Understanding ERM proteins—The awesome power of genetics finally brought to bear. *Curr. Opin. Cell Biol.* 19 (2007): 51.

Insall, R. H., and L. M. Machesky. Actin dynamics at the leading edge: From simple machinery to complex networks. *Dev. Cell.* 17 (2009): 310.

Jaffe, A. B., and A. Hall. Rho GTPases: Biochemistry and biology. *Annu. Rev. Cell Dev. Biol.* 21 (2005): 247.

Lambrechts, A., K. Gevaert, P. Cossart, J. Vandekerckhove, and M. Van Troys. Listeria comet tails: The actin-based motility machinery at work. *Trends Cell. Biol.* 18 (2008): 220.

Niggli, V. Regulation of protein activities by phosphoinositide phosphates. *Annu. Rev. Cell Dev. Biol.* 21 (2005): 57.

Pollard, T. D. Regulation of actin filament assembly by Arp2/3 complex and formins. *Annu. Rev. Biophys. Biomol. Struct.* 36 (2007): 451.

• Schroder, R. R. et al. Three-dimensional atomic model of F-actin decorated with *Dictyostelium* myosin S1. *Nature* 364 (1993): 171.

Stossel, T. P. et al. Filamins as integrators of cell mechanics and signalling. *Nature Rev. Mol. Cell Biol.* 2 (2001): 138–145.

Winder, S. J., and K. R. Ayscough. Actin-binding proteins. *J. Cell Sci.* 118 (2005): 651.

Intermediate Filaments

Fuchs, E., and D. W. Cleveland. A structural scaffolding of intermediate filaments in health and disease. *Science* 279 (1998): 514.

Goldman, R. D., B. Grin, M. G. Mendez, and E. R. Kuczmarski. Intermediate filaments: Versatile building blocks of cell structure. *Curr. Opin. Cell Biol.* 20 (2008): 28.

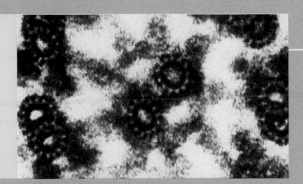

16

Cellular Movement: Motility and Contractility

In the previous chapter, we saw that the cytoskeleton of eukaryotic cells serves as an intracellular scaffold that organizes structures within the cell and shapes the cell itself. In this chapter, we will explore the role of these cytoskeletal elements in cellular **motility.** *This may involve the movement of a cell (or a whole organism) through its environment, the movement of the environment past or through the cell, the movement of components within the cell, or the shortening of the cell itself.* **Contractility,** *a related term often used to describe the shortening of muscle cells, is a specialized form of motility.*

Motile Systems

Motility occurs at the tissue, cellular, and subcellular levels. The most conspicuous examples of motility, particularly in the animal world, take place at the tissue level. The muscle tissues common to most animals consist of cells specifically adapted for contraction. The movements produced are often obvious, whether manifested as the bending of a limb, the beating of a heart, or a uterine contraction during childbirth.

At the cellular level, motility occurs in single cells or in organisms consisting of one or only a few cells. It occurs among cell types as diverse as ciliated protozoa and motile sperm, depending in each case on cilia or flagella, cellular appendages adapted for propulsion. Other examples include the actin-dependent migration of single cells, amoeboid movement, and the invasiveness of cancer cells in malignant tumors.

Equally important is the movement of *intracellular* components. For example, highly ordered microtubules of the mitotic spindle play a key role in the separation of chromosomes during cell division, as we will see in Chapter 19. Nondividing cells continuously shuttle components—such as RNAs, multiprotein complexes, and the membrane-bounded vesicles we learned about in Chapter 12—from one location to another.

Motility is an especially intriguing use of energy by cells because it often involves the conversion of chemical energy directly to mechanical energy. In contrast, most mechanical devices that produce movement from chemicals (such as an automobile engine, which depends on the combustion of gasoline) require an intermediate form of energy, (e.g., heated gasses). As we will see, the cellular energy for motility typically comes from ATP, whose hydrolysis is coupled to changes in the shape of specific proteins that mediate movement. To generate movement, the microfilaments and microtubules of the cytoskeleton provide a basic scaffold for specialized **motor proteins,** or **mechanoenzymes,** which interact with the cytoskeleton to produce motion at the molecular level. The combined effects of these molecular motions produce movement at the cellular level. In cases such as muscle contraction, the combined effects of many cells moving simultaneously produce motion at the tissue level.

In eukaryotes, there are two major motility systems. The first involves interactions between specialized motor proteins and microtubules. Microtubules are abundant in cells and are used for a variety of intracellular movements. A specific example of such microtubule-based movement is *fast axonal transport,* one of the processes used by a nerve cell to transport materials between its cell body and outlying regions. Another process is the sliding of microtubules in *cilia* and *flagella.* The second type of eukaryotic motility requires interactions between actin microfilaments and members of the *myosin* family of motor molecules. A familiar example of microfilament-based movement is *muscle contraction.* We begin our detailed examination of the two motility systems with two proteins essential for microtubule-based movement.

Intracellular Microtubule-Based Movement: Kinesin and Dynein

Microtubules (MTs) provide a rigid set of tracks for the transport of a variety of membrane-enclosed organelles and vesicles. As we saw in Chapter 15, the centrosome organizes and orients MTs because the minus ends of most MTs are embedded in the centrosome. The centrosome is generally located near the center of the cell, so traffic toward the minus ends of MTs might be considered "inbound" traffic. Traffic directed toward the plus ends might likewise be considered "outbound," meaning that it is directed toward the periphery of the cell.

While microtubules provide an organized set of tracks along which organelles can move, they do not directly generate the force necessary for movement. The mechanical work needed for movement depends on *microtubule-associated motor proteins,* which attach to vesicles or organelles and then "walk" along the MT, using ATP to provide the needed energy. Furthermore, MT motor proteins recognize the polarity of the MT, with each motor protein having a preferred direction of movement. At present, we are aware of two major families of MT motors: **kinesins** and **dyneins** (Table 16-1).

MT Motor Proteins Move Organelles Along Microtubules During Axonal Transport

A historically important cell type for studying microtubule-dependent intracellular movement is the squid giant axon Proteins or neurotransmitters synthesized in the cell body of the neuron must be transported over distances up to a meter between the cell body and the nerve ending. The need for such transport arises because ribosomes are present only in the cell body, so no protein synthesis occurs in the axons or synaptic knobs. Instead, proteins and membranous vesicles are synthesized in the cell body and transported along the axons to the synaptic knobs. Some form of energy-dependent transport is clearly required, and MT-based movement provides the mechanism. The process, called **fast axonal transport,** involves the movement of vesicles and other organelles along MTs. (We will not discuss slow axonal transport, which involves somewhat different processes.)

The role of microtubules in axonal transport was initially suggested because the process is inhibited by drugs that depolymerize MTs but is insensitive to drugs that affect microfilaments. Since then, MTs have been visualized along the axon and have been shown to be prominent features of the axonal cytoskeleton. Moreover, axonal MTs have small, membranous vesicles and mitochondria associated with them (**Figure 16-1**).

Evidence that a motor protein drives the movements of organelles was obtained when investigators found that organelles in the presence of ATP could move along fine filamentous structures present in exuded *axoplasm* (the

Motor Protein	Typical Function
Table 16-1 **Selected Motor Proteins of Eukaryotic Cells**	
Microtubule (MT)-Associated Motors	
Dyneins	
Cytoplasmic dynein	Moves cargo toward minus ends of MTs
Axonemal dynein	Activates sliding in flagellar MTs
*Kinesins**	
Kinesin 1 (classic kinesin)	Dimer; moves cargo toward plus ends of MTs
Kinesin 3	Monomer; movement of synaptic vesicles in neurons
Kinesin 5	Bipolar, tetrameric; bidirectional sliding of MTs during anaphase of mitosis
Kinesin 6	Completion of cytokinesis
Kinesin 13 ("catastrophins")	Dimer; destabilization of plus ends of MTs
Kinesin 14	Spindle dynamics in meiosis and mitosis; moves toward minus end of MTs
Microfilament (MF)-Associated Motors	
*Myosins**	
Myosin I	Motion of membranes along MFs; endocytosis
Myosin II	Slides MFs in muscle; other contractile events such as cytokinesis, cell migration
Myosin V	Vesicle positioning and trafficking
Myosin VI	Endocytosis; moves toward minus ends of MFs
Myosin VII	Base of stereocilia in inner ear
Myosin X	Tips of filopodia
Myosin XV	Tips of stereocilia in inner ear

*Kinesins and myosins comprise large families of proteins. There are many families of kinesins and myosins.

cytosol of axons), which could be visualized by video-enhanced differential interference contrast microscopy (see the Appendix for details). The rate of organelle movement was shown to be about 2 μm/sec, comparable to the axonal transport rate in intact neurons. A combination of immunofluorescence and electron microscopy demonstrated that the fine filaments the organelles move along are single microtubules.

Since that time, two MT motor proteins responsible for fast axonal transport, kinesin 1 and cytoplasmic dynein, have been purified and characterized. To determine the direction of transport by these motors, purified proteins were used experimentally to drive the transport of polystyrene beads along microtubules polymerized from purified centrosomes. When polystyrene beads, purified kinesin, and ATP were added to such MTs, the beads moved toward the plus ends (i.e., away from the centrosome). This finding means that in a nerve cell,

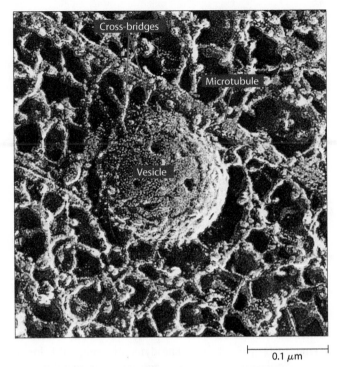

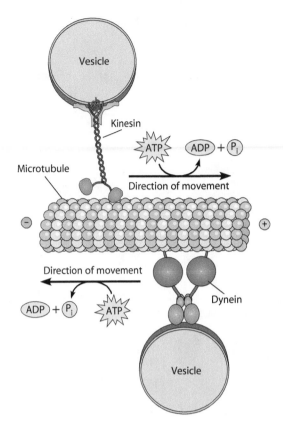

FIGURE 16-1 A Vesicle Attached to a Microtubule in a Crayfish Axon. Cross-bridges connect the membrane vesicle (round structure at center) to the microtubule (deep-etch TEM).

FIGURE 16-2 Microtubule-Based Motility. Kinesins and dyneins are motor proteins that couple ATP hydrolysis to conformational changes to "walk" along microtubules. Most kinesins move vesicles or organelles toward the plus ends of MTs. Dyneins move in the opposite direction, toward the minus ends of MTs.

VIDEOS www.thecellplace.com   *Movement of organelles in vivo*

kinesin mediates transport from the cell body down the axon to the nerve ending (called *anterograde axonal transport*). When similar experiments were carried out with purified cytoplasmic dynein, particles were moved in the opposite direction, toward the minus ends of the MTs (called *retrograde axonal transport* when it occurs in neurons). Thus these two motors transport their *cargo*, those organelles or components that they shuttle along microtubules, in opposite directions within the cytosol (**Figure 16-2**), a finding that has been abundantly confirmed by more recent molecular and genetic analysis.

Figure 16-2 may suggest that cargo always moves in one direction or another along MTs. In some cases, such as fast axonal transport, such unidirectional transport is the rule. However, some vesicles are capable of changing direction as they move along an MT. In these cases cargo is attached to both kinesins and dyneins; the direction of motion seems to be determined by which type of motor predominates.

Motor Proteins Move Along Microtubules by Hydrolyzing ATP

The first kinesins, originally identified in the cytoplasm of squid giant axons, consist of three parts: a globular *head* region that attaches to microtubules and is involved in hydrolysis of ATP, a coiled helical region, and a *light-chain* region that is involved in attaching the kinesin to other proteins or organelles (**Figure 16-3a**). The movements of single kinesin molecules along MTs have

been studied by tracking the movement of beads attached to kinesin or by measuring the force exerted by single kinesin molecules using calibrated glass fibers or beads trapped in a special type of laser beam known as an "optical tweezer" (see the Appendix). Classic kinesins move along MTs in 8-nm steps: One of the two globular heads moves forward to make an attachment to a new β-tubulin subunit, followed by detachment of the trailing globular head, which can now make an attachment to a new region of the MT. It is easiest to visualize this movement as analogous to walking, with the two globular heads taking turns as the front "foot" (Figure 16-3b). This movement is coupled to the hydrolysis of ATP bound at specific sites within the heads. The result is that kinesin moves toward the plus end of an MT in an ATP-dependent fashion. A single kinesin-1 molecule exhibits *processivity*. It can cover long distances before detaching from an MT. To do so, it releases its bound ADP and acquires a new molecule of ATP, allowing the cycle to repeat. A single kinesin molecule can move as far as 1 μm, which is a great distance relative to its size. As a molecular motor, kinesin appears to be quite efficient; estimates of its efficiency in converting the energy of ATP hydrolysis to useful work are on the order of 60–70%.

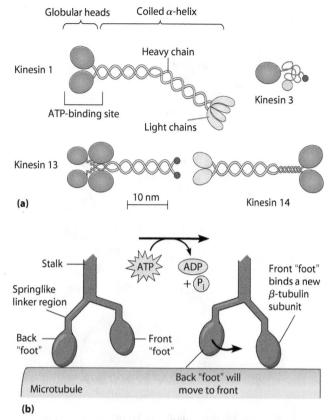

FIGURE 16-3 Movement of Kinesin. (a) The basic structure of several kinesin family members. (b) Kinesins "walk" along microtubules. The front "foot," one of kinesin's two globular heads, detaches from a β-tubulin subunit by hydrolyzing ATP and moves forward. The rear "foot" then releases by hydrolyzing ATP and springs forward, moving to the front.

Kinesins Are a Large Family of Proteins with Varying Structures and Functions

Since the discovery of the original kinesin involved in anterograde transport in neurons, many other kinesins have been discovered. They can be grouped into families based on their structure (Table 16-1). Some of these kinesins form dimers with another identical protein or with another, different kinesin. One family (kinesin 14) acts as minus-end-directed motors, rather than as plus-end motors. Biochemical and immunocytochemical studies, as well as analysis of mutant organisms, have shown that kinesins are involved in many different processes within cells. One important function for kinesin is moving and localizing substances within cells. These include RNAs, multiprotein complexes, and membranous organelles. (We will consider their role in organelle transport later in this chapter.) We saw another role for kinesins in Chapter 15: one family of kinesins, the catastrophins, aids depolymerization of MTs. Various kinesins localize to the mitotic or meiotic spindle or to kinetochores, where they play roles in various phases of mitosis and meiosis (see Chapter 19). Other kinesins are required for completion of mitosis and cytokinesis. For

example, cells in mutant fruit flies or nematode worms lacking one of these kinesins (called MKLP kinesins) initiate cytokinesis, but, because the cleavage furrow never deepens, cell division fails.

To attach to their cargo, kinesins often use their light chains. In some cases, the light chains attach directly to cargo. In other cases, such as mitochondria, adapter proteins allow the light chains to attach to cargo indirectly.

Dyneins Can Be Grouped into Two Major Classes: Axonemal and Cytoplasmic Dyneins

The dynein family of motor proteins consists of two basic types: cytoplasmic dynein and axonemal dynein (Table 16-1). In contrast to the kinesins, few cytoplasmic dyneins have been identified. **Cytoplasmic dynein** contains two heavy chains that interact with microtubules, two intermediate chains, two light intermediate chains, and various light chains. In contrast to most kinesins, cytoplasmic dynein moves toward the minus ends of MTs. Cytoplasmic dynein is associated with the protein complex known as **dynactin** (Figure 16-4). The dynactin complex helps to link cytoplasmic dynein to cargo (such as membranous vesicles) it transports along MTs, by binding to proteins such as spectrin attached to the membrane of its cargo.

At least four types of **axonemal dynein** have been identified. We will discuss the function of axonemal dynein in cilia and flagella in some detail later in this chapter.

Microtubule Motors Are Involved in Shaping the Endomembrane System and Vesicle Transport

In Chapter 12 we saw that the cell has an elaborate transportation system of vesicles and membranous organelles. First, recall that the endomembrane system is a complex

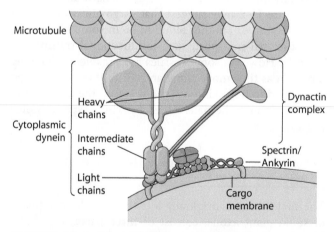

FIGURE 16-4 Schematic Representation of the Cytoplasmic Dynein/Dynactin Complex. Cytoplasmic dynein (brown) is linked with cargo membranes indirectly through the dynactin multiprotein complex (aqua). The dynactin complex binds to a complex containing spectrin and ankyrin, associated with the membrane of the cargo vesicle.

network of membrane-bounded tubules, important not only for export and processing of newly synthesized proteins but also for events such as calcium release. MT motors appear to be important for dynamically shaping this complicated network. Live imaging of MTs and endoplasmic reticulum (ER) membrane in vitro and in living cells indicates that extensions of the ER can be moved along MTs.

Second, recall that the Golgi complex is a series of flattened membrane stacks located in the region of the centrosome. The function of the Golgi is to receive proteins made in the ER and to process and package those proteins for distribution to the correct cellular destinations. At each step of this process, proteins are transported in vesicles. Thus, there is a continuous flow of vesicles to and from the Golgi. The vesicles are carried by MT motors on microtubule tracks (**Figure 16-5**).

Several experiments demonstrate that microtubule-based transport is crucial for maintenance of the Golgi stacks. For example, if MTs are depolymerized using the drug nocodazole (see Chapter 15, page 428), the Golgi complex disperses. When the nocodazole is washed out, the Golgi complex re-forms. Similarly, disruption of the function of the dynactin complex by inducing cells to produce too much of one of its subunits results in collapse of the Golgi complex and disruption of the transport of intermediates from the ER to the Golgi.

Proteins are processed as they move through the stacks of Golgi membranes. The finished proteins emerge—still packaged in vesicles—from the other side of the complex. Plus-end-directed MT motors carry the finished vesicles away from the Golgi complex toward the cell periphery. In organisms in which various kinesins are mutated, specific defects in vesicle transport have been observed, providing evidence that these motors are crucial for plus-end-directed vesicular transport.

Microtubule-Based Motility: Cilia and Flagella

Cilia and Flagella Are Common Motile Appendages of Eukaryotic Cells

Microtubules are crucial not only for movement within cells but also for the movements of *flagella* and *cilia*, the motile appendages of eukaryotic cells. The two appendages share a common structural basis and differ only in relative length, number per cell, and mode of beating. **Cilia** (singular: **cilium**) have a diameter of about 0.25 μm, are about 2–10 μm long, and tend to occur in large numbers on the surface of ciliated cells. Each cilium is bounded by an extension of the plasma membrane and is therefore an intracellular structure.

Cilia occur in both unicellular and multicellular eukaryotes. Unicellular organisms, such as *Paramecium,* a protozoan, use cilia for both locomotion and the collection of food particles. In multicellular organisms, cilia serve primarily to move the environment past the cell rather than to propel the cell through the environment. The cells that line the air passages of the human respiratory tract, for example, have several hundred cilia each, which means that every square centimeter of epithelial tissue lining the respiratory tract has about a billion cilia (**Figure 16-6a**)! The coordinated, wavelike beating of these cilia carries mucus, dust, dead cells, and other foreign matter out of the lungs. One of the health hazards of cigarette smoking lies in the inhibitory effect that smoke has on normal ciliary beating. Certain respiratory ailments can also be traced to defective cilia.

Cilia display an oarlike pattern of beating, with a power stroke perpendicular to the cilium, thereby generating a force parallel to the cell surface. The cycle of beating for an epithelial cilium is shown in Figure 16-6b. Each cycle requires about 0.1–0.2 sec and involves an active power stroke followed by a recovery stroke.

Flagella (singular: **flagellum**) move cells through a fluid environment. Although they have the same diameter as cilia, flagella are often much longer—from 1 μm to several millimeters, though usually in the range of 10–200 μm— and may be limited to one or a few per cell (Figure 16-6c). Flagella differ from cilia in the nature of their beat. Flagella

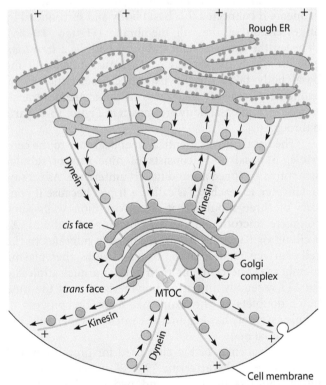

FIGURE 16-5 Microtubules and the Endomembrane System. Vesicles going to and from the Golgi complex are attached to microtubules and carried by MT motors. Vesicles derived from either the ER or the cell membrane are carried toward the Golgi complex and microtubule-organizing center (MTOC) by dynein, whereas vesicles derived from the Golgi complex are carried toward either the ER or the cell periphery by kinesins.

(a) Cilia on a mammalian tracheal cell

`1 μm`

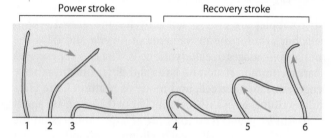

Power stroke   Recovery stroke

1   2   3   4   5   6

(b) Beating of a cilium

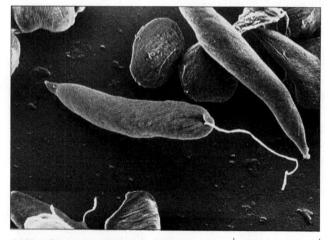

(c) Flagellum on unicellular alga *Euglena*

`1 μm`

(d) Movement of flagellated eukaryotic cell

move with a propagated bending motion that is usually symmetrical and undulatory and may even have a helical pattern. This type of beat generates a force parallel to the flagellum, such that the cell moves in approximately the same direction as the axis of the flagellum. The locomotory

FIGURE 16-6 Cilia and Flagella. (a) A micrograph of cilia on a mammalian tracheal cell (SEM). **(b)** The beating of a cilium on the surface of an epithelial cell from the human respiratory tract. A beat begins with a power stroke that sweeps fluid over the cell surface. A recovery stroke follows, leaving the cilium poised for the next beat. Each cycle requires about 0.1–0.2 sec. **(c)** A micrograph of the flagellated unicellular alga *Euglena* (SEM). **(d)** Movement of a eukaryotic flagellated cell through an aqueous environment.

VIDEOS www.thecellplace.com *Flagellum movement in swimming sperm*

pattern of most flagellated cells, such as many sperm cells, involves propulsion of the cell by the trailing flagellum. Examples are also known in which the flagellum actually precedes the cell. Figure 16-6d illustrates this type of swimming movement. The flagella of bacteria are constructed from an entirely different set of proteins, and their mechanism of movement is completely different. These flagella are fascinating, but we will not consider them further here.

Cilia and Flagella Consist of an Axoneme Connected to a Basal Body

Cilia and flagella share a common structure, known as the **axoneme,** that is about 0.25 μm in diameter. The axoneme is connected to a **basal body** and surrounded by an extension of the cell membrane (**Figure 16-7a**). Between the axoneme and the basal body is a *transition zone* in which the arrangement of microtubules in the basal body takes on the pattern characteristic of the axoneme. Cross-sectional views of the axoneme, transition zone, and basal body are shown in Figure 16-7, parts b through d.

The basal body is identical in appearance to the centriole. A basal body consists of nine sets of tubular structures arranged around its circumference. As we saw in Chapter 15, each set is called a *triplet* because it consists of three tubules that share common walls—one complete microtubule and two incomplete tubules. As a cilium or flagellum forms, a centriole migrates to the cell surface and makes contact with the plasma membrane. The centriole then acts as a nucleation site for MT assembly, initiating polymerization of the nine outer doublets of the axoneme. After the process of tubule assembly has begun, the centriole is then referred to as a basal body.

The axonemes of the cilia used for propulsion and flagella have a characteristic "9 + 2" pattern, with nine **outer doublets** of tubules and two additional microtubules in the center, often called the **central pair.** Another, specialized group of cilia, called *primary cilia,* are used in sensory structures and play an important role in animal embryos during their development. These cilia have a "9 + 0" structure; that is, they lack the central pair.

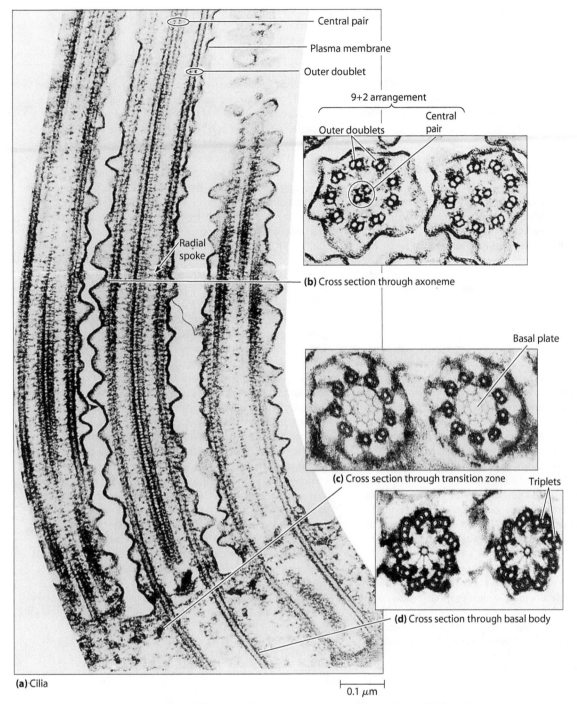

Central pair

Plasma membrane

Outer doublet

9+2 arrangement

Central pair

Outer doublets

(b) Cross section through axoneme

Radial spoke

Basal plate

(c) Cross section through transition zone

Triplets

(d) Cross section through basal body

(a) Cilia

0.1 μm

FIGURE 16-7 The Structure of a Cilium. (a) These longitudinal sections of three cilia from the protozoan *Tetrahymena thermophila* illustrate several structural features of cilia, including the central pair and outer doublet microtubules and the radial spokes. Cross-sectional views are shown for **(b)** axonemes, **(c)** the transition zone between cilia and basal bodies, and **(d)** basal bodies. Notice the triplet pattern of the basal body and the "9 + 2" pattern of tubule arrangement in the axoneme of the cilium. (All TEMs.)

ACTIVITIES www.thecellplace.com *Cilia and flagella*

Defects in these cilia can result in fascinating human syndromes (see **Box 16A**).

Figure 16-8 on p. 458 illustrates these structural features of a typical "9 + 2" cilium in greater detail. The nine outer doublets of the axoneme are thought to be extensions of two of the three subfibers from each of the nine triplets

of the basal body. Each outer doublet of the axoneme therefore consists of one complete MT, called the **A tubule,** and one incomplete MT, the **B tubule** (Figure 16-8b). The A tubule has 13 protofilaments, whereas the B tubule has only 10 or 11. The tubules of the central pair are both complete, with 13 protofilaments each. All of these structures

As it has become easier to isolate genes that are defective in many human genetic disorders, researchers have identified several human disorders that are due to defects in motor proteins. We will discuss two examples: reversal of body symmetry and genetic deafness.

Dyneins, Reversal of the Left-Right Body Axis, and Ciliopathies

In at least 1 in 20,000 live human births, organs in the body cavity are completely reversed left to right. This condition, known as *situs inversus viscerum,* has no medical consequences and is often not recognized until a patient undergoes medical tests for an unrelated condition. In contrast, when only some organs are reversed (*heterotaxia*), serious health complications result. In patients suffering from an autosomal recessive condition known as *Kartagener's triad,* there is a 50% probability of the complete reversal of the left-right location of internal organs. In addition, such patients suffer from male sterility and bronchial problems. The reason for these abnormalities is a defect in the outer dynein arms of cilia and flagella. Studies in mice support the idea that microtubule motor proteins are somehow involved in left-right asymmetry in the developing mammalian embryo. In *inversus viscerum (iv)* mutant mice, the internal organs are reversed in half of the newborn homozygotes. Surprisingly, *iv* encodes an axonemal dynein, which is required for the activity of primary cilia ("9 + 0" cilia) that are required for left-right asymmetry. Remarkably, similar cilia have been identified in all vertebrate embryos, and it is thought that they play a similar role in all of these cases. By beating in a rotary fashion, the cilia may create a flow of secreted components that shuttle signaling molecules across the midline of the embryo, or they may serve a sensory function. Current research is aimed at clarifying the role these fascinating cilia play in early embryonic development.

In addition to *situs inversus,* a growing number of human diseases are now known to be due to defects in cilia. These diseases, known as "ciliopathies," include a number of human syndromes, including *Bardet–Biedl syndrome (BBS)* and *polycystic kidney disease (PKD).* BBS is principally characterized by obesity, retinitis pigmentosa (which results in blindness), polydactyly (more than the usual number of fingers/toes), underdevelopment of the gonads, and mental retardation. At least twelve human genes, when mutated, can give rise to BBS. All of the proteins these genes encode localize to basal bodies or cilia. Analysis of the equivalent genes in the roundworm, *C. elegans,* has shown that BBS proteins are involved in intraflagellar transport, moving material into and along primary cilia. Retinal degeneration in BBS patients results from defects in the *connecting cilium* of rod cells. The connecting cilium carries components to rod outer segments using the same machinery as intraflagellar transport. PKD is characterized by multiple, fluid-filled cysts in the kidneys. An autosomal dominant form of PKD is associated with another protein that in worms has been shown to be involved in intraflagellar transport. How defects in such a protein lead to PKD is still poorly understood.

Myosins and Deafness

Recently, nonmuscle myosins have also been implicated in human genetic disorders. For example, mutations in a myosin VII result in *Usher's syndrome,* an autosomal recessive disorder characterized by congenital profound hearing loss, problems in the vestibular system (i.e., sensing where one is in space), and retinitis pigmentosa. Another type of deafness in humans is caused by recessive mutations in the *myosin XV* gene. The shaker-2 mouse is a model for this condition: when mice are genetically engineered to carry a functional copy of the *myosin XV* gene, their deafness is rescued. How do defects in myosins lead to deafness? Specialized cells known as *hair cells* are found in the organ of Corti (a specialized structure within the cochlea of the inner ear) and the vestibular system; they contain special actin-rich sensory structures known as *stereocilia* (**Figure 16A-1**). By sensing movements of fluid within the inner ear, hair cells carry out auditory and vestibular transduction. Myosin VII is concentrated in the cell body of hair cells and in stereocilia; another myosin (myosin IC) is localized to sites where hair cells are connected laterally. Myosin XV is concentrated at the tips of stereocilia. All of these myosins are thought to be involved in linking stereocilia into a mechanically integrated vibration sensor.

---

contain tubulin, together with a second protein called *tektin.* Tektin is related to intermediate filament proteins (see Chapter 15) and is a necessary component of the axoneme. The A and B tubules share a wall that appears to contain tektin as a major component.

In addition to microtubules, axonemes contain several other key components (Figure 16-8b). The most important of these are the sets of **sidearms** that project out from each of the A tubules of the nine outer doublets. Each sidearm reaches out clockwise toward the B tubules of the adjacent doublet. These arms consist of axonemal dynein, which is responsible for sliding MTs within the axoneme past one another to bend the axoneme. The dynein arms occur in pairs, one inner arm and one outer arm, spaced along the MT at regular intervals. At less frequent intervals, adjacent doublets are joined by **interdoublet links.** These links are thought to limit the extent to which doublets can move with respect to each other as the axoneme bends.

At regular intervals, **radial spokes** project inward from each of the nine MT doublets, terminating near a set of projections that extend outward from the central pair of microtubules. These spokes are thought to be important in translating the sliding motion of adjacent doublets into the bending motion that characterizes the beating of these

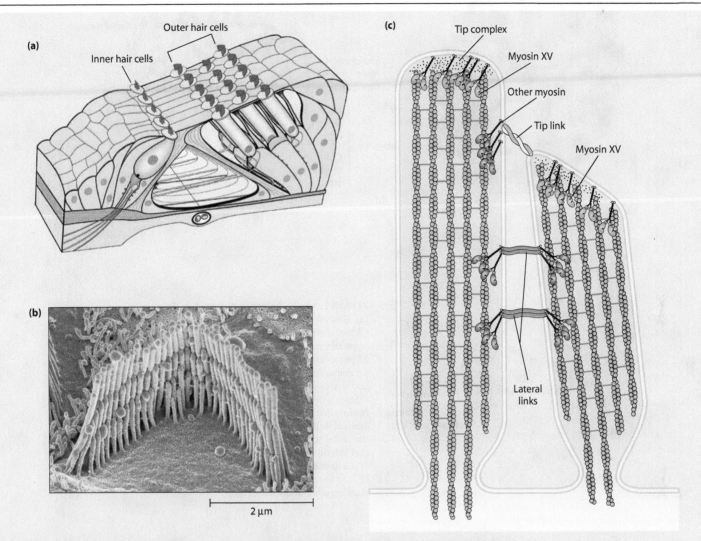

(a)

Outer hair cells

Inner hair cells

(c)

Tip complex

Myosin XV

Other myosin

Tip link

Myosin XV

Lateral links

(b)

2 μm

FIGURE 16A-1 Stereocilia and the Inner Ear. (a) Hair cells in the inner ear, including the organ of Corti in the cochlea, contain stereocilia. (b) A scanning electron micrograph of stereocilia in an outer hair cell. (c) Stereocilia are similar to microvilli but are much larger. They sense tiny movements caused by sound vibrations or fluid movement in the semicircular canals. Tip links, which are composed of cell surface proteins similar to cadherins, are associated with myosin XV. Lateral links are associated with other types of myosin. Such links connect one stereocilium to the next.

appendages. In addition to the radial spoke attachment to the central pair, a protein called **nexin** links adjacent doublets to one another and probably also plays a role in converting sliding into bending motion.

Microtubule Sliding Within the Axoneme Causes Cilia and Flagella to Bend

How does axonemal dynein act on this elaborate structure to generate the characteristic bending of cilia and flagella? The overall length of MTs in cilia and flagella does not change. Instead, the microtubules in adjacent outer doublets slide relative to one another in an ATP-dependent fashion. According to the **sliding-microtubule model** for cilia and flagella, this sliding movement is converted to a localized bending because the doublets of the axoneme are connected radially to the central pair and circumferentially to one another and therefore cannot slide past each other freely. The resultant bending takes the form of a wave that begins at the base of the organelle and proceeds toward the tip.

Dynein Arms Are Responsible for Sliding. The driving force for MT sliding is provided by ATP hydrolysis, catalyzed by the dynein arms. The importance of the dynein

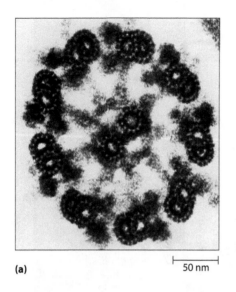

(a)

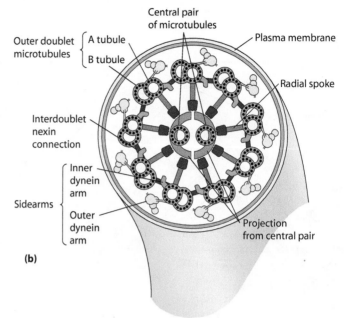

Central pair
of microtubules

Outer doublet
microtubules

A tubule

B tubule

Plasma membrane

Radial spoke

Interdoublet
nexin
connection

Sidearms

Inner
dynein
arm

Outer
dynein
arm

Projection
from central pair

(b)

50 nm

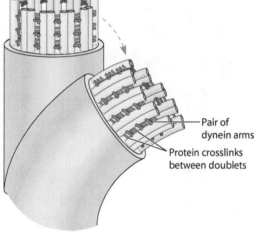

Pair of
dynein arms

Protein crosslinks
between doublets

(c)

FIGURE 16-8 Enlarged Views of an Axoneme.

(a) This micrograph shows an axoneme from a flagellum of *Chlamydomonas* (TEM). (b) Diagram of an axoneme in cross section. The microtubules of the central pair have 13 protofilaments each, as do the A tubules of the outer doublets. Each B tubule has 11 protofilaments of its own and shares 5 protofilaments with the A tubule. The dynein sidearms have ATPase activity and are thought to be responsible for the sliding of adjacent doublets. The inter-doublet links (nexin connections) join adjacent doublets, and the radial spokes project inward, terminating near projections that extend outward from the central pair of MTs. (c) Bending of the axoneme by dynein. Connection of the outer doublet MTs to the central pair converts sliding of adjacent MTs into local bending of the axoneme.

arms is indicated by two kinds of evidence. First, when dynein is selectively extracted from isolated axonemes, the arms disappear from the outer doublets, and the axonemes lose both their ability to hydrolyze ATP and their capacity to beat. Furthermore, the effect is reversible: If purified dynein is added to isolated outer doublets, the sidearms reappear, and ATP-dependent sliding is restored.

A second kind of evidence comes from studies of non-motile mutant flagella in such species as *Chlamydomonas*, a green alga. In some of these mutants, flagella are present but nonfunctional. Depending on the particular mutant, their nonmotile flagella lack dynein arms, radial spokes, or the central pair of microtubules. These structures are therefore essential for flagellar bending.

Axonemal dynein is a very large protein. It has multiple subunits, the three largest having ATPase activity and a molecular weight of about 450,000 each. During the sliding process, the stalk of the dynein arm apparently attaches to and detaches from the B tubule in a cyclic manner. Each cycle requires the hydrolysis of ATP and shifts the dynein

arm of one doublet relative to the adjacent doublet. In this way, the dynein arms of one doublet move the neighboring doublet, resulting in a relative displacement of the two.

Crosslinks and Spokes Are Responsible for Bending. To convert the dynein-mediated displacement of doublets to a bending motion, the doublets must be restrained in a way that resists sliding but allows deformation. This resistance is provided by the radial spokes that connect the doublets to the central pair of microtubules and possibly also by the nexin crosslinks between doublets (Figure 16-8b, c). If these crosslinks and spokes are removed (by partial digestion with proteolytic enzymes, for example), the resistance that translates doublet sliding into a bending action is absent, and sliding is uncoupled from bending. Under these conditions, the free doublets move with respect to each other, and the axonemes become longer and thinner as the MTs slide apart.

In addition to their role in flagellar and ciliary beating, axonemal dyneins have been implicated in a process that at first glance seems completely unrelated to its function in sliding microtubules: positioning the internal organs of the body (see Box 16A).

Intraflagellar Transport Adds Components to Growing Flagella. The elaborate structure of flagella and cilia raises an interesting question: How are tubulin subunits and other components added to the growing cilia or flagella? Based on the analysis of mutants in *Chlamydomonas* and nematodes, both plus- and minus-end-directed microtubule motors are involved in shuttling components to and from the tips of flagella. This process, known as **intraflagellar transport (IFT),** is somewhat analogous to the process of axonal transport in nerve cells: Kinesins move material out to the tips of flagella, and a dynein brings material back toward the base. Several adapter proteins, which form two different major protein complexes, are required to link these motors to IFT particles. Several human disease syndromes are now known to result from mutations in components of these protein complexes (see Box 16A).

Actin-Based Cell Movement: The Myosins

Myosins Are a Large Family of Actin-Based Motors with Diverse Roles in Cell Motility

Movements of molecules and other cellular components also occurs along another major filament system in the cell—the actin cytoskeleton. As with microtubules, ATP-dependent motors exert force on actin microfilaments within cells. These motors are all members of a large superfamily of proteins known as **myosins.** Currently, there are 24 known classes of myosins (for a list of some major types of myosins, see Table 16-1). All myosins have at least one polypeptide chain, called the *heavy chain,* with a globular head group at one end attached to a tail of varying length (**Figure 16-9**). The globular head binds to actin and uses the energy of ATP hydrolysis to move along an actin filament. Many myosins move toward the plus (barbed) ends of actin filaments. (Myosin VI is a well-studied exception: It moves toward the minus, or pointed, ends of actin filaments.)

The structure of the tail region varies among the different kinds of myosin, giving myosin molecules the ability to bind to various molecules or cell structures. The tail structure also determines the ability of myosins to bind to other identical myosins to form dimers or large arrays. Myosins typically contain small polypeptides bound to the globular head group. These polypeptides, referred to as the *light chains,* often play a role in regulating the activity of the myosin ATPase. Some myosins are unusual in that they have a binding site for actin in their tail region, as well as in the head. In addition, some myosins, such as myosin I and myosin V, appear to bind to membranes, suggesting that these forms of myosin play a role in movement

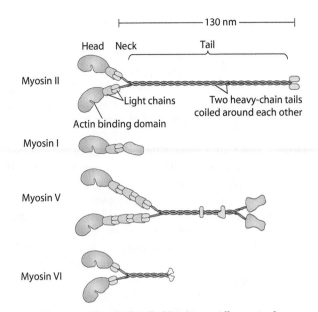

FIGURE 16-9 Myosin Family Members. All myosins have an actin- and ATP-binding heavy-chain "head" and typically have two or more regulatory light chains. Some myosins, like myosin I, have one head. Others, like myosin II, V, and VI, associate via their tails into two-stranded coils.

of the plasma membrane or in transporting membrane-enclosed organelles inside the cell.

Myosins have many functions in events as wide-ranging as muscle contraction (muscle myosin II), cell movement (nonmuscle myosin II), phagocytosis (myosin VI), and vesicle transport or other membrane-associated events (myosins I, V). One unexpected function for myosins is in maintaining the structures required for hearing in humans (see Box 16A).

The best-understood myosins are the **type II myosins.** They are composed of two heavy chains, each featuring a globular myosin head, a hinge region, a long rodlike tail, and four light chains. These myosins are found in skeletal, cardiac (heart), and smooth muscle cells, as well as in non-muscle cells. Type II myosins are distinctive in that they can assemble into long filaments such as the thick filaments of muscle cells. The basic function of myosin II in all cell types is to convert ATP hydrolysis to mechanical force that can cause actin filaments to slide past the myosin molecule, typically resulting in the contraction of a cell or group of cells. For example, in *Drosophila* embryos, analysis of mutants for a nonmuscle type II myosin indicates that it is required for the closure of tissue sheets. Non-muscle type II myosins are also involved in formation of the contractile ring during cytokinesis (see Chapter 19).

Many Myosins Move Along Actin Filaments in Short Steps

Like kinesins, myosins have been studied at the level of single molecules. These studies have shown that the force individual myosin heads exert on actin is similar to that measured for kinesins. Like kinesin, myosin II is an efficient motor. When myosins must pull against moderate loads, they are about 50% efficient.

It is useful to compare the two best-studied types of cytoskeletal motor proteins, "classic" kinesin and myosin II, because it is now possible to see how they function as biochemical motors at the level of single molecules. Both have two heads that they use to "walk" along a protein filament, and both utilize ATP hydrolysis to change their shape. Despite these similarities, there are profound differences as well. Conventional kinesins operate alone or in small numbers to transport vesicles over large distances, and a single kinesin can move hundreds of nanometers along a single microtubule. In contrast, a single myosin II molecule slides an actin filament about 12–15 nm per power stroke. Not all myosins move such short distances. Myosin V, for example, which is involved in organelle and vesicle transport, is much more processive.

If myosin II cannot move large distances along actin, how can it be involved in movement? Myosin II molecules often operate in large arrays. In the case of myosin II filaments in muscle, these arrays can contain billions of motors working together to mediate contraction of skeletal muscle, the process to which we now turn.

Filament-Based Movement in Muscle

Muscle contraction is the most familiar example of mechanical work mediated by intracellular filaments. Mammals have several kinds of muscles, including skeletal muscle, cardiac muscle, and smooth muscle. We will first consider skeletal muscle because much of our knowledge of the contractile process grew out of early investigations of its molecular structure and function.

Skeletal Muscle Cells Contain Thin and Thick Filaments

Skeletal muscles are responsible for voluntary movement. The structural organization of skeletal muscle is shown in **Figure 16-10**. A muscle consists of bundles of parallel **muscle fibers** joined by tendons to the bones that the muscle must move. Each fiber is actually a long, thin, multinucleate cell that is highly specialized for its contractile function. The multinucleate state arises from the fusion of embryonic cells called *myoblasts* during muscle differentiation to produce a *syncytium*. This cell fusion also accounts at least in part for the striking length of muscle cells, which may be many centimeters in length.

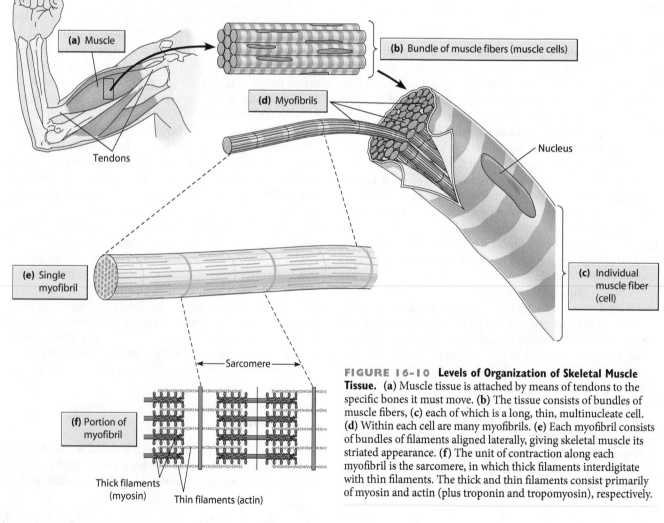

FIGURE 16-10 Levels of Organization of Skeletal Muscle Tissue. (**a**) Muscle tissue is attached by means of tendons to the specific bones it must move. (**b**) The tissue consists of bundles of muscle fibers, (**c**) each of which is a long, thin, multinucleate cell. (**d**) Within each cell are many myofibrils. (**e**) Each myofibril consists of bundles of filaments aligned laterally, giving skeletal muscle its striated appearance. (**f**) The unit of contraction along each myofibril is the sarcomere, in which thick filaments interdigitate with thin filaments. The thick and thin filaments consist primarily of myosin and actin (plus troponin and tropomyosin), respectively.

For muscles to exert force on other tissues, they use specialized structures to attach to other tissues. One such attachment is known as a *costamere*.

At the subcellular level, each muscle fiber (or cell) contains numerous **myofibrils.** Myofibrils are 1–2 μm in diameter and may extend the entire length of the cell. Each myofibril is subdivided along its length into repeating units called **sarcomeres.** The sarcomere is the fundamental contractile unit of the muscle cell. Each sarcomere of the myofibril contains bundles of **thick filaments** and **thin filaments.** Thick filaments consist of myosin, whereas thin filaments consist mainly of actin, tropomyosin, and troponin. The thin filaments are arranged around the thick filaments in a hexagonal pattern, as can be seen when the myofibril is viewed in cross section (**Figure 16-11**).

The filaments in skeletal muscle are aligned in lateral register, giving the myofibrils a pattern of alternating dark and light bands (**Figure 16-12a**). This pattern of bands, or *striations*, is characteristic of skeletal and cardiac muscle, which are therefore referred to as **striated muscle.** The dark bands are called **A bands,** and the light bands are called **I bands.** (The terminology for the structure and appearance of muscle myofibrils was developed from observations originally made with the polarizing light microscope. I stands for *isotropic* and A for *anisotropic*,

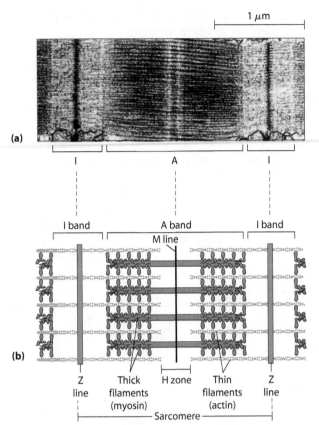

FIGURE 16-12 Appearance of and Nomenclature for Skeletal Muscle. (a) An electron micrograph of a single sarcomere (TEM). **(b)** A schematic diagram that can be used to interpret the repeating pattern of bands in striated muscle in terms of the interdigitation of thick and thin filaments. An A band corresponds to the length of the thick filaments, and an I band represents the portion of the thin filaments that does not overlap with thick filaments. The lighter area in the center of the A band is called the H zone; the line in the middle is known as the M line. The dense zone in the center of each I band is called the Z line. A sarcomere, the basic repeating unit along the myofibril, is the distance between two successive Z lines.

terms related to the appearance of these bands when illuminated with plane-polarized light.)

As illustrated in Figure 16-12b, the lighter region in the middle of each A band is called the **H zone** (from the German word *hell*, meaning "light"). Running down the center of the H zone is the **M line,** which contains *myomesin*, a protein that links myosin filaments together. In the middle of each I band appears a dense **Z line** (from the German word *zwischen*, meaning "between"). The distance from one Z line to the next defines a single sarcomere. A sarcomere is about 2.5–3.0 μm long in the relaxed state but shortens progressively as the muscle contracts.

Sarcomeres Contain Ordered Arrays of Actin, Myosin, and Accessory Proteins

The striated pattern of skeletal muscle and the observed shortening of the sarcomeres during contraction are due to the arrangement of thick and thin filaments in myofibrils. We will therefore look in some detail at both types of

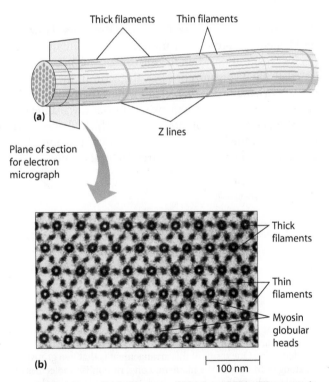

FIGURE 16-11 Arrangement of Thick and Thin Filaments in a Myofibril. (a) A myofibril consists of interdigitated thick and thin filaments. **(b)** The thin filaments are arranged around the thick filaments in a hexagonal pattern, as seen in this cross section of a flight muscle from the fruit fly *Drosophila melanogaster* viewed by high-voltage electron microscopy (HVEM).

filaments and then return to the contraction process in which they play so vital a role.

Thick Filaments. The thick filaments of myofibrils are about 15 nm in diameter and about 1.6 μm long. They lie parallel to one another in the middle of the sarcomere (see Figure 16-12). Each thick filament consists of many molecules of myosin, which are oriented in opposite directions in the two halves of the filament. Each myosin molecule is long and thin, with a molecular weight of about 525,000.

Every thick filament consists of hundreds of myosin molecules organized in a staggered array such that the heads of successive molecules protrude from the thick filament in a repeating pattern, facing away from the center (**Figure 16-13**). Projecting pairs of heads are spaced 14.3 nm apart along the thick filament, with each pair displaced one-third of the way around the filament from the previous pair. These protruding heads can make contact with adjacent thin filaments, forming the cross-bridges between thick and thin filaments that are essential for muscle contraction.

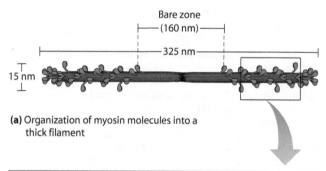

(a) Organization of myosin molecules into a thick filament

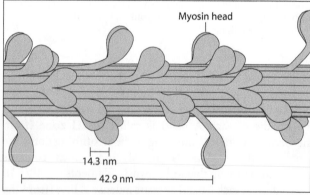

(b) Portion of a thick filament

FIGURE 16-13 The Thick Filament of Skeletal Muscle. (a) The thick filament of the myofibril consists of hundreds of myosin molecules organized in a repeating, staggered array. Only a portion of such a thick filament is shown here. A typical thick filament is about 1.6 μm long and about 15 nm in diameter. Individual myosin molecules are integrated into the filament longitudinally, with their ATPase-containing heads oriented away from the center of the filament. The central region of the filament is therefore a bare zone containing no heads. **(b)** This enlargement of a portion of the thick filament shows that pairs of myosin heads are spaced 14.3 nm apart.

Thin Filaments. The thin filaments of myofibrils interdigitate with the thick filaments. The thin filaments are about 7 nm in diameter and about 1 μm long. Each I band consists of *two* sets of thin filaments, one set on either side of the Z line, with each filament attached to the Z line and extending toward and into the A band in the center of the sarcomere. This accounts for the length of almost 2 μm for I bands in extended muscle.

The structure of thin filaments is shown in **Figure 16-14**. A thin filament consists of at least three proteins. The most important component of thin filaments is F-actin, intertwined with the proteins **tropomyosin** and **troponin**. Tropomyosin is a long, rodlike molecule, similar to the myosin tail, that fits in the groove of the actin helix. Each tropomyosin molecule stretches for about 38.5 nm along the filament and associates along its length with seven actin monomers.

Troponin is actually a complex of three polypeptide chains, called *TnT, TnC,* and *TnI.* TnT binds to tropomyosin and is thought to be responsible for positioning the complex on the tropomyosin molecule. TnC binds calcium ions, and TnI binds to actin. (*Tn* stands for troponin, *T* for tropomyosin, *C* for calcium, and *I* for inhibitory, because TnI inhibits muscle contraction.) One troponin complex is associated with each tropomyosin molecule, so the spacing between successive troponin complexes along the thin filament is 38.5 nm. Troponin and tropomyosin constitute a calcium-sensitive switch that activates contraction in both skeletal and cardiac muscle.

Organization of Muscle Filament Proteins. How can the filamentous proteins of muscle fibers maintain such a precise organization when the microfilaments in other cells are relatively disorganized? First, the actin in the thin filaments is oriented such that all of the plus (barbed) ends are anchored at Z lines. Since myosin II moves toward the plus end of F-actin, this guarantees that the thick filaments will move toward the Z lines. Second, structural proteins play a central role in maintaining the architectural relationships of

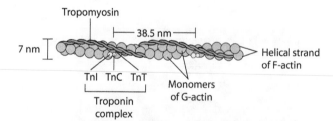

FIGURE 16-14 The Thin Filament of Striated Muscle. Each thin filament is a single strand of F-actin in which the G-actin monomers are staggered and give the appearance of a double-stranded helix. One result of this arrangement is that two grooves run along both sides of the filament. Long, ribbonlike molecules of tropomyosin lie in these grooves. Each tropomyosin molecule consists of two α helices wound about each other to form a ribbon about 2 nm in diameter and 38.5 nm long. Associated with each tropomyosin molecule is a troponin complex consisting of the three polypeptides TnT, TnC, and TnI.

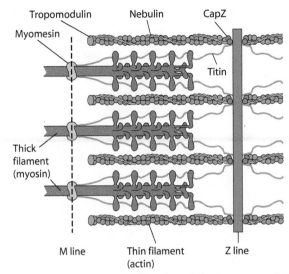

FIGURE 16-15 Structural Proteins of the Sarcomere. The thick and thin filaments require structural support to maintain their precise organization in the sarcomere. The support is provided by two proteins, α-actinin and myomesin, which bundle actin and myosin filaments, respectively. Titin attaches thick filaments to the Z line, thereby maintaining their position within the thin filament array. Nebulin stabilizes the organization of thin filaments. For clarity, tropomyosin is not shown.

muscle proteins (**Figure 16-15**). For instance, *α-actinin* keeps actin filaments bundled into parallel arrays. The capping protein, *CapZ*, maintains the attachment of the barbed (plus) ends of actin filaments to the Z line and simultaneously caps the actin in the thin filaments. At the other end of the thin filaments is *tropomodulin*, which helps to maintain the length and stability of thin filaments by binding their pointed (minus) ends. *Myomesin* is present at the H zone of the thick filament arrays and bundles the myosin molecules composing the arrays. A third structural protein, *titin*, attaches the thick filaments to the Z lines. Titin is highly flexible. During contraction-relaxation cycles, it can keep thick filaments in the correct position relative to thin filaments. This titin scaffolding also keeps the thick and

thin filament arrays from being pulled apart when a muscle is stretched. Another protein, *nebulin*, stabilizes the organization of thin filaments. The protein components involved in muscle contraction are summarized in **Table 16-2**. The contractile process involves the complex interaction of all these proteins.

The Sliding-Filament Model Explains Muscle Contraction

With our understanding of muscle structure, we can now consider what happens during the contraction process. Based on electron microscopic studies, it is clear that the A bands of the myofibrils remain fixed in length during contraction, whereas the I bands shorten progressively and virtually disappear in the fully contracted state. To explain these observations, the **sliding-filament model** illustrated in **Figure 16-16** was proposed in 1954 independently by Andrew Huxley and Rolf Niedergerke and by Hugh Huxley and Jean Hanson. According to this model, muscle contraction is due to thin filaments sliding past thick filaments, with no change in the length of either type of filament. The sliding-filament model not only proved to be correct but was instrumental in focusing attention on the molecular interactions between thick and thin filaments that underlie the sliding process.

As Figure 16-16a indicates, contraction involves the sliding of thin filaments such that they are drawn progressively into the spaces between adjacent thick filaments, overlapping more and more with the thick filaments and narrowing the I band in the process. The result is a shortening of the individual sarcomeres and myofibrils and a contraction of the muscle cell and the whole tissue. This, in turn, causes the movement of the body parts attached to the muscle.

The sliding of the thin and thick filaments past each other as a means of generating force suggests that there should be a relationship between the force generated during contraction and the degree of shortening of the sarcomere. In fact, when the relationship between shortening and

Table 16-2	Major Protein Components of Vertebrate Skeletal Muscle	
Protein	**Molecular Weight**	**Function**
Actin	42,000	Major component of thin filaments
Myosin	510,000	Major component of thick filaments
Tropomyosin	64,000	Binds along the length of thin filaments
Troponin	78,000	Positioned at regular intervals along thin filaments; mediates calcium regulation of contraction
Titin	2,500,000	Links thick filaments to Z line
Nebulin	700,000	Links thin filaments to Z line; stabilizes thin filaments
Myomesin	185,000	Myosin-binding protein present at the M line of thick filaments
α-actinin	190,000	Bundles actin filaments and attaches them to Z line
Ca^{2+} ATPase	115,000	Major protein of sarcoplasmic reticulum (SR); transports Ca^{2+} into SR to relax muscle
CapZ	68,000	Attaches actin filaments to Z line; caps actin
Tropomodulin	41,000	Maintains thin filament length and stability

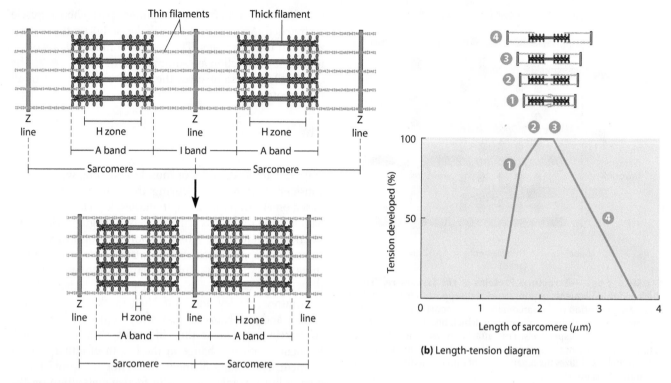

(a) Sliding filament model

(b) Length-tension diagram

FIGURE 16-16 **The Sliding-Filament Model of Muscle Contraction.** **(a)** Two sarcomeres of a myofibril during the contraction process. The extended configuration is shown at the top, while the bottom view represents a more contracted myofibril. A myofibril shortens by the progressive sliding of thick and thin filaments past each other. The result is a greater interdigitation of filaments with no change in length of individual filaments. The increasing overlap of thick and thin filaments leads to a progressive decrease in the length of the I band as interpenetration continues during contraction. **(b)** This graph shows that the amount of tension developed by the sarcomere is proportional to the amount of overlap between the thin filament and the region of the thick filament containing myosin heads. When the sarcomere begins to shorten, as during a muscle contraction, the Z lines move closer together, increasing the amount of overlap between thin and thick filaments. This overlap allows more of the thick filament to interact with the thin filament. Therefore, the muscle can develop more tension (see ❹ to ❸). This proportional relationship continues until the ends of the thin filaments move into the H zone. Here they encounter no further myosin heads, so tension remains constant (❸ to ❷). Any further shortening of the sarcomere results in a dramatic decline in tension (❷ to ❶) as the filaments crowd into one another.

force is measured, it is exactly what the sliding-filament model predicts (Figure 16-16b): The amount of force the muscle can generate during a contraction depends on the number of myosin heads from the thick filament that can make contact with the thin filament. When the sarcomere is stretched, there is relatively little overlap between thin and thick filaments, so the force generated is small. As the sarcomere shortens, the region of overlap increases and the force of contraction increases. Finally, a point is reached at which continued shortening no longer increases the amount of overlap between thin and thick filaments, and the force of contraction stays the same. Any further shortening of the sarcomere results in a dramatic decline in tension as the filaments crowd into one another.

The sliding of thin filaments past thick filaments depends on the elaborate structural features of the sarcomere, and it requires energy. These basic observations raise important questions. First, by what mechanism are the thin filaments pulled progressively into the spaces between thick filaments to cause contraction? Second, how is the energy of ATP used to drive this process? These questions are answered in the next section.

Cross-Bridges Hold Filaments Together, and ATP Powers Their Movement

Cross-Bridge Formation. Regions of overlap between thick and thin filaments, whether extensive (in contracted muscle) or minimal (in relaxed muscle), are always characterized by the presence of transient **cross-bridges.** The cross-bridges are formed from links between the F-actin of the thin filaments and the myosin heads of the thick filaments (**Figure 16-17**). For contraction, the cross-bridges must form and dissociate repeatedly, so that each cycle of cross-bridge formation causes the thin filaments to interdigitate with the thick filaments more and more, thereby shortening the individual sarcomeres and causing the muscle fiber to contract. A given myosin head on the thick filament thus undergoes a cycle of events in which it binds to specific actin subunits on the thin filament, undergoes an energy-requiring change in shape that pulls the thin filament, and then breaks its association with the thin filament and associates with another site farther along the thin filament toward the Z line. Muscle contraction is the net result of the repeated making and breaking of many such

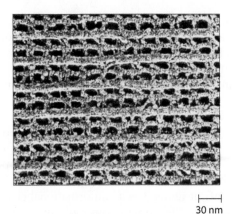

FIGURE 16-17 Cross-Bridges. The cross-bridges between thick and thin filaments formed by the projecting heads of myosin molecules can be readily seen in this high-resolution electron micrograph (TEM).

cross-bridges, with each cycle of cross-bridge formation causing the translocation of a small length of thin filament of a single fibril in a single cell.

ATP and the Contraction Cycle. The driving force for cross-bridge formation is the hydrolysis of ATP, catalyzed by the myosin heads. The requirement for ATP can be demonstrated in vitro because isolated muscle fibers contract in response to added ATP.

The mechanism of muscle contraction is depicted in **Figure 16-18** as a four-step cycle. In the high-energy configuration containing an ADP and a P_i molecule (a hydrolyzed ATP, in effect) shown in step ❶, a specific myosin head binds loosely to the actin filament. The myosin head then proceeds to a more tightly bound configuration that requires the loss of P_i. Step ❷ is the power stroke. The transition of myosin to the more tightly bound

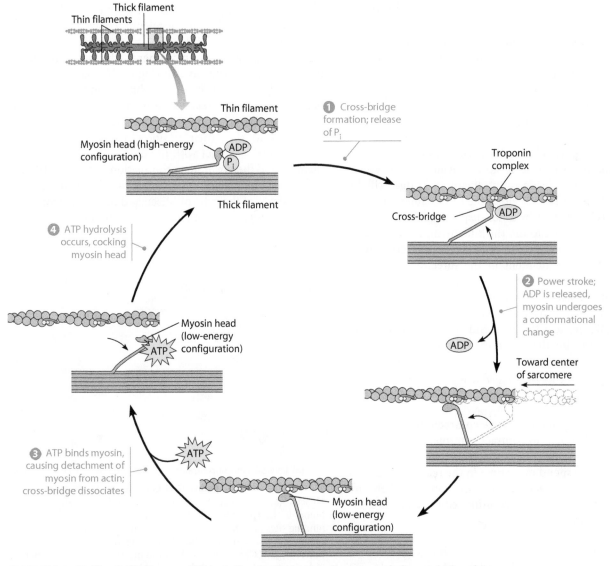

FIGURE 16-18 The Cyclic Process of Muscle Contraction. A small segment of adjacent thick and thin filaments (see the orienting inset at upper left) is used to illustrate the series of events in which the cross-bridge formed by a myosin head draws the thin filament toward the center of the sarcomere, thereby causing the myofibril to contract. Step ❶ shows the cross-bridge configuration of relaxed muscle, whereas the end of step ❷ shows the configuration of a muscle in rigor. A detailed description of all steps is given in the text.

state triggers a conformational change in myosin, which is associated with release of ADP. This conformational change is associated with a movement of the head, causing the thick filament to pull against the thin filament, which then moves with respect to the thick filament.

Cross-bridge dissociation follows in step ❸, as ATP binds to the myosin head in preparation for the next step. The binding of ATP causes the myosin head to change its conformation in a way that weakens its binding to actin. In the absence of adequate ATP, cross-bridge dissociation does not occur, and the muscle becomes locked in a stiff, rigid state called *rigor*. The *rigor mortis* associated with death results from the depletion of ATP and the progressive accumulation of cross-bridges in the configuration shown at the end of step ❷. Note that, once detached, the thick and thin filaments would be free to slip back to their previous positions, but they are held together at all times by the many other cross-bridges along their length at any given moment—just as at least some legs of a millipede are always in contact with the surface it is walking on. In fact, each thick filament has about 350 myosin heads, and each head attaches and detaches about five times per second during rapid contraction, so there are always many cross-bridges intact at any time.

Finally, in step ❹, ATP hydrolysis is used to return the myosin head to the high-energy configuration necessary for the next round of cross-bridge formation and filament sliding. This brings us back to where we started because the myosin head is now activated and ready to form a new cross-bridge. But the new bridge will be formed with actin farther along the thin filament because the first cycle resulted in a net displacement of the thin filament with respect to the thick filament. In succeeding cycles, the particular myosin head shown in Figure 16-18 will draw the thin filament in the direction of further contraction. And what about the direction of contraction? Recall that the actin in thin filaments is uniformly oriented, with plus ends anchored at Z lines. Myosin II always walks toward the *plus* end of the thin filament, thereby establishing the direction of contraction.

The Regulation of Muscle Contraction Depends on Calcium

So far, our description of muscle contraction implies that skeletal muscle ought to contract continuously, as long as there is sufficient ATP. Yet experience tells us that most skeletal muscles spend more time in the relaxed state than in contraction. Contraction and relaxation must therefore be regulated to result in the coordinated movements associated with muscle activity.

The Role of Calcium in Contraction. Regulation of muscle contraction depends on free calcium ions (Ca^{2+}) and on the muscle cell's ability to rapidly raise and lower calcium levels in the cytosol (called the *sarcoplasm* in muscle cells) around the myofibrils. The regulatory proteins *tropomyosin* and *troponin* act in concert to regulate the availability of myosin-binding sites on actin filaments in a way that depends critically on the level of calcium in the sarcoplasm.

To understand how this process works, we must first recognize that the myosin-binding sites on actin are normally blocked by tropomyosin. For myosin to bind to actin and initiate the cross-bridge cycle, the tropomyosin molecule must be moved out of the way. The calcium dependence of muscle contraction is due to troponin C (TnC), which binds calcium ions. When a calcium ion binds to TnC, it undergoes a conformational change that is transmitted to the tropomyosin molecule, causing it to move toward the center of the helical groove of the thin filament, out of the blocking position. The binding sites on actin are then accessible to the myosin heads, allowing contraction to proceed.

Figure 16-19 illustrates how the troponin-tropomyosin complex regulates the interaction between actin and myosin. When the calcium concentration in the sarcoplasm is low (<0.1 μM), tropomyosin blocks the binding sites on the actin filament, effectively preventing their interaction with myosin (Figure 16-19a). As a result, cross-bridge formation is inhibited, and the muscle becomes or remains relaxed. At higher calcium concentrations (>1 μM), calcium binds to TnC, causing tropomyosin molecules to shift their position, which allows myosin heads to make contact with the binding sites on the actin filament and thereby initiate contraction (Figure 16-19b).

When the calcium concentration falls again as it is pumped out of the cytosol (discussed next), the troponin-calcium complex dissociates, and the tropomyosin moves

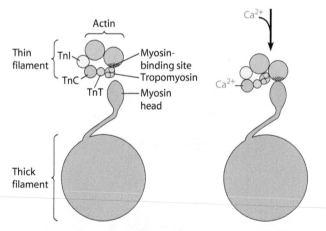

(a) Low calcium concentration   **(b)** High calcium concentration

FIGURE 16-19 Regulation of Contraction in Striated Muscle. **(a)** At low concentrations (<0.1 μM Ca^{2+}), calcium is not bound to the TnC subunit of troponin, and tropomyosin blocks the binding sites on actin, preventing access by myosin and thereby maintaining the muscle in the relaxed state. **(b)** At high concentrations (>1 μM Ca^{2+}), calcium binds to the TnC subunit of troponin, inducing a conformational change that is transmitted to tropomyosin. The tropomyosin molecule moves toward the center of the groove in the thin filament, allowing myosin to gain access to the binding sites on actin and thereby triggering contraction.

back to the blocking position. Myosin binding is therefore inhibited, further cross-bridge formation is prevented, and the contraction cycle ends.

Regulation of Calcium Levels in Skeletal Muscle Cells.

From the previous discussion, we know that muscle contraction is regulated by the concentration of calcium ions in the sarcoplasm. But how is the level of calcium controlled? Think for a moment about what must happen when we move any part of our bodies—when we flex an index finger, for instance. A nerve impulse is generated in the brain and transmitted down the spinal column to the nerve cells, or *motor neurons,* that control a small muscle in the forearm. The motor neurons activate the appropriate muscle cells, which contract and relax, all within about 100 msec. When nerve impulses to the muscle cell cease, calcium levels decline quickly, and the muscle relaxes. Therefore, to understand how muscle contraction is regulated, we need to know how nerve impulses cause calcium levels in the sarcoplasm to change and how these changes affect the contractile machinery. Muscle cells have many specialized features that facilitate a rapid change in the sarcoplasmic concentration of calcium ions and a rapid response of the contractile machinery. We discuss these features next.

Events at the Neuromuscular Junction.

Recall from the signal for a muscle cell to contract is conveyed by a nerve cell in the form of an electrical impulse called an *action potential.* The site where the nerve innervates, or makes contact with, the muscle cell is called the **neuromuscular junction.** At the neuromuscular junction, the axon branches out and forms *axon terminals* that make contact with the muscle cell. These terminals contain the transmitter chemical *acetylcholine,* which is stored in membrane-enclosed vesicles and secreted by axon terminals in response

to an action potential. The area of the muscle cell plasma membrane under the axon terminals is called the *motor end plate.* There, in the plasma membrane (called the *sarcolemma* in muscle cells), clusters of acetylcholine receptors are associated with each axon terminal. When the receptor binds acetylcholine, it opens a pore in the plasma membrane through which sodium ions can flow into the muscle cell. The sodium influx in turn causes a membrane depolarization to be transmitted away from the sarcolemma at the motor end plate.

Transmission of an Impulse to the Interior of the Muscle.

Once a membrane depolarization occurs at the motor end plate, it spreads throughout the sarcolemma via the **transverse (T) tubule system** (**Figure 16-20**), a series of regular inpocketings of the muscle membrane that penetrates the interior of a muscle cell. The T tubules carry action potentials into the muscle cell, and they are part of the reason that muscle cells can respond so quickly to a nerve impulse.

Inside the muscle cell, the T tubule system comes into contact with the **sarcoplasmic reticulum (SR),** a system of intracellular membranes in the form of flattened sacs or tubes. As the name suggests, the SR is similar to the endoplasmic reticulum (ER) found in nonmuscle cells except that it is highly specialized. The SR runs along the myofibrils, where it is poised to release calcium ions directly into the myofibril and cause contraction and then to remove calcium from the myofibril and cause relaxation. This close proximity of the SR to the myofibrils facilitates the rapid response of muscle cells to nerve signals.

SR Function in Calcium Release and Uptake.

The SR can be functionally divided into two components, referred to as the *medial element* and the *terminal cisternae* (singular: *terminal cisterna;* see Figure 16-20). The terminal

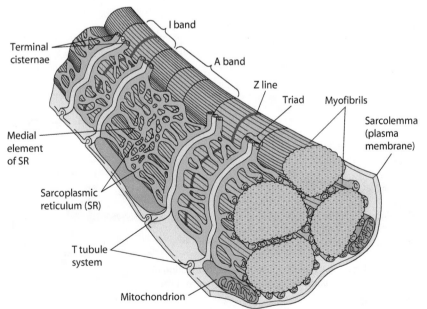

FIGURE 16-20 The Sarcoplasmic Reticulum and the Transverse Tubule System of Skeletal Muscle Cells. The sarcoplasmic reticulum (SR) is an extensive network of specialized ER that accumulates calcium ions and releases them in response to nerve signals. T tubules are invaginations of the sarcolemma (plasma membrane) that relay the membrane potential changes to the interior of the cell. Where the T tubule passes near the terminal cisternae of the SR, a triad structure is formed that appears in electron micrographs as the cross section of three adjacent tubes. The T tubule is in the middle, and on each side is one of the SR terminal cisternae. The triad contains the important junctional complex that regulates the release of calcium ions from the SR.

Labels on figure: I band; Terminal cisternae; A band; Z line; Triad; Myofibrils; Sarcolemma (plasma membrane); Medial element of SR; Sarcoplasmic reticulum (SR); T tubule system; Mitochondrion

cisternae of the SR contain a high concentration of ATP-dependent calcium pumps that continually pump calcium into the lumen of the SR. The ability of the SR to pump calcium ions is crucial for muscle relaxation, but it is also needed for muscle contraction. Calcium pumping produces a high calcium concentration in the lumen of the SR (up to several millimolar). This calcium can then be released from the terminal cisternae of the SR when needed. Figure 16-20 shows how the terminal cisternae of the SR are positioned adjacent to the contractile apparatus of each myofibril. Terminal cisternae are typically found right next to a T tubule, giving rise to a structure called a **triad.** In electron micrographs, a triad appears as three circles in a row. The central circle is the membrane of the T tubule, and the circles on each side are the membranes of the terminal cisternae. Close inspection of the triad reveals that the terminal cisternae appear to be connected to the T tubule by material between the two membranes. This material is referred to as the *junctional complex* (to which we will return shortly).

The proximity of the T tubule, the terminal cisternae of the SR, and the contractile machinery of the myofibril provides the basis for how muscle cells can respond so rapidly to a nerve impulse. The action potential travels from the motor end plate, spreads out over the sarcolemma, and enters the T tubule (**Figure 16-21**). As the action potential travels down the T tubule, it activates voltage-gated calcium channels in the T tubule that are adjacent to ryanodine receptors in the terminal cisternae of the SR, causing them to open. When the ryanodine receptor channels open, calcium rushes into the sarcoplasm immediately adjacent to the myofibrils, causing contraction.

Letting calcium out of the SR causes a muscle cell to contract. For the muscle cell to relax, calcium levels must be brought back down to the resting level. This is accomplished by pumping calcium back into the SR. The membrane of the SR contains an active transport protein, a **calcium ATPase,** which can pump calcium ions from the sarcoplasm into the cisternae of the SR. These pumps are concentrated in the medial element of the SR. The ATP-dependent mechanism by which calcium moves through the pump is similar for the Na^+/K^+ pump.

The pumping of calcium from the sarcoplasm back into the SR cisternae quickly lowers the sarcoplasmic calcium level to the point at which troponin releases calcium, tropomyosin moves back to the blocking position on actin, and further cross-bridge formation is prevented. Cross-bridges therefore disappear rapidly as actin dissociates from myosin and becomes blocked by tropomyosin. This leaves the muscle relaxed and free to be re-extended because the absence of cross-bridge contacts allows the thin filaments to slide out from between the thick filaments, due to passive stretching of the muscle by other tissues.

The Coordinated Contraction of Cardiac Muscle Cells Involves Electrical Coupling

Cardiac (heart) muscle is responsible for the beating of the heart and the pumping of blood through the body's circulatory system. Cardiac muscle functions continuously. In one year, your heart beats about 40 million times! Cardiac muscle is very similar to skeletal muscle in the organization of actin and myosin filaments and has the same striated appearance (**Figure 16-22**). In contrast to skeletal muscle, most of the energy required for the beating of the heart under resting conditions is provided not by blood glucose but by free fatty acids that are transported from adipose (fat storage) tissue to the heart by serum albumin, a blood protein.

1 An action potential moves down the axon of the neuron until it reaches the neuromuscular junction, where synapses exist between the neuron and the muscle cell.

2 Depolarization of the terminals of the axon causes the release of neurotransmitters, which bind acetylcholine receptors on the surface of the muscle cell, initiating depolarization of the muscle cell.

3 The depolarization spreads into the interior via the T tubules, stimulating calcium release via ryanodine receptors in the terminal cisternae of the SR.

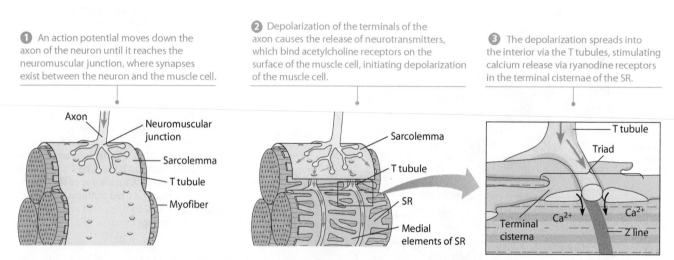

FIGURE 16-21 Stimulation of a Muscle Cell by a Nerve Impulse. The nerve causes a depolarization of the muscle cell, which spreads into the interior via the T tubule system, stimulating calcium release from the terminal cisternae of the sarcoplasmic reticulum (SR).

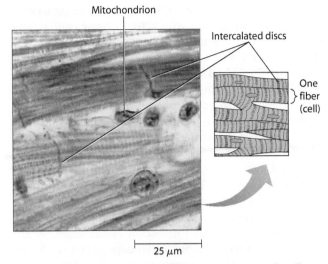

Mitochondrion

Intercalated discs

One fiber (cell)

25 μm

FIGURE 16-22 Cardiac Muscle Cells. Cardiac muscle cells have a contractile mechanism and sarcomeric structure similar to those of skeletal muscle cells. However, unlike skeletal muscle cells, cardiac muscle cells are joined together end to end at intercalated discs, which allow ions and electrical signals to pass from one cell to the next. This ionic permeability enables a contraction stimulus to spread evenly to all the cells of the heart (LM).

VIDEOS www.thecellplace.com *Cardiac muscle contraction*

A second difference between cardiac and skeletal muscle is that heart muscle cells are not multinucleate. Instead, cells are joined end to end through structures called **intercalated discs.** The discs have a high density of desmosomes and gap junctions; the gap junctions electrically couple neighboring cells, allowing depolarization waves to spread throughout the heart during its contraction cycle. The heart is not activated by nerve impulses, as skeletal muscle is, but contracts spontaneously once every second or so. The heart rate is controlled by a "pacemaker" region in an upper portion of the heart (right atrium). The depolarization wave initiated by the pacemaker then spreads to the rest of the heart to produce the heartbeat.

Smooth Muscle Is More Similar to Nonmuscle Cells than to Skeletal Muscle

Smooth muscle is responsible for involuntary contractions such as those of the stomach, intestines, uterus, and blood vessels. In general, such contractions are slow, taking up to five seconds to reach maximum tension. Smooth muscle contractions are also of greater duration than those of skeletal or cardiac muscle. Though smooth muscle is not able to contract rapidly, it is well adapted to maintain tension for long periods of time, as is required in these organs and tissues.

The Structure of Smooth Muscle. Smooth muscle cells are long and thin, with pointed ends. Unlike skeletal or heart muscle, smooth muscle has no striations (**Figure 16-23a**). Smooth muscle cells do not contain Z lines, which are

responsible for the periodic organization of the sarcomeres found in skeletal and cardiac muscle cells. Instead, smooth muscle cells contain *dense bodies,* plaque-like structures in the cytoplasm and on the cell membrane (Figure 16-23b), that contain intermediate filaments. Bundles of actin filaments are anchored at their ends to these dense bodies. As a result, actin filaments appear in a crisscross pattern, aligned obliquely to the long axis of the cell. Cross-bridges connect thick and thin filaments in smooth muscle but not in the regular, repeating pattern seen in skeletal muscle.

Regulation of Contraction in Smooth Muscle Cells. Smooth muscle cell contraction and nonmuscle cell contraction are regulated in a manner distinct from that of skeletal muscle cells. Although skeletal and smooth muscle cells are both stimulated to contract by an increase in the sarcoplasmic concentration of calcium ions, the mechanisms involved are quite different. When sarcoplasmic calcium concentrations increase in smooth muscle and nonmuscle cells, a cascade of events takes place

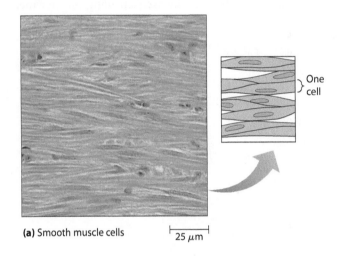

One cell

(a) Smooth muscle cells   25 μm

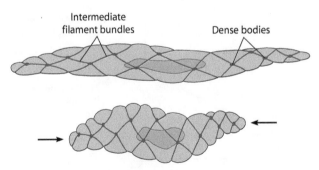

Intermediate filament bundles   Dense bodies

(b) Contraction of smooth muscle cell

FIGURE 16-23 Smooth Muscle and Its Contraction.
(a) Individual smooth muscle cells are long and spindle shaped, with no Z lines or sarcomeric structure (LM). **(b)** In the smooth muscle cell, contractile bundles of actin and myosin appear to be anchored to plaque-like structures called dense bodies. The dense bodies are connected to each other by intermediate filaments, thereby orienting the actin and myosin bundles obliquely to the long axis of the cell. When the actin and myosin bundles contract, they pull on the dense bodies and intermediate filaments, producing the cellular contraction shown here.

that includes the activation of **myosin light-chain kinase (MLCK).** Activated MLCK then phosphorylates one type of myosin light chain known as a **regulatory light chain** (see Figure 16-9, myosin II).

Myosin light-chain phosphorylation affects myosin in two ways. First, some myosin molecules are curled up so that they cannot assemble into filaments. When the myosin light chain is phosphorylated, the myosin tail uncurls and becomes capable of assembly. Second, the phosphorylation of the light chains activates myosin, enabling it to interact with actin filaments to undergo the cross-bridge cycle.

The cascade of events involved in the activation of smooth muscle and nonmuscle myosin is shown in **Figure 16-24a.** In response to a nerve impulse or hormonal signal reaching the smooth muscle cell, an influx of extracellular calcium ions occurs, increasing the intracellular calcium concentration and causing contraction. Elevation of intracellular calcium can activate the protein *calmodulin.* The resulting *calcium-calmodulin complex* can bind to myosin light-chain kinase, activating the enzyme.

As a result, myosin light chains become phosphorylated, and myosin can interact with actin to cause contractions. In addition, the tails of the myosins straighten out and can assemble with other myosin molecules into filaments (Figure 16-24b). As the calcium levels within smooth muscle cells drop again, the MLCK is inactivated, and a second enzyme, *myosin light-chain phosphatase,* removes the phosphate group from the myosin light chain. Since the dephosphorylated myosins can no longer bind to actin, the muscle cell relaxes.

Thus, both skeletal muscle and smooth muscle are activated to contract by calcium ions but from different sources and by different mechanisms. In skeletal muscle, the calcium comes from the sarcoplasmic reticulum. Its effect on actin-myosin interaction is mediated by troponin and is very rapid because it depends on conformational changes only. In smooth muscle, the calcium comes from outside the cell, and its effect is mediated by calmodulin. The effect is much slower in this case because it involves a covalent modification (phosphorylation) of the myosin molecule.

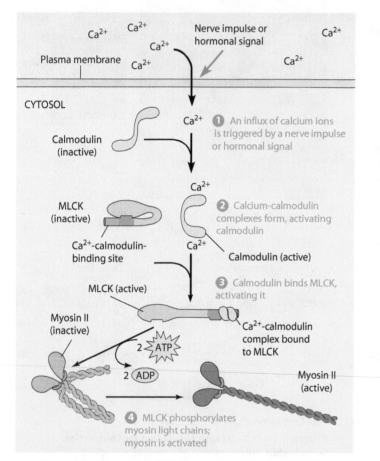

(a) Phosphorylation of myosin II by myosin light-chain kinase (MLCK)

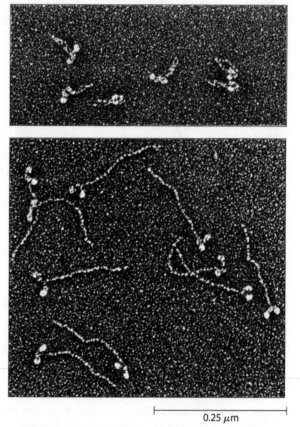

0.25 μm

(b) Curled and uncurled myosin II molecules

FIGURE 16-24 Phosphorylation of Smooth Muscle and Nonmuscle Myosin. (a) The functions of both smooth muscle and nonmuscle myosin II are regulated by phosphorylation of the regulatory light chains. An influx of calcium ions into the cell, triggered by a nerve impulse or a hormonal signal, allows the calcium-calmodulin complex to bind myosin light-chain kinase (MLCK), which in turn phosphorylates the myosin light chains. The activated (and uncurled) myosin can then bind to actin. **(b)** Electron micrographs of curled and uncurled myosin II molecules (TEMs).

Actin-Based Motility in Nonmuscle Cells

Actin and myosin are best known as the major components of the thin and thick filaments of muscle cells. In fact, muscle cells represent only one specialized case of cell movements driven by the interactions of actin and myosin. Actins and myosins have now been discovered in almost all eukaryotic cells and are known to play important roles in various types of nonmuscle motility. One example of actin-dependent, nonmuscle motility occurs during cytokinesis (see Chapter 19). In this section, we examine several other examples.

Cell Migration via Lamellipodia Involves Cycles of Protrusion, Attachment, Translocation, and Detachment

Actin microfilaments (MFs) are required for the movement of most nonmuscle cells in animals. Many nonmuscle cells, such as fibroblasts, the growth cones of neurons, and many embryonic cells in animals, are capable of crawling over a substrate using lamellipodia and/or filopodia, whose internal structure we explored in Chapter 15. (A scanning electron micrograph of a crawling cell in vitro is shown in **Figure 16-25.**) In this section, we will consider such cell crawling in more detail. In a later section, we will

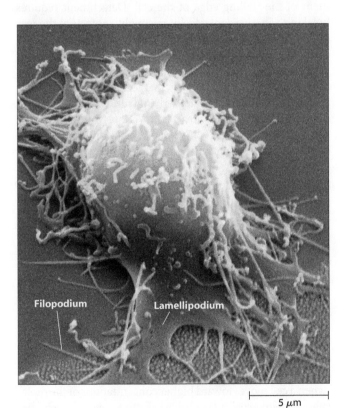

FIGURE 16-25 A Crawling Cell. A mouse fibroblast displays a lamellipodium and numerous filopodia extending from the cell surface (SEM).

VIDEOS www.thecellplace.com *Lamellipodia in cell migration*

consider a specialized form of crawling known as amoeboid movement.

Cell crawling involves several distinct events: (1) extension of a protrusion at the cell's leading edge; (2) attachment of the protrusion to the substrate; and (3) generation of tension, which pulls the cell forward as its "tail" releases its attachments and retracts. These events are summarized in **Figure 16-26.**

Extending Protrusions. To crawl, cells must produce specialized extensions, or *protrusions,* at their front or *leading edge.* One type of protrusion is a thin sheet of cytoplasm called a **lamellipodium** (plural: **lamellipodia**). Another type of protrusion is a thin, pointed structure known as a **filopodium** (plural: **filopodia**). Crawling cells often exhibit interconversion of these two types of protrusions as they migrate.

Fundamental to the dynamics of protrusions is the phenomenon of **retrograde flow** of F-actin. During normal retrograde flow, there is bulk movement of microfilaments toward the rear of the protrusion as it extends. Retrograde flow appears to result from two simultaneous processes: *actin assembly* at the tip of the growing lamellipodium or filopodium and *rearward translocation* of actin filaments toward the base of the protrusion. In a typical cell, forward assembly and rearward translocation balance one another; as one or the other occurs, a protrusion can be extended or retracted.

Actin polymerization, especially in lamellipodia, is driven by Arp2/3-dependent dendritic branching, a process we examined in some detail in Chapter 15. As actin polymerizes at the tip of a protrusion, the protrusion pushes forward. At the same time that extension of the tip of a protrusion is occurring, the polymerized actin is drawn toward the base of the protrusion, where it is disassembled. Released actin monomers are then available for addition to the barbed ends of new or growing microfilaments as the cell continues to crawl forward.

Microtubules are also involved in the polarized production of protrusions. Although how MTs are involved is not entirely clear, in cultured cells MTs can be seen polymerizing near the leading edge. Moreover, treating some cells with MT depolymerizing agents causes them to lose their polarized appearance, and they make protrusions simultaneously all around their perimeter.

Cell Attachment. If cells only polymerized actin at the tips of protrusions, pulled it rearward, and then depolymerized it, they would not be able to move. Something must couple retrograde flow to forward movement of the cell as a whole. Attachment, or adhesion of the cell to its substrate, is also necessary for cell crawling. New sites of attachment must be formed at the front of a cell, and contacts at the rear must be broken. Attachment sites between the cell and the substrate are complex structures involving the attachment of transmembrane proteins to other proteins both outside and inside the cell. One family of such

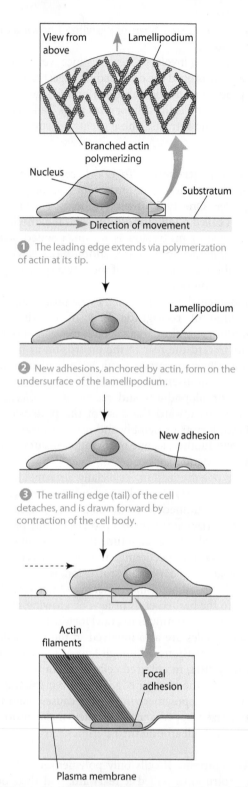

1 The leading edge extends via polymerization of actin at its tip.

2 New adhesions, anchored by actin, form on the undersurface of the lamellipodium.

3 The trailing edge (tail) of the cell detaches, and is drawn forward by contraction of the cell body.

FIGURE 16-26 The Steps of Cell Crawling. Several different processes are involved in cell crawling, including cell protrusion, attachment, and contractile activities. Protrusion is accompanied by Arp2/3-dependent actin polymerization at the leading edge. Attachment connects actin to the cell surface, typically via integrins, which cluster at focal adhesions.

attachment proteins is the *integrins*. On the outside of the cell, integrins attach to extracellular matrix proteins. Inside the cell, integrins are connected to actin filaments through

linker proteins. Such integrin-dependent attachments are known as *focal contacts* and are crucial for cell migration.

How firmly a cell is attached to the underlying substrate helps to determine whether a cell will move forward. In this sense, actin polymerization at the leading edge is analogous to a car with its transmission in neutral. Once the car is shifted into a forward gear, it rapidly moves forward. In the same way, firm attachment of the leading edge shifts the balance in favor of forward movement.

Translocation and Detachment. Cell crawling coordinates protrusion formation and attachment with forward movement of the entire cell body. Contraction of the rear of the cell squeezes the cell body forward and releases the cell from attachments at its rear. Evidence suggests that contraction is due to interactions between actin and myosins, and that contraction is under the control of the protein Rho. Rho is thought to regulate activation of nonmuscle myosin II, which is localized toward the rear of the cell. In mutant cells from the cellular slime mold *Dictyostelium* that lack myosin II, the ability of the trailing edge of the cell to retract is reduced. Similarly, when Rho activity is impaired in migrating monocytes, they are unable to withdraw attachments at their rear and contract their trailing edge. These and other results support the idea that Rho and myosin II are involved in tail retraction.

Contraction of the cell body must be linked to detachment of the trailing edge of the cell. Detachment requires breaking adhesive contacts. Interestingly, contacts at the rear of the cell are sometimes too tight to be detached, and the tail of the cell actually breaks off as the cell pulls the rear forward (see Figure 16-26). In general, how firmly a cell attaches to a substrate affects how quickly that cell can crawl. If cells adhere too tightly to the underlying substrate, they cannot dynamically make and break connections to the substrate, and motility is actually impeded. Thus for movement to occur, new attachments must be balanced by loss of old ones.

Chemotaxis Is a Directional Movement in Response to a Graded Chemical Stimulus

A key feature of migrating cells in the body and in embryos is *directional* migration. One way that directional migration occurs is through the formation of protrusions predominantly on one side of the cell. In this case, cells must be able to regulate not only whether they form protrusions but where they form them. Diffusible molecules can act as important cues for such directional migration. When a migrating cell moves toward a greater or lesser concentration of a diffusible chemical, the response is known as **chemotaxis.** The molecule(s) that elicit this response are called *chemoattractants* (when a cell moves toward higher concentrations of the molecule) or *chemorepellants* (when a cell moves away from higher concentrations of the molecule). In eukaryotes, chemotaxis has been studied most intensively in white blood cells and in the *Dictyostelium* amoeba. In both cases, increasing the local concentration of a chemoattractant (small peptides in the case of white blood cells and cyclic AMP in the case of *Dictyostelium*) results in dramatic changes in the actin cytoskeleton, including biochemical changes in actin-binding proteins and migration of the cell toward the source of chemoattractant. These changes occur through local activation of chemoattractant (or repellant) receptors on the cell surface. These receptors are G protein–linked receptors. Activation of these receptors leads to local accumulation of phosphoinositides (see Chapter 15), which in turn is thought to result in polarized recruitment of the cell's cytoskeletal machinery to form a protrusion in the direction of migration.

Amoeboid Movement Involves Cycles of Gelation and Solation of the Actin Cytoskeleton

Amoebas and white blood cells exhibit a type of crawling movement referred to as **amoeboid movement** (**Figure 16-27**). This type of movement is accompanied by protrusions of the cytosol called **pseudopodia** (singular: **pseudopodium,** from the Greek for "false foot"). Cells that undergo amoeboid movement have an outer layer of thick, gelatinous, actin-rich cytosol ("gel") and an inner, more fluid layer of cytosol ("sol"). In an amoeba, for example, as a pseudopodium is extended, more fluid material streams forward in the direction of extension and congeals at the tip of the pseudopodium (this event is often called gelation). Meanwhile, at the rear of the moving cell, gelatinous cytosol changes into a more fluid state and streams toward the pseudopodium (solation). Proteins such as gelsolin that are present within these gels may be activated by calcium to convert the gel to a more fluid state. Experiments have shown that the forward streaming in the pseudopodium does not require squeezing from the rear of the cell: When a pseudopodium's cell membrane is removed using detergent, the remaining components can still stream forward if the

appropriate mixture of ions and other chemicals is added. Pressure exerted on the endoplasm, possibly due to contraction of an actomyosin network in the trailing edge of the cell, may also squeeze the endoplasm forward, aiding formation of a protrusion at the leading edge.

Actin-Based Motors Move Components Within the Cytoplasm of Some Cells

Cytoplasmic streaming, an actomyosin-dependent movement of the cytosol within a cell, is seen in a variety of organisms that do not display amoeboid movement. In slime molds such as *Physarum polycephalum,* for example, cytosol streams back and forth in the branched network that constitutes the cell mass.

Many plant cells display a circular flow of cell contents around a central vacuole. This streaming process, called *cyclosis,* has been studied most extensively in the giant algal cell *Nitella.* In this case, the movement seems to circulate and mix cell contents (**Figure 16-28a**). Cytoplasmic streaming requires actin filaments, as it is inhibited in cells treated with cytochalasin. In *Nitella,* a dense set of aligned microfilaments are found near sites where cyclosis occurs (Figure 16-28b). Cyclosis involves specific myosins that provide the force for movement of components within the

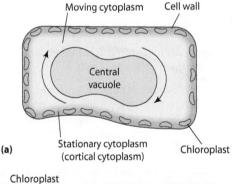

(a)

(b)　　　　　　　　　　　10 μm

FIGURE 16-28 Cytoplasmic Streaming. (**a**) Cyclosis in an algal cell. The cytoplasm moves in a circular path around a central vacuole, driven by myosin motors that interact with actin anchored to chloroplasts near the cell wall. (**b**) Chloroplasts and actin filaments in an algal cell. Actin filaments are arranged in parallel tracks (SEM).

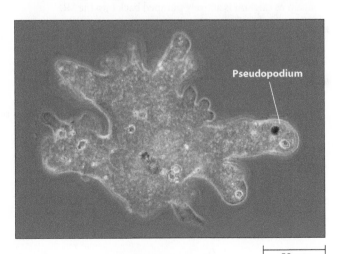

50 μm

FIGURE 16-27 Amoeboid Movement. A micrograph of *Amoeba proteus,* a protozoan that moves by extension of pseudopodia (LM).

VIDEOS www.thecellplace.com *A crawling amoeba*

VIDEOS www.thecellplace.com *Cytoplasmic streaming*

cytosol. When latex beads coated with various types of myosin are added to *Nitella* cells that have been broken open, the beads move along the actin filaments in an ATP-dependent manner in the same direction as normal organelle movement.

In animal cells, myosins may also be involved in vesicular transport. For example, by carefully observing vesicles from the cytoplasm of squid giant axons in vitro, it is clear that individual vesicles can jump from microtubules to microfilaments. This means that the vesicles have both MT motors, such as kinesins, and myosins attached to their surfaces. Myosin V may be particularly important for such actin-based vesicle movement. Myosin V may be able to physically interact with kinesins on the surface of such vesicles, and myosin V has been shown to interact with the plus ends of MTs, making it well suited to such a "handoff" between MTs and MF-based vesicle trafficking. A human disorder called *Griscelli's disease,* which involves partial albinism and neurological defects, has been shown to result from a mutation in this class of myosins.

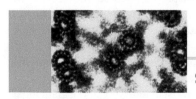

SUMMARY OF KEY POINTS

Motile Systems

- Cell motility and intracellular movements of cellular components are driven by motor proteins, which couple ATP hydrolysis to movements along microtubules (MTs) or microfilaments (MFs). ATP hydrolysis is coupled to conformational changes in the motor that allow the motor to move along a cytoskeletal element.

Microtubule-Based Movement

- Kinesins generally move toward the plus ends of MTs; dyneins move toward the minus ends.

- There are many families of kinesins, which can act as highly processive motors, moving great distances along MTs. One major function for kinesins is moving intracellular cargo. Kinesins connect to adapter proteins and/or their cargo mainly via their light chains.

- There are relatively few dyneins, which fall into two basic classes: cytoplasmic and axonemal. Cytoplasmic dyneins bind to the dynactin complex, which serves as an adapter between dyneins and their cargo.

- MT motors are important for the shaping and transport of the endomembrane system within cells and for intraflagellar transport.

- Axonemal dyneins mediate the bending of cilia and eukaryotic flagella. Dynein arms project out from one MT doublet to the next and slide one set of microtubules past the next. The nine outer doublets of the axoneme are connected laterally to one another and radially to the central pair of single MTs. These connections allow the sliding movement powered by dynein to be converted into bending of the cilium or flagellum.

Microfilament-Based Movement

- There are many families of myosins, and many of them move toward the plus ends of MFs. The best studied is myosin II, one form of which is found in skeletal muscle. Other myosins are involved in events as diverse as cytokinesis, vesicular trafficking, and endocytosis.

- Skeletal muscle contraction involves progressive sliding of thin filaments that contain actin past thick myosin filaments, driven by the interaction between the ATPase head of the myosins and successive myosin-binding sites on actin filaments. Contraction is triggered by the release of calcium from the sarcoplasmic reticulum (SR), which binds troponin, causing a conformational change in tropomyosin that in turn opens myosin-binding sites on the thin filament. Contraction ceases again as calcium is actively pumped back into the SR.

- In smooth muscle, the effect of calcium is mediated by calmodulin, which activates myosin light-chain kinase, leading to the phosphorylation of myosin.

- Actin and myosin are involved in various sorts of motility, including cell crawling, amoeboid movement, cytoplasmic streaming, and cytokinesis. In crawling cells, polymerization of actin extends cellular protrusions; attachment of the protrusions to the substrate and contraction of the cell drive forward movement.

MAKING CONNECTIONS

In Chapter 15 we saw how cytoskeletal polymers assemble and disassemble under tight control. In this chapter, we have examined how motor proteins move along these polymers. To accomplish cell movement, cells use cytoskeletal motor proteins. Like other mechanoenzymes we examined, such as the F1 subunit of the mitochondrial ATP synthase, eukaryotic motility is driven by a set of motor molecules (dyneins and kinesin in the case of microtubules, myosin in the case of actin) that also act as mechanoenzymes. In this case, movement is coupled to ATP hydrolysis. Cytoskeletal motors move intracellular components, such as the vesicles and endomembrane system we examined in Chapter 12, along cytoskeletal elements. Cell movements are also mediated by cytoskeletal motors. Indeed, motility is a major theme in cell biology.

In the case of smooth muscle and chemotaxis, we saw that such events are tightly controlled by cell signaling. In the case of skeletal muscle, movement is controlled by neuronal activity. Efficient cell movement requires cells to be attached to one another or the extracellular matrix, the topic of the next chapter.

PROBLEM SET

More challenging problems are marked with a •.

16-1 Kartegener's Triad. Sterility in human males with Kartegener's triad is due to nonmotile sperm. Upon cytological examination, the sperm of such individuals are found to have tails (that is, flagella) that lack one or more of the normal structural components. Such individuals are also likely to have histories of respiratory tract disease, especially recurrent bronchitis and sinusitis, caused by an inability to clear mucus from the lungs and sinuses.

(a) What is a likely mechanistic explanation for nonmotility of sperm in such cases of sterility?

(b) Why is respiratory tract disease linked with sterility in affected individuals?

16-2 A Moving Experience. For each of the following statements, indicate whether it is true of the motility system that you use to lift your arm (A), to cause your heart to beat (H), to move ingested food through your intestine (I), or to sweep mucus and debris out of your respiratory tract (R). More than one response may be appropriate in some cases.

(a) It depends on muscles that have a striated appearance when examined with an electron microscope.

(b) It would probably be affected by the same drugs that inhibit motility of a flagellated protozoan.

(c) It requires ATP.

(d) It involves calmodulin-mediated calcium signaling.

(e) It involves interaction between actin and myosin filaments.

(f) It depends heavily on fatty acid oxidation for energy.

(g) It is under the control of the voluntary nervous system.

16-3 Muscle Structure. Frog skeletal muscle consists of thick filaments that are about 1.6 μm long and thin filaments about 1 μm long.

(a) What is the length of the A band and the I band in a muscle with a sarcomere length of 3.2 μm? Describe what happens to the length of both bands as the sarcomere length decreases during contraction from 3.2 to 2.0 μm.

(b) The H zone is a specific portion of the A band. If the H zone of each A band decreases in length from 1.2 to 0 μm as the sarcomere length contracts from 3.2 to 2.0 μm, what can you deduce about the physical meaning of the H zone?

(c) What can you say about the distance from the Z line to the edge of the H zone during contraction?

16-4 Rigor Mortis and the Contraction Cycle. At death, the muscles of the body become very stiff and inextensible, and the corpse is said to go into rigor.

(a) Explain the basis of rigor. Where in the contraction cycle is the muscle arrested? Why?

(b) Would you be likely to go into rigor faster if you were to die while racing to class or while sitting in lecture? Explain.

(c) What effect do you think the addition of ATP might have on muscles in rigor?

• **16-5 AMPPNP and the Contraction Cycle.** AMPPNP is the abbreviation for a structural analogue of ATP in which the third phosphate group is linked to the second by a CH_2 group instead of an oxygen atom. AMPPNP binds to the ATP-binding site of virtually all ATPases, including myosin. It differs from ATP, however, in that its terminal phosphate cannot be removed by hydrolysis. When isolated myofibrils are placed in a flask containing a solution of calcium ions and AMPPNP, contraction is quickly arrested.

(a) Where in the contraction cycle will contraction be arrested by AMPPNP? Draw the arrangement of the thin filament, the thick filament, and a cross-bridge in the arrested configuration.

(b) Do you think contraction would resume if ATP were added to the flask containing the AMPPNP-arrested myofibrils? Explain.

(c) What other processes in a muscle cell do you think are likely to be inhibited by AMPPNP?

16-6 Pulled in Two Directions. The following questions deal with the arrangement of actin and myosin in contractile structures.

(a) In skeletal muscle sarcomeres, the H zone is in the middle and bounded on each side by a Z line. During contraction, the Z lines on either side move in opposite directions toward the H zone. Myosin, however, can crawl along an actin filament in only one direction. How can you reconcile movements of Z lines in opposite directions with the unidirectional movement of myosin along an actin filament?

(b) Stress fibers of nonmuscle cells contain contractile bundles of actin and myosin II. For stress fibers to contract or develop tension, how would actin and myosin have to be oriented within the stress fibers?

16-7 Nervous Twitching. Recent military conflicts have involved discussions of "weapons of mass destruction," including nerve gas. One such nerve gas contains the chemical sarin. Sarin inhibits reuptake of the neurotransmitter acetylcholine. What effect would you expect sarin to have on muscle function in individuals exposed to the nerve gas, and why? In your answer, discuss in detail how sarin would be expected to affect the neuromuscular junction, and how it would affect signaling and cytoskeletal events within affected muscle cells.

• 16-8 Tipped Off. Polarized cytoskeletal structures and intraflagellar transport (IFT) are involved in formation of cilia and flagella.

(a) Observation of flagella in the biflagellate alga, *Chlamydomonas reinhardtii*, indicates that particles move toward the tips of flagella at a rate of 2.5 μm/min., but the particles moving back toward the base of flagella move at 4 μm/min. How do you explain this difference in rate of movement?

(b) Temperature-sensitive mutations in a kinesin II required for intraflagellar transport (IFT) have been identified in *Chlamydomonas*. Such mutations only lead to defects when the temperature is raised above a certain threshold, called the *restrictive temperature*. When algae with fully formed flagella are grown at the restrictive temperature, their flagella degenerate. What can you conclude about the necessity of IFT from this experiment?

(c) Based on your knowledge of the directionality of microtubule motors and the information in (b), where would you predict that the plus ends of flagellar microtubules are? State your reasoning.

16-9 AMPPNP Again. AMPPNP can be used to study microtubule (MT) motors as well as myosins.

(a) What effects would you predict on a sperm flagellum to which AMPPNP was added? In your explanation, please be specific about what molecule's function would be inhibited and what the effect on overall flagellar function would be.

(b) When researchers incubated purified vesicles, nerve cytosol from squid giant axons, and MTs in the presence of AMPPNP, the vesicles bound tightly to the microtubules but did not move. Scientists then used AMPPNP to promote its tight binding to MTs, and the MTs with bound proteins were collected by centrifugation. The main protein purified in this way promotes movement of vesicles away from the cell body, where the nucleus resides. What was this protein?

SUGGESTED READING

References of historical importance are marked with a •.

General References

Bray, D. *Cell Movements: From Molecules to Motility*, 2nd ed. New York: Garland, 2001.

Vale, R. D. The molecular motor toolbox for intracellular transport. *Cell* 112 (2003): 467–480.

Microtubule-Based Motility

Gennerich, A., and R. D. Vale. Walking the walk: How kinesin and dynein coordinate their steps. *Curr. Opin. Cell Biol.* 21 (2009): 59.

Hirokawa, N., Y. Noda, Y. Tanaka, and S. Niwa. Kinesin superfamily motor proteins and intracellular transport. *Nature Rev. Mol. Cell Biol.* 10 (2009): 682.

Hook, P., and R. B. Vallee. The dynein family at a glance. *J. Cell Sci.* 119 (2006): 4369.

Cilia and Flagella

Brokaw, C. J. Thinking about flagellar oscillation. *Cell Motil. Cytoskeleton* 66 (2009): 425.

• Brokaw, C. J., D. J. L. Luck, and B. Huang. Analysis of the movement of *Chlamydomonas* flagella: The function of the radial-spoke system is revealed by comparison of wild-type and mutant flagella. *J. Cell Biol.* 92 (1982): 722.

• Goodenough, U. W., and J. E. Heuser. Substructure of the outer dynein arm. *J. Cell Biol.* 95 (1982): 795.

• Grigg, G. Discovery of the 9 + 2 subfibrillar structure of flagella/cilia. *BioEssays* 13 (1991): 363.

Nicastro, D. et al. The molecular architecture of axonemes revealed by cryoelectron tomography. *Science* 313 (2006): 944.

Silverman, M. A., and M. R. Leroux. Intraflagellar transport and the generation of dynamic, structurally and functionally diverse cilia. *Trends Cell Biol.* 19 (2009): 306.

Filament-Based Movement in Muscle

Geeves, M. A., and K. C. Holmes. The molecular mechanism of muscle contraction. *Adv. Protein Chem.* 71 (2005): 161.

• Huxley, A. F. *Reflections on Muscle*. Princeton, NJ: Princeton University Press, 1980.

• Huxley, H. E. The mechanism of muscular contraction. *Science* 164 (1969): 1356.

• Maruyama, K. Birth of the sliding filament concept in muscle contraction. *J. Biochem.* 117 (1995): 1.

Rossi, D., V. Barone, E. Giacomello, V. Cusimano, and V. Sorrentino. The sarcoplasmic reticulum: An organized patchwork of specialized domains. *Traffic* 9 (2008): 1044.

Spudich, J. A. The myosin swinging cross-bridge model. *Nature Rev. Mol. Cell Biol.* 2 (2001): 387.

Squire, J. M., H. A. Al-Khayat, C. Knupp, and P. K. Luther. Molecular architecture in muscle contractile assemblies. *Adv. Protein Chem.* 71 (2005): 17.

Nonmuscle Microfilament-Based Movement

Gillespie, P. G., and U. Müller. Mechanotransduction by hair cells: Models, molecules, and mechanisms. *Cell* 139 (2009): 33.

Hodge, T., and M. J. Cope. A myosin family tree. *J. Cell Sci.* (2000) 113: 3353.

Kay, R. R., P. Langridge, D. Traynor, and O. Hoeller. Changing directions in the study of chemotaxis. *Nature Rev. Mol. Cell Biol.* 9 (2008): 455.

Le Clainche, C., and M. F. Carlier. Regulation of actin assembly associated with protrusion and adhesion in cell migration. *Physiol. Rev.* 88 (2008): 489–513.

Ridley, A. J. et al. Cell migration: Integrating signals from front to back. *Science* 302 (2003): 1704.

• Taylor, D. L., and J. S. Condeelis. Cytoplasmic structure and contractility in amoeboid cells. *Int. Rev. Cytol.* 56 (1979): 57.

Vicente-Manzanares, M., X. Ma, R. S. Adelstein, and A. R. Horwitz. Non-muscle myosin II takes centre stage in cell adhesion and migration. *Nature Rev. Mol. Cell Biol.* 10 (2009): 778.

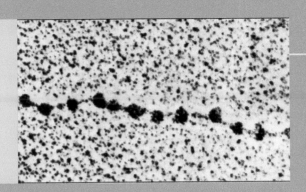

18

The Structural Basis of Cellular Information: DNA, Chromosomes, and the Nucleus

mplicit in our earlier discussions of cellular structure and function has been a sense of predictability, order, and control. We have come to expect that organelles and other cellular structures will have a predictable appearance and function, that metabolic pathways will proceed in an orderly fashion in specific intracellular locations, and that all of a cell's activities will be carried out in a carefully controlled, highly efficient, and heritable manner.

Such expectations express our confidence that cells possess a set of "instructions" that specify their structure, dictate their functions, and regulate their activities and that these instructions can be passed on faithfully to daughter cells. More than a hundred years ago, the Augustinian monk Gregor Mendel worked out rules accounting for the inheritance patterns he observed in pea plants, although he had little inkling of the cellular or molecular basis for these rules. These studies led Mendel to conclude that hereditary information is transmitted in the form of distinct units that we now call **genes.** *We also now know that genes consist of DNA sequences that code for functional products that are usually protein chains but may in some cases be RNA molecules that do not code for proteins.*

Figure 18-1 *presents a preview of how DNA carries out its instructional role in cells and, at the same time, provides a framework for describing how this set of chapters on information flow is organized. The figure highlights the fact that the information carried by DNA flows both between generations of cells and within each individual cell. During the first of these two processes (Figure 18-1a), the information stored in a cell's DNA molecules undergoes replication, generating two DNA copies that are distributed to the daughter cells when the cell divides. The initial three chapters in this section focus on the structures and events associated with this aspect of information flow. The present chapter covers the structural organization of DNA and the chromosomes in which it is packaged; it also discusses the nucleus, which is the organelle that houses the chromosomes*

of eukaryotic cells. Chapter 19 then discusses DNA replication and cell division, Considers the cellular and molecular events associated with information flow between generations of sexually reproducing organisms (including Mendel's work and its chromosomal basis).

Figure 18-1b summarizes how information residing in DNA is used within a cell. Instructions stored in DNA are transmitted in a two-stage process called transcription *and* translation. *During transcription, RNA is synthesized in an enzymatic reaction that copies information from DNA. During translation, the base sequences of the resulting messenger RNA molecules are used to determine the amino acid sequences of proteins.* Thus, the information initially stored in DNA base sequences is ultimately used to code for the synthesis of specific protein molecules. *It is the particular proteins synthesized by a cell that ultimately determine most of a cell's structural features as well as the functions it performs. Transcription and translation, which together constitute the expression of genetic information, are the subjects of Chapters 21–22.*

We open this chapter by describing the discovery of DNA, the molecule whose informational role lies at the heart of this group of six chapters.

Chemical Nature of the Genetic Material

When Mendel first postulated the existence of genes, he did not know the identity of the molecule that allows them to store and transmit inherited information. But a few years later, this molecule was unwittingly discovered by Johann Friedrich Miescher, a Swiss physician. Miescher reported the discovery of the substance now known as DNA in 1869, just a few years before the cell biologist Walther Flemming first observed chromosomes as he studied dividing cells under the microscope.

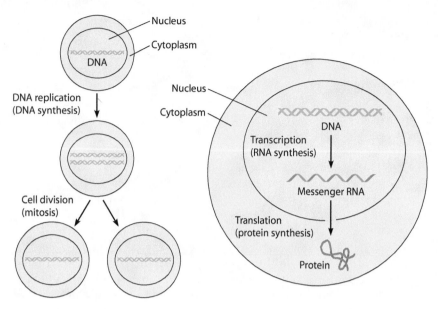

FIGURE 18-1 **The Flow of Information in Cells.** The diagrams here feature eukaryotic cells, but DNA replication, cell division, transcription, and translation are processes that occur in prokaryotic cells as well. **(a)** Genetic information encoded in DNA molecules is passed on to successive generations of cells by DNA replication and cell division (in eukaryotic cells, by means of mitosis). The DNA is first duplicated and then divided equally between the two daughter cells. In this way, each daughter cell is assured of having the same genetic information as the cell from which it arose. **(b)** Within each cell, genetic information encoded in the DNA is expressed through the processes of transcription (RNA synthesis) and translation (protein synthesis). Transcription involves the use of selected segments of DNA as templates for the synthesis of messenger RNA and other RNA molecules. Translation is the process whereby amino acids are joined together in a sequence dictated by the sequence of nucleotides in messenger RNA.

(a) The flow of genetic information between generations of cells

(b) The flow of genetic information within a cell: the expression of genetic information

Miescher's Discovery of DNA Led to Conflicting Proposals Concerning the Chemical Nature of Genes

Miescher was interested in studying the chemistry of the nucleus, which most scientists guessed was the site of the cell's genetic material. In his initial experiments, Miescher isolated nuclei from white blood cells obtained from pus found on surgical bandages. Extracting these nuclei with alkali led to the discovery of a novel substance that he called "nuclein," though we now know it to have been largely DNA. Miescher then went on to study DNA from a more pleasant source, salmon sperm. Fish sperm may seem a somewhat unusual source material until we realize that the nucleus accounts for more than 90% of the mass of a typical sperm cell and therefore that DNA accounts for most of the mass of sperm cells. For this reason, Miescher initially believed that DNA is involved in the transmission of hereditary information. He soon rejected this idea, however, because his crude measuring techniques incorrectly suggested that egg cells contain much more DNA than sperm cells do. Reasoning that the sperm and egg must contribute roughly equal amounts of hereditary information to the offspring, it seemed to him that DNA could not be carrying hereditary information.

Although Miescher was led astray concerning the role of DNA, in the early 1880s a botanist named Eduard Zacharias reported that extracting DNA from cells causes the staining of the chromosomes to disappear. Since evidence was already beginning to suggest a role for chromosomes in transmitting hereditary information, Zacharias and others inferred that DNA is the genetic material. This view prevailed until the early 1900s, when incorrectly interpreted staining experiments led to the false conclusion that the amount of

DNA changes dramatically within cells. Because cells would be expected to maintain a constant amount of the substance that stores their hereditary instructions, these mistaken observations led to a repudiation of the idea that DNA carries genetic information.

As a result, from around 1910 to the 1940s, most scientists believed that genes were made of protein rather than DNA. The chemical building blocks of both proteins and nucleic acids had been identified by the early 1900s, and proteins were perceived to be more complex and hence more likely to store genetic information. It was argued that proteins are constructed from 20 different amino acids that can be assembled in a vast number of combinations, thereby generating the sequence diversity and complexity expected of a molecule that stores and transmits genetic information. In contrast, DNA was widely perceived to be a simple polymer consisting of the same sequence of four bases (e.g., the tetranucleotide–ATCG–) repeated over and over, thereby lacking the variability expected of a genetic molecule. Such a simple polymer was thought to serve merely as a structural support for the genes, which were in turn made of protein. This view prevailed until two lines of evidence resolved the matter in favor of DNA as the genetic material, as we describe next.

Avery Showed That DNA Is the Genetic Material of Bacteria

A great surprise was in store for biologists who were studying protein molecules to determine how genetic information is stored and transmitted. The background was provided in 1928 by the British physician Frederick Griffith, who was studying a pathogenic strain of a bacterium, then called "pneumococcus," that causes a fatal pneumonia in animals. Griffith discovered that this bacterium (now called *Streptococcus pneumoniae*) exists in two forms called the *S strain* and the *R strain*. When grown on a solid agar medium, the S strain produces colonies that are smooth and shiny because of the mucous, polysaccharide coat each cell secretes, whereas the R strain lacks the ability to manufacture a mucous coat and therefore produces colonies exhibiting a rough boundary.

When injected into mice, S-strain (but not R-strain) bacteria trigger a fatal pneumonia. The S strain's ability to cause disease is directly related to the presence of its polysaccharide coat, which protects the bacterial cell from attack by the mouse's immune system. One of Griffith's most intriguing discoveries, however, was that pneumonia can also be induced by injecting animals with a mixture of live R-strain bacteria and dead S-strain bacteria (**Figure 18-2**). This finding was surprising because neither live R-strain nor dead S-strain organisms cause pneumonia if injected alone. When Griffith autopsied the animals that had been injected with the mixture of live R-strain and dead S-strain bacteria, he found them teeming with live S-strain bacteria. Since the animals had not been injected with any live S-strain cells, he concluded that the nonpathogenic R bacteria were somehow converted into pathogenic S bacteria by a substance present in the heat-killed S bacteria that had been co-injected. He called this phenomenon **genetic transformation** and referred to the active (though still unknown) substance in the S cells as the "transforming principle."

Griffith's discoveries set the stage for 14 years of work by Oswald Avery and his colleagues at the Rockefeller Institute in New York. These researchers pursued the investigation of bacterial transformation to its logical conclusion by asking which component of the heat-killed S bacteria was actually responsible for the transforming activity. They fractionated cell-free extracts of S-strain bacteria and found that only the nucleic acid fraction was capable of causing transformation. Moreover, the activity was specifically eliminated by treatment with deoxyribonuclease, an enzyme that degrades DNA. This and other evidence convinced them that the transforming substance of pneumococcus was DNA—a conclusion published by Avery, Colin MacLeod, and Maclyn McCarty in 1944.

It was the first rigorously documented assertion that DNA can carry genetic information. But despite the rigor of the experiments, the assignment of a genetic role to DNA was not immediately accepted. Skepticism was due partly to the persistent, widespread conviction that DNA was not complex enough for such a role. In addition, many scientists questioned whether genetic information in bacteria had anything to do with heredity in other organisms. However, most remaining doubts were alleviated eight years later when DNA was also shown to be the genetic material of a virus, the bacteriophage T2.

Hershey and Chase Showed That DNA Is the Genetic Material of Viruses

Bacteriophages—or **phages,** for short—are viruses that infect bacteria. They have been objects of scientific study since the 1930s, and much of our early understanding of molecular genetics came from experiments involving these viruses. **Box 18A** describes the anatomy and replication cycle of some phages and highlights their advantages for genetic studies.

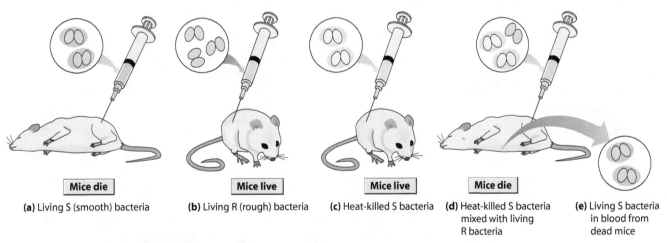

Mice die	Mice live	Mice live	Mice die
(a) Living S (smooth) bacteria	(b) Living R (rough) bacteria	(c) Heat-killed S bacteria	(d) Heat-killed S bacteria mixed with living R bacteria	(e) Living S bacteria in blood from dead mice

FIGURE 18-2 Griffith's Experiment on Genetic Transformation in Pneumococcus. S (smooth) cells of the pneumococcus bacterium *(Streptococcus pneumoniae)* are pathogenic in mice; R (rough) cells are not. **(a)** Injection of living S bacteria into mice causes pneumonia and death. **(b)** Injection of living R bacteria leaves mice healthy. **(c)** Heat-killed S bacteria have no effect when injected alone. **(d)** When a mixture of living R bacteria and heat-killed S bacteria is injected, the result is pneumonia and death. **(e)** The discovery of living S-strain bacteria in the blood of the mice in part d suggested to Griffith that a substance in the heat-killed S cells caused a heritable change (transformation) of nonpathogenic R bacteria into pathogenic S bacteria. The chemical substance was later identified as DNA.

From its inception in the mid-nineteenth century, genetics has drawn upon a wide variety of organisms for its experimental materials. Initially, attention focused on plants and animals, such as Mendel's peas and the fruit flies popularized by later investigators. Around 1940, however, bacteria and viruses came into their own, providing biologists with experimental systems that literally revolutionized the science of genetics by bringing it to the molecular level.

Bacteriophages have been especially important. Bacteriophages, or phages for short, are viruses that infect bacterial cells. It is easy to grow huge numbers of phage particles in a short time; this greatly facilitates screening for mutants—phages with heritable variations—and thereby enables geneticists to identify particular genes. Some of the most thoroughly studied phages are the T2, T4, and T6 (the so-called T-even) bacteriophages, which infect the bacterium *Escherichia coli*. The three T-even phages have similar structures, which are quite elaborate. T4 is shown in **Figure 18A-1**. The *head* of the phage is a protein capsule shaped like a hollow icosahedron (a 20-sided object) and filled with DNA. The head is attached to a protein *tail*, which consists of a hollow *tail core* surrounded by a contractile *tail sheath* and terminating in a hexagonal *baseplate,* to which six *tail fibers* are attached.

Figure 18A-2 depicts the main events in the replication cycle of the T4 phage. The drawings are not to scale; the bacterium is proportionately larger, as the electron micrograph indicates. The process begins with the adsorption of a phage particle to the wall of a bacterial cell. When the phage collides with the cell, it "squats" so that its baseplate attaches to a specific receptor protein in the wall (Figure 18A-2a, ❶). Next, the tail sheath contracts, driving the hollow tail core through the cell wall. The core forms a needle

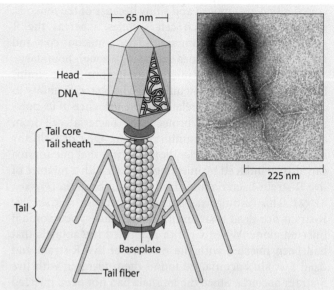

FIGURE 18A-1 The Structure of Bacteriophage T4. The drawing identifies the main structural components of this phage; not all of them are visible in the micrograph (TEM).

through which the bacteriophage DNA is injected into the bacterium (❷). Once this DNA has gained entry to the bacterial cell, the genetic information of the phage is transcribed and translated (❸). This gives rise to a few key proteins that subvert the metabolic machinery of the host cell for the phage's benefit, which is usually its own rapid multiplication. Since the phage consists simply

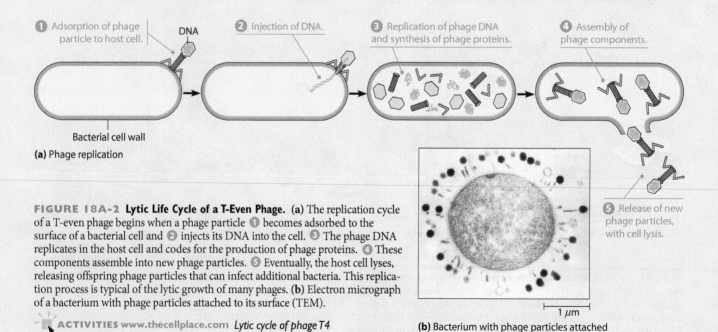

FIGURE 18A-2 Lytic Life Cycle of a T-Even Phage. (a) The replication cycle of a T-even phage begins when a phage particle ❶ becomes adsorbed to the surface of a bacterial cell and ❷ injects its DNA into the cell. ❸ The phage DNA replicates in the host cell and codes for the production of phage proteins. ❹ These components assemble into new phage particles. ❺ Eventually, the host cell lyses, releasing offspring phage particles that can infect additional bacteria. This replication process is typical of the lytic growth of many phages. **(b)** Electron micrograph of a bacterium with phage particles attached (TEM).

ACTIVITIES www.thecellplace.com *Lytic cycle of phage T4*

of a DNA molecule surrounded by a protein coat (its *capsid*), most of the metabolic activity in the infected cell is channeled toward the replication of phage DNA and the synthesis of capsid proteins. The phage DNA and capsid proteins then self-assemble into hundreds of new phage particles (④). Within about half an hour, the infected cell lyses (breaks open), releasing the new phage particles into the medium (⑤). Each new phage can now infect another bacterial cell, making it possible to obtain enormous populations of phage—as many as 10^{11} phage particles per milliliter in infected bacterial cultures.

To determine the number of phage particles in a sample, a measured volume is mixed with bacterial cells growing in liquid medium to allow adsorption of the phages to the bacteria. The mixture is then spread onto agar growth medium in a Petri dish. Upon incubation, the bacteria multiply to produce a dense "lawn" of cells on the surface of the nutrient medium. But wherever a virus particle has infected a bacterial cell, a clear spot appears in the lawn because the bacterial cells there have been killed by the multiplying phage population. Such clear spots are called *plaques*. The number of plaques reflects the number of phage particles present in the original phage-bacterium mixture, provided only that the initial number of phages was small enough to ensure that each gives rise to a separate plaque. **Figure 18A-3** shows plaques formed by T4 bacteriophage on a lawn of *E. coli* cells.

The course of events shown in Figure 18A-2a is called *lytic growth* and is characteristic of a *virulent phage*. Lytic growth results in lysis of the host cell and the production of many progeny phage particles. In contrast, a *temperate phage* can either produce lytic growth, as a virulent phage does, or integrate its DNA into the bacterial chromosome without causing any immediate harm to the host cell. An especially well-studied example of a temperate phage is bacteriophage λ *(lambda)*, which, like the T-even phages, infects

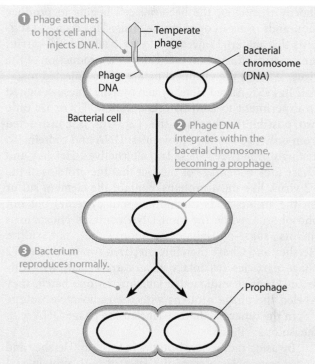

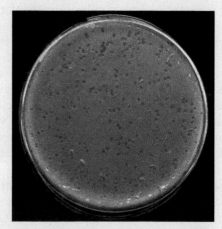

FIGURE 18A-3 Phage Plaques on a Lawn of Bacteria. Phage plaques have formed on a lawn of *E. coli* infected with phage T4. Each plaque arises from the reproduction of a single phage particle in the original mixture.

FIGURE 18A-4 Lysogenic State of a Prophage Within a Bacterial Chromosome. The DNA injected by a temperate phage can become integrated into the DNA of the bacterial chromosome. The integrated phage DNA, called a prophage, is replicated along with the bacterial DNA each time the bacterium reproduces.

E. coli cells. In the integrated or *lysogenic state,* the DNA of the temperate phage is called a *prophage*. The prophage is replicated along with the bacterial DNA, often through many generations of host cells (**Figure 18A-4**). During this time, the phage genes, though potentially lethal to the host, are inactive, or *repressed*. Under certain conditions, however, the prophage DNA is excised from the bacterial chromosome and again enters a lytic cycle, producing progeny phage particles and lysing the host cell.

One reason bacteriophages are so attractive to geneticists is that the small size of their genomes makes it relatively easy to identify and study their genes. The genome of bacteriophage λ, for example, is a single DNA molecule containing fewer than 60 genes, compared with several thousand genes in a bacterium such as *E. coli*. Other phages are still smaller; in some instances, they contain less than a dozen genes. Because of their simple genomes, their rapidity of multiplication, and the enormous numbers of progeny that can be produced in a small volume of culture medium, bacteriophages are among the best understood of all "organisms." They may have some practical benefits as well. Since phages are capable of destroying bacteria, some biotechnology companies are exploring the development of modified phages that might be useful in treating human bacterial infections, especially in cases where the bacteria have become resistant to antibiotics.

One of the most thoroughly studied of the phages that infect the bacterium *Escherichia coli* is bacteriophage T2. During infection, this virus attaches to the bacterial cell surface and injects material into the cell. Shortly thereafter, the bacterial cell begins to produce thousands of new copies of the virus. This scenario suggests that material injected into the bacterial cell carries the genetic information that guides the production of the virus. What is the chemical nature of the injected material? In 1952, Alfred Hershey and Martha Chase designed an experiment to address this question. There are only two possibilities because the T2 virus is constructed from only two kinds of molecules: DNA and protein. To distinguish between these two alternatives, Hershey and Chase took advantage of the fact that the proteins of the T2 virus, like most proteins, contain the element sulfur (in the amino acids methionine and cysteine) but not phosphorus, while the viral DNA contains phosphorus (in its sugar-phosphate backbone) but not sulfur. Hershey and Chase therefore prepared two batches of T2 phage particles (as intact phages are called) with different kinds of radioactive labeling. In one batch, they labeled the phage proteins with the radioactive isotope ^{35}S; in the other batch, they labeled the phage DNA with the isotope ^{32}P.

By using radioactive isotopes in this way, Hershey and Chase were able to trace the fates of both protein and DNA during the infection process (**Figure 18-3a**). They began the experiment by mixing radioactive phage with intact bacterial cells and allowing the phage particles to attach to the bacterial cell surface and inject their genetic material into the cells. At this point, Hershey and Chase found that the empty protein coats (or phage "ghosts") could be effectively removed from the surface of the bacterial cells by agitating the suspension in an ordinary kitchen blender and recovering the bacterial cells by centrifugation. They then measured the radioactivity in the supernatant liquid and in the pellet of bacteria at the bottom of the tube.

The data revealed that most (65%) of the ^{32}P remained with the bacterial cells, while the bulk (80%) of the ^{35}S was released into the surrounding medium (Figure 18-3b). Since the ^{32}P labeled the viral DNA and the ^{35}S labeled the viral protein, Hershey and Chase concluded that DNA, not protein, had been injected into the bacterial cells; hence, DNA must function as the genetic material of phage T2. This conclusion received further support from the following observation: When the infected, radioactive bacteria were resuspended in fresh liquid and incubated longer, the ^{32}P was transferred to some of the offspring phage particles, but the ^{35}S was not.

As a result of the experiments we have described, by the early 1950s most biologists came to accept the view that genes are made of DNA, not protein. Unfortunately, Oswald Avery, the visionary most responsible for the complete turnabout in views concerning the function of DNA, never received the credit he so richly deserved. The Nobel Prize Committee discussed Avery's work but decided he had not done enough. Perhaps Avery's modest and unassuming nature was responsible for this lack of recognition. After Avery died in 1955, the biochemist Erwin Chargaff wrote in tribute: "He was a quiet man; and it would have honored the world more, had it honored him more."

Why did the Hershey–Chase experiments receive a warmer welcome than Avery's earlier work on bacterial transformation, even though both led to the same conclusion? The main reason seems to have been simply the passage of time and the accumulation of additional, circumstantial evidence after Avery's 1944 publication. Perhaps most important was evidence that DNA is indeed variable enough in structure to serve as the genetic material. This evidence came from studies of DNA base composition, as we will see next.

Chargaff's Rules Reveal That A = T and G = C

Despite the initial lukewarm reaction to Avery's work, it had an important influence on several other scientists. Among them was Erwin Chargaff, who was interested in the base composition of DNA. Between 1944 and 1952, Chargaff used chromatographic methods to separate and quantify the relative amounts of the four bases—adenine (A), guanine (G), cytosine (C), and thymine (T)—found in DNA. Several important discoveries came from his analyses. First, he showed that DNA isolated from different cells of a given species has the same percentage of each of the four bases (**Table 18-1**, rows 1–4) and that this percentage does not vary with individual, tissue, age, nutritional state, or environment. This is exactly what would be expected of the chemical substance that stores genetic information because the cells of a given species would be expected to have similar genetic information. However, Chargaff did find that DNA base composition varies from species to species. This can be seen by examining the last column of Table 18-1, which shows the relative amounts of the bases A and T versus G and C in the DNAs of various organisms. The data also reveal that DNA preparations from closely related species have similar base compositions, whereas those from very different species tend to exhibit quite different base compositions. Again, this is what would be expected of a molecule that stores genetic information.

But Chargaff's most striking observation was his discovery that, for all DNA samples examined, the number of adenines is equal to the number of thymines (A = T), and the number of guanines is equal to the number of cytosines (G = C). This meant that the number of purines is equal to the number of pyrimidines (A + G = C + T). The significance of these equivalencies, known as **Chargaff's rules,** was an enigma and remained so until Watson and Crick proposed the double-helical model of DNA in 1953.

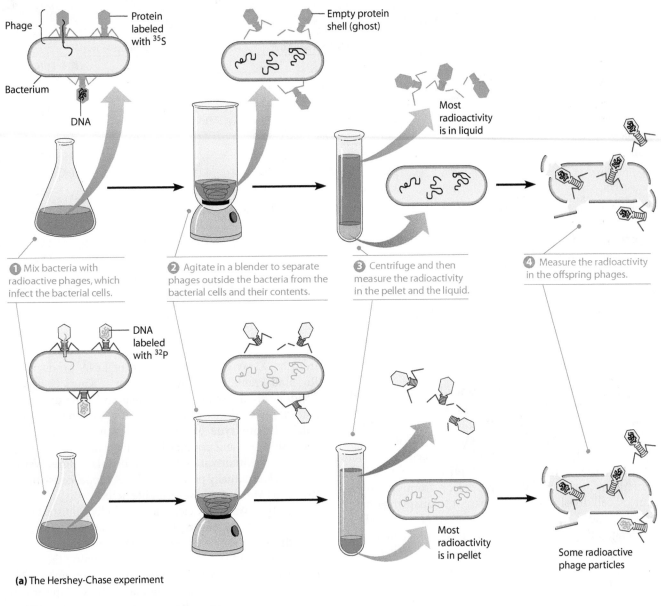

(a) The Hershey-Chase experiment

① Mix bacteria with radioactive phages, which infect the bacterial cells.

② Agitate in a blender to separate phages outside the bacteria from the bacterial cells and their contents.

③ Centrifuge and then measure the radioactivity in the pellet and the liquid.

④ Measure the radioactivity in the offspring phages.

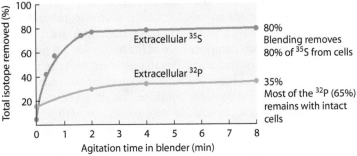

(b) Experimental data from part a, step 3

FIGURE 18-3 The Hershey–Chase Experiment: DNA as the Genetic Material of Phage T2. (a) ① T2 labeled with either ^{35}S (to label protein) or ^{32}P (to label DNA) is used to infect bacteria. The phages adsorb to the cell surface and inject their DNA. ② Agitation of the infected cells in a blender dislodges most of the ^{35}S from the cells, whereas most of the ^{32}P remains. ③ Centrifugation causes the cells to form a pellet; any free phage particles, including ghosts, remain in the supernatant liquid. ④ When the cells in each pellet are incubated further, the phage DNA within them dictates the synthesis and eventual release of new phage particles. Some of these phages contain ^{32}P in their DNA (because the old, labeled phage DNA is packaged into some of the new particles), but none contain ^{35}S in their coat proteins. (b) The graph shows the extent to which ^{35}S and ^{32}P are removed from the intact cells at step ③, as a function of time in the blender. A few minutes of blending is enough to remove most (80%) of the ^{35}S, while leaving most (65%) of the ^{32}P with the cells.

ACTIVITIES www.thecellplace.com *DNA as genetic material: The Hershey-Chase experiment*

Table 18-1 DNA Base Composition Data That Led to Chargaff's Rules

Source of DNA	Number of Each Type of Nucleotide*				Nucleotide Ratios**		
	A	T	G	C	A/T	G/C	(A + T)/(G + C)
Bovine thymus	28.4	28.4	21.1	22.1	1.00	0.95	1.31
Bovine liver	28.1	28.4	22.5	21.0	0.99	1.07	1.30
Bovine kidney	28.3	28.2	22.6	20.9	1.00	1.08	1.30
Bovine brain	28.0	28.1	22.3	21.6	1.00	1.03	1.28
Human liver	30.3	30.3	19.5	19.9	1.00	0.98	1.53
Locust	29.3	29.3	20.5	20.7	1.00	1.00	1.41
Sea urchin	32.8	32.1	17.7	17.3	1.02	1.02	1.85
Wheat germ	27.3	27.1	22.7	22.8	1.01	1.00	1.19
Marine crab	47.3	47.3	2.7	2.7	1.00	1.00	17.50
Aspergillus (mold)	25.0	24.9	25.1	25.0	1.00	1.00	1.00
Saccharomyces cerevisiae (yeast)	31.3	32.9	18.7	17.1	0.95	1.09	1.79
Clostridium (bacterium)	36.9	36.3	14.0	12.8	1.02	1.09	2.73

*The values in these four columns are the average number of each type of nucleotide found per 100 nucleotides in DNA.

**The A/T and G/C ratios are not all exactly 1.00 because of experimental error.

DNA Structure

As the scientific community gradually came to accept the conclusion that DNA stores genetic information, a new set of questions began to emerge concerning how DNA performs its genetic function. One of the first questions to be addressed was how do cells accurately replicate their DNA so that duplicate copies of the genetic information can be passed on from cell to cell during cell division and from parent to offspring during reproduction? Answering this question required an understanding of the three-dimensional structure of DNA, which was provided in 1953 when Watson and Crick formulated their double-helical model of DNA. We described the structure of the double helix in Chapter 3 and its discovery in Box 3A (page 60), but we return to it now for review and some further details.

Watson and Crick Discovered That DNA Is a Double Helix

In 1952, James Watson and Francis Crick were among a handful of scientists who were convinced that DNA is the genetic material and that knowing its three-dimensional structure would provide valuable clues to how it functions. Working at Cambridge University in England, Watson and Crick approached the puzzle by building wire models of possible structures. DNA had been known for years to be a long polymer having a backbone of repeating sugar (deoxyribose) and phosphate units, with a nitrogenous base attached to each sugar. These scientists were aided in their model building by knowing that the particular forms in which the bases A, G, C, and T exist at physiological pH permit specific hydrogen bonds to form between pairs of them. The crucial experimental evidence, however, came from an X-ray diffraction picture of DNA produced by Rosalind Franklin, who was working at King's College in London. Franklin's painstaking analysis of the diffraction pattern revealed that DNA was a long, thin, helical molecule with one type of structural feature being repeated every 0.34 nm and another being repeated every 3.4 nm. Based on the information provided by this picture, Watson and Crick eventually produced a DNA model consisting of two intertwined strands—a **double helix.**

In the Watson–Crick double helix, illustrated in **Figure 18-4,** the sugar-phosphate backbones of the two strands are on the outside of the helix, and the bases face inward toward the center of the helix, forming the "steps" of the "circular staircase" that the structure resembles. The helix is right-handed, meaning that it curves "upward" to the right (notice that this is true even if you turn the diagram upside down). It contains ten nucleotide pairs per turn and advances 0.34 nm per nucleotide pair. Consequently, each complete turn of the helix adds 3.4 nm to the length of the molecule. The diameter of the helix is 2 nm. This distance turns out to be too small for two purines and too great for two pyrimidines; but it accommodates a purine and a pyrimidine well, consistent with Chargaff's rules. Pyrimidine-purine pairing, in other words, was necessitated by their physical sizes. The two strands are held together by hydrogen bonding between the bases in opposite strands. Moreover, the hydrogen bonds holding together the two strands of the double helix fit *only when they form between the base adenine (A) in one chain and thymine (T) in the other or between the base guanine (G) in one chain and cytosine (C) in the other.* This means that the base sequence of one chain determines the base sequence of the opposing chain; the two chains of the DNA double helix are therefore said to be **complementary** to each other. Such a model explains why Chargaff had

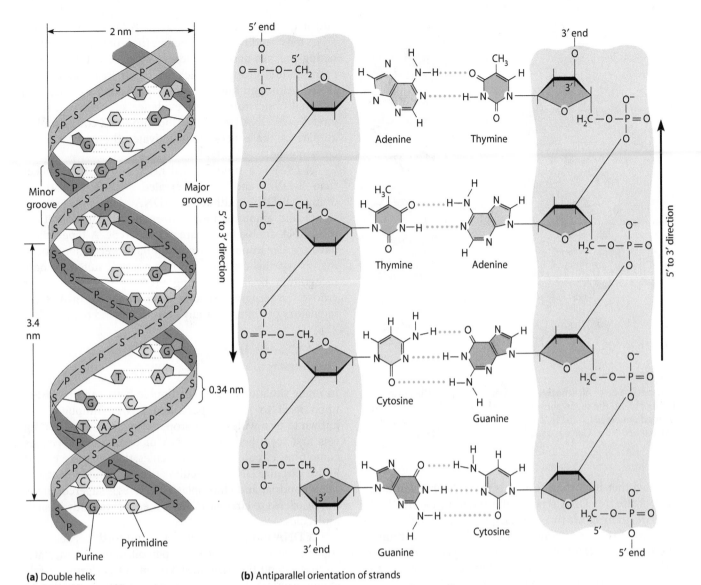

(a) Double helix

(b) Antiparallel orientation of strands

FIGURE 18-4 The DNA Double Helix. **(a)** This schematic illustration shows the sugar-phosphate chains of the DNA backbone, the complementary base pairs, the major and minor grooves, and several important dimensions. A = adenine, G = guanine, C = cytosine, T = thymine, P = phosphate, and S = sugar (deoxyribose). **(b)** One strand of a DNA molecule is oriented 5′→3′ in one direction, whereas its complement has a 5′→3′ orientation in the opposite direction. This diagram also shows the hydrogen bonds that connect the bases in AT and GC pairs.

observed that DNA molecules contain equal amounts of the bases A and T and equal amounts of the bases G and C.

The most profound implication of the Watson–Crick model was that it suggested a mechanism by which cells can replicate their genetic information: The two strands of the DNA double helix could simply separate from each other before cell division so that each strand could function as a *template,* dictating the synthesis of a new complementary DNA strand using the base-pairing rules. In other words, the base A in the template strand would specify insertion of the base T in the newly forming strand, the base G would specify insertion of the base C, the base T would specify insertion of the base A, and the base C would specify insertion of the base G. In the next

chapter, we will discuss the experimental evidence for this proposed mechanism and describe the molecular basis of DNA replication in detail.

Several other important features of the DNA double helix are illustrated in Figure 18-4. For example, notice that the two strands are twisted around each other so that there is a *major groove* and a *minor groove*. Base pairs viewed from the major groove yield more information than when viewed from the minor groove because more hydrogen bond donors (H) and acceptors (O, N), as well as the methyl group of the base T, are exposed to the major groove. As a result, regulatory proteins can bind to the major groove and recognize specific base sequences without unfolding the DNA double helix.

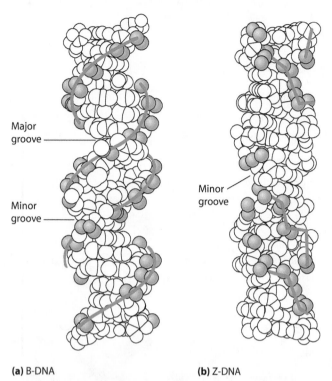

Major groove

Minor groove

Minor groove

(a) B-DNA

(b) Z-DNA

FIGURE 18-5 Alternative Forms of DNA. (a) In the normal B form of DNA, the sugar-phosphate backbone forms a smooth right-handed double helix. (b) In Z-DNA, the backbone forms a zigzag left-handed helix. Color is used to highlight the backbones.

Another important feature is the *antiparallel* orientation of the two DNA strands, illustrated in Figure 18-4b. This diagram shows that the phosphodiester bonds, which join the 5′ carbon of one nucleotide to the 3′ carbon of the adjacent nucleotide, are oriented in *opposite* directions in the two DNA strands. Starting at the top of the diagram, the strand on the left is said to exhibit a $5' \rightarrow 3'$ *orientation* because its first nucleotide has a free 5′ end and its final nucleotide has a free 3′ end. Conversely, the strand on the right exhibits a $3' \rightarrow 5'$ *orientation* starting from the top because its first nucleotide has a free 3′ end and its final nucleotide has a free 5′ end. The opposite orientation of the two strands has important implications for both DNA replication and DNA transcription, as we will see in Chapters 19 and 21.

The right-handed Watson–Crick helix is an idealized version of what is called *B-DNA* (**Figure 18-5a**). Naturally occurring B-DNA double helices are flexible molecules whose exact shapes and dimensions depend on the local nucleotide sequence. Although B-DNA is the main form of DNA in cells (and in test tube solutions of DNA), other forms may also exist, perhaps in short segments interspersed in molecules that are mostly B-DNA. The most important of these alternative forms are Z-DNA and A-DNA. As shown in Figure 18-5b, Z-DNA is a *left-handed* double helix. Its name derives from the zigzag pattern of its sugar-phosphate backbone,

and it is longer and thinner than B-DNA. The Z form arises most readily in DNA regions that contain either alternating purines and pyrimidines or have cytosines with extra methyl groups (which do occur in chromosomal DNA). Although the biological significance of Z-DNA is not well understood, some evidence suggests that short stretches of DNA transiently flip into the Z configuration as part of the process that activates the expression of certain genes.

A-DNA is a right-handed helix, shorter and thicker than B-DNA, and can be created artificially by dehydrating B-DNA. Although A-DNA does not exist in significant amounts under normal cellular condition, most RNA double helices are of the A type. A-type helices have a wider minor groove and a narrower major groove than B-type helices, so A-RNA is not well suited for base recognition by RNA-binding proteins from the major groove. To recognize specific base sequences in A-RNA, regulatory proteins generally need to unwind the duplex.

DNA Can Be Interconverted Between Relaxed and Supercoiled Forms

In many situations, the DNA double helix can be twisted upon itself to form **supercoiled DNA.** Although now known to be a widespread property of DNA, supercoiling was first identified in the DNA of certain small viruses containing circular DNA molecules that exist as closed loops. Circular DNA molecules are also found in bacteria, mitochondria, and chloroplasts. Although supercoiling is not restricted to circular DNA, it is easiest to study in such molecules.

A DNA molecule can go back and forth between the supercoiled state and the nonsupercoiled, or *relaxed*, state. To understand the basic idea, you might perform the following exercise. Start with a length of rope consisting of two strands twisted together into a right-handed coil; this is the equivalent of a relaxed, linear DNA molecule. Just joining the ends of the rope together changes nothing; the rope is now circular but still in a relaxed state. But before sealing the ends, if you first give the rope an extra twist in the direction in which the strands are already entwined around each other, the rope is thrown into a *positive supercoil.* Conversely, if before sealing, you give the rope an extra twist in the opposite direction, the rope is thrown into a *negative supercoil.* Like the rope in this example, a relaxed DNA molecule can be converted to a positive supercoil by twisting in the same direction as the double helix is wound and into a negative supercoil by twisting in the opposite direction (**Figure 18-6**). Circular DNA molecules found in nature, including those of bacteria, viruses, and eukaryotic organelles, are invariably negatively supercoiled.

Supercoiling also occurs in linear DNA molecules when regions of the molecule are anchored to some cell structure and so cannot freely rotate. At any given time,

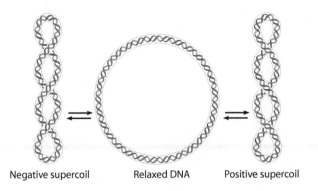

Negative supercoil   Relaxed DNA   Positive supercoil

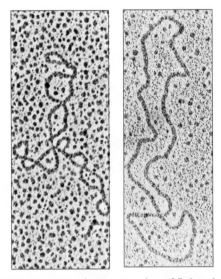

FIGURE 18-6 Interconversion of Relaxed and Supercoiled DNA. *(Top)* Conversion of a relaxed circular DNA molecule into a negatively supercoiled form (by twisting it in the opposite direction as the double helix is wound) and into a positively supercoiled form (by twisting it in the same direction as the double helix is wound). *(Bottom)* Electron micrographs of circular DNA molecules from a bacteriophage called PM2, showing a molecule with negative supercoils on the left and a relaxed molecule on the right (TEMs).

ACTIVITIES www.thecellplace.com *DNA supercoiling*

significant portions of the linear DNA in the nucleus of eukaryotic cells may be supercoiled; and, when DNA is packaged into chromosomes at the time of cell division, extensive supercoiling helps to make the DNA more compact.

By influencing both the spatial organization and the energy state of DNA, supercoiling affects the ability of a DNA molecule to interact with other molecules. Positive supercoiling involves tighter winding of the double helix and therefore reduces opportunities for interaction. In contrast, negative supercoiling is associated with unwinding of the double helix, which gives its strands increased access to proteins involved in DNA replication or transcription.

The interconversion between relaxed and supercoiled forms of DNA is catalyzed by enzymes known as **topoisomerases,** which are classified as either *type I* or *type II.* Both types catalyze the relaxation of supercoiled DNA; type I enzymes do so by introducing transient single-strand breaks in DNA, whereas type II enzymes introduce transient double-strand breaks. **Figure 18-7** shows how these temporary breaks affect DNA supercoiling. Type I topoisomerases induce DNA relaxation by cutting one strand of the double helix, thereby allowing the DNA to rotate and the uncut strand to be passed through the break before the broken strand is resealed. In contrast, type II topoisomerases induce relaxation by cutting both DNA strands and then passing a segment of uncut double helix through the break before resealing. Unlike the type I reaction, this action of type II topoisomerases requires energy derived from the hydrolysis of ATP.

Type I and type II topoisomerases are able to remove both positive and negative supercoils from DNA. In addition, bacteria have a type II topoisomerase called **DNA gyrase,** which can induce as well as relax supercoiling. As you will learn in Chapter 19, DNA gyrase is one of several enzymes involved in DNA replication. It can relax the positive supercoiling that results from partial unwinding of a double helix, or it can actively introduce negative supercoils that promote strand separation, thereby facilitating access of other proteins involved in DNA replication. DNA gyrase requires ATP to generate supercoiling but not to relax an already supercoiled molecule.

The Two Strands of a DNA Double Helix Can Be Separated Experimentally by Denaturation and Rejoined by Renaturation

Because the two strands of the DNA double helix are bound together by relatively weak, noncovalent bonds, the two strands can be readily separated from each other under appropriate conditions. As we will see in coming chapters, strand separation is an integral part of both DNA replication and RNA synthesis. Strand separation can also be induced experimentally, resulting in **DNA denaturation;** the reverse process, which reestablishes a double helix from separated DNA strands, is called **DNA renaturation.**

DNA is commonly denatured in the laboratory by raising either the temperature or the pH. When denaturation is induced by slowly raising the temperature, the DNA retains its double-stranded, or native, state until a critical temperature is reached; at that point the duplex rapidly denatures, or "melts," into its component strands. The melting process is easy to monitor because double-stranded and single-stranded DNA differ in their light-absorbing properties. All DNA absorbs ultraviolet light, with an absorption maximum around 260 nm. When the temperature of a DNA solution is slowly raised, the absorbance at 260 nm remains constant until the double helix begins to melt into its component strands. As the strands separate, the absorbance of the solution

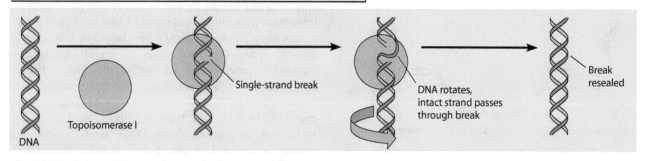

(a) Topoisomerase I. Supercoils are removed by transiently cleaving one strand of the DNA double helix and passing the unbroken strand through the break.

DNA

Topoisomerase I

Single-strand break

DNA rotates, intact strand passes through break

Break resealed

(b) Topoisomerase II. Supercoils are removed by transiently cleaving both strands of the DNA double helix and passing an unbroken region of the DNA double helix through the break.

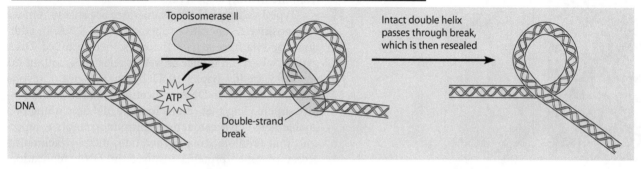

Topoisomerase II

DNA

ATP

Double-strand break

Intact double helix passes through break, which is then resealed

FIGURE 18-7 Reactions Catalyzed by Topoisomerases I and II. (a) Type I and (b) type II topoisomerases are used for removing both positive and negative supercoils from DNA.

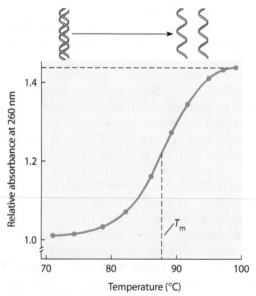

FIGURE 18-8 A Thermal Denaturation Profile for DNA. When the temperature of a solution of double-stranded (native) DNA is raised, the heat causes the DNA to denature. The conversion to single strands is accompanied by an increase in the absorbance of light at 260 nm. The temperature at which the midpoint of this increase occurs is called the melting temperature, T_m. For the sample shown, the T_m is about 87°C.

increases rapidly due to the higher intrinsic absorption of single-stranded DNA (**Figure 18-8**).

The temperature at which one-half of the absorbance change has been achieved is called the **DNA melting temperature (T_m).** The value of the melting temperature reflects how tightly the DNA double helix is held together. For example, GC base pairs, held together by three hydrogen bonds, are more resistant to separation than are AT base pairs, which have only two (see Figure 18-4b). The melting temperature therefore increases in direct proportion to the relative number of GC base pairs in the DNA (**Figure 18-9**). Likewise, DNA molecules in which the two strands of the double helix are properly base-paired at each position will melt at higher temperatures than will DNA in which the two strands are not perfectly complementary.

Denatured DNA can be renatured by lowering the temperature to permit hydrogen bonds between the two strands to be reestablished (**Figure 18-10**). The ability to renature nucleic acids has a variety of important scientific applications. Most importantly, it forms the basis for **nucleic acid hybridization,** a family of procedures for identifying nucleic acids based on the ability of single-stranded chains with complementary base sequences to bind, or *hybridize,* to each other. Nucleic acid hybridization can be applied to DNA–DNA, DNA–RNA, and even RNA–RNA interactions. In DNA–DNA hybridization, for

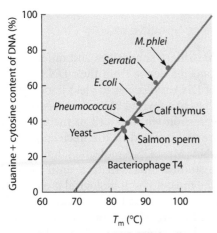

FIGURE 18-9 Dependence of DNA Melting Temperature on Base Composition. The melting temperature of DNA increases with its G + C content, as shown by the relationship between T_m and G + C content for DNA samples from a variety of sources.

example, the DNA being examined is denatured and then incubated with a purified, single-stranded radioactive DNA fragment, called a **probe,** whose sequence is complementary to the base sequence one is trying to detect. Box 18C provides an example of the use of a probe in DNA fingerprinting.

Nucleic acid sequences do not need to be perfectly complementary to be able to hybridize. Changing the temperature, salt concentration, and pH used during hybridization can permit pairing to take place between partially complementary sequences exhibiting numerous

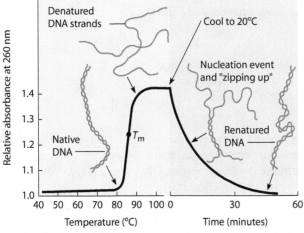

FIGURE 18-10 DNA Denaturation and Renaturation. If a solution of native (double-stranded) DNA is heated slowly under carefully controlled conditions, the DNA "melts" over a narrow temperature range, with an increase in absorbance at 260 nm. When the solution is allowed to cool, the separated DNA strands reassociate by random collisions, followed by a rapid "zipping up" of complementary base pairs in the two strands. The reassociation requires varying amounts of time, depending on both the DNA concentration in the solution and the length of the DNA strands.

mismatched bases. Under such conditions, hybridization will occur between DNAs that are related to one another but not identical. This approach is useful for identifying families of related genes, both within a given type of organism and among different kinds of organisms.

The Organization of DNA in Genomes

So far, we have considered several chemical and physical properties of DNA. But as cell biologists, we are primarily interested in its importance to the cell. We therefore want to know how much DNA cells have, how and where they store it, and how they utilize the genetic information it contains. We begin by inquiring about the amount of DNA present because that determines the maximum amount of information a cell can possibly possess.

The **genome** of an organism or virus consists of the DNA (or for some viruses, RNA) that contains one complete copy of all the genetic information of that organism or virus. For many viruses and prokaryotes, the genome resides in a single linear or circular DNA molecule or in a small number of them. Eukaryotic cells have a nuclear genome, a mitochondrial genome, and, in the case of plants and algae, a chloroplast genome as well. Mitochondrial and chloroplast genomes are single, usually circular DNA molecules resembling those of bacteria. The nuclear genome generally consists of multiple DNA molecules dispersed among a haploid set of chromosomes. (A *haploid* set of chromosomes consists of one representative of each type of chromosome, whereas a *diploid* set consists of two copies of each type of chromosome, one copy from the mother and one from the father. Sperm and egg cells each have a haploid set of chromosomes, whereas most other types of eukaryotic cells are diploid.)

Genome Size Generally Increases with an Organism's Complexity

Genome size is usually expressed as the total number of base-paired nucleotides, or **base pairs (bp).** For example, the circular DNA molecule that constitutes the genome of an *E. coli* cell has 4,639,221 bp. Since such numbers tend to be rather large, the abbreviations **Kb** (kilobases), **Mb** (megabases), and **Gb** (gigabases) are used to refer to a thousand, or million, or billion base pairs, respectively. Thus, the size of the *E. coli* genome can be expressed simply as 4.6 Mb. The range of genome sizes observed for various groups of organisms is summarized in **Figure 18-11.** These data reveal a spread of almost eight orders of magnitude in genome size, from a few thousand base pairs for the simplest viruses to more than 100 billion base pairs for certain plants, amphibians, and protists. Expressed in terms of total DNA length, this corresponds to a range of less than 2 μm of DNA for a small virus, such as SV40, to

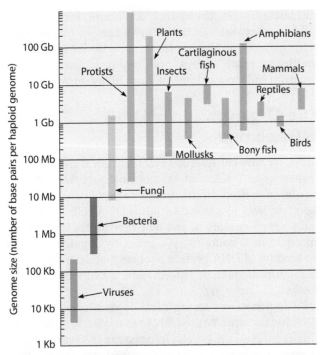

FIGURE 18-11 Relationship Between Genome Size and Type of Organism. For each group of organisms shown, the bar represents the approximate range in genome size measured as the number of base pairs per haploid genome. The same color (purple) is used for groups that involve members of the animal kingdom.

roughly 34 meters of DNA (more than 100 feet!) for certain plants, such as the wildflower *Trillium*.

Broadly speaking, genome size increases with the complexity of the organism. Viruses contain enough nucleic acid to code for only a few or a few dozen proteins, bacteria can specify a few thousand proteins, and eukaryotic cells have enough DNA (at least in theory) to encode hundreds of thousands of proteins. But closer examination of such data reveals some puzzling features. Most notably, the genome sizes of eukaryotes exhibit great variations that do not clearly correlate with any known differences in organismal complexity. Some amphibians and plants, for example, have gigantic genomes that are tens or even hundreds of times larger than those of other amphibians or plants or of mammalian species. *Trillium*, for example, is a member of the lily family that has no obvious need for exceptional amounts of genetic information. Yet its genome size is more than 20 times that of pea plants and 30 times that of humans. Moreover, a single-celled amoeba has a genome that is 200 times the size of the human genome. We have no idea why lily plants and amoebae possess so much DNA. Its presence highlights the fact that most eukaryotic genomes carry large amounts of DNA of no currently known function, a phenomenon we will discuss shortly. In the final analysis, genome size is less important than the number and identity of functional genes and the DNA sequences that control their expression.

Restriction Endonucleases Cleave DNA Molecules at Specific Sites

Since the hereditary similarities and differences observed among organisms derive from their DNA, we can expect the study of DNA molecules to yield important biological insights. Clues to a myriad of mysteries—from the control of gene expression within a cell to the evolution of new species—are to be found in the nucleotide sequences of genomic DNA. Most DNA molecules, however, are far too large to be studied intact. In fact, until the early 1970s, DNA was the most difficult biological molecule to analyze biochemically. Eukaryotic DNA seemed especially intimidating, given the size of most eukaryotic genomes, and no method was known for cutting DNA at specific sites to yield reproducible fragments. The prospect of ever being able to identify, isolate, sequence, or manipulate specific eukaryotic genes seemed unlikely. Yet in less than a decade, DNA became one of the easiest biological molecules to work with.

This breakthrough was made possible by the discovery of **restriction endonucleases** (also called *restriction enzymes*), which are proteins isolated from bacteria that cut foreign DNA molecules at specific internal sites. (**Box 18B** describes the biological role of restriction endonucleases and provides some details about the sites they cut; here we focus on their use as analytical tools.) The cutting action of a restriction enzyme generates a specific set of DNA pieces called *restriction fragments*. Each restriction enzyme cleaves double-stranded DNA only in places where it encounters a specific recognition sequence, called a **restriction site,** that is usually four or six (but may be eight or more) nucleotides long. For example, here is the restriction site recognized by the widely used *E. coli* restriction enzyme called *Eco*RI:

$$\downarrow$$
$$5'\ \text{G—A—A—T—T—C}\ 3'$$
$$3'\ \text{C—T—T—A—A—G}\ 5'$$
$$\uparrow$$

The arrows indicate where *Eco*RI cuts the DNA. This restriction enzyme, like many others, makes a *staggered* cut in the double-stranded DNA molecule, as you can see in Figure 18B-1b (Box 18B).

Restriction sites occur frequently enough in DNA to permit typical restriction enzymes to cleave DNA into fragments ranging from a few hundred to a few thousand base pairs in length. Fragments of these sizes are far more amenable to further manipulation than are the enormously long DNA molecules from which they are generated.

Separation of Restriction Fragments by Gel Electrophoresis. Incubating a DNA sample with a specific restriction enzyme yields a collection of restriction fragments of different sizes. To determine the number

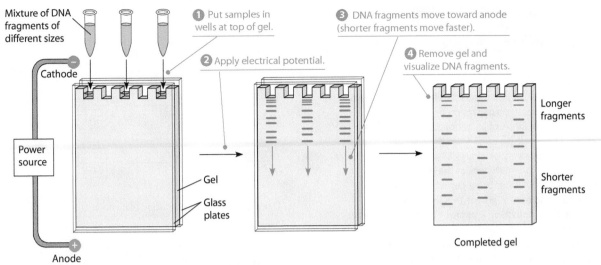

FIGURE 18-12 Gel Electrophoresis of DNA. The three test tubes contain mixtures of DNA fragments produced by incubating DNA with different restriction enzymes. A small sample of each is applied to the top of a gel, and an electrical potential of several hundred volts is applied. This causes the DNA fragments to migrate toward the anode, with shorter fragments migrating faster than larger ones. After allowing time for the fragments to separate from one another, the gel is removed and stained with a dye such as ethidium bromide, which binds to the DNA fragments and causes them to fluoresce under ultraviolet light. Alternatively, autoradiography can be used to locate the DNA bands in the gel, provided that the DNA is radioactively labeled.

and lengths of such fragments and to isolate individual fragments for further study, a researcher must be able to separate the fragments from one another. The technique of choice for this purpose is **gel electrophoresis,** essentially the same method used to separate proteins and polypeptides (see Figure 7-22). In fact, the procedure for DNA is even simpler than for proteins because DNA molecules have an inherent negative charge (due to their phosphate groups) and therefore do not need to be treated with a negatively charged detergent to make them move toward the anode. Small DNA fragments are usually separated in *polyacrylamide* gels, whereas larger DNA fragments are separated in more porous gels made of *agarose,* a polysaccharide.

Figure 18-12 illustrates the separation of restriction fragments of different sizes by gel electrophoresis. DNA samples are first incubated with the desired restriction enzyme; in the figure, three different restriction enzymes are used. The samples are then placed in separate compartments ("wells") at one end of the gel. Next, an electrical potential is applied across the gel, with the anode situated at the opposite end of the gel from the samples. Because their phosphate groups have a negative charge, DNA fragments migrate toward the anode. Smaller fragments (i.e., those with lower molecular weight) move through the gel with relative ease and therefore migrate rapidly, while larger fragments move more slowly. The current is left on until the fragments are well spaced out on the gel. The final result is a series of DNA fragments that have been separated based on differences in size.

DNA fragments in the gel can be visualized either by staining or by using radioactively labeled DNA. A common staining technique involves soaking the gel in the dye *ethidium bromide,* which binds to DNA and fluoresces orange when exposed to ultraviolet light. If the DNA fragments are radioactive, their locations can be determined by **autoradiography,** a technique for detecting radioactive molecules by overlaying a sample with X-ray film. When the film is developed, it yields an *autoradiogram* that is darkened wherever radioactivity has interacted with the film. After individual DNA fragments are located in this way, they can be removed from the gel for further study.

Restriction Mapping. How does a researcher determine the order in which a set of restriction fragments is arranged in a DNA molecule? One approach involves treating the DNA with two or more restriction enzymes, alone and in combination, followed by gel electrophoresis to determine the size of the resulting DNA fragments. **Figure 18-13** shows how it would work for a simple DNA molecule cleaved with the restriction enzymes *Eco*RI and *Hae*III. In this example, each individual restriction enzyme cleaves the DNA into two fragments, indicating that the DNA contains one restriction site for each enzyme. Based on such information alone, two possible restriction maps can be proposed (see maps A and B in Figure 18-13). To determine which of the two maps is correct, an experiment must be done in which the starting DNA molecule is cleaved *simultaneously* with *Eco*RI and *Hae*III. The size of the fragments produced by simultaneous digestion with both enzymes reveals that map A must be the correct one.

In practice, restriction mapping usually involves data that are considerably more complex than in our simple

Restriction enzymes are a type of endonuclease (an enzyme that cuts DNA internally) found in most bacteria. These enzymes help bacteria protect themselves against invasion by foreign DNA molecules, particularly the DNA of bacteriophages. In fact, the name "restriction" endonuclease came from the discovery that these enzymes *restrict* the ability of foreign DNA to take over the transcription and translation machinery of the bacterial cell.

To protect its own DNA from being degraded, the bacterial cell has enzymes that add methyl groups ($-CH_3$) to specific nucleotides that its own restriction enzymes would otherwise recognize. Once they have been methylated, the nucleotides are no longer recognized by the restriction enzymes, and so the bacterial DNA is not attacked by the cell's own restriction enzymes. Restriction enzymes are therefore said to be part of the cell's **restriction/methylation system:** Foreign DNA is cleaved by the restriction enzymes, while the bacterial genome is protected by prior methylation.

Restriction enzymes are named after the bacteria from which they are obtained. Each enzyme name is derived by combining the first letter of the bacterial genus with the first two letters of the species. The strain of the bacterium may also be indicated, and if two or more enzymes have been isolated from the same species, the enzymes are numbered (using Roman numerals) in order of discovery. Thus, the first restriction enzyme isolated from *E. coli* strain R is designated *Eco*RI, whereas the third enzyme isolated from *Hemophilus aegyptius* is called *Hae*III.

Restriction enzymes are specific for double-stranded DNA and cleave both strands. Each restriction enzyme recognizes a specific DNA sequence that is usually four or six (but may be eight or more) nucleotide pairs long. For example, the enzyme *Hae*III recognizes the tetranucleotide sequence GGCC and cleaves the DNA double helix as shown in **Figure 18B-1a**. The restriction sites for several other restriction enzymes are summarized in **Table 18B-1**. Some restriction enzymes, such as *Hae*III, cut both strands at the same point, generating restriction fragments with

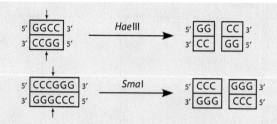

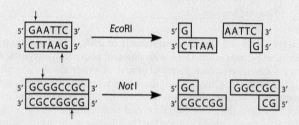

(a) Cleavage by enzymes producing blunt ends

(b) Cleavage by enzymes producing sticky ends

FIGURE 18B-1 Cleavage of DNA by Restriction Enzymes.
(a) *Hae*III and *Sma*I are examples of restriction enzymes that cut both DNA strands in the same location, generating fragments with blunt ends. (b) *Eco*RI and *Not*I are examples of enzymes that cut DNA in a staggered fashion, generating fragments with sticky ends. A genetic "engineer" can use such sticky ends for joining DNA fragments from different source.

blunt ends. Many other restriction enzymes cleave the two strands in a staggered manner, generating short, single-stranded tails or overhangs on both fragments. *Eco*RI is an example of such an enzyme; it recognizes the sequence GAATTC and cuts the DNA molecule in an offset manner, leaving an AATT tail on both

example. In such situations, the DNA fragments produced by each restriction enzyme can be physically isolated—for example, by cutting the gel into slices and extracting the DNA from each slice. The isolated fragments are then individually cleaved with the second restriction enzyme, allowing the cleavage sites in each fragment to be analyzed separately. Problem 18-4 provides an example of how this approach can be used to construct a **restriction map** depicting the location of all the restriction sites in the original DNA.

Rapid Procedures Exist for DNA Sequencing

At about the same time that techniques for preparing restriction fragments were developed, two methods were devised for rapid **DNA sequencing**—that is, determining the linear order of bases in DNA. One method was devised

by Allan Maxam and Walter Gilbert, the other by Frederick Sanger and his colleagues. The Maxam–Gilbert method, called the *chemical method,* is based on the use of (nonprotein) chemicals that cleave DNA preferentially at specific bases; the Sanger procedure, called the *chain termination method,* utilizes *dideoxynucleotides* (nucleotides lacking a 3' hydroxyl group) to interfere with the normal enzymatic synthesis of DNA. We will focus on Sanger's method because it has been adapted for use in automated machines that are now employed for most DNA sequencing tasks.

In this procedure, a single-stranded DNA fragment is employed as a template to guide the synthesis of new complementary DNA strands. DNA synthesis is carried out in the presence of the *deoxynucleotides* dATP, dCTP, dTTP, and dGTP, which are the normal substrates that provide the bases A, C, T, and G to growing DNA chains. Also included, at lower concentrations, are four dye-labeled

fragments (Figure 18B-1b). The restriction fragments generated by enzymes with this staggered cleavage pattern always have **sticky ends** (also called *cohesive ends*). These terms derive from the fact that the single-stranded tail at the end of each such fragment can base-pair with the tail at either end of any other fragment generated by the same enzyme, causing the fragments to stick to one another by hydrogen bonding. Enzymes that generate such fragments are particularly useful because they can be employed experimentally to create recombinant DNA molecules.

The restriction sites for most restriction enzymes are *palindromes*, which means that the sequence reads the same in either direction. (The English word *radar* is a palindrome, for example.) The palindromic nature of a restriction site is due to its twofold rotational symmetry, which means that rotating the double-stranded sequence 180° in the plane of the paper yields a sequence that reads the same as it did before rotation. Palindromic restriction sites have the same base sequence on both strands when each strand is read in the 5′→3′ direction.

The frequency with which any particular restriction site is likely to occur within a DNA molecule can be predicted statistically. For example, in a DNA molecule containing equal amounts of the four bases (A, T, C, and G), we can predict that, on average, a recognition site with four nucleotide pairs will occur once every 256 (i.e., 4^4) nucleotide pairs, whereas the likely frequency of a six-nucleotide sequence is once every 4096 (i.e., 4^6) nucleotide pairs. Restriction enzymes therefore tend to cleave DNA into fragments that typically vary in length from several hundred to a few thousand nucleotide pairs—gene-sized pieces, essentially. Such pieces are called *restriction fragments*. Because each restriction enzyme cleaves only a single, specific nucleotide sequence, it will always cut a given DNA molecule in the same predictable manner, generating a reproducible set of restriction fragments. This property makes restriction enzymes powerful tools for generating manageable-sized pieces of DNA for further study.

Table 18B-1	Some Common Restriction Enzymes and Their Recognition Sequences	
Enzyme	**Source Organism**	**Recognition Sequence***
*Bam*HI	*Bacillus amyloliquefaciens*	5′ G—G—A—T—C—C 3′ 3′ C—C—T—A—G—G 5′
*Eco*RI	*Escherichia coli*	5′ G—A—A—T—T—C 3′ 3′ C—T—T—A—A—G 5′
*Hae*III	*Hemophilus aegyptius*	5′ G—G—C—C 3′ 3′ C—C—G—G 5′
*Hind*III	*Hemophilus influenzae*	5′ A—A—G—C—T—T 3′ 3′ T—T—C—G—A—A 5′
*Pst*I	*Providencia stuartii* 164	5′ C—T—G—C—A—G 3′ 3′ G—A—C—G—T—C 5′
*Pvu*I	*Proteus vulgaris*	5′ C—G—A—T—C—G 3′ 3′ G—C—T—A—G—C 5′
*Pvu*II	*Proteus vulgaris*	5′ C—A—G—C—T—G 3′ 3′ G—T—C—G—A—C 5′
*Sal*I	*Streptomyces albus* G	5′ C—T—C—G—A—C 3′ 3′ C—A—G—C—T—G 5′

*The arrows within the recognition sequence indicate the points at which each restriction enzyme cuts the two strands of the DNA molecule.

dideoxynucleotides (ddATP, ddCTP, ddTTP, and ddGTP), which lack the hydroxyl group attached to the 3′ carbon of normal deoxynucleotides. When a dideoxynucleotide is incorporated into a growing DNA chain in place of the normal deoxynucleotide, *DNA synthesis is prematurely halted* because the absence of the 3′ hydroxyl group makes it impossible to form a bond with the next nucleotide. Hence, a series of incomplete DNA fragments are produced whose sizes provide information concerning the linear sequence of bases in the DNA.

Figure 18-14 illustrates how this procedure works. In step ❶, a reaction mixture is assembled that includes the dideoxynucleotides ddATP, ddCTP, ddTTP, and ddGTP, each labeled with a fluorescent dye of a different color (e.g., ddATP = red, ddCTP = blue, ddTTP = orange, and ddGTP = green). These colored dideoxynucleotides are mixed with the normal deoxynucleotide substrates for

DNA synthesis, along with a single-stranded DNA molecule to be sequenced and a short, single-stranded DNA *primer* that is complementary to the 3′ end of the DNA strand being sequenced. When DNA polymerase is added, it catalyzes the attachment of nucleotides, one by one, to the 3′ end of the primer, producing a growing DNA strand that is complementary to the template whose sequence is being determined. Most of the nucleotides inserted are the normal deoxynucleotides because they are the preferred substrates for DNA polymerase. But every so often, at random, a colored dideoxynucleotide is inserted instead of its normal equivalent. Each time a dideoxynucleotide is incorporated, it halts further DNA synthesis for that particular strand. Consequently, a mixture of strands of varying lengths is generated, each containing a colored base at the end where DNA synthesis was prematurely terminated by incorporation of a dideoxynucleotide (step ❷).

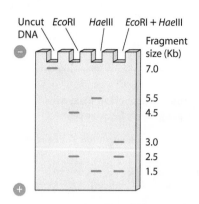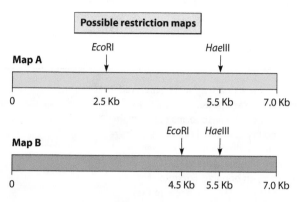

FIGURE 18-13 Restriction Mapping. In this hypothetical example, the location of restriction sites for *Eco*RI and *Hae*III is determined in a DNA fragment 7.0 Kb long. The gel on the left shows that *Eco*RI cleaves the DNA into two fragments measuring 2.5 Kb and 4.5 Kb, indicating that DNA has been cleaved at a single point located 2.5 Kb from one end. Treatment with *Hae*III cleaves the DNA into two fragments measuring 1.5 Kb and 5.5 Kb, indicating that DNA has been cleaved at a single point located 1.5 Kb from one end. Based on this information alone, two possible restriction maps can be proposed. If map A were correct, simultaneous digestion of the DNA with *Eco*RI and *Hae*III should yield three fragments measuring 3.0 Kb, 2.5 Kb, and 1.5 Kb. If map B were correct, simultaneous digestion of the DNA with *Eco*RI and *Hae*III should yield three fragments measuring 4.5 Kb, 1.5 Kb, and 1.0 Kb. The experimental data reveal that map A must be correct.

ACTIVITIES www.thecellplace.com *Restriction mapping*

Next, the sample is subjected to electrophoresis in a polyacrylamide gel, which allows the newly synthesized DNA fragments to be separated from one another because the shorter fragments migrate through the gel more quickly than the longer fragments (step ❸). As the fragments move through the gel, a special camera detects the color of each fragment as it passes by. Step ❹ shows how such information allows the DNA base sequence to be determined. In this particular example, the shortest DNA fragment is blue, and the next shortest fragment is green. Since blue and green are the colors of ddCTP and ddGTP, respectively, the first two bases added to the primer must have been C followed by G. In automatic sequencing machines, such information is collected for hundreds of bases in a row and fed into a computer, allowing the complete sequence of the initial DNA fragment to be quickly determined.

The Genomes of Many Organisms Have Been Sequenced

The significance of the technique we have just described can scarcely be overestimated. DNA sequencing is now so commonplace and automated that it is routinely applied not just to individual genes, but to entire genomes. Although DNA sequencing machines determine the sequence of only short pieces of DNA, usually 500–800 bases long, one at a time, computer programs search for overlapping sequences between such fragments and thereby allow data from hundreds or thousands of DNA pieces to be assembled into longer stretches that can reach millions of bases in length.

Many of the initial successes in genome sequencing involved bacteria because they have relatively small genomes, typically a few million bases. Complete DNA sequences are now available for over 2000 different bacteria, including those that cause a variety of human diseases. In fact, sequencing machines are so efficient that one research institute reported the sequences of 15 different bacterial genomes in a single month! But DNA sequencing has also been successfully applied to much larger genomes, including those from several dozen organisms that are most important in biological research (Table 18-2). For example, scientists have completed the genome sequences of the yeast *Saccharomyces cerevisiae* (12.1 million bases), the roundworm *Caenorhabditis elegans* (97 million bases), the mustard plant *Arabidopsis thaliana* (125 million bases), and the fruit fly *Drosophila melanogaster* (180 million bases).

To us as human beings, of course, the ultimate challenge of DNA sequencing is the human genome. How awesome a challenge was that? To answer this question, we need to realize that the human nuclear genome contains about 3.2 billion bases, which is roughly a thousandfold more DNA than is present in an *E. coli* cell. One way to comprehend the magnitude of such a challenge is to note that in the early 1990s, when genome sequencing efforts began in earnest, it required almost 6 years for the laboratory of Frederick Blattner to determine the complete base sequence of the *E. coli* genome. At this rate, it would have taken a single lab almost 6000 years to sequence the entire human genome! Consequently, scientists came together in 1990 to establish the *Human Genome Project,* a cooperative international effort involving hundreds of scientists who shared their data in an attempt to determine the entire sequence of the human genome. In the late 1990s a commercial company, Celera Genomics, tackled the job as well. Through these efforts,

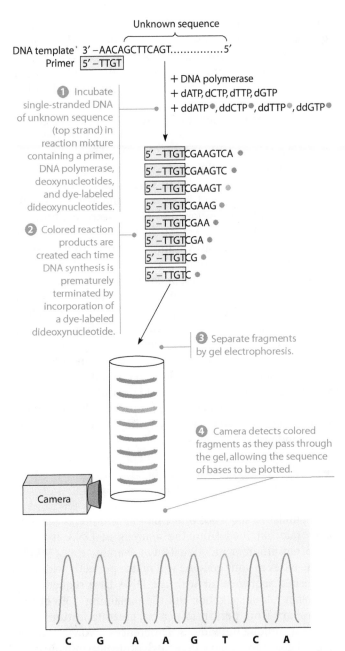

Unknown sequence

DNA template 3′ –AACAGCTTCAGT...............5′
Primer 5′ –TTGT

1 Incubate single-stranded DNA of unknown sequence (top strand) in reaction mixture containing a primer, DNA polymerase, deoxynucleotides, and dye-labeled dideoxynucleotides.

+ DNA polymerase
+ dATP, dCTP, dTTP, dGTP
+ ddATP●, ddCTP●, ddTTP●, ddGTP●

5′ –TTGT CGAAGTCA ●
5′ –TTGT CGAAGTC ●
5′ –TTGT CGAAGT ●
5′ –TTGT CGAAG ●
5′ –TTGT CGAA ●
5′ –TTGT CGA ●
5′ –TTGT CG ●
5′ –TTGT C ●

2 Colored reaction products are created each time DNA synthesis is prematurely terminated by incorporation of a dye-labeled dideoxynucleotide.

3 Separate fragments by gel electrophoresis.

4 Camera detects colored fragments as they pass through the gel, allowing the sequence of bases to be plotted.

Camera

C G A A G T C A

FIGURE 18-14 DNA Sequencing. The chain termination technique illustrated here, which employs dye-labeled dideoxynucleotides, has been adapted for use in high-speed, automated sequencing machines. Although this example summarizes the results obtained for only the first eight bases of a DNA sequence, experiments of this type typically determine the sequence of DNA fragments that are 500–800 bases long. The four main steps involved in the procedure are described in more detail in the text.

ACTIVITIES www.thecellplace.com *Dideoxy DNA sequencing*

the complete sequence of the human genome was determined by 2003, roughly two years ahead of schedule.

This monumental achievement took more than a decade to complete and cost nearly $3 billion. Today, continued improvements to the Sanger sequencing method have made it possible to sequence a comparable-sized genome for $20 million in less than a year, and rapid progress continues to be made. For example, a newly

developed sequencing approach permits a million DNA fragments to be sequenced simultaneously in microscopic reaction chambers, thereby making it possible to sequence a human genome for less than $100,000 in a month or less. And efforts are not stopping there. A prize has been established to spur the development of a technology that can sequence a human genome for $1000—a cost so affordable that doctors may one day be able to order a copy of a patient's own genome sequence to facilitate treatment decisions best suited to the genes found in that person.

The Field of Bioinformatics Has Emerged to Decipher Genomes, Transcriptomes, and Proteomes

Because of its sheer scale as well as its potential impact on our understanding of human evolution, physiology, and disease, sequencing the human genome is one of the crowning achievements of modern biology. And yet, unraveling the sequence of bases was the "easy" part. Next comes the hard part: figuring out the meaning of this sequence of 3 billion A's, G's, C's, and T's. For example, which stretches of DNA correspond to genes, when and in what tissues are these genes expressed, what kinds of proteins do they code for, and how do all these proteins interact with each other and function?

The prospect of analyzing such a vast amount of data has led to the emergence of a new discipline, called **bioinformatics,** which merges computer science and biology in an attempt to make sense of it all. For example, computer programs that analyze DNA for stretches that could code for amino acid sequences are used to estimate the number of protein-coding genes. Such analyses suggest the presence of about 25,000 protein-coding genes in the human genome, roughly half of which were not known to exist prior to genome sequencing. The fascinating

Table 18-2 Examples of Sequenced Genomes*

Organism	Genome Size	Estimated Gene Number
Bacteria		
Mycoplasma genitalium	0.6 Mb	470
Haemophilus influenza	1.8 Mb	1,740
Streptococcus pneumoniae	2.2 Mb	2,240
Escherichia coli	4.6 Mb	4,400
Yeast (*S. cerevisiae*)	12.1 Mb	6,200
Roundworm (*C. elegans*)	97 Mb	19,700
Mustard plant (*A. thaliana*)	125 Mb	25,500
Fruit fly (*D. melanogaster*)	180 Mb	13,600
Rice (*O. sativa*)	389 Mb	37,500
Mouse (*Mus musculus*)	2500 Mb	25,000
Human (*H. sapiens*)	3200 Mb	25,000

*As of November 2009, complete genome sequences had been published for 2351 organisms (2060 bacteria, 80 archaea, and 211 eukaryotes).

thing about this estimate is that it means humans have only about twice the number of genes as a fruit fly, barely more genes than a worm, and 12,000 fewer genes than a rice plant! Computer analysis has also revealed that less than 2% of the human genome actually codes for proteins. While the remaining 98% contains some important regulatory elements and some genes that code for RNA products instead of proteins, much of it has no obvious function. (For examples, see the discussions of repeated DNA in the following section and introns in Chapter 21). While the significance of this extra DNA is not clear, some evidence suggests that its presence may enhance the ability of the genome to evolve over time.

Determining the DNA sequence of an organism's genome can provide only a partial understanding of the functions a genome performs. Scientists must look beyond the genome to examine the molecules it produces. Because the first step in gene expression involves transcription of genome sequences into RNA, techniques have been developed for identifying **transcriptomes**— that is, the entire set of RNA molecules produced by a genome. You will see how the development of *DNA microarray* technology for identifying thousands of RNA molecules simultaneously has facilitated the study of transcriptomes.

Most RNAs, in turn, are used to guide the production of proteins, so scientists are also studying **proteomes**—the structure and properties of every protein produced by a genome. An organism's proteome is considerably more complex than its genome. For example, the roughly 25,000 genes in human cells produce hundreds of thousands of different proteins. In Chapter 21, we explain how cells can produce so many proteins from a smaller number of genes. You will see that this ability to produce so many proteins is made possible by a mechanism called *alternative splicing*, which allows each individual gene to be "read" in multiple ways to produce multiple versions of its protein product. Moreover, the resulting proteins are subject to subsequent biochemical modifications that produce either new proteins or multiple versions of the same protein.

Identifying the vast number of proteins produced by a genome has been facilitated by **mass spectrometry**, a high-speed, extremely sensitive technique that utilizes magnetic and electric fields to separate proteins or protein fragments based on differences in mass and charge. One application of mass spectrometry involves using it to identify peptides derived from proteins that have been separated by gel electrophoresis and then digested with specific proteases, such as trypsin. Comparing the resulting data to the predicted masses of peptides that would be produced by DNA sequences present in genomic databases permits the proteins produced by newly discovered genes to be identified. Other techniques make it feasible to study the interactions and functional properties of the vast number of proteins found in a proteome. For example, it is possible to immobilize thousands of different proteins (or other molecules

that bind to specific proteins) as tiny spots on a piece of glass smaller than a microscope slide. The resulting *protein microarrays* (or protein "chips") can then be used to study a variety of protein properties, such as the ability of each individual spot to bind to other molecules added to the surrounding solution.

The enormous amount of data being collected on DNA and protein sequences presents a daunting challenge to scientists who wish to locate information about a particular gene or protein. To cope with this problem, the most recent DNA and protein sequences from hundreds of organisms are stored in several online databases, and software has been developed to help researchers find the information they need. Among the more widely used tools is **BLAST (Basic Local Alignment Search Tool),** a software program that searches databases to locate DNA or protein sequences that resemble any known sequence of interest. For example, if you identify a new gene in an organism that has not been previously studied and determine its base sequence, a BLAST search could then determine whether humans (or any other organism in the database) possess a similar gene. Or if you are interested in the properties of a particular protein and know part of its amino acid sequence, you could do a BLAST search to identify related proteins. BLAST searching has therefore become a routine step when analyzing and characterizing genes and proteins.

Tiny Differences in Genome Sequence Distinguish People from One Another

The published sequence of the human genome is actually a mosaic obtained from the analysis of DNA isolated from ten different individuals. On average, about 99.7% of the bases in your genome will match perfectly with this published sequence, or with the DNA base sequence of your next-door neighbor. But the remaining 0.3% of the bases vary from person to person, creating features that make us unique individuals. Differences involving single base changes are called **single nucleotide polymorphisms,** or **SNPs** (pronounced "snips"). Although 0.3% might not sound like very much, 0.3% multiplied by the 3.2 billion bases in the human genome yields a total of roughly 10 million SNPs. Scientists have already created databases containing most of the common SNPs, which are thought to be important because some of these tiny genetic variations may influence your susceptibility to certain diseases or determine how well you respond to a particular treatment.

Most SNPs, however, are not located in the protein-coding regions of genes. So how do we find out which SNPs are related to important traits, such as susceptibility to a specific disease? Fortunately, it is not necessary to examine all 10 million SNPs separately because SNPs are not independent of one another. SNPs located near each other on the same chromosome tend to be inherited together in blocks called **haplotypes.** A database of these haplotypes, called the *HapMap*, provides a shortcut for scientists interested in the relationship between genes and disease: Only a few hundred thousand SNPs (each located in a different haplotype) need to be examined rather than 10 million. Once a trait has been linked to a particular haplotype, only the SNPs within that haplotype are studied to determine which one is responsible.

SNPs are not the only sources of genetic variation that define a person's individuality. DNA rearrangements, deletions, and duplications also contribute to variability among genomes. Such mechanisms have produced DNA segments thousands of bases long that are present in variable numbers of copies among different individuals. Each person's genome is thought to contain hundreds of such **copy number variations (CNVs)** involving millions of bases of DNA overall.

The impact of our rapidly growing understanding of the human genome is already becoming apparent as discoveries regarding the genetic basis of many human diseases—from breast cancer and colon cancer to diabetes and Alzheimer's disease—are being reported at a rapidly increasing pace. Such discoveries promise to revolutionize the future practice of medicine because having the ability to identify disease genes and investigate their function makes it possible to devise medical interventions for alleviating and even preventing disease.

But being able to identify potentially harmful genes also raises ethical concerns because all of us are likely to carry a few dozen genes that place us at risk for something. Such information possibly could be misused—for example, in genetic discrimination against individuals or groups of people by insurance companies, employers, or even government agencies. Moreover, detailed knowledge of the human genome increases the potential for using recombinant DNA techniques to *alter* people's genes, not only to correct diseases in malfunctioning body tissues but also to change genes in sperm and eggs, thereby altering the genetic makeup of future generations. What use to make of these abilities and how to regulate them are clearly questions that concern not only the scientific community but human society as a whole.

Repeated DNA Sequences Partially Explain the Large Size of Eukaryotic Genomes

Besides the difficulties it created for DNA sequencing studies, the enormous size of the human genome raises a more fundamental question: Does the large amount of DNA in human cells simply reflect the need for thousands of times more genes than are present in bacterial cells, or are other factors at play as well? The first breakthrough in answering this question occurred in the late 1960s, when DNA renaturation studies carried out by Roy Britten and David Kohne led to the discovery of repeated DNA sequences.

In these experiments, DNA was broken into small fragments and dissociated into single strands by heating.

The temperature was then lowered to permit the single-stranded fragments to renature. The renaturation rate depends on the concentration of each individual kind of DNA sequence; the higher the concentration of fragments exhibiting any given DNA sequence, the greater the probability that they will randomly collide with complementary strands and reassociate. As an example, let us consider DNA from a bacterial cell and from a typical mammalian cell containing a thousandfold more DNA. If this difference in DNA content reflects a thousandfold difference in the kinds of DNA sequences present, then bacterial DNA should renature 1000 times faster than mammalian DNA. The rationale for this prediction is that any particular DNA sequence should be present in a thousandfold lower concentration in the mammalian DNA sample because there are a thousand times more kinds of sequences present, and so each individual sequence represents a smaller fraction of the total population of sequences.

When Britten and Kohne compared the behavior of mammalian and bacterial DNAs, however, the results were not exactly as expected. In **Figure 18-15**, which summarizes their data obtained for calf and *E. coli* DNA, renaturation is plotted as a function of initial DNA concentration multiplied by the elapsed time because it facilitates comparison of data obtained from reactions run at different DNA concentrations. When graphed this way, the data reveal that calf DNA consists of two classes of sequences that renature at very different rates. One type of sequence, which accounts for about 40% of the calf DNA, renatures *more* rapidly than bacterial DNA does. The most straightforward explanation for this unexpected result is that calf DNA contains **repeated DNA** sequences that are present in multiple copies. The existence of multiple copies increases the concentration of such sequences, thereby generating more collisions and a faster rate of reassociation than would be expected if each sequence were present in only a single copy.

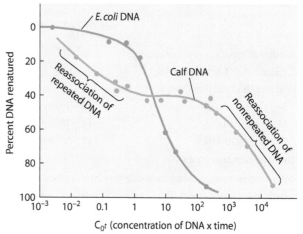

FIGURE 18-15 Renaturation of Calf and *E. coli* DNAs. The calf DNA that reassociates more rapidly than the bacterial DNA consists of repeated sequences.

The remaining 60% of the calf DNA renatures about a thousand times more slowly than *E. coli* DNA does, which is the behavior expected of sequences present as single copies. This fraction is therefore called **nonrepeated DNA** to distinguish it from the repeated sequences that renature more quickly. Nonrepeated DNA sequences are each present in one copy per genome. Most protein-coding genes consist of nonrepeated DNA, although this does not mean that all nonrepeated DNA codes for proteins.

In bacterial cells virtually all the DNA is nonrepeated, whereas eukaryotes exhibit large variations in their amounts of repeated versus nonrepeated DNA. This helps explain the mystery of the seemingly excess amount of DNA in species such as *Trillium*: This organism contains a relatively large amount of repeated DNA. Using the sequencing techniques described earlier, researchers have been able to determine the base sequences of various types of repeated DNAs and to classify them into two main categories: *tandemly repeated DNA* and *interspersed repeated DNA* (Table 18-3).

Tandemly Repeated DNA. One major category of repeated DNA is referred to as **tandemly repeated DNA** because the multiple copies are arranged next to each other in a row—that is, tandemly. Tandemly repeated DNA accounts for 10–15% of a typical mammalian genome and consists of many different types of DNA sequences that vary in both the length of the basic repeat unit and the number of times this unit is repeated in succession. The length of the repeated unit can measure anywhere from 1 to 2000 bp or so. Most of the time,

however, the repeated unit is shorter than 10 bp; consequently, this subcategory is called *simple-sequence repeated DNA*. Here is an example (showing one strand only) of a simple-sequence repeated DNA built from the five-base unit, GTTAC:

$$\ldots\text{GTTACGTTACGTTACGTTACGTTAC}\ldots$$

The number of sequential repetitions of the GTTAC unit can be as high as several hundred thousand at selected sites in the genome.

Tandemly repeated DNA of the simple-sequence type was originally called *satellite DNA* because its distinctive base composition often causes it to appear in a "satellite" band that separates from the rest of the genomic DNA during centrifugation procedures designed to separate molecules by density. This difference in density arises because adenine and guanine differ slightly in molecular weight, as do cytosine and thymine; hence, the densities of DNAs with differing base compositions will differ. In the procedures that reveal satellite bands, the genomic DNA is cleaved to short lengths, thus allowing DNA segments of differing densities to migrate freely to different positions during centrifugation.

What is the function of simple-sequence repeated DNA (satellite DNA)? Because such sequences are not usually transcribed, it has been proposed that they may instead be responsible for imparting special physical properties to certain regions of the chromosome. In most eukaryotes, chromosomal regions called **centromeres**—which play an important role in chromosome distribution during cell division (see Chapter 19)—are particularly rich in simple-sequence repeats, and these sequences may impart specialized structural properties to the centromere. **Telomeres,** which are DNA sequences located at the ends of chromosomes, also have simple-sequence repeats. In the next chapter, we will learn how telomeres protect chromosomes from degradation at their vulnerable ends during each round of replication (see Figure 19-16). Human telomeres contain 250–1500 copies of the sequence TTAGGG, which has been highly conserved over hundreds of millions of years of evolution. All vertebrates studied so far have this same identical sequence, and even unicellular eukaryotes possess similar sequences. Apparently, such sequences are critical to the survival of these organisms.

The amount of satellite DNA present at any given site can vary enormously. Typical satellite DNAs usually range from 10^5 to 10^7 bp in overall length. The term *minisatellite* DNA refers to shorter regions, about 10^2 to 10^5 bp in total length, composed of a tandem repeat unit of roughly 10–100 bp. *Microsatellite* DNAs, in which the repeat unit is only 1–10 bp, are even shorter (about 10–100 bp in length), although numerous sites in the genome may exhibit the same sequence. The short repeated sequences found in microsatellite and minisatellite DNAs are extremely useful in the laboratory for **DNA fingerprinting.** This procedure,

Table 18-3	**Categories of Repeated Sequences in Eukaryotic DNA**

I. Tandemly repeated DNA, including simple-sequence repeated DNA (satellite DNA)

10–15% of most mammalian genomes is this type of DNA

Length of each repeated unit:	1–2000 bp; typically 5–10 bp for simple-sequence repeated DNA
Number of repetitions per genome:	10^2–10^5
Arrangement of repeated units:	Tandem
Total length of satellite DNA at each site:	
Regular satellite DNA:	10^5–10^7 bp
Minisatellite DNA:	10^2–10^5 bp
Microsatellite DNA:	10^1–10^2 bp

II. Interspersed repeated DNA

25–50% of most mammalian genomes is this type of DNA

Length of each repeated unit:	10^2–10^4 bp
Arrangement of repeated units:	Scattered throughout the genome
Number of repetitions per genome:	10^1–10^6; "copies" not identical

described more fully in **Box 18C**, uses gel electrophoresis to compare DNA fragments derived from various regions of the genomes of two or more individuals. It is a means of identifying individuals that is as accurate as conventional fingerprinting.

Medical researchers have made the surprising discovery that more than a dozen inherited diseases of the nervous system involve simple changes in microsatellite DNAs. More specifically, these diseases are traceable to excessive numbers of repeated trinucleotide sequences within an otherwise normal gene. An example of this phenomenon, called *triplet repeat amplification,* is found in *Huntington's disease,* a devastating neurological disease that strikes in middle age and is invariably fatal. The normal version of the Huntington's gene contains the trinucleotide CAG tandemly repeated 11–34 times. The genes of afflicted individuals, however, possess up to 100 copies of the repeated unit. Neurological diseases resulting from the amplification of other triplet repeat sequences include *fragile X syndrome,* which is a major cause of mental retardation, and *myotonic dystrophy,* which affects the muscles. For some of these diseases, the repeated sequence is in a region of the affected gene that is not translated; for others, it is translated into a polypeptide segment consisting of a long string of the same amino acid. In both cases, the severity of the disease appears to correlate with the number of triplet repeats.

Interspersed Repeated DNA. The other main type of repeated DNA is **interspersed repeated DNA.** Rather than being clustered in tandem arrangements, the repeated units of this type of DNA are scattered around the genome. A single repeat unit tends to be hundreds or even thousands of base pairs long, and its dispersed "copies," which may number in the hundreds of thousands, are similar but usually not identical to one another. Interspersed repeated DNA typically accounts for 25–50% of mammalian genomes.

Most interspersed repeated DNA consists of families of **transposable elements (transposons),** also known as "jumping genes" because they can move around the genome and leave copies of themselves wherever they stop. Remarkably, in humans, roughly half the genome consists of these mobile elements. The most abundant, called **LINEs (long interspersed nuclear elements),** measure 6000–8000 bp in length and account for roughly 20% of the genome. LINEs possess genes coding for enzymes involved in copying LINE sequences (and other mobile elements) and inserting the copies elsewhere in the genome. Another class of mobile elements, called **SINEs (short interspersed nuclear elements),** consist of short repeated sequences less than 500 bp in length that do not contain genes, relying instead on enzymes made by other mobile elements for their movement. The most common SINEs in humans measure about 300 bp in length and are called *Alu sequences,* because the first ones identified all contained a restriction site for the restriction enzyme

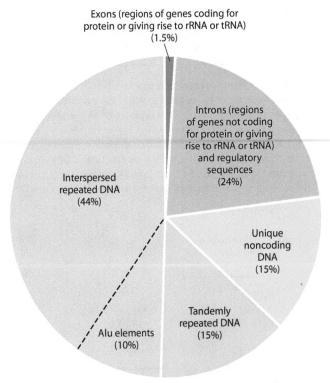

FIGURE 18-16 Types of DNA in the Human Genome. The DNA that encodes proteins or that is transcribed into ribosomal or transfer RNA accounts for only 1.5% of the DNA in the human genome. Interspersed repeat DNA accounts for 44% of the human genome; almost one quarter of this consists of *Alu* elements. Tandemly repeated DNA accounts for another 15% of the genome.

*Alu*I. Close to a million copies of the *Alu* sequence are spread throughout the human genome, accounting for approximately 10% of the DNA. DNA that encodes proteins or gives rise to ribosomal or transfer RNAs (such DNA is found in *exons,* as we will see in Chapter 21) accounts for surprisingly little of the DNA in the human genome (**Figure 18-16**).

The mobility of LINEs, SINEs, and other types of transposable elements is thought to create genomic variability that contributes to the evolutionary adaptability of organisms. In addition, the movement of some LINEs can occur during normal development and alter the expression of adjacent genes, suggesting a possible role in gene regulation. The origins of transposable elements and the mechanisms by which they move will be discussed more fully in Chapter 21.

DNA Packaging

Cells must accommodate an awesome amount of DNA, even in species with modestly sized genomes. For example, the typical *E. coli* cell measures about 1 μm in diameter and 2 μm in length, yet it must accommodate a (circular) DNA molecule with a length of about 1600 μm—enough DNA to encircle the cell more than 400 times! Eukaryotic cells face an even greater challenge. A human cell of average size

Analysis of the fragment patterns produced when DNA is digested with restriction enzymes has been exploited for a variety of purposes, ranging from research into genome organization to practical applications such as diagnosing genetic diseases and solving violent crimes. These practical applications are based on the fact that no two people (other than identical twins) have the same exact set of DNA base sequences. Although the differences in DNA sequence between any two people are quite small, they alter the lengths of some of the DNA fragments produced by restriction enzymes. These differences in fragment length, called **restriction fragment length polymorphisms (RFLPs)**, can be analyzed by gel electrophoresis. The resulting pattern of fragments serves as a "fingerprint" that identifies the individual from whom the DNA was obtained.

In practical usage, *DNA fingerprinting* is performed in a way that examines only a small, selected subset of restriction fragments. To illustrate this point, **Figure 18C-1** summarizes

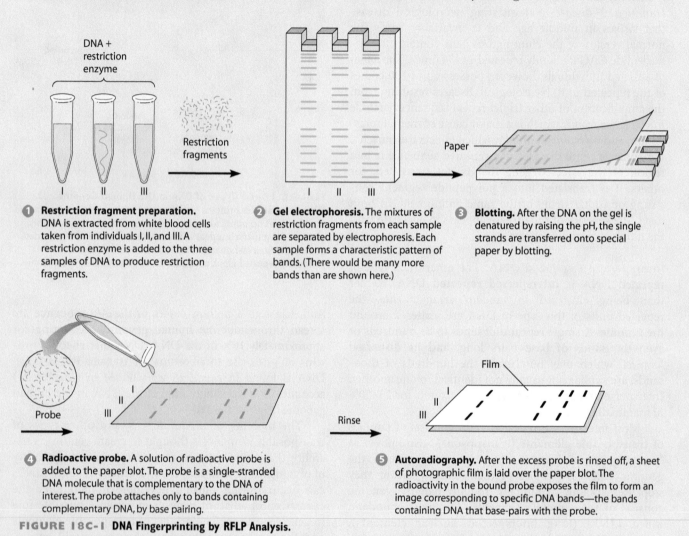

1 Restriction fragment preparation. DNA is extracted from white blood cells taken from individuals I, II, and III. A restriction enzyme is added to the three samples of DNA to produce restriction fragments.

2 Gel electrophoresis. The mixtures of restriction fragments from each sample are separated by electrophoresis. Each sample forms a characteristic pattern of bands. (There would be many more bands than are shown here.)

3 Blotting. After the DNA on the gel is denatured by raising the pH, the single strands are transferred onto special paper by blotting.

4 Radioactive probe. A solution of radioactive probe is added to the paper blot. The probe is a single-stranded DNA molecule that is complementary to the DNA of interest. The probe attaches only to bands containing complementary DNA, by base pairing.

5 Autoradiography. After the excess probe is rinsed off, a sheet of photographic film is laid over the paper blot. The radioactivity in the bound probe exposes the film to form an image corresponding to specific DNA bands—the bands containing DNA that base-pairs with the probe.

FIGURE 18C-1   DNA Fingerprinting by RFLP Analysis.

contains enough DNA to wrap around the cell more than 15,000 times. Somehow, all of this DNA must be efficiently packaged into cells and still be accessible to the cellular machinery for both DNA replication and the transcription of specific genes. Clearly, DNA packaging is a challenging problem for all forms of life. We will look first at how bacteria accomplish this task of organizing their DNA and then consider how eukaryotes address the same problem.

Bacteria Package DNA in Bacterial Chromosomes and Plasmids

The genome of a bacterium such as *E. coli* was once thought to be a "naked" DNA molecule lacking any elaborate organization and having only trivial amounts of protein associated with it. We now know that the organization of the bacterial genome is more like the

how DNA fingerprinting might be used to determine whether individuals carry a particular disease-causing gene even though they may not yet exhibit symptoms of the disease. In this example, imagine that individuals I, II, and III are members of a family in which the disease-causing gene is common. It is known that individual I carries the defective gene but individual II does not, and we want to determine the genetic status of their child, individual III.

The key step in DNA fingerprinting is called **Southern blotting** (after E. M. Southern, who developed it in 1975), but the fingerprinting procedure actually involves several distinct steps. In ❶ of Figure 18C-1, DNA obtained from the three individuals is digested with a restriction enzyme. In ❷, the resulting fragments are then separated from each other by gel electrophoresis. Because each person's DNA represents an entire genome, hundreds of thousands of bands would appear at this stage if all were made visible. Here is where Southern's stroke of brilliance comes in, with a technique that enables us to locate particular DNA sequences of interest within a complex mixture. In the Southern blotting process (❸), a special kind of "blotter" paper (nitrocellulose or nylon) is pressed against the completed gel, allowing the separated DNA fragments to be transferred to the paper. In ❹, a radioactive *probe* is added to the blot. The probe is simply a radioactive single-stranded DNA (or RNA) molecule whose base sequence is complementary to the DNA of interest—in this case, the DNA of the disease-causing gene. The probe binds to complementary DNA sequences by base pairing (the same process that occurs when denatured DNA renatures). In ❺, the bands that bind the radioactive probe are made visible by autoradiography. The results indicate that the child's version of the gene matches that of the *healthy* parent, individual II.

The autoradiogram in **Figure 18C-2** illustrates the use of DNA fingerprinting in a murder case. Here, RFLP analysis makes it clear that blood found on the defendant's clothes came from the victim, strongly implicating the defendant in the murder. Another practical application of DNA fingerprinting in the legal area is the determination of paternity or maternity.

For many DNA fingerprinting applications, scientists now analyze the length of short repeated sequences (microsatellite DNAs) called **short tandem repeats (STRs).** The STR sites chosen for DNA fingerprinting vary in length from person to person because of differences in the number of times the basic repeat unit is sequentially repeated. As a result, STR patterns in a person's DNA can be used to identify that individual uniquely. For example, the DNA of three suspects in a murder case might all

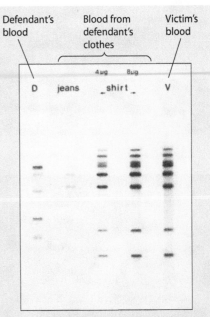

FIGURE 18C-2 DNA Fingerprints from a Murder Case. DNA was isolated from bloodstains on the defendant's clothes and compared, by RFLP analysis, with DNA from the defendant and DNA from the victim. The band pattern for the bloodstain DNA matches that for the victim, showing that the blood on the defendant's clothes came from the victim. (Courtesy of Cellmark Diagnostics.)

have different numbers of copies of the repeat sequence CTG at a particular place in the genome; one might have 19 copies, another 21 copies, and the third 32 copies. In criminal cases, the numbers of repeat copies present at 13 different STR sites in the genome are routinely examined. The chance that any two unrelated individuals would exhibit the same exact profile at all 13 sites is roughly one in a million billion.

The usefulness of DNA fingerprinting is further enhanced by the *polymerase chain reaction (PCR)*, a technique for making multiple DNA copies that will be described in Chapter 19. Starting with DNA isolated from a single cell, the PCR reaction can be used to selectively synthesize millions of copies of any given DNA sequence within a few hours, easily producing enough DNA for fingerprinting analysis of the 13 STR sites. In this way, a few skin cells left on a pen or car keys touched by a person may yield enough DNA to uniquely identify that individual.

chromosomes of eukaryotes than we previously realized. Bacterial geneticists therefore refer to the structure that contains the main bacterial genome as the **bacterial chromosome.**

Bacterial Chromosomes. Bacteria can have single or multiple, circular or linear chromosomes; the most common arrangement, however, is a single circular DNA molecule that is bound to small amounts of protein and localized to a special region of the bacterial cell called the **nucleoid** (**Figure 18-17**). Although the nucleoid is not surrounded by a membrane, the bacterial DNA residing in this region forms a threadlike mass of fibers packed together in a way that maintains a distinct boundary between the nucleoid and the rest of the cell. The DNA of the bacterial chromosome is negatively

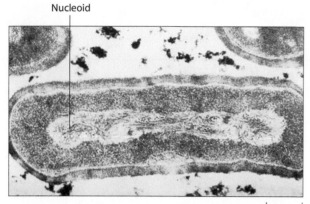

Nucleoid

0.25 µm

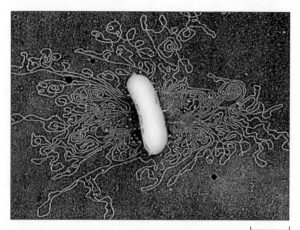

1 µm

FIGURE 18-17 The Bacterial Nucleoid. The electron micrograph at the top shows a bacterial cell with a distinct nucleoid, in which the bacterial chromosome resides. When bacterial cells are ruptured, their chromosomal DNA is released from the cell. The bottom micrograph shows that the released DNA forms a series of loops that remain attached to a structural framework within the nucleoid (TEMs).

supercoiled and folded into an extensive series of loops averaging about 20,000 bp in length. Because the two ends of each loop are anchored to structural components that lie within the nucleoid, the supercoiling of any individual loop can be altered without influencing the supercoiling of adjacent loops.

The loops are thought to be held in place by RNA and protein molecules. Evidence for a structural role for RNA in the bacterial chromosome has come from studies showing that treatment with ribonuclease, an enzyme that degrades RNA, releases some of the loops, although it does not relax the supercoiling. Nicking the DNA with a topoisomerase, on the other hand, relaxes the supercoiling but does not disrupt the loops. The supercoiled DNA that forms each loop is organized into beadlike packets containing small, basic protein molecules, analogous to the histones of eukaryotic cells (discussed below). Current evidence suggests that the DNA molecule is wrapped around particles of the basic protein. Thus, from what we

know so far, the bacterial chromosome consists of supercoiled DNA that is bound to small, basic proteins and then folded into looped domains.

Bacterial Plasmids. In addition to its chromosome, a bacterial cell may contain one or more plasmids. **Plasmids** are relatively small, usually circular molecules of DNA that carry genes both for their own replication and, often, for one or more cellular functions (usually nonessential ones). Most plasmids are supercoiled, giving them a condensed, compact form. Although plasmids replicate autonomously, the replication is usually sufficiently synchronized with the replication of the bacterial chromosome to ensure a roughly comparable number of plasmids from one cell generation to the next. In *E. coli* cells, several classes of plasmids are recognized: *F (fertility) factors* are involved in the process of conjugation, a sexual process ; *R (resistance) factors* carry genes that impart drug resistance to the bacterial cell; *col (colicinogenic) factors* allow the bacterium to secrete *colicins,* compounds that kill other bacteria lacking the col factor; *virulence factors* enhance the ability to cause disease by producing toxic proteins that cause tissue damage or enzymes that allow the bacteria to enter host cells; and *metabolic plasmids* produce enzymes required for certain metabolic reactions. Some strains of *E. coli* also possess *cryptic plasmids,* which have no known function and possess no genes other than those needed for the plasmid to replicate and spread to other cells.

Eukaryotes Package DNA in Chromatin and Chromosomes

When we turn from bacteria to eukaryotes, DNA packaging becomes more complicated. First, substantially larger amounts of DNA are involved. Each eukaryotic chromosome contains a single, linear DNA molecule of enormous size. In human cells, for example, just *one* of these DNA molecules may be 10 cm or more in length—roughly a hundred times the size of the DNA molecule found in a typical bacterial chromosome. Second, greater structural complexity is introduced by the association of eukaryotic DNA with greater amounts and numbers of proteins. When bound to these proteins, the DNA is converted into **chromatin** fibers 10–30 nm in diameter that are normally dispersed throughout the nucleus. At the time of cell division (and in a few other situations), these fibers condense and fold into much larger, compact structures that become recognizable as individual **chromosomes.**

The proteins with the most important role in chromatin structure are the **histones,** a group of relatively small proteins whose high content of the amino acids lysine and arginine gives them a strong positive charge. The binding of histones to DNA, which is negatively charged, is therefore stabilized by ionic bonds. In most cells, the mass of histones in chromatin is approximately equal to the mass of DNA. Histones are divided into five main types, designated H1, H2A, H2B, H3, and H4. Chromatin contains roughly equal numbers of H2A, H2B, H3, and H4 molecules, and about half that number of H1 molecules. These proportions are remarkably constant among different kinds of eukaryotic cells, regardless of the type of cell or its physiological state. In addition to histones, chromatin contains a diverse group of *nonhistone proteins* that play a variety of enzymatic, structural, and regulatory roles.

Nucleosomes Are the Basic Unit of Chromatin Structure

The DNA contained within a typical nucleus would measure a meter or more in length if it were completely extended, whereas the nucleus itself is usually no more than 5–10 μm in diameter. The folding of such an enormous length of DNA into a nucleus that is almost a million times smaller presents a significant topological problem. One of the first insights into the folding process emerged in the late 1960s, when X-ray diffraction studies carried out by Maurice Wilkins revealed that purified chromatin fibers have a repeating structural subunit that is seen in neither DNA nor histones alone. Wilkins therefore concluded that histones impose a repeating structural organization upon DNA. A clue to the nature of this structure was provided in 1974, when Ada Olins and Donald Olins published electron micrographs of chromatin fibers isolated from cells in a way that avoided the harsh solvents used in earlier procedures for preparing chromatin for microscopic examination. Chromatin fibers viewed in this way appear as a series of tiny particles attached to one another by thin filaments. This "beads-on-a-string" appearance led to the suggestion that the beads consist of protein (presumably histones) and the thin filaments connecting the beads correspond to DNA. We now refer to each bead, along with its associated short stretch of DNA, as a **nucleosome** (Figure 18-18).

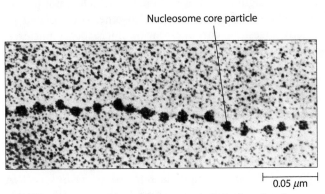

Nucleosome core particle

FIGURE 18-18 Nucleosomes. The core particles of nucleosomes appear as beadlike structures spaced at regular intervals along eukaryotic chromatin fibers. A nucleosome is defined to include both a core particle and the stretch of DNA that connects to the next core particle (TEM).

0.05 μm

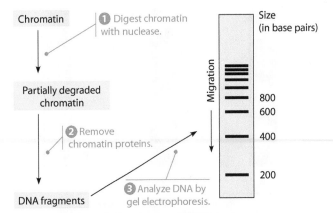

FIGURE 18-19 Evidence That Proteins Are Clustered at 200 Base-Pair Intervals Along the DNA Molecule in Chromatin Fibers. In these experiments, DNA fragments generated by nuclease digestion of rat liver chromatin were analyzed by gel electrophoresis. The discovery that the DNA fragments are multiples of 200 base pairs suggests that histones are clustered at 200 base-pair intervals along the DNA, thereby conferring a regular pattern of protection against nuclease digestion.

Based on electron microscopy alone, it would have been difficult to determine whether nucleosomes are a normal component of chromatin or an artifact generated during sample preparation. Fortunately, independent evidence for the existence of a repeating structure in chromatin was reported at about the same time by Dean Hewish and Leigh Burgoyne, who discovered that rat liver nuclei contain a nuclease that is capable of cleaving the DNA in chromatin fibers. In one crucial set of experiments, these investigators exposed chromatin to this nuclease and then purified the partially degraded DNA to remove chromatin proteins. Upon examining the purified DNA by gel electrophoresis, they found a distinctive pattern of fragments in which the smallest piece of DNA measured about 200 bp in length, and the remaining fragments were exact multiples of 200 bp (**Figure 18-19**). Since nuclease digestion of protein-free DNA does not generate this fragment pattern, they concluded that (1) chromatin proteins are clustered along the DNA molecule in a regular pattern that repeats at intervals of roughly 200 bp, and (2) the DNA located between these protein clusters is susceptible to nuclease digestion, yielding fragments that are multiples of 200 bp in length.

These observations raised the question of whether the protein clusters postulated to occur at 200-bp intervals correspond to the spherical particles observed in electron micrographs of chromatin fibers. Answering this question required a combination of the nuclease digestion and electron microscopic approaches. In these studies, chromatin was briefly exposed to *microccocal nuclease*—a bacterial enzyme that, like the rat liver nuclease, cleaves chromatin DNA at intervals of 200 bp. The fragmented chromatin was then separated into fractions of varying sizes by centrifugation and examined by electron microscopy. The smallest fraction was found to contain single spherical

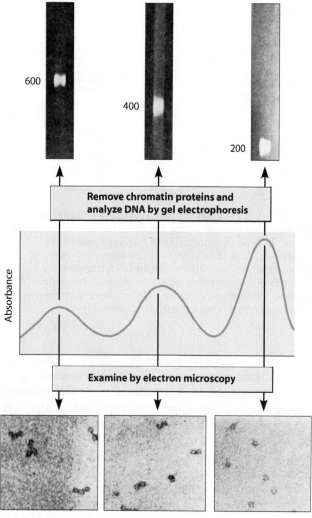

A Histone Octamer Forms the Nucleosome Core

The first insights into the molecular architecture of the nucleosome emerged from the work of Roger Kornberg, who was awarded a Nobel Prize in 2006 for a series of fundamental discoveries concerning DNA packaging and transcription in eukaryotes. In their early studies, Kornberg and his colleagues showed that chromatin fibers composed of nucleosomes can be generated by combining purified DNA with a mixture of all five histones. However, when they attempted to use individually purified histones, they discovered that nucleosomes could be assembled only when histones were isolated using gentle techniques that left histone H2A bound to histone H2B, and histone H3 bound to histone H4. When these H3–H4 and H2A–H2B complexes were mixed with DNA, chromatin fibers exhibiting normal nucleosomal structure were reconstituted. Kornberg therefore concluded that histone H3–H4 and H2A–H2B complexes are an integral part of the nucleosome.

To investigate the nature of these histone interactions in more depth, Kornberg and his colleague, Jean Thomas, treated isolated chromatin with a chemical reagent that forms covalent crosslinks between protein molecules that are located next to each other. After being treated with this reagent, the chemically crosslinked proteins were isolated and analyzed by polyacrylamide gel electrophoresis. Protein complexes the size of eight histone molecules were prominent in such gels, suggesting that the nucleosomal particle contains an *octamer* of eight histones. Given the knowledge that histones H3–H4 and histones H2A–H2B each form tight complexes and that these four histones are present in roughly equivalent amounts in chromatin, Kornberg and Thomas proposed that histone octamers are created by joining together two H2A–H2B dimers and two H3–H4 dimers and that the DNA double helix is then wrapped around the resulting octamer (**Figure 18-21**).

One issue not addressed by the preceding model concerns the significance of histone H1, which is not part of the octamer. If individual nucleosomes are isolated by briefly digesting chromatin with micrococcal nuclease, histone H1 is still present (along with the four other histones and 200 bp of DNA). When digestion is carried out for longer periods, the DNA fragment is further degraded until it reaches a length of about 146 bp; during the final stages of the digestion process, histone H1 is released. The remaining particle, consisting of a histone octamer associated with 146 bp of DNA, is referred to as a *core particle*. The DNA that is degraded during digestion from 200 to 146 bp in length is referred to as *linker DNA* because it joins one nucleosome to the next (Figure 18-21). Since histone H1 is released upon degradation of the linker DNA, histone H1 molecules are thought to be associated with the linker region. The length of the linker DNA varies somewhat among organisms, but the DNA

FIGURE 18-20 Evidence for the Existence of Nucleosomes. Chromatin that had been partially degraded by treatment with micrococcal nuclease was fractionated by density gradient centrifugation *(center graph)*. The individual peaks were then analyzed both by electron microscopy *(bottom)* and by gel electrophoresis after removal of chromatin proteins *(top)*. The peak on the right consists of single protein particles associated with 200 base pairs of DNA, the middle peak consists of clusters of two particles associated with 400 base pairs of DNA, and the peak on the left consists of clusters of three particles associated with 600 base pairs of DNA. This indicates that the basic repeat unit in chromatin is a protein particle associated with 200 base pairs of DNA.

particles, the next fraction contained clusters of two particles, the succeeding fraction contained clusters of three particles, and so forth (**Figure 18-20**). When DNA was isolated from these fractions and analyzed by gel electrophoresis, the DNA from the fraction containing single particles measured 200 bp in length, the DNA from the fraction containing clusters of two particles measured 400 bp in length, and so on. It was therefore concluded that the spherical particles observed in electron micrographs are each associated with 200 bp of DNA. This basic repeat unit, containing an average of 200 bp of DNA associated with a protein particle, is the nucleosome.

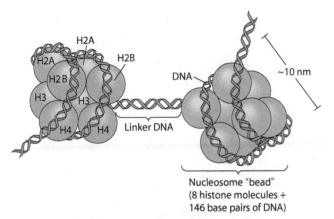

FIGURE 18-21 A Closer Look at Nucleosome Structure. Each nucleosome consists of eight histone molecules (two each of histones H2A, H2B, H3, and H4) associated with 146 base pairs of DNA and a stretch of linker DNA about 50 base pairs in length. The diameter of the nucleosome "bead," or core particle, is about 10 nm. Histone H1 (not shown) is thought to bind to the linker DNA and facilitate the packing of nucleosomes into 30-nm fibers.

ACTIVITIES www.thecellplace.com *Nucleosome structure*

associated with the core particle always measures close to 146 bp, which is enough to wrap around the core particle roughly 1.7 times.

Nucleosomes Are Packed Together to Form Chromatin Fibers and Chromosomes

The formation of nucleosomes is only the first step in the packaging of nuclear DNA (**Figure 18-22**). Isolated chromatin fibers exhibiting the beads-on-a-string appearance measure about 10 nm in diameter, but the chromatin of intact cells often forms a slightly thicker fiber, about 30 nm in diameter, called the **30-nm chromatin fiber.** In preparations of isolated chromatin, the 10-nm and 30-nm forms of the chromatin fiber can be interconverted by changing the salt concentration of the solution. However, the 30-nm fiber does not form in chromatin preparations whose histone H1 molecules have been removed, suggesting that histone H1 facilitates the packing of nucleosomes into the 30-nm fiber. Several models have been proposed to explain how individual nucleosomes are packed together to form a 30-nm fiber. Most early models postulated that the chain of nucleosomes is twisted upon itself to form some type of coiled structure. However, more recent studies suggest that the structure of the 30-nm fiber is much less uniform than a coiled model suggests. Instead, the nucleosomes of the 30-nm fiber seem to be packed together to form an irregular, three-dimensional zigzag structure that can interdigitate with its neighboring fibers.

The next level of chromatin packaging is the folding of the 30-nm fibers into **looped domains** averaging 50,000–100,000 bp in length. This looped arrangement is maintained by the periodic attachment of DNA to an insoluble network of nonhistone proteins that form a chromosomal *scaffold* to which the long loops of DNA are attached. The looped domains can be most clearly seen in electron micrographs of chromosomes isolated from dividing cells and treated to remove all the histones and most of the nonhistone proteins (**Figure 18-23**). Loops can also be seen in specialized types of chromosomes that are not associated with the process of cell division. In these cases, the chromatin loops turn out to contain "active" regions of DNA—that is, DNA that is being transcribed. It makes sense that active DNA would be less tightly packed than inactive DNA because it would allow easier access by proteins involved in gene transcription.

Even in cells where genes are being actively transcribed, significant amounts of chromatin may be further compacted (Figure 18-22d). The degree of folding in such cells varies over a continuum. Segments of chromatin so highly compacted that they show up as dark spots in micrographs are called **heterochromatin,** whereas the more loosely packed, diffuse form of chromatin is called **euchromatin** (see Figure 18-27a). The tightly packed heterochromatin contains DNA that is transcriptionally inactive, while the more loosely packed euchromatin is associated with DNA that is being actively transcribed. Much of the chromatin in metabolically active cells is loosely packed as euchromatin; but as a cell prepares to divide, *all* of its chromatin becomes highly compacted, generating a group of microscopically distinguishable chromosomes. Because the chromosomal DNA has recently been duplicated, each chromosome is composed of two duplicate units called *chromatids* (Figure 18-22e).

The extent to which a DNA molecule has been folded in chromatin and chromosomes can be quantified using the **DNA packing ratio,** which is calculated by determining the total extended length of a DNA molecule and dividing it by the length of the chromatin fiber or chromosome into which it has been packaged. The initial coiling of the DNA around the histone cores of the nucleosomes reduces the length by a factor of about seven, and formation of the 30-nm fiber results in a further sixfold condensation. The packing ratio of the 30-nm fiber is therefore about $7 \times 6 = 42$. Further folding and coiling brings the overall packing ratio of typical euchromatin to about 750. For heterochromatin and the chromosomes of dividing cells, the packing ratio is still higher. At the time of cell division, for example, a typical human chromosome measures about 4–5 μm in length, yet contains a DNA molecule that would measure almost 75 mm if completely extended. The packing ratio for such a chromosome therefore falls in the range of 15,000–20,000.

Eukaryotes Package Some of Their DNA in Mitochondria and Chloroplasts

A eukaryotic cell's DNA is not contained solely in the nucleus. Though nuclear DNA accounts for nearly all of a cell's genetic information, mitochondria and chloroplasts

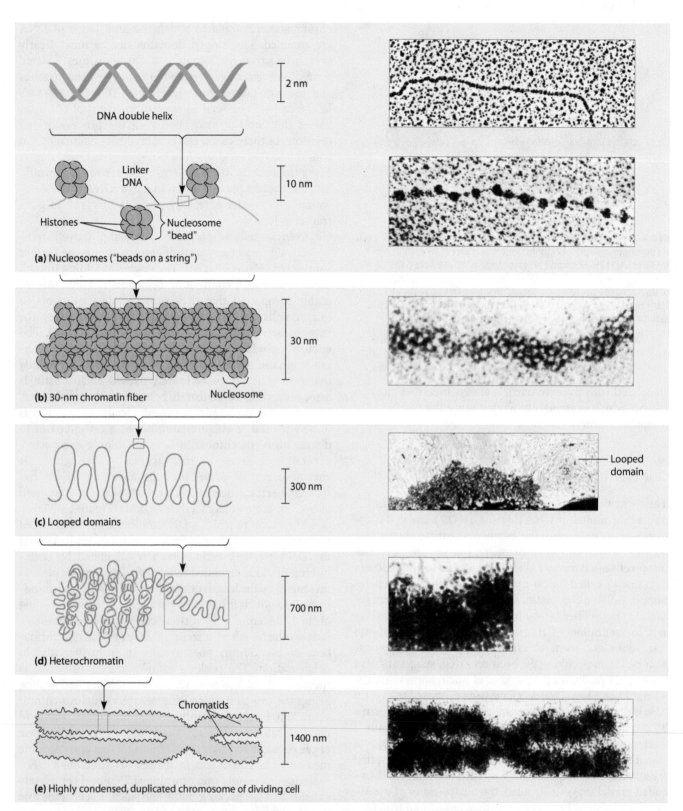

FIGURE 18-22 Levels of Chromatin Packing. These diagrams and TEMs show a current model for progressive stages of DNA coiling and folding, culminating in the highly compacted chromosome of a dividing cell. **(a)** "Beads on a string," an extended configuration of nucleosomes formed by the association of DNA with four types of histones. **(b)** The 30-nm chromatin fiber, shown here as a tightly packed collection of nucleosomes. The fifth histone, H1, may be located in the interior of the fiber. **(c)** Looped domains of 30-nm fibers, visible in the TEM here because a mitotic chromosome has been experimentally unraveled. **(d)** Heterochromatin, highly folded chromatin that is visible as discrete spots even in interphase cells. **(e)** A replicated chromosome (two attached chromatids) from a dividing cell, with all the DNA of the chromosome in the form of very highly compacted heterochromatin.

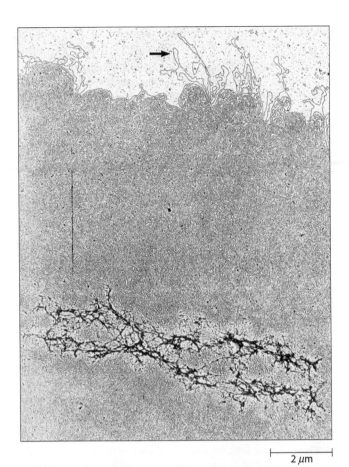

FIGURE 18-23 Electron Micrograph Showing the Protein Scaffold That Remains After Removing Histones from Human Chromosomes. The chromosomal DNA remains attached to the scaffold as a series of long loops. The arrow points to a region where a loop of the DNA molecule can be clearly seen (TEM).

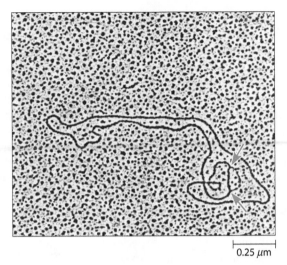

0.25 μm

FIGURE 18-24 Mitochondrial DNA. Mitochondrial DNA from most organisms is circular, as seen in this electron micrograph. This molecule was caught in the act of replication; the arrows indicate the points at which replication was proceeding when the molecule was fixed for electron microscopy (TEM).

required for mitochondrial protein synthesis, and 13 of the polypeptide subunits of the electron transport system. These include subunits of NADH dehydrogenase, cytochrome *b*, cytochrome *c* oxidase, and ATP synthase (**Figure 18-25**).

contain some DNA of their own—along with the machinery needed to replicate, transcribe, and translate the information encoded by this DNA. The DNA molecules residing in mitochondria and chloroplasts are devoid of histones and are usually circular (**Figure 18-24**). In other words, they resemble the genomes of bacteria, as we might expect from the likely endosymbiotic origin of these organelles. Mitochondrial and chloroplast genomes tend to be relatively small, comparable in size to a viral genome. Both organelles are therefore semiautonomous, able to code for some of their polypeptides but dependent on the nuclear genome to encode most of them.

The genome of the human mitochondrion, for example, consists of a circular DNA molecule containing 16,569 base pairs and measuring about 5 μm in length. It has been completely sequenced, and all of its 37 genes are known. The RNA and polypeptides encoded by this DNA are just a small fraction (about 5%) of the number of RNA molecules and proteins needed by the mitochondrion. This is nonetheless a vital genetic contribution, for these products include the RNA molecules present in mitochondrial ribosomes, all of the transfer RNA molecules

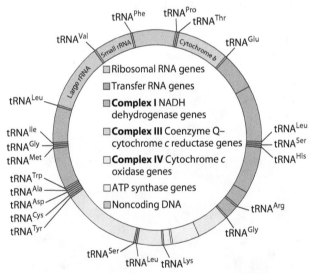

FIGURE 18-25 Genome of the Human Mitochondrion. The double-stranded DNA molecule of the human mitochondrion is circular and contains 16,569 base pairs. This genome codes for large and small ribosomal RNA molecules, transfer RNA (tRNA) molecules (each identified by a superscript with the three-letter abbreviation for the amino acid it carries), and subunits of a number of the proteins that make up the mitochondrial electron transport system complexes. The tRNA genes are very short because the RNA molecules they encode each contain only about 75 nucleotides. Notice that there are two tRNA genes for leucine and two for serine; they code for slightly different versions of tRNAs for these amino acids. The mitochondrial genome is extremely compact, with little noncoding DNA between genes.

DNA Packaging **535**

The size of the mitochondrial genome varies considerably among organisms. Mammalian mitochondria typically have about 16,500 bp of DNA, yeast mitochondrial DNA is five times larger, and plant mitochondrial DNA is larger yet. It is not clear, however, that larger mitochondrial genomes necessarily code for correspondingly more polypeptides. A comparison of yeast and human mitochondrial DNA, for example, suggests that most of the additional DNA present in the yeast mitochondrion consists of noncoding sequences. In addition to these species-specific differences in mitochondrial genome size, some mitochondrial DNA sequences are unique to a given species. For example, a 648-nucletotide sequence, sometimes called the "*DNA bar code*," can be used to precisely identify one closely related species from another.

Chloroplasts typically possess circular DNA molecules measuring around 120,000 bp in length and containing about 120 genes. Besides the ribosomal and transfer RNAs and polypeptides involved in protein synthesis, the chloroplast genome also codes for a few polypeptides involved in photosynthesis. These include several polypeptide components of photosystems I and II and one of the two subunits of ribulose-1,5-bisphosphate carboxylase, the carbon-fixing enzyme of the Calvin cycle.

Interestingly, most polypeptides encoded by mitochondrial or chloroplast genomes are components of multimeric proteins that also contain subunits encoded by the nuclear genome. In other words, organelle proteins that contain subunits encoded within the organelle are typically hybrid protein complexes containing polypeptides encoded and synthesized within the organelle plus polypeptides encoded by the nuclear genome and synthesized by cytoplasmic ribosomes. This raises intriguing questions about how polypeptides synthesized in the cytoplasm enter the organelle, a topic we will cover in Chapter 22.

The Nucleus

We have discussed DNA as the genetic material of the cell, the genome as a complete set of DNA instructions for the cells of a particular species, and the chromosome as the physical means of packaging DNA within cells. Now we come to the **nucleus,** the site within the eukaryotic cell where the chromosomes are localized and replicated and where the DNA they contain is transcribed. The nucleus is therefore both the repository of most of the cell's genetic information and the control center for the expression of that information.

The nucleus is one of the most prominent and distinguishing features of eukaryotic cells (**Figure 18-26**). In fact, the term *eukaryon* means "true nucleus." This means that the very essence of a eukaryotic cell is its membrane-bounded nucleus, which compartmentalizes the activities of the genome—both replication and transcription—from the rest of cellular metabolism. In the following discussion, we focus first on the membrane envelope that forms the boundary of the nucleus. Then we turn our attention to the pores that perforate the envelope, the structural

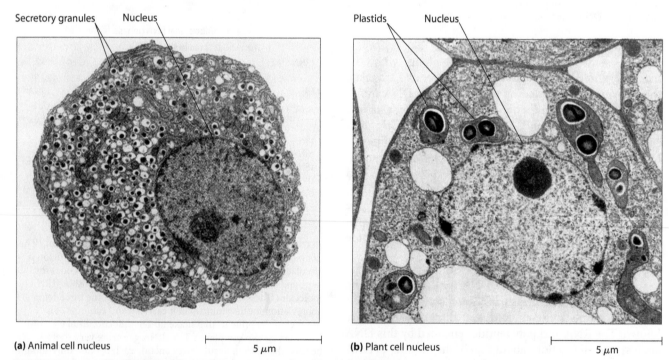

(a) Animal cell nucleus   5 μm   **(b)** Plant cell nucleus   5 μm

FIGURE 18-26 The Nucleus. The nucleus is a prominent structural feature in most eukaryotic cells. **(a)** The nucleus of an animal cell. This is an insulin-producing cell from a rat pancreas, hence the prominence of secretory granules in the cytoplasm. **(b)** The nucleus of a plant cell. This is a cell from a soybean root nodule. The prominence of plastids reflects their role in the storage of starch granules (TEMs).

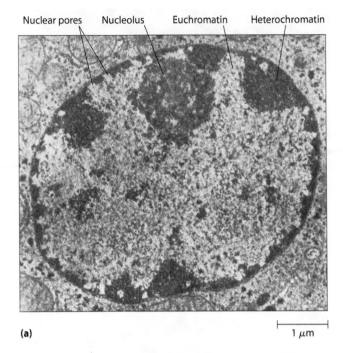

Nuclear pores Nucleolus Euchromatin Heterochromatin

(a)

| 1 μm

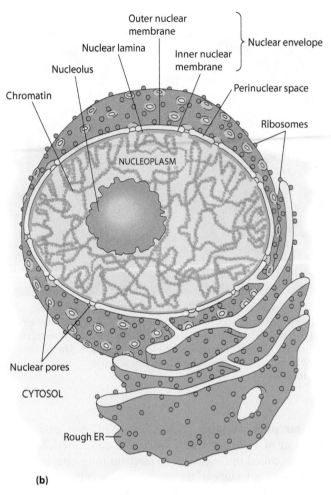

Outer nuclear
membrane
Nuclear lamina
Nucleolus
Inner nuclear
membrane
Chromatin
Nuclear envelope
Perinuclear space
Ribosomes

NUCLEOPLASM

Nuclear pores

CYTOSOL

Rough ER

(b)

FIGURE 18-27 Structural Organization of the Nucleus and Nuclear Envelope. (a) An electron micrograph of the nucleus from a mouse liver cell, with prominent structural features labeled (TEM). The nuclear envelope is a double membrane perforated by nuclear pores. Internal structures include the nucleolus, euchromatin, and heterochromatin. (b) A drawing of a typical nucleus. Structural features included here but not visible in the micrograph include the nuclear lamina, ribosomes on the outer nuclear membrane, and the continuity between the outer nuclear membrane and the rough ER.

matrix inside the nucleus, the arrangement of the chromatin fibers, and finally, the organization of the nucleolus. **Figure 18-27** provides an overview of some of these nuclear structures.

A Double-Membrane Nuclear Envelope Surrounds the Nucleus

The existence of a membrane around the nucleus was first suggested in the late nineteenth century, based primarily on the osmotic properties of the nucleus. Since light microscopy reveals only a narrow, fuzzy border at the outer surface of the nucleus, little was known about the structure of this membranous boundary before the advent of electron microscopy. Transmission electron microscopy revealed that the nucleus is bounded by a **nuclear envelope** composed of two membranes—the inner and outer nuclear membranes—separated by a **perinuclear space** measuring about 20–40 nm across (see Figure 18-27b). The outer nuclear membrane is continuous with the endoplasmic reticulum, making the perinuclear space continuous with the lumen of the ER. Like membranes of the rough ER, the outer membrane is often studded on its outer surface with ribosomes engaged in protein synthesis. Several proteins in the outer

membrane bind to actin and intermediate filaments of the cell's cytoskeleton, thereby anchoring the nucleus within the cell and providing a mechanism for nuclear movements. Tubular invaginations of the nuclear envelope, collectively known as the *nucleoplasmic reticulum,* may project into the internal nuclear space and increase the area of the nucleus that makes direct contact with the inner nuclear membrane.

One of the most distinctive features of the nuclear envelope is the presence of specialized channels called **nuclear pores,** which are especially easy to see when the nuclear envelope is examined by freeze-fracture microscopy (**Figure 18-28**). Each pore is a small cylindrical channel extending through both membranes of the nuclear envelope, thereby providing direct continuity between the cytosol and the **nucleoplasm** (the name for the interior space of the nucleus other than the region occupied by the nucleolus). The number of pores varies greatly with cell type and activity. A typical mammalian nucleus has about 3000–4000 pores, or about 10–20 pores per square micrometer of membrane surface area.

At each pore, the inner and outer membranes of the nuclear envelope are fused together, forming a channel that is lined with an intricate protein structure called the

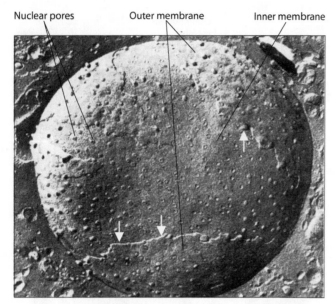

Nuclear pores   Outer membrane   Inner membrane

FIGURE 18-28 Nuclear Pores. Numerous nuclear pores are visible in this freeze-fracture micrograph of the nuclear envelope of an epithelial cell from a rat kidney. The fracture plane reveals faces of both the inner membrane and the outer membrane. The arrows point to ridges that represent the perinuclear space delimited by the two membranes (TEM).

nuclear pore complex (NPC). The NPC has an outer diameter of ~120 nm and is built from about 30 different proteins called *nucleoporins.* In electron micrographs, the most striking feature of the pore complex is its octagonal symmetry. Micrographs such as the one in **Figure 18-29a** show rings of eight subunits arranged in an octagonal pattern. In other views, the eight subunits are seen to protrude on both the cytoplasmic and nucleoplasmic sides of the envelope. Notice that central granules can be seen in some of the nuclear pore complexes in Figure 18-29a. Although these granules were once thought to consist solely of particles in transit through the pores, they are now thought to also contain components that are an integral part of the pore complex.

Figure 18-29b illustrates the main components of the nuclear pore complex. Examination of this diagram reveals that the pore complex as a whole is shaped somewhat like a wheel lying on its side within the nuclear envelope. Two parallel rings, outlining the rim of the wheel, each consist of the eight subunits seen in electron micrographs. Eight spokes (shown in green) extend from the rings to the wheel's hub (dark pink), which is the "central granule" seen in many electron micrographs. This granule is sometimes called the *transporter* because it is thought to contain components that are involved in moving macromolecules across the nuclear envelope. Proteins extending from the rim into the perinuclear space may help anchor the pore complex to the envelope. Fibers also extend from the rings into the cytosol and nucleoplasm, with those on the nucleoplasm side forming a basket (sometimes called a "cage" or "fishtrap").

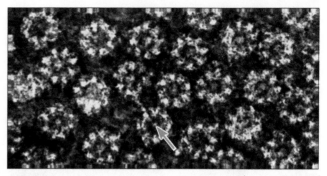

(a) Nuclear pores in the envelope   0.25 μm

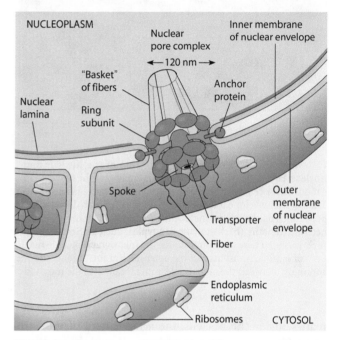

(b) Location of nuclear pores in nuclear membrane

FIGURE 18-29 Structure of the Nuclear Pore. (a) Negative staining of an oocyte nuclear envelope reveals the octagonal pattern of the nuclear pore complexes. The arrow shows a central granule. This nuclear envelope is from an oocyte of the newt *Taricha granulosa* (TEM). **(b)** A nuclear pore is formed by fusion of the inner and outer nuclear membranes and is lined by an intricate protein structure called the nuclear pore complex. The structure is roughly wheel-shaped and has octagonal symmetry. Two parallel rings, each consisting of eight subunits (dark purple), outline the rim of the wheel. Eight spokes (green) connect the two rings (two of the spokes are omitted from the drawing) and extend to the central transporter (dark pink) at the hub of the wheel; the transporter is thought to contain components involved in moving particles through the pore. Fibers extend above and below the complex, with those on the nucleoplasmic side forming a basket of unknown function.

VIDEOS www.thecellplace.com *Nuclear pore structure*

Molecules Enter and Exit the Nucleus Through Nuclear Pores

The nuclear envelope solves one problem but creates another. As a means of localizing chromosomes and their activities to one region of the cell, it is an example of the general eukaryotic strategy of compartmentalization.

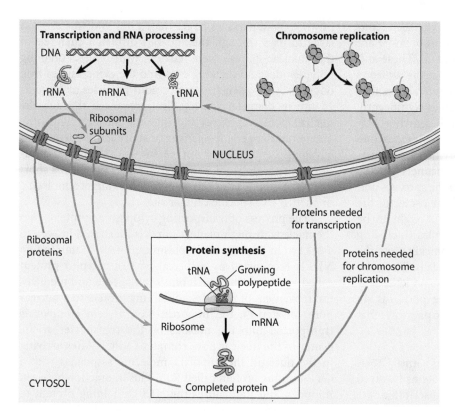

FIGURE 18-30 Macromolecular Transport into and out of the Nucleus. Because eukaryotic cells store their genetic information in the nucleus but synthesize proteins in the cytoplasm, all the proteins needed in the nucleus must be transported inward from the cytoplasm (purple arrows), and all the RNA molecules and ribosomal subunits needed for protein synthesis in the cytoplasm must be transported outward from the nucleus (red arrows). The three kinds of RNA molecules required for protein synthesis are ribosomal RNA (rRNA), messenger RNA (mRNA), and transfer RNA (tRNA).

Presumably, it is advantageous for a nucleus to possess a barrier that keeps in the chromosomes and keeps out organelles such as ribosomes, mitochondria, lysosomes, and microtubules. For example, the nuclear envelope protects newly synthesized RNA from being acted upon by cytoplasmic organelles or enzymes before it has been fully processed.

But in the act of separating immature RNA molecules and chromosomes from the cytoplasm, the nuclear envelope creates several formidable transport problems for eukaryotic cells that are unknown in prokaryotes. All the enzymes and other proteins required for chromosome replication and transcription of DNA in the nucleus must be imported from the cytoplasm, and all the RNA molecules and partially assembled ribosomes needed for protein synthesis in the cytoplasm must be obtained from the nucleus (**Figure 18-30**). In response to these transport problems, specialized pores have evolved that mediate virtually all transport into and out of the nucleus.

To get some idea of how much traffic must travel through the nuclear pores, consider the flow of ribosomal subunits from the nucleus to the cytoplasm. Ribosomes are partially assembled in the nucleus as two classes of subunits, each of which is a complex of RNA and proteins. These subunits move to the cytoplasm and, when needed for protein synthesis, are combined into functional ribosomes containing one of each type of subunit. An actively growing mammalian cell can easily be synthesizing 20,000 ribosomal subunits per minute. We already know that such a cell has about 3000–4000 nuclear pores, so ribosomal subunits must be transported to the cytosol at a rate

of about 5–6 subunits per minute per pore. Traffic in the opposite direction is, if anything, even heavier. When chromosomes are being replicated, histones are needed at the rate of about 300,000 molecules per minute. The rate of inward movement must therefore be about 100 histone molecules per minute per pore! In addition to all this macromolecular traffic, the pores mediate the transport of smaller particles, molecules, and ions.

Simple Diffusion of Small Molecules Through Nuclear Pores. The idea that small particles can diffuse freely back and forth through nuclear pores first received experimental support from studies in which colloidal gold particles of various sizes were injected into the cytoplasm of cells that were then examined by electron microscopy. Shortly after injection, the gold particles could be seen passing through the nuclear pores and into the nucleus. The rate of particle entry into the nucleus is inversely related to the particle's diameter—that is, the larger the gold particle, the slower it enters the nucleus. Particles larger than about 10 nm in diameter are excluded entirely. Since the overall diameter of a nuclear pore complex is much larger than such gold particles, it was concluded that the pore complex contains tiny, *aqueous diffusion channels* through which small particles and molecules can freely move.

To determine the diameter of these channels, investigators have injected radioactive proteins of various sizes into the cytoplasm of cells and observed how long it takes for the proteins to appear in the nucleus. A globular protein with a molecular weight of 20,000 takes only a few minutes to equilibrate between the cytoplasm and nucleus, but most proteins of 60,000 daltons or more are barely able to penetrate into the nucleus at all. These and other transport measurements indicate that the aqueous diffusion channels are about 9 nm in diameter, a size that creates a permeability barrier for molecules significantly larger than ~30,000 in molecular weight. Researchers initially assumed that each nuclear pore complex has one such channel. However, more recent evidence suggests there may be eight separate 9-nm channels at the periphery of the pore complex—between the spokes—and perhaps an additional 9-nm channel at the center of the transporter. These aqueous channels are thought to be freely permeable to ions and small molecules (including small proteins) because such substances quickly cross the nuclear envelope after being injected into cells. Thus, the nucleoside triphosphates required for DNA and RNA synthesis probably diffuse freely through the pores, as do other small molecules needed for metabolic pathways that function within the nucleus.

Active Transport of Large Proteins and RNA Through Nuclear Pores. Many of the proteins involved in DNA packaging, replication, and transcription are small enough to pass through a 9-nm-wide channel. Histones, for example, have molecular weights of 21,000 or less and should therefore passively diffuse through the nuclear pores with little problem. Some nuclear proteins are very large, however. The enzymes involved in DNA and RNA synthesis, for example, have subunits with molecular weights in excess of 100,000, which is too large to fit through a 9-nm opening. Messenger RNA molecules pose a challenge, too, because they leave the nucleus bound to proteins in the form of RNA-protein ("ribonucleoprotein") complexes that are quite large. Ribosomal subunits must also be exported to the cytoplasm after being assembled in the nucleus. Clearly, transporting all these particles through the nuclear pores is a significant challenge.

A large body of evidence suggests that such large molecules and particles are actively transported through nuclear pores by a selective process. Like active transport across single membranes, active transport through nuclear pores requires energy and involves specific binding of the transported substance to membrane proteins, which in this case are part of the pore complex. The underlying molecular mechanism is best understood for proteins that are actively transported from the cytosol into the nucleus. Such proteins possess one or more **nuclear localization signals (NLS),** which are amino acid sequences that enable the protein to be recognized and transported by the nuclear pore complex. An NLS is usually 8–30 amino acids in length and often contains proline as well as the positively charged (basic) amino acids lysine and arginine.

The role played by NLS sequences in targeting proteins for the nucleus has been established by experiments in which gold particles larger than 9 nm in diameter—too large to pass through the aqueous diffusion channels of the nuclear pores—were coated with NLS-containing polypeptides and then injected into the cytoplasm of frog oocytes. After such treatment, gold particles as large as 26 nm in diameter are rapidly transported through the nuclear pore complexes and into the nucleus. Thus, the maximum diameter for *active* transport across the nuclear envelope seems to be 26 nm (versus 9 nm for simple diffusion). This is only one of many examples in which a short stretch of amino acids has been found to target a molecule or particle to a specific cellular site.

The process of transporting cytoplasmic proteins into the nucleus through nuclear pores is illustrated in **Figure 18-31a.** In step ❶, a cytoplasmic protein containing an NLS is recognized by a special type of receptor protein called an **importin,** which binds to the NLS and mediates the movement of the NLS-containing protein to a nuclear pore. In step ❷, the importin-NLS protein complex is transported into the nucleus by the transporter at the center of the nuclear pore complex (NPC). After arriving in the nucleus, the importin molecule associates with a GTP-binding protein called *Ran*. This interaction between importin and Ran causes the NLS-containing protein to be released for use in the nucleus (step ❸). The Ran-GTP-importin complex is then transported back through a nuclear pore to the cytoplasm (step ❹), where the importin is released for reuse accompanied by hydrolysis of the Ran-bound GTP (step ❺). Evidence that this GTP hydrolysis step provides the energy for nuclear import has come from experiments showing that nuclear transport can be inhibited by exposing cells to nonhydrolyzable analogs of GTP but not by exposing cells to nonhydrolyzable analogs of ATP.

For exporting material out of the nucleus, comparable mechanisms operate. The main difference is that transport out of the nucleus is used mainly for RNA molecules that are synthesized in the nucleus but function in the cytoplasm, whereas nuclear import is devoted largely to importing proteins that are synthesized in the cytoplasm but function in the nucleus. Although the main cargo for nuclear export is RNA rather than protein, RNA export is mediated by proteins that bind to the RNA. These adaptor proteins contain amino acid sequences called **nuclear export signals (NES),** which target the protein—and hence its bound RNA—for export through the nuclear pores. NES sequences are recognized by nuclear transport receptor proteins called **exportins,** which bind to molecules containing NES sequences and mediate their transport out through the nuclear pores by a mechanism resembling that used by importins to transport cytoplasmic molecules into the nucleus (Figure 18-31b).

The difference in direction between importin- and exportin-mediated transport is governed by the interaction between Ran-GTP and these two classes of molecules, accompanied by a concentration gradient of Ran-GTP across the nuclear envelope. The Ran-GTP concentration

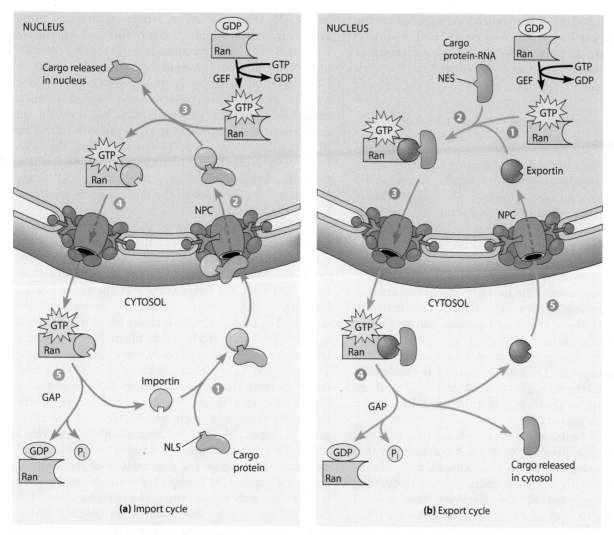

FIGURE 18-31 Transport Through the Nuclear Pore Complex. (a) Import cycle. Proteins made in the cytosol and destined for use in the nucleus contain a nuclear localization sequence (NLS) that targets them as "cargo" for transport through the nuclear pore complex. ❶ An NLS-containing cargo protein binds to importin, and ❷ the importin-cargo complex is then transported through the nuclear pore complex. ❸ Nuclear Ran-GTP binds to importin, triggering the release of the cargo protein in the nucleus. ❹ The Ran-GTP-importin complex is transported back to the cytosol, where ❺ the hydrolysis of GTP to GDP is accompanied by the release of importin. (b) Export cycle. The main cargo for nuclear export is RNA rather than protein, but RNAs are generally transported out of the nucleus by proteins containing a nuclear export signal (NES). During the export cycle, ❶ Ran-GTP binds to exportin in the nucleus, which ❷ promotes the binding of exportin to its cargo, in this case a protein-RNA complex. ❸ The exportin-cargo-Ran-GTP complex is exported through the nuclear pore to the cytosol, where ❹ the exportin and its cargo are released from Ran, accompanied by hydrolysis of GTP to GDP. ❺ Exportin then moves back into the nucleus, where it can repeat the export cycle. The import and export cycles are both driven by a concentration gradient of Ran-GTP that is maintained by the presence of a GEF (guanine-nucleotide exchange factor) in the nucleus and a GAP (GTPase activating protein) in the cytosol.

is maintained at high levels inside the nucleus by a *guanine-nucleotide exchange factor (GEF)* that promotes the binding of GTP to Ran in exchange for GDP. In contrast, the cytosol contains a *GTPase activating protein (GAP)* that promotes the hydrolysis of GTP by Ran, thereby lowering the Ran-GTP concentration outside the nucleus. The relatively high concentration of Ran-GTP inside the nucleus has two effects: first, nuclear Ran-GTP *promotes the release* of NLS-containing cargo from importin (Figure 18-31a, step ❸); second, nuclear Ran-

GTP *promotes the binding* of NES-containing cargo to exportin (Figure 18-31b, step ❷). The net result is that the direction of transport for any given cargo molecule is determined by the type of targeting sequence it contains (NLS or NES), which dictates whether importins will release the cargo in the nucleus and bind it in the cytoplasm or exportins will bind the cargo in the nucleus and release it in the cytoplasm.

The nuclear transport cycle poses a recycling problem for the cell: Ran-GTP is exported along with molecules that leave the nucleus. If Ran were not recycled back to the nucleus, nuclear Ran would soon be depleted. A specific nuclear transport protein, *NTF2* (for nuclear transport factor 2), solves this problem by shuttling Ran-GDP back into the nucleus.

The Nuclear Matrix and Nuclear Lamina Are Supporting Structures of the Nucleus

Roughly 80–90% of the nuclear mass is accounted for by chromatin fibers, so you might expect that removing the chromatin would cause the nucleus to collapse into a relatively structureless form. However, in the early 1970s researchers discovered that an insoluble fibrous network retaining the overall shape of the nucleus remains behind after more than 95% of the chromatin has been removed by a combination of nuclease and detergent treatments. This network, called the **nuclear matrix** or **nucleoskeleton,** is thought to help maintain the shape of the nucleus and provide an organizing skeleton for the chromatin fibers. The existence of such an organizing skeleton has not been accepted by all cell biologists, however. The fibrous network is visible only in certain micrographs (**Figure 18-32**), leading skeptics to question whether it is an artifact introduced during sample preparation.

In recent years, additional evidence has bolstered the case for the presence of a structural skeleton that organizes nuclear activities. For example, a close connection between chromatin fibers and an underlying matrix is suggested by the discovery that isolated nuclear matrix preparations always contain small amounts of tightly bound DNA and RNA. Nucleic acid hybridization techniques have revealed that the tightly bound DNA is enriched in sequences that are being actively transcribed into RNA. Moreover, when cells are incubated with ^{3}H-thymidine, a radioactive precursor for DNA synthesis, the newly synthesized radioactive DNA is found to be preferentially associated with the nuclear matrix. These observations suggest that an underlying skeletal network may be involved in anchoring chromatin fibers at locations where DNA or RNA is being synthesized, thereby organizing the DNA for orderly replication and transcription and perhaps even providing tracks that guide and propel newly formed messenger RNA to the nuclear pores for transport to the cytoplasm.

While the exact makeup and role of the nuclear matrix remain to be elucidated, the nucleus contains one skeletal structure that is well understood. This structure, called the **nuclear lamina,** is a thin, dense meshwork of fibers that lines the inner surface of the inner nuclear membrane and confers mechanical strength to the nucleus. The nuclear lamina is about 10–40 nm thick and is constructed from intermediate filaments made of proteins called *lamins* (described in more detail in Chapter 15). Inherited abnormalities in these proteins have been linked to more than a dozen human diseases, including several involving severe muscle wasting or premature aging. For example, a single base mutation in one lamin gene is responsible for *Hutchinson–Gilford progeria,* a disease in which symptoms of old age—such as hair loss, cardiovascular disease, and degeneration of skin, muscle, and bone—appear in young children and usually cause death by the early teenage years. The cells of such individuals exhibit severe abnormalities in nuclear shape, although it is not clear how such nuclear changes relate to the various disease symptoms.

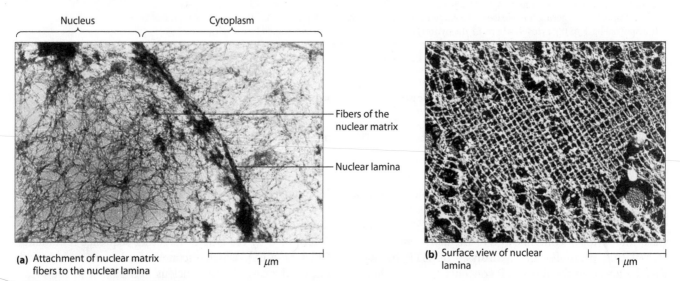

(a) Attachment of nuclear matrix fibers to the nuclear lamina

1 μm

(b) Surface view of nuclear lamina

1 μm

FIGURE 18-32 The Nuclear Matrix and the Nuclear Lamina. (a) This electron micrograph of part of a mammalian cell nucleus shows a branched network of nuclear matrix filaments traversing the nucleus. These filaments seem attached to the nuclear lamina, the dense layer of filaments that lines the nucleoplasm side of the nuclear envelope. **(b)** A surface view of the nuclear lamina of a frog oocyte (TEMs).

Chromatin Fibers Are Dispersed Within the Nucleus in a Nonrandom Fashion

Other than during cell division, a cell's chromatin fibers tend to be highly extended and dispersed throughout the nucleus. You might therefore guess that the chromatin threads corresponding to each individual chromosome are randomly distributed and highly intertwined within the nucleus. Perhaps surprisingly, this seems not to be the case. Instead, the chromatin of each chromosome has its own discrete location. This idea was first proposed in 1885, but evidence that it is true in a variety of cells awaited the techniques of modern molecular biology. Experiments using nucleic acid probes that hybridize to the DNA of specific chromosomes (one example of a technique known as *in situ hybridization*) have now shown that the chromatin fibers corresponding to individual chromosomes occupy discrete compartments within the nucleus, referred to as *chromosome territories* (**Figure 18-33**). The positions of these territories do not seem to be fixed, however. They vary from cell to cell of the same organism and change during a cell's life cycle, likely reflecting changes in gene activity of the different chromosomes.

The nuclear envelope helps organize chromatin by binding parts of it to the inner nuclear envelope at sites that are closely associated with the nuclear pores. These chromatin regions are highly compacted—that is, they are heterochromatin. In electron micrographs, this material appears as a dark irregular layer around the nuclear periphery, as we saw in Figure 18-27a. Most of it seems to be the type called **constitutive heterochromatin**, which exists in a highly condensed form at virtually all times in all cells of the organism. The DNA of constitutive heterochromatin consists of simple-sequence repeated DNA (recall that these are short sequences that repeat tandemly and are not transcribed). Two major chromosomal regions composed of constitutive heterochromatin are the centromere and the telomere. In many cases, it is chromosomal telomeres—the highly repeated DNA sequences located at the ends of chromosomes—that are attached to the nuclear envelope at times other than during cell division.

In contrast to constitutive heterochromatin, **facultative heterochromatin** varies with the particular activities carried out by the cell. Thus, this type of chromatin differs from tissue to tissue and can even vary from time to time within a given cell. Facultative heterochromatin appears to represent chromosomal regions that have become specifically inactivated in a specific cell type. The formation of facultative heterochromatin may be an important means of inactivating entire blocks of genetic information during embryonic development.

The Nucleolus Is Involved in Ribosome Formation

A prominent structural component of the eukaryotic nucleus is the **nucleolus** (plural **nucleoli**), the ribosome factory of the cell. Typical eukaryotic cells contain one or two nucleoli, but the occurrence of several more is not uncommon; in certain situations, hundreds or even thousands may be present. The nucleolus is usually spherical, measuring several micrometers in diameter, but wide variations in size and shape are observed. Because of their relatively large size, nucleoli are easily seen with the light microscope and were first observed more than 200 years ago. However, it was not until the advent of electron microscopy in the 1950s that the structural components of the nucleolus were clearly identified. In thin-section electron micrographs, each nucleolus appears as a membrane-free organelle consisting of fibrils and granules (**Figure 18-34**). The fibrils contain DNA that is being transcribed into *ribosomal RNA (rRNA)*, the RNA component of ribosomes. The granules are rRNA molecules being packaged with proteins (imported from the cytoplasm) to form ribosomal subunits. As we saw earlier, the ribosomal subunits are subsequently exported through the nuclear pores to the cytoplasm. Because of their role in synthesizing RNA, nucleoli become heavily radiolabeled when the cell is exposed to radioactive precursors of RNA (**Figure 18-35**).

The earliest evidence associating the nucleolus with ribosome formation was provided in the early 1960s by Robert Perry, who employed a microbeam of ultraviolet light to destroy the nucleoli of living cells. Such cells lost their ability to synthesize rRNA, suggesting that the nucleolus is involved in manufacturing ribosomes. Additional evidence emerged from studies carried out by Donald Brown and John Gurdon on the African clawed frog, *Xenopus laevis*. Through genetic crosses, it is possible to produce *Xenopus* embryos whose cells lack nucleoli. Brown and Gurdon discovered that such embryos, termed *anucleolate mutants,* cannot synthesize rRNA and therefore die during early development—again implicating the nucleolus in ribosome formation.

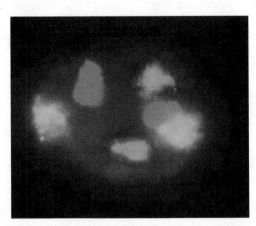

FIGURE 18-33 Chromosome Territories. Mouse lung cells were stained with fluorescent dyes linked to nucleic acid probes that specifically hybridize to the DNA of chromosome 12 (red), chromosome 14 (green), or chromosome 15 (blue). This view of a single nucleus observed by light microscopy shows that the DNA of each chromosome is localized to a specific region of the nucleus (each chromosome is present in two copies).

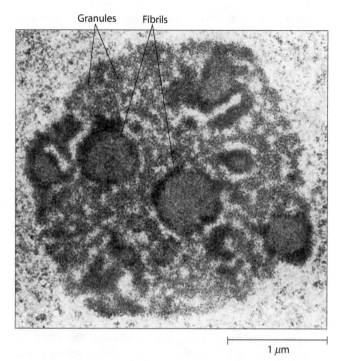

FIGURE 18-34 The Nucleolus. The nucleolus is a prominent intranuclear structure composed of a mass of fibrils and granules. The fibrils are DNA and rRNA; the granules are newly forming ribosomal subunits. Shown here is a nucleolus of a spermatogonium, a cell that gives rise to sperm cells (TEM).

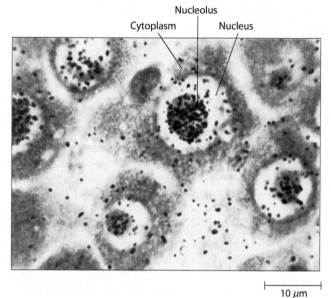

FIGURE 18-35 The Nucleolus as a Site of RNA Synthesis. To demonstrate the role of the nucleolus in RNA synthesis, a rat was injected with ^{3}H-cytidine, a radioactively labeled RNA precursor. Five hours later, liver tissue was removed and subjected to autoradiography. The black spots over the nucleoli in this autoradiograph indicate that the ^{3}H is concentrated in the nucleoli (TEM).

If rRNA is synthesized in the nucleolus, then the DNA sequences coding for this RNA must reside in the nucleolus as well. This prediction has been verified by showing that isolated nucleoli contain the **nucleolus organizer region (NOR)**—a stretch of DNA carrying multiple copies of rRNA genes. These multiple rRNA genes occur in all genomes and are thus an important example of repeated DNA that carries genetic information. The number of copies of the rRNA genes varies greatly from species to species, but animal cells generally contain hundreds of copies and plant cells often contain thousands. The multiple copies are grouped into one or more NORs, which may reside on more than one chromosome; in each NOR, the multiple gene copies are tandemly arranged. A single nucleolus may contain rRNA genes derived from more than one NOR. For example, the human genome has five NORs per haploid chromosome set—or ten per diploid nucleus—each located near the tip of a different chromosome. But instead of ten separate nucleoli, the typical human nucleus has a single large nucleolus containing loops of chromatin derived from ten separate chromosomes.

The size of the nucleolus is correlated with its level of activity. In cells having a high rate of protein synthesis and hence a need for many ribosomes, nucleoli tend to be large and can account for 20–25% of the total volume of the nucleus. In less-active cells, nucleoli are much smaller.

The nucleolus disappears during mitosis, at least in the cells of higher plants and animals. As the cell approaches division, chromatin condenses into compact chromosomes accompanied by the shrinkage and then disappearance of the nucleoli. With our current knowledge of nucleolar composition and function, this makes perfect sense: The extended chromatin loops of the nucleolus cease being transcribed as they are coiled and folded, and any remaining rRNA and ribosomal protein molecules disperse or are degraded. Then, as mitosis is ending, the chromatin uncoils, the NORs loop out again, and rRNA synthesis resumes. In human cells, this is the only time the ten NORs of the diploid nucleus are apparent; as rRNA synthesis begins again, ten tiny nucleoli become visible, one near the tip of each of ten chromosomes. As these nucleoli enlarge, they quickly fuse into the single large nucleolus found in human cells that are not in the process of dividing.

In addition to the nucleolus, microscopists have also identified several kinds of small, non-membrane-enclosed nuclear structures. These nuclear bodies are thought to play a variety of roles related to the processing and handling of RNA molecules produced in the nucleus. These include *Cajal bodies* (named for the scientist who discovered them), *Gemini of Cajal bodies* (*GEMs;* so named because they appear similar to Cajal bodies), *speckles,* and *promyelocytic leukemia bodies (PML bodies).* Cajal bodies and GEMs are involved in maturation and processing of small nucleolar RNA (snoRNA) and small nuclear RNA (snRNA). Speckles, sometimes called *interchromatin granule clusters,* are rich in RNAs and proteins necessary for splicing of messenger RNA precursors into mature messenger RNAs. Current research is aimed at clarifying the roles of these nuclear bodies.

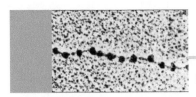

SUMMARY OF KEY POINTS

Chemical Nature of the Genetic Material

- DNA was discovered in the nineteenth century by Miescher, but it was not until the mid-twentieth century that studies with pneumococcal bacteria and bacteriophage T2 revealed that genes are made of DNA.

DNA Structure

- Watson and Crick discovered that DNA is a double helix in which the base A is paired with T, and the base G is paired with C. Supercoiling of the double helix affects the ability of DNA to interact with other molecules.

- Under experimental conditions, the two strands of the double helix can be separated from each other (denaturation) and rejoined (renaturation).

The Organization of DNA in Genomes

- The DNA (or RNA in some viruses) that contains one complete set of an organism's genetic information is called its genome. Viral or prokaryotic genomes consist of one or a small number of DNA molecules. Eukaryotes have a nuclear genome divided among multiple chromosomes, each containing one long DNA molecule, plus a mitochondrial genome; plants and algae possess a chloroplast genome as well.

- The study of genomes has been facilitated by the development of automated techniques for rapid DNA sequencing; these techniques have allowed the complete DNA sequences of numerous organisms, including humans, to be determined. Several online databases and software tools help researchers sort through the enormous amount of data being collected on DNA and protein sequences.

- In the nuclear genomes of multicellular eukaryotes, much of the DNA consists of repeated sequences that do not code for RNA or proteins. Some of this noncoding DNA performs structural or regulatory roles, but most of it has no obvious function.

DNA Packaging

- Due to their enormous size, DNA molecules need to be efficiently packaged by proteins that bind to the DNA. In eukaryotic chromosomes, short stretches of DNA are wrapped around protein particles composed of eight histone molecules to form a basic structural unit called the nucleosome. Chains of nucleosomes ("beads on a string") are packed together to form a 30-nm chromatin fiber, which can then loop and fold further.

- In eukaryotic cells that are actively transcribing DNA, much of the chromatin is in an extended, uncoiled form called euchromatin. Other portions are in a highly condensed, transcriptionally inactive state called heterochromatin. During cell division, all the chromatin becomes highly compacted, forming discrete chromosomes that can be seen with a light microscope.

The Nucleus

- Eukaryotic chromosomes are contained within a nucleus that is bounded by a double-membrane nuclear envelope.

- The nuclear envelope is perforated with nuclear pores that mediate two-way transport of materials between the nucleoplasm and the cytosol. Ions and small molecules diffuse passively through aqueous channels in the pore complex; larger molecules and particles are actively transported through it.

- The nucleolus is a specialized nuclear structure involved in the synthesis of ribosomal RNA and the assembly of ribosomal subunits. Other nuclear bodies perform functions related to processing of RNA.

- The nucleus appears to contain a fibrous skeleton that localizes certain activities, such as DNA replication and messenger RNA production, to discrete regions of the nucleus. One well-defined skeletal structure is the nuclear lamina—a thin, dense meshwork of fibers lining the inner surface of the inner nuclear membrane that confers mechanical strength to the nucleus.

MAKING CONNECTIONS

In this chapter we have introduced you to the properties of DNA—the molecule that stores genetic information—and to the cell nucleus, the site within eukaryotic cells where the bulk of the DNA is localized, replicated, and transcribed. In the next chapter, you will see how DNA replication is carried out by a process that unwinds the two strands of the double helix, thereby allowing each strand to guide the synthesis of a new complementary strand. You will also see how DNA replication is coordinated with mitosis, a type of cell division in which one cell gives rise to two daughter cells containing the same DNA as the original parental cell. Another type of cell division, called meiosis, in which the genetic information in DNA is recombined during formation of the sperm and egg cells that make sexual reproduction possible. In Chapters 21 and 22, you will see how the genetic information stored in DNA is used to guide the synthesis of specific protein molecules.

PROBLEM SET

More challenging problems are marked with a •.

18-1 Prior Knowledge. Virtually every experiment performed by biologists builds on knowledge provided by earlier experiments.

(a) Of what significance to Avery and his colleagues was the finding (made in 1932 by J. L. Alloway) that the same kind of transformation of R cells into S cells that Griffith observed to occur in mice could also be demonstrated in culture with isolated pneumococcus cells?

(b) Of what significance to Hershey and Chase was the following suggestion (made in 1951 by R. M. Herriott)? "A virus may act like a little hypodermic needle full of transforming principles; the virus as such never enters the cell; only the tail contacts the host and perhaps enzymatically cuts a small hole through the outer membrane and then the nucleic acid of the virus head flows into the cell."

(c) Of what significance to Watson and Crick were the data of their colleagues at Cambridge suggesting that the particular forms in which A, G, C, and T exist at physiologic pH permit the formation of specific hydrogen bonds?

(d) How did the findings of Hershey and Chase help explain an earlier report (by T. F. Anderson and R. M. Herriott) that bacteriophage T2 loses its ability to reproduce when it is burst open osmotically by suspending the viral particles in distilled water before adding them to a bacterial culture?

18-2 DNA Base Composition. Based on your understanding of the rules of complementary base pairing, answer the following questions:

(a) You analyze a DNA sample and find that its base composition is 30% A, 20% T, 30% G, and 20% C. What can you conclude about the structure of this DNA?

(b) For a double-stranded DNA molecule in which 40% of the bases are either G or C, what can you conclude about its content of the base A?

(c) For a double-stranded DNA molecule in which 40% of the bases are either G or T, what can you conclude about its content of the base A?

(d) For a double-stranded DNA molecule in which 15% of the bases are A, what can you conclude about its content of the base C? Would you expect the T_m of this DNA to be above or below 90°C? (Hint: Refer to Figure 18-9.)

18-3 DNA Structure. Carefully inspect the double-stranded DNA molecule shown here, and notice that it has twofold rotational symmetry:

3′ A—G—C—G—C—T—A—T—A—G—C—G—C—T 5′
5′ T—C—G—C—G—A—T—A—T—C—G—C—G—A 3′

Label each of the following statements as T if true or F if false.

(a) There is no way to distinguish the right end of the double helix from the left end.

(b) If a solution of these molecules were heated to denature them, every single-stranded molecule in the solution would be capable of hybridizing with every other molecule.

(c) If the molecule were cut at its midpoint into two halves, it would be possible to distinguish the left half from the right half.

(d) If the two single strands were separated from each other, it would not be possible to distinguish one strand from the other.

(e) In a single strand from this molecule, it would be impossible to determine which is the 3′ end and which is the 5′ end.

18-4 Restriction Mapping of DNA. The genome of a newly discovered bacteriophage is a linear DNA molecule 10,500 nucleotide pairs in length. One sample of this DNA has been incubated with restriction enzyme X and another sample with restriction enzyme Y. The lengths (in thousands of base pairs) of the restriction fragments produced by the two enzymes have been determined by gel electrophoresis to be as follows:

Enzyme X: Fragment X-1 = 4.5; X-2 = 3.6; X-3 = 2.4
Enzyme Y: Fragment Y-1 = 5.2; Y-2 = 3.8; Y-3 = 1.5

Next, the fragments from the enzyme X reaction are isolated and treated with enzyme Y, and the fragments from the enzyme Y reaction are treated with enzyme X. The results are as follows:

X fragments treated with Y: X-1 → 4.5 (unchanged)
X-2 → 2.1 + 1.5
X-3 → 1.7 + 0.7
Y fragments treated with X: Y-1 → 4.5 + 0.7
Y-2 → 2.1 + 1.7
Y-3 → 1.5 (unchanged)

Draw a restriction map of the phage DNA, indicating the positions of all enzyme X and enzyme Y restriction sites and the lengths of DNA between them.

18-5 DNA Sequencing. You have isolated the DNA fragment shown in Problem 18-3 but do not know its complete sequence. From knowledge of the specificity of the restriction enzyme used to prepare it, you know the first four bases at the left end and have prepared a single-stranded DNA primer of sequence 5′ T–C–G–C 3′. Explain how you would determine the rest of the sequence using dye-labeled dideoxynucleotides. Draw the gel pattern that would be observed, indicating the base sequence of the DNA in each band and the color pattern that would be detected by the camera in a DNA sequencing machine.

• 18-6 DNA Melting. Figure 18-36 shows the melting curves for two DNA samples that were thermally denatured under the same conditions.

(a) What conclusion can you draw concerning the base compositions of the two samples? Explain.

(b) How might you explain the steeper slope of the melting curve for sample A?

(c) Formamide and urea are agents known to form hydrogen bonds with pyrimidines and purines. What effect, if any,

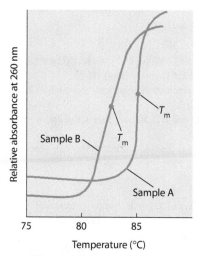

FIGURE 18-36 Thermal Denaturation of Two DNA Samples. See Problem 18-6.

would the inclusion of a small amount of formamide or urea in the incubation mixture have on the melting curves?

• **18-7 DNA Renaturation.** You are given two samples of DNA, each of which melts at 92°C during thermal denaturation. After denaturing the DNA, you mix the two samples together and then cool the mixture to allow the DNA strands to reassociate. When the newly reassociated DNA is denatured a second time, the sample now melts at 85°C.

(a) How might you explain the lowering of the melting temperature from 92°C to 85°C?

(b) What kind of experiment could be carried out to test your hypothesis?

(c) If the newly reassociated DNA had melted at 92°C instead of 85°C, what conclusions might you have drawn concerning the base sequences of the two initial DNA samples?

• **18-8 Nucleosomes.** You perform an experiment in which chromatin is isolated from sea urchin sperm cells and briefly digested with micrococcal nuclease. When the chromatin proteins are removed and the resulting purified DNA is analyzed by gel electrophoresis, you observe a series of DNA fragments that are multiples of 260 base pairs in length (that is, 260 bp, 520 bp, 780 bp, and so forth).

(a) Although these results differ somewhat from the typical results discussed in the chapter, explain why they still point to the likely existence of nucleosomes in this cell type.

(b) What can you conclude about the amount of DNA that is associated with each nucleosome?

(c) If the chromatin had been analyzed by density gradient centrifugation immediately after digestion with micrococcal nuclease, describe what you would expect to see.

(d) Suppose you perform an experiment in which the chromatin is digested for a much longer period of time with micrococcal nuclease before removal of chromatin proteins. When

the resulting DNA preparation is analyzed by electrophoresis, all of the DNA appears as fragments 146 bp in length. What does this suggest to you about the length of the linker DNA in this cell type?

18-9 Nuclear Structure and Function. Indicate the implications for nuclear structure or function of each of the following experimental observations.

(a) Sucrose crosses the nuclear envelope so rapidly that its rate of movement cannot be accurately measured.

(b) Colloidal gold particles with a diameter of 5.5 nm equilibrate rapidly between the nucleus and cytoplasm when injected into an amoeba, but gold particles with a diameter of 15 nm do not.

(c) Nuclear pore complexes sometimes stain heavily for RNA and protein.

(d) If gold particles up to 26 nm in diameter are coated with a polypeptide containing a nuclear localization signal (NLS) and are then injected into the cytoplasm of a living cell, they are transported into the nucleus. If they are injected into the nucleus, however, they remain there.

(e) Many of the proteins of the nuclear envelope appear from electrophoretic analysis to be the same as those found in the endoplasmic reticulum.

(f) Ribosomal proteins are synthesized in the cytoplasm but are packaged with rRNA into ribosomal subunits in the nucleus.

(g) If nucleoli are irradiated with a microbeam of ultraviolet light, synthesis of ribosomal RNA is inhibited.

(h) Treatment of nuclei with the nonionic detergent Triton X-100 dissolves the nuclear envelope but leaves an otherwise intact nucleus.

• **18-10 Nuclear Transport.** Budding yeast with temperature-sensitive mutations in NTF2 have been identified. In such mutants, NTF2 functions at 25°C. Raising the temperature to 37°C, however, causes the NTF2 protein to stop functioning. What effects would you predict raising these mutant yeast to 37°C would have on nuclear transport? Explain your answer.

18-11 Nucleoli. Indicate whether each of the following statements is true (T) or false (F). If false, reword the statement to make it true.

(a) Nucleoli are membrane-bounded structures present in the eukaryotic nucleus.

(b) The fibrils seen in electron micrographs of nucleoli contain DNA and RNA.

(c) The DNA of nucleoli carries the cell's tRNA genes, which are present in clusters of multiple copies.

(d) A single nucleolus always corresponds to a single nucleolus organizer region (NOR).

(e) Nucleoli become heavily radiolabeled when radioactive ribonucleotides are provided to the cell.

(f) In animals and plants, the disappearance of nucleoli during mitosis correlates with cessation of ribosome synthesis.

SUGGESTED READING

References of historical importance are marked with a •.

Chemical Nature of the Genetic Material

• Avery, O. T., C. M. MacLeod, and M. McCarty. Studies on the chemical nature of the substance inducing transformation of pneumococcal types. Induction of transformation by a desoxyribonucleic acid fraction isolated from *Pneumococcus* Type III. *J. Exp. Med.* 79 (1944): 137.

• Chargaff, E. Preface to a grammar of biology: A hundred years of nucleic acid research. *Science* 172 (1971): 637.

• Hershey, A. D., and M. Chase. Independent functions of viral protein and nucleic acid in growth of bacteriophage. *J. Gen. Physiol.* 36 (1952): 39.

• Portugal, F. H., and J. S. Cohen. *The Century of DNA: A History of the Discovery of the Structure and Function of the Genetic Substance.* Cambridge, MA: MIT Press, 1977.

DNA Structure

Arnott, S. Historical article: DNA polymorphism and the early history of the double helix. *Trends Biochem. Sci.* 31 (2006): 349.

• Bauer, W. R., F. H. C. Crick, and J. H. White. Supercoiled DNA. *Sci. Amer.* 243 (July 1980): 118.

Marmur, J. DNA strand separation, renaturation and hybridization. *Trends Biochem. Sci.* 19 (1994): 343.

• Watson, J. D., and F. H. C. Crick. Molecular structure of nucleic acids: A structure for deoxyribose nucleic acid. *Nature* 171 (1953): 737.

The Organization of DNA in Genomes

• Britten, R. J., and D. E. Kohne. Repeated sequences of DNA. *Science* 161 (1968): 529.

Church, G. M. Genomes for all. *Sci. Amer.* 294 (January 2006): 46.

Cox, J., and M. Mann. Is proteomics the new genomics? *Cell* 130 (2007): 395.

Feuk, L., A. R. Carson, and S. W. Scherer. Structural variation in the human genome. *Nature Rev. Genet.* 7 (2006): 85.

Jobling, M. A., and P. Gill. Encoded evidence: DNA in forensic analysis. *Nature Rev. Genet.* 5 (2004): 739.

Pollard, K. S. What makes us human? *Sci. Amer.* 300 (2009): 44.

Kung, L. A., and M. Snyder. Proteome chips for whole-organism assays. *Nature Rev. Mol. Cell Biol.* 7 (2006): 617.

• Lander, E. S. et al. Initial sequencing and analysis of the human genome. *Nature* 409 (2001): 860.

Mirkin, S. M. Expandable DNA repeats and human disease. *Nature* 447 (2007): 932.

Moxon, E. R., and C. Willis. DNA microsatellites: Agents of evolution? *Sci. Amer.* 280 (January 1999): 94.

• Sanger, F. Determination of nucleotide sequences in DNA. *Science* 214 (1981): 1205.

Stoeckle, M. Y., and P. D. Hebert. Barcode of life. *Sci. Amer.* 299 (2008): 82.

• Venter, J. C. et al. The sequence of the human genome. *Science* 291 (2001): 1304.

DNA Packaging

Kornberg, R. D., and Y. Lorch. Twenty-five years of the nucleosome, fundamental particle of the eukaryote chromosome. *Cell* 98 (1999): 285.

Tremethick, D. J. Higher-order structures of chromatin: The elusive 30 nm fiber. *Cell* 128 (2007): 651.

Wallace, D. C. Mitochondrial DNA in aging and disease. *Sci. Amer.* 277 (August 1997): 40.

Zlatanova, J., T., C. Bishop, J. M. Victor, and K. van Holde. The nucleosome family: Dynamic and growing. *Structure* 17 (2009): 160–71.

The Nucleus

Boisvert, F.-M. et al. The multifunctional nucleolus. *Nature Rev. Mol. Cell Biol.* 8 (2007): 574.

Capell, B. C., and F. S. Collins. Human laminopathies: Nuclei gone genetically awry. *Nature Rev. Genet.* 7 (2006): 940.

Cioce, M., and A. I. Lamond. Cajal bodies: A long history of discovery. *Annu. Rev. Cell Dev. Biol.* 21 (2005): 105.

Cook, A. et al. Structural biology of nucleocytoplasmic transport. *Annu. Rev. Biochem.* 76 (2007): 647.

Fedorova, E., and D. Zink. 2009. Nuclear genome organization: Common themes and individual patterns. *Curr. Opin. Genet. Dev.* 19 (2009): 166.

Gruenbaum, Y. et al. The nuclear lamina comes of age. *Nature Rev. Mol. Cell Biol.* 6 (2005): 21.

Handwerger, K. E., and J. G. Gall. Subnuclear organelles: New insights into form and function. *Trends Cell Biol.* 16 (2006): 19.

Hetzer, M. W., T. C. Walther, and I. W. Mattaj. Pushing the envelope: Structure, function, and dynamics of the nuclear periphery. *Annu. Rev. Cell Dev. Biol.* 21 (2005): 347.

Meaburn, K. J., and T. Misteli. Chromosome territories. *Nature* 445 (2007): 379.

Roderick, Y. H., and B. Fahrenkrog. The nuclear pore complex up close. *Curr. Opin. Cell Biol.* 18 (2006): 342.

Thiry, M., and D. L. J. Lafontaine. Birth of a nucleolus: The evolution of nucleolar compartments. *Trends Cell Biol.* 15 (2005): 194.

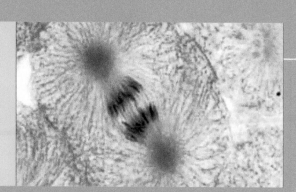

The Cell Cycle, DNA Replication, and Mitosis

The ability to grow and reproduce is a fundamental property of living organisms. However, growth of single cells is fundamentally limited. As new proteins, nucleic acids, carbohydrates, and lipids are synthesized, their accumulation causes the volume of a cell to increase, forcing the plasma membrane to expand to prevent the cell from bursting. But cells cannot continue to enlarge indefinitely; as a cell grows larger, there is an accompanying decrease in its surface area/volume ratio and hence in its capacity for effective exchange with the environment. Therefore, cell growth is generally accompanied by **cell division,** *whereby one cell gives rise to two new daughter cells. (The term* daughter *is used by convention and does not indicate that cells have gender.) For single-celled organisms, cell division increases the total number of individuals in a population. In multicellular organisms, cell division either increases the number of cells, leading to growth of the organism, or replaces cells that have died. In an adult human, for example, about 2 million stem cells in bone marrow divide every second to maintain a constant number of red blood cells in the body. Although often cell growth and cell division are coupled, there is a notable exception. A fertilized animal egg typically undergoes many divisions without the growth of its cells, dividing the volume of the egg into smaller and smaller parcels. Here as well, however, tight regulation of where and when cells divide is crucial.*

When cells grow and divide, the newly formed daughter cells are usually genetic duplicates of the parent cell, containing the same (or virtually the same) DNA sequences. Therefore, all the genetic information in the nucleus of the parent cell must be duplicated and carefully distributed to the daughter cells during the division process. In accomplishing this task, a cell passes through a series of discrete stages, collectively known as the cell cycle. In this chapter, we will examine the events associated with the cell cycle, focusing first on the mechanisms that ensure that each new cell receives a complete set of genetic instructions and then examining how the cell cycle is regulated to fit the needs of the organism.

Overview of the Cell Cycle

The **cell cycle** begins when two new cells are formed by the division of a single parental cell and ends when one of these cells divides again into two cells (**Figure 19-1**). To early cell biologists studying eukaryotic cells under the microscope, the most dramatic events in the life of a cell were those associated with the point in the cycle when cell actually divides. This division process, called **M phase,** involves two overlapping events in which nucleus divides first and the cytoplasm second. Nuclear division is called **mitosis,** and the division of the cytoplasm to produce two daughter cells is termed **cytokinesis.**

The stars of the mitotic drama are the chromosomes. As you can see in Figure 19-1a, the beginning of mitosis is marked by condensation (coiling and folding) of the cell's chromatin, which generates chromosomes that are thick enough to be individually discernible under the microscope. Because DNA replication has already taken place, each chromosome actually consists of two chromosome copies that remain attached to each other until the cell divides. As long as they remain attached, the two new chromosomes are referred to as **sister chromatids.** As the chromatids become visible, the nuclear envelope breaks into fragments. Then, in a stately ballet guided by the microtubules of the *mitotic spindle,* the sister chromatids separate and—each now a full-fledged chromosome—move to opposite ends of the cell. By this time, cytokinesis has usually begun, and new nuclear membranes envelop the two groups of daughter chromosomes as cell division is completed.

While visually striking, the events of M phase account for a relatively small portion of the total cell cycle; for a

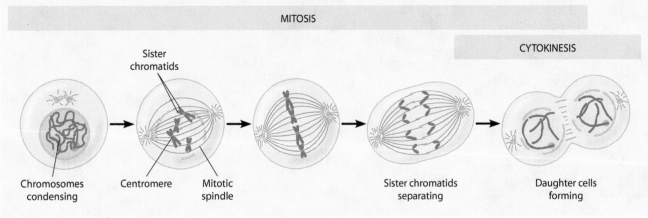

Sister chromatids

Chromosomes condensing

Centromere

Mitotic spindle

Sister chromatids separating

Daughter cells forming

(a) The M (mitotic) phase

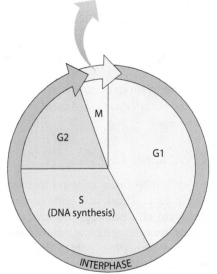

(b) The cell cycle

FIGURE 19-1 The Eukaryotic Cell Cycle. (a) The M (mitotic) phase, the process of cell division, is the most visually distinctive part of the cell cycle. It consists of two overlapping processes, mitosis and cytokinesis. In mitosis, the mitotic spindle segregates the duplicated, condensed chromosomes into two daughter nuclei; in cytokinesis, the cytoplasm divides to yield two genetically identical daughter cells. **(b)** Between divisions, the cell is said to be in interphase, which is made up of the S phase (the period of nuclear DNA replication) and two "gap" phases, called G1 and G2. The cell continues to grow throughout interphase, a time of high metabolic activity.

ACTIVITIES www.thecellplace.com *Cell cycle*

typical mammalian cell, M phase usually lasts less than an hour. Cells spend most of their time in the growth phase between divisions, called **interphase** (Figure 19-1b). Most cellular contents are synthesized continuously during interphase, so cell mass gradually increases as the cell approaches division. During interphase the amount of nuclear DNA doubles, and experiments using radioactive DNA precursors have shown that the new nuclear DNA is synthesized during a specific portion of interphase named the **S phase** (S for synthesis). A time gap called **G1 phase** separates S phase from the preceding M phase; a second gap, the **G2 phase,** separates the end of S phase from the onset of the next M phase.

Although the cells of a multicellular organism divide at varying rates, most studies of the cell cycle involve cells growing in culture, where the length of the cycle tends to be similar for different cell types. We can easily determine the overall length of the cell cycle—the *generation time*—for cultured cells by counting the cells under a microscope and determining how long it takes for the cell population to double. In cultured mammalian cells, for example, the total cycle usually takes about 18–24 hours. Once we know the total length of the cycle, it is possible to deter-

mine the length of specific phases. To determine the length of the S phase, we can expose cells to a radioactively labeled DNA precursor (usually ^{3}H-thymidine) for a short period of time and then examine the cells by autoradiography. The fraction of cells with silver grains over their nuclei represents the fraction of cells that were somewhere in S phase when the radioactive compound was available. When we multiply this fraction by the total length of the cell cycle, the result is an estimate of the average length of the S phase. For mammalian cells in culture, this fraction is often around 0.33, which indicates that S phase is about 6–8 hours in length. Similarly, we can estimate the length of M phase by multiplying the generation time by the percentage of the cells that are actually in mitosis at any given time. This percentage is called the **mitotic index.** The mitotic index for cultured mammalian cells is often about 3–5%, which means that M phase lasts less than an hour (usually 30–45 minutes).

In contrast to the S and M phases, whose lengths tend to be similar for different mammalian cells, the length of G1 is quite variable, depending on the cell type. Although a typical G1 phase lasts 8–10 hours, some cells spend only a few minutes or hours in G1, whereas others are delayed for long periods of time. During G1, a major "decision" is made as to whether and when the cell is to divide again. Cells that become arrested in G1, awaiting a signal that will trigger reentry into the cell cycle and a commitment to divide, are said to be in **G0 (G zero).** Other cells exit from the cell cycle entirely and undergo *terminal differentiation,* which means they are destined never to divide again; most of the nerve cells in your body are in this state. In some cells, transient arrest of the cell cycle can also occur in G2. In general, however, G2 is shorter than G1 and more uniform in duration, usually lasting 4–6 hours.

Cell cycle studies have been facilitated by the use of **flow cytometry,** a technique that permits automated analysis of the chemical makeup of millions of individual cells almost simultaneously. In this procedure, cells are first stained with one or more fluorescent dyes—for example, a red dye that stains DNA might be combined with a green dye that binds specifically to a particular cell protein. The dyed cells are then passed in a tiny, liquid stream through a beam of laser light. By analyzing fluctuations in the intensity and color of the fluorescent light emitted by each cell as it passes through the laser beam, researchers can assess the concentration of DNA and specific proteins in each individual cell. This information is then used to assess the chemical makeup of cells at different points in the cycle.

DNA Replication

Now that we have provided an overview of the cell cycle, we are ready to consider its workings in detail. Since DNA replication is a central event in the cycle, we begin by examining its underlying mechanism, which in turn depends on the double-helical structure of DNA. In fact, a month after Watson and Crick published their now-classic paper postulating a double helix for DNA, they followed it with an equally important paper suggesting how such a base-paired structure might duplicate itself. Here, in their own words, is the basis of that suggestion:

> *Now our model for deoxyribonucleic acid is, in effect, a pair of templates, each of which is complementary to the other. We imagine that prior to duplication the hydrogen bonds are broken, and the two chains unwind and separate. Each chain then acts as a template for the formation onto itself of a new companion chain, so that eventually we shall have two pairs of chains, where we only had one before. Moreover, the sequence of the pairs of bases will have been duplicated exactly. (Watson and Crick, 1953, p. 966)*

The model Watson and Crick proposed for DNA replication is shown in **Figure 19-2.** The essence of their suggestion is that one of the two strands of every newly formed DNA molecule is derived from the parent molecule, whereas the other strand is newly synthesized. This is called **semiconservative replication** because half of the parent molecule is retained by each daughter molecule.

Equilibrium Density Centrifugation Shows That DNA Replication Is Semiconservative

Within five years of its publication, the Watson–Crick model of semiconservative DNA replication was tested and proved correct by Matthew Meselson and Franklin

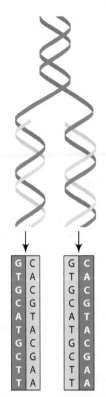

FIGURE 19-2 Watson–Crick Model of DNA Replication. In 1953, Watson and Crick proposed that the DNA double helix replicates semiconservatively, using a model like this one to illustrate the principle. The double-stranded helix unwinds, and each parent strand serves as a template for the synthesis of a complementary daughter strand, assembled according to the base-pairing rules. A, T, C, and G stand for the adenine, thymine, cytosine, and guanine nucleotides. A pairs with T, and G with C.

Stahl. The ingenuity of Meselson and Stahl's contribution lay in the method they devised, in collaboration with Jerome Vinograd, for distinguishing semiconservative replication from other possibilities. Their studies utilized two isotopic forms of nitrogen, ^{14}N and ^{15}N, to distinguish newly synthesized strands of DNA from old strands. Bacterial cells were first grown for many generations in a medium containing ^{15}N-labeled ammonium chloride to incorporate this *heavy* (but nonradioactive) isotope of nitrogen into their DNA molecules. Cells containing ^{15}N-labeled DNA were then transferred to a growth medium containing the normal *light* isotope of nitrogen, ^{14}N. Any new strands of DNA synthesized after this transfer would therefore incorporate ^{14}N rather than ^{15}N.

Since ^{15}N-labeled DNA is significantly denser than ^{14}N-labeled DNA, the old and new DNA strands can be distinguished from each other by **equilibrium density centrifugation,** a technique we encountered earlier when discussing the separation of organelles in Chapter 12 (see Box 12A, page 327). Briefly, this technique allows organelles or macromolecules with differing densities to be separated from each other by centrifugation in a solution containing a gradient of increasing density from the top of the tube to the bottom. In response to centrifugal force, the particles migrate "down" the tube (actually, they move *outward,* away from the axis of rotation) until they reach a density equal to their own. They then remain at this equilibrium density and can be recovered as a band at that position in the tube after centrifugation.

For DNA analysis, equilibrium density centrifugation often uses cesium chloride (CsCl), a heavy metal salt that forms solutions of very high density. The DNA to be analyzed is simply mixed with a solution of cesium chloride and then centrifuged at high speed (generating a centrifugal force of several hundred thousand times gravity for 8 hours, for example). As a density gradient of cesium chloride is established by the centrifugal force, the DNA molecules float "up" or sink "down" within the gradient to reach their equilibrium density positions. The difference in density between heavy (^{15}N-containing) DNA and light (^{14}N-containing) DNA causes them to come to rest at different positions in the gradient.

Using this approach, Meselson and Stahl analyzed DNA obtained from bacterial cells that were first grown for many generations in ^{15}N and then transferred to ^{14}N for additional cycles of replication (**Figure 19-3**). What results would be predicted for a semiconservative mechanism of DNA replication? After one replication cycle in ^{14}N, each DNA molecule should consist of one ^{15}N strand (the old strand) and one ^{14}N strand (the new strand), and so the overall density would be intermediate between heavy DNA and light DNA. The experiments clearly supported this model. After one replication cycle in the ^{14}N medium, centrifugation in cesium chloride revealed a single band of DNA whose density was *exactly halfway* between that of ^{15}N-DNA and ^{14}N-DNA (Figure 19-3b). Because they saw no band at the density expected for heavy DNA, Meselson and Stahl concluded that the original, double-stranded parental DNA was not preserved intact in the replication process. Similarly, the absence of a band at the density expected for light DNA indicated that no daughter DNA molecules consisted exclusively of new DNA. Instead, it appeared that a part of every daughter DNA molecule was newly synthesized and another part was derived from the parent molecule. In fact, the density halfway between that of ^{14}N-DNA and ^{15}N-DNA meant that the $^{14}N/^{15}N$ hybrid DNA molecules were one-half parental and one-half newly synthesized.

When the $^{14}N/^{15}N$ hybrid DNA was heated to separate its two strands, one strand exhibited the density of a ^{15}N-containing strand and the other exhibited the density of a ^{14}N-containing strand, just as predicted by the semiconservative model of replication. Data obtained from cells grown for additional generations in the presence of ^{14}N provided further confirmation. After the second cycle of DNA replication, for example, Meselson and Stahl saw two equal bands, one at the hybrid density of the previous cycle and one at the density of purely ^{14}N-DNA (Figure 19-3c). As the figure illustrates, this is also consistent with a semiconservative mode of replication.

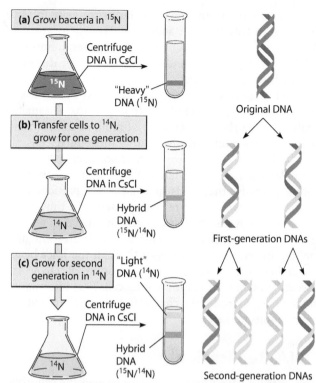

FIGURE 19-3 Semiconservative Replication of Density-Labeled DNA. Meselson and Stahl **(a)** grew bacteria for many generations on a ^{15}N-containing medium and then transferred the cells to a ^{14}N-containing medium for **(b)** one or **(c)** two further cycles of replication. In each case, DNA was extracted from the cells and centrifuged to equilibrium in cesium chloride (CsCl). As shown in the model on the right (where dark blue strands contain ^{15}N and light blue strands contain ^{14}N), the data are compatible with a semiconservative model of DNA replication.

ACTIVITIES www.thecellplace.com *The Meselson-Stahl experiment*

DNA Replication Is Usually Bidirectional

The Meselson–Stahl experiments provided strong support for the idea that, during DNA replication, each strand of the DNA double helix serves as a template for the synthesis of a new complementary strand. As biologists proceeded to unravel the molecular details of this process, it gradually became clear that DNA replication is a complex event involving numerous enzymes and other proteins—and even the participation of RNA. We will first examine the general features of this replication mechanism and then focus on some of its molecular details. In doing so, we will frequently refer to the bacterium *Escherichia coli,* for which DNA replication is especially well understood. However, studies of mammalian viruses such as SV40 and of the yeast *Saccharomyces cerevisiae* have revealed the details of eukaryotic DNA replication as well. DNA replication seems to be a drama whose plot and molecular actors are basically similar in bacterial and eukaryotic cells. This is perhaps not surprising for such a fundamental process—one that must have arisen early in the evolution of life.

FIGURE 19-4 Replication of Circular DNA. (a) This autoradiograph shows an *E. coli* DNA molecule caught in the act of replicating. The DNA molecule was isolated from a bacterium that had been grown in a medium containing ³H-thymidine, thereby allowing the DNA to be visualized by autoradiography. **(b)** Replication of a circular DNA molecule begins at a single origin and proceeds bidirectionally around the circle, with the two replication forks moving in opposite directions. The new strands are shown in light blue. The replication process generates intermediates that resemble the Greek letter theta (θ), from which this type of replication derives its name. **(c)** During the cell division cycle of bacteria containing a single circular chromosome, membrane growth between the attachment sites of the two replicating copies moves the daughter chromosomes toward opposite sides of the cell.

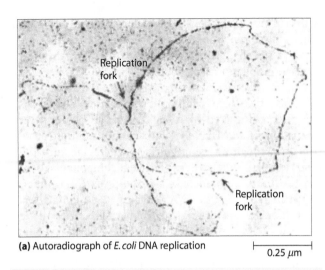

(a) Autoradiograph of *E. coli* DNA replication

0.25 µm

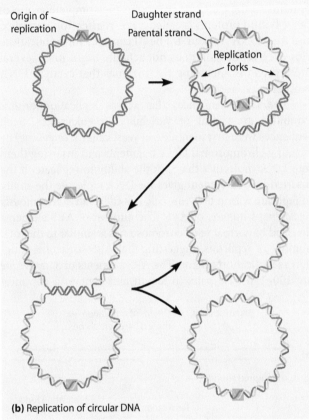

(b) Replication of circular DNA

The first experiments to directly visualize DNA replication were carried out by John Cairns, who grew *E. coli* cells in a medium containing the DNA precursor ³H-thymidine and then used autoradiography to examine the cell's single, circular DNA molecule caught in the act of replication. One such molecule is shown in **Figure 19-4a**. The two Y-shaped structures indicated by the arrows represent the sites where the DNA duplex is being replicated. These **replication forks** are created by a DNA replication mechanism that begins at a single point within the DNA and proceeds in a *bidirectional* fashion away from this origin. In other words, two replication forks are created that move in opposite directions away from the point of origin, unwinding the helix and copying both strands as they proceed. For circular DNA, this process is sometimes called *theta replication* because it generates intermediates that look like the Greek letter theta *(θ)*, as you can see in Figure 19-4b. Theta replication occurs not only in bacterial genomes such as that of *E. coli* but also in the circular DNAs of mitochondria, chloroplasts, plasmids, and some viruses. At the end of a round of theta replication the two resulting DNA circles remain interlinked, and the action of a topoisomerase (page 562) is required to disconnect the two circles from each other.

Figure 19-4c shows how these events relate to the cell division cycle of bacteria that contain a single circular chromosome. In such bacteria, the two copies of the replicating chromosome bind to the plasma membrane at their replication origins. As the cell grows in preparation for cell division, new plasma membrane is added to the region between these chromosome attachment sites, thereby pushing the chromosomes toward opposite ends of the cell. When DNA replication is complete and the cell has doubled in size, *binary fission* partitions the cell down the middle and segregates the two chromosomes into two daughter cells.

Eukaryotic DNA Replication Involves Multiple Replicons

In contrast to circular bacterial chromosomes—where DNA replication is initiated at a single origin—replication of the linear DNA molecules of eukaryotic chromosomes

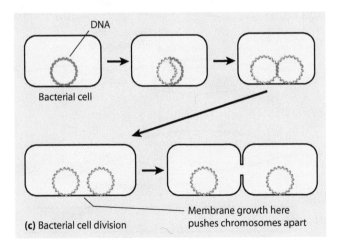

(c) Bacterial cell division

is initiated at multiple sites, creating multiple replication units called **replicons** (**Figure 19-5**). The DNA of a typical large eukaryotic chromosome may contain several thousand replicons, each about 50,000–300,000 base pairs in length. At the center of each replicon is a special DNA sequence, called an **origin of replication,** where DNA synthesis is initiated by a mechanism involving several groups of *initiator proteins*. First, a multisubunit protein complex known as the *origin recognition complex (ORC)* binds to a replication origin. The next components to bind are the *minichromosome maintenance (MCM) proteins,* which include several *DNA helicases* that facilitate DNA replication by unwinding the double helix. The recruitment of MCM proteins to the replication origin requires the participation of a third set of proteins, known as *helicase loaders,* which mediate the binding of the MCM proteins to the ORC. At this point the complete group of DNA-bound proteins is called a **pre-replication complex,** and the DNA is said to be "licensed" for replication. However, replication does not actually begin until several more proteins, including the enzymes that catalyze DNA synthesis, are added.

The DNA sequences that act as replication origins exhibit a great deal of variability in eukaryotes. Such sequences were first identified in yeast cells (*S. cerevisiae*) by isolating chromosomal DNA fragments and inserting them into DNA molecules that lack the ability to replicate. If the inserted DNA fragment gives the DNA molecule the ability to replicate within the yeast cell, it is called an *autonomously replicating sequence,* or *ARS*. The number of ARS elements detected in normal yeast chromosomes is similar to the total number of replicons, suggesting that ARS sequences function as replication origins. The ARS elements of *S. cerevisiae* are 100–150 base pairs in length and contain a common

11-nucleotide core sequence, consisting largely of AT base pairs, flanked by auxiliary sequences containing additional AT-rich regions. Since the DNA double helix must be unwound when replication is initiated, the presence of so many AT base pairs serves a useful purpose at replication origins because AT base pairs, held together by two hydrogen bonds, are easier to disrupt than GC base pairs, which have three hydrogen bonds. The replication origins of multicellular eukaryotes are generally larger and more variable in sequence than the ARS elements of *S. cerevisiae*, but they also tend to contain regions that are AT-rich.

After DNA synthesis has been initiated at an origin of replication, two replication forks begin to synthesize DNA in opposite directions away from the origin, creating a "replication bubble" that grows in size as replication proceeds in both directions (Figure 19-5). When the growing replication bubble of one replicon encounters the replication bubble of an adjacent replicon, the DNA synthesized by the two replicons is joined together. In this way, DNA synthesized at numerous replication sites is ultimately linked together to form two double-stranded daughter molecules, each composed of one parental strand and one new strand.

Why does DNA replication involve multiple replication sites in eukaryotes but not in bacteria? Since eukaryotic chromosomes contain more DNA than bacterial chromosomes do, it would take eukaryotes much longer to replicate their chromosomes if DNA synthesis were initiated from only a single replication origin. Moreover, the rate at which each replication fork synthesizes DNA is slower in eukaryotes than in bacteria (presumably because the presence of nucleosomes slows down the replication process). Measurements of the length of radioactive DNA synthesized by cells exposed to ^{3}H-thymidine for varying periods of time have revealed

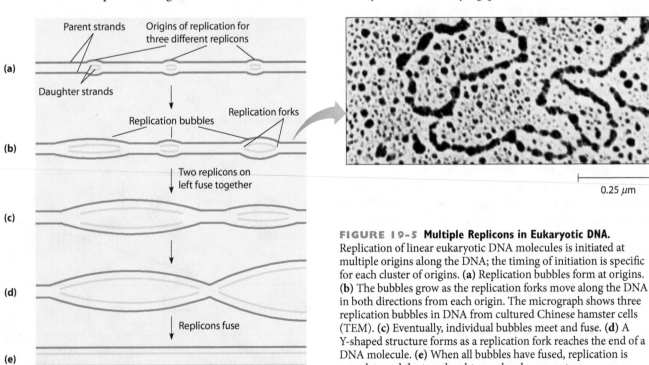

0.25 μm

FIGURE 19-5 Multiple Replicons in Eukaryotic DNA. Replication of linear eukaryotic DNA molecules is initiated at multiple origins along the DNA; the timing of initiation is specific for each cluster of origins. (**a**) Replication bubbles form at origins. (**b**) The bubbles grow as the replication forks move along the DNA in both directions from each origin. The micrograph shows three replication bubbles in DNA from cultured Chinese hamster cells (TEM). (**c**) Eventually, individual bubbles meet and fuse. (**d**) A Y-shaped structure forms as a replication fork reaches the end of a DNA molecule. (**e**) When all bubbles have fused, replication is complete and the two daughter molecules separate.

that eukaryotic replication forks synthesize DNA at a rate of about 2000 base pairs/minute, compared with 50,000 base pairs/minute in bacteria. Since the average human chromosome contains about 10^8 base pairs of DNA, it would take more than a month to duplicate a chromosome if there were only a single replication origin!

The relationship between the speed of chromosome replication and the number of replicons is nicely illustrated by comparing the rates of DNA synthesis in embryonic and adult cells of the fruit fly *Drosophila*. In the developing embryo, where cell divisions occur in quick succession, cells employ a large number of simultaneously active replicons measuring only a few thousand base pairs in length. As a result, DNA replication occurs very rapidly, and S phase takes only a few minutes. Adult cells, on the other hand, employ fewer replicons spaced at intervals of tens or hundreds of thousands of base pairs, generating an S phase that requires almost 10 hours to complete. Since the rate of DNA synthesis at any given replication fork is about the same in embryonic and adult cells, it is clear that the length of the S phase is determined by the number of replicons and the rate at which they are activated—not by the rate at which each replicon synthesizes DNA.

During the S phase of a typical eukaryotic cell cycle, replicons are not all activated at the same time. Instead, certain clusters of replicons tend to replicate early during S phase, whereas others replicate later. Information concerning the order in which replicons are activated has been obtained by incubating cells at various points during S phase with *5-bromodeoxyuridine (BrdU)*, a substance that is incorporated into DNA in place of thymidine. Because DNA that contains BrdU is denser than normal DNA, it can be separated from the remainder of the DNA by equilibrium density centrifugation. The BrdU-labeled DNA is then analyzed by hybridization with a series of DNA probes that are specific for individual genes. Such studies have revealed that the genes being actively expressed in a given tissue are replicated early during S phase, whereas inactive genes are replicated later during S phase. If the same gene is analyzed in two different cell types, one in which the gene is active and one in which it is inactive, early replication is observed only in the cell type where the gene is being transcribed.

Replication Licensing Ensures That DNA Molecules Are Duplicated Only Once Prior to Each Cell Division

During the eukaryotic cell cycle it is crucial that nuclear DNA molecules undergo replication once, and only once, prior to cell division. To enforce this restriction, a process called **licensing** ensures that after DNA is replicated at any given replication origin during S phase, the DNA at that site does not become competent (licensed) for a further round of DNA replication until the cell has first passed through mitosis. The license is provided by the binding of MCM proteins to replication origins, an event that requires both ORC and helicase loaders (page 554). Once

replication begins, the MCM proteins are displaced from the origins by the traveling replication fork, and re-replication from the same origins is prevented by mechanisms that stop MCM proteins from binding to replication origins again. Thus the license to replicate is never associated with replicated DNA.

A critical player in this mechanism is *cyclin-dependent kinase (Cdk)*, an enzyme whose many roles in the cell cycle will be described later in the chapter. One form of Cdk is produced at the beginning of S phase and functions both in activating DNA synthesis at licensed origins and in ensuring that these same origins cannot become licensed again. Cdk blocks relicensing by catalyzing the phosphorylation, and thereby inhibiting the function, of proteins required for licensing, such as ORC and the helicase loaders. Multicellular eukaryotes contain another inhibitor of relicensing called *geminin*, a protein made during S phase that blocks the binding of MCM proteins to DNA. After the cell completes mitosis, geminin is degraded and Cdk activity falls, so the proteins required for DNA licensing can function again for the next cell cycle (**Figure 19-6**).

DNA Polymerases Catalyze the Elongation of DNA Chains

When the semiconservative model of DNA replication was first proposed in the early 1950s, biologists thought that DNA replication was so complex that it could only be carried out by intact cells. But just a few years later, Arthur Kornberg showed that an enzyme he had isolated from bacteria can copy DNA molecules in a test tube. This enzyme, which he named **DNA polymerase,** requires that a small amount of DNA be initially present to act as a template. Guided by this template, DNA polymerase catalyzes the elongation of DNA chains using as substrates the triphosphate deoxynucleoside derivatives of the four bases

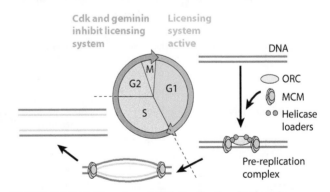

FIGURE 19-6 Licensing of DNA Replication During the Eukaryotic Cell Cycle. DNA is licensed for replication during G1 by the binding of MCM proteins to replication origins, an event that requires both ORC and helicase loaders. The licensing system is turned off at the end of G1 by the production of Cdks and/or geminin, whose activities block the functions of the proteins required for licensing (ORC, helicase loaders, and MCM). After the cell completes mitosis, geminin is degraded and Cdk activity falls, so the licensing system becomes active again for the next cell cycle.

found in DNA (dATP, dTTP, dGTP, and dCTP). As each of these substrates is incorporated into a newly forming DNA chain, its two terminal phosphate groups are released. Since deoxynucleoside triphosphates are high-energy compounds (comparable to ATP), the energy released as these phosphate bonds are broken drives what would otherwise be a thermodynamically unfavorable polymerization reaction.

In the DNA polymerase reaction, incoming nucleotides are covalently bonded to the 3′ hydroxyl end of the growing DNA chain. Each successive nucleotide is linked to the growing chain by a phosphoester bond between the phosphate group on its 5′ carbon and the hydroxyl group on the 3′ carbon of the nucleotide added in the previous step (Figure 19-7). In other words, chain elongation occurs at the 3′ end of a DNA strand, and the strand is therefore said to grow in the 5′ → 3′ direction.

Soon after Kornberg's initial discovery, several other forms of DNA polymerase were detected. (Table 19-1 lists the main DNA polymerases used in DNA replication, along with other key proteins involved in the process.) In *E. coli,* the enzyme discovered by Kornberg has turned out not to be responsible for DNA replication in intact cells. This fact first became apparent when Peter DeLucia and John Cairns reported that mutant strains of bacteria lacking the Kornberg enzyme can still replicate their DNA

and reproduce normally. With the Kornberg enzyme missing, it was possible to detect the presence of several other bacterial enzymes that synthesize DNA. These additional enzymes are named using Roman numerals (e.g., DNA polymerases II, III, IV, and V) to distinguish them from the original Kornberg enzyme, now called DNA polymerase I. When the rates at which the various DNA polymerases synthesize DNA in a test tube were first compared, only DNA polymerase III was found to work fast enough to account for the rate of DNA replication in intact cells, which averages about 50,000 base pairs/minute in bacteria.

Such observations suggested that DNA polymerase III is the main enzyme responsible for DNA replication in bacterial cells, but the evidence would be more convincing if it could be shown that cells lacking DNA polymerase III are unable to replicate their DNA. How is it possible to grow and study cells that have lost the ability to carry out an essential function such as DNA replication? One powerful approach involves the use of **temperature-sensitive mutants,** which are cells that produce proteins that function properly at normal temperatures but become seriously impaired when the temperature is altered slightly. For example, mutant bacteria have been isolated in which DNA polymerase III behaves normally at 37°C but loses its function when the temperature is raised to 42°C. Such

Table 19-1	Some Important DNA Replication Proteins in Bacteria and Eukaryotes	
Protein	**Cell Type**	**Main Activities and/or Functions**
DNA polymerase I	Bacteria	DNA synthesis; 3′ → 5′ exonuclease (for proofreading); 5′ → 3′ exonuclease; removes and replaces RNA primers used in DNA replication (also functions in excision repair of damaged DNA)
DNA polymerase III	Bacteria	DNA synthesis; 3′ → 5′ exonuclease (for proofreading); used in synthesis of both DNA strands
DNA polymerase α (alpha)	Eukaryotes	Nuclear DNA synthesis; forms complex with primase and begins DNA synthesis at the 3′ end of RNA primers for both leading and lagging strands (also functions in DNA repair)
DNA polymerase γ (gamma)	Eukaryotes	Mitochondrial DNA synthesis
DNA polymerase δ (delta)	Eukaryotes	Nuclear DNA synthesis; 3′ → 5′ exonuclease (for proofreading); involved in lagging and leading strand synthesis (also functions in DNA repair)
DNA polymerase ε (epsilon)	Eukaryotes	Nuclear DNA synthesis; 3′ → 5′ exonuclease (for proofreading); thought to be involved in leading and lagging strand synthesis (also functions in DNA repair)
Primase	Both	RNA synthesis; makes RNA oligonucleotides that are used as primers for DNA synthesis
DNA helicase	Both	Unwinds double-stranded DNA
Single-stranded DNA binding protein (SSB)	Both	Binds to single-stranded DNA; stabilizes strands of unwound DNA in an extended configuration that facilitates access by other proteins
DNA topoisomerase (type I and type II)	Both	Makes single-strand cuts (type I) or double-strand cuts (type II) in DNA; induces and/or relaxes DNA supercoiling; can serve as swivel to prevent overwinding ahead of the DNA replication fork; can separate linked DNA circles at the end of DNA replication
DNA gyrase	Bacteria	Type II DNA topoisomerase that serves as a swivel to relax supercoiling ahead of the DNA replication fork in *E. coli*
DNA ligase	Both	Makes covalent bonds to join together adjacent DNA strands, including the Okazaki fragments in lagging strand DNA synthesis and the new and old DNA segments in excision repair of DNA
Initiator proteins	Both	Bind to origin of replication and initiate unwinding of DNA double helix
Telomerase	Eukaryotes	Using an integral RNA molecule as template, synthesizes DNA for extension of telomeres (sequences at ends of chromosomal DNA)

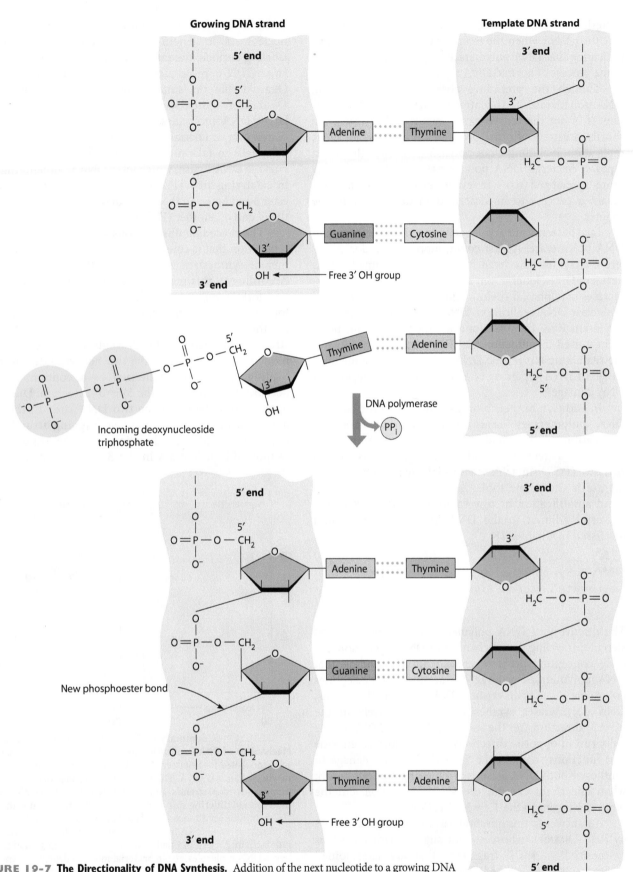

FIGURE 19-7 The Directionality of DNA Synthesis. Addition of the next nucleotide to a growing DNA strand is catalyzed by DNA polymerase and always occurs at the 3′ end of the strand. A phosphoester bond is formed between the 3′ hydroxyl group of the terminal nucleotide and the 5′ phosphate of the incoming deoxynucleoside triphosphate (here dTTP), extending the growing chain by one nucleotide, liberating pyrophosphate (PP$_i$) and leaving the 3′ end of the strand with a free hydroxyl group to accept the next nucleotide.

bacteria grow normally at 37°C but lose the ability to replicate their DNA when the temperature is elevated to 42°C, indicating that DNA polymerase III plays an essential role in the process of normal DNA replication.

Though the preceding observations indicate that DNA polymerase III is central to bacterial DNA replication, it is not the only enzyme involved. As we will see shortly, a variety of other proteins are required for DNA replication, including DNA polymerase I. The other main types of bacterial DNA polymerase (II, IV, and V) play more specialized roles in events associated with DNA repair, a process to be described in detail later in the chapter.

Like bacteria, eukaryotic cells contain several types of DNA polymerase. At last count, more than a dozen different enzymes have been identified, each named with a different Greek letter. From among this group, DNA polymerases α (alpha), δ (delta), and ε (epsilon) are involved in nuclear DNA replication. DNA polymerase γ (gamma) is present only in mitochondria and is the main polymerase used in mitochondrial DNA replication. Most of the remaining eukaryotic DNA polymerases are involved either in DNA repair or in replication across regions of DNA damage.

In addition to their biological functions inside cells, DNA polymerases have found important practical applications in the field of biotechnology. **Box 19A** describes a technique called the *polymerase chain reaction (PCR)*, in which a special type of DNA polymerase is the prime tool. Used experimentally for the rapid amplification of tiny samples of DNA, PCR is a powerful adjunct to the DNA fingerprinting method discussed in Chapter 18.

DNA Is Synthesized as Discontinuous Segments That Are Joined Together by DNA Ligase

The discovery of DNA polymerase was merely the first step in unraveling the mechanism of DNA replication. An early conceptual problem arose from the finding that DNA polymerases catalyze the addition of nucleotides *only to the 3′ end of an existing DNA chain;* in other words, DNA polymerases synthesize DNA exclusively in the 5′ → 3′ direction. Yet the two strands of the DNA double helix run in opposite directions. So how does an enzyme that functions solely in the 5′ → 3′ direction manage to synthesize both DNA strands at a moving replication fork when one chain runs in the 5′ → 3′ direction and the other chain runs in the 3′ → 5′ direction?

An answer to this question was first proposed in 1968 by Reiji Okazaki, whose studies suggested that DNA is synthesized as small fragments that are later joined together. Okazaki isolated DNA from bacterial cells that had been briefly exposed to a radioactive substrate that is incorporated into newly made DNA. Analysis of this DNA revealed that much of the radioactivity was located in small DNA fragments measuring about a thousand nucleotides in length (**Figure 19-8a**). After longer labeling periods, the radioactivity became associated with larger DNA molecules. These findings suggested to Okazaki that the smaller DNA pieces, now known as **Okazaki fragments,** are precursors of newly forming larger DNA molecules. Later research revealed that the conversion of Okazaki fragments into larger DNA molecules fails to take place in mutant bacteria that lack the enzyme **DNA ligase,** which joins DNA fragments together by catalyzing the ATP-dependent formation of a phosphoester bond between the 3′ end of one nucleotide chain and the 5′ end of another (Figure 19-8b).

The preceding observations suggest a model of DNA replication that is consistent with the fact that DNA polymerase synthesizes DNA only in the 5′ → 3′ direction. According to this model, DNA synthesis at each replication fork is *continuous* in the direction of fork movement for one strand but *discontinuous* in the opposite direction for the other strand (**Figure 19-9**). The two daughter strands can therefore be distinguished based on their mode of growth. One of the two new strands, called the **leading strand,** is synthesized as a continuous chain because it is growing in the 5′ → 3′ direction. Due to the opposite orientation of the two DNA strands, the other newly forming strand, called the **lagging strand,** must grow in the 3′ → 5′ direction. But DNA polymerase cannot add nucleotides in the 3′ → 5′ direction, so the

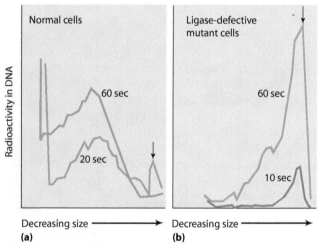

FIGURE 19-8 Summary of Okazaki's Experiments on the Mechanism of DNA Replication in Bacterial Cells. (a) Bacteria were incubated for brief periods with radioactive thymidine to label newly synthesized DNA. The DNA was then isolated, dissociated into its individual strands, and fractionated by centrifugation into molecules of differing size. In normal bacteria incubated with ^{3}H-thymidine for 20 seconds, a significant amount of radioactivity is present in small DNA fragments (arrow). By 60 seconds, the radioactivity present in small DNA fragments has all shifted to larger DNA molecules. (b) In bacterial mutants deficient in the enzyme DNA ligase, radioactivity remains in small DNA fragments even after 60 seconds of incubation. It was therefore concluded that DNA ligase normally functions to join small DNA fragments together into longer DNA chains.

lagging strand is instead formed as a series of short, discontinuous Okazaki fragments that are synthesized in the $5' \rightarrow 3'$ direction. These fragments are then joined together by DNA ligase to make a continuous new $3' \rightarrow 5'$ DNA strand. Okazaki fragments are generally about 1000–2000 nucleotides long in viral and bacterial systems but only about one-tenth this length in eukaryotic cells. In *E. coli*, the same DNA polymerase, polymerase III, is used for synthesizing the Okazaki fragments of the lagging strand and the continuous DNA chain of the leading strand. In eukaryotes, DNA polymerases δ and ε are both thought to be involved in synthesizing leading and lagging strands.

Proofreading Is Performed by the $3' \rightarrow 5'$ Exonuclease Activity of DNA Polymerase

Given the complexity of the preceding model, you might wonder why cells have not simply evolved an enzyme that synthesizes DNA in the $3' \rightarrow 5'$ direction. One possible answer is related to the need for error correction during DNA replication. About 1 out of every 100,000 nucleotides incorporated during DNA replication is incorrectly base-paired with the template DNA strand, an error rate that would yield more than 120,000 errors every time a human cell replicates its DNA. Fortunately, such mistakes are usually fixed by a **proofreading** mechanism that uses the same DNA polymerase molecules that catalyze DNA synthesis. Proofreading is made possible by the fact that almost all DNA polymerases possess $3' \rightarrow 5'$ exonuclease activity (in addition to their ability to catalyze DNA synthesis). **Exonucleases** are enzymes that degrade nucleic acids (usually DNA) from one end, rather than making internal cuts, as **endonucleases** do. A $3' \rightarrow 5'$ exonuclease is one that clips off nucleotides from the 3' end of a nucleotide chain. Hence, the $3' \rightarrow 5'$ exonuclease activity of DNA polymerase allows it to remove improperly base-paired nucleotides from the 3' end of a growing DNA chain (**Figure 19-10**). This ability to remove incorrect nucleotides improves the fidelity of DNA replication to an average of only a few errors for every billion base pairs replicated.

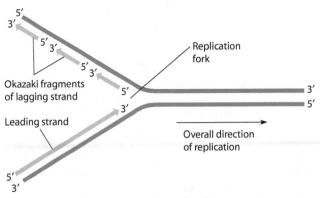

FIGURE 19-9 Directions of DNA Synthesis at a Replication Fork. Because DNA polymerases synthesize DNA chains only in the $5' \rightarrow 3'$ direction, synthesis at each replication fork is continuous in the direction of fork movement for the leading strand but discontinuous in the opposite direction for the lagging strand. Discontinuous synthesis involves short intermediates called Okazaki fragments, which are 1000–2000 nucleotides long in bacteria and about 100–200 nucleotides long in eukaryotic cells. The fragments are later joined together by the enzyme DNA ligase. Parental DNA is shown in dark blue, and newly synthesized DNA in lighter blue. Here and in subsequent figures, arrowheads indicate the direction in which the nucleic acid chain is being elongated.

ACTIVITIES www.thecellplace.com *Molecular model of DNA replication*

If cells did happen to possess an enzyme capable of synthesizing DNA in the $3' \rightarrow 5'$ direction, proofreading could not work because a DNA chain growing in the $3' \rightarrow 5'$ direction would have a nucleotide triphosphate at its growing 5' end. What if this 5' nucleotide contained an incorrect base that needed to be removed during proofreading? Removing this 5' nucleotide would eliminate the triphosphate group that provides the free energy that allows DNA polymerase to add nucleotides to a growing DNA chain, and hence the chain could not elongate further.

RNA Primers Initiate DNA Replication

Since DNA polymerase can only add nucleotides to an existing nucleotide chain, how is replication of a DNA double helix initiated? Shortly after Okazaki fragments were

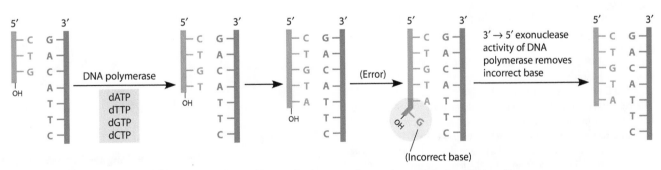

FIGURE 19-10 Proofreading by $3' \rightarrow 5'$ Exonuclease. If an incorrect base is inserted during DNA replication, the $3' \rightarrow 5'$ exonuclease activity that is part of the DNA polymerase molecule catalyzes its removal so that the correct base can be inserted.

The ability to work with minuscule amounts of DNA is invaluable in a wide range of endeavors, from paleontology to criminology. In Chapter 18, we described how DNA fingerprinting analysis can be used to identify and characterize particular sequences contained in as little as 1 μg of DNA, the amount in a small drop of blood (see Box 18C). But sometimes even that amount of DNA may not be available. In such cases another method, called the **polymerase chain reaction (PCR)**, can come to the rescue. With PCR, it is possible to rapidly replicate, or *amplify,* selected DNA segments that are initially present in extremely small amounts. In only a few hours, PCR can make millions or even billions of copies of a particular DNA sequence, thereby producing enough material for DNA fingerprinting, DNA sequencing, or other applications.

The complex multiprotein system that cells use for DNA replication is not required for the PCR method. Instead, PCR employs an unusual DNA polymerase coupled with synthetic primers to set up a chain reaction that produces an exponentially growing population of specific DNA molecules. Biochemist Kary Mullis received a Nobel Prize in 1993 for developing this technique. To perform PCR, you first need to know part of the base sequence of the DNA segment you wish to amplify. Based on this information, short single-stranded *DNA primers* are chemically synthesized; these primers generally consist of DNA segments 15–20 nucleotides long that are complementary to sequences located at opposite ends of the DNA segment being amplified. (If sequences that naturally flank the sequence of interest are not known, artificial ones can be attached before running the polymerase chain reaction.) DNA polymerase is then added to catalyze the synthesis of complementary DNA strands using the two primers as starting points. The DNA polymerase routinely used for this purpose was first isolated from the bacterium *Thermus aquaticus,* an inhabitant of thermal hot springs where the waters are normally 70–80°C. The optimal temperature for this enzyme, called *Taq* polymerase, is 72°C, and it is stable at even higher temperatures—a property that made possible the automation of PCR.

Figure 19A-1 summarizes how the PCR procedure works. The ingredients of the initial reaction mixture include the DNA containing the sequence to be amplified, *Taq* DNA polymerase, the synthetic DNA primers, and the four deoxynucleoside triphosphates (dATP, dTTP, dCTP, and dGTP). Each reaction cycle begins with a short period of heating to near boiling (95°C) to denature the DNA double helix into its two strands (❶). The DNA solution is then cooled to allow the primers to base-pair to complementary regions on the DNA strands being copied (❷). The temperature is then raised to 72°C, and the *Taq* DNA polymerase goes to work, adding nucleotides to the 3′ end of the primer (❸). The specificity of the primers ensures the selective copying of the stretches of template DNA downstream from the primers. It takes no more than a few minutes for the *Taq* polymerase to completely copy the targeted DNA sequence, thereby doubling the amount of DNA. The reaction mixture is then heated again to melt the new double helices, more primer is bound to the DNA, and the cycle is repeated to double the amount of DNA again (❶–❸).

This reaction cycle is repeated as many times as necessary, with each cycle doubling the amount of DNA from the previous cycle. After the third cycle, more and more of the product DNA molecules will be of a uniform length that consists only of the targeted

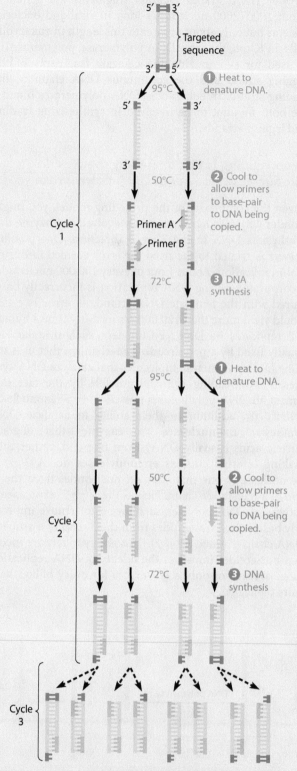

FIGURE 19A-1 DNA Amplification Using the Polymerase Chain Reaction. See the description in the box text. PCR works best when the DNA segment to be amplified—the region flanked by the two primers—is 50–2000 nucleotides long.

sequence (like the third and sixth molecules in the last line of the figure). Because heating to 95°C does not destroy the *Taq* polymerase, there is no need to add fresh enzyme for each round of the cycle. In most cases, 20–30 reaction cycles are sufficient to produce the desired quantity of DNA. The theoretical amplification accomplished by *n* cycles is 2^n, so 20 cycles yields an amplification of a millionfold or more ($2^{20} = 1,048,576$) and 30 cycles over a billion-fold ($2^{30} = 1,073,741,824$). Since each cycle takes less than 5 minutes, several hundred billion copies of the original DNA sequence can be produced within a few hours. This is considerably quicker than the several days required for amplifying DNA by cloning it in bacteria. Furthermore, PCR can be used with as little as one molecule of DNA, and it does not require the starting DNA sample to be purified because the primers select the DNA region that will be amplified.

PCR therefore makes it possible to identify a person from the minuscule amount of DNA that is left behind when that person touches an object, inadvertently leaving a few skin cells behind. By using PCR to amplify the tiny amount of DNA in such a sample and then performing a DNA fingerprinting analysis on the amplified DNA, it is possible to obtain a DNA fingerprint from a person's actual fingerprints! Although such techniques have enormous potential in helping to solve crimes, this extraordinary sensitivity can also cause problems. A few contaminating DNA molecules (such as from skin cells shed by a lab technician) might be amplified along with the DNA of interest, yielding misleading results.

Nevertheless, with proper precautions and controls, PCR is proving extremely valuable. As an aid in evolution research, it has been used to amplify DNA fragments recovered from ancient Egyptian mummies and a 40,000-year-old woolly mammoth frozen in a glacier, and to unravel the genome of Neanderthals. In medical diagnosis, PCR has been used to amplify DNA from single embryonic cells for rapid prenatal diagnosis, and it has made possible the detection of viral genes in cells infected with HIV or other viruses. Perhaps most importantly, PCR has revolutionized basic research in molecular genetics by allowing easy amplification of particular genes or sequences from among the thousands of genes in mammalian genomes.

first discovered, researchers implicated RNA in the initiation process through the following observations: (1) Okazaki fragments often have short stretches of RNA, usually 3–10 nucleotides in length, at their 5′ ends; (2) DNA polymerase can catalyze the addition of nucleotides to the 3′ end of RNA chains as well as to DNA chains; (3) cells contain an enzyme called **primase** that synthesizes RNA fragments about ten bases long using DNA as a template; and (4) unlike DNA polymerase, which adds nucleotides only to the ends of existing chains, primase can initiate RNA synthesis from scratch by joining two nucleotides together.

These observations led to the conclusion that DNA synthesis is initiated by the formation of short **RNA primers.** RNA primers are synthesized by primase, which uses a single DNA strand as a template to guide the synthesis of a complementary stretch of RNA (**Figure 19-11**, ❶). Primase is a specific kind of RNA polymerase used only in DNA replication. Like other RNA polymerases, but unlike DNA polymerases, primases can *initiate* the synthesis of a new polynucleotide strand complementary to a template strand; they do not themselves require a primer.

In *E. coli,* primase is relatively inactive unless it is accompanied by six other proteins, forming a complex called a **primosome.** The other primosome proteins function in unwinding the parental DNA and recognizing target DNA sequences where replication is to be initiated. The situation in eukaryotic cells is slightly different, so the term *primosome* is not used. The eukaryotic primase is not as closely associated with unwinding proteins, but it is very tightly bound to DNA polymerase α, the main DNA polymerase involved in initiating DNA replication.

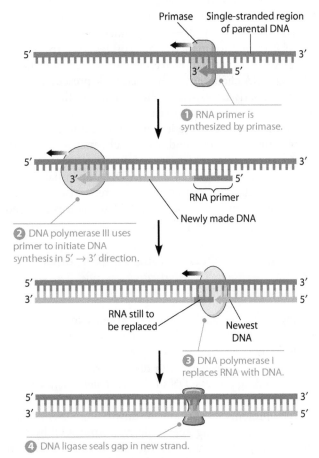

FIGURE 19-11 The Role of RNA Primers in DNA Replication. DNA synthesis is initiated with a short RNA primer in both bacteria and eukaryotes. This figure shows the process as it occurs for the lagging strand in *E. coli.*

Once an RNA primer has been created, DNA synthesis can proceed, with DNA polymerase III (or DNA polymerase α followed by polymerase δ or ε in eukaryotes) adding successive deoxynucleotides to the 3′ end of the primer (Figure 19-11, ❷). For the leading strand, initiation using an RNA primer needs to occur only once, when a replication fork first forms; DNA polymerase can then add nucleotides to the chain continuously in the 5′ → 3′ direction. In contrast, the lagging strand is synthesized as a series of discontinuous Okazaki fragments, and each of them must be initiated with a separate RNA primer. For each primer, DNA nucleotides are added by DNA polymerase III until the growing fragment reaches the adjacent Okazaki fragment. No longer needed at that point, the RNA segment is removed and DNA nucleotides are polymerized to fill its place. In *E. coli*, the RNA primers are removed by a 5′ → 3′ exonuclease activity inherent to the DNA polymerase I molecule (distinct from the 3′ → 5′ exonuclease activity involved in proofreading). At the same time, the DNA polymerase I molecule synthesizes DNA in the normal 5′ → 3′ direction to fill in the resulting gaps (Figure 19-11, ❸). Adjacent fragments are subsequently joined together by DNA ligase.

Why do cells employ RNA primers that must later be removed rather than simply using a DNA primer in the first place? Again, the answer may be related to the need for error correction. We have already seen that DNA polymerase possesses a 3′ → 5′ exonuclease activity that allows it to remove incorrect nucleotides from the 3′ end of a DNA chain. In fact, DNA polymerase will elongate an existing DNA chain only if the nucleotide present at the 3′ end is properly base-paired. But an enzyme that *initiates* the synthesis of a new chain cannot perform such a proofreading function because it is not adding a nucleotide to an existing base-paired end. As a result, enzymes that initiate nucleic acid synthesis are not very good at correcting errors. By using RNA rather than DNA to initiate DNA synthesis, cells ensure that any incorrect bases inserted during initiation are restricted to RNA sequences destined to be removed by DNA polymerase I.

Unwinding the DNA Double Helix Requires DNA Helicases, Topoisomerases, and Single-Stranded DNA Binding Proteins

During DNA replication, the two strands of the double helix must unwind at each replication fork to expose the single strands to the enzymes responsible for copying them. Three classes of proteins with distinct functions facilitate this unwinding process: *DNA helicases, topoisomerases,* and *single-stranded DNA binding proteins* (**Figure 19-12**).

The proteins responsible for unwinding DNA are the **DNA helicases.** Using energy derived from ATP hydrolysis, these proteins unwind the DNA double helix in advance of the replication fork, breaking the hydrogen bonds as they go. In *E. coli*, at least two different DNA helicases are involved in DNA replication; one attaches to the lagging strand template and moves in a 5′ → 3′ direction; the other attaches to the leading strand template and

moves 3′ → 5′. Both are part of the primosome, but the 5′ → 3′ helicase is more important for unwinding DNA at the replication fork.

The unwinding associated with DNA replication would create an intolerable amount of supercoiling and possibly tangling in the rest of the DNA were it not for the actions of **topoisomerases,** which we discussed in Chapter 18. These enzymes create swivel points in the DNA molecule by making and then quickly resealing single- or double-stranded breaks in the double helix. Of the ten or so topoisomerases found in *E. coli*, the key enzyme for DNA replication is *DNA gyrase,* a type II topoisomerase (an enzyme that cuts both DNA strands). Using energy derived from ATP, DNA gyrase introduces negative supercoils and thereby relaxes positive ones. DNA gyrase serves as the main swivel that prevents over-winding (positive supercoiling) of the DNA ahead of the replication fork. In addition, this enzyme has a role in both initiating and completing DNA replication in *E. coli*—in opening up the double helix at the origin of replication and in separating the linked circles of daughter DNA at the end. The situation in eukaryotic cells is not as well understood, although topoisomerases of both types have been isolated.

Once strand separation has begun, molecules of **single-stranded DNA binding protein (SSB)** quickly attach to the exposed single strands to keep the DNA unwound and therefore accessible to the DNA replication machinery. After a particular segment of DNA has been replicated, the SSB molecules fall off and are recycled, attaching to the next single-stranded segment.

Putting It All Together: DNA Replication in Summary

Figure 19-13 reviews the highlights of what we currently understand about the mechanics of DNA replication in

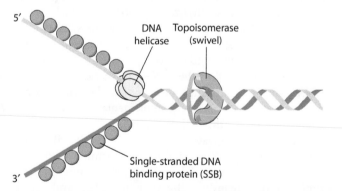

FIGURE 19-12 Proteins Involved in Unwinding DNA at the Replication Fork. Three types of proteins are involved in DNA unwinding. The actual unwinding proteins are the DNA helicases; the principal one in *E. coli*, which is part of the primosome, operates 5′ → 3′ along the template for the lagging strand, as shown here. Single-stranded DNA binding proteins (SSB) stabilize the unwound DNA in an extended position. A topoisomerase forms a swivel ahead of the replication fork; in *E. coli*, this topoisomerase is DNA gyrase.

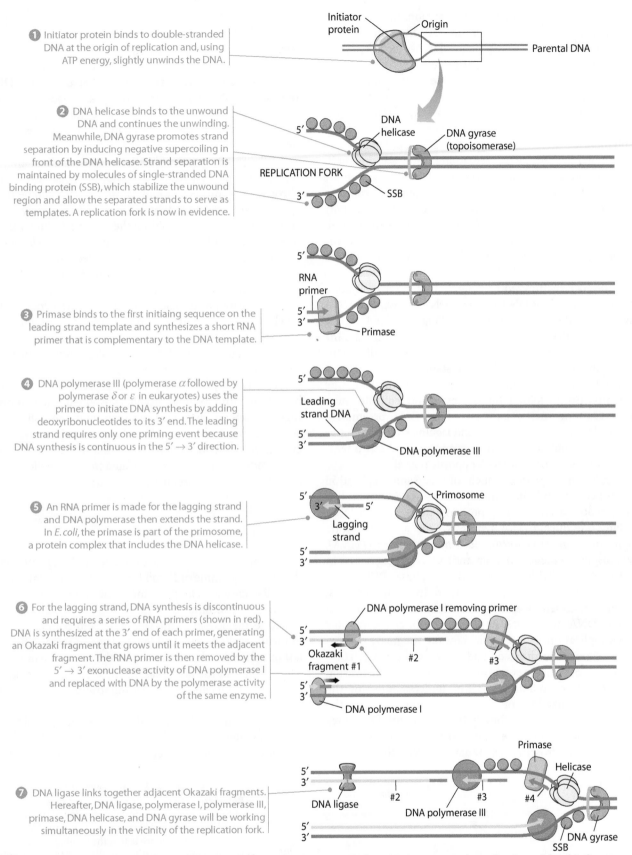

1 Initiator protein binds to double-stranded DNA at the origin of replication and, using ATP energy, slightly unwinds the DNA.

Initiator protein
Origin
Parental DNA

2 DNA helicase binds to the unwound DNA and continues the unwinding. Meanwhile, DNA gyrase promotes strand separation by inducing negative supercoiling in front of the DNA helicase. Strand separation is maintained by molecules of single-stranded DNA binding protein (SSB), which stabilize the unwound region and allow the separated strands to serve as templates. A replication fork is now in evidence.

DNA helicase
DNA gyrase (topoisomerase)
5′
REPLICATION FORK
3′
SSB

3 Primase binds to the first initiaing sequence on the leading strand template and synthesizes a short RNA primer that is complementary to the DNA template.

5′
RNA primer
5′
3′
Primase

4 DNA polymerase III (polymerase α followed by polymerase δ or ε in eukaryotes) uses the primer to initiate DNA synthesis by adding deoxyribonucleotides to its 3′ end. The leading strand requires only one priming event because DNA synthesis is continuous in the 5′ → 3′ direction.

5′
Leading strand DNA
5′
3′
DNA polymerase III

5 An RNA primer is made for the lagging strand and DNA polymerase then extends the strand. In *E. coli*, the primase is part of the primosome, a protein complex that includes the DNA helicase.

5′
3′   5′
Primosome
Lagging strand
5′
3′

6 For the lagging strand, DNA synthesis is discontinuous and requires a series of RNA primers (shown in red). DNA is synthesized at the 3′ end of each primer, generating an Okazaki fragment that grows until it meets the adjacent fragment. The RNA primer is then removed by the 5′ → 3′ exonuclease activity of DNA polymerase I and replaced with DNA by the polymerase activity of the same enzyme.

DNA polymerase I removing primer
5′
3′
Okazaki fragment #1
#2
#3
5′
3′
DNA polymerase I

7 DNA ligase links together adjacent Okazaki fragments. Hereafter, DNA ligase, polymerase I, polymerase III, primase, DNA helicase, and DNA gyrase will be working simultaneously in the vicinity of the replication fork.

Primase
Helicase
5′
3′
DNA ligase
#2
DNA polymerase III
#3
#4
5′
3′
DNA gyrase
SSB

FIGURE 19-13 A Summary of DNA Replication in Bacteria. Starting with the initiation event at the replication origin, this figure depicts DNA replication in *E. coli* in seven steps. Two replication forks move in opposite directions from the origin, but only one fork is illustrated for steps **2**–**7**. The various proteins shown here as separate entities are actually closely associated (along with others) in a single large complex called a replisome. The primase and DNA helicase are particularly closely bound and, together with other proteins, form a primosome. Parental DNA is shown in dark blue, newly synthesized DNA in light blue, and RNA in red. This series of diagrams does not show the topological arrangement of the DNA strands.

E. coli. Starting at the origin of replication, the machinery at the replication fork sequentially adds the different proteins required for synthesizing DNA—that is, DNA helicase, DNA gyrase, SSB, primase, DNA polymerase, and DNA ligase. Several other proteins (not illustrated) are also involved in improving the overall efficiency of DNA replication. For example, a ring-shaped *sliding clamp* protein encircles the DNA double helix and binds to DNA polymerase, thereby allowing the DNA polymerase to slide along the DNA while remaining firmly attached to it.

The various proteins involved in DNA replication are all closely associated in one large complex, called a **replisome,** that is about the size of a ribosome. The activity and movement of the replisome is powered by the hydrolysis of nucleoside triphosphates. These include both the nucleoside triphosphates (used by DNA polymerases and primase as building blocks for DNA and RNA synthesis) and the ATP hydrolyzed by several other DNA replication proteins (including DNA helicase, DNA gyrase, and DNA ligase). As the replisome moves along the DNA in the direction of the replication fork, it must accommodate the fact that DNA is being synthesized in opposite directions along the template on the two stands. **Figure 19-14** provides a schematic model illustrating how this might be accomplished by folding the lagging strand template into a loop. Creating such a loop allows the DNA polymerase molecules on both the leading and lagging strands to move in the same physical direction, even though the two template strands are oriented with opposite polarity.

Eukaryotes possess much of the same replication machinery found in prokaryotes. For example, like prokaryotes, a DNA clamp protein acts along with DNA polymerase during DNA synthesis. One such eukaryotic clamp protein, *proliferating nuclear cell antigen (PCNA),* was originally identified as an antigen that is expressed in the nuclei of dividing cells during S phase. PCNA is a clamp protein for DNA polymerase δ. In eukaryotic cells, the enormous length and elaborate folding of the chromosomal DNA molecules pose additional challenges for DNA replication. For example, how are the many replication origins coordinated, and how is their activation linked to other key events in the cell cycle? Answering such questions requires a better understanding of the spatial organization of DNA replication within the nucleus. When cells are briefly incubated with DNA precursors that make the most recently formed DNA fluorescent, microscopic examination reveals that the new,

fluorescent DNA is located in a series of discrete spots scattered throughout the nucleus. Such observations suggest the existence of apparently immobile structures, known as *replication factories,* where chromatin fibers are fed through stationary replisomes that carry out DNA replication. These sites are closely associated with the inner surface of the nuclear envelope, although it is not clear whether they are anchored in the nuclear membrane or to some other nuclear support.

When a chromatin fiber is fed through a stationary replication factory, how are the histones and other chromosomal proteins removed, so the DNA can be replicated, and then added back after the two new DNA strands are formed? Unfolding the chromatin fibers ahead of the replication fork is facilitated by *chromatin remodeling* proteins, which loosen nucleosome packing to give the replication machinery access to the DNA template. As the replication fork moves, old nucleosomes slide from the parental double helix ahead of the fork to the newly forming strands behind the fork. At the same time, new nucleosomes are assembled on the newly forming strands because the two DNA molecules produced by replication require twice as many nucleosomes as the single parental DNA possessed prior to replication. When and how other chromosomal proteins are added, what controls higher levels of chromatin packing, and how all this is accomplished without tangling the chromatin are areas of current research. Meanwhile, an answer has emerged to one of the most baffling questions related to DNA replication in eukaryotes—the end-replication problem.

Telomeres Solve the DNA End-Replication Problem

If we continue the process summarized in Figure 19-13 for the circular genome of *E. coli* (or any other circular DNA), we will eventually complete the circle. The leading strand can simply continue to grow 5′ → 3′ until its 3′ end is joined to the 5′ end of the lagging strand coming around in the other direction. And for the lagging strand, the very last bit of DNA to be synthesized—the replacement for the RNA primer of the last Okazaki fragment—can be added to the free 3′ OH end of the leading strand coming around in the opposite direction.

For linear DNA molecules, however, the fact that DNA polymerases can add nucleotides only to the 3′ OH end of a *preexisting* DNA chain creates a serious problem,

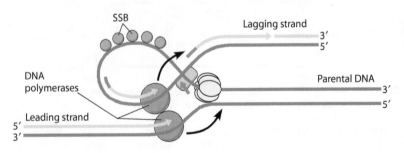

FIGURE 19-14 Arrangement of Proteins at the Replication Fork. This model shows how some of the key replication proteins illustrated in Figure 19-13 are organized at the replication fork. The main distinguishing feature is that the lagging strand DNA is folded into a loop, thereby allowing the DNA polymerase molecules on the leading and lagging strands to come together and move in the same physical direction (black arrows) even though the two template strands are oriented with opposite polarity in the parental DNA molecule.

which is depicted in **Figure 19-15.** When a growing lagging strand (lightest blue) reaches the end of the DNA molecule and the last RNA primer is removed by a $5' \rightarrow 3'$ exonuclease, the final gap cannot be filled because there is no 3' OH end that deoxynucleotides can be added to. As a result, linear DNA molecules are in danger of yielding shorter and shorter daughter DNA molecules each time they replicate. Clearly, if this trend continued indefinitely, we would not be here today!

Viruses with linear DNA genomes solve this problem in various ways. In some cases, such as bacteriophage 1, the linear DNA forms a closed circle before it replicates. In other cases, the viruses use more exotic reproduction strategies, although the DNA polymerases always progress 5' to 3', adding nucleotides to a 3' end.

Eukaryotes have solved the end-replication problem by locating highly repeated DNA sequences at the terminal ends, or **telomeres,** of each linear chromosome. These special telomeric elements consist of short, repeating sequences enriched in the base G in the $5' \rightarrow 3'$ strand. The sequence TTAGGG, located at the ends of human chromosomes, is an example of such a telomeric or *TEL sequence.* Human telomeres typically contain between 100 and 1500 copies of the TTAGGG sequence repeated in tandem. Such noncoding sequences at the ends of each chromosome ensure that the cell will not lose any important genetic information if a DNA molecule is shortened slightly during the process of DNA replication. Moreover, a special DNA polymerase called **telomerase** can catalyze the formation of additional copies of the telomeric repeat sequence, thereby compensating for the gradual shortening that occurs at both ends of the chromosome during DNA replication. Elizabeth Blackburn, Carol Greider, and Jack Szostak received the 2009 Nobel Prize in Physiology or Medicine for their fundamental contributions to our understanding of telomeres and telomerase.

Telomerase is an unusual enzyme in that it is composed of RNA as well as protein. In the protozoan *Tetrahymena,* whose telomerase was the first to be isolated, the RNA component contains the sequence $3' - AACCCC - 5'$, which is complementary to the $5' - TTGGGG - 3'$ repeat sequence that makes up *Tetrahymena* telomeres. As shown in **Figure 19-16,** this enzyme-bound RNA acts as a template for creating the DNA repeat sequence that is added to the telomere ends. After being lengthened by telomerase, the telomeres are protected by *telomere capping proteins* that bind to the exposed 3' end of the DNA. In many eukaryotes, the 3' end of the DNA can loop back and base-pair with the opposite DNA strand, generating a closed loop that likewise protects the end of the telomere (Figure 19-16, step ❺).

In multicellular organisms, telomerase resides mainly in the *germ cells* that give rise to sperm and eggs and in a few other types of actively proliferating cells. The presence

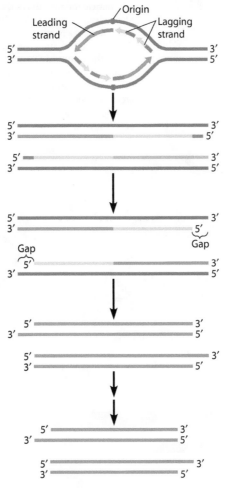

❶ DNA replication is initiated at the origin; the replication bubble grows as the two replication forks move in opposite directions.

❷ Finally only one primer (red) remains on each daughter DNA molecule.

❸ The last primers are removed by a $5' \rightarrow 3'$ exonuclease, but no DNA polymerase can fill the resulting gaps because there is no 3' OH available to which a nucleotide can be added.

❹ Each round of replication generates shorter and shorter DNA molecules.

FIGURE 19-15 The End-Replication Problem. For a linear DNA molecule, such as that of a eukaryotic chromosome, the usual DNA replication machinery is unable to replicate the ends. As a result, with each round of replication, the DNA molecules will get shorter, with potentially disastrous consequences for the cell. In this diagram, the initial parental DNA strands are dark blue, daughter DNA strands are lighter blue, and RNA primers are red. For simplicity, we show only one origin of replication and, in the last two steps, only the shortest of the progeny molecules. (The lagging strand daughter DNA is shown in the lightest blue in the first three steps to make a point unrelated to the end-replication problem—that each daughter strand is leading at one end and lagging at the other. This is apparent in this figure because it shows the entire replicating molecule, with both replication forks.)

of telomerase allows these cells to divide indefinitely without telomere shortening. Because telomerase is not found in most cells, their chromosomal telomeres get shorter and shorter with each cell division. As a result, telomere length is a counting device that reveals how many times a cell has divided. If a cell divides enough times, the telomeres are in danger of disappearing entirely, and the cell would then be at risk of eroding its coding DNA. This potential danger is averted by a cell destruction pathway set in motion by the shortened telomeric DNA. In essence, when the telomeric DNA becomes too short to bind telomeric capping proteins or generate a loop, it exposes a bare, double-stranded DNA end whose presence activates a signaling system that triggers *apoptosis*, an orchestrated type of cell death described later in this chapter.

Cell death triggered by a lifetime of telomere shortening is thought to contribute to some of the degenerative diseases associated with human aging—for example, increased susceptibility to infections due to the death of immune cells, inefficient wound healing caused by depletion of connective tissue cells, and ulcers triggered by loss of cells in the digestive tract. People who inherit mutations in telomerase (or in other proteins affecting telomere length) experience similar degenerative changes, show symptoms of premature aging, and usually die when they are relatively young. Based on these relationships, scientists have speculated that telomerase-based therapies may one day be used to combat the symptoms of human aging and thereby extend life span.

Besides being found in germ cells and a few other types of proliferating normal cells, telomerase has also been detected in human cancers. Because cancer cells divide an abnormally large number of times, their telomeres become unusually short. This progressive telomere shortening would lead to self-destruction of the cancer

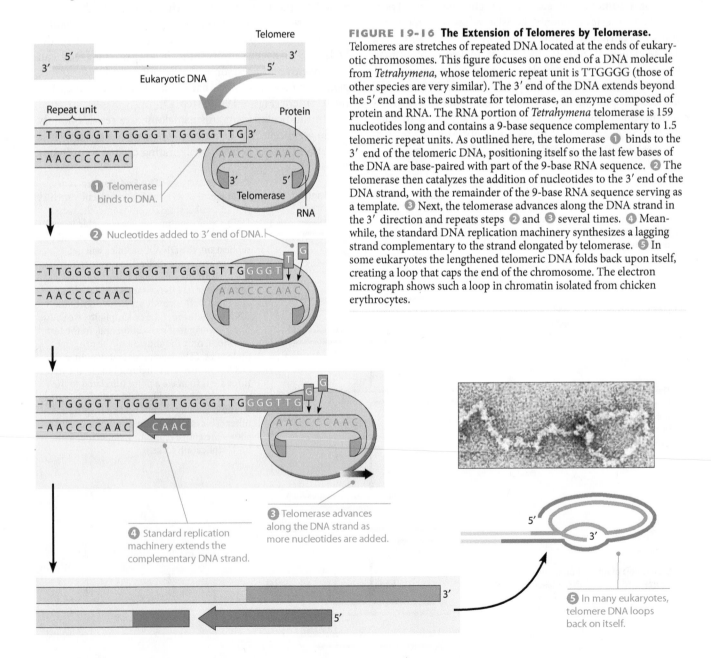

FIGURE 19-16 The Extension of Telomeres by Telomerase. Telomeres are stretches of repeated DNA located at the ends of eukaryotic chromosomes. This figure focuses on one end of a DNA molecule from *Tetrahymena*, whose telomeric repeat unit is TTGGGG (those of other species are very similar). The 3′ end of the DNA extends beyond the 5′ end and is the substrate for telomerase, an enzyme composed of protein and RNA. The RNA portion of *Tetrahymena* telomerase is 159 nucleotides long and contains a 9-base sequence complementary to 1.5 telomeric repeat units. As outlined here, the telomerase ❶ binds to the 3′ end of the telomeric DNA, positioning itself so the last few bases of the DNA are base-paired with part of the 9-base RNA sequence. ❷ The telomerase then catalyzes the addition of nucleotides to the 3′ end of the DNA strand, with the remainder of the 9-base RNA sequence serving as a template. ❸ Next, the telomerase advances along the DNA strand in the 3′ direction and repeats steps ❷ and ❸ several times. ❹ Meanwhile, the standard DNA replication machinery synthesizes a lagging strand complementary to the strand elongated by telomerase. ❺ In some eukaryotes the lengthened telomeric DNA folds back upon itself, creating a loop that caps the end of the chromosome. The electron micrograph shows such a loop in chromatin isolated from chicken erythrocytes.

unless telomerase were produced to stabilize telomere length. This is exactly what seems to happen. A survey of a large number of human cell samples—including more than 100 tumors—found telomerase activity in almost all of the cancer cells but in none of the samples from normal tissues. If telomerase is indeed an important factor in the development of cancer, it may eventually provide a useful target for anticancer drug therapy.

DNA Damage and Repair

The faithful transmission of genetic information from one generation of cells to the next requires not just that DNA be replicated accurately. Provision must also be made for repairing DNA alterations that arise both spontaneously and from exposure to DNA-damaging environmental agents. Of course, DNA alterations are occasionally beneficial because DNA base-sequence changes, or **mutations,** provide the genetic variability that is the raw material of evolution. Still, the net rate at which organisms accumulate mutations is quite low; by some estimates, an average gene retains only one mutation every 200,000 years. The underlying mutation rate is far greater than this number suggests, but most DNA damage is repaired shortly after it occurs so does not affect future generations. Moreover, since most mutations occur in cells other than sperm and eggs, they are never passed on to offspring.

DNA Damage Can Occur Spontaneously or in Response to Mutagens

During the normal process of DNA replication, several types of mutations occur spontaneously. The most common involve depurination and deamination reactions, which are spontaneous hydrolysis reactions caused by random interactions between DNA and the water molecules around it. *Depurination* refers to the loss of a purine base (either adenine or guanine) by spontaneous hydrolysis of the glycosidic bond that links it to deoxyribose (**Figure 19-17a**). This glycosidic bond is intrinsically unstable and is in fact so susceptible to hydrolysis that the DNA in a human cell may lose thousands of purine bases every day. *Deamination* is the removal of a base's amino group ($-NH_2$). This type of alteration, which can involve cytosine, adenine, or guanine, changes the base-pairing properties of the affected base. Of the three bases, cytosine is most susceptible to deamination, giving rise to uracil (Figure 19-17b). Like depurination, deamination is a hydrolytic reaction, usually caused by random collision of a water molecule with the bond that links the amino group of the base to the pyrimidine or purine ring. In a typical human cell, the rate of DNA damage by this means is about 100 deaminations per day.

If a DNA strand with missing purines or deaminated bases is not repaired, an erroneous base sequence may be propagated when the strand serves as a template in the next round of DNA replication. For example, where a cytosine has been converted to a uracil by deamination,

the uracil behaves like thymine in its base-pairing properties; that is, it directs the insertion of an adenine in the opposite strand, rather than guanine, the correct base. The ultimate effect of this change in base sequence may be a change in the amino acid sequence and function of a protein encoded by the affected gene.

In addition to spontaneous mutations, DNA damage can also be caused by mutation-causing agents, or *mutagens,* in the environment. Environmental mutagens fall into two major categories: chemicals and radiation. Mutagenic chemicals alter DNA structure by a variety of mechanisms. *Base analogs* resemble nitrogenous bases in structure and are incorporated into DNA; *base-modifying* agents react chemically with DNA bases to alter

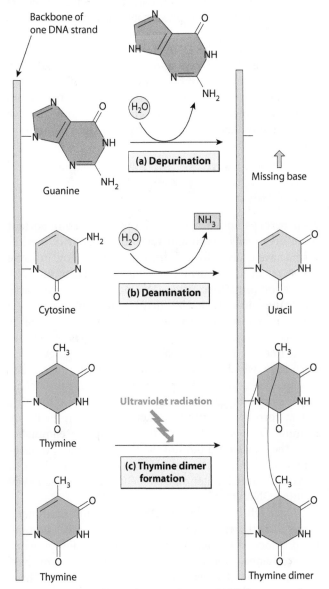

FIGURE 19-17 Some Common Types of DNA Damage. The most common kinds of chemical changes that can damage DNA are **(a)** depurination, **(b)** deamination, and **(c)** pyrimidine dimer formation (shown here are thymine dimers). Depurination and deamination are spontaneous hydrolytic reactions, whereas dimers result from covalent bonds induced to form by ultraviolet light.

their structure, forming what are sometimes known as *DNA adducts*; and *intercalating agents* insert themselves between adjacent bases of the double helix, thereby distorting DNA structure and increasing the chance that a base will be deleted or inserted during DNA replication. Not surprisingly mutagens can cause cancer. Analysis of DNA from heavy cigarette smokers, for example, shows a direct correlation between how much a patient smokes and how frequently the DNA of such patients has adducts.

DNA mutations can also be caused by several types of radiation. Sunlight is a strong source of ultraviolet radiation, which alters DNA by triggering *pyrimidine dimer formation*—that is, the formation of covalent bonds between adjacent pyrimidine bases, often two thymines (Figure 19-17c). Both replication and transcription are blocked by such dimers, presumably because the enzymes carrying out these functions cannot cope with the resulting bulge in the DNA double helix. Mutations can also be caused by X-rays and related forms of radiation emitted by radioactive substances. This type of radiation is called *ionizing radiation* because it removes electrons from biological molecules, thereby generating highly reactive intermediates that cause various types of DNA damage.

Translesion Synthesis and Excision Repair Correct Mutations Involving Abnormal Nucleotides

As is perhaps not surprising for a molecule so important to an organism's health and survival, a variety of mechanisms have evolved for repairing damaged DNA. In some cases, repair is performed during the process of DNA replication using specialized DNA polymerases that carry out **translesion synthesis**—that is, the synthesis of new DNA across regions in which the DNA template is damaged. While this type of DNA synthesis is sometimes prone to error, it is also capable of synthesizing new DNA strands in which the damage has been eliminated. For example, eukaryotic DNA polymerase η (eta) can catalyze DNA synthesis across a region containing a thymine dimer, correctly inserting two new adenines in the newly forming DNA strand. Since the mutation is eliminated from the new strand but not the template strand, translesion synthesis is a damage-tolerance mechanism that can prevent an initial mutation from being passed on to newly forming DNA strands.

Once left behind by the DNA replication machinery, errors that still remain (or that subsequently arise) become the province of a different group of enzymes and proteins. In *E. coli* alone, almost 100 genes code for proteins involved in removing and replacing abnormal nucleotides. These proteins are components of **excision repair** pathways, which correct DNA defects using a basic three-step process (**Figure 19-18**). In the first step, the defective nucleotides are cut out from one strand of the DNA double helix. This process is carried out by special enzymes called *repair endonucleases*, which are recruited to DNA by proteins that recognize sites of DNA damage. Repair endonucleases cleave the DNA backbone adjacent to the damage site, and other enzymes then facilitate removal of the defective nucleotide(s). For example, a DNA helicase might unwind the DNA located between two nicks to release the damaged DNA from the double helix; alternatively, an exonuclease might attach to an end created by a single nick and chew away the damaged strand one nucleotide at a time. During the second step in excision repair, the missing nucleotides are replaced with the correct ones by a DNA polymerase—in *E. coli*, usually DNA polymerase I. The nucleotide sequence of the complementary strand serves as a template to ensure correct base insertion, just as it does in DNA replication. Finally, in the third step, DNA ligase seals the remaining nick in the repaired strand by forming the missing phosphoester bond.

Excision repair pathways are classified into two main types, *base excision repair* and *nucleotide excision repair*. The first of these pathways, **base excision repair,** corrects single damaged bases in DNA. For example, deaminated bases are detected by specific *DNA glycosylases,* which recognize a specific deaminated base and remove it from the DNA molecule by cleaving the bond between the base and the sugar it is attached to. The sugar with the missing base is then recognized by a repair endonuclease that detects depurination. This repair endonuclease breaks the phosphodiester backbone on one side of the sugar lacking a

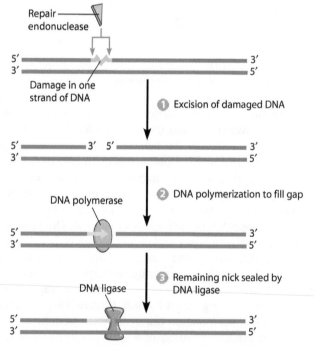

FIGURE 19-18 General Scheme for Excision Repair of DNA Damage. The three steps shown here are common to all types of excision repair of DNA damage in one strand. ❶ The damaged part of the DNA strand, and possibly some DNA on either side of it, is cut out (excised) from the double helix. An endonuclease, which nicks the DNA near the damage, is crucial for this step; a DNA helicase and/or exonuclease may help remove the damaged segment. ❷ A DNA polymerase fills in the gap by adding nucleotides to the strand's 3′ end; DNA polymerase I plays this role in *E. coli*. ❸ The remaining nick is sealed by DNA ligase.

base, and a second enzyme then completes the removal of the sugar-phosphate unit.

For removing pyrimidine dimers and other bulky lesions in DNA, cells employ the second type of excision repair, namely **nucleotide excision repair (NER).** This repair system utilizes proteins that recognize major distortions in the DNA double helix and recruit an enzyme, called an *NER endonuclease* (or *excinuclease*), that makes two cuts in the DNA backbone, one on either side of the distortion. Then a DNA helicase binds to the stretch of DNA between the nicks (12 nucleotides long in *E. coli*, 29 in humans) and unwinds it, freeing it from the rest of the DNA. Finally, the resulting gap is filled in by DNA polymerase and sealed by DNA ligase.

The NER system is the most versatile of a cell's DNA repair systems, recognizing and correcting many types of damage that cannot otherwise be repaired. In some cases, the NER system is specifically recruited to DNA regions where transcription has been halted because the transcription machinery encountered an area of DNA damage. This mechanism, known as *transcription-coupled repair,* permits active genes to be repaired faster than DNA sequences located elsewhere in the genome. The importance of NER is underscored by the plight of people who have mutations affecting the NER pathway. Individuals with the disease *xeroderma pigmentosum,* for example, usually carry a mutation in any of seven genes coding for components of the NER system. As a result, they cannot repair the DNA damage caused by the ultraviolet radiation in sunlight and so have a high risk of developing skin cancer.

Mismatch Repair Corrects Mutations That Involve Noncomplementary Base Pairs

Excision repair is a powerful mechanism for correcting damage involving the presence of abnormal nucleotides. This is not the only type of DNA error that cells can repair, however. An alternative repair pathway, called **mismatch repair,** targets errors made during DNA replication, when improperly base-paired nucleotides sometimes escape the normal proofreading mechanisms. Because mismatched base pairs do not hydrogen-bond properly, their presence can be detected and corrected by the mismatch repair system. But to operate properly, this repair system must solve a problem that puzzled biologists for many years: How is the *incorrect* member of an abnormal base pair distinguished from the *correct* member? Unlike the situation in excision repair, neither of the bases in a mismatched pair exhibits any structural alteration that would allow it to be recognized as an abnormal base. The pair is simply composed of two normal bases that are inappropriately paired with each other, such as the base A paired with C or G paired with T. If the incorrect member of an AC base pair were the base C and the repair system instead removed the base A, the repair system would create a permanent mutation instead of correcting a mismatched base pair!

To solve this problem, the mismatch repair system must be able to recognize which of the two DNA strands

was newly synthesized during the previous round of DNA replication (the new strand would be the one that contains the incorrectly inserted base). The bacterium *E. coli* employs a detection system that is based on the fact that a methyl group is normally added to the base adenine (A) wherever it appears in the sequence GATC in DNA. This process of *DNA methylation* does not take place until a short time after a new DNA strand has been synthesized; hence, the bacterial mismatch repair system can detect the new DNA strand by its unmethylated state. A repair endonuclease then introduces a single nick in the unmethylated strand, and an exonuclease removes the incorrect nucleotides from the nicked strand.

Although the initial evidence for the existence of mismatch repair came largely from studies of bacterial cells, comparable repair systems have been detected in eukaryotes as well. Eukaryotic mismatch repair differs from the bacterial process in that eukaryotes use mechanisms other than DNA methylation for distinguishing the newly synthesized DNA strand. The importance of mismatch repair for eukaryotes is highlighted by the discovery that one of the most common hereditary cancers, *hereditary nonpolyposis colon cancer (HNPCC),* results from mutations in genes coding for proteins involved in mismatch repair.

Damage Repair Helps Explain Why DNA Contains Thymine Instead of Uracil

For many years, it was not clear why DNA contains thymine instead of the uracil found in RNA. Both bases pair with adenine, but thymine has a methyl group not present on uracil (**Figure 19-19**). Because the methylation step used to create thymine is energetically expensive, it might seem more efficient for DNA to contain uracil. But now that we understand how deamination damage is repaired, we also understand why thymine, rather than uracil, is present in DNA.

When DNA is damaged through deamination reactions, cytosine is converted to uracil (see Figure 19-17b), which is then detected and removed by the DNA repair enzyme, *uracil-DNA glycosylase.* But if uracil were present as a normal component of DNA, DNA repair would not work because these normal uracils would not be distinguishable from the uracils generated by the accidental deamination of cytosine. By using thymine in DNA in place of uracil, cells ensure that DNA damage caused by the deamination of cytosine can be recognized and repaired without causing other changes in the DNA molecule.

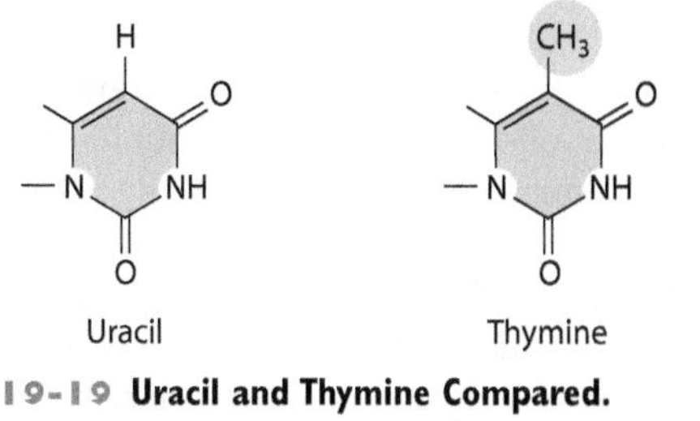

FIGURE 19-19 Uracil and Thymine Compared.

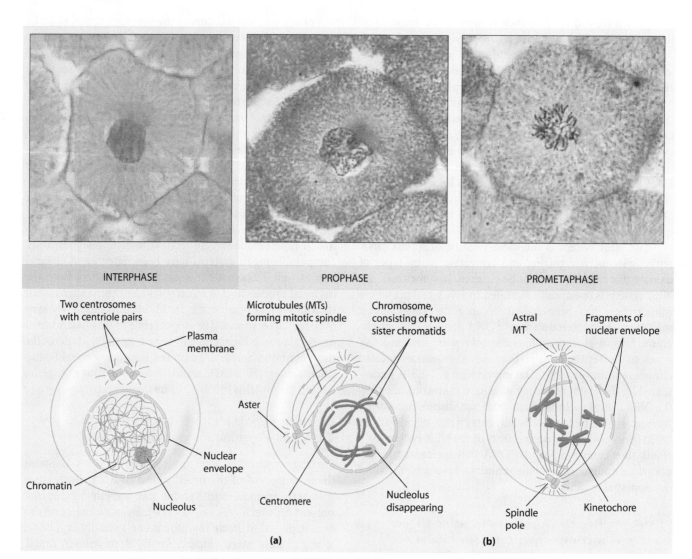

INTERPHASE

Two centrosomes
with centriole pairs

Plasma
membrane

Chromatin

Nuclear
envelope

Nucleolus

PROPHASE

Microtubules (MTs)
forming mitotic spindle

Chromosome,
consisting of two
sister chromatids

Aster

Centromere

Nucleolus
disappearing

(a)

PROMETAPHASE

Astral
MT

Fragments of
nuclear envelope

Spindle
pole

Kinetochore

(b)

FIGURE 19-20 The Phases of Mitosis in an Animal Cell. The micrographs show mitosis in cells from a fish embryo viewed by light microscopy. The mitotic spindle, including asters, is visible in the metaphase and anaphase micrographs. At this low magnification (about 600-fold), we see spindle "fibers" rather than individual microtubules; each fiber consists of a number of microtubules. The drawings are schematic and include details not visible in the micrographs; for simplicity, only four chromosomes are drawn (MT = microtubule).

ACTIVITIES www.thecellplace.com *Mitosis and cytokinesis*

Double-Strand DNA Breaks Are Repaired by Nonhomologous End-Joining or Homologous Recombination

The repair mechanisms described thus far—excision and mismatch repair—are effective in correcting DNA damage involving chemically altered or incorrect bases. In such cases a "cut-and-patch" pathway removes the damaged or incorrect nucleotides from one DNA strand, and the resulting gap is filled using the intact strand as template. But some types of damage, such as double-strand breaks in the DNA double helix, cannot be handled this way. Repair is more difficult for double-strand breaks because, with other types of DNA damage, one strand of the double helix remains undamaged and can serve as a template for aligning and repairing the defective strand. In contrast, double-strand breaks completely cleave the DNA double

helix into two separate fragments; the repair machinery is therefore confronted with the problem of identifying the correct two fragments and rejoining their broken ends without losing any nucleotides.

Two main pathways are employed in such cases. One, called **nonhomologous end-joining,** uses a set of proteins that bind to the ends of the two broken DNA fragments and join them together. Unfortunately, this mechanism is error-prone because it cannot prevent the loss of nucleotides from the broken ends and has no way of ensuring that the correct two DNA fragments are being joined to each other. A more precise method for fixing double-strand breaks, called **homologous recombination,** takes advantage of the fact that cells generally possess two copies of each chromosome; if the DNA molecule in one chromosome incurs a double-strand break, another intact copy of the chromosomal DNA is still available to

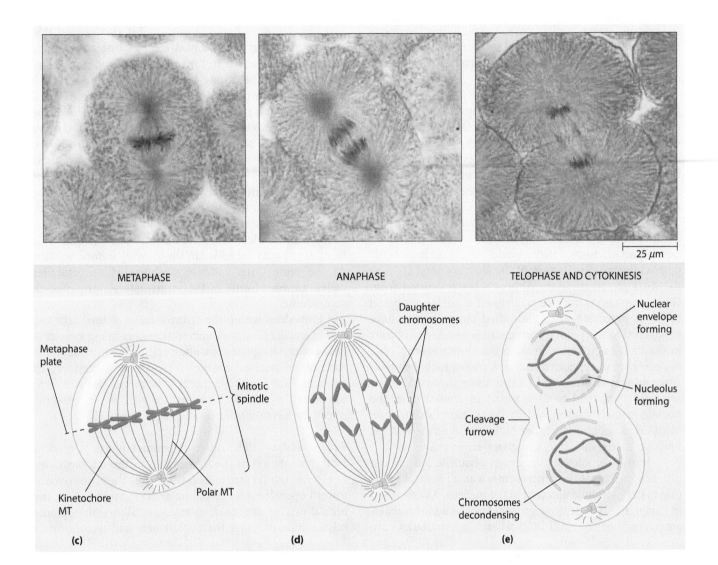

| METAPHASE | ANAPHASE | TELOPHASE AND CYTOKINESIS |

(c) Metaphase plate, Mitotic spindle, Kinetochore MT, Polar MT

(d) Daughter chromosomes

(e) Nuclear envelope forming, Nucleolus forming, Cleavage furrow, Chromosomes decondensing

25 μm

serve as a template for guiding the repair of the broken chromosome. Besides its role in repairing double-strand breaks, homologous recombination is involved in the exchange of genetic information between chromosomes during the meiotic cell divisions that are used to produce sperm and egg cells. We will therefore delay a discussion of the molecular mechanisms involved in homologous recombination until, where meiosis and genetic recombination are described in detail.

Now that we have considered the various types of DNA repair, it is important to emphasize that some of the same proteins are used in more than one repair pathway. Moreover, many of these "repair" proteins play additional roles in other important activities, including DNA replication, gene transcription, genetic recombination, and control of the cell cycle. In other words, the same molecular tool kit appears to be used for a variety of DNA-related activities.

Nuclear and Cell Division

Having examined the mechanisms involved in DNA replication and repair, we can now turn to the question of how the two copies of each chromosomal DNA molecule created during the S phase of the cell cycle are subsequently separated from each other and partitioned into daughter cells. These events occur during M phase, which encompasses both nuclear division (mitosis) and cytoplasmic division (cytokinesis).

Mitosis Is Subdivided into Prophase, Prometaphase, Metaphase, Anaphase, and Telophase

Mitosis has been studied for more than a century, but only in the past few decades has significant progress been made toward understanding the mitotic process at the molecular level. We will begin by surveying the morphological changes that occur in a cell as it undergoes mitosis, and we will then examine the underlying molecular mechanisms.

Mitosis is subdivided into five stages based on the changing appearance and behavior of the chromosomes. These five phases are *prophase, prometaphase, metaphase, anaphase,* and *telophase.* (An alternative term for prometaphase is simply *late prophase.*) The micrographs and schematic diagrams of **Figure 19-20** illustrate the phases in a typical animal cell; **Figure 19-21** depicts the comparable stages in plant cells. As you follow the events of each phase, keep in mind that the purpose of mitosis is to ensure that each of the two daughter nuclei receives one copy of each duplicated chromosome.

Prophase. After completing DNA replication, cells exit from S phase and enter into G2 phase (see Figure 19-1b), where final preparations are made for the onset of mitosis. Toward the end of G2, the chromosomes start to condense from the extended, highly diffuse form of interphase chromatin fibers into the compact, extensively folded structures that are typical of mitosis. Chromosome condensation is an important event because interphase chromatin fibers are so long and intertwined that in an uncompacted form, they would become impossibly tangled during distribution of the chromosomal DNA at the time of cell division. Although the transition from G2 to prophase is not sharply defined, a cell is considered to be in **prophase** when individual chromosomes have condensed to the point of being visible as discrete objects in the light microscope. Because the chromosomal DNA molecules have replicated during S phase, each prophase chromosome is composed of two sister chromatids that are tightly attached to each other. In animal cells, the nucleoli usually disperse as the chromosomes condense; plant cell nucleoli may either remain as discrete entities, undergo partial disruption, or disappear entirely.

Meanwhile, another important organelle has sprung into action. This is the **centrosome,** a small zone of granular material located adjacent to the nucleus. As described in Chapter 15, the centrosome functions as a *microtubule-organizing center (MTOC)* where microtubules are assembled and anchored. Some studies also suggest that centrosomes may be involved in orienting the spindle within the cell, which in turn determines the position of the cleavage plane during cell division. During each cell cycle, the centrosome is duplicated prior to mitosis, usually during S phase. At the beginning of prophase the two centrosomes then separate from each other and move toward opposite sides of the nucleus. As they move apart, each centrosome acts as a nucleation site for microtubule assembly and the region between the two centrosomes begins to fill with microtubules destined to form the **mitotic spindle,** the structure that distributes the chromosomes to the daughter cells later in mitosis. During this process, cytoskeletal microtubules disassemble and their tubulin subunits are added to the growing mitotic spindle. At the same time, a dense starburst of microtubules called an *aster* forms in the immediate vicinity of each centrosome.

Embedded within the centrosome of animal cells is a pair of small, cylindrical, microtubule-containing structures called *centrioles* (page 430), often oriented at right angles to each other. Because centrioles are absent in certain cell types, including most plant cells, they cannot be essential to the process of mitosis. They do, however, play an essential role in the formation of cilia and flagella (page 453).

Prometaphase. The onset of **prometaphase** is marked by fragmentation of the membranes of the nuclear envelope. As the centrosomes complete their movement toward opposite sides of the nucleus (Figure 19-20b), the breakdown of the nuclear envelope allows the spindle microtubules to enter the nuclear area and make contact

FIGURE 19-21 The Phases of Mitosis in a Plant Cell. These micrographs show mitosis in cells of an onion root viewed by light microscopy.

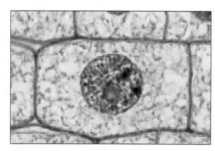
(a) Prophase

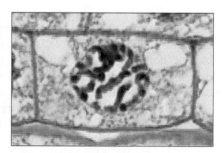
(b) Prometaphase

(c) Metaphase

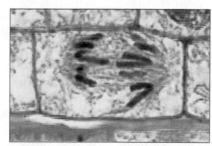
(d) Anaphase

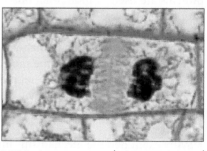
(e) Telophase

25 µm

with the chromosomes, which still consist of paired chromatids at this stage. The spindle microtubules are destined to attach to the chromatids in the region of the **centromere,** a constricted area where the two members of each chromatid pair are held together. The DNA of each centromere consists of simple-sequence, tandemly repeated *CEN sequences,* whose makeup varies considerably among species. Despite this diversity, a common feature of centromere regions is the presence of specialized nucleosomes in which histone H3 is replaced by a related protein, which in humans is called *CENP-A (centromere protein A).*

CENP-A plays a key role in recruiting additional proteins to the centromere to form the **kinetochore,** which is the structure that attaches the paired chromatids to the spindle microtubules. Kinetochore proteins begin to associate with the centromere shortly after DNA is replicated during S phase; additional proteins are sequentially added later until mature kinetochores, containing more than 50 different proteins, have been assembled. As shown in **Figure 19-22a,** each chromosome eventually acquires two kinetochores facing in opposite directions, one associated with each of the two chromatids. During prometaphase some spindle microtubules bind to these kinetochores, thereby attaching the chromosomes to the spindle. Forces exerted by these **kinetochore microtubules** then throw the chromosomes into agitated motion and gradually move them toward the center of the cell, in a process known as *congression* (Figure 19-22b).

In addition to kinetochore microtubules, there are two other kinds of microtubules in the spindle. Those that interact with microtubules from the opposite pole of the cell are called **polar microtubules;** the shorter ones that form the

asters (from the Greek word for "star") at each pole are called **astral microtubules.** Some of the astral microtubules appear to interact with proteins lining the plasma membrane.

Metaphase. A cell is said to be in **metaphase** when the fully condensed chromosomes all become aligned at the *metaphase plate,* the plane equidistant between the two poles of the mitotic spindle (Figure 19-20c). Agents that interfere with spindle function, such as the drug *colchicine,* can be used to arrest cells at metaphase. Microscopic examination of such cells allows individual chromosomes to be identified and classified based on differences in size and shape, generating an analysis known as a **karyotype** (**Figure 19-23**).

At metaphase the chromosomes appear to be relatively stationary, but this appearance is misleading. Actually, the two sister chromatids of each chromosome are already being actively tugged toward opposite poles. They appear stationary because the forces acting on them are equal in magnitude and opposite in direction; the chromatids are the prizes in a tug-of-war between two equally strong opponents. (We will discuss the source of these opposing forces shortly.)

Anaphase. Usually the shortest phase of mitosis, **anaphase** typically lasts only a few minutes. At the beginning of anaphase, the two sister chromatids of each chromosome abruptly separate and begin moving toward opposite spindle poles at a rate of about 1 μm/min (Figure 19-20d).

Anaphase is characterized by two kinds of movements, called anaphase A and anaphase B (**Figure 19-24**). In **anaphase A,** the chromosomes are pulled, centromere

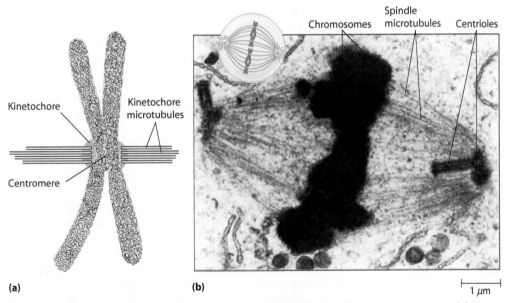

(a) **(b)** 1 μm

FIGURE 19-22 Attachment of Chromosomes to the Mitotic Spindle. (a) A schematic model summarizing the relationship between the centromere, kinetochores, and kinetochore microtubules. **(b)** This electron micrograph shows the mitotic spindle of a metaphase cell from a rooster. The centrioles at the two poles and the spindle between the poles are clearly visible. The chromosomes appear as a single mass aligned at the spindle equator. Although individual chromosomes cannot be distinguished in this type of micrograph, the individual chromosomes remain distinct from one another at this stage of mitosis (TEM).

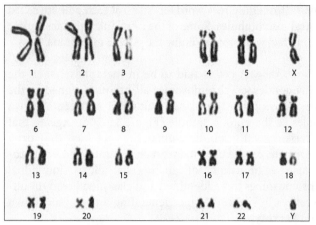

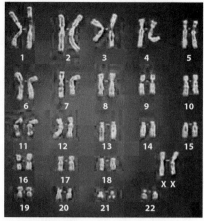

FIGURE 19-23 Mitotic Karyotype of Human Chromosomes from Metaphase-Arrested Cells. (Left) This set of human male chromosomes was stained with a dye that reacts uniformly with the entire body of the chromosome. Human males contain 22 pairs of chromosomes, plus one X and one Y chromosome. The chromosomes in the karyotype have been arranged according to size and centromere position. (Right) This set of human female chromosomes was stained with dyes that selectively react with certain chromosome regions, creating a unique banding pattern for each type of chromosome.

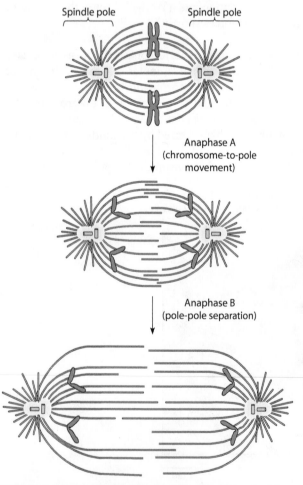

FIGURE 19-24 The Two Types of Movement Involved in Chromosome Separation During Anaphase. Anaphase A involves the movement of chromosomes toward the spindle poles. Anaphase B is the movement of the two spindle poles away from each other. Anaphase A and anaphase B may occur simultaneously.

VIDEOS www.thecellplace.com *Spindle formation during mitosis*

first, toward the spindle poles as the kinetochore microtubules get shorter and shorter. In **anaphase B,** the poles themselves move away from each other as the polar microtubules lengthen. Depending on the cell type involved, anaphase A and B may take place at the same time, or anaphase B may follow anaphase A.

Telophase. At the beginning of **telophase,** the daughter chromosomes have arrived at the poles of the spindle (Figure 19-20e). Next the chromosomes uncoil into the extended fibers typical of interphase chromatin, nucleoli develop at the nucleolar organizing sites on the DNA, the spindle disassembles, and nuclear envelopes form around the two groups of daughter chromosomes. During this period the cell usually undergoes cytokinesis, which divides the cell into two daughter cells.

The Mitotic Spindle Is Responsible for Chromosome Movements During Mitosis

The central purpose of mitosis is to separate the two sets of daughter chromosomes and partition them into the two newly forming daughter cells. To understand the mechanisms that allow this to be accomplished, we need to take a closer look at the microtubule-containing apparatus responsible for these events, the mitotic spindle.

Spindle Assembly and Chromosome Attachment. We saw in Chapter 15 that the tubulin subunits of a microtubule all face in the same direction, thereby giving microtubules an inherent *polarity;* that is, the two ends of each microtubule are chemically different (**Figure 19-25**). The end where microtubule assembly is initiated—located at the centrosome for spindle microtubules—is the minus (−) end. The end where most growth occurs, located away from the centrosome, is the plus (+) end. Microtubules are dynamic structures (see

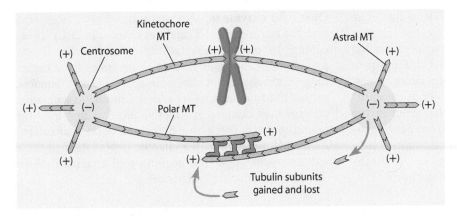

FIGURE 19-25 **Microtubule Polarity in the Mitotic Spindle.** This diagram shows only a few representatives of the many microtubules making up a spindle. The orientation of the tubulin subunits constituting a microtubule (MT) make the two ends of the MT different. The minus end is at the initiating centrosome; the plus end points away from the centrosome. MTs lengthen by adding tubulin subunits and shrink by losing subunits. In general, lengthening is due to addition at the plus ends and shortening to loss at the minus ends, but subunits can also be removed from the plus ends. The red structures between the plus ends of the polar MTs shown here represent proteins that crosslink them.

Chapter 15), in that tubulin subunits are continually being added and subtracted from both ends. When more subunits are being added than removed, the microtubule gets longer. In general, the plus end is the site favored for the addition of tubulin subunits and the minus end favored for subunit removal, so increases in microtubule length come mainly from addition of subunits to the plus end.

During late prophase, microtubule growth speeds up dramatically and initiation of new microtubules at the centrosomes increases. Once the nuclear envelope disintegrates at the beginning of prometaphase, contact between microtubules and chromosomal kinetochores becomes possible. When contact is made between a kinetochore and the plus end of a microtubule, they bind to each other and the microtubule becomes known as a kinetochore microtubule. This binding slows down depolymerization at the plus end of the microtubule, although polymerization and depolymerization can still occur there.

Figure 19-26 is an electron micrograph of a metaphase chromosome with two sets of attached microtubules, whose plus ends are embedded in the two kinetochores. Each kinetochore is a platelike, three-layered structure made of proteins attached to CEN sequences located in the centromere's DNA. Kinetochores of different species vary in size. In yeast, for example, they are small and bind only one spindle microtubule each, whereas the kinetochores of mammalian cells are much larger, each binding 30–40 microtubules.

Because the two kinetochores are located on opposite sides of a chromosome, they usually attach to microtubules emerging from centrosomes located at opposite poles of the cell. (The orientation of each chromosome is random; either kinetochore can end up facing either pole.) Meanwhile, the other main group of microtubules—the polar microtubules—make direct contact with polar microtubules coming from the opposite centrosome. When the plus-end regions of two microtubules of opposite polarity start to overlap, crosslinking proteins bind them to each other (Figure 19-25). Like the crosslinking between kinetochores and kinetochore microtubules, this crosslinking stabilizes the polar microtubules. Thus, we

can picture a barrage of microtubules rapidly shooting out from each centrosome during late prophase and prometaphase. The ones that successfully hit a kinetochore or a microtubule of opposite polarity are stabilized; the others retreat by disassembling.

One shortcoming of the preceding mechanism is that it does not explain how spindles are assembled in cells lacking centrosomes, which includes most of the cells of higher plants and the oocytes (immature eggs) of many animals. Moreover, experiments using a laser microbeam to destroy centrosomes have shown that animal cells that normally contain centrosomes can assemble spindles using a centrosome-independent mechanism. In cells lacking centrosomes, chromosomes rather than centrosomes promote microtubule assembly and spindle formation. Chromosome-induced microtubule assembly requires the involvement of *Ran*, the GTP-binding protein whose role in nuclear transport was described in Chapter 18 (see Figure 18-31). Mitotic chromosomes possess a

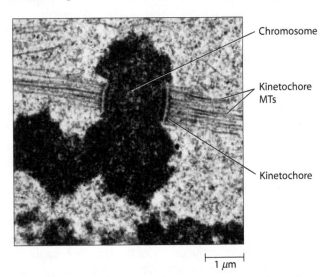

FIGURE 19-26 **Kinetochores and Their Microtubules.** The striped structures on either side of this metaphase chromosome are its kinetochores, each associated with one of the two sister chromatids. Numerous kinetochore MTs are attached to each kinetochore. The two sets of microtubules come from opposite poles of the cell (TEM).

protein that promotes the binding of GTP to Ran. The Ran-GTP complex then interacts with the protein *importin,* just as it does during nuclear transport, leading to the release of importin-bound proteins that promote microtubule assembly. So in cells lacking centrosomes, spindle formation is initiated in the vicinity of the chromosomes rather than at the spindle poles. Even in the more common case of cells that use centrosomes to generate spindle microtubules, Ran-GTP is thought to help organize the newly forming spindle and guide the attachment of microtubules to chromosomal kinetochores.

Chromosome Alignment and Separation. When spindle microtubules first become attached to chromosomal kinetochores during early prometaphase, the chromosomes are randomly distributed throughout the spindle. The chromosomes then migrate toward the central region of the spindle through a series of agitated, back-and-forth motions generated by at least two different kinds of forces. First, the kinetochore microtubules exert a "pulling" force, moving the chromosomes toward the pole that the microtubules are attached to. This force can be demonstrated experimentally by using glass microneedles to tear individual chromosomes away from the spindle. A chromosome that has been removed from the spindle remains motionless until new microtubules attach to its kinetochore, at which time the chromosome is drawn back into the spindle.

The second force tends to "push" chromosomes away if they approach either spindle pole. The existence of this pushing force has been demonstrated by studies in which a laser microbeam is used to break off one end of a chromosome. Once the broken chromosome fragment has been cut free from its associated centromere and kinetochore, the fragment tends to move away from the nearest spindle pole, even though it is no longer attached to the spindle by microtubules. The nature of the pushing force that propels chromosomes in the absence of microtubule attachments has not yet been clearly identified.

The combination of pulling and pushing forces exerted on the chromosomes drives them to the metaphase plate, their most stable location, where they line up in random order. Although the chromosomes appear to stop moving at this point, careful microscopic study of living cells reveals that they continue to make small jerking movements, indicating that the chromosomes are under constant tension in both directions. If the kinetochore on one side of a metaphase chromosome is severed using a laser microbeam, the chromosome promptly moves toward the opposite spindle pole. Hence, metaphase chromosomes remain at the center of the spindle because the forces pulling them toward opposite poles are precisely balanced.

At the beginning of anaphase, the two chromatids of each metaphase chromosome split apart and start moving toward opposite spindle poles. Several molecules have been implicated in this process of chromatid separation.

One is the enzyme topoisomerase II, which concentrates near the centromere and catalyzes changes in DNA supercoiling. In mutant cells lacking topoisomerase II, the paired chromatids still attempt to separate at the beginning of anaphase, but they tear apart and are damaged instead of being properly separated. Chromatid separation also involves changes in adhesive proteins that hold the paired chromatids together before the onset of anaphase. As we will see later in the chapter, degradation of these adhesive proteins at the beginning of anaphase allows the sister chromatids to separate.

Motor Proteins and Chromosome Movement. Once the two chromatids of each metaphase chromosome have split apart, they function as two independent chromosomes that move to opposite spindle poles. Studies of the mechanisms underlying this movement have led to the discovery of several **motor proteins** that play active roles in mitosis. As we saw in Chapters 15 and 16, motor proteins use energy derived from ATP to change shape in such a way that they exert force and cause attached structures to move. Motor proteins play at least three distinct roles in the movement of anaphase chromosomes.

The first role involves the mechanism that moves chromosomes, kinetochores first, toward the spindle poles during anaphase A. As shown in **Figure 19-27a** (❶), this type of chromosome movement is driven by motors associated with kinetochore microtubules. Considerable evidence suggests that these motors are specialized members of the *kinesin* family of proteins. In Chapter 16 we saw that some specialized kinesins can bind to the end of a microtubule and induce it to depolymerize. Two such kinesin-like motors are involved in moving chromosomes toward the spindle poles: One is located at the plus end of the kinetochore microtubules, and the other is located at the minus end. The motor located at the plus end is embedded in the kinetochore, where it induces microtubule depolymerization and thereby moves the chromosome toward the spindle pole as it "chews up" the plus end of the microtubule. At the same time, the motor located at the minus end is embedded in the spindle pole, where it induces microtubule depolymerization and thereby "reels in" the microtubules and their attached chromosomes.

Several lines of evidence support this view that microtubule depolymerization plays a crucial role in chromosome movement. For example, if cells are exposed to the drug *taxol,* which inhibits microtubule depolymerization, chromosomes do not move toward the spindle poles. Conversely, exposing cells to increased pressure, which increases the rate of microtubule depolymerization, causes chromosomes to move toward the poles more quickly. Finally, antibodies that inhibit the depolymerizing activity of either the motor protein located at the spindle pole or the motor protein located at the kinetochore have both been shown to interfere with chromosome movement.

The second role played by motor proteins during anaphase is associated with the movement of the spindle

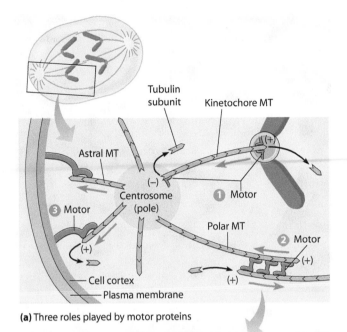

Tubulin subunit

Kinetochore MT

Astral MT

(+)

(−)

Centrosome (pole)

1 Motor

3 Motor

Polar MT

2 Motor

(+)

(+)

(+)

Cell cortex

Plasma membrane

(a) Three roles played by motor proteins

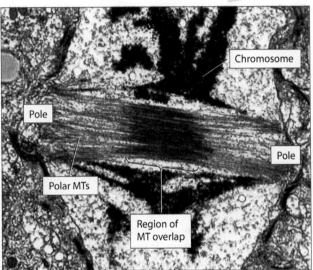

Chromosome

Pole

Pole

Polar MTs

Region of MT overlap

(b) Polar microtubules during metaphase

2 μm

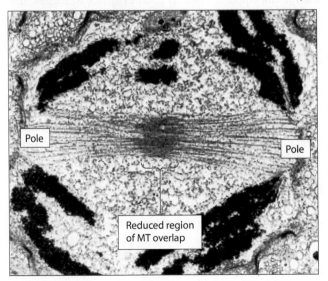

Pole

Pole

Reduced region of MT overlap

(c) Polar microtubules during anaphase

2 μm

FIGURE 19-27 Mitotic Motors. (**a**) A model for mitotic chromosome movement based on three roles played by motor proteins. Motor proteins are shown in red, and the small red arrows indicate the direction of movement generated by these motors. Motor proteins are associated with three types of microtubules: kinetochore MTs, polar MTs, and astral MTs. **1** Kinetochore MTs have motor proteins associated with both their plus ends (embedded in the chromosomal kinetochore) and their minus ends (located in the centrosome of the spindle pole). The motor proteins located at the kinetochore "chew up" (i.e., depolymerize) the plus ends of the kinetochore MTs. In this way, the chromosome is pulled toward the spindle pole as the kinetochore MTs are shortened through the loss of tubulin subunits. Simultaneously, motor proteins located at the spindle pole depolymerize the minus ends of the kinetochore MTs, reeling in the MTs and their attached chromosomes. **2** Motor proteins crosslink the polar MTs and cause them to slide apart, thereby forcing the spindle poles away from each other. As the polar MTs slide apart, they are lengthened by the addition of tubulin subunits to their plus ends where they overlap near the spindle center. **3** Astral MT motor proteins link the plus ends of astral MTs to the cell cortex and exert a pull on the spindle poles by inducing astral MT depolymerization at their plus ends. (**b, c**) The two electron micrographs provide evidence for the sliding of polar MTs driven by polar MT motors. During metaphase, the polar MTs from opposite ends of the cell overlap significantly. During anaphase, the polar MT motors cause these two groups of MTs to slide away from each other, thereby resulting in a reduced region of overlap (TEMs). (MT = microtubule)

poles away from each other during anaphase B. In this case, bipolar kinesin motors bind to overlapping polar microtubules coming from opposite spindle poles, causing the polar microtubules to slide apart, thereby forcing the spindle poles away from each other (Figure 19-27a, **2**). As the microtubules slide apart, they are lengthened by the addition of tubulin subunits to their plus ends near the center of the spindle, where microtubules coming from opposite spindle poles overlap. Microtubule sliding can be experimentally induced by exposing isolated spindles to ATP, indicating that the motor proteins use energy derived from ATP hydrolysis to cause the overlapping microtubules to slide away from one another. During anaphase B, this motor activity may be the primary force that elongates the spindle, while the lengthening of the polar microtubules is secondary. In Figure 19-27, parts b and c provide electron microscopic evidence for the sliding of overlapping polar microtubules during anaphase B.

The third type of motor-produced force detected during anaphase involves *cytoplasmic dynein*, which is associated with astral microtubules (Figure 19-27a, **3**). The plus ends of astral microtubules are connected to the *cell cortex*, a layer of actin microfilaments lining the inner surface of the plasma membrane. Cytoplasmic dynein, which moves toward the minus end of microtubules, appears to pull each spindle pole toward the cortex. Such pulling—in addition to the outward push generated by the motor proteins that crosslink the overlapping polar microtubules—helps to separate the spindle poles during anaphase B in some cell types.

Nuclear and Cell Division **577**

Mitosis therefore involves at least three separate groups of motor proteins, operating on kinetochore microtubules, polar microtubules, and astral microtubules, respectively (Figure 19-27a). The relative contributions of the pushing and pulling forces generated by these three sets of motor proteins differ among organisms. For example, in diatoms and yeast, the pushing (sliding) of microtubules against adjacent ones of opposite polarity is particularly important in anaphase B. In contrast, pulling at the asters is the main force in the cells of certain other fungi. In vertebrates both mechanisms are probably operative, although astral pulling may play a greater role, especially during spindle formation.

Cytokinesis Divides the Cytoplasm

After the two sets of chromosomes have separated during anaphase, cytokinesis divides the cytoplasm in two, thereby completing the process of cell division. Cytokinesis usually starts during late anaphase or early telophase, as the nuclear envelope and nucleoli are re-forming and the chromosomes are decondensing. Cytokinesis is not inextricably linked to mitosis, however. In some cases, a significant time lag may occur between nuclear division (mitosis) and cytokinesis, indicating that the two processes are not tightly coupled. Moreover, certain cell types can undergo many rounds of chromosome replication and nuclear division in the absence of cytokinesis, thereby producing a large, multinucleate cell known as a *syncytium*. Sometimes the multinucleate condition is permanent; in other situations, the multinucleate state is only a temporary phase in the organism's development. This is the case, for example, in the development of a plant seed tissue called *endosperm* in cereal grains. Here, nuclear division occurs for a time unaccompanied by cytokinesis, generating many nuclei in a common cytoplasm. Successive rounds of cytokinesis then occur without mitosis, walling off the many nuclei into separate endosperm cells. A similar process occurs in some insect embryos.

Despite these examples, in most cases cytokinesis does accompany or closely follow mitosis, thereby ensuring that each of the daughter nuclei acquires its own cytoplasm and becomes a separate cell.

Cytokinesis in Animal Cells. The mechanism of cytokinesis differs between animals and plants. In animal cells, cytoplasmic division is called **cleavage.** The process begins as a slight indentation or puckering of the cell surface, which deepens into a **cleavage furrow** that encircles the cell, as shown in **Figure 19-28** for a fertilized frog egg. The furrow continues to deepen until opposite surfaces make contact and the cell is split in two. The cleavage furrow divides the cell along a plane that passes through the central region of the spindle (the *spindle equator*), suggesting that the location of the spindle determines where the cytoplasm will be divided. This idea has been investigated experimentally by moving the mitotic spindle

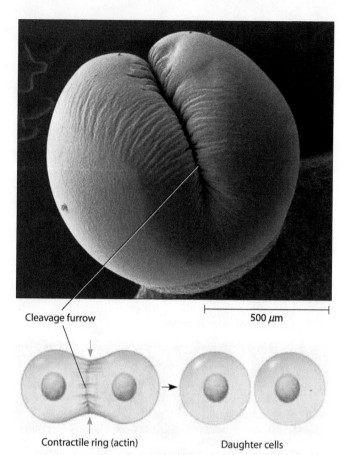

Cleavage furrow

500 μm

Contractile ring (actin)

Daughter cells

FIGURE 19-28 Cytokinesis in an Animal Cell. (Top) An electron micrograph of a fertilized frog egg caught in the act of dividing. The cleavage furrow is clearly visible as an inward constriction of the plasma membrane (SEM). (Bottom) A schematic diagram showing the position of the contractile ring during cytokinesis, which pinches the dividing cell in two (red arrows).

using either tiny glass needles or gravitational forces generated by centrifugation. If the spindle is moved before the end of metaphase, the orientation of the cleavage plane changes so that it passes through the new location of the spindle equator. There is good evidence to suggest that signals emanating from the central portion of the spindle, known as the *spindle midzone*, are important for completion of cytokinesis (**Figure 19-29a**). For example, in nematode worm or fruit fly cells lacking components of a multiprotein complex (known as *centralspindlin*) found in the spindle midzone, cytokinesis begins, but the cleavage furrow regresses. The activity of astral microtubules may complement the work of the spindle midzone by inhibiting formation of a cleavage furrow in other regions of the cortex.

Cleavage depends on a beltlike bundle of actin microfilaments called the **contractile ring,** which forms just beneath the plasma membrane during early anaphase (Figure 19-29a). Examination of the contractile ring with an electron microscope reveals large numbers of actin filaments oriented with their long axes parallel to the furrow. As cleavage progresses, this ring of microfilaments tightens around the cytoplasm, like a belt around the waist, eventually pinching the cell in two. Tightening of the contractile

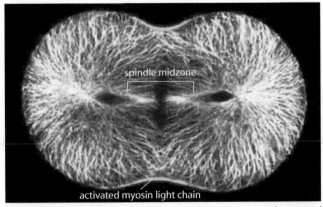

spindle midzone

activated myosin light chain

(a) Myosin and tubulin during cutokinesis

10 μm

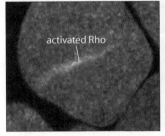

activated Rho

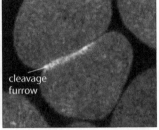

cleavage furrow

(b) Activated Rho during cytokinesis

25 μm

FIGURE 19-29 Myosin and Rho During Cytokinesis. (a) A confocal micrograph of a sea urchin zygote, showing microtubules in white and activated myosin regulatory light chain in blue. Active myosin accumulates at the cleavage furrow. **(b)** A fluorescent protein that binds active Rho accumulates in the cleavage furrow of cells in a *Xenopus* (frog) embryo. Accumulation of active Rho precedes furrowing (left); the same cell four minutes later has formed a furrow at the site where Rho accumulated (right).

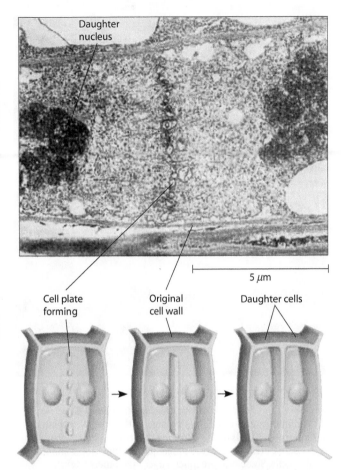

Daughter nucleus

5 μm

Cell plate forming

Original cell wall

Daughter cells

FIGURE 19-30 Cytokinesis and Cell Plate Formation in a Plant Cell. (Top) A cell from the sugar maple, *Acer saccharinum*, at late telophase. The daughter nuclei with their sets of chromosomes are partially visible as the dark material on the far right and far left of the micrograph, and the developing cell plate is seen as a line of vesicles in the midregion of the cell. The microtubules of the phragmoplast are oriented perpendicular to the cell plate (TEM). (Bottom) A schematic diagram showing the location of the cell plate and the original cell wall of a dividing plant cell.

ring is generated by interactions between the actin microfilaments and *myosin,* the motor protein whose role in muscle contraction was described in Chapter 16.

The contractile ring provides a dramatic example of how rapidly actin-myosin complexes can be assembled and disassembled in nonmuscle cells. Members of the *Rho* family of GTP-binding proteins play a central role in regulating the assembly and activation of the contractile ring. One family member, called RhoA, is recruited to the cleavage furrow (Figure 19-29b), where it helps orchestrate cytokinesis by activating proteins that promote actin polymerization. RhoA also stimulates protein kinases that phosphorylate myosin, the key step in activating myosin to perform its motor function in tightening the contractile ring.

Cytokinesis in Plant Cells. Cytokinesis in higher plants is fundamentally different from the corresponding process in animal cells. Because plant cells are surrounded by a rigid cell wall, they cannot form a contractile ring at the cell surface that pinches the cell in two. Instead, they divide by assembling a plasma membrane and a cell wall between the two daughter nuclei (**Figure 19-30**). In other words, rather than pinching the cytoplasm in half with a contractile ring

that moves from the outside of the cell toward the interior, the plant cell cytoplasm is divided by a process that begins in the cell interior and works toward the periphery.

Cytokinesis in plants is typically initiated during late anaphase or early telophase, when a group of small, membranous vesicles derived from the Golgi complex align themselves across the equatorial region of the spindle. These vesicles, which contain polysaccharides and glycoproteins required for cell wall formation, are guided to the spindle equator by the **phragmoplast,** a parallel array of microtubules derived from polar microtubules and oriented perpendicular to the direction in which the new cell wall is being formed. After arriving at the equator, the Golgi-derived vesicles fuse together to produce a large, flattened sac called the **cell plate,** which represents the cell wall in the process of formation. The contents of the sac assemble to form the noncellulose components of the primary cell wall, which expands outward as clusters of microtubules and vesicles form at the lateral edges of the

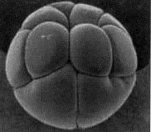

(a) Unequal cleavage in a frog embryo   500 μm

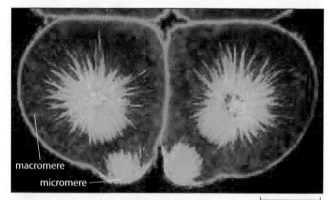

macromere
micromere

(b) Asymmetric spindles in a sea urchin embryo   10 μm

FIGURE 19-31 Asymmetric Cleavage in Animal Embryos.
(a) Amphibian eggs (left) are very large, with enough cytoplasm to sustain many rounds of cell division after fertilization. Each round of division during early development parcels the cytoplasm into smaller cells. Some cells are much larger than others (right). **(b)** Two cells of an 8-cell sea urchin embryo stained for microtubules (green) and actin (red). Each cell is about to divide to form a much larger cell (a "macromere") and a smaller cell ("micromere"). The spindle is highly asymmetric in its location.

advancing cell plate. Eventually, the expanding cell plate makes contact with the original cell wall, separating the two daughter cells from each other. The new cell wall is then completed by deposition of cellulose microfibrils. The plasmodesmata that provide channels of continuity between the cytoplasms of adjacent plant cells are also present in the cell plate and the new wall as it forms.

Cell Division Is Sometimes Asymmetric

The division plane passes through the spindle equator in both animal and plant cells. When the spindle is positioned across the middle of the cell, as is typically the case, there is a roughly even division of components between the two new cells. Cytoplasmic division is not always symmetric, however. In the budding yeast *Saccharomyces cerevisiae*, for example, the mitotic spindle forms in a highly asymmetric fashion, creating one large cell and one very small cell (see Figure 1B-1). Asymmetric divisions also occur frequently during embryonic development in animal embryos. Such asymmetric division often results in cells that not only vary dramatically in size but also acquire different developmental potential (**Figure 19-31**). Asymmetric divisions also take

place in female animals during the development of egg cells from precursor cells called *oocytes*. In this case, cytokinesis divides the cytoplasm unequally so that the cell destined to become the egg receives the bulk of the cytoplasm of the original oocyte, thereby maximizing the content of stored nutrients in each egg.

Cell division can also involve a more subtle type of asymmetry in which daughter cells look alike but have different fates. Such differences in cell fate are generated by mechanisms in which specific molecules located in certain regions of the parental cytoplasm are distributed unequally to the two daughter cells, thereby determining their unique fates.

Regulation of the Cell Cycle

Earlier in the chapter, we described a typical eukaryotic cell cycle in which G1, S, G2, and M phases are completed in orderly progression over a period of roughly 24 hours. Such a pattern is common in growing organisms and in cultured cells that have not run out of nutrients or space. But many variations are also observed, especially in the overall length of the cycle, the relative length of time spent in various phases, and how closely mitosis and cytokinesis are coupled. This variability tells us that the cell cycle must be regulated to meet the needs of each cell type and organism. The molecular basis of such cell cycle regulation is a subject of intense interest, not only for understanding the life cycles of normal cells but also for understanding how cancer cells manage to escape these normal control mechanisms.

The Length of the Cell Cycle Varies Among Different Cell Types

Some of the most commonly encountered variations in the cell cycle involve differences in how fast cells divide. In multicellular organisms, generation times vary markedly among cell types, depending on their role in the organism. At one extreme are cells that divide continuously as a means of replacing cells that are constantly being lost or destroyed. Included in this category are cells involved in sperm formation and the *stem cells* that give rise to blood cells, skin cells, and the epithelial cells that form the inner lining of body organs such as the lungs and intestines. Human stem cells may have generation times as short as 8 hours.

In contrast, cells located in slow-growing tissues may have generation times of several days or more, and some cells, such as those of mature nerve or muscle tissue, do not divide at all. Still other cell types do not divide under normal conditions but can be induced to start dividing again by an appropriate stimulus. Liver cells are in this category; they do not normally proliferate in the mature liver but can be induced to do so if a portion of the liver is removed surgically. Lymphocytes (white blood cells) are another example; when exposed to a foreign protein, they begin dividing as part of the immune response.

Most of these variations in generation time are based on differences in the length of G1, although S and G2 can also vary. Cells that divide slowly may spend days, months, or even years in the offshoot of G1 called G0, whereas cells that divide very rapidly have a short G1 phase or even eliminate G1 entirely. The embryonic cells of insects, amphibians, and several other nonmammalian animals are dramatic examples of cells that have very short cell cycles, with no G1 phase and a very short S phase. For example, during early embryonic development of the frog *Xenopus laevis,* each round of division simply subdivides the initial cytoplasm into smaller and smaller cells, until the cell size typical of adult tissues is reached (see Figure 19-31a). The cell cycle takes less than 30 minutes, even though the normal length of the cell cycle in adult tissues is about 20 hours. The rapid rate of DNA synthesis needed to sustain such a quick cell cycle is achieved in part by increasing the total number of replicons, thereby decreasing the amount of DNA that each replicon must synthesize. In addition, all replicons are activated at the same time, in contrast to the sequential activation observed in adult tissues. By increasing the number of replicons and activating them all simultaneously, S phase is completed in less than 3 minutes, at least 100 times faster than in adult tissues of the same organism.

Although we know from such examples that cell growth is not essential to the cell cycle, the two are generally linked so that cells can divide without getting progressively smaller. A protein kinase called *TOR (target of rapamycin)* plays a central role in the signaling network that controls cell size and coordinates it with cell cycle progression. This signaling network activates TOR in the presence of nutrients and growth factors, and the activated TOR then stimulates molecules that control the rate of protein synthesis. The resulting increase in protein production leads to an increase in cell mass. Some of the molecules activated by TOR also facilitate entry into S phase, making TOR an important regulator of both cell growth and cell cycle progression.

Progression Through the Cell Cycle Is Controlled at Several Key Transition Points

The control system that regulates progression through the cell cycle must accomplish several tasks. First, it must ensure that the events associated with each phase of the cell cycle are carried out at the appropriate time and in the appropriate sequence. Second, it must make sure that each phase of the cycle has been properly completed before the next phase is initiated. Finally, it must be able to respond to external conditions that indicate the need for cell proliferation (e.g., the quantity of nutrients available or the presence of growth-signaling molecules).

The preceding objectives are accomplished by a group of molecules that act at key transition points in the cell cycle (**Figure 19-32**). At each of these points, conditions within the cell determine whether the cell will proceed to

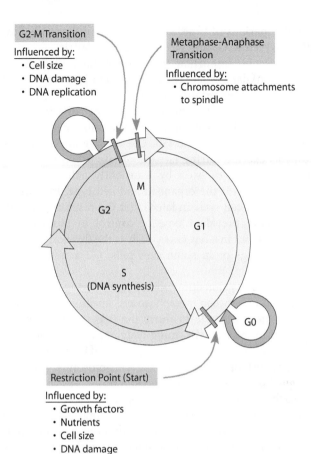

FIGURE 19-32 Key Transition Points in the Cell Cycle. The red bars mark three important transition points in the eukaryotic cell cycle where control mechanisms determine whether the cell will continue to proceed through the cycle. That determination is based on chemical signals reflecting both the cell's internal state and its external environment. The two circular, dark green arrows indicate locations in late G1 and late G2 where the cell can exit from the cycle and enter a nondividing state.

the next stage of the cycle. The first such control point occurs during late G1. We have already seen that G1 is the phase that varies most among cell types, and mammalian cells that have stopped dividing are almost always arrested during G1. For example, in cultured cells the process of cell division can be stopped or slowed by allowing the cells to run out of either nutrients or space or by adding inhibitors of vital processes such as protein synthesis. In all such cases, the cell cycle is halted in late G1, suggesting that progression from G1 into S is a critical control point in the cell cycle. In yeast, this control point is called **Start**; yeast cells must have sufficient nutrients and must reach a certain size before they can pass through Start. In animal cells, the comparable control point is called the **restriction point**. The ability to pass through the restriction point is influenced by the presence of extracellular *growth factors* (page 407), which are proteins used by multicellular organisms to stimulate or inhibit cell proliferation. Cells that have successfully passed through the restriction point are committed to S phase, whereas those that do not pass the restriction point enter into G0 and reside there for variable periods of time, awaiting a signal that will allow them to reenter G1 and pass through the restriction point.

A second important transition point occurs at the G2-M boundary, where the commitment is made to enter into mitosis. In certain cell types, the cell cycle can be indefinitely arrested at the end of G2 if cell division is not necessary; under such conditions, the cells enter a nondividing state analogous to G0. The relative importance of controls exerted during late G2 or late G1 in regulating the rate of cell division by transiently halting the cell cycle varies with the organism and cell type. In general, arresting the cell cycle in late G1 (at the restriction point) is the more prevalent type of control in multicellular organisms. But in a few cases, such as the division of fertilized frog eggs or in some skin cells, G2 arrest is more important.

A third key transition point occurs during M phase at the junction between metaphase and anaphase, where the commitment is made to move the two sets of chromosomes into the newly forming daughter cells. Before cells can pass through this transition point and begin anaphase, it is important to have all the chromosomes properly attached to the spindle. If the two chromatids that make up each chromosome are not properly attached to opposite spindle poles, the cell cycle is temporarily arrested to allow spindle attachment to occur. Without such a mechanism, there would be no guarantee that each of the newly forming daughter cells would receive a complete set of chromosomes.

Cell behavior at the various transition points is influenced both by successful completion of preceding events in the cycle (such as chromosome attachment to the spindle) and by factors in the cell's environment (such as nutrients and growth factors). But whatever the particular influences may be, their effects on cell cycle progression are mediated by a group of related control molecules that activate or inhibit one another in chains of interactions that can be quite elaborate. Let's now see how these control molecules were identified and what functions they perform.

Studies Involving Cell Fusion and Cell Cycle Mutants Led to the Identification of Molecules That Control the Cell Cycle

The first hints concerning the identity of the molecules that drive progression through the cell cycle came from cell fusion experiments performed in the early 1970s. In these studies, two cultured mammalian cells in different phases of the cell cycle were fused to form a single cell with two nuclei—a *heterokaryon*. As **Figure 19-33a** indicates, if one of the original cells is in S phase and the other is in G1, the G1 nucleus in the heterokaryon quickly initiates DNA synthesis, even if it would not normally have reached S phase until many hours later. Such observations indicate that S phase cells contain molecules that trigger progression from G1 into S. The controlling molecules are

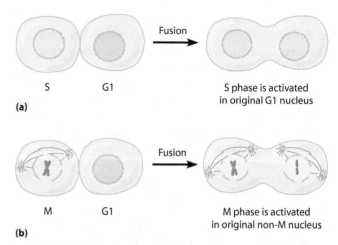

(a)

(b)

FIGURE 19-33 Evidence for the Role of Chemical Signals in Cell Cycle Regulation. Evidence was obtained from studies in which cells at two different points in the cell cycle were fused, forming a single cell with two nuclei. Cell fusion can be induced by adding certain viruses or polyethylene glycol or by applying a brief electrical pulse, which causes plasma membranes to destabilize momentarily (electroporation). **(a)** When cells in S phase and G1 phase are fused, DNA synthesis begins in the original G1 nucleus, suggesting that a substance that activates S phase is present in the S phase cell. **(b)** When a cell in M phase is fused with one in any other phase, the latter cell immediately enters mitosis. If the cell was in G1, the condensed chromosomes that appear have not replicated and therefore are analogous to single chromatids.

not simply the enzymes involved in DNA replication, since these enzymes can be present in high concentration in cells that do not enter S phase.

Cell fusion experiments have also been performed in which cells undergoing mitosis are fused with interphase cells in either G1, S, or G2. After fusion, the nucleus of such interphase cells is immediately driven into the early stages of mitosis, including chromatin condensation into visible chromosomes, spindle formation, and fragmentation of the nuclear envelope. If the interphase cell had been in G1, the condensed chromosomes will be unduplicated (Figure 19-33b).

Taken together, the preceding experiments suggested that molecules present in the cytoplasm are responsible for driving cells from G1 into S phase and from G2 into mitosis. Progress in identifying these cell cycle control molecules was facilitated by genetic studies of yeasts. Because they are single-celled organisms that can be readily grown and studied under defined laboratory conditions, yeasts are particularly convenient for investigating the genes involved in cell cycle control.

Working with the budding yeast *Saccharomyces cerevisiae*, geneticist Leland Hartwell pioneered the development of techniques for identifying yeast mutants that are "stuck" at some point in the cell cycle. It might be expected that most such mutants would be difficult or impossible to study because their blocked cell cycle would prevent them from reproducing. But Hartwell overcame this potential obstacle with a powerful strategy—the use of temperature-sensitive mutants. As mentioned earlier in the chapter, this is a type of mutation whose harmful effects are apparent only at temperatures above the normal range for the organism. Therefore, yeast cells carrying a temperature-sensitive mutation can be successfully grown at a lower ("permissive") temperature, even though their cell cycles would be blocked at higher temperatures. Presumably the protein encoded by the mutated cell cycle gene is close enough to the normal gene product to function at the lower temperature, while the increased thermal energy at higher temperatures disrupts its active conformation (the molecular shape needed for function) more readily than that of the normal protein.

Using this approach, Hartwell and his colleagues identified many genes involved in the cell cycle of *S. cerevisiae* and established where in the cycle their products operate. Predictably, it turned out that some of these genes produce DNA replication proteins, but others seemed to function in cell cycle regulation. A breakthrough discovery was made by Paul Nurse, who carried out similar research with the fission yeast *Schizosaccharomyces pombe*. He identified a gene called *cdc2*, whose activity is needed for initiating mitosis—that is, for moving cells through the G2-M transition. (The acronym *cdc* stands for cell division cycle.) The *cdc2* gene was soon found to have counterparts in all eukaryotic cells studied. When the properties of the protein produced by the *cdc2* gene were examined, it was discovered to be a *protein kinase*—that is, an enzyme that catalyzes the transfer of a phosphate group from ATP to other target proteins. This discovery opened the door to unraveling the mysteries of the cell cycle.

Progression Through the Cell Cycle Is Controlled by Cyclin-Dependent Kinases (Cdks)

The phosphorylation of target proteins by protein kinases, and their dephosphorylation by enzymes called *protein phosphatases,* is a common mechanism for regulating protein activity that turns out to be widely used in controlling the cell cycle. Progression through the cell cycle is driven by a series of protein kinases—including the protein kinase produced by the *cdc2* gene—that exhibit enzymatic activity only when they are bound to a special type of activator protein called a **cyclin.** Such protein kinases are therefore referred to as **cyclin-dependent kinases** or simply **Cdks.** The eukaryotic cell cycle is controlled by several different Cdks that bind to different cyclins, thereby creating a variety of Cdk-cyclin complexes.

As originally shown by Tim Hunt using sea urchin embryos, cyclins get their name because their concentration in the cell oscillates up and down with the different phases of the cell cycle. Cyclins required for the G2-M transition and the early events of mitosis are called *mitotic cyclins,* and the Cdks to which they bind are known as *mitotic Cdks.* Likewise, cyclins required for passage through the G1 restriction point (or Start) are called *G1 cyclins,* and the Cdks to which they bind are *G1*

Cdks. Yet another group of cyclins, called *S cyclins,* are required for events associated with DNA replication during S phase. The pioneering work of Hartwell, Nurse, and Hunt that led to our current understanding of Cdks and cyclins was honored by the Nobel Prize in Physiology or Medicine in 2001.

If progression through critical points in the cell cycle is controlled by an assortment of different Cdks and cyclins interacting in various combinations, how is the activity of these protein complexes regulated? One level of control is exerted by the availability of cyclin molecules, which are required for activating the protein kinase activity of Cdks, and a second type of regulation involves phosphorylation of Cdks. We will illustrate both types of control by taking a closer look at mitotic Cdk-cyclin, which controls progression from G2 into mitosis.

Mitotic Cdk-Cyclin Drives Progression Through the G2-M Transition by Phosphorylating Key Proteins Involved in the Early Stages of Mitosis

The earliest evidence for the existence of a control molecule that triggers the onset of mitosis came from experiments involving frog eggs. Mature eggs develop from precursor cells called *oocytes* through meiosis, a special type of cell division that reduces the chromosome number in half when eggs or sperm are being formed. During egg maturation, the cell cycle is halted shortly after the start of meiosis, where the oocyte waits until it is stimulated by an appropriate hormone. The oocyte then completes most of the phases of meiosis but is arrested during metaphase of the second of two meiotic divisions. It is now a "mature" egg cell, capable of being fertilized. Crucial experiments by Yoshio Masui and colleagues demonstrated that if cytoplasm taken from a mature egg cell is injected into the cytoplasm of an immature oocyte that is awaiting hormonal stimulation, the oocyte will immediately proceed through meiosis (**Figure 19-34**). Masui therefore hypothesized that a cytoplasmic chemical, which he named **MPF (maturation-promoting factor)**, induces oocyte maturation (i.e., meiotic division).

Subsequent experiments demonstrated that besides inducing meiosis, MPF also triggers mitosis when injected into fertilized frog eggs. Comparable molecules were soon detected in the cytoplasms of a broad range of dividing cell types, including yeasts, marine invertebrates, and mammals. Biochemical studies of these mitosis-inducing molecules revealed that they consist of two subunits: a Cdk and a cyclin. In other words, *MPF is a mitotic Cdk-cyclin complex.* Moreover, the mitotic Cdk portion of this complex is almost identical to the protein produced by the yeast *cdc2* gene. In fact, in yeast cells with a defective or missing *cdc2* gene, the human gene coding for mitotic Cdk can substitute perfectly well, even though the last ancestor common to yeasts and humans probably lived about a billion years ago!

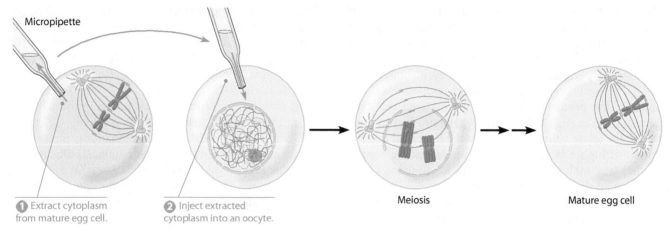

Micropipette

1 Extract cytoplasm from mature egg cell.

2 Inject extracted cytoplasm into an oocyte.

Meiosis

Mature egg cell

FIGURE 19-34 Evidence for the Existence of MPF. Hormones act on frog oocytes to trigger meiosis and development into mature frog eggs, which are arrested (until fertilization) in metaphase of the second meiotic division. The experiment shown here, performed by Y. Masui and C. L. Markert in 1971, established the existence of a substance involved in this process; they called it maturation-promoting factor (MPF). In their experiment, they used a micropipette to remove cytoplasm from a mature egg cell (arrested in metaphase of the second meiotic division) and injected it into an immature oocyte. The oocyte then proceeded through meiosis and became a mature egg cell. This experimental procedure could thus be used as an assay for detecting and eventually isolating MPF. The hormones that trigger oocyte maturation in the frog were presumed to act by stimulating the synthesis or activation of MPF. MPF is now known to be a mitotic Cdk-cyclin.

Having established that MPF is a mitotic Cdk-cyclin that triggers the onset of mitosis in a broad spectrum of cell types, the question arose as to how mitotic Cdk-cyclin is controlled so that it functions only at the proper moment—that is, at the end of G2. The answer is not to be found in the availability of mitotic Cdk itself because its concentration remains relatively constant throughout the cell cycle. However, mitotic Cdk is active as a protein kinase only when it is bound to mitotic cyclin, and mitotic cyclin is not always present in adequate amounts. Instead, the concentration of mitotic cyclin gradually increases during G1, S, and G2; eventually it reaches a critical threshold at the end of G2 that permits it to activate mitotic Cdk and thereby trigger the onset of mitosis (**Figure 19-35**). Halfway through mitosis, the mitotic cyclin molecules are abruptly destroyed. The resulting decline in mitotic Cdk activity prevents another mitosis from occurring until the mitotic cyclin concentration builds up again during the next cell cycle.

In addition to requiring mitotic cyclin, the activation of mitotic Cdk involves phosphorylation and dephosphorylation of the Cdk molecule itself. As shown in **Figure 19-36**, the binding of mitotic cyclin to mitotic Cdk yields a Cdk-cyclin complex that is initially inactive (step **1**). To trigger mitosis, the complex requires the addition of an activating phosphate group to a particular amino acid in the Cdk molecule. Before this phosphate is added, however, *inhibiting* kinases phosphorylate the Cdk molecule at two other locations, causing the active site to be blocked (step **2**). The activating phosphate group, highlighted with yellow in step **3**, is then added by a specific *activating* kinase. The last step in the activation sequence is the removal of the inhibiting phosphates by a specific *phosphatase* enzyme (step **4**). Once the phosphatase begins removing the inhibiting phosphates, a positive

feedback loop is set up: The activated mitotic Cdk generated by this reaction stimulates the phosphatase, thereby causing the activation process to proceed more rapidly.

After mitotic Cdk-cyclin has been activated through the preceding steps, its protein kinase activity triggers the onset of mitosis (**Figure 19-37**). We have already seen that the early events of mitosis include chromosome condensation, assembly of the mitotic spindle, and nuclear envelope breakdown. How are these changes triggered by mitotic Cdk-cyclin? In the case of nuclear envelope breakdown, the mitotic Cdk-cyclin phosphorylates (and stimulates other kinases to phosphorylate) the *lamin* proteins of the *nuclear*

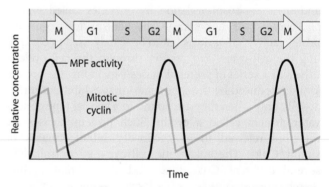

FIGURE 19-35 Fluctuating Levels of Mitotic Cyclin and MPF Activity During the Cell Cycle. Cellular levels of mitotic cyclin rise during interphase (G1, S, and G2), then fall abruptly during M phase. The peaks of MPF activity (assayed by testing for the ability to stimulate mitosis) and cyclin concentration correspond, although the rise in MPF activity is not significant until a threshold concentration of cyclin is reached. Active MPF has been found to consist of a combination of mitotic cyclin and mitotic Cdk. The mitotic Cdk itself is present at a constant concentration (not shown on the graph) because the amount of mitotic Cdk increases at a rate corresponding to the overall growth of the cell.

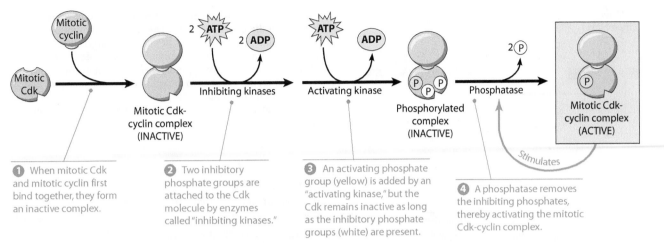

1. When mitotic Cdk and mitotic cyclin first bind together, they form an inactive complex.

2. Two inhibitory phosphate groups are attached to the Cdk molecule by enzymes called "inhibiting kinases."

3. An activating phosphate group (yellow) is added by an "activating kinase," but the Cdk remains inactive as long as the inhibitory phosphate groups (white) are present.

4. A phosphatase removes the inhibiting phosphates, thereby activating the mitotic Cdk-cyclin complex.

FIGURE 19-36 Regulation of Mitotic Cdk-Cyclin by Phosphorylation and Dephosphorylation. Activation of mitotic Cdk-cyclin involves the addition of inhibiting and activating phosphate groups, followed by removal of the inhibiting phosphate groups by a phosphatase. Once removal of the inhibiting phosphate groups has begun in step ❹, a positive feedback loop is set up: The activated Cdk-cyclin complex generated by this reaction stimulates the phosphatase, thereby causing the activation process to proceed more rapidly.

lamina, to which the inner nuclear membrane is attached (see Figure 18-32). Phosphorylation causes the lamins to depolymerize, resulting in a breakdown of the nuclear lamina and destabilization of the nuclear envelope. The integrity of the nuclear envelope is further disrupted by phosphorylation of envelope-associated proteins, and the membranes of the envelope are soon torn apart. Phosphorylation of additional target proteins by mitotic Cdk-cyclin has been implicated in other mitotic events. For example, phosphorylation of a multiprotein complex called *condensin* is involved in condensing chromatin fibers into compact chromosomes. Finally, phosphorylation of microtubule-associated proteins by mitotic Cdk-cyclin is thought to facilitate assembly of the mitotic spindle.

The Anaphase-Promoting Complex Coordinates Key Mitotic Events by Targeting Specific Proteins for Destruction

Besides triggering the onset of mitosis, mitotic Cdk-cyclin also plays an important role later in mitosis when the decision is made to separate the sister chromatids during anaphase. Mitotic Cdk-cyclin exerts its influence on this event by phosphorylating and thereby contributing to the activation of the **anaphase-promoting complex,** a multiprotein complex that coordinates mitotic events by promoting the destruction of several key proteins at specific points during mitosis. The anaphase-promoting complex functions as a *ubiquitin ligase,* a type of enzyme that targets specific proteins for degradation by joining them to the small protein *ubiquitin.* Proteins linked to ubiquitin are subsequently destroyed by a mechanism.

One crucial protein targeted for destruction by the anaphase-promoting complex is **securin,** an inhibitor of

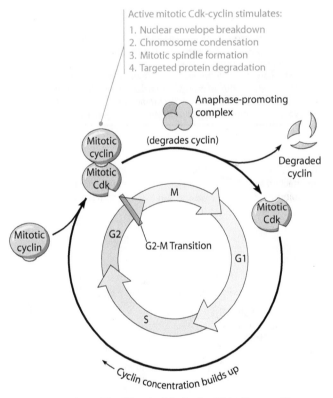

Active mitotic Cdk-cyclin stimulates:
1. Nuclear envelope breakdown
2. Chromosome condensation
3. Mitotic spindle formation
4. Targeted protein degradation

FIGURE 19-37 The Mitotic Cdk Cycle. This diagram illustrates the activation and inactivation of the mitotic Cdk protein during the cell cycle. In G1, S, and G2, mitotic Cdk is made at a steady rate as the cell grows, while the mitotic cyclin concentration gradually increases. Mitotic Cdk and cyclin form an active complex whose protein kinase activity drives the cell cycle through the G2-M transition and into mitosis by stimulating the mitotic events listed. By activating a protein-degradation pathway that degrades cyclin, the mitotic Cdk-cyclin complex also brings about its own demise, allowing the completion of mitosis and entry into G1 of the next cell cycle.

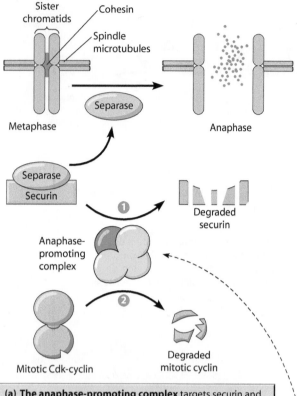

FIGURE 19-38 **The Anaphase-Promoting Complex and the Mitotic Spindle Checkpoint.** (a) The anaphase-promoting complex controls the final stages of mitosis by targeting selected proteins, including securin and mitotic cyclin, for destruction. (b) A model for the mitotic spindle checkpoint shows how chromosomes that are not attached to the spindle may organize Mad and Bub proteins into a complex that inhibits the anaphase-promoting complex, thereby delaying the onset of anaphase until all chromosomes are attached to the spindle.

(a) The anaphase-promoting complex targets securin and mitotic cyclin for degradation. ❶The destruction of securin allows separase to cleave the cohesins that hold sister chromatids together, thereby initiating anaphase. ❷The degradation of mitotic cyclin depresses mitotic Cdk activity, leading to cytokinesis, chromosome decondensation, and nuclear envelope reassembly.

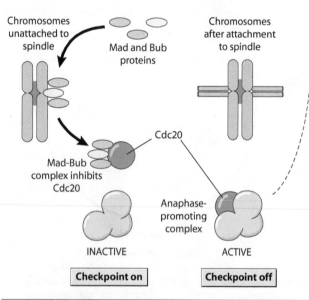

(b) The mitotic spindle checkpoint prevents anaphase from starting until all chromosomes are attached to the spindle. Unattached chromosomes keep the "checkpoint on" by organizing Mad and Bub proteins into a complex that prevents Cdc20 from activating the anaphase-promoting complex. After all chromosomes are attached, the Mad-Bub complex is not formed ("checkpoint off") and the anaphase-promoting complex is free to initiate anaphase.

sister chromatid separation. As shown in **Figure 19-38a**, sister chromatids are held together prior to anaphase by adhesive proteins called **cohesins**, which become bound to newly replicated chromosomal DNA in S phase following the movement of the replication forks. Securin maintains this sister chromatid attachment by inhibiting a protease called **separase**, which would otherwise degrade the cohesins. At the beginning of anaphase, however, the anaphase-promoting complex attaches ubiquitin to securin and thereby triggers its destruction, releasing separase from inhibition. The activated separase then cleaves cohesin, which frees sister chromatids to separate from each other and begin their anaphase movements toward the spindle poles.

Besides initiating anaphase by causing cohesins to be destroyed, the anaphase-promoting complex induces events associated with the end of mitosis by targeting another crucial protein for destruction, namely mitotic cyclin. The resulting loss of mitotic cyclin causes the protein kinase activity of mitotic Cdk to fall. Evidence suggests that many changes associated with the exit from mitosis—such as cytokinesis, chromosome decondensation, and reassembly of the nuclear envelope—depend on this cyclin degradation step and the associated reduction in Cdk activity. For example, it has been shown that introducing a nondegradable form of mitotic cyclin into cells inhibits cytokinesis, blocks nuclear envelope reassembly, and stops chromosomes from decondensing, thereby preventing mitosis from being completed.

G1 Cdk-Cyclin Regulates Progression Through the Restriction Point by Phosphorylating the Rb Protein

Now that we have examined the role played by mitotic Cdk-cyclin in controlling events associated with mitosis, let's briefly see how another type of Cdk-cyclin regulates entry into S phase. As mentioned earlier, the restriction point (Start in yeast) is a control mechanism located in late G1 that determines whether a cell will enter S phase, proceed through the rest of the cell cycle, and divide. Because passing through the restriction point is the main step that commits a cell to the cell division cycle, it is subject to control by a variety of factors such as cell size, the availability of nutrients, and the presence of growth factors that signal the need for cell proliferation.

Such signals exert their effects by activating G1 Cdk-cyclin, whose protein kinase activity triggers progression

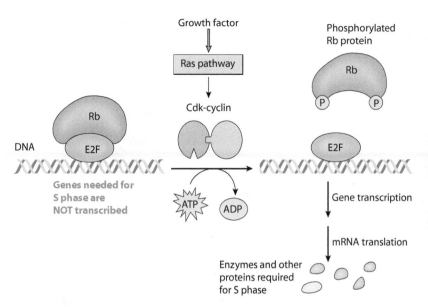

FIGURE 19-39 Role of the Rb Protein in Cell Cycle Control. In its dephosphorylated state, the Rb protein binds to the E2F transcription factor. This binding prevents E2F from activating the transcription of genes coding for proteins required for DNA replication, which are needed before the cell can pass through the restriction point into S phase. In cells stimulated by growth factors, the Ras pathway is activated (see Figure 19-41), which leads to the production and activation of a G1 Cdk-cyclin complex that phosphorylates the Rb protein. Phosphorylated Rb can no longer bind to E2F, thereby allowing E2F to activate gene transcription and trigger the onset of S phase. During the subsequent M phase (not shown), the Rb protein is dephosphorylated so that it can once again inhibit E2F.

through the restriction point by phosphorylating several target proteins. A key target is the **Rb protein,** a molecule that controls the expression of genes whose products are needed for moving through the restriction point and into S phase. The molecular mechanism by which Rb exerts this control is summarized in **Figure 19-39.** Prior to being phosphorylated by G1 Cdk-cyclin, Rb binds to and inhibits the **E2F transcription factor,** a protein that would otherwise activate the transcription of genes coding for products required for initiating DNA replication. As long as the Rb protein remains bound to E2F, the E2F molecule is inactive and these genes remain silent, thereby preventing the cell from entering into S phase. But when cells are stimulated to divide by the addition of growth factors, a pathway is triggered that produces and activates the G1 Cdk-cyclins that catalyze Rb phosphorylation. Phosphorylation of Rb abolishes its ability to bind to E2F, thereby freeing E2F to activate the transcription of genes whose products are needed for entry into S phase.

Since the Rb protein regulates such a key event—namely, the decision to proceed through the restriction point and commit to the cell division cycle—it is not surprising to discover that defects in Rb can have disastrous consequences. For example, how such defects can lead to both hereditary and environmentally induced forms of cancer.

Checkpoint Pathways Monitor Chromosome-to-Spindle Attachments, Completion of DNA Replication, and DNA Damage

It would obviously create problems if cells proceeded from one phase of the cell cycle to the next before the preceding phase had been properly completed. For example, if chromosomes start moving toward the spindle poles before they have all been properly attached to the spindle, the newly forming daughter cells might receive extra copies of some chromosomes and no copies of others, a situation known as **aneuploidy** (an = "not," eu = "good," and "ploidy" refers to chromosome number). Similarly, it would be potentially hazardous for a cell to begin mitosis before all of its chromosomal DNA had been replicated. To minimize the possibility of such errors, cells utilize a series of **checkpoint** mechanisms that monitor conditions within the cell and transiently halt the cell cycle if conditions are not suitable for continuing.

The checkpoint pathway that prevents anaphase chromosome movements from beginning before the chromosomes are all attached to the spindle is called the **mitotic spindle checkpoint.** It works through a mechanism in which chromosomes whose kinetochores remain *unattached* to spindle microtubules produce a "wait" signal that inhibits the anaphase-promoting complex. As long as the anaphase-promoting complex is inhibited, it cannot trigger destruction of the cohesins that hold sister chromatids together. The exact molecular basis of the wait signal remains an open question, but members of the *Mad* and *Bub protein families* are involved. One model proposes that Mad and Bub proteins accumulate at unattached chromosomal kinetochores, where they are converted into a multiprotein complex that inhibits the anaphase-promoting complex by blocking the action of one of its essential activators, the *Cdc20* protein (see Figure 19-38b). After all the chromosomes have become attached to the spindle, the Mad and Bub proteins are no longer converted into this inhibitory complex, thereby freeing the anaphase-promoting complex to initiate the onset of anaphase.

A second checkpoint mechanism, called the **DNA replication checkpoint,** monitors the state of DNA replication to help ensure that DNA synthesis is completed before the cell exits from G2 and begins mitosis. The existence of this checkpoint has been demonstrated by treating cells with inhibitors that prevent DNA replication from being finished. Under such conditions, the phosphatase that catalyzes the final dephosphorylation step involved in the activation of mitotic Cdk-cyclin (see

Figure 19-36, ❹) is inhibited through a series of events triggered by proteins associated with replicating DNA. The resulting lack of mitotic Cdk-cyclin activity halts the cell cycle at the end of G2 until all DNA replication is completed.

A third type of checkpoint mechanism is involved in preventing cells with damaged DNA from proceeding through the cell cycle unless the DNA damage is first repaired. In this case, a multiple series of **DNA damage checkpoints** exist that monitor for DNA damage and halt the cell cycle at various points—including late G1, S, and late G2—by inhibiting different Cdk-cyclin complexes. A protein called **p53,** sometimes referred to as the "guardian of the genome," plays a central role in these checkpoint pathways. As shown in **Figure 19-40,** when cells encounter agents that cause extensive double-stranded breaks in DNA, the altered DNA triggers the activation of an enzyme called *ATM protein kinase* (for *ataxia telangiectasia mutated;* mutations in the ATM gene can cause defects in the cerebellum that lead to uncoordinated movement, as well as prominent blood vessels that form in the whites of the eyes). ATM catalyzes the phosphorylation of kinases known as *checkpoint kinases,* which in turn phosphorylate p53 (and several other target proteins). Phosphorylation of p53 prevents it from interacting with *Mdm2,* a protein that would otherwise mark p53 for destruction by linking it to ubiquitin (just as the anaphase-promoting complex targets proteins for degradation by linking them to ubiquitin). ATM-catalyzed phosphorylation of p53 therefore protects it from degradation and leads to a buildup of p53 in the presence of damaged DNA. A protein related to ATM, called *ATR* (ATM-related) acts similarly but instead causes cell cycle arrest as a result of extensive single-stranded breaks in DNA.

The accumulating p53 in turn activates two types of events: *cell cycle arrest* and *cell death.* Both responses are based on the ability of p53 to bind to DNA and act as a transcription factor that stimulates the transcription of specific genes. One of the crucial genes activated by p53 is the gene coding for **p21,** a protein that halts progression through the cell cycle at multiple points by inhibiting the activity of several different Cdk-cyclins. Phosphorylated p53 also stimulates the production of enzymes involved in DNA repair. But if the damage cannot be successfully repaired, p53 then activates a group of genes coding for proteins involved in triggering cell death by apoptosis (page 591). A key protein in this pathway, called **Puma (p53 upregulated modulator of apoptosis),** promotes apoptosis by binding to and inactivating a normally occurring inhibitor of apoptosis known as *Bcl-2.*

The ability of p53 to trigger cell cycle arrest and cell death allows it to function as a molecular stoplight that protects cells with damaged DNA from proliferating and passing the damage to daughter cells. Where we describe how defects in the p53 pathway contribute to the development of cancer.

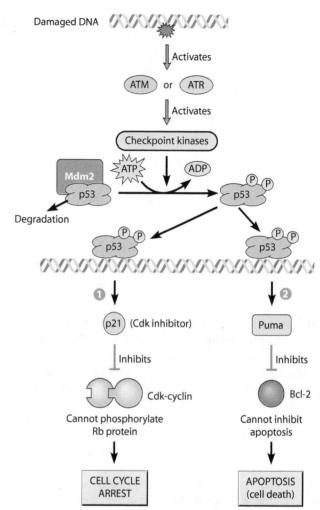

FIGURE 19-40 Role of the p53 Protein in Responding to DNA Damage. Damaged DNA activates the ATM or ATR protein kinase, leading to activation of checkpoint kinases, which leads to phosphorylation of the p53 protein. Phosphorylation stabilizes p53 by blocking its interaction with Mdm2, a protein that would otherwise mark p53 for degradation. (The degradation mechanism is not shown, but it involves Mdm2-catalyzed attachment of p53 to ubiquitin, which targets molecules to the cell's main protein destruction machine, the proteasome.) When the interaction between p53 and Mdm2 is blocked by p53 phosphorylation, the phosphorylated p53 protein accumulates and triggers two events. ❶ The p53 protein binds to DNA and activates transcription of the gene coding for the p21 protein, a Cdk inhibitor. The resulting inhibition of Cdk-cyclin prevents phosphorylation of the Rb protein, leading to cell cycle arrest at the restriction point. ❷ When the DNA damage cannot be repaired, p53 then activates genes coding for a group of proteins that trigger cell death by apoptosis. A key protein is Puma, which promotes apoptosis by binding to, and blocking the action of, the apoptosis inhibitor, Bcl-2.

Putting It All Together: The Cell Cycle Regulation Machine

Figure 19-41 is a generalized and simplified summary of the main features of the molecular "machine" that regulates the eukaryotic cell cycle. The operation of this machine can be described in terms of two fundamental, interacting mechanisms. One mechanism is an autonomous clock that

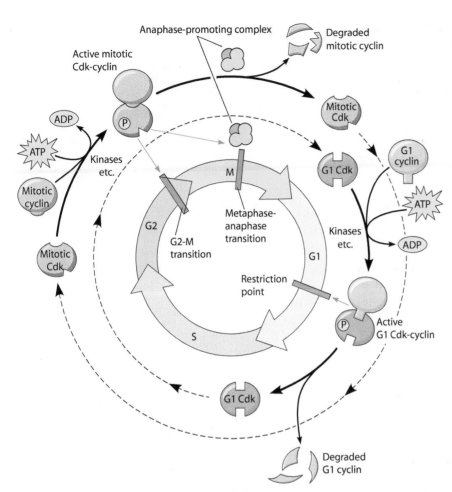

FIGURE 19-41 A General Model for Cell Cycle Regulation. Passage through the three main transition points in the cell cycle is triggered by protein complexes made of cyclin and Cdk, whose phosphorylation of other proteins induces progression through the cycle. G1 Cdk-cyclin acts at the restriction point by catalyzing phosphorylation of the Rb protein. Mitotic Cdk-cyclin acts at the G2-M boundary by catalyzing the phosphorylation of proteins involved in chromosome condensation, nuclear envelope breakdown, and spindle assembly. The same mitotic Cdk-cyclin also influences the metaphase-anaphase transition by catalyzing the phosphorylation of the anaphase-promoting complex, which in turn triggers chromosome separation and the breakdown of mitotic cyclin. Checkpoint pathways that monitor the cell for DNA damage, DNA replication, and chromosome attachment to the spindle can send signals that halt the cell cycle at one or more of these key transition points.

goes through a fixed cycle over and over again. The molecular basis of this clock is the synthesis and degradation of cyclins, alternating in a rhythmic fashion. These cyclins in turn bind to Cdk molecules, creating various Cdk-cyclin complexes that trigger the passage of cells through the main cell cycle transition points. The second mechanism adjusts the clock as needed, by providing feedback from the cell's internal and external environments. This mechanism makes use of additional proteins that, directly or indirectly, influence the activity of Cdks and cyclins. Many of these additional proteins are protein kinases or phosphatases. It is this part of the cell cycle machine that relays information about the state of the cell's metabolism—including DNA damage and replication—and about conditions outside the cell, thereby influencing whether or not the cell should commit to the process of cell division. As we will see next, growth-promoting and growth-inhibiting signaling molecules that come from outside the cell are prominent components of this regulatory mechanism.

Growth Factors and Cell Proliferation

Simple unicellular organisms, such as bacteria and yeast, live under conditions in which the presence of sufficient nutrients in the external environment is the primary factor

determining whether cells grow and divide. In multicellular organisms, the situation is usually reversed; cells are typically surrounded by nutrient-rich extracellular fluids, but the organism as a whole would be quickly destroyed if every cell were to continually grow and divide just because it had access to adequate nutrients. Cancer is a potentially lethal reminder of what happens when cell proliferation continues unabated without being coordinated with the needs of the organism as a whole. To overcome this potential problem, multicellular organisms utilize extracellular signaling proteins called *growth factors* to control the rate of cell proliferation. Most growth factors are *mitogens,* which means that they stimulate cells to pass through the restriction point and subsequently divide by mitosis.

Stimulatory Growth Factors Activate the Ras Pathway

If mammalian cells are placed in a culture medium containing nutrients and vitamins but lacking growth factors, they normally become arrested in G1 despite the presence of adequate nutrients. Growth and division can be triggered by adding small amounts of blood serum, which contains several stimulatory *growth factors.* Among them is **platelet-derived growth factor (PDGF),** a protein produced by blood platelets that stimulates the proliferation of connective tissue cells and smooth muscle cells. Another important growth factor, **epidermal growth factor (EGF),** is widely distributed in many tissues and body fluids. EGF was initially isolated from the salivary glands of mice by Stanley Cohen, who received a Nobel Prize in 1987 for his pioneering investigations of growth factors.

Growth factors such as PDGF and EGF act by binding to plasma membrane receptors located on the surface of target cells. You learned that receptors for these growth factors exhibit tyrosine kinase activity. The binding of a growth factor to its receptor activates this tyrosine kinase activity, leading to phosphorylation of tyrosine residues located in the portion of the receptor molecule protruding into the cytosol. Phosphorylation of these tyrosines in turn triggers a complex cascade of events that culminates in the cell passing through the restriction point and entering into S phase. The *Ras pathway* introduced in plays a central role in these events, as shown by studies involving cells that have stopped dividing because growth factor is not present. When mutant, hyperactive forms of the Ras protein are injected into such cells, the cells enter S phase and begin dividing, even in the absence of growth factor. Conversely, injecting cells with antibodies that inactivate the Ras protein prevents cells from entering S phase and dividing in response to growth factor stimulation.

How does the Ras pathway affect the cell cycle? As shown in **Figure 19-42,** the process involves several steps. ❶ First, binding of a growth factor to its receptor at the plasma membrane leads to activation of Ras. ❷ Next, activated Ras leads to phosphorylation and activation of a protein kinase called *Raf,* which sets in motion a cascade of phosphorylation events. Activated Raf phosphorylates serine and threonine residues in a protein kinase called *MEK,* which in turn phosphorylates threonine and tyrosine residues in a group of protein kinases called *MAP kinases (mitogen-activated protein kinases; MAPKs).* ❸ The activated MAPKs enter the nucleus and phosphorylate several regulatory proteins that activate the transcription of specific genes. Among these proteins are *Jun* (a component of the AP-1 transcription factor) and members of the *Ets family* of transcription factors. These activated transcription factors turn on the transcription of "early genes" that code for the production of other transcription factors, including Myc, Fos, and Jun, which then activate the transcription of a family of "delayed genes." One of these latter genes encodes the E2F transcription factor, whose role in controlling entry into S phase was described earlier in the chapter. ❹ Also included in the delayed genes are several genes coding for either Cdk or cyclin molecules, whose production leads to the formation of Cdk-cyclin complexes that phosphorylate Rb and hence trigger passage from G1 into S phase.

Thus in summary, the Ras pathway is a multistep signaling cascade in which the binding of a growth factor to a receptor on the cell surface ultimately causes the cell to pass through the restriction point and into S phase, thereby starting the cell on the road to cell division. The importance of this pathway for the control of cell proliferation has been

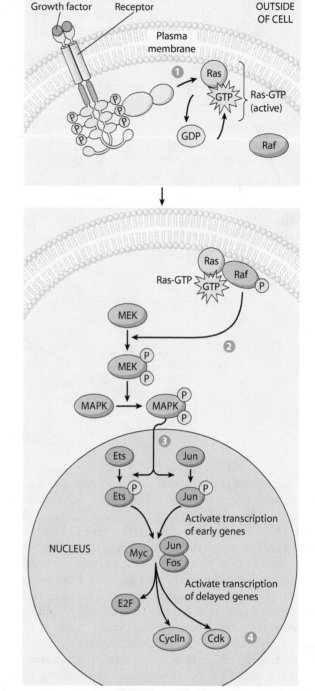

FIGURE 19-42 Regulation of the Cell Cycle via the Ras Pathway. Regulation of the cell cycle by Ras consists of four steps: ❶ binding of a growth factor to its receptor, leading to activation of Ras protein; ❷ activation of a cascade of cytoplasmic protein kinases (Raf, MEK, and MAPK); ❸ activation or production of nuclear transcription factors (Ets, Jun, Fos, Myc, E2F); and ❹ synthesis of cyclin and Cdk molecules. The resulting Cdk-cyclin complexes catalyze the phosphorylation of Rb and hence trigger passage from G1 into S phase (MAPK = Map kinases).

highlighted by the discovery that mutations affecting the Ras pathway appear frequently in cancer cells. For example, mutant Ras proteins that provide an ongoing stimulus for the cell to proliferate, independent of growth factor stimulation, are commonly encountered in pancreatic, colon, lung, and bladder cancers; and they occur in about 25–30% of all human cancers overall. The role played by such Ras pathway mutations in the development of cancer will be described in detail.

Stimulatory Growth Factors Can Also Activate the PI3K-Akt Pathway

When a growth factor binds to a receptor that triggers the Ras pathway, the activated receptor may simultaneously trigger other pathways as well. One example that we examined in the context of insulin signaling (page 417) is the *PI 3-kinase–Akt pathway*. This pathway begins with receptor-induced activation of phosphatidylinositol 3-kinase (abbreviated as *PI 3-kinase* or *PI3K*), which catalyzes formation of PIP_3 (phosphatidylinositol-3,4,5-trisphosphate), ultimately leading to phosphorylation and activation of *Akt*. Through its ability to catalyze the phosphorylation of several key target proteins, Akt suppresses apoptosis (see the next section of this chapter) and inhibits cell cycle arrest (**Figure 19-43**). One way in which the latter happens is through activation of a monomeric G protein called Rheb. Activation of Rheb leads to activation of TOR, a key regulator of cell growth mentioned earlier in this chapter. The net effect of the PI

3-kinase–Akt signaling pathway is therefore to promote cell survival and proliferation.

As in the case of the Ras pathway, mutations that disrupt the normal behavior of the PI 3-kinase–Akt pathway are associated with many cancers. In some cases, such mutations cause excessive activity of the Akt protein that leads to increased cell proliferation and survival. In other cases, hyperactivity of the PI 3-kinase–Akt pathway is caused by mutations that disable proteins that normally inhibit this pathway. One such protein is *PTEN*, a phosphatase that removes a phosphate group from PIP_3 and thereby prevents the activation of Akt (see page 417). When mutations disrupt PTEN, the cell cannot degrade PIP_3 efficiently, and its concentration rises. The accumulating PIP_3 activates Akt in an uncontrolled fashion, even in the absence of growth factors, leading to enhanced cell proliferation and survival. Mutations that reduce PTEN activity are found in up to 50% of prostate cancers, 35% of uterine cancers, and to varying extents in ovarian, breast, liver, lung, kidney, thyroid, and lymphoid cancers.

Inhibitory Growth Factors Act Through Cdk Inhibitors

Although we usually think of growth factors as being growth-stimulating molecules, the function of some growth factors is actually to inhibit cell proliferation. One example is **transforming growth factor β (TGFβ)**, a protein that can exhibit either growth-stimulating or growth-inhibiting properties, depending on the target cell type. When acting as a growth inhibitor, the binding of TGFβ to its cell surface receptor triggers a series of events in which the receptor catalyzes the phosphorylation of *Smad* proteins that move into the nucleus and regulate gene expression . Once inside the nucleus, Smads activate the expression of genes coding for proteins that inhibit cell proliferation. Two key genes produce proteins called *p15* and *p21*, which are **Cdk inhibitors** that suppress the activity of Cdk-cyclin complexes and thereby block progression through the cell cycle. (The p21 protein was already mentioned earlier in the chapter when we discussed the mechanism of p53-mediated cell cycle arrest.)

Growth-inhibiting signals that act on cells by triggering the production of Cdk inhibitors help protect normal tissues from excessive cell divisions that might otherwise produce more cells than are needed.

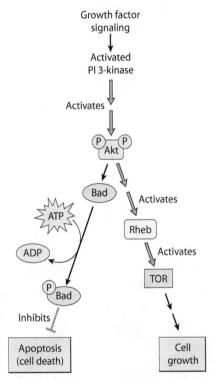

FIGURE 19-43 The PI 3-Kinase–Akt Signaling Pathway. Growth factors that bind to receptor tyrosine kinases activate several pathways in addition to the Ras pathway illustrated in Figure 19-42. The pathway shown here leads to activation of the protein kinase Akt. Akt suppresses apoptosis, in part by phosphorylating and inactivating a protein called Bad that normally promotes apoptosis. Akt also inhibits cell cycle arrest by leading to activation of TOR. Thus, the net effect of PI 3-kinase–Akt signaling is to promote cell survival and proliferation. The PI 3-kinase–Akt pathway is inhibited by PTEN.

Apoptosis

As you saw in previous sections of this chapter, organisms tightly regulate when their cells enter mitosis. When cells divide is often regulated by growth factors, which can stimulate or inhibit division, depending on the circumstances. At other times, however, organisms need to regulate whether cells stay alive. Damaged or diseased cells need to be killed, but this presents a challenge. Dismantling cells that are destined for death must occur in such a way that the internal contents of the dead cell—which include digestive enzymes in organelles such as lysosomes—do not wreak havoc on other cells around them. Multicellular organisms accomplish this feat through an important kind of programmed cell death—**apoptosis.** Apoptosis is a key event in many biological processes. In embryos, apoptosis occurs in a variety of circumstances. Examples include removal of the webbing between the digits (fingers and toes) during the development of hands and feet and the "pruning" of neurons that occurs in human infants during the first few months of life as connections mature within the developing brain. In adult humans, apoptosis occurs continually; when cells become infected by pathogens or when white blood cells reach the end of their life span, they are eliminated through apoptosis. When cells that should die via apoptosis do not, the consequences can be dire. Mutations in some of the proteins that participate in apoptosis can lead to cancer. For example, melanoma frequently results from a mutation in Apaf-1, a protein we discuss later in this section.

Apoptosis is very different from another type of cell death, known as *necrosis*, which sometimes follows massive tissue injury. Whereas necrosis involves the swelling and rupture of the injured cells, apoptosis involves a specific series of events that lead to the dismantling of the internal contents of the cell (**Figure 19-44**). During the early phases of apoptosis, the cell's DNA segregates near the periphery of the nucleus, and the volume of the cytoplasm decreases (❶). Next, the cell begins to produce small, bubble-like, cytoplasmic extensions ("blebs"), and the nucleus and organelles begin to fragment (❷). The cell's DNA is cleaved by an apoptosis-specific DNA endonuclease, or *DNase* (an enzyme that digests DNA), at regular intervals along the DNA. As a result, the DNA fragments, which are multiples of 200 base pairs in length, form a diagnostic "ladder" of fragments. (This precise size distribution of DNA reflects the susceptibility of DNA to cleavage between nucleosomes, structures you learned about in Chapter 18). Eventually the cell is dismantled into small pieces called *apoptotic bodies*. During apoptosis, inactivation of a phospholipid translocator, or flippase (see Chapter 7), results in accumulation of phosphatidylserine in the outer leaflet of the plasma membrane. The phosphatidylserine serves as an "eat-me" signal for the remnants of the affected cell to be engulfed by other nearby cells (typically macrophages) via phagocytosis (see Chapter 12; ❸). The macrophages act as scavengers to remove the resulting cellular debris.

That cells have a "death program" was first conclusively demonstrated in the nematode, *Caenorhabditis elegans*, where key genes that control apoptosis were first identified (**Box 19B**). Subsequent research showed that many other organisms, including mammals, use similar proteins during apoptosis. A key event in apoptosis is the

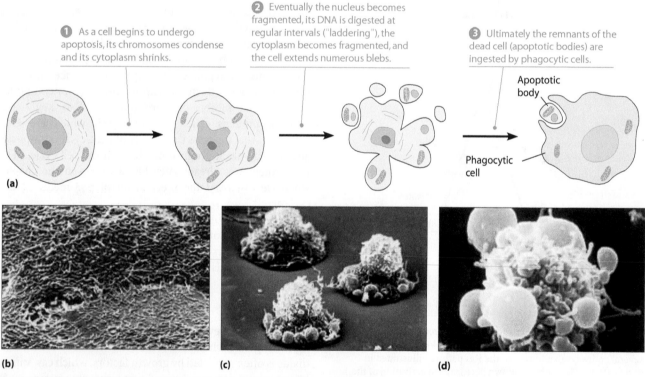

❶ As a cell begins to undergo apoptosis, its chromosomes condense and its cytoplasm shrinks.

❷ Eventually the nucleus becomes fragmented, its DNA is digested at regular intervals ("laddering"), the cytoplasm becomes fragmented, and the cell extends numerous blebs.

❸ Ultimately the remnants of the dead cell (apoptotic bodies) are ingested by phagocytic cells.

Apoptotic body

Phagocytic cell

(a)

(b)   (c)   (d)

FIGURE 19-44 Major Steps in Apoptosis. (a) Cells in the process of apoptosis undergo a series of characteristic changes. Ultimately the remnants of the dead cell (apoptotic bodies) are ingested by phagocytic cells. (b–d) SEMs of epithelial cells undergoing apoptosis. (b) Epithelial cells in contact with one another in culture form flat sheets. (c) As apoptosis ensues, the cells round up, withdraw their connections with one another, and bleb. (d) A single dead cell with many apoptotic bodies.

Key breakthroughs in the study of apoptosis came through analysis of the development of the nematode worm, *Caenorhabditis elegans*. *C. elegans* is uniquely suited to studying cell death. Its life cycle is very short, it is optically transparent, and its embryos are remarkably consistent in their development. In fact, they are so consistent that the lineage of every cell in the adult animal is known with *complete* precision. This means the sequence of cell divisions that results in each of the 1090 cells produced during development can be traced back to the single-celled fertilized egg! This feat was achieved largely through the work of John Sulston at the Medical Research Council in Cambridge, England. Sulston also showed that 131 cells undergo precisely timed apoptosis during normal embryonic development in *C. elegans*. Largely through the work of Robert Horvitz and colleagues at the Massachusetts Institute of Technology, mutants defective in various aspects of cell death, called *ced* mutants (for cell death abnormal), were identified. For example, Horvitz and colleagues identified several mutations that block phagocytosis of dead cells, so that their corpses persist, making them easy to see in the light microscope (**Figure 19B-1**). One of the first *ced* genes to be characterized at the molecular level was the gene *ced-3*, which encodes a member of the *caspase* family of proteins (see Figure 19-45). Another gene, *ced-9*, encodes the *C. elegans* version of *Bcl-2*, which plays a key role in regulating the leakage of molecules from mitochondria that can trigger apoptosis. Another gene, *ced-10*, encodes a member of the Rac family of proteins, which is required for phagocytosis of dead cells. In conjunction with work proceeding on cultured cells at about the same time, the work of Horvitz and

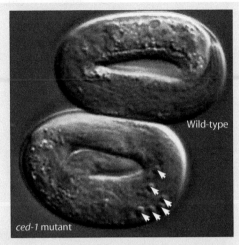

FIGURE 19B-1 Cell Death in *C. elegans*. Wild-type (top) and *ced-1* mutant (bottom) embryos (DIC microscopy). Although cell deaths can be seen in both embryos as small "buttons," these cell corpses accumulate only in the *ced-1* embryo because phagocytosis of dead cells fails (arrows).

colleagues provided key insights into apoptosis. For this work—and his work on cell signaling in the vulva—Horvitz, along with Sulston and geneticist Sydney Brenner, shared the Nobel Prize in Physiology or Medicine in 2002.

activation of a series of enzymes called **caspases.** (Caspases get their name because they contain a *cy*steine at their active site, and they cleave proteins at sites that contain an *asp*artic acid residue followed by four amino acids that are specific to each caspase). Caspases are produced as inactive precursors known as **procaspases,** which are subsequently cleaved to create active enzymes, often by other caspases, in a proteolytic cascade. Once they are activated, caspases cleave other proteins. The apoptosis-specific DNase is a good example; it is bound to an inhibitory protein that is cleaved by a caspase.

Apoptosis Is Triggered by Death Signals or Withdrawal of Survival Factors

There are two main routes by which cells can activate caspases and enter the apoptotic pathway. In some cases, activation of caspases occurs directly. For example, when cells in the human body are infected by certain viruses, a population of *cytotoxic T lymphocytes* are activated and induce the infected cells to initiate apoptosis. How do lymphocytes induce cells to initiate the process of apoptosis? Typically, such activation is triggered when cells receive *cell death signals*. Two well-known death signals are *tumor necrosis factor* and *CD95/Fas*. Here, we will

focus on CD95, a protein on the surface of infected cells. Lymphocytes have a protein on their surfaces that binds to CD95, causing the CD95 within the infected cell to aggregate (**Figure 19-45, ❶**). CD95 aggregation results in the attachment of adaptor proteins to the clustered CD95, which in turn recruits a procaspase (*procaspase-8*) to sites of receptor clustering. When the procaspase is activated (**❷**), it acts as an initiator of the caspase cascade. A key action of such *initiator caspases* is the activation of an *executioner caspase*, known as *caspase-3* (**❸**). Active caspase-3 is important for activating many steps in apoptosis.

In other cases, apoptosis is triggered indirectly. One of the best-studied cases of this second type of apoptosis involves **survival factors.** When such factors are withdrawn, a cell may enter apoptosis (**❹**). Surprisingly, a key site of action of this second pathway is the mitochondrion. The connection between mitochondria and cell death may be surprising, but it is clear that, in addition to their role in energy production, mitochondria are important in apoptosis. If withdrawal of survival factors is the sentence of execution, then the executioners are mitochondria.

How do mitochondria hasten cell death? In a healthy cell that is not committed to apoptosis, there are several *anti-apoptotic* proteins in the outer mitochondrial membrane

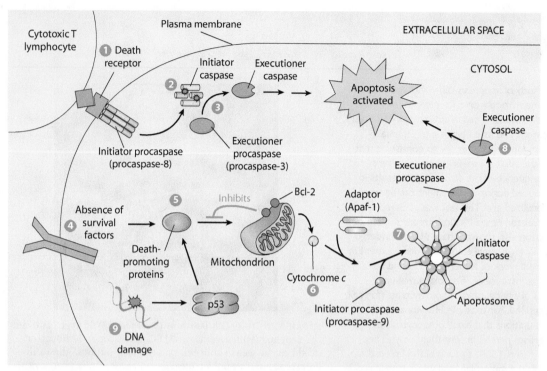

FIGURE 19-45 Induction of Apoptosis by Cell Death Signals or by Withdrawal of Survival Factors. Cell death signals, such as ligands on the surface of a cytotoxic T lymphocyte, can lead to apoptosis. ❶ Ligand binds to a "death receptor" on the surface of a target cell. Binding causes clustering of receptors and recruitment of adaptor proteins in the target cell, resulting in clustering of initiator procaspase (procaspase-8) protein. ❷ Initiator caspases then become activated. ❸ The initiator caspases in turn activate the executioner caspase, caspase-3, a key initiator of apoptosis. ❹ When survival factors are no longer present, ❺ death-promoting (pro-apoptotic) proteins accumulate, counterbalancing anti-apoptotic proteins (such as Bcl-2) at the mitochondrial outer membrane, ❻ causing release of cytochrome *c*. ❼ Cytochrome *c* forms a complex with other proteins, resulting in activation of an initiator caspase (caspase-9). ❽ The initiator caspase in turn activates the executioner caspase, caspase-3, triggering apoptosis. ❾ DNA damage can also lead to apoptosis through the activity of the p53 protein.

that prevent apoptosis, but only as long as a cell continues to be exposed to survival factors. These proteins are structurally related to a protein known as **Bcl-2,** the best understood of these anti-apoptotic proteins. Bcl-2 and other anti-apoptotic proteins exert their effects by counteracting other proteins that are themselves structurally similar to Bcl-2. These proteins, however, *promote* apoptosis, and so they are collectively referred to as *pro-apoptotic* proteins. Thus, pro- and anti-apoptotic proteins, influenced by cell signals, wage an ongoing battle; when the balance shifts toward pro-apoptotic proteins, a cell is more likely to undergo apoptosis (❺). For example, stimulation of the Akt pathway, which you learned about earlier in this chapter, can lead to phosphorylation and inactivation of a pro-apoptotic protein called *Bad* (for Bcl-2-associated death promoter; Figure 19-43).

Surprisingly, mitochondria trigger apoptosis by releasing **cytochrome *c*** into the cytosol (Figure 19-45, ❻). Although the details by which this happens are currently under debate, eventually the accumulation of pro-apoptotic protein at the surface of the mitochondrion leads to the formation of channels in the outer mitochondrial membrane, allowing cytochrome *c* to escape into the cytosol. Although cytochrome *c* is normally involved in electron transport it is

important in triggering apoptosis in at least two ways. First, cytochrome *c* stimulates calcium release from adjacent mitochondria and from the endoplasmic reticulum, where it binds inositol-1-4-5-trisphosphate (IP_3) receptors. Second, it can activate an initiator procaspase associated with mitochondria, known as *procaspase-9*. It does this by recruiting a cytosolic adaptor protein (known as *Apaf-1*) that assembles procaspase-9 into a complex sometimes called an *apoptosome*; the apoptosome promotes the production of active caspase-9 (❼). Like other initiator caspases, caspase-9 activates the executioner caspase, caspase-3 (❽). Thus, in the end, both cell death mechanisms lead to the activation of a common caspase that sets apoptosis in motion.

There is another situation that can trigger the mitochondrial pathway to apoptosis. When a cell suffers so much damage that it is unable to repair itself, it may trigger its own demise. In particular, when a cell's DNA is damaged (for example, by radiation or ultraviolet light), it can enter apoptosis via the activity of *p53* (❾). As we saw earlier in this chapter, p53 acts through the protein Puma, which binds to and inhibits Bcl-2 (see Figure 19-40, step ❷). In the end, just like withdrawal of survival factors, the p53 pathway activates pro-apoptotic proteins to trigger apoptosis.

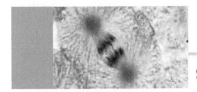

SUMMARY OF KEY POINTS

Overview of the Cell Cycle

- The eukaryotic cell cycle is divided into G1, S, G2, and M phases. Chromosomal DNA replication takes place during S phase, whereas cell division (mitosis and cytokinesis) occurs in M phase. Interphase (G1, S, and G2) is a time of cell growth and metabolism that typically occupies about 95% of the cycle.

- The length of the cell cycle varies greatly, ranging from cells that divide rapidly and continuously to cells that do not divide at all.

DNA Replication

- DNA is replicated by a semiconservative mechanism in which the two strands of the double helix unwind and each strand serves as a template for the synthesis of a complementary strand.

- Bacterial chromosome replication is typically initiated at a single point and moves in both directions around a circular DNA molecule. In contrast, eukaryotes initiate DNA replication at multiple replicons, and replication proceeds bidirectionally at each replicon. A licensing mechanism involving the binding of MCM proteins to replication origins allows eukaryotes to ensure that DNA is replicated only once prior to each mitosis.

- During replication, DNA polymerases synthesize DNA in the $5' \rightarrow 3'$ direction. Synthesis is continuous along the leading strand but discontinuous along the lagging strand, generating small Okazaki fragments that are subsequently joined by DNA ligase.

- DNA replication is initiated by primase, which synthesizes short RNA primers that are later removed and replaced with DNA. During replication, the double helix is unwound through the combined action of DNA helicases, topoisomerases, and single-stranded DNA binding proteins. As replication proceeds, a proofreading mechanism based on the $3' \rightarrow 5'$ exonuclease activity of DNA polymerase allows incorrectly base-paired nucleotides to be removed and replaced.

- The ends of linear chromosomal DNA molecules are synthesized by telomerase, an enzyme that uses an RNA template for creating short, repeated DNA sequences at the ends of each chromosome.

DNA Damage and Repair

- DNA damage arises both spontaneously and through the action of mutagenic chemicals and radiation.

- Some forms of DNA polymerase carry out translesion synthesis of new DNA across regions where the template DNA is damaged.

- Excision repair is used to correct DNA damage involving abnormal bases, whereas mismatch repair fixes improperly base-paired nucleotides. Nonhomologous end-joining and homologous recombination are used to repair double-strand DNA breaks.

Nuclear and Cell Division

- Mitosis is subdivided into prophase, prometaphase, metaphase, anaphase, and telophase. During prophase, replicated chromosomes condense into paired sister chromatids while centrosomes initiate assembly of the mitotic spindle. In prometaphase, the nuclear envelope breaks down and chromosomes then attach to spindle microtubules and move to the spindle equator, where they line up at metaphase. At anaphase, sister chromatids separate and the resulting daughter chromosomes move toward opposite spindle poles. During telophase the chromosomes decondense, and a nuclear envelope reassembles around each daughter nucleus.

- Chromosome movements are driven by three groups of motor proteins. Motor proteins located at the kinetochores and spindle poles move chromosomes toward the spindle poles, accompanied by disassembly of the microtubules at their plus and minus ends. Motor proteins that crosslink the polar microtubules move overlapping microtubules in opposite directions, thereby pushing the spindle poles apart. The final group of motor proteins move astral microtubules toward the plasma membrane, thereby pulling the spindle poles apart.

- Cytokinesis usually begins before mitosis is complete. In animal cells, an actomyosin filament network forms a cleavage furrow that constricts the cell at the midline and separates the cytoplasm into two daughter cells. In plant cells, a cell wall forms through the middle of the dividing cell.

Regulation of the Cell Cycle

- Progression through the eukaryotic cell cycle is regulated by Cdk-cyclin complexes.

- At the restriction point (Start in yeast), a Cdk-cyclin complex catalyzes the phosphorylation of the Rb protein to trigger passage into S phase.

- At the G2-M boundary, another Cdk-cyclin complex triggers entry into mitosis by catalyzing the phosphorylation of proteins that promote nuclear envelope breakdown, chromosome condensation, and spindle formation.

- At the metaphase-anaphase boundary, activation of the anaphase-promoting complex triggers a protein degradation pathway that initiates chromatid separation and targets mitotic cyclin for breakdown. The resulting loss of mitotic Cdk activity leads to events associated with the exit from mitosis, including cytokinesis, chromatin decondensation, and reassembly of the nuclear envelope.

- Checkpoint pathways monitor intracellular conditions and temporarily halt the cell cycle if conditions are not suitable for proceeding. The DNA replication checkpoint verifies that DNA synthesis has been completed before allowing the cell to exit from G2 and begin mitosis. DNA damage checkpoints involving the p53 protein halt the cell cycle at various points if

DNA damage is detected. Finally, the mitotic spindle checkpoint prevents chromosomes from moving to the spindle poles before all chromosomes are attached to the spindle.

Growth Factors and Cell Proliferation

- The cells of multicellular organisms do not normally proliferate unless they are stimulated by an appropriate growth factor.

- Many growth factors bind to receptors that activate the Ras pathway, which culminates in passage through the restriction point and into S phase. Growth factor receptors also activate the P1 3-kinase–Akt pathway, which promotes cell survival and proliferation by phosphorylating and thereby activating target proteins that suppress apoptosis and inhibit cell cycle arrest.

- Some growth factors inhibit (rather than stimulate) cell proliferation by triggering the production of Cdk inhibitors.

Apoptosis

- Apoptosis is a form of cellular death triggered by activation of death receptors, withdrawal of survival factors, or as a result of DNA damage.

- Apoptosis involves the orderly dismantling of a dying cell's contents.

- Proteases called caspases are key mediators of apoptosis. Initiator caspases activate executioner caspases, which in turn activate other apoptosis proteins.

- Initiator caspases can be activated in several ways, including through the release of cytochrome c from mitochondria. Pro- and anti-apoptotic proteins at the mitochondrion regulate release of cytochrome c.

MAKING CONNECTIONS

In this chapter, you have seen how DNA is replicated by a mechanism that unwinds the two strands of the DNA double helix and uses each strand as a template to guide the synthesis of a new complementary strand. The two sets of replicated DNA molecules are then parceled out to the two daughter cells during mitosis. Cell signaling, a topic you learned in regulates mitosis. The processes of mitosis and cytokinesis involve intricate regulation of the cytoskeleton, which you learned about in Chapters 15 and 16. You will learn how a different type of cell division, meiosis, allows genetic information in replicated DNA molecules to be recombined during formation of the sperm and egg cells that make sexual reproduction possible. After learning about the replication and distribution of DNA molecules during mitosis in this chapter and meiosis in the following chapter, you will see in Chapters 21–22 how the information stored in DNA molecules is expressed and regulated.

PROBLEM SET

More challenging problems are marked with a •.

19-1 Cell Cycle Phases. Indicate whether each of the following statements is true of the G1 phase of the cell cycle, S phase, G2 phase, or M phase. A given statement may be true of any, all, or none of the phases.

(a) The amount of nuclear DNA in the cell doubles.

(b) The nuclear envelope breaks into fragments.

(c) Sister chromatids separate from each other.

(d) Cells that will never divide again are likely to be arrested in this phase.

(e) The primary cell wall of a plant cell forms.

(f) Chromosomes are present as diffuse, extended chromatin.

(g) This phase is part of interphase.

(h) Mitotic cyclin is at its lowest level.

(i) A Cdk protein is present in the cell.

(j) A cell cycle checkpoint has been identified in this phase.

19-2 The Mitotic Index and the Cell Cycle. The mitotic index is a measure of the mitotic activity of a population of cells. It is calculated as the percentage of cells in mitosis at any one time. Assume that upon examining a sample of 1000 cells, you find 30 cells in prophase, 20 in prometaphase, 20 in metaphase, 10 in anaphase, 20 in telophase, and 900 in interphase. Of those in interphase, 400 are found (by staining the cells with a DNA-specific stain) to have X amount of DNA, 200 to have $2X$, and 300 cells to be somewhere in between. Autoradiographic analysis indicates that the G2 phase lasted 4 hours.

(a) What is the mitotic index for this population of cells?

(b) Specify the proportion of the cell cycle spent in each of the following phases: prophase, prometaphase, metaphase, anaphase, telophase, G1, S, and G2.

(c) What is the total length of the cell cycle?

(d) What is the actual amount of time (in hours) spent in each of the phases of part b?

(e) To measure the G2 phase, radioactive thymidine (a DNA precursor) is added to the culture at some time t, and samples of the culture are analyzed autoradiographically for labeled nuclei at regular intervals thereafter. What specific observation would have to be made to assess the length of the G2 phase?

(f) What proportion of the interphase cells would you expect to exhibit labeled nuclei in autoradiographs prepared shortly after exposure to the labeled thymidine? (Assume a labeling period just long enough to allow the thymidine to get into the cells and begin to be incorporated into DNA.)

19-3 Meselson and Stahl Revisited. Although the Watson–Crick structure for DNA suggested a semiconservative model for DNA replication, at least two other models are conceivable.

In a *conservative model,* the parental DNA double helix remains intact and a second, all-new copy is made. In a *dispersive model,* each strand of both daughter molecules contains a mixture of old and newly synthesized segments.

(a) Starting with one parental double helix, sketch the progeny molecules for two rounds of replication according to each of these alternative models. Use one color for the original parent strands and another color for all the DNA synthesized thereafter (as is done in Figure 19-3 for the semiconservative model).

(b) For each of the alternative models, indicate the distribution of DNA bands that Meselson and Stahl would have found in their cesium chloride gradients after one and two rounds of replication.

19-4 DNA Replication. Sketch a replication fork of bacterial DNA in which one strand is being replicated discontinuously and the other is being replicated continuously. List six different enzyme activities associated with the replication process, identify the function of each activity, and show where each would be located on the replication fork. In addition, identify the following features on your sketch: DNA template, RNA primer, Okazaki fragments, and single-stranded DNA binding protein.

• **19-5 More DNA Replication.** The following are observations from five experiments carried out to determine the mechanism of DNA replication in the hypothetical organism *Fungus mungus.* For each experiment, indicate whether the results support (S), refute (R), or have no bearing (NB) on the hypothesis that this fungus replicates its DNA by the same mechanism as that known for *E. coli.* Explain your reasoning in each case.

(a) Neither of the two DNA polymerases of *F. mungus* appears to have an exonuclease activity.

(b) Replicating DNA from *F. mungus* shows discontinuous synthesis on both strands of the replication fork.

(c) Some of the DNA sequences from *F. mungus* are present in multiple copies per genome, whereas other sequences are unique.

(d) Short fragments of *F. mungus* DNA isolated during replication contain both ribose and deoxyribose.

(e) *F. mungus* cells are grown in the presence of the heavy isotopes ^{15}N and ^{13}C for several generations and then grown for one generation in normal (^{14}N, ^{12}C) medium; then DNA is isolated from these cells and denatured. The single strands yield a single band in a cesium chloride density gradient.

19-6 Still More DNA Replication. Suppose you are given a new temperature-sensitive bacterial mutant that grows normally at 37°C but cannot replicate its chromosomes properly at 42°C. To investigate the nature of the underlying defect, you incubate the cells at 42°C with radioactive substrates required for DNA synthesis. After one hour you find that the cell population has doubled its DNA content, suggesting that DNA replication can still occur at 42°C. Moreover, centrifugation reveals that all of this DNA has the same large molecular weight as does the original DNA present in the cells. When the DNA is denatured, however, you discover that 75% of the resulting single-stranded DNA has a molecular weight that is half that of the original double-stranded DNA, and the remaining 25% of the DNA has a much lower molecular weight. Based on the preceding results, what gene do you think is defective in these cells? Explain how such a defect would account for the experimental results that you observed.

19-7 The Minimal Chromosome. To enable it to be transmitted intact from one cell generation to the next, the linear DNA molecule of a eukaryotic chromosome must have appropriate nucleotide sequences making up three special kinds of regions: Origins of replication (at least one), a centromere, and two telomeres. What would happen if such a chromosomal DNA molecule somehow lost:

(a) all of its origins of replication?

(b) all of the DNA constituting its centromere?

(c) one of its telomeres?

19-8 DNA Damage and Repair. Indicate whether each of the following statements is true of depurination (DP), deamination (DA), or pyrimidine dimer formation (DF). A given statement may be true of any, all, or none of these processes.

(a) This process is caused by spontaneous hydrolysis of a glycosidic bond.

(b) This process is induced by ultraviolet light.

(c) This can happen to guanine but not to cytosine.

(d) This can happen to thymine but not to adenine.

(e) This can happen to thymine but not to cytosine.

(f) Repair involves a DNA glycosylase.

(g) Repair involves an endonuclease.

(h) Repair involves DNA ligase.

(i) Repair depends on the existence of separate copies of the genetic information in the two strands of the double helix.

(j) Repair depends on cleavage of both strands of the double helix.

19-9 Nonstandard Purines and Pyrimidines. Shown in **Figure 19-46a** are three nonstandard nitrogenous bases that are formed by the deamination of naturally occurring bases in DNA.

(a) Indicate which base in DNA must be deaminated to form each of these bases.

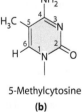

Uracil   Hypoxanthine   Xanthine
(a)

5-Methylcytosine
(b)

FIGURE 19-46 Structures of Several Nonstandard Purines and Pyrimidines. See Problem 19-9.

(b) Why are there only three bases shown, when DNA contains four bases?

(c) Why is it important that none of the bases shown in Figure 19-46a occurs naturally in DNA?

(d) Figure 19-46b shows 5-methylcytosine, a pyrimidine that arises naturally in DNA when cellular enzymes methylate cytosine. Why is the presence of this base likely to increase the probability of a mutation?

• 19-10 Chromosome Movement in Mitosis. It is possible to mark the microtubules of a spindle by photobleaching with a laser microbeam (**Figure 19-47**). When this is done, chromosomes move *toward* the bleached area during anaphase. Are the following statements consistent (C) or inconsistent (I) with this experimental result?

(a) Microtubules move chromosomes solely by disassembling at the spindle poles.

(b) Chromosomes move by disassembling microtubules at their kinetochore ends.

(c) Chromosomes are moved along microtubules by a kinetochore motor protein that moves along the surface of the microtubule and "pulls" the chromosome with it.

19-11 Cytokinesis. Predict what will happen in each of the following situations, based on your knowledge of cytokinesis. In each case, explain your answer.

(a) A fertilized sea urchin egg is injected with C3 transferase, a bacterial toxin that ADP ribosylates and inhibits Rho, 30 minutes prior to first cleavage.

(b) A one-celled *C. elegans* zygote lacks *anillin*, a protein that is required to assemble myosin efficiently at the cell surface.

19-12 More on Cell Cycle Phases. For each of the following pairs of phases from the cell cycle, indicate how you could tell in which of the two phases a specific cell is located.

(a) G1 and G2   **(c)** G2 and M

(b) G1 and S   **(d)** G1 and M

• 19-13 Cell Cycle Regulation. Recall that one approach to the study of cell cycle regulation has been to fuse cultured cells that are at different stages of the cell cycle and observe the effect of the fusion on the nuclei of the fused cells (heterokaryons). When cells in G1 are fused with cells in S, the nuclei from the G1 cells begin DNA replication earlier than they would have if they had not been fused. In fusions of cells in G2 and S, however, nuclei continue their previous activities, apparently uninfluenced by the fusion. Fusions between mitotic cells and interphase cells always lead to chromatin condensation in the nonmitotic nuclei. Based on these results, identify each of the following statements about cell cycle regulation as probably true (T), probably false (F), or not possible to conclude from the data (NP).

(a) The activation of DNA synthesis may result from the stimulatory activity of one or more cytoplasmic factors.

(b) The transition from S to G2 may result from the presence of a cytoplasmic factor that inhibits DNA synthesis.

(c) The transition from G2 to mitosis may result from the presence in the G2 cytoplasm of one or more factors that induce chromatin condensation.

(d) G1 is not an obligatory phase of all cell cycles.

(e) The transition from mitosis to G1 appears to result from the disappearance or inactivation of a cytoplasmic factor present during M phase.

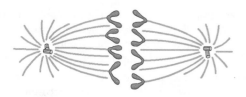

Microtubules are labeled with a fluorescent dye during anaphase.

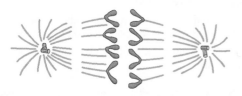

A laser microbeam is used to mark two areas by bleaching the fluorescent dye.

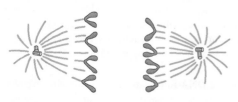

The chromosomes are observed to move toward the bleached areas.

FIGURE 19-47 Use of Laser Photobleaching to Study Chromosome Movement During Mitosis. See Problem 19-10.

• 19-14 Role of Cyclin-Dependent Protein Kinases. Based on your understanding of the regulation of the eukaryotic cell cycle, how could you explain each of the following experimental observations?

(a) When mitotic Cdk-cyclin is injected into cells that have just emerged from S phase, chromosome condensation and nuclear envelope breakdown occur immediately, rather than after the normal G2 delay of several hours.

(b) When an abnormal, indestructible form of mitotic cyclin is introduced into cells, they enter into mitosis but cannot emerge from it and reenter G1 phase.

(c) Mutations that inactivate the main protein phosphatase used to catalyze protein dephosphorylations cause a long delay in the reconstruction of the nuclear envelope that normally takes place at the end of mitosis.

• 19-15 Apoptosis and Medicine. A current focus of molecular medicine is to trigger or prevent apoptosis in specific cells. Several components of the apoptotic pathway are being targeted using this approach. For each of the following, state specifically how the treatment would be expected to stimulate or inhibit apoptosis.

(a) Cells are treated with a small molecule called pifithrin-α, which was originally isolated for its ability to reversibly block p53-dependent transcriptional activation.

(b) Exposing cells to recombinant TRAIL protein, a ligand for the tumor necrosis factor family of receptors.

(c) Treatment of cells with organic compounds that enter the cell and bind with high affinity to the active site of caspase-3.

SUGGESTED READING

References of historical importance are marked with a •.

Overview of the Cell Cycle

Darzynkiewicz, Z., H. Crissman, and J. W. Jacobberger. Cytometry of the cell cycle: Cycling through history. *Cytometry* 58A (2004): 21.

DNA Replication

Aladjem, M. I. Replication in context: Dynamic regulation of DNA replication patterns in metazoans. *Nature Rev. Genet.* 8 (2007): 588.

Alberts, B. DNA replication and recombination. *Nature* 421 (2003): 431.

Blow, J. J., and A. Dutta. Preventing re-replication of chromosomal DNA. *Nature Rev. Mol. Cell Biol.* 6 (2005): 476.

• Friedberg, E. C. The eureka enzyme: The discovery of DNA polymerase. *Nature Rev. Mol. Cell Biol.* 7 (2006): 143.

Gilbert, D. M. In search of the holy replicator. *Nature Rev. Mol. Cell Biol.* 5 (2004): 848.

Gilson, E., and V. Géli. How telomeres are replicated. *Nature Rev. Mol. Cell Biol.* 8 (2007): 825.

• Greider, C. W., and E. H. Blackburn. Telomeres, telomerase, and cancer. *Sci. Amer.* 274 (February 1996): 92.

Johnson, A., and M. O'Donnell. Cellular DNA replicases: Components and dynamics at the replication fork. *Annu. Rev. Biochem.* 74 (2005): 283.

Méndez, J., and B. Stillman. Perpetuating the double helix: Molecular machines at eukaryotic DNA replication origins. *BioEssays* 25 (2003): 1158.

• Meselson, M., and F. W. Stahl. The replication of DNA in *E. coli. Proc. Natl. Acad. Sci. USA* 44 (1958): 671.

• Mullis, K. B. The unusual origin of the polymerase chain reaction. *Sci. Amer.* 262 (April 1990): 56.

• Ogawa, T., and R. Okazaki. Discontinuous DNA replication. *Annu. Rev. Biochem.* 49 (1980): 421.

Remus, D., and J. F. Diffley. Eukaryotic DNA replication control: Lock and load, then fire. *Curr. Opin. Cell Biol.* 21 (2009): 771.

Stewart, S. A., and R. A. Weinberg. Telomeres: Cancer to human aging. *Annu. Rev. Cell Dev. Biol.* 22 (2006): 531.

• Watson, J. D., and F. H. C. Crick. Genetical implications of the structure of deoxyribonucleic acid. *Nature* 171 (1953): 964.

DNA Repair

Clarke, P. R., and L. A. Allan. Cell-cycle control in the face of damage— A matter of life or death. *Trends Cell Biol.* 19 (2009): 89

Friedberg, E. C. DNA damage and repair. *Nature* 421 (2003): 436.

Jiricny, J. The multifaceted mismatch-repair system. *Nature Rev. Mol. Cell Biol.* 7 (2006): 335.

Lainé, J.-P., and J.-M. Egly. When transcription and repair meet: A complex system. *Trends Genet.* 22 (2006): 430.

Lieber, M. R. et al. Mechanism and regulation of human non-homologous DNA end-joining. *Nature Rev. Mol. Cell Biol.* 4 (2003): 712.

Nuclear and Cell Division

Davis, T. N., and L. Wordeman. Rings, bracelets, sleeves, and chevrons: New structures of kinetochore proteins. *Trends Cell Biol.* 17 (2007): 377.

Glotzer, M. The 3Ms of central spindle assembly: Microtubules, motors and MAPs. *Nat. Rev. Mol. Cell Biol.* 10 (2009): 9.

• Mitchison, T. J., and E. D. Salmon. Mitosis: A history of division. *Nature Cell Biol.* 3 (2001): E17.

Muller, S., A. J. Wright, and L. G. Smith. Division plane control in plants: New players in the band. *Trends Cell Biol.* 19 (2009): 180.

Nigg, E. A. Centrosome duplication: Of rules and licenses. *Trends Cell Biol.* 17 (2007): 215.

Nigg, E. A., ed. *Centrosomes in Development and Disease.* Weinheim: Wiley-VCH, 2004.

Scholey, J. M., I. Brust-Mascher, and A. Mogilner. Cell division. *Nature* 422 (2003): 746.

Siller, K. H., and C. Q. Doe. Spindle orientation during asymmetric cell division. *Nat. Cell Biol* 11 (2009): 365.

von Dassow, G. Concurrent cues for cytokinetic furrow induction in animal cells. *Trends Cell Biol* 19 (2009): 165.

Wadsworth, P., and A. Khodjakov. *E pluribus unum:* Towards a universal mechanism for spindle assembly. *Trends Cell Biol.* 14 (2004): 413.

Regulation of the Cell Cycle

Bloom, J., and F. R. Cross. Multiple levels of cyclin specificity in cell-cycle control. *Nature Rev. Mol. Cell Biol.* 8 (2007): 149.

Chan, G. K., S.-T. Liu, and T. J. Yen. Kinetochore structure and function. *Trends Cell Biol.* 15 (2005): 589.

Clarke, P. R., and C. Zhang. Spatial and temporal coordination of mitosis by Ran GTPase. *Nat. Rev. Mol. Cell.* 9 (2008): 464.

Coller, H. A., What's taking so long? S-phase entry from quiescence versus proliferation. *Nature Rev. Mol. Cell Biol.* 8 (2007): 667.

De Veylder, L., T. Beeckman, and D. Inzé. The ins and outs of the plant cell cycle. *Nature Rev. Mol. Cell. Biol.* 8 (2007): 655.

Jiang, B. H., and L. Z. Liu. PI3K/PTEN signaling in angiogenesis and tumorigenesis. *Adv. Cancer Res.* 102 (2009): 19.

• Nasmyth, K. A prize for proliferation. *Cell* 107 (2001): 689.

Nigg, E. A. Mitotic kinases as regulators of cell division and its checkpoints. *Nature Rev. Mol. Cell Biol.* 2 (2001): 21.

Nurse, P. A long twentieth century of the cell cycle and beyond. *Cell* 100 (2000): 71.

Onn, I., J. M. Heidinger-Pauli, V. Guacci, E. Unal, and D. E. Koshland. Sister chromatid cohesion: A simple concept with a complex reality. *Ann. Rev. Cell Dev. Biol.* 24 (2008): 105.

Peters, J.-M. The anaphase promoting complex/cyclosome: A machine designed to destroy. *Nature Rev. Mol. Cell Biol.* 7 (2006): 644.

Pines, J. Mitosis: A matter of getting rid of the right protein at the right time. *Trends Cell Biol.* 16 (2006): 55.

van den Heuvel, S., and N. J. Dyson. Conserved functions of the pRB and E2F families. *Nat. Rev. Mol. Cell. Biol.* 9 (2008): 713.

Apoptosis

Brenner, D., and T. W. Mak. Mitochondrial cell death effectors. *Curr. Opin. Cell Biol.* 21 (2009): 871.

Brunelle, J. K., and A. Letai. Control of mitochondrial apoptosis by the Bcl-2 family. *J. Cell Sci.* 122 (2009): 437.

Danial, N. N., and S. J. Korsmeyer. Cell death: Critical control points. *Cell* 116 (2004): 205.

Horvitz, H. R. Worms, life, and death (Nobel lecture). *Chembiochem.* 4 (2003): 697.

Ow, Y. P., D. R. Green, Z. Hao, and T. W. Mak. Cytochrome *c:* Functions beyond respiration. *Nat. Rev. Mol. Cell. Biol.* 9 (2008): 532.

Vaseva, A. V., and U. M. Moll. The mitochondrial p53 pathway. *Biochim. Biophys. Acta* 1787 (2009): 414.

Gene Expression: I. The Genetic Code and Transcription

So far, we have described DNA as the genetic material of cells and organisms. We have come to understand its structure, chemistry, and replication, as well as the way it is packaged into chromosomes and parceled out to daughter cells during mitotic and meiotic cell divisions. Now we are ready to explore how DNA is expressed—that is, how the coded information it contains is used to guide the production of RNA and protein molecules. Our discussion of this important subject is divided among three chapters. The present chapter deals with the nature of the genetic code and how information stored in DNA guides the synthesis of RNA molecules in the process we call transcription. Chapter 22 describes how RNA molecules are then used to guide the synthesis of specific proteins in the process known as translation. n. To put these topics in context, we start here with an overview of the roles played by DNA, RNA, and proteins in gene expression.

The Directional Flow of Genetic Information

As mentioned at the beginning of this series of chapters, the flow of genetic information in cells generally proceeds from DNA to RNA to protein (see Figure 18-1). DNA (more precisely, a segment of one DNA strand) first serves as a template for the synthesis of an RNA molecule, which in most cases then directs the synthesis of a particular protein. (In a few cases, the RNA is the final product of gene expression and functions as such within the cell.) The principle of directional information flow from DNA to RNA to protein is known as the *central dogma of molecular biology*, a term coined by Francis Crick soon after the double-helical model of DNA was first proposed. This principle is summarized as follows:

Thus, the flow of genetic information involves replication of DNA, transcription of information carried by DNA into the form of RNA, and translation of this information from RNA into protein. The term **transcription** is used when referring to RNA synthesis using DNA as a template to emphasize that this phase of gene expression is simply a transfer of information from one nucleic acid to another, so the basic "language" remains the same. In contrast, protein synthesis is called **translation** because it involves a language change—from the nucleotide sequence of an RNA molecule to the amino acid sequence of a polypeptide chain.

RNA that is translated into protein is called **messenger RNA (mRNA)** because it carries a genetic message from DNA to the ribosomes, where protein synthesis actually takes place. In addition to mRNA, two other types of RNA are involved in protein synthesis: **ribosomal RNA (rRNA)** molecules, which are integral components of the ribosome, and **transfer RNA (tRNA)** molecules, which serve as intermediaries that translate the coded base sequence of messenger RNA and bring the appropriate amino acids to the ribosome. Note that ribosomal and transfer RNAs do not themselves code for proteins; genes coding for these two types of RNA are examples of genes whose final products are RNA molecules rather than protein chains. The involvement of all three major classes of RNA in the overall flow of information from DNA to protein is outlined in **Figure 21-1**.

In the years since it was first formulated by Crick, the central dogma has been refined in various ways. For example, many viruses with RNA genomes have been found to synthesize RNA molecules using RNA as a

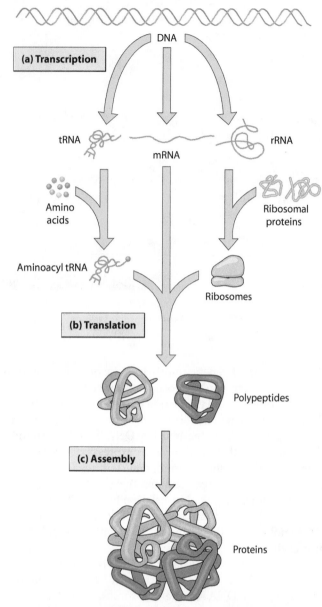

FIGURE 21-1 RNAs as Intermediates in the Flow of Genetic Information. All three major classes of RNA—tRNA, mRNA, and rRNA—are **(a)** synthesized by transcription of the appropriate DNA sequences (genes) and **(b)** involved in the subsequent process of translation (polypeptide synthesis). The appropriate amino acids are brought to the mRNA and ribosome by tRNA. A tRNA molecule carrying an amino acid is called an aminoacyl tRNA. Polypeptides then fold and **(c)** assemble into functional proteins. The specific polypeptides shown here are the globin chains of the protein hemoglobin. For simplicity, this figure omits many details that will be described in this chapter and the next.

template. Other RNA viruses, such as HIV, carry out *reverse transcription*, whereby the viral RNA is used as a template for DNA synthesis—a "backward" flow of genetic information. (**Box 21A** discusses these viruses and the role of reverse transcription in rearranging DNA sequences.) But despite these variations on the original model, the principle that information flows from DNA to RNA to protein remains the main operating principle by which all cells use their genetic information.

The Genetic Code

The essence of gene expression lies in the relationship between the nucleotide base sequence of DNA molecules and the linear order of amino acids in protein molecules. This relationship is based on a set of rules known as the **genetic code.** The cracking of that code, which tells us how DNA can code for proteins, is one of the major landmarks of twentieth-century biology.

During the flow of information from DNA to RNA to protein, it is easy to envision how information residing in a DNA base sequence could be passed to mRNA through the mechanism of complementary base pairing. But how does a base sequence in mRNA use its "message" to guide the synthesis of a protein molecule, which consists of a sequence of amino acids? What is needed, of course, is knowledge of the appropriate code—the set of rules that determines which nucleotides in mRNA correspond to which amino acids. Until it was cracked in the early 1960s, this genetic code was a secret code in a double sense: Before scientists could figure out the exact coding relationship between the base sequence of a DNA molecule and the amino acid sequence of a protein, they first had to become aware that such a relationship existed at all. That awareness arose from the discovery that mutations in DNA can lead to changes in proteins.

Experiments on *Neurospora* Revealed That Genes Can Code for Enzymes

The link between gene mutations and proteins was first detected experimentally by George Beadle and Edward Tatum in the early 1940s using the common bread mold, *Neurospora crassa. Neurospora* is a relatively self-sufficient organism that can grow in a *minimal medium* containing only sugar, inorganic salts, and the vitamin biotin. From these few ingredients, *Neurospora*'s metabolic pathways produce everything else the organism requires. To investigate the influence of genes on these metabolic pathways, Beadle and Tatum treated a *Neurospora* culture with X-rays to induce genetic mutations. Such treatments generated mutant strains that had lost the ability to survive in the minimal culture medium, although they could be grown on a *complete medium* supplemented with a variety of amino acids, nucleosides, and vitamins.

Such observations suggested that the *Neurospora* mutants had lost the ability to synthesize certain amino acids or vitamins and could survive only when these nutrients were added to the growth medium. To determine exactly which nutrients were required, Beadle and Tatum transferred the mutant cells to a variety of growth media, each containing a single amino acid or vitamin added as a supplement to the minimal medium. This approach led to the discovery that one mutant strain would grow only in a medium supplemented with vitamin B_6, a second mutant would grow only when the medium was supplemented with the amino acid arginine, and so forth. A large number of different mutants were eventually characterized, each impaired in its ability to synthesize a particular amino acid or vitamin.

Because amino acids and vitamins are synthesized by metabolic pathways involving multiple steps, Beadle and Tatum set out to identify the particular step in each pathway that had become defective. They approached this task by supplementing the minimal medium with metabolic precursors of a given amino acid or vitamin rather than with the amino acid or vitamin itself. By finding out which precursors supported the growth of each mutant strain, they were able to infer that each mutation disabled a single enzyme-catalyzed step in a pathway for making a particular compound. There was, in other words, a one-to-one correspondence between each genetic mutation and the lack of a specific enzyme required in a metabolic pathway. From these findings, Beadle and Tatum formulated the *one gene–one enzyme hypothesis*, which stated that each gene controls the production of a single type of enzyme.

Most Genes Code for the Amino Acid Sequences of Polypeptide Chains

The theory that genes direct the production of enzyme molecules represented a major advance in our understanding of gene action, but it provided little insight into the question of how genes accomplish this task. The first clue to the underlying mechanism emerged a few years later in the laboratory of Linus Pauling, who was studying the inherited disease *sickle-cell anemia*. The red blood cells of individuals suffering from sickle-cell anemia exhibit an abnormal, "sickle" shape that causes the cells to become trapped and damaged when they pass through small blood vessels (**Figure 21-2**). In trying to identify the reason for this behavior, Pauling decided to analyze the properties of *hemoglobin*, the major protein of red blood cells. Because hemoglobin is a charged molecule, he used the technique of *electrophoresis*, which separates charged molecules from one another by placing them in an electric field. Pauling found that hemoglobin from

sickle cells migrated at a different rate than normal hemoglobin, suggesting that the two proteins differ in electric charge. Since some amino acids have charged side chains, Pauling proposed that the difference between normal and sickle-cell hemoglobin lay in their amino acid compositions.

One way to test this hypothesis would be to determine the amino acid sequence of the normal and mutant forms of hemoglobin. At the time of Pauling's discovery in the early 1950s, the largest protein to have been sequenced was less than one-tenth the size of hemoglobin, so determining the complete amino acid sequence of hemoglobin would have been a monumental undertaking. Fortunately, an ingenious shortcut devised by Vernon Ingram made it possible to identify the amino acid abnormality in sickle-cell hemoglobin without determining the protein's complete amino acid sequence. Ingram used the protease *trypsin* to cleave hemoglobin into peptide fragments, which were then separated from each other as shown in **Figure 21-3** (page 650). When Ingram examined the peptide patterns of normal and sickle-cell hemoglobin, he discovered that only one peptide differed between the two proteins. Analysis of the amino acid makeup of the altered peptide revealed that a glutamic acid in normal hemoglobin had been replaced by a valine in sickle-cell hemoglobin. Since glutamic acid is negatively charged and valine is neutral, this substitution explains the difference in electrophoretic behavior between normal and sickle-cell hemoglobin originally observed by Pauling.

This single change from a glutamic acid to valine (caused by a single base-pair change in DNA) is enough to alter the way that hemoglobin molecules pack into red blood cells. Normal hemoglobin is jellylike in consistency, but sickle-cell hemoglobin tends to form a kind of crystal when it delivers oxygen to and picks up carbon dioxide from tissues. The crystalline array deforms the red blood cell into a sickled shape that blocks blood flow in capillaries and leads to a debilitating, potentially fatal, disease.

Following Ingram's discovery that a gene mutation alters a single amino acid in sickle-cell hemoglobin, subsequent studies revealed the existence of other abnormal forms of hemoglobin, some of which involve mutations in a different gene. Two different genes are able to influence the amino acid sequence of the same protein because hemoglobin is a multisubunit protein containing two different kinds of polypeptide chains. The amino acid sequences of the two types of chains, called the α and β chains, are specified by two different genes.

The discoveries by Pauling and Ingram necessitated several refinements in the one gene–one enzyme concept of Beadle and Tatum. First, the fact that hemoglobin is not an enzyme indicates that genes encode the amino acid sequences of proteins in general, not just enzymes. In addition, the discovery that different genes code for the α and β chains of hemoglobin reveals that each gene encodes the sequence of a polypeptide chain, not necessarily a complete protein. Thus, the original hypothesis was refined into the *one gene–one polypeptide theory*.

├─────── 2 μm ───────┤

FIGURE 21-2 Normal and Sickled Red Blood Cells. The micrograph on the right reveals the abnormal shape of a sickled cell. This distorted shape, which is caused by a mutated form of hemoglobin, allows sickled cells to become trapped and damaged when passing through small blood vessels (SEMs).

Transcription generally proceeds in the direction described in the central dogma, with DNA serving as a template for RNA synthesis. In certain cases, however, the process can be reversed and RNA serves as a template for DNA synthesis. This process of *reverse transcription* is catalyzed by the enzyme **reverse transcriptase,** first discovered by Howard Temin and David Baltimore in certain viruses with RNA genomes. Viruses that carry out reverse transcription are called **retroviruses.** Examples of retroviruses include some important pathogens, such as the *human immunodeficiency virus (HIV)*, which causes *aquired immune deficiency syndrome (AIDS)*, and a number of viruses that cause cancers in animals.

Retroviruses

Figure 21A-1 depicts the reproductive cycle of a typical retrovirus. In the virus particle, two copies of the RNA genome are enclosed within a protein capsid that is surrounded by a membranous envelope. Each RNA copy has a molecule of reverse transcriptase attached to it. The virus first (**1**) binds to the surface of the host cell, and its envelope fuses with the plasma membrane, releasing the capsid and its contents into the cytoplasm. Once inside the cell, the viral reverse transcriptase (**2**) catalyzes the synthesis of a DNA strand that is complementary to the viral RNA and then (**3**) catalyzes the formation of a second DNA strand complementary to the first. The result is a double-stranded DNA version of the viral genome. (**4**) This double-stranded DNA then enters the nucleus and integrates into the host cell's chromosomal DNA, much as the DNA genome of a lysogenic phage integrates into the DNA of the bacterial chromosome (see Box 18A). Like a prophage, the integrated viral genome, called a *provirus*, is replicated every time the cell replicates its own DNA. (**5**) Transcription of the proviral DNA (by cellular enzymes) produces RNA transcripts that function in two ways. First, they serve as (**6**) mRNA molecules that direct the synthesis of viral proteins (capsid protein, envelope protein, and reverse transcriptase). Second, (**7**) some of these same RNA transcripts are packaged with the viral proteins into new virus particles. (**8**) The new viruses then "bud" from the plasma membrane without necessarily killing the cell.

The ability of a retroviral genome to integrate into host cell DNA helps explain how some retroviruses can cause cancer. These viruses, called RNA tumor viruses, are of two types. Viruses of the first type carry a cancer-causing *oncogene* in their genomes, along with the genes coding for viral proteins. An oncogene is a mutated version of a normal cellular gene (a proto-oncogene) that codes for proteins used to regulate cell growth and division. For example, the oncogene carried by the Rous sarcoma virus (a chicken virus that was the first RNA tumor virus to be

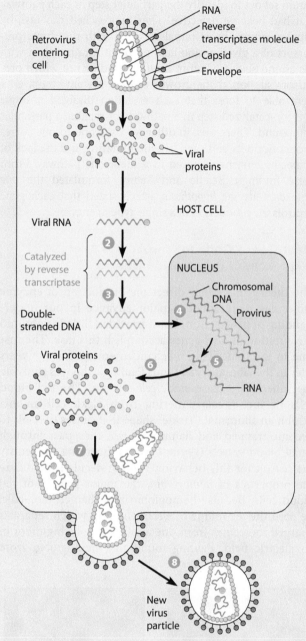

FIGURE 21A-1 **The Reproductive Cycle of a Retrovirus.**

ACTIVITIES www.thecellplace.com *Retrovirus (HIV) reproductive cycle*

According to this theory, the nucleotide sequence of a gene determines the sequence of amino acids in a polypeptide chain. In the mid-1960s, this prediction was confirmed in the laboratory of Charles Yanofsky, where the locations of dozens of mutations in the bacterial gene coding for a subunit of the enzyme tryptophan syn-thase were determined. As predicted, the positions of the mutations within the gene correlated with the positions of the resulting amino acid substitutions in the tryptophan synthase polypeptide chain.

Showing that a gene's base sequence specifies the amino acid sequence of a polypeptide chain represented a

discovered) is a modified version of a cellular gene for a protein kinase. The protein product of the viral gene is hyperactive, and the cell cannot control it in the normal way. As a result, cells expressing this gene proliferate wildly, producing cancerous tumors called *sarcomas*. RNA tumor viruses of the second type do not themselves carry oncogenes, but integration of their genomes into the host chromosome alters the cellular DNA in such a way that a normal proto-oncogene is converted into an oncogene.

Retrotransposons

Reverse transcription also occurs in normal eukaryotic cells in the absence of viral infection. Much of it involves DNA elements called **retrotransposons.** In Chapter 18, we saw that *transposable elements* are DNA segments that can move themselves from one site to another within the genome. Retrotransposons are a special type of transposable element that use reverse transcription to carry out this movement. As outlined in **Figure 21A-2,** the transposition mechanism begins with ❶ transcription of the retrotransposon DNA followed by ❷ translation of the resulting RNA, which produces a protein exhibiting both reverse transcriptase and endonuclease activities. ❸ Next, the retrotransposon RNA and protein bind to chromosomal DNA at some other location, and ❹ the endonuclease cuts one of the DNA strands. ❺ The reverse transcriptase then uses the retrotransposon RNA as a template to make a DNA copy that is ❻ integrated into the target DNA site.

Although retrotransposons do not transpose themselves very often, they can attain very high copy numbers within a genome. We encountered one example in Chapter 18—the *Alu* family of sequences. *Alu* sequences are only 300 base pairs long, and they do not encode a reverse transcriptase. But by using a reverse transcriptase encoded elsewhere in the genome, they have sent copies of themselves throughout the genomes of humans and other primates. The human genome contains about a million *Alu* sequences that together represent about 11% of the total DNA. Another type of retrotransposon, called an *L1 element,* is even more prevalent, accounting for roughly 17% of human DNA. The L1 retrotransposon is larger than *Alu* and encodes its own reverse transcriptase and endonuclease, as illustrated in Figure 21A-2. The reason that genomes retain so many copies of retrotransposon sequences such as L1 and *Alu* is not well understood, but they are thought to contribute to evolutionary flexibility and variability.

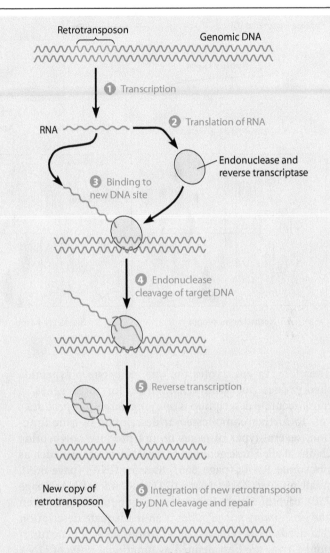

FIGURE 21A-2 Movement of a Retrotransposon.

major milestone, but subsequent developments have revealed that gene function is often more complicated than this, especially in eukaryotes. As we will see later in the chapter, most eukaryotic genes contain noncoding sequences interspersed among the coding regions and so do not exhibit a complete linear correspondence with their polypeptide product. Moreover, the coding sequences in such genes can be read in various combinations to produce different mRNAs, each coding for a unique polypeptide chain. This phenomenon, called *alternative splicing* (page 673), allows dozens or even hundreds of different polypeptides to be produced from a single gene.

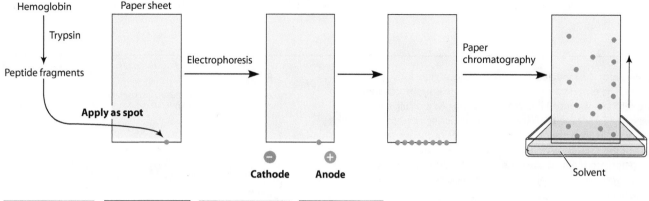

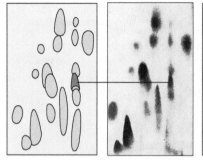 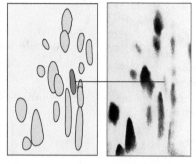

Normal hemoglobin   Sickle-cell hemoglobin

FIGURE 21-3 Peptide Patterns of Normal and Sickle-Cell Hemoglobin. *(Top)* Normal and sickle-cell hemoglobin were digested with trypsin, and the resulting peptide fragments were separated by electrophoresis followed by paper chromatography (movement of a solvent up a sheet of paper by capillary action). *(Bottom)* The colored spots in the drawings next to each photograph represent peptide fragments that differ in the two types of hemoglobin. In the altered fragment present in sickle-cell hemoglobin, a single glutamic acid has been replaced by valine.

Therefore, in eukaryotes the one gene–one polypeptide theory does not always hold true; for most genes, a more accurate description is *one gene–many polypeptides.*

To further complicate our description of gene function, several types of genes do not produce polypeptide chains at all. These genes code for RNA molecules such as ribosomal RNAs (page 666), transfer RNAs (page 665), small nuclear RNAs (page 671), and microRNAs (page 750), each of which performs a unique function. So even *one gene–many polypeptides* is an inadequate description that needs to be replaced by a broader view of gene function: **Genes** are best defined as functional units of DNA that code for the amino acid sequence of one or more polypeptide chains or, alternatively, for one of several types of RNA that perform functions other than specifying the amino acid sequence of polypeptide chains.

The Genetic Code Is a Triplet Code

Given a sequence relationship between DNA and proteins, the next question is: How many nucleotides in DNA are needed to specify each amino acid in a protein? We know that the information in DNA must reside in the sequence of the four nucleotides that constitute the DNA: A, T, G, and C. These are the only "letters" of the DNA alphabet. Because the DNA language has to contain at least 20 "words," one for each of the 20 amino acids found in protein molecules, the DNA word coding for each amino acid must consist of more than one nucleotide. A doublet code involving two adjacent nucleotides would not be adequate, as four

kinds of nucleotides taken two at a time can generate only $4^2 = 16$ different combinations.

But with three nucleotides per word, the number of different words that can be produced with an alphabet of just four letters is $4^3 = 64$. This number is more than sufficient to code for 20 different amino acids. In the early 1950s, such mathematical arguments led biologists to suspect the existence of a **triplet code**—that is, a code in which three base pairs in double-stranded DNA are required to specify each amino acid in a polypeptide. But direct evidence for the triplet nature of the code was not provided until ten years later. To understand the nature of that evidence, we first need to become acquainted with frameshift mutations.

Frameshift Mutations. In 1961, Francis Crick, Sydney Brenner, and their colleagues provided genetic evidence for the triplet nature of the code by studying the mutagenic effects of the chemical *proflavin* on bacteriophage T4. Their work is well worth considering, not just for the critical evidence it provided concerning the nature of the code but also because of the ingenuity that was needed to understand the significance of their observations.

Proflavin is one of several *acridine dyes* commonly used as **mutagens** (mutation-inducing agents) in genetic research. Acridines are interesting mutagens because they act by causing the addition or deletion of single base pairs in DNA. Sometimes, mutants generated by acridine treatment of a wild-type ("normal") virus or organism appear to revert to wild-type when treated with more of the same type of mutagen. Closer examination often reveals, however, that the reversion is not a true reversal of the original mutation but the acquisition of a second mutation that maps very close to the first.

Such mutations display an interesting kind of arithmetic. If the first alteration is called a plus (+) mutation, then the second can be called a minus (−) mutation. By itself, each creates a mutant phenotype. But when they occur close together as a double mutation, they cancel each other out and the virus or organism exhibits the normal, wild-type phenotype. (Properly speaking, the phenotype is said to be *pseudo wild-type* because, despite its wild-type appearance, two mutations are present.) Such behavior can be explained using the analogy in **Figure 21-4**. Suppose that line 1 represents a wild-type "gene" written in a language that uses three-letter words. When we "translate" the line by starting at the beginning and reading three letters at a time, the message of the gene is readily comprehensible. A plus mutation is the addition of a single letter within the message (line 2). That change may seem minor, but since the message is always read three letters at a time, the insertion of an extra letter early in the sequence means that all the remaining letters are read out of phase. There is, in other words, a shift in the *reading frame,* and the result is a garbled message from the point of the insertion onward. A minus mutation can be explained in a similar way because the deletion of a single letter also causes the reading frame to shift, resulting in another garbled message (line 3). Such **frameshift mutations** are typical effects of acridine dyes and other mutagens that cause the insertion or deletion of individual base pairs.

Individually, plus and minus mutations always change the reading frame and garble the message. But when a plus and a minus mutation occur in close proximity within the same gene, they can largely cancel out each other's effect. In such cases, the insertion caused by the plus mutation compensates for the deletion caused by the minus mutation, and the message is intelligible from that point on (line 4). Notice, however, that double mutations with either two additions (+/+; line 5) or two deletions (−/−; line 6) do not cancel in this way. They remain out of phase for the remainder of the message.

Evidence for a Triplet Code. When Crick and Brenner generated T4 phage mutants with proflavin, they obtained results similar to those in the hypothetical example illustrated in Figure 21-4 involving a language that uses three-letter words. They found that minus mutants, which exhibited an abnormal phenotype, could acquire a second mutation that caused them to revert to the wild-type (or more properly, pseudo wild-type) phenotype. The second mutation was always a plus mutation located at a site different from, but close to, the original minus mutation. In other words, mutants reverting to the wild-type phenotype exhibited a −/+ pattern of mutations. Crick and Brenner observed many examples of −/+ (or +/−) mutants exhibiting the wild-type phenotype in their experiments. But when they generated +/+ or −/− double mutants by recombination, no wild-type phenotypes were ever seen.

Crick and Brenner also constructed triple mutants of the same types (+/+/+ or −/−/−) and found that many of them now reverted to wild-type phenotypes. This finding, of course, can be readily understood by consulting lines 7 and 8 of Figure 21-4: The reading frame (based on three-letter words) at the beginning and end of that hypothetical message remains the same when three letters are either added or removed. The portion of the message between the first and third mutations is garbled, but provided these are close enough to each other, enough of the sentence may remain to convey an intelligible message.

FIGURE 21-4 Frameshift Mutations. The effect of frameshift mutations can be illustrated with an English sentence. The wild-type sentence (line 1) consists of three-letter words. When read in the correct frame, it is fully comprehensible. The insertion (line 2) or deletion (line 3) of a single letter shifts the reading frame and garbles the message from that point onward. (Garbled words due to shifts in the reading frame are underscored.) Double mutants containing a deletion that "cancels" a prior insertion have a restored reading frame from the point of the second mutation onward (line 4). However, double insertions (line 5) or double deletions (line 6) produce garbled messages. Triple insertions (line 7) or deletions (line 8) garble part of the message but restore the reading frame with the net addition or deletion of a single word.

Applying this concept of a three-letter code to DNA, Crick and Brenner concluded that adding or deleting a single base pair will shift the reading frame of the gene from that point onward, and a second, similar change shifts the reading frame yet again. Therefore, from the site of the first mutation onward, the message is garbled. But after a third change of the same type, the original reading frame is restored, and the only segment of the gene translated incorrectly is the segment between the first and third mutations. Such errors can often be tolerated when the genetic message is translated into the amino acid sequence of a protein, provided the affected region is short and the changes in amino acid sequence do not destroy protein function. This is why the individual mutations in a triple mutant with wild-type phenotype map so closely together. Subsequent sequencing of wild-type polypeptides from such triple mutants confirmed the slightly altered sequences of amino acids that would be expected.

Based on their finding that wild-type phenotypes are often maintained in the presence of three base-pair additions (or deletions) but not in the presence of one or two, Crick and Brenner concluded that the nucleotides making up a DNA strand are read in groups of three. In other words, the genetic code is a triplet code in which the reading of a message begins at a specific starting place (to ensure the proper reading frame) and then proceeds three nucleotides at a time, with each such triplet translated into the appropriate amino acid, until the end of the message is reached. Keep in mind that in establishing the triplet nature of the code, Crick and Brenner did not have Figure 21-4 to assist them. Their ability to deduce the correct explanation from their analysis of proflavin-induced mutations is an especially inspiring example of the careful, often ingenious reasoning that almost always accompanies significant advances in science.

The Genetic Code Is Degenerate and Nonoverlapping

From the fact that so many of their triple mutants were viable, Crick and Brenner drew an additional conclusion: Most of the 64 possible nucleotide triplets must specify amino acids, even though proteins have only 20 different kinds of amino acids. If only 20 of the 64 possible combinations of nucleotides "made sense" to the cell, the chances of a meaningless triplet appearing in the out-of-phase stretches would be high. Such triplets would surely interfere with protein synthesis, and frameshift mutants would revert to wild-type behavior only rarely.

But Crick and Brenner frequently detected reversion to wild-type behavior, so they reasoned that most of the 64 possible triplets must code for amino acids. Since there are only 20 amino acids, this told them that the genetic code is a **degenerate code**—that is, a given amino acid can be specified by more than one nucleotide triplet. Degeneracy serves a useful function in enhancing the adaptability of the coding system. If only 20 triplets were assigned a coding function (one for each of the 20 amino acids), any

mutation in DNA that led to the formation of any of the other 44 possible triplets would interrupt the genetic message at that point. Therefore, the susceptibility of such a coding system to disruption would be very great.

A further conclusion from Crick and Brenner's work—which we have implicitly assumed—is that the genetic code is *nonoverlapping*. In an *overlapping* code, the reading frame would advance only one or two nucleotides at a time along a DNA strand so that each nucleotide would be read two or three times. **Figure 21-5** compares a nonoverlapping code with an overlapping code in which the reading frame advances one nucleotide at a time. With such an overlapping code, the insertion or deletion of a single base pair in the gene would lead to the insertion or deletion of one amino acid at one point in the polypeptide and would change several adjacent amino acids, but it would not affect the reading frame of the remainder of the gene. This means that if the genetic code were overlapping, Crick and Brenner would not have observed their frameshift mutations. Thus, their results clearly indicated the nonoverlapping nature of the code: Each nucleotide is a part of one, and only one, triplet.

Interestingly, although the genetic code is always translated in a nonoverlapping way, there are cases where a particular segment of DNA is translated in more than one reading frame. For example, certain viruses with very small genomes have overlapping genes, as was first discovered in 1977 for phage ƒX174. In this phage's DNA, one gene is completely embedded within another gene, and, to complicate matters further, a third gene overlaps them both! The three genes are translated in different reading frames. Other instances of overlapping genes are found in bacteria, where some genes overlap by a few nucleotides at their boundaries.

Messenger RNA Guides the Synthesis of Polypeptide Chains

After the publication of Crick and Brenner's historic findings in 1961, it took only five years for the meaning of each of the 64 triplets in the genetic code to be elucidated. Before we look at how that was done, let us first describe the role of RNA in the coding system. As we usually describe it, the genetic code refers not to the order of nucleotides in double-stranded DNA but to their order in the single-stranded mRNA molecules that actually direct protein synthesis. As indicated at the top of Figure 21-5, mRNA molecules are transcribed from DNA using a base-pairing mechanism similar to DNA replication, with two significant differences.

1. In contrast to DNA replication, where both DNA strands are copied, only one of the two DNA strands—the **template strand**—serves as a template for mRNA formation during transcription. The nontemplate DNA strand, although not directly involved in transcription, is by convention called the **coding strand** because it is similar in sequence to the single-stranded mRNA molecules that carry the coded message.

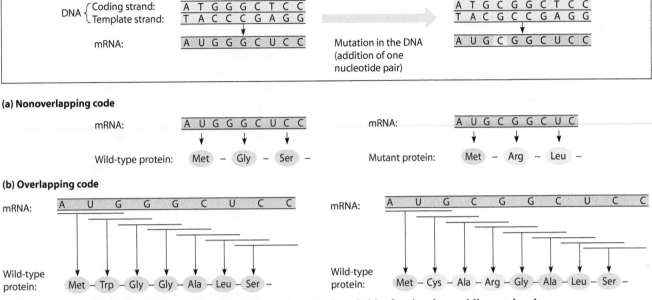

(a) Nonoverlapping code

(b) Overlapping code

FIGURE 21-5 Effect of Inserting a Single Base Pair on Proteins Encoded by Overlapping and Nonoverlapping Genetic Codes. One strand of the DNA duplex at the top, called the *template strand*, is transcribed into the nine-nucleotide segment of mRNA shown, according to the same base-pairing rules used in DNA replication, except the base U is used in RNA in place of T. (The complementary DNA strand, with a sequence essentially identical to that of the mRNA, is called the *coding strand*.) **(a)** With a nonoverlapping code, the reading frame advances three nucleotides at a time, and this mRNA segment is therefore read as three successive triplets, coding for the amino acids methionine, glycine, and serine. (See Figure 21-6 for amino acid coding rules.) If the DNA duplex is mutated by insertion of a single base pair (the yellow-shaded CG pair in the top box), the mRNA will have an additional nucleotide. This insertion alters the reading frame beyond that point, so the remainder of the mRNA is read incorrectly and all amino acids are wrong. In the example shown, the insertion occurs near the beginning of the message, and the only similarity between the wild-type protein and the mutant protein is the first amino acid (methionine). **(b)** In one type of overlapping code, the reading frame advances only one nucleotide at a time. The wild-type protein will therefore contain three times as many amino acids as would a protein generated from the same mRNA using a nonoverlapping code. Insertion of a single base pair in the DNA again results in an mRNA molecule with one extra nucleotide. However, in this case the effect of the insertion on the protein is modest; two amino acids in the wild-type protein are replaced by three different amino acids in the mutant protein, but the remainder of the protein is normal. The frameshift mutations that Crick and Brenner found in their studies with the mutagen proflavin would not have been observed if the genetic code were overlapping. Accordingly, their data indicated the code to be nonoverlapping.

2. The mechanism used to copy sequence information from a DNA template strand to a complementary molecule of RNA utilizes the same base-pairing rules as DNA replication, with the single exception that the base uracil (U) is employed in RNA where the base thymine (T) would have been incorporated into DNA. This substitution is permitted because U and T can both form hydrogen bonds with the base A. During DNA replication the base A pairs with T, whereas in transcription the base A pairs with U. Hence the sequence of an mRNA molecule is not exactly the same as the DNA coding strand, in that mRNA contains the base U anywhere the coding DNA strand has the base T.

How do we know that mRNA molecules, produced by this transcription process, are responsible for directing the order in which amino acids are linked together during protein synthesis? This relationship was first demonstrated experimentally in 1961 by Marshall Nirenberg and J. Heinrich Matthei, who pioneered the use of *cell-free*

systems for studying protein synthesis. In such systems, protein synthesis can be studied outside living cells by mixing together isolated ribosomes, amino acids, an energy source, and an extract containing soluble components of the cytoplasm. Nirenberg and Matthei found that adding RNA to cell-free systems increased the rate of protein synthesis, raising the question of whether the added RNA molecules were functioning as messages that determined the amino acid sequences of the proteins being manufactured. To address this question, they decided to add synthetic RNA molecules of known base composition to the cell-free system to see if such RNA molecules would influence the type of protein being made.

Their initial experiments took advantage of an enzyme called *polynucleotide phosphorylase*, which can be used to make synthetic RNA molecules of predictable base composition. Unlike the enzymes involved in cellular transcription, polynucleotide phosphorylase does not require a template but simply assembles available nucleotides randomly into a linear chain. If only one or two of the four ribonucleotides (ATP, GTP, CTP, and

UTP) are provided, the enzyme will synthesize RNA molecules with a restricted base composition. The simplest RNA molecule results when a single kind of nucleotide is used because the only possible product is an RNA *homopolymer*—that is, a polymer consisting of a single repeating nucleotide. For example, when polynucleotide phosphorylase is incubated with UTP as the sole substrate, the product is a homopolymer of uracil, called poly(U). When Nirenberg and Matthei added poly(U) to a cell-free protein-synthesizing system, they observed a marked increase in the incorporation of one particular amino acid, phenylalanine, into polypeptide chains. Synthetic RNA molecules containing bases other than uracil did not stimulate phenylalanine incorporation, whereas poly(U) enhanced the incorporation of only phenylalanine.

From these observations, Nirenberg and Matthei concluded that poly(U) directs the synthesis of polypeptide chains consisting solely of phenylalanine. This observation represented a crucial milestone in the development of the messenger RNA concept, for it was the first demonstration that the base sequence of an RNA molecule determines the order in which amino acids are linked together during protein synthesis.

The Codon Dictionary Was Established Using Synthetic RNA Polymers and Triplets

Once it had been shown that RNA functions as a messenger that guides the process of protein synthesis, the exact nature of the triplet coding system could be elucidated. Nucleotide triplets in mRNA, called **codons,** are the actual coding units read by the translational machinery during protein synthesis. The four bases present in RNA are the purines adenine (A) and guanine (G) and the pyrimidines cytosine (C) and uracil (U), so the 64 triplet codons consist of all 64 possible combinations of these four "letters" taken three at a time. And since mRNA molecules are synthesized in the $5' \rightarrow 3'$ direction (like DNA) and are translated starting at the $5'$ end, the 64 codons by convention are always written in the $5' \rightarrow 3'$ order.

These triplet codons in mRNA determine the amino acids that will be incorporated during protein synthesis, but which amino acid does each of the 64 triplets code for? The discovery that poly(U) directs the incorporation of phenylalanine during protein synthesis allowed Nirenberg and Matthei to make the first codon assignment: The triplet UUU in mRNA must code for the amino acid phenylalanine. Subsequent studies on the coding properties of other synthetic homopolymers, such as poly(A) and poly(C), quickly revealed that AAA codes for lysine and CCC codes for proline. (Because of unexpected structural complications, poly(G) is not a good messenger and was not tested.)

After the homopolymers had been tested, polynucleotide phosphorylase was employed to create *copolymers* containing a mixture of two nucleotides. For example, incubating polynucleotide phosphorylase with the precur-

sors CTP and ATP yielded a copolymer built from C's and A's but in no predictable order. Such a copolymer contains a random mixture of eight different codons: CCC, CCA, CAC, ACC, AAC, ACA, CAA, and AAA. When this copolymer was used to direct protein synthesis, the resulting polypeptides incorporated 6 of the 20 possible amino acids. It was already known from the homopolymer studies that two of these amino acids were specified by the codons CCC and AAA, but the codons for the other four amino acids could not be unambiguously assigned.

Further progress depended on an alternative means of codon assignment devised by Nirenberg's group. Instead of using long polymers, they synthesized 64 very short RNA molecules, each only three nucleotides long. They then conducted studies to see which amino acid bound to the ribosome in response to each of these triplets. (In such experiments, tRNA molecules actually carry the amino acids to the ribosome.) With this approach, they were able to determine most of the codon assignments.

Meanwhile, a refined method of polymer synthesis had been devised in the laboratory of H. Gobind Khorana. Khorana's approach was similar to that of Nirenberg and Matthei but with the important difference that the polymers he synthesized had defined sequences. Thus, he could produce a synthetic mRNA molecule with the strictly alternating sequence UAUA.... Such an RNA copolymer has only two codons, UAU and AUA, and they alternate in strict sequence. When Khorana added this particular RNA to a cell-free protein-synthesizing system, a polypeptide containing only tyrosine and isoleucine was produced. Khorana was therefore able to narrow the possible codon assignments for UAU and AUA to these two particular amino acids. When the results obtained with such synthetic polymers were combined with the findings of Nirenberg's binding studies, most of the codons could be assigned unambiguously.

Of the 64 Possible Codons in Messenger RNA, 61 Code for Amino Acids

By 1966, just five years after the first codon was identified, the approaches we have just described allowed all 64 codons to be assigned—that is, the entire genetic code had been worked out, as shown in **Figure 21-6.** The elucidation of the code confirmed several properties that had been deduced earlier from indirect evidence. All 64 codons are in fact used in the translation of mRNA. Sixty-one of the codons specify the addition of specific amino acids to the growing polypeptide, and one of these (AUG) also plays a prominent role as a **start codon** that initiates the process of protein synthesis. The remaining three codons (UAA, UAG, and UGA) are **stop codons** that instruct the cell to terminate synthesis of the polypeptide chain.

It is clear from examining Figure 21-6 that the genetic code is *unambiguous:* Every codon has one and only one meaning. The figure also shows the *degenerate* nature of the code—that is, many of the amino acids are specified by

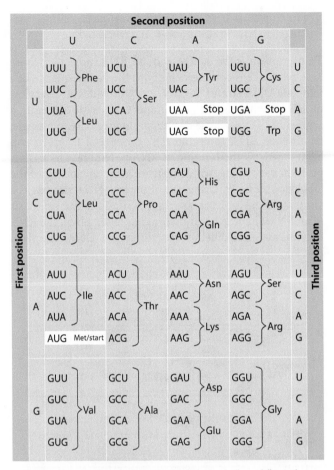

Second position

	U	C	A	G	
U	UUU ⎤ Phe / UUC ⎦ / UUA ⎤ Leu / UUG ⎦	UCU ⎤ / UCC / UCA ⎥ Ser / UCG ⎦	UAU ⎤ Tyr / UAC ⎦ / UAA Stop / UAG Stop	UGU ⎤ Cys / UGC ⎦ / UGA Stop / UGG Trp	U / C / A / G
C	CUU ⎤ / CUC / CUA ⎥ Leu / CUG ⎦	CCU ⎤ / CCC / CCA ⎥ Pro / CCG ⎦	CAU ⎤ His / CAC ⎦ / CAA ⎤ Gln / CAG ⎦	CGU ⎤ / CGC / CGA ⎥ Arg / CGG ⎦	U / C / A / G
A	AUU ⎤ / AUC ⎥ Ile / AUA ⎦ / AUG Met/start	ACU ⎤ / ACC / ACA ⎥ Thr / ACG ⎦	AAU ⎤ Asn / AAC ⎦ / AAA ⎤ Lys / AAG ⎦	AGU ⎤ Ser / AGC ⎦ / AGA ⎤ Arg / AGG ⎦	U / C / A / G
G	GUU ⎤ / GUC / GUA ⎥ Val / GUG ⎦	GCU ⎤ / GCC / GCA ⎥ Ala / GCG ⎦	GAU ⎤ Asp / GAC ⎦ / GAA ⎤ Glu / GAG ⎦	GGU ⎤ / GGC / GGA ⎥ Gly / GGG ⎦	U / C / A / G

First position (left edge) / **Third position** (right edge)

FIGURE 21-6 The Genetic Code. The code "words" are three-letter codons present in the nucleotide sequence of mRNA, as read in the 5′ → 3′ direction. Letters represent the nucleotide bases uracil (U), cytosine (C), adenine (A), and guanine (G). Each codon specifies either an amino acid or a stop signal. To decode a codon, read down the left edge for the first letter, then across the grid for the second letter, and then down the right edge for the third letter. For example, the codon AUG represents methionine. (As we will see in Chapter 22, AUG is also a start signal.)

The validity of the codon assignments summarized in Figure 21-6 has been confirmed by analyzing the amino acid sequences of mutant proteins. For example, we learned earlier in the chapter that sickle-cell hemoglobin differs from normal hemoglobin at a single amino acid position, where valine is substituted for glutamic acid. The genetic code table reveals that glutamic acid may be encoded by either GAA or GAG. Whichever triplet is employed, a single base change could create a codon for valine. For example, GAA might have been changed to GUA, or GAG might have been changed to GUG. In either case, a glutamic acid codon would be converted into a valine codon. Many other mutant proteins have been examined in a similar way. In nearly all cases, the amino acid substitutions are consistent with a single base change in a triplet codon.

The Genetic Code Is (Nearly) Universal

A final property of the genetic code worth noting is its near universality. Except for a few cases, all organisms studied so far—prokaryotes as well as eukaryotes—use the same basic genetic code. Even viruses, though they are nonliving entities, employ this same code. In other words, the 64 codons almost always stand for the same amino acids or stop signals specified in Figure 21-6, suggesting that this coding system was established early in the history of life on Earth and has remained largely unchanged over billions of years of evolution.

However, several exceptions to the standard genetic code do exist, most notably in mitochondria and in a few bacteria and other unicellular organisms. In the case of mitochondria, which contain their own DNA and carry out both transcription and translation, the genetic code can differ in several ways from the standard code. One difference involves the codon UGA, which is a stop codon in the standard code but is translated as tryptophan in mammalian and yeast mitochondria. Conversely, AGA is a stop codon in mammalian mitochondria, even though in most other systems (including yeast mitochondria) it codes for arginine. Such anomalies result from alterations in the properties of transfer RNA (tRNA) molecules found in mitochondria. As you will learn in the next chapter, tRNA molecules play a key role in the genetic code because they recognize codons in mRNA and bring the appropriate amino acid to each codon during the process of protein synthesis. Differences in the types of tRNA molecules present in mitochondria appear to underlie the ability to read codons such as UAG and AGA differently than in the standard genetic code.

Some bacteria also employ a few codons in a nonstandard way, as do the nuclear genomes of certain protozoa and fungi. For example, the fungus *Candida* produces an unusual tRNA that brings serine to mRNAs containing the codon CUG rather than bringing the normally expected amino acid, leucine. In an especially interesting case, observed in organisms as diverse as bacteria and mammals, a variation of the genetic code allows the incorporation of

more than one codon. There are, for example, two codons for histidine (His), four for threonine (Thr), and six for leucine (Leu). Although degeneracy may sound wasteful, it serves a useful function in enhancing the adaptability of the coding system. As we noted earlier, if there were only one codon for each of the 20 amino acids, then any mutation that created one of the remaining 44 codons would terminate synthesis of the growing polypeptide chain at that point. But with a degenerate code, most mutations simply cause codon changes that alter the specified amino acid. The change in a protein's behavior that results from a single amino acid alteration is often quite small, and in some cases may even be advantageous. Moreover, mutations in the third base of a codon frequently do not change the specified amino acid at all, as you can see in Figure 21-6. For example, a mutation that changes the codon ACU to ACC, ACA, or ACG does not alter the corresponding amino acid, which is threonine (Thr) in all four cases.

a 21st amino acid, *selenocysteine*, in which the sulfur atom of cysteine is replaced by an atom of selenium. In mRNAs coding for the few rare proteins that contain selenocysteine, the meaning of a UGA codon is changed from a stop codon to a codon specifying selenocysteine. In such cases, folding of the mRNA molecule causes specific UGA codons to bind to a special tRNA carrying selenocysteine, rather than functioning as stop codons that terminate protein synthesis. A similar mechanism permits another stop codon, UAG, to specify incorporation of a 22nd amino acid, *pyrrolysine*.

Transcription in Bacterial Cells

Now that you have been introduced to the genetic code that governs the relationship between nucleotide sequences in DNA and the amino acid sequences of protein molecules, we can discuss the specific steps involved in the flow of genetic information from DNA to protein. The first stage in this process is the transcription of a nucleotide sequence in DNA into a sequence of nucleotides in RNA. RNA is chemically similar to DNA, but it contains ribose instead of deoxyribose as its sugar, has the base uracil (U) in place of thymine (T), and is usually single stranded. As in other areas of molecular genetics, the fundamental principles of RNA synthesis were first elucidated in bacteria, where the molecules and mechanisms are relatively simple. For that reason, we will start with transcription in bacteria.

Transcription Is Catalyzed by RNA Polymerase, Which Synthesizes RNA Using DNA as a Template

Transcription of DNA is carried out by the enzyme **RNA polymerase,** which catalyzes the synthesis of RNA using DNA as a template. Bacterial cells have a single kind of RNA polymerase that synthesizes all three major classes of RNA—mRNA, tRNA, and rRNA. The enzymes from different bacteria are quite similar, and the RNA polymerase from *Escherichia coli* has been especially well characterized. It is a large protein consisting of two α subunits, two β subunits that differ enough to be identified as β and β', and a dissociable subunit called the **sigma (σ) factor.** Although the *core enzyme* lacking the sigma subunit is competent to carry out RNA synthesis, the *holoenzyme* (complete enzyme containing all of its subunits) is required to ensure initiation at the proper sites within a DNA molecule. The sigma subunit plays a critical role in this process by promoting the binding of RNA polymerase to specific DNA sequences, called *promoters,* found at the beginnings of genes. Bacteria contain a variety of different sigma factors that selectively initiate the transcription of specific categories of genes. After the sigma factor guides RNA polymerase to an appropriate promoter site, the sigma factor is usually released during the early stages of transcription.

Transcription Involves Four Stages: Binding, Initiation, Elongation, and Termination

Transcription is the synthesis of an RNA molecule whose base sequence is complementary to the base sequence of a template DNA strand. **Figure 21-7** provides an overview of RNA synthesis from a single **transcription unit,** a segment of DNA whose transcription gives rise to a single, continuous RNA molecule. The process of transcription begins with ❶ the binding of RNA polymerase to a DNA promoter sequence, which triggers local unwinding of the DNA double helix. Using one of the two DNA strands as a template, RNA polymerase then ❷ initiates the synthesis of an RNA chain. After initiation has taken place, the RNA polymerase molecule moves along the DNA template,

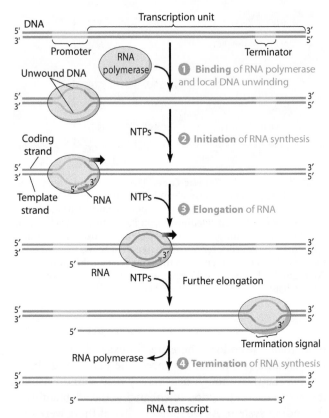

FIGURE 21-7 An Overview of Transcription. Transcription of DNA occurs in four main stages: ❶ binding of RNA polymerase to DNA at a promoter, ❷ initiation of transcription on the template DNA strand, ❸ subsequent elongation of the RNA chain, and ❹ eventual termination of transcription, accompanied by the release of RNA polymerase and the completed RNA product from the DNA template. RNA polymerase moves along the template strand of the DNA in the $3' \rightarrow 5'$ direction, and the RNA molecule grows in the $5' \rightarrow 3'$ direction. The supercoiling generated by DNA unwinding ahead of the moving RNA polymerase is relieved through the action of topoisomerases (not shown). The general scheme illustrated here holds for transcription in all organisms. NTPs (ribonucleoside triphosphate molecules) = ATP, GTP, CTP, and UTP.

unwinding the double helix and ❸ elongating the RNA chain as it goes. During this process, the enzyme catalyzes the polymerization of nucleotides in an order determined by their base pairing with the DNA template strand. Eventually the enzyme transcribes a special base sequence called a *termination signal*, which ❹ terminates RNA synthesis and causes the completed RNA molecule to be released and RNA polymerase to dissociate from the DNA template.

Although transcription is a complicated process, it can be thought of in four distinct stages: binding, initiation, elongation, and termination. We will now look at each stage in detail, as it occurs in *E. coli*. You can refer back to Figure 21-7 throughout this discussion to see how each step fits into the overall process.

Binding of RNA Polymerase to a Promoter Sequence. The first step in RNA synthesis is the *binding* of RNA polymerase to a DNA **promoter site**—a specific sequence of several dozen base pairs that determines where RNA synthesis starts and which DNA strand is to serve as the template strand. Each transcription unit has a promoter site located near the beginning of the DNA sequence to be transcribed. By convention, promoter sequences are described in the 5′→3′ direction on the coding strand, which is the strand that lies opposite the template strand. The terms **upstream** and **downstream** are used to refer to DNA sequences located toward the 5′ or 3′ end of the coding strand, respectively. Therefore the region where the promoter is located is said to be upstream of the transcribed sequence. Binding of RNA polymerase to the promoter is mediated by the sigma subunit and leads to unwinding of a short stretch of DNA in the area where transcription will begin, exposing the two separate strands of the double helix.

Promoter sequences were initially identified by *DNA footprinting* and *electrophoretic mobility shift assays,* techniques for locating the DNA region to which a DNA-binding protein has become bound (**Box 21B**). More recently, *chromatin immunoprecipitation (ChIP)* has been used to assess binding of proteins to specific genomic DNA sequences in eukaryotes. Sequences essential to the promoter region have also been identified by deleting or adding specific base sequences to cloned genes and then testing the ability of the altered DNA to be transcribed by RNA polymerase. Such techniques have revealed that DNA promoter sites differ significantly among bacterial transcription units. How, then, does a single kind of RNA polymerase recognize them all? Enzyme recognition and binding, it turns out, depend only on several very short sequences located at specific positions within each promoter site. The identities of the nucleotides making up the rest of the promoter are irrelevant for this purpose.

Figure 21-8 highlights the essential sequences in a typical bacterial promoter. The point where transcription will begin, called the *startpoint,* is almost always a purine and often an adenine. Approximately 10 bases upstream of the startpoint is the six-nucleotide sequence TATAAT, called the *−10 sequence* or the *Pribnow box,* after its discoverer. By convention, the nucleotides are numbered from the startpoint (+1), with positive numbers to the right (downstream) and negative ones to the left (upstream). The −1 nucleotide is immediately upstream of the startpoint (there is no "0"). At or near the −35 position is the six-nucleotide sequence TTGACA, called the *−35 sequence.*

The −10 and the −35 sequences (and their positions relative to the startpoint) have been conserved during evolution, but they are not identical in all bacterial promoters or even in all the promoters in a single genome. For example, the −10 sequence in the promoter for one of the *E. coli* tRNA genes is TATGAT, whereas the −10 sequence for a group of genes needed for lactose breakdown in the same organism is TATGTT, and the sequence given in Figure 21-8 is TATAAT. The particular promoter sequences shown in the figure are **consensus sequences,** which consist of the most common nucleotides at each position within a given sequence. Mutations that cause significant deviations from the consensus sequences tend

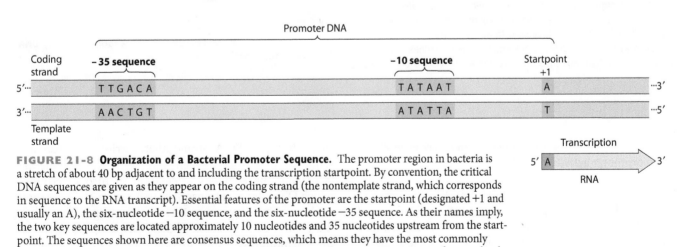

FIGURE 21-8 Organization of a Bacterial Promoter Sequence. The promoter region in bacteria is a stretch of about 40 bp adjacent to and including the transcription startpoint. By convention, the critical DNA sequences are given as they appear on the coding strand (the nontemplate strand, which corresponds in sequence to the RNA transcript). Essential features of the promoter are the startpoint (designated +1 and usually an A), the six-nucleotide −10 sequence, and the six-nucleotide −35 sequence. As their names imply, the two key sequences are located approximately 10 nucleotides and 35 nucleotides upstream from the startpoint. The sequences shown here are consensus sequences, which means they have the most commonly found base at each position. The numbers of nucleotides separating the consensus sequences from each other and from the startpoint are important for promoter function, but the identity of these nucleotides is not.

The initiation of transcription depends on the interactions of proteins with specific DNA sequences. Thus, the researcher seeking to understand transcription needs to know about transcriptional proteins and the DNA sequences they bind to.

DNA footprinting is one technique that has been used to locate the DNA sites where specific proteins attach. The underlying principle is that the binding of a protein to a particular DNA sequence should protect that sequence from degradation by enzymes or chemicals. A version of footprinting, outlined in **Figure 21B-1**, employs a DNA-degrading enzyme called DNase I, which attacks the bonds between nucleotides more or less at random. In this example, the starting material is a DNA fragment that has been labeled at its 5' end with radioactive phosphate (indicated with red stars).

In step ❶, a sample of the radioactive DNA is first mixed with the DNA-binding protein under study. Another sample, without the added protein, serves as the control. ❷ Both samples are briefly incubated with a low concentration of DNase I—conditions ensuring that most of the DNA molecules will be cleaved only once. The arrowheads indicate possible cleavage sites in the DNA. ❸ The two incubation mixtures are submitted to electrophoresis and visualized by autoradiography. The control lane (on the right) has nine bands because every possible cleavage site has been cut. However, the other lane (on the left) is missing some of the bands because the protein that was bound to the DNA protected some of the cleavage sites during DNase treatment. The blank region in this lane is the "footprint" that identifies the location and length of the DNA sequence in contact with the DNA-binding protein.

Along with DNA footprinting, a technique known as an *electrophoretic mobility shift assay (EMSA)* (also called a *gel shift assay*) has been used to confirm DNA-protein binding. In this approach, a specific DNA sequence is mixed with a DNA-binding protein or a cellular extract containing such a protein. If the protein binds to the DNA sequence, it will result in the DNA sequence moving more slowly when subjected to gel electrophoresis. This shift in mobility indicates that the protein binds to the DNA sequences of interest.

A newer approach, called the *chromatin immunoprecipitation (ChIP) assay*, is now widely used to study protein-binding sites in the DNA of eukaryotic chromatin. In the ChIP assay, cells are first treated with formaldehyde to generate stable crosslinks between proteins and the DNA sites they are bound to. Next, the cells are disrupted to shear chromatin into small fragments, and the chromatin fragments are treated with an antibody directed against a protein of interest. DNA fragments bound to that particular protein will be precipitated by the antibody, and the sequence of the precipitated DNA can then be analyzed.

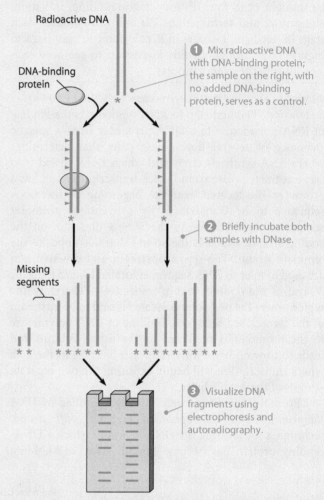

FIGURE 21B-1 DNase Footprinting as a Tool to Identify DNA Sites That Bind Specific Proteins.

to interfere with promoter function and may even eliminate promoter activity entirely.

Initiation of RNA Synthesis. Once an RNA polymerase molecule has bound to a promoter site and locally unwound the DNA double helix, *initiation* of RNA synthesis can take place. One of the two exposed segments of single-stranded DNA serves as the template for the synthesis of RNA, using incoming ribonucleoside triphosphate molecules (NTPs) as substrates. The DNA strand that carries the promoter sequence determines which way the RNA polymerase faces, and the enzyme's orientation in turn determines which DNA strand it transcribes (see Figure 21-7). As soon as the first two incoming NTPs are hydrogen-bonded to the complementary bases of the DNA template strand at the startpoint, RNA polymerase catalyzes the formation of a phosphodiester bond between the 3'-hydroxyl group of the first NTP and the 5'-phosphate of the second,

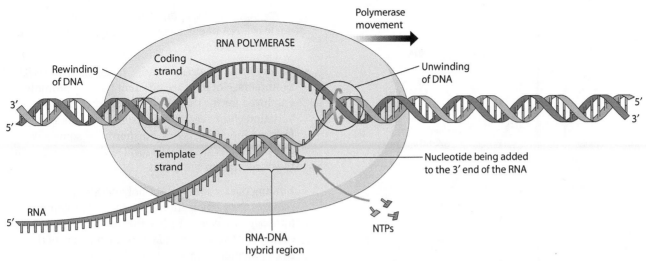

FIGURE 21-9 Closeup of a Bacterial Elongation Complex. During elongation, RNA polymerase binds to about 30 bp of DNA. (Recall that each complete turn of the DNA double helix is about 10 bp.) At any given moment, about 18 bp of DNA are unwound, and the most recently synthesized RNA is still hydrogen-bonded to the DNA, forming a short RNA–DNA hybrid about 8–9 bp long. The total length of growing RNA bound to the enzyme and/or DNA is about 25 nucleotides.

accompanied by the release of pyrophosphate (PP$_i$). The polymerase then advances along the template strand as additional nucleotides are added one by one, the 5'-phosphate of each new nucleotide joining to the 3'-hydroxyl group of the growing RNA chain, until the chain is about nine nucleotides long. At this point the sigma factor generally detaches from the RNA polymerase molecule, and the initiation stage is complete.

Elongation of the RNA Chain. Chain *elongation* (**Figure 21-9**) now continues as RNA polymerase moves along the DNA molecule, untwisting the helix bit by bit and adding one complementary nucleotide at a time to the growing RNA chain. The enzyme moves along the template DNA strand from the 3' toward the 5' end. Because complementary base pairing between the DNA template strand and the newly forming RNA chain is antiparallel, *the RNA strand is elongated in the 5' → 3' direction* as each successive nucleotide is added to the 3' end of the growing chain. (This is the same direction in which DNA strands are synthesized during DNA replication.) As the RNA chain grows, the most recently added nucleotides remain base-paired with the DNA template strand, forming a short RNA–DNA hybrid about 8–9 bp long. As the polymerase moves forward, the DNA ahead of the enzyme is unwound to permit the RNA–DNA hybrid to form. At the same time, the DNA behind the moving enzyme is rewound into a double helix. The supercoiling that would otherwise be generated by this unwinding and rewinding is released through the action of topoisomerases, just as in DNA replication (page 562).

Like DNA polymerase, RNA polymerases possess a 3' → 5' exonuclease activity that might in theory allow improperly base-paired nucleotides to be removed from the 3' end of a growing RNA chain after an incorrect base

has been incorporated. However, this intrinsic exonuclease activity is relatively weak, and an alternative mechanism for correcting errors is used instead. When a noncomplementary nucleotide is incorporated into a growing RNA chain by mistake, the RNA polymerase backs up slightly, and the noncomplementary nucleotide participates in catalyzing its own removal along with removal of the previously incorporated nucleotide. Such *RNA proofreading* appears to be sufficient for correcting mistakes that arise during transcription, especially since occasional errors in RNA molecules are not as critical as errors in DNA replication because numerous RNA copies are transcribed from each gene; hence a few inaccurate copies can be tolerated. In contrast, only one copy of each DNA molecule is made when DNA is replicated prior to cell division. Since each newly forming cell receives only one set of DNA molecules, it is crucial that the copying mechanism used in DNA replication be extremely accurate.

Termination of RNA Synthesis. Elongation of the growing RNA chain proceeds until RNA polymerase copies a special sequence, called a **termination signal,** that triggers the end of transcription. In bacteria, two classes of termination signals can be distinguished based on whether they require the participation of a protein called **rho (ρ) factor.** RNA molecules terminated without the aid of the rho factor contain a short GC-rich sequence followed by several U residues near their 3' end (**Figure 21-10**). Since GC base pairs are held together by three hydrogen bonds, whereas AU base pairs are joined by only two hydrogen bonds, this configuration promotes termination in the following way: First, the GC region contains sequences that are complementary to each other, causing the RNA to spontaneously fold into a **hairpin loop** that tends to pull the RNA molecule away from the DNA.

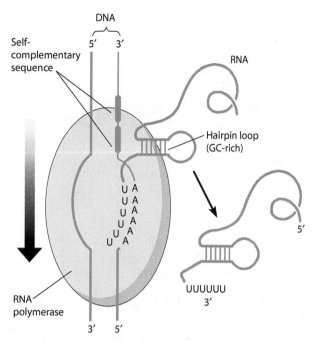

FIGURE 21-10 Termination of Transcription in Bacterial Genes That Do Not Require the Rho Termination Factor. A short self-complementary sequence near the end of the gene allows the newly formed RNA molecule to form a hairpin loop structure that helps dissociate the RNA from the DNA template.

Then the weaker bonds between the sequence of U residues and the DNA template are broken, releasing the newly formed RNA molecule.

In contrast, RNA molecules that do not form a GC-rich hairpin loop require participation of the rho factor for termination. Genes coding for such RNAs were first discovered in experiments in which purified DNA obtained from bacteriophage λ was transcribed with purified RNA polymerase. Some genes were found to be transcribed into RNA molecules that are longer than the RNAs produced in living cells, suggesting that transcription was not terminating properly. This problem could be corrected by adding rho factor, which binds to specific termination sequences 50–90 bases long located near the 3′ end of newly forming RNA molecules. The rho factor acts as an ATP-dependent unwinding enzyme, moving along the newly forming RNA molecule toward its 3′ end and unwinding it from the DNA template as it proceeds.

Whether termination depends on rho or on the formation of a hairpin loop, it results in the release of the newly transcribed RNA molecule and of the core RNA polymerase. The core polymerase can then bind sigma factor again and reinitiate RNA synthesis at another promoter.

Transcription in Eukaryotic Cells

Transcription in eukaryotic cells involves the same four stages described in Figure 21-7, but the process in eukaryotes is more complicated than that in bacteria. The main differences are as follows:

- *Three different RNA polymerases* transcribe the nuclear DNA of eukaryotes. Each synthesizes one or more classes of RNA.

- *Eukaryotic promoters* are more varied than bacterial promoters. Not only are different types of promoters employed for the three polymerases, but there is great variation within each type—especially among the ones for protein-coding genes. Furthermore, some eukaryotic promoters are actually located *downstream* from the transcription startpoint.

- Binding of eukaryotic RNA polymerases to DNA requires the participation of additional proteins, called *transcription factors*. Unlike the bacterial sigma factor, eukaryotic transcription factors are not part of the RNA polymerase molecule. Rather, some of them must bind to DNA *before* RNA polymerase can bind to the promoter and initiate transcription. Thus, transcription factors, rather than RNA polymerase itself, determine the specificity of transcription in eukaryotes. In this chapter, we limit our discussion to the class of factors that are essential for the transcription of all genes transcribed by an RNA polymerase. We defer discussion of the regulatory class of transcription factors, which selectively act on specific genes.

- *Protein–protein interactions* play a prominent role in the first stage of eukaryotic transcription. Although some transcription factors bind directly to DNA, many attach to other proteins—either to other transcription factors or to RNA polymerase itself.

- *RNA cleavage* is more important than the site where transcription is terminated in determining the location of the 3′ end of the RNA product.

- Newly forming eukaryotic RNA molecules typically undergo extensive *RNA processing* (chemical modification) both during and, to a larger extent, after transcription.

We will now examine these various aspects of eukaryotic transcription, starting with the existence of multiple forms of RNA polymerase.

RNA Polymerases I, II, and III Carry Out Transcription in the Eukaryotic Nucleus

Table 21-1 summarizes some properties of the three RNA polymerases that function in the nucleus of the eukaryotic cell, along with two other polymerases found in mitochondria and chloroplasts. The nuclear enzymes are designated RNA polymerases I, II, and III. As the table indicates, these enzymes differ in their location within the nucleus and in the kinds of RNA they synthesize. The nuclear RNA polymerases also differ in their sensitivity to various inhibitors, such as α-*amanitin*, a deadly toxin produced by the mushroom *Amanita phalloides* (the "death

Table 21-1 Properties of Eukaryotic RNA Polymerases

RNA Polymerase	Location	Main Products	α-Amanitin Sensitivity
I	Nucleolus	Precursor for 28S rRNA, 18S rRNA, and 5.8S rRNA	Resistant
II	Nucleoplasm	Pre-mRNA, most snRNA, and microRNA	Very sensitive
III	Nucleoplasm	Pre-tRNA, 5S rRNA, and other small RNAs	Moderately sensitive*
Mitochondrial	Mitochondrion	Mitochondrial RNA	Resistant
Chloroplast	Chloroplast	Chloroplast RNA	Resistant

*In mammals.

cap" fungus; the F-actin binding drug phalloidin, introduced in Chapter 15, also comes from this organism).

RNA polymerase I resides in the nucleolus and is responsible for synthesizing an RNA molecule that serves as a precursor for three of the four types of rRNA found in eukaryotic ribosomes (28S rRNA, 18S rRNA, and 5.8S rRNA). This enzyme is not sensitive to α-amanitin. Its association with the nucleolus is understandable, for the nucleolus is the site of ribosomal RNA synthesis and ribosomal subunit assembly (page 543).

RNA polymerase II is found in the nucleoplasm and synthesizes precursors to mRNA, the class of RNA molecules that code for proteins. Rather than being diffusely distributed throughout the nucleus, active molecules of polymerase II are located in discrete clusters, called *transcription factories,* that represent sites where active genes come together to be transcribed. In addition to producing mRNA precursors, RNA polymerase II synthesizes most of the *snRNAs*—small nuclear RNAs involved in posttranscriptional RNA processing—and the *microRNAs,* which regulate the translation and stability of specific mRNAs and, to a lesser extent, control the transcription of certain genes. Polymerase II is responsible for producing the greatest variety of RNA molecules and is extremely sensitive to α-amanitin, which explains the toxicity of this compound to humans and other animals.

RNA polymerase II differs from polymerases I and III at its C terminus, where it has extra amino acids. The C terminus of RNA polymerase II can be phosphorylated at a variety of locations, to produce what is sometimes called a phosphorylation "code." This "code" dramatically affects the functions of polymerase II, and correlates with where the enzyme is located along the DNA as it continues transcription. As a result, this most versatile of the RNA polymerases is also the most tightly regulated.

RNA polymerase III is also a nucleoplasmic enzyme, but it synthesizes a variety of small RNAs, including tRNA precursors and the smallest type of ribosomal RNA, 5S rRNA. Mammalian RNA polymerase III is sensitive to α-amanitin but only at higher levels of the toxin than are required to inhibit RNA polymerase II. (The comparable enzymes of some other eukaryotes, such as insects and yeasts, are insensitive to α-amanitin.)

Structurally, RNA polymerases I, II, and III are somewhat similar to each other as well as to bacterial core RNA polymerase. The three enzymes are all quite large, with multiple polypeptide subunits and molecular weights around 500,000. RNA polymerase II, for example, has more than ten subunits of at least eight different types. The three biggest subunits are evolutionarily related to the bacterial RNA polymerase subunits α, β, and β′. Three of the smaller subunits lack that relationship but are also found in RNA polymerases II and III. The RNA polymerases of mitochondria and chloroplasts resemble their bacterial counterparts closely, as you might expect from the probable origins of these organelles as endosymbiotic bacteria. Like bacterial RNA polymerase, the mitochondrial and chloroplast enzymes are resistant to α-amanitin.

Three Classes of Promoters Are Found in Eukaryotic Nuclear Genes, One for Each Type of RNA Polymerase

The promoters that eukaryotic RNA polymerases bind to are even more varied than bacterial promoters, but they can be grouped into three main categories, one for each type of polymerase. **Figure 21-11** shows examples of the three types of promoters.

The promoter used by RNA polymerase I—that is, the promoter of the transcription unit that produces the precursor for the three largest rRNAs—has two parts (Figure 21-11a). The part called the **core promoter**—defined as the smallest set of DNA sequences able to direct the accurate initiation of transcription by RNA polymerase—actually extends into the nucleotide sequence to be transcribed. The core promoter is sufficient for proper initiation of transcription, but transcription is made more efficient by the presence of an *upstream control element,* which for RNA polymerase I is a fairly long sequence similar (though not identical) to the core promoter. Attachment of transcription factors to both parts of the promoter facilitates the binding of RNA polymerase I to the core promoter and enables it to initiate transcription at the startpoint.

In the case of RNA polymerase II, at least four types of DNA sequences are involved in core promoter function (Figure 21-11b). These four elements are (1) a short **initiator (Inr)** sequence surrounding the transcription startpoint (which is often an A, as in bacteria); (2) the **TATA box,** which consists of a consensus sequence of

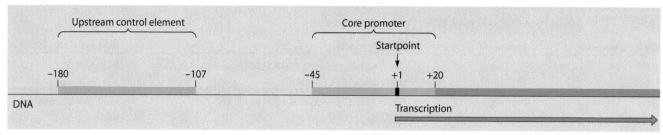

(a) Promoter for RNA polymerase I

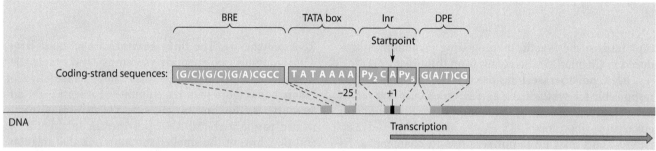

(b) Core promoter elements for RNA polymerase II

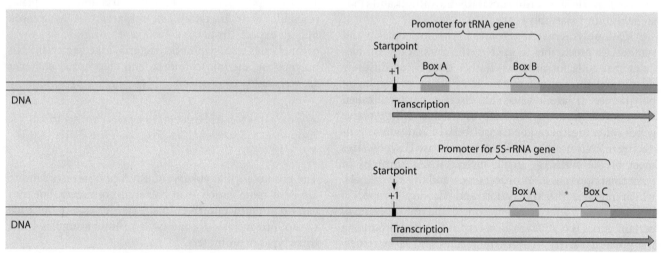

(c) Two types of promoters for RNA polymerase III

FIGURE 21-11 Examples of Eukaryotic Promoters For RNA Polymerases I, II, and III. **(a)** The promoter for RNA polymerase I has two parts, a core promoter surrounding the startpoint and an upstream control element. After the binding of appropriate transcription factors to both parts, the RNA polymerase binds to the core promoter. **(b)** The typical promoter for RNA polymerase II has a short initiator (Inr) sequence, consisting mostly of pyrimidines (Py), combined with either a TATA box or a downstream promoter element (DPE). Promoters containing a TATA box may also include a TFIIB recognition element (BRE) as part of the core promoter. **(c)** The promoters for RNA polymerase III vary in structure, but the ones for tRNA genes and 5S-rRNA genes are located entirely downstream of the startpoint, within the transcribed sequence. Boxes A, B, and C are DNA consensus sequences, each about 10 bp long. In tRNA genes, about 30–60 bp of DNA separate boxes A and B. In 5S-rRNA genes, about 10–30 bp separate boxes A and C.

TATA followed by two or three more A's, usually located about 25 nucleotides upstream from the startpoint; (3) the **TFIIB recognition element (BRE)** located slightly upstream of the TATA box; and (4) the **downstream promoter element (DPE)** located about 30 nucleotides downstream from the startpoint. These four elements are organized into two general types of core promoters: *TATA-driven promoters,* which contain an Inr sequence and a TATA box with or without an associated BRE, and *DPE-driven promoters,* which contain DPE and Inr sequences but no TATA box or BRE. Besides being found

in eukaryotes, TATA-driven promoters are also present in archaea, a key piece of evidence supporting the idea that in some ways, archaea resemble eukaryotes more closely than they resemble bacteria (page 76).

By itself, a core promoter (TATA-driven or DPE-driven) is capable of supporting only a *basal* (low) level of transcription. However, most protein-coding genes have additional short sequences further upstream—*upstream control elements*—that improve the promoter's efficiency. Some of these upstream elements are common to many different genes; examples include the *CAAT box* (consensus sequence GCCCAATCT in animals and yeasts) and the *GC box* (consensus sequence GGGCGG). The locations of these elements relative to a gene's startpoint vary from gene to gene. The elements within 100–200 nucleotides of the startpoint are often called *proximal control elements* to distinguish them from *enhancer* elements, which tend to be farther away and can even be located downstream of the gene. We will return to proximal control elements and enhancers.

The sequences important in promoter activity are often identified by deleting specific sequences from a cloned DNA molecule, which is then tested for its ability to serve as a template for gene transcription, either in a test tube or after introduction of the DNA into cultured cells. For example, when transcription of the gene for β-globin (the β chain of hemoglobin) is investigated in this way, deletion of either the TATA box or an upstream CAAT box reduces the rate of transcription at least tenfold.

In contrast to RNA polymerases I and II, the RNA polymerase III molecule uses promoters that are entirely *downstream* of the transcription unit's startpoint when transcribing genes for tRNAs and 5S rRNA. The promoters used by tRNA and 5S-rRNA genes are different, but in both cases the consensus sequences fall into two blocks of about 10 bp each (Figure 21-11c). The tRNA promoter has consensus sequences called *box A* and *box B*. The promoters for 5S-rRNA genes have box A (positioned farther from the startpoint than in tRNA-gene promoters) and another critical sequence, called *box C*. (Not shown in the figure is a third type of RNA polymerase III promoter, an upstream promoter that is used for the synthesis of other kinds of small RNA molecules.)

The promoters used by all the eukaryotic RNA polymerases must be recognized and bound by transcription factors before the RNA polymerase molecule can bind to DNA. We turn now to these transcription factors.

General Transcription Factors Are Involved in the Transcription of All Nuclear Genes

A **general transcription factor** is a protein that is always required for an RNA polymerase molecule to bind to its promoter and initiate RNA synthesis, regardless of the identity of the gene involved. Eukaryotes have many such transcription factors; their names usually include "TF" (for transcription factor), a roman numeral identifying the

polymerase they aid, and a capital letter that identifies each individual factor (for example, TFIIA, TFIIB, and so forth).

Using RNA polymerase II as an example, **Figure 21-12** illustrates the involvement of general transcription factors in the binding of RNA polymerase to a TATA-containing promoter site in DNA. General transcription

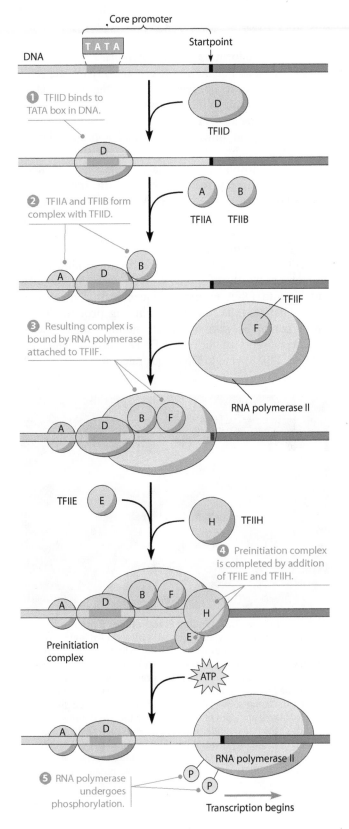

FIGURE 21-12 Role of General Transcription Factors in Binding RNA Polymerase II to DNA. This figure outlines the sequential binding of six general transcription factors (called TFII_, where _ is a letter identifying the particular factor) and RNA polymerase. After the final activation step involving ATP-dependent phosphorylation of the RNA polymerase molecule, the polymerase can initiate transcription. In intact chromatin, the efficient binding of general transcription factors and RNA polymerase to DNA requires the participation of additional regulatory proteins that open up chromatin structure and facilitate assembly of the preinitiation complex at specific genes.

Transcription in Eukaryotic Cells   **663**

factors bind to promoters in a defined order, starting with TFIID. Notice that while TFIID binds directly to a DNA sequence (the TATA box in this example or the DPE sequence in the case of DPE-driven promoters), the other transcription factors interact primarily with each other. Hence, protein-protein interactions play a crucial role in the binding stage of eukaryotic transcription. RNA polymerase II does not bind to the DNA until several steps into the process. Eventually, a large complex of proteins, including RNA polymerase, becomes bound to the promoter region to form a *preinitiation complex.*

Before RNA polymerase II can actually initiate RNA synthesis, it must be released from the preinitiation complex. A key role in this process is played by the general transcription factor TFIIH, which possesses both a helicase activity that unwinds DNA and a protein kinase activity that catalyzes the phosphorylation of RNA polymerase II. Phosphorylation changes the shape of RNA polymerase, thereby releasing it from the transcription factors so that it can initiate RNA synthesis at the startpoint. At the same time, the helicase activity of TFIIH is thought to unwind the DNA so that the RNA polymerase molecule can begin to move.

TFIID, the initial transcription factor to bind to the promoter, is worthy of special note. Its ability to recognize and bind to DNA promoter sequences is conferred by one of its subunits, the **TATA-binding protein (TBP),** which combines with a variable number of additional protein subunits to form TFIID. Despite its name, the ability of TBP to bind to DNA, illustrated in **Figure 21-13,**

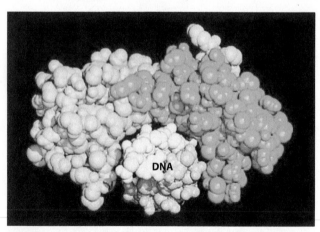

FIGURE 21-13 TATA-Binding Protein (TBP) Bound to DNA. In this computer graphic model, TBP is shown bound to DNA (white and gray, viewed looking down its axis). TBP differs from most DNA-binding proteins in that it interacts with the minor groove of DNA, rather than the major groove, and imparts a sharp bend to the DNA. The TBP molecule shown here is from the plant *Arabidopsis thaliana,* but TBP has been highly conserved during evolution. Dark and light blue differentiate the two symmetrical domains of the polypeptide, and light green is used for its nonconserved N-terminal segment. When TBP is bound to DNA, other transcription factors can interact with the convex surface of the TBP "saddle." TBP is involved in transcription initiation for all types of eukaryotic promoters.

is not restricted to TATA-containing promoters. TBP can also bind to promoters lacking a TATA box, including promoters used by RNA polymerases I and III. Depending on the type of promoter, TBP associates with different proteins, and for promoters lacking a TATA box, much of TBP's specificity is probably derived from its interaction with these associated proteins.

In addition to general transcription factors and RNA polymerase II, several other kinds of proteins are required for the efficient transcription and regulated activation of specific genes. Some of these proteins are involved in opening up chromatin structure to facilitate the binding of RNA polymerase to DNA. Others are *regulatory transcription factors,* which activate specific genes by binding to upstream control elements and recruiting *coactivator proteins* that in turn facilitate assembly of the RNA polymerase preinitiation complex. The identities and roles of these additional proteins, which covers the regulation of gene expression.

Elongation, Termination, and RNA Cleavage Are Involved in Completing Eukaryotic RNA Synthesis

After initiating transcription, RNA polymerases move along the DNA and synthesize a complementary RNA copy of the DNA template strand. Special proteins facilitate the disassembly of nucleosomes in front of the moving polymerase and their immediate reassembly after the enzyme passes. If an area of DNA damage is encountered, RNA polymerase may become stalled temporarily while the damage is corrected by proteins that carry out DNA excision repair (page 568).

Termination of transcription is governed by an assortment of signals that differ for each type of RNA polymerase. For example, transcription by RNA polymerase I is terminated by a protein factor that recognizes an 18-nucleotide termination signal in the growing RNA chain. Termination signals for RNA polymerase III are also known; they always include a short run of U's (as in bacterial termination signals), and no ancillary protein factors are needed for their recognition. Hairpin structures do not appear to be involved in termination by either polymerase I or polymerase III.

For RNA polymerase II, transcripts destined to become mRNA are often cleaved at a specific site before transcription is actually terminated. The cleavage site is 10–35 nucleotides downstream from a special AAUAAA sequence in the growing RNA chain. The polymerase may continue transcription for hundreds or even thousands of nucleotides beyond the cleavage site, but this additional RNA is quickly degraded. The cleavage site is also the site for the addition of a *poly(A) tail,* a string of adenine nucleotides found at the 3′ end of almost all eukaryotic mRNAs. Addition of the poly(A) tail is part of RNA processing, our next topic.

RNA Processing

An RNA molecule newly produced by transcription, called a **primary transcript,** frequently must undergo chemical changes before it can function in the cell. We use the term **RNA processing** to mean all the chemical modifications necessary to generate a final RNA product from the primary transcript that serves as its precursor. Processing typically involves removal of portions of the primary transcript, and it may also include the addition or chemical modification of specific nucleotides. For example, methylation of bases or ribose groups is a common modification of individual nucleotides. In addition to chemical modifications, other posttranscriptional events, such as association with specific proteins or (in eukaryotes) passage from the nucleus to the cytoplasm, are often necessary before the RNA can function.

In this section, we examine the most important processing steps involved in the production of rRNA, tRNA, and mRNA from their respective primary transcripts. Although the term *RNA processing* is most often associated with eukaryotic systems, bacteria process some of their RNA as well. We therefore include examples involving both eukaryotic and bacterial RNAs.

Ribosomal RNA Processing Involves Cleavage of Multiple rRNAs from a Common Precursor

Ribosomal RNA (rRNA) is by far the most abundant and most stable form of RNA found in cells. Typically, rRNA represents about 70–80% of the total cellular RNA, tRNA represents about 10–20%, and mRNA accounts for less than 10%. In eukaryotes, cytoplasmic ribosomes contain four types of rRNA, usually identified by their differing sedimentation rates during centrifugation (page 95). Table 21-2 lists the sedimentation coefficients (S values) of these different types of rRNA. The smaller of the two ribosomal subunits has a single 18S rRNA molecule. The larger subunit contains three rRNA molecules, one of about 28S (as low as 25S in some species) and the other two of about 5.8S and 5S. In bacterial ribosomes, only three species of rRNA are present: a 16S molecule associated with the small subunit and molecules of 23S and 5S associated with the large subunit.

Of the four kinds of rRNA in eukaryotic ribosomes, the three larger ones (28S, 18S, and 5.8S) are encoded by a single transcription unit that is transcribed by RNA polymerase I in the nucleolus to produce a single primary transcript called **pre-rRNA** (**Figure 21-14**). The DNA sequences that code for these three rRNAs are separated within the transcription unit by segments of DNA called *transcribed spacers*. The presence of three different rRNA genes within a single transcription unit ensures that the cell makes these three rRNAs in equal quantities. Most eukaryotic genomes have multiple copies of the pre-rRNA transcription unit, arranged in one or more tandem arrays (Figure 21-14a). These multiple copies facilitate production of the large amounts of ribosomal RNA typically needed by cells. The human haploid genome, for example, has 150–200 copies of the pre-rRNA transcription unit, distributed among five chromosomes. *Nontranscribed spacers* separate the transcription units within each cluster.

After RNA polymerase I has transcribed the pre-rRNA transcription unit, the resulting pre-rRNA molecule is processed by a series of cleavage reactions that remove the transcribed spacers and release the mature rRNAs (Figure 21-14c, d). The transcribed spacer sequences are then degraded. The pre-rRNA is also processed by the addition of methyl groups. The main site of methylation is the $2'$-hydroxyl group of the sugar ribose, although a few bases are methylated as well. The methylation process, as well as pre-rRNA cleavage, are guided by a special group of RNA molecules, called **snoRNAs** (small nucleolar RNAs), which bind to complementary regions of the pre-rRNA molecule and target specific sites for methylation or cleavage.

Pre-rRNA methylation has been studied by incubating cells with radioactive *S-adenosyl methionine,* which is the methyl group donor for cellular methylation reactions. When human cells are incubated with radioactive S-adenosyl methionine, all of the radioactive methyl groups initially incorporated into the pre-rRNA molecule are eventually found in the finished 28S, 18S, and 5.8S rRNA products, indicating that the methylated segments are selectively conserved during rRNA processing. Methylation may help to guide RNA processing by protecting specific regions of the pre-rRNA molecule from cleavage. In support of this hypothesis, it has been shown that depriving cells of one of the essential components required for the addition of methyl groups leads to disruption of pre-rRNA cleavage patterns.

In mammalian cells, the pre-rRNA molecule has about 13,000 nucleotides and a sedimentation coefficient of 45S. The three mature rRNA molecules generated by cleavage of this precursor contain only about 52% of the original RNA. The remaining 48% (about 6200 nucleotides) consists of transcribed spacer sequences that are removed and degraded during the cleavage steps. The rRNA precursors of some other eukaryotes contain smaller amounts of spacer sequences, but in all cases the pre-rRNA is larger

		rRNA	
Source	Ribosomal Subunit	Sedimentation Coefficient	Nucleotides
Bacterial cells	Large (50S)	23S	2900
		5S	120
	Small (30S)	16S	1540
Eukaryotic cells	Large (60S)	25–28S	≤4700
		5.8S	160
		5S	120
	Small (40S)	18S	1900

Table 21-2 **RNA Components of Cytoplasmic Ribosomes**

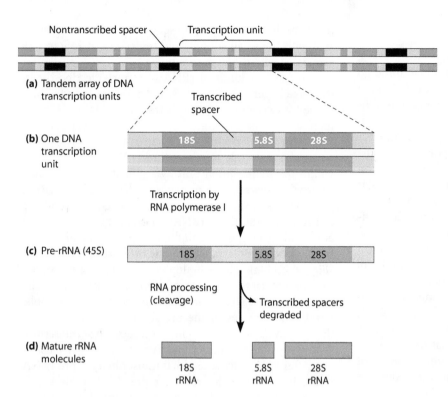

(a) Tandem array of DNA transcription units

Nontranscribed spacer

Transcription unit

Transcribed spacer

(b) One DNA transcription unit

18S   5.8S   28S

Transcription by RNA polymerase I

(c) Pre-rRNA (45S)

18S   5.8S   28S

RNA processing (cleavage)

Transcribed spacers degraded

(d) Mature rRNA molecules

18S rRNA   5.8S rRNA   28S rRNA

FIGURE 21-14 Eukaryotic rRNA Genes: Processing of Primary Transcripts. (a) The eukaryotic transcription unit that includes the genes for the three largest rRNAs occurs in multiple copies, arranged in tandem arrays. Nontranscribed spacers (black) separate the units. **(b)** Each transcription unit includes the genes for the three rRNAs (darker blue) and four transcribed spacers (lighter blue). **(c)** The transcription unit is transcribed by RNA polymerase I into a single long transcript (pre-rRNA) with a sedimentation coefficient of about 45S. **(d)** RNA processing yields mature 18S, 5.8S, and 28S rRNA molecules. RNA cleavage actually occurs in a series of steps. The order of steps varies with the species and cell type, but the final products are always the same three types of rRNA molecules.

than the aggregate size of the three rRNA molecules made from it. Thus, some processing is always required.

Processing of pre-rRNA in the nucleolus is accompanied by assembly of the RNA with proteins to form ribosomal subunits. In addition to the 28S, 18S, and 5.8S rRNAs generated by pre-rRNA processing, the ribosome assembly process also requires 5S rRNA. The gene for 5S rRNA constitutes a separate transcription unit that is transcribed by RNA polymerase III rather than RNA polymerase I. It, too, occurs in multiple copies arranged in long, tandem arrays. However, 5S-rRNA genes are not usually located near the genes for the larger rRNAs and so do not tend to be associated with the nucleolus. Unlike pre-rRNA, the RNA molecules generated during transcription of 5S-rRNA genes require little or no processing.

As in eukaryotes, ribosome formation in prokaryotic cells involves processing of multiple rRNAs from a larger precursor. *E. coli*, for example, has seven rRNA transcription units scattered about its genome. Each contains genes for all three bacterial rRNAs—23S rRNA, 16S rRNA, and 5S rRNA—plus several tRNA genes. Processing of the primary transcripts produced from these transcription units involves two sets of enzymes, one for the rRNAs and one for the tRNAs.

Transfer RNA Processing Involves Removal, Addition, and Chemical Modification of Nucleotides

Cells synthesize several dozen kinds of tRNA molecules, each designed to bring a particular amino acid to one or more codons in mRNA. However, all tRNA molecules share a common general structure, as illustrated in **Figure 21-15**. A mature tRNA molecule contains only 70–90 nucleotides, some of which are chemically modified. Base pairing between complementary sequences located in different regions causes each tRNA molecule to fold into a secondary structure containing several *hairpin loops*, illustrated in the figure. Most tRNAs have four base-paired regions, indicated by the light blue dots in part b of the figure. In some tRNAs, a fifth such region is present at the *variable loop*. Each of these base-paired regions is a short stretch of RNA double helix. Molecular biologists call the tRNA secondary structure a *cloverleaf* structure because it resembles a cloverleaf when drawn in two dimensions. However, in its normal three-dimensional tertiary structure, the molecule is folded so that the overall shape actually resembles the letter "L" (see Figure 22-3b).

Like ribosomal RNA, transfer RNA is synthesized in a precursor form in both eukaryotic and prokaryotic cells. Processing of these **pre-tRNA** molecules involves several different events, as shown in Figure 21-15a for yeast tyrosine tRNA: ➊ At the 5' end, a short *leader sequence* of 16 nucleotides is removed from the pre-tRNA. ➋ At the 3' end, the two terminal nucleotides of the pre-tRNA are removed and replaced with the trinucleotide CCA, which is a common structural feature of all tRNA molecules. (Some tRNAs already have CCA in their primary transcripts and therefore do not require modification at the 3' end.) ➌ In a typical tRNA molecule, about 10–15% of the nucleotides are chemically modified during pre-tRNA processing. The principal modifications include methylation of bases and sugars and creation of unusual bases such as dihydrouracil, ribothymine, pseudouridine, and inosine.

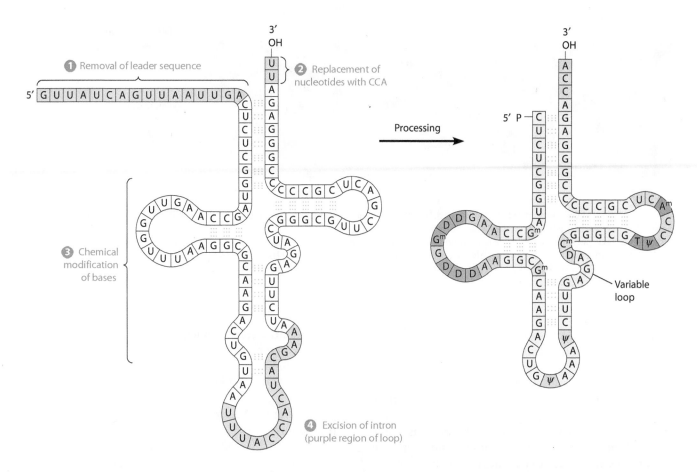

(a) Primary transcript (precursor) for yeast tyrosine tRNA

(b) Mature tRNA, secondary structure

FIGURE 21-15 Processing and Secondary Structure of Transfer RNA. (a) Every tRNA gene is transcribed as a precursor that must be processed into a mature tRNA molecule. In this primary transcript for yeast tyrosine tRNA, all regions highlighted in purple are removed during processing. Processing for this tRNA involves ❶ removal of the leader sequence at the 5′ end, ❷ replacement of two nucleotides at the 3′ end by the sequence CCA (which serves as an attachment site for amino acids in all mature tRNAs), ❸ chemical modification of certain bases, and ❹ excision of an intron. (b) The mature tRNA in a flattened, cloverleaf representation, which clearly shows the base pairing between self-complementary stretches in the molecule. Modified bases (darker colors) are abbreviated as A^m for methyladenine, G^m for methylguanine, C^m for methylcytosine, D for dihydrouracil, T for ribothymine, and c for pseudouridine.

The processing of yeast tyrosine tRNA is also characterized by the removal of an internal 14-nucleotide sequence (❹), although the transcripts for most tRNAs do not require this kind of excision. An internal segment of an RNA transcript that must be removed to create a mature RNA product is called an RNA *intron*. We will consider introns in more detail during our discussion of mRNA processing because they are a nearly universal feature of mRNA precursors in eukaryotic cells. For the present, we simply note that some eukaryotic tRNA precursors contain introns that must be eliminated by a precise mechanism that cuts and splices the precursor molecule at exactly the same location every time. The cutting-splicing mechanism involves two separate enzymes, an RNA endonuclease and an RNA ligase, which are similar from species to species, even among organisms that are evolutionarily distant from one another. In an experiment that demonstrates this point vividly, cloned genes for the yeast tyrosine tRNA shown in Figure 21-15

were microinjected into eggs of *Xenopus laevis,* the African clawed frog. Despite the long evolutionary divergence between fungi and amphibians, the yeast genes placed in the frog eggs were transcribed and processed properly, including removal of the 14-nucleotide intron.

Messenger RNA Processing in Eukaryotes Involves Capping, Addition of Poly(A), and Removal of Introns

Bacterial mRNA is, in almost all cases, an exception to the generalization that RNA requires processing before it can be used by the cell. Most bacterial mRNA is synthesized in a form that is ready for translation, even before the entire RNA molecule has been completed. Moreover, transcription in bacteria is not separated by a membrane barrier from the ribosomes responsible for translation, so bacterial mRNA molecules in the process of being synthesized by RNA polymerase often have ribosomes already associated

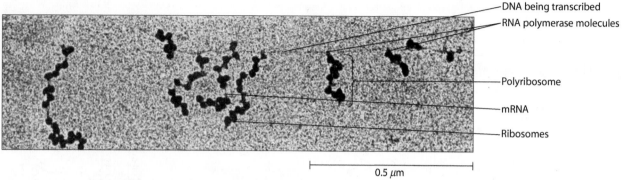

DNA being transcribed
RNA polymerase molecules
Polyribosome
mRNA
Ribosomes

0.5 μm

FIGURE 21-16 Coupling of Transcription and Translation in Bacterial Cells. This electron micrograph shows *E. coli* DNA being transcribed by RNA polymerase molecules that are moving from right to left. Attached to each polymerase molecule is a strand of mRNA still in the process of being transcribed. The large dark particles attached to each growing mRNA strand are ribosomes that are actively translating the partially complete mRNA. (The polypeptides being synthesized are not visible.) A cluster of ribosomes attached to a single mRNA strand is called a polyribosome (TEM).

with them. The electron micrograph in **Figure 21-16** shows this coupling of transcription and translation in a bacterial cell.

In contrast, transcription and translation in eukaryotic cells are separated in both time and space: Transcription takes place in the nucleus, whereas translation occurs mainly in the cytoplasm. Substantial processing is required in the nucleus to convert primary transcripts into mature mRNA molecules that are ready to be transported to the cytoplasm and translated. Primary transcripts are often very long, typically ranging from 2000 to 20,000 nucleotides. This size heterogeneity is reflected in the term *heterogeneous nuclear RNA (hnRNA)*, which refers to the nonribosomal, nontransfer RNA found in eukaryotic nuclei. HnRNA consists of a mixture of mRNA molecules and their precursors, **pre-mRNA.** Conversion of pre-mRNA molecules into functional mRNAs usually requires the removal of nucleotide sequences and the addition of 5′ caps and 3′ tails, as will be described in the following sections. The C-terminal domain of one of the subunits of RNA polymerase II plays a key role in coupling these RNA processing events to transcription, presumably by acting as a platform for the assembly of the protein complexes involved in pre-mRNA processing.

5′ Caps and 3′ Poly(A) Tails. Most eukaryotic mRNA molecules bear distinctive modifications at both ends. At the 5′ end, they all possess a modified nucleotide called a **5′ cap,** and at the 3′ end they usually have a long stretch of adenine ribonucleotides known as a **poly(A) tail.**

A 5′ cap is simply a guanosine nucleotide that has been methylated at position 7 of the purine ring and is "backward"—that is, the bond joining it to the 5′ end of the RNA molecule is a 5′→5′ linkage rather than the usual 3′→5′ bond (**Figure 21-17**). This distinctive feature of eukaryotic mRNA is added to the primary transcript shortly after initiation of RNA synthesis. As part of the capping process, the ribose rings of the first,

and often the second, nucleotides of the RNA chain can also become methylated, as shown in Figure 21-17. The 5′ cap contributes to mRNA stability by protecting the molecule from degradation by nucleases that attack RNA at the 5′ end. The cap also plays an important role in positioning mRNA on the ribosome for the initiation of translation.

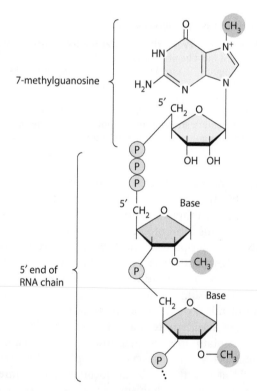

7-methylguanosine
5′ end of RNA chain

FIGURE 21-17 Cap Structure Located at the 5′ End of Eukaryotic Pre-mRNA and mRNA Molecules. The methyl groups attached to the first two riboses at the 5′ end of the RNA chain are not always present. Notice that the bond joining the RNA to 7-methylguanosine is a 5′-to-5′ linkage rather than the usual 5′-to-3′ linkage.

In addition to the 5′ cap, a poly(A) tail ranging from 50–250 nucleotides in length is present at the 3′ end of most eukaryotic mRNA molecules. (In animal cells, mRNAs coding for the major histones are among the few mRNAs known to lack such a poly(A) tail.) It is clear that poly(A) must be added after transcription because genes do not contain long stretches of thymine (T) nucleotides that could serve as a template for the addition of poly(A). Direct support for this conclusion has come from the isolation of the enzyme *poly(A) polymerase,* which catalyzes the addition of poly(A) sequences to RNA without requiring a DNA template.

The addition of poly(A) is part of the process that creates the 3′ end of most eukaryotic mRNA molecules. Unlike bacteria, where specific termination sequences halt transcription at the 3′ end of newly forming mRNAs, the transcription of eukaryotic pre-mRNAs often proceeds hundreds or even thousands of nucleotides beyond the site destined to become the 3′ end of the final mRNA molecule. A special signal—consisting of an AAUAAA sequence located slightly upstream from this site and a GU-rich and/or U-rich element downstream from the site—determines where the poly(A) tail should be added. As shown in **Figure 21-18**, this signaling element triggers cleavage of the primary transcript 10–35 nucleotides downstream from the AAUAAA sequence, and poly(A) polymerase catalyzes formation of the poly(A) tail. In addition to creating the poly(A) tail, the processing events associated with the AAUAAA signal may also help to trigger the termination of transcription.

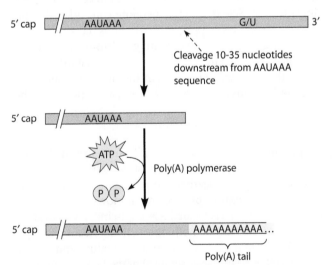

FIGURE 21-18 Addition of a Poly(A) Tail to Pre-mRNA. Transcription of eukaryotic pre-mRNAs often proceeds beyond the 3′ end of the mature mRNA. The RNA chain is then cleaved about 10–35 nucleotides downstream from a special AAUAAA sequence, followed by the addition of a poly(A) tail catalyzed by poly(A) polymerase. The proper AAUAAA sequence is distinguished by the presence of an accompanying downstream GU-rich and/or U-rich element (designated "G/U" in the diagram).

The poly(A) tail seems to have several functions. Like the 5′ cap, it protects mRNA from nuclease attack and, as a result, the length of the poly(A) influences mRNA stability (the longer the tail, the longer the life span of the mRNA in the cytoplasm). In addition, poly(A) is recognized by specific proteins involved in exporting mRNA from the nucleus to the cytoplasm, and it may also help ribosomes recognize mRNA as a molecule to be translated. In the laboratory, poly(A) tails can be used to isolate mRNA from the more prevalent rRNA and tRNA. RNA extracted from cells is simply passed through a column packed with particles coated with poly(dT), which are single strands of DNA consisting solely of thymine nucleotides. Molecules with poly(A) tails bind to the poly(dT) via complementary base pairing, while other RNA molecules pass through. The poly(A)-containing mRNA can then be removed from the column by changing the ionic conditions.

The Discovery of Introns. In eukaryotic cells, the precursors for most mRNAs (and for some tRNAs and rRNAs) contain **introns,** which are *sequences within the primary transcript that do not appear in the mature, functional RNA.* The discovery of introns was a great surprise to biologists. It had already been shown for numerous bacterial genes that the amino acid sequence of the polypeptide chain produced by a gene corresponds exactly with a sequence of contiguous nucleotides in DNA. This relationship was first demonstrated by Charles Yanofsky in the early 1960s and, as better methods for sequencing DNA and proteins became available, was confirmed by direct comparison of nucleotide and amino acid sequences. Biologists naturally assumed the same would turn out to be true for eukaryotes.

It was therefore a shock in 1977 when Philip Sharp and Richard Roberts independently reported the identification of eukaryotic genes that do not follow this pattern but are instead interrupted by stretches of nucleotides—introns—that are not represented in either the functional mRNA or its protein product. The widespread importance of introns in eukaryotes led to the awarding of the 1993 Nobel Prize in Medicine to Sharp and Roberts. The existence of introns was first shown by *R looping,* a technique in which single-stranded RNA is hybridized to double-stranded DNA under conditions that favor the formation of *heteroduplexes,* hybrids between complementary regions of RNA and DNA. The mRNA hybridizes to the template strand of the DNA, leaving the other, displaced strand as a single-stranded DNA loop that can be easily identified using electron microscopy. With eukaryotic mRNAs coding for such proteins as human β-globin and chick ovalbumin, the surprising result was that *multiple* loops were seen (**Figure 21-19**). This unexpected result indicated that the DNA sequences coding for a typical eukaryotic mRNA are not continuous with each other but instead are separated by intervening sequences that do not appear in the final mRNA. The intervening sequences that disrupt the linear continuity

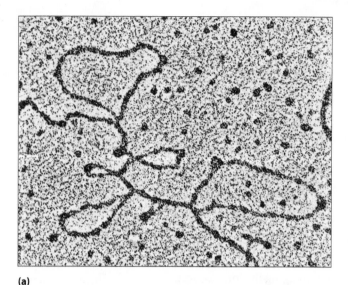

(a)

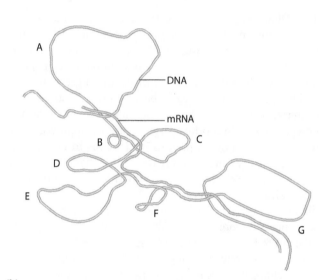

(b)

FIGURE 21-19 Demonstration of Introns in Protein-Coding Genes. Mature mRNA molecules were allowed to hydrogen-bond to the DNA (gene) from which they had been transcribed, forming a hybrid molecule (heteroduplex). The resulting hybrid molecules were then examined with an electron microscope. The example shown here is the chicken ovalbumin gene. **(a)** An electron micrograph showing the loops produced in a heteroduplex (TEM). **(b)** An interpretive diagram showing the positions of the mRNA and the unpaired loops of DNA, which correspond to introns (A-G).

Table 21-3 Examples of Genes with Introns

Gene	Organism	Number of Introns	Number of Exons
Actin	*Drosophila*	1	2
β-Globin	Human	2	3
Insulin	Human	2	3
Actin	Chicken	3	4
Albumin	Human	14	15
Thyroglobulin	Human	36	37
Collagen	Chicken	50	51
Titin	Human	233	234

introns, one of 120 bp and the other of 550 bp. Together, these account for about 40% of the total length of the gene. For many mammalian genes, an even larger fraction of the gene consists of introns. An extreme example is the human dystrophin gene, a mutant form of which causes Duchenne muscular dystrophy. This gene is over 2 million bp long and has 85 introns, representing more than 99% of the gene's DNA!

The discovery of introns that do not appear in mature mRNA molecules raises the question of whether the introns present in DNA are actually transcribed into the primary transcript (pre-mRNA). This question has been addressed by experiments in which pre-mRNA and DNA were mixed together and the resulting hybrids examined by electron microscopy. In contrast to the appearance of hybrids between mRNA and DNA, which exhibit multiple R loops where the DNA molecule contains sequences that are not present in the mRNA (Figure 21-19), pre-mRNA hybridizes in one continuous stretch to the DNA molecule, forming a single R loop. Scientists have therefore concluded that pre-mRNA molecules represent continuous copies of their corresponding genes, containing introns as well as sequences destined to become part of the final mRNA. This means that converting pre-mRNA into mRNA requires specific mechanisms for removing introns, as we now describe.

Spliceosomes Remove Introns from Pre-mRNA

To produce a functional mRNA from a pre-mRNA that contains introns, eukaryotes must somehow remove the introns and splice together the remaining RNA segments (exons). The entire process of removing introns and rejoining the exons is termed **RNA splicing**. As an example, **Figure 21-20** shows both the primary transcript (pre-mRNA) of the β-globin gene and the mature end-product (mRNA) that results after removal of the two introns.

The relevance of RNA splicing for human health has become apparent from the discovery that roughly 15% of inherited human diseases involve splicing errors in pre-mRNA. Precise splicing is critical because a single nucleotide error would alter the mRNA reading frame and render it useless. Splicing precision can be disrupted by altering short base sequences at either end of an intron,

of the message-encoding regions of a gene are the introns (*intervening* sequences), and the sequences destined to appear in the final mRNA are referred to as **exons** (because they are *ex*pressed).

Once they had been reported for a few genes, introns began popping up everywhere. The use of restriction mapping and DNA sequencing techniques has led to the conclusion that introns are present in most protein-coding genes of multicellular eukaryotes, although the size and number of the introns can vary considerably (**Table 21-3**). The human β-globin gene, for example, has only two

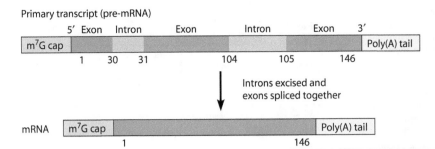

Primary transcript (pre-mRNA)

| 5' Exon | Intron | Exon | Intron | Exon | 3' |

Introns excised and
exons spliced together

mRNA

FIGURE 21-20 An Overview of RNA Splicing.
The capped and tailed primary transcript of the
human gene for β-globin contains three exons
(dark red) and two introns (light red). The numbers
refer to codon positions in the final mRNA. In the
mature mRNA that results from RNA splicing, the
introns have been excised and the exons joined
together to form a molecule with a continuous
coding sequence. The cell's ribosomes will translate
this message into a polypeptide of 146 amino acids.

ACTIVITIES www.thecellplace.com *RNA
splicing*

suggesting that these sequences determine the location of
the *5' and 3' splice sites*—that is, the points where the two
ends of an intron are cleaved during its removal. Analysis
of the base sequences of hundreds of different introns has
revealed that the 5' end of an intron typically starts with
the sequence GU and the 3' end terminates with AG. In
addition, a short stretch of bases adjacent to these GU and
AG sequences tends to be similar among different introns.
The base sequence of the remainder of the intron appears
to be largely irrelevant to the splicing process. Though
introns vary from a few dozen to thousands of nucleotides
in length, most of the intron can be artificially removed
without altering the splicing process. One exception is
a special sequence located several dozen nucleotides
upstream from the 3' end of the intron and referred to as
the *branch-point*. The branch-point plays an important
role in the mechanism that removes introns.

Intron removal is catalyzed by **spliceosomes,** which
are large, molecular complexes consisting of five kinds of
RNA combined with more than 200 proteins. Electron
microscopy has revealed that spliceosomes assemble on
pre-mRNA molecules while the pre-mRNA is still being
synthesized (**Figure 21-21**), indicating that intron
removal can begin before transcription of pre-mRNA is
completed. Spliceosomes are assembled on pre-mRNAs
from a group of smaller RNA-protein complexes called
snRNPs (small nuclear ribonucleoproteins) and additional
proteins. Each snRNP (pronounced "snurp") contains one
or two small molecules of a special type of RNA known as
snRNA (small nuclear RNA).

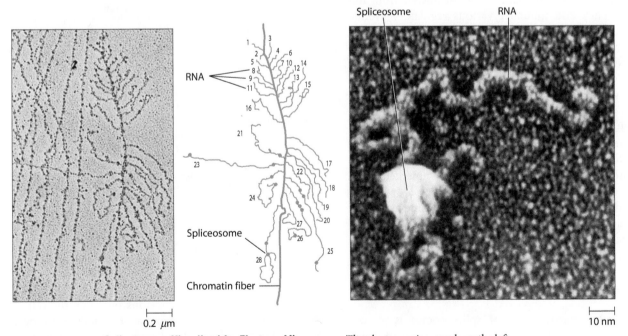

FIGURE 21-21 Spliceosomes Visualized by Electron Microscopy. The electron micrograph on the left
shows chromatin fibers in the process of being transcribed. Many newly forming RNA transcripts (each numbered separately in the diagram) protrude from one of the chromatin fibers. The darker granules on the RNA
transcripts represent snRNPs that are beginning the process of spliceosome assembly. In the case of RNA transcript number 28, a mature spliceosome has formed. The higher-magnification electron micrograph on the
right shows a single RNA molecule with an attached spliceosome (TEMs).

RNA Processing 671

FIGURE 21-22 Intron Removal by Spliceosomes. The spliceo-some is an RNA-protein complex that splices intron-containing pre-mRNA in the eukaryotic nucleus. The substrate here is a mole-cule of pre-mRNA with two exons and one intron. In a stepwise fashion, the pre-mRNA assembles with the U1 snRNP, U2 snRNP, and U4/U6 and U5 snRNPs (along with some non-snRNP splicing factors), forming a mature spliceosome. The pre-mRNA is then cleaved at the 5′ splice site and the newly released 5′ end is linked to an adenine (A) nucleotide located at the branch-point sequence, cre-ating a looped lariat structure. Finally, the 3′ splice site is cleaved and the two ends of the exon are joined together, releasing the intron for subsequent degradation.

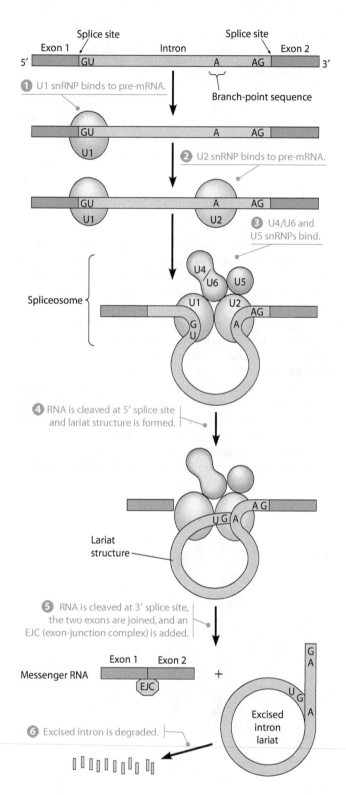

Figure 21-22 summarizes how spliceosomes are assembled by the sequential binding of snRNPs to pre-mRNA. The first step is the binding of a snRNP called U1, whose RNA contains a nucleotide sequence that allows it to base-pair with the 5′ splice site. A second snRNP, called U2, then binds to the branch-point sequence. Finally, another group of snRNPs (U4/U6 and U5) brings the two ends of the intron together to form a mature spliceosome, a massive complex comparable in size to a ribosome. At this stage the pre-mRNA is cleaved at the 5′ splice site, and the newly released 5′ end of the intron is covalently joined to an adenine residue located at the branch-point sequence, creating a looped structure called a *lariat*. The 3′ splice site is then cleaved, and the two ends of the exon are joined together, releasing the intron for subsequent degradation. A multiprotein complex called an **exon junction complex (EJC)** is deposited near the boundary of each newly formed exon-exon junction. EJCs are required for the efficient export of mRNA from the nucleus. They also influence various regulatory events, including mRNA localization and translation.

In addition to the main class of introns containing GU and AG sequences at their 5′ and 3′ boundaries, respectively, a second class of introns with AU and AC at these two sites has been identified. These "AU-AC" introns are often excised by a second type of spliceosome that differs in snRNP composition from the spliceosome illustrated in Figure 21-22. But despite the complexities raised by the existence of multiple types of introns and spliceosomes, a unifying principle has emerged: The snRNA molecules present in spliceosomes are directly involved in splice-site recognition, spliceosome assembly, and the catalytic mechanism of splicing. The idea of a catalytic role for snRNAs arose from the discovery of self-splicing RNA introns, our next topic.

Some Introns Are Self-Splicing

Although the participation of spliceosomes is almost always required for intron removal, a few types of genes have *self-splicing RNA introns*. The RNA transcript of such a gene can carry out the entire process of RNA splicing in the absence of any protein (for example, in a test tube); the intron RNA itself catalyzes the process. As we described in Chapter 6, such RNA molecules that function as catalysts in the absence of protein are called *ribozymes*.

There are two classes of introns in which the intron RNA can function as a ribozyme to catalyze its own removal. The first class, called *Group I introns*, is present in the mitochondrial genome of fungi (e.g., yeast) in rRNA genes and in genes coding for components of the electron transport system. Group I introns also occur in plant mito-chondrial genes, in some rRNA and tRNA genes of chloroplasts, in nuclear rRNA genes of some unicellular eukaryotes, in some tRNA genes in bacteria, and in a few bacteriophage genes coding for mRNAs. Group I RNA introns are excised in the form of linear RNA fragments.

In contrast, *Group II introns* are excised as lariats in which an adenine within the intron forms the branch-point, just as in the spliceosome mechanism. Group II introns are found in some mitochondrial and chloroplast genes of plants and unicellular eukaryotes and in the genomes of some archaea and bacteria. Biologists think that today's prevailing splicing mechanism, based on spliceosomes, evolved from Group II introns, with the intron RNA's catalytic role being taken over by the snRNA molecules of the spliceosome. Support for this idea has come from the discovery that protein-free RNA molecules isolated from spliceosomes are capable of catalyzing the first step in the splicing reaction involving the branch-point adenine.

The Existence of Introns Permits Alternative Splicing and Exon Shuffling

The burning questions about introns are: Why do nearly all genes in multicellular eukaryotes have them? Why do cells have so much DNA that seems to serve no coding function? Why, in generation after generation of cells, is so much energy invested in synthesizing segments of DNA—and their RNA transcripts—that appear to serve no useful function and are destined only for the splicing scrap heap?

In fact, it is not true that introns never perform any functions of their own. In a few cases, intron RNAs are processed to yield functional products rather than being degraded. For example, some types of snoRNA—whose role in guiding pre-rRNA methylation and cleavage was discussed earlier in the chapter—are derived from introns that are first removed from pre-mRNA and then processed to form snoRNA. And in a few cases, introns are even translated into proteins.

Despite these exceptions, most introns are destroyed without serving any obvious function. One benefit to such a seemingly wasteful arrangement is that the presence of introns allows each pre-mRNA molecule to be spliced in multiple ways, thereby generating anywhere from 2 or 3 to more than 100 different mRNAs (and hence polypeptides) from the same gene. This phenomenon, called **alternative splicing,** is made possible by mechanisms that allow certain splice sites to be either activated or skipped (**Figure 21-23**). Control over these splice sites is exerted by various molecules, including regulatory proteins and snoRNAs, that bind to *splicing enhancer* or *splicing silencer* sequences in pre-mRNAs. Binding of the appropriate regulatory molecule to a splicing enhancer or silencer leads to activation or skipping of individual splice sites, respectively.

The existence of alternative splicing may help explain how the biological complexity of vertebrates is achieved without a major increase in the number of genes compared to simpler organisms. (Recall from Chapter 18 that humans have barely more genes than a nematode worm does and 12,000 fewer genes than a rice plant does.) Instead of increasing the number of genes, humans transcribe the majority of their genes into pre-mRNAs that can be spliced in more than one way. As a result, the roughly 25,000 human genes produce mRNAs coding for hundreds of thousands of different polypeptides.

Another function of introns is that they allow the evolution of new protein-coding genes through recombination events that bring together new combinations of exons. At least two different mechanisms are involved, both based on the fact that introns are long stretches of DNA where genetic recombination can occur without harming coding sequences. First, genetic recombination between the introns of different genes will produce genes containing new combinations of exons—*exon shuffling*. Second, recombination

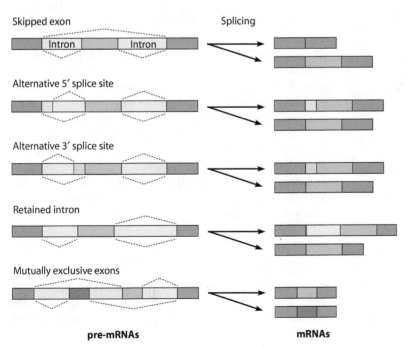

FIGURE 21-23 Some Examples of Alternative Splicing. This diagram illustrates five alternative splicing mechanisms that allow different mRNAs to be produced from the same pre-mRNA by activating or skipping individual splice sites. The thin dashed lines above and below each pre-mRNA represent the splice sites that are used to generate the two different mRNAs shown for each example.

can also create duplicate copies of an individual exon within a single gene. The two copies could continue as exact duplicates, or one copy might mutate to a sequence that produces a new activity in the polypeptide encoded by that gene.

RNA Editing Allows mRNA Coding Sequences to Be Altered

About a decade after introns and RNA splicing were first discovered, molecular biologists were surprised by the discovery of yet another type of mRNA processing, called **RNA editing.** During RNA editing, anywhere from a single nucleotide to hundreds of nucleotides may be inserted, removed, or chemically altered within the coding sequence of an mRNA. Such changes can create new start or stop codons, or they can alter the reading frame of the message.

Some of the best-studied examples of RNA editing occur in the mitochondrial mRNAs of trypanosomes, which are parasitic protozoa. In these mRNAs, editing involves the insertion and deletion of multiple uracil nucleotides at various points in the mRNA. The information for this editing is located in small RNA molecules called *guide RNAs,* which are encoded by mitochondrial genes separate from the mRNA genes. In one proposed editing mechanism, hydrogen bonding causes short complementary regions of the guide RNA and mRNA to come together, and nearby sequences of U's in the guide RNA are then spliced into the mRNA.

A different type of editing occurs in the mitochondrial and chloroplast mRNAs of flowering plants. In these cases, nucleotides are neither inserted nor deleted, but C's are converted to U's (and vice versa) by deamination (and amination) reactions. Similar base conversions have also been discovered in mRNAs transcribed from nuclear genes in animal cells. For example, a single codon in the mRNA transcribed from the mammalian apolipoprotein-B gene undergoes a C-to-U conversion during RNA editing. Another type of editing detected in animal cell nuclei converts adenosine (A) to inosine (I), which resembles guanosine (G) in its base-pairing properties. Such A-to-I editing has been detected in mRNAs produced by more than 1600 human genes, mostly in noncoding regions. The reason for putting I's in the untranslated regions of mRNAs is a mystery, but roles in regulating RNA stability, localization, and translation rate have been suggested.

The existence of RNA editing provides a reason to be cautious in inferring either polypeptide or RNA sequences from genomic DNA sequences. For example, many discrepancies were observed when the amino acid sequences of proteins produced by plant mitochondrial genes were first compared with the amino acid sequences that would be predicted based on the base sequence of mitochondrial DNA. Although some of these discrepancies can be explained by nonstandard codon usage in mitochondria (described earlier in the chapter), most of the unexpected amino acids arise because RNA editing alters the base sequence of various mRNA codons, leading to the incor-

poration of amino acids that would not have been expected based on a gene's DNA sequence.

Nucleic acid editing is not restricted to mRNAs. *MicroRNAs*—whose role in regulating gene expression—are another class of RNAs that can be edited. And DNA is also subject to editing. For example, eukaryotes possess a DNA-editing enzyme called *APOBEC3G,* which inactivates retroviruses by catalyzing C-to-U conversions in the initial DNA strand produced when viral RNA is copied by reverse transcriptase (step ❷ in Figure 21A-1). The C-to-U conversions in the first strand lead to G-to-A conversions in the complementary DNA strand, thereby introducing mutations that debilitate the virus. To defend against this attack, HIV and other retroviruses produce a protein called *Vif,* which targets APOBEC3G for destruction. Because suppression of APOBEC3G is essential for successful retroviral infection, blocking the action of Vif might be a useful strategy for developing novel new treatments for HIV/AIDS.

Key Aspects of mRNA Metabolism

Before ending this chapter, we should note two key aspects of mRNA metabolism that are important to our overall understanding of how mRNA molecules behave within cells. These are the short life span of most mRNAs and the ability of mRNA to amplify genetic information.

Most mRNA Molecules Have a Relatively Short Life Span

Most mRNA molecules have a high *turnover rate*—that is, the rate at which molecules are degraded and then replaced with newly synthesized versions. In this respect, mRNA contrasts with the other major forms of RNA in the cell, rRNA and tRNA, which are notable for their stability. Because of its short life span, mRNA accounts for most of the transcriptional activity in many cells, even though it represents only a small fraction of the total RNA content. Turnover is usually measured in terms of a molecule's *half-life,* which is the length of time required for 50% of the molecules present at any given moment to degrade. The mRNA molecules of bacterial cells generally have half-lives of only a few minutes, whereas the half-lives of eukaryotic mRNAs range from several hours to a few days.

Since the rate at which a given mRNA is degraded determines the length of time it is available for translation, alterations in mRNA life span can affect the amount of protein a given message will produce. Regulation of mRNA life span is one of the mechanisms cells use to exert control over gene expression.

The Existence of mRNA Allows Amplification of Genetic Information

Because mRNA molecules can be synthesized again and again from the same stretch of template DNA, cells are provided with an important opportunity for *amplification* of the genetic message. If DNA gene sequences were used directly in protein synthesis, the number of protein molecules that could be translated from any gene within a given time period would be strictly limited by the rate of polypeptide synthesis. But in a system using mRNA as an intermediate, multiple copies of a gene's informational content can be made, and each of these can be used in turn to direct the synthesis of the protein product.

As an especially dramatic example of this amplification effect, consider the synthesis of *fibroin,* the major protein of silk. The haploid genome of the silkworm has only one fibroin gene, but about 10^4 copies of fibroin mRNA are transcribed from the two copies of the gene in each diploid cell of the silk gland. Each of these mRNA molecules, in turn, directs the synthesis of about 10^5 fibroin molecules, resulting in the production of more than 10^9 molecules of fibroin per cell—all within the four-day period it takes the worm to make its cocoon! Without mRNA as an intermediate, the genome of the silkworm would need 10^4 copies of the fibroin gene (or about 40,000 days!) to make a cocoon.

Significantly, most genes that code for proteins occur in only one or a few copies per haploid genome. In contrast, genes that code for rRNA and tRNA are always present in multiple copies. It is advantageous for cells to have many copies of genes whose final products are RNA (rather than protein) because in this case there is no opportunity for amplifying each gene's effect by repeated translation.

SUMMARY OF KEY POINTS

The Directional Flow of Genetic Information

- Instructions stored in DNA are transcribed and processed into molecules of mRNA, rRNA, and tRNA for use in protein synthesis.

- The base sequence of each mRNA molecule dictates the sequence of amino acids in a polypeptide chain.

The Genetic Code

- When guiding the synthesis of a polypeptide chain, mRNA is read in units of three bases called codons.

- The table of the genetic code indicates which amino acid (or stop signal) is specified by each codon. The code is unambiguous, nonoverlapping, degenerate, and nearly universal.

Transcription in Bacterial Cells

- Transcription is the process by which a DNA template strand is copied by RNA polymerase to produce a complementary molecule of RNA.

- The molecular mechanism of transcription involves four stages: (1) binding of RNA polymerase to promoter sequences in the DNA template strand, (2) initiation of RNA synthesis, (3) elongation of the RNA chain, and (4) termination.

Transcription in Eukaryotic Cells

- Transcription in eukaryotes involves the same general principles as in bacteria but is more complex. One major difference is that eukaryotic cells have multiple forms of RNA polymerase that are specialized for synthesizing different types of RNA.

- The three nuclear RNA polymerases recognize different families of DNA promoter sequences. These eukaryotic promoters are usually bound by transcription factors that associate with RNA polymerase rather than by RNA polymerase itself.

RNA Processing

- Newly forming RNA molecules must generally undergo some type of processing, both during and after transcription, before the RNA can perform its normal function. The major exception is bacterial mRNA, whose translation often begins before transcription is completed.

- RNA processing involves chemical alterations such as cleavage of multigene transcription units, removal of noncoding sequences, addition of sequences to the 3' and 5' ends, and insertion, removal, and chemical modification of individual nucleotides.

- Processing of eukaryotic pre-mRNA is especially elaborate, involving the addition of a 5' cap and a 3' poly(A) tail, as well as the removal of introns by spliceosomes or, in some cases, by a process catalyzed by intron RNA.

- The presence of introns and exons allows pre-mRNA molecules to be spliced in more than one way, thereby permitting a single gene to produce multiple mRNAs coding for different polypeptides.

- Various editing mechanisms allow the base sequence of mRNA molecules to be altered, thereby creating mRNAs that code for polypeptides whose amino acid sequences could not have been predicted by knowing the base sequence of the corresponding genes.

Key Aspects of mRNA Metabolism

- Most mRNAs have a relatively short life span.

- Active protein-coding genes are transcribed multiple times to produce many molecules of their corresponding mRNAs, thereby amplifying the amount of protein that each gene can produce.

MAKING CONNECTIONS

How does DNA—whose structure, replication, and sorting into daughter cells during mitosis and meiosis were described in Chapters 18 and 19—perform its role as the source of the genetic information that specifies cellular structure and behavior? In this chapter, you learned that the DNA base sequence of protein-coding genes specifies the amino acid sequence of polypeptide chains using a triplet code. The first step in the decoding process involves transcription of DNA base sequences into molecules of messenger RNA (mRNA). The principle underlying transcription is relatively easy to understand because it involves the transfer of information from one nucleic acid to another by complementary base pairing, thereby keeping the basic "language" (i.e., nucleotide sequences) the same. But how, you may ask, does the sequence of nucleotides in an mRNA molecule specify the sequence of amino acids in a polypeptide chain? The answer will be provided in Chapter 22, where you will see how nucleotide sequences are translated into amino acid sequences during protein synthesis, a complex process involving ribosomes, transfer RNAs, and dozens of enzymes and protein factors. After Chapter 22 answers the question of how proteins are manufactured, folded, and distributed throughout the cell, the mechanisms responsible for regulating the production of protein molecules will be explored.

PROBLEM SET

More challenging problems are marked with a •.

21-1 Triplets or Sextuplets? In his Nobel Prize lecture in 1962, Francis Crick pointed out that while the pioneering experiments he performed with Barnett, Brenner, and Watts-Tobin suggested that the DNA "code" is a triplet, their experiments did not rule out the possibility that the code could require six or nine bases.

(a) Assuming the code is a triplet, what effect would adding or removing six or nine bases have on the reading frame of a piece of DNA?

(b) If the code actually were a sextuplet, how would addition of three, six, or nine nucleotides affect the reading frame of a piece of DNA?

21-2 The Genetic Code in a T-Even Phage. A portion of a polypeptide produced by bacteriophage T4 was found to have the following sequence of amino acids:

...Lys-Ser-Pro-Ser-Leu-Asn-Ala...

Deletion of a single nucleotide from one location in the T4 DNA template strand with subsequent insertion of a different nucleotide nearby changed the sequence to:

...Lys-Val-His-His-Leu-Met-Ala...

(a) What was the nucleotide sequence of the mRNA segment that encoded this portion of the original polypeptide?

(b) What was the nucleotide sequence of the mRNA encoding this portion of the mutant polypeptide?

(c) Can you determine which nucleotide was deleted and which was inserted? Explain your answer.

21-3 Frameshift Mutations. Each of the mutants listed below this paragraph has a different mutant form of the gene encoding protein X. Each mutant gene contains one or more nucleotide insertions (+) or deletions (−) of the type caused by acridine dyes. Assume that all the mutations are located very near the beginning of the gene for protein X. In each case, indicate with an "OK" if you would expect the mutant protein to be nearly normal and with a "Not OK" if you would expect it to be obviously abnormal.

(a) −   (b) −/+   (c) −/−   (d) +/−/+

(e) +/−/+/−   (f) +/+/+   (g) +/+/−/+   (h) −/−/+/−/−

(i) −/−/−/−/−/−

21-4 Amino Acid Substitutions in Mutant Proteins. Although the codon assignments summarized in Figure 21-7 were originally deduced from experiments involving synthetic RNA polymers and triplets, their validity was subsequently confirmed by examining the amino acid sequences of normally occurring mutant proteins. The table below lists some examples of amino acid substitutions seen in mutant forms of hemoglobin, tryptophan synthase, and the tobacco mosaic virus coat protein. For each amino acid alteration, list the corresponding single-base changes in mRNA that could have caused that particular amino acid substitution.

Protein	Amino Acid Substitution
Hemoglobin	Glu → Val
	His → Tyr
	Asn → Lys
Coat protein of tobacco mosaic virus	Glu → Gly
	Ile → Val
Tryptophan synthase	Tyr → Cys
	Gly → Arg
	Lys → Stop

• 21-5 Locating Promoters. The following table provides data concerning the effects of various deletions in a eukaryotic gene coding for 5S rRNA on the ability of this gene to be transcribed by RNA polymerase III.

Nucleotides Deleted	Ability of 5S-rRNA Gene to Be Transcribed by RNA Polymerase III
−45 through −1	Yes
+1 through +47	Yes
+10 through +47	Yes
+10 through +63	No
+80 through +123	No
+83 through +123	Yes

(a) What do these data tell you about the probable location of the promoter for this particular 5S-rRNA gene?

(b) If a similar experiment were carried out for a gene transcribed by RNA polymerase I, what kinds of results would you expect?

(c) If a similar experiment were carried out for a gene transcribed by RNA polymerase II, what kinds of results would you expect?

21-6 RNA Polymerases and Promoters. For each of the following statements about RNA polymerases, indicate with a B if the statement is true of the bacterial enzyme and with a I, II, or III if it is true of the respective eukaryotic RNA polymerase. A given statement may be true of any, all, or none (N) of these enzymes.

(a) The enzyme is insensitive to α-amanitin.

(b) The enzyme catalyzes an exergonic reaction.

(c) All the primary transcripts must be processed before being used in translation.

(d) The enzyme may sometimes be found attached to an RNA molecule that also has ribosomes bound to it.

(e) The enzyme synthesizes rRNA.

(f) Transcription factors must bind to the promoter before the polymerase can bind.

(g) The enzyme adds a poly(A) sequence to mRNA.

(h) The enzyme moves along the DNA template strand in the $3' \rightarrow 5'$ direction.

(i) The enzyme synthesizes a product likely to acquire a 5′ cap.

(j) All promoters used by the enzyme lie mostly upstream of the transcriptional startpoint and are only partially transcribed.

(k) The specificity of transcription by the enzyme is determined by a subunit of the holoenzyme.

21-7 RNA Processing. The three major classes of RNA found in the cytoplasm of a typical eukaryotic cell are rRNA, tRNA, and mRNA. For each, indicate the following:

(a) Two or more kinds of processing that the RNA has almost certainly been subjected to.

(b) A processing event unique to that RNA species.

(c) A processing event that you would also expect to find for the same species of RNA from a bacterial cell.

21-8 Spliceosomes. The RNA processing carried out by spliceosomes in the eukaryotic nucleus involves many different kinds of protein and RNA molecules. For each of the following five components of the splicing process, indicate whether it is protein (P), RNA (R), or both (PR). Then briefly explain how each of the five fits into the process.

(a) snRNA   (b) Spliceosome   (c) snRNP

(d) Splice sites   (e) Lariat

• **21-9 Antibiotic Inhibitors of Transcription.** Rifamycin and actinomycin D are two antibiotics derived from the bacterium *Streptomyces*. Rifamycin binds to the β subunit of *E. coli* RNA polymerase and interferes with the formation of the first phosphodiester bond in the RNA chain. Actinomycin D binds to double-stranded DNA by intercalation (slipping between neighboring base pairs).

(a) Which of the four stages in transcription would you expect rifamycin to affect primarily?

(b) Which of the four stages in transcription would you expect actinomycin D to affect primarily?

(c) Which of the two inhibitors is more likely to affect RNA synthesis in cultured human liver cells?

(d) Which of the two inhibitors would be more useful for an experiment that requires the initiation of new RNA chains to be blocked without interfering with the elongation of chains that are already being synthesized?

(e) When fertilized sea urchin eggs are treated with actinomycin D, they develop for many hours but eventually arrest as hollow balls of several hundred cells (called blastulae). Propose an explanation for why such embryos arrest, but also why they progress as far as they do.

• **21-10 Copolymer Analysis.** In their initial attempts to determine codon assignments, Nirenberg and Matthei first used RNA homopolymers and then used RNA copolymers synthesized by the enzyme polynucleotide phosphorylase. This enzyme adds nucleotides randomly to the growing chain but in proportion to their presence in the incubation mixture. By varying the ratio of precursor molecules in the synthesis of copolymers, Nirenberg and Matthei were able to deduce base compositions (but usually not actual sequences) of the codons that code for various amino acids. Suppose you carry out two polynucleotide phosphorylase incubations, with UTP and CTP present in both but in different ratios. In incubation A, the precursors are present in equal concentrations. In incubation B, there is three times as much UTP as CTP. The copolymers generated in both incubation mixtures are then used in a cell-free protein-synthesizing system, and the resulting polypeptides are analyzed for amino acid composition.

(a) What are the eight possible codons represented by the nucleotide sequences of the resulting copolymers in both incubation mixtures? What amino acids do these codons code for?

(b) For every 64 codons in the copolymer formed in incubation A, how many of each of the 8 possible codons would you expect on average? How many for incubation B?

(c) What can you say about the expected frequency of occurrence of the possible amino acids in the polypeptides obtained upon translation of the copolymers from incubation A? What about the polypeptides that result from translation of the incubation B copolymers?

(d) Explain what sort of information can be obtained by this technique.

(e) Would it be possible by this technique to determine that codons with 2 U's and 1 C code for phenylalanine, leucine, and serine? Why or why not?

(f) Would it be possible by this technique to decide which of the three codons with 2 U's and 1 C (UUC, UCU, CUU) correspond to each of the three amino acids mentioned in part e? Why or why not?

(g) Suggest a way to assign the three codons of part f to the appropriate amino acids of part e.

• **21-11 Introns.** To investigate the possible presence of introns in three newly discovered genes (*X, Y,* and *Z*), you perform an experiment in which the restriction enzyme *Hae*III is used to cleave either the DNA of each gene or the cDNA made by copying its mRNA with reverse transcriptase. The resulting DNA fragments are separated by gel electrophoresis, and the presence of fragments in the gels is detected by hybridizing to a radioactive DNA probe made by copying the intact gene with DNA polymerase in the presence of radioactive substrates. The following results are obtained:

Source of DNA	Number of Fragments After Electrophoresis
Gene *X* DNA	3
cDNA made from mRNA *X*	2
Gene *Y* DNA	4
cDNA made from mRNA *Y*	2
Gene *Z* DNA	2
cDNA made from mRNA *Z*	2

(a) What can you conclude about the number of introns present in gene *X*?

(b) What can you conclude about the number of introns present in gene *Y*?

(c) What can you conclude about the number of introns present in gene *Z*?

21-12 Cloning Conundrum. Using established recombinant DNA technology, you insert a gene from a human liver cell into a bacterium. The bacterium then expresses a protein corresponding to the inserted DNA. To your dismay, you discover that the protein produced is useless and is found to contain many more amino acids than does the protein made by the eukaryotic cell. Assuming there is no mutation in the human gene, explain why this happened.

SUGGESTED READING

References of historical importance are marked with a •.

Information Flow and the Genetic Code

Atkins, J. F., and P. V. Baranov. Duality in the genetic code. *Nature* 448 (2007): 1004.

Chiu, Y. L., and W. C. Greene. APOBEC3G: An intracellular centurion. *Philos. Trans. R. Soc. Lond. B Biol. Sci.* 364 (2009): 689.

• Crick, F. H. C. The genetic code. *Sci. Amer.* 207 (October 1962): 66.

• Crick, F. H. C. The genetic code III. *Sci. Amer.* 215 (October 1966): 55.

Kazazian, H. H. Jr. Mobile elements: Drivers of genome evolution. *Science* 303 (2004): 1626.

Lobanov, A. V. et al. Is there a twenty third amino acid in the genetic code? *Trends Genet.* 22 (2006): 357.

• Nirenberg, M. Historical review: Deciphering the genetic code—A personal account. *Trends Biochem. Sci.* 29 (2004): 46.

• Nirenberg, M. W. The genetic code II. *Sci. Amer.* 208 (March 1963): 80.

• Sarkar, S. Forty years under the central dogma. *Trends Biochem. Sci.* 23 (1998): 312.

Yanofsky, C. Establishing the triplet nature of the genetic code. *Cell* 128 (2007): 815.

Transcription in Bacterial Cells

Landick, R. Shifting RNA polymerase into overdrive. *Science* 284 (1999): 598.

Mooney, R. A., S. A. Darst, and R. Landick. Sigma and RNA polymerase: An on-again, off-again relationship? *Mol. Cell* 20 (2005): 335.

Roberts, J. W., S. Shankar, and J. J. Filter. RNA polymerase elongation factors. *Annu. Rev. Microbiol.* 62 (2008): 211.

Young, B. A., T. M. Gruber, and C. A. Gross. Views of transcription initiation. *Cell* 109 (2002): 417.

Transcription in Eukaryotic Cells

Buratowski, S. Connections between mRNA 3′ end processing and transcription termination. *Curr. Opin. Cell Biol.* 17 (2005): 257.

Cramer, P. Self-correcting messages. *Science* 313 (2006): 447.

Egloff, S., and S. Murphy. Cracking the RNA polymerase II CTD code. *Trends Genet.* 24 (2008): 280.

Juven-Gershon, T., J. Y. Hsu, J. W. Theisen, and J. T. Kadonaga. The RNA polymerase II core promoter—The gateway to transcription. *Curr. Opin. Cell Biol.* 20 (2008): 253.

Nudler, E. RNA polymerase active center: The molecular engine of transcription. *Annu. Rev. Biochem.* 78 (2009): 335.

Saunders, A., L. J. Core, and J. T. Lis. Breaking barriers to transcription elongation. *Nature Rev. Mol. Cell Biol.* 7 (2006): 557.

Sutherland, H., and W. A. Bickmore. Transcription factories: Gene expression in unions? *Nat. Rev. Genet.* 10 (2009): 457.

Tjian, R. Molecular machines that control genes. *Sci. Amer.* 272 (February 1995): 54.

RNA Processing

Blencowe, B. J. Alternative splicing: New insights from global analysis. *Cell* 126 (2006): 37.

Eisenberg, E. et al. Is abundant A-to-I editing primate-specific? *Trends Genet.* 21 (2005): 77.

Perales, R., and D. Bentley. "Cotranscriptionality": The transcription elongation complex as a nexus for nuclear transactions. *Mol. Cell* 36 (2009): 178.

Roy, S. W., and W. Gilbert. The evolution of spliceosomal introns: Patterns, puzzles and progress. *Nature Rev. Genet.* 7 (2006): 211.

Samuel, C. E. et al. RNA editing minireview series. *J. Biol. Chem.* 278 (2003): 1389.

Scherrer, K. Historical review: The discovery of "giant" RNA and RNA processing: 40 years of enigma. *Trends Biochem. Sci.* 28 (2003): 566.

Sharp, P. The discovery of split genes and RNA splicing. *Trends Biochem. Sci.* 30 (2005): 279.

Steitz, J. A. Snurps. *Sci. Amer.* 258 (June 1988): 58.

Wahl, M. C., C. L. Will, and R. Luhrmann. The spliceosome: Design principles of a dynamic RNP machine. *Cell* 136 (2009): 701.

Wang, G.-S., and T. A. Cooper. Splicing in disease: Disruption of the splicing code and the decoding machinery. *Nature Rev. Genet.* 8 (2007): 749.

Xing, Y., and C. Lee. Alternative splicing and RNA selection pressure—Evolutionary consequences for eukaryotic genomes. *Nature Rev. Genet.* 7 (2006): 499.

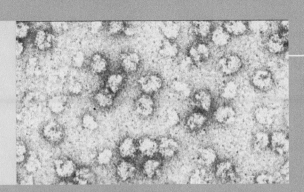

Gene Expression: II. Protein Synthesis and Sorting

n the preceding chapter we took gene expression from DNA to RNA, covering DNA transcription followed by processing of the resulting RNA transcripts. For genes encoding ribosomal and transfer RNAs (and some other small RNAs), RNA is the final product of gene expression. But for the thousands of other genes in an organism's genome, the ultimate gene product is protein. This chapter describes how the messenger RNAs (mRNAs) produced by these protein-coding genes are translated into polypeptides, how polypeptides become functional proteins, and how proteins reach the destinations where they carry out their functions.

Translation, the key step in the production of protein molecules, involves a change in language from the nucleotide base sequence of an mRNA molecule to the amino acid sequence of a polypeptide chain. During this process, a sequence of mRNA nucleotides, read as triplet codons, specifies the order in which amino acids are added to a growing polypeptide chain. Ribosomes serve as the intracellular sites for translation, while RNA molecules are the agents that ensure insertion of the correct amino acids at each position in the polypeptide. We will start by surveying the cell's cast of characters for performing translation, and then we will examine each of its steps in detail.

Translation: The Cast of Characters

The cellular machinery for translating mRNAs into polypeptides involves five major components: *ribosomes* that carry out the process of polypeptide synthesis, *tRNA* molecules that align amino acids in the correct order along the mRNA template, *aminoacyl-tRNA synthetases* that attach amino acids to their appropriate tRNA molecules, *mRNA* molecules that encode the amino acid sequence information for the polypeptides being synthesized, and *protein factors* that facilitate several steps in the translation process. In introducing this cast of characters, let's begin with the ribosomes.

The Ribosome Carries Out Polypeptide Synthesis

Ribosomes play a central role in protein synthesis, orienting the mRNA and amino acid-carrying tRNAs so the genetic code can be read accurately and catalyzing peptide bond formation to link the amino acids into a polypeptide. As we saw in Chapter 4, **ribosomes** are particles made of ribosomal RNA (rRNA) and protein that reside in the cytoplasm and, in eukaryotes, in the mitochondrial matrix and chloroplast stroma. In the eukaryotic cytoplasm, ribosomes occur both free in the cytosol and bound to membranes of the endoplasmic reticulum and the outer membrane of the nuclear envelope. The ribosomes of prokaryotes (archaea and bacteria) are smaller than those of eukaryotes, although many of the ribosomal proteins, translation factors, and tRNAs used by archaea resemble their eukaryotic counterparts more closely than do the comparable components of bacteria.

The shape of a typical bacterial ribosome revealed by electron microscopy is shown in **Figure 22-1**. Like all ribosomes, it is built from two dissociable subunits called the *large* and *small subunits*. The bacterial ribosome has a sedimentation coefficient of about 70S and is built from a 30S small subunit and a 50S large subunit. Its eukaryotic equivalent is an 80S ribosome consisting of a 40S subunit and a 60S subunit. **Table 22-1** lists some of the properties of bacterial and eukaryotic ribosomes and their subunits. The bacterial ribosome contains fewer proteins, is sensitive to different inhibitors of protein synthesis, and has smaller RNA molecules (and one fewer RNA) than eukaryotic ribosomes have. In Chapter 21, we saw that rRNAs are produced from larger precursor molecules by cleavage and processing reactions that, in eukaryotes, take place within the nucleolus (page 543). During these processing events, the rRNAs become associated with ribosomal proteins and self-assemble into small and large subunits, which come together only after binding to mRNA. X-ray crystallography has allowed the

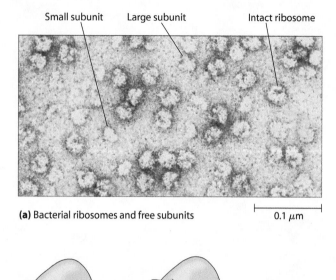

Small subunit   Large subunit   Intact ribosome

(a) Bacterial ribosomes and free subunits

0.1 μm

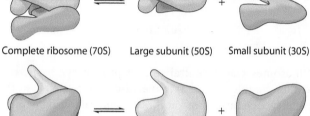

Complete ribosome (70S)   Large subunit (50S)   Small subunit (30S)

(b) Two views of a bacterial ribosome and its subunits

FIGURE 22-1 The Bacterial Ribosome. (a) The electron micrograph shows intact ribosomes as well as individual subunits (TEM). **(b)** The two structural models, based on such micrographs, show two views in which the ribosome has been rotated by 90 degrees. Bacterial ribosomes are about 25 nm in diameter. (Eukaryotic cytoplasmic ribosomes are roughly similar in shape and about 30 nm in diameter.)

3-D STRUCTURE TUTORIALS *An introduction to ribosome*
www.thecellplace.com   *structure*

arrangement of all the individual proteins and RNA molecules of the small and large subunits of bacterial ribosomes to be pinpointed down to the atomic level. Venkatraman Ramakrishnan, Thomas A. Steitz, and Ada E. Yonath were awarded the Nobel Prize in Chemistry in 2009 for their contributions to this monumental achievement.

Functionally, ribosomes have sometimes been called the "workbenches" of protein synthesis, but their active role in polypeptide synthesis makes "machine" a more apt label. In essence, the role of the ribosome in polypeptide synthesis resembles that of a large, complicated enzyme constructed from more than 50 different proteins and several kinds of rRNA. For many years it was thought that the rRNA simply provided a structural scaffold for the ribosomal proteins, with the latter actually carrying out the steps in polypeptide synthesis. But today we know that the reverse is closer to the truth—rRNA performs many of the ribosome's key functions.

Four sites on the ribosome are particularly important for protein synthesis (**Figure 22-2**). These are an **mRNA-binding site** and three sites where tRNA can bind: an **A (aminoacyl) site** that binds each newly arriving tRNA with its attached amino acid, a **P (peptidyl) site** where the tRNA carrying the growing polypeptide chain resides, and an **E (exit) site,** from which tRNAs leave the ribosome after they have discharged their amino acids. How these sites function in the process of translation will become clear in a few pages.

Transfer RNA Molecules Bring Amino Acids to the Ribosome

Since the sequence of codons in mRNA ultimately determines the amino acid sequence of polypeptide chains, a mechanism must exist that enables codons to arrange amino acids in the proper order. The general nature of this mechanism was first proposed in 1957 by Francis Crick. With remarkable foresight, Crick postulated that amino acids cannot directly recognize nucleotide base sequences and that some kind of hypothetical "adaptor" molecule must therefore mediate the interaction between amino acids and mRNA. He further predicted that each adaptor molecule possesses two sites, one that binds to a specific amino acid and the other that recognizes an mRNA base sequence coding for this amino acid.

In the year following Crick's adaptor proposal, Mahlon Hoagland discovered a family of adaptor molecules exhibiting these predicted properties. While investigating the process of protein synthesis in cell-free systems, Hoagland found that radioactive amino acids first become

Table 22-1   Properties of Bacterial and Eukaryotic Cytoplasmic Ribosomes

Source	Size of Ribosomes		Subunit	Subunit Size		Subunit Proteins	Subunit RNA	
	S Value*	Mol. Wt.		S Value	Mol. Wt.		S Value	Nucleotides
Bacterial cells	70S	2.5×10^6	Large	50S	1.6×10^6	34	23S	2900
							5S	120
			Small	30S	0.9×10^6	21	16S	1540
Eukaryotic cells	80S	4.2×10^6	Large	60S	2.8×10^6	About 46	25–28S	≤4700
							5.8S	160
							5S	120
			Small	40S	1.43×10^6	About 32	18S	1900

*If you are surprised that the S values of the subunits do not add up to that of the whole ribosome, recall that an S value is a measure of the velocity at which a particle sediments upon centrifugation and is only indirectly related to the mass of the particle.

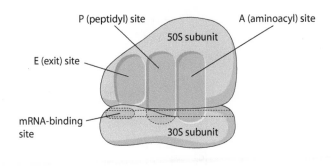

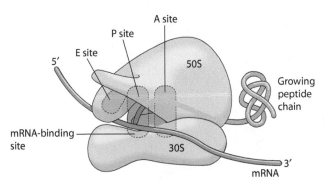

FIGURE 22-2 Binding Sites on a Ribosome. Ribosomes contain A and P sites where amino acid-carrying tRNA molecules bind during polypeptide synthesis, and an E site from which empty tRNAs leave the ribosome. The mRNA-binding site binds a specific nucleotide sequence near the 5′ end of mRNA, placing the mRNA in proper position for translation of its first codon. The binding sites are all located at or near the interface between the large and small subunits. In the top diagram, which is a schematic representation of a bacterial ribosome used in this chapter, the pair of horizontal dashed lines indicates where the mRNA molecule lies. The bottom diagram is a more realistic representation.

covalently attached to small RNA molecules. Adding these amino acid–RNA complexes to ribosomes led to the onset of protein synthesis and the incorporation of radioactive amino acids into new proteins. Hoagland therefore concluded that amino acids are initially bound to small RNA molecules, which then bring the amino acids to the ribosome for subsequent insertion into newly forming polypeptide chains.

The small RNA molecules that Hoagland discovered were named **transfer RNAs (tRNAs).** Appropriate to their role as intermediaries between mRNA and amino acids, tRNA molecules have two kinds of specificity. Each tRNA binds to one specific amino acid, and each recognizes one or more mRNA codons specifying that particular amino acid, as indicated by the genetic code. Transfer RNAs are linked to their corresponding amino acids by an ester bond that joins the amino acid to the 2′- or 3′-hydroxyl group of the adenine (A) nucleotide located at the 3′ end of all tRNA molecules (**Figure 22-3a**). Selection of the correct amino acid for each tRNA is the responsibility of the enzymes that catalyze formation of the ester bond, as we will discuss shortly. By convention, the name of the amino acid that attaches to a given tRNA is indicated by a superscript. For example, tRNA molecules specific for alanine are identified as tRNA[Ala]. Once the amino acid is

attached, the tRNA is called an **aminoacyl tRNA** (e.g., alanyl tRNA[Ala]). The tRNA is said to be in its *charged* form, and the amino acid is said to be *activated.*

Transfer RNA molecules can recognize codons in mRNA because each tRNA possesses an **anticodon,** a special trinucleotide sequence located within one of the loops of the tRNA molecule (see Figure 22-3a). The anticodon of each tRNA is complementary to one or more mRNA codons that specify the amino acid being carried by that tRNA. Therefore, *anticodons permit tRNA molecules to recognize codons in mRNA by complementary base pairing.* Take careful note of the convention used in representing codons and anticodons: Codons in mRNA are written in the 5′ → 3′ direction, whereas anticodons in tRNA are usually represented in the 3′ → 5′ orientation. Thus, one of the codons for alanine is 5′-GCC-3′, and the corresponding anticodon in tRNA is 3′-CGG-5′.

Since the genetic code employs 61 codons to specify amino acids (page 655), you might expect to find 61 different tRNA molecules involved in protein synthesis, each recognizing a different codon. However, the number of different tRNAs is significantly less than 61 because many tRNA molecules recognize more than one codon. You can see why this is possible by examining the table of the genetic code (see Figure 21-6). Codons differing in the third base often code for the same amino acid. For example, UUU and UUC both code for phenylalanine; UCU, UCC, UCA, and UCG all code for serine; and so forth. In such cases, the same tRNA can bind to more than one codon without introducing mistakes. For example, a single tRNA can recognize the codons UUU and UUC because both code for the same amino acid, phenylalanine.

Such considerations led Francis Crick to propose that mRNA and tRNA line up on the ribosome in a way that permits flexibility or "wobble" in the pairing between the third base of the codon and the corresponding base in the anticodon. According to this **wobble hypothesis,** the flexibility in codon-anticodon binding allows some unexpected base pairs to form (**Figure 22-4**). The unusual base inosine (I), which is extremely rare in other RNA molecules, occurs often in the wobble position of tRNA anticodons (see Figure 22-3a). Inosine is the "wobbliest" of all third-position bases, since it can pair with U, C, or A. For example, a tRNA with the anticodon 3′-UAI-5′ can recognize the codons AUU, AUC, and AUA, all of which code for the amino acid isoleucine.

It is because of wobble that fewer tRNA molecules are required for some amino acids than the number of codons that specify those amino acids. In the case of isoleucine, for example, a cell can translate all three codons with a single tRNA molecule containing 3′-UAI-5′ as its anticodon. Similarly, the six codons for the amino acid leucine (UUA, UUG, CUU, CUC, CUA, and CUG) require only three tRNAs because of wobble. Although the existence of wobble means that a single tRNA molecule can recognize more than one codon, the different codons recognized by a given tRNA always code for the same amino acid, so wobble does not cause insertion of incorrect amino acids.

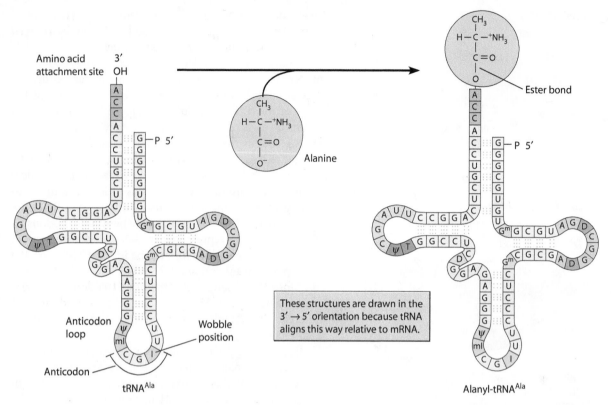

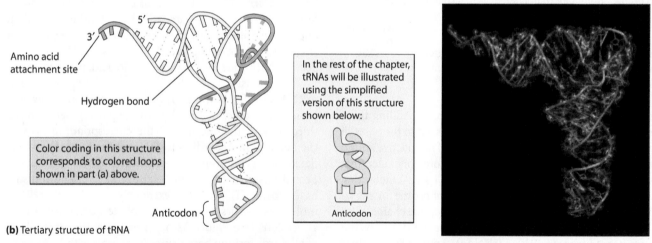

FIGURE 22-3 Structure and Aminoacylation of a tRNA. (a) Yeast alanine tRNA, like all tRNA molecules, contains three major loops, four base-paired regions, an anticodon triplet, and a 3' terminal sequence of CCA, to which the appropriate amino acid can be attached by an ester bond. Modified bases are dark colored, and their names (as nucleosides) are abbreviated I for inosine, mI for methylinosine, D for dihydrouridine, T for ribothymidine, ψ for pseudouridine, and G^m for methylguanosine. (For the significance of the wobble position in the anticodon, see Figure 22-4.) **(b)** In the L-shaped tertiary structure of a tRNA the amino acid attachment site is at one end and the anticodon at the other. The image on the right shows a three-dimensional model of the yeast phenylalanine tRNA, with the molecular surface in transparent gray, and the RNA backbone in orange.

VIDEOS www.thecellplace.com *A stick-and-ribbon rendering of a tRNA*

Aminoacyl-tRNA Synthetases Link Amino Acids to the Correct Transfer RNAs

Before a tRNA molecule can bring its amino acid to the ribosome, that amino acid must be attached covalently to the tRNA. The enzymes responsible for linking amino

acids to their corresponding tRNAs are called **aminoacyl-tRNA synthetases.** Cells typically have 20 different aminoacyl-tRNA synthetases, one for each of the 20 amino acids commonly used in protein synthesis. Cells that utilize the unusual 21st and 22nd amino acids, *selenocysteine* and

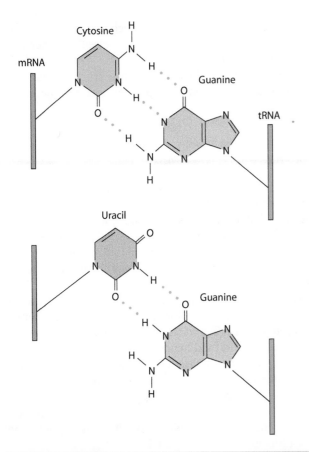

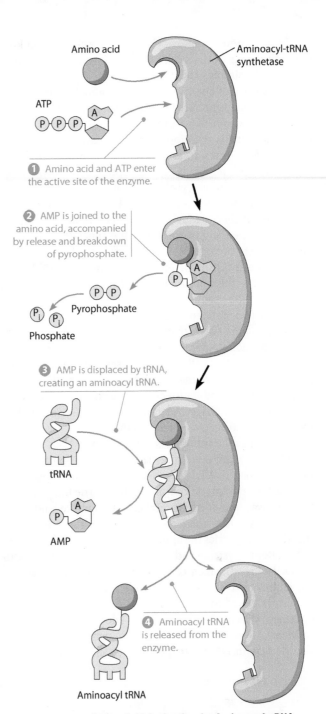

Bases Recognized in Codon (third position only)	Base in Anticodon
U	A
G	C
A or G	U
C or U	G
U, C, or A	I (Inosine)

FIGURE 22-4 The Wobble Hypothesis. The two diagrams illustrate how a slight shift or "wobble" in the position of the base guanine in a tRNA anticodon would permit it to pair with uracil (*bottom*) instead of its normal complementary base, cytosine (*top*). The table summarizes the base pairs permitted at the third position of a codon by the wobble hypothesis.

FIGURE 22-5 Amino Acid Activation by Aminoacyl-tRNA Synthetase. This enzyme catalyzes the formation of an ester bond between the carboxyl group of an amino acid and the 3′ OH of the appropriate tRNA, generating an aminoacyl tRNA.

pyrrolysine (page 656), contain special tRNAs and aminoacyl-tRNA synthetases for these amino acids as well. When more than one tRNA exists for a given amino acid, the aminoacyl-tRNA synthetase specific for that particular amino acid recognizes each of the tRNAs. Some cells possess less than 20 aminoacyl-tRNA synthetases. In such cases, the same aminoacyl-tRNA synthetase may catalyze the attachment of two different amino acids to their corresponding tRNAs, or it may attach an incorrect amino acid to a tRNA molecule. These latter "errors" are corrected by a second enzyme that alters the incorrect amino acid after it has been attached to the tRNA.

Aminoacyl-tRNA synthetases catalyze the attachment of amino acids to their corresponding tRNAs via an ester bond, accompanied by the hydrolysis of ATP to AMP and pyrophosphate:

Figure 22-5 outlines the steps by which this reaction occurs. The driving force for the reaction is provided by the hydrolysis of pyrophosphate to 2 P_i.

In the product, aminoacyl tRNA, the ester bond linking the amino acid to the tRNA is said to be a "high-energy" bond. This simply means that hydrolysis of the bond releases sufficient energy to drive formation of the peptide bond that will eventually join the amino acid to a growing polypeptide chain. The process of aminoacylation of a tRNA molecule is therefore also called *amino acid activation* because it links an amino acid to its proper tRNA as well as activates it for subsequent peptide bond formation.

How do aminoacyl-tRNA synthetases identify the correct tRNA for each amino acid? Differences in the base sequences of the various tRNA molecules allow them to be distinguished and, surprisingly, the anticodon is not the only feature to be recognized. Changes in the base sequence of either the anticodon triplet or the 3′ end of a tRNA molecule can alter the amino acid that a tRNA attaches to. Thus, aminoacyl-tRNA synthetases recognize nucleotides located in at least two different regions of tRNA molecules when they pick out the tRNA that is to become linked to a particular amino acid. After linking an amino acid to a tRNA molecule, aminoacyl-tRNA synthetases proofread the final product to make sure that the correct amino acid has been used. This proofreading function is performed by a site on the aminoacyl-tRNA synthetase molecule that recognizes incorrect amino acids and releases them by hydrolyzing the bond that links the amino acid to the tRNA.

Once the correct amino acid has been joined to its tRNA, it is the tRNA itself (and not the amino acid) that recognizes the appropriate codon in mRNA. The first evidence for this was provided by François Chapeville and Fritz Lipmann, who designed an elegant experiment involving the tRNA that carries the amino acid cysteine. They took the tRNA after its cysteine had been attached and treated it with a nickel catalyst, which converts the attached cysteine into the amino acid alanine. The result was therefore alanine covalently linked to a tRNA molecule that normally carries cysteine. When the researchers added this abnormal aminoacyl tRNA to a cell-free protein-synthesizing system, alanine was inserted into polypeptide chains in locations normally occupied by cysteine. Such results proved that codons in mRNA recognize tRNA molecules rather than their bound amino acids. Hence, the specificity of the aminoacyl-tRNA synthetase reaction is crucial to the accuracy of gene expression because it ensures that the proper amino acid is linked to each tRNA.

Messenger RNA Brings Polypeptide Coding Information to the Ribosome

As you learned in Chapter 21, the sequence of codons in mRNA directs the order in which amino acids are linked together during protein synthesis. Hence, the mRNA that happens to bind to a given ribosome will determine which polypeptide that ribosome will manufacture. In eukaryotes, where transcription takes place in the nucleus and protein synthesis is mainly a cytoplasmic event, the mRNA must first be exported from the nucleus. Export is mediated by mRNA-binding proteins that contain amino acid sequences called *nuclear export signals (NES)*, which target the protein (and hence its bound mRNA) for transport through the nuclear pores (page 540). This step is not required in prokaryotes, which by definition have no nucleus. As a result, transcription and translation are often coupled in prokaryotic cells—that is, ribosomes can begin translating an mRNA before its transcription from DNA is completed (see Figure 21-16).

At the heart of each messenger RNA molecule is, of course, its message—the sequence of nucleotides that encodes a polypeptide. However, mRNAs also possess sequences at either end that are not translated (**Figure 22-6**). The untranslated sequence at the 5′ end of an mRNA precedes the **start codon**, which is the first codon to be translated. AUG is the most common start codon, although a few other triplets are occasionally used for this purpose. The untranslated sequence at the 3′ end follows the **stop codon**, which signals the end of translation and can be UAG, UAA, or UGA. The 5′ and 3′ untranslated regions range from a few dozen to hundreds of nucleotides in length. Although these

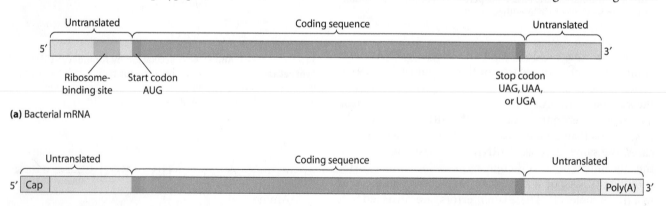

(a) Bacterial mRNA

(b) Eukaryotic mRNA

FIGURE 22-6 Comparison of Bacterial and Eukaryotic Messenger RNA. **(a)** A bacterial mRNA molecule encoding a single polypeptide has the features shown here. (A polycistronic bacterial mRNA would generally have a set of these features for each gene.) **(b)** A eukaryotic mRNA molecule has, in addition, a 5′ cap and a 3′ poly(A) tail. It lacks a ribosome-binding site (a nucleotide sequence also called a Shine–Dalgarno sequence, after its discoverers).

sequences are not translated, their presence is essential for proper mRNA function. Included in the untranslated regions of eukaryotic mRNAs are a 5′ cap and a 3′ poly(A) tail, both of which were described in Chapter 21. As we will see, the 5′ cap is important in initiating translation in eukaryotes.

In eukaryotes, most mRNA molecules are *monocistronic* (i.e., they encode a single polypeptide). In bacteria and archaea, however, some mRNAs are *polycistronic*—meaning they encode several polypeptides, usually with related functions in the cell. The clusters of genes that give rise to polycistronic mRNAs are single transcription units called *operons* Although most often thought of as a feature of prokaryotes, eukaryotes also produce polycistronic RNAs. In some cases, such as the nematode, *Caenorhabditis elegans,* it is only the pre-mRNA that is polycistronic; subsequent RNA processing results in individual mRNAs that are monocistronic and translated separately. In other eukaryotes, dicistronic RNAs (i.e., RNAs that encode two proteins) remain joined and are translated together.

Protein Factors Are Required for the Initiation, Elongation, and Termination of Polypeptide Chains

In addition to aminoacyl-tRNA synthetases and the protein components of the ribosome, translation requires the participation of several other kinds of protein molecules. Some of these *protein factors* are required for initiating the translation process, others for elongating the growing polypeptide chain, and still others for terminating polypeptide synthesis. The exact roles played by these factors will become apparent as we now proceed to a discussion of the mechanism of translation.

The Mechanism of Translation

The translation of mRNAs into polypeptides is an ordered, stepwise process that begins the synthesis of a polypeptide chain at its amino-terminal end, or *N-terminus,* and sequentially adds amino acids to the growing chain until the carboxyl-terminal end, or *C-terminus,* is reached. The first experimental evidence for such a mechanism was provided in 1961 by Howard Dintzis, who investigated hemoglobin synthesis in developing red blood cells that had been incubated briefly with radioactive amino acids. Dintzis reasoned that if the time of incubation is kept relatively brief, then the radioactivity present in completed hemoglobin chains should be concentrated at the most recently synthesized end of the molecule. He found that the highest concentration of radioactivity in completed hemoglobin chains was at the C-terminal end, indicating that the C-terminus is the last part of the polypeptide chain to be synthesized. This allowed him to conclude that during mRNA translation, *amino acids are added to the growing polypeptide chain beginning at the N-terminus and proceeding toward the C-terminus.*

In theory, mRNA could be read in either the 5′ → 3′ direction or the 3′ → 5′ direction during this process. The

first attempts to determine the direction in which mRNA is actually read involved the use of artificial RNA molecules. A typical example is the synthetic RNA that can be made by adding the base C to the 3′ end of poly(A), yielding the molecule 5′-AAAAAAAAAAAA…AAC-3′. When added to a cell-free protein-synthesizing system, this RNA stimulates the synthesis of a polypeptide consisting of a stretch of lysine residues with an asparagine at the C-terminus. Because AAA codes for lysine and AAC codes for asparagine, this means that *mRNA is translated in the 5′ → 3′ direction.* Confirming evidence has come from many studies in which the base sequences of naturally occurring mRNAs have been compared with the amino acid sequences of the polypeptide chains they encode. In all cases, the amino acid sequence of the polypeptide chain corresponds to the order of mRNA codons read in the 5′ → 3′ direction.

To understand how translation of mRNA in the 5′ → 3′ direction leads to the synthesis of polypeptides in the N-terminal to C-terminal direction, it is helpful to subdivide the translation process into three stages, as shown in **Figure 22-7**: ❶ an *initiation* stage, in which mRNA is bound to the ribosome and positioned for proper translation; ❷ an *elongation* stage, in which amino acids are sequentially joined together via peptide bonds in an order specified by the arrangement of codons in mRNA; and ❸ a *termination* stage, in which the mRNA and the newly formed polypeptide chain are released from the ribosome.

In the following sections we examine each of these stages in detail. Although our discussion focuses mainly on translation in bacterial cells, where the mechanisms are especially well understood, the comparable events in eukaryotic cells are rather similar. The aspects of translation that differ between bacteria and eukaryotes are confined mostly to the initiation stage, as we describe in the next section.

The Initiation of Translation Requires Initiation Factors, Ribosomal Subunits, mRNA, and Initiator tRNA

Bacterial Initiation. The initiation of translation in bacteria is illustrated in **Figure 22-8**, which shows that initiation can be subdivided into three distinct steps. In step ❶, three **initiation factors**—called *IF1, IF2,* and *IF3*—bind to the small (30S) ribosomal subunit, with GTP attaching to IF2. The presence of IF3 at this early stage prevents the 30S subunit from prematurely associating with the 50S subunit.

In step ❷, mRNA and the tRNA carrying the first amino acid bind to the 30S ribosomal subunit. The mRNA is bound to the 30S subunit in its proper orientation by means of a special nucleotide sequence called the mRNA's *ribosome-binding site* (also known as the *Shine–Dalgarno sequence,* after its discoverers). This sequence consists of a stretch of 3–9 purine nucleotides (often AGGA) located slightly upstream of the start codon. These purines in the mRNA form complementary base pairs with a pyrimidine-rich sequence at the 3′ end of 16S rRNA, which forms the ribosome's *mRNA-binding site.* The importance of the

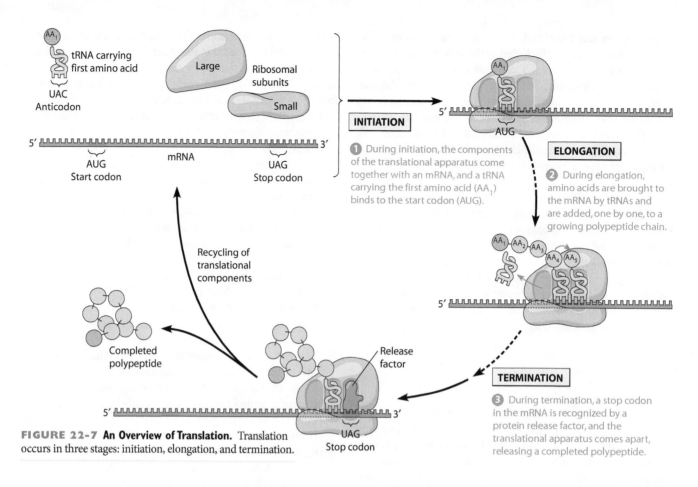

FIGURE 22-7 An Overview of Translation. Translation occurs in three stages: initiation, elongation, and termination.

Within the figure:

- AA₁ / tRNA carrying first amino acid
- UAC Anticodon
- Large / Small Ribosomal subunits
- 5′ mRNA 3′
- AUG Start codon
- UAG Stop codon
- **INITIATION**
- ❶ During initiation, the components of the translational apparatus come together with an mRNA, and a tRNA carrying the first amino acid (AA₁) binds to the start codon (AUG).
- **ELONGATION**
- ❷ During elongation, amino acids are brought to the mRNA by tRNAs and are added, one by one, to a growing polypeptide chain.
- **TERMINATION**
- ❸ During termination, a stop codon in the mRNA is recognized by a protein release factor, and the translational apparatus comes apart, releasing a completed polypeptide.
- Release factor
- Completed polypeptide
- Recycling of translational components

mRNA-binding site has been shown by studies involving *colicins*, which are proteins produced by certain strains of *Escherichia coli* that can kill other types of bacteria. One such protein, colicin E3, kills bacteria by destroying their ability to synthesize proteins. Upon entering the cytoplasm of susceptible bacteria, colicin E3 catalyzes the removal of a 49-nucleotide fragment from the 3′ end of 16S rRNA. This action destroys the mRNA-binding site, thereby creating ribosomes that can no longer initiate polypeptide synthesis.

The binding of mRNA to the mRNA-binding site of the small ribosomal subunit places the mRNA's AUG start codon at the ribosome's P site, where it can bind to the anticodon of the appropriate tRNA. The first clue that a special kind of tRNA is involved in this step emerged when it was discovered that roughly half the proteins in *E. coli* contain methionine at their N-terminal ends. This was surprising because methionine is a relatively uncommon amino acid, accounting for no more than a few percent of the amino acids in bacterial proteins. The explanation for such a pattern became apparent when it was discovered that bacterial cells contain two different methionine-specific tRNAs. One, designated tRNA^Met, carries a normal methionine destined for insertion into the internal regions of polypeptide chains. The other, called tRNA^fMet, carries a methionine that is converted to the derivative *N-formylmethionine (fMet)* after linkage to the tRNA (**Figure 22-9**). In *N*-formylmethionine, the amino group of methionine is blocked by the addition of a formyl group and so cannot form a peptide bond with another amino acid; only the carboxyl group is available for

bonding to another amino acid. Hence *N*-formylmethionine can be situated only at the N-terminal end of a polypeptide chain—suggesting that tRNA^fMet functions as an **initiator tRNA** that starts the process of translation. This idea was soon confirmed by the discovery that bacterial polypeptide chains in the early stages of synthesis always contain *N*-formylmethionine at their N-terminus. Following completion of the polypeptide chain (and in some cases while it is still being synthesized), the formyl group, and often the methionine itself, is enzymatically removed.

During initiation, the initiator tRNA with its attached *N*-formylmethionine is bound to the P site of the 30S ribosomal subunit by the action of initiation factor IF2 (plus GTP), which can distinguish initiator tRNA^fMet from other kinds of tRNA. This attribute of IF2 helps explain why AUG start codons bind to the initiator tRNA^fMet, whereas AUG codons located elsewhere in mRNA bind to the noninitiating tRNA^Met. Once tRNA^fMet enters the P site, its anticodon becomes base-paired with the AUG start codon in the mRNA, and IF3 is released. At this point the 30S subunit with its associated IF1, IF2-GTP, mRNA, and *N*-formylmethionyl tRNA^fMet is referred to as the **30S initiation complex.**

Once IF3 has been released, the 30S initiation complex can bind to a free 50S ribosomal subunit, generating the **70S initiation complex** (step ❸ of Figure 22-8). The 50S subunit then promotes hydrolysis of the IF2-bound GTP, leading to the release of IF2 and IF1. At this stage, all three initiation factors have been released.

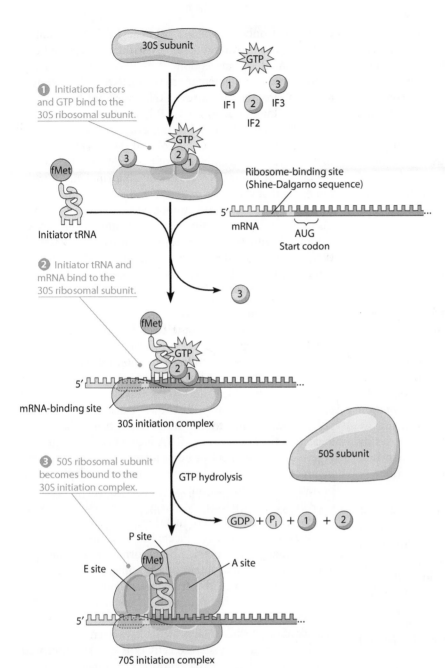

FIGURE 22-8 Initiation of Translation in Bacteria. Assembly of the 70S translation initiation complex occurs in three steps. ❶ Three initiation factors (IF1, IF2, and IF3) plus GTP bind to the small ribosomal subunit. ❷ The initiator aminoacyl tRNA and mRNA are attached. The mRNA-binding site is composed, at least in part, of a portion of the 16S rRNA of the small ribosomal subunit. ❸ The large ribosomal subunit joins the complex. The resulting 70S initiation complex has fMet-tRNA^{fMet} residing in the ribosome's P site.

FIGURE 22-8 Initiation of Translation in Bacteria. Assembly of the 70S translation initiation complex occurs in three steps. ❶ Three initiation factors (IF1, IF2, and IF3) plus GTP bind to the small ribosomal subunit. ❷ The initiator aminoacyl tRNA and mRNA are attached. The mRNA-binding site is composed, at least in part, of a portion of the 16S rRNA of the small ribosomal subunit. ❸ The large ribosomal subunit joins the complex. The resulting 70S initiation complex has fMet-tRNA^{fMet} residing in the ribosome's P site.

ACTIVITIES www.thecellplace.com

Initiation of translation

Eukaryotic Initiation. Unlike the situation in bacteria, the AUG start codon in eukaryotes (and archaea) specifies the amino acid methionine rather than *N*-formylmethionine. Other differences in eukaryotes include the use of a different set of initiation factors known as *eIFs* (roughly

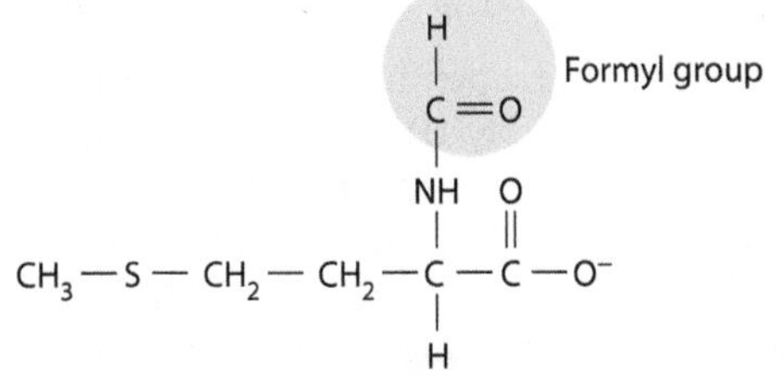

FIGURE 22-9 The Structure of *N*-Formylmethionine. *N*-formylmethionine (fMet) is the modified amino acid with which every polypeptide is initiated in bacteria.

a dozen proteins with names such as eIF1, eIF2, and so forth), a somewhat different pathway for assembling the initiation complex, and a special initiator tRNA^{Met} that—like the normal tRNA for methionine but unlike the initiator tRNA of bacteria—carries methionine that does not become formylated.

At the beginning of eukaryotic initiation, the initiation factor *eIF2* (with GTP attached) binds to the initiator methionyl tRNA^{Met} *before* the tRNA then binds to the small ribosomal subunit along with other initiation factors, including *eIF1A* (the eukaryotic counterpart of bacterial IF1). The resulting complex next binds to the 5′ end of an mRNA, recognizing the 5′ cap with the aid of a cap-binding initiation factor, *eIF4F.* (In some cases the complex may instead bind to an *internal ribosome entry sequence,* or *IRES,* which lies directly upstream of the start codon of certain types of mRNA, especially viral mRNAs.)

After binding to mRNA, the small ribosomal subunit, with the initiator tRNA in tow, scans along the mRNA and usually begins translation at the first AUG triplet it encounters. The nucleotides on either side of the eukaryotic start codon appear to be involved in its recognition. A common start sequence is ACCAUGG (also called a *Kozak sequence*, after the scientist who discovered that many eukaryotic mRNAs have this sequence), where the underlined triplet is the actual start codon. After the initiator tRNA^{Met} becomes base-paired with the start codon, the large ribosomal subunit joins the complex in a reaction facilitated by the hydrolysis of GTP bound to initiation factor *eIF5B*.

Chain Elongation Involves Sequential Cycles of Aminoacyl tRNA Binding, Peptide Bond Formation, and Translocation

Once the initiation complex has been completed, a polypeptide chain is synthesized by the successive addition of amino acids in a sequence specified by codons in mRNA. As summarized in **Figure 22-10**, this *elongation stage* of polypeptide synthesis involves a repetitive three-step cycle in which ❶ *binding of an aminoacyl tRNA* to the ribosome brings a new amino acid into position to be joined to the polypeptide chain, ❷ *peptide bond formation* links this amino acid to the growing polypeptide, and ❸ the mRNA is advanced a distance of three nucleotides by the process of *translocation* to bring the next codon into position for translation. Each of these steps is described in more detail in the following paragraphs.

Binding of Aminoacyl tRNA. At the onset of the elongation stage, the AUG start codon in the mRNA is located at the ribosomal P site and the second codon (the codon immediately downstream from the start codon) is located at the A site. Elongation begins when an aminoacyl tRNA whose anticodon is complementary to the second codon binds to the ribosomal A site (see Figure 22-10, ❶). The binding of this new aminoacyl tRNA to the codon in the A site requires two protein **elongation factors,** *EF-Tu* and *EF-Ts,* and is driven by the hydrolysis of GTP. From now on, every incoming aminoacyl tRNA will bind first to the A (aminoacyl) site—hence the site's name.

The function of EF-Tu, along with its bound GTP, is to convey the aminoacyl tRNA to the A site of the ribosome. The EF-Tu–GTP complex promotes the binding of all aminoacyl tRNAs *except the initiator tRNA* to the ribosome, thus ensuring that AUG codons located downstream from the start codon do not mistakenly recruit an initiator tRNA to the ribosome. As the aminoacyl tRNA is transferred to the ribosome, the GTP is hydrolyzed and the EF-Tu–GDP complex is released. The role of EF-Ts is to regenerate EF-Tu–GTP from EF-Tu–GDP for the next round of the elongation cycle (see Figure 22-10, ❶).

Elongation factors do not recognize individual anticodons, which means that aminoacyl tRNAs of all types (other than initiator tRNAs) are randomly brought to the A site of the ribosome. Some mechanism must therefore ensure that only the correct aminoacyl tRNA is retained by the ribosome for subsequent use during peptide bond formation. If the anticodon of an incoming aminoacyl tRNA is not complementary to the mRNA codon exposed at the A site, the aminoacyl tRNA does not bind to the ribosome long enough for GTP hydrolysis to take place. When the match is close but not exact, transient binding may occur, and GTP is hydrolyzed. However, the mismatch between the anticodon of the aminoacyl tRNA and the codon of the mRNA creates an abnormal structure at the A site that is usually detected by the ribosome, leading to rejection of the bound aminoacyl tRNA. These mechanisms for selecting against incorrect aminoacyl tRNAs, combined with the proofreading capacity of aminoacyl-tRNA synthetases described earlier, ensure that the final error rate in translation is usually no more than 1 incorrect amino acid per 10,000 incorporated.

Peptide Bond Formation. After the appropriate aminoacyl tRNA has become bound to the ribosomal A site, the next step is formation of a peptide bond between the amino group of the amino acid bound at the A site and the carboxyl group that links the initiating amino acid (or growing polypeptide chain) to the tRNA at the P site. The formation of this peptide bond causes the growing polypeptide chain to be transferred from the tRNA located at the P site to the tRNA located at the A site (see Figure 22-10, ❷). Peptide bond formation is the only step in protein synthesis that requires neither nonribosomal protein factors nor an outside source of energy such as GTP or ATP. The necessary energy is provided by cleavage of the high-energy bond that joins the amino acid or peptide chain to the tRNA located at the P site.

For many years, peptide bond formation was thought to be catalyzed by a hypothetical ribosomal protein that was given the name **peptidyl transferase.** However, in 1992 Harry Noller and his colleagues showed that the large subunit of bacterial ribosomes retains peptidyl transferase activity after all ribosomal proteins have been removed. In contrast, peptidyl transferase activity is quickly destroyed when rRNA is degraded by exposing ribosomes to ribonuclease. Such observations suggested that rRNA rather than a ribosomal protein is responsible for catalyzing peptide bond formation. In bacterial ribosomes, peptidyl transferase activity has been localized to the 23S rRNA of the large ribosomal subunit, and high-resolution X-ray data have pinpointed the catalytic site to a specific region of the RNA chain. Hence 23S rRNA is an example of a *ribozyme,* an enzyme made entirely of RNA (see Chapter 6, page 150).

Translocation. After a peptide bond has been formed, the P site contains an empty tRNA and the A site contains a peptidyl tRNA (the tRNA to which the growing polypeptide chain is attached). The mRNA now advances a distance of three nucleotides relative to the small subunit, bringing the next codon into proper position for translation. During this process of **translocation**—which requires that an elongation factor called *EF-G* plus GTP become

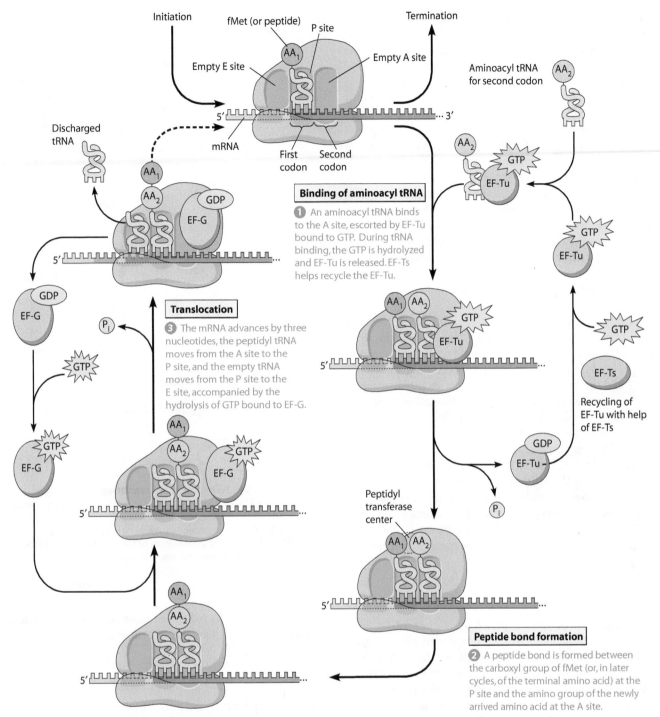

FIGURE 22-10 Polypeptide Chain Elongation in Bacteria. Chain elongation requires the presence of a peptidyl tRNA or, in the first elongation cycle shown here, an fMet-tRNA^{fMet} at the ribosomal P site. Binding of aminoacyl tRNA (❶) is followed by peptide bond formation (❷) catalyzed by the peptidyl transferase activity of the 23S rRNA of the large ribosomal subunit. During translocation (❸), the peptidyl tRNA moves from the A site to the P site, taking the mRNA along with it, and the empty tRNA moves from the P site to the E site and leaves the ribosome. The next mRNA codon is now located in the A site, where the same cycle of events can be repeated for the next amino acid.

ACTIVITIES www.thecellplace.com *Elongation of the polypeptide chain*

transiently associated with the ribosome—the peptidyl tRNA moves from the A site to the P site and the empty tRNA moves from the P site to the E (exit) site. Although these movements are shown in Figure 22-10 as occurring in a

single step (❸), an intermediate "hybrid" state exists in which the anticodon of the peptidyl tRNA still resides at the A site while its aminoacyl end has rotated into the P site, and the anticodon of the empty tRNA still resides at the P site while its other end has rotated into the E site. Hydrolysis of the GTP bound to EF-G triggers a conformational change in the ribosome that completes the movement of the peptidyl tRNA from the A site to the P site, and the empty tRNA from the P site to the E site.

During translocation, the peptidyl tRNA remains hydrogen-bonded to the mRNA as the mRNA advances by three nucleotides. The central role played by peptidyl tRNA in the translocation process has been demonstrated using mutant tRNA molecules that have *four*-nucleotide anticodons. These tRNAs hydrogen-bond to four nucleotides in mRNA; and, when translocation occurs, the mRNA advances by four nucleotides rather than the usual three. Although this observation indicates that the size of the anticodon loop of the peptidyl tRNA bound to the A site determines how far the mRNA advances during translocation, the physical basis for the mechanism that actually translocates the mRNA over the surface of the ribosome is not well understood.

The net effect of translocation is to bring the next mRNA codon into the A site, so the ribosome is now set to receive the next aminoacyl tRNA and repeat the elongation cycle. The only difference between succeeding elongation cycles and the first cycle is that an initiator tRNA occupies the P site at the beginning of the first elongation cycle, and peptidyl tRNA occupies the P site at the beginning of all subsequent cycles. As each successive amino acid is added, the mRNA is progressively read in the $5' \rightarrow 3'$ direction. The amino-terminal end of the growing polypeptide passes out of the ribosome through an *exit tunnel* in the 50S subunit, where it is met by molecular chaperones that help fold the polypeptide into its proper three-dimensional shape. Polypeptide synthesis is very rapid; in a growing *E. coli* cell, a polypeptide of 400 amino acids can be made in 10 seconds.

Termination of Polypeptide Synthesis Is Triggered by Release Factors That Recognize Stop Codons

The elongation process depicted in Figure 22-10 continues in cyclic fashion, reading one codon after another and adding successive amino acids to the polypeptide chain, until one of the three possible stop codons (UAG, UAA, or UGA) in the mRNA arrives at the ribosome's A site (**Figure 22-11**). Unlike other codons, stop codons are not recognized by tRNA molecules. Instead, the stop codons are recognized by proteins called **release factors**, which possess special regions ("peptide anticodons") that bind to mRNA stop codons present at the ribosomal A site. After binding to the A site along with GTP, the release factors terminate translation by triggering release of the completed polypeptide from the peptidyl tRNA. In essence, the reaction is a hydrolytic cleavage: The polypeptide transfers to a water molecule instead of to an activated amino acid, producing a free carboxyl group at the end of the polypeptide—its C-terminus. After the polypeptide is released accompanied by GTP hydrolysis, the ribosome dissociates into its subunits and the tRNAs

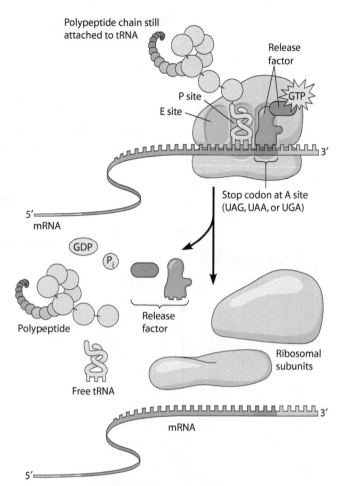

FIGURE 22-11 Termination of Translation. When a stop codon—UAG, UAA, or UGA—arrives at the A site, it is recognized and bound by protein release factors associated with GTP. Hydrolysis of the GTP is accompanied by release of the completed polypeptide, followed by dissociation of the tRNA, mRNA, ribosomal subunits, and release factors.

ACTIVITIES www.thecellplace.com *Translation termination*

and mRNAs are released. All of these components are now available for reuse in a new cycle of protein synthesis.

Polypeptide Folding Is Facilitated by Molecular Chaperones

Before newly synthesized polypeptides can function properly, they must fold into the correct three-dimensional shape. As discussed in Chapter 3, the primary sequence of a protein is sufficient to specify its three-dimensional structure, and some polypeptides spontaneously fold into the proper shape in a test tube. However, protein folding inside cells is usually facilitated by proteins called **molecular chaperones** (p. 33). In fact, proper folding often requires the action of several chaperones acting in sequence, beginning when the growing polypeptide chain first emerges from the ribosome's exit tunnel.

A key function of molecular chaperones is to bind to polypeptide chains during the early stages of folding, thereby preventing them from interacting with other polypeptides before the newly folding chains have acquired the proper conformation. If the folding process goes awry, chaperones can sometimes rescue improperly folded proteins and help them fold properly, or the improperly folded proteins may be destroyed. However, some kinds of incorrectly folded polypeptides tend to bind to each other and form insoluble aggregates that become deposited both within and between cells. Such protein deposits disrupt cell function and may even lead to tissue degeneration and cell death. In **Box 22A**, we discuss how such events can contribute to the development of ailments such as Alzheimer disease and mad cow disease.

Chaperones are found throughout the living world, from archaea and bacteria to the various compartments of eukaryotic cells. Two of the most widely occurring chaperone families are *Hsp70* and *Hsp60*. The "Hsp" comes from the original designation of these proteins as "heat-shock proteins" because cells produce them in response to stressful conditions, such as exposure to high temperatures; under these conditions, chaperones facilitate the refolding of heat-damaged proteins. Members of the Hsp70 and Hsp60 chaperone families operate by somewhat different mechanisms, but both involve ATP-dependent cycles of binding and releasing their protein substrates. (It is the release step that requires ATP hydrolysis.) Molecular chaperones are also involved in activities other than protein folding. For example, they help assemble folded polypeptides into multisubunit proteins and—as we will see later in this chapter—they facilitate protein transport into mitochondria and chloroplasts by maintaining polypeptides in an unfolded state prior to their transport into these organelles.

Protein Synthesis Typically Utilizes a Substantial Fraction of a Cell's Energy Budget

Polypeptide elongation involves the hydrolysis of at least four "high-energy" phosphoanhydride bonds per amino acid added. Two of these bonds are broken in the aminoacyl-tRNA synthetase reaction, where ATP is hydrolyzed to AMP accompanied by the release of two free phosphate groups (see Figure 22-5). The rest are supplied by two molecules of GTP: one used in binding the incoming aminoacyl tRNA at the A site, and the other in the translocation step. Assuming each phosphoanhydride bond has a $\Delta G^{o\prime}$ (standard free energy) of 7.3 kcal/mol, the four bonds represent a standard free energy input of 29.2 kcal/mol of amino acid inserted. Thus, the elongation steps required to synthesize a polypeptide 100 amino acids long have a $\Delta G^{o\prime}$ value of about 2920 kcal/mol. Moreover, additional GTPs are utilized during formation of the initiation complex, during the transient binding of incorrect aminoacyl tRNAs to the ribosome, and during the termination step of polypeptide synthesis. Clearly, protein synthesis is an expensive process energetically. In fact, it accounts for a substantial fraction of the total energy budget of most cells. When we also consider the energy required to synthesize messenger RNA and the components of the translational apparatus, as well as the use of ATP by chaperone proteins, the cost of protein synthesis becomes even greater.

It is important to note that during translation, GTP does not function as a typical ATP-like energy donor: Its hydrolysis is not directly linked to the formation of a covalent bond. Instead, GTP appears to induce conformational changes in initiation and elongation factors by binding to them and releasing from them, just as we saw for heterotrimeric and monomeric G proteins. These shape changes, in turn, allow the factors to bind (noncovalently) to, and be released from, the ribosome. In addition, hydrolysis of the GTP attached to EF-Tu apparently contributes to the accuracy of translation by playing a role in the proofreading mechanism that ejects incorrect aminoacyl tRNAs when they enter the A site.

A Summary of Translation

We have now seen that translation serves as the mechanism that converts information stored in strings of mRNA codons into a chain of amino acids linked by peptide bonds. For a visual summary of the process, refer back to Figure 22-7. As the ribosome reads the mRNA codon by codon in the $5' \rightarrow 3'$ direction, successive amino acids are brought into place by complementary base pairing between the codons in the mRNA and the anticodons of aminoacyl-tRNA molecules. When a stop codon is encountered, the completed polypeptide is released, and the mRNA and ribosomal subunits become available for further use.

Most messages are read by many ribosomes simultaneously, each ribosome following closely behind the next on the same mRNA molecule. A cluster of such ribosomes attached to a single mRNA molecule is called a **polyribosome** (see Figure 21-16). By allowing many polypeptides to be synthesized at the same time from a single mRNA molecule, polyribosomes maximize the efficiency of mRNA utilization.

RNA molecules play especially important roles in translation. The mRNA plays a central role, of course, as the carrier of the genetic message. The tRNA molecules serve as the adaptors that bring the amino acids to the appropriate codons. Last but not least, the rRNA molecules have multiple functions. Not only do they serve as structural components of the ribosomes, but one (the 16S rRNA of the small subunit) provides the binding site for incoming mRNA, and another (the 23S rRNA of the large subunit) catalyzes the formation of the peptide bond. The fundamental roles played by RNA may be a vestige of the way that living organisms first evolved on Earth. As we discussed in Chapter 6, the discovery of RNA catalysts (ribozymes) has fostered the idea that the first catalysts on Earth may have been self-replicating RNA molecules rather than proteins. Hence, the present-day ribosome may have evolved from a primitive translational apparatus that was based entirely on RNA molecules.

Polypeptide chains must be folded properly before they can perform their normal functions. In humans, more than a dozen diseases have been linked to defects in this folding process. Among the best known is *Alzheimer disease,* the memory disorder that affects one in ten Americans over 65 years old. The symptoms of Alzheimer's are caused by the degeneration of brain cells that exhibit two kinds of structural abnormalities—intracellular *tangles* of a polymerized form of a microtubule accessory protein called *tau,* and extracellular *amyloid plaques* containing fibrils made of a protein fragment 40 to 42 amino acids long called *amyloid-β* (Aβ). Evidence that Aβ accumulation is the primary cause of Alzheimer's emerged in the early 1990s, when it was discovered that some forms of Alzheimer's are triggered by inherited mutations in APP, a plasma membrane precursor protein whose cleavage gives rise to Aβ. Cleavage of the mutant APP yields a misfolded form of Aβ that aggregates into long fibrils instead of remaining soluble, thereby creating amyloid plaques that accumulate in the brain. Inherited mutations in the enzymes responsible for cleaving APP into Aβ can also produce hereditary forms of Alzheimer's, again characterized by the presence of amyloid plaques. Amyloid accumulation leads to a series of events, including the alteration of tau proteins inside cells, that cause brain cell death and memory loss.

Most people with Alzheimer disease do not inherit mutations in APP or in the enzymes that cleave it, and so they produce a normal version of Aβ. Though this normal Aβ usually causes no problems, in some individuals these same Aβ molecules aggregate into fibrils that accumulate and form amyloid plaques. A possible reason for this aberrant behavior is suggested by the discovery that people who inherit different forms of the protein *apolipoprotein E (apoE)* have differing risks of developing Alzheimer's. ApoE functions primarily in cholesterol transport, but some forms of apoE stimulate the accumulation and aggregation of Aβ into the fibrils that form amyloid plaques. Thus any factor that promotes Aβ accumulation may increase a person's risk for Alzheimer's.

Our growing understanding of the relationship between Aβ and Alzheimer's suggests that the disease might eventually be treated using drugs that either inhibit the formation of Aβ or promote its elimination from the brain. It has already been shown that animals can be protected against Aβ buildup by using experimental treatments such as (1) enzyme inhibitors that block the cleavage of Aβ from its precursor APP, (2) small molecules that disrupt amyloid plaques or prevent their formation, and (3) Aβ-containing vaccines that stimulate the immune system to clean up amyloid plaques and/or prevent them from forming. Such vaccines are capable of protecting mice with Alzheimer's symptoms from suffering further memory loss, providing hope that this devastating illness will be conquered in the not-too-distant future.

Abnormalities in protein folding also lie at the heart of a group of brain-destroying infectious diseases that include *scrapie* in sheep and *mad cow disease* in cattle. Stanley Prusiner, who received a Nobel Prize in 1997 for his pioneering work in this field, has proposed that such diseases are transmitted by protein-containing particles called **prions** (briefly discussed in Chapter 4). Because prions do not appear to contain DNA or RNA, Prusiner formulated a unique theory to explain how prions might transmit disease by triggering the infectious spread of abnormal protein folding. According to this theory, a

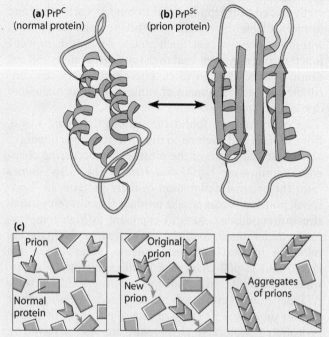

FIGURE 22A-1 A Model for How Prions Promote Their Own Formation. (a) A normal prion protein (PrP^C) contains several α-helices. (b) A misfolded prion protein (PrP^{Sc}) contains β-pleated sheets. (c) The interaction of the prion form of the protein with the normal form can induce the normal protein to misfold. The resulting chain reaction can cause aggregation of the prion form of the protein, leading to degeneration of the brain.

normally folded prion protein (designated PrP^C, **Figure 22-A1a**) can adopt a misfolded conformation (designated PrP^{Sc}, Figure 22-A1b). When the misfolded PrP^{Sc} encounters a normal PrP^C polypeptide in the process of folding, it causes the normal polypeptide to fold improperly (Figure 22-A1c). The resulting, abnormally folded protein triggers extensive nerve cell damage in the brain, leading to uncontrolled muscle movements and eventual death. The presence of even a tiny bit of prion protein can initiate a chain reaction that causes a cell's normal PrP^C polypeptide chains to fold into more and more of the improperly folded prion protein (PrP^{Sc}). In this way, prion proteins are able to reproduce themselves without the need for nucleic acid.

Even more surprising has been the discovery of different "strains" of prions that cause slightly different forms of disease. When researchers mix tiny quantities of different PrP^{Sc} strains in separate test tubes with large amounts of the same, normal PrP^C polypeptide, each tube produces more of the specific PrP^{Sc} strain than was initially added to that tube. This ability to identify different strains of prions has helped investigators show that almost 200 people in Great Britain were infected with mad cow prions by eating meat derived from diseased cattle, resulting in a fatal, human form of mad cow disease known as *variant Creutzfeldt-Jakob disease (vCJD).* More than 1 million cattle have already been destroyed in the United Kingdom in an effort to halt the spread of this disease, but people may continue to die from vCJD as a result of having ingested tainted beef over the past two decades.

Mutations and Translation

Having described the *normal* process of translation, let us now consider what happens when mRNAs containing *mutant* codons are translated. **Box 22B** provides an overview of the main types of mutations that arise in DNA and their impact on the polypeptide chains produced by mRNAs. Most codon mutations simply alter a single amino acid, and mutations in the third base of a codon frequently do not change the amino acid at all. However, mutations that add or remove stop codons, or alter the reading frame, can severely disrupt mRNA translation. In this section, we will examine some of the ways in which cells can respond to such disruptive mutations.

Suppressor tRNAs Overcome the Effects of Some Mutations

Mutations that convert amino acid-coding codons into stop codons are referred to as **nonsense mutations. Figure 22-12** shows a case in which mutation of a single base pair in DNA converts an AAG lysine codon in mRNA to a UAG stop signal. Nonsense mutations like this one typically lead to production of incomplete, nonfunctional polypeptides that have been prematurely terminated at the mutant stop codon.

Nonsense mutations in essential genes are often lethal, but sometimes their detrimental effects can be overcome by an independent mutation affecting a tRNA gene. Such mutant tRNA genes produce mutant tRNAs that recognize what would otherwise be a stop codon and insert an amino acid at that point. In the example shown in Figure 22-12c, a mutant tRNA has an altered anticodon that allows it to read the stop codon UAG as a codon for tyrosine. The inserted amino acid is almost always different from the amino acid that would be present at that position in the wild-type protein, but the important point is that chain termination is averted and a full-length polypeptide can be made.

A tRNA molecule that somehow negates the effect of a mutation is called a **suppressor tRNA.** As you might expect, suppressor tRNAs exist that negate the effects of various types of mutations in addition to nonsense mutations (see Problem 22-8 at the end of the chapter). For a cell to survive, suppressor tRNAs must be rather inefficient; otherwise, the protein-synthesizing apparatus would produce too many abnormal proteins. An overly efficient nonsense suppressor, for example, would cause normal stop codons to be read as if they coded for an amino acid, thereby preventing normal termination. In fact, the synthesis of most polypeptides is terminated properly in cells containing nonsense suppressor tRNAs, indicating that a stop codon located in its proper place at the end of an mRNA coding sequence still triggers termination, whereas the same codon in an internal location does not. The most likely explanation is based on the behavior of the release factors that trigger normal termination (page 690). When a stop codon occurs in its proper location near the end of an RNA, release factors trigger termination because they are more efficient than suppressor tRNAs in binding to

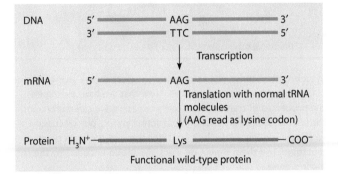

(a) Normal gene, normal tRNA molecules

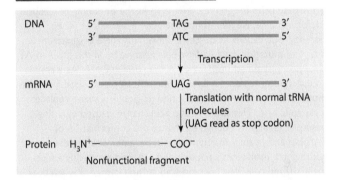

(b) Mutant gene, normal tRNA molecules

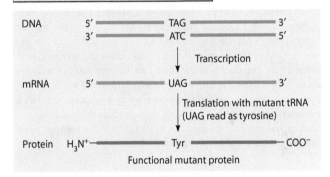

(c) Mutant gene, mutant (suppressor) tRNA molecule

FIGURE 22-12 Nonsense Mutations and Suppressor tRNAs. **(a)** A wild-type (normal) gene is transcribed into an mRNA molecule that contains the codon AAG at one point. Upon translation, this codon specifies the amino acid lysine (Lys) at this point in the functional, wild-type protein. **(b)** If a DNA mutation occurs that changes the AAG codon in the mRNA to UAG, the UAG codon will be read as a stop signal, and the translation product will be a short, nonfunctional polypeptide. Mutations of this sort are called nonsense mutations. **(c)** In the presence of a mutant tRNA that reads UAG as an amino acid codon instead of a stop signal, an amino acid will be inserted and polypeptide synthesis will continue. In the example shown, UAG is read as a codon for tyrosine because the mutant tyrosine tRNA has as its anticodon 3'-AUC-5' instead of the usual 3'-AUG-5' (which recognizes the tyrosine codon 5'-UAC-3'). The resulting protein will be mutant because a lysine has been replaced by a tyrosine at one point along the chain. However, the protein may still be functional if its biological activity is not significantly affected by the amino acid substitution.

In its broadest sense, the term *mutation* refers to any change in the nucleotide sequence of a genome. Now that we have examined the processes of transcription and translation, we can understand the effects of several kinds of mutations. Limiting our discussion to protein-coding genes, let's consider some of the main types of mutations and their impact on the polypeptide encoded by the mutant gene.

In this and the previous chapter, we have encountered several types of mutations in which the DNA change involves only one or a few base pairs (**Figure 22B-1a**). At the beginning of Chapter 21, for instance, we mentioned the genetic allele that, when homozygous, causes sickle-cell anemia. This allele originated from a type of mutation called a *base-pair substitution*. In this case, an AT base pair was substituted for a TA base pair in DNA. As a result, a GUA codon replaces a GAA in the mRNA transcribed from the mutant allele, and in the polypeptide (*β*-globin) a valine replaces a glutamic acid. This single amino acid change, caused by a single base-pair change, is enough to change the conformation of *β*-globin and, in turn, the hemoglobin tetramer, altering the way hemoglobin molecules pack into red cells and producing abnormally shaped cells that become trapped and damaged when they pass through small blood vessels (see Figure 21-2). Such a base-pair substitution is called a *missense mutation* because the mutated codon continues to code for an amino acid—but the "wrong" one.

Alternatively, a base-pair substitution can create a *nonstop mutation* by converting a normal stop codon into an amino acid codon, or conversely, it can create a *nonsense mutation* by converting an amino acid codon into a stop codon. In the latter case, the translation machinery will terminate the polypeptide prematurely. Unless the nonsense mutation is close to the end of the message or a suppressor tRNA is present, the polypeptide is not likely to be functional. Nonsense, nonstop, and missense codons can also arise from the *base-pair insertions* and *deletions* that cause *frameshift mutations*.

A single amino acid change (or even a change in several amino acids) does not always affect a protein's function in a major way. As long as the protein's three-dimensional conformation remains relatively unchanged, biological activity may be unaffected. Substitution of one amino acid for another of the same type—for example, valine for isoleucine—is especially unlikely to affect protein function. The nature of the genetic code actually reduces the effects of single base-pair alterations because many turn out to be *silent mutations* that change the nucleotide sequence without changing the genetic message. For example, changing the third base of a codon often produces a new codon that still codes for the same amino acid. Here, the "mutant" polypeptide is exactly the same as the wild-type.

In addition to mutations affecting one or a few base pairs, some alterations involve longer stretches of DNA (Figure 22B-1b). A few affect genome segments so large that the DNA changes can be detected by light microscopic examination of chromosomes. Some of these large-scale mutations are created by *insertions* or *deletions* of long DNA segments, but several other mechanisms also exist. In a *duplication*, a section of DNA is tandemly repeated. In an *inversion*, a chromosome segment is cut out and reinserted in its original position but in the reverse direction. A *translocation* involves the movement of a DNA segment from its normal location in the genome to another place, either in the same chromosome or a different one. Because these large-scale mutations may or may not affect the expression of many genes, they have a wide range of phenotypic effects, from no effect at all to lethality.

When we think about the potential effects of mutations, it is useful to remember that genes have important noncoding components and that these, too, can be mutated in ways that seriously affect gene products. A mutation in a promoter, for example, can result in more or less frequent transcription of the gene. Even a mutation in an intron can affect the gene product in a major way if it touches a critical part of a splice-site sequence.

stop codons in this location—perhaps because release factor action is stimulated by a special sequence or three-dimensional configuration near the end of the mRNA.

Nonsense-Mediated Decay and Nonstop Decay Promote the Destruction of Defective mRNAs

In the absence of an appropriate suppressor tRNA, a nonsense stop codon will cause mRNA translation to stop prematurely, thereby generating an incomplete polypeptide chain that cannot function properly and may even harm the cell. To avoid wasting energy on the production of such useless products, eukaryotic cells invoke a quality control mechanism called **nonsense-mediated decay** to destroy mRNAs containing premature stop codons. In mammals, the method for identifying premature stop codons involves the *exon junction complex (EJC),* a multiprotein complex deposited during mRNA splicing at each point where an intron is removed from pre-mRNA (see Figure 21-22). Thus, every newly spliced mRNA molecule will have one or more

EJCs bound to it, one at each exon-exon junction. During translation, the distinction between normal and premature stop codons is made on the basis of their relationship to EJCs. If a stop codon is encountered in an mRNA prior to the last EJC—in other words, before the last exon—it must be a premature stop codon. The presence of such a stop codon will cause translation to be terminated while the mRNA still has one or more EJCs bound to it, and the presence of these remaining EJCs marks the mRNA for degradation.

How do cells handle the opposite situation, namely an mRNA with no stop codons? In eukaryotic cells, translation becomes stalled when a ribosome reaches the end of an mRNA without encountering a stop codon. An RNA-degrading enzyme complex then binds to the empty A site of the ribosome and degrades the defective mRNA in a process called **nonstop decay.** The same problem is handled a bit differently in bacteria. When translation halts at the end of a bacterial mRNA lacking a stop codon, an unusual type of RNA called *tmRNA* ("transfer-messenger RNA") binds to the A site of the ribosome and directs the addition of about a

Finally, mutations in genes that encode regulatory proteins—that is, proteins that control the expression of other genes—can have far-reaching effects on many other proteins.

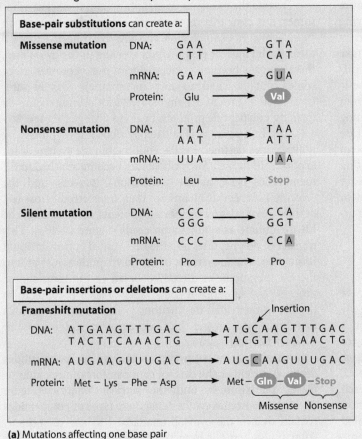

Base-pair substitutions can create a:

Missense mutation

DNA: GAA → GTA
     CTT → CAT

mRNA: GAA → GUA

Protein: Glu → Val

Nonsense mutation

DNA: TTA → TAA
     AAT → ATT

mRNA: UUA → UAA

Protein: Leu → Stop

Silent mutation

DNA: CCC → CCA
     GGG → GGT

mRNA: CCC → CCA

Protein: Pro → Pro

Base-pair insertions or deletions can create a:

Frameshift mutation

DNA: ATGAAGTTTGAC → ATGCAAGTTTGAC
     TACTTCAAACTG → TACGTTCAAACTG

mRNA: AUGAAGUUUGAC → AUGCAAGUUUGAC

Protein: Met – Lys – Phe – Asp → Met – Gln – Val – Stop

Missense Nonsense

(a) Mutations affecting one base pair

FIGURE 22B-1 Types of Mutations. Mutations can affect **(a)** one base pair or **(b)** long DNA segments.

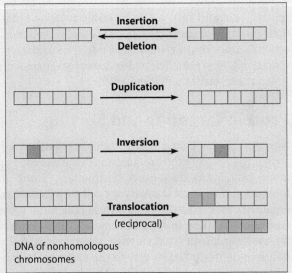

Insertion

Deletion

Duplication

Inversion

Translocation
(reciprocal)

DNA of nonhomologous chromosomes

(b) Mutations affecting long DNA segments

dozen more amino acids to the growing polypeptide chain. This amino acid sequence creates a signal that targets the protein for destruction. At the same time, the mRNA is degraded by a ribonuclease associated with the tmRNA.

Posttranslational Processing

After polypeptide chains have been synthesized, they often must be chemically modified before they can perform their normal functions. Such modifications are known collectively as **posttranslational modifications.** In bacteria, for example, the *N*-formyl group located at the N-terminus of polypeptide chains is always removed. The methionine it was attached to is often removed also, as is the methionine that starts eukaryotic polypeptides. As a result, relatively few mature polypeptides have methionine at their N-terminus, even though they all started out that way. Sometimes whole blocks of amino acids are removed from the polypeptide. Certain enzymes, for example, are synthesized as inactive precursors that must be activated by the removal of a spe-

cific sequence at one end or the other. The transport of proteins across membranes also may involve the removal of a terminal *signal sequence*, as we will see shortly, and some polypeptides have internal stretches of amino acids that must be removed to produce an active protein. For instance, insulin is synthesized as a single polypeptide and then processed to remove an internal segment; the two end segments remain linked by disulfide bonds between cysteine residues in the active hormone (see Figure 3-7).

Other common processing events include chemical modifications of individual amino acid groups—by methylation, phosphorylation, or acetylation reactions, for example. In addition, a polypeptide may undergo glycosylation (the addition of carbohydrate side chains; see Chapter 12) or binding to prosthetic groups. Finally, in the case of proteins composed of multiple subunits, individual polypeptide chains must bind to one another to form the appropriate multisubunit proteins or multiprotein complexes.

In addition to the preceding posttranslational events, some proteins undergo a relatively unusual type of processing called *protein splicing*, which is analogous to the phenomenon of *RNA splicing* discussed in Chapter 21. As we saw, intron sequences are removed from RNA molecules during RNA splicing, and the remaining exon sequences are simultaneously spliced together. Likewise, during protein splicing, specific amino acid sequences called *inteins* are removed from a polypeptide chain and the remaining segments, called *exteins,* are spliced together to form the mature protein. Protein splicing is usually intramolecular, involving the excision of an intein from a single polypeptide chain by a self-catalytic mechanism. However, splicing can also take place between two polypeptide chains arising from two different mRNAs. For example, in some photosynthetic bacteria a subunit of DNA polymerase III is produced from two separate genes, each coding for an intein-containing polypeptide that includes part of the DNA polymerase subunit. In some cases, the inteins removed by protein splicing reactions turn out to be stable proteins exhibiting their own biological functions (usually endonuclease activity). Once considered to be an oddity of nature, protein splicing has now been detected in dozens of different organisms, prokaryotes as well as eukaryotes.

Protein Targeting and Sorting

Now that we have seen how proteins are synthesized, we are ready to explore the mechanisms that route each newly made protein to its correct destination. Think for a moment about a typical eukaryotic cell with its diversity of organelles, each containing its own unique set of proteins. Such a cell is likely to have billions of protein molecules, representing at least 10,000 kinds of polypeptides. And each polypeptide must find its way to the appropriate location within the cell, or even out of the cell altogether. A limited number of these polypeptides are encoded by the genome of the mitochondrion (and, for plant cells, by the chloroplast genome as well), but most are encoded by nuclear genes and are synthesized by a process beginning in the cytosol. Each of these polypeptides must then be directed to its proper destination and must therefore have some sort of molecular "zip code" ensuring its delivery to the correct place. As our final topic for this chapter, we will consider this process of protein targeting and sorting.

We can begin by grouping the various compartments of eukaryotic cells into three categories: (1) the endomembrane system, the interrelated system of membrane compartments that includes the endoplasmic reticulum (ER), the Golgi complex, lysosomes, secretory vesicles, the nuclear envelope, and the plasma membrane; (2) the cytosol; and (3) mitochondria, chloroplasts, peroxisomes (and related organelles), and the interior of the nucleus.

Polypeptides encoded by nuclear genes are routed to these compartments using several different mechanisms. The process begins with transcription of DNA into RNAs that are processed in the nucleus and then transported through nuclear pores for translation in the cytoplasm, where most ribosomes occur. Although translation is largely a cytoplasmic process, some evidence suggests that up to 10% of a cell's ribosomes may actually reside in the nucleus, where they can translate newly synthesized RNAs. Nuclear translation appears to function mainly as a quality control mechanism that checks new mRNAs for the presence of errors (see the discussion of nonsense-mediated decay on page 694).

Despite the existence of these functioning nuclear ribosomes, it is clear that most polypeptide synthesis occurs on cytoplasmic ribosomes after mRNAs have been exported through the nuclear pores. Upon arriving in the cytoplasm, these mRNAs become associated with *free ribosomes* (ribosomes not attached to any membrane). Shortly after translation begins, two main pathways for routing the newly forming polypeptide products begin to diverge (**Figure 22-13**). The first pathway is utilized by ribosomes synthesizing polypeptides destined for the endomembrane system or for export from the cell. Such ribosomes become attached to ER membranes early in the translational process, and the growing polypeptide chains are then transferred across (or, in the case of integral membrane proteins, inserted into) the ER membrane as synthesis proceeds (Figure 22-13a). This transfer of polypeptides into the ER is called **cotranslational import** because movement of the polypeptide across or into the ER membrane is directly coupled to the translational process. The subsequent conveyance of such proteins from the ER to their final destinations is carried out by various membrane vesicles and the Golgi complex, as discussed in Chapter 12 (see Figure 12-8).

An alternative pathway is employed for polypeptides destined for either the cytosol or for mitochondria, chloroplasts, peroxisomes, and the nuclear interior (Figure 22-13b). Ribosomes synthesizing these types of polypeptides remain free in the cytosol, unattached to any membrane. After translation has been completed, the polypeptides are released from the ribosomes and either remain in the cytosol as their final destination or are taken up by the appropriate organelle. The uptake by organelles of such completed polypeptides requires the presence of special targeting signals and is called **posttranslational import.** In the case of the nucleus, polypeptides enter through the nuclear pores, as discussed in Chapter 18 (see Figure 18-31). Polypeptide entrance into mitochondria, chloroplasts, and peroxisomes involves a different kind of mechanism, as we will see shortly.

With this general overview in mind, we are now ready to examine the mechanisms of cotranslational import and posttranslational import in detail.

Cotranslational Import Allows Some Polypeptides to Enter the ER as They Are Being Synthesized

Cotranslational import into the ER is the first step in the pathway for delivering newly synthesized proteins to various locations within the endomembrane system. Proteins handled in this way are synthesized on ribosomes that become attached to the ER shortly after translation begins.

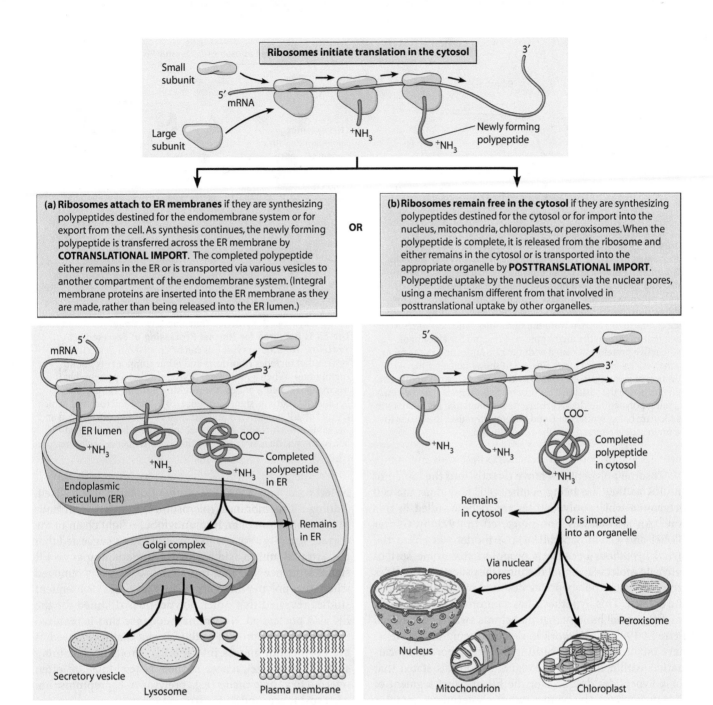

FIGURE 22-13 Intracellular Sorting of Proteins. Polypeptide synthesis begins in the cytosol but takes one of two alternative routes when the polypeptide is about 30 amino acids long. **(a)** Polypeptides destined for the endomembrane system, or for export from the cell, are transferred across the ER membrane by cotranslational import as they are being made. **(b)** Other polypeptides are synthesized in the cytosol and either remain there or are transferred by posttranslational import into the nucleus, mitochondria, chloroplasts, or peroxisomes.

The role of the ER in this process was first suggested by experiments in which Colvin Redman and David Sabatini studied protein synthesis in isolated vesicles of rough ER (ER vesicles with attached ribosomes). Such vesicles, known as *microsomes,* can be isolated using subcellular fractionation and centrifugation (see Box 12A). After briefly incubating the rough ER vesicles in the presence of radioactive amino acids and other components needed for protein synthesis, they stopped the reaction by adding *puromycin,*

an antibiotic that causes partially completed polypeptide chains to be released from ribosomes. When the ribosomes and membrane vesicles were then separated and analyzed to see where the newly made, radioactive polypeptide chains were located, a substantial fraction of the radioactivity was found inside the ER lumen (**Figure 22-14**). Such results suggested that newly forming polypeptides pass into the lumen of the ER *as they are being synthesized,* allowing them to be routed through the ER to their correct destinations.

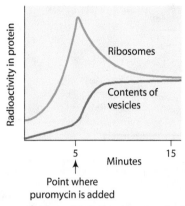

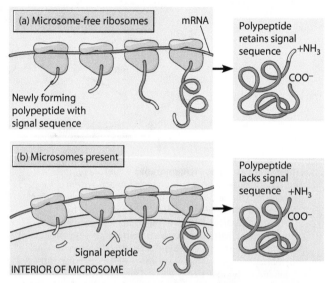

FIGURE 22-14 Evidence That Proteins Synthesized on Ribosomes Attached to ER Membranes Pass Directly into the ER Lumen. ER vesicles containing attached ribosomes were isolated and incubated with radioactive amino acids to label newly made polypeptide chains. Next, protein synthesis was halted by adding puromycin, which also causes the newly forming polypeptide chains to be released from the ribosomes. The ribosomes were then removed from the membrane vesicles, and the amount of radioactive protein associated with the ribosomes and in the membrane vesicles was measured. The graph shows that after the addition of puromycin, radioactivity is lost from the ribosomes and appears inside the vesicles. This observation suggests that the newly forming polypeptide chains are inserted through the ER membrane as they are being synthesized, and puromycin causes the chains to be prematurely released into the vesicle lumen.

FIGURE 22-15 Evidence That Cotranslational Insertion into the ER Is Required for Normal Processing of Secreted Proteins. (a) Protein synthesis can be carried out in a cell-free system that includes ribosomes and other components but no membranes. When a messenger RNA encoding a protein that is normally secreted is added, the resulting protein is abnormally large because it retains its signal sequence. (b) When microsomes, which consist of ER membranes and attached ribosomes, are isolated and the same mRNA is added, the resulting protein is transported across the vesicle membrane and the signal sequence is cleaved.

If some polypeptides move directly into the lumen of the ER as they are being synthesized, how does the cell determine which polypeptides are to be handled in this way? An answer was first suggested in 1971 by Günter Blobel and David Sabatini, whose model was called the *signal hypothesis* because it proposed that some sort of intrinsic molecular signal distinguishes such polypeptides from the many polypeptides destined to be released into the cytosol. This hypothesis has so profoundly influenced the field of cell biology that Blobel was awarded the Nobel Prize in 1999 for his work in demonstrating that proteins have intrinsic signals governing their transport and localization within the cell. The signal hypothesis stated that for polypeptides destined for the ER, the first segment of the polypeptide to be synthesized, the N-terminus, contains an **ER signal sequence** that directs the ribosome-mRNA-polypeptide complex to the surface of the rough ER, where the complex anchors at a protein "dock" on the ER surface. Then, as the polypeptide chain elongates during mRNA translation, it progressively crosses the ER membrane and enters the ER lumen.

Shortly after the signal hypothesis was first proposed, evidence for the actual existence of ER signal sequences was obtained by César Milstein and his associates, who were studying the synthesis of the small subunit, or *light chain,* of the protein *immunoglobulin G.* In cell-free systems containing purified ribosomes and the components required for protein synthesis, the mRNA coding for the immunoglobulin light chain directs the synthesis of a polypeptide product that is 20 amino acids longer at its N-terminal end than the authentic light chain itself. Adding ER membranes (microsomes) to this system leads to the production of an immunoglobulin light chain of the correct size (**Figure 22-15**). Such findings suggested that the extra 20-amino acid segment is functioning as an ER signal sequence and that this signal sequence is removed when the polypeptide moves into the ER. Subsequent studies revealed that other polypeptides destined for the ER also possess an N-terminal sequence that is required for targeting the protein to the ER and that is removed as the polypeptide moves into the ER. Proteins containing such ER signal sequences at their N-terminus are often referred to as *preproteins* (e.g., prelysozyme, preproinsulin, pretrypsinogen, and so forth).

Sequencing studies have revealed that the amino acid compositions of ER signal sequences are surprisingly variable, but several unifying features have been noted. ER signal sequences are typically 15–30 amino acids long and consist of three domains: a positively charged N-terminal region, a central hydrophobic region, and a polar region adjoining the site where cleavage from the mature protein will take place. The positively charged end may promote interaction with the hydrophilic exterior of the ER membrane, and the hydrophobic region may facilitate interaction of the signal sequence with the membrane's lipid interior. In any case, it is now established that only polypeptides with ER signal sequences can be inserted into or across the ER membrane as their synthesis proceeds. In fact, when recombinant DNA methods are used to add ER signal sequences to polypeptides that do not usually have them, the recombinant polypeptides are directed to the ER.

The Signal Recognition Particle (SRP) Binds the Ribosome-mRNA-Polypeptide Complex to the ER Membrane

Once the existence of ER signal sequences was established, it quickly became clear that newly forming polypeptides must become attached to the ER membrane before very much of the polypeptide has emerged from the ribosome. If translation were to continue without attachment to the ER, the folding of the growing polypeptide chain might bury the signal sequence. To understand what prevents this from happening, we need to look at the signal mechanism in further detail.

Contrary to the original signal hypothesis, the ER signal sequence does not itself initiate contact with the ER. Instead, the contact is mediated by a **signal recognition particle (SRP),** which recognizes and binds to the ER signal sequence of the newly forming polypeptide and then binds to the ER membrane (**Figure 22-16**). At first the SRP was thought to be purely protein (the *P* in its name originally stood for protein). Later, however, the SRP was shown to consist of six different polypeptides complexed with a 300-nucleotide (7S) molecule of RNA. The protein components have three main active sites: one that recognizes and binds to the ER signal sequence, one that interacts with the ribosome to block further translation, and one that binds to the ER membrane.

Figure 22-16 illustrates the role played by the SRP in cotranslational import. The process begins when an mRNA coding for a polypeptide destined for the ER starts to be translated on a free ribosome. Polypeptide synthesis proceeds until the ER signal sequence has been formed and emerges from the surface of the ribosome. At this stage, SRP (shown in orange) binds to the signal sequence and blocks further translation (step ❶). The SRP then binds the ribosome to a special structure in the ER membrane called a **translocon** because it carries out the translocation of polypeptides across the ER membrane. (Note that the term *translocation,* which literally means "a change of location," is used to describe both the movement of proteins through membranes and, earlier in the chapter, the movement of mRNA across the ribosome.)

The translocon is a protein complex composed of several components involved in cotranslational import, including an *SRP receptor* to which the SRP binds, a *ribosome receptor* that holds the ribosome in place, a *pore protein* that forms a channel through which the growing polypeptide can enter the ER lumen, and *signal peptidase,* an enzyme that removes the ER signal sequence. As ❷ shows, SRP (bringing an attached ribosome) first binds to the SRP receptor, allowing the ribosome to become attached to the ribosome receptor. Next, GTP binds to both SRP and the SRP receptor, unblocking translation and causing transfer of the signal sequence to the pore protein, whose central channel opens as the signal sequence is inserted (❸). GTP is then hydrolyzed, accompanied by release of the SRP (❹). As the polypeptide elongates, it passes into the ER lumen and signal peptidase cleaves the signal sequence, which is quickly degraded (❺). After polypeptide synthesis is completed, the final polypeptide is released into the ER lumen, the translocon channel is closed, and the ribosome detaches from the ER membrane and dissociates into its subunits, releasing the mRNA (❻).

Protein Folding and Quality Control Take Place Within the ER

After polypeptides are released into the ER lumen, they fold into their final shape and, in some cases, assemble with other polypeptides to form multisubunit proteins. As we mentioned earlier in the chapter, molecular chaperones facilitate these folding and assembly events. The most abundant chaperone in the ER lumen is a member of the Hsp70 family of chaperones known as **BiP** (an abbreviation for *Binding Protein*). BiP acts by binding to *hydrophobic regions* of polypeptide chains, especially to regions enriched in the amino acids tryptophan, phenylalanine, and leucine.

In a mature, fully folded protein, such hydrophobic regions are buried in the interior of the protein molecule. In an unfolded polypeptide, these same hydrophobic regions are exposed to the surrounding aqueous environment, creating an unstable situation in which polypeptides tend to aggregate with one another. BiP prevents this aggregation by transiently binding to the hydrophobic regions of unfolded polypeptides as they emerge into the ER lumen, stabilizing them and preventing them from interacting with other unfolded polypeptides. BiP then releases the polypeptide chain, accompanied by ATP hydrolysis, giving the polypeptide a brief opportunity to fold (perhaps aided by other chaperones). If the polypeptide folds correctly, its hydrophobic regions become buried in the molecule's interior and can no longer bind to BiP. But if the hydrophobic segments fail to fold properly, BiP binds again to the polypeptide and the cycle is repeated. In this way, BiP uses energy released by ATP hydrolysis to promote proper protein folding.

Folding is often accompanied by the formation of disulfide bonds between cysteines located in different regions of a polypeptide chain. This reaction is facilitated by **protein disulfide isomerase,** an enzyme present in the ER lumen that catalyzes the formation and breakage of disulfide bonds between cysteine residues. Protein disulfide isomerase starts acting before the synthesis of a newly forming polypeptide has been completed, allowing various disulfide bond combinations to be tested until the most stable arrangement is found.

Proteins that repeatedly fail to fold properly can activate several types of quality control mechanisms. One such mechanism, called the **unfolded protein response (UPR),** uses sensor molecules in the ER membrane to detect misfolded proteins. These sensors activate signaling

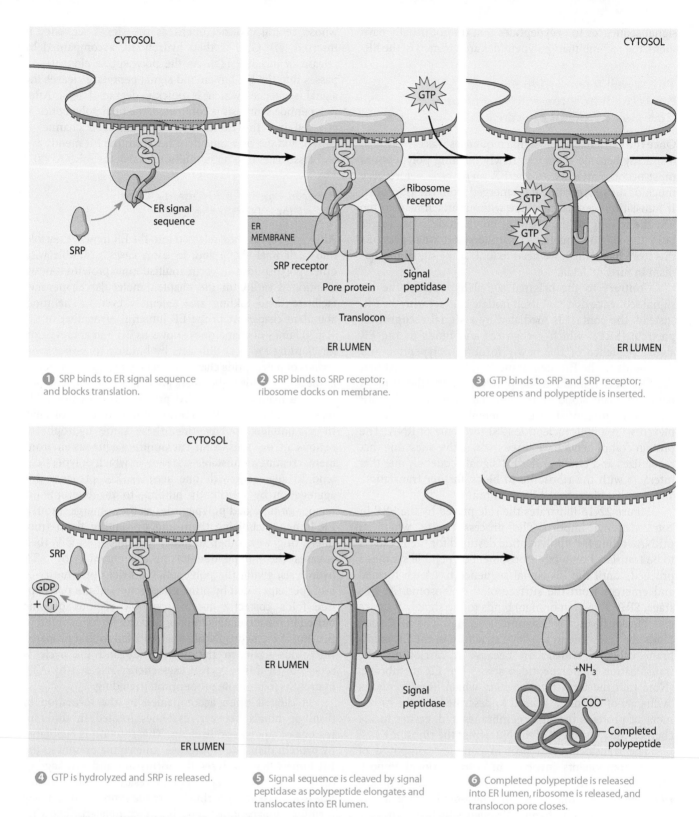

① SRP binds to ER signal sequence and blocks translation.

② SRP binds to SRP receptor; ribosome docks on membrane.

③ GTP binds to SRP and SRP receptor; pore opens and polypeptide is inserted.

④ GTP is hydrolyzed and SRP is released.

⑤ Signal sequence is cleaved by signal peptidase as polypeptide elongates and translocates into ER lumen.

⑥ Completed polypeptide is released into ER lumen, ribosome is released, and translocon pore closes.

FIGURE 22-16 A Model for the Signal Mechanism of Cotranslational Import. This figure shows a schematic model for the signal mechanism. It is now well established that the growing polypeptide translocates through a hydrophilic pore created by one or more membrane proteins. The complex of membrane proteins that carry out translocation is called the *translocon.*

pathways that shut down the synthesis of most proteins while enhancing the production of those required for protein folding and degradation. Another type of quality control, known as **ER-associated degradation (ERAD)**, recognizes misfolded or unassembled proteins and exports or "retrotranslocates" them back across the ER membrane to the cytosol, where they are degraded by *proteasomes*.

Proteins Released into the ER Lumen Are Routed to the Golgi Complex, Secretory Vesicles, Lysosomes, or Back to the ER

Most of the proteins synthesized on ribosomes attached to the ER are *glycoproteins*—that is, proteins with covalently bound carbohydrate groups. As you learned in Chapter 12, the initial glycosylation reactions that add these carbohydrate side chains take place in the ER, often while the growing polypeptide is still being synthesized. After polypeptides have been released into the ER lumen, glycosylated, and folded, they are delivered by various types of transport vesicles to their destinations within the cell (see Figure 12-8). The first stop in this transport pathway is the Golgi complex, where further glycosylation and processing of carbohydrate side chains may occur. The Golgi complex then serves as a site for sorting and distributing proteins to other locations.

For soluble proteins, the default pathway takes them from the Golgi complex to secretory vesicles that move to the cell surface and fuse with the plasma membrane, leading to secretion of such proteins from the cell. Soluble proteins entering the Golgi complex and that are not destined for secretion from the cell possess specific carbohydrate side chains and/or short amino acid signal sequences that target each protein to its appropriate location within the endomembrane system. For example, we saw in Chapter 12 that many lysosomal enzymes possess carbohydrate side chains exhibiting the unusual sugar *mannose-6-phosphate*. This sugar serves as a recognition device that allows the Golgi complex to selectively package such proteins into newly forming lysosomes (see Figure 12-9). As we also saw in Chapter 12, a different signaling mechanism is used for proteins whose final destination is the ER. The C-terminus of these proteins usually contains a *KDEL sequence,* which consists of the amino acids Lys-Asp-Glu-Leu or a closely related sequence. The Golgi complex employs a receptor protein that binds to the KDEL sequence and delivers the targeted protein back to the ER. Protein disulfide isomerase—the ER-resident enzyme whose role in protein folding was described in the preceding section—is an example of a protein possessing a KDEL sequence that confines the molecule to the ER.

Stop-Transfer Sequences Mediate the Insertion of Integral Membrane Proteins

So far, we have focused on the cotranslational import and sorting of *soluble proteins* that are destined either for secretion from the cell or for the lumen of endomembrane components, such as the ER, the Golgi complex, lyso-somes, and related vesicles. The other major group of polypeptides synthesized on ER-attached ribosomes consists of molecules destined to become integral *membrane proteins.* Polypeptides of this type are synthesized by a mechanism similar to the one illustrated in Figure 22-16 for soluble proteins except that the completed polypeptide chain remains embedded in the ER membrane rather than being released into the ER lumen.

Recall from Chapter 7 that integral membrane proteins are typically anchored to the lipid bilayer by one or more α-helical *transmembrane segments* consisting of 20–30 hydrophobic amino acids. In considering the mechanism that allows such proteins to be retained as part of the ER membrane after synthesis rather than being released into the ER lumen, we focus here on the simplest case: proteins with only a single such transmembrane segment. The principles involved, however, extend to proteins with more complicated configurations. Researchers postulate two main mechanisms by which hydrophobic transmembrane segments anchor newly forming polypeptide chains to the lipid bilayer of the ER membrane.

The first of these mechanisms involves polypeptides with a typical ER signal sequence at their N-terminus, which allows an SRP to bind the ribosome-mRNA complex to the ER membrane. Elongation of the polypeptide chain then continues until the hydrophobic transmembrane segment of the polypeptide is synthesized. As shown in **Figure 22-17a**, this stretch of amino acids functions as a **stop-transfer sequence** that halts translocation of the polypeptide through the ER membrane. Translation continues, but the rest of the polypeptide chain remains on the cytosolic side of the ER membrane, resulting in a transmembrane protein with its N-terminus in the ER lumen and its C-terminus in the cytosol. Meanwhile, the hydrophobic stop-transfer signal moves laterally out through a side opening in the translocon and into the lipid bilayer, forming the permanent transmembrane segment that anchors the protein to the membrane.

The second mechanism involves membrane proteins that lack a typical signal sequence at their N-terminus and instead possess an *internal* **start-transfer sequence** that performs two functions: It first acts as an ER signal sequence that allows an SRP to bind the ribosome-mRNA complex to the ER membrane, and then its hydrophobic region functions as a membrane anchor that moves out through a side opening in the translocon and permanently attaches the polypeptide to the lipid bilayer (Figure 22-17b). The orientation of the start-transfer sequence at the time of insertion determines which terminus of the polypeptide ends up in the ER lumen and which in the cytosol. Transmembrane proteins with multiple membrane-spanning regions are formed in a similar way, except that an alternating pattern of start-transfer and stop-transfer sequences creates a polypeptide containing multiple transmembrane segments that pass back and forth across the membrane.

Once a newly formed polypeptide has been incorporated into the ER membrane by one of the preceding

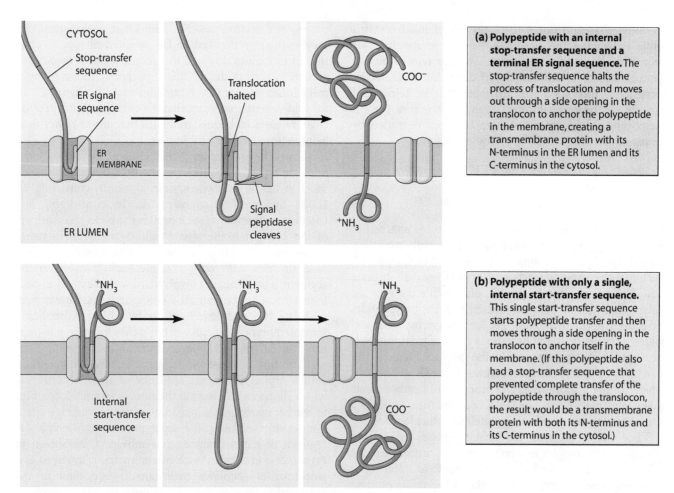

(a) Polypeptide with an internal stop-transfer sequence and a terminal ER signal sequence. The stop-transfer sequence halts the process of translocation and moves out through a side opening in the translocon to anchor the polypeptide in the membrane, creating a transmembrane protein with its N-terminus in the ER lumen and its C-terminus in the cytosol.

(b) Polypeptide with only a single, internal start-transfer sequence. This single start-transfer sequence starts polypeptide transfer and then moves through a side opening in the translocon to anchor itself in the membrane. (If this polypeptide also had a stop-transfer sequence that prevented complete transfer of the polypeptide through the translocon, the result would be a transmembrane protein with both its N-terminus and its C-terminus in the cytosol.)

FIGURE 22-17 Cotranslational Insertion of Transmembrane Proteins into the ER Membrane. This figure shows two mechanisms for inserting integral membrane proteins containing a single transmembrane segment. For clarity, the SRP, ribosome, and most other parts of the translocational apparatus have been omitted. Transmembrane proteins whose N- and C-termini are oriented in opposite directions from those shown here can be created using a start-transfer sequence that has the opposite orientation when it first inserts into the translocation apparatus.

mechanisms, it can either remain in place to function as an ER membrane protein or be transported to other components of the endomembrane system, such as the Golgi complex, lysosomes, nuclear envelope, or plasma membrane. Transport is carried out by a series of membrane budding and fusing events in which membrane vesicles pinch off from one compartment of the endomembrane system and fuse with another compartment, as we described in Figure 12-8.

Posttranslational Import Allows Some Polypeptides to Enter Organelles After They Have Been Synthesized

In contrast to the cotranslational import of proteins into the ER discussed in the preceeding several pages, proteins destined for the nuclear interior, mitochondrion, chloroplast, or peroxisome are imported into these organelles *after* translation has been completed. Because such proteins are synthesized on free ribosomes and released into the cytosol, each protein must carry a targeting signal that directs it to

the correct organelle. In Chapter 12, you learned that a serine-lysine-leucine sequence (SKL in single-letter code) located near the C-terminus of a protein targets it for uptake into peroxisomes. And in Chapter 18, you learned that posttranslational import of proteins into the nucleus depends on *nuclear localization signals* that target proteins for transport through nuclear pore complexes (see Figure 18-31). Here, we focus on protein import into mitochondria and chloroplasts, which involves signal sequences similar to those used in cotranslational import.

Importing Polypeptides into Mitochondria and Chloroplasts. Although mitochondria and chloroplasts contain their own DNA and protein-synthesizing machinery, they synthesize few of the polypeptides they require. More than 95% of the proteins residing in these two organelles, like all proteins found in the nucleus and peroxisomes, are encoded by nuclear genes and synthesized on cytosolic ribosomes. The small number of polypeptides synthesized within mitochondria are targeted mainly to the inner mitochondrial membrane, and the polypeptides synthesized within chloroplasts are targeted mainly to thylakoid membranes. Almost without exception, such polypeptides encoded by mitochondrial or chloroplast genes are subunits of multimeric proteins, with one or more of the other subunits being encoded by nuclear genes and imported from the cytosol. For example, mammalian cytochrome *c* oxidase consists of 13 polypeptides, 3 of which are encoded by the mitochondrial genome and synthesized within mitochondria. The other 10 subunits are synthesized in the cytosol and imported into mitochondria.

Most mitochondrial and chloroplast polypeptides are synthesized on cytosolic ribosomes, released into the cytosol, and taken up by the appropriate organelle (mitochondrion or chloroplast) within a few minutes. The targeting signal for such polypeptides is a special sequence called a **transit sequence.** Like the ER signal sequence of ER-targeted polypeptides, the transit sequence is located at the N-terminus of the polypeptide. Once inside the mitochondrion or chloroplast, the transit sequence is removed by a *transit peptidase* located within the organelle. Removal of the transit sequence often occurs before transport is complete.

The transit sequences of mitochondrial or chloroplast polypeptides typically contain both hydrophobic and hydrophilic amino acids. The presence of positively charged amino acids is critical, although the secondary structure of the sequence may be more important than the specific amino acids. For example, some mitochondrial transit sequences have positively charged amino acids interspersed with hydrophobic amino acids in such a way that, when the sequence is coiled into an a α helix, most of the positively charged amino acids are on one side of the helix and the hydrophobic amino acids are on the other.

The uptake of polypeptide chains possessing transit sequences is mediated by specialized transport complexes located in the outer and inner membranes of mitochondria and chloroplasts. As shown in **Figure 22-18,** the mitochondrial transport complexes are called **TOM** (translocase of the outer mitochondrial membrane) and **TIM** (translocase of the inner mitochondrial membrane). The comparable chloroplast complexes are **TOC** (translocase of the outer chloroplast membrane) and **TIC** (translocase of the inner chloroplast membrane). Polypeptides are initially selected for transport into mitochondria or chloroplasts by components of TOM or TOC known as *transit sequence receptors.* After a transit sequence has bound to its receptor, the polypeptide containing this sequence is translocated across the outer membrane through a *pore* in the TOM or TOC complex. If the polypeptide is destined for the interior of the organelle, movement through the TOM or TOC complex is quickly followed by passage through the TIM or TIC complex of the inner membrane, presumably at a *contact site* where the outer and inner membranes lie close together.

Evidence supporting this model has come both from electron microscopy, which reveals many sites of close contact between outer and inner membranes, and from

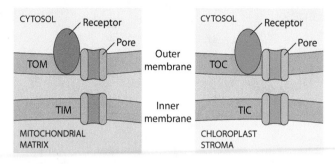

Mitochondrion   **Chloroplast**

FIGURE 22-18 Polypeptide Transport Complexes of the Outer and Inner Mitochondrial and Chloroplast Membranes. Mitochondrial and chloroplast polypeptides synthesized in the cytosol are transported into these organelles by specialized transport complexes located in their outer and inner membranes. In mitochondria, the outer and inner membrane complexes are called TOM and TIM, respectively. The comparable chloroplast structures are TOC and TIC. The transport complexes of the outer membranes (TOM and TOC) consist of two types of components: receptor proteins that recognize and bind to polypeptides targeted for uptake and pore proteins that form channels through which the polypeptides are translocated.

biochemical experiments, in which cell-free mitochondrial import systems are incubated on ice to trap polypeptides in the act of being translocated (**Figure 22-19**). The low temperature causes polypeptide movement across the membranes to halt shortly after it starts. At this point the polypeptides have already had their transit sequences removed by the transit peptidase enzyme located in the mitochondrial matrix, but they can still be attacked by externally added proteolytic enzymes. Such results indicate that polypeptides can transiently span both membranes during import. In other words, the N-terminus can enter the matrix of the mitochondrion while the rest of the molecule is still outside the organelle.

Polypeptides entering mitochondria and chloroplasts must generally be in an unfolded state before they can pass across the membranes bounding these organelles. This requirement has been demonstrated experimentally by attaching polypeptides containing a mitochondrial transit sequence to agents that maintain the polypeptide chain in a tightly folded state. Such polypeptides bind to the outer surface of mitochondria but will not move across the membrane, apparently because the size of the folded polypeptide exceeds the diameter of the membrane pore it must pass through.

To maintain the necessary unfolded state, polypeptides targeted for mitochondria and chloroplasts are usually bound to *chaperone proteins* similar to those that help newly synthesized polypeptides fold correctly. **Figure 22-20** shows a current model for this chaperone-mediated import of polypeptides into the mitochondrial matrix. To start the process, chaperones of the Hsp70 class bind to a newly forming polypeptide that is still in the process of being synthesized in the cytosol, keeping it in a loosely folded state (step ❶). Next, the transit sequence at the N-terminus of the

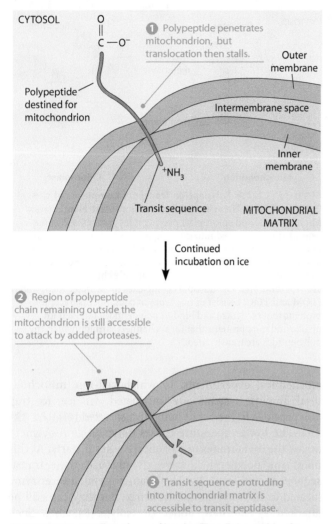

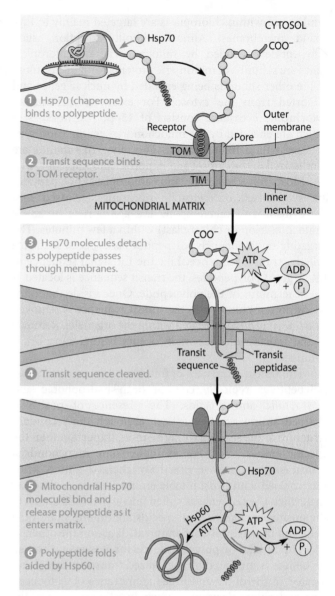

Continued
incubation on ice

FIGURE 22-19 Experiment Showing That Polypeptides Span Both Mitochondrial Membranes During Import. To demonstrate that polypeptides being imported into mitochondria span both membranes at the same time, a cell-free import system was incubated on ice instead of at the usual temperature of 37°C. At low temperature, polypeptides start to enter the mitochondrion, but their translocation soon stalls. Under these conditions, the transit sequence is cleaved by transit peptidase in the matrix, indicating that the N-terminus of the polypeptide is inside the mitochondrion. At the same time, most of the polypeptide chain is accessible to attack by proteolytic enzymes added to the outside of the mitochondrion. This means that the polypeptide must span both membranes during import, presumably at a contact site between the two membranes.

FIGURE 22-20 Posttranslational Import of Polypeptides into the Mitochondrion. Like cotranslational import into the ER, posttranslational import into a mitochondrion involves a signal sequence (called a transit sequence in this case), a membrane receptor, pore-forming membrane proteins, and a peptidase. However, in the mitochondrion, the membrane receptor recognizes the signal sequence directly, without the intervention of a cytosolic SRP. Furthermore, chaperone proteins play several crucial roles in the mitochondrial process: They keep the polypeptide partially unfolded after synthesis in the cytosol so that binding of the transit sequence and translocation can occur (steps ❶– ❸); they drive the translocation itself by binding to and releasing from the polypeptide *within* the matrix, which is an ATP-requiring process (step ❺); and they help the polypeptide fold into its final conformation (step ❻). The chaperones included here are cytosolic and mitochondrial versions of Hsp70 (light blue) and a mitochondrial Hsp60 (not illustrated).

polypeptide binds to the receptor component of TOM, which protrudes from the surface of the outer mitochondrial membrane (❷). The chaperone proteins then are released, accompanied by ATP hydrolysis, as the polypeptide is translocated through the TOM and TIM pores and into the mitochondrial matrix (❸). When the transit sequence emerges into the matrix, it is removed by transit peptidase (❹). As the rest of the polypeptide subsequently enters the matrix, *mitochondrial* Hsp70 molecules bind to it temporarily. The subsequent release of Hsp70 requires ATP hydrolysis (❺), which is thought to drive the translocation process. Finally, in many cases mitochondrial Hsp60 chap-

erone molecules bind to the polypeptide and help it achieve its fully folded conformation (❻).

Both chloroplasts and mitochondria require energy for the import of polypeptides. Mitochondrial import is driven both by ATP hydrolysis and by the electrochemical gradient across the inner membrane. The electrochemical gradient seems to be necessary only for the binding and penetration of the transit sequence. Once this step has occurred, experimental abolition of the membrane potential does not interfere with the rest of the transfer process. Chloroplasts, on the other hand, maintain an electrochemical gradient across the thylakoid membrane but not across the inner membrane. Presumably the energy requirement for import into the chloroplast stroma is met by ATP alone.

Targeting Polypeptides to the Proper Compartments Within Mitochondria and Chloroplasts. Due to the structural complexity of mitochondria and chloroplasts, proteins to be imported from the cytosol must be targeted not only to the right organelle but also to the appropriate compartment within the organelle. Mitochondria have four compartments: the outer membrane, the intermembrane space, the inner membrane, and the matrix. Chloroplasts have four similar compartments (with the stroma substituted for matrix) plus two additional compartments: the thylakoid membrane and the thylakoid lumen. Thus, a polypeptide may have to cross one, two, or even three membranes to reach its final destination.

Given the structural complexity of both organelles, it is perhaps not surprising that many mitochondrial and chloroplast polypeptides require more than one signal to arrive at their proper destinations. For example, targeting a polypeptide to the outer or inner mitochondrial membrane requires an N-terminal transit sequence to direct the polypeptide to the mitochondrion, plus an additional internal sequence, called a *hydrophobic sorting signal,* to target the polypeptide to its final destination. In such cases the hydrophobic sorting signal acts as a stop-transfer sequence that halts translocation of the polypeptide through either the outer or inner membrane translocase and promotes its lateral movement out through a side opening in the translocase and into the lipid bilayer of the membrane. The hydrophobic signal sequence then remains embedded in the membrane, anchoring the polypeptide to the lipid bilayer, while the N-terminal transit sequence is usually removed. A combination of transit and hydrophobic sorting sequences is also used for targeting polypeptides to the intermembrane space. In this case the polypeptide passes through the outer membrane and the signal sequences are then removed, leaving the polypeptide in the space between the two membranes.

Multiple signals are also involved in directing some chloroplast polypeptides to their final destination. Polypeptides intended for insertion into (or transport across) the thylakoid membrane, for example, must first be targeted to the chloroplast and transported into the stroma, presumably crossing the inner and outer membranes at a contact site. In the stroma, the transit sequence used for this first step is cleaved from the polypeptide, unmasking a hydrophobic *thylakoid signal sequence* that targets the polypeptide for either the thylakoid membrane or thylakoid lumen. For polypeptides destined for the thylakoid membrane, the hydrophobic signal sequence may spontaneously insert and anchor the polypeptide within the lipid bilayer of the thylakoid membrane. Alternatively, the insertion of some polypeptides into thylakoid membranes requires the participation of a GTP-dependent protein resembling the signal recognition particle (SRP) that directs and binds polypeptides to ER membranes.

Polypeptides destined for the thylakoid lumen are translocated completely across the thylakoid membrane, accompanied by cleavage of the thylakoid signal sequence as the polypeptide is released into the lumen. Most polypeptides targeted to the lumen are translocated across the thylakoid membrane in an unfolded state by an ATP-dependent process that resembles the mechanism employed for translocating polypeptides across the outer chloroplast or mitochondrial membranes. However, some extensively folded proteins can also be transported across thylakoid membranes using an alternative mechanism driven by energy derived from the proton gradient. Although translocation of extensively folded proteins across membranes is relatively unusual, similar mechanisms have been detected in peroxisomes and in the bacterial plasma membrane.

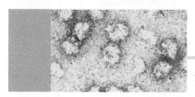

SUMMARY OF KEY POINTS

Translation: The Cast of Characters

- Translation refers to the synthesis of polypeptide chains on ribosomes using a process that employs mRNA to determine the amino acid sequence.

- The rRNA component of the ribosome helps position the mRNA and catalyzes peptide bond formation; aminoacyl-tRNA synthetases link amino acids to the tRNA molecules that bring amino acids to the ribosome; and various protein factors trigger specific events associated with the translation cycle.

The Mechanism of Translation

- Translation involves initiation, elongation, and termination stages.

- During the initiation stage, initiation factors trigger the assembly of mRNA, ribosomal subunits, and initiator aminoacyl tRNA into an initiation complex.

- Chain elongation involves sequential cycles of aminoacyl tRNA binding, peptide bond formation, and translocation, with each cycle driven by the action of elongation factors. The net result is that aminoacyl tRNAs add their amino acids to the growing polypeptide chain in an order specified by the codon sequence in mRNA.

- Chain termination occurs when a stop codon in mRNA is recognized by release factors, which cause the mRNA and newly formed polypeptide to be released from the ribosome.

- GTP binding and hydrolysis are required for the action of several initiation, elongation, and release factors.

- Proper folding of newly produced polypeptide chains is assisted by molecular chaperones. Abnormalities in protein folding can lead to various health problems, including Alzheimer disease and mad cow disease.

Mutations and Translation

- Nonsense mutations, which change an amino acid codon to a stop codon, can be overcome by suppressor mutations that allow a tRNA anticodon to read the stop codon as an amino acid.

- Defective mRNAs containing premature stop codons are destroyed by nonsense-mediated decay; defective mRNAs containing no stop codon are destroyed by nonstop decay.

Posttranslational Processing

- Newly made polypeptide chains often require chemical modification before they can function properly. Such modifications include cleavage of peptide bonds, phosphorylation, acetylation, methylation, glycosylation, and protein splicing.

Protein Targeting and Sorting

- Many polypeptides possess special amino acid sequences that target them to their appropriate location.

- Polypeptides destined for the endomembrane system, or for secretion from the cell, have an N-terminal ER signal sequence that causes them to enter translocon channels in the ER membrane while the polypeptide chain is still being synthesized.

- Some of these polypeptides pass completely through the translocon and are released into the ER lumen. Others possess one or more internal stop-transfer sequences that cause the polypeptide to remain anchored to the membrane. In either case the resulting proteins may stay in the ER or be transported to other locations within the endomembrane system, such as the Golgi complex, lysosomes, plasma membrane, or secretory vesicles that expel the protein from the cell.

- The unfolded protein response (UPR) and ER-associated degradation (ERAD) help prevent the endomembrane system from accumulating unfolded proteins.

- Polypeptides destined for the nuclear interior, mitochondria, chloroplasts, or peroxisomes are synthesized on cytosolic ribosomes (as are polypeptides that remain in the cytosol) and are then imported posttranslationally into the targeted organelle. Polypeptides destined for peroxisomes contain a special targeting sequence near the C-terminus, whereas those targeted to the nucleus contain nuclear localization signals that promote their uptake through the nuclear pores.

- Some mitochondrial and chloroplast polypeptides require more than one signal to arrive at their proper destinations. Such polypeptides usually possess an N-terminal transit sequence to direct the polypeptide into mitochondria or chloroplasts plus a hydrophobic sorting signal to target the polypeptide to its final destination within each organelle.

MAKING CONNECTIONS

In this chapter you learned how mRNA molecules determine the amino acid sequence of newly forming polypeptide chains, which are then folded and assembled into functional proteins destined for various subcellular locations. The protein molecules produced and delivered by the mechanisms described in this chapter are responsible for most of the properties we associate with living cells. The events responsible for creating the mRNAs that guide polypeptide synthesis were described in Chapter 21, and the role of the endomembrane system in delivering the resulting proteins to their appropriate subcellular locations was covered in Chapter 12. Now that you understand how a cell's protein molecules are produced and distributed, the next chapter will describe how the production of specific proteins is regulated to meet the changing needs of individual cells.

PROBLEM SET

More challenging problems are marked with a •.

22-1 The Genetic Code and Two Human Hormones. The following is the actual sequence of a small stretch of human DNA:

3′ AATTATACACGATGAAGCTTGTGACAGGGTTTCCAATCATTAA 5′

5′ TTAATATGTGCTACTTCGAACACTGTCCCAAAGGTTAGTAATT 3′

(a) What are the two possible RNA molecules that could be transcribed from this DNA?

(b) Only one of these two RNA molecules can actually be translated. Explain why.

(c) The RNA molecule that can be translated is the mRNA for the hormone vasopressin. What is the apparent amino acid sequence for vasopressin? (The genetic code is given in Figure 21-6.)

(d) In its active form, vasopressin is a nonapeptide (that is, it has nine amino acids) with cysteine at the N-terminus. How can you explain this in light of your answer to part c?

(e) A related hormone, oxytocin, has the following amino acid sequence:

Cys-Tyr-Ile-Glu-Asp-Cys-Pro-Leu-Gly

Where and how would you change the DNA that codes for vasopressin so that it would code for oxytocin instead? Does your answer suggest a possible evolutionary relationship between the genes for vasopressin and oxytocin?

22-2 Tracking a Series of Mutations. The following diagram shows the amino acids that result from mutations in the codon for a particular amino acid in a bacterial polypeptide:

$$Arg \nearrow^{Ile}_{\searrow Lys \rightarrow Thr \rightarrow Ser \searrow Stop}$$

Assume that each arrow denotes a single base-pair substitution in the bacterial DNA.

(a) Referring to the genetic code table in Figure 21-6, determine the most likely codons for each of the amino acids and the stop signal in the diagram.

(b) Starting with a population of mutant cells carrying the nonsense mutation, another mutant is isolated in which the premature stop signal is suppressed. Assuming wobble does not occur and assuming a single base change in the tRNA anticodon, what are all the possible amino acids that might be found in this mutant at the amino acid position in question?

• 22-3 Sleuthing Using Mutants. You identify three independent missense mutations that all affect the same gene. In fact, all three mutations affect the same codon but do not cause the same amino acid substitution. The first mutation results in substitution of arginine (Arg), the second results in substitution of tyrosine (Tyr), and the third results in substitution of glutamine (Gln). Each mutation affects just a single base within this codon *but not necessarily the same base*. What was the original amino acid?

22-4 Initiation of Translation. Figure 22-8 diagrams the initiation of translation in bacterial cells. Using the text on pages 687–688 as a guide, draw a similar sketch outlining the steps in *eukaryotic* initiation of translation. What are the main differences between bacterial and eukaryotic initiation?

22-5 Bacterial and Eukaryotic Protein Synthesis Compared. For each of the following statements, indicate whether it applies to protein synthesis in bacteria (Ba), in eukaryotes (E), in both (Bo), or in neither (N).

(a) The mRNA has a ribosome-binding site within its leader region.

(b) AUG is a start codon.

(c) The enzyme that catalyzes peptide bond formation is an RNA molecule.

(d) The mRNA is translated in the $3' \rightarrow 5'$ direction.

(e) The C-terminus of the polypeptide is synthesized last.

(f) Translation is terminated by special tRNA molecules that recognize stop codons.

(g) GTP hydrolysis functions to induce conformational changes in various proteins involved in polypeptide elongation.

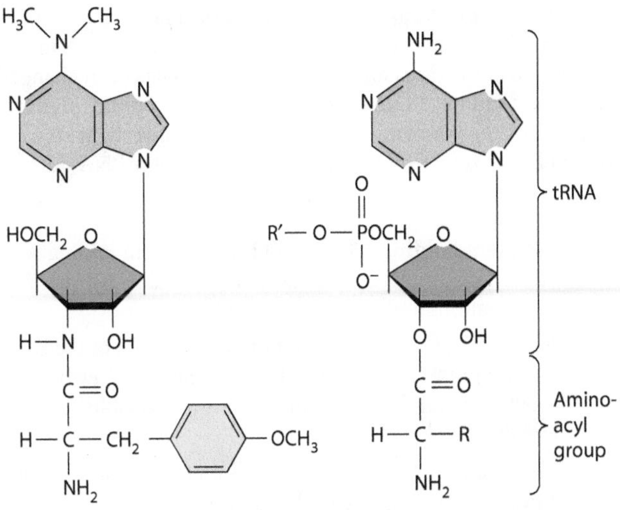

FIGURE 22-21 The Structure of Puromycin. See Problem 22-6.

(h) ATP hydrolysis is required to attach an amino acid to a tRNA molecule.

(i) The specificity required to link the right amino acids to the right tRNA molecules is a property of the enzymes called aminoacyl-tRNA synthetases.

• 22-6 An Antibiotic Inhibitor of Translation. Puromycin is a powerful inhibitor of protein synthesis (see page 697). It is an analog of the 3' end of aminoacyl tRNA, as **Figure 22-21** reveals. (R represents the functional group of the amino acid; R′ represents the remainder of the tRNA molecule.) When puromycin is added to a cell-free system containing all the necessary machinery for protein synthesis, incomplete polypeptide chains are released from the ribosomes. Each such chain has puromycin covalently attached to one end.

(a) Explain these results.

(b) To which end of the polypeptide chains would you expect the puromycin to be attached? Explain.

(c) Would you expect puromycin to bind to the A or P site on the ribosome or to both? Explain.

(d) Assuming that it can penetrate into the cell equally well in both cases, would you expect puromycin to be a better inhibitor of protein synthesis in eukaryotes or bacteria? Explain.

• 22-7 A Fictional Antibiotic. In a study involving a cell-free protein synthesizing system from *E. coli*, the polyribonucleotide AUGUUUUUUUUUUUU directs the synthesis of the oligopeptide fMet-Phe-Phe-Phe-Phe. In the presence of Rambomycin, a new antibiotic just developed by Macho Pharmaceuticals, only the dipeptide fMet-Phe is made.

(a) What step in polypeptide synthesis does Rambomycin inhibit? Explain your answer.

(b) Will the oligopeptide product be found attached to tRNA at the end of the uninhibited reaction? Will the dipeptide product be found attached to tRNA at the end of the Rambomycin-inhibited reaction? Explain.

22-8 Frameshift Suppression. As discussed in the chapter, a nonsense mutation can be suppressed by a mutant tRNA in which one of the three anticodon nucleotides has been changed. Describe a mutant tRNA that could suppress a *frameshift* mutation. (Hint: Such a mutant tRNA was used to investigate the role played by peptidyl tRNA in the translocation of mRNA during protein synthesis.)

• **22-9 Protein Folding.** The role of BiP in protein folding was briefly described in this chapter. Answer the following questions about observations and situations involving BiP.

(a) BiP is found in high concentration in the lumen of the ER but is not present in significant concentrations elsewhere in the cell. How do you think this condition is established and maintained?

(b) If the gene coding for BiP acquires a mutation that disrupts the protein's binding site for hydrophobic amino acids, what kind of impact might this have on the cell?

• **22-10 Cotranslational Import.** You perform a series of experiments on the synthesis of the pituitary hormone prolactin, which is a single polypeptide chain 199 amino acids long. The mRNA coding for prolactin is translated in a cell-free protein synthesizing system containing ribosomes, amino acids, tRNAs, aminoacyl-tRNA synthetases, ATP, GTP, and the appropriate initiation, elongation, and termination factors. Under these conditions, a polypeptide chain 227 amino acids long is produced.

(a) How might you explain the discrepancy between the normal length of prolactin (199 amino acids) and the length of the polypeptide synthesized in your experiment (227 amino acids)?

(b) You perform a second experiment, in which you add SRP to your cell-free protein-synthesizing system, and find that translation stops after a polypeptide about 70 amino acids long has been produced. How can you explain this result? Can you think of any purpose this phenomenon might serve for the cell?

(c) You perform a third experiment, in which you add both SRP and ER membrane vesicles to your protein-synthesizing system, and find that translation of the prolactin mRNA now produces a polypeptide 199 amino acids long. How can you explain this result? Where would you expect to find this polypeptide?

22-11 Two Types of Posttranslational Import. The mechanism by which proteins synthesized in the cytosol are imported into the mitochondrial matrix is different from the mechanism by which proteins enter the nucleus, yet the two mechanisms do share some features. Indicate whether each of the following statements applies to nuclear import (Nu), mitochondrial import (M), both (B), or neither (N). You may want to review the discussion of nuclear import in Chapter 18 before answering this question (see especially Figure 18-31).

(a) The polypeptide to be transported into the organelle has a specific short stretch of amino acids that targets the polypeptide to the organelle.

(b) The signal sequence is always at the polypeptide's N-terminus and is cut off by a peptidase within the organelle.

(c) The signal sequence is recognized and bound by a receptor protein in the organelle's outer membrane.

(d) ATP hydrolysis is known to be required for the translocation process.

(e) GTP hydrolysis is known to be required for the translocation process.

(f) There is strong evidence for the involvement of chaperone proteins during translocation of the protein.

(g) The imported protein enters the organelle through some sort of protein pore.

(h) The pore complex consists of more than two dozen proteins and is large enough to be readily seen with the electron microscope.

SUGGESTED READING

References of historical importance are marked with a •.

Translation

Blumenthal, T. Operons in eukaryotes. *Brief. Funct. Genomic Proteomic* 3 (2004): 199.

Cech, T. R. The ribosome is a ribozyme. *Science* 289 (2000): 878.

Chang, Y.-F., J. S. Imam, and M. F. Wilkinson. The nonsense-mediated decay RNA surveillance pathway. *Annu. Rev. Biochem.* 76 (2007): 51.

• Frank, J. How the ribosome works. *Amer. Scientist* 86 (1998): 428.

Hoagland, M. Enter transfer RNA. *Nature* 431 (2004): 249.

Isken, O., and L. E. Maquat. Quality control of eukaryotic mRNA: Safeguarding cells from abnormal mRNA function. *Genes Dev.* 21 (2007): 1833.

Moore, S. D., and R. T. Sauer. The tmRNA system for translational surveillance and ribosome rescue. *Annu. Rev. Biochem.* 76 (2007): 101.

Myasnikov, A. G., A. Simonetti, S. Marzi, and B. P. Klaholz. Structure-function insights into prokaryotic and eukaryotic translation initiation. *Curr. Opin. Struct. Biol.* 19 (2009): 300.

Rodnina, M. V., M. Beringer, and W. Wintermeyer. How ribosomes make peptide bonds. *Trends Biochem. Sci.* 32 (2007): 20.

Schmeing, T. M., and V. Ramakrishnan. What recent ribosome structures have revealed about the mechanism of translation. *Nature* 461 (2009): 1234.

Van Noorden, R. Structural biology bags chemistry prize. *Nature* 461 (2009): 860.

Warner, J. R., and P. M. Knopf. The discovery of polyribosomes. *Trends Biochem. Sci.* 27 (2002): 376.

Youngman, E. M., M. E. McDonald, and R. Green. Peptide release on the ribosome: Mechanism and implications for translational control. *Annu. Rev. Microbiol.* 62 (2008): 353.

Zaher, H. S., and R. Green. Fidelity at the molecular level: lessons from protein synthesis. *Cell* 136 (2009): 746.

Protein Folding and Processing

Aguzzi, A., M. Heikenwalder, and M. Polymenidou. Insights into prion strains and neurotoxicity. *Nature Rev. Mol. Cell Biol.* 8 (2007): 552.

Buku, B., J. Weissman, and A. Horwich. Molecular chaperones and protein quality control. *Cell* 125 (2006): 443.

Caughey, B., G. S. Baron, B. Chesebro, and M. Jeffrey. Getting a grip on prions: Oligomers, amyloids, and pathological membrane interactions. *Annu. Rev. Biochem.* 78 (2009): 177.

Paulus, H. Protein splicing and related forms of protein autoprocessing. *Annu. Rev. Biochem.* 69 (2000): 447.

Prusiner, S. B. Detecting mad cow disease. *Sci. Amer.* 291 (July 2004): 86.

Smith, B., ed. Nature insight: Protein misfolding. *Nature* 426 (2003): 883–909.

Wolfe, M. S. Shutting down Alzheimer's. *Sci. Amer.* 294 (May 2006): 72.

Cotranslational Protein Import

Anderson, D., and P. Walter. Blobel's Nobel: A vision validated. *Cell* 99 (1999): 557.

Cross, B. C., I. Sinning, J. Luirink, and S. High. Delivering proteins for export from the cytosol. *Nat. Rev. Mol. Cell Biol.* 10 (2009): 255.

Kramer, G., D. Boehringer, N. Ban, and B. Bukau. The ribosome as a platform for co-translational processing, folding and targeting of newly synthesized proteins. *Nat. Struct. Mol. Biol.* 16 (2009): 589.

Matlin, K. S. The strange case of the signal recognition particle. *Nature Rev. Mol. Cell. Biol.* 3 (2002): 538.

Meusser, B. et al. ERAD: The long road to destruction. *Nature Cell Biol.* 7 (2005): 766.

Ron, D., and P. Walter. Signal integration in the endoplasmic reticulum unfolded protein response. *Nature Rev. Mol. Cell Biol.* 8 (2007): 519.

Schnell, D. J., and D. N. Hebert. Protein translocons: Multifunctional mediators of protein translocation across membranes. *Cell* 112 (2003): 491.

Shental-Bechor, D., S. J. Fleishman, and N. Ben-Tal. Has the code for protein translocation been broken? *Trends Biochem. Sci.* 31 (2006): 192.

Tsai, B., Y. Ye, and T. A. Rapoport. Retro-translocation of proteins from the endoplasmic reticulum into the cytosol. *Nature Rev. Mol. Cell. Biol.* 3 (2002): 246.

Posttranslational Protein Import

Chacinska, A., C. M. Koehler, D. Milenkovic, T. Lithgow, and N. Pfanner. Importing mitochondrial proteins: Machineries and mechanisms. *Cell* 138 (2009): 628.

Dolezal, P. et al. Evolution of the molecular machines for protein import into mitochondria. *Science* 313 (2006): 314.

Kessler, F., and D. Schnell. Chloroplast biogenesis: Diversity and regulation of the protein import apparatus. *Curr. Opin. Cell Biol.* 21 (2009): 494.

Neupert, W., and J. M. Herrmann. Translocation of proteins into mitochondria. *Annu. Rev. Biochem.* 76 (2007): 723.

Soll, J., and E. Schleiff. Protein import into chloroplasts. *Nature Rev. Mol. Cell Biol.* 5 (2004): 198.

Teter, S. A., and D. J. Klionsky. How to get a folded protein across a membrane. *Trends Cell Biol.* 9 (1999): 428.

Wickner, W., and R. Schekman. Protein translocation across biological membranes. *Science* 310 (2005): 1452.

*C*ell biologists often need to examine the
structure of cells and their components,
and they need to see specific structures or
molecules amid a complicated mixture of
cellular components. The microscope is an indispensable
tool for this purpose because most cellular structures
are too small to be seen by the unaided eye. In fact, the
beginnings of cell biology can be traced to the invention of
the **light microscope,** which made it possible for scientists
to see enlarged images of cells for the first time. The first
generally useful light microscope was developed in 1590 by
Z. Janssen and his nephew, H. Janssen. Many important
microscopic observations were reported during the next
century, notably those of Robert Hooke, who observed the
first cells, and Antonie van Leeuwenhoek, whose improved
microscopes provided our first glimpses of internal cell
structure. Since then, the light microscope has undergone
numerous improvements and modifications, right up to
the present time.

Just as the invention of the light microscope heralded a
wave of scientific achievement by allowing us to see cells for
the first time, the development of the **electron microscope**
in the 1930s revolutionized our ability to explore cell structure and function. Because it is at least a hundred times
better at visualizing objects than the light microscope is, the
electron microscope ushered in a new era in cell biology,
opening our eyes to an exquisite subcellular architecture
never before seen and changing forever the way we think
about cells.

Light microscopy has experienced a renaissance in recent
years as the development of specialized new techniques allows
researchers to explore aspects of cell structure and behavior
that cannot be readily studied by electron microscopy. These
advances have involved the merging of technologies from
physics, engineering, chemistry, and molecular biology, and
they have greatly expanded our ability to study cells using the
light microscope.

In this appendix, we explore the fundamental principles
of light and electron microscopy, emphasizing the various
specialized techniques used to adapt these two types of
microscopy for a variety of specialized purposes. We also
examine other related technologies that extend the range
of view beyond the microscope to visualization of single
molecules at high resolution.

Optical Principles of Microscopy

Although light and electron microscopes differ in many
ways, they make use of similar optical principles to form
images. Therefore, we begin our discussion of microscopy
by examining these underlying common principles,
placing special emphasis on the factors that determine how
small an object can be seen with current technologies.

The Illuminating Wavelength Sets a Limit on How Small an Object Can Be Seen

Regardless of the type of microscope being used, three elements are always needed to form an image: a *source
of illumination,* a *specimen* to be examined, and a system of
lenses that focuses the illumination on the specimen and
forms the image. **Figure A-1** illustrates these features for a
light microscope and an electron microscope. In a light
microscope, the source of illumination is *visible light* (wavelength approximately 400–700 nm), and the lens system
consists of a series of glass lenses. The image can either be
viewed directly through an eyepiece or focused on a
detector, such as photographic film or an electronic camera.
In an electron microscope, the illumination source is a
beam of electrons emitted by a heated tungsten filament, and
the lens system consists of a series of electromagnets. The
electron beam is focused on either a fluorescent screen or
photographic film, or it is digitally imaged using a detector.

Despite these differences in illumination source and
instrument design, both types of microscopes depend on
the same principles of optics and form images in a similar
manner. When a specimen is placed in the path of a light
or electron beam, physical characteristics of the beam are
changed in a way that creates an image that can be interpreted by the human eye or recorded on a photographic
detector. To understand this interaction between the illumination source and the specimen, we need to understand
the concept of wavelength, which is illustrated in **Figure
A-2** using the following simple analogy.

If two people hold onto opposite ends of a slack rope
and wave the rope with a rhythmic up-and-down motion,
they will generate a long, regular pattern of movement in
the rope called a *waveform* (Figure A-2a). The distance
from the crest of one wave to the crest of the next is called
the **wavelength.** If someone standing to one side of the
rope tosses a large object such as a beach ball toward the

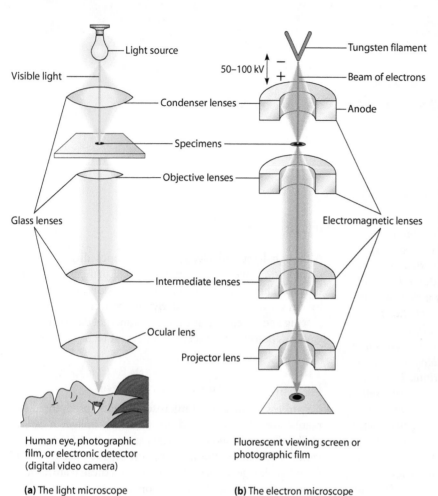

(a) The light microscope uses visible light (wavelength approximately 400–700 nm) and glass lenses to form an image of the specimen that can be seen by the eye, focused on photographic film, or received by an electronic detector such as a digital camera. (b) The electron microscope uses a beam of electrons emitted by a tungsten filament and focused by electromagnetic lenses to form an image of the specimen on a fluorescent screen, a digital detector, or photographic film. (These diagrams have been drawn to emphasize the similarities in overall design between the two types of microscope. In reality, a light microscope is designed with the light source at the bottom and the ocular lens at the top, as shown in Figure A-5b.)

(a) The light microscope

(b) The electron microscope

rope, the ball may interfere with, or perturb, the waveform of the rope's motion (Figure A-2b). However, if a small object, such as a softball, is tossed toward the rope, the movement of the rope will probably not be affected at all (Figure A-2c). If the rope holders move the rope faster, the motion of the rope will still have a waveform, but the wavelength will be shorter (Figure A-2d). In this case, a softball tossed toward the rope is quite likely to perturb the rope's movement (Figure A-2e).

This simple analogy illustrates an important principle: The ability of an object to perturb a wave's motion depends crucially on the size of the object in relation to the wavelength of the motion. This principle is of great importance in microscopy because it means that the wavelength of the illumination source sets a limit on how small an object can be seen. To understand this relationship, we need to recognize that the moving rope of Figure A-2 is analogous to the beam of light (photons) or the electrons used as an illumination source in a light or electron microscope, respectively. In other words, both light and electrons behave as waves. When a beam of light (or electrons) encounters a specimen, the specimen alters the physical characteristics of the illuminating beam, just as the beach ball or softball alters the motion of the rope. And because an object can be detected only by its effect on the wave, the wavelength must be comparable in size to the object that is to be detected.

Once we understand this relationship between wavelength and object size, we can readily appreciate why very small objects can be seen only by electron microscopy: The wavelengths of electrons are very much shorter than those of photons. Thus, objects such as viruses and ribosomes are too small to perturb the waveform of photons, but they can readily interact with electrons. As we discuss different types of microscopes and specimen preparation techniques, you might find it helpful to ask yourself how the source and specimen are interacting and how the characteristics of both are modified to produce an image.

Resolution Refers to the Ability to Distinguish Adjacent Objects as Separate from One Another

When waves of light or electrons pass through a lens and are focused, the image that is formed results from a property of waves called **interference**—the process by which two or more waves combine to reinforce or cancel one another, producing a wave equal to the sum of the two combining waves. Thus, the image that you see when you look at a specimen through a series of lenses is really just a pattern of either additive or canceling interference of the waves that went through the lenses, a phenomenon known as **diffraction.**

In a light microscope, glass lenses are used to direct photons, whereas an electron microscope uses electro-

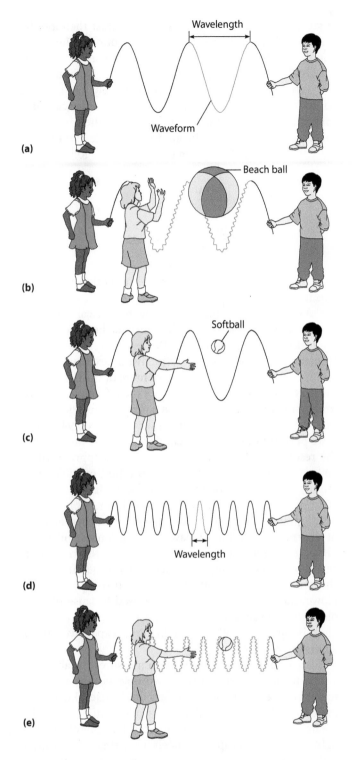

(a)

Wavelength

Waveform

(b)

Beach ball

(c)

Softball

(d)

Wavelength

(e)

FIGURE A-2 Wave Motion, Wavelength, and Perturbations. The wave motion of a rope held between two people is analogous to the waveform of both photons and electrons, and it can be used to illustrate the effect of the size of an object on its ability to perturb wave motion. **(a)** Moving a slack rope up and down rhythmically will generate a waveform with a characteristic wavelength. **(b)** When thrown against a rope, an object with a diameter comparable to the wavelength of the rope (e.g., a beach ball) will perturb the motion of the rope. **(c)** An object with a diameter significantly less than the wavelength of the rope (e.g., a softball) will probably cause little or no perturbation of the rope because, with its smaller diameter, it is not likely to strike the rope when tossed toward it. **(d)** If the rope is moved more rapidly, the wavelength will be reduced substantially. **(e)** A softball can now perturb the motion of the rope because its diameter is comparable to the wavelength of the rope.

lens of the microscope from the specimen (**Figure A-4**). Angular aperture is therefore a measure of how much of the illumination that leaves the specimen actually passes through the lens. This in turn determines the sharpness of the interference pattern and therefore the ability of the lens to convey information about the specimen. In the best light microscopes, the angular aperture is about 70°.

The angular aperture of a lens is one of the factors influencing a microscope's **resolution,** which is defined as the minimum distance that can separate two points that still remain identifiable as separate points when viewed through the microscope.

Resolution is governed by three factors: the wavelength of the light used to illuminate the specimen, the angular aperture, and the refractive index of the medium surrounding the specimen. (**Refractive index** is a measure of the change in the velocity of light as it passes from one medium to another.) The effect of these three variables on resolution is described quantitatively by an equation known as the *Abbé equation:*

$$r = \frac{0.61\,\lambda}{n \sin \alpha} \qquad \text{(A-1)}$$

where r is the resolution, λ is the wavelength of the light used for illumination, n is the refractive index of the

magnets as lenses to direct electrons. Yet both kinds of lenses have two fundamental properties in common: focal length and angular aperture. The **focal length** is the distance between the midline of the lens and the point at which rays passing through the lens converge to a focus (**Figure A-3**). The focal length is determined by the index of refraction of the lens itself, the medium in which it is immersed, and the geometry of the lens. The lens magnifying strength, measured in diopters, is the inverse of the focal length, measured in meters. The **angular aperture** is the half-angle α of the cone of light entering the objective

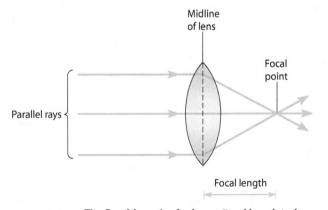

Midline of lens

Focal point

Parallel rays

Focal length

FIGURE A-3 The Focal Length of a Lens. Focal length is the distance from the midline of a lens to the point where parallel rays passing through the lens converge to a focus.

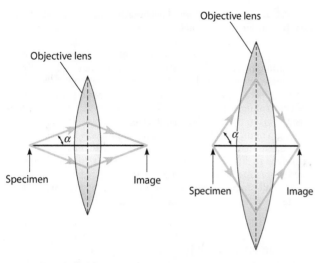

(a) Low-aperture lens   **(b)** High-aperture lens

FIGURE A-4 The Angular Aperture of a Lens. The angular aperture is the half-angle α of the cone of light entering the objective lens of the microscope from the specimen. **(a)** A low-aperture lens (α is small). **(b)** A high-aperture lens (α is large). The larger the angular aperture, the more information the lens can transmit. The best glass lenses have an angular aperture of about 70°.

medium between the specimen and the objective lens of the microscope, and α is the angular aperture as previously defined. The constant 0.61 represents the degree to which image points can overlap and still be recognized as separate points by an observer.

In the preceding equation, the quantity $n \sin \alpha$ is called the **numerical aperture** of the objective lens, abbreviated **NA**. An alternative expression for resolution is therefore

$$r = \frac{0.61\lambda}{NA} \qquad \text{(A-2)}$$

The Practical Limit of Resolution Is Roughly 200 nm for Light Microscopy and 2 nm for Electron Microscopy

Maximizing resolution is an important goal in both light and electron microscopy. Because r is a measure of how close two points can be and still be distinguished from each other, resolution improves as r becomes smaller. Thus, for the best resolution, the numerator of equation A-2 should be as small as possible and the denominator should be as large as possible.

Consider a glass lens that uses visible light as an illumination source. First, we need to make the numerator as small as possible. The wavelength for visible light falls in the range of 400–700 nm, so the minimum value for λ is set by the shortest wavelength in this range that is practical to use for illumination, which turns out to be blue light of approximately 450 nm. To maximize the denominator of Equation A-2, recall that the numerical aperture is the product of the refractive index and the sine of the

angular aperture. Both of these values must therefore be maximized to achieve optimal resolution. Since the angular aperture for the best objective lenses is approximately 70°, the maximum value for $\sin \alpha$ is about 0.94. The refractive index of air is approximately 1.0, so for a lens designed for use in air, the maximum numerical aperture is approximately 0.94. Putting all of these numbers together, the resolution in air for a sample illuminated with blue light of 450 nm can be calculated as follows:

$$r = \frac{0.61\lambda}{NA}$$
$$= \frac{(0.61)(450)}{0.94} = 292 \text{ nm} \qquad \text{(A-3)}$$

As a rule of thumb, then, the limit of resolution for a glass lens in air is roughly 300 nm.

As a means of increasing the numerical aperture, some microscope lenses are designed to be used with a layer of *immersion oil* between the lens and the specimen. Immersion oil has a higher refractive index than air and therefore allows the lens to receive more of the light transmitted through the specimen. Since the refractive index of immersion oil is about 1.5, the maximum numerical aperture for an oil immersion lens is about $1.5 \times 0.94 = 1.4$. If we perform the same calculations as before, we find that the resolution of an oil immersion lens is approximately 200 nm. Thus, the **limit of resolution** (best possible resolution) for a microscope that uses visible light is roughly 300 nm in air and 200 nm with an oil immersion lens. In actual practice, such limits can rarely be reached because of aberrations (technical flaws) in the lenses. By using ultraviolet light as an illumination source, the resolution can be enhanced to approximately 100 nm because of the shorter wavelength (200–300 nm) of this type of light. However, special cameras must be used because ultraviolet light is invisible to the human eye. Moreover, ordinary glass is opaque to ultraviolet light, so expensive quartz lenses must be used.

Because the limit of resolution measures the ability of a lens to distinguish between two objects that are close together, it sets an upper boundary on the **useful magnification** that is possible with any given lens. In practice, the greatest useful magnification that can be achieved with a light microscope is approximately 1000 times the numerical aperture of the lens being used. Since numerical aperture ranges from approximately 1.0 to 1.4, this means that the useful magnification of a light microscope is limited to roughly 1000× in air and 1400× with immersion oil. Magnification greater than these limits is referred to as "empty magnification" because it provides no additional information about the object being studied.

The most effective way to achieve better magnification is to switch from visible light to electrons as the illumination source. Because the wavelength of an electron is approximately 100,000 times shorter than that of a photon of visible light, the theoretical limit of resolution of the electron microscope (0.002 nm) is orders of magnitude better than that of the light microscope (200 nm). However, practical problems in the design of the electromagnetic lenses used to focus the electron beam prevent the electron microscope from achieving this theoretical potential. The main problem is that electromagnets produce considerable distortion when the angular aperture is more than a few tenths of a degree. This tiny angle is several orders of magnitude less than that of a good glass lens (about 70°), giving the electron microscope a numerical aperture considerably smaller than that of the light microscope. The limit of resolution for the best electron microscope is therefore only approximately 0.2 nm, far from the theoretical limit of 0.002 nm. Moreover, when viewing biological samples, problems with specimen preparation and contrast are such that the practical limit of resolution is often closer to 2 nm. Practically speaking, therefore, resolution in an electron microscope is generally about 100 times better than that of the light microscope. As a result, the useful magnification of an electron microscope is approximately 100 times that of a light microscope, or approximately 100,000×.

The Light Microscope

It was the light microscope that first opened our eyes to the existence of cells. A pioneering name in the history of light microscopy is that of Antonie van Leeuwenhoek, the Dutch shopkeeper who is generally regarded as the father of light microscopy. Leeuwenhoek's lenses, which he manufactured himself during the late 1600s, were of surprisingly high quality for his time. They were capable of 300-fold magnification—a tenfold improvement over previous instruments. This improved magnification made the interior of cells visible for the first time, and Leeuwenhoek's observations over a period of more than 25 years led to the discovery of cells in various types of biological specimens and set the stage for the formulation of the cell theory.

Compound Microscopes Use Several Lenses in Combination

In the 300 years since Leeuwenhoek's pioneering work, considerable advances in the construction and application of light microscopes have been made. Today, the instrument of choice for light microscopy uses several lenses in combination and is therefore called a **compound microscope** (**Figure A-5**). The optical path through a compound microscope, illustrated in Figure A-5b, begins with a source of illumination, often a light source located in the base of the instrument. The light from the source first passes through **condenser lenses,** which direct the light toward a specimen mounted on a glass slide and positioned on the **stage** of the microscope. The **objective lens,** located immediately above the specimen, is responsible for forming the *primary image.* Most compound microscopes have several objective lenses of differing magnifications mounted on a rotatable turret.

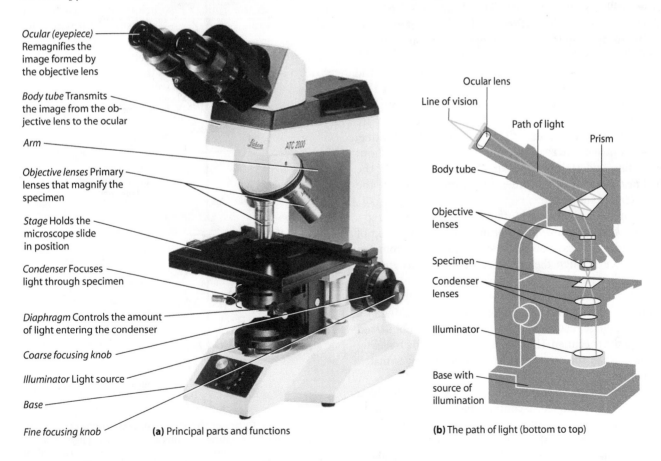

Ocular (eyepiece) Remagnifies the image formed by the objective lens

Body tube Transmits the image from the objective lens to the ocular

Arm

Objective lenses Primary lenses that magnify the specimen

Stage Holds the microscope slide in position

Condenser Focuses light through specimen

Diaphragm Controls the amount of light entering the condenser

Coarse focusing knob

Illuminator Light source

Base

Fine focusing knob

(a) Principal parts and functions

Ocular lens

Line of vision

Path of light

Prism

Body tube

Objective lenses

Specimen

Condenser lenses

Illuminator

Base with source of illumination

(b) The path of light (bottom to top)

The primary image is further enlarged by the **ocular lens,** or *eyepiece.* In some microscopes, an **intermediate lens** is positioned between the objective and ocular lenses to accomplish still further enlargement. Overall magnification of the image can be calculated by multiplying the enlarging powers of the objective lens, the ocular lens, and the intermediate lens (if present). Thus, a microscope with a $10\times$ objective lens, a $2.5\times$ intermediate lens, and a $10\times$ ocular lens will magnify a specimen 250-fold.

The elements of the microscope described so far create a basic form of light microscopy called **brightfield microscopy.** Compared with other microscopes, the brightfield microscope is inexpensive and simple to align and use. However, the only specimens that can be seen directly by brightfield microscopy are those possessing color or some other property that affects the amount of light that passes through. Many biological specimens lack these characteristics and must therefore be stained with dyes or examined with specialized types of light microscopes. These special microscopes have various advantages that make them especially well suited for visualizing specific types of specimens. These include phase-contrast, differential interference contrast, fluorescence, and confocal microscopes. We will look at these and several other important techniques in the following sections.

Phase-Contrast Microscopy Detects Differences in Refractive Index and Thickness

As we will describe in more detail later, cells are often killed, sliced into thin sections, and stained before being examined by brightfield microscopy. While such procedures are useful for visualizing the details of a cell's internal architecture, little can be learned about the dynamic aspects of cell behavior by examining cells that have been killed, sliced, and stained. Therefore, various techniques have been developed to observe cells that are intact and, in many cases, still living. One such technique, **phase-contrast microscopy,** improves contrast without sectioning and staining by exploiting differences in the thickness and refractive index of various regions of the cells being examined.

To understand the basis of phase-contrast microscopy, we must first recognize that a beam of light is made up of many individual rays of light. As the rays pass from the light source through the specimen, their velocity may be affected by the physical properties of the specimen. Usually, the velocity of the rays is slowed down to varying extents by different regions of the specimen, resulting in a change in phase relative to light waves that have not passed through the specimen. (Light waves are said to be traveling *in phase* when the crests and troughs of the waves match each other.)

Although the human eye cannot detect such phase changes directly, the phase-contrast microscope overcomes this problem by converting phase differences into alterations in brightness. This conversion is accomplished using a *phase plate* (**Figure A-6**), which is an optical material inserted into the light path above the objective lens. On average, light passing through transparent specimens is retarded by approximately $\frac{1}{4}$ wavelength. The direct, undiffracted light passes through a portion of the phase plate that speeds it up by approximately $\frac{1}{4}$ wavelength. Now the two types of light interfere with one another, producing an image with highly contrasting bright and dark areas against an evenly illuminated background (**Figure A-7**). As a result, internal structures of cells are often better visualized by phase-contrast microscopy than with brightfield optics.

This approach to light microscopy is particularly useful for examining living, unstained specimens because biological materials almost inevitably diffract light. Phase-contrast microscopy is widely used in microbiology and tissue culture research to detect bacteria, cellular organelles, and other small entities in living specimens.

Differential Interference Contrast (DIC) Microscopy Utilizes a Split Light Beam to Detect Phase Differences

Differential interference contrast (DIC) microscopy, or *Nomarski* microscopy (named for its inventor), resembles phase-contrast microscopy in principle but is more sensitive because it employs a special prism to split the

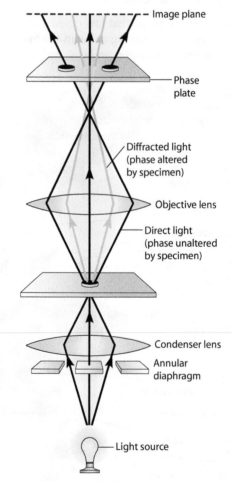

FIGURE A-6 Optics of the Phase-Contrast Microscope. Configuration of the optical elements and the paths of light rays through the phase-contrast microscope. Orange lines represent light diffracted by the specimen, and black lines represent direct light.

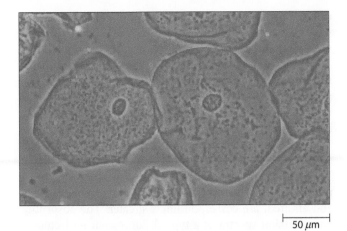

FIGURE A-7 **Phase-Contrast Microscopy.** A phase-contrast micrograph of epithelial cells. The cells were observed in an unprocessed and unstained state, which is a major advantage of phase-contrast microscopy.

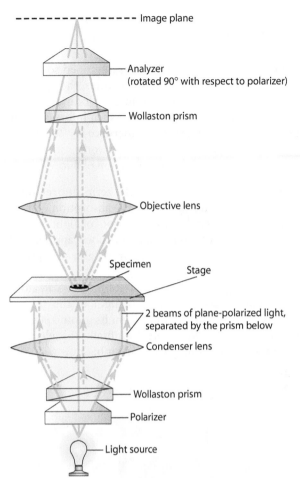

FIGURE A-8 **Optics of the Differential Interference Contrast (DIC) Microscope.** Configuration of the optical elements and the paths of light rays through the DIC microscope.

illuminating light beam into two separate rays (**Figure A-8**). When the two beams are recombined, any changes that occurred in the phase of one beam as it passed through the specimen cause it to interfere with the second beam. Because the largest phase changes usually occur at cell edges (the refractive index is more constant within the cell), the outline of the cell typically gives a strong signal. The image appears three-dimensional due to a shadow-casting illusion that arises because differences in phase are positive on one side of the cell but negative on the opposite side of the cell (**Figure A-9**).

The optical components required for DIC microscopy consist of a *polarizer,* an *analyzer,* and a pair of *Wollaston prisms* (see Figure A-8). The polarizer and the first Wollaston prism split a beam of light, creating two beams that are separated by a small distance along one direction. After traveling through the specimen, the beams are recombined by the second Wollaston prism. If no specimen is present, the beams recombine to form one beam that is identical to the one that initially entered the polarizer and first Wollaston prism. In the presence of a specimen, the two beams do not recombine in the same way (i.e., they interfere with each other), and the resulting beam's polarization becomes rotated slightly compared with the original. The net effect is a remarkable enhancement in resolution that makes this technique especially useful for studying living, unstained specimens. As we will soon see, combining this technique with digital microscopy is an especially effective approach for studying dynamic events within cells as they take place.

Other contrast enhancement methods are also used by cell biologists. *Hoffman modulation contrast,* developed by Robert Hoffman, increases contrast by detecting optical gradients across a transparent specimen using special filters and a rotating polarizer. Hoffman modulation contrast results in a shadow-casting effect similar to that in DIC microscopy.

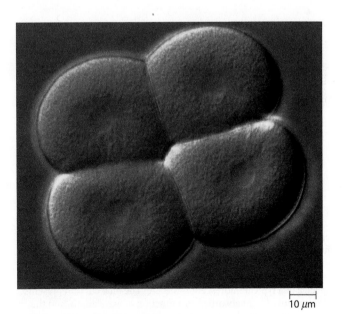

FIGURE A-9 **DIC Microscopy.** A DIC micrograph of a four-cell sea urchin embryo. Notice the shadow-casting effect that makes these cells appear dark at the bottom and light at the top.

Fluorescence Microscopy Can Detect the Presence of Specific Molecules or Ions Within Cells

Although the microscopic techniques described so far are quite effective for visualizing cell structures, they provide relatively little information concerning the location of specific molecules. One way of obtaining such information is through the use of **fluorescence microscopy.** To understand how fluorescence microscopy works, it is first necessary to understand the phenomenon of fluorescence.

The Nature of Fluorescence. The term **fluorescence** refers to a process that begins with the absorption of light by a molecule and ends with emission of light with a longer wavelength. This phenomenon is best approached by considering the quantum behavior of light, as opposed to its wavelike behavior. **Figure A-10a** is a diagram of the various energy levels of a simple atom. When an atom absorbs a photon (or *quantum*) of light of the proper energy, one of its electrons jumps from its ground state to a higher-energy, or *excited,* state. Eventually, this electron often loses some of its energy and drops back down to the

original ground state, emitting another photon as it does so. The emitted photon is always of less energy (longer wavelength) than the original photon that was absorbed. Thus, for example, shining blue light on the atom may result in green light being emitted. (The energy of a photon is inversely proportional to its wavelength; therefore, green light, being longer in wavelength than blue light, is lower in energy.)

Real fluorescent molecules have energy diagrams that are more complicated than that depicted in Figure A-10a. The number of possible energy levels in real molecules is much greater, so the different energies that can be absorbed, and emitted, are correspondingly greater. The absorption and emission spectra of a typical fluorescent molecule are shown in Figure A-10b. Every fluorescent molecule has its own characteristic absorption and emission spectra.

The Fluorescence Microscope. Fluorescence microscopy is a specialized type of light microscopy that employs light to excite fluorescence in the specimen. A standard fluorescence microscope has an *excitation filter* between the light source and the rest of the light path that transmits only light of a particular wavelength (**Figure A-11**). A *dichroic mirror,* which reflects light below a certain wavelength and transmits light above a certain wavelength, deflects the incoming light toward the objective lens, which focuses the light onto the specimen (because

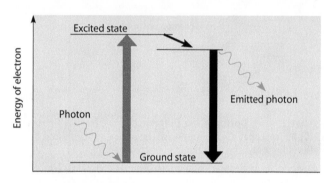

(a) Energy diagram

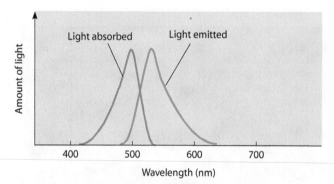

(b) Absorption and emission spectra

FIGURE A-10 Principles of Fluorescence. (a) An energy diagram of fluorescence from a simple atom. Light of a certain energy is absorbed (e.g., the blue light shown here). The electron jumps from its ground state to an excited state. It returns to the ground state by emitting a photon of lower energy and hence longer wavelength (e.g., green light). (b) The absorption and emission spectra of a typical fluorescent molecule. The blue curve represents the amount of light absorbed as a function of wavelength, and the green curve shows the amount of emitted light as a function of wavelength.

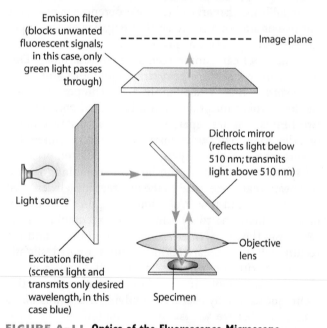

FIGURE A-11 Optics of the Fluorescence Microscope. Configuration of the optical elements and the paths of light rays through the fluorescence microscope. Light from the source passes through an excitation filter that transmits only excitation light (solid blue lines). Illumination of the specimen with this light induces fluorescent molecules in the specimen to emit longer-wavelength light (green lines). The emission filter subsequently removes the excitation light, while allowing passage of the emitted light. The image is therefore formed exclusively by light emitted by fluorescent molecules in the specimen.

the light is routed through the objective lens onto the specimen in this way, this technique is often called *epifluorescence microscopy*, from the Greek *epi-*, "upon"). The incoming light causes fluorescent compounds in the specimen to emit light of longer wavelength, which passes back through the objective lens. The longer wavelength light, instead of being reflected, passes through the dichroic mirror and encounters an *emission filter* that specifically prevents light that does not match the emission wavelength of the fluorescent molecules of interest from exiting the microscope. This leaves only the emission wavelengths to form the final fluorescent image, which therefore appears bright against a dark background.

Fluorescent Antibodies. To use fluorescence microscopy for locating specific molecules or ions within cells, researchers must employ special indicator molecules called *fluorescent probes*. A fluorescent probe is a molecule capable of emitting fluorescent light that can be used to indicate the presence of a specific molecule or ion.

One of the most common applications of fluorescent probes is in **immunostaining,** a technique based on the ability of antibodies to recognize and bind to specific molecules. (The molecules that antibodies bind to are called *antigens*.) Antibodies can be generated in the laboratory by injecting a foreign protein or other macromolecule into an animal such as a rabbit or mouse. In this way, it is possible to produce antibodies that will bind selectively to virtually any protein that a scientist wishes to study. Antibodies are not directly visible using light microscopy, however, so they are linked to a fluorescent dye such as *fluorescein*, which emits green light, or to *rhodamine*, which emits red light. More recently, antibodies have been linked to *quantum dots*—tiny, light-emitting crystals that are chemically more stable than traditional dyes, can be tuned to very specific wavelengths, and have other useful properties. To identify the subcellular location of a specific protein, cells are simply stained with a fluorescent antibody directed against that protein. The location of the fluorescence is then detected by viewing the cells with light of the appropriate wavelength.

Immunofluorescence microscopy can be performed using antibodies that are directly labeled with a fluorescent dye (**Figure A-12a**). However, immunofluorescence microscopy is more commonly performed using **indirect immunofluorescence** (Figure A-12b). In indirect immunofluorescence, a tissue or cell is treated with an antibody that is not labeled with dye. This antibody, called the *primary antibody*, attaches to specific antigenic sites within the tissue or cell. A second type of antibody, called the *secondary antibody*, is then added. The secondary antibody is labeled with a fluorescent dye, and it attaches to the primary antibody. Because more than one primary antibody molecule can attach to an antigen and more than one secondary antibody molecule can attach to each primary antibody, more fluorescent molecules are concentrated near each molecule that we seek to detect. As

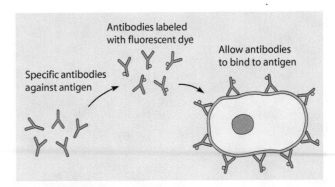

(a) Immunofluorescence

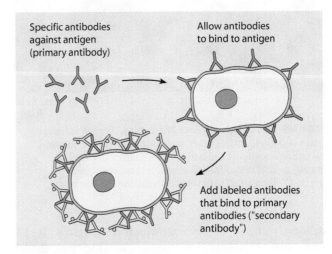

(b) Indirect immunofluorescence

FIGURE A-12 Immunostaining Using Fluorescent Antibodies. Immunofluorescence microscopy relies on the use of fluorescently labeled antibodies to detect specific molecular components (antigens) within a tissue sample. **(a)** In direct immunofluorescence, an antibody that binds to a molecular component in a tissue sample is labeled with a fluorescent dye. The labeled antibody is then added to the tissue sample, and it binds to the tissue in specific locations. The pattern of fluorescence that results is visualized using fluorescence or confocal microscopy. **(b)** In indirect immunofluorescence, a primary antibody is added to the tissue. Then a secondary antibody that carries a fluorescent label is added. The secondary antibody binds to the primary antibody. Because more than one fluorescent secondary antibody can bind to each primary antibody, indirect immunofluorescence effectively amplifies the fluorescent signal, making it more sensitive than direct immunofluorescence.

a result, indirect immunofluorescence results in signal amplification, and it is much more sensitive than the use of a primary antibody alone. The method is "indirect" because it does not examine where antibodies are bound to antigens; technically, the fluorescence reflects where the secondary antibody is located. This, of course, provides an indirect measure of where the original molecule of interest is located.

By using different combinations of antibodies or other fluorescent probes, more than one molecule in a cell can be labeled at the same time. Different probes can be imaged using different combinations of fluorescent filters, and the different images can be combined to generate

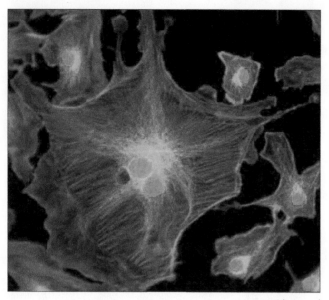

FIGURE A-13 **Fluorescence Microscopy.** Bovine pulmonary artery endothelial cells stained with an anti–β-tubulin mouse monoclonal antibody and a BODIPY FL secondary antibody (green) to label microtubules, Texas Red phalloidin (red) for labeling F-actin, and DAPI (blue) for labeling DNA in nuclei.

striking pictures of cellular structures. **Figure A-13** shows one example of this approach, in which endothelial cells are labeled with antibodies against β-tubulin (green), actin (red), and DNA (blue).

Other Fluorescent Probes. Naturally occurring proteins that selectively bind to specific cell components are also used in fluorescence microscopy. For example, the red structures in Figure A-13 are stained with a Texas Red-tagged mushroom toxin, *phalloidin*, which binds specifically to actin microfilaments. Another powerful fluorescence technique utilizes the **green fluorescent protein (GFP)**, a naturally fluorescent protein made by the jellyfish *Aequoria victoria*. Using recombinant DNA techniques, scientists can fuse DNA encoding GFP to a gene coding for a particular cellular protein. The resulting recombinant DNA can then be introduced into cells, where it is expressed to produce a fluorescently tagged version of the normal cellular protein. In many cases, the fusion of GFP to the end of a protein does not interfere with its function, allowing the use of fluorescence microscopy to view the GFP-fusion protein as it functions in a living cell (**Figure A-14**). Molecular biologists have produced mutated forms of GFP that absorb and emit light at a variety of wavelengths. Other naturally fluorescent proteins have also been identified, such as a red fluorescent protein from coral. These tools have expanded the repertoire of fluorescent molecules at the disposal of cell biologists.

Besides detecting macromolecules such as proteins, fluorescence microscopy can be used to monitor the subcellular distribution of various ions. To accomplish this task, chemists have synthesized molecules whose fluorescent properties are sensitive to the concentrations of ions such as Ca^{2+}, H^+, Na^+, Zn^{2+}, and Mg^{2+}, as well as to the electrical potential across the plasma membrane or the membranes of organelles. For example, a fluorescent probe called *fura-2* is commonly used to track the Ca^{2+} concentration inside living cells, because fura-2 emits a yellow fluorescence in the presence of low concentrations of Ca^{2+} and a green and then blue fluorescence in the presence of progressively higher concentrations of this ion. Therefore, monitoring the color of the fluorescence in living cells stained with this probe allows scientists to observe changes in the intracellular Ca^{2+} concentration as they occur.

Confocal Microscopy Minimizes Blurring by Excluding Out-of-Focus Light from an Image

When biologists use fluorescence microscopy to view intact cells, the resolution is limited. This occurs because, although fluorescence is emitted throughout the entire depth of the specimen, the viewer can focus the objective lens on only a single plane at any given time. As a result, light emitted from regions of the specimen above and below the focal plane causes a blurring of the image

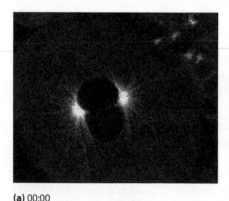

(a) 00:00

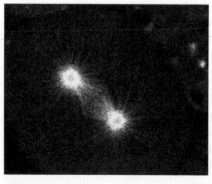

(b) 03:40

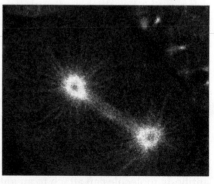

(c) 05:08

FIGURE A-14 **Using Green Fluorescent Protein to Visualize Proteins.** An image series of a living, one-cell nematode worm embryo undergoing mitosis. The embryo is expressing β-tubulin that is tagged with green fluorescent protein (GFP). Elapsed time from the first frame is shown in minutes:seconds.

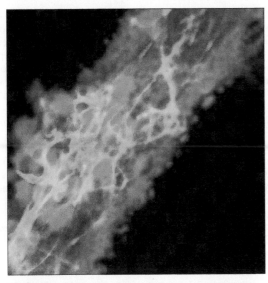

(a) Traditional fluorescence microscopy

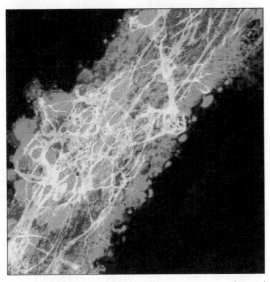

(b) Confocal fluorescence microscopy

$\overline{}$ 25 μm

FIGURE A-15 Comparison of Confocal Fluorescence Microscopy with Traditional Fluorescence Microscopy. These fluorescence micrographs show fluorescently labeled glial cells (red) and nerve cells (green) stained with two different fluorescent markers. **(a)** In traditional fluorescence microscopy, the entire specimen is illuminated, so fluorescent material above and below the plane of focus tends to blur the image. **(b)** In confocal fluorescence microscopy, incoming light is focused on a single plane, and out-of-focus fluorescence from the specimen is excluded. The resulting image is therefore much sharper.

(Figure A-15a). To overcome this problem, cell biologists often turn to the **confocal microscope**—a specialized type of light microscope that employs a laser beam to produce an image of a single plane of the specimen at a time (Figure A-15b). This approach improves the resolution along the optical axis of the microscope—that is, structures in the middle of a cell may be distinguished from those on the top or bottom. Likewise, a cell in the middle of a piece of tissue can be distinguished from cells above or below it.

To understand this type of microscopy, it is first necessary to consider the paths of light taken through a simple lens. **Figure A-16** illustrates how a simple lens forms an image of a point source of light. To understand what your eye would see, imagine placing a piece of photographic film in the plane of focus (image plane). Now ask how the images of other points of light placed further away or closer to the lens contribute to the original image (Figure A-16b). As you might guess, there is a precise relationship between the distance of the object from the lens (o), the distance from the lens to the image of that object brought into focus (i), and the focal length of the lens (f). This relationship is given by the equation

$$\frac{1}{f} = \frac{1}{o} + \frac{1}{i} \qquad \text{(A-4)}$$

As Figure A-16b shows, light arising from the points that are not in focus covers a greater surface area on the film because the rays are still either converging or diverging. Thus, the image on the film now has the original point source that is in focus, with a superimposed halo of light from the out-of-focus objects.

If we were interested only in seeing the original point source, we could mask out the extraneous light by placing an aperture, or *pinhole,* in the same plane as the film. This principle is used in a confocal microscope to discriminate against out-of-focus rays. In a real specimen, of course, we have more than one extraneous source of light on each side of the object we wish to see; in fact, we have a continuum of points. To understand how this affects our image, imagine that instead of three points of light, our specimen consists of a long, thin tube of light, as in Figure A-16c. Now consider obtaining an image of some arbitrary small section, dx. If the tube sends out the same amount of light per unit length, then even with a pinhole, the image of interest will be obscured by the halos arising from other parts of the tube. This occurs because there is a small contribution from each out-of-focus section, and the sheer number of small sections will create a large background over the section of interest.

This situation is very close to the one we face when dealing with real biological samples that have been stained with a fluorescent probe. In general, the distribution of the probe is three-dimensional, and the image is often marred by the halo of background light that arises mostly from probes above and below the plane of interest. To circumvent this, we can preferentially illuminate the plane of interest, thereby biasing the contributions in the image plane so that they arise mostly from a single plane (Figure A-16d). Thus, the essence of confocal microscopy is to bring the illumination beam that excites the fluorescence into focus in a single plane, and to use a pinhole to ensure that the light we collect in the image plane arises mainly from that plane of focus.

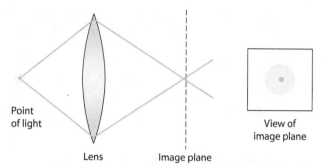

(a) Formation of an image of a single point of light by a lens

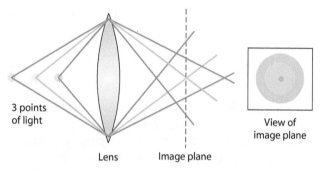

(b) Formation of an image of a point of light in the presence of two other points

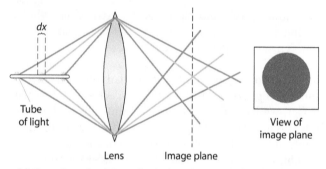

(c) Formation of an image of a section of an equally bright tube of light

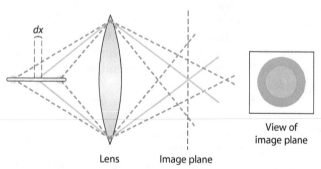

(d) Formation of an image of a brightened section of a tube of light

Figure A-17 illustrates how these principles are put to work in a laser scanning confocal microscope, which illuminates specimens using a laser beam focused by an objective lens down to a diffraction-limited spot. The position of the spot is controlled by scanning mirrors, which allow the beam to be swept over the specimen in a precise pattern. As the beam is scanned over the spec-

FIGURE A-16 Paths of Light Through a Single Lens. (a) The image of a single point of light formed by a lens. **(b)** The paths of light from three points of light at different distances from the lens. In the image plane, the in-focus image of the central point is superimposed on the out-of-focus rays of the other points. A pinhole or aperture around the central point can be used to discriminate against out-of-focus rays and maximize the contributions from the central point. **(c)** The paths of light originating from a continuum of points, represented as a tube of light. This is similar to a uniformly illuminated sample. In the image plane, the contributions from an arbitrarily small in-focus section, *dx*, are completely obscured by the other out-of-focus rays; here a pinhole does not help. **(d)** By illuminating only a single section of the tube strongly and the rest weakly, we can recover information in the image plane about the section *dx*. Now a pinhole placed around the spot will reject out-of-focus rays. Because the rays in the middle are almost all from *dx*, we have a means of discriminating against the dimmer, out-of-focus points.

imen, an image of the specimen is formed in the following way. First, the fluorescent light emitted by the specimen is collected by the objective lens and returned along the same path as the original incoming light. The path of the fluorescent light is then separated from the laser light using a dichroic mirror, which reflects one color but transmits another. Because the fluorescent light has a longer wavelength than the excitation beam, the fluorescence color is shifted (for example, from blue to green). The fluorescent light passes through a pinhole placed at an image plane in front of a photomultiplier tube, which acts as a detector. The signal from the photomultiplier tube is then digitized and displayed by a computer. To see the enhanced resolution that results from confocal microscopy, look back to Figure A-15, which shows images of the same cell visualized by conventional fluorescence microscopy and by laser scanning confocal microscopy.

As an alternative to laser scanning confocal microscopy, a *spinning disc confocal microscope* uses rapidly spinning discs containing a series of small lenses and a corresponding series of pinholes. Although it cannot produce optical sections as thin as those produced by laser scanning microscopes, it can generate confocal images that can be acquired rapidly using sensitive digital cameras. Such speed is useful for visualizing very rapid events within living cells.

In confocal microscopy, a pinhole is used to exclude out-of-focus light. The result is a sharp image, but molecules above and below the focal plane of the objective lens are still being excited by the incoming light. This can result in rapid bleaching of the fluorescent molecules. In some cases, especially when viewing living cells that contain fluorescent molecules, such bleaching releases toxic radicals that can cause the cells to die. To reduce such "photodamage," it would be desirable if only the fluorescent molecules very close to the focal plane being examined were excited. This is possible using **multiphoton excitation microscopy,** in which a laser that rapidly emits pulses of high-amplitude light is used to irradiate the specimen. When two (or in some cases, three or more) photons arrive at the specimen almost simultaneously,

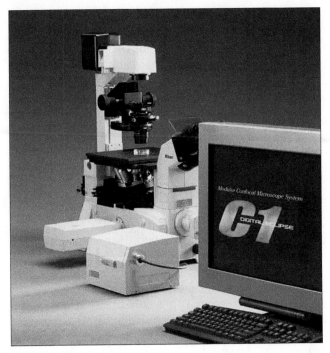

(a)

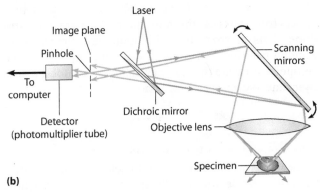

(b)

FIGURE A-17 A Laser Scanning Confocal Microscope.
(a) A photograph and (b) a schematic of a laser scanning confocal microscope (LSCM). A laser is used to illuminate one spot at a time in the specimen (blue lines). Scanning mirrors move the spot in a given plane of focus through a precise pattern. The fluorescent light being emitted from the specimen (green lines) bounces off the same scanning mirrors and returns along the original path of the illumination beam. The emitted light does not return to the laser, but instead is transmitted through the dichroic mirror (which in this example reflects blue light but transmits green light). A pinhole in the image plane blocks the extraneous rays that are out of focus. The light is detected by a photomultiplier tube, whose signal is digitized and stored by a computer.

the physics of light indicates that these photons can combine to effectively approximate a photon of shorter wavelength. When this approximate wavelength is near the absorption wavelength for a fluorescent molecule, the fluorescent molecule absorbs the light and fluoresces (Figure A-18). The likelihood of this happening is very low, except near the focal plane of the objective lens. As a result, only the fluorescent molecules that are in focus fluoresce. The result is very similar in sharpness to confocal

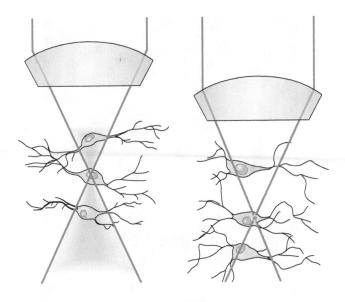

(a) Confocal microscopy **(b)** Multiphoton microscopy

FIGURE A-18 Multiphoton Excitation Microscopy. (a) In a standard LSCM, the laser results in fluorescence in an hourglass-shaped path throughout the specimen. Because a large area fluoresces, photodamage is much more likely to occur than in multiphoton excitation microscopy. (b) In a multiphoton excitation microscope, fluorescence is limited to a spot at the focus of the pulsed infrared laser beam, resulting in much less damage. The infrared illumination also penetrates more deeply into the specimen than visible light does.

microscopy, but no pinhole is needed since there is no out-of-focus light that needs to be excluded. Photodamage is also dramatically reduced. As an example, multiphoton excitation microscopy was used to image the living embryo shown in Figure A-14.

A third technique, **digital deconvolution microscopy,** can be used to provide very sharp images. Digital deconvolution relies on a completely different principle. In this case, normal fluorescence microscopy is used to acquire a series of images throughout the thickness of a specimen. Then a computer is used to digitally process, or *deconvolve,* each focal plane to mathematically remove the contribution due to the out-of-focus light. In many cases, digital deconvolution can produce images comparable to those obtained by confocal microscopy (Figure A-19). One advantage of deconvolution is that the microscope is not restricted to the specific wavelengths of light used in the lasers commonly found in confocal microscopes.

Digital Microscopy Can Record Enhanced Time-Lapse Images

The advent of solid-state light detectors has, in many circumstances, made it possible to replace photographic film with an electronic equivalent—that is, with a video camera or digital imaging camera. These developments have given rise to the technique of **digital microscopy,** in which microscopic images are recorded and stored electronically by placing a video or digital camera in the image plane produced by the ocular lens. The resulting digital

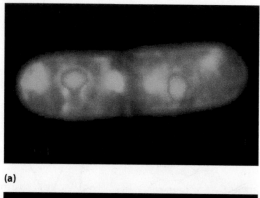

(a)

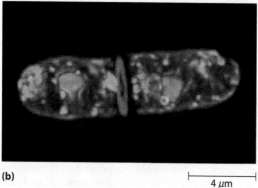

(b)

$\vdash\!\!-\!\!\dashv$
4 μm

FIGURE A-19 Digital Deconvolution Microscopy. A fission yeast cell stained with a dye specific for DNA (red) and a membrane-specific dye (green). The image in **(a)** is an unprocessed optical section through the center of the cell, while the image in **(b)** is a projection of all the sections following three-dimensional image processing. The ring of the developing medial septum (red) is forming between the two nuclei (red) that arose by nuclear division during the previous mitosis.

that can be seen with a conventional light microscope. Digital techniques can be applied to conventional brightfield light microscopy, as well as to DIC and fluorescence microscopy, thereby creating a powerful set of approaches for improving the effectiveness of light microscopy.

An additional advantage of digital microscopy is that the specimen does not need to be killed by fixation, as is required with electron microscopy, so dynamic events can be monitored as they take place. Moreover, special, sensitive cameras have been developed that can detect extremely dim images, thereby facilitating the ability to record a rapid series of time-lapse pictures of cellular events as they proceed. This technique has allowed scientists to obtain information on the changes in concentration and subcellular distribution of such cytosolic components as second messengers during cellular signaling and to study the role of cytoskeletal structures in intracellular movements.

Digital microscopy is not only useful for examining events in one focal plane. In a variation of this technique, a computer is used to control a focus motor attached to a microscope. Images are then collected throughout the thickness of a specimen. When such a series of images is collected at specific time intervals, such microscopy is called *four-dimensional microscopy* (this phrase is borrowed from physics; the four dimensions are the three dimensions of space plus the additional dimension of time). Analyzing four-dimensional data requires special computer software that can navigate between focal planes over time to display specific images.

Optical Methods Can Be Used to Measure the Movements and Properties of Proteins and Other Macromolecules

Optical microscopy can be used to help us visualize where molecules reside within cells and to study the dynamic movements and properties of biological molecules. We briefly consider these modern techniques in this section.

images can then be *enhanced* by a computer to increase contrast and remove background features that obscure the image of interest (**Figure A-20**).

The resulting enhancement allows the visualization of structures that are an order of magnitude smaller than those

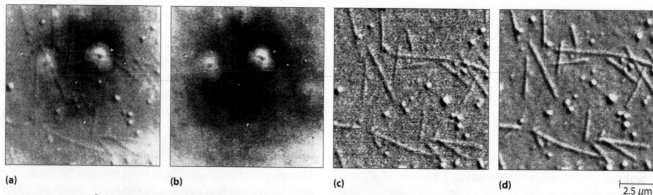

(a)   **(b)**   **(c)**   **(d)**

$\vdash\!\!-\!\!\dashv$
2.5 μm

FIGURE A-20 Computer-Enhanced Digital Microscopy. This series of micrographs shows how computers can be used to enhance images obtained with light microscopy. In this example, an image of several microtubules—too small to be seen with unenhanced light microscopy—are processed to make them visible in detail. **(a)** The image resulting from electronic contrast enhancement of the original image (which appeared to be empty). **(b)** The background of the enhanced image in (a), which is then **(c)** subtracted from image (a), leaving only the microtubules. **(d)** The final, detailed image resulting from electronic averaging of the separate images processed as shown in parts a–c.

Photobleaching, Photoactivation, and Photoconversion. When fluorescent molecules are irradiated with light at the appropriate excitation wavelength for long periods of time, they undergo **photobleaching** (i.e., the irradiation induces the molecules to cease fluorescing). If a cell is exposed to intense light in only a small region, such bleaching results in a characteristic decrease in fluorescence (**Figure A-21a**). As unbleached molecules move into the bleach zone, the fluorescence gradually returns to normal levels. Such *fluorescence recovery after photobleaching (FRAP)* is therefore one useful measure of how fast molecules diffuse or undergo directed transport (see Figure 7-11 for a classic example of the use of FRAP).

In other cases, fluorescent molecules are chemically modified so that they do not fluoresce until they are irradiated with a specific wavelength of light, usually ultraviolet light. The UV light induces the release of the chemical modifier, allowing the molecule of interest to fluoresce. Both chemically modified dyes and forms of GFP have been produced that behave in this way. Such compounds are often called *caged compounds* because they are "freed" only by this light-induced cleavage. Uncaging, or **photoactivation,** produces the converse situation to photobleaching: Local uncaging of a fluorescent molecule produces a bright spot of fluorescence that can be followed as the molecules diffuse throughout the cell (Figure A-21b). Uncaging via photoactivation can also be used to convert other kinds of inert molecules to their active state. For example, "caged calcium" is actually a calcium chelator that is bound to calcium ions. When the caged compound is irradiated, it gives up its calcium, causing a local elevation of calcium within the cell. A third technique causes a fluorescent molecule to permanently change its fluorescence properties after it is exposed to ultraviolet or other short wavelengths of light. Such *photoconversion* can, for example, cause a green fluorescent protein to become a red fluorescent protein and has uses that are similar to photoactivation. Other fluorescent molecules can be temporarily switched "off" so that they do not fluoresce and then back "on" again, a process called *"photoswitching."*

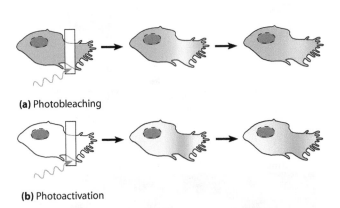

(a) Photobleaching

(b) Photoactivation

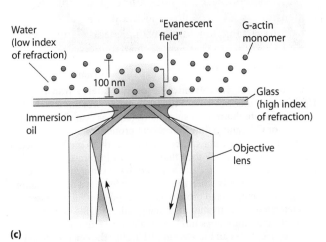

(c)

FIGURE A-21 Techniques for Studying Dynamic Movements of Molecules Within Cells. **(a)** Photobleaching of fluorescent molecules. A well-defined area of a cell is irradiated, causing bleaching of fluorescent molecules. Gradually, new, unbleached molecules invade the bleached zone. **(b)** Photoactivation of fluorescent proteins. Photoactivation of a selected region (indicated by the box) results in an increase in fluorescence. Subsequent movements of the fluorescent molecules can then be monitored. **(c)** Total internal reflection fluorescence (TIRF) microscopy. This procedure is often performed using an inverted microscope, which places the objective lens under the specimen. The example shown here involves fluorescent G-actin monomers (see Chapter 15). When a parallel beam of light in a medium of high refractive index (such as glass) strikes an interface with a medium of lower refractive index (such as a cell or water) at an angle that exceeds the critical angle, it undergoes total internal reflection. Total internal reflection results in an "evanescent field" in the medium of lower refractive index, which falls off quickly with distance. This allows only a very small number of fluorescent molecules to be seen.

Total Internal Reflection Fluorescence Microscopy. An even more spatially precise method for observing fluorescent molecules involves **total internal reflection fluorescence (TIRF) microscopy.** TIRF relies on a useful property of light: When light moves from a medium with a high refractive index (such as glass) to a medium with a lower refractive index (such as water or a cell), if the angle of incidence of the light exceeds a certain angle (called the *critical angle*), the light is reflected. You may be familiar with fiber-optic cables, which rely on the same physical principle. The curvature of the fiber causes almost all of the light that passes into the cable to be internally reflected, allowing such fibers to serve as "light pipes." Microscopists can use special lenses to exploit total internal reflection as well. When fluorescent light shines on a cell such that all of the light exceeds the critical angle, it will undergo total internal reflection. If all of the light is reflected, why is TIRF useful? It turns out that a very small layer of light, called the "evanescent field," extends into the water or cell (Figure A-21c). This layer is very thin, about 100 nm, making TIRF up to ten times better than a confocal microscope for resolving small objects very close to the surface of a coverslip. This makes TIRF extremely useful for studying the release of secretory vesicles or for observing the polymerization of actin.

Fluorescence Resonance Energy Transfer. Fluorescence microscopy is useful not only for observing the movements of proteins but also for measuring their physical interactions with one another. When two fluorescent molecules whose fluorescence properties are matched are brought very close to one another, it is possible for them to experience **fluorescence resonance energy transfer (FRET).** In FRET, illuminating a cell at the excitation wavelength of the first, or *donor,* fluorophore results in energy transfer to the second, or *acceptor,* fluorophore. This energy transfer does not itself involve a photon of light; however, once it occurs, it causes the acceptor to emit light at its characteristic wavelength. A commonly used pair of fluorescent molecules used in FRET is derived from GFP: One glows with bluish (cyan) fluorescence (so it is called *cyan fluorescent protein,* or *CFP*); the other is excited by bluish light and glows with a yellowish color (so it is called *yellow fluorescent protein,* or *YFP*). FRET can be measured between two separate proteins (*inter*molecular FRET; **Figure A-22a**), or between fluorescent side chains on the same protein (*intra*molecular FRET; Figure A-22b). FRET acts only at a very short range (100 Ångstroms or less); as a result, intermolecular FRET provides a readout regarding where within a cell the two fluorescent proteins are essentially touching one another.

Intramolecular FRET is used in several kinds of "molecular biosensors." When we considered "cameleons" (the spelling is correct; the name comes from the abbreviation for the protein calmodulin, CaM, part of which is used to make these types of sensors). These engineered proteins change shape to bring blue and yellow fluorescent protein subunits into contact only when calcium levels rise. The resulting FRET can be used to measure local calcium levels. Similar biosensors are being used to measure the local activation of small G proteins, such as Ras (Figure A-22c).

"Optical Tweezers." The final application of light microscopy we will discuss relies on well-established ways in which light interacts with small objects. When photons strike small objects, they exert "light pressure" on them. When a small object is highly curved, such as a small plastic bead, the differential forces exerted by a tightly focused laser beam channeled through a microscope tend to cause the bead to remain in the center of the beam, trapping it via light pressure. Such **optical tweezers** can be used to move objects, or they can be used to exert exceedingly small forces on beads that are attached to proteins or other molecules. By measuring the forces exerted on beads coupled to myosin, for example, scientists have been able to measure the forces produced by the power stroke of a single myosin protein (**Figure A-23**).

Superresolution Microscopy Has Broken the Diffraction Limit

The wavelength of visible light seems to place a limit on what can be resolved in the light microscope. We described this limit, due to diffraction, using the Abbé

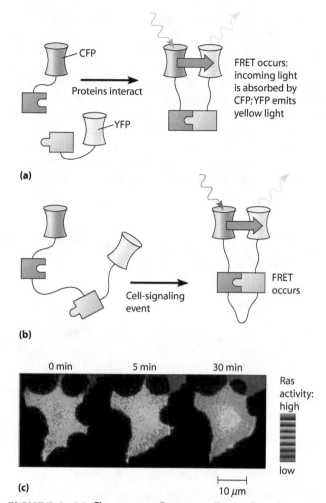

(a)

(b)

(c)

FIGURE A-22 Fluorescence Resonance Energy Transfer (FRET). **(a)** Intermolecular FRET. When two proteins attached to two different fluorescent side chains (such as cyan fluorescent protein, or CFP, and yellow fluorescent protein, or YFP) are in close proximity, the CFP can transfer energy directly to the YFP when the CFP is excited. The YFP then fluoresces. **(b)** Intramolecular FRET. In this case, CFP and YFP are attached to the same molecule, but they can interact only when the protein undergoes a conformational change. Such engineered proteins can be used as cellular "biosensors." **(c)** Detecting Ras activation in a living cell. A COS-1 cell expressing a protein that undergoes intramolecular FRET in regions where Ras is active shows an increase in FRET after the cell is exposed to epidermal growth factor (EGF), which activates Ras.

equation. Recent ingenious techniques, collectively called **superresolution microscopy,** have broken this "diffraction barrier." One of these techniques is called *stimulated emission depletion (STED) microscopy.* Like confocal microscopy, STED uses very short pulses of laser light to cause molecules in a specimen to fluoresce. The first pulse is immediately followed by a ring-shaped "depletion" pulse, which causes stimulated emission, moving electrons from the excited state (which causes fluorescence to occur) to a lower energy state before they can fluoresce. The interaction of the two pulses effectively results in a smaller spot size than could be achieved with a conventional microscope (**Figure A-24a**). Two other

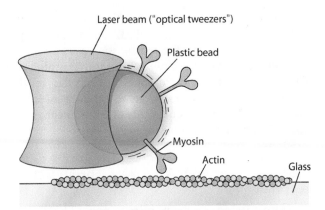

FIGURE A-23 "Optical Tweezers." A small plastic bead can be held in place by a laser beam focused through the objective lens of a microscope. When the bead is attached to a molecule such as myosin, the force produced by the myosin as it pulls on an actin filament attached to a microscope slide can be precisely measured.

techniques take a different approach. These techniques, called *photoactivated localization microscopy (PALM)* and *stochastic optical reconstruction microscopy (STORM)*, use photoactivatable or photoswitchable probes, respectively. A specimen containing these probes is scanned many times but in a way that the fluorescence of individual molecules against a dark background can be pinpointed with improved precision using computers. These calculations are then combined to generate an image (**Figure A-24b**). As technology continues to improve, STED, PALM, STORM, and other superresolution techniques will continue to push the limits of resolution of the light microscope.

Sample Preparation Techniques for Light Microscopy

One attractive feature of using light microscopy is how easily most specimens can be prepared for examination. In some cases, preparing a sample involves nothing more than mounting a small piece of the specimen in a suitable liquid on a glass slide and covering it with a glass coverslip. The slide is then positioned on the specimen stage of the microscope and examined through the ocular lens, or with a camera. However, to take maximum advantage of the resolving power of the light microscope, samples are usually prepared in a way designed to enhance *contrast*— that is, differences in the darkness or color of the structures being examined. A common means for enhancing contrast is to apply specific dyes that color or otherwise alter the light-transmitting properties of cell constituents.

Specimen Preparation Often Involves Fixation, Sectioning, and Staining

To prepare cells for staining, tissues are often first treated with **fixatives** that kill the cells while preserving their structural appearance. The most widely employed fixatives are acids and aldehydes such as acetic acid, picric acid, formaldehyde, and glutaraldehyde. One way of fixing

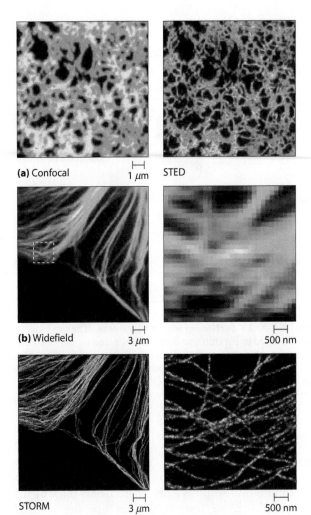

(a) Confocal   1 μm   STED

(b) Widefield   3 μm   500 nm

STORM   3 μm   500 nm

FIGURE A-24 Superresolution Microscopy Breaks the Diffraction Barrier. (a) A yellow fluorescent protein fused to a sequence that targets it to the endoplasmic reticulum was used to image the same specimen using confocal microscopy (left) and STED (right). **(b)** Comparison of immunostaining of microtubules using widefield (i.e., standard, non-confocal) fluorescence microscopy (top) and STORM (bottom). The right-hand panels zoom in on the boxed region. The zoomed confocal image, but not the STORM image, is blurry, because STORM imaging can identify fluorescent molecules with much higher spatial resolution.

tissues is simply to immerse them in the fixative solution. An alternative approach for animal tissues is to inject the fixative into the bloodstream of the animal before removing the organs—a technique known as *perfusion*.

In most cases, the next step is to slice the specimen into sections that are thin enough to transmit light. To prepare such *thin sections,* the specimen is embedded in a medium (such as plastic or paraffin wax) that can hold it rigidly in position while sections are cut. Since paraffin is insoluble in water, any water in the specimen must first be removed (by dehydration in alcohol, usually) and replaced by an organic solvent, such as xylene, in which paraffin is soluble. The processed tissue is then placed in warm, liquefied paraffin and allowed to harden. Dehydration is less critical if the specimen is embedded in a water-soluble medium instead of paraffin. Specimens may also be

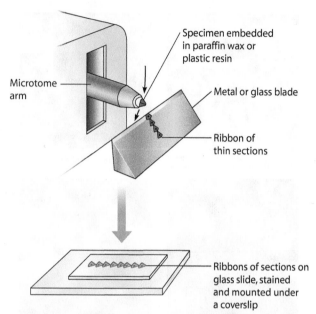

Microtome arm

Specimen embedded in paraffin wax or plastic resin

Metal or glass blade

Ribbon of thin sections

Ribbons of sections on glass slide, stained and mounted under a coverslip

FIGURE A-25 Sectioning with a Microtome. The fixed specimen is embedded in paraffin wax or plastic resin and mounted on the arm of the microtome. As the arm moves up and down through a circular arc, the blade cuts successive sections. The sections adhere to each other, forming a ribbon of thin sections that can be mounted on a glass slide, stained, and protected with a coverslip.

embedded in epoxy plastic resin, or, as an alternative way of providing support, the tissue can simply be quick-frozen.

After embedding or quick-freezing, the specimen is sliced into thin sections a few micrometers thick by using a **microtome,** an instrument that operates somewhat like a meat slicer (**Figure A-25**). The specimen is simply mounted on the arm of the microtome, which advances the specimen by small increments toward a metal or glass blade that slices the tissue into thin sections. The sections are then mounted on a glass slide and subjected to **staining** with any of various dyes or antibodies that have been adapted for this purpose. Often a series of treatments are applied, each with an affinity for a different kind of cellular component. Once stained, the specimen is covered with a glass coverslip for protection.

A historically important approach for localizing specific components within cells is *microscopic autoradiography,* a technique that uses photographic emulsion to determine where a specific radioactive compound is located within a cell at the time the cell is fixed and sectioned for microscopy. When the emulsion is later developed and the specimen is examined under the microscope, *silver grains* appear directly above the specimen wherever radiation had bombarded the emulsion.

The Electron Microscope

The impact of electron microscopy on our understanding of cells can only be described as revolutionary. Yet, like light microscopy, electron microscopy has both strengths and weaknesses. In electron microscopy, resolution is much better; but specimen preparation and instrument operation are often more difficult. Electron microscopes are of two basic designs: the *transmission electron microscope* and the *scanning electron microscope*. Scanning and transmission electron microscopes are similar in that each employs a beam of electrons to produce an image. However, the instruments use quite different mechanisms to form the final image, as we see next.

Transmission Electron Microscopy Forms an Image from Electrons That Pass Through the Specimen

The **transmission electron microscope (TEM)** is so named because it forms an image from electrons that are *transmitted* through the specimen being examined. As shown in **Figure A-26**, most of the parts of the TEM are similar in name and function to their counterparts in the light microscope, although their physical orientation is reversed. We will look briefly at each of the major features.

The Vacuum System and Electron Gun. Because electrons cannot travel very far in air, a strong vacuum must be maintained along the entire path of the electron beam. Two types of vacuum pumps work together to create this vacuum. On some TEMs, a device called a *cold trap* is incorporated into the vacuum system to help establish a high vacuum. The cold trap is a metal insert in the column of the microscope that is cooled by liquid nitrogen. The cold trap attracts gases and random contaminating molecules, which then solidify on the cold metal surface.

The electron beam in a TEM is generated by an **electron gun,** an assembly of several components. The *cathode,* a tungsten filament similar to a light bulb filament, emits electrons from its surface when it is heated. The cathode tip is near a circular opening in a metal cylinder. A negative voltage on the cylinder helps control electron emission and shape the beam. At the other end of the cylinder is the *anode.* The anode is kept at 0 V, while the cathode is usually maintained at 50–100 kV. This difference in voltage causes the electrons to accelerate as they pass through the cylinder and hence is called the **accelerating voltage.**

Electromagnetic Lenses and Image Formation. The formation of an image using electron microscopy depends on both the wavelike and the particle-like properties of electrons. Because electrons are negatively charged particles, their movement can be altered by magnetic forces. This means that the trajectory of an electron beam can be controlled using electromagnets, just as a glass lens can bend rays of light that pass through it.

As the electron beam leaves the electron gun, it enters a series of electromagnetic lenses (Figure A-26b). Each lens is simply a space influenced by an electromagnetic field. The focal length of each lens can be increased or decreased by varying the amount of electric current

(a)

Cathode (tungsten filament)

Electron gun (inside cylinder, not shown)

Anode

First condenser lens

Second condenser lens

Condenser lens system

Specimen

Specimen stage

Objective lens

Intermediate lens

Projector lens

Detector

(b)

FIGURE A-26 **A Transmission Electron Microscope.** (a) A photograph and (b) a schematic diagram of a TEM.

applied to its energizing coils. Thus, when several lenses are arranged together, they can control illumination, focus, and magnification.

The **condenser lens** is the first lens to affect the electron beam. It functions in the same fashion as its counterpart in the light microscope to focus the beam on the specimen. Most electron microscopes actually use a condenser lens system with two lenses to achieve better focus of the electron beam. The next component, the **objective lens,** is the most important part of the electron microscope's sophisticated lens system. The specimen is positioned on the specimen stage within the objective lens. The objective lens, in concert with the **intermediate lens** and the **projector lens,** produces a final image on a *viewing screen* that fluoresces when struck by electrons or that is produced directly by a detector.

How is an image formed from the action of these electromagnetic lenses on an electron beam? When the beam strikes the specimen, some electrons are scattered by the sample, whereas others continue in their paths relatively unimpeded. This scattering of electrons is the result of properties created in the specimen by preparation procedures we will describe shortly. Specimen preparation, in other words, imparts selective *electron density* to the specimen. That is, some areas become more opaque to electrons than others do. Electron-dense areas of the specimen will appear dark because few electrons pass through, whereas other areas will appear lighter because they permit the passage of more electrons.

The contrasting light, dark, and intermediate areas of the specimen create the final image. The image is formed by differing extents of electron transmission through the specimen, thus the name *transmission electron microscope.*

The Image Capture System. Since electrons are not visible to the human eye, the final image is detected in the transmission electron microscope by allowing the transmitted electrons to strike a fluorescent screen or photographic film. The use of film allows one to create a photographic print called an **electron micrograph,** which then becomes a permanent photographic record of the specimen (**Figure A-27a**). In many modern microscopes, a digital camera records the screen or a digital detector directly detects incoming electrons.

Voltage. An electron beam is too weak to penetrate very far into biological samples, so specimens examined by conventional transmission electron microscopy must be extremely thin (usually no more than 100 nm). Otherwise, the electrons will not be able to pass through the specimen, and the image will be entirely opaque. Examination of thicker sections requires a special **high-voltage electron microscope (HVEM),** which is similar to a transmission electron microscope but utilizes an accelerating voltage that is much higher—about 200–1000 kV compared with the 50–100 kV of a TEM. Because the penetrating power of the resulting electron beam is roughly ten times as great as that of conventional electron microscopes, relatively

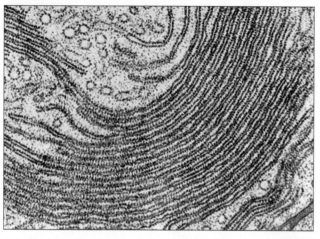

(a) Transmission electron micrograph

0.5 μm

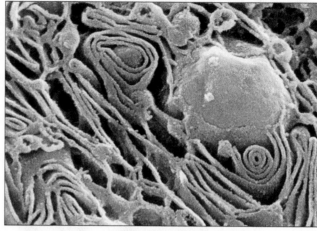

(b) Scanning electron micrograph

1 μm

FIGURE A-27 Comparison of Transmission and Scanning Electron Micrographs. (a) The transmission electron micrograph shows membranes of rough endoplasmic reticulum in the cytoplasm of a rat pancreas cell. The "rough" appearance of the membranes in this specimen is caused by the presence of numerous membrane-bound ribosomes. (b) A similar specimen viewed by scanning electron microscopy reveals the three-dimensional appearance of the rough endoplasmic reticulum, although individual ribosomes cannot be resolved.

thick specimens can be examined with good resolution. As a result, cellular structure can be studied in sections as thick as 1 μm, or about ten times the thickness possible with an ordinary TEM.

Scanning Electron Microscopy Reveals the Surface Architecture of Cells and Organelles

Scanning electron microscopy is a fundamentally different type of electron microscopy that produces images from electrons deflected from a specimen's outer surface (rather than electrons transmitted through the specimen). It is an especially spectacular technique because of the sense of depth it gives to biological structures, thereby allowing surface topography to be studied (Figure A-27b). As the name implies, a **scanning electron microscope (SEM)** generates such an image by scanning the specimen's surface with a beam of electrons.

An SEM and its optical system are shown in **Figure A-28**. The vacuum system and electron source are similar to those found in the TEM, although the accelerating voltage is lower (about 5–30 kV). The main difference between the two kinds of instruments lies in the way the image is formed. In an SEM, the electromagnetic lens system focuses the beam of electrons into an intense spot that is moved back and forth over the specimen's surface by charged plates called *beam deflectors,* which are located between the condenser lens and the specimen. The beam deflectors attract or repel the beam according to the signals sent to them by the deflector circuitry (Figure A-28b).

As the electron beams sweep rapidly over the specimen, molecules in the specimen are excited to high energy levels and emit *secondary electrons.* These emitted electrons are captured by a detector located immediately above and to one side of the specimen, thereby generating an image of the specimen's surface. The essential component of the detector is a *scintillator,* which emits photons of light when excited by electrons that impinge upon it. The photons are used to generate an electronic signal to a video screen. The image then develops point by point, line by line on the screen as the primary electron beam sweeps over the specimen.

Sample Preparation Techniques for Electron Microscopy

Specimens to be examined by electron microscopy can be prepared in several different ways, depending on the type of microscope and the kind of information the microscopist wants to obtain. In each case, however, the method is complicated, time-consuming, and costly compared with methods used for light microscopy. Moreover, living cells cannot be examined because the electron microscope requires specimens to be subjected to a vacuum.

Ultrathin Sectioning and Staining Are Common Preparation Techniques for Transmission Electron Microscopy

The most common way of preparing specimens for transmission electron microscopy involves slicing tissues and cells into ultrathin sections no more than 50–100 nm in thickness (less than one-tenth the thickness of the typical sections used for light microscopy). Specimens must first be chemically fixed and stabilized. The fixation step kills the cells but keeps the cellular components much as they were in the living cell. The fixatives employed are usually buffered solutions of aldehydes, most commonly glutaraldehyde. Following fixation, the specimen is often stained with a 1–2% solution of buffered osmium tetroxide (OsO_4), which binds to various components of the cell, making them more electron dense.

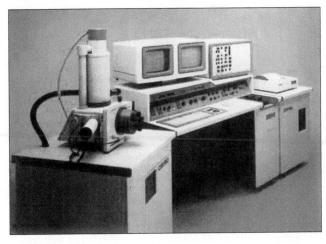

(a)

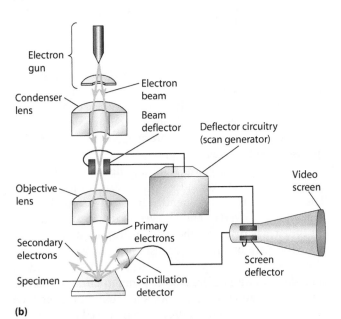

(b)

FIGURE A-28 A Scanning Electron Microscope. (a) A photograph and (b) a schematic diagram of an SEM. The image is generated by secondary electrons (short orange lines) emitted by the specimen as a focused beam of primary electrons (long orange lines) sweeps rapidly over it. The signal to the video screen is synchronized to the movement of the primary electron beam over the specimen by the deflector circuitry of the scan generator.

Chemical fixatives are very good at stabilizing many structures within cells, but they suffer from two drawbacks. First, they are slow; it takes a minimum amount of time for the fixative to diffuse into the sample to fix its structures. Second, chemical fixatives often extract cellular components (i.e., fine structures within the cell are often lost during fixation). **Cryofixation,** which typically involves extremely rapid freezing (within 20 msec) of a specimen under very high pressure, avoids these problems. Such *high-pressure freezing* is necessary; without it, water ice crystals form within the specimen, causing extensive damage to its fine structures. In most applications, high-pressure freezing is followed by *freeze substitution.* During freeze substitution, the water in the

sample is slowly replaced by an organic solvent, such as acetone, over a period of days. The resulting specimen can be processed for embedding and sectioning in the same way as chemically fixed specimens are processed.

The tissue is next passed through a series of alcohol solutions to dehydrate it, and then it is placed in a solvent such as acetone or propylene oxide to prepare it for embedding in liquefied plastic epoxy resin. After the plastic has infiltrated the specimen, it is put into a mold and heated in an oven to harden the plastic. The embedded specimen is then sliced into ultrathin sections by an instrument called an **ultramicrotome** (**Figure A-29a**). The specimen is mounted firmly on the arm of the ultramicrotome, which

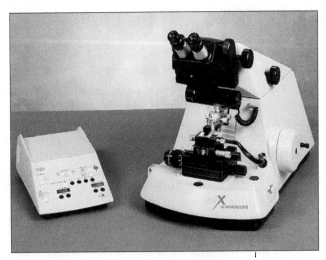

(a) Ultramicrotome

(b) Microtome arm of ultramicrotome

FIGURE A-29 An Ultramicrotome. (a) A photograph of an ultramicrotome. (b) A close-up view of the ultramicrotome arm, showing the specimen in a plastic block mounted on the end of the arm. As the ultramicrotome arm moves up and down, the block is advanced in small increments, and ultrathin sections are cut from the block face by the diamond knife.

advances the specimen in small increments toward a glass or diamond knife (Figure A-29). When the block reaches the knife blade, ultrathin sections are cut from the block face. The sections float from the blade onto a water surface, where they can be picked up on a circular copper specimen grid. The grid consists of a meshwork of very thin copper strips, which support the specimen while still allowing openings between adjacent strips through which the specimen can be observed.

Once in place on the grid, the sections are usually stained again, this time with solutions containing lead and uranium. This step enhances the contrast of the specimen because the lead and uranium give still greater electron density to specific parts of the cell. After poststaining, the specimen is ready for viewing or photography with the TEM.

Radioisotopes and Antibodies Can Localize Molecules in Electron Micrographs

In our discussion of light microscopy, we described how microscopic autoradiography can be used to locate radioactive molecules inside cells. Autoradiography can also be applied to transmission electron microscopy, with only minor differences. For the TEM, the specimen containing the radioactively labeled compounds is simply examined in ultrathin sections on copper specimen grids instead of in thin sections on glass slides.

We also described how fluorescently labeled antibodies can be used in conjunction with light microscopy to locate specific cellular components. Antibodies are likewise used in the electron microscopic technique called **immunoelectron microscopy (immunoEM)**; fluorescence cannot be seen in the electron microscope, so antibodies are instead visualized by linking them to substances that are electron dense and therefore visible as opaque dots. One of the most common approaches is to couple antibody molecules to colloidal gold particles. When ultrathin tissue sections are stained with gold-labeled antibodies directed against various proteins, electron microscopy can reveal the subcellular location of these proteins with great precision (**Figure A-30**).

A powerful approach that unites light microscopy and immunoEM is **correlative microscopy.** In correlative microscopy, dynamic images of a cell are acquired using the light microscope, often using antibodies and/or GFP. The very same cell is then processed and viewed using electron microscopy (EM). Commonly, immunoEM is used to determine where a protein is found at very high resolution. Correlative microscopy thus bridges the gap between dynamic imaging using the light microscope and the detailed images that can be acquired only via EM.

Negative Staining Can Highlight Small Objects in Relief Against a Stained Background

Although cutting tissues into ultrathin sections is the most common way of preparing specimens for transmission electron microscopy, other techniques are suitable for particular purposes. For example, the shape and surface

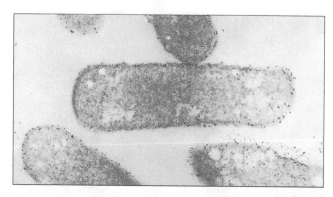

0.25 μm

FIGURE A-30 The Use of Gold-Labeled Antibodies in Electron Microscopy. Cells of the bacterium *E. coli* were stained with gold-labeled antibodies directed against a plasma membrane protein. The small, dark granules distributed around the periphery of the cell are the gold-labeled antibody molecules.

appearance of very small objects, such as viruses or isolated organelles, can be examined without cutting the specimen into sections. In the **negative staining** technique, which is one of the simplest techniques in transmission electron microscopy, intact specimens are simply visualized in relief against a darkly stained background.

To carry out negative staining, the copper specimen grid must first be overlaid with an ultrathin plastic film. The specimen is then suspended in a small drop of liquid, applied to the overlay, and allowed to dry in air. After the specimen has dried on the grid, a drop of stain such as uranyl acetate or phosphotungstic acid is applied to the film surface. The edges of the grid are then blotted in several places with a piece of filter paper to absorb the excess stain. This draws the stain down and around the specimen and its ultrastructural features. When viewed in the TEM, the specimen is seen in *negative contrast* because the background is dark and heavily stained, whereas the specimen itself is lightly stained (**Figure A-31**).

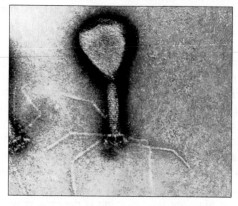

25 nm

FIGURE A-31 Negative Staining. An electron micrograph of a bacteriophage as seen in a negatively stained preparation. This specimen was simply suspended in an electron-dense stain, allowing it to be visualized in relief against a darkly stained background (TEM).

FIGURE A-32 Shadowing. An electron micrograph of tobacco mosaic virus particles visualized by shadowing. In this technique, heavy metal vapor was sprayed at an angle across the specimen, causing an accumulation of metal on one side of each virus particle and a shadow region lacking metal on the other side (TEM).

0.1 μm

Shadowing Techniques Use Metal Vapor Sprayed Across a Specimen's Surface

Isolated particles or macromolecules can also be visualized by the technique of **shadowing** (Figure A-32), which involves spraying a thin layer of an electron-dense metal such as gold or platinum at an angle across the surface of a biological specimen. **Figure A-33a** illustrates the shadowing technique. The specimen is first spread on a clean mica surface and dried (step ❶). It is then placed in a **vacuum evaporator,** a bell jar in which a vacuum is created by a system similar to that of an electron microscope (Figure A-33b). Also within the evaporator are two electrodes, one consisting of a carbon rod located directly over the specimen and the other consisting of a metal wire positioned at an angle of approximately 10–45° relative to the specimen.

After a vacuum is created in the evaporator, current is applied to the metal electrode, causing the metal to evaporate from the electrode and spray over the surface of the specimen (Figure A-33a, ❷). Because the metal-emitting electrode is positioned at an angle to the specimen, metal is deposited on only one side of the specimen, generating

FIGURE A-33 The Technique of Shadowing. (a) The specimen is spread on a mica surface and shadowed by coating it with atoms of a heavy metal (platinum or gold, shown in orange). This generates a metal replica (orange) whose thickness reflects the surface contours of the specimen. The replica is coated with carbon atoms to strengthen it, and it is then floated away and washed before viewing in the TEM. **(b)** The vacuum evaporator in which shadowing is done. The carbon electrode is located directly over the specimen; the heavy metal electrode is off to the side.

❶ The specimen is spread on a mica surface and dried.

Specimen

Mica surface

❷ The specimen is shadowed by coating it with atoms of a heavy metal that are evaporated from a heated filament.

Metal wire

Heated filament

Metal atoms

Metal replica

❸ The specimen is coated with carbon atoms evaporated from an overhead electrode.

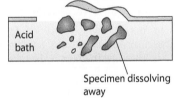

Carbon atoms

Metal replica

❹ The replica is floated onto the surface of an acid bath to dissolve away the specimen, leaving a clean metal replica.

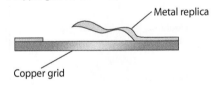

Acid bath

Specimen dissolving away

❺ The replica is washed and picked up on a copper grid for examination in the TEM.

Metal replica

Copper grid

(a) Shadowing technique

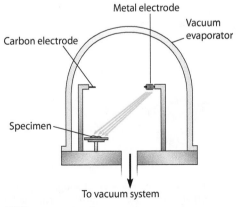

Metal electrode

Vacuum evaporator

Carbon electrode

Specimen

To vacuum system

(b) Vacuum evaporator

a metal *replica* of the surface. The opposite side of the specimen remains unstained; it is this unstained region that creates the "shadow" effect.

An overhead carbon-emitting electrode is then used to coat the specimen with evaporated carbon, thereby providing stability and support to the metal replicas (❸). Next, the mica support containing the specimen is removed from the vacuum evaporator and lowered gently onto a water surface, causing the replica to float away from the mica surface. The replica is transferred into an acid bath, which dissolves any remaining bits of specimen, leaving a clean metal replica of the specimen (❹). The replica is then transferred to a standard copper specimen grid (❺) for viewing by transmission electron microscopy.

A related procedure is commonly used for visualizing purified molecules such as DNA and RNA. In this technique, a solution of DNA and/or RNA is spread on an air-water interface, creating a molecular monolayer that is collected on a thin film and visualized by uniformly depositing heavy metal on all sides.

Freeze Fracturing and Freeze Etching Are Useful for Examining the Interior of Membranes

Freeze fracturing is an approach to sample preparation that is fundamentally different from the methods described so far. Instead of cutting uniform slices through a tissue sample (or staining unsectioned material), specimens are rapidly frozen at the temperature of liquid nitrogen or liquid helium, placed in a vacuum, and struck with a sharp knife edge. Samples frozen at such low temperatures are too hard to be cut. Instead, they fracture along lines of natural weakness—the hydrophobic interior of membranes, in most cases. Platinum/carbon shadowing is then used to create a replica of the fractured surface.

Freeze fracturing is illustrated in **Figure A-34**. It takes place in a modified vacuum evaporator with an internal microtome knife for fracturing the frozen specimen. The temperature of the specimen support and the microtome arm and knife is precisely controlled. Specimens are generally fixed prior to freeze fracturing, although some living tissues can be frozen fast enough to keep them in almost lifelike condition. Because cells contain large amounts of water, fixed specimens are usually treated with an antifreeze such as glycerol to provide *cryoprotection*—that is, to reduce the formation of ice crystals during freezing.

The cryoprotected specimen is mounted on a metal specimen support (Figure A-34, step ❶) and immersed rapidly in freon cooled with liquid nitrogen (❷). This procedure also reduces the formation of ice crystals in the cells. With the frozen specimen positioned on the specimen table in the vacuum evaporator (❸), a high vacuum is established, the stage temperature is adjusted to around −100°C, and the frozen specimen is fractured with a blow from the microtome knife (❹). A replica of the fractured specimen is made by shadowing with platinum and carbon as described in the previous section (❺), and the replica is then ready to be viewed in the TEM (❻).

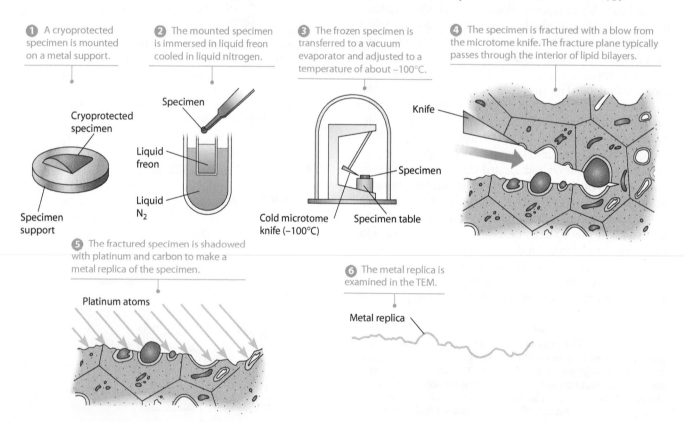

❶ A cryoprotected specimen is mounted on a metal support.

❷ The mounted specimen is immersed in liquid freon cooled in liquid nitrogen.

❸ The frozen specimen is transferred to a vacuum evaporator and adjusted to a temperature of about –100°C.

❹ The specimen is fractured with a blow from the microtome knife. The fracture plane typically passes through the interior of lipid bilayers.

Cryoprotected specimen

Specimen support

Specimen

Liquid freon

Liquid N₂

Knife

Specimen

Cold microtome knife (–100°C)

Specimen table

❺ The fractured specimen is shadowed with platinum and carbon to make a metal replica of the specimen.

Platinum atoms

❻ The metal replica is examined in the TEM.

Metal replica

FIGURE A-34 The Technique of Freeze Fracturing. The result is a replica of a specimen, fractured through its lipid bilayer, that can be viewed in the TEM. The shadowing is performed as in Figure A-33.

Freeze-fractured membranes appear as smooth surfaces studded with **intramembranous particles (IMPs).** These particles are integral membrane proteins that have remained with one lipid monolayer or the other as the fracture plane passes through the interior of the membrane.

The electron micrograph in **Figure A-35** shows the two faces of a plasma membrane revealed by freeze fracturing. The **P face** is the interior face of the inner monolayer; it is called the P face because this monolayer is on the *protoplasmic* side of the membrane. The **E face** is the interior face of the outer monolayer; it is called the E face because this monolayer is on the *exterior* side of the membrane. Notice that the P face has far more intramembranous particles than does the E face. In general, most of the particles in the membrane stay with the inner monolayer when the fracture plane passes down the middle of a membrane.

To have a P face and an E face appear side by side as in Figure A-35, the fracture plane must pass through two neighboring cells, such that one cell has its cytoplasm and the inner monolayer of its plasma membrane removed to reveal the E face, while the other cell has the outer monolayer of its plasma membrane and the associated intercellular space removed to reveal the P face. Accordingly, E faces are always separated from P faces of adjacent cells by a "step" (marked by the arrows in Figure A-35) that represents the thickness of the intercellular space.

In a closely related technique called **freeze etching,** a further step is added to the conventional freeze-fracture procedure. Following the fracture of the specimen but prior to shadowing, the microtome arm is placed directly over the specimen for a short period of time (a few seconds to several minutes). This maneuver causes a small amount of water to evaporate (sublime) from the surface of the specimen to the cold knife surface, and this sublimation produces an *etching* effect—that is, an accentuation of surface detail. By using ultrarapid freezing techniques to minimize the formation of ice crystals during freezing, and by including a volatile cryoprotectant such as aqueous methanol, which sublimes very readily to a cold surface, the etching period can be extended and a deeper layer of ice can be removed, thereby exposing structures that are located deep within the cell interior. This modification, called **deep etching,** provides a fascinating look at cellular structure. Deep etching has been especially useful in exploring the cytoskeleton and examining its connections with other structures of the cell.

Stereo Electron Microscopy and 3-D Electron Tomography Allow Specimens to Be Viewed in Three Dimensions

Electron microscopists frequently want to visualize specimens in three dimensions. Shadowing, freeze fracturing, and scanning electron microscopy are useful for this purpose, as is another specialized technique called **stereo electron microscopy.** In stereoelectron microscopy, three-dimensional information is obtained by photographing the same specimen at two slightly different angles. This is accomplished using a special specimen stage that can be tilted relative to the electron beam. The specimen is first tilted in one direction and photographed, then tilted an equal amount in the opposite direction and photographed again. The two micrographs are then mounted side by side as a *stereo pair.* When you view a stereo pair through a stereoscopic viewer, your brain uses the two independent images to construct a three-dimensional view that gives a striking sense of depth. **Figure A-36a** is a stereo pair of a *Drosophila* polytene chromosome imaged by high-voltage electron microscopy. Using a stereo viewer or allowing your eyes to fuse the two images visually creates a striking, three-dimensional view of the chromosome.

More recently, electron microscopists have used computer-based methods to make three-dimensional reconstructions of structures imaged in the TEM. In a process known as **3-D electron tomography,** serial thin sections containing a specimen are rotated and imaged at several different orientations; the resulting rotated views are then used to construct very thin, computer-generated "slices" of the specimen. Structures within these highly resolved slices can then be traced and reconstructed to provide three-dimensional information about the specimen. 3-D electron tomography has revolutionized our view of cellular structures, such as the organelles shown in

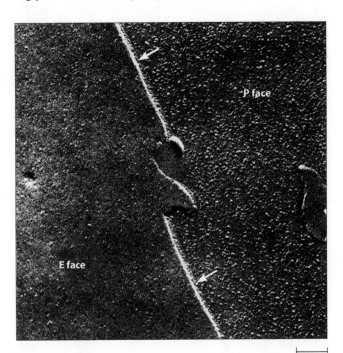

0.1 µm

FIGURE A-35 Freeze Fracturing of the Plasma Membrane. This electron micrograph shows the exposed faces of the plasma membranes of two adjacent endocrine cells from a rat pancreas as revealed by freeze fracturing. The P face is the inner surface of the lipid monolayer on the protoplasmic side of the plasma membrane. The E face is the inner surface of the lipid monolayer on the exterior side of the plasma membrane. The P face is much more richly studded with intramembranous particles than the E face. The arrows indicate the "step" along which the fracture plane passed from the interior of the plasma membrane of one cell to the interior of the plasma membrane of a neighboring cell. The step therefore represents the thickness of the intercellular space (TEM).

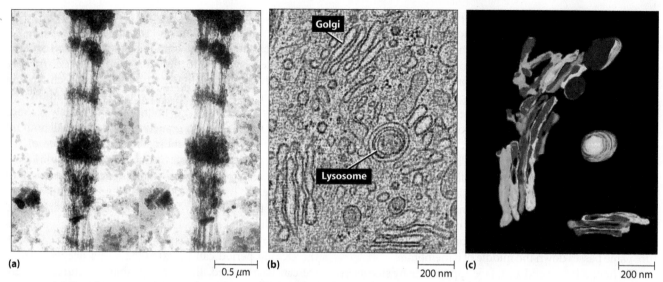

(a)   ⊢ 0.5 μm ⊣   **(b)**   ⊢ 200 nm ⊣   **(c)**   ⊢ 200 nm ⊣

FIGURE A-36 Stereo Electron Microscopy and 3-D Electron Tomography. **(a)** The polytene chromosome in this micrograph is shown as a stereo pair. The two photographs were taken by tilting the specimen stage first 5° to the right and then 5° to the left of the electron beam. For a three-dimensional view, the stereo pair can be examined with a stereoscopic viewer. Alternatively, simply let your eyes cross slightly, fusing the two micrographs into a single image (HVEM). **(b)** A thin (3.2 nm) digital slice computed from a series of tilted images of a dendritic cell (TEM). A region of the Golgi apparatus and a lysosome are clearly visible. **(c)** A contour model of some of the structures visible in the tomogram shown in part b.

Figure A-36b, c, effectively extending the type of topographical data obtained by SEM to the level of TEM.

Specimen Preparation for Scanning Electron Microscopy Involves Fixation but Not Sectioning

When preparing a specimen for scanning electron microscopy, the biologist's goal is to preserve the structural features of the cell surface and to treat the tissue in a way that minimizes damage by the electron beam. The procedure is actually similar to preparing ultrathin sections for transmission electron microscopy but without the sectioning step. The tissue is fixed in aldehyde, postfixed in osmium tetroxide, and dehydrated by processing through a series of alcohol solutions. The tissue is then placed in a fluid such as liquid carbon dioxide in a heavy metal canister called a **critical point dryer,** which is used to dry the specimen under conditions of controlled temperature and pressure. This helps keep structures on the surfaces of the tissue in almost the same condition as they were before dehydration.

The dried specimen is then attached to a metal specimen mount with a metallic paste. The mounted specimen is coated with a layer of gold or a mixture of gold and palladium, using a modified form of vacuum evaporation called **sputter coating.** Once the specimen has been mounted and coated, it is ready to be examined in the SEM.

Other Imaging Methods

Light and electron microscopy are direct imaging techniques in that they use photons or electrons to produce actual images of a specimen. However, some imaging techniques are indirect. To understand what we mean by indirect imaging, suppose you are given an object to handle with your eyes closed. You might feel 6 flat surfaces, 12 edges, and 8 corners. If you then draw what you have felt, it would turn out to be a box. This is an example of an indirect imaging procedure.

The two indirect imaging methods we describe here are *scanning probe microscopy* and *X-ray crystallography.* Both approaches have the potential for showing molecular structures at near-atomic resolution, ten times better than the best electron microscope. They do have some shortcomings that limit their usefulness with biological specimens. But when these techniques can be applied successfully, the resulting images provide unique information about molecular structure that cannot be obtained using conventional microscopic techniques.

Scanning Probe Microscopy Reveals the Surface Features of Individual Molecules

Although "scanning" is involved in both scanning electron microscopy and scanning probe microscopy, the two methods are in fact quite different. The first example of a **scanning probe microscope,** called the *scanning tunneling microscope (STM),* was developed in the early 1980s for the purpose of exploring the surface structure of specimens at the atomic level. The STM utilizes a tiny probe that does not emit an electron beam, but instead possesses a tip made of a conducting material such as platinum-iridium. The tip of the probe is extremely sharp; ideally, its point is composed of a single atom. It is under the precise control of an electronic circuit that can move it in three dimensions over a surface. The *x* and *y* dimensions scan

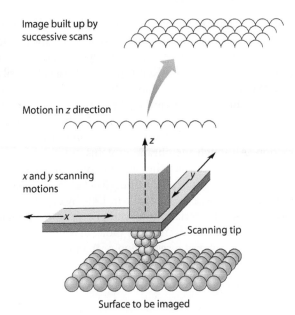

Image built up by successive scans

Motion in *z* direction

z

x and *y* scanning motions

x

y

Scanning tip

Surface to be imaged

FIGURE A-37 Scanning Tunneling Electron Microscopy.
The scanning tunneling microscope (STM) uses electronic methods to move a metallic tip across the surface of a specimen. The tip is not drawn to scale in this illustration; the point of the tip is ideally composed of only one or a few atoms, shown here as balls. An electrical voltage is produced between the tip and the specimen surface. As the tip scans the specimen in the *x* and *y* directions, electron tunneling occurs at a rate dependent on the distance between the tip and the first layer of atoms in the surface. The instrument is designed to move the tip in the *z* direction to maintain a constant current flow. The movement is therefore a function of the tunneling current and is presented on a computer screen. Successive scans then build up an image of the surface at atomic resolution.

the surface, while the *z* dimension governs the distance of the tip above the surface (**Figure A-37**).

As the tip of the STM is moved across the surface of a specimen, voltages from a few millivolts to several volts are applied. If the tip is close enough to the surface and the surface is electrically conductive, electrons will begin to leak or "tunnel" across the gap between the probe and the sample. The tunneling is highly dependent on the distance, so that even small irregularities in the size range of single atoms will affect the rate of electron tunneling. As the probe scans the sample, the tip of the probe is automatically moved up and down to maintain a constant rate of electron tunneling across the gap. A computer measures this movement and uses the information to generate a map of the sample's surface, which is viewed on a computer screen.

Despite the enormous power of the STM, it suffers from two limitations: The specimen must be an electrical conductor, and the technique provides information only about electrons associated with the specimen's surface. Researchers have therefore begun to develop other kinds of scanning probe microscopes that scan a sample just like the STM but measure different kinds of interactions between the tip and the sample surface. For example, in the *atomic force microscope (AFM),* the scanning tip is pushed right up against the surface of the sample. When it

scans, it moves up and down as it runs into the microscopic hills and valleys formed by the atoms present at the sample's surface. A variety of scanning probe microscopes have been designed to detect other properties, such as friction, magnetic force, electrostatic force, van der Waals forces, heat, and sound.

One of the most important potential applications of scanning probe microscopy is the measurement of dynamic changes in the conformation of functioning biomolecules. Recently, it has become possible to visualize the movements of single myosin proteins as they change their shape during their power stroke. Such "molecular eavesdropping" is now entirely within the realm of possibility. It is even possible to use a modified form of atomic force microscopy to directly stretch large biomolecules to measure their mechanical properties.

X-Ray Crystallography Allows the Three-Dimensional Structure of Macromolecules to Be Determined

Though **X-ray crystallography** does not involve microscopy, it is such an important method for investigating the three-dimensional structure of individual molecules that we include it here. This method reconstructs images from the diffraction patterns of X-rays passing through a crystalline or fibrous specimen, thereby revealing molecular structure at the atomic level of resolution.

A good way to understand X-ray crystallography is to draw an analogy with visible light. As discussed earlier, light has certain properties that are best described as wavelike. If waves from two sources come into phase with one another, their total amplitude is additive (*constructive interference*); if they are out of phase, their amplitude is reduced (*destructive interference*). This effect can be seen when light passes through two pinholes in a piece of opaque material and then falls onto a white surface. Interference patterns result, with dark regions where light waves are out of phase and bright regions where they are in phase (**Figure A-38**). If the wavelength of the light (λ) is known, one can measure the angle α between the original beam and the first diffraction peak and then calculate the distance *d* between the two holes with the formula

$$d = \frac{\lambda}{\sin \alpha} \qquad (A\text{-}5)$$

The same approach can be used to calculate the distance between atoms in crystals or fibers of proteins and nucleic acids. Instead of a sheet of paper with two holes in it, imagine that we have multiple layers of atoms organized in a crystal or fiber. And instead of visible light, which has much too long a wavelength to interact with atoms, we will use a narrow beam of X-rays with wavelengths in the range of interatomic distances. As the X-rays pass through the specimen, they reflect off planes of atoms, and the reflected beams come into constructive and destructive interference. The reflected beams then fall onto photographic plates

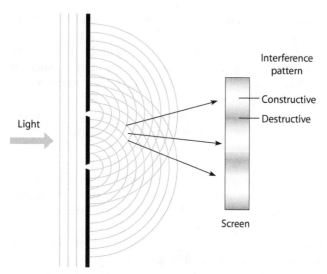

FIGURE A-38 Understanding Diffraction Patterns. Any energy in the form of waves will produce interference patterns if the waves from two or more sources are superimposed in space. One of the simplest patterns can be seen when monochromatic light passes through two neighboring pinholes and is allowed to fall on a screen. When the light passes through the two pinholes, the holes act as light sources, with waves radiating from each and falling on a white surface. Where the waves are in the same phase, a bright area appears (constructive interference). Where the waves are out of phase, they cancel each other out and produce dark areas (destructive interference).

behind the specimen, generating distinctive diffraction patterns. These patterns are then analyzed mathematically to deduce the three-dimensional structure of the original molecule. **Figure A-39** illustrates the use of this procedure to deduce the double-helical structure of DNA.

The technique of X-ray diffraction was developed in 1912 by Sir William Bragg, who used it to establish the structures of relatively simple mineral crystals. Forty years later, Max Perutz and John Kendrew found ways to apply X-ray crystallography to crystals of hemoglobin and myoglobin, providing our first view of the intricacies of protein structure. Since then, many proteins and other biological molecules have been crystallized and analyzed by X-ray diffraction. Although membrane proteins are much more difficult to crystallize than the proteins typically analyzed by X-ray crystallography, Hartmut Michel and Johann Deisenhofer overcame this obstacle in 1985 by crystallizing the proteins of a bacterial photosynthetic reaction center. They then went on to describe the molecular organization of the reaction center at a resolution of 0.3 nm, an accomplishment that earned them a Nobel Prize.

CryoEM Bridges the Gap Between X-Ray Crystallography and Electron Microscopy

X-ray crystallography has provided unprecedented views of biological molecules down to the atomic level. However, crystallography requires large amounts of purified molecules. In addition, X-ray crystallography is not currently well suited for analyzing very large macromolecular assemblies, such as the ribosome (see Figure 22-1). For such large structures, another technique is needed. A technique that helps to bridge this gap is **cryoEM.** In cryoEM, purified molecules or macromolecular assemblies are rapidly frozen via

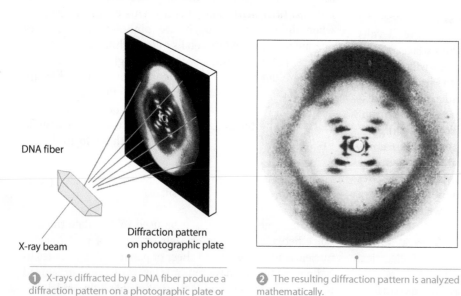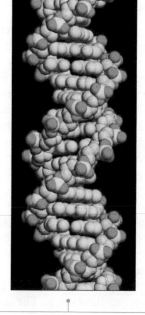

① X-rays diffracted by a DNA fiber produce a diffraction pattern on a photographic plate or other detector.

② The resulting diffraction pattern is analyzed mathematically.

③ The three-dimensional structure of the molecule is deduced.

FIGURE A-39 X-Ray Crystallography. X-ray crystallography can be used to analyze molecular structure at near-atomic resolution. The specific example illustrated in this figure is a DNA fiber. The photograph in **②** depicts the actual X-ray diffraction pattern used by James Watson and Francis Crick to deduce the molecular structure of double-stranded DNA. The photograph in **③** is a computer graphic model of the DNA double helix.

cryofixation. The rapid freezing prevents ice crystals from forming. Instead, the molecules are embedded in *vitreous ice*, noncrystalline frozen water, which better preserves the structures of the embedded molecules. The sample is then directly imaged at a very low temperature (−170°C) in an electron microscope. Often the specimens are imaged using three-dimensional electron tomography. To see how cryoEM can work together with X-ray crystallography, consider **Figure A-40**, in which a cryoEM image of the 30S and 50S ribosomal subunits and a releasing factor protein known as RF2 have been combined with a detailed structure of RF2 obtained from X-ray data. By using the two techniques together, cell biologists can see how the structure of the protein enables it to fit neatly within the overall structure of the ribosome to perform its function.

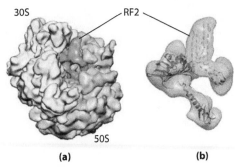

FIGURE A-40 CryoEM Bridges the Gap Between the Atomic and Molecular Levels. (a) A three-dimensional reconstruction of the 30S (yellow) and 50S (blue) ribosomal subunits bound to a releasing factor (RF2, in pink) obtained via cryoEM. X-ray crystallography provides a more detailed view of RF2 (b). Adapted by permission from Macmillan Publishers Ltd: *Nature*. From Urmila B. S. Rawat et al., "A Cryo-Electron Microscopic Study of Ribosome-Bound Termination factor RF2," (2 January 2003), 421: 87-90, Copyright 2003.

SUGGESTED READING

References of historical importance are marked with a •.

General References

Bradbury, S., B. Bracegirdle, and S. Bradbury. *Introduction to Light Microscopy*. Oxford, UK: BIOS Scientific Publishers, 1998.

Inoue, S., and K. R. Spring. *Video Microscopy: The Fundamentals*. New York: Springer, 1997.

Murphy, D. B. *Fundamentals of Light Microscopy and Electronic Imaging*. New York: Wiley-Liss, 2001.

Pawley, J. B., ed. *Handbook of Biological Confocal Microscopy*, 3rd ed. New York: Springer, 2006.

Stoffler, D., M. O. Steinmetz, and U. Aebi. Imaging biological matter across dimensions: From cells to molecules and atoms. *FASEB J.* 13 (1999, Suppl. 2): S195.

Light Microscopy

Bates, M., B. Huang, G. T. Dempsey, and X. Zhuang. Multicolor super-resolution imaging with photo-switchable fluorescent probes. *Science* 317 (2007): 1749.

Fernandez-Suarez, M., and A. Y. Ting. Fluorescent probes for super-resolution imaging in living cells. *Nature Rev. Mol. Cell Biol.* 9 (2008): 929.

• Ford, B. J. The earliest views. *Sci. Amer.* 278 (April 1998): 50.

Hein, B., K. I. Willig, and S. W. Hell. Stimulated emission depletion (STED) nanoscopy of a fluorescent protein-labeled organelle inside a living cell. *Proc. Natl. Acad. Sci. USA* 105 (2008): 14271.

Gerlich, D., and J. Ellenberg. 4D imaging to assay complex dynamics in live specimens. *Nature Cell. Biol.* (2003, Suppl.): S14.

Giepmans, B. N., S. R. Adams, M. H. Ellisman, and R. Y. Tsien. The fluorescent toolbox for assessing protein location and function. *Science* 312 (2006): 217.

Lippincott-Schwartz, J., and G. H. Patterson. Development and use of fluorescent protein markers in living cells. *Science* 300 (2003): 87.

Matsumoto, B., ed. *Cell Biological Applications of Confocal Microscopy*, 2nd ed. New York: Academic Press, 2002.

Piston, D. W. (1999). Imaging living cells and tissues by two-photon excitation microscopy. *Trends Cell Biol.* 9 (1999): 66.

Stephens, D. J., and V. J. Allan. Light microscopy techniques for live cell imaging. *Science* 300 (2003): 82.

Steyer, J. A., and W. Almers. A real-time view of life within 100 nm of the plasma membrane. *Nature Rev. Mol. Cell Biol.* 2 (2001): 268.

Walker, S. A., and P. J. Lockyer. Visualizing Ras signaling in real time. *J. Cell Sci.* 117 (2004): 2879.

Wang, Y. L. Digital deconvolution of fluorescence images for biologists. *Methods Cell Biol.* 56 (1998): 305.

Electron Microscopy

Bozzola, J. J., and L. D. Russell. *Electron Microscopy: Principles and Techniques for Biologists*, 2nd ed. Boston: Jones and Bartlett, 1998.

• Heuser, J. Quick-freeze, deep-etch preparation of samples for 3-D electron microscopy. *Trends Biochem. Sci.* 6 (1981): 64.

Hoenger, A., and J. R. McIntosh. Probing the macromolecular organization of cells by electron tomography. *Curr. Opin. Cell Biol.* 21 (2009): 89.

Koster, A. J., and J. Klumperman. Electron microscopy in cell biology: Integrating structure and function. *Nature Rev. Mol. Cell Biol.* (2003, Suppl.): SS6.

Maunsbach, A. B., and B. A. Afzelius. *Biomedical Electron Microscopy: Illustrated Methods and Interpretations*. San Diego, CA: Academic Press, 1999.

• Orci, L., and A. Perrelet. *Freeze-Etch Histology: A Comparison between Thin Sections and Freeze-Etch Replicas*. New York: Springer-Verlag, 1975.

• Satir, P. Keith R. Porter and the first electron micrograph of a cell. *Trends Cell Biol.* 7 (1997): 330.

Other Imaging Methods

Horber, J. K., and M. J. Miles. Scanning probe evolution in biology. *Science* 302 (2003): 1002.

Lucic, V., F. Forster, and W. Baumeister. Structural studies by electron tomography: From cells to molecules. *Annu. Rev. Biochem.* 74 (2005): 833.

Muller, D. J., J. Helenius, D. Alsteens, and Y. F. Dufrene. Force probing surfaces of living cells to molecular resolution. *Nat. Chem. Biol.* 5 (2009): 383.

Woolfson, M. M. *An Introduction to X-ray Crystallography*, 2nd ed. Cambridge: Cambridge University Press, 2003.

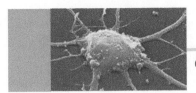

GLOSSARY

A

A: see *adenine.*

A band: region of a striated muscle myofibril that appears as a dark band when viewed by microscopy; contains thick myosin filaments and those regions of the thin actin filaments that overlap the thick filaments.

A site (aminoacyl site): site on the ribosome that binds each newly arriving tRNA with its attached amino acid.

A tubule: a complete microtubule that is fused to an incomplete microtubule (the B tubule) to make up an outer doublet in the axoneme of a eukaryotic cilium or flagellum.

ABC transporter: see *ABC-type ATPase.*

ABC-type ATPase: type of transport ATPase characterized by an "ATP-binding cassette" (hence the "ABC"), with the term *cassette* used to describe catalytic domains of the protein that bind ATP as an integral part of the transport process; also called ABC transporters. Also see *multidrug resistance transport protein.*

absolute refractory period: brief time during which the sodium channels of a nerve cell are inactivated and cannot be opened by depolarization.

absorption spectrum (plural, **spectra**): relative extent to which light of different wavelengths is absorbed by a pigment.

accelerating voltage: difference in voltage between the cathode and anode of an electron microscope, responsible for accelerating electrons prior to their emission from the electron gun.

accessory pigments: molecules such as carotenoids and phycobilins that confer enhanced light-gathering properties on photosynthetic tissue by absorbing light of wavelengths not absorbed by chlorophyll; accessory pigments give distinctive colors to plant tissue, depending on their specific absorption properties.

acetyl CoA: high-energy, two-carbon compound generated by glycolysis and fatty acid oxidation; employed for transferring carbon atoms to the tricarboxylic acid cycle.

acetylcholine: the most common excitatory neurotransmitter used at synapses between neurons outside the central nervous system.

actin: principal protein of the microfilaments found in the cytoskeleton of nonmuscle cells and in the thin filaments of skeletal muscle; synthesized as a globular monomer (G-actin) that polymerizes into long, linear filaments (F-actin).

actin-binding proteins: proteins that bind to actin microfilaments, thereby regulating the length or assembly of microfilaments or mediating their association with each other or with other cellular structures, such as the plasma membrane.

action potential: brief change in membrane potential involving an initial depolarization followed by a rapid return to the normal resting potential; caused by the inward movement of Na^+ followed by the subsequent outward movement of K^+; serves as the means of transmission of a nerve impulse.

activated monomer: a monomer whose free energy has been increased by being linked to a carrier molecule.

activation domain: region of a transcription factor, distinct from the DNA-binding domain, that is responsible for activating transcription.

activation energy (E_A): energy required to initiate a chemical reaction.

activator (transcription): regulatory protein whose binding to DNA leads to an increase in the transcription rate of specific nearby genes.

active site: region of an enzyme molecule at which the substrate binds and the catalytic event occurs; also called the catalytic site.

active transport: membrane protein-mediated movement of a substance across a membrane against a concentration or electrochemical gradient; an energy-requiring process.

active zone: region of the presynaptic membrane of an axon where neurosecretory vesicles dock.

adaptor protein (AP): protein found along with clathrin in the coats of clathrin-coated vesicles.

adenine (A): nitrogen-containing aromatic base, chemically designated as a purine, that serves as an informational monomeric unit when present in nucleic acids with other bases in a specific sequence; forms a complementary base pair with thymine (T) or uracil (U) by hydrogen bonding.

adenosine diphosphate (ADP): adenosine with two phosphates linked to each other by a phosphoanhydride bond and to the 5′ carbon of the ribose by a phosphoester bond.

adenosine monophosphate (AMP): adenosine with a phosphate linked to the 5′ carbon of ribose by a phosphoester bond.

adenosine triphosphate (ATP): adenosine with three phosphates linked to each other by phosphoanhydride bonds and to the 5′ carbon of the ribose by a phosphoester bond; principal energy storage compound of most cells, with energy stored in the high-energy phosphoanhydride bonds.

adenylyl cyclase: enzyme that catalyzes the formation of cyclic AMP from ATP; located on the inner surface of the plasma membrane of many eukaryotic cells and activated by specific ligand-receptor interactions on the outer surface of the membrane.

adherens junction: junction for cell-cell adhesion that is connected to the cytoskeleton by actin microfilaments.

adhesive (anchoring) junction: type of cell junction that links the cytoskeleton of one cell either to the cytoskeleton of neighboring cells or to the extracellular matrix; examples include desmosomes, hemidesmosomes, and adherens junctions.

ADP: see *adenosine diphosphate.*

ADP ribosylation factor (ARF): a protein associated with COPI in the "fuzzy" coats of COPI-coated vesicles.

adrenergic hormone: epinephrine or norepinephrine.

adrenergic receptor: any of a family of G protein-linked receptors that bind to one or both of the adrenergic hormones, epinephrine and norepinephrine.

adrenergic synapse: a synapse that uses norepinephrine or epinephrine as the neurotransmitter.

aerobic respiration: exergonic process by which cells oxidize glucose to carbon dioxide and water using oxygen as the ultimate electron acceptor, with a significant portion of the released energy conserved as ATP.

agonist: substance that binds to a receptor and activates it.

Akt: protein kinase involved in the PI3K-Akt pathway; catalyzes the phosphorylation of several target proteins that suppress apoptosis and inhibit cell cycle arrest.

alcoholic fermentation: anaerobic catabolism of carbohydrates with ethanol and carbon dioxide as the end products.

allele: one of two or more alternative forms of a gene.

allosteric activator: a small molecule whose binding to an enzyme's allosteric site shifts the equilibrium to favor the high-affinity state of the enzyme.

allosteric effector: small molecule that causes a change in the state of an allosteric protein by binding to a site other than the active site.

allosteric enzyme: an enzyme exhibiting two alternative forms, each with a different biological property; interconversion of the two states is mediated by the reversible binding of a specific small molecule (allosteric effector) to a regulatory site called the allosteric site.

allosteric inhibitor: a small molecule whose binding to an enzyme's allosteric site shifts the equilibrium to favor the low-affinity state of the enzyme.

allosteric regulation: control of a reaction pathway by the effector-mediated reversible interconversion of the two forms of an allosteric enzyme.

allosteric (regulatory) site: region of a protein molecule that is distinct from the active site at which the catalytic event occurs and that binds selectively to a small molecule, thereby regulating the protein's activity.

alpha beta heterodimer ($\alpha\beta$-heterodimer): protein dimer composed of one α-tubulin molecule and one β-tubulin molecule that forms the basic building block of microtubules.

alpha helix (α helix): spiral-shaped secondary structure of protein molecules, consisting of a backbone of peptide bonds with R groups of amino acids jutting out.

alpha tubulin (α-tubulin): protein that joins with β-tubulin to form a heterodimer that is the basic building block of microtubules.

alternating conformation model: membrane transport model in which a carrier protein alternates between two conformational states, such that the solute-binding site of the protein is open or accessible first to one side of the membrane and then to the other.

alternation of generations: occurrence of alternating haploid and diploid multicellular forms within the life cycle of an organism.

alternative splicing: utilization of different combinations of intron/exon splice junctions in pre-mRNA to produce messenger RNAs that differ in exon composition, thereby allowing production of more than one type of polypeptide from the same gene.

Ames test: screening test for potential carcinogens that assesses whether a substance causes mutations in bacteria.

amino acid: monomeric unit of proteins, consisting of a carboxylic acid with an amino group and one of a variety of R groups attached to the α carbon; 20 different kinds of amino acids are normally found in proteins.

amino terminus: see *N-terminus*.

aminoacyl site: see *A site*.

aminoacyl tRNA: a tRNA molecule containing an amino acid attached to its 3′ end.

aminoacyl-tRNA synthetase: enzyme that joins an amino acid to its appropriate tRNA molecule using energy provided by the hydrolysis of ATP.

amoeboid movement: mode of cell locomotion that depends on pseudopodia and involves cycles of gelation and solation of the actin cytoskeleton.

AMP: see *adenosine monophosphate*.

amphibolic pathway: series of reactions that can function both in a catabolic mode and as a source of precursors for anabolic pathways.

amphipathic molecule: molecule having spatially separated hydrophilic and hydrophobic regions.

amylopectin: branched-chain form of starch consisting of repeating glucose subunits linked together by $\alpha(1 \rightarrow 4)$ glycosidic bonds, with occasional $\alpha(1 \rightarrow 6)$ linkages creating branches every 12 to 25 units that commonly consist of 20 to 25 glucose units.

amylose: straight-chain form of starch consisting of repeating glucose subunits linked together by $\alpha(1 \rightarrow 4)$ glycosidic bonds.

anabolic pathway: series of reactions that results in the synthesis of cellular components.

anaerobic respiration: cellular respiration in which the ultimate electron acceptor is a molecule other than oxygen.

anaphase: stage during mitosis (or meiosis) when the sister chromatids (or homologous chromo-

somes) separate and move to opposite spindle poles.

anaphase A: movement of sister chromatids toward opposite spindle poles during anaphase.

anaphase B: movement of the spindle poles away from each other during anaphase.

anaphase-promoting complex: large multiprotein complex that targets selected proteins (e.g., securin and mitotic cyclin) for degradation, thereby initiating anaphase and the subsequent completion of mitosis.

anchorage-dependent growth: requirement that cells be attached to a solid surface such as the extracellular matrix before they can grow and divide.

anchorage-independent growth: a trait exhibited by cancer cells, which grow well not just when they are attached to a solid surface, but also when they are freely suspended in a liquid or semisolid medium.

anchoring junction: see *adhesive junction*.

aneuploidy: abnormal state in which a cell possesses an incorrect number of chromosomes.

angiogenesis: growth of new blood vessels.

angular aperture: half-angle of the cone of light entering the objective lens of a microscope from the specimen.

anion exchange protein: antiport carrier protein that facilitates the reciprocal exchange of chloride and bicarbonate ions across the plasma membrane.

anoxygenic phototroph: a photosynthetic organism that uses an oxidizable substrate other than water as the electron donor in photosynthetic electron transduction.

antagonist: substance that binds to a receptor and prevents it from being activated.

antenna pigment: light-absorbing molecule of a photosystem that absorbs photons and passes the energy to a neighboring chlorophyll molecule or accessory pigment by resonance energy transfer.

anterograde transport: movement of material from the ER through the Golgi complex toward the plasma membrane.

antibody: class of proteins produced by lymphocytes that bind with extraordinary specificity to substances, referred to as antigens, that provoke an immune response.

anticodon: triplet of nucleotides located in one of the loops of a tRNA molecule that recognizes the appropriate codon in mRNA by complementary base pairing.

antigen: a foreign or abnormal substance that can trigger an immune response.

antiport: coupled transport of two solutes across a membrane in opposite directions.

AP: see *adaptor protein*.

***APC* gene:** a tumor suppressor gene, frequently mutated in colon cancers, that codes for a protein involved in the Wnt pathway.

apoptosis: cell suicide mediated by a group of protein-degrading enzymes called caspases; involves a programmed series of events that leads to the dismantling of the internal contents of the cell.

AQP: see *aquaporin*.

aquaporin (AQP): any of a family of membrane channel proteins that facilitate the rapid movement of water molecules into or out of cells in tissues that require this capability, such as the proximal tubules of the kidneys.

archaea: one of the two groups of prokaryotes, the other being bacteria; many archaea thrive

under harsh conditions, such as salty, acidic, or hot environments, that would be fatal to most other organisms. Also see *bacteria*.

ARF: see *ADP ribosylation factor*.

Arp2/3 complex: complex of actin-related proteins that allows actin monomers to polymerize as new "branches" on the sides of existing microfilaments.

asexual reproduction: form of reproduction in which a single parent is the only contributor of genetic information to the new organism.

assisted self-assembly: folding and assembly of proteins and protein-containing structures in which the appropriate molecular chaperone is required to ensure that correct assembly will predominate over incorrect assembly.

astral microtubule: type of microtubule that forms asters, which are dense starbursts of microtubules that radiate in all directions from each spindle pole.

asymmetric carbon atom: carbon atom that has four different substituents. Two different stereoisomers are possible for each asymmetric carbon atom in an organic molecule.

ATP: see *adenosine triphosphate*.

ATP synthase: alternative name for an F-type ATPase when it catalyzes the reverse process in which the exergonic flow of protons down their electrochemical gradient is used to drive ATP synthesis; examples include the CF_oCF_1 complex found in chloroplast thylakoid membranes, and the $F_o F_1$ complex found in mitochondrial inner membranes and bacterial plasma membranes.

attenuation: mechanism for regulating bacterial gene expression based on the prematuretermination of transcription.

autophagic lysosome: mature lysosome containing hydrolytic enzymes involved in the digestion of materials of intracellular origin. Also see *heterophagic lysosome*.

autophagic vacuole (autophagosome): vacuole formed when an old or unwanted organelle or other cellular structure is wrapped in membranes derived from the endoplasmic reticulum prior to digestion by lysosomal enzymes.

autophagosome: see *autophagic vacuole*.

autophagy: intracellular digestion of old or unwanted organelles or other cell structures as it occurs within autophagic lysosomes; "self-eating."

autophosphorylation: phosphorylation of a receptor molecule by a receptor molecule of the same type.

autoradiography: procedure for detecting the location of radioactive molecules by overlaying a sample with photographic film, which becomes darkened upon exposure to radioactivity.

axon: extension of a nerve cell that conducts impulses away from the cell body.

axon hillock: region at the base of an axon where action potentials are initiated most easily.

axonal transport: see *fast axonal transport*.

axonemal dynein: motor protein in the axonemes of cilia and flagella that generates axonemal motility by moving along the surface of microtubules driven by energy derived from ATP hydrolysis.

axonemal microtubules: microtubules present in highly ordered bundles in the axonemes of eukaryotic cilia and flagella.

axoneme: group of interconnected microtubules that form the backbone of a eukaryotic cilium or flagellum, usually arranged as nine outer doublet microtubules surrounding a pair of central microtubules.

axoplasm: cytoplasm within the axon of a nerve cell.

B

B tubule: an incomplete microtubule that is fused to a complete microtubule (the A tubule) to make up an outer doublet in the axoneme of a eukaryotic cilium or flagellum.

BAC: see *bacterial artificial chromosome.*

backcrossing: process in a genetic breeding experiment in which a heterozygote is cross-fertilized with one of the original homozygous parental organisms.

bacteria (singular, bacterium): one of the two groups of prokaryotes, the other being archaea; include most of the commonly encountered single-celled organisms with no nucleus that have traditionally been called bacteria. Also see *archaea.*

bacterial artificial chromosome (BAC): bacterial cloning vector derived from the F-factor plasmid that is useful in cloning large DNA fragments.

bacterial chromosome: circular (or linear) DNA molecule with bound proteins that contains the main genome of a bacterial cell.

bacteriochlorophyll: type of chlorophyll found in bacteria that is able to extract electrons from donors other than water.

bacteriophage (phage): virus that infects bacterial cells.

bacteriorhodopsin: transmembrane protein complexed with rhodopsin, capable of transporting protons across the bacterial cell membrane to create a light-dependent electrochemical proton gradient.

basal body: microtubule-containing structure located at the base of a eukaryotic flagellum or cilium that consists of nine sets of triplet microtubules; identical in appearance to a centriole.

basal lamina: thin sheet of specialized extracellular matrix material that separates epithelial cells from underlying connective tissues.

base excision repair: DNA repair mechanism that removes and replaces single damaged bases in DNA.

base pair (bp): pair of nucleotides joined together by complementary hydrogen bonding.

base pairing: complementary relationship between purines and pyrimidines based on hydrogen bonding that provides a mechanism for nucleic acids to recognize and bind to each other; involves the pairing of A with T or U, and the pairing of G with C.

Bcl-2: protein located in the outer mitochondrial membrane that blocks cell death by apoptosis.

benign tumor: tumor that grows only locally, unable to invade neighboring tissues or spread to other parts of the body.

beta oxidation (β oxidation): pathway involving successive cycles of fatty acid oxidation in which the fatty acid chain is shortened each time by two carbon atoms released as acetyl CoA.

beta sheet (β sheet): extended sheetlike secondary structure of proteins in which adjacent polypeptides are linked by hydrogen bonds between amino and carbonyl groups.

beta tubulin (β-tubulin): protein that joins with α-tubulin to form a heterodimer that is the basic building block of microtubules.

bimetallic iron-copper (Fe-Cu) center: a complex formed between a single copper atom and the iron atom bound to the heme group of an oxygen-binding cytochrome such as cytochrome a_3; important in keeping an O_2 molecule bound to the cytochrome until it picks up four electrons and four protons, resulting in the release of two molecules of water.

binding change model: a mechanism involving the physical rotation of the γ subunit of an $F_o F_1$ ATP synthase postulated to explain how the exergonic flow of protons through the F_o component of the complex drives the otherwise endergonic phosphorylation of ADP to ATP by the F_1 component.

biochemistry: study of the chemistry of living systems; same as biological chemistry.

bioenergetics: area of science that deals with the application of thermodynamic principles to reactions and processes in the biological world.

bioinformatics: using computers to analyze the vast amounts of data generated by sequencing and expression studies on genomes and proteomes.

biological chemistry: study of the chemistry of living systems; called biochemistry for short.

bioluminescence: production of light by an organism as a result of the reaction of ATP with specific luminescent compounds.

biosynthesis: generation of new molecules through a series of chemical reactions within the cell.

BiP: member of the Hsp70 family of chaperones; present in the ER lumen, where it facilitates protein folding by reversibly binding to the hydrophobic regions of polypeptide chains.

bivalent: pair of homologous chromosomes that have synapsed during the first meiotic division; contains four chromatids, two from each chromosome.

BLAST (Basic Local Alignment Search Tool): software program that can search databases and locate DNA or protein sequences that resemble any known sequence of interest.

bond energy: amount of energy required to break one mole of a particular chemical bond.

bp: see *base pair.*

BRCA1 and BRCA2 genes: tumor suppressor genes in which inheritance of a single mutant copy creates a high risk for breast and ovarian cancer; code for proteins involved in repairing double-strand DNA breaks.

BRE (TFIIB recognition element): component of core promoters for RNA polymerase II, located immediately upstream from the TATA box.

brightfield microscopy: light microscopy of specimen that possesses color, has been stained, or has some other property that affects the amount of light that passes through, thereby allowing an image to be formed.

bundle sheath cell: internal cell of the leaf of a C4 plant located in close proximity to the vascular bundle (vein) of the leaf; site of the Calvin cycle in such plants.

buoyant density centrifugation: see *equilibrium density centrifugation.*

Burkitt lymphoma: a lymphocyte cancer associated with infection by Epstein-Barr virus along with a chromosome translocation in which the *MYC* gene is activated by moving it from chromosome 8 to 14.

C

C: see *cytosine.*

C value: amount of DNA in a single (haploid) set of chromosomes.

C₃ plant: plant that depends solely on the Calvin cycle for carbon dioxide fixation, creating the three-carbon compound 3-phosphoglycerate as the initial product.

C₄ plant: plant that uses the Hatch-Slack pathway in mesophyll cells to carry out the initial fixation of carbon dioxide, creating the four-carbon compound oxaloacetate; the assimilated carbon is subsequently released again in bundle sheath cells and recaptured by the Calvin cycle.

cadherin: any of a family of plasma membrane glycoproteins that mediate Ca^{2+}-dependent adhesion between cells.

cal: see *calorie.*

calcium ATPase: membrane protein that transports calcium ions across a membrane using energy derived from ATP hydrolysis; prominent example occurs in the sarcoplasmic reticulum (SR), where it pumps calcium ions into the SR lumen.

calcium indicator: a dye or genetically engineered protein whose fluorescence changes in response to the local cytosolic calcium concentration.

calcium ionophore: a molecule that increases the permeability of membranes to calcium ions.

calmodulin: calcium-binding protein involved in mediating many of the intracellular effects of calcium ions in eukaryotic cells.

calnexin: a membrane-bound ER protein that forms a protein complex with a newly synthesized glycoprotein and assists in its proper folding.

calorie (cal): unit of energy; amount of energy needed to raise the temperature of 1 gram of water 1°C.

calreticulin: a soluble ER protein that forms a protein complex with a newly synthesized glycoprotein and assists in its proper folding.

Calvin cycle: cyclic series of reactions used by photosynthetic organisms for the fixation of carbon dioxide and its reduction to form carbohydrates.

CAM: see *crassulacean acid metabolism.*

CAM plant: plant that carries out crassulacean acid metabolism.

cAMP: see *cyclic AMP.*

cancer: uncontrolled, growing mass of cells that is capable of invading neighboring tissues and spreading via body fluids, especially the bloodstream, to other parts of the body; also called a *malignant tumor.*

CAP: see *catabolite activator protein.*

cap (5′cap): methylated structure at the 5′ end of eukaryotic mRNAs created by adding 7-methylguanosine and methylating the ribose rings of the first, and often the second, nucleotides of the RNA chain.

capping protein: protein that binds to the end of an actin microfilament, thereby preventing the further addition or loss of subunits.

carbohydrate: general name given to molecules that contain carbon, hydrogen, and oxygen in a ratio $C_n(H_2O)n$; examples include starch, glycogen, and cellulose.

carbon assimilation reactions: portion of the photosynthetic pathway in which fully oxidized carbon atoms from carbon dioxide are fixed (covalently attached) to organic acceptor molecules and then reduced and rearranged to form carbohydrates and other organic compounds required for building a living cell.

carbon atom: the most important atom in biological molecules, capable of forming up to four covalent bonds.

carboxyl terminus: see *C-terminus*.

carcinogen: any cancer-causing agent.

carcinoma: a malignant tumor (cancer) arising from the epithelial cells that cover external and internal body surfaces.

cardiac (heart) muscle: striated muscle of the heart, highly dependent on aerobic respiration.

caretaker gene: a tumor suppressor gene involved in DNA repair or chromosome sorting; loss-of-function mutations in such genes contribute to genetic instability.

carotenoid: any of several accessory pigments found in most plant species that absorb in the blue region of the visible spectrum (420–480 nm) and are therefore yellow or orange in color.

carrier molecule: a molecule that joins to a monomer, thereby activating the monomer for a subsequent reaction.

carrier protein: membrane protein that transports solutes across the membrane by binding to the solute on one side of the membrane and then undergoing a conformational change that transfers the solute to the other side of the membrane.

caspase: any of a family of proteases that degrade other cellular proteins as part of the process of apoptosis.

cassette mechanism: process of DNA rearrangement in which alternative alleles for yeast mating type are inserted into the *MAT* locus for transcription.

catabolic pathway: series of reactions that results in the breakdown of cellular components.

catabolite activator protein (CAP): bacterial protein that binds cyclic AMP and then activates the transcription of catabolite-repressible genes.

catalyst: agent that enhances the rate of a reaction by lowering the activation energy without itself being consumed; catalysts change the rate at which a reaction approaches equilibrium, but not the position of equilibrium.

catalytic subunit: a subunit of a multisubunit enzyme that contains the enzyme's catalytic site.

catecholamine: any of several compounds derived from the amino acid tyrosine that functions as a hormone and/or neurotransmitter.

caveolae: small invaginations of the plasma membrane that are coated with the protein caveolin; a type of lipid raft enriched in cholesterol that may be involved in cholesterol uptake or signal transduction.

CBP: transcriptional coactivator that exhibits histone acetyltransferase activity and associates with RNA polymerase to facilitate assembly of the transcription machinery at gene promoters.

Cdc42: member of a family of monomeric G proteins, which also includes Rac and Rho, that stimulate formation of various actin-containing structures within cells.

Cdk: see *cyclin-dependent kinase*.

Cdk inhibitor: any of several proteins that restrain cell growth and division by inhibiting Cdk-cyclin complexes.

cDNA: see *complementary DNA*.

cDNA library: collection of recombinant DNA clones produced by copying the entire mRNA population of a particular cell type with reverse transcriptase and then cloning the resulting cDNAs.

cell: the basic structural and functional unit of living organisms; the smallest structure capable of performing the essential functions characteristic of life.

cell body: portion of a nerve cell that contains the nucleus and other organelles and has extensions called axons and dendrites projecting from it.

cell-cell junction: specialized connection between the plasma membranes of adjoining cells for the purpose of adhesion, sealing, or communication.

cell cycle: stages involved in preparing for and carrying out cell division; begins when two new cells are formed by the division of a single parental cell and is completed when one of these cells divides again into two cells.

cell differentiation: process by which cells acquire the specialized properties that distinguish different types of cells from each other.

cell division: process by which one cell gives rise to two.

cell membrane: see *plasma membrane*.

cell plate: flattened sac representing a stage in plant cell wall formation, leading to separation of the two daughter nuclei during plant cell division.

cell theory: theory of cellular organization stating that all organisms consist of one or more cells, that the cell is the basic unit of structure for all organisms, and that all cells arise only from preexisting cells.

cell wall: rigid, nonliving structure exterior to the plasma membrane of bacterial, algal, fungal, and plant cells; plant cell walls consist of cellulose microfibrils embedded in a noncellulosic matrix.

cellular respiration: oxidation-driven flow of electrons from reduced coenzymes to an electron acceptor, usually accompanied by the generation of ATP.

cellulose: structural polysaccharide present in plant cell walls, consisting of repeating glucose units linked by $\beta(1 \rightarrow 4)$ bonds.

central pair: two parallel microtubules located in the center of the axoneme of a eukaryotic cilium or flagellum.

central vacuole: large membrane-bounded organelle present in many plant cells; helps maintain turgor pressure of the plant cell, plays a limited storage role, and is also capable of a lysosome-like function in intracellular digestion.

centrifugation: process of rapidly spinning a tube containing a fluid to subject its contents to a centrifugal force.

centrifuge: machine for rapidly spinning a tube containing a fluid to subject its contents to a centrifugal force.

centriole: structure consisting of nine sets of triplet microtubules embedded within the centrosome of animal cells, where two centrioles lie at right angles to each other; identical in structure to the basal body of eukaryotic cilia and flagella.

centromere: chromosome region where sister chromatids are held together prior to anaphase and where kinetochores are attached; contains simple-sequence, tandemly repeated DNA.

centrosome: small zone of granular material surrounding two centrioles located adjacent to the nucleus of animal cells; functions as a cell's main microtubule-organizing center.

cerebroside: an uncharged glycolipid containing the amino alcohol sphingosine.

CF: see *cystic fibrosis*.

CF₁: component of the chloroplast ATP synthase complex that protrudes from the stromal side

of thylakoid membranes and contains the catalytic site for ATP synthesis.

CF₀: component of the chloroplast ATP synthase complex that is embedded in thylakoid membranes and serves as the proton translocator.

CF₀CF₁ complex: ATP synthase complex found in chloroplast thylakoid membranes; catalyzes the process by which the exergonic flow of protons down their electrochemical gradient is used to drive ATP synthesis.

CFTR: see *cystic fibrosis transmembrane conductance regulator*.

CGN: see *cis-Golgi network*.

channel gating: closing of a membrane ion channel in such a way that it can reopen immediately in response to an appropriate stimulus.

channel inactivation: closing of a membrane ion channel in such a way that it cannot reopen immediately.

channel protein: membrane protein that forms a hydrophilic channel through which solutes can pass across the membrane without any change in the conformation of the channel protein.

chaperone: see *molecular chaperone*.

Chargaff's rules: observation, first made by Erwin Chargaff, that in DNA the number of adenines is equal to the number of thymines (A = T) and the number of guanines is equal to the number of cytosines (G = C).

charge repulsion: force driving apart two ions, molecules, or regions of molecules of the same electric charge.

checkpoint: pathway that monitors conditions within the cell and transiently halts the cell cycle if conditions are not suitable for continuing. Also see *DNA damage checkpoint, DNA replication checkpoint*, and *mitotic spindle checkpoint*.

chemical synapse: junction between two nerve cells where a nerve impulse is transmitted between the cells by neurotransmitters that diffuse across the synaptic cleft from the presynaptic cell to the postsynaptic cell.

chemiosmotic coupling model: model postulating that electron transport pathways establish proton gradients across membranes and that the energy stored in such gradients can then be used to drive ATP synthesis.

chemotaxis: cell movement toward a chemical attractant or away from a chemical repellent.

chemotroph: organism that is dependent on the bond energies of organic molecules such as carbohydrates, fats, and proteins to satisfy energy requirements.

chemotrophic energy metabolism: reactions and pathways by which cells catabolize nutrients such as carbohydrates, fats, and proteins, conserving as ATP some of the free energy that is released in the process.

chiasma (plural, chiasmata): connection between homologous chromosomes produced by crossing over during prophase I of meiosis.

chitin: structural polysaccharide found in insect exoskeletons and crustacean cells; consists of N-acetylglucosamine units linked by $\beta(1 \rightarrow 4)$ bonds.

chlorophyll: light-absorbing molecule that donates photoenergized electrons to organic molecules, initiating photochemical events that lead to the generation of the NADPH and ATP required for the Calvin cycle; because of its absorption properties, chlorophyll gives plants their characteristic green color.

chlorophyll-binding protein: any of several proteins that bind to and stabilize the arrangement of chlorophyll molecules within a photosystem.

chloroplast: double membrane-enclosed cytoplasmic organelle of plants and algae that contains chlorophyll and the enzymes needed to carry out photosynthesis.

cholesterol: lipid constituent of animal cell plasma membrane; serves as a precursor to the steroid hormones.

cholinergic synapse: a synapse that uses acetylcholine as the neurotransmitter.

chromatid: see *sister chromatid*.

chromatin: DNA-protein fibers that make up chromosomes; constructed from nucleosomes spaced regularly along a DNA chain.

chromatin fiber (30 nm): fiber formed by packing together the nucleosomes of a 10-nm chromatin fiber.

chromatin remodeling protein: protein that induces alterations in nucleosome structure, packing, and/or position designed to give transcription factors access to DNA target sites in the promoter region of a gene.

chromatography: a group of related techniques that utilize the flow of a fluid phase over a non-mobile absorbing phase to separate molecules based on their relative affinities for the two phases, which in turn reflect differences in size, charge, hydrophobicity, or affinity for a particular chemical group.

chromosome: in eukaryotes a single DNA molecule, complexed with histones and other proteins, that becomes condensed into a compact structure at the time of mitosis or meiosis. Also see *bacterial chromosome*.

chromosome puff: uncoiled region of a polytene chromosome that is undergoing transcription.

chromosome theory of heredity: theory stating that hereditary factors are located in the chromosomes within the nucleus.

cilium (plural, cilia): membrane-bounded appendage on the surface of a eukaryotic cell, composed of a specific arrangement of microtubules and responsible for motility of the cell or the fluids around cells; shorter and more numerous than closely related organelles called flagella. Also see *flagellum*.

cis-acting element: a DNA sequence to which a regulatory protein can bind.

cis-Golgi network (CGN): region of the Golgi complex consisting of a network of membrane-bounded tubules that are located closest to the transitional elements.

cisterna (plural, cisternae): membrane-bounded flattened sac, such as in the endoplasmic reticulum or Golgi complex.

cisternal maturation model: model postulating that Golgi cisternae are transient compartments that gradually change from *cis*-Golgi network cisternae into medial cisternae and then into *trans*-Golgi network cisternae.

cis-trans test: analysis used to determine whether a mutation in a bacterial operon affects a regulatory protein or the DNA sequence to which it binds.

clathrin: large protein that forms a "cage" around the coated vesicles and coated pits involved in endocytosis and other intracellular transport processes.

clathrin-dependent endocytosis: see *receptor-mediated endocytosis*.

claudin: transmembrane protein that forms the main structural component of a tight junction.

cleavage: process of cytoplasmic division in animal cells, in which a band of actin microfilaments lying beneath the plasma membrane constricts the cell at the midline and eventually divides it in two.

cleavage furrow: groove formed during the division of an animal cell that encircles the cell and deepens progressively, leading to cytoplasmic division.

clone: organism (or cell or molecule) that is genetically identical to another organism (or cell or molecule) from which it is derived.

cloning vector: DNA molecule to which a selected DNA fragment can be joined prior to rapid replication of the vector in a host cell (usually a bacterium); phage and plasmid DNA are the most common cloning vectors.

CNVs: see *copy number variations*.

CoA: see *coenzyme A*.

coactivator: class of proteins that mediate interactions between activators and the genes they regulate; include histone-modifying enzymes such as HAT, chromatin-remodeling proteins such as SWI/SNF, and Mediator.

coated vesicle: any of several types of membrane vesicles involved in vesicular traffic within the endomembrane system; surrounded by a coat protein such as clathrin, COPI, COPII, or caveolin.

coding strand: the nontemplate strand of a DNA double helix, which is base-paired to the template strand; identical in sequence to the single-stranded RNA molecules transcribed from the template strand, except that RNA has uracil (U) where the coding strand has thymine (T).

codon: triplet of nucleotides in an mRNA molecule that serves as a coding unit for an amino acid (or a start or stop signal) during protein synthesis.

coenzyme: small organic molecule that functions along with an enzyme by serving as a carrier of electrons or functional groups.

coenzyme A (CoA): organic molecule that serves as a carrier of acyl groups by forming a high-energy thioester bond with an organic acid.

coenzyme Q (CoQ): nonprotein (quinone) component of the mitochondrial electron transport system that serves as the collection point for electrons from both FMN- and FAD-linked dehydrogenases; also called ubiquinone.

coenzyme Q-cytochrome c oxidoreductase: see *complex III*.

cohesin: protein that holds sister chromatids together prior to anaphase.

colchicine: plant-derived drug that binds to tubulin and prevents its polymerization into microtubules.

collagen: a family of closely related proteins that form high-strength fibers found in high concentration in the extracellular matrix of animals.

collagen fiber: extremely strong fibers measuring several micrometers in diameter found in the extracellular matrix; constructed from collagen fibrils that are, in turn, composed of collagen molecules lined up in a staggered array.

combinatorial model for gene regulation: model proposing that complex patterns of tissue-specific gene expression can be achieved by a relatively small number of DNA control elements and their respective transcription factors acting in different combinations.

complementary: in nucleic acids, the ability of guanine (G) to form a hydrogen-bonded base pair with cytosine (C), and adenine (A) to form a hydrogen-bonded base pair with thymine (T) or uracil (U).

complementary DNA (cDNA): DNA molecule copied from an mRNA template by the enzyme reverse transcriptase.

complex I (NADH-coenzyme Q oxidoreductase): multiprotein complex of the electron transport system that catalyzes the transfer of electrons from NADH to coenzyme Q.

complex II (succinate-coenzyme Q oxidoreductase): multiprotein complex of the electron transport system that catalyzes the transfer of electrons from succinate to coenzyme Q.

complex III (coenzyme Q-cytochrome c oxidoreductase): multiprotein complex of the electron transport system that catalyzes the transfer of electrons from coenzyme Q to cytochrome c.

complex IV (cytochrome c oxidase): multiprotein complex of the electron transport system that catalyzes the transfer of electrons from cytochrome c to oxygen.

compound microscope: light microscope that uses several lenses in combination; usually has a condenser lens, an objective lens, and an ocular lens.

concentration gradient: transmembrane gradient in concentration of a molecule or ion, expressed as a ratio of the concentration of the substance on one side of the membrane to its concentration on the other side of the membrane; the sole driving force for transport of molecules across a membrane, but only one of two components of the electrochemical potential that serves as the driving force for transport of ions across a membrane.

concentration work: use of energy to transport ions or molecules across a membrane against an electrochemical or concentration gradient.

condensation reaction: chemical reaction that results in the joining of two molecules by the removal of a water molecule.

condenser lens: lens of a light microscope (or electron microscope) that is the first lens to direct the light rays (or electron beam) from the source toward the specimen.

confocal microscope: specialized type of light microscope that employs a laser beam to illuminate a single plane of the specimen at a time.

conformation: three-dimensional shape of a polypeptide or other biological macromolecule.

conjugation: cellular mating process by which DNA is transferred from one bacterial cell to another.

connexon: assembly of six protein subunits with a hollow center that forms a channel through the plasma membrane at a gap junction.

consensus sequence: the most common version of a DNA base sequence when that sequence occurs in slightly different forms at different sites.

constitutive heterochromatin: chromosomal regions that are condensed in all cells of an organism at virtually all times and are therefore genetically inactive. Also see *facultative heterochromatin*.

constitutive secretion: continuous fusion of secretory vesicles with the plasma membrane and expulsion of their contents to the cell exterior, independent of specific extracellular signals.

constitutively active mutation: mutation that causes a receptor to be active even when no activating ligand is present.

contractile ring: beltlike bundle of actin microfilaments that forms beneath the plasma membrane and acts to constrict the cleavage furrow during the division of an animal cell.

contractility: shortening of muscle cells.

cooperativity: property of enzymes possessing multiple catalytic sites in which the binding of a substrate molecule to one catalytic site causes conformational changes that influence the affinity of the remaining sites for substrate.

COPI: main protein component of the "fuzzy" coats of COPI-coated vesicles, which are involved in retrograde transport from the Golgi complex back to the ER and between Golgi complex cisternae.

COPII: main protein component of COPII-coated vesicles, which are involved in transport from the ER to the Golgi complex.

copy number variations (CNVs): variations in the number of copies of DNA segments, thousands of bases long, that occur among individuals of the same species.

CoQ: see *coenzyme Q*.

core oligosaccharide: initial oligosaccharide segment joined to an asparagine residue during N-glycosylation of a polypeptide chain; consists of two N-acetylglucosamine units, nine mannose units, and three glucose units.

core promoter: minimal set of DNA sequences sufficient to direct the accurate initiation of transcription by RNA polymerase.

core protein: a protein molecule to which numerous glycosaminoglycan chains are attached to form a proteoglycan.

corepressor: effector molecule required along with the repressor to prevent transcription of a bacterial operon.

correlative microscopy: combination of light and electron-based microscopy that allows the fine structure associated with a fluorescent signal to be examined at high resolution, often using immunoelectron microscopy.

cotranslational import: transfer of a growing polypeptide chain across (or, in the case of integral membrane proteins, into) the ER membrane as polypeptide synthesis proceeds.

coupled transport: coordinated transport of two solutes across a membrane in such a way that transport of either stops if the other is stopped or interrupted; the two solutes may move in the same direction (symport) or in opposite directions (antiport).

covalent bond: strong chemical bond in which two atoms share two or more electrons.

covalent modification: type of regulation in which the activity of an enzyme (or other protein) is altered by the addition or removal of specific chemical groups.

crassulacean acid metabolism (CAM): pathway in which plants use PEP carboxylase to fix CO_2 at night, generating the four-carbon acid, malate. The malate is then decarboxylated during the day to release CO_2, which is fixed by the Calvin cycle.

CREB: transcription factor that activates the transcription of cyclic AMP-inducible genes by binding to cAMP response elements in DNA.

crista (plural, **cristae**): infolding of the inner mitochondrial membrane into the matrix of the mitochondrion, thereby increasing the total surface area of the inner membrane; contains the enzymes of electron transport and oxidative phosphorylation.

critical concentration: tubulin concentration at which the rate of assembly of tubulin subunits into a polymer is exactly balanced with the rate of disassembly.

critical point dryer: heavy metal canister used to dry a specimen under conditions of controlled temperature and pressure.

cross-bridge: structure formed by contact between the myosin heads of thick filaments and the thin filaments in muscle myofibrils.

crossing over: exchange of DNA segments between homologous chromosomes.

cryoEM: technique in which cryofixed biological samples are directly imaged in a transmission electron microscope at low temperature; often used to examine suspensions of isolated macromolecules.

cryofixation: rapid freezing of small samples so that cellular structures can be immobilized in milliseconds; often followed by freeze substitution, in which an organic solvent replaces the frozen water in the sample.

C-terminus (carboxyl terminus): the end of a polypeptide chain that contains the last amino acid to be incorporated during mRNA translation; usually retains a free carboxyl group.

current: movement of positive or negative ions.

cyclic AMP (cAMP): adenosine monophosphate with the phosphate group linked to both the 3′ and 5′ carbons by phosphodiester bonds; functions in both prokaryotic and eukaryotic gene regulation; in eukaryotes, acts as a second messenger that mediates the effects of various signaling molecules by activating protein kinase A.

cyclic electron flow: light-driven transfer of electrons from photosystem I through a sequence of electron carries that returns them to a chlorophyll molecule of the same photosystem, with the released energy used to drive ATP synthesis.

cyclin: any of a group of proteins that activate the cyclin-dependent kinases (Cdks) involved in regulating progression through the eukaryotic cell cycle.

cyclin-dependent kinase (Cdk): any of several protein kinases that are activated by different cyclins and that control progression through the eukaryotic cell cycle by phosphorylating various target proteins.

cyclosis: see *cytoplasmic streaming*.

cystic fibrosis (CF): a disease whose symptoms result from an inability to secrete chloride ions that is, in turn, caused by a genetic defect in a membrane protein that functions as a chloride ion channel.

cystic fibrosis transmembrane conductance regulator (CFTR): a membrane protein that functions as a chloride ion channel, a mutant form of which can lead to cystic fibrosis.

cytochalasins: family of drugs produced by certain fungi that inhibit a variety of cell movements by preventing actin polymerization.

cytochrome: family of heme-containing proteins of the electron transport system; involved in the transfer of electrons from coenzyme Q to oxygen by the oxidation and reduction of the central iron atom of the heme group.

cytochrome b_6/f complex: multiprotein complex within the thylakoid membrane that transfers electrons from a plastoquinol to plastocyanin as part of the energy transduction reactions of photosynthesis.

cytochrome c: heme-containing protein of the electron transport system that also plays a role in triggering apoptosis when released from mitochondria.

cytochrome c oxidase: see *complex IV*.

cytochrome P-450: family of heme-containing proteins, located mainly in the liver, that catalyze hydroxylation reactions involved in drug detoxification and steroid biosynthesis.

cytokinesis: division of the cytoplasm of a parent cell into two daughter cells; usually follows mitosis.

cytology: study of cellular structure, based primarily on microscopic techniques.

cytoplasm: that portion of the interior of a eukaryotic cell that is not occupied by the nucleus; includes organelles, such as mitochondria and components of the endomembrane system, as well as the cytosol.

cytoplasmic dynein: cytoplasmic motor protein that moves along the surface of microtubules in the plus-to-minus direction, driven by energy derived from ATP hydrolysis; associated with dynactin, which links cytoplasmic dynein to cargo vesicles.

cytoplasmic microtubules: microtubules arranged in loosely organized, dynamic networks in the cytoplasm of eukaryotic cells.

cytoplasmic streaming: movement of the cytoplasm driven by interactions between actin filaments and specific types of myosin; also called cyclosis in plant cells.

cytosine (C): nitrogen-containing aromatic base, chemically designated as a pyrimidine, that serves as an informational monomeric unit when present in nucleic acids with other bases in a specific sequence; forms a complementary base pair with guanine (G) by hydrogen bonding.

cytoskeleton: three-dimensional, interconnected network of microtubules, microfilaments, and intermediate filaments that provides structure to the cytoplasm of a eukaryotic cell and plays an important role in cell movement.

cytosol: the semifluid substance in which the organelles of the cytoplasm are suspended.

D

DAG: see *diacylglycerol*.

deep etching: modification of freeze-etching technique in which ultrarapid freezing and a volatile cryoprotectant are used to extend the etching period, thereby removing a deeper layer of ice and allowing the interior of a cell to be examined in depth.

degenerate code: ability of the genetic code to use more than one triplet code to specify the same amino acid.

degron: amino acid sequence within a protein that is used in targeting the protein for destruction.

dehydrogenation: removal of electrons plus hydrogen ions (protons) from an organic molecule; oxidation.

denaturation: loss of the natural three-dimensional structure of a macromolecule, usually resulting in a loss of its biological activity; caused by agents such as heat, extremes of pH, urea, salt, and other chemicals. Also see *DNA denaturation*.

dendrite: extension of a nerve cell that receives impulses and transmits them inward toward the cell body.

density-dependent inhibition of growth: tendency of cell division to stop when cells growing in culture reach a high population density.

density gradient (rate-zonal) centrifugation: type of centrifugation in which the sample is applied as a thin layer on top of a gradient of solute, and centrifugation is stopped before the particles reach the bottom of the tube; separates organelles and molecules based mainly on differences in size.

deoxyribonucleic acid: see *DNA*.

deoxyribose: five-carbon sugar present in DNA.

dephosphorylation: removal of a phosphate group.

depolarization: change in membrane potential to a less-negative value.

desmosome: junction for cell-cell adhesion that is connected to the cytoskeleton by intermediate filaments; creates buttonlike points of strong adhesion between adjacent animal cells that give tissue structural integrity and allow the cells to function as a unit and resist stress.

diacylglycerol (DAG): glycerol esterified to two fatty acids; formed, along with inositol trisphosphate (IP$_3$), upon hydrolysis of phosphatidylinositol-4,5-bisphosphate by phospholipase C; remains membrane-bound after hydrolysis and functions as a second messenger by activating protein kinase C, which then phosphorylates specific serine and threonine groups in a variety of target proteins.

diakinesis: final stage of prophase I of meiosis; associated with chromosome condensation, disappearance of nucleoli, breakdown of the nuclear envelope, and initiation of spindle formation.

DIC microscopy: see *differential interference contrast microscopy.*

Dicer: enzyme that cleaves double-stranded RNAs into short fragments about 21–22 base pairs in length.

differential centrifugation: technique for separating organelles or molecules that differ in size and/or density by subjecting cellular fractions to centrifugation at high speeds and separating particles based on their different rates of sedimentation.

differential interference contrast (DIC) microscopy: technique that resembles phase-contrast microscopy in principle, but is more sensitive because it employs a special prism to split the illuminating light beam into two separate rays.

differential scanning calorimetry: technique for determining a membrane's transition temperature by monitoring the uptake of heat during the transition of the membrane from the gel to fluid state.

differentiation: see *cell differentiation.*

diffraction: pattern of either additive or canceling interference exhibited by light waves.

diffusion: free, unassisted movement of a solute, with direction and rate dictated by the difference in solute concentration between two different regions.

digital deconvolution microscopy: technique in which fluorescence microscopy is used to acquire a series of images through the thickness of a specimen, followed by computer analysis to remove the contribution of out-of-focus light to the image in each focal plane.

digital microscopy: technique in which microscopic images are recorded and stored electronically by placing a video camera in the image plane produced by the ocular lens.

diploid: containing two sets of chromosomes and therefore two copies of each gene; can describe a cell, nucleus, or organism composed of such cells.

diplotene: stage during prophase I of meiosis when the two homologous chromosomes of each bivalent begin to separate from each other, revealing the chiasmata that connect them.

direct active transport: membrane transport in which the movement of solute molecules or ions across a membrane is coupled directly to an exergonic chemical reaction, most commonly the hydrolysis of ATP.

directionality: having two ends that are chemically different from each other; used to describe a polymer chain such as a protein, nucleic acid, or carbohydrate; also used to describe membrane transport systems that selectively transport solutes across a membrane in one direction.

disaccharide: carbohydrate consisting of two covalently linked monosaccharide units.

dissociation constant (K_d): the concentration of free ligand needed to produce a state in which half the receptors are bound to ligand.

disulfide bond: covalent bond formed between two sulfur atoms by oxidation of sulfhydryl groups. The disulfide bond formed between two cysteines is important in stabilizing the tertiary structure of proteins.

DNA (deoxyribonucleic acid): macromolecule that serves as the repository of genetic information in all cells; constructed from nucleotides consisting of deoxyribose phosphate linked to either adenine, thymine, cytosine, or guanine; forms a double helix held together by complementary base pairing between adenine and thymine, and between cytosine and guanine.

DNA cloning: generating multiple copies of a specific DNA sequence, either by replication of a recombinant plasmid or bacteriophage within bacterial cells or by use of the polymerase chain reaction.

DNA damage checkpoint: mechanism that monitors for DNA damage and halts the cell cycle at various points, including late G1, S, and late G2, if damage is detected.

DNA denaturation: separation of the two strands of the DNA double helix caused by disruption of complementary base pairing.

DNA fingerprinting: technique for identifying individuals based on small differences in DNA fragment patterns detected by electrophoresis.

DNA gyrase: a type II topoisomerase that can relax positive supercoiling and induce negative supercoiling of DNA; involved in unwinding the DNA double helix during DNA replication.

DNA helicase: any of several enzymes that unwind the DNA double helix, driven by energy derived from ATP hydrolysis.

DNA ligase: enzyme that joins two DNA fragments together by catalyzing the formation of a phosphoester bond between the 3' end of one fragment and the 5' end of the other fragment.

DNA melting temperature (T_m): temperature at which the transition from double-stranded to single-stranded DNA is halfway complete when DNA is denatured by increasing the temperature.

DNA methylation: addition of methyl groups to nucleotides in DNA; associated with suppression of gene transcription when selected cytosine groups are methylated in eukaryotic DNA.

DNA microarray: tiny chip that has been spotted at fixed locations with thousands of different DNA fragments for use in gene expression studies.

DNA packing ratio: ratio of the length of a DNA molecule to the length of the chromosome or fiber into which it is packaged; used to quantify the extent of DNA coiling and folding.

DNA polymerase: any of a group of enzymes involved in DNA replication and repair that catalyze the addition of successive nucleotides to the 3' end of a growing DNA strand, using an existing DNA strand as template.

DNA rearrangement: movement of DNA segments from one location to another within the genome.

DNA renaturation: binding together of the two separated strands of a DNA double helix by complementary base pairing, thereby regenerating the double helix.

DNA replication checkpoint: mechanism that monitors the state of DNA replication to help ensure that DNA synthesis is completed prior to permitting the cell to exit from G2 and begin mitosis.

DNA sequencing: technology used to determine the linear order of bases in DNA molecules or fragments.

DNA-binding domain: region of a transcription factor that recognizes and binds to a specific DNA base sequence.

DNase I hypersensitive site: location near an active gene that shows extreme sensitivity to digestion by the nuclease DNase I; thought to correlate with binding sites for transcriptional factors or other regulatory proteins.

domain: a discrete, locally folded unit of protein tertiary structure, often containing regions of α helices and β sheets packed together compactly.

dominant (allele): allele that determines how the trait will appear in an organism, whether present in the heterozygous or homozygous form.

dominant negative mutation: a loss-of-function mutation involving proteins consisting of more than one copy of the same polypeptide chain, in which a single mutant polypeptide chain disrupts the function of the protein even though the other polypeptide chains are normal.

double bond: chemical bond formed between two atoms as a result of the sharing of two pairs of electrons.

double helix (model): two intertwined helical chains of a DNA molecule, held together by complementary base pairing between adenine (A) and thymine (T) and between cytosine (C) and guanine (G).

double-reciprocal plot: graphic method for analyzing enzyme kinetic data by plotting $1/v$ versus $1/[S]$.

downstream: located toward the 3' end of the DNA coding strand.

downstream promoter element: see *DPE.*

DPE (downstream promoter element): component of core promoters for RNA polymerase II, located about 30 nucleotides downstream from the transcriptional startpoint.

Drosha: nuclear enzyme that cleaves the primary transcript of microRNA genes (pri-microRNAs) to form the smaller precursor microRNAs (pre-microRNAs).

dynactin: protein complex that helps link cytoplasmic dynein to the cargo (e.g., a vesicle) that it transports along microtubules.

dynamic instability model: model for microtubule behavior that presumes two populations of microtubules, one growing in length by continued polymerization at their plus ends and the other shrinking in length by depolymerization.

dynamin: cytosolic GTPase required for coated pit constriction and the closing of a budding, clathrin-coated vesicle.

dynein: motor protein that moves along the surface of microtubules in the plus-to-minus direction, driven by energy derived from ATP hydrolysis; present both in the cytoplasm and in the arms that reach between adjacent microtubule doublets in the axoneme of a flagellum or cilium.

dystrophin: a large protein found at muscle costameres that is part of a complex of proteins that attaches the muscle cell plasma membrane to the extracellular matrix

E

E: see *internal energy.*

E face: interior face of the outer monolayer of a membrane as revealed by the technique of freeze fracturing; called the E face because this monolayer is on the *exterior* side of the membrane.

E site (exit site): site on the ribosome to which the empty tRNA is moved during translocation prior to its release from the ribosome.

E'_0: see *standard reduction potential.*

E2F transcription factor: protein that, when not bound to the Rb protein, activates the transcription of genes coding for proteins required for DNA replication and entrance into the S phase of the cell cycle.

E_A: see *activation energy.*

Eadie–Hofstee equation: alternative to the Lineweaver-Burk equation in which enzyme kinetic data are analyzed by plotting $v/[S]$ versus v.

early endosome: vesicles budding off the *trans*-Golgi network that are sites for the sorting and recycling of extracellular material brought into the cell by endocytosis.

EBV: see *Epstein-Barr virus.*

ECM: see *extracellular matrix.*

effector: see *allosteric effector.*

EGF: see *epidermal growth factor.*

egg (ovum): haploid female gamete, usually a relatively large cell with many stored nutrients.

EJC: see *exon junction complex.*

elastin: protein subunit of the elastic fibers that impart elasticity and flexibility to the extracellular matrix.

electrical excitability: ability to respond to certain types of stimuli with a rapid series of changes in membrane potential known as an action potential.

electrical potential (voltage): tendency of oppositely charged ions to flow toward each other.

electrical synapse: junction between two nerve cells where nerve impulses are transmitted by direct movement of ions through gap junctions without the involvement of chemical neurotransmitters.

electrical work: use of energy to transport ions across a membrane against a potential gradient.

electrochemical equilibrium: condition in which a transmembrane concentration gradient of a specific ion is balanced with an electrical potential across the same membrane, such that there is no net movement of the ion across the membrane.

electrochemical gradient: see *electrochemical potential.*

electrochemical potential: transmembrane gradient of an ion, with both an electrical component due to the charge separation quantified by the membrane potential and a concentration component; also called electrochemical gradient.

electrochemical proton gradient: transmembrane gradient of protons, with both an electrical component due to charge separation and a chemical component due to a difference in proton concentration (pH) across the membrane.

electron gun: assembly of several components that generates the electron beam in an electron microscope.

electron micrograph: photographic image of a specimen produced by the exposure of a photographic plate to the image-forming electron beam of an electron microscope.

electron microscope: instrument that uses a beam of electrons to visualize cellular

structures and thereby examine cellular architecture; the resolution is much greater than that of the light microscope, allowing detailed ultrastructural examination.

electron shuttle system: any of several mechanisms whereby electrons from a reduced coenzyme such as NADH are moved across a membrane; consists of one or more electron carriers that can be reversibly reduced, with transport proteins present in the membrane for both the oxidized and reduced forms of the carrier.

electron tomography: see *three-dimensional electron tomography.*

electron transport: process of coenzyme reoxidation under aerobic conditions, involving stepwise transfer of electrons to oxygen by means of a series of electron carriers.

electron transport system (ETS): group of membrane-bound electron carriers that transfer electrons from the coenzymes NADH and $FADH_2$ to oxygen.

electronegative: property of an atom that tends to draw electrons toward it.

electrophoresis: a group of related techniques that utilize an electrical field to separate electrically charged molecules.

elongation (of microtubules): growth of microtubules by addition of tubulin heterodimers to either end.

elongation factors: group of proteins that catalyze steps involved in the elongation phase of protein synthesis; examples include EF-Tu and EF-Ts.

embryonic stem (ES) cells: see *stem cells.*

Emerson enhancement effect: achievement of greater photosynthetic activity with red light of two slightly different wavelengths than is possible by summing the activities obtained with the individual wavelengths separately.

endergonic: an energy-requiring reaction characterized by a positive free energy change ($\Delta G > 0$).

endocytic vesicle: membrane vesicle formed by pinching off of a small segment of plasma membrane during the process of endocytosis.

endocytosis: uptake of extracellular materials by infolding of the plasma membrane, followed by pinching off of a membrane-bound vesicle containing extracellular fluid and materials.

endomembrane system: interconnected system of cytoplasmic membranes in eukaryotic cells composed of the endoplasmic reticulum, Golgi complex, endosomes, lysosomes, and nuclear envelope.

endonuclease: an enzyme that degrades a nucleic acid (usually DNA) by cutting the molecule internally. Also see *restriction endonuclease.*

endoplasmic reticulum (ER): network of interconnected membranes distributed throughout the cytoplasm and involved in the synthesis, processing, and transport of proteins in eukaryotic cells.

endosome: see *early endosome* or *late endosome.*

endosymbiont theory: theory postulating that mitochondria and chloroplasts arose from ancient bacteria that were ingested by ancestral eukaryotic cells about a billion years ago.

endothermic: a reaction or process that absorbs heat.

end-product inhibition: see *feedback inhibition.*

end-product repression: regulation of an anabolic pathway based on the ability of an end product to repress further synthesis of enzymes involved in production of that end product.

energy: capacity to do work; ability to cause specific changes.

energy transduction reactions: portion of the photosynthetic pathway in which light energy is converted to chemical energy in the form of ATP and the coenzyme NADPH, which subsequently provide energy and reducing power for the carbon assimilation reactions.

enhancer: DNA sequence containing a binding site for transcription factors that stimulates transcription and whose position and orientation relative to the promoter can vary significantly without interfering with the ability to regulate transcription.

enthalpy (H): the heat content of a substance, quantified as the sum of its internal energy, E, plus the product of pressure and volume: $H = E + PV$.

entropy (S): measure of the randomness or disorder in a system.

enzyme: biological catalyst; protein (or in certain cases, RNA) molecule that acts on one or more specific substrates, converting them to products with different molecular structures. Also see *ribozyme.*

enzyme catalysis: involvement of an organic molecule, usually a protein but in some cases RNA, in speeding up the rate of a specific chemical reaction or class of reactions. Also see *catalyst.*

enzyme kinetics: quantitative analysis of enzyme reaction rates and the manner in which they are influenced by a variety of factors.

epidermal growth factor (EGF): protein that stimulates the growth and division of a wide variety of epithelial cell types.

epigenetic change: alteration in the expression of a gene rather than a change in the structure of the gene itself.

EPSP: see *excitatory postsynaptic potential.*

Epstein–Barr virus (EBV): virus associated with Burkitt lymphoma (as well as the noncancerous condition, infectious mononucleosis).

equilibrium constant (K_{eq}): ratio of product concentrations to reactant concentrations for a given chemical reaction when the reaction has reached equilibrium.

equilibrium density (buoyant density) centrifugation: technique used to separate cellular components by subjecting them to centrifugation in a solution that increases in density from the top to the bottom of the centrifuge tube; during centrifugation, an organelle or molecule sediments to the density layer equal to its own density, at which point movement stops because no further net force acts on the material.

equilibrium (or reversal) potential: membrane potential that exactly offsets the effect of the concentration gradient for a given ion.

ER: see *endoplasmic reticulum.*

ER-associated degradation (ERAD): quality control mechanism in the ER that recognizes misfolded or unassembled proteins and exports or "retrotranslocates" them back across the ER membrane to the cytosol, where they are degraded by proteasomes.

ER cisterna (plural, cisternae): flattened sac of the endoplasmic reticulum.

ER lumen: the internal space enclosed by membranes of the endoplasmic reticulum.

ER signal sequence: amino acid sequence in a newly forming polypeptide chain that directs the ribosome-mRNA-polypeptide complex to the surface of the rough ER, where the complex becomes anchored.

ERAD: see *ER-associated degradation.*

ETS: see *electron transport system.*

euchromatin: loosely packed, uncondensed form of chromatin present during interphase;

contains DNA that is being actively transcribed. Also see *heterochromatin*.

eukarya: one of the three domains of organisms, the other two being bacteria and archaea; the domain consisting of one-celled and multicellular organisms called eukaryotes whose cells are characterized by a membrane-bounded nucleus and other membrane-bounded organelles.

eukaryote: category of organisms whose cells are characterized by the presence of a membrane-bounded nucleus and other membrane-bounded organelles; includes plants, animals, fungi, algae, and protozoa.

excision repair: DNA repair mechanism that removes and replaces abnormal nucleotides.

excitatory postsynaptic potential (EPSP): small depolarization of the postsynaptic membrane triggered by binding of an excitatory neurotransmitter to its receptor; if the EPSP exceeds a threshold level, it can trigger an action potential. Also see *inhibitory postsynaptic potential*.

exergonic: an energy-releasing reaction characterized by a negative free energy change ($\Delta G < 0$)

exit site: see *E site*.

exocytosis: fusion of vesicle membranes with the plasma membrane so that contents of the vesicle can be expelled or secreted to the extracellular environment.

exon: nucleotide sequence in a primary RNA transcript that is preserved in the mature, functional RNA molecule. Also see *intron*.

exon junction complex (EJC): protein complex deposited at exon-exon junctions created by pre-mRNA splicing.

exonuclease: an enzyme that degrades a nucleic acid (usually DNA) from one end, rather than cutting the molecule internally.

exosome: macromolecular complex involved in mRNA degradation in eukaryotic cells; contains multiple $3' \rightarrow 5'$ exonucleases.

exothermic: a reaction or process that releases heat.

exportin: nuclear receptor protein that binds to the nuclear export signal of proteins in the nucleus and then transports the bound protein out through the nuclear pore complex and into the cytosol.

extensin: group of related glycoproteins that form rigid, rodlike molecules tightly woven into the cell walls of plants and fungi.

extracellular digestion: degradation of components outside a cell, usually by lysosomal enzymes that are released from the cell by exocytosis.

extracellular matrix (ECM): material secreted by animal cells that fills the spaces between neighboring cells; consists of a mixture of structural proteins (e.g., collagen, elastin) and adhesive glycoproteins (e.g., fibronectin, laminin) embedded in a matrix composed of protein-polysaccharide complexes called proteoglycans.

F

F factor: DNA sequence that enables an *E. coli* cell to act as a DNA donor during bacterial conjugation.

F_1 complex: knoblike sphere protruding into the matrix from mitochondrial inner membranes (or into the cytosol from the bacterial plasma membrane) that contains the ATP-synthesizing site of aerobic respiration.

F_1 generation: offspring of the P_1 generation in a genetic breeding experiment.

F_2 generation: offspring of the F_1 generation in a genetic breeding experiment.

F2,6BP: see *fructose-2,6-bisphosphate*.

facilitated diffusion: membrane protein-mediated movement of a substance across a membrane that does not require energy because the ion or molecule being transported is moving down an electrochemical gradient.

F-actin: component of microfilaments consisting of G-actin monomers that have been polymerized into long, linear strands.

facultative heterochromatin: chromosomal regions that have become specifically condensed and inactivated in a particular cell type at a specific time. Also see *constitutive heterochromatin*.

facultative organism: organism that can function in either an anaerobic or aerobic mode.

FAD: see *flavin adenine dinucleotide*.

familial hypercholesterolemia (FH): genetic predisposition to high blood cholesterol levels and heart disease caused by an inherited defect in the gene coding for the LDL receptor.

fast axonal transport: microtubule-mediated movement of vesicles and organelles back and forth along a nerve cell axon.

fatty acid: long, unbranched hydrocarbon chain that has a carboxyl group at one end and is therefore amphipathic; usually contains an even number of carbon atoms and may be of varying degrees of unsaturation.

fatty acid-anchored membrane protein: protein located on a membrane surface that is covalently bound to a fatty acid embedded with the lipid bilayer.

Fd: see *ferredoxin*.

feedback (end-product) inhibition: ability of the end product of a biosynthetic pathway to inhibit the activity of the first enzyme in the pathway, thereby ensuring that the functioning of the pathway is sensitive to the intracellular concentration of its product.

fermentation: partial oxidation of carbohydrates by oxygen-independent (anaerobic) pathways, resulting often (but not always) in the production of either ethanol and carbon dioxide or lactate.

ferredoxin (Fd): iron-sulfur protein in the chloroplast stroma involved in the transfer of electrons from photosystem I to $NADP^+$ during the energy transduction reactions of photosynthesis.

ferredoxin-NADP$^+$ reductase (FNR): enzyme located on the stroma side of the thylakoid membrane that catalyzes the transfer of electrons from ferredoxin to $NADP^+$.

fertilization: union of two haploid gametes to form a diploid cell, the zygote, that develops into a new organism.

FGF: see *fibroblast growth factor*.

FH: see *familial hypercholesterolemia*.

fibroblast growth factor (FGF): any of several related signaling proteins that stimulate growth and cell division in fibroblasts as well as numerous other cell types, both in adults and during embryonic development.

fibronectin: adhesive glycoprotein found in the extracellular matrix and loosely associated with the cell surface; binds cells to the extracellular matrix and is important in determining cell shape and guiding cell migration.

fibrous protein: protein with extensive α helix or β sheet structure that confers a highly ordered, repetitive structure.

filopodium (plural, filopodia): thin, pointed cytoplasmic protrusion that transiently emerges from the surface of eukaryotic cells during cell movements.

first law of thermodynamics: law of conservation of energy; principle that energy can be converted from one form to another but can never be created or destroyed.

Fischer projection: model depicting the chemical structure of a molecule as a chain drawn vertically with the most oxidized atom on top and horizontal projections that are understood to be coming out of the plane of the paper.

fixative: chemical that kills cells while preserving their structural appearance for microscopic examination.

flagellum (plural, flagella): membrane-bounded appendage on the surface of a eukaryotic cell composed of a specific arrangement of microtubules and responsible for motility of the cell; longer and less numerous (usually limited to one or a few per cell) than closely related organelles called cilia. Also see *cilium*.

flavin adenine dinucleotide (FAD): coenzyme that accepts two electrons and two protons from an oxidizable organic molecule to generate the reduced form, FADH$_2$; important electron carrier in energy metabolism.

flavoprotein: protein that has a tightly bound flavin coenzyme (FAD or FMN) and that serves as a biological electron donor or acceptor. Several examples occur in the mitochondrial electron transport system.

flippase: see *phospholipid translocator*.

flow cytometry: technique for automated rapid analysis of cells stained with fluorescent dyes as they pass in a narrow stream through a laser beam.

fluid mosaic model: model for membrane structure consisting of a lipid bilayer with proteins associated as discrete globular entities that penetrate the bilayer to various extents and are free to move laterally in the membrane.

fluid-phase endocytosis: nonspecific uptake of extracellular fluid by infolding of the plasma membrane, followed by budding off of a membrane vesicle.

fluorescence: property of molecules that absorb light and then reemit the energy as light of a longer wavelength.

fluorescence microscopy: light microscopic technique that focuses ultraviolet rays on the specimen, thereby causing fluorescent compounds in the specimen to emit visible light.

fluorescence recovery after photobleaching: technique for measuring the lateral diffusion rate of membrane lipids or proteins in which such molecules are linked to a fluorescent dye and a tiny membrane region is then bleached with a laser.

fluorescence resonance energy transfer (FRET): an extremely short-distance interaction between two fluorescent molecules in which excitation is transferred from a donor molecule to an acceptor molecule directly; can be used to determine whether two molecules are in contact, or to produce "biosensors" that detect where proteins are activated or identify changes in local ion concentration.

fluorescent antibody: antibody containing covalently linked fluorescent dye molecules that allow the antibody to be used to locate antigen molecules microscopically.

FNR: see *ferredoxin-NADP$^+$ reductase*.

F$_0$ complex: group of hydrophobic membrane proteins that anchor the F$_1$ complex to either the inner mitochondrial membrane or the bacterial plasma membrane; serves as the proton translocator channel through which protons flow when the electrochemical gradient across the membrane is used to drive ATP synthesis.

F_oF_1 complex: protein complex in the mitochondrial inner membrane and the bacterial plasma membrane that consists of the F_1 complex bound to the F_o complex; the flow of protons through the F_o component leads to the synthesis of ATP by the F_1 component.

focal adhesion: localized points of attachment between cell surface integrin molecules and the extracellular matrix; contain clustered integrin molecules that interact with bundles of cytoskeletal actin microfilaments via several linker proteins.

focal length: distance between the midline of a lens and the point at which rays passing through the lens converge to a focus.

frameshift mutation: insertion or deletion of one or more base pairs in a DNA molecule, causing a change in the reading frame of the mRNA molecule that usually garbles the message.

free energy (G): thermodynamic function that measures the extractable energy content of a molecule; under conditions of constant temperature and pressure, the change in free energy is a measure of the system's ability to do work.

free energy change (ΔG): thermodynamic parameter used to quantify the net free energy liberated or required by a reaction or process; measure of thermodynamic spontaneity.

freeze etching: cleaving a quick-frozen specimen, as in freeze fracturing, followed by the subsequent sublimation of ice from the specimen surface to expose small areas of the true cell surface.

freeze fracturing: sample preparation technique for electron microscopy in which a frozen specimen is cleaved by a sharp blow followed by examination of the fractured surface, often the interior of a membrane.

FRET: see *fluorescence resonance energy transfer.*

fructose-2,6-bisphosphate (F2,6BP): a doubly phosphorylated fructose molecule, formed by the action of phosphofructokinase-2 on fructose-6-phosphate, that plays an important role in regulating both glycolysis and gluconeogenesis.

F-type ATPase: type of transport ATPase found in bacteria, mitochondria, and chloroplasts that can use the energy of ATP hydrolysis to pump protons against their electrochemical gradient; can also catalyze the reverse process, in which the exergonic flow of protons down their electrochemical gradient is used to drive ATP synthesis. Also see *ATP synthase.*

functional group: group of chemical elements covalently bonded to each other that confers characteristic chemical properties upon any molecule to which it is covalently linked.

G

G: see *guanine* or *free energy.*

ΔG: see *free energy change.*

$\Delta G^{o'}$: see *standard free energy change.*

G protein: any of numerous GTP-binding regulatory proteins located in the plasma membrane that mediate signal transduction pathways, usually by activating a specific target protein such as an enzyme or channel protein.

G protein-linked receptor family: group of plasma membrane receptors that activate a specific G protein upon binding of the appropriate ligand.

G protein-linked receptor kinase (GRK): any of several protein kinases that catalyze the phosphorylation of activated G protein-linked receptors, thereby leading to receptor desensitization.

G0 (G zero): designation applied to eukaryotic cells that have become arrested in the G1 phase of the cell cycle and thus are no longer proliferating.

G1 phase: stage of the eukaryotic cell cycle between the end of the previous division and the onset of chromosomal DNA synthesis.

G2 phase: stage of the eukaryotic cell cycle between the completion of chromosomal DNA replication and the onset of cell division.

G-actin: globular monomeric form of actin that polymerizes to form F-actin.

GAG: see *glycosaminoglycan.*

gamete: haploid cells produced by each parent that fuse together to form the diploid offspring; for example, sperm or egg.

gametogenesis: the process that produces gametes.

gametophyte: haploid generation in the life cycle of an organism that alternates between haploid and diploid forms; form that produces gametes.

gamma tubulin (γ-tubulin): form of tubulin located in the centrosome, where it functions in the nucleation of microtubules.

gamma tubulin ring complexes (γ-TuRCs): rings of γ-tubulin that emerge from centrosomes and nucleate the assembly of new microtubules.

gamma-TuRCs (γ-TuRCs): see *gamma tubulin ring complexes.*

ganglioside: a charged glycolipid containing the amino alcohol sphingosine and negatively charged sialic acid residues.

GAP: see *GTPase activating protein.*

gap junction: type of cell junction that provides a point of intimate contact between two adjacent cells through which ions and small molecules can pass.

gatekeeper gene: a tumor suppressor gene directly involved in restraining cell proliferation; loss-of-function mutations in such genes can lead to excessive cell proliferation and tumor formation.

Gb: gigabases; a billion base pairs

GEF: see *guanine-nucleotide exchange factor.*

gel electrophoresis: technique in which proteins or nucleic acids are separated in gels made of polyacrylamide or agarose by placing the gel in an electric field.

gene: "hereditary factor" that specifies an inherited trait; consists of a DNA base sequence that codes for the amino acid sequence of one or more polypeptide chains, or alternatively, for one of several types of RNA that perform functions other than coding for polypeptide chains (e.g., rRNA, tRNA, snRNA, or microRNA).

gene amplification: mechanism for creating extra copies of individual genes by selectively replicating specific DNA sequences.

gene conversion: phenomenon in which genes undergo nonreciprocal recombination during meiosis, such that one of the recombining genes ends up on both chromosomes of a homologous pair rather than being exchanged from one chromosome to the other.

gene deletion: selective removal within a cell of specific DNA sequences whose products are not required.

gene locus (plural, **loci**): location within a chromosome that contains the DNA sequence for a particular gene.

general transcription factor: a protein that is always required for RNA polymerase to bind to its promoter and initiate RNA synthesis, regardless of the identity of the gene involved.

genetic code: set of rules specifying the relationship between the sequence of bases in a DNA or mRNA molecule and the order of amino acids in the polypeptide chain encoded by that DNA or mRNA.

genetic engineering: application of recombinant DNA technology to practical problems, primarily in medicine and agriculture.

genetic instability: trait of cancer cells in which abnormally high mutation rates are caused by defects in DNA repair and/or chromosome sorting mechanisms.

genetic mapping: determining the sequential order and spacing of genes on a chromosome based on recombination frequencies.

genetic recombination: exchange of DNA segments between two different DNA molecules.

genetics: study of the behavior of genes, which are the chemical units involved in the storage and transmission of hereditary information.

genome: the DNA (or for some viruses, RNA) that contains one complete copy of all the genetic information of an organism or virus.

genomic control: a regulatory change in the makeup or structural organization of the genome.

genomic library: collection of recombinant DNA clones produced by cleaving an organism's entire genome into fragments, usually using restriction endonucleases, and then cloning all the fragments in an appropriate cloning vector.

genotype: genetic makeup of an organism.

globular protein: protein whose polypeptide chains are folded into compact structures rather than extended filaments.

glucagon: peptide hormone, produced by the islets of Langerhans in the pancreas, that acts to increase blood glucose by promoting the breakdown of glycogen.

gluconeogenesis: synthesis of glucose from precursors such as amino acids, glycerol, or lactate; occurs in the liver via a pathway that is essentially the reverse of glycolysis.

glucose: a six-carbon sugar that is widely used as the starting molecule in cellular energy metabolism.

glucose transporter (GLUT): membrane carrier protein responsible for the facilitated diffusion of glucose.

GLUT: see *glucose transporter.*

glycerol: three-carbon alcohol with a hydroxyl group on each carbon; serves as the backbone for triacylglycerols.

glycerol phosphate shuttle: mechanism for carrying electrons from cytosolic NADH into the mitochondrion, where the electrons are delivered to FAD in the respiratory complexes.

glycocalyx: carbohydrate-rich zone located at the outer boundary of many animal cells.

glycogen: highly branched storage polysaccharide in animal cells; consists of glucose repeating subunits linked by $\alpha(1 \rightarrow 4)$ bonds and $\alpha(1 \rightarrow 6)$ bonds.

glycolate pathway: light-dependent pathway that decreases the efficiency of photosynthesis by oxidizing reduced carbon compounds without capturing the released energy; occurs when oxygen substitutes for carbon dioxide in the reaction catalyzed by rubisco, thereby generating phosphoglycolate that is then converted to 3-phosphoglycerate in the peroxisome and mitochondrion; also called photorespiration.

glycolipid: lipid molecule containing a bound carbohydrate group.

glycolysis (glycolytic pathway): series of reactions by which glucose or some other monosaccharide is catabolized to pyruvate without the involvement of oxygen, generating two molecules of ATP per molecule of monosaccharide metabolized.

glycolytic pathway: see *glycolysis*.

glycoprotein: protein with one or more carbohydrate groups linked covalently to amino acid side chains.

glycosaminoglycan (GAG): polysaccharide constructed from a repeating disaccharide unit containing one sugar with an amino group and one sugar that usually has a negatively charged sulfate or carboxyl group; component of the extracellular matrix.

glycosidic bond: bond linking a sugar to another molecule, which may be another sugar molecule.

glycosylation: addition of carbohydrate side chains to specific amino acid residues of proteins, usually beginning in the lumen of the endoplasmic reticulum and completed in the Golgi complex.

glyoxylate cycle: modified version of the TCA cycle occurring in plant glyoxysomes; an anabolic pathway that converts two molecules of acetyl CoA to one molecule of succinate, thereby permitting the synthesis of carbohydrates from lipids.

glyoxysome: specialized type of plant peroxisome that contains some of the enzymes responsible for the conversion of stored fat to carbohydrate in germinating seeds.

Goldman equation: modification of the Nernst equation that calculates the resting membrane potential by adding together the effects of all relevant ions, each weighted for its relative permeability.

Golgi complex: stacks of flattened, disk-shaped membrane cisternae in eukaryotic cells that are important in the processing and packaging of secretory proteins and in the synthesis of complex polysaccharides.

golgin: one of a class of tethering proteins that connect vesicles to the Golgi and Golgi cisternae to each other.

GPI-anchored membrane protein: protein bound to the outer surface of the plasma membrane by linkage to glycosylphosphatidylinositol (GPI), a glycolipid found in the external monolayer of the plasma membrane.

grading: see *tumor grading*.

granum (plural, grana): stack of thylakoid membranes in a chloroplast.

green fluorescent protein (GFP): a protein that exhibits bright green fluorescence when exposed to blue light. Using genetic engineering techniques, GFP can be fused to non-fluorescent proteins, allowing them to be followed using fluorescence microscopy.

GRK: see *G protein-linked receptor kinase*.

group specificity: ability of an enzyme to act on any of a whole group of substrates as long as they possess some common structural feature.

group transfer reaction: chemical reaction that involves the movement of a chemical group from one molecule to another.

growth factor: any of a number of extracellular signaling proteins that stimulate cell division in specific types of target cells; examples include platelet-derived growth factor (PDGF) and epidermal growth factor (EGF).

GTPase activating protein (GAP): a protein that speeds up the inactivation of Ras by facilitating the hydrolysis of bound GTP.

guanine (G): nitrogen-containing aromatic base, chemically designated as a purine, which serves as an informational monomeric unit when present in nucleic acids with other bases in a specific sequence; forms a complementary base pair with cytosine (C) by hydrogen bonding.

guanine-nucleotide exchange factor (GEF): a protein that triggers the release of GDP from the Ras protein, thereby permitting Ras to acquire a molecule of GTP.

gyrase: see *DNA gyrase*.

H

H: see *enthalpy*.

H zone: light region located in the middle of the A band of striated muscle myofibrils.

hairpin loop: looped structure formed when two adjacent segments of a nucleic acid chain are folded back on one another and held in that conformation by base pairing between complementary base sequences.

haploid: containing a single set of chromosomes and therefore a single copy of the genome; can describe a cell, nucleus, or organism composed of such cells.

haploid spore: haploid product of meiosis in organisms that display an alternation of generations; gives rise upon spore germination to the haploid form of the organism (the gametophyte, in the case of higher plants).

haplotype: group of SNPs located near one another on the same chromosome that tend to be inherited as a unit.

HAT: see *histone acetyl transferase*.

Hatch–Slack cycle: series of reactions in C₄ plants in which carbon dioxide is fixed in the mesophyll cells and transported as a four-carbon compound to the bundle sheath cells, where subsequent decarboxylation results in a higher concentration of carbon dioxide and therefore a higher rate of carbon fixation by rubisco.

Haworth projection: model that depicts the chemical structure of a molecule in a way that suggests the spatial relationship of different parts of the molecule.

HCI: see *heme-controlled inhibitor*.

HDL: see *high-density lipoprotein*.

heart muscle: see *cardiac muscle*.

heat: transfer of energy as a result of a temperature difference.

heat-shock gene: gene whose transcription is activated when cells are exposed to elevated temperatures or other stressful conditions; some heat-shock genes code for molecular chaperones that, in addition to guiding normal protein folding, can facilitate the refolding of heat-damaged proteins.

heat-shock response element: DNA base sequence located adjacent to heat-shock genes that functions as a binding site for the heat-shock transcription factor.

helicase: see *DNA helicase*.

helix: see *alpha helix* or *double helix*.

helix-loop-helix: DNA-binding motif found in transcription factors that is composed of a short α helix connected by a loop to a longer α helix.

helix-turn-helix: DNA-binding motif found in many regulatory transcription factors; consists of two regions of α helix separated by a bend in the polypeptide chain.

hemicellulose: heterogeneous group of polysaccharides deposited along with cellulose in the cell walls of plants and fungi to provide added strength; each consists of a long, linear chain of a single kind of sugar with short side chains.

hemidesmosome: point of attachment between cell surface integrin molecules of epithelial cells and the basal lamina; contains integrin molecules that are anchored via linker proteins to intermediate filaments of the cytoskeleton.

heterochromatin: highly compacted form of chromatin present during interphase; contains DNA that is not being transcribed. Also see *euchromatin*.

heterodimer (αβ-heterodimer): see *alpha beta heterodimer*.

heterophagic lysosome: mature lysosome containing hydrolytic enzymes involved in the digestion of materials of extracellular origin. Also see *autophagic lysosome*.

heterophilic interaction: binding of two different molecules to each other. Also see *homophilic interaction*.

heterozygous: having two different alleles for a given gene. Also see *homozygous*.

Hfr cell: bacterial cell in which the F factor has become integrated into the bacterial chromosome, allowing the cell to transfer genomic DNA during conjugation.

hierarchical assembly: synthesis of biological structures from simple starting molecules to progressively more complex structures, usually by self-assembly.

high-density lipoprotein (HDL): cholesterol-containing protein-lipid complex that transports cholesterol through the bloodstream and is taken up by cells; exhibits high density because of its low cholesterol content.

high-voltage electron microscope (HVEM): an electron microscope that uses accelerating voltages up to a thousand or more kilovolts, thereby allowing the examination of thicker samples than is possible with a conventional electron microscope.

histone: class of basic proteins found in eukaryotic chromosomes; an octamer of histones forms the core of nucleosomes.

histone acetyltransferase (HAT): enzyme that catalyzes the addition of acetyl groups to histones.

histone deacetylase (HDAC): enzyme that catalyzes removal of acetyl groups from histones.

Holliday junction: X-shaped structure produced when two DNA molecules are joined together by single-strand crossovers during genetic recombination.

homeobox: highly conserved DNA sequence found in homeotic genes; codes for a DNA-binding protein domain present in transcription factors that are important regulators of gene expression during development.

homeodomain: amino acid sequence, about 60 amino acids long, found in transcription factors encoded by homeotic genes; contains a helix-turn-helix DNA-binding motif.

homeotic gene: family of genes that control formation of the body plan during embryonic development; they code for transcription factors possessing homeodomains.

homeoviscous adaptation: alterations in membrane lipid composition that keep the viscosity of membranes approximately the same despite changes in environmental temperature.

homogenate: suspension of cell organelles, smaller cellular components, and molecules produced by disrupting cells or tissues using techniques such as grinding, ultrasonic vibration, or osmotic shock.

homogenization: disruption of cells or tissues using techniques such as grinding, ultrasonic vibration, or osmotic shock.

homologous chromosomes: two copies of a specific chromosome, one derived from each parent, that pair with each other and exchange genetic information during meiosis.

homologous recombination: exchange of genetic information between two DNA molecules exhibiting extensive sequence similarity; also used in repairing double-strand DNA breaks.

homophilic interaction: binding of two identical molecules to each other. Also see *heterophilic interaction.*

homozygous: having two identical alleles for a given gene. Also see *heterozygous.*

hormone: chemical that is synthesized in one organ, secreted into the blood, and able to cause a physiological change in cells or tissues of another organ.

hormone response element: DNA base sequence that selectively binds to a hormone-receptor complex, resulting in the activation (or inhibition) of transcription of nearby genes.

HPV: see *human papillomavirus.*

human papillomavirus (HPV): virus responsible for cervical cancer; possesses oncogenes that block the actions of the proteins produced by the *RB* and *p53* tumor suppressor genes.

HVEM: see *high-voltage electron microscope.*

hyaluronate: a glycosaminoglycan found in high concentration in the extracellular matrix where cells are actively proliferating or migrating, and in the joints between movable bones.

hybrid: product of the cross of two genetically different parents.

hybridization: see *nucleic acid hybridization.*

hydrocarbon: an organic molecule consisting only of carbon and hydrogen atoms; not generally compatible with living cells.

hydrogen bond: weak attractive interaction between an electronegative atom and a hydrogen atom that is covalently linked to a second electronegative atom.

hydrogenation: addition of electrons plus hydrogen ions (protons) to an organic molecule; reduction.

hydrolysis: reaction in which a chemical bond is broken by the addition of a water molecule.

hydropathy index: a value representing the average of the hydrophobicity values for a short stretch of contiguous amino acids within a protein.

hydropathy (hydrophobicity) plot: graph showing the location of hydrophobic amino acid clusters within the primary sequence of a protein molecule; used to determine the likely locations of transmembrane segments within integral membrane proteins.

hydrophilic: describing molecules or regions of molecules that readily associate with or dissolve in water because of a preponderance of polar groups; "water-loving."

hydrophobic: describing molecules or regions of molecules that are poorly soluble in water because of a preponderance of nonpolar groups; "water-hating."

hydrophobic interaction: tendency of hydrophobic groups to be excluded from interactions with water molecules.

hydrophobicity plot: see *hydropathy plot.*

hydroxylation: chemical reaction in which a hydroxyl group is added to an organic molecule.

hyperpolarization (undershoot): state in which the membrane potential is more negative than the normal membrane potential.

hypothesis: a statement or explanation that is consistent with most of the observational and experimental evidence to date.

I

I band: region of a striated muscle myofibril that appears as a light band when viewed by microscopy; contains those regions of the thin actin filaments that do not overlap the thick myosin filaments.

IF: see *intermediate filament.*

IgSF: see *immunoglobulin superfamily.*

immunoelectron microscopy (immunoEM): electron microscopic technique for visualizing antibodies within cells by linking them to substances that are electron dense and therefore visible as opaque dots.

immunoEM: see *immunoelectron microscopy.*

immunoglobulin superfamily (IgSF): family of cell surface proteins involved in cell-cell adhesion that are structurally related to the immunoglobulin subunits of antibody molecules.

immunostaining: technique in which antibodies are labeled with a fluorescent dye to enable them to be identified and localized microscopically based on their fluorescence.

immunotherapy: treatment of a disease, such as cancer, by stimulating the immune system or administering antibodies made by the immune system.

IMP: see *intramembranous particle.*

importin: receptor protein that binds to the nuclear localization signal of proteins in the cytosol and then transports the bound protein through the nuclear pore complex and into the nucleus.

imprinting: a process that causes some genes to be expressed differently depending on whether they are inherited from a person's mother or father; such behavior can be caused by differences in DNA methylation.

indirect active transport: membrane transport involving the cotransport of two solutes in which the movement of one solute down its gradient drives the movement of the other solute up its gradient.

indirect immunofluorescence: type of fluorescence microscopy in which a specimen is first exposed to an unlabeled antibody that attaches to specific antigenic sites within the specimen and is then stained with a secondary, fluorescent antibody that binds to the first antibody.

induced-fit model: model postulating that the active site of an enzyme is relatively specific for its substrate before it binds, but even more so thereafter because of a conformational change in the enzyme induced by the substrate.

induced pluripotent stem (IPS) cells: differentiated cells forced to express transcription factor proteins found in embryonic stem cells, allowing them to become many different types of cells

inducer: any effector molecule that activates the transcription of an inducible operon.

inducible enzyme: enzyme whose synthesis is regulated by the presence or absence of its substrate.

inducible operon: group of adjoining genes whose transcription is activated in the presence of an inducer.

informational macromolecule: polymer of non-identical subunits ordered in a nonrandom sequence that stores and transmits information important to the function or utilization of the macromolecule; DNA and RNA are informational macromolecules.

inhibition (of enzyme activity): decreasing the catalytic activity of an enzyme, either by a change in conformation or by chemical modification of one of its functional groups.

inhibitory postsynaptic potential (IPSP): small hyperpolarization of the postsynaptic membrane triggered by binding of an inhibitory neurotransmitter to its receptor, thereby reducing the amplitude of subsequent excitatory postsynaptic potentials and possibly preventing the firing of an action potential. Also see *excitatory postsynaptic potential.*

initial reaction velocity (v): Reaction rate measured over a period of time during which the substrate concentration has not decreased enough to affect the rate and the accumulation of product is still too small to cause any measurable back reaction.

initiation complex (30S): complex formed by the association of mRNA, the 30S ribosomal subunit, an initiator aminoacyl tRNA molecule, and initiation factor IF2.

initiation complex (70S): complex formed by the association of a 30S initiation complex with a 50S ribosomal subunit; contains an initiator aminoacyl tRNA at the P site and is ready to commence mRNA translation.

initiation factors: group of proteins that promote the binding of ribosomal subunits to mRNA and initiator tRNA, thereby initiating the process of protein synthesis.

initiation (stage of carcinogenesis): irreversible conversion of a cell to a precancerous state by agents that cause DNA mutation.

initiator (Inr): short DNA sequence surrounding the transcription startpoint that forms part of the promoter for RNA polymerase II.

initiator tRNA: type of transfer RNA molecule that starts the process of translation; recognizes the AUG start codon and carries formylmethionine in prokaryotes or methionine in eukaryotes.

inner membrane: the inner of the two membranes that surround a mitochondrion, chloroplast, or nucleus.

inositol-1,4,5-trisphosphate (IP$_3$): triply phosphorylated inositol molecule formed as a product of the cleavage of phosphatidylinositol-4,5-bisphosphate catalyzed by phospholipase C; functions as a second messenger by triggering the release of calcium ions from storage sites within the endoplasmic reticulum.

Inr: see *initiator.*

insertional mutagenesis: change in gene structure or activity resulting from the integration of DNA derived from another source, usually a virus.

insulin: peptide hormone, produced by the islets of Langerhans in the pancreas, that acts to decrease blood glucose by stimulating glucose uptake into muscle and adipose cells and by stimulating glycogen synthesis.

integral membrane protein: hydrophobic protein localized within the interior of a membrane but possessing hydrophilic regions that protrude from one or both membrane surfaces.

integral monotopic protein: an integral membrane protein embedded in only one side of the lipid bilayer.

integrin: any of several plasma membrane receptors that bind to extracellular matrix components at the outer membrane surface and interact with cytoskeletal components at the inner membrane surface; includes receptors for fibronectin, laminin, and collagen.

intercalated disc: membrane partition enriched in gap junctions that divides cardiac muscle into separate cells containing single nuclei.

interdoublet link: link between adjacent doublets in the axoneme of a eukaryotic cilium or flagellum; believed to limit the extent of doublet movement with respect to each other as the axoneme bends.

interference: process by which two or more waves of light combine to reinforce or cancel one another, producing a wave equal to the sum of the combining waves.

intermediate filament (IF): group of protein filaments that are the most stable components of the cytoskeleton of eukaryotic cells; exhibits a diameter of 8–12 nm, which is intermediate between the diameters of actin microfilaments and microtubules.

intermediate lens (electron microscope): electromagnetic lens positioned between the objective and projector lenses in a transmission electron microscope.

intermediate lens (light microscope): lens positioned between the ocular and objective lenses in a light microscope.

intermembrane space: region of a mitochondrion or chloroplast between the inner and outer membranes.

internal energy (E): total energy stored within a system; cannot be measured directly, but the change in internal energy, ΔE, is measurable.

interphase: growth phase of the eukaryotic cell cycle situated between successive division phases (M phases); composed of G1, S, and G2 phases.

interspersed repeated DNA: repeated DNA sequences whose multiple copies are scattered around the genome.

intracellular membrane: any cellular membrane internal to the plasma membrane; suchmembranes serve to compartmentalize functions within eukaryotic cells.

intraflagellar transport (IFT): movement of components to and from the tips of flagella driven by both plus- and minus-end directed microtubule motor proteins.

intramembranous particle (IMP): integral membrane protein that is visible as a particle when the interior of a membrane is visualized by freeze-fracture microscopy.

intron: nucleotide sequence in an RNA molecule that is part of the primary transcript but not the mature, functional RNA molecule. Also see *exon*.

invasion: direct spread of cancer cells into neighboring tissues.

inverted repeat: DNA segment containing two copies of the same base sequence oriented in opposite directions.

ion channel: membrane protein that allows the passage of specific ions through the membrane; generally regulated by either changes in membrane potential (voltage-gated channels) or binding of a specific ligand (ligand-gated channels).

ionic bond: attractive force between a positively charged chemical group and a negatively charged chemical group.

ionizing radiation: high-energy forms of radiation that remove electrons from molecules, thereby generating highly reactive ions that cause DNA damage; includes X-rays and radiation emitted by radioactive elements.

IP$_3$: see *inositol-1,4,5-trisphosphate*.

IP$_3$ receptor: ligand-gated calcium channel in the ER membrane that opens when bound to IP$_3$, allowing calcium ions to flow from the ER lumen into the cytosol.

IPSP: see *inhibitory postsynaptic potential*.

IRE: see *iron-response element*.

iron-response element (IRE): short base sequence found in mRNAs whose translation or stability is controlled by iron; binding site for an IRE-binding protein.

iron-sulfur protein: protein that contains iron and sulfur atoms complexed with four cysteine groups and that serves as an electron carrier in the electron transport system.

irreversible inhibitor: molecule that binds to an enzyme covalently, causing an irrevocable loss of catalytic activity.

isoenzyme: any of several, physically distinct proteins that catalyze the same reaction.

isoprenylated membrane protein: protein located on a membrane surface that is covalently bound to a prenyl group embedded within the lipid bilayer.

J

J: see *joule*.

Jak: see *Janus activated kinase*.

Janus kinase (Jak): cytoplasmic protein kinase that, after activation by cell surface receptors, catalyzes the phosphorylation and activation of STAT transcription factors.

joule (J): a unit of energy corresponding to 0.239 calories.

K

karyotype: picture of the complete set of chromosomes for a particular cell type, organized as homologous pairs arranged on the basis of differences in size and shape.

Kb: kilobases; a thousand base pairs

k$_{cat}$: see *turnover number*.

K$_d$: see *dissociation constant*.

K$_{eq}$: see *equilibrium constant*.

kilocalorie (kcal): unit of energy; 1 kcal = 1000 calories.

kinesin: family of motor proteins that generate movement along microtubules using energy derived from ATP hydrolysis.

kinetochore: multiprotein complex located at the centromere region of a chromosome thatprovides the attachment site for spindle microtubules during mitosis or meiosis.

kinetochore microtubule: spindle microtubule that attaches to chromosomal kinetochores.

K$_m$: see *Michaelis constant*.

Knockout mice: Mice that have been genetically engineered to contain a deletion of DNA sequences in a particular gene using homologous recombination in embryonic stem cells.

Krebs cycle: see *tricarboxylic acid cycle*.

L

lac operon: group of adjoining bacterial genes that code for enzymes involved in lactose metabolism and whose transcription is inhibited by the *lac* repressor.

lactate fermentation: anaerobic catabolism of carbohydrates with lactate as the end product.

lagging strand: strand of DNA that grows in the $3' \rightarrow 5'$ direction during DNA replication by discontinuous synthesis of short fragments in the $5' \rightarrow 3'$ direction, followed by ligation of adjacent fragments. Also see *leading strand*.

lamellipodium (plural, lamellipodia): thin sheet of flattened cytoplasm that transiently protrudes from the surface of eukaryotic cells during cell crawling; supported by actin filaments.

laminin: adhesive glycoprotein of the extracellular matrix, localized predominantly in the basal lamina of epithelial cells.

large ribosomal subunit: component of a ribosome with a sedimentation coefficient of 60S in eukaryotes and 50S in prokaryotes; associates with a small ribosomal subunit to form a functional ribosome.

late endosome: vesicle containing newly synthesized acid hydrolases plus material fated for digestion; activated either by lowering the pH of the late endosome or transferring its material to an existing lysosome.

lateral diffusion: diffusion of a membrane lipid or protein in the plane of the membrane.

latrunculin A: chemical compound derived from marine sponges that causes depolymerization of actin microfilaments.

law: a theory that has been so thoroughly tested and confirmed over a long period of time by a large number of investigators that virtually no doubt remains as to its validity.

law of independent assortment: principle stating that the alleles of each gene separate independently of the alleles of other genes during gamete formation.

law of segregation: principle stating that the alleles of each gene separate from each other during gamete formation.

LDL: see *low-density lipoprotein*.

LDL receptor: plasma membrane protein that serves as a receptor for binding extracellular LDL, which is then taken into the cell by receptor-mediated endocytosis.

leading strand: strand of DNA that grows as a continuous chain in the $5' \rightarrow 3'$ direction during DNA replication. Also see *lagging strand*.

leaf peroxisome: special type of peroxisome found in the leaves of photosynthetic plant cells that contains some of the enzymes involved in photorespiration.

lectin: any of numerous carbohydrate-binding proteins that can be isolated from plant or animal cells and that promote cell-cell adhesion.

leptotene: first stage of prophase I of meiosis, characterized by condensation of chromatin fibers into visible chromosomes.

leucine zipper: DNA-binding motif found in many transcription factors; formed by an interaction between α helices in two polypeptide chains that are "zippered" together by hydrophobic interactions between leucine residues.

leukemia: cancer of blood or lymphatic origin in which the cancer cells proliferate and reside mainly in the bloodstream rather than growing as solid masses of tissue.

LHC: see *light-harvesting complex*.

LHCI: see *light-harvesting complex I*.

LHCII: see *light-harvesting complex II*.

licensing: process of making DNA competent for replication; normally occurs only once per cell cycle.

ligand: substance that binds to a specific receptor, thereby initiating the particular event or series of events for which that receptor is responsible.

ligand-gated ion channel: an integral membrane protein that forms an ion-conducting pore that opens when a specific molecule (ligand) binds to the channel.

light microscope: instrument consisting of a source of visible light and a system of glass lenses that allows an enlarged image of a specimen to be viewed.

light-harvesting complex (LHC): collection of light-absorbing pigments, usually chlorophylls and carotenoids, linked together by proteins; unlike a photosystem, does not contain a reaction center, but absorbs photons of light and funnels the energy to a nearby photosystem.

light-harvesting complex I (LHCI): the light-harvesting complex associated with photosystem I.

light-harvesting complex II (LHCII): the light-harvesting complex associated with photosystem II.

lignin: insoluble polymers of aromatic alcohols that occur mainly in woody plant tissues, where they contribute to the hardening of the cell wall and the structural strength we associate with wood.

limit of resolution: measurement of how far apart adjacent objects must be in order to be distinguished as separate entities.

LINEs (long interspersed nuclear elements): class of interspersed repeated DNA sequences 6000–8000 base pairs in length that function as transposable elements and account for roughly 20% of the human genome; contain genes coding for enzymes needed for copying LINE sequences (and other mobile elements) and inserting the copies elsewhere in the genome.

Lineweaver-Burk equation: linear equation obtained by inverting the Michaelis-Menten equation, useful in determining parameters V_{max} and K_m and in the analysis of enzyme inhibition.

linkage group: group of genes that are transmitted, inherited, and assorted together.

linked genes: genes that are usually inherited together because they are located relatively close to each other on the same chromosome.

lipid: any of a large and chemically diverse class of organic compounds that are poorly soluble or insoluble in water but soluble in organic solvents.

lipid bilayer: unit of membrane structure, consisting of two layers of lipid molecules (mainly phospholipid) arranged so that their hydrophobic tails face toward each other and the polar region of each faces the aqueous environment on one side or the other of the bilayer.

lipid raft: localized region of membrane lipids, often characterized by elevated levels of cholesterol and glycosphingolipids, that sequester proteins involved in cell signaling; also called lipid microdomain.

lipid-anchored membrane protein: protein located on a membrane surface that is covalently bound to one or more lipid molecules residing within the lipid bilayer. Also see *fatty acid-anchored membrane protein, prenylated membrane protein,* and *GPI-anchored membrane protein.*

looped domain: folding of a 30-nm chromatin fiber into loops 50,000–100,000 bp in length by periodic attachment of the DNA to an insoluble network of nonhistone proteins.

low-density lipoprotein (LDL): cholesterol-containing protein-lipid complex that transports cholesterol through the bloodstream and is taken up by cells; exhibits low density because of its high cholesterol content.

lumen: internal space enclosed by a membrane, usually the endoplasmic reticulum or related membrane systems.

lymphoma: cancer of lymphatic origin in which the cancer cells grow as solid masses of tissue.

lysosomal storage disease: disease resulting from a deficiency of one or more lysosomal enzymes and characterized by the undesirable accumulation of excessive amounts of specific substances that would normally be degraded by the deficient enzymes.

lysosome: membrane-bounded organelle containing digestive enzymes capable of degrading all the major classes of biological macromolecules.

M

M line: dark line running down the middle of the H zone of a striated muscle myofibril.

M phase: stage of the eukaryotic cell cycle when the nucleus and the rest of the cell divide.

macromolecule: polymer built from small repeating monomer units, with molecular weights ranging from a few thousand to hundreds of millions.

macrophagy: process by which an organelle becomes wrapped in a double membrane derived from the endoplasmic reticulum, creating an autophagic vacuole that acquires lysosomal enzymes which degrade the organelle.

malignant tumor: tumor that can invade neighboring tissues and spread through the body via fluids, especially the bloodstream, to other parts of the body; also called a cancer.

MAP: see *microtubule-associated protein.*

MAP kinase: see *mitogen-activated protein kinase.*

MAPK: see *mitogen-activated protein kinase.*

mass spectrometry: high-speed, extremely sensitive technique that uses magnetic and electric fields to separate proteins or protein fragments based on differences in mass and charge.

MAT locus: site in the yeast genome where the active allele for mating type resides.

mating bridge: transient cytoplasmic connection through which DNA is transferred from a male bacterial cell to a female cell during conjugation.

mating type: equivalent of sexuality (male or female) in lower organisms, where the molecular properties of a gamete determine the type of gamete it can fuse with.

matrix: unstructured semifluid substance that fills the interior of a mitochondrion.

maximum ATP yield: maximum amount of ATP produced per molecule of glucose oxidized by aerobic respiration; usually 38 molecules of ATP for prokaryotic cells and either 36 or 38 for eukaryotic cells.

maximum velocity (V_{max}): upper limiting reaction rate approached by an enzyme-catalyzed reaction as the substrate concentration approaches infinity.

Mb: megabases; a million base pairs.

MDR: see *multidrug resistance transport protein.*

mechanical work: use of energy to bring about a physical change in the position or orientation of a cell or some part of it.

mechanoenzyme: see *motor protein.*

medial cisterna: flattened membrane sac of the Golgi complex located between the membrane tubules of the *cis*-Golgi network and the *trans*-Golgi network.

Mediator: large multiprotein complex that functions as a transcriptional coactivator by binding both to activator proteins associated with an enhancer and to RNA polymerase; acts as a central coordinating unit of gene regulation, receiving both positive and negative inputs and transmitting the information to the transcription machinery.

meiosis: series of two cell divisions, preceded by a single round of DNA replication, that converts a single diploid cell into four haploid cells (or haploid nuclei).

meiosis I: the first meiotic division, which produces two haploid cells with chromosomes composed of sister chromatids.

meiosis II: the second meiotic division, which separates the sister chromatids of the haploid cell generated by the first meiotic division.

membrane: permeability barrier surrounding and delineating cells and organelles; consists of a lipid bilayer with associated proteins.

membrane asymmetry: a membrane property based on differences between the molecular compositions of the two lipid monolayers and the proteins associated with each.

membrane potential: voltage across a membrane created by ion gradients; usually the inside of a cell is negatively charged with respect to the outside.

Mendel's laws of inheritance: principles derived by Mendel from his work on the inheritance of traits in pea plants. . Also see *law of segregation* and *law of independent assortment.*

mesophyll cell: outer cell in the leaf of a C_4 plant that serves as the site of carbon fixation by the Hatch-Slack cycle.

messenger RNA (mRNA): RNA molecule containing the information that specifies the amino acid sequence of one or more polypeptides.

metabolic pathway: series of cellular enzymatic reactions that convert one molecule to another via a series of intermediates.

metabolism: all chemical reactions occurring within a cell.

metaphase: stage during mitosis or meiosis when the chromosomes become aligned at the spindle equator.

metastable state: condition where potential reactants are thermodynamically unstable but have insufficient energy to exceed the activation energy barrier for the reaction.

metastasis: spread of tumor cells to distant organs via the bloodstream or other body fluids.

MF: see *microfilament.*

Michaelis constant (K_m): substrate concentration at which an enzyme-catalyzed reaction is proceeding at one-half of its maximum velocity.

Michaelis-Menten equation: widely used equation describing the relationship between velocity and substrate concentration for an enzyme-catalyzed reaction:
$V = V_{max}[S]/(K_m + [S])$.

microautophagy: process by which lysosomes take up and degrade cytosolic proteins.

microfibril: aggregate of several dozen cellulose molecules laterally crosslinked by hydrogen bonds; serves as a structural component of plant and fungal cell walls.

microfilament (MF): polymer of actin, with a diameter of about 7 nm, that is an integral part of the cytoskeleton, contributing to the support, shape, and mobility of eukaryotic cells.

micrometer (μm): unit of measure: 1 micrometer $= 10^{-6}$ meters.

microphagy: process by which small bits of cytoplasm are surrounded by ER membrane to form an autophagic vesicle whose contents are then digested either by accumulation of lysosomal enzymes or by fusion of the vesicle with a late endosome.

microRNA (miRNA): class of single-stranded RNAs, about 21–22 nucleotides long, produced by cellular genes for the purpose of inhibiting the translation of mRNAs produced by other genes.

microsome: vesicle formed by fragments of endoplasmic reticulum when tissue is homogenized.

microtome: instrument used to slice an embedded biological specimen into thin sections for light microscopy.

microtubule (MT): polymer of the protein tubulin, with a diameter of about 25 nm, that is an integral part of the cytoskeleton and that contributes to the support, shape, and motility of eukaryotic cells; also found in eukaryotic cilia and flagella.

microtubule-associated protein (MAP): any of various accessory proteins that bind to microtubules and modulate their assembly, structure, and/or function.

microtubule-organizing center (MTOC): structure that initiates the assembly of microtubules, the primary example being the centrosome.

microvillus (plural, **microvilli**): fingerlike projection from the cell surface that increases membrane surface area; important in cells that have an absorption function, such as those that line the intestine.

middle lamella: first layer of the plant cell wall to be synthesized; ends up farthest away from the plasma membrane, where it functions to hold adjacent cells together.

minus end (of microtubule): slower-growing (or non-growing or shrinking) end of a microtubule.

miRISC: complex between microRNA and several proteins that together silence the expression of messenger RNAs containing sequences complementary to those of the microRNA. . Also see *siRISC* and *RISC*.

miRNA: see *microRNA*.

mismatch repair: DNA repair mechanism that detects and corrects base pairs that are improperly hydrogen-bonded.

mitochondrion (plural, **mitochondria**): double membrane-enclosed cytoplasmic organelle of eukaryotic cells that is the site of aerobic respiration and hence of ATP generation.

mitogen-activated protein kinase (MAP kinase, or MAPK): a family of protein kinases that are activated when cells receive a signal to grow and divide.

mitosis: process by which two genetically identical daughter nuclei are produced from one nucleus as the duplicated chromosomes of the parent cell segregate into separate nuclei; usually followed by cell division.

mitotic index: percentage of cells in a population that are in any stage of mitosis at a certain point in time; used to estimate the relative length of the M phase of the cell cycle.

mitotic spindle: microtubular structure responsible for separating chromosomes during mitosis.

mitotic spindle checkpoint: mechanism that halts mitosis at the junction between metaphase and anaphase if chromosomes are not properly attached to the spindle.

MLCK: see *myosin light-chain kinase*.

model organism: an organism that is widely studied, well characterized, easy to manipulate, and has particular advantages for various experimental studies; examples include *E. coli*, yeast, *Drosophila, C. elegans, Arabipsis,* and mice

molecular chaperone: a protein that facilitates the folding of other proteins but is not acomponent of the final folded structure.

molecular targeting: development of drugs designed to specifically target molecules that are critical to cancer cells.

monoclonal antibody: a highly purified antibody, directed against a single antigen, that is produced by a cloned population of antibody-producing cells.

monomer: small organic molecule that serves as a subunit in the assembly of a macromolecule.

monomeric protein: protein that consists of a single polypeptide chain.

monosaccharide: simple sugar; the repeating unit of polysaccharides.

motif: region of protein secondary structure consisting of small segments of α helix and/or β sheet connected by looped regions of varying length.

motility (cellular): movement or shortening of a cell, movement of components within a cell, or movement of environmental components past or through a cell.

motor protein (mechanoenzyme): protein that uses energy derived from ATP to change shape in a way that exerts force and causes attached structures to move; includes three families of proteins (myosin, dynein, and kinesin) that interact with cytoskeletal elements (microtubules and microfilaments) to produce movements.

MPF: a mitotic Cdk-cyclin complex that drives progression from G2 into mitosis by phosphorylating proteins involved in key stages of mitosis.

mRNA: see *messenger RNA*.

mRNA-binding site: place on the ribosome where mRNA binds during protein synthesis.

MT: see *microtubule*.

MTOC: see *microtubule-organizing center*.

multidrug resistance (MDR) transport protein: an ABC-type ATPase that uses the energy of ATP hydrolysis to pump hydrophobic drugs out of cells.

multimeric protein: protein that consists of two or more polypeptide chains.

multiphoton excitation microscopy: specialized type of fluorescence light microscope employing a laser beam that emits rapid pulses of light; images are similar in sharpness to confocal microscopy, but photodamage is minimized because there is little out-of-focus light.

multiprotein complex: two or more proteins (usually enzymes) bound together in a way that allows each protein to play a sequential role in the same multistep process.

muscle contraction: generation of tension in muscle cells by the sliding of thin (actin) filaments past thick (myosin) filaments.

muscle fiber: long, thin, multinucleate cell specialized for contraction.

mutagen: chemical or physical agent capable of inducing mutations.

mutation: change in the base sequence of a DNA molecule.

myelin sheath: concentric layers of membrane that surround an axon and serve as electrical insulation that allows rapid transmission of nerve impulses.

myofibril: cylindrical structure composed of an organized array of thin actin filaments and thick myosin filaments; found in the cytoplasm of skeletal muscle cells.

myosin: family of motor proteins that create movements by exerting force on actin microfilaments using energy derived from ATP hydrolysis; makes up the thick filaments that move the actin thin filaments during muscle contraction.

myosin light-chain kinase (MLCK): enzyme that phosphorylates myosin light chains, thereby triggering smooth muscle contraction.

myosin subfragment 1 (S1): proteolytic fragment of myosin that binds to actin microfilaments in a way that yields a distinctive arrowhead pattern, with all the S1 molecules pointing in the same direction.

N

NA: see *numerical aperture*.

Na$^+$/glucose symporter: a membrane transport protein that simultaneously transports glucose and sodium ions into cells, with the movement of sodium ions down their electrochemical gradient driving the transport of glucose against its concentration gradient.

Na$^+$/K$^+$ ATPase: see *Na$^+$/K$^+$ pump*.

Na$^+$/K$^+$ pump: membrane carrier protein that couples ATP hydrolysis to the inward transport of potassium ions and the outward transport of sodium ions to maintain the Na$^+$ and K$^+$ gradients that exist across the plasma membrane of most animal cells.

NAD$^+$: see *nicotinamide adenine dinucleotide*.

NADH-coenzyme Q oxidoreductase: see *complex I*.

NADP$^+$: see *nicotinamide adenine dinucleotide phosphate*.

nanometer (nm): unit of measure: 1 nanometer $= 10^{-9}$ meters.

native conformation: three-dimensional folding of a polypeptide chain into a shape that represents the most stable state for that particular sequence of amino acids.

negative staining: technique in which an unstained specimen is visualized in a transmission electron microscope against a darkly stained background.

NER: see *nucleotide excision repair*.

Nernst equation: equation for calculating the equilibrium membrane potential for a given ion: $E_x = (RT/zF) \ln[X]_{outside}/[X]_{inside}$.

nerve: a tissue composed of bundles of axons.

nerve impulse: signal transmitted along nerve cells by a wave of depolarization-repolarization events propagated along the axonal membrane.

NES: see *nuclear export signal*.

N-ethylmaleimide-sensitive factor (NSF): soluble cytoplasmic protein that acts in conjunction with several soluble NSF attachment proteins (SNAPs) to mediate the fusion of membranes brought together by interactions between v-SNAREs and t-SNAREs.

neuromuscular junction: site where a nerve cell axon makes contact with a skeletal muscle cell for the purpose of transmitting electrical impulses.

neuron: specialized cell directly involved in the conduction and transmission of nerve impulses; nerve cell.

neuropeptide: a molecule consisting of a short chain of amino acids that is involved in transmitting signals from neurons to other cells (neurons as well as other cell types).

neurosecretory vesicle: a small vesicle containing neurotransmitter molecules; located in theterminal bulb of an axon.

neurotoxin: toxic substance that disrupts the transmission of nerve impulses.

neurotransmitter: chemical released by a neuron that transmits nerve impulses across a synapse.

neurotransmitter reuptake: mechanism for removing neurotransmitters from the synaptic cleft by pumping them back into the presynaptic axon terminals or nearby support cells.

nexin: protein that connects and maintains the spatial relationship of adjacent outer doublets in the axoneme of eukaryotic cilia and flagella.

N-glycosylation: see *N-linked glycosylation*.

nicotinamide adenine dinucleotide (NAD$^+$): coenzyme that accepts two electrons and one proton to generate the reduced form, NADH; important electron carrier in energy metabolism.

nicotinamide adenine dinucleotide phosphate (NADP⁺): coenzyme that accepts two electrons and one proton to generate the reduced form, NADPH; important electron carrier in the Calvin cycle and other biosynthetic pathways.

nitric oxide (NO): a gas molecule that transmits signals to neighboring cells by stimulating guanylyl cyclase.

N-linked glycosylation (N-glycosylation): addition of oligosaccharide units to the terminal amino group of asparagine residues in protein molecules.

NLS: see *nuclear localization signal.*

NO: see *nitric oxide.*

nocodazole: synthetic drug that inhibits microtubule assembly; frequently used instead of colchicine because its effects are more readily reversible when the drug is removed.

nodes of Ranvier: small segments of bare axon between successive segments of myelin sheath.

noncovalent bonds and interactions: binding forces that do not involve the sharing of electrons; examples include ionic bonds, hydrogen bonds, van der Waals interactions, and hydrophobic interactions.

noncyclic electron flow: continuous, unidirectional flow of electrons from water to NADP¹ during the energy transduction reactions of photosynthesis, with light providing the energy that drives the transfer.

nondisjunction: failure of the two members of a homologous chromosome pair to separate during anaphase I of meiosis, resulting in a joined chromosome pair that moves into one of the two daughter cells.

nonhomologous end-joining: mechanism for repairing double-strand DNA breaks that uses proteins that bind to the ends of the two broken DNA fragments and join the ends together.

nonreceptor protein kinase: any protein kinase that is not an intrinsic part of a cell surface receptor.

nonrepeated DNA: DNA sequences present in single copies within an organism's genome.

nonsense-mediated decay: mechanism for destroying mRNAs containing premature stop codons.

nonsense mutation: change in base sequence converting a codon that previously coded for an amino acid into a stop codon.

nonstop decay: mechanism for destroying mRNAs containing no stop codons.

NOR: see *nucleolus organizer region.*

Northern blotting: technique in which RNA molecules are size-fractionated by gelelectrophoresis and then transferred to a special type of "blotter" paper (nitrocellulose or nyon), which is then hybridized with a radioactive DNA probe.

NPC: see *nuclear pore complex.*

NSF: see *N-ethylmaleimide-sensitive factor.*

N-terminus (amino terminus): the end of a polypeptide chain that contains the first amino acid to be incorporated during mRNA translation; usually retains a free amino group.

nuclear envelope: double membrane around the nucleus that is interrupted by numerous small pores.

nuclear export signal (NES): amino acid sequence that targets a protein for export from the nucleus.

nuclear lamina: thin, dense meshwork of fibers that lines the inner surface of the inner nuclear membrane and helps support the nuclear envelope.

nuclear localization signal (NLS): amino acid sequence that targets a protein for transport into the nucleus.

nuclear matrix (nucleoskeleton): insoluble fibrous network that provides a supporting framework for the nucleus.

nuclear pore: small opening in the nuclear envelope through which molecules enter and exit the nucleus; lined by an intricate protein structure called the nuclear pore complex (NPC).

nuclear pore complex (NPC): intricate protein structure, composed of 30 or more different polypeptide subunits, that lines the nuclear pores through which molecules enter and exit the nucleus, both by simple diffusion of smaller molecules and active transport of larger molecules.

nuclear transfer: experimental technique in which the nucleus from one cell is transferred into another cell (usually an egg cell) whose own nucleus has been removed.

nucleation: act of providing a small aggregate of molecules from which a polymer can grow.

nucleic acid: a linear polymer of nucleotides joined together in a genetically determined order. Each nucleotide is composed of ribose or deoxyribose, a phosphate group, and the nitrogenous base guanine, cytosine, adenosine, or thymine (for DNA) or uracil (for RNA). Also see *DNA* and *RNA.*

nucleic acid hybridization: family of techniques in which single-stranded nucleic acids are allowed to bind to each other by complementary base pairing; used for assessing whether two nucleic acids contain similar base sequences

nucleic acid probe: see *probe.*

nucleoid: region of cytoplasm in which the genetic material of a prokaryotic cell is located.

nucleolus (plural, nucleoli): large, spherical structure present in the nucleus of a eukaryotic cell; the site of ribosomal RNA synthesis and processing and of the assembly of ribosomal subunits.

nucleolus organizer region (NOR): stretch of DNA in certain chromosomes where multiple copies of the genes for ribosomal RNA are located and where nucleoli form.

nucleoplasm: the interior space of the nucleus, other than that occupied by the nucleolus.

nucleoside: molecule consisting of a nitrogen-containing base (purine or pyrimidine) linked to a five-carbon sugar (ribose or deoxyribose); a nucleotide with the phosphate removed.

nucleoside monophosphate: see *nucleotide.*

nucleoskeleton (nuclear matrix): insoluble fibrous network that provides a supporting framework for the nucleus.

nucleosome: basic structural unit of eukaryotic chromosomes, consisting of about 200 base pairs of DNA associated with an octamer of histones.

nucleotide: molecule consisting of a nitrogen-containing base (purine or pyrimidine) linked to a five-carbon sugar (ribose or deoxyribose) attached to a phosphate group; also called a nucleoside monophosphate.

nucleotide excision repair (NER): DNA repair mechanism that recognizes and repairs damage involving major distortions of the DNA double helix, such as that caused by pyrimidine dimers.

nucleus: large, double membrane-enclosed organelle that contains the chromosomal DNA of a eukaryotic cell.

numerical aperture (NA): property of a microscope corresponding to the quantity $n \sin \alpha$, where n is the refractive index of the medium between the specimen and the objective lens and α is the aperture angle.

O

objective lens (electron microscope): electromagnetic lens within which the specimen is placed in a transmission electron microscope.

objective lens (light microscope): lens located immediately above the specimen in a light microscope.

obligate aerobe: organism that has an absolute requirement for oxygen as an electron acceptor and therefore cannot live under anaerobic conditions.

obligate anaerobe: organism that cannot use oxygen as an electron acceptor and therefore has an absolute requirement for an electron acceptor other than oxygen.

ocular lens: lens through which the observer looks in a light microscope; also called the eyepiece.

OEC: see *oxygen-evolving complex.*

Okazaki fragments: short fragments of newly synthesized, lagging-strand DNA that are joined together by DNA ligase during DNA replication.

oligodendrocyte: cell type in the central nervous system that forms the myelin sheath around nerve axons.

O-linked glycosylation: addition of oligosaccharide units to hydroxyl groups of serine or threonine residues in protein molecules.

oncogene: any gene whose presence can cause cancer; arises by mutation from normal cellular genes called proto-oncogenes.

oncogenic virus: a virus that can cause cancer.

operator (O): base sequence in an operon to which a repressor protein can bind.

operon: cluster of genes with related functions that is under the control of a single operator and promoter, thereby allowing transcription of these genes to be turned on and off together.

optical tweezers: technique in which laser light focused through the objective lens of a microscope traps a small plastic bead, which is then used to manipulate the molecules it is attached to.

organelle: any membrane-bounded, intracellular structure that is specialized for carrying out a particular function. Eukaryotic cells contain several kinds of membrane-enclosed organelles, including the nucleus, mitochondria, Golgi complex, endoplasmic reticulum, lysosomes, peroxisomes, secretory vesicles, and, in the case of plants, chloroplasts.

organic chemistry: the study of carbon-containing compounds.

origin of replication: specific base sequence within a DNA molecule where replication is initiated.

origin of transfer: point on an F-factor plasmid where the transfer of the plasmid from an F⁺ donor bacterial cell to an F⁻ recipient cell begins during conjugation.

osmolarity: solute concentration on one side of a membrane relative to that on the other side of the membrane; drives the osmotic movement of water across the membrane.

osmosis: movement of water through a semipermeable membrane driven by a difference in solute concentration on the two sides of the membrane.

outer doublet: pair of fused microtubules, arranged in groups of nine around the periphery of the axoneme of a eukaryotic cilium or flagellum.

outer membrane: the outer of the two membranes that surround a mitochondrion, chloroplast, or nucleus.

ovum (plural, ova): see *egg*.

oxidation: chemical reaction involving the removal of electrons; oxidation of organic molecules frequently involves the removal of both electrons and hydrogen ions (protons) and is therefore also called a dehydrogenation reaction. Also see *beta oxidation*.

oxidative phosphorylation: formation of ATP from ADP and inorganic phosphate by coupling the exergonic oxidation of reduced coenzyme molecules by oxygen to the phosphorylation of ADP, with an electrochemical proton gradient as the intermediate.

oxygen-evolving complex (OEC): assembly of manganese ions and proteins included within photosystem II that catalyzes the oxidation of water to oxygen.

oxygenic phototroph: organism that utilizes water as the electron donor in photosynthesis, with release of oxygen.

P

P face: interior face of the inner, or cytoplasmic, monolayer of a membrane as revealed by the technique of freeze fracturing; called the P face because this monolayer is on the *protoplasmic* side of the membrane.

P site (peptidyl site): site on the ribosome that contains the growing polypeptide chain at the beginning of each elongation cycle.

P_1 generation: the first parental generation of a genetic breeding experiment.

p21 protein: Cdk inhibitor that halts progression through the cell cycle by inhibiting severaldifferent Cdk-cyclins.

p53 gene: tumor suppressor gene that codes for the p53 protein, a transcription factor involved in preventing genetically damaged cells from proliferating; most frequently mutated gene in human cancers.

p53 protein: transcription factor that accumulates in the presence of damaged DNA and activates genes whose products halt the cell cycle and trigger apoptosis.

P680: the pair of chloroplast molecules that make up the reaction center of photosystem II.

P700: the pair of chloroplast molecules that make up the reaction center of photosystem I.

pachytene: stage during prophase I of meiosis when crossing over between homologous chromosomes takes place.

packing ratio: see *DNA packing ratio*.

Pap smear: screening technique for early detection of cervical cancer in which cells obtained from a sample of vaginal secretions are examined with a microscope.

paracellular transport: a type of cellular transport in which ions move between, rather than through, cells.

passive spread of depolarization: process in which cations (mostly K^+) move away from the site of membrane depolarization to regions of membrane where the potential is more negative.

patch clamping: technique in which a tiny micropipette placed on the surface of a cell is used to measure the movement of ions through individual ion channels.

P bodies: microscopic structures present in the cytoplasm of eukaryotic cells that are involved in the storage and degradation of mRNAs.

PC: see *plastocyanin*.

PCR: see *polymerase chain reaction*.

PDGF: see *platelet-derived growth factor*.

pectin: branched polysaccharides, rich in galacturonic acid and rhamnose; found in plant cell walls, where they form a matrix in which cellulose microfibrils are embedded.

pellet: material that sediments to the bottom of a centrifuge tube during centrifugation.

peptide bond: a covalent bond between the amino group of one amino acid and the carboxyl group of a second amino acid.

peptidyl site: see *P site*.

peptidyl transferase: enzymatic activity, exhibited by the rRNA of the large ribosomal subunit, that catalyzes peptide bond formation during protein synthesis.

perinuclear space: space between the inner and outer nuclear membranes that is continuous with the lumen of the endoplasmic reticulum.

peripheral membrane protein: hydrophilic protein bound through weak ionic interactions and hydrogen bonds to a membrane surface.

peroxisome: single membrane-bounded organelle that contains catalase and one or more hydrogen peroxide-generating oxidases and is therefore involved in the metabolism of hydrogen peroxide. Also see *leaf peroxisome*.

PFK-2: see *phosphofructokinase-2*.

phage: see *bacteriophage*.

phagocyte: specialized white blood cell that carries out phagocytosis as a defense mechanism.

phagocytic vacuole: membrane-bounded structure containing ingested particulate matter that fuses with a late endosome or matures directly into a lysosome, forming a large vesicle in which the ingested material is digested.

phagocytosis: type of endocytosis in which particulate matter or even an entire cell is taken up from the environment and incorporated into vesicles for digestion.

pharmacogenetics: study of how inherited differences in genes cause people to respond differently to drugs and medications.

phase transition: change in the state of a membrane between a fluid state and a gel state.

phase-contrast microscopy: light microscopic technique that improves contrast without sectioning and staining by exploiting differences in thickness and refractive index; produces an image using an optical material that is capable of bringing undiffracted rays into phase with those that have been diffracted by the specimen.

phenotype: observable physical characteristics of an organism attributable to the expression of its genotype.

phosphatidic acid: basic component of phosphoglycerides; consists of two fatty acids and a phosphate group linked by ester bonds to glycerol; key intermediate in the synthesis of other phosphoglycerides.

phosphoanhydride bond: high-energy bond between phosphate groups.

phosphodiester bridge (3′, 5′ phosphodiester bridge): covalent linkage in which two parts of a molecule are joined through oxygen atoms to the same phosphate group.

phosphodiesterase: enzyme that catalyzes the hydrolysis of cyclic AMP to AMP.

phosphoester bond: covalent linkage in which a molecule is joined through an oxygen atom to a phosphate group.

phosphofructokinase-2 (PFK-2): an enzyme that catalyzes the ATP-dependent phosphorylation of fructose-6-phosphate on carbon atom 2 to form fructose-2,6-bisphosphate (F2,6BP), an important regulator of both glycolysis and gluconeogenesis.

phosphoglyceride: predominant phospholipid component of cell membranes, consisting of a glycerol molecule esterified to two fatty acids and a phosphate group.

phosphoglycolate: two-carbon compound produced by the oxygenase activity of rubisco. Because it cannot be metabolized during the next step of the Calvin cycle, the production of phosphoglycolate decreases photosynthetic efficiency.

phospholipase C: enzyme that catalyzes the hydrolysis of phosphatidylinositol-4,5-bisphosphate into inositol-1,4,5-trisphosphate (IP_3) and diacylglycerol (DAG).

phospholipid: lipid possessing a covalently attached phosphate group and therefore exhibiting both hydrophilic and hydrophobic properties; main component of the lipid bilayer that forms the structural backbone of all cell membranes.

phospholipid exchange protein: any of a group of proteins located in the cytosol that transfer specific phospholipid molecules from the ER membrane to the outer mitochondrial, chloroplast, or plasma membranes.

phospholipid translocator (flippase): a membrane protein that catalyzes the flip-flop of membrane phospholipids from one monolayer to the other.

phosphorylation: addition of a phosphate group.

photoactivation: light-induced activation of an inert molecule to an active state; generally associated with the ultraviolet light-induced release of a caging group that had blocked the fluorescence of a molecule that it had been attached to.

photoautotroph: organism capable of obtaining energy from the sun and using this energy to drive the synthesis of energy-rich organic molecules, using carbon dioxide as a source of carbon.

photobleaching: technique in which an intense beam of light within a well-defined area is used to render fluorescent molecules non-fluorescent; the rate at which unbleached fluorescent molecules repopulate the bleached area provides information about the dynamic movements of the molecule of interest.

photochemical reduction: transfer of photoexcited electrons from one molecule to another.

photoexcitation: excitation of an electron to a higher energy level by the absorption of a photon of light.

photoheterotroph: organism capable of obtaining energy from the sun but dependent on organic compounds, rather than carbon dioxide, for carbon.

photon: fundamental particle of light with an energy content that is inversely proportional to its wavelength.

photophosphorylation: light-dependent generation of ATP driven by an electrochemical proton gradient established and maintained as excited electrons of chlorophyll return to their ground state via an electron transport system.

photoreduction: light-dependent generation of NADPH by the transfer of energized electrons from photoexcited chlorophyll molecules to $NADP^+$ via a series of electron carriers.

photorespiration: light-dependent pathway that decreases the efficiency of photosynthesis by oxidizing reduced carbon compounds without capturing the released energy; occurs when oxygen substitutes for carbon dioxide in the reaction catalyzed by rubisco, thereby generating phosphoglycolate that is then converted to 3-phosphoglycerate in the peroxisome and mitochondrion; also called the glycolate pathway.

photosynthesis: process by which plants and certain bacteria convert light energy to chemical energy that is then used in synthesizing organic molecules.

photosystem: assembly of chlorophyll molecules, accessory pigments, and associated proteins embedded in thylakoid membranes or bacterial photosynthetic membranes; functions in the light-requiring reactions of photosynthesis.

photosystem I (PSI): photosystem containing a pair of chlorophyll molecules (P700) that absorbs 700-nm red light maximally; light of this wavelength can excite electrons derived from plastocyanin to an energy level that allows them to reduce ferredoxin, from which the electrons are then used to reduce NADP$^+$ to NADPH.

photosystem II (PSII): photosystem containing a pair of chlorophyll molecules (P680) that absorb 680-nm red light maximally; light of this wavelength can excite electrons donated by water to an energy level that allows them to reduce plastoquinone.

photosystem complex: a photosystem plus its associated light-harvesting complexes.

phototroph: organism that is capable of utilizing the radiant energy of the sun to satisfy its energy requirements.

phragmoplast: parallel array of microtubules that guides vesicles containing polysaccharides and glycoproteins toward the spindle equator during cell wall formation in dividing plant cells.

phycobilin: accessory pigment found in red algae and cyanobacteria that absorbs visible light in the green-to-orange range of the spectrum, giving these cells their characteristic colors.

phycobilisome: light-harvesting complex found in red algae and cyanobacteria that contains phycobilins rather than chlorophyll and carotenoids.

phytosterol: any of several sterols that are found uniquely, or primarily, in the membranes of plant cells; examples include campesterol, sitosterol, and stigmasterol.

PI 3-kinase (PI3K): enzyme that adds a phosphate group to PIP$_2$ (phosphatidylinositol-4,5-bisphosphate), thereby converting it to PIP$_3$ (phosphatidylinositol-3,4,5-trisphosphate); key component of the PI3K-Akt pathway, which is activated in response to the binding of certain growth factors to their receptors.

PI3K: see *PI 3-kinase*.

pigment: light-absorbing molecule responsible for the color of a substance.

pilus: see *sex pilus*.

PKA: see *protein kinase A*.

PKC: see *protein kinase C*.

plakin: family of proteins involved in linking the integrin molecules of a hemidesmosome to intermediate filaments of the cytoskeleton.

plaque: dense layer of fibrous material located on the cytoplasmic side of adhesive junctions such as desmosomes, hemidesmosomes, and adherens junctions; composed of intracellular attachment proteins that link the junction to the appropriate type of cytoskeletal filament. The same term can also refer to the clear zone produced when bacterial cells in a small region

of a culture dish are destroyed by infection with a bacteriophage.

plasma membrane: bilayer of lipids and proteins that defines the boundary of the cell and regulates the flow of materials into and out of the cell; also called the cell membrane.

plasmid: small circular DNA molecule in bacteria that can replicate independent of chromosomal DNA; useful as cloning vectors.

plasmodesma (plural, **plasmodesmata**): cytoplasmic channel through pores in the cell walls of two adjacent plant cells, allowing fusion of the plasma membranes and chemical communication between the cells.

plasmolysis: outward movement of water that causes the plasma membrane to pull away from the cell wall in cells that have been exposed to a hypertonic solution.

plastid: any of several types of plant cytoplasmic organelles derived from proplastids, including chloroplasts, amyloplasts, chromoplasts, proteinoplasts, and elaioplasts.

plastocyanin (PC): copper-containing protein that donates electrons to chlorophyll P700 of photosystem I in the light-requiring reactions of photosynthesis.

plastoquinol: fully reduced form of plastoquinone, involved in the light-requiring reactions of photosynthesis; present in the lipid phase of the photosynthetic membrane, where it transfers electrons to the cytochrome b_6/f complex.

plastoquinone: nonprotein (quinone) molecule associated with photosystem II, where it receives electrons from a modified type of chlorophyll called pheophytin during the light-requiring reactions of photosynthesis.

platelet-derived growth factor (PDGF): protein produced by blood platelets that stimulates the proliferation of connective tissue and smooth muscle cells.

plus end (of microtubule): rapidly growing end of a microtubule.

plus-end tubulin interacting proteins (+ −TIP proteins): proteins that stabilize the plus ends of microtubules, decreasing the likelihood that microtubules will undergo catastrophic subunit loss.

pmf: see *proton motive force*.

polar body: tiny haploid cell produced during the meiotic divisions that create egg cells. Polar bodies receive a disproportionately small amount of cytoplasm and usually degenerate.

polar microtubule: spindle microtubule that interacts with spindle microtubules from the opposite spindle pole.

polarity: property of a molecule that results from part of the molecule having a partial positive charge and another part having a partial negative charge, usually because one region of the molecule possesses one or more electronegative atoms that draw electrons toward that region.

polarized secretion: fusion of secretory vesicles with the plasma membrane and expulsion of their contents to the cell exterior specifically localized at one end of a cell.

poly(A) tail: stretch of about 50–250 adenine nucleotides added to the 3′ end of most eukaryotic mRNAs after transcription is completed.

polycistronic mRNA: an mRNA molecule that codes for more than one polypeptide.

polymerase chain reaction (PCR): reaction in which a specific segment of DNA is amplified by repeated cycles of (1) heat treatment to separate the two strands of the DNA double helix, (2) incubation with primers that are

complementary to sequences located at the two ends of the DNA segment being amplified, and (3) incubation with DNA polymerase to synthesize DNA using the primers as starting points.

polynucleotide: linear chain of nucleotides linked by phosphodiester bonds.

polypeptide: linear chain of amino acids linked by peptide bonds.

polyribosome: cluster of two or more ribosomes simultaneously translating a single mRNA molecule.

polysaccharide: polymer consisting of sugars and sugar derivatives linked together by glycosidic bonds.

polytene chromosome: giant chromosome containing multiple copies of the same DNA molecule generated by successive rounds of DNA replication in the absence of cell division.

porin: transmembrane protein that forms pores for the facilitated diffusion of small hydrophilic molecules; found in the outer membranes of mitochondria, chloroplasts, and many bacteria.

postsynaptic neuron: a neuron that receives a signal from another neuron through a synapse.

posttranslational control: mechanisms of gene regulation involving selective alterations in polypeptides that have already been synthesized; includes covalent modifications, proteolytic cleavage, protein folding and assembly, import into organelles, and protein degradation.

posttranslational import: uptake by organelles of completed polypeptide chains after they have been synthesized, mediated by specific targeting signals within the polypeptide.

posttranslational modifications: alterations in polypeptides that have already been synthesized; includes covalent modifications such as glycosylation, phosphorylation, or ubiquitylation, as well as proteolytic cleavage and folding.

precarcinogen: substance capable of causing cancer only after it has been metabolically activated by enzymes in the liver.

pre-mRNA: primary transcript whose processing yields a mature mRNA.

pre-replication complex: group of proteins that bind to eukaryotic DNA and license it for replication; includes the Origin Recognition Complex, MCM complex, and helicase loaders.

pre-rRNA: primary transcript whose processing yields mature rRNAs.

presynaptic neuron: a neuron that transmits a signal to another neuron through a synapse.

pre-tRNA: primary transcript whose processing yields a mature tRNA.

primary cell wall: flexible portion of the plant cell wall that develops beneath the middle lamella while cell growth is still occurring; contains a loosely organized network of cellulose microfibrils.

primary structure: sequence of amino acids in a polypeptide chain.

primary transcript: any RNA molecule newly produced by transcription, before any processing has occurred.

primase: enzyme that uses a single DNA strand as a template to guide the synthesis of the RNA primers that are required for initiation of replication of both the lagging and leading strands of a DNA double helix.

primosome: complex of proteins in bacterial cells that includes primase plus six other proteins involved in unwinding DNA and recognizing base sequences where replication is to be initiated.

prion: infectious, protein-containing particle responsible for neurological diseases such as scrapie in sheep and goats, kuru in humans, and mad cow disease in cattle—and its human form, vCJD.

probe (nucleic acid): single-stranded nucleic acid that is used in hybridization experiments to identify nucleic acids containing sequences that are complementary to the probe.

procaspase: an inactive precursor form of a caspase.

procollagen: a precursor molecule that is converted to collagen by proteolytic cleavage of sequences at both the N- and C-terminal ends.

progression: see *tumor progression.*

projector lens: electromagnetic lens located between the intermediate lens and the viewing screen in a transmission electron microscope.

prokaryote: category of organisms characterized by the absence of a true nucleus and other membrane-bounded organelles; includes bacteria and archaea.

prometaphase: stage of mitosis characterized by nuclear envelope breakdown and attachment of chromosomes to spindle microtubules; also called late prophase.

promoter (site): base sequence in DNA to which RNA polymerase binds when initiating transcription[PPA6].

promotion (stage of carcinogenesis): gradual process by which cells previously exposed to an initiating carcinogen are subsequently converted into cancer cells by agents that stimulate cell proliferation.

proofreading: removal of mismatched base pairs during DNA replication by the exonuclease activity of DNA polymerase.

propagation: movement of an action potential along a membrane away from the site of origin.

prophase: initial phase of mitosis, characterized by chromosome condensation and the beginning of spindle assembly. Prophase I of meiosis is more complex, consisting of stages called leptotene, zygotene, pachytene, diplotene, and diakinesis.

proplastid: small, double-membrane-enclosed, plant cytoplasmic organelle that can develop into several kinds of plastids, including chloroplasts.

prosthetic group: small organic molecule or metal ion component of an enzyme that plays an indispensable role in the catalytic activity of the enzyme.

proteasome: multiprotein complex that catalyzes the ATP-dependent degradation of proteins linked to ubiquitin.

protein: macromolecule that consists of one or more polypeptides folded into a conformation specified by the linear sequence of amino acids. Proteins play important roles as enzymes, structural proteins, motility proteins, and regulatory proteins.

protein disulfide isomerase: enzyme in the ER lumen that catalyzes the formation and breakage of disulfide bonds between cysteine residues in polypeptide chains.

protein kinase: any of numerous enzymes that catalyze the phosphorylation of proteinmolecules.

protein kinase A (PKA): a protein kinase, activated by the second messenger cyclic AMP, that catalyzes the phosphorylation of serine or threonine residues in target proteins.

protein kinase C (PKC): enzyme that phosphorylates serine and threonine groups in a variety of target proteins when activated by diacylglycerol.

protein phosphatase: any of numerous enzymes that catalyze the dephosphorylation, or

removal by hydrolysis, of phosphate groups from a variety of target proteins.

proteoglycan: complex between proteins and glycosaminoglycans found in the extracellular matrix.

proteolysis: degradation of proteins by hydrolysis of the peptide bonds between amino acids.

proteolytic cleavage: removal of a portion of a polypeptide chain, or cutting a polypeptide chain into two fragments, by an enzyme that cleaves peptide bonds.

proteome: the structure and properties of all the proteins produced by a genome.

protoeukaryote: hypothetical evolutionary ancestor of present-day eukaryotic cells whose ability to carry out phagocytosis allowed it to engulf and establish an endosymbiotic relationship with primitive bacteria.

protofilament: linear polymer of tubulin subunits; usually arranged in groups of 13 to form the wall of a microtubule.

proton motive force (pmf): force across a membrane exerted by an electrochemical proton gradient that tends to drive protons back down their concentration gradient.

proton translocator: channel through which protons flow across a membrane driven by an electrochemical gradient; examples include CF_0 in thylakoid membranes and F_0 in mitochondrial inner membranes.

proto-oncogene: normal cellular gene that can be converted into an oncogene by point mutation, gene amplification, chromosomal translocation, local DNA rearrangement, or insertional mutagenesis.

provacuole: vesicle in plant cells comparable to an endosome in animal cells; arises either from the Golgi complex or by autophagy.

proximal control element: DNA regulatory sequence located upstream of the core promoter but within about 100–200 base pairs of it.

PSA test: screening technique for early detection of prostate cancer that measures how much prostate-specific antigen (PSA) is present in the blood.

pseudopodium (plural, **pseudopodia**): large, blunt-ended cytoplasmic protrusion involved in cell crawling by amoebas, slime molds, and leukocytes.

PSI: see *photosystem I.*

PSII: see *photosystem II.*

PTEN: phosphatase that removes a phosphate group from PIP_3 (phosphatidylinositol-3,4, 5-trisphosphate), thereby converting it to PIP_2 (phosphatidylinositol-4,5-bisphosphate); component of the PI3K-Akt pathway.

P-type ATPase: type of transport ATPase that is reversibly phosphorylated by ATP as part of the transport mechanism.

Puma (p53 upregulated modulator of apoptosis): protein that triggers apoptosis by binding to and inactivating Bcl-2, an inhibitor of apoptosis.

purine: two-ringed nitrogen-containing molecule; parent compound of the bases adenine and guanine.

pyrimidine: single-ringed nitrogen-containing molecule; parent compound of the bases cytosine, thymine, and uracil.

Q

Q cycle: proposed pathway for recycling electrons during mitochondrial or chloroplast electron transport to allow additional proton pumping across the membrane containing the electron carriers.

quantum: indivisible packet of energy carried by a photon of light.

quaternary structure: level of protein structure involving interactions between two or more polypeptide chains to form a single multimeric protein.

R

Rab GTPase: GTP-hydrolyzing protein involved in locking v-SNAREs and t-SNAREs together during the binding of a transport vesicle to an appropriate target membrane.

Rac: member of a family of monomeric G proteins, which also includes Rho and Cdc42, that stimulate formation of various actin-containing structures within cells.

radial spokes: inward projections from each of the nine outer doublets to the center pair of microtubules in the axoneme of a eukaryotic cilium or flagellum, believed to be important in converting the sliding of the doublets into a bending of the axoneme.

Ras (protein): a small, monomeric G protein bound to the inner surface of the plasma membrane; Ras is a key intermediate in transmitting signals from receptor tyrosine kinases to the cell interior.

rate-zonal centrifugation: see *density gradient centrifugation.*

RB gene: tumor suppressor gene coding for the Rb protein.

Rb protein: protein whose phosphorylation controls passage through the restriction point of the cell cycle.

reaction center: portion of a photosystem containing the two chlorophyll molecules that initiate electron transfer, utilizing the energy gathered by other chlorophyll molecules and accessory pigments. Also see *P680* and *P700.*

reactive oxygen species: highly reactive oxygen-containing compounds such as H_2O_2, superoxide anion, and hydroxyl radical that are formed in the presence of molecular oxygen and can damage cells by oxidizing cellular components

receptor: a protein that contains a binding site for a specific signaling molecule.

receptor affinity: a measure of the chemical attraction between a receptor and its ligand.

receptor tyrosine kinase (RTK): a receptor whose activation causes it to catalyze the phosphorylation of tyrosine residues in proteins, thereby triggering a chain of signal transduction events inside cells that can lead to cell growth, proliferation, and differentiation.

receptor-mediated (clathrin-dependent) endocytosis: type of endocytosis initiated at coated pits and resulting in coated vesicles; believed to be a major mechanism for selective uptake of macromolecules and peptide hormones.

recessive (allele): allele that is present in the genome but is phenotypically expressed only in the homozygous form; masked by a dominant allele when heterozygous.

recombinant DNA molecule: DNA molecule containing DNA sequences derived from two different sources.

recombinant DNA technology: group of laboratory techniques for joining DNA fragments derived from two or more sources.

redox pair: two molecules or ions that are interconvertible by the loss or gain of electrons; also called a reduction-oxidation pair.

reduction: chemical reaction involving the addition of electrons; reduction of organic molecules frequently involves the addition of both electrons and hydrogen ions (protons) and is therefore also called a hydrogenation reaction.

reduction-oxidation pair: see *redox pair*.

refractive index: measure of the change in the velocity of light as it passes from one medium to another.

regulated secretion: fusion of secretory vesicles with the plasma membrane and expulsion of their contents to the cell exterior in response to specific extracellular signals.

regulators of G protein signaling (RGS) proteins: group of proteins that stimulate GTP hydrolysis by the G_a subunit of G proteins.

regulatory light chain: type of myosin light chain that is phosphorylated by myosin light-chain kinase in smooth muscle cells, thereby enabling myosin to interact with actin filaments and triggering muscle contraction.

regulatory site: see *allosteric site*.

regulatory subunit: a subunit of a multisubunit enzyme that contains an allosteric site.

regulatory transcription factor: protein that controls the rate at which one or more specific genes are transcribed by binding to DNA control elements located outside the core promoter.

relative refractory period: time during the hyperpolarization phase of an action potential when the sodium channels of a nerve cell are capable of opening again, but it is difficult to trigger an action potential because Na^+ currents are opposed by larger K^+ currents.

release factors: group of proteins that terminate translation by triggering the release of a completed polypeptide chain from peptidyl tRNA bound to a ribosome's P site.

renaturation: return of a protein from a denatured state to the native conformation determined by its amino acid sequence, usually accompanied by restoration of physiological function. Also see *DNA renaturation*.

repeated DNA: DNA sequences present in multiple copies within an organism's genome.

replication fork: Y-shaped structure that represents the site at which replication of a DNA double helix is occurring.

replicon: total length of DNA replicated from a single origin of replication.

replisome: large complex of proteins that work together to carry out DNA replication at the replication fork; about the size of a ribosome.

repressible operon: group of adjoining genes that are normally transcribed, but whose transcription is inhibited in the presence of a corepressor.

repressor protein (eukaryotic): regulatory transcription factor whose binding to DNA control elements leads to a reduction in the transcription rate of nearby genes.

repressor protein (bacterial): protein that binds to the operator site of an operon and prevents transcription of adjacent structural genes.

residual body: mature lysosome in which digestion has ceased and only indigestible material remains.

resolution: minimum distance that can separate two points that still remain identifiable as separate points when viewed through a microscope.

resolving power: ability of a microscope to distinguish adjacent objects as separate entities.

resonance energy transfer: mechanism whereby the excitation energy of a photoexcited molecule is transferred to an electron in an adjacent molecule, exciting that electron to a high-energy orbital; important means of passing energy from one pigment molecule to another in photosynthetic energy transduction.

resonance hybrid: the actual structure of functional groups such as carboxylate or phosphate groups that are written formally as two or more structures with one double bond and one or more single bonds to oxygen when the unshared electron pair is, in fact, delocalized over all of the possible bonds to oxygen; written as single bonds to all possible oxygen atoms and dashed lines indicating delocalization of one electron pair.

resonance stabilization: achievement of the most stable configuration of a molecule by maximal delocalization of an unshared electron pair over all possible bonds.

respirasome: group of respiratory complexes associated together in defined ratios.

respiratory complex: subset of carriers of the electron transport system consisting of a distinctive assembly of polypeptides and prosthetic groups, organized together to play a specific role in the electron transport process.

respiratory control: regulation of oxidative phosphorylation and electron transport by the availability of ADP.

response element: DNA base sequence located adjacent to physically separate genes whose expression can then be coordinated by binding a regulatory transcription factor to the response element wherever it occurs.

resting membrane potential (V_m): electrical potential (voltage) across the plasma membrane of an unstimulated nerve cell.

restriction endonuclease: any of a large family of enzymes isolated from bacteria that cut foreign DNA molecules at or near a palindromic recognition sequence that is usually 4 or 6 (but may be 8 or more) base pairs long; used in recombinant DNA technology to cleave DNA molecules at specific sites.

restriction fragment length polymorphism (RFLP): difference in restriction maps between individuals caused by small differences in the base sequences of their DNA.

restriction map: map of a DNA molecule indicating the location of cleavage sites for various restriction endonucleases.

restriction/methylation system: pathway in bacterial cells by which foreign DNA is cleaved by restriction endonucleases while the bacterial genome is protected from cleavage by prior methylation.

restriction point: control point near the end of G1 phase of the cell cycle where the cycle can be halted until conditions are suitable for progression into S phase; regulated to a large extent by the presence or absence of extracellular growth factors; called *Start* in yeast.

restriction site: DNA base sequence, usually 4 or 6 (but may be 8 or more base pairs long, that is cleaved by a specific restriction endonuclease.

retrograde flow (of F-actin): bulk movement of actin microfilaments toward the rear of a cell protrusion (e.g., lamellipodium) as the protrusion extends.

retrograde transport: movement of vesicles from Golgi cisternae back toward the endoplasmic reticulum.

retrotransposon: type of transposable element that moves from one chromosomal site to another by a process in which the retrotransposon DNA is first transcribed into RNA, and reverse transcriptase then uses the RNA as a template to make a DNA copy that is integrated into the chromosomal DNA at another site.

retrovirus: any RNA virus that uses reverse transcriptase to make a DNA copy of its RNA.

reverse transcriptase: enzyme that uses an RNA template to synthesize a complementary molecule of double-stranded DNA.

reversible inhibitor: molecule that causes a reversible loss of catalytic activity when bound to an enzyme; upon dissociation of the inhibitor, the enzyme regains biological function.

RFLP: see *restriction fragment length polymorphism*.

RGS proteins: see *regulators of G protein signaling proteins*.

Rho GTPases: a family of monomeric G proteins, which includes Rho, Rac and Cdc42, that stimulate formation of various actin-containing structures within cells.

Rho: member of a family of monomeric G proteins, which also includes Rac and Cdc42, that stimulate formation of various actin-containing structures within cells.

rho (ρ) factor: bacterial protein that binds to the 3′ end of newly forming RNA molecules, triggering the termination of transcription.

ribonucleic acid: see *RNA*.

ribose: five-carbon sugar present in RNA and in important nucleoside triphosphates such as ATP and GTP.

ribosomal RNA (rRNA): any of several types of RNA molecules used in the construction of ribosomes.

ribosome: small particle composed of rRNA and protein that functions as the site of protein synthesis in the cytoplasm of prokaryotes and in the cytoplasm, mitochondria, and chloroplasts of eukaryotes; composed of large and small subunits.

riboswitch: site in mRNA to which a small molecule can bind, triggering changes in mRNA conformation that impact either transcription or translation.

ribozyme: an RNA molecule with catalytic activity.

ribulose-1,5-bisphosphate carboxylase/oxygenase: see *rubisco*.

RISC: complex between either siRNA or microRNA and several proteins that together silence the expression of messenger RNAs or genes containing sequences complementary to those of these RNAs; abbreviation for RNA-induced silencing complex. Also see *miRISC* and *siRISC*.

RNA (ribonucleic acid): nucleic acid that plays several different roles in the expression of genetic information; constructed from nucleotides consisting of ribose phosphate linked to adenine, uracil, cytosine, or guanine. Also see *messenger RNA, ribosomal RNA, transfer RNA, microRNA, snRNA,* and *snoRNA*.

RNA editing: altering the base sequence of an mRNA molecule by the insertion, removal, or modification of nucleotides.

RNA interference (RNAi): ability of short RNA molecules (siRNAs or microRNAs) to inhibit gene expression by triggering the degradation or inhibiting the translation of specific mRNAs, or inhibiting transcription of the gene coding for a particular mRNA.

RNA polymerase: any of a group of enzymes that catalyze the synthesis of RNA using DNA as a template; function by adding successive nucleotides to the 3′ end of the growing RNA strand.

RNA polymerase I: type of eukaryotic RNA polymerase present in the nucleolus that synthesizes an RNA precursor for three of the four types of rRNA.

RNA polymerase II: type of eukaryotic RNA polymerase present in the nucleoplasm that synthesizes pre-mRNA, microRNA, and most of the snRNAs.

RNA polymerase III: type of eukaryotic RNA polymerase present in the nucleoplasm that synthesizes a variety of small RNAs, including pre-tRNAs and 5S rRNA.

RNA primer: short RNA fragment, synthesized by DNA primase, that serves as an initiation site for DNA synthesis.

RNA processing: conversion of an initial RNA transcript into a final RNA product by the removal, addition, and/or chemical modification of nucleotide sequences.

RNA splicing: excision of introns from a primary RNA transcript to generate the mature, functional form of the RNA molecule.

RNAi: see *RNA interference.*

rotation (of lipid molecules): turning of a molecule about its long axis; occurs freely and rapidly in membrane phospholipids.

rough endoplasmic reticulum (rough ER): endoplasmic reticulum that is studded with ribosomes on its cytosolic side because of its involvement in protein synthesis.

rough ER: see *rough endoplasmic reticulum.*

rRNA: see *ribosomal RNA.*

RTK: see *receptor tyrosine kinase.*

rubisco (ribulose-1,5-bisphosphate carboxylase/oxygenase): enzyme that catalyzes the CO_2-capturing step of the Calvin cycle; joins CO_2 to ribulose-1,5-bisphosphate, forming two molecules of 3-phosphoglycerate.

rubisco activase: protein that stimulates photosynthetic carbon fixation by rubisco by removing inhibitory sugar phosphates from the rubisco active site.

S

S: see *entropy.*

S: see *substrate concentration* and *Svedberg unit.*

S phase: stage of the eukaryotic cell cycle in which DNA is synthesized.

S1: see *myosin subfragment 1.*

sarcoma: any cancer arising from a supporting tissue, such as bone, cartilage, fat, connective tissue, and muscle.

sarcomere: fundamental contractile unit of striated muscle myofibrils that extends from one Z line to the next and that consists of two sets of thin (actin) and one set of thick (myosin) filaments.

sarcoplasmic reticulum (SR): endoplasmic reticulum of a muscle cell, specialized for accumulating, storing, and releasing calcium ions.

saturated fatty acid: fatty acid without double or triple bonds such that every carbon atom in the chain has the maximum number of hydrogen atoms bonded to it.

saturation: inability of higher substrate concentrations to increase the velocity of an enzyme-catalyzed reaction beyond a fixed upper limit determined by the finite number of enzyme molecules available.

scanning electron microscope (SEM): microscope in which an electron beam scans across the surface of a specimen and forms an image from electrons that are deflected from the outer surface of the specimen.

scanning probe microscope: instrument that visualizes the surface features of individual molecules by using a tiny probe that moves over the surface of a specimen.

Schwann cell: cell type in the peripheral nervous system that forms the myelin sheath around nerve axons.

second law of thermodynamics: the law of thermodynamic spontaneity; principle stating that all physical and chemical changes proceed in a manner such that the entropy of the universe increases.

second messenger: any of several substances, including cyclic AMP, calcium ion, inositol trisphosphate, and diacylglycerol, that transmit signals from extracellular signaling ligands to the cell interior.

secondary cell wall: rigid portion of the plant cell wall that develops beneath the primary cell wall after cell growth has ceased; contains densely packed, highly organized bundles of cellulose microfibrils.

secondary structure: level of protein structure involving hydrogen bonding between atoms in the peptide bonds along the polypeptide backbone, creating two main patterns called the α helix and β sheet conformations.

secretory granule: a large, dense secretory vesicle.

secretory pathway: pathway by which newly synthesized proteins move from the ER through the Golgi complex to secretory vesicles and secretory granules, which then discharge their contents to the exterior of the cell.

secretory vesicle: membrane-bounded compartment of a eukaryotic cell that carries secretory proteins from the Golgi complex to the plasma membrane for exocytosis and that may serve as a storage compartment for such proteins before they are released; large, dense vesicles are sometimes referred to as secretory granules.

securin: protein that prevents sister chromatid separation by inhibiting separase, the enzyme that would otherwise degrade the cohesins that hold sister chromatids together.

sedimentation coefficient: a measure of the rate at which a particle or macromolecule moves in a centrifugal force field; expressed in Svedberg units.

sedimentation rate: rate of movement of a molecule or particle through a solution when subjected to a centrifugal force.

selectable marker: gene whose expression allows cells to grow under specific conditions that prevent the growth of cells lacking this gene.

selectin: plasma membrane glycoprotein that mediates cell-cell adhesion by binding to specific carbohydrate groups located on the surface of target cells.

self-assembly: principle that the information required to specify the folding of macromolecules and their interactions to form more complicated structures with specific biological functions is inherent in the polymers themselves.

SEM: see *scanning electron microscope.*

semiautonomous organelle: organelle, either a mitochondrion or a chloroplast, that contains DNA and is therefore able to encode some of its polypeptides, although it is dependent on the nuclear genome to encode most of them.

semiconservative replication: mode of DNA replication in which each newly formed DNA molecule consists of one old strand and one newly synthesized strand.

separase: protease that initiates anaphase by degrading the cohesins that hold sister chromatids together.

serine-threonine kinase receptor: a receptor that, upon activation, catalyzes the phosphorylation of serine and threonine residues in target protein molecules.

70S initiation complex: complex formed by the association of a 30S initiation complex with a 50S ribosomal subunit; contains an initiator aminoacyl tRNA at the P site and is ready to commence mRNA translation.

sex chromosome: chromosome involved in determining whether an individual is male or female.

sex pilus (plural, pili): projection emerging from the surface of a bacterial donor cell that binds to the surface of a recipient cell, leading to the formation of a transient cytoplasmic mating bridge through which DNA is transferred from donor cell to recipient cell during bacterial conjugation.

sexual reproduction: form of reproduction in which two parent organisms each contribute genetic information to the new organism; reproduction by the fusion of gametes.

SH2 domain: a region of a protein molecule that recognizes and binds to phosphorylated tyrosines in another protein.

shadowing: deposition of a thin layer of an electron-dense metal on a biological specimen from a heated electrode, such that surfaces facing toward the electrode are coated while surfaces facing away are not.

sheet (β sheet): see *beta sheet.*

short interfering RNA: see *siRNA.*

short tandem repeat (STR): short repeated DNA sequences whose variation in length between individuals forms the basis for DNA fingerprinting.

sidearm: structure composed of axonemal dynein that projects out from each of the A tubules of the nine outer doublets in the axoneme of a eukaryotic cilium or flagellum.

sigma (s) factor: subunit of bacterial RNA polymerase that ensures the initiation of RNA synthesis at the correct site on the DNA strand.

signal recognition particle (SRP): cytoplasmic RNA-protein complex that binds to the ER signal sequence located at the N-terminus of a newly forming polypeptide chain and directs the ribosome-mRNA-polypeptide complex to the surface of the ER membrane.

signal transduction: mechanisms by which signals detected at the cell surface are transmitted into the cell's interior, resulting in changes in cell behavior and/or gene expression.

silencer: DNA sequence containing a binding site for transcription factors that inhibit transcription and whose position and orientation relative to the promoter can vary significantly without interfering with the ability to regulate transcription.

simple diffusion: unassisted net movement of a solute from a region where its concentration is higher to a region where its concentration is lower.

SINEs (short interspersed nuclear elements): class of interspersed, repeated DNA sequences less than 500 base pairs in length that function as transposable elements, relying on enzymes made by other mobile elements for their movement; include *Alu* sequences, the most prevalent SINE in humans.

single bond: chemical bond formed between two atoms as a result of sharing a pair of electrons.

single nucleotide polymorphisms (SNPs): variations in DNA base sequence involving single base changes that occur among individuals of the same species.

single-stranded DNA binding protein (SSB): protein that binds to single strands of DNA at the replication fork to keep the DNA unwound and therefore accessible to the DNA replication machinery.

siRISC: complex between siRNA and several proteins that together silence the expression of messenger RNAs or genes containing sequences complementary to those of the siRNA. Also see *miRISC* and *RISC*.

siRNA: class of double-stranded RNAs about 21–22 nucleotides in length that silence gene expression; act by either promoting the degradation of mRNAs with precisely complementary sequences or by inhibiting the transcription of genes containing precisely complementary sequences.

sister chromatids: the two replicated copies of each chromosome that remain attached to each other prior to anaphase of mitosis.

site-specific mutagenesis: technique for altering the DNA base sequence at a particular location in the genome, thereby creating a specific mutation whose effects can be studied.

skeletal muscle: type of muscle, striated in microscopic appearance, that is responsible for voluntary movements.

Slicer: ribonuclease present in RISC that cleaves mRNA at the site where the RISC has become bound.

sliding-filament model: model stating that muscle contraction is caused by thin actin filaments sliding past thick myosin filaments, with no change in the length of either type of filament.

sliding-microtubule model: model of motility in eukaryotic cilia and flagella which proposes that microtubule length remains unchanged but adjacent outer doublets slide past each other, thereby causing a localized bending because lateral connections between adjacent doublets and radial links to the center pair prevent free sliding of the microtubules past each other.

Smad (protein): class of proteins involved in the signaling pathway triggered by transforming growth factor β; upon activation, Smads enter the nucleus and regulate gene expression.

small ribosomal subunit: component of a ribosome with a sedimentation coefficient of 40S in eukaryotes and 30S in prokaryotes; associates with a large ribosomal subunit to form a functional ribosome.

smooth endoplasmic reticulum (smooth ER): endoplasmic reticulum that has no attached ribosomes and plays no direct role in protein synthesis; involved in packaging of secretory proteins and synthesis of lipids.

smooth ER: see *smooth endoplasmic reticulum*.

smooth muscle: muscle lacking striations that is responsible for involuntary contractions such as those of the stomach, intestines, uterus, and blood vessels.

SNAP: see *soluble NSF attachment protein*.

SNAP receptor protein: see *SNARE protein*.

SNARE (SNAP receptor) protein: two families of proteins involved in targeting and sorting membrane vesicles; include the v-SNAREs found on transport vesicles and the t-SNAREs found on target membranes.

SNARE hypothesis: model explaining how membrane vesicles fuse with the proper target membrane; based on specific interactions between v-SNAREs (vesicle-SNAP receptors) and t-SNAREs (target-SNAP receptors).

snoRNA: group of small nucleolar RNAs that bind to complementary regions of pre-rRNA and target specific sites for methylation or cleavage.

SNPs: see *single nucleotide polymorphisms*.

snRNA: a small nuclear RNA molecule that binds to specific proteins to form a snRNP, which in turn assembles with other snRNPs to form a spliceosome.

snRNP: RNA-protein complex that assembles with other snRNPs to form a spliceosome; pronounced "snurp."

sodium/potassium pump: see Na^+/K^+ *pump*.

soluble NSF attachment protein (SNAP): soluble cytoplasmic protein that acts in conjunction with NSF (N-ethylmaleimide-sensitive factor) to mediate the fusion of membranes brought together by interactions between v-SNAREs and t-SNAREs.

solute: substance that is dissolved in a solvent, forming a solution.

solvent: substance, usually liquid, in which other substances are dissolved, forming a solution.

Sos (protein): a guanine-nucleotide exchange factor that activates Ras by triggering the release of GDP, thereby permitting Ras to acquire a molecule of GTP. The Sos protein is activated by interacting with a GRB2 protein molecule that has become bound to phosphorylated tyrosines in an activated tyrosine kinase receptor.

Southern blotting: technique in which DNA fragments separated by gel electrophoresis are transferred to a special type of "blotter" paper (nitrocellulose or nylon), which is then hybridized with a radioactive DNA probe.

special pair: two chlorophyll *a* molecules, located in the reaction center of a photosystem, that catalyze the conversion of solar energy into chemical energy.

specific heat: amount of heat needed to raise the temperature of 1 gram of a substance 1°C.

sperm: haploid male gamete, usually flagellated.

sphingolipid: class of lipids containing the amine alcohol sphingosine as a backbone.

sphingosine: amine alcohol that serves as the backbone for sphingolipids; contains an amino group that can form an amide bond with a long-chain fatty acid; also contains a hydroxyl group that can attach to a phosphate group.

spliceosome: protein-RNA complex that catalyzes the removal of introns from pre-mRNA.

spore: see *haploid spore*.

sporophyte: diploid generation in the life cycle of an organism that alternates between haploid and diploid forms; form that produces spores by meiosis.

sputter coating: vacuum evaporation process used to coat the surface of a specimen with a layer of gold or a mixture of gold and palladium prior to examining the specimen by scanningelectron microscopy.

squid giant axon: an exceptionally large axon emerging from certain squid nerve cells; its wide diameter (0.5–1.0 mm) makes it relatively easy to insert microelectrodes that can measure and control electrical potentials and ionic currents.

SR: see *sarcoplasmic reticulum*.

SRP: see *signal recognition particle*.

SSB: see *single-stranded DNA binding protein*.

stage: platform on which the specimen is placed in a microscope.

staining: incubation of tissue specimens in a solution of dye, heavy metal, or other substance that binds specifically to selected cellular constituents, thereby giving those constituents a distinctive color or electron density.

standard free energy change ($\Delta G°9$): free energy change accompanying the conversion of 1 mole of reactants to 1 mole of products, with the temperature, pressure, pH, and concentration of all relevant species maintained at standard values.

standard reduction potential (E'_0): convention used to quantify the electron transport potential of oxidation-reduction couples relative to the H^+/H_2 redox pair, which is assigned an E'_0 value of 0.0 V at pH 7.0.

standard state: set of arbitrary conditions defined for convenience in reporting free energy changes in chemical reactions. For systems consisting of dilute aqueous solutions, these conditions are usually a temperature of 25°C (298 K), a pressure of 1 atmosphere, and reactants other than water present at a concentration of 1 *M*.

starch: storage polysaccharide in plants consisting of repeating glucose subunits linked together by $\alpha(1 \rightarrow 4)$ bonds and, in some cases, $\alpha(1 \rightarrow 6)$ bonds. The two main forms of starch are the unbranched polysaccharide, amylose, and the branched polysaccharide, amylopectin.

Start: control point near the end of G1 phase of the yeast cell cycle where the cycle can be halted until conditions are suitable for progression into S phase; known as the *restriction point* in other eukaryotes.

start codon: the codon AUG in mRNA when it functions as the starting point for protein synthesis.

start-transfer sequence: amino acid sequence in a newly forming polypeptide that acts as both an ER signal sequence that directs the ribosome-mRNA-polypeptide complex to the ER membrane and as a membrane anchor that permanently attaches the polypeptide to the lipid bilayer.

STAT: type of transcription factor activated by phosphorylation in the cytoplasm catalyzed by Janus activated kinase, followed by migration of the activated STAT molecules to the nucleus.

state: condition of a system defined by various properties, such as temperature, pressure, and volume.

stationary cisternae model: model postulating that each compartment of the Golgi stack is a stable structure, and that traffic between successive cisternae is mediated by shuttle vesicles that bud from one cisterna and fuse with another.

steady state: nonequilibrium condition of an open system through which matter is flowing, such that all components of the system are present at constant, nonequilibrium concentrations.

stem cell: a cell capable of unlimited division that can differentiate into a variety of other cell types.

stereo electron microscopy: microscopic technique for obtaining a three-dimensional view of a specimen by photographing it at two slightly different angles.

stereoisomers: two molecules that have the same structural formula but are not superimposable; stereoisomers are mirror images of each other.

steroid: any of numerous lipid molecules that are derived from a four-membered ring compound called phenanthrene.

steroid hormone: any of several steroids derived from cholesterol that function as signaling molecules, moving via the circulatory system to target tissues, where they cross the plasma membrane and interact with intracellular receptors to form hormone-receptor complexes that are capable of activating (or inhibiting) the transcription of specific genes.

steroid receptor: protein that functions as a transcription factor after binding to a specific steroid hormone.

sterol: any of numerous compounds consisting of a 17-carbon four-ring system with at least one hydroxyl group and a variety of other possible side groups; includes cholesterol and a variety of other biologically important compounds, such as the male and female sex hormones, that are related to cholesterol.

sticky end: single-stranded end of a DNA fragment generated by cleavage with a restriction endonuclease that tends to reassociate with another fragment generated by the same restriction endonuclease because of base complementarity.

stomata (singular, stoma): pores on the surface of a plant leaf that can be opened or closed to control gas and water exchange between the atmosphere and the interior of the leaf.

stop codon: sequence of three bases in mRNA that instructs the ribosome to terminate protein synthesis. UAG, UAA, and UGA generally function as stop codons.

stop-transfer sequence: hydrophobic amino acid sequence in a newly forming polypeptide that halts translocation of the chain through the ER membrane, thereby anchoring the polypeptide within the membrane.

storage macromolecule: polymer that consists of one or a few kinds of subunits in no specific order and that serves as a storage form of monosaccharides; examples include starch and glycogen.

STR: see *short tandem repeat*.

striated muscle: muscle whose myofibrils exhibit a pattern of alternating dark and light bands when viewed microscopically; includes both skeletal and cardiac muscle.

stroma: unstructured semifluid matrix that fills the interior of the chloroplast.

stroma thylakoid: membrane that interconnects stacks of grana thylakoids with each other.

structural macromolecule: polymer that consists of one or a few kinds of subunits in no specific order and that provides structure and mechanical strength to the cell; examples include cellulose and pectin.

subcellular fractionation: technique for isolating organelles from cell homogenates using various types of centrifugation.

substrate activation: role of an enzyme's active site in making a substrate molecule maximally reactive by subjecting it to the appropriate chemical environment for catalysis.

substrate concentration (S): amount of substrate present per unit volume at the beginning of a chemical reaction.

substrate induction: regulatory mechanism for catabolic pathways in which the synthesis of enzymes involved in the pathway is stimulated in the presence of the substrate and inhibited in the absence of the substrate.

substrate specificity: ability of an enzyme to discriminate between very similar molecules.

substrate-level phosphorylation: formation of ATP by direct transfer to ADP of a high-energy phosphate group derived from a phosphorylated substrate.

substrate-level regulation: enzyme regulation that depends directly on the interactions of substrates and products with the enzyme.

succinate-coenzyme Q oxidoreductase: see *complex II*.

supercoiled DNA: twisting of a DNA double helix upon itself, either in a circular DNA molecule or in a DNA loop anchored at both ends.

supernatant: material that remains in solution after particles of a given size and density are removed as a pellet during centrifugation.

superresolution microscopy: a set of related techniques, including stimulated emission depletion (STED) microscopy, photoactivated localization microscopy (PALM) and stochastic optical reconstruction microscopy (STORM), that allows objects to be visualized in the light microscope at a resolution greater than the theoretical limit predicted due to diffraction by the Abbé equation

suppressor tRNA: mutant tRNA molecule that inserts an amino acid where a stop codon generated by another mutation would otherwise have caused premature termination of protein synthesis.

surface area/volume ratio: mathematical ratio of the surface area of a cell to its volume; decreases with increasing linear dimension of the cell (length or radius), thereby increasing the difficulty of maintaining adequate surface area for import of nutrients and export of waste products as cell size increases.

surroundings: the remainder of the universe when one is studying the distribution of energy within a given system.

survival factor: a secreted molecule whose presence prevents a cell from undergoing apoptosis.

Svedberg unit (S): unit for expressing the sedimentation coefficient of biological macromolecules: One Svedberg unit $(S) = 10^{-13}$ second. In general, the greater the mass of a particle, the greater the sedimentation rate, though the relationship is not linear.

SWI/SNF: family of chromatin-remodeling proteins.

synaptic boutons: regions near the end of an axon where neurotransmitter molecules are stored for use in transmitting signals across the synapse.

symbiotic relationship: a mutually beneficial association between cells (or organisms) of two different species.

symport: coupled transport of two solutes across a membrane in the same direction.

synapse: tiny gap between a neuron and another cell (neuron, muscle fiber, or gland cell), across which the nerve impulse is transferred by direct electrical connection or by chemicals called neurotransmitters.

synapsis: close pairing between homologous chromosomes during the zygotene phase of prophase I of meiosis.

synaptic bouton: region near the end of an axon where neurotransmitter molecules are stored for use in transmitting signals across the synapse.

synaptic cleft: gap between the presynaptic and postsynaptic membranes at the junction between two nerve cells.

synaptonemal complex: zipperlike, protein-containing structure that joins homologous chromosomes together during prophase I of meiosis.

system: the restricted portion of the universe that one decides to study at any given time when investigating the principles that govern the distribution of energy.

T

T: see *thymine*.

T tubule system: see *transverse tubule system*.

tandemly repeated DNA: repeated DNA sequences whose multiple copies are adjacent to one another.

target-SNAP receptor: see *t-SNARE*.

TATA box: part of the core promoter for many eukaryotic genes transcribed by RNA polymerase II; consists of a consensus sequence of TATA followed by two or three more A's, located about 25 nucleotides upstream from the transcriptional startpoint.

TATA-binding protein (TBP): component of transcription factor TFIID that confers the ability to recognize and bind the TATA box sequence in DNA; also involved in regulating transcription initiation at promoters lacking a TATA box.

taxol: drug that binds tightly to microtubules and stabilizes them, causing much of the free tubulin in the cell to assemble into microtubules.

TBP: see *TATA-binding protein*.

TCA cycle: see *tricarboxylic acid cycle*.

TE: see *transitional element*.

telomerase: special type of DNA polymerase that catalyzes the formation of additional copies of a telomeric repeat sequence.

telomere: DNA sequence located at either end of a linear chromosome; contains simple-sequence, tandemly repeated DNA.

telophase: final stage of mitosis or meiosis, when daughter chromosomes arrive at the poles of the spindle accompanied by reappearance of the nuclear envelope.

TEM: see *transmission electron microscope*.

temperature-sensitive mutant: cell that produces a protein that functions properly at normal temperatures but becomes seriously impaired when the temperature is altered slightly.

template: a nucleic acid whose base sequence serves as a pattern for the synthesis of another (complementary) nucleic acid.

template strand: the strand of a DNA double helix that serves as the template for RNA synthesis via complementary base pairing.

terminal bulb: see *synaptic bouton*.

terminal glycosylation: modification of glycoproteins in the Golgi complex involving removal and/or addition of sugars to the carbohydrate side chains formed by prior core glycosylation in the endoplasmic reticulum.

terminal oxidase: electron transfer complex that is capable of transferring electrons directly to oxygen. Complex IV (cytochrome *c* oxidase) of the mitochondrial electron transport system is an example.

terminal web: dense meshwork of spectrin and myosin molecules located at the base of a microvillus; the bundle of actin microfilaments that make up the core of the microvillus is anchored to the terminal web.

termination signal: DNA sequence located near the end of a gene that triggers the termination of transcription.

terpene: a lipid constructed from the five-carbon compound isoprene and its derivatives, joined together in various combinations.

tertiary structure: level of protein structure involving interactions between amino acid side chains of a polypeptide, regardless of where along the primary sequence they happen to be located; results in three-dimensional folding of a polypeptide chain.

tethering protein: a coiled-coil protein or a multisubunit protein complex that recognizes and binds vesicles to their target membranes.

tetrahedral (carbon atom): an atom of carbon from which four single bonds extend to other atoms, each bond equidistant from all other bonds, causing the atom to resemble a tetrahedron with its four equal faces.

TFIIB recognition element: see *BRE*.

TGFβ: see *transforming growth factor β*.

TGN: see *trans-Golgi network*.

theory: a hypothesis that has been tested critically under many different conditions—usually by many different investigators using a variety of approaches—and is consistently supported by the evidence.

thermodynamic spontaneity: a measure of whether a reaction can occur, but it says nothing about whether the reaction actually will occur. Reactions with a negative free energy change are thermodynamically spontaneous.

thermodynamics: area of science that deals with the laws governing the energy transactions that accompany all physical processes and chemical reactions.

thick filament: myosin-containing filament, found in the myofibrils of striated muscle cells, in which individual myosin molecules are arranged in a staggered array with the heads of the myosin molecules projecting out in a repeating pattern.

thin filament: actin-containing filament, found in the myofibrils of striated muscle cells, in which two F-actin molecules are arranged in a helix associated with tropomyosin and troponin.

thin-layer chromatography (TLC): procedure for separating compounds by chromatography in a medium, such as silicic acid, that is bound as a thin layer to a glass or metal surface.

30-nm chromatin fiber: fiber formed by packing together the nucleosomes of a 10-nm chromatin fiber.

30S initiation complex: complex formed by the association of mRNA, the 30S ribosomal subunit, an initiator aminoacyl tRNA molecule, and initiation factor IF2.

three-dimensional (3-D) electron tomography: computer-based method for making three-dimensional reconstructions of structures visualized in serial thin sections by transmission electron microscopy.

threshold potential: value of the membrane potential that must be reached before an action potential is triggered.

thylakoid: flattened membrane sac suspended in the chloroplast stroma, usually arranged in stacks called grana; contains the pigments, enzymes, and electron carriers involved in the light-requiring reactions of photosynthesis.

thylakoid lumen: compartment enclosed by an interconnected network of grana and stroma thylakoids.

thymine (T): nitrogen-containing aromatic base, chemically designated as a pyrimidine, which serves as an informational monomeric unit when present in DNA with other bases in a specific sequence; forms a complementary base pair with adenine (A) by hydrogen bonding.

Ti plasmid: DNA molecule that causes crown gall tumors when transferred into plants by bacteria; used as a cloning vector for introducing foreign genes into plant cells.

TIC: translocase of the inner chloroplast membrane, a transport complex involved in the uptake of specific polypeptides into the chloroplast.

tight junction: type of cell junction in which the adjacent plasma membranes of neighboring animal cells are tightly sealed, thereby preventing molecules from diffusing from one side of an epithelial cell layer to the other by passing through the spaces between adjoining cells.

TIM: translocase of the inner mitochondrial membrane, a transport complex involved in the uptake of specific polypeptides into the mitochondrion.

+−TIP proteins: see *plus-end tubulin interacting proteins*.

TIRF: see *total internal reflection fluorescence microscopy*.

TLC: see *thin-layer chromatography*.

T_m: see *transition temperature* or *DNA melting temperature*.

TOC: translocase of the outer chloroplast membrane, a transport complex involved in the uptake of specific polypeptides into the chloroplast.

TOM: translocase of the outer mitochondrial membrane, a transport complex involved in the uptake of specific polypeptides into the mitochondrion.

topoisomerase: enzyme that catalyzes the interconversion of the relaxed and supercoiled forms of DNA by making transient breaks in one or both DNA strands.

total internal reflection fluorescence (TIRF) microscopy: technique in which a light beam strikes the interface of two media of different indices of refraction at an angle beyond the critical angle, causing all the light to be reflected back into the incident medium; an "evanescent field" that develops at the interface allows selective excitation of fluorescent molecules located within ∼100 nm of the interface.

***trans*-acting factor:** regulatory protein that exerts its function by binding to specific DNA sequences.

transcription: process by which RNA polymerase utilizes one DNA strand as a template for guiding the synthesis of a complementary RNA molecule.

transcription factor: protein required for the binding of RNA polymerase to a promoter and for the optimal initiation of transcription. Also see *general transcription factor* and *regulatory transcription factor*.

transcription regulation domain: region of a transcription factor, distinct from the DNA-binding domain, that is responsible for regulating transcription.

transcription unit: segment of DNA whose transcription gives rise to a single, continuous RNA molecule.

transcriptional control: group of regulatory mechanisms involved in controlling the rates at which specific genes are transcribed.

transcriptome: the entire set of RNA molecules produced by a genome.

transcytosis: endocytosis of material into vesicles that move to the opposite side of the cell and fuse with the plasma membrane, releasing the material into the extracellular space.

transduction: transfer of bacterial DNA sequences from one bacterium to another by a bacteriophage.

transfection: introduction of foreign DNA into cells under artificial conditions.

transfer RNA (tRNA): family of small RNA molecules, each binding a specific amino acid and possessing an anticodon that recognizes a specific codon in mRNA.

transformation: change in the hereditary properties of a cell brought about by the uptake of foreign DNA.

transforming growth factor β (TGFβ): family of growth factors that can exhibit either growth-stimulating or growth-inhibiting properties, depending on the target cell type; regulate a wide range of activities in both embryos and adult animals, including effects on cell growth, division, differentiation, and death.

transgenic: any organism whose genome contains a gene that has been experimentally introduced from another organism using the techniques of genetic engineering.

***trans*-Golgi network (TGN):** region of the Golgi complex consisting of a network of membrane-bounded tubules that are located on the opposite side of the Golgi complex from the *cis*-Golgi network.

transit sequence: amino acid sequence that targets a completed polypeptide chain to either mitochondria or chloroplasts.

transition state: intermediate stage in a chemical reaction, of higher free energy than the initial state, through which reactants must pass before giving rise to products.

transition temperature (T_m): temperature at which a membrane will undergo a sharp decrease in fluidity ("freezing") as the temperature is decreased and becomes more fluid again ("melts") when it is then warmed; determined by the kinds of fatty acid side chains present in the membrane.

transition vesicle: membrane vesicle that shuttles lipids and proteins from the endoplasmic reticulum to the Golgi complex.

transitional element (TE): region of the endoplasmic reticulum that is involved in the formation of transition vesicles.

translation: process by which the base sequence of an mRNA molecule guides the sequence of amino acids incorporated into a polypeptide chain; occurs on ribosomes.

translational control: mechanisms that regulate the rate at which mRNA molecules are translated into their polypeptide products; includes control of translation rates by initiation factors, selective inhibition of specific mRNAs by translational repressor proteins or microRNAs, and control of mRNA degradation rates.

translational repressor: regulatory protein that selectively inhibits the translation of a particular mRNA.

translesion synthesis: DNA replication across regions where the DNA template is damaged.

translocation: movement of mRNA across a ribosome by a distance of three nucleotides, bringing the next codon into position for translation. (*Note:* The same term, *translocation*, which literally means "a change of location," can also refer to the movement of a protein molecule through a membrane channel or to the transfer of a segment of one chromosome to another nonhomologous chromosome.)

translocon: structure in the ER membrane that carries out the translocation of newly forming polypeptides across (or into) the ER membrane.

transmembrane protein: an integral membrane protein possessing one or more hydrophobic regions that span the membrane plus hydrophilic regions that protrude from the membrane on both sides.

transmembrane segment: hydrophobic segment about 20–30 amino acids long that crosses the lipid bilayer in a transmembrane protein.

transmission electron microscope (TEM): type of electron microscope in which an image is formed by electrons that are transmitted through a specimen.

transport: selective movement of substances across membranes, both into and out of cells and into and out of organelles.

transport protein: membrane protein that recognizes substances with great specificity and assists their movement across a membrane; includes both carrier proteins and channel proteins.

transport vesicle: vesicle that buds off from a membrane in one region of the cell and fuses with other membranes; includes vesicles that convey lipids and proteins from the ER to the Golgi complex, between the Golgi stack cisternae, and from the Golgi complex to various destinations in the cell, including secretory vesicles, endosomes, and lysosomes.

transposable element (transposon): DNA sequence that can move from one chromosomal location to another.

transposon: see *transposable element*.

transverse diffusion: movement of a lipid molecule from one monolayer of a membrane to the other, a thermodynamically unfavorable and therefore infrequent event; also called "flip-flop."

transverse (T) tubule system: invaginations of the plasma membrane that penetrate into a muscle cell and conduct electrical impulses into the cell interior, where T tubules make close contact with the sarcoplasmic reticulum and trigger the release of calcium ions.

triacylglycerol: a glycerol molecule with three fatty acids linked to it; also called a triglyceride.

triad: region where a T tubule passes between the terminal cisternae of the sarcoplasmic reticulum in skeletal muscle.

tricarboxylic acid cycle (TCA cycle): cyclic metabolic pathway that oxidizes acetyl CoA to carbon dioxide in the presence of oxygen, generating ATP and the reduced coenzymes NADH and $FADH_2$; a component of aerobic respiration; also called the Krebs cycle.

triglyceride: see *triacylglycerol*.

triple bond: chemical bond formed between two atoms as a result of sharing three pairs of electrons.

triplet code: a coding system in which three units of information are read as a unit; a reference to the genetic code, which is read from mRNA in units of three bases called *codons*.

triskelion: structure formed by clathrin molecules consisting of three polypeptides radiating from a central vertex; the basic unit of assembly for clathrin coats.

tRNA: see *transfer RNA*.

tropomyosin: long, rodlike protein associated with the thin actin filaments of muscle cells, functioning as a component of the calcium-sensitive switch that activates muscle contraction; blocks the interaction between actin and myosin in the absence of calcium ions.

troponin: complex of three polypeptides (TnT, TnC, and TnI) that functions as a component of the calcium-sensitive switch that activates muscle contraction; displaces tropomyosin in the presence of calcium ions, thereby activating contraction.

trp operon: group of adjoining bacterial genes that code for enzymes involved in tryptophan biosynthesis and whose transcription is selectively inhibited in the presence of tryptophan.

true-breeding (plant strain): organism that, upon self-fertilization, produces only offspring of the same kind for a given genetic trait.

t-SNARE (target-SNAP receptor): protein associated with the outer surface of a target membrane that binds to a v-SNARE protein associated with the outer surface of an appropriate transport vesicle.

tubulin: family of related proteins that form the main building block of microtubules. Also see

alpha tubulin, beta tubulin, gamma tubulin, and gamma tubulin ring complexes.

tumor: growing mass of cells caused by uncontrolled cell proliferation. Also see *benign tumor* and *malignant tumor*.

tumor grading: assignment of numerical grades to tumors based on differences in their microscopic appearance; higher-grade cancers tend to grow and spread more aggressively, and to be less responsive to therapy, than lower-grade cancers.

tumor progression: gradual changes in tumor properties observed over time as cancer cells acquire more aberrant traits and become increasingly aggressive.

tumor suppressor gene: gene whose loss or inactivation by deletion or mutation can lead to cancer. Also see *gatekeeper gene* and *caretaker gene*.

γ-TuRCs: see *gamma tubulin ring complexes*.

turgor pressure: pressure that builds up in a cell due to the inward movement of water that occurs because of a higher solute concentration inside the cell than outside; accounts for the firmness, or turgidity, of fully hydrated cells or tissues of plants and other organisms.

turnover number (k_{cat}): rate at which substrate molecules are converted to product by a single enzyme molecule when the enzyme is operating at its maximum velocity.

type II myosin: form of myosin composed of four light chains and two heavy chains, each having a globular myosin head, a hinge region, and a long rodlike tail; found in skeletal, cardiac, and smooth muscle cells, as well as in nonmuscle cells.

U

U: see *uracil*.

ubiquitin: small protein that is linked to other proteins as a way of marking the targeted protein for degradation by proteasomes.

ultracentrifuge: instrument capable of generating centrifugal forces that are large enough to separate subcellular structures and macromolecules on the basis of size, shape, and density.

ultramicrotome: instrument used to slice an embedded biological specimen into ultrathin sections for electron microscopy.

ultraviolet radiation (UV): mutagenic type of radiation present in sunlight that triggers the formation of pyrimidine dimers in DNA.

undershoot: see *hyperpolarization*.

unfolded protein response (UPR): quality control mechanism in which sensor molecules in the ER membrane detect misfolded proteins and trigger a response that inhibits the synthesis of most proteins while enhancing the production of those required for protein folding and degradation.

unidirectional pumping of protons: the active and directional transport of protons across a membrane such that they accumulate preferentially on one side of the membrane, establishing an electrochemical proton gradient across the membrane; a central component of electron transport and ATP generation in both respiration and photosynthesis.

uniport: membrane protein that transports a single solute from one side of a membrane to the other.

unsaturated fatty acid: fatty acid molecule containing one or more double bonds.

UPR: see *unfolded protein response*.

upstream: located toward the 5′ end of the DNA coding strand.

uracil (U): nitrogen-containing aromatic base, chemically designated as a pyrimidine, that serves as an informational monomeric unit when present in RNA with other bases in a specific sequence; forms a complementary base pair with adenine (A) by hydrogen bonding.

useful magnification: measurement of how much an image can be enlarged before additional enlargement provides no additional information.

UV: see *ultraviolet radiation*.

V

v: see *initial reaction velocity*.

vacuole: membrane-bounded organelle in the cytoplasm of a cell, used for temporary storage or transport; acidic membrane-enclosed compartment in plant cells.

vacuum evaporator: bell jar containing a metal electrode and a carbon electrode in which a vacuum can be created; used in preparing metal replicas of the surfaces of biological specimens.

valence: a number indicating the number of other atoms with which a given atom can combine.

van der Waals interaction: weak attractive interaction between two atoms caused by transient asymmetries in the distribution of charge in each atom.

vesicle-SNAP receptor: see *v-SNARE*.

viroid: small, circular RNA molecule that can infect and replicate in host cells even though it does not code for any protein.

virus: subcellular parasite composed of a protein coat and DNA or RNA, incapable of independent existence; invades and infects cells and redirects the host cell's synthetic machinery toward the production of more virus.

V_m: see *resting membrane potential*.

V_{max}: see *maximum velocity*.

voltage: see *electrical potential*.

voltage sensor: amino acid segment of a voltage-gated ion channel that makes the channel responsive to changes in membrane potential.

voltage-gated calcium channel: an integral membrane protein in the terminal bulb of presynaptic neurons that forms a calcium ion-conducting pore whose permeability is regulated by the membrane potential; action potentials cause the calcium channel to open and calcium ions rush into the cell, stimulating the release of neurotransmitters.

voltage-gated ion channel: an integral membrane protein that forms an ion-conducting pore whose permeability is regulated by changes in the membrane potential.

v-SNARE (vesicle-SNAP receptor): protein associated with the outer surface of a transport vesicle that binds to a t-SNARE protein associated with the outer surface of the appropriate target membrane.

V-type ATPase: type of transport ATPase that pumps protons into such organelles as vesicles, vacuoles, lysosomes, endosomes, and the Golgi complex.

W

wavelength: distance between the crests of two successive waves.

Western blotting: technique in which polypeptides separated by gel electrophoresis are transferred to a special type of "blotter" paper (nitrocellulose or nylon), which is then reacted with labeled antibodies that are known to bind to specific polypeptides.

wild type: normal, nonmutant form of an organism, usually the form found in nature.

Wnt pathway: signaling pathway that plays a prominent role in controlling cell proliferation and differentiation during embryonic development; abnormalities in this pathway occur in some cancers.

wobble hypothesis: flexibility in base pairing between the third base of a codon and the corresponding base in its anticodon.

work: transfer of energy from one place or form to another place or form by any process other than heat flow.

X

xenobiotic: chemical compound that is foreign to biological organisms.

xeroderma pigmentosum: inherited susceptibility to cancer (mainly skin cancer) caused by defects in DNA excision repair or translesion synthesis of DNA.

X-ray crystallography: technique for determining the three-dimensional structure of macromolecules based on the pattern produced when a beam of X-rays is passed through a sample, usually a crystal or fiber.

Y

YAC: see *yeast artificial chromosome.*

yeast artificial chromosome (YAC): yeast cloning vector consisting of a "minimalist" chromosome that contains all the DNA sequences needed for normal chromosome replication and segregation to daughter cells, and very little else.

yeast two-hybrid system: Technique for determing whether two proteins interact by introducing DNA encoding one protein fused to DNA encoding the DNA binding domain of a transcription factor (bait), and another DNA encoding the second protein plus sequence encoding the activation domain of the transcirption factor (prey), followed by assessing expression of a reporter.

Z

Z line: dark line in the middle of the I band of a striated muscle myofibril; defines the boundary of a sarcomere.

zinc finger: DNA-binding motif found in some transcription factors; consists of an α helix and a two-segment β sheet held in place by the interaction of precisely positioned cysteine or histidine residues with a zinc atom.

zygote: diploid cell formed by the union of two haploid gametes.

zygotene: stage during prophase I of meiosis when homologous chromosomes become closely paired by the process of synapsis.

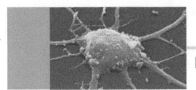

Photo Credits

Chapter 3 3-CO Dr. Jeremy Burgess/SPL/Photo Researchers, Inc. 3-24a Dr. Jeremy Burgess/SPL/Photo Researchers, Inc. 3-24b Don W. Fawcett/Photo Researchers, Inc. 3-25 Eva Frei and R. D. Preston. 3A-1 National Cancer Institute.

Chapter 4 4-CO Dr. Mary Olson. 4-2 Susumu Ito. 4-3b Gregory J. Brewer, Southern Illinois University. 4-4 Eldon H. Newcomb 4-5b Richard Rodewald/Biological Photo Service. 4-6b W. P. Wergin. 4-7 Hans Ris. 4-8 Oscar L. Miller Jr., University of Virginia. 4-10b Richard Rodewald/Biological Photo Service. 4-10c From J. P. Strafstrom and L. A. Staehelin, *The Journal of Cell Biology* 98 (1984): 699. Reproduced by copyright permission of The Rockefeller University Press. 4-11c Keith R. Porter/Photo Researchers, Inc. 4-12b From J.B. Rattner and B.R. Brinkley, *J. Ultrastructure Res.* 32 (1970): 316. © 1970 by Academic Press. 4-13 S. M. Wang. 4-14b W. P. Wergin. 4-15c H. Stuart Pankratz/Biological Photo Service. 4-15d Barry F. King/Biological Photo Service. 4-16b Eldon H. Newcomb. 4-18b M. Simionescu and N. Simionescu, *J. Cell Biol.* 70 (1976): 608. Reproduced by copyright permission of The Rockefeller University Press. 4-19 Barry F. King/Biological Photo Service. 4-20b From S.E. Frederick and E.H. Newcomb, *Journal of Cell Biology* 43 (1969): 343. Reproduced by copyright permission of The Rockefeller University Press. 4-21b P. J. Gruber. 4-23 Dr. Mary Olson. 4-25 Bottom From P.H. Raven, R.F. Evert, and H.A. Curtis, *Biology of Plants,* 2nd ed. New York: Worth Publishers, Inc., 1999. Used with permission of Worth Publishers. 4-26a Left, Middle, Right R.C. Williams and H.W. Fisher. 4-26b Left, Middle, Right R.C. Williams and H.W. Fisher. 4-26c Left, Middle, Right R.C. Williams and H.W. Fisher.

Chapter 6 6-CO Barry F. King/Biological Photo Service. 6-5 Richard J. Feldmann, National Institute of Health.

Chapter 7 7-CO M. Simionescu and N. Simionescu, *J. Cell Biol.* 70 (1976): 622. Reproduced by copyright permission of The Rockefeller University Press. 7-1a M. Simionescu and N. Simionescu, *J. Cell Biol.* 70 (1976): 622. Reproduced by copyright permission of The Rockefeller University Press. 7-1b Eldon H. Newcomb. 7-3e J. David Robertson. 7-4 Don W. Fawcett, Harvard Medical School. 7-16b Philippa Claude. 7-17a Daniel Branton. 7-17b R. B. Park. 7-18a,b David Deamer, University of California, Santa Cruz. 7-20a Ken Eward/Science Source/Photo Researchers, Inc. 7-27 Susumu Ito. 7-29a,b Arthur E. Sowers.

Chapter 12 12-CO Don W. Fawcett, Harvard Medical School. 12-2a Don W. Fawcett, Harvard Medical School. 12-2b M. Bielinska. 12-3a Barry F. King/Biological Photo Service. 12-4b Michael J. Wynne. 12-5 William G. Dunphy with Ruud Brands and James E. Rothman, *Cell* 40 (1985): 467, Fig. 6, Panel B. 12-10a–d J. D. Jamieson. 12-11 From L. Orci and A. Perrelet, *Freeze-Etch Histology,* Heidelberg: Springer-Verlag, 1975. 12-12b Holger Jastrow. 12-14b H. S. Pankratz & R. N. Band/Biological Photo Service. 12-16a–d From M.M. Perry and A.B. Gilbert, *The Journal of Cell Science* 39 (1979):257. © 1979 by The Company of Biologists Limited. 12-17a John E. Heuser. 12-18a John E. Heuser. 12-18b N. Hirokawa and J. E. Heuser. 12-20 Pierre Baudhuin. 12-22 Zdenek Hruban. 12-23 H. Shio and Paul B. Lazarow. 12-24 Eldon H. Newcomb/Biological Photo Service. 12B-2a,b R.G.W. Anderson, M.S. Brown, and J.L. Goldstein, *Cell* 10 (1977): 351–64.

Chapter 15 15-CO John E. Heuser. 15-2b L.E. Roth, Y. Shigenaka, and D.J. Pihlaja/Biological Photo Service. 15-4 Lester Binder and Joel Rosenbaum, *Journal of Cell Biology* 79 (1978): 510. Reproduced by permission of The Rockefeller University Press. 15-7 Andrew Matus and Beat Ludin. 15-8b Kent L. McDonald. 15-8c Mitchison and Kirschner, *Nature* 312 (1984): 235, Fig. 4c. 15-9b T.J. Keating and G.G. Borisy, "Immunostructural Evidence for the Template Mechanism of Microtubule Nucleation." *Nat Cell Biol.* 2(6):352–357, fig.2A, 2000. 15-11 Adapted from C.E. Schutt et al., *Nature* 365 (1993): 810; Courtesy of M. Rozycki. 15-12c R. Niederman and J. Hartwig. 15-13c Roger W. Craig. 15-15 John H. Hartwig. 15-17a M. S. Mooseker and L.G. Tilney, *Journal of Cell Biology* 67 (1975): 725–43, Fig 2. Reproduced by permission of The Rockefeller University Press. 15-18 John E. Heuser. 15-19b Daniel Branton. 15-20a Borisylab, Northwestern University Medical School. 15-21a–d Alan Hall, University College, London, and Kate Nobes, University of Bristol. 15-22 P. A. Coulombe et al., "The 'ins' and 'outs' of intermediate filament organization," from *Trends in Cell Biology* 10: 420–28, Fig. 1. Reprinted with permission from Elsevier Science. Image courtesy Pierre A. Coulombe, Johns Hopkins University. 15-24 Reprinted by permission from E. Fuchs, *Science* 279: 518, Fig. D. Images: T. Svitkina and G. Borisy. © 1998 American Association for the Advancement of Science. 15A-1b Lewis J. Tilney with Daniel Portnoy and Pat Connelly, *Journal of Cell Biology* 109: 1604, Fig. 18. Table 15-1 Left Mary Osborn. Table 15-1 Middle Frank Solomon. Table 15-1 Right Mark S. Ladinsky and J. Richard McIntosh, University of Colorado. Table 15-2 Row 1 Thomas D. Pollard. Table 15-2 Row 2 Summak and Borisy, *Nature* 332 (1988): 724–36, Fig. 1b. Table 15-2 Row 3 Left and Right Reprinted from E.D. Salmon, *Trends in Cell Biology* 5: 154–58, Fig. 3, with permission from Elsevier Science. Table 15-2 Row 4 John Heuser.

Chapter 16 16-CO Lewis Tilney, University of Pennsylvania. 16-1 Nobutaka Hirokawa. 16-6a W. L. Dentler/Biological Photo Service. 16-6c Biophoto Associates/Photo Researchers, Inc. 16-7a–d William L. Dentler. 16A-1b From I.A. Belyantseva et al. Gamma-actin is required for cytoskeletal maintenance but not development. *Proc. Natl. Acad. Sci. USA.* (2009) 106:9703–9708. 16-8a Lewis Tilney, University of Pennsylvania. 16-11b Hans Ris. 16-12a Clara Franzini-Armstrong. 16-17 John E. Heuser. 16-22a Allen Bell, University of New England. 16-23a A. Hall, Rho GTPasses at the actin cytoskeleton. *Science* 279:509–14, 1998. Figs a, c, e, g. Reprinted with permission from the American Association for the Advancement of Science. 16-24b Adapted from K.M. Trybus and S. Lowey, *Journal of Biological Chemistry* 259 (1984): 8564–71. 16-25 G. Albrecht-Buehler. 16-27 Melba/AGE Fotostock. 16-28b N. K. Wessels.

Chapter 18 18-CO Jack Griffith. 18-6 Left, Right James C. Wang. 18-17 Top Reproduced from H. Kobayashi, K. Kobayashi, and Y. Kobayashi, *Journal of Bacteriology* 132 (1977): 262–269 by copyright permission of the American Society for Microbiology. 18-17 Bottom Gopal Murti/SPL/Photo Researchers, Inc. 18-18 Jack Griffith. 18-20a,b Roger D. Kornberg. 18-22a, Top Jack Griffith. 18-22a, Bottom Stanley C. Holt/Biological Photo Service. 18-22b Barbara Hamkalo. 18-22c J. R. Paulsen and U.K. Laemmli, Cell. © Cell Press. 18-22d,e Armed Forces Institute of Pathology. 18-23 Ulrich K. Laemmli. 18-24 D. L. Robberson. 18-26a From L. Orci and A. Perrelet, *Freeze-Etch Histology.* Heidelberg: Springer-Verlag, 1975. 18-26b S.R. Tandon. 18-27a From L. Orci and A. Perrelet, *Freeze-Etch Histology.* Heidelberg: Springer-Verlag, 1975. 18-28 From L. Orci and A. Perrelet, *Freeze-Etch Histology.* Heidelberg: Springer-Verlag, 1975. 18-29a From A. C. Faberge, *Cell Tiss. Res.* 15 (1974): 403. Heidelberg: Springer-Verlag, 1974. 18-32a Jeffrey A. Nickerson, Sheldon Penman, and Gariela Krockmalnic. 18-32b Ueli Aebi. 18-33 Luis Parada and Tom Misteli, National Cancer Institute, NIH. 18-34 David Phillips/Photo Researchers, Inc. 18-35 Sasha Koulish and Ruth G. Kleinfeld, *Journal of Cell Biology* 23 (1964): 39. Reproduced by permission of The Rockefeller University Press. 18A-1b Lee D. Simon/Science Source/Photo Researchers, Inc. 18A-2b Orchid Cellmark, Inc., Germantown, MD. 18A-3 Madboy via Wikipedia, http://creativecommons.org/licenses/by-sa/1.0/deed.en. 18C-2 Orchid Cellmark, Inc., Germantown, MD.

Chapter 19 19-CO Ed Reschke. 19-4a *Cold Spring Harbor Symposium Quantitative Biology* 28 (1963):44. 19-5b From D.J. Burks and P.J. Stambrook, *Journal of Cell Biology* 77 (1978): 766, fig 6. Reproduced with permission of the Rockefeller University Press. Photos provided by

P.J. Stambrook. 19-16 Nikitina T and Woodcock CL. Closed chromatin loops at the ends of chromosomes. *JCB*, Volume 166, Number 2, 161–165. © The Rockefeller University Press. 19-20 Ed Reschke. 19-21a–e PhotoLibrary. 19-22b J. Richard McIntosh. 19-23 Left J. F. Gennaro/Photo Researchers, Inc. 19-23 Right CNRI/SPL/Photo Researchers, Inc. 19-26 Matthew Schibler, from *Protoplasma* 137 (1987): 29–44. Springer-Verlag. 19-27b Jeremy Pickett-Heaps, University of Melbourne. 19-27c Jeremy Pickett-Heaps, University of Melbourne. 19-28a Michael Danilchik, Dept. of Cell and Developmental Biology, Oregon Health & Science University. 19-29a George Von Dassow, University of Oregon. 19-29b Bill Bement, University of Wisconsin. 19-30a B.A. Palevitz. 19-31a Left and Right Michael Danilchik, Dept. of Cell and Developmental Biology, Oregon Health & Science University. 19-31b George Von Dassow, University of Oregon. 19-44b–d Walter Malorni et al., from "Morphological aspects of apoptosis," Image courtesy Walter Malorni, Instituto Superiore de Sanita Rome. 19B-1 Bob Goldstein, University of North Carolina.

Chapter 21 21-CO Jack Griffith. 21-2 Left and Right Janice Carr/Centers for Disease Control 21-3 Left and Right Vernon Ingram. 21-13 D. B. Nikolov and S. K. Burley from Nikolov et al., *Nature* 360 (1992): 40–46. 21-16 From O.L. Miller, Jr., B.A. Hamkalo, and C.A. Thomas, Jr. Reprinted with permission from *Science* 169 (1970): 392, Fig. 3. © American Association for the Advancement of Science. 21-19a Bert W. O'Malley, Baylor College of Medicine. 21-21 Left Ann L. Beyer. 21-21 Right Jack Griffith.

Chapter 22 22-CO James A. Lake. 22-1a James A. Lake.

Appendix A-CO Timothy Ryan. A-5a Leica Microsystems Inc. A-7 M.I. Walker/Photo Researchers, Inc. A-9 Tim Ryan. A-13 © Molecular Probes, Inc. (probes.invitrogen.com). A-14a–c S. Strome et al., "Spindle dynamics and the role of b-tubulin in early Caenohabditis elegans embryos," from *Molecular Biology of the Cell* 12: 1751–64, Fig. 8. Reprinted with permission by the American Society for Cell Biology. A-15a,b Karl Garsha, Digital Light Microscopy Specialist, Imaging Technology Group, Beckman Institute for Advanced Science and Technology, University of Illinois at Urbana–Champaign, Urbana, IL. A-17a Nikon USA. A-19a,b Shelly Sazor, Baylor College of Medicine. A-20a–d Reprinted from "Trends in Cell Biology" Vol 5, pp 154–158, Salmon: Figure 3. Copyright © 2002, with permission from Elsevier Science. A-22c Mochizuki et al, "Spatio-temporal images of growth factor-induced activation of Ras and Rap 1," from *Nature* 411 (2001): 1065–68. Courtesy of M. Matsuda. Reprinted by permission of Nature Publishing Group. A-24a Reprinted from Hein et al. Stimulated emission depletion (STED) nanoscopy of a fluorescent protein-labeled organelle inside a living cell. *Proc. Natl. Acad. Sci.* 105 (2008): 14271–14276. A-24b Reprinted from Bates et al., Multicolor Super-Resolution Imaging with Photo-Switchable Fluorescent Probes. *Science* 317 (2007): 1749–1753. A-26a Carl Zeiss, Inc./LEO Electron Microscopy, Inc. A-27a Don W. Fawcett, Harvard Medical School. A-27b Keiichi Tanaka. A-28a Carl Zeiss, Inc./LEO

Electron Microscopy, Inc. A-29a,b Ventana Medical Systems Inc. A-30 Janine R. Maddock. A-31 Michael F. Moody. A-32 Omikron/Photo Researchers, Inc. A-35 From L. Orci and A. Perrelet, *Freeze-Etch Histology*, Heidelberg: Springer-Verlag, 1975. A-36a Hans Ris. A-36b Koster AJ, Klumperman J. Electron microscopy in cell biology: integrating structure and function. *Nat Rev Mol Cell Biol.* 2003 Sep; Suppl: SS6–10, Fig 1. A-36c Koster AJ, Klumperman J. Electron microscopy in cell biology: integrating structure and function. *Nat Rev Mol Cell Biol.* 2003 Sep; Suppl: SS6–10, Fig 1. A-39 Left and Middle Reprinted with permission from *Nature* 171 (1953): 740; Copyright 1953 Macmillan Magazines Limited. A-39 Right Sonia DiVittorio, Pearson Education. A-40 Reprinted by permission of Nature Publishing Group.

Images used in Human Applications, Deeper Insights, and Tools of Discovery titles are by permission of Duncan Smith/Photodisc/Getty Images.

Illustration and Text Credits

The following illustrations are taken from L. J. Kleinsmith and V. M. Kish, *Principles of Cell and Molecular Biology*, 2d ed. (New York, NY: HarperCollins, 1995). Reprinted by permission of Pearson Education, Inc.

Figs. 3-7, 3-9, 3-13, 3-27, 7-6, 7-7, 7-8, 7-11, 7-19, 7-23, 7-24, 12-9, 12-14, 12-17c,d, 12-18b, 15-6, 16-2, 16-26, 18-15, 18-19, 19-2, 19-8, 19-10, 19-22a, 19-24, 21-3, 21-4, 21-11, 21-18, 21-19, 21-21, 21-23, 21-24, 22-4

Fig. 3-4 Illustration, Irving Geis. Image from Irving Geis Collection, Howard Hughes Medical Institute. Rights owned by HHMI. Not to be reproduced without permission. Used by permission of Sandy Geis.

Fig. 3-6 Illustration, Irving Geis. Image from Irving Geis Collection, Howard Hughes Medical Institute. Rights owned by HHMI. Not to be reproduced without permission. Used by permission of Sandy Geis.

Fig. 4-22 From P. J. Russell, *Genetics*, 5th ed., Fig. 13.18. Copyright © 1998. Reprinted by permission of Pearson Education, Inc.

Fig. 6-7 From N. A. Campbell and J. B. Reece, *Biology*, 6th ed., Fig. 6-15, p. 99. Copyright © 2002. Reprinted by permission of Pearson Education, Inc.

Box 6A Source: Cech, *Science* 236: 1532 (1987).

Fig. 7-30 Reprinted from *Journal of Molecular Biology*, vol. 157, no. 1, J. Kyte and R. F. Doolittle, "A Simple Method for Displaying the Hydropathic Character of a Protein," pp. 105–132, Copyright 1982, with permission from Elsevier.

Fig. 15-1a–d Adapted by permission of Macmillan Publishers Ltd: From M. T. Cabeen and C. Jacobs-Wagner, "Bacterial Cell Shape," *Nature Reviews Microbiology* (August 2005), 3 (8): 601–10 (Fig. 4), Copyright 2005. Adapted by permission of Macmillan Publishers Ltd: From W. Margolin, "FtsZ and the Division of Prokaryotic Cells and Organelles," *Nature Reviews Molecular Cell Biology* (November 2005), 6 (11): 862–71 (Fig. 6), Copyright 2005.

Fig. 15-3 Adapted from Bruce Alberts et al., *Molecular Biology of the Cell*, 3rd ed., Fig. 16.33,

p. 810. Copyright 1994 by Garland Science-Books. Reproduced with permission of Garland Science-Books via Copyright Clearance Center.

Fig. 15-14 Adapted from Bruce Alberts et al., *Molecular Biology of the Cell*, 3rd ed., Fig. 16.65, p. 835. Copyright 1994 by Garland Science-Books. Reproduced with permission of Garland Science-Books via Copyright Clearance Center.

Fig. 16A-1a I. A. Belyantseva et al., "gamma-Actin Is Required for Cytoskeletal Maintenance but Not Development," *Proceedings of the National Academy of Sciences* 106 (24): 9703–9708 (Fig. 2A). Copyright 2009 National Academy of Sciences, U.S.A.

Fig. 16A-1c Reprinted from *Current Opinion in Cell Biology*, 17 (1), H. W. Lin, M. E. Schneider, & B. Kachar, "When Size Matters: The Dynamic Regulation of Stereocilia Lengths," pp. 55–61 (Fig. 3), with permission from Elsevier.

Fig. 16-3a Adapted by permission from Macmillan Publishers Ltd: *Nature Reviews Neuroscience*. From N. Hirokawa and R. Takemura, "Molecular Motors and Mechanisms of Directional Transport in Neurons," (March 2005), 6:201–214, Fig. 1. Copyright © 2005.

Fig. 16-3b From *Molecular Cell Biology*, 3rd ed. by H. Lodish, A. Berk, S. L. Zipursky, P. Matsudaira, D. Baltimore, and J. Darnell, Fig. 23-11. © 1995 by W. H. Freeman and Company. Used with permission.

Fig. 16-5 Source: Corthesy-Theulaz et al., "Cytoplasm Dynein Participates in the Centrosomal Localization of the Golgi Complex," *Journal of Cell Biology* (September 1992), 118 (6): 1333–45.

Fig. 16-9 From T. Hodge and M. J. Cope, "The Myosin Family Tree," *Journal of Cell Science* (2000), 113 (19): 3353–3354, Fig. 1. Copyright © 2000. Reproduced with permission of The Company of Biologists, Ltd.

Fig. 16-21 *Cell Movements* by Dennis Bray, p. 166. Copyright 1992 by Taylor & Francis Group LLC-Books. Reproduced with permission of Taylor & Francis Group LLC-Books via Copyright Clearance Center.

Fig. 16-27a Adapted from C. H. Lin, E. M. Espreafico, M. S. Mooseker, and P. Forscher, "Myosin Drives Retrograde F-Actin Flow in Neuronal Growth Cones," *Neuron*, April 1996, 16 (4): 769–782, Fig. B. Used by permission of Paul Forscher.

Fig. 18-12 From N. A. Campbell, J. B. Reece, and L. G. Mitchell, *Biology*, 5th ed., p. 377. Copyright © 1999. Reprinted by permission of Pearson Education, Inc.

Fig. 19-28 From N. A. Campbell and J. B. Reece, *Biology*, 8th ed., Fig. 12-9, p. 235. Copyright © 2008. Reprinted by permission of Pearson Education, Inc.

Fig. 19-30 From N. A. Campbell and J. B. Reece, *Biology*, 8th ed., Fig. 12-9, p. 235. Copyright © 2008. Reprinted by permission of Pearson Education, Inc.

Fig. 22A-1c From N. A. Campbell and J. B. Reece, *Biology*, 8th ed., Fig. 19-11, p. 394. Copyright © 2008. Reprinted by permission of Pearson Education, Inc.

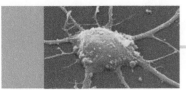

INDEX

Phosphorylase a and, 149
Phosphorylase kinase, 149, 416
Phosphorylase phosphatase, 149
Phosphorylation, 148–49, 149*f*
    of mitotic Cdk-cyclin complex, 584–85, 585*f*
    of myosin II, 470*f*
    oxidative, 254, **276**, 277, 278
    protein, gene regulation and, 742–43, 746–47
    of Rb protein, regulation of GI checkpoint and, 586–87
    in receptor down-regulation, 394
    and regulation of G protein-linked receptors, 396
    substrate-level, **235**, 276
Photoactivated localization microscopy (PALM), A17
Photoactivation, **A15**, A15*f*
Photoautotrophs, **109**, 293
Photobleaching, **A15**, A15*f*
Photochemical reduction, **298**
Photoconversion, A15
Photoexcitation, **297**–98
Photoheterotrophs, **109**, 293
Photolysis, water, 305
Photon, **297**
    transfer of energy from, to photosystem reaction center, 300, 302*b*
Photophosphorylation, 295, **307**
Photoreactions of photosynthetic energy transduction, 305
Photoreduction, 295, **302–7**, 302*f*
Photorespiration (glycolate pathway), **316–20**, 359
    in C₄ versus C₃ plants, 317–18
    CAM plants and, 320
    leaf peroxisomes in, 93, 94*f*, 316–17
Photorespiration pathway, 359
Photosswitching, A15
Photosynthesis, 107*f*, **293–323**
    ATP synthesis in, 307–9
    Calvin cycle and carbon assimilation, 293, 309–13
    Calvin cycle and energy transduction, 311–12
    in carbohydrate synthesis, 313–15
    chloroplast as site of, 87–88, 295
    energy transduction in, 295, 297–309
    evolution of chloroplasts and mitochondria, 297
    light harvesting in, 297–301
    NADPH synthesis in, 302–7
    overview of, 293–97, 294*f*
    photosynthetic reaction center from purple bacterium, 302*b*
    rubisco oxygenase activity and reduction of efficiency in, 315–20
Photosynthetic membranes, 297
Photosystem, **300–301**, 301*f*
Photosystem complex, **301**
Photosystem II (PSII) complex, **301**, 302*b*, 308
    electron transfer from water to plastoquinone by, 303–5
Photosystem I (PSI) complex, **301**, 302*b*, 308
    electron transfer from plastocyanin to ferredoxin by, 304*f*, 306
Phototrophs, 108, **109**, 110–11, 110*f*, 224, **293**
    anoxygenic, **295**
    oxygenic, 293, **295**
    oxygenic, noncyclic electron flow in, 303*f*
Ph (pheophytin), 304
Phragmoplast, **579**
Phycobilins, **300**
Phycobilisome, **301**
Phycocyanin, 300
Phycoerythrin, 300
Phylloquinone, 306
Physostigmine (eserine), 387*b*
Phytohormone synthesis, 331
Phytol side chain, 299, 300*f*
Phytosterols, 25, 164*f*, **165**–66

PI3K-Akt pathway
    activation by stimulatory growth factors, 591, 591*f*
    activation during insulin signaling, 417, 418*f*
PI3K or PI 3-kinase (phosphatidylinositol 3-kinase), 410, **417**, 591
    activation by stimulatory growth factors, 591, 591*f*
    activation during insulin signaling, 417, 418*f*
Pigment, **297**
    accessory, **300**–301
    antenna, **301**, 301*f*
    chlorophyll, 298–300. *See also* Chlorophyll
Ping-pong mechanism, 205
Pinocytosis, 343
PIP₂ (phosphatidylinositol-4,5-bisphosphate), 401, 417, 440
PIP₃ (phosphatidylinositol-3,4,5-trisphosphate), 417, 418*f*, 591, 591*f*
PKA. *See* Protein kinase A
PKC (protein kinase C), **401**
PKD (polycystic kidney disease), 456*b*
Plakin proteins, 444, **495**
Plakoglobin, 483, 484
Plant cell(s), 497–501
    cellulose in, 65, 65*f*
    cristae in mitochondria of, 257
    cytokinesis in, 579–80, 579*f*
    leaf peroxisomes in, 93, 94*f*
    membrane receptors in, 158
    membranes of, 157*f*, 158, 165
    mitosis in, 572*f*
    peroxisomes in, 93, 94*f*, 357*f*, 358–59
    starch in, 29, 30, 63, 64*f*
    structure of typical, 80*f*
    surface of, 497–501
    telophase in, 572*f*
    vacuoles in, 93–94, 94*f*, 355–56
Plant cell wall, 35, 63, 98, 99*f*, 488*t*, 497–501
    as permeability barrier, 497–98
    plasmodesmata and cell-cell communication through, 99, 500–501, 501*f*
    structure of, 99*f*, 498*f*
    synthesis of, 499
Plant diseases
    cadang-cadang as, 101
    tobacco mosaic virus as, 35*f*, 36*f*, 100*f*
    viral and viroid, 99, 101
Plant(s)
    absorption spectra of common pigments in, 300*f*
    C₃ compared to C₄, 318, 320
    CAM, **320**
    genetically engineered, using Ti plasmid, 636, 637*f*
    genetically modified, 636–37
    glyoxylate cycle, glyoxysomes, and seed germination of, 268–69*b*
    homeoviscous adaptation in, 172–73
    photosynthesis in. *See* Photosynthesis
    transgenic, 636–37
    turgor pressure in, 94, 200*b*
Plaque, 483–84, **495**, 632
    bacteriophage, 509*b*
Plasma, blood, 407
Plasma (cell) membrane, 82–83, **156**
    biosynthesis of, endoplasmic reticulum in, 331–32
    clathrin-coated vesicles and, 349–50
    composition of, in rat liver cells, 332*t*
    glycoproteins in, 83, 83*f*
    G protein-linked receptors in, 396–406
    linkage of actin to, 438–39
    lipids in, 163–73. *See also* Membrane lipids
    membrane potential in, 367–72
    membrane proteins of. *See* Membrane protein(s)
    models of, 158–63
    neurosecretory vesicle fusion with, secretion of neurotransmitters and, 385, 385*f*

organization of, 83*f*
    phospholipid composition of select, 165*f*
    protein kinase-associated receptors in, 406–14
    protein, lipid, and carbohydrate content of, 161*t*
    proteins of, 83, 83*f*, 173–89
    transport across. *See* Transport across membranes
Plasma fibronectin, 493
Plasma membrane GTP-binding protein oncogene-produced, 775*t*, 776
Plasma membrane receptors, 396
    apoptosis and, 592–94
    G protein-linked, 396–406
    for growth factors, 407
    for hormones, 414–18
    protein kinase-associated, 406–14
Plasmid(s), **530**
    as cloning vectors, 629–30, 630*f*, 631*f*, 636, 637*f*
    col (colicinogenic) factors, 530
    cryptic, 530
    F (fertility) factors, 530, **622**, 623*f*, 634
    metabolic, 530
    pUC19, 629–30, 631*f*
    recombinant, 631–32
    R (resistance) factors, 530
    Ti, 636, 637*f*
    virulence factors, 530
Plasmin, 763
Plasminogen, 763
Plasminogen activator, 763
Plasmodesma(ta), **98**, 99*f*, 158, 184, 481, **500–501**
    structure of, 500–501, 501*f*
Plasmolysis, 200*b*
Plastid, **88**, 295
Plastocyanin (PC), **305**–6
    electron transfer from plastoquinol to, 305–6
    electron transfer from, to ferredoxin, 304*f*, 306
Plastoquinol, 305
    electron transfer from, to plastocyanin, 305
Plastoquinone, 70, 304–5
    photosystem and transfer of electrons to, 303–5
Plateau phase of MT assembly, 427, 427*f*
Platelet. *See* Blood platelets
Platelet-derived growth factor (PDGF), 407, 440, **589**
    oncogene related to, 775
Platinum, 133
Pleated β sheets, 50
Plectin, 444–45, 445*f*, 495, 496*f*
Plus end (barbed end), microtubule, 427–28, 428*f*
pmf (proton motive force), **279**
PML bodies (promyelocytic leukemia bodies), 544
PNS (peripheral nervous system), 365
Poikilotherms, 172
Point mutations, 772
Pointed end. *See* Minus end
Poisoning, food, 483*b*
Poisons
    enzyme inhibitors as, 144
    neurotoxins as, 385, 386, 387*b*
Polar body, 602, **611**
Polar bond, 21
Polar groups in hydrophilic amino acids, 42, 43*f*
Polar head, 25*f*, 26
Polarity, **23**
    in Golgi stacks, 333
    of microtubules, 97, 430–31, 432*f*, 574–75, 575*f*
    of solutes, 199, 201
    of water molecules, 23, 23*f*
Polarized cells, 189
Polarized epithelium, 478, 478*f*
Polarized secretion, **342**
Polarizer in DIC microscopy, A7, A7*f*

Polar microtubules, **573**, 574–75, 575*f*, 577*f*, 578
Polar pores, 160
Poliovirus, 100*f*
Polyacrylamide gels, 519
Poly(A) polymerase, 669
Poly(A) tail, 664, **668**–69
    addition of, to pre-mRNA, 669, 669*f*
Polycistronic mRNA, 685, **712**
Polycyclic aromatic hydrocarbons, 330, 768
Polycystic kidney disease (PKD), 456*b*
Polyhistidine tagging, 635
Polyisoprenoids, 70
Polymerase chain reaction (PCR), 529*b*, **560–61***b*
    to clone genes from sequenced genomes, 635
Polymerization, synthesis by, 27–32, 31*f*
Polymer(s), 18
    elongation of, 31–32, 31*f*
    hydrolysis of, 32
    nucleic acid (DNA, RNA), 57–60
    as polypeptides and proteins, 44
    polysaccharides, 63–65
Polynucleotide, **58**
Polynucleotide phosphorylase, 653–54
Polypeptide exit tunnel, 690
Polypeptide(s), **32**, **44**. *See also* Protein(s); Protein synthesis
    chaperone-mediated import of, into mitochondrial matrix, 703–4, 705*f*
    gene coding for amino acid sequence of, 647–50
    hydrophobic regions of chains of, 699
    insulin A subunit and B subunit of, 48
    light and heavy chains of, 726–27
    molecular chaperones and folding of, 32–34, 690–91, 699, 701
    polymers as, 44
    posttranslational import of, into organelles, 697–98, 697*f*, 702–5
    spanning both mitochondrial membranes during import, 704*f*
    synthesis of, chain elongation in, 685, 688–90, 689*f*
    synthesis of chains of, messenger RNA and, 652–54
    synthesis of, energy budget for, 691
    synthesis of, initiation of, 685–86
    synthesis of, messenger RNA and, 652–54, 684–85
    synthesis of, protein factors in, 679, 685
    synthesis of, ribosomes and, 679–80
    synthesis of, termination of, 690
Polyphosphoinositides, 440
Polyps, 780
Polyribosome, **691**
Polysaccharide(s), 27, **60**–65. *See also* Carbohydrate(s)
    monosaccharide monomers of, 61–63
    storage and structural polymers of, 30, 30*f*, 66*f*
    storage and structural, polymers as, 63–65
    storage, phosphorolytic cleavage of, 238, 240*f*
    structural, cellulose as, 65, 65*f*
    structure of, glycosidic bonds and, 65
    as substrates for glycolysis, 238, 240*f*
    subunits of, 66*f*
    synthesis of, 29*f*
Polyspermy, blocks to, 402
Polytene chromosome, **728**
    puffs in, 728*f*
    transcriptional activity of, 728*f*
Poly(U), 654
Pore complex, nuclear, 84
Pore protein, 699
Pore(s)
    membrane, 202
    nuclear, 84, 84*f*
Porins, 177, 202, **205**–6, 208*f*, 255, 297
Porphyrin ring, 133, 298–99
Porter, Keith, 348
Portis, Archie, 313
Positive control of transcription, 716
Positive cooperativity, **148**